Emile Watson

10/04/04 - Staff
3C 11/30/04

The Phrase concordance of the Bible

THE

PHRASE CONCORDANCE

OF THE BIBLE

THE PHRASE CONCORDANCE OF THE BIBLE

THOMAS NELSON PUBLISHERS
NASHVILLE • CAMDEN • NEW YORK

Published in Nashville, Tennessee, by Thomas Nelson, Inc., Publishers, and distributed in Canada by Lawson Falle, Ltd., Cambridge, Ontario.

Library of Congress Cataloging-in-Publication Data

Phrase concordance of the Bible.

1. Bible—Concordances, English. I. Thomas Nelson Publishers.
BS425.P47 1986 220.5′2033 86–16314

Printed in the United States of America

1 2 3 4 5 6 7 8 9 10—89 88 87 86

A NEW KIND OF CONCORDANCE

This book springs from the conviction that there is a new and different way to organize a concordance. For years, concordances have used the individual-word format to help Bible students find familiar passages of Scripture. But this book departs from that standard procedure by using important Bible *phrases* as the reference key. This system has several distinct advantages over the old approach.

First, this organization by phrases reduces the bulk of a concordance considerably, making it easier to handle and use. Suppose a Bible student is searching for a specific passage that mentions "word of God." With a standard exhaustive word concordance, he would have to labor through more than 900 references to "word" or about 4,500 occurrences of the word "God." But with the *Phrase Concordance,* he looks under "word of God" and its 48 occurrences to find exactly the passage he is searching for in a fraction of the time.

Another advantage of the phrase format is that it allows the user to trace an important theme or topic throughout the entire Bible. For example, the concept of the "Day of the Lord"—a time of God's approaching judgment on an evil world—was a prominent theme of the prophet Joel. But a careful study of this phrase in the *Phrase Concordance* shows the idea was also mentioned by other Old Testament prophets as well as several New Testament writers. Other key biblical themes and phrases, such as "Spirit of God," "Kingdom of Heaven," and "Lord of Lords," are easy to research by using the information in the *Phrase Concordance.*

Finally, a concordance arranged by familiar Bible phrases is an excellent sourcebook of Scriptural quotations. New Testament writers often quoted from the Old Testament to support an argument or drive home an important point. Turn to the phrase, "Calls upon the name of the Lord," in this concordance for a good example of this quoting technique.

In this particular case, the apostle Peter quoted from the prophet Joel to impress his Jewish audience with the credentials of Christ. The careful Bible student will find many cases like this in the *Phrase Concordance* that show how often the New Testament draws upon the riches of the Old.

To use this handy concordance, try to recall a memorable phrase from the specific Bible passage you are searching for. Then look under that phrase in the book. The 5,200 phrases in the *Phrase Concordance* are arranged in alphabetical order according to the first words of the entries.

If you can recall only one important word of a Bible passage, look in the Key Word Index at the back of the concordance. This index will help you locate the exact phrase you have in mind.

The *Phrase Concordance* uses the New King James Version (NKJV) as the text on which the phrases are based. However, handy cross-references within the text make the book usable with four additional English translations—King James Version (KJV), Revised Standard Version (RSV), New American Standard Bible (NASB), and New International Version (NIV). For example, "Verily, verily, I say unto you—a KJV phrase—refers the reader to its NKJV equivalent, "Most assuredly, I say to you."

This book is the work of a team of editors, computer programmers, lay Bible students, and educators. Many people were consulted about which Bible phrases were familiar to them, and some were asked to submit their own lists. The publisher also sought the contributions of New Testament Professor William L. Lane and Old Testament Professor Ronald Youngblood. These two scholars insured that general users would be exposed to phrases of scholarly interest and that the overall list of phrases was comprehensive.

Our thanks to all these people for their contribution. We hope the *Phrase Concordance* will cultivate and promote a more discriminating study of God's Word.

—The Publisher

Abbreviations Used
for Books of the Bible

Old Testament

Gen..Genesis
Ex ....Exodus
Lev ....Leviticus
Num ....Numbers
Deut ....Deuteronomy
Josh..Joshua
Judg ....Judges
Ruth..Ruth
1Sam ....1 Samuel
2Sam ....2 Samuel
1Kin..1 Kings
2Kin..2 Kings
1Chr ....1 Chronicles
2Chr ....2 Chronicles
Ezra..Ezra
Neh..Nehemiah
Esth ....Esther
Job..Job
Ps..Psalms
Prov..Proverbs
Eccl ....Ecclesiastes
Song..Song of Solomon
Is..Isaiah
Jer..Jeremiah
Lam ....Lamentations
Ezek ....Ezekiel
Dan..Daniel
Hos ....Hosea
Joel..Joel
Amos..Amos
Obad..Obadiah
Jon..Jonah
Mic ....Micah
Nah..Nahum
Hab..Habakkuk
Zeph ....Zephaniah
Hag..Haggai
Zech ....Zechariah
Mal ....Malachi

New Testament

Matt ....Matthew
Mark ....Mark
Luke..Luke
John ....John
Acts..Acts
Rom..Romans
1Cor ....1 Corinthians
2Cor ....2 Corinthians
Gal..Galatians
Eph ....Ephesians
Phil ....Philippians
Col..Colossians
1Th ....1 Thessalonians
2Th ....2 Thessalonians
1Tim ....1 Timothy
2Tim ....2 Timothy
Tit ....Titus
Phm..Philemon
Heb ....Hebrews
Jas ....James
1Pet ....1 Peter
2Pet ....2 Peter
1Jn ....1 John
2Jn ....2 John
3Jn..3 John
Jude..Jude
Rev ....Revelation

PHRASE CONCORDANCE

ABBA, FATHER
Mark 14:36 And He said, "*Abba, Father*, all things are possible for You
Rom 8:15 For you did not receive the spirit of bondage again to fear, but you received the Spirit of adoption by whom we cry out, "*Abba, Father*
Gal 4:6 And because you are sons, God has sent forth the Spirit of His Son into your hearts, crying out, "*Abba, Father*

ABIDE IN HIM
1Jn 2:27 but as the same anointing teaches you concerning all things, and is true, and is not a lie, and just as it has taught you, you will *abide in Him*
1Jn 2:28 And now, little children, *abide in Him*, that when He appears, we may have confidence and not be ashamed before Him at His coming
1Jn 3:17 But whoever has this world's goods, and sees his brother in need, and shuts up his heart from him, how does the love of God *abide in him*
1Jn 4:13 By this we know that we *abide in Him*, and He in us, because He has given us of His Spirit

ABIDE IN MAN (RSV)
(See *STRIVE WITH MAN*)

ABIDE IN ME
John 15:4 *Abide in Me*, and I in you. As the branch cannot bear fruit of itself, unless it abides in the vine, neither can you, unless you *abide in Me*
John 15:6 If anyone does not *abide in Me*, he is cast out as a branch and is withered
John 15:7 If you *abide in Me*, and My words abide in you, you will ask what you desire, and it shall be done for you

ABIDE IN MY LOVE
John 15:9 As the Father loved Me, I also have loved you; *abide in My love*
John 15:10 If you keep My commandments, you will *abide in My love*, just as I have kept My Father's commandments and abide in His love

ABIDE IN MY WORD
John 8:31 Then Jesus said to those Jews who believed Him, "If you *abide in My word*, you are My disciples indeed

ABIDE IN THE SON
1Jn 2:24 If what you heard from the beginning abides in you, you also will *abide in the Son* and in the Father

ABIDE WITH YOU
John 14:16 And I will pray the Father, and He will give you another Helper, that He may *abide with you* forever

ABIDES FOREVER
Ps 125:1 Those who trust in the Lord are like Mount Zion, which cannot be moved, but *abides forever*
Eccl 1:4 One generation passes away, and another generation comes; but the earth *abides forever*
John 8:35 And a slave does not abide in the house forever, but a son *abides forever*
1Pet 1:23 having been born again, not of corruptible seed but incorruptible, through the word of God which lives and *abides forever*
1Jn 2:17 but he who does the will of God *abides forever*

ABIDES IN HIM
1Jn 2:6 He who says he *abides in Him* ought himself also to walk just as He walked
1Jn 3:6 Whoever *abides in Him* does not sin. Whoever sins has neither seen Him nor known Him
1Jn 3:24 Now he who keeps His commandments *abides in Him*, and He in him
1Jn 4:15 Whoever confesses that Jesus is the Son of God, God *abides in him*, and he in God

ABIDES IN LOVE
1Jn 4:16 God is love, and he who *abides in love* abides in God, and God in him

ABIDES IN ME
John 6:56 He who eats My flesh and drinks My blood *abides in Me*, and I in him
John 15:5 He who *abides in Me*, and I in him, bears much fruit

ABIDETH A PRIEST CONTINUALLY (KJV)
(See *REMAINS A PRIEST CONTINUALLY*)

ABLE TO DELIVER
2Kin 18:29 Do not let Hezekiah deceive you, for he shall not be *able to deliver* you from his hand
2Chr 32:13 Were the gods of the nations of those lands in any way *able to deliver* their lands out of my hand
2Chr 32:14 Who was there among all the gods of those nations that my fathers utterly destroyed that could deliver his people from my hand, that your God should be *able to deliver* you from my hand
2Chr 32:15 for no god of any nation or kingdom was *able to deliver* his people from my hand or the hand of my fathers

Is 36:14 Do not let Hezekiah deceive you, for he will not be *able to deliver* you
Ezek 7:19 their silver and their gold will not be *able to deliver* them in the day of the wrath of the Lord
Dan 3:17 If that is the case, our God whom we serve is *able to deliver* us from the burning fiery furnace, and He will deliver us from your hand, O king
Dan 6:20 The king spoke, saying to Daniel, "Daniel, servant of the living God, has your God, whom you serve continually, been *able to deliver* you from the lions
Zeph 1:18 Neither their silver nor their gold shall be *able to deliver* them in the day of the Lord's wrath

ABLE TO GO TO WAR
Num 1:3 from twenty years old and above all who are *able to go to war* in Israel
Num 1:20 Now the children of Reuben, Israel's oldest son, their genealogies by their families, by their fathers' house, according to the number of names, every male individually, from twenty years old and above, all who were *able to go to war*
Num 1:22 From the children of Simeon, their genealogies by their families, by their fathers' house, of those who were numbered, according to the number of names, every male individually, from twenty years old and above, all who were *able to go to war*
Num 1:24 From the children of Gad, their genealogies by their families, by their fathers' house, according to the number of names, from twenty years old and above, all who were *able to go to war*
Num 1:26 From the children of Judah, their genealogies by their families, by their fathers' house, according to the number of names, from twenty years old and above, all who were *able to go to war*
Num 1:28 From the children of Issachar, their genealogies by their families, by their fathers' house, according to the number of names, from twenty years old and above, all who were *able to go to war*
Num 1:30 From the children of Zebulun, their genealogies by their families, by their fathers' house, according to the number of names, from twenty years old and above, all who were *able to go to war*
Num 1:32 From the sons of Joseph, the children of Ephraim, their genealogies by their families, by their fathers' house, according to the number of names, from twenty years old and above, all who were *able to go to war*
Num 1:34 From the children of Manasseh, their genealogies by their families, by their fathers' house, according to the number of names, from twenty years old and above, all who were *able to go to war*
Num 1:36 From the children of Benjamin, their genealogies by their families, by their fathers' house, according to the number of names, from twenty years old and above, all who were *able to go to war*
Num 1:38 From the children of Dan, their genealogies by their families, by their fathers' house, according to the number of names, from twenty years old and above, all who were *able to go to war*
Num 1:40 From the children of Asher, their genealogies by their families, by their fathers' house, according to the number of names, from twenty years old and above, all who were *able to go to war*
Num 1:42 From the children of Naphtali, their genealogies by their families, by their fathers' house, according to the number of names, from twenty years old and above, all who were *able to go to war*
Num 1:45 So all who were numbered of the children of Israel, by their fathers' houses, from twenty years old and above, all who were *able to go to war* in Israel
Num 26:2 Take a census of all the congregation of the children of Israel from twenty years old and above, by their fathers' houses, all who are *able to go to war* in Israel
2Chr 25:5 and he numbered them from twenty years old and above, and found them to be three hundred thousand choice men, *able to go to war*, who could handle spear and shield

ABLE TO SAVE
Heb 5:7 who, in the days of His flesh, when He had offered up prayers and supplications, with vehement cries and tears to Him who was *able to save* Him from death, and was heard because of His godly fear
Heb 7:25 Therefore He is also *able to save* to the uttermost those who come to God through Him, since He ever lives to make intercession for them
Jas 1:21 Therefore lay aside all filthiness and overflow of wickedness, and receive with meekness the implanted word, which is *able to save* your souls
Jas 4:12 There is one Lawgiver, who is *able to save* and to destroy

ABLE TO SERVE IN THE ARMY (NIV)
(See *ABLE TO GO TO WAR*)

ABLE TO STAND
Deut 7:24 no one shall be *able to stand* against you until you have destroyed them
Deut 11:25 No man shall be *able to stand* against you; the Lord your God will put the dread of you and the fear of you upon all the land where you tread, just as He has said to you
Josh 1:5 No man shall be *able to stand* before you all the days of your life
Josh 23:9 but as for you, no one has been *able to stand* against you to this day
1Sam 6:20 And the men of Beth Shemesh said, "Who is *able to stand* before this holy Lord God
Ezra 10:13 it is the season for heavy rain, and we are not *able to stand* outside
Job 41:10 No one is so fierce that he would dare stir him up. Who then is *able to stand* against Me
Prov 27:4 Wrath is cruel and anger a torrent, but who is *able to stand* before jealousy
Eph 6:11 Put on the whole armor of God, that you may be *able to stand* against the wiles of the devil
Rev 6:17 For the great day of His wrath has come, and who is *able to stand*

ABNORMALLY BORN (NIV)
(See *BORN OUT OF DUE TIME*)

ABOLISH THE LAW (RSV)
(See *DESTROY THE LAW*)

ABOMINATION OF DESOLATION
Dan 11:31 then they shall take away the daily sacrifices, and place there the *abomination of desolation*
Dan 12:11 And from the time that the daily sacrifice is taken away, and the *abomination of desolation* is set up, there shall be one thousand two hundred and ninety days
Matt 24:15 Therefore when you see the '*abomination of desolation*,' spoken of by Daniel the prophet, standing in the holy place

Mark 13:14 But when you see the '*abomination of desolation*,' spoken of by Daniel the prophet, standing where it ought not

ABOMINATION TO THE LORD
Deut 7:25 for it is an *abomination to the Lord* your God
Deut 12:31 for every *abomination to the Lord* which He hates they have done to their gods
Deut 17:1 You shall not sacrifice to the Lord your God a bull or sheep which has any blemish or defect, for that is an *abomination to the Lord* your God
Deut 18:12 For all who do these things are an *abomination to the Lord*, and because of these abominations the Lord your God drives them out from before you
Deut 22:5 A woman shall not wear anything that pertains to a man, nor shall a man put on a woman's garment, for all who do so are an *abomination to the Lord* your God
Deut 23:18 You shall not bring the hire of a harlot or the price of a dog to the house of the Lord your God for any vowed offering, for both of these are an *abomination to the Lord* your God
Deut 25:16 For all who do such things, and all who behave unrighteously, are an *abomination to the Lord* your God
Deut 27:15 Cursed is the one who makes any carved or molded image, an *abomination to the Lord*, the work of the hands of the craftsman, and sets it up in secret
Prov 3:32 for the perverse person is an *abomination to the Lord*, but His secret counsel is with the upright
Prov 11:1 A false balance is an *abomination to the Lord*, but a just weight is His delight
Prov 11:20 Those who are of a perverse heart are an *abomination to the Lord*, but such as are blameless in their ways are His delight
Prov 12:22 Lying lips are an *abomination to the Lord*, but those who deal truthfully are His delight
Prov 15:8 The sacrifice of the wicked is an *abomination to the Lord*, but the prayer of the upright is His delight
Prov 15:9 The way of the wicked is an *abomination to the Lord*, but He loves him who follows righteousness
Prov 15:26 The thoughts of the wicked are an *abomination to the Lord*, but the words of the pure are pleasant
Prov 16:5 Everyone who is proud in heart is an *abomination to the Lord*
Prov 17:15 He who justifies the wicked, and he who condemns the just, both of them alike are an *abomination to the Lord*
Prov 20:10 Diverse weights and diverse measures, they are both alike, an *abomination to the Lord*
Prov 20:23 Diverse weights are an *abomination to the Lord*, and a false balance is not good

ABOUNDING IN LOVE (NIV)
(See *ABUNDANT IN MERCY*)

ABOUNDING IN MERCY
Ps 103:8 The Lord is merciful and gracious, slow to anger, and *abounding in mercy*

ABOUNDING IN STEADFAST LOVE (RSV)
(See *ABOUNDING IN MERCY*)

ABOVE ALL GODS
1Chr 16:25 For the Lord is great and greatly to be praised; He is also to be feared *above all gods*
Ps 95:3 For the Lord is the great God, and the great King *above all gods*
Ps 96:4 For the Lord is great and greatly to be praised; He is to be feared *above all gods*
Ps 97:9 For You, Lord, are most high above all the earth; You are exalted far *above all gods*
Ps 135:5 For I know that the Lord is great, and our Lord is *above all gods*

ABRAHAM, ISAAC, AND JACOB
Ex 6:8 And I will bring you into the land which I swore to give to *Abraham, Isaac, and Jacob*
Ex 33:1 Then the Lord said to Moses, "Depart and go up from here, you and the people whom you have brought out of the land of Egypt, to the land of which I swore to *Abraham, Isaac, and Jacob*, saying
Num 32:11 Surely none of the men who came up from Egypt, from twenty years old and above, shall see the land of which I swore to *Abraham, Isaac, and Jacob*, because they have not wholly followed Me
Deut 1:8 go in and possess the land which the Lord swore to your fathers to *Abraham, Isaac, and Jacob* to give to them and their descendants after them
Deut 6:10 And it shall be, when the Lord your God brings you into the land of which He swore to your fathers, to *Abraham, Isaac, and Jacob*, to give you large and beautiful cities which you did not build
Deut 9:5 It is not because of your righteousness or the uprightness of your heart that you go in to possess their land, but because of the wickedness of these nations that the Lord your God drives them out from before you, and that He may fulfill the word which the Lord swore to your fathers, to *Abraham, Isaac, and Jacob*
Deut 9:27 Remember Your servants, *Abraham, Isaac, and Jacob;* do not look on the stubbornness of this people, or on their wickedness or their sin
Deut 29:13 that He may establish you today as a people for Himself, and that He may be God to you, just as He has spoken to you, and just as He has sworn to your fathers, to *Abraham, Isaac, and Jacob*
Deut 30:20 and that you may dwell in the land which the Lord swore to your fathers, to *Abraham, Isaac, and Jacob*, to give them
Deut 34:4 Then the Lord said to him, "This is the land of which I swore to give *Abraham, Isaac, and Jacob*, saying
2Kin 13:23 But the Lord was gracious to them, had compassion on them, and regarded them, because of His covenant with *Abraham, Isaac, and Jacob*, and would not yet destroy them or cast them from His presence
Jer 33:26 then I will cast away the descendants of Jacob and David My servant, so that I will not take any of his descendants to be rulers over the descendants of *Abraham, Isaac, and Jacob*
Matt 8:11 And I say to you that many will come from east and west, and sit down with *Abraham, Isaac, and Jacob* in the kingdom of heaven
Acts 3:13 The God of *Abraham, Isaac, and Jacob*, the God of our fathers, glorified His Servant Jesus, whom you delivered up and denied in the presence of Pilate, when he was determined to let Him go

ABRAHAM MY FRIEND
Is 41:8 But you, Israel, are My servant, Jacob, whom I have chosen, the descendants of *Abraham My friend*

ABRAHAM YOUR FATHER
Gen 26:3 for to you and your descendants I give all these lands, and I will perform the oath which I swore to *Abraham your father*

ABRAHAM'S BOSOM

Gen 28:13 I am the Lord God of *Abraham your father* and the God of Isaac
Is 51:2 Look to *Abraham your father*, and to Sarah who bore you

ABRAHAM'S BOSOM
Luke 16:22 So it was that the beggar died, and was carried by the angels to *Abraham's bosom*

ABRAHAM'S CHILDREN
John 8:39 Jesus said to them, "If you were *Abraham's children*, you would do the works of Abraham

ABRAHAM'S SIDE (NIV)
(See *ABRAHAM'S BOSOM*)

ABSENT FROM THE LORD
2Cor 5:6 Therefore we are always confident, knowing that while we are at home in the body we are *absent from the Lord*

ABSTAIN FROM
Deut 23:22 But if you *abstain from* vowing, it shall not be sin to you
Acts 15:20 but that we write to them to *abstain from* things polluted by idols, from sexual immorality, from things strangled, and from blood
Acts 15:29 that you *abstain from* things offered to idols, from blood, from things strangled, and from sexual immorality
1Th 4:3 For this is the will of God, your sanctification: that you should *abstain from* sexual immorality
1Th 5:22 *Abstain from* every form of evil
1Tim 4:3 forbidding to marry, and commanding to *abstain from* foods which God created to be received with thanksgiving by those who believe and know the truth
1Pet 2:11 Beloved, I beg you as sojourners and pilgrims, *abstain from* fleshly lusts which war against the soul

ABUNDANCE OF PEACE
Ps 37:11 But the meek shall inherit the earth, and shall delight themselves in the *abundance of peace*
Ps 72:7 In His days the righteous shall flourish, and *abundance of peace*, until the moon is no more
Jer 33:6 I will heal them and reveal to them the *abundance of peace* and truth

ABUNDANCE OF THE HEART
Matt 12:34 For out of the *abundance of the heart* the mouth speaks
Luke 6:45 For out of the *abundance of the heart* his mouth speaks

ABUNDANT IN MERCY
Num 14:18 The Lord is longsuffering and *abundant in mercy*, forgiving iniquity and transgression
Ps 86:5 For You, Lord, are good, and ready to forgive, and *abundant in mercy* to all those who call upon You
Ps 86:15 But You, O Lord, are a God full of compassion, and gracious, longsuffering and *abundant in mercy* and truth

ABUNDANT PROSPERITY (RSV)
(See *ABUNDANCE OF PEACE*)

ACCEPT HIM WHOSE FAITH IS WEAK (NIV)
(See *RECEIVE ONE WHO IS WEAK*)

ACCEPT HIS PERSON (RSV)
(See *SHOW PARTIALITY*)

ACCEPT MY WORDS (RSV)
(See *RECEIVE MY SAYINGS*)

ACCEPT THIS ATONEMENT (NIV)
(See *PROVIDE ATONEMENT*)

ACCEPT WHAT I SAY (NIV)
(See *RECEIVE MY SAYINGS*)

ACCEPTABLE TO THE LORD
Prov 21:3 To do righteousness and justice is more *acceptable to the Lord* than sacrifice
Eph 5:10 proving what is *acceptable to the Lord*

ACCEPTABLE YEAR
Is 61:2 to proclaim the *acceptable year* of the Lord, and the day of vengeance of our God
Luke 4:19 to preach the *acceptable year* of the Lord

ACCEPTED TIME
2Cor 6:2 Behold, now is the *accepted time;* behold, now is the day of salvation

ACCEPTS MY PRAYER (RSV)
(See *RECEIVE MY PRAYER*)

ACCOMPLISH HIS VOW (KJV)
(See *FULFILL HIS VOW*)

ACCORDING TO HIS DEEDS
Prov 24:12 and will He not render to each man *according to his deeds*
Hos 12:2 The Lord also brings a charge against Judah, and will punish Jacob according to his ways; *according to his deeds* He will recompense him
Rom 2:6 who "will render to each one *according to his deeds*

ACCORDING TO HIS FOLLY
Prov 26:4 Do not answer a fool *according to his folly*, lest you also be like him
Prov 26:5 Answer a fool *according to his folly*, lest he be wise in his own eyes

ACCORDING TO HIS OWN WILL
Dan 11:16 But he who comes against him shall do *according to his own will*, and no one shall stand against him
Dan 11:36 Then the king shall do *according to his own will*
Heb 2:4 God also bearing witness both with signs and wonders, with various miracles, and gifts of the Holy Spirit, *according to His own will*

ACCORDING TO HIS WILL
Dan 4:35 He does *according to His will* in the army of heaven and among the inhabitants of the earth
Dan 8:4 nor was there any that could deliver from his hand, but he did *according to his will* and became great
Dan 11:3 Then a mighty king shall arise, who shall rule with great dominion, and do *according to his will*
Luke 12:47 And that servant who knew his master's will, and did not prepare himself or do *according to his will*, shall be beaten with many stripes
1Jn 5:14 Now this is the confidence that we have in Him, that if we ask anything *according to His will*, He hears us

ACCORDING TO ITS KIND
Gen 1:11 Then God said, "Let the earth bring forth grass, the herb that yields seed, and the fruit tree that yields fruit *according to its kind*, whose seed is in itself, on the earth

Gen 1:12 And the earth brought forth grass, the herb that yields seed *according to its kind*, and the tree that yields fruit, whose seed is in itself *according to its kind*
Gen 1:21 So God created great sea creatures and every living thing that moves, with which the waters abounded, according to their kind, and every winged bird *according to its kind*
Gen 1:24 Then God said, "Let the earth bring forth the living creature *according to its kind:* cattle and creeping thing and beast of the earth, each *according to its kind*
Gen 1:25 And God made the beast of the earth *according to its kind*, cattle *according to its kind*, and everything that creeps on the earth *according to its kind*

ACCORDING TO OUR DEEDS
Zech 1:6 Just as the Lord of hosts determined to do to us, according to our ways and *according to our deeds*, so He has dealt with us

ACCORDING TO THE COMMAND OF THE LORD
Num 9:20 *according to the command of the Lord* they would remain encamped, and *according to the command of the Lord* they would journey
Num 10:13 So they started out for the first time *according to the command of the Lord* by the hand of Moses
Num 13:3 So Moses sent them from the Wilderness of Paran *according to the command of the Lord*, all of them men who were heads of the children of Israel

ACCORDING TO THE FLESH
John 8:15 You judge *according to the flesh;* I judge no one
Acts 2:30 Therefore, being a prophet, and knowing that God had sworn with an oath to him that of the fruit of his body, *according to the flesh*, He would raise up the Christ to sit on his throne
Rom 1:3 concerning His Son Jesus Christ our Lord, who was born of the seed of David *according to the flesh*
Rom 4:1 What then shall we say that Abraham our father has found *according to the flesh*
Rom 8:1 There is therefore now no condemnation to those who are in Christ Jesus, who do not walk *according to the flesh*, but according to the Spirit
Rom 8:4 that the righteous requirement of the law might be fulfilled in us who do not walk *according to the flesh* but according to the Spirit
Rom 8:5 For those who live *according to the flesh* set their minds on the things of the flesh, but those who live according to the Spirit, the things of the Spirit
Rom 8:12 Therefore, brethren, we are debtors not to the flesh, to live *according to the flesh*
Rom 8:13 For if you live *according to the flesh* you will die
Rom 9:3 For I could wish that I myself were accursed from Christ for my brethren, my kinsmen *according to the flesh*
Rom 9:5 of whom are the fathers and from whom, *according to the flesh*, Christ came, who is over all, the eternally blessed God
1Cor 1:26 For you see your calling, brethren, that not many wise *according to the flesh*, not many mighty, not many noble, are called
2Cor 1:17 Or the things I plan, do I plan *according to the flesh*, that with me there should be Yes, Yes, and No, No
2Cor 5:16 Therefore, from now on, we regard no one *according to the flesh*. Even though we have known Christ *according to the flesh*, yet now we know Him thus no longer
2Cor 10:2 But I beg you that when I am present I may not be bold with that confidence by which I intend to be bold against some, who think of us as if we walked *according to the flesh*
2Cor 10:3 For though we walk in the flesh, we do not war *according to the flesh*
2Cor 11:18 Seeing that many boast *according to the flesh*, I also will boast
Gal 4:23 But he who was of the bondwoman was born *according to the flesh*, and he of the freewoman through promise
Gal 4:29 But, as he who was born *according to the flesh* then persecuted him who was born according to the Spirit, even so it is now
Eph 6:5 Servants, be obedient to those who are your masters *according to the flesh*, with fear and trembling, in sincerity of heart, as to Christ
Col 3:22 Servants, obey in all things your masters *according to the flesh*, not with eyeservice, as men-pleasers, but in sincerity of heart, fearing God
2Pet 2:10 and especially those who walk *according to the flesh* in the lust of uncleanness and despise authority

ACCORDING TO THE LAW
Num 6:21 according to the vow which he takes, so he must do *according to the law* of his separation
2Chr 30:16 They stood in their place according to their custom, *according to the Law* of Moses the man of God
Ezra 10:3 Now therefore, let us make a covenant with our God to put away all these wives and those who have been born to them, according to the counsel of my master and of those who tremble at the commandment of our God; and let it be done *according to the law*
Jer 32:11 So I took the purchase deed, both that which was sealed *according to the law* and custom, and that which was open
Dan 6:8 Now, O king, establish the decree and sign the writing, so that it cannot be changed, *according to the law* of the Medes and Persians, which does not alter
Dan 6:12 The king answered and said, "The thing is true, *according to the law* of the Medes and Persians, which does not alter
Luke 2:22 Now when the days of her purification *according to the law* of Moses were completed, they brought Him to Jerusalem to present Him to the Lord
Luke 2:39 So when they had performed all things *according to the law* of the Lord, they returned to Galilee, to their own city, Nazareth
Acts 22:12 Then one, Ananias, a devout man *according to the law*, having a good testimony with all the Jews who dwelt there
Acts 23:3 For you sit to judge me *according to the law*, and do you command me to be struck contrary to the law
Heb 7:5 And indeed those who are of the sons of Levi, who receive the priesthood, have a commandment to receive tithes from the people *according to the law*, that is, from their brethren, though they have come from the loins of Abraham
Heb 7:16 who has come, not *according to the law* of a fleshly commandment, but according to the power of an endless life
Heb 8:4 For if He were on earth, He would not be a priest, since there are priests who offer the gifts *according to the law*
Heb 9:19 For when Moses had spoken every precept to all the people *according to the law*, he took the blood of calves and goats, with water, scarlet wool, and hyssop, and sprinkled both the book itself and all the people
Heb 9:22 And *according to the law* almost all

things are purged with blood, and without shedding of blood there is no remission

Heb 10:8 Previously saying, "Sacrifice and offering, burnt offerings, and offerings for sin You did not desire, nor had pleasure in them" (which are offered *according to the law*

ACCORDING TO THE PATTERN

Ex 25:40 And see to it that you make them *according to the pattern* which was shown you on the mountain

Num 8:4 *According to the pattern* which the Lord had shown Moses, so he made the lampstand

Acts 7:44 Our fathers had the tabernacle of witness in the wilderness, as He appointed, instructing Moses to make it *according to the pattern* that he had seen

Heb 8:5 For He said, "See that you make all things *according to the pattern* shown you on the mountain

ACCORDING TO THE SCRIPTURES

1Cor 15:3 that Christ died for our sins *according to the Scriptures*

1Cor 15:4 and that He was buried, and that He rose again the third day *according to the Scriptures*

ACCORDING TO THE WORD OF THE LORD

Num 3:16 So Moses numbered them *according to the word of the Lord*, as he was commanded

Num 3:51 And Moses gave their redemption money to Aaron and his sons, *according to the word of the Lord*, as the Lord commanded Moses

Num 4:45 These are the ones who were numbered of the families of the sons of Merari, whom Moses and Aaron numbered *according to the word of the Lord* by the hand of Moses

Num 36:5 Then Moses commanded the children of Israel *according to the word of the Lord*, saying

Deut 34:5 So Moses the servant of the Lord died there in the land of Moab, *according to the word of the Lord*

Josh 8:27 Only the livestock and the spoil of that city Israel took as booty for themselves, *according to the word of the Lord* which He had commanded Joshua

Josh 19:50 *According to the word of the Lord* they gave him the city which he asked for, Timnath Serah in the mountains of Ephraim

Josh 22:9 So the children of Reuben, the children of Gad, and half the tribe of Manasseh returned, and departed from the children of Israel at Shiloh, which is in the land of Canaan, to go to the country of Gilead, to the land of their possession, which they possessed *according to the word of the Lord* by the hand of Moses

1Kin 12:24 Therefore they obeyed the word of the Lord, and turned back, *according to the word of the Lord*

1Kin 13:26 Therefore the Lord has delivered him to the lion, which has torn him and killed him, *according to the word of the Lord* which He spoke to him

1Kin 14:18 and all Israel mourned for him, *according to the word of the Lord* which He spoke through His servant Ahijah the prophet

1Kin 15:29 He did not leave to Jeroboam anyone that breathed, until he had destroyed him, *according to the word of the Lord* which He had spoken by His servant Ahijah the Shilonite

1Kin 16:12 Thus Zimri destroyed all the household of Baasha, *according to the word of the Lord*, which He spoke against Baasha by Jehu the prophet

1Kin 16:34 He laid its foundation with Abiram his firstborn, and with his youngest son Segub he set up its gates, *according to the word of the Lord*, which He had spoken through Joshua the son of Nun

1Kin 17:5 So he went and did *according to the word of the Lord*, for he went and stayed by the Brook Cherith, which flows into the Jordan

1Kin 17:16 The bin of flour was not used up, nor did the jar of oil run dry, *according to the word of the Lord* which He spoke by Elijah

1Kin 22:38 Then someone washed the chariot at a pool in Samaria, and the dogs licked up his blood while the harlots bathed, *according to the word of the Lord* which He had spoken

2Kin 1:17 So Ahaziah died *according to the word of the Lord* which Elijah had spoken

2Kin 4:44 and they ate and had some left over, *according to the word of the Lord*

2Kin 7:16 So a seah of fine flour was sold for a shekel, and two seahs of barley for a shekel, *according to the word of the Lord*

2Kin 9:26 Now therefore, take and throw him on the plot of ground, *according to the word of the Lord*

2Kin 10:17 And when he came to Samaria, he killed all who remained to Ahab in Samaria, till he had destroyed them, *according to the word of the Lord* which He spoke to Elijah

2Kin 14:25 He restored the territory of Israel from the entrance of Hamath to the Sea of the Arabah, *according to the word of the Lord* God of Israel, which He had spoken through His servant Jonah the son of Amittai, the prophet who was from Gath Hepher

2Kin 23:16 And he sent and took the bones out of the tombs and burned them on the altar, and defiled it *according to the word of the Lord* which the man of God proclaimed, who proclaimed these words

2Kin 24:2 He sent them against Judah to destroy it, *according to the word of the Lord* which He had spoken by His servants the prophets

1Chr 11:3 Then they anointed David king over Israel, *according to the word of the Lord* by Samuel

1Chr 11:10 Now these were the heads of the mighty men whom David had, who strengthened themselves with him in his kingdom, with all Israel, to make him king, *according to the word of the Lord* concerning Israel

1Chr 12:23 Now these were the numbers of the divisions that were equipped for the war, and came to David at Hebron to turn over the kingdom of Saul to him, *according to the word of the Lord*

1Chr 15:15 And the children of the Levites bore the ark of God on their shoulders, by its poles, as Moses had commanded *according to the word of the Lord*

2Chr 35:6 So slaughter the Passover offerings, sanctify yourselves, and prepare them for your brethren, that they may do *according to the word of the Lord* by the hand of Moses

Jer 13:2 So I got a sash *according to the word of the Lord*, and put it around my waist

Jer 32:8 Then Hanameel my uncle's son came to me in the court of the prison *according to the word of the Lord*, and said to me

Jon 3:3 So Jonah arose and went to Nineveh, *according to the word of the Lord*

ACCORDING TO THEIR DEEDS

Ps 28:4 Give to them *according to their deeds*, and according to the wickedness of their endeavors

Is 59:18 *According to their deeds*, accordingly He will repay, fury to His adversaries, recompense to His enemies

Jer 25:14 and I will repay them *according to their deeds* and according to the works of their own hands

ACCORDING TO THEIR FATHERS' HOUSES (RSV)
(See *HOUSE OF HIS FATHER*)

ACCORDING TO THEIR WORK (NAS, RSV)
(See *ACCORDING TO THEIR DEEDS*)

ACCORDING TO THY STEADFAST LOVE (RSV)
(See *ACCORDING TO YOUR LOVINGKINDNESS*)

ACCORDING TO WHAT HE HAS DONE
2Cor 5:10 For we must all appear before the judgment seat of Christ, that each one may receive the things done in the body, *according to what he has done*, whether good or bad

ACCORDING TO YOUR DEEDS
Ezek 24:14 according to your ways and *according to your deeds* they will judge you

ACCORDING TO YOUR FAITH
Matt 9:29 Then He touched their eyes, saying, *"According to your faith* let it be to you

ACCORDING TO YOUR LOVINGKINDNESS
Ps 51:1 Have mercy upon me, O God, *according to Your lovingkindness*
Ps 119:88 Revive me *according to Your lovingkindness*, so that I may keep the testimony of Your mouth
Ps 119:149 Hear my voice *according to Your lovingkindness;* O Lord, revive me according to Your justice
Ps 119:159 Consider how I love Your precepts; revive me, O Lord, *according to Your lovingkindness*

ACCORDING TO YOUR UNFAILING LOVE (NIV)
(See *ACCORDING TO YOUR LOVINGKINDNESS*)

ACCOUNTED TO HIM
Ps 106:31 And that was *accounted to him* for righteousness to all generations forevermore
Rom 4:3 Abraham believed God, and it was *accounted to him* for righteousness
Rom 4:22 And therefore "it was *accounted to him* for righteousness
Gal 3:6 just as Abraham "believed God, and it was *accounted to him* for righteousness
Jas 2:23 And the Scripture was fulfilled which says, "Abraham believed God, and it was *accounted to him* for righteousness

ACCOUNTING FOR THE LIFE OF HIS FELLOW MAN (NIV)
(See *REQUIRE THE LIFE OF MAN*)

ACCREDITED BY GOD (NIV)
(See *ATTESTED BY GOD*)

ACKNOWLEDGE AND TAKE TO HEART THIS DAY (NIV)
(See *KNOW THIS DAY*)

ACKNOWLEDGES THE SON
1Jn 2:23 Whoever denies the Son does not have the Father either; he who *acknowledges the Son* has the Father also

ACQUIRE SKILL (RSV)
(See *WISE COUNSEL*)

ACT AS KING (NIV)
(See *EXERCISE AUTHORITY*)

ACTED LIKE A FOOL (NIV)
(See *PLAYED THE FOOL*)

ACTS OF THE SINFUL NATURE (NIV)
(See *WORKS OF THE FLESH*)

ADAM KNEW EVE
Gen 4:1 Now *Adam knew Eve* his wife, and she conceived and bore Cain, and said

ADAM WAS FORMED FIRST
1Tim 2:13 For *Adam was formed first*, then Eve

ADD FIELD TO FIELD
Is 5:8 Woe to those who join house to house, who *add field to field*, till there is no place Where they may dwell alone in the midst of the land

ADD SIN TO SIN
Is 30:1 Woe to the rebellious children," says the Lord, "Who take counsel, but not of Me, and who devise plans, but not of My Spirit, that they may *add sin to sin*

ADD TO IT NOR TAKE AWAY FROM IT
Deut 12:32 you shall not *add to it nor take away from it*

ADD TO YOUR FAITH
2Pet 1:5 But also for this very reason, giving all diligence, *add to your faith* virtue, to virtue knowledge

ADDED TO THE CHURCH
Acts 2:47 And the Lord *added to the church* daily those who were being saved

ADDED TO THEIR NUMBER (RSV)
(See *ADDED TO THE CHURCH*)

ADMINISTER JUDGMENT (NIV)
(See *EXECUTE JUDGMENT*)

ADOPTION AS SONS
Gal 4:5 to redeem those who were under the law, that we might receive the *adoption as sons*
Eph 1:5 having predestined us to *adoption as sons* by Jesus Christ to Himself, according to the good pleasure of His will

ADORNED THE HEAVENS
Job 26:13 By His Spirit He *adorned the heavens;* His hand pierced the fleeing serpent

ADULTEROUS GENERATION
Matt 12:39 But He answered and said to them, "An evil and *adulterous generation* seeks after a sign, and no sign will be given to it except the sign of the prophet Jonah
Matt 16:4 A wicked and *adulterous generation* seeks after a sign, and no sign shall be given to it except the sign of the prophet Jonah

ADVANCED IN YEARS
Josh 13:1 Now Joshua was old, *advanced in years*. And the Lord said to him: "You are old, *advanced in years*, and there remains very much land yet to be possessed
1Sam 17:12 And the man was old, *advanced in years*, in the days of Saul
1Kin 1:1 Now King David was old, *advanced in years;* and they put covers on him, but he could not get warm
Luke 1:7 But they had no child, because Elizabeth was barren, and they were both well *advanced in years*
Luke 1:18 For I am an old man, and my wife is well *advanced in years*

AFFAIRS OF THIS LIFE
2Tim 2:4 No one engaged in warfare entangles himself with the *affairs of this life*, that he may please him who enlisted him as a soldier

AFFLICT HIS SOUL
Is 58:5 Is it a fast that I have chosen, a day for a man to *afflict his soul*

AFFLICT YOUR SOULS
Lev 16:29 In the seventh month, on the tenth day of the month, you shall *afflict your souls*, and do no work at all, whether a native of your own country or a stranger who sojourns among you
Lev 16:31 It is a sabbath of solemn rest for you, and you shall *afflict your souls*
Lev 23:27 you shall *afflict your souls*, and offer an offering made by fire to the Lord
Lev 23:32 It shall be to you a sabbath of solemn rest, and you shall *afflict your souls*
Num 29:7 You shall *afflict your souls;* you shall not do any work

AFFLICT YOURSELVES (RSV)
(See *AFFLICT YOUR SOULS*)

AFFLICTED THEIR RIGHT (RSV)
(See *JUSTICE TO THE OPPRESSED*)

AFFLICTION OF MY PEOPLE (KJV, NAS, RSV)
(See *OPPRESSION OF MY PEOPLE*)

AFFLICTION OF OUR FATHERS
Neh 9:9 You saw the *affliction of our fathers* in Egypt, and heard their cry by the Red Sea

AFFLICTION OF YOUR MAIDSERVANT
1Sam 1:11 Then she made a vow and said, "O Lord of hosts, if You will indeed look on the *affliction of your maidservant* and remember me, and not forget your maidservant, but will give your maidservant a male child, then I will give him to the Lord all the days of his life, and no razor shall come upon his head

AFLAME WITH PASSION (RSV)
(See *BURN WITH PASSION*)

AFTER THE DEATH OF
Gen 25:11 And it came to pass, *after the death of* Abraham, that God blessed his son Isaac
Gen 26:18 And Isaac dug again the wells of water which they had dug in the days of Abraham his father, for the Philistines had stopped them up *after the death of* Abraham
Lev 16:1 Now the Lord spoke to Moses *after the death of* the two sons of Aaron, when they offered profane fire before the Lord, and died
Num 35:28 But *after the death of* the high priest the manslayer may return to the land of his possession
Josh 1:1 *After the death of* Moses the servant of the Lord, it came to pass that the Lord spoke to Joshua the son of Nun, Moses' assistant
Judg 1:1 Now *after the death of* Joshua it came to pass that the children of Israel asked the Lord, saying
2Sam 1:1 Now it came to pass *after the death of* Saul, when David had returned from the slaughter of the Amalekites, and David had stayed two days in Ziklag
2Kin 1:1 Moab rebelled against Israel *after the death of* Ahab
2Kin 14:17 Amaziah the son of Joash, king of Judah, lived fifteen years *after the death of* Jehoash the son of Jehoahaz, king of Israel
2Chr 22:4 for they were his counselors *after the death of* his father, to his destruction
2Chr 24:17 Now *after the death of* Jehoiada the leaders of Judah came and bowed down to the king
2Chr 25:25 Amaziah the son of Joash, king of Judah, lived fifteen years *after the death of* Joash the son of Jehoahaz, king of Israel

AFTER THE FLESH (KJV)
(See *ACCORDING TO THE FLESH*)

AFTER THE PATTERN (RSV)
(See *ACCORDING TO THE PATTERN*)

AGAINST JERUSALEM
Judg 1:8 Now the children of Judah fought *against Jerusalem* and took it
1Kin 14:25 Now it happened, in the fifth year of King Rehoboam, that Shishak king of Egypt came up *against Jerusalem*
2Kin 18:17 Then the king of Assyria sent the Tartan, the Rabsaris, and the Rabshakeh from Lachish, with a great army *against Jerusalem*, to King Hezekiah
2Kin 24:10 At that time the servants of Nebuchadnezzar king of Babylon came up *against Jerusalem*, and the city was besieged
2Kin 25:1 Now it came to pass in the ninth year of his reign, in the tenth month, on the tenth day of the month, that Nebuchadnezzar king of Babylon and all his army came *against Jerusalem* and encamped against it
2Chr 12:2 And it happened, in the fifth year of King Rehoboam, that Shishak king of Egypt came up *against Jerusalem*, because they had transgressed against the Lord
2Chr 12:9 So Shishak king of Egypt came up *against Jerusalem*, and took away the treasures of the house of the Lord and the treasures of the king's house
2Chr 32:2 And when Hezekiah saw that Sennacherib had come, and that his purpose was to make war *against Jerusalem*
Ezra 4:8 Rehum the commander and Shimshai the scribe wrote a letter *against Jerusalem* to King Artaxerxes in this fashion
Jer 4:16 Make mention to the nations, yes, proclaim *against Jerusalem*, that watchers come from a far country and raise their voice against the cities of Judah
Jer 6:6 Hew down trees, and build a mound *against Jerusalem*. This is the city to be punished
Jer 34:1 The word which came to Jeremiah from the Lord, when Nebuchadnezzar king of Babylon and all his army, all the kingdoms of the earth under his dominion, and all the people, fought *against Jerusalem* and all its cities, saying
Jer 34:7 when the king of Babylon's army fought *against Jerusalem* and all the cities of Judah that were left, against Lachish and Azekah
Jer 39:1 In the ninth year of Zedekiah king of Judah, in the tenth month, Nebuchadnezzar king of Babylon and all his army came *against Jerusalem*, and besieged it
Jer 52:4 Now it came to pass in the ninth year of his reign, in the tenth month, on the tenth day of the month, that Nebuchadnezzar king of Babylon and all his army came *against Jerusalem* and encamped against it
Ezek 24:2 Son of man, write down the name of the day, this very day the king of Babylon started his siege *against Jerusalem* this very day
Ezek 26:2 Son of man, because Tyre has said *against Jerusalem*, 'Aha
Zech 12:9 It shall be in that day that I will seek to destroy all the nations that come *against Jerusalem*
Zech 14:2 For I will gather all the nations to battle *against Jerusalem*

Zech 14:12 And this shall be the plague with which the Lord will strike all the people who fought *against Jerusalem*

Zech 14:16 And it shall come to pass that everyone who is left of all the nations which came *against Jerusalem* shall go up from year to year to worship the King, the Lord of hosts, and to keep the Feast of Tabernacles

AGAINST THE JEWS

Ezra 4:23 Now when the copy of King Artaxerxes' letter was read before Rehum, Shimshai the scribe, and their companions, they went up in haste to Jerusalem *against the Jews*, and by force of arms made them cease

Esth 8:3 Now Esther spoke again to the king, fell down at his feet, and implored him with tears to counteract the evil plot of Haman the Agagite, and the scheme which he had devised *against the Jews*

Esth 9:24 because Haman, the son of Hammedatha the Agagite, the enemy of all the Jews, had plotted *against the Jews* to annihilate them, and had cast Pur (that is, the lot

Esth 9:25 but when Esther came before the king, he commanded by letter that this wicked plot which Haman had devised *against the Jews* should return on his own head, and that he and his sons should be hanged on the gallows

AGE TO COME

Matt 12:32 but whoever speaks against the Holy Spirit, it will not be forgiven him, either in this age or in the *age to come*

Mark 10:30 who shall not receive a hundredfold now in this time houses and brothers and sisters and mothers and children and lands, with persecutions and in the *age to come*, eternal life

Luke 18:30 who shall not receive many times more in this present time, and in the *age to come* everlasting life

Heb 6:5 and have tasted the good word of God and the powers of the *age to come*

AGONY IN THIS FIRE (NIV)
(See *TORMENTED IN THIS FLAME*)

AGREE WITH YOUR ADVERSARY

Matt 5:25 *Agree with your adversary* quickly, while you are on the way with him, lest your adversary deliver you to the judge, the judge hand you over to the officer, and you are thrown into prison

ALIEN IN A FOREIGN LAND (NIV)
(See *STRANGER IN A FOREIGN LAND*)

ALIEN LIVING AMONG YOU (NIV)
(See *STRANGER WHO SOJOURNS AMONG YOU*)

ALIENS AND STRANGERS (NIV)
(See *STRANGERS AND PILGRIMS*)

ALIENS WHO HAVE SETTLED AMONG YOU (NIV)
(See *STRANGERS WHO SOJOURN AMONG YOU*)

ALIVE BY THE SPIRIT

1Pet 3:18 For Christ also suffered once for sins, the just for the unjust, that He might bring us to God, being put to death in the flesh but made *alive by the Spirit*

ALIVE TOGETHER WITH HIM

Col 2:13 And you, being dead in your trespasses and the uncircumcision of your flesh, He has made *alive together with Him*, having forgiven you all trespasses

ALIVE WITH CHRIST (NIV)
(See *ALIVE TOGETHER WITH HIM*)

ALL AT ONE TIME (NIV)
(See *AS ONE MAN*)

ALL DAY LONG

Deut 28:32 Your sons and your daughters shall be given to another people, and your eyes shall look and fail with longing for them *all day long*

Ps 42:10 As with a breaking of my bones, my enemies reproach me, while they say to me *all day long*

Ps 44:8 In God we boast *all day long*, and praise Your name forever

Ps 44:22 Yet for Your sake we are killed *all day long*

Ps 73:14 For *all day long* I have been plagued, and chastened every morning

Ps 86:3 Be merciful to me, O Lord, for I cry to You *all day long*

Ps 88:17 They came around me *all day long* like water; they engulfed me altogether

Ps 89:16 In Your name they rejoice *all day long*, and in Your righteousness they are exalted

Ps 102:8 My enemies reproach me *all day long*, and those who deride me swear an oath against me

Prov 21:26 He covets greedily *all day long*, but the righteous gives and does not spare

Prov 23:17 Do not let your heart envy sinners, but in the fear of the Lord continue *all day long*

Is 65:2 I have stretched out My hands *all day long* to a rebellious people, who walk in a way that is not good, according to their own thoughts

Rom 8:36 For Your sake we are killed *all day long;* we are accounted as sheep for the slaughter

Rom 10:21 *All day long* I have stretched out My hands to a disobedient and contrary people

ALL FLESH IS GRASS

Is 40:6 *All flesh is grass*, and all its loveliness is like the flower of the field

ALL GENERATIONS

Ex 3:15 This is My name forever, and this is My memorial to *all generations*

Ps 33:11 The counsel of the Lord stands forever, the plans of His heart to *all generations*

Ps 45:17 I will make Your name to be remembered in *all generations*

Ps 49:11 Their inner thought is that their houses will continue forever, and their dwelling places to *all generations*

Ps 72:5 They shall fear You as long as the sun and moon endure, throughout *all generations*

Ps 79:13 So we, Your people and sheep of Your pasture, will give You thanks forever; we will show forth Your praise to *all generations*

Ps 85:5 Will You be angry with us forever? Will You prolong Your anger to *all generations*

Ps 89:1 With my mouth will I make known Your faithfulness to *all generations*

Ps 89:4 Your seed I will establish forever, and build up your throne to *all generations*

Ps 90:1 Lord, You have been our dwelling place in *all generations*

Ps 100:5 His mercy is everlasting, and His truth endures to *all generations*

Ps 102:12 But You, O Lord, shall endure forever, and the remembrance of Your name to *all generations*

Ps 102:24 I said, "O my God, do not take me away in the midst of my days; Your years are throughout *all generations*

Ps 106:31 And that was accounted to him for righteousness to *all generations* forevermore
Ps 119:90 Your faithfulness endures to *all generations;* You established the earth, and it abides
Ps 135:13 Your name, O Lord, endures forever, Your fame, O Lord, throughout *all generations*
Ps 145:13 Your kingdom is an everlasting kingdom, and Your dominion endures throughout *all generations*
Ps 146:10 The Lord shall reign forever Your God, O Zion, to *all generations*
Prov 27:24 for riches are not forever, nor does a crown endure to *all generations*
Luke 1:48 For He has regarded the lowly state of His maidservant; for behold, henceforth *all generations* will call me blessed

ALL HAVE COME TO PASS
Josh 23:14 *All have come to pass* for you, and not one word of them has failed

ALL IS VANITY
Eccl 1:2 Vanity of vanities," says the Preacher; "Vanity of vanities, *all is vanity*
Eccl 1:14 and indeed, *all is vanity* and grasping for the wind
Eccl 2:17 Therefore I hated life because the work that was done under the sun was grievous to me, for *all is vanity* and grasping for the wind
Eccl 3:19 man has no advantage over beasts, for *all is vanity*
Eccl 12:8 Vanity of vanities," says the Preacher, "*All is vanity*

ALL ISRAEL
Ex 18:25 And Moses chose able men out of *all Israel*, and made them heads over the people
Num 16:34 Then *all Israel* who were around them fled at their cry, for they said
Deut 1:1 These are the words which Moses spoke to *all Israel* on this side of the Jordan in the wilderness, in the plain opposite Suph, between Paran, Tophel, Laban, Hazeroth, and Dizahab
Deut 5:1 And Moses called *all Israel*, and said to them: "Hear, O Israel, the statutes and judgments which I speak in your hearing today, that you may learn them and be careful to observe them
Deut 11:6 how the earth opened its mouth and swallowed them up, their households, their tents, and all the substance that was in their possession, in the midst of *all Israel*
Deut 13:11 So *all Israel* shall hear and fear, and not again do such wickedness as this among you
Deut 18:6 And if a Levite comes from any of your gates, from where he sojourns among *all Israel*, and comes with all the desire of his mind to the place which the Lord chooses
Deut 21:21 so you shall put away the evil person from among you, and *all Israel* shall hear and fear
Deut 27:9 Then Moses and the priests, the Levites, spoke to *all Israel*, saying
Deut 29:2 Now Moses called *all Israel* and said to them: 'You have seen all that the Lord did before your eyes in the land of Egypt, to Pharaoh and to all his servants and to all his land
Deut 31:1 Then Moses went and spoke these words to *all Israel*
Deut 31:7 Then Moses called Joshua and said to him in the sight of *all Israel*
Deut 31:11 when *all Israel* comes to appear before the Lord your God in the place which He chooses, you shall read this law before *all Israel* in their hearing
Deut 32:45 Moses finished speaking all these words to *all Israel*
Deut 34:12 and by all that mighty power and all the great terror which Moses performed in the sight of *all Israel*
Josh 3:7 And the Lord said to Joshua, "This day I will begin to magnify you in the sight of *all Israel*, that they may know that, as I was with Moses, so I will be with you
Josh 3:17 and *all Israel* crossed over on dry ground, until all the people had crossed completely over the Jordan
Josh 4:14 On that day the Lord magnified Joshua in the sight of *all Israel*
Josh 7:24 Then Joshua, and *all Israel* with him, took Achan the son of Zerah, the silver, the garment, the wedge of gold, his sons, his daughters, his oxen, his donkeys, his sheep, his tent, and all that he had, and they brought them to the Valley of Achor
Josh 7:25 So *all Israel* stoned him with stones; and they burned them with fire after they had stoned them with stones
Josh 8:15 And Joshua and *all Israel* made as if they were beaten before them, and fled by the way of the wilderness
Josh 8:21 Now when Joshua and *all Israel* saw that the ambush had taken the city and that the smoke of the city ascended, they turned back and struck down the men of Ai
Josh 8:33 Then *all Israel*, with their elders and officers and judges, stood on either side of the ark before the priests, the Levites, who bore the ark of the covenant of the Lord, the stranger as well as he who was born among them
Josh 10:15 Then Joshua returned, and *all Israel* with him, to the camp at Gilgal
Josh 10:29 Then Joshua passed from Makkedah, and *all Israel* with him, to Libnah
Josh 10:31 Then Joshua passed from Libnah, and *all Israel* with him, to Lachish
Josh 10:34 From Lachish Joshua passed to Eglon, and *all Israel* with him
Josh 10:36 Then Joshua went up from Eglon, and *all Israel* with him, to Hebron
Josh 10:38 Then Joshua returned, and *all Israel* with him, to Debir
Josh 10:43 Then Joshua returned, and *all Israel* with him, to the camp at Gilgal
Josh 23:2 And Joshua called for *all Israel*, for their elders, for their heads, for their judges, and for their officers, and said to them
Judg 8:27 And *all Israel* played the harlot with it there. It became a snare to Gideon and to his house
Judg 20:34 And ten thousand select men from *all Israel* came against Gibeah, and the battle was fierce
1Sam 2:22 and he heard everything his sons did to *all Israel*, and how they lay with the women who assembled at the door of the tabernacle of meeting
1Sam 3:20 And *all Israel* from Dan to Beersheba knew that Samuel had been established as a prophet of the Lord
1Sam 4:1 And the word of Samuel came to *all Israel*. Now Israel went out to battle against the Philistines, and encamped beside Ebenezer
1Sam 4:5 And when the ark of the covenant of the Lord came into the camp, *all Israel* shouted so loudly that the earth shook
1Sam 7:5 And Samuel said, "Gather *all Israel* to Mizpah, and I will pray to the Lord for you
1Sam 11:2 And Nahash the Ammonite answered them, "On this condition I will make a covenant with you, that I may put out all your right eyes, and bring reproach on *all Israel*
1Sam 12:1 Now Samuel said to *all Israel:* "Indeed I have heeded your voice in all that you said to me, and have made a king over you
1Sam 13:4 Now *all Israel* heard it said that Saul

had attacked a garrison of the Philistines, and that Israel had also become an abomination to the Philistines
1Sam 14:40 Then he said to *all Israel*, "You be on one side, and my son Jonathan and I will be on the other side
1Sam 17:11 When Saul and *all Israel* heard these words of the Philistine, they were dismayed and greatly afraid
1Sam 18:16 But *all Israel* and Judah loved David, because he went out and came in before them
1Sam 19:5 For he took his life in his hands and killed the Philistine, and the Lord brought about a great salvation for *all Israel*
1Sam 24:2 Then Saul took three thousand chosen men from *all Israel*, and went to seek David and his men on the Rocks of the Wild Goats
1Sam 28:3 Now Samuel had died, and *all Israel* had lamented for him and buried him in Ramah, in his own city
1Sam 28:4 So Saul gathered *all Israel* together, and they encamped at Gilboa
2Sam 2:9 and he made him king over Gilead, over the Ashurites, over Jezreel, over Ephraim, over Benjamin, and over *all Israel*
2Sam 3:12 saying also, "Make your covenant with me, and indeed my hand shall be with you to bring *all Israel* to you
2Sam 3:21 Then Abner said to David, "I will arise and go, and gather *all Israel* to my lord the king, that they may make a covenant with you, and that you may reign over all that your heart desires
2Sam 3:37 For all the people and *all Israel* understood that day that it had not been the king's intent to kill Abner the son of Ner
2Sam 4:1 And when Saul's son heard that Abner had died in Hebron, he lost heart, and *all Israel* was troubled
2Sam 5:5 In Hebron he reigned over Judah seven years and six months, and in Jerusalem he reigned thirty-three years over *all Israel* and Judah
2Sam 8:15 So David reigned over *all Israel;* and David administered judgment and justice to all his people
2Sam 10:17 When it was told David, he gathered *all Israel*, crossed over the Jordan, and came to Helam
2Sam 11:1 Now it came to pass in the spring of the year, at the time when kings go out to battle, that David sent Joab and his servants with him, and *all Israel*
2Sam 12:12 For you did it secretly, but I will do this thing before *all Israel*, before the sun
2Sam 14:25 Now in *all Israel* there was no one who was praised as much as Absalom for his good looks
2Sam 15:6 In this manner Absalom acted toward *all Israel* who came to the king for judgment
2Sam 16:21 and *all Israel* will hear that you are abhorred by your father
2Sam 16:22 So they pitched a tent for Absalom on the top of the house, and Absalom went in to his father's concubines in the sight of *all Israel*
2Sam 17:10 For *all Israel* knows that your father is a mighty man, and those who are with him are valiant men
2Sam 17:11 Therefore I counsel that *all Israel* be fully gathered to you, from Dan to Beersheba, like the sand that is by the sea for multitude, and that you go to battle in person
2Sam 17:13 Moreover, if he has withdrawn into a city, then *all Israel* shall bring ropes to that city
2Sam 18:17 And they took Absalom and cast him into a large pit in the woods, and laid a very large heap of stones over him. Then *all Israel* fled, everyone to his tent
2Sam 19:11 Then King David sent to Zadok and Abiathar the priests, saying, "Speak to the elders of Judah, saying, 'Why are you the last to bring the king back to his house, since the words of *all Israel* have come to the king, even to his house
1Kin 1:20 And as for you, my lord, O king, the eyes of *all Israel* are on you, that you should tell them who will sit on the throne of my lord the king after him
1Kin 2:15 Then he said, "You know that the kingdom was mine, and *all Israel* had set their expectations on me, that I should reign
1Kin 3:28 And *all Israel* heard of the judgment which the king had rendered
1Kin 4:1 So King Solomon was king over *all Israel*
1Kin 4:7 And Solomon had twelve governors over *all Israel*, who provided food for the king and his household
1Kin 5:13 Then King Solomon raised up a labor force out of *all Israel*
1Kin 8:62 Then the king and *all Israel* with him offered sacrifices before the Lord
1Kin 8:65 At that time Solomon held a feast, and *all Israel* with him, a great congregation from the entrance of Hamath to the Brook of Egypt, before the Lord our God, seven days and seven more days fourteen days
1Kin 11:16 (because for six months Joab remained there with *all Israel*, until he had cut down every male in Edom
1Kin 11:42 And the period that Solomon reigned in Jerusalem over *all Israel* was forty years
1Kin 12:1 Now Rehoboam went to Shechem, for *all Israel* had gone to Shechem to make him king
1Kin 12:16 Now when *all Israel* saw that the king did not listen to them, the people answered the king, saying
1Kin 12:18 but *all Israel* stoned him with stones, and he died
1Kin 12:20 Now it came to pass when *all Israel* heard that Jeroboam had come back, they sent for him and called him to the congregation, and made him king over *all Israel*
1Kin 14:13 And *all Israel* shall mourn for him and bury him, for he is the only one of Jeroboam who shall come to the grave, because in him there is found something good toward the Lord God of Israel in the house of Jeroboam
1Kin 14:18 and *all Israel* mourned for him, according to the word of the Lord which He spoke through His servant Ahijah the prophet
1Kin 15:27 And Baasha killed him at Gibbethon, which belonged to the Philistines, while Nadab and *all Israel* laid siege to Gibbethon
1Kin 15:33 In the third year of Asa king of Judah, Baasha the son of Ahijah became king over *all Israel* in Tirzah, and reigned twenty-four years
1Kin 16:16 So *all Israel* made Omri, the commander of the army, king over Israel that day in the camp
1Kin 16:17 Then Omri and *all Israel* with him went up from Gibbethon, and they besieged Tirzah
1Kin 18:19 Now therefore, send and gather *all Israel* to me on Mount Carmel, the four hundred and fifty prophets of Baal, and the four hundred prophets of Asherah, who eat at Jezebel's table
1Kin 22:17 Then he said, "I saw *all Israel* scattered on the mountains, as sheep that have no shepherd
2Kin 3:6 So King Jehoram went out of Samaria at that time and mustered *all Israel*
2Kin 9:14 (Now Joram had been defending Ramoth Gilead, he and *all Israel*, against Hazael king of Syria
2Kin 10:21 Then Jehu sent throughout *all Israel;* and all the worshipers of Baal came, so that there was not a man left who did not come

1Chr 9:1 So *all Israel* was recorded by genealogies, and indeed, they were inscribed in the book of the kings of Israel

1Chr 11:1 Then *all Israel* came together to David at Hebron, saying

1Chr 11:4 And David and *all Israel* went to Jerusalem, which is Jebus, where the Jebusites were, the inhabitants of the land

1Chr 11:10 Now these were the heads of the mighty men whom David had, who strengthened themselves with him in his kingdom, with *all Israel*, to make him king, according to the word of the Lord concerning Israel

1Chr 12:38 All these men of war, who could keep ranks, came to Hebron with a loyal heart, to make David king over *all Israel*

1Chr 13:5 So David gathered *all Israel* together, from Shihor in Egypt to as far as the entrance of Hamath, to bring the ark of God from Kirjath Jearim

1Chr 13:6 And David and *all Israel* went up to Baalah, to Kirjath Jearim, which belonged to Judah, to bring up from there the ark of God the Lord, who dwells between the cherubim, where His name is proclaimed

1Chr 13:8 Then David and *all Israel* played music before God with all their might, with singing, on harps, on stringed instruments, on tambourines, on cymbals, and with trumpets

1Chr 14:8 Now when the Philistines heard that David had been anointed king over *all Israel*, all the Philistines went up to search for David

1Chr 15:3 And David gathered *all Israel* together at Jerusalem, to bring up the ark of the Lord to its place, which he had prepared for it

1Chr 15:28 Thus *all Israel* brought up the ark of the covenant of the Lord with shouting and with the sound of the horn, with trumpets and with cymbals, making music with stringed instruments and harps

1Chr 17:6 Wherever I have moved about with *all Israel*, have I ever spoken a word to any of the judges of Israel, whom I commanded to shepherd My people, saying

1Chr 18:14 So David reigned over *all Israel*, and administered judgment and justice to all his people

1Chr 19:17 When it was told David, he gathered *all Israel*, crossed over the Jordan and came upon them, and set up in battle array against them

1Chr 21:4 Therefore Joab departed and went throughout *all Israel* and came to Jerusalem

1Chr 21:5 *All Israel* had one million one hundred thousand men who drew the sword, and Judah had four hundred and seventy thousand men who drew the sword

1Chr 28:4 and of the house of Judah, the house of my father, and among the sons of my father, He was pleased with me to make me king over *all Israel*

1Chr 28:8 Now therefore, in the sight of *all Israel*, the congregation of the Lord, and in the hearing of our God, be careful to seek out all the commandments of the Lord your God, that you may possess this good land, and leave it as an inheritance for your children after you forever

1Chr 29:21 a thousand bulls, a thousand rams, a thousand lambs, with their drink offerings, and sacrifices in abundance for *all Israel*

1Chr 29:23 Then Solomon sat on the throne of the Lord as king instead of David his father, and prospered; and *all Israel* obeyed him

1Chr 29:25 So the Lord exalted Solomon exceedingly in the sight of *all Israel*, and bestowed on him such royal majesty as had not been on any king before him in Israel

1Chr 29:26 Thus David the son of Jesse reigned over *all Israel*

2Chr 1:2 And Solomon spoke to *all Israel*, to the captains of thousands and of hundreds, to the judges, and to every leader in *all Israel*, the heads of the fathers' houses

2Chr 7:6 The priests sounded trumpets opposite them, while *all Israel* stood

2Chr 7:8 At that time Solomon kept the feast seven days, and *all Israel* with him, a very great congregation from the entrance of Hamath to the Brook of Egypt

2Chr 9:30 Solomon reigned in Jerusalem over *all Israel* forty years

2Chr 10:1 And Rehoboam went to Shechem, for *all Israel* had gone to Shechem to make him king

2Chr 10:3 And Jeroboam and *all Israel* came and spoke to Rehoboam, saying

2Chr 10:16 Now when *all Israel* saw that the king did not listen to them, the people answered the king, saying: "What portion have we in David? We have no inheritance in the son of Jesse. Every man to your tents, O Israel! Now see to your own house, O David!" So *all Israel* departed to their tents

2Chr 11:3 Speak to Rehoboam the son of Solomon, king of Judah, and to *all Israel* in Judah and Benjamin, saying

2Chr 11:13 And from all their territories the priests and the Levites who were in *all Israel* took their stand with him

2Chr 12:1 Now it came to pass, when Rehoboam had established the kingdom and had strengthened himself, that he forsook the law of the Lord, and *all Israel* along with him

2Chr 13:4 Then Abijah stood on Mount Zemaraim, which is in the mountains of Ephraim, and said, "Hear me, Jeroboam and *all Israel*

2Chr 13:15 and as the men of Judah shouted, it happened that God struck Jeroboam and *all Israel* before Abijah and Judah

2Chr 18:16 Then he said, "I saw *all Israel* scattered on the mountains, as sheep that have no shepherd

2Chr 24:5 Then he gathered the priests and the Levites, and said to them, "Go out to the cities of Judah, and gather from *all Israel* money to repair the house of your God from year to year, and see that you do it quickly

2Chr 28:23 But they were the ruin of him and of *all Israel*

2Chr 29:24 and they presented their blood on the altar as a sin offering to make an atonement for *all Israel*, for the king commanded that the burnt offering and the sin offering be made for *all Israel*

2Chr 30:1 And Hezekiah sent to *all Israel* and Judah, and also wrote letters to Ephraim and Manasseh, that they should come to the house of the Lord at Jerusalem, to keep the Passover to the Lord God of Israel

2Chr 30:5 So they resolved to make a proclamation throughout *all Israel*, from Beersheba to Dan, that they should come to keep the Passover to the Lord God of Israel at Jerusalem, since they had not done it for a long time in the prescribed manner

2Chr 30:6 Then the runners went throughout *all Israel* and Judah with the letters from the king and his leaders, and spoke according to the commandment of the king

2Chr 31:1 Now when all this was finished, *all Israel* who were present went out to the cities of Judah and broke the sacred pillars in pieces, cut down the wooden images, and threw down the high places and the altars from all Judah, Benjamin, Ephraim, and Manasseh until they had utterly destroyed them all

2Chr 35:3 Then he said to the Levites who taught *all Israel*, who were holy to the Lord

Ezra 2:70 So the priests and the Levites, some of

the people, the singers, the gatekeepers, and the Nethinim, dwelt in their cities, and *all Israel* in their cities

Ezra 6:17 And they offered sacrifices at the dedication of this house of God, one hundred bulls, two hundred rams, four hundred lambs, and as a sin offering for *all Israel* twelve male goats, according to the number of the tribes of Israel

Ezra 8:25 and weighed out to them the silver, the gold, and the articles, the offering for the house of our God which the king and his counselors and his princes, and *all Israel* who were present, had offered

Ezra 8:35 twelve bulls for *all Israel*, ninety-six rams, seventy-seven lambs, and twelve male goats as a sin offering

Ezra 10:5 Then Ezra arose, and made the leaders of the priests, the Levites, and *all Israel* swear an oath that they would do according to this word

Neh 7:73 So the priests, the Levites, the gatekeepers, the singers, some of the people, the Nethinim, and *all Israel* dwelt in their cities

Neh 12:47 In the days of Zerubbabel and in the days of Nehemiah *all Israel* gave the portions for the singers and the gatekeepers, a portion for each day

Neh 13:26 and God made him king over *all Israel*. Nevertheless pagan women caused even him to sin

Dan 9:7 O Lord, righteousness belongs to You, but to us shame of face, as it is this day to the men of Judah, to the inhabitants of Jerusalem and *all Israel*, those near and those far off in all the countries to which You have driven them, because of the unfaithfulness which they have committed against You

Dan 9:11 Yes, *all Israel* has transgressed Your law, and has departed so as not to obey Your voice

Mal 4:4 Remember the Law of Moses, My servant, which I commanded him in Horeb for *all Israel*, with the statutes and judgments

Rom 9:6 For they are not *all Israel* who are of Israel

Rom 11:26 And so *all Israel* will be saved, as it is written

ALL ISRAEL WILL BE SAVED

Rom 11:26 And so *all Israel will be saved*, as it is written

ALL KINGS SHALL FALL DOWN BEFORE HIM

Ps 72:11 Yes, *all kings shall fall down before Him;* all nations shall serve Him

ALL LOVE BRIBES (NIV)

(See *EVERYONE LOVES BRIBES*)

ALL MEN ARE LIKE GRASS (NIV)

(See *ALL FLESH IS GRASS*)

ALL NATIONS SHALL SERVE HIM

Ps 72:11 Yes, all kings shall fall down before Him; *all nations shall serve Him*

Jer 27:7 So *all nations shall serve him* and his son and his son's son, until the time of his land comes

ALL RETURN TO DUST

Eccl 3:20 all are from the dust, and *all return to dust*

ALL SCRIPTURE IS GIVEN BY INSPIRATION

2Tim 3:16 *All Scripture is given by inspiration* of God, and is profitable for doctrine, for reproof, for correction, for instruction in righteousness

ALL SHOULD COME TO REPENTANCE

2Pet 3:9 The Lord is not slack concerning His promise, as some count slackness, but is longsuffering toward us, not willing that any should perish but that *all should come to repentance*

ALL THAT GOD COMMANDED

Gen 6:22 according to *all that God commanded* him, so he did

ALL THAT THE LORD COMMANDED

Gen 7:5 And Noah did according to *all that the Lord commanded* him

Num 1:54 according to *all that the Lord commanded* Moses, so they did

Num 2:34 Thus the children of Israel did according to *all that the Lord commanded* Moses

Num 8:20 according to *all that the Lord commanded* Moses concerning the Levites, so the children of Israel did to them

Num 9:5 according to *all that the Lord commanded* Moses, so the children of Israel did

ALL THE COUNSEL OF GOD (KJV)

(See *WHOLE COUNSEL OF GOD*)

ALL THE DAYS OF HIS LIFE

Deut 17:19 And it shall be with him, and he shall read it *all the days of his life*, that he may learn to fear the Lord his God and be careful to observe all the words of this law and these statutes

Josh 4:14 and they feared him, as they had feared Moses, *all the days of his life*

1Sam 1:11 Then she made a vow and said, "O Lord of hosts, if You will indeed look on the affliction of your maidservant and remember me, and not forget your maidservant, but will give your maidservant a male child, then I will give him to the Lord *all the days of his life*, and no razor shall come upon his head

1Sam 7:15 So Samuel judged Israel *all the days of his life*

1Kin 4:21 They brought tribute and served Solomon *all the days of his life*

1Kin 11:34 However I will not take the whole kingdom out of his hand, because I have made him ruler *all the days of his life* for the sake of My servant David, whom I chose because he kept My commandments and My statutes

1Kin 15:5 because David did what was right in the eyes of the Lord, and had not turned aside from anything that He commanded him *all the days of his life*, except in the matter of Uriah the Hittite

1Kin 15:6 And there was war between Rehoboam and Jeroboam *all the days of his life*

2Kin 25:29 So Jehoiachin changed from his prison garments, and he ate bread regularly before the king *all the days of his life*

2Kin 25:30 And as for his provisions, there was a regular ration given him by the king, a portion for each day, *all the days of his life*

Eccl 5:18 It is good and fitting for one to eat and drink, and to enjoy the good of all his labor in which he toils under the sun *all the days of his life* which God gives him

Jer 52:33 So Jehoiachin changed from his prison garments, and he ate bread regularly before the king *all the days of his life*

Jer 52:34 And as for his provisions, there was a regular ration given him by the king of Babylon, a portion for each day until the day of his death, *all the days of his life*

ALL THE DAYS OF MY LIFE

Ps 23:6 Surely goodness and mercy shall follow me *all the days of my life*

Ps 27:4 That I may dwell in the house of the Lord *all the days of my life*, to behold the beauty of the Lord, and to inquire in His temple

ALL THE DAYS OF OUR LIFE
Is 38:20 therefore we will sing my songs with stringed instruments *all the days of our life*, in the house of the Lord
Luke 1:75 in holiness and righteousness before Him *all the days of our life*

ALL THE DESCENDANTS (NIV, RSV)
(See *ALL THE SEED*)

ALL THE EARTH
Gen 1:26 let them have dominion over the fish of the sea, over the birds of the air, and over the cattle, over *all the earth* and over every creeping thing that creeps on the earth
Gen 1:29 And God said, "See, I have given you every herb that yields seed which is on the face of *all the earth*, and every tree whose fruit yields seed
Gen 7:3 also seven each of birds of the air, male and female, to keep the species alive on the face of *all the earth*
Gen 11:8 So the Lord scattered them abroad from there over the face of *all the earth*, and they ceased building the city
Gen 11:9 Therefore its name is called Babel, because there the Lord confused the language of *all the earth;* and from there the Lord scattered them abroad over the face of *all the earth*
Gen 18:25 Shall not the Judge of *all the earth* do right
Gen 19:31 Now the firstborn said to the younger, "Our father is old, and there is no man on the earth to come in to us as is the custom of *all the earth*
Ex 9:14 for at this time I will send all My plagues to your very heart, and on your servants and on your people, that you may know that there is none like Me in *all the earth*
Ex 9:16 But indeed for this purpose I have raised you up, that I may show My power in you, and that My name may be declared in *all the earth*
Ex 19:5 Now therefore, if you will indeed obey My voice and keep My covenant, then you shall be a special treasure to Me above all people; for *all the earth* is Mine
Ex 34:10 Before all your people I will do marvels such as have not been done in *all the earth*, nor in any nation
Num 14:21 but truly, as I live, *all the earth* shall be filled with the glory of the Lord
Josh 3:11 Behold, the ark of the covenant of the Lord of *all the earth* is crossing over before you into the Jordan
Josh 3:13 And it shall come to pass, as soon as the soles of the feet of the priests who bear the ark of the Lord, the Lord of *all the earth*, shall rest in the waters of the Jordan, that the waters of the Jordan shall be cut off, the waters that come down from upstream, and they shall stand as a heap
Josh 23:14 Behold, this day I am going the way of *all the earth*
1Sam 17:46 And this day I will give the carcasses of the camp of the Philistines to the birds of the air and the wild beasts of the earth, that *all the earth* may know that there is a God in Israel
1Kin 2:2 I go the way of *all the earth;* be strong, therefore, and prove yourself a man
1Kin 10:24 And *all the earth* sought the presence of Solomon to hear his wisdom, which God had put in his heart
2Kin 5:15 and he said, "Indeed, now I know that there is no God in *all the earth*, except in Israel
1Chr 16:14 He is the Lord our God; His judgments are in *all the earth*
1Chr 16:23 Sing to the Lord, *all the earth;* proclaim the good news of His salvation from day to day
1Chr 16:30 Tremble before Him, *all the earth*. The world also is firmly established, it shall not be moved
Ps 8:1 O Lord, our Lord, how excellent is Your name in *all the earth*, You who set Your glory above the heavens
Ps 8:9 O Lord, our Lord, how excellent is Your name in *all the earth*
Ps 19:4 Their line has gone out through *all the earth*, and their words to the end of the world
Ps 33:8 Let *all the earth* fear the Lord; let all the inhabitants of the world stand in awe of Him
Ps 45:16 Instead of Your fathers shall be Your sons, whom You shall make princes in *all the earth*
Ps 47:2 For the Lord Most High is awesome; He is a great King over *all the earth*
Ps 47:7 For God is the King of *all the earth;* sing praises with understanding
Ps 57:5 Be exalted, O God, above the heavens; let Your glory be above *all the earth*
Ps 57:11 Be exalted, O God, above the heavens; let Your glory be above *all the earth*
Ps 66:1 Make a joyful shout to God, *all the earth*
Ps 66:4 *All the earth* shall worship You and sing praises to You
Ps 83:18 That men may know that You, whose name alone is the Lord, are the Most High over *all the earth*
Ps 96:1 Oh, sing to the Lord a new song! Sing to the Lord, *all the earth*
Ps 96:9 Oh, worship the Lord in the beauty of holiness! Tremble before Him, *all the earth*
Ps 97:9 For You, Lord, are most high above *all the earth*
Ps 98:4 Shout joyfully to the Lord, *all the earth;* break forth in song, rejoice, and sing praises
Ps 105:7 He is the Lord our God; His judgments are in *all the earth*
Ps 108:5 Be exalted, O God, above the heavens, and Your glory above *all the earth*
Is 10:14 My hand has found like a nest the riches of the people, and as one gathers eggs that are left, I have gathered *all the earth*
Is 12:5 Sing to the Lord, For He has done excellent things; this is known in *all the earth*
Is 25:8 the rebuke of His people He will take away from *all the earth*
Jer 51:7 Babylon was a golden cup in the Lord's hand, that made *all the earth* drunk
Jer 51:25 Behold, I am against you, O destroying mountain, who destroys *all the earth*
Jer 51:49 As Babylon has caused the slain of Israel to fall, so at Babylon the slain of *all the earth* shall fall
Dan 2:39 then another, a third kingdom of bronze, which shall rule over *all the earth*
Dan 4:1 Nebuchadnezzar the king, To all peoples, nations and languages that dwell in *all the earth*
Dan 4:11 its height reached to the heavens, and it could be seen to the ends of *all the earth*
Dan 4:20 The tree that you saw, which grew and became strong, whose height reached to the heavens and which could be seen by *all the earth*
Dan 6:25 To all peoples, nations, and languages that dwell in *all the earth*
Hab 2:20 But the Lord is in His holy temple. Let *all the earth* keep silence before Him
Zeph 3:8 *all the earth* shall be devoured with the fire of My jealousy
Zech 1:11 So they answered the Angel of the Lord, who stood among the myrtle trees, and said, "We have walked to and fro throughout the earth, and behold, *all the earth* is resting quietly
Zech 6:5 And the angel answered and said to me,

"These are four spirits of heaven, who go out from their station before the Lord of *all the earth*
Zech 14:9 And the Lord shall be King over *all the earth*
Luke 23:44 And it was about the sixth hour, and there was darkness over *all the earth* until the ninth hour
Rom 9:17 For the Scripture says to Pharaoh, "Even for this same purpose I have raised you up, that I might show My power in you, and that My name might be declared in *all the earth*
Rom 10:18 Their sound has gone out to *all the earth*, and their words to the ends of the world
Rev 5:6 And I looked, and behold, in the midst of the throne and of the four living creatures, and in the midst of the elders, stood a Lamb as though it had been slain, having seven horns and seven eyes, which are the seven Spirits of God sent out into *all the earth*

ALL THE FAMILIES OF THE EARTH SHALL BE BLESSED
Gen 12:3 and in you *all the families of the earth shall be blessed*
Gen 28:14 and in you and in your seed *all the families of the earth shall be blessed*
Acts 3:25 You are sons of the prophets, and of the covenant which God made with our fathers, saying to Abraham, 'And in your seed *all the families of the earth shall be blessed*

ALL THE FULLNESS OF GOD
Eph 3:19 that you may be filled with *all the fullness of God*

ALL THE HOLY ONES (NIV, NAS, RSV)
(See *ALL THE SAINTS*)

ALL THE KINGDOMS OF THE EARTH
Deut 28:25 and you shall become troublesome to *all the kingdoms of the earth*
2Kin 19:15 O Lord God of Israel, the One who dwells between the cherubim, You are God, You alone, of *all the kingdoms of the earth*
2Kin 19:19 Now therefore, O Lord our God, I pray, save us from his hand, that *all the kingdoms of the earth* may know that You are the Lord God, You alone
2Chr 36:23 *All the kingdoms of the earth* the Lord God of heaven has given me
Ezra 1:2 *All the kingdoms of the earth* the Lord God of heaven has given me
Is 37:16 O Lord of hosts, God of Israel, the One who dwells between the cherubim, You are God, You alone, of *all the kingdoms of the earth*
Is 37:20 Now therefore, O Lord our God, save us from his hand, that *all the kingdoms of the earth* may know that You are the Lord, You alone
Jer 24:9 I will deliver them to trouble into *all the kingdoms of the earth*, for their harm, to be a reproach and a byword, a taunt and a curse, in all places where I shall drive them
Jer 29:18 and I will deliver them to trouble among *all the kingdoms of the earth* to be a curse, an astonishment, a hissing, and a reproach among all the nations where I have driven them
Jer 34:1 The word which came to Jeremiah from the Lord, when Nebuchadnezzar king of Babylon and all his army, *all the kingdoms of the earth* under his dominion, and all the people, fought against Jerusalem and all its cities, saying
Jer 34:17 And I will deliver you to trouble among *all the kingdoms of the earth*

ALL THE MIGHT OF ISRAEL (RSV)
(See *HORN OF ISRAEL*)

ALL THE NATIONS WILL BE GATHERED
Matt 25:32 *All the nations will be gathered* before Him, and He will separate them one from another, as a shepherd divides his sheep from the goats

ALL THE PEOPLE OF THE WORLD (NIV)
(See *INHABITANTS OF THE WORLD*)

ALL THE SAINTS
Zech 14:5 Thus the Lord my God will come, and *all the saints* with You
Rom 16:15 Greet Philologus and Julia, Nereus and his sister, and Olympas, and *all the saints* who are with them
2Cor 1:1 Paul, an apostle of Jesus Christ by the will of God, and Timothy our brother, To the church of God which is at Corinth, with *all the saints* who are in all Achaia
2Cor 13:13 *All the saints* greet you
Eph 1:15 Therefore I also, after I heard of your faith in the Lord Jesus and your love for *all the saints*
Eph 3:8 To me, who am less than the least of *all the saints*, this grace was given, that I should preach among the Gentiles the unsearchable riches of Christ
Eph 3:18 may be able to comprehend with *all the saints* what is the width and length and depth and height
Eph 6:18 praying always with all prayer and supplication in the Spirit, being watchful to this end with all perseverance and supplication for *all the saints*
Phil 1:1 Paul and Timothy, servants of Jesus Christ, To *all the saints* in Christ Jesus who are in Philippi, with the bishops and deacons
Phil 4:22 *All the saints* greet you, but especially those who are of Caesar's household
Col 1:4 since we heard of your faith in Christ Jesus and of your love for *all the saints*
Phm 5 hearing of your love and faith which you have toward the Lord Jesus and toward *all the saints*
Heb 13:24 Greet all those who rule over you, and *all the saints*
Rev 8:3 And he was given much incense, that he should offer it with the prayers of *all the saints* upon the golden altar which was before the throne

ALL THE SEED
Jer 31:37 If heaven above can be measured, and the foundations of the earth searched out beneath, I will also cast off *all the seed* of Israel for all that they have done
Rom 4:16 Therefore it is of faith that it might be according to grace, so that the promise might be sure to *all the seed*, not only to those who are of the law, but also to those who are of the faith of Abraham, who is the father of us all

ALL THE SURFACE OF THE EARTH (NIV)
(See *WHOLE EARTH*)

ALL THE WORDS OF THIS LAW
Deut 17:19 And it shall be with him, and he shall read it all the days of his life, that he may learn to fear the Lord his God and be careful to observe *all the words of this law* and these statutes
Deut 27:3 You shall write on them *all the words of this law*, when you have crossed over, that you may enter the land which the Lord your God is giving you
Deut 27:8 And you shall write very plainly on the stones *all the words of this law*
Deut 27:26 Cursed is the one who does not confirm *all the words of this law*
Deut 28:58 If you do not carefully observe *all the*

words of this law that are written in this book, that you may fear this glorious and awesome name, THE LORD YOUR GOD
Deut 29:29 The secret things belong to the Lord our God, but those things which are revealed belong to us and to our children forever, that we may do *all the words of this law*
Deut 31:12 Gather the people together, men and women and little ones, and the stranger who is within your gates, that they may hear and that they may learn to fear the Lord your God and carefully observe *all the words of this law*
Deut 32:46 Set your hearts on all the words which I testify among you today, which you shall command your children to be careful to observe *all the words of this law*

ALL THE WORK WHICH THE LORD DID (RSV)
(See *WORKS OF THE LORD*)

ALL THINGS
Gen 9:3 I have given you *all things*, even as the green herbs
Gen 24:1 Now Abraham was old, well-advanced in age; and the Lord had blessed Abraham in *all things*
Ex 25:22 And there I will meet with you, and I will speak with you from above the mercy seat, from between the two cherubim which are on the ark of the Testimony, of *all things* which I will give you in commandment to the children of Israel
Num 1:50 but you shall appoint the Levites over the tabernacle of the Testimony, over all its furnishings, and over *all things* that belong to it
Deut 28:47 Because you did not serve the Lord your God with joy and gladness of heart, for the abundance of *all things*
Deut 28:48 therefore you shall serve your enemies, whom the Lord will send against you, in hunger, in thirst, in nakedness, and in need of *all things*
Deut 28:57 for she will eat them secretly for lack of *all things* in the siege and desperate straits in which your enemy shall distress you at all your gates
Josh 1:17 Just as we heeded Moses in *all things*, so we will heed you
2Sam 14:20 but my lord is wise, according to the wisdom of the angel of God, to know *all things* that are in the earth
2Sam 23:5 Although my house is not so with God, yet He has made with me an everlasting covenant, ordered in *all things* and secure
1Chr 29:14 For *all things* come from You, and of Your own we have given You
Neh 9:6 You have made heaven, the heaven of heavens, with all their host, the earth and *all things* on it, the seas and all that is in them, and You preserve them all
Ps 8:6 You have made him to have dominion over the works of Your hands; You have put *all things* under his feet
Ps 57:2 I will cry out to God Most High, to God who performs *all things* for me
Ps 119:128 Therefore all Your precepts concerning *all things* I consider to be right
Prov 16:4 The Lord has made *all things* for Himself, yes, even the wicked for the day of doom
Prov 26:10 The great God who formed *all things* gives the fool his hire and the transgressor his wages
Eccl 1:8 *All things* are full of labor; man cannot express it
Eccl 7:15 I have seen *all things* in my days of vanity
Eccl 11:5 As you do not know what is the way of the wind, or how the bones grow in the womb of her who is with child, so you do not know the works of God who makes *all things*
Is 34:1 Let the earth hear, and all that is in it, the world and *all things* that come forth from it
Is 44:24 I am the Lord, who makes *all things*, Who stretches out the heavens all alone, Who spreads abroad the earth by Myself
Jer 10:16 The Portion of Jacob is not like them, for He is the Maker of *all things*, and Israel is the tribe of His inheritance
Jer 17:9 The heart is deceitful above *all things*, and desperately wicked
Jer 21:14 I will kindle a fire in its forest, and it shall devour *all things* around it
Jer 51:19 The Portion of Jacob is not like them, for He is the Maker of *all things*
Dan 2:40 And the fourth kingdom shall be as strong as iron, inasmuch as iron breaks in pieces and shatters *all things*
Zeph 1:2 I will utterly consume *all things* from the face of the land
Matt 11:27 *All things* have been delivered to Me by My Father, and no one knows the Son except the Father
Matt 13:41 The Son of Man will send out His angels, and they will gather out of His kingdom *all things* that offend, and those who practice lawlessness
Matt 17:11 Then Jesus answered and said to them, "Elijah truly is coming first and will restore *all things*
Matt 19:26 But Jesus looked at them and said to them, "With men this is impossible, but with God *all things* are possible
Matt 21:22 And *all things*, whatever you ask in prayer, believing, you will receive
Matt 22:4 my oxen and fatted cattle are killed, and *all things* are ready
Matt 23:20 Therefore he who swears by the altar, swears by it and by *all things* on it
Matt 28:20 teaching them to observe *all things* that I have commanded you
Mark 4:11 but to those who are outside, *all things* come in parables
Mark 4:34 And when they were alone, He explained *all things* to His disciples
Mark 6:30 Then the apostles gathered to Jesus and told Him *all things*, both what they had done and what they had taught
Mark 7:37 And they were astonished beyond measure, saying, "He has done *all things* well
Mark 9:12 Then He answered and told them, "Elijah does come first, and restores *all things*
Mark 9:23 Jesus said to him, "If you can believe, *all things* are possible to him who believes
Mark 10:27 But looking at them, Jesus said, "With men it is impossible, but not with God; for with God *all things* are possible
Mark 11:11 So when He had looked around at *all things*, as the hour was already late, He went out to Bethany with the twelve
Mark 13:23 But take heed; see, I have told you *all things* beforehand
Mark 14:36 And He said, "Abba, Father, *all things* are possible for You
Luke 1:3 it seemed good to me also, having had perfect understanding of *all things* from the very first, to write to you an orderly account, most excellent Theophilus
Luke 2:39 So when they had performed *all things* according to the law of the Lord, they returned to Galilee, to their own city, Nazareth
Luke 10:22 *All things* have been delivered to Me by My Father, and no one knows who the Son is but the Father, and who the Father is but the Son, and the one to whom the Son wills to reveal Him
Luke 11:41 But rather give alms of such things as you have; then indeed *all things* are clean to you
Luke 14:17 and sent his servant at supper time to

say to those who were invited, 'Come, for *all things* are now ready
Luke 18:31 Then He took the twelve aside and said to them, "Behold, we are going up to Jerusalem, and *all things* that are written by the prophets concerning the Son of Man will be accomplished
Luke 21:22 For these are the days of vengeance, that *all things* which are written may be fulfilled
Luke 21:32 Assuredly, I say to you, this generation will by no means pass away till *all things* are fulfilled
Luke 24:44 Then He said to them, "These are the words which I spoke to you while I was still with you, that *all things* must be fulfilled which were written in the Law of Moses and the Prophets and the Psalms concerning Me
John 1:3 *All things* were made through Him, and without Him nothing was made that was made
John 3:35 The Father loves the Son, and has given *all things* into His hand
John 4:25 The woman said to Him, "I know that Messiah is coming" (who is called Christ). "When He comes, He will tell us *all things*
John 4:29 Come, see a Man who told me *all things* that I ever did
John 5:20 For the Father loves the Son, and shows Him *all things* that He Himself does
John 13:3 Jesus, knowing that the Father had given *all things* into His hands, and that He had come from God and was going to God
John 14:26 But the Helper, the Holy Spirit, whom the Father will send in My name, He will teach you *all things*, and bring to your remembrance *all things* that I said to you
John 15:15 but I have called you friends, for *all things* that I heard from My Father I have made known to you
John 16:15 *All things* that the Father has are Mine. Therefore I said that He will take of Mine and declare it to you
John 16:30 Now we are sure that You know *all things*, and have no need that anyone should question You
John 17:7 Now they have known that *all things* which You have given Me are from You
John 18:4 Jesus therefore, knowing *all things* that would come upon Him, went forward and said to them
John 19:28 After this, Jesus, knowing that *all things* were now accomplished, that the Scripture might be fulfilled, said
John 21:17 And he said to Him, "Lord, You know *all things*
Acts 2:44 Now all who believed were together, and had *all things* in common
Acts 3:21 whom heaven must receive until the times of restoration of *all things*, which God has spoken by the mouth of all His holy prophets since the world began
Acts 3:22 Him you shall hear in *all things*, whatever He says to you
Acts 4:32 neither did anyone say that any of the things he possessed was his own, but they had *all things* in common
Acts 10:39 And we are witnesses of *all things* which He did both in the land of the Jews and in Jerusalem, whom they killed by hanging on a tree
Acts 13:39 and by Him everyone who believes is justified from *all things* from which you could not be justified by the law of Moses
Acts 14:15 We also are men with the same nature as you, and preach to you that you should turn from these vain things to the living God, who made the heaven, the earth, the sea, and *all things* that are in them
Acts 15:4 and they reported *all things* that God had done with them
Acts 17:22 Then Paul stood in the midst of the Areopagus and said, "Men of Athens, I perceive that in *all things* you are very religious
Acts 17:25 Nor is He worshiped with men's hands, as though He needed anything, since He gives to all life, breath, and *all things*
Acts 22:10 And the Lord said to me, 'Arise and go into Damascus, and there you will be told *all things* which are appointed for you to do
Acts 24:14 But this I confess to you, that according to the Way which they call a sect, so I worship the God of my fathers, believing *all things* which are written in the Law and in the Prophets
Rom 8:28 And we know that *all things* work together for good to those who love God, to those who are the called according to His purpose
Rom 8:32 He who did not spare His own Son, but delivered Him up for us all, how shall He not with Him also freely give us *all things*
Rom 11:36 For of Him and through Him and to Him are *all things*, to whom be glory forever
Rom 14:2 For one believes he may eat *all things*, but he who is weak eats only vegetables
Rom 14:20 *All things* indeed are pure, but it is evil for the man who eats with offense
1Cor 2:10 For the Spirit searches *all things*, yes, the deep things of God
1Cor 2:15 But he who is spiritual judges *all things*, yet he himself is rightly judged by no one
1Cor 3:21 Therefore let no one glory in men. For *all things* are yours
1Cor 4:13 We have been made as the filth of the world, the offscouring of *all things* until now
1Cor 6:12 *All things* are lawful for me, but *all things* are not helpful. *All things* are lawful for me, but I will not be brought under the power of any
1Cor 8:6 yet for us there is only one God, the Father, of whom are *all things*, and we for Him; and one Lord Jesus Christ, through whom are *all things*, and through whom we live
1Cor 9:12 Nevertheless we have not used this right, but endure *all things* lest we hinder the gospel of Christ
1Cor 9:22 I have become *all things* to all men, that I might by all means save some
1Cor 9:25 And everyone who competes for the prize is temperate in *all things*
1Cor 10:23 *All things* are lawful for me, but *all things* are not helpful; *all things* are lawful for me, but *all things* do not edify
1Cor 10:33 just as I also please all men in *all things*, not seeking my own profit, but the profit of many, that they may be saved
1Cor 11:2 Now I praise you, brethren, that you remember me in *all things* and keep the traditions as I delivered them to you
1Cor 11:12 For as the woman was from the man, even so the man also is through the woman; but *all things* are from God
1Cor 13:7 bears *all things*, believes *all things*, hopes *all things*, endures *all things*
1Cor 14:26 Whenever you come together, each of you has a psalm, has a teaching, has a tongue, has a revelation, has an interpretation. Let *all things* be done for edification
1Cor 14:40 Let *all things* be done decently and in order
1Cor 15:27 For "He has put *all things* under His feet." But when He says "*all things* are put under Him," it is evident that He who put *all things* under Him is excepted
1Cor 15:28 Now when *all things* are made subject to Him, then the Son Himself will also be subject to Him who put *all things* under Him, that God may be all in all
2Cor 2:9 For to this end I also wrote, that I might

put you to the test, whether you are obedient in *all things*

2Cor 4:15 For *all things* are for your sakes, that grace, having spread through the many, may cause thanksgiving to abound to the glory of God

2Cor 5:17 old things have passed away; behold, *all things* have become new

2Cor 5:18 Now *all things* are of God, who has reconciled us to Himself through Jesus Christ, and has given us the ministry of reconciliation

2Cor 6:4 But in *all things* we commend ourselves as ministers of God

2Cor 6:10 as poor, yet making many rich; as having nothing, and yet possessing *all things*

2Cor 7:11 In *all things* you proved yourselves to be clear in this matter

2Cor 7:14 But as we spoke *all things* to you in truth, even so our boasting to Titus was found true

2Cor 9:8 And God is able to make all grace abound toward you, that you, always having all sufficiency in *all things*, have an abundance for every good work

2Cor 11:6 But we have been thoroughly made manifest among you in *all things*

2Cor 12:19 We speak before God in Christ. But we do *all things*, beloved, for your edification

Gal 3:10 for it is written, "Cursed is everyone who does not continue in *all things* which are written in the book of the law, to do them

Eph 1:10 that in the dispensation of the fullness of the times He might gather together in one *all things* in Christ, both which are in heaven and which are on earth in Him

Eph 1:11 in whom also we have obtained an inheritance, being predestined according to the purpose of Him who works *all things* according to the counsel of His will

Eph 1:22 And He put *all things* under His feet, and gave Him to be head over *all things* to the church

Eph 3:9 and to make all people see what is the fellowship of the mystery, which from the beginning of the ages has been hidden in God who created *all things* through Jesus Christ

Eph 4:10 He who descended is also the One who ascended far above all the heavens, that He might fill *all things*

Eph 4:15 but, speaking the truth in love, may grow up in *all things* into Him who is the head Christ

Eph 5:13 But *all things* that are exposed are made manifest by the light, for whatever makes manifest is light

Eph 5:20 giving thanks always for *all things* to God the Father in the name of our Lord Jesus Christ

Eph 6:21 But that you also may know my affairs and how I am doing, Tychicus, a beloved brother and faithful minister in the Lord, will make *all things* known to you

Phil 2:14 Do *all things* without murmuring and disputing

Phil 3:8 But indeed I also count *all things* loss for the excellence of the knowledge of Christ Jesus my Lord, for whom I have suffered the loss of *all things*, and count them as rubbish, that I may gain Christ

Phil 3:21 who will transform our lowly body that it may be conformed to His glorious body, according to the working by which He is able even to subdue *all things* to Himself

Phil 4:12 Everywhere and in *all things* I have learned both to be full and to be hungry, both to abound and to suffer need

Phil 4:13 I can do *all things* through Christ who strengthens me

Col 1:16 For by Him *all things* were created that are in heaven and that are on earth, visible and invisible, whether thrones or dominions or principalities or powers. *All things* were created through Him and for Him

Col 1:17 And He is before *all things*, and in Him *all things* consist

Col 1:18 And He is the head of the body, the church, who is the beginning, the firstborn from the dead, that in *all things* He may have the preeminence

Col 1:20 and by Him to reconcile *all things* to Himself, by Him, whether things on earth or things in heaven, having made peace through the blood of His cross

Col 3:20 Children, obey your parents in *all things*, for this is well pleasing to the Lord

Col 3:22 Servants, obey in *all things* your masters according to the flesh, not with eyeservice, as men-pleasers, but in sincerity of heart, fearing God

Col 4:9 They will make known to you *all things* which are happening here

1Th 5:21 Test *all things;* hold fast what is good

1Tim 3:11 Likewise their wives must be reverent, not slanderers, temperate, faithful in *all things*

1Tim 4:8 For bodily exercise profits a little, but godliness is profitable for *all things*, having promise of the life that now is and of that which is to come

1Tim 6:13 I urge you in the sight of God who gives life to *all things*, and before Christ Jesus who witnessed the good confession before Pontius Pilate

1Tim 6:17 Command those who are rich in this present age not to be haughty, nor to trust in uncertain riches but in the living God, who gives us richly *all things* to enjoy

2Tim 2:7 Consider what I say, and may the Lord give you understanding in *all things*

2Tim 2:10 Therefore I endure *all things* for the sake of the elect, that they also may obtain the salvation which is in Christ Jesus with eternal glory

2Tim 4:5 But you be watchful in *all things*, endure afflictions, do the work of an evangelist, fulfill your ministry

Tit 1:15 To the pure *all things* are pure, but to those who are defiled and unbelieving nothing is pure

Tit 2:7 in *all things* showing yourself to be a pattern of good works

Tit 2:9 Exhort servants to be obedient to their own masters, to be well pleasing in *all things*, not answering back

Tit 2:10 not pilfering, but showing all good fidelity, that they may adorn the doctrine of God our Savior in *all things*

Heb 1:2 has in these last days spoken to us by His Son, whom He has appointed heir of *all things*, through whom also He made the worlds

Heb 1:3 who being the brightness of His glory and the express image of His person, and upholding *all things* by the word of His power, when He had by Himself purged our sins, sat down at the right hand of the Majesty on high

Heb 2:8 You have put *all things* in subjection under his feet." For in that He put all in subjection under him, He left nothing that is not put under him. But now we do not yet see *all things* put under him

Heb 2:10 For it was fitting for Him, for whom are *all things* and by whom are *all things*, in bringing many sons to glory, to make the author of their salvation perfect through sufferings

Heb 2:17 Therefore, in *all things* He had to be made like His brethren, that He might be a merciful and faithful High Priest in things pertaining to God, to make propitiation for the sins of the people

Heb 3:4 For every house is built by someone, but He who built *all things* is God
Heb 4:13 And there is no creature hidden from His sight, but *all things* are naked and open to the eyes of Him to whom we must give account
Heb 8:5 For He said, "See that you make *all things* according to the pattern shown you on the mountain
Heb 9:22 And according to the law almost *all things* are purged with blood, and without shedding of blood there is no remission
Heb 13:18 for we are confident that we have a good conscience, in *all things* desiring to live honorably
1Pet 4:7 But the end of *all things* is at hand; therefore be serious and watchful in your prayers
1Pet 4:8 And above *all things* have fervent love for one another, for
1Pet 4:11 If anyone ministers, let him do it as with the ability which God supplies, that in *all things* God may be glorified through Jesus Christ, to whom belong the glory and the dominion forever and ever
2Pet 1:3 as His divine power has given to us *all things* that pertain to life and godliness, through the knowledge of Him who called us by glory and virtue
2Pet 3:4 For since the fathers fell asleep, *all things* continue as they were from the beginning of creation
1Jn 2:20 But you have an anointing from the Holy One, and you know *all things*
1Jn 2:27 but as the same anointing teaches you concerning *all things*, and is true, and is not a lie, and just as it has taught you, you will abide in Him
1Jn 3:20 For if our heart condemns us, God is greater than our heart, and knows *all things*
3Jn 2 Beloved, I pray that you may prosper in *all things* and be in health, just as your soul prospers
Rev 1:2 who bore witness to the word of God, and to the testimony of Jesus Christ, and to *all things* that he saw
Rev 4:11 for You created *all things*, and by Your will they exist and were created
Rev 21:5 Then He who sat on the throne said, "Behold, I make *all things* new
Rev 21:7 He who overcomes shall inherit *all things*, and I will be his God and he shall be My son

ALL THINGS ARE LAWFUL FOR ME
1Cor 6:12 *All things are lawful for me*, but all things are not helpful. *All things are lawful for me*, but I will not be brought under the power of any
1Cor 10:23 *All things are lawful for me*, but all things are not helpful; *all things are lawful for me*, but all things do not edify

ALL THINGS ARE POSSIBLE
Matt 19:26 But Jesus looked at them and said to them, "With men this is impossible, but with God *all things are possible*
Mark 9:23 Jesus said to him, "If you can believe, *all things are possible* to him who believes
Mark 10:27 But looking at them, Jesus said, "With men it is impossible, but not with God; for with God *all things are possible*
Mark 14:36 And He said, "Abba, Father, *all things are possible* for You

ALL THINGS IN SUBJECTION
Heb 2:8 You have put *all things in subjection* under his feet

ALL THINGS UNDER HIS FEET
Ps 8:6 You have made him to have dominion over the works of Your hands; You have put *all things under his feet*
1Cor 15:27 For "He has put *all things under His feet*." But when He says
Eph 1:22 And He put *all things under His feet*, and gave Him to be head over all things to the church

ALL WE LIKE SHEEP
Is 53:6 *All we like sheep* have gone astray; we have turned, every one, to his own way

ALL WHO LIVE ON EARTH (NIV)
(See *INHABITANTS OF THE EARTH*)

ALL WHO RECIEVED HIM (NIV, RSV)
(See *AS MANY AS RECEIVED HIM*)

ALL WHO TAKE THE SWORD
Matt 26:52 Then Jesus said to him, "Put your sword in its place, for *all who take the sword* will perish by the sword

ALL WORK MIRACLES (NIV, RSV)
(See *WORKERS OF MIRACLES*)

ALL YOU WHO ARE THIRSTY (NIV)
(See *EVERYONE WHO THIRSTS*)

ALLIED WITH (NAS)
(See *HAVE FELLOWSHIP WITH*)

ALLOWED OF GOD (KJV)
(See *APPROVED BY GOD*)

ALMIGHTY GOD
Gen 17:1 When Abram was ninety-nine years old, the Lord appeared to Abram and said to him, "I am *Almighty God*
Ezek 10:5 And the sound of the wings of the cherubim was heard even in the outer court, like the voice of *Almighty God* when He speaks
Rev 19:15 He Himself treads the winepress of the fierceness and wrath of *Almighty God*

ALMIGHTY HAS AFFLICTED ME
Ruth 1:21 Why do you call me Naomi, since the Lord has testified against me, and the *Almighty has afflicted me*

ALMIGHTY HAS BROUGHT MISFORTUNE UPON ME (NIV)
(See *ALMIGHTY HAS AFFLICTED ME*)

ALMIGHTY UNTO PERFECTION (KJV)
(See *LIMITS OF THE ALMIGHTY*)

ALMOND BLOSSOMS
Ex 25:33 Three bowls shall be made like *almond blossoms* on one branch, with an ornamental knob and a flower, and three bowls made like *almond blossoms* on the other branch, with an ornamental knob and a flower and so for the six branches that come out of the lampstand
Ex 25:34 On the lampstand itself four bowls shall be made like *almond blossoms*, each with its ornamental knob and flower
Ex 37:19 There were three bowls made like *almond blossoms* on one branch, with an ornamental knob and a flower, and three bowls made like *almond blossoms* on the other branch, with an ornamental knob and a flower and so for the six branches coming out of the lampstand
Ex 37:20 And on the lampstand itself were four bowls made like *almond blossoms*, each with its ornamental knob and flower

ALPHA AND THE OMEGA
Rev 1:8 I am the *Alpha and the Omega*, the Beginning and the End
Rev 1:11 saying, "I am the *Alpha and the Omega*, the First and the Last
Rev 21:6 I am the *Alpha and the Omega*, the Beginning and the End
Rev 22:13 I am the *Alpha and the Omega*, the Beginning and the End, the First and the Last

ALREADY GETTING LATE (NIV)
(See *HOUR IS ALREADY LATE*)

ALTAR OF BURNT OFFERING
Ex 30:28 the *altar of burnt offering* with all its utensils, and the laver and its base
Ex 31:9 the *altar of burnt offering* with all its utensils, and the laver and its base
Ex 35:16 the *altar of burnt offering* with its bronze grating, its poles, all its utensils, and the laver and its base
Ex 38:1 He made the *altar of burnt offering* of acacia wood
Ex 40:29 And he put the *altar of burnt offering* before the door of the tabernacle of the tent of meeting, and offered upon it the burnt offering and the grain offering, as the Lord had commanded Moses
Lev 4:18 and he shall pour the remaining blood at the base of the *altar of burnt offering*, which is at the door of the tabernacle of meeting
Lev 4:25 The priest shall take some of the blood of the sin offering with his finger, put it on the horns of the *altar of burnt offering*, and pour its blood at the base of the *altar of burnt offering*
Lev 4:30 Then the priest shall take some of its blood with his finger, put it on the horns of the *altar of burnt offering*, and pour all the remaining blood at the base of the altar
Lev 4:34 The priest shall take some of the blood of the sin offering with his finger, put it on the horns of the *altar of burnt offering*, and pour all the remaining blood at the base of the altar
1Chr 6:49 But Aaron and his sons offered sacrifices on the *altar of burnt offering* and on the altar of incense, for all the work of the Most Holy Place, and to make atonement for Israel, according to all that Moses the servant of God had commanded
1Chr 16:40 to offer burnt offerings to the Lord on the *altar of burnt offering* regularly morning and evening, and to do according to all that is written in the Law of the Lord which He commanded Israel
1Chr 21:26 and He answered him from heaven by fire on the *altar of burnt offering*
1Chr 22:1 Then David said, "This is the house of the Lord God, and this is the *altar of burnt offering* for Israel

ALTAR OF INCENSE
Ex 30:27 the table and all its utensils, the lampstand and its utensils, and the *altar of incense*
Ex 31:8 the table and its utensils, the pure gold lampstand with all its utensils, the *altar of incense*
1Chr 6:49 But Aaron and his sons offered sacrifices on the altar of burnt offering and on the *altar of incense*, for all the work of the Most Holy Place, and to make atonement for Israel, according to all that Moses the servant of God had commanded
1Chr 28:18 and refined gold by weight for the *altar of incense*, and for the construction of the chariot, that is, the gold cherubim that spread their wings and overshadowed the ark of the covenant of the Lord
2Chr 26:16 But when he was strong his heart was lifted up, to his destruction, for he transgressed against the Lord his God by entering the temple of the Lord to burn incense on the *altar of incense*
Luke 1:11 Then an angel of the Lord appeared to him, standing on the right side of the *altar of incense*
Heb 9:4 which had the golden *altar of incense* and the ark of the covenant overlaid on all sides with gold, in which were the golden pot that had the manna, Aaron's rod that budded, and the tablets of the covenant

ALTAR OF THE LORD
Lev 17:6 And the priest shall sprinkle the blood on the *altar of the Lord* at the door of the tabernacle of meeting, and burn the fat for a sweet aroma to the Lord
Deut 12:27 And you shall offer your burnt offerings, the meat and the blood, on the *altar of the Lord* your God; and the blood of your sacrifices shall be poured out on the *altar of the Lord* your God, and you shall eat the meat
Deut 26:4 Then the priest shall take the basket out of your hand and set it down before the *altar of the Lord* your God
Deut 27:6 You shall build with whole stones the *altar of the Lord* your God, and offer burnt offerings on it to the Lord your God
Josh 9:27 And that day Joshua made them woodcutters and water carriers for the congregation and for the *altar of the Lord*, in the place which He would choose, even to this day
Josh 22:19 but do not rebel against the Lord, nor rebel against us, by building yourselves an altar besides the *altar of the Lord* our God
Josh 22:28 Therefore we said that it will be, when they say this to us or to our generations in time to come, that we may say, 'Here is the replica of the *altar of the Lord* which our fathers made, though not for burnt offerings nor for sacrifices
Josh 22:29 Far be it from us that we should rebel against the Lord, and turn from following the Lord this day, to build an altar for burnt offerings, for grain offerings, or for sacrifices, besides the *altar of the Lord* our God which is before His tabernacle
1Kin 8:22 Then Solomon stood before the *altar of the Lord* in the presence of all the congregation of Israel, and spread out his hands toward heaven
1Kin 8:54 And so it was, when Solomon had finished praying all this prayer and supplication to the Lord, that he arose from before the *altar of the Lord*, from kneeling on his knees with his hands spread up to heaven
1Kin 18:30 And he repaired the *altar of the Lord* that was broken down
2Kin 23:9 Nevertheless the priests of the high places did not come up to the *altar of the Lord* in Jerusalem, but they ate unleavened bread among their brethren
2Chr 6:12 Then Solomon stood before the *altar of the Lord* in the presence of all the congregation of Israel, and spread out his hands
2Chr 8:12 Then Solomon offered burnt offerings to the Lord on the *altar of the Lord* which he had built before the vestibule
2Chr 15:8 and he restored the *altar of the Lord* that was before the vestibule of the Lord
2Chr 29:19 and there they are, before the *altar of the Lord*
2Chr 29:21 Then he commanded the priests, the sons of Aaron, to offer them on the *altar of the Lord*
2Chr 33:16 He also repaired the *altar of the Lord*, sacrificed peace offerings and thank offerings on it, and commanded Judah to serve the Lord God of Israel
2Chr 35:16 So all the service of the Lord was pre-

pared the same day, to keep the Passover and to offer burnt offerings on the *altar of the Lord*, according to the command of King Josiah
Neh 10:34 We cast lots among the priests, the Levites, and the people, for bringing the wood offering into the house of our God, according to our fathers' houses, at the appointed times year by year, to burn on the *altar of the Lord* our God as it is written in the Law
Mal 2:13 you cover the *altar of the Lord* with tears, with weeping and crying

ALTAR TO THE LORD
Gen 8:20 Then Noah built an *altar to the Lord*, and took of every clean animal and of every clean bird, and offered burnt offerings on the altar
Gen 12:7 And there he built an *altar to the Lord*, who had appeared to him
Gen 12:8 there he built an *altar to the Lord* and called on the name of the Lord
Lev 22:22 Those that are blind or broken or maimed, or have an ulcer or eczema or scabs, you shall not offer to the Lord, nor make an offering by fire of them on the *altar to the Lord*
Deut 27:5 And there you shall build an *altar to the Lord* your God, an altar of stones
Josh 8:30 Now Joshua built an *altar to the Lord* God of Israel in Mount Ebal
Judg 6:26 and build an *altar to the Lord* your God on top of this rock in the proper arrangement, and take the second bull and offer a burnt sacrifice with the wood of the image which you shall cut down
1Sam 7:17 There he judged Israel, and there he built an *altar to the Lord*
1Sam 14:35 Then Saul built an *altar to the Lord*. This was the first altar that he built to the Lord
2Sam 24:18 And Gad came that day to David and said to him, "Go up, erect an *altar to the Lord* on the threshing floor of Araunah the Jebusite
2Sam 24:21 And David said, "To buy the threshing floor from you, to build an *altar to the Lord*, that the plague may be withdrawn from the people
2Sam 24:25 And David built there an *altar to the Lord*, and offered burnt offerings and peace offerings
1Chr 21:18 Then the angel of the Lord commanded Gad to say to David that David should go and erect an *altar to the Lord* on the threshing floor of Ornan the Jebusite
1Chr 21:26 And David built there an *altar to the Lord*, and offered burnt offerings and peace offerings, and called on the Lord
Is 19:19 In that day there will be an *altar to the Lord* in the midst of the land of Egypt, and a pillar to the Lord at its border

ALWAYS BE POOR PEOPLE (NIV)
(See *POOR WILL NEVER CEASE*)

ALWAYS HAVE THE POOR AMONG YOU (NIV)
(See *POOR YOU HAVE WITH YOU*)

ALWAYS PERSEVERES (NIV)
(See *ENDURES ALL THINGS*)

ALWAYS PROTECTS (NIV)
(See *BEARS ALL THINGS*)

AM I A JEW
John 18:35 Pilate answered, "*Am I a Jew?* Your own nation and the chief priests have delivered You to me

AMAZED AT HIS TEACHING (NIV, NAS)
(See *ASTONISHED AT HIS TEACHING*)

AMBASSADORS FOR CHRIST
2Cor 5:20 Therefore we are *ambassadors for Christ*, as though God were pleading through us

AMEN AND AMEN
Ps 41:13 Blessed be the Lord God of Israel from everlasting to everlasting! *Amen and Amen*
Ps 72:19 And let the whole earth be filled with His glory. *Amen and Amen*
Ps 89:52 Blessed be the Lord forevermore! *Amen and Amen*

AMONG THE HERDSMEN OF TEKOA
Amos 1:1 The words of Amos, who was *among the herdsmen of Tekoa*, which he saw concerning Israel in the days of Uzziah king of Judah, and in the days of Jeroboam the son of Joash, king of Israel, two years before the earthquake

AMONG THE NATIONS
Lev 26:33 I will scatter you *among the nations* and draw out a sword after you
Lev 26:38 You shall perish *among the nations*, and the land of your enemies shall eat you up
Num 23:9 A people dwelling alone, not reckoning itself *among the nations*
Num 24:20 Amalek was first *among the nations*, but shall be last until he perishes
Deut 4:27 And the Lord will scatter you among the peoples, and you will be left few in number *among the nations* where the Lord will drive you
1Chr 16:24 Declare His glory *among the nations*, His wonders among all peoples
1Chr 16:31 and let them say *among the nations*, "The Lord reigns
Neh 1:8 Remember, I pray, the word that You commanded Your servant Moses, saying, 'If you are unfaithful, I will scatter you *among the nations*
Neh 6:6 It is reported *among the nations*, and Geshem says, that you and the Jews plan to rebel
Ps 44:11 You have given us up like sheep intended for food, and have scattered us *among the nations*
Ps 44:14 You make us a byword *among the nations*, a shaking of the head among the peoples
Ps 46:10 I will be exalted *among the nations*, I will be exalted in the earth
Ps 57:9 I will praise You, O Lord, among the peoples; I will sing to You *among the nations*
Ps 79:10 Let there be known *among the nations* in our sight the avenging of the blood of Your servants which has been shed
Ps 96:3 Declare His glory *among the nations*, His wonders among all peoples
Ps 96:10 Say *among the nations*, "The Lord reigns; the world also is firmly established, it shall not be moved
Ps 106:27 To overthrow their descendants *among the nations*, and to scatter them in the lands
Ps 108:3 I will praise You, O Lord, among the peoples, and I will sing praises to You *among the nations*
Ps 110:6 He shall judge *among the nations*, He shall fill the places with dead bodies, He shall execute the heads of many countries
Ps 126:2 Then they said *among the nations*, "The Lord has done great things for them
Jer 50:2 Declare *among the nations*, proclaim, and set up a standard
Jer 50:23 How Babylon has become a desolation *among the nations!* I have laid a snare for you
Jer 50:46 At the noise of the taking of Babylon the earth trembles, and the cry is heard *among the nations*
Jer 51:27 Set up a banner in the land, blow the trumpet *among the nations*
Jer 51:41 Oh, how the praise of the whole earth is

seized! How Babylon has become desolate *among the nations*
Lam 1:1 How like a widow is she, who was great *among the nations*
Lam 1:3 she dwells *among the nations*, she finds no rest; all her persecutors overtake her in dire straits
Lam 2:9 Her king and her princes are *among the nations;* the Law is no more, and her prophets find no vision from the Lord
Lam 4:15 When they fled and wandered, those *among the nations* said
Lam 4:20 The breath of our nostrils, the anointed of the Lord, was caught in their pits, of whom we said, "Under his shadow we shall live *among the nations*
Ezek 5:14 Moreover I will make you a waste and a reproach *among the nations* that are all around you, in the sight of all who pass by
Ezek 6:8 Yet I will leave a remnant, so that you may have some who escape the sword *among the nations*, when you are scattered through the countries
Ezek 6:9 Then those of you who escape will remember Me *among the nations* where they are carried captive, because I was crushed by their adulterous heart which has departed from Me, and by their eyes which play the harlot after their idols
Ezek 12:15 Then they shall know that I am the Lord, when I scatter them *among the nations* and disperse them throughout the countries
Ezek 16:14 Your fame went out *among the nations* because of your beauty, for it was perfect through My splendor which I had bestowed on you
Ezek 22:15 I will scatter you *among the nations*, disperse you throughout the countries, and remove your filthiness completely from you
Ezek 25:10 To the men of the East I will give it as a possession, together with the Ammonites, that the Ammonites may not be remembered *among the nations*
Ezek 29:12 and I will scatter the Egyptians *among the nations* and disperse them throughout the countries
Ezek 30:23 I will scatter the Egyptians *among the nations*, and disperse them throughout the countries
Ezek 30:26 I will scatter the Egyptians *among the nations* and disperse them throughout the countries
Ezek 31:17 and those who were its strong arm dwelt in its shadows *among the nations*
Ezek 32:2 You are like a young lion *among the nations*, and you are like a monster in the seas, bursting forth in your rivers, troubling the waters with your feet, and fouling their rivers
Ezek 32:9 I will also trouble the hearts of many peoples, when I bring your destruction *among the nations*, into the countries which you have not known
Ezek 36:19 So I scattered them *among the nations*, and they were dispersed throughout the countries
Ezek 36:21 But I had concern for My holy name, which the house of Israel had profaned *among the nations* wherever they went
Ezek 36:22 I do not do this for your sake, O house of Israel, but for My holy name's sake, which you have profaned *among the nations* wherever you went
Ezek 36:23 And I will sanctify My great name, which has been profaned *among the nations*, which you have profaned in their midst
Ezek 36:24 For I will take you from *among the nations*, gather you out of all countries, and bring you into your own land
Ezek 36:30 And I will multiply the fruit of your trees and the increase of your fields, so that you need never again bear the reproach of famine *among the nations*
Ezek 37:21 Surely I will take the children of Israel from *among the nations*, wherever they have gone, and will gather them from every side and bring them into their own land
Ezek 39:21 I will set My glory *among the nations;* all the nations shall see My judgment which I have executed, and My hand which I have laid on them
Ezek 39:28 then they shall know that I am the Lord their God, who sent them into captivity *among the nations*, but also brought them back to their own land, and left none of them captive any longer
Hos 8:10 Yes, though they have hired *among the nations*, now I will gather them
Hos 9:17 My God will cast them away, because they did not obey Him; and they shall be wanderers *among the nations*
Joel 2:19 I will no longer make you a reproach *among the nations*
Joel 3:2 and I will enter into judgment with them there on account of My people, My heritage Israel, whom they have scattered *among the nations*
Joel 3:9 Proclaim this *among the nations:* Prepare for war! Wake up the mighty men, let all the men of war draw near, let them come up
Obad 1 Thus says the Lord God concerning Edom (We have heard a report from the Lord, and a messenger has been sent *among the nations*, saying
Obad 2 Behold, I will make you small *among the nations;* you shall be greatly despised
Hab 1:5 Look *among the nations* and watch be utterly astounded! For I will work a work in your days which you would not believe, though it were told you
Zech 8:13 And it shall come to pass that just as you were a curse *among the nations*, O house of Judah and house of Israel, so I will save you, and you shall be a blessing
Mal 1:11 For My name shall be great *among the nations*," says the Lord of hosts
Mal 1:14 But cursed be the deceiver who has in his flock a male, and makes a vow, but sacrifices to the Lord what is blemished for I am a great King," says the Lord of hosts, "And My name is to be feared *among the nations*

ANCESTRAL INHERITANCE (NIV)
(See *INHERITANCE OF THE*)

ANCIENT OF DAYS
Dan 7:9 I watched till thrones were put in place, and the *Ancient of Days* was seated
Dan 7:13 He came to the *Ancient of Days*, and they brought Him near before Him
Dan 7:22 until the *Ancient of Days* came, and a judgment was made in favor of the saints of the Most High, and the time came for the saints to possess the kingdom

ANCIENT PATHS
Jer 18:15 And they have caused themselves to stumble in their ways, from the *ancient paths*, to walk in pathways and not on a highway

ANCIENT SERPENT (RSV)
(See *SERPENT OF OLD*)

AND IMMEDIATELY
Matt 4:22 *and immediately* they left the boat and their father, and followed Him
Matt 8:3 Then Jesus put out His hand and touched

him, saying, "I am willing; be cleansed." *And immediately* his leprosy was cleansed
Matt 13:20 But he who received the seed on stony places, this is he who hears the word *and immediately* receives it with joy
Matt 14:31 *And immediately* Jesus stretched out His hand and caught him, and said to him
Matt 20:34 *And immediately* their eyes received sight, and they followed Him
Matt 21:2 saying to them, "Go into the village opposite you, *and immediately* you will find a donkey tied, and a colt with her
Matt 21:3 And if anyone says anything to you, you shall say, 'The Lord has need of them,' *and immediately* he will send them
Matt 21:19 And seeing a fig tree by the road, He came to it and found nothing on it but leaves, and said to it, "Let no fruit grow on you ever again." *And immediately* the fig tree withered away
Matt 25:15 And to one he gave five talents, to another two, and to another one, to each according to his own ability; *and immediately* he went on a journey
Matt 26:74 Then he began to curse and swear, saying, "I do not know the Man!" *And immediately* a rooster crowed
Mark 1:10 *And immediately*, coming up from the water, He saw the heavens parting and the Spirit descending upon Him like a dove
Mark 1:12 *And immediately* the Spirit drove Him into the wilderness
Mark 1:18 *And immediately* they left their nets and followed Him
Mark 1:20 *And immediately* He called them, and they left their father Zebedee in the boat with the hired servants, and went after Him
Mark 1:21 Then they went into Capernaum, *and immediately* on the Sabbath He entered the synagogue and taught
Mark 1:28 *And immediately* His fame spread throughout all the region around Galilee
Mark 1:31 So He came and took her by the hand and lifted her up, *and immediately* the fever left her
Mark 2:8 *And immediately*, when Jesus perceived in His spirit that they reasoned thus within themselves, He said to them
Mark 2:12 *And immediately* he arose, took up the bed, and went out in the presence of them all, so that all were amazed and glorified God, saying
Mark 3:6 Then the Pharisees went out *and immediately* plotted with the Herodians against Him, how they might destroy Him
Mark 4:5 *and immediately* it sprang up because it had no depth of earth
Mark 6:27 *And immediately* the king sent an executioner and commanded his head to be brought
Mark 6:50 *And immediately* He talked with them and said to them
Mark 8:10 *And immediately* He got into the boat with His disciples and came to the region of Dalmanutha
Mark 10:52 *And immediately* he received his sight and followed Jesus on the road
Mark 11:3 say, 'The Lord has need of it,' *and immediately* he will send it here
Mark 14:43 *And immediately*, while He was still speaking, Judas, one of the twelve, with a great multitude with swords and clubs, came from the chief priests and the scribes and the elders
Luke 4:39 So He stood over her and rebuked the fever, and it left her. *And immediately* she arose and served them
Luke 5:13 Then He put out His hand and touched him, saying, "I am willing; be cleansed." *And immediately* the leprosy left him
Luke 6:49 *and immediately* it fell. And the ruin of that house was great
Luke 8:44 came from behind and touched the border of His garment. *And immediately* her flow of blood stopped
Luke 13:13 And He laid His hands on her, *and immediately* she was made straight, and glorified God
Luke 18:43 *And immediately* he received his sight, and followed Him, glorifying God
Luke 22:60 *And immediately*, while he was still speaking, the rooster crowed
John 5:9 *And immediately* the man was made well, took up his bed, and walked
John 6:21 Then they willingly received Him into the boat, *and immediately* the boat was at the land where they were going
John 18:27 Peter then denied again; *and immediately* a rooster crowed
John 19:34 But one of the soldiers pierced His side with a spear, *and immediately* blood and water came out
John 21:3 They went out *and immediately* got into the boat, and that night they caught nothing
Acts 3:7 And he took him by the right hand and lifted him up, *and immediately* his feet and ankle bones received strength
Acts 12:10 and they went out and went down one street, *and immediately* the angel departed from him
Acts 13:11 *And immediately* a dark mist fell on him, and he went around seeking someone to lead him by the hand
Acts 16:26 *and immediately* all the doors were opened and everyone's chains were loosed
Acts 16:33 And he took them the same hour of the night and washed their stripes. *And immediately* he and all his family were baptized
Acts 21:30 and the people ran together, seized Paul, and dragged him out of the temple; *and immediately* the doors were shut
Jas 1:24 for he observes himself, goes away, *and immediately* forgets what kind of man he was

ANGEL OF GOD

Gen 21:17 Then the *angel of God* called to Hagar out of heaven, and said to her
Gen 31:11 Then the *Angel of God* spoke to me in a dream, saying
Ex 14:19 And the *Angel of God*, who went before the camp of Israel, moved and went behind them
Judg 6:20 The *Angel of God* said to him, "Take the meat and the unleavened bread and lay them on this rock, and pour out the broth
Judg 13:6 So the woman came and told her husband, saying, "A Man of God came to me, and His countenance was like the countenance of the *Angel of God*, very awesome
Judg 13:9 And God listened to the voice of Manoah, and the *Angel of God* came to the woman again as she was sitting in the field
1Sam 29:9 But Achish answered and said to David, "I know that you are as good in my sight as an *angel of God*
2Sam 14:17 for as the *angel of God*, so is my lord the king in discerning good and evil
2Sam 14:20 but my lord is wise, according to the wisdom of the *angel of God*, to know all things that are in the earth
2Sam 19:27 And he has slandered your servant to my lord the king, but my lord the king is like the *angel of God*
Acts 10:3 About the ninth hour of the day he saw clearly in a vision an *angel of God* coming in and saying to him
Gal 4:14 And my trial which was in my flesh you did not despise or reject, but you received me as an *angel of God*, even as Christ Jesus

ANGEL OF HIS PRESENCE
Is 63:9 In all their affliction He was afflicted, and the *Angel of His Presence* saved them

ANGEL OF LIGHT
2Cor 11:14 For Satan himself transforms himself into an *angel of light*

ANGEL OF THE CHURCH
Rev 2:1 To the *angel of the church* of Ephesus write, 'These things says He who holds the seven stars in His right hand, who walks in the midst of the seven golden lampstands
Rev 2:8 And to the *angel of the church* in Smyrna write
Rev 2:12 And to the *angel of the church* in Pergamos write
Rev 2:18 And to the *angel of the church* in Thyatira write
Rev 3:1 And to the *angel of the church* in Sardis write
Rev 3:7 And to the *angel of the church* in Philadelphia write
Rev 3:14 And to the *angel of the church* of the Laodiceans write

ANGEL OF THE LORD
Gen 16:7 Now the *Angel of the Lord* found her by a spring of water in the wilderness, by the spring on the way to Shur
Gen 16:9 So the *Angel of the Lord* said to her, "Return to your mistress, and submit yourself under her hand
Gen 16:10 Then the *Angel of the Lord* said to her, "I will multiply your descendants exceedingly, so that they shall not be counted for multitude
Gen 16:11 And the *Angel of the Lord* said to her: "Behold, you are with child, and you shall bear a son
Gen 22:11 But the *Angel of the Lord* called to him from heaven and said
Gen 22:15 Then the *Angel of the Lord* called to Abraham a second time out of heaven
Ex 3:2 And the *Angel of the Lord* appeared to him in a flame of fire from the midst of a bush
Num 22:22 Then God's anger was aroused because he went, and the *Angel of the Lord* took His stand in the way as an adversary against him
Num 22:23 Now the donkey saw the *Angel of the Lord* standing in the way with His drawn sword in His hand, and the donkey turned aside out of the way and went into the field
Num 22:24 Then the *Angel of the Lord* stood in a narrow path between the vineyards, with a wall on this side and a wall on that side
Num 22:25 And when the donkey saw the *Angel of the Lord*, she pushed herself against the wall and crushed Balaam's foot against the wall
Num 22:26 Then the *Angel of the Lord* went further, and stood in a narrow place where there was no way to turn either to the right hand or to the left
Num 22:27 And when the donkey saw the *Angel of the Lord*, she lay down under Balaam
Num 22:31 Then the Lord opened Balaam's eyes, and he saw the *Angel of the Lord* standing in the way with His drawn sword in His hand
Num 22:32 And the *Angel of the Lord* said to him, "Why have you struck your donkey these three times
Num 22:34 And Balaam said to the *Angel of the Lord*, "I have sinned, for I did not know You stood in the way against me
Num 22:35 Then the *Angel of the Lord* said to Balaam, "Go with the men, but only the word that I speak to you, that you shall speak
Judg 2:1 Then the *Angel of the Lord* came up from Gilgal to Bochim, and said
Judg 2:4 And so it was, when the *Angel of the Lord* spoke these words to all the children of Israel, that the people lifted up their voice and wept
Judg 5:23 Curse Meroz,' said the *angel of the Lord*, 'curse its inhabitants bitterly, because they did not come to the help of the Lord, to the help of the Lord against the mighty
Judg 6:11 Now the *Angel of the Lord* came and sat under the terebinth tree which was in Ophrah, which belonged to Joash the Abiezrite, while his son Gideon threshed wheat in the winepress, in order to hide it from the Midianites
Judg 6:12 And the *Angel of the Lord* appeared to him, and said to him
Judg 6:21 Then the *Angel of the Lord* put out the end of the staff that was in His hand, and touched the meat and the unleavened bread; and fire rose out of the rock and consumed the meat and the unleavened bread. And the *Angel of the Lord* departed out of his sight
Judg 6:22 Now Gideon perceived that He was the *Angel of the Lord*. So Gideon said, "Alas, O Lord God! For I have seen the *Angel of the Lord* face to face
Judg 13:3 And the *Angel of the Lord* appeared to the woman and said to her
Judg 13:13 So the *Angel of the Lord* said to Manoah, "Of all that I said to the woman let her be careful
Judg 13:15 Then Manoah said to the *Angel of the Lord*, "Please let us detain You, and we will prepare a young goat for You
Judg 13:16 And the *Angel of the Lord* said to Manoah, "Though you detain Me, I will not eat your food. But if you offer a burnt offering, you must offer it to the Lord." (For Manoah did not know He was the *Angel of the Lord*
Judg 13:17 Then Manoah said to the *Angel of the Lord*, "What is Your name, that when Your words come to pass we may honor You
Judg 13:18 And the *Angel of the Lord* said to him, "Why do you ask My name, seeing it is wonderful
Judg 13:20 as the flame went up toward heaven from the altar, it happened that the *Angel of the Lord* ascended in the flame of the altar
Judg 13:21 When the *Angel of the Lord* appeared no more to Manoah and his wife, then Manoah knew that He was the *Angel of the Lord*
2Sam 24:16 And the *angel of the Lord* was by the threshing floor of Araunah the Jebusite
1Kin 19:7 And the *angel of the Lord* came back the second time, and touched him, and said
2Kin 1:3 But the *angel of the Lord* said to Elijah the Tishbite
2Kin 1:15 And the *angel of the Lord* said to Elijah, "Go down with him
2Kin 19:35 And it came to pass on a certain night that the *angel of the Lord* went out, and killed in the camp of the Assyrians one hundred and eighty-five thousand
1Chr 21:12 either three years of famine, or three months to be defeated by your foes with the sword of your enemies overtaking you, or else for three days the sword of the Lord the plague in the land, with the *angel of the Lord* destroying throughout all the territory of Israel
1Chr 21:15 And the *angel of the Lord* stood by the threshing floor of Ornan the Jebusite
1Chr 21:16 Then David lifted his eyes and saw the *angel of the Lord* standing between earth and heaven, having in his hand a drawn sword stretched out over Jerusalem
1Chr 21:18 Then the *angel of the Lord* commanded Gad to say to David that David should go and erect an altar to the Lord on the threshing floor of Ornan the Jebusite
1Chr 21:30 But David could not go before it to inquire of God, for he was afraid of the sword of the *angel of the Lord*

Ps 34:7 The *angel of the Lord* encamps all around those who fear Him, and delivers them
Ps 35:5 Let them be like chaff before the wind, and let the *angel of the Lord* chase them
Ps 35:6 Let their way be dark and slippery, and let the *angel of the Lord* pursue them
Is 37:36 Then the *angel of the Lord* went out, and killed in the camp of the Assyrians one hundred and eighty-five thousand
Zech 1:11 So they answered the *Angel of the Lord*, who stood among the myrtle trees, and said
Zech 1:12 Then the *Angel of the Lord* answered and said, "O Lord of hosts, how long will You not have mercy on Jerusalem and on the cities of Judah, against which You were angry these seventy years
Zech 3:1 Then he showed me Joshua the high priest standing before the *Angel of the Lord*, and Satan standing at his right hand to oppose him
Zech 3:5 So they put a clean turban on his head, and they put the clothes on him. And the *Angel of the Lord* stood by
Zech 3:6 Then the *Angel of the Lord* admonished Joshua, saying
Zech 12:8 the one who is feeble among them in that day shall be like David, and the house of David shall be like God, like the *Angel of the Lord* before them
Matt 1:20 But while he thought about these things, behold, an *angel of the Lord* appeared to him in a dream, saying
Matt 1:24 Then Joseph, being aroused from sleep, did as the *angel of the Lord* commanded him and took to him his wife
Matt 2:13 Now when they had departed, behold, an *angel of the Lord* appeared to Joseph in a dream, saying
Matt 2:19 But when Herod was dead, behold, an *angel of the Lord* appeared in a dream to Joseph in Egypt
Matt 28:2 for an *angel of the Lord* descended from heaven, and came and rolled back the stone from the door, and sat on it
Luke 1:11 Then an *angel of the Lord* appeared to him, standing on the right side of the altar of incense
Luke 2:9 And behold, an *angel of the Lord* stood before them, and the glory of the Lord shone around them, and they were greatly afraid
Acts 5:19 But at night an *angel of the Lord* opened the prison doors and brought them out, and said
Acts 7:30 And when forty years had passed, an *Angel of the Lord* appeared to him in a flame of fire in a bush, in the wilderness of Mount Sinai
Acts 8:26 Now an *angel of the Lord* spoke to Philip, saying
Acts 12:7 Now behold, an *angel of the Lord* stood by him, and a light shone in the prison
Acts 12:23 Then immediately an *angel of the Lord* struck him, because he did not give glory to God

ANGELS IN HEAVEN
Mark 12:25 For when they rise from the dead, they neither marry nor are given in marriage, but are like *angels in heaven*
Mark 13:32 But of that day and hour no one knows, neither the *angels in heaven*, nor the Son, but only the Father

ANGELS OF GOD
Gen 28:12 and there the *angels of God* were ascending and descending on it
Gen 32:1 So Jacob went on his way, and the *angels of God* met him
Matt 22:30 For in the resurrection they neither marry nor are given in marriage, but are like *angels of God* in heaven
Luke 12:8 Also I say to you, whoever confesses Me before men, him the Son of Man also will confess before the *angels of God*
Luke 12:9 But he who denies Me before men will be denied before the *angels of God*
Luke 15:10 Likewise, I say to you, there is joy in the presence of the *angels of God* over one sinner who repents
John 1:51 And He said to him, "Most assuredly, I say to you, hereafter you shall see heaven open, and the *angels of God* ascending and descending upon the Son of Man
Heb 1:6 But when He again brings the firstborn into the world, He says: "Let all the *angels of God* worship Him

ANGELS' FOOD
Ps 78:25 Men ate *angels' food;* He sent them food to the full

ANGER BURNS (NIV)
(See *KINDLED HIS WRATH*)

ANGER IS NOT TURNED AWAY
Is 5:25 For all this His *anger is not turned away*, but His hand is stretched out still
Is 9:12 For all this His *anger is not turned away*, but His hand is stretched out still
Is 9:17 For all this His *anger is not turned away*, but His hand is stretched out still
Is 9:21 For all this His *anger is not turned away*, but His hand is stretched out still
Is 10:4 For all this His *anger is not turned away*, but His hand is stretched out still

ANGER OF GOD (RSV)
(See *WRATH OF GOD*)

ANGER OF THE LORD
Ex 4:14 So the *anger of the Lord* was kindled against Moses, and He said
Num 11:10 and the *anger of the Lord* was greatly aroused; Moses also was displeased
Num 12:9 So the *anger of the Lord* was aroused against them, and He departed
Num 25:3 So Israel was joined to Baal of Peor, and the *anger of the Lord* was aroused against Israel
Num 25:4 Then the Lord said to Moses, "Take all the leaders of the people and hang the offenders before the Lord, out in the sun, that the fierce *anger of the Lord* may turn away from Israel
Num 32:14 You have risen in your father's place, a brood of sinful men, to increase still more the fierce *anger of the Lord* against Israel
Deut 6:15 lest the *anger of the Lord* your God be aroused against you and destroy you from the face of the earth
Deut 7:4 so the *anger of the Lord* will be aroused against you and destroy you suddenly
Deut 29:20 for then the *anger of the Lord* and His jealousy would burn against that man, and every curse that is written in this book would settle on him, and the Lord would blot out his name from under heaven
Deut 29:27 Then the *anger of the Lord* was aroused against this land, to bring on it every curse that is written in this book
Josh 7:1 so the *anger of the Lord* burned against the children of Israel
Josh 23:16 When you have transgressed the covenant of the Lord your God, which He commanded you, and have gone and served other gods, and bowed down to them, then the *anger of the Lord* will burn against you, and you shall perish quickly from the good land which He has given you
Judg 2:14 And the *anger of the Lord* was hot against Israel

Judg 2:20 Then the *anger of the Lord* was hot against Israel
Judg 3:8 Therefore the *anger of the Lord* was hot against Israel, and He sold them into the hand of Cushan-Rishathaim king of Mesopotamia
Judg 10:7 So the *anger of the Lord* was hot against Israel
2Sam 6:7 Then the *anger of the Lord* was aroused against Uzzah, and God struck him there for his error
2Sam 24:1 Again the *anger of the Lord* was aroused against Israel, and He moved David against them to say
2Kin 13:3 Then the *anger of the Lord* was aroused against Israel, and He delivered them into the hand of Hazael king of Syria, and into the hand of Ben-Hadad the son of Hazael, all their days
2Kin 24:20 For because of the *anger of the Lord* this happened in Jerusalem and Judah, that He finally cast them out from His presence
1Chr 13:10 Then the *anger of the Lord* was aroused against Uzza, and He struck him because he put his hand to the ark
2Chr 25:15 Therefore the *anger of the Lord* was aroused against Amaziah, and He sent him a prophet who said to him
Is 5:25 Therefore the *anger of the Lord* is aroused against His people
Jer 4:8 For the fierce *anger of the Lord* has not turned back from us
Jer 12:13 But be ashamed of your harvest because of the fierce *anger of the Lord*
Jer 23:20 The *anger of the Lord* will not turn back until He has executed and performed the thoughts of His heart
Jer 25:37 and the peaceful habitations are cut down because of the fierce *anger of the Lord*
Jer 30:24 The fierce *anger of the Lord* will not return until He has done it, and until He has performed the intents of His heart
Jer 51:45 And let everyone deliver himself from the fierce *anger of the Lord*
Jer 52:3 For because of the *anger of the Lord* this happened in Jerusalem and Judah, till He finally cast them out from His presence

ANGER WAS AROUSED
Gen 30:2 And Jacob's *anger was aroused* against Rachel, and he said
Gen 39:19 So it was, when his master heard the words which his wife spoke to him, saying, "Your servant did to me after this manner," that his *anger was aroused*
Num 11:1 for the Lord heard it, and His *anger was aroused*
Num 22:22 Then God's *anger was aroused* because he went, and the Angel of the Lord took His stand in the way as an adversary against him
Num 22:27 so Balaam's *anger was aroused*, and he struck the donkey with his staff
Num 24:10 Then Balak's *anger was aroused* against Balaam, and he struck his hands together
Num 32:10 So the Lord's *anger was aroused* on that day, and He swore an oath, saying
Num 32:13 So the Lord's *anger was aroused* against Israel, and He made them wander in the wilderness forty years, until all the generation that had done evil in the sight of the Lord was gone
Judg 9:30 When Zebul, the ruler of the city, heard the words of Gaal the son of Ebed, his *anger was aroused*
Judg 14:19 So his *anger was aroused*, and he went back up to his father's house
1Sam 17:28 and Eliab's *anger was aroused* against David, and he said
1Sam 20:30 Then Saul's *anger was aroused* against Jonathan, and he said to him
2Kin 23:26 Nevertheless the Lord did not turn from the fierceness of His great wrath, with which His *anger was aroused* against Judah, because of all the provocations with which Manasseh had provoked Him

ANGER WAS GREATLY AROUSED
1Sam 11:6 Then the Spirit of God came upon Saul when he heard this news, and his *anger was greatly aroused*
2Sam 12:5 Then David's *anger was greatly aroused* against the man, and he said to Nathan
2Chr 25:10 Therefore their *anger was greatly aroused* against Judah, and they returned home in great anger

ANGER WAS KINDLED (RSV)
(See *ANGER WAS AROUSED*)

ANGRY FOREVER
Ps 79:5 Will You be *angry forever?* Will Your jealousy burn like fire
Jer 3:5 Will He remain *angry forever?* Will He keep it to the end
Jer 3:12 For I am merciful,' says the Lord, 'and I will not remain *angry forever*

ANGUISH IN THIS FLAME (RSV)
(See *TORMENTED IN THIS FLAME*)

ANGUISH OF HEART (NIV, RSV)
(See *SORROW OF HEART*)

ANGUISH OF SOUL
Deut 28:65 but there the Lord will give you a trembling heart, failing eyes, and *anguish of soul*

ANOINT HIM KING OVER ISRAEL
1Kin 1:34 There let Zadok the priest and Nathan the prophet *anoint him king over Israel*

ANOINT MY HEAD WITH OIL
Ps 23:5 You *anoint my head with oil;* my cup runs over
Luke 7:46 You did not *anoint My head with oil*, but this woman has anointed My feet with fragrant oil

ANOINTED HIM KING
1Kin 1:45 So Zadok the priest and Nathan the prophet have *anointed him king* at Gihon
1Kin 5:1 Now Hiram king of Tyre sent his servants to Solomon, because he heard that they had *anointed him king* in place of his father, for Hiram had always loved David

ANOINTED OF THE LORD
1Sam 24:6 And he said to his men, "The Lord forbid that I should do this thing to my master, the Lord's anointed, to stretch out my hand against him, seeing he is the *anointed of the Lord*
Lam 4:20 The breath of our nostrils, the *anointed of the Lord*, was caught in their pits, of whom we said

ANOINTED WITH OIL
Ex 29:2 and unleavened bread, unleavened cakes mixed with oil, and unleavened wafers *anointed with oil* (you shall make them of wheat flour
Lev 2:4 And if you bring as an offering a grain offering baked in the oven, it shall be unleavened cakes of fine flour mixed with oil, or unleavened wafers *anointed with oil*
Lev 7:12 If he offers it for a thanksgiving, then he shall offer, with the sacrifice of thanksgiving, unleavened cakes mixed with oil, unleavened wafers *anointed with oil*, or cakes of finely blended flour mixed with oil

Lev 8:26 and from the basket of unleavened bread that was before the Lord he took one unleavened cake, a cake of bread *anointed with oil*, and one wafer, and put them on the fat and on the right thigh

Num 6:15 a basket of unleavened bread, cakes of fine flour mixed with oil, unleavened wafers *anointed with oil*, and their grain offering with their drink offerings

2Sam 1:21 For the shield of the mighty is cast away there! The shield of Saul, not *anointed with oil*

Mark 6:13 And they cast out many demons, and *anointed with oil* many who were sick, and healed them

ANOTHER COUNSELOR (NIV, RSV)
(See *ANOTHER HELPER*)

ANOTHER GOSPEL (KJV)
(See *DIFFERENT GOSPEL*)

ANOTHER HELPER

John 14:16 And I will pray the Father, and He will give you *another Helper*, that He may abide with you forever

ANOTHER MAN'S WIFE

Lev 20:10 The man who commits adultery with *another man's wife*, he who commits adultery with his neighbor's wife, the adulterer and the adulteress, shall surely be put to death

Deut 24:2 when she has departed from his house, and goes and becomes *another man's wife*

ANSWER A FOOL ACCORDING TO HIS FOLLY

Prov 26:4 Do not *answer a fool according to his folly*, lest you also be like him

Prov 26:5 *Answer a fool according to his folly*, lest he be wise in his own eyes

ANSWER ME (NIV)
(See *ATTEND TO ME*)

ANSWERED HIS PRAYER (NIV)
(See *GRANTED HIS PLEA*)

ANSWERED OUR PRAYER

Ezra 8:23 So we fasted and entreated our God for this, and He *answered our prayer*

ANXIETIES OF LIFE (NIV)
(See *CARES OF THIS LIFE*)

ANY OTHER GOSPEL

Gal 1:8 But even if we, or an angel from heaven, preach *any other gospel* to you than what we have preached to you, let him be accursed

Gal 1:9 As we have said before, so now I say again, if anyone preaches *any other gospel* to you than what you have received, let him be accursed

ANYONE WHO HAS SEEN ME (NIV)
(See *HE WHO HAS SEEN ME*)

APART FROM THE LAW

Rom 3:21 But now the righteousness of God *apart from the law* is revealed, being witnessed by the Law and the Prophets

Rom 7:8 But sin, taking opportunity by the commandment, produced in me all manner of evil desire. For *apart from the law* sin was dead

APOSTLE OF JESUS CHRIST

1Cor 1:1 Paul, called to be an *apostle of Jesus Christ* through the will of God, and Sosthenes our brother

2Cor 1:1 Paul, an *apostle of Jesus Christ* by the will of God, and Timothy our brother, To the church of God which is at Corinth, with all the saints who are in all Achaia

Eph 1:1 Paul, an *apostle of Jesus Christ* by the will of God, to the saints who are in Ephesus, and faithful in Christ Jesus

Col 1:1 Paul, an *apostle of Jesus Christ* by the will of God, and Timothy our brother

1Tim 1:1 Paul, an *apostle of Jesus Christ*, by the commandment of God our Savior and the Lord Jesus Christ, our hope

2Tim 1:1 Paul, an *apostle of Jesus Christ* by the will of God, according to the promise of life which is in Christ Jesus

Tit 1:1 Paul, a servant of God and an *apostle of Jesus Christ*, according to the faith of God's elect and the acknowledgment of the truth which is according to godliness

1Pet 1:1 Peter, an *apostle of Jesus Christ*, To the pilgrims of the Dispersion in Pontus, Galatia, Cappadocia, Asia, and Bithynia

2Pet 1:1 Simon Peter, a servant and *apostle of Jesus Christ*, to those who have obtained like precious faith with us by the righteousness of our God and Savior Jesus Christ

APOSTLE TO THE GENTILES

Rom 11:13 inasmuch as I am an *apostle to the Gentiles*, I magnify my ministry

APOSTLES AND ELDERS

Acts 15:2 Therefore, when Paul and Barnabas had no small dissension and dispute with them, they determined that Paul and Barnabas and certain others of them should go up to Jerusalem, to the *apostles and elders*, about this question

Acts 15:6 So the *apostles and elders* came together to consider this matter

Acts 15:22 Then it pleased the *apostles and elders*, with the whole church, to send chosen men of their own company to Antioch with Paul and Barnabas, namely, Judas who was also named Barsabas, and Silas, leading men among the brethren

Acts 16:4 And as they went through the cities, they delivered to them the decrees to keep, which were determined by the *apostles and elders* at Jerusalem

APOSTLES OF CHRIST

2Cor 11:13 For such are false apostles, deceitful workers, transforming themselves into *apostles of Christ*

1Th 2:6 Nor did we seek glory from men, either from you or from others, when we might have made demands as *apostles of Christ*

APPEAL TO CAESAR

Acts 25:11 but if there is nothing in these things of which these men accuse me, no one can deliver me to them. I *appeal to Caesar*

Acts 28:19 But when the Jews spoke against it, I was compelled to *appeal to Caesar*, not that I had anything of which to accuse my nation

APPEAL TO THE LORD (NIV)
(See *CRY OUT TO THE LORD*)

APPEALED TO CAESAR

Acts 25:12 Then Festus, when he had conferred with the council, answered, "You have *appealed to Caesar*

Acts 26:32 Then Agrippa said to Festus, "This man might have been set free if he had not *appealed to Caesar*

APPEAR BEFORE GOD
Ps 42:2 My soul thirsts for God, for the living God. When shall I come and *appear before God*

APPEAR BEFORE ME
Ex 23:15 You shall keep the Feast of Unleavened Bread (you shall eat unleavened bread seven days, as I commanded you, at the time appointed in the month of Abib, for in it you came out of Egypt; none shall *appear before Me* empty)
Ex 34:20 All the firstborn of your sons you shall redeem. And none shall *appear before Me* empty-handed
Is 1:12 When you come to *appear before Me*, who has required this from your hand, to trample My courts

APPEAR BEFORE THE LORD
Ex 23:17 Three times in the year all your males shall *appear before the Lord* God
Ex 34:23 Three times in the year all your men shall *appear before the Lord*, the Lord God of Israel
Ex 34:24 neither will any man covet your land when you go up to *appear before the Lord* your God three times in the year
Deut 16:16 Three times a year all your males shall *appear before the Lord* your God in the place which He chooses: at the Feast of Unleavened Bread, at the Feast of Weeks, and at the Feast of Tabernacles; and they shall not *appear before the Lord* empty-handed
Deut 31:11 when all Israel comes to *appear before the Lord* your God in the place which He chooses, you shall read this law before all Israel in their hearing
1Sam 1:22 then I will take him, that he may *appear before the Lord* and remain there forever

APPEARANCE WAS LIKE LIGHTNING (NAS, NIV, RSV)
(See *COUNTENANCE WAS LIKE LIGHTNING*)

APPEARED IN A BODY (NIV)
(See *MANIFESTED IN THE FLESH*)

APPLE OF HIS EYE
Deut 32:10 He encircled him, He instructed him, He kept him as the *apple of His eye*
Zech 2:8 for he who touches you touches the *apple of His eye*

APPLE OF YOUR EYE
Ps 17:8 Keep me as the *apple of Your eye;* hide me under the shadow of Your wings
Prov 7:2 Keep my commands and live, and my law as the *apple of your eye*

APPLES OF GOLD
Prov 25:11 A word fitly spoken is like *apples of gold* in settings of silver

APPLY THEMSELVES TO GOOD DEEDS (RSV)
(See *MAINTAIN GOOD WORKS*)

APPLY YOUR HEART
Prov 2:2 so that you incline your ear to wisdom, and *apply your heart* to understanding
Prov 22:17 Incline your ear and hear the words of the wise, and *apply your heart* to my knowledge
Prov 23:12 *Apply your heart* to instruction, and your ears to words of knowledge

APPOINTED FEASTS
Num 10:10 Also in the day of your gladness, in your *appointed feasts*, and at the beginning of your months, you shall blow the trumpets over your burnt offerings and over the sacrifices of your peace offerings
Num 15:3 and you make an offering by fire to the Lord, a burnt offering or a sacrifice, to fulfill a vow or as a freewill offering or in your *appointed feasts*, to make a sweet aroma to the Lord, from the herd or the flock
Num 29:39 These things you shall present to the Lord at your *appointed feasts* (besides your vowed offerings and your freewill offerings
Ezra 3:5 and afterward they offered the regular burnt offering, and those for New Moons and for all the *appointed feasts* of the Lord that were consecrated, and those of everyone who willingly offered a freewill offering to the Lord
Is 1:14 Your New Moons and your *appointed feasts* my soul hates
Is 33:20 Look upon Zion, the city of our *appointed feasts;* your eyes will see Jerusalem, a quiet habitation, a tabernacle that will not be taken down
Lam 2:6 the Lord has caused the *appointed feasts* and Sabbaths to be forgotten in Zion
Hos 2:11 I will also cause all her mirth to cease, her feast days, her New Moons, her Sabbaths all her *appointed feasts*
Nah 1:15 O Judah, keep your *appointed feasts*, perform your vows. For the wicked one shall no more pass through you

APPOINTED TIME
Gen 18:14 At the *appointed time* I will return to you, according to the time of life, and Sarah shall have a son
Ex 34:18 Seven days you shall eat unleavened bread, as I commanded you, in the *appointed time* of the month of Abib
Num 9:2 Let the children of Israel keep the Passover at its *appointed time*
Num 9:3 On the fourteenth day of this month, at twilight, you shall keep it at its *appointed time*
Num 9:7 Why are we kept from presenting the offering of the Lord at its *appointed time* among the children of Israel
Num 9:13 But the man who is clean and is not on a journey, and ceases to keep the Passover, that same person shall be cut off from among his people, because he did not bring the offering of the Lord at its *appointed time*
Num 28:2 Command the children of Israel, and say to them, 'My offering, My food for My offerings made by fire as a sweet aroma to Me, you shall be careful to offer to Me at their *appointed time*
Deut 31:10 At the end of every seven years, at the *appointed time* in the year of release, at the Feast of Tabernacles
2Sam 24:15 So the Lord sent a plague upon Israel from the morning till the *appointed time*
2Kin 4:17 And the woman conceived, and bore a son when the *appointed time* had come, of which Elisha had told her
Esth 9:31 to confirm these days of Purim at their *appointed time*, as Mordecai the Jew and Queen Esther had prescribed for them, and as they had decreed for themselves and their descendants concerning matters of their fasting and lamenting
Jer 46:17 They cried there, 'Pharaoh, king of Egypt, is but a noise. He has passed by the *appointed time*
Dan 8:19 And he said, "Look, I am making known to you what shall happen in the latter time of the indignation; for at the *appointed time* the end shall be
Dan 10:1 The message was true, but the *appointed time* was long
Dan 11:27 but it shall not prosper, for the end will still be at the *appointed time*
Dan 11:29 At the *appointed time* he shall return and go toward the south
Dan 11:35 And some of those of understanding

shall fall, to refine them, purge them, and make them white, until the time of the end; because it is still for the *appointed time*
Hab 2:3 For the vision is yet for an *appointed time;* but at the end it will speak, and it will not lie

APPROVED BY GOD
1Th 2:4 But as we have been *approved by God* to be entrusted with the gospel, even so we speak, not as pleasing men, but God who tests our hearts

APPROVED OF GOD (KJV)
(See *ATTESTED BY GOD*)

APPROVED TO GOD
2Tim 2:15 Be diligent to present yourself *approved to God*, a worker who does not need to be ashamed, rightly dividing the word of truth

APPROVING OURSELVES (KJV)
(See *WE COMMEND OURSELVES*)

ARE ALL PROPHETS
1Cor 12:29 *Are all prophets?* Are all teachers? Are all workers of miracles

ARE YOU ELIJAH
John 1:21 *Are you Elijah?*" He said, "I am not." "Are you the Prophet

ARGUE YOUR CASE (NAS, NIV, RSV)
(See *DEBATE YOUR CASE*)

ARISE, O LORD
2Chr 6:41 Now therefore, *arise, O Lord* God, to Your resting place, You and the ark of Your strength
Ps 3:7 *Arise, O Lord;* Save me, O my God! For You have struck all my enemies on the cheekbone
Ps 7:6 *Arise, O Lord*, in Your anger; lift Yourself up because of the rage of my enemies, and awake for me to the judgment You have commanded
Ps 9:19 *Arise, O Lord*, do not let man prevail; let the nations be judged in Your sight
Ps 10:12 *Arise, O Lord!* O God, lift up Your hand
Ps 17:13 *Arise, O Lord*, confront him, cast him down; deliver my life from the wicked with Your sword
Ps 132:8 *Arise, O Lord*, to Your resting place, You and the ark of Your strength

ARK OF CYPRESS WOOD (NIV)
(See *ARK OF GOPHERWOOD*)

ARK OF GOD
1Sam 3:3 and before the lamp of God went out in the tabernacle of the Lord where the *ark of God* was, and while Samuel was lying down to sleep
1Sam 4:11 Also the *ark of God* was captured; and the two sons of Eli, Hophni and Phinehas, died
1Sam 4:13 Now when he came, there was Eli, sitting on a seat by the wayside watching, for his heart trembled for the *ark of God*
1Sam 4:17 Also your two sons, Hophni and Phinehas, are dead; and the *ark of God* has been captured
1Sam 4:18 Then it happened, when he made mention of the *ark of God*, that Eli fell off the seat backward by the side of the gate
1Sam 4:19 and when she heard the news that the *ark of God* was captured, and that her father-in-law and her husband were dead, she bowed herself and gave birth, for her labor pains came upon her
1Sam 4:21 because the *ark of God* had been captured and because of her father-in-law and her husband
1Sam 4:22 And she said, "The glory has departed from Israel, for the *ark of God* has been captured
1Sam 5:1 Then the Philistines took the *ark of God* and brought it from Ebenezer to Ashdod
1Sam 5:2 When the Philistines took the *ark of God*, they brought it into the temple of Dagon and set it by Dagon
1Sam 5:10 Therefore they sent the *ark of God* to Ekron. So it was, as the *ark of God* came to Ekron, that the Ekronites cried out, saying
1Sam 14:18 And Saul said to Ahijah, "Bring the *ark of God* here" (for at that time the *ark of God* was with the children of Israel
2Sam 6:2 And David arose and went with all the people who were with him from Baale Judah to bring up from there the *ark of God*, whose name is called by the Name, the Lord of Hosts, who dwells between the cherubim
2Sam 6:3 So they set the *ark of God* on a new cart, and brought it out of the house of Abinadab, which was on the hill
2Sam 6:4 And they brought it out of the house of Abinadab, which was on the hill, accompanying the *ark of God*
2Sam 6:6 And when they came to Nachon's threshingfloor, Uzzah put out his hand to the *ark of God* and took hold of it, for the oxen stumbled
2Sam 6:7 Then the anger of the Lord was aroused against Uzzah, and God struck him there for his error; and he died there by the *ark of God*
2Sam 6:12 And it was told King David, saying, "The Lord has blessed the house of Obed-Edom and all that belongs to him, because of the *ark of God*." So David went and brought up the *ark of God* from the house of Obed-Edom to the City of David with gladness
2Sam 7:2 that the king said to Nathan the prophet, "See now, I dwell in a house of cedar, but the *ark of God* dwells inside tent curtains
2Sam 15:24 And they set down the *ark of God*, and Abiathar went up until all the people had finished crossing over from the city
2Sam 15:25 Then the king said to Zadok, "Carry the *ark of God* back into the city
2Sam 15:29 Therefore Zadok and Abiathar carried the *ark of God* back to Jerusalem
1Chr 13:5 So David gathered all Israel together, from Shihor in Egypt to as far as the entrance of Hamath, to bring the *ark of God* from Kirjath Jearim
1Chr 13:6 And David and all Israel went up to Baalah, to Kirjath Jearim, which belonged to Judah, to bring up from there the *ark of God* the Lord, who dwells between the cherubim, where His name is proclaimed
1Chr 13:7 So they carried the *ark of God* on a new cart from the house of Abinadab, and Uzza and Ahio drove the cart
1Chr 13:12 David was afraid of God that day, saying, "How can I bring the *ark of God* to me
1Chr 13:14 The *ark of God* remained with the family of Obed-Edom in his house three months
1Chr 15:1 and he prepared a place for the *ark of God*, and pitched a tent for it
1Chr 15:2 Then David said, "No one may carry the *ark of God* but the Levites, for the Lord has chosen them to carry the *ark of God* and to minister before Him forever
1Chr 15:15 And the children of the Levites bore the *ark of God* on their shoulders, by its poles, as Moses had commanded according to the word of the Lord
1Chr 15:24 Shebaniah, Joshaphat, Nethaneel, Amasai, Zechariah, Benaiah, and Eliezer, the priests, were to blow the trumpets before the *ark of God*

1Chr 16:1 So they brought the *ark of God*, and set it in the midst of the tabernacle that David had erected for it

2Chr 1:4 But David had brought up the *ark of God* from Kirjath Jearim to the place David had prepared for it, for he had pitched a tent for it at Jerusalem

ARK OF GOPHERWOOD

Gen 6:14 Make yourself an *ark of gopherwood;* make rooms in the ark, and cover it inside and outside with pitch

ARK OF HIS COVENANT

Rev 11:19 Then the temple of God was opened in heaven, and the *ark of His covenant* was seen in His temple

ARK OF THE COVENANT

Num 10:33 and the *ark of the covenant* of the Lord went before them for the three days

Num 14:44 nevertheless, neither the *ark of the covenant* of the Lord nor Moses departed from the camp

Deut 10:8 At that time the Lord separated the tribe of Levi to bear the *ark of the covenant* of the Lord, to stand before the Lord to minister to Him and to bless in His name, to this day

Deut 31:9 So Moses wrote this law and delivered it to the priests, the sons of Levi, who bore the *ark of the covenant* of the Lord, and to all the elders of Israel

Deut 31:25 that Moses commanded the Levites, who bore the *ark of the covenant* of the Lord, saying

Deut 31:26 Take this Book of the Law, and put it beside the *ark of the covenant* of the Lord your God, that it may be there as a witness against you

Josh 3:3 and they commanded the people, saying, "When you see the *ark of the covenant* of the Lord your God, and the priests, the Levites, bearing it, then you shall set out from your place and go after it

Josh 3:6 Then Joshua spoke to the priests, saying, "Take up the *ark of the covenant* and cross over before the people." So they took up the *ark of the covenant* and went before the people

Josh 3:8 You shall command the priests who bear the *ark of the covenant*, saying

Josh 3:11 Behold, the *ark of the covenant* of the Lord of all the earth is crossing over before you into the Jordan

Josh 3:14 So it was, when the people set out from their camp to cross over the Jordan, with the priests bearing the *ark of the covenant* before the people

Josh 3:17 Then the priests who bore the *ark of the covenant* of the Lord stood firm on dry ground in the midst of the Jordan

Josh 4:7 Then you shall answer them that the waters of the Jordan were cut off before the *ark of the covenant* of the Lord

Josh 4:9 Then Joshua set up twelve stones in the midst of the Jordan, in the place where the feet of the priests who bore the *ark of the covenant* stood

Josh 4:18 And it came to pass, when the priests who bore the *ark of the covenant* of the Lord had come from the midst of the Jordan, and the soles of the priests' feet touched the dry land, that the waters of the Jordan returned to their place and flowed over all its banks as before

Josh 6:6 So Joshua the son of Nun called the priests and said to them, "Take up the *ark of the covenant*, and let seven priests bear seven trumpets of rams' horns before the ark of the Lord

Josh 6:8 So it was, when Joshua had spoken to the people, that the seven priests bearing the seven trumpets of rams' horns before the Lord advanced and blew the trumpets, and the *ark of the covenant* of the Lord followed them

Josh 8:33 Then all Israel, with their elders and officers and judges, stood on either side of the ark before the priests, the Levites, who bore the *ark of the covenant* of the Lord, the stranger as well as he who was born among them

Judg 20:27 So the children of Israel inquired of the Lord (the *ark of the covenant* of God was there in those days

1Sam 4:3 Let us bring the *ark of the covenant* of the Lord from Shiloh to us, that when it comes among us it may save us from the hand of our enemies

1Sam 4:4 So the people sent to Shiloh, that they might bring from there the *ark of the covenant* of the Lord of hosts, who dwells between the cherubim. And the two sons of Eli, Hophni and Phinehas, were there with the *ark of the covenant* of God

1Sam 4:5 And when the *ark of the covenant* of the Lord came into the camp, all Israel shouted so loudly that the earth shook

2Sam 15:24 There was Zadok also, and all the Levites with him, bearing the *ark of the covenant* of God

1Kin 3:15 And he came to Jerusalem and stood before the *ark of the covenant* of the Lord, offered up burnt offerings, offered peace offerings, and made a feast for all his servants

1Kin 6:19 And he prepared the inner sanctuary inside the temple, to set the *ark of the covenant* of the Lord there

1Kin 8:1 Now Solomon assembled the elders of Israel and all the heads of the tribes, the chief fathers of the children of Israel, to King Solomon in Jerusalem, that they might bring up the *ark of the covenant* of the Lord from the City of David, which is Zion

1Kin 8:6 Then the priests brought in the *ark of the covenant* of the Lord to its place, into the inner sanctuary of the temple, to the Most Holy Place, under the wings of the cherubim

1Chr 15:25 So David, the elders of Israel, and the captains over thousands went to bring up the *ark of the covenant* of the Lord from the house of Obed-Edom with joy

1Chr 15:26 And so it was, when God helped the Levites who bore the *ark of the covenant* of the Lord, that they offered seven bulls and seven rams

1Chr 15:28 Thus all Israel brought up the *ark of the covenant* of the Lord with shouting and with the sound of the horn, with trumpets and with cymbals, making music with stringed instruments and harps

1Chr 15:29 And it happened, as the *ark of the covenant* of the Lord came to the City of David, that Michal the daughter of Saul, looking through a window, saw King David whirling and playing music

1Chr 16:6 Benaiah and Jahaziel the priests regularly blew the trumpets before the *ark of the covenant* of God

1Chr 16:37 So he left Asaph and his brothers there before the *ark of the covenant* of the Lord to minister before the ark regularly, as every day's work required

1Chr 17:1 Now it came to pass, when David was dwelling in his house, that David said to Nathan the prophet, "See now, I dwell in a house of cedar, but the *ark of the covenant* of the Lord is under tent curtains

1Chr 22:19 Therefore arise and build the sanctuary of the Lord God, to bring the *ark of the covenant* of the Lord and the holy articles of God into the house that is to be built for the name of the Lord

1Chr 28:2 I had it in my heart to build a house of rest for the *ark of the covenant* of the Lord, and for the footstool of our God, and had made preparations to build it

1Chr 28:18 and refined gold by weight for the altar of incense, and for the construction of the chariot, that is, the gold cherubim that spread their wings and overshadowed the *ark of the covenant* of the Lord

2Chr 5:2 Now Solomon assembled the elders of Israel and all the heads of the tribes, the chief fathers of the children of Israel, in Jerusalem, that they might bring the *ark of the covenant* of the Lord up from the City of David, which is Zion

2Chr 5:7 Then the priests brought in the *ark of the covenant* of the Lord to its place, into the inner sanctuary of the temple, to the Most Holy Place, under the wings of the cherubim

Jer 3:16 Then it shall come to pass, when you are multiplied and increased in the land in those days," says the Lord, "that they will say no more, 'The *ark of the covenant* of the Lord

Heb 9:4 which had the golden altar of incense and the *ark of the covenant* overlaid on all sides with gold, in which were the golden pot that had the manna, Aaron's rod that budded, and the tablets of the covenant

ARK OF THE LORD

Josh 3:13 And it shall come to pass, as soon as the soles of the feet of the priests who bear the *ark of the Lord*, the Lord of all the earth, shall rest in the waters of the Jordan, that the waters of the Jordan shall be cut off, the waters that come down from upstream, and they shall stand as a heap

Josh 4:5 Cross over before the *ark of the Lord* your God into the midst of the Jordan, and each one of you take up a stone on his shoulder, according to the number of the tribes of the children of Israel

Josh 4:11 Then it came to pass, when all the people had completely crossed over, that the *ark of the Lord* and the priests crossed over in the presence of the people

Josh 6:6 So Joshua the son of Nun called the priests and said to them, "Take up the ark of the covenant, and let seven priests bear seven trumpets of rams' horns before the *ark of the Lord*

Josh 6:7 And he said to the people, "Proceed, and march around the city, and let him who is armed advance before the *ark of the Lord*

Josh 6:11 So he had the *ark of the Lord* circle the city, going around it once

Josh 6:12 And Joshua rose early in the morning, and the priests took up the *ark of the Lord*

Josh 6:13 Then seven priests bearing seven trumpets of rams' horns before the *ark of the Lord* went on continually and blew with the trumpets. And the armed men went before them. But the rear guard came after the *ark of the Lord*, while the priests continued blowing the trumpets

Josh 7:6 Then Joshua tore his clothes, and fell to the earth on his face before the *ark of the Lord* until evening, both he and the elders of Israel

1Sam 4:6 Then they understood that the *ark of the Lord* had come into the camp

1Sam 5:3 And when the people of Ashdod arose early in the morning, there was Dagon, fallen on its face to the earth before the *ark of the Lord*

1Sam 5:4 And when they arose early the next morning, there was Dagon, fallen on its face to the ground before the *ark of the Lord*

1Sam 6:1 Now the *ark of the Lord* was in the country of the Philistines seven months

1Sam 6:2 And the Philistines called for the priests and the diviners, saying, "What shall we do with the *ark of the Lord*

1Sam 6:8 Then take the *ark of the Lord* and set it on the cart

1Sam 6:11 And they set the *ark of the Lord* on the cart, and the chest with the gold rats and the images of their tumors

1Sam 6:15 The Levites took down the *ark of the Lord* and the chest that was with it, in which were the articles of gold, and put them on the large stone

1Sam 6:18 and the gold rats, according to the number of all the cities of the Philistines belonging to the five lords, both fortified cities and country villages, even as far as the large stone of Abel on which they set the *ark of the Lord*, which stone remains to this day in the field of Joshua of Beth Shemesh

1Sam 6:19 Then He struck the men of Beth Shemesh, because they had looked into the *ark of the Lord*

1Sam 6:21 So they sent messengers to the inhabitants of Kirjath Jearim, saying, "The Philistines have brought back the *ark of the Lord*

1Sam 7:1 Then the men of Kirjath Jearim came and took the *ark of the Lord*, and brought it into the house of Abinadab on the hill, and consecrated Eleazar his son to keep the *ark of the Lord*

2Sam 6:9 and he said, "How can the *ark of the Lord* come to me

2Sam 6:10 So David would not move the *ark of the Lord* with him into the City of David

2Sam 6:11 The *ark of the Lord* remained in the house of Obed-Edom the Gittite three months

2Sam 6:13 And so it was, when those bearing the *ark of the Lord* had gone six paces, that he sacrificed oxen and fatted sheep

2Sam 6:15 So David and all the house of Israel brought up the *ark of the Lord* with shouting and with the sound of the trumpet

2Sam 6:16 And as the *ark of the Lord* came into the City of David, Michal, Saul's daughter, looked through a window and saw King David leaping and whirling before the Lord

2Sam 6:17 So they brought the *ark of the Lord*, and set it in its place in the midst of the tabernacle that David had erected for it

1Kin 2:26 but I will not put you to death at this time, because you carried the *ark of the Lord* God before my father David, and because you were afflicted every time my father was afflicted

1Kin 8:4 And they brought up the *ark of the Lord*, the tabernacle of meeting, and all the holy furnishings that were in the tabernacle

1Chr 15:3 And David gathered all Israel together at Jerusalem, to bring up the *ark of the Lord* to its place, which he had prepared for it

1Chr 15:12 sanctify yourselves, you and your brethren, that you may bring up the *ark of the Lord* God of Israel to the place I have prepared for it

1Chr 15:14 So the priests and the Levites sanctified themselves to bring up the *ark of the Lord* God of Israel

1Chr 16:4 And he appointed some of the Levites to minister before the *ark of the Lord*, to commemorate, to thank, and to praise the Lord God of Israel

2Chr 8:11 Now Solomon brought the daughter of Pharaoh up from the City of David to the house he had built for her, for he said, "My wife shall not dwell in the house of David king of Israel, because the places to which the *ark of the Lord* has come are holy

ARK OF THE TESTIMONY

Ex 25:22 And there I will meet with you, and I will speak with you from above the mercy seat, from

between the two cherubim which are on the *ark of the Testimony*, of all things which I will give you in commandment to the children of Israel
Ex 26:33 Then you shall bring the *ark of the Testimony* in there, behind the veil
Ex 26:34 You shall put the mercy seat upon the *ark of the Testimony* in the Most Holy
Ex 30:6 And you shall put it before the veil that is before the *ark of the Testimony*, before the mercy seat that is over the Testimony, where I will meet with you
Ex 30:26 With it you shall anoint the tabernacle of meeting and the *ark of the Testimony*
Ex 31:7 the tabernacle of meeting, the *ark of the Testimony* and the mercy seat that is on it, and all the furniture of the tabernacle
Ex 39:35 the *ark of the Testimony* with its poles, and the mercy seat
Ex 40:3 You shall put in it the *ark of the Testimony*, and partition off the ark with the veil
Ex 40:5 You shall also set the altar of gold for the incense before the *ark of the Testimony*, and put up the screen for the door of the tabernacle
Ex 40:21 And he brought the ark into the tabernacle, hung up the veil of the covering, and partitioned off the *ark of the Testimony*, as the Lord had commanded Moses
Num 4:5 When the camp prepares to journey, Aaron and his sons shall come, and they shall take down the covering veil and cover the *ark of the Testimony* with it
Num 7:89 Now when Moses went into the tabernacle of meeting to speak with Him, he heard the voice of One speaking to him from above the mercy seat that was on the *ark of the Testimony*, from between the two cherubim
Josh 4:16 Command the priests who bear the *ark of the Testimony* to come up from the Jordan

ARM BROUGHT SALVATION
Is 59:16 therefore His own *arm brought salvation* for Him; and His own righteousness, it sustained Him
Is 63:5 therefore My own *arm brought salvation* for Me; and My own fury, it sustained Me

ARM OF THE LORD
Is 51:9 Awake, awake, put on strength, O *arm of the Lord*
Is 53:1 and to whom has the *arm of the Lord* been revealed
John 12:38 And to whom has the *arm of the Lord* been revealed

ARMED FOR BATTLE
Num 32:29 If the children of Gad and the children of Reuben cross over the Jordan with you, every man *armed for battle* before the Lord, and the land is subdued before you, then you shall give them the land of Gilead as a possession
1Chr 12:37 of the Reubenites and the Gadites and the half-tribe of Manasseh, from the other side of the Jordan, one hundred and twenty thousand *armed for battle* with every kind of weapon of war

ARMOR OF GOD
Eph 6:11 Put on the whole *armor of God*, that you may be able to stand against the wiles of the devil
Eph 6:13 Therefore take up the whole *armor of God*, that you may be able to withstand in the evil day, and having done all, to stand

ARMOR OF LIGHT
Rom 13:12 Therefore let us cast off the works of darkness, and let us put on the *armor of light*

ARMOR OF RIGHTEOUSNESS
2Cor 6:7 by the word of truth, by the power of God, by the *armor of righteousness* on the right hand and on the left

ARMY OF THE LORD
Josh 5:14 So He said, "No, but as Commander of the *army of the Lord* I have now come

AROMA PLEASING TO THE LORD (NIV)
(See *SWEET AROMA TO THE LORD*)

ARROGANCE OF THE PROUD
Is 13:11 I will halt the *arrogance of the proud*, and will lay low the haughtiness of the terrible

ARTICLES OF POTTERY (NIV)
(See *EARTHEN VESSELS*)

AS A FOOL
2Sam 3:33 And the king sang a lament over Abner and said: "Should Abner die *as a fool* dies
Prov 7:22 Immediately he went after her, as an ox goes to the slaughter, or *as a fool* to the correction of the stocks
2Cor 11:16 If otherwise, at least receive me *as a fool*, that I also may boast a little
2Cor 11:23 I speak *as a fool* I am more: in labors more abundant, in stripes above measure, in prisons more frequently, in deaths often

AS A HEN GATHERS HER BROOD
Luke 13:34 How often I wanted to gather your children together, *as a hen gathers her brood* under her wings, but you were not willing

AS A HEN GATHERS HER CHICKS
Matt 23:37 How often I wanted to gather your children together, *as a hen gathers her chicks* under her wings, but you were not willing

AS A HERITAGE
Ex 6:8 and I will give it to you *as a heritage*
Deut 4:19 And take heed, lest you lift your eyes to heaven, and when you see the sun, the moon, and the stars, all the host of heaven, you feel driven to worship them and serve them, which the Lord your God has given to all the peoples under the whole heaven *as a heritage*
Ps 119:111 Your testimonies I have taken *as a heritage* forever, for they are the rejoicing of my heart
Ps 135:12 And gave their land *as a heritage*, a heritage to Israel His people
Ps 136:21 And gave their land *as a heritage*, for His mercy endures forever

AS A LAMB TO THE SLAUGHTER
Is 53:7 He was led *as a lamb to the slaughter*, and as a sheep before its shearers is silent, so He opened not his mouth

AS A LITTLE CHILD
Mark 10:15 Assuredly, I say to you, whoever does not receive the kingdom of God *as a little child* will by no means enter it
Luke 18:17 Assuredly, I say to you, whoever does not receive the kingdom of God *as a little child* will by no means enter it

AS A POSSESSION (NIV)
(See *AS A HERITAGE*)

AS WITH A SWARM OF LOCUSTS (NIV)
(See *AS WITH LOCUSTS*)

AS A THIEF IN THE NIGHT
1Th 5:2 For you yourselves know perfectly that the day of the Lord so comes *as a thief in the night*
2Pet 3:10 But the day of the Lord will come *as a thief in the night*, in which the heavens will pass away with a great noise, and the elements will melt with fervent heat

AS A WOMAN IN CHILDBIRTH
Is 13:8 they will be in pain *as a woman in childbirth*

AS AN ASHERAH (RSV)
(See *WOODEN IMAGE*)

AS AN INHERITANCE
Lev 25:46 And you may take them *as an inheritance* for your children after you, to inherit them as a possession
Num 18:21 Behold, I have given the children of Levi all the tithes in Israel *as an inheritance* in return for the work which they perform, the work of the tabernacle of meeting
Num 18:24 For the tithes of the children of Israel, which they offer up as a heave offering to the Lord, I have given to the Levites *as an inheritance*
Num 26:53 To these the land shall be divided *as an inheritance*, according to the number of names
Num 33:54 And you shall divide the land by lot *as an inheritance* among your families
Num 34:2 When you come into the land of Canaan, this is the land that shall fall to you *as an inheritance* the land of Canaan to its boundaries
Num 34:17 These are the names of the men who shall divide the land among you *as an inheritance*
Num 36:2 The Lord commanded my lord Moses to give the land *as an inheritance* by lot to the children of Israel, and my lord was commanded by the Lord to give the inheritance of our brother Zelophehad to his daughters
Deut 4:21 Furthermore the Lord was angry with me for your sakes, and swore that I would not cross over the Jordan, and that I would not enter the good land which the Lord your God is giving you *as an inheritance*
Deut 4:38 driving out from before you nations greater and mightier than you, to bring you in, to give you their land *as an inheritance*, as it is this day
Deut 15:4 for the Lord will greatly bless you in the land which the Lord your God is giving you to possess *as an inheritance*
Deut 19:10 lest innocent blood be shed in the midst of your land which the Lord your God is giving you *as an inheritance*, and thus bloodguiltiness be upon you
Deut 20:16 But of the cities of these peoples which the Lord your God gives you *as an inheritance* , you shall let nothing that breathes remain alive
Deut 21:23 his body shall not remain overnight on the tree, but you shall surely bury him that day, so that you do not defile the land which the Lord your God is giving you *as an inheritance*
Deut 24:4 for that is an abomination before the Lord, and you shall not bring sin on the land which the Lord your God is giving you *as an inheritance*
Deut 25:19 Therefore it shall be, when the Lord your God has given you rest from your enemies all around, in the land which the Lord your God is giving you to possess *as an inheritance*, that you will blot out the remembrance of Amalek from under heaven
Deut 26:1 And it shall be, when you come into the land which the Lord your God is giving you *as an inheritance*, and you possess it and dwell in it
Deut 29:8 We took their land and gave it *as an inheritance* to the Reubenites, to the Gadites, and to half the tribe of Manasseh
Josh 1:6 Be strong and of good courage, for to this people you shall divide *as an inheritance* the land which I swore to their fathers to give them
Josh 11:23 and Joshua gave it *as an inheritance* to Israel according to their divisions by their tribes
Josh 13:6 only divide it by lot to Israel *as an inheritance*, as I have commanded you
Josh 13:7 Now therefore, divide this land *as an inheritance* to the nine tribes and half the tribe of Manasseh
Josh 13:32 These are the areas which Moses had distributed *as an inheritance* in the plains of Moab on the other side of the Jordan, by Jericho eastward
Josh 14:1 These are the areas which the children of Israel inherited in the land of Canaan, which Eleazar the priest, Joshua the son of Nun, and the heads of the fathers of the tribes of the children of Israel distributed *as an inheritance* to them
Josh 14:13 And Joshua blessed him, and gave Hebron to Caleb the son of Jephunneh *as an inheritance*
Josh 19:49 When they had made an end of dividing the land *as an inheritance* according to their borders, the children of Israel gave an inheritance among them to Joshua the son of Nun
Josh 19:51 These were the inheritances which Eleazar the priest, Joshua the son of Nun, and the heads of the fathers of the tribes of the children of Israel divided *as an inheritance* by lot in Shiloh before the Lord, at the door of the tabernacle of meeting
1Kin 8:36 and give rain on Your land which You have given to Your people *as an inheritance*
1Chr 28:8 Now therefore, in the sight of all Israel, the congregation of the Lord, and in the hearing of our God, be careful to seek out all the commandments of the Lord your God, that you may possess this good land, and leave it *as an inheritance* for your children after you forever
2Chr 6:27 and send rain on Your land which You have given to Your people *as an inheritance*
Ezra 9:12 and never seek their peace or prosperity, that you may be strong and eat the good of the land, and leave it *as an inheritance* to your children forever
Jer 3:18 In those days the house of Judah shall walk with the house of Israel, and they shall come together out of the land of the north to the land that I have given *as an inheritance* to your fathers
Ezek 47:13 These are the borders by which you shall divide the land *as an inheritance* among the twelve tribes of Israel
Ezek 47:22 It shall be that you will divide it by lot *as an inheritance* for yourselves, and for the strangers who sojourn among you and who bear children among you
Ezek 48:29 This is the land which you shall divide by lot *as an inheritance* among the tribes of Israel, and these are their portions
Heb 11:8 By faith Abraham obeyed when he was called to go out to the place which he would afterward receive *as an inheritance*

AS COLD WATER TO A WEARY SOUL
Prov 25:25 *As cold water to a weary soul*, so is good news from a far country

AS FOR ME AND MY HOUSE
Josh 24:15 But *as for me and my house*, we will serve the Lord

AS GOOD AS DEAD
Heb 11:12 Therefore from one man, and him *as good as dead*, were born as many as the stars of

the sky in multitude innumerable as the sand which is by the seashore

AS GOODS INCREASE (NIV)
(See *WHEN GOODS INCREASE*)

AS HE PROMISED
Ex 12:25 It will come to pass when you come to the land which the Lord will give you, just *as He promised*, that you shall keep this service
Deut 15:6 For the Lord your God will bless you just *as He promised* you
Josh 22:4 And now the Lord your God has given rest to your brethren, *as He promised* them
1Kin 2:24 Now therefore, as the Lord lives, who has established me and set me on the throne of David my father, and who has made me a house, *as He promised*, Adonijah shall be put to death today
2Kin 8:19 Yet the Lord would not destroy Judah, for the sake of his servant David, *as He promised* him to give a lamp to him and his sons forever

AS HE SAW FIT (NIV)
(See *WHAT WAS RIGHT IN HIS OWN EYES*)

AS I LIVE
Num 14:21 but truly, *as I live*, all the earth shall be filled with the glory of the Lord
Num 14:28 Say to them, '*As I live*,' says the Lord, 'just as you have spoken in My hearing, so I will do to you
Deut 32:40 For I lift My hand to heaven, and say, "*As I live* forever
Job 27:6 my heart shall not reproach me as long *as I live*
Ps 104:33 I will sing to the Lord as long *as I live*
Ps 116:2 Because He has inclined His ear to me, therefore I will call upon Him as long *as I live*
Is 49:18 *As I live*," says the Lord, "You shall surely clothe yourselves with them all as an ornament, and bind them on you as a bride does
Jer 22:24 *As I live*," says the Lord, "though Coniah the son of Jehoiakim, king of Judah, were the signet on My right hand, yet I would pluck you off
Jer 46:18 *As I live*," says the King, whose name is the Lord of hosts
Ezek 5:11 Therefore, *as I live*,' says the Lord God, 'surely, because you have defiled My sanctuary with all your detestable things and with all your abominations, therefore I will also diminish you
Ezek 14:16 even though these three men were in it, *as I live*
Ezek 14:18 even though these three men were in it, *as I live*
Ezek 14:20 even though Noah, Daniel, and Job were in it, *as I live*
Ezek 16:48 *As I live*," says the Lord God, "neither your sister Sodom nor her daughters have done as you and your daughters have done
Ezek 17:16 *As I live*,' says the Lord God, 'surely in the place where the king dwells who made him king, whose oath he despised and whose covenant he broke with him in the midst of Babylon he shall die
Ezek 17:19 *As I live*, surely My oath which he despised, and My covenant which he broke, I will recompense on his own head
Ezek 18:3 *As I live*," says the Lord God, "you shall no longer use this proverb in Israel
Ezek 20:3 *As I live*," says the Lord God, "I will not be inquired of by you
Ezek 20:31 *As I live*," says the Lord God, "I will not be inquired of by you
Ezek 20:33 *As I live*," says the Lord God, "surely with a mighty hand, with an outstretched arm, and with fury poured out, I will rule over you
Ezek 33:11 *As I live*,' says the Lord God, 'I have no pleasure in the death of the wicked, but that the wicked turn from his way and live
Ezek 33:27 *As I live*, surely those who are in the ruins shall fall by the sword, and the one who is in the open field I will give to the beasts to be devoured, and those who are in the strongholds and caves shall die of the pestilence
Ezek 34:8 *as I live*," says the Lord God, "surely because My flock became a prey, and My flock became food for every beast of the field, because there was no shepherd, nor did My shepherds search for My flock, but the shepherds fed themselves and did not feed My flock
Ezek 35:6 therefore, *as I live*," says the Lord God, "I will prepare you for blood, and blood shall pursue you
Ezek 35:11 therefore, *as I live*," says the Lord God, "I will do according to your anger and according to the envy which you showed in your hatred against them
Zeph 2:9 Therefore, *as I live*," says the Lord of hosts, the God of Israel
Rom 14:11 *As I live*, says the Lord, every knee shall bow to Me, and every tongue shall confess to God

AS INHERITED PROPERTY (NIV)
(See *AS AN INHERITANCE*)

AS IT IS WRITTEN
Josh 8:31 as Moses the servant of the Lord had commanded the children of Israel, *as it is written* in the Book of the Law of Moses
1Kin 2:3 to walk in His ways, to keep His statutes, His commandments, His judgments, and His testimonies, *as it is written* in the Law of Moses, that you may prosper in all that you do and wherever you turn
2Kin 23:21 Then the king commanded all the people, saying, "Keep the Passover to the Lord your God, *as it is written* in this Book of the Covenant
2Chr 23:18 Also Jehoiada appointed the oversight of the house of the Lord to the hand of the priests, the Levites, whom David had assigned in the house of the Lord, to offer the burnt offerings of the Lord, *as it is written* in the Law of Moses, with rejoicing and with singing, as it was established by David
2Chr 25:4 However he did not execute their children, but did *as it is written* in the Law in the Book of Moses, where the Lord commanded, saying
2Chr 31:3 for the morning and evening burnt offerings, the burnt offerings for the Sabbaths and the New Moons and the set feasts, *as it is written* in the Law of the Lord
2Chr 35:12 Then they removed the burnt offerings that they might give them to the divisions of the fathers' houses of the lay people, to offer to the Lord, *as it is written* in the Book of Moses
Ezra 3:2 Then Jeshua the son of Jozadak and his brethren the priests, and Zerubbabel the son of Shealtiel and his brethren, arose and built the altar of the God of Israel, to offer burnt offerings on it, *as it is written* in the Law of Moses the man of God
Ezra 3:4 They also kept the Feast of Tabernacles, *as it is written*, and offered the daily burnt offerings in the number required by ordinance for each day
Ezra 6:18 They assigned the priests to their divisions and the Levites to their divisions, over the service of God in Jerusalem, *as it is written* in the Book of Moses
Neh 8:15 and that they should announce and proclaim in all their cities and in Jerusalem, saying, "Go out to the mountain, and bring olive

branches, branches of oil trees, myrtle branches, palm branches, and branches of leafy trees, to make booths, *as it is written*
Neh 10:34 We cast lots among the priests, the Levites, and the people, for bringing the wood offering into the house of our God, according to our fathers' houses, at the appointed times year by year, to burn on the altar of the Lord our God *as it is written* in the Law
Neh 10:36 to bring the firstborn of our sons and our cattle, *as it is written* in the Law, and the firstlings of our herds and our flocks, to the house of our God, to the priests who minister in the house of our God
Dan 9:13 *As it is written* in the Law of Moses, all this disaster has come upon us
Matt 26:24 The Son of Man goes *as it is written* of Him, but woe to that man by whom the Son of Man is betrayed
Mark 1:2 *As it is written* in the Prophets: Behold, I send My messenger before Your face, who will prepare Your way before You
Mark 7:6 He answered and said to them, "Well did Isaiah prophesy of you hypocrites, *as it is written*
Mark 9:13 But I say to you that Elijah has also come, and they did to him whatever they wished, *as it is written* of him
Mark 14:21 The Son of Man indeed goes just *as it is written* of Him, but woe to that man by whom the Son of Man is betrayed
Luke 2:23 (*as it is written* in the law of the Lord
Luke 3:4 *as it is written* in the book of the words of Isaiah the prophet, saying
John 6:31 *as it is written*, 'He gave them bread from heaven to eat
John 12:14 Then Jesus, when He had found a young donkey, sat on it; *as it is written*
Acts 7:42 Then God turned and gave them up to worship the host of heaven, *as it is written* in the book of the Prophets
Acts 15:15 And with this the words of the prophets agree, just *as it is written*
Rom 1:17 *as it is written*, "The just shall live by faith
Rom 2:24 For "The name of God is blasphemed among the Gentiles because of you," *as it is written*
Rom 3:4 *As it is written:* "That you may be justified in Your words, and may overcome when You are judged
Rom 3:10 *As it is written:* "There is none righteous, no, not one
Rom 4:17 (*as it is written*, "I have made you a father of many nations
Rom 8:36 *As it is written:* "For your sake we are killed all day long
Rom 9:13 *As it is written*, "Jacob I have loved, but Esau I have hated
Rom 9:33 *As it is written:* "Behold, I lay in Zion a stumbling stone and rock of offense, and whoever believes on Him will not be put to shame
Rom 10:15 *As it is written:* "How beautiful are the feet of those who preach the gospel of peace, who bring glad tidings of good things
Rom 11:8 Just *as it is written:* "God has given them a spirit of stupor, eyes that they should not see and ears that they should not hear, to this very day
Rom 11:26 And so all Israel will be saved, *as it is written*
Rom 15:3 but *as it is written*, "The reproaches of those who reproached You fell on Me
Rom 15:9 and that the Gentiles might glorify God for His mercy, *as it is written*
Rom 15:21 but *as it is written:* "To whom He was not announced, they shall see
1Cor 1:31 that, *as it is written*, "He who glories, let him glory in the Lord
1Cor 2:9 But *as it is written:* "Eye has not seen, nor ear heard, nor have entered into the heart of man the things which God has prepared for those who love Him
1Cor 10:7 *As it is written*, "The people sat down to eat and drink, and rose up to play
2Cor 8:15 *As it is written*, "He who gathered much had nothing left over, and he who gathered little had no lack
2Cor 9:9 *As it is written:* "He has dispersed abroad, He has given to the poor

AS LIGHTNING FALL FROM HEAVEN (KJV)
(See *LIKE LIGHTNING FROM HEAVEN*)

AS LIGHTS IN THE WORLD
Phil 2:15 that you may become blameless and harmless, children of God without fault in the midst of a crooked and perverse generation, among whom you shine *as lights in the world*

AS LONG AS I LIVE
Job 27:6 my heart shall not reproach me *as long as I live*
Ps 104:33 I will sing to the Lord *as long as I live*
Ps 116:2 Because He has inclined His ear to me, therefore I will call upon Him *as long as I live*

AS LONG AS YOU LIVE
Deut 12:19 Take heed to yourself that you do not forsake the Levite *as long as you live* in your land
Deut 31:13 and that their children, who have not known it, may hear and learn to fear the Lord your God *as long as you live* in the land which you cross the Jordan to possess

AS MANY AS RECEIVED HIM
John 1:12 But *as many as received Him*, to them He gave the right to become children of God, even to those who believe in His name

AS ONE APPROVED (NIV, RSV)
(See *APPROVED TO GOD*)

AS ONE HAVING AUTHORITY
Matt 7:29 for He taught them *as one having authority*, and not as the scribes
Mark 1:22 And they were astonished at His teaching, for He taught them *as one having authority*, and not as the scribes

AS ONE MAN
Num 14:15 Now if You kill these people *as one man*, then the nations which have heard of Your fame will speak, saying
Judg 6:16 And the Lord said to him, "Surely I will be with you, and you shall defeat the Midianites *as one man*
Judg 20:1 Then all the children of Israel came out, from Dan to Beersheba, as well as from the land of Gilead, and the congregation gathered together *as one man* before the Lord at Mizpah
Judg 20:8 Then all the people arose *as one man*, saying, "None of us will go to his tent, nor will any of us turn back to his house
Judg 20:11 So all the men of Israel were gathered against the city, united together *as one man*
Ezra 3:1 And when the seventh month had come, and the children of Israel were in the cities, the people gathered together *as one man* to Jerusalem
Neh 8:1 Now all the people gathered together *as one man* in the open square that was in front of the Water Gate

AS SOUNDING BRASS
1Cor 13:1 Though I speak with the tongues of men and of angels, but have not love, I have become *as sounding brass* or a clanging cymbal

AS SURELY AS YOU LIVE (NIV)
(See *AS YOUR SOUL LIVES*)

AS SWEET AS HONEY
Rev 10:9 and it will make your stomach bitter, but it will be *as sweet as honey* in your mouth
Rev 10:10 And I took the little book out of the angel's hand and ate it, and it was *as sweet as honey* in my mouth

AS THE CLOUD DISAPPEARS
Job 7:9 *As the cloud disappears* and vanishes away, so he who goes down to the grave does not come up

AS THE FATHER LOVED ME
John 15:9 *As the Father loved Me*, I also have loved you

AS THE HEAVENS ARE HIGHER THAN THE EARTH
Is 55:9 For *as the heavens are higher than the earth*, so are My ways higher than your ways, and My thoughts than your thoughts

AS THE LAWLESS (NIV)
(See *AS A FOOL*)

AS THE LORD HAS SAID
Num 32:31 *As the Lord has said* to your servants, so we will do
Deut 9:3 so you shall drive them out and destroy them quickly, *as the Lord has said* to you
Deut 31:3 Joshua himself crosses over before you, just *as the Lord has said*
2Chr 23:3 And he said to them, "Behold, the king's son shall reign, *as the Lord has said* of the sons of David
Joel 2:32 For in Mount Zion and in Jerusalem there shall be deliverance, *as the Lord has said*, among the remnant whom the Lord calls

AS THE LORD LIVES
Judg 8:19 *As the Lord lives*, if you had let them live, I would not kill you
Ruth 3:13 But if he does not want to perform the duty for you, then I will perform the duty for you, *as the Lord lives*
1Sam 14:39 For *as the Lord lives*, who saves Israel, though it be in Jonathan my son, he shall surely die
1Sam 14:45 *As the Lord lives*, not one hair of his head shall fall to the ground, for he has worked with God this day
1Sam 19:6 So Saul heeded the voice of Jonathan, and Saul swore, "*As the Lord lives*, he shall not be killed
1Sam 20:3 But truly, *as the Lord lives* and as your soul lives, there is but a step between me and death
1Sam 20:21 get them and come then, *as the Lord lives*, there is safety for you and no harm
1Sam 25:26 Now therefore, my lord, *as the Lord lives* and as your soul lives, since the Lord has held you back from coming to bloodshed and from avenging yourself with your own hand, now then, let your enemies and those who seek harm for my lord be as Nabal
1Sam 26:10 David said furthermore, "*As the Lord lives*, the Lord shall strike him, or his day shall come to die, or he shall go out to battle and perish
1Sam 26:16 *As the Lord lives*, you are worthy to die, because you have not guarded your master, the Lord's anointed
1Sam 28:10 And Saul swore to her by the Lord, saying, "*As the Lord lives*, no punishment shall come upon you for this thing
1Sam 29:6 Then Achish called David and said to him, "Surely, *as the Lord lives*, you have been upright, and your going out and your coming in with me in the army is good in my sight
2Sam 4:9 Then David answered Rechab and Baanah his brother, the sons of Rimmon the Beerothite, and said to them, "*As the Lord lives*, who has redeemed my life from all adversity
2Sam 12:5 Then David's anger was greatly aroused against the man, and he said to Nathan, "*As the Lord lives*, the man who has done this shall surely die
2Sam 14:11 And he said, "*As the Lord lives*, not one hair of your son shall fall to the ground
2Sam 15:21 And Ittai answered the king and said, "*As the Lord lives*, and as my lord the king lives, surely in whatever place my lord the king shall be, whether in death or life, even there also your servant will be
1Kin 1:29 And the king took an oath and said, "*As the Lord lives*, who has redeemed my life from every distress
1Kin 2:24 Now therefore, *as the Lord lives*, who has established me and set me on the throne of David my father, and who has made me a house, as He promised, Adonijah shall be put to death today
1Kin 22:14 And Micaiah said, "*As the Lord lives*, whatever the Lord says to me, that I will speak
2Kin 2:2 And Elisha said, "*As the Lord lives*, and as your soul lives, I will not leave you
2Kin 2:4 And he said, "*As the Lord lives*, and as your soul lives, I will not leave you
2Kin 2:6 And he said, "*As the Lord lives*, and as your soul lives, I will not leave you
2Kin 4:30 And the mother of the child said, "*As the Lord lives*, and as your soul lives, I will not leave you
2Kin 5:16 But he said, "*As the Lord lives*, before whom I stand, I will receive nothing
2Kin 5:20 but *as the Lord lives*, I will run after him and take something from him
2Chr 18:13 And Micaiah said, "*As the Lord lives*, whatever my God says, that I will speak
Jer 5:2 Though they say, '*As the Lord lives*,' surely they swear falsely
Jer 12:16 And it shall be, if they will diligently learn the ways of My people, to swear by My name, '*As the Lord lives*
Jer 23:7 Therefore, behold, the days are coming," says the Lord, "that they shall no longer say, '*As the Lord lives* who brought up the children of Israel from the land of Egypt
Jer 23:8 but, '*As the Lord lives* who brought up and led the descendants of the house of Israel from the north country and from all the countries where I had driven them
Jer 38:16 So Zedekiah the king swore secretly to Jeremiah, saying, "*As the Lord lives*, who made our very souls, I will not put you to death, nor will I give you into the hand of these men who seek your life
Hos 4:15 Do not come up to Gilgal, nor go up to Beth Aven, nor swear an oath, saying, '*As the Lord lives*

AS THE SPIRIT ENABLED THEM (NIV)
(See *AS THE SPIRIT GAVE THEM UTTERANCE*)

AS THE SPIRIT GAVE THEM UTTERANCE
Acts 2:4 And they were all filled with the Holy Spirit and began to speak with other tongues, *as the Spirit gave them utterance*

AS WATER DISAPPEARS
Job 14:11 *As water disappears* from the sea, and a river becomes parched and dries up

AS WATERS FAIL FROM A LAKE (RSV)
(See *AS WATER DISAPPEARS*)

AS WITH LOCUSTS
Jer 51:14 Surely I will fill you with men, *as with locusts*, and they shall lift up a shout against you

AS YOU LIVE (RSV)
(See *AS YOUR SOUL LIVES*)

AS YOUR SOUL LIVES
1Sam 1:26 *As your soul lives*, my lord, I am the woman who stood by you here, praying to the Lord
1Sam 17:55 And Abner said, "*As your soul lives*, O king, I do not know
1Sam 20:3 But truly, as the Lord lives and *as your soul lives*, there is but a step between me and death
1Sam 25:26 Now therefore, my lord, as the Lord lives and *as your soul lives*, since the Lord has held you back from coming to bloodshed and from avenging yourself with your own hand, now then, let your enemies and those who seek harm for my lord be as Nabal
2Sam 11:11 As you live, and *as your soul lives*, I will not do this thing
2Kin 2:2 And Elisha said, "As the Lord lives, and *as your soul lives*, I will not leave you
2Kin 2:4 And he said, "As the Lord lives, and *as your soul lives*, I will not leave you
2Kin 2:6 And he said, "As the Lord lives, and *as your soul lives*, I will not leave you
2Kin 4:30 And the mother of the child said, "As the Lord lives, and *as your soul lives*, I will not leave you

ASCEND INTO HEAVEN
Deut 30:12 It is not in heaven, that you should say, 'Who will *ascend into heaven* for us and bring it to us, that we may hear it and do it
Ps 139:8 If I *ascend into heaven*, You are there; if I make my bed in hell, behold, You are there
Is 14:13 I will *ascend into heaven*, I will exalt my throne above the stars of God
Rom 10:6 But the righteousness of faith speaks in this way, "Do not say in your heart, 'Who will *ascend into heaven*

ASCEND INTO THE HEAVENS
Acts 2:34 For David did not *ascend into the heavens*, but he says himself

ASCENDED INTO HEAVEN
Prov 30:4 Who has *ascended into heaven*, or descended? Who has gathered the wind in His fists

ASCENDED TO HEAVEN
Josh 8:20 And when the men of Ai looked behind them, they saw, and behold, the smoke of the city *ascended to heaven*
John 3:13 No one has *ascended to heaven* but He who came down from heaven, that is, the Son of Man who is in heaven
Rev 11:12 And they *ascended to heaven* in a cloud, and their enemies saw them

ASHAMED OF ME
Mark 8:38 For whoever is *ashamed of Me* and My words in this adulterous and sinful generation, of him the Son of Man also will be ashamed when He comes in the glory of His Father with the holy angels
Luke 9:26 For whoever is *ashamed of Me* and My words, of him the Son of Man will be ashamed when He comes in His own glory, and in His Father's, and of the holy angels

ASHERAH POLES (NIV)
(See *WOODEN IMAGES*)

ASK WHAT YOU DESIRE
John 15:7 If you abide in Me, and My words abide in you, you will *ask what you desire*, and it shall be done for you

ASPIRE TO LIVE QUIETLY (RSV)
(See *LEAD A QUIET LIFE*)

ASSEMBLY OF EVILDOERS (NIV)
(See *CONGREGATION OF EVILDOERS*)

ASSEMBLY OF THE SAINTS
Ps 89:7 God is greatly to be feared in the *assembly of the saints*, and to be held in reverence by all those who are around Him

ASSIGN THE INHERITANCE (NIV)
(See *DIVIDE THE INHERITANCE*)

ASSURANCE OF THINGS (NAS)
(See *SUBSTANCE OF THINGS*)

ASSUREDLY, I SAY TO YOU
Matt 5:18 For *assuredly, I say to you*, till heaven and earth pass away, one jot or one tittle will by no means pass from the law till all is fulfilled
Matt 5:26 *Assuredly, I say to you*, you will by no means get out of there till you have paid the last penny
Matt 6:2 *Assuredly, I say to you*, they have their reward
Matt 6:5 *Assuredly, I say to you*, they have their reward
Matt 6:16 *Assuredly, I say to you*, they have their reward
Matt 8:10 When Jesus heard it, He marveled, and said to those who followed, "*Assuredly, I say to you*, I have not found such great faith, not even in Israel
Matt 10:15 *Assuredly, I say to you*, it will be more tolerable for the land of Sodom and Gomorrah in the day of judgment than for that city
Matt 10:23 For *assuredly, I say to you*, you will not have gone through the cities of Israel before the Son of Man comes
Matt 10:42 And whoever gives one of these little ones only a cup of cold water in the name of a disciple, *assuredly, I say to you*, he shall by no means lose his reward
Matt 11:11 *Assuredly, I say to you*, among those born of women there has not risen one greater than John the Baptist
Matt 13:17 for *assuredly, I say to you* that many prophets and righteous men desired to see what you see, and did not see it, and to hear what you hear, and did not hear it
Matt 16:28 *Assuredly, I say to you*, there are some standing here who shall not taste death till they see the Son of Man coming in His kingdom
Matt 17:20 for *assuredly, I say to you*, if you have faith as a mustard seed, you will say to this mountain
Matt 18:3 and said, "*Assuredly, I say to you*, unless you are converted and become as little children, you will by no means enter the kingdom of heaven
Matt 18:13 And if he should find it, *assuredly, I say to you*, he rejoices more over that sheep than over the ninety-nine that did not go astray
Matt 18:18 *Assuredly, I say to you*, whatever you

bind on earth will be bound in heaven, and whatever you loose on earth will be loosed in heaven

Matt 19:23 Then Jesus said to His disciples, "*Assuredly, I say to you* that it is hard for a rich man to enter the kingdom of heaven

Matt 21:21 So Jesus answered and said to them, "*Assuredly, I say to you*, if you have faith and do not doubt, you will not only do what was done to the fig tree, but also if you say to this mountain

Matt 21:31 Jesus said to them, "*Assuredly, I say to you* that tax collectors and harlots enter the kingdom of God before you

Matt 23:36 *Assuredly, I say to you*, all these things will come upon this generation

Matt 24:2 *Assuredly, I say to you*, not one stone shall be left here upon another, that shall not be thrown down

Matt 24:34 *Assuredly, I say to you*, this generation will by no means pass away till all these things are fulfilled

Matt 24:47 *Assuredly, I say to you* that he will make him ruler over all his goods

Matt 25:12 But he answered and said, '*Assuredly, I say to you*, I do not know you

Matt 25:40 And the King will answer and say to them, '*Assuredly, I say to you*, inasmuch as you did it to one of the least of these My brethren, you did it to Me

Matt 25:45 Then He will answer them, saying, '*Assuredly, I say to you*, inasmuch as you did not do it to one of the least of these, you did not do it to Me

Matt 26:13 *Assuredly, I say to you*, wherever this gospel is preached in the whole world, what this woman has done will also be told as a memorial to her

Matt 26:21 Now as they were eating, He said, "*Assuredly, I say to you*, one of you will betray Me

Matt 26:34 Jesus said to him, "*Assuredly, I say to you* that this night, before the rooster crows, you will deny Me three times

Mark 3:28 *Assuredly, I say to you*, all sins will be forgiven the sons of men, and whatever blasphemies they may utter

Mark 6:11 *Assuredly, I say to you*, it will be more tolerable for Sodom and Gomorrah in the day of judgment than for that city

Mark 8:12 *Assuredly, I say to you*, no sign shall be given to this generation

Mark 9:1 And He said to them, "*Assuredly, I say to you* that there are some standing here who will not taste death till they see the kingdom of God present with power

Mark 9:41 For whoever gives you a cup of water to drink in My name, because you belong to Christ, *assuredly, I say to you*, he will by no means lose his reward

Mark 10:15 *Assuredly, I say to you*, whoever does not receive the kingdom of God as a little child will by no means enter it

Mark 10:29 So Jesus answered and said, "*Assuredly, I say to you*, there is no one who has left house or brothers or sisters or father or mother or wife or children or lands, for My sake and the gospel's

Mark 11:23 For *assuredly, I say to you*, whoever says to this mountain

Mark 12:43 So He called His disciples to Him and said to them, "*Assuredly, I say to you* that this poor widow has put in more than all those who have given to the treasury

Mark 13:30 *Assuredly, I say to you*, this generation will by no means pass away till all these things take place

Mark 14:9 *Assuredly, I say to you*, wherever this gospel is preached throughout the whole world, what this woman did will also be spoken of as a memorial to her

Mark 14:18 Now as they sat and ate, Jesus said, "*Assuredly, I say to you*, one of you who eats with Me will betray Me

Mark 14:25 *Assuredly, I say to you*, I will no longer drink of the fruit of the vine until that day when I drink it new in the kingdom of God

Mark 14:30 And Jesus said to him, "*Assuredly, I say to you* that today, even this night, before the rooster crows twice, you will deny Me three times

Luke 4:24 Then He said, "*Assuredly, I say to you*, no prophet is accepted in his own country

Luke 12:37 *Assuredly, I say to you* that he will gird himself and have them sit down to eat, and will come and serve them

Luke 13:35 and *assuredly, I say to you*, you shall not see Me until the time comes when you say

Luke 18:17 *Assuredly, I say to you*, whoever does not receive the kingdom of God as a little child will by no means enter it

Luke 18:29 So He said to them, "*Assuredly, I say to you*, there is no one who has left house or parents or brothers or wife or children, for the sake of the kingdom of God

Luke 21:32 *Assuredly, I say to you*, this generation will by no means pass away till all things are fulfilled

Luke 23:43 And Jesus said to him, "*Assuredly, I say to you*, today you will be with Me in Paradise

John 1:51 And He said to him, "Most *assuredly, I say to you*, hereafter you shall see heaven open, and the angels of God ascending and descending upon the Son of Man

John 3:3 Jesus answered and said to him, "Most *assuredly, I say to you*, unless one is born again, he cannot see the kingdom of God

John 3:5 Jesus answered, "Most *assuredly, I say to you*, unless one is born of water and the Spirit, he cannot enter the kingdom of God

John 3:11 Most *assuredly, I say to you*, We speak what We know and testify what We have seen, and you do not receive Our witness

John 5:19 Then Jesus answered and said to them, "Most *assuredly, I say to you*, the Son can do nothing of Himself, but what He sees the Father do

John 5:24 Most *assuredly, I say to you*, he who hears My word and believes in Him who sent Me has everlasting life, and shall not come into judgment, but has passed from death into life

John 5:25 Most *assuredly, I say to you*, the hour is coming, and now is, when the dead will hear the voice of the Son of God

John 6:26 Jesus answered them and said, "Most *assuredly, I say to you*, you seek Me, not because you saw the signs, but because you ate of the loaves and were filled

John 6:32 Then Jesus said to them, "Most *assuredly, I say to you*, Moses did not give you the bread from heaven, but My Father gives you the true bread from heaven

John 6:47 Most *assuredly, I say to you*, he who believes in Me has everlasting life

John 6:53 Then Jesus said to them, "Most *assuredly, I say to you*, unless you eat the flesh of the Son of Man and drink His blood, you have no life in you

John 8:34 Jesus answered them, "Most *assuredly, I say to you*, whoever commits sin is a slave of sin

John 8:51 Most *assuredly, I say to you*, if anyone keeps My word he shall never see death

John 8:58 Jesus said to them, "Most *assuredly, I say to you*, before Abraham was, I AM

John 10:1 Most *assuredly, I say to you*, he who does not enter the sheepfold by the door, but

climbs up some other way, the same is a thief and a robber
John 10:7 Then Jesus said to them again, "Most *assuredly, I say to you*, I am the door of the sheep
John 12:24 Most *assuredly, I say to you*, unless a grain of wheat falls into the ground and dies, it remains alone
John 13:16 Most *assuredly, I say to you*, a servant is not greater than his master
John 13:20 Most *assuredly, I say to you*, he who receives whomever I send receives Me
John 13:21 When Jesus had said these things, He was troubled in spirit, and testified and said, "Most *assuredly, I say to you*, one of you will betray Me
John 13:38 Most *assuredly, I say to you*, the rooster shall not crow till you have denied Me three times
John 14:12 Most *assuredly, I say to you*, he who believes in Me, the works that I do he will do also
John 16:20 Most *assuredly, I say to you* that you will weep and lament, but the world will rejoice
John 16:23 Most *assuredly, I say to you*, whatever you ask the Father in My name He will give you
John 21:18 Most *assuredly, I say to you*, when you were younger, you girded yourself and walked where you wished

ASTONISHED AT HIS TEACHING
Matt 7:28 And so it was, when Jesus had ended these sayings, that the people were *astonished at His teaching*
Matt 22:33 And when the multitudes heard this, they were *astonished at His teaching*
Mark 1:22 And they were *astonished at His teaching*, for He taught them as one having authority, and not as the scribes
Mark 11:18 for they feared Him, because all the people were *astonished at His teaching*
Luke 4:32 And they were *astonished at His teaching*, for His word was with authority

AT EASE IN ZION
Amos 6:1 Woe to you who are *at ease in Zion*, and trust in Mount Samaria, notable persons in the chief nation, to whom the house of Israel comes

AT HIS COMING
1Sam 16:4 And the elders of the town trembled *at his coming*, and said
1Cor 15:23 Christ the firstfruits, afterward those who are Christ's *at His coming*
1Th 2:19 Is it not even you in the presence of our Lord Jesus Christ *at His coming*
1Jn 2:28 And now, little children, abide in Him, that when He appears, we may have confidence and not be ashamed before Him *at His coming*

AT HIS PRESENCE (KJV, NIV, NAS, RSV)
(See *IN HIS PRESENCE*)

AT HIS RIGHT HAND (KJV)
(See *IN HIS RIGHT HAND*)

AT THE APOSTLES' FEET
Acts 4:35 and laid them *at the apostles' feet;* and they distributed to each as anyone had need
Acts 4:37 having land, sold it, and brought the money and laid it *at the apostles' feet*
Acts 5:2 And he kept back part of the proceeds, his wife also being aware of it, and brought a certain part and laid it *at the apostles' feet*

AT THE CLOSE OF THE AGE (RSV)
(See *AT THE END OF THE AGE*)

AT THE COMING
1Th 3:13 so that He may establish your hearts blameless in holiness before our God and Father *at the coming* of our Lord Jesus Christ with all His saints
1Th 5:23 and may your whole spirit, soul, and body be preserved blameless *at the coming* of our Lord Jesus Christ

AT THE END OF THE AGE
Matt 13:49 So it will be *at the end of the age*

AT THE FEET OF GAMALIEL
Acts 22:3 I am indeed a Jew, born in Tarsus of Cilicia, but brought up in this city *at the feet of Gamaliel*, taught according to the strictness of our fathers' law, and was zealous toward God as you all are today

AT THE HEAD OF THE TWO WAYS (KJV, RSV)
(See *FORK OF THE TWO ROADS*)

AT THE LAST DAY
John 6:39 This is the will of the Father who sent Me, that of all He has given Me I should lose nothing, but should raise it up *at the last day*
John 6:40 and I will raise him up *at the last day*
John 6:44 and I will raise him up *at the last day*
John 6:54 Whoever eats My flesh and drinks My blood has eternal life, and I will raise him up *at the last day*
John 11:24 Martha said to Him, "I know that he will rise again in the resurrection *at the last day*

AT THE MOUNTAIN, OUT OF THE MIDST OF THE FIRE (RSV)
(See *ON THE MOUNTAIN FROM THE MIDST OF THE FIRE*)

AT THE RIGHT HAND
Ps 109:31 For He shall stand *at the right hand* of the poor, to save him from those who condemn him
Matt 26:64 Nevertheless, I say to you, hereafter you will see the Son of Man sitting *at the right hand* of the Power, and coming on the clouds of heaven
Mark 14:62 And you will see the Son of Man sitting *at the right hand* of the Power, and coming with the clouds of heaven
Mark 16:19 So then, after the Lord had spoken to them, He was received up into heaven, and sat down *at the right hand* of God
Acts 7:55 But he, being full of the Holy Spirit, gazed into heaven and saw the glory of God, and Jesus standing *at the right hand* of God
Acts 7:56 I see the heavens opened and the Son of Man standing *at the right hand* of God
Rom 8:34 It is Christ who died, and furthermore is also risen, who is even *at the right hand* of God, who also makes intercession for us
Col 3:1 If then you were raised with Christ, seek those things which are above, where Christ is, sitting *at the right hand* of God
Heb 1:3 who being the brightness of His glory and the express image of His person, and upholding all things by the word of His power, when He had by Himself purged our sins, sat down *at the right hand* of the Majesty on high
Heb 8:1 We have such a High Priest, who is seated *at the right hand* of the throne of the Majesty in the heavens
Heb 10:12 But this Man, after He had offered one sacrifice for sins forever, sat down *at the right hand* of God
Heb 12:2 looking unto Jesus, the author and finisher of our faith, who for the joy that was set before Him endured the cross, despising the

shame, and has sat down *at the right hand* of the throne of God
1Pet 3:22 who has gone into heaven and is *at the right hand* of God, angels and authorities and powers having been made subject to Him

AT THE RIGHT HAND OF GOD
Mark 16:19 So then, after the Lord had spoken to them, He was received up into heaven, and sat down *at the right hand of God*
Acts 7:55 But he, being full of the Holy Spirit, gazed into heaven and saw the glory of God, and Jesus standing *at the right hand of God*
Acts 7:56 I see the heavens opened and the Son of Man standing *at the right hand of God*
Rom 8:34 It is Christ who died, and furthermore is also risen, who is even *at the right hand of God*, who also makes intercession for us
Col 3:1 If then you were raised with Christ, seek those things which are above, where Christ is, sitting *at the right hand of God*
Heb 10:12 But this Man, after He had offered one sacrifice for sins forever, sat down *at the right hand of God*
1Pet 3:22 who has gone into heaven and is *at the right hand of God*, angels and authorities and powers having been made subject to Him

ATE MANNA FORTY YEARS
Ex 16:35 And the children of Israel *ate manna forty years*, until they came to an inhabited land

ATONEMENT COVER (NIV)
(See *MERCY SEAT*)

ATONEMENT FOR OUR SINS
Ps 79:9 And deliver us, and provide *atonement for our sins*, For Your name's sake

ATONEMENT THROUGH FAITH IN HIS BLOOD (NIV)
(See *PROPITIATION BY HIS BLOOD*)

ATONING SACRIFICE FOR OUR SINS (NIV)
(See *PROPITIATION FOR OUR SINS*)

ATTACKED JERUSALEM (NIV)
(See *AGAINST JERUSALEM*)

ATTACKED THE ISRAELITES (NIV)
(See *FOUGHT AGAINST ISRAEL*)

ATTEND TO ME
Ps 55:2 *Attend to me*, and hear me; I am restless in my complaint, and moan noisily

ATTEND TO MY CRY
Ps 17:1 Hear a just cause, O Lord, *attend to my cry*
Ps 142:6 *Attend to my cry*, for I am brought very low

ATTEND TO MY PRAYER
Ps 61:1 Hear my cry, O God; *attend to my prayer*

ATTESTED BY GOD
Acts 2:22 Jesus of Nazareth, a Man *attested by God* to you by miracles, wonders, and signs which God did through Him in your midst, as you yourselves also know

ATTITUDES OF THE HEART (NIV)
(See *INTENTS OF THE HEART*)

AUDIENCE OF THE PEOPLE (KJV)
(See *HEARING OF THE PEOPLE*)

AUTHOR AND FINISHER OF OUR FAITH
Heb 12:2 looking unto Jesus, the *author and finisher of our faith*, who for the joy that was set before Him endured the cross, despising the shame, and has sat down at the right hand of the throne of God

AUTHOR OF CONFUSION
1Cor 14:33 For God is not the *author of confusion* but of peace, as in all the churches of the saints

AUTHOR OF LIFE (NIV, RSV)
(See *PRINCE OF LIFE*)

AUTHORITY ON EARTH (NAS, NIV, RSV)
(See *POWER ON EARTH*)

AUTHORITY OVER UNCLEAN SPIRITS (NAS, RSV)
(See *POWER OVER UNCLEAN SPIRITS*)

AUTUMN AND SPRING RAINS (NIV)
(See *LATTER RAIN*)

AVENGE HIMSELF ON HIS ADVERSARIES
Jer 46:10 For this is the day of the Lord God of hosts, a day of vengeance, that He may *avenge Himself on His adversaries*

AVENGE THE BLOOD OF
Deut 32:43 for He will *avenge the blood of* His servants, and render vengeance to His adversaries
2Kin 9:7 You shall strike down the house of Ahab your master, that I may *avenge the blood of* My servants the prophets, and the blood of all the servants of the Lord, at the hand of Jezebel

AVENGER OF BLOOD
Num 35:19 The *avenger of blood* himself shall put the murderer to death
Num 35:21 the *avenger of blood* shall put the murderer to death when he meets him
Num 35:24 then the congregation shall judge between the manslayer and the *avenger of blood* according to these judgments
Num 35:25 So the congregation shall deliver the manslayer from the hand of the *avenger of blood*, and the congregation shall return him to the city of refuge where he had fled, and he shall remain there until the death of the high priest who was anointed with the holy oil
Num 35:27 and the *avenger of blood* finds him outside the limits of his city of refuge, and the *avenger of blood* kills the manslayer, he shall not be guilty of blood
Deut 19:6 lest the *avenger of blood*, while his anger is hot, pursue the manslayer and overtake him, because the way is long, and kill him, though he was not worthy of death, since he had not hated the victim in time past
Deut 19:12 then the elders of his city shall send and bring him from there, and deliver him over to the hand of the *avenger of blood*, that he may die
Josh 20:3 and they shall be your refuge from the *avenger of blood*
Josh 20:5 Then if the *avenger of blood* pursues him, they shall not deliver the slayer into his hand, because he struck his neighbor unintentionally, but did not hate him beforehand
Josh 20:9 These were the cities appointed for all the children of Israel and for the stranger who sojourned among them, that whoever killed any person accidentally might flee there, and not die by the hand of the *avenger of blood* until he stood before the congregation
2Sam 14:11 Then she said, "Please let the king remember the Lord your God, and do not permit

the *avenger of blood* to destroy anymore, lest they destroy my son

AWAKEN THE DAWN
Ps 57:8 Awake, my glory! Awake, lute and harp! I will *awaken the dawn*
Ps 108:2 Awake, lute and harp! I will *awaken the dawn*

AWAY FROM THE LORD (NIV, RSV)
(See *ABSENT FROM THE LORD*)

AWAY WITH HIM
John 19:15 But they cried out, "*Away with Him, away with Him*
Acts 21:36 For the multitude of the people followed after, crying out, "*Away with him*

AWAY WITH YOU
Matt 4:10 Then Jesus said to him, "*Away with you*, Satan! For it is written

AX HEAD
2Kin 6:5 But as one was cutting down a tree, the iron *ax head* fell into the water

AX IS LAID TO THE ROOT
Matt 3:10 And even now the *ax is laid to the root* of the trees
Luke 3:9 And even now the *ax is laid to the root* of the trees

B

BAALS AND ASHTORETHS
1Sam 12:10 Then they cried out to the Lord, and said, 'We have sinned, because we have forsaken the Lord and served the *Baals and Ashtoreths*

BABE LYING IN A MANGER
Luke 2:16 And they came with haste and found Mary and Joseph, and the *Babe lying in a manger*

BABE WRAPPED IN SWADDLING CLOTHS
Luke 2:12 You will find a *Babe wrapped in swaddling cloths*, lying in a manger

BABYLON IS FALLEN
Is 21:9 and he answered and said, "*Babylon is fallen*, is fallen
Rev 14:8 And another angel followed, saying, "*Babylon is fallen*, is fallen, that great city, because she has made all nations drink of the wine of the wrath of her fornication

BABYLON THE GREAT
Rev 17:5 MYSTERY, *BABYLON THE GREAT*, THE MOTHER OF HARLOTS AND OF THE ABOMINATIONS OF THE EARTH
Rev 18:2 And he cried mightily with a loud voice, saying, "*Babylon the great* is fallen, is fallen, and has become a habitation of demons, a prison for every foul spirit, and a cage for every unclean and hated bird

BACKSLIDING ISRAEL
Jer 3:6 Have you seen what *backsliding Israel* has done? She has gone up on every high mountain and under every green tree, and there played the harlot
Jer 3:8 Then I saw that for all the causes for which *backsliding Israel* had committed adultery, I had put her away and given her a certificate of divorce
Jer 3:11 Then the Lord said to me, "*Backsliding Israel* has shown herself more righteous than treacherous Judah
Jer 3:12 Return, *backsliding Israel*,' says the Lord, 'and I will not cause My anger to fall on you

BAD TREE
Matt 7:17 Even so, every good tree bears good fruit, but a *bad tree* bears bad fruit
Matt 7:18 A good tree cannot bear bad fruit, nor can a *bad tree* bear good fruit
Luke 6:43 For a good tree does not bear bad fruit, nor does a *bad tree* bear good fruit

BAKED WITH LEAVEN
Lev 6:17 It shall not be *baked with leaven*. I have given it to them as their portion of My offerings made by fire
Lev 23:17 they shall be *baked with leaven*. They are the firstfruits to the Lord

BAKED WITH YEAST (NIV)
(See *BAKED WITH LEAVEN*)

BALM IN GILEAD
Jer 8:22 Is there no *balm in Gilead*, is there no physician there

BAND OF PROPHETS (RSV)
(See *GROUP OF PROPHETS*)

BANNER FOR THE NATIONS
Is 11:12 He will set up a *banner for the nations*, and will assemble the outcasts of Israel, and gather together the dispersed of Judah from the four corners of the earth

BANNER ON A HILL
Is 30:17 One thousand shall flee at the threat of one, at the threat of five you shall flee, till you are left as a pole on top of a mountain and as a *banner on a hill*

BAPTISM INTO DEATH
Rom 6:4 Therefore we were buried with Him through *baptism into death*, that just as Christ was raised from the dead by the glory of the Father, even so we also should walk in newness of life

BAPTISM OF JOHN
Matt 21:25 The *baptism of John*, where was it from? From heaven or from men
Mark 11:30 The *baptism of John* was it from heaven or from men
Luke 7:29 And when all the people heard Him, even the tax collectors justified God, having been baptized with the *baptism of John*
Luke 20:4 The *baptism of John* was it from heaven or from men
Acts 1:22 beginning from the *baptism of John* to that day when He was taken up from us, one of these must become a witness with us of His resurrection
Acts 18:25 and being fervent in spirit, he spoke and taught accurately the things of the Lord, though he knew only the *baptism of John*

BAPTISM OF REPENTANCE
Mark 1:4 John came baptizing in the wilderness and preaching a *baptism of repentance* for the remission of sins
Luke 3:3 And he went into all the region around the Jordan, preaching a *baptism of repentance* for the remission of sins
Acts 13:24 after John had first preached, before His coming, the *baptism of repentance* to all the people of Israel
Acts 19:4 Then Paul said, "John indeed baptized

with a *baptism of repentance*, saying to the people that they should believe on Him who would come after him, that is, on Christ Jesus

BAPTIZE WITH WATER
John 1:26 John answered them, saying, "I *baptize with water*, but there stands One among you whom you do not know
John 1:33 I did not know Him, but He who sent me to *baptize with water* said to me

BAPTIZE YOU WITH THE HOLY SPIRIT
Matt 3:11 He will *baptize you with the Holy Spirit* and fire
Mark 1:8 I indeed baptized you with water, but He will *baptize you with the Holy Spirit*
Luke 3:16 He will *baptize you with the Holy Spirit* and with fire

BAPTIZE YOU WITH WATER
Matt 3:11 I indeed *baptize you with water* unto repentance, but He who is coming after me is mightier than I, whose sandals I am not worthy to carry
Luke 3:16 John answered, saying to them all, "I indeed *baptize you with water*

BAPTIZED BY JOHN
Mark 1:9 It came to pass in those days that Jesus came from Nazareth of Galilee, and was *baptized by John* in the Jordan

BAPTIZED FOR THE DEAD
1Cor 15:29 Otherwise, what will they do who are *baptized for the dead*, if the dead do not rise at all? Why then are they *baptized for the dead*

BAPTIZED IN THE NAME OF
Acts 2:38 Then Peter said to them, "Repent, and let every one of you be *baptized in the name of* Jesus Christ for the remission of sins
Acts 8:16 They had only been *baptized in the name of* the Lord Jesus
Acts 10:48 And he commanded them to be *baptized in the name of* the Lord
Acts 19:5 When they heard this, they were *baptized in the name of* the Lord Jesus
1Cor 1:13 Was Paul crucified for you? Or were you *baptized in the name of* Paul

BAPTIZED INTO CHRIST
Rom 6:3 Or do you not know that as many of us as were *baptized into Christ* Jesus were baptized into His death
Gal 3:27 For as many of you as were *baptized into Christ* have put on Christ

BAPTIZED INTO MOSES
1Cor 10:2 all were *baptized into Moses* in the cloud and in the sea

BAPTIZED INTO ONE BODY
1Cor 12:13 For by one Spirit we were all *baptized into one body* whether Jews or Greeks, whether slaves or free and have all been made to drink into one Spirit

BAPTIZED WITH THE HOLY SPIRIT
Acts 1:5 for John truly baptized with water, but you shall be *baptized with the Holy Spirit* not many days from now
Acts 11:16 Then I remembered the word of the Lord, how He said, 'John indeed baptized with water, but you shall be *baptized with the Holy Spirit*

BAPTIZED WITH WATER
Acts 1:5 for John truly *baptized with water*, but you shall be baptized with the Holy Spirit not many days from now
Acts 11:16 Then I remembered the word of the Lord, how He said, 'John indeed *baptized with water*, but you shall be baptized with the Holy Spirit

BAPTIZED YOU WITH WATER
Mark 1:8 I indeed *baptized you with water*, but He will baptize you with the Holy Spirit

BARE HEIGHTS (RSV)
(See *DESOLATE HEIGHTS*)

BARE HILL (RSV)
(See *HIGH MOUNTAIN*)

BARE HILLTOP (NIV)
(See *HIGH MOUNTAIN*)

BARREN HEIGHTS (NIV)
(See *DESOLATE HEIGHTS*)

BASED ON WORKS (RSV)
(See *WORKS OF THE LAW*)

BASIC PRINCIPLES OF THE WORLD
Col 2:8 Beware lest anyone cheat you through philosophy and empty deceit, according to the tradition of men, according to the *basic principles of the world*, and not according to Christ
Col 2:20 Therefore, if you died with Christ from the *basic principles of the world*, why, as though living in the world, do you subject yourselves to regulations

BATHED IN BLOOD (NIV)
(See *FILLED WITH BLOOD*)

BATHED MY FEET (RSV)
(See *WASHED MY FEET*)

BATTLE IS THE LORD'S
1Sam 17:47 for the *battle is the Lord's*, and He will give you into our hands

BATTLES OF THE LORD
1Sam 25:28 For the Lord will certainly make for my lord an enduring house, because my lord fights the *battles of the Lord*, and evil is not found in you throughout your days

BE ACCURSED
Is 65:20 for the child shall die one hundred years old, but the sinner being one hundred years old shall *be accursed*
1Cor 16:22 If anyone does not love the Lord Jesus Christ, let him *be accursed*
Gal 1:8 But even if we, or an angel from heaven, preach any other gospel to you than what we have preached to you, let him *be accursed*
Gal 1:9 As we have said before, so now I say again, if anyone preaches any other gospel to you than what you have received, let him *be accursed*

BE ANXIOUS FOR NOTHING
Phil 4:6 *Be anxious for nothing*, but in everything by prayer and supplication, with thanksgiving, let your requests be made known to God

BE CAREFUL
Gen 31:24 But God had come to Laban the Syrian in a dream by night, and said to him, "*Be careful* that you speak to Jacob neither good nor bad
Gen 31:29 It is in my power to do you harm, but the God of your father spoke to me last night, saying, '*Be careful* that you speak to Jacob neither good nor bad

Num 28:2 Command the children of Israel, and say to them, 'My offering, My food for My offerings made by fire as a sweet aroma to Me, you shall *be careful* to offer to Me at their appointed time

Deut 4:6 Therefore *be careful* to observe them; for this is your wisdom and your understanding in the sight of the peoples who will hear all these statutes, and say

Deut 5:1 Hear, O Israel, the statutes and judgments which I speak in your hearing today, that you may learn them and *be careful* to observe them

Deut 5:32 Therefore you shall *be careful* to do as the Lord your God has commanded you

Deut 6:3 Therefore hear, O Israel, and *be careful* to observe it, that it may be well with you, and that you may multiply greatly as the Lord God of your fathers has promised you

Deut 8:1 Every commandment which I command you today you must *be careful* to observe, that you may live and multiply, and go in and possess the land of which the Lord swore to your fathers

Deut 11:32 And you shall *be careful* to observe all the statutes and judgments which I set before you today

Deut 12:1 These are the statutes and judgments which you shall *be careful* to observe in the land which the Lord God of your fathers is giving you to possess, all the days that you live on the earth

Deut 12:32 Whatever I command you, *be careful* to observe it; you shall not add to it nor take away from it

Deut 16:12 And you shall remember that you were a slave in Egypt, and you shall *be careful* to observe these statutes

Deut 17:10 And you shall *be careful* to do according to all that they order you

Deut 17:19 And it shall be with him, and he shall read it all the days of his life, that he may learn to fear the Lord his God and *be careful* to observe all the words of this law and these statutes

Deut 24:8 just as I commanded them, so you shall *be careful* to do

Deut 26:16 therefore you shall *be careful* to observe them with all your heart and with all your soul

Deut 32:46 Set your hearts on all the words which I testify among you today, which you shall command your children to *be careful* to observe all the words of this law

Judg 13:4 Now therefore, please *be careful* not to drink wine or similar drink, and not to eat any unclean thing

Judg 13:13 So the Angel of the Lord said to Manoah, "Of all that I said to the woman let her *be careful*

2Kin 17:37 And the statutes, the ordinances, the law, and the commandment which He wrote for you, you shall *be careful* to observe forever

1Chr 28:8 Now therefore, in the sight of all Israel, the congregation of the Lord, and in the hearing of our God, *be careful* to seek out all the commandments of the Lord your God, that you may possess this good land, and leave it as an inheritance for your children after you forever

Ezra 7:17 now therefore, *be careful* to buy with this money bulls, rams, and lambs, with their grain offerings and their drink offerings, and offer them on the altar of the house of your God in Jerusalem

Tit 3:8 This is a faithful saying, and these things I want you to affirm constantly, that those who have believed in God should *be careful* to maintain good works

2Pet 1:15 Moreover I will *be careful* to ensure that you always have a reminder of these things after my decease

BE CAREFUL FOR NOTHING (KJV)
(See *BE ANXIOUS FOR NOTHING*)

BE CAREFUL NOT TO NEGLECT (NIV)
(See *DO NOT FORSAKE*)

BE CLEAN (KJV)
(See *PURIFY YOURSELVES*)

BE EAGER TO PROPHESY (NIV)
(See *DESIRE EARNESTLY TO PROPHESY*)

BE EXALTED

Num 24:7 His king shall be higher than Agag, and his kingdom shall *be exalted*

2Sam 22:47 Blessed be my Rock! Let God *be exalted*, the Rock of my salvation

1Kin 9:8 And this house will *be exalted;* yet everyone who passes by it will be astonished and will hiss, and say

Ps 13:2 How long shall I take counsel in my soul, having sorrow in my heart daily? How long will my enemy *be exalted* over me

Ps 18:46 Blessed be my Rock! Let the God of my salvation *be exalted*

Ps 21:13 *Be exalted*, O Lord, in Your own strength! We will sing and praise Your power

Ps 46:10 I will *be exalted* among the nations, I will *be exalted* in the earth

Ps 57:5 *Be exalted*, O God, above the heavens; let Your glory be above all the earth

Ps 57:11 *Be exalted*, O God, above the heavens; let Your glory be above all the earth

Ps 75:10 All the horns of the wicked I will also cut off, but the horns of the righteous shall *be exalted*

Ps 89:24 But My faithfulness and My mercy shall be with him, and in My name his horn shall *be exalted*

Ps 108:5 *Be exalted*, O God, above the heavens, and Your glory above all the earth

Ps 112:9 His righteousness endures forever; His horn will *be exalted* with honor

Ps 140:8 Do not further his wicked scheme, lest they *be exalted*

Is 2:2 Now it shall come to pass in the latter days that the mountain of the Lord's house shall be established on the top of the mountains, and shall *be exalted* above the hills

Is 2:11 The lofty looks of man shall be humbled, the haughtiness of men shall be bowed down, and the Lord alone shall *be exalted* in that day

Is 2:17 The loftiness of man shall be bowed down, and the haughtiness of men shall be brought low; the Lord alone will *be exalted* in that day

Is 5:16 But the Lord of hosts shall *be exalted* in judgment, and God who is holy shall be hallowed in righteousness

Is 30:18 and therefore He will *be exalted*, that He may have mercy on you

Is 33:10 Now I will *be exalted*, now I will lift Myself up

Is 40:4 Every valley shall *be exalted*, and every mountain and hill shall be made low

Is 52:13 Behold, My Servant shall deal prudently, He shall *be exalted* and extolled and be very high

Mic 4:1 Now it shall come to pass in the latter days that the mountain of the Lord's house shall be established on the top of the mountains, and shall *be exalted* above the hills

Matt 23:12 And whoever exalts himself will be abased, and he who humbles himself will *be exalted*

Luke 14:11 For whoever exalts himself will be abased, and he who humbles himself will *be exalted*

Luke 18:14 for everyone who exalts himself will be

abased, and he who humbles himself will *be exalted*
2Cor 11:7 Did I commit sin in abasing myself that you might *be exalted*, because I preached the gospel of God to you free of charge
2Cor 12:7 And lest I should *be exalted* above measure by the abundance of the revelations, a thorn in the flesh was given to me, a messenger of Satan to buffet me, lest I *be exalted* above measure

BE FRUITFUL AND MULTIPLY
Gen 1:22 And God blessed them, saying, "*Be fruitful and multiply*, and fill the waters in the seas, and let birds multiply on the earth
Gen 1:28 Then God blessed them, and God said to them, "*Be fruitful and multiply*
Gen 8:17 birds and cattle and every creeping thing that creeps on the earth, so that they may abound on the earth, and *be fruitful and multiply* on the earth
Gen 9:1 So God blessed Noah and his sons, and said to them: "*Be fruitful and multiply* and fill the earth
Gen 9:7 And as for you, *be fruitful and multiply;* bring forth abundantly in the earth and multiply in it
Gen 35:11 *Be fruitful and multiply;* a nation and a company of nations shall proceed from you, and kings shall come from your body

BE GLAD AND REJOICE
Ps 9:2 I will *be glad and rejoice* in You; I will sing praise to Your name, O Most High
Ps 31:7 I will *be glad and rejoice* in Your mercy, for You have considered my trouble
Song 1:4 The Daughters of Jerusalem we will *be glad and rejoice* in you
Is 25:9 we have waited for Him; we will *be glad and rejoice* in His salvation
Is 65:18 But *be glad and rejoice* forever in what I create
Joel 2:21 *be glad and rejoice*, for the Lord has done marvelous things
Zeph 3:14 *Be glad and rejoice* with all your heart, O daughter of Jerusalem
Phil 2:18 For the same reason you also *be glad and rejoice* with me
Rev 19:7 Let us *be glad and rejoice* and give Him glory, for the marriage of the Lamb has come, and His wife has made herself ready

BE GONE (RSV)
(See *GO YOUR WAY*)

BE GRACIOUS (NAS, RSV)
(See *HAVE MERCY*)

BE HELD RESPONSIBLE (NIV)
(See *BEAR THEIR GUILT*)

BE HOLY
Ex 22:31 And you shall *be holy* men to Me: you shall not eat any meat which is torn by beasts in the field
Ex 29:37 And the altar shall be most holy. Whatever touches the altar must *be holy*
Ex 30:29 You shall consecrate them, that they may be most holy; whatever touches them must *be holy*
Ex 30:32 It is holy, and it shall *be holy* to you
Ex 40:9 and you shall hallow it and all its utensils, and it shall *be holy*
Lev 6:18 It shall be a statute forever in your generations concerning the offerings made by fire to the Lord. Everyone who touches them must *be holy*
Lev 6:27 Everyone who touches its flesh must *be holy*. And when its blood is sprinkled on any garment, you shall wash that on which it was sprinkled, in a holy place
Lev 11:44 You shall therefore sanctify yourselves, and you shall *be holy*
Lev 11:45 For I am the Lord who brings you up out of the land of Egypt, to be your God. You shall therefore *be holy*, for I am holy
Lev 19:2 You shall *be holy*, for I the Lord your God am holy
Lev 19:24 But in the fourth year all its fruit shall *be holy*, a praise to the Lord
Lev 20:7 Sanctify yourselves therefore, and *be holy*, for I am the Lord your God
Lev 20:26 And you shall *be holy* to Me, for I the Lord am holy, and have separated you from the peoples, that you should be Mine
Lev 21:6 They shall *be holy* to their God and not profane the name of their God, for they offer the offerings of the Lord made by fire, and the bread of their God; therefore they shall *be holy*
Lev 21:8 He shall *be holy* to you, for I the Lord, who sanctify you, am holy
Lev 23:2 The feasts of the Lord, which you shall proclaim to *be holy* convocations, these are My feasts
Lev 23:20 They shall *be holy* to the Lord for the priest
Lev 23:37 These are the feasts of the Lord which you shall proclaim to *be holy* convocations, to offer an offering made by fire to the Lord, a burnt offering and a grain offering, a sacrifice and drink offerings, everything on its day
Lev 25:12 it shall *be holy* to you; you shall eat its produce from the field
Lev 27:9 And if it is a beast such as men may bring as an offering to the Lord, all such that any man gives to the Lord shall *be holy*
Lev 27:10 and if he at all exchanges beast for beast, then both it and the one exchanged for it shall *be holy*
Lev 27:14 And when a man sanctifies his house to *be holy* to the Lord, then the priest shall set a value for it, whether it is good or bad
Lev 27:21 but the field, when it is released in the Jubilee, shall *be holy* to the Lord, as a devoted field
Lev 27:32 And concerning the tithe of the herd or the flock, of whatever passes under the rod, the tenth one shall *be holy* to the Lord
Lev 27:33 and if he exchanges it at all, then both it and the one exchanged for it shall *be holy*
Num 6:5 until the days are fulfilled for which he separated himself to the Lord, he shall *be holy*
Num 6:8 All the days of his separation he shall *be holy* to the Lord
Num 15:40 and that you may remember and do all My commandments, and *be holy* for your God
Num 18:10 every male shall eat it. It shall *be holy* to you
Deut 23:14 therefore your camp shall *be holy*, that He may see no unclean thing among you, and turn away from you
Jer 31:40 And the whole valley of the dead bodies and of the ashes, and all the fields as far as the Brook Kidron, to the corner of the Horse Gate toward the east, shall *be holy* to the Lord
Ezek 45:1 its length shall be twenty-five thousand cubits, and the width ten thousand. It shall *be holy* throughout its territory all around
Joel 3:17 then Jerusalem shall *be holy*, and no aliens shall ever pass through her again
1Cor 7:34 The unmarried woman cares about the things of the Lord, that she may *be holy* both in body and in spirit
Eph 1:4 just as He chose us in Him before the foundation of the world, that we should *be holy* and without blame before Him in love
Eph 5:27 that He might present it to Himself a glo-

rious church, not having spot or wrinkle or any such thing, but that it should *be holy* and without blemish
1Pet 1:15 but as He who called you is holy, you also *be holy* in all your conduct
1Pet 1:16 because it is written, "*Be holy*, for I am holy
Rev 22:11 he who is righteous, let him be righteous still; he who is holy, let him *be holy* still

BE IN SUBJECTION TO YOUR OWN HUSBANDS (KJV)
(See *SUBMISSIVE TO YOUR OWN HUSBANDS*)

BE INSTANT IN SEASON (KJV)
(See *BE READY IN SEASON*)

BE IT FAR FROM ME (KJV)
(See *FAR BE IT FROM ME*)

BE KIND TO ONE ANOTHER
Eph 4:32 And *be kind to one another*, tenderhearted, forgiving one another, just as God in Christ also forgave you

BE MERCIFUL
Ps 26:11 But as for me, I will walk in my integrity; redeem me and *be merciful* to me
Ps 41:4 I said, "Lord, *be merciful* to me; heal my soul, for I have sinned against You
Ps 41:10 But You, O Lord, *be merciful* to me, and raise me up, that I may repay them
Ps 56:1 *Be merciful* to me, O God, for man would swallow me up
Ps 57:1 *Be merciful* to me, O God, *be merciful* to me
Ps 59:5 You therefore, O Lord God of hosts, the God of Israel, awake to punish all the nations; do not *be merciful* to any wicked transgressors.
Ps 67:1 God *be merciful* to us and bless us, and cause His face to shine upon us
Ps 86:3 *Be merciful* to me, O Lord, for I cry to You all day long
Ps 119:58 I entreated Your favor with my whole heart; *be merciful* to me according to Your word
Ps 119:132 Look upon me and *be merciful* to me, as Your custom is toward those who love Your name
Luke 6:36 Therefore *be merciful*, just as your Father also is merciful
Luke 18:13 And the tax collector, standing afar off, would not so much as raise his eyes to heaven, but beat his breast, saying, 'God *be merciful* to me a sinner
Heb 8:12 For I will *be merciful* to their unrighteousness, and their sins and their lawless deeds I will remember no more

BE NOT AFRAID
Is 40:9 O Jerusalem, you who bring good tidings, lift up your voice with strength, lift it up, *be not afraid*

BE NOT DECEIVED (KJV)
(See *DO NOT BE DECEIVED*)

BE OF GOOD CHEER
Matt 9:2 And Jesus, seeing their faith, said to the paralytic, "Son, *be of good cheer*
Matt 9:22 But Jesus turned around, and when He saw her He said, "*Be of good cheer*, daughter
Matt 14:27 But immediately Jesus spoke to them, saying, "*Be of good cheer*
Mark 6:50 And immediately He talked with them and said to them, "*Be of good cheer*
Mark 10:49 Then they called the blind man, saying to him, "*Be of good cheer*
Luke 8:48 And He said to her, "Daughter, *be of good cheer*
John 16:33 but *be of good cheer*, I have overcome the world
Acts 23:11 But the following night the Lord stood by him and said, "*Be of good cheer*, Paul

BE OF GOOD COURAGE
Num 13:20 *Be of good courage*. And bring some of the fruit of the land
2Sam 10:12 *Be of good courage*, and let us be strong for our people and for the cities of our God
1Chr 19:13 *Be of good courage*, and let us be strong for our people and for the cities of our God
Ezra 10:4 We also will be with you. *Be of good courage*, and do it
Ps 27:14 *Be of good courage*, and He shall strengthen your heart
Ps 31:24 *Be of good courage*, and He shall strengthen your heart, all you who hope in the Lord
Is 41:6 Everyone helped his neighbor, and said to his brother, "*Be of good courage*

BE ON YOUR GUARD
1Sam 19:2 Therefore please *be on your guard* until morning, and stay in a secret place and hide

BE ON YOUR GUARD AGAINST THE YEAST (NIV)
(See *BEWARE OF THE LEAVEN*)

BE PARTIAL (NAS, RSV)
(See *SHOW PARTIALITY*)

BE PREPARED IN SEASON (NIV)
(See *BE READY IN SEASON*)

BE PUT TO DEATH
Gen 26:11 So Abimelech charged all his people, saying, "He who touches this man or his wife shall surely *be put to death*
Ex 19:12 Whoever touches the mountain shall surely *be put to death*
Ex 21:12 He who strikes a man so that he dies shall surely *be put to death*
Ex 21:15 And he who strikes his father or his mother shall surely *be put to death*
Ex 21:16 He who kidnaps a man and sells him, or if he is found in his hand, shall surely *be put to death*
Ex 21:17 And he who curses his father or his mother shall surely *be put to death*
Ex 21:29 But if the ox tended to thrust with its horn in times past, and it has been made known to his owner, and he has not kept it confined, so that it has killed a man or a woman, the ox shall be stoned and its owner also shall *be put to death*
Ex 22:19 Whoever lies with an animal shall surely *be put to death*
Ex 31:14 Everyone who profanes it shall surely *be put to death*
Ex 31:15 Whoever does any work on the Sabbath day, he shall surely *be put to death*
Ex 35:2 Whoever does any work on it shall *be put to death*
Lev 19:20 but they shall not *be put to death*, because she was not free
Lev 20:2 Whoever of the children of Israel, or of the strangers who sojourn in Israel, who gives any of his descendants to Molech, he shall surely *be put to death*
Lev 20:9 For everyone who curses his father or his mother shall surely *be put to death*
Lev 20:10 The man who commits adultery with another man's wife, he who commits adultery with his neighbor's wife, the adulterer and the adulteress, shall surely *be put to death*

Lev 20:11 both of them shall surely *be put to death*. Their blood shall be upon them
Lev 20:12 If a man lies with his daughter-in-law, both of them shall surely *be put to death*
Lev 20:13 They shall surely *be put to death*. Their blood shall be upon them
Lev 20:15 If a man mates with a beast, he shall surely *be put to death*, and you shall kill the beast
Lev 20:16 They shall surely *be put to death*. Their blood is upon them
Lev 20:27 A man or a woman who is a medium, or who has familiar spirits, shall surely *be put to death*
Lev 24:16 And whoever blasphemes the name of the Lord shall surely *be put to death*, and all the congregation shall certainly stone him, the stranger as well as him who is born in the land. When he blasphemes the name of the Lord, he shall *be put to death*
Lev 24:17 Whoever kills any man shall surely *be put to death*
Lev 24:21 but whoever kills a man shall *be put to death*
Lev 27:29 No person under the ban, who may become doomed to destruction among men, shall be redeemed, but shall surely *be put to death*
Num 1:51 The outsider who comes near shall *be put to death*
Num 3:10 but the outsider who comes near shall *be put to death*
Num 3:38 but the outsider who came near was to *be put to death*
Num 15:35 Then the Lord said to Moses, "The man must surely *be put to death*
Num 18:7 I give your priesthood to you as a gift for service, but the outsider who comes near shall *be put to death*
Num 35:16 But if he strikes him with an iron implement, so that he dies, he is a murderer; the murderer shall surely *be put to death*
Num 35:17 And if he strikes him with a stone in the hand, by which one could die, and he does die, he is a murderer; the murderer shall surely *be put to death*
Num 35:18 Or if he strikes him with a wooden hand weapon, by which one could die, and he does die, he is a murderer; the murderer shall surely *be put to death*
Num 35:21 or in enmity he strikes him with his hand so that he dies, the one who struck him shall surely *be put to death*, for he is a murderer
Num 35:30 Whoever kills a person, the murderer shall *be put to death* on the testimony of witnesses
Num 35:31 Moreover you shall take no ransom for the life of a murderer who is guilty of death, but he shall surely *be put to death*
Deut 13:5 But that prophet or that dreamer of dreams shall *be put to death*, because he has spoken in order to turn you away from the Lord your God, who brought you out of the land of Egypt and redeemed you from the house of bondage, to entice you from the way in which the Lord your God commanded you to walk
Deut 17:6 Whoever is worthy of death shall *be put to death* on the testimony of two or three witnesses, but he shall not *be put to death* on the testimony of one witness
Deut 24:16 The fathers shall not *be put to death* for their children, nor shall the children *be put to death* for their fathers; a person shall *be put to death* for his own sin
Josh 1:18 Whoever rebels against your command and does not heed your words, in all that you command him, shall *be put to death*
Judg 6:31 Let the one who would plead for him *be put to death* by morning
Judg 21:5 For they had made a great oath concerning anyone who had not come up to the Lord at Mizpah, saying, "He shall surely *be put to death*
1Sam 11:13 But Saul said, "Not a man shall *be put to death* this day, for today the Lord has accomplished salvation in Israel
2Sam 8:2 With two lines he measured off those to *be put to death*, and with one full line those to be kept alive
2Sam 19:21 But Abishai the son of Zeruiah answered and said, "Shall not Shimei *be put to death* for this, because he cursed the Lord's anointed
2Sam 19:22 Shall any man *be put to death* today in Israel
1Kin 2:24 Now therefore, as the Lord lives, who has established me and set me on the throne of David my father, and who has made me a house, as He promised, Adonijah shall *be put to death* today
2Kin 11:8 and whoever comes within range, let him *be put to death*
2Kin 14:6 But the children of the murderers he did not execute, according to what is written in the Book of the Law of Moses, in which the Lord commanded, saying, "The fathers shall not *be put to death* for the children, nor shall the children *be put to death* for the fathers; but a person shall *be put to death* for his own sin
2Chr 15:13 and whoever would not seek the Lord God of Israel was to *be put to death*, whether small or great, whether man or woman
2Chr 23:7 and whoever comes into the house, let him *be put to death*
2Chr 25:4 However he did not execute their children, but did as it is written in the Law in the Book of Moses, where the Lord commanded, saying, "The fathers shall not *be put to death* for their children, nor shall the children *be put to death* for their fathers
Jer 18:21 Let their men *be put to death*, their young men be slain by the sword in battle
Jer 38:4 Therefore the princes said to the king, "Please, let this man *be put to death*, for thus he weakens the hands of the men of war who remain in this city, and the hands of all the people, by speaking such words to them
Matt 10:21 and children will rise up against parents and cause them to *be put to death*
Matt 15:4 and, 'He who curses father or mother, let him *be put to death*
Mark 7:10 and, 'He who curses father or mother, let him *be put to death*
Mark 13:12 and children will rise up against parents and cause them to *be put to death*
Luke 23:32 There were also two others, criminals, led with Him to *be put to death*
Acts 12:19 But when Herod had searched for him and not found him, he examined the guards and commanded that they should *be put to death*
Acts 13:28 And though they found no cause for death in Him, they asked Pilate that He should *be put to death*

BE READY

Ex 19:11 And let them *be ready* for the third day. For on the third day the Lord will come down upon Mount Sinai in the sight of all the people
Ex 19:15 And he said to the people, "*Be ready* for the third day
Ex 34:2 So *be ready* in the morning, and come up in the morning to Mount Sinai, and present yourself to Me there on the top of the mountain
Josh 8:4 Do not go very far from the city, but all of you *be ready*
Esth 3:14 A copy of the document was to be issued as law in every province, being published for all people, that they should *be ready* for that day

Esth 8:13 A copy of the document was to be issued as a decree in every province and published to all people, so that the Jews would *be ready* on that day to avenge themselves on their enemies
Is 32:4 Also the heart of the rash will understand knowledge, and the tongue of the stammerers will *be ready* to speak plainly
Ezek 38:7 Prepare yourself and *be ready*, you and all your companies that are gathered about you
Matt 24:44 Therefore you also *be ready*, for the Son of Man is coming at an hour when you do not expect Him
Luke 12:40 Therefore you also *be ready*, for the Son of Man is coming at an hour you do not expect
2Cor 9:3 Yet I have sent the brethren, lest our boasting of you should be in vain in this respect, that, as I said, you may *be ready*
2Cor 9:5 Therefore I thought it necessary to exhort the brethren to go to you ahead of time, and prepare your bountiful gift beforehand, which you had previously promised, that it may *be ready* as a matter of generosity and not as a grudging obligation
2Tim 4:2 *Be ready* in season and out of season. Convince, rebuke, exhort, with all longsuffering and teaching
Tit 3:1 Remind them to be subject to rulers and authorities, to obey, to *be ready* for every good work
1Pet 3:15 But sanctify the Lord God in your hearts, and always *be ready* to give a defense to everyone who asks you a reason for the hope that is in you, with meekness and fear

BE READY IN SEASON
2Tim 4:2 *Be ready in season* and out of season. Convince, rebuke, exhort, with all longsuffering and teaching

BE RECONCILED TO GOD
2Cor 5:20 we implore you on Christ's behalf, *be reconciled to God*

BE SHEPHERDS OF GOD'S FLOCK (NIV)
(See *SHEPHERD THE FLOCK OF GOD*)

BE STRONG
Deut 11:8 Therefore you shall keep every commandment which I command you today, that you may *be strong*, and go in and possess the land which you cross over to possess
Deut 31:6 *Be strong* and of good courage, do not fear nor be afraid of them
Deut 31:7 Then Moses called Joshua and said to him in the sight of all Israel, "*Be strong* and of good courage, for you must go with this people to the land which the Lord has sworn to their fathers to give them, and you shall cause them to inherit it
Deut 31:23 Then He inaugurated Joshua the son of Nun, and said, "*Be strong* and of good courage
Josh 1:6 *Be strong* and of good courage, for to this people you shall divide as an inheritance the land which I swore to their fathers to give them
Josh 1:7 Only *be strong* and very courageous, that you may observe to do according to all the law which Moses My servant commanded you
Josh 1:9 *Be strong* and of good courage; do not be afraid, nor be dismayed, for the Lord your God is with you wherever you go
Josh 1:18 Whoever rebels against your command and does not heed your words, in all that you command him, shall be put to death. Only *be strong* and of good courage
Josh 10:25 *be strong* and of good courage, for thus the Lord will do to all your enemies against whom you fight
1Sam 4:9 *Be strong* and conduct yourselves like men, you Philistines, that you do not become servants of the Hebrews, as they have been to you
2Sam 10:12 Be of good courage, and let us *be strong* for our people and for the cities of our God
2Sam 16:21 Then the hands of all who are with you will *be strong*
1Kin 2:2 I go the way of all the earth; *be strong*, therefore, and prove yourself a man
1Chr 19:13 Be of good courage, and let us *be strong* for our people and for the cities of our God
1Chr 22:13 *Be strong* and of good courage; do not fear nor be dismayed
1Chr 28:10 Consider now, for the Lord has chosen you to build a house for the sanctuary; *be strong*, and do it
1Chr 28:20 And David said to his son Solomon, "*Be strong* and of good courage, and do it
2Chr 15:7 But you, *be strong* and do not let your hands be weak, for your work shall be rewarded
2Chr 25:8 *Be strong* in battle! Even so, God shall make you fall before the enemy
2Chr 32:7 *Be strong* and courageous; do not be afraid nor dismayed before the king of Assyria, nor before all the multitude that is with him
Ezra 9:12 and never seek their peace or prosperity, that you may *be strong* and eat the good of the land, and leave it as an inheritance to your children forever
Is 35:4 Say to those who are fearful-hearted, "*Be strong*, do not fear
Dan 10:19 *be strong*, yes, *be strong*
Dan 11:32 but the people who know their God shall *be strong*, and carry out great exploits
Hag 2:4 Yet now *be strong*, Zerubbabel,' says the Lord; 'and *be strong*, Joshua, son of Jehozadak, the high priest; and *be strong*, all you people of the land
Zech 8:9 Let your hands *be strong*, you who have been hearing in these days these words by the mouth of the prophets, who were in the day that the foundation was laid for the house of the Lord of hosts, that the temple might be built
Zech 8:13 And it shall come to pass that just as you were a curse among the nations, O house of Judah and house of Israel, so I will save you, and you shall be a blessing. Do not fear, let your hands *be strong*
1Cor 16:13 Watch, stand fast in the faith, be brave, *be strong*
Eph 6:10 Finally, my brethren, *be strong* in the Lord and in the power of His might
2Tim 2:1 You therefore, my son, *be strong* in the grace that is in Christ Jesus

BE STRONG AND LET YOUR HEART TAKE COURAGE (NAS, RSV)
(See *STRENGTHEN YOUR HEART*)

BE STRONG AND TAKE HEART (NIV)
(See *STRENGTHEN YOUR HEART*)

BE SUBJECT TO (RSV)
(See *SUBMIT TO*)

BE URGENT IN SEASON (RSV)
(See *BE READY IN SEASON*)

BE WITH ME IN PARADISE
Luke 23:43 And Jesus said to him, "Assuredly, I say to you, today you will *be with Me in Paradise*

BE YE MINDFUL ALWAYS OF HIS COVENANT (KJV)
(See *REMEMBER HIS COVENANT ALWAYS*)

BEAM IS IN THINE OWN EYE (KJV)
(See *PLANK IN YOUR OWN EYE*)

BEAR DEPRIVED OF HER CUBS
Hos 13:8 I will meet them like a *bear deprived of her cubs*

BEAR FALSE WITNESS
Ex 20:16 You shall not *bear false witness* against your neighbor
Deut 5:20 You shall not *bear false witness* against your neighbor
Matt 19:18 Jesus said, "'You shall not murder,' 'You shall not commit adultery,' 'You shall not steal,' 'You shall not *bear false witness*
Mark 10:19 Do not commit adultery,' 'Do not murder,' 'Do not steal,' 'Do not *bear false witness*
Luke 18:20 Do not commit adultery,' 'Do not murder,' 'Do not steal,' 'Do not *bear false witness*
Rom 13:9 For the commandments, "You shall not commit adultery," "You shall not murder," "You shall not steal," "You shall not *bear false witness*

BEAR FRUIT
2Kin 19:30 And the remnant who have escaped of the house of Judah shall again take root downward, and *bear fruit* upward
Ps 92:14 They shall still *bear fruit* in old age; they shall be fresh and flourishing
Is 37:31 And the remnant who have escaped of the house of Judah shall again take root downward, and *bear fruit* upward
Jer 12:2 they grow, yes, they *bear fruit*. You are near in their mouth but far from their mind
Ezek 17:8 It was planted in good soil by many waters, to bring forth branches, *bear fruit*, and become a majestic vine
Ezek 17:23 and it will bring forth boughs, and *bear fruit*, and be a majestic cedar
Ezek 47:12 They will *bear fruit* every month, because their water flows from the sanctuary
Mal 3:11 And I will rebuke the devourer for your sakes, so that he will not destroy the fruit of your ground, nor shall the vine fail to *bear fruit* for you in the field
Mark 4:20 But these are the ones sown on good ground, those who hear the word, accept it, and *bear fruit*
Luke 8:15 But the ones that fell on the good ground are those who, having heard the word with a noble and good heart, keep it and *bear fruit* with patience
John 15:2 Every branch in Me that does not *bear fruit* He takes away
John 15:4 As the branch cannot *bear fruit* of itself, unless it abides in the vine, neither can you, unless you abide in Me
John 15:16 You did not choose Me, but I chose you and appointed you that you should go and *bear fruit*, and that your fruit should remain, that whatever you ask the Father in My name He may give you
Rom 7:4 Therefore, my brethren, you also have become dead to the law through the body of Christ, that you may be married to another, even to Him who was raised from the dead, that we should *bear fruit* to God
Rom 7:5 For when we were in the flesh, the passions of sins which were aroused by the law were at work in our members to *bear fruit* to death

BEAR FRUITS
Matt 3:8 Therefore *bear fruits* worthy of repentance
Luke 3:8 Therefore *bear fruits* worthy of repentance, and do not begin to say to yourselves

BEAR GOOD FRUIT
Matt 3:10 Therefore every tree which does not *bear good fruit* is cut down and thrown into the fire
Matt 7:18 A good tree cannot bear bad fruit, nor can a bad tree *bear good fruit*
Matt 7:19 Every tree that does not *bear good fruit* is cut down and thrown into the fire
Luke 3:9 Therefore every tree which does not *bear good fruit* is cut down and thrown into the fire
Luke 6:43 For a good tree does not bear bad fruit, nor does a bad tree *bear good fruit*

BEAR HER GUILT
Num 5:31 Then the man shall be free from iniquity, but that woman shall *bear her guilt*
Num 30:15 But if he does make them void after he has heard them, then he shall *bear her guilt*

BEAR HER INIQUITY (KJV, RSV)
(See *BEAR HER GUILT*)

BEAR HIS CROSS
Matt 27:32 Now as they came out, they found a man of Cyrene, Simon by name. Him they compelled to *bear His cross*
Mark 15:21 Now they compelled a certain man, Simon a Cyrenian, the father of Alexander and Rufus, as he was coming out of the country and passing by, to *bear His cross*
Luke 14:27 And whoever does not *bear his cross* and come after Me cannot be My disciple

BEAR HIS GUILT
Lev 17:16 But if he does not wash or bathe his body, then he shall *bear his guilt*
Lev 20:17 He has uncovered his sister's nakedness. He shall *bear his guilt*

BEAR HIS INIQUITY (KJV, RSV)
(See *BEAR HIS GUILT*)

BEAR IT IN MIND (RSV)
(See *TAKE IT TO HEART*)

BEAR MUCH FRUIT
John 15:8 By this My Father is glorified, that you *bear much fruit*

BEAR ROBBED OF HER CUBS
2Sam 17:8 For," said Hushai, "you know your father and his men, that they are mighty men, and they are enraged in their minds, like a *bear robbed of her cubs* in the field
Prov 17:12 Let a man meet a *bear robbed of her cubs*, rather than a fool in his folly

BEAR SIN BECAUSE OF HIM
Lev 19:17 You shall surely rebuke your neighbor, and not *bear sin because of him*

BEAR THE CONSEQUENCES OF HER SIN (NIV)
(See *BEAR HER GUILT*)

BEAR THE GUILT
Lev 10:17 Why have you not eaten the sin offering in a holy place, since it is most holy, and God has given it to you to *bear the guilt* of the congregation, to make atonement for them before the Lord
Lev 22:16 or allow them to *bear the guilt* of trespass when they eat their holy offerings
Ezek 18:19 Yet you say, 'Why should the son not *bear the guilt* of the father
Ezek 18:20 The son shall not *bear the guilt* of the father, nor the father *bear the guilt* of the son

BEAR THE INIQUITY
Ex 28:38 So it shall be on Aaron's forehead, that Aaron may *bear the iniquity* of the holy things which the children of Israel hallow in all their holy gifts
Num 18:1 You and your sons and your father's house with you shall *bear the iniquity* related to the sanctuary, and you and your sons with you shall *bear the iniquity* associated with your priesthood
Ezek 4:5 so you shall *bear the iniquity* of the house of Israel
Ezek 4:6 then you shall *bear the iniquity* of the house of Judah forty days

BEAR THE RESPONSIBILITY (NIV)
(See *BEAR THEIR INIQUITY*)

BEAR THEIR GUILT
Lev 20:19 You shall not uncover the nakedness of your mother's sister nor of your father's sister, for that would uncover his near of kin. They shall *bear their guilt*

BEAR THEIR INIQUITY
Num 18:23 But the Levites shall perform the work of the tabernacle of meeting, and they shall *bear their iniquity*
Ezek 4:4 According to the number of the days that you lie on it, you shall *bear their iniquity*
Ezek 14:10 And they shall *bear their iniquity;* the punishment of the prophet shall be the same as the punishment of the one who inquired
Ezek 44:10 And the Levites who went far from Me, when Israel went astray, who strayed away from Me after their idols, they shall *bear their iniquity*
Ezek 44:12 Because they ministered to them before their idols and caused the house of Israel to fall into iniquity, therefore I have lifted My hand in an oath against them," says the Lord God, "that they shall *bear their iniquity*

BEAR WITNESS
1Kin 21:10 and seat two men, scoundrels, before him to *bear witness* against him, saying
Luke 11:48 In fact, you *bear witness* that you approve the deeds of your fathers
John 1:7 This man came for a witness, to *bear witness* of the Light, that all through him might believe
John 1:8 He was not that Light, but was sent to *bear witness* of that Light
John 5:31 If I *bear witness* of Myself, My witness is not true
John 5:36 for the works which the Father has given Me to finish the very works that I do *bear witness* of Me, that the Father has sent Me
John 8:13 The Pharisees therefore said to Him, "You *bear witness* of Yourself
John 8:14 Jesus answered and said to them, "Even if I *bear witness* of Myself, My witness is true, for I know where I came from and where I am going
John 10:25 The works that I do in My Father's name, they *bear witness* of Me
John 15:27 And you also will *bear witness*, because you have been with Me from the beginning
John 18:23 Jesus answered him, "If I have spoken evil, *bear witness* of the evil
John 18:37 For this cause I was born, and for this cause I have come into the world, that I should *bear witness* to the truth
Acts 23:11 for as you have testified for Me in Jerusalem, so you must also *bear witness* at Rome
2Cor 8:3 For I *bear witness* that according to their ability, yes, and beyond their ability, they were freely willing
1Jn 1:2 the life was manifested, and we have seen, and *bear witness*, and declare to you that eternal life which was with the Father and was manifested to us
1Jn 5:7 For there are three who *bear witness* in heaven: the Father, the Word, and the Holy Spirit
1Jn 5:8 And there are three that *bear witness* on earth: the Spirit, the water, and the blood
3Jn 12 And we also *bear witness*, and you know that our testimony is true

BEAR YOUR GUILT
Num 14:34 According to the number of the days in which you spied out the land, forty days, for each day you shall *bear your guilt* one year, namely forty years, and you shall know My rejection

BEAR YOUR INIQUITIES (KJV)
(See *BEAR YOUR GUILT*)

BEARING WITNESS
Acts 14:3 Therefore they stayed there a long time, speaking boldly in the Lord, who was *bearing witness* to the word of His grace, granting signs and wonders to be done by their hands
Rom 2:15 who show the work of the law written in their hearts, their conscience also *bearing witness*, and between themselves their thoughts accusing or else excusing them
Heb 2:4 God also *bearing witness* both with signs and wonders, with various miracles, and gifts of the Holy Spirit, according to His own will

BEARS ALL THINGS
1Cor 13:7 *bears all things*, believes all things, hopes all things, endures all things

BEARS BAD FRUIT
Matt 7:17 Even so, every good tree bears good fruit, but a bad tree *bears bad fruit*

BEARS FALSE WITNESS
Prov 25:18 A man who *bears false witness* against his neighbor is like a club, a sword, and a sharp arrow

BEARS GOOD FRUIT
Matt 7:17 Even so, every good tree *bears good fruit*, but a bad tree bears bad fruit

BEARS ME WITNESS
Acts 22:5 as also the high priest *bears me witness*, and all the council of the elders, from whom I also received letters to the brethren, and went to Damascus to bring in chains even those who were there to Jerusalem to be punished

BEARS MUCH FRUIT
John 15:5 He who abides in Me, and I in him, *bears much fruit*

BEARS THE VERY STAMP OF HIS NATURE (RSV)
(See *EXPRESS IMAGE OF HIS PERSON*)

BEARS WITNESS
Job 16:8 my leanness rises up against me and *bears witness* to my face
John 5:32 There is another who *bears witness* of Me, and I know that the witness which He witnesses of Me is true
John 8:18 I am One who *bears witness* of Myself, and the Father who sent Me *bears witness* of Me
Rom 8:16 The Spirit Himself *bears witness* with our spirit that we are children of God
1Jn 5:6 And it is the Spirit who *bears witness*, because the Spirit is truth

BEAST OF THE EARTH
Gen 1:24 cattle and creeping thing and *beast of the earth*, each according to its kind
Gen 1:25 And God made the *beast of the earth* according to its kind, cattle according to its kind, and everything that creeps on the earth according to its kind
Gen 1:30 Also, to every *beast of the earth*, to every bird of the air, and to everything that creeps on the earth, in which there is life, I have given every green herb for food
Gen 9:2 And the fear of you and the dread of you shall be on every *beast of the earth*, on every bird of the air, on all that moves on the earth, and on all the fish of the sea
Gen 9:10 the birds, the cattle, and every *beast of the earth* with you, of all that go out of the ark, every *beast of the earth*

BEAST OF THE FIELD
Gen 2:19 Out of the ground the Lord God formed every *beast of the field* and every bird of the air, and brought them to Adam to see what he would call them
Gen 2:20 So Adam gave names to all cattle, to the birds of the air, and to every *beast of the field*
Gen 3:1 Now the serpent was more cunning than any *beast of the field* which the Lord God had made
Gen 3:14 Because you have done this, you are cursed more than all cattle, and more than every *beast of the field*
Ex 23:29 I will not drive them out from before you in one year, lest the land become desolate and the *beast of the field* become too numerous for you
Ps 80:13 The boar out of the woods uproots it, and the wild *beast of the field* devours it
Ps 104:11 They give drink to every *beast of the field;* the wild donkeys quench their thirst
Is 43:20 The *beast of the field* will honor Me, the jackals and the ostriches, because I give waters in the wilderness and rivers in the desert, to give drink to My people, My chosen
Ezek 34:8 as I live," says the Lord God, "surely because My flock became a prey, and My flock became food for every *beast of the field*, because there was no shepherd, nor did My shepherds search for My flock, but the shepherds fed themselves and did not feed My flock
Ezek 39:17 And as for you, son of man, thus says the Lord God, 'Speak to every sort of bird and to every *beast of the field*

BEASTS OF THE EARTH
Deut 28:26 Your carcasses shall be food for all the birds of the air and the *beasts of the earth*, and no one shall frighten them away
1Sam 17:46 And this day I will give the carcasses of the camp of the Philistines to the birds of the air and the wild *beasts of the earth*, that all the earth may know that there is a God in Israel
Job 5:22 You shall laugh at destruction and famine, and you shall not be afraid of the *beasts of the earth*
Job 35:11 Who teaches us more than the *beasts of the earth*, and makes us wiser than the birds of heaven
Ps 79:2 The dead bodies of Your servants they have given as food for the birds of the heavens, the flesh of Your saints to the *beasts of the earth*
Is 18:6 They will be left together for the mountain birds of prey and for the *beasts of the earth;* the birds of prey will summer on them, and all the *beasts of the earth* will winter on them
Jer 7:33 The corpses of this people will be food for the birds of the heaven and for the *beasts of the earth*
Jer 15:3 the sword to slay, the dogs to drag, the birds of the heavens and the *beasts of the earth* to devour and destroy
Jer 16:4 They shall be consumed by the sword and by famine, and their corpses shall be meat for the birds of heaven and for the *beasts of the earth*
Jer 19:7 their corpses I will give as meat for the birds of the heaven and for the *beasts of the earth*
Jer 34:20 Their dead bodies shall be for meat for the birds of the heaven and the *beasts of the earth*
Rev 6:8 And power was given to them over a fourth of the earth, to kill with sword, with hunger, with death, and by the *beasts of the earth*

BEASTS OF THE FIELD
Ex 23:11 and what they leave, the *beasts of the field* may eat
Deut 7:22 you will be unable to destroy them at once, lest the *beasts of the field* become too numerous for you
1Sam 17:44 And the Philistine said to David, "Come to me, and I will give your flesh to the birds of the air and the *beasts of the field*
2Sam 21:10 And she did not allow the birds of the air to rest on them by day nor the *beasts of the field* by night
Job 5:23 For you shall have a covenant with the stones of the field, and the *beasts of the field* shall be at peace with you
Job 40:20 Surely the mountains yield food for him, and all the *beasts of the field* play there
Ps 8:7 All sheep and oxen even the *beasts of the field*
Ps 50:11 I know all the birds of the mountains, and the wild *beasts of the field* are Mine
Is 56:9 All you *beasts of the field*, come to devour, all you beasts in the forest
Jer 12:9 Come, assemble all the *beasts of the field*, bring them to devour
Jer 27:6 and the *beasts of the field* I have also given him to serve him
Jer 28:14 I have given him the *beasts of the field* also
Ezek 29:5 I have given you as food to the *beasts of the field* and to the birds of the heavens
Ezek 31:6 under its branches all the *beasts of the field* brought forth their young
Ezek 31:13 On its ruin will remain all the birds of the heavens, and all the *beasts of the field* will come to its branches
Ezek 34:5 and they became food for all the *beasts of the field* when they were scattered
Ezek 38:20 so that the fish of the sea, the birds of the heavens, the *beasts of the field*, all creeping things that creep on the earth, and all men who are on the face of the earth shall shake at My presence
Ezek 39:4 I will give you to birds of prey of every sort and to the *beasts of the field* to be devoured
Dan 2:38 and wherever the children of men dwell, or the *beasts of the field* and the birds of the heaven, He has given them into your hand, and has made you ruler over them all you are this head of gold
Dan 4:12 The *beasts of the field* found shade under it, the birds of the heavens dwelt in its branches, and all flesh was fed from it
Dan 4:21 whose leaves were lovely and its fruit abundant, in which was food for all, under which the *beasts of the field* dwelt, and on whose branches the birds of the heaven had their habitation
Dan 4:23 let it be wet with the dew of heaven, and let him graze with the *beasts of the field*, till seven times pass over him
Dan 4:25 They shall drive you from men, your

dwelling shall be with the *beasts of the field*, and they shall make you eat grass like oxen
Dan 4:32 And they shall drive you from men, and your dwelling shall be with the *beasts of the field*
Hos 2:12 So I will make them a forest, and the *beasts of the field* shall eat them
Hos 2:18 In that day I will make a covenant for them with the *beasts of the field*, with the birds of the air, and with the creeping things of the ground
Hos 4:3 and everyone who dwells there will waste away with the *beasts of the field* and the birds of the air
Joel 1:20 The *beasts of the field* also cry out to You, for the water brooks are dried up, and fire has devoured the open pastures
Joel 2:22 Do not be afraid, you *beasts of the field;* for the open pastures are springing up, and the tree bears its fruit

BEAT THEIR SWORDS INTO PLOWSHARES
Is 2:4 they shall *beat their swords into plowshares*, and their spears into pruning hooks
Mic 4:3 they shall *beat their swords into plowshares*, and their spears into pruning hooks

BEAT YOUR PLOWSHARES INTO SWORDS
Joel 3:10 *Beat your plowshares into swords* and your pruninghooks into spears

BEAUTIFUL BEFORE GOD (RSV)
(See *PLEASING TO GOD*)

BEAUTIFUL CROWN (RSV)
(See *CROWN OF GLORY*)

BEAUTIFUL LAND (NAS, NIV)
(See *GLORIOUS LAND*)

BEAUTIFUL UPON THE MOUNTAINS
Is 52:7 How *beautiful upon the mountains* are the feet of him who brings good news, who proclaims peace, who brings glad tidings of good things, who proclaims salvation, who says to Zion

BEAUTY IS FLEETING (NIV)
(See *BEAUTY IS VAIN*)

BEAUTY IS VAIN
Prov 31:30 Charm is deceitful and *beauty is vain*, but a woman who fears the Lord, she shall be praised

BEAUTY OF HOLINESS
1Chr 16:29 bring an offering, and come before Him. Oh, worship the Lord in the *beauty of holiness*
2Chr 20:21 And when he had consulted with the people, he appointed those who should sing to the Lord, and who should praise the *beauty of holiness*, as they went out before the army and were saying
Ps 29:2 Give unto the Lord the glory due to His name; worship the Lord in the *beauty of holiness*
Ps 96:9 Oh, worship the Lord in the *beauty of holiness!* Tremble before Him, all the earth

BEAUTY OF THE LORD
Ps 27:4 That I may dwell in the house of the Lord all the days of my life, to behold the *beauty of the Lord*, and to inquire in His temple
Ps 90:17 And let the *beauty of the Lord* our God be upon us, and establish the work of our hands for us

BECAME ANGRY (NIV)
(See *ANGER WAS AROUSED*)

BECAUSE OF THEIR UNBELIEF
Matt 13:58 And He did not do many mighty works there *because of their unbelief*
Mark 6:6 And He marveled *because of their unbelief*. Then He went about the villages in a circuit, teaching

BECAUSE OF UNBELIEF
Rom 11:20 *Because of unbelief* they were broken off, and you stand by faith
Heb 3:19 So we see that they could not enter in *because of unbelief*

BECAUSE OF YOUR TRADITION
Matt 15:3 But He answered and said to them, "Why do you also transgress the commandment of God *because of your tradition*

BECOME A STENCH (NIV)
(See *BECOME AN ABOMINATION*)

BECOME A WITNESS (NAS, NIV)
(See *BEARS WITNESS*)

BECOME AN ABOMINATION
1Sam 13:4 Now all Israel heard it said that Saul had attacked a garrison of the Philistines, and that Israel had also *become an abomination* to the Philistines

BECOME AS LITTLE CHILDREN
Matt 18:3 and said, "Assuredly, I say to you, unless you are converted and *become as little children*, you will by no means enter the kingdom of heaven

BECOME DRUNK (RSV)
(See *DRUNK WITH THE WINE*)

BECOME MATURE (NIV)
(See *PERFECT MAN*)

BECOME ODIOUS (NAS, RSV)
(See *BECOME AN ABOMINATION*)

BECOMING LIKE HIM IN DEATH (NIV)
(See *CONFORMED TO HIS DEATH*)

BEDS OF IVORY
Amos 6:4 who lie on *beds of ivory*, stretch out on your couches, eat lambs from the flock and calves from the midst of the stall

BEDS OF SPICES
Song 6:2 My beloved has gone to his garden, to the *beds of spices*, to feed his flock in the gardens, and to gather lilies

BEFITS REPENTANCE (RSV)
(See *WORTHY OF REPENTANCE*)

BEFORE ABRAHAM WAS
John 8:58 Jesus said to them, "Most assuredly, I say to you, *before Abraham was*, I AM

BEFORE GOD
Gen 6:11 The earth also was corrupt *before God*, and the earth was filled with violence
Ex 18:12 And Aaron came with all the elders of Israel to eat bread with Moses' father-in-law *before God*
Ex 18:19 Stand *before God* for the people, so that you may bring the difficulties to God
Josh 24:1 Then Joshua gathered all the tribes of Israel to Shechem and called for the elders of Israel, for their heads, for their judges, and for their officers; and they presented themselves *before God*

Judg 21:2 Then the people came to the house of God, and remained there *before God* till evening
1Chr 13:8 Then David and all Israel played music *before God* with all their might, with singing, on harps, on stringed instruments, on tambourines, on cymbals, and with trumpets
1Chr 13:10 Then the anger of the Lord was aroused against Uzza, and He struck him because he put his hand to the ark; and he died there *before God*
1Chr 16:1 Then they offered burnt offerings and peace offerings *before God*
2Chr 34:27 because your heart was tender, and you humbled yourself *before God* when you heard His words against this place and against its inhabitants, and you humbled yourself before Me, and you tore your clothes and wept before Me, I also have heard you
Job 9:2 Truly I know it is so, but how can a man be righteous *before God*
Job 15:4 Yes, you cast off fear, and restrain prayer *before God*
Job 25:4 How then can man be righteous *before God?* Or how can he be pure who is born of a woman
Job 33:6 Truly I am as your spokesman *before God;* I also have been formed out of clay
Job 34:23 For He need not further consider a man, that he should go *before God* in judgment
Ps 42:2 My soul thirsts for God, for the living God. When shall I come and appear *before God*
Ps 56:13 Have You not delivered my feet from falling, that I may walk *before God* in the light of the living
Ps 61:7 He shall abide *before God* forever. Oh, prepare mercy and truth, which may preserve him
Ps 68:3 Let them rejoice *before God;* yes, let them rejoice exceedingly
Ps 84:7 They go from strength to strength; every one of them appears *before God* in Zion
Eccl 2:26 but to the sinner He gives the work of gathering and collecting, that he may give to him who is good *before God*
Eccl 5:2 Do not be rash with your mouth, and let not your heart utter anything hastily *before God*
Eccl 8:13 nor will he prolong his days, which are as a shadow, because he does not fear *before God*
Luke 1:6 And they were both righteous *before God*, walking in all the commandments and ordinances of the Lord blameless
Luke 1:8 So it was, that while he was serving as priest *before God* in the order of his division
Luke 12:6 Are not five sparrows sold for two copper coins? And not one of them is forgotten *before God*
Luke 24:19 And they said to Him, "The things concerning Jesus of Nazareth, who was a Prophet mighty in deed and word *before God* and all the people
Acts 7:46 who found favor *before God* and asked to find a dwelling for the God of Jacob
Acts 10:4 So he said to him, "Your prayers and your alms have come up for a memorial *before God*
Acts 10:33 Now therefore, we are all present *before God*, to hear all the things commanded you by God
Acts 23:1 Then Paul, looking earnestly at the council, said, "Men and brethren, I have lived in all good conscience *before God* until this day
Rom 3:19 Now we know that whatever the law says, it says to those who are under the law, that every mouth may be stopped, and all the world may become guilty *before God*
Rom 4:2 For if Abraham was justified by works, he has something of which to boast, but not *before God*
Rom 14:22 Have it to yourself *before God*. Happy is he who does not condemn himself in what he approves
2Cor 12:19 We speak *before God* in Christ. But we do all things, beloved, for your edification
Gal 1:20 (Now concerning the things which I write to you, indeed, *before God*, I do not lie
1Tim 5:4 But if any widow has children or grandchildren, let them first learn to show piety at home and to repay their parents; for this is good and acceptable *before God*
1Tim 5:21 I charge you *before God* and the Lord Jesus Christ and the elect angels that you observe these things without prejudice, doing nothing with partiality
2Tim 4:1 I charge you therefore *before God* and the Lord Jesus Christ, who will judge the living and the dead at His appearing and His kingdom
Jas 1:27 Pure and undefiled religion *before God* and the Father is this
1Pet 2:20 But when you do good and suffer for it, if you take it patiently, this is commendable *before God*
Rev 3:2 Be watchful, and strengthen the things which remain, that are ready to die, for I have not found your works perfect *before God*
Rev 8:2 And I saw the seven angels who stand *before God*, and to them were given seven trumpets
Rev 8:4 And the smoke of the incense, with the prayers of the saints, ascended *before God* from the angel's hand
Rev 9:13 And I heard a voice from the four horns of the golden altar which is *before God*
Rev 11:16 And the twenty-four elders who sat *before God* on their thrones fell on their faces and worshiped God
Rev 16:19 And great Babylon was remembered *before God*, to give her the cup of the wine of the fierceness of His wrath
Rev 20:12 And I saw the dead, small and great, standing *before God*, and books were opened

BEFORE MANY WITNESSES (KJV)
(See *IN THE PRESENCE OF MANY WITNESSES*)

BEFORE THE CREATION OF THE WORLD (NIV)
(See *BEFORE THE FOUNDATION OF THE WORLD*)

BEFORE THE FOUNDATION OF THE WORLD
John 17:24 for You loved Me *before the foundation of the world*
Eph 1:4 just as He chose us in Him *before the foundation of the world*, that we should be holy and without blame before Him in love
1Pet 1:20 He indeed was foreordained *before the foundation of the world*, but was manifest in these last times for you

BEFORE THE ROOSTER CROWS TWICE
Mark 14:30 And Jesus said to him, "Assuredly, I say to you that today, even this night, *before the rooster crows twice*, you will deny Me three times
Mark 14:72 And Peter called to mind the word that Jesus had said to him, "*Before the rooster crows twice*, you will deny Me three times

BEFORE THE THRONE OF GOD
Rev 7:15 Therefore they are *before the throne of God*, and serve Him day and night in His temple
Rev 14:5 And in their mouth was found no guile, for they are without fault *before the throne of God*

BEFORE THE WORLD WAS
John 17:5 And now, O Father, glorify Me together with Yourself, with the glory which I had with You *before the world was*

BEFORE YOUR EYES
Gen 47:19 Why should we die *before your eyes*, both we and our land
Deut 1:30 The Lord your God, who goes before you, He will fight for you, according to all He did for you in Egypt *before your eyes*
Deut 4:34 Or did God ever try to go and take for Himself a nation from the midst of another nation, by trials, by signs, by wonders, by war, by a mighty hand and an outstretched arm, and by great terrors, according to all that the Lord your God did for you in Egypt *before your eyes*
Deut 9:17 Then I took the two tablets and threw them out of my two hands and broke them *before your eyes*
Deut 28:31 Your ox shall be slaughtered *before your eyes*, but you shall not eat of it
Deut 29:2 You have seen all that the Lord did *before your eyes* in the land of Egypt, to Pharaoh and to all his servants and to all his land
1Sam 12:16 Now therefore, stand and see this great thing which the Lord will do *before your eyes*
2Sam 12:11 and I will take your wives *before your eyes* and give them to your neighbor, and he shall lie with your wives in the sight of this sun
Ps 31:22 For I said in my haste, "I am cut off from *before Your eyes*
Ps 50:21 But I will reprove you, and set them in order *before your eyes*
Jer 16:9 Behold, I will cause to cease from this place, *before your eyes* and in your days, the voice of mirth and the voice of gladness, the voice of the bridegroom and the voice of the bride
Jer 29:21 Behold, I will deliver them into the hand of Nebuchadnezzar king of Babylon, and he shall slay them *before your eyes*
Zeph 3:20 for I will give you fame and praise among all the peoples of the earth, when I return your captives *before your eyes*

BEFORE YOUR FACE
Deut 28:7 The Lord will cause your enemies who rise against you to be defeated *before your face*
Ps 41:12 As for me, You uphold me in my integrity, and set me *before Your face* forever
Ps 89:14 Righteousness and justice are the foundation of Your throne; mercy and truth go *before Your face*
Nah 2:1 He who scatters has come up *before your face*. Man the fort
Matt 11:10 Behold, I send My messenger *before Your face*, who will prepare Your way before You
Mark 1:2 Behold, I send My messenger *before Your face*, who will prepare Your way before You
Luke 7:27 Behold, I send My messenger *before Your face*, who will prepare Your way before You

BEGINNING OF CREATION
Mark 13:19 For in those days there will be tribulation, such as has not been from the *beginning of creation* which God created until this time, nor ever shall be
2Pet 3:4 For since the fathers fell asleep, all things continue as they were from the *beginning of creation*

BEGINNING OF KNOWLEDGE
Prov 1:7 The fear of the Lord is the *beginning of knowledge*, but fools despise wisdom and instruction

BEGINNING OF THE CREATION
Mark 10:6 But from the *beginning of the creation*, God 'made them male and female
Rev 3:14 And to the angel of the church of the Laodiceans write, 'These things says the Amen, the Faithful and True Witness, the *Beginning of the creation* of God

BEGINNING OF THE GOSPEL
Mark 1:1 The *beginning of the gospel* of Jesus Christ, the Son of God
Phil 4:15 Now you Philippians know also that in the *beginning of the gospel*, when I departed from Macedonia, no church shared with me concerning giving and receiving but you only

BEGINNING OF WISDOM
Ps 111:10 The fear of the Lord is the *beginning of wisdom*
Prov 9:10 The fear of the Lord is the *beginning of wisdom*, and the knowledge of the Holy One is understanding

BEGOTTEN US AGAIN
1Pet 1:3 Blessed be the God and Father of our Lord Jesus Christ, who according to His abundant mercy has *begotten us again* to a living hope through the resurrection of Jesus Christ from the dead

BEHIND THE CURTAIN (NIV)
(See *INSIDE THE VEIL*)

BEHIND THE VEIL
Ex 26:33 Then you shall bring the ark of the Testimony in there, *behind the veil*
Num 18:7 Therefore you and your sons with you shall attend to your priesthood for everything at the altar and *behind the veil*
Heb 6:19 This hope we have as an anchor of the soul, both sure and steadfast, and which enters the Presence *behind the veil*

BEHOLD MY HANDS AND MY FEET
Luke 24:39 *Behold My hands and My feet*, that it is I Myself

BEHOLD THE FACE OF GOD (RSV)
(See *APPEAR BEFORE GOD*)

BEHOLD THE LAMB
John 1:36 And looking at Jesus as He walked, he said, "*Behold the Lamb* of God

BEHOLD THE MAN
John 19:5 Then Jesus came out, wearing the crown of thorns and the purple robe. And Pilate said to them, "*Behold the Man*

BEHOLD YOUR KING
John 19:14 Now it was the Preparation Day of the Passover, and about the sixth hour. And he said to the Jews, "*Behold your King*

BEHOLD YOUR MOTHER
John 19:27 Then He said to the disciple, "*Behold your mother!*" And from that hour that disciple took her to his own home

BEHOLD YOUR SON
John 19:26 When Jesus therefore saw His mother, and the disciple whom He loved standing by, He said to His mother, "Woman, *behold your son*

BEING SURE (NIV)
(See *SUBSTANCE OF THINGS*)

BELIEVE HIS PROMISE (NIV)
(See *BELIEVE HIS WORD*)

BELIEVE HIS WORD
Ps 106:24 Then they despised the pleasant land; they did not *believe His word*

BELIEVE IN GOD
Ps 78:22 Because they did not *believe in God*, and did not trust in His salvation
John 14:1 Let not your heart be troubled; you *believe in God*, believe also in Me
1Pet 1:21 who through Him *believe in God*, who raised Him from the dead and gave Him glory, so that your faith and hope are in God

BELIEVE IN THE GOSPEL
Mark 1:15 and saying, "The time is fulfilled, and the kingdom of God is at hand. Repent, and *believe in the gospel*

BELIEVE IN THE LORD
2Kin 17:14 Nevertheless they would not hear, but stiffened their necks, like the necks of their fathers, who did not *believe in the Lord* their God
2Chr 20:20 *Believe in the Lord* your God, and you shall be established

BELIEVE IN YOUR HEART
Rom 10:9 that if you confess with your mouth the Lord Jesus and *believe in your heart* that God has raised Him from the dead, you will be saved

BELIEVE MY WORDS
Luke 1:20 But behold, you will be mute and not able to speak until the day these things take place, because you did not *believe my words* which will be fulfilled in their own time
John 5:47 But if you do not believe his writings, how will you *believe My words*

BELIEVE THE LORD
Deut 1:32 Yet, for all that, you did not *believe the Lord* your God

BELIEVED AND WERE BAPTIZED
Acts 18:8 And many of the Corinthians, hearing, *believed and were baptized*

BELIEVED GOD
Jon 3:5 So the people of Nineveh *believed God*, proclaimed a fast, and put on sackcloth, from the greatest to the least of them
Rom 4:3 Abraham *believed God*, and it was accounted to him for righteousness
Gal 3:6 just as Abraham "*believed God*, and it was accounted to him for righteousness
Jas 2:23 And the Scripture was fulfilled which says, "Abraham *believed God*, and it was accounted to him for righteousness

BELIEVED IN GOD
Acts 16:34 and he rejoiced, having *believed in God* with all his household
Tit 3:8 This is a faithful saying, and these things I want you to affirm constantly, that those who have *believed in God* should be careful to maintain good works

BELIEVED IN HIM
John 2:11 This beginning of signs Jesus did in Cana of Galilee, and manifested His glory; and His disciples *believed in Him*
John 4:39 And many of the Samaritans of that city *believed in Him* because of the word of the woman who testified
John 7:31 And many of the people *believed in Him*, and said
John 7:48 Have any of the rulers or the Pharisees *believed in Him*
John 8:30 As He spoke these words, many *believed in Him*
John 10:42 And many *believed in Him* there
John 11:45 Then many of the Jews who had come to Mary, and had seen the things Jesus did, *believed in Him*
John 12:42 Nevertheless even among the rulers many *believed in Him*, but because of the Pharisees they did not confess Him, lest they should be put out of the synagogue

BELIEVED IN HIS GOD
Dan 6:23 So Daniel was taken up out of the den, and no injury whatever was found on him, because he *believed in his God*

BELIEVED IN HIS NAME
John 2:23 Now when He was in Jerusalem at the Passover, during the feast, many *believed in His name* when they saw the signs which He did

BELIEVED IN THE LORD
Gen 15:6 And he *believed in the Lord*, and He accounted it to him for righteousness

BELIEVED ON THE LORD
Acts 9:42 And it became known throughout all Joppa, and many *believed on the Lord*
Acts 11:17 If therefore God gave them the same gift as He gave us when we *believed on the Lord* Jesus Christ, who was I that I could withstand God
Acts 18:8 Then Crispus, the ruler of the synagogue, *believed on the Lord* with all his household

BELIEVES AND IS BAPTIZED
Mark 16:16 He who *believes and is baptized* will be saved; but he who does not believe will be condemned

BELIEVETH ON THE SON (KJV)
(See *WHO BELIEVES IN THE SON*)

BELLY OF THE FISH
Jon 1:17 And Jonah was in the *belly of the fish* three days and three nights

BELONGED TO THE CIRCUMCISION GROUP (NIV)
(See *THOSE WHO WERE OF THE CIRCUMCISION*)

BELOVED SON
Matt 3:17 And suddenly a voice came from heaven, saying, "This is My *beloved Son*, in whom I am well pleased
Matt 17:5 and suddenly a voice came out of the cloud, saying, "This is My *beloved Son*, in whom I am well pleased
Mark 1:11 Then a voice came from heaven, "You are My *beloved Son*, in whom I am well pleased
Mark 9:7 and a voice came out of the cloud, saying, "This is My *beloved Son*
Luke 3:22 And the Holy Spirit descended in bodily form like a dove upon Him, and a voice came from heaven which said, "You are My *beloved Son*
Luke 9:35 Then a voice came out of the cloud, saying, "This is My *beloved Son*
Luke 20:13 I will send my *beloved son*. Probably they will respect him when they see him
2Tim 1:2 To Timothy, my *beloved son:* Grace, mercy, and peace from God the Father and Christ Jesus our Lord

2Pet 1:17 This is My *beloved Son*, in whom I am well pleased

BELT OF TRUTH BUCKLED ABOUT YOUR WAIST (NIV)
(See *GIRDED YOUR WAIST WITH TRUTH*)

BESIDE THE STILL WATERS
Ps 23:2 He makes me to lie down in green pastures; He leads me *beside the still waters*

BESOUGHT GOD (KJV, RSV)
(See *PLEADED WITH GOD*)

BEST OF THE FIRSTFRUITS (NIV)
(See *FIRST OF THE FIRSTFRUITS*)

BETHINK THEMSELVES (KJV)
(See *COME TO THEMSELVES*)

BETRAYED INTO THE HANDS OF (NIV)
(See *DELIVERED INTO THE HANDS OF*)

BETRAYED INTO THE HANDS OF MEN
Matt 17:22 Now while they were staying in Galilee, Jesus said to them, "The Son of Man is about to be *betrayed into the hands of men*

BETRAYED TO BE CRUCIFIED (KJV)
(See *DELIVERED UP TO BE CRUCIFIED*)

BETTER COVENANT
Heb 7:22 by so much more Jesus has become a surety of a *better covenant*
Heb 8:6 But now He has obtained a more excellent ministry, inasmuch as He is also Mediator of a *better covenant*, which was established on better promises

BETTER IS OPEN REBUKE (NAS, NIV, RSV)
(See *OPEN REBUKE IS BETTER*)

BETTER SACRIFICE (NAS, NIV)
(See *MORE EXCELLENT SACRIFICE*)

BETTER TO MARRY THAN TO BURN
1Cor 7:9 For it is *better to marry than to burn* with passion

BETWEEN HEAVEN AND EARTH
2Sam 18:9 so he was left hanging *between heaven and earth*. And the mule which was under him went on

BETWEEN THE CHERUBIM
1Sam 4:4 So the people sent to Shiloh, that they might bring from there the ark of the covenant of the Lord of hosts, who dwells *between the cherubim*
2Sam 6:2 And David arose and went with all the people who were with him from Baale Judah to bring up from there the ark of God, whose name is called by the Name, the Lord of Hosts, who dwells *between the cherubim*
2Kin 19:15 O Lord God of Israel, the One who dwells *between the cherubim*, You are God, You alone, of all the kingdoms of the earth
1Chr 13:6 And David and all Israel went up to Baalah, to Kirjath Jearim, which belonged to Judah, to bring up from there the ark of God the Lord, who dwells *between the cherubim*, where His name is proclaimed
Ps 80:1 Give ear, O Shepherd of Israel, You who lead Joseph like a flock; You who dwell *between the cherubim*, shine forth
Ps 99:1 He dwells *between the cherubim;* let the earth be moved
Is 37:16 O Lord of hosts, God of Israel, the One who dwells *between the cherubim*, You are God, You alone, of all the kingdoms of the earth

BEWARE OF FALSE PROPHETS
Matt 7:15 *Beware of false prophets*, who come to you in sheep's clothing, but inwardly they are ravenous wolves

BEWARE OF THE LEAVEN
Matt 16:6 Then Jesus said to them, "Take heed and *beware of the leaven* of the Pharisees and the Sadducees
Matt 16:11 but you should *beware of the leaven* of the Pharisees and Sadducees
Matt 16:12 Then they understood that He did not tell them to *beware of the leaven* of bread, but of the doctrine of the Pharisees and Sadducees
Mark 8:15 Then He charged them, saying, "Take heed, *beware of the leaven* of the Pharisees and the leaven of Herod
Luke 12:1 In the meantime, when an innumerable multitude of people had gathered together, so that they trampled one another, He began to say to His disciples first of all, "*Beware of the leaven* of the Pharisees, which is hypocrisy

BEWARE OF THE SCRIBES
Mark 12:38 Then He said to them in His teaching, "*Beware of the scribes*, who desire to go around in long robes, love greetings in the marketplaces
Luke 20:46 *Beware of the scribes*, who desire to walk in long robes, love greetings in the marketplaces, the best seats in the synagogues, and the best places at feasts

BEYOND THE JORDAN
Gen 50:10 Then they came to the threshing floor of Atad, which is *beyond the Jordan*, and they mourned there with a great and very solemn lamentation
Gen 50:11 Therefore its name was called Abel Mizraim, which is *beyond the Jordan*
Deut 3:20 until the Lord has given rest to your brethren as to you, and they also possess the land which the Lord your God is giving them *beyond the Jordan*
Deut 3:25 I pray, let me cross over and see the good land *beyond the Jordan*, those pleasant mountains, and Lebanon
Josh 9:10 and all that He did to the two kings of the Amorites who were *beyond the Jordan* to Sihon king of Heshbon, and Og king of Bashan, who was at Ashtaroth
Josh 13:8 With the other half tribe the Reubenites and the Gadites received their inheritance, which Moses had given them, *beyond the Jordan* eastward, as Moses the servant of the Lord had given them
Josh 18:7 And Gad, Reuben, and half the tribe of Manasseh have received their inheritance *beyond the Jordan* on the east, which Moses the servant of the Lord gave them
Judg 5:17 Gilead stayed *beyond the Jordan*, and why did Dan remain on ships
Is 9:1 Nevertheless the gloom will not be upon her who is distressed, as when at first He lightly esteemed the land of Zebulun and the land of Naphtali, and afterward more heavily oppressed her, by the way of the sea, *beyond the Jordan*, in Galilee of the Gentiles
Matt 4:15 The land of Zebulun and the land of Naphtali, the way of the sea, *beyond the Jordan*, Galilee of the Gentiles
Matt 4:25 And great multitudes followed Him from Galilee, and from Decapolis, Jerusalem, Judea, and *beyond the Jordan*
Matt 19:1 Now it came to pass, when Jesus had finished these sayings, that He departed from

Galilee and came to the region of Judea *beyond the Jordan*
Mark 3:8 and Jerusalem and Idumea and *beyond the Jordan;* and those from Tyre and Sidon, a great multitude, when they heard how many things He was doing, came to Him
John 1:28 These things were done in Bethabara *beyond the Jordan*, where John was baptizing
John 3:26 And they came to John and said to him, "Rabbi, He who was with you *beyond the Jordan*, to whom you have testified behold, He is baptizing, and all are coming to Him
John 10:40 And He went away again *beyond the Jordan* to the place where John was baptizing at first, and there He stayed

BEYOND THE RIVER
2Sam 10:16 Then Hadadezer sent and brought out the Syrians who were *beyond the River*, and they came to Helam
1Kin 14:15 He will uproot Israel from this good land which He gave to their fathers, and will scatter them *beyond the River*, because they have made their wooden images, provoking the Lord to anger
1Chr 19:16 Now when the Syrians saw that they had been defeated by Israel, they sent messengers and brought the Syrians who were *beyond the River*, and Shophach the commander of Hadadezer's army went before them
Ezra 4:10 and the rest of the nations whom the great and noble Osnapper took captive and settled in the cities of Samaria and the rest of the region *beyond the River* and so forth
Ezra 4:11 This is a copy of the letter that they sent him To King Artaxerxes from your servants the men of the region *beyond the River*, and so forth
Ezra 4:16 We inform the king that if this city is rebuilt and its walls are completed, the result will be that you will have no dominion over the region *beyond the River*
Ezra 4:17 To Rehum the commander, to Shimshai the scribe, to the rest of their companions who dwell in Samaria, and to the rest in the region *beyond the River*
Ezra 4:20 There have also been mighty kings over Jerusalem, who have ruled over all the provinces *beyond the River*
Ezra 5:3 At the same time Tattenai the governor of the region *beyond the River* and Shethar-Bozenai and their companions came to them and spoke thus to them
Ezra 5:6 The governor of the region *beyond the River*, and Shethar-Baznai, and his companions, the Persians who were in the region *beyond the River*, to Darius the king
Ezra 6:6 Now therefore, Tattenai, governor of the region *beyond the River*, and Shethar-Boznai, and your companions the Persians who are *beyond the River*, keep yourselves far from there
Ezra 6:8 Let the cost be paid at the king's expense from taxes on the region *beyond the River*
Ezra 6:13 Then Tattenai, governor of the region *beyond the River*, Shethar-Boznai, and their companions diligently did according to what King Darius had sent
Ezra 7:21 And I, even I, Artaxerxes the king, do issue a decree to all the treasurers who are in the region *beyond the River*, that whatever Ezra the priest, the scribe of the Law of the God of heaven, may require of you, let it be done diligently
Ezra 7:25 And you, Ezra, according to your God-given wisdom, set magistrates and judges who may judge all the people who are in the region *beyond the River*, all such as know the laws of your God
Ezra 8:36 And they delivered the king's orders to the king's satraps and the governors in the region *beyond the River*
Neh 2:7 Furthermore I said to the king, "If it pleases the king, let letters be given to me for the governors of the region *beyond the River*, that they must permit me to pass through till I come to Judah
Neh 2:9 Then I went to the governors in the region *beyond the River*, and gave them the king's letters
Neh 3:7 And next to them Melatiah the Gibeonite, Jadon the Meronothite, the men of Gibeon and Mizpah, repaired the residence of the governor of the region *beyond the River*
Is 7:20 In the same day the Lord will shave with a hired razor, with those from *beyond the River*, with the king of Assyria, the head and the hair of the legs, and will also remove the beard

BIND THEM AS A SIGN
Deut 6:8 You shall *bind them as a sign* on your hand, and they shall be as frontlets between your eyes
Deut 11:18 Therefore you shall lay up these words of mine in your heart and in your soul, and *bind them as a sign* on your hand, and they shall be as frontlets between your eyes

BIND UP THE BROKENHEARTED (KJV, NAS, NIV, RSV)
(See *HEAL THE BROKENHEARTED*)

BIND UP THE TESTIMONY
Is 8:16 *Bind up the testimony*, seal the law among my disciples

BIND US UP
Hos 6:1 for He has torn, but He will heal us; He has stricken, but He will *bind us up*

BINDS EVERYTHING TOGETHER IN PERFECT HARMONY (RSV)
(See *BOND OF PERFECTION*)

BINDS THEM ALL TOGETHER IN PERFECT UNITY (NIV)
(See *BOND OF PERFECTION*)

BIRDS OF THE AIR
Gen 1:26 let them have dominion over the fish of the sea, over the *birds of the air*, and over the cattle, over all the earth and over every creeping thing that creeps on the earth
Gen 1:28 have dominion over the fish of the sea, over the *birds of the air*, and over every living thing that moves on the earth
Gen 2:20 So Adam gave names to all cattle, to the *birds of the air*, and to every beast of the field
Gen 6:7 So the Lord said, "I will destroy man whom I have created from the face of the earth, both man and beast, creeping thing and *birds of the air*, for I am sorry that I have made them
Gen 7:3 also seven each of *birds of the air*, male and female, to keep the species alive on the face of all the earth
Deut 28:26 Your carcasses shall be food for all the *birds of the air* and the beasts of the earth, and no one shall frighten them away
1Sam 17:44 And the Philistine said to David, "Come to me, and I will give your flesh to the *birds of the air* and the beasts of the field
1Sam 17:46 And this day I will give the carcasses of the camp of the Philistines to the *birds of the air* and the wild beasts of the earth, that all the earth may know that there is a God in Israel
2Sam 21:10 And she did not allow the *birds of the air* to rest on them by day nor the beasts of the field by night

1Kin 14:11 The dogs shall eat whoever belongs to Jeroboam and dies in the city, and the *birds of the air* shall eat whoever dies in the field
1Kin 16:4 The dogs shall eat whoever belongs to Baasha and dies in the city, and the *birds of the air* shall eat whoever dies in the fields
1Kin 21:24 The dogs shall eat whoever belongs to Ahab and dies in the city, and the *birds of the air* shall eat whoever dies in the field
Job 12:7 and the *birds of the air*, and they will tell you
Job 28:21 It is hidden from the eyes of all living, and concealed from the *birds of the air*
Ps 8:8 The *birds of the air*, and the fish of the sea that pass through the paths of the seas
Hos 2:18 In that day I will make a covenant for them with the beasts of the field, with the *birds of the air*, and with the creeping things of the ground
Hos 4:3 and everyone who dwells there will waste away with the beasts of the field and the *birds of the air*
Hos 7:12 I will bring them down like *birds of the air*
Matt 6:26 Look at the *birds of the air*, for they neither sow nor reap nor gather into barns
Matt 8:20 And Jesus said to him, "Foxes have holes and *birds of the air* have nests, but the Son of Man has nowhere to lay His head
Matt 13:32 but when it is grown it is greater than the herbs and becomes a tree, so that the *birds of the air* come and nest in its branches
Mark 4:4 and the *birds of the air* came and devoured it
Mark 4:32 but when it is sown, it grows up and becomes greater than all herbs, and shoots out large branches, so that the *birds of the air* may nest under its shade
Luke 8:5 and it was trampled down, and the *birds of the air* devoured it
Luke 9:58 And Jesus said to him, "Foxes have holes and *birds of the air* have nests, but the Son of Man has nowhere to lay His head
Luke 13:19 and it grew and became a large tree, and the *birds of the air* nested in its branches
Acts 10:12 In it were all kinds of four-footed animals of the earth, wild beasts, creeping things, and *birds of the air*
Acts 11:6 When I observed it intently and considered, I saw four-footed animals of the earth, wild beasts, creeping things, and *birds of the air*

BIRTH PANGS
Jer 48:41 the mighty men's hearts in Moab on that day shall be like the heart of a woman in *birth pangs*
Jer 49:22 The heart of the mighty men of Edom in that day shall be like the heart of a woman in *birth pangs*
Mic 4:10 Be in pain, and labor to bring forth, O daughter of Zion, like a woman in *birth pangs*
Rom 8:22 For we know that the whole creation groans and labors with *birth pangs* together until now

BITTER AS GALL (NIV)
(See *BITTER AS WORMWOOD*)

BITTER AS WORMWOOD
Prov 5:4 but in the end she is *bitter as wormwood*, sharp as a two-edged sword

BITTER HERBS
Ex 12:8 roasted in fire, with unleavened bread and with *bitter herbs* they shall eat it
Num 9:11 They shall eat it with unleavened bread and *bitter herbs*

BITTERNESS OF HIS SOUL
Job 21:25 Another man dies in the *bitterness of his soul*, never having eaten with pleasure

BITTERNESS OF MY SOUL
Job 7:11 I will speak in the anguish of my spirit; I will complain in the *bitterness of my soul*
Job 10:1 I will give free course to my complaint, I will speak in the *bitterness of my soul*
Is 38:15 I shall walk carefully all my years in the *bitterness of my soul*

BITTERNESS OF SOUL
1Sam 1:10 And she was in *bitterness of soul*, and prayed to the Lord and wept in anguish

BLAMELESS AND UPRIGHT MAN
Job 1:8 Then the Lord said to Satan, "Have you considered My servant Job, that there is none like him on the earth, a *blameless and upright man*, one who fears God and shuns evil
Job 2:3 Then the Lord said to Satan, "Have you considered My servant Job, that there is none like him on the earth, a *blameless and upright man*, one who fears God and shuns evil

BLASPHEMES AGAINST THE HOLY SPIRIT
Mark 3:29 but he who *blasphemes against the Holy Spirit* never has forgiveness, but is subject to eternal condemnation
Luke 12:10 but to him who *blasphemes against the Holy Spirit*, it will not be forgiven

BLASPHEMY AGAINST GOD
Rev 13:6 Then he opened his mouth in *blasphemy against God*, to blaspheme His name, His tabernacle, and those who dwell in heaven

BLASPHEMY AGAINST THE SPIRIT
Matt 12:31 Therefore I say to you, every sin and blasphemy will be forgiven men, but the *blasphemy against the Spirit* will not be forgiven men

BLAST OF THE BREATH
2Sam 22:16 Then the channels of the sea were seen, the foundations of the world were uncovered, at the rebuke of the Lord, at the *blast of the breath* of His nostrils
Ps 18:15 Then the channels of waters were seen, and the foundations of the world were uncovered at Your rebuke, O Lord, at the *blast of the breath* of Your nostrils

BLAZING FURNACE (NIV)
(See *FIERY FURNACE*)

BLEMISHES ON YOUR LOVE FEASTS (RSV)
(See *SPOTS IN YOUR LOVE FEASTS*)

BLESS GOD
Ps 68:26 *Bless God* in the congregations, the Lord, from the fountain of Israel

BLESS HIS HOLY NAME
Ps 103:1 And all that is within me, *bless His holy name*
Ps 145:21 My mouth shall speak the praise of the Lord, and all flesh shall *bless His holy name* forever and ever

BLESS THE LORD
Deut 8:10 When you have eaten and are full, then you shall *bless the Lord* your God for the good land which He has given you
Judg 5:2 When leaders lead in Israel, when the people willingly offer themselves, *bless the Lord*
Judg 5:9 My heart is with the rulers of Israel who

offered themselves willingly with the people. *Bless the Lord*
1Chr 29:20 Then David said to all the congregation, "Now *bless the Lord* your God
Neh 9:5 Stand up and *bless the Lord* your God forever and ever
Ps 16:7 I will *bless the Lord* who has given me counsel
Ps 26:12 My foot stands in an even place; in the congregations I will *bless the Lord*
Ps 34:1 I will *bless the Lord* at all times; His praise shall continually be in my mouth
Ps 103:1 *Bless the Lord*, O my soul; and all that is within me, bless His holy name
Ps 103:2 *Bless the Lord*, O my soul, and forget not all His benefits
Ps 103:20 *Bless the Lord*, you His angels, Who excel in strength, who do His word, heeding the voice of His word
Ps 103:21 *Bless the Lord*, all you His hosts, you ministers of His, who do His pleasure
Ps 103:22 *Bless the Lord*, all His works, in all places of His dominion. *Bless the Lord*, O my soul
Ps 104:1 *Bless the Lord*, O my soul! O Lord my God, You are very great
Ps 104:35 May sinners be consumed from the earth, and the wicked be no more. *Bless the Lord*, O my soul! Praise the Lord
Ps 115:18 But we will *bless the Lord* from this time forth and forevermore
Ps 134:1 Behold, *bless the Lord*, all you servants of the Lord, who by night stand in the house of the Lord
Ps 134:2 Lift up your hands in the sanctuary, and *bless the Lord*
Ps 135:19 *Bless the Lord*, O house of Israel! *Bless the Lord*, O house of Aaron
Ps 135:20 *Bless the Lord*, O house of Levi! You who fear the Lord, *bless the Lord*

BLESS THOSE WHO BLESS YOU
Gen 12:3 I will *bless those who bless you*, and I will curse him who curses you

BLESS THOSE WHO PERSECUTE YOU
Rom 12:14 *Bless those who persecute you;* bless and do not curse

BLESSED AND ONLY POTENTATE
1Tim 6:15 which He will manifest in His own time, He who is the *blessed and only Potentate*, the King of kings and Lord of lords

BLESSED ARE
Ruth 3:10 Then he said, "*Blessed are* you of the Lord, my daughter
1Sam 15:13 Then Samuel went to Saul, and Saul said to him, "*Blessed are* you of the Lord
1Sam 23:21 And Saul said, "*Blessed are* you of the Lord, for you have compassion on me
1Sam 25:33 And blessed is your advice and *blessed are* you, because you have kept me this day from coming to bloodshed and from avenging myself with my own hand
1Chr 29:10 *Blessed are* You, Lord God of Israel, our Father, forever and ever
Ps 2:12 *Blessed are* all those who put their trust in Him
Ps 84:4 *Blessed are* those who dwell in Your house; they will still be praising You
Ps 89:15 *Blessed are* the people who know the joyful sound! They walk, O Lord, in the light of Your countenance
Ps 106:3 *Blessed are* those who keep justice, and he who does righteousness at all times
Ps 119:1 *Blessed are* the undefiled in the way, who walk in the law of the Lord
Ps 119:2 *Blessed are* those who keep His testimonies, who seek Him with the whole heart
Ps 119:12 *Blessed are* You, O Lord! Teach me Your statutes
Prov 8:32 Now therefore, listen to me, my children, for *blessed are* those who keep my ways
Eccl 10:17 *Blessed are* you, O land, when your king is the son of nobles, and your princes feast at the proper time for strength and not for drunkenness
Is 30:18 For the Lord is a God of justice; *blessed are* all those who wait for Him
Is 32:20 *Blessed are* you who sow beside all waters, who send out freely the feet of the ox and the donkey
Matt 5:3 *Blessed are* the poor in spirit, for theirs is the kingdom of heaven
Matt 5:4 *Blessed are* those who mourn, for they shall be comforted
Matt 5:5 *Blessed are* the meek, for they shall inherit the earth
Matt 5:6 *Blessed are* those who hunger and thirst for righteousness, for they shall be filled
Matt 5:7 *Blessed are* the merciful, for they shall obtain mercy
Matt 5:8 *Blessed are* the pure in heart, for they shall see God
Matt 5:9 *Blessed are* the peacemakers, for they shall be called sons of God
Matt 5:10 *Blessed are* those who are persecuted for righteousness' sake, for theirs is the kingdom of heaven
Matt 5:11 *Blessed are* you when they revile and persecute you, and say all kinds of evil against you falsely for My sake
Matt 13:16 But *blessed are* your eyes for they see, and your ears for they hear
Matt 16:17 Jesus answered and said to him, "*Blessed are* you, Simon Bar-Jonah, for flesh and blood has not revealed this to you, but My Father who is in heaven
Luke 1:28 And having come in, the angel said to her, "Rejoice, highly favored one, the Lord is with you; *blessed are* you among women
Luke 1:42 Then she spoke out with a loud voice and said, "*Blessed are* you among women, and blessed is the fruit of your womb
Luke 6:20 *Blessed are* you poor, for yours is the kingdom of God
Luke 6:21 *Blessed are* you who hunger now, for you shall be filled. *Blessed are* you who weep now, for you shall laugh
Luke 6:22 *Blessed are* you when men hate you, and when they exclude you, and revile you, and cast out your name as evil, for the Son of Man's sake
Luke 10:23 And He turned to His disciples and said privately, "*Blessed are* the eyes which see the things you see
Luke 11:28 But He said, "More than that, *blessed are* those who hear the word of God and keep it
Luke 12:37 *Blessed are* those servants whom the master, when he comes, will find watching
Luke 12:38 And if he should come in the second watch, or come in the third watch, and find them so, *blessed are* those servants
Luke 23:29 For indeed the days are coming in which they will say, '*Blessed are* the barren, the wombs that never bore, and the breasts which never nursed
John 20:29 *Blessed are* those who have not seen and yet have believed
Rom 4:7 *Blessed are* those whose lawless deeds are forgiven, and whose sins are covered
1Pet 4:14 If you are reproached for the name of Christ, *blessed are* you, for the Spirit of glory and of God rests upon you

Rev 14:13 *Blessed are* the dead who die in the Lord from now on
Rev 19:9 *Blessed are* those who are called to the marriage supper of the Lamb
Rev 22:14 *Blessed are* those who do His commandments, that they may have the right to the tree of life, and may enter through the gates into the city

BLESSED ARE THE PEACEMAKERS
Matt 5:9 *Blessed are the peacemakers*, for they shall be called sons of God

BLESSED ARE YOU AMONG WOMEN
Luke 1:28 And having come in, the angel said to her, "Rejoice, highly favored one, the Lord is with you; *blessed are you among women*
Luke 1:42 Then she spoke out with a loud voice and said, "*Blessed are you among women*, and blessed is the fruit of your womb

BLESSED BE GOD
Gen 14:20 And *blessed be God* Most High, Who has delivered your enemies into your hand
Ps 66:20 *Blessed be God*, Who has not turned away my prayer, nor His mercy from me
Ps 68:35 The God of Israel is He who gives strength and power to His people. *Blessed be God*

BLESSED BE THE GOD
Dan 3:28 Nebuchadnezzar spoke, saying, *Blessed be the God* of Shadrach, Meshach, and Abed-Nego, who sent His Angel and delivered His servants who trusted in Him, and they have frustrated the king's word, and yielded their bodies, that they should not serve nor worship any god except their own God
2Cor 1:3 *Blessed be the God* and Father of our Lord Jesus Christ, the Father of mercies and God of all comfort
Eph 1:3 *Blessed be the God* and Father of our Lord Jesus Christ, who has blessed us with every spiritual blessing in the heavenly places in Christ
1Pet 1:3 *Blessed be the God* and Father of our Lord Jesus Christ, who according to His abundant mercy has begotten us again to a living hope through the resurrection of Jesus Christ from the dead

BLESSED BE THE LORD
Gen 9:26 *Blessed be the Lord*, the God of Shem, and may Canaan be his servant
Gen 24:27 And he said, "*Blessed be the Lord* God of my master Abraham, who has not forsaken His mercy and His truth toward my master
Ex 18:10 And Jethro said, "*Blessed be the Lord*, who has delivered you out of the hand of the Egyptians and out of the hand of Pharaoh, and who has delivered the people from under the hand of the Egyptians
Ruth 4:14 Then the women said to Naomi, "*Blessed be the Lord*, who has not left you this day without a near kinsman
1Sam 25:32 *Blessed be the Lord* God of Israel, who sent you this day to meet me
1Sam 25:39 So when David heard that Nabal was dead, he said, "*Blessed be the Lord*, who has pleaded the cause of my reproach from the hand of Nabal, and has kept His servant from evil
2Sam 18:28 Then he bowed down with his face to the earth before the king, and said, "*Blessed be the Lord* your God, who has delivered up the men who raised their hand against my lord the king
1Kin 1:48 Also the king said thus, '*Blessed be the Lord* God of Israel, who has given one to sit on my throne this day, while my eyes see it
1Kin 5:7 So it was, when Hiram heard the words of Solomon, that he rejoiced greatly and said, "*Blessed be the Lord* this day, for He has given David a wise son over this great people
1Kin 8:15 *Blessed be the Lord* God of Israel, who spoke with His mouth to my father David, and with His hand has fulfilled it, saying
1Kin 8:56 *Blessed be the Lord*, who has given rest to His people Israel, according to all that He promised
1Kin 10:9 *Blessed be the Lord* your God, who delighted in you, setting you on the throne of Israel
1Chr 16:36 *Blessed be the Lord* God of Israel from everlasting to everlasting
2Chr 2:12 *Blessed be the Lord* God of Israel, who made heaven and earth, for He has given King David a wise son, endowed with prudence and understanding, who will build a temple for the Lord and a royal house for himself
2Chr 6:4 *Blessed be the Lord* God of Israel, who has fulfilled with His hands what He spoke with His mouth to my father David, saying
2Chr 9:8 *Blessed be the Lord* your God, who delighted in you, setting you on His throne to be king for the Lord your God
Ezra 7:27 *Blessed be the Lord* God of our fathers, who has put such a thing as this in the king's heart, to beautify the house of the Lord which is in Jerusalem
Ps 28:6 *Blessed be the Lord*, because He has heard the voice of my supplications
Ps 31:21 *Blessed be the Lord*, for He has shown me His marvelous kindness in a strong city
Ps 41:13 *Blessed be the Lord* God of Israel from everlasting to everlasting
Ps 68:19 *Blessed be the Lord*, Who daily loads us with benefits, the God of our salvation
Ps 72:18 *Blessed be the Lord* God, the God of Israel, Who only does wondrous things
Ps 89:52 *Blessed be the Lord* forevermore! Amen and Amen
Ps 106:48 *Blessed be the Lord* God of Israel from everlasting to everlasting
Ps 124:6 *Blessed be the Lord*, Who has not given us as prey to their teeth
Ps 135:21 *Blessed be the Lord* out of Zion, Who dwells in Jerusalem
Ps 144:1 *Blessed be the Lord* my Rock, Who trains my hands for war, and my fingers for battle
Zech 11:5 those who sell them say, '*Blessed be the Lord*, for I am rich

BLESSED IS
Num 24:9 *Blessed is* he who blesses you, and cursed is he who curses you
Deut 33:20 *Blessed is* he who enlarges Gad; He dwells as a lion, and tears the arm and the crown of his head
Judg 5:24 Most blessed among women is Jael, the wife of Heber the Kenite; *blessed is* she among women in tents
1Sam 25:33 And *blessed is* your advice and blessed are you, because you have kept me this day from coming to bloodshed and from avenging myself with my own hand
Ps 1:1 *Blessed is* the man who walks not in the counsel of the ungodly, nor stands in the path of sinners, nor sits in the seat of the scornful
Ps 32:1 *Blessed is* he whose transgression is forgiven, whose sin is covered
Ps 32:2 *Blessed is* the man to whom the Lord does not impute iniquity, and in whose spirit there is no guile
Ps 33:12 *Blessed is* the nation whose God is the Lord, and the people whom He has chosen as His own inheritance
Ps 34:8 Oh, taste and see that the Lord is good; *blessed is* the man who trusts in Him
Ps 40:4 *Blessed is* that man who makes the Lord

his trust, and does not respect the proud, nor such as turn aside to lies

Ps 41:1 *Blessed is* he who considers the poor; the Lord will deliver him in time of trouble

Ps 65:4 *Blessed is* the man whom You choose, and cause to approach You, that he may dwell in Your courts

Ps 84:5 *Blessed is* the man whose strength is in You, whose heart is set on pilgrimage

Ps 84:12 O Lord of hosts, *blessed is* the man who trusts in You

Ps 94:12 *Blessed is* the man whom You instruct, O Lord, and teach out of Your law

Ps 112:1 *Blessed is* the man who fears the Lord, who delights greatly in His commandments

Ps 118:26 *Blessed is* he who comes in the name of the Lord

Ps 128:1 *Blessed is* every one who fears the Lord, who walks in His ways

Prov 8:34 *Blessed is* the man who listens to me, watching daily at my gates, waiting at the posts of my doors

Is 19:25 whom the Lord of hosts shall bless, saying, "*Blessed is* Egypt My people, and Assyria the work of My hands, and Israel My inheritance

Is 56:2 *Blessed is* the man who does this, and the son of man who lays hold on it

Jer 17:7 *Blessed is* the man who trusts in the Lord, and whose hope is the Lord

Ezek 3:12 *Blessed is* the glory of the Lord from His place

Dan 12:12 *Blessed is* he who waits, and comes to the one thousand three hundred and thirty-five days

Matt 11:6 And *blessed is* he who is not offended because of Me

Matt 21:9 *Blessed is* He who comes in the name of the Lord

Matt 23:39 for I say to you, you shall see Me no more till you say, '*Blessed is* He who comes in the name of the Lord

Matt 24:46 *Blessed is* that servant whom his master, when he comes, will find so doing

Mark 11:9 *Blessed is* He who comes in the name of the Lord

Mark 11:10 *Blessed is* the kingdom of our father David that comes in the name of the Lord

Luke 1:42 Then she spoke out with a loud voice and said, "Blessed are you among women, and *blessed is* the fruit of your womb

Luke 1:45 *Blessed is* she who believed, for there will be a fulfillment of those things which were told her from the Lord

Luke 1:68 *Blessed is* the Lord God of Israel, for He has visited and redeemed His people

Luke 7:23 And *blessed is* he who is not offended because of Me

Luke 11:27 And it happened, as He spoke these things, that a certain woman from the crowd raised her voice and said to Him, "*Blessed is* the womb that bore You, and the breasts which nursed You

Luke 12:43 *Blessed is* that servant whom his master will find so doing when he comes

Luke 13:35 and assuredly, I say to you, you shall not see Me until the time comes when you say, '*Blessed is* He who comes in the name of the Lord

Luke 14:15 Now when one of those who sat at the table with Him heard these things, he said to Him, "*Blessed is* he who shall eat bread in the kingdom of God

Luke 19:38 *Blessed is* the King who comes in the name of the Lord

John 12:13 *Blessed is* He who comes in the name of the Lord

Rom 4:8 *blessed is* the man to whom the Lord shall not impute sin

Jas 1:12 *Blessed is* the man who endures temptation; for when he has been proved, he will receive the crown of life which the Lord has promised to those who love Him

Rev 1:3 *Blessed is* he who reads and those who hear the words of this prophecy, and keep those things which are written in it

Rev 16:15 *Blessed is* he who watches, and keeps his garments, lest he walk naked and they see his shame

Rev 22:7 *Blessed is* he who keeps the words of the prophecy of this book

BLESSED IS THE MAN

Ps 1:1 *Blessed is the man* who walks not in the counsel of the ungodly, nor stands in the path of sinners, nor sits in the seat of the scornful

Ps 32:2 *Blessed is the man* to whom the Lord does not impute iniquity, and in whose spirit there is no guile

Ps 34:8 Oh, taste and see that the Lord is good; *blessed is the man* who trusts in Him

Ps 65:4 *Blessed is the man* whom You choose, and cause to approach You, that he may dwell in Your courts

Ps 84:5 *Blessed is the man* whose strength is in You, whose heart is set on pilgrimage

Ps 84:12 O Lord of hosts, *blessed is the man* who trusts in You

Ps 94:12 *Blessed is the man* whom You instruct, O Lord, and teach out of Your law

Ps 112:1 *Blessed is the man* who fears the Lord, who delights greatly in His commandments

Prov 8:34 *Blessed is the man* who listens to me, watching daily at my gates, waiting at the posts of my doors

Is 56:2 *Blessed is the man* who does this, and the son of man who lays hold on it

Jer 17:7 *Blessed is the man* who trusts in the Lord, and whose hope is the Lord

Rom 4:8 *blessed is the man* to whom the Lord shall not impute sin

Jas 1:12 *Blessed is the man* who endures temptation; for when he has been proved, he will receive the crown of life which the Lord has promised to those who love Him

BLESSING AND A CURSE

Deut 11:26 Behold, I set before you today a *blessing and a curse*

BLESSING OF ABRAHAM

Gen 28:4 and give you the *blessing of Abraham*, to you and your descendants with you, that you may inherit the land in which you are a stranger, which God gave to Abraham

Gal 3:14 that the *blessing of Abraham* might come upon the Gentiles in Christ Jesus, that we might receive the promise of the Spirit through faith

BLESSING OF THE LORD

Gen 39:5 and the *blessing of the Lord* was on all that he had in the house and in the field

Deut 12:15 However, you may slaughter and eat meat within all your gates, whatever your heart desires, according to the *blessing of the Lord* your God which He has given you

Deut 16:17 Every man shall give as he is able, according to the *blessing of the Lord* your God which He has given you

Deut 33:23 O Naphtali, satisfied with favor, and full of the *blessing of the Lord*, possess the west and the south

Ps 129:8 Neither let those who pass by them say, "The *blessing of the Lord* be upon you

Prov 10:22 The *blessing of the Lord* makes one rich, and He adds no sorrow with it

BLESSINGS OF HEAVEN
Gen 49:25 by the God of your father who will help you, and by the Almighty who will bless you with *blessings of heaven* above, blessings of the deep that lies beneath, blessings of the breasts and of the womb

BLESSINGS OF YOUR FATHER
Gen 49:26 The *blessings of your father* have excelled the blessings of my ancestors, up to the utmost bound of the everlasting hills

BLEW A TRUMPET
2Sam 2:28 So Joab *blew a trumpet;* and all the people stood still and did not pursue Israel anymore, nor did they fight anymore
2Sam 20:1 And he *blew a trumpet*, and said: We have no part in David, nor do we have inheritance in the son of Jesse
2Sam 20:22 Then he *blew a trumpet*, and they withdrew from the city, every man to his tent

BLIGHT AND MILDEW
Amos 4:9 I blasted you with *blight and mildew*. When your gardens increased, your vineyards, your fig trees, and your olive trees, the locust devoured them
Hag 2:17 I struck you with *blight and mildew* and hail in all the labors of your hands

BLIGHT OR MILDEW
1Kin 8:37 When there is famine in the land, or pestilence, *blight or mildew*, locusts or grasshoppers
2Chr 6:28 When there is famine in the land, pestilence or *blight or mildew*, locusts or grasshoppers

BLIND AND THE LAME
2Sam 5:6 but the *blind and the lame* will repel you," thinking
2Sam 5:8 Therefore they say, "The *blind and the lame* shall not come into the house
Jer 31:8 Behold, I will bring them from the north country, and gather them from the ends of the earth, among them the *blind and the lame*, the woman with child and the one who labors with child, together
Matt 21:14 Then the *blind and the lame* came to Him in the temple, and He healed them

BLIND GUIDES
Matt 23:16 Woe to you, *blind guides*, who say, 'Whoever swears by the temple, it is nothing
Matt 23:24 *Blind guides*, who strain out a gnat and swallow a camel

BLIND LEAD THE BLIND
Luke 6:39 Can the *blind lead the blind?* Will they not both fall into the ditch

BLOOD BE ON US
Matt 27:25 And all the people answered and said, "His *blood be on us* and on our children

BLOOD BE UPON YOUR OWN HEADS
Acts 18:6 But when they opposed him and blasphemed, he shook his garments and said to them, "Your *blood be upon your own heads*

BLOOD CRIES OUT
Gen 4:10 The voice of your brother's *blood cries out* to Me from the ground

BLOOD IS ON THEIR HANDS
Ezek 23:37 For they have committed adultery, and *blood is on their hands*
Ezek 23:45 But righteous men will judge them after the manner of adulteresses, and after the manner of women who shed blood, because they are adulteresses, and *blood is on their hands*

BLOOD OF ABEL
Luke 11:51 from the *blood of Abel* to the blood of Zechariah who perished between the altar and the temple

BLOOD OF ALL THE PROPHETS
Luke 11:50 that the *blood of all the prophets* which was shed from the foundation of the world may be required of this generation

BLOOD OF CHRIST
1Cor 10:16 The cup of blessing which we bless, is it not the communion of the *blood of Christ*
Eph 2:13 But now in Christ Jesus you who once were far off have been made near by the *blood of Christ*
Heb 9:14 how much more shall the *blood of Christ*, who through the eternal Spirit offered Himself without spot to God, purge your conscience from dead works to serve the living God
1Pet 1:19 but with the precious *blood of Christ*, as of a lamb without blemish and without spot

BLOOD OF JESUS
Heb 10:19 Therefore, brethren, having boldness to enter the Holiest by the *blood of Jesus*
1Pet 1:2 elect according to the foreknowledge of God the Father, in sanctification of the Spirit, for obedience and sprinkling of the *blood of Jesus* Christ
1Jn 1:7 But if we walk in the light as He is in the light, we have fellowship with one another, and the *blood of Jesus* Christ His Son cleanses us from all sin

BLOOD OF PROPHETS
Rev 18:24 And in her was found the *blood of prophets* and saints, and of all who were slain on the earth

BLOOD OF SPRINKLING
Heb 12:24 to Jesus the Mediator of the new covenant, and to the *blood of sprinkling* that speaks better things than that of Abel

BLOOD OF THE COVENANT
Ex 24:8 And Moses took the blood, sprinkled it on the people, and said, "Behold, the *blood of the covenant* which the Lord has made with you according to all these words
Heb 9:20 saying, "This is the *blood of the covenant* which God has commanded you
Heb 10:29 Of how much worse punishment, do you suppose, will he be thought worthy who has trampled the Son of God underfoot, counted the *blood of the covenant* by which he was sanctified a common thing, and insulted the Spirit of grace

BLOOD OF THE LAMB
Rev 7:14 So he said to me, "These are the ones who come out of the great tribulation, and washed their robes and made them white in the *blood of the Lamb*
Rev 12:11 And they overcame him by the *blood of the Lamb* and by the word of their testimony, and they did not love their lives to the death

BLOOD OF THE MARTYRS
Rev 17:6 And I saw the woman, drunk with the blood of the saints and with the *blood of the martyrs* of Jesus

BLOOD OF THE NEW COVENANT
Matt 26:28 For this is My *blood of the new covenant*, which is shed for many for the remission of sins
Mark 14:24 And He said to them, "This is My

blood of the new covenant, which is shed for many

BLOOD OF THE PROPHETS
Matt 23:30 and say, 'If we had lived in the days of our fathers, we would not have been partakers with them in the *blood of the prophets*

BLOOD OF THE SAINTS
Rev 17:6 And I saw the woman, drunk with the *blood of the saints* and with the blood of the martyrs of Jesus

BLOOD SHALL BE UPON THEM
Lev 20:11 both of them shall surely be put to death. Their *blood shall be upon them*
Lev 20:12 They have committed perversion. Their *blood shall be upon them*
Lev 20:13 They shall surely be put to death. Their *blood shall be upon them*
Lev 20:27 they shall stone them with stones. Their *blood shall be upon them*

BLOODSHED AFTER BLOODSHED
Hos 4:2 By swearing and lying, killing and stealing and committing adultery, they break all restraint, with *bloodshed after bloodshed*

BLOODY CITY
Ezek 22:2 Now, son of man, will you judge, will you judge the *bloody city*
Ezek 24:6 Woe to the *bloody city*, to the pot whose scum is in it, and whose scum is not gone from it
Ezek 24:9 Woe to the *bloody city!* I too will make the pyre great
Nah 3:1 Woe to the *bloody city!* It is all full of lies and robbery

BLOSSOM AND BUD
Is 27:6 Israel shall *blossom and bud*, and fill the face of the world with fruit

BLOT OUT ALL MY INIQUITIES
Ps 51:9 Hide Your face from my sins, and *blot out all my iniquities*

BLOT OUT HIS NAME
Deut 29:20 for then the anger of the Lord and His jealousy would burn against that man, and every curse that is written in this book would settle on him, and the Lord would *blot out his name* from under heaven
Rev 3:5 He who overcomes shall be clothed in white garments, and I will not *blot out his name* from the Book of Life

BLOT OUT MY TRANSGRESSIONS
Ps 51:1 According to the multitude of Your tender mercies, *blot out my transgressions*

BLOT OUT THEIR NAME
Deut 9:14 Let Me alone, that I may destroy them and *blot out their name* from under heaven

BLOT OUT THEIR SIN
Jer 18:23 Provide no atonement for their iniquity, nor *blot out their sin* from Your sight

BLOTTED OUT THEIR NAME
Ps 9:5 You have rebuked the nations, You have destroyed the wicked; You have *blotted out their name* forever and ever

BLOW THE TRUMPET
Judg 7:18 When I *blow the trumpet*, I and all who are with me, then you also blow the trumpets on every side of the whole camp, and say
Ps 81:3 *Blow the trumpet* at the time of the New Moon, at the full moon, on our solemn feast day
Jer 4:5 *Blow the trumpet* in the land; cry, 'Gather together,' and say
Jer 6:1 *Blow the trumpet* in Tekoa, and set up a signal-fire in Beth Haccherem
Jer 51:27 Set up a banner in the land, *blow the trumpet* among the nations
Ezek 33:6 But if the watchman sees the sword coming and does not *blow the trumpet*, and the people are not warned, and the sword comes and takes any person from among them, he is taken away in his iniquity
Joel 2:1 *Blow the trumpet* in Zion, and sound an alarm in My holy mountain
Joel 2:15 *Blow the trumpet* in Zion, consecrate a fast, call a sacred assembly
Zech 9:14 The Lord God will *blow the trumpet*, and go with whirlwinds from the south

BLOWING OF A VIOLENT WIND (NIV)
(See *RUSHING MIGHTY WIND*)

BLOWN HERE AND THERE (NIV)
(See *TOSSED TO AND FRO*)

BOAST ABOUT TOMORROW
Prov 27:1 Do not *boast about tomorrow*, for you do not know what a day may bring forth

BOAST IN THE LAW
Rom 2:23 You who make your *boast in the law*, do you dishonor God through breaking the law

BOAST NOT THYSELF OF TOMORROW (KJV)
(See *DO NOT BOAST ABOUT TOMORROW*)

BOASTING OF WHAT HE HAS AND DOES (NIV)
(See *PRIDE OF LIFE*)

BODIES WASHED WITH PURE WATER
Heb 10:22 let us draw near with a true heart in full assurance of faith, having our hearts sprinkled from an evil conscience and our *bodies washed with pure water*

BODILY EXERCISE PROFITS A LITTLE
1Tim 4:8 For *bodily exercise profits a little*, but godliness is profitable for all things, having promise of the life that now is and of that which is to come

BODY IS FULL OF LIGHT
Luke 11:36 If then your whole *body is full of light*, having no part dark, the whole body will be full of light, as when the bright shining of a lamp gives you light

BODY IS THE TEMPLE
1Cor 6:19 Or do you not know that your *body is the temple* of the Holy Spirit who is in you, whom you have from God, and you are not your own

BODY IS WEAK (NIV)
(See *FLESH IS WEAK*)

BODY OF CHRIST
Rom 7:4 Therefore, my brethren, you also have become dead to the law through the *body of Christ*, that you may be married to another, even to Him who was raised from the dead, that we should bear fruit to God
1Cor 10:16 The bread which we break, is it not the communion of the *body of Christ*
1Cor 12:27 Now you are the *body of Christ*, and members individually

Eph 4:12 for the equipping of the saints for the work of ministry, for the edifying of the *body of Christ*

BODY OF JESUS
Matt 27:58 This man went to Pilate and asked for the *body of Jesus*
Mark 15:43 Joseph of Arimathea, a prominent council member, who was himself waiting for the kingdom of God, coming and taking courage, went in to Pilate and asked for the *body of Jesus*
Luke 23:52 This man went to Pilate and asked for the *body of Jesus*
John 19:38 After this, Joseph of Arimathea, being a disciple of Jesus, but secretly, for fear of the Jews, asked Pilate that he might take away the *body of Jesus;* and Pilate gave him permission. So he came and took the *body of Jesus*
John 19:40 Then they took the *body of Jesus*, and bound it in strips of linen with the spices, as the custom of the Jews is to bury
John 20:12 And she saw two angels in white sitting, one at the head and the other at the feet, where the *body of Jesus* had lain
Heb 10:10 By that will we have been sanctified through the offering of the *body of Jesus* Christ once for all

BODY OF THE LORD
Luke 24:3 Then they went in and did not find the *body of the Lord* Jesus

BODY TREMBLED
Hab 3:16 When I heard, my *body trembled;* my lips quivered at the voice

BOLD IN OUR GOD
1Th 2:2 But even after we had suffered before and were spitefully treated at Philippi, as you know, we were *bold in our God* to speak to you the gospel of God in much conflict

BOND AND FREE
1Kin 14:10 I will bring disaster on the house of Jeroboam, and will cut off from Jeroboam every male in Israel, *bond and free*
1Kin 21:21 I will take away your posterity, and will cut off from Ahab every male in Israel, both *bond and free*
2Kin 9:8 and I will cut off from Ahab all the males in Israel, both *bond and free*

BOND OF PEACE
Eph 4:3 endeavoring to keep the unity of the Spirit in the *bond of peace*

BOND OF PERFECTION
Col 3:14 But above all these things put on love, which is the *bond of perfection*

BOND OR FREE
Deut 32:36 For the Lord will judge His people and have compassion on His servants, when He sees that their power is gone, and there is no one remaining, *bond or free*
2Kin 14:26 and whether *bond or free*, there was no helper for Israel

BONE OF MY BONES
Gen 2:23 This is now *bone of my bones* and flesh of my flesh

BONES CLING TO MY SKIN
Ps 102:5 Because of the sound of my groaning my *bones cling to my skin*

BOOK OF GAD
1Chr 29:29 Now the acts of King David, first and last, indeed they are written in the book of Samuel the seer, in the book of Nathan the prophet, and in the *book of Gad* the seer

BOOK OF JASHER
Josh 10:13 Is this not written in the *Book of Jasher?* So the sun stood still in the midst of heaven, and did not hasten to go down for about a whole day
2Sam 1:18 and he told them to teach the children of Judah the Song of the Bow; indeed it is written in the *Book of Jasher*

BOOK OF LIFE
Phil 4:3 And I urge you also, true companion, help these women who labored with me in the gospel, with Clement also, and the rest of my fellow workers, whose names are in the *Book of Life*
Rev 3:5 He who overcomes shall be clothed in white garments, and I will not blot out his name from the *Book of Life*
Rev 13:8 And all who dwell on the earth will worship him, whose names have not been written in the *Book of Life* of the Lamb slain from the foundation of the world
Rev 17:8 And those who dwell on the earth will marvel, whose names are not written in the *Book of Life* from the foundation of the world, when they see the beast that was, and is not, and yet is
Rev 20:12 And another book was opened, which is the *Book of Life*
Rev 20:15 And anyone not found written in the *Book of Life* was cast into the lake of fire
Rev 21:27 But there shall by no means enter it anything that defiles, or causes an abomination or a lie, but only those who are written in the Lamb's *Book of Life*
Rev 22:19 and if anyone takes away from the words of the book of this prophecy, God shall take away his part from the *Book of Life*, from the holy city, and from the things which are written in this book

BOOK OF MOSES
2Chr 25:4 However he did not execute their children, but did as it is written in the Law in the *Book of Moses*, where the Lord commanded, saying
2Chr 35:12 Then they removed the burnt offerings that they might give them to the divisions of the fathers' houses of the lay people, to offer to the Lord, as it is written in the *Book of Moses*
Ezra 6:18 They assigned the priests to their divisions and the Levites to their divisions, over the service of God in Jerusalem, as it is written in the *Book of Moses*
Neh 13:1 On that day they read from the *Book of Moses* in the hearing of the people, and in it was found written that no Ammonite or Moabite should ever come into the congregation of God
Mark 12:26 But concerning the dead, that they rise, have you not read in the *book of Moses*, in the burning bush passage, how God spoke to him, saying

BOOK OF NATHAN
1Chr 29:29 Now the acts of King David, first and last, indeed they are written in the book of Samuel the seer, in the *book of Nathan* the prophet, and in the book of Gad the seer
2Chr 9:29 Now the rest of the acts of Solomon, first and last, are they not written in the *book of Nathan* the prophet, in the prophecy of Ahijah the Shilonite, and in the visions of Iddo the seer concerning Jeroboam the son of Nebat

BOOK OF PSALMS
Luke 20:42 Now David himself said in the *Book of Psalms*, 'The Lord said to my Lord
Acts 1:20 For it is written in the *book of Psalms:* 'Let his habitation be desolate, and let no one live in it

BOOK OF SAMUEL
1Chr 29:29 Now the acts of King David, first and last, indeed they are written in the *book of Samuel* the seer, in the book of Nathan the prophet, and in the book of Gad the seer

BOOK OF SHEMAIAH
2Chr 12:15 The acts of Rehoboam, first and last, are they not written in the *book of Shemaiah* the prophet, and of Iddo the seer concerning genealogies

BOOK OF THE ACTS OF SOLOMON
1Kin 11:41 Now the rest of the acts of Solomon, all that he did, and his wisdom, are they not written in the *book of the acts of Solomon*

BOOK OF THE CHRONICLES
1Kin 14:19 Now the rest of the acts of Jeroboam, how he made war and how he reigned, indeed they are written in the *book of the chronicles* of the kings of Israel
1Kin 14:29 Now the rest of the acts of Rehoboam, and all that he did, are they not written in the *book of the chronicles* of the kings of Judah
1Kin 15:7 Now the rest of the acts of Abijam, and all that he did, are they not written in the *book of the chronicles* of the kings of Judah
1Kin 15:23 The rest of all the acts of Asa, all his might, all that he did, and the cities which he built, are they not written in the *book of the chronicles* of the kings of Judah
1Kin 15:31 Now the rest of the acts of Nadab, and all that he did, are they not written in the *book of the chronicles* of the kings of Israel
1Kin 16:5 Now the rest of the acts of Baasha, what he did, and his might, are they not written in the *book of the chronicles* of the kings of Israel
1Kin 16:14 Now the rest of the acts of Elah, and all that he did, are they not written in the *book of the chronicles* of the kings of Israel
1Kin 16:20 Now the rest of the acts of Zimri, and the treason he committed, are they not written in the *book of the chronicles* of the kings of Israel
1Kin 16:27 Now the rest of the acts of Omri which he did, and the might that he showed, are they not written in the *book of the chronicles* of the kings of Israel
1Kin 22:39 Now the rest of the acts of Ahab and all that he did, the ivory house which he built and all the cities that he built, are they not written in the *book of the chronicles* of the kings of Israel
1Kin 22:45 Now the rest of the acts of Jehoshaphat, the might that he showed, and how he made war, are they not written in the *book of the chronicles* of the kings of Judah
2Kin 1:18 Now the rest of the acts of Ahaziah which he did, are they not written in the *book of the chronicles* of the kings of Israel
2Kin 8:23 Now the rest of the acts of Joram, and all that he did, are they not written in the *book of the chronicles* of the kings of Judah
2Kin 10:34 Now the rest of the acts of Jehu, all that he did, and all his might, are they not written in the *book of the chronicles* of the kings of Israel
2Kin 12:19 Now the rest of the acts of Joash, and all that he did, are they not written in the *book of the chronicles* of the kings of Judah
2Kin 13:8 Now the rest of the acts of Jehoahaz, all that he did, and his might, are they not written in the *book of the chronicles* of the kings of Israel
2Kin 13:12 Now the rest of the acts of Joash, all that he did, and his might with which he fought against Amaziah king of Judah, are they not written in the *book of the chronicles* of the kings of Israel
2Kin 14:15 Now the rest of the acts of Jehoash which he did his might, and how he fought with Amaziah king of Judah are they not written in the *book of the chronicles* of the kings of Israel
2Kin 14:18 Now the rest of the acts of Amaziah, are they not written in the *book of the chronicles* of the kings of Judah
2Kin 14:28 Now the rest of the acts of Jeroboam, and all that he did his might, how he made war, and how he recaptured for Israel, from Damascus and Hamath, what had belonged to Judah are they not written in the *book of the chronicles* of the kings of Israel
2Kin 15:6 Now the rest of the acts of Azariah, and all that he did, are they not written in the *book of the chronicles* of the kings of Judah
2Kin 15:11 Now the rest of the acts of Zechariah, indeed they are written in the *book of the chronicles* of the kings of Israel
2Kin 15:15 Now the rest of the acts of Shallum, and the conspiracy which he led, indeed they are written in the *book of the chronicles* of the kings of Israel
2Kin 15:21 Now the rest of the acts of Menahem, and all that he did, are they not written in the *book of the chronicles* of the kings of Israel
2Kin 15:26 Now the rest of the acts of Pekahiah, and all that he did, indeed they are written in the *book of the chronicles* of the kings of Israel
2Kin 15:31 Now the rest of the acts of Pekah, and all that he did, indeed they are written in the *book of the chronicles* of the kings of Israel
2Kin 15:36 Now the rest of the acts of Jotham, and all that he did, are they not written in the *book of the chronicles* of the kings of Judah
2Kin 16:19 Now the rest of the acts of Ahaz which he did, are they not written in the *book of the chronicles* of the kings of Judah
2Kin 20:20 Now the rest of the acts of Hezekiah all his might, and how he made a pool and a tunnel and brought water into the city are they not written in the *book of the chronicles* of the kings of Judah
2Kin 21:17 Now the rest of the acts of Manasseh all that he did, and the sin that he committed are they not written in the *book of the chronicles* of the kings of Judah
2Kin 21:25 Now the rest of the acts of Amon which he did, are they not written in the *book of the chronicles* of the kings of Judah
2Kin 23:28 Now the rest of the acts of Josiah, and all that he did, are they not written in the *book of the chronicles* of the kings of Judah
2Kin 24:5 Now the rest of the acts of Jehoiakim, and all that he did, are they not written in the *book of the chronicles* of the kings of Judah
Neh 12:23 The sons of Levi, the heads of the fathers' houses until the days of Johanan the son of Eliashib, were written in the *book of the chronicles*
Esth 2:23 and it was written in the *book of the chronicles* in the presence of the king
Esth 10:2 Now all the acts of his power and his might, and the account of the greatness of Mordecai, to which the king advanced him, are they not written in the *book of the chronicles* of the kings of Media and Persia

BOOK OF THE COVENANT
Ex 24:7 Then he took the *Book of the Covenant* and read in the hearing of the people
2Kin 23:2 and he read in their hearing all the

words of the *Book of the Covenant* which had been found in the house of the Lord
2Kin 23:21 Then the king commanded all the people, saying, "Keep the Passover to the Lord your God, as it is written in this *Book of the Covenant*
2Chr 34:30 and he read in their hearing all the words of the *book of the covenant* which had been found in the house of the Lord

BOOK OF THE KINGS
1Chr 9:1 So all Israel was recorded by genealogies, and indeed, they were inscribed in the *book of the kings* of Israel
2Chr 16:11 Note that the acts of Asa, first and last, are indeed written in the *book of the kings* of Judah and Israel
2Chr 20:34 Now the rest of the acts of Jehoshaphat, first and last, indeed they are written in the book of Jehu the son of Hanani, which is mentioned in the *book of the kings* of Israel
2Chr 24:27 Now concerning his sons, and the many oracles about him, and the repairing of the house of God, indeed they are written in the annals of the *book of the kings*
2Chr 25:26 Now the rest of the acts of Amaziah, from first to last, indeed are they not written in the *book of the kings* of Judah and Israel
2Chr 27:7 Now the rest of the acts of Jotham, and all his wars and his ways, indeed they are written in the *book of the kings* of Israel and Judah
2Chr 28:26 Now the rest of his acts and all his ways, from first to last, indeed they are written in the *book of the kings* of Judah and Israel
2Chr 32:32 Now the rest of the acts of Hezekiah, and his goodness, indeed they are written in the vision of Isaiah the prophet, the son of Amoz, and in the *book of the kings* of Judah and Israel
2Chr 33:18 Now the rest of the acts of Manasseh, his prayer to his God, and the words of the seers who spoke to him in the name of the Lord God of Israel, indeed they are written in the *book of the kings* of Israel
2Chr 35:27 and his deeds from first to last, indeed they are written in the *book of the kings* of Israel and Judah
2Chr 36:8 Now the rest of the acts of Jehoiakim, the abominations which he did, and what was found against him, indeed they are written in the *book of the kings* of Israel and Judah

BOOK OF THE LAW
Deut 29:21 And the Lord would separate him from all the tribes of Israel for adversity, according to all the curses of the covenant that are written in this *Book of the Law*
Deut 30:10 if you obey the voice of the Lord your God, to keep His commandments and His statutes which are written in this *Book of the Law*, and if you turn to the Lord your God with all your heart and with all your soul
Deut 31:26 Take this *Book of the Law*, and put it beside the ark of the covenant of the Lord your God, that it may be there as a witness against you
Josh 1:8 This *Book of the Law* shall not depart from your mouth, but you shall meditate in it day and night, that you may observe to do according to all that is written in it
Josh 8:31 as Moses the servant of the Lord had commanded the children of Israel, as it is written in the *Book of the Law* of Moses
Josh 8:34 And afterward he read all the words of the law, the blessings and the cursings, according to all that is written in the *Book of the Law*
Josh 23:6 Therefore be very courageous to keep and to do all that is written in the *Book of the Law* of Moses, lest you turn aside from it to the right hand or to the left
Josh 24:26 Then Joshua wrote these words in the *Book of the Law* of God
2Kin 14:6 But the children of the murderers he did not execute, according to what is written in the *Book of the Law* of Moses, in which the Lord commanded
2Kin 22:8 Then Hilkiah the high priest said to Shaphan the scribe, "I have found the *Book of the Law* in the house of the Lord
2Kin 22:11 Now it happened, when the king heard the words of the *Book of the Law*, that he tore his clothes
2Chr 17:9 So they taught in Judah, and had the *Book of the Law* of the Lord with them
2Chr 34:14 Now when they brought out the money that was brought into the house of the Lord, Hilkiah the priest found the *Book of the Law* of the Lord given by Moses
2Chr 34:15 Then Hilkiah answered and said to Shaphan the scribe, "I have found the *Book of the Law* in the house of the Lord
Neh 8:1 and they told Ezra the scribe to bring the *Book of the Law* of Moses, which the Lord had commanded Israel
Neh 8:3 and the ears of all the people were attentive to the *Book of the Law*
Neh 8:18 Also day by day, from the first day until the last day, he read from the *Book of the Law* of God
Neh 9:3 And they stood up in their place and read from the *Book of the Law* of the Lord their God for one-fourth of the day
Gal 3:10 for it is written, "Cursed is everyone who does not continue in all things which are written in the *book of the law*, to do them

BOOK OF THE PROPHETS
Acts 7:42 Then God turned and gave them up to worship the host of heaven, as it is written in the *book of the Prophets*

BOOK OF THE WARS
Num 21:14 Therefore it is said in the *Book of the Wars* of the Lord

BORDER OF HIS GARMENT
Mark 6:56 Wherever He entered, into villages, cities, or the country, they laid the sick in the marketplaces, and begged Him that they might just touch the *border of His garment*
Luke 8:44 came from behind and touched the *border of His garment*

BORE A SON
Gen 4:25 And Adam knew his wife again, and she *bore a son* and named him Seth
Gen 19:37 The firstborn *bore a son* and called his name Moab
Gen 19:38 And the younger, she also *bore a son* and called his name Ben-Ammi
Gen 24:36 And Sarah my master's wife *bore a son* to my master when she was old
Gen 29:32 So Leah conceived and *bore a son*, and she called his name Reuben
Gen 29:33 Then she conceived again and *bore a son*, and said
Gen 29:34 She conceived again and *bore a son*, and said, "Now this time my husband will become attached to me, because I have borne him three sons
Gen 29:35 And she conceived again and *bore a son*, and said
Gen 30:23 And she conceived and *bore a son*, and said, "God has taken away my reproach
Gen 38:3 So she conceived and *bore a son*, and he called his name Er
Gen 38:4 She conceived again and *bore a son*, and she called his name Onan

BORE UP

Gen 38:5 And she conceived yet again and *bore a son*, and called his name Shelah
Ex 2:2 So the woman conceived and *bore a son*. And when she saw that he was a beautiful child, she hid him three months
Judg 13:24 So the woman *bore a son* and called his name Samson
Ruth 4:13 and when he went in to her, the Lord gave her conception, and she *bore a son*
1Sam 1:20 So it came to pass in the process of time that Hannah conceived and *bore a son*, and called his name Samuel, saying
2Sam 12:24 So she *bore a son*, and he called his name Solomon
2Kin 4:17 And the woman conceived, and *bore a son* when the appointed time had come, of which Elisha had told her
1Chr 7:16 (Maachah the wife of Machir *bore a son*, and she called his name Peresh
1Chr 7:23 And when he went in to his wife, she conceived and *bore a son*
Is 8:3 Then I went to the prophetess, and she conceived and *bore a son*
Hos 1:8 Now when she had weaned Lo-Ruhamah, she conceived and *bore a son*

BORE UP (RSV)
(See *LIFTED UP*)

BORE WITNESS (RSV)
(See *BEARING WITNESS*)

BORE YOU ON EAGLES' WINGS
Ex 19:4 You have seen what I did to the Egyptians, and how I *bore you on eagles' wings* and brought you to Myself

BORN ACCORDING TO THE SPIRIT
Gal 4:29 But, as he who was born according to the flesh then persecuted him who was *born according to the Spirit*, even so it is now

BORN AGAIN
John 3:3 Jesus answered and said to him, "Most assuredly, I say to you, unless one is *born again*, he cannot see the kingdom of God
John 3:7 Do not marvel that I said to you, 'You must be *born again*
1Pet 1:23 having been *born again*, not of corruptible seed but incorruptible, through the word of God which lives and abides forever

BORN ANEW (RSV)
(See *BEGOTTEN US AGAIN*)

BORN FOR ADVERSITY
Prov 17:17 A friend loves at all times, and a brother is *born for adversity*

BORN IN SINS
John 9:34 They answered and said to him, "You were completely *born in sins*, and are you teaching us

BORN OF A WOMAN
Job 15:14 And he who is *born of a woman*, that he could be righteous
Job 25:4 Or how can he be pure who is *born of a woman*
Gal 4:4 But when the fullness of the time had come, God sent forth His Son, *born of a woman*, born under the law

BORN OF GOD
1Jn 3:9 Whoever has been *born of God* does not sin, for His seed remains in him; and he cannot sin, because he has been *born of God*
1Jn 4:7 and everyone who loves is *born of God* and knows God
1Jn 5:1 Whoever believes that Jesus is the Christ is *born of God*, and everyone who loves Him who begot also loves him who is begotten of Him
1Jn 5:4 For whatever is *born of God* overcomes the world. And this is the victory that has overcome the world our faith
1Jn 5:18 We know that whoever is *born of God* does not sin; but he who has been *born of God* keeps himself, and the wicked one does not touch him

BORN OF THE FLESH
John 3:6 That which is *born of the flesh* is flesh, and that which is born of the Spirit is spirit

BORN OF THE SPIRIT
John 3:6 That which is born of the flesh is flesh, and that which is *born of the Spirit* is spirit
John 3:8 The wind blows where it wishes, and you hear the sound of it, but cannot tell where it comes from and where it goes. So is everyone who is *born of the Spirit*

BORN OF WATER AND THE SPIRIT
John 3:5 Jesus answered, "Most assuredly, I say to you, unless one is *born of water and the Spirit*, he cannot enter the kingdom of God

BORN OUT OF DUE TIME
1Cor 15:8 Then last of all He was seen by me also, as by one *born out of due time*

BORN UNDER THE LAW
Gal 4:4 But when the fullness of the time had come, God sent forth His Son, born of a woman, *born under the law*

BORNE WITNESS
3Jn 6 who have *borne witness* of your love before the church

BOTH SMALL AND GREAT (NAS)
(See *FROM THE LEAST TO THE GREATEST*)

BOTTOM OF THE SEA (KJV)
(See *DEPTHS OF THE SEA*)

BOTTOMLESS PIT
Rev 9:1 And to him was given the key to the *bottomless pit*
Rev 9:2 And he opened the *bottomless pit*, and smoke arose out of the pit like the smoke of a great furnace
Rev 9:11 And they had as king over them the angel of the *bottomless pit*, whose name in Hebrew is Abaddon, but in Greek he has the name Apollyon
Rev 11:7 Now when they finish their testimony, the beast that ascends out of the *bottomless pit* will make war against them, overcome them, and kill them
Rev 17:8 The beast that you saw was, and is not, and will ascend out of the *bottomless pit* and go to perdition
Rev 20:1 Then I saw an angel coming down from heaven, having the key to the *bottomless pit* and a great chain in his hand
Rev 20:3 and he cast him into the *bottomless pit*, and shut him up, and set a seal on him, so that he should deceive the nations no more till the thousand years were finished

BOUGHT AT A PRICE
1Cor 6:20 For you were *bought at a price;* therefore glorify God in your body and in your spirit, which are God's

1Cor 7:23 You were *bought at a price;* do not become slaves of men

BOUGHT WITH HIS OWN BLOOD (NIV)
(See *PURCHASED WITH HIS OWN BLOOD*)

BOUND IN HEAVEN
Matt 16:19 And I will give you the keys of the kingdom of heaven, and whatever you bind on earth will be *bound in heaven*, and whatever you loose on earth will be loosed in heaven
Matt 18:18 Assuredly, I say to you, whatever you bind on earth will be *bound in heaven*, and whatever you loose on earth will be loosed in heaven

BOW DOWN THINE EAR (KJV)
(See *INCLINE YOUR EAR*)

BOW DOWN TO HIM
1Sam 2:36 And it shall come to pass that everyone who is left in your house will come and *bow down to him* for a piece of silver and a morsel of bread, and say
2Sam 15:5 And so it was, whenever anyone came near him to *bow down to him*, that he would put out his hand and take him and kiss him

BOW DOWN YOUR EAR
Ps 31:2 *Bow down Your ear* to me, deliver me speedily; be my rock of refuge, a fortress of defense to save me
Ps 86:1 *Bow down Your ear*, O Lord, hear me; for I am poor and needy

BOW IN THE CLOUD (KJV, RSV)
(See *RAINBOW IN THE CLOUD*)

BOWED DOWN AND WORSHIPED (NIV)
(See *FELL DOWN AND WORSHIPED*)

BOWED DOWN TO THE GROUND
Ruth 2:10 Then she fell on her face, *bowed down to the ground*, and said to him
1Sam 25:23 Now when Abigail saw David, she hastened to dismount from the donkey, fell on her face before David, and *bowed down to the ground*

BOWED LOW (NIV)
(See *BOWED THEIR HEADS*)

BOWED MY HEAD AND WORSHIPED
Gen 24:48 And I *bowed my head and worshiped* the Lord, and blessed the Lord God of my master Abraham, who had led me in the way of truth to take the daughter of my master's brother for his son

BOWED THE HEAVENS
2Sam 22:10 He *bowed the heavens* also, and came down with darkness under His feet
Ps 18:9 He *bowed the heavens* also, and came down with darkness under His feet

BOWED THE KNEE
Matt 27:29 And they *bowed the knee* before Him and mocked Him, saying
Rom 11:4 I have reserved for Myself seven thousand men who have not *bowed the knee* to Baal

BOWED THEIR FACES
2Chr 7:3 When all the children of Israel saw how the fire came down, and the glory of the Lord on the temple, they *bowed their faces* to the ground on the pavement, and worshiped and praised the Lord, saying
Luke 24:5 Then, as they were afraid and *bowed their faces* to the earth, they said to them

BOWED THEIR HEADS
Gen 43:28 he is still alive." And they *bowed their heads* down and prostrated themselves
Ex 4:31 and when they heard that the Lord had visited the children of Israel and that He had looked on their affliction, then they *bowed their heads* and worshiped
Ex 12:27 that you shall say, 'It is the Passover sacrifice of the Lord, who passed over the houses of the children of Israel in Egypt when He struck the Egyptians and delivered our households.'" So the people *bowed their heads* and worshiped
1Chr 29:20 So all the congregation blessed the Lord God of their fathers, and *bowed their heads* and prostrated themselves before the Lord and the king
2Chr 29:30 So they sang praises with gladness, and they *bowed their heads* and worshiped
Neh 8:6 And they *bowed their heads* and worshiped the Lord with their faces to the ground

BOWELS ARE TROUBLED (KJV)
(See *SOUL IS TROUBLED*)

BOWING IN WORSHIP OVER THE HEAD OF HIS STAFF (RSV)
(See *LEANING ON THE TOP OF HIS STAFF*)

BRAG ABOUT THE LAW (NIV)
(See *BOAST IN THE LAW*)

BRANCH AND RUSH (KJV)
(See *PALM BRANCH AND BULRUSH*)

BRANCH OF RIGHTEOUSNESS
Jer 23:5 Behold, the days are coming," says the Lord, "That I will raise to David a *Branch of righteousness*
Jer 33:15 In those days and at that time I will cause to grow up to David a *Branch of righteousness*

BRANCH OF THE LORD
Is 4:2 In that day the *Branch of the Lord* shall be beautiful and glorious

BRAND PLUCKED FROM THE FIRE
Zech 3:2 The Lord who has chosen Jerusalem rebuke you! Is this not a *brand plucked from the fire*

BRAWLING WOMAN (KJV)
(See *CONTENTIOUS WOMAN*)

BREAD AND WATER
Deut 23:4 because they did not meet you with *bread and water* on the road when you came out of Egypt, and because they hired against you Balaam the son of Beor from Pethor of Mesopotamia, to curse you
1Kin 18:4 For so it was, while Jezebel massacred the prophets of the Lord, that Obadiah had taken one hundred prophets and hidden them, fifty to a cave, and had fed them with *bread and water*
1Kin 18:13 Was it not reported to my lord what I did when Jezebel killed the prophets of the Lord, how I hid one hundred men of the Lord's prophets, fifty to a cave, and fed them with *bread and water*
Neh 13:2 because they had not met the children of Israel with *bread and water*, but hired Balaam against them to curse them
Ezek 4:17 that they may lack *bread and water*, and be dismayed with one another, and waste away because of their iniquity

BREAD AND WINE
Gen 14:18 Then Melchizedek king of Salem brought out *bread and wine*
Judg 19:19 although we have both straw and fodder for our donkeys, and *bread and wine* for myself, for your maidservant, and for the young man who is with your servant
Neh 5:15 But the former governors who had been before me laid burdens on the people, and took from them *bread and wine*, besides forty shekels of silver

BREAD EATEN IN SECRET
Prov 9:17 Stolen water is sweet, and *bread eaten in secret* is pleasant

BREAD FROM HEAVEN
Ex 16:4 Then the Lord said to Moses, "Behold, I will rain *bread from heaven* for you
Neh 9:15 You gave them *bread from heaven* for their hunger, and brought them water out of the rock for their thirst, and told them to go in to possess the land which You had sworn to give them
John 6:31 as it is written, 'He gave them *bread from heaven* to eat
John 6:32 Then Jesus said to them, "Most assuredly, I say to you, Moses did not give you the *bread from heaven*, but My Father gives you the true *bread from heaven*

BREAD OF ADVERSITY
Is 30:20 And though the Lord gives you the *bread of adversity* and the water of affliction, yet your teachers will not be moved into a corner anymore, but your eyes shall see your teachers

BREAD OF GOD
John 6:33 For the *bread of God* is He who comes down from heaven and gives life to the world

BREAD OF HEAVEN
Ps 78:24 Had rained down manna on them to eat, and given them of the *bread of heaven*
Ps 105:40 The people asked, and He brought quail, and satisfied them with the *bread of heaven*

BREAD OF IDLENESS
Prov 31:27 She watches over the ways of her household, and does not eat the *bread of idleness*

BREAD OF LIFE
John 6:35 And Jesus said to them, "I am the *bread of life*
John 6:48 I am the *bread of life*

BREAD OF SORROWS
Ps 127:2 It is vain for you to rise up early, to sit up late, to eat the *bread of sorrows*

BREAD OF THE ANGELS (RSV)
(See *ANGELS' FOOD*)

BREAD OF WICKEDNESS
Prov 4:17 For they eat the *bread of wickedness*, and drink the wine of violence

BREAD TO THE HUNGRY
Ezek 18:7 has robbed no one by violence, but has given his *bread to the hungry* and covered the naked with clothing
Ezek 18:16 has not oppressed anyone, nor withheld a pledge, nor robbed by violence, but has given his *bread to the hungry* and covered the naked with clothing

BREAD WHICH COMES DOWN FROM HEAVEN
John 6:50 This is the *bread which comes down from heaven*, that one may eat of it and not die

BREAD WITHOUT YEAST (NIV)
(See *UNLEAVENED BREAD*)

BREAK BREAD
Jer 16:7 Nor shall men *break bread* in mourning for them, to comfort them for the dead
Acts 20:7 Now on the first day of the week, when the disciples came together to *break bread*, Paul, ready to depart the next day, spoke to them and continued his message until midnight

BREAK DOWN THEIR ALTARS (NIV)
(See *DESTROY THEIR ALTARS*)

BREAK FORTH INTO SINGING
Is 14:7 The whole earth is at rest and quiet; they *break forth into singing*
Is 44:23 *break forth into singing*, you mountains, O forest, and every tree in it
Is 54:1 *Break forth into singing*, and cry aloud, you who have not travailed with child
Is 55:12 the mountains and the hills shall *break forth into singing* before you, and all the trees of the field shall clap their hands

BREAK MY COVENANT
Lev 26:15 and if you despise My statutes, or if your soul abhors My judgments, so that you do not perform all My commandments, but *break My covenant*
Lev 26:44 Yet for all that, when they are in the land of their enemies, I will not cast them away, nor shall I abhor them, to utterly destroy them and *break My covenant* with them
Deut 31:16 and this people will rise and play the harlot with the gods of the foreigners of the land, where they go to be among them, and they will forsake Me and *break My covenant* which I have made with them
Deut 31:20 When I have brought them to the land flowing with milk and honey, of which I swore to their fathers, and they have eaten and filled themselves and grown fat, then they will turn to other gods and serve them; and they will provoke Me and *break My covenant*
Judg 2:1 and I said, 'I will never *break My covenant* with you
Jer 33:20 If you can *break My covenant* with the day and My covenant with the night, so that there will not be day and night in their season

BREAK THE YOKE
Jer 28:4 And I will bring back to this place Jeconiah the son of Jehoiakim, king of Judah, with all the captives of Judah who went to Babylon,' says the Lord, 'for I will *break the yoke* of the king of Babylon
Jer 28:11 Even so I will *break the yoke* of Nebuchadnezzar king of Babylon from the neck of all nations within the space of two full years

BREAK THEM WITH A ROD OF IRON
Ps 2:9 You shall *break them with a rod of iron;* You shall dash them in pieces like a potter's vessel

BREAKER OF THE LAW
Rom 2:25 but if you are a *breaker of the law*, your circumcision has become uncircumcision

BREAKING BREAD
Acts 2:46 So continuing daily with one accord in the temple, and *breaking bread* from house to house, they ate their food with gladness and simplicity of heart

BREAKING OF BREAD
Luke 24:35 And they told about the things that had happened on the road, and how He was known to them in the *breaking of bread*
Acts 2:42 And they continued steadfastly in the apostles' doctrine and fellowship, in the *breaking of bread*, and in prayers

BREAKING THE SABBATH (NAS, NIV)
(See *BROKE THE SABBATH*)

BREASTPLATE OF RIGHTEOUSNESS
Eph 6:14 Stand therefore, having girded your waist with truth, having put on the *breastplate of righteousness*

BREATH OF GOD
Job 27:3 as long as my breath is in me, and the *breath of God* in my nostrils
Job 37:10 By the *breath of God* ice is given, and the broad waters are frozen

BREATH OF HIS ANGER
Job 4:9 By the blast of God they perish, and by the *breath of His anger* they are consumed

BREATH OF LIFE
Gen 2:7 And the Lord God formed man of the dust of the ground, and breathed into his nostrils the *breath of life*
Gen 6:17 And behold, I Myself am bringing floodwaters on the earth, to destroy from under heaven all flesh in which is the *breath of life*
Gen 7:15 And they went into the ark to Noah, two by two, of all flesh in which is the *breath of life*
Rev 11:11 Now after the three and a half days the *breath of life* from God entered them, and they stood on their feet, and great fear fell on those who saw them

BREATH OF THE ALMIGHTY
Job 32:8 But there is a spirit in man, and the *breath of the Almighty* gives him understanding
Job 33:4 The Spirit of God has made me, and the *breath of the Almighty* gives me life

BREATH OF THE LORD
Is 30:33 the *breath of the Lord*, like a stream of brimstone, kindles it
Is 40:7 The grass withers, the flower fades, because the *breath of the Lord* blows upon it

BREATHED HIS LAST
Gen 25:8 Then Abraham *breathed his last* and died in a good old age, an old man and full of years, and was gathered to his people
Gen 25:17 and he *breathed his last* and died, and was gathered to his people
Gen 35:29 So Isaac *breathed his last* and died, and was gathered to his people, being old and full of days
Gen 49:33 And when Jacob had finished commanding his sons, he drew his feet up into the bed and *breathed his last*, and was gathered to his people
Mark 15:37 And Jesus cried out with a loud voice, and *breathed His last*
Mark 15:39 Now when the centurion, who stood opposite Him, saw that He cried out like this and *breathed His last*, he said
Luke 23:46 And when Jesus had cried out with a loud voice, He said, "Father, 'into Your hands I commend My spirit.'" And having said this, He *breathed His last*
Acts 5:5 Then Ananias, hearing these words, fell down and *breathed his last*

BREATHED INTO HIS NOSTRILS
Gen 2:7 And the Lord God formed man of the dust of the ground, and *breathed into his nostrils* the breath of life

BRETHREN TO DWELL TOGETHER
Ps 133:1 Behold, how good and how pleasant it is for *brethren to dwell together* in unity

BRIBE BLINDS THE EYES
Deut 16:19 you shall not show partiality, nor take a bribe, for a *bribe blinds the eyes* of the wise and twists the words of the righteous

BRIBE DEBASES THE HEART
Eccl 7:7 Surely oppression destroys a wise man's reason, and a *bribe debases the heart*

BRIERS AND THORNS
Is 5:6 it shall not be pruned or dug, but there shall come up *briers and thorns*
Is 7:23 It shall happen in that day, that wherever there could be a thousand vines worth a thousand shekels of silver, it will be for *briers and thorns*
Is 7:24 With arrows and bows men will come there, because all the land will become *briers and thorns*
Is 7:25 And to any hill which could be dug with the hoe, you will not go there for fear of *briers and thorns*
Is 9:18 it shall devour the *briers and thorns*, and kindle in the thickets of the forest
Is 27:4 who would set *briers and thorns* against Me in battle
Ezek 2:6 And you, son of man, do not be afraid of them nor be afraid of their words, though *briers and thorns* are with you and you dwell among scorpions

BRIGHT AND MORNING STAR
Rev 22:16 I am the Root and the Offspring of David, the *Bright and Morning Star*

BRIGHT AS THE SUN (NIV, RSV)
(See *CLEAR AS THE SUN*)

BRING ALL THE TITHES
Mal 3:10 *Bring all the tithes* into the storehouse, that there may be food in My house, and prove Me now in this

BRING BACK FROM CAPTIVITY
Jer 30:3 For behold, the days are coming,' says the Lord, 'that I will *bring back from captivity* My people Israel and Judah

BRING BACK OUR CAPTIVITY
Ps 126:4 *Bring back our captivity*, O Lord, as the streams in the South

BRING BACK THE CAPTIVITY
Jer 30:18 Behold, I will *bring back the captivity* of Jacob's tents, and have mercy on his dwelling places

BRING FIRE ON THE EARTH (NIV)
(See *SEND FIRE ON THE EARTH*)

BRING GOOD NEWS (NAS)
(See *PREACH GOOD TIDINGS*)

BRING GOOD TIDINGS
1Kin 1:42 And Adonijah said to him, "Come in, for you are a prominent man, and *bring good tidings*
Is 40:9 O Zion, you who *bring good tidings*, get up into the high mountain; O Jerusalem, you who *bring good tidings*, lift up your voice with strength, lift it up, be not afraid

BRING JUDGMENT (NIV)
(See *EXECUTE JUDGMENT*)

BRING JUDGMENT ON
Jer 51:47 therefore behold, the days are coming that I will *bring judgment on* the carved images of Babylon
Jer 51:52 Therefore behold, the days are coming," says the Lord, "That I will *bring judgment on* her carved images, and throughout all her land the wounded shall groan
Rom 13:2 Therefore whoever resists the authority resists the ordinance of God, and those who resist will *bring judgment on* themselves

BRING THEM LIFE (NIV)
(See *LEADS TO LIFE*)

BRING TO YOUR REMEMBRANCE
John 14:26 But the Helper, the Holy Spirit, whom the Father will send in My name, He will teach you all things, and *bring to your remembrance* all things that I said to you

BRING YOUR SERVANT INTO JUDGMENT (NIV)
(See *ENTER INTO JUDGMENT*)

BRINGETH FORTH GOOD FRUIT (KJV)
(See *BEARS GOOD FRUIT*)

BRINGETH FORTH MUCH FRUIT (KJV)
(See *BEARS MUCH FRUIT*)

BRINGING IN SHEAVES
Neh 13:15 In those days I saw in Judah some people treading wine presses on the Sabbath, and *bringing in sheaves*, and loading donkeys with wine, grapes, figs, and all kinds of burdens, which they brought into Jerusalem on the Sabbath day

BRINGS ON MISERY (NIV)
(See *DEVISES EVIL*)

BROAD IS THE WAY
Matt 7:13 for wide is the gate and *broad is the way* that leads to destruction, and there are many who go in by it

BROKE DOWN THE ALTARS
2Chr 34:4 They *broke down the altars* of the Baals in his presence, and the incense altars which were above them he cut down

BROKE DOWN THE HIGH PLACES
2Kin 23:8 also he *broke down the high places* at the gates which were at the entrance of the Gate of Joshua the governor of the city, which were to the left of the city gate

BROKE DOWN THE SACRED PILLARS
2Chr 14:3 for he removed the altars of the foreign gods and the high places, and *broke down the sacred pillars* and cut down the wooden images

BROKE MY COVENANT
Ezek 44:7 When you brought in foreigners, uncircumcised in heart and uncircumcised in flesh, to be in My sanctuary to defile it My house and when you offered My food, the fat and the blood, then they *broke My covenant* because of all your abominations

BROKE THE BREAD (NIV)
(See *BREAKING OF BREAD*)

BROKE THE SABBATH
John 5:18 Therefore the Jews sought all the more to kill Him, because He not only *broke the Sabbath*, but also said that God was His Father, making Himself equal with God

BROKEN AND A CONTRITE HEART
Ps 51:17 The sacrifices of God are a broken spirit, a *broken and a contrite heart*—these, O God, You will not despise

BROKEN CISTERNS
Jer 2:13 they have forsaken Me, the fountain of living waters, and hewn themselves cisterns *broken cisterns* that can hold no water

BROKEN DOWN THE ALTARS
2Chr 34:7 When he had *broken down the altars* and the wooden images, had beaten the carved images into powder, and cut down all the incense altars throughout all the land of Israel, he returned to Jerusalem

BROKEN FOR YOU
1Cor 11:24 this is My body which is *broken for you;* do this in remembrance of Me

BROKEN HIS COMMANDMENT
Num 15:31 Because he has despised the word of the Lord, and has *broken His commandment*, that person shall be completely cut off

BROKEN MY COVENANT
Gen 17:14 And the uncircumcised male child, who is not circumcised in the flesh of his foreskin, that person shall be cut off from his people; he has *broken My covenant*
Jer 11:10 the house of Israel and the house of Judah have *broken My covenant* which I made with their fathers

BROKEN THE EVERLASTING COVENANT
Is 24:5 The earth is also defiled under its inhabitants, because they have transgressed the laws, changed the ordinance, *broken the everlasting covenant*

BROOD OF VIPERS
Matt 3:7 But when he saw many of the Pharisees and Sadducees coming to his baptism, he said to them, "*Brood of vipers*
Matt 12:34 *Brood of vipers!* How can you, being evil, speak good things
Matt 23:33 Serpents, *brood of vipers!* How can you escape the condemnation of hell
Luke 3:7 Then he said to the multitudes that came out to be baptized by him, "*Brood of vipers*

BROOKS OF WATER (NAS, RSV)
(See *RIVERS OF WATER*)

BROTHERLY COVENANT (KJV)
(See *COVENANT OF BROTHERHOOD*)

BROTHER'S KEEPER
Gen 4:9 And he said, "I do not know. Am I my *brother's keeper*

BROTHERS LIVE TOGETHER (NIV)
(See *BRETHREN TO DWELL TOGETHER*)

BROUGHT ME INTO DARKNESS (KJV, RSV)
(See *WALK IN DARKNESS*)

BROUGHT UP IN THE TRUTHS OF FAITH (NIV)
(See *NOURISHED IN THE WORDS OF FAITH*)

BROUGHT YOU OUT OF EGYPT
Ex 13:9 for with a strong hand the Lord has *brought you out of Egypt*
Deut 4:37 and He *brought you out of Egypt* with His Presence, with His mighty power
Deut 16:1 Observe the month of Abib, and keep the Passover to the Lord your God, for in the month of Abib the Lord your God *brought you out of Egypt* by night

BROUGHT YOU UP FROM EGYPT (RSV)
(See *LED YOU UP FROM EGYPT*)

BRUISE HIS HEEL
Gen 3:15 He shall bruise your head, and you shall *bruise His heel*

BRUISE YOUR HEAD
Gen 3:15 He shall *bruise your head*, and you shall bruise His heel

BRUISED FOR OUR INIQUITIES
Is 53:5 But He was wounded for our transgressions, He was *bruised for our iniquities*

BRUISED REED
Is 42:3 A *bruised reed* He will not break, and smoking flax He will not quench
Matt 12:20 A *bruised reed* He will not break, and smoking flax He will not quench, till He sends forth justice to victory

BUILD A MOUND
Jer 6:6 Hew down trees, and *build a mound* against Jerusalem. This is the city to be punished

BUILD A TEMPLE
2Chr 2:1 Then Solomon determined to *build a temple* for the name of the Lord, and a royal house for himself
2Chr 2:12 Blessed be the Lord God of Israel, who made heaven and earth, for He has given King David a wise son, endowed with prudence and understanding, who will *build a temple* for the Lord and a royal house for himself
2Chr 6:7 Now it was in the heart of my father David to *build a temple* for the name of the Lord God of Israel
2Chr 6:8 But the Lord said to my father David, 'Whereas it was in your heart to *build a temple* for My name, you did well in that it was in your heart

BUILD AND TO PLANT
Jer 1:10 See, I have this day set you over the nations and over the kingdoms, to root out and to pull down, to destroy and to throw down, to *build and to plant*
Jer 18:9 And the instant I speak concerning a nation and concerning a kingdom, to *build and to plant* it
Jer 31:28 And it shall come to pass, that as I have watched over them to pluck up, to break down, to throw down, to destroy, and to afflict, so I will watch over them to *build and to plant*

BUILD HIM A SURE HOUSE
1Sam 2:35 I will *build him a sure house*, and he shall walk before My anointed forever

BUILD HIM A TEMPLE
2Chr 2:6 But who is able to *build Him a temple*, since heaven and the heaven of heavens cannot contain Him? Who am I then, that I should *build Him a temple*, except to burn sacrifice before Him

BUILD ME A HOUSE
1Chr 17:4 You shall not *build Me a house* to dwell in
1Chr 17:12 He shall *build Me a house*, and I will establish his throne forever

BUILD MY CHURCH
Matt 16:18 And I also say to you that you are Peter, and on this rock I will *build My church*, and the gates of Hades shall not prevail against it

BUILD MY HOUSE
1Chr 28:6 Now He said to me, 'It is your son Solomon who shall *build My house* and My courts

BUILD OURSELVES A CITY
Gen 11:4 And they said, "Come, let us *build ourselves a city*, and a tower whose top is in the heavens

BUILD SIEGE RAMPS (NIV)
(See *BUILD A MOUND*)

BUILD THE HOUSE
1Kin 5:5 And behold, I propose to build a house for the name of the Lord my God, as the Lord spoke to my father David, saying, 'Your son, whom I will set on your throne in your place, he shall *build the house* for My name
1Kin 6:1 And it came to pass in the four hundred and eightieth year after the children of Israel had come out of the land of Egypt, in the fourth year of Solomon's reign over Israel, in the month of Ziv, which is the second month, that he began to *build the house* of the Lord
1Kin 8:19 Nevertheless you shall not *build the house*, but your son, who shall come from your loins, he shall *build the house* for My name
1Kin 9:15 to *build the house* of the Lord, his own house, the Millo, the wall of Jerusalem, Hazor, Megiddo, and Gezer
1Chr 22:2 and he appointed masons to cut hewn stones to *build the house* of God
1Chr 22:11 and may you prosper, and *build the house* of the Lord your God, as He has said to you
2Chr 3:1 Now Solomon began to *build the house* of the Lord at Jerusalem on Mount Moriah, where the Lord had appeared to his father David, at the place that David had prepared on the threshing floor of Ornan the Jebusite
2Chr 6:9 Nevertheless you shall not *build the house*, but your son who will come forth from your own loins, he shall build the temple for My name
Ezra 1:3 Now let him go up to Jerusalem, which is in Judah, and *build the house* of the Lord God of Israel (He is God
Ezra 1:5 Then the heads of the fathers' houses of Judah and Benjamin, and the priests and the Levites, with all those whose spirits God had moved, arose to go up and *build the house* of the Lord which is in Jerusalem
Ezra 5:2 So Zerubbabel the son of Shealtiel and Jeshua the son of Jozadak rose up and began to *build the house* of God which is in Jerusalem

BUILD THE OLD WASTE PLACES
Is 58:12 Those from among you shall *build the old waste places*

BUILD THE TEMPLE
1Kin 5:18 and they prepared timber and stones to *build the temple*
1Chr 29:19 And give my son Solomon a loyal heart to keep Your commandments and Your testimonies and Your statutes, to do all these things, and to *build the temple* for which I have made provision

2Chr 6:9 Nevertheless you shall not build the house, but your son who will come forth from your own loins, he shall *build the temple* for My name
Hag 1:8 Go up to the mountains and bring wood and *build the temple*, that I may take pleasure in it and be glorified
Zech 6:12 From His place He shall branch out, and He shall *build the temple* of the Lord
Zech 6:13 yes, He shall *build the temple* of the Lord. He shall bear the glory, and shall sit and rule on His throne
Zech 6:15 Even those who are far away shall come and *build the temple* of the Lord

BUILD UP (NAS, NIV, RSV)
(See *HEAP IT UP*)

BUILD UP YOUR THRONE
Ps 89:4 Your seed I will establish forever, and *build up your throne* to all generations

BUILDER AND MAKER IS GOD
Heb 11:10 for he waited for the city which has foundations, whose *builder and maker is God*

BUILDING A TEMPLE
2Chr 2:4 Behold, I am *building a temple* for the name of the Lord my God, to dedicate it to Him, to burn before Him sweet incense, for the continual showbread, for the burnt offerings morning and evening, on the Sabbaths, on the New Moons, and on the set feasts of the Lord our God

BUILDING THE HOUSE
1Kin 9:1 And it came to pass, when Solomon had finished *building the house* of the Lord and the king's house, and all Solomon's desire which he wanted to do
2Chr 3:3 This is the foundation which Solomon laid for *building the house* of God

BUILDING UP THE CHURCH (RSV)
(See *EDIFICATION OF THE CHURCH*)

BUILT AN ALTAR
Gen 8:20 Then Noah *built an altar* to the Lord, and took of every clean animal and of every clean bird, and offered burnt offerings on the altar
Gen 12:7 And there he *built an altar* to the Lord, who had appeared to him
Gen 12:8 there he *built an altar* to the Lord and called on the name of the Lord
Gen 13:18 Then Abram moved his tent, and went and dwelt by the terebinth trees of Mamre, which are in Hebron, and *built an altar* there to the Lord
Gen 22:9 And Abraham *built an altar* there and placed the wood in order
Gen 26:25 So he *built an altar* there and called on the name of the Lord, and he pitched his tent there
Gen 35:7 And he *built an altar* there and called the place El Bethel, because there God appeared to him when he fled from the face of his brother
Ex 17:15 And Moses *built an altar* and called its name, The-Lord-Is-My-Banner
Ex 24:4 And he rose early in the morning, and *built an altar* at the foot of the mountain, and twelve pillars according to the twelve tribes of Israel
Ex 32:5 So when Aaron saw it, he *built an altar* before it
Josh 8:30 Now Joshua *built an altar* to the Lord God of Israel in Mount Ebal
Josh 22:10 And when they came to the region of the Jordan which is in the land of Canaan, the children of Reuben, the children of Gad, and half the tribe of Manasseh *built an altar* there by the Jordan a great, impressive altar
Josh 22:11 Now the children of Israel heard someone say, "Behold, the children of Reuben, the children of Gad, and half the tribe of Manasseh have *built an altar* on the frontier of the land of Canaan, in the region of the Jordan, on the side occupied by the children of Israel
Judg 6:24 So Gideon *built an altar* there to the Lord, and called it The-Lord-Shalom
Judg 21:4 So it was, on the next morning, that the people rose early and *built an altar* there, and offered burnt offerings and peace offerings
1Sam 7:17 There he judged Israel, and there he *built an altar* to the Lord
1Sam 14:35 Then Saul *built an altar* to the Lord. This was the first altar that he built to the Lord
1Kin 18:32 Then with the stones he *built an altar* in the name of the Lord
2Kin 16:11 Then Urijah the priest *built an altar* according to all that King Ahaz had sent from Damascus

BULLS AND GOATS
Heb 9:13 For if the blood of *bulls and goats* and the ashes of a heifer, sprinkling the unclean, sanctifies for the purifying of the flesh
Heb 10:4 For it is not possible that the blood of *bulls and goats* could take away sins

BULLS OF BASHAN
Ps 22:12 Many bulls have surrounded Me; strong *bulls of Bashan* have encircled Me

BURDEN AGAINST
Is 13:1 The *burden against* Babylon which Isaiah the son of Amoz saw
Is 15:1 The *burden against* Moab. Because in the night Ar of Moab is laid waste and destroyed, because in the night Kir of Moab is laid waste and destroyed
Is 17:1 The *burden against* Damascus. "Behold, Damascus will cease from being a city, and it will be a ruinous heap
Is 19:1 The *burden against* Egypt. Behold, the Lord rides on a swift cloud, and will come into Egypt
Is 21:1 The *burden against* the Wilderness of the Sea. As whirlwinds in the South pass through, so it comes from the desert, from a terrible land
Is 21:11 The *burden against* Dumah. He calls to me out of Seir
Is 21:13 The *burden against* Arabia. In the forest in Arabia you will lodge, O you traveling companies of Dedanites
Is 22:1 The *burden against* the Valley of Vision. What ails you now, that you have all gone up to the housetops
Is 23:1 The *burden against* Tyre. Wail, you ships of Tarshish! For it is laid waste, so that there is no house, no harbor
Is 30:6 The *burden against* the beasts of the South. Through a land of trouble and anguish, from which came the lioness and lion, the viper and fiery flying serpent, they will carry their riches on the backs of young donkeys, and their treasures on the humps of camels, to a people who shall not benefit them
Nah 1:1 The *burden against* Nineveh. The book of the vision of Nahum the Elkoshite

BURDEN IS TOO HEAVY FOR ME
Num 11:14 I am not able to bear all these people alone, because the *burden is too heavy for me*

BURDEN OF THE LORD (KJV, RSV)
(See *ORACLE OF THE LORD*)

BURIED HIM IN THE CITY OF DAVID
1Kin 15:8 So Abijam rested with his fathers, and they *buried him in the City of David*
2Chr 14:1 So Abijah rested with his fathers, and they *buried him in the City of David*
2Chr 21:20 However they *buried him in the City of David*, but not in the tombs of the kings
2Chr 24:16 And they *buried him in the City of David* among the kings, because he had done good in Israel, both toward God and His house
2Chr 24:25 And they *buried him in the City of David*, but they did not bury him in the tombs of the kings
2Chr 27:9 So Jotham rested with his fathers, and they *buried him in the City of David*

BURIED IN THE CITY OF DAVID
1Kin 2:10 So David rested with his fathers, and was *buried in the City of David*
1Kin 11:43 Then Solomon rested with his fathers, and was *buried in the City of David* his father
2Chr 9:31 Then Solomon rested with his fathers, and was *buried in the City of David* his father
2Chr 12:16 So Rehoboam rested with his fathers, and was *buried in the City of David*

BURIED WITH HIM IN BAPTISM
Col 2:12 *buried with Him in baptism*, in which you also were raised with Him through faith in the working of God, who raised Him from the dead

BURN INCENSE
Ex 30:1 You shall make an altar to *burn incense* on; you shall make it of acacia wood
Ex 30:7 when he tends the lamps, he shall *burn incense* on it
Ex 30:8 And when Aaron lights the lamps at twilight, he shall *burn incense* on it, a perpetual incense before the Lord throughout your generations
1Sam 2:28 Did I not choose him out of all the tribes of Israel to be My priest, to offer upon My altar, to *burn incense*, and to wear an ephod before Me
1Kin 13:1 And behold, a man of God went from Judah to Bethel by the word of the Lord, and Jeroboam stood by the altar to *burn incense*
1Kin 13:2 and on you he shall sacrifice the priests of the high places who *burn incense* on you, and men's bones shall be burned on you
2Kin 23:5 Then he removed the idolatrous priests whom the kings of Judah had ordained to *burn incense* on the high places in the cities of Judah and in the places all around Jerusalem, and those who burned incense to Baal, to the sun, to the moon, to the constellations, and to all the host of heaven
1Chr 23:13 and Aaron was set apart, he and his sons forever, that he should sanctify the most holy things, to *burn incense* before the Lord, to minister to Him, and to give the blessing in His name forever
2Chr 26:16 But when he was strong his heart was lifted up, to his destruction, for he transgressed against the Lord his God by entering the temple of the Lord to *burn incense* on the altar of incense
2Chr 26:18 And they withstood King Uzziah, and said to him, "It is not for you, Uzziah, to *burn incense* to the Lord, but for the priests, the sons of Aaron, who are consecrated to *burn incense*
2Chr 26:19 and he had a censer in his hand to *burn incense*
2Chr 28:25 And in every single city of Judah he made high places to *burn incense* to other gods, and provoked to anger the Lord God of his fathers
2Chr 29:11 My sons, do not be negligent now, for the Lord has chosen you to stand before Him, to serve Him, and that you should minister to Him and *burn incense*
2Chr 32:12 Has not the same Hezekiah taken away His high places and His altars, and commanded Judah and Jerusalem, saying, "You shall worship before one altar and *burn incense* on it
Is 65:3 who sacrifice in gardens, and *burn incense* on altars of brick
Jer 7:9 Will you steal, murder, commit adultery, swear falsely, *burn incense* to Baal, and walk after other gods whom you do not know
Jer 11:13 and according to the number of the streets of Jerusalem you have set up altars to that shameful thing, altars to *burn incense* to Baal
Jer 34:5 as in the ceremonies of your fathers, the former kings who were before you, so they shall *burn incense* for you and lament for you, saying
Jer 44:3 because of their wickedness which they have committed to provoke Me to anger, in that they went to *burn incense* and to serve other gods whom they did not know, they nor you nor your fathers
Jer 44:17 But we will certainly do whatever has gone out of our own mouth, to *burn incense* to the queen of heaven and pour out drink offerings to her, as we have done, we and our fathers, our kings and our princes, in the cities of Judah and in the streets of Jerusalem
Jer 44:25 You and your wives have spoken with your mouths and fulfilled with your hands, saying, "We will surely perform our vows that we have made, to *burn incense* to the queen of heaven and pour out drink offerings to her
Hos 4:13 They offer sacrifices on the mountaintops, and *burn incense* on the hills, under oaks, poplars, and terebinths, because their shade is good
Hab 1:16 Therefore they sacrifice to their net, and *burn incense* to their dragnet
Luke 1:9 according to the custom of the priesthood, his lot fell to *burn incense* when he went into the temple of the Lord

BURN WITH PASSION
1Cor 7:9 For it is better to marry than to *burn with passion*

BURNED INCENSE
1Kin 3:3 And Solomon loved the Lord, walking in the statutes of his father David, except that he sacrificed and *burned incense* at the high places
1Kin 9:25 Now three times a year Solomon offered burnt offerings and peace offerings on the altar which he had built for the Lord, and he *burned incense* with them on the altar that was before the Lord
1Kin 11:8 And he did likewise for all his foreign wives, who *burned incense* and sacrificed to their gods
1Kin 12:33 And he ordained a feast for the children of Israel, and offered sacrifices on the altar and *burned incense*
1Kin 22:43 Nevertheless the high places were not taken away, for the people offered sacrifices and *burned incense* on the high places
2Kin 12:3 the people still sacrificed and *burned incense* on the high places
2Kin 14:4 However the high places were not taken away, and the people still sacrificed and *burned incense* on the high places
2Kin 15:4 the people still sacrificed and *burned incense* on the high places
2Kin 15:35 the people still sacrificed and *burned incense* on the high places
2Kin 16:4 And he sacrificed and *burned incense* on the high places, on the hills, and under every green tree

2Kin 17:11 and there they *burned incense* on all the high places, as the nations had done whom the Lord had carried away before them
2Kin 18:4 for until those days the children of Israel *burned incense* to it, and called it Nehushtan
2Kin 22:17 because they have forsaken Me and *burned incense* to other gods, that they might provoke Me to anger with all the works of their hands
2Kin 23:5 Then he removed the idolatrous priests whom the kings of Judah had ordained to burn incense on the high places in the cities of Judah and in the places all around Jerusalem, and those who *burned incense* to Baal, to the sun, to the moon, to the constellations, and to all the host of heaven
2Kin 23:8 And he brought all the priests from the cities of Judah, and defiled the high places where the priests had *burned incense*, from Geba to Beersheba
2Chr 25:14 Now it was so, after Amaziah came from the slaughter of the Edomites, that he brought the gods of the people of Seir, set them up to be his gods, and bowed down before them and *burned incense* to them
2Chr 28:3 He *burned incense* in the Valley of the Son of Hinnom, and burned his children in the fire, according to the abominations of the nations whom the Lord had cast out before the children of Israel
2Chr 28:4 And he sacrificed and *burned incense* on the high places, on the hills, and under every green tree
2Chr 29:7 They have also shut up the doors of the vestibule, put out the lamps, and have not *burned incense* or offered burnt offerings in the holy place to the God of Israel
2Chr 34:25 because they have forsaken Me and *burned incense* to other gods, that they might provoke Me to anger with all the works of their hands
Is 65:7 your iniquities and the iniquities of your fathers together," says the Lord, "Who have *burned incense* on the mountains and blasphemed Me on the hills
Jer 1:16 I will utter My judgments against them concerning all their wickedness, because they have forsaken Me, *burned incense* to other gods, and worshiped the works of their own hands
Jer 18:15 Because My people have forgotten Me, they have *burned incense* to worthless idols
Jer 19:4 Because they have forsaken Me and made this an alien place, because they have *burned incense* in it to other gods whom neither they, their fathers, nor the kings of Judah have known, and have filled this place with the blood of the innocents
Jer 19:13 And the houses of Jerusalem and the houses of the kings of Judah shall be defiled like the place of Tophet, because of all the houses on whose roofs they have *burned incense* to all the host of heaven, and poured out drink offerings to other gods
Jer 44:15 Then all the men who knew that their wives had *burned incense* to other gods, with all the women who stood by, a great multitude, and all the people who dwelt in the land of Egypt, in Pathros, answered Jeremiah, saying
Jer 44:19 The women also said, "And when we *burned incense* to the queen of heaven and poured out drink offerings to her, did we make cakes for her, to worship her, and pour out drink offerings to her without our husbands' permission
Jer 44:23 Because you have *burned incense* and because you have sinned against the Lord, and have not obeyed the voice of the Lord or walked in His law, in His statutes or in His testimonies, therefore this calamity has happened to you, as at this day
Hos 2:13 I will punish her for the days of the Baals to which she *burned incense*
Hos 11:2 so they went from them, they sacrificed to the Baals, and *burned incense* to carved images

BURNED WITH ANGER (NIV)
(See *ANGER WAS GREATLY AROUSED*)

BURNING COALS
Lev 16:12 Then he shall take a censer full of *burning coals* of fire from the altar before the Lord, with his hands full of sweet incense beaten fine, and bring it inside the veil
Ps 140:10 Let *burning coals* fall upon them; let them be cast into the fire, into deep pits, that they rise not up again
Prov 26:21 As charcoal is to *burning coals*, and wood to fire, so is a contentious man to kindle strife
Ezek 1:13 As for the likeness of the living creatures, their appearance was like *burning coals* of fire, and like the appearance of torches

BURNING STICK SNATCHED FROM THE FIRE (NIV)
(See *BRAND PLUCKED FROM THE FIRE*)

BURNS INCENSE
Is 66:3 he who *burns incense*, as if he blesses an idol
Jer 48:35 Moreover," says the Lord, "I will cause to cease in Moab the one who offers sacrifices in the high places and *burns incense* to his gods

BURNT OFFERING
Gen 22:2 And He said, "Take now your son, your only son Isaac, whom you love, and go to the land of Moriah, and offer him there as a *burnt offering* on one of the mountains of which I shall tell you
Gen 22:3 and he split the wood for the *burnt offering*, and arose and went to the place of which God had told him
Gen 22:6 So Abraham took the wood of the *burnt offering* and laid it on Isaac his son
Gen 22:7 And he said, "Look, the fire and the wood, but where is the lamb for a *burnt offering*
Gen 22:8 And Abraham said, "My son, God will provide for Himself the lamb for a *burnt offering*
Gen 22:13 So Abraham went and took the ram, and offered it up for a *burnt offering* instead of his son
Ex 18:12 Then Jethro, Moses' father-in-law, took a *burnt offering* and other sacrifices to offer to God
Ex 29:18 It is a *burnt offering* to the Lord; it is a sweet aroma, an offering made by fire to the Lord
Ex 29:25 You shall receive them back from their hands and burn them on the altar as a *burnt offering*, as a sweet aroma before the Lord
Ex 29:42 This shall be a continual *burnt offering* throughout your generations at the door of the tabernacle of meeting before the Lord, where I will meet you to speak with you
Ex 30:9 You shall not offer strange incense on it, or a *burnt offering*, or a grain offering
Ex 30:28 the altar of *burnt offering* with all its utensils, and the laver and its base
Ex 31:9 the altar of *burnt offering* with all its utensils, and the laver and its base
Ex 35:16 the altar of *burnt offering* with its bronze grating, its poles, all its utensils, and the laver and its base
Ex 38:1 He made the altar of *burnt offering* of acacia wood
Ex 40:6 Then you shall set the altar of the *burnt*

offering before the door of the tabernacle of the tent of meeting
Ex 40:10 You shall anoint the altar of the *burnt offering* and all its utensils, and consecrate the altar
Ex 40:29 And he put the altar of *burnt offering* before the door of the tabernacle of the tent of meeting, and offered upon it the *burnt offering* and the grain offering, as the Lord had commanded Moses
Lev 1:4 Then he shall put his hand on the head of the *burnt offering*, and it will be accepted on his behalf to make atonement for him
Lev 1:6 And he shall skin the *burnt offering* and cut it into its pieces
Lev 4:7 and he shall pour the remaining blood of the bull at the base of the altar of the *burnt offering*, which is at the door of the tabernacle of meeting
Lev 4:10 and the priest shall burn them on the altar of the *burnt offering*
Lev 4:18 and he shall pour the remaining blood at the base of the altar of *burnt offering*, which is at the door of the tabernacle of meeting
Lev 4:24 And he shall lay his hand on the head of the goat, and kill it at the place where they kill the *burnt offering* before the Lord
Lev 4:25 The priest shall take some of the blood of the sin offering with his finger, put it on the horns of the altar of *burnt offering*, and pour its blood at the base of the altar of *burnt offering*
Lev 4:29 And he shall lay his hand on the head of the sin offering, and kill the sin offering at the place of the *burnt offering*
Lev 4:30 Then the priest shall take some of its blood with his finger, put it on the horns of the altar of *burnt offering*, and pour all the remaining blood at the base of the altar
Lev 4:33 Then he shall lay his hand on the head of the sin offering, and kill it as a sin offering at the place where they kill the *burnt offering*
Lev 4:34 The priest shall take some of the blood of the sin offering with his finger, put it on the horns of the altar of *burnt offering*, and pour all the remaining blood at the base of the altar
Lev 5:7 one as a sin offering and the other as a *burnt offering*
Lev 5:10 And he shall offer the second as a *burnt offering* according to the prescribed manner
Lev 6:9 Command Aaron and his sons, saying, 'This is the law of the *burnt offering:* The *burnt offering* shall be on the hearth upon the altar all night until morning, and the fire of the altar shall be kept burning on it
Lev 6:10 And the priest shall put on his linen garment, and his linen trousers he shall put on his body, and take up the ashes of the *burnt offering* which the fire has consumed on the altar, and he shall put them beside the altar
Lev 6:12 And the priest shall burn wood on it every morning, and lay the *burnt offering* in order on it
Lev 6:25 In the place where the *burnt offering* is killed, the sin offering shall be killed before the Lord
Lev 7:2 In the place where they kill the *burnt offering* they shall kill the trespass offering
Lev 7:8 And the priest who offers anyone's *burnt offering*, that priest shall have for himself the skin of the *burnt offering* which he has offered
Lev 7:37 This is the law of the *burnt offering*, the grain offering, the sin offering, the trespass offering, the consecrations, and the sacrifice of the peace offering
Lev 8:18 Then he brought the ram as the *burnt offering*. And Aaron and his sons laid their hands on the head of the ram
Lev 8:28 Then Moses took them from their hands and burned them on the altar, on the *burnt offering*
Lev 9:2 And he said to Aaron, "Take for yourself a young bull as a sin offering and a ram as a *burnt offering*, without blemish, and offer them before the Lord
Lev 9:3 And to the children of Israel you shall speak, saying, 'Take a kid of the goats as a sin offering, and a calf and a lamb, both of the first year, without blemish, as a *burnt offering*
Lev 9:7 And Moses said to Aaron, "Go to the altar, offer your sin offering and your *burnt offering*, and make atonement for yourself and for the people
Lev 9:12 And he killed the *burnt offering;* and Aaron's sons presented to him the blood, which he sprinkled all around on the altar
Lev 9:13 Then they presented the *burnt offering* to him, with its pieces and head, and he burned them on the altar
Lev 9:14 And he washed the entrails and the legs, and burned them with the *burnt offering* on the altar
Lev 9:16 And he brought the *burnt offering* and offered it according to the prescribed manner
Lev 9:22 Then Aaron lifted his hand toward the people, blessed them, and came down from offering the sin offering, the *burnt offering*, and peace offerings
Lev 9:24 and fire came out from before the Lord and consumed the *burnt offering* and the fat on the altar
Lev 10:19 And Aaron said to Moses, "Look, this day they have offered their sin offering and their *burnt offering* before the Lord, and such things have befallen me
Lev 12:6 When the days of her purification are fulfilled, whether for a son or a daughter, she shall bring to the priest a lamb of the first year as a *burnt offering*, and a young pigeon or a turtledove as a sin offering, to the door of the tabernacle of meeting
Lev 12:8 And if she is not able to bring a lamb, then she may bring two turtledoves or two young pigeons one as a *burnt offering* and the other as a sin offering
Lev 14:13 Then he shall kill the lamb in the place where he kills the sin offering and the *burnt offering*, in a holy place
Lev 14:19 Then the priest shall offer the sin offering, and make atonement for him who is to be cleansed from his uncleanness. Afterward he shall kill the *burnt offering*
Lev 14:20 And the priest shall offer the *burnt offering* and the grain offering on the altar
Lev 14:22 one shall be a sin offering and the other a *burnt offering*
Lev 14:31 such as he is able to afford, the one as a sin offering and the other as a *burnt offering*, with the grain offering
Lev 15:15 Then the priest shall offer them, the one as a sin offering and the other as a *burnt offering*
Lev 15:30 Then the priest shall offer the one as a sin offering and the other as a *burnt offering*, and the priest shall make atonement for her before the Lord for the discharge of her uncleanness
Lev 16:3 with the blood of a young bull as a sin offering, and of a ram as a *burnt offering*
Lev 16:5 And he shall take from the congregation of the children of Israel two kids of the goats as a sin offering, and one ram as a *burnt offering*
Lev 16:24 And he shall wash his body with water in a holy place, put on his garments, come out and offer his *burnt offering* and the *burnt offering* of the people, and make atonement for himself and for the people
Lev 17:8 Whatever man of the house of Israel, or

of the strangers who sojourn among you, who offers a *burnt offering* or sacrifice

Lev 22:18 Whatever man of the house of Israel, or of the strangers in Israel, who offers his sacrifice for any of his vows or for any of his freewill offerings, which they offer to the Lord as a *burnt offering*

Lev 23:12 And you shall offer on that day, when you wave the sheaf, a male lamb of the first year, without blemish, as a *burnt offering* to the Lord

Lev 23:18 They shall be as a *burnt offering* to the Lord, with their grain offering and their drink offerings, an offering made by fire for a sweet aroma to the Lord

Lev 23:37 These are the feasts of the Lord which you shall proclaim to be holy convocations, to offer an offering made by fire to the Lord, a *burnt offering* and a grain offering, a sacrifice and drink offerings, everything on its day

Num 6:11 and the priest shall offer one as a sin offering and the other as a *burnt offering*, and make atonement for him, because he sinned by reason of the dead body

Num 6:14 one male lamb in its first year without blemish as a *burnt offering*, one ewe lamb in its first year without blemish as a sin offering, one ram without blemish as a peace offering

Num 6:16 Then the priest shall bring them before the Lord and offer his sin offering and his *burnt offering*

Num 7:15 one young bull, one ram, and one male lamb in its first year, as a *burnt offering*

Num 7:21 one young bull, one ram, and one male lamb in its first year, as a *burnt offering*

Num 7:27 one young bull, one ram, and one male lamb in its first year, as a *burnt offering*

Num 7:33 one young bull, one ram, and one male lamb in its first year, as a *burnt offering*

Num 7:39 one young bull, one ram, and one male lamb in its first year, as a *burnt offering*

Num 7:45 one young bull, one ram, and one male lamb in its first year, as a *burnt offering*

Num 7:51 one young bull, one ram, and one male lamb in its first year, as a *burnt offering*

Num 7:57 one young bull, one ram, and one male lamb in its first year, as a *burnt offering*

Num 7:63 one young bull, one ram, and one male lamb in its first year, as a *burnt offering*

Num 7:69 one young bull, one ram, and one male lamb in its first year, as a *burnt offering*

Num 7:75 one young bull, one ram, and one male lamb in its first year, as a *burnt offering*

Num 7:81 one young bull, one ram, and one male lamb in its first year, as a *burnt offering*

Num 7:87 All the oxen for the *burnt offering* were twelve young bulls, the rams twelve, the male lambs in their first year twelve, with their grain offering, and the kids of the goats as a sin offering twelve

Num 8:12 Then the Levites shall lay their hands on the heads of the young bulls, and you shall offer one as a sin offering and the other as a *burnt offering* to the Lord, to make atonement for the Levites

Num 15:3 and you make an offering by fire to the Lord, a *burnt offering* or a sacrifice, to fulfill a vow or as a freewill offering or in your appointed feasts, to make a sweet aroma to the Lord, from the herd or the flock

Num 15:5 and one-fourth of a hin of wine as a drink offering you shall prepare with the *burnt offering* or the sacrifice, for each lamb

Num 15:8 And when you prepare a young bull as a *burnt offering*, or as a sacrifice to fulfill a vow, or as a peace offering to the Lord

Num 15:24 then it will be, if it is unintentionally committed, without the knowledge of the congregation, that the whole congregation shall offer one young bull as a *burnt offering*, as a sweet aroma to the Lord, with its grain offering and its drink offering, according to the ordinance, and one kid of the goats as a sin offering

Num 23:3 Then Balaam said to Balak, "Stand by your *burnt offering*, and I will go

Num 23:6 So he returned to him, and there he was, standing by his *burnt offering*, he and all the princes of Moab

Num 23:15 And he said to Balak, "Stand here by your *burnt offering* while I meet the Lord over there

Num 23:17 So he came to him, and there he was, standing by his *burnt offering*, and the princes of Moab were with him

Num 28:3 two male lambs in their first year without blemish, day by day, as a regular *burnt offering*

Num 28:6 It is a regular *burnt offering* which was ordained at Mount Sinai for a sweet aroma, an offering made by fire to the Lord

Num 28:10 this is the *burnt offering* for every Sabbath, besides the regular *burnt offering* with its drink offering

Num 28:11 At the beginnings of your months you shall present a *burnt offering* to the Lord

Num 28:13 and one-tenth of an ephah of fine flour, mixed with oil, as a grain offering for each lamb, as a *burnt offering* of sweet aroma, an offering made by fire to the Lord

Num 28:14 this is the *burnt offering* for each month throughout the months of the year

Num 28:15 Also one kid of the goats as a sin offering to the Lord shall be offered, besides the regular *burnt offering* and its drink offering

Num 28:19 And you shall present an offering made by fire as a *burnt offering* to the Lord

Num 28:23 You shall offer these besides the *burnt offering* of the morning, which is for a regular *burnt offering*

Num 28:24 it shall be offered besides the regular *burnt offering* and its drink offering

Num 28:27 You shall present a *burnt offering* as a sweet aroma to the Lord

Num 28:31 You shall present them with their drink offerings, besides the regular *burnt offering* with its grain offering

Num 29:2 You shall offer a *burnt offering* as a sweet aroma to the Lord

Num 29:6 besides the *burnt offering* with its grain offering for the New Moon, the regular *burnt offering* with its grain offering, and their drink offerings, according to their ordinance, as a sweet aroma, an offering made by fire to the Lord

Num 29:8 You shall present a *burnt offering* to the Lord as a sweet aroma

Num 29:11 also one kid of the goats as a sin offering, besides the sin offering for atonement, the regular *burnt offering* with its grain offering, and their drink offerings

Num 29:13 You shall present a *burnt offering*, an offering made by fire as a sweet aroma to the Lord

Num 29:16 also one kid of the goats as a sin offering, besides the regular *burnt offering*, its grain offering, and its drink offering

Num 29:19 also one kid of the goats as a sin offering, besides the regular *burnt offering* with its grain offering, and their drink offerings

Num 29:22 also one goat as a sin offering, besides the regular *burnt offering*, its grain offering, and its drink offering

Num 29:25 also one kid of the goats as a sin offering, besides the regular *burnt offering*, its grain offering, and its drink offering

Num 29:28 also one goat as a sin offering, besides the regular *burnt offering*, its grain offering, and its drink offering

Num 29:31 also one goat as a sin offering, besides the regular *burnt offering*, its grain offering, and its drink offering
Num 29:34 also one goat as a sin offering, besides the regular *burnt offering*, its grain offering, and its drink offering
Num 29:36 You shall present a *burnt offering*, an offering made by fire as a sweet aroma to the Lord
Num 29:38 also one goat as a sin offering, besides the regular *burnt offering*, its grain offering, and its drink offering
Josh 22:26 Therefore we said, 'Let us now prepare to build ourselves an altar, not for *burnt offering* nor for sacrifice
Judg 11:31 then it will be that whatever comes out of the doors of my house to meet me, when I return in peace from the people of Ammon, shall surely be the Lord's, and I will offer it up as a *burnt offering*
Judg 13:16 But if you offer a *burnt offering*, you must offer it to the Lord
Judg 13:23 Then his wife said to him, "If the Lord had desired to kill us, He would not have accepted a *burnt offering* and a grain offering from our hands, nor would He have shown us all these things, nor would He have told us such things as these at this time
1Sam 6:14 So they split the wood of the cart and offered the cows as a *burnt offering* to the Lord
1Sam 7:9 And Samuel took a suckling lamb and offered it as a whole *burnt offering* to the Lord
1Sam 7:10 Now as Samuel was offering up the *burnt offering*, the Philistines drew near to battle against Israel
1Sam 13:9 So Saul said, "Bring a *burnt offering* and peace offerings here to me." And he offered the *burnt offering*
1Sam 13:10 Now it happened, as soon as he had finished offering the *burnt offering*, that Samuel came
1Sam 13:12 Therefore I felt compelled, and offered a *burnt offering*
2Kin 3:27 Then he took his eldest son who would have reigned in his place, and offered him as a *burnt offering* upon the wall
2Kin 5:17 for your servant will no longer offer either *burnt offering* or sacrifice to other gods, but to the Lord
2Kin 10:25 Now it was so, as soon as he had made an end of offering the *burnt offering*, that Jehu said to the guard and to the captains
2Kin 16:13 So he burned his *burnt offering* and his grain offering
2Kin 16:15 Then King Ahaz commanded Urijah the priest, saying, "On the great new altar burn the morning *burnt offering*, the evening grain offering, the king's burnt sacrifice, and his grain offering, with the *burnt offering* of all the people of the land, their grain offering, and their drink offerings; and sprinkle on it all the blood of the *burnt offering* and all the blood of the sacrifice
1Chr 6:49 But Aaron and his sons offered sacrifices on the altar of *burnt offering* and on the altar of incense, for all the work of the Most Holy Place, and to make atonement for Israel, according to all that Moses the servant of God had commanded
1Chr 16:40 to offer burnt offerings to the Lord on the altar of *burnt offering* regularly morning and evening, and to do according to all that is written in the Law of the Lord which He commanded Israel
1Chr 21:26 and He answered him from heaven by fire on the altar of *burnt offering*
1Chr 21:29 For the tabernacle of the Lord and the altar of the *burnt offering*, which Moses had made in the wilderness, were at that time at the high place in Gibeon
1Chr 22:1 Then David said, "This is the house of the Lord God, and this is the altar of *burnt offering* for Israel
1Chr 23:31 and at every presentation of a *burnt offering* to the Lord on the Sabbaths and on the New Moons and on the set feasts, by number according to the ordinance governing them, regularly before the Lord
2Chr 4:6 such things as they offered for the *burnt offering* they would wash in them, but the Sea was for the priests to wash in
2Chr 7:1 Now when Solomon had finished praying, fire came down from heaven and consumed the *burnt offering* and the sacrifices
2Chr 29:24 and they presented their blood on the altar as a sin offering to make an atonement for all Israel, for the king commanded that the *burnt offering* and the sin offering be made for all Israel
2Chr 29:27 Then Hezekiah commanded them to offer the *burnt offering* on the altar. And when the *burnt offering* began, the song of the Lord also began, with the trumpets and with the instruments of David king of Israel
2Chr 29:28 So all the congregation worshiped, the singers sang, and the trumpeters sounded; all this continued until the *burnt offering* was finished
2Chr 29:32 all these were for a *burnt offering* to the Lord
2Chr 29:35 Also the burnt offerings were in abundance, with the fat of the peace offerings and with the drink offerings for every *burnt offering*
Ezra 3:5 and afterward they offered the regular *burnt offering*, and those for New Moons and for all the appointed feasts of the Lord that were consecrated, and those of everyone who willingly offered a freewill offering to the Lord
Ezra 8:35 twelve bulls for all Israel, ninety-six rams, seventy-seven lambs, and twelve male goats as a sin offering. All this was a *burnt offering* to the Lord
Neh 10:33 for the showbread, for the regular grain offering, for the regular *burnt offering* of the Sabbaths, the New Moons, and the set feasts
Job 42:8 Now therefore, take for yourselves seven bulls and seven rams, go to My servant Job, and offer up for yourselves a *burnt offering*
Ps 40:6 My ears You have opened; *burnt offering* and sin offering You did not require
Ps 51:16 For You do not desire sacrifice, or else I would give it; You do not delight in *burnt offering*
Ps 51:19 Then You shall be pleased with the sacrifices of righteousness, with *burnt offering* and whole *burnt offering*
Is 40:16 And Lebanon is not sufficient to burn, nor its beasts sufficient for a *burnt offering*
Is 61:8 I hate robbery for *burnt offering;* I will direct their work in truth, and will make with them an everlasting covenant
Jer 14:12 and when they offer *burnt offering* and grain offering, I will not accept them
Ezek 40:38 There was a chamber and its entrance by the gateposts of the gateway, where they washed the *burnt offering*
Ezek 40:39 In the vestibule of the gateway were two tables on this side and two tables on that side, on which to slay the *burnt offering*, the sin offering, and the trespass offering
Ezek 40:42 There were also four tables of hewn stone for the *burnt offering*, one cubit and a half long, one cubit and a half wide, and one cubit high; on these they laid the instruments with which they slaughtered the *burnt offering* and the sacrifice
Ezek 43:24 When you offer them before the Lord,

the priests shall throw salt on them, and they will offer them up as a *burnt offering* to the Lord
Ezek 44:11 they shall slay the *burnt offering* and the sacrifice for the people, and they shall stand before them to minister to them
Ezek 45:17 He shall prepare the sin offering, the grain offering, the *burnt offering*, and the peace offerings to make atonement for the house of Israel
Ezek 45:23 On the seven days of the feast he shall prepare a *burnt offering* to the Lord, seven bulls and seven rams without blemish, daily for seven days, and a kid of the goats daily for a sin offering
Ezek 45:25 In the seventh month, on the fifteenth day of the month, at the feast, he shall do likewise for seven days, according to the sin offering, the *burnt offering*, the grain offering, and the oil
Ezek 46:2 The priests shall prepare his *burnt offering* and his peace offerings
Ezek 46:4 The *burnt offering* that the prince offers to the Lord on the Sabbath day shall be six lambs without blemish, and a ram without blemish
Ezek 46:12 Now when the prince makes a voluntary *burnt offering* or voluntary peace offering to the Lord, the gate that faces toward the east shall then be opened for him; and he shall prepare his *burnt offering* and his peace offerings as he did on the Sabbath day
Ezek 46:13 You shall daily make a *burnt offering* to the Lord of a lamb of the first year without blemish
Ezek 46:15 Thus they shall prepare the lamb, the grain offering, and the oil, as a regular *burnt offering* every morning

BURNT OFFERINGS
Gen 8:20 Then Noah built an altar to the Lord, and took of every clean animal and of every clean bird, and offered *burnt offerings* on the altar
Ex 10:25 But Moses said, "You must also give us sacrifices and *burnt offerings*, that we may sacrifice to the Lord our God
Ex 20:24 An altar of earth you shall make for Me, and you shall sacrifice on it your *burnt offerings* and your peace offerings, your sheep and your oxen
Ex 24:5 Then he sent young men of the children of Israel, who offered *burnt offerings* and sacrificed peace offerings of oxen to the Lord
Ex 32:6 Then they rose early on the next day, offered *burnt offerings*, and brought peace offerings
Num 10:10 Also in the day of your gladness, in your appointed feasts, and at the beginning of your months, you shall blow the trumpets over your *burnt offerings* and over the sacrifices of your peace offerings
Num 29:39 as your *burnt offerings* and your grain offerings, as your drink offerings and your peace offerings
Deut 12:6 There you shall take your *burnt offerings*, your sacrifices, your tithes, the heave offerings of your hand, your vowed offerings, your freewill offerings, and the firstlings of your herds and flocks
Deut 12:11 your *burnt offerings*, your sacrifices, your tithes, the heave offerings of your hand, and all your choice offerings which you vow to the Lord
Deut 12:13 Take heed to yourself that you do not offer your *burnt offerings* in every place that you see
Deut 12:14 but in the place which the Lord chooses, in one of your tribes, there you shall offer your *burnt offerings*, and there you shall do all that I command you
Deut 12:27 And you shall offer your *burnt offerings*, the meat and the blood, on the altar of the Lord your God
Deut 27:6 You shall build with whole stones the altar of the Lord your God, and offer *burnt offerings* on it to the Lord your God
Josh 8:31 And they offered on it *burnt offerings* to the Lord, and sacrificed peace offerings
Josh 22:23 If we have built ourselves an altar to turn from following the Lord, or if to offer on it *burnt offerings* or grain offerings, or if to offer peace offerings on it, let the Lord Himself require an account
Josh 22:27 but that it may be a witness between you and us and our generations after us, that we may perform the service of the Lord before Him with our *burnt offerings*, with our sacrifices, and with our peace offerings
Josh 22:28 Therefore we said that it will be, when they say this to us or to our generations in time to come, that we may say, 'Here is the replica of the altar of the Lord which our fathers made, though not for *burnt offerings* nor for sacrifices
Josh 22:29 Far be it from us that we should rebel against the Lord, and turn from following the Lord this day, to build an altar for *burnt offerings*, for grain offerings, or for sacrifices, besides the altar of the Lord our God which is before His tabernacle
Judg 20:26 and they offered *burnt offerings* and peace offerings before the Lord
Judg 21:4 So it was, on the next morning, that the people rose early and built an altar there, and offered *burnt offerings* and peace offerings
1Sam 6:15 Then the men of Beth Shemesh offered *burnt offerings* and made sacrifices the same day to the Lord
1Sam 10:8 and surely I will come down to you to offer *burnt offerings* and make sacrifices of peace offerings
1Sam 15:22 Has the Lord as great delight in *burnt offerings* and sacrifices, as in obeying the voice of the Lord
2Sam 6:17 Then David offered *burnt offerings* and peace offerings before the Lord
2Sam 6:18 And when David had finished offering *burnt offerings* and peace offerings, he blessed the people in the name of the Lord of hosts
2Sam 24:24 nor will I offer *burnt offerings* to the Lord my God with that which costs me nothing
2Sam 24:25 And David built there an altar to the Lord, and offered *burnt offerings* and peace offerings
1Kin 3:4 Now the king went to Gibeon to sacrifice there, for that was the great high place: Solomon offered a thousand *burnt offerings* on that altar
1Kin 3:15 And he came to Jerusalem and stood before the ark of the covenant of the Lord, offered up *burnt offerings*, offered peace offerings, and made a feast for all his servants
1Kin 8:64 for there he offered *burnt offerings*, grain offerings, and the fat of the peace offerings, because the bronze altar that was before the Lord was too small to receive the *burnt offerings*, the grain offerings, and the fat of the peace offerings
1Kin 9:25 Now three times a year Solomon offered *burnt offerings* and peace offerings on the altar which he had built for the Lord, and he burned incense with them on the altar that was before the Lord
2Kin 10:24 So they went in to offer sacrifices and *burnt offerings*
1Chr 16:1 Then they offered *burnt offerings* and peace offerings before God
1Chr 16:2 And when David had finished offering the *burnt offerings* and the peace offerings, he blessed the people in the name of the Lord
1Chr 16:40 to offer *burnt offerings* to the Lord on the altar of burnt offering regularly morning and

evening, and to do according to all that is written in the Law of the Lord which He commanded Israel

1Chr 21:23 Look, I also give you the oxen for *burnt offerings*, the threshing implements for wood, and the wheat for the grain offering

1Chr 21:24 Then King David said to Ornan, "No, but I will surely buy it for the full price, for I will not take what is yours for the Lord, nor offer *burnt offerings* with that which costs me nothing

1Chr 21:26 And David built there an altar to the Lord, and offered *burnt offerings* and peace offerings, and called on the Lord

1Chr 29:21 And they made sacrifices to the Lord and offered *burnt offerings* to the Lord on the next day

2Chr 1:6 And Solomon went up there to the bronze altar before the Lord, which was at the tabernacle of meeting, and offered a thousand *burnt offerings* on it

2Chr 2:4 Behold, I am building a temple for the name of the Lord my God, to dedicate it to Him, to burn before Him sweet incense, for the continual showbread, for the *burnt offerings* morning and evening, on the Sabbaths, on the New Moons, and on the set feasts of the Lord our God

2Chr 7:7 for there he offered *burnt offerings* and the fat of the peace offerings, because the bronze altar which Solomon had made was not able to receive the *burnt offerings*, the grain offerings, and the fat

2Chr 8:12 Then Solomon offered *burnt offerings* to the Lord on the altar of the Lord which he had built before the vestibule

2Chr 23:18 Also Jehoiada appointed the oversight of the house of the Lord to the hand of the priests, the Levites, whom David had assigned in the house of the Lord, to offer the *burnt offerings* of the Lord, as it is written in the Law of Moses, with rejoicing and with singing, as it was established by David

2Chr 24:14 And they offered *burnt offerings* in the house of the Lord continually all the days of Jehoiada

2Chr 29:7 They have also shut up the doors of the vestibule, put out the lamps, and have not burned incense or offered *burnt offerings* in the holy place to the God of Israel

2Chr 29:18 Then they went in to King Hezekiah and said, "We have cleansed all the house of the Lord, the altar of *burnt offerings* with all its articles, and the table of the showbread with all its articles

2Chr 29:31 So the congregation brought in sacrifices and thank offerings, and as many as were of a willing heart brought *burnt offerings*

2Chr 29:32 And the number of the *burnt offerings* which the congregation brought was seventy bulls, one hundred rams, and two hundred lambs

2Chr 29:34 But the priests were too few, so that they could not skin all the *burnt offerings*

2Chr 29:35 Also the *burnt offerings* were in abundance, with the fat of the peace offerings and with the drink offerings for every burnt offering

2Chr 30:15 The priests and the Levites were ashamed, and sanctified themselves, and brought the *burnt offerings* to the house of the Lord

2Chr 31:2 And Hezekiah appointed the divisions of the priests and the Levites according to their divisions, each man according to his service, the priests and Levites for *burnt offerings* and peace offerings, to serve, to give thanks, and to praise in the gates of the camp of the Lord

2Chr 31:3 The king also appointed a portion of his possessions for the *burnt offerings:* for the morning and evening *burnt offerings*, the *burnt offerings* for the Sabbaths and the New Moons and the set feasts, as it is written in the Law of the Lord

2Chr 35:12 Then they removed the *burnt offerings* that they might give them to the divisions of the fathers' houses of the lay people, to offer to the Lord, as it is written in the Book of Moses

2Chr 35:14 Then afterward they prepared portions for themselves and for the priests, because the priests, the sons of Aaron, were busy in offering *burnt offerings* and fat until night

2Chr 35:16 So all the service of the Lord was prepared the same day, to keep the Passover and to offer *burnt offerings* on the altar of the Lord, according to the command of King Josiah

Ezra 3:2 Then Jeshua the son of Jozadak and his brethren the priests, and Zerubbabel the son of Shealtiel and his brethren, arose and built the altar of the God of Israel, to offer *burnt offerings* on it, as it is written in the Law of Moses the man of God

Ezra 3:3 and they offered *burnt offerings* on it to the Lord, both the morning and evening *burnt offerings*

Ezra 3:4 They also kept the Feast of Tabernacles, as it is written, and offered the daily *burnt offerings* in the number required by ordinance for each day

Ezra 3:6 From the first day of the seventh month they began to offer *burnt offerings* to the Lord

Ezra 6:9 And whatever they need young bulls, rams, and lambs for the *burnt offerings* of the God of heaven, wheat, salt, wine, and oil, according to the request of the priests who are in Jerusalem let it be given them day by day without fail

Ezra 8:35 The children of those who had been carried away captive, who had come from the captivity, offered *burnt offerings* to the God of Israel

Job 1:5 So it was, when the days of feasting had run their course, that Job would send and sanctify them, and he would rise early in the morning and offer *burnt offerings* according to the number of them all

Ps 50:8 I will not reprove you for your sacrifices or your *burnt offerings*, which are continually before Me

Ps 66:13 I will go into Your house with *burnt offerings;* I will pay You my vows

Is 1:11 I have had enough of *burnt offerings* of rams and the fat of fed cattle

Is 43:23 You have not brought Me the sheep for your *burnt offerings*, nor have you honored Me with your sacrifices

Is 56:7 Their *burnt offerings* and their sacrifices will be accepted on My altar

Jer 6:20 Your *burnt offerings* are not acceptable, nor your sacrifices sweet to Me

Jer 7:21 Add your *burnt offerings* to your sacrifices and eat meat

Jer 7:22 For I did not speak to your fathers, or command them in the day that I brought them out of the land of Egypt, concerning *burnt offerings* or sacrifices

Jer 17:26 And they shall come from the cities of Judah and from the places around Jerusalem, from the land of Benjamin and from the lowland, from the mountains and from the South, bringing *burnt offerings* and sacrifices, grain offerings and incense, bringing sacrifices of praise to the house of the Lord

Jer 19:5 (they have also built the high places of Baal, to burn their sons with fire for *burnt offerings* to Baal, which I did not command or speak, nor did it come into My mind

Jer 33:18 nor shall the priests, the Levites, lack a man to offer *burnt offerings* before Me, to kindle grain offerings, and to sacrifice continually

Ezek 43:18 These are the ordinances for the altar

on the day when it is made, for sacrificing *burnt offerings* on it, and for sprinkling blood on it

Ezek 43:27 When these days are over it shall be, on the eighth day and thereafter, that the priests shall offer your *burnt offerings* and your peace offerings on the altar

Ezek 45:15 These shall be for grain offerings, *burnt offerings*, and peace offerings, to make atonement for them

Ezek 45:17 Then it shall be the prince's part to give *burnt offerings*, grain offerings, and drink offerings, at the feasts, the New Moons, the Sabbaths, and at all the appointed seasons of the house of Israel

Hos 6:6 For I desire mercy and not sacrifice, and the knowledge of God more than *burnt offerings*

Amos 5:22 Though you offer Me *burnt offerings* and your grain offerings, I will not accept them, nor will I regard your fattened peace offerings

Mic 6:6 Shall I come before Him with *burnt offerings*, with calves a year old

Mark 12:33 And to love Him with all the heart, with all the understanding, with all the soul, and with all the strength, and to love one's neighbor as oneself, is more than all the whole *burnt offerings* and sacrifices

Heb 10:6 In *burnt offerings* and sacrifices for sin you had no pleasure

Heb 10:8 Previously saying, "Sacrifice and offering, *burnt offerings*, and offerings for sin You did not desire, nor had pleasure in them

BURNT SACRIFICE

Lev 1:3 If his offering is a *burnt sacrifice* of the herd, let him offer a male without blemish

Lev 1:9 And the priest shall burn all on the altar as a *burnt sacrifice*, an offering made by fire, a sweet aroma to the Lord

Lev 1:10 And if his offering is of the flocks of the sheep or of the goats as a *burnt sacrifice*, he shall bring a male without blemish

Lev 1:13 it is a *burnt sacrifice*, an offering made by fire, a sweet aroma to the Lord

Lev 1:14 And if the *burnt sacrifice* of his offering to the Lord is of birds, then he shall bring his offering of turtledoves or young pigeons

Lev 1:17 It is a *burnt sacrifice*, an offering made by fire, a sweet aroma to the Lord

Lev 3:5 and Aaron's sons shall burn it on the altar upon the *burnt sacrifice*, which is on the wood that is on the fire, as an offering made by fire, a sweet aroma to the Lord

Lev 8:21 It was a *burnt sacrifice* for a sweet aroma, and an offering made by fire to the Lord, as the Lord had commanded Moses

Lev 9:17 Then he brought the grain offering, took a handful of it, and burned it on the altar, besides the *burnt sacrifice* of the morning

Deut 33:10 They shall put incense before You, and a whole *burnt sacrifice* on Your altar

Judg 6:26 and build an altar to the Lord your God on top of this rock in the proper arrangement, and take the second bull and offer a *burnt sacrifice* with the wood of the image which you shall cut down

2Sam 24:22 Look, here are oxen for *burnt sacrifice*, and threshing implements and the yokes of the oxen for wood

1Kin 18:33 And he put the wood in order, cut the bull in pieces, and laid it on the wood, and said, "Fill four waterpots with water, and pour it on the *burnt sacrifice* and on the wood

1Kin 18:38 Then the fire of the Lord fell and consumed the *burnt sacrifice*, and the wood and the stones and the dust, and it licked up the water that was in the trench

2Kin 16:15 Then King Ahaz commanded Urijah the priest, saying, "On the great new altar burn the morning burnt offering, the evening grain offering, the king's *burnt sacrifice*, and his grain offering, with the burnt offering of all the people of the land, their grain offering, and their drink offerings

Ps 20:3 May He remember all your offerings, and accept your *burnt sacrifice*

BURST THE WINESKINS

Luke 5:37 or else the new wine will *burst the wineskins* and be spilled, and the wineskins will be ruined

BURSTS THE WINESKINS

Mark 2:22 or else the new wine *bursts the wineskins*, the wine is spilled, and the wineskins are ruined

BURYING PLACE OF MANOAH HIS FATHER (KJV)

(See *TOMB OF HIS FATHER*)

BUSH WAS BURNING WITH FIRE

Ex 3:2 So he looked, and behold, the *bush was burning with fire*, but the bush was not consumed

BUT I SAY TO YOU

Matt 5:22 *But I say to you* that whoever is angry with his brother without a cause shall be in danger of the judgment

Matt 5:28 *But I say to you* that whoever looks at a woman to lust for her has already committed adultery with her in his heart

Matt 5:32 *But I say to you* that whoever divorces his wife for any reason except sexual immorality causes her to commit adultery

Matt 5:34 *But I say to you*, do not swear at all

Matt 5:44 *But I say to you*, love your enemies, bless those who curse you, do good to those who hate you, and pray for those who spitefully use you and persecute you

Matt 11:22 *But I say to you*, it will be more tolerable for Tyre and Sidon in the day of judgment than for you

Matt 11:24 *But I say to you* that it shall be more tolerable for the land of Sodom in the day of judgment than for you

Matt 12:6 *But I say to you* that in this place there is One greater than the temple

Matt 12:36 *But I say to you* that for every idle word men may speak, they will give account of it in the day of judgment

Matt 17:12 *But I say to you* that Elijah has come already, and they did not know him but did to him whatever they wished

Matt 26:29 *But I say to you*, I will not drink of this fruit of the vine from now on until that day when I drink it new with you in My Father's kingdom

Mark 9:13 *But I say to you* that Elijah has also come, and they did to him whatever they wished, as it is written of him

Luke 6:27 *But I say to you* who hear: Love your enemies, do good to those who hate you

Luke 10:12 *But I say to you* that it will be more tolerable in that Day for Sodom than for that city

BUY THE TRUTH

Prov 23:23 *Buy the truth*, and do not sell it, also wisdom and instruction and understanding

BY A PARABLE

Luke 8:4 And when a great multitude had gathered, and others had come to Him from every city, He spoke *by a parable*

BY BREAD ALONE

Deut 8:3 So He humbled you, allowed you to hunger, and fed you with manna which you did not know nor did your fathers know, that He might make you know that man shall not live *by bread alone*

Matt 4:4 But He answered and said, "It is written, 'Man shall not live *by bread alone*, but by every word that proceeds from the mouth of God

Luke 4:4 But Jesus answered him, saying, "It is written, 'Man shall not live *by bread alone*, but by every word of God

BY FAITH

Acts 15:9 and made no distinction between us and them, purifying their hearts *by faith*

Acts 26:18 to open their eyes and to turn them from darkness to light, and from the power of Satan to God, that they may receive forgiveness of sins and an inheritance among those who are sanctified *by faith* in Me

Rom 1:17 as it is written, "The just shall live *by faith*

Rom 3:28 Therefore we conclude that a man is justified *by faith* apart from the deeds of the law

Rom 3:30 since there is one God who will justify the circumcised *by faith* and the uncircumcised through faith

Rom 5:1 Therefore, having been justified *by faith*, we have peace with God through our Lord Jesus Christ

Rom 5:2 through whom also we have access *by faith* into this grace in which we stand, and rejoice in hope of the glory of God

Rom 9:32 Because they did not seek it *by faith*, but as it were, by the works of the law

Rom 11:20 Because of unbelief they were broken off, and you stand *by faith*

2Cor 1:24 Not that we have dominion over your faith, but are fellow workers for your joy; for *by faith* you stand

2Cor 5:7 For we walk *by faith*, not by sight

Gal 2:16 knowing that a man is not justified by the works of the law but *by faith* in Jesus Christ, even we have believed in Christ Jesus, that we might be justified *by faith* in Christ and not by the works of the law

Gal 2:20 and the life which I now live in the flesh I live *by faith* in the Son of God, who loved me and gave Himself for me

Gal 3:8 And the Scripture, foreseeing that God would justify the nations *by faith*, preached the gospel to Abraham beforehand, saying

Gal 3:11 But that no one is justified by the law in the sight of God is evident, for "The just shall live *by faith*

Gal 3:22 But the Scripture has confined all under sin, that the promise *by faith* in Jesus Christ might be given to those who believe

Gal 3:24 Therefore the law was our tutor to bring us to Christ, that we might be justified *by faith*

Gal 5:5 For we through the Spirit eagerly wait for the hope of righteousness *by faith*

Phil 3:9 and be found in Him, not having my own righteousness, which is from the law, but that which is through faith in Christ, the righteousness which is from God *by faith*

Heb 10:38 Now the just shall live *by faith;* but if anyone draws back, my soul has no pleasure in him

Heb 11:3 *By faith* we understand that the worlds were framed by the word of God, so that the things which are seen were not made of things which are visible

Heb 11:4 *By faith* Abel offered to God a more excellent sacrifice than Cain, through which he obtained witness that he was righteous, God testifying of his gifts

Heb 11:5 *By faith* Enoch was translated so that he did not see death

Heb 11:7 *By faith* Noah, being divinely warned of things not yet seen, moved with godly fear, prepared an ark for the saving of his household, by which he condemned the world and became heir of the righteousness which is according to faith

Heb 11:8 *By faith* Abraham obeyed when he was called to go out to the place which he would afterward receive as an inheritance

Heb 11:9 *By faith* he sojourned in the land of promise as in a foreign country, dwelling in tents with Isaac and Jacob, the heirs with him of the same promise

Heb 11:11 *By faith* Sarah herself also received strength to conceive seed, and she bore a child when she was past the age, because she judged Him faithful who had promised

Heb 11:17 *By faith* Abraham, when he was tested, offered up Isaac, and he who had received the promises offered up his only begotten son

Heb 11:20 *By faith* Isaac blessed Jacob and Esau concerning things to come

Heb 11:21 *By faith* Jacob, when he was dying, blessed each of the sons of Joseph, and worshiped, leaning on the top of his staff

Heb 11:22 *By faith* Joseph, when he was dying, made mention of the departure of the children of Israel, and gave instructions concerning his bones

Heb 11:23 *By faith* Moses, when he was born, was hidden three months by his parents, because they saw he was a beautiful child

Heb 11:24 *By faith* Moses, when he became of age, refused to be called the son of Pharaoh's daughter

Heb 11:27 *By faith* he forsook Egypt, not fearing the wrath of the king

Heb 11:28 *By faith* he kept the Passover and the sprinkling of blood, lest he who destroyed the firstborn should touch them

Heb 11:29 *By faith* they passed through the Red Sea as by dry land, whereas the Egyptians, attempting to do so, were drowned

Heb 11:30 *By faith* the walls of Jericho fell down after they were encircled for seven days

Heb 11:31 *By faith* the harlot Rahab did not perish with those who did not believe, when she had received the spies with peace

Jas 2:24 You see then that a man is justified by works, and not *by faith* only

BY GRACE

Rom 11:6 And if *by grace*, then it is no longer of works

Eph 2:5 even when we were dead in trespasses, made us alive together with Christ (*by grace* you have been saved

Eph 2:8 For *by grace* you have been saved through faith, and that not of yourselves

2Th 2:16 Now may our Lord Jesus Christ Himself, and our God and Father, who has loved us and given us everlasting consolation and good hope *by grace*

Heb 13:9 For it is good that the heart be established *by grace*, not with foods which have not profited those who have been occupied with them

BY HIM ALL THINGS WERE CREATED (NAS)
(See *CREATED THROUGH HIM*)

BY HIS BLOOD

Rom 3:25 whom God set forth to be a propitiation *by His blood*, through faith, to demonstrate His righteousness, because in His forbearance God had passed over the sins that were previously committed

Rom 5:9 Much more then, having now been justified *by His blood*, we shall be saved from wrath through Him

BY HIS STRIPES WE ARE HEALED
Is 53:5 the chastisement for our peace was upon Him, and *by His stripes we are healed*

BY HUMAN STANDARDS (NIV)
(See *ACCORDING TO THE FLESH*)

BY MY SPIRIT
Is 26:9 With my soul I have desired You in the night, yes, *by my spirit* within me I will seek You early
Zech 4:6 Not by might nor by power, but *by My Spirit*

BY NO MEANS (NIV, RSV)
(See *CERTAINLY NOT*)

BY RESURRECTION (NAS, RSV)
(See *RAISED TO LIFE*)

BY THE MOUTH OF BABES (RSV)
(See *OUT OF THE MOUTH OF BABES*)

BY THE ONE MAN'S OFFENSE
Rom 5:15 For if *by the one man's offense* many died, much more the grace of God and the gift by the grace of the one Man, Jesus Christ, abounded to many
Rom 5:17 For if *by the one man's offense* death reigned through the one, much more those who receive abundance of grace and of the gift of righteousness will reign in life through the One, Jesus Christ

BY THE POWER OF GOD
2Cor 6:7 by the word of truth, *by the power of God*, by the armor of righteousness on the right hand and on the left
2Cor 13:4 For though He was crucified in weakness, yet He lives *by the power of God*. For we also are weak in Him, but we shall live with Him *by the power of God* toward you
1Pet 1:5 who are kept *by the power of God* through faith for salvation ready to be revealed in the last time

BY THE PROPHETS
1Sam 28:6 And when Saul inquired of the Lord, the Lord did not answer him, either by dreams or by Urim or *by the prophets*
Hos 6:5 Therefore I have hewn them *by the prophets*, I have slain them by the words of My mouth
Hos 12:10 I have also spoken *by the prophets*, and have multiplied visions
Matt 2:23 And he came and dwelt in a city called Nazareth, that it might be fulfilled which was spoken *by the prophets*
Luke 18:31 Then He took the twelve aside and said to them, "Behold, we are going up to Jerusalem, and all things that are written *by the prophets* concerning the Son of Man will be accomplished
Heb 1:1 God, who at various times and in different ways spoke in time past to the fathers *by the prophets*

BY THE RIGHT WAY (RSV)
(See *WAY OF TRUTH*)

BY THE SPIRIT (NAS, NIV, RSV)
(See *IN THE SPIRIT*)

BY THE SWORD
Lev 26:7 You will chase your enemies, and they shall fall *by the sword* before you
Lev 26:8 Five of you shall chase a hundred, and a hundred of you shall put ten thousand to flight; your enemies shall fall *by the sword* before you
Num 14:3 Why has the Lord brought us to this land to fall *by the sword*, that our wives and children should become victims
Num 14:43 For the Amalekites and the Canaanites are there before you, and you shall fall *by the sword*
2Sam 1:12 And they mourned and wept and fasted until evening for Saul and for Jonathan his son, for the people of the Lord and for the house of Israel, because they had fallen *by the sword*
2Sam 3:29 and let there never fail to be in the house of Joab one who has a discharge or is a leper, who leans on a staff or falls *by the sword*, or who lacks bread
2Kin 19:7 and I will cause him to fall *by the sword* in his own land
2Chr 29:9 For indeed, because of this our fathers have fallen *by the sword*
Job 33:18 He keeps back his soul from the Pit, and his life from perishing *by the sword*
Job 36:12 But if they do not obey, they shall perish *by the sword*, and they shall die without knowledge
Ps 63:10 They shall fall *by the sword;* they shall be a portion for jackals
Ps 78:64 Their priests fell *by the sword*, and their widows made no lamentation
Is 1:20 but if you refuse and rebel, you shall be devoured *by the sword*
Is 3:25 Your men shall fall *by the sword*, and your mighty in the war
Is 13:15 Everyone who is found will be thrust through, and everyone who is captured will fall *by the sword*
Is 37:7 and I will cause him to fall *by the sword* in his own land
Jer 11:22 The young men shall die *by the sword*, their sons and their daughters shall die by famine
Jer 14:12 But I will consume them *by the sword*, by the famine, and by the pestilence
Jer 16:4 They shall be consumed *by the sword* and by famine, and their corpses shall be meat for the birds of heaven and for the beasts of the earth
Jer 18:21 Let their men be put to death, their young men be slain *by the sword* in battle
Jer 19:7 And I will make void the counsel of Judah and Jerusalem in this place, and I will cause them to fall *by the sword* before their enemies and by the hands of those who seek their lives
Jer 20:4 and they shall fall *by the sword* of their enemies, and your eyes shall see it
Jer 21:9 He who remains in this city shall die *by the sword*, by famine, and by pestilence
Jer 27:13 Why will you die, you and your people, *by the sword*, by the famine, and by the pestilence, as the Lord has spoken against the nation that will not serve the king of Babylon
Jer 32:36 Now therefore, thus says the Lord, the God of Israel, concerning this city of which you say, 'It shall be delivered into the hand of the king of Babylon *by the sword*, by the famine, and by the pestilence
Jer 34:4 Thus says the Lord concerning you: "You shall not die *by the sword*
Jer 38:2 He who remains in this city shall die *by the sword*, by famine, and by pestilence
Jer 39:18 For I will surely deliver you, and you shall not fall *by the sword*
Jer 42:17 They shall die *by the sword*, by famine, and by pestilence
Jer 42:22 Now therefore, know certainly that you shall die *by the sword*, by famine, and by pestilence in the place where you desire to go to sojourn
Jer 44:12 They shall be consumed *by the sword*

and by famine. They shall die, from the least to the greatest, *by the sword* and by famine
Jer 44:13 For I will punish those who dwell in the land of Egypt, as I have punished Jerusalem, *by the sword*, by famine, and by pestilence
Jer 44:18 But since we stopped burning incense to the queen of heaven and pouring out drink offerings to her, we have lacked everything and have been consumed *by the sword* and by famine
Jer 44:27 And all the men of Judah who are in the land of Egypt shall be consumed *by the sword* and by famine, until there is an end to them
Lam 2:21 my virgins and my young men have fallen *by the sword*
Lam 4:9 Those slain *by the sword* are better off than those who die of hunger
Ezek 5:12 and one-third shall fall *by the sword* all around you
Ezek 6:11 For they shall fall *by the sword*, by famine, and by pestilence
Ezek 6:12 He who is far off shall die by the pestilence, he who is near shall fall *by the sword*, and he who remains and is besieged shall die by the famine
Ezek 7:15 Whoever is in the field will die *by the sword*
Ezek 11:10 You shall fall *by the sword*. I will judge you at the border of Israel
Ezek 17:21 All his fugitives with all his troops shall fall *by the sword*, and those who remain shall be scattered to every wind
Ezek 23:25 they shall remove your nose and your ears, and your remnant shall fall *by the sword*
Ezek 24:21 and your sons and daughters whom you left behind shall fall *by the sword*
Ezek 25:13 I will also stretch out My hand against Edom, cut off man and beast from it, and make it desolate from Teman; Dedan shall fall *by the sword*
Ezek 26:6 Also her daughter villages which are in the fields shall be slain *by the sword*
Ezek 26:11 he will slay your people *by the sword*, and your strong pillars will fall to the ground
Ezek 28:23 the wounded shall be judged in her midst *by the sword* against her on every side
Ezek 30:5 Ethiopia, Libya, Lydia, all the mingled people, Chub, and the men of the lands who are allied, shall fall with them *by the sword*
Ezek 30:6 From Migdol to Syene those within her shall fall *by the sword*
Ezek 30:17 The young men of Aven and Pi Beseth shall fall *by the sword*, and these cities shall go into captivity
Ezek 31:17 They also went down to hell with it, with those slain *by the sword*
Ezek 31:18 you shall lie in the midst of the uncircumcised, with those slain *by the sword*
Ezek 32:20 They shall fall in the midst of those slain *by the sword*
Ezek 32:21 They have gone down, they lie with the uncircumcised, slain *by the sword*
Ezek 32:22 Assyria is there, and all her company, with their graves all around her, all of them slain, fallen *by the sword*
Ezek 32:23 Her graves are set in the recesses of the Pit, and her company is all around her grave, all of them slain, fallen *by the sword*, who caused terror in the land of the living
Ezek 32:24 There is Elam and all her multitude, all around her grave, all of them slain, fallen *by the sword*, who have gone down uncircumcised to the lower parts of the earth, who caused their terror in the land of the living
Ezek 32:25 They have set her bed in the midst of the slain, with all her multitude, with her graves all around it, all of them uncircumcised, slain *by the sword*
Ezek 32:26 There are Meshech and Tubal and all their multitudes, with all their graves around it, all of them uncircumcised, slain *by the sword*, though they caused their terror in the land of the living
Ezek 32:28 Yes, you shall be broken in the midst of the uncircumcised, and lie with those slain *by the sword*
Ezek 32:29 There is Edom, her kings and all her princes, who despite their might are laid beside those who were slain *by the sword*
Ezek 32:30 they lie uncircumcised with those slain *by the sword*, and bear their shame with those who go down to the Pit
Ezek 32:31 Pharaoh will see them and be comforted over all his multitude, Pharaoh and all his army, slain *by the sword*
Ezek 32:32 and he shall be placed in the midst of the uncircumcised with those slain *by the sword*, Pharaoh and all his multitude
Ezek 33:27 As I live, surely those who are in the ruins shall fall *by the sword*, and the one who is in the open field I will give to the beasts to be devoured, and those who are in the strongholds and caves shall die of the pestilence
Ezek 35:8 on your hills and in your valleys and in all your ravines those who are slain *by the sword* shall fall
Ezek 39:23 I gave them into the hand of their enemies, and they all fell *by the sword*
Hos 7:16 their princes shall fall *by the sword* for the cursings of their tongue
Hos 13:16 They shall fall *by the sword*, their infants shall be dashed in pieces, and their women with child ripped open
Amos 7:11 Jeroboam shall die *by the sword*, and Israel shall surely be led away captive from their own land
Amos 7:17 your sons and daughters shall fall *by the sword;* your land shall be divided by survey line
Amos 9:10 All the sinners of My people shall die *by the sword*, who say
Hag 2:22 the horses and their riders shall come down, every one *by the sword* of his brother
Matt 26:52 Then Jesus said to him, "Put your sword in its place, for all who take the sword will perish *by the sword*
Rev 13:14 And he deceives those who dwell on the earth by those signs which he was granted to do in the sight of the beast, telling those who dwell on the earth to make an image to the beast who was wounded *by the sword* and lived

BY THE SWORD, BY THE FAMINE, AND BY THE PESTILENCE
Jer 14:12 But I will consume them *by the sword, by the famine, and by the pestilence*
Jer 27:13 Why will you die, you and your people, *by the sword, by the famine, and by the pestilence*, as the Lord has spoken against the nation that will not serve the king of Babylon
Jer 32:36 Now therefore, thus says the Lord, the God of Israel, concerning this city of which you say, 'It shall be delivered into the hand of the king of Babylon *by the sword, by the famine, and by the pestilence*

BY THE WILL OF GOD
Acts 13:36 For David, after he had served his own generation *by the will of God*, fell asleep, was buried with his fathers, and saw corruption
Rom 15:32 that I may come to you with joy *by the will of God*, and may be refreshed together with you
2Cor 1:1 Paul, an apostle of Jesus Christ *by the will of God*, and Timothy our brother, To the church of God which is at Corinth, with all the saints who are in all Achaia

2Cor 8:5 And this they did, not as we had hoped, but first gave themselves to the Lord, and then to us *by the will of God*
Eph 1:1 Paul, an apostle of Jesus Christ *by the will of God*, To the saints who are in Ephesus, and faithful in Christ Jesus
Col 1:1 Paul, an apostle of Jesus Christ *by the will of God*, and Timothy our brother
2Tim 1:1 Paul, an apostle of Jesus Christ *by the will of God*, according to the promise of life which is in Christ Jesus

BY WATER AND BLOOD
1Jn 5:6 This is He who came *by water and blood* Jesus Christ; not only by water, but *by water and blood*

BY WHAT AUTHORITY
Matt 21:23 Now when He came into the temple, the chief priests and the elders of the people confronted Him as He was teaching, and said, "*By what authority* are You doing these things
Matt 21:24 But Jesus answered and said to them, "I also will ask you one thing, which if you tell Me, I likewise will tell you *by what authority* I do these things
Matt 21:27 And He said to them, "Neither will I tell you *by what authority* I do these things
Mark 11:28 And they said to Him, "*By what authority* are You doing these things
Mark 11:29 then answer Me, and I will tell you *by what authority* I do these things
Mark 11:33 And Jesus answered and said to them, "Neither will I tell you *by what authority* I do these things
Luke 20:2 and spoke to Him, saying, "Tell us, *by what authority* are You doing these things
Luke 20:8 And Jesus said to them, "Neither will I tell you *by what authority* I do these things

BY YOUR DESCENDANTS (RSV)
(See *IN YOUR SEED*)

BY YOUR TRADITION (KJV)
(See *BECAUSE OF YOUR TRADITION*)

BYWORD AMONG ALL NATIONS
Deut 28:37 And you shall become an astonishment, a proverb, and a *byword among all nations* where the Lord will lead you
2Chr 7:20 and this house which I have sanctified for My name I will cast out of My sight, and will make it to be a proverb and a *byword among all nations*

C

CALL A SACRED ASSEMBLY
Joel 1:14 Consecrate a fast, *call a sacred assembly;* gather the elders and all the inhabitants of the land into the house of the Lord your God, and cry out to the Lord
Joel 2:15 Blow the trumpet in Zion, consecrate a fast, *call a sacred assembly*

CALL AN ASSEMBLY (NIV)
(See *PROCLAIM A SOLEMN ASSEMBLY*)

CALL OF GOD (RSV)
(See *CALLING OF GOD*)

CALL ON THE LORD
Ps 14:4 Have all the workers of iniquity no knowledge, who eat up my people as they eat bread, and do not *call on the Lord*
2Tim 2:22 but pursue righteousness, faith, love, peace with those who *call on the Lord* out of a pure heart

CALL ON THE NAME OF THE LORD
Gen 4:26 Then men began to *call on the name of the Lord*
1Kin 18:24 Then you call on the name of your gods, and I will *call on the name of the Lord*
2Kin 5:11 But Naaman became furious, and went away and said, "Indeed, I said to myself, 'He will surely come out to me, and stand and *call on the name of the Lord* his God, and wave his hand over the place, and heal the leprosy
Zeph 3:9 For then I will restore to the peoples a pure language, that they all may *call on the name of the Lord*, to serve Him with one accord

CALL UPON HIS NAME
1Chr 16:8 *Call upon His name;* make known His deeds among the peoples
Ps 105:1 *Call upon His name;* make known His deeds among the peoples
Is 12:4 Praise the Lord, *call upon His name;* declare His deeds among the peoples, make mention that His name is exalted

CALLED BY GOD
Heb 5:4 And no man takes this honor to himself, but he who is *called by God*, just as Aaron was
Heb 5:10 *called by God* as High Priest "according to the order of Melchizedek

CALLED BY MY NAME
2Chr 7:14 if My people who are *called by My name* will humble themselves, and pray and seek My face, and turn from their wicked ways, then I will hear from heaven, and will forgive their sin and heal their land
Is 43:7 everyone who is *called by My name*, whom I have created for My glory
Is 65:1 I said, 'Here I am, here I am,' to a nation that was not *called by My name*
Jer 7:10 and then come and stand before Me in this house which is *called by My name*, and say
Jer 7:11 Has this house, which is *called by My name*, become a den of thieves in your eyes
Jer 7:14 therefore I will do to this house which is *called by My name*, in which you trust, and to this place which I gave to you and your fathers, as I have done to Shiloh
Jer 7:30 They have set their abominations in the house which is *called by My name*, to pollute it
Jer 25:29 For behold, I begin to bring calamity on the city which is *called by My name*, and should you be utterly unpunished
Jer 32:34 But they set their abominations in the house which is *called by My name*, to defile it
Jer 34:15 and you made a covenant before Me in the house which is *called by My name*
Amos 9:12 that they may possess the remnant of Edom, and all the Gentiles who are *called by My name*
Acts 15:17 so that the rest of mankind may seek the Lord, even all the Gentiles who are *called by My name*, says the Lord who does all these things

CALLED BY NAME
Ex 31:2 See, I have *called by name* Bezalel the son of Uri, the son of Hur, of the tribe of Judah
Ex 35:30 And Moses said to the children of Israel, "See, the Lord has *called by name* Bezalel the son of Uri, the son of Hur, of the tribe of Judah

CALLED BY YOUR NAME
1Kin 8:43 hear in heaven Your dwelling place, and do according to all for which the foreigner calls to You, that all peoples of the earth may know Your

name and fear You, as do Your people Israel, and that they may know that this temple which I have built is *called by Your name*

2Chr 6:33 then hear from heaven Your dwelling place, and do according to all for which the foreigner calls to You, that all people of the earth may know Your name and fear You, as do Your people Israel, and that they may know that this temple which I have built is *called by Your name*

Is 4:1 only let us be *called by your name*, to take away our reproach

Is 63:19 We have become like those of old, over whom You never ruled, those who were never *called by Your name*

Jer 14:9 Yet You, O Lord, are in our midst, and we are *called by Your name*

Jer 15:16 for I am *called by Your name*, O Lord God of hosts

Dan 9:18 open Your eyes and see our desolations, and the city which is *called by Your name*

Dan 9:19 Do not delay for Your own sake, my God, for Your city and Your people are *called by Your name*

CALLED OUT IN MY HEARING

Ezek 9:1 Then He *called out in my hearing* with a loud voice, saying

CALLED THE NAME OF THE PLACE

Gen 22:14 And Abraham *called the name of the place*, The-Lord-Will-Provide; as it is said to this day

Gen 32:30 And Jacob *called the name of the place* Peniel: "For I have seen God face to face, and my life is preserved

Gen 35:15 And Jacob *called the name of the place* where God spoke with him, Bethel

Ex 17:7 So he *called the name of the place* Massah and Meribah, because of the contention of the children of Israel, and because they tempted the Lord

Num 11:3 So he *called the name of the place* Taberah, because the fire of the Lord had burned among them

2Sam 6:8 and he *called the name of the place* Perez Uzzah to this day

CALLED TO BE AN APOSTLE

Rom 1:1 Paul, a servant of Jesus Christ, *called to be an apostle*, separated to the gospel of God

1Cor 1:1 Paul, *called to be an apostle* of Jesus Christ through the will of God, and Sosthenes our brother

CALLED TO BE SAINTS

Rom 1:7 To all who are in Rome, beloved of God, *called to be saints*

1Cor 1:2 To the church of God which is at Corinth, to those who are sanctified in Christ Jesus, *called to be saints*, with all who in every place call on the name of Jesus Christ our Lord, both theirs and ours

CALLED TO FREEDOM (NAS, RSV)
(See *CALLED TO LIBERTY*)

CALLED TO LIBERTY

Gal 5:13 For you, brethren, have been *called to liberty;* only do not use liberty as an opportunity for the flesh, but through love serve one another

CALLED UPON THE LORD

2Sam 22:7 In my distress I *called upon the Lord*, and cried to my God

Ps 18:6 In my distress I *called upon the Lord*, and cried out to my God

Ps 99:6 Moses and Aaron were among His priests, and Samuel was among those who called upon His name; they *called upon the Lord*, and He answered them

CALLED UPON THE NAME OF THE LORD

Ps 116:4 Then I *called upon the name of the Lord:* "O Lord, I implore You, deliver my soul

CALLING OF GOD

Rom 11:29 For the gifts and the *calling of God* are irrevocable

CALLS ON THE NAME OF THE LORD

Joel 2:32 And it shall come to pass that whoever *calls on the name of the Lord* shall be saved

Acts 2:21 And it shall come to pass that whoever *calls on the name of the Lord* shall be saved

CALLS ON YOUR NAME

Is 64:7 And there is no one who *calls on Your name*, who stirs himself up to take hold of You

CALVES OF GOLD

1Kin 12:28 Therefore the king took counsel and made two *calves of gold*, and said to the people

CAME TO JESUS BY NIGHT

John 3:2 This man *came to Jesus by night* and said to Him

John 7:50 Nicodemus (he who *came to Jesus by night*, being one of them

John 19:39 And Nicodemus, who at first *came to Jesus by night*, also came, bringing a mixture of myrrh and aloes, about a hundred pounds

CAN TESTIFY (NAS, NIV)
(See *BEARS ME WITNESS*)

CAN THE ETHIOPIAN CHANGE HIS SKIN

Jer 13:23 *Can the Ethiopian change his skin* or the leopard its spots

CAN THESE BONES LIVE

Ezek 37:3 And He said to me, "Son of man, *can these bones live*

CAN TWO WALK TOGETHER

Amos 3:3 *can two walk together*, unless they are agreed

CANDLE OF THE WICKED (KJV)
(See *LAMP OF THE WICKED*)

CANNOT BE GREEK AND JEW (RSV)
(See *NEITHER GREEK NOR JEW*)

CANNOT DISCERN BETWEEN

Jon 4:11 And should I not pity Nineveh, that great city, in which are more than one hundred and twenty thousand persons who *cannot discern between* their right hand and their left, and also much livestock

CAPABLE MAN (NIV)
(See *MAN OF UNDERSTANDING*)

CAPTAIN OF THE GUARD

Gen 37:36 Now the Midianites had sold him in Egypt to Potiphar, an officer of Pharaoh and *captain of the guard*

Gen 39:1 And Potiphar, an officer of Pharaoh, *captain of the guard*, an Egyptian, bought him from the Ishmaelites who had taken him down there

Gen 40:3 So he put them in custody in the house of the *captain of the guard*, in the prison, the place where Joseph was confined

Gen 40:4 And the *captain of the guard* charged Joseph with them, and he served them

Gen 41:10 When Pharaoh was angry with his ser-

vants, and put me in custody in the house of the *captain of the guard*, both me and the chief baker
Gen 41:12 Now there was a young Hebrew man with us there, a servant of the *captain of the guard*
2Kin 25:8 Nebuzaradan the *captain of the guard*, a servant of the king of Babylon, came to Jerusalem
2Kin 25:10 And all the army of the Chaldeans who were with the *captain of the guard* broke down the walls of Jerusalem all around
2Kin 25:11 Then Nebuzaradan the *captain of the guard* carried away captive the rest of the people who remained in the city and the defectors who had deserted to the king of Babylon, with the rest of the multitude
2Kin 25:12 But the *captain of the guard* left some of the poor of the land as vinedressers and farmers
2Kin 25:15 The firepans and the basins, the things made of solid gold and solid silver, the *captain of the guard* took away
2Kin 25:18 And the *captain of the guard* took Seraiah the chief priest, Zephaniah the second priest, and the three doorkeepers
2Kin 25:20 So Nebuzaradan, *captain of the guard*, took these and brought them to the king of Babylon at Riblah
Jer 37:13 And when he was in the gate of Benjamin, a *captain of the guard* was there whose name was Irijah the son of Shelemiah, the son of Hananiah
Jer 39:9 Then Nebuzaradan the *captain of the guard* carried away captive to Babylon the remnant of the people who remained in the city and those who defected to him, with the rest of the people who remained
Jer 39:10 But Nebuzaradan the *captain of the guard* left in the land of Judah the poor people, who had nothing, and gave them vineyards and fields at the same time
Jer 39:11 Now Nebuchadnezzar king of Babylon gave charge concerning Jeremiah to Nebuzaradan the *captain of the guard*
Jer 39:13 So Nebuzaradan the *captain of the guard* sent Nebushasban, Rabsaris, Nergal-Sharezer, Rabmag, and all the king of Babylon's chief officers
Jer 40:1 The word that came to Jeremiah from the Lord after Nebuzaradan the *captain of the guard* had let him go from Ramah, when he had taken him bound in chains among all who were carried away captive from Jerusalem and Judah, who were carried away captive to Babylon
Jer 40:2 And the *captain of the guard* took Jeremiah and said to him
Jer 40:5 So the *captain of the guard* gave him rations and a gift and let him go
Jer 41:10 Then Ishmael carried away captive all the rest of the people who were in Mizpah, the king's daughters and all the people who remained in Mizpah, whom Nebuzaradan the *captain of the guard* had committed to Gedaliah the son of Ahikam
Jer 43:6 men, women, children, the king's daughters, and every person whom Nebuzaradan the *captain of the guard* had left with Gedaliah the son of Ahikam, the son of Shaphan, and Jeremiah the prophet and Baruch the son of Neriah
Jer 52:12 Nebuzaradan, the *captain of the guard*, who served the king of Babylon, came to Jerusalem
Jer 52:14 And all the army of the Chaldeans who were with the *captain of the guard* broke down all the walls of Jerusalem all around
Jer 52:15 Then Nebuzaradan the *captain of the guard* carried away captive some of the poor people, the rest of the people who remained in the city, the defectors who had deserted to the king of Babylon, and the rest of the craftsmen
Jer 52:16 But Nebuzaradan the *captain of the guard* left some of the poor of the land as vinedressers and farmers
Jer 52:19 The basins, the firepans, the bowls, the pots, the lampstands, the spoons, and the cups, whatever was of solid gold and whatever was of solid silver, the *captain of the guard* took away
Jer 52:24 The *captain of the guard* took Seraiah the chief priest, Zephaniah the second priest, and the three doorkeepers
Jer 52:26 And Nebuzaradan the *captain of the guard* took these and brought them to the king of Babylon at Riblah
Jer 52:30 in the twenty-third year of Nebuchadnezzar, Nebuzaradan the *captain of the guard* carried away captive of the Jews seven hundred and forty-five persons
Acts 28:16 Now when we came to Rome, the centurion delivered the prisoners to the *captain of the guard*

CAPTIVITY OF THE LAND
Judg 18:30 and Jonathan the son of Gershom, the son of Manasseh, and his sons were priests to the tribe of Dan until the day of the *captivity of the land*

CAREFUL TO OBSERVE
Deut 4:6 Therefore be *careful to observe* them; for this is your wisdom and your understanding in the sight of the peoples who will hear all these statutes, and say
Deut 5:1 Hear, O Israel, the statutes and judgments which I speak in your hearing today, that you may learn them and be *careful to observe* them
Deut 6:3 Therefore hear, O Israel, and be *careful to observe* it, that it may be well with you, and that you may multiply greatly as the Lord God of your fathers has promised you
Deut 6:25 Then it will be righteousness for us, if we are *careful to observe* all these commandments before the Lord our God, as He has commanded us
Deut 8:1 Every commandment which I command you today you must be *careful to observe*, that you may live and multiply, and go in and possess the land of which the Lord swore to your fathers
Deut 11:32 And you shall be *careful to observe* all the statutes and judgments which I set before you today
Deut 12:1 These are the statutes and judgments which you shall be *careful to observe* in the land which the Lord God of your fathers is giving you to possess, all the days that you live on the earth
Deut 12:32 Whatever I command you, be *careful to observe* it; you shall not add to it nor take away from it
Deut 16:12 And you shall remember that you were a slave in Egypt, and you shall be *careful to observe* these statutes
Deut 17:19 And it shall be with him, and he shall read it all the days of his life, that he may learn to fear the Lord his God and be *careful to observe* all the words of this law and these statutes
Deut 26:16 therefore you shall be *careful to observe* them with all your heart and with all your soul
Deut 28:13 you shall be above only, and not be beneath, if you heed the commandments of the Lord your God, which I command you today, and are *careful to observe* them
Deut 32:46 Set your hearts on all the words which I testify among you today, which you shall command your children to be *careful to observe* all the words of this law

2Kin 17:37 And the statutes, the ordinances, the law, and the commandment which He wrote for you, you shall be *careful to observe* forever
Ezek 20:21 they did not walk in My statutes, and were not *careful to observe* My judgments

CARES OF THIS LIFE
Luke 21:34 But take heed to yourselves, lest your hearts be weighed down with carousing, drunkenness, and *cares of this life*, and that day come on you unexpectedly

CARES OF THIS WORLD
Matt 13:22 Now he who received seed among the thorns is he who hears the word, and the *cares of this world* and the deceitfulness of riches choke the word, and he becomes unfruitful
Mark 4:19 and the *cares of this world*, the deceitfulness of riches, and the desires for other things entering in choke the word, and it becomes unfruitful

CARNALLY MINDED
Rom 8:6 For to be *carnally minded* is death, but to be spiritually minded is life and peace

CARRIED AWAY CAPTIVE
2Kin 25:11 Then Nebuzaradan the captain of the guard *carried away captive* the rest of the people who remained in the city and the defectors who had deserted to the king of Babylon, with the rest of the multitude
2Kin 25:21 Thus Judah was *carried away captive* from its own land
1Chr 9:1 But Judah was *carried away captive* to Babylon because of their unfaithfulness
2Chr 28:8 And the children of Israel *carried away captive* of their brethren two hundred thousand women, sons, and daughters
Ezra 8:35 The children of those who had been *carried away captive*, who had come from the captivity, offered burnt offerings to the God of Israel
Ezra 9:4 Then everyone who trembled at the words of the God of Israel assembled to me, because of the transgression of those who had been *carried away captive*, and I sat astonished until the evening sacrifice
Neh 7:6 These are the people of the province who came back from the captivity, of those who had been carried away, whom Nebuchadnezzar the king of Babylon had *carried away captive*, and who returned to Jerusalem and Judah, everyone to his own city
Jer 13:19 Judah shall be *carried away captive*, all of it; it shall be wholly *carried away captive*
Jer 24:1 The Lord showed me, and there were two baskets of figs set before the temple of the Lord, after Nebuchadnezzar king of Babylon had *carried away captive* Jeconiah the son of Jehoiakim, king of Judah, and the princes of Judah with the craftsmen and smiths, from Jerusalem, and had brought them to Babylon
Jer 24:5 Like these good figs, so will I acknowledge those who are *carried away captive* from Judah, whom I have sent out of this place for their own good, into the land of the Chaldeans
Jer 27:20 which Nebuchadnezzar king of Babylon did not take, when he *carried away captive* Jeconiah the son of Jehoiakim, king of Judah, from Jerusalem to Babylon, and all the nobles of Judah and Jerusalem
Jer 28:6 the Lord perform your words which you have prophesied, to bring back the vessels of the Lord's house and all who were *carried away captive*, from Babylon to this place
Jer 29:1 Now these are the words of the letter that Jeremiah the prophet sent from Jerusalem to the remainder of the elders who were *carried away captive* to the priests, the prophets, and all the people whom Nebuchadnezzar had *carried away captive* from Jerusalem to Babylon
Jer 29:4 Thus says the Lord of hosts, the God of Israel, to all who were *carried away captive*, whom I have caused to be carried away from Jerusalem to Babylon
Jer 29:7 And seek the peace of the city where I have caused you to be *carried away captive*, and pray to the Lord for it
Jer 29:14 I will gather you from all the nations and from all the places where I have driven you, says the Lord, and I will bring you to the place from which I cause you to be *carried away captive*
Jer 39:9 Then Nebuzaradan the captain of the guard *carried away captive* to Babylon the remnant of the people who remained in the city and those who defected to him, with the rest of the people who remained
Jer 40:1 The word that came to Jeremiah from the Lord after Nebuzaradan the captain of the guard had let him go from Ramah, when he had taken him bound in chains among all who were *carried away captive* from Jerusalem and Judah, who were *carried away captive* to Babylon
Jer 40:7 Now when all the captains of the armies who were in the fields, they and their men, heard that the king of Babylon had made Gedaliah the son of Ahikam governor in the land, and had committed to him men, women, children, and the poorest of the land who had not been *carried away captive* to Babylon
Jer 41:10 Then Ishmael *carried away captive* all the rest of the people who were in Mizpah, the king's daughters and all the people who remained in Mizpah, whom Nebuzaradan the captain of the guard had committed to Gedaliah the son of Ahikam
Jer 41:14 Then all the people whom Ishmael had *carried away captive* from Mizpah turned around and came back, and went to Johanan the son of Kareah
Jer 52:15 Then Nebuzaradan the captain of the guard *carried away captive* some of the poor people, the rest of the people who remained in the city, the defectors who had deserted to the king of Babylon, and the rest of the craftsmen
Jer 52:27 Thus Judah was *carried away captive* from its own land
Jer 52:28 These are the people whom Nebuchadnezzar *carried away captive:* in the seventh year, three thousand and twenty-three Jews
Jer 52:29 in the eighteenth year of Nebuchadnezzar he *carried away captive* from Jerusalem eight hundred and thirty-two persons
Jer 52:30 in the twenty-third year of Nebuchadnezzar, Nebuzaradan the captain of the guard *carried away captive* of the Jews seven hundred and forty-five persons

CARRIED INTO CAPTIVITY
2Kin 24:14 Also he *carried into captivity* all Jerusalem: all the captains and all the mighty men of valor, ten thousand captives, and all the craftsmen and smiths
2Kin 24:15 The king's mother, the king's wives, his officers, and the mighty of the land he *carried into captivity* from Jerusalem to Babylon
1Chr 5:6 and Beerah his son, whom Tiglath-Pileser king of Assyria *carried into captivity*

CARRIED INTO EXILE (NIV, RSV)
(See *CARRIED AWAY CAPTIVE*)

CARRIED YOU ON EAGLES' WINGS (NIV)
(See *BORE YOU ON EAGLES' WINGS*)

CARRY THE ARK
2Sam 15:25 Then the king said to Zadok, "*Carry the ark* of God back into the city
1Chr 15:2 Then David said, "No one may *carry the ark* of God but the Levites, for the Lord has chosen them to *carry the ark* of God and to minister before Him forever

CARVED IMAGE
Ex 20:4 You shall not make for yourself a *carved image*, or any likeness of anything that is in heaven above, or that is in the earth beneath, or that is in the water under the earth
Lev 26:1 neither a *carved image* nor a sacred pillar shall you rear up for yourselves
Deut 4:16 lest you act corruptly and make for yourselves a *carved image* in the form of any figure
Deut 4:23 Take heed to yourselves, lest you forget the covenant of the Lord your God which He made with you, and make for yourselves a *carved image* in the form of anything which the Lord your God has forbidden you
Deut 4:25 When you beget children and grandchildren and have grown old in the land, act corruptly and make a *carved image* in the form of anything, and do evil in the sight of the Lord your God to provoke Him to anger
Deut 5:8 You shall not make for yourself any *carved image*, or any likeness of anything that is in heaven above, or that is in the earth beneath, or that is in the water under the earth
Judg 17:3 So when he had returned the eleven hundred shekels of silver to his mother, his mother said, "I had wholly dedicated the silver from my hand to the Lord for my son, to make a *carved image* and a molded image
Judg 17:4 Then his mother took two hundred shekels of silver and gave them to the silversmith, and he made it into a *carved image* and a molded image
Judg 18:14 Then the five men who had gone to spy out the country of Laish answered and said to their brethren, "Do you know that there are in these houses an ephod, household idols, a *carved image*, and a molded image
Judg 18:17 Then the five men who had gone to spy out the land went up, and entering there, they took the *carved image*, the ephod, the household idols, and the molded image
Judg 18:20 and he took the ephod, the household idols, and the *carved image*, and took his place among the people
Judg 18:30 Then the children of Dan set up for themselves the *carved image*
Judg 18:31 So they set up for themselves Micah's *carved image* which he made, all the time that the house of God was in Shiloh
2Kin 21:7 He even set a *carved image* of Asherah that he had made, in the house of which the Lord had said to David and to Solomon his son
2Chr 33:7 He even set a *carved image*, the idol which he had made, in the house of God, of which God had said to David and to Solomon his son
Is 40:20 He seeks for himself a skillful workman to prepare a *carved image* that will not totter
Is 44:15 he makes it a *carved image*, and falls down to it
Is 44:17 And the rest of it he makes into a god, his *carved image*
Is 45:20 They have no knowledge, who carry the wood of their *carved image*, and pray to a god that cannot save
Is 48:5 before it came to pass I proclaimed it to you, lest you should say, 'My idol has done them, and my *carved image* and my molded image have commanded them
Jer 51:17 every metalsmith is put to shame by the *carved image*
Nah 1:14 Out of the house of your gods I will cut off the *carved image* and the molded image

CARVED IMAGES
Deut 7:5 you shall destroy their altars, and break down their sacred pillars, and cut down their wooden images, and burn their *carved images* with fire
Deut 7:25 You shall burn the *carved images* of their gods with fire
Deut 12:3 you shall cut down the *carved images* of their gods and destroy their names from that place
2Kin 17:41 So these nations feared the Lord, yet served their *carved images*
2Chr 33:19 Also his prayer and how God received his entreaty, and all his sin and trespass, and the sites where he built high places and set up wooden images and *carved images*, before he was humbled, indeed they are written among the sayings of Hozai
2Chr 33:22 for Amon sacrificed to all the *carved images* which his father Manasseh had made, and served them
2Chr 34:3 and in the twelfth year he began to purge Judah and Jerusalem of the high places, the wooden images, the *carved images*, and the molded images
2Chr 34:4 and the wooden images, the *carved images*, and the molded images he broke in pieces, and made dust of them and scattered it on the graves of those who had sacrificed to them
2Chr 34:7 When he had broken down the altars and the wooden images, had beaten the *carved images* into powder, and cut down all the incense altars throughout all the land of Israel, he returned to Jerusalem
Ps 78:58 For they provoked Him to anger with their high places, and moved Him to jealousy with their *carved images*
Ps 97:7 Let all be put to shame who serve *carved images*, who boast of idols
Is 10:10 As my hand has found the kingdoms of the idols, whose *carved images* excelled those of Jerusalem and Samaria
Is 21:9 And all the *carved images* of her gods he has broken to the ground
Is 42:17 They shall be turned back, they shall be greatly ashamed, who trust in *carved images*, who say to the molded images
Jer 8:19 Why have they provoked Me to anger with their *carved images*, and with foreign idols
Jer 50:38 For it is the land of *carved images*, and they are insane with their idols
Jer 51:47 therefore behold, the days are coming that I will bring judgment on the *carved images* of Babylon
Jer 51:52 Therefore behold, the days are coming," says the Lord, "That I will bring judgment on her *carved images*, and throughout all her land the wounded shall groan
Hos 11:2 so they went from them, they sacrificed to the Baals, and burned incense to *carved images*
Mic 1:7 All her *carved images* shall be beaten to pieces, and all her pay as a harlot shall be burned with the fire
Mic 5:13 Your *carved images* I will also cut off, and your sacred pillars from your midst

CAST DUST ON THEIR HEADS
Ezek 27:30 they will cry bitterly and *cast dust on their heads*

CAST FIRE UPON THE EARTH (NAS, RSV)
(See *SEND FIRE ON THE EARTH*)

CAST IDOL (NIV)
(See *MOLDED IMAGE*)

CAST INTO THE FIRE
Ps 140:10 Let them be *cast into the fire*, into deep pits, that they rise not up again

CAST INTO THE LAKE OF FIRE
Rev 20:10 And the devil, who deceived them, was *cast into the lake of fire* and brimstone where the beast and the false prophet are
Rev 20:14 Then Death and Hades were *cast into the lake of fire*
Rev 20:15 And anyone not found written in the Book of Life was *cast into the lake of fire*

CAST LOTS
Lev 16:8 Then Aaron shall *cast lots* for the two goats: One lot for the Lord and the other lot for the scapegoat
Josh 18:6 You shall therefore survey the land in seven parts and bring the survey here to me, that I may *cast lots* for you here before the Lord our God
Josh 18:8 and Joshua charged those who went to survey the land, saying, "Go, walk through the land, survey it, and come back to me, that I may *cast lots* for you here before the Lord in Shiloh
Josh 18:10 Then Joshua *cast lots* for them in Shiloh before the Lord, and there Joshua divided the land to the children of Israel according to their divisions
1Sam 14:42 And Saul said, "*Cast lots* between my son Jonathan and me
1Chr 24:31 These also *cast lots* just as their brothers the sons of Aaron did, in the presence of King David, Zadok, Ahimelech, and the heads of the fathers' houses of the priests and Levites
1Chr 25:8 And they *cast lots* for their duty, the small as well as the great, the teacher with the student
1Chr 26:13 And they *cast lots* for each gate, the small as well as the great, according to their father's house
1Chr 26:14 Then they *cast lots* for his son Zechariah, a wise counselor, and his lot came out for the North Gate
Neh 10:34 We *cast lots* among the priests, the Levites, and the people, for bringing the wood offering into the house of our God, according to our fathers' houses, at the appointed times year by year, to burn on the altar of the Lord our God as it is written in the Law
Neh 11:1 the rest of the people *cast lots* to bring one out of ten to dwell in Jerusalem, the holy city, and nine-tenths were to dwell in other cities
Ps 22:18 They divide My garments among them, and for My clothing they *cast lots*
Joel 3:3 They have *cast lots* for My people, have given a boy in exchange for a harlot, and sold a girl for wine, that they may drink
Obad 11 In the day that you stood on the other side in the day that strangers carried captive his forces, when foreigners entered his gates and *cast lots* for Jerusalem even you were as one of them
Jon 1:7 And they said to one another, "Come, let us *cast lots*, that we may know for whose cause this trouble has come upon us." So they *cast lots*, and the lot fell on Jonah
Nah 3:10 they *cast lots* for her honorable men, and all her great men were bound in chains
Matt 27:35 They divided My garments among them, and for My clothing they *cast lots*
Luke 23:34 Then Jesus said, "Father, forgive them, for they do not know what they do." And they divided His garments and *cast lots*
John 19:24 They said therefore among themselves, "Let us not tear it, but *cast lots* for it, whose it shall be," that the Scripture might be fulfilled which says: "They divided My garments among them, and for My clothing they *cast lots*

CAST OUT DEMONS
Matt 7:22 Many will say to Me in that day, 'Lord, Lord, have we not prophesied in Your name, *cast out demons* in Your name, and done many wonders in Your name
Matt 10:8 Heal the sick, cleanse the lepers, raise the dead, *cast out demons*
Matt 12:24 But when the Pharisees heard it they said, "This fellow does not *cast out demons* except by Beelzebub, the ruler of the demons
Matt 12:27 And if I *cast out demons* by Beelzebub, by whom do your sons cast them out
Matt 12:28 But if I *cast out demons* by the Spirit of God, surely the kingdom of God has come upon you
Mark 3:15 and to have power to heal sicknesses and to *cast out demons*
Mark 16:17 In My name they will *cast out demons;* they will speak with new tongues
Luke 11:18 If Satan also is divided against himself, how will his kingdom stand? Because you say I *cast out demons* by Beelzebub
Luke 11:19 And if I *cast out demons* by Beelzebub, by whom do your sons cast them out
Luke 11:20 But if I *cast out demons* with the finger of God, surely the kingdom of God has come upon you
Luke 13:32 And He said to them, "Go, tell that fox, 'Behold, I *cast out demons* and perform cures today and tomorrow, and the third day I shall be perfected

CAST OUT DEVILS (KJV)
(See *CASTING OUT DEMONS*)

CAST YE UP (KJV)
(See *HEAP IT UP*)

CAST YOU OFF
1Chr 28:9 but if you forsake Him, He will *cast you off* forever

CAST YOUR BREAD UPON THE WATERS
Eccl 11:1 *Cast your bread upon the waters*, for you will find it after many days

CAST YOUR BURDEN
Ps 55:22 *Cast your burden* on the Lord, and He shall sustain you

CAST YOUR CARES (NIV)
(See *CAST YOUR BURDEN*)

CAST YOUR PEARLS BEFORE SWINE
Matt 7:6 nor *cast your pearls before swine*, lest they trample them under their feet, and turn and tear you in pieces

CASTING ALL YOUR CARE UPON HIM
1Pet 5:7 *casting all your care upon Him*, for He cares for you

CASTING OUT DEMONS
Mark 1:39 And He was preaching in their synagogues throughout all Galilee, and *casting out demons*
Mark 9:38 Now John answered Him, saying, "Teacher, we saw someone who does not follow us *casting out demons* in Your name, and we forbade him because he does not follow us
Luke 9:49 Then John answered and said, "Master, we saw someone *casting out demons* in Your name, and we forbade him because he does not follow with us

CASTS OUT DEMONS
Matt 9:34 But the Pharisees said, "He *casts out demons* by the ruler of the demons
Mark 3:22 And the scribes who came down from Jerusalem said, "He has Beelzebub," and, "By the ruler of the demons He *casts out demons*
Luke 11:15 But some of them said, "He *casts out demons* by Beelzebub, the ruler of the demons

CATTLE ON A THOUSAND HILLS
Ps 50:10 For every beast of the forest is Mine, and the *cattle on a thousand hills*

CAUGHT UP INTO PARADISE
2Cor 12:4 how he was *caught up into Paradise* and heard inexpressible words, which it is not lawful for a man to utter

CAUSE HIM TO SWEAR (KJV)
(See *TAKE AN OATH*)

CAUSE LIFE TO PINE AWAY (RSV)
(See *SORROW OF HEART*)

CAUSE OF THE POOR
Prov 29:7 The righteous considers the *cause of the poor*, but the wicked does not understand such knowledge
Prov 31:9 Open your mouth, judge righteously, and plead the *cause of the poor* and needy
Jer 22:16 He judged the *cause of the poor* and needy; then it was well

CAUSED MY PEOPLE ISRAEL TO ERR
Jer 23:13 they prophesied by Baal and *caused My people Israel to err*

CAUSETH US TO TRIUMPH (KJV)
(See *LEADS US IN TRIUMPH*)

CEDARS OF LEBANON
Judg 9:15 but if not, let fire come out of the bramble and devour the *cedars of Lebanon*
Ps 29:5 The voice of the Lord breaks the cedars, yes, the Lord splinters the *cedars of Lebanon*
Ps 104:16 The trees of the Lord are full of sap, the *cedars of Lebanon* which He planted
Is 2:13 upon all the *cedars of Lebanon* that are high and lifted up, and upon all the oaks of Bashan
Is 14:8 Indeed the cypress trees rejoice over you, and the *cedars of Lebanon*, saying

CELEBRATE THE LORD'S PASSOVER (NIV)
(See *KEEP THE PASSOVER*)

CELESTIAL BODIES
1Cor 15:40 There are also *celestial bodies* and terrestrial bodies; but the glory of the celestial is one, and the glory of the terrestrial is another

CENTER OF THE LAND
Judg 9:37 So Gaal spoke again and said, "See, people are coming down from the *center of the land*, and another company is coming from the Diviners' Terebinth Tree

CENTER OF THE NATIONS (NAS, RSV)
(See *MIDST OF THE NATIONS*)

CERTAIN MAN
Gen 37:15 Now a *certain man* found him, and there he was, wandering in the field
Judg 13:2 Now there was a *certain man* from Zorah, of the family of the Danites, whose name was Manoah
Ruth 1:1 And a *certain man* of Bethlehem, Judah, went to sojourn in the country of Moab, he and his wife and his two sons
1Sam 1:1 Now there was a *certain man* of Ramathaim Zophim, of the mountains of Ephraim, and his name was Elkanah the son of Jeroham, the son of Elihu, the son of Tohu, the son of Zuph, an Ephraimite
1Sam 21:7 Now a *certain man* of the servants of Saul was there that day, detained before the Lord
2Sam 18:10 Now a *certain man* saw it and told Joab, and said
1Kin 20:35 Now a *certain man* of the sons of the prophets said to his neighbor by the word of the Lord
1Kin 22:34 Now a *certain man* drew a bow at random, and struck the king of Israel between the joints of his armor
2Chr 18:33 Now a *certain man* drew a bow at random, and struck the king of Israel between the joints of his armor
Dan 10:5 I lifted my eyes and looked, and behold, a *certain man* clothed in linen, whose waist was girded with gold of Uphaz
Matt 26:18 And He said, "Go into the city to a *certain man*, and say to him
Mark 15:21 Now they compelled a *certain man*, Simon a Cyrenian, the father of Alexander and Rufus, as he was coming out of the country and passing by, to bear His cross
Luke 8:27 And when He stepped out on the land, there met Him a *certain man* from the city who had demons for a long time
Luke 10:30 A *certain man* went down from Jerusalem to Jericho, and fell among thieves, who stripped him of his clothing, wounded him, and departed, leaving him half dead
Luke 13:6 A *certain man* had a fig tree planted in his vineyard, and he came seeking fruit on it and found none
Luke 14:2 And behold, there was a *certain man* before Him who had dropsy
Luke 14:16 Then He said to him, "A *certain man* gave a great supper and invited many
Luke 15:11 Then He said: "A *certain man* had two sons.
Luke 20:9 A *certain man* planted a vineyard, leased it to vinedressers, and went into a far country for a long time
Luke 23:26 Now as they led Him away, they laid hold of a *certain man*, Simon a Cyrenian, who was coming from the country, and on him they laid the cross that he might bear it after Jesus
John 5:5 Now a *certain man* was there who had an infirmity thirty-eight years
John 11:1 Now a *certain man* was sick, Lazarus of Bethany, the town of Mary and her sister Martha
Acts 3:2 And a *certain man* lame from his mother's womb was carried, whom they laid daily at the gate of the temple which is called Beautiful, to ask alms from those who entered the temple
Acts 5:1 But a *certain man* named Ananias, with Sapphira his wife, sold a possession
Acts 8:9 But there was a *certain man* called Simon, who previously practiced sorcery in the city and astonished the people of Samaria, claiming that he was someone great
Acts 9:33 There he found a *certain man* named Aeneas, who had been bedridden eight years and was paralyzed
Acts 10:1 There was a *certain man* in Caesarea called Cornelius, a centurion of what was called the Italian Regiment
Acts 14:8 And in Lystra a *certain man* without strength in his feet was sitting, a cripple from his mother's womb, who had never walked
Acts 18:7 And he departed from there and entered the house of a *certain man* named Justus, one

who worshiped God, whose house was next door to the synagogue
Acts 19:24 For a *certain man* named Demetrius, a silversmith, who made silver shrines of Diana, brought no small profit to the craftsmen
Acts 25:14 There is a *certain man* left a prisoner by Felix

CERTAIN OF WHAT WE DO NOT SEE (NIV)
(See *EVIDENCE OF THINGS NOT SEEN*)

CERTAINLY NOT
1Sam 14:45 *Certainly not!* As the Lord lives, not one hair of his head shall fall to the ground, for he has worked with God this day
Luke 20:16 He will come and destroy those vinedressers and give the vineyard to others." And when they heard it they said, "*Certainly not*
Rom 3:4 *Certainly not!* Indeed, let God be true but every man a liar
Rom 3:6 *Certainly not!* For then how will God judge the world
Rom 3:31 Do we then make void the law through faith? *Certainly not!* On the contrary, we establish the law
Rom 6:2 *Certainly not!* How shall we who died to sin live any longer in it
Rom 6:15 Shall we sin because we are not under law but under grace? *Certainly not*
Rom 7:7 *Certainly not!* On the contrary, I would not have known sin except through the law
Rom 7:13 *Certainly not!* But sin, that it might appear sin, was producing death in me through what is good, so that sin through the commandment might become exceedingly sinful
Rom 9:14 What shall we say then? Is there unrighteousness with God? *Certainly not*
Rom 11:1 *Certainly not!* For I also am an Israelite, of the seed of Abraham, of the tribe of Benjamin
Rom 11:11 *Certainly not!* But through their fall, to provoke them to jealousy, salvation has come to the Gentiles
1Cor 6:15 Shall I then take the members of Christ and make them members of a harlot? *Certainly not*
Gal 2:17 But if, while we seek to be justified by Christ, we ourselves also are found sinners, is Christ therefore a minister of sin? *Certainly not*
Gal 3:21 *Certainly not!* For if there had been a law given which could have given life, truly righteousness would have been by the law

CERTIFICATE OF DIVORCE
Deut 24:1 When a man takes a wife and marries her, and it happens that she finds no favor in his eyes because he has found some uncleanness in her, and he writes her a *certificate of divorce*, puts it in her hand, and sends her out of his house
Deut 24:3 if the latter husband detests her and writes her a *certificate of divorce*, puts it in her hand, and sends her out of his house, or if the latter husband dies who took her to be his wife
Jer 3:8 Then I saw that for all the causes for which backsliding Israel had committed adultery, I had put her away and given her a *certificate of divorce*
Matt 5:31 Furthermore it has been said, 'Whoever divorces his wife, let him give her a *certificate of divorce*
Matt 19:7 They said to Him, "Why then did Moses command to give a *certificate of divorce*, and to put her away
Mark 10:4 They said, "Moses permitted a man to write a *certificate of divorce*, and to dismiss her

CHAFF BEFORE THE WIND
Ps 35:5 Let them be like *chaff before the wind*, and let the angel of the Lord chase them
Ps 83:13 O my God, make them like the whirling dust, like the *chaff before the wind*

CHANGE LIKE SHIFTING SHADOWS (NIV)
(See *VARIATION OR SHADOW OF TURNING*)

CHANGE OF HEART (NIV)
(See *COME TO THEMSELVES*)

CHANGED THE TRUTH (KJV)
(See *EXCHANGED THE TRUTH*)

CHARIOT OF FIRE
2Kin 2:11 Then it happened, as they continued on and talked, that suddenly a *chariot of fire* appeared with horses of fire, and separated the two of them

CHARIOTS AND HORSEMEN
Gen 50:9 And there went up with him both *chariots and horsemen*, and it was a very great gathering
Josh 24:6 and the Egyptians pursued your fathers with *chariots and horsemen* to the Red Sea
2Sam 1:6 and indeed the *chariots and horsemen* followed hard after him
1Kin 1:5 and he prepared for himself *chariots and horsemen*, and fifty men to run before him
1Kin 10:26 And Solomon gathered *chariots and horsemen;* he had one thousand four hundred chariots and twelve thousand horsemen, whom he stationed in the chariot cities and with the king in Jerusalem
2Kin 18:24 How then will you repel one captain of the least of my master's servants, and put your trust in Egypt for *chariots and horsemen*
1Chr 19:6 When the people of Ammon saw that they had made themselves repulsive to David, Hanun and the people of Ammon sent a thousand talents of silver to hire for themselves *chariots and horsemen* from Mesopotamia, from Syrian Maachah, and from Zobah
2Chr 1:14 And Solomon gathered *chariots and horsemen;* he had one thousand four hundred chariots and twelve thousand horsemen, whom he stationed in the chariot cities and with the king in Jerusalem
2Chr 16:8 Were the Ethiopians and the Lubim not a huge army with very many *chariots and horsemen*
Is 36:9 How then will you repel one captain of the least of my master's servants, and put your trust in Egypt for *chariots and horsemen*

CHARIOTS OF FIRE
2Kin 6:17 And behold, the mountain was full of horses and *chariots of fire* all around Elisha

CHARITY EDIFIETH (KJV)
(See *LOVE EDIFIES*)

CHARITY ENVIETH NOT (KJV)
(See *LOVE DOES NOT ENVY*)

CHARITY NEVER FAILETH (KJV)
(See *LOVE NEVER FAILS*)

CHARITY SUFFERETH LONG (KJV)
(See *LOVE SUFFERS LONG*)

CHASING AFTER THE WIND (NIV)
(See *GRASPING FOR THE WIND*)

CHERISH ANGER (RSV)
(See *STORE UP WRATH*)

CHEW THE CUD
Lev 11:4 Nevertheless these you shall not eat

among those that *chew the cud* or those that have cloven hooves
Lev 11:7 and the swine, though it divides the hoof, having cloven hooves, yet does not *chew the cud*, is unclean to you
Lev 11:26 The carcass of any beast which divides the foot, but is not cloven-hoofed or does not *chew the cud*, is unclean to you
Deut 14:7 Nevertheless, of those that *chew the cud* or have cloven hooves, you shall not eat, such as these: the camel, the hare, and the rock hyrax; for they *chew the cud* but do not have cloven hooves
Deut 14:8 Also the swine is unclean for you, because it has cloven hooves, yet does not *chew the cud*

CHEWING THE CUD
Lev 11:3 Among the beasts, whatever divides the hoof, having cloven hooves and *chewing the cud* that you may eat

CHEWS THE CUD
Lev 11:4 the camel, because it *chews the cud* but does not have cloven hooves, is unclean to you
Lev 11:5 the rock hyrax, because it *chews the cud* but does not have cloven hooves, is unclean to you
Lev 11:6 the hare, because it *chews the cud* but does not have cloven hooves, is unclean to you
Deut 14:6 And you may eat every animal with cloven hooves, having the hoof split into two parts, and that *chews the cud*, among the animals

CHIDE YE WITH ME (KJV)
(See *CONTEND WITH ME*)

CHIEF CORNERSTONE
Ps 118:22 The stone which the builders rejected has become the *chief cornerstone*
Matt 21:42 The stone which the builders rejected has become the *chief cornerstone*
Mark 12:10 The stone which the builders rejected has become the *chief cornerstone*
Luke 20:17 The stone which the builders rejected has become the *chief cornerstone*
Acts 4:11 This is the 'stone which was rejected by you builders, which has become the *chief cornerstone*
Eph 2:20 having been built on the foundation of the apostles and prophets, Jesus Christ Himself being the *chief cornerstone*
1Pet 2:6 Therefore it is also contained in the Scripture, "Behold, I lay in Zion a *chief cornerstone*, elect, precious, and he who believes on Him will by no means be put to shame
1Pet 2:7 but to those who are disobedient, "The stone which the builders rejected has become the *chief cornerstone*

CHIEF FATHERS (KJV)
(See *HEADS OF FATHERS' HOUSES*)

CHIEF PRIEST
2Kin 25:18 And the captain of the guard took Seraiah the *chief priest*, Zephaniah the second priest, and the three doorkeepers
2Chr 19:11 Amariah the *chief priest* is over you in all matters of the Lord
2Chr 24:6 So the king called Jehoiada the *chief priest*, and said to him
2Chr 26:20 And Azariah the *chief priest* and all the priests looked at him, and there, on his forehead, he was leprous
2Chr 31:10 And Azariah the *chief priest*, from the house of Zadok, answered him and said
Ezra 7:5 the son of Abishua, the son of Phinehas, the son of Eleazar, the son of Aaron the *chief priest*
Jer 52:24 The captain of the guard took Seraiah the *chief priest*, Zephaniah the second priest, and the three doorkeepers
Acts 19:14 Also there were seven sons of Sceva, a Jewish *chief priest*, who did so

CHIEF PRIESTS
Matt 2:4 And when he had gathered all the *chief priests* and scribes of the people together, he inquired of them where the Christ was to be born
Matt 16:21 From that time Jesus began to show to His disciples that He must go to Jerusalem, and suffer many things from the elders and *chief priests* and scribes, and be killed, and be raised again the third day
Matt 20:18 Behold, we are going up to Jerusalem, and the Son of Man will be betrayed to the *chief priests* and to the scribes
Matt 21:15 But when the *chief priests* and scribes saw the wonderful things that He did, and the children crying out in the temple and saying
Matt 21:23 Now when He came into the temple, the *chief priests* and the elders of the people confronted Him as He was teaching, and said
Matt 21:45 Now when the *chief priests* and Pharisees heard His parables, they perceived that He was speaking of them
Matt 26:3 Then the *chief priests*, the scribes, and the elders of the people assembled at the palace of the high priest, who was called Caiaphas
Matt 26:14 Then one of the twelve, called Judas Iscariot, went to the *chief priests*
Matt 26:47 And while He was still speaking, behold, Judas, one of the twelve, with a great multitude with swords and clubs, came from the *chief priests* and elders of the people
Matt 26:59 Now the *chief priests*, the elders, and all the council sought false testimony against Jesus to put Him to death
Matt 27:1 When morning came, all the *chief priests* and elders of the people took counsel against Jesus to put Him to death
Matt 27:3 Then Judas, His betrayer, seeing that He had been condemned, was remorseful and brought back the thirty pieces of silver to the *chief priests* and elders
Matt 27:6 But the *chief priests* took the silver pieces and said
Matt 27:12 And while He was being accused by the *chief priests* and elders, He answered nothing
Matt 27:20 But the *chief priests* and elders persuaded the multitudes that they should ask for Barabbas and destroy Jesus
Matt 27:41 Likewise the *chief priests*, also mocking with the scribes and elders, said
Matt 27:62 On the next day, which followed the Day of Preparation, the *chief priests* and Pharisees gathered together to Pilate
Matt 28:11 Now while they were going, behold, some of the guard came into the city and reported to the *chief priests* all the things that had happened
Mark 8:31 And He began to teach them that the Son of Man must suffer many things, and be rejected by the elders and *chief priests* and scribes, and be killed, and after three days rise again
Mark 10:33 Behold, we are going up to Jerusalem, and the Son of Man will be delivered to the *chief priests* and to the scribes, and they will condemn Him to death and deliver Him to the Gentiles
Mark 11:18 And the scribes and *chief priests* heard it and sought how they might destroy Him
Mark 11:27 And as He was walking in the temple, the *chief priests*, the scribes, and the elders came to Him
Mark 14:1 And the *chief priests* and the scribes

sought how they might take Him by trickery and put Him to death
Mark 14:10 Then Judas Iscariot, one of the twelve, went to the *chief priests* to betray Him to them
Mark 14:43 And immediately, while He was still speaking, Judas, one of the twelve, with a great multitude with swords and clubs, came from the *chief priests* and the scribes and the elders
Mark 14:53 and with him were assembled all the *chief priests*, the elders, and the scribes
Mark 14:55 And the *chief priests* and all the council sought testimony against Jesus to put Him to death, and found none
Mark 15:1 Immediately, in the morning, the *chief priests* held a consultation with the elders and scribes and the whole council
Mark 15:3 And the *chief priests* accused Him of many things, but He answered nothing
Mark 15:10 For he knew that the *chief priests* had handed Him over because of envy
Mark 15:11 But the *chief priests* stirred up the crowd, so that he should rather release Barabbas to them
Mark 15:31 Likewise the *chief priests* also, together with the scribes, mocked and said among themselves
Luke 9:22 saying, "The Son of Man must suffer many things, and be rejected by the elders and *chief priests* and scribes, and be killed, and be raised the third day
Luke 19:47 But the *chief priests*, the scribes, and the leaders of the people sought to destroy Him
Luke 20:1 Now it happened on one of those days, as He taught the people in the temple and preached the gospel, that the *chief priests* and the scribes, together with the elders, confronted Him
Luke 20:19 And the *chief priests* and the scribes that very hour sought to lay hands on Him, but they feared the people for they knew that He had spoken this parable against them
Luke 22:2 And the *chief priests* and the scribes sought how they might kill Him, for they feared the people
Luke 22:4 So he went his way and conferred with the *chief priests* and captains, how he might betray Him to them
Luke 22:52 Then Jesus said to the *chief priests*, captains of the temple, and the elders who had come to Him
Luke 22:66 As soon as it was day, the elders of the people, both *chief priests* and scribes, came together and led Him into their council, saying
Luke 23:4 Then Pilate said to the *chief priests* and the crowd
Luke 23:10 And the *chief priests* and scribes stood and vehemently accused Him
Luke 23:13 Then Pilate, when he had called together the *chief priests*, the rulers, and the people
Luke 23:23 And the voices of these men and of the *chief priests* prevailed
Luke 24:20 and how the *chief priests* and our rulers delivered Him to be condemned to death, and crucified Him
John 7:32 The Pharisees heard the crowd murmuring these things concerning Him, and the Pharisees and the *chief priests* sent officers to take Him
John 7:45 Then the officers came to the *chief priests* and Pharisees, who said to them
John 11:47 Then the *chief priests* and the Pharisees gathered a council and said
John 11:57 Now both the *chief priests* and the Pharisees had given a command, that if anyone knew where He was, he should report it, that they might seize Him
John 12:10 But the *chief priests* took counsel that they might also put Lazarus to death
John 18:3 Then Judas, having received a detachment of troops, and officers from the *chief priests* and Pharisees, came there with lanterns, torches, and weapons
John 18:35 Your own nation and the *chief priests* have delivered You to me
John 19:6 Therefore, when the *chief priests* and officers saw Him, they cried out, saying
John 19:15 The *chief priests* answered, "We have no king but Caesar
John 19:21 Then the *chief priests* of the Jews said to Pilate
Acts 4:23 And being let go, they went to their own companions and reported all that the *chief priests* and elders had said to them
Acts 5:24 Now when the high priest, the captain of the temple, and the *chief priests* heard these things, they wondered what the outcome would be
Acts 9:14 And here he has authority from the *chief priests* to bind all who call on Your name
Acts 9:21 Then all who heard were amazed, and said, "Is this not he who destroyed those who called on this name in Jerusalem, and has come here for that purpose, so that he might bring them bound to the *chief priests*
Acts 22:30 The next day, because he wanted to know for certain why he was accused by the Jews, he released him from his bonds, and commanded the *chief priests* and all their council to appear, and brought Paul down and set him before them
Acts 23:14 They came to the *chief priests* and elders, and said
Acts 25:15 about whom the *chief priests* and the elders of the Jews informed me, when I was in Jerusalem, asking for a judgment against him
Acts 26:10 This I also did in Jerusalem, and many of the saints I shut up in prison, having received authority from the *chief priests*
Acts 26:12 While thus occupied, as I journeyed to Damascus with authority and commission from the *chief priests*

CHIEF PRIESTS AND ELDERS
Matt 26:47 And while He was still speaking, behold, Judas, one of the twelve, with a great multitude with swords and clubs, came from the *chief priests and elders* of the people
Matt 27:1 When morning came, all the *chief priests and elders* of the people took counsel against Jesus to put Him to death
Matt 27:3 Then Judas, His betrayer, seeing that He had been condemned, was remorseful and brought back the thirty pieces of silver to the *chief priests and elders*
Matt 27:12 And while He was being accused by the *chief priests and elders*, He answered nothing
Matt 27:20 But the *chief priests and elders* persuaded the multitudes that they should ask for Barabbas and destroy Jesus
Acts 4:23 And being let go, they went to their own companions and reported all that the *chief priests and elders* had said to them
Acts 23:14 They came to the *chief priests and elders*, and said

CHILD AND HIS MOTHER
Matt 2:13 Now when they had departed, behold, an angel of the Lord appeared to Joseph in a dream, saying, "Arise, take the young *Child and His mother*, flee to Egypt, and stay there until I bring you word
Matt 2:14 When he arose, he took the young *Child and His mother* by night and departed for Egypt
Matt 2:20 saying, "Arise, take the young *Child and His mother*, and go to the land of Israel, for those who sought the young Child's life are dead

Matt 2:21 Then he arose, took the young *Child and His mother*, and came into the land of Israel

CHILDREN ARE A HERITAGE
Ps 127:3 Behold, *children are a heritage* from the Lord, the fruit of the womb is His reward

CHILDREN OF ABRAHAM (NIV)
(See *FAMILY OF ABRAHAM*)

CHILDREN OF DISOBEDIENCE (KJV)
(See *SONS OF DISOBEDIENCE*)

CHILDREN OF GOD
John 1:12 But as many as received Him, to them He gave the right to become *children of God*, even to those who believe in His name
John 11:52 and not for that nation only, but also that He would gather together in one the *children of God* who were scattered abroad
Rom 8:16 The Spirit Himself bears witness with our spirit that we are *children of God*
Rom 8:21 because the creation itself also will be delivered from the bondage of corruption into the glorious liberty of the *children of God*
Rom 9:8 That is, those who are the children of the flesh, these are not the *children of God*
Phil 2:15 that you may become blameless and harmless, *children of God* without fault in the midst of a crooked and perverse generation, among whom you shine as lights in the world
1Jn 3:1 Behold what manner of love the Father has bestowed on us, that we should be called *children of God*
1Jn 3:2 Beloved, now we are *children of God;* and it has not yet been revealed what we shall be, but we know that when He is revealed, we shall be like Him, for we shall see Him as He is
1Jn 3:10 In this the *children of God* and the children of the devil are manifest
1Jn 5:2 By this we know that we love the *children of God*, when we love God and keep His commandments

CHILDREN OF ISRAEL
Gen 32:32 Therefore to this day the *children of Israel* do not eat the muscle that shrank, which is on the hip socket, because He touched the socket of Jacob's hip in the muscle that shrank
Gen 36:31 Now these were the kings who reigned in the land of Edom before any king reigned over the *children of Israel*
Gen 46:8 Now these were the names of the *children of Israel*, Jacob and his sons, who went to Egypt
Gen 50:25 Then Joseph took an oath from the *children of Israel*, saying
Ex 1:1 Now these are the names of the *children of Israel* who came to Egypt
Ex 1:7 But the *children of Israel* were fruitful and increased abundantly, multiplied and grew exceedingly mighty
Ex 1:9 And he said to his people, "Look, the people of the *children of Israel* are more and mightier than we
Ex 1:12 And they were in dread of the *children of Israel*
Ex 1:13 So the Egyptians made the *children of Israel* serve with rigor
Ex 2:23 Then the *children of Israel* groaned because of the bondage, and they cried out
Ex 2:25 And God looked upon the *children of Israel*, and God acknowledged them
Ex 3:9 Now therefore, behold, the cry of the *children of Israel* has come to Me, and I have also seen the oppression with which the Egyptians oppress them
Ex 3:10 Come now, therefore, and I will send you to Pharaoh that you may bring My people, the *children of Israel*, out of Egypt
Ex 3:11 But Moses said to God, "Who am I that I should go to Pharaoh, and that I should bring the *children of Israel* out of Egypt
Ex 3:13 Then Moses said to God, "Indeed, when I come to the *children of Israel* and say to them
Ex 3:14 And He said, "Thus you shall say to the *children of Israel*
Ex 3:15 Moreover God said to Moses, "Thus you shall say to the *children of Israel*
Ex 4:29 Then Moses and Aaron went and gathered together all the elders of the *children of Israel*
Ex 4:31 and when they heard that the Lord had visited the *children of Israel* and that He had looked on their affliction, then they bowed their heads and worshiped
Ex 5:14 Also the officers of the *children of Israel*, whom Pharaoh's taskmasters had set over them, were beaten and were asked
Ex 5:15 Then the officers of the *children of Israel* came and cried out to Pharaoh, saying
Ex 5:19 And the officers of the *children of Israel* saw that they were in trouble after it was said
Ex 6:5 And I have also heard the groaning of the *children of Israel* whom the Egyptians keep in bondage, and I have remembered My covenant
Ex 6:6 Therefore say to the *children of Israel:* 'I am the Lord
Ex 6:9 So Moses spoke thus to the *children of Israel;* but they would not heed Moses, because of anguish of spirit and cruel bondage
Ex 6:11 Go in, speak to Pharaoh king of Egypt, that he must let the *children of Israel* go out of his land
Ex 6:12 And Moses spoke before the Lord, saying, "The *children of Israel* have not heeded me
Ex 6:13 Then the Lord spoke to Moses and Aaron, and gave them a command for the *children of Israel* and for Pharaoh king of Egypt, to bring the *children of Israel* out of the land of Egypt
Ex 6:26 These are the same Aaron and Moses to whom the Lord said, "Bring out the *children of Israel* from the land of Egypt according to their armies
Ex 6:27 These are the ones who spoke to Pharaoh king of Egypt, to bring out the *children of Israel* from Egypt
Ex 7:2 And Aaron your brother shall speak to Pharaoh, that he must send the *children of Israel* out of his land
Ex 7:4 But Pharaoh will not heed you, so that I may lay My hand on Egypt and bring My armies and My people, the *children of Israel*, out of the land of Egypt by great judgments
Ex 7:5 And the Egyptians shall know that I am the Lord, when I stretch out My hand on Egypt and bring out the *children of Israel* from among them
Ex 9:4 So nothing shall die of all that belongs to the *children of Israel*
Ex 9:6 but of the livestock of the *children of Israel*, not one died
Ex 9:26 Only in the land of Goshen, where the *children of Israel* were, there was no hail
Ex 9:35 neither would he let the *children of Israel* go, as the Lord had spoken by Moses
Ex 10:20 But the Lord hardened Pharaoh's heart, and he did not let the *children of Israel* go
Ex 10:23 But all the *children of Israel* had light in their dwellings
Ex 11:7 But against none of the *children of Israel* shall a dog move its tongue, against man or beast, that you may know that the Lord does make a difference between the Egyptians and Israel
Ex 11:10 and the Lord hardened Pharaoh's heart, and he did not let the *children of Israel* go out of his land

Ex 12:27 that you shall say, 'It is the Passover sacrifice of the Lord, who passed over the houses of the *children of Israel* in Egypt when He struck the Egyptians and delivered our households
Ex 12:28 Then the *children of Israel* went away and did so
Ex 12:31 Then he called for Moses and Aaron by night, and said, "Rise and go out from among my people, both you and the *children of Israel*
Ex 12:35 Now the *children of Israel* had done according to the word of Moses, and they had asked from the Egyptians articles of silver, articles of gold, and clothing
Ex 12:37 Then the *children of Israel* journeyed from Rameses to Succoth, about six hundred thousand men on foot, besides children
Ex 12:40 Now the sojourn of the *children of Israel* who lived in Egypt was four hundred and thirty years
Ex 12:42 This is that night of the Lord, a solemn observance for all the *children of Israel* throughout their generations
Ex 12:50 Thus all the *children of Israel* did; as the Lord commanded Moses and Aaron, so they did
Ex 12:51 So it came to pass, on that very same day, that the Lord brought the *children of Israel* out of the land of Egypt according to their armies
Ex 13:2 Consecrate to Me all the firstborn, whatever opens the womb among the *children of Israel*, both of man and beast
Ex 13:18 And the *children of Israel* went up in orderly ranks out of the land of Egypt
Ex 13:19 And Moses took the bones of Joseph with him, for he had placed the *children of Israel* under solemn oath, saying
Ex 14:2 Speak to the *children of Israel*, that they turn and camp before Pi Hahiroth, between Migdol and the sea, opposite Baal Zephon
Ex 14:3 For Pharaoh will say of the *children of Israel*, 'They are bewildered by the land
Ex 14:8 And the Lord hardened the heart of Pharaoh king of Egypt, and he pursued the *children of Israel;* and the *children of Israel* went out with boldness
Ex 14:10 And when Pharaoh drew near, the *children of Israel* lifted their eyes, and behold, the Egyptians marched after them. So they were very afraid, and the *children of Israel* cried out to the Lord
Ex 14:15 And the Lord said to Moses, "Why do you cry to Me? Tell the *children of Israel* to go forward
Ex 14:16 And the *children of Israel* shall go on dry ground through the midst of the sea
Ex 14:22 So the *children of Israel* went into the midst of the sea on the dry ground, and the waters were a wall to them on their right hand and on their left
Ex 14:29 But the *children of Israel* had walked on dry land in the midst of the sea, and the waters were a wall to them on their right hand and on their left
Ex 15:1 Then Moses and the *children of Israel* sang this song to the Lord, and spoke, saying
Ex 15:19 But the *children of Israel* went on dry land in the midst of the sea
Ex 16:1 And they journeyed from Elim, and all the congregation of the *children of Israel* came to the Wilderness of Sin, which is between Elim and Sinai, on the fifteenth day of the second month after they departed from the land of Egypt
Ex 16:2 Then the whole congregation of the *children of Israel* complained against Moses and Aaron in the wilderness
Ex 16:3 And the *children of Israel* said to them, "Oh, that we had died by the hand of the Lord in the land of Egypt, when we sat by the pots of meat and when we ate bread to the full
Ex 16:6 Then Moses and Aaron said to all the *children of Israel*
Ex 16:9 Then Moses spoke to Aaron, "Say to all the congregation of the *children of Israel*
Ex 16:10 Now it came to pass, as Aaron spoke to the whole congregation of the *children of Israel*, that they looked toward the wilderness, and behold, the glory of the Lord appeared in the cloud
Ex 16:12 I have heard the complaints of the *children of Israel*
Ex 16:15 So when the *children of Israel* saw it, they said to one another
Ex 16:17 And the *children of Israel* did so and gathered, some more, some less
Ex 16:35 And the *children of Israel* ate manna forty years, until they came to an inhabited land
Ex 17:1 Then all the congregation of the *children of Israel* set out on their journey from the Wilderness of Sin, according to the commandment of the Lord, and camped in Rephidim
Ex 17:7 So he called the name of the place Massah and Meribah, because of the contention of the *children of Israel*, and because they tempted the Lord, saying
Ex 19:1 In the third month after the *children of Israel* had gone out of the land of Egypt, on the same day, they came to the Wilderness of Sinai
Ex 19:3 And Moses went up to God, and the Lord called to him from the mountain, saying, "Thus you shall say to the house of Jacob, and tell the *children of Israel*
Ex 19:6 These are the words which you shall speak to the *children of Israel*
Ex 20:22 Then the Lord said to Moses, "Thus you shall say to the *children of Israel*
Ex 24:5 Then he sent young men of the *children of Israel*, who offered burnt offerings and sacrificed peace offerings of oxen to the Lord
Ex 24:11 But on the nobles of the *children of Israel* He did not lay His hand
Ex 24:17 The sight of the glory of the Lord was like a consuming fire on the top of the mountain in the eyes of the *children of Israel*
Ex 25:2 Speak to the *children of Israel*, that they bring Me an offering
Ex 25:22 And there I will meet with you, and I will speak with you from above the mercy seat, from between the two cherubim which are on the ark of the Testimony, of all things which I will give you in commandment to the *children of Israel*
Ex 27:20 And you shall command the *children of Israel* that they bring you pure oil of pressed olives for the light, to cause the lamp to burn continually
Ex 27:21 It shall be a statute forever to their generations on behalf of the *children of Israel*
Ex 28:1 Now take Aaron your brother, and his sons with him, from among the *children of Israel*, that he may minister to Me as priest, Aaron and Aaron's sons
Ex 28:30 So Aaron shall bear the judgment of the *children of Israel* over his heart before the Lord continually
Ex 28:38 So it shall be on Aaron's forehead, that Aaron may bear the iniquity of the holy things which the *children of Israel* hallow in all their holy gifts
Ex 29:28 It shall be from the *children of Israel* for Aaron and his sons by a statute forever. For it is a heave offering; it shall be a heave offering from the *children of Israel* from the sacrifices of their peace offerings, that is, their heave offering to the Lord
Ex 29:43 And there I will meet with the *children of Israel*, and the tabernacle shall be sanctified by My glory
Ex 29:45 I will dwell among the *children of Israel* and will be their God

Ex 30:12 When you take the census of the *children of Israel* for their number, then every man shall give a ransom for himself to the Lord, when you number them, that there may be no plague among them when you number them
Ex 30:16 And you shall take the atonement money of the *children of Israel*, and shall appoint it for the service of the tabernacle of meeting, that it may be a memorial for the *children of Israel* before the Lord, to make atonement for yourselves
Ex 30:31 And you shall speak to the *children of Israel*, saying
Ex 31:13 Speak also to the *children of Israel*, saying: "Surely My Sabbaths you shall keep for it is a sign between Me and you throughout your generations, that you may know that I am the Lord who sanctifies you
Ex 31:16 Therefore the *children of Israel* shall keep the Sabbath, to observe the Sabbath throughout their generations as a perpetual covenant
Ex 31:17 It is a sign between Me and the *children of Israel* forever
Ex 32:20 and he scattered it on the water and made the *children of Israel* drink it
Ex 33:5 For the Lord had said to Moses, "Say to the *children of Israel*
Ex 33:6 So the *children of Israel* stripped themselves of their ornaments by Mount Horeb
Ex 34:30 So when Aaron and all the *children of Israel* saw Moses, behold, the skin of his face shone, and they were afraid to come near him
Ex 34:32 Afterward all the *children of Israel* came near, and he gave them as commandments all that the Lord had spoken with him on Mount Sinai
Ex 34:34 and he would come out and speak to the *children of Israel* whatever he had been commanded
Ex 34:35 And whenever the *children of Israel* saw the face of Moses, that the skin of Moses' face shone, then Moses would put the veil on his face again, until he went in to speak with Him
Ex 35:1 Then Moses gathered all the congregation of the *children of Israel* together, and said to them
Ex 35:4 And Moses spoke to all the congregation of the *children of Israel*, saying
Ex 35:20 And all the congregation of the *children of Israel* departed from the presence of Moses
Ex 35:29 The *children of Israel* brought a freewill offering to the Lord, all the men and women whose hearts were willing to bring material for all kinds of work which the Lord, by the hand of Moses, had commanded to be done
Ex 35:30 And Moses said to the *children of Israel*, "See, the Lord has called by name Bezalel the son of Uri, the son of Hur, of the tribe of Judah
Ex 36:3 And they received from Moses all the offering which the *children of Israel* had brought for the work of the service of making the sanctuary
Ex 39:32 And the *children of Israel* did according to all that the Lord had commanded Moses
Ex 39:42 According to all that the Lord had commanded Moses, so the *children of Israel* did all the work
Ex 40:36 When the cloud was taken up from above the tabernacle, the *children of Israel* went onward in all their journeys
Lev 1:2 Speak to the *children of Israel*, and say to them
Lev 4:2 Speak to the *children of Israel*, saying: "If a person sins unintentionally against any of the commandments of the Lord in anything which ought not to be done, and does any of them
Lev 7:23 Speak to the *children of Israel*, saying: "You shall not eat any fat, of ox or sheep or goat
Lev 7:29 Speak to the *children of Israel*, saying: "He who offers the sacrifice of his peace offering to the Lord shall bring his offering to the Lord from the sacrifice of his peace offering
Lev 7:34 For the breast of the wave offering and the thigh of the heave offering I have taken from the *children of Israel*, from the sacrifices of their peace offerings, and I have given them to Aaron the priest and to his sons from the *children of Israel* by a statute forever
Lev 7:36 The Lord commanded this to be given to them by the *children of Israel*, on the day that He anointed them, by a statute forever throughout their generations
Lev 7:38 which the Lord commanded Moses on Mount Sinai, on the day when He commanded the *children of Israel* to offer their offerings to the Lord in the Wilderness of Sinai
Lev 9:3 And to the *children of Israel* you shall speak, saying
Lev 10:11 and that you may teach the *children of Israel* all the statutes which the Lord has spoken to them by the hand of Moses
Lev 10:14 for they are your due and your sons' due, which are given from the sacrifices of peace offerings of the *children of Israel*
Lev 11:2 Speak to the *children of Israel*, saying, 'These are the animals which you may eat among all the beasts that are on the earth
Lev 12:2 Speak to the *children of Israel*, saying: "If a woman has conceived, and borne a male child, then she shall be unclean seven days
Lev 15:2 Speak to the *children of Israel*, and say to them
Lev 15:31 Thus you shall separate the *children of Israel* from their uncleanness, lest they die in their uncleanness when they defile My tabernacle that is among them
Lev 16:5 And he shall take from the congregation of the *children of Israel* two kids of the goats as a sin offering, and one ram as a burnt offering
Lev 16:16 So he shall make atonement for the Holy Place, because of the uncleanness of the *children of Israel*, and because of their transgressions, for all their sins
Lev 16:19 Then he shall sprinkle some of the blood on it with his finger seven times, cleanse it, and sanctify it from the uncleanness of the *children of Israel*
Lev 16:21 and Aaron shall lay both his hands on the head of the live goat, confess over it all the iniquities of the *children of Israel*, and all their transgressions, concerning all their sins, putting them on the head of the goat, and shall send it away into the wilderness by the hand of a suitable man
Lev 16:34 This shall be an everlasting statute for you, to make atonement for the *children of Israel*, for all their sins, once a year
Lev 17:2 Speak to Aaron, to his sons, and to all the *children of Israel*, and say to them
Lev 17:5 to the end that the *children of Israel* may bring their sacrifices which they offer in the open field, that they may bring them to the Lord at the door of the tabernacle of meeting, to the priest, and offer them as peace offerings to the Lord
Lev 17:12 Therefore I said to the *children of Israel*, 'No one among you shall eat blood, nor shall any stranger who sojourns among you eat blood
Lev 17:13 And whatever man of the *children of Israel*, or of the strangers who sojourn among you, who hunts and catches any animal or bird that may be eaten, he shall pour out its blood and cover it with dust
Lev 17:14 Therefore I said to the *children of Israel*, 'You shall not eat the blood of any flesh, for the life of all flesh is its blood

Lev 18:2 Speak to the *children of Israel*, and say to them
Lev 19:2 Speak to all the congregation of the *children of Israel*, and say to them
Lev 20:2 Again, you shall say to the *children of Israel:* "Whoever of the *children of Israel*, or of the strangers who sojourn in Israel, who gives any of his descendants to Molech, he shall surely be put to death
Lev 21:24 And Moses told it to Aaron and his sons, and to all the *children of Israel*
Lev 22:2 Speak to Aaron and his sons, that they separate themselves from the holy things of the *children of Israel*, and that they do not profane My holy name in those things which they sanctify to Me
Lev 22:3 Whoever of all your descendants throughout your generations, who goes near the holy things which the *children of Israel* sanctify to the Lord, while he has uncleanness upon him, that person shall be cut off from My presence
Lev 22:15 They shall not profane the holy offerings of the *children of Israel*, which they offer to the Lord
Lev 22:18 Speak to Aaron and his sons, and to all the *children of Israel*, and say to them
Lev 22:32 You shall not profane My holy name, but I will be hallowed among the *children of Israel*
Lev 23:2 Speak to the *children of Israel*, and say to them
Lev 23:10 Speak to the *children of Israel*, and say to them
Lev 23:24 Speak to the *children of Israel*, saying: "In the seventh month, on the first day of the month, you shall have a sabbath-rest, a memorial of blowing of trumpets, a holy convocation
Lev 23:34 Speak to the *children of Israel*, saying: "The fifteenth day of this seventh month shall be the Feast of Tabernacles for seven days to the Lord
Lev 23:43 that your generations may know that I made the *children of Israel* dwell in booths when I brought them out of the land of Egypt
Lev 23:44 So Moses declared to the *children of Israel* the feasts of the Lord
Lev 24:2 Command the *children of Israel* that they bring to you pure oil of pressed olives for the light, to make the lamps burn continually
Lev 24:8 Every Sabbath he shall set it in order before the Lord continually, being taken from the *children of Israel* by an everlasting covenant
Lev 24:10 Now the son of an Israelite woman, whose father was an Egyptian, went out among the *children of Israel*
Lev 24:15 Then you shall speak to the *children of Israel*, saying
Lev 24:23 Then Moses spoke to the *children of Israel;* and they took outside the camp him who had cursed, and stoned him with stones. So the *children of Israel* did as the Lord commanded Moses
Lev 25:2 Speak to the *children of Israel*, and say to them
Lev 25:33 for the houses in the cities of the Levites are their possession among the *children of Israel*
Lev 25:46 But regarding your brethren, the *children of Israel*, you shall not rule over one another with rigor
Lev 25:55 For the *children of Israel* are servants to Me; they are My servants whom I brought out of the land of Egypt
Lev 26:46 These are the statutes and judgments and laws which the Lord made between Himself and the *children of Israel* on Mount Sinai by the hand of
Lev 27:2 Speak to the *children of Israel*, and say to them
Lev 27:34 These are the commandments which the Lord commanded Moses for the *children of Israel* on Mount Sinai
Num 1:2 Take a census of all the congregation of the *children of Israel*, by their families, by their fathers' houses, according to the number of names, every male individually
Num 1:45 So all who were numbered of the *children of Israel*, by their fathers' houses, from twenty years old and above, all who were able to go to war in Israel
Num 1:49 Only the tribe of Levi you shall not number, nor take a census of them among the *children of Israel*
Num 1:52 The *children of Israel* shall pitch their tents, everyone by his own camp, everyone by his own standard, according to their armies
Num 1:53 but the Levites shall camp around the tabernacle of the Testimony, that there may be no wrath on the congregation of the *children of Israel*
Num 1:54 Thus the *children of Israel* did; according to all that the Lord commanded Moses, so they did
Num 2:2 Everyone of the *children of Israel* shall camp by his own standard, beside the emblems of his father's house
Num 2:32 These are the ones who were numbered of the *children of Israel* by their fathers' houses
Num 2:33 But the Levites were not numbered among the *children of Israel*, just as the Lord commanded Moses
Num 2:34 Thus the *children of Israel* did according to all that the Lord commanded Moses
Num 3:8 Also they shall attend to all the furnishings of the tabernacle of meeting, and to the needs of the *children of Israel*, to do the work of the tabernacle
Num 3:9 they are given entirely to him from among the *children of Israel*
Num 3:12 Now behold, I Myself have taken the Levites from among the *children of Israel* instead of every firstborn who opens the womb among the *children of Israel*
Num 3:38 Moreover those who were to camp before the tabernacle on the east, before the tabernacle of meeting, were Moses, Aaron, and his sons, keeping charge of the sanctuary, to meet the needs of the *children of Israel*
Num 3:40 Number all the firstborn males of the *children of Israel* from a month old and above, and take the number of their names
Num 3:41 And you shall take the Levites for Me I am the Lord instead of all the firstborn among the *children of Israel*, and the livestock of the Levites instead of all the firstborn among the livestock of the *children of Israel*
Num 3:42 So Moses numbered all the firstborn among the *children of Israel*, as the Lord commanded him
Num 3:45 Take the Levites instead of all the firstborn among the *children of Israel*, and the livestock of the Levites instead of their livestock
Num 3:46 And for the redemption of the two hundred and seventy-three of the firstborn of the *children of Israel*, who are more than the number of the Levites
Num 3:50 From the firstborn of the *children of Israel* he took the money, one thousand three hundred and sixty-five shekels, according to the shekel of the sanctuary
Num 5:2 Command the *children of Israel* that they put out of the camp every leper, everyone who has a discharge, and whoever becomes defiled by a dead body
Num 5:4 And the *children of Israel* did so, and put them outside the camp; as the Lord spoke to Moses, so the *children of Israel* did

Num 5:6 Speak to the *children of Israel:* When a man or woman commits any sin that men commit in unfaithfulness against the Lord, and that person is guilty
Num 5:9 Every offering of all the holy things of the *children of Israel*, which they bring to the priest, shall be his
Num 5:12 Speak to the *children of Israel*, and say to them
Num 6:2 Speak to the *children of Israel*, and say to them
Num 6:23 Speak to Aaron and his sons, saying, 'This is the way you shall bless the *children of Israel*
Num 6:27 So they shall put My name on the *children of Israel*, and I will bless them
Num 8:6 Take the Levites from among the *children of Israel* and cleanse them ceremonially
Num 8:9 And you shall bring the Levites before the tabernacle of meeting, and you shall gather together the whole assembly of the *children of Israel*
Num 8:10 So you shall bring the Levites before the Lord, and the *children of Israel* shall lay their hands on the Levites
Num 8:11 and Aaron shall offer the Levites before the Lord, as though a wave offering from the *children of Israel*, that they may perform the work of the Lord
Num 8:14 Thus you shall separate the Levites from among the *children of Israel*, and the Levites shall be Mine
Num 8:16 For they are wholly given to Me from among the *children of Israel;* I have taken them for Myself instead of all who open the womb, the firstborn of all the *children of Israel*
Num 8:17 For all the firstborn among the *children of Israel* are Mine, both man and beast
Num 8:18 I have taken the Levites instead of all the firstborn of the *children of Israel*
Num 8:19 And I have given the Levites as a gift to Aaron and his sons from among the *children of Israel*, to do the work for the *children of Israel* in the tabernacle of meeting, and to make atonement for the *children of Israel*, that there be no plague among the *children of Israel* when the *children of Israel* come near the sanctuary
Num 8:20 Thus Moses and Aaron and all the congregation of the *children of Israel* did to the Levites; according to all that the Lord commanded Moses concerning the Levites, so the *children of Israel* did to them
Num 9:2 Let the *children of Israel* keep the Passover at its appointed time
Num 9:4 So Moses told the *children of Israel* that they should keep the Passover
Num 9:5 according to all that the Lord commanded Moses, so the *children of Israel* did
Num 9:7 Why are we kept from presenting the offering of the Lord at its appointed time among the *children of Israel*
Num 9:10 Speak to the *children of Israel*, saying: "If anyone of you or your posterity is unclean because of a dead body, or is far away on a journey, he may still keep the Lord's Passover
Num 9:17 Whenever the cloud was taken up from above the tabernacle, after that the *children of Israel* would journey; and in the place where the cloud settled, there the *children of Israel* would pitch their tents
Num 9:18 At the command of the Lord the *children of Israel* would journey, and at the command of the Lord they would camp
Num 9:19 Even when the cloud continued long, many days above the tabernacle, the *children of Israel* kept the charge of the Lord and did not journey
Num 9:22 Whether it was two days, a month, or a year that the cloud remained above the tabernacle, the *children of Israel* would remain encamped and not journey
Num 10:12 And the *children of Israel* set out from the Wilderness of Sinai on their journeys
Num 10:28 Thus was the order of march of the *children of Israel*, according to their armies, when they began their journey
Num 11:4 so the *children of Israel* also wept again and said
Num 13:2 Send men to spy out the land of Canaan, which I am giving to the *children of Israel*
Num 13:3 So Moses sent them from the Wilderness of Paran according to the command of the Lord, all of them men who were heads of the *children of Israel*
Num 13:26 So they departed and came back to Moses and Aaron and all the congregation of the *children of Israel* in the Wilderness of Paran, at Kadesh
Num 13:32 And they gave the *children of Israel* a bad report of the land which they had spied out, saying
Num 14:2 And all the *children of Israel* murmured against Moses and Aaron, and the whole congregation said to them
Num 14:5 Then Moses and Aaron fell on their faces before all the assembly of the congregation of the *children of Israel*
Num 14:7 and they spoke to all the congregation of the *children of Israel*, saying
Num 14:10 Now the glory of the Lord appeared in the tabernacle of meeting before all the *children of Israel*
Num 14:27 I have heard the murmurings which the *children of Israel* murmur against Me
Num 14:39 Then Moses told these words to all the *children of Israel*, and the people mourned greatly
Num 15:2 Speak to the *children of Israel*, and say to them
Num 15:18 Speak to the *children of Israel*, and say to them
Num 15:25 So the priest shall make atonement for the whole congregation of the *children of Israel*, and it shall be forgiven them, for it was unintentional
Num 15:26 It shall be forgiven the whole congregation of the *children of Israel* and the stranger who sojourns among them, because all the people did it unintentionally
Num 15:29 You shall have one law for him who sins unintentionally, both for him who is native-born among the *children of Israel* and for the stranger who sojourns among them
Num 15:32 Now while the *children of Israel* were in the wilderness, they found a man gathering sticks on the Sabbath day
Num 15:38 Speak to the *children of Israel:* Tell them to make tassels on the corners of their garments throughout their generations, and to put a blue thread in the tassels of the corners
Num 16:2 and they rose up before Moses with some of the *children of Israel*, two hundred and fifty leaders of the congregation, representatives of the congregation, men of renown
Num 16:38 and they shall be a sign to the *children of Israel*
Num 16:40 to be a memorial to the *children of Israel* that no outsider, who is not a descendant of Aaron, should come near to offer incense before the Lord, that he might not become like Korah and his companions, just as the Lord had said to him through Moses
Num 16:41 On the next day all the congregation of the *children of Israel* murmured against Moses and Aaron, saying
Num 17:2 Speak to the *children of Israel*, and get

from them a rod from each father's house, all their leaders according to their fathers' houses twelve rods
Num 17:5 thus I will rid Myself of the murmurings of the *children of Israel*, which they murmur against you
Num 17:6 So Moses spoke to the *children of Israel*, and each of their leaders gave him a rod apiece, for each leader according to their fathers' houses, twelve rods
Num 17:9 Then Moses brought out all the rods from before the Lord to all the *children of Israel*
Num 17:12 And the *children of Israel* spoke to Moses, saying, "Surely we die, we perish, we all perish
Num 18:5 And you shall attend to the duties of the sanctuary and the duties of the altar, that there may be no more wrath on the *children of Israel*
Num 18:6 Behold, I Myself have taken your brethren the Levites from among the *children of Israel*
Num 18:8 Here, I Myself have also given you charge of My heave offerings, all the holy gifts of the *children of Israel*
Num 18:11 the heave offering of their gift, with all the wave offerings of the *children of Israel*
Num 18:19 All the heave offerings of the holy things, which the *children of Israel* offer to the Lord, I have given to you and your sons and daughters with you as an ordinance forever
Num 18:20 I am your portion and your inheritance among the *children of Israel*
Num 18:22 Hereafter the *children of Israel* shall not come near the tabernacle of meeting, lest they bear sin and die
Num 18:23 it shall be a statute forever, throughout your generations, that among the *children of Israel* they shall have no inheritance
Num 18:24 For the tithes of the *children of Israel*, which they offer up as a heave offering to the Lord, I have given to the Levites as an inheritance; therefore I have said to them, 'Among the *children of Israel* they shall have no inheritance
Num 18:26 When you take from the *children of Israel* the tithes which I have given you from them as your inheritance, then you shall offer up a heave offering of it to the Lord, a tenth of the tithe
Num 18:28 Thus you shall also offer a heave offering to the Lord from all your tithes which you receive from the *children of Israel*, and you shall give the Lord's heave offering from it to Aaron the priest
Num 18:32 But you shall not profane the holy gifts of the *children of Israel*, lest you die
Num 19:2 Speak to the *children of Israel*, that they bring you a red heifer without blemish, in which there is no defect and on which a yoke has never come
Num 19:9 and they shall be kept for the congregation of the *children of Israel* for the water of purification
Num 19:10 It shall be a statute forever to the *children of Israel* and to the stranger who sojourns among them
Num 20:1 Then the *children of Israel*, the whole congregation, came into the Wilderness of Zin in the first month, and the people stayed in Kadesh
Num 20:12 Then the Lord spoke to Moses and Aaron, "Because you did not believe Me, to hallow Me in the eyes of the *children of Israel*, therefore you shall not bring this congregation into the land which I have given them
Num 20:13 This was the water of Meribah, because the *children of Israel* contended with the Lord, and He was hallowed among them
Num 20:19 So the *children of Israel* said to him, "We will go by the Highway, and if I or my livestock drink any of your water, then I will pay for it
Num 20:22 Then the *children of Israel*, the whole congregation, journeyed from Kadesh and came to Mount Hor
Num 20:24 Aaron shall be gathered to his people, for he shall not enter the land which I have given to the *children of Israel*, because you rebelled against My word at the water of Meribah
Num 21:10 Now the *children of Israel* moved on and camped in Oboth
Num 22:1 Then the *children of Israel* moved, and camped in the plains of Moab on the side of the Jordan across from Jericho
Num 22:3 And Moab was exceedingly afraid of the people because they were many, and Moab was sick with dread because of the *children of Israel*
Num 25:6 And indeed, one of the *children of Israel* came and presented to his brethren a Midianite woman in the sight of Moses and in the sight of all the congregation of the *children of Israel*, who were weeping at the door of the tabernacle of meeting
Num 25:8 So the plague was stopped among the *children of Israel*
Num 25:11 Phinehas the son of Eleazar, the son of Aaron the priest, has turned back My wrath from the *children of Israel*, because he was zealous with My zeal among them, so that I did not consume the *children of Israel* in My zeal
Num 25:13 and it shall be to him and his descendants after him a covenant of an everlasting priesthood, because he was zealous for his God, and made atonement for the *children of Israel*
Num 26:2 Take a census of all the congregation of the *children of Israel* from twenty years old and above, by their fathers' houses, all who are able to go to war in Israel
Num 26:4 Take a census of the people from twenty years old and above, just as the Lord commanded Moses and the *children of Israel* who came out of the land of Egypt
Num 26:51 These are those who were numbered of the *children of Israel*
Num 26:62 for they were not numbered among the other *children of Israel*, because there was no inheritance given to them among the *children of Israel*
Num 26:63 These are those who were numbered by Moses and Eleazar the priest, who numbered the *children of Israel* in the plains of Moab by the Jordan, across from Jericho
Num 26:64 But among these there was not a man of those who were numbered by Moses and Aaron the priest when they numbered the *children of Israel* in the Wilderness of Sinai
Num 27:8 And you shall speak to the *children of Israel*, saying
Num 27:11 And it shall be to the *children of Israel* a statute of judgment, just as the Lord commanded Moses
Num 27:12 Go up into this Mount Abarim, and see the land which I have given to the *children of Israel*
Num 27:20 And you shall give some of your authority to him, that all the congregation of the *children of Israel* may be obedient
Num 27:21 at his word they shall go out, and at his word they shall come in, both he and all the *children of Israel* with him, all the congregation
Num 28:2 Command the *children of Israel*, and say to them, 'My offering, My food for My offerings made by fire as a sweet aroma to Me, you shall be careful to offer to Me at their appointed time
Num 29:40 So Moses told the *children of Israel* everything, just as the Lord commanded Moses

Num 30:1 Then Moses spoke to the heads of the tribes concerning the *children of Israel*, saying
Num 31:2 Take vengeance for the *children of Israel* on the Midianites
Num 31:9 And the *children of Israel* took all the women of Midian captive, with their little ones, and took as spoil all their cattle, all their flocks, and all their goods
Num 31:12 Then they brought the captives, the booty, and the spoil to Moses, to Eleazar the priest, and to the congregation of the *children of Israel*, to the camp in the plains of Moab by the Jordan, across from Jericho
Num 31:16 Look, these women caused the *children of Israel*, through the counsel of Balaam, to trespass against the Lord in the incident of Peor, and there was a plague among the congregation of the Lord
Num 31:54 And Moses and Eleazar the priest received the gold from the captains of thousands and of hundreds, and brought it into the tabernacle of meeting as a memorial for the *children of Israel* before the Lord
Num 32:7 Now why will you discourage the heart of the *children of Israel* from going over into the land which the Lord has given them
Num 32:9 For when they went up to the Valley of Eshcol and saw the land, they discouraged the heart of the *children of Israel*, so that they did not go into the land which the Lord had given them
Num 32:17 but we ourselves will be armed, ready to go before the *children of Israel* until we have brought them to their place
Num 32:18 We will not return to our homes until every one of the *children of Israel* has received his inheritance
Num 32:28 So Moses gave command concerning them to Eleazar the priest, to Joshua the son of Nun, and to the chief fathers of the tribes of the *children of Israel*
Num 33:1 These are the journeys of the *children of Israel*, who went out of the land of Egypt by their armies under the hand of Moses and Aaron
Num 33:3 on the day after the Passover the *children of Israel* went out with boldness in the sight of all the Egyptians
Num 33:5 Then the *children of Israel* moved from Rameses and camped at Succoth
Num 33:38 Then Aaron the priest went up to Mount Hor at the command of the Lord, and died there in the fortieth year after the *children of Israel* had come out of the land of Egypt, on the first day of the fifth month
Num 33:40 Now the king of Arad, the Canaanite, who dwelt in the South in the land of Canaan, heard of the coming of the *children of Israel*
Num 33:51 Speak to the *children of Israel*, and say to them
Num 34:2 Command the *children of Israel*, and say to them: "When you come into the land of Canaan, this is the land that shall fall to you as an inheritance the land of Canaan to its boundaries
Num 34:13 Then Moses commanded the *children of Israel*, saying: "This is the land which you shall inherit by lot, which the Lord has commanded to give to the nine tribes and to the half-tribe
Num 34:29 These are the ones the Lord commanded to divide the inheritance among the *children of Israel* in the land of Canaan
Num 35:2 Command the *children of Israel* that they give the Levites cities to dwell in from the inheritance of their possession, and you shall also give the Levites common-land around the cities
Num 35:8 And the cities which you will give shall be from the possession of the *children of Israel*
Num 35:10 Speak to the *children of Israel*, and say to them
Num 35:15 These six cities shall be for refuge for the *children of Israel*, for the stranger, and for the sojourner among them, that anyone who kills a person accidentally may flee there
Num 35:34 for I the Lord dwell among the *children of Israel*
Num 36:1 Now the chief fathers of the families of the children of Gilead the son of Machir, the son of Manasseh, of the families of the sons of Joseph, came near and spoke before Moses and before the leaders, the chief fathers of the *children of Israel*
Num 36:2 The Lord commanded my lord Moses to give the land as an inheritance by lot to the *children of Israel*, and my lord was commanded by the Lord to give the inheritance of our brother Zelophehad to his daughters
Num 36:3 Now if they are married to any of the sons of the other tribes of the *children of Israel*, then their inheritance will be taken from the inheritance of our fathers, and it will be added to the inheritance of the tribe into which they marry
Num 36:4 And when the Jubilee of the *children of Israel* comes, then their inheritance will be added to the inheritance of the tribe into which they marry
Num 36:5 Then Moses commanded the *children of Israel* according to the word of the Lord, saying
Num 36:7 So the inheritance of the *children of Israel* shall not change hands from tribe to tribe, for every one of the *children of Israel* shall keep the inheritance of the tribe of his fathers
Num 36:8 And every daughter who possesses an inheritance in any tribe of the *children of Israel* shall be the wife of one of the family of her father's tribe, so that the *children of Israel* each may possess the inheritance of his fathers
Num 36:9 Thus no inheritance shall change hands from one tribe to another, but every tribe of the *children of Israel* shall keep its own inheritance
Num 36:13 These are the commandments and the judgments which the Lord commanded the *children of Israel* by the hand of Moses in the plains of Moab by the Jordan, across from Jericho
Deut 1:3 Now it came to pass in the fortieth year, in the eleventh month, on the first day of the month, that Moses spoke to the *children of Israel* according to all that the Lord had given him as commandments to them
Deut 3:18 All you men of valor shall cross over armed before your brethren, the *children of Israel*
Deut 4:44 And this is the law which Moses set before the *children of Israel*
Deut 4:45 These are the testimonies, the statutes, and the judgments which Moses spoke to the *children of Israel* after they came out of Egypt
Deut 4:46 on this side of the Jordan, in the valley opposite Beth Peor, in the land of Sihon king of the Amorites, who dwelt at Heshbon, whom Moses and the *children of Israel* defeated after they came out of Egypt
Deut 10:6 (Now the *children of Israel* journeyed from the wells of Bene Jaakan to Moserah
Deut 24:7 If a man is found kidnapping any of his brethren of the *children of Israel*, and mistreats him or sells him, then that kidnapper shall die
Deut 29:1 These are the words of the covenant which the Lord commanded Moses to make with the *children of Israel* in the land of Moab, besides the covenant which He made with them in Horeb
Deut 31:19 Now therefore, write down this song for yourselves, and teach it to the *children of Israel;* put it in their mouths, that this song may be a witness for Me against the *children of Israel*
Deut 31:22 Therefore Moses wrote this song the same day, and taught it to the *children of Israel*

Deut 31:23 for you shall bring the *children of Israel* into the land of which I swore to them, and I will be with you
Deut 32:8 when the Most High divided their inheritance to the nations, when He separated the sons of Adam, He set the boundaries of the peoples according to the number of the *children of Israel*
Deut 32:49 view the land of Canaan, which I give to the *children of Israel* as a possession
Deut 32:51 because you trespassed against Me among the *children of Israel* at the waters of Meribah Kadesh, in the Wilderness of Zin, because you did not hallow Me in the midst of the *children of Israel*
Deut 32:52 Yet you shall see the land before you, though you shall not go there, into the land which I am giving to the *children of Israel*
Deut 33:1 Now this is the blessing with which Moses the man of God blessed the *children of Israel* before his death
Deut 34:8 And the *children of Israel* wept for Moses in the plains of Moab thirty days
Deut 34:9 so the *children of Israel* heeded him, and did as the Lord had commanded Moses
Josh 1:2 Now therefore, arise, go over this Jordan, you and all this people, to the land which I am giving to them the *children of Israel*
Josh 2:2 And it was told the king of Jericho, saying, "Behold, men have come here tonight from the *children of Israel* to search out the country
Josh 3:1 and they set out from Acacia Grove and came to the Jordan, he and all the *children of Israel*, and lodged there before they crossed over
Josh 3:9 So Joshua said to the *children of Israel*, "Come here, and hear the words of the Lord your God
Josh 4:4 Then Joshua called the twelve men whom he had appointed from the *children of Israel*, one man from every tribe
Josh 4:5 Cross over before the ark of the Lord your God into the midst of the Jordan, and each one of you take up a stone on his shoulder, according to the number of the tribes of the *children of Israel*
Josh 4:7 And these stones shall be for a memorial to the *children of Israel* forever
Josh 4:8 And the *children of Israel* did so, just as Joshua commanded, and took up twelve stones from the midst of the Jordan, as the Lord had spoken to Joshua, according to the number of the tribes of the *children of Israel*, and carried them over with them to the place where they lodged, and laid them down there
Josh 4:12 And the men of Reuben, the men of Gad, and half the tribe of Manasseh crossed over armed before the *children of Israel*, as Moses had spoken to them
Josh 4:21 Then he spoke to the *children of Israel*, saying: "When your children ask their fathers in time to come, saying
Josh 5:1 So it was, when all the kings of the Amorites who were on the west side of the Jordan, and all the kings of the Canaanites who were by the sea, heard that the Lord had dried up the waters of the Jordan from before the *children of Israel* until we had crossed over, that their heart melted; and there was no spirit in them any longer because of the *children of Israel*
Josh 5:6 For the *children of Israel* walked forty years in the wilderness, till all the people who were men of war, who came out of Egypt, were consumed, because they did not obey the voice of the Lord to whom the Lord swore that He would not show them the land which the Lord had sworn to their fathers that He would give us
Josh 5:10 So the *children of Israel* camped in Gilgal, and kept the Passover on the fourteenth day of the month at twilight on the plains of Jericho
Josh 5:12 and the *children of Israel* no longer had manna, but they ate the food of the land of Canaan that year
Josh 6:1 Now Jericho was securely shut up because of the *children of Israel*
Josh 7:1 But the *children of Israel* committed a trespass regarding the accursed things, for Achan the son of Carmi, the son of Zabdi, the son of Zerah, of the tribe of Judah, took of the accursed things; so the anger of the Lord burned against the *children of Israel*
Josh 7:12 Therefore the *children of Israel* could not stand before their enemies, but turned their backs before their enemies, because they have become doomed to destruction
Josh 7:23 And they took them from the midst of the tent, brought them to Joshua and to all the *children of Israel*, and laid them out before the Lord
Josh 8:31 as Moses the servant of the Lord had commanded the *children of Israel*, as it is written in the Book of the Law of Moses
Josh 8:32 And there, in the presence of the *children of Israel*, he wrote on the stones a copy of the law of Moses, which he had written
Josh 9:17 Then the *children of Israel* journeyed and came to their cities on the third day
Josh 9:18 But the *children of Israel* did not attack them, because the rulers of the congregation had sworn to them by the Lord God of Israel
Josh 9:26 So he did to them, and delivered them out of the hand of the *children of Israel*, so that they did not kill them
Josh 10:4 Come up to me and help me, that we may attack Gibeon, for it has made peace with Joshua and with the *children of Israel*
Josh 10:11 There were more who died from the hailstones than those whom the *children of Israel* killed with the sword
Josh 10:12 Then Joshua spoke to the Lord in the day when the Lord delivered up the Amorites before the *children of Israel*, and he said in the sight of Israel
Josh 10:20 Then it happened, while Joshua and the *children of Israel* made an end of slaying them with a very great slaughter, till they had finished, that those who escaped entered fortified cities
Josh 10:21 No one moved his tongue against any of the *children of Israel*
Josh 11:14 And all the spoil of these cities and the livestock, the *children of Israel* took as booty for themselves
Josh 11:19 There was not a city that made peace with the *children of Israel*, except the Hivites, the inhabitants of Gibeon
Josh 11:22 None of the Anakim were left in the land of the *children of Israel*
Josh 12:1 These are the kings of the land whom the *children of Israel* defeated, and whose land they possessed on the other side of the Jordan toward the rising of the sun, from the River Arnon to Mount Hermon, and all the eastern Jordan plain
Josh 12:6 These Moses the servant of the Lord and the *children of Israel* had conquered
Josh 12:7 And these are the kings of the country which Joshua and the *children of Israel* conquered on this side of the Jordan, on the west, from Baal Gad in the Valley of Lebanon as far as Mount Halak and the ascent to Seir, which Joshua gave to the tribes of Israel as a possession according to their divisions
Josh 13:6 all the inhabitants of the mountains from Lebanon as far as the Brook Misrephoth, and all the Sidonians them I will drive out from before the *children of Israel*
Josh 13:13 Nevertheless the *children of Israel* did

not drive out the Geshurites or the Maachathites, but the Geshurites and the Maachathites dwell among the Israelites until this day

Josh 13:22 The *children of Israel* also killed with the sword Balaam the son of Beor, the soothsayer, among those who were killed by them

Josh 14:1 These are the areas which the *children of Israel* inherited in the land of Canaan, which Eleazar the priest, Joshua the son of Nun, and the heads of the fathers of the tribes of the *children of Israel* distributed as an inheritance to them

Josh 14:5 As the Lord had commanded Moses, so the *children of Israel* did

Josh 17:13 And it happened, when the *children of Israel* grew strong, that they put the Canaanites to forced labor, but did not utterly drive them out

Josh 18:1 Then the whole congregation of the *children of Israel* assembled together at Shiloh, and set up the tabernacle of meeting there

Josh 18:2 But there remained among the *children of Israel* seven tribes which had not yet received their inheritance

Josh 18:3 Then Joshua said to the *children of Israel:* "How long will you neglect to go and possess the land which the Lord God of your fathers has given you

Josh 18:10 Then Joshua cast lots for them in Shiloh before the Lord, and there Joshua divided the land to the *children of Israel* according to their divisions

Josh 19:49 When they had made an end of dividing the land as an inheritance according to their borders, the *children of Israel* gave an inheritance among them to Joshua the son of Nun

Josh 19:51 These were the inheritances which Eleazar the priest, Joshua the son of Nun, and the heads of the fathers of the tribes of the *children of Israel* divided as an inheritance by lot in Shiloh before the Lord, at the door of the tabernacle of meeting

Josh 20:2 Speak to the *children of Israel*, saying: "Appoint for yourselves cities of refuge, of which I spoke to you through Moses

Josh 20:9 These were the cities appointed for all the *children of Israel* and for the stranger who sojourned among them, that whoever killed any person accidentally might flee there, and not die by the hand of the avenger of blood until he stood before the congregation

Josh 21:1 Now the heads of the fathers of the Levites came near to Eleazar the priest, to Joshua the son of Nun, and to the heads of the fathers of the tribes of the *children of Israel*

Josh 21:3 So the *children of Israel* gave to the Levites from their inheritance, at the commandment of the Lord, these cities and their common-lands

Josh 21:8 And the *children of Israel* gave these cities with their common-lands by lot to the Levites, as the Lord had commanded by the hand of Moses

Josh 21:41 All the cities of the Levites within the possession of the *children of Israel* were forty-eight cities with their common-lands

Josh 22:9 So the children of Reuben, the children of Gad, and half the tribe of Manasseh returned, and departed from the *children of Israel* at Shiloh, which is in the land of Canaan, to go to the country of Gilead, to the land of their possession, which they possessed according to the word of the Lord by the hand of Moses

Josh 22:11 Now the *children of Israel* heard someone say, "Behold, the children of Reuben, the children of Gad, and half the tribe of Manasseh have built an altar on the frontier of the land of Canaan, in the region of the Jordan, on the side occupied by the *children of Israel*

Josh 22:12 And when the *children of Israel* heard of it, the whole congregation of the *children of Israel* gathered together at Shiloh to go to war against them

Josh 22:13 Then the *children of Israel* sent Phinehas the son of Eleazar the priest to the children of Reuben, to the children of Gad, and to half the tribe of Manasseh, into the land of Gilead

Josh 22:31 Now you have delivered the *children of Israel* out of the hand of the Lord

Josh 22:32 And Phinehas the son of Eleazar the priest, and the rulers, returned from the children of Reuben and the children of Gad, from the land of Gilead to the land of Canaan, to the *children of Israel*, and brought back word to them

Josh 22:33 So the thing pleased the *children of Israel*, and the *children of Israel* blessed God

Josh 24:32 The bones of Joseph, which the *children of Israel* had brought up out of Egypt, they buried at Shechem, in the plot of ground which Jacob had bought from the sons of Hamor the father of Shechem for one hundred pieces of silver, and which had become an inheritance of the children of Joseph

Judg 1:1 Now after the death of Joshua it came to pass that the *children of Israel* asked the Lord, saying

Judg 2:4 And so it was, when the Angel of the Lord spoke these words to all the *children of Israel*, that the people lifted up their voice and wept

Judg 2:6 And when Joshua had dismissed the people, the *children of Israel* went each to his own inheritance to possess the land

Judg 2:11 Then the *children of Israel* did evil in the sight of the Lord, and served the Baals

Judg 3:2 (this was only so that the generations of the *children of Israel* might be taught to know war, at least those who had not formerly known it

Judg 3:5 So the *children of Israel* dwelt among the Canaanites, the Hittites, the Amorites, the Perizzites, the Hivites, and the Jebusites

Judg 3:7 So the *children of Israel* did evil in the sight of the Lord

Judg 3:8 Therefore the anger of the Lord was hot against Israel, and He sold them into the hand of Cushan-Rishathaim king of Mesopotamia; and the *children of Israel* served Cushan-Rishathaim eight years

Judg 3:9 When the *children of Israel* cried out to the Lord, the Lord raised up a deliverer for the *children of Israel*, who delivered them

Judg 3:12 And the *children of Israel* again did evil in the sight of the Lord

Judg 3:14 So the *children of Israel* served Eglon king of Moab eighteen years

Judg 3:15 And when the *children of Israel* cried out to the Lord, the Lord raised up a deliverer for them: Ehud, the son of Gera, a left-handed man. By him the *children of Israel* sent tribute to Eglon king of Moab

Judg 3:27 And it happened, when he arrived, that he blew the trumpet in the mountains of Ephraim, and the *children of Israel* went down with him from the mountains

Judg 4:1 When Ehud was dead, the *children of Israel* again did evil in the sight of the Lord

Judg 4:3 And the *children of Israel* cried out to the Lord; for Jabin had nine hundred chariots of iron, and for twenty years he harshly oppressed the *children of Israel*

Judg 4:5 And the *children of Israel* came up to her for judgment

Judg 4:23 So on that day God subdued Jabin king of Canaan in the presence of the *children of Israel*

Judg 4:24 And the hand of the *children of Israel* grew stronger and stronger against Jabin king of

Canaan, until they had destroyed Jabin king of Canaan

Judg 6:1 And the *children of Israel* did evil in the sight of the Lord

Judg 6:2 Because of the Midianites, the *children of Israel* made for themselves the dens, the caves, and the strongholds which are in the mountains

Judg 6:6 So Israel was greatly impoverished because of the Midianites, and the *children of Israel* cried out to the Lord

Judg 6:7 And it came to pass, when the *children of Israel* cried out to the Lord because of the Midianites

Judg 6:8 that the Lord sent a prophet to the *children of Israel*, who said to them

Judg 8:28 Thus Midian was subdued before the *children of Israel*, so that they lifted their heads no more

Judg 8:33 And it was so, as soon as Gideon was dead, that the *children of Israel* again played the harlot with the Baals, and made Baal-Berith their god

Judg 8:34 Thus the *children of Israel* did not remember the Lord their God, who had delivered them from the hands of all their enemies on every side

Judg 10:6 Then the *children of Israel* again did evil in the sight of the Lord, and served the Baals and the Ashtoreths, the gods of Syria, the gods of Sidon, the gods of Moab, the gods of the people of Ammon, and the gods of the Philistines

Judg 10:8 From that year they harassed and oppressed the *children of Israel* for eighteen years all the *children of Israel* who were on the other side of the Jordan in the land of the Amorites, in Gilead

Judg 10:10 And the *children of Israel* cried out to the Lord, saying

Judg 10:11 So the Lord said to the *children of Israel*, "Did I not deliver you from the Egyptians and from the Amorites and from the people of Ammon and from the Philistines

Judg 10:15 Then the *children of Israel* said to the Lord, "We have sinned

Judg 10:17 And the *children of Israel* assembled together and encamped in Mizpah

Judg 11:27 May the Lord, the Judge, render judgment this day between the *children of Israel* and the people of Ammon

Judg 11:33 Thus the people of Ammon were subdued before the *children of Israel*

Judg 13:1 Again the *children of Israel* did evil in the sight of the Lord, and the Lord delivered them into the hand of the Philistines for forty years

Judg 19:12 But his master said to him, "We will not turn aside here into a city of foreigners, who are not of the *children of Israel*

Judg 19:30 And so it was that all who saw it said, "No such deed has been done or seen from the day that the *children of Israel* came up from the land of Egypt until this day

Judg 20:1 Then all the *children of Israel* came out, from Dan to Beersheba, as well as from the land of Gilead, and the congregation gathered together as one man before the Lord at Mizpah

Judg 20:3 (Now the children of Benjamin heard that the *children of Israel* had gone up to Mizpah.) Then the *children of Israel* said

Judg 20:7 All of you are *children of Israel;* give your advice and counsel here and now

Judg 20:13 But the children of Benjamin would not listen to the voice of their brethren, the *children of Israel*

Judg 20:14 Instead, the children of Benjamin gathered together from their cities to Gibeah, to go to battle against the *children of Israel*

Judg 20:18 And the *children of Israel* arose and went up to the house of God to ask counsel of God

Judg 20:19 So the *children of Israel* rose in the morning and encamped against Gibeah

Judg 20:23 Then the *children of Israel* went up and wept before the Lord until evening, and asked counsel of the Lord, saying

Judg 20:24 So the *children of Israel* approached the children of Benjamin on the second day

Judg 20:25 And Benjamin went out against them from Gibeah on the second day, and cut down to the ground eighteen thousand more of the *children of Israel*

Judg 20:26 Then all the *children of Israel*, that is, all the people, went up and came to the house of God and wept

Judg 20:27 So the *children of Israel* inquired of the Lord (the ark of the covenant of God was there in those days

Judg 20:30 And the *children of Israel* went up against the children of Benjamin on the third day, and put themselves in battle array against Gibeah as at the other times

Judg 20:32 But the *children of Israel* said, "Let us flee and draw them away from the city to the highways

Judg 20:35 And the *children of Israel* destroyed that day twenty-five thousand one hundred Benjamites

Judg 21:5 The *children of Israel* said, "Who is there among all the tribes of Israel who did not come up with the assembly to the Lord

Judg 21:6 And the *children of Israel* grieved for Benjamin their brother, and said

Judg 21:18 However, we cannot give them wives from our daughters, for the *children of Israel* have sworn an oath, saying

Judg 21:24 So the *children of Israel* departed from there at that time, every man to his tribe and family

1Sam 2:28 And did I not give to the house of your father all the offerings of the *children of Israel* made by fire

1Sam 7:4 So the *children of Israel* put away the Baals and the Ashtoreths, and served the Lord only

1Sam 7:6 And they fasted that day, and said there, "We have sinned against the Lord." And Samuel judged the *children of Israel* at Mizpah

1Sam 7:7 Now when the Philistines heard that the *children of Israel* had gathered together at Mizpah, the lords of the Philistines went up against Israel. And when the *children of Israel* heard of it, they were afraid of the Philistines

1Sam 7:8 So the *children of Israel* said to Samuel, "Do not cease to cry out to the Lord our God for us, that He may save us from the hand of the Philistines

1Sam 9:2 There was not a more handsome person than he among the *children of Israel*

1Sam 10:18 and said to the *children of Israel*, "Thus says the Lord God of Israel

1Sam 11:8 When he numbered them in Bezek, the *children of Israel* were three hundred thousand, and the men of Judah thirty thousand

1Sam 14:18 And Saul said to Ahijah, "Bring the ark of God here" (for at that time the ark of God was with the *children of Israel*

1Sam 15:6 For you showed kindness to all the *children of Israel* when they came up out of Egypt

1Sam 17:53 Then the *children of Israel* returned from chasing the Philistines, and they plundered their tents

2Sam 7:6 For I have not dwelt in a house since the time that I brought the *children of Israel* up from Egypt, even to this day, but have moved about in a tent and in a tabernacle

2Sam 7:7 In all the places where I have walked with all the *children of Israel*, have I ever spoken a word to anyone from the tribes of Israel, whom I commanded to shepherd My people Israel, saying

2Sam 21:2 Now the Gibeonites were not of the *children of Israel*, but of the remnant of the Amorites; the *children of Israel* had sworn protection to them, but Saul had sought to kill them in his zeal for the *children of Israel* and Judah

1Kin 6:1 And it came to pass in the four hundred and eightieth year after the *children of Israel* had come out of the land of Egypt, in the fourth year of Solomon's reign over Israel, in the month of Ziv, which is the second month, that he began to build the house of the Lord

1Kin 6:13 And I will dwell among the *children of Israel*, and will not forsake My people Israel

1Kin 8:1 Now Solomon assembled the elders of Israel and all the heads of the tribes, the chief fathers of the *children of Israel*, to King Solomon in Jerusalem, that they might bring up the ark of the covenant of the Lord from the City of David, which is Zion

1Kin 8:9 There was nothing in the ark except the two tablets of stone which Moses put there at Horeb, when the Lord made a covenant with the *children of Israel*, when they came out of the land of Egypt

1Kin 8:63 So the king and all the *children of Israel* dedicated the house of the Lord

1Kin 9:20 All the people who were left of the Amorites, Hittites, Perizzites, Hivites, and Jebusites, who were not of the *children of Israel*

1Kin 9:21 that is, their descendants who were left in the land after them, whom the *children of Israel* had not been able to destroy completely from these Solomon raised forced labor, as it is to this day

1Kin 9:22 But of the *children of Israel* Solomon made no forced laborers, because they were men of war and his servants

1Kin 11:2 from the nations of whom the Lord had said to the *children of Israel*

1Kin 12:17 But Rehoboam reigned over the *children of Israel* who dwelt in the cities of Judah

1Kin 12:24 You shall not go up nor fight against your brethren the *children of Israel*

1Kin 12:33 And he ordained a feast for the *children of Israel*, and offered sacrifices on the altar and burned incense

1Kin 14:24 They did according to all the abominations of the nations which the Lord had cast out before the *children of Israel*

1Kin 18:20 So Ahab sent for all the *children of Israel*, and gathered the prophets together on Mount Carmel

1Kin 19:10 for the *children of Israel* have forsaken Your covenant, torn down Your altars, and killed Your prophets with the sword

1Kin 19:14 because the *children of Israel* have forsaken Your covenant, torn down Your altars, and killed Your prophets with the sword

1Kin 20:15 and after them he mustered all the people, all the *children of Israel* seven thousand

1Kin 20:27 And the *children of Israel* were mustered and given provisions, and they went against them. Now the *children of Israel* encamped before them like two little flocks of goats, while the Syrians filled the countryside

1Kin 20:29 and the *children of Israel* killed one hundred thousand foot soldiers of the Syrians in one day

1Kin 21:26 And he behaved very abominably in following idols, according to all that the Amorites had done, whom the Lord had cast out before the *children of Israel*

2Kin 8:12 And he answered, "Because I know the evil that you will do to the *children of Israel*

2Kin 13:5 and the *children of Israel* dwelt in their tents as before

2Kin 16:3 indeed he made his son pass through the fire, according to the abominations of the nations whom the Lord had cast out from before the *children of Israel*

2Kin 17:7 For so it was that the *children of Israel* had sinned against the Lord their God, who had brought them up out of the land of Egypt, from under the hand of Pharaoh king of Egypt

2Kin 17:8 and had walked in the statutes of the nations whom the Lord had cast out from before the *children of Israel*, and of the kings of Israel, which they had made

2Kin 17:9 Also the *children of Israel* secretly did against the Lord their God things that were not right, and they built for themselves high places in all their cities, from watchtower to fortified city

2Kin 17:22 For the *children of Israel* walked in all the sins of Jeroboam which he did

2Kin 17:24 Then the king of Assyria brought people from Babylon, Cuthah, Ava, Hamath, and from Sepharvaim, and placed them in the cities of Samaria instead of the *children of Israel*

2Kin 18:4 for until those days the *children of Israel* burned incense to it, and called it Nehushtan

2Kin 21:2 And he did evil in the sight of the Lord, according to the abominations of the nations whom the Lord had cast out before the *children of Israel*

2Kin 21:9 But they paid no attention, and Manasseh seduced them to do more evil than the nations whom the Lord had destroyed before the *children of Israel*

1Chr 1:43 Now these were the kings who reigned in the land of Edom before any king reigned over the *children of Israel*

1Chr 6:64 So the *children of Israel* gave these cities with their common-lands to the Levites

1Chr 27:1 And the *children of Israel*, according to their number, the heads of fathers' houses, the captains of thousands and hundreds and their officers, served the king in every matter of the military divisions

2Chr 5:2 Now Solomon assembled the elders of Israel and all the heads of the tribes, the chief fathers of the *children of Israel*, in Jerusalem, that they might bring the ark of the covenant of the Lord up from the City of David, which is Zion

2Chr 5:10 There was nothing in the ark except the two tablets which Moses put there at Horeb, when the Lord made a covenant with the *children of Israel*, when they had come out of Egypt

2Chr 6:11 And there I have put the ark, in which is the covenant of the Lord which He made with the *children of Israel*

2Chr 7:3 When all the *children of Israel* saw how the fire came down, and the glory of the Lord on the temple, they bowed their faces to the ground on the pavement, and worshiped and praised the Lord, saying

2Chr 8:2 that the cities which Hiram had given to Solomon, Solomon built them; and he settled the *children of Israel* there

2Chr 8:8 (that is, their descendants who were left in the land after them, whom the *children of Israel* did not destroy

2Chr 8:9 But Solomon did not make the *children of Israel* servants for his work

2Chr 10:17 But Rehoboam reigned over the *children of Israel* who dwelt in the cities of Judah

2Chr 10:18 but the *children of Israel* stoned him with stones, and he died

2Chr 13:12 O *children of Israel*, do not fight against the Lord God of your fathers, for you shall not prosper

2Chr 13:16 And the *children of Israel* fled before Judah, and God delivered them into their hand
2Chr 13:18 Thus the *children of Israel* were subdued at that time
2Chr 28:3 He burned incense in the Valley of the Son of Hinnom, and burned his children in the fire, according to the abominations of the nations whom the Lord had cast out before the *children of Israel*
2Chr 28:8 And the *children of Israel* carried away captive of their brethren two hundred thousand women, sons, and daughters
2Chr 30:6 *Children of Israel*, return to the Lord God of Abraham, Isaac, and Israel
2Chr 30:21 So the *children of Israel* who were present at Jerusalem kept the Feast of Unleavened Bread seven days with great gladness
2Chr 31:1 Then all the *children of Israel* returned to their own cities, every man to his possession
2Chr 31:5 As soon as the commandment was circulated, the *children of Israel* brought in abundance the firstfruits of grain and wine, oil and honey, and of all the produce of the field
2Chr 31:6 And the *children of Israel* and Judah, who dwelt in the cities of Judah, brought the tithe of oxen and sheep
2Chr 33:2 But he did evil in the sight of the Lord, according to the abominations of the nations whom the Lord had cast out before the *children of Israel*
2Chr 33:9 So Manasseh seduced Judah and the inhabitants of Jerusalem to do more evil than the nations whom the Lord had destroyed before the *children of Israel*
2Chr 34:33 Thus Josiah removed all the abominations from all the country that belonged to the *children of Israel*, and made all who were present in Israel diligently serve the Lord their God
2Chr 35:17 And the *children of Israel* who were present kept the Passover at that time, and the Feast of Unleavened Bread for seven days
Ezra 3:1 And when the seventh month had come, and the *children of Israel* were in the cities, the people gathered together as one man to Jerusalem
Ezra 6:16 Then the *children of Israel*, the priests and the Levites and the rest of the descendants of the captivity, celebrated the dedication of this house of God with joy
Ezra 6:21 Then the *children of Israel* who had returned from the captivity ate together with all who had separated themselves from the filth of the nations of the land in order to seek the Lord God of Israel
Ezra 7:7 Some of the *children of Israel*, the priests, the Levites, the singers, the gatekeepers, and the Nethinim came up to Jerusalem in the seventh year of King Artaxerxes
Neh 1:6 please let Your ear be attentive and Your eyes open, that You may hear the prayer of Your servant which I pray before You now, day and night, for the *children of Israel* Your servants, and confess the sins of the *children of Israel* which we have sinned against You
Neh 2:10 When Sanballat the Horonite and Tobiah the Ammonite official heard of it, they were deeply disturbed that a man had come to seek the well-being of the *children of Israel*
Neh 7:73 When the seventh month came, the *children of Israel* were in their cities
Neh 8:14 And they found written in the Law, which the Lord had commanded by Moses, that the *children of Israel* should dwell in booths during the feast of the seventh month
Neh 8:17 for since the days of Joshua the son of Nun until that day the *children of Israel* had not done so
Neh 9:1 Now on the twenty-fourth day of this month the *children of Israel* were assembled with fasting, in sackcloth, and with dust on their heads
Neh 10:39 For the *children of Israel* and the children of Levi shall bring the offering of the grain, of the new wine and the oil, to the storerooms where the articles of the sanctuary are, where the priests who minister and the gatekeepers and the singers are
Neh 13:2 because they had not met the *children of Israel* with bread and water, but hired Balaam against them to curse them
Ps 103:7 He made known His ways to Moses, His acts to the *children of Israel*
Ps 148:14 And He has exalted the horn of His people, the praise of all His saints of the *children of Israel*, a people near to Him
Is 17:3 they will be as the glory of the *children of Israel*
Is 17:9 In that day his strong cities will be as a forsaken bough and an uppermost branch, which they left because of the *children of Israel*
Is 27:12 and you will be gathered one by one, O you *children of Israel*
Is 31:6 Return to Him against whom the *children of Israel* have deeply revolted
Is 66:20 Then they shall bring all your brethren for an offering to the Lord out of all nations, on horses and in chariots and in litters, on mules and on camels, to My holy mountain Jerusalem," says the Lord, "as the *children of Israel* bring an offering in a clean vessel into the house of the Lord
Jer 3:21 A voice was heard on the desolate heights, weeping and supplications of the *children of Israel*
Jer 16:14 Therefore behold, the days are coming," says the Lord, "that it shall no more be said, 'The Lord lives who brought up the *children of Israel* from the land of Egypt
Jer 16:15 but, 'The Lord lives who brought up the *children of Israel* from the land of the north and from all the lands where He had driven them
Jer 23:7 Therefore, behold, the days are coming," says the Lord, "that they shall no longer say, 'As the Lord lives who brought up the *children of Israel* from the land of Egypt
Jer 32:30 because the *children of Israel* and the children of Judah have done only evil before Me from their youth. For the *children of Israel* have provoked Me only to anger with the work of their hands
Jer 32:32 because of all the evil of the *children of Israel* and the children of Judah, which they have done to provoke Me to anger they, their kings, their princes, their priests, their prophets, the men of Judah, and the inhabitants of Jerusalem
Jer 50:4 In those days and in that time," says the Lord, "The *children of Israel* shall come, they and the children of Judah together
Jer 50:33 The *children of Israel* were oppressed, along with the children of Judah
Ezek 2:3 Son of man, I am sending you to the *children of Israel*, to a rebellious nation that has rebelled against Me
Ezek 4:13 Then the Lord said, "So shall the *children of Israel* eat their defiled bread among the Gentiles, where I will drive them
Ezek 6:5 And I will lay the corpses of the *children of Israel* before their idols, and I will scatter your bones all around your altars
Ezek 35:5 Because you have had an ancient hatred, and have shed the blood of the *children of Israel* by the power of the sword at the time of their calamity, when their iniquity came to an end
Ezek 37:16 For Judah and for the *children of Israel*, his companions
Ezek 37:21 Surely I will take the *children of Israel* from among the nations, wherever they have

gone, and will gather them from every side and bring them into their own land
Ezek 43:7 And He said to me, "Son of man, this is the place of My throne and the place of the soles of My feet, where I will dwell in the midst of the *children of Israel* forever
Ezek 44:9 No foreigner, uncircumcised in heart or uncircumcised in flesh, shall enter My sanctuary, including any foreigner who is among the *children of Israel*
Ezek 44:15 But the priests, the Levites, the sons of Zadok, who kept charge of My sanctuary when the *children of Israel* went astray from Me, they shall come near Me to minister to Me
Ezek 47:22 They shall be to you as native-born among the *children of Israel*
Ezek 48:11 It shall be for the priests of the sons of Zadok, who are sanctified, who have kept My charge, who did not go astray when the *children of Israel* went astray, as the Levites went astray
Dan 1:3 Then the king instructed Ashpenaz, the master of his eunuchs, to bring some of the *children of Israel* and some of the king's descendants and some of the nobles
Hos 1:10 Yet the number of the *children of Israel* shall be as the sand of the sea, which cannot be measured or numbered
Hos 1:11 Then the children of Judah and the *children of Israel* shall be gathered together, and appoint for themselves one head
Hos 3:1 Then the Lord said to me, "Go again, love a woman who is loved by a lover and is committing adultery, just like the love of the Lord for the *children of Israel*, who look to other gods and love the raisin cakes of the pagans
Hos 3:4 For the *children of Israel* shall abide many days without king or prince, without sacrifice or sacred pillar, without ephod or teraphim
Hos 3:5 Afterward the *children of Israel* shall return, seek the Lord their God and David their king, and fear the Lord and His goodness in the latter days
Hos 4:1 Hear the word of the Lord, you *children of Israel*, for the Lord brings a charge against the inhabitants of the land
Joel 3:16 but the Lord will be a shelter for His people, and the strength of the *children of Israel*
Amos 2:11 Is it not so, O you *children of Israel?*" says the Lord
Amos 3:1 Hear this word that the Lord has spoken against you, O *children of Israel*, against the whole family which I brought up from the land of Egypt, saying
Amos 3:12 As a shepherd takes from the mouth of a lion two legs or a piece of an ear, so shall the *children of Israel* be taken out who dwell in Samaria in the corner of a bed and on the edge of a couch
Amos 4:5 for this you love, you *children of Israel!*" says the Lord God
Amos 9:7 Are you not like the people of Ethiopia to Me, O *children of Israel*
Obad 20 And the captives of this host of the *children of Israel* shall possess the land of the Canaanites as far as Zarephath
Mic 5:3 then the remnant of His brethren shall return to the *children of Israel*
Matt 27:9 Then was fulfilled what was spoken by Jeremiah the prophet, saying, "And they took the thirty pieces of silver, the value of Him who was priced, whom they of the *children of Israel* priced
Luke 1:16 And he will turn many of the *children of Israel* to the Lord their God
Acts 5:21 But the high priest and those with him came and called the council together, with all the elders of the *children of Israel*, and sent to the prison to have them brought
Acts 7:23 But when he was forty years old, it came into his heart to visit his brethren, the *children of Israel*
Acts 7:37 This is that Moses who said to the *children of Israel*
Acts 9:15 But the Lord said to him, "Go, for he is a chosen vessel of Mine to bear My name before Gentiles, kings, and the *children of Israel*
Acts 10:36 The word which God sent to the *children of Israel*, preaching peace through Jesus Christ He is Lord of all
Rom 9:27 Though the number of the *children of Israel* be as the sand of the sea, the remnant will be saved
2Cor 3:7 But if the ministry of death, written and engraved on stones, was glorious, so that the *children of Israel* could not look steadily at the face of Moses because of the glory of his countenance, which glory was passing away
2Cor 3:13 unlike Moses, who put a veil over his face so that the *children of Israel* could not look steadily at the end of what was passing away
Heb 11:22 By faith Joseph, when he was dying, made mention of the departure of the *children of Israel*, and gave instructions concerning his bones
Rev 2:14 But I have a few things against you, because you have there those who hold the doctrine of Balaam, who taught Balak to put a stumbling block before the *children of Israel*, to eat things sacrificed to idols, and to commit sexual immorality
Rev 7:4 One hundred and forty-four thousand of all the tribes of the *children of Israel* were sealed
Rev 21:12 Also she had a great and high wall with twelve gates, and twelve angels at the gates, and names written on them, which are the names of the twelve tribes of the *children of Israel*

CHILDREN OF LIGHT
Eph 5:8 For you were once darkness, but now you are light in the Lord. Walk as *children of light*

CHILDREN OF MEN (KJV)
(See *SONS OF MEN*)

CHILDREN OF THE PROPHETS (KJV)
(See *SONS OF THE PROPHETS*)

CHILDREN OF THE RESURRECTION (KJV)
(See *SONS OF THE RESURRECTION*)

CHILDREN OF THIS WORLD (KJV)
(See *SONS OF THIS AGE*)

CHILDREN'S TEETH ARE SET ON EDGE
Jer 31:29 The fathers have eaten sour grapes, and the *children's teeth are set on edge*
Ezek 18:2 The fathers have eaten sour grapes, and the *children's teeth are set on edge*

CHOKE THE WORD
Matt 13:22 Now he who received seed among the thorns is he who hears the word, and the cares of this world and the deceitfulness of riches *choke the word*, and he becomes unfruitful
Mark 4:19 and the cares of this world, the deceitfulness of riches, and the desires for other things entering in *choke the word*, and it becomes unfruitful

CHOOSE FOR YOURSELVES THIS DAY WHOM YOU WILL SERVE
Josh 24:15 And if it seems evil to you to serve the Lord, *choose for yourselves this day whom you will serve*, whether the gods which your fathers served that were on the other side of the River, or the gods of the Amorites, in whose land you dwell

CHOOSE JUSTICE
Job 34:4 Let us *choose justice* for ourselves; let us know among ourselves what is good

CHOOSE LIFE
Deut 30:19 therefore *choose life*, that both you and your descendants may live

CHOOSE MY INSTRUCTION (NIV)
(See *RECEIVE MY INSTRUCTION*)

CHOOSE THE GOOD
Is 7:15 Curds and honey He shall eat, that He may know to refuse the evil and *choose the good*
Is 7:16 For before the Child shall know to refuse the evil and *choose the good*, the land that you dread will be forsaken by both her kings

CHOOSE THE RIGHT (NIV)
(See *CHOOSE THE GOOD*)

CHOOSE WHAT IS RIGHT (RSV)
(See *CHOOSE JUSTICE*)

CHOSEN OF GOD
Luke 23:35 let Him save Himself if He is the Christ, the *chosen of God*

CHOSEN ONE (NIV, RSV)
(See *CHOSEN OF GOD*)

CHOSEN ONES
1Chr 16:13 O seed of Israel His servant, you children of Jacob, His *chosen ones*
Ps 105:6 O seed of Abraham His servant, you children of Jacob, His *chosen ones*
Ps 105:43 He brought out His people with joy, His *chosen ones* with gladness
Ps 106:5 That I may see the benefit of Your *chosen ones*, that I may rejoice in the gladness of Your nation, that I may glory with Your inheritance

CHRIST ALWAYS LEADS US IN TRIUMPH (RSV)
(See *TRIUMPH IN CHRIST*)

CHRIST DIED FOR THE UNGODLY
Rom 5:6 For when we were still without strength, in due time *Christ died for the ungodly*

CHRIST DIED FOR US
Rom 5:8 But God demonstrates His own love toward us, in that while we were still sinners, *Christ died for us*

CHRIST HAS REDEEMED US
Gal 3:13 *Christ has redeemed us* from the curse of the law, having become a curse for us (for it is written

CHRIST IS FORMED IN YOU
Gal 4:19 My little children, for whom I labor in birth again until *Christ is formed in you*

CHRIST IS IN YOU
Rom 8:10 And if *Christ is in you*, the body is dead because of sin, but the Spirit is life because of righteousness
2Cor 13:5 Do you not know yourselves, that Jesus *Christ is in you*

CHRIST IS RISEN
1Cor 15:20 But now *Christ is risen* from the dead, and has become the firstfruits of those who have fallen asleep

CHRIST JESUS
Acts 19:4 Then Paul said, "John indeed baptized with a baptism of repentance, saying to the people that they should believe on Him who would come after him, that is, on *Christ Jesus*
Rom 3:24 being justified freely by His grace through the redemption that is in *Christ Jesus*
Rom 6:3 Or do you not know that as many of us as were baptized into *Christ Jesus* were baptized into His death
Rom 6:11 Likewise you also, reckon yourselves to be dead indeed to sin, but alive to God in *Christ Jesus* our Lord
Rom 6:23 For the wages of sin is death, but the gift of God is eternal life in *Christ Jesus* our Lord
Rom 8:1 There is therefore now no condemnation to those who are in *Christ Jesus*, who do not walk according to the flesh, but according to the Spirit
Rom 8:2 For the law of the Spirit of life in *Christ Jesus* has made me free from the law of sin and death
Rom 8:39 nor height nor depth, nor any other created thing, shall be able to separate us from the love of God which is in *Christ Jesus* our Lord
Rom 15:5 Now may the God of patience and comfort grant you to be like-minded toward one another, according to *Christ Jesus*
Rom 15:17 Therefore I have reason to glory in *Christ Jesus* in the things which pertain to God
Rom 16:3 Greet Priscilla and Aquila, my fellow workers in *Christ Jesus*
1Cor 1:2 To the church of God which is at Corinth, to those who are sanctified in *Christ Jesus*, called to be saints, with all who in every place call on the name of Jesus Christ our Lord, both theirs and ours
1Cor 1:4 I thank my God always concerning you for the grace of God which was given to you by *Christ Jesus*
1Cor 1:30 But of Him you are in *Christ Jesus*, who became for us wisdom from God and righteousness and sanctification and redemption
1Cor 4:15 for in *Christ Jesus* I have begotten you through the gospel
1Cor 15:31 I affirm, by the boasting in you which I have in *Christ Jesus* our Lord, I die daily
1Cor 16:24 My love be with you all in *Christ Jesus*. Amen
2Cor 4:5 For we do not preach ourselves, but *Christ Jesus* the Lord, and ourselves your servants for Jesus' sake
Gal 2:4 But this occurred because of false brethren secretly brought in (who came in by stealth to spy out our liberty which we have in *Christ Jesus*, that they might bring us into bondage
Gal 2:16 knowing that a man is not justified by the works of the law but by faith in Jesus Christ, even we have believed in *Christ Jesus*, that we might be justified by faith in Christ and not by the works of the law
Gal 3:14 that the blessing of Abraham might come upon the Gentiles in *Christ Jesus*, that we might receive the promise of the Spirit through faith
Gal 3:26 For you are all sons of God through faith in *Christ Jesus*
Gal 3:28 There is neither Jew nor Greek, there is neither slave nor free, there is neither male nor female; for you are all one in *Christ Jesus*
Gal 4:14 And my trial which was in my flesh you did not despise or reject, but you received me as an angel of God, even as *Christ Jesus*
Gal 5:6 For in *Christ Jesus* neither circumcision nor uncircumcision avails anything, but faith working through love
Gal 6:15 For in *Christ Jesus* neither circumcision nor uncircumcision avails anything, but a new creation
Eph 1:1 Paul, an apostle of Jesus Christ by the will

of God, To the saints who are in Ephesus, and faithful in *Christ Jesus*
Eph 2:6 and raised us up together, and made us sit together in the heavenly places in *Christ Jesus*
Eph 2:7 that in the ages to come He might show the exceeding riches of His grace in His kindness toward us in *Christ Jesus*
Eph 2:10 For we are His workmanship, created in *Christ Jesus* for good works, which God prepared beforehand that we should walk in them
Eph 2:13 But now in *Christ Jesus* you who once were far off have been made near by the blood of Christ
Eph 3:11 according to the eternal purpose which He accomplished in *Christ Jesus* our Lord
Eph 3:21 to Him be glory in the church by *Christ Jesus* throughout all ages, world without end
Phil 1:1 Paul and Timothy, servants of Jesus Christ, to all the saints in *Christ Jesus* who are in Philippi, with the bishops and deacons
Phil 2:5 Let this mind be in you which was also in *Christ Jesus*
Phil 2:21 For all seek their own, not the things which are of *Christ Jesus*
Phil 3:3 For we are the circumcision, who worship God in the Spirit, rejoice in *Christ Jesus*, and have no confidence in the flesh
Phil 3:8 But indeed I also count all things loss for the excellence of the knowledge of *Christ Jesus* my Lord, for whom I have suffered the loss of all things, and count them as rubbish, that I may gain Christ
Phil 3:12 but I press on, that I may lay hold of that for which *Christ Jesus* has also laid hold of me
Phil 3:14 I press toward the goal for the prize of the upward call of God in *Christ Jesus*
Phil 4:7 and the peace of God, which surpasses all understanding, will guard your hearts and minds through *Christ Jesus*
Phil 4:19 And my God shall supply all your need according to His riches in glory by *Christ Jesus*
Phil 4:21 Greet every saint in *Christ Jesus*. The brethren who are with me greet you
Col 1:4 since we heard of your faith in *Christ Jesus* and of your love for all the saints
Col 1:28 Him we preach, warning every man and teaching every man in all wisdom, that we may present every man perfect in *Christ Jesus*
Col 2:6 As you have therefore received *Christ Jesus* the Lord, so walk in Him
1Th 2:14 For you, brethren, became imitators of the churches of God which are in Judea in *Christ Jesus*
1Th 5:18 for this is the will of God in *Christ Jesus* for you
1Tim 1:12 And I thank *Christ Jesus* our Lord who has enabled me, because He counted me faithful, putting me into the ministry
1Tim 1:14 And the grace of our Lord was exceedingly abundant, with faith and love which are in *Christ Jesus*
1Tim 1:15 This is a faithful saying and worthy of all acceptance, that *Christ Jesus* came into the world to save sinners, of whom I am chief
1Tim 2:5 For there is one God and one Mediator between God and men, the Man *Christ Jesus*
1Tim 3:13 For those who have served well as deacons obtain for themselves a good standing and great boldness in the faith which is in *Christ Jesus*
1Tim 6:13 I urge you in the sight of God who gives life to all things, and before *Christ Jesus* who witnessed the good confession before Pontius Pilate
2Tim 1:1 Paul, an apostle of Jesus Christ by the will of God, according to the promise of life which is in *Christ Jesus*
2Tim 1:2 Grace, mercy, and peace from God the Father and *Christ Jesus* our Lord
2Tim 1:9 who has saved us and called us with a holy calling, not according to our works, but according to His own purpose and grace which was given to us in *Christ Jesus* before time began
2Tim 1:13 Hold fast the pattern of sound words which you have heard from me, in faith and love which are in *Christ Jesus*
2Tim 2:1 You therefore, my son, be strong in the grace that is in *Christ Jesus*
2Tim 2:10 Therefore I endure all things for the sake of the elect, that they also may obtain the salvation which is in *Christ Jesus* with eternal glory
2Tim 3:12 Yes, and all who desire to live godly in *Christ Jesus* will suffer persecution
2Tim 3:15 and that from childhood you have known the Holy Scriptures, which are able to make you wise for salvation through faith which is in *Christ Jesus*
Phm 1 Paul, a prisoner of *Christ Jesus*, and Timothy our brother, to Philemon our beloved friend and fellow laborer
Phm 6 that the sharing of your faith may become effective by the acknowledgment of every good thing which is in you in *Christ Jesus*
Phm 23 Epaphras, my fellow prisoner in *Christ Jesus*, greets you
Heb 3:1 Therefore, holy brethren, partakers of the heavenly calling, consider the Apostle and High Priest of our confession, *Christ Jesus*
1Pet 5:10 But may the God of all grace, who called us to His eternal glory by *Christ Jesus*, after you have suffered a while, perfect, establish, strengthen, and settle you
1Pet 5:14 Peace to you all who are in *Christ Jesus*. Amen

CHRIST LIVES IN ME
Gal 2:20 it is no longer I who live, but *Christ lives in me*

CHRIST SUFFERED FOR US
1Pet 4:1 Therefore, since *Christ suffered for us* in the flesh, arm yourselves also with the same mind, for he who has suffered in the flesh has ceased from sin

CHRIST WAS OFFERED ONCE
Heb 9:28 so *Christ was offered once* to bear the sins of many

CHRIST WAS SACRIFICED ONCE (NIV)
(See *CHRIST WAS OFFERED ONCE*)

CHRIST'S AMBASSADORS (NIV)
(See *AMBASSADORS FOR CHRIST*)

CHRIST'S SUFFERINGS (NAS)
(See *SUFFERINGS OF CHRIST*)

CHRONICLES OF THE KINGS OF ISRAEL
1Kin 14:19 Now the rest of the acts of Jeroboam, how he made war and how he reigned, indeed they are written in the book of the *chronicles of the kings of Israel*
1Kin 15:31 Now the rest of the acts of Nadab, and all that he did, are they not written in the book of the *chronicles of the kings of Israel*
1Kin 16:5 Now the rest of the acts of Baasha, what he did, and his might, are they not written in the book of the *chronicles of the kings of Israel*
1Kin 16:14 Now the rest of the acts of Elah, and all that he did, are they not written in the book of the *chronicles of the kings of Israel*
1Kin 16:20 Now the rest of the acts of Zimri, and the treason he committed, are they not written in the book of the *chronicles of the kings of Israel*
1Kin 16:27 Now the rest of the acts of Omri which he did, and the might that he showed, are they

not written in the book of the *chronicles of the kings of Israel*
1Kin 22:39 Now the rest of the acts of Ahab and all that he did, the ivory house which he built and all the cities that he built, are they not written in the book of the *chronicles of the kings of Israel*
2Kin 1:18 Now the rest of the acts of Ahaziah which he did, are they not written in the book of the *chronicles of the kings of Israel*
2Kin 10:34 Now the rest of the acts of Jehu, all that he did, and all his might, are they not written in the book of the *chronicles of the kings of Israel*
2Kin 13:8 Now the rest of the acts of Jehoahaz, all that he did, and his might, are they not written in the book of the *chronicles of the kings of Israel*
2Kin 13:12 Now the rest of the acts of Joash, all that he did, and his might with which he fought against Amaziah king of Judah, are they not written in the book of the *chronicles of the kings of Israel*
2Kin 14:15 Now the rest of the acts of Jehoash which he did his might, and how he fought with Amaziah king of Judah are they not written in the book of the *chronicles of the kings of Israel*
2Kin 14:28 Now the rest of the acts of Jeroboam, and all that he did his might, how he made war, and how he recaptured for Israel, from Damascus and Hamath, what had belonged to Judah are they not written in the book of the *chronicles of the kings of Israel*
2Kin 15:11 Now the rest of the acts of Zechariah, indeed they are written in the book of the *chronicles of the kings of Israel*
2Kin 15:15 Now the rest of the acts of Shallum, and the conspiracy which he led, indeed they are written in the book of the *chronicles of the kings of Israel*
2Kin 15:21 Now the rest of the acts of Menahem, and all that he did, are they not written in the book of the *chronicles of the kings of Israel*
2Kin 15:26 Now the rest of the acts of Pekahiah, and all that he did, indeed they are written in the book of the *chronicles of the kings of Israel*
2Kin 15:31 Now the rest of the acts of Pekah, and all that he did, indeed they are written in the book of the *chronicles of the kings of Israel*

CHRONICLES OF THE KINGS OF JUDAH
1Kin 14:29 Now the rest of the acts of Rehoboam, and all that he did, are they not written in the book of the *chronicles of the kings of Judah*
1Kin 15:7 Now the rest of the acts of Abijam, and all that he did, are they not written in the book of the *chronicles of the kings of Judah*
1Kin 15:23 The rest of all the acts of Asa, all his might, all that he did, and the cities which he built, are they not written in the book of the *chronicles of the kings of Judah*
1Kin 22:45 Now the rest of the acts of Jehoshaphat, the might that he showed, and how he made war, are they not written in the book of the *chronicles of the kings of Judah*
2Kin 8:23 Now the rest of the acts of Joram, and all that he did, are they not written in the book of the *chronicles of the kings of Judah*
2Kin 12:19 Now the rest of the acts of Joash, and all that he did, are they not written in the book of the *chronicles of the kings of Judah*
2Kin 14:18 Now the rest of the acts of Amaziah, are they not written in the book of the *chronicles of the kings of Judah*
2Kin 15:6 Now the rest of the acts of Azariah, and all that he did, are they not written in the book of the *chronicles of the kings of Judah*
2Kin 15:36 Now the rest of the acts of Jotham, and all that he did, are they not written in the book of the *chronicles of the kings of Judah*
2Kin 16:19 Now the rest of the acts of Ahaz which he did, are they not written in the book of the *chronicles of the kings of Judah*
2Kin 20:20 Now the rest of the acts of Hezekiah all his might, and how he made a pool and a tunnel and brought water into the city are they not written in the book of the *chronicles of the kings of Judah*
2Kin 21:17 Now the rest of the acts of Manasseh all that he did, and the sin that he committed are they not written in the book of the *chronicles of the kings of Judah*
2Kin 21:25 Now the rest of the acts of Amon which he did, are they not written in the book of the *chronicles of the kings of Judah*
2Kin 23:28 Now the rest of the acts of Josiah, and all that he did, are they not written in the book of the *chronicles of the kings of Judah*
2Kin 24:5 Now the rest of the acts of Jehoiakim, and all that he did, are they not written in the book of the *chronicles of the kings of Judah*

CHURCH OF GOD
Acts 20:28 Therefore take heed to yourselves and to all the flock, among which the Holy Spirit has made you overseers, to shepherd the *church of God* which He purchased with His own blood
1Cor 1:2 To the *church of God* which is at Corinth, to those who are sanctified in Christ Jesus, called to be saints, with all who in every place call on the name of Jesus Christ our Lord, both theirs and ours
1Cor 10:32 Give no offense, either to the Jews or to the Greeks or to the *church of God*
1Cor 11:22 Or do you despise the *church of God* and shame those who have nothing
1Cor 15:9 For I am the least of the apostles, who am not worthy to be called an apostle, because I persecuted the *church of God*
2Cor 1:1 Paul, an apostle of Jesus Christ by the will of God, and Timothy our brother, To the *church of God* which is at Corinth, with all the saints who are in all Achaia
Gal 1:13 For you have heard of my former conduct in Judaism, how I persecuted the *church of God* beyond measure and tried to destroy it
1Tim 3:5 (for if a man does not know how to rule his own house, how will he take care of the *church of God*

CHURCHES OF CHRIST
Rom 16:16 Greet one another with a holy kiss. The *churches of Christ* greet you

CIRCLE OF HEAVEN
Job 22:14 Thick clouds cover Him, so that He cannot see, and He walks above the *circle of heaven*

CIRCLE OF THE EARTH
Is 40:22 It is He who sits above the *circle of the earth*, and its inhabitants are like grasshoppers, Who stretches out the heavens like a curtain, and spreads them out like a tent to dwell in

CIRCUMCISE THE FORESKIN
Deut 10:16 Therefore *circumcise the foreskin* of your heart, and be stiff-necked no longer

CIRCUMCISE YOUR HEART
Deut 30:6 And the Lord your God will *circumcise your heart* and the heart of your descendants, to love the Lord your God with all your heart and with all your soul, that you may live

CIRCUMCISION NOR UNCIRCUMCISION
Gal 5:6 For in Christ Jesus neither *circumcision nor uncircumcision* avails anything, but faith working through love

CIRCUMCISION OF CHRIST

Gal 6:15 For in Christ Jesus neither *circumcision nor uncircumcision* avails anything, but a new creation

CIRCUMCISION OF CHRIST
Col 2:11 In Him you were also circumcised with the circumcision made without hands, by putting off the body of the sins of the flesh, by the *circumcision of Christ*

CITIES OF REFUGE
Num 35:6 Now among the cities which you will give to the Levites you shall appoint six *cities of refuge*, to which a manslayer may flee
Num 35:11 then you shall appoint cities to be *cities of refuge* for you, that the manslayer who kills any person accidentally may flee there
Num 35:12 They shall be *cities of refuge* for you from the avenger, that the manslayer may not die until he stands before the congregation in judgment
Num 35:13 And of the cities which you give, you shall have six *cities of refuge*
Num 35:14 You shall appoint three cities on this side of the Jordan, and three cities you shall appoint in the land of Canaan, which will be *cities of refuge*
Josh 20:2 Appoint for yourselves *cities of refuge*, of which I spoke to you through Moses
1Chr 6:57 And to the sons of Aaron they gave one of the *cities of refuge*, Hebron
1Chr 6:67 And they gave them one of the *cities of refuge*, Shechem with its common-lands, in the mountains of Ephraim, also Gezer with its common-lands

CITIES OF THE LEVITES
Lev 25:32 Nevertheless the *cities of the Levites*, and the houses in the cities of their possession, the Levites may redeem at any time
Lev 25:33 for the houses in the *cities of the Levites* are their possession among the children of Israel
Josh 21:41 All the *cities of the Levites* within the possession of the children of Israel were forty-eight cities with their common-lands

CITIES OF THE PLAIN
Gen 13:12 Abram dwelt in the land of Canaan, and Lot dwelt in the *cities of the plain* and pitched his tent even as far as Sodom
Gen 19:29 And it came to pass, when God destroyed the *cities of the plain*, that God remembered Abraham, and sent Lot out of the midst of the overthrow, when He overthrew the cities in which Lot had dwelt
Deut 3:10 all the *cities of the plain*, all Gilead, and all Bashan, as far as Salcah and Edrei, cities of the kingdom of Og in Bashan
Josh 13:21 all the *cities of the plain* and all the kingdom of Sihon king of the Amorites, who reigned in Heshbon, whom Moses had struck with the princes of Midian

CITIZENSHIP IN ISRAEL (NIV)
(See *COMMONWEALTH OF ISRAEL*)

CITIZENSHIP IS IN HEAVEN
Phil 3:20 For our *citizenship is in heaven*, from which we also eagerly wait for the Savior, the Lord Jesus Christ

CITY A HEAP (NIV)
(See *CITY A RUIN*)

CITY A RUIN
Is 25:2 For You have made a *city a ruin*, a fortified *city a ruin*, a palace of foreigners to be a city no more

CITY GATE
Judg 9:35 When Gaal the son of Ebed went out and stood in the entrance to the *city gate*, Abimelech and the people who were with him rose from lying in wait
2Kin 23:8 also he broke down the high places at the gates which were at the entrance of the Gate of Joshua the governor of the city, which were to the left of the *city gate*
2Chr 32:6 Then he set military captains over the people, gathered them together to him in the open square of the *city gate*, and gave them encouragement, saying

CITY OF BLOODSHED (NIV)
(See *BLOODY CITY*)

CITY OF DAVID
2Sam 5:7 Nevertheless David took the stronghold of Zion (that is, the *City of David*
2Sam 5:9 So David dwelt in the stronghold, and called it the *City of David*
2Sam 6:10 So David would not move the ark of the Lord with him into the *City of David*
2Sam 6:12 So David went and brought up the ark of God from the house of Obed-Edom to the *City of David* with gladness
2Sam 6:16 And as the ark of the Lord came into the *City of David*, Michal, Saul's daughter, looked through a window and saw King David leaping and whirling before the Lord
1Kin 2:10 So David rested with his fathers, and was buried in the *City of David*
1Kin 3:1 then he brought her to the *City of David* until he had finished building his own house, and the house of the Lord, and the wall all around Jerusalem
1Kin 8:1 Now Solomon assembled the elders of Israel and all the heads of the tribes, the chief fathers of the children of Israel, to King Solomon in Jerusalem, that they might bring up the ark of the covenant of the Lord from the *City of David*, which is Zion
1Kin 9:24 But Pharaoh's daughter came up from the *City of David* to her house which Solomon had built for her
1Kin 11:27 Solomon had built the Millo and repaired the damages to the *City of David* his father
1Kin 11:43 Then Solomon rested with his fathers, and was buried in the *City of David* his father
1Kin 14:31 So Rehoboam rested with his fathers, and was buried with his fathers in the *City of David*
1Kin 15:8 So Abijam rested with his fathers, and they buried him in the *City of David*
1Kin 15:24 So Asa rested with his fathers, and was buried with his fathers in the *City of David* his father
1Kin 22:50 And Jehoshaphat rested with his fathers, and was buried with his fathers in the *City of David* his father
2Kin 8:24 So Joram rested with his fathers, and was buried with his fathers in the *City of David*
2Kin 9:28 And his servants carried him in the chariot to Jerusalem, and buried him in his tomb with his fathers in the *City of David*
2Kin 12:21 So he died, and they buried him with his fathers in the *City of David*
2Kin 14:20 Then they brought him on horses, and he was buried at Jerusalem with his fathers in the *City of David*
2Kin 15:7 So Azariah rested with his fathers, and

they buried him with his fathers in the *City of David*
2Kin 15:38 So Jotham rested with his fathers, and was buried with his fathers in the *City of David* his father
2Kin 16:20 So Ahaz rested with his fathers, and was buried with his fathers in the *City of David*
1Chr 11:5 Nevertheless David took the stronghold of Zion (that is, the *City of David*
1Chr 11:7 Then David dwelt in the stronghold; therefore they called it the *City of David*
1Chr 13:13 And David would not move the ark with him into the *City of David*, but took it aside into the house of Obed-Edom the Gittite
1Chr 15:1 David built houses for himself in the *City of David*
1Chr 15:29 And it happened, as the ark of the covenant of the Lord came to the *City of David*, that Michal the daughter of Saul, looking through a window, saw King David whirling and playing music
2Chr 5:2 Now Solomon assembled the elders of Israel and all the heads of the tribes, the chief fathers of the children of Israel, in Jerusalem, that they might bring the ark of the covenant of the Lord up from the *City of David*, which is Zion
2Chr 8:11 Now Solomon brought the daughter of Pharaoh up from the *City of David* to the house he had built for her, for he said
2Chr 9:31 Then Solomon rested with his fathers, and was buried in the *City of David* his father
2Chr 12:16 So Rehoboam rested with his fathers, and was buried in the *City of David*
2Chr 14:1 So Abijah rested with his fathers, and they buried him in the *City of David*
2Chr 16:14 They buried him in his own tomb, which he had made for himself in the *City of David*
2Chr 21:1 And Jehoshaphat rested with his fathers, and was buried with his fathers in the *City of David*
2Chr 21:20 However they buried him in the *City of David*, but not in the tombs of the kings
2Chr 24:16 And they buried him in the *City of David* among the kings, because he had done good in Israel, both toward God and His house
2Chr 24:25 And they buried him in the *City of David*, but they did not bury him in the tombs of the kings
2Chr 27:9 So Jotham rested with his fathers, and they buried him in the *City of David*
2Chr 32:5 also he repaired the Millo in the *City of David*, and made weapons and shields in abundance
2Chr 32:30 This same Hezekiah also stopped the water outlet of Upper Gihon, and brought the water by tunnel to the west side of the *City of David*
2Chr 33:14 After this he built a wall outside the *City of David* on the west side of Gihon, in the valley, as far as the entrance of the Fish Gate
Neh 3:15 he built it, covered it, hung its doors with its bolts and bars, and repaired the wall of the Pool of Shelah by the King's Garden, as far as the stairs that go down from the *City of David*
Neh 12:37 By the Fountain Gate, in front of them, they went up the stairs of the *City of David*, on the stairway of the wall, beyond the house of David, as far as the Water Gate eastward
Is 22:9 You also saw the damage to the *city of David*, that it was great
Luke 2:4 And Joseph also went up from Galilee, out of the city of Nazareth, into Judea, to the *city of David*, which is called Bethlehem, because he was of the house and lineage of David
Luke 2:11 For there is born to you this day in the *city of David* a Savior, who is Christ the Lord

CITY OF DESTRUCTION
Is 19:18 In that day five cities in the land of Egypt will speak the language of Canaan and swear by the Lord of hosts; one will be called the *City of Destruction*

CITY OF GOD
Ps 46:4 There is a river whose streams shall make glad the *city of God*, the holy place of the tabernacle of the Most High
Ps 87:3 Glorious things are spoken of you, O *city of God*

CITY OF OUR GOD
Ps 48:1 Great is the Lord, and greatly to be praised In the *city of our God*, in His holy mountain
Ps 48:8 As we have heard, so we have seen in the city of the Lord of hosts, in the *city of our God*

CITY OF REFUGE
Num 35:25 So the congregation shall deliver the manslayer from the hand of the avenger of blood, and the congregation shall return him to the *city of refuge* where he had fled, and he shall remain there until the death of the high priest who was anointed with the holy oil
Num 35:26 But if the manslayer at any time goes outside the limits of the *city of refuge* where he fled
Num 35:27 and the avenger of blood finds him outside the limits of his *city of refuge*, and the avenger of blood kills the manslayer, he shall not be guilty of blood
Num 35:28 because he should have remained in his *city of refuge* until the death of the high priest
Num 35:32 And you shall take no ransom for him who has fled to his *city of refuge*, that he may return to dwell in the land before the death of the priest
Josh 21:13 Thus to the children of Aaron the priest they gave Hebron with its common-land (a *city of refuge* for the slayer
Josh 21:21 For they gave them Shechem with its common-land in the mountains of Ephraim (a *city of refuge* for the slayer
Josh 21:27 And to the children of Gershon, of the families of the Levites, from the other half-tribe of Manasseh, they gave Golan in Bashan with its common-land (a *city of refuge* for the slayer
Josh 21:32 and from the tribe of Naphtali, Kedesh in Galilee with its common-land (a *city of refuge* for the slayer
Josh 21:38 and from the tribe of Gad, Ramoth in Gilead with its common-land (a *city of refuge* for the slayer

CITY OF THE LIVING GOD
Heb 12:22 But you have come to Mount Zion and to the *city of the living God*, the heavenly Jerusalem, to an innumerable company of angels

CITY OF THE LORD
Ps 48:8 As we have heard, so we have seen in the *city of the Lord* of hosts, in the city of our God
Ps 101:8 Early I will destroy all the wicked of the land, that I may cut off all the evildoers from the *city of the Lord*
Is 60:14 and they shall call you the *City of the Lord*, Zion of the Holy One of Israel

CITY THAT IS SET ON A HILL
Matt 5:14 A *city that is set on a hill* cannot be hidden

CIVILIAN AFFAIRS (NIV)
(See *AFFAIRS OF THIS LIFE*)

CIVILIAN PURSUITS (RSV)
(See *AFFAIRS OF THIS LIFE*)

CLAIMED TO BE WISE (NIV)
(See *PROFESSING TO BE WISE*)

CLAIMING TO BE WISE (RSV)
(See *PROFESSING TO BE WISE*)

CLAP YOUR HANDS
Ps 47:1 Oh, *clap your hands*, all you peoples! Shout to God with the voice of triumph

CLAPS HIS HANDS
Job 34:37 he *claps his hands* among us, and multiplies his words against God

CLEAN, AND THE UNCLEAN
Eccl 9:2 to the good, the *clean, and the unclean;* to him who sacrifices and him who does not sacrifice

CLEAN HANDS
Job 17:9 Yet the righteous will hold to his way, and he who has *clean hands* will be stronger and stronger
Ps 24:4 He who has *clean hands* and a pure heart, who has not lifted up his soul to an idol, nor sworn deceitfully

CLEAN HEART
Ps 51:10 Create in me a *clean heart*, O God, and renew a steadfast spirit within me

CLEANSE ME FROM MY SIN
Ps 51:2 Wash me thoroughly from my iniquity, and *cleanse me from my sin*

CLEANSE ME WITH HYSSOP (NIV)
(See *PURGE ME WITH HYSSOP*)

CLEANSE OUT THE OLD LEAVEN (RSV)
(See *PURGE OUT THE OLD LEAVEN*)

CLEANSE THE ALTAR
Ex 29:36 You shall *cleanse the altar* when you make atonement for it, and you shall anoint it to sanctify it
Ezek 43:22 and they shall *cleanse the altar*, as they cleansed it with the bull

CLEANSES US FROM ALL SIN
1Jn 1:7 But if we walk in the light as He is in the light, we have fellowship with one another, and the blood of Jesus Christ His Son *cleanses us from all sin*

CLEAR AS CRYSTAL
Rev 21:11 And her light was like a most precious stone, like a jasper stone, *clear as crystal*
Rev 22:1 And he showed me a pure river of water of life, *clear as crystal*, proceeding from the throne of God and of the Lamb

CLEAR AS THE SUN
Song 6:10 Who is she who looks forth as the morning, fair as the moon, *clear as the sun*, awesome as an army with banners

CLEAR CONSCIENCE (NIV)
(See *INTEGRITY OF YOUR HEART*)

CLEAR FROM THIS OATH (KJV)
(See *RELEASED FROM THIS OATH*)

CLEAVE TO WHAT IS GOOD (KJV)
(See *CLING TO WHAT IS GOOD*)

CLEFT OF THE ROCK
Ex 33:22 So it shall be, while My glory passes by, that I will put you in the *cleft of the rock*, and will cover you with My hand while I pass by
Judg 15:8 then he went down and dwelt in the *cleft of the rock* of Etam
Judg 15:11 Then three thousand men of Judah went down to the *cleft of the rock* of Etam, and said to Samson

CLEFTS OF THE ROCK
Song 2:14 O my dove, in the *clefts of the rock*, in the secret places of the cliff, let me see your countenance, let me hear your voice
Jer 49:16 Your fierceness has deceived you, the pride of your heart, O you who dwell in the *clefts of the rock*, who hold the height of the hill
Obad 3 The pride of your heart has deceived you, you who dwell in the *clefts of the rock*, whose habitation is high

CLING TO WHAT IS GOOD
Rom 12:9 Let love be without hypocrisy. Abhor what is evil. *Cling to what is good*

CLOAK AS A PLEDGE (NAS, NIV)
(See *GARMENT AS A PLEDGE*)

CLOAK THAT HAD FALLEN FROM ELIJAH (NIV)
(See *MANTLE OF ELIJAH*)

CLOSED HER WOMB
1Sam 1:5 But to Hannah he would give a double portion, for he loved Hannah, although the Lord had *closed her womb*
1Sam 1:6 And her rival also provoked her severely, to make her miserable, because the Lord had *closed her womb*

CLOSING ASSEMBLY (NIV)
(See *SACRED ASSEMBLY*)

CLOTHED IN PURPLE
Ezek 23:6 who were *clothed in purple*, captains and rulers, all of them desirable young men, horsemen riding on horses
Luke 16:19 There was a certain rich man who was *clothed in purple* and fine linen and fared sumptuously every day

CLOTHED IN SOFT GARMENTS
Matt 11:8 A man *clothed in soft garments?* Indeed, those who wear soft clothing are in kings' houses
Luke 7:25 A man *clothed in soft garments?* Indeed those who are gorgeously appareled and live in luxury are in kings' courts

CLOTHED IN WHITE
2Chr 5:12 and the Levites who were the singers, all those of Asaph and Heman and Jeduthun, with their sons and their brethren, stood at the east end of the altar, *clothed in white* linen, having cymbals, stringed instruments and harps, and with them one hundred and twenty priests sounding with trumpets
Rev 3:5 He who overcomes shall be *clothed in white* garments, and I will not blot out his name from the Book of Life
Rev 4:4 Around the throne were twenty-four thrones, and on the thrones I saw twenty-four elders sitting, *clothed in white* robes

CLOTHED WITH HONOR
Ps 104:1 O Lord my God, You are very great: You are *clothed with honor* and majesty

CLOTHED WITH MAJESTY
Ps 93:1 The Lord reigns, He is *clothed with majesty;* the Lord is clothed, He has girded Himself with strength

CLOTHED WITH PURPLE
Dan 5:7 And the king spoke, saying to the wise men of Babylon, "Whoever reads this writing, and tells me its interpretation, shall be *clothed with purple* and have a chain of gold around his neck
Dan 5:16 Now if you can read the writing and make known to me its interpretation, you shall be *clothed with purple* and have a chain of gold around your neck, and shall be the third ruler in the kingdom

CLOTHED WITH RIGHTEOUSNESS
Ps 132:9 Let Your priests be *clothed with righteousness*, and let Your saints shout for joy

CLOTHED WITH SACKCLOTH
Esth 4:2 He went as far as the square in front of the king's gate, for no one might enter the king's gate *clothed with sackcloth*

CLOTHED WITH SHAME
Job 8:22 Those who hate you will be *clothed with shame*, and the dwelling place of the wicked will come to nothing
Ps 35:26 Let them be *clothed with shame* and dishonor who magnify themselves against me
Ps 109:29 Let my accusers be *clothed with shame*, and let them cover themselves with their own disgrace as with a mantle

CLOTHED WITH SPLENDOR (NAS, NIV)
(See *CLOTHED WITH HONOR*)

CLOUD, AS SMALL AS A MAN'S HAND
1Kin 18:44 Then it came to pass the seventh time, that he said, "There is a *cloud, as small as a man's hand*, rising out of the sea

CLOUD FILLED THE HOUSE OF THE LORD
1Kin 8:10 And it came to pass, when the priests came out of the holy place, that the *cloud filled the house of the Lord*

CLOUD OF THE LORD
Ex 40:38 For the *cloud of the Lord* was above the tabernacle by day, and fire was over it by night, in the sight of all the house of Israel, throughout all their journeys
Num 10:34 And the *cloud of the Lord* was above them by day when they went out from the camp

CLOUD OF WITNESSES
Heb 12:1 Therefore we also, since we are surrounded by so great a *cloud of witnesses*, let us lay aside every weight, and the sin which so easily ensnares us, and let us run with endurance the race that is set before us

CLOUDS WITHOUT WATER
Jude 12 they are *clouds without water*, carried about by the winds

CO-HEIRS WITH CHRIST (NIV)
(See *JOINT HEIRS WITH CHRIST*)

COAT OF MANY COLORS (KJV)
(See *TUNIC OF MANY COLORS*)

COLLECTION FOR THE SAINTS
1Cor 16:1 Now concerning the *collection for the saints*, as I have given orders to the churches of Galatia, so you must do also

COLOR IN THE CUP (KJV)
(See *SPARKLES IN THE CUP*)

COME AFTER ME
Eccl 2:18 Then I hated all my labor in which I had toiled under the sun, because I must leave it to the man who will *come after me*
Matt 16:24 Then Jesus said to His disciples, "If anyone desires to *come after Me*, let him deny himself, and take up his cross, and follow Me
Mark 1:17 Then Jesus said to them, "*Come after Me*, and I will make you become fishers of men
Mark 8:34 And when He had called the people to Him, with His disciples also, He said to them, "Whoever desires to *come after Me*, let him deny himself, and take up his cross, and follow Me
Luke 9:23 Then He said to them all, "If anyone desires to *come after Me*, let him deny himself, and take up his cross daily, and follow Me
Luke 14:27 And whoever does not bear his cross and *come after Me* cannot be My disciple

COME AND SHARE YOUR MASTER'S HAPPINESS (RSV)
(See *ENTER INTO THE JOY*)

COME BEFORE THE LORD
Lev 15:14 On the eighth day he shall take for himself two turtledoves or two young pigeons, and *come before the Lord*, to the door of the tabernacle of meeting, and give them to the priest
Ezek 46:9 But when the people of the land *come before the Lord* on the appointed feast days, whoever enters by way of the north gate to worship shall go out by way of the south gate
Mic 6:6 With what shall I *come before the Lord*, and bow myself before the High God

COME CRINGING (RSV)
(See *SUBMIT TO*)

COME DOWN FROM HEAVEN (NIV)
(See *DESCEND FROM HEAVEN*)

COME DOWN FROM YOUR THRONES (NIV)
(See *HUMBLE YOURSELVES*)

COME FAWNING (RSV)
(See *SUBMIT TO*)

COME FROM DAVID'S FAMILY (NIV)
(See *SEED OF DAVID*)

COME IN PEACE
1Kin 22:27 Put this fellow in prison, and feed him with bread of affliction and water of affliction, until I *come in peace*

COME IN THE FLESH
1Jn 4:2 Every spirit that confesses that Jesus Christ has *come in the flesh* is of God
1Jn 4:3 and every spirit that does not confess that Jesus Christ has *come in the flesh* is not of God

COME INTO YOUR RIGHTEOUSNESS
Ps 69:27 Add iniquity to their iniquity, and let them not *come into Your righteousness*

COME, LORD JESUS
Rev 22:20 He who testifies to these things says, "Surely I am coming quickly." Amen. Even so, *come, Lord Jesus*

COME TO THE WATERS
Is 55:1 Everyone who thirsts, *come to the waters;* and you who have no money, come, buy and eat

COME TO THEMSELVES
1Kin 8:47 yet when they *come to themselves* in the land where they were carried captive, and repent, and make supplication to You in the land of those who took them captive
2Chr 6:37 yet when they *come to themselves* in the land where they were carried captive, and repent, and make supplication to You in the land of their captivity

COMES IN THE NAME OF THE LORD
Ps 118:26 Blessed is he who *comes in the name of the Lord*
Matt 21:9 Blessed is He who *comes in the name of the Lord*
Matt 23:39 for I say to you, you shall see Me no more till you say, 'Blessed is He who *comes in the name of the Lord*
Mark 11:9 Blessed is He who *comes in the name of the Lord*
Mark 11:10 Blessed is the kingdom of our father David that *comes in the name of the Lord*
Luke 13:35 and assuredly, I say to you, you shall not see Me until the time comes when you say, 'Blessed is He who *comes in the name of the Lord*
Luke 19:38 Blessed is the King who *comes in the name of the Lord*
John 12:13 Blessed is He who *comes in the name of the Lord*

COMES TO POVERTY (NIV)
(See *LEADS TO POVERTY*)

COMFORT ME
Job 7:13 When I say, 'My bed will *comfort me*, my couch will ease my complaint
Job 21:34 How then can you *comfort me* with empty words, since falsehood remains in your answers
Ps 23:4 For You are with me; Your rod and Your staff, they *comfort me*
Ps 71:21 You shall increase my greatness, and *comfort me* on every side
Ps 119:82 My eyes fail from seeking Your word, saying, "When will You *comfort me*
Is 12:1 though You were angry with me, Your anger is turned away, and You *comfort me*
Is 22:4 do not labor to *comfort me* because of the plundering of the daughter of my people
Lam 1:21 They have heard that I sigh, with no one to *comfort me*

COMFORT MY PEOPLE
Is 40:1 Comfort, yes, *comfort My people!*" says your God

COMING AND GOING
Jer 37:4 Now Jeremiah was *coming and going* among the people, for they had not yet put him in prison
Mark 6:31 For there were many *coming and going*, and they did not even have time to eat

COMING IN A CLOUD
Luke 21:27 Then they will see the Son of Man *coming in a cloud* with power and great glory

COMING OF THE LORD
1Th 4:15 For this we say to you by the word of the Lord, that we who are alive and remain until the *coming of the Lord* will by no means precede those who are asleep
Jas 5:7 Therefore be patient, brethren, until the *coming of the Lord*
Jas 5:8 Establish your hearts, for the *coming of the Lord* is at hand

COMING OF THE SON OF MAN
Matt 24:27 For as the lightning comes from the east and flashes to the west, so also will the *coming of the Son of Man* be
Matt 24:37 But as the days of Noah were, so also will the *coming of the Son of Man* be
Matt 24:39 and did not know until the flood came and took them all away, so also will the *coming of the Son of Man* be

COMING ON THE CLOUDS
Matt 24:30 Then the sign of the Son of Man will appear in heaven, and then all the tribes of the earth will mourn, and they will see the Son of Man *coming on the clouds* of heaven with power and great glory
Matt 26:64 Nevertheless, I say to you, hereafter you will see the Son of Man sitting at the right hand of the Power, and *coming on the clouds* of heaven

COMING WITH THE CLOUDS
Dan 7:13 I was watching in the night visions, and behold, One like the Son of Man, *coming with the clouds* of heaven
Mark 14:62 And you will see the Son of Man sitting at the right hand of the Power, and *coming with the clouds* of heaven

COMING WRATH (NIV)
(See *WRATH TO COME*)

COMMAND OF THE LORD
Num 9:18 At the *command of the Lord* the children of Israel would journey, and at the *command of the Lord* they would camp
Num 9:20 according to the *command of the Lord* they would remain encamped, and according to the *command of the Lord* they would journey
Num 9:23 At the *command of the Lord* they remained encamped, and at the *command of the Lord* they journeyed; they kept the charge of the Lord, at the *command of the Lord* by the hand of Moses
Num 10:13 So they started out for the first time according to the *command of the Lord* by the hand of Moses
Num 13:3 So Moses sent them from the Wilderness of Paran according to the *command of the Lord*, all of them men who were heads of the children of Israel
Num 14:41 Then Moses said, "Now why do you transgress the *command of the Lord*
Num 33:2 Now Moses wrote down the starting points of their journeys at the *command of the Lord*
Num 33:38 Then Aaron the priest went up to Mount Hor at the *command of the Lord*, and died there in the fortieth year after the children of Israel had come out of the land of Egypt, on the first day of the fifth month
Deut 1:26 Nevertheless you would not go up, but rebelled against the *command of the Lord* your God
Deut 1:43 yet you would not listen, but rebelled against the *command of the Lord*, and presumptuously went up into the mountain
2Chr 13:11 for we keep the *command of the Lord* our God, but you have forsaken Him

COMMANDED BY THE WORD OF THE LORD (NIV)
(See *ACCORDING TO THE WORD OF THE LORD*)

COMMANDER OF THE LORD'S ARMY
Josh 5:15 Then the *Commander of the Lord's army* said to Joshua

COMMANDMENT OF GOD

Matt 15:3 But He answered and said to them, "Why do you also transgress the *commandment of God* because of your tradition

Matt 15:6 Thus you have made the *commandment of God* of no effect by your tradition

Mark 7:8 For laying aside the *commandment of God*, you hold the tradition of men the washing of pitchers and cups, and many other such things you do

Mark 7:9 And He said to them, "All too well you reject the *commandment of God*, that you may keep your tradition

1Tim 1:1 Paul, an apostle of Jesus Christ, by the *commandment of God* our Savior and the Lord Jesus Christ, our hope

Tit 1:3 but has in due time manifested His word through preaching, which was committed to me according to the *commandment of God* our Savior

COMMANDMENT OF THE LORD

Ex 17:1 Then all the congregation of the children of Israel set out on their journey from the Wilderness of Sin, according to the *commandment of the Lord*, and camped in Rephidim

Num 3:39 All who were numbered of the Levites, whom Moses and Aaron numbered at the *commandment of the Lord*, by their families, all the males from a month old and above, were twenty-two thousand

Num 4:37 These were the ones who were numbered of the families of the Kohathites, all who might serve in the tabernacle of meeting, whom Moses and Aaron numbered according to the *commandment of the Lord* by the hand of Moses

Num 4:41 These are the ones who were numbered of the families of the sons of Gershon, of all who might serve in the tabernacle of meeting, whom Moses and Aaron numbered according to the *commandment of the Lord*

Num 4:49 According to the *commandment of the Lord* they were numbered by the hand of Moses, each according to his service and according to his task

Deut 9:23 Likewise, when the Lord sent you from Kadesh Barnea, saying, 'Go up and possess the land which I have given you,' then you rebelled against the *commandment of the Lord* your God, and you did not believe Him nor obey His voice

Josh 8:8 According to the *commandment of the Lord* you shall do

Josh 15:13 Now to Caleb the son of Jephunneh he gave a portion among the children of Judah, according to the *commandment of the Lord* to Joshua, namely, Kirjath Arba, which is Hebron

Josh 17:4 Therefore, according to the *commandment of the Lord*, he gave them an inheritance among their father's brothers

Josh 21:3 So the children of Israel gave to the Levites from their inheritance, at the *commandment of the Lord*, these cities and their common-lands

Josh 22:3 You have not left your brethren these many days, up to this day, but have kept the charge of the *commandment of the Lord* your God

1Sam 12:14 If you fear the Lord and serve Him and obey His voice, and do not rebel against the *commandment of the Lord*, then both you and the king who reigns over you will continue following the Lord your God

1Sam 12:15 However, if you do not obey the voice of the Lord, but rebel against the *commandment of the Lord*, then the hand of the Lord will be against you, as it was against your fathers

1Sam 13:13 You have not kept the *commandment of the Lord* your God, which He commanded you

1Sam 15:13 Then Samuel went to Saul, and Saul said to him, "Blessed are you of the Lord! I have performed the *commandment of the Lord*

1Sam 15:24 Then Saul said to Samuel, "I have sinned, for I have transgressed the *commandment of the Lord* and your words, because I feared the people and obeyed their voice

2Sam 12:9 Why have you despised the *commandment of the Lord*, to do evil in His sight

2Kin 24:3 Surely at the *commandment of the Lord* this came upon Judah, to remove them from His sight because of the sins of Manasseh, according to all that he had done

2Chr 29:25 for thus was the *commandment of the Lord* by his prophets

Ps 19:8 The *commandment of the Lord* is pure, enlightening the eyes

COMMANDMENTS OF GOD

1Cor 7:19 Circumcision is nothing and uncircumcision is nothing, but keeping the *commandments of God* is what matters

Rev 12:17 And the dragon was enraged with the woman, and he went to make war with the rest of her offspring, who keep the *commandments of God* and have the testimony of Jesus Christ

Rev 14:12 here are those who keep the *commandments of God* and the faith of Jesus

COMMANDMENTS OF MEN

Matt 15:9 And in vain they worship Me, teaching as doctrines the *commandments of men*

Mark 7:7 And in vain they worship Me, teaching as doctrines the *commandments of men*

Tit 1:14 not giving heed to Jewish fables and *commandments of men* who turn from the truth

COMMANDMENTS OF THE LORD

Lev 4:2 If a person sins unintentionally against any of the *commandments of the Lord* in anything which ought not to be done, and does any of them

Lev 4:13 Now if the whole congregation of Israel sins unintentionally, and the thing is hidden from the eyes of the assembly, and they have done something against any of the *commandments of the Lord* in anything which should not be done, and are guilty

Lev 4:22 When a ruler has sinned, and done something unintentionally against any of the *commandments of the Lord* his God in anything which should not be done, and is guilty

Lev 4:27 If anyone of the common people sins unintentionally by doing something against any of the *commandments of the Lord* in anything which ought not to be done, and is guilty

Lev 5:17 If a person sins, and commits any of these things which are forbidden to be done by the *commandments of the Lord*, though he does not know it, yet he is guilty and shall bear his iniquity

Num 15:39 And you shall have the tassel, that you may look upon it and remember all the *commandments of the Lord* and do them, and that you may not follow the harlotry to which your own heart and your own eyes are inclined

Deut 4:2 You shall not add to the word which I command you, nor take anything from it, that you may keep the *commandments of the Lord* your God which I command you

Deut 6:17 You shall diligently keep the *commandments of the Lord* your God, His testimonies, and His statutes which He has commanded you

Deut 8:6 Therefore you shall keep the *commandments of the Lord* your God, to walk in His ways and to fear Him

Deut 10:13 and to keep the *commandments of the Lord* and His statutes which I command you today for your good

Deut 11:27 the blessing, if you obey the *commandments of the Lord* your God which I command you today
Deut 11:28 and the curse, if you do not obey the *commandments of the Lord* your God, but turn aside from the way which I command you today, to go after other gods which you have not known
Deut 28:9 The Lord will establish you as a holy people to Himself, just as He has sworn to you, if you keep the *commandments of the Lord* your God and walk in His ways
Deut 28:13 you shall be above only, and not be beneath, if you heed the *commandments of the Lord* your God, which I command you today, and are careful to observe them
Judg 2:17 They turned quickly from the way in which their fathers walked, in obeying the *commandments of the Lord*
Judg 3:4 And they were left, that He might test Israel by them, to know whether they would obey the *commandments of the Lord*, which He had commanded their fathers by the hand of Moses
1Kin 18:18 And he answered, "I have not troubled Israel, but you and your father's house have, in that you have forsaken the *commandments of the Lord*, and you have followed the Baals
2Kin 17:16 So they left all the *commandments of the Lord* their God, made for themselves a molded image and two calves, made a wooden image and worshiped all the host of heaven, and served Baal
2Kin 17:19 Also Judah did not keep the *commandments of the Lord* their God, but walked in the statutes of Israel which they made
1Chr 28:8 Now therefore, in the sight of all Israel, the congregation of the Lord, and in the hearing of our God, be careful to seek out all the *commandments of the Lord* your God, that you may possess this good land, and leave it as an inheritance for your children after you forever
2Chr 24:20 Why do you transgress the *commandments of the Lord*, so that you cannot prosper
Ezra 7:11 Now this is the copy of the letter that King Artaxerxes gave Ezra the priest, the scribe, expert in the words of the *commandments of the Lord*, and of His statutes to Israel
Neh 10:29 they joined with their brethren, their nobles, and entered into a curse and an oath to walk in God's Law, which was given by Moses the servant of God, and to observe and do all the *commandments of the Lord* our Lord, and His ordinances and His statutes
1Cor 14:37 If anyone thinks himself to be a prophet or spiritual, let him acknowledge that the things which I write to you are the *commandments of the Lord*

COMMANDS AND DECREES (NIV)
(See *MY COMMANDMENTS AND MY STATUTES*)

COMMIT ADULTERY
Ex 20:14 You shall not *commit adultery*
Deut 5:18 You shall not *commit adultery*
Jer 7:9 Will you steal, murder, *commit adultery*, swear falsely, burn incense to Baal, and walk after other gods whom you do not know
Jer 23:14 they *commit adultery* and walk in lies; they also strengthen the hands of evildoers, so that no one turns back from his wickedness
Hos 4:13 Therefore your daughters commit harlotry, and your brides *commit adultery*
Hos 4:14 I will not punish your daughters when they commit harlotry, nor your brides when they *commit adultery*
Matt 5:27 You have heard that it was said to those of old, 'You shall not *commit adultery*
Matt 5:32 But I say to you that whoever divorces his wife for any reason except sexual immorality causes her to *commit adultery*
Matt 19:18 Jesus said, "'You shall not murder,' 'You shall not *commit adultery*
Mark 10:19 Do not *commit adultery*,' 'Do not murder,' 'Do not steal
Luke 18:20 Do not *commit adultery*,' 'Do not murder,' 'Do not steal
Rom 2:22 You who say, "Do not *commit adultery*," do you *commit adultery*
Rom 13:9 For the commandments, "You shall not *commit adultery*," "You shall not murder
Jas 2:11 For He who said, "Do not *commit adultery*," also said, "Do not murder." Now if you do not *commit adultery*, but you do murder, you have become a transgressor of the law
Rev 2:22 Indeed I will cast her into a sickbed, and those who *commit adultery* with her into great tribulation, unless they repent of their deeds

COMMIT YOUR WAY
Ps 37:5 *Commit your way* to the Lord, trust also in Him, and He shall bring it to pass

COMMITS ADULTERY
Lev 20:10 The man who *commits adultery* with another man's wife, he who *commits adultery* with his neighbor's wife, the adulterer and the adulteress, shall surely be put to death
Prov 6:32 Whoever *commits adultery* with a woman lacks understanding; he who does so destroys his own soul
Matt 5:32 and whoever marries a woman who is divorced *commits adultery*
Matt 19:9 And I say to you, whoever divorces his wife, except for sexual immorality, and marries another, *commits adultery;* and whoever marries her who is divorced *commits adultery*
Mark 10:11 So He said to them, "Whoever divorces his wife and marries another *commits adultery* against her
Mark 10:12 And if a woman divorces her husband and marries another, she *commits adultery*
Luke 16:18 Whoever divorces his wife and marries another *commits adultery;* and whoever marries her who is divorced from her husband *commits adultery*

COMMITTED ADULTERY
Jer 3:8 Then I saw that for all the causes for which backsliding Israel had *committed adultery*, I had put her away and given her a certificate of divorce
Jer 3:9 So it came to pass, through her casual harlotry, that she defiled the land and *committed adultery* with stones and trees
Jer 5:7 When I had fed them to the full, then they *committed adultery* and assembled themselves by troops in the harlots
Jer 29:23 because they have done disgraceful things in Israel, have *committed adultery* with their neighbors' wives, and have spoken lying words in My name, which I have not commanded them
Ezek 23:37 For they have *committed adultery*, and blood is on their hands. They have *committed adultery* with their idols, and even sacrificed their sons whom they bore to Me, passing them through the fire, to devour them
Matt 5:28 But I say to you that whoever looks at a woman to lust for her has already *committed adultery* with her in his heart

COMMITTING ADULTERY
Hos 3:1 Then the Lord said to me, "Go again, love a woman who is loved by a lover and is *committing adultery*, just like the love of the Lord for

the children of Israel, who look to other gods and love the raisin cakes of the pagans
Hos 4:2 By swearing and lying, killing and stealing and *committing adultery*, they break all restraint, with bloodshed after bloodshed

COMMON OR UNCLEAN
Acts 10:14 But Peter said, "Not so, Lord! For I have never eaten anything *common or unclean*
Acts 10:28 But God has shown me that I should not call any man *common or unclean*
Acts 11:8 For nothing *common or unclean* has at any time entered my mouth

COMMON PEOPLE
Lev 4:27 If anyone of the *common people* sins unintentionally by doing something against any of the commandments of the Lord in anything which ought not to be done, and is guilty
2Kin 23:6 And he brought out the wooden image from the house of the Lord, to the Brook Kidron outside Jerusalem, burned it at the Brook Kidron and ground it to ashes, and threw its ashes on the graves of the *common people*
Jer 26:23 And they brought Urijah from Egypt and brought him to Jehoiakim the king, who killed him with the sword and cast his dead body into the graves of the *common people*
Ezek 7:27 The king will mourn, the prince will be clothed with desolation, and the hands of the *common people* will tremble
Mark 12:37 how is He then his Son?" And the *common people* heard Him gladly

COMMONWEALTH IS IN HEAVEN (RSV)
(See *CITIZENSHIP IS IN HEAVEN*)

COMMONWEALTH OF ISRAEL
Eph 2:12 that at that time you were without Christ, being aliens from the *commonwealth of Israel* and strangers from the covenants of promise, having no hope and without God in the world

COMMUNION OF THE BLOOD
1Cor 10:16 The cup of blessing which we bless, is it not the *communion of the blood* of Christ

COMMUNION OF THE BODY
1Cor 10:16 The bread which we break, is it not the *communion of the body* of Christ

COMMUNION OF THE HOLY SPIRIT
2Cor 13:14 The grace of the Lord Jesus Christ, and the love of God, and the *communion of the Holy Spirit* be with you all

COMMUNITY OF ISRAEL (NIV)
(See *CONGREGATION OF ISRAEL*)

COMPANY OF PROPHETS (KJV)
(See *GROUP OF PROPHETS*)

COMPASSED THE CITY (KJV)
(See *MARCHED AROUND THE CITY*)

COMPEL THEM TO COME IN
Luke 14:23 Then the master said to the servant, 'Go out into the highways and hedges, and *compel them to come in*, that my house may be filled

COMPLACENT IN ZION (NIV)
(See *AT EASE IN ZION*)

CONCEAL A MATTER
Prov 25:2 It is the glory of God to *conceal a matter*, but the glory of kings is to search out a matter

CONCEIVED AND BORE
Gen 4:1 Now Adam knew Eve his wife, and she *conceived and bore* Cain, and said
Gen 4:17 And Cain knew his wife, and she *conceived and bore* Enoch
Gen 21:2 For Sarah *conceived and bore* Abraham a son in his old age, at the set time of which God had spoken to him
Gen 29:32 So Leah *conceived and bore* a son, and she called his name Reuben
Gen 30:5 And Bilhah *conceived and bore* Jacob a son
Gen 30:17 And God listened to Leah, and she *conceived and bore* Jacob a fifth son
Gen 30:23 And she *conceived and bore* a son, and said, "God has taken away my reproach
Gen 38:3 So she *conceived and bore* a son, and he called his name Er
Ex 2:2 So the woman *conceived and bore* a son. And when she saw that he was a beautiful child, she hid him three months
1Sam 1:20 So it came to pass in the process of time that Hannah *conceived and bore* a son, and called his name Samuel, saying
1Sam 2:21 And the Lord visited Hannah, so that she *conceived and bore* three sons and two daughters
1Chr 7:23 And when he went in to his wife, she *conceived and bore* a son
Is 8:3 Then I went to the prophetess, and she *conceived and bore* a son
Hos 1:3 So he went and took Gomer the daughter of Diblaim, and she *conceived and bore* him a son
Hos 1:8 Now when she had weaned Lo-Ruhamah, she *conceived and bore* a son

CONCERNING THE TRUTH HAVE ERRED (KJV)
(See *STRAYED CONCERNING THE TRUTH*)

CONFESS HIS NAME
Rev 3:5 but I will *confess his name* before My Father and before His angels

CONFESS MY TRANSGRESSIONS
Ps 32:5 I said, "I will *confess my transgressions* to the Lord

CONFESS YOUR NAME
1Kin 8:33 When Your people Israel are defeated before an enemy because they have sinned against You, and when they turn back to You and *confess Your name*, and pray and make supplication to You in this temple
1Kin 8:35 When the heavens are shut up and there is no rain because they have sinned against You, when they pray toward this place and *confess Your name*, and turn from their sin because You afflict them
2Chr 6:24 Or if Your people Israel are defeated before an enemy because they have sinned against You, and return and *confess Your name*, and pray and make supplication before You in this temple
2Chr 6:26 When heaven is shut up and there is no rain because they have sinned against You, when they pray toward this place and *confess Your name*, and turn from their sin because You afflict them

CONFESS YOUR TRESPASSES
Jas 5:16 *Confess your trespasses* to one another, and pray for one another, that you may be healed

CONFESSES ME BEFORE MEN
Matt 10:32 Therefore whoever *confesses Me before men*, him I will also confess before My Father who is in heaven

CONFESSES THE SON

Luke 12:8 Also I say to you, whoever *confesses Me before men*, him the Son of Man also will confess before the angels of God

CONFESSES THE SON (NAS, RSV)
(See *ACKNOWLEDGES THE SON*)

CONFESSING THEIR SINS
Matt 3:6 and were baptized by him in the Jordan, *confessing their sins*
Mark 1:5 And all the land of Judea, and those from Jerusalem, went out to him and were all baptized by him in the Jordan River, *confessing their sins*

CONFIDENCE IN THE FLESH
Phil 3:3 For we are the circumcision, who worship God in the Spirit, rejoice in Christ Jesus, and have no *confidence in the flesh*
Phil 3:4 though I also might have *confidence in the flesh*. If anyone else thinks he may have *confidence in the flesh*, I more so

CONFIDENCE IN THE LORD
2Th 3:4 And we have *confidence in the Lord* concerning you, both that you do and will do the things we command you

CONFIDENT OF BETTER THINGS
Heb 6:9 But, beloved, we are *confident of better things* concerning you, yes, things that accompany salvation, though we speak in this manner

CONFIRMED THE MESSAGE (NIV)
(See *BEARING WITNESS*)

CONFORMED TO HIS DEATH
Phil 3:10 that I may know Him and the power of His resurrection, and the fellowship of His sufferings, being *conformed to His death*

CONFORMED TO THE IMAGE OF HIS SON
Rom 8:29 For whom He foreknew, He also predestined to be *conformed to the image of His Son*, that He might be the firstborn among many brethren

CONFORMED TO THIS WORLD
Rom 12:2 And do not be *conformed to this world*, but be transformed by the renewing of your mind, that you may prove what is that good and acceptable and perfect will of God

CONGREGATION OF EVILDOERS
Ps 26:5 I have hated the *congregation of evildoers*, and will not sit with the wicked

CONGREGATION OF ISRAEL
Ex 12:3 Speak to all the *congregation of Israel*, saying: "On the tenth day of this month every man shall take for himself a lamb, according to the house of his father, a lamb for a household
Ex 12:6 Then the whole assembly of the *congregation of Israel* shall kill it at twilight
Ex 12:19 For seven days no leaven shall be found in your houses, since whoever eats what is leavened, that same person shall be cut off from the *congregation of Israel*, whether he is a stranger or a native of the land
Ex 12:47 All the *congregation of Israel* shall keep it
Lev 4:13 Now if the whole *congregation of Israel* sins unintentionally, and the thing is hidden from the eyes of the assembly, and they have done something against any of the commandments of the Lord in anything which should not be done, and are guilty
Lev 16:17 There shall be no man in the tabernacle of meeting when he goes in to make atonement in the Holy Place, until he comes out, that he may make atonement for himself, for his household, and for all the *congregation of Israel*
Num 16:9 Is it a small thing to you that the God of Israel has separated you from the *congregation of Israel*, to bring you near to Himself, to do the work of the tabernacle of the Lord, and to stand before the congregation to serve them
Num 32:4 the country which the Lord defeated before the *congregation of Israel*, is a land for livestock, and your servants have livestock
Deut 31:30 Then Moses spoke in the hearing of all the *congregation of Israel* the words of this song until they were ended
Josh 8:35 There was not a word of all that Moses had commanded which Joshua did not read before all the *congregation of Israel*, with the women, the little ones, and the strangers who were living among them
Josh 22:18 And it shall be, if you rebel today against the Lord, that tomorrow He will be angry with the whole *congregation of Israel*
Josh 22:20 Did not Achan the son of Zerah commit a trespass in the accursed thing, and wrath fell on all the *congregation of Israel*
1Kin 8:5 Also King Solomon, and all the *congregation of Israel* who were assembled to him, were with him before the ark, sacrificing sheep and oxen that could not be counted or numbered for multitude
1Kin 8:14 And the king turned around and blessed the whole *congregation of Israel*, while all the *congregation of Israel* was standing
1Kin 8:22 Then Solomon stood before the altar of the Lord in the presence of all the *congregation of Israel*, and spread out his hands toward heaven
1Kin 8:55 Then he stood and blessed all the *congregation of Israel* with a loud voice, saying
1Kin 12:3 Then Jeroboam and the whole *congregation of Israel* came and spoke to Rehoboam, saying
1Chr 13:2 And David said to all the *congregation of Israel*, "If it seems good to you, and if it is of the Lord our God, let us send out to our brethren everywhere who are left in all the land of Israel, and with them to the priests and Levites who are in their cities and their common-lands, that they may gather together to us
2Chr 5:6 Also King Solomon, and all the *congregation of Israel* who were assembled with him before the ark, were sacrificing sheep and oxen that could not be counted or numbered for multitude
2Chr 6:3 Then the king turned around and blessed the whole *congregation of Israel*, while all the *congregation of Israel* stood
2Chr 6:12 Then Solomon stood before the altar of the Lord in the presence of all the *congregation of Israel*, and spread out his hands
2Chr 6:13 and he stood on it, knelt down on his knees before all the *congregation of Israel*, and spread out his hands toward heaven
2Chr 24:6 So the king called Jehoiada the chief priest, and said to him, "Why have you not required the Levites to bring in from Judah and from Jerusalem the collection, according to the commandment of Moses the servant of the Lord and of the *congregation of Israel*, for the tabernacle of witness

CONGREGATION OF THE CHILDREN OF ISRAEL
Ex 16:1 And they journeyed from Elim, and all the *congregation of the children of Israel* came to the Wilderness of Sin, which is between Elim and Si-

nai, on the fifteenth day of the second month after they departed from the land of Egypt
Ex 16:2 Then the whole *congregation of the children of Israel* complained against Moses and Aaron in the wilderness
Ex 16:9 Then Moses spoke to Aaron, "Say to all the *congregation of the children of Israel*
Ex 16:10 Now it came to pass, as Aaron spoke to the whole *congregation of the children of Israel*, that they looked toward the wilderness, and behold, the glory of the Lord appeared in the cloud
Ex 17:1 Then all the *congregation of the children of Israel* set out on their journey from the Wilderness of Sin, according to the commandment of the Lord, and camped in Rephidim
Ex 35:1 Then Moses gathered all the *congregation of the children of Israel* together, and said to them
Ex 35:4 And Moses spoke to all the *congregation of the children of Israel*, saying
Ex 35:20 And all the *congregation of the children of Israel* departed from the presence of Moses
Lev 16:5 And he shall take from the *congregation of the children of Israel* two kids of the goats as a sin offering, and one ram as a burnt offering
Lev 19:2 Speak to all the *congregation of the children of Israel*, and say to them
Num 1:2 Take a census of all the *congregation of the children of Israel*, by their families, by their fathers' houses, according to the number of names, every male individually
Num 1:53 but the Levites shall camp around the tabernacle of the Testimony, that there may be no wrath on the *congregation of the children of Israel*
Num 8:20 Thus Moses and Aaron and all the *congregation of the children of Israel* did to the Levites
Num 13:26 So they departed and came back to Moses and Aaron and all the *congregation of the children of Israel* in the Wilderness of Paran, at Kadesh
Num 14:5 Then Moses and Aaron fell on their faces before all the assembly of the *congregation of the children of Israel*
Num 14:7 and they spoke to all the *congregation of the children of Israel*, saying
Num 15:25 So the priest shall make atonement for the whole *congregation of the children of Israel*, and it shall be forgiven them, for it was unintentional
Num 15:26 It shall be forgiven the whole *congregation of the children of Israel* and the stranger who sojourns among them, because all the people did it unintentionally
Num 16:41 On the next day all the *congregation of the children of Israel* murmured against Moses and Aaron, saying
Num 19:9 and they shall be kept for the *congregation of the children of Israel* for the water of purification
Num 25:6 And indeed, one of the children of Israel came and presented to his brethren a Midianite woman in the sight of Moses and in the sight of all the *congregation of the children of Israel*, who were weeping at the door of the tabernacle of meeting
Num 26:2 Take a census of all the *congregation of the children of Israel* from twenty years old and above, by their fathers' houses, all who are able to go to war in Israel
Num 27:20 And you shall give some of your authority to him, that all the *congregation of the children of Israel* may be obedient
Num 31:12 Then they brought the captives, the booty, and the spoil to Moses, to Eleazar the priest, and to the *congregation of the children of Israel*, to the camp in the plains of Moab by the Jordan, across from Jericho
Josh 18:1 Then the whole *congregation of the children of Israel* assembled together at Shiloh, and set up the tabernacle of meeting there
Josh 22:12 And when the children of Israel heard of it, the whole *congregation of the children of Israel* gathered together at Shiloh to go to war against them

CONGREGATION OF THE LORD
Num 16:3 Why then do you exalt yourselves above the *congregation of the Lord*
Num 20:4 Why have you brought up the *congregation of the Lord* into this wilderness, that we and our animals should die here
Num 27:17 who may go out before them and go in before them, who may lead them out and bring them in, that the *congregation of the Lord* may not be like sheep which have no shepherd
Num 31:16 Look, these women caused the children of Israel, through the counsel of Balaam, to trespass against the Lord in the incident of Peor, and there was a plague among the *congregation of the Lord*
Deut 23:1 He who is emasculated by crushing or mutilation shall not enter the *congregation of the Lord*
Deut 23:2 One of illegitimate birth shall not enter the *congregation of the Lord;* even to the tenth generation none of his descendants shall enter the *congregation of the Lord*
Deut 23:3 An Ammonite or Moabite shall not enter the *congregation of the Lord;* even to the tenth generation none of his descendants shall enter the *congregation of the Lord* forever
Deut 23:8 The children of the third generation born to them may enter the *congregation of the Lord*
Josh 22:16 Thus says the whole *congregation of the Lord:* "What treachery is this that you have committed against the God of Israel, to turn away this day from following the Lord, in that you have built for yourselves an altar, that you might rebel this day against the Lord
Josh 22:17 Is the iniquity of Peor not enough for us, from which we are not cleansed until this day, although there was a plague in the *congregation of the Lord*
1Chr 28:8 Now therefore, in the sight of all Israel, the *congregation of the Lord*, and in the hearing of our God, be careful to seek out all the commandments of the Lord your God, that you may possess this good land, and leave it as an inheritance for your children after you forever
Mic 2:5 Therefore you will have no one to determine boundaries by lot in the *congregation of the Lord*

CONSCIENCE WHEN IT IS WEAK (NAS, RSV)
(See *WEAK CONSCIENCE*)

CONSECRATE YOURSELVES
Ex 32:29 Then Moses said, "*Consecrate yourselves* today to the Lord, that He may bestow on you a blessing this day, for every man has opposed his son and his brother

CONSECRATED TO THE LORD
Josh 6:19 But all the silver and gold, and vessels of bronze and iron, are *consecrated to the Lord*
2Chr 31:6 also the tithe of holy things which were *consecrated to the Lord* their God they laid in heaps

CONSIDER MY CAUSE (NIV)
(See *PLEAD MY CASE*)

CONSIDER THE LILIES
Matt 6:28 *Consider the lilies* of the field, how they grow: they neither toil nor spin
Luke 12:27 *Consider the lilies*, how they grow: they neither toil nor spin

CONSIDER YOUR WAYS
Hag 1:5 Now therefore, thus says the Lord of hosts: *Consider your ways*
Hag 1:7 Thus says the Lord of hosts: *Consider your ways*

CONSOLATION IN CHRIST
Phil 2:1 Therefore if there is any *consolation in Christ*, if any comfort of love, if any fellowship of the Spirit, if any affection and mercy

CONSOLATION OF ISRAEL
Luke 2:25 And behold, there was a man in Jerusalem whose name was Simeon, and this man was just and devout, waiting for the *Consolation of Israel*, and the Holy Spirit was upon him

CONSTRAINED BY THE SPIRIT
Acts 18:5 When Silas and Timothy had come from Macedonia, Paul was *constrained by the Spirit*, and testified to the Jews that Jesus is the Christ

CONSUME HER FORTRESSES (NIV)
(See *DEVOUR ITS PALACES*)

CONSUMING FIRE
Ex 24:17 The sight of the glory of the Lord was like a *consuming fire* on the top of the mountain in the eyes of the children of Israel
Deut 4:24 For the Lord your God is a *consuming fire*, a jealous God
Deut 9:3 Therefore understand today that the Lord your God is He who goes over before you as a *consuming fire*
Heb 12:29 For our God is a *consuming fire*

CONSUMPTION DECREED (KJV)
(See *DESTRUCTION DECREED*)

CONTEMPT OF THE PROUD
Ps 123:4 Our soul is exceedingly filled with the scorn of those who are at ease, with the *contempt of the proud*

CONTEND EARNESTLY FOR THE FAITH
Jude 3 Beloved, while I was very diligent to write to you concerning our common salvation, I found it necessary to write to you exhorting you to *contend earnestly for the faith* which was once for all delivered to the saints

CONTEND WITH HIM
Job 9:3 If one wished to *contend with Him*, he could not answer Him one time out of a thousand
Job 33:13 Why do you *contend with Him?* For He does not give an accounting of any of His words
Eccl 6:10 and he cannot *contend with Him* who is mightier than he
Is 49:25 for I will *contend with him* who contends with you, and I will save your children

CONTEND WITH MAN (NIV)
(See *STRIVE WITH MAN*)

CONTEND WITH ME
Ex 17:2 And Moses said to them, "Why do you *contend with me*
Job 10:2 I will say to God, 'Do not condemn me; show me why You *contend with me*
Job 13:19 Who is he who will *contend with me?* If now I hold my tongue, I perish
Job 23:6 Would He *contend with me* in His great power? No
Is 50:8 who will *contend with Me?* Let us stand together.
Jer 18:19 Give heed to me, O Lord, and listen to the voice of those who *contend with me*

CONTENDED AGAINST THE LORD
Num 26:9 These are the Dathan and Abiram, representatives of the congregation, who contended against Moses and Aaron in the company of Korah, when they *contended against the Lord*
Jer 50:24 you have been found and also caught, because you have *contended against the Lord*

CONTENDING AGAINST FLESH (RSV)
(See *WRESTLE AGAINST FLESH*)

CONTENTIOUS MAN
Prov 26:21 As charcoal is to burning coals, and wood to fire, so is a *contentious man* to kindle strife

CONTENTIOUS WOMAN
Prov 21:9 It is better to dwell in a corner of a housetop, than in a house shared with a *contentious woman*
Prov 25:24 It is better to dwell in a corner of a housetop, than in a house shared with a *contentious woman*
Prov 27:15 A continual dripping on a very rainy day and a *contentious woman* are alike

CONTINUE EARNESTLY IN PRAYER
Col 4:2 *Continue earnestly in prayer*, being vigilant in it with thanksgiving

CONTINUE IN FAITH
1Tim 2:15 Nevertheless she will be saved in childbearing if they *continue in faith*, love, and holiness, with self-control

CONTINUE IN THE FAITH
Acts 14:22 strengthening the souls of the disciples, exhorting them to *continue in the faith*, and saying
Col 1:23 if indeed you *continue in the faith*, grounded and steadfast, and are not moved away from the hope of the gospel which you heard, which was preached to every creature under heaven, of which I, Paul, became a minister

CONTINUES A PRIEST FOR EVER (RSV)
(See *REMAINS A PRIEST CONTINUALLY*)

CONTRARY TO THE LAW
Acts 18:13 saying, "This fellow persuades men to worship God *contrary to the law*
Acts 23:3 For you sit to judge me according to the law, and do you command me to be struck *contrary to the law*

CONTRITE AND HUMBLE SPIRIT
Is 57:15 I dwell in the high and holy place, with him who has a *contrite and humble spirit*, to revive the spirit of the humble, and to revive the heart of the contrite ones

CONVERSATION IS IN HEAVEN (KJV)
(See *CITIZENSHIP IS IN HEAVEN*)

CONVERTING THE SOUL
Ps 19:7 The law of the Lord is perfect, *converting the soul*

CONVICT THE WORLD OF SIN
John 16:8 And when He has come, He will *convict the world of sin*, and of righteousness, and of judgment

CONVICTED BY THE LAW
Jas 2:9 but if you show partiality, you commit sin, and are *convicted by the law* as transgressors

CONVICTION OF THINGS NOT SEEN (NAS, RSV)
(See *EVIDENCE OF THINGS NOT SEEN*)

CONVINCE THE WORLD CONCERNING SIN (RSV)
(See *CONVICT THE WORLD OF SIN*)

CONVINCED OF THE LAW (KJV)
(See *CONVICTED BY THE LAW*)

COOL OF THE DAY
Gen 3:8 And they heard the sound of the Lord God walking in the garden in the *cool of the day*, and Adam and his wife hid themselves from the presence of the Lord God among the trees of the garden

CORDS OF AFFLICTION
Job 36:8 And if they are bound in fetters, held in the *cords of affliction*

CORDS OF DEATH (NAS, RSV)
(See *PANGS OF DEATH*)

CORDS OF SHEOL (NAS, RSV)
(See *SORROWS OF SHEOL*)

CORDS OF THE GRAVE (NIV)
(See *SORROWS OF SHEOL*)

CORNER OF A HOUSETOP
Prov 21:9 It is better to dwell in a *corner of a housetop*, than in a house shared with a contentious woman
Prov 25:24 It is better to dwell in a *corner of a housetop*, than in a house shared with a contentious woman

CORRECT OPPRESSION (RSV)
(See *REPROVE THE OPPRESSOR*)

CORRECTION OF FOOLS
Prov 16:22 Understanding is a wellspring of life to him who has it. But the *correction of fools* is folly

CORRECTLY HANDLES THE WORD OF TRUTH (NIV)
(See *RIGHTLY DIVIDING THE WORD OF TRUTH*)

CORRUPT TREE (KJV)
(See *BAD TREE*)

CORRUPTION OF THE WORLD (NIV)
(See *POLLUTIONS OF THE WORLD*)

CORRUPTS GOOD HABITS
1Cor 15:33 Do not be deceived: Evil company *corrupts good habits*

COST HIM HIS LIFE (RSV)
(See *TAKE HIS LIFE*)

COUCHED AS A LION (RSV)
(See *LIES DOWN AS A LION*)

COUNCIL OF THE HOLY ONES (NAS, NIV, RSV)
(See *ASSEMBLY OF THE SAINTS*)

COUNSEL OF THE ELDERS
2Chr 10:13 Then the king answered them roughly. King Rehoboam rejected the *counsel of the elders*

COUNSEL OF THE LORD
Josh 9:14 Then the men of Israel took some of their provisions; but they did not ask *counsel of the Lord*
Judg 20:23 Then the children of Israel went up and wept before the Lord until evening, and asked *counsel of the Lord*, saying
Ps 33:11 The *counsel of the Lord* stands forever, the plans of His heart to all generations
Is 19:17 everyone who makes mention of it will be afraid in himself, because of the *counsel of the Lord* of hosts which He has determined against it
Jer 23:18 For who has stood in the *counsel of the Lord*, and has perceived and heard His word
Jer 49:20 Therefore hear the *counsel of the Lord* that He has taken against Edom, and His purposes that He has proposed against the inhabitants of Teman
Jer 50:45 Therefore hear the *counsel of the Lord* that He has taken against Babylon, and His purposes that He has proposed against the land of the Chaldeans

COUNT THE COST
Luke 14:28 For which of you, intending to build a tower, does not sit down first and *count the cost*, whether he has enough to finish it

COUNTED LOSS FOR CHRIST
Phil 3:7 But what things were gain to me, these I have *counted loss for Christ*

COUNTED UNTO HIM (KJV)
(See *ACCOUNTED TO HIM*)

COUNTENANCE A POOR MAN IN HIS CAUSE (KJV)
(See *SHOW PARTIALITY*)

COUNTENANCE WAS LIKE LIGHTNING
Matt 28:3 His *countenance was like lightning*, and his clothing as white as snow

COURSE OF THE JUST (NIV)
(See *PATHS OF JUSTICE*)

COURSE OF THIS WORLD
Eph 2:2 in which you once walked according to the *course of this world*, according to the prince of the power of the air, the spirit who now works in the sons of disobedience

COURT OF THE HOUSE OF THE LORD
1Kin 7:12 So were the inner *court of the house of the Lord* and the vestibule of the temple
2Chr 24:21 So they conspired against him, and at the commandment of the king they stoned him with stones in the *court of the house of the Lord*
2Chr 29:16 Then the priests went into the inner part of the house of the Lord to cleanse it, and brought out all the debris that they found in the temple of the Lord to the *court of the house of the Lord*

COURTS OF THE HOUSE OF THE LORD
2Kin 21:5 And he built altars for all the host of heaven in the two *courts of the house of the Lord*
2Kin 23:12 The altars that were on the roof, the upper chamber of Ahaz, which the kings of Judah had made, and the altars which Manasseh had made in the two *courts of the house of the Lord*, the king broke down and pulverized there, and threw their dust into the Brook Kidron

1Chr 28:12 and the plans for all that he had by the Spirit, of the *courts of the house of the Lord*, of all the chambers all around, of the treasuries of the house of God, and of the treasuries for the dedicated things
2Chr 23:5 All the people shall be in the *courts of the house of the Lord*
2Chr 33:5 And he built altars for all the host of heaven in the two *courts of the house of the Lord*

COURTS OF THE TEMPLE OF THE LORD (NIV)
(See *COURTS OF THE HOUSE OF THE LORD*)

COURTYARD OF THE TEMPLE OF THE LORD (NIV)
(See *COURT OF THE HOUSE OF THE LORD*)

COVENANT AND MERCY
Deut 7:9 Therefore know that the Lord your God, He is God, the faithful God who keeps *covenant and mercy* for a thousand generations with those who love Him and keep His commandments
1Kin 8:23 Lord God of Israel, there is no God in heaven above or on earth below like You, who keep Your *covenant and mercy* with Your servants who walk before You with all their heart
2Chr 6:14 Lord God of Israel, there is no God in heaven or on earth like You, who keep Your *covenant and mercy* with Your servants who walk before You with all their hearts
Neh 1:5 I pray, Lord God of heaven, O great and awesome God, You who keep Your *covenant and mercy* with those who love You and observe Your commandments
Neh 9:32 Now therefore, our God, the great, the mighty, and awesome God, Who keeps *covenant and mercy*
Dan 9:4 And I prayed to the Lord my God, and made confession, and said, "O Lord, great and awesome God, who keeps His *covenant and mercy* with those who love Him, and with those who keep His commandments

COVENANT AND STEADFAST LOVE (RSV)
(See *COVENANT AND MERCY*)

COVENANT OF BROTHERHOOD
Amos 1:9 For three transgressions of Tyre, and for four, I will not turn away its punishment, because they delivered up the whole captivity to Edom, and did not remember the *covenant of brotherhood*

COVENANT OF CIRCUMCISION
Acts 7:8 Then He gave him the *covenant of circumcision;* and so Abraham begot Isaac and circumcised him on the eighth day

COVENANT OF GOD
Judg 20:27 So the children of Israel inquired of the Lord (the ark of the *covenant of God* was there in those days
1Sam 4:4 And the two sons of Eli, Hophni and Phinehas, were there with the ark of the *covenant of God*
2Sam 15:24 There was Zadok also, and all the Levites with him, bearing the ark of the *covenant of God*
1Chr 16:6 Benaiah and Jahaziel the priests regularly blew the trumpets before the ark of the *covenant of God*
2Chr 34:32 So the inhabitants of Jerusalem did according to the *covenant of God*, the God of their fathers
Ps 78:10 They did not keep the *covenant of God;* they refused to walk in His law

COVENANT OF LOVE (NIV)
(See *COVENANT AND MERCY*)

COVENANT OF PEACE
Num 25:12 Therefore say, 'Behold, I give to him My *covenant of peace*
Is 54:10 For the mountains shall depart and the hills be removed, but My kindness shall not depart from you, nor shall My *covenant of peace* be removed
Ezek 34:25 I will make a *covenant of peace* with them, and cause wild beasts to cease from the land
Ezek 37:26 Moreover I will make a *covenant of peace* with them, and it shall be an everlasting covenant with them

COVENANT OF SALT
Num 18:19 it is a *covenant of salt* forever before the Lord with you and your descendants with you
2Chr 13:5 Should you not know that the Lord God of Israel gave the dominion over Israel to David forever, to him and his sons, by a *covenant of salt*

COVENANT OF THE LORD
Num 10:33 and the ark of the *covenant of the Lord* went before them for the three days
Num 14:44 nevertheless, neither the ark of the *covenant of the Lord* nor Moses departed from the camp
Deut 4:23 Take heed to yourselves, lest you forget the *covenant of the Lord* your God which He made with you, and make for yourselves a carved image in the form of anything which the Lord your God has forbidden you
Deut 10:8 At that time the Lord separated the tribe of Levi to bear the ark of the *covenant of the Lord*, to stand before the Lord to minister to Him and to bless in His name, to this day
Deut 29:25 Because they have forsaken the *covenant of the Lord* God of their fathers, which He made with them when He brought them out of the land of Egypt
Deut 31:9 So Moses wrote this law and delivered it to the priests, the sons of Levi, who bore the ark of the *covenant of the Lord*, and to all the elders of Israel
Deut 31:25 that Moses commanded the Levites, who bore the ark of the *covenant of the Lord*, saying
Deut 31:26 Take this Book of the Law, and put it beside the ark of the *covenant of the Lord* your God, that it may be there as a witness against you
Josh 3:3 and they commanded the people, saying, "When you see the ark of the *covenant of the Lord* your God, and the priests, the Levites, bearing it, then you shall set out from your place and go after it
Josh 3:11 Behold, the ark of the *covenant of the Lord* of all the earth is crossing over before you into the Jordan
Josh 3:17 Then the priests who bore the ark of the *covenant of the Lord* stood firm on dry ground in the midst of the Jordan
Josh 4:7 Then you shall answer them that the waters of the Jordan were cut off before the ark of the *covenant of the Lord*
Josh 4:18 And it came to pass, when the priests who bore the ark of the *covenant of the Lord* had come from the midst of the Jordan, and the soles of the priests' feet touched the dry land, that the waters of the Jordan returned to their place and flowed over all its banks as before
Josh 6:8 So it was, when Joshua had spoken to the people, that the seven priests bearing the seven trumpets of rams' horns before the Lord advanced and blew the trumpets, and the ark of the *covenant of the Lord* followed them
Josh 7:15 Then it shall be that he who is taken

with the accursed thing shall be burned with fire, he and all that he has, because he has transgressed the *covenant of the Lord*, and because he has done a disgraceful thing in Israel

Josh 8:33 Then all Israel, with their elders and officers and judges, stood on either side of the ark before the priests, the Levites, who bore the ark of the *covenant of the Lord*, the stranger as well as he who was born among them

Josh 23:16 When you have transgressed the *covenant of the Lord* your God, which He commanded you, and have gone and served other gods, and bowed down to them, then the anger of the Lord will burn against you, and you shall perish quickly from the good land which He has given you

1Sam 4:3 Let us bring the ark of the *covenant of the Lord* from Shiloh to us, that when it comes among us it may save us from the hand of our enemies

1Sam 4:4 So the people sent to Shiloh, that they might bring from there the ark of the *covenant of the Lord* of hosts, who dwells between the cherubim

1Sam 4:5 And when the ark of the *covenant of the Lord* came into the camp, all Israel shouted so loudly that the earth shook

1Sam 20:8 Therefore you shall deal kindly with your servant, for you have brought your servant into a *covenant of the Lord* with you

1Kin 3:15 And he came to Jerusalem and stood before the ark of the *covenant of the Lord*, offered up burnt offerings, offered peace offerings, and made a feast for all his servants

1Kin 6:19 And he prepared the inner sanctuary inside the temple, to set the ark of the *covenant of the Lord* there

1Kin 8:1 Now Solomon assembled the elders of Israel and all the heads of the tribes, the chief fathers of the children of Israel, to King Solomon in Jerusalem, that they might bring up the ark of the *covenant of the Lord* from the City of David, which is Zion

1Kin 8:6 Then the priests brought in the ark of the *covenant of the Lord* to its place, into the inner sanctuary of the temple, to the Most Holy Place, under the wings of the cherubim

1Kin 8:21 And there I have made a place for the ark, in which is the *covenant of the Lord* which He made with our fathers, when He brought them out of the land of Egypt

1Chr 15:25 So David, the elders of Israel, and the captains over thousands went to bring up the ark of the *covenant of the Lord* from the house of Obed-Edom with joy

1Chr 15:26 And so it was, when God helped the Levites who bore the ark of the *covenant of the Lord*, that they offered seven bulls and seven rams

1Chr 15:28 Thus all Israel brought up the ark of the *covenant of the Lord* with shouting and with the sound of the horn, with trumpets and with cymbals, making music with stringed instruments and harps

1Chr 15:29 And it happened, as the ark of the *covenant of the Lord* came to the City of David, that Michal the daughter of Saul, looking through a window, saw King David whirling and playing music

1Chr 16:37 So he left Asaph and his brothers there before the ark of the *covenant of the Lord* to minister before the ark regularly, as every day's work required

1Chr 17:1 Now it came to pass, when David was dwelling in his house, that David said to Nathan the prophet, "See now, I dwell in a house of cedar, but the ark of the *covenant of the Lord* is under tent curtains

1Chr 22:19 Therefore arise and build the sanctuary of the Lord God, to bring the ark of the *covenant of the Lord* and the holy articles of God into the house that is to be built for the name of the Lord

1Chr 28:2 I had it in my heart to build a house of rest for the ark of the *covenant of the Lord*, and for the footstool of our God, and had made preparations to build it

1Chr 28:18 and refined gold by weight for the altar of incense, and for the construction of the chariot, that is, the gold cherubim that spread their wings and overshadowed the ark of the *covenant of the Lord*

2Chr 5:2 Now Solomon assembled the elders of Israel and all the heads of the tribes, the chief fathers of the children of Israel, in Jerusalem, that they might bring the ark of the *covenant of the Lord* up from the City of David, which is Zion

2Chr 5:7 Then the priests brought in the ark of the *covenant of the Lord* to its place, into the inner sanctuary of the temple, to the Most Holy Place, under the wings of the cherubim

2Chr 6:11 And there I have put the ark, in which is the *covenant of the Lord* which He made with the children of Israel

Jer 3:16 Then it shall come to pass, when you are multiplied and increased in the land in those days," says the Lord, "that they will say no more, 'The ark of the *covenant of the Lord*

Jer 22:9 Then they will answer, 'Because they have forsaken the *covenant of the Lord* their God, and worshiped other gods and served them

COVENANT WHICH THEY BROKE

Jer 31:32 not according to the covenant that I made with their fathers in the day that I took them by the hand to bring them out of the land of Egypt, My *covenant which they broke*, though I was a husband to them

COVENANT WITH DEATH

Is 28:15 because you have said, "We have made a *covenant with death*, and with Sheol we are in agreement

Is 28:18 Your *covenant with death* will be annulled, and your agreement with Sheol will not stand

COVERED MY HEAD

Ps 140:7 O God the Lord, the strength of my salvation, You have *covered my head* in the day of battle

COVERED THE NAKED WITH CLOTHING

Ezek 18:7 has robbed no one by violence, but has given his bread to the hungry and *covered the naked with clothing*

Ezek 18:16 has not oppressed anyone, nor withheld a pledge, nor robbed by violence, but has given his bread to the hungry and *covered the naked with clothing*

COVERED THEIR HEADS

2Sam 15:30 And all the people who were with him *covered their heads* and went up, weeping as they went up

Jer 14:3 They returned with their vessels empty; they were ashamed and confounded and *covered their heads*

Jer 14:4 Because the ground is parched, for there was no rain in the land, the plowmen were ashamed; they *covered their heads*

COVERT OF THY WINGS (KJV)
(See *SHELTER OF YOUR WINGS*)

COVET TO PROPHESY (KJV)
(See *DESIRE EARNESTLY TO PROPHESY*)

COVET YOUR NEIGHBOR'S HOUSE
Ex 20:17 You shall not *covet your neighbor's house;* you shall not covet your neighbor's wife, nor his male servant, nor his female servant, nor his ox, nor his donkey, nor anything that is your neighbor's

COWS OF BASHAN
Amos 4:1 Hear this word, you *cows of Bashan*, who are on the mountain of Samaria, who oppress the poor, who crush the needy, who say to your husbands

CRAVE PURE SPIRITUAL MILK (NIV)
(See *DESIRE THE PURE MILK*)

CRAVINGS OF OUR SINFUL NATURE (NIV)
(See *DESIRES OF THE FLESH*)

CREATE IN ME
Ps 51:10 *Create in me* a clean heart, O God, and renew a steadfast spirit within me

CREATE NEW HEAVENS
Is 65:17 For behold, I *create new heavens* and a new earth

CREATED BY THE WORD OF GOD (RSV)
(See *FRAMED BY THE WORD OF GOD*)

CREATED IN CHRIST JESUS
Eph 2:10 For we are His workmanship, *created in Christ Jesus* for good works, which God prepared beforehand that we should walk in them

CREATED THE HEAVENS
Gen 1:1 In the beginning God *created the heavens* and the earth
Is 42:5 Thus says God the Lord, Who *created the heavens* and stretched them out, Who spread forth the earth and that which comes from it, Who gives breath to the people on it, and spirit to those who walk on it
Is 45:18 For thus says the Lord, Who *created the heavens*, Who is God, Who formed the earth and made it, Who has established it, Who did not create it in vain, Who formed it to be inhabited

CREATED THROUGH HIM
Col 1:16 For by Him all things were created that are in heaven and that are on earth, visible and invisible, whether thrones or dominions or principalities or powers. All things were *created through Him* and for Him

CREATION OF THE WORLD
Rom 1:20 For since the *creation of the world* His invisible attributes are clearly seen, being understood by the things that are made, even His eternal power and Godhead, so that they are without excuse

CREATOR OF HEAVEN AND EARTH (NIV)
(See *POSSESSOR OF HEAVEN AND EARTH*)

CREDITED TO HIM (NIV)
(See *ACCOUNTED TO HIM*)

CREEPING THINGS
Lev 5:2 Or if a person touches any unclean thing, whether it is the carcass of an unclean beast, or the carcass of unclean livestock, or the carcass of unclean *creeping things*, and it is hidden from him, he also shall be unclean and guilty
Lev 11:29 These also shall be unclean to you among the *creeping things* that creep on the earth
Lev 11:42 Whatever crawls on its belly, whatever goes on all fours, or whatever has many feet among all *creeping things* that creep on the earth these you shall not eat, for they are an abomination
1Kin 4:33 he spoke also of animals, of birds, of *creeping things*, and of fish
Ps 148:10 Beasts and all cattle; *creeping things* and flying fowl
Ezek 38:20 so that the fish of the sea, the birds of the heavens, the beasts of the field, all *creeping things* that creep on the earth, and all men who are on the face of the earth shall shake at My presence
Hos 2:18 In that day I will make a covenant for them with the beasts of the field, with the birds of the air, and with the *creeping things* of the ground
Hab 1:14 Why do You make men like fish of the sea, like *creeping things* that have no ruler over them
Acts 10:12 In it were all kinds of four-footed animals of the earth, wild beasts, *creeping things*, and birds of the air
Acts 11:6 When I observed it intently and considered, I saw four-footed animals of the earth, wild beasts, *creeping things*, and birds of the air
Rom 1:23 and changed the glory of the incorruptible God into an image made like corruptible man and birds and four-footed beasts and *creeping things*

CRIED OUT TO GOD
1Chr 5:20 And they were helped against them, and the Hagrites were delivered into their hand, and all who were with them, for they *cried out to God* in the battle
Ps 77:1 I *cried out to God* with my voice to God with my voice

CRIED OUT TO THE LORD
Ex 8:12 And Moses *cried out to the Lord* concerning the frogs which He had brought against Pharaoh
Ex 14:10 So they were very afraid, and the children of Israel *cried out to the Lord*
Ex 15:25 So he *cried out to the Lord*, and the Lord showed him a tree
Ex 17:4 So Moses *cried out to the Lord*, saying, "What shall I do with this people
Num 12:13 So Moses *cried out to the Lord*, saying, "Please heal her, O God, I pray
Num 20:16 When we *cried out to the Lord*, He heard our voice and sent the Angel and brought us up out of Egypt
Deut 26:7 Then we *cried out to the Lord* God of our fathers, and the Lord heard our voice and looked on our affliction and our labor and our oppression
Josh 24:7 So they *cried out to the Lord;* and He put darkness between you and the Egyptians, brought the sea upon them, and covered them
Judg 3:9 When the children of Israel *cried out to the Lord*, the Lord raised up a deliverer for the children of Israel, who delivered them
Judg 3:15 And when the children of Israel *cried out to the Lord*, the Lord raised up a deliverer for them
Judg 4:3 And the children of Israel *cried out to the Lord*
Judg 6:6 So Israel was greatly impoverished because of the Midianites, and the children of Israel *cried out to the Lord*
Judg 6:7 And it came to pass, when the children of Israel *cried out to the Lord* because of the Midianites

Judg 10:10 And the children of Israel *cried out to the Lord*, saying
Judg 15:18 so he *cried out to the Lord* and said, "You have given this great deliverance by the hand of Your servant
1Sam 7:9 Then Samuel *cried out to the Lord* for Israel, and the Lord answered him
1Sam 12:8 When Jacob had gone into Egypt, and your fathers *cried out to the Lord*, then the Lord sent Moses and Aaron, who brought your fathers out of Egypt and made them dwell in this place
1Sam 12:10 Then they *cried out to the Lord*, and said, 'We have sinned, because we have forsaken the Lord and served the Baals and Ashtoreths
1Sam 15:11 And it grieved Samuel, and he *cried out to the Lord* all night
1Kin 17:20 Then he *cried out to the Lord* and said, "O Lord my God, have You also brought tragedy on the widow with whom I lodge, by killing her son
1Kin 17:21 And he stretched himself out on the child three times, and *cried out to the Lord* and said
2Kin 20:11 So Isaiah the prophet *cried out to the Lord*, and He brought the shadow ten degrees backward, by which it had gone down on the sundial of Ahaz
2Chr 13:14 and they *cried out to the Lord*, and the priests sounded the trumpets
2Chr 14:11 And Asa *cried out to the Lord* his God, and said
Ps 107:6 Then they *cried out to the Lord* in their trouble, and He delivered them out of their distresses
Ps 107:13 Then they *cried out to the Lord* in their trouble, and He saved them out of their distresses
Ps 107:19 Then they *cried out to the Lord* in their trouble, and He saved them out of their distresses
Lam 2:18 Their heart *cried out to the Lord*, "O wall of the daughter of Zion, let tears run down like a river day and night
Jon 1:14 Therefore they *cried out to the Lord* and said, "We pray, O Lord, please do not let us perish for this man's life, and do not charge us with innocent blood
Jon 2:2 I *cried out to the Lord* because of my affliction, and He answered me

CRIED TO THE LORD
Ps 3:4 I *cried to the Lord* with my voice, and He heard me from His holy hill
Ps 120:1 In my distress I *cried to the Lord*, and He heard me

CROOKED GENERATION
Deut 32:5 they are not His children, because of their blemish: A perverse and *crooked generation*

CROOKED PATHS
Is 59:8 they have made themselves *crooked paths;* whoever takes that way shall not know peace

CROSS OF CHRIST
1Cor 1:17 For Christ did not send me to baptize, but to preach the gospel, not with wisdom of words, lest the *cross of Christ* should be made of no effect
Gal 6:12 As many as desire to make a good showing in the flesh, these try to compel you to be circumcised, only that they may not suffer persecution for the *cross of Christ*
Phil 3:18 For many walk, of whom I have told you often, and now tell you even weeping, that they are the enemies of the *cross of Christ*

CROSS OF JESUS
John 19:25 Now there stood by the *cross of Jesus* His mother, and His mother's sister, Mary the wife of Clopas, and Mary Magdalene

CROSS OF OUR LORD
Gal 6:14 But God forbid that I should glory except in the *cross of our Lord* Jesus Christ, by whom the world has been crucified to me, and I to the world

CROSS OVER THE JORDAN
Num 32:21 and all your armed men *cross over the Jordan* before the Lord until He has driven out His enemies from before Him
Num 32:29 If the children of Gad and the children of Reuben *cross over the Jordan* with you, every man armed for battle before the Lord, and the land is subdued before you, then you shall give them the land of Gilead as a possession
Deut 4:21 Furthermore the Lord was angry with me for your sakes, and swore that I would not *cross over the Jordan*, and that I would not enter the good land which the Lord your God is giving you as an inheritance
Deut 4:22 But I must die in this land, I must not *cross over the Jordan*
Deut 4:26 I call heaven and earth to witness against you this day, that you will soon utterly perish from the land which you *cross over the Jordan* to possess
Deut 9:1 You are to *cross over the Jordan* today, and go in to dispossess nations greater and mightier than yourself, cities great and fortified up to heaven
Deut 11:31 For you will *cross over the Jordan* and go in to possess the land which the Lord your God is giving you, and you will possess it and dwell in it
Deut 12:10 But when you *cross over the Jordan* and dwell in the land which the Lord your God is giving you to inherit, and when He gives you rest from all your enemies round about, so that you dwell in safety
Deut 27:2 And it shall be, on the day when you *cross over the Jordan* to the land which the Lord your God is giving you, that you shall set up for yourselves large stones, and whitewash them with lime
Deut 30:18 you shall not prolong your days in the land which you *cross over the Jordan* to go in and possess
Deut 32:47 For it is not a futile thing for you, because it is your life, and by this word you shall prolong your days in the land which you *cross over the Jordan* to possess
Josh 3:14 So it was, when the people set out from their camp to *cross over the Jordan*, with the priests bearing the ark of the covenant before the people

CROSSED OVER ON DRY GROUND
Josh 3:17 and all Israel *crossed over on dry ground*, until all the people had crossed completely over the Jordan
2Kin 2:8 and it was divided this way and that, so that the two of them *crossed over on dry ground*

CROSSED OVER THE JORDAN
Deut 27:4 Therefore it shall be, when you have *crossed over the Jordan*, that on Mount Ebal you shall set up these stones, which I command you today, and you shall whitewash them with lime
Deut 27:12 These shall stand on Mount Gerizim to bless the people, when you have *crossed over the Jordan*
Josh 4:1 And it came to pass, when all the people had completely *crossed over the Jordan*, that the Lord spoke to Joshua, saying

Josh 4:7 when it *crossed over the Jordan*, the waters of the Jordan were cut off
Judg 10:9 Moreover the people of Ammon *crossed over the Jordan* to fight against Judah also, against Benjamin, and against the house of Ephraim, so that Israel was severely distressed
1Sam 13:7 And some of the Hebrews *crossed over the Jordan* to the land of Gad and Gilead
2Sam 2:29 Then Abner and his men went on all that night through the plain, *crossed over the Jordan*, and went through all Bithron
2Sam 10:17 When it was told David, he gathered all Israel, *crossed over the Jordan*, and came to Helam
2Sam 17:22 So David and all the people who were with him arose and *crossed over the Jordan*
2Sam 17:24 And Absalom *crossed over the Jordan*, he and all the men of Israel with him
2Sam 24:5 And they *crossed over the Jordan* and camped in Aroer, on the right side of the town which is in the midst of the ravine of Gad, and toward Jazer
1Chr 19:17 When it was told David, he gathered all Israel, *crossed over the Jordan* and came upon them, and set up in battle array against them

CROSSED THE RED SEA (RSV)
(See *THROUGH THE RED SEA*)

CROWN OF GLORY
Prov 4:9 She will place on your head an ornament of grace; a *crown of glory* she will deliver to you
Prov 16:31 The silver-haired head is a *crown of glory*, if it is found in the way of righteousness
Is 28:5 In that day the Lord of hosts will be for a *crown of glory* and a diadem of beauty to the remnant of His people
Is 62:3 You shall also be a *crown of glory* in the hand of the Lord, and a royal diadem in the hand of your God
1Pet 5:4 and when the Chief Shepherd appears, you will receive the *crown of glory* that does not fade away

CROWN OF LIFE
Jas 1:12 for when he has been proved, he will receive the *crown of life* which the Lord has promised to those who love Him
Rev 2:10 Be faithful until death, and I will give you the *crown of life*

CROWN OF RIGHTEOUSNESS
2Tim 4:8 Finally, there is laid up for me the *crown of righteousness*, which the Lord, the righteous Judge, will give to me on that Day, and not to me only but also to all who have loved His appearing

CROWN OF SPLENDOR (NIV)
(See *CROWN OF GLORY*)

CROWN OF THORNS
Matt 27:29 When they had twisted a *crown of thorns*, they put it on His head, and a reed in His right hand
Mark 15:17 and they twisted a *crown of thorns*, put it on His head
John 19:2 And the soldiers twisted a *crown of thorns* and put it on His head, and they put on Him a purple robe
John 19:5 Then Jesus came out, wearing the *crown of thorns* and the purple robe

CROWN THAT WILL LAST FOREVER (NIV)
(See *IMPERISHABLE CROWN*)

CROWNED HIM WITH GLORY
Ps 8:5 For You have made him a little lower than the angels, and You have *crowned him with glory* and honor
Heb 2:7 You *crowned him with glory* and honor, and set him over the works of Your hands

CRUCIFIED THE FLESH
Gal 5:24 And those who are Christ's have *crucified the flesh* with its passions and desires

CRUCIFIED WITH CHRIST
Gal 2:20 I have been *crucified with Christ;* it is no longer I who live, but Christ lives in me

CRUCIFY HIM
Mark 15:13 So they cried out again, "*Crucify Him*
Mark 15:14 Then Pilate said to them, "Why, what evil has He done?" And they cried out more exceedingly, "*Crucify Him*
Mark 15:20 And when they had mocked Him, they took the purple off Him, put His own clothes on Him, and led Him out to *crucify Him*
Luke 23:21 But they shouted, saying, "*Crucify Him, crucify Him*
John 19:6 Therefore, when the chief priests and officers saw Him, they cried out, saying, "*Crucify Him, crucify Him!*" Pilate said to them, "You take Him and *crucify Him*, for I find no fault in Him
John 19:15 *Crucify Him!*" Pilate said to them, "Shall I crucify your King

CRUSE OF OIL (RSV)
(See *JAR OF OIL*)

CRUSH THE NEEDY (NAS, RSV)
(See *OPPRESS THE POOR*)

CRUSH YOUR HEAD (NIV)
(See *BRUISE YOUR HEAD*)

CRUSHED FOR OUR INIQUITIES (NAS, NIV)
(See *BRUISED FOR OUR INIQUITIES*)

CRY FOR HELP
Job 36:13 they do not *cry for help* when He binds them
Ps 119:147 I rise before the dawning of the morning, and *cry for help*
Lam 3:56 Do not hide Your ear from my sighing, from my *cry for help*

CRY OF THE AFFLICTED
Job 34:28 so that they caused the cry of the poor to come to Him; for He hears the *cry of the afflicted*

CRY OF THE POOR
Job 34:28 so that they caused the *cry of the poor* to come to Him
Prov 21:13 Whoever shuts his ears to the *cry of the poor* will also cry himself and not be heard

CRY OUT TO GOD
Ps 57:2 I will *cry out to God* Most High, to God who performs all things for me

CRY OUT TO THE LORD
Deut 15:9 Beware lest there be a wicked thought in your heart, saying, 'The seventh year, the year of release, is at hand,' and your eye be evil against your poor brother and you give him nothing, and he *cry out to the Lord* against you, and it become sin among you
1Sam 7:8 So the children of Israel said to Samuel,"Do not cease to *cry out to the Lord* our God for us, that He may save us from the hand of the Philistines
Ps 107:28 Then they *cry out to the Lord* in their

trouble, and He brings them out of their distresses
Ps 142:1 I *cry out to the Lord* with my voice; with my voice to the Lord I make my supplication
Joel 1:14 gather the elders and all the inhabitants of the land into the house of the Lord your God, and *cry out to the Lord*

CRYING IN THE WILDERNESS
Is 40:3 The voice of one *crying in the wilderness:* "Prepare the way of the Lord
Matt 3:3 The voice of one *crying in the wilderness:* 'Prepare the way of the Lord, make His paths straight
Mark 1:3 The voice of one *crying in the wilderness:* 'Prepare the way of the Lord, make His paths straight
Luke 3:4 The voice of one *crying in the wilderness:* 'Prepare the way of the Lord, make His paths straight
John 1:23 I am 'The voice of one *crying in the wilderness*

CUNNING PLAYER ON AN HARP (KJV)
(See *SKILLFUL PLAYER ON THE HARP*)

CUP OF
Ps 116:13 I will take up the *cup of* salvation, and call upon the name of the Lord
Is 51:17 Stand up, O Jerusalem, you who have drunk at the hand of the Lord the *cup of* His fury; you have drunk the dregs of the *cup of* trembling, and drained it out
Is 51:22 See, I have taken out of your hand the *cup of* trembling, the dregs of the *cup of* My fury
Jer 16:7 nor shall men give them the *cup of* consolation to drink for their father or their mother
Jer 25:15 Take this wine *cup of* fury from My hand, and cause all the nations, to whom I send you, to drink it
Ezek 23:33 You will be filled with drunkenness and sorrow, the *cup of* horror and desolation, the *cup of* your sister Samaria
Hab 2:16 The *cup of* the Lord's right hand will be turned against you, and utter shame will be on your glory
Zech 12:2 Behold, I will make Jerusalem a *cup of* drunkenness to all the surrounding peoples, when they lay siege against Judah and Jerusalem
Matt 10:42 And whoever gives one of these little ones only a *cup of* cold water in the name of a disciple, assuredly, I say to you, he shall by no means lose his reward
Mark 9:41 For whoever gives you a *cup of* water to drink in My name, because you belong to Christ, assuredly, I say to you, he will by no means lose his reward
1Cor 10:16 The *cup of* blessing which we bless, is it not the communion of the blood of Christ
1Cor 10:21 You cannot drink the *cup of* the Lord and the *cup of* demons
1Cor 11:27 Therefore whoever eats this bread or drinks this *cup of* the Lord in an unworthy manner will be guilty of the body and blood of the Lord
Rev 14:10 he himself shall also drink of the wine of the wrath of God, which is poured out full strength into the *cup of* His indignation
Rev 16:19 And great Babylon was remembered before God, to give her the *cup of* the wine of the fierceness of His wrath

CUP OF BLESSING
1Cor 10:16 The *cup of blessing* which we bless, is it not the communion of the blood of Christ

CUP OF DEMONS
1Cor 10:21 You cannot drink the cup of the Lord and the *cup of demons*

CUP OF HIS FURY
Is 51:17 Stand up, O Jerusalem, you who have drunk at the hand of the Lord the *cup of His fury*

CUP OF HIS WRATH (NIV, RSV)
(See *CUP OF HIS FURY*)

CUP OF MY FURY
Is 51:22 See, I have taken out of your hand the cup of trembling, the dregs of the *cup of My fury*

CUP OF SALVATION
Ps 116:13 I will take up the *cup of salvation*, and call upon the name of the Lord

CUP THAT I DRINK
Mark 10:38 Can you drink the *cup that I drink*, and be baptized with the baptism that I am baptized with
Mark 10:39 And Jesus said to them, "You will indeed drink the *cup that I drink*, and with the baptism I am baptized with you will be baptized

CURDS AND HONEY
Is 7:15 *Curds and honey* He shall eat, that He may know to refuse the evil and choose the good
Is 7:22 for *curds and honey* everyone will eat who is left in the land

CURSE GOD AND DIE
Job 2:9 Then his wife said to him, "Do you still hold to your integrity? *Curse God and die*

CURSE HIM WHO CURSES YOU
Gen 12:3 I will bless those who bless you, and I will *curse him who curses you*

CURSE OF THE LAW
Gal 3:13 Christ has redeemed us from the *curse of the law*, having become a curse for us (for it is written

CURSED BE CANAAN
Gen 9:25 *Cursed be Canaan;* a servant of servants he shall be to his brethren

CURSED IS THE GROUND
Gen 3:17 *Cursed is the ground* for your sake; in toil you shall eat of it all the days of your life

CURSED IS THE ONE
Deut 27:15 *Cursed is the one* who makes any carved or molded image, an abomination to the Lord, the work of the hands of the craftsman, and sets it up in secret
Deut 27:16 *Cursed is the one* who treats his father or his mother with contempt
Deut 27:17 *Cursed is the one* who moves his neighbor's landmark.' And all the people shall say
Deut 27:18 *Cursed is the one* who makes the blind to wander off the road
Deut 27:19 *Cursed is the one* who perverts the justice due the stranger, the fatherless, and widow
Deut 27:20 *Cursed is the one* who lies with his father's wife, because he has uncovered his father's bed
Deut 27:21 *Cursed is the one* who lies with any kind of animal
Deut 27:22 *Cursed is the one* who lies with his sister, the daughter of his father or the daughter of his mother
Deut 27:23 *Cursed is the one* who lies with his mother-in-law.' And all the people shall say

Deut 27:24 *Cursed is the one* who attacks his neighbor secretly.' And all the people shall say
Deut 27:25 *Cursed is the one* who takes a bribe to slay an innocent person
Deut 27:26 *Cursed is the one* who does not confirm all the words of this law

CURTAIN OF THE TEMPLE (RSV)
(See *VEIL OF THE TEMPLE*)

CUT OFF FROM HIS PEOPLE
Gen 17:14 And the uncircumcised male child, who is not circumcised in the flesh of his foreskin, that person shall be *cut off from his people*
Ex 30:33 Whoever compounds any like it, or whoever puts any of it on an outsider, shall be *cut off from his people*
Ex 30:38 Whoever makes any like it, to smell it, he shall be *cut off from his people*
Lev 7:20 But the person who eats the flesh of the sacrifice of the peace offering that belongs to the Lord, while he is unclean, that person shall be *cut off from his people*
Lev 7:21 Moreover the person who touches any unclean thing, such as human uncleanness, any unclean beast, or any abominable unclean thing, and who eats the flesh of the sacrifice of the peace offering that belongs to the Lord, that person shall be *cut off from his people*
Lev 7:25 For whoever eats the fat of the beast of which men offer an offering made by fire to the Lord, the person who eats it shall be *cut off from his people*
Lev 7:27 Whoever eats any blood, that person shall be *cut off from his people*
Lev 19:8 and that person shall be *cut off from his people*
Lev 23:29 For any person who is not afflicted of soul on that same day, he shall be *cut off from his people*

D

DAILY BREAD
Matt 6:11 Give us this day our *daily bread*
Luke 11:3 Give us day by day our *daily bread*

DANCED BEFORE THE LORD
2Sam 6:14 Then David *danced before the Lord* with all his might

DARKNESS DID NOT COMPREHEND IT
John 1:5 And the light shines in the darkness, and the *darkness did not comprehend it*

DASH YOUR FOOT AGAINST A STONE
Ps 91:12 They shall bear you up in their hands, lest you *dash your foot against a stone*
Matt 4:6 He shall give His angels charge concerning you,' and, 'In their hands they shall bear you up, lest you *dash your foot against a stone*
Luke 4:11 and, 'In their hands they shall bear You up, lest You *dash Your foot against a stone*

DAUGHTER OF JERUSALEM
2Kin 19:21 the *daughter of Jerusalem* has shaken her head behind your back
Is 37:22 the *daughter of Jerusalem* has shaken her head behind your back
Lam 2:13 To what shall I liken you, O *daughter of Jerusalem*
Lam 2:15 they hiss and shake their heads at the *daughter of Jerusalem*
Mic 4:8 And you, O tower of the flock, the stronghold of the daughter of Zion, to you shall it come, even the former dominion shall come, the kingdom of the *daughter of Jerusalem*
Zeph 3:14 Be glad and rejoice with all your heart, O *daughter of Jerusalem*
Zech 9:9 Shout, O *daughter of Jerusalem!* Behold, your King is coming to you

DAUGHTER OF ZION
2Kin 19:21 The virgin, the *daughter of Zion*, has despised you, laughed you to scorn
Ps 9:14 That I may tell of all Your praise in the gates of the *daughter of Zion*
Is 1:8 So the *daughter of Zion* is left as a booth in a vineyard, as a hut in a garden of cucumbers, as a besieged city
Is 10:32 he will shake his fist at the mount of the *daughter of Zion*, the hill of Jerusalem
Is 16:1 Send the lamb to the ruler of the land, from Sela to the wilderness, to the mount of the *daughter of Zion*
Is 37:22 The virgin, the *daughter of Zion*, has despised you, laughed you to scorn
Is 52:2 loose yourself from the bonds of your neck, O captive *daughter of Zion*
Is 62:11 Say to the *daughter of Zion*, 'Surely your salvation is coming
Jer 4:31 For I have heard a voice as of a woman in labor, the anguish as of her who brings forth her first child, the voice of the *daughter of Zion* bewailing herself, who spreads her hands, saying
Jer 6:2 I have likened the *daughter of Zion* to a lovely and delicate woman
Jer 6:23 and they ride on horses, as men of war set in array against you, O *daughter of Zion*
Lam 1:6 And from the *daughter of Zion* all her splendor has departed
Lam 2:1 How the Lord has covered the *daughter of Zion* with a cloud in His anger
Lam 2:4 on the tent of the *daughter of Zion*, he has poured out His fury like fire
Lam 2:8 The Lord has purposed to destroy the wall of the *daughter of Zion*
Lam 2:10 The elders of the *daughter of Zion* sit on the ground and keep silence
Lam 2:13 what shall I compare with you, that I may comfort you, O virgin *daughter of Zion*
Lam 2:18 Their heart cried out to the Lord, "O wall of the *daughter of Zion*, let tears run down like a river day and night
Lam 4:22 The punishment of your iniquity is accomplished, O *daughter of Zion*
Mic 1:13 O inhabitant of Lachish, harness the chariot to the swift steeds (She was the beginning of sin to the *daughter of Zion*
Mic 4:8 And you, O tower of the flock, the stronghold of the *daughter of Zion*, to you shall it come, even the former dominion shall come, the kingdom of the daughter of Jerusalem
Mic 4:10 Be in pain, and labor to bring forth, O *daughter of Zion*, like a woman in birth pangs
Mic 4:13 Arise and thresh, O *daughter of Zion;* for I will make your horn iron, and I will make your hooves bronze
Zeph 3:14 Sing, O *daughter of Zion!* Shout, O Israel! Be glad and rejoice with all your heart, O daughter of Jerusalem
Zech 2:10 Sing and rejoice, O *daughter of Zion!* For behold, I am coming and I will dwell in your midst
Zech 9:9 Rejoice greatly, O *daughter of Zion!* Shout, O daughter of Jerusalem
Matt 21:5 Tell the *daughter of Zion*, 'Behold, your King is coming to you, lowly, and sitting on a donkey, a colt, the foal of a donkey
John 12:15 Fear not, *daughter of Zion;* behold, your King is coming, sitting on a donkey's colt

DAUGHTERS OF JOB
Job 42:15 In all the land were found no women so beautiful as the *daughters of Job*

DAUGHTERS OF ZION
Song 3:11 Go forth, O *daughters of Zion*, and see King Solomon with the crown with which his mother crowned him on the day of his espousals, the day of the gladness of his heart
Is 3:16 Because the *daughters of Zion* are haughty, and walk with outstretched necks and wanton eyes, walking and mincing as they go, making a jingling with their feet
Is 3:17 therefore the Lord will strike with a scab the crown of the head of the *daughters of Zion*, and the Lord will uncover their secret parts
Is 4:4 When the Lord has washed away the filth of the *daughters of Zion*, and purged the blood of Jerusalem from her midst, by the spirit of judgment and by the spirit of burning

DAUGHTERS SHALL PROPHESY
Joel 2:28 your sons and your *daughters shall prophesy*, your old men shall dream dreams, your young men shall see visions
Acts 2:17 your sons and your *daughters shall prophesy* , your young men shall see visions, your old men shall dream dreams

DAVID AND HIS DESCENDANTS
2Sam 22:51 He is the tower of salvation to His king, and shows mercy to His anointed, to *David and his descendants* forevermore
1Kin 2:33 But upon *David and his descendants*, upon his house and his throne, there shall be peace forever from the Lord
Ps 18:50 Great deliverance He gives to His king, and shows mercy to His anointed, to *David and his descendants* forevermore

DAVID MY SERVANT
Jer 33:21 then My covenant may also be broken with *David My servant*, so that he shall not have a son to reign on his throne, and with the Levites, the priests, My ministers
Jer 33:22 As the host of heaven cannot be numbered, nor the sand of the sea measured, so will I multiply the descendants of *David My servant* and the Levites who minister to Me
Jer 33:26 then I will cast away the descendants of Jacob and *David My servant*, so that I will not take any of his descendants to be rulers over the descendants of Abraham, Isaac, and Jacob
Ezek 37:24 *David My servant* shall be king over them, and they shall all have one shepherd

DAVID'S DESCENDANTS (NIV)
(See *DESCENDANTS OF DAVID*)

DAVID'S SON (RSV)
(See *SON OF DAVID*)

DAVID'S SONS (RSV)
(See *SONS OF DAVID*)

DAVID'S THRONE
Jer 13:13 Behold, I will fill all the inhabitants of this land even the kings who sit on *David's throne*, the priests, the prophets, and all the inhabitants of Jerusalem with drunkenness

DAY AFTER DAY (NIV)
(See *ALL DAY LONG*)

DAY AFTER DAY THEY POUR FORTH SPEECH (NIV)
(See *DAY UNTO DAY UTTERS SPEECH*)

DAY AND HOUR NO ONE KNOWS
Matt 24:36 But of that *day and hour no one knows*, no, not even the angels of heaven, but My Father only
Mark 13:32 But of that *day and hour no one knows*, neither the angels in heaven, nor the Son, but only the Father

DAY AND NIGHT
Gen 8:22 While the earth remains, seedtime and harvest, and cold and heat, and winter and summer, and *day and night* shall not cease
Ex 13:21 And the Lord went before them by day in a pillar of cloud to lead the way, and by night in a pillar of fire to give them light, so as to go by *day and night*
Lev 8:35 Therefore you shall abide at the door of the tabernacle of meeting *day and night* for seven days, and keep the charge of the Lord, so that you may not die
Deut 28:66 you shall fear *day and night*, and have no assurance of life
Josh 1:8 This Book of the Law shall not depart from your mouth, but you shall meditate in it *day and night*, that you may observe to do according to all that is written in it
1Kin 8:59 And may these words of mine, with which I have made supplication before the Lord, be near the Lord our God *day and night*, that He may maintain the cause of His servant and the cause of His people Israel, as each day may require
1Chr 9:33 for they were employed in that work *day and night*
2Chr 6:20 that Your eyes may be open toward this temple *day and night*, toward the place where You said You would put Your name, that You may hear the prayer which Your servant prays toward this place
Neh 1:6 please let Your ear be attentive and Your eyes open, that You may hear the prayer of Your servant which I pray before You now, *day and night*, for the children of Israel Your servants, and confess the sins of the children of Israel which we have sinned against You
Neh 4:9 Nevertheless we made our prayer to our God, and because of them we set a watch against them *day and night*
Ps 1:2 But his delight is in the law of the Lord, and in His law he meditates *day and night*
Ps 32:4 For *day and night* Your hand was heavy upon me
Ps 42:3 My tears have been my food *day and night*, while they continually say to me
Ps 55:10 *Day and night* they go around it on its walls
Ps 88:1 O Lord, God of my salvation, I have cried out *day and night* before You
Jer 9:1 Oh, that my head were waters, and my eyes a fountain of tears, that I might weep *day and night* for the slain of the daughter of my people
Jer 16:13 and there you shall serve other gods *day and night*, where I will not show you favor
Jer 33:20 If you can break My covenant with the day and My covenant with the night, so that there will not be *day and night* in their season
Jer 33:25 If My covenant is not with *day and night*, and if I have not appointed the ordinances of heaven and earth
Lam 2:18 Their heart cried out to the Lord, "O wall of the daughter of Zion, let tears run down like a river *day and night*
Luke 18:7 And shall God not avenge His own elect who cry out *day and night* to Him, though He bears long with them
Acts 9:24 And they watched the gates *day and night*, to kill him

Rev 7:15 Therefore they are before the throne of God, and serve Him *day and night* in His temple
Rev 12:10 Then I heard a loud voice saying in heaven, "Now salvation, and strength, and the kingdom of our God, and the power of His Christ have come, for the accuser of our brethren, who accused them before our God *day and night*, has been cast down
Rev 20:10 And they will be tormented *day and night* forever and ever

DAY HE VISITS US (NIV)
(See *DAY OF VISITATION*)

DAY IS NOW OVER (RSV)
(See *HOUR IS ALREADY LATE*)

DAY OF AFFLICTION
Jer 16:19 O Lord, my strength and my fortress, my refuge in the *day of affliction*, the Gentiles shall come to You from the ends of the earth and say

DAY OF ATONEMENT
Lev 23:27 Also the tenth day of this seventh month shall be the *Day of Atonement*
Lev 23:28 And you shall do no work on that same day, for it is the *Day of Atonement*, to make atonement for you before the Lord your God
Lev 25:9 on the *Day of Atonement* you shall make the trumpet to sound throughout all your land

DAY OF BATTLE
1Sam 13:22 So it came about, on the *day of battle*, that there was neither sword nor spear found in the hand of any of the people who were with Saul and Jonathan
Job 38:23 Which I have reserved for the time of trouble, for the *day of battle* and war
Ps 78:9 The children of Ephraim, being armed and carrying bows, turned back in the *day of battle*
Ps 140:7 O God the Lord, the strength of my salvation, You have covered my head in the *day of battle*
Prov 21:31 The horse is prepared for the *day of battle*, but deliverance is of the Lord
Hos 10:14 Therefore tumult shall arise among your people, and all your fortresses shall be plundered as Shalman plundered Beth Arbel in the *day of battle* a mother dashed in pieces upon her children
Amos 1:14 But I will kindle a fire in the wall of Rabbah, and it shall devour its palaces, amid shouting in the *day of battle*, and a tempest in the day of the whirlwind
Zech 14:3 Then the Lord will go forth and fight against those nations, as He fights in the *day of battle*

DAY OF CALAMITY (NAS, NIV, RSV)
(See *DAY OF DOOM*)

DAY OF CHRIST
Phil 1:10 that you may approve the things that are excellent, that you may be sincere and without offense till the *day of Christ*
Phil 2:16 holding fast the word of life, so that I may rejoice in the *day of Christ* that I have not run in vain or labored in vain
2Th 2:2 not to be soon shaken in mind or troubled, either by spirit or by word or by letter, as if from us, as though the *day of Christ* had come

DAY OF CLOUDS
Ezek 30:3 it will be a *day of clouds*, the time of the Gentiles
Joel 2:2 a day of darkness and gloominess, a *day of clouds* and thick darkness, like the morning clouds spread over the mountains
Zeph 1:15 That day is a day of wrath, a day of trouble and distress, a day of devastation and desolation, a day of darkness and gloominess, a *day of clouds* and thick darkness

DAY OF DARKNESS
Job 15:23 He knows that a *day of darkness* is ready at his hand
Joel 2:2 a *day of darkness* and gloominess, a day of clouds and thick darkness, like the morning clouds spread over the mountains
Zeph 1:15 That day is a day of wrath, a day of trouble and distress, a day of devastation and desolation, a *day of darkness* and gloominess, a day of clouds and thick darkness

DAY OF DESTRUCTION (KJV)
(See *DAY OF DOOM*)

DAY OF DEVASTATION
Zeph 1:15 That day is a day of wrath, a day of trouble and distress, a *day of devastation* and desolation, a day of darkness and gloominess, a day of clouds and thick darkness

DAY OF DISTRESS (NAS, RSV)
(See *DAY OF TROUBLE*)

DAY OF DOOM
Job 21:30 For the wicked are reserved for the *day of doom*
Prov 16:4 The Lord has made all things for Himself, yes, even the wicked for the *day of doom*
Jer 17:17 Do not be a terror to me; You are my hope in the *day of doom*
Jer 17:18 Bring on them the *day of doom*, and destroy them with double destruction
Jer 51:2 For in the *day of doom* they shall be against her all around
Amos 6:3 Woe to you who put far off the *day of doom*, who cause the seat of violence to come near

DAY OF GOD'S WRATH (NIV, RSV)
(See *DAY OF HIS WRATH*)

DAY OF HIS DEATH
Judg 13:7 Now drink no wine or similar drink, nor eat anything unclean, for the child shall be a Nazirite to God from the womb to the *day of his death*
1Sam 15:35 And Samuel went no more to see Saul until the *day of his death*
2Kin 15:5 Then the Lord struck the king, so that he was a leper until the *day of his death*
2Chr 26:21 King Uzziah was a leper until the *day of his death*
Jer 52:11 and the king of Babylon bound him in bronze fetters, took him to Babylon, and put him in prison till the *day of his death*
Jer 52:34 And as for his provisions, there was a regular ration given him by the king of Babylon, a portion for each day until the *day of his death*, all the days of his life

DAY OF HIS WRATH
Job 20:28 The increase of his house will depart, and his goods will flow away in the *day of His wrath*
Ps 110:5 He shall execute kings in the *day of His wrath*
Rev 6:17 For the great *day of His wrath* has come, and who is able to stand

DAY OF JUDGMENT
Matt 10:15 Assuredly, I say to you, it will be more tolerable for the land of Sodom and Gomorrah in the *day of judgment* than for that city

Matt 11:22 But I say to you, it will be more tolerable for Tyre and Sidon in the *day of judgment* than for you

Matt 11:24 But I say to you that it shall be more tolerable for the land of Sodom in the *day of judgment* than for you

Matt 12:36 But I say to you that for every idle word men may speak, they will give account of it in the *day of judgment*

Mark 6:11 Assuredly, I say to you, it will be more tolerable for Sodom and Gomorrah in the *day of judgment* than for that city

2Pet 2:9 then the Lord knows how to deliver the godly out of temptations and to reserve the unjust under punishment for the *day of judgment*

2Pet 3:7 But the heavens and the earth which now exist are kept in store by the same word, reserved for fire until the *day of judgment* and perdition of ungodly men

1Jn 4:17 that we may have boldness in the *day of judgment*

DAY OF OUR LORD JESUS CHRIST

1Cor 1:8 who will also confirm you to the end, that you may be blameless in the *day of our Lord Jesus Christ*

DAY OF PENTECOST

Acts 2:1 Now when the *Day of Pentecost* had fully come, they were all with one accord in one place

Acts 20:16 for he was hurrying to be at Jerusalem, if possible, on the *Day of Pentecost*

DAY OF PUNISHMENT

Is 10:3 What will you do in the *day of punishment*, and in the desolation which will come from afar

DAY OF REST (NIV)
(See *SABBATH REST*)

DAY OF SALVATION

Is 49:8 In an acceptable time I have heard You, and in the *day of salvation* I have helped You

2Cor 6:2 In an acceptable time I have heard you, and in the *day of salvation* I have helped you." Behold, now is the accepted time; behold, now is the *day of salvation*

DAY OF THE LORD

Is 2:12 For the *day of the Lord* of hosts shall come upon everything proud and lofty, upon everything lifted up and it shall be brought low

Is 13:6 Wail, for the *day of the Lord* is at hand

Is 13:9 Behold, the *day of the Lord* comes, cruel, with both wrath and fierce anger, to lay the land desolate

Is 58:13 If you turn away your foot from the Sabbath, from doing your pleasure on My holy day, and call the Sabbath a delight, the holy *day of the Lord* honorable, and shall honor Him, not doing your own ways, nor finding your own pleasure, nor speaking your own words

Jer 46:10 For this is the *day of the Lord* God of hosts, a day of vengeance, that He may avenge Himself on His adversaries

Ezek 13:5 You have not gone up into the gaps to build a wall for the house of Israel to stand in battle on the *day of the Lord*

Ezek 30:3 For the day is near, even the *day of the Lord* is near

Joel 1:15 For the *day of the Lord* is at hand; it shall come as destruction from the Almighty

Joel 2:1 for the *day of the Lord* is coming, for it is at hand

Joel 2:11 For the *day of the Lord* is great and very terrible

Joel 2:31 The sun shall be turned into darkness, and the moon into blood, before the coming of the great and terrible *day of the Lord*

Joel 3:14 For the *day of the Lord* is near in the valley of decision

Amos 5:18 Woe to you who desire the *day of the Lord!* For what good is the *day of the Lord* to you

Amos 5:20 Is not the *day of the Lord* darkness, and not light

Obad 15 For the *day of the Lord* upon all the nations is near

Zeph 1:7 for the *day of the Lord* is at hand, for the Lord has prepared a sacrifice

Zeph 1:14 The great *day of the Lord* is near; it is near and hastens quickly. The noise of the *day of the Lord* is bitter

Zech 14:1 Behold, the *day of the Lord* is coming, and your spoil will be divided in your midst

Mal 4:5 Behold, I will send you Elijah the prophet before the coming of the great and dreadful *day of the Lord*

Acts 2:20 The sun shall be turned into darkness, and the moon into blood, before the coming of the great and notable *day of the Lord*

1Cor 5:5 deliver such a one to Satan for the destruction of the flesh, that his spirit may be saved in the *day of the Lord* Jesus

2Cor 1:14 that we are your boast as you also are ours, in the *day of the Lord* Jesus

1Th 5:2 For you yourselves know perfectly that the *day of the Lord* so comes as a thief in the night

2Pet 3:10 But the *day of the Lord* will come as a thief in the night, in which the heavens will pass away with a great noise, and the elements will melt with fervent heat

DAY OF THEIR DEATH

2Sam 20:3 So they were shut up to the *day of their death*, living in widowhood

DAY OF TROUBLE

2Kin 19:3 This day is a *day of trouble*, and rebuke, and blasphemy

Ps 20:1 May the Lord answer you in the *day of trouble*

Ps 50:15 Call upon Me in the *day of trouble;* I will deliver you, and you shall glorify Me

Is 22:5 For it is a *day of trouble* and treading down and perplexity by the Lord God of hosts in the Valley of Vision breaking down the walls and of crying to the mountain

Is 37:3 This day is a *day of trouble* and rebuke and blasphemy

Ezek 7:7 The time has come, a *day of trouble* is near, and not of rejoicing in the mountains

Nah 1:7 The Lord is good, a stronghold in the *day of trouble*

Hab 3:16 and I trembled in myself, that I might rest in the *day of trouble*

Zeph 1:15 That day is a day of wrath, a *day of trouble* and distress, a day of devastation and desolation, a day of darkness and gloominess, a day of clouds and thick darkness

DAY OF VENGEANCE

Prov 6:34 therefore he will not spare in the *day of vengeance*

Is 61:2 to proclaim the acceptable year of the Lord, and the *day of vengeance* of our God

Is 63:4 For the *day of vengeance* is in My heart, and the year of My redeemed has come

Jer 46:10 For this is the day of the Lord God of hosts, a *day of vengeance*, that He may avenge Himself on His adversaries

DAY OF VISITATION

1Pet 2:12 having your conduct honorable among the Gentiles, that when they speak against you as evildoers, they may, by your good works which they observe, glorify God in the *day of visitation*

DAY OF WRATH
Job 21:30 they shall be brought out on the *day of wrath*
Prov 11:4 Riches do not profit in the *day of wrath*, but righteousness delivers from death
Zeph 1:15 That day is a *day of wrath*, a day of trouble and distress, a day of devastation and desolation, a day of darkness and gloominess, a day of clouds and thick darkness
Rom 2:5 But in accordance with your hardness and your impenitent heart you are treasuring up for yourself wrath in the *day of wrath* and revelation of the righteous judgment of God

DAY STAR (KJV)
(See *MORNING STAR*)

DAY TO DAY POURS FORTH SPEECH (NAS, RSV)
(See *DAY UNTO DAY UTTERS SPEECH*)

DAY UNTO DAY UTTERS SPEECH
Ps 19:2 *Day unto day utters speech*, and night unto night reveals knowledge

DAY WHICH THE LORD HAS MADE
Ps 118:24 This is the *day which the Lord has made;* we will rejoice and be glad in it

DAY YOUR LORD WILL COME (NIV)
(See *HOUR YOUR LORD IS COMING*)

DAYS ARE AS A SHADOW (KJV)
(See *DAYS ARE LIKE A PASSING SHADOW*)

DAYS ARE COMING
1Sam 2:31 Behold, the *days are coming* that I will cut off your arm and the arm of your father's house, so that there will not be an old man in your house
2Kin 20:17 Behold, the *days are coming* when all that is in your house, and what your fathers have accumulated until this day, shall be carried to Babylon
Is 39:6 Behold, the *days are coming* when all that is in your house, and what your fathers have accumulated until this day, shall be carried to Babylon
Jer 7:32 Therefore behold, the *days are coming*," says the Lord, "when it will no more be called Tophet, or the Valley of the Son of Hinnom, but the Valley of Slaughter
Jer 9:25 Behold, the *days are coming*," says the Lord, "that I will punish all those who are circumcised with the uncircumcised
Jer 16:14 Therefore behold, the *days are coming*," says the Lord, "that it shall no more be said
Jer 19:6 therefore behold, the *days are coming*," says the Lord, "that this place shall no more be called Tophet or the Valley of the Son of Hinnom, but the Valley of Slaughter
Jer 23:5 Behold, the *days are coming*," says the Lord, "That I will raise to David a Branch of righteousness
Jer 23:7 Therefore, behold, the *days are coming*," says the Lord, "that they shall no longer say
Jer 30:3 For behold, the *days are coming*,' says the Lord, 'that I will bring back from captivity My people Israel and Judah
Jer 31:27 Behold, the *days are coming*," says the Lord, "that I will sow the house of Israel and the house of Judah with the seed of man and the seed of beast
Jer 31:31 Behold, the *days are coming*," says the Lord, "when I will make a new covenant with the house of Israel and with the house of Judah
Jer 31:38 Behold, the *days are coming*," says the Lord, "that the city shall be built for the Lord from the Tower of Hananeel to the Corner Gate
Jer 33:14 Behold, the *days are coming*,' says the Lord, 'that I will perform that good thing which I have promised to the house of Israel and to the house of Judah
Jer 48:12 Therefore behold, the *days are coming*," says the Lord, "That I shall send him wine-workers who will tip him over and empty his vessels and break the bottles
Jer 49:2 Therefore behold, the *days are coming*," says the Lord, "That I will cause to be heard an alarm of war in Rabbah of the Ammonites
Jer 51:47 therefore behold, the *days are coming* that I will bring judgment on the carved images of Babylon
Jer 51:52 Therefore behold, the *days are coming*," says the Lord, "That I will bring judgment on her carved images, and throughout all her land the wounded shall groan
Amos 8:11 Behold, the *days are coming*," says the Lord God, "That I will send a famine on the land, not a famine of bread, nor a thirst for water, but of hearing the words of the Lord
Amos 9:13 Behold, the *days are coming*," says the Lord, "When the plowman shall overtake the reaper, and the treader of grapes him who sows seed
Luke 23:29 For indeed the *days are coming* in which they will say
Heb 8:8 Behold, the *days are coming*," says the Lord, "when I will make a new covenant with the house of Israel and with the house of Judah

DAYS ARE LIKE A PASSING SHADOW
Ps 144:4 Man is like a breath; his *days are like a passing shadow*

DAYS ARE LIKE A SHADOW
Ps 102:11 My *days are like a shadow* that lengthens, and I wither away like grass

DAYS AS NUMEROUS AS THE GRAINS OF SAND (NIV)
(See *MULTIPLY MY DAYS AS THE SAND*)

DAYS COME (KJV)
(See *DAYS ARE COMING*)

DAYS OF AFFLICTION
Job 30:16 And now my soul is poured out because of my plight; the *days of affliction* take hold of me
Job 30:27 My heart is in turmoil and cannot rest; *days of affliction* confront me

DAYS OF ELIJAH
Luke 4:25 But I tell you truly, many widows were in Israel in the *days of Elijah*, when the heaven was shut up three years and six months, and there was a great famine throughout all the land

DAYS OF NOAH
Gen 9:29 So all the *days of Noah* were nine hundred and fifty years
Matt 24:37 But as the *days of Noah* were, so also will the coming of the Son of Man be
Luke 17:26 And as it was in the *days of Noah*, so it will be also in the days of the Son of Man
1Pet 3:20 who formerly were disobedient, when once the longsuffering of God waited in the *days of Noah*, while the ark was being prepared, in which a few, that is, eight souls, were saved through water

DAYS OF PURIFICATION
Acts 21:26 Then Paul took the men, and the next day, having been purified with them, entered the temple to announce the expiration of the *days of purification*, at which time an offering should be made for each one of them

DAYS OF SUFFERING (NIV)
(See *DAYS OF AFFLICTION*)

DAYS OF VENGEANCE
Luke 21:22 For these are the *days of vengeance*, that all things which are written may be fulfilled

DAYS OF YOUR YOUTH
Eccl 11:9 Rejoice, O young man, in your youth, and let your heart cheer you in the *days of your youth*
Eccl 12:1 Remember now your Creator in the *days of your youth*, before the difficult days come, and the years draw near when you say
Ezek 16:22 And in all your abominations and acts of harlotry you did not remember the *days of your youth*, when you were naked and bare, struggling in your blood
Ezek 16:43 Because you did not remember the *days of your youth*, but agitated Me with all these things, surely I will also recompense your deeds on your own head
Ezek 16:60 Nevertheless I will remember My covenant with you in the *days of your youth*, and I will establish an everlasting covenant with you

DAYS ON EARTH ARE A SHADOW
Job 8:9 for we are but of yesterday, and know nothing, because our *days on earth are a shadow*

DAYS ON EARTH ARE AS A SHADOW
1Chr 29:15 our *days on earth are as a shadow*, and without hope

DAYS THAT WERE BEFORE (KJV)
(See *FORMER DAYS*)

DAYS TO COME (NAS, NIV, RSV)
(See *LAST DAYS*)

DEAD IN CHRIST
1Th 4:16 For the Lord Himself will descend from heaven with a shout, with the voice of an archangel, and with the trumpet of God. And the *dead in Christ* will rise first

DEAD IN TRESPASSES
Eph 2:1 And you He made alive, who were *dead in trespasses* and sins
Eph 2:5 even when we were *dead in trespasses*, made us alive together with Christ (by grace you have been saved

DEAD IN YOUR TRANSGRESSIONS (NIV)
(See *DEAD IN TRESPASSES*)

DEAD RISE (NIV)
(See *RISE FROM THE DEAD*)

DEAD SHALL LIVE
Is 26:19 Your *dead shall live;* together with my dead body they shall arise

DEAD THROUGH THE TRESPASSES (RSV)
(See *DEAD IN TRESPASSES*)

DEAD TO THE LAW
Rom 7:4 Therefore, my brethren, you also have become *dead to the law* through the body of Christ, that you may be married to another, even to Him who was raised from the dead, that we should bear fruit to God

DEAD WITH CHRIST (KJV)
(See *DIED WITH CHRIST*)

DEADLY PESTILENCE (NAS, NIV, RSV)
(See *PERILOUS PESTILENCE*)

DEADLY WEAPONS (NAS, NIV, RSV)
(See *INSTRUMENTS OF DEATH*)

DEAF AND DUMB SPIRIT
Mark 9:25 When Jesus saw that the people came running together, He rebuked the unclean spirit, saying to him, "You *deaf and dumb spirit*, I command you, come out of him, and enter him no more

DEAL DIFFERENTLY (NIV)
(See *SET APART*)

DEAL LOYALLY (RSV)
(See *SHOW KINDNESS*)

DEAL THY BREAD TO THE HUNGRY (KJV)
(See *SHARE YOUR BREAD*)

DEAL TREACHEROUSLY
Ps 25:3 Indeed, let no one who waits on You be ashamed; let those be ashamed who *deal treacherously* without cause
Is 33:1 and you who *deal treacherously*, though they have not dealt treacherously with you! When you cease plundering, you will be plundered; and when you make an end of dealing treacherously, they will *deal treacherously* with you
Hab 1:13 Why do You look on those who *deal treacherously*, and hold Your tongue when the wicked devours one more rightous than he
Mal 2:10 Why do we *deal treacherously* with one another by profaning the covenant of the fathers
Mal 2:15 Therefore take heed to your spirit, and let none *deal treacherously* with the wife of his youth
Mal 2:16 Therefore take heed to your spirit, that you do not *deal treacherously*

DEATH AND DESTRUCTION (NIV)
(See *HELL AND DESTRUCTION*)

DEATH IS SWALLOWED UP
1Cor 15:54 So when this corruptible has put on incorruption, and this mortal has put on immortality, then shall be brought to pass the saying that is written: *Death is swallowed up* in victory

DEATH OF HIS SAINTS
Ps 116:15 Precious in the sight of the Lord is the *death of His saints*

DEATH OF THE ONE WHO MADE IT (NAS, NIV, RSV)
(See *DEATH OF THE TESTATOR*)

DEATH OF THE TESTATOR
Heb 9:16 For where there is a testament, there must also of necessity be the *death of the testator*

DEATH REIGNED FROM ADAM TO MOSES
Rom 5:14 Nevertheless *death reigned from Adam to Moses*, even over those who had not sinned according to the likeness of the transgression of Adam, who is a type of Him who was to come

DEATH SHALL NOT PREVAIL (RSV)
(See *HADES SHALL NOT PREVAIL*)

DEBATE YOUR CASE
Prov 25:9 *Debate your case* with your neighbor himself, and do not disclose the secret to another

DEBATER OF THIS AGE (NAS, RSV)
(See *DISPUTER OF THIS AGE*)

DECAY IN HIS BONES (NIV)
(See *ROTTENNESS IN HIS BONES*)

DECEIT OF THEIR HEART
Jer 14:14 they prophesy to you a false vision, divination, a worthless thing, and the *deceit of their heart*

DECEITFUL BROOK (RSV)
(See *UNRELIABLE STREAM*)

DECEITFUL LIPS
Ps 17:1 Give ear to my prayer that is not from *deceitful lips*

DECEITFUL TONGUE
Ps 52:4 You love all devouring words, you *deceitful tongue*
Ps 120:2 Deliver my soul, O Lord, from lying lips and from a *deceitful tongue*
Zeph 3:13 The remnant of Israel shall do no unrighteousness and speak no lies, nor shall a *deceitful tongue* be found in their mouth

DECEITFULNESS OF RICHES
Matt 13:22 Now he who received seed among the thorns is he who hears the word, and the cares of this world and the *deceitfulness of riches* choke the word, and he becomes unfruitful
Mark 4:19 and the cares of this world, the *deceitfulness of riches*, and the desires for other things entering in choke the word, and it becomes unfruitful

DECEIVED BY THE SERPENT'S CUNNING (NIV)
(See *SERPENT DECEIVED EVE*)

DECEIVER AND AN ANTICHRIST
2Jn 7 For many deceivers have gone out into the world who do not confess Jesus Christ as coming in the flesh. This is a *deceiver and an antichrist*

DECEIVES HIS OWN HEART
Jas 1:26 If anyone among you thinks he is religious, and does not bridle his tongue but *deceives his own heart*, this one's religion is useless

DECEPTIVE BROOK (NIV)
(See *UNRELIABLE STREAM*)

DECLARE IT BOLDLY (RSV)
(See *SPEAK BOLDLY*)

DECLARE IT FEARLESSLY (NIV)
(See *SPEAK BOLDLY*)

DECLARE THE WORK OF GOD
Ps 64:9 All men shall fear, and shall *declare the work of God*

DECLARE UNTO US THE PARABLE (KJV)
(See *EXPLAIN TO US THE PARABLE*)

DECLARES THE LORD (NAS, NIV)
(See *SAYS THE LORD*)

DECREE AND A LAW (NIV)
(See *STATUTE AND AN ORDINANCE*)

DECREES, THE LAWS AND THE REGULATIONS (NIV)
(See *STATUTES AND JUDGMENTS*)

DEDICATED THE HOUSE OF THE LORD
1Kin 8:63 So the king and all the children of Israel *dedicated the house of the Lord*

DEDICATED THE TEMPLE OF THE LORD (NIV)
(See *DEDICATED THE HOUSE OF THE LORD*)

DEDICATED TO THE LORD (RSV)
(See *GIVEN BY THE LORD*)

DEEDS OF THE LAW
Rom 3:20 Therefore by the *deeds of the law* no flesh will be justified in His sight, for by the law is the knowledge of sin
Rom 3:28 Therefore we conclude that a man is justified by faith apart from the *deeds of the law*

DEEDS WILL BE SIGNED, SEALED (NIV)
(See *SIGN DEEDS AND SEAL THEM*)

DEEDS WORTHY OF THEIR REPENTANCE (RSV)
(See *WORKS BEFITTING REPENTANCE*)

DEEP CALLS UNTO DEEP
Ps 42:7 *Deep calls unto deep* at the noise of Your waterfalls

DEEP DARKNESS (RSV)
(See *SHADOW OF DEATH*)

DEEP SHADOW (NIV)
(See *SHADOW OF DEATH*)

DEEP SLEEP
Gen 2:21 And the Lord God caused a *deep sleep* to fall on Adam, and he slept
Gen 15:12 Now when the sun was going down, a *deep sleep* fell upon Abram
1Sam 26:12 For they were all asleep, because a *deep sleep* from the Lord had fallen on them
Job 4:13 In disquieting thoughts from the visions of the night, when *deep sleep* falls on men
Job 33:15 In a dream, in a vision of the night, when *deep sleep* falls upon men, while slumbering on their beds
Prov 19:15 Slothfulness casts one into a *deep sleep*, and an idle person will suffer hunger
Is 29:10 For the Lord has poured out on you the spirit of *deep sleep*, and has closed your eyes, namely, the prophets
Dan 8:18 Now, as he was speaking with me, I was in a *deep sleep* with my face to the ground
Dan 10:9 and while I heard the sound of his words I was in a *deep sleep* on my face, with my face to the ground
Acts 20:9 And in a window sat a certain young man named Eutychus, who was sinking into a *deep sleep*

DEEP THINGS OF GOD
Job 11:7 Can you search out the *deep things of God?* Can you find out the limits of the Almighty
1Cor 2:10 For the Spirit searches all things, yes, the *deep things of God*

DEEPER THAN HELL (KJV)
(See *DEEPER THAN SHEOL*)

DEEPER THAN SHEOL
Job 11:8 They are higher than heaven what can you do? *Deeper than Sheol* what can you know

DEEPER THAN THE DEPTHS OF THE GRAVE (NIV)
(See *DEEPER THAN SHEOL*)

DEFEND THE AFFLICTED (NIV)
(See *JUSTICE TO THE POOR*)

DEFEND THE CAUSE OF THE POOR (RSV)
(See *JUSTICE TO THE POOR*)

DEFEND THE FATHERLESS
Is 1:17 seek justice, reprove the oppressor; *defend the fatherless*, plead for the widow
Is 1:23 They do not *defend the fatherless*, nor does the cause of the widow come before them

DEFEND YOUR CAUSE (NIV)
(See *PLEAD YOUR CASE*)

DEFENDED THE CAUSE OF THE POOR (NIV)
(See *JUDGED THE CAUSE OF THE POOR*)

DEFENDER OF WIDOWS
Ps 68:5 A father of the fatherless, a *defender of widows*, is God in His holy habitation

DEFENSE OF THE GOSPEL
Phil 1:17 but the latter out of love, knowing that I am appointed for the *defense of the gospel*

DEFILE THE HOUSE (KJV, RSV)
(See *DEFILE THE TEMPLE*)

DEFILE THE LAND
Num 35:34 Therefore do not *defile the land* which you inhabit, in the midst of which I dwell
Deut 21:23 his body shall not remain overnight on the tree, but you shall surely bury him that day, so that you do not *defile the land* which the Lord your God is giving you as an inheritance

DEFILE THE SANCTUARY
Dan 11:31 And forces shall be mustered by him, and they shall *defile the sanctuary* fortress

DEFILE THE TEMPLE
Ezek 9:7 Then He said to them, "*Defile the temple*, and fill the courts with the slain

DEFILED MY LAND
Jer 2:7 But when you entered, you *defiled My land* and made My heritage an abomination
Jer 16:18 And first I will repay double for their iniquity and their sin, because they have *defiled My land*

DEFILED MY SANCTUARY
Ezek 5:11 Therefore, as I live,' says the Lord God, 'surely, because you have *defiled My sanctuary* with all your detestable things and with all your abominations, therefore I will also diminish you
Ezek 23:38 They have *defiled My sanctuary* on the same day and profaned My Sabbaths

DEFILEMENTS OF THE WORLD (NAS, RSV)
(See *POLLUTIONS OF THE WORLD*)

DEFILES THE LAND
Num 35:33 for blood *defiles the land*, and no atonement can be made for the land, for the blood that is shed on it, except by the blood of him who shed it

DEFILING THE SABBATH
Is 56:2 who keeps from *defiling the Sabbath*, and keeps his hand from doing any evil
Is 56:6 Also the sons of the foreigner who join themselves to the Lord, to serve Him, and to love the name of the Lord, to be His servants everyone who keeps from *defiling the Sabbath*, and holds fast My covenant

DELIGHT IN BURNT OFFERINGS
1Sam 15:22 Has the Lord as great *delight in burnt offerings* and sacrifices, as in obeying the voice of the Lord

DELIGHT IN RICHES (RSV)
(See *DECEITFULNESS OF RICHES*)

DELIGHT IN YOUR LAW
Ps 119:70 Their heart is as fat as grease, but I *delight in Your law*

DELIGHT OF YOUR SOUL
Ezek 24:21 Behold, I will profane My sanctuary, your arrogant boast, the desire of your eyes, the *delight of your soul*

DELIGHT TO THE EYES (NAS, RSV)
(See *PLEASANT TO THE EYES*)

DELIVER ME
Gen 32:11 *Deliver me*, I pray, from the hand of my brother, from the hand of Esau
Judg 12:2 and when I called you, you did not *deliver me* out of their hands
Judg 12:3 So when I saw that you would not *deliver me*, I took my life in my hands and crossed over against the people of Ammon
1Sam 17:37 Moreover David said, "The Lord, who delivered me from the paw of the lion and from the paw of the bear, He will *deliver me* from the hand of this Philistine
1Sam 23:11 Will the men of Keilah *deliver me* into his hand
1Sam 23:12 Then David said, "Will the men of Keilah *deliver me* and my men into the hand of Saul
1Sam 24:15 Therefore let the Lord be judge, and judge between you and me, and see and plead my case, and *deliver me* out of your hand
1Sam 26:24 And indeed, as your life was valued much this day in my eyes, so let my life be valued much in the eyes of the Lord, and let Him *deliver me* out of all tribulation
1Sam 30:15 And he said, "Swear to me by God that you will neither kill me nor *deliver me* into the hands of my master, and I will take you down to this troop
Job 6:23 or, '*Deliver me* from the enemy's hand'? or, 'Redeem me from the hand of oppressors
Ps 6:4 Return, O Lord, *deliver me!* Oh, save me for Your mercies' sake
Ps 7:1 Save me from all those who persecute me; and *deliver me*
Ps 22:20 *Deliver me* from the sword, my precious life from the power of the dog
Ps 25:20 Oh, keep my soul, and *deliver me;* let me not be ashamed, for I put my trust in You
Ps 27:12 Do not *deliver me* to the will of my adversaries
Ps 31:1 Let me never be ashamed; *deliver me* in Your righteousness
Ps 31:2 Bow down Your ear to me, *deliver me* speedily; be my rock of refuge, a fortress of defense to save me
Ps 31:15 *Deliver me* from the hand of my enemies, and from those who persecute me
Ps 39:8 *Deliver me* from all my transgressions; do not make me the reproach of the foolish
Ps 40:13 Be pleased, O Lord, to *deliver me;* O Lord, make haste to help me
Ps 43:1 Vindicate me, O God, and plead my cause against an ungodly nation; oh, *deliver me* from the deceitful and unjust man

Ps 51:14 *Deliver me* from bloodguiltiness, O God, the God of my salvation, and my tongue shall sing aloud of Your righteousness
Ps 59:1 *Deliver me* from my enemies, O my God; defend me from those who rise up against me
Ps 59:2 *Deliver me* from the workers of iniquity, and save me from bloodthirsty men
Ps 69:14 *Deliver me* out of the mire, and let me not sink
Ps 69:18 Draw near to my soul, and redeem it; *deliver me* because of my enemies
Ps 70:1 Make haste, O God, to *deliver me!* Make haste to help me, O Lord
Ps 71:2 *Deliver me* in Your righteousness, and cause me to escape
Ps 71:4 *Deliver me*, O my God, out of the hand of the wicked, out of the hand of the unrighteous and cruel man
Ps 109:21 But You, O God the Lord, deal with me for Your name's sake; because Your mercy is good, *deliver me*
Ps 119:153 Consider my affliction and *deliver me*, for I do not forget Your law
Ps 119:170 Let my supplication come before You; *deliver me* according to Your word
Ps 140:1 *Deliver me*, O Lord, from evil men; preserve me from violent men
Ps 142:6 *Deliver me* from my persecutors, for they are stronger than I
Ps 143:9 *Deliver me*, O Lord, from my enemies; in You I take shelter
Ps 144:7 Rescue me and *deliver me* out of great waters, from the hand of foreigners
Ps 144:11 Rescue me and *deliver me* from the hand of foreigners, whose mouth speaks vain words, and whose right hand is a right hand of falsehood
Is 44:17 he falls down before it and worships it, prays to it and says, "*Deliver me*, for you are my god
Jer 38:19 And Zedekiah the king said to Jeremiah, "I am afraid of the Jews who have defected to the Chaldeans, lest they *deliver me* into their hand, and they abuse me
Acts 25:11 but if there is nothing in these things of which these men accuse me, no one can *deliver me* to them
Rom 7:24 O wretched man that I am! Who will *deliver me* from this body of death
2Tim 4:18 And the Lord will *deliver me* from every evil work and preserve me for His heavenly kingdom

DELIVER SUCH A ONE TO SATAN
1Cor 5:5 *deliver such a one to Satan* for the destruction of the flesh, that his spirit may be saved in the day of the Lord Jesus

DELIVER US
Deut 1:27 and you murmured in your tents, and said, 'Because the Lord hates us, He has brought us out of the land of Egypt to *deliver us* into the hand of the Amorites, to destroy us
Josh 7:7 And Joshua said, "Alas, Lord God, why have You brought this people over the Jordan at all to *deliver us* into the hand of the Amorites, to destroy us
Judg 10:15 Do to us whatever seems best to You; only *deliver us* this day, we pray
1Sam 4:8 Who will *deliver us* from the hand of these mighty gods
1Sam 12:10 but now *deliver us* from the hand of our enemies, and we will serve You
2Kin 18:30 nor let Hezekiah make you trust in the Lord, saying, "The Lord will surely *deliver us*
2Kin 18:32 But do not listen to Hezekiah, lest he persuade you, saying, "The Lord will *deliver us*
1Chr 16:35 gather us together, and *deliver us* from the Gentiles, to give thanks to Your holy name, to triumph in Your praise
2Chr 32:11 Does not Hezekiah persuade you to give yourselves over to die by famine and by thirst, saying, "The Lord our God will *deliver us* from the hand of the king of Assyria
Ps 79:9 And *deliver us*, and provide atonement for our sins, for Your name's sake
Is 36:15 nor let Hezekiah make you trust in the Lord, saying, "The Lord will surely *deliver us*
Is 36:18 Beware lest Hezekiah persuade you, saying, "The Lord will *deliver us*
Jer 43:3 But Baruch the son of Neriah has set you against us, to *deliver us* into the hand of the Chaldeans, that they may put us to death or carry us away captive to Babylon
Lam 5:8 Servants rule over us; there is none to *deliver us* from their hand
Dan 3:17 If that is the case, our God whom we serve is able to *deliver us* from the burning fiery furnace, and He will *deliver us* from your hand, O king
Mic 5:6 thus He shall *deliver us* from the Assyrian, when he comes into our land and when he treads within our borders
Matt 6:13 And do not lead us into temptation, but *deliver us* from the evil one
Luke 11:4 And do not lead us into temptation, but *deliver us* from the evil one
2Cor 1:10 who delivered us from so great a death, and does *deliver us;* in whom we trust that He will still *deliver us*
Gal 1:4 who gave Himself for our sins, that He might *deliver us* from this present evil age, according to the will of our God and Father

DELIVERANCE BELONGS TO THE LORD (RSV)
(See *SALVATION BELONGS TO THE LORD*)

DELIVERANCE IS OF THE LORD
Prov 21:31 The horse is prepared for the day of battle, but *deliverance is of the Lord*

DELIVERANCE THE LORD WILL BRING (NIV)
(See *SALVATION OF THE LORD*)

DELIVERANCE TO THE CAPTIVES
Luke 4:18 He has sent Me to heal the brokenhearted, to preach *deliverance to the captives* and recovery of sight to the blind, to set at liberty those who are oppressed

DELIVERED INTO THE HANDS OF
Mark 9:31 For He taught His disciples and said to them, "The Son of Man is being *delivered into the hands of* men, and they will kill Him
Luke 9:44 Let these words sink down into your ears, for the Son of Man is about to be *delivered into the hands of* men
Luke 24:7 saying, 'The Son of Man must be *delivered into the hands of* sinful men, and be crucified, and the third day rise again

DELIVERED INTO THE HANDS OF MEN (NAS, RSV)
(See *BETRAYED INTO THE HANDS OF MEN*)

DELIVERED UP TO BE CRUCIFIED
Matt 26:2 You know that after two days is the Passover, and the Son of Man will be *delivered up to be crucified*

DELIVERS THE KINGDOM
1Cor 15:24 Then comes the end, when He *delivers the kingdom* to God the Father, when He puts an end to all rule and all authority and power

DELUSIONS OF THEIR OWN MINDS (NIV)
(See *DECEIT OF THEIR HEART*)

DEMONSTRATE HIS JUSTICE (NIV)
(See *DEMONSTRATE HIS RIGHTEOUSNESS*)

DEMONSTRATE HIS RIGHTEOUSNESS
Rom 3:25 whom God set forth to be a propitiation by His blood, through faith, to *demonstrate His righteousness*, because in His forbearance God had passed over the sins that were previously committed

DEN OF LIONS
Dan 6:7 All the governors of the kingdom, the administrators and satraps, the counselors and advisors, have consulted together to establish a royal statute and to make a firm decree, that whoever petitions any god or man for thirty days, except you, O king, shall be cast into the *den of lions*
Dan 6:12 Have you not signed a decree that every man who petitions any god or man within thirty days, except you, O king, shall be cast into the *den of lions*
Dan 6:16 So the king gave the command, and they brought Daniel and cast him into the *den of lions*
Dan 6:19 Then the king arose very early in the morning and went in haste to the *den of lions*
Dan 6:24 And the king gave the command, and they brought those men who had accused Daniel, and they cast them into the *den of lions* them, their children, and their wives

DEN OF THIEVES
Jer 7:11 Has this house, which is called by My name, become a *den of thieves* in your eyes
Matt 21:13 And He said to them, "It is written, 'My house shall be called a house of prayer,' but you have made it a'*den of thieves*
Mark 11:17 Then He taught, saying to them, "Is it not written, 'My house shall be called a house of prayer for all nations'? But you have made it a '*den of thieves*
Luke 19:46 saying to them, "It is written, 'My house is a house of prayer,' but you have made it a '*den of thieves*

DENIED ME THREE TIMES
John 13:38 Most assuredly, I say to you, the rooster shall not crow till you have *denied Me three times*

DENSE CLOUD (NIV)
(See *THICK CLOUD*)

DENY HIMSELF
Matt 16:24 Then Jesus said to His disciples, "If anyone desires to come after Me, let him *deny himself*, and take up his cross, and follow Me
Mark 8:34 And when He had called the people to Him, with His disciples also, He said to them, "Whoever desires to come after Me, let him *deny himself*, and take up his cross, and follow Me
Luke 9:23 Then He said to them all, "If anyone desires to come after Me, let him *deny himself*, and take up his cross daily, and follow Me
2Tim 2:13 If we are faithless, He remains faithful; He cannot *deny Himself*

DENY YOURSELVES (NIV)
(See *AFFLICT YOUR SOULS*)

DEPART FROM EVIL
Job 28:28 And to man He said, 'Behold, the fear of the Lord, that is wisdom, and to *depart from evil* is understanding
Ps 34:14 *Depart from evil*, and do good; seek peace, and pursue it
Ps 37:27 *Depart from evil*, and do good; and dwell forevermore
Prov 3:7 Do not be wise in your own eyes; fear the Lord and *depart from evil*
Prov 13:19 A desire accomplished is sweet to the soul, but it is an abomination to fools to *depart from evil*
Prov 16:17 The highway of the upright is to *depart from evil*

DEPART FROM ME
1Kin 20:36 Then he said to him, "Because you have not obeyed the voice of the Lord, surely, as soon as you *depart from me*, a lion shall kill you
Ps 6:8 *Depart from me*, all you workers of iniquity; for the Lord has heard the voice of my weeping
Ps 101:4 A perverse heart shall *depart from me;* I will not know wickedness
Ps 119:115 *Depart from me*, you evildoers, for I will keep the commandments of my God
Ps 139:19 Oh, that You would slay the wicked, O God! *Depart from me*, therefore, you bloodthirsty men
Jer 17:13 Those who *depart from Me* shall be written in the earth, because they have forsaken the Lord, the fountain of living waters
Jer 32:40 but I will put My fear in their hearts so that they will not *depart from Me*
Matt 7:23 And then I will declare to them, 'I never knew you; *depart from Me*, you who practice lawlessness
Matt 25:41 Then He will also say to those on the left hand, '*Depart from Me*, you cursed, into the everlasting fire prepared for the devil and his angels
Luke 5:8 When Simon Peter saw it, he fell down at Jesus' knees, saying, "*Depart from me*, for I am a sinful man, O Lord
Luke 13:27 But He will say, 'I tell you I do not know you, where you are from. *Depart from Me*, all you workers of iniquity
2Cor 12:8 Concerning this thing I pleaded with the Lord three times that it might *depart from me*

DEPART TO SHEOL (RSV)
(See *INTO HELL*)

DEPARTED AS A SCROLL (KJV)
(See *RECEDED AS A SCROLL*)

DEPENDING ON THE LORD (NIV)
(See *TRUST IN THE LORD*)

DEPTH OF THE RICHES
Rom 11:33 Oh, the *depth of the riches* both of the wisdom and knowledge of God

DEPTHS OF SHEOL
Ps 86:13 For great is Your mercy toward me, and You have delivered my soul from the *depths of Sheol*

DEPTHS OF THE EARTH
Ps 71:20 You, who have shown me great and severe troubles, shall revive me again, and bring me up again from the *depths of the earth*
Ezek 31:14 For they have all been delivered to death, to the *depths of the earth*, among the children of men who go down to the Pit
Ezek 31:16 and all the trees of Eden, the choice and best of Lebanon, all that drink water, were comforted in the *depths of the earth*
Ezek 31:18 Yet you shall be brought down with the trees of Eden to the *depths of the earth*
Ezek 32:18 Son of man, wail over the multitude of Egypt, and cast them down to the *depths of the*

earth, her and the daughters of the famous nations, with those who go down to the Pit

DEPTHS OF THE GRAVE (NIV)
(See *DEPTHS OF SHEOL*)

DEPTHS OF THE PIT
Is 14:15 Yet you shall be brought down to Sheol, to the lowest *depths of the Pit*

DEPTHS OF THE SEA
Job 36:30 Look, He scatters his light upon it, and covers the *depths of the sea*
Ps 68:22 The Lord said, "I will bring back from Bashan, I will bring them back from the *depths of the sea*
Is 51:10 that made the *depths of the sea* a road for the redeemed to cross over
Mic 7:19 You will cast all our sins into the *depths of the sea*

DESCEND FROM HEAVEN
1Th 4:16 For the Lord Himself will *descend from heaven* with a shout, with the voice of an archangel, and with the trumpet of God

DESCENDANTS OF ABRAHAM (NIV)
(See *SEED OF ABRAHAM*)

DESCENDANTS OF DAVID
1Kin 11:39 And I will afflict the *descendants of David* because of this, but not forever
Jer 33:22 As the host of heaven cannot be numbered, nor the sand of the sea measured, so will I multiply the *descendants of David* My servant and the Levites who minister to Me

DESCENDANTS OF LEVI (NIV)
(See *SONS OF LEVI*)

DESCENDED FROM DAVID (RSV)
(See *SEED OF DAVID*)

DESECRATE THE TEMPLE (NIV)
(See *DEFILE THE TEMPLE*)

DESECRATED MY SABBATHS (NIV)
(See *PROFANED MY SABBATHS*)

DESERT OF JUDAH (NIV)
(See *WILDERNESS OF JUDAH*)

DESERTED PLACE
Matt 14:13 When Jesus heard it, He departed from there by boat to a *deserted place* by Himself
Matt 14:15 When it was evening, His disciples came to Him, saying, "This is a *deserted place*, and the hour is already late
Mark 6:31 And He said to them, "Come aside by yourselves to a *deserted place* and rest a while
Mark 6:32 So they departed to a *deserted place* in the boat by themselves
Mark 6:35 And when the day was now far spent, His disciples came to Him and said, "This is a *deserted place*, and already the hour is late
Luke 4:42 Now when it was day, He departed and went into a *deserted place*
Luke 9:10 And He took them and went aside privately into a *deserted place* belonging to the city called Bethsaida
Luke 9:12 When the day began to wear away, the twelve came and said to Him, "Send the multitude away, that they may go into the surrounding towns and country, and lodge and get provisions; for we are in a *deserted place* here

DESERVE TO DIE (NAS, NIV)
(See *WORTHY OF DEATH*)

DESERVES TO DIE
Jer 26:11 And the priests and the prophets spoke to the princes and all the people, saying, "This man *deserves to die*

DESIRE EARNESTLY TO PROPHESY
1Cor 14:39 Therefore, brethren, *desire earnestly to prophesy*, and do not forbid to speak with tongues

DESIRE MERCY AND NOT SACRIFICE
Hos 6:6 For I *desire mercy and not sacrifice*, and the knowledge of God more than burnt offerings
Matt 9:13 I *desire mercy and not sacrifice*.' For I did not come to call the righteous, but sinners, to repentance
Matt 12:7 But if you had known what this means, 'I *desire mercy and not sacrifice*

DESIRE OF ALL NATIONS
Hag 2:7 and I will shake all nations, and they shall come to the *Desire of All Nations*, and I will fill this temple with glory

DESIRE OF YOUR EYES
Ezek 24:16 Son of man, behold, I take away from you the *desire of your eyes* with one stroke
Ezek 24:21 Behold, I will profane My sanctuary, your arrogant boast, the *desire of your eyes*, the delight of your soul

DESIRE OF YOUR SOUL (RSV)
(See *DELIGHT OF YOUR SOUL*)

DESIRE SPIRITUAL GIFTS
1Cor 14:1 Pursue love, and *desire spiritual gifts*, but especially that you may prophesy

DESIRE STEADFAST LOVE AND NOT SACRIFICE (RSV)
(See *DESIRE MERCY AND NOT SACRIFICE*)

DESIRE THE PURE MILK
1Pet 2:2 as newborn babes, *desire the pure milk* of the word, that you may grow thereby

DESIRE THE SINCERE MILK (KJV)
(See *DESIRE THE PURE MILK*)

DESIRES OF BODY AND MIND (RSV)
(See *DESIRES OF THE FLESH*)

DESIRES OF THE FLESH
Eph 2:3 among whom also we all once conducted ourselves in the lusts of our flesh, fulfilling the *desires of the flesh* and of the mind, and were by nature children of wrath, just as the others

DESIRES OF THE SINFUL NATURE (NIV)
(See *LUST OF THE FLESH*)

DESOLATE HEIGHTS
Is 41:18 I will open rivers in *desolate heights*, and fountains in the midst of the valleys
Is 49:9 They shall feed along the roads, and their pastures shall be on all *desolate heights*
Jer 3:2 Lift up your eyes to the *desolate heights* and see
Jer 3:21 A voice was heard on the *desolate heights*, weeping and supplications of the children of Israel
Jer 4:11 At that time it will be said to this people and to Jerusalem, "A dry wind of the *desolate heights* blows in the wilderness toward the daughter of My people not to fan or to cleanse
Jer 7:29 Cut off your hair and cast it away, and take up a lamentation on the *desolate heights*
Jer 12:12 The plunderers have come on all the

desolate heights in the wilderness, for the sword of the Lord shall devour from one end of the land to the other end of the land
Jer 14:6 And the wild donkeys stood in the *desolate heights;* they sniffed at the wind like jackals

DESOLATE WASTE
Job 38:27 To satisfy the *desolate waste*, and cause to spring forth the growth of tender grass

DESPAIRING HEART (NIV)
(See *ANGUISH OF SOUL*)

DESPISE ME (RSV)
(See *PROVOKE ME*)

DESPISE MY LIFE
Job 9:21 I am blameless, yet I do not know myself; I *despise my life*

DESPISE MY STATUTES
Lev 26:15 and if you *despise My statutes*, or if your soul abhors My judgments, so that you do not perform all My commandments, but break My covenant

DESPISED AND REJECTED
Is 53:3 He is *despised and rejected* by men, a man of sorrows and acquainted with grief

DESPISED THE LAW
Amos 2:4 For three transgressions of Judah, and for four, I will not turn away its punishment, because they have *despised the law* of the Lord, and have not kept His commandments

DESPISED THE POOR (KJV)
(See *DISHONORED THE POOR MAN*)

DESPISED THE WORD
Num 15:31 Because he has *despised the word* of the Lord, and has broken His commandment, that person shall be completely cut off
Is 5:24 because they have rejected the law of the Lord of hosts, and *despised the word* of the Holy One of Israel

DESPISES THE WORD
Prov 13:13 He who *despises the word* will be destroyed, but he who fears the commandment will be rewarded

DESPISING THE SHAME
Heb 12:2 looking unto Jesus, the author and finisher of our faith, who for the joy that was set before Him endured the cross, *despising the shame*, and has sat down at the right hand of the throne of God

DESTROY AND TO THROW DOWN
Jer 1:10 See, I have this day set you over the nations and over the kingdoms, to root out and to pull down, to *destroy and to throw down*, to build and to plant

DESTROY THE LAW
Matt 5:17 Do not think that I came to *destroy the Law* or the Prophets

DESTROY THEIR ALTARS
Ex 34:13 But you shall *destroy their altars*, break their sacred pillars, and cut down their wooden images
Deut 7:5 you shall *destroy their altars*, and break down their sacred pillars, and cut down their wooden images, and burn their carved images with fire
Deut 12:3 And you shall *destroy their altars*, break their sacred pillars, and burn their wooden images with fire

DESTROY THIS TEMPLE
Mark 14:58 We heard Him say, 'I will *destroy this temple* that is made with hands, and within three days I will build another made without hands
John 2:19 Jesus answered and said to them, "*Destroy this temple*, and in three days I will raise it up

DESTROYED BY FIRE (NIV)
(See *MELT WITH FERVENT HEAT*)

DESTROYED FOR LACK OF KNOWLEDGE
Hos 4:6 My people are *destroyed for lack of knowledge*. Because you have rejected knowledge, I also will reject you from being priest for Me

DESTRUCTION AND DEATH
Job 28:22 *Destruction and Death* say, 'We have heard a report about it with our ears

DESTRUCTION COMES
Prov 1:27 when your terror comes like a storm, and your *destruction comes* like a whirlwind, when distress and anguish come upon you
Jer 46:20 Egypt is like a very pretty heifer, but *destruction comes*, it comes from the north
Ezek 7:25 *Destruction comes;* they will seek peace, but there shall be none
1Th 5:3 then sudden *destruction comes* upon them, as labor pains upon a pregnant woman

DESTRUCTION DECREED
Is 10:22 For though your people, O Israel, be as the sand of the sea, yet a remnant of them will return; the *destruction decreed* shall overflow with righteousness

DESTRUCTION FROM THE ALMIGHTY
Is 13:6 Wail, for the day of the Lord is at hand! It will come as *destruction from the Almighty*
Joel 1:15 For the day of the Lord is at hand; it shall come as *destruction from the Almighty*

DESTRUCTION OF THE DAUGHTER OF MY PEOPLE (NAS, RSV)
(See *PLUNDERING OF THE DAUGHTER OF MY PEOPLE*)

DETESTABLE TO THE LORD (NIV)
(See *ABOMINATION TO THE LORD*)

DEVIL'S SCHEMES (NIV)
(See *WILES OF THE DEVIL*)

DEVIL'S TRAP (NIV)
(See *SNARE OF THE DEVIL*)

DEVISE EVIL
Prov 3:29 Do not *devise evil* against your neighbor, for he dwells by you for safety's sake
Prov 12:20 Deceit is in the heart of those who *devise evil*, but counselors of peace have joy
Prov 14:22 Do they not go astray who *devise evil?* But mercy and truth belong to those who devise good
Hos 7:15 Though I disciplined and strengthened their arms, yet they *devise evil* against Me

DEVISED EVIL
Prov 30:32 If you have been foolish in exalting yourself, or if you have *devised evil*, put your hand on your mouth
Jer 48:2 In Heshbon they have *devised evil*

against her: "Come, and let us cut her off as a nation

DEVISES EVIL
Ps 94:20 Shall the throne of iniquity, which *devises evil* by law, have fellowship with You
Prov 6:14 perversity is in his heart, he *devises evil* continually, he sows discord

DEVOID OF UNDERSTANDING
Prov 7:7 and saw among the simple, I perceived among the youths, a young man *devoid of understanding*
Prov 10:13 Wisdom is found on the lips of him who has understanding, but a rod is for the back of him who is *devoid of understanding*
Prov 12:11 He who tills his land will be satisfied with bread, but he who follows frivolity is *devoid of understanding*
Prov 17:18 A man *devoid of understanding* shakes hands in a pledge, and becomes surety for his friend
Prov 24:30 I went by the field of the slothful, and by the vineyard of the man *devoid of understanding*

DEVOTE THEMSELVES TO DOING WHAT IS GOOD (NIV)
(See *MAINTAIN GOOD WORKS*)

DEVOTE YOURSELF TO PRAYER (NIV)
(See *CONTINUE EARNESTLY IN PRAYER*)

DEVOUR HER STRONGHOLDS (RSV)
(See *DEVOUR ITS PALACES*)

DEVOUR ITS PALACES
Amos 1:7 But I will send a fire upon the wall of Gaza, which shall *devour its palaces*
Amos 1:10 But I will send a fire upon the wall of Tyre, which shall *devour its palaces*
Amos 1:14 But I will kindle a fire in the wall of Rabbah, and it shall *devour its palaces*, amid shouting in the day of battle, and a tempest in the day of the whirlwind

DEVOUR THE PALACES
Jer 17:27 But if you will not heed Me to hallow the Sabbath day, such as not carrying a burden when entering the gates of Jerusalem on the Sabbath day, then I will kindle a fire in its gates, and it shall *devour the palaces* of Jerusalem, and it shall not be quenched
Amos 1:4 But I will send a fire into the house of Hazael, which shall *devour the palaces* of Ben-Hadad
Amos 1:12 But I will send a fire upon Teman, which shall *devour the palaces* of Bozrah
Amos 2:2 But I will send a fire upon Moab, and it shall *devour the palaces* of Kerioth
Amos 2:5 but I will send a fire upon Judah, and it shall *devour the palaces* of Jerusalem

DEVOUR WIDOWS' HOUSES
Matt 23:14 For you *devour widows' houses*, and for a pretense make long prayers
Mark 12:40 who *devour widows' houses*, and for a pretense make long prayers
Luke 20:47 who *devour widows' houses*, and for a pretense make long prayers

DEW OF HEAVEN
Gen 27:28 Therefore may God give you of the *dew of heaven*, of the fatness of the earth, and plenty of grain and wine
Gen 27:39 Behold, your dwelling shall be of the fatness of the earth, and of the *dew of heaven* from above
Dan 4:15 let it be wet with the *dew of heaven*, and let him graze with the beasts on the grass of the earth
Dan 4:23 let it be wet with the *dew of heaven*, and let him graze with the beasts of the field, till seven times pass over him
Dan 4:25 They shall wet you with the *dew of heaven*, and seven times shall pass over you, till you know that the Most High rules in the kingdom of men, and gives it to whomever He chooses
Dan 4:33 his body was wet with the *dew of heaven* till his hair had grown like eagles' feathers and his nails like birds' claws
Dan 5:21 They fed him with grass like oxen, and his body was wet with the *dew of heaven*, till he knew that the Most High God rules in the kingdom of men, and appoints over it whomever He chooses

DEW THAT GOES EARLY (RSV)
(See *EARLY DEW*)

DID EVIL IN THE EYES OF THE LORD
1Kin 16:25 Omri *did evil in the eyes of the Lord*, and did worse than all who were before him

DID NOT REMEMBER THE LORD
Judg 8:34 Thus the children of Israel *did not remember the Lord* their God, who had delivered them from the hands of all their enemies on every side

DIE BY THE SWORD
Jer 11:22 The young men shall *die by the sword*, their sons and their daughters shall die by famine
Jer 21:9 He who remains in this city shall *die by the sword*, by famine, and by pestilence
Jer 34:4 Thus says the Lord concerning you: "You shall not *die by the sword*
Jer 38:2 He who remains in this city shall *die by the sword*, by famine, and by pestilence
Jer 42:17 They shall *die by the sword*, by famine, and by pestilence
Jer 42:22 Now therefore, know certainly that you shall *die by the sword*, by famine, and by pestilence in the place where you desire to go to sojourn
Ezek 7:15 Whoever is in the field will *die by the sword*
Amos 7:11 Jeroboam shall *die by the sword*, and Israel shall surely be led away captive from their own land
Amos 9:10 All the sinners of My people shall *die by the sword*, who say

DIE FOR HIS OWN SIN
2Chr 25:4 However he did not execute their children, but did as it is written in the Law in the Book of Moses, where the Lord commanded, saying, "The fathers shall not be put to death for their children, nor shall the children be put to death for their fathers; but a person shall *die for his own sin*

DIE FOR HIS SIN (NIV)
(See *DIE IN HIS INIQUITY*)

DIE FOR THE PEOPLE
John 11:50 nor do you consider that it is expedient for us that one man should *die for the people*, and not that the whole nation should perish
John 18:14 Now it was Caiaphas who gave counsel to the Jews that it was expedient that one man should *die for the people*

DIE IN HIS INIQUITY
Ezek 3:18 When I say to the wicked, 'You shall surely die,' and you give him no warning, nor

speak to warn the wicked from his wicked way, to save his life, that same wicked man shall *die in his iniquity*
Ezek 3:19 Yet, if you warn the wicked, and he does not turn from his wickedness, nor from his wicked way, he shall *die in his iniquity*
Ezek 33:8 and you do not speak to warn the wicked from his way, that wicked man shall *die in his iniquity*
Ezek 33:9 Nevertheless if you warn the wicked to turn from his way, and he does not turn from his way, he shall *die in his iniquity*

DIE IN PEACE
Jer 34:5 But you shall *die in peace;* as in the ceremonies of your fathers, the former kings who were before you, so they shall burn incense for you and lament for you, saying

DIE IN THE WILDERNESS
Ex 14:11 Then they said to Moses, "Because there were no graves in Egypt, have you taken us away to *die in the wilderness*
Ex 14:12 For it would have been better for us to serve the Egyptians than that we should *die in the wilderness*
Num 21:5 Why have you brought us up out of Egypt to *die in the wilderness*
Num 26:65 For the Lord had said of them, "They shall surely *die in the wilderness*

DIE IN YOUR SINS
John 8:24 Therefore I said to you that you will *die in your sins;* for if you do not believe that I am He, you will *die in your sins*

DIE PEACEFULLY (NIV)
(See *DIE IN PEACE*)

DIE TO THE LORD
Rom 14:8 and if we die, we *die to the Lord*. Therefore, whether we live or die, we are the Lord's

DIED AT A GOOD OLD AGE
Judg 8:32 Now Gideon the son of Joash *died at a good old age*, and was buried in the tomb of Joash his father, in Ophrah of the Abiezrites

DIED FOR SINS (NAS, NIV, RSV)
(See *SUFFERED ONCE FOR SINS*)

DIED TO SIN ONCE
Rom 6:10 For the death that He died, He *died to sin once* for all

DIED TO THE LAW (NIV, RSV)
(See *DEAD TO THE LAW*)

DIED WITH CHRIST
Rom 6:8 Now if we *died with Christ*, we believe that we shall also live with Him
Col 2:20 Therefore, if you *died with Christ* from the basic principles of the world, why, as though living in the world, do you subject yourselves to regulations

DIFFERENT GOSPEL
2Cor 11:4 For if he who comes preaches another Jesus whom we have not preached, or if you receive a different spirit which you have not received, or a *different gospel* which you have not accepted, you may well put up with it
Gal 1:6 I marvel that you are turning away so soon from Him who called you in the grace of Christ, to a *different gospel*

DIFFERENT KINDS OF GIFTS (NIV)
(See *DIVERSITIES OF GIFTS*)

DIGGED THROUGH THE WALL (KJV)
(See *DUG THROUGH THE WALL*)

DILIGENTLY STUDY THE SCRIPTURES (NIV)
(See *SEARCH THE SCRIPTURES*)

DIMLY BURNING WICK (NAS, RSV)
(See *SMOKING FLAX*)

DIRECT HIS OWN STEPS
Jer 10:23 it is not in man who walks to *direct his own steps*

DIRECTION FROM THE LORD (RSV)
(See *COUNSEL OF THE LORD*)

DIRT FROM THE BODY (NIV, RSV)
(See *FILTH OF THE FLESH*)

DISASTER FROM THE NORTH
Jer 4:6 For I will bring *disaster from the north*, and great destruction

DISASTER SWEEPS OVER YOU (NIV)
(See *DESTRUCTION COMES*)

DISCERN FOR OURSELVES WHAT IS RIGHT (NIV)
(See *CHOOSE JUSTICE*)

DISCERN THE SIGNS
Matt 16:3 You know how to discern the face of the sky, but you cannot *discern the signs* of the times

DISCERNER OF THE THOUGHTS
Heb 4:12 For the word of God is living and powerful, and sharper than any two-edged sword, piercing even to the division of soul and spirit, and of joints and marrow, and is a *discerner of the thoughts* and intents of the heart

DISCERNING THE LORD'S BODY
1Cor 11:29 For he who eats and drinks in an unworthy manner eats and drinks judgment to himself, not *discerning the Lord's body*

DISCIPLE WHOM JESUS LOVED
John 21:7 Therefore that *disciple whom Jesus loved* said to Peter, "It is the Lord
John 21:20 Then Peter, turning around, saw the *disciple whom Jesus loved* following, who also had leaned on His breast at the supper, and said

DISCIPLES ASKED
Matt 17:10 And His *disciples asked* Him, saying, "Why then do the scribes say that Elijah must come first
Mark 7:17 And when He had entered a house away from the crowd, His *disciples asked* Him concerning the parable
Mark 9:28 And when He had come into the house, His *disciples asked* Him privately
Mark 10:10 And in the house His *disciples asked* Him again about the same matter
Luke 8:9 Then His *disciples asked* Him, saying, "What does this parable mean
John 9:2 And His *disciples asked* Him, saying, "Rabbi, who sinned, this man or his parents, that he was born blind

DISCIPLES CAME
Matt 5:1 And seeing the multitudes, He went up on a mountain, and when He was seated His *disciples came* to Him

Matt 8:25 Then His *disciples came* to Him and awoke Him, saying
Matt 13:10 And the *disciples came* and said to Him, "Why do You speak to them in parables
Matt 13:36 And His *disciples came* to Him, saying, "Explain to us the parable of the tares of the field
Matt 14:12 Then his *disciples came* and took away the body and buried it, and went and told Jesus
Matt 14:15 When it was evening, His *disciples came* to Him, saying
Matt 15:12 Then His *disciples came* and said to Him, "Do You know that the Pharisees were offended when they heard this saying
Matt 15:23 And His *disciples came* and urged Him, saying, "Send her away, for she cries out after us
Matt 17:19 Then the *disciples came* to Jesus privately and said, "Why could we not cast him out
Matt 18:1 At that time the *disciples came* to Jesus, saying, "Who then is greatest in the kingdom of heaven
Matt 24:1 Then Jesus went out and departed from the temple, and His *disciples came* to Him to show Him the buildings of the temple
Matt 24:3 Now as He sat on the Mount of Olives, the *disciples came* to Him privately, saying
Matt 26:17 Now on the first day of the Feast of the Unleavened Bread the *disciples came* to Jesus, saying to Him
Matt 28:13 saying, "Tell them, 'His *disciples came* at night and stole Him away while we slept
Mark 6:35 And when the day was now far spent, His *disciples came* to Him and said
John 3:22 After these things Jesus and His *disciples came* into the land of Judea, and there He remained with them and baptized
John 4:27 And at this point His *disciples came*, and they marveled that He talked with a woman
John 21:8 But the other *disciples came* in the little boat (for they were not far from land, but about two hundred cubits
Acts 20:7 Now on the first day of the week, when the *disciples came* together to break bread, Paul, ready to depart the next day, spoke to them and continued his message until midnight

DISCORD AMONG BRETHREN
Prov 6:19 a false witness who speaks lies, and one who sows *discord among brethren*

DISCOVER THY SKIRTS UPON THY FACE (KJV)
(See *LIFT YOUR SKIRTS OVER YOUR FACE*)

DISGRACEFUL THING
Gen 34:7 and the men were grieved and very angry, because he had done a *disgraceful thing* in Israel by lying with Jacob's daughter, a thing which ought not to be done
Deut 22:21 then they shall bring out the young woman to the door of her father's house, and the men of her city shall stone her to death with stones, because she has done a *disgraceful thing* in Israel, to play the harlot in her father's house
Josh 7:15 Then it shall be that he who is taken with the accursed thing shall be burned with fire, he and all that he has, because he has transgressed the covenant of the Lord, and because he has done a *disgraceful thing* in Israel
2Sam 13:12 And she answered him, "No, my brother, do not force me, for no such thing should be done in Israel. Do not this *disgraceful thing*

DISHONEST MANAGER (NIV)
(See *UNJUST STEWARD*)

DISHONEST STEWARD (RSV)
(See *UNJUST STEWARD*)

DISHONORED THE POOR MAN
Jas 2:6 But you have *dishonored the poor man*. Do not the rich oppress you and drag you into the courts

DISHONORS HER HEAD
1Cor 11:5 But every woman who prays or prophesies with her head uncovered *dishonors her head*, for that is one and the same as if her head were shaved

DISHONORS HIS HEAD
1Cor 11:4 Every man praying or prophesying, having his head covered, *dishonors his head*

DISOBEDIENT TO PARENTS
Rom 1:30 backbiters, haters of God, violent, proud, boasters, inventors of evil things, *disobedient to parents*
2Tim 3:2 For men will be lovers of themselves, lovers of money, boasters, proud, blasphemers, *disobedient to parents*, unthankful, unholy

DISOBEY THEIR PARENTS (NIV)
(See *DISOBEDIENT TO PARENTS*)

DISOWN HIMSELF (NIV)
(See *DENY HIMSELF*)

DISOWN ME THREE TIMES (NIV)
(See *DENIED ME THREE TIMES*)

DISPENSATION OF THE FULLNESS
Eph 1:10 that in the *dispensation of the fullness* of the times He might gather together in one all things in Christ, both which are in heaven and which are on earth in Him

DISPENSATION OF THE SPIRIT (RSV)
(See *MINISTRY OF THE SPIRIT*)

DISPUTE WITH HIM (NAS, NIV)
(See *CONTEND WITH HIM*)

DISPUTER OF THIS AGE
1Cor 1:20 Where is the *disputer of this age?* Has not God made foolish the wisdom of this world

DISSENSION AMONG BROTHERS (NIV)
(See *DISCORD AMONG BRETHEN*)

DISSENSIONS AMONG YOU (RSV)
(See *DIVISIONS AMONG YOU*)

DISSOLVED WITH FIRE (RSV)
(See *MELT WITH FERVENT HEAT*)

DISTANT COUNTRY (NIV)
(See *FAR COUNTRY*)

DISTRESSING SPIRIT FROM GOD
1Sam 16:15 And Saul's servants said to him, "Surely, a *distressing spirit from God* is troubling you
1Sam 16:16 and it shall be that he will play it with his hand when the *distressing spirit from God* is upon you, and you shall be well
1Sam 18:10 And it happened on the next day that the *distressing spirit from God* came upon Saul, and he prophesied inside the house

DISTRESSING SPIRIT FROM THE LORD
1Sam 16:14 But the Spirit of the Lord departed from Saul, and a *distressing spirit from the Lord* troubled him
1Sam 19:9 Now the *distressing spirit from the Lord* came upon Saul as he sat in his house with his spear in his hand

DISTRIBUTE TO THE POOR
Luke 18:22 Sell all that you have and *distribute to the poor*, and you will have treasure in heaven

DIVERSITIES OF GIFTS
1Cor 12:4 Now there are *diversities of gifts*, but the same Spirit

DIVIDE MY GARMENTS
Ps 22:18 They *divide My garments* among them, and for My clothing they cast lots

DIVIDE THE DAY FROM THE NIGHT
Gen 1:14 Then God said, "Let there be lights in the firmament of the heavens to *divide the day from the night*

DIVIDE THE INHERITANCE
Num 34:29 These are the ones the Lord commanded to *divide the inheritance* among the children of Israel in the land of Canaan
Luke 12:13 Then one from the crowd said to Him, "Teacher, tell my brother to *divide the inheritance* with me

DIVIDED HIS GARMENTS
Matt 27:35 Then they crucified Him, and *divided His garments*, casting lots, that it might be fulfilled which was spoken by the prophet
Mark 15:24 And when they crucified Him, they *divided His garments*, casting lots for them to determine what every man should take
Luke 23:34 Then Jesus said, "Father, forgive them, for they do not know what they do." And they *divided His garments* and cast lots

DIVIDED MY GARMENTS
Matt 27:35 They *divided My garments* among them, and for My clothing they cast lots
John 19:24 They *divided My garments* among them, and for My clothing they cast lots

DIVIDED THE SEA
Neh 9:11 And You *divided the sea* before them, so that they went through the midst of the sea on the dry land
Ps 74:13 You *divided the sea* by Your strength; You broke the heads of the sea serpents in the waters
Ps 78:13 He *divided the sea* and caused them to pass through
Is 51:15 But I am the Lord your God, who *divided the sea* whose waves roared the Lord of hosts is His name

DIVIDED THE WATERS
Gen 1:7 Thus God made the firmament, and *divided the waters* which were under the firmament from the waters which were above the firmament

DIVIDED UP HIS CLOTHES (NIV)
(See *DIVIDED HIS GARMENTS*)

DIVISION AMONG THEM
John 9:16 Others said, "How can a man who is a sinner do such miracles?" And there was a *division among them*

DIVISIONS AMONG YOU
1Cor 1:10 Now I plead with you, brethren, by the name of our Lord Jesus Christ, that you all speak the same thing, and that there be no *divisions among you*, but that you be perfectly joined together in the same mind and in the same judgment
1Cor 3:3 For where there are envy, strife, and *divisions among you*, are you not carnal and behaving like mere men
1Cor 11:18 For first of all, when you come together as a church, I hear that there are *divisions among you*, and in part I believe it

DO GOOD
Lev 5:4 Or if a person swears, speaking thoughtlessly with his lips to do evil or to *do good*, whatever it is that a man may pronounce by an oath, and it is hidden from him when he realizes it, then he shall be guilty in any of these matters
Ps 34:14 Depart from evil, and *do good;* seek peace, and pursue it
Ps 36:3 He has ceased to be wise and to *do good*
Ps 37:3 Trust in the Lord, and *do good;* dwell in the land, and feed on His faithfulness
Ps 37:27 Depart from evil, and *do good;* and dwell forevermore
Ps 51:18 *Do good* in Your good pleasure to Zion; build the walls of Jerusalem
Ps 119:68 You are good, and *do good;* teach me Your statutes
Ps 125:4 *Do good*, O Lord, to those who are good, and to those who are upright in their hearts
Eccl 3:12 I know that there is nothing better for them than to rejoice, and to *do good* in their lives
Is 1:17 learn to *do good;* seek justice, reprove the oppressor; defend the fatherless, plead for the widow
Is 41:23 yes, *do good* or do evil, that we may be dismayed and see it together
Jer 4:22 They are wise to do evil, but to *do good* they have no knowledge
Jer 13:23 Then may you also *do good* who are accustomed to do evil
Mic 2:7 Do not My words *do good* to him who walks uprightly
Zeph 1:12 And it shall come to pass at that time that I will search Jerusalem with lamps, and punish the men who are settled in complacency, who say in their heart, 'The Lord will not *do good*, nor will He do evil
Zech 8:15 so again in these days I am determined to *do good* to Jerusalem and to the house of Judah
Matt 5:44 But I say to you, love your enemies, bless those who curse you, *do good* to those who hate you, and pray for those who spitefully use you and persecute you
Matt 12:12 Therefore it is lawful to *do good* on the Sabbath
Mark 3:4 And He said to them, "Is it lawful on the Sabbath to *do good* or to do evil, to save life or to kill
Luke 6:9 Is it lawful on the Sabbath to *do good* or to do evil, to save life or to destroy it
Luke 6:27 Love your enemies, *do good* to those who hate you
Luke 6:33 And if you *do good* to those who *do good* to you, what credit is that to you
Luke 6:35 But love your enemies, *do good*, and lend, hoping for nothing in return
Rom 7:21 I find then a law, that evil is present with me, the one who wills to *do good*
Gal 6:10 Therefore, as we have opportunity, let us *do good* to all, especially to those who are of the household of faith
1Tim 6:18 Let them *do good*, that they be rich in good works, ready to give, willing to share
Heb 13:16 But do not forget to *do good* and to share, for with such sacrifices God is well pleased
Jas 4:17 Therefore, to him who knows to *do good* and does not do it, to him it is sin
1Pet 2:14 or to governors, as to those who are sent by him for the punishment of evildoers and for the praise of those who *do good*
1Pet 2:20 But when you *do good* and suffer for it,

if you take it patiently, this is commendable before God
1Pet 3:6 as Sarah obeyed Abraham, calling him lord, whose daughters you are if you *do good* and are not afraid with any terror
1Pet 3:11 let him turn away from evil and *do good;* let him seek peace and pursue it

DO JUDGMENT AND JUSTICE (KJV)
(See *DO JUSTICE AND RIGHTEOUSNESS*)

DO JUSTICE AND RIGHTEOUSNESS
1Kin 10:9 Because the Lord has loved Israel forever, therefore He made you king, to *do justice and righteousness*
2Chr 9:8 Because your God has loved Israel, to establish them forever, therefore He made you king over them, to *do justice and righteousness*
Jer 22:15 Did not your father eat and drink, and *do justice and righteousness*

DO ME THE KINDNESS (RSV)
(See *SHOW KINDNESS*)

DO MY ORDINANCES AND KEEP MY STATUES (RSV)
(See *MY STATUTES AND MY JUDGMENTS*)

DO NOT ACCEPT A BRIBE (NIV)
(See *TAKE NO BRIBE*)

DO NOT BE AFRAID
Gen 15:1 After these things the word of the Lord came to Abram in a vision, saying, "*Do not be afraid*, Abram
Gen 43:23 But he said, "Peace be with you, *do not be afraid*
Gen 50:19 Joseph said to them, "*Do not be afraid*, for am I in the place of God
Gen 50:21 Now therefore, *do not be afraid;* I will provide for you and your little ones
Ex 14:13 And Moses said to the people, "*Do not be afraid*
Deut 20:1 When you go out to battle against your enemies, and see horses and chariots and people more numerous than you, *do not be afraid* of them
Deut 20:3 do not let your heart faint, *do not be afraid*, and do not tremble or be terrified because of them
Josh 1:9 *do not be afraid*, nor be dismayed, for the Lord your God is with you wherever you go
Josh 8:1 *Do not be afraid*, nor be dismayed; take all the people of war with you, and arise, go up to Ai
Josh 10:25 Then Joshua said to them, "*Do not be afraid*, nor be dismayed
Josh 11:6 But the Lord said to Joshua, "*Do not be afraid* because of them, for tomorrow about this time I will deliver all of them slain before Israel
1Sam 28:13 And the king said to her, "*Do not be afraid*
2Sam 13:28 *Do not be afraid*. Have I not commanded you? Be courageous and valiant
2Kin 1:15 *do not be afraid* of him." So he arose and went down with him to the king
2Kin 19:6 *Do not be afraid* of the words which you have heard, with which the servants of the king of Assyria have blasphemed Me
2Kin 25:24 And Gedaliah took an oath before them and their men, and said to them, "*Do not be afraid* of the servants of the Chaldeans
2Chr 20:15 *Do not be afraid* nor dismayed because of this great multitude, for the battle is not yours, but God's
2Chr 32:7 *do not be afraid* nor dismayed before the king of Assyria, nor before all the multitude that is with him
Neh 4:14 And I looked, and arose and said to the nobles, to the leaders, and to the rest of the people, "*Do not be afraid* of them
Ps 49:16 *Do not be afraid* when one becomes rich, when the glory of his house is increased
Prov 3:25 *Do not be afraid* of sudden terror, nor of trouble from the wicked when it comes
Is 10:24 O My people, who dwell in Zion, *do not be afraid* of the Assyrian
Is 37:6 *Do not be afraid* of the words which you have heard, with which the servants of the king of Assyria have blasphemed Me
Jer 1:8 *Do not be afraid* of their faces, for I am with you to deliver you
Jer 10:5 *Do not be afraid* of them, for they cannot do evil, nor can they do any good
Jer 40:9 And Gedaliah the son of Ahikam, the son of Shaphan, took an oath before them and thcir men, saying, "*Do not be afraid* to serve the Chaldeans
Jer 42:11 *Do not be afraid* of the king of Babylon, of whom you are afraid; *do not be afraid* of him
Ezek 2:6 And you, son of man, *do not be afraid* of them nor be afraid of their words, though briers and thorns are with you and you dwell among scorpions; *do not be afraid* of their words or dismayed by their looks, though they are a rebellious house
Ezek 3:9 *do not be afraid* of them, nor be dismayed at their looks, though they are a rebellious house
Joel 2:22 *Do not be afraid*, you beasts of the field; for the open pastures are springing up, and the tree bears its fruit
Matt 1:20 But while he thought about these things, behold, an angel of the Lord appeared to him in a dream, saying, "Joseph, son of David, *do not be afraid* to take to you Mary your wife, for that which is conceived in her is of the Holy Spirit
Matt 14:27 But immediately Jesus spoke to them, saying, "Be of good cheer! It is I; *do not be afraid*
Matt 17:7 But Jesus came and touched them and said, "Arise, and *do not be afraid*
Matt 28:5 But the angel answered and said to the women, "*Do not be afraid*, for I know that you seek Jesus who was crucified
Matt 28:10 Then Jesus said to them, "*Do not be afraid*. Go and tell My brethren to go to Galilee, and there they will see Me
Mark 5:36 As soon as Jesus heard the word that was spoken, He said to the ruler of the synagogue, "*Do not be afraid*
Mark 6:50 And immediately He talked with them and said to them, "Be of good cheer! It is I; *do not be afraid*
Luke 1:13 But the angel said to him, "*Do not be afraid*, Zacharias, for your prayer is heard
Luke 1:30 Then the angel said to her, "*Do not be afraid*, Mary, for you have found favor with God
Luke 2:10 Then the angel said to them, "*Do not be afraid*, for behold, I bring you good tidings of great joy which will be to all people
Luke 5:10 And Jesus said to Simon, "*Do not be afraid*. From now on you will catch men
Luke 8:50 But when Jesus heard it, He answered him, saying, "*Do not be afraid*
Luke 12:4 And I say to you, My friends, *do not be afraid* of those who kill the body, and after that have no more that they can do
John 6:20 But He said to them, "It is I; *do not be afraid*
Acts 18:9 Now the Lord spoke to Paul in the night by a vision, "*Do not be afraid*, but speak, and do not keep silent
Acts 27:24 saying, '*Do not be afraid*, Paul; you must be brought before Caesar

1Pet 3:14 And *do not be afraid* of their threats, nor be troubled
Rev 1:17 But He laid His right hand on me, saying to me, "*Do not be afraid*

DO NOT BE DECEIVED
1Cor 6:9 *Do not be deceived.* Neither fornicators, nor idolaters, nor adulterers, nor homosexuals, nor sodomites
1Cor 15:33 *Do not be deceived:* "Evil company corrupts good habits
Gal 6:7 *Do not be deceived,* God is not mocked; for whatever a man sows, that he will also reap
Jas 1:16 *Do not be deceived,* my beloved brethren

DO NOT BE MISMATED (RSV)
(See *UNEQUALLY YOKED*)

DO NOT BE UNWISE
Eph 5:17 Therefore *do not be unwise,* but understand what the will of the Lord is

DO NOT BE YOKED TOGETHER (NIV)
(See *UNEQUALLY YOKED*)

DO NOT BELONG TO THE WORLD (NIV)
(See *NOT OF THE WORLD*)

DO NOT BOAST ABOUT TOMORROW
Prov 27:1 *Do not boast about tomorrow,* for you do not know what a day may bring forth

DO NOT ENVY A VIOLENT MAN (NIV)
(See *DO NOT ENVY THE OPPRESSOR*)

DO NOT ENVY THE OPPRESSOR
Prov 3:31 *Do not envy the oppressor,* and choose none of his ways

DO NOT FEAR
Gen 26:24 *do not fear,* for I am with you. I will bless you and multiply your descendants for My servant Abraham's sake
Gen 35:17 Now it came to pass, when she was in hard labor, that the midwife said to her, "*Do not fear*
Gen 46:3 *do not fear* to go down to Egypt, for I will make of you a great nation there
Ex 20:20 And Moses said to the people, "*Do not fear;* for God has come to test you, and that His fear may be before you, so that you may not sin
Num 14:9 their protection has departed from them, and the Lord is with us. *Do not fear* them
Num 21:34 Then the Lord said to Moses, "*Do not fear* him, for I have delivered him into your hand, with all his people and his land
Deut 1:21 go up and possess it, as the Lord God of your fathers has spoken to you; *do not fear* or be discouraged
Deut 3:2 And the Lord said to me, '*Do not fear* him, for I have delivered him and all his people and his land into your hand
Deut 31:6 Be strong and of good courage, *do not fear* nor be afraid of them
Deut 31:8 He will be with you, He will not leave you nor forsake you; *do not fear* nor be dismayed
Josh 10:8 And the Lord said to Joshua, "*Do not fear* them, for I have delivered them into your hand
Judg 4:18 *do not fear.*" And when he had turned aside with her into the tent, she covered him with a blanket
Judg 6:10 *do not fear* the gods of the Amorites, in whose land you dwell
Judg 6:23 Then the Lord said to him, "Peace be with you; *do not fear,* you shall not die
Ruth 3:11 And now, my daughter, *do not fear.* I will do for you all that you request, for all the people of my town know that you are a virtuous woman
1Sam 4:20 And about the time of her death the women who stood by her said to her, "*Do not fear,* for you have borne a son
1Sam 12:20 Then Samuel said to the people, "*Do not fear.* You have done all this wickedness
1Sam 22:23 *do not fear.* For he who seeks my life seeks your life, but with me you shall be safe
1Sam 23:17 And he said to him, "*Do not fear,* for the hand of Saul my father shall not find you
2Sam 9:7 So David said to him, "*Do not fear,* for I will surely show you kindness for Jonathan your father's sake, and will restore to you all the land of Saul your grandfather
1Kin 17:13 And Elijah said to her, "*Do not fear;* go and do as you have said, but make me a small cake from it first, and bring it to me
2Kin 6:16 So he answered, "*Do not fear,* for those who are with us are more than those who are with them
2Kin 17:34 they *do not fear* the Lord, nor do they follow their statutes or their ordinances, or the law and commandment which the Lord had commanded the children of Jacob, whom He named Israel
1Chr 22:13 Be strong and of good courage; *do not fear* nor be dismayed
1Chr 28:20 *do not fear* nor be dismayed, for the Lord God my God will be with you
2Chr 20:17 *Do not fear* or be dismayed; tomorrow go out against them, for the Lord is with you
Ps 55:19 Because they do not change, therefore they *do not fear* God
Ps 64:4 That they may shoot in secret at the blameless; suddenly they shoot at him and *do not fear*
Is 7:4 *do not fear* or be fainthearted for these two stubs of smoking firebrands, for the fierce anger of Rezin and Syria, and the son of Remaliah
Is 35:4 Say to those who are fearful-hearted, "Be strong, *do not fear*
Is 44:8 *Do not fear,* nor be afraid; have I not told you from that time, and declared it
Is 51:7 *do not fear* the reproach of men, nor be afraid of their revilings
Is 54:4 *Do not fear,* for you will not be ashamed; nor be disgraced, for you will not be put to shame
Is 57:11 Is it not because I have held My peace from of old that you *do not fear* Me
Jer 30:10 Therefore *do not fear,* O My servant Jacob,' says the Lord
Jer 46:27 But *do not fear,* O My servant Jacob, and do not be dismayed, O Israel
Jer 46:28 *Do not fear,* O Jacob My servant," says the Lord
Lam 3:57 You drew near on the day I called on You, and said, "*Do not fear*
Dan 10:12 Then he said to me, "*Do not fear,* Daniel, for from the first day that you set your heart to understand, and to humble yourself before your God, your words were heard
Zeph 3:16 *Do not fear;* Zion, let not your hands be weak
Hag 2:5 According to the word that I covenanted with you when you came out of Egypt, so My Spirit remains among you; *do not fear*
Zech 8:13 And it shall come to pass that just as you were a curse among the nations, O house of Judah and house of Israel, so I will save you, and you shall be a blessing. *Do not fear,* let your hands be strong
Zech 8:15 so again in these days I am determined to do good to Jerusalem and to the house of Judah. *Do not fear*
Mal 3:5 I will be a swift witness against sorcerers, against adulterers, against perjurers, against those who exploit wage earners and widows and

the fatherless, and against those who turn away an alien because they *do not fear* Me
Matt 10:26 Therefore *do not fear* them. For there is nothing covered that will not be revealed, and hidden that will not be known
Matt 10:28 And *do not fear* those who kill the body but cannot kill the soul
Matt 10:31 *Do not fear* therefore; you are of more value than many sparrows
Luke 12:7 *Do not fear* therefore; you are of more value than many sparrows
Luke 12:32 *Do not fear*, little flock, for it is your Father's good pleasure to give you the kingdom
Luke 18:4 but afterward he said within himself, 'Though I *do not fear* God nor regard man
Rev 2:10 *Do not fear* any of those things which you are about to suffer

DO NOT FORBID
Matt 19:14 But Jesus said, "Let the little children come to Me, and *do not forbid* them
Mark 9:39 But Jesus said, "*Do not forbid* him, for no one who works a miracle in My name can soon afterward speak evil of Me
Mark 10:14 But when Jesus saw it, He was greatly displeased and said to them, "Let the little children come to Me, and *do not forbid* them
Luke 9:50 But Jesus said to him, "*Do not forbid* him, for he who is not against us is for us
Luke 18:16 But Jesus called them to Him and said, "Let the little children come to Me, and *do not forbid* them
1Cor 14:39 Therefore, brethren, desire earnestly to prophesy, and *do not forbid* to speak with tongues

DO NOT FORGET
Deut 8:11 Beware that you *do not forget* the Lord your God by not keeping His commandments, His judgments, and His statutes which I command you today
Deut 9:7 Remember and *do not forget* how you provoked the Lord your God to wrath in the wilderness
Ps 10:12 O God, lift up Your hand! *Do not forget* the humble
Ps 74:19 Oh, do not deliver the life of Your turtledove to the wild beast! *Do not forget* the life of Your poor forever
Ps 74:23 *Do not forget* the voice of your enemies; the tumult of those who rise up against you increases continually
Ps 119:83 For I have become like a wineskin in smoke, yet I *do not forget* Your statutes
Ps 119:109 My life is continually in my hand, yet I *do not forget* Your law
Ps 119:141 I am small and despised, yet I *do not forget* Your precepts
Ps 119:153 Consider my affliction and deliver me, for I *do not forget* Your law
Ps 119:176 Seek Your servant, for I *do not forget* Your commandments
Prov 3:1 My son, *do not forget* my law, but let your heart keep my commands
Prov 4:5 *Do not forget*, nor turn away from the words of my mouth
Heb 13:2 *Do not forget* to entertain strangers, for by so doing some have unwittingly entertained angels
Heb 13:16 But *do not forget* to do good and to share, for with such sacrifices God is well pleased
2Pet 3:8 But, beloved, *do not forget* this one thing, that with the Lord one day is as a thousand years, and a thousand years as one day

DO NOT FORSAKE
Deut 12:19 Take heed to yourself that you *do not forsake* the Levite as long as you live in your land
Josh 10:6 And the men of Gibeon sent to Joshua at the camp at Gilgal, saying, "*Do not forsake* your servants
Ps 38:21 *Do not forsake* me, O Lord; O my God, be not far from me
Ps 71:9 Do not cast me off in the time of old age; *do not forsake* me when my strength fails
Ps 71:18 Now also when I am old and grayheaded, O God, *do not forsake* me, until I declare Your strength to this generation, Your power to everyone who is to come
Ps 119:8 I will keep Your statutes; oh, *do not forsake* me utterly
Ps 138:8 Your mercy, O Lord, endures forever; *do not forsake* the works of Your hands
Prov 1:8 My son, hear the instruction of your father, and *do not forsake* the law of your mother
Prov 4:2 for I give you good doctrine: *Do not forsake* my law
Prov 4:6 *Do not forsake* her, and she will preserve you; love her, and she will keep you
Prov 6:20 My son, keep your father's command, and *do not forsake* the law of your mother
Prov 27:10 *Do not forsake* your own friend or your father's friend, nor go to your brother's house in the day of your calamity

DO NOT HARDEN YOUR HEARTS
Ps 95:8 *Do not harden your hearts*, as in the rebellion, and as in the day of trial in the wilderness
Heb 3:8 *do not harden your hearts* as in the rebellion, in the day of trial in the wilderness
Heb 3:15 Today, if you will hear His voice, *do not harden your hearts* as in the rebellion
Heb 4:7 Today, if you will hear His voice, *do not harden your hearts*

DO NOT HINDER THEM (NAS, NIV, RSV)
(See *DO NOT FORBID*)

DO NOT LOSE HEART
2Cor 4:1 Therefore, since we have this ministry, as we have received mercy, we *do not lose heart*
2Cor 4:16 Therefore we *do not lose heart*. Even though our outward man is perishing, yet the inward man is being renewed day by day
Gal 6:9 And let us not grow weary while doing good, for in due season we shall reap if we *do not lose heart*
Eph 3:13 Therefore I ask that you *do not lose heart* at my tribulations for you, which is your glory

DO NOT PUT OUT THE SPIRIT'S FIRE (NIV)
(See *QUENCH THE SPIRIT*)

DO NOT SPEAK OF IT (NIV)
(See *KEEP SILENT*)

DO NOT YET KNOW (NIV)
(See *HAVE NO KNOWLEDGE*)

DO THE WHOLE LAW (KJV)
(See *KEEP THE WHOLE LAW*)

DO THIS AND LIVE
Gen 42:18 Then Joseph said to them the third day, "*Do this and live*, for I fear God

DO TWO WALK TOGETHER (NIV, RSV)
(See *CAN TWO WALK TOGETHER*)

DO WHAT IS RIGHT IN THE EYES OF THE LORD
Deut 13:18 because you have listened to the voice of the Lord your God, to keep all His commandments which I command you today, to *do what is right in the eyes of the Lord* your God

DO YOU LOVE ME
John 21:15 So when they had eaten breakfast, Jesus said to Simon Peter, "Simon, son of Jonah, *do you love Me* more than these
John 21:16 He said to him again a second time, "Simon, son of Jonah, *do you love Me*
John 21:17 He said to him the third time, "Simon, son of Jonah, *do you love Me?*" Peter was grieved because He said to him the third time, "*Do you love Me*

DO YOU NOT KNOW
Judg 15:11 Then three thousand men of Judah went down to the cleft of the rock of Etam, and said to Samson, "*Do you not know* that the Philistines rule over us
2Sam 2:26 *Do you not know* that it will be bitter in the latter end
2Sam 3:38 Then the king said to his servants, "*Do you not know* that a prince and a great man has fallen this day in Israel
2Chr 32:13 *Do you not know* what I and my fathers have done to all the peoples of other lands
Job 20:4 *Do you not know* this of old, since man was placed on earth
Job 21:29 Have you not asked those who travel the road? And *do you not know* their signs
Ezek 17:12 *Do you not know* what these things mean?' Tell them
Zech 4:5 Then the angel who talked with me answered and said to me, "*Do you not know* what these are
Zech 4:13 Then he answered me and said, "*Do you not know* what these are
John 19:10 *Do You not know* that I have power to crucify You, and power to release You
Rom 6:3 Or *do you not know* that as many of us as were baptized into Christ Jesus were baptized into His death
Rom 6:16 *Do you not know* that to whom you present yourselves slaves to obey, you are that one's slaves whom you obey, whether of sin to death, or of obedience to righteousness
Rom 7:1 Or *do you not know*, brethren (for I speak to those who know the law
Rom 11:2 Or *do you not know* what the Scripture says of Elijah, how he pleads with God against Israel, saying
1Cor 3:16 *Do you not know* that you are the temple of God and that the Spirit of God dwells in you
1Cor 5:6 *Do you not know* that a little leaven leavens the whole lump
1Cor 6:2 *Do you not know* that the saints will judge the world
1Cor 6:3 *Do you not know* that we shall judge angels? How much more, things that pertain to this life
1Cor 6:9 *Do you not know* that the unrighteous will not inherit the kingdom of God
1Cor 6:15 *Do you not know* that your bodies are members of Christ
1Cor 6:16 Or *do you not know* that he who is joined to a harlot is one body with her
1Cor 6:19 Or *do you not know* that your body is the temple of the Holy Spirit who is in you, whom you have from God, and you are not your own
1Cor 9:13 *Do you not know* that those who minister the holy things eat of the things of the temple, and those who serve at the altar partake of the offerings of the altar
1Cor 9:24 *Do you not know* that those who run in a race all run, but one receives the prize
2Cor 13:5 *Do you not know* yourselves, that Jesus Christ is in you
Jas 4:4 *Do you not know* that friendship with the world is enmity with God

DO YOU TRULY LOVE ME (NIV)
(See *DO YOU LOVE ME*)

DOCTORS OF THE LAW (KJV)
(See *TEACHERS OF THE LAW*)

DOCTRINE OF CHRIST
2Jn 9 Whoever transgresses and does not abide in the *doctrine of Christ* does not have God. He who abides in the *doctrine of Christ* has both the Father and the Son

DOERS OF THE WORD
Jas 1:22 But be *doers of the word*, and not hearers only, deceiving yourselves

DOES WHAT IS RIGHT (RSV)
(See *WORKS RIGHTEOUSNESS*)

DOES WHAT IS RIGHTEOUS (NIV)
(See *WORKS RIGHTEOUSNESS*)

DOG RETURNS TO HIS OWN VOMIT
Prov 26:11 As a *dog returns to his own vomit*, so a fool repeats his folly
2Pet 2:22 A *dog returns to his own vomit*," and, "a sow, having washed, to her wallowing in the mire

DOING A KINDNESS (NIV)
(See *SHOW MERCY*)

DOING WHAT IS RIGHT IN THE SIGHT OF THE LORD (NAS, RSV)
(See *DO WHAT IS RIGHT IN THE EYES OF THE LORD*)

DON'T YOU REALIZE (NIV)
(See *DO YOU NOT KNOW*)

DOOMED TO DESTRUCTION
Lev 27:29 No person under the ban, who may become *doomed to destruction* among men, shall be redeemed, but shall surely be put to death
Deut 7:26 Nor shall you bring an abomination into your house, lest you be *doomed to destruction* like it
Josh 7:12 Therefore the children of Israel could not stand before their enemies, but turned their backs before their enemies, because they have become *doomed to destruction*

DOOR OF HOPE
Hos 2:15 I will give her her vineyards from there, and the Valley of Achor as a *door of hope*

DOORKEEPER IN THE HOUSE OF MY GOD
Ps 84:10 I would rather be a *doorkeeper in the house of my God* than dwell in the tents of wickedness

DOORS OF HEAVEN
Ps 78:23 Yet He had commanded the clouds above, and opened the *doors of heaven*

DOORS OF THE TEMPLE
2Kin 18:16 At that time Hezekiah stripped the gold from the *doors of the temple* of the Lord, and from the pillars which Hezekiah king of Judah had overlaid, and gave it to the king of Assyria
Neh 6:10 and he said, "Let us meet together in the house of God, within the temple, and let us close the *doors of the temple*, for they are coming to kill you
Ezek 41:25 Cherubim and palm trees were carved on the *doors of the temple* just as they were carved on the walls

DOUBLE PORTION
Deut 21:17 But he shall acknowledge the son of the unloved wife as the firstborn by giving him a *double portion* of all that he has, for he is the beginning of his strength
1Sam 1:5 But to Hannah he would give a *double portion*, for he loved Hannah, although the Lord had closed her womb
2Kin 2:9 And Elisha said, "Please let a *double portion* of your spirit be upon me

DOUBLE-EDGED SWORD (NIV)
(See *TWO-EDGED SWORD*)

DOUBLE-MINDED MAN
Jas 1:8 he is a *double-minded man*, unstable in all his ways

DOWN TO THE SEA IN SHIPS
Ps 107:23 Those who go *down to the sea in ships*, who do business on great waters

DRAIN AWAY YOUR LIFE (NIV)
(See *SORROW OF HEART*)

DRAW ALL PEOPLES TO MYSELF
John 12:32 And I, if I am lifted up from the earth, will *draw all peoples to Myself*

DRAW NEAR TO GOD
1Sam 14:36 Then the priest said, "Let us *draw near to God* here
Ps 73:28 But it is good for me to *draw near to God*
Heb 7:19 on the other hand, there is the bringing in of a better hope, through which we *draw near to God*
Jas 4:8 *Draw near to God* and He will draw near to you

DRAW OUT A SWORD AFTER THEM
Ezek 5:2 then you shall take one-third and strike around it with the sword, and one-third you shall scatter in the wind: I will *draw out a sword after them*
Ezek 5:12 and I will scatter another third to all the winds, and I will *draw out a sword after them*

DREAD OF THE LORD (NIV)
(See *TERROR OF THE LORD*)

DRENCH MY COUCH WITH MY TEARS
Ps 6:6 All night I make my bed swim; I *drench my couch with my tears*

DRENCHED WITH BLOOD (NIV)
(See *SOAKED WITH BLOOD*)

DRESS MODESTLY (NIV)
(See *MODEST APPAREL*)

DRINK AT MY TABLE
Luke 22:30 that you may eat and *drink at My table* in My kingdom, and sit on thrones judging the twelve tribes of Israel

DRINK HIS BLOOD
John 6:53 Then Jesus said to them, "Most assuredly, I say to you, unless you eat the flesh of the Son of Man and *drink His blood*, you have no life in you

DRINK INTO ONE SPIRIT
1Cor 12:13 For by one Spirit we were all baptized into one body whether Jews or Greeks, whether slaves or free and have all been made to *drink into one Spirit*

DRINK NO WINE
Judg 13:7 Now *drink no wine* or similar drink, nor eat anything unclean, for the child shall be a Nazirite to God from the womb to the day of his death
Jer 35:6 But they said, "We will *drink no wine*, for Jonadab the son of Rechab, our father, commanded us, saying, 'You shall *drink no wine*, you nor your sons, forever
Jer 35:8 Thus we have obeyed the voice of Jonadab the son of Rechab, our father, in all that he charged us, to *drink no wine* all our days, we, our wives, our sons, or our daughters

DRINK OFFERING
Gen 35:14 and he poured a *drink offering* on it, and he poured oil on it
Ex 29:40 With the one lamb shall be one-tenth of an ephah of flour mixed with one-fourth of a hin of pressed oil, and one-fourth of a hin of wine as a *drink offering*
Ex 29:41 and you shall offer with it the grain offering and the *drink offering*, as in the morning, for a sweet aroma, an offering made by fire to the Lord
Ex 30:9 You shall not offer strange incense on it, or a burnt offering, or a grain offering; nor shall you pour a *drink offering* on it
Lev 23:13 and its *drink offering* shall be of wine, one-fourth of a hin
Num 6:17 the priest shall also offer its grain offering and its *drink offering*
Num 15:5 and one-fourth of a hin of wine as a *drink offering* you shall prepare with the burnt offering or the sacrifice, for each lamb
Num 15:7 and as a *drink offering* you shall offer one-third of a hin of wine as a sweet aroma to the Lord
Num 15:10 and you shall bring as the *drink offering* half a hin of wine as an offering made by fire, a sweet aroma to the Lord
Num 15:24 then it will be, if it is unintentionally committed, without the knowledge of the congregation, that the whole congregation shall offer one young bull as a burnt offering, as a sweet aroma to the Lord, with its grain offering and its *drink offering*, according to the ordinance, and one kid of the goats as a sin offering
Num 28:7 And its *drink offering* shall be one-fourth of a hin for each lamb
Num 28:8 as the morning grain offering and its *drink offering*, you shall offer it as an offering made by fire, a sweet aroma to the Lord
Num 28:9 And on the Sabbath day two lambs in their first year, without blemish, and two-tenths of an ephah of fine flour as a grain offering, mixed with oil, with its *drink offering*
Num 28:10 this is the burnt offering for every Sabbath, besides the regular burnt offering with its *drink offering*
Num 28:14 Their *drink offering* shall be half a hin of wine for a bull, one-third of a hin for a ram, and one-fourth of a hin for a lamb
Num 28:15 Also one kid of the goats as a sin offering to the Lord shall be offered, besides the regular burnt offering and its *drink offering*
Num 28:24 it shall be offered besides the regular burnt offering and its *drink offering*
Num 29:16 also one kid of the goats as a sin offering, besides the regular burnt offering, its grain offering, and its *drink offering*
Num 29:22 also one goat as a sin offering, besides the regular burnt offering, its grain offering, and its *drink offering*
Num 29:25 also one kid of the goats as a sin offering, besides the regular burnt offering, its grain offering, and its *drink offering*
Num 29:28 also one goat as a sin offering, besides

the regular burnt offering, its grain offering, and its *drink offering*
Num 29:31 also one goat as a sin offering, besides the regular burnt offering, its grain offering, and its *drink offering*
Num 29:34 also one goat as a sin offering, besides the regular burnt offering, its grain offering, and its *drink offering*
Num 29:38 also one goat as a sin offering, besides the regular burnt offering, its grain offering, and its *drink offering*
Deut 32:38 Who ate the fat of their sacrifices, and drank the wine of their *drink offering*
2Kin 16:13 and he poured his *drink offering* and sprinkled the blood of his peace offerings on the altar
Is 57:6 Even to them you have poured a *drink offering*, you have offered a grain offering
Is 65:11 But you are those who forsake the Lord, who forget My holy mountain, who prepare a table for Gad, and who furnish a *drink offering* for Meni
Joel 1:9 The grain offering and the *drink offering* have been cut off from the house of the Lord
Joel 1:13 for the grain offering and the *drink offering* are withheld from the house of your God
Joel 2:14 Who knows if He will turn and relent, and leave a blessing behind Him a grain offering and a *drink offering* for the Lord your God
Phil 2:17 Yes, and if I am being poured out as a *drink offering* on the sacrifice and service of your faith, I am glad and rejoice with you all
2Tim 4:6 For I am already being poured out as a *drink offering*, and the time of my departure is at hand

DRINK OFFERINGS
Lev 23:18 They shall be as a burnt offering to the Lord, with their grain offering and their *drink offerings*, an offering made by fire for a sweet aroma to the Lord
Lev 23:37 These are the feasts of the Lord which you shall proclaim to be holy convocations, to offer an offering made by fire to the Lord, a burnt offering and a grain offering, a sacrifice and *drink offerings*, everything on its day
Num 6:15 a basket of unleavened bread, cakes of fine flour mixed with oil, unleavened wafers anointed with oil, and their grain offering with their *drink offerings*
Num 28:31 You shall present them with their *drink offerings*, besides the regular burnt offering with its grain offering
Num 29:6 besides the burnt offering with its grain offering for the New Moon, the regular burnt offering with its grain offering, and their *drink offerings*, according to their ordinance, as a sweet aroma, an offering made by fire to the Lord
Num 29:11 also one kid of the goats as a sin offering, besides the sin offering for atonement, the regular burnt offering with its grain offering, and their *drink offerings*
Num 29:18 and their grain offering and their *drink offerings* for the bulls, for the rams, and for the lambs, by their number, according to the ordinance
Num 29:19 also one kid of the goats as a sin offering, besides the regular burnt offering with its grain offering, and their *drink offerings*
Num 29:21 and their grain offering and their *drink offerings* for the bulls, for the rams, and for the lambs, by their number, according to the ordinance
Num 29:24 and their grain offering and their *drink offerings* for the bulls, for the rams, and for the lambs, by their number, according to the ordinance
Num 29:27 and their grain offering and their *drink offerings* for the bulls, for the rams, and for the lambs, by their number, according to the ordinance
Num 29:30 and their grain offering and their *drink offerings* for the bulls, for the rams, and for the lambs, by their number, according to the ordinance
Num 29:33 and their grain offering and their *drink offerings* for the bulls, for the rams, and for the lambs, by their number, according to the ordinance
Num 29:37 and their grain offering and their *drink offerings* for the bull, for the ram, and for the lambs, by their number, according to the ordinance
Num 29:39 as your burnt offerings and your grain offerings, as your *drink offerings* and your peace offerings
2Kin 16:15 Then King Ahaz commanded Urijah the priest, saying, "On the great new altar burn the morning burnt offering, the evening grain offering, the king's burnt sacrifice, and his grain offering, with the burnt offering of all the people of the land, their grain offering, and their *drink offerings*
1Chr 29:21 a thousand bulls, a thousand rams, a thousand lambs, with their *drink offerings*, and sacrifices in abundance for all Israel
2Chr 29:35 Also the burnt offerings were in abundance, with the fat of the peace offerings and with the *drink offerings* for every burnt offering
Ezra 7:17 now therefore, be careful to buy with this money bulls, rams, and lambs, with their grain offerings and their *drink offerings*, and offer them on the altar of the house of your God in Jerusalem
Ps 16:4 Their *drink offerings* of blood I will not offer, nor take up their names on my lips
Jer 7:18 and they pour out *drink offerings* to other gods, that they may provoke Me to anger
Jer 19:13 And the houses of Jerusalem and the houses of the kings of Judah shall be defiled like the place of Tophet, because of all the houses on whose roofs they have burned incense to all the host of heaven, and poured out *drink offerings* to other gods
Jer 32:29 And the Chaldeans who fight against this city shall come and set fire to this city and burn it, with the houses on whose roofs they have offered incense to Baal and poured out *drink offerings* to other gods, to provoke Me to anger
Jer 44:17 But we will certainly do whatever has gone out of our own mouth, to burn incense to the queen of heaven and pour out *drink offerings* to her, as we have done, we and our fathers, our kings and our princes, in the cities of Judah and in the streets of Jerusalem
Jer 44:18 But since we stopped burning incense to the queen of heaven and pouring out *drink offerings* to her, we have lacked everything and have been consumed by the sword and by famine
Jer 44:19 The women also said, "And when we burned incense to the queen of heaven and poured out *drink offerings* to her, did we make cakes for her, to worship her, and pour out *drink offerings* to her without our husbands' permission
Jer 44:25 You and your wives have spoken with your mouths and fulfilled with your hands, saying, "We will surely perform our vows that we have made, to burn incense to the queen of heaven and pour out *drink offerings* to her
Ezek 20:28 There they also sent up their sweet aroma and poured out their *drink offerings*
Ezek 45:17 Then it shall be the prince's part to give burnt offerings, grain offerings, and *drink offerings*, at the feasts, the New Moons, the Sab-

baths, and at all the appointed seasons of the house of Israel

DRINK THE CUP
Matt 20:22 Are you able to *drink the cup* that I am about to drink, and be baptized with the baptism that I am baptized with
Mark 10:38 Can you *drink the cup* that I drink, and be baptized with the baptism that I am baptized with
Mark 10:39 And Jesus said to them, "You will indeed *drink the cup* that I drink, and with the baptism I am baptized with you will be baptized
John 18:11 Shall I not *drink the cup* which My Father has given Me
1Cor 10:21 You cannot *drink the cup* of the Lord and the cup of demons

DRINK THE WINE
Ps 60:3 You have shown Your people hard things; You have made us *drink the wine* of confusion
Prov 4:17 For they eat the bread of wickedness, and *drink the wine* of violence
Amos 2:8 They lie down by every altar on clothes taken in pledge, and *drink the wine* of the condemned in the house of their god

DRINK WINE
Gen 19:32 Come, let us make our father *drink wine*, and we will lie with him, that we may preserve the lineage of our father
Gen 19:33 So they made their father *drink wine* that night. And the firstborn went in and lay with her father, and he did not know when she lay down or when she arose
Gen 19:34 let us make him *drink wine* tonight also, and you go in and lie with him, that we may preserve the lineage of our father
Gen 19:35 Then they made their father *drink wine* that night also
Lev 10:9 Do not *drink wine* or intoxicating drink, you, nor your sons with you, when you go into the tabernacle of meeting, lest you die
Num 6:20 they are holy for the priest, together with the breast of the wave offering and the thigh of the heave offering. After that the Nazirite may *drink wine*
Judg 13:4 Now therefore, please be careful not to *drink wine* or similar drink, and not to eat any unclean thing
Judg 13:14 She may not eat anything that comes from the vine, nor may she *drink wine* or similar drink, nor eat anything unclean
Prov 31:4 It is not for kings, O Lemuel, it is not for kings to *drink wine*, nor for princes intoxicating drink
Is 24:9 They shall not *drink wine* with a song; strong drink is bitter to those who drink it
Jer 35:5 Then I set before the sons of the house of the Rechabites bowls full of wine, and cups; and I said to them, "*Drink wine*
Jer 35:14 The words of Jonadab the son of Rechab, which he commanded his sons, not to *drink wine*, are performed
Ezek 44:21 No priest shall *drink wine* when he enters the inner court
Amos 5:11 you have planted pleasant vineyards, but you shall not *drink wine* from them
Amos 6:6 who *drink wine* from bowls, and anoint yourselves with the best ointments, but are not grieved for the affliction of Joseph
Amos 9:14 they shall plant vineyards and *drink wine* from them; they shall also make gardens and eat fruit from them
Mic 6:15 you shall tread the olives, but not anoint yourselves with oil; and make sweet wine, but not *drink wine*
Rom 14:21 It is good neither to eat meat nor *drink wine* nor do anything by which your brother stumbles or is offended or is made weak

DRINKS MY BLOOD
John 6:54 Whoever eats My flesh and *drinks My blood* has eternal life, and I will raise him up at the last day
John 6:56 He who eats My flesh and *drinks My blood* abides in Me, and I in him

DRINKS THIS CUP
1Cor 11:27 Therefore whoever eats this bread or *drinks this cup* of the Lord in an unworthy manner will be guilty of the body and blood of the Lord

DRIVE OUT EVIL SPIRITS (NIV)
(See *POWER OVER UNCLEAN SPIRITS*)

DRIVE THEM OUT
Ex 6:1 For with a strong hand he will let them go, and with a strong hand he will *drive them out* of his land
Ex 23:29 I will not *drive them out* from before you in one year, lest the land become desolate and the beast of the field become too numerous for you
Ex 23:30 Little by little I will *drive them out* from before you, until you have increased, and you inherit the land
Ex 23:31 For I will deliver the inhabitants of the land into your hand, and you shall *drive them out* before you
Num 22:6 Perhaps I shall be able to defeat them and *drive them out* of the land, for I know that he whom you bless is blessed, and he whom you curse is cursed
Num 22:11 perhaps I shall be able to overpower them and *drive them out*
Deut 9:3 so you shall *drive them out* and destroy them quickly, as the Lord has said to you
Josh 14:12 It may be that the Lord will be with me, and I shall be able to *drive them out* as the Lord said
Josh 15:63 As for the Jebusites, the inhabitants of Jerusalem, the children of Judah could not *drive them out*
Josh 17:13 And it happened, when the children of Israel grew strong, that they put the Canaanites to forced labor, but did not utterly *drive them out*
Josh 23:5 And the Lord your God will expel them from before you and *drive them out* of your sight
Judg 1:28 And it came to pass, when Israel was strong, that they put the Canaanites under tribute, but did not completely *drive them out*
Judg 1:32 So the Asherites dwelt among the Canaanites, the inhabitants of the land; for they did not *drive them out*
Judg 2:3 Therefore I also said, 'I will not *drive them out* before you

DRIVES OUT DEMONS (NIV)
(See *CASTS OUT DEMONS*)

DRIVING OUT DEMONS (NIV)
(See *CASTING OUT DEMONS*)

DROP IN A BUCKET
Is 40:15 Behold, the nations are as a *drop in a bucket*, and are counted as the small dust on the balance

DROPS OF BLOOD
Luke 22:44 And His sweat became like great *drops of blood* falling down to the ground

DRUNK WITH BLOOD
Deut 32:42 I will make My arrows *drunk with blood*, and My sword shall devour flesh, with the

blood of the slain and the captives, from the heads of the leaders of the enemy

DRUNK WITH THE BLOOD
Rev 17:6 And I saw the woman, *drunk with the blood* of the saints and with the blood of the martyrs of Jesus

DRUNK WITH THE WINE
Rev 17:2 with whom the kings of the earth committed fornication, and the inhabitants of the earth were made *drunk with the wine* of her fornication

DRUNK WITH WINE
Eph 5:18 And do not be *drunk with wine*, in which is dissipation

DRUNKARD AND THE GLUTTON
Prov 23:21 for the *drunkard and the glutton* will come to poverty, and drowsiness will clothe a man with rags

DRUNKEN MAN STAGGERS
Is 19:14 and they have caused Egypt to err in all her work, as a *drunken man staggers* in his vomit

DRUNKEN WITH THE BLOOD (KJV)
(See *DRUNK WITH THE BLOOD*)

DRY AND THIRSTY LAND
Ps 63:1 My flesh longs for You in a *dry and thirsty land* where there is no water
Ezek 19:13 And now she is planted in the wilderness, in a *dry and thirsty land*

DRY AND WEARY LAND (NIV, RSV)
(See *DRY AND THIRSTY LAND*)

DRY BONES
Ezek 37:4 Again He said to me, "Prophesy to these bones, and say to them, 'O *dry bones*, hear the word of the Lord

DUG THROUGH THE WALL
Ezek 12:7 I brought out my belongings by day, as though going into captivity, and at evening I *dug through the wall* with my hand

DULL OF HEARING
Heb 5:11 of whom we have much to say, and hard to explain, since you have become *dull of hearing*

DUMB AND DEAF SPIRIT (KJV, RSV)
(See *DEAF AND DUMB SPIRIT*)

DUST AND ASHES
Gen 18:27 Then Abraham answered and said, "Indeed now, I who am but *dust and ashes* have taken it upon myself to speak to the Lord
Job 30:19 He has cast me into the mire, and I have become like *dust and ashes*
Job 42:6 Therefore I abhor myself, and repent in *dust and ashes*

DUST FROM YOUR FEET
Matt 10:14 And whoever will not receive you nor hear your words, when you depart from that house or city, shake off the *dust from your feet*
Luke 9:5 And whoever will not receive you, when you go out of that city, shake off the very *dust from your feet* as a testimony against them

DUST OF DEATH
Ps 22:15 My strength is dried up like a potsherd, and My tongue clings to My jaws; You have brought Me to the *dust of death*

DUST OF THE EARTH
Gen 13:16 And I will make your descendants as the *dust of the earth;* so that if a man could number the *dust of the earth*, then your descendants also could be numbered
Gen 28:14 Also your descendants shall be as the *dust of the earth*
Ex 8:17 For Aaron stretched out his hand with his rod and struck the *dust of the earth*, and it became lice on man and beast
2Sam 22:43 Then I beat them as fine as the *dust of the earth*
2Chr 1:9 Now, O Lord God, let Your promise to David my father be established, for You have made me king over a people like the *dust of the earth* in multitude
Is 40:12 Who has measured the waters in the hollow of his hand, measured heaven with a span and calculated the *dust of the earth* in a measure
Dan 12:2 And many of those who sleep in the *dust of the earth* shall awake, some to everlasting life, some to shame and everlasting contempt
Amos 2:7 They pant after the *dust of the earth* which is on the head of the poor, and pervert the way of the humble

DUST OF THE GROUND
Gen 2:7 And the Lord God formed man of the *dust of the ground*, and breathed into his nostrils the breath of life

DUST ON HIS HEAD
2Sam 1:2 on the third day, behold, it happened that a man came from Saul's camp with his clothes torn and *dust on his head*
2Sam 15:32 Now it happened when David had come to the top of the mountain, where he worshiped God, that there was Hushai the Archite, coming to meet him with his robe torn and *dust on his head*
Job 2:12 and each one tore his robe and sprinkled *dust on his head* toward heaven

DUST ON THEIR HEADS
Josh 7:6 Then Joshua tore his clothes, and fell to the earth on his face before the ark of the Lord until evening, both he and the elders of Israel; and they put *dust on their heads*
Neh 9:1 Now on the twenty-fourth day of this month the children of Israel were assembled with fasting, in sackcloth, and with *dust on their heads*
Lam 2:10 they throw *dust on their heads* and gird themselves with sackcloth
Ezek 27:30 they will cry bitterly and cast *dust on their heads*
Rev 18:19 And they threw *dust on their heads* and cried out, weeping and wailing, and saying

DWELL IN THE HOUSE OF THE LORD
Ps 23:6 And I will *dwell in the house of the Lord* forever
Ps 27:4 That I may *dwell in the house of the Lord* all the days of my life, to behold the beauty of the Lord, and to inquire in His temple

DWELL IN THE LAND
Gen 34:21 Therefore let them *dwell in the land* and trade in it
Gen 45:10 You shall *dwell in the land* of Goshen, and you shall be near to me, you and your children, your children's children, your flocks and your herds, and all that you have
Gen 46:34 that you shall say, 'Your servants' occupation has been with livestock from our youth even till now, both we and also our fathers,' that you may *dwell in the land* of Goshen
Gen 47:4 And they said to Pharaoh, "We have

come to *dwell in the land*, because your servants have no pasture for their flocks, for the famine is severe in the land of Canaan. Now therefore, please let your servants *dwell in the land* of Goshen

Gen 47:6 let them *dwell in the land* of Goshen. And if you know any competent men among them, then make them chief herdsmen over my livestock

Lev 25:18 So you shall observe My statutes and keep My judgments, and perform them; and you will *dwell in the land* in safety

Num 13:28 Nevertheless the people who *dwell in the land* are strong

Num 13:29 The Amalekites *dwell in the land* of the South; the Hittites, the Jebusites, and the Amorites dwell in the mountains

Num 35:32 And you shall take no ransom for him who has fled to his city of refuge, that he may return to *dwell in the land* before the death of the priest

Deut 12:10 But when you cross over the Jordan and *dwell in the land* which the Lord your God is giving you to inherit, and when He gives you rest from all your enemies round about, so that you dwell in safety

Deut 30:20 and that you may *dwell in the land* which the Lord swore to your fathers, to Abraham, Isaac, and Jacob, to give them

Josh 17:16 and all the Canaanites who *dwell in the land* of the valley have chariots of iron, both those who are of Beth Shean and its towns and those who are of the Valley of Jezreel

2Kin 25:24 *Dwell in the land* and serve the king of Babylon, and it shall be well with you

Ps 37:3 Trust in the Lord, and do good; *dwell in the land*, and feed on His faithfulness

Prov 2:21 For the upright will *dwell in the land*, and the blameless will remain in it

Jer 24:8 And as the bad figs which cannot be eaten, they are so bad' surely thus says the Lord 'so will I give up Zedekiah the king of Judah, his princes, the residue of Jerusalem who remain in this land, and those who *dwell in the land* of Egypt

Jer 25:5 They said, 'Repent now everyone of his evil way and his evil doings, and *dwell in the land* that the Lord has given to you and your fathers forever and ever

Jer 35:15 then you will *dwell in the land* which I have given you and your fathers

Jer 40:9 *Dwell in the land* and serve the king of Babylon, and it shall be well with you

Jer 43:5 But Johanan the son of Kareah and all the captains of the forces took all the remnant of Judah who had returned to *dwell in the land* of Judah, from all nations where they had been driven

Jer 44:1 The word that came to Jeremiah concerning all the Jews who *dwell in the land* of Egypt, who dwell at Migdol, at Tahpanhes, at Noph, and in the country of Pathros, saying

Jer 44:13 For I will punish those who *dwell in the land* of Egypt, as I have punished Jerusalem, by the sword, by famine, and by pestilence

Jer 44:26 Therefore hear the word of the Lord, all Judah who *dwell in the land* of Egypt

Lam 4:21 Rejoice and be glad, O daughter of Edom, you who *dwell in the land* of Uz

Ezek 7:7 Doom has come to you, you who *dwell in the land*

Ezek 36:28 Then you shall *dwell in the land* that I gave to your fathers

Ezek 37:25 Then they shall *dwell in the land* that I have given to Jacob My servant, where your fathers dwelt

Zeph 1:18 but the whole land shall be devoured by the fire of His jealousy, for He will make speedy riddance of all those who *dwell in the land*

DWELL IN YOU RICHLY

Col 3:16 Let the word of Christ *dwell in you richly* in all wisdom, teaching and admonishing one another in psalms and hymns and spiritual songs, singing with grace in your hearts to the Lord

DWELLING FOR MY NAME

Neh 1:9 but if you return to Me, and keep My commandments and do them, though some of you were cast out to the farthest part of the heavens, yet I will gather them from there, and bring them to the place which I have chosen as a *dwelling for My name*

DWELLING IN WHICH GOD LIVES (NIV)
(See *HABITATION OF GOD*)

DWELLING PLACE OF GOD (RSV)
(See *HABITATION OF GOD*)

DWELLING PLACE OF THE WICKED

Job 8:22 Those who hate you will be clothed with shame, and the *dwelling place of the wicked* will come to nothing

Job 21:28 And where is the tent, the *dwelling place of the wicked*

DWELLS BETWEEN THE CHERUBIM

1Sam 4:4 So the people sent to Shiloh, that they might bring from there the ark of the covenant of the Lord of hosts, who *dwells between the cherubim*

2Sam 6:2 And David arose and went with all the people who were with him from Baale Judah to bring up from there the ark of God, whose name is called by the Name, the Lord of Hosts, who *dwells between the cherubim*

2Kin 19:15 O Lord God of Israel, the One who *dwells between the cherubim*, You are God, You alone, of all the kingdoms of the earth

1Chr 13:6 And David and all Israel went up to Baalah, to Kirjath Jearim, which belonged to Judah, to bring up from there the ark of God the Lord, who *dwells between the cherubim*, where His name is proclaimed

Ps 99:1 He *dwells between the cherubim;* let the earth be moved

Is 37:16 O Lord of hosts, God of Israel, the One who *dwells between the cherubim*, You are God, You alone, of all the kingdoms of the earth

DWELLS IN ZION

Ps 9:11 Sing praises to the Lord, who *dwells in Zion!* Declare His deeds among the people

Joel 3:21 For I will acquit them of bloodguilt, whom I had not acquitted; for the Lord *dwells in Zion*

DWELLS ON HIGH

Ps 113:5 Who is like the Lord our God, Who *dwells on high*

Is 33:5 The Lord is exalted, for He *dwells on high;* He has filled Zion with justice and righteousness

DWELT AMONG US

John 1:14 And the Word became flesh and *dwelt among us*, and we beheld His glory, the glory as of the only begotten of the Father, full of grace and truth

DWELT THERE

Gen 11:2 And it came to pass, as they journeyed from the east, that they found a plain in the land of Shinar, and they *dwelt there*

Gen 11:31 And Terah took his son Abram and his grandson Lot, the son of Haran, and his daughter-in-law Sarai, his son Abram's wife, and they went out with them from Ur of the Chaldeans to

go to the land of Canaan; and they came to Haran and *dwelt there*
Gen 26:17 Then Isaac departed from there and pitched his tent in the Valley of Gerar, and *dwelt there*
Deut 2:10 (The Emim had *dwelt there* in times past, a people as great and numerous and tall as the Anakim
Deut 2:20 giants formerly *dwelt there*. But the Ammonites call them Zamzummim
Judg 9:21 and he went to Beer and *dwelt there*, for fear of Abimelech his brother
Judg 18:28 It was in the valley that belongs to Beth Rehob. So they rebuilt the city and *dwelt there*
Ruth 1:4 the name of the one was Orpah, and the name of the other Ruth. And they *dwelt there* about ten years
1Kin 11:24 And they went to Damascus and *dwelt there*, and reigned in Damascus
1Kin 12:25 Then Jeroboam built Shechem in the mountains of Ephraim, and *dwelt there*
1Chr 4:43 And they defeated the rest of the Amalekites who had escaped. They have *dwelt there* to this day
2Chr 28:18 The Philistines also had invaded the cities of the lowland and of the South of Judah, and had taken Beth Shemesh, Aijalon, Gederoth, Sochoh with its villages, Timnah with its villages, and Gimzo with its villages; and they *dwelt there*
Neh 13:16 Men of Tyre *dwelt there* also, who brought in fish and all kinds of goods, and sold them on the Sabbath to the children of Judah, and in Jerusalem
Acts 22:12 Then one, Ananias, a devout man according to the law, having a good testimony with all the Jews who *dwelt there*

E

EACH ACCORDING TO HIS ABILITY
Acts 11:29 Then the disciples, *each according to his ability*, determined to send relief to the brethren dwelling in Judea

EACH MAN UNDER HIS VINE AND HIS FIG TREE
1Kin 4:25 And Judah and Israel dwelt safely, *each man under his vine and his fig tree*, from Dan as far as Beersheba, all the days of Solomon

EACH MEMBER BELONGS TO ALL THE OTHERS (NIV)
(See *MEMBERS OF ONE ANOTHER*)

EACH TO HIS OWN INHERITANCE
Josh 24:28 So Joshua let the people depart, *each to his own inheritance*
Judg 2:6 And when Joshua had dismissed the people, the children of Israel went *each to his own inheritance* to possess the land

EAGER TO DO WHAT IS GOOD (NIV)
(See *ZEALOUS FOR GOOD WORKS*)

EARLIER PROPHETS (NIV)
(See *FORMER PROPHETS*)

EARLY AND LATTER RAIN
Jas 5:7 See how the farmer waits for the precious fruit of the earth, waiting patiently for it until it receives the *early and latter rain*

EARLY DAYS OF YOUR ACQUAINTANCE WITH THE GOSPEL (NIV)
(See *BEGINNING OF THE GOSPEL*)

EARLY DEW
Hos 6:4 For your faithfulness is like a morning cloud, and like the *early dew* it goes away
Hos 13:3 Therefore they shall be like the morning cloud and like the *early dew* that passes away, like chaff blown off from a threshing floor and like smoke from a chimney

EARLY IN THE MORNING
Gen 19:27 And Abraham went *early in the morning* to the place where he had stood before the Lord
Gen 20:8 So Abimelech rose *early in the morning*, called all his servants, and told all these things in their hearing
Gen 21:14 So Abraham rose *early in the morning*, and took bread and a skin of water
Gen 22:3 So Abraham rose *early in the morning* and saddled his donkey, and took two of his young men with him, and Isaac his son
Gen 26:31 Then they arose *early in the morning* and swore an oath with one another
Gen 28:18 Then Jacob rose *early in the morning*, and took the stone that he had put at his head, set it up as a pillar, and poured oil on top of it
Gen 31:55 And *early in the morning* Laban arose, and kissed his sons and daughters and blessed them
Ex 8:20 And the Lord said to Moses, "Rise *early in the morning* and stand before Pharaoh as he comes out to the water
Ex 9:13 Then the Lord said to Moses, "Rise *early in the morning* and stand before Pharaoh, and say to him
Ex 24:4 And he rose *early in the morning*, and built an altar at the foot of the mountain, and twelve pillars according to the twelve tribes of Israel
Ex 34:4 Then Moses rose *early in the morning* and went up Mount Sinai, as the Lord had commanded him
Num 14:40 And they rose *early in the morning* and went up to the top of the mountain, saying
Josh 3:1 Then Joshua rose *early in the morning;* and they set out from Acacia Grove and came to the Jordan, he and all the children of Israel, and lodged there before they crossed over
Josh 6:12 And Joshua rose *early in the morning*, and the priests took up the ark of the Lord
Josh 7:16 So Joshua rose *early in the morning* and brought Israel by their tribes, and the tribe of Judah was taken
Josh 8:10 Then Joshua rose up *early in the morning* and mustered the people, and went up, he and the elders of Israel, before the people to Ai
Judg 6:28 And when the men of the city arose *early in the morning*, there was the altar of Baal, torn down
Judg 19:5 Then it came to pass on the fourth day that they arose *early in the morning*, and he stood to depart
Judg 19:8 Then he arose *early in the morning* on the fifth day to depart, but the young woman's father said
1Sam 1:19 Then they rose *early in the morning* and worshiped before the Lord, and returned and came to their house at Ramah
1Sam 5:3 And when the people of Ashdod arose *early in the morning*, there was Dagon, fallen on its face to the earth before the ark of the Lord
1Sam 15:12 So when Samuel rose *early in the morning* to meet Saul, it was told Samuel, saying
1Sam 17:20 So David rose *early in the morning*, left the sheep with a keeper, and took the things and went as Jesse had commanded him
1Sam 29:10 Now therefore, rise *early in the morn-*

ing with your master's servants who have come with you. And as soon as you are up *early in the morning* and have light, depart

2Kin 3:22 Then they rose up *early in the morning*, and the sun was shining on the water

2Kin 19:35 and when people arose *early in the morning*, there were the corpses all dead

2Chr 20:20 And they rose *early in the morning* and went out into the Wilderness of Tekoa

Job 1:5 So it was, when the days of feasting had run their course, that Job would send and sanctify them, and he would rise *early in the morning* and offer burnt offerings according to the number of them all

Prov 27:14 He who blesses his friend with a loud voice, rising *early in the morning*, it will be counted a curse to him

Is 5:11 Woe to those who rise *early in the morning*, that they may follow intoxicating drink

Is 37:36 and when people arose *early in the morning*, there were the corpses all dead

Dan 6:19 Then the king arose very *early in the morning* and went in haste to the den of lions

Matt 20:1 For the kingdom of heaven is like a landowner who went out *early in the morning* to hire laborers for his vineyard

Mark 16:2 Very *early in the morning*, on the first day of the week, they came to the tomb when the sun had risen

Luke 21:38 Then *early in the morning* all the people came to Him in the temple to hear Him

Luke 24:1 Now on the first day of the week, very *early in the morning*, they, and certain other women with them, came to the tomb bringing the spices which they had prepared

John 8:2 But *early in the morning* He came again into the temple, and all the people came to Him

Acts 5:21 And when they heard that, they entered the temple *early in the morning* and taught

EARLY THE NEXT MORNING

Judg 6:38 When he rose *early the next morning* and squeezed the fleece together, he wrung the dew out of the fleece, a bowl full of water

1Sam 5:4 And when they arose *early the next morning*, there was Dagon, fallen on its face to the ground before the ark of the Lord

EARNEST OF THE SPIRIT IN OUR HEARTS (KJV)
(See *SPIRIT IN OUR HEARTS AS A DEPOSIT*)

EARNESTLY DESIRE TO PROPHESY (RSV)
(See *DESIRE EARNESTLY TO PROPHESY*)

EARS TO HEAR

Deut 29:4 Yet the Lord has not given you a heart to perceive and eyes to see and *ears to hear*, to this very day

Ezek 12:2 Son of man, you dwell in the midst of a rebellious house, which has eyes to see but does not see, and *ears to hear* but does not hear

Matt 11:15 He who has *ears to hear*, let him hear

Matt 13:9 He who has *ears to hear*, let him hear

Matt 13:43 Then the righteous will shine forth as the sun in the kingdom of their Father. He who has *ears to hear*, let him hear

Mark 4:9 And He said to them, "He who has *ears to hear*, let him hear

Mark 4:23 If anyone has *ears to hear*, let him hear

Mark 7:16 If anyone has *ears to hear*, let him hear

Luke 8:8 When He had said these things He cried, "He who has *ears to hear*, let him hear

Luke 14:35 It is neither fit for the land nor for the dunghill, but men throw it out. He who has *ears to hear*, let him hear

EARS WILL TINGLE

2Kin 21:12 Behold, I am bringing such calamity upon Jerusalem and Judah, that whoever hears of it, both his *ears will tingle*

Jer 19:3 Behold, I will bring such a catastrophe on this place, that whoever hears of it, his *ears will tingle*

EARTH ABIDES FOREVER

Eccl 1:4 One generation passes away, and another generation comes; but the *earth abides forever*

EARTH BELOW

1Kin 8:23 Lord God of Israel, there is no God in heaven above or on *earth below* like You, who keep Your covenant and mercy with Your servants who walk before You with all their heart

EARTH HELPED THE WOMAN

Rev 12:16 But the *earth helped the woman*, and the earth opened its mouth and swallowed up the flood which the dragon had spewed out of his mouth

EARTH IS FULL

Ps 33:5 The *earth is full* of the goodness of the Lord

Ps 104:24 In wisdom You have made them all. The *earth is full* of Your possessions

Is 6:3 Holy, holy, holy is the Lord of hosts; the whole *earth is full* of His glory

EARTH IS MY FOOTSTOOL

Is 66:1 Heaven is My throne, and *earth is My footstool*. Where is the house that you will build Me

Acts 7:49 Heaven is My throne, and *earth is My footstool*. What house will you build for Me

EARTH IS THE LORD'S

Ex 9:29 the thunder will cease, and there will be no more hail, that you may know that the *earth is the Lord's*

Ps 24:1 The *earth is the Lord's*, and all its fullness, the world and those who dwell therein

1Cor 10:26 for "The *earth is the Lord's*, and all its fullness

1Cor 10:28 for "The *earth is the Lord's*, and all its fullness

EARTH MOURNS AND LANGUISHES

Is 33:9 The *earth mourns and languishes*, Lebanon is shamed and shriveled

EARTH OPENS ITS MOUTH

Num 16:30 But if the Lord creates a new thing, and the *earth opens its mouth* and swallows them up with all that belongs to them, and they go down alive into the pit, then you will understand that these men have rejected the Lord

EARTH REELED AND ROCKED (RSV)
(See *EARTH SHOOK AND TREMBLED*)

EARTH REMAINS FOREVER (NAS, NIV, RSV)
(See *EARTH ABIDES FOREVER*)

EARTH SHOOK AND TREMBLED

2Sam 22:8 Then the *earth shook and trembled;* the foundations of heaven moved and shook, because He was angry

Ps 18:7 Then the *earth shook and trembled;* the foundations of the hills also quaked and were shaken, because He was angry

EARTH UPON HIS HEAD (KJV, RSV)
(See *DUST ON HIS HEAD*)

EARTH WAS WITHOUT FORM
Gen 1:2 The *earth was without form*, and void; and darkness was on the face of the deep

EARTH WILL PASS AWAY
Matt 24:35 Heaven and *earth will pass away*, but My words will by no means pass away
Mark 13:31 Heaven and *earth will pass away*, but My words will by no means pass away
Luke 21:33 Heaven and *earth will pass away*, but My words will by no means pass away

EARTH'S FOUNDATION (NIV)
(See *FOUNDATIONS OF THE EARTH*)

EARTHEN VESSELS
2Sam 17:28 brought beds and basins, *earthen vessels* and wheat, barley and flour, parched grain and beans, lentils and parched seeds
2Cor 4:7 But we have this treasure in *earthen vessels*, that the excellence of the power may be of God and not of us

EARTHLY THINGS
John 3:12 If I have told you *earthly things* and you do not believe, how will you believe if I tell you heavenly things
Phil 3:19 whose end is destruction, whose god is their belly, and whose glory is in their shame who set their mind on *earthly things*

EARTHY MAN (NIV)
(See *MAN OF DUST*)

EAST AND WEST
Matt 8:11 many will come from *east and west*, and sit down with Abraham, Isaac, and Jacob

EAST OF EDEN
Gen 4:16 Then Cain went out from the presence of the Lord and dwelt in the land of Nod on the *east of Eden*

EAST WIND
Gen 41:6 Then behold, seven thin heads, blighted by the *east wind*, sprang up after them
Gen 41:23 Then behold, seven heads, withered, thin, and blighted by the *east wind*, sprang up after them
Gen 41:27 And the seven thin and ugly cows which came up after them are seven years, and the seven empty heads blighted by the *east wind* are seven years of famine
Ex 10:13 So Moses stretched out his rod over the land of Egypt, and the Lord brought an *east wind* on the land all that day and all that night. When it was morning, the *east wind* brought the locusts
Ex 14:21 and the Lord caused the sea to go back by a strong *east wind* all that night, and made the sea into dry land, and the waters were divided
Job 15:2 Should a wise man answer with empty knowledge, and fill himself with the *east wind*
Job 27:21 The *east wind* carries him away, and he is gone
Job 38:24 By what way is light diffused, or the *east wind* scattered over the earth
Ps 48:7 As when You break the ships of Tarshish with an *east wind*
Ps 78:26 He caused an *east wind* to blow in the heavens
Is 27:8 He removes it by His rough wind in the day of the *east wind*
Jer 18:17 I will scatter them as with an *east wind* before the enemy
Ezek 17:10 will it not utterly wither when the *east wind* touches it
Ezek 19:12 But she was plucked up in fury, she was cast down to the ground, and the *east wind* dried her fruit
Ezek 27:26 Your oarsmen brought you into many waters, but the *east wind* broke you in the midst of the seas
Hos 12:1 Ephraim feeds on the wind, and pursues the *east wind*
Hos 13:15 Though he is fruitful among his brethren, an *east wind* shall come
Jon 4:8 And it happened, when the sun arose, that God prepared a vehement *east wind*
Hab 1:9 Their faces are set like the *east wind*. They gather captives like sand

EAT AS DOTH A CANKER (KJV)
(See *SPREAD LIKE CANCER*)

EAT AT HOME
1Cor 11:34 But if anyone is hungry, let him *eat at home*, lest you come together for judgment

EAT BEFORE THE LORD
Deut 12:7 And there you shall *eat before the Lord* your God, and you shall rejoice in all to which you have put your hand, you and your households, in which the Lord your God has blessed you
Deut 14:23 And you shall *eat before the Lord* your God, in the place where He chooses to make His name abide, the tithe of your grain and your new wine and your oil, of the firstlings of your herds and your flocks, that you may learn to fear the Lord your God always

EAT BREAD MADE WITHOUT YEAST (NIV)
(See *EAT UNLEAVENED BREAD*)

EAT, DRINK, AND BE MERRY
Eccl 8:15 So I commended enjoyment, because a man has nothing better under the sun than to *eat, drink, and be merry*
Luke 12:19 take your ease; *eat, drink, and be merry*

EAT ITS WAY LIKE GANGRENE (RSV)
(See *SPREAD LIKE CANCER*)

EAT THE FRUIT
Gen 3:2 And the woman said to the serpent, "We may *eat the fruit* of the trees of the garden
Deut 28:33 A nation whom you have not known shall *eat the fruit* of your land and the produce of your labor, and you shall be only oppressed and crushed continually
Deut 28:53 You shall *eat the fruit* of your own body, the flesh of your sons and your daughters whom the Lord your God has given you, in the siege and desperate straits in which your enemy shall distress you
2Kin 19:29 also in the third year sow and reap, plant vineyards and *eat the fruit* of them
Prov 1:31 therefore they shall *eat the fruit* of their own way, and be filled to the full with their own fancies
Is 3:10 Say to the righteous that it shall be well with them, for they shall *eat the fruit* of their doings
Is 37:30 also in the third year sow and reap, plant vineyards, and *eat the fruit* of them

EAT THE LORD'S SUPPER
1Cor 11:20 Therefore when you come together in one place, it is not to *eat the Lord's Supper*

EAT THE PASSOVER
Matt 26:17 Now on the first day of the Feast of the Unleavened Bread the disciples came to Jesus,

saying to Him, "Where do You want us to prepare for You to *eat the Passover*

Mark 14:12 Now on the first day of Unleavened Bread, when they killed the Passover lamb, His disciples said to Him, "Where do You want us to go and prepare, that You may *eat the Passover*

Mark 14:14 And wherever he goes in, say to the master of the house, 'The Teacher says, "Where is the guest room in which I may *eat the Passover* with My disciples

Luke 22:11 Then you shall say to the master of the house, 'The Teacher says to you, "Where is the guest room in which I may *eat the Passover* with My disciples

John 18:28 But they themselves did not go into the Praetorium, lest they should be defiled, but that they might *eat the Passover*

EAT UNLEAVENED BREAD

Ex 12:15 Seven days you shall *eat unleavened bread*. On the first day you shall remove leaven from your houses

Ex 12:18 In the first month, on the fourteenth day of the month at evening, you shall *eat unleavened bread*, until the twenty-first day of the month at evening

Ex 12:20 You shall eat nothing leavened; in all your dwellings you shall *eat unleavened bread*

Ex 13:6 Seven days you shall *eat unleavened bread*, and on the seventh day there shall be a feast to the Lord

Ex 23:15 You shall keep the Feast of Unleavened Bread (you shall *eat unleavened bread* seven days, as I commanded you, at the time appointed in the month of Abib, for in it you came out of Egypt

Ex 34:18 Seven days you shall *eat unleavened bread*, as I commanded you, in the appointed time of the month of Abib

Lev 23:6 And on the fifteenth day of the same month is the Feast of Unleavened Bread to the Lord; seven days you must *eat unleavened bread*

Deut 16:3 seven days you shall *eat unleavened bread* with it, that is, the bread of affliction (for you came out of the land of Egypt in haste

Deut 16:8 Six days you shall *eat unleavened bread*, and on the seventh day there shall be a sacred assembly to the Lord your God

EATING AND DRINKING

Ruth 3:3 but do not make yourself known to the man until he has finished *eating and drinking*

1Sam 1:9 So Hannah arose after they had finished *eating and drinking* in Shiloh

1Sam 30:16 So when he had brought him down, there they were, spread out over all the land, *eating and drinking* and dancing, because of all the great spoil which they had taken from the land of the Philistines and from the land of Judah

1Kin 1:25 They are *eating and drinking* before him; and they say

1Kin 4:20 Judah and Israel were as numerous as the sand by the sea in multitude, *eating and drinking* and rejoicing

1Chr 12:39 And they were there with David three days, *eating and drinking*, for their brethren had prepared for them

Job 1:13 Now there was a day when his sons and daughters were *eating and drinking* wine in their oldest brother's house

Job 1:18 While he was still speaking, another also came and said, "Your sons and daughters were *eating and drinking* wine in their oldest brother's house

Matt 11:19 The Son of Man came *eating and drinking*, and they say

Matt 24:38 For as in the days before the flood, they were *eating and drinking*, marrying and giving in marriage, until the day that Noah entered the ark

Luke 7:34 The Son of Man has come *eating and drinking*, and you say

Luke 10:7 And remain in the same house, *eating and drinking* such things as they give, for the laborer is worthy of his wages

EDGE OF HIS CLOAK (NIV)
(See *BORDER OF HIS GARMENT*)

EDGE OF THE SWORD

Gen 34:26 And they killed Hamor and Shechem his son with the *edge of the sword*, and took Dinah from Shechem's house, and went out

Ex 17:13 So Joshua defeated Amalek and his people with the *edge of the sword*

Num 21:24 Then Israel defeated him with the *edge of the sword*, and took possession of his land from the Arnon to the Jabbok, as far as the people of Ammon

Deut 13:15 you shall surely strike the inhabitants of that city with the *edge of the sword* utterly destroying it, all that is in it and its livestock, with the *edge of the sword*

Deut 20:13 And when the Lord your God delivers it into your hands, you shall strike every male in it with the *edge of the sword*

Josh 6:21 And they utterly destroyed all that was in the city, both man and woman, young and old, ox and sheep and donkey, with the *edge of the sword*

Josh 8:24 And it came to pass when Israel had made an end of slaying all the inhabitants of Ai in the field, in the wilderness where they pursued them, and when they all had fallen by the *edge of the sword* until they were consumed, that all the Israelites returned to Ai and struck it with the *edge of the sword*

Josh 10:28 On that day Joshua took Makkedah, and struck it and its king with the *edge of the sword*

Josh 10:30 he struck it and all the people who were in it with the *edge of the sword*

Josh 10:32 And the Lord delivered Lachish into the hand of Israel, who took it on the second day, and struck it and all the people who were in it with the *edge of the sword*, according to all that he had done to Libnah

Josh 10:35 They took it on that day and struck it with the *edge of the sword*

Josh 10:37 And they took it and struck it with the *edge of the sword* its king, all its cities, and all the people who were in it

Josh 10:39 they struck them with the *edge of the sword* and utterly destroyed all the people who were in it

Josh 11:11 And they struck all the people who were in it with the *edge of the sword*, utterly destroying them

Josh 11:12 So all the cities of those kings, and all their kings, Joshua took and struck with the *edge of the sword*

Josh 11:14 but they struck every man with the *edge of the sword* until they had destroyed them, and they left none breathing

Josh 19:47 and they struck it with the *edge of the sword*, took possession of it, and dwelt in it

Judg 1:8 they struck it with the *edge of the sword* and set the city on fire

Judg 1:25 So he showed them the entrance to the city, and they struck the city with the *edge of the sword*

Judg 4:15 And the Lord routed Sisera and all his chariots and all his army with the *edge of the sword* before Barak

Judg 4:16 But Barak pursued the chariots and the

army as far as Harosheth Hagoyim, and all the army of Sisera fell by the *edge of the sword*
Judg 18:27 and they struck them with the *edge of the sword* and burned the city with fire
Judg 20:37 the men in ambush spread out and struck the whole city with the *edge of the sword*
Judg 20:48 And the men of Israel turned back against the children of Benjamin, and struck them down with the *edge of the sword* from every city, men and beasts, all who were found
Judg 21:10 So the congregation sent out there twelve thousand of their most valiant men, and commanded them, saying, "Go and strike the inhabitants of Jabesh Gilead with the *edge of the sword*, including the women and children
1Sam 15:8 He also took Agag king of the Amalekites alive, and utterly destroyed all the people with the *edge of the sword*
1Sam 22:19 Also Nob, the city of the priests, he struck with the *edge of the sword*, both men and women, children and nursing infants, oxen and donkeys and sheep with the *edge of the sword*
2Sam 15:14 Make haste to depart, lest he overtake us suddenly and bring disaster upon us, and strike the city with the *edge of the sword*
2Kin 10:25 And they killed them with the *edge of the sword*
Job 1:15 when the Sabeans raided them and took them away indeed they have killed the servants with the *edge of the sword*
Job 1:17 While he was still speaking, another also came and said, "The Chaldeans formed three bands, raided the camels and took them away, yes, and killed the servants with the *edge of the sword*
Jer 21:7 and he shall strike them with the *edge of the sword*
Luke 21:24 And they will fall by the *edge of the sword*, and be led away captive into all nations
Heb 11:34 quenched the violence of fire, escaped the *edge of the sword*, out of weakness were made strong, became valiant in battle, turned to flight the armies of the aliens

EDIFICATION OF THE CHURCH
1Cor 14:12 Even so you, since you are zealous for spiritual gifts, let it be for the *edification of the church* that you seek to excel

ELDERS OF ISRAEL
Ex 3:16 Go and gather the *elders of Israel* together, and say to them
Ex 3:18 and you shall come, you and the *elders of Israel*, to the king of Egypt
Ex 12:21 Then Moses called for all the *elders of Israel* and said to them
Ex 17:5 And the Lord said to Moses, "Go on before the people, and take with you some of the *elders of Israel*
Ex 17:6 And Moses did so in the sight of the *elders of Israel*
Ex 18:12 And Aaron came with all the *elders of Israel* to eat bread with Moses' father-in-law before God
Ex 24:1 Now He said to Moses, "Come up to the Lord, you and Aaron, Nadab and Abihu, and seventy of the *elders of Israel*, and worship from afar
Ex 24:9 Then Moses went up, also Aaron, Nadab, and Abihu, and seventy of the *elders of Israel*
Lev 9:1 It came to pass on the eighth day that Moses called Aaron and his sons and the *elders of Israel*
Num 11:16 Gather to Me seventy men of the *elders of Israel*, whom you know to be the elders of the people and officers over them
Num 11:30 And Moses returned to the camp, both he and the *elders of Israel*
Num 16:25 Then Moses rose and went to Dathan and Abiram, and the *elders of Israel* followed him
Deut 27:1 Then Moses, with the *elders of Israel*, commanded the people, saying
Deut 31:9 So Moses wrote this law and delivered it to the priests, the sons of Levi, who bore the ark of the covenant of the Lord, and to all the *elders of Israel*
Josh 7:6 Then Joshua tore his clothes, and fell to the earth on his face before the ark of the Lord until evening, both he and the *elders of Israel*
Josh 8:10 Then Joshua rose up early in the morning and mustered the people, and went up, he and the *elders of Israel*, before the people to Ai
Josh 24:1 Then Joshua gathered all the tribes of Israel to Shechem and called for the *elders of Israel*, for their heads, for their judges, and for their officers
1Sam 4:3 And when the people had come into the camp, the *elders of Israel* said
1Sam 8:4 Then all the *elders of Israel* gathered together and came to Samuel at Ramah
2Sam 3:17 Now Abner had communicated with the *elders of Israel*, saying
2Sam 5:3 So all the *elders of Israel* came to the king at Hebron, and King David made a covenant with them at Hebron before the Lord
2Sam 17:4 And the saying pleased Absalom and all the *elders of Israel*
2Sam 17:15 Then Hushai said to Zadok and Abiathar the priests, "Thus and so Ahithophel counseled Absalom and the *elders of Israel*, and thus and so I have counseled
1Kin 8:1 Now Solomon assembled the *elders of Israel* and all the heads of the tribes, the chief fathers of the children of Israel, to King Solomon in Jerusalem, that they might bring up the ark of the covenant of the Lord from the City of David, which is Zion
1Kin 8:3 Then all the *elders of Israel* came, and the priests took up the ark
1Chr 11:3 Therefore all the *elders of Israel* came to the king at Hebron, and David made a covenant with them at Hebron before the Lord
1Chr 15:25 So David, the *elders of Israel*, and the captains over thousands went to bring up the ark of the covenant of the Lord from the house of Obed-Edom with joy
2Chr 5:2 Now Solomon assembled the *elders of Israel* and all the heads of the tribes, the chief fathers of the children of Israel, in Jerusalem, that they might bring the ark of the covenant of the Lord up from the City of David, which is Zion
2Chr 5:4 So all the *elders of Israel* came, and the Levites took up the ark
Ezek 14:1 Now some of the *elders of Israel* came to me and sat before me
Ezek 20:1 It came to pass in the seventh year, in the fifth month, on the tenth day of the month, that certain of the *elders of Israel* came to inquire of the Lord, and sat before me
Ezek 20:3 Son of man, speak to the *elders of Israel*, and say to them
Acts 4:8 Then Peter, filled with the Holy Spirit, said to them, "Rulers of the people and *elders of Israel*

ELDERS OF THE CHURCH
Acts 20:17 From Miletus he sent to Ephesus and called for the *elders of the church*
Jas 5:14 Let him call for the *elders of the church*, and let them pray over him, anointing him with oil in the name of the Lord

ELDERS OF THE HOUSE OF ISRAEL
Ezek 8:11 And there stood before them seventy men of the *elders of the house of Israel*, and in their midst stood Jaazaniah the son of Shaphan

Ezek 8:12 Then He said to me, "Son of man, have you seen what the *elders of the house of Israel* do in the dark, every man in the room of his idols

ELECT OF GOD
Col 3:12 Therefore, as the *elect of God*, holy and beloved, put on tender mercies, kindness, humbleness of mind, meekness, longsuffering

ELEMENTAL SPIRITS OF THE UNIVERSE (RSV)
(See *BASIC PRINCIPLES OF THE WORLD*)

ELEMENTS OF THE WORLD
Gal 4:3 Even so we, when we were children, were in bondage under the *elements of the world*

ELEVENTH HOUR
Matt 20:6 And about the *eleventh hour* he went out and found others standing idle, and said to them
Matt 20:9 And when those came who were hired about the *eleventh hour*, they each received a denarius

EMISSION OF SEMEN
Lev 15:16 If any man has an *emission of semen*, then he shall wash all his body in water, and be unclean until evening
Lev 15:18 Also, when a woman lies with a man, and there is an *emission of semen*, they both shall bathe in water, and be unclean until evening
Lev 22:4 And whoever touches anything made unclean by a corpse, or a man who has had an *emission of semen*

EMPTIED HIMSELF (NAS, RSV)
(See *MADE HIMSELF OF NO REPUTATION*)

EMPTY NOTHINGS (RSV)
(See *EMPTY WORDS*)

EMPTY PHRASES (RSV)
(See *VAIN REPETITIONS*)

EMPTY WORDS
Job 21:34 How then can you comfort me with *empty words*, since falsehood remains in your answers
Is 59:4 they trust in *empty words* and speak lies; they conceive evil and bring forth iniquity
Eph 5:6 Let no one deceive you with *empty words*, for because of these things the wrath of God comes upon the sons of disobedience

ENCOURAGE THE OPPRESSED (NIV)
(See *REPROVE THE OPPRESSOR*)

ENCOURAGEMENT IN CHRIST (NAS, RSV)
(See *CONSOLATION IN CHRIST*)

END OF A MATTER (NAS, NIV)
(See *END OF A THING*)

END OF A THING
Eccl 7:8 The *end of a thing* is better than its beginning, and the patient in spirit is better than the proud in spirit

END OF ALL FLESH
Gen 6:13 And God said to Noah, "The *end of all flesh* has come before Me, for the earth is filled with violence through them

END OF ALL THINGS
1Pet 4:7 But the *end of all things* is at hand; therefore be serious and watchful in your prayers

END OF THE AGE
Matt 13:39 The enemy who sowed them is the devil, the harvest is the *end of the age*, and the reapers are the angels
Matt 13:49 So it will be at the *end of the age*
Matt 24:3 And what will be the sign of Your coming, and of the *end of the age*
Matt 28:20 and lo, I am with you always, even to the *end of the age*

END OF THE EARTH
Deut 13:7 of the gods of the people which are all around you, near to you or far off from you, from one *end of the earth* to the other *end of the earth*
Deut 28:49 The Lord will bring a nation against you from afar, from the *end of the earth*, as swift as the eagle flies, a nation whose language you will not understand
Deut 28:64 Then the Lord will scatter you among all peoples, from one *end of the earth* to the other, and there you shall serve other gods, which neither you nor your fathers have known
Ps 46:9 He makes wars cease to the *end of the earth*
Ps 61:2 From the *end of the earth* I will cry to You, when my heart is overwhelmed
Is 5:26 He will lift up a banner to the nations from afar, and will whistle to them from the *end of the earth*
Is 48:20 With a voice of singing, declare, proclaim this, utter it even to the *end of the earth*
Jer 25:33 And at that day the slain of the Lord shall be from one *end of the earth* even to the other *end of the earth*
Dan 4:22 for your greatness has grown and reaches to the heavens, and your dominion to the *end of the earth*
Acts 1:8 and you shall be witnesses to Me in Jerusalem, and in all Judea and Samaria, and to the *end of the earth*

END OF THE LAND (NIV)
(See *END OF THE EARTH*)

END OF THE WORLD
Ps 19:4 Their line has gone out through all the earth, and their words to the *end of the world*
Is 62:11 Indeed the Lord has proclaimed to the *end of the world*

END OF THIS AGE
Matt 13:40 Therefore as the tares are gathered and burned in the fire, so it will be at the *end of this age*

END WAS NEAR
Lam 4:18 Our *end was near;* our days were over, for our end had come

ENDS OF HEAVEN (RSV)
(See *FARTHEST PART OF HEAVEN*)

ENDS OF THE EARTH
Deut 33:17 together with them He shall push the peoples to the *ends of the earth*
1Sam 2:10 The Lord will judge the *ends of the earth*. "He will give strength to His king, and exalt the horn of His anointed
Job 28:24 For He looks to the *ends of the earth*, and sees under the whole heavens
Job 37:3 He sends it forth under the whole heaven, His lightning to the *ends of the earth*
Job 38:13 that it might take hold of the *ends of the earth*, and the wicked be shaken out of it
Ps 2:8 Ask of Me, and I will give you the nations for your inheritance, and the *ends of the earth* for your possession

Ps 48:10 According to Your name, O God, so is Your praise to the *ends of the earth*
Ps 59:13 And let them know that God rules in Jacob to the *ends of the earth*
Ps 65:5 By awesome deeds in righteousness You will answer us, O God of our salvation, You who are the confidence of all the *ends of the earth*, and of the far-off seas
Ps 67:7 God shall bless us, and all the *ends of the earth* shall fear Him
Ps 72:8 He shall have dominion also from sea to sea, and from the River to the *ends of the earth*
Ps 98:3 All the *ends of the earth* have seen the salvation of our God
Ps 135:7 He causes the vapors to ascend from the *ends of the earth*
Prov 17:24 Wisdom is in the sight of him who has understanding, but the eyes of a fool are on the *ends of the earth*
Prov 30:4 Who has established all the *ends of the earth?* What is His name, and what is His Son's name, if you know
Is 24:16 From the *ends of the earth* we have heard songs
Is 40:28 The everlasting God, the Lord, the Creator of the *ends of the earth*, neither faints nor is weary
Is 41:5 The coastlands saw it and feared, the *ends of the earth* were afraid
Is 41:9 You whom I have taken from the *ends of the earth*, and called from its farthest regions, and said to You
Is 42:10 Sing to the Lord a new song, and His praise from the *ends of the earth*, you who go down to the sea, and all that is in it, you coastlands and you inhabitants of them
Is 43:6 Bring My sons from afar, and My daughters from the *ends of the earth*
Is 45:22 Look to Me, and be saved, all you *ends of the earth*
Is 49:6 I will also give You as a light to the Gentiles, that You should be My salvation to the *ends of the earth*
Is 52:10 and all the *ends of the earth* shall see the salvation of our God
Jer 10:13 And He causes the vapors to ascend from the *ends of the earth*
Jer 16:19 O Lord, my strength and my fortress, my refuge in the day of affliction, the Gentiles shall come to You from the *ends of the earth* and say
Jer 25:31 A noise will come to the *ends of the earth* for the Lord has a controversy with the nations
Jer 31:8 Behold, I will bring them from the north country, and gather them from the *ends of the earth*, among them the blind and the lame, the woman with child and the one who labors with child, together
Jer 50:41 Behold, a people shall come from the north, and a great nation and many kings shall be raised up from the *ends of the earth*
Jer 51:16 He causes the vapors to ascend from the *ends of the earth*
Mic 5:4 and they shall abide, for now He shall be great to the *ends of the earth*
Zech 9:10 His dominion shall be 'from sea to sea, and from the River to the *ends of the earth*
Matt 12:42 The queen of the South will rise up in the judgment with this generation and condemn it, for she came from the *ends of the earth* to hear the wisdom of Solomon
Luke 11:31 The queen of the South will rise up in the judgment with the men of this generation and condemn them, for she came from the *ends of the earth* to hear the wisdom of Solomon
Acts 13:47 I have set you to be a light to the Gentiles, that you should be for salvation to the *ends of the earth*

ENDURES ALL THINGS
1Cor 13:7 bears all things, believes all things, hopes all things, *endures all things*

ENEMIES OF THE CROSS
Phil 3:18 For many walk, of whom I have told you often, and now tell you even weeping, that they are the *enemies of the cross* of Christ

ENEMY OF THE JEWS
Esth 3:10 So the king took his signet ring from his hand and gave it to Haman, the son of Hammedatha the Agagite, the *enemy of the Jews*
Esth 8:1 On that day King Ahasuerus gave Queen Esther the house of Haman, the *enemy of the Jews*
Esth 9:10 the ten sons of Haman the son of Hammedatha, the *enemy of the Jews* they killed

ENFLAMING YOURSELVES WITH IDOLS (KJV)
(See *INFLAMING YOURSELVES WITH GODS*)

ENGULFING WATERS THREATENED ME (NIV)
(See *WATERS ENCOMPASSED ME*)

ENJOY GOOD
Eccl 2:24 There is nothing better for a man than that he should eat and drink, and that his soul should *enjoy good* in his labor

ENJOY THE GOOD
Eccl 3:13 and also that every man should eat and drink and *enjoy the good* of all his labor it is the gift of God
Eccl 5:18 It is good and fitting for one to eat and drink, and to *enjoy the good* of all his labor in which he toils under the sun all the days of his life which God gives him

ENMITY BETWEEN YOU
Gen 3:15 And I will put *enmity between you* and the woman, and between your seed and her Seed

ENMITY WITH GOD
Jas 4:4 Do you not know that friendship with the world is *enmity with God*

ENORMOUS RED DRAGON (NIV)
(See *FIERY RED DRAGON*)

ENSIGN FOR THE NATIONS (KJV, RSV)
(See *BANNER FOR THE NATIONS*)

ENSIGN ON A HILL (KJV)
(See *BANNER ON A HILL*)

ENSLAVED TO SIN (RSV)
(See *SLAVES OF SIN*)

ENTER A STRONG MAN'S HOUSE
Matt 12:29 Or else how can one *enter a strong man's house* and plunder his goods, unless he first binds the strong man
Mark 3:27 No one can *enter a strong man's house* and plunder his goods, unless he first binds the strong man, and then he will plunder his house

ENTER HIS REST
Heb 3:18 And to whom did He swear that they would not *enter His rest*, but to those who did not obey

ENTER INTO JUDGMENT
Ps 143:2 Do not *enter into judgment* with Your servant, for in Your sight no one living is righteous
Is 3:14 The Lord will *enter into judgment* with the elders of His people and His princes

Joel 3:2 and I will *enter into judgment* with them there on account of My people, My heritage Israel, whom they have scattered among the nations

ENTER INTO LIFE
Matt 18:8 It is better for you to *enter into life* lame or maimed, rather than having two hands or two feet, to be cast into the everlasting fire
Matt 18:9 It is better for you to *enter into life* with one eye, rather than having two eyes, to be cast into hell fire
Matt 19:17 But if you want to *enter into life*, keep the commandments
Mark 9:43 It is better for you to *enter into life* maimed, than having two hands, to go to hell, into the fire that shall never be quenched

ENTER INTO TEMPTATION
Matt 26:41 Watch and pray, lest you *enter into temptation*. The spirit indeed is willing, but the flesh is weak
Mark 14:38 Watch and pray, lest you *enter into temptation*. The spirit truly is ready, but the flesh is weak
Luke 22:40 When He came to the place, He said to them, "Pray that you may not *enter into temptation*
Luke 22:46 Then He said to them, "Why do you sleep? Rise and pray, lest you *enter into temptation*

ENTER INTO THE JOY
Matt 25:21 you were faithful over a few things, I will make you ruler over many things. *Enter into the joy* of your lord
Matt 25:23 you have been faithful over a few things, I will make you ruler over many things. *Enter into the joy* of your lord

ENTER LIFE (NAS, NIV, RSV)
(See *ENTER INTO LIFE*)

ENTER MY REST
Ps 95:11 So I swore in My wrath, 'They shall not *enter My rest*
Heb 3:11 So I swore in My wrath, 'They shall not *enter My rest*
Heb 4:3 So I swore in My wrath, "They shall not *enter My rest*
Heb 4:5 and again in this place: "They shall not *enter My rest*

ENTER THE KINGDOM OF GOD
Matt 19:24 And again I say to you, it is easier for a camel to go through the eye of a needle than for a rich man to *enter the kingdom of God*
Matt 21:31 Jesus said to them, "Assuredly, I say to you that tax collectors and harlots *enter the kingdom of God* before you
Mark 9:47 It is better for you to *enter the kingdom of God* with one eye, than having two eyes, to be cast into hell fire
Mark 10:23 Then Jesus looked around and said to His disciples, "How hard it is for those who have riches to *enter the kingdom of God*
Mark 10:24 But Jesus answered again and said to them, "Children, how hard it is for those who trust in riches to *enter the kingdom of God*
Mark 10:25 It is easier for a camel to go through the eye of a needle than for a rich man to *enter the kingdom of God*
Luke 18:24 And when Jesus saw that he became very sorrowful, He said, "How hard it is for those who have riches to *enter the kingdom of God*
Luke 18:25 For it is easier for a camel to go through a needle's eye than for a rich man to *enter the kingdom of God*
John 3:5 Jesus answered, "Most assuredly, I say to you, unless one is born of water and the Spirit, he cannot *enter the kingdom of God*
Acts 14:22 strengthening the souls of the disciples, exhorting them to continue in the faith, and saying, "We must through many tribulations *enter the kingdom of God*

ENTER THE LAND
Num 14:30 Except for Caleb the son of Jephunneh and Joshua the son of Nun, you shall by no means *enter the land* which I swore I would make you dwell in
Num 20:24 Aaron shall be gathered to his people, for he shall not *enter the land* which I have given to the children of Israel, because you rebelled against My word at the water of Meribah
Deut 27:3 You shall write on them all the words of this law, when you have crossed over, that you may *enter the land* which the Lord your God is giving you
Judg 6:5 both they and their camels were without number; and they would *enter the land* to destroy it
Ezek 20:38 I will bring them out of the country where they sojourn, but they shall not *enter the land* of Israel

ENTERED INTO A COVENANT
2Chr 15:12 Then they *entered into a covenant* to seek the Lord God of their fathers with all their heart and with all their soul
Ezek 16:8 Yes, I swore an oath to you and *entered into a covenant* with you, and you became Mine

ENTERED SATAN INTO JUDAS (KJV)
(See *SATAN ENTERED JUDAS*)

ENTERED THE SYNAGOGUE AND TAUGHT
Mark 1:21 Then they went into Capernaum, and immediately on the Sabbath He *entered the synagogue and taught*
Luke 6:6 Now it happened on another Sabbath, also, that He *entered the synagogue and taught*

ENTERTAINED ANGELS
Heb 13:2 Do not forget to entertain strangers, for by so doing some have unwittingly *entertained angels*

ENTHRONED BETWEEN THE CHERUBIM (NIV)
(See *DWELLS BETWEEN THE CHERUBIM*)

ENTHRONED IN ZION (NIV)
(See *DWELLS IN ZION*)

ENTHRONED ON HIGH (NAS, NIV)
(See *DWELLS ON HIGH*)

ENTICING WORDS (KJV)
(See *PERSUASIVE WORDS*)

ENTREAT NOW THE FACE (KJV)
(See *ENTREAT THE FAVOR*)

ENTREAT THE FAVOR
1Kin 13:6 Then the king answered and said to the man of God, "Please *entreat the favor* of the Lord your God, and pray for me, that my hand may be restored to me
Prov 19:6 Many *entreat the favor* of the nobility, and every man is a friend to one who gives gifts

ENTREAT THE LORD
Ex 8:8 Then Pharaoh called for Moses and Aaron, and said, "*Entreat the Lord* that He may take away the frogs from me and from my people
Ex 8:29 Then Moses said, "Indeed I am going out

from you, and I will *entreat the Lord*, that the swarms of flies may depart tomorrow from Pharaoh, from his servants, and from his people
Ex 9:28 *Entreat the Lord*, that there may be no more mighty thundering and hail, for it is enough
Ex 10:17 Now therefore, please forgive my sin only this once, and *entreat the Lord* your God, that He may take away from me this death only

ENTREATED OF HIM (KJV)
(See *GRANTED HIS PLEA*)

ENTREATED THE FAVOR OF THE LORD (RSV)
(See *SUPPLICATION TO THE LORD*)

ENTREATED THE LORD
Ex 8:30 So Moses went out from Pharaoh and *entreated the Lord*
Ex 10:18 So he went out from Pharaoh and *entreated the Lord*
1Kin 13:6 So the man of God *entreated the Lord*, and the king's hand was restored to him, and became as it was before

ENTRUSTED WITH THE GOSPEL
1Th 2:4 But as we have been approved by God to be *entrusted with the gospel*, even so we speak, not as pleasing men, but God who tests our hearts

ENVY IS ROTTENNESS
Prov 14:30 A sound heart is life to the body, but *envy is rottenness* to the bones

ENVY SLAYS
Job 5:2 For wrath kills a foolish man, and *envy slays* a simple one

ENVY THOU NOT THE OPPRESSOR (KJV)
(See *DO NOT ENVY THE OPPRESSOR*)

EQUAL TO THE ANGELS
Luke 20:36 nor can they die anymore, for they are *equal to the angels* and are sons of God, being sons of the resurrection

EQUAL WITH GOD
John 5:18 Therefore the Jews sought all the more to kill Him, because He not only broke the Sabbath, but also said that God was His Father, making Himself *equal with God*
Phil 2:6 who, being in the form of God, did not consider it robbery to be *equal with God*

EQUIPPED FOR BATTLE (RSV)
(See *EXPERT IN WAR*)

ERR IN HEART (RSV)
(See *GO ASTRAY IN THEIR HEARTS*)

ERRED CONCERNING THE FAITH (KJV)
(See *STRAYED CONCERNING THE FAITH*)

ERROR OF HIS WAY
Jas 5:20 let him know that he who turns a sinner from the *error of his way* will save a soul from death and cover a multitude of sins

ESAU I HAVE HATED
Mal 1:3 but *Esau I have hated*, and laid waste his mountains and his heritage for the jackals of the wilderness
Rom 9:13 As it is written, "Jacob I have loved, but *Esau I have hated*

ESTABLISH HIS KINGDOM
2Sam 7:12 When your days are fulfilled and you rest with your fathers, I will set up your seed after you, who will come from your body, and I will *establish his kingdom*
1Chr 17:11 And it shall be, when your days are fulfilled, when you must go to be with your fathers, that I will set up your seed after you, who will be of your sons; and I will *establish his kingdom*
1Chr 28:7 Moreover I will *establish his kingdom* forever, if he is steadfast to observe My commandments and My judgments, as it is this day

ESTABLISH HIS THRONE FOREVER
1Chr 17:12 He shall build Me a house, and I will *establish his throne forever*

ESTABLISH JUSTICE
Amos 5:15 *establish justice* in the gate. It may be that the Lord God of hosts will be gracious to the remnant of Joseph

ESTABLISH MY COVENANT
Gen 6:18 But I will *establish My covenant* with you; and you shall go into the ark you, your sons, your wife, and your sons' wives with you
Gen 9:9 And as for Me, behold, I *establish My covenant* with you and with your descendants after you
Gen 9:11 Thus I *establish My covenant* with you: Never again shall all flesh be cut off by the waters of the flood
Gen 17:7 And I will *establish My covenant* between Me and you and your descendants after you in their generations, for an everlasting covenant, to be God to you and your descendants after you
Gen 17:19 I will *establish My covenant* with him for an everlasting covenant, and with his descendants after him
Ezek 16:62 And I will *establish My covenant* with you. Then you shall know that I am the Lord

ESTABLISHED HIS THRONE (NAS, NIV, RSV)
(See *PREPARED HIS THRONE*)

ESTABLISHED IN LOVE (NIV)
(See *GROUNDED IN LOVE*)

ESTABLISHED JUSTICE
Is 42:4 He will not fail nor be discouraged, till He has *established justice* in the earth

ESTABLISHED MY COVENANT
Ex 6:4 I have also *established My covenant* with them, to give them the land of Canaan, the land of their pilgrimage, in which they were strangers

ESTABLISHED THE WORLD
Jer 10:12 He has made the earth by His power, He has *established the world* by His wisdom, And has stretched out the heavens at His discretion
Jer 51:15 He has *established the world* by His wisdom, and stretched out the heaven by His understanding

ESTIMATE THE COST (NIV)
(See *COUNT THE COST*)

ETERNAL FIRE
Jude 7 as Sodom and Gomorrah, and the cities around them in a similar manner to these, having given themselves over to sexual immorality and gone after strange flesh, are set forth as an example, suffering the vengeance of *eternal fire*

ETERNAL GOD IS YOUR DWELLING PLACE (RSV)
(See *ETERNAL GOD IS YOUR REFUGE*)

ETERNAL GOD IS YOUR REFUGE
Deut 33:27 The *eternal God is your refuge*, and underneath are the everlasting arms

ETERNAL INHERITANCE
Heb 9:15 And for this reason He is the Mediator of the new covenant, by means of death, for the redemption of the transgressions under the first covenant, that those who are called may receive the promise of the *eternal inheritance*

ETERNAL LIFE
Matt 19:16 Now behold, one came and said to Him, "Good Teacher, what good thing shall I do that I may have *eternal life*
Matt 25:46 And these will go away into everlasting punishment, but the righteous into *eternal life*
Mark 10:17 Now as He was going out on the road, one came running, knelt before Him, and asked Him, "Good Teacher, what shall I do that I may inherit *eternal life*
Mark 10:30 who shall not receive a hundredfold now in this time houses and brothers and sisters and mothers and children and lands, with persecutions and in the age to come, *eternal life*
Luke 10:25 And behold, a certain lawyer stood up and tested Him, saying, "Teacher, what shall I do to inherit *eternal life*
Luke 18:18 Now a certain ruler asked Him, saying, "Good Teacher, what shall I do to inherit *eternal life*
John 3:15 that whoever believes in Him should not perish but have *eternal life*
John 4:36 And he who reaps receives wages, and gathers fruit for *eternal life*, that both he who sows and he who reaps may rejoice together
John 5:39 You search the Scriptures, for in them you think you have *eternal life*
John 6:54 Whoever eats My flesh and drinks My blood has *eternal life*, and I will raise him up at the last day
John 6:68 Then Simon Peter answered Him, "Lord, to whom shall we go? You have the words of *eternal life*
John 10:28 And I give them *eternal life*, and they shall never perish
John 12:25 He who loves his life will lose it, and he who hates his life in this world will keep it for *eternal life*
John 17:2 as You have given Him authority over all flesh, that He should give *eternal life* to as many as You have given Him
John 17:3 And this is *eternal life*, that they may know You, the only true God, and Jesus Christ whom You have sent
Acts 13:48 And as many as had been appointed to *eternal life* believed
Rom 2:7 *eternal life* to those who by patient continuance in doing good seek for glory, honor, and immortality
Rom 5:21 so that as sin reigned in death, even so grace might reign through righteousness to *eternal life* through Jesus Christ our Lord
Rom 6:23 For the wages of sin is death, but the gift of God is *eternal life* in Christ Jesus our Lord
1Tim 6:12 Fight the good fight of faith, lay hold on *eternal life*, to which you were also called and have confessed the good confession in the presence of many witnesses
1Tim 6:19 storing up for themselves a good foundation for the time to come, that they may lay hold on *eternal life*
Tit 1:2 in hope of *eternal life* which God, who cannot lie, promised before time began
Tit 3:7 that having been justified by His grace we should become heirs according to the hope of *eternal life*
1Jn 1:2 the life was manifested, and we have seen, and bear witness, and declare to you that *eternal life* which was with the Father and was manifested to us
1Jn 2:25 And this is the promise that He has promised us *eternal life*
1Jn 3:15 Whoever hates his brother is a murderer, and you know that no murderer has *eternal life* abiding in him
1Jn 5:11 that God has given us *eternal life*, and this life is in His Son
1Jn 5:13 These things I have written to you who believe in the name of the Son of God, that you may know that you have *eternal life*, and that you may continue to believe in the name of the Son of God
1Jn 5:20 and we are in Him who is true, in His Son Jesus Christ. This is the true God and *eternal life*
Jude 21 keep yourselves in the love of God, looking for the mercy of our Lord Jesus Christ unto *eternal life*

ETERNAL PUNISHMENT (NAS, NIV, RSV)
(See *EVERLASTING PUNISHMENT*)

ETERNAL REDEMPTION
Heb 9:12 Not with the blood of goats and calves, but with His own blood He entered the Most Holy Place once for all, having obtained *eternal redemption*

EVEN AS HE IS PURE (KJV)
(See *JUST AS HE IS PURE*)

EVEN AS HE IS RIGHTEOUS (KJV)
(See *JUST AS HE IS RIGHTEOUS*)

EVEN BALANCE (KJV)
(See *JUST BALANCE*)

EVEN GIVEN THEE TO THE HALF OF MY KINGDOM (KJV)
(See *UP TO HALF MY KINGDOM*)

EVENING AND MORNING
Ps 55:17 *Evening and morning* and at noon I will pray, and cry aloud, and He shall hear my voice

EVENING AND THE MORNING
Gen 1:5 So the *evening and the morning* were the first day
Gen 1:8 So the *evening and the morning* were the second day
Gen 1:13 So the *evening and the morning* were the third day
Gen 1:19 So the *evening and the morning* were the fourth day
Gen 1:23 So the *evening and the morning* were the fifth day
Gen 1:31 So the *evening and the morning* were the sixth day

EVENING SACRIFICE
1Kin 18:29 And it was so, when midday was past, that they prophesied until the time of the offering of the *evening sacrifice*
1Kin 18:36 And it came to pass, at the time of the offering of the *evening sacrifice*, that Elijah the prophet came near and said
Ezra 9:4 Then everyone who trembled at the words of the God of Israel assembled to me, because of the transgression of those who had been carried away captive, and I sat astonished until the *evening sacrifice*
Ezra 9:5 At the *evening sacrifice* I arose from my fasting; and having torn my garment and my robe, I fell on my knees and spread out my hands to the Lord my God

Ps 141:2 Let my prayer be set before You as incense, the lifting up of my hands as the *evening sacrifice*

EVENING WOLVES
Hab 1:8 Their horses also are swifter than leopards, and more fierce than *evening wolves*
Zeph 3:3 her judges are *evening wolves* that leave not a bone till morning

EVERLASTING COVENANT
Gen 9:16 The rainbow shall be in the cloud, and I will look on it to remember the *everlasting covenant* between God and every living creature of all flesh that is on the earth
Gen 17:7 And I will establish My covenant between Me and you and your descendants after you in their generations, for an *everlasting covenant*, to be God to you and your descendants after you
Gen 17:13 He who is born in your house and he who is bought with your money must be circumcised, and My covenant shall be in your flesh for an *everlasting covenant*
Gen 17:19 I will establish My covenant with him for an *everlasting covenant*, and with his descendants after him
Lev 24:8 Every Sabbath he shall set it in order before the Lord continually, being taken from the children of Israel by an *everlasting covenant*
2Sam 23:5 Although my house is not so with God, yet He has made with me an *everlasting covenant*, ordered in all things and secure
1Chr 16:17 and confirmed it to Jacob for a statute, to Israel for an *everlasting covenant*
Ps 105:10 And confirmed it to Jacob for a statute, to Israel for an *everlasting covenant*
Is 24:5 The earth is also defiled under its inhabitants, because they have transgressed the laws, changed the ordinance, broken the *everlasting covenant*
Is 55:3 and I will make an *everlasting covenant* with you the sure mercies of David
Is 61:8 I will direct their work in truth, and will make with them an *everlasting covenant*
Jer 32:40 And I will make an *everlasting covenant* with them, that I will not turn away from doing them good
Ezek 16:60 Nevertheless I will remember My covenant with you in the days of your youth, and I will establish an *everlasting covenant* with you
Ezek 37:26 Moreover I will make a covenant of peace with them, and it shall be an *everlasting covenant* with them
Heb 13:20 Now may the God of peace who brought up our Lord Jesus from the dead, that great Shepherd of the sheep, through the blood of the *everlasting covenant*

EVERLASTING FATHER
Is 9:6 And His name will be called Wonderful, Counselor, Mighty God, *Everlasting Father*, Prince of Peace

EVERLASTING KINGDOM
Ps 145:13 Your kingdom is an *everlasting kingdom*, and Your dominion endures throughout all generations
Dan 4:3 His kingdom is an *everlasting kingdom*, and His dominion is from generation to generation
Dan 7:27 His kingdom is an *everlasting kingdom*, and all dominions shall serve and obey Him
2Pet 1:11 for so an entrance will be supplied to you abundantly into the *everlasting kingdom* of our Lord and Savior Jesus Christ

EVERLASTING LIFE
Dan 12:2 And many of those who sleep in the dust of the earth shall awake, some to *everlasting life*, some to shame and everlasting contempt
Matt 19:29 And everyone who has left houses or brothers or sisters or father or mother or wife or children or lands, for My name's sake, shall receive a hundredfold, and inherit *everlasting life*
Luke 18:30 who shall not receive many times more in this present time, and in the age to come *everlasting life*
John 3:16 For God so loved the world that He gave His only begotten Son, that whoever believes in Him should not perish but have *everlasting life*
John 3:36 He who believes in the Son has *everlasting life;* and he who does not believe the Son shall not see life, but the wrath of God abides on him
John 4:14 But the water that I shall give him will become in him a fountain of water springing up into *everlasting life*
John 5:24 Most assuredly, I say to you, he who hears My word and believes in Him who sent Me has *everlasting life*, and shall not come into judgment, but has passed from death into life
John 6:27 Do not labor for the food which perishes, but for the food which endures to *everlasting life*, which the Son of Man will give you, because God the Father has set His seal on Him
John 6:40 And this is the will of Him who sent Me, that everyone who sees the Son and believes in Him may have *everlasting life*
John 6:47 Most assuredly, I say to you, he who believes in Me has *everlasting life*
John 12:50 And I know that His command is *everlasting life*. Therefore, whatever I speak, just as the Father has told Me, so I speak
Acts 13:46 but since you reject it, and judge yourselves unworthy of *everlasting life*, behold, we turn to the Gentiles
Rom 6:22 But now having been set free from sin, and having become slaves of God, you have your fruit to holiness, and the end, *everlasting life*
Gal 6:8 For he who sows to his flesh will of the flesh reap corruption, but he who sows to the Spirit will of the Spirit reap *everlasting life*
1Tim 1:16 However, for this reason I obtained mercy, that in me first Jesus Christ might show all longsuffering, as a pattern to those who are going to believe on Him for *everlasting life*

EVERLASTING LIGHT
Is 60:19 but the Lord will be to you an *everlasting light*, and your God your glory
Is 60:20 for the Lord will be your *everlasting light*, and the days of your mourning shall be ended

EVERLASTING ORDINANCE
Ex 12:14 You shall keep it as a feast by an *everlasting ordinance*
Ex 12:17 Therefore you shall observe this day throughout your generations as an *everlasting ordinance*

EVERLASTING POSSESSION
Gen 17:8 Also I give to you and your descendants after you the land in which you are a stranger, all the land of Canaan, as an *everlasting possession*
Gen 48:4 and said to me, 'Behold, I will make you fruitful and multiply you, and I will make of you a multitude of people, and give this land to your descendants after you as an *everlasting possession*

EVERLASTING PUNISHMENT
Matt 25:46 And these will go away into *everlasting punishment*, but the righteous into eternal life

EVERLASTING RUINS (NIV)
(See *PERPETUAL DESOLATIONS*)

EVERY DAY HE WAS TEACHING AT THE TEMPLE (NIV)
(See *TEACHING DAILY IN THE TEMPLE*)

EVERY EYE WILL SEE HIM
Rev 1:7 Behold, He is coming with clouds, and *every eye will see Him*, and they also who pierced Him

EVERY GOOD WORK
2Cor 9:8 And God is able to make all grace abound toward you, that you, always having all sufficiency in all things, have an abundance for *every good work*
Col 1:10 that you may have a walk worthy of the Lord, fully pleasing Him, being fruitful in *every good work* and increasing in the knowledge of God
1Tim 5:10 if she has brought up children, if she has lodged strangers, if she has washed the saints' feet, if she has relieved the afflicted, if she has diligently followed *every good work*
2Tim 2:21 Therefore if anyone cleanses himself from the latter, he will be a vessel for honor, sanctified and useful for the Master, prepared for *every good work*
2Tim 3:17 that the man of God may be complete, thoroughly equipped for *every good work*
Tit 1:16 They profess to know God, but in works they deny Him, being abominable, disobedient, and disqualified for *every good work*
Tit 3:1 Remind them to be subject to rulers and authorities, to obey, to be ready for *every good work*
Heb 13:21 make you complete in *every good work* to do His will, working in you what is well pleasing in His sight, through Jesus Christ, to whom be glory forever and ever

EVERY GREEN TREE
Deut 12:2 You shall utterly destroy all the places where the nations which you shall dispossess served their gods, on the high mountains and on the hills and under *every green tree*
1Kin 14:23 For they also built for themselves high places, sacred pillars, and wooden images on every high hill and under *every green tree*
2Kin 16:4 And he sacrificed and burned incense on the high places, on the hills, and under *every green tree*
2Kin 17:10 They set up for themselves sacred pillars and wooden images on every high hill and under *every green tree*
2Chr 28:4 And he sacrificed and burned incense on the high places, on the hills, and under *every green tree*
Is 57:5 inflaming yourselves with gods under *every green tree*, slaying the children in the valleys, under the clefts of the rocks
Jer 2:20 and you said, 'I will not transgress,' when on every high hill and under *every green tree* you lay down, playing the harlot
Jer 3:6 She has gone up on every high mountain and under *every green tree*, and there played the harlot
Jer 3:13 Only acknowledge your iniquity, that you have transgressed against the Lord your God, and have scattered your charms to alien deities under *every green tree*, and you have not obeyed My voice
Ezek 6:13 Then you shall know that I am the Lord, when their slain men are among their idols all around their altars, on every high hill, on all the mountaintops, under *every green tree*, and under every thick oak, wherever they offered sweet incense to all their idols
Ezek 20:47 Behold, I will kindle a fire in you, and it shall devour *every green tree* and every dry tree in you

EVERY HIGH HILL
1Kin 14:23 For they also built for themselves high places, sacred pillars, and wooden images on *every high hill* and under every green tree
2Kin 17:10 They set up for themselves sacred pillars and wooden images on *every high hill* and under every green tree
Is 30:25 There will be on every high mountain and on *every high hill* rivers and streams of waters, in the day of the great slaughter, when the towers fall
Jer 2:20 and you said, 'I will not transgress,' when on *every high hill* and under every green tree you lay down, playing the harlot
Ezek 6:13 Then you shall know that I am the Lord, when their slain men are among their idols all around their altars, on *every high hill*, on all the mountaintops, under every green tree, and under every thick oak, wherever they offered sweet incense to all their idols
Ezek 34:6 My sheep wandered through all the mountains, and on *every high hill*

EVERY KNEE SHALL BOW
Is 45:23 the word has gone out of My mouth in righteousness, and shall not return, that to Me *every knee shall bow*, every tongue shall take an oath
Rom 14:11 As I live, says the Lord, *every knee shall bow* to Me, and every tongue shall confess to God

EVERY KNEE SHOULD BOW
Phil 2:10 that at the name of Jesus *every knee should bow*, of those in heaven, and of those on earth, and of those under the earth

EVERY MAN TO HIS INHERITANCE (RSV)
(See *EACH TO HIS OWN INHERITANCE*)

EVERY MAN UNDER HIS VINE (KJV, RSV)
(See *EACH MAN UNDER HIS VINE AND HIS FIG TREE*)

EVERY NATION, TRIBE, TONGUE, AND PEOPLE
Rev 14:6 Then I saw another angel flying in the midst of heaven, having the everlasting gospel to preach to those who dwell on the earth to *every nation, tribe, tongue, and people*

EVERY ONE LOVETH GIFTS (KJV)
(See *EVERYONE LOVES BRIBES*)

EVERY PROMISE HAS BEEN FULFILLED (NIV)
(See *ALL HAVE COME TO PASS*)

EVERY SPREADING TREE (NIV)
(See *EVERY GREEN TREE*)

EVERY TONGUE SHOULD CONFESS
Phil 2:11 and that *every tongue should confess* that Jesus Christ is Lord, to the glory of God the Father

EVERY WIND OF DOCTRINE
Eph 4:14 that we should no longer be children, tossed to and fro and carried about with *every wind of doctrine*, by the trickery of men, in the cunning craftiness by which they lie in wait to deceive

EVERYONE AS HE SEES FIT (NIV)
(See *RIGHT IN HIS OWN EYES*)

EVERYONE LOVES BRIBES
Is 1:23 *Everyone loves bribes*, and follows after rewards. They do not defend the fatherless, nor does the cause of the widow come before them

EVERYONE WHO BELIEVES (NIV)
(See *WHOEVER BELIEVES IN HIM*)

EVERYONE WHO THIRSTS
Is 55:1 *Everyone who thirsts*, come to the waters; and you who have no money, come, buy and eat

EVERYTHING IN SUBJECTION (RSV)
(See *ALL THINGS IN SUBJECTION*)

EVERYTHING IS MEANINGLESS (NIV)
(See *ALL IS VANITY*)

EVERYTHING IS PERMISSIBLE FOR ME (NIV)
(See *ALL THINGS ARE LAWFUL FOR ME*)

EVERYTHING JUST AS GOD COMMANDED (NIV)
(See *ALL THAT GOD COMMANDED*)

EVERYTHING THE LORD HAD DONE (NIV)
(See *WORKS OF THE LORD*)

EVERYTHING UNDER HIS FEET (NIV)
(See *ALL THINGS UNDER HIS FEET*)

EVIDENCE OF THINGS NOT SEEN
Heb 11:1 Now faith is the substance of things hoped for, the *evidence of things not seen*

EVIL AND ADULTEROUS GENERATION
Matt 12:39 But He answered and said to them, "An *evil and adulterous generation* seeks after a sign, and no sign will be given to it except the sign of the prophet Jonah

EVIL CONSCIENCE
Heb 10:22 let us draw near with a true heart in full assurance of faith, having our hearts sprinkled from an *evil conscience* and our bodies washed with pure water

EVIL FROM THE NORTH (KJV, NAS, RSV)
(See *DISASTER FROM THE NORTH*)

EVIL IN HIS SIGHT (NIV)
(See *EVIL IN THE SIGHT OF THE LORD*)

EVIL IN THE EYES OF THE LORD
1Kin 16:25 Omri did *evil in the eyes of the Lord*, and did worse than all who were before him
2Chr 29:6 For our fathers have trespassed and done *evil in the eyes of the Lord* our God

EVIL IN THE SIGHT OF THE LORD
Num 32:13 So the Lord's anger was aroused against Israel, and He made them wander in the wilderness forty years, until all the generation that had done *evil in the sight of the Lord* was gone
Deut 4:25 When you beget children and grandchildren and have grown old in the land, act corruptly and make a carved image in the form of anything, and do *evil in the sight of the Lord* your God to provoke Him to anger
Deut 31:29 and evil will befall you in the latter days, because you will do *evil in the sight of the Lord*, to provoke Him to anger through the work of your hands
Judg 2:11 Then the children of Israel did *evil in the sight of the Lord*, and served the Baals
Judg 3:7 So the children of Israel did *evil in the sight of the Lord*
Judg 3:12 And the children of Israel again did *evil in the sight of the Lord*. So the Lord strengthened Eglon king of Moab against Israel, because they had done *evil in the sight of the Lord*
Judg 4:1 When Ehud was dead, the children of Israel again did *evil in the sight of the Lord*
Judg 6:1 And the children of Israel did *evil in the sight of the Lord*
Judg 10:6 Then the children of Israel again did *evil in the sight of the Lord*, and served the Baals and the Ashtoreths, the gods of Syria, the gods of Sidon, the gods of Moab, the gods of the people of Ammon, and the gods of the Philistines
Judg 13:1 Again the children of Israel did *evil in the sight of the Lord*, and the Lord delivered them into the hand of the Philistines for forty years
1Sam 15:19 Why did you swoop down on the spoil, and do *evil in the sight of the Lord*
1Kin 11:6 Solomon did *evil in the sight of the Lord*, and did not fully follow the Lord, as did his father David
1Kin 14:22 Now Judah did *evil in the sight of the Lord*, and they provoked Him to jealousy with their sins which they committed, more than all that their fathers had done
1Kin 15:26 And he did *evil in the sight of the Lord*, and walked in the way of his father, and in his sin by which he had made Israel sin
1Kin 15:34 He did *evil in the sight of the Lord*, and walked in the way of Jeroboam, and in his sin by which he had made Israel sin
1Kin 16:19 because of the sins which he had sinned in doing *evil in the sight of the Lord*, in walking in the way of Jeroboam, and in his sin which he had committed to make Israel sin
1Kin 16:30 Now Ahab the son of Omri did *evil in the sight of the Lord*, more than all who were before him
1Kin 21:20 And he answered, "I have found you, because you have sold yourself to do *evil in the sight of the Lord*
1Kin 22:52 He did *evil in the sight of the Lord*, and walked in the way of his father and in the way of his mother and in the way of Jeroboam the son of Nebat, who had made Israel sin
2Kin 3:2 And he did *evil in the sight of the Lord*, but not like his father and mother
2Kin 8:18 and he did *evil in the sight of the Lord*
2Kin 8:27 And he walked in the way of the house of Ahab, and did *evil in the sight of the Lord*, as the house of Ahab had done, for he was the son-in-law of the house of Ahab
2Kin 13:2 And he did *evil in the sight of the Lord*, and followed the sins of Jeroboam the son of Nebat, who had made Israel sin
2Kin 13:11 And he did *evil in the sight of the Lord*
2Kin 14:24 And he did *evil in the sight of the Lord*
2Kin 15:9 And he did *evil in the sight of the Lord*, as his fathers had done
2Kin 15:18 And he did *evil in the sight of the Lord*
2Kin 15:24 And he did *evil in the sight of the Lord*
2Kin 15:28 And he did *evil in the sight of the Lord*
2Kin 17:2 And he did *evil in the sight of the Lord*, but not as the kings of Israel who were before him
2Kin 17:17 And they caused their sons and daughters to pass through the fire, practiced witchcraft and soothsaying, and sold themselves to do *evil in the sight of the Lord*, to provoke Him to anger
2Kin 21:2 And he did *evil in the sight of the Lord*, according to the abominations of the nations whom the Lord had cast out before the children of Israel

2Kin 21:6 He did much *evil in the sight of the Lord*, to provoke Him to anger
2Kin 21:16 Moreover Manasseh shed very much innocent blood, till he had filled Jerusalem from one end to another, besides his sin with which he made Judah sin, in doing *evil in the sight of the Lord*
2Kin 21:20 And he did *evil in the sight of the Lord*, as his father Manasseh had done
2Kin 23:32 And he did *evil in the sight of the Lord*, according to all that his fathers had done
2Kin 23:37 And he did *evil in the sight of the Lord*, according to all that his fathers had done
2Kin 24:9 And he did *evil in the sight of the Lord*, according to all that his father had done
2Kin 24:19 He also did *evil in the sight of the Lord*, according to all that Jehoiakim had done
2Chr 21:6 and he did *evil in the sight of the Lord*
2Chr 22:4 Therefore he did *evil in the sight of the Lord*, like the house of Ahab
2Chr 33:2 But he did *evil in the sight of the Lord*, according to the abominations of the nations whom the Lord had cast out before the children of Israel
2Chr 33:6 He did much *evil in the sight of the Lord*, to provoke Him to anger
2Chr 33:22 But he did *evil in the sight of the Lord*, as his father Manasseh had done
2Chr 36:5 And he did *evil in the sight of the Lord* his God
2Chr 36:9 And he did *evil in the sight of the Lord*
2Chr 36:12 He also did *evil in the sight of the Lord* his God, and did not humble himself before Jeremiah the prophet, who spoke from the mouth of the Lord
Jer 52:2 He also did *evil in the sight of the Lord*, according to all that Jehoiakim had done

EVIL ONE
Matt 5:37 For whatever is more than these is from the *evil one*
Matt 6:13 And do not lead us into temptation, but deliver us from the *evil one*
Luke 11:4 And do not lead us into temptation, but deliver us from the *evil one*
John 17:15 I do not pray that You should take them out of the world, but that You should keep them from the *evil one*
2Th 3:3 But the Lord is faithful, who will establish you and guard you from the *evil one*

EVIL SPIRIT
Acts 19:15 And the *evil spirit* answered and said, "Jesus I know, and Paul I know
Acts 19:16 Then the man in whom the *evil spirit* was leaped on them, overpowered them, and prevailed against them, so that they fled out of that house naked and wounded

EVIL SPIRIT FROM GOD (KJV, NAS, NIV, RSV)
(See *DISTRESSING SPIRIT FROM GOD*)

EVIL SPIRIT FROM THE LORD (KJV, NAS, NIV, RSV)
(See *DISTRESSING SPIRIT FROM THE LORD*)

EVIL SPIRITS
Luke 7:21 And that very hour He cured many people of their infirmities, afflictions, and *evil spirits*
Luke 8:2 and certain women who had been healed of *evil spirits* and infirmities Mary called Magdalene, out of whom had come seven demons
Acts 19:12 so that even handkerchiefs or aprons were brought from his body to the sick, and the diseases left them and the *evil spirits* went out of them
Acts 19:13 Then some of the itinerant Jewish exorcists took it upon themselves to call the name of the Lord Jesus over those who had *evil spirits*, saying

EVIL WILL RISE TO BE CONDEMNED (NIV)
(See *RESURRECTION OF CONDEMNATION*)

EXACT REPRESENTATION OF HIS BEING (NIV)
(See *EXPRESS IMAGE OF HIS PERSON*)

EXALT OUR HORN (NIV)
(See *HORN IS EXALTED*)

EXALT THE HORN
1Sam 2:10 He will give strength to His king, and *exalt the horn* of His anointed

EXALT THE LORD
Ps 99:5 *Exalt the Lord* our God, and worship at His footstool
Ps 99:9 *Exalt the Lord* our God, and worship at His holy hill

EXALT THE POWER (RSV)
(See *EXALT THE HORN*)

EXALTED ABOVE THE HEAVENS (NAS, NIV, RSV)
(See *HIGHER THAN THE HEAVENS*)

EXALTED IN MY BODY (NAS, NIV)
(See *MAGNIFIED IN MY BODY*)

EXAMINED THE SCRIPTURES EVERY DAY (NIV)
(See *SEARCHED THE SCRIPTURES DAILY*)

EXAMINING THE SCRIPTURES DAILY (NAS, RSV)
(See *SEARCHED THE SCRIPTURES DAILY*)

EXCEEDING FAIR (KJV)
(See *PLEASING TO GOD*)

EXCELLENT IS YOUR NAME
Ps 8:1 O Lord, our Lord, how *excellent is Your name* in all the earth, You who set Your glory above the heavens
Ps 8:9 O Lord, our Lord, how *excellent is Your name* in all the earth

EXCEPT A CORN OF WHEAT FALL (KJV)
(See *UNLESS A GRAIN OF WHEAT FALLS*)

EXCEPT THE LORD BUILD THE HOUSE (KJV)
(See *UNLESS THE LORD BUILDS THE HOUSE*)

EXCEPT YE BE CONVERTED (KJV)
(See *UNLESS YOU ARE CONVERTED*)

EXCEPT YE REPENT (KJV)
(See *UNLESS YOU REPENT*)

EXCHANGED THE TRUTH
Rom 1:25 who *exchanged the truth* of God for the lie, and worshiped and served the creature rather than the Creator, who is blessed forever

EXCLUDE ME FROM (NIV)
(See *SEPARATED ME FROM*)

EXECUTE JUDGMENT
Ex 12:12 and against all the gods of Egypt I will *execute judgment*
Ps 119:84 When will You *execute judgment* on those who persecute me
Is 16:3 Take counsel, *execute judgment;* make

your shadow like the night in the middle of the day
Jer 7:5 For if you thoroughly amend your ways and your doings, if you thoroughly *execute judgment* between a man and his neighbor
Jer 21:12 *Execute judgment* in the morning; and deliver him who is plundered out of the hand of the oppressor, lest My fury go out like fire and burn so that no one can quench it, because of the evil of your doings
Jer 22:3 *Execute judgment* and righteousness, and deliver the plundered out of the hand of the oppressor
Jer 23:5 a King shall reign and prosper, and *execute judgment* and righteousness in the earth
Jer 33:15 In those days and at that time I will cause to grow up to David a Branch of righteousness; He shall *execute judgment* and righteousness in the earth
John 5:27 and has given Him authority to *execute judgment* also, because He is the Son of Man
Jude 15 to *execute judgment* on all, to convict all who are ungodly among them of all their ungodly deeds which they have committed in an ungodly way, and of all the harsh things which ungodly sinners have spoken against Him

EXECUTE JUDGMENTS
Ezek 5:8 Indeed I, even I, am against you and will *execute judgments* in your midst in the sight of the nations
Ezek 5:10 and I will *execute judgments* among you, and all of you who remain I will scatter to all the winds
Ezek 5:15 So it shall be a reproach, a taunt, a lesson, and an astonishment to the nations that are all around you, when I *execute judgments* among you in anger and in fury and in furious rebukes
Ezek 11:9 And I will bring you out of its midst, and deliver you into the hands of strangers, and *execute judgments* on you
Ezek 16:41 They shall burn your houses with fire, and *execute judgments* on you in the sight of many women
Ezek 25:11 And I will *execute judgments* upon Moab, and they shall know that I am the Lord
Ezek 28:22 and they shall know that I am the Lord, when I *execute judgments* in her and am hallowed in her
Ezek 28:26 yes, they will dwell securely, when I *execute judgments* on all those around them who despise them
Ezek 30:14 I will make Pathros desolate, set fire to Zoan, and *execute judgments* in No
Ezek 30:19 Thus I will *execute judgments* on Egypt, then they shall know that I am the Lord

EXECUTE JUSTICE AND RIGHTEOUSNESS (RSV)
(See *DO JUSTICE AND RIGHTEOUSNESS*)

EXERCISE AUTHORITY
1Kin 21:7 Then Jezebel his wife said to him, "You now *exercise authority* over Israel
Matt 20:25 But Jesus called them to Himself and said, "You know that the rulers of the Gentiles lord it over them, and those who are great *exercise authority* over them
Mark 10:42 But Jesus called them to Himself and said to them, "You know that those who are considered rulers over the Gentiles lord it over them, and their great ones *exercise authority* over them
Luke 22:25 And He said to them, "The kings of the Gentiles exercise lordship over them, and those who *exercise authority* over them are called

EXILES OF ISRAEL (NIV)
(See *OUTCASTS OF ISRAEL*)

EXILES ON THE EARTH (NAS)
(See *PILGRIMS ON THE EARTH*)

EXPANSE OF THE SKY (NIV)
(See *FIRMAMENT OF THE HEAVENS*)

EXPECTATION OF THE POOR
Ps 9:18 For the needy shall not always be forgotten; the *expectation of the poor* shall not perish forever

EXPECTATION OF THE WICKED
Prov 10:28 The hope of the righteous will be gladness, but the *expectation of the wicked* will perish
Prov 11:23 The desire of the righteous is only good, but the *expectation of the wicked* is wrath

EXPERIENCED IN BATTLE (NIV)
(See *EXPERT IN WAR*)

EXPERT IN WAR
1Chr 12:33 of Zebulun there were fifty thousand who went out to battle, *expert in war* with all weapons of war, stouthearted men who could keep ranks
Song 3:8 They all hold swords, being *expert in war*. Every man has his sword on his thigh because of fear in the night

EXPIATION BY HIS BLOOD (RSV)
(See *PROPITIATION BY HIS BLOOD*)

EXPIATION FOR OUR SINS (RSV)
(See *PROPITIATION FOR OUR SINS*)

EXPLAIN THE RIDDLE
Judg 14:14 Now for three days they could not *explain the riddle*
Judg 14:15 So it came to pass on the seventh day that they said to Samson's wife, "Entice your husband, that he may *explain the riddle* to us, or else we will burn you and your father's house with fire

EXPLAIN THIS PARABLE
Matt 15:15 Then Peter answered and said to Him, "*Explain this parable* to us

EXPLAIN TO US THE PARABLE
Matt 13:36 And His disciples came to Him, saying, "*Explain to us the parable* of the tares of the field

EXPLORE THE LAND (NIV)
(See *SPY OUT THE LAND*)

EXPLORED THE LAND (NIV)
(See *SPIED OUT THE LAND*)

EXPOUND THE RIDDLE (KJV)
(See *EXPLAIN THE RIDDLE*)

EXPRESS IMAGE OF HIS PERSON
Heb 1:3 who being the brightness of His glory and the *express image of His person*, and upholding all things by the word of His power, when He had by Himself purged our sins, sat down at the right hand of the Majesty on high

EXTOL HIM (NIV)
(See *SHOUT JOYFULLY*)

EXTORTION TURNS (NIV)
(See *OPPRESSION DESTROYS*)

EYE FOR AN EYE
Matt 5:38 You have heard that it was said, 'An *eye for an eye* and a tooth for a tooth

EYE FOR EYE, TOOTH FOR TOOTH
Ex 21:24 *eye for eye, tooth for tooth*, hand for hand, foot for foot
Lev 24:20 fracture for fracture, *eye for eye, tooth for tooth*
Deut 19:21 but life shall be for life, *eye for eye, tooth for tooth*, hand for hand, foot for foot

EYE HAS NOT SEEN
1Cor 2:9 *Eye has not seen*, nor ear heard, nor have entered into the heart of man the things which God has prepared for those who love Him

EYE IS THE LAMP (NIV, RSV)
(See *LAMP OF THE BODY*)

EYE OF A NEEDLE
Matt 19:24 And again I say to you, it is easier for a camel to go through the *eye of a needle* than for a rich man to enter the kingdom of God
Mark 10:25 It is easier for a camel to go through the *eye of a needle* than for a rich man to enter the kingdom of God

EYES OF THE LORD
Gen 6:8 But Noah found grace in the *eyes of the Lord*
Deut 11:12 the *eyes of the Lord* your God are always on it, from the beginning of the year to the very end of the year
Deut 13:18 because you have listened to the voice of the Lord your God, to keep all His commandments which I command you today, to do what is right in the *eyes of the Lord* your God
1Sam 26:24 And indeed, as your life was valued much this day in my eyes, so let my life be valued much in the *eyes of the Lord*, and let Him deliver me out of all tribulation
2Sam 15:25 If I find favor in the *eyes of the Lord*, He will bring me back and show me both it and His habitation
1Kin 15:5 because David did what was right in the *eyes of the Lord*, and had not turned aside from anything that He commanded him all the days of his life, except in the matter of Uriah the Hittite
1Kin 15:11 Asa did what was right in the *eyes of the Lord*, as did his father David
1Kin 16:25 Omri did evil in the *eyes of the Lord*, and did worse than all who were before him
1Kin 22:43 He did not turn aside from them, doing what was right in the *eyes of the Lord*
2Chr 14:2 Asa did what was good and right in the *eyes of the Lord* his God
2Chr 16:9 For the *eyes of the Lord* run to and fro throughout the whole earth, to show Himself strong on behalf of those whose heart is loyal to Him
2Chr 29:6 For our fathers have trespassed and done evil in the *eyes of the Lord* our God
Ps 34:15 The *eyes of the Lord* are on the righteous, and His ears are open to their cry
Prov 5:21 For the ways of man are before the *eyes of the Lord*, and He ponders all his paths
Prov 15:3 The *eyes of the Lord* are in every place, keeping watch on the evil and the good
Prov 22:12 The *eyes of the Lord* preserve knowledge, but He overthrows the words of the faithless
Is 49:5 And now the Lord says, who formed Me from the womb to be His Servant, to bring Jacob back to Him, so that Israel is gathered to Him (for I shall be glorious in the *eyes of the Lord*, and My God shall be My strength
Amos 9:8 Behold, the *eyes of the Lord* God are on the sinful kingdom, and I will destroy it from the face of the earth
Zech 4:10 They are the *eyes of the Lord*, which scan to and fro throughout the whole earth
1Pet 3:12 For the *eyes of the Lord* are on the righteous, and his ears are open to their prayers

F

FACE OF AN ANGEL
Acts 6:15 And all who sat in the council, looking steadfastly at him, saw his face as the *face of an angel*

FACE OF GOD
Gen 33:10 And Jacob said, "No, please, if I have now found favor in your sight, then receive my present from my hand, inasmuch as I have seen your face as though I had seen the *face of God*, and you were pleased with me

FACE OF THE DEEP
Gen 1:2 and darkness was on the *face of the deep*. And the Spirit of God was hovering over the face of the waters
Prov 8:27 When He prepared the heavens, I was there, when He drew a circle on the *face of the deep*

FACE OF THE EARTH
Gen 6:1 Now it came to pass, when men began to multiply on the *face of the earth*, and daughters were born to them
Gen 6:7 So the Lord said, "I will destroy man whom I have created from the *face of the earth*, both man and beast, creeping thing and birds of the air, for I am sorry that I have made them
Gen 7:4 For after seven more days I will cause it to rain on the earth forty days and forty nights, and I will destroy from the *face of the earth* all living things that I have made
Gen 41:56 The famine was over all the *face of the earth*, and Joseph opened all the storehouses and sold to the Egyptians
Ex 10:5 And they shall cover the *face of the earth*, so that no one will be able to see the earth
Ex 32:12 Why should the Egyptians speak, and say, 'He brought them out to harm them, to kill them in the mountains, and to consume them from the *face of the earth*
Ex 33:16 So we shall be separate, Your people and I, from all the people who are upon the *face of the earth*
Num 12:3 (Now the man Moses was very humble, more than all men who were on the *face of the earth*
Num 22:5 See, they cover the *face of the earth*, and are settling next to me
Num 22:11 Look, a people has come out of Egypt, and they cover the *face of the earth*
Deut 6:15 lest the anger of the Lord your God be aroused against you and destroy you from the *face of the earth*
Deut 7:6 the Lord your God has chosen you to be a people for Himself, a special treasure above all the peoples on the *face of the earth*
Deut 14:2 For you are a holy people to the Lord your God, and the Lord has chosen you to be a people for Himself, a special treasure above all the peoples who are on the *face of the earth*
1Sam 20:15 but you shall not cut off your kindness from my house forever, no, not when the Lord has cut off every one of the enemies of David from the *face of the earth*
1Kin 13:34 And this thing was the sin of the house

of Jeroboam, so as to exterminate and destroy it from the *face of the earth*
Ps 104:30 You send forth Your Spirit, they are created; and You renew the *face of the earth*
Is 23:17 She will return to her pay, and commit fornication with all the kingdoms of the world on the *face of the earth*
Jer 8:2 they shall be like refuse on the *face of the earth*
Jer 16:4 they shall not be lamented nor shall they be buried, but they shall be like refuse on the *face of the earth*
Jer 25:26 and all the kingdoms of the world which are on the *face of the earth*
Jer 28:16 Behold, I will cast you from the *face of the earth*
Ezek 34:6 yes, My flock was scattered over the whole *face of the earth*, and no one was seeking or searching for them
Ezek 38:20 so that the fish of the sea, the birds of the heavens, the beasts of the field, all creeping things that creep on the earth, and all men who are on the *face of the earth* shall shake at My presence
Amos 5:8 He calls for the waters of the sea and pours them out on the *face of the earth*
Amos 9:6 who calls for the waters of the sea, and pours them out on the *face of the earth* the Lord is His name
Amos 9:8 Behold, the eyes of the Lord God are on the sinful kingdom, and I will destroy it from the *face of the earth*
Acts 17:26 And He has made from one blood every nation of men to dwell on all the *face of the earth*, and has determined their preappointed times and the boundaries of their habitation

FACE OF THE LORD
Gen 19:13 For we will destroy this place, because the outcry against them has grown great before the *face of the Lord*, and the Lord has sent us to destroy it
1Sam 26:20 Now therefore, do not let my blood fall to the earth before the *face of the Lord*
Ps 34:16 The *face of the Lord* is against those who do evil, to cut off the remembrance of them from the earth
Lam 2:19 pour out your heart like water before the *face of the Lord*
Lam 4:16 The *face of the Lord* scattered them; He no longer regards them
Luke 1:76 for you will go before the *face of the Lord* to prepare His ways
1Pet 3:12 but the *face of the Lord* is against those who do evil

FACE SHINE UPON YOU
Num 6:25 the Lord make His *face shine upon you*, and be gracious to you

FACE TO FACE
Gen 32:30 For I have seen God *face to face*, and my life is preserved
Ex 33:11 So the Lord spoke to Moses *face to face*, as a man speaks to his friend
Num 12:8 I speak with him *face to face*, even plainly, and not in dark sayings
Num 14:14 that You, Lord, are seen *face to face* and that Your cloud stands above them
Deut 5:4 The Lord talked with you *face to face* on the mountain from the midst of the fire
Deut 34:10 But since then there has not arisen in Israel a prophet like Moses, whom the Lord knew *face to face*
Judg 6:22 For I have seen the Angel of the Lord *face to face*
Jer 32:4 and Zedekiah king of Judah shall not escape from the hand of the Chaldeans, but shall surely be delivered into the hand of the king of Babylon, and shall speak with him *face to face*, and see him eye to eye
Jer 34:3 your eyes shall see the eyes of the king of Babylon, he shall speak with you *face to face*, and you shall go to Babylon
Ezek 20:35 And I will bring you into the wilderness of the peoples, and there I will plead My case with you *face to face*
Acts 25:16 To them I answered, 'It is not the custom of the Romans to deliver any man to destruction before the accused meets the accusers *face to face*, and has opportunity to answer for himself concerning the charge against him
1Cor 13:12 For now we see in a mirror, dimly, but then *face to face*
2Jn 12 but I hope to come to you and speak *face to face*, that our joy may be full
3Jn 14 but I hope to see you shortly, and we shall speak *face to face*

FACULTIES TRAINED BY PRACTICE TO DISTINGUISH GOOD FROM EVIL (RSV)
(See *SENSES EXERCISED TO DISCERN BOTH GOOD AND EVIL*)

FADE AS A LEAF
Is 64:6 we all *fade as a leaf*, and our iniquities, like the wind, have taken us away

FAILINGS OF THE WEAK (NIV, RSV)
(See *SCRUPLES OF THE WEAK*)

FAINT AND WEARY (KJV, NAS, RSV)
(See *TIRED AND WEARY*)

FAINT FROM HUNGER
Lam 2:19 Lift your hands toward Him for the life of your young children, who *faint from hunger* at the head of every street

FAINT NOT (KJV)
(See *DO NOT LOSE HEART*)

FAIR SPEECHES (KJV)
(See *FLATTERING SPEECH*)

FAIREST AMONG WOMEN
Song 1:8 If you do not know, O *fairest among women*, follow in the footsteps of the flock, and feed your little goats beside the shepherds' tents
Song 5:9 What is your beloved more than another beloved, O *fairest among women*
Song 6:1 Where has your beloved gone, O *fairest among women?* Where has your beloved turned aside, that we may seek him with you

FAITH AS A MUSTARD SEED
Matt 17:20 for assuredly, I say to you, if you have *faith as a mustard seed*, you will say to this mountain
Luke 17:6 So the Lord said, "If you have *faith as a mustard seed*, you can say to this mulberry tree

FAITH COMES BY
Rom 10:17 So then *faith comes by* hearing, and hearing by the word of God

FAITH FROM FIRST TO LAST (NIV)
(See *FAITH TO FAITH*)

FAITH HAS MADE YOU WELL
Matt 9:22 your *faith has made you well.*" And the woman was made well from that hour
Mark 5:34 And He said to her, "Daughter, your *faith has made you well*
Mark 10:52 your *faith has made you well.*" And

immediately he received his sight and followed Jesus on the road
Luke 8:48 And He said to her, "Daughter, be of good cheer; your *faith has made you well*. Go in peace
Luke 17:19 And He said to him, "Arise, go your way. Your *faith has made you well*

FAITH HAS NO VALUE (NIV)
(See *FAITH IS MADE VOID*)

FAITH HAS SAVED YOU
Luke 7:50 Then He said to the woman, "Your *faith has saved you*
Luke 18:42 Then Jesus said to him, "Receive your sight; your *faith has saved you*

FAITH, HOPE, LOVE
1Cor 13:13 And now abide *faith, hope, love*, these three

FAITH IN CHRIST
Acts 24:24 And after some days, when Felix came with his wife Drusilla, who was Jewish, he sent for Paul and heard him concerning the *faith in Christ*
Gal 2:16 knowing that a man is not justified by the works of the law but by faith in Jesus Christ, even we have believed in Christ Jesus, that we might be justified by *faith in Christ* and not by the works of the law
Gal 3:26 For you are all sons of God through *faith in Christ* Jesus
Phil 3:9 and be found in Him, not having my own righteousness, which is from the law, but that which is through *faith in Christ*, the righteousness which is from God by faith
Col 1:4 since we heard of your *faith in Christ* Jesus and of your love for all the saints
Col 2:5 For though I am absent in the flesh, yet I am with you in spirit, rejoicing to see your good order and the steadfastness of your *faith in Christ*

FAITH IN GOD
Mark 11:22 So Jesus answered and said to them, "Have *faith in God*

FAITH IN JESUS
Rom 3:22 even the righteousness of God which is through *faith in Jesus* Christ to all and on all who believe
Rom 3:26 to demonstrate at the present time His righteousness, that He might be just and the justifier of the one who has *faith in Jesus*
Gal 2:16 knowing that a man is not justified by the works of the law but by *faith in Jesus* Christ, even we have believed in Christ Jesus, that we might be justified by faith in Christ and not by the works of the law
Gal 3:22 But the Scripture has confined all under sin, that the promise by *faith in Jesus* Christ might be given to those who believe

FAITH IN THE LORD
Eph 1:15 Therefore I also, after I heard of your *faith in the Lord* Jesus and your love for all the saints

FAITH IS MADE VOID
Rom 4:14 For if those who are of the law are heirs, *faith is made void* and the promise made of no effect

FAITH IS NULL (RSV)
(See *FAITH IS MADE VOID*)

FAITH TO FAITH
Rom 1:17 For in it the righteousness of God is revealed from *faith to faith*

FAITH UNFEIGNED (KJV)
(See *SINCERE FAITH*)

FAITH WITHOUT WORKS
Jas 2:20 But do you want to know, O foolish man, that *faith without works* is dead
Jas 2:26 For as the body without the spirit is dead, so *faith without works* is dead also

FAITHFUL AND TRUE
Rev 3:14 And to the angel of the church of the Laodiceans write, 'These things says the Amen, the *Faithful and True* Witness, the Beginning of the creation of God
Rev 19:11 And He who sat on him was called *Faithful and True*, and in righteousness He judges and makes war
Rev 22:6 Then he said to me, "These words are *faithful and true*

FAITHFUL AND WISE SERVANT
Matt 24:45 Who then is a *faithful and wise servant*, whom his master made ruler over his household, to give them food in due season

FAITHFUL, EVEN TO THE POINT OF DEATH (NIV)
(See *FAITHFUL UNTIL DEATH*)

FAITHFUL LOVE PROMISED TO DAVID (NIV)
(See *SURE MERCIES OF DAVID*)

FAITHFUL MAN
Neh 7:2 that I gave the charge of Jerusalem to my brother Hanani, and Hananiah the leader of the citadel, for he was a *faithful man* and feared God more than many
Prov 20:6 Most men will proclaim each his own goodness, but who can find a *faithful man*
Prov 28:20 A *faithful man* will abound with blessings, but he who hastens to be rich will not go unpunished
Mic 7:2 The *faithful man* has perished from the earth, and there is no one upright among men

FAITHFUL SAYING
1Tim 1:15 This is a *faithful saying* and worthy of all acceptance, that Christ Jesus came into the world to save sinners, of whom I am chief
1Tim 3:1 This is a *faithful saying:* If a man desires the position of a bishop, he desires a good work
1Tim 4:9 This is a *faithful saying* and worthy of all acceptance
2Tim 2:11 This is a *faithful saying:* For if we died with Him, we shall also live with Him
Tit 3:8 This is a *faithful saying*, and these things I want you to affirm constantly, that those who have believed in God should be careful to maintain good works

FAITHFUL UNTIL DEATH
Rev 2:10 Be *faithful until death*, and I will give you the crown of life

FAITHFUL WITNESS
Ps 89:37 It shall be established forever like the moon, even like the *faithful witness* in the sky
Prov 14:5 A *faithful witness* does not lie, but a false witness will utter lies
Jer 42:5 Then they said to Jeremiah, "Let the Lord be a true and *faithful witness* between us, if we do not do according to everything which the Lord your God sends us by you
Rev 1:5 and from Jesus Christ, the *faithful wit-*

ness, the firstborn from the dead, and the ruler over the kings of the earth

FAITHLESS ISRAEL (NAS, NIV)
(See *BACKSLIDING ISRAEL*)

FAITHLESS ONE, ISRAEL (RSV)
(See *BACKSLIDING ISRAEL*)

FAITHLESS TO THE LORD (RSV)
(See *UNFAITHFUL TO THE LORD*)

FALL AWAY
Ps 101:3 I hate the work of those who *fall away;* it shall not cling to me
Luke 8:13 and these have no root, who believe for a while and in time of temptation *fall away*
Heb 6:6 if they *fall away*, to renew them again to repentance, since they crucify again for themselves the Son of God, and put Him to an open shame

FALL BEFORE YOU BY THE SWORD (KJV, NAS, RSV)
(See *FALL BY THE SWORD*)

FALL BY THE SWORD
Lev 26:7 You will chase your enemies, and they shall *fall by the sword* before you
Lev 26:8 Five of you shall chase a hundred, and a hundred of you shall put ten thousand to flight; your enemies shall *fall by the sword* before you
Num 14:3 Why has the Lord brought us to this land to *fall by the sword*, that our wives and children should become victims
Num 14:43 For the Amalekites and the Canaanites are there before you, and you shall *fall by the sword*
2Kin 19:7 and I will cause him to *fall by the sword* in his own land
Ps 63:10 They shall *fall by the sword;* they shall be a portion for jackals
Is 3:25 Your men shall *fall by the sword*, and your mighty in the war
Is 13:15 Everyone who is found will be thrust through, and everyone who is captured will *fall by the sword*
Is 37:7 and I will cause him to *fall by the sword* in his own land
Jer 19:7 And I will make void the counsel of Judah and Jerusalem in this place, and I will cause them to *fall by the sword* before their enemies and by the hands of those who seek their lives
Jer 20:4 and they shall *fall by the sword* of their enemies, and your eyes shall see it
Jer 39:18 For I will surely deliver you, and you shall not *fall by the sword*
Ezek 5:12 and one-third shall *fall by the sword* all around you
Ezek 6:11 For they shall *fall by the sword*, by famine, and by pestilence
Ezek 6:12 He who is far off shall die by the pestilence, he who is near shall *fall by the sword*, and he who remains and is besieged shall die by the famine
Ezek 11:10 You shall *fall by the sword*. I will judge you at the border of Israel
Ezek 17:21 All his fugitives with all his troops shall *fall by the sword*, and those who remain shall be scattered to every wind
Ezek 23:25 they shall remove your nose and your ears, and your remnant shall *fall by the sword*
Ezek 24:21 and your sons and daughters whom you left behind shall *fall by the sword*
Ezek 25:13 I will also stretch out My hand against Edom, cut off man and beast from it, and make it desolate from Teman; Dedan shall *fall by the sword*
Ezek 30:6 From Migdol to Syene those within her shall *fall by the sword*
Ezek 30:17 The young men of Aven and Pi Beseth shall *fall by the sword*, and these cities shall go into captivity
Ezek 33:27 As I live, surely those who are in the ruins shall *fall by the sword*, and the one who is in the open field I will give to the beasts to be devoured, and those who are in the strongholds and caves shall die of the pestilence
Hos 7:16 their princes shall *fall by the sword* for the cursings of their tongue
Hos 13:16 They shall *fall by the sword*, their infants shall be dashed in pieces, and their women with child ripped open
Amos 7:17 your sons and daughters shall *fall by the sword;* your land shall be divided by survey line

FALL INTO TEMPTATION (NIV)
(See *ENTER INTO TEMPTATION*)

FALL SHORT OF THE GLORY OF GOD
Rom 3:23 for all have sinned and *fall short of the glory of God*

FALL UPON THE HEAD (NIV, RSV)
(See *LET IT REST ON THE HEAD*)

FALLEN ASLEEP
Matt 27:52 and many bodies of the saints who had *fallen asleep* were raised
1Cor 15:6 After that He was seen by over five hundred brethren at once, of whom the greater part remain to the present, but some have *fallen asleep*
1Cor 15:18 Then also those who have *fallen asleep* in Christ have perished
1Cor 15:20 But now Christ is risen from the dead, and has become the firstfruits of those who have *fallen asleep*
1Th 4:13 But I do not want you to be ignorant, brethren, concerning those who have *fallen asleep*, lest you sorrow as others who have no hope

FALLEN FROM GRACE
Gal 5:4 You have become estranged from Christ, you who attempt to be justified by law; you have *fallen from grace*

FALLEN FROM HEAVEN
Is 14:12 How you are *fallen from heaven*, O Lucifer, son of the morning
Rev 9:1 And I saw a star *fallen from heaven* to the earth

FALLING AT HIS FEET (NIV)
(See *FELL DOWN AT HIS FEET*)

FALSE APOSTLES
2Cor 11:13 For such are *false apostles*, deceitful workers, transforming themselves into apostles of Christ

FALSE CHRISTS
Matt 24:24 For *false christs* and false prophets will arise and show great signs and wonders, so as to deceive, if possible, even the elect
Mark 13:22 For *false christs* and false prophets will rise and show signs and wonders to deceive, if possible, even the elect

FALSE GODS (RSV)
(See *WORTHLESS IDOLS*)

FALSE PROPHETS
Matt 7:15 Beware of *false prophets*, who come to you in sheep's clothing, but inwardly they are ravenous wolves
Matt 24:11 Then many *false prophets* will rise up and deceive many
Matt 24:24 For false christs and *false prophets* will arise and show great signs and wonders, so as to deceive, if possible, even the elect
Mark 13:22 For false christs and *false prophets* will rise and show signs and wonders to deceive, if possible, even the elect
Luke 6:26 Woe to you when all men speak well of you, For so did their fathers to the *false prophets*
2Pet 2:1 But there were also *false prophets* among the people, even as there will be false teachers among you, who will secretly bring in destructive heresies, even denying the Lord who bought them, and bring on themselves swift destruction
1Jn 4:1 because many *false prophets* have gone out into the world

FALSE TESTIMONY
Matt 26:59 Now the chief priests, the elders, and all the council sought *false testimony* against Jesus to put Him to death

FALSE WITNESS
Ex 20:16 You shall not bear *false witness* against your neighbor
Deut 5:20 You shall not bear *false witness* against your neighbor
Deut 19:16 If a *false witness* rises against any man to testify against him of wrongdoing
Deut 19:18 And the judges shall make diligent inquiry, and indeed, if the witness is a *false witness*, who has testified falsely against his brother
Prov 6:19 a *false witness* who speaks lies, and one who sows discord among brethren
Prov 12:17 He who speaks truth declares righteousness, but a *false witness*, deceit
Prov 14:5 A faithful witness does not lie, but a *false witness* will utter lies
Prov 19:5 A *false witness* will not go unpunished, and he who speaks lies will not escape
Prov 19:9 A *false witness* will not go unpunished, and he who speaks lies shall perish
Prov 21:28 A *false witness* shall perish, but the man who hears him will speak endlessly
Prov 25:18 A man who bears *false witness* against his neighbor is like a club, a sword, and a sharp arrow
Matt 15:19 For out of the heart proceed evil thoughts, murders, adulteries, fornications, thefts, *false witness*, blasphemies
Matt 19:18 Jesus said, "'You shall not murder,' 'You shall not commit adultery,' 'You shall not steal,' 'You shall not bear *false witness*
Mark 10:19 Do not commit adultery,' 'Do not murder,' 'Do not steal,' 'Do not bear *false witness*
Mark 14:56 For many bore *false witness* against Him, but their testimonies did not agree
Mark 14:57 And some rose up and bore *false witness* against Him, saying
Luke 18:20 Do not commit adultery,' 'Do not murder,' 'Do not steal,' 'Do not bear *false witness*
Rom 13:9 For the commandments, "You shall not commit adultery," "You shall not murder," "You shall not steal," "You shall not bear *false witness*

FALTER BETWEEN TWO OPINIONS
1Kin 18:21 And Elijah came to all the people, and said, "How long will you *falter between two opinions*

FALTERING KNEES (NIV)
(See *FEEBLE KNEES*)

FALTERING LIPS (NIV)
(See *UNCIRCUMCISED LIPS*)

FAME AND PRAISE
Zeph 3:20 for I will give you *fame and praise* among all the peoples of the earth, when I return your captives before your eyes

FAMILIAR SPIRITS
Lev 19:31 Give no regard to mediums and *familiar spirits;* do not seek after them, to be defiled by them
Lev 20:6 And the person who turns after mediums and *familiar spirits*, to prostitute himself with them, I will set My face against that person and cut him off from his people
Lev 20:27 A man or a woman who is a medium, or who has *familiar spirits*, shall surely be put to death

FAMILIES OF THE EARTH
Gen 12:3 and in you all the *families of the earth* shall be blessed
Gen 28:14 and in you and in your seed all the *families of the earth* shall be blessed
Amos 3:2 You only have I known of all the *families of the earth*
Zech 14:17 And it shall be that whichever of the *families of the earth* do not come up to Jerusalem to worship the King, the Lord of hosts, on them there will be no rain
Acts 3:25 You are sons of the prophets, and of the covenant which God made with our fathers, saying to Abraham, 'And in your seed all the *families of the earth* shall be blessed

FAMILY OF ABRAHAM
Acts 13:26 Men and brethren, sons of the *family of Abraham*, and those among you who fear God, to you the word of this salvation has been sent

FAMILY OF BELIEVERS (NIV)
(See *HOUSEHOLD OF FAITH*)

FAMINE IN THE LAND
Gen 12:10 Now there was a *famine in the land*, and Abram went down to Egypt to dwell there, for the famine was severe in the land
Gen 26:1 There was a *famine in the land*, besides the first famine that was in the days of Abraham
Ruth 1:1 Now it came to pass, in the days when the judges ruled, that there was a *famine in the land*
1Kin 8:37 When there is *famine in the land*, or pestilence, blight or mildew, locusts or grasshoppers
2Kin 4:38 And Elisha returned to Gilgal, and there was a *famine in the land*
2Chr 6:28 When there is *famine in the land*, pestilence or blight or mildew, locusts or grasshoppers
Ps 105:16 Moreover He called for a *famine in the land;* He destroyed all the provision of bread

FAR BE IT FROM ME
Gen 44:17 But he said, "*Far be it from me* that I should do so
1Sam 2:30 *Far be it from Me;* for those who honor Me I will honor, and those who despise Me shall be lightly esteemed
1Sam 12:23 Moreover, as for me, *far be it from me* that I should sin against the Lord in ceasing to pray for you
1Sam 22:15 *Far be it from me!* Let not the king impute anything to his servant, or to any in the house of my father
2Sam 20:20 And Joab answered and said, "Far be it, *far be it from me*, that I should swallow up or destroy

2Sam 23:17 And he said, "*Far be it from me*, O Lord, that I should do this
1Chr 11:19 And he said, "*Far be it from me*, O my God, that I should do this
Job 27:5 *Far be it from me* that I should say you are right

FAR COUNTRY
Josh 9:6 And they went to Joshua, to the camp at Gilgal, and said to him and to the men of Israel, "We have come from a *far country*
Josh 9:9 From a very *far country* your servants have come, because of the name of the Lord your God
1Kin 8:41 Moreover, concerning a foreigner, who is not of Your people Israel, but has come from a *far country* for Your name's sake
2Kin 20:14 And Hezekiah said, "They came from a *far country*, from Babylon
2Chr 6:32 Moreover, concerning a foreigner, who is not of Your people Israel, but who comes from a *far country* for the sake of Your great name and Your mighty hand and Your outstretched arm, when they come and pray in this temple
Prov 25:25 As cold water to a weary soul, so is good news from a *far country*
Is 13:5 They come from a *far country*, from the end of heaven, even the Lord and His weapons of indignation, to destroy the whole land
Is 39:3 And Hezekiah said, "They came to me from a *far country*, from Babylon
Is 46:11 calling a bird of prey from the east, the man who executes My counsel, from a *far country*
Jer 4:16 Make mention to the nations, yes, proclaim against Jerusalem, that watchers come from a *far country* and raise their voice against the cities of Judah
Jer 6:20 For what purpose to Me comes frankincense from Sheba, and sweet cane from a *far country*
Jer 8:19 The voice, the cry of the daughter of my people from a *far country*
Matt 21:33 And he leased it to vinedressers and went into a *far country*
Matt 25:14 For the kingdom of heaven is like a man traveling to a *far country*, who called his own servants and delivered his goods to them
Mark 12:1 And he leased it to vinedressers and went into a *far country*
Mark 13:34 It is like a man going to a *far country*, who left his house and gave authority to his servants, and to each his work, and commanded the doorkeeper to watch
Luke 15:13 And not many days after, the younger son gathered all together, journeyed to a *far country*, and there wasted his possessions with prodigal living
Luke 19:12 A certain nobleman went into a *far country* to receive for himself a kingdom and to return
Luke 20:9 A certain man planted a vineyard, leased it to vinedressers, and went into a *far country* for a long time

FARTHEST HORIZON (NIV)
(See *FARTHEST PART OF THE HEAVENS*)

FARTHEST PART OF HEAVEN
Mark 13:27 And then He will send His angels, and gather together His elect from the four winds, from the farthest part of earth to the *farthest part of heaven*

FARTHEST PART OF THE HEAVENS
Neh 1:9 but if you return to Me, and keep My commandments and do them, though some of you were cast out to the *farthest part of the heavens*, yet I will gather them from there, and bring them to the place which I have chosen as a dwelling for My name

FARTHEST PARTS OF THE EARTH
Jer 6:22 Behold, a people comes from the north country, and a great nation will be raised from the *farthest parts of the earth*
Jer 25:32 Behold, disaster shall go forth from nation to nation, and a great whirlwind shall be raised up from the *farthest parts of the earth*

FARTHEST SKIES (RSV)
(See *FARTHEST PART OF THE HEAVENS*)

FASTED AND PRAYED
Acts 13:3 Then, having *fasted and prayed*, and laid hands on them, they sent them away

FASTED FORTY DAYS
Matt 4:2 And when He had *fasted forty days* and forty nights, afterward He was hungry

FASTING AND LAMENTING
Esth 9:31 to confirm these days of Purim at their appointed time, as Mordecai the Jew and Queen Esther had prescribed for them, and as they had decreed for themselves and their descendants concerning matters of their *fasting and lamenting*

FAT OF THE LAND
Gen 45:18 I will give you the best of the land of Egypt, and you will eat the *fat of the land*

FATHER, FORGIVE THEM
Luke 23:34 Then Jesus said, "*Father, forgive them*, for they do not know what they do

FATHER, I THANK YOU
John 11:41 And Jesus lifted up His eyes and said, "*Father, I thank You* that You have heard Me

FATHER IN HEAVEN
Matt 5:16 Let your light so shine before men, that they may see your good works and glorify your *Father in heaven*
Matt 5:45 that you may be sons of your *Father in heaven*
Matt 5:48 Therefore you shall be perfect, just as your *Father in heaven* is perfect
Matt 6:1 Otherwise you have no reward from your *Father in heaven*
Matt 6:9 In this manner, therefore, pray: Our *Father in heaven*, hallowed be Your name
Matt 7:21 Not everyone who says to Me, 'Lord, Lord,' shall enter the kingdom of heaven, but he who does the will of My *Father in heaven*
Matt 12:50 For whoever does the will of My *Father in heaven* is My brother and sister and mother
Matt 18:19 Again I say to you that if two of you agree on earth concerning anything that they ask, it will be done for them by My *Father in heaven*
Mark 11:25 And whenever you stand praying, if you have anything against anyone, forgive him, that your *Father in heaven* may also forgive you your trespasses
Mark 11:26 But if you do not forgive, neither will your *Father in heaven* forgive your trespasses
Luke 11:2 Our *Father in heaven*, hallowed be Your name. Your kingdom come

FATHER IS GLORIFIED
John 15:8 By this My *Father is glorified*, that you bear much fruit

FATHER OF A MULTITUDE OF NATIONS (NAS, RSV)
(See *FATHER OF MANY NATIONS*)

FATHER OF LIGHTS
Jas 1:17 Every good gift and every perfect gift is from above, and comes down from the *Father of lights*, with whom there is no variation or shadow of turning

FATHER OF MANY NATIONS
Gen 17:4 As for Me, behold, My covenant is with you, and you shall be a *father of many nations*
Gen 17:5 for I have made you a *father of many nations*
Rom 4:17 (as it is written, "I have made you a *father of many nations*
Rom 4:18 who, contrary to hope, in hope believed, so that he became the *father of many nations*, according to what was spoken

FATHER OF OUR LORD
Rom 15:6 that you may with one mind and one mouth glorify the God and *Father of our Lord* Jesus Christ
2Cor 1:3 Blessed be the God and *Father of our Lord* Jesus Christ, the Father of mercies and God of all comfort
2Cor 11:31 The God and *Father of our Lord* Jesus Christ, who is blessed forever, knows that I am not lying
Eph 1:3 Blessed be the God and *Father of our Lord* Jesus Christ, who has blessed us with every spiritual blessing in the heavenly places in Christ
Eph 3:14 For this reason I bow my knees to the *Father of our Lord* Jesus Christ
Col 1:3 We give thanks to the God and *Father of our Lord* Jesus Christ, praying always for you
1Pet 1:3 Blessed be the God and *Father of our Lord* Jesus Christ, who according to His abundant mercy has begotten us again to a living hope through the resurrection of Jesus Christ from the dead

FATHER WHO SENT ME
John 5:30 and My judgment is righteous, because I do not seek My own will but the will of the *Father who sent Me*
John 6:39 This is the will of the *Father who sent Me*, that of all He has given Me I should lose nothing, but should raise it up at the last day
John 6:44 No one can come to Me unless the *Father who sent Me* draws him
John 8:16 for I am not alone, but I am with the *Father who sent Me*
John 8:18 I am One who bears witness of Myself, and the *Father who sent Me* bears witness of Me
John 12:49 but the *Father who sent Me* gave Me a command, what I should say and what I should speak

FATHER'S BLESSING (NIV)
(See *BLESSINGS OF YOUR FATHER*)

FATHER'S HOUSE
Gen 12:1 Get out of your country, from your family and from your *father's house*, to a land that I will show you
Gen 20:13 And it came to pass, when God caused me to wander from my *father's house*, that I said to her
Gen 24:7 The Lord God of heaven, who took me from my *father's house* and from the land of my family, and who spoke to me and swore to me, saying
Gen 24:23 Tell me, please, is there room in your *father's house* for us to lodge
Gen 24:38 but you shall go to my *father's house* and to my family, and take a wife for my son
Gen 24:40 and you shall take a wife for my son from my family and from my *father's house*
Gen 28:21 so that I come back to my *father's house* in peace, then the Lord shall be my God
Gen 31:14 Then Rachel and Leah answered and said to him, "Is there still any portion or inheritance for us in our *father's house*
Gen 31:30 And now you have surely gone because you greatly long for your *father's house*, but why did you steal my gods
Gen 38:11 Then Judah said to Tamar his daughter-in-law, "Remain a widow in your *father's house* till my son Shelah is grown." For he said, "Lest he also die as his brothers did." And Tamar went and dwelt in her *father's house*
Gen 41:51 For God has made me forget all my toil and all my *father's house*
Gen 46:31 Then Joseph said to his brothers and to his father's household, "I will go up and tell Pharaoh, and say to him, 'My brothers and those of my *father's house*, who were in the land of Canaan, have come to me
Gen 50:8 as well as all the house of Joseph, his brothers, and his *father's house*
Lev 22:13 But if the priest's daughter is a widow or divorced, and has no child, and has returned to her *father's house* as in her youth, she may eat her father's food
Num 1:4 And with you there shall be a man from every tribe, each one the head of his *father's house*
Num 1:44 These are the ones who were numbered, whom Moses and Aaron numbered, with the leaders of Israel, twelve men, each one representing his *father's house*
Num 2:2 Everyone of the children of Israel shall camp by his own standard, beside the emblems of his *father's house*
Num 17:2 Speak to the children of Israel, and get from them a rod from each *father's house*, all their leaders according to their fathers' houses twelve rods
Num 17:3 For there shall be one rod for the head of each *father's house*
Num 18:1 You and your sons and your *father's house* with you shall bear the iniquity related to the sanctuary, and you and your sons with you shall bear the iniquity associated with your priesthood
Num 25:14 Now the name of the Israelite who was killed, who was killed with the Midianite woman, was Zimri the son of Salu, a leader of a *father's house* among the Simeonites
Num 25:15 he was head of the people of a *father's house* in Midian
Num 30:3 Or if a woman vows a vow to the Lord, and binds herself by some agreement while in her *father's house* in her youth
Num 30:16 These are the statutes which the Lord commanded Moses, between a man and his wife, and between a father and his daughter in her youth in her *father's house*
Deut 22:21 then they shall bring out the young woman to the door of her *father's house*, and the men of her city shall stone her to death with stones, because she has done a disgraceful thing in Israel, to play the harlot in her *father's house*
Josh 2:12 Now therefore, I beg you, swear to me by the Lord, since I have shown you kindness, that you also will show kindness to my *father's house*, and give me a true token
Judg 6:15 Indeed my clan is the weakest in Manasseh, and I am the least in my *father's house*
Judg 9:5 Then he went to his *father's house* at Ophrah and killed his brothers, the seventy sons of Jerubbaal, on one stone

Judg 9:18 but you have risen up against my *father's house* this day, and killed his seventy sons on one stone, and made Abimelech, the son of his maidservant, king over the men of Shechem, because he is your brother
Judg 11:2 and when his wife's sons grew up, they drove Jephthah out, and said to him, "You shall have no inheritance in our *father's house*, for you are the son of another woman
Judg 11:7 So Jephthah said to the elders of Gilead, "Did you not hate me, and expel me from my *father's house*
Judg 14:15 So it came to pass on the seventh day that they said to Samson's wife, "Entice your husband, that he may explain the riddle to us, or else we will burn you and your *father's house* with fire
Judg 14:19 So his anger was aroused, and he went back up to his *father's house*
Judg 19:2 But his concubine played the harlot against him, and went away from him to her *father's house* at Bethlehem in Judah, and was there four whole months
Judg 19:3 So she brought him into her *father's house;* and when the father of the young woman saw him, he was glad to meet him
1Sam 2:31 Behold, the days are coming that I will cut off your arm and the arm of your *father's house*, so that there will not be an old man in your house
1Sam 9:20 Is it not on you and on all your *father's house*
1Sam 17:25 and it shall be that the man who kills him the king will enrich with great riches, will give him his daughter, and give his *father's house* exemption in Israel
1Sam 18:2 Saul took him that day, and would not let him go home to his *father's house* anymore
1Sam 22:1 And when his brothers and all his *father's house* heard it, they went down there to him
1Sam 22:11 Then the king sent to call Ahimelech the priest, the son of Ahitub, and all his *father's house*, the priests who were in Nob
1Sam 22:16 And the king said, "You shall surely die, Ahimelech, you and all your *father's house*
1Sam 22:22 I have caused the death of all the persons of your *father's house*
1Sam 24:21 Therefore swear now to me by the Lord that you will not cut off my descendants after me, and that you will not destroy my name from my *father's house*
2Sam 3:29 Let it rest on the head of Joab and on all his *father's house*
2Sam 14:9 And the woman of Tekoa said to the king, "My lord, O king, let the iniquity be on me and on my *father's house*, and the king and his throne be guiltless
2Sam 19:28 For all of my *father's house* were but dead men before my lord the king
2Sam 24:17 Let Your hand, I pray, be against me and against my *father's house*
1Kin 18:18 And he answered, "I have not troubled Israel, but you and your *father's house* have, in that you have forsaken the commandments of the Lord, and you have followed the Baals
1Chr 4:38 these mentioned by name were leaders in their families, and their *father's house* increased greatly
1Chr 5:13 and their brethren of their *father's house:* Michael, Meshullam, Sheba, Jorai, Jachan, Zia, and Heber seven in all
1Chr 5:15 Ahi the son of Abdiel, the son of Guni, was chief of their *father's house*
1Chr 7:2 The sons of Tola were Uzzi, Rephaiah, Jeriel, Jahmai, Jibsam, and Shemuel, heads of their *father's house*
1Chr 9:9 All these men were heads of a *father's house* in their fathers' houses
1Chr 9:19 Shallum the son of Kore, the son of Ebiasaph, the son of Korah, and his brethren, from his *father's house*, the Korahites, were in charge of the work of the service, gatekeepers of the tabernacle
1Chr 12:28 Zadok, a young man, a valiant warrior, and from his *father's house* twenty-two captains
1Chr 12:30 of the children of Ephraim twenty thousand eight hundred, mighty men of valor, famous men throughout their *father's house*
1Chr 21:17 Let Your hand, I pray, O Lord my God, be against me and my *father's house*, but not against Your people that they should be plagued
1Chr 23:11 But Jeush and Beriah did not have many sons; therefore they were assigned as one *father's house*
1Chr 24:6 And the scribe, Shemaiah the son of Nethaneel, one of the Levites, wrote them down before the king, the leaders, Zadok the priest, Ahimelech the son of Abiathar, and the heads of the fathers' houses of the priests and Levites, one *father's house* taken for Eleazar and one for Ithamar
1Chr 26:13 And they cast lots for each gate, the small as well as the great, according to their *father's house*
2Chr 31:17 and to the priests who were written in the genealogy according to their *father's house*, and to the Levites from twenty years old and up according to their work, by their divisions
2Chr 35:5 And stand in the holy place according to the divisions of the fathers' houses of your brethren the lay people, and according to the division of the *father's house* of the Levites
Ezra 2:59 but they could not identify their *father's house* or their genealogy, whether they were of Israel
Neh 1:6 please let Your ear be attentive and Your eyes open, that You may hear the prayer of Your servant which I pray before You now, day and night, for the children of Israel Your servants, and confess the sins of the children of Israel which we have sinned against You. Both my *father's house* and I have sinned
Neh 7:61 And these were the ones who came up from Tel Melah, Tel Harsha, Cherub, Addon, and Immer, but they could not identify their *father's house* nor their lineage, whether they were of Israel
Esth 4:14 For if you remain completely silent at this time, relief and deliverance will arise for the Jews from another place, but you and your *father's house* will perish
Ps 45:10 Listen, O daughter, consider and incline your ear; forget your own people also, and your *father's house*
Is 7:17 The Lord will bring the king of Assyria upon you and your people and your *father's house* days that have not come since the day that Ephraim departed from Judah
Is 22:23 I will fasten him as a peg in a secure place, and he will become a glorious throne to his *father's house*
Is 22:24 They will hang on him all the glory of his *father's house*, the offspring and the issue, all vessels of small quantity, from the cups to all the pitchers
Luke 16:27 Then he said, 'I beg you therefore, father, that you would send him to my *father's house*
John 2:16 Do not make My *Father's house* a house of merchandise
John 14:2 In My *Father's house* are many mansions; if it were not so, I would have told you
Acts 7:20 and he was brought up in his *father's house* for three months

FATHER'S NAKEDNESS
Gen 9:23 Their faces were turned away, and they did not see their *father's nakedness*
Lev 18:8 The nakedness of your father's wife you shall not uncover; it is your *father's nakedness*
Lev 20:11 The man who lies with his father's wife has uncovered his *father's nakedness*

FATHERLESS AND THE WIDOW
Deut 10:18 He administers justice for the *fatherless and the widow*, and loves the stranger, giving him food and clothing
Deut 14:29 And the Levite, because he has no portion nor inheritance with you, and the stranger and the *fatherless and the widow* who are within your gates, may come and eat and be satisfied, that the Lord your God may bless you in all the work of your hand which you do
Deut 16:11 You shall rejoice before the Lord your God, you and your son and your daughter, your manservant and your maidservant, the Levite who is within your gates, the stranger and the *fatherless and the widow* who are among you, at the place where the Lord your God chooses to make His name abide
Deut 16:14 and you shall rejoice in your feast, you and your son and your daughter, your manservant and your maidservant and the Levite, the stranger and the *fatherless and the widow*, who are within your gates
Ezek 22:7 in you they have mistreated the *fatherless and the widow*

FATHERLESS, AND THE WIDOW
Deut 24:19 it shall be for the stranger, the *fatherless, and the widow*, that the Lord your God may bless you in all the work of your hands
Deut 24:20 it shall be for the stranger, the *fatherless, and the widow*
Deut 24:21 it shall be for the stranger, the *fatherless, and the widow*
Deut 26:12 When you have finished laying aside all the tithe of your increase in the third year, which is the year of tithing, and have given it to the Levite, the stranger, the *fatherless, and the widow*, so that they may eat within your gates and be filled
Deut 26:13 I have removed the holy tithe from my house, and also have given them to the Levite, the stranger, the *fatherless, and the widow*, according to all Your commandments which You have commanded me
Jer 7:6 if you do not oppress the stranger, the *fatherless, and the widow*, and do not shed innocent blood in this place, or walk after other gods to your hurt

FATHERS HAVE EATEN SOUR GRAPES
Jer 31:29 The *fathers have eaten sour grapes*, and the children's teeth are set on edge
Ezek 18:2 The *fathers have eaten sour grapes*, and the children's teeth are set on edge

FATHERS' LABOR (NIV)
(See *LABOR OF OUR FATHERS*)

FAVOR WITH GOD
Luke 1:30 Then the angel said to her, "Do not be afraid, Mary, for you have found *favor with God*
Luke 2:52 And Jesus increased in wisdom and stature, and in *favor with God* and men

FEAR AND THE PIT AND THE SNARE
Is 24:17 *Fear and the pit and the snare* are upon you, O inhabitant of the earth
Jer 48:43 *Fear and the pit and the snare* shall be upon you, O inhabitant of Moab

FEAR AND TREMBLING
2Cor 7:15 And his affections are greater for you as he remembers the obedience of you all, how with *fear and trembling* you received him
Eph 6:5 Servants, be obedient to those who are your masters according to the flesh, with *fear and trembling*, in sincerity of heart, as to Christ
Phil 2:12 Therefore, my beloved, as you have always obeyed, not as in my presence only, but now much more in my absence, work out your own salvation with *fear and trembling*

FEAR BEFORE HIM (KJV)
(See *TREMBLE BEFORE HIM*)

FEAR GOD AND KEEP HIS COMMANDMENTS
Eccl 12:13 *Fear God and keep His commandments*, for this is the whole duty of man

FEAR HAS TO DO WITH PUNISHMENT (NIV, RSV)
(See *FEAR INVOLVES TORMENT*)

FEAR HATH TORMENT (KJV)
(See *FEAR INVOLVES TORMENT*)

FEAR INVOLVES TORMENT
1Jn 4:18 but perfect love casts out fear, because *fear involves torment*

FEAR IS ON EVERY SIDE
Ps 31:13 *Fear is on every side;* while they take counsel together against me, they scheme to take away my life
Jer 6:25 Because of the sword of the enemy, *fear is on every side*
Jer 49:29 and they shall cry out to them, '*Fear is on every side*

FEAR NOT
Gen 21:17 *Fear not*, for God has heard the voice of the lad where he is
Is 41:10 *Fear not*, for I am with you; be not dismayed, for I am your God
Is 41:13 For I, the Lord your God, will hold your right hand, saying to you, '*Fear not*, I will help you
Is 41:14 *Fear not*, you worm Jacob, you men of Israel! I will help you
Is 43:1 *Fear not*, for I have redeemed you; I have called you by your name
Is 43:5 *Fear not*, for I am with you; I will bring your descendants from the east, and gather you from the west
Is 44:2 *Fear not*, O Jacob My servant; and you, Jeshurun, whom I have chosen
Dan 10:19 And he said, "O man greatly beloved, *fear not!* Peace be to you
Joel 2:21 *Fear not*, O land; be glad and rejoice, for the Lord has done marvelous things
John 12:15 *Fear not*, daughter of Zion; behold, your King is coming, sitting on a donkey's colt

FEAR OF DEATH
Heb 2:15 and release those who through *fear of death* were all their lifetime subject to bondage

FEAR OF GOD
Gen 20:11 And Abraham said, "Because I thought, surely the *fear of God* is not in this place
2Sam 23:4 ruling in the *fear of God*. And he shall be like the light of the morning when the sun rises, a morning without clouds, like the tender grass springing out of the earth, by clear shining after rain
2Chr 20:29 And the *fear of God* was on all the kingdoms of those countries when they heard

that the Lord had fought against the enemies of Israel

Neh 5:15 yes, even their servants bore rule over the people, but I did not do so, because of the *fear of God*

Ps 36:1 An oracle within my heart concerning the transgression of the wicked: There is no *fear of God* before his eyes

Rom 3:18 There is no *fear of God* before their eyes

2Cor 7:1 Therefore, having these promises, beloved, let us cleanse ourselves from all filthiness of the flesh and spirit, perfecting holiness in the *fear of God*

Eph 5:21 submitting to one another in the *fear of God*

FEAR OF THE LORD

1Sam 11:7 And the *fear of the Lord* fell on the people, and they came out with one consent

2Chr 14:14 Then they defeated all the cities around Gerar, for the *fear of the Lord* came upon them

2Chr 17:10 And the *fear of the Lord* fell on all the kingdoms of the lands that were around Judah, so that they did not make war against Jehoshaphat

2Chr 19:7 Now therefore, let the *fear of the Lord* be upon you

2Chr 19:9 And he commanded them, saying, "Thus you shall act in the *fear of the Lord*, faithfully and with a loyal heart

Job 28:28 And to man He said, 'Behold, the *fear of the Lord*, that is wisdom, and to depart from evil is understanding

Ps 19:9 The *fear of the Lord* is clean, enduring forever; the judgments of the Lord are true and righteous altogether

Ps 34:11 Come, you children, listen to me; I will teach you the *fear of the Lord*

Ps 111:10 The *fear of the Lord* is the beginning of wisdom

Prov 1:7 The *fear of the Lord* is the beginning of knowledge, but fools despise wisdom and instruction

Prov 1:29 Because they hated knowledge and did not choose the *fear of the Lord*

Prov 2:5 then you will understand the *fear of the Lord*, and find the knowledge of God

Prov 8:13 The *fear of the Lord* is to hate evil; pride and arrogance and the evil way and the perverse mouth I hate

Prov 9:10 The *fear of the Lord* is the beginning of wisdom, and the knowledge of the Holy One is understanding

Prov 10:27 The *fear of the Lord* prolongs days, but the years of the wicked will be shortened

Prov 14:26 In the *fear of the Lord* there is strong confidence, and His children will have a place of refuge

Prov 14:27 The *fear of the Lord* is a fountain of life, to avoid the snares of death

Prov 15:16 Better is a little with the *fear of the Lord*, than great treasure with trouble

Prov 15:33 The *fear of the Lord* is the instruction of wisdom, and before honor is humility

Prov 16:6 and by the *fear of the Lord* one departs from evil

Prov 19:23 The *fear of the Lord* leads to life, and he who has it will abide in satisfaction

Prov 22:4 By humility and the *fear of the Lord* are riches and honor and life

Prov 23:17 Do not let your heart envy sinners, but in the *fear of the Lord* continue all day long

Is 11:2 The Spirit of the Lord shall rest upon Him, the Spirit of wisdom and understanding, the Spirit of counsel and might, the Spirit of knowledge and of the *fear of the Lord*

Is 11:3 His delight is in the *fear of the Lord*, and He shall not judge by the sight of His eyes, nor decide by the hearing of His ears

Is 33:6 Wisdom and knowledge will be the stability of your times, and the strength of salvation; the *fear of the Lord* is His treasure

Acts 9:31 And walking in the *fear of the Lord* and in the comfort of the Holy Spirit, they were multiplied

FEAR THE LORD

Ex 9:30 But as for you and your servants, I know that you will not yet *fear the Lord* God

Deut 6:2 that you may *fear the Lord* your God, to keep all His statutes and His commandments which I command you, you and your son and your grandson, all the days of your life, and that your days may be prolonged

Deut 6:13 You shall *fear the Lord* your God and serve Him, and shall take oaths in His name

Deut 6:24 And the Lord commanded us to observe all these statutes, to *fear the Lord* our God, for our good always, that He might preserve us alive, as it is this day

Deut 10:12 And now, Israel, what does the Lord your God require of you, but to *fear the Lord* your God, to walk in all His ways and to love Him, to serve the Lord your God with all your heart and with all your soul

Deut 10:20 You shall *fear the Lord* your God; you shall serve Him, and to Him you shall hold fast, and take oaths in His name

Deut 14:23 And you shall eat before the Lord your God, in the place where He chooses to make His name abide, the tithe of your grain and your new wine and your oil, of the firstlings of your herds and your flocks, that you may learn to *fear the Lord* your God always

Deut 17:19 And it shall be with him, and he shall read it all the days of his life, that he may learn to *fear the Lord* his God and be careful to observe all the words of this law and these statutes

Deut 31:12 Gather the people together, men and women and little ones, and the stranger who is within your gates, that they may hear and that they may learn to *fear the Lord* your God and carefully observe all the words of this law

Deut 31:13 and that their children, who have not known it, may hear and learn to *fear the Lord* your God as long as you live in the land which you cross the Jordan to possess

Josh 4:24 that all the peoples of the earth may know the hand of the Lord, that it is mighty, that you may *fear the Lord* your God forever

Josh 24:14 Now therefore, *fear the Lord*, serve Him in sincerity and in truth, and put away the gods which your fathers served on the other side of the River and in Egypt

1Sam 12:14 If you *fear the Lord* and serve Him and obey His voice, and do not rebel against the commandment of the Lord, then both you and the king who reigns over you will continue following the Lord your God

1Sam 12:24 Only *fear the Lord*, and serve Him in truth with all your heart

2Kin 17:25 And it was so, at the beginning of their dwelling there, that they did not *fear the Lord*

2Kin 17:28 Then one of the priests whom they had carried away from Samaria came and dwelt in Bethel, and taught them how they should *fear the Lord*

2Kin 17:34 they do not *fear the Lord*, nor do they follow their statutes or their ordinances, or the law and commandment which the Lord had commanded the children of Jacob, whom He named Israel

Ps 15:4 In whose eyes a vile person is despised, but he honors those who *fear the Lord*

Ps 22:23 You who *fear the Lord*, praise Him! All

you descendants of Jacob, glorify Him, and fear Him, all you offspring of Israel
Ps 33:8 Let all the earth *fear the Lord;* let all the inhabitants of the world stand in awe of Him
Ps 34:9 Oh, *fear the Lord*, you His saints! There is no want to those who fear Him
Ps 115:11 You who *fear the Lord*, trust in the Lord; He is their help and their shield
Ps 115:13 He will bless those who *fear the Lord*, both small and great
Ps 118:4 Let those who *fear the Lord* now say, "His mercy endures forever
Ps 135:20 Bless the Lord, O house of Levi! You who *fear the Lord*, bless the Lord
Prov 3:7 Do not be wise in your own eyes; *fear the Lord* and depart from evil
Prov 24:21 My son, *fear the Lord* and the king; do not associate with those given to change
Jer 5:24 They do not say in their heart, "Let us now *fear the Lord* our God, Who gives rain, both the former and the latter, in its season
Jer 26:19 Did he not *fear the Lord* and seek the Lord's favor
Hos 3:5 Afterward the children of Israel shall return, seek the Lord their God and David their king, and *fear the Lord* and His goodness in the latter days
Hos 10:3 For now they say, "We have no king, because we did not *fear the Lord*
Jon 1:9 and I *fear the Lord*, the God of heaven, who made the sea and the dry land
Mal 3:16 so a book of remembrance was written before Him for those who *fear the Lord* and who meditate on His name

FEAR THE NAME OF THE LORD
Ps 102:15 So the nations shall *fear the name of the Lord*, and all the kings of the earth Your glory
Is 59:19 So shall they *fear the name of the Lord* from the west, and His glory from the rising of the sun

FEAR YOUR NAME
Neh 1:11 O Lord, I pray, please let Your ear be attentive to the prayer of Your servant, and to the prayer of Your servants who desire to *fear Your name*
Ps 61:5 You have given me the heritage of those who *fear Your name*
Ps 86:11 I will walk in Your truth; unite my heart to *fear Your name*
Rev 11:18 The nations were angry, and Your wrath has come, and the time of the dead, that they should be judged, and that You should reward Your servants the prophets and the saints, and those who *fear Your name*, small and great, and should destroy those who destroy the earth

FEARED GOD
Ex 1:17 But the midwives *feared God*, and did not do as the king of Egypt commanded them, but saved the male children alive
Ex 1:21 And so it was, because the midwives *feared God*, that He provided households for them
Neh 7:2 that I gave the charge of Jerusalem to my brother Hanani, and Hananiah the leader of the citadel, for he was a faithful man and *feared God* more than many
Job 1:1 and that man was blameless and upright, and one who *feared God* and shunned evil
Acts 10:2 a devout man and one who *feared God* with all his household, who gave alms generously to the people, and prayed to God always

FEARED THE LORD
Ex 14:31 so the people *feared the Lord*, and believed the Lord and His servant Moses
1Sam 12:18 and all the people greatly *feared the Lord* and Samuel
1Kin 18:3 And Ahab had called Obadiah, who was in charge of his house. (Now Obadiah *feared the Lord* greatly
1Kin 18:12 But I your servant have *feared the Lord* from my youth
2Kin 4:1 A certain woman of the wives of the sons of the prophets cried out to Elisha, saying, "Your servant my husband is dead, and you know that your servant *feared the Lord*
2Kin 17:32 So they *feared the Lord*, and from every class they appointed for themselves priests of the high places, who sacrificed for them in the shrines of the high places
2Kin 17:33 They *feared the Lord*, yet served their own gods according to the rituals of the nations from among whom they were carried away
2Kin 17:41 So these nations *feared the Lord*, yet served their carved images
Jon 1:16 Then the men *feared the Lord* exceedingly, and offered a sacrifice to the Lord and made vows
Mal 3:16 Then those who *feared the Lord* spoke to one another, and the Lord listened and heard them

FEARFULLY AND WONDERFULLY MADE
Ps 139:14 I will praise You, for I am *fearfully and wonderfully made*

FEARS GOD
Job 1:8 Then the Lord said to Satan, "Have you considered My servant Job, that there is none like him on the earth, a blameless and upright man, one who *fears God* and shuns evil
Job 2:3 Then the Lord said to Satan, "Have you considered My servant Job, that there is none like him on the earth, a blameless and upright man, one who *fears God* and shuns evil
Eccl 7:18 It is good that you grasp this, and also not remove your hand from the other; for he who *fears God* will escape them all
Acts 10:22 And they said, "Cornelius the centurion, a just man, one who *fears God* and has a good reputation among all the nation of the Jews, was divinely instructed by a holy angel to summon you to his house, and to hear words from you

FEAST OF DEDICATION
John 10:22 Now it was the *Feast of Dedication* in Jerusalem, and it was winter

FEAST OF HARVEST
Ex 23:16 and the *Feast of Harvest*, the firstfruits of your labors which you have sown in the field

FEAST OF INGATHERING
Ex 23:16 and the *Feast of Ingathering* at the end of the year, when you have gathered in the fruit of your labors from the field
Ex 34:22 And you shall observe the Feast of Weeks, of the firstfruits of wheat harvest, and the *Feast of Ingathering* at the year's end

FEAST OF TABERNACLES
Lev 23:34 The fifteenth day of this seventh month shall be the *Feast of Tabernacles* for seven days to the Lord
Deut 16:13 You shall observe the *Feast of Tabernacles* seven days, when you have gathered from your threshing floor and from your winepress
Deut 16:16 at the Feast of Unleavened Bread, at the Feast of Weeks, and at the *Feast of Tabernacles*
Deut 31:10 At the end of every seven years, at the

appointed time in the year of release, at the *Feast of Tabernacles*
2Chr 8:13 according to the daily rate, offering according to the commandment of Moses, for the Sabbaths, the New Moons, and the three appointed yearly feasts the Feast of Unleavened Bread, the Feast of Weeks, and the *Feast of Tabernacles*
Ezra 3:4 They also kept the *Feast of Tabernacles*, as it is written, and offered the daily burnt offerings in the number required by ordinance for each day
Zech 14:16 And it shall come to pass that everyone who is left of all the nations which came against Jerusalem shall go up from year to year to worship the King, the Lord of hosts, and to keep the *Feast of Tabernacles*
Zech 14:18 they shall receive the plague with which the Lord strikes the nations who do not come up to keep the *Feast of Tabernacles*
Zech 14:19 This shall be the punishment of Egypt and the punishment of all the nations that do not come up to keep the *Feast of Tabernacles*
John 7:2 Now the Jews' *Feast of Tabernacles* was at hand

FEAST OF THE PASSOVER
Ex 34:25 You shall not offer the blood of My sacrifice with leaven, nor shall the sacrifice of the *Feast of the Passover* be left until morning
Luke 2:41 His parents went to Jerusalem every year at the *Feast of the Passover*
John 13:1 Now before the *feast of the Passover*, when Jesus knew that His hour had come that He should depart from this world to the Father, having loved His own who were in the world, He loved them to the end

FEAST OF THE UNLEAVENED BREAD
Matt 26:17 Now on the first day of the *Feast of the Unleavened Bread* the disciples came to Jesus, saying to Him

FEAST OF UNLEAVENED BREAD
Ex 12:17 So you shall observe the *Feast of Unleavened Bread*, for on this same day I will have brought your armies out of the land of Egypt
Ex 23:15 You shall keep the *Feast of Unleavened Bread* (you shall eat unleavened bread seven days, as I commanded you, at the time appointed in the month of Abib, for in it you came out of Egypt
Ex 34:18 The *Feast of Unleavened Bread* you shall keep. Seven days you shall eat unleavened bread, as I commanded you, in the appointed time of the month of Abib
Lev 23:6 And on the fifteenth day of the same month is the *Feast of Unleavened Bread* to the Lord
Deut 16:16 at the *Feast of Unleavened Bread*, at the Feast of Weeks, and at the Feast of Tabernacles
2Chr 8:13 according to the daily rate, offering according to the commandment of Moses, for the Sabbaths, the New Moons, and the three appointed yearly feasts the *Feast of Unleavened Bread*, the Feast of Weeks, and the Feast of Tabernacles
2Chr 30:13 Now many people, a very great congregation, assembled at Jerusalem to keep the *Feast of Unleavened Bread* in the second month
2Chr 30:21 So the children of Israel who were present at Jerusalem kept the *Feast of Unleavened Bread* seven days with great gladness
2Chr 35:17 And the children of Israel who were present kept the Passover at that time, and the *Feast of Unleavened Bread* for seven days
Ezra 6:22 And they kept the *Feast of Unleavened Bread* seven days with joy
Mark 14:1 After two days it was the Passover and the *Feast of Unleavened Bread*
Luke 22:1 Now the *Feast of Unleavened Bread* drew near, which is called Passover

FEAST OF WEEKS
Ex 34:22 And you shall observe the *Feast of Weeks*, of the firstfruits of wheat harvest, and the Feast of Ingathering at the year's end
Num 28:26 Also on the day of the firstfruits, when you bring a new grain offering to the Lord at your *Feast of Weeks*, you shall have a holy convocation
Deut 16:10 Then you shall keep the *Feast of Weeks* to the Lord your God with the tribute of a freewill offering from your hand, which you shall give as the Lord your God blesses you
Deut 16:16 at the Feast of Unleavened Bread, at the *Feast of Weeks*, and at the Feast of Tabernacles
2Chr 8:13 according to the daily rate, offering according to the commandment of Moses, for the Sabbaths, the New Moons, and the three appointed yearly feasts the Feast of Unleavened Bread, the *Feast of Weeks*, and the Feast of Tabernacles

FEASTS OF THE LORD
Lev 23:2 The *feasts of the Lord*, which you shall proclaim to be holy convocations, these are My feasts
Lev 23:4 These are the *feasts of the Lord*, holy convocations which you shall proclaim at their appointed times
Lev 23:37 These are the *feasts of the Lord* which you shall proclaim to be holy convocations, to offer an offering made by fire to the Lord, a burnt offering and a grain offering, a sacrifice and drink offerings, everything on its day
Lev 23:44 So Moses declared to the children of Israel the *feasts of the Lord*
2Chr 2:4 Behold, I am building a temple for the name of the Lord my God, to dedicate it to Him, to burn before Him sweet incense, for the continual showbread, for the burnt offerings morning and evening, on the Sabbaths, on the New Moons, and on the set *feasts of the Lord* our God
Ezra 3:5 and afterward they offered the regular burnt offering, and those for New Moons and for all the appointed *feasts of the Lord* that were consecrated, and those of everyone who willingly offered a freewill offering to the Lord

FEEBLE HANDS (NIV)
(See *WEAK HANDS*)

FEEBLE KNEES
Job 4:4 Your words have upheld him who was stumbling, and you have strengthened the *feeble knees*
Is 35:3 Strengthen the weak hands, and make firm the *feeble knees*
Heb 12:12 Therefore strengthen the hands which hang down, and the *feeble knees*

FEED MY LAMBS
John 21:15 You know that I love You." He said to him, "*Feed My lambs*

FEED MY PEOPLE (KJV)
(See *SHEPHERD MY PEOPLE*)

FEED MY SHEEP
John 21:17 You know that I love You." Jesus said to him, "*Feed My sheep*

FEED THE FLOCK OF GOD (KJV)
(See *SHEPHERD THE FLOCK OF GOD*)

FEEDS ON THE WIND
Hos 12:1 Ephraim *feeds on the wind*, and pursues the east wind

FEET HAVE NOT SLIPPED (NAS, NIV, RSV)
(See *FOOTSTEPS MAY NOT SLIP*)

FEET OF IRON
Dan 2:34 You watched while a stone was cut out without hands, which struck the image on its *feet of iron* and clay, and broke them in pieces

FEET OF THE POOR
Is 26:6 The foot shall tread it down the *feet of the poor* and the steps of the needy

FEET RUN TO EVIL
Prov 1:16 for their *feet run to evil*, and they make haste to shed blood
Is 59:7 Their *feet run to evil*, and they make haste to shed innocent blood

FEET THAT ARE SWIFT IN RUNNING TO EVIL
Prov 6:18 a heart that devises wicked plans, *feet that are swift in running to evil*

FEIGNED LIPS (KJV)
(See *DECEITFUL LIPS*)

FELL AMONG THIEVES
Luke 10:30 A certain man went down from Jerusalem to Jericho, and *fell among thieves*, who stripped him of his clothing, wounded him, and departed, leaving him half dead

FELL AT HIS FEET
1Sam 25:24 So she *fell at his feet* and said: "On me, my lord, on me let this iniquity be
2Kin 4:37 So she went in, *fell at his feet*, and bowed to the ground
Mark 5:22 And when he saw Him, he *fell at His feet*
Mark 7:25 For a woman whose young daughter had an unclean spirit heard about Him, and she came and *fell at His feet*
Rev 1:17 And when I saw Him, I *fell at His feet* as dead
Rev 19:10 And I *fell at his feet* to worship him. But he said to me

FELL DOWN AND WORSHIPED
Dan 3:7 So at that time, when all the people heard the sound of the horn, flute, harp, and lyre, in symphony with all kinds of music, all the people, nations, and languages *fell down and worshiped* the gold image which King Nebuchadnezzar had set up
Matt 2:11 And when they had come into the house, they saw the young Child with Mary His mother, and *fell down and worshiped* Him
Rev 5:14 And the twenty-four elders *fell down and worshiped* Him who lives forever and ever
Rev 19:4 And the twenty-four elders and the four living creatures *fell down and worshiped* God who sat on the throne, saying

FELL DOWN AT HIS FEET
Esth 8:3 Now Esther spoke again to the king, *fell down at his feet*, and implored him with tears to counteract the evil plot of Haman the Agagite, and the scheme which he had devised against the Jews
Matt 18:29 So his fellow servant *fell down at his feet* and begged him, saying
John 11:32 Then, when Mary came where Jesus was, and saw Him, she *fell down at His feet*, saying to Him
Acts 5:10 Then immediately she *fell down at his feet* and breathed her last
Acts 10:25 As Peter was coming in, Cornelius met him and *fell down at his feet* and worshiped him

FELL DOWN ON HIS FACE
Luke 17:16 and *fell down on his face* at His feet, giving Him thanks

FELL FACEDOWN (NIV)
(See *FELL ON MY FACE*)

FELL INTO THE HANDS OF ROBBERS (NIV)
(See *FELL AMONG THIEVES*)

FELL ON HIS KNEES
2Kin 1:13 And the third captain of fifty went up, and came and *fell on his knees* before Elijah, and pleaded with him, and said to him

FELL ON MY FACE
Ezek 1:28 So when I saw it, I *fell on my face*, and I heard a voice of One speaking
Ezek 3:23 So I arose and went out into the plain, and behold, the glory of the Lord stood there, like the glory which I saw by the River Chebar; and I *fell on my face*
Ezek 9:8 and I *fell on my face* and cried out, and said
Ezek 11:13 Then I *fell on my face* and cried with a loud voice, and said
Ezek 43:3 The visions were like the vision which I saw by the River Chebar; and I *fell on my face*
Ezek 44:4 so I looked, and behold, the glory of the Lord filled the house of the Lord; and I *fell on my face*
Dan 8:17 So he came near where I stood, and when he came I was afraid and *fell on my face*

FELL ON THE GROUND
Mark 9:20 And when he saw Him, immediately the spirit convulsed him, and he *fell on the ground* and wallowed, foaming at the mouth
Mark 14:35 He went a little farther, and *fell on the ground*, and prayed that if it were possible, the hour might pass from Him

FELL ON THEIR FACES
Lev 9:24 When all the people saw it, they shouted and *fell on their faces*
Num 14:5 Then Moses and Aaron *fell on their faces* before all the assembly of the congregation of the children of Israel
Num 16:22 Then they *fell on their faces*, and said, "O God, the God of the spirits of all flesh, shall one man sin, and You be angry with all the congregation
Num 16:45 Get away from among this congregation, that I may consume them in a moment." And they *fell on their faces*
Num 20:6 So Moses and Aaron went from the presence of the assembly to the door of the tabernacle of meeting, and they *fell on their faces*
Judg 13:20 When Manoah and his wife saw this, they *fell on their faces* to the ground
1Kin 18:39 Now when all the people saw it, they *fell on their faces*
1Chr 21:16 So David and the elders, clothed in sackcloth, *fell on their faces*
Matt 17:6 And when the disciples heard it, they *fell on their faces* and were greatly afraid
Rev 7:11 And all the angels stood around the throne and the elders and the four living creatures, and *fell on their faces* before the throne and worshiped God
Rev 11:16 And the twenty-four elders who sat be-

fore God on their thrones *fell on their faces* and worshiped God

FELLOW HEIRS WITH CHRIST (NAS, RSV)
(See *JOINT HEIRS WITH CHRIST*)

FELLOWSHIP OF HIS SON
1Cor 1:9 God is faithful, by whom you were called into the *fellowship of His Son*, Jesus Christ our Lord

FELLOWSHIP OF HIS SUFFERINGS
Phil 3:10 that I may know Him and the power of His resurrection, and the *fellowship of His sufferings*, being conformed to His death

FELLOWSHIP OF THE HOLY SPIRIT (NAS, NIV, RSV)
(See *COMMUNION OF THE HOLY SPIRIT*)

FELLOWSHIP OF THE SPIRIT
Phil 2:1 Therefore if there is any consolation in Christ, if any comfort of love, if any *fellowship of the Spirit*, if any affection and mercy

FELLOWSHIP OFFERING (NIV)
(See *SACRIFICE OF PEACE OFFERINGS*)

FELLOWSHIP WITH ONE ANOTHER
1Jn 1:7 But if we walk in the light as He is in the light, we have *fellowship with one another*, and the blood of Jesus Christ His Son cleanses us from all sin

FENCED CITIES (KJV)
(See *FORTIFIED CITIES*)

FEW DAYS AND FULL OF TROUBLE
Job 14:1 Man who is born of woman is of *few days and full of trouble*

FIELD OF BLOOD
Matt 27:8 Therefore that field has been called the *Field of Blood* to this day
Acts 1:19 so that field is called in their own language, Akel Dama, that is, *Field of Blood*

FIELDS AND VINEYARDS
Num 16:14 Moreover you have not brought us into a land flowing with milk and honey, nor given us inheritance of *fields and vineyards*
1Sam 22:7 Will the son of Jesse give every one of you *fields and vineyards*, and make you all captains of thousands and captains of hundreds
Jer 32:15 Houses and *fields and vineyards* shall be possessed again in this land

FIERCE ANGER
Num 25:4 Then the Lord said to Moses, "Take all the leaders of the people and hang the offenders before the Lord, out in the sun, that the *fierce anger* of the Lord may turn away from Israel
Num 32:14 You have risen in your father's place, a brood of sinful men, to increase still more the *fierce anger* of the Lord against Israel
1Sam 20:34 So Jonathan arose from the table in *fierce anger*, and ate no food the second day of the month, for he was grieved for David, because his father had treated him shamefully
Is 7:4 do not fear or be fainthearted for these two stubs of smoking firebrands, for the *fierce anger* of Rezin and Syria, and the son of Remaliah
Is 13:9 Behold, the day of the Lord comes, cruel, with both wrath and *fierce anger*, to lay the land desolate
Is 13:13 Therefore I will shake the heavens, and the earth will move out of her place, in the wrath of the Lord of hosts and in the day of His *fierce anger*
Jer 4:8 For the *fierce anger* of the Lord has not turned back from us
Jer 4:26 I beheld, and indeed the fruitful land was a wilderness, and all its cities were broken down at the presence of the Lord, by His *fierce anger*
Jer 12:13 But be ashamed of your harvest because of the *fierce anger* of the Lord
Jer 25:37 and the peaceful habitations are cut down because of the *fierce anger* of the Lord
Jer 25:38 for their land is desolate because of the fierceness of the Oppressor, and because of His *fierce anger*
Jer 30:24 The *fierce anger* of the Lord will not return until He has done it, and until He has performed the intents of His heart
Jer 49:37 I will bring disaster upon them, my *fierce anger*,' says the Lord
Jer 51:45 And let everyone deliver himself from the *fierce anger* of the Lord
Lam 1:12 Behold and see if there is any sorrow like my sorrow, which has been brought on me, which the Lord has inflicted on me in the day of His *fierce anger*
Lam 2:3 He has cut off in *fierce anger* every horn of Israel
Lam 4:11 The Lord has fulfilled His fury, He has poured out His *fierce anger*
Jon 3:9 Who can tell if God will turn and relent, and turn away from His *fierce anger*, so that we may not perish
Zeph 2:2 before the decree is issued, before the day passes like chaff, before the Lord's *fierce anger* comes upon you, before the day of the Lord's anger comes upon you
Zeph 3:8 My determination is to gather the nations to My assembly of kingdoms, to pour on them My indignation, all my *fierce anger*

FIERCE WOLVES (RSV)
(See *SAVAGE WOLVES*)

FIERCE WRATH
Ex 32:12 Turn from Your *fierce wrath*, and repent from this harm to Your people
1Sam 28:18 Because you did not obey the voice of the Lord nor execute His *fierce wrath* upon Amalek, therefore the Lord has done this thing to you this day
2Chr 28:11 Now hear me, therefore, and return the captives, whom you have taken captive from your brethren, for the *fierce wrath* of the Lord is upon you
2Chr 28:13 for our guilt is great, and there is *fierce wrath* against Israel
2Chr 29:10 Now it is in my heart to make a covenant with the Lord God of Israel, that His *fierce wrath* may turn away from us
Ezra 10:14 and let all those in our cities who have taken pagan wives come at appointed times, together with the elders and judges of their cities, until the *fierce wrath* of our God is turned away from us in this matter
Ps 88:16 Your *fierce wrath* has gone over me; Your terrors have cut me off

FIERY DARTS OF THE WICKED ONE
Eph 6:16 above all, taking the shield of faith with which you will be able to quench all the *fiery darts of the wicked one*

FIERY FURNACE
Dan 3:6 and whoever does not fall down and worship shall be cast immediately into the midst of a burning *fiery furnace*
Dan 3:11 and whoever does not fall down and

worship shall be cast into the midst of a burning *fiery furnace*
Dan 3:15 But if you do not worship, you shall be cast immediately into the midst of a burning *fiery furnace*
Dan 3:17 If that is the case, our God whom we serve is able to deliver us from the burning *fiery furnace*, and He will deliver us from your hand, O king
Dan 3:20 And he commanded certain mighty men of valor who were in his army to bind Shadrach, Meshach, and Abed-Nego, and cast them into the burning *fiery furnace*
Dan 3:21 Then these men were bound in their coats, their trousers, their turbans, and their other garments, and were cast into the midst of the burning *fiery furnace*
Dan 3:23 And these three men, Shadrach, Meshach, and Abed-Nego, fell down bound into the midst of the burning *fiery furnace*
Dan 3:26 Then Nebuchadnezzar went near the mouth of the burning *fiery furnace* and spoke, saying

FIERY RED DRAGON
Rev 12:3 behold, a great, *fiery red dragon* having seven heads and ten horns, and seven diadems on his heads

FIG LEAVES
Gen 3:7 and they sewed *fig leaves* together and made themselves coverings

FIGHT FOR YOU
Ex 14:14 The Lord will *fight for you*, and you shall hold your peace
Deut 1:30 The Lord your God, who goes before you, He will *fight for you*, according to all He did for you in Egypt before your eyes
Deut 20:4 for the Lord your God is He who goes with you, to *fight for you* against your enemies, to save you

FIGHT THE GOOD FIGHT
1Tim 6:12 *Fight the good fight* of faith, lay hold on eternal life, to which you were also called and have confessed the good confession in the presence of many witnesses

FIGHTING MEN (NIV)
(See *MIGHTY MEN OF VALOR*)

FILL ME WITH JOY (NIV)
(See *FULLNESS OF JOY*)

FILL THE EARTH
Gen 1:28 *fill the earth* and subdue it; have dominion over the fish of the sea, over the birds of the air, and over every living thing that moves on the earth
Gen 9:1 So God blessed Noah and his sons, and said to them: "Be fruitful and multiply and *fill the earth*

FILL YOUR HORN WITH OIL
1Sam 16:1 *Fill your horn with oil*, and go; I am sending you to Jesse the Bethlehemite

FILLED THE HOUSE OF THE LORD
1Kin 8:10 And it came to pass, when the priests came out of the holy place, that the cloud *filled the house of the Lord*
1Kin 8:11 for the glory of the Lord *filled the house of the Lord*
Ezek 44:4 so I looked, and behold, the glory of the Lord *filled the house of the Lord*

FILLED THE TEMPLE
2Chr 7:1 Now when Solomon had finished praying, fire came down from heaven and consumed the burnt offering and the sacrifices; and the glory of the Lord *filled the temple*
Is 6:1 In the year that King Uzziah died, I saw the Lord sitting on a throne, high and lifted up, and the train of His robe *filled the temple*
Ezek 43:5 and behold, the glory of the Lord *filled the temple*

FILLED THE TEMPLE OF THE LORD (NIV)
(See *FILLED THE HOUSE OF THE LORD*)

FILLED TO OVERFLOWING (NIV)
(See *FILLED WITH PLENTY*)

FILLED WITH AWE (NIV, RSV)
(See *FILLED WITH FEAR*)

FILLED WITH BLOOD
Is 34:6 The sword of the Lord is *filled with blood*, it is made overflowing with fatness, and with the blood of lambs and goats, with the fat of the kidneys of rams
Zech 9:15 they shall be *filled with blood* like basins, like the corners of the altar

FILLED WITH ENVY
Acts 13:45 But when the Jews saw the multitudes, they were *filled with envy*

FILLED WITH FEAR
Luke 5:26 And they were all amazed, and they glorified God and were *filled with fear*, saying

FILLED WITH FURY (RSV)
(See *FILLED WITH RAGE*)

FILLED WITH HIS GLORY
Ps 72:19 And let the whole earth be *filled with His glory*

FILLED WITH INDIGNATION
Esth 5:9 but when Haman saw Mordecai in the king's gate, and that he did not stand or tremble before him, he was *filled with indignation* against Mordecai
Acts 5:17 Then the high priest rose up, and all those who were with him (which is the sect of the Sadducees), and they were *filled with indignation*

FILLED WITH JOY
Acts 13:52 And the disciples were *filled with joy* and with the Holy Spirit
2Tim 1:4 greatly desiring to see you, being mindful of your tears, that I may be *filled with joy*

FILLED WITH LAUGHTER
Ps 126:2 Then our mouth was *filled with laughter*, and our tongue with singing

FILLED WITH MADNESS (KJV)
(See *FILLED WITH RAGE*)

FILLED WITH PLENTY
Prov 3:10 so your barns will be *filled with plenty*, and your vats will overflow with new wine

FILLED WITH RAGE
Luke 6:11 But they were *filled with rage*, and discussed with one another what they might do to Jesus

FILLED WITH SMOKE
Is 6:4 And the posts of the door were shaken by the voice of him who cried out, and the house was *filled with smoke*

Rev 15:8 The temple was *filled with smoke* from the glory of God and from His power, and no one was able to enter the temple till the seven plagues of the seven angels were completed

FILLED WITH THE HOLY SPIRIT
Luke 1:15 He will also be *filled with the Holy Spirit*, even from his mother's womb
Luke 1:41 And it happened, when Elizabeth heard the greeting of Mary, that the babe leaped in her womb; and Elizabeth was *filled with the Holy Spirit*
Luke 1:67 Now his father Zacharias was *filled with the Holy Spirit*, and prophesied, saying
Luke 4:1 Then Jesus, being *filled with the Holy Spirit*, returned from the Jordan and was led by the Spirit into the wilderness
Acts 2:4 And they were all *filled with the Holy Spirit* and began to speak with other tongues, as the Spirit gave them utterance
Acts 4:8 Then Peter, *filled with the Holy Spirit*, said to them
Acts 4:31 and they were all *filled with the Holy Spirit*, and they spoke the word of God with boldness
Acts 9:17 and laying his hands on him he said, "Brother Saul, the Lord Jesus, who appeared to you on the road as you came, has sent me that you may receive your sight and be *filled with the Holy Spirit*
Acts 13:9 Then Saul, who also is called Paul, *filled with the Holy Spirit*, looked intently at him

FILLED WITH THE SPIRIT
Ex 28:3 So you shall speak to all who are gifted artisans, whom I have *filled with the spirit* of wisdom, that they may make Aaron's garments, to consecrate him, that he may minister to Me as priest
Eph 5:18 And do not be drunk with wine, in which is dissipation; but be *filled with the Spirit*

FILLED WITH VIOLENCE
Gen 6:11 The earth also was corrupt before God, and the earth was *filled with violence*
Gen 6:13 And God said to Noah, "The end of all flesh has come before Me, for the earth is *filled with violence* through them
Ezek 28:16 By the abundance of your trading you became *filled with violence* within, and you sinned

FILLED WITH WINE
Jer 13:12 Every bottle shall be *filled with wine*.'" And they will say to you, 'Do we not certainly know that every bottle will be *filled with wine*

FILLED WITH WISDOM
1Kin 7:14 he was *filled with wisdom* and understanding and skill in working with all kinds of bronze work
Luke 2:40 And the Child grew and became strong in spirit, *filled with wisdom*

FILLED WITH WONDER
Acts 3:10 and they were *filled with wonder* and amazement at what had happened to him

FILLED WITH WRATH
Esth 3:5 When Haman saw that Mordecai did not bow or pay him homage, Haman was *filled with wrath*
Luke 4:28 Then all those in the synagogue, when they heard these things, were *filled with wrath*

FILTH OF THE FLESH
1Pet 3:21 There is also an antitype which now saves us, namely baptism (not the removal of the *filth of the flesh*, but the answer of a good conscience toward God

FILTHY RAGS
Is 64:6 But we are all like an unclean thing, and all our righteousnesses are like *filthy rags*

FIND ENJOYMENT (RSV)
(See *ENJOY GOOD*)

FIND FAULT WITH ME (RSV)
(See *CONTEND WITH ME*)

FIND FAVOR IN THE EYES OF
2Sam 15:25 If I *find favor in the eyes of* the Lord, He will bring me back and show me both it and His habitation

FIND FAVOR IN THE SIGHT OF
Gen 33:8 And he said, "These are to *find favor in the sight of* my lord
Gen 33:15 Let me *find favor in the sight of* my lord
Gen 47:25 let us *find favor in the sight of* my lord, and we will be Pharaoh's servants

FIND FAVOR IN YOUR EYES (NIV)
(See *FIND FAVOR IN THE SIGHT OF*)

FIND GRACE IN THE SIGHT OF (KJV)
(See *FIND FAVOR IN THE SIGHT OF*)

FIND SATISFACTION (NIV)
(See *ENJOY GOOD*)

FINE OIL (NIV)
(See *PRECIOUS OINTMENT*)

FINGER OF GOD
Ex 8:19 Then the magicians said to Pharaoh, "This is the *finger of God*
Ex 31:18 And when He had made an end of speaking with him on Mount Sinai, He gave Moses two tablets of the Testimony, tablets of stone, written with the *finger of God*
Deut 9:10 Then the Lord delivered to me two tablets of stone written with the *finger of God*, and on them were all the words which the Lord had spoken to you on the mountain from the midst of the fire in the day of the assembly
Luke 11:20 But if I cast out demons with the *finger of God*, surely the kingdom of God has come upon you

FINISH OUR YEARS LIKE A SIGH
Ps 90:9 For all our days have passed away in Your wrath; we *finish our years like a sigh*

FINISHER OF OUR FAITH
Heb 12:2 looking unto Jesus, the author and *finisher of our faith*, who for the joy that was set before Him endured the cross, despising the shame, and has sat down at the right hand of the throne of God

FIRE AND BRIMSTONE
Ps 11:6 Upon the wicked He will rain coals, *fire and brimstone* and a burning wind
Luke 17:29 but on the day that Lot went out of Sodom it rained *fire and brimstone* from heaven and destroyed them all
Rev 14:10 And he shall be tormented with *fire and brimstone* in the presence of the holy angels and in the presence of the Lamb
Rev 20:10 And the devil, who deceived them, was cast into the lake of *fire and brimstone* where the beast and the false prophet are
Rev 21:8 But the cowardly, unbelieving, abomina-

ble, murderers, sexually immoral, sorcerers, idolaters, and all liars shall have their part in the lake which burns with *fire and brimstone*, which is the second death

FIRE BE QUENCHED (KJV, NIV)
(See *FIRE IS NOT QUENCHED*)

FIRE CAME DOWN FROM HEAVEN
2Kin 1:10 And *fire came down from heaven* and consumed him and his fifty
2Chr 7:1 Now when Solomon had finished praying, *fire came down from heaven* and consumed the burnt offering and the sacrifices

FIRE IS NOT QUENCHED
Is 66:24 For their worm does not die, and their *fire is not quenched*
Mark 9:44 where 'their worm does not die and the *fire is not quenched*
Mark 9:46 where 'their worm does not die and the *fire is not quenched*
Mark 9:48 where 'their worm does not die and the *fire is not quenched*

FIRE OF GOD
2Kin 1:12 And the *fire of God* came down from heaven and consumed him and his fifty
Job 1:16 While he was still speaking, another also came and said, "The *fire of God* fell from heaven and burned up the sheep and the servants, and consumed them

FIRE OF HELL (NIV)
(See *HELL FIRE*)

FIRE OF THE LORD
Num 11:1 So the *fire of the Lord* burned among them, and consumed some in the outskirts of the camp
Num 11:3 So he called the name of the place Taberah, because the *fire of the Lord* had burned among them
1Kin 18:38 Then the *fire of the Lord* fell and consumed the burnt sacrifice, and the wood and the stones and the dust, and it licked up the water that was in the trench

FIRE SHALL NOT BE QUENCHED (RSV)
(See *FIRE IS NOT QUENCHED*)

FIRE TO THE LORD
Ex 29:18 it is a sweet aroma, an offering made by *fire to the Lord*
Ex 29:25 It is an offering made by *fire to the Lord*
Ex 29:41 and you shall offer with it the grain offering and the drink offering, as in the morning, for a sweet aroma, an offering made by *fire to the Lord*
Ex 30:20 When they go into the tabernacle of meeting, or when they come near the altar to minister, to burn an offering made by *fire to the Lord*, they shall wash with water, lest they die
Lev 2:16 part of its beaten grain and part of its oil, with all the frankincense, as an offering made by *fire to the Lord*
Lev 3:3 Then he shall offer from the sacrifice of the peace offering an offering made by *fire to the Lord*
Lev 3:9 Then he shall offer from the sacrifice of the peace offering, as an offering made by *fire to the Lord*, its fat and the whole fat tail which he shall remove close to the backbone
Lev 3:11 and the priest shall burn them on the altar as food, an offering made by *fire to the Lord*
Lev 3:14 Then he shall offer from it his offering, as an offering made by *fire to the Lord*
Lev 4:35 Then the priest shall burn it on the altar, according to the offerings made by *fire to the Lord*
Lev 5:12 Then he shall bring it to the priest, and the priest shall take his handful of it as a memorial portion, and burn it on the altar according to the offerings made by *fire to the Lord*
Lev 6:18 It shall be a statute forever in your generations concerning the offerings made by *fire to the Lord*
Lev 7:5 and the priest shall burn them on the altar as an offering made by *fire to the Lord*
Lev 7:25 For whoever eats the fat of the beast of which men offer an offering made by *fire to the Lord*, the person who eats it shall be cut off from his people
Lev 7:30 His own hands shall bring the offerings made by *fire to the Lord*
Lev 7:35 This is the consecrated portion for Aaron and his sons, from the offerings made by *fire to the Lord*, on the day when Moses presented them to minister to the Lord as priests
Lev 8:21 It was a burnt sacrifice for a sweet aroma, and an offering made by *fire to the Lord*, as the Lord had commanded Moses
Lev 8:28 That was an offering made by *fire to the Lord*
Lev 10:12 Take the grain offering that remains of the offerings made by *fire to the Lord*, and eat it without leaven beside the altar
Lev 10:13 And you shall eat it in a holy place, because it is your due and your sons' due, of the sacrifices made by *fire to the Lord*
Lev 21:21 No man of the descendants of Aaron the priest, who has a defect, shall come near to offer the offerings made by *fire to the Lord*
Lev 22:27 and from the eighth day and thereafter it shall be accepted as an offering made by *fire to the Lord*
Lev 23:8 But you shall offer an offering made by *fire to the Lord* for seven days
Lev 23:13 Its grain offering shall be two-tenths of an ephah of fine flour mixed with oil, an offering made by *fire to the Lord*, for a sweet aroma
Lev 23:25 and you shall offer an offering made by *fire to the Lord*
Lev 23:27 you shall afflict your souls, and offer an offering made by *fire to the Lord*
Lev 23:36 For seven days you shall offer an offering made by *fire to the Lord*. On the eighth day you shall have a holy convocation, and you shall offer an offering made by *fire to the Lord*
Lev 23:37 These are the feasts of the Lord which you shall proclaim to be holy convocations, to offer an offering made by *fire to the Lord*, a burnt offering and a grain offering, a sacrifice and drink offerings, everything on its day
Lev 24:7 And you shall put pure frankincense on each row, that it may be on the bread for a memorial, an offering made by *fire to the Lord*
Num 15:3 and you make an offering by *fire to the Lord*, a burnt offering or a sacrifice, to fulfill a vow or as a freewill offering or in your appointed feasts, to make a sweet aroma to the Lord, from the herd or the flock
Num 15:25 they shall bring their offering, an offering made by *fire to the Lord*, and their sin offering before the Lord, for their unintended sin
Num 28:6 It is a regular burnt offering which was ordained at Mount Sinai for a sweet aroma, an offering made by *fire to the Lord*
Num 28:13 and one-tenth of an ephah of fine flour, mixed with oil, as a grain offering for each lamb, as a burnt offering of sweet aroma, an offering made by *fire to the Lord*
Num 29:6 besides the burnt offering with its grain offering for the New Moon, the regular burnt offering with its grain offering, and their drink of-

ferings, according to their ordinance, as a sweet aroma, an offering made by *fire to the Lord*

FIRM TO THE END
Heb 3:6 but Christ as a Son over His own house, whose house we are if we hold fast the confidence and the rejoicing of the hope *firm to the end*

FIRMAMENT OF THE HEAVENS
Gen 1:14 Then God said, "Let there be lights in the *firmament of the heavens* to divide the day from the night
Gen 1:15 and let them be for lights in the *firmament of the heavens* to give light on the earth
Gen 1:17 God set them in the *firmament of the heavens* to give light on the earth
Gen 1:20 Then God said, "Let the waters abound with an abundance of living creatures, and let birds fly above the earth across the face of the *firmament of the heavens*

FIRMLY ESTABLISH HIS HOUSE (NIV)
(See *BUILD HIM A SURE HOUSE*)

FIRMLY FIXED IN THE HEAVENS (RSV)
(See *SETTLED IN HEAVEN*)

FIRST AND THE LAST
Rev 1:11 saying, "I am the Alpha and the Omega, the *First and the Last*
Rev 1:17 But He laid His right hand on me, saying to me, "Do not be afraid; I am the *First and the Last*
Rev 2:8 And to the angel of the church in Smyrna write, 'These things says the *First and the Last*, who was dead, and came to life
Rev 22:13 I am the Alpha and the Omega, the Beginning and the End, the *First and the Last*

FIRST CALLED CHRISTIANS
Acts 11:26 So it was that for a whole year they assembled with the church and taught a great many people. And the disciples were *first called Christians* in Antioch

FIRST COMMANDMENT
Mark 12:28 Then one of the scribes came, and having heard them reasoning together, perceiving that He had answered them well, asked Him, "Which is the *first commandment* of all
Mark 12:30 And you shall love the Lord your God with all your heart, with all your soul, with all your mind, and with all your strength.' This is the *first commandment*
Eph 6:2 Honor your father and mother," which is the *first commandment* with promise

FIRST COVENANT
Heb 8:7 For if that *first covenant* had been faultless, then no place would have been sought for a second
Heb 9:1 Then indeed, even the *first covenant* had ordinances of divine service and the earthly sanctuary
Heb 9:15 And for this reason He is the Mediator of the new covenant, by means of death, for the redemption of the transgressions under the *first covenant*, that those who are called may receive the promise of the eternal inheritance
Heb 9:18 Therefore not even the *first covenant* was dedicated without blood

FIRST DAY
Gen 1:5 So the evening and the morning were the *first day*
Gen 8:5 In the tenth month, on the *first day* of the month, the tops of the mountains were seen
Gen 8:13 And it came to pass in the six hundred and first year, in the first month, the *first day* of the month, that the waters were dried up from the earth
Ex 12:15 On the *first day* you shall remove leaven from your houses. For whoever eats leavened bread from the *first day* until the seventh day, that person shall be cut off from Israel
Ex 12:16 On the *first day* there shall be a holy convocation, and on the seventh day there shall be a holy convocation for you
Ex 40:2 On the *first day* of the first month you shall set up the tabernacle of the tent of meeting
Ex 40:17 And it came to pass in the first month of the second year, on the *first day* of the month, that the tabernacle was raised up
Lev 23:7 On the *first day* you shall have a holy convocation
Lev 23:24 In the seventh month, on the *first day* of the month, you shall have a sabbath-rest, a memorial of blowing of trumpets, a holy convocation
Lev 23:35 On the *first day* there shall be a holy convocation
Lev 23:39 on the *first day* there shall be a sabbath-rest, and on the eighth day a sabbath-rest
Lev 23:40 And you shall take for yourselves on the *first day* the fruit of beautiful trees, branches of palm trees, the boughs of leafy trees, and willows of the brook
Num 1:1 Now the Lord spoke to Moses in the Wilderness of Sinai, in the tabernacle of meeting, on the *first day* of the second month, in the second year after they had come out of the land of Egypt, saying
Num 1:18 and they assembled all the congregation together on the *first day* of the second month
Num 7:12 And the one who offered his offering on the *first day* was Nahshon the son of Amminadab, from the tribe of Judah
Num 28:18 On the *first day* you shall have a holy convocation
Num 29:1 And in the seventh month, on the *first day* of the month, you shall have a holy convocation
Num 33:38 Then Aaron the priest went up to Mount Hor at the command of the Lord, and died there in the fortieth year after the children of Israel had come out of the land of Egypt, on the *first day* of the fifth month
Deut 1:3 Now it came to pass in the fortieth year, in the eleventh month, on the *first day* of the month, that Moses spoke to the children of Israel according to all that the Lord had given him as commandments to them
Deut 16:4 And no leaven shall be seen among you in all your territory for seven days, nor shall any of the meat which you sacrifice the *first day* at twilight remain overnight until morning
Judg 20:22 And the people, that is, the men of Israel, encouraged themselves and again formed the battle line at the place where they had put themselves in array on the *first day*
2Chr 29:17 Now they began to sanctify on the *first day* of the first month, and on the eighth day of the month they came to the vestibule of the Lord
Ezra 3:6 From the *first day* of the seventh month they began to offer burnt offerings to the Lord
Ezra 7:9 On the *first day* of the first month he began his journey from Babylon, and on the *first day* of the fifth month he came to Jerusalem, according to the good hand of his God upon him
Ezra 10:16 and they sat down on the *first day* of the tenth month to examine the matter
Ezra 10:17 By the *first day* of the first month they finished questioning all the men who had taken pagan wives
Neh 8:2 So Ezra the priest brought the Law before

the congregation, of men and women and all who could hear with understanding, on the *first day* of the seventh month

Neh 8:18 Also day by day, from the *first day* until the last day, he read from the Book of the Law of God

Ezek 26:1 And it came to pass in the eleventh year, on the *first day* of the month, that the word of the Lord came to me, saying

Ezek 29:17 And it came to pass in the twenty-seventh year, in the first month, on the *first day* of the month, that the word of the Lord came to me, saying

Ezek 31:1 Now it came to pass in the eleventh year, in the third month, on the *first day* of the month, that the word of the Lord came to me, saying

Ezek 32:1 And it came to pass in the twelfth year, in the twelfth month, on the *first day* of the month, that the word of the Lord came to me, saying

Ezek 45:18 In the first month, on the *first day* of the month, you shall take a young bull without blemish and cleanse the sanctuary

Dan 10:12 Then he said to me, "Do not fear, Daniel, for from the *first day* that you set your heart to understand, and to humble yourself before your God, your words were heard

Hag 1:1 In the second year of King Darius, in the sixth month, on the *first day* of the month, the word of the Lord came by Haggai the prophet to Zerubbabel the son of Shealtiel, governor of Judah, and to Joshua the son of Jehozadak, the high priest, saying

Matt 26:17 Now on the *first day* of the Feast of the Unleavened Bread the disciples came to Jesus, saying to Him

Matt 28:1 Now after the Sabbath, as the *first day* of the week began to dawn, Mary Magdalene and the other Mary came to see the tomb

Mark 14:12 Now on the *first day* of Unleavened Bread, when they killed the Passover lamb, His disciples said to Him

Mark 16:2 Very early in the morning, on the *first day* of the week, they came to the tomb when the sun had risen

Mark 16:9 Now when He rose early on the *first day* of the week, He appeared first to Mary Magdalene, out of whom He had cast seven demons

Luke 24:1 Now on the *first day* of the week, very early in the morning, they, and certain other women with them, came to the tomb bringing the spices which they had prepared

John 20:1 On the *first day* of the week Mary Magdalene came to the tomb early, while it was still dark, and saw that the stone had been taken away from the tomb

John 20:19 Then, the same day at evening, being the *first day* of the week, when the doors were shut where the disciples were assembled, for fear of the Jews, Jesus came and stood in the midst, and said to them

Acts 20:7 Now on the *first day* of the week, when the disciples came together to break bread, Paul, ready to depart the next day, spoke to them and continued his message until midnight

Acts 20:18 You know, from the *first day* that I came to Asia, in what manner I always lived among you

1Cor 16:2 On the *first day* of the week let each one of you lay something aside, storing up as he may prosper, that there be no collections when I come

Phil 1:5 for your fellowship in the gospel from the *first day* until now

FIRST DAY OF THE WEEK

Matt 28:1 Now after the Sabbath, as the *first day of the week* began to dawn, Mary Magdalene and the other Mary came to see the tomb

Mark 16:2 Very early in the morning, on the *first day of the week*, they came to the tomb when the sun had risen

Mark 16:9 Now when He rose early on the *first day of the week*, He appeared first to Mary Magdalene, out of whom He had cast seven demons

Luke 24:1 Now on the *first day of the week*, very early in the morning, they, and certain other women with them, came to the tomb bringing the spices which they had prepared

John 20:1 On the *first day of the week* Mary Magdalene came to the tomb early, while it was still dark, and saw that the stone had been taken away from the tomb

John 20:19 Then, the same day at evening, being the *first day of the week*, when the doors were shut where the disciples were assembled, for fear of the Jews, Jesus came and stood in the midst, and said to them

Acts 20:7 Now on the *first day of the week*, when the disciples came together to break bread, Paul, ready to depart the next day, spoke to them and continued his message until midnight

1Cor 16:2 On the *first day of the week* let each one of you lay something aside, storing up as he may prosper, that there be no collections when I come

FIRST FOR THE JEW (NIV)
(See *FOR THE JEW FIRST*)

FIRST FOR THE JEW, THEN FOR THE GENTILE (NIV)
(See *JEW FIRST AND ALSO FOR THE GREEK*)

FIRST MAN

Job 15:7 Are you the *first man* who was born? Or were you made before the hills

1Cor 15:45 And so it is written, "The *first man* Adam became a living being

1Cor 15:47 The *first man* was of the earth, made of dust

FIRST OF THE FIRSTFRUITS

Ex 23:19 The *first of the firstfruits* of your land you shall bring into the house of the Lord your God

Ex 34:26 The *first of the firstfruits* of your land you shall bring to the house of the Lord your God

FIRST RESURRECTION

Rev 20:5 But the rest of the dead did not live again until the thousand years were finished. This is the *first resurrection*

Rev 20:6 Blessed and holy is he who has part in the *first resurrection*

FIRST WHO WILL BE LAST

Luke 13:30 And indeed there are last who will be first, and there are *first who will be last*

FIRST WILL BE LAST

Matt 19:30 But many who are *first will be last*, and the last first

Mark 10:31 But many who are *first will be last*, and the last first

FIRSTBORN AMONG MANY BRETHREN

Rom 8:29 For whom He foreknew, He also predestined to be conformed to the image of His Son, that He might be the *firstborn among many brethren*

FIRSTBORN FROM THE DEAD
Col 1:18 And He is the head of the body, the church, who is the beginning, the *firstborn from the dead*, that in all things He may have the preeminence
Rev 1:5 and from Jesus Christ, the faithful witness, the *firstborn from the dead*, and the ruler over the kings of the earth

FIRSTBORN MALES
Num 3:40 Number all the *firstborn males* of the children of Israel from a month old and above, and take the number of their names
Num 3:43 And all the *firstborn males*, according to the number of names from a month old and above, of those who were numbered of them, were twenty-two thousand two hundred and seventy-three
Deut 15:19 All the *firstborn males* that come from your herd and your flock you shall sanctify to the Lord your God

FIRSTBORN OF EVERY CREATURE (KJV)
(See *FIRSTBORN OVER ALL CREATION*)

FIRSTBORN OF ISRAEL
Ex 6:14 The sons of Reuben, the *firstborn of Israel*, were Hanoch, Pallu, Hezron, and Carmi
Num 26:5 Reuben was the *firstborn of Israel*. The children of Reuben were
1Chr 5:1 Now the sons of Reuben the *firstborn of Israel* he was indeed the firstborn, but because he defiled his father's bed, his birthright was given to the sons of Joseph, the son of Israel, so that the genealogy is not listed according to the birthright
1Chr 5:3 the sons of Reuben the *firstborn of Israel* were Hanoch, Pallu, Hezron, and Carmi

FIRSTBORN OF THE POOR
Is 14:30 The *firstborn of the poor* will feed, and the needy will lie down in safety

FIRSTBORN OVER ALL CREATION
Col 1:15 He is the image of the invisible God, the *firstborn over all creation*

FIRSTBORN SON
Gen 36:15 The sons of Eliphaz, the *firstborn son* of Esau, were Chief Teman, Chief Omar, Chief Zepho, Chief Kenaz
Deut 21:15 If a man has two wives, one loved and the other unloved, and they have borne him children, both the loved and the unloved, and if the *firstborn son* is of her who is unloved
Deut 25:6 And it shall be that the *firstborn son* which she bears will succeed to the name of his dead brother, that his name may not be blotted out of Israel
1Chr 8:30 And his *firstborn son* was Abdon, then Zur, Kish, Baal, Nadab
1Chr 9:36 His *firstborn son* was Abdon, then Zur, Kish, Baal, Ner, Nadab
Matt 1:25 and did not know her till she had brought forth her *firstborn Son*
Luke 2:7 And she brought forth her *firstborn Son*, and wrapped Him in swaddling cloths, and laid Him in a manger, because there was no room for them in the inn

FIRSTBORN SON OF ISRAEL (NIV)
(See *FIRSTBORN OF ISRAEL*)

FIRSTFRUITS OF THE CROPS (NIV)
(See *FIRSTFRUITS OF YOUR LABORS*)

FIRSTFRUITS OF THE SPIRIT
Rom 8:23 And not only they, but we also who have the *firstfruits of the Spirit*, even we ourselves groan within ourselves, eagerly waiting for the adoption, the redemption of our body

FIRSTFRUITS OF YOUR LABORS
Ex 23:16 and the Feast of Harvest, the *firstfruits of your labors* which you have sown in the field

FISHERS OF MEN
Matt 4:19 And He said to them, "Follow Me, and I will make you *fishers of men*
Mark 1:17 Then Jesus said to them, "Come after Me, and I will make you become *fishers of men*

FIVE BARLEY LOAVES AND TWO SMALL FISH
John 6:9 There is a lad here who has *five barley loaves and two small fish*, but what are they among so many

FIVE LOAVES AND TWO FISH
Matt 14:17 And they said to Him, "We have here only *five loaves and two fish*
Luke 9:13 And they said, "We have no more than *five loaves and two fish*, unless we go and buy food for all these people

FIX OUR EYES ON JESUS (NIV)
(See *LOOKING UNTO JESUS*)

FLAMING ARROWS OF THE EVIL ONE (NIV)
(See *FIERY DARTS OF THE WICKED ONE*)

FLAMING DARTS OF THE EVIL ONE (RSV)
(See *FIERY DARTS OF THE WICKED ONE*)

FLAMING FIRE
Ps 105:32 He gave them hail for rain, and *flaming fire* in their land
Is 4:5 then the Lord will create above every dwelling place of Mount Zion, and above her assemblies, a cloud and smoke by day and the shining of a *flaming fire* by night
Lam 2:3 He has blazed against Jacob like a *flaming fire* which devours all around
Hos 7:6 their baker sleeps all night; in the morning it burns like a *flaming fire*
Joel 2:5 With a noise like chariots over mountaintops they leap, like the noise of a *flaming fire* that devours the stubble, like a strong people set in battle array
2Th 1:8 in *flaming fire* taking vengeance on those who do not know God, and on those who do not obey the gospel of our Lord Jesus Christ

FLAMING SWORD
Gen 3:24 and He placed cherubim at the east of the garden of Eden, and a *flaming sword* which turned every way, to guard the way to the tree of life

FLATTERING LIPS
Ps 12:2 They speak idly everyone with his neighbor; with *flattering lips* and a double heart they speak
Ps 12:3 May the Lord cut off all *flattering lips*, and the tongue that speaks proud things
Prov 7:21 With her enticing speech she caused him to yield, with her *flattering lips* she seduced him

FLATTERING SPEECH
Rom 16:18 For those who are such do not serve our Lord Jesus Christ, but their own belly, and by smooth words and *flattering speech* deceive the hearts of the simple

FLEE FROM IDOLATRY
1Cor 10:14 Therefore, my beloved, *flee from idolatry*

FLEE TO THE MOUNTAINS
Matt 24:16 then let those who are in Judea *flee to the mountains*
Mark 13:14 then let those who are in Judea *flee to the mountains*
Luke 21:21 Then let those in Judea *flee to the mountains*, let those who are in the midst of her depart, and let not those who are in the country enter her

FLESH AND BLOOD
Matt 16:17 Jesus answered and said to him, "Blessed are you, Simon Bar-Jonah, for *flesh and blood* has not revealed this to you, but My Father who is in heaven
1Cor 15:50 Now this I say, brethren, that *flesh and blood* cannot inherit the kingdom of God
Gal 1:16 to reveal His Son in me, that I might preach Him among the Gentiles, I did not immediately confer with *flesh and blood*
Eph 6:12 For we do not wrestle against *flesh and blood*, but against principalities, against powers, against the rulers of the darkness of this age, against spiritual hosts of wickedness in the heavenly places
Heb 2:14 Inasmuch then as the children have partaken of *flesh and blood*, He Himself likewise shared in the same, that through death He might destroy him who had the power of death, that is, the devil

FLESH AND BONES
Luke 24:39 Handle Me and see, for a spirit does not have *flesh and bones* as you see I have

FLESH AND SPIRIT
2Cor 7:1 Therefore, having these promises, beloved, let us cleanse ourselves from all filthiness of the *flesh and spirit*, perfecting holiness in the fear of God

FLESH COUNTS FOR NOTHING (NIV)
(See *FLESH PROFITS NOTHING*)

FLESH IS CONSUMED AWAY (KJV)
(See *FLESH WASTES AWAY*)

FLESH IS OF NO AVAIL (RSV)
(See *FLESH PROFITS NOTHING*)

FLESH IS SO WASTED AWAY (RSV)
(See *FLESH WASTES AWAY*)

FLESH IS WEAK
Matt 26:41 The spirit indeed is willing, but the *flesh is weak*
Mark 14:38 The spirit truly is ready, but the *flesh is weak*

FLESH OF MY FLESH
Gen 2:23 This is now bone of my bones and *flesh of my flesh*

FLESH OF PIGS (NIV)
(See *SWINE'S FLESH*)

FLESH PROFITS NOTHING
John 6:63 the *flesh profits nothing*. The words that I speak to you are spirit, and they are life

FLESH WASTES AWAY
Job 33:21 His *flesh wastes away* from sight, and his bones stick out which once were not seen

FLOCK OF GOD
1Pet 5:2 Shepherd the *flock of God* which is among you, serving as overseers, not by constraint but willingly, not for dishonest gain but eagerly

FLOCK OF THY PASTURE (RSV)
(See *SHEEP OF YOUR PASTURE*)

FLOCKS AND HERDS
Gen 13:5 Lot also, who went with Abram, had *flocks and herds* and tents
Gen 24:35 and He has given him *flocks and herds*, silver and gold, male and female servants, and camels and donkeys
Gen 32:7 and he divided the people that were with him, and the *flocks and herds* and camels, into two companies
Gen 33:13 But Jacob said to him, "My lord knows that the children are weak, and the *flocks and herds* which are nursing are with me
Ex 12:38 A mixed multitude went up with them also, and *flocks and herds* a great deal of livestock
Num 11:22 Shall *flocks and herds* be slaughtered for them, to provide enough for them
1Sam 30:20 Then David took all the *flocks and herds* which they had driven before those other livestock, and said
2Sam 12:2 The rich man had exceedingly many *flocks and herds*
2Chr 32:29 Moreover he provided cities for himself, and possessions of *flocks and herds* in abundance
Hos 5:6 With their *flocks and herds* they shall go to seek the Lord, but they will not find Him

FLOODGATES OF THE HEAVENS (NIV)
(See *WINDOWS FROM ON HIGH*)

FLOW OF BLOOD
Matt 9:20 And suddenly, a woman who had a *flow of blood* for twelve years came from behind and touched the hem of His garment
Mark 5:25 Now a certain woman had a *flow of blood* for twelve years
Luke 8:43 Now a woman, having a *flow of blood* for twelve years, who had spent all her livelihood on physicians and could not be healed by any
Luke 8:44 came from behind and touched the border of His garment. And immediately her *flow of blood* stopped

FLOWER FADES
Is 40:7 The grass withers, the *flower fades*, because the breath of the Lord blows upon it
Is 40:8 The grass withers, the *flower fades*, but the word of our God stands forever

FLOWER OF HER YOUTH
1Cor 7:36 But if any man thinks he is behaving improperly toward his virgin, if she is past the *flower of her youth*, and thus it must be, let him do what he wishes

FLOWER OF THEIR AGE
1Sam 2:33 And all the descendants of your house shall die in the *flower of their age*

FLOWING WITH MILK AND HONEY
Ex 3:8 So I have come down to deliver them out of the hand of the Egyptians, and to bring them up from that land to a good and large land, to a land *flowing with milk and honey*, to the place of the Canaanites and the Hittites and the Amorites and the Perizzites and the Hivites and the Jebusites
Ex 3:17 and I have said I will bring you up out of the affliction of Egypt to the land of the Canaanites and the Hittites and the Amorites and the Perizzites and the Hivites and the Jebusites, to a land *flowing with milk and honey*
Ex 13:5 And it shall be, when the Lord brings you

into the land of the Canaanites and the Hittites and the Amorites and the Hivites and the Jebusites, which He swore to your fathers to give you, a land *flowing with milk and honey*, that you shall keep this service in this month

Ex 33:3 Go up to a land *flowing with milk and honey*

Lev 20:24 But I have said to you, "You shall inherit their land, and I will give it to you to possess, a land *flowing with milk and honey*

Num 16:13 Is it a small thing that you have brought us up out of a land *flowing with milk and honey*, to kill us in the wilderness, that you should keep acting like a prince over us

Num 16:14 Moreover you have not brought us into a land *flowing with milk and honey*, nor given us inheritance of fields and vineyards

Deut 6:3 Therefore hear, O Israel, and be careful to observe it, that it may be well with you, and that you may multiply greatly as the Lord God of your fathers has promised you 'a land *flowing with milk and honey*

Deut 11:9 and that you may prolong your days in the land which the Lord swore to give your fathers, to them and their descendants, 'a land *flowing with milk and honey*

Deut 26:9 He has brought us to this place and has given us this land, "a land *flowing with milk and honey*

Deut 26:15 Look down from Your holy habitation, from heaven, and bless Your people Israel and the land which You have given us, just as You swore to our fathers, "a land *flowing with milk and honey*

Deut 27:3 You shall write on them all the words of this law, when you have crossed over, that you may enter the land which the Lord your God is giving you, 'a land *flowing with milk and honey*

Deut 31:20 When I have brought them to the land *flowing with milk and honey*, of which I swore to their fathers, and they have eaten and filled themselves and grown fat, then they will turn to other gods and serve them

Josh 5:6 For the children of Israel walked forty years in the wilderness, till all the people who were men of war, who came out of Egypt, were consumed, because they did not obey the voice of the Lord to whom the Lord swore that He would not show them the land which the Lord had sworn to their fathers that He would give us, "a land *flowing with milk and honey*

Jer 11:5 that I may establish the oath which I have sworn to your fathers, to give them a land *flowing with milk and honey*, as it is this day

Jer 32:22 You have given them this land, of which You swore to their fathers to give them "a land *flowing with milk and honey*

Ezek 20:6 On that day I lifted My hand in an oath to them, to bring them out of the land of Egypt into a land that I had searched out for them, *flowing with milk and honey*, the glory of all lands

Ezek 20:15 So I also lifted My hand in an oath to them in the wilderness, that I would not bring them into the land which I had given them, *flowing with milk and honey*, the glory of all lands

FLYING BACK AND FORTH (NIV)
(See *GOING TO AND FRO*)

FOAL OF A DONKEY

Zech 9:9 He is just and having salvation, lowly and riding on a donkey, a colt, the *foal of a donkey*

Matt 21:5 Tell the daughter of Zion, 'Behold, your King is coming to you, lowly, and sitting on a donkey, a colt, the *foal of a donkey*

FOAL OF AN ASS (KJV, RSV)
(See *FOAL OF A DONKEY*)

FOLLOW ME

Gen 24:5 And the servant said to him, "Perhaps the woman will not be willing to *follow me* to this land

Gen 24:39 And I said to my master, 'Perhaps the woman will not *follow me*

Judg 3:28 Then he said to them, "*Follow me*, for the Lord has delivered your enemies the Moabites

Judg 8:5 Then he said to the men of Succoth, "Please give loaves of bread to the people who *follow me*, for they are exhausted, and I am pursuing Zebah and Zalmunna, kings of Midian

1Kin 20:10 Then Ben-Hadad sent to him and said, "The gods do so to me, and more also, if enough dust is left of Samaria for a handful for each of the people who *follow me*

2Kin 6:19 *Follow me*, and I will bring you to the man whom you seek

2Kin 9:18 Turn around and *follow me*." And the watchman reported, saying

2Kin 9:19 And Jehu answered, "What have you to do with peace? Turn around and *follow me*

Ps 23:6 Surely goodness and mercy shall *follow me* all the days of my life

Matt 4:19 And He said to them, "*Follow Me*, and I will make you fishers of men

Matt 8:22 But Jesus said to him, "*Follow Me*, and let the dead bury their own dead

Matt 9:9 And He said to him, "*Follow Me.*" And he arose and followed Him

Matt 16:24 Then Jesus said to His disciples, "If anyone desires to come after Me, let him deny himself, and take up his cross, and *follow Me*

Matt 19:21 Jesus said to him, "If you want to be perfect, go, sell what you have and give to the poor, and you will have treasure in heaven; and come, *follow Me*

Mark 2:14 And as He passed by, He saw Levi the son of Alphaeus sitting at the tax office, and said to him, "*Follow Me*

Mark 8:34 And when He had called the people to Him, with His disciples also, He said to them, "Whoever desires to come after Me, let him deny himself, and take up his cross, and *follow Me*

Mark 10:21 Go your way, sell whatever you have and give to the poor, and you will have treasure in heaven; and come, take up the cross, and *follow Me*

Luke 5:27 After these things He went out and saw a tax collector named Levi, sitting at the tax office. And He said to him, "*Follow Me*

Luke 9:23 Then He said to them all, "If anyone desires to come after Me, let him deny himself, and take up his cross daily, and *follow Me*

Luke 9:59 Then He said to another, "*Follow Me.*" But he said

Luke 18:22 Sell all that you have and distribute to the poor, and you will have treasure in heaven; and come, *follow Me*

John 1:43 The following day Jesus wanted to go to Galilee, and He found Philip and said to him, "*Follow Me*

John 10:27 My sheep hear My voice, and I know them, and they *follow Me*

John 12:26 If anyone serves Me, let him *follow Me;* and where I am, there My servant will be also

John 13:36 Jesus answered him, "Where I am going you cannot *follow Me* now, but you shall *follow Me* afterward

John 21:19 And when He had spoken this, He said to him, "*Follow Me*

John 21:22 Jesus said to him, "If I will that he remain till I come, what is that to you? You *follow Me*

Acts 12:8 And he said to him, "Put on your garment and *follow me*

FOLLOW MY DECREES (NIV)
(See *WALK IN MY STATUTES*)

FOLLOW MY EXAMPLE (NIV)
(See *IMITATE ME*)

FOLLOW THE EXAMPLE OF CHRIST (NIV)
(See *IMITATE CHRIST*)

FOLLOW THE TRUTH (RSV)
(See *WALK IN THE TRUTH*)

FOLLOWED ME FULLY
Num 14:24 But My servant Caleb, because he has a different spirit in him and has *followed Me fully*, I will bring into the land where he went, and his descendants shall inherit it

FOLLOWED NOT AFTER RIGHTEOUSNESS (KJV)
(See *PURSUE RIGHTEOUSNESS*)

FOLLOWERS OF ME (KJV)
(See *IMITATE ME*)

FOLLOWING HIS LAWS (RSV)
(See *WALK IN HIS LAWS*)

FOLLOWING THE LORD
Josh 22:16 What treachery is this that you have committed against the God of Israel, to turn away this day from *following the Lord*, in that you have built for yourselves an altar, that you might rebel this day against the Lord
Josh 22:18 but that you must turn away this day from *following the Lord*
Josh 22:23 If we have built ourselves an altar to turn from *following the Lord*, or if to offer on it burnt offerings or grain offerings, or if to offer peace offerings on it, let the Lord Himself require an account
Josh 22:29 Far be it from us that we should rebel against the Lord, and turn from *following the Lord* this day, to build an altar for burnt offerings, for grain offerings, or for sacrifices, besides the altar of the Lord our God which is before His tabernacle
1Sam 12:14 If you fear the Lord and serve Him and obey His voice, and do not rebel against the commandment of the Lord, then both you and the king who reigns over you will continue *following the Lord* your God
1Sam 12:20 yet do not turn aside from *following the Lord*, but serve the Lord with all your heart
2Kin 17:21 Then Jeroboam drove Israel from *following the Lord*, and made them commit a great sin
2Chr 25:27 After the time that Amaziah turned away from *following the Lord*, they made a conspiracy against him in Jerusalem, and he fled to Lachish
2Chr 34:33 All his days they did not depart from *following the Lord* God of their fathers
Zeph 1:6 those who have turned back from *following the Lord*, and have not sought the Lord, nor inquired of Him

FOLLY IS BOUND UP (NIV, RSV)
(See *FOOLISHNESS IS BOUND UP*)

FOOD AND CLOTHING
Deut 10:18 He administers justice for the fatherless and the widow, and loves the stranger, giving him *food and clothing*
1Tim 6:8 And having *food and clothing*, with these we shall be content

FOOD DOES NOT COMMEND US
1Cor 8:8 But *food does not commend us* to God; for neither if we eat are we the better, nor if we do not eat are we the worse

FOOD EATEN IN SECRET (NIV)
(See *BREAD EATEN IN SECRET*)

FOOD SACRIFICED TO IDOLS (NIV)
(See *THINGS OFFERED TO IDOLS*)

FOOD TO THE HUNGRY (NIV)
(See *BREAD TO THE HUNGRY*)

FOOD WHICH PERISHES
John 6:27 Do not labor for the *food which perishes*, but for the food which endures to everlasting life, which the Son of Man will give you, because God the Father has set His seal on Him

FOOL'S WORK (NIV)
(See *LABOR OF FOOLS*)

FOOLISH MAN
Job 5:2 For wrath kills a *foolish man*, and envy slays a simple one
Ps 74:22 Arise, O God, plead Your own cause; remember how the *foolish man* reproaches You daily
Prov 14:7 Go from the presence of a *foolish man*, when you do not perceive in him the lips of knowledge
Prov 15:20 A wise son makes a father glad, but a *foolish man* despises his mother
Prov 21:20 There is desirable treasure, and oil in the dwelling of the wise, but a *foolish man* squanders it
Prov 29:9 If a wise man contends with a *foolish man*, whether the fool rages or laughs, there is no peace
Matt 7:26 Now everyone who hears these sayings of Mine, and does not do them, will be like a *foolish man* who built his house on the sand
Jas 2:20 But do you want to know, O *foolish man*, that faith without works is dead

FOOLISH MEN
1Pet 2:15 For this is the will of God, that by doing good you may put to silence the ignorance of *foolish men*

FOOLISH WOMAN
Prov 9:13 A *foolish woman* is clamorous; she is simple, and knows nothing

FOOLISH WOMEN
Job 2:10 But he said to her, "You speak as one of the *foolish women* speaks

FOOLISHNESS IS BOUND UP
Prov 22:15 *Foolishness is bound up* in the heart of a child, but the rod of correction will drive it far from him

FOOLISHNESS OF GOD
1Cor 1:25 Because the *foolishness of God* is wiser than men, and the weakness of God is stronger than men

FOOLS FOR CHRIST'S SAKE
1Cor 4:10 We are *fools for Christ's sake*, but you are wise in Christ

FOOT OF THE MOUNTAIN
Ex 19:17 And Moses brought the people out of the camp to meet with God, and they stood at the *foot of the mountain*

Ex 24:4 And he rose early in the morning, and built an altar at the *foot of the mountain*, and twelve pillars according to the twelve tribes of Israel
Ex 32:19 So Moses' anger became hot, and he cast the tablets out of his hands and broke them at the *foot of the mountain*
Deut 4:11 Then you came near and stood at the *foot of the mountain*, and the mountain burned with fire to the midst of heaven, with darkness, cloud, and thick darkness

FOOTSTEPS MAY NOT SLIP
Ps 17:5 Uphold my steps in Your paths, that my *footsteps may not slip*

FOR A POSSESSION (NAS, RSV)
(See *AS A HERITAGE*)

FOR A SEASON (KJV)
(See *OPPORTUNE TIME*)

FOR ALL NATIONS
Is 56:7 for My house shall be called a house of prayer *for all nations*
Mark 11:17 Then He taught, saying to them, "Is it not written, 'My house shall be called a house of prayer *for all nations*
Rev 15:4 *For all nations* shall come and worship before You, for Your judgments have been manifested

FOR ALL PEOPLE (KJV)
(See *FOR ALL NATIONS*)

FOR AN HERITAGE (KJV)
(See *AS A HERITAGE*)

FOR DUST YOU ARE
Gen 3:19 *for dust you are*, and to dust you shall return

FOR FEAR OF THE JEWS
John 7:13 However, no one spoke openly of Him *for fear of the Jews*
John 19:38 After this, Joseph of Arimathea, being a disciple of Jesus, but secretly, *for fear of the Jews*, asked Pilate that he might take away the body of Jesus
John 20:19 Then, the same day at evening, being the first day of the week, when the doors were shut where the disciples were assembled, *for fear of the Jews*, Jesus came and stood in the midst, and said to them

FOR GOD SO LOVED THE WORLD
John 3:16 *For God so loved the world* that He gave His only begotten Son, that whoever believes in Him should not perish but have everlasting life

FOR HIS NAME'S SAKE
Ps 23:3 He leads me in the paths of righteousness *for His name's sake*
Ps 106:8 Nevertheless He saved them *for His name's sake*, that He might make His mighty power known
1Jn 2:12 I write to you, little children, because your sins are forgiven you *for His name's sake*
3Jn 7 because they went forth *for His name's sake*, taking nothing from the Gentiles

FOR JUDGMENT I HAVE COME
John 9:39 And Jesus said, "*For judgment I have come* into this world, that those who do not see may see, and that those who see may be made blind

FOR MY NAME
Ex 23:21 do not provoke Him, for He will not pardon your transgressions; *for My name* is in Him
2Sam 7:13 He shall build a house *for My name*, and I will establish the throne of his kingdom forever
1Kin 5:5 And behold, I propose to build a house for the name of the Lord my God, as the Lord spoke to my father David, saying, 'Your son, whom I will set on your throne in your place, he shall build the house *for My name*
1Kin 8:18 But the Lord said to my father David, 'Whereas it was in your heart to build a house *for My name*, you did well that it was in your heart
1Kin 8:19 Nevertheless you shall not build the house, but your son, who shall come from your loins, he shall build the house *for My name*
1Kin 9:7 and this house which I have sanctified *for My name* I will cast out of My sight
1Chr 22:8 you shall not build a house *for My name*, because you have shed much blood on the earth in My sight
1Chr 22:10 He shall build a house *for My name*, and he shall be My son, and I will be his Father
1Chr 28:3 But God said to me, 'You shall not build a house *for My name*, because you have been a man of war and have shed blood
2Chr 6:8 But the Lord said to my father David, 'Whereas it was in your heart to build a temple *for My name*, you did well in that it was in your heart
2Chr 6:9 Nevertheless you shall not build the house, but your son who will come forth from your own loins, he shall build the temple *for My name*
2Chr 7:20 and this house which I have sanctified *for My name* I will cast out of My sight, and will make it to be a proverb and a byword among all nations
Neh 1:9 but if you return to Me, and keep My commandments and do them, though some of you were cast out to the farthest part of the heavens, yet I will gather them from there, and bring them to the place which I have chosen as a dwelling *for My name*
Mal 1:11 *For My name* shall be great among the nations," says the Lord of hosts

FOR MY SAKE
Num 11:29 Then Moses said to him, "Are you zealous *for my sake*
1Sam 23:10 Then David said, "O Lord God of Israel, Your servant has certainly heard that Saul seeks to come to Keilah to destroy the city *for my sake*
2Sam 18:5 Now the king had commanded Joab, Abishai, and Ittai, saying, "Deal gently *for my sake* with the young man Absalom
Matt 5:11 Blessed are you when they revile and persecute you, and say all kinds of evil against you falsely *for My sake*
Matt 10:18 And you will be brought before governors and kings *for My sake*, as a testimony to them and to the Gentiles
Matt 10:39 He who finds his life will lose it, and he who loses his life *for My sake* will find it
Matt 16:25 For whoever desires to save his life will lose it, and whoever loses his life *for My sake* will find it
Mark 8:35 For whoever desires to save his life will lose it, but whoever loses his life *for My sake* and the gospel's will save it
Mark 10:29 So Jesus answered and said, "Assuredly, I say to you, there is no one who has left house or brothers or sisters or father or mother or

wife or children or lands, *for My sake* and the gospel's
Mark 13:9 And you will be brought before rulers and kings *for My sake*, for a testimony to them
Luke 9:24 For whoever desires to save his life will lose it, but whoever loses his life *for My sake* will save it
John 13:38 Jesus answered him, "Will you lay down your life *for My sake*

FOR SUCH A TIME AS THIS
Esth 4:14 Yet who knows whether you have come to the kingdom *for such a time as this*

FOR THE GLORY OF GOD (RSV)
(See *TO THE GLORY OF GOD*)

FOR THE GOSPEL'S SAKE
1Cor 9:23 Now this I do *for the gospel's sake*, that I may be partaker of it with you

FOR THE JEW FIRST
Rom 1:16 For I am not ashamed of the gospel of Christ, for it is the power of God to salvation for everyone who believes, *for the Jew first* and also for the Greek

FOR THE SAKE OF THE GOSPEL (NIV, RSV)
(See *FOR THE GOSPEL'S SAKE*)

FOR THE SAKE OF THE NAME (NIV)
(See *FOR HIS NAME'S SAKE*)

FOR THE SAKE OF YOUR TRADITION (NIV, RSV)
(See *BECAUSE OF YOUR TRADITION*)

FOR THE THINGS DONE (NIV)
(See *ACCORDING TO WHAT HE HAS DONE*)

FOR THEIR DEEDS (NIV)
(See *ACCORDING TO THEIR DEEDS*)

FOR THIS CAUSE
Judg 8:7 So Gideon said, "*For this cause*, when the Lord has delivered Zebah and Zalmunna into my hand, then I will tear your flesh with the thorns of the wilderness and with briers
2Chr 32:20 Now *for this cause* King Hezekiah and the prophet Isaiah, the son of Amoz, prayed and cried out to heaven
Ps 32:6 *For this cause* everyone who is godly shall pray to You in a time when You may be found
John 18:37 *For this cause* I was born, and *for this cause* I have come into the world, that I should bear witness to the truth

FOR THIS PURPOSE
Ex 9:16 But indeed *for this purpose* I have raised you up, that I may show My power in you, and that My name may be declared in all the earth
Mark 1:38 But He said to them, "Let us go into the next towns, that I may preach there also, because *for this purpose* I have come forth
Luke 4:43 but He said to them, "I must preach the kingdom of God to the other cities also, because *for this purpose* I have been sent
John 12:27 Father, save Me from this hour'? But *for this purpose* I came to this hour
Acts 26:16 for I have appeared to you *for this purpose*, to make you a minister and a witness both of the things which you have seen and of the things which I will yet reveal to you
Phm 15 For perhaps he departed for a while *for this purpose*, that you might receive him forever
1Jn 3:8 *For this purpose* the Son of God was manifested, that He might destroy the works of the devil

FOR THIS VERY REASON (NIV)
(See *FOR THIS PURPOSE*)

FOR THREE TRANSGRESSIONS
Amos 1:3 *For three transgressions* of Damascus, and for four, I will not turn away its punishment, because they have threshed Gilead with implements of iron
Amos 1:6 *For three transgressions* of Gaza, and for four, I will not turn away its punishment, because they took captive the whole captivity to deliver them up to Edom
Amos 1:9 *For three transgressions* of Tyre, and for four, I will not turn away its punishment, because they delivered up the whole captivity to Edom, and did not remember the covenant of brotherhood
Amos 1:11 *For three transgressions* of Edom, and for four, I will not turn away its punishment, because he pursued his brother with the sword, and cast off all pity
Amos 1:13 *For three transgressions* of the people of Ammon, and for four, I will not turn away its punishment, because they ripped open the women with child in Gilead, that they might enlarge their territory
Amos 2:1 *For three transgressions* of Moab, and for four, I will not turn away its punishment, because he burned the bones of the king of Edom to lime
Amos 2:4 *For three transgressions* of Judah, and for four, I will not turn away its punishment, because they have despised the law of the Lord, and have not kept His commandments
Amos 2:6 *For three transgressions* of Israel, and for four, I will not turn away its punishment, because they sell the righteous for silver, and the poor for a pair of sandals

FOR US
Gen 24:23 Tell me, please, is there room in your father's house *for us* to lodge
Gen 26:22 So he called its name Rehoboth, because he said, "For now the Lord has made room *for us*, and we shall be fruitful in the land
Gen 31:14 Then Rachel and Leah answered and said to him, "Is there still any portion or inheritance *for us* in our father's house
Gen 41:12 And we told him, and he interpreted our dreams *for us*
Gen 41:13 And it came to pass, just as he interpreted *for us*, so it happened
Gen 42:2 go down to that place and buy *for us* there, that we may live and not die
Ex 2:19 And they said, "An Egyptian delivered us from the hand of the shepherds, and he also drew enough water *for us* and watered the flock
Ex 14:12 For it would have been better *for us* to serve the Egyptians than that we should die in the wilderness
Ex 24:14 And he said to the elders, "Wait here *for us* until we come back to you
Num 14:3 Would it not be better *for us* to return to Egypt
Deut 1:22 And everyone of you came near to me and said, 'Let us send men before us, and let them search out the land *for us*, and bring back word to us of the way by which we should go up, and of the cities into which we shall come
Deut 2:36 From Aroer, which is on the bank of the River Arnon, and from the city that is in the ravine, as far as Gilead, there was not one city too strong *for us*
Deut 6:25 Then it will be righteousness *for us*, if we are careful to observe all these commandments before the Lord our God, as He has commanded us
Deut 30:12 It is not in heaven, that you should

say, 'Who will ascend into heaven *for us* and bring it to us, that we may hear it and do it

Deut 30:13 Nor is it beyond the sea, that you should say, 'Who will go over the sea *for us* and bring it to us, that we may hear it and do it

Deut 33:4 Moses commanded a law *for us*, a heritage of the congregation of Jacob

Josh 5:13 And Joshua went to Him and said to Him, "Are You *for us* or for our adversaries

Josh 17:16 But the children of Joseph said, "The mountain country is not enough *for us*

Josh 22:17 Is the iniquity of Peor not enough *for us*, from which we are not cleansed until this day, although there was a plague in the congregation of the Lord

Judg 1:1 Now after the death of Joshua it came to pass that the children of Israel asked the Lord, saying, "Who shall be first to go up *for us* against the Canaanites to fight against them

Judg 16:25 So it happened, when their hearts were merry, that they said, "Call for Samson, that he may perform *for us*

1Sam 7:8 So the children of Israel said to Samuel, "Do not cease to cry out to the Lord our God *for us*, that He may save us from the hand of the Philistines

1Sam 8:5 Now make *for us* a king to judge us like all the nations

1Sam 14:6 it may be that the Lord will work *for us*

2Sam 21:4 And the Gibeonites said to him, "We will have no silver or gold from Saul or from his house, nor shall you kill any man in Israel *for us*

2Kin 4:13 And he said to him, "Say now to her, 'Look, you have been concerned *for us* with all this care

2Kin 6:1 And the sons of the prophets said to Elisha, "See now, the place where we dwell with you is too small *for us*

2Chr 13:10 But as *for us*, the Lord is our God, and we have not forsaken Him

Ezra 4:14 Now because we receive support from the palace, it was not proper *for us* to see the king's dishonor

Ezra 8:21 Then I proclaimed a fast there at the river of Ahava, that we might humble ourselves before our God, to seek from Him the right way *for us* and our little ones and all our possessions

Neh 4:20 Therefore, wherever you hear the sound of the trumpet, rally to us there. Our God will fight *for us*

Ps 47:4 He will choose our inheritance *for us*, the excellence of Jacob whom He loves

Ps 62:8 Pour out your heart before Him; God is a refuge *for us*

Ps 68:28 Your God has commanded your strength; strengthen, O God, what You have done *for us*

Ps 90:17 And let the beauty of the Lord our God be upon us, and establish the work of our hands *for us*

Ps 126:3 The Lord has done great things *for us*, whereof we are glad

Is 6:8 Whom shall I send, and who will go *for us*

Is 26:12 Lord, You will establish peace *for us*, for You have also done all our works in us

Is 33:21 But there the majestic Lord will be *for us* a place of broad rivers and streams, in which no galley with oars will sail, nor majestic ships pass by

Jer 5:24 He reserves *for us* the appointed weeks of the harvest

Jer 9:18 Let them make haste and take up a wailing *for us*, that our eyes may run with tears, and our eyelids gush with water

Jer 14:19 Why have You stricken us so that there is no healing *for us*

Jer 21:2 Please inquire of the Lord *for us*, for Nebuchadnezzar king of Babylon makes war against us

Jer 29:15 Because you have said, "The Lord has raised up prophets *for us* in Babylon

Jer 37:3 And Zedekiah the king sent Jehucal the son of Shelemiah, and Zephaniah the son of Maaseiah, the priest, to the prophet Jeremiah, saying, "Pray now to the Lord our God *for us*

Jer 42:2 and said to Jeremiah the prophet, "Please, let our petition be acceptable to you, and pray *for us* to the Lord your God, for all this remnant (since we are left but a few of many, as you can see

Jer 42:20 For you were hypocrites in your hearts when you sent me to the Lord your God, saying, 'Pray *for us* to the Lord our God, and according to all that the Lord your God says, so declare to us and we will do it

Lam 4:19 They pursued us on the mountains and lay in wait *for us* in the wilderness

Hos 10:3 and as for a king, what would he do *for us*

Jon 1:11 Then they said to him, "What shall we do to you that the sea may be calm *for us*

Matt 3:15 But Jesus answered and said to him, "Permit it to be so now, for thus it is fitting *for us* to fulfill all righteousness

Matt 17:4 Then Peter answered and said to Jesus, "Lord, it is good *for us* to be here

Matt 25:9 But the wise answered, saying, 'No, lest there should not be enough *for us* and you

Mark 9:5 Then Peter answered and said to Jesus, "Rabbi, it is good *for us* to be here

Mark 10:35 Then James and John, the sons of Zebedee, came to Him, saying, "Teacher, we want You to do *for us* whatever we ask

Mark 14:15 Then he will show you a large upper room, furnished and prepared; there make ready *for us*

Mark 16:3 And they said among themselves, "Who will roll away the stone from the door of the tomb *for us*

Luke 1:69 and has raised up a horn of salvation *for us* in the house of His servant David

Luke 9:33 And it happened, as they were parting from Him, that Peter said to Jesus, "Master, it is good *for us* to be here

Luke 9:50 But Jesus said to him, "Do not forbid him, for he who is not against us is *for us*

Luke 13:25 When once the Master of the house has risen up and shut the door, and you begin to stand outside and knock at the door, saying, 'Lord, Lord, open *for us*

Luke 20:22 Is it lawful *for us* to pay taxes to Caesar or not

Luke 22:8 And He sent Peter and John, saying, "Go and prepare the Passover *for us*, that we may eat

John 11:50 nor do you consider that it is expedient *for us* that one man should die for the people, and not that the whole nation should perish

John 14:8 Philip said to Him, "Lord, show us the Father, and it is sufficient *for us*

John 18:31 Therefore the Jews said to him, "It is not lawful *for us* to put anyone to death

Acts 13:33 God has fulfilled this *for us* their children, in that He has raised up Jesus

Acts 16:21 and they teach customs which are not lawful *for us*, being Romans, to receive or observe

Acts 20:5 These men, going ahead, waited *for us* at Troas

Rom 4:24 but also *for us*. It shall be imputed to us who believe in Him who raised up Jesus our Lord from the dead

Rom 5:8 But God demonstrates His own love toward us, in that while we were still sinners, Christ died *for us*

Rom 8:26 For we do not know what we should pray for as we ought, but the Spirit Himself makes intercession *for us* with groanings which cannot be uttered

Rom 8:31 If God is *for us*, who can be against us

Rom 8:32 He who did not spare His own Son, but delivered Him up *for us* all, how shall He not with Him also freely give us all things

Rom 8:34 It is Christ who died, and furthermore is also risen, who is even at the right hand of God, who also makes intercession *for us*

Rom 16:6 Greet Mary, who labored much *for us*

1Cor 1:30 But of Him you are in Christ Jesus, who became *for us* wisdom from God and righteousness and sanctification and redemption

1Cor 5:7 Therefore purge out the old leaven, that you may be a new lump, since you truly are unleavened. For indeed Christ, our Passover, was sacrificed *for us*

1Cor 8:6 yet *for us* there is only one God, the Father, of whom are all things, and we for Him

2Cor 1:11 you also helping together in prayer *for us*, that thanks may be given by many persons on our behalf for the gift granted to us through many

2Cor 4:17 For our light affliction, which is but for a moment, is working *for us* a far more exceeding and eternal weight of glory

2Cor 5:21 For He made Him who knew no sin to be sin *for us*, that we might become the righteousness of God in Him

2Cor 8:7 But as you abound in everything in faith, in speech, in knowledge, in all diligence, and in your love *for us* see that you abound in this grace also

Gal 3:13 Christ has redeemed us from the curse of the law, having become a curse *for us* (for it is written

Eph 5:2 And walk in love, as Christ also has loved us and given Himself *for us*, an offering and a sacrifice to God for a sweet-smelling aroma

Col 4:3 meanwhile praying also *for us*, that God would open to us a door for the word, to speak the mystery of Christ, for which I am also in chains

1Th 5:10 who died *for us*, that whether we wake or sleep, we should live together with Him

1Th 5:25 Brethren, pray *for us*

2Th 3:1 Finally, brethren, pray *for us*, that the word of the Lord may have free course and be glorified, just as it is with you

Tit 2:14 who gave Himself *for us*, that He might redeem us from every lawless deed and purify for Himself His own special people, zealous for good works

Heb 6:20 where the forerunner has entered *for us*, even Jesus, having become High Priest forever according to the order of Melchizedek

Heb 7:26 For such a High Priest was fitting *for us*, who is holy, harmless, undefiled, separate from sinners, and has become higher than the heavens

Heb 9:24 For Christ has not entered the holy places made with hands, which are copies of the true, but into heaven itself, now to appear in the presence of God *for us*

Heb 10:20 by a new and living way which He consecrated *for us*, through the veil, that is, His flesh

Heb 11:40 God having provided something better *for us*, that they should not be made perfect apart from us

Heb 13:18 Pray *for us;* for we are confident that we have a good conscience, in all things desiring to live honorably

1Pet 2:21 For to this you were called, because Christ also suffered *for us*, leaving us an example, that you should follow His steps

1Pet 4:1 Therefore, since Christ suffered *for us* in the flesh, arm yourselves also with the same mind, for he who has suffered in the flesh has ceased from sin

1Jn 3:16 By this we know love, because He laid down His life *for us*

1Jn 4:16 And we have known and believed the love that God has *for us*

FOR YOUR STOMACH'S SAKE

1Tim 5:23 No longer drink only water, but use a little wine *for your stomach's sake* and your frequent infirmities

FORBID THEM NOT (KJV)

(See *DO NOT FORBID*)

FORCED LABOR

Josh 17:13 And it happened, when the children of Israel grew strong, that they put the Canaanites to *forced labor*, but did not utterly drive them out

1Kin 9:21 that is, their descendants who were left in the land after them, whom the children of Israel had not been able to destroy completely from these Solomon raised *forced labor*, as it is to this day

2Chr 8:8 from these Solomon raised *forced labor*, as it is to this day

Prov 12:24 The hand of the diligent will rule, but the slothful will be put to *forced labor*

Is 31:8 But he shall flee from the sword, and his young men shall become *forced labor*

FOREIGN GODS

Gen 35:2 And Jacob said to his household and to all who were with him, "Put away the *foreign gods* that are among you, purify yourselves, and change your garments

Gen 35:4 So they gave Jacob all the *foreign gods* which were in their hands, and all their earrings which were in their ears

Deut 32:16 They provoked Him to jealousy with *foreign gods;* with abominations they provoked Him to anger

Josh 24:20 If you forsake the Lord and serve *foreign gods*, then He will turn and do you harm and consume you, after He has done you good

Josh 24:23 Now therefore," he said, "put away the *foreign gods* which are among you, and incline your heart to the Lord God of Israel

Judg 10:16 So they put away the *foreign gods* from among them and served the Lord

1Sam 7:3 Then Samuel spoke to all the house of Israel, saying, "If you return to the Lord with all your hearts, then put away the *foreign gods* and the Ashtoreths from among you, and prepare your hearts for the Lord, and serve Him only

2Chr 14:3 for he removed the altars of the *foreign gods* and the high places, and broke down the sacred pillars and cut down the wooden images

2Chr 33:15 He took away the *foreign gods* and the idol from the house of the Lord, and all the altars that he had built in the mount of the house of the Lord and in Jerusalem

Jer 5:19 then you shall answer them, 'Just as you have forsaken Me and served *foreign gods* in your land, so you shall serve aliens in a land that is not yours

Acts 17:18 Others said, "He seems to be a proclaimer of *foreign gods*

FOREKNOWLEDGE OF GOD

Acts 2:23 Him, being delivered by the determined counsel and *foreknowledge of God*, you have taken by lawless hands, have crucified, and put to death

1Pet 1:2 elect according to the *foreknowledge of God* the Father, in sanctification of the Spirit, for obedience and sprinkling of the blood of Jesus Christ

FOREVER IN YOUR GENERATIONS
Lev 6:18 It shall be a statute *forever in your generations* concerning the offerings made by fire to the Lord
Lev 23:41 It shall be a statute *forever in your generations*. You shall celebrate it in the seventh month
Lev 24:3 Outside the veil of the Testimony, in the tabernacle of meeting, Aaron shall be in charge of it from evening until morning before the Lord continually; it shall be a statute *forever in your generations*

FOREVER THROUGHOUT YOUR GENERATIONS
Lev 10:9 Do not drink wine or intoxicating drink, you, nor your sons with you, when you go into the tabernacle of meeting, lest you die. It shall be a statute *forever throughout your generations*
Lev 23:14 it shall be a statute *forever throughout your generations* in all your dwellings
Lev 23:31 it shall be a statute *forever throughout your generations* in all your dwellings
Num 10:8 and these shall be to you as an ordinance *forever throughout your generations*
Num 15:15 One ordinance shall be for you of the congregation and for the stranger who sojourns with you, an ordinance *forever throughout your generations*

FORGET GOD
Job 8:13 So are the paths of all who *forget God;* and the hope of the hypocrite shall perish
Ps 9:17 The wicked shall be turned into hell, and all the nations that *forget God*
Ps 50:22 Now consider this, you who *forget God*, lest I tear you in pieces, and there be none to deliver

FORGET NOT (KJV)
(See *DO NOT FORGET*)

FORGET YOUR PRECEPTS
Ps 119:93 I will never *forget Your precepts*, for by them You have given me life
Ps 119:141 I am small and despised, yet I do not *forget Your precepts*

FORGETFUL HEARER
Jas 1:25 But he who looks into the perfect law of liberty and continues in it, and is not a *forgetful hearer* but a doer of the work, this one will be blessed in what he does

FORGETTING THOSE THINGS
Phil 3:13 but one thing I do, *forgetting those things* which are behind and reaching forward to those things which are ahead

FORGIVE, O LORD (RSV)
(See *PROVIDE ATONEMENT*)

FORGIVE OUR SINS (NAS, RSV)
(See *ATONEMENT FOR OUR SINS*)

FORGIVE THEM
Is 2:9 People bow down, and each man humbles himself; therefore do not *forgive them*
Luke 23:34 Then Jesus said, "Father, *forgive them*, for they do not know what they do

FORGIVE US OUR DEBTS
Matt 6:12 And *forgive us our debts*, as we forgive our debtors

FORGIVE US OUR SINS
Luke 11:4 and *forgive us our sins*, for we also forgive everyone who is indebted to us
1Jn 1:9 If we confess our sins, He is faithful and just to *forgive us our sins* and to cleanse us from all unrighteousness

FORGIVENESS OF SINS
Acts 5:31 Him God has exalted to His right hand to be Prince and Savior, to give repentance to Israel and *forgiveness of sins*
Acts 13:38 Therefore let it be known to you, brethren, that through this Man is preached to you the *forgiveness of sins*
Acts 26:18 to open their eyes and to turn them from darkness to light, and from the power of Satan to God, that they may receive *forgiveness of sins* and an inheritance among those who are sanctified by faith in Me
Eph 1:7 In Him we have redemption through His blood, the *forgiveness of sins*, according to the riches of His grace
Col 1:14 in whom we have redemption through His blood, the *forgiveness of sins*

FORGOT THE LORD
Judg 3:7 They *forgot the Lord* their God, and served the Baals and Asherahs
1Sam 12:9 And when they *forgot the Lord* their God, He sold them into the hand of Sisera, commander of the army of Hazor, into the hand of the Philistines, and into the hand of the king of Moab

FORGOTTEN THE GOD
Deut 32:18 Of the Rock who begot you, you are unmindful, and have *forgotten the God* who fathered you
Is 17:10 Because you have *forgotten the God* of your salvation, and have not been mindful of the Rock of your stronghold, therefore you will plant pleasant plants and set out foreign seedlings

FORGOTTEN THE LORD
Jer 3:21 for they have perverted their way, and they have *forgotten the Lord* their God

FORK OF THE TWO ROADS
Ezek 21:21 For the king of Babylon stands at the parting of the road, at the *fork of the two roads*, to use divination

FORM OF A SERVANT
Phil 2:7 but made Himself of no reputation, taking the *form of a servant*, and coming in the likeness of men

FORM OF GOD
Phil 2:6 who, being in the *form of God*, did not consider it robbery to be equal with God

FORM OF GODLINESS
2Tim 3:5 having a *form of godliness* but denying its power. And from such people turn away

FORMED AT GOD'S COMMAND (NIV)
(See *FRAMED BY THE WORD OF GOD*)

FORMED ME FROM THE WOMB
Is 49:5 And now the Lord says, who *formed Me from the womb* to be His Servant, to bring Jacob back to Him, so that Israel is gathered to Him (for I shall be glorious in the eyes of the Lord, and My God shall be My strength

FORMED MY INWARD PARTS
Ps 139:13 For You have *formed my inward parts;* You have covered me in my mother's womb

FORMED YOU FROM THE WOMB
Is 44:2 Thus says the Lord who made you and *formed you from the womb*, who will help you

FORMED YOU IN THE WOMB

Is 44:24 Thus says the Lord, your Redeemer, and He who *formed you from the womb*

FORMED YOU IN THE WOMB
Jer 1:5 Before I *formed you in the womb* I knew you

FORMER DAYS
Num 6:12 but the *former days* shall be lost, because his separation was defiled
Eccl 7:10 Do not say, "Why were the *former days* better than these
Ezek 38:17 Are you he of whom I have spoken in *former days* by My servants the prophets of Israel, who prophesied for years in those days that I would bring you against them
Zech 8:11 But now I will not treat the remnant of this people as in the *former days*
Heb 10:32 But recall the *former days* in which, after you were illuminated, you endured a great struggle with sufferings

FORMER PROPHETS
Zech 1:4 Do not be like your fathers, to whom the *former prophets* preached, saying
Zech 7:7 Should you not have obeyed the words which the Lord proclaimed through the *former prophets* when Jerusalem and the cities around it were inhabited and prosperous, and the South and the Lowland were inhabited
Zech 7:12 Yes, they made their hearts like flint, refusing to hear the law and the words which the Lord of hosts had sent by His Spirit through the *former prophets*

FORMER RAIN
Hos 6:3 He will come to us like the rain, like the latter and *former rain* to the earth
Joel 2:23 for He has given you the *former rain* faithfully, and He will cause the rain to come down for you the *former rain*, and the latter rain in the first month

FORMER THINGS
Eccl 1:11 There is no remembrance of *former things*, nor will there be any remembrance of things that are to come by those who will come after
Is 41:22 let them show the *former things*, what they were, that we may consider them, and know the latter end of them
Is 42:9 Behold, the *former things* have come to pass, and new things I declare
Is 43:9 Who among them can declare this, and show us *former things*
Is 43:18 Do not remember the *former things*, nor consider the things of old
Is 46:9 Remember the *former things* of old, for I am God, and there is no other
Is 48:3 I have declared the *former things* from the beginning; they went forth from My mouth, and I caused them to hear it
Rev 21:4 and there shall be no more pain, for the *former things* have passed away

FORMER TIME (RSV)
(See *FORMER DAYS*)

FORMLESS AND EMPTY (NIV)
(See *WITHOUT FORM, AND VOID*)

FORSAKE NOT (KJV)
(See *DO NOT FORSAKE*)

FORSAKEN THE LORD
1Sam 12:10 Then they cried out to the Lord, and said, 'We have sinned, because we have *forsaken the Lord* and served the Baals and Ashtoreths
2Chr 21:10 At that time Libnah revolted against his rule, because he had *forsaken the Lord* God of his fathers
2Chr 24:20 Because you have *forsaken the Lord*, He also has forsaken you
2Chr 24:24 but the Lord delivered a very great army into their hand, because they had *forsaken the Lord* God of their fathers
2Chr 28:6 For Pekah the son of Remaliah killed one hundred and twenty thousand in Judah in one day, all valiant men, because they had *forsaken the Lord* God of their fathers
Is 1:4 They have *forsaken the Lord*, they have provoked to anger the Holy One of Israel, they have turned away backward
Jer 2:17 Have you not brought this on yourself, in that you have *forsaken the Lord* your God when He led you in the way
Jer 2:19 Know therefore and see that it is an evil and bitter thing that you have *forsaken the Lord* your God, and the fear of Me is not in you
Jer 17:13 Those who depart from Me shall be written in the earth, because they have *forsaken the Lord*, the fountain of living waters

FORSOOK THE LORD
Judg 2:12 and they *forsook the Lord* God of their fathers, who had brought them out of the land of Egypt
Judg 2:13 They *forsook the Lord* and served Baal and the Ashtoreths
Judg 10:6 and they *forsook the Lord* and did not serve Him
1Kin 9:9 Then they will answer, 'Because they *forsook the Lord* their God, who brought their fathers out of the land of Egypt, and have embraced other gods, and worshiped them and served them
2Kin 21:22 He *forsook the Lord* God of his fathers, and did not walk in the way of the Lord
2Chr 7:22 Then they will answer, 'Because they *forsook the Lord* God of their fathers, who brought them out of the land of Egypt, and embraced other gods, and worshiped them and served them

FORTIFIED CITIES
Num 32:17 and our little ones will dwell in the *fortified cities* because of the inhabitants of the land
Num 32:36 Beth Nimrah and Beth Haran, *fortified cities*, and folds for sheep
Josh 10:20 Then it happened, while Joshua and the children of Israel made an end of slaying them with a very great slaughter, till they had finished, that those who escaped entered *fortified cities*
Josh 19:35 And the *fortified cities* are Ziddim, Zer, Hammath, Rakkath, Chinnereth
1Sam 6:18 and the gold rats, according to the number of all the cities of the Philistines belonging to the five lords, both *fortified cities* and country villages, even as far as the large stone of Abel on which they set the ark of the Lord, which stone remains to this day in the field of Joshua of Beth Shemesh
2Sam 20:6 Take your lord's servants and pursue him, lest he find for himself *fortified cities*, and escape us
2Kin 18:13 And in the fourteenth year of King Hezekiah, Sennacherib king of Assyria came up against all the *fortified cities* of Judah and took them
2Kin 19:25 Now I have brought it to pass, that you should be for crushing *fortified cities* into heaps of ruins
2Chr 8:5 He built Upper Beth Horon and Lower

Beth Horon, *fortified cities* with walls, gates, and bars
2Chr 11:10 Zorah, Aijalon, and Hebron, which are in Judah and Benjamin, *fortified cities*
2Chr 12:4 And he took the *fortified cities* of Judah and came to Jerusalem
2Chr 14:6 And he built *fortified cities* in Judah, for the land had rest
2Chr 17:2 And he placed troops in all the *fortified cities* of Judah, and set garrisons in the land of Judah and in the cities of Ephraim which Asa his father had taken
2Chr 17:19 These served the king, besides those whom the king put in the *fortified cities* throughout all Judah
2Chr 19:5 Then he set judges in the land throughout all the *fortified cities* of Judah, city by city
2Chr 21:3 Their father gave them great gifts of silver and gold and precious things, with *fortified cities* in Judah
2Chr 32:1 he encamped against the *fortified cities*, thinking to win them over to himself
2Chr 33:14 Then he put military captains in all the *fortified cities* of Judah
Is 36:1 Now it came to pass in the fourteenth year of King Hezekiah that Sennacherib king of Assyria came up against all the *fortified cities* of Judah and took them
Is 37:26 Now I have brought it to pass, that you should be for crushing *fortified cities* into heaps of ruins
Jer 4:5 cry, 'Gather together,' and say, 'Assemble yourselves, and let us go into the *fortified cities*
Jer 5:17 they shall destroy your *fortified cities*, in which you trust, with the sword
Jer 8:14 Assemble yourselves, and let us enter the *fortified cities*, and let us be silent there
Jer 34:7 for only these *fortified cities* remained of the cities of Judah
Hos 8:14 Judah also has multiplied *fortified cities;* but I will send fire upon his cities, and it shall devour his palaces
Mic 7:12 In that day they shall come to you from Assyria and the *fortified cities*, from the fortress to the River, from sea to sea, and mountain to mountain
Zeph 1:16 a day of trumpet and alarm against the *fortified cities* and against the high towers

FORTIFIED CITY
Josh 19:29 And the border turned to Ramah and to the *fortified city* of Tyre
2Kin 3:19 Also you shall attack every *fortified city* and every choice city, and shall cut down every good tree, and stop up every spring of water, and ruin every good piece of land with stones
2Kin 10:2 Now as soon as this letter comes to you, since your master's sons are with you, and you have chariots and horses, a *fortified city* also, and weapons
2Kin 17:9 Also the children of Israel secretly did against the Lord their God things that were not right, and they built for themselves high places in all their cities, from watchtower to *fortified city*
2Kin 18:8 He subdued the Philistines, as far as Gaza and its territory, from watchtower to *fortified city*
2Chr 11:23 He dealt wisely, and dispersed some of his sons throughout all the territories of Judah and Benjamin, to every *fortified city*
Is 25:2 For You have made a city a ruin, a *fortified city* a ruin, a palace of foreigners to be a city no more
Is 27:10 Yet the *fortified city* will be desolate, the habitation forsaken and left like a wilderness
Jer 1:18 For behold, I have made you this day a *fortified city* and an iron pillar, and bronze walls against the whole land against the kings of Judah, against its princes, against its priests, and against the people of the land
Dan 11:15 So the king of the North shall come and build a siege mound, and take a *fortified city*

FORTY DAYS
Gen 7:4 For after seven more days I will cause it to rain on the earth *forty days* and forty nights, and I will destroy from the face of the earth all living things that I have made
Gen 7:12 And the rain was on the earth *forty days* and forty nights
Gen 7:17 Now the flood was on the earth *forty days*. The waters increased and lifted up the ark, and it rose high above the earth
Gen 8:6 So it came to pass, at the end of *forty days*, that Noah opened the window of the ark which he had made
Gen 50:3 *Forty days* were required for him, for such are the days required for those who are embalmed
Ex 24:18 And Moses was on the mountain *forty days* and forty nights
Ex 34:28 So he was there with the Lord *forty days* and forty nights
Num 13:25 And they returned from spying out the land after *forty days*
Num 14:34 According to the number of the days in which you spied out the land, *forty days*, for each day you shall bear your guilt one year, namely forty years, and you shall know My rejection
Deut 9:9 When I went up into the mountain to receive the tablets of stone, the tablets of the covenant which the Lord made with you, then I stayed on the mountain *forty days* and forty nights
Deut 9:11 And it came to pass, at the end of *forty days* and forty nights, that the Lord gave me the two tablets of stone, the tablets of the covenant
Deut 9:18 And I fell down before the Lord, as at the first, *forty days* and forty nights
Deut 9:25 *forty days* and forty nights I kept prostrating myself, because the Lord had said He would destroy you
Deut 10:10 As at the first time, I stayed in the mountain *forty days* and forty nights
1Sam 17:16 And the Philistine drew near and presented himself *forty days*, morning and evening
1Kin 19:8 and he went in the strength of that food *forty days* and forty nights as far as Horeb, the mountain of God
Ezek 4:6 then you shall bear the iniquity of the house of Judah *forty days*
Jon 3:4 Then he cried out and said, "Yet *forty days*, and Nineveh shall be overthrown
Matt 4:2 And when He had fasted *forty days* and forty nights, afterward He was hungry
Mark 1:13 And He was there in the wilderness *forty days*, tempted by Satan, and was with the wild beasts
Luke 4:2 being tempted for *forty days* by the devil. And in those days He ate nothing, and afterward, when they had ended, He was hungry
Acts 1:3 to whom He also presented Himself alive after His suffering by many infallible proofs, being seen by them during *forty days* and speaking of the things pertaining to the kingdom of God

FORTY DAYS AND FORTY NIGHTS
Gen 7:4 For after seven more days I will cause it to rain on the earth *forty days and forty nights*, and I will destroy from the face of the earth all living things that I have made
Gen 7:12 And the rain was on the earth *forty days and forty nights*
Ex 24:18 And Moses was on the mountain *forty days and forty nights*

Ex 34:28 So he was there with the Lord *forty days and forty nights*
Deut 9:9 When I went up into the mountain to receive the tablets of stone, the tablets of the covenant which the Lord made with you, then I stayed on the mountain *forty days and forty nights*
Deut 9:11 And it came to pass, at the end of *forty days and forty nights*, that the Lord gave me the two tablets of stone, the tablets of the covenant
Deut 9:18 And I fell down before the Lord, as at the first, *forty days and forty nights*
Deut 9:25 *forty days and forty nights* I kept prostrating myself, because the Lord had said He would destroy you
Deut 10:10 As at the first time, I stayed in the mountain *forty days and forty nights*
1Kin 19:8 and he went in the strength of that food *forty days and forty nights* as far as Horeb, the mountain of God
Matt 4:2 And when He had fasted *forty days and forty nights*, afterward He was hungry

FORTY YEARS
Gen 25:20 Isaac was *forty years* old when he took Rebekah as wife, the daughter of Bethuel the Syrian of Padan Aram, the sister of Laban the Syrian
Gen 26:34 When Esau was *forty years* old, he took as wives Judith the daughter of Beeri the Hittite, and Basemath the daughter of Elon the Hittite
Ex 16:35 And the children of Israel ate manna *forty years*, until they came to an inhabited land
Num 14:33 And your sons shall be shepherds in the wilderness *forty years*, and bear the brunt of your infidelity, until your carcasses are consumed in the wilderness
Num 14:34 According to the number of the days in which you spied out the land, forty days, for each day you shall bear your guilt one year, namely *forty years*, and you shall know My rejection
Num 32:13 So the Lord's anger was aroused against Israel, and He made them wander in the wilderness *forty years*, until all the generation that had done evil in the sight of the Lord was gone
Deut 2:7 These *forty years* the Lord your God has been with you
Deut 8:2 And you shall remember that the Lord your God led you all the way these *forty years* in the wilderness, to humble you and test you, to know what was in your heart, whether you would keep His commandments or not
Deut 8:4 Your garments did not wear out on you, nor did your foot swell these *forty years*
Deut 29:5 And I have led you *forty years* in the wilderness
Josh 5:6 For the children of Israel walked *forty years* in the wilderness, till all the people who were men of war, who came out of Egypt, were consumed, because they did not obey the voice of the Lord to whom the Lord swore that He would not show them the land which the Lord had sworn to their fathers that He would give us
Josh 14:7 I was *forty years* old when Moses the servant of the Lord sent me from Kadesh Barnea to spy out the land, and I brought back word to him as it was in my heart
Judg 3:11 So the land had rest for *forty years*. Then Othniel the son of Kenaz died
Judg 5:31 But let those who love Him be like the sun when it comes out in full strength." So the land had rest for *forty years*
Judg 8:28 And the country was quiet for *forty years* in the days of Gideon
Judg 13:1 Again the children of Israel did evil in the sight of the Lord, and the Lord delivered them into the hand of the Philistines for *forty years*
1Sam 4:18 and his neck was broken and he died, for the man was old and heavy. And he had judged Israel *forty years*
2Sam 2:10 Ishbosheth, Saul's son, was *forty years* old when he began to reign over Israel, and he reigned two years
2Sam 5:4 David was thirty years old when he began to reign, and he reigned *forty years*
2Sam 15:7 And it came to pass after *forty years* that Absalom said to the king
1Kin 2:11 The period that David reigned over Israel was *forty years*
1Kin 11:42 And the period that Solomon reigned in Jerusalem over all Israel was *forty years*
2Kin 12:1 In the seventh year of Jehu, Jehoash became king, and he reigned *forty years* in Jerusalem
1Chr 29:27 And the period that he reigned over Israel was *forty years*
2Chr 9:30 Solomon reigned in Jerusalem over all Israel *forty years*
2Chr 24:1 Joash was seven years old when he became king, and he reigned *forty years* in Jerusalem
Neh 9:21 *Forty years* You sustained them in the wilderness, so that they lacked nothing
Ps 95:10 For *forty years* I was grieved with that generation, and said
Ezek 29:11 Neither foot of man shall pass through it nor foot of beast pass through it, and it shall be uninhabited *forty years*
Ezek 29:12 and among the cities that are laid waste, her cities shall be desolate *forty years*
Ezek 29:13 At the end of *forty years* I will gather the Egyptians from the peoples among whom they were scattered
Amos 2:10 Also it was I who brought you up from the land of Egypt, and led you *forty years* through the wilderness, to possess the land of the Amorite
Amos 5:25 Did you offer Me sacrifices and offerings in the wilderness *forty years*, O house of Israel
Acts 4:22 For the man was over *forty years* old on whom this miracle of healing had been performed
Acts 7:23 But when he was *forty years* old, it came into his heart to visit his brethren, the children of Israel
Acts 7:30 And when *forty years* had passed, an Angel of the Lord appeared to him in a flame of fire in a bush, in the wilderness of Mount Sinai
Acts 7:36 He brought them out, after he had shown wonders and signs in the land of Egypt, and in the Red Sea, and in the wilderness *forty years*
Acts 7:42 Did you offer Me slaughtered animals and sacrifices during *forty years* in the wilderness, O house of Israel
Acts 13:18 Now for a time of about *forty years* He put up with their ways in the wilderness
Acts 13:21 so God gave them Saul the son of Kish, a man of the tribe of Benjamin, for *forty years*
Heb 3:9 where your fathers tested Me, proved Me, and saw My works *forty years*
Heb 3:17 Now with whom was He angry *forty years?* Was it not with those who sinned, whose corpses fell in the wilderness

FOUGHT AGAINST ISRAEL
Num 21:1 When the king of Arad, the Canaanite, who dwelt in the South, heard that Israel was coming on the road to Atharim, then he *fought against Israel* and took some of them prisoners
Num 21:23 So Sihon gathered all his people together and went out against Israel in the wilderness, and he came to Jahaz and *fought against Israel*
Judg 11:20 So Sihon gathered all his people to-

gether, encamped in Jahaz, and *fought against Israel*

1Sam 31:1 So the Philistines *fought against Israel;* and the men of Israel fled from before the Philistines, and fell slain on Mount Gilboa

1Chr 10:1 Now the Philistines *fought against Israel;* and the men of Israel fled from before the Philistines, and fell slain on Mount Gilboa

FOUND FAVOR IN YOUR EYES

Gen 30:27 And Laban said to him, "Please stay, if I have *found favor in your eyes*, for I have learned by experience that the Lord has blessed me for your sake

Gen 50:4 And when the days of his mourning were past, Joseph spoke to the household of Pharaoh, saying, "If now I have *found favor in your eyes*, please speak in the hearing of Pharaoh, saying

Ruth 2:10 Then she fell on her face, bowed down to the ground, and said to him, "Why have I *found favor in your eyes*, that you should take notice of me, since I am a foreigner

1Sam 20:3 Then David took an oath again, and said, "Your father certainly knows that I have *found favor in your eyes*, and he says

1Sam 20:29 And now, if I have *found favor in your eyes*, please let me get away and see my brothers

1Sam 27:5 Then David said to Achish, "If I have now *found favor in your eyes*, let them give me a place in some town in the country, that I may dwell there

FOUND FAVOR IN YOUR SIGHT

Gen 18:3 and said, "My Lord, if I have now *found favor in Your sight*, do not pass on by Your servant

Gen 19:19 Indeed now, your servant has *found favor in your sight*, and you have increased your mercy which you have shown me by saving my life

Gen 33:10 And Jacob said, "No, please, if I have now *found favor in your sight*, then receive my present from my hand, inasmuch as I have seen your face as though I had seen the face of God, and you were pleased with me

Gen 47:29 When the time drew near that Israel must die, he called his son Joseph and said to him, "Now if I have *found favor in your sight*, please put your hand under my thigh, and deal kindly and truly with me

Num 11:11 And why have I not *found favor in Your sight*, that You have laid the burden of all these people on me

Num 11:15 If You treat me like this, please kill me here and now if I have *found favor in Your sight* and do not let me see my wretchedness

Num 32:5 Therefore they said, "If we have *found favor in your sight*, let this land be given to your servants as a possession, and do not take us over the Jordan

Judg 6:17 Then he said to Him, "If now I have *found favor in Your sight*, then show me a sign that it is You who talk with me

2Sam 14:22 And Joab said, "Today your servant knows that I have *found favor in your sight*, my lord, O king, in that the king has fulfilled the request of his servant

Neh 2:5 And I said to the king, "If it pleases the king, and if your servant has *found favor in your sight*, I ask that you send me to Judah, to the city of my fathers' tombs, that I may rebuild it

Esth 7:3 Then Queen Esther answered and said, "If I have *found favor in your sight*, O king, and if it pleases the king, let my life be given me at my petition, and my people at my request

FOUND FAVOR WITH GOD

Luke 1:30 Then the angel said to her, "Do not be afraid, Mary, for you have *found favor with God*

FOUND GRACE IN THE EYES OF

Gen 6:8 But Noah *found grace in the eyes of* the Lord

FOUND GRACE IN YOUR SIGHT

Ex 33:13 Now therefore, I pray, if I have *found grace in Your sight*, show me now Your way, that I may know You and that I may find grace in Your sight

Ex 33:16 For how then will it be known that Your people and I have *found grace in Your sight*, except You go with us

Ex 34:9 Then he said, "If now I have *found grace in Your sight*, O Lord, let my Lord, I pray, go among us, even though we are a stiff-necked people

FOUND LIARS UNTO THEE (KJV)
(See *SUBMIT TO*)

FOUND THE EARTH (NAS)
(See *FOUNDATIONS OF THE EARTH*)

FOUND WANTING

Dan 5:27 You have been weighed in the balances, and *found wanting*

FOUNDATION OF THE EARTH

Ps 102:25 Of old You laid the *foundation of the earth*, and the heavens are the work of Your hands

Is 48:13 Indeed My hand has laid the *foundation of the earth*, and My right hand has stretched out the heavens

Zech 12:1 Thus says the Lord, who stretches out the heavens, lays the *foundation of the earth*, and forms the spirit of man within him

Heb 1:10 You, Lord, in the beginning laid the *foundation of the earth*, and the heavens are the work of Your hands

FOUNDATION OF THE HOUSE (KJV, NAS, RSV)
(See *FOUNDATION OF THE TEMPLE*)

FOUNDATION OF THE LORD'S TEMPLE (NIV)
(See *FOUNDATION OF THE TEMPLE*)

FOUNDATION OF THE TEMPLE

1Kin 5:17 And the king commanded them to quarry large stones, costly stones, and hewn stones, to lay the *foundation of the temple*

Ezra 3:6 But the *foundation of the temple* of the Lord had not yet been laid

Ezra 3:10 When the builders laid the *foundation of the temple* of the Lord, the priests stood in their apparel with trumpets, and the Levites, the sons of Asaph, with cymbals, to praise the Lord, according to the ordinance of David king of Israel

FOUNDATION OF THE WORLD

Matt 13:35 I will utter things which have been kept secret from the *foundation of the world*

Matt 25:34 Then the King will say to those on His right hand, 'Come, you blessed of My Father, inherit the kingdom prepared for you from the *foundation of the world*

Luke 11:50 that the blood of all the prophets which was shed from the *foundation of the world* may be required of this generation

John 17:24 for You loved Me before the *foundation of the world*

Eph 1:4 just as He chose us in Him before the *foundation of the world*, that we should be holy and without blame before Him in love

Heb 4:3 So I swore in My wrath, they shall not

enter My rest," although the works were finished from the *foundation of the world*
Heb 9:26 He then would have had to suffer often since the *foundation of the world*
1Pet 1:20 He indeed was foreordained before the *foundation of the world*, but was manifest in these last times for you
Rev 13:8 And all who dwell on the earth will worship him, whose names have not been written in the Book of Life of the Lamb slain from the *foundation of the world*
Rev 17:8 And those who dwell on the earth will marvel, whose names are not written in the Book of Life from the *foundation of the world*, when they see the beast that was, and is not, and yet is

FOUNDATION OF THIS HOUSE (KJV, NAS, RSV)
(See *FOUNDATION OF THIS TEMPLE*)

FOUNDATION OF THIS TEMPLE
Ezra 3:12 But many of the priests and Levites and heads of the fathers' houses, who were old men, who had seen the first temple, wept with a loud voice when the *foundation of this temple* was laid before their eyes
Zech 4:9 The hands of Zerubbabel have laid the *foundation of this temple*

FOUNDATION ON THE ROCK (NIV)
(See *FOUNDED ON THE ROCK*)

FOUNDATIONS OF THE EARTH
Job 38:4 Where were you when I laid the *foundations of the earth*
Ps 82:5 They walk about in darkness; all the *foundations of the earth* are unstable
Ps 104:5 You who laid the *foundations of the earth*, so that it should not be moved forever
Prov 8:29 When He assigned to the sea its limit, so that the waters would not transgress His command, when He marked out the *foundations of the earth*
Is 24:18 for the windows from on high are open, and the *foundations of the earth* are shaken
Is 40:21 Have you not understood from the *foundations of the earth*
Is 51:13 And you forget the Lord your Maker, Who stretched out the heavens and laid the *foundations of the earth*
Is 51:16 I have covered you with the shadow of My hand, that I may plant the heavens, lay the *foundations of the earth*, and say to Zion
Jer 31:37 If heaven above can be measured, and the *foundations of the earth* searched out beneath, I will also cast off all the seed of Israel for all that they have done
Mic 6:2 Hear, O you mountains, the Lord's complaint, and you strong *foundations of the earth*

FOUNDATIONS OF THE WORLD
2Sam 22:16 Then the channels of the sea were seen, the *foundations of the world* were uncovered, at the rebuke of the Lord, at the blast of the breath of His nostrils
Ps 18:15 Then the channels of waters were seen, and the *foundations of the world* were uncovered at Your rebuke, O Lord, at the blast of the breath of Your nostrils

FOUNDED ON THE ROCK
Matt 7:25 and it did not fall, for it was *founded on the rock*
Luke 6:48 And when the flood arose, the stream beat vehemently against that house, and could not shake it, for it was *founded on the rock*

FOUNDED THE WORLD (NIV)
(See *ESTABLISHED THE WORLD*)

FOUNTAIN OF LIFE
Ps 36:9 For with You is the *fountain of life;* in Your light we see light
Prov 13:14 The law of the wise is a *fountain of life*, to turn one away from the snares of death
Prov 14:27 The fear of the Lord is a *fountain of life*, to avoid the snares of death

FOUNTAIN OF LIVING WATERS
Jer 2:13 they have forsaken Me, the *fountain of living waters*, and hewn themselves cisterns broken cisterns that can hold no water
Jer 17:13 Those who depart from Me shall be written in the earth, because they have forsakèn the Lord, the *fountain of living waters*

FOUR CORNERS OF THE EARTH
Is 11:12 He will set up a banner for the nations, and will assemble the outcasts of Israel, and gather together the dispersed of Judah from the *four corners of the earth*
Rev 7:1 After these things I saw four angels standing at the *four corners of the earth*, holding the four winds of the earth, that the wind should not blow on the earth, on the sea, or on any tree
Rev 20:8 and will go out to deceive the nations which are in the *four corners of the earth*, Gog and Magog, to gather them together to battle, whose number is as the sand of the sea

FOUR LIVING CREATURES
Ezek 1:5 Also from within it came the likeness of *four living creatures*
Rev 4:6 And in the midst of the throne, and around the throne, were *four living creatures* full of eyes in front and in back
Rev 4:8 And the *four living creatures*, each having six wings, were full of eyes around and within
Rev 5:6 And I looked, and behold, in the midst of the throne and of the *four living creatures* , and in the midst of the elders, stood a Lamb as though it had been slain, having seven horns and seven eyes, which are the seven Spirits of God sent out into all the earth
Rev 5:8 Now when He had taken the scroll, the *four living creatures* and the twenty-four elders fell down before the Lamb, each having a harp, and golden bowls full of incense, which are the prayers of the saints
Rev 5:14 Then the *four living creatures* said, "Amen!" And the twenty-four elders fell down and worshiped Him who lives forever and ever
Rev 6:1 and I heard one of the *four living creatures* saying with a voice like thunder
Rev 6:6 And I heard a voice in the midst of the *four living creatures* saying
Rev 7:11 And all the angels stood around the throne and the elders and the *four living creatures*, and fell on their faces before the throne and worshiped God
Rev 14:3 And they sang as it were a new song before the throne, before the *four living creatures*, and the elders
Rev 15:7 Then one of the *four living creatures* gave to the seven angels seven golden bowls full of the wrath of God who lives forever and ever
Rev 19:4 And the twenty-four elders and the *four living creatures* fell down and worshiped God who sat on the throne, saying

FOUR QUARTERS OF THE EARTH (NIV)
(See *FOUR CORNERS OF THE EARTH*)

FOURTH GENERATION
Gen 15:16 But in the *fourth generation* they shall return here, for the iniquity of the Amorites is not yet complete
Ex 34:7 keeping mercy for thousands, forgiving iniquity and transgression and sin, by no means clearing the guilty, visiting the iniquity of the fathers upon the children and the children's children to the third and the *fourth generation*
Num 14:18 but He by no means clears the guilty, visiting the iniquity of the fathers on the children to the third and *fourth generation*
2Kin 10:30 And the Lord said to Jehu, "Because you have done well in doing what is right in My sight, and have done to the house of Ahab all that was in My heart, your sons shall sit on the throne of Israel to the *fourth generation*
2Kin 15:12 This was the word of the Lord which He spoke to Jehu, saying, "Your sons shall sit on the throne of Israel to the *fourth generation*

FOWLER'S SNARE
Hos 9:8 but the prophet is a *fowler's snare* in all his ways, and enmity in the house of his God

FOXES HAVE HOLES
Matt 8:20 And Jesus said to him, "*Foxes have holes* and birds of the air have nests, but the Son of Man has nowhere to lay His head
Luke 9:58 And Jesus said to him, "*Foxes have holes* and birds of the air have nests, but the Son of Man has nowhere to lay His head

FRAGRANT INCENSE (NAS, NIV, RSV)
(See *SWEET INCENSE*)

FRAME MISCHIEF (RSV)
(See *DEVISES EVIL*)

FRAMED BY THE WORD OF GOD
Heb 11:3 By faith we understand that the worlds were *framed by the word of God*, so that the things which are seen were not made of things which are visible

FREE FROM SIN
Rom 6:18 And having been set *free from sin*, you became slaves of righteousness
Rom 6:22 But now having been set *free from sin*, and having become slaves of God, you have your fruit to holiness, and the end, everlasting life

FREE FROM THIS OATH (RSV)
(See *RELEASED FROM THIS OATH*)

FREE WOMAN'S SON (NIV)
(See *SON OF THE FREEWOMAN*)

FREED FROM SIN
Rom 6:7 For he who has died has been *freed from sin*

FREEDOM FOR THE PRISONERS (NIV)
(See *DELIVERANCE TO THE CAPTIVES*)

FREEDOM OF THE CHILDREN OF GOD (NIV)
(See *LIBERTY OF THE CHILDREN OF GOD*)

FREEDOM WE HAVE IN CHRIST (NIV)
(See *LIBERTY WHICH WE HAVE IN CHRIST*)

FREEING HIM FROM THE AGONY OF DEATH (NIV)
(See *LOOSED THE PAINS OF DEATH*)

FREELY EAT
Gen 2:16 And the Lord God commanded the man, saying, "Of every tree of the garden you may *freely eat*

FREEWILL OFFERING
Ex 35:29 The children of Israel brought a *freewill offering* to the Lord, all the men and women whose hearts were willing to bring material for all kinds of work which the Lord, by the hand of Moses, had commanded to be done
Lev 22:21 And whoever offers a sacrifice of peace offering to the Lord, to fulfill his vow, or a *freewill offering* from the cattle or the sheep, it must be perfect to be accepted
Lev 22:23 Either a bull or a lamb that has any limb too long or too short you may offer as a *freewill offering*, but for a vow it shall not be accepted
Num 15:3 and you make an offering by fire to the Lord, a burnt offering or a sacrifice, to fulfill a vow or as a *freewill offering* or in your appointed feasts, to make a sweet aroma to the Lord, from the herd or the flock
Deut 16:10 Then you shall keep the Feast of Weeks to the Lord your God with the tribute of a *freewill offering* from your hand, which you shall give as the Lord your God blesses you
Ezra 3:5 and afterward they offered the regular burnt offering, and those for New Moons and for all the appointed feasts of the Lord that were consecrated, and those of everyone who willingly offered a *freewill offering* to the Lord
Ezra 7:16 and whereas all the silver and gold that you may find in all the province of Babylon, along with the *freewill offering* of the people and the priests, are to be freely offered for the house of their God in Jerusalem
Ezra 8:28 and the silver and the gold are a *freewill offering* to the Lord God of your fathers

FREEWILL OFFERINGS
Ex 36:3 So they continued bringing to him *freewill offerings* every morning
Lev 22:18 Whatever man of the house of Israel, or of the strangers in Israel, who offers his sacrifice for any of his vows or for any of his *freewill offerings*, which they offer to the Lord as a burnt offering
Lev 23:38 besides the Sabbaths of the Lord, besides your gifts, besides all your vows, and besides all your *freewill offerings* which you give to the Lord
Num 29:39 These things you shall present to the Lord at your appointed feasts (besides your vowed offerings and your *freewill offerings*
Deut 12:6 There you shall take your burnt offerings, your sacrifices, your tithes, the heave offerings of your hand, your vowed offerings, your *freewill offerings*, and the firstlings of your herds and flocks
Deut 12:17 You may not eat within your gates the tithe of your grain or your new wine or your oil, of the firstlings of your herd or your flock, of any of your offerings which you vow, of your *freewill offerings*, or of the heave offering of your hand
2Chr 31:14 Kore the son of Imnah the Levite, the keeper of the East Gate, was over the *freewill offerings* to God, to distribute the offerings of the Lord and the most holy things
Ezra 1:4 And whoever remains in any place where he sojourns, let the men of his place help him with silver and gold, with goods and livestock, besides the *freewill offerings* for the house of God which is in Jerusalem
Ps 119:108 Accept, I pray, the *freewill offerings* of my mouth, O Lord, and teach me Your judgments
Amos 4:5 Offer a sacrifice of thanksgiving with leaven, proclaim and announce the *freewill offerings*

FRIEND LOVES AT ALL TIMES
Prov 17:17 A *friend loves at all times*, and a brother is born for adversity

FRIEND OF GOD
Jas 2:23 And the Scripture was fulfilled which says, "Abraham believed God, and it was accounted to him for righteousness." And he was called the *friend of God*

FRIEND OF PUBLICANS AND SINNERS (KJV)
(See *FRIEND OF TAX COLLECTORS AND SINNERS*)

FRIEND OF TAX COLLECTORS AND SINNERS
Matt 11:19 The Son of Man came eating and drinking, and they say, 'Look, a gluttonous man and a winebibber, a *friend of tax collectors and sinners*
Luke 7:34 The Son of Man has come eating and drinking, and you say, 'Look, a glutton and a winebibber, a *friend of tax collectors and sinners*

FRIEND OF THE BRIDEGROOM
John 3:29 but the *friend of the bridegroom*, who stands and hears him, rejoices greatly because of the bridegroom's voice

FRIENDS OF THE BRIDEGROOM
Matt 9:15 And Jesus said to them, "Can the *friends of the bridegroom* mourn as long as the bridegroom is with them
Mark 2:19 So Jesus said to them, "Can the *friends of the bridegroom* fast while the bridegroom is with them
Luke 5:34 And He said to them, "Can you make the *friends of the bridegroom* fast while the bridegroom is with them

FRINGE OF HIS GARMENT (RSV)
(See *BORDER OF HIS GARMENT*)

FROM BEGINNING TO END
1Sam 3:12 In that day I will perform against Eli all that I have spoken concerning his house, *from beginning to end*
Eccl 3:11 Also He has put eternity in their hearts, except that no one can find out the work that God does *from beginning to end*

FROM DAN TO BEERSHEBA
Judg 20:1 Then all the children of Israel came out, *from Dan to Beersheba*, as well as from the land of Gilead, and the congregation gathered together as one man before the Lord at Mizpah
1Sam 3:20 And all Israel *from Dan to Beersheba* knew that Samuel had been established as a prophet of the Lord
2Sam 3:10 to transfer the kingdom from the house of Saul, and set up the throne of David over Israel and over Judah, *from Dan to Beersheba*
2Sam 17:11 Therefore I counsel that all Israel be fully gathered to you, *from Dan to Beersheba*, like the sand that is by the sea for multitude, and that you go to battle in person
2Sam 24:2 So the king said to Joab the commander of the army who was with him, "Now go throughout all the tribes of Israel, *from Dan to Beersheba*, and count the people, that I may know the number of the people
2Sam 24:15 *From Dan to Beersheba* seventy thousand men of the people died

FROM DARKNESS TO LIGHT
Acts 26:18 to open their eyes and to turn them *from darkness to light*, and from the power of Satan to God, that they may receive forgiveness of sins and an inheritance among those who are sanctified by faith in Me

FROM EGYPT TO THE EUPHRATES (NIV)
(See *FROM THE FORTRESS TO THE RIVER*)

FROM EVERLASTING TO EVERLASTING
1Chr 16:36 Blessed be the Lord God of Israel *from everlasting to everlasting*
Ps 41:13 Blessed be the Lord God of Israel *from everlasting to everlasting*
Ps 90:2 Before the mountains were brought forth, or ever You had formed the earth and the world, even *from everlasting to everlasting*, You are God
Ps 103:17 But the mercy of the Lord is *from everlasting to everlasting* on those who fear Him, and His righteousness to children's children
Ps 106:48 Blessed be the Lord God of Israel *from everlasting to everlasting*

FROM GENERATION TO GENERATION
Ex 17:16 the Lord will have war with Amalek *from generation to generation*
Is 13:20 It will never be inhabited, nor will it be settled *from generation to generation*
Is 34:10 *from generation to generation* it shall lie waste; no one shall pass through it forever and ever
Is 34:17 they shall possess it forever; *from generation to generation* they shall dwell in it
Is 51:8 but My righteousness will be forever, and My salvation *from generation to generation*
Jer 50:39 It shall be inhabited no more forever, nor shall it be dwelt in *from generation to generation*
Lam 5:19 You, O Lord, remain forever; Your throne *from generation to generation*
Dan 4:3 His kingdom is an everlasting kingdom, and His dominion is *from generation to generation*
Dan 4:34 For His dominion is an everlasting dominion, and His kingdom is *from generation to generation*
Joel 3:20 But Judah shall abide forever, and Jerusalem *from generation to generation*
Luke 1:50 And His mercy is on those who fear Him *from generation to generation*

FROM GOD
Judg 3:20 Then Ehud said, "I have a message *from God* for you
1Sam 16:15 And Saul's servants said to him, "Surely, a distressing spirit *from God* is troubling you
1Sam 16:16 and it shall be that he will play it with his hand when the distressing spirit *from God* is upon you, and you shall be well
1Sam 16:23 And so it was, whenever the spirit *from God* was upon Saul, that David would take a harp and play it with his hand
1Sam 18:10 And it happened on the next day that the distressing spirit *from God* came upon Saul, and he prophesied inside the house
2Chr 10:15 for the turn of affairs was *from God*, that the Lord might fulfill His word, which He had spoken by the hand of Ahijah the Shilonite to Jeroboam the son of Nebat
2Chr 25:20 But Amaziah would not heed, for it came *from God*, that He might give them into the hand of their enemies, because they sought the gods of Edom
Job 2:10 Shall we indeed accept good *from God*, and shall we not accept adversity
Job 20:29 This is the portion *from God* for a wicked man, the heritage appointed to him by God
Job 31:23 For destruction *from God* is a terror to me, and because of His magnificence I could not endure
Job 34:10 far be it *from God* to do wickedness, and from the Almighty to commit iniquity

Ps 104:21 The young lions roar after their prey, and seek their food *from God*
Mic 3:7 indeed they shall all cover their lips; for there is no answer *from God*
John 1:6 There was a man sent *from God*, whose name was John
John 3:2 This man came to Jesus by night and said to Him, "Rabbi, we know that You are a teacher come *from God*
John 6:46 Not that anyone has seen the Father, except He who is *from God*
John 7:17 If anyone wants to do His will, he shall know concerning the doctrine, whether it is *from God* or whether I speak on My own authority
John 8:40 But now you seek to kill Me, a Man who has told you the truth which I heard *from God*
John 8:42 Jesus said to them, "If God were your Father, you would love Me, for I proceeded forth and came *from God*
John 9:16 Therefore some of the Pharisees said, "This Man is not *from God*, because He does not keep the Sabbath
John 9:33 If this Man were not *from God*, He could do nothing
John 13:3 Jesus, knowing that the Father had given all things into His hands, and that He had come *from God* and was going to God
John 16:27 for the Father Himself loves you, because you have loved Me, and have believed that I came forth *from God*
John 16:30 By this we believe that You came forth *from God*
Acts 26:22 Therefore, having obtained help *from God*, to this day I stand, witnessing both to small and great, saying no other things than those which the prophets and Moses said would come
Rom 1:7 Grace to you and peace *from God* our Father and the Lord Jesus Christ
Rom 2:29 but he is a Jew who is one inwardly, and circumcision is that of the heart, in the Spirit, and not in the letter; whose praise is not from men but *from God*
Rom 13:1 For there is no authority except *from God*, and the authorities that exist are appointed by God
1Cor 1:3 Grace to you and peace *from God* our Father and the Lord Jesus Christ
1Cor 1:30 But of Him you are in Christ Jesus, who became for us wisdom *from God* and righteousness and sanctification and redemption
1Cor 2:12 Now we have received, not the spirit of the world, but the Spirit who is *from God*, that we might know the things that have been freely given to us by God
1Cor 4:5 Therefore judge nothing before the time, until the Lord comes, who will both bring to light the hidden things of darkness and reveal the counsels of the hearts; and then each one's praise will come *from God*
1Cor 6:19 Or do you not know that your body is the temple of the Holy Spirit who is in you, whom you have *from God*, and you are not your own
1Cor 7:7 But each one has his own gift *from God*, one in this manner and another in that
1Cor 11:12 For as the woman was from the man, even so the man also is through the woman; but all things are *from God*
2Cor 1:2 Grace to you and peace *from God* our Father and the Lord Jesus Christ
2Cor 2:17 but as of sincerity, but as *from God*, we speak in the sight of God in Christ
2Cor 3:5 Not that we are sufficient of ourselves to think of anything as being from ourselves, but our sufficiency is *from God*
2Cor 5:1 For we know that if our earthly house, this tent, is destroyed, we have a building *from God*, a house not made with hands, eternal in the heavens
Gal 1:3 Grace to you and peace *from God* the Father and our Lord Jesus Christ
Eph 1:2 Grace to you and peace *from God* our Father and the Lord Jesus Christ
Eph 6:23 Peace to the brethren, and love with faith, *from God* the Father and the Lord Jesus Christ
Phil 1:2 Grace to you and peace *from God* our Father and the Lord Jesus Christ
Phil 1:28 and not in any way terrified by your adversaries, which is to them a proof of perdition, but to you of salvation, and that *from God*
Phil 3:9 and be found in Him, not having my own righteousness, which is from the law, but that which is through faith in Christ, the righteousness which is *from God* by faith
Col 1:2 Grace to you and peace *from God* our Father and the Lord Jesus Christ
Col 1:25 of which I became a minister according to the stewardship *from God* which was given to me for you, to fulfill the word of God
Col 2:19 and not holding fast to the Head, from whom all the body, nourished and knit together by joints and ligaments, grows with the increase which is *from God*
1Th 1:1 Grace to you and peace *from God* our Father and the Lord Jesus Christ
2Th 1:2 Grace to you and peace *from God* our Father and the Lord Jesus Christ
1Tim 1:2 Grace, mercy, and peace *from God* our Father and Jesus Christ our Lord
2Tim 1:2 Grace, mercy, and peace *from God* the Father and Christ Jesus our Lord
Tit 1:4 Grace, mercy, and peace *from God* the Father and the Lord Jesus Christ our Savior
Phm 3 Grace to you and peace *from God* our Father and the Lord Jesus Christ
Heb 6:7 For the earth which drinks in the rain that often comes upon it, and bears herbs useful for those by whom it is cultivated, receives blessing *from God*
2Pet 1:17 For He received *from God* the Father honor and glory when such a voice came to Him from the Excellent Glory
2Jn 3 Grace, mercy, and peace will be with you *from God* the Father and from the Lord Jesus Christ, the Son of the Father, in truth and love
Rev 11:11 Now after the three and a half days the breath of life *from God* entered them, and they stood on their feet, and great fear fell on those who saw them
Rev 20:9 And fire came down *from God* out of heaven and devoured them
Rev 21:2 Then I, John, saw the holy city, New Jerusalem, coming down out of heaven *from God*, prepared as a bride adorned for her husband
Rev 21:10 And he carried me away in the Spirit to a great and high mountain, and showed me the great city, the holy Jerusalem, descending out of heaven *from God*

FROM HEAVEN THE LORD LOOKS DOWN
(NIV)
(See *LORD LOOKS FROM HEAVEN*)

FROM HOUSE TO HOUSE
Luke 10:7 And remain in the same house, eating and drinking such things as they give, for the laborer is worthy of his wages. Do not go *from house to house*
Acts 2:46 So continuing daily with one accord in the temple, and breaking bread *from house to house*, they ate their food with gladness and simplicity of heart
Acts 20:20 and how I kept back nothing that was helpful, but proclaimed it to you, and taught you publicly and *from house to house*
1Tim 5:13 And besides they learn to be idle, wan-

dering about *from house to house*, and not only idle but also gossips and busybodies, saying things which they ought not

FROM MIGDOL TO SYENE

Ezek 29:10 Indeed, therefore, I am against you and against your rivers, and I will make the land of Egypt utterly waste and desolate, *from Migdol to Syene*, as far as the border of Ethiopia

Ezek 30:6 *From Migdol to Syene* those within her shall fall by the sword

FROM ONE MAN

Heb 11:12 Therefore *from one man*, and him as good as dead, were born as many as the stars of the sky in multitude innumerable as the sand which is by the seashore

FROM STRENGTH TO STRENGTH

Ps 84:7 They go *from strength to strength;* every one of them appears before God in Zion

FROM THE BEGINNING

Deut 11:12 the eyes of the Lord your God are always on it, *from the beginning* of the year to the very end of the year

2Sam 21:10 Now Rizpah the daughter of Aiah took sackcloth and spread it for herself on the rock, *from the beginning* of harvest until the late rains poured on them from heaven

Prov 8:23 I have been established from everlasting, *from the beginning*, before there was ever an earth

Is 40:21 Has it not been told you *from the beginning*? Have you not understood from the foundations of the earth

Is 41:4 Who has performed and done it, calling the generations *from the beginning*

Is 41:26 Who has declared *from the beginning*, that we may know

Is 46:10 Declaring the end *from the beginning*, and from ancient times things that are not yet done, saying

Is 48:3 I have declared the former things *from the beginning;* they went forth from My mouth, and I caused them to hear it

Is 48:5 even *from the beginning* I have declared it to you

Is 48:7 They are created now and not *from the beginning;* and before this day you have not heard them, lest you should say

Is 48:16 I have not spoken in secret *from the beginning;* from the time that it was, I was there

Jer 17:12 A glorious high throne *from the beginning* is the place of our sanctuary

Matt 19:8 He said to them, "Moses, because of the hardness of your hearts, permitted you to divorce your wives, but *from the beginning* it was not so

Mark 10:6 But *from the beginning* of the creation, God 'made them male and female

Mark 13:19 For in those days there will be tribulation, such as has not been *from the beginning* of creation which God created until this time, nor ever shall be

Luke 1:2 just as those who *from the beginning* were eyewitnesses and ministers of the word delivered them to us

John 6:64 For Jesus knew *from the beginning* who they were who did not believe, and who would betray Him

John 8:25 And Jesus said to them, "Just what I have been saying to you *from the beginning*

John 8:44 He was a murderer *from the beginning*, and does not stand in the truth, because there is no truth in him

John 15:27 And you also will bear witness, because you have been with Me *from the beginning*

Acts 11:4 But Peter explained it to them in order *from the beginning*, saying

Acts 26:4 My manner of life from my youth, which was spent *from the beginning* among my own nation at Jerusalem, all the Jews know

Eph 3:9 and to make all people see what is the fellowship of the mystery, which *from the beginning* of the ages has been hidden in God who created all things through Jesus Christ

2Th 2:13 But we are bound to give thanks to God always for you, brethren beloved by the Lord, because God *from the beginning* chose you for salvation through sanctification by the Spirit and belief in the truth

2Pet 3:4 For since the fathers fell asleep, all things continue as they were *from the beginning* of creation

1Jn 1:1 That which was *from the beginning*, which we have heard, which we have seen with our eyes, which we have looked upon, and our hands have handled, concerning the Word of life

1Jn 2:7 Brethren, I write no new commandment to you, but an old commandment which you have had *from the beginning*. The old commandment is the word which you heard *from the beginning*

1Jn 2:13 I write to you, fathers, because you have known Him who is *from the beginning*

1Jn 2:14 I have written to you, fathers, because you have known Him who is *from the beginning*

1Jn 2:24 Therefore let that abide in you which you heard *from the beginning*. If what you heard *from the beginning* abides in you, you also will abide in the Son and in the Father

1Jn 3:8 He who sins is of the devil, for the devil has sinned *from the beginning*

1Jn 3:11 For this is the message that you heard *from the beginning*, that we should love one another

2Jn 5 And now I plead with you, lady, not as though I wrote a new commandment to you, but that which we have had *from the beginning*

2Jn 6 This is the commandment, that as you have heard *from the beginning*, you should walk in it

FROM THE BROOK OF EGYPT

2Kin 24:7 And the king of Egypt did not come out of his land anymore, for the king of Babylon had taken all that belonged to the king of Egypt *from the Brook of Egypt* to the River Euphrates

FROM THE FATHER

John 6:45 Therefore everyone who has heard and learned *from the Father* comes to Me

John 15:26 But when the Helper comes, whom I shall send to you *from the Father*, the Spirit of truth who proceeds *from the Father*, He will testify of Me

John 16:28 I came forth *from the Father* and have come into the world

Acts 2:33 Therefore being exalted to the right hand of God, and having received *from the Father* the promise of the Holy Spirit, He poured out this which you now see and hear

Jas 1:17 Every good gift and every perfect gift is from above, and comes down *from the Father* of lights, with whom there is no variation or shadow of turning

2Jn 4 I rejoiced greatly that I have found some of your children walking in truth, as we received commandment *from the Father*

FROM THE FORTRESS TO THE RIVER

Mic 7:12 In that day they shall come to you from Assyria and the fortified cities, *from the fortress to the River*, from sea to sea, and mountain to mountain

FROM THE GRAVE (NIV)
(See *POWER OF THE GRAVE*)

FROM THE LEAST TO THE GREATEST
Jer 42:1 Then all the captains of the forces, Johanan the son of Kareah, Jezaniah the son of Hoshaiah, and all the people, *from the least to the greatest*, came near
Jer 44:12 They shall die, *from the least to the greatest*, by the sword and by famine
Acts 8:10 to whom they all gave heed, *from the least to the greatest*, saying

FROM THE LIPS OF CHILDREN (NIV)
(See *OUT OF THE MOUTH OF BABES*)

FROM THE LORD
Gen 4:1 Now Adam knew Eve his wife, and she conceived and bore Cain, and said, "I have gotten a man *from the Lord*
Gen 19:24 Then the Lord rained brimstone and fire on Sodom and Gomorrah, *from the Lord* out of the heavens
Gen 24:50 Then Laban and Bethuel answered and said, "The thing comes *from the Lord*
Lev 10:2 So fire went out *from the Lord* and devoured them, and they died before the Lord
Num 11:31 Now a wind went out *from the Lord*, and it brought quail from the sea and left them fluttering near the camp, about a day's journey on this side and about a day's journey on the other side, all around the camp, and about two cubits above the surface of the ground
Num 14:43 because you have turned away *from the Lord*, the Lord will not be with you
Num 16:35 And a fire came out *from the Lord* and consumed the two hundred and fifty men who were offering incense
Num 16:46 for wrath has gone out *from the Lord*. The plague has begun
Deut 13:5 But that prophet or that dreamer of dreams shall be put to death, because he has spoken in order to turn you away *from the Lord* your God, who brought you out of the land of Egypt and redeemed you from the house of bondage, to entice you from the way in which the Lord your God commanded you to walk
Deut 13:10 And you shall stone him with stones until he dies, because he sought to entice you away *from the Lord* your God, who brought you out of the land of Egypt, from the house of bondage
Deut 29:18 so that there may not be among you man or woman or family or tribe, whose heart turns away today *from the Lord* our God, to go and serve the gods of these nations, and that there may not be among you a root bearing bitterness or wormwood
1Sam 1:20 So it came to pass in the process of time that Hannah conceived and bore a son, and called his name Samuel, saying, "Because I have asked for him *from the Lord*
1Sam 16:14 But the Spirit of the Lord departed from Saul, and a distressing spirit *from the Lord* troubled him
1Sam 19:9 Now the distressing spirit *from the Lord* came upon Saul as he sat in his house with his spear in his hand
1Sam 26:12 For they were all asleep, because a deep sleep *from the Lord* had fallen on them
1Kin 2:15 However, the kingdom has been turned over, and has become my brother's; for it was his *from the Lord*
1Kin 2:33 But upon David and his descendants, upon his house and his throne, there shall be peace forever *from the Lord*
1Kin 11:9 So the Lord became angry with Solomon, because his heart had turned *from the Lord* God of Israel, who had appeared to him twice
1Kin 12:15 for the turn of affairs was *from the Lord*, that He might fulfill His word, which the Lord had spoken by Ahijah the Shilonite to Jeroboam the son of Nebat
1Kin 22:24 Then Zedekiah the son of Chenaanah went near and struck Micaiah on the cheek, and said, "Which way did the spirit *from the Lord* go from me to speak to you
2Kin 6:33 and then he said, "Surely this calamity is *from the Lord*
2Kin 20:9 Then Isaiah said, "This is the sign to you *from the Lord*, that the Lord will do the thing which He has spoken
2Chr 18:23 Then Zedekiah the son of Chenaanah went near and struck Micaiah on the cheek, and said, "Which way did the spirit *from the Lord* go from me to speak to you
2Chr 20:4 So Judah gathered together to ask help *from the Lord*
2Chr 26:18 Get out of the sanctuary, for you have trespassed! You shall have no honor *from the Lord* God
Ezra 9:8 And now for a little while grace has been shown *from the Lord* our God, to leave us a remnant to escape, and to give us a peg in His holy place, that our God may enlighten our eyes and give us a measure of revival in our bondage
Ps 24:5 He shall receive blessing *from the Lord*, and righteousness from the God of his salvation
Ps 37:39 But the salvation of the righteous is *from the Lord*
Ps 121:2 My help comes *from the Lord*, Who made heaven and earth
Ps 127:3 Behold, children are a heritage *from the Lord*, the fruit of the womb is His reward
Prov 8:35 For whoever finds me finds life, and obtains favor *from the Lord*
Prov 12:2 A good man obtains favor *from the Lord*, but a man of wicked devices He will condemn
Prov 16:1 The preparations of the heart belong to man, but the answer of the tongue is *from the Lord*
Prov 16:33 The lot is cast into the lap, but its every decision is *from the Lord*
Prov 18:22 He who finds a wife finds a good thing, and obtains favor *from the Lord*
Prov 19:14 Houses and riches are an inheritance from fathers, but a prudent wife is *from the Lord*
Prov 29:26 Many seek the ruler's favor, but justice for man comes *from the Lord*
Is 7:11 Ask a sign for yourself *from the Lord* your God
Is 8:18 We are for signs and wonders in Israel *from the Lord* of hosts, Who dwells in Mount Zion
Is 21:10 That which I have heard *from the Lord* of hosts, the God of Israel, I have declared to you
Is 28:22 for I have heard *from the Lord* God of hosts, a destruction determined even upon the whole earth
Is 28:29 This also comes *from the Lord* of hosts, Who is wonderful in counsel and excellent in guidance
Is 29:15 Woe to those who seek deep to hide their counsel far *from the Lord*, and their works are in the dark
Is 38:7 And this is the sign to you *from the Lord*, that the Lord will do this thing which He has spoken
Is 40:27 My way is hidden *from the Lord*, and my just claim is passed over by my God
Jer 7:1 The word that came to Jeremiah *from the Lord*, saying
Jer 11:1 The word that came to Jeremiah *from the Lord*, saying
Jer 17:5 Cursed is the man who trusts in man and

makes flesh his strength, whose heart departs *from the Lord*

Jer 18:1 The word which came to Jeremiah *from the Lord*, saying

Jer 21:1 The word which came to Jeremiah *from the Lord* when King Zedekiah sent to him Pashhur the son of Melchiah, and Zephaniah the son of Maaseiah, the priest, saying

Jer 26:1 In the beginning of the reign of Jehoiakim the son of Josiah, king of Judah, this word came *from the Lord*, saying

Jer 27:1 In the beginning of the reign of Jehoiakim the son of Josiah, king of Judah, this word came to Jeremiah *from the Lord*, saying

Jer 30:1 The word that came to Jeremiah *from the Lord*, saying

Jer 32:1 The word that came to Jeremiah *from the Lord* in the tenth year of Zedekiah king of Judah, which was the eighteenth year of Nebuchadnezzar

Jer 34:1 The word which came to Jeremiah *from the Lord*, when Nebuchadnezzar king of Babylon and all his army, all the kingdoms of the earth under his dominion, and all the people, fought against Jerusalem and all its cities, saying

Jer 34:8 This is the word that came to Jeremiah *from the Lord*, after King Zedekiah had made a covenant with all the people who were at Jerusalem to proclaim liberty to them

Jer 34:12 Therefore the word of the Lord came to Jeremiah *from the Lord*, saying

Jer 35:1 The word which came to Jeremiah *from the Lord* in the days of Jehoiakim the son of Josiah, king of Judah, saying

Jer 36:1 Now it came to pass in the fourth year of Jehoiakim the son of Josiah, king of Judah, that this word came to Jeremiah *from the Lord*, saying

Jer 37:17 The king asked him secretly in his house, and said, "Is there any word *from the Lord*

Jer 40:1 The word that came to Jeremiah *from the Lord* after Nebuzaradan the captain of the guard had let him go from Ramah, when he had taken him bound in chains among all who were carried away captive from Jerusalem and Judah, who were carried away captive to Babylon

Jer 49:14 I have heard a message *from the Lord*, and an ambassador has been sent to the nations

Lam 2:9 the Law is no more, and her prophets find no vision *from the Lord*

Lam 3:18 And I said, "My strength and my hope have perished *from the Lord*

Ezek 11:15 Son of man, your brethren, your relatives, your kinsmen, and all the house of Israel in its entirety, are those about whom the inhabitants of Jerusalem have said, 'Get far away *from the Lord*

Ezek 33:30 and they speak to one another, everyone saying to his brother, 'Please come and hear what the word is that comes *from the Lord*

Hos 1:2 Go, take yourself a wife of harlotry and children of harlotry, for the land has committed great harlotry by departing *from the Lord*

Obad 1 Thus says the Lord God concerning Edom (We have heard a report *from the Lord*, and a messenger has been sent among the nations, saying

Mic 1:12 For the inhabitant of Maroth pined for good, but disaster came down *from the Lord* to the gate of Jerusalem

Mic 5:7 Then the remnant of Jacob shall be in the midst of many peoples, like dew *from the Lord*, like showers on the grass, that tarry for no man nor wait for the sons of men

Zech 7:12 Yes, they made their hearts like flint, refusing to hear the law and the words which the Lord of hosts had sent by His Spirit through the former prophets. Thus great wrath came *from the Lord* of hosts

Zech 14:13 It shall come to pass in that day that a great panic *from the Lord* will be among them

Luke 1:45 Blessed is she who believed, for there will be a fulfillment of those things which were told her *from the Lord*

Acts 20:24 nor do I count my life dear to myself, so that I may finish my race with joy, and the ministry which I received *from the Lord* Jesus, to testify to the gospel of the grace of God

1Cor 7:25 I have no commandment *from the Lord;* yet I give judgment as one whom the Lord in His mercy has made trustworthy

1Cor 11:23 For I received *from the Lord* that which I also delivered to you

2Cor 5:6 Therefore we are always confident, knowing that while we are at home in the body we are absent *from the Lord*

Eph 6:8 knowing that whatever good anyone does, he will receive the same *from the Lord*, whether he is a slave or free

Col 3:24 knowing that *from the Lord* you will receive the reward of the inheritance

2Tim 1:18 The Lord grant to him that he may find mercy *from the Lord* in that Day and you know very well how many ways he ministered to me at Ephesus

Jas 1:7 For let not that man suppose that he will receive anything *from the Lord*

2Jn 3 Grace, mercy, and peace will be with you from God the Father and *from the Lord* Jesus Christ, the Son of the Father, in truth and love

FROM THE LORD COMES DELIVERANCE (NIV)
(See *SALVATION BELONGS TO THE LORD*)

FROM THE RISING OF THE SUN TO ITS SETTING

Is 45:6 That they may know *from the rising of the sun to its setting* that there is none besides Me

FROM THE RIVER OF EGYPT (KJV)
(See *FROM THE BROOK OF EGYPT*)

FROM THE RIVER, THE RIVER EUPHRATES

Deut 11:24 from the wilderness and Lebanon, *from the river, the River Euphrates*, even to the Western Sea, shall be your territory

FROM THE RIVER TO THE ENDS OF THE EARTH

Ps 72:8 He shall have dominion also from sea to sea, and *from the River to the ends of the earth*

Zech 9:10 His dominion shall be 'from sea to sea, and *from the River to the ends of the earth*

FROM THE SOLE OF YOUR FOOT

Deut 28:35 The Lord will strike you in the knees and on the legs with severe boils which cannot be healed, and *from the sole of your foot* to the top of your head

FROM THE WADI OF EGYPT (NIV)
(See *FROM THE BROOK OF EGYPT*)

FROM THEIR RIGHT (KJV)
(See *JUSTICE AT THE GATE*)

FRONTLETS BETWEEN YOUR EYES

Ex 13:16 It shall be as a sign on your hand and as *frontlets between your eyes*, for by strength of hand the Lord brought us out of Egypt

Deut 6:8 You shall bind them as a sign on your hand, and they shall be as *frontlets between your eyes*

Deut 11:18 Therefore you shall lay up these words of mine in your heart and in your soul, and bind them as a sign on your hand, and they shall be as *frontlets between your eyes*

FROWARD GENERATION (KJV)
(See *PERVERSE GENERATION*)

FRUIT ABOVE AND HIS ROOTS BENEATH
Amos 2:9 yet I destroyed his *fruit above and his roots beneath*

FRUIT IN KEEPING WITH REPENTANCE (NAS, NIV)
(See *FRUITS WORTHY OF REPENTANCE*)

FRUIT OF RIGHTEOUSNESS
Amos 6:12 Yet you have turned justice into gall, and the *fruit of righteousness* into wormwood
Heb 12:11 nevertheless, afterward it yields the peaceable *fruit of righteousness* to those who have been trained by it
Jas 3:18 Now the *fruit of righteousness* is sown in peace by those who make peace

FRUIT OF THE SPIRIT
Gal 5:22 But the *fruit of the Spirit* is love, joy, peace, longsuffering, kindness, goodness, faithfulness
Eph 5:9 (for the *fruit of the Spirit* is in all goodness, righteousness, and truth

FRUIT OF THE VINE
Matt 26:29 But I say to you, I will not drink of this *fruit of the vine* from now on until that day when I drink it new with you in My Father's kingdom
Mark 14:25 Assuredly, I say to you, I will no longer drink of the *fruit of the vine* until that day when I drink it new in the kingdom of God
Luke 22:18 for I say to you, I will not drink of the *fruit of the vine* until the kingdom of God comes

FRUIT OF THE WOMB
Gen 30:2 And Jacob's anger was aroused against Rachel, and he said, "Am I in the place of God, who has withheld from you the *fruit of the womb*
Ps 127:3 Behold, children are a heritage from the Lord, the *fruit of the womb* is His reward
Is 13:18 Also their bows will dash the young men to pieces, and they will have no pity on the *fruit of the womb*

FRUIT THAT BEFITS REPENTANCE (RSV)
(See *FRUITS WORTHY OF REPENTANCE*)

FRUITFUL VINEYARD (NIV)
(See *VINEYARD OF RED WINE*)

FRUITLESS DEEDS OF DARKNESS (NIV)
(See *UNFRUITFUL WORKS OF DARKNESS*)

FRUITS MEET FOR REPENTANCE (KJV)
(See *FRUITS WORTHY OF REPENTANCE*)

FRUITS OF YOUR RIGHTEOUSNESS
2Cor 9:10 Now may He who supplies seed to the sower, and bread for food, supply and multiply the seed you have sown and increase the *fruits of your righteousness*

FRUITS WORTHY OF REPENTANCE
Matt 3:8 Therefore bear *fruits worthy of repentance*
Luke 3:8 Therefore bear *fruits worthy of repentance,* and do not begin to say to yourselves

FUEL FOR THE FIRE
Is 9:19 Through the wrath of the Lord of hosts the land is burned up, and the people shall be as *fuel for the fire*
Ezek 21:32 You shall be *fuel for the fire;* your blood shall be in the midst of the land

FULFIL WHAT THE LORD HAD SPOKEN (RSV)
(See *THAT IT MIGHT BE FULFILLED*)

FULFILL HIS VOW
Lev 22:21 And whoever offers a sacrifice of peace offering to the Lord, to *fulfill his vow*, or a freewill offering from the cattle or the sheep, it must be perfect to be accepted

FULFILL MY VOWS (NIV)
(See *PAY MY VOWS*)

FULFILL THE WORD OF THE LORD
1Kin 2:27 So Solomon removed Abiathar from being priest to the Lord, that he might *fulfill the word of the Lord* which He spoke concerning the house of Eli at Shiloh
2Chr 36:21 to *fulfill the word of the Lord* by the mouth of Jeremiah, until the land had enjoyed her Sabbaths

FULFILL WHAT THE LORD HAD SAID (NIV)
(See *THAT IT MIGHT BE FULFILLED*)

FULL ARMOR OF GOD (NAS, NIV)
(See *WHOLE ARMOR OF GOD*)

FULL ASSURANCE
Col 2:2 that their hearts may be encouraged, being knit together in love, and attaining to all riches of the *full assurance* of understanding, to the knowledge of the mystery of God, both of the Father and of Christ
Heb 6:11 And we desire that each one of you show the same diligence to the *full assurance* of hope until the end
Heb 10:22 let us draw near with a true heart in *full assurance* of faith, having our hearts sprinkled from an evil conscience and our bodies washed with pure water

FULL OF EXTORTION (RSV)
(See *FULL OF GREED*)

FULL OF GRACE AND TRUTH
John 1:14 And the Word became flesh and dwelt among us, and we beheld His glory, the glory as of the only begotten of the Father, *full of grace and truth*

FULL OF GREED
Luke 11:39 But the Lord said to him, "Now you Pharisees make the outside of the cup and dish clean, but your inward part is *full of greed* and wickedness

FULL OF HIS GLORY
Is 6:3 Holy, holy, holy is the Lord of hosts; the whole earth is *full of His glory*

FULL OF INDIGNATION (KJV)
(See *FILLED WITH INDIGNATION*)

FULL OF JOY THROUGH THE HOLY SPIRIT (NIV)
(See *REJOICED IN THE SPIRIT*)

FULL OF RAVENING (KJV)
(See *FULL OF GREED*)

FULL OF THE HOLY SPIRIT
Acts 6:3 Therefore, brethren, seek out from among you seven men of good reputation, *full of the Holy Spirit* and wisdom, whom we may appoint over this business

Acts 7:55 But he, being *full of the Holy Spirit*, gazed into heaven and saw the glory of God, and Jesus standing at the right hand of God
Acts 11:24 For he was a good man, *full of the Holy Spirit* and of faith

FULL OF TROUBLE
Job 14:1 Man who is born of woman is of few days and *full of trouble*

FULL OF VIOLENCE (NIV)
(See *FILLED WITH VIOLENCE*)

FULL OF WISDOM (RSV)
(See *FILLED WITH WISDOM*)

FULL OF WRATH (KJV)
(See *FILLED WITH WRATH*)

FULL RIGHTS OF SONS (NIV)
(See *ADOPTION AS SONS*)

FULLNESS OF CHRIST
Eph 4:13 till we all come to the unity of the faith and the knowledge of the Son of God, to a perfect man, to the measure of the stature of the *fullness of Christ*

FULLNESS OF GOD
Eph 3:19 that you may be filled with all the *fullness of God*

FULLNESS OF JOY
Ps 16:11 In Your presence is *fullness of joy;* at Your right hand are pleasures forevermore

FULLNESS OF THE DEITY (NIV)
(See *FULLNESS OF THE GODHEAD*)

FULLNESS OF THE GODHEAD
Col 2:9 For in Him dwells all the *fullness of the Godhead* bodily

FULLNESS OF THE TIMES
Eph 1:10 that in the dispensation of the *fullness of the times* He might gather together in one all things in Christ, both which are in heaven and which are on earth in Him

FURNACE OF AFFLICTION
Is 48:10 Behold, I have refined you, but not as silver; I have tested you in the *furnace of affliction*

G

GAIN CHRIST
Phil 3:8 But indeed I also count all things loss for the excellence of the knowledge of Christ Jesus my Lord, for whom I have suffered the loss of all things, and count them as rubbish, that I may *gain Christ*

GAIN WITH INJUSTICE (NIV)
(See *REVENUES WITHOUT JUSTICE*)

GALILEE OF THE GENTILES
Is 9:1 Nevertheless the gloom will not be upon her who is distressed, as when at first He lightly esteemed the land of Zebulun and the land of Naphtali, and afterward more heavily oppressed her, by the way of the sea, beyond the Jordan, in *Galilee of the Gentiles*
Matt 4:15 The land of Zebulun and the land of Naphtali, the way of the sea, beyond the Jordan, *Galilee of the Gentiles*

GALILEE OF THE NATIONS (KJV, RSV)
(See *GALILEE OF THE GENTILES*)

GARDEN OF EDEN
Gen 2:15 Then the Lord God took the man and put him in the *garden of Eden* to tend and keep it
Gen 3:23 therefore the Lord God sent him out of the *garden of Eden* to till the ground from which he was taken
Gen 3:24 and He placed cherubim at the east of the *garden of Eden*, and a flaming sword which turned every way, to guard the way to the tree of life
Ezek 36:35 So they will say, 'This land that was desolate has become like the *garden of Eden*
Joel 2:3 the land is like the *Garden of Eden* before them, and behind them a desolate wilderness

GARDEN OF THE LORD
Gen 13:10 like the *garden of the Lord*, like the land of Egypt as you go toward Zoar
Is 51:3 He will make her wilderness like Eden, and her desert like the *garden of the Lord*

GARMENT AS A PLEDGE
Ex 22:26 If you ever take your neighbor's *garment as a pledge*, you shall return it to him before the sun goes down
Deut 24:17 You shall not pervert justice due the stranger or the fatherless, nor take a widow's *garment as a pledge*

GARMENT IN PLEDGE (NAS, RSV)
(See *GARMENT AS A PLEDGE*)

GARMENTS ARE MOTH-EATEN
Jas 5:2 Your riches are corrupted, and your *garments are moth-eaten*

GARNISHED THE HEAVENS (KJV)
(See *ADORNED THE HEAVENS*)

GATE IS NARROW (RSV)
(See *NARROW IS THE GATE*)

GATE IS WIDE (RSV)
(See *BROAD IS THE WAY*)

GATE OF THE CITY
Josh 8:29 And as soon as the sun was down, Joshua commanded that they should take his corpse down from the tree, cast it at the entrance of the *gate of the city*, and raise over it a great heap of stones that remains to this day
Josh 20:4 And when he flees to one of those cities, and stands at the entrance of the *gate of the city*, and declares his case in the hearing of the elders of that city, they shall take him into the city as one of them, and give him a place, that he may dwell among them
Judg 9:44 Then Abimelech and the company that was with him rushed forward and stood at the entrance of the *gate of the city*
Judg 16:2 they surrounded the place and lay in wait for him all night at the *gate of the city*
Judg 16:3 then he arose at midnight, took hold of the doors of the *gate of the city* and the two gateposts, pulled them up, bar and all, put them on his shoulders, and carried them to the top of the hill that faces Hebron
1Kin 17:10 And when he came to the *gate of the city*, indeed a widow was there gathering sticks
1Chr 19:9 Then the people of Ammon came out and put themselves in battle array before the *gate of the city*, and the kings who had come were by themselves in the field
Luke 7:12 And when He came near the *gate of the*

city, behold, a dead man was being carried out, the only son of his mother

GATES ARE DESOLATE
Lam 1:4 All her *gates are desolate;* her priests sigh, her virgins are afflicted, and she is in bitterness

GATES OF DEATH
Job 38:17 Have the *gates of death* been revealed to you? Or have you seen the doors of the shadow of death
Ps 9:13 Consider my trouble from those who hate me, You who lift me up from the *gates of death*
Ps 107:18 Their soul abhorred all manner of food, and they drew near to the *gates of death*

GATES OF HADES
Matt 16:18 And I also say to you that you are Peter, and on this rock I will build My church, and the *gates of Hades* shall not prevail against it

GATES OF SHEOL
Job 17:16 Will they go down to the *gates of Sheol?* Shall we have rest together in the dust
Is 38:10 I said, "In the prime of my life I shall go to the *gates of Sheol*

GATHER ALL THE NATIONS
Zech 14:2 For I will *gather all the nations* to battle against Jerusalem

GATHER HER THAT WAS DRIVEN OUT (RSV)
(See *GATHER THOSE WHO WERE DRIVEN OUT*)

GATHER INTO BARNS
Matt 6:26 Look at the birds of the air, for they neither sow nor reap nor *gather into barns*

GATHER THE OUTCAST (RSV)
(See *GATHER THOSE WHO WERE DRIVEN OUT*)

GATHER THEM FROM THE ENDS OF THE EARTH
Jer 31:8 Behold, I will bring them from the north country, and *gather them from the ends of the earth*, among them the blind and the lame, the woman with child and the one who labors with child, together

GATHER THOSE WHO WERE DRIVEN OUT
Zeph 3:19 I will save the lame, and *gather those who were driven out*

GATHER YOU FROM ALL THE NATIONS
Jer 29:14 I will *gather you from all the nations* and from all the places where I have driven you, says the Lord, and I will bring you to the place from which I cause you to be carried away captive

GATHER YOU FROM THE NATIONS (NIV)
(See *GATHER YOU FROM THE PEOPLES*)

GATHER YOU FROM THE PEOPLES
Ezek 11:17 I will *gather you from the peoples*, assemble you from the countries where you have been scattered, and I will give you the land of Israel

GATHER YOU OUT OF THE COUNTRIES
Ezek 20:34 I will bring you out from the peoples and *gather you out of the countries* where you are scattered, with a mighty hand, with an outstretched arm, and with fury poured out
Ezek 20:41 I will accept you as a sweet aroma when I bring you out from the peoples and *gather you out of the countries* where you have been scattered

GATHER YOU TO YOUR FATHERS
2Kin 22:20 Surely, therefore, I will *gather you to your fathers*, and you shall be gathered to your grave in peace
2Chr 34:28 Surely I will *gather you to your fathers*, and you shall be gathered to your grave in peace

GATHERED FROM THE NATIONS
Ezek 38:12 to take plunder and to take booty, to stretch out your hand against the waste places that are again inhabited, and against a people *gathered from the nations*, who have acquired livestock and goods, who dwell in the midst of the land

GATHERS HER BROOD
Luke 13:34 How often I wanted to gather your children together, as a hen *gathers her brood* under her wings, but you were not willing

GATHERS HER CHICKS
Matt 23:37 How often I wanted to gather your children together, as a hen *gathers her chicks* under her wings, but you were not willing

GATHERS THE EXILES (NIV)
(See *GATHERS THE OUTCASTS*)

GATHERS THE OUTCASTS
Is 56:8 The Lord God, who *gathers the outcasts* of Israel, says

GATHERS TOGETHER THE OUTCASTS
Ps 147:2 The Lord builds up Jerusalem; He *gathers together the outcasts* of Israel

GAVE BIRTH TO A SON (NAS, NIV)
(See *BORE A SON*)

GAVE HIMSELF
Gal 1:4 who *gave Himself* for our sins, that He might deliver us from this present evil age, according to the will of our God and Father
Gal 2:20 and the life which I now live in the flesh I live by faith in the Son of God, who loved me and *gave Himself* for me
Eph 5:25 Husbands, love your wives, just as Christ also loved the church and *gave Himself* for it
1Tim 2:6 who *gave Himself* a ransom for all, to be testified in due time
Tit 2:14 who *gave Himself* for us, that He might redeem us from every lawless deed and purify for Himself His own special people, zealous for good works

GAVE TESTIMONY (KJV)
(See *BEARING WITNESS*)

GAZING UP INTO HEAVEN
Acts 1:11 who also said, "Men of Galilee, why do you stand *gazing up into heaven*

GENEALOGY OF JESUS CHRIST
Matt 1:1 The book of the *genealogy of Jesus Christ*, the Son of David, the Son of Abraham

GENERATION OF JESUS CHRIST (KJV)
(See *GENEALOGY OF JESUS CHRIST*)

GENERATION TO GENERATION (NIV)
(See *ALL GENERATIONS*)

GENERATIONS TO COME (NIV)
(See *THROUGHOUT THEIR GENERATIONS*)

GENTLE AND LOWLY IN HEART
Matt 11:29 Take My yoke upon you and learn from Me, for I am *gentle and lowly in heart*, and you will find rest for your souls

GENTLE AND RIDING ON A DONKEY (NIV)
(See *LOWLY, AND SITTING ON A DONKEY*)

GENTLE ANSWER (NIV)
(See *SOFT ANSWER*)

GENTLE WHISPER (NIV)
(See *STILL SMALL VOICE*)

GENUINENESS OF YOUR FAITH
1Pet 1:7 that the *genuineness of your faith*, being much more precious than gold that perishes, though it is tested by fire, may be found to praise, honor, and glory at the revelation of Jesus Christ

GET BEHIND ME, SATAN
Matt 16:23 But He turned and said to Peter, "*Get behind Me, Satan*
Mark 8:33 But when He had turned around and looked at His disciples, He rebuked Peter, saying, "*Get behind Me, Satan*
Luke 4:8 And Jesus answered and said to him, "*Get behind Me, Satan*

GET GUIDANCE (NIV)
(See *WISE COUNSEL*)

GET HIM UP (NIV)
(See *RAISE HIM UP*)

GET INSIGHT (RSV)
(See *GET UNDERSTANDING*)

GET ME A DRINK (NIV)
(See *GIVE ME A DRINK*)

GET OUT OF YOUR COUNTRY
Gen 12:1 *Get out of your country*, from your family and from your father's house, to a land that I will show you
Acts 7:3 and said to him, '*Get out of your country* and from your relatives, and come to a land that I will show you

GET RID OF THE OLD YEAST (NIV)
(See *PURGE OUT THE OLD LEAVEN*)

GET UNDERSTANDING
Ps 119:104 Through Your precepts I *get understanding;* therefore I hate every false way
Prov 4:5 *Get understanding!* Do not forget, nor turn away from the words of my mouth
Prov 4:7 therefore get wisdom. And in all your getting, *get understanding*
Prov 16:16 And to *get understanding* is to be chosen rather than silver

GIFT FROM GOD
1Cor 7:7 But each one has his own *gift from God*, one in this manner and another in that

GIFT OF GOD
Eccl 3:13 and also that every man should eat and drink and enjoy the good of all his labor it is the *gift of God*
Eccl 5:19 As for every man to whom God has given riches and wealth, and given him power to eat of it, to receive his heritage and rejoice in his labor this is the *gift of God*
John 4:10 Jesus answered and said to her, "If you knew the *gift of God*, and who it is who says to you
Acts 8:20 But Peter said to him, "Your money perish with you, because you thought that the *gift of God* could be purchased with money
Rom 6:23 For the wages of sin is death, but the *gift of God* is eternal life in Christ Jesus our Lord
Eph 2:8 For by grace you have been saved through faith, and that not of yourselves; it is the *gift of God*
2Tim 1:6 Therefore I remind you to stir up the *gift of God* which is in you through the laying on of my hands

GIFT OF THE HOLY SPIRIT
Acts 2:38 and you shall receive the *gift of the Holy Spirit*
Acts 10:45 And those of the circumcision who believed were astonished, as many as came with Peter, because the *gift of the Holy Spirit* had been poured out on the Gentiles also

GIFTS AND SACRIFICES
Heb 5:1 For every priest taken from among men is appointed for men in things pertaining to God, that he may offer both *gifts and sacrifices* for sins
Heb 8:3 For every high priest is appointed to offer both *gifts and sacrifices*
Heb 9:9 It was symbolic for the present time in which both *gifts and sacrifices* are offered which cannot make him who performed the service perfect in regard to the conscience

GIFTS OF THE HOLY SPIRIT
Heb 2:4 God also bearing witness both with signs and wonders, with various miracles, and *gifts of the Holy Spirit*, according to His own will

GIFTS TO THE POOR (NIV)
(See *GIVEN TO THE POOR*)

GIRD UP THE LOINS
1Pet 1:13 Therefore *gird up the loins* of your mind, be sober, and rest your hope fully upon the grace that is to be brought to you at the revelation of Jesus Christ

GIRD UP YOUR MINDS (RSV)
(See *GIRD UP THE LOINS*)

GIRD YOURSELVES
2Sam 3:31 Then David said to Joab and to all the people who were with him, "Tear your clothes, *gird yourselves* with sackcloth, and mourn for Abner
Is 8:9 *Gird yourselves*, but be broken in pieces; *gird yourselves*, but be broken in pieces
Jer 49:3 Cry, you daughters of Rabbah, *gird yourselves* with sackcloth! Lament and run to and fro by the walls
Joel 1:13 *Gird yourselves* and lament, you priests; wail, you who minister before the altar

GIRDED YOUR WAIST WITH TRUTH
Eph 6:14 Stand therefore, having *girded your waist with truth*, having put on the breastplate of righteousness

GIVE ATTENTION TO YOUR SERVANT'S PRAYER (NIV)
(See *REGARD THE PRAYER*)

GIVE CAREFUL THOUGHT TO YOUR WAYS (NIV)
(See *CONSIDER YOUR WAYS*)

GIVE EAR
Ex 15:26 and said, "If you diligently heed the voice of the Lord your God and do what is right

in His sight, *give ear* to His commandments and keep all His statutes, I will put none of the diseases on you which I have brought on the Egyptians
Deut 1:45 Then you returned and wept before the Lord, but the Lord would not listen to your voice nor *give ear* to you
Deut 32:1 *Give ear*, O heavens, and I will speak; and hear, O earth, the words of my mouth
Judg 5:3 *Give ear*, O princes! I, even I, will sing to the Lord
Job 33:31 *Give ear*, Job, listen to me; hold your peace, and I will speak
Job 34:2 Hear my words, you wise men; *give ear* to me, you who have knowledge
Ps 5:1 *Give ear* to my words, O Lord, consider my meditation
Ps 17:1 *Give ear* to my prayer that is not from deceitful lips
Ps 39:12 Hear my prayer, O Lord, and *give ear* to my cry
Ps 49:1 Hear this, all you peoples; *give ear*, all you inhabitants of the world
Ps 54:2 Hear my prayer, O God; *give ear* to the words of my mouth
Ps 55:1 *Give ear* to my prayer, O God, and do not hide Yourself from my supplication
Ps 78:1 *Give ear*, O my people, to my law; incline your ears to the words of my mouth
Ps 80:1 *Give ear*, O Shepherd of Israel, You who lead Joseph like a flock
Ps 84:8 O Lord God of hosts, hear my prayer; *give ear*, O God of Jacob
Ps 86:6 *Give ear*, O Lord, to my prayer; and attend to the voice of my supplications
Ps 141:1 *Give ear* to my voice when I cry out to You
Ps 143:1 Hear my prayer, O Lord, *give ear* to my supplications
Is 1:2 Hear, O heavens, and *give ear*, O earth! For the Lord has spoken
Is 1:10 *give ear* to the law of our God, you people of Gomorrah
Is 8:9 *Give ear*, all you from far countries. Gird yourselves, but be broken in pieces
Is 28:23 *Give ear* and hear my voice, listen and hear my speech
Is 32:9 Rise up, you women who are at ease, hear my voice; you complacent daughters, *give ear* to my speech
Is 42:23 Who among you will *give ear* to this? Who will listen and hear for the time to come
Is 51:4 and *give ear* to Me, O My nation: For law will proceed from Me, and I will make My justice rest as a light of the peoples
Jer 13:15 Hear and *give ear:* Do not be proud for the Lord has spoken
Hos 5:1 *Give ear*, O house of the king! For yours is the judgment, because you have been a snare to Mizpah and a net spread on Tabor
Joel 1:2 Hear this, you elders, and *give ear*, all you inhabitants of the land

GIVE EAR TO ME
Job 34:2 Hear my words, you wise men; *give ear to me*, you who have knowledge
Is 51:4 and *give ear to Me*, O My nation: For law will proceed from Me, and I will make My justice rest as a light of the peoples

GIVE HEED (RSV)
(See *GIVE EAR*)

GIVE HELP BY THY RIGHT HAND (RSV)
(See *SAVE WITH YOUR RIGHT HAND*)

GIVE ME A DRINK
2Sam 23:15 And David said with longing, "Oh, that someone would *give me a drink* of the water from the well of Bethlehem, which is by the gate
1Chr 11:17 And David said with longing, "Oh, that someone would *give me a drink* of water from the well of Bethlehem, which is by the gate
John 4:7 A woman of Samaria came to draw water. Jesus said to her, "*Give Me a drink*
John 4:10 Jesus answered and said to her, "If you knew the gift of God, and who it is who says to you, '*Give Me a drink*

GIVE ME A SIGN (NIV)
(See *SHOW ME A SIGN*)

GIVE ME WATER TO DRINK (NAS, RSV)
(See *GIVE ME A DRINK*)

GIVE OVER (NIV)
(See *SET APART*)

GIVE THANKS
2Sam 22:50 Therefore I will *give thanks* to You, O Lord, among the Gentiles, and sing praises to Your name
1Chr 16:8 Oh, *give thanks* to the Lord! Call upon His name
1Chr 16:34 Oh, *give thanks* to the Lord, for He is good
1Chr 16:35 gather us together, and deliver us from the Gentiles, to *give thanks* to Your holy name, to triumph in Your praise
1Chr 16:41 and with them Heman and Jeduthun and the rest who were chosen, who were designated by name, to *give thanks* to the Lord, because His mercy endures forever
1Chr 25:3 Gedaliah, Zeri, Jeshaiah, Shimei, Hashabiah, and Mattithiah, six, under the direction of their father Jeduthun, who prophesied with a harp to *give thanks* and to praise the Lord
2Chr 31:2 And Hezekiah appointed the divisions of the priests and the Levites according to their divisions, each man according to his service, the priests and Levites for burnt offerings and peace offerings, to serve, to *give thanks*, and to praise in the gates of the camp of the Lord
Neh 12:24 And the heads of the Levites were Hashabiah, Sherebiah, and Jeshua the son of Kadmiel, with their brothers across from them, to praise and *give thanks*, group alternating with group, according to the command of David the man of God
Ps 18:49 Therefore I will *give thanks* to You, O Lord, among the Gentiles, and sing praises to Your name
Ps 30:4 Sing praise to the Lord, you saints of His, and *give thanks* at the remembrance of His holy name
Ps 30:12 O Lord my God, I will *give thanks* to You forever
Ps 75:1 We *give thanks* to You, O God, we *give thanks*
Ps 92:1 It is good to *give thanks* to the Lord, and to sing praises to Your name, O Most High
Ps 97:12 Rejoice in the Lord, you righteous, and *give thanks* at the remembrance of His holy name
Ps 105:1 Oh, *give thanks* to the Lord! Call upon His name
Ps 106:1 Oh, *give thanks* to the Lord, for He is good
Ps 106:47 Save us, O Lord our God, and gather us from among the Gentiles, to *give thanks* to Your holy name, and to triumph in Your praise
Ps 107:1 Oh, *give thanks* to the Lord, for He is good
Ps 107:8 Oh, that men would *give thanks* to the

Lord for His goodness, and for His wonderful works to the children of men
Ps 107:15 Oh, that men would *give thanks* to the Lord for His goodness, and for His wonderful works to the children of men
Ps 107:21 Oh, that men would *give thanks* to the Lord for His goodness, and for His wonderful works to the children of men
Ps 107:31 Oh, that men would *give thanks* to the Lord for His goodness, and for His wonderful works to the children of men
Ps 118:1 Oh, *give thanks* to the Lord, for He is good
Ps 118:29 Oh, *give thanks* to the Lord, for He is good
Ps 119:62 At midnight I will rise to *give thanks* to You, because of Your righteous judgments
Ps 122:4 Where the tribes go up, the tribes of the Lord, to the Testimony of Israel, to *give thanks* to the name of the Lord
Ps 136:1 Oh, *give thanks* to the Lord, for He is good
Ps 136:2 Oh, *give thanks* to the God of gods! For His mercy endures forever
Ps 136:3 Oh, *give thanks* to the Lord of lords! For His mercy endures forever
Ps 136:26 Oh, *give thanks* to the God of heaven! For His mercy endures forever
Ps 140:13 Surely the righteous shall *give thanks* to Your name; the upright shall dwell in Your presence
Rom 16:4 who risked their own necks for my life, to whom not only I *give thanks*, but also all the churches of the Gentiles
1Cor 10:30 But if I partake with thanks, why am I evil spoken of for the food over which I *give thanks*
1Cor 14:17 For you indeed *give thanks* well, but the other is not edified
Eph 1:16 do not cease to *give thanks* for you, making mention of you in my prayers
Col 1:3 We *give thanks* to the God and Father of our Lord Jesus Christ, praying always for you
1Th 1:2 We *give thanks* to God always for you all, making mention of you in our prayers
1Th 5:18 in everything *give thanks;* for this is the will of God in Christ Jesus for you
2Th 2:13 But we are bound to *give thanks* to God always for you, brethren beloved by the Lord, because God from the beginning chose you for salvation through sanctification by the Spirit and belief in the truth

GIVE THANKS TO THE LORD
1Chr 16:8 Oh, *give thanks to the Lord!* Call upon His name
1Chr 16:34 Oh, *give thanks to the Lord*, for He is good
1Chr 16:41 and with them Heman and Jeduthun and the rest who were chosen, who were designated by name, to *give thanks to the Lord*, because His mercy endures forever
Ps 92:1 It is good to *give thanks to the Lord*, and to sing praises to Your name, O Most High
Ps 105:1 Oh, *give thanks to the Lord!* Call upon His name
Ps 106:1 Oh, *give thanks to the Lord*, for He is good
Ps 107:1 Oh, *give thanks to the Lord*, for He is good
Ps 107:8 Oh, that men would *give thanks to the Lord* for His goodness, and for His wonderful works to the children of men
Ps 107:15 Oh, that men would *give thanks to the Lord* for His goodness, and for His wonderful works to the children of men
Ps 107:21 Oh, that men would *give thanks to the Lord* for His goodness, and for His wonderful works to the children of men
Ps 107:31 Oh, that men would *give thanks to the Lord* for His goodness, and for His wonderful works to the children of men
Ps 118:1 Oh, *give thanks to the Lord*, for He is good
Ps 118:29 Oh, *give thanks to the Lord*, for He is good
Ps 136:1 Oh, *give thanks to the Lord*, for He is good
Ps 136:3 Oh, *give thanks to the Lord* of lords! For His mercy endures forever

GIVE THE ANSWER (NIV)
(See *EXPLAIN THE RIDDLE*)

GIVE TO CAESAR (NIV)
(See *RENDER TO CAESAR*)

GIVE TO THE LORD
Lev 23:38 besides the Sabbaths of the Lord, besides your gifts, besides all your vows, and besides all your freewill offerings which you *give to the Lord*
Num 15:21 Of the first of your ground meal you shall *give to the Lord* a heave offering throughout your generations
1Chr 16:28 *Give to the Lord*, O kindreds of the peoples, *give to the Lord* glory and strength
1Chr 16:29 *Give to the Lord* the glory due His name; bring an offering, and come before Him
Ps 96:7 *Give to the Lord*, O kindreds of the peoples, *give to the Lord* glory and strength
Ps 96:8 *Give to the Lord* the glory due His name; bring an offering, and come into His courts

GIVE TO THE POOR (NIV)
(See *DISTRIBUTE TO THE POOR*)

GIVE TO THEM ACCORDING TO THEIR DEEDS
Ps 28:4 *Give to them according to their deeds*, and according to the wickedness of their endeavors

GIVE US THIS DAY
Matt 6:11 *Give us this day* our daily bread

GIVE VICTORY BY THY RIGHT HAND (RSV)
(See *SAVE WITH YOUR RIGHT HAND*)

GIVEN AS A GIFT FOR THE LORD (KJV)
(See *GIVEN BY THE LORD*)

GIVEN BY THE LORD
Num 18:6 they are a gift to you, *given by the Lord*, to do the work of the tabernacle of meeting

GIVEN IN MARRIAGE
Ps 78:63 The fire consumed their young men, and their maidens were not *given in marriage*
Matt 22:30 For in the resurrection they neither marry nor are *given in marriage*, but are like angels of God in heaven
Mark 12:25 For when they rise from the dead, they neither marry nor are *given in marriage*, but are like angels in heaven
Luke 17:27 They ate, they drank, they married wives, they were *given in marriage*, until the day that Noah entered the ark, and the flood came and destroyed them all
Luke 20:34 And Jesus answered and said to them, "The sons of this age marry and are *given in marriage*
Luke 20:35 But those who are counted worthy to attain that age, and the resurrection from the dead, neither marry nor are *given in marriage*

GIVEN TO HOSPITALITY
Rom 12:13 distributing to the needs of the saints, *given to hospitality*

GIVEN TO THE FIRE (RSV)
(See *THROWN INTO THE FIRE*)

GIVEN TO THE LORD (RSV)
(See *GIVEN BY THE LORD*)

GIVEN TO THE POOR
Ps 112:9 He has dispersed abroad, He has *given to the poor*
Matt 26:9 For this fragrant oil might have been sold for much and *given to the poor*
Mark 14:5 For it might have been sold for more than three hundred denarii and *given to the poor*
John 12:5 Why was this fragrant oil not sold for three hundred denarii and *given to the poor*
2Cor 9:9 He has dispersed abroad, He has *given to the poor*

GIVEN TO WINE
1Tim 3:3 not *given to wine*, not violent, not greedy for money, but gentle, not quarrelsome, not covetous
Tit 1:7 For a bishop must be blameless, as a steward of God, not self-willed, not quick-tempered, not *given to wine*, not violent, not greedy for money

GIVEN UNTO US THE EARNEST OF THE SPIRIT (KJV)
(See *SPIRIT AS A GUARANTEE*)

GIVEN US NEW BIRTH (NIV)
(See *BEGOTTEN US AGAIN*)

GIVEN YOU FROM ABOVE
John 19:11 Jesus answered, "You could have no power at all against Me unless it had been *given you from above*

GIVES GRACE TO THE HUMBLE
Prov 3:34 Surely He scorns the scornful, but *gives grace to the humble*
Jas 4:6 God resists the proud, but *gives grace to the humble*
1Pet 5:5 Yes, all of you be submissive to one another, and be clothed with humility, for "God resists the proud, but *gives grace to the humble*

GIVES LIFE TO THE DEAD
Rom 4:17 in the presence of Him whom he believed, even God, who *gives life to the dead* and calls those things which do not exist as though they did

GIVETH GRACE UNTO THE LOWLY (KJV)
(See *GIVES GRACE TO THE HUMBLE*)

GIVING OF THE LAW
Rom 9:4 who are Israelites, to whom pertain the adoption, the glory, the covenants, the *giving of the law*, the service of God, and the promises

GLAD TIDINGS OF GOOD THINGS
Is 52:7 How beautiful upon the mountains are the feet of him who brings good news, who proclaims peace, who brings *glad tidings of good things*, who proclaims salvation, who says to Zion
Rom 10:15 How beautiful are the feet of those who preach the gospel of peace, who bring *glad tidings of good things*

GLAD TIDINGS OF THE KINGDOM OF GOD
Luke 8:1 Now it came to pass, afterward, that He went through every city and village, preaching and bringing the *glad tidings of the kingdom of God*

GLEANING GRAPES
Is 17:6 Yet *gleaning grapes* will be left in it, like the shaking of an olive tree, two or three olives at the top of the uppermost bough, four or five in its most fruitful branches
Jer 49:9 If grape-gatherers came to you, would they not leave some *gleaning grapes*

GLEANING OF THE GRAPES
Judg 8:2 Is not the *gleaning of the grapes* of Ephraim better than the vintage of Abiezer

GLORIFIED GOD
Matt 9:8 Now when the multitudes saw it, they marveled and *glorified God* who had given such power to men
Mark 2:12 And immediately he arose, took up the bed, and went out in the presence of them all, so that all were amazed and *glorified God*, saying
Luke 5:26 And they were all amazed, and they *glorified God* and were filled with fear, saying
Luke 7:16 Then fear came upon all, and they *glorified God*, saying
Luke 13:13 And He laid His hands on her, and immediately she was made straight, and *glorified God*
Luke 17:15 Now one of them, when he saw that he was healed, returned, and with a loud voice *glorified God*
Luke 23:47 Now when the centurion saw what had happened, he *glorified God*, saying
Acts 4:21 So when they had further threatened them, they let them go, finding no way of punishing them, because of the people, since they all *glorified God* for what had been done
Acts 11:18 and they *glorified God*, saying, "Then God has also granted to the Gentiles repentance to life
Gal 1:24 And they *glorified God* in me

GLORIFY GOD
John 21:19 This He spoke, signifying by what death he would *glorify God*
Rom 15:9 and that the Gentiles might *glorify God* for His mercy, as it is written
1Cor 6:20 therefore *glorify God* in your body and in your spirit, which are God's
2Cor 9:13 while, through the proof of this ministry, they *glorify God* for the obedience of your confession to the gospel of Christ, and for your liberal sharing with them and all men
1Pet 2:12 having your conduct honorable among the Gentiles, that when they speak against you as evildoers, they may, by your good works which they observe, *glorify God* in the day of visitation
1Pet 4:16 Yet if anyone suffers as a Christian, let him not be ashamed, but let him *glorify God* in this matter

GLORIFY THE LORD (NIV)
(See *MAGNIFY THE LORD*)

GLORIFY YOUR NAME
Ps 86:9 All nations whom You have made shall come and worship before You, O Lord, and shall *glorify Your name*
Ps 86:12 I will praise You, O Lord my God, with all my heart, and I will *glorify Your name* forevermore
John 12:28 Father, *glorify Your name*." Then a voice came from heaven, saying
Rev 15:4 Who shall not fear You, O Lord, and *glorify Your name*

GLORIFYING AND PRAISING GOD
Luke 2:20 Then the shepherds returned, *glorifying and praising God* for all the things that they had heard and seen, as it was told them

GLORIFYING GOD
Luke 5:25 Immediately he rose up before them, took up what he had been lying on, and departed to his own house, *glorifying God*
Luke 18:43 And immediately he received his sight, and followed Him, *glorifying God*

GLORIOUS DEEDS OF THE LORD (RSV)
(See *PRAISES OF THE LORD*)

GLORIOUS LAND
Dan 8:9 And out of one of them came a little horn which grew exceedingly great toward the south, toward the east, and toward the *Glorious Land*
Dan 11:16 He shall stand in the *Glorious Land* with destruction in his power
Dan 11:41 He shall also enter the *Glorious Land*, and many countries shall be overthrown

GLORIOUS RICHES (NIV)
(See *RICHES IN GLORY*)

GLORIOUS THINGS
Ps 87:3 *Glorious things* are spoken of you, O city of God
Luke 13:17 and all the multitude rejoiced for all the *glorious things* that were done by Him

GLORY AND HONOR
Ps 8:5 For You have made him a little lower than the angels, and You have crowned him with *glory and honor*
Dan 5:18 O king, the Most High God gave Nebuchadnezzar your father a kingdom and majesty, *glory and honor*
Heb 2:7 You crowned him with *glory and honor*, and set him over the works of Your hands
Heb 2:9 But we see Jesus, who was made a little lower than the angels, for the suffering of death crowned with *glory and honor*, that He, by the grace of God, might taste death for everyone
Rev 4:9 Whenever the living creatures give *glory and honor* and thanks to Him who sits on the throne, who lives forever and ever
Rev 4:11 You are worthy, O Lord, to receive *glory and honor* and power
Rev 19:1 Salvation and *glory and honor* and power to the Lord our God
Rev 21:24 And the nations of those who are saved shall walk in its light, and the kings of the earth bring their *glory and honor* into it

GLORY HAS DEPARTED
1Sam 4:21 Then she named the child Ichabod, saying, "The *glory has departed* from Israel
1Sam 4:22 And she said, "The *glory has departed* from Israel, for the ark of God has been captured
Hos 10:5 For its people mourn for it, and its priests shriek for it because its *glory has departed* from it

GLORY OF CHRIST
2Cor 4:4 whose minds the god of this age has blinded, who do not believe, lest the light of the gospel of the *glory of Christ*, who is the image of God, should shine on them
2Cor 8:23 Or if our brethren are inquired about, they are messengers of the churches, the *glory of Christ*

GLORY OF GOD
Ps 19:1 The heavens declare the *glory of God;* and the firmament shows His handiwork
Prov 25:2 It is the *glory of God* to conceal a matter, but the glory of kings is to search out a matter
John 11:4 When Jesus heard that, He said, "This sickness is not unto death, but for the *glory of God*, that the Son of God may be glorified through it
John 11:40 Jesus said to her, "Did I not say to you that if you would believe you would see the *glory of God*
Acts 7:55 But he, being full of the Holy Spirit, gazed into heaven and saw the *glory of God*, and Jesus standing at the right hand of God
Rom 3:23 for all have sinned and fall short of the *glory of God*
Rom 5:2 through whom also we have access by faith into this grace in which we stand, and rejoice in hope of the *glory of God*
Rom 15:7 Therefore receive one another, just as Christ also received us, to the *glory of God*
1Cor 10:31 Therefore, whether you eat or drink, or whatever you do, do all to the *glory of God*
1Cor 11:7 For a man indeed ought not to cover his head, since he is the image and *glory of God*
2Cor 1:20 For all the promises of God in Him are Yes, and in Him Amen, to the *glory of God* through us
2Cor 4:6 For it is the God who commanded light to shine out of darkness who has shone in our hearts to give the light of the knowledge of the *glory of God* in the face of Jesus Christ
2Cor 4:15 For all things are for your sakes, that grace, having spread through the many, may cause thanksgiving to abound to the *glory of God*
Phil 2:11 and that every tongue should confess that Jesus Christ is Lord, to the *glory of God* the Father
Rev 15:8 The temple was filled with smoke from the *glory of God* and from His power, and no one was able to enter the temple till the seven plagues of the seven angels were completed
Rev 21:11 having the *glory of God*. And her light was like a most precious stone, like a jasper stone, clear as crystal
Rev 21:23 And the city had no need of the sun or of the moon to shine in it, for the *glory of God* illuminated it, and the Lamb is its light

GLORY OF HIS MAJESTY
Is 2:10 Enter into the rock, and hide in the dust, from the terror of the Lord and the *glory of His majesty*
Is 2:19 They shall go into the holes of the rocks, and into the caves of the earth, from the terror of the Lord and the *glory of His majesty*, when He arises to shake the earth mightily
Is 2:21 to go into the clefts of the rocks, and into the crags of the rugged rocks, from the terror of the Lord and the *glory of His majesty*, when He arises to shake the earth mightily

GLORY OF HIS NAME (NAS, NIV, RSV)
(See *HONOR OF HIS NAME*)

GLORY OF KINGDOMS
Is 13:19 And Babylon, the *glory of kingdoms*, the beauty of the Chaldeans' pride, will be as when God overthrew Sodom and Gomorrah

GLORY OF THE IMMORTAL (NIV, RSV)
(See *GLORY OF THE INCORRUPTIBLE*)

GLORY OF THE INCORRUPTIBLE
Rom 1:23 and changed the *glory of the incorruptible* God into an image made like corruptible man and birds and four-footed beasts and creeping things

GLORY OF THE LORD
Ex 16:7 And in the morning you shall see the *glory of the Lord*
Ex 16:10 Now it came to pass, as Aaron spoke to the whole congregation of the children of Israel, that they looked toward the wilderness, and behold, the *glory of the Lord* appeared in the cloud
Ex 24:16 Now the *glory of the Lord* rested on Mount Sinai, and the cloud covered it six days
Ex 24:17 The sight of the *glory of the Lord* was like a consuming fire on the top of the mountain in the eyes of the children of Israel
Ex 40:34 Then the cloud covered the tabernacle of meeting, and the *glory of the Lord* filled the tabernacle
Ex 40:35 And Moses was not able to enter the tabernacle of meeting, because the cloud rested above it, and the *glory of the Lord* filled the tabernacle
Lev 9:6 Then Moses said, "This is the thing which the Lord commanded you to do, and the *glory of the Lord* will appear to you
Lev 9:23 Then the *glory of the Lord* appeared to all the people
Num 14:10 Now the *glory of the Lord* appeared in the tabernacle of meeting before all the children of Israel
Num 14:21 but truly, as I live, all the earth shall be filled with the *glory of the Lord*
Num 16:19 Then the *glory of the Lord* appeared to all the congregation
Num 16:42 and suddenly the cloud covered it, and the *glory of the Lord* appeared
Num 20:6 So Moses and Aaron went from the presence of the assembly to the door of the tabernacle of meeting, and they fell on their faces. And the *glory of the Lord* appeared to them
1Kin 8:11 for the *glory of the Lord* filled the house of the Lord
2Chr 5:14 for the *glory of the Lord* filled the house of God
2Chr 7:1 Now when Solomon had finished praying, fire came down from heaven and consumed the burnt offering and the sacrifices; and the *glory of the Lord* filled the temple
2Chr 7:2 And the priests could not enter the house of the Lord, because the *glory of the Lord* had filled the Lord's house
2Chr 7:3 When all the children of Israel saw how the fire came down, and the *glory of the Lord* on the temple, they bowed their faces to the ground on the pavement, and worshiped and praised the Lord, saying
Ps 104:31 May the *glory of the Lord* endure forever; may the Lord rejoice in His works
Ps 138:5 Yes, they shall sing of the ways of the Lord, for great is the *glory of the Lord*
Is 35:2 They shall see the *glory of the Lord*, the excellency of our God
Is 40:5 the *glory of the Lord* shall be revealed, and all flesh shall see it together
Is 58:8 the *glory of the Lord* shall be your rear guard
Is 60:1 and the *glory of the Lord* is risen upon you
Ezek 1:28 This was the appearance of the likeness of the *glory of the Lord*
Ezek 3:12 Blessed is the *glory of the Lord* from His place
Ezek 3:23 So I arose and went out into the plain, and behold, the *glory of the Lord* stood there, like the glory which I saw by the River Chebar
Ezek 10:4 Then the *glory of the Lord* went up from the cherub, and paused over the threshold of the temple
Ezek 10:18 Then the *glory of the Lord* departed from the threshold of the temple and stood over the cherubim
Ezek 11:23 And the *glory of the Lord* went up from the midst of the city and stood on the mountain, which is on the east side of the city
Ezek 43:4 And the *glory of the Lord* came into the temple by way of the gate which faces toward the east
Ezek 43:5 and behold, the *glory of the Lord* filled the temple
Ezek 44:4 so I looked, and behold, the *glory of the Lord* filled the house of the Lord
Hab 2:14 For the earth will be filled with the knowledge of the *glory of the Lord*, as the waters cover the sea
Luke 2:9 And behold, an angel of the Lord stood before them, and the *glory of the Lord* shone around them, and they were greatly afraid
2Cor 3:18 But we all, with unveiled face, beholding as in a mirror the *glory of the Lord*, are being transformed into the same image from glory to glory, just as by the Spirit of the Lord
2Cor 8:19 and not only that, but who was also chosen by the churches to travel with us with this gift, which is administered by us to the *glory of the Lord* Himself and to show your ready mind

GLORY OF THE UNCORRUPTIBLE (KJV)
(See *GLORY OF THE INCORRUPTIBLE*)

GLORY OF YOUR NAME
Ps 79:9 Help us, O God of our salvation, for the *glory of Your name*

GLORY THAT WILL BE REVEALED IN US (NIV)
(See *GLORY WHICH SHALL BE REVEALED IN US*)

GLORY TO GOD
Luke 2:14 *Glory to God* in the highest, and on earth peace, good will toward men
Luke 17:18 Were there not any found who returned to give *glory to God* except this foreigner
Acts 12:23 Then immediately an angel of the Lord struck him, because he did not give *glory to God*
Rom 4:20 He did not waver at the promise of God through unbelief, but was strengthened in faith, giving *glory to God*

GLORY TO YOUR NAME (NIV)
(See *GLORIFY YOUR NAME*)

GLORY WHICH SHALL BE REVEALED IN US
Rom 8:18 For I consider that the sufferings of this present time are not worthy to be compared with the *glory which shall be revealed in us*

GLUTTON AND A DRUNKARD (NIV, RSV)
(See *GLUTTON AND A WINEBIBBER*)

GLUTTON AND A WINEBIBBER
Luke 7:34 The Son of Man has come eating and drinking, and you say, 'Look, a *glutton and a winebibber*, a friend of tax collectors and sinners

GNASHING OF TEETH
Matt 8:12 But the sons of the kingdom will be cast out into outer darkness. There will be weeping and *gnashing of teeth*
Matt 13:42 and will cast them into the furnace of fire. There will be wailing and *gnashing of teeth*
Matt 13:50 and cast them into the furnace of fire. There will be wailing and *gnashing of teeth*
Matt 22:13 Then the king said to the servants, 'Bind him hand and foot, take him away, and cast him into outer darkness; there will be weeping and *gnashing of teeth*
Matt 24:51 and will cut him in two and appoint him his portion with the hypocrites. There shall be weeping and *gnashing of teeth*

Matt 25:30 And cast the unprofitable servant into the outer darkness. There will be weeping and *gnashing of teeth*
Luke 13:28 There will be weeping and *gnashing of teeth*, when you see Abraham and Isaac and Jacob and all the prophets in the kingdom of God, and yourselves thrust out

GO A-WHORING (KJV)
(See *PLAY THE HARLOT*)

GO AND SIN NO MORE
John 8:11 And Jesus said to her, "Neither do I condemn you; *go and sin no more*

GO ASTRAY AFTER FALSE GODS (RSV)
(See *TURN ASIDE TO LIES*)

GO ASTRAY IN THEIR HEARTS
Ps 95:10 For forty years I was grieved with that generation, and said, 'It is a people who *go astray in their hearts*, and they do not know My ways

GO DOWN TO SHEOL (RSV)
(See *GO DOWN TO THE GRAVE*)

GO DOWN TO THE GRAVE
1Kin 2:6 Therefore do according to your wisdom, and do not let his gray hair *go down to the grave* in peace
Job 21:13 They spend their days in wealth, and in a moment *go down to the grave*

GO DOWN TO THE PIT
Ps 28:1 Do not be silent to me, lest, if You are silent to me, I become like those who *go down to the pit*
Ps 30:3 You have kept me alive, that I should not *go down to the pit*
Ps 30:9 What profit is there in my blood, when I *go down to the pit*
Ps 88:4 I am counted with those who *go down to the pit*
Prov 1:12 let us swallow them alive like Sheol, and whole, like those who *go down to the Pit*
Is 38:18 those who *go down to the pit* cannot hope for Your truth
Ezek 26:20 then I will bring you down with those who descend into the Pit, to the people of old, and I will make you dwell in the lowest part of the earth, in places desolate from antiquity, with those who *go down to the Pit*, so that you may never be inhabited
Ezek 31:14 For they have all been delivered to death, to the depths of the earth, among the children of men who *go down to the Pit*
Ezek 32:18 Son of man, wail over the multitude of Egypt, and cast them down to the depths of the earth, her and the daughters of the famous nations, with those who *go down to the Pit*
Ezek 32:24 now they bear their shame with those who *go down to the Pit*
Ezek 32:25 though their terror was caused in the land of the living, yet they bear their shame with those who *go down to the Pit*
Ezek 32:29 they shall lie with the uncircumcised, and with those who *go down to the Pit*
Ezek 32:30 they lie uncircumcised with those slain by the sword, and bear their shame with those who *go down to the Pit*

GO FROM YOUR COUNTRY (RSV)
(See *GET OUT OF YOUR COUNTRY*)

GO IN PEACE
Ex 4:18 So Moses went and returned to Jethro his father-in-law, and said to him, "Please let me go and return to my brethren who are in Egypt, and see whether they are still alive." And Jethro said to Moses, "*Go in peace*
Judg 18:6 And the priest said to them, "*Go in peace*. May the presence of the Lord be with you on your way
1Sam 1:17 Then Eli answered and said, "*Go in peace*, and the God of Israel grant your petition which you have asked of Him
1Sam 20:42 Then Jonathan said to David, "*Go in peace*, since we have both sworn in the name of the Lord, saying
1Sam 29:7 Therefore return now, and *go in peace*, that you may not displease the lords of the Philistines
2Sam 15:9 And the king said to him, "*Go in peace*." So he arose and went to Hebron
2Kin 5:19 Then he said to him, "*Go in peace*." So he departed from him a short distance
Mark 5:34 And He said to her, "Daughter, your faith has made you well. *Go in peace*, and be healed of your affliction
Luke 7:50 Then He said to the woman, "Your faith has saved you. *Go in peace*
Luke 8:48 And He said to her, "Daughter, be of good cheer; your faith has made you well. *Go in peace*
Acts 16:36 So the keeper of the prison reported these words to Paul, saying, "The magistrates have sent to let you go. Now therefore depart, and *go in peace*

GO INTO CAPTIVITY
Deut 28:41 You shall beget sons and daughters, but they shall not be yours; for they shall *go into captivity*
Jer 20:6 And you, Pashhur, and all who dwell in your house, shall *go into captivity*
Jer 22:22 The wind shall eat up all your rulers, and your lovers shall *go into captivity*
Jer 30:16 and all your adversaries, every one of them, shall *go into captivity*
Jer 46:19 O you daughter dwelling in Egypt, prepare yourself to *go into captivity*
Jer 49:3 for Milcham shall *go into captivity* with his priests and his princes together
Ezek 12:3 Therefore, son of man, prepare your belongings for captivity, and *go into captivity* by day in their sight
Ezek 12:4 and at evening you shall go in their sight, like those who *go into captivity*
Ezek 30:17 The young men of Aven and Pi Beseth shall fall by the sword, and these cities shall *go into captivity*
Ezek 30:18 as for her, a cloud shall cover her, and her daughters shall *go into captivity*
Amos 1:15 Their king shall *go into captivity*, he and his princes together
Amos 5:5 for Gilgal shall surely *go into captivity*, and Bethel shall come to nothing
Amos 9:4 Though they *go into captivity* before their enemies, from there I will command the sword, and it shall slay them
Zech 14:2 Half of the city shall *go into captivity*, but the remnant of the people shall not be cut off from the city
Rev 13:10 He who leads into captivity shall *go into captivity;* he who kills with the sword must be killed with the sword

GO INTO EXILE (NAS, NIV, RSV)
(See *GONE INTO CAPTIVITY*)

GO LIMPING WITH TWO DIFFERENT OPINIONS (RSV)
(See *FALTER BETWEEN TWO OPINIONS*)

GO OVER (NIV)
(See *TURN ASIDE*)

GO, PROPHESY
Amos 7:15 Then the Lord took me as I followed the flock, and the Lord said to me, '*Go, prophesy* to My people Israel

GO THE WAY OF ALL THE EARTH
1Kin 2:2 I *go the way of all the earth;* be strong, therefore, and prove yourself a man

GO TO MY FATHER
Luke 15:18 I will arise and *go to my father*, and will say to him
John 14:12 and greater works than these he will do, because I *go to My Father*
John 16:10 of righteousness, because I *go to My Father* and you see Me no more

GO TO THE ANT
Prov 6:6 *Go to the ant*, you sluggard! Consider her ways and be wise

GO TO THE FATHER
John 16:16 and again a little while, and you will see Me, because I *go to the Father*
John 16:17 and again a little while, and you will see Me'; and, 'because I *go to the Father*
John 16:28 Again, I leave the world and *go to the Father*

GO YOUR WAY
Gen 12:19 Now therefore, here is your wife; take her and *go your way*
Josh 2:16 Hide there three days, until the pursuers have returned. Afterward you may *go your way*
Judg 19:5 but the young woman's father said to his son-in-law, "Refresh your heart with a morsel of bread, and afterward *go your way*
Judg 19:9 Tomorrow *go your way* early, so that you may get home
Ruth 1:12 Turn back, my daughters, *go your way;* for I am too old to have a husband
1Sam 20:22 But if I say thus to the young man, 'Look, the arrows are beyond you' *go your way*, for the Lord has sent you away
Neh 8:10 Then he said to them, "*Go your way*, eat the fat, drink the sweet, and send portions to those for whom nothing is prepared
Dan 12:9 And he said, "*Go your way*, Daniel, for the words are closed up and sealed till the time of the end
Dan 12:13 But you, *go your way* till the end; for you shall rest, and will arise to your inheritance at the end of the days
Matt 5:24 leave your gift there before the altar, and *go your way*
Matt 8:4 but *go your way*, show yourself to the priest, and offer the gift that Moses commanded, as a testimony to them
Matt 8:13 Then Jesus said to the centurion, "*Go your way;* and as you have believed, so let it be done for you
Matt 20:14 Take what is yours and *go your way*. I wish to give to this last man the same as to you
Matt 27:65 *go your way*, make it as secure as you know how
Mark 1:44 but *go your way*, show yourself to the priest, and offer for your cleansing those things which Moses commanded, as a testimony to them
Mark 2:11 I say to you, arise, take up your bed, and *go your way* to your house
Mark 7:29 Then He said to her, "For this saying *go your way*
Mark 10:21 *Go your way*, sell whatever you have and give to the poor, and you will have treasure in heaven
Mark 10:52 Then Jesus said to him, "*Go your way;* your faith has made you well
Luke 10:3 *Go your way;* behold, I send you out as lambs among wolves
Luke 17:19 And He said to him, "Arise, *go your way*. Your faith has made you well
John 4:50 Jesus said to him, "*Go your way;* your son lives

GOBLET OF MY WRATH (NIV)
(See *CUP OF MY FURY*)

GOD ALMIGHTY
Gen 28:3 May *God Almighty* bless you, and make you fruitful and multiply you, that you may be an assembly of peoples
Gen 35:11 I am *God Almighty*. Be fruitful and multiply; a nation and a company of nations shall proceed from you, and kings shall come from your body
Gen 43:14 And may *God Almighty* give you mercy before the man, that he may release your other brother and Benjamin
Gen 48:3 *God Almighty* appeared to me at Luz in the land of Canaan and blessed me
Ex 6:3 I appeared to Abraham, to Isaac, and to Jacob, as *God Almighty*, but by My name, Lord, I was not known to them
Rev 4:8 Holy, holy, holy, Lord *God Almighty*, Who was and is and is to come
Rev 11:17 We give You thanks, O Lord *God Almighty*, the One who is and who was and who is to come, because You have taken Your great power and reigned
Rev 15:3 Great and marvelous are Your works, Lord *God Almighty!* Just and true are Your ways, O King of the saints
Rev 16:7 And I heard another from the altar saying, "Even so, Lord *God Almighty*, true and righteous are Your judgments
Rev 16:14 For they are spirits of demons, performing signs, which go out to the kings of the earth and of the whole world, to gather them to the battle of that great day of *God Almighty*
Rev 21:22 But I saw no temple in it, for the Lord *God Almighty* and the Lamb are its temple

GOD AND FATHER OF OUR LORD JESUS CHRIST
Rom 15:6 that you may with one mind and one mouth glorify the *God and Father of our Lord Jesus Christ*
2Cor 1:3 Blessed be the *God and Father of our Lord Jesus Christ*, the Father of mercies and God of all comfort
2Cor 11:31 The *God and Father of our Lord Jesus Christ*, who is blessed forever, knows that I am not lying
Eph 1:3 Blessed be the *God and Father of our Lord Jesus Christ*, who has blessed us with every spiritual blessing in the heavenly places in Christ
Col 1:3 We give thanks to the *God and Father of our Lord Jesus Christ*, praying always for you
1Pet 1:3 Blessed be the *God and Father of our Lord Jesus Christ*, who according to His abundant mercy has begotten us again to a living hope through the resurrection of Jesus Christ from the dead

GOD AND MAMMON
Matt 6:24 for either he will hate the one and love the other, or else he will be loyal to the one and despise the other. You cannot serve *God and mammon*
Luke 16:13 for either he will hate the one and love the other, or else he will be loyal to the one and despise the other. You cannot serve *God and mammon*

GOD AND MEN
Judg 9:9 But the olive tree said to them, 'Should I cease giving my oil, with which they honor *God and men*, and go to sway over trees
Judg 9:13 But the vine said to them, 'Should I cease my new wine, which cheers both *God and men*, and go to sway over trees
Luke 2:52 And Jesus increased in wisdom and stature, and in favor with *God and men*
Acts 24:16 This being so, I myself always strive to have a conscience without offense toward *God and men*
1Tim 2:5 For there is one God and one Mediator between *God and men*, the Man Christ Jesus

GOD APPEARED TO
Gen 35:7 And he built an altar there and called the place El Bethel, because there *God appeared to* him when he fled from the face of his brother
Gen 35:9 Then *God appeared to* Jacob again, when he came from Padan Aram, and blessed him
2Chr 1:7 On that night *God appeared to* Solomon, and said to him

GOD COMES IN AWESOME MAJESTY (NIV)
(See *GOD IS AWESOME MAJESTY*)

GOD COMMANDED
Gen 2:16 And the Lord *God commanded* the man, saying, "Of every tree of the garden you may freely eat
Gen 6:22 according to all that *God commanded* him, so he did
Deut 1:41 we will go up and fight, just as the Lord our *God commanded* us
Deut 4:5 Surely I have taught you statutes and judgments, just as the Lord my *God commanded* me, that you should act according to them in the land which you go to possess
Deut 5:12 Observe the Sabbath day, to keep it holy, as the Lord your *God commanded* you
Deut 5:15 therefore the Lord your *God commanded* you to keep the Sabbath day
Deut 13:5 But that prophet or that dreamer of dreams shall be put to death, because he has spoken in order to turn you away from the Lord your God, who brought you out of the land of Egypt and redeemed you from the house of bondage, to entice you from the way in which the Lord your *God commanded* you to walk
Josh 9:24 So they answered Joshua and said, "Because it was certainly told your servants that the Lord your *God commanded* His servant Moses to give you all the land, and to destroy all the inhabitants of the land from before you
1Kin 13:21 Because you have disobeyed the word of the Lord, and have not kept the commandment which the Lord your *God commanded* you
1Chr 14:16 So David did as *God commanded* him, and they drove back the army of the Philistines from Gibeon as far as Gezer
2Chr 35:21 for *God commanded* me to make haste. Refrain from meddling with God, who is with me, lest He destroy you
Matt 15:4 For *God commanded*, saying, 'Honor your father and your mother

GOD CREATED
Gen 1:1 In the beginning *God created* the heavens and the earth
Gen 1:21 So *God created* great sea creatures and every living thing that moves, with which the waters abounded, according to their kind, and every winged bird according to its kind
Gen 1:27 So *God created* man in His own image; in the image of God He created him
Gen 5:1 In the day that *God created* man, He made him in the likeness of God
Deut 4:32 For ask now concerning the days that are past, which were before you, since the day that *God created* man on the earth, and ask from one end of heaven to the other, whether any great thing like this has happened, or anything like it has been heard
Mal 2:10 Has not one *God created* us? Why do we deal treacherously with one another by profaning the covenant of the fathers
Mark 13:19 For in those days there will be tribulation, such as has not been from the beginning of creation which *God created* until this time, nor ever shall be
1Tim 4:3 forbidding to marry, and commanding to abstain from foods which *God created* to be received with thanksgiving by those who believe and know the truth

GOD DOES NOT HEAR SINNERS
John 9:31 Now we know that *God does not hear sinners;* but if anyone is a worshiper of God and does His will, He hears him

GOD DOES NOT SHOW FAVORITISM (NIV)
(See *GOD SHOWS NO PARTIALITY*)

GOD EXALTETH (KJV)
(See *GOD IS EXALTED*)

GOD FORBID
Gal 6:14 But *God forbid* that I should glory except in the cross of our Lord Jesus Christ, by whom the world has been crucified to me, and I to the world

GOD FORBID THAT I (KJV)
(See *FAR BE IT FROM ME*)

GOD FORMED MAN
Gen 2:7 And the Lord *God formed man* of the dust of the ground, and breathed into his nostrils the breath of life

GOD GIVES WISDOM AND KNOWLEDGE
Eccl 2:26 For *God gives wisdom and knowledge* and joy to a man who is good in His sight

GOD HAS APPOINTED (RSV)
(See *ORDINANCE OF GOD*)

GOD HAS COMMANDED
Deut 5:16 Honor your father and your mother, as the Lord your *God has commanded* you, that your days may be long, and that it may be well with you in the land which the Lord your God is giving you
Deut 5:32 Therefore you shall be careful to do as the Lord your *God has commanded* you
Deut 5:33 You shall walk in all the ways which the Lord your *God has commanded* you, that you may live and that it may be well with you, and that you may prolong your days in the land which you shall possess
Deut 6:1 Now this is the commandment, and these are the statutes and judgments which the Lord your *God has commanded* to teach you, that you may observe them in the land which you are crossing over to possess
Deut 6:20 When your son asks you in time to come, saying, 'What is the meaning of the testimonies, the statutes, and the judgments which the Lord our *God has commanded* you
Deut 20:17 the Hittite and the Amorite and the Canaanite and the Perizzite and the Hivite and the Jebusite, just as the Lord your *God has commanded* you
Ps 68:28 Your *God has commanded* your strength; strengthen, O God, what You have done for us

Heb 9:20 saying, "This is the blood of the covenant which *God has commanded* you

GOD HAS GIVEN YOU REST
Deut 25:19 Therefore it shall be, when the Lord your *God has given you rest* from your enemies all around, in the land which the Lord your God is giving you to possess as an inheritance, that you will blot out the remembrance of Amalek from under heaven

GOD HAS INSTITUTED (NIV)
(See *ORDINANCE OF GOD*)

GOD HAS MADE YOU ALSO AN HEIR (NIV)
(See *HEIR OF GOD*)

GOD HAS POWER
2Chr 25:8 Even so, God shall make you fall before the enemy; for *God has power* to help and to overthrow

GOD HEARETH NOT SINNERS (KJV)
(See *GOD DOES NOT HEAR SINNERS*)

GOD IN HEAVEN WHO REVEALS SECRETS
Dan 2:28 But there is a *God in heaven who reveals secrets*, and He has made known to King Nebuchadnezzar what will be in the latter days

GOD IS A CONSUMING FIRE
Deut 4:24 For the Lord your *God is a consuming fire*, a jealous God
Heb 12:29 For our *God is a consuming fire*

GOD IS A JEALOUS GOD
Deut 6:15 (for the Lord your *God is a jealous God* among you

GOD IS A JUST JUDGE
Ps 7:11 *God is a just judge*, and God is angry with the wicked every day

GOD IS A REFUGE
Ps 62:8 Pour out your heart before Him; *God is a refuge* for us

GOD IS A RIGHTEOUS JUDGE (NAS, NIV, RSV)
(See *GOD IS A JUST JUDGE*)

GOD IS A SUN AND SHIELD
Ps 84:11 For the Lord *God is a sun and shield;* the Lord will give grace and glory

GOD IS A TERROR
Job 31:23 For destruction from *God is a terror* to me, and because of His magnificence I could not endure

GOD IS AWESOME MAJESTY
Job 37:22 He comes from the north as golden splendor; with *God is awesome majesty*

GOD IS CLOTHED WITH TERRIBLE MAJESTY (RSV)
(See *GOD IS AWESOME MAJESTY*)

GOD IS EXALTED
Job 36:22 Behold, *God is exalted* by His power; who teaches like Him

GOD IS FAITHFUL
1Cor 1:9 *God is faithful*, by whom you were called into the fellowship of His Son, Jesus Christ our Lord
1Cor 10:13 but *God is faithful*, who will not allow you to be tempted beyond what you are able, but with the temptation will also make the way of escape, that you may be able to bear it
2Cor 1:18 But as *God is faithful*, our word to you was not Yes and No

GOD IS FULL OF COMPASSION (NIV)
(See *GOD IS MERCIFUL*)

GOD IS GLORIFIED
John 13:31 So, when he had gone out, Jesus said, "Now the Son of Man is glorified, and *God is glorified* in Him
John 13:32 If *God is glorified* in Him, God will also glorify Him in Himself, and glorify Him immediately

GOD IS GREAT
Job 36:26 Behold, *God is great*, and we do not know Him

GOD IS GREATER THAN MAN
Job 33:12 I will answer you, for *God is greater than man*

GOD IS IN HEAVEN
Ps 115:3 But our *God is in heaven;* He does whatever He pleases
Eccl 5:2 For *God is in heaven*, and you on earth; therefore let your words be few

GOD IS LOVE
1Jn 4:8 He who does not love does not know God, for *God is love*
1Jn 4:16 *God is love*, and he who abides in love abides in God, and God in him

GOD IS MERCIFUL
Ps 116:5 Gracious is the Lord, and righteous; yes, our *God is merciful*

GOD IS MIGHTY
Job 36:5 Behold, *God is mighty*, but despises no one; He is mighty in strength of understanding

GOD IS MINE HELPER (KJV)
(See *GOD IS MY HELPER*)

GOD IS MY DEFENSE
Ps 59:9 O You his Strength, I will wait for You. For *God is my defense*
Ps 59:17 For *God is my defense*, the God of my mercy

GOD IS MY HELPER
Ps 54:4 Behold, *God is my helper;* the Lord is with those who uphold my life

GOD IS MY SALVATION
Ps 62:7 In *God is my salvation* and my glory; the rock of my strength, and my refuge, is in God
Is 12:2 Behold, *God is my salvation*, I will trust and not be afraid

GOD IS MY STRENGTH
2Sam 22:33 *God is my strength* and power, and He makes my way perfect
Hab 3:19 The Lord *God is my strength;* he will make my feet like deer's feet, and He will make me walk on my high hills

GOD IS MY STRONG REFUGE (RSV)
(See *GOD IS MY STRENGTH*)

GOD IS NO RESPECTER (KJV)
(See *GOD SHOWS NO PARTIALITY*)

GOD IS NOT A MAN
Num 23:19 *God is not a man*, that He should lie, nor a son of man, that He should repent

GOD IS OUR REFUGE
Ps 46:1 *God is our refuge* and strength, a very present help in trouble

GOD IS OUR WITNESS (NIV)
(See *GOD IS WITNESS*)

GOD IS SPIRIT
John 4:24 *God is Spirit*, and those who worship Him must worship in spirit and truth

GOD IS TERRIBLE MAJESTY (KJV)
(See *GOD IS AWESOME MAJESTY*)

GOD IS THE JUDGE
Ps 75:7 But *God is the Judge:* He puts down one, and exalts another

GOD IS THE KING
Ps 47:7 For *God is the King* of all the earth; sing praises with understanding

GOD IS THE LORD
Ps 33:12 Blessed is the nation whose *God is the Lord*, and the people whom He has chosen as His own inheritance
Ps 118:27 *God is the Lord*, and He has given us light
Ps 144:15 Happy are the people who are in such a state; happy are the people whose *God is the Lord*

GOD IS THEIR BELLY
Phil 3:19 whose end is destruction, whose *god is their belly*, and whose glory is in their shame who set their mind on earthly things

GOD IS WITNESS
Gen 31:50 If you afflict my daughters, or if you take other wives besides my daughters, although no man is with us see, *God is witness* between you and me
1Th 2:5 For neither at any time did we use flattering words, as you know, nor a cloak for covetousness *God is witness*

GOD JUDGETH THE RIGHTEOUS (KJV)
(See *GOD IS A JUST JUDGE*)

GOD KNOWS YOUR HEARTS
Luke 16:15 And He said to them, "You are those who justify yourselves before men, but *God knows your hearts*

GOD LOVES A CHEERFUL GIVER
2Cor 9:7 So let each one give as he purposes in his heart, not grudgingly or of necessity; for *God loves a cheerful giver*

GOD MADE
Gen 1:7 Thus *God made* the firmament, and divided the waters which were under the firmament from the waters which were above the firmament
Gen 1:16 Then *God made* two great lights: the greater light to rule the day, and the lesser light to rule the night
Gen 1:25 And *God made* the beast of the earth according to its kind, cattle according to its kind, and everything that creeps on the earth according to its kind
Gen 2:4 This is the history of the heavens and the earth when they were created, in the day that the Lord *God made* the earth and the heavens
Gen 2:9 And out of the ground the Lord *God made* every tree grow that is pleasant to the sight and good for food
Gen 3:21 Also for Adam and his wife the Lord *God made* tunics of skin, and clothed them
Gen 8:1 And *God made* a wind to pass over the earth, and the waters subsided
Deut 5:2 The Lord our *God made* a covenant with us in Horeb
2Chr 26:5 and as long as he sought the Lord, *God made* him prosper
Neh 13:26 and *God made* him king over all Israel. Nevertheless pagan women caused even him to sin
Job 23:16 For *God made* my heart weak, and the Almighty terrifies me
Eccl 7:29 that *God made* man upright, but they have sought out many schemes
Acts 3:25 You are sons of the prophets, and of the covenant which *God made* with our fathers, saying to Abraham
1Cor 1:20 Has not *God made* foolish the wisdom of this world
Heb 6:13 For when *God made* a promise to Abraham, because He could swear by no one greater, He swore by Himself

GOD MOST HIGH
Gen 14:18 Then Melchizedek king of Salem brought out bread and wine; he was the priest of *God Most High*
Gen 14:19 Blessed be Abram of *God Most High*, Possessor of heaven and earth
Gen 14:20 And blessed be *God Most High*, Who has delivered your enemies into your hand
Gen 14:22 But Abram said to the king of Sodom, "I have lifted my hand to the Lord, *God Most High*, the Possessor of heaven and earth
Ps 57:2 I will cry out to *God Most High*, to God who performs all things for me

GOD OF ABRAHAM, ISAAC, AND JACOB
Acts 3:13 The *God of Abraham, Isaac, and Jacob*, the God of our fathers, glorified His Servant Jesus, whom you delivered up and denied in the presence of Pilate, when he was determined to let Him go

GOD OF ALL THE EARTH (NAS, NIV)
(See *GOD OF THE WHOLE EARTH*)

GOD OF ANY NATION (NIV)
(See *GODS OF THE NATIONS*)

GOD OF CONFUSION (NAS, RSV)
(See *AUTHOR OF CONFUSION*)

GOD OF DISORDER (NIV)
(See *AUTHOR OF CONFUSION*)

GOD OF GODS
Deut 10:17 For the Lord your God is *God of gods* and Lord of lords, the great God, mighty and awesome, who shows no partiality nor takes a bribe
Josh 22:22 The Lord *God of gods*, the Lord *God of gods*, He knows, and let Israel itself know if it is in rebellion, or if in treachery against the Lord, do not save us this day
Ps 136:2 Oh, give thanks to the *God of gods!* For His mercy endures forever
Dan 2:47 The king answered Daniel, and said, "Truly your God is the *God of gods*, the Lord of kings, and a revealer of secrets, since you could reveal this secret
Dan 11:36 he shall exalt and magnify himself above every god, shall speak blasphemies against the *God of gods*, and shall prosper till the wrath has been accomplished

GOD OF HEAVEN

Gen 24:3 and I will make you swear by the Lord, the *God of heaven* and the God of the earth, that you will not take a wife for my son from the daughters of the Canaanites, among whom I dwell

Gen 24:7 The Lord *God of heaven*, who took me from my father's house and from the land of my family, and who spoke to me and swore to me, saying

2Chr 36:23 All the kingdoms of the earth the Lord *God of heaven* has given me

Ezra 1:2 All the kingdoms of the earth the Lord *God of heaven* has given me

Ezra 5:11 We are the servants of the *God of heaven* and earth, and we are rebuilding the temple that was built many years ago, which a great king of Israel built and completed

Ezra 5:12 But because our fathers provoked the *God of heaven* to wrath, He gave them into the hand of Nebuchadnezzar king of Babylon, the Chaldean, who destroyed this temple and carried the people away to Babylon

Ezra 6:9 And whatever they need young bulls, rams, and lambs for the burnt offerings of the *God of heaven*, wheat, salt, wine, and oil, according to the request of the priests who are in Jerusalem let it be given them day by day without fail

Ezra 6:10 that they may offer sacrifices of sweet aroma to the *God of heaven*, and pray for the life of the king and his sons

Ezra 7:12 Artaxerxes, king of kings, to Ezra the priest, a scribe of the Law of the *God of heaven*

Ezra 7:21 And I, even I, Artaxerxes the king, do issue a decree to all the treasurers who are in the region beyond the River, that whatever Ezra the priest, the scribe of the Law of the *God of heaven*, may require of you, let it be done diligently

Ezra 7:23 Whatever is commanded by the *God of heaven*, let it diligently be done for the house of the *God of heaven*

Neh 1:4 I was fasting and praying before the *God of heaven*

Neh 1:5 I pray, Lord *God of heaven*, O great and awesome God, You who keep Your covenant and mercy with those who love You and observe Your commandments

Neh 2:4 Then the king said to me, "What do you request?" So I prayed to the *God of heaven*

Neh 2:20 So I answered them, and said to them, "The *God of heaven* Himself will prosper us

Ps 136:26 Oh, give thanks to the *God of heaven!* For His mercy endures forever

Dan 2:18 that they might seek mercies from the *God of heaven* concerning this secret, so that Daniel and his companions might not perish with the rest of the wise men of Babylon

Dan 2:19 Then the secret was revealed to Daniel in a night vision. So Daniel blessed the *God of heaven*

Dan 2:37 For the *God of heaven* has given you a kingdom, power, strength, and glory

Dan 2:44 And in the days of these kings the *God of heaven* will set up a kingdom which shall never be destroyed

Jon 1:9 and I fear the Lord, the *God of heaven*, who made the sea and the dry land

Rev 11:13 In the earthquake seven thousand men were killed, and the rest were afraid and gave glory to the *God of heaven*

Rev 16:11 And they blasphemed the *God of heaven* because of their pains and their sores, and did not repent of their deeds

GOD OF HEAVEN AND EARTH

Ezra 5:11 We are the servants of the *God of heaven and earth*, and we are rebuilding the temple that was built many years ago, which a great king of Israel built and completed

GOD OF HOPE

Rom 15:13 Now may the *God of hope* fill you with all joy and peace in believing, that you may abound in hope by the power of the Holy Spirit

GOD OF ISRAEL

Ex 5:1 Afterward Moses and Aaron went in and told Pharaoh, "Thus says the Lord *God of Israel*

Ex 24:10 and they saw the *God of Israel*. And there was under His feet as it were a paved work of sapphire stone, and it was like the very heavens in its clarity

Ex 32:27 And he said to them, "Thus says the Lord *God of Israel*

Ex 34:23 Three times in the year all your men shall appear before the Lord, the Lord *God of Israel*

Num 16:9 Is it a small thing to you that the *God of Israel* has separated you from the congregation of Israel, to bring you near to Himself, to do the work of the tabernacle of the Lord, and to stand before the congregation to serve them

Josh 7:13 Get up, sanctify the people, and say, 'Sanctify yourselves for tomorrow, because thus says the Lord *God of Israel*

Josh 7:19 So Joshua said to Achan, "My son, I beg you, give glory to the Lord *God of Israel*, and make confession to Him, and tell me now what you have done

Josh 7:20 And Achan answered Joshua and said, "Indeed I have sinned against the Lord *God of Israel*, and this is what I have done

Josh 8:30 Now Joshua built an altar to the Lord *God of Israel* in Mount Ebal

Josh 9:18 But the children of Israel did not attack them, because the rulers of the congregation had sworn to them by the Lord *God of Israel*

Josh 9:19 Then all the rulers said to all the congregation, "We have sworn to them by the Lord *God of Israel*

Josh 10:40 he left none remaining, but utterly destroyed all that breathed, as the Lord *God of Israel* had commanded

Josh 10:42 All these kings and their land Joshua took at one time, because the Lord *God of Israel* fought for Israel

Josh 13:14 the sacrifices of the Lord *God of Israel* made by fire are their inheritance, as He said to them

Josh 13:33 the Lord *God of Israel* was their inheritance, as He had said to them

Josh 14:14 Hebron therefore became the inheritance of Caleb the son of Jephunneh the Kenizzite to this day, because he wholly followed the Lord *God of Israel*

Josh 22:16 What treachery is this that you have committed against the *God of Israel*, to turn away this day from following the Lord, in that you have built for yourselves an altar, that you might rebel this day against the Lord

Josh 22:24 But in fact we have done it for fear, for a reason, saying, 'In time to come your descendants may speak to our descendants, saying, "What have you to do with the Lord *God of Israel*

Josh 24:2 And Joshua said to all the people, "Thus says the Lord *God of Israel*

Josh 24:23 Now therefore," he said, "put away the foreign gods which are among you, and incline your heart to the Lord *God of Israel*

Judg 4:6 Then she sent and called for Barak the son of Abinoam from Kedesh in Naphtali, and said to him, "Has not the Lord *God of Israel* commanded, saying

Judg 5:3 I will sing praise to the Lord *God of Israel*
Judg 5:5 the mountains gushed before the Lord, this Sinai, before the Lord *God of Israel*
Judg 6:8 that the Lord sent a prophet to the children of Israel, who said to them, "Thus says the Lord *God of Israel*
Judg 11:21 And the Lord *God of Israel* delivered Sihon and all his people into the hand of Israel, and they defeated them
Judg 11:23 So now the Lord *God of Israel* has dispossessed the Amorites from before His people Israel
Judg 21:3 and said, "O Lord *God of Israel*, why has this come to pass in Israel, that today there should be one tribe missing in Israel
Ruth 2:12 The Lord repay your work, and a full reward be given you by the Lord *God of Israel*, under whose wings you have come for refuge
1Sam 1:17 Then Eli answered and said, "Go in peace, and the *God of Israel* grant your petition which you have asked of Him
1Sam 2:30 Therefore the Lord *God of Israel* says: 'I said indeed that your house and the house of your father would walk before Me forever
1Sam 5:7 And when the men of Ashdod saw how it was, they said, "The ark of the *God of Israel* must not remain with us, for His hand is harsh toward us and Dagon our god
1Sam 5:8 Therefore they sent and gathered to themselves all the lords of the Philistines, and said, "What shall we do with the ark of the *God of Israel?*" And they answered, "Let the ark of the *God of Israel* be carried away to Gath." So they carried the ark of the *God of Israel* away
1Sam 5:10 So it was, as the ark of God came to Ekron, that the Ekronites cried out, saying, "They have brought the ark of the *God of Israel* to us, to kill us and our people
1Sam 5:11 So they sent and gathered together all the lords of the Philistines, and said, "Send away the ark of the *God of Israel*, and let it go back to its own place, so that it does not kill us and our people
1Sam 6:3 So they said, "If you send away the ark of the *God of Israel*, do not send it empty
1Sam 6:5 Therefore you shall make images of your tumors and images of your rats that ravage the land, and you shall give glory to the *God of Israel*
1Sam 10:18 and said to the children of Israel, "Thus says the Lord *God of Israel*
1Sam 14:41 Therefore Saul said to the Lord *God of Israel*, "Give a perfect lot
1Sam 20:12 The Lord *God of Israel* is witness! When I have sounded out my father sometime tomorrow, or the third day, and indeed there is good toward David, and I do not send to you and tell you
1Sam 23:10 Then David said, "O Lord *God of Israel*, Your servant has certainly heard that Saul seeks to come to Keilah to destroy the city for my sake
1Sam 23:11 O Lord *God of Israel*, I pray, tell Your servant
1Sam 25:32 Blessed be the Lord *God of Israel*, who sent you this day to meet me
1Sam 25:34 For indeed, as the Lord *God of Israel* lives, who has kept me back from hurting you, unless you had hastened and come to meet me, surely by morning light no males would have been left to Nabal
2Sam 7:27 For You, O Lord of hosts, *God of Israel*, have revealed this to Your servant, saying
2Sam 12:7 Thus says the Lord *God of Israel:* 'I anointed you king over Israel, and I delivered you from the hand of Saul
2Sam 23:3 The *God of Israel* said, the Rock of Israel spoke to me
1Kin 1:30 just as I swore to you by the Lord *God of Israel*, saying
1Kin 1:48 Also the king said thus, 'Blessed be the Lord *God of Israel*, who has given one to sit on my throne this day, while my eyes see it
1Kin 8:15 Blessed be the Lord *God of Israel*, who spoke with His mouth to my father David, and with His hand has fulfilled it, saying
1Kin 8:17 Now it was in the heart of my father David to build a house for the name of the Lord *God of Israel*
1Kin 8:20 and I have built a house for the name of the Lord *God of Israel*
1Kin 8:23 Lord *God of Israel*, there is no God in heaven above or on earth below like You, who keep Your covenant and mercy with Your servants who walk before You with all their heart
1Kin 8:25 Therefore, Lord *God of Israel*, now keep what You promised Your servant David my father, saying
1Kin 8:26 And now I pray, O *God of Israel*, let Your word come true, which You have spoken to Your servant David my father
1Kin 11:9 So the Lord became angry with Solomon, because his heart had turned from the Lord *God of Israel*, who had appeared to him twice
1Kin 11:31 And he said to Jeroboam, "Take for yourself ten pieces, for thus says the Lord, the *God of Israel*
1Kin 14:7 Go, tell Jeroboam, 'Thus says the Lord *God of Israel*
1Kin 14:13 And all Israel shall mourn for him and bury him, for he is the only one of Jeroboam who shall come to the grave, because in him there is found something good toward the Lord *God of Israel* in the house of Jeroboam
1Kin 15:30 because of the sins of Jeroboam, which he had sinned and by which he had made Israel sin, because of his provocation with which he had provoked the Lord *God of Israel* to anger
1Kin 16:13 for all the sins of Baasha and the sins of Elah his son, by which they had sinned and by which they had made Israel sin, in provoking the Lord *God of Israel* to anger with their idols
1Kin 16:26 For he walked in all the ways of Jeroboam the son of Nebat, and in his sin by which he had made Israel sin, provoking the Lord *God of Israel* to anger with their idols
1Kin 16:33 Ahab did more to provoke the Lord *God of Israel* to anger than all the kings of Israel who were before him
1Kin 17:1 And Elijah the Tishbite, of the inhabitants of Gilead, said to Ahab, "As the Lord *God of Israel* lives, before whom I stand, there shall not be dew nor rain these years, except at my word
1Kin 17:14 For thus says the Lord *God of Israel:* 'The bin of flour shall not be used up, nor shall the jar of oil run dry, until the day the Lord sends rain on the earth
1Kin 22:53 for he served Baal and worshiped him, and provoked the Lord *God of Israel* to anger, according to all that his father had done
2Kin 9:6 And he poured the oil on his head, and said to him, "Thus says the Lord *God of Israel*
2Kin 10:31 But Jehu took no heed to walk in the law of the Lord *God of Israel* with all his heart
2Kin 14:25 He restored the territory of Israel from the entrance of Hamath to the Sea of the Arabah, according to the word of the Lord *God of Israel*, which He had spoken through His servant Jonah the son of Amittai, the prophet who was from Gath Hepher
2Kin 18:5 He trusted in the Lord *God of Israel*, so that after him was none like him among all the kings of Judah, nor any who were before him

2Kin 19:15 O Lord *God of Israel*, the One who dwells between the cherubim, You are God, You alone, of all the kingdoms of the earth
2Kin 19:20 Then Isaiah the son of Amoz sent to Hezekiah, saying, "Thus says the Lord *God of Israel*
2Kin 21:12 therefore thus says the Lord *God of Israel:* 'Behold, I am bringing such calamity upon Jerusalem and Judah, that whoever hears of it, both his ears will tingle
2Kin 22:15 Then she said to them, "Thus says the Lord *God of Israel*
2Kin 22:18 But to the king of Judah, who sent you to inquire of the Lord, in this manner you shall speak to him, 'Thus says the Lord *God of Israel*
1Chr 4:10 And Jabez called on the *God of Israel* saying, "Oh, that You would bless me indeed, and enlarge my territory, that Your hand would be with me, and that You would keep me from evil, that I may not cause pain
1Chr 5:26 So the *God of Israel* stirred up the spirit of Pul king of Assyria, that is, Tiglath-Pileser king of Assyria
1Chr 15:12 sanctify yourselves, you and your brethren, that you may bring up the ark of the Lord *God of Israel* to the place I have prepared for it
1Chr 15:14 So the priests and the Levites sanctified themselves to bring up the ark of the Lord *God of Israel*
1Chr 16:4 And he appointed some of the Levites to minister before the ark of the Lord, to commemorate, to thank, and to praise the Lord *God of Israel*
1Chr 16:36 Blessed be the Lord *God of Israel* from everlasting to everlasting
1Chr 17:24 So let it be established, that Your name may be magnified forever, saying, 'The Lord of hosts, the *God of Israel*, is Israel's God
1Chr 22:6 Then he called for his son Solomon, and charged him to build a house for the Lord *God of Israel*
1Chr 23:25 For David said, "The Lord *God of Israel* has given rest to His people, that they may dwell in Jerusalem forever
1Chr 24:19 This was the schedule of their service for coming into the house of the Lord according to their ordinance by the hand of Aaron their father, as the Lord *God of Israel* had commanded him
1Chr 28:4 However the Lord *God of Israel* chose me above all the house of my father to be king over Israel forever, for He has chosen Judah to be the ruler
1Chr 29:10 Blessed are You, Lord *God of Israel*, our Father, forever and ever
2Chr 2:12 Blessed be the Lord *God of Israel*, who made heaven and earth, for He has given King David a wise son, endowed with prudence and understanding, who will build a temple for the Lord and a royal house for himself
2Chr 6:4 Blessed be the Lord *God of Israel*, who has fulfilled with His hands what He spoke with His mouth to my father David, saying
2Chr 6:7 Now it was in the heart of my father David to build a temple for the name of the Lord *God of Israel*
2Chr 6:10 and I have built the temple for the name of the Lord *God of Israel*
2Chr 6:14 Lord *God of Israel*, there is no God in heaven or on earth like You, who keep Your covenant and mercy with Your servants who walk before You with all their hearts
2Chr 6:16 Therefore, Lord *God of Israel*, now keep what You promised Your servant David my father, saying
2Chr 6:17 Now then, O Lord *God of Israel*, let Your word come true, which You have spoken to Your servant David
2Chr 11:16 And after the Levites left, those from all the tribes of Israel, such as set their heart to seek the Lord *God of Israel*, came to Jerusalem to sacrifice to the Lord God of their fathers
2Chr 13:5 Should you not know that the Lord *God of Israel* gave the dominion over Israel to David forever, to him and his sons, by a covenant of salt
2Chr 15:4 but when in their trouble they turned to the Lord *God of Israel*, and sought Him, He was found by them
2Chr 15:13 and whoever would not seek the Lord *God of Israel* was to be put to death, whether small or great, whether man or woman
2Chr 20:19 Then the Levites of the children of the Kohathites and of the children of the Korahites stood up to praise the Lord *God of Israel* with voices loud and high
2Chr 29:7 They have also shut up the doors of the vestibule, put out the lamps, and have not burned incense or offered burnt offerings in the holy place to the *God of Israel*
2Chr 29:10 Now it is in my heart to make a covenant with the Lord *God of Israel*, that His fierce wrath may turn away from us
2Chr 30:1 And Hezekiah sent to all Israel and Judah, and also wrote letters to Ephraim and Manasseh, that they should come to the house of the Lord at Jerusalem, to keep the Passover to the Lord *God of Israel*
2Chr 30:5 So they resolved to make a proclamation throughout all Israel, from Beersheba to Dan, that they should come to keep the Passover to the Lord *God of Israel* at Jerusalem, since they had not done it for a long time in the prescribed manner
2Chr 32:17 He also wrote letters to revile the Lord *God of Israel*, and to speak against Him, saying
2Chr 33:16 He also repaired the altar of the Lord, sacrificed peace offerings and thank offerings on it, and commanded Judah to serve the Lord *God of Israel*
2Chr 33:18 Now the rest of the acts of Manasseh, his prayer to his God, and the words of the seers who spoke to him in the name of the Lord *God of Israel*, indeed they are written in the book of the kings of Israel
2Chr 34:23 Then she answered them, "Thus says the Lord *God of Israel*
2Chr 34:26 And as for the king of Judah, who sent you to inquire of the Lord, in this manner you shall speak to him, 'Thus says the Lord *God of Israel*
2Chr 36:13 but he stiffened his neck and hardened his heart against turning to the Lord *God of Israel*
Ezra 1:3 Now let him go up to Jerusalem, which is in Judah, and build the house of the Lord *God of Israel* (He is God
Ezra 3:2 Then Jeshua the son of Jozadak and his brethren the priests, and Zerubbabel the son of Shealtiel and his brethren, arose and built the altar of the *God of Israel*, to offer burnt offerings on it, as it is written in the Law of Moses the man of God
Ezra 4:1 Now when the adversaries of Judah and Benjamin heard that the descendants of the captivity were building the temple of the Lord *God of Israel*
Ezra 4:3 but we alone will build to the Lord *God of Israel*, as King Cyrus the king of Persia has commanded us
Ezra 5:1 Then the prophet Haggai and Zechariah the son of Iddo, prophets, prophesied to the Jews who were in Judah and Jerusalem, in the name of the *God of Israel*, who was over them
Ezra 6:14 And they built and finished it, according

to the commandment of the *God of Israel*, and according to the command of Cyrus, Darius, and Artaxerxes king of Persia

Ezra 6:21 Then the children of Israel who had returned from the captivity ate together with all who had separated themselves from the filth of the nations of the land in order to seek the Lord *God of Israel*

Ezra 6:22 for the Lord made them joyful, and turned the heart of the king of Assyria toward them, to strengthen their hands in the work of the house of God, the *God of Israel*

Ezra 7:6 and he was a skilled scribe in the Law of Moses, which the Lord *God of Israel* had given

Ezra 7:15 and whereas you are to carry the silver and gold which the king and his counselors have freely offered to the *God of Israel*, whose dwelling is in Jerusalem

Ezra 8:35 The children of those who had been carried away captive, who had come from the captivity, offered burnt offerings to the *God of Israel*

Ezra 9:4 Then everyone who trembled at the words of the *God of Israel* assembled to me, because of the transgression of those who had been carried away captive, and I sat astonished until the evening sacrifice

Ezra 9:15 O Lord *God of Israel*, You are righteous, for we are left as a remnant, as it is this day

Ps 41:13 Blessed be the Lord *God of Israel* from everlasting to everlasting

Ps 59:5 You therefore, O Lord God of hosts, the *God of Israel*, awake to punish all the nations

Ps 68:8 Sinai itself was moved at the presence of God, the *God of Israel*

Ps 68:35 The *God of Israel* is He who gives strength and power to His people

Ps 69:6 Let not those who seek You be confounded because of me, O *God of Israel*

Ps 72:18 Blessed be the Lord God, the *God of Israel*, Who only does wondrous things

Ps 106:48 Blessed be the Lord *God of Israel* from everlasting to everlasting

Is 17:6 Yet gleaning grapes will be left in it, like the shaking of an olive tree, two or three olives at the top of the uppermost bough, four or five in its most fruitful branches," says the Lord *God of Israel*

Is 21:10 That which I have heard from the Lord of hosts, the *God of Israel*, I have declared to you

Is 21:17 and the remainder of the number of archers, the mighty men of the people of Kedar, will be diminished; for the Lord *God of Israel* has spoken it

Is 24:15 Therefore glorify the Lord in the dawning light, the name of the Lord *God of Israel* in the coastlands of the sea

Is 29:23 but when he sees his children, the work of My hands, in his midst, they will hallow My name, and hallow the Holy One of Jacob, and fear the *God of Israel*

Is 37:16 O Lord of hosts, *God of Israel*, the One who dwells between the cherubim, You are God, You alone, of all the kingdoms of the earth

Is 37:21 Then Isaiah the son of Amoz sent to Hezekiah, saying, "Thus says the Lord *God of Israel*

Is 41:17 When the poor and needy seek water, and there is none, and their tongues fail for thirst, I, the Lord, will hear them; I, the *God of Israel*, will not forsake them

Is 45:3 I will give you the treasures of darkness and hidden riches of secret places, that you may know that I, the Lord, Who call you by your name, am the *God of Israel*

Is 45:15 Truly You are God, who hide Yourself, O *God of Israel*, the Savior

Is 48:1 who swear by the name of the Lord, and make mention of the *God of Israel*, but not in truth or in righteousness

Is 48:2 for they call themselves after the holy city, and lean on the *God of Israel*

Is 52:12 for the Lord will go before you, and the *God of Israel* will be your rear guard

Jer 7:3 Thus says the Lord of hosts, the *God of Israel*

Jer 7:21 Thus says the Lord of hosts, the *God of Israel*

Jer 9:15 therefore thus says the Lord of hosts, the *God of Israel*

Jer 11:3 and say to them, 'Thus says the Lord *God of Israel*

Jer 13:12 Thus says the Lord *God of Israel:* "Every bottle shall be filled with wine

Jer 16:9 For thus says the Lord of hosts, the *God of Israel*

Jer 19:3 Thus says the Lord of hosts, the *God of Israel*

Jer 19:15 Thus says the Lord of hosts, the *God of Israel*

Jer 21:4 Thus says the Lord *God of Israel:* "Behold, I will turn back the weapons of war that are in your hands, with which you fight against the king of Babylon and the Chaldeans who besiege you outside the walls

Jer 23:2 Therefore thus says the Lord *God of Israel* against the shepherds who feed My people

Jer 24:5 Thus says the Lord, the *God of Israel:* 'Like these good figs, so will I acknowledge those who are carried away captive from Judah, whom I have sent out of this place for their own good, into the land of the Chaldeans

Jer 25:15 For thus says the Lord *God of Israel* to me

Jer 25:27 Therefore you shall say to them, 'Thus says the Lord of hosts, the *God of Israel*

Jer 27:4 And command them to say to their masters, "Thus says the Lord of hosts, the *God of Israel* thus you shall say to your masters

Jer 27:21 yes, thus says the Lord of hosts, the *God of Israel*, concerning the vessels that remain in the house of the Lord, and in the house of the king of Judah and of Jerusalem

Jer 28:2 Thus speaks the Lord of hosts, the *God of Israel*

Jer 28:14 For thus says the Lord of hosts, the *God of Israel*

Jer 29:4 Thus says the Lord of hosts, the *God of Israel*, to all who were carried away captive, whom I have caused to be carried away from Jerusalem to Babylon

Jer 29:8 For thus says the Lord of hosts, the *God of Israel*

Jer 29:21 Thus says the Lord of hosts, the *God of Israel*, concerning Ahab the son of Kolaiah, and Zedekiah the son of Maaseiah, who prophesy a lie to you in My name

Jer 29:25 Thus speaks the Lord of hosts, the *God of Israel*

Jer 30:2 Thus speaks the Lord *God of Israel*, saying: 'Write in a book for yourself all the words that I have spoken to you

Jer 31:23 Thus says the Lord of hosts, the *God of Israel*

Jer 32:14 Thus says the Lord of hosts, the *God of Israel*

Jer 32:15 For thus says the Lord of hosts, the *God of Israel*

Jer 32:36 Now therefore, thus says the Lord, the *God of Israel*, concerning this city of which you say

Jer 33:4 For thus says the Lord, the *God of Israel*, concerning the houses of this city and the houses of the kings of Judah, which have been pulled down to fortify against the siege mounds and the sword

Jer 34:2 Thus says the Lord, the *God of Israel:* 'Go and speak to Zedekiah king of Judah and tell him

Jer 34:13 Thus says the Lord, the *God of Israel:* 'I made a covenant with your fathers in the day that I brought them out of the land of Egypt, out of the house of bondage, saying
Jer 35:13 Thus says the Lord of hosts, the *God of Israel*
Jer 35:17 Therefore thus says the Lord God of hosts, the *God of Israel*
Jer 35:18 And Jeremiah said to the house of the Rechabites, "Thus says the Lord of hosts, the *God of Israel*
Jer 35:19 therefore thus says the Lord of hosts, the *God of Israel*
Jer 37:7 Thus says the Lord, the *God of Israel*, 'Thus you shall say to the king of Judah, who sent you to Me to inquire of Me
Jer 38:17 Then Jeremiah said to Zedekiah, "Thus says the Lord, the God of hosts, the *God of Israel*
Jer 39:16 Go and speak to Ebed-Melech the Ethiopian, saying, 'Thus says the Lord of hosts, the *God of Israel*
Jer 42:9 and said to them, "Thus says the Lord, the *God of Israel*, to whom you sent me to present your petition before Him
Jer 42:15 Thus says the Lord of hosts, the *God of Israel*
Jer 42:18 For thus says the Lord of hosts, the *God of Israel*
Jer 43:10 and say to them, 'Thus says the Lord of hosts, the *God of Israel*
Jer 44:2 Thus says the Lord of hosts, the *God of Israel*
Jer 44:7 Now therefore, thus says the Lord, the God of hosts, the *God of Israel*
Jer 44:11 Therefore thus says the Lord of hosts, the *God of Israel*
Jer 44:25 Thus says the Lord of hosts, the *God of Israel*, saying
Jer 45:2 Thus says the Lord, the *God of Israel*, to you, O Baruch
Jer 46:25 The Lord of hosts, the *God of Israel*, says: "Behold, I will bring punishment on Amon of No, and Pharaoh and Egypt, with their gods and their kings Pharaoh and those who trust in him
Jer 48:1 Thus says the Lord of hosts, the *God of Israel*
Jer 50:18 Therefore thus says the Lord of hosts, the *God of Israel*
Jer 51:33 For thus says the Lord of hosts, the *God of Israel*
Ezek 8:4 And behold, the glory of the *God of Israel* was there, like the vision that I saw in the plain
Ezek 9:3 Now the glory of the *God of Israel* had gone up from the cherub, where it had been, to the threshold of the temple
Ezek 10:19 and they stood at the door of the east gate of the Lord's house, and the glory of the *God of Israel* was above them
Ezek 10:20 This is the living creature I saw under the *God of Israel* by the River Chebar, and I knew they were cherubim
Ezek 11:22 Then the cherubim lifted up their wings, with the wheels beside them, and the glory of the *God of Israel* was high above them
Ezek 43:2 And behold, the glory of the *God of Israel* came from the way of the east
Ezek 44:2 it shall not be opened, and no man shall enter by it, because the Lord *God of Israel* has entered by it
Zeph 2:9 Therefore, as I live," says the Lord of hosts, the *God of Israel*
Mal 2:16 For the Lord *God of Israel* says that He hates divorce, for it covers one's garment with violence
Matt 15:31 So the multitude marveled when they saw the mute speaking, the maimed made whole, the lame walking, and the blind seeing; and they glorified the *God of Israel*
Luke 1:68 Blessed is the Lord *God of Israel*, for He has visited and redeemed His people

GOD OF JUSTICE
Is 30:18 For the Lord is a *God of justice;* blessed are all those who wait for Him
Mal 2:17 In that you say, "Everyone who does evil is good in the sight of the Lord, and He delights in them," or, "Where is the *God of justice*

GOD OF MY SALVATION
Ps 18:46 Blessed be my Rock! Let the *God of my salvation* be exalted
Ps 25:5 Lead me in Your truth and teach me, for You are the *God of my salvation*
Ps 27:9 Do not leave me nor forsake me, O *God of my salvation*
Ps 51:14 Deliver me from bloodguiltiness, O God, the *God of my salvation*, and my tongue shall sing aloud of Your righteousness
Ps 88:1 O Lord, *God of my salvation*, I have cried out day and night before You
Mic 7:7 I will wait for the *God of my salvation;* my God will hear me
Hab 3:18 Yet I will rejoice in the Lord, I will joy in the *God of my salvation*

GOD OF OUR FATHERS
Deut 26:7 Then we cried out to the Lord *God of our fathers*, and the Lord heard our voice and looked on our affliction and our labor and our oppression
1Chr 12:17 but if to betray me to my enemies, since there is no wrong in my hands, may the *God of our fathers* look and bring judgment
2Chr 20:6 O Lord *God of our fathers*, are You not God in heaven, and do You not rule over all the kingdoms of the nations, and in Your hand is there not power and might, so that no one is able to withstand You
Ezra 7:27 Blessed be the Lord *God of our fathers*, who has put such a thing as this in the king's heart, to beautify the house of the Lord which is in Jerusalem
Acts 3:13 The God of Abraham, Isaac, and Jacob, the *God of our fathers*, glorified His Servant Jesus, whom you delivered up and denied in the presence of Pilate, when he was determined to let Him go
Acts 5:30 The *God of our fathers* raised up Jesus whom you murdered by hanging on a tree
Acts 22:14 Then he said, 'The *God of our fathers* has chosen you that you should know His will, and see the Just One, and hear the voice of His mouth

GOD OF OUR SALVATION
1Chr 16:35 And say, "Save us, O *God of our salvation;* gather us together, and deliver us from the Gentiles, to give thanks to Your holy name, to triumph in Your praise
Ps 65:5 By awesome deeds in righteousness You will answer us, O *God of our salvation*, You who are the confidence of all the ends of the earth, and of the far-off seas
Ps 68:19 Blessed be the Lord, Who daily loads us with benefits, the *God of our salvation*
Ps 79:9 Help us, O *God of our salvation*, for the glory of Your name
Ps 85:4 Restore us, O *God of our salvation*, and cause Your anger toward us to cease

GOD OF PEACE
Rom 15:33 Now the *God of peace* be with you all
Rom 16:20 And the *God of peace* will crush Satan under your feet shortly

Phil 4:9 The things which you learned and received and heard and saw in me, these do, and the *God of peace* will be with you
1Th 5:23 Now may the *God of peace* Himself sanctify you completely
Heb 13:20 Now may the *God of peace* who brought up our Lord Jesus from the dead, that great Shepherd of the sheep, through the blood of the everlasting covenant

GOD OF SALVATION
Ps 68:20 Our God is the *God of salvation;* and to God the Lord belong escapes from death

GOD OF THE ARMIES OF ISRAEL
1Sam 17:45 But I come to you in the name of the Lord of hosts, the *God of the armies of Israel*, whom you have defied

GOD OF THE DEAD
Matt 22:32 God is not the *God of the dead*, but of the living
Mark 12:27 He is not the *God of the dead*, but the God of the living
Luke 20:38 For He is not the *God of the dead* but of the living, for all live to Him

GOD OF THE HEBREWS
Ex 3:18 and you shall say to him, 'The Lord *God of the Hebrews* has met with us
Ex 5:3 So they said, "The *God of the Hebrews* has met with us
Ex 7:16 And you shall say to him, 'The Lord *God of the Hebrews* has sent me to you, saying
Ex 9:1 Then the Lord said to Moses, "Go in to Pharaoh and tell him, 'Thus says the Lord *God of the Hebrews*
Ex 9:13 Then the Lord said to Moses, "Rise early in the morning and stand before Pharaoh, and say to him, 'Thus says the Lord *God of the Hebrews*
Ex 10:3 So Moses and Aaron came in to Pharaoh and said to him, "Thus says the Lord *God of the Hebrews*

GOD OF THE HILLS
1Kin 20:28 Because the Syrians have said, "The Lord is *God of the hills*, but He is not God of the valleys

GOD OF THE LIVING
Mark 12:27 He is not the God of the dead, but the *God of the living*

GOD OF THE SPIRITS
Num 16:22 Then they fell on their faces, and said, "O God, the *God of the spirits* of all flesh, shall one man sin, and You be angry with all the congregation
Num 27:16 Let the Lord, the *God of the spirits* of all flesh, set a man over the congregation

GOD OF THE WHOLE EARTH
Is 54:5 and your Redeemer is the Holy One of Israel; He is called the *God of the whole earth*

GOD OF THEIR FATHERS
Ex 4:5 that they may believe that the Lord *God of their fathers*, the God of Abraham, the God of Isaac, and the God of Jacob, has appeared to you
Deut 29:25 Because they have forsaken the covenant of the Lord *God of their fathers*, which He made with them when He brought them out of the land of Egypt
Judg 2:12 and they forsook the Lord *God of their fathers*, who had brought them out of the land of Egypt
1Chr 5:25 And they were unfaithful to the *God of their fathers*, and played the harlot after the gods of the peoples of the land, whom God had destroyed before them
1Chr 29:20 So all the congregation blessed the Lord *God of their fathers*, and bowed their heads and prostrated themselves before the Lord and the king
2Chr 7:22 Then they will answer, 'Because they forsook the Lord *God of their fathers*, who brought them out of the land of Egypt, and embraced other gods, and worshiped them and served them
2Chr 11:16 And after the Levites left, those from all the tribes of Israel, such as set their heart to seek the Lord God of Israel, came to Jerusalem to sacrifice to the Lord *God of their fathers*
2Chr 13:18 and the children of Judah prevailed, because they relied on the Lord *God of their fathers*
2Chr 14:4 He commanded Judah to seek the Lord *God of their fathers*, and to observe the law and the commandment
2Chr 15:12 Then they entered into a covenant to seek the Lord *God of their fathers* with all their heart and with all their soul
2Chr 19:4 and he went out again among the people from Beersheba to the mountains of Ephraim, and brought them back to the Lord *God of their fathers*
2Chr 20:33 Nevertheless the high places were not taken away, for as yet the people had not directed their hearts to the *God of their fathers*
2Chr 24:18 Therefore they left the house of the Lord *God of their fathers*, and served wooden images and idols
2Chr 24:24 but the Lord delivered a very great army into their hand, because they had forsaken the Lord *God of their fathers*
2Chr 28:6 For Pekah the son of Remaliah killed one hundred and twenty thousand in Judah in one day, all valiant men, because they had forsaken the Lord *God of their fathers*
2Chr 30:7 And do not be like your fathers and your brethren, who trespassed against the Lord *God of their fathers*, so that He gave them up to astonishment, as you see
2Chr 30:22 and they ate throughout the feast seven days, offering peace offerings and making confession to the Lord *God of their fathers*
2Chr 34:32 So the inhabitants of Jerusalem did according to the covenant of God, the *God of their fathers*
2Chr 34:33 All his days they did not depart from following the Lord *God of their fathers*
2Chr 36:15 And the Lord *God of their fathers* sent warnings to them by His messengers, rising up early and sending them, because He had compassion on His people and on His dwelling place

GOD OF TRUTH
Deut 32:4 for all His ways are justice, a *God of truth* and without injustice
Ps 31:5 Into Your hand I commit my spirit; You have redeemed me, O Lord *God of truth*
Is 65:16 So that he who blesses himself in the earth shall bless himself in the *God of truth;* and he who swears in the earth shall swear by the *God of truth*

GOD OF YOUR FATHER
Gen 26:24 And the Lord appeared to him the same night and said, "I am the *God of your father* Abraham
Gen 31:29 It is in my power to do you harm, but the *God of your father* spoke to me last night, saying
Gen 43:23 Your God and the *God of your father* has given you treasure in your sacks

Gen 46:3 And He said, "I am God, the *God of your father*
Gen 49:25 by the *God of your father* who will help you, and by the Almighty who will bless you with blessings of heaven above, blessings of the deep that lies beneath, blessings of the breasts and of the womb
Gen 50:17 Now, please, forgive the trespass of the servants of the *God of your father*
Ex 3:6 Moreover He said, "I am the *God of your father* the God of Abraham, the God of Isaac, and the God of Jacob
1Chr 28:9 As for you, my son Solomon, know the *God of your father*, and serve Him with a loyal heart and with a willing mind
2Chr 21:12 And a letter came to him from Elijah the prophet, saying, Thus says the Lord *God of your father* David

GOD OF YOUR FATHERS
Ex 3:13 Then Moses said to God, "Indeed, when I come to the children of Israel and say to them, 'The *God of your fathers* has sent me to you
Ex 3:15 The Lord *God of your fathers*, the God of Abraham, the God of Isaac, and the God of Jacob, has sent me to you
Ex 3:16 Go and gather the elders of Israel together, and say to them, 'The Lord *God of your fathers*, the God of Abraham, of Isaac, and of Jacob, appeared to me, saying
Deut 1:11 May the Lord *God of your fathers* make you a thousand times more numerous than you are, and bless you as He has promised you
Deut 1:21 go up and possess it, as the Lord *God of your fathers* has spoken to you
Deut 4:1 Now, O Israel, listen to the statutes and the judgments which I teach you to observe, that you may live, and go in and possess the land which the Lord *God of your fathers* is giving you
Deut 6:3 Therefore hear, O Israel, and be careful to observe it, that it may be well with you, and that you may multiply greatly as the Lord *God of your fathers* has promised you
Deut 12:1 These are the statutes and judgments which you shall be careful to observe in the land which the Lord *God of your fathers* is giving you to possess, all the days that you live on the earth
Deut 27:3 You shall write on them all the words of this law, when you have crossed over, that you may enter the land which the Lord your God is giving you, 'a land flowing with milk and honey,' just as the Lord *God of your fathers* has promised you
Josh 18:3 How long will you neglect to go and possess the land which the Lord *God of your fathers* has given you
2Chr 13:12 O children of Israel, do not fight against the Lord *God of your fathers*, for you shall not prosper
2Chr 28:9 Look, because the Lord *God of your fathers* was angry with Judah, He has delivered them into your hand
2Chr 29:5 Now sanctify yourselves, sanctify the house of the Lord *God of your fathers*, and carry out the rubbish from the holy place
Ezra 8:28 and the silver and the gold are a freewill offering to the Lord *God of your fathers*
Ezra 10:11 Now therefore, make confession to the Lord *God of your fathers*, and do His will
Acts 7:32 saying, 'I am the *God of your fathers* the God of Abraham, the God of Isaac, and the God of Jacob

GOD OPPOSES THE PROUD (NIV, RSV)
(See *GOD RESISTS THE PROUD*)

GOD OUR SAVIOR
1Tim 1:1 Paul, an apostle of Jesus Christ, by the commandment of *God our Savior* and the Lord Jesus Christ, our hope
1Tim 2:3 For this is good and acceptable in the sight of *God our Savior*
Tit 1:3 but has in due time manifested His word through preaching, which was committed to me according to the commandment of *God our Savior*
Tit 2:10 not pilfering, but showing all good fidelity, that they may adorn the doctrine of *God our Savior* in all things
Tit 3:4 But when the kindness and the love of *God our Savior* toward man appeared
Jude 25 to *God our Savior*, who alone is wise, be glory and majesty, dominion and power, both now and forever

GOD RESISTS THE PROUD
Jas 4:6 *God resists the proud*, but gives grace to the humble
1Pet 5:5 Yes, all of you be submissive to one another, and be clothed with humility, for "*God resists the proud*, but gives grace to the humble

GOD RESTS MY DELIVERANCE (RSV)
(See *GOD IS MY SALVATION*)

GOD REVEALED (NIV)
(See *GOD APPEARED TO*)

GOD SAVE THE KING (KJV)
(See *LONG LIVE THE KING*)

GOD SENT A SPIRIT OF ILL
Judg 9:23 *God sent a spirit of ill* will between Abimelech and the men of Shechem

GOD SENT FORTH HIS SON
Gal 4:4 But when the fullness of the time had come, *God sent forth His Son*, born of a woman, born under the law

GOD SENT ME
Gen 45:5 But now, do not therefore be grieved nor angry with yourselves because you sold me here; for *God sent me* before you to preserve life
Gen 45:7 And *God sent me* before you to preserve a posterity for you in the earth, and to save your lives by a great deliverance

GOD SHOWS NO PARTIALITY
Acts 10:34 Then Peter opened his mouth and said: "In truth I perceive that *God shows no partiality*

GOD SO LOVED THE WORLD
John 3:16 For *God so loved the world* that He gave His only begotten Son, that whoever believes in Him should not perish but have everlasting life

GOD SPOKE ALL THESE WORDS
Ex 20:1 And *God spoke all these words*, saying

GOD TESTS THE HEARTS
Ps 7:9 Oh, let the wickedness of the wicked come to an end, but establish the just; for the righteous *God tests the hearts* and minds

GOD THAT PERFORMETH ALL THINGS (KJV)
(See *GOD WHO PERFORMS ALL THINGS*)

GOD THE FATHER
John 6:27 Do not labor for the food which perishes, but for the food which endures to everlasting life, which the Son of Man will give you, because *God the Father* has set His seal on Him
1Cor 15:24 Then comes the end, when He delivers

the kingdom to *God the Father*, when He puts an end to all rule and all authority and power
Gal 1:1 Paul, an apostle (not from men nor through man, but through Jesus Christ and *God the Father* who raised Him from the dead
Gal 1:3 Grace to you and peace from *God the Father* and our Lord Jesus Christ
Eph 5:20 giving thanks always for all things to *God the Father* in the name of our Lord Jesus Christ
Eph 6:23 Peace to the brethren, and love with faith, from *God the Father* and the Lord Jesus Christ
Phil 2:11 and that every tongue should confess that Jesus Christ is Lord, to the glory of *God the Father*
Col 3:17 And whatever you do in word or deed, do all in the name of the Lord Jesus, giving thanks to *God the Father* through Him
1Th 1:1 Paul, Silvanus, and Timothy, to the church of the Thessalonians in *God the Father* and the Lord Jesus Christ
2Tim 1:2 Grace, mercy, and peace from *God the Father* and Christ Jesus our Lord
Tit 1:4 Grace, mercy, and peace from *God the Father* and the Lord Jesus Christ our Savior
1Pet 1:2 elect according to the foreknowledge of *God the Father*, in sanctification of the Spirit, for obedience and sprinkling of the blood of Jesus Christ
2Pet 1:17 For He received from *God the Father* honor and glory when such a voice came to Him from the Excellent Glory
2Jn 3 Grace, mercy, and peace will be with you from *God the Father* and from the Lord Jesus Christ, the Son of the Father, in truth and love
Jude 1 Jude, a servant of Jesus Christ, and brother of James, to those who are called, sanctified by *God the Father*, and preserved in Jesus Christ

GOD TRIETH THE HEARTS (KJV)
(See *GOD TESTS THE HEARTS*)

GOD WAITED PATIENTLY (NIV)
(See *LONGSUFFERING OF GOD*)

GOD WAS A TERROR (KJV)
(See *GOD IS A TERROR*)

GOD WAS IN CHRIST
2Cor 5:19 that is, that *God was in Christ* reconciling the world to Himself, not imputing their trespasses to them, and has committed to us the word of reconciliation

GOD WHO ARMS ME WITH STRENGTH (NIV)
(See *GOD IS MY STRENGTH*)

GOD WHO DOES WONDERS
Ps 77:14 You are the *God who does wonders;* You have declared Your strength among the peoples

GOD WHO FULFILLS HIS PURPOSE (NIV, RSV)
(See *GOD WHO PERFORMS ALL THINGS*)

GOD WHO JUDGES (NIV)
(See *GOD IS THE JUDGE*)

GOD WHO JUSTIFIES
Rom 8:33 Who shall bring a charge against God's elect? It is *God who justifies*

GOD WHO PERFORMS ALL THINGS
Ps 57:2 I will cry out to God Most High, to *God who performs all things* for me

GOD WHO PERFORMS MIRACLES (NIV)
(See *GOD WHO DOES WONDERS*)

GOD WHO SAVES (NIV)
(See *GOD OF SALVATION*)

GOD, WHO SEARCHES MINDS AND HEARTS (NIV)
(See *GOD TESTS THE HEARTS*)

GOD WHO WORKEST WONDERS (NAS, RSV)
(See *GOD WHO DOES WONDERS*)

GOD WILL CAST THEM AWAY
Hos 9:17 My *God will cast them away*, because they did not obey Him

GOD'S ANGER (NIV)
(See *WRATH OF GOD*)

GOD'S CHOSEN PEOPLE (NIV)
(See *ELECT OF GOD*)

GOD'S COMMAND (NIV)
(See *MOUTH OF GOD*)

GOD'S ELECT
Rom 8:33 Who shall bring a charge against *God's elect?* It is God who justifies
Tit 1:1 Paul, a servant of God and an apostle of Jesus Christ, according to the faith of *God's elect* and the acknowledgment of the truth which is according to godliness

GOD'S FELLOW WORKER (NAS, NIV)
(See *MINISTER OF GOD*)

GOD'S FLOCK (NIV)
(See *FLOCK OF GOD*)

GOD'S HOUSEHOLD (NAS, NIV)
(See *HOUSEHOLD OF GOD*)

GOD'S KINDNESS (NIV)
(See *KINDNESS OF GOD*)

GOD'S MERCY (NIV)
(See *MERCIES OF GOD*)

GOD'S MINISTERS
Rom 13:6 For because of this you also pay taxes, for they are *God's ministers* attending continually to this very thing

GOD'S MYSTERY (NAS, RSV)
(See *MYSTERY OF GOD*)

GOD'S NAME (NIV)
(See *NAME OF GOD*)

GOD'S OFFSPRING (NIV, RSV)
(See *OFFSPRING OF GOD*)

GOD'S PATIENCE (RSV)
(See *LONGSUFFERING OF GOD*)

GOD'S PURPOSE (NAS, NIV, RSV)
(See *PURPOSE OF GOD*)

GOD'S RIGHTEOUS DECREE (NIV)
(See *JUDGMENT OF GOD*)

GOD'S SERVANT (RSV)
(See *MINISTER OF GOD*)

GOD'S SERVANTS (NIV)
(See *GOD'S MINISTERS*)

GOD'S THRONE (NIV)
(See *THRONE OF GOD*)

GOD'S UNFAILING LOVE (NIV)
(See *MERCY OF GOD*)

GOD'S WILL (NIV)
(See *WILL OF GOD*)

GOD'S WONDERS (NIV)
(See *WORKS OF GOD*)

GODLY MAN (NIV)
(See *WORSHIPER OF GOD*)

GODLY SORROW
2Cor 7:10 For *godly sorrow* produces repentance to salvation, not to be regretted

GODS OF THE NATIONS
2Kin 18:33 Has any of the *gods of the nations* at all delivered its land from the hand of the king of Assyria
2Kin 19:12 Have the *gods of the nations* delivered those whom my fathers have destroyed, Gozan and Haran and Rezeph, and the people of Eden who were in Telassar
2Chr 32:13 Were the *gods of the nations* of those lands in any way able to deliver their lands out of my hand
2Chr 32:17 He also wrote letters to revile the Lord God of Israel, and to speak against Him, saying, "As the *gods of the nations* of other lands have not delivered their people from my hand, so the God of Hezekiah will not deliver His people from my hand
Is 36:18 Has any one of the *gods of the nations* delivered its land from the hand of the king of Assyria
Is 37:12 Have the *gods of the nations* delivered those whom my fathers have destroyed, Gozan and Haran and Rezeph, and the people of Eden who were in Telassar

GOG AND MAGOG
Rev 20:8 and will go out to deceive the nations which are in the four corners of the earth, *Gog and Magog*, to gather them together to battle, whose number is as the sand of the sea

GOING DOWN TO THE PIT
Job 33:24 then He is gracious to him, and says, 'Deliver him from *going down to the Pit*
Job 33:28 He will redeem his soul from *going down to the Pit*, and his life shall see the light

GOING TO AND FRO
Gen 8:7 Then he sent out a raven, which kept *going to and fro* until the waters had dried up from the earth
Job 1:7 So Satan answered the Lord and said, "From *going to and fro* on the earth, and from walking back and forth on it
Job 2:2 So Satan answered the Lord and said, "From *going to and fro* on the earth, and from walking back and forth on it

GOING UP TO JERUSALEM
Matt 20:17 Then Jesus, *going up to Jerusalem*, took the twelve disciples aside on the road and said to them
Matt 20:18 Behold, we are *going up to Jerusalem*, and the Son of Man will be betrayed to the chief priests and to the scribes
Mark 10:32 Now they were on the road, *going up to Jerusalem*, and Jesus was going before them
Mark 10:33 Behold, we are *going up to Jerusalem*, and the Son of Man will be delivered to the chief priests and to the scribes, and they will condemn Him to death and deliver Him to the Gentiles
Luke 18:31 Then He took the twelve aside and said to them, "Behold, we are *going up to Jerusalem*, and all things that are written by the prophets concerning the Son of Man will be accomplished
Luke 19:28 When He had said this, He went on ahead, *going up to Jerusalem*

GOINGS OF MY GOD (KJV)
(See *PROCESSION OF MY GOD*)

GOLD, FRANKINCENSE, AND MYRRH
Matt 2:11 And when they had opened their treasures, they presented gifts to Him: *gold, frankincense, and myrrh*

GOLD LAMPSTAND
Ex 31:8 the table and its utensils, the pure *gold lampstand* with all its utensils, the altar of incense
Lev 24:4 He shall be in charge of the lamps on the pure *gold lampstand* before the Lord continually

GOLD OF OPHIR
1Chr 29:4 three thousand talents of gold, of the *gold of Ophir*, and seven thousand talents of refined silver, to overlay the walls of the houses
Job 22:24 Then you will lay your gold in the dust, and the *gold of Ophir* among the stones of the brooks
Job 28:16 It cannot be valued in the *gold of Ophir*, in precious onyx or sapphire

GOLD RINGS (NAS, NIV)
(See *RINGS OF GOLD*)

GOLDEN CALVES
2Kin 10:29 However Jehu did not turn away from the sins of Jeroboam the son of Nebat, who had made Israel sin, that is, from the *golden calves* that were at Bethel and Dan

GOLDEN LAMPSTANDS
Rev 1:12 Then I turned to see the voice that spoke with me. And having turned I saw seven *golden lampstands*
Rev 1:20 The mystery of the seven stars which you saw in My right hand, and the seven *golden lampstands*
Rev 2:1 To the angel of the church of Ephesus write, 'These things says He who holds the seven stars in His right hand, who walks in the midst of the seven *golden lampstands*

GONE DOWN INTO THE PIT (KJV)
(See *GO DOWN TO THE PIT*)

GONE FROM ME (RSV)
(See *DEPART FROM ME*)

GONE INTO CAPTIVITY
Is 5:13 Therefore my people have *gone into captivity*, because they have no knowledge
Is 46:2 they could not deliver the burden, but have themselves *gone into captivity*
Jer 48:11 he has settled on his dregs, and has not been emptied from vessel to vessel, nor has he *gone into captivity*
Lam 1:3 Judah has *gone into captivity*, under affliction and hard servitude
Lam 1:5 for the Lord has afflicted her because of the multitude of her transgressions. Her children have *gone into captivity* before the enemy
Lam 1:18 my virgins and my young men have *gone into captivity*

GONE UP TO HEAVEN (NIV)
(See *ASCENDED INTO HEAVEN*)

GOOD AND FAITHFUL SERVANT

Matt 25:21 His lord said to him, 'Well done, *good and faithful servant*

Matt 25:23 His lord said to him, 'Well done, *good and faithful servant*

GOOD CONFESSION

1Tim 6:12 Fight the good fight of faith, lay hold on eternal life, to which you were also called and have confessed the *good confession* in the presence of many witnesses

1Tim 6:13 I urge you in the sight of God who gives life to all things, and before Christ Jesus who witnessed the *good confession* before Pontius Pilate

GOOD CONSCIENCE

Acts 23:1 Then Paul, looking earnestly at the council, said, "Men and brethren, I have lived in all *good conscience* before God until this day

1Tim 1:5 Now the purpose of the commandment is love from a pure heart, from a *good conscience*, and from sincere faith

1Tim 1:19 having faith and a *good conscience*, which some having rejected, concerning the faith have suffered shipwreck

Heb 13:18 for we are confident that we have a *good conscience*, in all things desiring to live honorably

1Pet 3:16 having a *good conscience*, that when they defame you as evildoers, those who revile your good conduct in Christ may be ashamed

1Pet 3:21 There is also an antitype which now saves us, namely baptism (not the removal of the filth of the flesh, but the answer of a *good conscience* toward God

GOOD COURAGE

Num 13:20 Be of *good courage*. And bring some of the fruit of the land

Deut 31:6 Be strong and of *good courage*, do not fear nor be afraid of them

Deut 31:7 Then Moses called Joshua and said to him in the sight of all Israel, "Be strong and of *good courage*, for you must go with this people to the land which the Lord has sworn to their fathers to give them, and you shall cause them to inherit it

Deut 31:23 Then He inaugurated Joshua the son of Nun, and said, "Be strong and of *good courage*

Josh 1:6 Be strong and of *good courage*, for to this people you shall divide as an inheritance the land which I swore to their fathers to give them

Josh 1:9 Be strong and of *good courage;* do not be afraid, nor be dismayed, for the Lord your God is with you wherever you go

Josh 1:18 Whoever rebels against your command and does not heed your words, in all that you command him, shall be put to death. Only be strong and of *good courage*

Josh 10:25 be strong and of *good courage*, for thus the Lord will do to all your enemies against whom you fight

2Sam 10:12 Be of *good courage*, and let us be strong for our people and for the cities of our God

1Chr 19:13 Be of *good courage*, and let us be strong for our people and for the cities of our God

1Chr 22:13 Be strong and of *good courage;* do not fear nor be dismayed

1Chr 28:20 And David said to his son Solomon, "Be strong and of *good courage*, and do it

Ezra 10:4 We also will be with you. Be of *good courage*, and do it

Ps 27:14 Be of *good courage*, and He shall strengthen your heart

Ps 31:24 Be of *good courage*, and He shall strengthen your heart, all you who hope in the Lord

Is 41:6 Everyone helped his neighbor, and said to his brother, "Be of *good courage*

GOOD DEEDS

Neh 6:19 Also they reported his *good deeds* before me, and reported my words to him

Neh 13:14 Remember me, O my God, concerning this, and do not wipe out my *good deeds* that I have done for the house of my God, and for its services

GOOD IN THE SIGHT OF THE LORD

Deut 6:18 And you shall do what is right and *good in the sight of the Lord*, that it may be well with you, and that you may go in and possess the good land of which the Lord swore to your fathers

Mal 2:17 In that you say, "Everyone who does evil is *good in the sight of the Lord*, and He delights in them

GOOD JUDGMENT AND KNOWLEDGE

Ps 119:66 Teach me *good judgment and knowledge*, for I believe Your commandments

GOOD MAN

2Sam 18:27 And the king said, "He is a *good man*, and comes with good news

Ps 37:23 The steps of a *good man* are ordered by the Lord, and He delights in his way

Ps 112:5 A *good man* deals graciously and lends; he will guide his affairs with discretion

Prov 12:2 A *good man* obtains favor from the Lord, but a man of wicked devices He will condemn

Prov 13:22 A *good man* leaves an inheritance to his children's children, but the wealth of the sinner is stored up for the righteous

Prov 14:14 The backslider in heart will be filled with his own ways, but a *good man* will be satisfied from above

Matt 12:35 A *good man* out of the good treasure of his heart brings forth good things, and an evil man out of the evil treasure brings forth evil things

Luke 6:45 A *good man* out of the good treasure of his heart brings forth good

Acts 11:24 For he was a *good man*, full of the Holy Spirit and of faith

Rom 5:7 yet perhaps for a *good man* someone would even dare to die

GOOD NEWS

2Sam 4:10 when someone told me, saying, 'Look, Saul is dead,' thinking to have brought *good news*, I arrested him and had him executed in Ziklag the one who thought I would give him a reward for his news

2Sam 18:27 And the king said, "He is a good man, and comes with *good news*

2Sam 18:31 Just then the Cushite came, and the Cushite said, "There is *good news*, my lord the king

2Kin 7:9 This day is a day of *good news*, and we remain silent

1Chr 16:23 proclaim the *good news* of His salvation from day to day

Ps 40:9 I have proclaimed the *good news* of righteousness in the great congregation

Ps 96:2 Proclaim the *good news* of His salvation from day to day

Prov 25:25 As cold water to a weary soul, so is *good news* from a far country

Is 52:7 How beautiful upon the mountains are the feet of him who brings *good news*, who proclaims peace, who brings glad tidings of good things, who proclaims salvation, who says to Zion

1Th 3:6 But now that Timothy has come to us from you, and brought us *good news* of your faith and love, and that you always have good remembrance of us, greatly desiring to see us, as we also to see you

GOOD NEWS OF GREAT JOY (NIV)
(See *GOOD TIDINGS OF GREAT JOY*)

GOOD NEWS OF THE KINGDOM OF GOD (NIV, RSV)
(See *GLAD TIDINGS OF THE KINGDOM OF GOD*)

GOOD OLD AGE
Gen 15:15 Now as for you, you shall go to your fathers in peace; you shall be buried at a *good old age*
Gen 25:8 Then Abraham breathed his last and died in a *good old age*, an old man and full of years, and was gathered to his people
Judg 8:32 Now Gideon the son of Joash died at a *good old age*, and was buried in the tomb of Joash his father, in Ophrah of the Abiezrites
1Chr 29:28 So he died in a *good old age*, full of days and riches and honor

GOOD PLEASURE (NIV)
(See *SEEMED GOOD IN YOUR SIGHT*)

GOOD PROFESSION (KJV)
(See *GOOD CONFESSION*)

GOOD SHEPHERD
John 10:11 I am the *good shepherd*. The *good shepherd* gives His life for the sheep
John 10:14 I am the *good shepherd;* and I know My sheep, and am known by My own

GOOD TEACHER
Matt 19:16 Now behold, one came and said to Him, "*Good Teacher*, what good thing shall I do that I may have eternal life
Mark 10:17 Now as He was going out on the road, one came running, knelt before Him, and asked Him, "*Good Teacher*, what shall I do that I may inherit eternal life
Luke 18:18 Now a certain ruler asked Him, saying, "*Good Teacher*, what shall I do to inherit eternal life

GOOD TIDINGS (KJV)
(See *GOOD NEWS*)

GOOD TIDINGS OF GREAT JOY
Luke 2:10 Then the angel said to them, "Do not be afraid, for behold, I bring you *good tidings of great joy* which will be to all people

GOOD TREE
2Kin 3:19 Also you shall attack every fortified city and every choice city, and shall cut down every *good tree*, and stop up every spring of water, and ruin every good piece of land with stones
Matt 7:17 Even so, every *good tree* bears good fruit, but a bad tree bears bad fruit
Matt 7:18 A *good tree* cannot bear bad fruit, nor can a bad tree bear good fruit
Luke 6:43 For a *good tree* does not bear bad fruit, nor does a bad tree bear good fruit

GOOD WILL TOWARD MEN
Luke 2:14 Glory to God in the highest, and on earth peace, *good will toward men*

GOOD WORKS
Matt 5:16 Let your light so shine before men, that they may see your *good works* and glorify your Father in heaven
John 10:32 Jesus answered them, "Many *good works* I have shown you from My Father
Acts 9:36 This woman was full of *good works* and charitable deeds which she did
Rom 13:3 For rulers are not a terror to *good works*, but to evil
Eph 2:10 For we are His workmanship, created in Christ Jesus for *good works*, which God prepared beforehand that we should walk in them
1Tim 2:10 but, which is proper for women professing godliness, with *good works*
1Tim 5:10 well reported for *good works:* if she has brought up children, if she has lodged strangers, if she has washed the saints' feet, if she has relieved the afflicted, if she has diligently followed every good work
1Tim 5:25 Likewise, the *good works* of some are clearly evident, and those that are otherwise cannot be hidden
1Tim 6:18 Let them do good, that they be rich in *good works*, ready to give, willing to share
Tit 2:7 in all things showing yourself to be a pattern of *good works*
Tit 2:14 who gave Himself for us, that He might redeem us from every lawless deed and purify for Himself His own special people, zealous for *good works*
Tit 3:8 This is a faithful saying, and these things I want you to affirm constantly, that those who have believed in God should be careful to maintain *good works*
Tit 3:14 And let our people also learn to maintain *good works*, to meet urgent needs, that they may not be unfruitful
Heb 10:24 And let us consider one another in order to stir up love and *good works*
1Pet 2:12 having your conduct honorable among the Gentiles, that when they speak against you as evildoers, they may, by your *good works* which they observe, glorify God in the day of visitation

GOODNESS AND LOVE (NIV)
(See *GOODNESS AND MERCY*)

GOODNESS AND MERCY
Ps 23:6 Surely *goodness and mercy* shall follow me all the days of my life

GOODNESS OF GOD
Ps 52:1 Why do you boast in evil, O mighty man? The *goodness of God* endures continually
Rom 2:4 Or do you despise the riches of His goodness, forbearance, and longsuffering, not knowing that the *goodness of God* leads you to repentance

GOSPEL OF CHRIST
Rom 1:16 For I am not ashamed of the *gospel of Christ*, for it is the power of God to salvation for everyone who believes, for the Jew first and also for the Greek
Rom 15:19 in mighty signs and wonders, by the power of the Spirit of God, so that from Jerusalem and round about to Illyricum I have fully preached the *gospel of Christ*
Rom 15:29 But I know that when I come to you, I shall come in the fullness of the blessing of the *gospel of Christ*
1Cor 9:12 Nevertheless we have not used this right, but endure all things lest we hinder the *gospel of Christ*
1Cor 9:18 That when I preach the gospel, I may present the *gospel of Christ* without charge, that I may not abuse my authority in the gospel
2Cor 9:13 while, through the proof of this ministry, they glorify God for the obedience of your confession to the *gospel of Christ*, and for your liberal sharing with them and all men

2Cor 10:14 for it was to you that we came with the *gospel of Christ*
Gal 1:7 but there are some who trouble you and want to pervert the *gospel of Christ*
Phil 1:27 Only let your conduct be worthy of the *gospel of Christ*, so that whether I come and see you or am absent, I may hear of your affairs, that you stand fast in one spirit, with one mind striving together for the faith of the gospel
1Th 3:2 and sent Timothy, our brother and minister of God, and our fellow laborer in the *gospel of Christ*, to establish you and encourage you concerning your faith

GOSPEL OF GOD
Rom 1:1 Paul, a servant of Jesus Christ, called to be an apostle, separated to the *gospel of God*
Rom 15:16 that I might be a minister of Jesus Christ to the Gentiles, ministering the *gospel of God*, that the offering of the Gentiles might be acceptable, sanctified by the Holy Spirit
2Cor 11:7 Did I commit sin in abasing myself that you might be exalted, because I preached the *gospel of God* to you free of charge
1Th 2:2 But even after we had suffered before and were spitefully treated at Philippi, as you know, we were bold in our God to speak to you the *gospel of God* in much conflict
1Th 2:8 So, affectionately longing for you, we were well pleased to impart to you not only the *gospel of God*, but also our own lives, because you had become dear to us
1Th 2:9 for laboring night and day, that we might not be a burden to any of you, we preached to you the *gospel of God*
1Pet 4:17 and if it begins with us first, what will be the end of those who do not obey the *gospel of God*

GOSPEL OTHER THAN THE ONE (NIV)
(See *ANY OTHER GOSPEL*)

GOVERN MY PEOPLE (RSV)
(See *SHEPHERD MY PEOPLE*)

GOVERN THE KINGDOM (KJV)
(See *EXERCISE AUTHORITY*)

GOVERNMENT WILL BE UPON HIS SHOULDER
Is 9:6 and the *government will be upon His shoulder*. And His name will be called Wonderful, Counselor, Mighty God, Everlasting Father, Prince of Peace

GOVERNOR AMONG THE NATIONS (KJV)
(See *RULES OVER THE NATIONS*)

GRACE AND PEACE
2Pet 1:2 *Grace and peace* be multiplied to you in the knowledge of God and of Jesus our Lord

GRACE AND TRUTH
John 1:14 And the Word became flesh and dwelt among us, and we beheld His glory, the glory as of the only begotten of the Father, full of *grace and truth*
John 1:17 For the law was given through Moses, but *grace and truth* came through Jesus Christ

GRACE BE WITH YOU
Col 4:18 This salutation by my own hand Paul. Remember my chains. *Grace be with you*. Amen
1Tim 6:21 by professing it, some have strayed concerning the faith. *Grace be with you*. Amen
2Tim 4:22 The Lord Jesus Christ be with your spirit. *Grace be with you*. Amen
Tit 3:15 Greet those who love us in the faith. *Grace be with you* all. Amen
Heb 13:25 *Grace be with you* all. Amen

GRACE MAY ABOUND
Rom 6:1 What shall we say then? Shall we continue in sin that *grace may abound*

GRACE, MERCY, AND PEACE
1Tim 1:2 *Grace, mercy, and peace* from God our Father and Jesus Christ our Lord
2Tim 1:2 *Grace, mercy, and peace* from God the Father and Christ Jesus our Lord
Tit 1:4 *Grace, mercy, and peace* from God the Father and the Lord Jesus Christ our Savior
2Jn 3 *Grace, mercy, and peace* will be with you from God the Father and from the Lord Jesus Christ, the Son of the Father, in truth and love

GRACE OF GOD
Luke 2:40 And the Child grew and became strong in spirit, filled with wisdom; and the *grace of God* was upon Him
Acts 11:23 When he came and had seen the *grace of God*, he was glad, and encouraged them all that with purpose of heart they should continue with the Lord
Acts 13:43 Now when the congregation had broken up, many of the Jews and devout proselytes followed Paul and Barnabas, who, speaking to them, persuaded them to continue in the *grace of God*
Acts 14:26 From there they sailed to Antioch, where they had been commended to the *grace of God* for the work which they had completed
Acts 15:40 but Paul chose Silas and departed, being commended by the brethren to the *grace of God*
Acts 20:24 nor do I count my life dear to myself, so that I may finish my race with joy, and the ministry which I received from the Lord Jesus, to testify to the gospel of the *grace of God*
Rom 5:15 For if by the one man's offense many died, much more the *grace of God* and the gift by the grace of the one Man, Jesus Christ, abounded to many
1Cor 1:4 I thank my God always concerning you for the *grace of God* which was given to you by Christ Jesus
1Cor 3:10 According to the *grace of God* which was given to me, as a wise master builder I have laid the foundation, and another builds on it
1Cor 15:10 But by the *grace of God* I am what I am, and His grace toward me was not in vain; but I labored more abundantly than they all, yet not I, but the *grace of God* which was with me
2Cor 1:12 the testimony of our conscience that we conducted ourselves in the world in simplicity and godly sincerity, not with fleshly wisdom but by the *grace of God*, and more abundantly toward you
2Cor 6:1 We then, as workers together with Him also plead with you not to receive the *grace of God* in vain
2Cor 8:1 Moreover, brethren, we make known to you the *grace of God* bestowed on the churches of Macedonia
2Cor 9:14 and by their prayer for you, who long for you because of the exceeding *grace of God* in you
Gal 2:21 I do not set aside the *grace of God;* for if righteousness comes through the law, then Christ died in vain
Eph 3:2 if indeed you have heard of the dispensation of the *grace of God* which was given to me for you
Eph 3:7 of which I became a minister according to the gift of the *grace of God* given to me by the effective working of His power
Col 1:6 which has come to you, as it has also in all

the world, and is bringing forth fruit, as it is also among you since the day you heard and knew the *grace of God* in truth
Tit 2:11 For the *grace of God* that brings salvation has appeared to all men
Heb 2:9 But we see Jesus, who was made a little lower than the angels, for the suffering of death crowned with glory and honor, that He, by the *grace of God*, might taste death for everyone
Heb 12:15 looking diligently lest anyone fall short of the *grace of God*
1Pet 4:10 As each one has received a gift, minister it to one another, as good stewards of the manifold *grace of God*
1Pet 5:12 By Silvanus, our faithful brother as I consider him, I have written to you briefly, exhorting and testifying that this is the true *grace of God* in which you stand

GRACE OF OUR LORD
Rom 16:20 The *grace of our Lord* Jesus Christ be with you
Rom 16:24 The *grace of our Lord* Jesus Christ be with you all
1Cor 16:23 The *grace of our Lord* Jesus Christ be with you
2Cor 8:9 For you know the *grace of our Lord* Jesus Christ, that though He was rich, yet for your sakes He became poor, that you through His poverty might become rich
Gal 6:18 Brethren, the *grace of our Lord* Jesus Christ be with your spirit
Phil 4:23 The *grace of our Lord* Jesus Christ be with you all
1Th 5:28 The *grace of our Lord* Jesus Christ be with you
2Th 3:18 The *grace of our Lord* Jesus Christ be with you all
1Tim 1:14 And the *grace of our Lord* was exceedingly abundant, with faith and love which are in Christ Jesus
Phm 25 The *grace of our Lord* Jesus Christ be with your spirit
Rev 22:21 The *grace of our Lord* Jesus Christ be with you all

GRACE OF THE LORD
Acts 15:11 But we believe that through the *grace of the Lord* Jesus Christ we shall be saved in the same manner as they
2Cor 13:14 The *grace of the Lord* Jesus Christ, and the love of God, and the communion of the Holy Spirit be with you all

GRACIOUS AND COMPASSIONATE (NAS, NIV)
(See *GRACIOUS AND MERCIFUL*)

GRACIOUS AND MERCIFUL
2Chr 30:9 for the Lord your God is *gracious and merciful*, and will not turn His face from you if you return to Him
Neh 9:17 But You are God, ready to pardon, *gracious and merciful*, slow to anger, abundant in kindness, and did not forsake them
Neh 9:31 Nevertheless in Your great mercy You did not utterly consume them nor forsake them; for You are God, *gracious and merciful*
Joel 2:13 return to the Lord your God, for He is *gracious and merciful*, slow to anger, and of great kindness
Jon 4:2 for I know that You are a *gracious and merciful* God, slow to anger and abundant in lovingkindness, One who relents from doing harm

GRAIN OFFERING
Ex 29:41 and you shall offer with it the *grain offering* and the drink offering, as in the morning, for a sweet aroma, an offering made by fire to the Lord
Ex 30:9 You shall not offer strange incense on it, or a burnt offering, or a *grain offering*
Ex 40:29 And he put the altar of burnt offering before the door of the tabernacle of the tent of meeting, and offered upon it the burnt offering and the *grain offering*, as the Lord had commanded Moses
Lev 2:1 When anyone offers a *grain offering* to the Lord, his offering shall be of fine flour
Lev 2:3 The rest of the *grain offering* shall be Aaron's and his sons'
Lev 2:4 And if you bring as an offering a *grain offering* baked in the oven, it shall be unleavened cakes of fine flour mixed with oil, or unleavened wafers anointed with oil
Lev 2:5 But if your offering is a *grain offering* baked in a pan, it shall be of fine flour, unleavened, mixed with oil
Lev 2:6 You shall break it in pieces and pour oil on it; it is a *grain offering*
Lev 2:7 And if your offering is a *grain offering* baked in a covered pan, it shall be made of fine flour with oil
Lev 2:8 You shall bring the *grain offering* that is made of these things to the Lord
Lev 2:9 Then the priest shall take from the *grain offering* a memorial portion, and burn it on the altar
Lev 2:10 And what is left of the *grain offering* shall be Aaron's and his sons'
Lev 2:11 No *grain offering* which you bring to the Lord shall be made with leaven, for you shall burn no leaven nor any honey in any offering to the Lord made by fire
Lev 2:13 And every offering of your *grain offering* you shall season with salt; you shall not allow the salt of the covenant of your God to be lacking from your *grain offering*
Lev 2:14 If you offer a *grain offering* of your firstfruits to the Lord, you shall offer for the *grain offering* of your firstfruits green heads of grain roasted on the fire, grain beaten from full heads
Lev 2:15 And you shall put oil on it, and lay frankincense on it. It is a *grain offering*
Lev 5:13 The rest shall be the priest's as a *grain offering*
Lev 6:14 This is the law of the *grain offering:* The sons of Aaron shall offer it on the altar before the Lord
Lev 6:15 He shall take from it his handful of the fine flour of the *grain offering*, with its oil, and all the frankincense which is on the *grain offering*, and shall burn it on the altar for a sweet aroma, as a memorial to the Lord
Lev 6:20 one-tenth of an ephah of fine flour as a daily *grain offering*, half of it in the morning and half of it at night
Lev 6:21 And the baked pieces of the *grain offering* you shall offer for a sweet aroma to the Lord
Lev 6:23 For every *grain offering* for the priest shall be wholly burned
Lev 7:9 Also every *grain offering* that is baked in the oven and all that is prepared in the covered pan, or in a pan, shall be the priest's who offers it
Lev 7:10 Every *grain offering* mixed with oil, or dry, shall belong to all the sons of Aaron, to one as much as the other
Lev 7:37 This is the law of the burnt offering, the *grain offering*, the sin offering, the trespass offering, the consecrations, and the sacrifice of the peace offering
Lev 9:4 also a bull and a ram as peace offerings, to sacrifice before the Lord, and a *grain offering* mixed with oil
Lev 9:17 Then he brought the *grain offering*, took

a handful of it, and burned it on the altar, besides the burnt sacrifice of the morning

Lev 10:12 Take the *grain offering* that remains of the offerings made by fire to the Lord, and eat it without leaven beside the altar

Lev 14:10 And on the eighth day he shall take two male lambs without blemish, one ewe lamb of the first year without blemish, three-tenths of an ephah of fine flour mixed with oil as a *grain offering*, and one log of oil

Lev 14:20 And the priest shall offer the burnt offering and the *grain offering* on the altar

Lev 14:21 But if he is poor and cannot afford it, then he shall take one male lamb as a trespass offering to be waved, to make atonement for him, one-tenth of an ephah of fine flour mixed with oil as a *grain offering*, a log of oil

Lev 14:31 such as he is able to afford, the one as a sin offering and the other as a burnt offering, with the *grain offering*

Lev 23:13 Its *grain offering* shall be two-tenths of an ephah of fine flour mixed with oil, an offering made by fire to the Lord, for a sweet aroma

Lev 23:16 then you shall offer a new *grain offering* to the Lord

Lev 23:18 They shall be as a burnt offering to the Lord, with their *grain offering* and their drink offerings, an offering made by fire for a sweet aroma to the Lord

Lev 23:37 These are the feasts of the Lord which you shall proclaim to be holy convocations, to offer an offering made by fire to the Lord, a burnt offering and a *grain offering*, a sacrifice and drink offerings, everything on its day

Num 4:16 The appointed duty of Eleazar the son of Aaron the priest is the oil for the light, the sweet incense, the daily *grain offering*, the anointing oil, the oversight of all the tabernacle, of all that is in it, with the sanctuary and its furnishings

Num 5:15 he shall pour no oil on it and put no frankincense on it, because it is a *grain offering* of jealousy, an offering for remembering, for bringing iniquity to remembrance

Num 5:18 Then the priest shall stand the woman before the Lord, uncover the woman's head, and put the offering for remembering in her hands, which is the *grain offering* of jealousy

Num 5:25 Then the priest shall take the *grain offering* of jealousy from the woman's hand, shall wave the offering before the Lord, and bring it to the altar

Num 6:15 a basket of unleavened bread, cakes of fine flour mixed with oil, unleavened wafers anointed with oil, and their *grain offering* with their drink offerings

Num 6:17 the priest shall also offer its *grain offering* and its drink offering

Num 7:13 His offering was one silver platter, the weight of which was one hundred and thirty shekels, and one silver bowl of seventy shekels, according to the shekel of the sanctuary, both of them full of fine flour mixed with oil as a *grain offering*

Num 7:19 For his offering he offered one silver platter, the weight of which was one hundred and thirty shekels, and one silver bowl of seventy shekels, according to the shekel of the sanctuary, both of them full of fine flour mixed with oil as a *grain offering*

Num 7:25 His offering was one silver platter, the weight of which was one hundred and thirty shekels, and one silver bowl of seventy shekels, according to the shekel of the sanctuary, both of them full of fine flour mixed with oil as a *grain offering*

Num 7:31 His offering was one silver platter, the weight of which was one hundred and thirty shekels, and one silver bowl of seventy shekels, according to the shekel of the sanctuary, both of them full of fine flour mixed with oil as a *grain offering*

Num 7:37 His offering was one silver platter, the weight of which was one hundred and thirty shekels, and one silver bowl of seventy shekels, according to the shekel of the sanctuary, both of them full of fine flour mixed with oil as a *grain offering*

Num 7:43 His offering was one silver platter, the weight of which was one hundred and thirty shekels, and one silver bowl of seventy shekels, according to the shekel of the sanctuary, both of them full of fine flour mixed with oil as a *grain offering*

Num 7:49 His offering was one silver platter, the weight of which was one hundred and thirty shekels, and one silver bowl of seventy shekels, according to the shekel of the sanctuary, both of them full of fine flour mixed with oil as a *grain offering*

Num 7:55 His offering was one silver platter, the weight of which was one hundred and thirty shekels, and one silver bowl of seventy shekels, according to the shekel of the sanctuary, both of them full of fine flour mixed with oil as a *grain offering*

Num 7:61 His offering was one silver platter, the weight of which was one hundred and thirty shekels, and one silver bowl of seventy shekels, according to the shekel of the sanctuary, both of them full of fine flour mixed with oil as a *grain offering*

Num 7:67 His offering was one silver platter, the weight of which was one hundred and thirty shekels, and one silver bowl of seventy shekels, according to the shekel of the sanctuary, both of them full of fine flour mixed with oil as a *grain offering*

Num 7:73 His offering was one silver platter, the weight of which was one hundred and thirty shekels, and one silver bowl of seventy shekels, according to the shekel of the sanctuary, both of them full of fine flour mixed with oil as a *grain offering*

Num 7:79 His offering was one silver platter, the weight of which was one hundred and thirty shekels, and one silver bowl of seventy shekels, according to the shekel of the sanctuary, both of them full of fine flour mixed with oil as a *grain offering*

Num 7:87 All the oxen for the burnt offering were twelve young bulls, the rams twelve, the male lambs in their first year twelve, with their *grain offering*, and the kids of the goats as a sin offering twelve

Num 8:8 Then let them take a young bull with its *grain offering* of fine flour mixed with oil, and you shall take another young bull as a sin offering

Num 15:4 then he who presents his offering to the Lord shall bring a *grain offering* of one-tenth of an ephah of fine flour mixed with one-fourth of a hin of oil

Num 15:6 Or for a ram you shall prepare as a *grain offering* two-tenths of an ephah of fine flour mixed with one-third of a hin of oil

Num 15:9 then shall be offered with the young bull a *grain offering* of three-tenths of an ephah of fine flour mixed with half a hin of oil

Num 15:24 then it will be, if it is unintentionally committed, without the knowledge of the congregation, that the whole congregation shall offer one young bull as a burnt offering, as a sweet aroma to the Lord, with its *grain offering* and its drink offering, according to the ordinance, and one kid of the goats as a sin offering

Num 18:9 every offering of theirs, every *grain offering* and every sin offering and every trespass offering which they render to Me, shall be most holy for you and your sons
Num 28:5 and one-tenth of an ephah of fine flour as a *grain offering* mixed with one-fourth of a hin of pressed oil
Num 28:8 as the morning *grain offering* and its drink offering, you shall offer it as an offering made by fire, a sweet aroma to the Lord
Num 28:9 And on the Sabbath day two lambs in their first year, without blemish, and two-tenths of an ephah of fine flour as a *grain offering*, mixed with oil, with its drink offering
Num 28:12 three-tenths of an ephah of fine flour as a *grain offering*, mixed with oil, for each bull; two-tenths of an ephah of fine flour as a *grain offering*, mixed with oil, for the one ram
Num 28:13 and one-tenth of an ephah of fine flour, mixed with oil, as a *grain offering* for each lamb, as a burnt offering of sweet aroma, an offering made by fire to the Lord
Num 28:20 Their *grain offering* shall be of fine flour mixed with oil
Num 28:26 Also on the day of the firstfruits, when you bring a new *grain offering* to the Lord at your Feast of Weeks, you shall have a holy convocation
Num 28:28 with their *grain offering* of fine flour mixed with oil
Num 28:31 You shall present them with their drink offerings, besides the regular burnt offering with its *grain offering*
Num 29:3 Their *grain offering* shall be fine flour mixed with oil
Num 29:6 besides the burnt offering with its *grain offering* for the New Moon, the regular burnt offering with its *grain offering*, and their drink offerings, according to their ordinance, as a sweet aroma, an offering made by fire to the Lord
Num 29:9 Their *grain offering* shall be of fine flour mixed with oil
Num 29:11 also one kid of the goats as a sin offering, besides the sin offering for atonement, the regular burnt offering with its *grain offering*, and their drink offerings
Num 29:14 Their *grain offering* shall be of fine flour mixed with oil
Num 29:16 also one kid of the goats as a sin offering, besides the regular burnt offering, its *grain offering*, and its drink offering
Num 29:18 and their *grain offering* and their drink offerings for the bulls, for the rams, and for the lambs, by their number, according to the ordinance
Num 29:19 also one kid of the goats as a sin offering, besides the regular burnt offering with its *grain offering*, and their drink offerings
Num 29:21 and their *grain offering* and their drink offerings for the bulls, for the rams, and for the lambs, by their number, according to the ordinance
Num 29:22 also one goat as a sin offering, besides the regular burnt offering, its *grain offering*, and its drink offering
Num 29:24 and their *grain offering* and their drink offerings for the bulls, for the rams, and for the lambs, by their number, according to the ordinance
Num 29:25 also one kid of the goats as a sin offering, besides the regular burnt offering, its *grain offering*, and its drink offering
Num 29:27 and their *grain offering* and their drink offerings for the bulls, for the rams, and for the lambs, by their number, according to the ordinance
Num 29:28 also one goat as a sin offering, besides the regular burnt offering, its *grain offering*, and its drink offering
Num 29:30 and their *grain offering* and their drink offerings for the bulls, for the rams, and for the lambs, by their number, according to the ordinance
Num 29:31 also one goat as a sin offering, besides the regular burnt offering, its *grain offering*, and its drink offering
Num 29:33 and their *grain offering* and their drink offerings for the bulls, for the rams, and for the lambs, by their number, according to the ordinance
Num 29:34 also one goat as a sin offering, besides the regular burnt offering, its *grain offering*, and its drink offering
Num 29:37 and their *grain offering* and their drink offerings for the bull, for the ram, and for the lambs, by their number, according to the ordinance
Num 29:38 also one goat as a sin offering, besides the regular burnt offering, its *grain offering*, and its drink offering
Judg 13:19 So Manoah took the young goat with the *grain offering*, and offered it upon the rock to the Lord
Judg 13:23 Then his wife said to him, "If the Lord had desired to kill us, He would not have accepted a burnt offering and a *grain offering* from our hands, nor would He have shown us all these things, nor would He have told us such things as these at this time
2Kin 3:20 Now it happened in the morning, when the *grain offering* was offered, that suddenly water came by way of Edom, and the land was filled with water
2Kin 16:13 So he burned his burnt offering and his *grain offering*
2Kin 16:15 Then King Ahaz commanded Urijah the priest, saying, "On the great new altar burn the morning burnt offering, the evening *grain offering*, the king's burnt sacrifice, and his *grain offering*, with the burnt offering of all the people of the land, their *grain offering*, and their drink offerings
1Chr 21:23 Look, I also give you the oxen for burnt offerings, the threshing implements for wood, and the wheat for the *grain offering*
1Chr 23:29 both with the showbread and the fine flour for the *grain offering*, with the unleavened cakes and what is baked in the pan, with what is mixed and with all kinds of measures and sizes
Neh 10:33 for the showbread, for the regular *grain offering*, for the regular burnt offering of the Sabbaths, the New Moons, and the set feasts
Neh 13:9 and I brought back into them the articles of the house of God, with the *grain offering* and the frankincense
Is 57:6 Even to them you have poured a drink offering, you have offered a *grain offering*
Is 66:3 he who offers a *grain offering*, as if he offers swine's blood
Jer 14:12 and when they offer burnt offering and *grain offering*, I will not accept them
Ezek 42:13 There they shall lay the most holy offerings the *grain offering*, the sin offering, and the trespass offering for the place is holy
Ezek 44:29 They shall eat the *grain offering*, the sin offering, and the trespass offering
Ezek 45:17 He shall prepare the sin offering, the *grain offering*, the burnt offering, and the peace offerings to make atonement for the house of Israel
Ezek 45:24 And he shall prepare a *grain offering* of one ephah for each bull and one ephah for each ram, together with a hin of oil for each ephah
Ezek 45:25 In the seventh month, on the fifteenth

day of the month, at the feast, he shall do likewise for seven days, according to the sin offering, the burnt offering, the *grain offering*, and the oil

Ezek 46:5 and the *grain offering* shall be one ephah for a ram, and the *grain offering* for the lambs, as much as he wants to give, as well as a hin of oil with every ephah

Ezek 46:7 He shall prepare a *grain offering* of an ephah for a bull, an ephah for a ram, as much as he wants to give for the lambs, and a hin of oil with every ephah

Ezek 46:11 At the festivals and the appointed feast days the *grain offering* shall be an ephah for a bull, an ephah for a ram, as much as he wants to give for the lambs, and a hin of oil with every ephah

Ezek 46:14 And you shall prepare a *grain offering* with it every morning, a sixth of an ephah, and a third of a hin of oil to moisten the fine flour. This *grain offering* is a perpetual ordinance, to be made regularly to the Lord

Ezek 46:15 Thus they shall prepare the lamb, the *grain offering*, and the oil, as a regular burnt offering every morning

Ezek 46:20 And he said to me, "This is the place where the priests shall boil the trespass offering and the sin offering, and where they shall bake the *grain offering*, so that they do not bring them out into the outer court to sanctify the people

Joel 1:9 The *grain offering* and the drink offering have been cut off from the house of the Lord

Joel 1:13 for the *grain offering* and the drink offering are withheld from the house of your God

Joel 2:14 Who knows if He will turn and relent, and leave a blessing behind Him a *grain offering* and a drink offering for the Lord your God

GRANT ME THIS ONE REQUEST (NIV)
(See *LET THIS THING BE DONE FOR ME*)

GRANTED HIS PLEA

Gen 25:21 and the Lord *granted his plea*, and Rebekah his wife conceived

GRASPING FOR THE WIND

Eccl 1:14 and indeed, all is vanity and *grasping for the wind*

Eccl 1:17 I perceived that this also is *grasping for the wind*

Eccl 2:11 and indeed all was vanity and *grasping for the wind*

Eccl 2:17 Therefore I hated life because the work that was done under the sun was grievous to me, for all is vanity and *grasping for the wind*

Eccl 2:26 but to the sinner He gives the work of gathering and collecting, that he may give to him who is good before God. This also is vanity and *grasping for the wind*

Eccl 4:4 Again, I saw that for all toil and every skillful work a man is envied by his neighbor. This also is vanity and *grasping for the wind*

Eccl 4:6 Better is a handful with quietness than both hands full, together with toil and *grasping for the wind*

Eccl 4:16 Surely this also is vanity and *grasping for the wind*

Eccl 6:9 Better is the sight of the eyes than the wandering of desire. This also is vanity and *grasping for the wind*

GRASS OF THE FIELD

Num 22:4 So Moab said to the elders of Midian, "Now this company will lick up all that is around us, as an ox licks up the *grass of the field*

2Kin 19:26 they were as the *grass of the field* and the green herb, as the grass on the housetops and grain blighted before it is grown

Is 37:27 they were as the *grass of the field* and as the green herb, as the grass on the housetops and as grain blighted before it is grown

Dan 4:15 Nevertheless leave the stump and roots in the earth, bound with a band of iron and bronze, in the tender *grass of the field*

Dan 4:23 And inasmuch as the king saw a watcher, a holy one, coming down from heaven and saying, 'Chop down the tree and destroy it, but leave its stump and roots in the earth, bound with a band of iron and bronze in the tender *grass of the field*

Matt 6:30 Now if God so clothes the *grass of the field*, which today is, and tomorrow is thrown into the oven, will He not much more clothe you, O you of little faith

GRASS WITHERS, AND ITS FLOWER FALLS AWAY

1Pet 1:24 because "All flesh is as grass, and all the glory of man as the flower of the grass. The *grass withers, and its flower falls away*

GRAVE'S MOUTH (KJV)
(See *MOUTH OF THE GRAVE*)

GRAVEN IMAGE

Judg 18:18 When these went into Micah's house and took the *graven image*, the ephod, the household idols, and the molded image, the priest said to them

Is 40:19 The workman molds a *graven image*, the goldsmith overspreads it with gold, and the silversmith casts silver chains

Is 44:9 Those who make a *graven image*, all of them are useless, and their precious things shall not profit

Is 44:10 Who would form a god or cast a *graven image* that profits him nothing

Jer 10:14 every metalsmith is put to shame by the *graven image*

GRAVEN IMAGES

Is 30:22 You will also defile the covering of your *graven images* of silver, and the ornament of your molded images of gold

Is 42:8 and My glory I will not give to another, nor My praise to *graven images*

GREAT ACTS OF JUDGMENTS (RSV)
(See *GREAT JUDGMENTS*)

GREAT AND AWESOME DEEDS (NIV)
(See *GREAT TERRORS*)

GREAT AND AWESOME GOD

Deut 7:21 for the Lord your God, the *great and awesome God*, is among you

Neh 1:5 I pray, Lord God of heaven, O *great and awesome God*, You who keep Your covenant and mercy with those who love You and observe Your commandments

Dan 9:4 And I prayed to the Lord my God, and made confession, and said, "O Lord, *great and awesome God*, who keeps His covenant and mercy with those who love Him, and with those who keep His commandments

GREAT AND DREADFUL DAY OF THE LORD

Mal 4:5 Behold, I will send you Elijah the prophet before the coming of the *great and dreadful day of the Lord*

GREAT AND TERRIBLE GOD (RSV)
(See *GREAT AND AWESOME GOD*)

GREAT ASSEMBLY

Neh 5:7 After serious thought, I rebuked the nobles and rulers, and said to them, "Each of you is exacting usury from his brother." So I called a *great assembly* against them

GREAT CHASM (NAS, NIV, RSV)
(See *GREAT GULF*)

GREAT CITY
Josh 10:2 that they feared greatly, because Gibeon was a *great city*, like one of the royal cities, and because it was greater than Ai, and all its men were mighty
Jer 22:8 and everyone will say to his neighbor, 'Why has the Lord done so to this *great city*
Jon 1:2 Arise, go to Nineveh, that *great city*, and cry out against it
Jon 3:2 Arise, go to Nineveh, that *great city*, and preach to it the message that I tell you
Jon 3:3 Now Nineveh was an exceedingly *great city*, a three-day journey in extent
Jon 4:11 And should I not pity Nineveh, that *great city*, in which are more than one hundred and twenty thousand persons who cannot discern between their right hand and their left, and also much livestock
Rev 11:8 And their dead bodies will lie in the street of the *great city* which spiritually is called Sodom and Egypt, where also our Lord was crucified
Rev 14:8 And another angel followed, saying, "Babylon is fallen, is fallen, that *great city*, because she has made all nations drink of the wine of the wrath of her fornication
Rev 16:19 Now the *great city* was divided into three parts, and the cities of the nations fell
Rev 17:18 And the woman whom you saw is that *great city* which reigns over the kings of the earth
Rev 18:10 standing at a distance for fear of her torment, saying, 'Alas, alas, that *great city* Babylon, that mighty city
Rev 18:16 and saying, 'Alas, alas, that *great city* that was clothed in fine linen, purple, and scarlet, and adorned with gold and precious stones and pearls
Rev 18:18 and cried out when they saw the smoke of her burning, saying, 'What is like this *great city*
Rev 18:19 And they threw dust on their heads and cried out, weeping and wailing, and saying, 'Alas, alas, that *great city*, in which all who had ships on the sea became rich by her wealth
Rev 18:21 Then a mighty angel took up a stone like a great millstone and threw it into the sea, saying, "Thus with violence the *great city* Babylon shall be thrown down, and shall not be found anymore
Rev 21:10 And he carried me away in the Spirit to a great and high mountain, and showed me the *great city*, the holy Jerusalem, descending out of heaven from God

GREAT COMMANDMENT
Matt 22:36 Teacher, which is the *great commandment* in the law
Matt 22:38 This is the first and *great commandment*

GREAT COMPANY OF THE HEAVENLY HOST (NIV)
(See *MULTITUDE OF THE HEAVENLY HOST*)

GREAT CROWDS (RSV)
(See *GREAT MULTITUDES*)

GREAT DELIVERANCE (NAS, NIV)
(See *GREAT SALVATION*)

GREAT DISTRESS (NIV)
(See *GREAT TRIBULATION*)

GREAT FAITH
Matt 8:10 When Jesus heard it, He marveled, and said to those who followed, "Assuredly, I say to you, I have not found such *great faith*, not even in Israel
Luke 7:9 When Jesus heard these things, He marveled at him, and turned around and said to the crowd that followed Him, "I say to you, I have not found such *great faith*, not even in Israel

GREAT GULF
Luke 16:26 And besides all this, between us and you there is a *great gulf* fixed, so that those who want to pass from here to you cannot, nor can those from there pass to us

GREAT HIGH PRIEST
Heb 4:14 Seeing then that we have a *great High Priest* who has passed through the heavens, Jesus the Son of God, let us hold fast our confession

GREAT IS ARTEMIS (NAS, NIV, RSV)
(See *GREAT IS DIANA*)

GREAT IS DIANA
Acts 19:28 And when they heard this, they were full of wrath and cried out, saying, "*Great is Diana* of the Ephesians
Acts 19:34 But when they found out that he was a Jew, all with one voice cried out for about two hours, "*Great is Diana* of the Ephesians

GREAT IS THE LORD
Ps 48:1 *Great is the Lord*, and greatly to be praised in the city of our God, in His holy mountain
Ps 145:3 *Great is the Lord*, and greatly to be praised; and His greatness is unsearchable

GREAT IS YOUR FAITHFULNESS
Lam 3:23 They are new every morning; *great is Your faithfulness*

GREAT JUDGMENTS
Ex 6:6 I will bring you out from under the burdens of the Egyptians, I will rescue you from their bondage, and I will redeem you with an outstretched arm and with *great judgments*
Ex 7:4 But Pharaoh will not heed you, so that I may lay My hand on Egypt and bring My armies and My people, the children of Israel, out of the land of Egypt by *great judgments*

GREAT KING
2Kin 18:19 Then the Rabshakeh said to them, "Say now to Hezekiah, 'Thus says the *great king*, the king of Assyria
2Kin 18:28 Then the Rabshakeh stood and called out with a loud voice in Hebrew, and spoke, saying, "Hear the word of the *great king*, the king of Assyria
Ezra 5:11 We are the servants of the God of heaven and earth, and we are rebuilding the temple that was built many years ago, which a *great king* of Israel built and completed
Ps 47:2 For the Lord Most High is awesome; He is a *great King* over all the earth
Ps 48:2 Beautiful in elevation, the joy of the whole earth, is Mount Zion on the sides of the north, the city of the *great King*
Ps 95:3 For the Lord is the great God, and the *great King* above all gods
Eccl 9:14 and a *great king* came against it, besieged it, and built great snares around it
Is 36:4 Then the Rabshakeh said to them, "Say

now to Hezekiah, 'Thus says the *great king*, the king of Assyria
Is 36:13 Then the Rabshakeh stood and called out with a loud voice in Hebrew, and said, "Hear the words of the *great king*, the king of Assyria
Mal 1:14 But cursed be the deceiver who has in his flock a male, and makes a vow, but sacrifices to the Lord what is blemished for I am a *great King*
Matt 5:35 nor by Jerusalem, for it is the city of the *great King*

GREAT LEARNING IS DRIVING YOU INSANE (NIV)
(See *MUCH LEARNING IS DRIVING YOU MAD*)

GREAT LEARNING IS TURNING YOU MAD (RSV)
(See *MUCH LEARNING IS DRIVING YOU MAD*)

GREAT MERCY (NIV)
(See *TENDER MERCIES*)

GREAT MIRACLES (KJV)
(See *GREAT WONDERS*)

GREAT MULTITUDES
Matt 4:25 And *great multitudes* followed Him from Galilee, and from Decapolis, Jerusalem, Judea, and beyond the Jordan
Matt 8:1 When He had come down from the mountain, *great multitudes* followed Him
Matt 8:18 Now when Jesus saw *great multitudes* about Him, He gave a command to depart to the other side
Matt 12:15 and *great multitudes* followed Him, and He healed them all
Matt 13:2 And *great multitudes* were gathered together to Him, so that He got into a boat and sat
Matt 15:30 Then *great multitudes* came to Him, having with them those who were lame, blind, mute, maimed, and many others
Matt 19:2 And *great multitudes* followed Him, and He healed them there
Luke 5:15 and *great multitudes* came together to hear, and to be healed by Him of their infirmities
Luke 14:25 And *great multitudes* went with Him. And He turned and said to them

GREAT NATION
Gen 12:2 I will make you a *great nation;* I will bless you and make your name great
Gen 17:20 He shall beget twelve princes, and I will make him a *great nation*
Gen 21:18 Arise, lift up the lad and hold him with your hand, for I will make him a *great nation*
Gen 46:3 do not fear to go down to Egypt, for I will make of you a *great nation* there
Ex 32:10 Now therefore, let Me alone, that My wrath may burn hot against them and I may consume them. And I will make of you a *great nation*
Deut 4:6 for this is your wisdom and your understanding in the sight of the peoples who will hear all these statutes, and say, 'Surely this *great nation* is a wise and understanding people
Deut 4:7 For what *great nation* is there that has God so near to it, as the Lord our God is to us, for whatever reason we may call upon Him
Deut 4:8 And what *great nation* is there that has such statutes and righteous judgments as are in all this law which I set before you this day
Jer 6:22 Behold, a people comes from the north country, and a *great nation* will be raised from the farthest parts of the earth
Jer 50:41 Behold, a people shall come from the north, and a *great nation* and many kings shall be raised up from the ends of the earth

GREAT PEACE (NIV)
(See *ABUNDANCE OF PEACE*)

GREAT RED DRAGON (KJV, NAS, RSV)
(See *FIERY RED DRAGON*)

GREAT SALVATION
1Sam 14:45 But the people said to Saul, "Shall Jonathan die, who has accomplished this *great salvation* in Israel
1Sam 19:5 For he took his life in his hands and killed the Philistine, and the Lord brought about a *great salvation* for all Israel

GREAT SIGNS FROM HEAVEN
Luke 21:11 and there will be fearful sights and *great signs from heaven*

GREAT TERRORS
Deut 4:34 Or did God ever try to go and take for Himself a nation from the midst of another nation, by trials, by signs, by wonders, by war, by a mighty hand and an outstretched arm, and by *great terrors*, according to all that the Lord your God did for you in Egypt before your eyes

GREAT THINGS (NIV)
(See *GREAT WORKS*)

GREAT THRONG (RSV)
(See *COMMON PEOPLE*)

GREAT TRIBULATION
Matt 24:21 For then there will be *great tribulation*, such as has not been since the beginning of the world until this time, no, nor ever shall be
Rev 2:22 Indeed I will cast her into a sickbed, and those who commit adultery with her into *great tribulation*, unless they repent of their deeds
Rev 7:14 So he said to me, "These are the ones who come out of the *great tribulation*, and washed their robes and made them white in the blood of the Lamb

GREAT VICTORY (RSV)
(See *GREAT SALVATION*)

GREAT WHITE THRONE
Rev 20:11 Then I saw a *great white throne* and Him who sat on it, from whose face the earth and the heaven fled away

GREAT WONDERS
Deut 29:3 the great trials which your eyes have seen, the signs, and those *great wonders*
Ps 136:4 To Him who alone does *great wonders*, for His mercy endures forever
Acts 6:8 And Stephen, full of faith and power, did *great wonders* and signs among the people

GREAT WORKS
Judg 2:7 So the people served the Lord all the days of Joshua, and all the days of the elders who outlived Joshua, who had seen all the *great works* of the Lord which He had done for Israel

GREATER LIGHT TO RULE THE DAY
Gen 1:16 the *greater light to rule the day*, and the lesser light to rule the night

GREATER LOVE
John 15:13 *Greater love* has no one than this, than to lay down one's life for his friends

GREATER THAN JOHN THE BAPTIST
Matt 11:11 Assuredly, I say to you, among those born of women there has not risen one *greater than John the Baptist*

GREATER THAN JONAH
Matt 12:41 The men of Nineveh will rise in the judgment with this generation and condemn it, because they repented at the preaching of Jonah; and indeed a *greater than Jonah* is here
Luke 11:32 The men of Nineveh will rise up in the judgment with this generation and condemn it, for they repented at the preaching of Jonah; and indeed a *greater than Jonah* is here

GREATEST AMONG YOU
Matt 23:11 But he who is *greatest among you* shall be your servant
Luke 22:26 on the contrary, he who is *greatest among you*, let him be as the younger, and he who governs as he who serves

GREATEST IN THE KINGDOM OF HEAVEN
Matt 18:1 At that time the disciples came to Jesus, saying, "Who then is *greatest in the kingdom of heaven*
Matt 18:4 Therefore whoever humbles himself as this little child is the *greatest in the kingdom of heaven*

GREATEST OF THESE IS LOVE
1Cor 13:13 And now abide faith, hope, love, these three; but the *greatest of these is love*

GREATNESS OF GOD (NAS, NIV)
(See *MAJESTY OF GOD*)

GREEDY FOR GAIN
Prov 1:19 So are the ways of everyone who is *greedy for gain*
Prov 15:27 He who is *greedy for gain* troubles his own house, but he who hates bribes will live

GREEDY FOR MONEY
1Tim 3:3 not given to wine, not violent, not *greedy for money*, but gentle, not quarrelsome, not covetous
1Tim 3:8 Likewise deacons must be reverent, not double-tongued, not given to much wine, not *greedy for money*
Tit 1:7 For a bishop must be blameless, as a steward of God, not self-willed, not quick-tempered, not given to wine, not violent, not *greedy for money*

GREEDY OF FILTHY LUCRE (KJV)
(See *GREEDY FOR MONEY*)

GREEN PASTURES
Ps 23:2 He makes me to lie down in *green pastures;* He leads me beside the still waters

GRIEF OF HIS MOTHER
Prov 10:1 A wise son makes a glad father, but a foolish son is the *grief of his mother*

GRIEF TO HIS FATHER
Prov 17:25 A foolish son is a *grief to his father*, and bitterness to her who bore him

GRIEVE THE HOLY SPIRIT
Eph 4:30 And do not *grieve the Holy Spirit* of God, by whom you were sealed for the day of redemption

GRIEVOUS WOLVES (KJV)
(See *SAVAGE WOLVES*)

GRINDING AT THE MILL
Matt 24:41 Two women will be *grinding at the mill:* one will be taken and the other left

GROAN WITHIN OURSELVES
Rom 8:23 And not only they, but we also who have the firstfruits of the Spirit, even we ourselves *groan within ourselves*, eagerly waiting for the adoption, the redemption of our body

GROPE IN THE DARK
Job 12:25 They *grope in the dark* without light, and He makes them stagger like a drunken man

GROUND OPENS ITS MOUTH (NAS, RSV)
(See *EARTH OPENS ITS MOUTH*)

GROUNDED IN LOVE
Eph 3:17 that Christ may dwell in your hearts through faith; that you, being rooted and *grounded in love*

GROUP OF PROPHETS
1Sam 10:5 And it will happen, when you have come there to the city, that you will meet a *group of prophets* coming down from the high place with a stringed instrument, a tambourine, a flute, and a harp before them
1Sam 10:10 When they came there to the hill, there was a *group of prophets* to meet him
1Sam 19:20 And when they saw the *group of prophets* prophesying, and Samuel standing as leader over them, the Spirit of God came upon the messengers of Saul, and they also prophesied

GROW OLD LIKE A GARMENT
Ps 102:26 Yes, all of them will *grow old like a garment*
Is 50:9 Indeed they will all *grow old like a garment;* the moth will eat them up
Is 51:6 For the heavens will vanish away like smoke, the earth will *grow old like a garment*, and those who dwell in it will die in like manner
Heb 1:11 They will perish, but You remain; and they will all *grow old like a garment*

GROWLING OF A LION (RSV)
(See *ROARING OF A LION*)

GRUMBLED AGAINST MOSES (NAS, NIV)
(See *MURMURED AGAINST MOSES*)

GUARD YOUR HEARTS
Phil 4:7 and the peace of God, which surpasses all understanding, will *guard your hearts* and minds through Christ Jesus

GUARD YOUR STEPS (NAS, NIV, RSV)
(See *WALK PRUDENTLY*)

GUEST OF A SINNER (NIV)
(See *GUEST WITH A MAN WHO IS A SINNER*)

GUEST WITH A MAN WHO IS A SINNER
Luke 19:7 But when they saw it, they all murmured, saying, "He has gone to be a *guest with a man who is a sinner*

GUIDE YOU INTO ALL TRUTH
John 16:13 However, when He, the Spirit of truth, has come, He will *guide you into all truth*

GUILT IS SO GREAT (NIV)
(See *MULTITUDE OF YOUR INIQUITIES*)

GUILT OF THE FATHER
Ezek 18:19 Yet you say, 'Why should the son not bear the *guilt of the father*

Ezek 18:20 The son shall not bear the *guilt of the father*, nor the father bear the guilt of the son

GUILT OFFERING (NAS, NIV)
(See *OFFERING FOR SIN*)

GUILTY BEFORE THE LORD (RSV)
(See *TRESPASSED AGAINST THE LORD*)

GUILTY CONSCIENCE (NIV)
(See *EVIL CONSCIENCE*)

GUILTY OF DEATH
Num 35:31 Moreover you shall take no ransom for the life of a murderer who is *guilty of death*, but he shall surely be put to death

GUILTY OF PROSTITUTION (NIV)
(See *PLAYED THE HARLOT*)

H

HABITATION OF GOD
Eph 2:22 in whom you also are being built together for a *habitation of God* in the Spirit

HABITATION OF JACKALS
Is 34:13 it shall be a *habitation of jackals*, a courtyard for ostriches
Is 35:7 in the *habitation of jackals*, where each lay, there shall be grass with reeds and rushes

HABITATION OF THE LORD
2Chr 29:6 they have forsaken Him, have turned their faces away from the *habitation of the Lord*, and turned their backs on Him

HAD COMPASSION ON THEM (NIV)
(See *MOVED WITH COMPASSION*)

HAD NO SIN (NIV)
(See *KNEW NO SIN*)

HADES SHALL NOT PREVAIL
Matt 16:18 And I also say to you that you are Peter, and on this rock I will build My church, and the gates of *Hades shall not prevail* against it

HAIL, KING OF THE JEWS
Matt 27:29 And they bowed the knee before Him and mocked Him, saying, "*Hail, King of the Jews*
Mark 15:18 and began to salute Him, "*Hail, King of the Jews*
John 19:3 Then they said, "*Hail, King of the Jews!*" And they struck Him with their hands

HAIR OF HIS HEAD
Num 6:5 Then he shall let the locks of the *hair of his head* grow
Judg 16:22 However, the *hair of his head* began to grow again after it had been shaven
1Sam 14:45 As the Lord lives, not one *hair of his head* shall fall to the ground, for he has worked with God this day
2Sam 14:26 And when he cut the *hair of his head* at the end of every year he cut it because it was heavy on him when he cut it, he weighed the *hair of his head* at two hundred shekels according to the king's standard
Dan 7:9 His garment was white as snow, and the *hair of His head* was like pure wool

HAIRS OF MY HEAD
Ps 40:12 They are more than the *hairs of my head;* therefore my heart fails me
Ps 69:4 Those who hate me without a cause are more than the *hairs of my head*

HAIRS OF YOUR HEAD
Matt 10:30 But the very *hairs of your head* are all numbered
Luke 12:7 But the very *hairs of your head* are all numbered

HALF MY KINGDOM
Esth 5:3 It shall be given to you up to *half my kingdom*
Esth 5:6 What is your request, up to *half my kingdom?* It shall be done
Esth 7:2 And what is your request, up to *half my kingdom*

HALLOWED BE YOUR NAME
Matt 6:9 In this manner, therefore, pray: Our Father in heaven, *hallowed be Your name*
Luke 11:2 Our Father in heaven, *hallowed be Your name*. Your kingdom come

HALT YE BETWEEN TWO OPINIONS (KJV)
(See *FALTER BETWEEN TWO OPINIONS*)

HAMMER AND NAILS (NIV, RSV)
(See *NAILS AND HAMMERS*)

HAND ME OVER (NAS, NIV)
(See *DELIVER ME*)

HAND OF GOD
1Sam 5:11 For there was a deadly destruction throughout all the city; the *hand of God* was very heavy there
2Chr 30:12 Also the *hand of God* was on Judah to give them singleness of heart to do the commandment of the king and the leaders, at the word of the Lord
Job 19:21 Have pity on me, have pity on me, O you my friends, for the *hand of God* has struck me
Job 27:11 I will teach you about the *hand of God;* what is with the Almighty I will not conceal
Eccl 2:24 This also, I saw, was from the *hand of God*
Eccl 9:1 that the righteous and the wise and their works are in the *hand of God*
Mark 16:19 So then, after the Lord had spoken to them, He was received up into heaven, and sat down at the right *hand of God*
Acts 2:33 Therefore being exalted to the right *hand of God*, and having received from the Father the promise of the Holy Spirit, He poured out this which you now see and hear
Acts 7:55 But he, being full of the Holy Spirit, gazed into heaven and saw the glory of God, and Jesus standing at the right *hand of God*
Acts 7:56 I see the heavens opened and the Son of Man standing at the right *hand of God*
Rom 8:34 It is Christ who died, and furthermore is also risen, who is even at the right *hand of God*, who also makes intercession for us
Col 3:1 If then you were raised with Christ, seek those things which are above, where Christ is, sitting at the right *hand of God*
Heb 10:12 But this Man, after He had offered one sacrifice for sins forever, sat down at the right *hand of God*
1Pet 3:22 who has gone into heaven and is at the right *hand of God*, angels and authorities and powers having been made subject to Him
1Pet 5:6 Therefore humble yourselves under the mighty *hand of God*, that He may exalt you in due time

HAND OF HIS ENEMIES
Jer 44:30 Behold, I will give Pharaoh Hophra king of Egypt into the *hand of his enemies* and into

the hand of those who seek his life, as I gave Zedekiah king of Judah into the hand of Nebuchadnezzar king of Babylon, his enemy who sought his life

HAND OF MY ENEMIES
Ps 31:15 Deliver me from the *hand of my enemies*, and from those who persecute me

HAND OF THE LORD
Ex 9:3 behold, the *hand of the Lord* will be on your cattle in the field, on the horses, on the donkeys, on the camels, on the oxen, and on the sheep
Ex 16:3 And the children of Israel said to them, "Oh, that we had died by the *hand of the Lord* in the land of Egypt, when we sat by the pots of meat and when we ate bread to the full
Deut 2:15 For indeed the *hand of the Lord* was against them, to destroy them from the midst of the camp until they were consumed
Josh 4:24 that all the peoples of the earth may know the *hand of the Lord*, that it is mighty, that you may fear the Lord your God forever
Josh 22:31 Now you have delivered the children of Israel out of the *hand of the Lord*
Judg 2:15 Wherever they went out, the *hand of the Lord* was against them for calamity, as the Lord had said, and as the Lord had sworn to them
Ruth 1:13 for it grieves me very much for your sakes that the *hand of the Lord* has gone out against me
1Sam 5:6 But the *hand of the Lord* was heavy on the people of Ashdod, and He ravaged them and struck them with tumors, both Ashdod and its territory
1Sam 5:9 And so it was, after they had carried it away, that the *hand of the Lord* was against the city with a very great destruction
1Sam 7:13 And the *hand of the Lord* was against the Philistines all the days of Samuel
1Sam 12:15 However, if you do not obey the voice of the Lord, but rebel against the commandment of the Lord, then the *hand of the Lord* will be against you, as it was against your fathers
2Sam 24:14 Please let us fall into the *hand of the Lord*, for His mercies are great
1Kin 18:46 Then the *hand of the Lord* came upon Elijah; and he girded up his loins and ran ahead of Ahab to the entrance of Jezreel
2Kin 3:15 And it happened, when the musician played, that the *hand of the Lord* came upon him
1Chr 21:13 Please let me fall into the *hand of the Lord*, for His mercies are very great
Ezra 7:6 The king granted him all his request, according to the *hand of the Lord* his God upon him
Ezra 7:28 So I was encouraged, as the *hand of the Lord* my God was upon me
Job 12:9 Who among all these does not know that the *hand of the Lord* has done this
Ps 75:8 For in the *hand of the Lord* there is a cup, and the wine is red
Ps 118:15 The voice of rejoicing and salvation is in the tents of the righteous; the right *hand of the Lord* does valiantly
Ps 118:16 The right *hand of the Lord* is exalted; the right *hand of the Lord* does valiantly
Prov 21:1 The king's heart is in the *hand of the Lord*, like the rivers of water
Is 19:16 In that day Egypt will be like women, and will be afraid and fear because of the waving of the *hand of the Lord* of hosts, which He waves over it
Is 25:10 For on this mountain the *hand of the Lord* will rest, and Moab shall be trampled down under Him, as straw is trampled down for the refuse heap
Is 41:20 That they may see and know, and consider and understand together, that the *hand of the Lord* has done this, and the Holy One of Israel has created it
Is 51:17 Stand up, O Jerusalem, you who have drunk at the *hand of the Lord* the cup of His fury
Is 62:3 You shall also be a crown of glory in the *hand of the Lord*, and a royal diadem in the hand of your God
Is 66:14 the *hand of the Lord* shall be known to His servants, and His indignation to His enemies
Ezek 1:3 and the *hand of the Lord* was upon him there
Ezek 3:14 but the *hand of the Lord* was strong upon me
Ezek 3:22 Then the *hand of the Lord* was upon me there, and He said to me
Ezek 8:1 And it came to pass in the sixth year, in the sixth month, on the fifth day of the month, as I sat in my house with the elders of Judah sitting before me, that the *hand of the Lord* God fell upon me there
Ezek 33:22 Now the *hand of the Lord* had been upon me the evening before the man came who had escaped
Ezek 37:1 The *hand of the Lord* came upon me and brought me out in the Spirit of the Lord, and set me down in the midst of the valley
Ezek 40:1 In the twenty-fifth year of our captivity, at the beginning of the year, on the tenth day of the month, in the fourteenth year after the city was captured, on the very same day the *hand of the Lord* was upon me
Luke 1:66 And all those who heard them kept them in their hearts, saying, "What kind of child will this be?" And the *hand of the Lord* was with him
Acts 11:21 And the *hand of the Lord* was with them, and a great number believed and turned to the Lord
Acts 13:11 And now, indeed, the *hand of the Lord* is upon you, and you shall be blind, not seeing the sun for a time

HAND THIS MAN OVER TO SATAN (NIV)
(See *DELIVER SUCH A ONE TO SATAN*)

HANDED OVER TO BE CRUCIFIED (NIV)
(See *DELIVERED UP TO BE CRUCIFIED*)

HANDMAID OF THE LORD (RSV)
(See *MAIDSERVANT OF THE LORD*)

HANDS OF THE LIVING GOD
Heb 10:31 It is a fearful thing to fall into the *hands of the living God*

HANDS OVER THE KINGDOM (NIV)
(See *DELIVERS THE KINGDOM*)

HANGED ON A GALLOWS
Esth 2:23 And when an inquiry was made into the matter, it was confirmed, and both were *hanged on a gallows*

HANGS ON A TREE
Gal 3:13 Christ has redeemed us from the curse of the law, having become a curse for us (for it is written, "Cursed is everyone who *hangs on a tree*

HANGS THE EARTH ON NOTHING
Job 26:7 He stretches out the north over empty space; he *hangs the earth on nothing*

HAPPY IS HE
Ps 146:5 *Happy is he* who has the God of Jacob for his help, whose hope is in the Lord his God
Prov 14:21 but he who has mercy on the poor, *happy is he*
Prov 16:20 He who heeds the word wisely will find good, and whoever trusts in the Lord, *happy is he*
Prov 29:18 Where there is no revelation, the people cast off restraint; but *happy is he* who keeps the law
Rom 14:22 *Happy is he* who does not condemn himself in what he approves

HAPPY IS THE MAN
Job 5:17 Behold, *happy is the man* whom God corrects; therefore do not despise the chastening of the Almighty
Ps 127:5 *Happy is the man* who has his quiver full of them
Prov 3:13 *Happy is the man* who finds wisdom, and the man who gains understanding
Prov 28:14 *Happy is the man* who is always reverent, but he who hardens his heart will fall into calamity

HARBOR RESENTMENT (NIV)
(See *STORE UP WRATH*)

HARD SAYING
John 6:60 Therefore many of His disciples, when they heard this, said, "This is a *hard saying*

HARD-WORKING FARMER
2Tim 2:6 The *hard-working farmer* must be first to partake of the crops

HARDEN NOT YOUR HEARTS (RSV)
(See *DO NOT HARDEN YOUR HEARTS*)

HARDEN YOUR HEARTS
1Sam 6:6 Why then do you *harden your hearts* as the Egyptians and Pharaoh hardened their hearts
Ps 95:8 Do not *harden your hearts*, as in the rebellion, and as in the day of trial in the wilderness
Heb 3:8 do not *harden your hearts* as in the rebellion, in the day of trial in the wilderness
Heb 3:15 Today, if you will hear His voice, do not *harden your hearts* as in the rebellion
Heb 4:7 Today, if you will hear His voice, do not *harden your hearts*

HARDENED PHARAOH'S HEART (KJV)
(See *PHARAOH'S HEART GREW HARD*)

HARDNESS OF HEART
Mark 16:14 and He rebuked their unbelief and *hardness of heart*, because they did not believe those who had seen Him after He had risen

HARM THE EARTH
Rev 7:2 And he cried with a loud voice to the four angels to whom it was granted to *harm the earth* and the sea
Rev 7:3 saying, "Do not *harm the earth*, the sea, or the trees till we have sealed the servants of our God on their foreheads

HARMLESS AS DOVES
Matt 10:16 Behold, I send you out as sheep in the midst of wolves. Therefore be wise as serpents and *harmless as doves*

HARPS OF GOD
Rev 15:2 And I saw something like a sea of glass mingled with fire, and those who have the victory over the beast, over his image and over his mark and over the number of his name, standing on the sea of glass, having *harps of God*

HARVEST IS PAST
Jer 8:20 The *harvest is past*, the summer is ended, and we are not saved

HARVEST OF YOUR RIGHTEOUSNESS (NAS, NIV, RSV)
(See *FRUITS OF YOUR RIGHTEOUSNESS*)

HAS ENOUGH TROUBLE (NAS, NIV)
(See *SUFFICIENT FOR THE DAY*)

HAS GIVEN YOU THIS LAND
Deut 3:18 The Lord your God *has given you this land* to possess

HAST THOU POWER WITH GOD (KJV)
(See *STRUGGLED WITH GOD*)

HATE DISCIPLINE (NAS, RSV)
(See *HATE INSTRUCTION*)

HATE EVIL
Ps 97:10 You who love the Lord, *hate evil!* He preserves the souls of His saints
Prov 8:13 The fear of the Lord is to *hate evil;* pride and arrogance and the evil way and the perverse mouth I hate
Amos 5:15 *Hate evil*, love good; establish justice in the gate. It may be that the Lord God of hosts will be gracious to the remnant of Joseph

HATE INSTRUCTION
Ps 50:17 Seeing you *hate instruction* and cast My words behind you

HATE YOUR ENEMY
Matt 5:43 You have heard that it was said, 'You shall love your neighbor and *hate your enemy*

HATED BY ALL
Matt 10:22 And you will be *hated by all* for My name's sake
Matt 24:9 Then they will deliver you up to tribulation and kill you, and you will be *hated by all* nations for My name's sake
Mark 13:13 And you will be *hated by all* men for My name's sake
Luke 21:17 And you will be *hated by all* for My name's sake

HATED OF ALL MEN (KJV)
(See *HATED BY ALL*)

HATERS OF GOD
Rom 1:30 backbiters, *haters of God*, violent, proud, boasters, inventors of evil things, disobedient to parents

HATH NOT WHERE TO LAY HIS HEAD (KJV)
(See *NOWHERE TO LAY HIS HEAD*)

HATH TAKEN AN OATH OF HIM (KJV)
(See *PUT HIM UNDER OATH*)

HATRED STIRS UP STRIFE
Prov 10:12 *Hatred stirs up strife*, but love covers all sins

HATRED TOWARD GOD (NIV)
(See *ENMITY WITH GOD*)

HAUGHTINESS OF HIS HEART
Jer 48:29 of his loftiness and arrogance and pride, and of the *haughtiness of his heart*

HAUNT FOR JACKALS (NIV)
(See *HABITATION OF JACKALS*)

HAVE COMPASSION (KJV, NAS, RSV)
(See *SHOW COMPASSION*)

HAVE DOMINION OVER
Gen 1:26 let them *have dominion over* the fish of the sea, over the birds of the air, and over the cattle, over all the earth and over every creeping thing that creeps on the earth
Gen 1:28 *have dominion over* the fish of the sea, over the birds of the air, and over every living thing that moves on the earth
Gen 37:8 Or shall you indeed *have dominion over* us?" So they hated him even more for his dreams and for his words
Neh 9:37 also they *have dominion over* our bodies and our cattle at their pleasure
Ps 8:6 You have made him to *have dominion over* the works of Your hands
Ps 19:13 Let them not *have dominion over* me. Then I shall be blameless, and I shall be innocent of great transgression
Ps 49:14 The upright shall *have dominion over* them in the morning
Ps 119:133 Direct my steps by Your word, and let no iniquity *have dominion over* me
Rom 6:14 For sin shall not *have dominion over* you, for you are not under law but under grace
2Cor 1:24 Not that we *have dominion over* your faith, but are fellow workers for your joy

HAVE DRIVEN THEM AWAY (NIV)
(See *SCATTERED THEM ABROAD*)

HAVE FAITH
Matt 17:20 for assuredly, I say to you, if you *have faith* as a mustard seed, you will say to this mountain
Matt 21:21 So Jesus answered and said to them, "Assuredly, I say to you, if you *have faith* and do not doubt, you will not only do what was done to the fig tree, but also if you say to this mountain
Mark 11:22 So Jesus answered and said to them, "*Have faith* in God
Luke 17:6 So the Lord said, "If you *have faith* as a mustard seed, you can say to this mulberry tree
Rom 14:22 Do you *have faith?* Have it to yourself before God
2Th 3:2 and that we may be delivered from unreasonable and wicked men; for not all *have faith*
Jas 2:18 But someone will say, "You *have faith*, and I have works

HAVE FELLOWSHIP WITH
Ps 94:20 Shall the throne of iniquity, which devises evil by law, *have fellowship with* You
1Cor 10:20 But I say that the things which the Gentiles sacrifice they sacrifice to demons and not to God, and I do not want you to *have fellowship with* demons
1Jn 1:3 that which we have seen and heard we declare to you, that you also may *have fellowship with* us
1Jn 1:6 If we say that we *have fellowship with* Him, and walk in darkness, we lie and do not practice the truth
1Jn 1:7 But if we walk in the light as He is in the light, we *have fellowship with* one another, and the blood of Jesus Christ His Son cleanses us from all sin

HAVE GIVEN YOU THE LAND
Num 33:53 you shall dispossess the inhabitants of the land and dwell in it, for I *have given you the land* to possess

HAVE MERCY
Ps 4:1 You have relieved me when I was in distress; *have mercy* on me, and hear my prayer
Ps 6:2 *Have mercy* on me, O Lord, for I am weak
Ps 9:13 *Have mercy* on me, O Lord! Consider my trouble from those who hate me, You who lift me up from the gates of death
Ps 25:16 Turn Yourself to me, and *have mercy* on me, for I am desolate and afflicted
Ps 27:7 Hear, O Lord, when I cry with my voice! *Have mercy* also upon me, and answer me
Ps 30:10 Hear, O Lord, and *have mercy* on me; Lord, be my helper
Ps 31:9 *Have mercy* on me, O Lord, for I am in trouble
Ps 51:1 *Have mercy* upon me, O God, according to Your lovingkindness
Ps 86:16 Oh, turn to me, and *have mercy* on me! Give Your strength to Your servant, and save the son of Your maidservant
Ps 102:13 You will arise and *have mercy* on Zion; for the time to favor her, yes, the set time, has come
Ps 123:3 *Have mercy* on us, O Lord, *have mercy* on us
Prov 28:13 He who covers his sins will not prosper, but whoever confesses and forsakes them will *have mercy*
Is 9:17 Therefore the Lord will have no joy in their young men, nor *have mercy* on their fatherless and widows
Is 14:1 For the Lord will *have mercy* on Jacob, and will still choose Israel, and settle them in their own land
Is 27:11 therefore He who made them will not *have mercy* on them, and He who formed them will show them no favor
Is 30:18 and therefore He will be exalted, that He may *have mercy* on you
Is 49:13 For the Lord has comforted His people, and will *have mercy* on His afflicted
Is 54:8 but with everlasting kindness I will *have mercy* on you
Is 55:7 let him return to the Lord, and He will *have mercy* on him
Jer 13:14 I will not pity nor spare nor *have mercy*, but will destroy them
Jer 30:18 Behold, I will bring back the captivity of Jacob's tents, and *have mercy* on his dwelling places
Jer 31:20 I will surely *have mercy* on him," says the Lord
Jer 33:26 For I will cause their captives to return, and will *have mercy* on them
Jer 42:12 And I will show you mercy, that he may *have mercy* on you and cause you to return to your own land
Ezek 39:25 Now I will bring back the captives of Jacob, and *have mercy* on the whole house of Israel
Hos 1:6 Call her name Lo-Ruhamah, for I will no longer *have mercy* on the house of Israel, but I will utterly take them away
Hos 1:7 Yet I will *have mercy* on the house of Judah, will save them by the Lord their God, and will not save them by bow, nor by sword or battle, by horses or horsemen
Hos 2:4 I will not *have mercy* on her children, for they are the children of harlotry
Hos 2:23 Then I will sow her for Myself in the earth, and I will *have mercy* on her who had not obtained mercy
Zech 1:12 Then the Angel of the Lord answered and said, "O Lord of hosts, how long will You not *have mercy* on Jerusalem and on the cities of Judah, against which You were angry these seventy years
Zech 10:6 I will bring them back, because I *have mercy* on them
Matt 9:27 When Jesus departed from there, two

blind men followed Him, crying out and saying, "Son of David, *have mercy* on us
Matt 15:22 And behold, a woman of Canaan came from that region and cried out to Him, saying, "*Have mercy* on me, O Lord, Son of David
Matt 17:15 Lord, *have mercy* on my son, for he is an epileptic and suffers severely
Matt 20:30 And behold, two blind men sitting by the road, when they heard that Jesus was passing by, cried out, saying, "*Have mercy* on us, O Lord, Son of David
Matt 20:31 but they cried out all the more, saying, "*Have mercy* on us, O Lord, Son of David
Mark 10:47 And when he heard that it was Jesus of Nazareth, he began to cry out and say, "Jesus, Son of David, *have mercy* on me
Mark 10:48 but he cried out all the more, "Son of David, *have mercy* on me
Luke 16:24 Then he cried and said, 'Father Abraham, *have mercy* on me, and send Lazarus that he may dip the tip of his finger in water and cool my tongue
Luke 17:13 And they lifted up their voices and said, "Jesus, Master, *have mercy* on us
Luke 18:38 And he cried out, saying, "Jesus, Son of David, *have mercy* on me
Luke 18:39 but he cried out all the more, "Son of David, *have mercy* on me
Rom 9:15 For He says to Moses, "I will *have mercy* on whomever I will *have mercy*, and I will have compassion on whomever I will have compassion
Rom 11:32 For God has committed them all to disobedience, that He might *have mercy* on all

HAVE NO ANXIETY ABOUT ANYTHING (RSV)
(See *BE ANXIOUS FOR NOTHING*)

HAVE NO KNOWLEDGE
Deut 1:39 Moreover your little ones and your children, who you say will be victims, who today *have no knowledge* of good and evil, they shall go in there
Is 5:13 Therefore my people have gone into captivity, because they *have no knowledge*
Is 45:20 They *have no knowledge*, who carry the wood of their carved image, and pray to a god that cannot save
Jer 4:22 They are wise to do evil, but to do good they *have no knowledge*

HAVE NO PLEASURE IN THE DEATH
Ezek 18:32 For I *have no pleasure in the death* of one who dies
Ezek 33:11 As I live,' says the Lord God, 'I *have no pleasure in the death* of the wicked, but that the wicked turn from his way and live

HAVE PITY ON ME
Job 19:21 *Have pity on me, have pity on me*, O you my friends, for the hand of God has struck me

HAVE RECEIVED THEIR REWARD (NIV, RSV)
(See *HAVE THEIR REWARD*)

HAVE THEIR REWARD
Matt 6:2 Therefore, when you do a charitable deed, do not sound a trumpet before you as the hypocrites do in the synagogues and in the streets, that they may have glory from men. Assuredly, I say to you, they *have their reward*
Matt 6:5 For they love to pray standing in the synagogues and on the corners of the streets, that they may be seen by men. Assuredly, I say to you, they *have their reward*
Matt 6:16 For they disfigure their faces that they may appear to men to be fasting. Assuredly, I say to you, they *have their reward*

HAVE YOU NOT HEARD
1Kin 1:11 So Nathan spoke to Bathsheba the mother of Solomon, saying, "*Have you not heard* that Adonijah the son of Haggith has become king, and David our lord does not know it
Is 40:21 *Have you not heard?* Has it not been told you from the beginning
Is 40:28 *Have you not heard?* The everlasting God, the Lord, the Creator of the ends of the earth, neither faints nor is weary

HAVE YOU NOT READ
Matt 12:3 Then He said to them, "*Have you not read* what David did when he was hungry, he and those who were with him
Matt 12:5 Or *have you not read* in the law that on the Sabbath the priests in the temple profane the Sabbath, and are blameless
Matt 19:4 And He answered and said to them, "*Have you not read* that He who made them at the beginning
Matt 22:31 But concerning the resurrection of the dead, *have you not read* what was spoken to you by God, saying
Mark 12:10 *Have you not read* this Scripture: 'The stone which the builders rejected has become the chief cornerstone
Mark 12:26 But concerning the dead, that they rise, *have you not read* in the book of Moses, in the burning bush passage, how God spoke to him, saying

HAVING OUR HEARTS SPRINKLED
Heb 10:22 let us draw near with a true heart in full assurance of faith, *having our hearts sprinkled* from an evil conscience and our bodies washed with pure water

HAZARDED THEIR LIVES (KJV)
(See *RISKED THEIR LIVES*)

HE FEARED GOD (NIV)
(See *ONE WHO FEARED GOD*)

HE HAS RISEN (NAS, NIV)
(See *HE IS RISEN*)

HE IS COMING
1Chr 16:33 Then the trees of the woods shall rejoice before the Lord, for *He is coming* to judge the earth
Ps 96:13 For *He is coming*, for *He is coming* to judge the earth
Ps 98:9 For *He is coming* to judge the earth. With righteousness He shall judge the world, and the peoples with equity
Mal 3:1 And the Lord, whom you seek, will suddenly come to His temple, even the Messenger of the covenant, in whom you delight. Behold, *He is coming*," says the Lord of hosts
Rev 1:7 Behold, *He is coming* with clouds, and every eye will see Him, and they also who pierced Him

HE IS NOT HERE
1Kin 18:10 and when they said, '*He is not here*,' he took an oath from the kingdom or nation that they could not find you
Matt 28:6 *He is not here;* for He is risen, as He said
Mark 16:6 *He is not here*. See the place where they laid Him
Luke 24:6 *He is not here*, but is risen! Remember how He spoke to you when He was still in Galilee

HE IS RISEN
Matt 14:2 *he is risen* from the dead, and therefore these powers are at work in him
Matt 28:6 for *He is risen*, as He said. Come, see the place where the Lord lay
Matt 28:7 And go quickly and tell His disciples that *He is risen* from the dead, and indeed He is going before you into Galilee
Mark 16:6 *He is risen!* He is not here. See the place where they laid Him

HE IS THE LORD
1Chr 16:14 *He is the Lord* our God; His judgments are in all the earth
Ps 105:7 *He is the Lord* our God; His judgments are in all the earth

HE MAKES ME TO LIE DOWN
Ps 23:2 *He makes me to lie down* in green pastures; He leads me beside the still waters

HE MUST INCREASE
John 3:30 *He must increase*, but I must decrease

HE REMEMBERED
Esth 2:1 After these things, when the wrath of King Ahasuerus subsided, *he remembered* Vashti, what she had done, and what had been decreed against her
Ps 78:39 For *He remembered* that they were but flesh, a breath that passes away and does not come again
Ps 105:42 For *He remembered* His holy promise, and Abraham His servant
Ps 106:45 And for their sake *He remembered* His covenant, and relented according to the multitude of His mercies
Is 63:11 Then *he remembered* the days of old, Moses and his people, saying

HE THAT BETRAYETH ME IS AT HAND (KJV)
(See *MY BETRAYER IS AT HAND*)

HE THAT HATETH HIS BROTHER (KJV)
(See *HE WHO HATES HIS BROTHER*)

HE THAT HATH SEEN ME (KJV)
(See *HE WHO HAS SEEN ME*)

HE THAT IS BORN IN HIS HOUSE (KJV)
(See *ONE WHO IS BORN IN HIS HOUSE*)

HE THAT IS WITHOUT SIN (KJV)
(See *HE WHO IS WITHOUT SIN*)

HE WAS BEFORE ME
John 1:15 John bore witness of Him and cried out, saying, "This was He of whom I said, 'He who comes after me is preferred before me, for *He was before me*
John 1:30 This is He of whom I said, 'After me comes a Man who is preferred before me, for *He was before me*

HE WAS OPPRESSED
Is 53:7 *He was oppressed* and He was afflicted, yet He opened not His mouth

HE WAS TAKEN UP
Acts 1:2 until the day in which *He was taken up*, after He through the Holy Spirit had given commandments to the apostles whom He had chosen
Acts 1:9 Now when He had spoken these things, while they watched, *He was taken up*, and a cloud received Him out of their sight
Acts 1:22 beginning from the baptism of John to that day when *He was taken up* from us, one of these must become a witness with us of His resurrection

HE WHO BELIEVES
Mark 16:16 *He who believes* and is baptized will be saved; but he who does not believe will be condemned
John 3:18 *He who believes* in Him is not condemned; but he who does not believe is condemned already, because he has not believed in the name of the only begotten Son of God
John 3:36 *He who believes* in the Son has everlasting life; and he who does not believe the Son shall not see life, but the wrath of God abides on him
John 6:35 He who comes to Me shall never hunger, and *he who believes* in Me shall never thirst
John 6:47 Most assuredly, I say to you, *he who believes* in Me has everlasting life
John 7:38 *He who believes* in Me, as the Scripture has said, out of his heart will flow rivers of living water
John 11:25 *He who believes* in Me, though he may die, he shall live
John 12:44 Then Jesus cried out and said, "*He who believes* in Me, believes not in Me but in Him who sent Me
John 14:12 Most assuredly, I say to you, *he who believes* in Me, the works that I do he will do also
1Pet 2:6 Therefore it is also contained in the Scripture, "Behold, I lay in Zion a chief cornerstone, elect, precious, and *he who believes* on Him will by no means be put to shame
1Jn 5:5 Who is he who overcomes the world, but *he who believes* that Jesus is the Son of God
1Jn 5:10 *He who believes* in the Son of God has the witness in himself

HE WHO HAS AN EAR
Rev 2:7 *He who has an ear*, let him hear what the Spirit says to the churches
Rev 2:11 *He who has an ear*, let him hear what the Spirit says to the churches
Rev 2:17 *He who has an ear*, let him hear what the Spirit says to the churches
Rev 2:29 *He who has an ear*, let him hear what the Spirit says to the churches
Rev 3:6 *He who has an ear*, let him hear what the Spirit says to the churches
Rev 3:13 *He who has an ear*, let him hear what the Spirit says to the churches
Rev 3:22 *He who has an ear*, let him hear what the Spirit says to the churches

HE WHO HAS EARS
Matt 11:15 *He who has ears* to hear, let him hear
Matt 13:9 *He who has ears* to hear, let him hear
Matt 13:43 Then the righteous will shine forth as the sun in the kingdom of their Father. *He who has ears* to hear, let him hear
Mark 4:9 And He said to them, "*He who has ears* to hear, let him hear
Luke 8:8 When He had said these things He cried, "*He who has ears* to hear, let him hear
Luke 14:35 It is neither fit for the land nor for the dunghill, but men throw it out. *He who has ears* to hear, let him hear

HE WHO HAS SEEN ME
John 14:9 *He who has seen Me* has seen the Father; so how can you say

HE WHO HATES HIS BROTHER
1Jn 2:11 But *he who hates his brother* is in darkness and walks in darkness, and does not know where he is going, because the darkness has blinded his eyes

HE WHO IS WITHOUT SIN
John 8:7 So when they continued asking Him, He raised Himself up and said to them, "*He who is*

without sin among you, let him throw a stone at her first

HE WHO LOSES HIS LIFE
Matt 10:39 He who finds his life will lose it, and *he who loses his life* for My sake will find it

HE WHO LOVES ME
John 14:21 He who has My commandments and keeps them, it is *he who loves Me*. And *he who loves Me* will be loved by My Father, and I will love him and manifest Myself to him

HE WHO SEARCHES
Rom 8:27 Now *He who searches* the hearts knows what the mind of the Spirit is, because He makes intercession for the saints according to the will of God
Rev 2:23 And all the churches shall know that I am *He who searches* the minds and hearts

HE WHO SENT ME
John 1:33 I did not know Him, but *He who sent me* to baptize with water said to me
John 7:28 and I have not come of Myself, but *He who sent Me* is true, whom you do not know
John 8:26 I have many things to say and to judge concerning you, but *He who sent Me* is true
John 8:29 And *He who sent Me* is with Me. The Father has not left Me alone, for I always do those things that please Him

HE WILL BE HELD RESPONSIBLE (NIV)
(See *BEAR HIS GUILT*)

HE WILL REIGN
Luke 1:33 And *He will reign* over the house of Jacob forever, and of His kingdom there will be no end

HEAD COVERED
2Sam 15:30 and he had his *head covered* and went barefoot. And all the people who were with him covered their heads and went up, weeping as they went up
Esth 6:12 But Haman hastened to his house, mourning and with his *head covered*
1Cor 11:4 Every man praying or prophesying, having his *head covered*, dishonors his head

HEAD OF A FAMILY (NIV, RSV)
(See *HOUSE OF HIS FATHER*)

HEAD OF CHRIST
1Cor 11:3 But I want you to know that the head of every man is Christ, the head of woman is man, and the *head of Christ* is God

HEAD OF EVERY MAN
1Cor 11:3 But I want you to know that the *head of every man* is Christ, the head of woman is man, and the head of Christ is God

HEAD OF EVERY STREET
Lam 2:19 Lift your hands toward Him for the life of your young children, who faint from hunger at the *head of every street*
Lam 4:1 The stones of the sanctuary are scattered at the *head of every street*
Nah 3:10 her young children also were dashed to pieces at the *head of every street*

HEAD OF THE BODY
Col 1:18 And He is the *head of the body*, the church, who is the beginning, the firstborn from the dead, that in all things He may have the preeminence

HEAD OF THE CHURCH
Eph 5:23 For the husband is head of the wife, as also Christ is *head of the church*

HEAD OF WOMAN
1Cor 11:3 But I want you to know that the head of every man is Christ, the *head of woman* is man, and the head of Christ is God

HEAD UNCOVERED
1Cor 11:5 But every woman who prays or prophesies with her *head uncovered* dishonors her head, for that is one and the same as if her head were shaved
1Cor 11:13 Is it proper for a woman to pray to God with her *head uncovered*

HEADS OF FAMILIES (NIV)
(See *HEADS OF FATHERS' HOUSES*)

HEADS OF FATHERS' HOUSES
1Chr 26:26 This Shelomith and his brethren were over all the treasuries of the dedicated things which King David and the *heads of fathers' houses*, the captains over thousands and hundreds, and the captains of the army, had dedicated
1Chr 26:32 And his brethren were two thousand seven hundred able men, *heads of fathers' houses*, whom King David made officials over the Reubenites, the Gadites, and the half-tribe of Manasseh, for every matter pertaining to God and the affairs of the king
1Chr 27:1 And the children of Israel, according to their number, the *heads of fathers' houses*, the captains of thousands and hundreds and their officers, served the king in every matter of the military divisions

HEADS OF THE FATHERS
Ex 6:25 These are the *heads of the fathers* of the Levites according to their families
Josh 14:1 These are the areas which the children of Israel inherited in the land of Canaan, which Eleazar the priest, Joshua the son of Nun, and the *heads of the fathers* of the tribes of the children of Israel distributed as an inheritance to them
Josh 19:51 These were the inheritances which Eleazar the priest, Joshua the son of Nun, and the *heads of the fathers* of the tribes of the children of Israel divided as an inheritance by lot in Shiloh before the Lord, at the door of the tabernacle of meeting
Josh 21:1 Now the *heads of the fathers* of the Levites came near to Eleazar the priest, to Joshua the son of Nun, and to the *heads of the fathers* of the tribes of the children of Israel

HEADS OF THE FATHERS' HOUSES
1Chr 8:6 And these are the sons of Ehud, who were the *heads of the fathers' houses* of the inhabitants of Geba, and who forced them to move to Manahath
1Chr 8:28 These were *heads of the fathers' houses* by their generations, chief men
1Chr 9:33 These are the singers, *heads of the fathers' houses* of the Levites, who lodged in the chambers, and were free from other duties
1Chr 9:34 These *heads of the fathers' houses* of the Levites were heads throughout their generations
1Chr 15:12 Then he said to them, "You are the *heads of the fathers' houses* of the Levites
1Chr 23:9 These were the *heads of the fathers' houses* of Laadan

1Chr 23:24 These were the sons of Levi by their fathers' houses the *heads of the fathers' houses* as they were counted individually by the number of their names, who did the work for the service of the house of the Lord, from the age of twenty years and above
1Chr 24:6 And the scribe, Shemaiah the son of Nethaneel, one of the Levites, wrote them down before the king, the leaders, Zadok the priest, Ahimelech the son of Abiathar, and the *heads of the fathers' houses* of the priests and Levites, one father's house taken for Eleazar and one for Ithamar
1Chr 24:31 These also cast lots just as their brothers the sons of Aaron did, in the presence of King David, Zadok, Ahimelech, and the *heads of the fathers' houses* of the priests and Levites
2Chr 1:2 And Solomon spoke to all Israel, to the captains of thousands and of hundreds, to the judges, and to every leader in all Israel, the *heads of the fathers' houses*
Ezra 1:5 Then the *heads of the fathers' houses* of Judah and Benjamin, and the priests and the Levites, with all those whose spirits God had moved, arose to go up and build the house of the Lord which is in Jerusalem
Ezra 2:68 Some of the *heads of the fathers' houses*, when they came to the house of the Lord which is in Jerusalem, offered freely for the house of God, to erect it in its place
Ezra 3:12 But many of the priests and Levites and *heads of the fathers' houses*, who were old men, who had seen the first temple, wept with a loud voice when the foundation of this temple was laid before their eyes
Ezra 4:2 they came to Zerubbabel and the *heads of the fathers' houses*, and said to them
Ezra 4:3 But Zerubbabel and Jeshua and the rest of the *heads of the fathers' houses* of Israel said to them
Ezra 8:29 Watch and keep them until you weigh them before the leaders of the priests and the Levites and *heads of the fathers' houses* of Israel in Jerusalem, in the chambers of the house of the Lord
Neh 7:70 And some of the *heads of the fathers' houses* gave to the work
Neh 7:71 Some of the *heads of the fathers' houses* gave to the treasury of the work twenty thousand gold drachmas, and two thousand two hundred silver minas
Neh 8:13 Now on the second day the *heads of the fathers' houses* of all the people, with the priests and Levites, were gathered to Ezra the scribe, in order to understand the words of the Law
Neh 11:13 and his brethren, *heads of the fathers' houses*, were two hundred and forty-two
Neh 12:12 Now in the days of Joiakim, the priests, the *heads of the fathers' houses* were
Neh 12:23 The sons of Levi, the *heads of the fathers' houses* until the days of Johanan the son of Eliashib, were written in the book of the chronicles

HEADS OF THE LEVITE FAMILIES (NIV)
(See *HEADS OF THE FATHERS*)

HEADS OF THE TRIBES
Num 30:1 Then Moses spoke to the *heads of the tribes* concerning the children of Israel, saying
1Kin 8:1 Now Solomon assembled the elders of Israel and all the *heads of the tribes*, the chief fathers of the children of Israel, to King Solomon in Jerusalem, that they might bring up the ark of the covenant of the Lord from the City of David, which is Zion
2Chr 5:2 Now Solomon assembled the elders of Israel and all the *heads of the tribes*, the chief fathers of the children of Israel, in Jerusalem, that they might bring the ark of the covenant of the Lord up from the City of David, which is Zion

HEAL MY SOUL
Ps 41:4 I said, "Lord, be merciful to me; *heal my soul*, for I have sinned against You

HEAL ON THE SABBATH
Matt 12:10 And they asked Him, saying, "Is it lawful to *heal on the Sabbath*
Luke 6:7 And the scribes and Pharisees watched Him closely, whether He would *heal on the Sabbath*, that they might find an accusation against Him
Luke 14:3 And Jesus, answering, spoke to the lawyers and Pharisees, saying, "Is it lawful to *heal on the Sabbath*

HEAL THE BROKENHEARTED
Is 61:1 He has sent Me to *heal the brokenhearted*, to proclaim liberty to the captives, and the opening of the prison to those who are bound
Luke 4:18 He has sent Me to *heal the brokenhearted*, to preach deliverance to the captives and recovery of sight to the blind, to set at liberty those who are oppressed

HEAL THE SICK
Matt 10:8 *Heal the sick*, cleanse the lepers, raise the dead, cast out demons
Luke 9:2 He sent them to preach the kingdom of God and to *heal the sick*
Luke 10:9 And *heal the sick* who are there, and say to them

HEALING SHALL SPRING FORTH
Is 58:8 Then your light shall break forth like the morning, your *healing shall spring forth* speedily, and your righteousness shall go before you

HEAP COALS OF FIRE
Prov 25:22 For so you will *heap coals of fire* on his head, and the Lord will reward you
Rom 12:20 for in so doing you will *heap coals of fire* on his head

HEAP IT UP
Is 57:14 And one shall say, "*Heap it up! Heap it up*

HEAP UP WRATH (KJV)
(See *STORE UP WRATH*)

HEAPING SIN UPON SIN (NIV)
(See *ADD SIN TO SIN*)

HEAR A JUST CAUSE
Ps 17:1 *Hear a just cause*, O Lord, attend to my cry

HEAR FROM HEAVEN
2Chr 6:23 then *hear from heaven*, and act, and judge Your servants, bringing retribution on the wicked by bringing his way on his own head, and justifying the righteous by giving him according to his righteousness
2Chr 6:25 then *hear from heaven* and forgive the sin of Your people Israel, and bring them back to the land which You gave to them and their fathers
2Chr 6:30 then *hear from heaven* Your dwelling place, and forgive, and give to everyone according to all his ways, whose heart You know (for You alone know the hearts of the sons of men
2Chr 6:33 then *hear from heaven* Your dwelling place, and do according to all for which the foreigner calls to You, that all people of the earth

may know Your name and fear You, as do Your people Israel, and that they may know that this temple which I have built is called by Your name
2Chr 6:35 then *hear from heaven* their prayer and their supplication, and maintain their cause
2Chr 6:39 then *hear from heaven* Your dwelling place their prayer and their supplications, and maintain their cause, and forgive Your people who have sinned against You
2Chr 7:14 if My people who are called by My name will humble themselves, and pray and seek My face, and turn from their wicked ways, then I will *hear from heaven*, and will forgive their sin and heal their land

HEAR HIM
Matt 17:5 and suddenly a voice came out of the cloud, saying, "This is My beloved Son, in whom I am well pleased. *Hear Him*
Mark 9:7 and a voice came out of the cloud, saying, "This is My beloved Son. *Hear Him*
Luke 6:17 And He came down with them and stood on a level place with a crowd of His disciples and a great multitude of people from all Judea and Jerusalem, and from the seacoast of Tyre and Sidon, who came to *hear Him* and be healed of their diseases
Luke 9:35 Then a voice came out of the cloud, saying, "This is My beloved Son. *Hear Him*
Luke 15:1 Then all the tax collectors and the sinners drew near to Him to *hear Him*
Luke 19:48 for all the people were very attentive to *hear Him*
Luke 21:38 Then early in the morning all the people came to Him in the temple to *hear Him*
Acts 25:22 Then Agrippa said to Festus, "I also would like to hear the man myself." "Tomorrow," he said, "you shall *hear him*

HEAR HIS VOICE
Deut 4:36 Out of heaven He let you *hear His voice*, that He might instruct you
Ps 95:7 For He is our God, and we are the people of His pasture, and the sheep of His hand. Today, if you will *hear His voice*
Matt 12:19 He will not quarrel nor cry out, nor will anyone *hear His voice* in the streets
John 5:28 for the hour is coming in which all who are in the graves will *hear His voice*
John 10:3 To him the doorkeeper opens, and the sheep *hear his voice*
Heb 3:7 Therefore, as the Holy Spirit says: "Today, if you will *hear His voice*
Heb 3:15 Today, if you will *hear His voice*, do not harden your hearts as in the rebellion
Heb 4:7 Today, if you will *hear His voice*, do not harden your hearts

HEAR MY CRY
Ps 61:1 *Hear my cry*, O God; attend to my prayer

HEAR MY PRAYER
Ps 4:1 You have relieved me when I was in distress; have mercy on me, and *hear my prayer*
Ps 39:12 *Hear my prayer*, O Lord, and give ear to my cry
Ps 54:2 *Hear my prayer*, O God; give ear to the words of my mouth
Ps 84:8 O Lord God of hosts, *hear my prayer;* give ear, O God of Jacob
Ps 102:1 *Hear my prayer*, O Lord, and let my cry come to You
Ps 143:1 *Hear my prayer*, O Lord, give ear to my supplications

HEAR, MY SON, YOUR FATHER'S INSTRUCTION (NAS, RSV)
(See *MY SON, HEAR THE INSTRUCTION*)

HEAR MY VOICE WHEN I CALL (NIV)
(See *HEAR, O LORD*)

HEAR, O HEAVENS
Is 1:2 *Hear, O heavens*, and give ear, O earth! For the Lord has spoken

HEAR, O ISRAEL
Deut 5:1 *Hear, O Israel*, the statutes and judgments which I speak in your hearing today, that you may learn them and be careful to observe them
Deut 6:3 Therefore *hear, O Israel*, and be careful to observe it, that it may be well with you, and that you may multiply greatly as the Lord God of your fathers has promised you
Deut 6:4 *Hear, O Israel:* The Lord our God, the Lord is one
Deut 9:1 *Hear, O Israel:* You are to cross over the Jordan today, and go in to dispossess nations greater and mightier than yourself, cities great and fortified up to heaven
Deut 20:3 And he shall say to them, '*Hear, O Israel*
Mark 12:29 *Hear, O Israel*, the Lord our God, the Lord is one

HEAR, O LORD
Ps 27:7 *Hear, O Lord*, when I cry with my voice
Ps 30:10 *Hear, O Lord*, and have mercy on me; Lord, be my helper
Ps 38:15 For in You, O Lord, I hope; You will *hear, O Lord* my God

HEAR, O LORD, MY RIGHTEOUS PLEA (NIV)
(See *HEAR A JUST CAUSE*)

HEAR THE PRAYER
1Kin 8:29 that Your eyes may be open toward this temple night and day, toward the place of which You said, 'My name shall be there,' that You may *hear the prayer* which Your servant makes toward this place
2Chr 6:20 that Your eyes may be open toward this temple day and night, toward the place where You said You would put Your name, that You may *hear the prayer* which Your servant prays toward this place
Neh 1:6 please let Your ear be attentive and Your eyes open, that You may *hear the prayer* of Your servant which I pray before You now, day and night, for the children of Israel Your servants, and confess the sins of the children of Israel which we have sinned against You
Dan 9:17 Now therefore, our God, *hear the prayer* of Your servant, and his supplications, and for the Lord's sake cause Your face to shine on Your sanctuary, which is desolate

HEAR THE RIGHT (KJV)
(See *HEAR A JUST CAUSE*)

HEAR THE WORD OF THE LORD
1Kin 22:19 Then Micaiah said, "Therefore *hear the word of the Lord*
2Kin 7:1 Then Elisha said, "*Hear the word of the Lord*. Thus says the Lord
2Kin 20:16 Then Isaiah said to Hezekiah, "*Hear the word of the Lord*
2Chr 18:18 Then Micaiah said, "Therefore *hear the word of the Lord*
Is 1:10 *Hear the word of the Lord*, you rulers of Sodom
Is 28:14 Therefore *hear the word of the Lord*, you scornful men, who rule this people who are in Jerusalem
Is 39:5 Then Isaiah said to Hezekiah, "*Hear the word of the Lord* of hosts

Is 66:5 *Hear the word of the Lord*, you who tremble at His word
Jer 2:4 *Hear the word of the Lord*, O house of Jacob and all the families of the house of Israel
Jer 7:2 Stand in the gate of the Lord's house, and proclaim there this word, and say, '*Hear the word of the Lord*, all you of Judah who enter in at these gates to worship the Lord
Jer 9:20 Yet *hear the word of the Lord*, O women, and let your ear receive the word of His mouth
Jer 17:20 and say to them, '*Hear the word of the Lord*, you kings of Judah, and all Judah, and all the inhabitants of Jerusalem, who enter by these gates
Jer 19:3 and say, '*Hear the word of the Lord*, O kings of Judah and inhabitants of Jerusalem
Jer 21:11 And concerning the house of the king of Judah, say, '*Hear the word of the Lord*
Jer 22:2 and say, '*Hear the word of the Lord*, O king of Judah, you who sit on the throne of David, you and your servants and your people who enter these gates
Jer 22:29 O earth, earth, earth, *hear the word of the Lord*
Jer 29:20 Therefore *hear the word of the Lord*, all you of the captivity, whom I have sent from Jerusalem to Babylon
Jer 31:10 *Hear the word of the Lord*, O nations, and declare it in the isles afar off, and say
Jer 34:4 Yet *hear the word of the Lord*, O Zedekiah king of Judah
Jer 44:24 Moreover Jeremiah said to all the people and to all the women, "*Hear the word of the Lord*, all Judah who are in the land of Egypt
Jer 44:26 Therefore *hear the word of the Lord*, all Judah who dwell in the land of Egypt
Ezek 6:3 and say, 'O mountains of Israel, *hear the word of the Lord* God
Ezek 13:2 Son of man, prophesy against the prophets of Israel who prophesy, and say to those who prophesy out of their own heart, '*Hear the word of the Lord*
Ezek 16:35 Now then, O harlot, *hear the word of the Lord*
Ezek 20:47 and say to the forest of the South, '*Hear the word of the Lord*
Ezek 25:3 Say to the Ammonites, '*Hear the word of the Lord* God
Ezek 34:7 Therefore, you shepherds, *hear the word of the Lord*
Ezek 34:9 therefore, O shepherds, *hear the word of the Lord*
Ezek 36:1 And you, son of man, prophesy to the mountains of Israel, and say, 'O mountains of Israel, *hear the word of the Lord*
Ezek 36:4 therefore, O mountains of Israel, *hear the word of the Lord* God
Ezek 37:4 Again He said to me, "Prophesy to these bones, and say to them, 'O dry bones, *hear the word of the Lord*
Hos 4:1 *Hear the word of the Lord*, you children of Israel, for the Lord brings a charge against the inhabitants of the land
Amos 7:16 Now therefore, *hear the word of the Lord:* you say

HEARD HIM CALL OUT (NIV)
(See *CALLED OUT IN MY HEARING*)

HEARD MY CRY
Ps 40:1 I waited patiently for the Lord; and He inclined to me, and *heard my cry*

HEARD THEIR CRY
Ex 3:7 I have surely seen the oppression of My people who are in Egypt, and have *heard their cry* because of their taskmasters, for I know their sorrows
Neh 9:9 You saw the affliction of our fathers in Egypt, and *heard their cry* by the Red Sea
Ps 106:44 Nevertheless He regarded their affliction, when He *heard their cry*

HEARD YOUR PRAYER
1Kin 9:3 I have *heard your prayer* and your supplication that you have made before Me
2Kin 20:5 I have *heard your prayer*, I have seen your tears
2Chr 7:12 I have *heard your prayer*, and have chosen this place for Myself as a house of sacrifice
Is 38:5 I have *heard your prayer*, I have seen your tears

HEARER OF THE WORD
Jas 1:23 For if anyone is a *hearer of the word* and not a doer, he is like a man observing his natural face in a mirror

HEARERS OF THE LAW
Rom 2:13 (for not the *hearers of the law* are just in the sight of God, but the doers of the law will be justified

HEARING OF FAITH
Gal 3:2 Did you receive the Spirit by the works of the law, or by the *hearing of faith*
Gal 3:5 Therefore He who supplies the Spirit to you and works miracles among you, does He do it by the works of the law, or by the *hearing of faith*

HEARING OF THE PEOPLE
Gen 23:13 and he spoke to Ephron in the *hearing of the people* of the land, saying
Ex 11:2 Speak now in the *hearing of the people*, and let every man ask from his neighbor and every woman from her neighbor, articles of silver and articles of gold
Ex 24:7 Then he took the Book of the Covenant and read in the *hearing of the people*
Deut 32:44 So Moses came with Joshua the son of Nun and spoke all the words of this song in the *hearing of the people*
Judg 7:3 Now therefore, proclaim in the *hearing of the people*, saying
1Sam 11:4 So the messengers came to Gibeah of Saul and told the news in the *hearing of the people*
2Kin 18:26 and do not speak to us in Hebrew in the *hearing of the people* who are on the wall
Neh 13:1 On that day they read from the Book of Moses in the *hearing of the people*, and in it was found written that no Ammonite or Moabite should ever come into the congregation of God
Is 36:11 and do not speak to us in Hebrew in the *hearing of the people* who are on the wall
Jer 36:6 You go, therefore, and read from the scroll which you have written at my instruction, the words of the Lord, in the *hearing of the people* in the Lord's house on the day of fasting
Jer 36:13 Then Michaiah declared to them all the words that he had heard when Baruch read the book in the *hearing of the people*
Jer 36:14 Therefore all the princes sent Jehudi the son of Nethaniah, the son of Shelemiah, the son of Cushi, to Baruch, saying, "Take in your hand the scroll from which you have read in the *hearing of the people*, and come
Luke 7:1 Now when He concluded all His sayings in the *hearing of the people*, He entered Capernaum

HEARKEN UNTO ME (KJV)
(See *LISTEN TO ME*)

HEARKEN UNTO MY VOICE (KJV)
(See *LISTEN TO MY VOICE*)

HEARKEN UNTO THE PRAYER (KJV)
(See *HEAR THE PRAYER*)

HEART BURN WITHIN US
Luke 24:32 And they said to one another, "Did not our *heart burn within us* while He talked with us on the road, and while He opened the Scriptures to us

HEART CONDEMNS US
1Jn 3:20 For if our *heart condemns us*, God is greater than our heart, and knows all things

HEART EXULTS (NAS, RSV)
(See *HEART GREATLY REJOICES*)

HEART FAILS ME
Ps 40:12 They are more than the hairs of my head; therefore my *heart fails me*

HEART GREATLY REJOICES
Ps 28:7 Therefore my *heart greatly rejoices*, and with my song I will praise Him

HEART GROWS FAINT (NIV)
(See *HEART IS OVERWHELMED*)

HEART HAS TURNED TO WAX (NIV)
(See *HEART IS LIKE WAX*)

HEART IS DECEITFUL
Jer 17:9 The *heart is deceitful* above all things, and desperately wicked

HEART IS FAINT
Jer 8:18 I would comfort myself in sorrow; my *heart is faint* in me
Lam 1:22 for my sighs are many, and my *heart is faint*
Lam 5:17 Because of this our *heart is faint;* because of these things our eyes grow dim

HEART IS FAR FROM ME
Matt 15:8 These people draw near to Me with their mouth, and honor Me with their lips, but their *heart is far from Me*
Mark 7:6 This people honors Me with their lips, but their *heart is far from Me*

HEART IS LIKE WAX
Ps 22:14 My *heart is like wax;* it has melted within Me

HEART IS OVERWHELMED
Ps 61:2 From the end of the earth I will cry to You, when my *heart is overwhelmed*

HEART IS SICK (RSV)
(See *HEART IS FAINT*)

HEART IS TROUBLED (NIV)
(See *SOUL IS TROUBLED*)

HEART LEAPS FOR JOY (NIV)
(See *HEART GREATLY REJOICES*)

HEART OF A CHILD
Prov 22:15 Foolishness is bound up in the *heart of a child*, but the rod of correction will drive it far from him

HEART OF FLESH
Ezek 11:19 Then I will give them one heart, and I will put a new spirit within them, and take the stony heart out of their flesh, and give them a *heart of flesh*
Ezek 36:26 I will take the heart of stone out of your flesh and give you a *heart of flesh*

HEART OF FOOLS
Prov 12:23 A prudent man conceals knowledge, but the *heart of fools* proclaims foolishness
Prov 14:33 Wisdom rests quietly in the heart of him who has understanding, but what is in the *heart of fools* is made known
Eccl 7:4 The heart of the wise is in the house of mourning, but the *heart of fools* is in the house of mirth

HEART OF STONE
Ezek 36:26 I will take the *heart of stone* out of your flesh and give you a heart of flesh

HEART OF THE FOOL
Prov 15:7 The lips of the wise disperse knowledge, but the *heart of the fool* does not do so

HEART OF THE FOOLISH (KJV)
(See *HEART OF THE FOOL*)

HEART POUNDED (NIV)
(See *BODY TREMBLED*)

HEART WAS HARDENED
Mark 6:52 For they had not understood about the loaves, because their *heart was hardened*

HEARTS ARE FAR FROM ME (NIV)
(See *HEART IS FAR FROM ME*)

HEARTS BURNING WITHIN US (NAS, NIV)
(See *HEART BURN WITHIN US*)

HEARTS CONDEMN US (NIV, RSV)
(See *HEART CONDEMNS US*)

HEARTS GO ASTRAY (NIV)
(See *GO ASTRAY IN THEIR HEARTS*)

HEARTS OF FOOLS (NAS, NIV)
(See *HEART OF THE FOOL*)

HEARTS OF MEN (NIV)
(See *HEARTS OF THE SONS OF MEN*)

HEARTS OF THE PEOPLE MELTED
Josh 7:5 therefore the *hearts of the people melted* and became like water

HEARTS OF THE SONS OF MEN
2Chr 6:30 then hear from heaven Your dwelling place, and forgive, and give to everyone according to all his ways, whose heart You know (for You alone know the *hearts of the sons of men*
Prov 15:11 so how much more the *hearts of the sons of men*
Eccl 9:3 Truly the *hearts of the sons of men* are full of evil

HEARTS WERE HARDENED (NIV, RSV)
(See *HEART WAS HARDENED*)

HEAT OF THE DAY
Gen 18:1 Then the Lord appeared to him by the terebinth trees of Mamre, as he was sitting in the tent door in the *heat of the day*
1Sam 11:11 and they came into the midst of the camp in the morning watch, and killed Ammonites until the *heat of the day*
2Sam 4:5 Then the sons of Rimmon the Beerothite, Rechab and Baanah, set out and came at about the *heat of the day* to the house of Ishbosheth, who was lying on his bed at noon
Jer 36:30 He shall have no one to sit on the throne

of David, and his dead body shall be cast out to the *heat of the day* and the frost of the night
Matt 20:12 saying, 'These last men have worked only one hour, and you made them equal to us who have borne the burden and the *heat of the day*

HEATHEN, WHOM THE LORD CAST OUT (KJV)
(See *NATIONS WHOM THE LORD HAD CAST OUT*)

HEAVE OFFERING
Ex 29:27 And from the ram of the consecration you shall consecrate the breast of the wave offering which is waved, and the thigh of the *heave offering* which is raised, of that which is for Aaron and of that which is for his sons
Ex 29:28 For it is a *heave offering;* it shall be a *heave offering* from the children of Israel from the sacrifices of their peace offerings, that is, their *heave offering* to the Lord
Lev 7:14 And from it he shall offer one cake from each offering as a *heave offering* to the Lord
Lev 7:32 Also the right thigh you shall give to the priest as a *heave offering* from the sacrifices of your peace offerings
Lev 7:34 For the breast of the wave offering and the thigh of the *heave offering* I have taken from the children of Israel, from the sacrifices of their peace offerings, and I have given them to Aaron the priest and to his sons from the children of Israel by a statute forever
Lev 10:14 The breast of the wave offering and the thigh of the *heave offering* you shall eat in a clean place, you, your sons, and your daughters with you
Lev 10:15 The thigh of the *heave offering* and the breast of the wave offering they shall bring with the offerings of fat made by fire, to offer as a wave offering before the Lord
Num 6:20 they are holy for the priest, together with the breast of the wave offering and the thigh of the *heave offering*
Num 15:19 then it will be, when you eat of the bread of the land, that you shall offer up a *heave offering* to the Lord
Num 15:20 You shall offer up a cake of the first of your ground meal as a *heave offering;* as a *heave offering* of the threshing floor, so shall you offer it up
Num 15:21 Of the first of your ground meal you shall give to the Lord a *heave offering* throughout your generations
Num 18:11 the *heave offering* of their gift, with all the wave offerings of the children of Israel
Num 18:24 For the tithes of the children of Israel, which they offer up as a *heave offering* to the Lord, I have given to the Levites as an inheritance
Num 18:26 When you take from the children of Israel the tithes which I have given you from them as your inheritance, then you shall offer up a *heave offering* of it to the Lord, a tenth of the tithe
Num 18:27 And your *heave offering* shall be reckoned to you as though it were the grain of the threshing floor and as the fullness of the winepress
Num 18:28 Thus you shall also offer a *heave offering* to the Lord from all your tithes which you receive from the children of Israel, and you shall give the Lord's *heave offering* from it to Aaron the priest
Num 18:29 Of all your gifts you shall offer up every *heave offering* due to the Lord, from all the best of them, the sanctified part of them
Num 31:29 take it from their half, and give it to Eleazar the priest as a *heave offering* to the Lord
Num 31:41 So Moses gave the tribute which was the Lord's *heave offering* to Eleazar the priest, as the Lord commanded Moses
Deut 12:17 You may not eat within your gates the tithe of your grain or your new wine or your oil, of the firstlings of your herd or your flock, of any of your offerings which you vow, of your freewill offerings, or of the *heave offering* of your hand

HEAVEN ABOVE
Gen 49:25 by the God of your father who will help you, and by the Almighty who will bless you with blessings of *heaven above*, blessings of the deep that lies beneath, blessings of the breasts and of the womb
Ex 20:4 You shall not make for yourself a carved image, or any likeness of anything that is in *heaven above*, or that is in the earth beneath, or that is in the water under the earth
Deut 4:39 Therefore know this day, and consider it in your heart, that the Lord Himself is God in *heaven above* and on the earth beneath
Deut 5:8 You shall not make for yourself any carved image, or any likeness of anything that is in *heaven above*, or that is in the earth beneath, or that is in the water under the earth
Josh 2:11 neither did there remain any more courage in anyone because of you, for the Lord your God, He is God in *heaven above* and on earth beneath
1Kin 8:23 Lord God of Israel, there is no God in *heaven above* or on earth below like You, who keep Your covenant and mercy with Your servants who walk before You with all their heart
Jer 31:37 If *heaven above* can be measured, and the foundations of the earth searched out beneath, I will also cast off all the seed of Israel for all that they have done
Acts 2:19 I will show wonders in *heaven above* and signs in the earth beneath

HEAVEN AND EARTH
Gen 14:19 Blessed be Abram of God Most High, Possessor of *heaven and earth*
Gen 14:22 But Abram said to the king of Sodom, "I have lifted my hand to the Lord, God Most High, the Possessor of *heaven and earth*
Deut 4:26 I call *heaven and earth* to witness against you this day, that you will soon utterly perish from the land which you cross over the Jordan to possess
Deut 30:19 I call *heaven and earth* as witnesses today against you, that I have set before you life and death, blessing and cursing
Deut 31:28 Gather to me all the elders of your tribes, and your officers, that I may speak these words in their hearing and call *heaven and earth* to witness against them
2Sam 18:9 so he was left hanging between *heaven and earth*. And the mule which was under him went on
2Kin 19:15 O Lord God of Israel, the One who dwells between the cherubim, You are God, You alone, of all the kingdoms of the earth. You have made *heaven and earth*
2Chr 2:12 Blessed be the Lord God of Israel, who made *heaven and earth*, for He has given King David a wise son, endowed with prudence and understanding, who will build a temple for the Lord and a royal house for himself
Ezra 5:11 We are the servants of the God of *heaven and earth*, and we are rebuilding the temple that was built many years ago, which a great king of Israel built and completed
Ps 69:34 Let *heaven and earth* praise Him, the seas and everything that moves in them
Ps 115:15 May you be blessed by the Lord, Who made *heaven and earth*

Ps 121:2 My help comes from the Lord, Who made *heaven and earth*
Ps 124:8 Our help is in the name of the Lord, Who made *heaven and earth*
Ps 134:3 The Lord who made *heaven and earth* bless you from Zion
Ps 146:6 Who made *heaven and earth*, the sea, and all that is in them
Is 37:16 O Lord of hosts, God of Israel, the One who dwells between the cherubim, You are God, You alone, of all the kingdoms of the earth. You have made *heaven and earth*
Jer 23:24 do I not fill *heaven and earth?"* says the Lord
Jer 33:25 If My covenant is not with day and night, and if I have not appointed the ordinances of *heaven and earth*
Hag 2:6 I will shake *heaven and earth*, the sea and dry land
Hag 2:21 Speak to Zerubbabel, governor of Judah, saying: "I will shake *heaven and earth*
Matt 5:18 For assuredly, I say to you, till *heaven and earth* pass away, one jot or one tittle will by no means pass from the law till all is fulfilled
Matt 11:25 At that time Jesus answered and said, "I thank You, Father, Lord of *heaven and earth*, because You have hidden these things from the wise and prudent and have revealed them to babes
Matt 24:35 *Heaven and earth* will pass away, but My words will by no means pass away
Mark 13:31 *Heaven and earth* will pass away, but My words will by no means pass away
Luke 10:21 In that hour Jesus rejoiced in the Spirit and said, "I praise You, Father, Lord of *heaven and earth*, that You have hidden these things from the wise and prudent and revealed them to babes
Luke 16:17 And it is easier for *heaven and earth* to pass away than for one tittle of the law to fail
Luke 21:33 *Heaven and earth* will pass away, but My words will by no means pass away
Acts 4:24 Lord, You are God, who made *heaven and earth* and the sea, and all that is in them
Acts 17:24 God, who made the world and everything in it, since He is Lord of *heaven and earth*, does not dwell in temples made with hands
Eph 3:15 from whom the whole family in *heaven and earth* is named
Rev 14:7 and worship Him who made *heaven and earth*, the sea and springs of water

HEAVEN IS MY THRONE
Is 66:1 *Heaven is My throne*, and earth is My footstool. Where is the house that you will build Me
Acts 7:49 *Heaven is My throne*, and earth is My footstool. What house will you build for Me

HEAVEN IS SHUT UP (KJV, RSV)
(See *HEAVENS ARE SHUT UP*)

HEAVEN OF HEAVENS
1Kin 8:27 Behold, heaven and the *heaven of heavens* cannot contain You
2Chr 2:6 But who is able to build Him a temple, since heaven and the *heaven of heavens* cannot contain Him
2Chr 6:18 Behold, heaven and the *heaven of heavens* cannot contain You
Neh 9:6 You have made heaven, the *heaven of heavens*, with all their host, the earth and all things on it, the seas and all that is in them, and You preserve them all
Ps 68:33 To Him who rides on the *heaven of heavens*, which were of old

HEAVEN, THE EARTH, THE SEA, AND ALL THINGS THAT ARE IN THEM
Acts 14:15 We also are men with the same nature as you, and preach to you that you should turn from these vain things to the living God, who made the *heaven, the earth, the sea, and all things that are in them*

HEAVEN YOUR DWELLING PLACE
1Kin 8:30 When they pray toward this place, then hear in *heaven Your dwelling place*
1Kin 8:39 then hear in *heaven Your dwelling place*, and forgive, and act, and give to everyone according to all his ways, whose heart You know (for You, only You, know the hearts of all the sons of men
1Kin 8:43 hear in *heaven Your dwelling place*, and do according to all for which the foreigner calls to You, that all peoples of the earth may know Your name and fear You, as do Your people Israel, and that they may know that this temple which I have built is called by Your name
1Kin 8:49 then hear in *heaven Your dwelling place* their prayer and their supplication, and maintain their cause
2Chr 6:30 then hear from *heaven Your dwelling place*, and forgive, and give to everyone according to all his ways, whose heart You know (for You alone know the hearts of the sons of men
2Chr 6:33 then hear from *heaven Your dwelling place*, and do according to all for which the foreigner calls to You, that all people of the earth may know Your name and fear You, as do Your people Israel, and that they may know that this temple which I have built is called by Your name
2Chr 6:39 then hear from *heaven Your dwelling place* their prayer and their supplications, and maintain their cause, and forgive Your people who have sinned against You

HEAVEN'S DEW (NIV)
(See *DEW OF HEAVEN*)

HEAVENLY ARRAY (NIV)
(See *HOST OF HEAVEN*)

HEAVENLY BODIES (NAS, NIV)
(See *CELESTIAL BODIES*)

HEAVENLY FATHER
Matt 6:14 For if you forgive men their trespasses, your *heavenly Father* will also forgive you
Matt 6:26 yet your *heavenly Father* feeds them. Are you not of more value than they
Matt 6:32 For your *heavenly Father* knows that you need all these things
Matt 15:13 But He answered and said, "Every plant which My *heavenly Father* has not planted will be uprooted
Matt 18:35 So My *heavenly Father* also will do to you if each of you, from his heart, does not forgive his brother his trespasses
Luke 11:13 If you then, being evil, know how to give good gifts to your children, how much more will your *heavenly Father* give the Holy Spirit to those who ask Him

HEAVENLY HOST
Luke 2:13 And suddenly there was with the angel a multitude of the *heavenly host* praising God and saying

HEAVENLY JERUSALEM
Heb 12:22 But you have come to Mount Zion and to the city of the living God, the *heavenly Jerusalem*, to an innumerable company of angels

HEAVENLY MAN
1Cor 15:48 and as is the *heavenly Man*, so also are those who are heavenly

1Cor 15:49 And as we have borne the image of the man of dust, we shall also bear the image of the *heavenly Man*

HEAVENLY PLACES
Eph 1:3 Blessed be the God and Father of our Lord Jesus Christ, who has blessed us with every spiritual blessing in the *heavenly places* in Christ
Eph 1:20 which He worked in Christ when He raised Him from the dead and seated Him at His right hand in the *heavenly places*
Eph 2:6 and raised us up together, and made us sit together in the *heavenly places* in Christ Jesus
Eph 3:10 to the intent that now the manifold wisdom of God might be made known by the church to the principalities and powers in the *heavenly places*
Eph 6:12 For we do not wrestle against flesh and blood, but against principalities, against powers, against the rulers of the darkness of this age, against spiritual hosts of wickedness in the *heavenly places*

HEAVENLY REALMS (NIV)
(See *HEAVENLY PLACES*)

HEAVENS AND THE EARTH
Gen 1:1 In the beginning God created the *heavens and the earth*
Gen 2:1 Thus the *heavens and the earth*, and all the host of them, were finished
Gen 2:4 This is the history of the *heavens and the earth* when they were created, in the day that the Lord God made the earth and the heavens
Ex 20:11 For in six days the Lord made the *heavens and the earth*, the sea, and all that is in them, and rested the seventh day
Ex 31:17 for in six days the Lord made the *heavens and the earth*, and on the seventh day He rested and was refreshed
Jer 10:11 The gods that have not made the *heavens and the earth* shall perish from the earth and from under these heavens
Jer 32:17 Behold, You have made the *heavens and the earth* by Your great power and outstretched arm
Jer 51:48 Then the *heavens and the earth* and all that is in them shall sing joyously over Babylon
2Pet 3:7 But the *heavens and the earth* which now exist are kept in store by the same word, reserved for fire until the day of judgment and perdition of ungodly men

HEAVENS ARE SHUT UP
1Kin 8:35 When the *heavens are shut up* and there is no rain because they have sinned against You, when they pray toward this place and confess Your name, and turn from their sin because You afflict them

HEAVENS ARE TELLING (NAS, RSV)
(See *HEAVENS DECLARE*)

HEAVENS DECLARE
Ps 19:1 The *heavens declare* the glory of God; and the firmament shows His handiwork
Ps 50:6 Let the *heavens declare* His righteousness, for God Himself is Judge
Ps 97:6 The *heavens declare* His righteousness, and all the peoples see His glory

HEAVENS WERE MADE FAIR (RSV)
(See *ADORNED THE HEAVENS*)

HEAVENS WERE OPENED
Ezek 1:1 Now it came to pass in the thirtieth year, in the fourth month, on the fifth day of the month, as I was among the captives by the River Chebar, that the *heavens were opened* and I saw visions of God
Matt 3:16 and behold, the *heavens were opened* to Him, and He saw the Spirit of God descending like a dove and alighting upon Him

HEAVINESS OF HIS MOTHER (KJV)
(See *GRIEF OF HIS MOTHER*)

HEBREW OF THE HEBREWS
Phil 3:5 circumcised the eighth day, of the stock of Israel, of the tribe of Benjamin, a *Hebrew of the Hebrews*

HEIGHTS OF THE EARTH (RSV)
(See *HIGH PLACES OF THE EARTH*)

HEIR OF ALL THINGS
Heb 1:2 has in these last days spoken to us by His Son, whom He has appointed *heir of all things*, through whom also He made the worlds

HEIR OF GOD
Gal 4:7 Therefore you are no longer a slave but a son, and if a son, then an *heir of God* through Christ

HEIRS ACCORDING TO THE PROMISE
Gal 3:29 And if you are Christ's, then you are Abraham's seed, and *heirs according to the promise*

HEIRS OF PROMISE
Heb 6:17 Thus God, determining to show more abundantly to the *heirs of promise* the immutability of His counsel, confirmed it by an oath

HEIRS OF THE KINGDOM
Jas 2:5 Has God not chosen the poor of this world to be rich in faith and *heirs of the kingdom* which He promised to those who love Him

HEIRS OF THE PROPHETS (NIV)
(See *SONS OF THE PROPHETS*)

HELD FOR JUDGMENT (NIV)
(See *RESERVED FOR JUDGMENT*)

HELD OUT MY HANDS (NIV, RSV)
(See *STRETCHED OUT MY HANDS*)

HELL AND DESTRUCTION
Prov 15:11 *Hell and Destruction* are before the Lord; so how much more the hearts of the sons of men
Prov 27:20 *Hell and Destruction* are never full; so the eyes of man are never satisfied

HELL FIRE
Matt 5:22 But whoever says, 'You fool!' shall be in danger of *hell fire*
Matt 18:9 It is better for you to enter into life with one eye, rather than having two eyes, to be cast into *hell fire*
Mark 9:47 It is better for you to enter the kingdom of God with one eye, than having two eyes, to be cast into *hell fire*

HELL SHALL NOT PREVAIL (KJV)
(See *HADES SHALL NOT PREVAIL*)

HELMET OF SALVATION
Is 59:17 For He put on righteousness as a breastplate, and a *helmet of salvation* on His head
Eph 6:17 And take the *helmet of salvation*, and the sword of the Spirit, which is the word of God

HELP AND THEIR SHIELD

Ps 115:9 O Israel, trust in the Lord; He is their *help and their shield*

Ps 115:10 O house of Aaron, trust in the Lord; He is their *help and their shield*

Ps 115:11 You who fear the Lord, trust in the Lord; He is their *help and their shield*

HELP ME

Josh 10:4 Come up to me and *help me*, that we may attack Gibeon, for it has made peace with Joshua and with the children of Israel

2Sam 10:11 Then he said, "If the Syrians are too strong for me, then you shall *help me*

1Chr 12:17 And David went out to meet them, and answered and said to them, "If you have come peaceably to me to *help me*, my heart will be united with you

1Chr 19:12 Then he said, "If the Syrians are too strong for me, then you shall *help me*

2Chr 28:23 For he sacrificed to the gods of Damascus which had defeated him, saying, "Because the gods of the kings of Syria help them, I will sacrifice to them that they may *help me*

Ps 22:19 But You, O Lord, do not be far from Me; O My Strength, hasten to *help Me*

Ps 38:22 Make haste to *help me*, O Lord, my salvation

Ps 40:13 Be pleased, O Lord, to deliver me; O Lord, make haste to *help me*

Ps 59:4 They run and prepare themselves through no fault of mine. Awake to *help me*, and behold

Ps 70:1 Make haste, O God, to deliver me! Make haste to *help me*, O Lord

Ps 71:12 O God, do not be far from me; O my God, make haste to *help me*

Ps 109:26 *Help me*, O Lord my God! Oh, save me according to Your mercy

Ps 118:7 The Lord is for me among those who *help me*

Ps 119:86 All Your commandments are faithful; they persecute me wrongfully; *help me*

Ps 119:175 Let my soul live, and it shall praise You; and let Your judgments *help me*

Is 50:7 For the Lord God will *help Me;* therefore I will not be disgraced

Is 50:9 Surely the Lord God will *help Me;* who is he who will condemn Me

Dan 10:13 and behold, Michael, one of the chief princes, came to *help me*, for I had been left alone there with the kings of Persia

Matt 15:25 Then she came and worshiped Him, saying, "Lord, *help me*

Luke 10:40 But Martha was distracted with much serving, and she approached Him and said, "Lord, do You not care that my sister has left me to serve alone? Therefore tell her to *help me*

HEM OF HIS GARMENT

Matt 9:20 And suddenly, a woman who had a flow of blood for twelve years came from behind and touched the *hem of His garment*

Matt 14:36 and begged Him that they might only touch the *hem of His garment*

HERALD OF GOOD TIDINGS (RSV)
(See *ONE WHO BRINGS GOOD TIDINGS*)

HERDS THE WIND (RSV)
(See *FEEDS ON THE WIND*)

HERE A LITTLE, THERE A LITTLE

Is 28:10 For precept must be upon precept, precept upon precept, line upon line, line upon line, *here a little, there a little*

Is 28:13 But the word of the Lord was to them, "Precept upon precept, precept upon precept, line upon line, line upon line, *here a little, there a little*

HERE AM I

Is 6:8 Whom shall I send, and who will go for Us?" Then I said, "*Here am I!* Send me

Is 8:18 *Here am I* and the children whom the Lord has given me

Heb 2:13 *Here am I* and the children whom God has given Me

HERE COMES MY BETRAYER (NIV)
(See *MY BETRAYER IS AT HAND*)

HERE I AM

Gen 22:1 Now it came to pass after these things that God tested Abraham, and said to him, "Abraham!" And he said, "*Here I am*

Gen 22:7 And he said, "*Here I am*, my son." And he said

Gen 22:11 But the Angel of the Lord called to him from heaven and said, "Abraham, Abraham!" And he said, "*Here I am*

Gen 27:1 Now it came to pass, when Isaac was old and his eyes were so dim that he could not see, that he called Esau his older son and said to him, "My son." And he answered him, "*Here I am*

Gen 27:18 and he said, "*Here I am*. Who are you, my son

Gen 31:11 Then the Angel of God spoke to me in a dream, saying, 'Jacob.' And I said, '*Here I am*

Gen 37:13 Come, I will send you to them." So he said to him, "*Here I am*

Gen 46:2 Then God spoke to Israel in the visions of the night, and said, "Jacob, Jacob!" And he said, "*Here I am*

Ex 3:4 So when the Lord saw that he turned aside to look, God called to him from the midst of the bush and said, "Moses, Moses!" And he said, "*Here I am*

Josh 14:10 and now, *here I am* this day, eighty-five years old

1Sam 3:4 that the Lord called Samuel. And he answered, "*Here I am*

1Sam 3:5 So he ran to Eli and said, "*Here I am*, for you called me

1Sam 3:6 So Samuel arose and went to Eli, and said, "*Here I am*, for you called me

1Sam 3:8 Then he arose and went to Eli, and said, "*Here I am*, for you did call me

1Sam 3:16 Then Eli called Samuel and said, "Samuel, my son!" And he answered, "*Here I am*

1Sam 12:3 *Here I am*. Witness against me before the Lord and before His anointed

1Sam 14:7 Go then; *here I am* with you, according to your heart

1Sam 22:12 And Saul said, "Hear now, son of Ahitub!" And he answered, "*Here I am*, my lord

2Sam 1:7 Now when he looked behind him, he saw me and called to me. And I answered, '*Here I am*

2Sam 15:26 I have no delight in you,' *here I am*, let Him do to me as seems good to Him

2Sam 19:20 Therefore *here I am*, the first to come today of all the house of Joseph to go down to meet my lord the king

Is 56:3 nor let the eunuch say, "*Here I am*, a dry tree

Is 58:9 you shall cry, and He will say, '*Here I am*

Is 65:1 I said, '*Here I am*, *here I am*

Jer 26:14 As for me, *here I am*, in your hand; do with me as seems good and proper to you

Acts 9:10 and to him the Lord said in a vision, "Ananias." And he said, "*Here I am*, Lord

HERITAGE FROM THE LORD

Ps 127:3 Behold, children are a *heritage from the Lord*, the fruit of the womb is His reward

HID MY FACE
Is 54:8 With a little wrath I *hid My face* from you for a moment
Ezek 39:23 because they were unfaithful to Me, therefore I *hid My face* from them

HID THEMSELVES
Gen 3:8 And they heard the sound of the Lord God walking in the garden in the cool of the day, and Adam and his wife *hid themselves* from the presence of the Lord God among the trees of the garden
1Chr 21:20 and his four sons who were with him *hid themselves*, but Ornan continued threshing wheat
Rev 6:15 And the kings of the earth, the great men, the rich men, the commanders, the mighty men, every slave and every free man, *hid themselves* in the caves and in the rocks of the mountains

HID WITH CHRIST (KJV, RSV)
(See *HIDDEN WITH CHRIST*)

HIDDEN HIS FACE
Ps 22:24 Nor has He *hidden His face* from Him; but when He cried to Him, He heard
Is 59:2 and your sins have *hidden His face* from you, so that He will not hear

HIDDEN LOVE (NIV, RSV)
(See *LOVE CAREFULLY CONCEALED*)

HIDDEN MY FACE
Jer 33:5 They come to fight with the Chaldeans, but only to fill their places with the dead bodies of men whom I will slay in My anger and My fury, all for whose wickedness I have *hidden My face* from this city
Ezek 39:24 According to their uncleanness and according to their transgressions I have dealt with them, and *hidden My face* from them

HIDDEN WITH CHRIST
Col 3:3 For you died, and your life is *hidden with Christ* in God

HIDE HIS FACE
Mic 3:4 He will even *hide His face* from them at that time, because they have been evil in their deeds

HIDE MY FACE
Deut 31:17 Then My anger shall be aroused against them in that day, and I will forsake them, and I will *hide My face* from them, and they shall be devoured
Deut 31:18 And I will surely *hide My face* in that day because of all the evil which they have done, in that they have turned to other gods
Deut 32:20 I will *hide My face* from them, I will see what their end will be, for they are a perverse generation, children in whom is no faith
Is 50:6 I did not *hide My face* from shame and spitting
Ezek 39:29 And I will not *hide My face* from them anymore

HIDE YOUR FACE
Job 13:24 Why do You *hide Your face*, and regard me as Your enemy
Ps 13:1 Will You forget me forever? How long will You *hide Your face* from me
Ps 27:9 Do not *hide Your face* from me; do not turn Your servant away in anger
Ps 44:24 Why do You *hide Your face*, and forget our affliction and our oppression
Ps 51:9 *Hide Your face* from my sins, and blot out all my iniquities
Ps 69:17 And do not *hide Your face* from Your servant, for I am in trouble
Ps 88:14 Lord, why do You cast off my soul? Why do You *hide Your face* from me
Ps 102:2 Do not *hide Your face* from me in the day of my trouble
Ps 104:29 You *hide Your face*, they are troubled; You take away their breath, they die and return to their dust
Ps 143:7 Do not *hide Your face* from me, lest I be like those who go down into the pit

HIDES HIS FACE
Job 34:29 And when He *hides His face*, who then can see Him, whether it is against a nation or a man alone
Ps 10:11 He has said in his heart, "God has forgotten; He *hides His face;* He will never see it
Is 8:17 And I will wait on the Lord, Who *hides His face* from the house of Jacob

HIGH AND LIFTED UP
Is 2:13 upon all the cedars of Lebanon that are *high and lifted up*, and upon all the oaks of Bashan
Is 6:1 In the year that King Uzziah died, I saw the Lord sitting on a throne, *high and lifted up*, and the train of His robe filled the temple

HIGH AS THE HEAVENS (NAS)
(See *HIGHER THAN HEAVEN*)

HIGH GOD (KJV)
(See *MOST HIGH GOD*)

HIGH MOUNTAIN
Is 13:2 Lift up a banner on the *high mountain*, raise your voice to them
Is 30:25 There will be on every *high mountain* and on every high hill rivers and streams of waters, in the day of the great slaughter, when the towers fall
Is 40:9 O Zion, you who bring good tidings, get up into the *high mountain*
Is 57:7 On a lofty and *high mountain* you have set your bed
Jer 3:6 She has gone up on every *high mountain* and under every green tree, and there played the harlot
Ezek 40:2 In the visions of God He took me into the land of Israel and set me on a very *high mountain*
Matt 4:8 Again, the devil took Him up on an exceedingly *high mountain*, and showed Him all the kingdoms of the world and their glory
Matt 17:1 Now after six days Jesus took Peter, James, and John his brother, brought them up on a *high mountain* by themselves
Mark 9:2 Now after six days Jesus took Peter, James, and John, and led them up on a *high mountain* apart by themselves
Luke 4:5 Then the devil, taking Him up on a *high mountain*, showed Him all the kingdoms of the world in a moment of time
Rev 21:10 And he carried me away in the Spirit to a great and *high mountain*, and showed me the great city, the holy Jerusalem, descending out of heaven from God

HIGH PLACE
1Sam 9:12 for today he came to this city, because there is a sacrifice of the people today on the *high place*
1Sam 9:13 As soon as you come into the city, you will surely find him before he goes up to the *high place* to eat
1Sam 9:14 And as they were coming into the city,

there was Samuel, coming out toward them on his way up to the *high place*
1Sam 9:19 Go up before me to the *high place*, for you shall eat with me today
1Sam 9:25 When they had come down from the *high place* into the city, Samuel spoke with Saul on the top of the house
1Sam 10:5 And it will happen, when you have come there to the city, that you will meet a group of prophets coming down from the *high place* with a stringed instrument, a tambourine, a flute, and a harp before them
1Sam 10:13 And when he had finished prophesying, he went to the *high place*
1Kin 3:4 Now the king went to Gibeon to sacrifice there, for that was the great *high place*
1Kin 11:7 Then Solomon built a *high place* for Chemosh the abomination of Moab, on the hill that is east of Jerusalem, and for Molech the abomination of the people of Ammon
2Kin 23:15 Moreover the altar that was at Bethel, and the *high place* which Jeroboam the son of Nebat, who made Israel sin, had made, both that altar and the *high place* he broke down; and he burned the *high place* and crushed it to powder, and burned the wooden image
1Chr 16:39 and Zadok the priest and his brethren the priests, before the tabernacle of the Lord at the *high place* that was at Gibeon
1Chr 21:29 For the tabernacle of the Lord and the altar of the burnt offering, which Moses had made in the wilderness, were at that time at the *high place* in Gibeon
2Chr 1:3 Then Solomon, and all the congregation with him, went to the *high place* that was at Gibeon
2Chr 1:13 So Solomon came to Jerusalem from the *high place* that was at Gibeon, from before the tabernacle of meeting, and reigned over Israel
Is 16:12 And it shall come to pass, when it is seen that Moab is weary on the *high place*, that he will come to his sanctuary to pray
Ezek 16:24 that you also built for yourself a shrine, and made a *high place* for yourself in every street
Ezek 16:31 You erected your shrine at the head of every road, and built your *high place* in every street
Ezek 20:29 Then I said to them, 'What is this *high place* to which you go

HIGH PLACES
Lev 26:30 I will destroy your *high places*, cut down your incense altars, and cast your carcasses on the lifeless forms of your idols
Num 22:41 So it was the next day, that Balak took Balaam and brought him up to the *high places* of Baal, that from there he might observe the extent of the people
Num 33:52 then you shall drive out all the inhabitants of the land from before you, destroy all their engraved stones, destroy all their molded images, and demolish all their *high places*
Deut 33:29 Your enemies shall submit to you, and you shall tread down their *high places*
2Sam 1:19 The beauty of Israel is slain on your *high places*
2Sam 1:25 How the mighty have fallen in the midst of the battle! Jonathan was slain in your *high places*
2Sam 22:34 He makes my feet like the feet of deer, and sets me on my *high places*
1Kin 3:2 Meanwhile the people sacrificed at the *high places*, because there was no house built for the name of the Lord until those days
1Kin 3:3 And Solomon loved the Lord, walking in the statutes of his father David, except that he sacrificed and burned incense at the *high places*
1Kin 12:31 He made shrines on the *high places*, and made priests from every class of people, who were not of the sons of Levi
1Kin 12:32 And at Bethel he installed the priests of the *high places* which he had made
1Kin 13:2 and on you he shall sacrifice the priests of the *high places* who burn incense on you, and men's bones shall be burned on you
1Kin 13:32 For the saying which he cried out by the word of the Lord against the altar in Bethel, and against all the shrines on the *high places* which are in the cities of Samaria, will surely come to pass
1Kin 13:33 After this event Jeroboam did not turn from his evil way, but again he made priests from every class of people for the *high places;* whoever wished, he consecrated him, and he became one of the priests of the *high places*
1Kin 14:23 For they also built for themselves *high places*, sacred pillars, and wooden images on every high hill and under every green tree
1Kin 15:14 But the *high places* were not removed. Nevertheless Asa's heart was loyal to the Lord all his days
1Kin 22:43 Nevertheless the *high places* were not taken away, for the people offered sacrifices and burned incense on the *high places*
2Kin 12:3 But the *high places* were not taken away; the people still sacrificed and burned incense on the *high places*
2Kin 14:4 However the *high places* were not taken away, and the people still sacrificed and burned incense on the *high places*
2Kin 15:4 except that the *high places* were not removed; the people still sacrificed and burned incense on the *high places*
2Kin 15:35 However the *high places* were not removed; the people still sacrificed and burned incense on the *high places*
2Kin 16:4 And he sacrificed and burned incense on the *high places*, on the hills, and under every green tree
2Kin 17:9 Also the children of Israel secretly did against the Lord their God things that were not right, and they built for themselves *high places* in all their cities, from watchtower to fortified city
2Kin 17:11 and there they burned incense on all the *high places*, as the nations had done whom the Lord had carried away before them
2Kin 17:29 However every nation continued to make gods of its own, and put them in the houses of the *high places* which the Samaritans had made, every nation in the cities where they dwelt
2Kin 17:32 So they feared the Lord, and from every class they appointed for themselves priests of the *high places*, who sacrificed for them in the shrines of the *high places*
2Kin 18:4 He removed the *high places* and broke the sacred pillars, cut down the wooden images and broke in pieces the bronze serpent that Moses had made
2Kin 18:22 But if you say to me, 'We trust in the Lord our God,' is it not He whose *high places* and whose altars Hezekiah has taken away, and said to Judah and Jerusalem
2Kin 21:3 For he rebuilt the *high places* which Hezekiah his father had destroyed
2Kin 23:5 Then he removed the idolatrous priests whom the kings of Judah had ordained to burn incense on the *high places* in the cities of Judah and in the places all around Jerusalem, and those who burned incense to Baal, to the sun, to the moon, to the constellations, and to all the host of heaven
2Kin 23:8 And he brought all the priests from the cities of Judah, and defiled the *high places* where the priests had burned incense, from Geba to Beersheba; also he broke down the *high places* at

the gates which were at the entrance of the Gate of Joshua the governor of the city, which were to the left of the city gate

2Kin 23:9 Nevertheless the priests of the *high places* did not come up to the altar of the Lord in Jerusalem, but they ate unleavened bread among their brethren

2Kin 23:13 Then the king defiled the *high places* that were east of Jerusalem, which were on the south of the Mount of Corruption, which Solomon king of Israel had built for Ashtoreth the abomination of the Sidonians, for Chemosh the abomination of the Moabites, and for Milcom the abomination of the people of Ammon

2Kin 23:19 Then Josiah also took away all the shrines of the *high places* that were in the cities of Samaria, which the kings of Israel had made to provoke the Lord to anger

2Kin 23:20 He executed all the priests of the *high places* who were there on the altars, and burned men's bones on them

2Chr 11:15 Then he appointed for himself priests for the *high places*, for the demons, and the calf idols which he had made

2Chr 14:3 for he removed the altars of the foreign gods and the *high places*, and broke down the sacred pillars and cut down the wooden images

2Chr 14:5 He also removed the *high places* and the incense altars from all the cities of Judah, and the kingdom was quiet under him

2Chr 15:17 But the *high places* were not removed from Israel. Nevertheless the heart of Asa was loyal all his days

2Chr 17:6 moreover he removed the *high places* and wooden images from Judah

2Chr 20:33 Nevertheless the *high places* were not taken away, for as yet the people had not directed their hearts to the God of their fathers

2Chr 21:11 Moreover he made *high places* in the mountains of Judah, and caused the inhabitants of Jerusalem to commit harlotry, and led Judah astray

2Chr 28:4 And he sacrificed and burned incense on the *high places*, on the hills, and under every green tree

2Chr 28:25 And in every single city of Judah he made *high places* to burn incense to other gods, and provoked to anger the Lord God of his fathers

2Chr 31:1 Now when all this was finished, all Israel who were present went out to the cities of Judah and broke the sacred pillars in pieces, cut down the wooden images, and threw down the *high places* and the altars from all Judah, Benjamin, Ephraim, and Manasseh until they had utterly destroyed them all

2Chr 32:12 Has not the same Hezekiah taken away His *high places* and His altars, and commanded Judah and Jerusalem, saying

2Chr 33:3 For he rebuilt the *high places* which Hezekiah his father had broken down

2Chr 33:17 Nevertheless the people still sacrificed on the *high places*, but only to the Lord their God

2Chr 33:19 Also his prayer and how God received his entreaty, and all his sin and trespass, and the sites where he built *high places* and set up wooden images and carved images, before he was humbled, indeed they are written among the sayings of Hozai

2Chr 34:3 and in the twelfth year he began to purge Judah and Jerusalem of the *high places*, the wooden images, the carved images, and the molded images

Job 25:2 Dominion and fear belong to Him; He makes peace in His *high places*

Ps 18:33 He makes my feet like the feet of deer, and sets me on my *high places*

Ps 78:58 For they provoked Him to anger with their *high places*, and moved Him to jealousy with their carved images

Is 15:2 he has gone up to the temple and Dibon, to the *high places* to weep

Is 36:7 But if you say to me, 'We trust in the Lord our God,' is it not He whose *high places* and whose altars Hezekiah has taken away, and said to Judah and Jerusalem

Jer 7:31 And they have built the *high places* of Tophet, which is in the Valley of the Son of Hinnom, to burn their sons and their daughters in the fire, which I did not command, nor did it come into My heart

Jer 17:3 O My mountain in the field, I will give as plunder your wealth, all your treasures, and your *high places* of sin within all your borders

Jer 19:5 (they have also built the *high places* of Baal, to burn their sons with fire for burnt offerings to Baal, which I did not command or speak, nor did it come into My mind

Jer 32:35 And they built the *high places* of Baal which are in the Valley of the Son of Hinnom, to cause their sons and their daughters to pass through the fire to Molech, which I did not command them, nor did it come into My mind that they should do this abomination, to cause Judah to sin

Jer 48:35 Moreover," says the Lord, "I will cause to cease in Moab the one who offers sacrifices in the *high places* and burns incense to his gods

Ezek 6:3 Indeed I, even I, will bring a sword against you, and I will destroy your *high places*

Ezek 6:6 In all your dwelling places the cities shall be laid waste, and the *high places* shall be desolate, so that your altars may be laid waste and made desolate, your idols may be broken and made to cease, your incense altars may be cut down, and your works may be abolished

Ezek 16:16 You took some of your garments and adorned multicolored *high places* for yourself, and played the harlot on them

Ezek 16:25 You built your *high places* at the head of every road, and made your beauty to be abhorred

Ezek 16:39 I will also give you into their hand, and they shall throw down your shrines and break down your *high places*

Ezek 43:7 No more shall the house of Israel defile My holy name, they nor their kings, by their harlotry or with the carcasses of their kings on their *high places*

Hos 10:8 Also the *high places* of Aven, the sin of Israel, shall be destroyed

Amos 4:13 For behold, He who forms mountains, and creates the wind, who declares to man what his thought is, and makes the morning darkness, who treads the *high places* of the earth. The Lord God of hosts is His name

Amos 7:9 The *high places* of Isaac shall be desolate, and the sanctuaries of Israel shall be laid waste

Mic 1:3 He will come down and tread on the *high places* of the earth

Mic 1:5 And what are the *high places* of Judah? Are they not Jerusalem

HIGH PLACES OF THE EARTH

Amos 4:13 For behold, He who forms mountains, and creates the wind, who declares to man what his thought is, and makes the morning darkness, who treads the *high places of the earth* The Lord God of hosts is His name

Mic 1:3 He will come down and tread on the *high places of the earth*

HIGH PRIEST

Lev 21:10 And he who is the *high priest* among his brethren, on whose head the anointing oil was

poured and who is consecrated to wear the garments, shall not uncover his head nor tear his clothes
Num 35:25 So the congregation shall deliver the manslayer from the hand of the avenger of blood, and the congregation shall return him to the city of refuge where he had fled, and he shall remain there until the death of the *high priest* who was anointed with the holy oil
Num 35:28 because he should have remained in his city of refuge until the death of the *high priest*. But after the death of the *high priest* the manslayer may return to the land of his possession
Josh 20:6 And he shall dwell in that city until he stands before the congregation for judgment, and until the death of the one who is *high priest* in those days
2Kin 12:10 So it was, whenever they saw that there was much money in the chest, that the king's scribe and the *high priest* came up and put it in bags, and counted the money that was found in the house of the Lord
2Kin 22:4 Go up to Hilkiah the *high priest*, that he may count the money which has been brought into the house of the Lord, which the doorkeepers have gathered from the people
2Kin 22:8 Then Hilkiah the *high priest* said to Shaphan the scribe
2Kin 23:4 And the king commanded Hilkiah the *high priest*, the priests of the second order, and the doorkeepers, to bring out of the temple of the Lord all the articles that were made for Baal, for Asherah, and for all the host of heaven
2Chr 34:9 When they came to Hilkiah the *high priest*, they delivered the money that was brought into the house of God, which the Levites who kept the doors had gathered from the hand of Manasseh and Ephraim, from all the remnant of Israel, from all Judah and Benjamin, and which they had brought back to Jerusalem
Neh 3:1 Then Eliashib the *high priest* rose up with his brethren the priests and built the Sheep Gate
Neh 3:20 After him Baruch the son of Zabbai diligently repaired the other section, from the buttress to the door of the house of Eliashib the *high priest*
Neh 13:28 And one of the sons of Joiada, the son of Eliashib the *high priest*, was a son-in-law of Sanballat the Horonite
Hag 1:1 In the second year of King Darius, in the sixth month, on the first day of the month, the word of the Lord came by Haggai the prophet to Zerubbabel the son of Shealtiel, governor of Judah, and to Joshua the son of Jehozadak, the *high priest*, saying
Hag 1:12 Then Zerubbabel the son of Shealtiel, and Joshua the son of Jehozadak, the *high priest*, with all the remnant of the people, obeyed the voice of the Lord their God, and the words of Haggai the prophet, as the Lord their God had sent him
Hag 1:14 So the Lord stirred up the spirit of Zerubbabel the son of Shealtiel, governor of Judah, and the spirit of Joshua the son of Jehozadak, the *high priest*, and the spirit of all the remnant of the people
Hag 2:2 Speak now to Zerubbabel the son of Shealtiel, governor of Judah, and to Joshua the son of Jehozadak, the *high priest*, and to the remnant of the people, saying
Hag 2:4 and be strong, Joshua, son of Jehozadak, the *high priest*
Zech 3:1 Then he showed me Joshua the *high priest* standing before the Angel of the Lord, and Satan standing at his right hand to oppose him
Zech 3:8 Hear, O Joshua, the *high priest*, you and your companions who sit before you, for they are a wondrous sign
Zech 6:11 Take the silver and gold, make an elaborate crown, and set it on the head of Joshua the son of Jehozadak, the *high priest*
Matt 26:3 Then the chief priests, the scribes, and the elders of the people assembled at the palace of the *high priest*, who was called Caiaphas
Matt 26:51 And suddenly, one of those who were with Jesus stretched out his hand and drew his sword, struck the servant of the *high priest*, and cut off his ear
Matt 26:57 And those who had laid hold of Jesus led Him away to Caiaphas the *high priest*, where the scribes and the elders were assembled
Matt 26:62 And the *high priest* arose and said to Him, "Do You answer nothing
Matt 26:63 And the *high priest* answered and said to Him, "I adjure You by the living God that You tell us if You are the Christ, the Son of God
Matt 26:65 Then the *high priest* tore his clothes, saying, "He has spoken blasphemy
Mark 2:26 how he went into the house of God in the days of Abiathar the *high priest*, and ate the showbread, which is not lawful to eat, except for the priests, and also gave some to those who were with him
Mark 14:47 And one of those who stood by drew his sword and struck the servant of the *high priest*, and cut off his ear
Mark 14:53 And they led Jesus away to the *high priest;* and with him were assembled all the chief priests, the elders, and the scribes
Mark 14:54 But Peter followed Him at a distance, right into the courtyard of the *high priest*
Mark 14:60 And the *high priest* stood up in the midst and asked Jesus, saying
Mark 14:61 Again the *high priest* asked Him, saying to Him, "Are You the Christ, the Son of the Blessed
Mark 14:63 Then the *high priest* tore his clothes and said, "What further need do we have of witnesses
Mark 14:66 Now as Peter was below in the courtyard, one of the servant girls of the *high priest* came
Luke 22:50 And one of them struck the servant of the *high priest* and cut off his right ear
John 11:49 And one of them, Caiaphas, being *high priest* that year, said to them
John 11:51 but being *high priest* that year he prophesied that Jesus would die for the nation
John 18:13 And they led Him away to Annas first, for he was the father-in-law of Caiaphas who was *high priest* that year
John 18:15 Now that disciple was known to the *high priest*, and went with Jesus into the courtyard of the *high priest*
John 18:16 Then the other disciple, who was known to the *high priest*, went out and spoke to her who kept the door, and brought Peter in
John 18:19 The *high priest* then asked Jesus about His disciples and His doctrine
John 18:22 And when He had said these things, one of the officers who stood by struck Jesus with the palm of his hand, saying, "Do You answer the *high priest* like that
John 18:24 Then Annas sent Him bound to Caiaphas the *high priest*
John 18:26 One of the servants of the *high priest*, a relative of him whose ear Peter cut off, said
Acts 4:6 as well as Annas the *high priest*, Caiaphas, John, and Alexander, and as many as were of the family of the *high priest*, were gathered together at Jerusalem
Acts 5:17 Then the *high priest* rose up, and all those who were with him (which is the sect of the Sadducees

Acts 5:21 But the *high priest* and those with him came and called the council together, with all the elders of the children of Israel, and sent to the prison to have them brought
Acts 5:24 Now when the *high priest*, the captain of the temple, and the chief priests heard these things, they wondered what the outcome would be
Acts 5:27 And when they had brought them, they set them before the council. And the *high priest* asked them
Acts 7:1 Then the *high priest* said, "Are these things so
Acts 9:1 Then Saul, still breathing threats and murder against the disciples of the Lord, went to the *high priest*
Acts 22:5 as also the *high priest* bears me witness, and all the council of the elders, from whom I also received letters to the brethren, and went to Damascus to bring in chains even those who were there to Jerusalem to be punished
Acts 23:2 And the *high priest* Ananias commanded those who stood by him to strike him on the mouth
Acts 23:4 And those who stood by said, "Do you revile God's *high priest*
Acts 23:5 Then Paul said, "I did not know, brethren, that he was the *high priest*
Acts 24:1 Now after five days Ananias the *high priest* came down with the elders and a certain orator named Tertullus
Acts 25:2 Then the *high priest* and the chief men of the Jews informed him against Paul
Heb 2:17 Therefore, in all things He had to be made like His brethren, that He might be a merciful and faithful *High Priest* in things pertaining to God, to make propitiation for the sins of the people
Heb 3:1 Therefore, holy brethren, partakers of the heavenly calling, consider the Apostle and *High Priest* of our confession, Christ Jesus
Heb 4:14 Seeing then that we have a great *High Priest* who has passed through the heavens, Jesus the Son of God, let us hold fast our confession
Heb 4:15 For we do not have a *High Priest* who cannot sympathize with our weaknesses, but was in all points tempted as we are, yet without sin
Heb 5:5 So also Christ did not glorify Himself to become *High Priest*, but it was He who said to Him
Heb 5:10 called by God as *High Priest* "according to the order of Melchizedek
Heb 6:20 where the forerunner has entered for us, even Jesus, having become *High Priest* forever according to the order of Melchizedek
Heb 7:26 For such a *High Priest* was fitting for us, who is holy, harmless, undefiled, separate from sinners, and has become higher than the heavens
Heb 8:1 We have such a *High Priest*, who is seated at the right hand of the throne of the Majesty in the heavens
Heb 8:3 For every *high priest* is appointed to offer both gifts and sacrifices
Heb 9:7 But into the second part the *high priest* went alone once a year, not without blood, which he offered for himself and for the people's sins committed in ignorance
Heb 9:11 But Christ came as *High Priest* of the good things to come, with the greater and more perfect tabernacle not made with hands, that is, not of this creation
Heb 9:25 not that He should offer Himself often, as the *high priest* enters the Most Holy Place every year with blood of another
Heb 10:21 and having a *High Priest* over the house of God
Heb 13:11 For the bodies of those beasts, whose blood is brought into the sanctuary by the *high priest* for sin, are burned outside the camp

HIGHER THAN HEAVEN
Job 11:8 They are *higher than heaven* what can you do? Deeper than Sheol what can you know

HIGHER THAN THE HEAVENS
Heb 7:26 For such a High Priest was fitting for us, who is holy, harmless, undefiled, separate from sinners, and has become *higher than the heavens*

HIGHEST HEAVENS
Deut 10:14 Indeed heaven and the *highest heavens* belong to the Lord your God, also the earth with all that is in it

HIGHEST POINT OF THE TEMPLE (NIV)
(See *PINNACLE OF THE TEMPLE*)

HIGHLY FAVORED ONE
Luke 1:28 And having come in, the angel said to her, "Rejoice, *highly favored one*, the Lord is with you

HIGHLY SKILLED AND EXPERIENCED (NIV)
(See *FILLED WITH WISDOM*)

HIGHWAY FOR OUR GOD
Is 40:3 make straight in the desert a *highway for our God*

HIGHWAY OF HOLINESS
Is 35:8 A highway shall be there, and a road, and it shall be called the *Highway of Holiness*

HIGHWAYS AND HEDGES
Luke 14:23 Then the master said to the servant, 'Go out into the *highways and hedges*, and compel them to come in, that my house may be filled

HILL COUNTRY OF EPHRAIM (NAS, NIV, RSV)
(See *MOUNTAINS OF EPHRAIM*)

HILL OF THE LORD
Ps 24:3 Who may ascend into the *hill of the Lord?* Or who may stand in His holy place

HILL OF ZION
Ps 2:6 Yet I have set My King On My holy *hill of Zion*

HILLS LIKE LAMBS (NAS, NIV, RSV)
(See *LITTLE HILLS LIKE LAMBS*)

HILLS MELTED LIKE WAX (KJV)
(See *MOUNTAINS MELT LIKE WAX*)

HIM THAT IS WEAK IN THE FAITH RECEIVE YE (KJV)
(See *RECEIVE ONE WHO IS WEAK*)

HINDER THE GOSPEL
1Cor 9:12 Nevertheless we have not used this right, but endure all things lest we *hinder the gospel* of Christ

HINNOM VALLEY (NIV)
(See *VALLEY OF HINNOM*)

HIS COMMANDMENTS, HIS JUDGMENTS, AND HIS STATUTES
Deut 8:11 Beware that you do not forget the Lord your God by not keeping *His commandments, His judgments, and His statutes* which I command you today

HIS COMMANDMENTS, HIS STATUTES, AND HIS JUDGMENTS
Deut 30:16 in that I command you today to love the Lord your God, to walk in His ways, and to keep *His commandments, His statutes, and His judgments*, that you may live and multiply

HIS FATHER'S HOUSE
Gen 50:8 as well as all the house of Joseph, his brothers, and *his father's house*
Num 1:4 And with you there shall be a man from every tribe, each one the head of *his father's house*
Num 1:44 These are the ones who were numbered, whom Moses and Aaron numbered, with the leaders of Israel, twelve men, each one representing *his father's house*
Num 2:2 Everyone of the children of Israel shall camp by his own standard, beside the emblems of *his father's house*
Judg 9:5 Then he went to *his father's house* at Ophrah and killed his brothers, the seventy sons of Jerubbaal, on one stone
Judg 14:19 So his anger was aroused, and he went back up to *his father's house*
1Sam 17:25 and it shall be that the man who kills him the king will enrich with great riches, will give him his daughter, and give *his father's house* exemption in Israel
1Sam 18:2 Saul took him that day, and would not let him go home to *his father's house* anymore
1Sam 22:1 And when his brothers and all *his father's house* heard it, they went down there to him
1Sam 22:11 Then the king sent to call Ahimelech the priest, the son of Ahitub, and all *his father's house*, the priests who were in Nob
2Sam 3:29 Let it rest on the head of Joab and on all *his father's house*
1Chr 9:19 Shallum the son of Kore, the son of Ebiasaph, the son of Korah, and his brethren, from *his father's house*, the Korahites, were in charge of the work of the service, gatekeepers of the tabernacle
1Chr 12:28 Zadok, a young man, a valiant warrior, and from *his father's house* twenty-two captains
Is 22:23 I will fasten him as a peg in a secure place, and he will become a glorious throne to *his father's house*
Is 22:24 They will hang on him all the glory of *his father's house*, the offspring and the issue, all vessels of small quantity, from the cups to all the pitchers
Acts 7:20 and he was brought up in *his father's house* for three months

HIS FEET DO NOT SLIP (NIV)
(See *NONE OF HIS STEPS SHALL SLIDE*)

HIS FOOTSTOOL
Ps 99:5 Exalt the Lord our God, and worship at *His footstool*
Ps 132:7 Let us go into His tabernacle; let us worship at *His footstool*
Lam 2:1 He cast down from heaven to the earth the beauty of Israel, and did not remember *His footstool* in the day of His anger
Matt 5:35 nor by the earth, for it is *His footstool;* nor by Jerusalem, for it is the city of the great King
Heb 10:13 from that time waiting till His enemies are made *His footstool*

HIS HOLY HILL
Ps 3:4 I cried to the Lord with my voice, and He heard me from *His holy hill*
Ps 99:9 Exalt the Lord our God, and worship at *His holy hill*

HIS LOVE ENDURES FOREVER (NIV)
(See *HIS MERCY ENDURES FOREVER*)

HIS LOVINGKINDNESS
Ps 42:8 The Lord will command *His lovingkindness* in the daytime, and in the night His song shall be with me a prayer to the God of my life

HIS MERCY ENDURES FOREVER
1Chr 16:34 Oh, give thanks to the Lord, for He is good! For *His mercy endures forever*
1Chr 16:41 and with them Heman and Jeduthun and the rest who were chosen, who were designated by name, to give thanks to the Lord, because *His mercy endures forever*
2Chr 5:13 For He is good, for *His mercy endures forever*," that the house, the house of the Lord, was filled with a cloud
2Chr 7:3 When all the children of Israel saw how the fire came down, and the glory of the Lord on the temple, they bowed their faces to the ground on the pavement, and worshiped and praised the Lord, saying: "For He is good, for *His mercy endures forever*
2Chr 7:6 the Levites also with instruments of the music of the Lord, which King David had made to praise the Lord, saying, "For *His mercy endures forever*
2Chr 20:21 And when he had consulted with the people, he appointed those who should sing to the Lord, and who should praise the beauty of holiness, as they went out before the army and were saying: "Praise the Lord, for *His mercy endures forever*
Ezra 3:11 For He is good, for *His mercy endures forever* toward Israel
Ps 106:1 Oh, give thanks to the Lord, for He is good! For *His mercy endures forever*
Ps 107:1 Oh, give thanks to the Lord, for He is good! For *His mercy endures forever*
Ps 118:1 Oh, give thanks to the Lord, for He is good! Because *His mercy endures forever*
Ps 118:2 Let Israel now say, "*His mercy endures forever*
Ps 118:3 Let the house of Aaron now say, "*His mercy endures forever*
Ps 118:4 Let those who fear the Lord now say, "*His mercy endures forever*
Ps 118:29 Oh, give thanks to the Lord, for He is good! For *His mercy endures forever*
Ps 136:1 Oh, give thanks to the Lord, for He is good! For *His mercy endures forever*
Ps 136:2 Oh, give thanks to the God of gods! For *His mercy endures forever*
Ps 136:3 Oh, give thanks to the Lord of lords! For *His mercy endures forever*
Ps 136:4 To Him who alone does great wonders, for *His mercy endures forever*
Ps 136:5 To Him who by wisdom made the heavens, for *His mercy endures forever*
Ps 136:6 To Him who laid out the earth above the waters, for *His mercy endures forever*
Ps 136:7 To Him who made great lights, for *His mercy endures forever*
Ps 136:8 The sun to rule by day, for *His mercy endures forever*
Ps 136:9 The moon and stars to rule by night, for *His mercy endures forever*
Ps 136:10 To Him who struck Egypt in their firstborn, for *His mercy endures forever*
Ps 136:11 And brought out Israel from among them, for *His mercy endures forever*
Ps 136:12 With a strong hand, and with an outstretched arm, for *His mercy endures forever*
Ps 136:13 To Him who divided the Red Sea in two, for *His mercy endures forever*
Ps 136:14 And made Israel pass through the midst of it, for *His mercy endures forever*

Ps 136:15 But overthrew Pharaoh and his army in the Red Sea, for *His mercy endures forever*
Ps 136:16 To Him who led His people through the wilderness, for *His mercy endures forever*
Ps 136:17 To Him who struck down great kings, for *His mercy endures forever*
Ps 136:18 And slew famous kings, for *His mercy endures forever*
Ps 136:19 Sihon king of the Amorites, for *His mercy endures forever*
Ps 136:20 And Og king of Bashan, for *His mercy endures forever*
Ps 136:21 And gave their land as a heritage, for *His mercy endures forever*
Ps 136:22 A heritage to Israel His servant, for *His mercy endures forever*
Ps 136:23 Who remembered us in our lowly state, for *His mercy endures forever*
Ps 136:24 And rescued us from our enemies, for *His mercy endures forever*
Ps 136:25 Who gives food to all flesh, for *His mercy endures forever*
Ps 136:26 Oh, give thanks to the God of heaven! For *His mercy endures forever*
Jer 33:11 Praise the Lord of hosts, for the Lord is good, for *His mercy endures forever*

HIS MIND WAS TROUBLED (NIV)
(See *HIS SPIRIT WAS TROUBLED*)

HIS OWN DID NOT RECEIVE HIM
John 1:11 He came to His own, and *His own did not receive Him*

HIS RIGHT HAND
Gen 48:13 And Joseph took them both, Ephraim with *his right hand* toward Israel's left hand, and Manasseh with his left hand toward Israel's right hand, and brought them near him
Gen 48:14 Then Israel stretched out *his right hand* and laid it on Ephraim's head, who was the younger, and his left hand on Manasseh's head, guiding his hands knowingly, for Manasseh was the firstborn
Gen 48:17 Now when Joseph saw that his father laid *his right hand* on the head of Ephraim, it displeased him
Lev 8:23 And he took some of its blood and put it on the tip of Aaron's right ear, on the thumb of *his right hand*, and on the big toe of his right foot
Lev 14:14 The priest shall take some of the blood of the trespass offering, and the priest shall put it on the tip of the right ear of him who is to be cleansed, on the thumb of *his right hand*, and on the big toe of his right foot
Lev 14:17 And of the rest of the oil in his hand, the priest shall put some on the tip of the right ear of him who is to be cleansed, on the thumb of *his right hand*, and on the big toe of his right foot, on the blood of the trespass offering
Lev 14:25 Then he shall kill the lamb of the trespass offering, and the priest shall take some of the blood of the trespass offering and put it on the tip of the right ear of him who is to be cleansed, on the thumb of *his right hand*, and on the big toe of his right foot
Deut 33:2 from *His right hand* came a fiery law for them
2Sam 16:6 And all the people and all the mighty men were on *his right hand* and on his left
2Sam 20:9 And Joab took Amasa by the beard with *his right hand* to kiss him
1Kin 2:19 And the king rose up to meet her and bowed down to her, and sat down on his throne and had a throne set for the king's mother; so she sat at *his right hand*
1Kin 22:19 I saw the Lord sitting on His throne, and all the host of heaven standing by, on *His right hand* and on His left
1Chr 6:39 And his brother Asaph, who stood at *his right hand*, was Asaph the son of Berachiah, the son of Shimea
2Chr 18:18 I saw the Lord sitting on His throne, and all the host of heaven standing on *His right hand* and on His left
Neh 8:4 and beside him, at *his right hand*, stood Mattithiah, Shema, Anaiah, Urijah, Hilkiah, and Maaseiah
Ps 20:6 He will answer him from His holy heaven with the saving strength of *His right hand*
Ps 78:54 And He brought them to His holy border, this mountain which *His right hand* had acquired
Ps 89:25 Also I will set his hand over the sea, and *his right hand* over the rivers
Ps 98:1 *His right hand* and His holy arm have gained Him the victory
Ps 109:6 Set a wicked man over him, and let an accuser stand at *his right hand*
Prov 27:16 whoever restrains her restrains the wind, and grasps oil with *his right hand*
Eccl 10:2 A wise man's heart is at *his right hand*, but a fool's heart at his left
Song 2:6 His left hand is under my head, and *his right hand* embraces me
Song 8:3 His left hand is under my head, and *his right hand* embraces me
Is 62:8 The Lord has sworn by *His right hand* and by the arm of His strength
Lam 2:3 He has drawn back *His right hand* from before the enemy
Lam 2:4 with *His right hand*, like an adversary, He has slain all who were pleasing to His eye
Ezek 21:22 In *his right hand* is the divination for Jerusalem: to set up battering rams, to call for a slaughter, to lift the voice with shouting, to set battering rams against the gates, to heap up a siege mound, and to build a wall
Dan 12:7 Then I heard the man clothed in linen, who was above the waters of the river, when he held up *his right hand* and his left hand to heaven, and swore by Him who lives forever, that it shall be for a time, times, and half a time
Zech 3:1 Then he showed me Joshua the high priest standing before the Angel of the Lord, and Satan standing at *his right hand* to oppose him
Matt 25:33 And He will set the sheep on *His right hand*, but the goats on the left
Matt 25:34 Then the King will say to those on *His right hand*
Matt 27:29 When they had twisted a crown of thorns, they put it on His head, and a reed in *His right hand*
Acts 5:31 Him God has exalted to *His right hand* to be Prince and Savior, to give repentance to Israel and forgiveness of sins
Eph 1:20 which He worked in Christ when He raised Him from the dead and seated Him at *His right hand* in the heavenly places
Rev 1:16 He had in *His right hand* seven stars, out of His mouth went a sharp two-edged sword, and His countenance was like the sun shining in its strength
Rev 1:17 But He laid *His right hand* on me, saying to me
Rev 2:1 To the angel of the church of Ephesus write, 'These things says He who holds the seven stars in *His right hand*, who walks in the midst of the seven golden lampstands

HIS SERVANTS THE PROPHETS
2Kin 17:23 until the Lord removed Israel out of His sight, as He had said by all *His servants the prophets*
2Kin 21:10 And the Lord spoke by *His servants the prophets*, saying

2Kin 24:2 He sent them against Judah to destroy it, according to the word of the Lord which He had spoken by *His servants the prophets*
Jer 25:4 And the Lord has sent to you all *His servants the prophets*, rising early and sending them, but you have not listened nor inclined your ear to hear
Dan 9:10 We have not obeyed the voice of the Lord our God, to walk in His laws, which He set before us by *His servants the prophets*
Amos 3:7 Surely the Lord God does nothing, unless He reveals His secret to *His servants the prophets*
Rev 10:7 but in the days of the sounding of the seventh angel, when he is about to sound, the mystery of God would be finished, as He declared to *His servants the prophets*

HIS SON REIGNED IN HIS PLACE
2Sam 10:1 And it happened after this that the king of the people of Ammon died, and Hanun *his son reigned in his place*
1Kin 11:43 Then Solomon rested with his fathers, and was buried in the City of David his father. And Rehoboam *his son reigned in his place*
1Kin 14:20 So he rested with his fathers. Then Nadab *his son reigned in his place*
1Kin 14:31 His mother's name was Naamah, an Ammonitess. Then Abijam *his son reigned in his place*
1Kin 15:8 So Abijam rested with his fathers, and they buried him in the City of David. Then Asa *his son reigned in his place*
1Kin 15:24 So Asa rested with his fathers, and was buried with his fathers in the City of David his father. Then Jehoshaphat *his son reigned in his place*
1Kin 16:6 So Baasha rested with his fathers and was buried in Tirzah. Then Elah *his son reigned in his place*
1Kin 16:28 So Omri rested with his fathers and was buried in Samaria. Then Ahab *his son reigned in his place*
1Kin 22:40 So Ahab rested with his fathers. Then Ahaziah *his son reigned in his place*
1Kin 22:50 And Jehoshaphat rested with his fathers, and was buried with his fathers in the City of David his father. Then Jehoram *his son reigned in his place*
2Kin 8:24 So Joram rested with his fathers, and was buried with his fathers in the City of David. Then Ahaziah *his son reigned in his place*
2Kin 10:35 So Jehu rested with his fathers, and they buried him in Samaria. Then Jehoahaz *his son reigned in his place*
2Kin 12:21 So he died, and they buried him with his fathers in the City of David. Then Amaziah *his son reigned in his place*
2Kin 13:9 So Jehoahaz rested with his fathers, and they buried him in Samaria. Then Joash *his son reigned in his place*
2Kin 13:24 Now Hazael king of Syria died. Then Ben-Hadad *his son reigned in his place*
2Kin 14:16 So Jehoash rested with his fathers, and was buried in Samaria with the kings of Israel. Then Jeroboam *his son reigned in his place*
2Kin 14:29 So Jeroboam rested with his fathers, the kings of Israel. Then Zechariah *his son reigned in his place*
2Kin 15:7 So Azariah rested with his fathers, and they buried him with his fathers in the City of David. Then Jotham *his son reigned in his place*
2Kin 15:22 So Menahem rested with his fathers. Then Pekahiah *his son reigned in his place*
2Kin 15:38 So Jotham rested with his fathers, and was buried with his fathers in the City of David his father. Then Ahaz *his son reigned in his place*
2Kin 16:20 So Ahaz rested with his fathers, and was buried with his fathers in the City of David. Then Hezekiah *his son reigned in his place*
2Kin 19:37 and they escaped into the land of Ararat. Then Esarhaddon *his son reigned in his place*
2Kin 20:21 So Hezekiah rested with his fathers. Then Manasseh *his son reigned in his place*
2Kin 21:26 And he was buried in his tomb in the garden of Uzza. Then Josiah *his son reigned in his place*
2Kin 24:6 So Jehoiakim rested with his fathers. Then Jehoiachin *his son reigned in his place*
1Chr 19:1 Now it happened after this that Nahash the king of the people of Ammon died, and *his son reigned in his place*
1Chr 29:28 So he died in a good old age, full of days and riches and honor; and Solomon *his son reigned in his place*
2Chr 9:31 Then Solomon rested with his fathers, and was buried in the City of David his father. And Rehoboam *his son reigned in his place*
2Chr 12:16 So Rehoboam rested with his fathers, and was buried in the City of David. Then Abijah *his son reigned in his place*
2Chr 14:1 Then Asa *his son reigned in his place*. In his days the land was quiet for ten years
2Chr 17:1 Then Jehoshaphat *his son reigned in his place*, and strengthened himself against Israel
2Chr 21:1 And Jehoshaphat rested with his fathers, and was buried with his fathers in the City of David. Then Jehoram *his son reigned in his place*
2Chr 24:27 Now concerning his sons, and the many oracles about him, and the repairing of the house of God, indeed they are written in the annals of the book of the kings. Then Amaziah *his son reigned in his place*
2Chr 26:23 So Uzziah rested with his fathers, and they buried him with his fathers in the field of burial which belonged to the kings, for they said, "He is a leper." Then Jotham *his son reigned in his place*
2Chr 27:9 So Jotham rested with his fathers, and they buried him in the City of David. Then Ahaz *his son reigned in his place*
2Chr 28:27 but they did not bring him into the tombs of the kings of Israel. Then Hezekiah *his son reigned in his place*
2Chr 32:33 and all Judah and the inhabitants of Jerusalem honored him at his death. Then Manasseh *his son reigned in his place*
2Chr 36:8 Now the rest of the acts of Jehoiakim, the abominations which he did, and what was found against him, indeed they are written in the book of the kings of Israel and Judah. Then Jehoiachin *his son reigned in his place*
Is 37:38 and they escaped into the land of Ararat. Then Esarhaddon *his son reigned in his place*

HIS SPIRIT WAS TROUBLED
Gen 41:8 Now it came to pass in the morning that *his spirit was troubled*, and he sent and called for all the magicians of Egypt and all its wise men

HIS STEADFAST LOVE (RSV)
(See *HIS LOVINGKINDNESS*)

HIS STEADFAST LOVE ENDURES FOREVER (RSV)
(See *HIS MERCY ENDURES FOREVER*)

HIS STEPS DO NOT SLIP (NAS, RSV)
(See *NONE OF HIS STEPS SHALL SLIDE*)

HO ARIEL (RSV)
(See *WOE TO ARIEL*)

HOLD FAST TO WHAT IS GOOD (RSV)
(See *CLING TO WHAT IS GOOD*)

HOLD HIM UP TO CONTEMPT (RSV)
(See *PUT HIM TO AN OPEN SHAME*)

HOLD MY TONGUE
Job 6:24 Teach me, and I will *hold my tongue;* cause me to understand wherein I have erred
Job 13:19 Who is he who will contend with me? If now I *hold my tongue*, I perish

HOLD YOUR PEACE (RSV)
(See *KEEP SILENT*)

HOLD YOUR TONGUE
Amos 6:10 And he will say, "*Hold your tongue!* For we dare not mention the name of the Lord
Hab 1:13 Why do You look on those who deal treacherously, and *hold Your tongue* when the wicked devours one more rightous than he

HOLDS THE SEVEN STARS
Rev 2:1 To the angel of the church of Ephesus write, 'These things says He who *holds the seven stars* in His right hand, who walks in the midst of the seven golden lampstands

HOLLOW OF HIS HAND
Is 40:12 Who has measured the waters in the *hollow of his hand*, measured heaven with a span and calculated the dust of the earth in a measure

HOLY AND THE UNHOLY
Ezek 44:23 And they shall teach My people the difference between the *holy and the unholy*, and cause them to discern between the unclean and the clean

HOLY ASSEMBLY (NAS, RSV)
(See *HOLY CONVOCATION*)

HOLY CHILD JESUS (KJV)
(See *HOLY SERVANT JESUS*)

HOLY CITY
Neh 11:1 the rest of the people cast lots to bring one out of ten to dwell in Jerusalem, the *holy city*, and nine-tenths were to dwell in other cities
Neh 11:18 All the Levites in the *holy city* were two hundred and eighty-four
Is 48:2 for they call themselves after the *holy city*, and lean on the God of Israel
Is 52:1 put on your beautiful garments, O Jerusalem, the *holy city*
Dan 9:24 Seventy weeks are determined for your people and for your *holy city*, to finish the transgression, to make an end of sins, to make reconciliation for iniquity, to bring in everlasting righteousness, to seal up vision and prophecy, and to anoint the Most Holy
Matt 4:5 Then the devil took Him up into the *holy city*, set Him on the pinnacle of the temple
Matt 27:53 and coming out of the graves after His resurrection, they went into the *holy city* and appeared to many
Rev 11:2 And they will tread the *holy city* under foot for forty-two months
Rev 21:2 Then I, John, saw the *holy city*, New Jerusalem, coming down out of heaven from God, prepared as a bride adorned for her husband
Rev 22:19 and if anyone takes away from the words of the book of this prophecy, God shall take away his part from the Book of Life, from the *holy city*, and from the things which are written in this book

HOLY CONVOCATION
Ex 12:16 On the first day there shall be a *holy convocation*, and on the seventh day there shall be a *holy convocation* for you
Lev 23:3 Six days shall work be done, but the seventh day is a Sabbath of solemn rest, a *holy convocation*
Lev 23:7 On the first day you shall have a *holy convocation*
Lev 23:8 The seventh day shall be a *holy convocation;* you shall do no customary work on it
Lev 23:21 And you shall proclaim on the same day that it is a *holy convocation* to you
Lev 23:24 In the seventh month, on the first day of the month, you shall have a sabbath-rest, a memorial of blowing of trumpets, a *holy convocation*
Lev 23:27 It shall be a *holy convocation* for you; you shall afflict your souls, and offer an offering made by fire to the Lord
Lev 23:35 On the first day there shall be a *holy convocation*
Lev 23:36 On the eighth day you shall have a *holy convocation*, and you shall offer an offering made by fire to the Lord
Num 28:18 On the first day you shall have a *holy convocation*
Num 28:25 And on the seventh day you shall have a *holy convocation*
Num 28:26 Also on the day of the firstfruits, when you bring a new grain offering to the Lord at your Feast of Weeks, you shall have a *holy convocation*
Num 29:1 And in the seventh month, on the first day of the month, you shall have a *holy convocation*
Num 29:7 On the tenth day of this seventh month you shall have a *holy convocation*
Num 29:12 On the fifteenth day of the seventh month you shall have a *holy convocation*

HOLY COVENANT
Dan 11:28 While returning to his land with great riches, his heart shall be moved against the *holy covenant*
Dan 11:30 therefore he shall be grieved, and return in rage against the *holy covenant*, and do damage. So he shall return and show regard for those who forsake the *holy covenant*
Luke 1:72 to perform the mercy promised to our fathers and to remember His *holy covenant*

HOLY DWELLING
2Chr 30:27 and their prayer came up to His *holy dwelling* place, to heaven

HOLY GHOST DESCENDED (KJV)
(See *SPIRIT DESCENDED*)

HOLY GROUND
Ex 3:5 Take your sandals off your feet, for the place where you stand is *holy ground*
Acts 7:33 Then the Lord said to him, "Take your sandals off your feet, for the place where you stand is *holy ground*

HOLY HABITATION (RSV)
(See *HOLY DWELLING*)

HOLY HILL
Ps 2:6 Yet I have set My King on My *holy hill* of Zion
Ps 3:4 I cried to the Lord with my voice, and He heard me from His *holy hill*
Ps 15:1 Lord, who may abide in Your tabernacle? Who may dwell in Your *holy hill*
Ps 43:3 Let them bring me to Your *holy hill* and to Your tabernacle
Ps 99:9 Exalt the Lord our God, and worship at His *holy hill*

HOLY, HOLY, HOLY
Is 6:3 *Holy, holy, holy* is the Lord of hosts
Rev 4:8 *Holy, holy, holy*, Lord God Almighty, Who was and is and is to come

HOLY IS HIS NAME
Luke 1:49 For He who is mighty has done great things for me, and *holy is His name*

HOLY KISS
Rom 16:16 Greet one another with a *holy kiss*. The churches of Christ greet you
1Cor 16:20 All the brethren greet you. Greet one another with a *holy kiss*
2Cor 13:12 Greet one another with a *holy kiss*
1Th 5:26 Greet all the brethren with a *holy kiss*

HOLY LAND
Zech 2:12 And the Lord will take possession of Judah as His inheritance in the *Holy Land*, and will again choose Jerusalem

HOLY MOUNTAIN
Ps 48:1 Great is the Lord, and greatly to be praised in the city of our God, in His *holy mountain*
Is 11:9 They shall not hurt nor destroy in all My *holy mountain*, for the earth shall be full of the knowledge of the Lord as the waters cover the sea
Is 56:7 even them I will bring to My *holy mountain*, and make them joyful in My house of prayer
Is 57:13 But he who puts his trust in Me shall possess the land, and shall inherit My *holy mountain*
Is 65:11 But you are those who forsake the Lord, who forget My *holy mountain*, who prepare a table for Gad, and who furnish a drink offering for Meni
Is 65:25 They shall not hurt nor destroy in all My *holy mountain*
Is 66:20 Then they shall bring all your brethren for an offering to the Lord out of all nations, on horses and in chariots and in litters, on mules and on camels, to My *holy mountain* Jerusalem
Ezek 20:40 For on My *holy mountain*, on the mountain height of Israel
Ezek 28:14 you were on the *holy mountain* of God; you walked back and forth in the midst of fiery stones
Dan 9:16 O Lord, according to all Your righteousness, I pray, let Your anger and Your fury be turned away from Your city Jerusalem, Your *holy mountain*
Dan 9:20 Now while I was speaking, praying, and confessing my sin and the sin of my people Israel, and presenting my supplication before the Lord my God for the *holy mountain* of my God
Dan 11:45 And he shall plant the tents of his palace between the seas and the glorious *holy mountain*
Joel 2:1 Blow the trumpet in Zion, and sound an alarm in My *holy mountain*
Joel 3:17 So you shall know that I am the Lord your God, dwelling in Zion My *holy mountain*
Obad 16 For as you drank on my *holy mountain*, so shall all the nations drink continually
Zeph 3:11 for then I will take away from your midst those who rejoice in your pride, and you shall no longer be haughty in My *holy mountain*
Zech 8:3 Jerusalem shall be called the City of Truth, the Mountain of the Lord of hosts, the *Holy Mountain*
2Pet 1:18 And we heard this voice which came from heaven when we were with Him on the *holy mountain*

HOLY MOUNTAINS
Ps 87:1 His foundation is in the *holy mountains*

HOLY NAME
Lev 20:3 I will set My face against that man, and will cut him off from his people, because he has given some of his descendants to Molech, to defile My sanctuary and profane My *holy name*
Lev 22:2 Speak to Aaron and his sons, that they separate themselves from the holy things of the children of Israel, and that they do not profane My *holy name* in those things which they sanctify to Me
Lev 22:32 You shall not profane My *holy name*, but I will be hallowed among the children of Israel
1Chr 16:10 Glory in His *holy name;* let the hearts of those rejoice who seek the Lord
1Chr 16:35 gather us together, and deliver us from the Gentiles, to give thanks to Your *holy name*, to triumph in Your praise
1Chr 29:16 O Lord our God, all this abundance that we have prepared to build You a house for Your *holy name* is from Your hand, and is all Your own
Ps 30:4 Sing praise to the Lord, You saints of His, and give thanks at the remembrance of His *holy name*
Ps 33:21 For our heart shall rejoice in Him, because we have trusted in His *holy name*
Ps 97:12 Rejoice in the Lord, you righteous, and give thanks at the remembrance of His *holy name*
Ps 103:1 And all that is within me, bless His *holy name*
Ps 105:3 Glory in His *holy name;* let the hearts of those rejoice who seek the Lord
Ps 106:47 Save us, O Lord our God, and gather us from among the Gentiles, to give thanks to Your *holy name*, and to triumph in Your praise
Ps 145:21 My mouth shall speak the praise of the Lord, and all flesh shall bless His *holy name* forever and ever
Ezek 20:39 but profane My *holy name* no more with your gifts and your idols
Ezek 36:20 When they came to the nations, wherever they went, they profaned My *holy name* when they said of them
Ezek 36:21 But I had concern for My *holy name*, which the house of Israel had profaned among the nations wherever they went
Ezek 39:7 So I will make My *holy name* known in the midst of My people Israel, and I will not let them profane My *holy name* anymore
Ezek 39:25 Now I will bring back the captives of Jacob, and have mercy on the whole house of Israel; and I will be jealous for My *holy name*
Ezek 43:7 No more shall the house of Israel defile My *holy name*, they nor their kings, by their harlotry or with the carcasses of their kings on their high places
Ezek 43:8 When they set their threshold by My threshold, and their doorpost by My doorpost, with a wall between them and Me, they defiled My *holy name* by the abominations which they committed
Amos 2:7 a man and his father go in to the same girl, to defile My *holy name*

HOLY NATION
Ex 19:6 And you shall be to Me a kingdom of priests and a *holy nation*
1Pet 2:9 But you are a chosen generation, a royal priesthood, a *holy nation*, His own special people, that you may proclaim the praises of Him who called you out of darkness into His marvelous light

HOLY ONE OF GOD
Mark 1:24 I know who You are the *Holy One of God*

Luke 4:34 I know You, who You are the *Holy One of God*

HOLY ONE OF ISRAEL

2Kin 19:22 Against whom have you raised your voice, and lifted up your eyes on high? Against the *Holy One of Israel*

Ps 71:22 To You I will sing with the harp, O *Holy One of Israel*

Ps 78:41 Yes, again and again they tempted God, and limited the *Holy One of Israel*

Ps 89:18 For our shield belongs to the Lord, and our king to the *Holy One of Israel*

Is 1:4 They have forsaken the Lord, they have provoked to anger the *Holy One of Israel*, they have turned away backward

Is 5:19 and let the counsel of the *Holy One of Israel* draw near and come, that we may know it

Is 5:24 because they have rejected the law of the Lord of hosts, and despised the word of the *Holy One of Israel*

Is 10:20 And it shall come to pass in that day that the remnant of Israel, and such as have escaped of the house of Jacob, will never again depend on him who defeated them, but will depend on the Lord, the *Holy One of Israel*, in truth

Is 12:6 Cry out and shout, O inhabitant of Zion, for great is the *Holy One of Israel* in your midst

Is 17:7 In that day a man will look to his Maker, and his eyes will have respect for the *Holy One of Israel*

Is 29:19 The humble also shall increase their joy in the Lord, and the poor among men shall rejoice in the *Holy One of Israel*

Is 30:11 Get out of the way, turn aside from the path, cause the *Holy One of Israel* to cease from before us

Is 30:12 Therefore thus says the *Holy One of Israel:* "Because you despise this word, and trust in oppression and perversity, and rely on them

Is 30:15 For thus says the Lord God, the *Holy One of Israel*

Is 31:1 Woe to those who go down to Egypt for help, and rely on horses, who trust in chariots because they are many, and in horsemen because they are very strong, but who do not look to the *Holy One of Israel*, nor seek the Lord

Is 37:23 Against whom have you raised your voice, and lifted up your eyes on high? Against the *Holy One of Israel*

Is 41:14 I will help you," says the Lord and your Redeemer, the *Holy One of Israel*

Is 41:16 you shall rejoice in the Lord, and glory in the *Holy One of Israel*

Is 41:20 That they may see and know, and consider and understand together, that the hand of the Lord has done this, and the *Holy One of Israel* has created it

Is 43:3 For I am the Lord your God, the *Holy One of Israel*, your Savior

Is 43:14 Thus says the Lord, your Redeemer, the *Holy One of Israel*

Is 45:11 Thus says the Lord, the *Holy One of Israel*, and his Maker

Is 47:4 As for our Redeemer, the Lord of hosts is His name, the *Holy One of Israel*

Is 48:17 Thus says the Lord, your Redeemer, the *Holy One of Israel*

Is 49:7 Kings shall see and arise, princes also shall worship, because of the Lord who is faithful, the *Holy One of Israel*

Is 54:5 and your Redeemer is the *Holy One of Israel;* He is called the God of the whole earth

Is 55:5 Surely you shall call a nation you do not know, and nations who do not know you shall run to you, because of the Lord your God, and the *Holy One of Israel*

Is 60:9 and the ships of Tarshish will come first, to bring your sons from afar, their silver and their gold with them, to the name of the Lord your God, and to the *Holy One of Israel*, because He has glorified you

Is 60:14 and they shall call you the City of the Lord, Zion of the *Holy One of Israel*

Jer 50:29 for she has been proud against the Lord, against the *Holy One of Israel*

Jer 51:5 For Israel is not forsaken, nor Judah, by his God, the Lord of hosts, though their land was filled with sin against the *Holy One of Israel*

HOLY PLACE

Ex 26:33 The veil shall be a divider for you between the *holy place* and the Most Holy

Ex 28:29 So Aaron shall bear the names of the sons of Israel on the breastplate of judgment over his heart, when he goes into the *holy place*, as a memorial before the Lord continually

Ex 28:35 And it shall be upon Aaron when he ministers, and its sound will be heard when he goes into the *holy place* before the Lord and when he comes out, that he may not die

Ex 28:43 They shall be on Aaron and on his sons when they come into the tabernacle of meeting, or when they come near the altar to minister in the *holy place*, that they do not incur iniquity and die

Ex 29:30 That son who becomes priest in his place shall put them on for seven days, when he enters the tabernacle of meeting to minister in the *holy place*

Ex 29:31 And you shall take the ram of the consecration and boil its flesh in the *holy place*

Ex 31:11 and the anointing oil and sweet incense for the *holy place*

Ex 35:19 the garments of ministry, for ministering in the *holy place* the holy garments for Aaron the priest and the garments of his sons, to minister as priests

Ex 38:24 All the gold that was used in all the work of the *holy place*, that is, the gold of the offering, was twenty-nine talents and seven hundred and thirty shekels, according to the shekel of the sanctuary

Ex 39:1 Of the blue, purple, and scarlet thread they made garments of ministry, for ministering in the *holy place*, and made the holy garments for Aaron, as the Lord had commanded Moses

Ex 39:41 and the garments of ministry, to minister in the *holy place*

Lev 6:16 with unleavened bread it shall be eaten in a *holy place*

Lev 6:26 In a *holy place* it shall be eaten, in the court of the tabernacle of meeting

Lev 6:27 And when its blood is sprinkled on any garment, you shall wash that on which it was sprinkled, in a *holy place*

Lev 6:30 But no sin offering from which any of the blood is brought into the tabernacle of meeting, to make atonement in the *holy place*, shall be eaten

Lev 7:6 It shall be eaten in a *holy place*. It is most holy

Lev 10:13 And you shall eat it in a *holy place*, because it is your due and your sons' due, of the sacrifices made by fire to the Lord

Lev 10:17 Why have you not eaten the sin offering in a *holy place*, since it is most holy, and God has given it to you to bear the guilt of the congregation, to make atonement for them before the Lord

Lev 10:18 Its blood was not brought inside the *holy place;* indeed you should have eaten it in a *holy place*, as I commanded

Lev 14:13 Then he shall kill the lamb in the place where he kills the sin offering and the burnt offering, in a *holy place*

Lev 16:2 Tell Aaron your brother not to come at simply any time into the *Holy Place* inside the veil, before the mercy seat which is on the ark, lest he die

Lev 16:3 Thus Aaron shall come into the *Holy Place:* with the blood of a young bull as a sin offering, and of a ram as a burnt offering

Lev 16:16 So he shall make atonement for the *Holy Place*, because of the uncleanness of the children of Israel, and because of their transgressions, for all their sins

Lev 16:17 There shall be no man in the tabernacle of meeting when he goes in to make atonement in the *Holy Place*, until he comes out, that he may make atonement for himself, for his household, and for all the congregation of Israel

Lev 16:20 And when he has made an end of atoning for the *Holy Place*, the tabernacle of meeting, and the altar, he shall bring the live goat

Lev 16:23 Then Aaron shall come into the tabernacle of meeting, shall take off the linen garments which he put on when he went into the *Holy Place*, and shall leave them there

Lev 16:24 And he shall wash his body with water in a *holy place*, put on his garments, come out and offer his burnt offering and the burnt offering of the people, and make atonement for himself and for the people

Lev 16:27 The bull for the sin offering and the goat for the sin offering, whose blood was brought in to make atonement in the *Holy Place*, shall be carried outside the camp

Lev 24:9 And it shall be for Aaron and his sons, and they shall eat it in a *holy place*

Num 18:10 In a most *holy place* you shall eat it; every male shall eat it

Num 28:7 in a *holy place* you shall pour out the drink to the Lord as an offering

1Kin 6:16 he built it inside as the inner sanctuary, as the Most *Holy Place*

1Kin 7:50 and the hinges of gold, both for the doors of the inner room (the Most *Holy Place*

1Kin 8:6 Then the priests brought in the ark of the covenant of the Lord to its place, into the inner sanctuary of the temple, to the Most *Holy Place*, under the wings of the cherubim

1Kin 8:8 And the poles extended so that the ends of the poles could be seen from the *holy place*, in front of the inner sanctuary

1Kin 8:10 And it came to pass, when the priests came out of the *holy place*, that the cloud filled the house of the Lord

1Chr 6:49 But Aaron and his sons offered sacrifices on the altar of burnt offering and on the altar of incense, for all the work of the Most *Holy Place*, and to make atonement for Israel, according to all that Moses the servant of God had commanded

1Chr 23:32 and that they should attend to the needs of the tabernacle of meeting, the needs of the *holy place*, and the needs of the sons of Aaron their brethren in the work of the house of the Lord

2Chr 3:8 And he made the Most *Holy Place*. Its length was according to the width of the house, twenty cubits, and its width twenty cubits

2Chr 3:10 In the Most *Holy Place* he made two cherubim, fashioned by carving, and overlaid them with gold

2Chr 4:22 As for the entry of the sanctuary, its inner doors to the Most *Holy Place*, and the doors of the main hall of the temple, were of gold

2Chr 5:7 Then the priests brought in the ark of the covenant of the Lord to its place, into the inner sanctuary of the temple, to the Most *Holy Place*, under the wings of the cherubim

2Chr 5:9 And the poles extended so that the ends of the poles of the ark could be seen from the *holy place*, in front of the inner sanctuary

2Chr 5:11 And it came to pass when the priests came out of the Most *Holy Place* (for all the priests who were present had sanctified themselves, without keeping to their divisions

2Chr 29:5 Now sanctify yourselves, sanctify the house of the Lord God of your fathers, and carry out the rubbish from the *holy place*

2Chr 29:7 They have also shut up the doors of the vestibule, put out the lamps, and have not burned incense or offered burnt offerings in the *holy place* to the God of Israel

2Chr 35:5 And stand in the *holy place* according to the divisions of the fathers' houses of your brethren the lay people, and according to the division of the father's house of the Levites

Ezra 9:8 And now for a little while grace has been shown from the Lord our God, to leave us a remnant to escape, and to give us a peg in His *holy place*, that our God may enlighten our eyes and give us a measure of revival in our bondage

Ps 24:3 Who may ascend into the hill of the Lord? Or who may stand in His *holy place*

Ps 46:4 There is a river whose streams shall make glad the city of God, the *holy place* of the tabernacle of the Most High

Ps 68:17 The Lord is among them as in Sinai, in the *Holy Place*

Is 57:15 I dwell in the high and *holy place*, with him who has a contrite and humble spirit, to revive the spirit of the humble, and to revive the heart of the contrite ones

Ezek 41:4 and he said to me, "This is the Most *Holy Place*

Ezek 44:13 And they shall not come near Me to minister to Me as priest, nor come near any of My holy things, nor into the Most *Holy Place*

Ezek 45:3 in it shall be the sanctuary, the Most *Holy Place*

Ezek 45:4 it shall be a place for their houses and a *holy place* for the sanctuary

Matt 24:15 Therefore when you see the 'abomination of desolation,' spoken of by Daniel the prophet, standing in the *holy place*

Acts 6:13 They also set up false witnesses who said, "This man does not cease to speak blasphemous words against this *holy place* and the law

Acts 21:28 and furthermore he also brought Greeks into the temple and has defiled this *holy place*

Heb 9:12 Not with the blood of goats and calves, but with His own blood He entered the Most *Holy Place* once for all, having obtained eternal redemption

Heb 9:25 not that He should offer Himself often, as the high priest enters the Most *Holy Place* every year with blood of another

HOLY SABBATH TO THE LORD

Ex 16:23 Tomorrow is a Sabbath rest, a *holy Sabbath to the Lord*

HOLY SERVANT JESUS

Acts 4:27 For truly against Your *holy Servant Jesus*, whom You anointed, both Herod and Pontius Pilate, with the Gentiles and the people of Israel, were gathered together

Acts 4:30 by stretching out Your hand to heal, and that signs and wonders may be done through the name of Your *holy Servant Jesus*

HOLY SPIRIT

Ps 51:11 Do not cast me away from Your presence, and do not take Your *Holy Spirit* from me

Is 63:10 But they rebelled and grieved His *Holy Spirit;* so He turned Himself against them as an enemy, and He fought against them

Is 63:11 Where is He who put His *Holy Spirit* within them

Matt 1:18 After His mother Mary was betrothed to Joseph, before they came together, she was found with child of the *Holy Spirit*

Matt 1:20 But while he thought about these things, behold, an angel of the Lord appeared to him in a dream, saying, "Joseph, son of David, do not be afraid to take to you Mary your wife, for that which is conceived in her is of the *Holy Spirit*

Matt 3:11 He will baptize you with the *Holy Spirit* and fire

Matt 12:32 but whoever speaks against the *Holy Spirit,* it will not be forgiven him, either in this age or in the age to come

Matt 28:19 Go therefore and make disciples of all the nations, baptizing them in the name of the Father and of the Son and of the *Holy Spirit*

Mark 1:8 I indeed baptized you with water, but He will baptize you with the *Holy Spirit*

Mark 3:29 but he who blasphemes against the *Holy Spirit* never has forgiveness, but is subject to eternal condemnation

Mark 12:36 For David himself said by the *Holy Spirit:* 'The Lord said to my Lord

Mark 13:11 for it is not you who speak, but the *Holy Spirit*

Luke 1:15 He will also be filled with the *Holy Spirit*, even from his mother's womb

Luke 1:35 And the angel answered and said to her, "The *Holy Spirit* will come upon you, and the power of the Highest will overshadow you

Luke 1:41 And it happened, when Elizabeth heard the greeting of Mary, that the babe leaped in her womb; and Elizabeth was filled with the *Holy Spirit*

Luke 1:67 Now his father Zacharias was filled with the *Holy Spirit*, and prophesied, saying

Luke 2:25 And behold, there was a man in Jerusalem whose name was Simeon, and this man was just and devout, waiting for the Consolation of Israel, and the *Holy Spirit* was upon him

Luke 2:26 And it had been revealed to him by the *Holy Spirit* that he would not see death before he had seen the Lord's Christ

Luke 3:16 He will baptize you with the *Holy Spirit* and with fire

Luke 3:22 And the *Holy Spirit* descended in bodily form like a dove upon Him, and a voice came from heaven which said

Luke 4:1 Then Jesus, being filled with the *Holy Spirit*, returned from the Jordan and was led by the Spirit into the wilderness

Luke 11:13 If you then, being evil, know how to give good gifts to your children, how much more will your heavenly Father give the *Holy Spirit* to those who ask Him

Luke 12:10 but to him who blasphemes against the *Holy Spirit*, it will not be forgiven

Luke 12:12 For the *Holy Spirit* will teach you in that very hour what you ought to say

John 1:33 I did not know Him, but He who sent me to baptize with water said to me, 'Upon whom you see the Spirit descending, and remaining on Him, this is He who baptizes with the *Holy Spirit*

John 7:39 for the *Holy Spirit* was not yet given, because Jesus was not yet glorified

John 14:26 But the Helper, the *Holy Spirit*, whom the Father will send in My name, He will teach you all things, and bring to your remembrance all things that I said to you

John 20:22 And when He had said this, He breathed on them, and said to them, "Receive the *Holy Spirit*

Acts 1:2 until the day in which He was taken up, after He through the *Holy Spirit* had given commandments to the apostles whom He had chosen

Acts 1:5 for John truly baptized with water, but you shall be baptized with the *Holy Spirit* not many days from now

Acts 1:8 But you shall receive power when the *Holy Spirit* has come upon you

Acts 1:16 Men and brethren, this Scripture had to be fulfilled, which the *Holy Spirit* spoke before by the mouth of David concerning Judas, who became a guide to those who arrested Jesus

Acts 2:4 And they were all filled with the *Holy Spirit* and began to speak with other tongues, as the Spirit gave them utterance

Acts 2:33 Therefore being exalted to the right hand of God, and having received from the Father the promise of the *Holy Spirit*, He poured out this which you now see and hear

Acts 2:38 and you shall receive the gift of the *Holy Spirit*

Acts 4:8 Then Peter, filled with the *Holy Spirit*, said to them

Acts 4:31 and they were all filled with the *Holy Spirit*, and they spoke the word of God with boldness

Acts 5:3 But Peter said, "Ananias, why has Satan filled your heart to lie to the *Holy Spirit* and keep back part of the price of the land for yourself

Acts 5:32 And we are His witnesses to these things, and so also is the *Holy Spirit* whom God has given to those who obey Him

Acts 6:3 Therefore, brethren, seek out from among you seven men of good reputation, full of the *Holy Spirit* and wisdom, whom we may appoint over this business

Acts 6:5 And they chose Stephen, a man full of faith and the *Holy Spirit*, and Philip, Prochorus, Nicanor, Timon, Parmenas, and Nicolas, a proselyte from Antioch

Acts 7:51 You always resist the *Holy Spirit;* as your fathers did, so do you

Acts 7:55 But he, being full of the *Holy Spirit*, gazed into heaven and saw the glory of God, and Jesus standing at the right hand of God

Acts 8:15 who, when they had come down, prayed for them that they might receive the *Holy Spirit*

Acts 8:17 Then they laid hands on them, and they received the *Holy Spirit*

Acts 8:18 Now when Simon saw that through the laying on of the apostles' hands the *Holy Spirit* was given, he offered them money

Acts 8:19 saying, "Give me this power also, that anyone on whom I lay hands may receive the *Holy Spirit*

Acts 9:17 and laying his hands on him he said, "Brother Saul, the Lord Jesus, who appeared to you on the road as you came, has sent me that you may receive your sight and be filled with the *Holy Spirit*

Acts 9:31 And walking in the fear of the Lord and in the comfort of the *Holy Spirit*, they were multiplied

Acts 10:38 how God anointed Jesus of Nazareth with the *Holy Spirit* and with power, who went about doing good and healing all who were oppressed by the devil, for God was with Him

Acts 10:44 While Peter was still speaking these words, the *Holy Spirit* fell upon all those who heard the word

Acts 10:45 And those of the circumcision who believed were astonished, as many as came with Peter, because the gift of the *Holy Spirit* had been poured out on the Gentiles also

Acts 10:47 Can anyone forbid water, that these should not be baptized who have received the *Holy Spirit* just as we have

Acts 11:15 And as I began to speak, the *Holy Spirit* fell upon them, as upon us at the beginning

Acts 11:16 Then I remembered the word of the Lord, how He said, 'John indeed baptized with

water, but you shall be baptized with the *Holy Spirit*
Acts 11:24 For he was a good man, full of the *Holy Spirit* and of faith
Acts 13:2 As they ministered to the Lord and fasted, the *Holy Spirit* said
Acts 13:4 So, being sent out by the *Holy Spirit*, they went down to Seleucia, and from there they sailed to Cyprus
Acts 13:9 Then Saul, who also is called Paul, filled with the *Holy Spirit*, looked intently at him
Acts 13:52 And the disciples were filled with joy and with the *Holy Spirit*
Acts 15:8 So God, who knows the heart, acknowledged them, by giving them the *Holy Spirit* just as He did to us
Acts 15:28 For it seemed good to the *Holy Spirit*, and to us, to lay upon you no greater burden than these necessary things
Acts 16:6 Now when they had gone through Phrygia and the region of Galatia, they were forbidden by the *Holy Spirit* to preach the word in Asia
Acts 19:2 he said to them, "Did you receive the *Holy Spirit* when you believed?" And they said to him, "We have not so much as heard whether there is a *Holy Spirit*
Acts 19:6 And when Paul had laid hands on them, the *Holy Spirit* came upon them, and they spoke with tongues and prophesied
Acts 20:23 except that the *Holy Spirit* testifies in every city, saying that chains and tribulations await me
Acts 20:28 Therefore take heed to yourselves and to all the flock, among which the *Holy Spirit* has made you overseers, to shepherd the church of God which He purchased with His own blood
Acts 21:11 When he had come to us, he took Paul's belt, bound his own hands and feet, and said, "Thus says the *Holy Spirit*
Acts 28:25 The *Holy Spirit* spoke rightly through Isaiah the prophet to our fathers
Rom 5:5 Now hope does not disappoint, because the love of God has been poured out in our hearts by the *Holy Spirit* who was given to us
Rom 9:1 I tell the truth in Christ, I am not lying, my conscience also bearing me witness in the *Holy Spirit*
Rom 14:17 for the kingdom of God is not food and drink, but righteousness and peace and joy in the *Holy Spirit*
Rom 15:13 Now may the God of hope fill you with all joy and peace in believing, that you may abound in hope by the power of the *Holy Spirit*
Rom 15:16 that I might be a minister of Jesus Christ to the Gentiles, ministering the gospel of God, that the offering of the Gentiles might be acceptable, sanctified by the *Holy Spirit*
1Cor 2:13 These things we also speak, not in words which man's wisdom teaches but which the *Holy Spirit* teaches, comparing spiritual things with spiritual
1Cor 6:19 Or do you not know that your body is the temple of the *Holy Spirit* who is in you, whom you have from God, and you are not your own
1Cor 12:3 Therefore I make known to you that no one speaking by the Spirit of God calls Jesus accursed, and no one can say that Jesus is Lord except by the *Holy Spirit*
2Cor 6:6 by purity, by knowledge, by longsuffering, by kindness, by the *Holy Spirit*, by sincere love
2Cor 13:14 The grace of the Lord Jesus Christ, and the love of God, and the communion of the *Holy Spirit* be with you all
Eph 1:13 in whom also, having believed, you were sealed with the *Holy Spirit* of promise
Eph 4:30 And do not grieve the *Holy Spirit* of God, by whom you were sealed for the day of redemption
1Th 1:5 For our gospel did not come to you in word only, but also in power, and in the *Holy Spirit* and in much assurance, as you know what kind of men we were among you for your sake
1Th 1:6 And you became followers of us and of the Lord, having received the word in much affliction, with joy of the *Holy Spirit*
1Th 4:8 Therefore he who rejects this does not reject man, but God, who has also given us His *Holy Spirit*
2Tim 1:14 That good thing which was committed to you, keep by the *Holy Spirit* who dwells in us
Tit 3:5 not by works of righteousness which we have done, but according to His mercy He saved us, through the washing of regeneration and renewing of the *Holy Spirit*
Heb 2:4 God also bearing witness both with signs and wonders, with various miracles, and gifts of the *Holy Spirit*, according to His own will
Heb 3:7 Therefore, as the *Holy Spirit* says: "Today, if you will hear His voice
Heb 6:4 For it is impossible for those who were once enlightened, and have tasted the heavenly gift, and have become partakers of the *Holy Spirit*
Heb 9:8 the *Holy Spirit* indicating this, that the way into the Holiest of All was not yet made manifest while the first tabernacle was still standing
Heb 10:15 And the *Holy Spirit* also witnesses to us; for after He had said before
1Pet 1:12 To them it was revealed that, not to themselves, but to us they were ministering the things which now have been reported to you through those who have preached the gospel to you by the *Holy Spirit* sent from heaven things which angels desire to look into
2Pet 1:21 for prophecy never came by the will of man, but holy men of God spoke as they were moved by the *Holy Spirit*
1Jn 5:7 the Father, the Word, and the *Holy Spirit;* and these three are one
Jude 20 But you, beloved, building yourselves up on your most holy faith, praying in the *Holy Spirit*

HOLY SPIRIT OF PROMISE

Eph 1:13 in whom also, having believed, you were sealed with the *Holy Spirit of promise*

HOLY TEMPLE

Ps 5:7 In fear of You I will worship toward Your *holy temple*
Ps 11:4 The Lord is in His *holy temple*, the Lord's throne is in heaven
Ps 65:4 We shall be satisfied with the goodness of Your house, of Your *holy temple*
Ps 79:1 Your *holy temple* they have defiled; they have laid Jerusalem in heaps
Ps 138:2 I will worship toward Your *holy temple*, and praise Your name for Your lovingkindness and Your truth
Jon 2:4 Then I said, 'I have been cast out of Your sight; yet I will look again toward Your *holy temple*
Jon 2:7 and my prayer went up to You, into Your *holy temple*
Mic 1:2 Let the Lord God be a witness against you, the Lord from His *holy temple*
Hab 2:20 But the Lord is in His *holy temple*. Let all the earth keep silence before Him
Eph 2:21 in whom the whole building, being joined together, grows into a *holy temple* in the Lord

HOLY TO THE LORD
Ex 30:10 once a year he shall make atonement upon it throughout your generations. It is most *holy to the Lord*
Ex 31:15 Work shall be done for six days, but the seventh is the Sabbath of rest, *holy to the Lord*
Lev 23:20 They shall be *holy to the Lord* for the priest
Lev 27:14 And when a man sanctifies his house to be *holy to the Lord*, then the priest shall set a value for it, whether it is good or bad
Lev 27:21 but the field, when it is released in the Jubilee, shall be *holy to the Lord*, as a devoted field
Lev 27:28 Nevertheless no devoted offering that a man may devote to the Lord of all that he has, both man and beast, or the field of his possession, shall be sold or redeemed; every devoted offering is most *holy to the Lord*
Lev 27:30 And all the tithe of the land, whether of the seed of the land or of the fruit of the tree, is the Lord's. It is *holy to the Lord*
Lev 27:32 And concerning the tithe of the herd or the flock, of whatever passes under the rod, the tenth one shall be *holy to the Lord*
Num 6:8 All the days of his separation he shall be *holy to the Lord*
2Chr 35:3 Then he said to the Levites who taught all Israel, who were *holy to the Lord*
Ezra 8:28 And I said to them, "You are *holy to the Lord*
Neh 8:9 And Nehemiah, who was the governor, Ezra the priest and scribe, and the Levites who taught the people said to all the people, "This day is *holy to the Lord* your God
Jer 31:40 And the whole valley of the dead bodies and of the ashes, and all the fields as far as the Brook Kidron, to the corner of the Horse Gate toward the east, shall be *holy to the Lord*
Ezek 48:14 they may not alienate this best part of the land, for it is *holy to the Lord*
Luke 2:23 (as it is written in the law of the Lord, "every male who opens the womb shall be called *holy to the Lord*

HOLY WAY (RSV)
(See *HIGHWAY OF HOLINESS*)

HONEST SCALES (NIV)
(See *JUST BALANCE*)

HONEST WEIGHTS (NIV)
(See *JUST WEIGHT*)

HONEY FROM THE ROCK
Deut 32:13 He made him to draw *honey from the rock*, and oil from the flinty rock
Ps 81:16 And with *honey from the rock* I would have satisfied you

HONOR AND MAJESTY
1Chr 16:27 *Honor and majesty* are before Him; strength and gladness are in His place
Ps 21:5 His glory is great in Your salvation; *honor and majesty* You have placed upon him
Ps 96:6 *Honor and majesty* are before Him; strength and beauty are in His sanctuary
Ps 104:1 O Lord my God, You are very great: You are clothed with *honor and majesty*

HONOR AND PRAISE (NIV)
(See *FAME AND PRAISE*)

HONOR ME WITH THEIR LIPS
Is 29:13 Inasmuch as these people draw near to Me with their mouths and *honor Me with their lips*, but have removed their hearts far from Me, and their fear toward Me is taught by the commandment of men
Matt 15:8 These people draw near to Me with their mouth, and *honor Me with their lips*, but their heart is far from Me

HONOR OF HIS NAME
Ps 66:2 Sing out the *honor of His name;* make His praise glorious

HONOR YOUR FATHER AND YOUR MOTHER
Ex 20:12 *Honor your father and your mother*, that your days may be long upon the land which the Lord your God is giving you
Deut 5:16 *Honor your father and your mother*, as the Lord your God has commanded you, that your days may be long, and that it may be well with you in the land which the Lord your God is giving you
Matt 15:4 For God commanded, saying, '*Honor your father and your mother*
Matt 19:19 *Honor your father and your mother*,' and, 'You shall love your neighbor as yourself
Mark 7:10 For Moses said, '*Honor your father and your mother*'
Mark 10:19 Do not commit adultery, Do not murder, Do not steal, Do not bear false witness, Do not defraud, *Honor your father and your mother*
Luke 18:20 Do not commit adultery, Do not murder, Do not steal, Do not bear false witness, *Honor your father and your mother*

HONORED IN MY BODY (RSV)
(See *MAGNIFIED IN MY BODY*)

HOPE DEFERRED
Prov 13:12 *Hope deferred* makes the heart sick, but when the desire comes, it is a tree of life

HOPE DOES NOT DISAPPOINT
Rom 5:5 Now *hope does not disappoint*, because the love of God has been poured out in our hearts by the Holy Spirit who was given to us

HOPE HELD OUT IN THE GOSPEL (NIV)
(See *HOPE OF THE GOSPEL*)

HOPE IN CHRIST
1Cor 15:19 If in this life only we have *hope in Christ*, we are of all men the most pitiable

HOPE IN GOD
Ps 42:5 *Hope in God*, for I shall yet praise Him for the help of His countenance
Ps 42:11 *Hope in God;* for I shall yet praise Him, the help of my countenance and my God
Ps 43:5 *Hope in God;* for I shall yet praise Him, the help of my countenance and my God
Ps 78:7 That they may set their *hope in God*, and not forget the works of God, but keep His commandments
Acts 24:15 I have *hope in God*, which they themselves also accept, that there will be a resurrection of the dead, both of the just and the unjust

HOPE IN THE LORD
Ps 31:24 Be of good courage, and He shall strengthen your heart, all you who *hope in the Lord*
Ps 130:7 O Israel, *hope in the Lord;* for with the Lord there is mercy, and with Him is abundant redemption
Ps 131:3 O Israel, *hope in the Lord* from this time forth and forever

HOPE MAKETH NOT ASHAMED (KJV)
(See *HOPE DOES NOT DISAPPOINT*)

HOPE OF ETERNAL LIFE
Tit 1:2 in *hope of eternal life* which God, who cannot lie, promised before time began
Tit 3:7 that having been justified by His grace we should become heirs according to the *hope of eternal life*

HOPE OF GLORY
Col 1:27 To them God willed to make known what are the riches of the glory of this mystery among the Gentiles: which is Christ in you, the *hope of glory*

HOPE OF SALVATION
1Th 5:8 But let us who are of the day be sober, putting on the breastplate of faith and love, and as a helmet the *hope of salvation*

HOPE OF THE GOSPEL
Col 1:23 if indeed you continue in the faith, grounded and steadfast, and are not moved away from the *hope of the gospel* which you heard, which was preached to every creature under heaven, of which I, Paul, became a minister

HOPE THAT IS SEEN
Rom 8:24 For we were saved in this hope, but *hope that is seen* is not hope

HOPED IN CHRIST (NAS, RSV)
(See *HOPE IN CHRIST*)

HOPES OF THE WICKED (NIV)
(See *EXPECTATION OF THE WICKED*)

HORN IS EXALTED
1Sam 2:1 my *horn is exalted* in the Lord. I smile at my enemies, because I rejoice in Your salvation
Ps 89:17 For You are the glory of their strength, and in Your favor our *horn is exalted*

HORN IS LIFTED HIGH (NIV)
(See *HORN IS EXALTED*)

HORN OF DAVID
Ps 132:17 There I will make the *horn of David* grow; I will prepare a lamp for My Anointed

HORN OF ISRAEL
Lam 2:3 He has cut off in fierce anger every *horn of Israel*

HORN OF MY SALVATION
2Sam 22:3 the God of my strength, in Him I will trust, my shield and the *horn of my salvation*, my stronghold and my refuge
Ps 18:2 My shield and the *horn of my salvation*, my stronghold

HORN OF OIL
1Sam 16:13 Then Samuel took the *horn of oil* and anointed him in the midst of his brothers
1Kin 1:39 Then Zadok the priest took a *horn of oil* from the tabernacle and anointed Solomon

HORN OF SALVATION
Luke 1:69 and has raised up a *horn of salvation* for us in the house of His servant David

HORNS OF THE ALTAR
Ex 29:12 You shall take some of the blood of the bull and put it on the *horns of the altar* with your finger, and pour all the blood beside the base of the altar
Lev 4:7 And the priest shall put some of the blood on the *horns of the altar* of sweet incense before the Lord, which is in the tabernacle of meeting
Lev 4:18 And he shall put some of the blood on the *horns of the altar* which is before the Lord, which is in the tabernacle of meeting
Lev 4:25 The priest shall take some of the blood of the sin offering with his finger, put it on the *horns of the altar* of burnt offering, and pour its blood at the base of the altar of burnt offering
Lev 4:30 Then the priest shall take some of its blood with his finger, put it on the *horns of the altar* of burnt offering, and pour all the remaining blood at the base of the altar
Lev 4:34 The priest shall take some of the blood of the sin offering with his finger, put it on the *horns of the altar* of burnt offering, and pour all the remaining blood at the base of the altar
Lev 8:15 Then he took the blood, and put some on the *horns of the altar* all around with his finger, and purified the altar
Lev 9:9 And he dipped his finger in the blood, put it on the *horns of the altar*, and poured the blood at the base of the altar
Lev 16:18 And he shall go out to the altar that is before the Lord, and make atonement for it, and shall take some of the blood of the bull and some of the blood of the goat, and put it on the *horns of the altar* all around
1Kin 1:50 so he arose, and went and took hold of the *horns of the altar*
1Kin 1:51 for look, he has taken hold of the *horns of the altar*, saying
1Kin 2:28 So Joab fled to the tabernacle of the Lord, and took hold of the *horns of the altar*
Ps 118:27 Bind the sacrifice with cords to the *horns of the altar*
Ezek 43:20 You shall take some of its blood and put it on the four *horns of the altar*, on the four corners of the ledge, and on the rim around it
Amos 3:14 and the *horns of the altar* shall be cut off and fall to the ground

HORSE AND ITS RIDER
Ex 15:1 The *horse and its rider* He has thrown into the sea
Ex 15:21 The *horse and its rider* He has thrown into the sea
Job 39:18 When she lifts herself on high, she scorns the *horse and its rider*
Jer 51:21 with you I will break in pieces the *horse and its rider*

HORSES ARE FLESH
Is 31:3 and their *horses are flesh*, and not spirit. When the Lord stretches out His hand, both he who helps will fall, and he who is helped will fall down

HOSANNA IN THE HIGHEST
Matt 21:9 Blessed is He who comes in the name of the Lord!' *Hosanna in the highest*
Mark 11:10 Blessed is the kingdom of our father David that comes in the name of the Lord! *Hosanna in the highest*

HOST OF HEAVEN
Deut 4:19 And take heed, lest you lift your eyes to heaven, and when you see the sun, the moon, and the stars, all the *host of heaven*, you feel driven to worship them and serve them, which the Lord your God has given to all the peoples under the whole heaven as a heritage
Deut 17:3 who has gone and served other gods and worshiped them, either the sun or moon or any of the *host of heaven*, which I have not commanded
1Kin 22:19 I saw the Lord sitting on His throne, and all the *host of heaven* standing by, on His right hand and on His left
2Kin 17:16 So they left all the commandments of the Lord their God, made for themselves a

molded image and two calves, made a wooden image and worshiped all the *host of heaven*, and served Baal
2Kin 21:3 and he worshiped all the *host of heaven* and served them
2Kin 21:5 And he built altars for all the *host of heaven* in the two courts of the house of the Lord
2Kin 23:4 And the king commanded Hilkiah the high priest, the priests of the second order, and the doorkeepers, to bring out of the temple of the Lord all the articles that were made for Baal, for Asherah, and for all the *host of heaven*
2Kin 23:5 Then he removed the idolatrous priests whom the kings of Judah had ordained to burn incense on the high places in the cities of Judah and in the places all around Jerusalem, and those who burned incense to Baal, to the sun, to the moon, to the constellations, and to all the *host of heaven*
2Chr 18:18 I saw the Lord sitting on His throne, and all the *host of heaven* standing on His right hand and on His left
2Chr 33:3 and he worshiped all the *host of heaven* and served them
2Chr 33:5 And he built altars for all the *host of heaven* in the two courts of the house of the Lord
Neh 9:6 You have made heaven, the heaven of heavens, with all their host, the earth and all things on it, the seas and all that is in them, and You preserve them all. The *host of heaven* worships You
Is 34:4 All the *host of heaven* shall be dissolved, and the heavens shall be rolled up like a scroll
Jer 8:2 They shall spread them before the sun and the moon and all the *host of heaven*, which they have loved and which they have served and after which they have walked, which they have sought and which they have worshiped
Jer 19:13 And the houses of Jerusalem and the houses of the kings of Judah shall be defiled like the place of Tophet, because of all the houses on whose roofs they have burned incense to all the *host of heaven*, and poured out drink offerings to other gods
Jer 33:22 As the *host of heaven* cannot be numbered, nor the sand of the sea measured, so will I multiply the descendants of David My servant and the Levites who minister to Me
Dan 8:10 And it grew up to the *host of heaven;* and it cast down some of the host and some of the stars to the ground, and trampled them
Zeph 1:5 those who worship the *host of heaven* on the housetops
Acts 7:42 Then God turned and gave them up to worship the *host of heaven*, as it is written in the book of the Prophets

HOUNDED TO DEATH THE POOR (NIV)
(See *PERSECUTED THE POOR*)

HOUR HAS COME
Mark 14:41 The *hour has come;* behold, the Son of Man is being betrayed into the hands of sinners
John 12:23 But Jesus answered them, saying, "The *hour has come* that the Son of Man should be glorified
John 16:21 A woman, when she is in labor, has sorrow because her *hour has come*
John 17:1 Father, the *hour has come*. Glorify Your Son, that Your Son also may glorify You

HOUR IS ALREADY LATE
Matt 14:15 When it was evening, His disciples came to Him, saying, "This is a deserted place, and the *hour is already late*

HOUR IS COMING
John 4:21 Jesus said to her, "Woman, believe Me, the *hour is coming* when you will neither on this mountain, nor in Jerusalem, worship the Father
John 4:23 But the *hour is coming*, and now is, when the true worshipers will worship the Father in spirit and truth
John 5:25 Most assuredly, I say to you, the *hour is coming*, and now is, when the dead will hear the voice of the Son of God
John 5:28 for the *hour is coming* in which all who are in the graves will hear His voice
John 16:32 Indeed the *hour is coming*, yes, has now come, that you will be scattered, each to his own, and will leave Me alone

HOUR IS LATE
Mark 6:35 And when the day was now far spent, His disciples came to Him and said, "This is a deserted place, and already the *hour is late*

HOUR OF PRAYER
Acts 3:1 Now Peter and John went up together to the temple at the *hour of prayer*, the ninth hour

HOUR OF TRIAL
Rev 3:10 Because you have kept My command to persevere, I also will keep you from the *hour of trial* which shall come upon the whole world, to test those who dwell on the earth

HOUR YOUR LORD IS COMING
Matt 24:42 Watch therefore, for you do not know what *hour your Lord is coming*

HOUSE DIVIDED AGAINST ITSELF
Matt 12:25 Every kingdom divided against itself is brought to desolation, and every city or *house divided against itself* will not stand

HOUSE FOR MY NAME
2Sam 7:13 He shall build a *house for My name*, and I will establish the throne of his kingdom forever
1Kin 5:5 And behold, I propose to build a house for the name of the Lord my God, as the Lord spoke to my father David, saying, 'Your son, whom I will set on your throne in your place, he shall build the *house for My name*
1Kin 8:18 But the Lord said to my father David, 'Whereas it was in your heart to build a *house for My name*, you did well that it was in your heart
1Kin 8:19 Nevertheless you shall not build the house, but your son, who shall come from your loins, he shall build the *house for My name*
1Chr 22:8 you shall not build a *house for My name*, because you have shed much blood on the earth in My sight
1Chr 22:10 He shall build a *house for My name*, and he shall be My son, and I will be his Father
1Chr 28:3 But God said to me, 'You shall not build a *house for My name*, because you have been a man of war and have shed blood

HOUSE OF BONDAGE
Ex 13:3 Remember this day in which you went out of Egypt, out of the *house of bondage*
Ex 13:14 that you shall say to him, 'By strength of hand the Lord brought us out of Egypt, out of the *house of bondage*
Ex 20:2 I am the Lord your God, who brought you out of the land of Egypt, out of the *house of bondage*
Deut 5:6 I am the Lord your God who brought you out of the land of Egypt, out of the *house of bondage*
Deut 6:12 then beware, lest you forget the Lord who brought you out of the land of Egypt, from the *house of bondage*

Deut 7:8 but because the Lord loves you, and because He would keep the oath which He swore to your fathers, the Lord has brought you out with a mighty hand, and redeemed you from the *house of bondage*, from the hand of Pharaoh king of Egypt
Deut 8:14 when your heart is lifted up, and you forget the Lord your God who brought you out of the land of Egypt, from the *house of bondage*
Deut 13:5 But that prophet or that dreamer of dreams shall be put to death, because he has spoken in order to turn you away from the Lord your God, who brought you out of the land of Egypt and redeemed you from the *house of bondage*, to entice you from the way in which the Lord your God commanded you to walk
Deut 13:10 And you shall stone him with stones until he dies, because he sought to entice you away from the Lord your God, who brought you out of the land of Egypt, from the *house of bondage*
Josh 24:17 for the Lord our God is He who brought us and our fathers up out of the land of Egypt, from the *house of bondage*, who did those great signs in our sight, and preserved us in all the way that we went and among all the people through whom we passed
Judg 6:8 I brought you up from Egypt and brought you out of the *house of bondage*
Jer 34:13 I made a covenant with your fathers in the day that I brought them out of the land of Egypt, out of the *house of bondage*, saying
Mic 6:4 For I brought you up from the land of Egypt, I redeemed you from the *house of bondage*

HOUSE OF DAVID
1Sam 20:16 So Jonathan made a covenant with the *house of David*, saying
2Sam 3:1 Now there was a long war between the house of Saul and the *house of David*
2Sam 3:6 Now it was so, while there was war between the house of Saul and the *house of David*, that Abner was strengthening his hold on the house of Saul
1Kin 12:19 So Israel has been in rebellion against the *house of David* to this day
1Kin 12:20 There was none who followed the *house of David*, but the tribe of Judah only
1Kin 12:26 And Jeroboam said in his heart, "Now the kingdom may return to the *house of David*
1Kin 13:2 Behold, a child, Josiah by name, shall be born to the *house of David*
1Kin 14:8 and tore the kingdom away from the *house of David*, and gave it to you
2Kin 17:21 For He tore Israel from the *house of David*, and they made Jeroboam the son of Nebat king
2Chr 8:11 Now Solomon brought the daughter of Pharaoh up from the City of David to the house he had built for her, for he said, "My wife shall not dwell in the *house of David* king of Israel, because the places to which the ark of the Lord has come are holy
2Chr 10:19 So Israel has been in rebellion against the *house of David* to this day
2Chr 21:7 Yet the Lord would not destroy the *house of David*, because of the covenant that He had made with David, and since He had promised to give a lamp to him and to his sons forever
Neh 12:37 By the Fountain Gate, in front of them, they went up the stairs of the City of David, on the stairway of the wall, beyond the *house of David*, as far as the Water Gate eastward
Ps 122:5 For thrones are set there for judgment, the thrones of the *house of David*
Is 7:2 And it was told to the *house of David*, saying
Is 7:13 Then he said, "Hear now, O *house of David!* Is it a small thing for you to weary men, but will you weary my God also
Is 22:22 The key of the *house of David* I will lay on his shoulder
Jer 21:12 O *house of David!* Thus says the Lord: "Execute judgment in the morning
Zech 12:7 The Lord will save the tents of Judah first, so that the glory of the *house of David* and the glory of the inhabitants of Jerusalem shall not become greater than that of Judah
Zech 12:8 the one who is feeble among them in that day shall be like David, and the *house of David* shall be like God, like the Angel of the Lord before them
Zech 12:10 And I will pour on the *house of David* and on the inhabitants of Jerusalem the Spirit of grace and supplication
Zech 12:12 the family of the *house of David* by itself, and their wives by themselves
Zech 13:1 In that day a fountain shall be opened for the *house of David* and for the inhabitants of Jerusalem, for sin and for uncleanness
Luke 1:27 to a virgin betrothed to a man whose name was Joseph, of the *house of David*

HOUSE OF GOD
Gen 28:17 This is none other than the *house of God*, and this is the gate of heaven
Judg 18:31 So they set up for themselves Micah's carved image which he made, all the time that the *house of God* was in Shiloh
Judg 20:18 And the children of Israel arose and went up to the *house of God* to ask counsel of God
Judg 20:26 Then all the children of Israel, that is, all the people, went up and came to the *house of God* and wept
Judg 21:2 Then the people came to the *house of God*, and remained there before God till evening
1Chr 6:48 And their brethren, the Levites, were appointed to every kind of service of the tabernacle of the *house of God*
1Chr 9:11 Azariah the son of Hilkiah, the son of Meshullam, the son of Zadok, the son of Meraioth, the son of Ahitub, the officer over the *house of God*
1Chr 9:13 They were very able men for the work of the service of the *house of God*
1Chr 9:26 And they had charge over the chambers and treasuries of the *house of God*
1Chr 9:27 And they lodged all around the *house of God* because they had the responsibility, and they were in charge of opening it every morning
1Chr 22:2 and he appointed masons to cut hewn stones to build the *house of God*
1Chr 23:28 because their duty was to help the sons of Aaron in the service of the house of the Lord, in the courts and in the chambers, in the purifying of all holy things and the work of the service of the *house of God*
1Chr 24:5 Thus they were divided by lot, one group as another, for there were officials of the sanctuary and officials of the *house of God*, from the sons of Eleazar and from the sons of Ithamar
1Chr 25:6 All these were under the direction of their father for the music in the house of the Lord, with cymbals, stringed instruments, and harps, for the service of the *house of God*
1Chr 26:20 Of the Levites, Ahijah was over the treasuries of the *house of God* and over the treasuries of the dedicated things
1Chr 28:12 and the plans for all that he had by the Spirit, of the courts of the house of the Lord, of all the chambers all around, of the treasuries of the *house of God*, and of the treasuries for the dedicated things
1Chr 28:21 Here are the divisions of the priests

and the Levites for all the service of the *house of God*

1Chr 29:7 They gave for the work of the *house of God* five thousand talents and ten thousand darics of gold, ten thousand talents of silver, eighteen thousand talents of bronze, and one hundred thousand talents of iron

2Chr 3:3 This is the foundation which Solomon laid for building the *house of God*

2Chr 4:11 So Huram finished doing the work that he was to do for King Solomon for the *house of God*

2Chr 4:19 Thus Solomon had all the furnishings made for the *house of God*

2Chr 5:1 And he put them in the treasuries of the *house of God*

2Chr 5:14 for the glory of the Lord filled the *house of God*

2Chr 7:5 So the king and all the people dedicated the *house of God*

2Chr 15:18 He also brought into the *house of God* the things that his father had dedicated and that he himself had dedicated

2Chr 22:12 And he was hidden with them in the *house of God* for six years, while Athaliah reigned over the land

2Chr 23:3 Then all the congregation made a covenant with the king in the *house of God*

2Chr 24:7 For the sons of Athaliah, that wicked woman, had broken into the *house of God*, and had also presented all the dedicated things of the house of the Lord to the Baals

2Chr 24:13 they restored the *house of God* to its original condition and reinforced it

2Chr 24:27 Now concerning his sons, and the many oracles about him, and the repairing of the *house of God*, indeed they are written in the annals of the book of the kings

2Chr 25:24 And he took all the gold and silver, all the articles that were found in the *house of God* with Obed-Edom, the treasures of the king's house, and hostages, and returned to Samaria

2Chr 28:24 So Ahaz gathered the articles of the *house of God*, cut in pieces the articles of the *house of God*, shut up the doors of the house of the Lord, and made for himself altars in every corner of Jerusalem

2Chr 31:13 Jehiel, Azaziah, Nahath, Asahel, Jerimoth, Jozabad, Eliel, Ismachiah, Mahath, and Benaiah were overseers under the hand of Cononiah and Shimei his brother, at the commandment of Hezekiah the king and Azariah the ruler of the *house of God*

2Chr 31:21 And in every work that he began in the service of the *house of God*, in the law and in the commandment, to seek his God, he did it with all his heart

2Chr 33:7 He even set a carved image, the idol which he had made, in the *house of God*, of which God had said to David and to Solomon his son

2Chr 34:9 When they came to Hilkiah the high priest, they delivered the money that was brought into the *house of God*, which the Levites who kept the doors had gathered from the hand of Manasseh and Ephraim, from all the remnant of Israel, from all Judah and Benjamin, and which they had brought back to Jerusalem

2Chr 35:8 Hilkiah, Zechariah, and Jehiel, rulers of the *house of God*, gave to the priests for the Passover offerings two thousand six hundred from the flock, and three hundred cattle

2Chr 36:18 And all the articles from the *house of God*, great and small, the treasures of the house of the Lord, and the treasures of the king and of his leaders, all these he took to Babylon

2Chr 36:19 Then they burned the *house of God*, broke down the wall of Jerusalem, burned all its palaces with fire, and destroyed all its precious possessions

Ezra 1:4 And whoever remains in any place where he sojourns, let the men of his place help him with silver and gold, with goods and livestock, besides the freewill offerings for the *house of God* which is in Jerusalem

Ezra 2:68 Some of the heads of the fathers' houses, when they came to the house of the Lord which is in Jerusalem, offered freely for the *house of God*, to erect it in its place

Ezra 3:8 Now in the second month of the second year of their coming to the *house of God* at Jerusalem, Zerubbabel the son of Shealtiel, Jeshua the son of Jozadak, and the rest of their brethren the priests and the Levites, and all those who had come out of the captivity to Jerusalem, began work and appointed the Levites from twenty years old and above to oversee the work of the house of the Lord

Ezra 3:9 Then Jeshua with his sons and brothers, Kadmiel with his sons, and the sons of Judah, arose as one to oversee those working on the *house of God*

Ezra 4:24 Thus the work of the *house of God* which is at Jerusalem ceased, and it was discontinued until the second year of the reign of Darius king of Persia

Ezra 5:2 So Zerubbabel the son of Shealtiel and Jeshua the son of Jozadak rose up and began to build the *house of God* which is in Jerusalem

Ezra 5:13 However, in the first year of Cyrus king of Babylon, King Cyrus issued a decree to build this *house of God*

Ezra 5:14 Also, the gold and silver articles of the *house of God*, which Nebuchadnezzar had taken from the temple that was in Jerusalem and carried into the temple of Babylon those King Cyrus took from the temple of Babylon, and they were given to one named Sheshbazzar, whom he had made governor

Ezra 5:15 go, carry them to the temple site that is in Jerusalem, and let the *house of God* be rebuilt on its former site

Ezra 5:16 Then the same Sheshbazzar came and laid the foundation of the *house of God* which is in Jerusalem

Ezra 5:17 Now therefore, if it seems good to the king, let a search be made in the king's treasure house, which is there in Babylon, whether it is so that a decree was issued by King Cyrus to build this *house of God* at Jerusalem, and let the king send us his pleasure concerning this matter

Ezra 6:3 In the first year of King Cyrus, King Cyrus issued a decree concerning the *house of God* at Jerusalem

Ezra 6:5 Also let the gold and silver articles of the *house of God*, which Nebuchadnezzar took from the temple which is in Jerusalem and brought to Babylon, be restored and taken back to the temple which is in Jerusalem, each to its place; and deposit them in the *house of God*

Ezra 6:7 Let the work of this *house of God* alone; let the governor of the Jews and the elders of the Jews build this *house of God* on its site

Ezra 6:8 Moreover I issue a decree as to what you shall do for the elders of these Jews, for the building of this *house of God*

Ezra 6:12 And may the God who causes His name to dwell there destroy any king or people who put their hand to alter it, or to destroy this *house of God* which is in Jerusalem

Ezra 6:16 Then the children of Israel, the priests and the Levites and the rest of the descendants of the captivity, celebrated the dedication of this *house of God* with joy

Ezra 6:17 And they offered sacrifices at the dedication of this *house of God*, one hundred bulls, two hundred rams, four hundred lambs, and as a sin offering for all Israel twelve male goats, according to the number of the tribes of Israel

Ezra 6:22 for the Lord made them joyful, and turned the heart of the king of Assyria toward them, to strengthen their hands in the work of the *house of God*, the God of Israel

Ezra 7:24 Also we inform you that it shall not be lawful to impose tax, tribute, or custom on any of the priests, Levites, singers, gatekeepers, Nethinim, or servants of this *house of God*

Ezra 8:36 So they gave support to the people and the *house of God*

Ezra 10:1 Now while Ezra was praying, and while he was confessing, weeping, and bowing down before the *house of God*, a very large congregation of men, women, and children assembled to him from Israel

Ezra 10:6 Then Ezra rose up from before the *house of God*, and went into the chamber of Jehohanan the son of Eliashib

Ezra 10:9 and all the people sat in the open square of the *house of God*, trembling because of this matter and because of heavy rain

Neh 6:10 and he said, "Let us meet together in the *house of God*, within the temple, and let us close the doors of the temple, for they are coming to kill you

Neh 8:16 Then the people went out and brought them and made themselves booths, each one on the roof of his house, or in their courtyards or the courts of the *house of God*, and in the open square of the Water Gate and in the open square of the Gate of Ephraim

Neh 11:11 Seraiah the son of Hilkiah, the son of Meshullam, the son of Zadok, the son of Meraioth, the son of Ahitub, was the leader of the *house of God*

Neh 11:16 Shabbethai and Jozabad, of the heads of the Levites, had the oversight of the business outside of the *house of God*

Neh 11:22 Also the overseer of the Levites at Jerusalem was Uzzi the son of Bani, the son of Hashabiah, the son of Mattaniah, the son of Micha, of the sons of Asaph, the singers in charge of the service of the *house of God*

Neh 12:40 So the two thanksgiving choirs stood in the *house of God*, likewise I and the half of the rulers with me

Neh 13:7 and I came to Jerusalem and discovered the evil that Eliashib had done for Tobiah, in preparing a room for him in the courts of the *house of God*

Neh 13:9 and I brought back into them the articles of the *house of God*, with the grain offering and the frankincense

Neh 13:11 So I contended with the rulers, and said, "Why is the *house of God* forsaken

Ps 42:4 I went with them to the *house of God*, with the voice of joy and praise, with a multitude that kept a pilgrim feast

Ps 52:8 But I am like a green olive tree in the *house of God*

Ps 55:14 We took sweet counsel together, and walked to the *house of God* in the throng

Eccl 5:1 Walk prudently when you go to the *house of God*

Dan 1:2 And the Lord gave Jehoiakim king of Judah into his hand, with some of the articles of the *house of God*, which he carried into the land of Shinar to the house of his god

Dan 5:3 Then they brought the gold vessels that had been taken from the temple of the *house of God* which had been in Jerusalem

Zech 7:2 when the people sent Sherezer, with Regem-Melech and his men, to the *house of God*, to pray before the Lord

Matt 12:4 how he entered the *house of God* and ate the showbread which was not lawful for him to eat, nor for those who were with him, but only for the priests

Mark 2:26 how he went into the *house of God* in the days of Abiathar the high priest, and ate the showbread, which is not lawful to eat, except for the priests, and also gave some to those who were with him

Luke 6:4 how he went into the *house of God*, took and ate the showbread, and also gave some to those who were with him, which is not lawful for any but the priests to eat

1Tim 3:15 but if I am delayed, I write so that you may know how you ought to conduct yourself in the *house of God*, which is the church of the living God, the pillar and ground of the truth

Heb 10:21 and having a High Priest over the *house of God*

1Pet 4:17 For the time has come for judgment to begin at the *house of God*

HOUSE OF HIS FATHER

Ex 12:3 On the tenth day of this month every man shall take for himself a lamb, according to the *house of his father*, a lamb for a household

Josh 22:14 and each one was the head of the *house of his father* among the divisions of Israel

Is 3:6 When a man takes hold of his brother in the *house of his father*, saying

HOUSE OF ISRAEL

Ex 16:31 And the *house of Israel* called its name Manna. And it was like white coriander seed, and the taste of it was like wafers made with honey

Ex 40:38 For the cloud of the Lord was above the tabernacle by day, and fire was over it by night, in the sight of all the *house of Israel*, throughout all their journeys

Lev 10:6 But let your brethren, the whole *house of Israel*, bewail the burning which the Lord has kindled

Lev 17:3 Whatever man of the *house of Israel*, kills an ox or lamb or goat in the camp, or who kills it outside the camp

Lev 17:8 Whatever man of the *house of Israel*, or of the strangers who sojourn among you, who offers a burnt offering or sacrifice

Lev 17:10 And whatever man of the *house of Israel*, or of the strangers who sojourn among you, who eats any blood, I will set My face against that person who eats blood, and will cut him off from among his people

Lev 22:18 Whatever man of the *house of Israel*, or of the strangers in Israel, who offers his sacrifice for any of his vows or for any of his freewill offerings, which they offer to the Lord as a burnt offering

Num 20:29 Now when all the congregation saw that Aaron was dead, all the *house of Israel* mourned for Aaron thirty days

Josh 21:45 Not a word failed of any good thing which the Lord had spoken to the *house of Israel*

Ruth 4:11 The Lord make the woman who is coming to your house like Rachel and Leah, the two who built the *house of Israel*

1Sam 7:2 And all the *house of Israel* lamented after the Lord

1Sam 7:3 Then Samuel spoke to all the *house of Israel*, saying

2Sam 1:12 And they mourned and wept and fasted until evening for Saul and for Jonathan his son, for the people of the Lord and for the *house of Israel*, because they had fallen by the sword

2Sam 6:5 Then David and all the *house of Israel* played music before the Lord on all kinds of instruments made of fir wood, on harps, on stringed instruments, on tambourines, on sistrums, and on cymbals

2Sam 6:15 So David and all the *house of Israel* brought up the ark of the Lord with shouting and with the sound of the trumpet
2Sam 12:8 I gave you your master's house and your master's wives into your keeping, and gave you the *house of Israel* and Judah
2Sam 16:3 And Ziba said to the king, "Indeed he is staying in Jerusalem, for he said, 'Today the *house of Israel* will restore the kingdom of my father to me
1Kin 12:21 And when Rehoboam came to Jerusalem, he assembled all the house of Judah with the tribe of Benjamin, one hundred and eighty thousand chosen men who were warriors, to fight against the *house of Israel*, that he might restore the kingdom to Rehoboam the son of Solomon
1Kin 20:31 And his servants said to him, "Look now, we have heard that the kings of the *house of Israel* are merciful kings
Ps 98:3 He has remembered His mercy and His faithfulness to the *house of Israel*
Ps 115:12 He will bless the *house of Israel;* He will bless the house of Aaron
Ps 135:19 Bless the Lord, O *house of Israel!* Bless the Lord, O house of Aaron
Is 5:7 For the vineyard of the Lord of hosts is the *house of Israel*, and the men of Judah are His pleasant plant
Is 14:2 Then people will take them and bring them to their place, and the *house of Israel* will possess them for servants and maids in the land of the Lord
Is 46:3 Listen to Me, O house of Jacob, and all the remnant of the *house of Israel*, who have been upheld by Me from birth, who have been carried from the womb
Is 63:7 I will mention the lovingkindnesses of the Lord and the praises of the Lord, according to all that the Lord has bestowed on us, and the great goodness toward the *house of Israel*, which He has bestowed on them according to His mercies, according to the multitude of His lovingkindnesses
Jer 2:4 Hear the word of the Lord, O house of Jacob and all the families of the *house of Israel*
Jer 2:26 As the thief is ashamed when he is found out, so is the *house of Israel* ashamed
Jer 3:18 In those days the house of Judah shall walk with the *house of Israel*, and they shall come together out of the land of the north to the land that I have given as an inheritance to your fathers
Jer 3:20 Surely, as a wife treacherously departs from her husband, so have you dealt treacherously with Me, O *house of Israel*
Jer 5:11 For the *house of Israel* and the house of Judah have dealt very treacherously with Me
Jer 5:15 Behold, I will bring a nation against you from afar, O *house of Israel*
Jer 9:26 For all these nations are uncircumcised, and all the *house of Israel* are uncircumcised in the heart
Jer 10:1 Hear the word which the Lord speaks to you, O *house of Israel*
Jer 11:10 the *house of Israel* and the house of Judah have broken My covenant which I made with their fathers
Jer 11:17 For the Lord of hosts, who planted you, has pronounced doom against you for the evil of the *house of Israel* and of the house of Judah, which they have done against themselves to provoke Me to anger in offering incense to Baal
Jer 13:11 For as the sash clings to the waist of a man, so I have caused the whole *house of Israel* and the whole house of Judah to cling to Me
Jer 18:6 O *house of Israel*, can I not do with you as this potter?" says the Lord. "Look, as the clay is in the potter's hand, so are you in My hand, O *house of Israel*
Jer 23:8 but, 'As the Lord lives who brought up and led the descendants of the *house of Israel* from the north country and from all the countries where I had driven them
Jer 31:27 Behold, the days are coming," says the Lord, "that I will sow the *house of Israel* and the house of Judah with the seed of man and the seed of beast
Jer 31:31 Behold, the days are coming," says the Lord, "when I will make a new covenant with the *house of Israel* and with the house of Judah
Jer 31:33 But this is the covenant that I will make with the *house of Israel*
Jer 33:14 Behold, the days are coming,' says the Lord, 'that I will perform that good thing which I have promised to the *house of Israel* and to the house of Judah
Jer 33:17 David shall never lack a man to sit on the throne of the *house of Israel*
Jer 48:13 Moab shall be ashamed of Chemosh, as the *house of Israel* was ashamed of Bethel, their confidence
Ezek 3:1 eat this scroll, and go, speak to the *house of Israel*
Ezek 3:4 Son of man, go to the *house of Israel* and speak with My words to them
Ezek 3:5 For you are not sent to a people of unfamiliar speech and of hard language, but to the *house of Israel*
Ezek 3:7 But the *house of Israel* will not listen to you, because they will not listen to Me; for all the *house of Israel* are impudent and hard-hearted
Ezek 3:17 Son of man, I have made you a watchman for the *house of Israel*
Ezek 4:3 This will be a sign to the *house of Israel*
Ezek 4:4 Lie also on your left side, and lay the iniquity of the *house of Israel* upon it
Ezek 4:5 so you shall bear the iniquity of the *house of Israel*
Ezek 5:4 for from there a fire will go out into all the *house of Israel*
Ezek 6:11 Pound your fists and stamp your feet, and say, 'Alas, for all the evil abominations of the *house of Israel*
Ezek 8:6 Furthermore He said to me, "Son of man, do you see what they are doing, the great abominations that the *house of Israel* commits here, to make Me go far away from My sanctuary
Ezek 8:10 So I went in and saw, and there every sort of creeping thing, abominable beasts, and all the idols of the *house of Israel*, portrayed all around on the walls
Ezek 8:11 And there stood before them seventy men of the elders of the *house of Israel*, and in their midst stood Jaazaniah the son of Shaphan
Ezek 8:12 Then He said to me, "Son of man, have you seen what the elders of the *house of Israel* do in the dark, every man in the room of his idols
Ezek 9:9 Then He said to me, "The iniquity of the *house of Israel* and Judah is exceedingly great, and the land is full of bloodshed, and the city full of perversity
Ezek 11:5 Thus you have said, O *house of Israel;* for I know the things that come into your mind
Ezek 11:15 Son of man, your brethren, your relatives, your kinsmen, and all the *house of Israel* in its entirety, are those about whom the inhabitants of Jerusalem have said
Ezek 12:6 you shall cover your face, so that you cannot see the ground, for I have made you a sign to the *house of Israel*
Ezek 12:9 Son of man, has not the *house of Israel*, the rebellious house, said to you
Ezek 12:10 This burden concerns the prince in Jerusalem and all the *house of Israel* who are among them

Ezek 12:24 For no more shall there be any false vision or flattering divination within the *house of Israel*
Ezek 12:27 Son of man, look, the *house of Israel* is saying
Ezek 13:5 You have not gone up into the gaps to build a wall for the *house of Israel* to stand in battle on the day of the Lord
Ezek 13:9 they shall not be in the assembly of My people, nor be written in the record of the *house of Israel*, nor shall they enter into the land of Israel
Ezek 14:4 Everyone of the *house of Israel* who sets up his idols in his heart, and puts before him what causes him to stumble into iniquity, and then comes to the prophet, I the Lord will answer him who comes, according to the multitude of his idols
Ezek 14:5 that I may seize the *house of Israel* by their heart, because they are all estranged from Me by their idols
Ezek 14:6 Therefore say to the *house of Israel*, 'Thus says the Lord God
Ezek 14:7 For anyone of the *house of Israel*, or of the strangers who sojourn in Israel, who separates himself from Me and sets up his idols in his heart and puts before him what causes him to stumble into iniquity, then comes to a prophet to inquire of him concerning Me, I the Lord will answer him by Myself
Ezek 14:11 that the *house of Israel* may no longer stray from Me, nor be profaned anymore with all their transgressions, but that they may be My people and I may be their God
Ezek 17:2 Son of man, pose a riddle, and speak a parable to the *house of Israel*
Ezek 18:6 if he has not eaten on the mountains, nor lifted up his eyes to the idols of the *house of Israel*, nor defiled his neighbor's wife, nor approached a woman during her impurity
Ezek 18:15 Who has not eaten on the mountains, nor lifted his eyes to the idols of the *house of Israel*, Nor defiled his neighbor's wife
Ezek 18:25 Hear now, O *house of Israel*, is it not My way which is fair, and your ways which are not fair
Ezek 18:29 Yet the *house of Israel* says, 'The way of the Lord is not fair.' O *house of Israel*, is it not My ways which are fair, and your ways which are not fair
Ezek 18:30 Therefore I will judge you, O *house of Israel*, every one according to his ways
Ezek 18:31 Cast away from you all the transgressions which you have committed, and get yourselves a new heart and a new spirit. For why should you die, O *house of Israel*
Ezek 20:13 Yet the *house of Israel* rebelled against Me in the wilderness
Ezek 20:27 Therefore, son of man, speak to the *house of Israel*, and say to them
Ezek 20:30 Therefore say to the *house of Israel*, 'Thus says the Lord God
Ezek 20:31 So shall I be inquired of by you, O *house of Israel*
Ezek 20:39 As for you, O *house of Israel*," thus says the Lord God
Ezek 20:40 For on My holy mountain, on the mountain height of Israel," says the Lord God, "there all the *house of Israel*, all of them in the land, shall serve Me
Ezek 20:44 Then you shall know that I am the Lord, when I have dealt with you for My name's sake, not according to your wicked ways nor according to your corrupt doings, O *house of Israel*
Ezek 22:18 Son of man, the *house of Israel* has become dross to Me
Ezek 24:21 Speak to the *house of Israel*, "Thus says the Lord God
Ezek 28:24 And there shall no longer be a pricking brier or a painful thorn for the *house of Israel* from among all who are around them, who despise them
Ezek 28:25 When I have gathered the *house of Israel* from the peoples among whom they are scattered, and am hallowed in them in the sight of the Gentiles, then they will dwell in their own land which I gave to My servant Jacob
Ezek 29:6 Then all the inhabitants of Egypt shall know that I am the Lord, because they have been a staff of reed to the *house of Israel*
Ezek 29:16 No longer shall it be the confidence of the *house of Israel*, but will remind them of their iniquity when they turned to follow them
Ezek 29:21 In that day I will cause the horn of the *house of Israel* to spring forth, and I will open your mouth to speak in their midst
Ezek 33:7 I have made you a watchman for the *house of Israel*
Ezek 33:10 Therefore you, O son of man, say to the *house of Israel*
Ezek 33:11 Turn, turn from your evil ways! For why should you die, O *house of Israel*
Ezek 33:20 O *house of Israel*, I will judge every one of you according to his own ways
Ezek 34:30 Thus they shall know that I, the Lord their God, am with them, and that they, the *house of Israel*, are My people
Ezek 35:15 As you rejoiced because the inheritance of the *house of Israel* was desolate, so I will do to you
Ezek 36:10 I will multiply men upon you, all the *house of Israel*, all of it
Ezek 36:17 Son of man, when the *house of Israel* dwelt in their own land, they defiled it by their own ways and deeds
Ezek 36:21 But I had concern for My holy name, which the *house of Israel* had profaned among the nations wherever they went
Ezek 36:22 Therefore say to the *house of Israel*, 'Thus says the Lord God: "I do not do this for your sake, O *house of Israel*, but for My holy name's sake, which you have profaned among the nations wherever you went
Ezek 36:32 Be ashamed and confounded for your own ways, O *house of Israel*
Ezek 36:37 I will also let the *house of Israel* inquire of Me to do this for them
Ezek 37:11 Then He said to me, "Son of man, these bones are the whole *house of Israel*
Ezek 37:16 Then take another stick and write on it, 'For Joseph, the stick of Ephraim, and for all the *house of Israel*, his companions
Ezek 39:12 For seven months the *house of Israel* will be burying them, in order to cleanse the land
Ezek 39:22 So the *house of Israel* shall know that I am the Lord their God from that day forward
Ezek 39:23 The Gentiles shall know that the *house of Israel* went into captivity for their iniquity
Ezek 39:25 Now I will bring back the captives of Jacob, and have mercy on the whole *house of Israel*
Ezek 39:29 for I shall have poured out My Spirit on the *house of Israel*
Ezek 40:4 for you were brought here so that I might show them to you. Declare to the *house of Israel* everything you see
Ezek 43:7 No more shall the *house of Israel* defile My holy name, they nor their kings, by their harlotry or with the carcasses of their kings on their high places
Ezek 43:10 Son of man, describe the temple to the *house of Israel*, that they may be ashamed of their iniquities
Ezek 44:6 Now say to the rebellious, to the *house of Israel*, 'Thus says the Lord God: "O *house of*

Israel, let us have no more of all your abominations

Ezek 44:12 Because they ministered to them before their idols and caused the *house of Israel* to fall into iniquity, therefore I have lifted My hand in an oath against them

Ezek 44:22 They shall not take as wife a widow or a divorced woman, but take virgins of the descendants of the *house of Israel*, or widows of priests

Ezek 45:6 You shall appoint as the property of the city an area five thousand cubits wide and twenty-five thousand long, adjacent to the district of the holy portion; it shall belong to the whole *house of Israel*

Ezek 45:8 and My princes shall no more oppress My people, but they shall give the rest of the land to the *house of Israel*, according to their tribes

Ezek 45:17 Then it shall be the prince's part to give burnt offerings, grain offerings, and drink offerings, at the feasts, the New Moons, the Sabbaths, and at all the appointed seasons of the *house of Israel*. He shall prepare the sin offering, the grain offering, the burnt offering, and the peace offerings to make atonement for the *house of Israel*

Hos 1:4 Call his name Jezreel, for in a little while I will avenge the bloodshed of Jezreel on the house of Jehu, and bring an end to the kingdom of the *house of Israel*

Hos 1:6 Call her name Lo-Ruhamah, for I will no longer have mercy on the *house of Israel*, but I will utterly take them away

Hos 5:1 Take heed, O *house of Israel!* Give ear, O house of the king

Hos 6:10 I have seen a horrible thing in the *house of Israel*

Hos 11:12 Ephraim has encompassed Me with lies, and the *house of Israel* with deceit

Amos 5:1 Hear this word which I take up against you, this lamentation, O *house of Israel*

Amos 5:3 The city that goes out by a thousand shall have a hundred left, and that which goes out by a hundred shall have ten left to the *house of Israel*

Amos 5:4 For thus says the Lord to the *house of Israel*

Amos 5:25 Did you offer Me sacrifices and offerings in the wilderness forty years, O *house of Israel*

Amos 6:1 Woe to you who are at ease in Zion, and trust in Mount Samaria, notable persons in the chief nation, to whom the *house of Israel* comes

Amos 6:14 But, behold, I will raise up a nation against you, O *house of Israel*

Amos 7:10 Then Amaziah the priest of Bethel sent to Jeroboam king of Israel, saying, "Amos has conspired against you in the midst of the *house of Israel*

Amos 9:9 For surely I will command, and will sift the *house of Israel* among all nations, as grain is sifted in a sieve

Mic 1:5 All this is for the transgression of Jacob and for the sins of the *house of Israel*

Mic 3:1 Hear now, O heads of Jacob, and you rulers of the *house of Israel*

Mic 3:9 Now hear this, you heads of the house of Jacob and rulers of the *house of Israel*, who abhor justice and pervert all equity

Zech 8:13 And it shall come to pass that just as you were a curse among the nations, O house of Judah and *house of Israel*, so I will save you, and you shall be a blessing

Matt 10:6 But go rather to the lost sheep of the *house of Israel*

Matt 15:24 But He answered and said, "I was not sent except to the lost sheep of the *house of Israel*

Acts 2:36 Therefore let all the *house of Israel* know assuredly that God has made this Jesus, whom you crucified, both Lord and Christ

Acts 7:42 Did you offer Me slaughtered animals and sacrifices during forty years in the wilderness, O *house of Israel*

Heb 8:8 Behold, the days are coming," says the Lord, "when I will make a new covenant with the *house of Israel* and with the house of Judah

Heb 8:10 For this is the covenant that I will make with the *house of Israel*

HOUSE OF JUDAH

2Sam 2:4 Then the men of Judah came, and there they anointed David king over the *house of Judah*

2Sam 2:7 for your master Saul is dead, and also the *house of Judah* has anointed me king over them

2Sam 2:10 Ishbosheth, Saul's son, was forty years old when he began to reign over Israel, and he reigned two years. Only the *house of Judah* followed David

2Sam 2:11 And the time that David was king in Hebron over the *house of Judah* was seven years and six months

1Kin 12:21 And when Rehoboam came to Jerusalem, he assembled all the *house of Judah* with the tribe of Benjamin, one hundred and eighty thousand chosen men who were warriors, to fight against the house of Israel, that he might restore the kingdom to Rehoboam the son of Solomon

1Kin 12:23 Speak to Rehoboam the son of Solomon, king of Judah, to all the *house of Judah* and Benjamin, and to the rest of the people, saying

2Kin 19:30 And the remnant who have escaped of the *house of Judah* shall again take root downward, and bear fruit upward

1Chr 28:4 and of the *house of Judah*, the house of my father, and among the sons of my father, He was pleased with me to make me king over all Israel

2Chr 11:1 Now when Rehoboam came to Jerusalem, he assembled from the *house of Judah* and Benjamin one hundred and eighty thousand chosen men who were warriors, to fight against Israel, that he might restore the kingdom to Rehoboam

2Chr 19:11 and Zebadiah the son of Ishmael, the ruler of the *house of Judah*, for all the king's matters

2Chr 22:10 Now when Athaliah the mother of Ahaziah saw that her son was dead, she arose and destroyed all the royal heirs of the *house of Judah*

Neh 4:16 and the leaders were behind all the *house of Judah*

Is 22:21 He shall be a father to the inhabitants of Jerusalem and to the *house of Judah*

Is 37:31 And the remnant who have escaped of the *house of Judah* shall again take root downward, and bear fruit upward

Jer 3:18 In those days the *house of Judah* shall walk with the house of Israel, and they shall come together out of the land of the north to the land that I have given as an inheritance to your fathers

Jer 5:11 For the house of Israel and the *house of Judah* have dealt very treacherously with Me

Jer 11:10 the house of Israel and the *house of Judah* have broken My covenant which I made with their fathers

Jer 11:17 For the Lord of hosts, who planted you, has pronounced doom against you for the evil of the house of Israel and of the *house of Judah*, which they have done against themselves to provoke Me to anger in offering incense to Baal

Jer 12:14 Against all My evil neighbors who touch

the inheritance which I have caused My people Israel to inherit behold, I will pluck them out of their land and pluck out the *house of Judah* from among them

Jer 13:11 For as the sash clings to the waist of a man, so I have caused the whole house of Israel and the whole *house of Judah* to cling to Me

Jer 31:27 Behold, the days are coming," says the Lord, "that I will sow the house of Israel and the *house of Judah* with the seed of man and the seed of beast

Jer 31:31 Behold, the days are coming," says the Lord, "when I will make a new covenant with the house of Israel and with the *house of Judah*

Jer 33:14 Behold, the days are coming,' says the Lord, 'that I will perform that good thing which I have promised to the house of Israel and to the *house of Judah*

Jer 36:3 It may be that the *house of Judah* will hear all the adversities which I purpose to bring upon them, that everyone may turn from his evil way, that I may forgive their iniquity and their sin

Ezek 4:6 then you shall bear the iniquity of the *house of Judah* forty days

Ezek 8:17 Is it a trivial thing to the *house of Judah* to commit the abominations which they commit here

Ezek 25:3 against My sanctuary when it was profaned, and against the land of Israel when it was desolate, and against the *house of Judah* when they went into captivity

Ezek 25:8 Because Moab and Seir say, 'Look! The *house of Judah* is like all the nations

Ezek 25:12 Because of what Edom did against the *house of Judah* by taking vengeance, and has greatly offended by avenging itself on them

Hos 1:7 Yet I will have mercy on the *house of Judah*, will save them by the Lord their God, and will not save them by bow, nor by sword or battle, by horses or horsemen

Hos 5:12 Therefore I will be to Ephraim like a moth, and to the *house of Judah* like rottenness

Hos 5:14 For I will be like a lion to Ephraim, and like a young lion to the *house of Judah*

Zeph 2:7 The coast shall be for the remnant of the *house of Judah*

Zech 8:13 And it shall come to pass that just as you were a curse among the nations, O *house of Judah* and house of Israel, so I will save you, and you shall be a blessing

Zech 8:15 so again in these days I am determined to do good to Jerusalem and to the *house of Judah*

Zech 8:19 The fast of the fourth month, the fast of the fifth, the fast of the seventh, and the fast of the tenth, shall be joy and gladness and cheerful feasts for the *house of Judah*

Zech 10:3 For the Lord of hosts will visit His flock, the *house of Judah*, and will make them as His royal horse in the battle

Zech 10:6 I will strengthen the *house of Judah*, and I will save the house of Joseph

Zech 12:4 I will open My eyes on the *house of Judah*, and will strike every horse of the peoples with blindness

Heb 8:8 Behold, the days are coming," says the Lord, "when I will make a new covenant with the house of Israel and with the *house of Judah*

HOUSE OF PRAYER

Is 56:7 even them I will bring to My holy mountain, and make them joyful in My *house of prayer*. Their burnt offerings and their sacrifices will be accepted on My altar; for My house shall be called a *house of prayer* for all nations

Matt 21:13 And He said to them, "It is written, 'My house shall be called a *house of prayer*

Mark 11:17 Then He taught, saying to them, "Is it not written, 'My house shall be called a *house of prayer* for all nations

Luke 19:46 saying to them, "It is written, 'My house is a *house of prayer*

HOUSE OF THE LORD

Ex 23:19 The first of the firstfruits of your land you shall bring into the *house of the Lord* your God

Ex 34:26 The first of the firstfruits of your land you shall bring to the *house of the Lord* your God

Deut 23:18 You shall not bring the hire of a harlot or the price of a dog to the *house of the Lord* your God for any vowed offering, for both of these are an abomination to the Lord your God

Josh 6:24 Only the silver and gold, and the vessels of bronze and iron, they put into the treasury of the *house of the Lord*

Judg 19:18 I went to Bethlehem in Judah, and now I am going to the *house of the Lord*

1Sam 1:7 So it was, year by year, when she went up to the *house of the Lord*, that she provoked her

1Sam 1:24 Now when she had weaned him, she took him up with her, with three bulls, one ephah of flour, and a skin of wine, and brought him to the *house of the Lord* in Shiloh

1Sam 3:15 So Samuel lay down until morning, and opened the doors of the *house of the Lord*

2Sam 12:20 and he went into the *house of the Lord* and worshiped

1Kin 3:1 then he brought her to the City of David until he had finished building his own house, and the *house of the Lord*, and the wall all around Jerusalem

1Kin 6:1 And it came to pass in the four hundred and eightieth year after the children of Israel had come out of the land of Egypt, in the fourth year of Solomon's reign over Israel, in the month of Ziv, which is the second month, that he began to build the *house of the Lord*

1Kin 6:37 In the fourth year the foundation of the *house of the Lord* was laid, in the month of Ziv

1Kin 7:12 So were the inner court of the *house of the Lord* and the vestibule of the temple

1Kin 7:40 So Hiram finished doing all the work that he was to do for King Solomon on the *house of the Lord*

1Kin 7:45 All these articles which Hiram made for King Solomon for the *house of the Lord* were of burnished bronze

1Kin 7:48 Solomon had all the furnishings made for the *house of the Lord*

1Kin 7:51 Thus all the work that King Solomon had done for the *house of the Lord* was finished; and Solomon brought in the things which his father David had dedicated: the silver and the gold and the furnishings. And he put them in the treasuries of the *house of the Lord*

1Kin 8:10 And it came to pass, when the priests came out of the holy place, that the cloud filled the *house of the Lord*

1Kin 8:11 for the glory of the Lord filled the *house of the Lord*

1Kin 8:63 So the king and all the children of Israel dedicated the *house of the Lord*

1Kin 8:64 On the same day the king consecrated the middle of the court that was in front of the *house of the Lord*

1Kin 9:1 And it came to pass, when Solomon had finished building the *house of the Lord* and the king's house, and all Solomon's desire which he wanted to do

1Kin 9:10 Now it happened at the end of twenty years, when Solomon had built the two houses, the *house of the Lord* and the king's house

1Kin 9:15 to build the *house of the Lord*, his own

house, the Millo, the wall of Jerusalem, Hazor, Megiddo, and Gezer

1Kin 10:5 the food on his table, the seating of his servants, the service of his waiters and their apparel, his cupbearers, and his entryway by which he went up to the *house of the Lord*, there was no more spirit in her

1Kin 10:12 And the king made steps of the almug wood for the *house of the Lord* and for the king's house, also harps and stringed instruments for singers

1Kin 12:27 If these people go up to offer sacrifices in the *house of the Lord* at Jerusalem, then the heart of this people will turn back to their lord, Rehoboam king of Judah, and they will kill me and go back to Rehoboam king of Judah

1Kin 14:26 And he took away the treasures of the *house of the Lord* and the treasures of the king's house

1Kin 14:28 And so it was, whenever the king went into the *house of the Lord*, that the guards carried them, then brought them back into the guard chamber

1Kin 15:15 He also brought into the *house of the Lord* the things which his father had dedicated, and the things which he himself had dedicated

1Kin 15:18 Then Asa took all the silver and gold that was left in the treasuries of the *house of the Lord* and the treasuries of the king's house, and delivered them into the hand of his servants

2Kin 11:3 So he was hidden with her in the *house of the Lord* for six years, while Athaliah reigned over the land

2Kin 11:4 In the seventh year Jehoiada sent and brought the captains of hundreds, of the bodyguards and the escorts, and brought them into the *house of the Lord* to him. And he made a covenant with them and took an oath from them in the *house of the Lord*, and showed them the king's son

2Kin 11:7 The two contingents of you who go off duty on the Sabbath shall keep the watch of the *house of the Lord* for the king

2Kin 11:15 For the priest had said, "Do not let her be killed in the *house of the Lord*

2Kin 11:18 And the priest appointed officers over the *house of the Lord*

2Kin 11:19 and they brought the king down from the *house of the Lord*, and went by way of the gate of the escorts to the king's house

2Kin 12:4 And Jehoash said to the priests, "All the money of the dedicated gifts that are brought into the *house of the Lord* each man's census money, each man's assessment money and all the money that a man purposes in his heart to bring into the *house of the Lord*

2Kin 12:9 Then Jehoiada the priest took a chest, bored a hole in its lid, and set it beside the altar, on the right side as one comes into the *house of the Lord;* and the priests who kept the door put there all the money that was brought into the *house of the Lord*

2Kin 12:10 So it was, whenever they saw that there was much money in the chest, that the king's scribe and the high priest came up and put it in bags, and counted the money that was found in the *house of the Lord*

2Kin 12:11 Then they gave the money, which had been apportioned, into the hands of those who did the work, who had the oversight of the *house of the Lord;* and they paid it out to the carpenters and builders who worked on the *house of the Lord*

2Kin 12:12 and to masons and stonecutters, and for buying timber and hewn stone, to repair the damage of the *house of the Lord*, and for all that was paid out to repair the temple

2Kin 12:13 However there were not made for the *house of the Lord* basins of silver, trimmers, sprinkling-bowls, trumpets, any articles of gold, or articles of silver, from the money that was brought into the *house of the Lord*

2Kin 12:14 But they gave that to the workmen, and they repaired the *house of the Lord* with it

2Kin 12:16 The money from the trespass offerings and the money from the sin offerings was not brought into the *house of the Lord*

2Kin 12:18 And Jehoash king of Judah took all the sacred things that his fathers, Jehoshaphat and Jehoram and Ahaziah, kings of Judah, had dedicated, and his own sacred things, and all the gold found in the treasuries of the *house of the Lord* and in the king's house, and sent them to Hazael king of Syria

2Kin 14:14 And he took all the gold and silver, all the articles that were found in the *house of the Lord* and in the treasuries of the king's house, and hostages, and returned to Samaria

2Kin 15:35 He built the Upper Gate of the *house of the Lord*

2Kin 16:8 And Ahaz took the silver and gold that was found in the *house of the Lord*, and in the treasuries of the king's house, and sent it as a present to the king of Assyria

2Kin 16:14 He also brought the bronze altar which was before the Lord, from the front of the temple from between the new altar and the *house of the Lord* and put it on the north side of the new altar

2Kin 16:18 Also he removed the Sabbath pavilion which they had built in the temple, and he removed the king's outer entrance from the *house of the Lord*, on account of the king of Assyria

2Kin 18:15 So Hezekiah gave him all the silver that was found in the *house of the Lord* and in the treasuries of the king's house

2Kin 19:1 And so it was, when King Hezekiah heard it, that he tore his clothes, covered himself with sackcloth, and went into the *house of the Lord*

2Kin 19:14 and Hezekiah went up to the *house of the Lord*, and spread it before the Lord

2Kin 20:5 On the third day you shall go up to the *house of the Lord*

2Kin 20:8 And Hezekiah said to Isaiah, "What is the sign that the Lord will heal me, and that I shall go up to the *house of the Lord* the third day

2Kin 21:4 He also built altars in the *house of the Lord*, of which the Lord had said

2Kin 21:5 And he built altars for all the host of heaven in the two courts of the *house of the Lord*

2Kin 22:3 Now it came to pass, in the eighteenth year of King Josiah, that the king sent Shaphan the scribe, the son of Azaliah, the son of Meshullam, to the *house of the Lord*, saying

2Kin 22:4 Go up to Hilkiah the high priest, that he may count the money which has been brought into the *house of the Lord*, which the doorkeepers have gathered from the people

2Kin 22:5 And let them deliver it into the hand of those doing the work, who are the overseers in the *house of the Lord;* let them give it to those who are in the *house of the Lord* doing the work, to repair the damages of the house

2Kin 22:8 Then Hilkiah the high priest said to Shaphan the scribe, "I have found the Book of the Law in the *house of the Lord*

2Kin 22:9 So Shaphan the scribe went to the king, bringing the king word, saying, "Your servants have gathered the money that was found in the house, and have delivered it into the hand of those who do the work, who oversee the *house of the Lord*

2Kin 23:2 And the king went up to the *house of the Lord* with all the men of Judah, and with him all the inhabitants of Jerusalem the priests and the prophets and all the people, both small and great; and he read in their hearing all the words of the Book of the Covenant which had been found in the *house of the Lord*

2Kin 23:6 And he brought out the wooden image from the *house of the Lord*, to the Brook Kidron outside Jerusalem, burned it at the Brook Kidron and ground it to ashes, and threw its ashes on the graves of the common people

2Kin 23:7 Then he tore down the ritual booths of the perverted persons that were in the *house of the Lord*, where the women wove hangings for the wooden image

2Kin 23:11 Then he removed the horses that the kings of Judah had dedicated to the sun, at the entrance to the *house of the Lord*, by the chamber of Nathan-Melech, the officer who was in the court

2Kin 23:12 The altars that were on the roof, the upper chamber of Ahaz, which the kings of Judah had made, and the altars which Manasseh had made in the two courts of the *house of the Lord*, the king broke down and pulverized there, and threw their dust into the Brook Kidron

2Kin 23:24 Moreover Josiah put away those who consulted mediums and spiritists, the household gods and idols, all the abominations that were seen in the land of Judah and in Jerusalem, that he might perform the words of the law which were written in the book that Hilkiah the priest found in the *house of the Lord*

2Kin 24:13 And he carried out from there all the treasures of the *house of the Lord* and the treasures of the king's house, and he cut in pieces all the articles of gold which Solomon king of Israel had made in the temple of the Lord, as the Lord had said

2Kin 25:9 He burned the *house of the Lord* and the king's house

2Kin 25:13 The bronze pillars that were in the *house of the Lord*, and the carts and the bronze Sea that were in the *house of the Lord*, the Chaldeans broke in pieces, and carried their bronze to Babylon

2Kin 25:16 The two pillars, one Sea, and the carts, which Solomon had made for the *house of the Lord*, the bronze of all these articles was beyond measure

1Chr 6:31 Now these are the men whom David appointed over the service of song in the *house of the Lord*, after the ark came to rest

1Chr 6:32 They were ministering with music before the dwelling place of the tabernacle of meeting, until Solomon had built the *house of the Lord* in Jerusalem, and they served in their office according to their order

1Chr 9:23 So they and their children were in charge of the gates of the *house of the Lord*, the house of the tabernacle, by assignment

1Chr 22:1 Then David said, "This is the *house of the Lord* God, and this is the altar of burnt offering for Israel

1Chr 22:11 and may you prosper, and build the *house of the Lord* your God, as He has said to you

1Chr 22:14 Indeed I have taken much trouble to prepare for the *house of the Lord* one hundred thousand talents of gold and one million talents of silver, and bronze and iron beyond measure, for it is so abundant

1Chr 23:4 Of these, twenty-four thousand were to look after the work of the *house of the Lord*, six thousand were officers and judges

1Chr 23:24 These were the sons of Levi by their fathers' houses the heads of the fathers' houses as they were counted individually by the number of their names, who did the work for the service of the *house of the Lord*, from the age of twenty years and above

1Chr 23:28 because their duty was to help the sons of Aaron in the service of the *house of the Lord*, in the courts and in the chambers, in the purifying of all holy things and the work of the service of the house of God

1Chr 23:32 and that they should attend to the needs of the tabernacle of meeting, the needs of the holy place, and the needs of the sons of Aaron their brethren in the work of the *house of the Lord*

1Chr 24:19 This was the schedule of their service for coming into the *house of the Lord* according to their ordinance by the hand of Aaron their father, as the Lord God of Israel had commanded him

1Chr 25:6 All these were under the direction of their father for the music in the *house of the Lord*, with cymbals, stringed instruments, and harps, for the service of the house of God

1Chr 26:12 Among these were the divisions of the gatekeepers, among the chief men, having duties just like their brethren, to serve in the *house of the Lord*

1Chr 26:22 The sons of Jehieli, Zetham and Joel his brother, were over the treasuries of the *house of the Lord*

1Chr 26:27 Some of the spoils won in battles they dedicated to maintain the *house of the Lord*

1Chr 28:12 and the plans for all that he had by the Spirit, of the courts of the *house of the Lord*, of all the chambers all around, of the treasuries of the house of God, and of the treasuries for the dedicated things

1Chr 28:13 also for the division of the priests and the Levites, for all the work of the service of the *house of the Lord*, and for all the articles of service in the *house of the Lord*

1Chr 28:20 He will not leave you nor forsake you, until you have finished all the work for the service of the *house of the Lord*

1Chr 29:8 And whoever had precious stones gave them to the treasury of the *house of the Lord*, into the hand of Jehiel the Gershonite

2Chr 3:1 Now Solomon began to build the *house of the Lord* at Jerusalem on Mount Moriah, where the Lord had appeared to his father David, at the place that David had prepared on the threshing floor of Ornan the Jebusite

2Chr 4:16 also the pots, the shovels, the forks and all their articles Huram his master craftsman made of burnished bronze for King Solomon for the *house of the Lord*

2Chr 5:1 So all the work that Solomon had done for the *house of the Lord* was finished

2Chr 5:13 For He is good, for His mercy endures forever," that the house, the *house of the Lord*, was filled with a cloud

2Chr 7:2 And the priests could not enter the *house of the Lord*, because the glory of the Lord had filled the Lord's house

2Chr 7:7 Furthermore Solomon consecrated the middle of the court that was in front of the *house of the Lord*

2Chr 7:11 Thus Solomon finished the *house of the Lord* and the king's house; and Solomon successfully accomplished all that came into his heart to make in the *house of the Lord* and in his own house

2Chr 8:1 It came to pass at the end of twenty years, in which Solomon had built the *house of the Lord* and his own house

2Chr 8:16 Now all the work of Solomon was well-ordered from the day of the foundation of the *house of the Lord* until it was finished. So the *house of the Lord* was completed

2Chr 9:4 the food on his table, the seating of his servants, the service of his waiters and their apparel, his cupbearers and their apparel, and his entryway by which he went up to the *house of the Lord*, there was no more spirit in her

2Chr 9:11 And the king made walkways of the algum wood for the *house of the Lord* and for the king's house, also harps and stringed instruments for singers

2Chr 12:9 So Shishak king of Egypt came up against Jerusalem, and took away the treasures of the *house of the Lord* and the treasures of the king's house

2Chr 12:11 And whenever the king entered the *house of the Lord*, the guard would go and bring them out

2Chr 16:2 Then Asa brought silver and gold from the treasuries of the *house of the Lord* and of the king's house, and sent to Ben-Hadad king of Syria, who dwelt in Damascus, saying

2Chr 20:5 Then Jehoshaphat stood in the congregation of Judah and Jerusalem, in the *house of the Lord*, before the new court

2Chr 20:28 So they came to Jerusalem, with stringed instruments and harps and trumpets, to the *house of the Lord*

2Chr 23:5 All the people shall be in the courts of the *house of the Lord*

2Chr 23:6 But let no one come into the *house of the Lord* except the priests and those of the Levites who serve

2Chr 23:14 For the priest said, "Do not kill her in the *house of the Lord*

2Chr 23:18 Also Jehoiada appointed the oversight of the *house of the Lord* to the hand of the priests, the Levites, whom David had assigned in the *house of the Lord*, to offer the burnt offerings of the Lord, as it is written in the Law of Moses, with rejoicing and with singing, as it was established by David

2Chr 23:19 And he set the gatekeepers at the gates of the *house of the Lord*, so that no one who was in any way unclean should enter

2Chr 23:20 Then he took the captains of hundreds, the nobles, the governors of the people, and all the people of the land, and brought the king down from the *house of the Lord*

2Chr 24:4 Now it happened after this that Joash set his heart on repairing the *house of the Lord*

2Chr 24:7 For the sons of Athaliah, that wicked woman, had broken into the house of God, and had also presented all the dedicated things of the *house of the Lord* to the Baals

2Chr 24:8 Then at the king's commandment they made a chest, and set it outside at the gate of the *house of the Lord*

2Chr 24:12 Then the king and Jehoiada gave it to those who did the work of the service of the *house of the Lord;* and they hired masons and carpenters to repair the *house of the Lord*, and also those who worked in iron and bronze to restore the *house of the Lord*

2Chr 24:14 they made from it articles for the *house of the Lord*, articles for serving and offering, spoons and vessels of gold and silver. And they offered burnt offerings in the *house of the Lord* continually all the days of Jehoiada

2Chr 24:18 Therefore they left the *house of the Lord* God of their fathers, and served wooden images and idols

2Chr 24:21 So they conspired against him, and at the commandment of the king they stoned him with stones in the court of the *house of the Lord*

2Chr 26:19 And while he was angry with the priests, leprosy broke out on his forehead, before the priests in the *house of the Lord*, beside the incense altar

2Chr 26:21 for he was cut off from the *house of the Lord*

2Chr 27:3 He built the Upper Gate of the *house of the Lord*, and he built extensively on the wall of Ophel

2Chr 28:21 For Ahaz took part of the treasures from the *house of the Lord*, from the house of the king, and from the leaders, and he gave it to the king of Assyria

2Chr 28:24 So Ahaz gathered the articles of the house of God, cut in pieces the articles of the house of God, shut up the doors of the *house of the Lord*, and made for himself altars in every corner of Jerusalem

2Chr 29:3 In the first year of his reign, in the first month, he opened the doors of the *house of the Lord* and repaired them

2Chr 29:5 Now sanctify yourselves, sanctify the *house of the Lord* God of your fathers, and carry out the rubbish from the holy place

2Chr 29:15 And they gathered their brethren, sanctified themselves, and went according to the commandment of the king, at the words of the Lord, to cleanse the *house of the Lord*

2Chr 29:16 Then the priests went into the inner part of the *house of the Lord* to cleanse it, and brought out all the debris that they found in the temple of the Lord to the court of the *house of the Lord*

2Chr 29:17 Then they sanctified the *house of the Lord* in eight days, and on the sixteenth day of the first month they finished

2Chr 29:18 Then they went in to King Hezekiah and said, "We have cleansed all the *house of the Lord*, the altar of burnt offerings with all its articles, and the table of the showbread with all its articles

2Chr 29:20 Then King Hezekiah rose early, gathered the rulers of the city, and went up to the *house of the Lord*

2Chr 29:25 Then he stationed the Levites in the *house of the Lord* with cymbals, with stringed instruments, and with harps, according to the commandment of David, of Gad the king's seer, and of Nathan the prophet

2Chr 29:31 Then Hezekiah answered and said, "Now that you have consecrated yourselves to the Lord, come near, and bring sacrifices and thank offerings into the *house of the Lord*

2Chr 29:35 So the service of the *house of the Lord* was set in order

2Chr 30:1 And Hezekiah sent to all Israel and Judah, and also wrote letters to Ephraim and Manasseh, that they should come to the *house of the Lord* at Jerusalem, to keep the Passover to the Lord God of Israel

2Chr 30:15 The priests and the Levites were ashamed, and sanctified themselves, and brought the burnt offerings to the *house of the Lord*

2Chr 31:10 And Azariah the chief priest, from the house of Zadok, answered him and said, "Since the people began to bring the offerings into the *house of the Lord*, we have had enough to eat and have plenty left, for the Lord has blessed His people

2Chr 31:11 Now Hezekiah commanded them to prepare rooms in the *house of the Lord*, and they prepared them

2Chr 31:16 Besides those males from three years old and up who were written in the genealogy, they distributed to everyone who entered the *house of the Lord* his daily portion for the work of his service, by his division

2Chr 33:4 He also built altars in the *house of the Lord*, of which the Lord had said

2Chr 33:5 And he built altars for all the host of heaven in the two courts of the *house of the Lord*

2Chr 33:15 He took away the foreign gods and the idol from the *house of the Lord*, and all the altars that he had built in the mount of the *house of the Lord* and in Jerusalem

2Chr 34:8 Now in the eighteenth year of his reign, when he had purged the land and the temple, he sent Shaphan the son of Azaliah, Maaseiah the governor of the city, and Joah the son of Joahaz the recorder, to repair the *house of the Lord* his God

2Chr 34:10 Then they put it in the hand of the workmen who had the oversight of the *house of the Lord;* and they gave it to the workmen who worked in the *house of the Lord*, to repair and restore the house

2Chr 34:14 Now when they brought out the money that was brought into the *house of the Lord*, Hilkiah the priest found the Book of the Law of the Lord given by Moses

2Chr 34:15 Then Hilkiah answered and said to Shaphan the scribe, "I have found the Book of the Law in the *house of the Lord*

2Chr 34:17 And they have gathered the money that was found in the *house of the Lord*, and have delivered it into the hand of the overseers and the workmen

2Chr 34:30 And the king went up to the *house of the Lord*, with all the men of Judah and the inhabitants of Jerusalem: the priests and the Levites, and all the people, great and small; and he read in their hearing all the words of the book of the covenant which had been found in the *house of the Lord*

2Chr 35:2 And he set the priests in their duties and encouraged them for the service of the *house of the Lord*

2Chr 36:7 Nebuchadnezzar also carried off some of the articles from the *house of the Lord* to Babylon, and put them in his temple at Babylon

2Chr 36:10 At the turn of the year King Nebuchadnezzar summoned him and took him to Babylon, with the costly articles from the *house of the Lord*, and made Zedekiah, Jehoiakim's brother, king over Judah and Jerusalem

2Chr 36:14 Moreover all the leaders of the priests and the people transgressed more and more, according to all the abominations of the nations, and defiled the *house of the Lord* which He had consecrated in Jerusalem

2Chr 36:18 And all the articles from the house of God, great and small, the treasures of the *house of the Lord*, and the treasures of the king and of his leaders, all these he took to Babylon

Ezra 1:3 Now let him go up to Jerusalem, which is in Judah, and build the *house of the Lord* God of Israel (He is God

Ezra 1:5 Then the heads of the fathers' houses of Judah and Benjamin, and the priests and the Levites, with all those whose spirits God had moved, arose to go up and build the *house of the Lord* which is in Jerusalem

Ezra 1:7 King Cyrus also brought out the articles of the *house of the Lord*, which Nebuchadnezzar had taken from Jerusalem and put in the temple of his gods

Ezra 2:68 Some of the heads of the fathers' houses, when they came to the *house of the Lord* which is in Jerusalem, offered freely for the house of God, to erect it in its place

Ezra 3:8 Now in the second month of the second year of their coming to the house of God at Jerusalem, Zerubbabel the son of Shealtiel, Jeshua the son of Jozadak, and the rest of their brethren the priests and the Levites, and all those who had come out of the captivity to Jerusalem, began work and appointed the Levites from twenty years old and above to oversee the work of the *house of the Lord*

Ezra 3:11 Then all the people shouted with a great shout, when they praised the Lord, because the foundation of the *house of the Lord* was laid

Ezra 7:27 Blessed be the Lord God of our fathers, who has put such a thing as this in the king's heart, to beautify the *house of the Lord* which is in Jerusalem

Ezra 8:29 Watch and keep them until you weigh them before the leaders of the priests and the Levites and heads of the fathers' houses of Israel in Jerusalem, in the chambers of the *house of the Lord*

Neh 10:35 And we made ordinances to bring the firstfruits of our ground and the firstfruits of all fruit of all trees, year by year, to the *house of the Lord*

Ps 23:6 And I will dwell in the *house of the Lord* forever

Ps 27:4 That I may dwell in the *house of the Lord*. all the days of my life, to behold the beauty of the Lord, and to inquire in His temple

Ps 92:13 Those who are planted in the *house of the Lord* shall flourish in the courts of our God

Ps 118:26 We have blessed you from the *house of the Lord*

Ps 122:1 I was glad when they said to me, "Let us go into the *house of the Lord*

Ps 122:9 Because of the *house of the Lord* our God I will seek your good

Ps 134:1 Behold, bless the Lord, all you servants of the Lord, who by night stand in the *house of the Lord*

Ps 135:2 You who stand in the *house of the Lord*, in the courts of the house of our God

Is 37:1 And so it was, when King Hezekiah heard it, that he tore his clothes, covered himself with sackcloth, and went into the *house of the Lord*

Is 37:14 and Hezekiah went up to the *house of the Lord*, and spread it before the Lord

Is 38:20 therefore we will sing my songs with stringed instruments all the days of our life, in the *house of the Lord*

Is 38:22 And Hezekiah had said, "What is the sign that I shall go up to the *house of the Lord*

Is 66:20 Then they shall bring all your brethren for an offering to the Lord out of all nations, on horses and in chariots and in litters, on mules and on camels, to My holy mountain Jerusalem," says the Lord, "as the children of Israel bring an offering in a clean vessel into the *house of the Lord*

Jer 17:26 And they shall come from the cities of Judah and from the places around Jerusalem, from the land of Benjamin and from the lowland, from the mountains and from the South, bringing burnt offerings and sacrifices, grain offerings and incense, bringing sacrifices of praise to the *house of the Lord*

Jer 20:1 Now Pashhur the son of Immer, the priest who was also chief governor in the *house of the Lord*, heard that Jeremiah prophesied these things

Jer 20:2 Then Pashhur struck Jeremiah the prophet, and put him in the stocks that were in the high gate of Benjamin, which was by the *house of the Lord*

Jer 26:7 So the priests and the prophets and all the people heard Jeremiah speaking these words in the *house of the Lord*

Jer 26:9 And all the people were gathered against Jeremiah in the *house of the Lord*

Jer 26:10 When the princes of Judah heard these things, they came up from the king's house to the *house of the Lord* and sat down in the entry of the new gate of the Lord's house

Jer 27:18 But if they are prophets, and if the word of the Lord is with them, let them now make intercession to the Lord of hosts, that the vessels which are left in the *house of the Lord*, in the house of the king of Judah, and at Jerusalem, do not go to Babylon

Jer 27:21 yes, thus says the Lord of hosts, the God of Israel, concerning the vessels that remain in the *house of the Lord*, and in the house of the king of Judah and of Jerusalem

Jer 28:1 And it happened in the same year, at the beginning of the reign of Zedekiah king of Judah, in the fourth year and in the fifth month, that Hananiah the son of Azur the prophet, who was from Gibeon, spoke to me in the *house of the Lord* in the presence of the priests and of all the people, saying

Jer 28:5 Then the prophet Jeremiah spoke to the prophet Hananiah in the presence of the priests and in the presence of all the people who stood in the *house of the Lord*

Jer 29:26 The Lord has made you priest instead of Jehoiada the priest, so that there should be officers in the *house of the Lord* over every man who is demented and considers himself a prophet, that you should put him in prison and in the stocks

Jer 33:11 Praise the Lord of hosts, for the Lord is good, for His mercy endures forever" and of those who will bring the sacrifice of praise into the *house of the Lord*

Jer 35:2 Go to the house of the Rechabites, speak to them, and bring them into the *house of the Lord*, into one of the chambers, and give them wine to drink

Jer 35:4 and I brought them into the *house of the Lord*, into the chamber of the sons of Hanan the son of Igdaliah, a man of God, which was by the chamber of the princes, above the chamber of Maaseiah the son of Shallum, the keeper of the door

Jer 36:5 And Jeremiah commanded Baruch, saying, "I am confined, I cannot go into the *house of the Lord*

Jer 36:10 Then Baruch read from the book the words of Jeremiah in the *house of the Lord*, in the chamber of Gemariah the son of Shaphan the scribe, in the upper court at the entry of the New Gate of the Lord's house, in the hearing of all the people

Jer 38:14 Then Zedekiah the king sent and had Jeremiah the prophet brought to him at the third entrance of the *house of the Lord*

Jer 41:5 that certain men came from Shechem, from Shiloh, and from Samaria, eighty men with their beards shaved and their clothes torn, having cut themselves, with offerings and incense in their hand, to bring them to the *house of the Lord*

Jer 52:13 He burned the *house of the Lord* and the king's house

Jer 52:17 The bronze pillars that were in the *house of the Lord*, and the carts and the bronze Sea that were in the *house of the Lord*, the Chaldeans broke in pieces, and carried all their bronze to Babylon

Jer 52:20 The two pillars, one Sea, the twelve bronze bulls which were under it, and the carts, which King Solomon had made for the *house of the Lord* the bronze of all these articles was beyond measure

Lam 2:7 They have made a noise in the *house of the Lord* as on the day of a set feast

Ezek 44:4 so I looked, and behold, the glory of the Lord filled the *house of the Lord*

Ezek 44:5 And the Lord said to me, "Son of man, mark well, see with your eyes and hear with your ears, all that I say to you concerning all the ordinances of the *house of the Lord* and all its laws

Hos 8:1 He shall come like an eagle against the *house of the Lord*, Because they have transgressed My covenant and rebelled against My law

Hos 9:4 it shall not come into the *house of the Lord*

Joel 1:9 The grain offering and the drink offering have been cut off from the *house of the Lord*

Joel 1:14 gather the elders and all the inhabitants of the land into the *house of the Lord* your God, and cry out to the Lord

Joel 3:18 a fountain shall flow from the *house of the Lord* and water the Valley of Acacias

Hag 1:14 and they came and worked on the *house of the Lord* of hosts, their God

Zech 7:3 and to ask the priests who were in the *house of the Lord* of hosts, and the prophets, saying

Zech 8:9 Let your hands be strong, you who have been hearing in these days these words by the mouth of the prophets, who were in the day that the foundation was laid for the *house of the Lord* of hosts, that the temple might be built

Zech 11:13 So I took the thirty pieces of silver and threw them into the *house of the Lord* for the potter

Zech 14:21 In that day there shall no longer be a Canaanite in the *house of the Lord* of hosts

HOUSE OF THEIR FATHERS (KJV)
(See *HOUSE OF HIS FATHER*)

HOUSEHOLD GODS

2Kin 23:24 Moreover Josiah put away those who consulted mediums and spiritists, the *household gods* and idols, all the abominations that were seen in the land of Judah and in Jerusalem, that he might perform the words of the law which were written in the book that Hilkiah the priest found in the house of the Lord

HOUSEHOLD OF FAITH

Gal 6:10 Therefore, as we have opportunity, let us do good to all, especially to those who are of the *household of faith*

HOUSEHOLD OF GOD

Eph 2:19 Now, therefore, you are no longer strangers and foreigners, but fellow citizens with the saints and members of the *household of God*

HOUSES OF IVORY

Amos 3:15 the *houses of ivory* shall perish, and the great houses shall have an end

HOW ARE THE MIGHTY FALLEN (KJV, RSV)
(See *HOW THE MIGHTY HAVE FALLEN*)

HOW CAN WE PROVIDE (NIV)
(See *WHAT SHALL WE DO*)

HOW GOOD IT IS

Prov 15:23 A man has joy by the answer of his mouth, and a word spoken in due season, *how good it is*

HOW LONG

Ex 10:3 *How long* will you refuse to humble yourself before Me

Ex 10:7 Then Pharaoh's servants said to him, "*How long* shall this man be a snare to us

Ex 16:28 And the Lord said to Moses, "*How long* do you refuse to keep My commandments and My laws

Num 14:11 *How long* will these people reject Me? And *how long* will they not believe Me, with all the signs which I have performed among them

Num 14:27 *How long* shall I bear with this evil congregation who murmur against Me

Num 24:22 nevertheless Kain shall be burned. *How long* until Asshur carries you away captive

Josh 18:3 *How long* will you neglect to go and possess the land which the Lord God of your fathers has given you

1Sam 1:14 So Eli said to her, "*How long* will you be drunk

1Sam 16:1 Then the Lord said to Samuel, "*How*

long will you mourn for Saul, seeing I have rejected him from reigning over Israel
2Sam 2:26 *How long* will it be then until you tell the people to return from pursuing their brethren
2Sam 19:34 But Barzillai said to the king, "*How long* have I to live, that I should go up with the king to Jerusalem
1Kin 18:21 And Elijah came to all the people, and said, "*How long* will you falter between two opinions
Neh 2:6 *How long* will your journey be? And when will you return
Job 7:19 *How long?* Will You not look away from me, and let me alone till I swallow my saliva
Job 8:2 *How long* will you speak these things, and the words of your mouth be like a strong wind
Job 18:2 *How long* till you put an end to words? Gain understanding, and afterward we will speak
Job 19:2 *How long* will you torment my soul, and break me in pieces with words
Ps 4:2 *How long*, O you sons of men, will you turn my glory to shame? *How long* will you love worthlessness and seek falsehood
Ps 6:3 My soul also is greatly troubled; but You, O Lord *how long*
Ps 13:1 *How long*, O Lord? Will You forget me forever? *How long* will You hide Your face from me
Ps 13:2 *How long* shall I take counsel in my soul, having sorrow in my heart daily? *How long* will my enemy be exalted over me
Ps 35:17 Lord, *how long* will You look on? Rescue me from their destructions, my precious life from the lions
Ps 62:3 *How long* will you attack a man? You shall be slain, all of you, like a leaning wall and a tottering fence
Ps 74:9 Nor is there any among us who knows *how long*
Ps 74:10 O God, *how long* will the adversary reproach? Will the enemy blaspheme Your name forever
Ps 79:5 *How long*, Lord? Will You be angry forever? Will Your jealousy burn like fire
Ps 80:4 O Lord God of hosts, *how long* will You be angry against the prayer of Your people
Ps 82:2 *How long* will you judge unjustly, and show partiality to the wicked
Ps 89:46 *How long*, Lord? Will You hide Yourself forever? Will Your wrath burn like fire
Ps 90:13 Return, O Lord! *How long?* And have compassion on Your servants
Ps 94:3 Lord, *how long* will the wicked, *how long* will the wicked triumph
Prov 1:22 *How long*, you simple ones, will you love simplicity? For scorners delight in their scorning, and fools hate knowledge
Prov 6:9 *How long* will you slumber, O sluggard? When will you rise from your sleep
Is 6:11 Then I said, "Lord, *how long?*" And He answered: "Until the cities are laid waste and without inhabitant, the houses are without a man, the land is utterly desolate
Jer 4:14 O Jerusalem, wash your heart from wickedness, that you may be saved. *How long* shall your evil thoughts lodge within you
Jer 4:21 *How long* will I see the standard, and hear the sound of the trumpet
Jer 12:4 *How long* will the land mourn, and the herbs of every field wither
Jer 23:26 *How long* will this be in the heart of the prophets who prophesy lies
Jer 31:22 *How long* will you gad about, O you backsliding daughter
Jer 47:5 Baldness has come upon Gaza, Ashkelon is cut off with the remnant of their valley. *How long* will you cut yourself
Jer 47:6 O you sword of the Lord, *how long* until you are quiet
Dan 8:13 and another holy one said to that certain one who was speaking, "*How long* will the vision be, concerning the daily sacrifices and the transgression of desolation, the giving of both the sanctuary and the host to be trampled under foot
Dan 12:6 And one said to the man clothed in linen, who was above the waters of the river, "*How long* shall the fulfillment of these wonders be
Hos 8:5 *How long* will it be until they attain to innocence
Hab 1:2 O Lord, *how long* shall I cry, and You will not hear
Hab 2:6 Shall not all these take up a proverb against him, and a taunting riddle against him, and say, 'Woe to him who increases what is not his *how long*
Zech 1:12 Then the Angel of the Lord answered and said, "O Lord of hosts, *how long* will You not have mercy on Jerusalem and on the cities of Judah, against which You were angry these seventy years
Matt 17:17 Then Jesus answered and said, "O faithless and perverse generation, *how long* shall I be with you? *How long* shall I bear with you
Mark 9:19 He answered him and said, "O faithless generation, *how long* shall I be with you? *How long* shall I bear with you
Mark 9:21 So He asked his father, "*How long* has this been happening to him
Luke 9:41 Then Jesus answered and said, "O faithless and perverse generation, *how long* shall I be with you and bear with you
John 10:24 Then the Jews surrounded Him and said to Him, "*How long* do You keep us in doubt
Rev 6:10 And they cried with a loud voice, saying, "*How long*, O Lord, holy and true, until You judge and avenge our blood on those who dwell on the earth

HOW SHALL WE DO (KJV)
(See *WHAT SHALL WE DO*)

HOW SHALL WE ESCAPE
Is 20:6 And the inhabitant of this territory will say in that day, 'Surely such is our expectation, wherever we flee for help to be delivered from the king of Assyria; and *how shall we escape*
Heb 2:3 *how shall we escape* if we neglect so great a salvation, which at the first began to be spoken by the Lord, and was confirmed to us by those who heard Him

HOW THE MIGHTY HAVE FALLEN
2Sam 1:19 The beauty of Israel is slain on your high places! *How the mighty have fallen*
2Sam 1:25 *How the mighty have fallen* in the midst of the battle
2Sam 1:27 *How the mighty have fallen*, and the weapons of war perished

HUMAN DECISION (NIV)
(See *WILL OF MAN*)

HUMBLE, AND MOUNTED ON AN ASS (RSV)
(See *LOWLY, AND SITTING ON A DONKEY*)

HUMBLE HIMSELF (NIV, RSV)
(See *AFFLICT HIS SOUL*)

HUMBLE IN HEART (NAS, NIV)
(See *LOWLY IN HEART*)

HUMBLE STATE OF HIS SERVANT (NIV)
(See *LOWLY STATE OF HIS MAIDSERVANT*)

HUMBLE YOURSELVES
Jer 13:18 Say to the king and to the queen mother, "*Humble yourselves*

Jas 4:10 *Humble yourselves* in the sight of the Lord, and He will lift you up
1Pet 5:6 Therefore *humble yourselves* under the mighty hand of God, that He may exalt you in due time

HURT THE EARTH (KJV)
(See *HARM THE EARTH*)

HUSBAND IS HEAD
Eph 5:23 For the *husband is head* of the wife, as also Christ is head of the church

HUSBAND'S WILL (NIV)
(See *WILL OF THE FLESH*)

I

I AM A YOUTH
Jer 1:6 Ah, Lord God! Behold, I cannot speak, for *I am a youth*
Jer 1:7 Do not say, '*I am a youth*,' for you shall go to all to whom I send you, and whatever I command you, you shall speak

I AM ALMIGHTY GOD
Gen 17:1 When Abram was ninety-nine years old, the Lord appeared to Abram and said to him, "*I am Almighty God*

I AM ASCENDING
John 20:17 but go to My brethren and say to them, '*I am ascending* to My Father and your Father, and to My God and your God

I AM ASTONISHED (NIV, RSV)
(See *I MARVEL*)

I AM COMING QUICKLY
Rev 22:7 Behold, *I am coming quickly!* Blessed is he who keeps the words of the prophecy of this book
Rev 22:12 And behold, *I am coming quickly*, and My reward is with Me, to give to every one according to his work
Rev 22:20 He who testifies to these things says, "Surely *I am coming quickly*

I AM COMING SOON (NIV, RSV)
(See *I COME QUICKLY*)

I AM GOD
Gen 35:11 *I am God* Almighty. Be fruitful and multiply; a nation and a company of nations shall proceed from you, and kings shall come from your body
Gen 46:3 And He said, "*I am God*, the God of your father
Ps 46:10 Be still, and know that *I am God;* I will be exalted among the nations, I will be exalted in the earth
Ps 50:7 Hear, O My people, and I will speak, O Israel, and I will testify against you; *I am God*, your God
Is 43:12 therefore you are My witnesses," says the Lord, "that *I am God*
Is 45:22 Look to Me, and be saved, all you ends of the earth! For *I am God*, and there is no other
Is 46:9 Remember the former things of old, for *I am God*, and there is no other; *I am God*, and there is none like Me
Hos 11:9 For *I am God*, and not man, the Holy One in your midst

I AM GOD ALMIGHTY
Gen 35:11 *I am God Almighty*. Be fruitful and multiply; a nation and a company of nations shall proceed from you, and kings shall come from your body

I AM HE
1Sam 4:16 Then the man said to Eli, "*I am he* who came from the battle
Is 41:4 I, the Lord, am the first; and with the last *I am He*
Is 43:10 You are My witnesses," says the Lord, "And My servant whom I have chosen, that you may know and believe Me, and understand that *I am He*
Is 43:13 Indeed before the day was, *I am He;* and there is no one who can deliver out of My hand
Is 46:4 even to your old age, *I am He*, and even to gray hairs I will carry you
Is 48:12 *I am He*, I am the First, I am also the Last
Is 52:6 therefore they shall know in that day that *I am He* who speaks
Mark 13:6 For many will come in My name, saying, '*I am He*
Luke 21:8 For many, will come in My name, saying, '*I am He*
John 8:24 for if you do not believe that *I am He*, you will die in your sins
John 8:28 Then Jesus said to them, "When you lift up the Son of Man, then you will know that *I am He*, and that I do nothing of Myself
John 9:9 Others said, "He is like him." He said, "*I am he*
John 13:19 Now I tell you before it comes, that when it does come to pass, you may believe that *I am He*
John 18:5 Jesus said to them, "*I am He*." And Judas, who betrayed Him, also stood with them
John 18:6 Then when He said to them, "*I am He*," they drew back and fell to the ground
John 18:8 Jesus answered, "I have told you that *I am He*
Acts 10:21 Then Peter went down to the men who had been sent to him from Cornelius, and said, "Yes, *I am he* whom you seek
Rev 1:18 *I am He* who lives, and was dead, and behold, I am alive forevermore
Rev 2:23 And all the churches shall know that *I am He* who searches the minds and hearts

I AM HOLY
Lev 11:44 for *I am holy*. Neither shall you defile yourselves with any creeping thing that creeps on the earth
Lev 11:45 For I am the Lord who brings you up out of the land of Egypt, to be your God. You shall therefore be holy, for *I am holy*
Ps 86:2 Preserve my life, for *I am holy;* You are my God
1Pet 1:16 because it is written, "Be holy, for *I am holy*

I AM NOT WORTHY
Gen 32:10 *I am not worthy* of the least of all the mercies and of all the truth which You have shown Your servant
Matt 3:11 I indeed baptize you with water unto repentance, but He who is coming after me is mightier than I, whose sandals *I am not worthy* to carry
Matt 8:8 The centurion answered and said, "Lord, *I am not worthy* that You should come under my roof
Mark 1:7 And he preached, saying, "There comes One after me who is mightier than I, whose sandal strap *I am not worthy* to stoop down and loose
Luke 3:16 but One mightier than I is coming, whose sandal strap *I am not worthy* to loose

Luke 7:6 And when He was already not far from the house, the centurion sent friends to Him, saying to Him, "Lord, do not trouble Yourself, for *I am not worthy* that You should enter under my roof

John 1:27 It is He who, coming after me, is preferred before me, whose sandal strap *I am not worthy* to loose

Acts 13:25 But behold, there comes One after me, the sandals of whose feet *I am not worthy* to loose

I AM RETURNING (NIV)
(See *I AM ASCENDING*)

I AM THAT I AM (KJV)
(See *I AM WHO I AM*)

I AM THE BREAD

John 6:35 And Jesus said to them, "*I am the bread* of life

John 6:41 The Jews then murmured against Him, because He said, "*I am the bread* which came down from heaven

John 6:48 *I am the bread* of life

I AM THE DOOR

John 10:7 Then Jesus said to them again, "Most assuredly, I say to you, *I am the door* of the sheep

John 10:9 *I am the door*. If anyone enters by Me, he will be saved, and will go in and out and find pasture

I AM THE FIRST

Is 44:6 *I am the First* and I am the Last; besides Me there is no God

Is 48:12 I am He, *I am the First*, I am also the Last

Rev 1:17 But He laid His right hand on me, saying to me, "Do not be afraid; *I am the First* and the Last

I AM THE GOD OF BETHEL

Gen 31:13 *I am the God of Bethel*, where you anointed the pillar and where you made a vow to Me

I AM THE GOOD SHEPHERD

John 10:11 *I am the good shepherd*. The good shepherd gives His life for the sheep

John 10:14 *I am the good shepherd;* and I know My sheep, and am known by My own

I AM THE LIGHT

John 8:12 Then Jesus spoke to them again, saying, "*I am the light* of the world

John 9:5 As long as I am in the world, *I am the light* of the world

I AM THE LORD

Gen 15:7 Then He said to him, "*I am the Lord*, who brought you out of Ur of the Chaldeans, to give you this land to inherit it

Gen 28:13 *I am the Lord* God of Abraham your father and the God of Isaac

Ex 6:2 And God spoke to Moses and said to him: "*I am the Lord*

Ex 6:6 *I am the Lord;* I will bring you out from under the burdens of the Egyptians, I will rescue you from their bondage, and I will redeem you with an outstretched arm and with great judgments

Ex 6:7 Then you shall know that *I am the Lord* your God who brings you out from under the burdens of the Egyptians

Ex 6:8 and I will give it to you as a heritage: *I am the Lord*

Ex 6:29 that the Lord spoke to Moses, saying, "*I am the Lord*

Ex 7:5 And the Egyptians shall know that *I am the Lord*, when I stretch out My hand on Egypt and bring out the children of Israel from among them

Ex 7:17 By this you shall know that *I am the Lord*

Ex 8:22 And in that day I will set apart the land of Goshen, in which My people dwell, that no swarms of flies shall be there, in order that you may know that *I am the Lord* in the midst of the land

Ex 10:2 and that you may tell in the hearing of your son and your son's son the mighty things I have done in Egypt, and My signs which I have done among them, that you may know that *I am the Lord*

Ex 12:12 and against all the gods of Egypt I will execute judgment: *I am the Lord*

Ex 14:4 and I will gain honor over Pharaoh and over all his army, that the Egyptians may know that *I am the Lord*

Ex 14:18 Then the Egyptians shall know that *I am the Lord*, when I have gained honor for Myself over Pharaoh, his chariots, and his horsemen

Ex 15:26 and said, "If you diligently heed the voice of the Lord your God and do what is right in His sight, give ear to His commandments and keep all His statutes, I will put none of the diseases on you which I have brought on the Egyptians. For *I am the Lord* who heals you

Ex 16:12 And you shall know that *I am the Lord* your God

Ex 20:2 *I am the Lord* your God, who brought you out of the land of Egypt, out of the house of bondage

Ex 29:46 And they shall know that *I am the Lord* their God, who brought them up out of the land of Egypt, that I may dwell among them. *I am the Lord* their God

Ex 31:13 Surely My Sabbaths you shall keep, for it is a sign between Me and you throughout your generations, that you may know that *I am the Lord* who sanctifies you

Lev 11:44 For *I am the Lord* your God. You shall therefore sanctify yourselves, and you shall be holy

Lev 11:45 For *I am the Lord* who brings you up out of the land of Egypt, to be your God

Lev 18:2 Speak to the children of Israel, and say to them: '*I am the Lord* your God

Lev 18:4 You shall observe My judgments and keep My ordinances, to walk in them: *I am the Lord* your God

Lev 18:5 You shall therefore keep My statutes and My judgments, which if a man does, he shall live by them: *I am the Lord*

Lev 18:6 None of you shall approach anyone who is near of kin to him, to uncover his nakedness: *I am the Lord*

Lev 18:21 And you shall not let any of your descendants pass through the fire to Molech, nor shall you profane the name of your God: *I am the Lord*

Lev 18:30 Therefore you shall keep My ordinance, so that you do not commit any of these abominable customs which were committed before you, and that you do not defile yourselves by them: *I am the Lord* your God

Lev 19:3 Every one of you shall revere his mother and his father, and keep My Sabbaths: *I am the Lord* your God

Lev 19:4 Do not turn to idols, nor make for yourselves molded gods: *I am the Lord* your God

Lev 19:10 you shall leave them for the poor and the stranger: *I am the Lord* your God

Lev 19:12 And you shall not swear by My name

falsely, nor shall you profane the name of your God: *I am the Lord*

Lev 19:14 You shall not curse the deaf, nor put a stumblingblock before the blind, but shall fear your God: *I am the Lord*

Lev 19:16 nor shall you take a stand against the life of your neighbor: *I am the Lord*

Lev 19:18 You shall not take vengeance, nor bear any grudge against the children of your people, but you shall love your neighbor as yourself: *I am the Lord*

Lev 19:25 And in the fifth year you may eat its fruit, that it may yield to you its increase: *I am the Lord* your God

Lev 19:28 You shall not make any cuttings in your flesh for the dead, nor tattoo any marks on you: *I am the Lord*

Lev 19:30 You shall keep My Sabbaths and reverence My sanctuary: *I am the Lord*

Lev 19:31 do not seek after them, to be defiled by them: *I am the Lord* your God

Lev 19:32 You shall rise before the gray headed and honor the presence of an old man, and fear your God: *I am the Lord*

Lev 19:34 for you were strangers in the land of Egypt: *I am the Lord* your God

Lev 19:36 *I am the Lord* your God, who brought you out of the land of Egypt

Lev 19:37 Therefore you shall observe all My statutes and all My judgments, and perform them: *I am the Lord*

Lev 20:7 Sanctify yourselves therefore, and be holy, for *I am the Lord* your God

Lev 20:8 And you shall keep My statutes, and perform them: *I am the Lord* who sanctifies you

Lev 20:24 *I am the Lord* your God, who has separated you from the peoples

Lev 21:12 for the consecration of the anointing oil of his God is upon him: *I am the Lord*

Lev 22:2 Speak to Aaron and his sons, that they separate themselves from the holy things of the children of Israel, and that they do not profane My holy name in those things which they sanctify to Me: *I am the Lord*

Lev 22:3 Whoever of all your descendants throughout your generations, who goes near the holy things which the children of Israel sanctify to the Lord, while he has uncleanness upon him, that person shall be cut off from My presence: *I am the Lord*

Lev 22:8 Whatever dies naturally or is torn by beasts he shall not eat, to defile himself with it: *I am the Lord*

Lev 22:30 you shall leave none of it until morning: *I am the Lord*

Lev 22:31 Therefore you shall keep My commandments, and perform them: *I am the Lord*

Lev 22:32 You shall not profane My holy name, but I will be hallowed among the children of Israel. *I am the Lord* who sanctifies you

Lev 22:33 who brought you out of the land of Egypt, to be your God: *I am the Lord*

Lev 23:22 You shall leave them for the poor and for the stranger: *I am the Lord* your God

Lev 23:43 that your generations may know that I made the children of Israel dwell in booths when I brought them out of the land of Egypt: *I am the Lord* your God

Lev 24:22 You shall have the same law for the stranger and for one from your own country; for *I am the Lord* your God

Lev 25:17 Therefore you shall not oppress one another, but you shall fear your God; for *I am the Lord* your God

Lev 25:38 *I am the Lord* your God, who brought you out of the land of Egypt, to give you the land of Canaan and to be your God

Lev 25:55 they are My servants whom I brought out of the land of Egypt: *I am the Lord* your God

Lev 26:1 nor shall you set up an engraved stone in your land, to bow down to it; for *I am the Lord* your God

Lev 26:2 You shall keep My Sabbaths and reverence My sanctuary: *I am the Lord*

Lev 26:13 *I am the Lord* your God, who brought you out of the land of Egypt, that you should not be their slaves

Lev 26:44 Yet for all that, when they are in the land of their enemies, I will not cast them away, nor shall I abhor them, to utterly destroy them and break My covenant with them; for *I am the Lord* their God

Lev 26:45 But for their sake I will remember the covenant of their ancestors, whom I brought out of the land of Egypt in the sight of the nations, that I might be their God: *I am the Lord*

Num 3:13 On the day that I struck all the firstborn in the land of Egypt, I sanctified to Myself all the firstborn in Israel, both man and beast. They shall be Mine: *I am the Lord*

Num 3:41 And you shall take the Levites for Me *I am the Lord* instead of all the firstborn among the children of Israel, and the livestock of the Levites instead of all the firstborn among the livestock of the children of Israel

Num 3:45 Take the Levites instead of all the firstborn among the children of Israel, and the livestock of the Levites instead of their livestock. The Levites shall be Mine: *I am the Lord*

Num 10:10 and they shall be a memorial for you before your God: *I am the Lord* your God

Num 15:41 *I am the Lord* your God, who brought you out of the land of Egypt, to be your God: *I am the Lord* your God

Deut 5:6 *I am the Lord* your God who brought you out of the land of Egypt, out of the house of bondage

Deut 29:6 that you may know that *I am the Lord* your God

Judg 6:10 Also I said to you, "*I am the Lord* your God

1Kin 20:13 Behold, I will deliver it into your hand today, and you shall know that *I am the Lord*

1Kin 20:28 Because the Syrians have said, "The Lord is God of the hills, but He is not God of the valleys," therefore I will deliver all this great multitude into your hand, and you shall know that *I am the Lord*

Ps 81:10 *I am the Lord* your God, Who brought you out of the land of Egypt

Is 42:8 *I am the Lord*, that is My name; and My glory I will not give to another, nor My praise to graven images

Is 43:3 For *I am the Lord* your God, the Holy One of Israel, your Savior

Is 43:15 *I am the Lord*, your Holy One, the Creator of Israel, your King

Is 44:24 *I am the Lord*, who makes all things, Who stretches out the heavens all alone, Who spreads abroad the earth by Myself

Is 45:5 *I am the Lord*, and there is no other; there is no God besides Me

Is 45:6 That they may know from the rising of the sun to its setting that there is none besides Me. *I am the Lord*, and there is no other

Is 45:18 For thus says the Lord, Who created the heavens, Who is God, Who formed the earth and made it, Who has established it, Who did not create it in vain, Who formed it to be inhabited: "*I am the Lord*, and there is no other

Is 48:17 *I am the Lord* your God, Who teaches you to profit, Who leads you by the way you should go

Is 49:23 Then you will know that *I am the Lord*, for they shall not be ashamed who wait for Me

Is 51:15 But *I am the Lord* your God, who divided the sea whose waves roared the Lord of hosts is His name
Jer 9:24 but let him who glories glory in this, that he understands and knows Me, that *I am the Lord*, exercising lovingkindness, judgment, and righteousness in the earth
Jer 24:7 Then I will give them a heart to know Me, that *I am the Lord*
Jer 32:27 Behold, *I am the Lord*, the God of all flesh
Ezek 6:7 The slain shall fall in your midst, and you shall know that *I am the Lord*
Ezek 6:10 And they shall know that *I am the Lord*, and that I have not said in vain that I would bring this calamity upon them
Ezek 6:13 Then you shall know that *I am the Lord*, when their slain men are among their idols all around their altars, on every high hill, on all the mountaintops, under every green tree, and under every thick oak, wherever they offered sweet incense to all their idols
Ezek 6:14 So I will stretch out My hand against them and make the land desolate, yes, more desolate than the wilderness toward Diblah, in all their habitations. Then they shall know that *I am the Lord*
Ezek 7:4 but I will repay your ways, and your abominations shall be in your midst; then you shall know that *I am the Lord*
Ezek 7:9 Then you will know that *I am the Lord* who strikes
Ezek 7:27 I will do to them according to their way, and according to what they deserve I will judge them; then they shall know that *I am the Lord*
Ezek 11:10 I will judge you at the border of Israel. Then you shall know that *I am the Lord*
Ezek 11:12 And you shall know that *I am the Lord;* for you have not walked in My statutes nor executed My judgments, but have done according to the customs of the Gentiles which are all around you
Ezek 12:15 Then they shall know that *I am the Lord*, when I scatter them among the nations and disperse them throughout the countries
Ezek 12:16 But I will spare a few of their men from the sword, from famine, and from pestilence, that they may declare all their abominations among the Gentiles wherever they go. Then they shall know that *I am the Lord*
Ezek 12:20 Then the cities that are inhabited shall be laid waste, and the land shall become desolate; and you shall know that *I am the Lord*
Ezek 12:25 For *I am the Lord*. I speak, and the word which I speak will come to pass
Ezek 13:9 Then you shall know that *I am the Lord* God
Ezek 13:14 it will fall, and you shall be consumed in the midst of it. Then you shall know that *I am the Lord*
Ezek 13:21 I will also tear off your veils and deliver My people out of your hand, and they shall no longer be as prey in your hand. Then you shall know that *I am the Lord*
Ezek 13:23 for I will deliver My people out of your hand, and you shall know that *I am the Lord*
Ezek 14:8 I will set My face against that man and make him a sign and a proverb, and I will cut him off from the midst of My people. Then you shall know that *I am the Lord*
Ezek 15:7 Then you shall know that *I am the Lord*, when I set My face against them
Ezek 16:62 And I will establish My covenant with you. Then you shall know that *I am the Lord*
Ezek 20:5 On the day when I chose Israel and lifted My hand in an oath to the descendants of the house of Jacob, and made Myself known to them in the land of Egypt, I lifted My hand in an oath to them, saying, '*I am the Lord* your God
Ezek 20:7 Then I said to them, 'Each of you, throw away the abominations which are before his eyes, and do not defile yourselves with the idols of Egypt. *I am the Lord* your God
Ezek 20:12 Moreover I also gave them My Sabbaths, to be a sign between them and Me, that they might know that *I am the Lord* who sanctifies them
Ezek 20:19 *I am the Lord* your God: Walk in My statutes, keep My judgments, and do them
Ezek 20:20 hallow My Sabbaths, and they will be a sign between Me and you, that you may know that *I am the Lord* your God
Ezek 20:26 and I pronounced them unclean because of their ritual gifts, in that they caused all their firstborn to pass through the fire, that I might make them desolate and that they might know that *I am the Lord*
Ezek 20:38 I will bring them out of the country where they sojourn, but they shall not enter the land of Israel. Then you will know that *I am the Lord*
Ezek 20:42 Then you shall know that *I am the Lord*, when I bring you into the land of Israel, into the country for which I lifted My hand in an oath to give to your fathers
Ezek 20:44 Then you shall know that *I am the Lord*, when I have dealt with you for My name's sake, not according to your wicked ways nor according to your corrupt doings, O house of Israel
Ezek 22:16 You shall defile yourself in the sight of the nations; then you shall know that *I am the Lord*
Ezek 23:49 Then you shall know that *I am the Lord* God
Ezek 24:24 and when this comes, you shall know that *I am the Lord* God
Ezek 24:27 Thus you will be a sign to them, and they will know that *I am the Lord*
Ezek 25:5 And I will make Rabbah a stable for camels and Ammon a resting place for flocks. Then you shall know that *I am the Lord*
Ezek 25:7 I will destroy you, and you shall know that *I am the Lord*
Ezek 25:11 And I will execute judgments upon Moab, and they shall know that *I am the Lord*
Ezek 25:17 and they shall know that *I am the Lord*, when I lay My vengeance upon them
Ezek 26:6 Also her daughter villages which are in the fields shall be slain by the sword. Then they shall know that *I am the Lord*
Ezek 28:22 and they shall know that *I am the Lord*, when I execute judgments in her and am hallowed in her
Ezek 28:23 the wounded shall be judged in her midst by the sword against her on every side; then they shall know that *I am the Lord*
Ezek 28:24 Then they shall know that *I am the Lord* God
Ezek 28:26 Then they shall know that *I am the Lord* their God
Ezek 29:6 Then all the inhabitants of Egypt shall know that *I am the Lord*, because they have been a staff of reed to the house of Israel
Ezek 29:9 then they will know that *I am the Lord*, because he said
Ezek 29:16 Then they shall know that *I am the Lord* God
Ezek 29:21 In that day I will cause the horn of the house of Israel to spring forth, and I will open your mouth to speak in their midst. Then they shall know that *I am the Lord*
Ezek 30:8 Then they will know that *I am the Lord*, when I have set a fire in Egypt and all her helpers are destroyed

Ezek 30:19 Thus I will execute judgments on Egypt, then they shall know that *I am the Lord*
Ezek 30:25 they shall know that *I am the Lord*, when I put My sword into the hand of the king of Babylon and he stretches it out against the land of Egypt
Ezek 30:26 I will scatter the Egyptians among the nations and disperse them throughout the countries. Then they shall know that *I am the Lord*
Ezek 32:15 When I make the land of Egypt desolate, and the country is destitute of all that once filled it, when I strike all who dwell in it, then they shall know that *I am the Lord*
Ezek 33:29 Then they shall know that *I am the Lord*, when I have made the land most desolate because of all their abominations which they have committed
Ezek 34:27 and they shall know that *I am the Lord*, when I have broken the bands of their yoke and delivered them from the hand of those who enslaved them
Ezek 35:4 I shall lay your cities waste, and you shall be desolate. Then you shall know that *I am the Lord*
Ezek 35:9 I will make you perpetually desolate, and your cities shall be uninhabited; then you shall know that *I am the Lord*
Ezek 35:12 Then you shall know that *I am the Lord*. I have heard all your blasphemies which you have spoken against the mountains of Israel, saying
Ezek 35:15 you shall be desolate, O Mount Seir, as well as all of Edom all of it! Then they shall know that *I am the Lord*
Ezek 36:11 I will make you inhabited as in former times, and do better for you than at your beginnings. Then you shall know that *I am the Lord*
Ezek 36:23 and the nations shall know that *I am the Lord*
Ezek 36:38 Like a flock offered as holy sacrifices, like the flock at Jerusalem on its feast days, so shall the ruined cities be filled with flocks of men. Then they shall know that *I am the Lord*
Ezek 37:6 and you shall live. Then you shall know that *I am the Lord*
Ezek 37:13 Then you shall know that *I am the Lord*, when I have opened your graves, O My people, and brought you up from your graves
Ezek 38:23 Thus I will magnify Myself and sanctify Myself, and I will be known in the eyes of many nations. Then they shall know that *I am the Lord*
Ezek 39:6 And I will send fire on Magog and on those who live in security in the coastlands. Then they shall know that *I am the Lord*
Ezek 39:7 Then the nations shall know that *I am the Lord*, the Holy One in Israel
Ezek 39:22 So the house of Israel shall know that *I am the Lord* their God from that day forward
Ezek 39:28 then they shall know that *I am the Lord* their God, who sent them into captivity among the nations, but also brought them back to their own land, and left none of them captive any longer
Hos 12:9 But *I am the Lord* your God, ever since the land of Egypt
Hos 13:4 Yet *I am the Lord* your God ever since the land of Egypt, and you shall know no God but Me
Joel 2:27 Then you shall know that I am in the midst of Israel, and that *I am the Lord* your God and there is no other
Joel 3:17 So you shall know that *I am the Lord* your God, dwelling in Zion My holy mountain
Zech 10:6 for *I am the Lord* their God, and I will hear them
Mal 3:6 For *I am the Lord*, I do not change; therefore you are not consumed, O sons of Jacob

I AM THE RESURRECTION
John 11:25 Jesus said to her, "*I am the resurrection* and the life

I AM THE SON OF GOD
Matt 27:43 let Him deliver Him now if He will have Him; for He said, '*I am the Son of God*
John 10:36 do you say of Him whom the Father sanctified and sent into the world, 'You are blaspheming,' because I said, '*I am the Son of God*

I AM THE TRUE VINE
John 15:1 *I am the true vine*, and My Father is the vinedresser

I AM THE VINE
John 15:5 *I am the vine*, you are the branches. He who abides in Me, and I in him, bears much fruit

I AM THE WAY
John 14:6 Jesus said to him, "*I am the way*, the truth, and the life

I AM THIRSTY (NAS, NIV)
(See *I THIRST*)

I AM UNWORTHY (NAS, NIV)
(See *I AM NOT WORTHY*)

I AM WHO I AM
Ex 3:14 And God said to Moses, "*I AM WHO I AM*

I AM WITH YOU
Gen 26:24 do not fear, for *I am with you*. I will bless you and multiply your descendants for My servant Abraham's sake
Gen 28:15 Behold, *I am with you* and will keep you wherever you go, and will bring you back to this land
1Sam 14:7 Go then; here *I am with you*, according to your heart
Is 41:10 Fear not, for *I am with you;* be not dismayed, for I am your God
Is 43:5 Fear not, for *I am with you;* I will bring your descendants from the east, and gather you from the west
Jer 1:8 Do not be afraid of their faces, for *I am with you* to deliver you
Jer 1:19 For *I am with you*," says the Lord, "to deliver you
Jer 15:20 for *I am with you* to save you and deliver you
Jer 30:11 For *I am with you*,' says the Lord, 'to save you
Jer 42:11 do not be afraid of him,' says the Lord, 'for *I am with you*, to save you and deliver you from his hand
Jer 46:28 Do not fear, O Jacob My servant," says the Lord, "For *I am with you*
Hag 1:13 Then Haggai, the Lord's messenger, spoke the Lord's message to the people, saying, "*I am with you*, says the Lord
Hag 2:4 for *I am with you*,' says the Lord of hosts
Matt 28:20 and lo, *I am with you* always, even to the end of the age
Acts 18:10 for *I am with you*, and no one will attack you to hurt you
Col 2:5 For though I am absent in the flesh, yet *I am with you* in spirit, rejoicing to see your good order and the steadfastness of your faith in Christ

I AM YOUR SERVANT
1Kin 18:36 And it came to pass, at the time of the offering of the evening sacrifice, that Elijah the prophet came near and said, "Lord God of Abraham, Isaac, and Israel, let it be known this day that You are God in Israel, and that *I am Your*

servant, and that I have done all these things at Your word
2Kin 16:7 So Ahaz sent messengers to Tiglath-Pileser king of Assyria, saying, "*I am your servant* and your son
Ps 116:16 O Lord, truly *I am Your servant; I am Your servant*, the son of Your maidservant
Ps 119:125 *I am Your servant;* give me understanding, that I may know Your testimonies
Ps 143:12 In Your mercy cut off my enemies, and destroy all those who afflict my soul; for *I am Your servant*

I AM YOUR SHIELD
Gen 15:1 After these things the word of the Lord came to Abram in a vision, saying, "Do not be afraid, Abram. *I am your shield*, your exceedingly great reward

I AND MY FATHER ARE ONE
John 10:30 *I and My Father are one*

I APPEAL TO CAESAR
Acts 25:11 but if there is nothing in these things of which these men accuse me, no one can deliver me to them. *I appeal to Caesar*

I ASCEND (KJV, NAS)
(See *I AM ASCENDING*)

I CALLED MY SON
Hos 11:1 When Israel was a child, I loved him, and out of Egypt *I called My son*
Matt 2:15 and was there until the death of Herod, that it might be fulfilled which was spoken by the Lord through the prophet, saying, "Out of Egypt *I called My Son*

I COME QUICKLY
Rev 3:11 Behold, *I come quickly!* Hold fast what you have, that no one may take your crown

I COMMIT MY SPIRIT
Ps 31:5 Into Your hand *I commit my spirit;* You have redeemed me, O Lord God of truth

I DESPISE MY LIFE
Job 9:21 I am blameless, yet I do not know myself; *I despise my life*

I FIND NO FAULT
Luke 23:4 Then Pilate said to the chief priests and the crowd, "*I find no fault* in this Man
John 18:38 And when he had said this, he went out again to the Jews, and said to them, "*I find no fault* in Him at all
John 19:4 Pilate then went out again, and said to them, "Behold, I am bringing Him out to you, that you may know that *I find no fault* in Him
John 19:6 Pilate said to them, "You take Him and crucify Him, for *I find no fault* in Him

I GO AWAY
Ps 39:13 Remove Your gaze from me, that I may regain strength, before *I go away* and am no more
John 16:5 But now *I go away* to Him who sent Me, and none of you asks Me
John 16:7 It is to your advantage that *I go away;* for if I do not go away, the Helper will not come to you

I HAVE LOVED YOU
Is 43:4 Since you were precious in My sight, you have been honored, and *I have loved you*
Jer 31:3 Yes, *I have loved you* with an everlasting love; therefore with lovingkindness I have drawn you
Mal 1:2 *I have loved you*," says the Lord. "Yet you say
John 13:34 as *I have loved you*, that you also love one another
John 15:12 This is My commandment, that you love one another as *I have loved you*
Rev 3:9 Indeed I will make those of the synagogue of Satan, who say they are Jews and are not, but lie indeed I will make them come and worship before your feet, and to know that *I have loved you*

I KNOW YOU BY NAME
Ex 33:12 Yet You have said, '*I know you by name*, and you have also found grace in My sight
Ex 33:17 for you have found grace in My sight, and *I know you by name*

I LAY DOWN MY LIFE
John 10:15 As the Father knows Me, even so I know the Father; and *I lay down My life* for the sheep
John 10:17 Therefore My Father loves Me, because *I lay down My life* that I may take it again

I LOATHE MY LIFE (RSV)
(See *I DESPISE MY LIFE*)

I MARVEL
Gal 1:6 *I marvel* that you are turning away so soon from Him who called you in the grace of Christ, to a different gospel

I, NOT THE LORD
1Cor 7:12 But to the rest *I, not the Lord*, say

I SAY, NOT THE LORD (RSV)
(See *I, NOT THE LORD*)

I SAY TO YOU, ARISE
Mark 2:11 *I say to you, arise*, take up your bed, and go your way to your house
Mark 5:41 Then He took the child by the hand, and said to her, "Talitha, cumi," which is translated, "Little girl, *I say to you, arise*
Luke 5:24 But that you may know that the Son of Man has power on earth to forgive sins" He said to the man who was paralyzed, "*I say to you, arise*, take up your bed, and go to your house
Luke 7:14 And He said, "Young man, *I say to you, arise*

I SEND MY MESSENGER
Mal 3:1 Behold, *I send My messenger*, and he will prepare the way before Me
Matt 11:10 Behold, *I send My messenger* before Your face, who will prepare Your way before You
Mark 1:2 Behold, *I send My messenger* before Your face, who will prepare Your way before You
Luke 7:27 Behold, *I send My messenger* before Your face, who will prepare Your way before You

I SHALL NOT BE MOVED
Ps 10:6 He has said in his heart, "*I shall not be moved*
Ps 16:8 Because He is at my right hand *I shall not be moved*
Ps 62:6 He only is my rock and my salvation; He is my defense; *I shall not be moved*

I TELL YOU, GET UP (NIV)
(See *I SAY TO YOU, ARISE*)

I TELL YOU THE TRUTH
John 16:7 Nevertheless *I tell you the truth*. It is to your advantage that I go away
Gal 4:16 Have I therefore become your enemy because *I tell you the truth*

I THIRST
John 19:28 After this, Jesus, knowing that all things were now accomplished, that the Scripture might be fulfilled, said, "*I thirst*

I WAS HUNGRY
Matt 25:35 for *I was hungry* and you gave Me food; I was thirsty and you gave Me drink
Matt 25:42 for *I was hungry* and you gave Me no food

I WAS THIRSTY
Matt 25:35 *I was thirsty* and you gave Me drink; I was a stranger and you took Me in
Matt 25:42 for I was hungry and you gave Me no food; *I was thirsty* and you gave Me no drink

I WILL BE WITH YOU
Gen 26:3 Dwell in this land, and *I will be with you* and bless you
Gen 31:3 Then the Lord said to Jacob, "Return to the land of your fathers and to your family, and *I will be with you*
Deut 31:23 for you shall bring the children of Israel into the land of which I swore to them, and *I will be with you*
Josh 1:5 as I was with Moses, so *I will be with you*
Josh 3:7 And the Lord said to Joshua, "This day I will begin to magnify you in the sight of all Israel, that they may know that, as I was with Moses, so *I will be with you*
Judg 6:16 And the Lord said to him, "Surely *I will be with you*, and you shall defeat the Midianites as one man
1Kin 11:38 Then it shall be, if you heed all that I command you, walk in My ways, and do what is right in My sight, to keep My statutes and My commandments, as My servant David did, then *I will be with you* and build for you an enduring house, as I built for David, and will give Israel to you
Is 43:2 When you pass through the waters, *I will be with you*

I WILL BE YOUR GOD
Ex 6:7 I will take you as My people, and *I will be your God*
Jer 7:23 But this is what I commanded them, saying, 'Obey My voice, and *I will be your God*, and you shall be My people
Jer 11:4 so shall you be My people, and *I will be your God*
Jer 30:22 You shall be My people, and *I will be your God*
Ezek 36:28 you shall be My people, and *I will be your God*

I WILL BLESS
Gen 12:2 *I will bless* you and make your name great; and you shall be a blessing
Gen 12:3 *I will bless* those who bless you, and I will curse him who curses you
Gen 17:16 And *I will bless* her and also give you a son by her; then *I will bless* her, and she shall be a mother of nations
Gen 22:17 in blessing *I will bless* you, and in multiplying I will multiply your descendants as the stars of the heaven and as the sand which is on the seashore
Gen 26:24 *I will bless* you and multiply your descendants for My servant Abraham's sake
Gen 48:9 And he said, "Please bring them to me, and *I will bless* them
Ex 20:24 In every place where I record My name I will come to you, and *I will bless* you
Num 6:27 So they shall put My name on the children of Israel, and *I will bless* them
Ps 16:7 *I will bless* the Lord who has given me counsel
Ps 26:12 My foot stands in an even place; in the congregations *I will bless* the Lord
Ps 34:1 *I will bless* the Lord at all times; His praise shall continually be in my mouth
Ps 63:4 Thus *I will bless* You while I live; I will lift up my hands in Your name
Ps 145:1 I will extol You, my God, O King; and *I will bless* Your name forever and ever
Ps 145:2 Every day *I will bless* You, and I will praise Your name forever and ever
Hag 2:19 As yet the vine, the fig tree, the pomegranate, and the olive tree have not yielded fruit. But from this day forward *I will bless* you
Heb 6:14 saying, "Surely blessing *I will bless* you, and multiplying I will multiply you

I WILL BOAST
2Cor 11:30 If I must boast, *I will boast* in the things which concern my infirmity
2Cor 12:5 Of such a one *I will boast;* yet of myself I will not boast, except in my infirmities

I WILL GIVE YOU REST
Ex 33:14 And He said, "My Presence will go with you, and *I will give you rest*
Matt 11:28 Come to Me, all you who labor and are heavy laden, and *I will give you rest*

I WILL RAISE IT UP
John 2:19 Jesus answered and said to them, "Destroy this temple, and in three days *I will raise it up*

I WILL REMEMBER MY COVENANT
Gen 9:15 and *I will remember My covenant* which is between Me and you and every living creature of all flesh
Lev 26:42 then *I will remember My covenant* with Jacob, and My covenant with Isaac and My covenant with Abraham I will remember
Ezek 16:60 Nevertheless *I will remember My covenant* with you in the days of your youth, and I will establish an everlasting covenant with you

I WILL REPAY
2Kin 9:26 Surely I saw yesterday the blood of Naboth and the blood of his sons,' says the Lord, 'and *I will repay* you in this plot
Jer 16:18 And first *I will repay* double for their iniquity and their sin, because they have defiled My land
Jer 25:14 and *I will repay* them according to their deeds and according to the works of their own hands
Jer 51:24 And *I will repay* Babylon and all the inhabitants of Chaldea for all the evil they have done in Zion in your sight
Ezek 7:3 I will judge you according to your ways, and *I will repay* you for all your abominations
Ezek 7:4 but *I will repay* your ways, and your abominations shall be in your midst
Ezek 7:8 I will judge you according to your ways, and *I will repay* you for all your abominations
Ezek 7:9 *I will repay* you according to your ways, and your abominations will be in your midst
Luke 10:35 and whatever more you spend, when I come again, *I will repay* you
Rom 12:19 for it is written, "Vengeance is Mine, *I will repay*
Phm 19 *I will repay* not to mention to you that you owe me even your own self besides
Heb 10:30 *I will repay*, says the Lord." And again, "The Lord will judge His people

I WILL REQUITE (KJV, RSV)
(See *I WILL REPAY*)

I WILL SEND MY MESSENGER (KJV, NIV)
(See *I SEND MY MESSENGER*)

I WOULD DESPISE MY LIFE (KJV)
(See *I DESPISE MY LIFE*)

IDOLATROUS PRIESTS
2Kin 23:5 Then he removed the *idolatrous priests* whom the kings of Judah had ordained to burn incense on the high places in the cities of Judah and in the places all around Jerusalem, and those who burned incense to Baal, to the sun, to the moon, to the constellations, and to all the host of heaven
Zeph 1:4 I will cut off every trace of Baal from this place, the names of the *idolatrous priests* with the pagan priests

IDOLS OF GOLD
Is 2:20 In that day a man will cast away his idols of silver and his *idols of gold*, which they made, each for himself to worship, to the moles and bats
Is 31:7 For in that day every man shall throw away his idols of silver and his *idols of gold* sin, which your own hands have made for yourselves
Rev 9:20 But the rest of mankind, who were not killed by these plagues, did not repent of the works of their hands, that they should not worship demons, and *idols of gold*, silver, brass, stone, and wood, which can neither see nor hear nor walk

IDOLS OF SILVER
Is 2:20 In that day a man will cast away his *idols of silver* and his idols of gold, which they made, each for himself to worship, to the moles and bats
Is 31:7 For in that day every man shall throw away his *idols of silver* and his idols of gold sin, which your own hands have made for yourselves

IF A MAN DIES
Num 27:8 *If a man dies* and has no son, then you shall cause his inheritance to pass to his daughter
Job 14:14 *If a man dies*, shall he live again? All the days of my hard service I will wait, till my change comes
Matt 22:24 Teacher, Moses said that *if a man dies*, having no children, his brother shall marry his wife and raise up offspring for his brother

IF A MAN MARRIES
Lev 20:14 *If a man marries* a woman and her mother, it is wickedness

IF A SLAVE IS BORN IN HIS HOUSEHOLD (NIV)
(See *ONE WHO IS BORN IN HIS HOUSE*)

IF ANY MAN WOULD COME (RSV)
(See *WHOEVER DESIRES TO COME*)

IF ANY ONE OF YOU IS WITHOUT SIN (NIV)
(See *HE WHO IS WITHOUT SIN*)

IF ANYONE HAS EARS
Mark 4:23 *If anyone has ears* to hear, let him hear
Mark 7:16 *If anyone has ears* to hear, let him hear

IF ANYONE SERVES ME
John 12:26 *If anyone serves Me*, let him follow Me; and where I am, there My servant will be also. *If anyone serves Me*, him My Father will honor

IF GOD SO LOVED US
1Jn 4:11 Beloved, *if God so loved us*, we also ought to love one another

IF IT PLEASES THE KING
Neh 2:5 And I said to the king, "*If it pleases the king*, and if your servant has found favor in your sight, I ask that you send me to Judah, to the city of my fathers' tombs, that I may rebuild it
Neh 2:7 Furthermore I said to the king, "*If it pleases the king*, let letters be given to me for the governors of the region beyond the River, that they must permit me to pass through till I come to Judah
Esth 1:19 *If it pleases the king*, let a royal decree go out from him, and let it be recorded in the laws of the Persians and the Medes, so that it will not be altered, that Vashti shall come no more before King Ahasuerus
Esth 3:9 *If it pleases the king*, let a decree be written that they be destroyed, and I will pay ten thousand talents of silver into the hands of those who do the work, to bring it into the king's treasuries
Esth 5:4 So Esther answered, "*If it pleases the king*, let the king and Haman come today to the banquet that I have prepared for him
Esth 5:8 If I have found favor in the sight of the king, and *if it pleases the king* to grant my petition and fulfill my request, then let the king and Haman come to the banquet which I will prepare for them, and tomorrow I will do as the king has said
Esth 7:3 Then Queen Esther answered and said, "If I have found favor in your sight, O king, and *if it pleases the king*, let my life be given me at my petition, and my people at my request
Esth 8:5 and said, "*If it pleases the king*, and if I have found favor in his sight and the thing seems right to the king and I am pleasing in his eyes, let it be written to revoke the letters devised by Haman, the son of Hammedatha the Agagite, which he wrote to annihilate the Jews who are in all the king's provinces
Esth 9:13 Then Esther said, "*If it pleases the king*, let it be granted to the Jews who are in Shushan to do again tomorrow according to today's decree, and let Haman's ten sons be hanged on the gallows

IF OUR HEART CONDEMNS US
1Jn 3:20 For *if our heart condemns us*, God is greater than our heart, and knows all things

IF SINNERS ENTICE YOU
Prov 1:10 My son, *if sinners entice you*, do not consent

IF THE DEAD DO NOT RISE
1Cor 15:16 For *if the dead do not rise*, then Christ is not risen
1Cor 15:29 Otherwise, what will they do who are baptized for the dead, *if the dead do not rise* at all
1Cor 15:32 *If the dead do not rise*, "Let us eat and drink, for tomorrow we die

IF THE LORD PERMITS
1Cor 16:7 but I hope to stay a while with you, *if the Lord permits*

IF THE SALT LOSES ITS FLAVOR
Matt 5:13 but *if the salt loses its flavor*, how shall it be seasoned
Mark 9:50 Salt is good, but *if the salt loses its flavor*, how will you season it

IF THE SON MAKES YOU FREE
John 8:36 Therefore *if the Son makes you free*, you shall be free indeed

IF THY FOOT OFFEND THEE (KJV)
(See *IF YOUR FOOT MAKES YOU SIN*)

IF THY HAND OFFEND THEE (KJV)
(See *IF YOUR HAND MAKES YOU SIN*)

IF THY RIGHT EYE OFFEND THEE (KJV)
(See *IF YOUR RIGHT EYE CAUSES YOU TO SIN*)

IF YOU DO NOT FORGIVE THEM (NIV)
(See *IF YOU RETAIN THE SINS*)

IF YOU FORGIVE THE SINS
John 20:23 *If you forgive the sins* of any, they are forgiven them

IF YOU LOVE ME
John 14:15 *If you love Me*, keep My commandments

IF YOU LOVED ME
John 14:28 *If you loved Me*, you would rejoice because I said

IF YOU RETAIN THE SINS
John 20:23 *if you retain the sins* of any, they are retained

IF YOUR BROTHER SINS
Matt 18:15 Moreover *if your brother sins* against you, go and tell him his fault between you and him alone
Luke 17:3 *If your brother sins* against you, rebuke him; and if he repents, forgive him

IF YOUR ENEMY HUNGERS
Rom 12:20 Therefore *if your enemy hungers*, feed him; if he thirsts, give him a drink

IF YOUR ENEMY IS HUNGRY
Prov 25:21 *If your enemy is hungry*, give him bread to eat

IF YOUR FOOT MAKES YOU SIN
Mark 9:45 And *if your foot makes you sin*, cut it off

IF YOUR HAND MAKES YOU SIN
Mark 9:43 And *if your hand makes you sin*, cut it off

IF YOUR RIGHT EYE CAUSES YOU TO SIN
Matt 5:29 And *if your right eye causes you to sin*, pluck it out and cast it from you

ILL-GOTTEN GAIN (NIV)
(See *GREEDY FOR GAIN*)

ILLNESS IS NOT UNTO DEATH (RSV)
(See *SICKNESS IS NOT UNTO DEATH*)

IMAGE OF GOD
Gen 1:27 in the *image of God* He created him; male and female He created them
Gen 9:6 Whoever sheds man's blood, by man his blood shall be shed; for in the *image of God* He made man
2Cor 4:4 whose minds the god of this age has blinded, who do not believe, lest the light of the gospel of the glory of Christ, who is the *image of God*, should shine on them

IMAGE OF HIS SON
Rom 8:29 For whom He foreknew, He also predestined to be conformed to the *image of His Son*, that He might be the firstborn among many brethren

IMAGINATION OF THEIR EVIL HEART (KJV)
(See *STUBBORNNESS OF THEIR EVIL HEART*)

IMITATE CHRIST
1Cor 11:1 Imitate me, just as I also *imitate Christ*

IMITATE ME
1Cor 4:16 Therefore I urge you, *imitate me*
1Cor 11:1 *Imitate me*, just as I also imitate Christ

IMPERISHABLE CROWN
1Cor 9:25 Now they do it to obtain a perishable crown, but we for an *imperishable crown*

IMPORTANT CITY (NIV)
(See *GREAT CITY*)

IMPORTANT MATTERS OF THE LAW (NIV)
(See *WEIGHTIER MATTERS OF THE LAW*)

IMPOSSIBLE FOR GOD TO LIE
Heb 6:18 that by two immutable things, in which it is *impossible for God to lie*, we might have strong consolation, who have fled for refuge to lay hold of the hope set before us

IMPOSSIBLE TO PLEASE HIM
Heb 11:6 But without faith it is *impossible to please Him*, for he who comes to God must believe that He is, and that He is a rewarder of those who diligently seek Him

IMPURE OR UNCLEAN (NIV)
(See *COMMON OR UNCLEAN*)

IMPUTED TO US
Rom 4:24 It shall be *imputed to us* who believe in Him who raised up Jesus our Lord from the dead

IN A DREAM BY NIGHT
Gen 20:3 But God came to Abimelech *in a dream by night*, and said to him
Gen 31:24 But God had come to Laban the Syrian *in a dream by night*, and said to him
1Kin 3:5 At Gibeon the Lord appeared to Solomon *in a dream by night*

IN A GREAT STRAIT (KJV)
(See *IN GREAT DISTRESS*)

IN A MANGER
Luke 2:7 And she brought forth her firstborn Son, and wrapped Him in swaddling cloths, and laid Him *in a manger*, because there was no room for them in the inn
Luke 2:12 You will find a Babe wrapped in swaddling cloths, lying *in a manger*
Luke 2:16 And they came with haste and found Mary and Joseph, and the Babe lying *in a manger*

IN A PARABLE (RSV)
(See *BY A PARABLE*)

IN ACCORDANCE WITH THE SCRIPTURES (RSV)
(See *ACCORDING TO THE SCRIPTURES*)

IN ADAM
1Cor 15:22 For as *in Adam* all die, even so in Christ all shall be made alive

IN ALL THE CHURCHES
1Cor 7:17 But as God has distributed to each one, as the Lord has called each one, so let him walk. And so I ordain *in all the churches*
1Cor 14:33 For God is not the author of confusion but of peace, as *in all the churches* of the saints

IN AN INSTANT

Is 29:5 Moreover the multitude of your foes shall be like fine dust, and the multitude of the terrible ones shall be as chaff that passes away; yes, it shall be *in an instant*, suddenly

Is 30:13 therefore this iniquity shall be to you like a breach ready to fall, a bulge in a high wall, whose breaking comes suddenly, *in an instant*

IN BROAD DAYLIGHT

Amos 8:9 And it shall come to pass in that day," says the Lord God, "That I will make the sun go down at noon, and I will darken the earth *in broad daylight*

IN CHRIST

Acts 24:24 And after some days, when Felix came with his wife Drusilla, who was Jewish, he sent for Paul and heard him concerning the faith *in Christ*

Rom 3:24 being justified freely by His grace through the redemption that is *in Christ* Jesus

Rom 6:11 Likewise you also, reckon yourselves to be dead indeed to sin, but alive to God *in Christ* Jesus our Lord

Rom 6:23 For the wages of sin is death, but the gift of God is eternal life *in Christ* Jesus our Lord

Rom 8:1 There is therefore now no condemnation to those who are *in Christ* Jesus, who do not walk according to the flesh, but according to the Spirit

Rom 8:2 For the law of the Spirit of life *in Christ* Jesus has made me free from the law of sin and death

Rom 8:39 nor height nor depth, nor any other created thing, shall be able to separate us from the love of God which is *in Christ* Jesus our Lord

Rom 9:1 I tell the truth *in Christ*, I am not lying, my conscience also bearing me witness in the Holy Spirit

Rom 12:5 so we, being many, are one body *in Christ*, and individually members of one another

Rom 15:17 Therefore I have reason to glory *in Christ* Jesus in the things which pertain to God

Rom 16:3 Greet Priscilla and Aquila, my fellow workers *in Christ* Jesus

Rom 16:7 Greet Andronicus and Junia, my kinsmen and my fellow prisoners, who are of note among the apostles, who also were *in Christ* before me

Rom 16:9 Greet Urbanus, our fellow worker *in Christ*, and Stachys, my beloved

Rom 16:10 Greet Apelles, approved *in Christ*. Greet those who are of the household of Aristobulus

1Cor 1:2 To the church of God which is at Corinth, to those who are sanctified *in Christ* Jesus, called to be saints, with all who in every place call on the name of Jesus Christ our Lord, both theirs and ours

1Cor 1:30 But of Him you are *in Christ* Jesus, who became for us wisdom from God and righteousness and sanctification and redemption

1Cor 3:1 And I, brethren, could not speak to you as to spiritual people but as to carnal, as to babes *in Christ*

1Cor 4:10 We are fools for Christ's sake, but you are wise *in Christ*

1Cor 4:15 For though you might have ten thousand instructors *in Christ*, yet you do not have many fathers; for *in Christ* Jesus I have begotten you through the gospel

1Cor 4:17 For this reason I have sent Timothy to you, who is my beloved and faithful son in the Lord, who will remind you of my ways *in Christ*, as I teach everywhere in every church

1Cor 15:18 Then also those who have fallen asleep *in Christ* have perished

1Cor 15:19 If in this life only we have hope *in Christ*, we are of all men the most pitiable

1Cor 15:22 For as in Adam all die, even so *in Christ* all shall be made alive

1Cor 15:31 I affirm, by the boasting in you which I have *in Christ* Jesus our Lord, I die daily

1Cor 16:24 My love be with you all *in Christ* Jesus. Amen

2Cor 1:21 Now He who establishes us with you *in Christ* and has anointed us is God

2Cor 2:14 Now thanks be to God who always leads us in triumph *in Christ*, and through us diffuses the fragrance of His knowledge in every place

2Cor 2:17 but as of sincerity, but as from God, we speak in the sight of God *in Christ*

2Cor 3:14 For until this day the same veil remains unlifted in the reading of the Old Testament, because the veil is taken away *in Christ*

2Cor 5:17 Therefore, if anyone is *in Christ*, he is a new creation

2Cor 5:19 that is, that God was *in Christ* reconciling the world to Himself, not imputing their trespasses to them, and has committed to us the word of reconciliation

2Cor 11:3 But I fear, lest somehow, as the serpent deceived Eve by his craftiness, so your minds may be corrupted from the simplicity that is *in Christ*

2Cor 12:2 I know a man *in Christ* who fourteen years ago whether in the body I do not know, or whether out of the body I do not know, God knows such a one was caught up to the third heaven

2Cor 12:19 We speak before God *in Christ*. But we do all things, beloved, for your edification

Gal 1:22 and I was unknown by face to the churches of Judea which were *in Christ*

Gal 2:4 But this occurred because of false brethren secretly brought in (who came in by stealth to spy out our liberty which we have *in Christ* Jesus, that they might bring us into bondage

Gal 2:16 knowing that a man is not justified by the works of the law but by faith in Jesus Christ, even we have believed *in Christ* Jesus, that we might be justified by faith *in Christ* and not by the works of the law

Gal 3:14 that the blessing of Abraham might come upon the Gentiles *in Christ* Jesus, that we might receive the promise of the Spirit through faith

Gal 3:17 And this I say, that the law, which was four hundred and thirty years later, cannot annul the covenant that was confirmed before by God *in Christ*, that it should make the promise of no effect

Gal 3:26 For you are all sons of God through faith *in Christ* Jesus

Gal 3:28 There is neither Jew nor Greek, there is neither slave nor free, there is neither male nor female; for you are all one *in Christ* Jesus

Gal 5:6 For *in Christ* Jesus neither circumcision nor uncircumcision avails anything, but faith working through love

Gal 6:15 For *in Christ* Jesus neither circumcision nor uncircumcision avails anything, but a new creation

Eph 1:1 Paul, an apostle of Jesus Christ by the will of God, To the saints who are in Ephesus, and faithful *in Christ* Jesus

Eph 1:3 Blessed be the God and Father of our Lord Jesus Christ, who has blessed us with every spiritual blessing in the heavenly places *in Christ*

Eph 1:10 that in the dispensation of the fullness of the times He might gather together in one all things *in Christ*, both which are in heaven and which are on earth in Him

Eph 1:12 that we who first trusted *in Christ* should be to the praise of His glory

Eph 1:20 which He worked *in Christ* when He

raised Him from the dead and seated Him at His right hand in the heavenly places
Eph 2:6 and raised us up together, and made us sit together in the heavenly places *in Christ* Jesus
Eph 2:7 that in the ages to come He might show the exceeding riches of His grace in His kindness toward us *in Christ* Jesus
Eph 2:10 For we are His workmanship, created *in Christ* Jesus for good works, which God prepared beforehand that we should walk in them
Eph 2:13 But now *in Christ* Jesus you who once were far off have been made near by the blood of Christ
Eph 3:6 that the Gentiles should be fellow heirs, of the same body, and partakers of His promise *in Christ* through the gospel
Eph 3:11 according to the eternal purpose which He accomplished *in Christ* Jesus our Lord
Eph 4:32 And be kind to one another, tenderhearted, forgiving one another, just as God *in Christ* also forgave you
Phil 1:1 Paul and Timothy, servants of Jesus Christ, to all the saints *in Christ* Jesus who are in Philippi, with the bishops and deacons
Phil 1:13 so that it has become evident to the whole palace guard, and to all the rest, that my chains are *in Christ*
Phil 2:1 Therefore if there is any consolation *in Christ*, if any comfort of love, if any fellowship of the Spirit, if any affection and mercy
Phil 2:5 Let this mind be in you which was also *in Christ* Jesus
Phil 3:3 For we are the circumcision, who worship God in the Spirit, rejoice *in Christ* Jesus, and have no confidence in the flesh
Phil 3:9 and be found in Him, not having my own righteousness, which is from the law, but that which is through faith *in Christ*, the righteousness which is from God by faith
Phil 3:14 I press toward the goal for the prize of the upward call of God *in Christ* Jesus
Phil 4:21 Greet every saint *in Christ* Jesus. The brethren who are with me greet you
Col 1:2 To the saints and faithful brethren *in Christ* who are in Colosse
Col 1:4 since we heard of your faith *in Christ* Jesus and of your love for all the saints
Col 1:28 Him we preach, warning every man and teaching every man in all wisdom, that we may present every man perfect *in Christ* Jesus
Col 2:5 For though I am absent in the flesh, yet I am with you in spirit, rejoicing to see your good order and the steadfastness of your faith *in Christ*
1Th 2:14 For you, brethren, became imitators of the churches of God which are in Judea *in Christ* Jesus
1Th 4:16 For the Lord Himself will descend from heaven with a shout, with the voice of an archangel, and with the trumpet of God. And the dead *in Christ* will rise first
1Th 5:18 for this is the will of God *in Christ* Jesus for you
1Tim 1:14 And the grace of our Lord was exceedingly abundant, with faith and love which are *in Christ* Jesus
1Tim 2:7 for which I was appointed a preacher and an apostle I am speaking the truth *in Christ* and not lying a teacher of the Gentiles in faith and truth
1Tim 3:13 For those who have served well as deacons obtain for themselves a good standing and great boldness in the faith which is *in Christ* Jesus
2Tim 1:1 Paul, an apostle of Jesus Christ by the will of God, according to the promise of life which is *in Christ* Jesus
2Tim 1:9 who has saved us and called us with a holy calling, not according to our works, but according to His own purpose and grace which was given to us *in Christ* Jesus before time began
2Tim 1:13 Hold fast the pattern of sound words which you have heard from me, in faith and love which are *in Christ* Jesus
2Tim 2:1 You therefore, my son, be strong in the grace that is *in Christ* Jesus
2Tim 2:10 Therefore I endure all things for the sake of the elect, that they also may obtain the salvation which is *in Christ* Jesus with eternal glory
2Tim 3:12 Yes, and all who desire to live godly *in Christ* Jesus will suffer persecution
2Tim 3:15 and that from childhood you have known the Holy Scriptures, which are able to make you wise for salvation through faith which is *in Christ* Jesus
Phm 6 that the sharing of your faith may become effective by the acknowledgment of every good thing which is in you *in Christ* Jesus
Phm 8 Therefore, though I might be very bold *in Christ* to command you what is fitting
Phm 23 Epaphras, my fellow prisoner *in Christ* Jesus, greets you
1Pet 3:16 having a good conscience, that when they defame you as evildoers, those who revile your good conduct *in Christ* may be ashamed
1Pet 5:14 Peace to you all who are *in Christ* Jesus. Amen

IN CHRIST GOD WAS (RSV)
(See *GOD WAS IN CHRIST*)

IN DAYS TO COME (NIV)
(See *IN THE LATTER DAYS*)

IN ELIJAH'S TIME (NIV)
(See *DAYS OF ELIJAH*)

IN GOD I HAVE PUT MY TRUST
Ps 56:4 *In God I have put my trust;* I will not fear
Ps 56:11 *In God I have put my trust;* I will not be afraid

IN GOD WE BOAST
Ps 44:8 *In God we boast* all day long, and praise Your name forever

IN GOD'S SIGHT (NIV, RSV)
(See *BEFORE GOD*)

IN GREAT DISTRESS
2Sam 24:14 And David said to Gad, "I am *in great distress*
1Chr 21:13 And David said to Gad, "I am *in great distress*
Neh 1:3 And they said to me, "The survivors who are left from the captivity in the province are there *in great distress* and reproach
Neh 9:37 also they have dominion over our bodies and our cattle at their pleasure; And we are *in great distress*

IN HER PANGS (KJV, RSV)
(See *BIRTH PANGS*)

IN HIM WAS LIFE
John 1:4 *In Him was life*, and the life was the light of men

IN HIS BLOOD (KJV, NAS, NIV)
(See *BY HIS BLOOD*)

IN HIS PRESENCE
Gen 45:3 But his brothers could not answer him, for they were dismayed *in his presence*
Deut 25:2 then it shall be, if the wicked man de-

serves to be beaten, that the judge will cause him to lie down and be beaten *in his presence*, according to his guilt, with a certain number of blows
1Sam 19:7 So Jonathan brought David to Saul, and he was *in his presence* as in times past
2Chr 34:4 They broke down the altars of the Baals *in his presence*, and the incense altars which were above them he cut down
Neh 2:1 Now I had never been sad *in his presence* before
1Cor 1:29 that no flesh should glory *in His presence*
Rev 13:12 And he exercises all the authority of the first beast *in his presence*, and causes the earth and those who dwell in it to worship the first beast, whose deadly wound was healed
Rev 19:20 Then the beast was captured, and with him the false prophet who worked signs *in his presence*, by which he deceived those who received the mark of the beast and those who worshiped his image

IN HIS RIGHT HAND
Ezek 21:22 *In his right hand* is the divination for Jerusalem: to set up battering rams, to call for a slaughter, to lift the voice with shouting, to set battering rams against the gates, to heap up a siege mound, and to build a wall
Matt 27:29 When they had twisted a crown of thorns, they put it on His head, and a reed *in His right hand*
Rev 1:16 He had *in His right hand* seven stars, out of His mouth went a sharp two-edged sword, and His countenance was like the sun shining in its strength
Rev 2:1 To the angel of the church of Ephesus write, 'These things says He who holds the seven stars *in His right hand*, who walks in the midst of the seven golden lampstands

IN LABOR (NAS, NIV)
(See *BIRTH PANGS*)

IN LIKE MANNER
Ex 7:11 so the magicians of Egypt, they also did *in like manner* with their enchantments
Ex 23:11 *In like manner* you shall do with your vineyard and your olive grove
Judg 11:17 And *in like manner* they sent to the king of Moab, but he would not consent
1Sam 19:24 And he also stripped off his clothes and prophesied before Samuel *in like manner*, and lay down naked all that day and all that night
Is 51:6 For the heavens will vanish away like smoke, the earth will grow old like a garment, and those who dwell in it will die *in like manner*
Luke 6:23 for indeed your reward is great in heaven, for *in like manner* their fathers did to the prophets
Luke 20:31 Then the third took her, and *in like manner* the seven also
John 5:19 for whatever He does, the Son also does *in like manner*
Acts 1:11 This same Jesus, who was taken up from you into heaven, will so come *in like manner* as you saw Him go into heaven
1Tim 2:9 *in like manner* also, that the women adorn themselves in modest apparel, with propriety and moderation, not with braided hair or gold or pearls or costly clothing

IN ME
Gen 41:16 So Joseph answered Pharaoh, saying, "It is not *in me*
1Sam 20:8 Nevertheless, if there is iniquity *in me*, kill me yourself, for why should you bring me to your father
2Sam 1:9 He said to me again, 'Please stand over me and kill me, for anguish has come upon me, but my life still remains *in me*
2Sam 14:32 but if there is any iniquity *in me*, let him execute me
2Sam 22:20 He also brought me out into a broad place; He delivered me, because He delighted *in me*
Job 19:28 Since the root of the matter is found *in me*
Job 27:3 as long as my breath is *in me*, and the breath of God in my nostrils
Job 28:14 The deep says, 'It is not *in me*'; and the sea says
Job 30:17 My bones are pierced *in me* at night, and my gnawing pains take no rest
Job 33:9 I am innocent, and there is no iniquity *in me*
Ps 18:19 He also brought me out into a broad place; He delivered me because He delighted *in me*
Ps 51:10 Create *in me* a clean heart, O God, and renew a steadfast spirit within me
Ps 139:24 And see if there is any wicked way *in me*, and lead me in the way everlasting
Is 27:4 Fury is not *in Me*. Who would set briers and thorns against Me in battle
Is 57:13 But he who puts his trust *in Me* shall possess the land, and shall inherit My holy mountain
Jer 2:5 What injustice have your fathers found *in Me*, that they have gone far from Me, have followed idols, and have become idolaters
Jer 4:19 My heart makes a noise *in me;* I cannot hold my peace, because you have heard, O my soul, the sound of the trumpet, the alarm of war
Jer 8:18 I would comfort myself in sorrow; my heart is faint *in me*
Jer 39:18 but your life shall be as a prize to you, because you have put your trust *in Me*
Jer 49:11 Leave your fatherless children, I will preserve them alive; and let your widows trust *in Me*
Dan 10:8 Therefore I was left alone when I saw this great vision, and no strength remained *in me;* for my vigor was turned to frailty *in me*, and I retained no strength
Dan 10:17 As for me, no strength remains *in me* now, nor is any breath left *in me*
Hos 12:8 in all my labors they shall find *in me* no iniquity that is sin
Hos 14:8 I am like a green cypress tree; Your fruit is found *in Me*
Matt 18:6 But whoever causes one of these little ones who believe *in Me* to sin, it would be better for him if a millstone were hung around his neck, and he were drowned in the depth of the sea
Mark 9:42 And whoever causes one of these little ones who believe *in Me* to stumble, it would be better for him if a millstone were hung around his neck, and he were thrown into the sea
Luke 22:37 For I say to you that this which is written must still be accomplished *in Me*
John 6:35 He who comes to Me shall never hunger, and he who believes *in Me* shall never thirst
John 6:47 Most assuredly, I say to you, he who believes *in Me* has everlasting life
John 6:56 He who eats My flesh and drinks My blood abides *in Me*, and I in him
John 7:38 He who believes *in Me*, as the Scripture has said, out of his heart will flow rivers of living water
John 10:38 but if I do, though you do not believe Me, believe the works, that you may know and believe that the Father is *in Me*, and I in Him
John 11:25 He who believes *in Me*, though he may die, he shall live
John 11:26 And whoever lives and believes *in Me* shall never die
John 12:44 Then Jesus cried out and said, "He

who believes *in Me*, believes not *in Me* but in Him who sent Me
John 12:46 I have come as a light into the world, that whoever believes *in Me* should not abide in darkness
John 14:1 Let not your heart be troubled; you believe in God, believe also *in Me*
John 14:10 Do you not believe that I am in the Father, and the Father *in Me?* The words that I speak to you I do not speak on My own authority; but the Father who dwells *in Me* does the works
John 14:11 Believe Me that I am in the Father and the Father *in Me*, or else believe Me for the sake of the works themselves
John 14:12 Most assuredly, I say to you, he who believes *in Me*, the works that I do he will do also
John 14:20 At that day you will know that I am in My Father, and you *in Me*, and I in you
John 14:30 I will no longer talk much with you, for the ruler of this world is coming, and he has nothing *in Me*
John 15:2 Every branch *in Me* that does not bear fruit He takes away
John 15:4 Abide *in Me*, and I in you. As the branch cannot bear fruit of itself, unless it abides in the vine, neither can you, unless you abide *in Me*
John 15:5 He who abides *in Me*, and I in him, bears much fruit
John 15:6 If anyone does not abide *in Me*, he is cast out as a branch and is withered
John 15:7 If you abide *in Me*, and My words abide in you, you will ask what you desire, and it shall be done for you
John 16:9 of sin, because they do not believe *in Me*
John 16:33 These things I have spoken to you, that *in Me* you may have peace
John 17:20 I do not pray for these alone, but also for those who will believe *in Me* through their word
John 17:21 that they all may be one, as You, Father, are *in Me*, and I in You
John 17:23 I in them, and You *in Me;* that they may be made perfect in one, and that the world may know that You have sent Me, and have loved them as You have loved Me
Acts 24:20 Or else let those who are here themselves say if they found any wrongdoing *in me* while I stood before the council
Acts 26:18 to open their eyes and to turn them from darkness to light, and from the power of Satan to God, that they may receive forgiveness of sins and an inheritance among those who are sanctified by faith *in Me*
Rom 1:15 So, as much as is *in me*, I am ready to preach the gospel to you who are in Rome also
Rom 7:8 But sin, taking opportunity by the commandment, produced *in me* all manner of evil desire
Rom 7:13 But sin, that it might appear sin, was producing death *in me* through what is good, so that sin through the commandment might become exceedingly sinful
Rom 7:17 But now, it is no longer I who do it, but sin that dwells *in me*
Rom 7:18 For I know that *in me* (that is, in my flesh
Rom 7:20 Now if I do what I will not to do, it is no longer I who do it, but sin that dwells *in me*
2Cor 11:10 As the truth of Christ is *in me*, no one shall stop me from this boasting in the regions of Achaia
2Cor 13:3 since you seek a proof of Christ speaking *in me*, who is not weak toward you, but mighty in you
Gal 1:16 to reveal His Son *in me*, that I might preach Him among the Gentiles, I did not immediately confer with flesh and blood
Gal 1:24 And they glorified God *in me*
Gal 2:8 (for He who worked effectively in Peter for the apostleship to the circumcised also worked effectively *in me* toward the Gentiles
Gal 2:20 it is no longer I who live, but Christ lives *in me*
Phil 1:30 having the same conflict which you saw *in me* and now hear is *in me*
Phil 4:9 The things which you learned and received and heard and saw *in me*, these do, and the God of peace will be with you
Col 1:29 To this end I also labor, striving according to His working which works *in me* mightily
1Tim 1:16 However, for this reason I obtained mercy, that *in me* first Jesus Christ might show all longsuffering, as a pattern to those who are going to believe on Him for everlasting life

IN MY DISTRESS
2Sam 22:7 *In my distress* I called upon the Lord, and cried to my God
Ps 18:6 *In my distress* I called upon the Lord, and cried out to my God
Ps 120:1 *In my distress* I cried to the Lord, and He heard me
Phil 4:14 Nevertheless you have done well that you shared *in my distress*

IN MY MEMBERS ANOTHER LAW (RSV)
(See *LAW IN MY MEMBERS*)

IN MY NAME
Deut 18:19 And it shall be that whoever will not hear My words, which He speaks *in My name*, I will require it of him
Deut 18:20 But the prophet who presumes to speak a word *in My name*, which I have not commanded him to speak, or who speaks in the name of other gods, that prophet shall die
1Sam 25:5 and David said to the young men, "Go up to Carmel, go to Nabal, and greet him *in my name*
Ps 89:24 But My faithfulness and My mercy shall be with him, and *in My name* his horn shall be exalted
Jer 14:14 And the Lord said to me, "The prophets prophesy lies *in My name*
Jer 14:15 Therefore thus says the Lord concerning the prophets who prophesy *in My name*, whom I did not send, and who say
Jer 23:25 I have heard what the prophets have said who prophesy lies *in My name*, saying
Jer 27:15 for I have not sent them," says the Lord, "yet they prophesy a lie *in My name*, that I may drive you out, and that you may perish, you and the prophets who prophesy to you
Jer 29:9 For they prophesy falsely to you *in My name;* I have not sent them, says the Lord
Jer 29:21 Thus says the Lord of hosts, the God of Israel, concerning Ahab the son of Kolaiah, and Zedekiah the son of Maaseiah, who prophesy a lie to you *in My name*
Jer 29:23 because they have done disgraceful things in Israel, have committed adultery with their neighbors' wives, and have spoken lying words *in My name*, which I have not commanded them
Matt 18:5 And whoever receives one little child like this *in My name* receives Me
Matt 18:20 For where two or three are gathered together *in My name*, I am there in the midst of them
Matt 24:5 For many will come *in My name*, saying, 'I am the Christ
Mark 9:37 Whoever receives one of these little children *in My name* receives Me

Mark 9:39 But Jesus said, "Do not forbid him, for no one who works a miracle *in My name* can soon afterward speak evil of Me
Mark 9:41 For whoever gives you a cup of water to drink *in My name*, because you belong to Christ, assuredly, I say to you, he will by no means lose his reward
Mark 13:6 For many will come *in My name*, saying, 'I am He
Mark 16:17 *In My name* they will cast out demons; they will speak with new tongues
Luke 9:48 and said to them, "Whoever receives this little child *in My name* receives Me
Luke 21:8 For many, will come *in My name*, saying, 'I am He
John 14:13 And whatever you ask *in My name*, that I will do, that the Father may be glorified in the Son
John 14:14 If you ask anything *in My name*, I will do it
John 14:26 But the Helper, the Holy Spirit, whom the Father will send *in My name*, He will teach you all things, and bring to your remembrance all things that I said to you
John 15:16 You did not choose Me, but I chose you and appointed you that you should go and bear fruit, and that your fruit should remain, that whatever you ask the Father *in My name* He may give you
John 16:23 Most assuredly, I say to you, whatever you ask the Father *in My name* He will give you
John 16:24 Until now you have asked nothing *in My name*. Ask, and you will receive, that your joy may be full
John 16:26 In that day you will ask *in My name*, and I do not say to you that I shall pray the Father for you

IN REMEMBRANCE OF ME
Luke 22:19 And He took bread, gave thanks and broke it, and gave it to them, saying, "This is My body which is given for you; do this *in remembrance of Me*
1Cor 11:24 this is My body which is broken for you; do this *in remembrance of Me*
1Cor 11:25 This do, as often as you drink it, *in remembrance of Me*

IN SIN
Ps 51:5 Behold, I was brought forth in iniquity, and *in sin* my mother conceived me
Rom 6:1 What shall we say then? Shall we continue *in sin* that grace may abound

IN THAT DAY
Ex 8:22 And *in that day* I will set apart the land of Goshen, in which My people dwell, that no swarms of flies shall be there, in order that you may know that I am the Lord in the midst of the land
Ex 13:8 And you shall tell your son *in that day*, saying
Deut 31:17 Then My anger shall be aroused against them *in that day*, and I will forsake them, and I will hide My face from them, and they shall be devoured. And many evils and troubles shall befall them, so that they will say *in that day*
Deut 31:18 And I will surely hide My face *in that day* because of all the evil which they have done, in that they have turned to other gods
Josh 14:12 Now therefore, give me this mountain of which the Lord spoke *in that day;* for you heard *in that day* how the Anakim were there, and that the cities were great and fortified
1Sam 3:12 *In that day* I will perform against Eli all that I have spoken concerning his house, from beginning to end
1Sam 8:18 And you will cry out *in that day* because of your king whom you have chosen for yourselves, and the Lord will not hear you *in that day*
Is 2:11 The lofty looks of man shall be humbled, the haughtiness of men shall be bowed down, and the Lord alone shall be exalted *in that day*
Is 2:17 The loftiness of man shall be bowed down, and the haughtiness of men shall be brought low; the Lord alone will be exalted *in that day*
Is 2:20 *In that day* a man will cast away his idols of silver and his idols of gold, which they made, each for himself to worship, to the moles and bats
Is 3:7 *in that day* he will protest, saying, "I cannot cure your ills, for in my house is neither food nor clothing
Is 3:18 *In that day* the Lord will take away the finery
Is 4:1 And *in that day* seven women shall take hold of one man, saying
Is 4:2 *In that day* the Branch of the Lord shall be beautiful and glorious
Is 5:30 *In that day* they will roar against them like the roaring of the sea
Is 7:18 And it shall come to pass *in that day* that the Lord will whistle for the fly that is in the farthest part of the rivers of Egypt, and for the bee that is in the land of Assyria
Is 7:21 It shall be *in that day* that a man will keep alive a young cow and two sheep
Is 7:23 It shall happen *in that day*, that wherever there could be a thousand vines worth a thousand shekels of silver, it will be for briers and thorns
Is 10:20 And it shall come to pass *in that day* that the remnant of Israel, and such as have escaped of the house of Jacob, will never again depend on him who defeated them, but will depend on the Lord, the Holy One of Israel, in truth
Is 10:27 It shall come to pass *in that day* that his burden will be taken away from your shoulder, and his yoke from your neck, and the yoke will be destroyed because of the anointing oil
Is 11:10 And *in that day* there shall be a Root of Jesse, who shall stand as a banner to the people
Is 11:11 It shall come to pass *in that day* that the Lord shall set His hand again the second time to recover the remnant of His people who are left, from Assyria and Egypt, from Pathros and Cush, from Elam and Shinar, from Hamath and the islands of the sea
Is 12:1 And *in that day* you will say: "O Lord, I will praise You
Is 12:4 And *in that day* you will say: "Praise the Lord, call upon His name
Is 17:4 *In that day* it shall come to pass that the glory of Jacob will wane, and the fatness of his flesh grow lean
Is 17:7 *In that day* a man will look to his Maker, and his eyes will have respect for the Holy One of Israel
Is 17:9 *In that day* his strong cities will be as a forsaken bough and an uppermost branch, which they left because of the children of Israel
Is 19:16 *In that day* Egypt will be like women, and will be afraid and fear because of the waving of the hand of the Lord of hosts, which He waves over it
Is 19:18 *In that day* five cities in the land of Egypt will speak the language of Canaan and swear by the Lord of hosts
Is 19:19 *In that day* there will be an altar to the Lord in the midst of the land of Egypt, and a pillar to the Lord at its border
Is 19:21 Then the Lord will be known to Egypt, and the Egyptians will know the Lord *in that day*, and will make sacrifice and offering
Is 19:23 *In that day* there will be a highway from Egypt to Assyria, and the Assyrian will come into

Egypt and the Egyptian into Assyria, and the Egyptians will serve with the Assyrians

Is 19:24 *In that day* Israel will be one of three with Egypt and Assyria, even a blessing in the midst of the land

Is 20:6 And the inhabitant of this territory will say *in that day*

Is 22:8 You looked *in that day* to the armor of the House of the Forest

Is 22:12 And *in that day* the Lord God of hosts called for weeping and for mourning, for baldness and for girding with sackcloth

Is 22:20 Then it shall be *in that day*, that I will call My servant Eliakim the son of Hilkiah

Is 22:25 *In that day*,' says the Lord of hosts, 'the peg that is fastened in the secure place will be removed and be cut down and fall, and the burden that was on it will be cut off

Is 23:15 Now it shall come to pass *in that day* that Tyre will be forgotten seventy years, according to the days of one king

Is 24:21 It shall come to pass *in that day* that the Lord will punish on high the host of exalted ones, and on the earth the kings of the earth

Is 25:9 And it will be said *in that day*: "Behold, this is our God

Is 26:1 *In that day* this song will be sung in the land of Judah

Is 27:1 *In that day* the Lord with His severe sword, great and strong, will punish Leviathan the fleeing serpent, Leviathan that twisted serpent

Is 27:2 *In that day* sing to her, "A vineyard of red wine

Is 27:12 And it shall come to pass *in that day* that the Lord will thresh, from the channel of the River to the Brook of Egypt

Is 27:13 So it shall be *in that day*. that the great trumpet will be blown

Is 28:5 *In that day* the Lord of hosts will be for a crown of glory and a diadem of beauty to the remnant of His people

Is 29:18 *In that day* the deaf shall hear the words of the book, and the eyes of the blind shall see out of obscurity and out of darkness

Is 30:23 *In that day* your cattle will feed in large pastures

Is 31:7 For *in that day* every man shall throw away his idols of silver and his idols of gold sin, which your own hands have made for yourselves

Is 52:6 therefore they shall know *in that day* that I am He who speaks

Jer 4:9 And it shall come to pass *in that day*," says the Lord

Jer 30:8 For it shall come to pass *in that day*,' says the Lord of hosts

Jer 39:16 Behold, I will bring My words upon this city for adversity and not for good, and they shall be performed *in that day* before you

Jer 39:17 But I will deliver you *in that day*," says the Lord

Jer 49:22 The heart of the mighty men of Edom *in that day* shall be like the heart of a woman in birth pangs

Jer 49:26 Therefore her young men shall fall in her streets, and all the men of war shall be cut off *in that day*

Jer 50:30 Therefore her young men shall fall in the streets, and all her men of war shall be cut off *in that day*

Ezek 29:21 *In that day* I will cause the horn of the house of Israel to spring forth, and I will open your mouth to speak in their midst

Ezek 38:19 Surely *in that day* there shall be a great earthquake in the land of Israel

Ezek 39:11 It will come to pass *in that day* that I will give Gog a burial place there in Israel, the valley of those who pass by east of the sea

Hos 1:5 It shall come to pass *in that day* that I will break the bow of Israel in the Valley of Jezreel

Hos 2:16 And it shall be, *in that day*," says the Lord

Hos 2:18 *In that day* I will make a covenant for them with the beasts of the field, with the birds of the air, and with the creeping things of the ground

Hos 2:21 It shall come to pass *in that day* that I will answer

Joel 3:18 And it will come to pass *in that day* that the mountains shall drip with new wine, the hills shall flow with milk, and all the brooks of Judah shall be flooded with water

Amos 2:16 The most courageous men of might shall flee naked *in that day*

Amos 8:3 And the songs of the temple shall be wailing *in that day*

Amos 8:9 And it shall come to pass *in that day*," says the Lord God

Amos 8:13 *In that day* the fair virgins and strong young men shall faint from thirst

Obad 8 Will I not *in that day*," says the Lord, "Even destroy the wise men from Edom, and understanding from the mountains of Esau

Mic 2:4 *In that day* one shall take up a proverb against you, and lament with a bitter lamentation, and say

Mic 4:6 *In that day*," says the Lord, "I will assemble the lame, I will gather the outcast and those whom I have afflicted

Mic 5:10 And it shall be *in that day*," says the Lord

Mic 7:11 In the day when your walls are to be built, *in that day* the decree shall go far and wide

Mic 7:12 *In that day* they shall come to you from Assyria and the fortified cities, from the fortress to the River, from sea to sea, and mountain to mountain

Zeph 3:11 *In that day* you shall not be shamed for any of your deeds in which you transgress against Me

Zeph 3:16 *In that day* it shall be said to Jerusalem: "Do not fear

Hag 2:23 *In that day*,' says the Lord of hosts, 'I will take you, Zerubbabel My servant, the son of Shealtiel

Zech 2:11 Many nations shall be joined to the Lord *in that day*, and they shall become My people

Zech 3:10 *In that day*,' says the Lord of hosts, 'Everyone will invite his neighbor under his vine and under his fig tree

Zech 9:16 The Lord their God will save them *in that day*, as the flock of His people

Zech 12:3 And it shall happen *in that day* that I will make Jerusalem a very heavy stone for all peoples

Zech 12:4 *In that day*," says the Lord, "I will strike every horse with confusion, and its rider with madness

Zech 12:6 *In that day* I will make the governors of Judah like a firepan in the woodpile, and like a fiery torch in the sheaves

Zech 12:8 *In that day* the Lord will defend the inhabitants of Jerusalem; the one who is feeble among them *in that day* shall be like David, and the house of David shall be like God, like the Angel of the Lord before them

Zech 12:9 It shall be *in that day* that I will seek to destroy all the nations that come against Jerusalem

Zech 12:11 *In that day* there shall be a great mourning in Jerusalem, like the mourning at Hadad Rimmon in the plain of Megiddo

Zech 13:1 *In that day* a fountain shall be opened for the house of David and for the inhabitants of Jerusalem, for sin and for uncleanness

Zech 13:2 It shall be *in that day*," says the Lord of hosts
Zech 13:4 And it shall be *in that day* that every prophet will be ashamed of his vision when he prophesies
Zech 14:4 And *in that day* His feet will stand on the Mount of Olives, which faces Jerusalem on the east
Zech 14:6 It shall come to pass *in that day* that there will be no light
Zech 14:8 And *in that day* it shall be that living waters shall flow from Jerusalem, half of them toward the eastern sea and half of them toward the western sea
Zech 14:9 *In that day* it shall be "the Lord is one
Zech 14:13 It shall come to pass *in that day* that a great panic from the Lord will be among them
Zech 14:20 *In that day* "HOLINESS TO THE LORD" shall be engraved on the bells of the horses
Zech 14:21 *In that day* there shall no longer be a Canaanite in the house of the Lord of hosts
Matt 7:22 Many will say to Me *in that day*, 'Lord, Lord, have we not prophesied in Your name, cast out demons in Your name, and done many wonders in Your name
Luke 6:23 Rejoice *in that day* and leap for joy! for indeed your reward is great in heaven, for in like manner their fathers did to the prophets
Luke 10:12 But I say to you that it will be more tolerable *in that Day* for Sodom than for that city
Luke 17:31 *In that day*, he who is on the housetop, and his goods are in the house, let him not come down to take them away
John 16:23 And *in that day* you will ask Me nothing. Most assuredly, I say to you, whatever you ask the Father in My name He will give you
John 16:26 *In that day* you will ask in My name, and I do not say to you that I shall pray the Father for you
2Th 1:10 when He comes, *in that Day*, to be glorified in His saints and to be admired among all those who believe, because our testimony among you was believed
2Tim 1:18 The Lord grant to him that he may find mercy from the Lord *in that Day* and you know very well how many ways he ministered to me at Ephesus

IN THE BEGINNING
Gen 1:1 *In the beginning* God created the heavens and the earth
2Sam 21:9 So they fell, all seven together, and were put to death in the days of harvest, in the first days, *in the beginning* of barley harvest
Ezra 4:6 Now in the reign of Ahasuerus, *in the beginning* of his reign, they wrote an accusation against the inhabitants of Judah and Jerusalem
Jer 26:1 *In the beginning* of the reign of Jehoiakim the son of Josiah, king of Judah, this word came from the Lord, saying
Jer 27:1 *In the beginning* of the reign of Jehoiakim the son of Josiah, king of Judah, this word came to Jeremiah from the Lord, saying
Jer 49:34 The word of the Lord that came to Jeremiah the prophet against Elam, *in the beginning* of the reign of Zedekiah king of Judah, saying
John 1:1 *In the beginning* was the Word, and the Word was with God, and the Word was God
John 1:2 He was *in the beginning* with God
Phil 4:15 Now you Philippians know also that *in the beginning* of the gospel, when I departed from Macedonia, no church shared with me concerning giving and receiving but you only
Heb 1:10 You, Lord, *in the beginning* laid the foundation of the earth, and the heavens are the work of Your hands

IN THE CLEAR DAY (KJV)
(See *IN BROAD DAYLIGHT*)

IN THE DARKNESS
Job 17:13 If I wait for the grave as my house, if I make my bed *in the darkness*
Job 28:3 Man puts an end to darkness, and searches every recess for ore *in the darkness* and the shadow of death
Ps 112:4 Unto the upright there arises light *in the darkness;* He is gracious, and full of compassion, and righteous
Is 58:10 If you extend your soul to the hungry and satisfy the afflicted soul, then your light shall dawn *in the darkness*, and your darkness shall be as the noonday
Jer 23:12 *in the darkness* they shall be driven on and fall in them
Dan 2:22 He knows what is *in the darkness*, and light dwells with Him
John 1:5 And the light shines *in the darkness*, and the darkness did not comprehend it

IN THE DAY OF TROUBLE (RSV)
(See *IN TIME OF TROUBLE*)

IN THE DESERT (NIV)
(See *IN THE WILDERNESS*)

IN THE DISPERSION (RSV)
(See *SCATTERED ABROAD*)

IN THE FAITH
Acts 14:22 strengthening the souls of the disciples, exhorting them to continue *in the faith*, and saying
Acts 16:5 So the churches were strengthened *in the faith*, and increased in number daily
Rom 14:1 Receive one who is weak *in the faith*, but not to disputes over doubtful things
1Cor 16:13 Watch, stand fast *in the faith*, be brave, be strong
2Cor 13:5 Examine yourselves as to whether you are *in the faith*
Col 1:23 if indeed you continue *in the faith*, grounded and steadfast, and are not moved away from the hope of the gospel which you heard, which was preached to every creature under heaven, of which I, Paul, became a minister
Col 2:7 rooted and built up in Him and established *in the faith*, as you have been taught, abounding in it with thanksgiving
1Tim 1:2 To Timothy, my true son *in the faith:* Grace, mercy, and peace from God our Father and Jesus Christ our Lord
1Tim 3:13 For those who have served well as deacons obtain for themselves a good standing and great boldness *in the faith* which is in Christ Jesus
Tit 1:13 Therefore rebuke them sharply, that they may be sound *in the faith*
Tit 3:15 Greet those who love us *in the faith*. Grace be with you all
1Pet 5:9 Resist him, steadfast *in the faith*, knowing that the same sufferings are experienced by your brotherhood in the world

IN THE FAR NORTH (NAS, RSV)
(See *SIDES OF THE NORTH*)

IN THE FATHER
John 14:10 Do you not believe that I am *in the Father*, and the Father in Me
John 14:11 Believe Me that I am *in the Father* and the Father in Me, or else believe Me for the sake of the works themselves

1Jn 2:24 If what you heard from the beginning abides in you, you also will abide in the Son and *in the Father*

IN THE FEAR OF THE LORD
2Chr 19:9 And he commanded them, saying, "Thus you shall act *in the fear of the Lord*, faithfully and with a loyal heart
Prov 14:26 *In the fear of the Lord* there is strong confidence, and His children will have a place of refuge
Prov 23:17 Do not let your heart envy sinners, but *in the fear of the Lord* continue all day long
Is 11:3 His delight is *in the fear of the Lord*, and He shall not judge by the sight of His eyes, nor decide by the hearing of His ears
Acts 9:31 And walking *in the fear of the Lord* and in the comfort of the Holy Spirit, they were multiplied

IN THE FUTURE (NIV)
(See *TIME TO COME*)

IN THE HEAVENLY PLACES
Eph 1:3 Blessed be the God and Father of our Lord Jesus Christ, who has blessed us with every spiritual blessing *in the heavenly places* in Christ
Eph 1:20 which He worked in Christ when He raised Him from the dead and seated Him at His right hand *in the heavenly places*
Eph 2:6 and raised us up together, and made us sit together *in the heavenly places* in Christ Jesus
Eph 3:10 to the intent that now the manifold wisdom of God might be made known by the church to the principalities and powers *in the heavenly places*
Eph 6:12 For we do not wrestle against flesh and blood, but against principalities, against powers, against the rulers of the darkness of this age, against spiritual hosts of wickedness *in the heavenly places*

IN THE LAST DAYS
Gen 49:1 And Jacob called his sons and said, "Gather together, that I may tell you what shall befall you *in the last days*
Acts 2:17 And it shall come to pass *in the last days*, says God, That I will pour out of My Spirit on all flesh
2Tim 3:1 But know this, that *in the last days* perilous times will come
Jas 5:3 Your gold and silver are corroded, and their corrosion will be a witness against you and will eat your flesh like fire. You have heaped up treasure *in the last days*
2Pet 3:3 that scoffers will come *in the last days*, walking according to their own lusts

IN THE LAST TIME
1Pet 1:5 who are kept by the power of God through faith for salvation ready to be revealed *in the last time*
Jude 18 how they told you that there would be mockers *in the last time* who would walk according to their own ungodly lusts

IN THE LATTER DAYS
Num 24:14 Come, I will advise you what this people will do to your people *in the latter days*
Deut 4:30 When you are in distress, and all these things come upon you *in the latter days*, when you turn to the Lord your God and obey His voice
Deut 31:29 and evil will befall you *in the latter days*, because you will do evil in the sight of the Lord, to provoke Him to anger through the work of your hands
Is 2:2 Now it shall come to pass *in the latter days* that the mountain of the Lord's house shall be established on the top of the mountains, and shall be exalted above the hills
Jer 23:20 The anger of the Lord will not turn back until He has executed and performed the thoughts of His heart. *In the latter days* you will understand it perfectly
Jer 30:24 The fierce anger of the Lord will not return until He has done it, and until He has performed the intents of His heart. *In the latter days* you will consider it
Jer 48:47 Yet I will bring back the captives of Moab *in the latter days*
Jer 49:39 But it shall come to pass *in the latter days*
Ezek 38:16 It will be *in the latter days* that I will bring you against My land, so that the nations may know Me, when I am hallowed in you, O Gog, before their eyes
Dan 2:28 But there is a God in heaven who reveals secrets, and He has made known to King Nebuchadnezzar what will be *in the latter days*
Dan 10:14 Now I have come to make you understand what will happen to your people *in the latter days*, for the vision refers to many days yet to come
Hos 3:5 Afterward the children of Israel shall return, seek the Lord their God and David their king, and fear the Lord and His goodness *in the latter days*
Mic 4:1 Now it shall come to pass *in the latter days* That the mountain of the Lord's house shall be established on the top of the mountains, and shall be exalted above the hills

IN THE LIGHT
Ps 56:13 Have You not delivered my feet from falling, that I may walk before God *in the light* of the living
Ps 89:15 They walk, O Lord, *in the light* of Your countenance
Ps 90:8 You have set our iniquities before You, our secret sins *in the light* of Your countenance
Prov 16:15 *In the light* of the king's face is life, and his favor is like a cloud of the latter rain
Is 2:5 O house of Jacob, come and let us walk *in the light* of the Lord
Is 50:11 walk *in the light* of your fire and in the sparks you have kindled this you shall have from My hand
Matt 10:27 Whatever I tell you in the dark, speak *in the light*
Luke 12:3 Therefore whatever you have spoken in the dark will be heard *in the light*, and what you have spoken in the ear in inner rooms will be proclaimed on the housetops
John 12:36 While you have the light, believe *in the light*, that you may become sons of light
Col 1:12 giving thanks to the Father who has qualified us to be partakers of the inheritance of the saints *in the light*
1Jn 1:7 But if we walk *in the light* as He is *in the light*, we have fellowship with one another, and the blood of Jesus Christ His Son cleanses us from all sin
1Jn 2:9 He who says he is *in the light*, and hates his brother, is in darkness until now
1Jn 2:10 He who loves his brother abides *in the light*, and there is no cause for stumbling in him

IN THE LORD'S NAME (NIV)
(See *IN THE NAME OF THE LORD*)

IN THE LORD'S SIGHT (NIV)
(See *IN THE SIGHT OF THE LORD*)

IN THE MOUNT OUT OF THE MIDST OF THE FIRE (KJV)
(See *ON THE MOUNTAIN FROM THE MIDST OF THE FIRE*)

IN THE NAME OF JESUS

Acts 2:38 Then Peter said to them, "Repent, and let every one of you be baptized *in the name of Jesus* Christ for the remission of sins

Acts 3:6 *In the name of Jesus* Christ of Nazareth, rise up and walk

Acts 4:18 And they called them and commanded them not to speak at all nor teach *in the name of Jesus*

Acts 5:40 And they agreed with him, and when they had called for the apostles and beaten them, they commanded that they should not speak *in the name of Jesus*, and let them go

Acts 9:27 And he declared to them how he had seen the Lord on the road, and that He had spoken to him, and how he had preached boldly at Damascus *in the name of Jesus*

Acts 16:18 But Paul, greatly annoyed, turned and said to the spirit, "I command you *in the name of Jesus* Christ to come out of her

IN THE NAME OF THE LORD

Deut 18:5 For the Lord your God has chosen him out of all your tribes to stand to minister *in the name of the Lord*, him and his sons forever

Deut 18:7 then he may serve *in the name of the Lord* his God as all his brethren the Levites do, who stand there before the Lord

Deut 18:22 when a prophet speaks *in the name of the Lord*, if the thing does not happen or come to pass, that is the thing which the Lord has not spoken

Deut 21:5 Then the priests, the sons of Levi, shall come near, for the Lord your God has chosen them to minister to Him and to bless *in the name of the Lord*

1Sam 17:45 But I come to you *in the name of the Lord* of hosts, the God of the armies of Israel, whom you have defied

1Sam 20:42 Then Jonathan said to David, "Go in peace, since we have both sworn *in the name of the Lord*, saying

2Sam 6:18 And when David had finished offering burnt offerings and peace offerings, he blessed the people *in the name of the Lord* of hosts

1Kin 18:32 Then with the stones he built an altar *in the name of the Lord*

1Kin 22:16 So the king said to him, "How many times shall I make you swear that you tell me nothing but the truth *in the name of the Lord*

2Kin 2:24 So he turned around and looked at them, and pronounced a curse on them *in the name of the Lord*

1Chr 16:2 And when David had finished offering the burnt offerings and the peace offerings, he blessed the people *in the name of the Lord*

1Chr 21:19 So David went up at the word of Gad, which he had spoken *in the name of the Lord*

2Chr 18:15 So the king said to him, "How many times shall I make you swear that you tell me nothing but the truth *in the name of the Lord*

2Chr 33:18 Now the rest of the acts of Manasseh, his prayer to his God, and the words of the seers who spoke to him *in the name of the Lord* God of Israel, indeed they are written in the book of the kings of Israel

Ps 118:10 All nations surrounded me, but *in the name of the Lord* I will destroy them

Ps 118:11 But *in the name of the Lord* I will destroy them

Ps 118:12 For *in the name of the Lord* I will destroy them

Ps 118:26 Blessed is he who comes *in the name of the Lord*

Ps 124:8 Our help is *in the name of the Lord*, Who made heaven and earth

Ps 129:8 Neither let those who pass by them say, "The blessing of the Lord be upon you; we bless you *in the name of the Lord*

Is 50:10 Let him trust *in the name of the Lord* and rely upon his God

Jer 11:21 Therefore thus says the Lord concerning the men of Anathoth who seek your life, saying, 'Do not prophesy *in the name of the Lord*, lest you die by our hand

Jer 26:9 Why have you prophesied *in the name of the Lord*, saying

Jer 26:16 For he has spoken to us *in the name of the Lord* our God

Jer 26:20 Now there was also a man who prophesied *in the name of the Lord*, Urijah the son of Shemaiah of Kirjath Jearim, who prophesied against this city and against this land according to all the words of Jeremiah

Jer 44:16 As for the word that you have spoken to us *in the name of the Lord*, we will not listen to you

Mic 4:5 For all people walk each in the name of his god, but we will walk *in the name of the Lord* our God forever and ever

Zeph 3:12 I will leave in your midst a meek and humble people, and they shall trust *in the name of the Lord*

Zech 13:3 It shall come to pass that if anyone still prophesies, then his father and mother who begot him will say to him, 'You shall not live, because you have spoken lies *in the name of the Lord*

Matt 21:9 Blessed is He who comes *in the name of the Lord*

Matt 23:39 for I say to you, you shall see Me no more till you say, 'Blessed is He who comes *in the name of the Lord*

Mark 11:9 Blessed is He who comes *in the name of the Lord*

Mark 11:10 Blessed is the kingdom of our father David that comes *in the name of the Lord*

Luke 13:35 and assuredly, I say to you, you shall not see Me until the time comes when you say, 'Blessed is He who Comes *in the name of the Lord*

Luke 19:38 Blessed is the King who comes *in the name of the Lord*

John 12:13 Blessed is He who comes *in the name of the Lord*

Acts 8:16 They had only been baptized *in the name of the Lord* Jesus

Acts 9:29 And he spoke boldly *in the name of the Lord* Jesus and disputed against the Hellenists, but they attempted to kill him

Acts 10:48 And he commanded them to be baptized *in the name of the Lord*

Acts 19:5 When they heard this, they were baptized *in the name of the Lord* Jesus

1Cor 6:11 But you were washed, but you were sanctified, but you were justified *in the name of the Lord* Jesus and by the Spirit of our God

Col 3:17 And whatever you do in word or deed, do all *in the name of the Lord* Jesus, giving thanks to God the Father through Him

Jas 5:10 My brethren, take the prophets, who spoke *in the name of the Lord*, as an example of suffering and patience

Jas 5:14 Let him call for the elders of the church, and let them pray over him, anointing him with oil *in the name of the Lord*

IN THE POWER OF GOD (NAS, NIV)
(See *BY THE POWER OF GOD*)

IN THE PRESENCE OF MANY WITNESSES

1Tim 6:12 Fight the good fight of faith, lay hold on eternal life, to which you were also called and have confessed the good confession *in the presence of many witnesses*

IN THE RIGHT WAY (KJV, NAS)
(See *WAY OF TRUTH*)

IN THE SIGHT OF GOD
Prov 3:4 and so find favor and high esteem *in the sight of God* and man
Luke 16:15 For what is highly esteemed among men is an abomination *in the sight of God*
Acts 4:19 But Peter and John answered and said to them, "Whether it is right *in the sight of God* to listen to you more than to God, you judge
Acts 8:21 You have neither part nor portion in this matter, for your heart is not right *in the sight of God*
Acts 10:31 and said, 'Cornelius, your prayer has been heard, and your alms are remembered *in the sight of God*
Rom 2:13 (for not the hearers of the law are just *in the sight of God*, but the doers of the law will be justified
2Cor 2:17 but as of sincerity, but as from God, we speak *in the sight of God* in Christ
2Cor 4:2 But we have renounced the hidden things of shame, not walking in craftiness nor handling the word of God deceitfully, but by manifestation of the truth commending ourselves to every man's conscience *in the sight of God*
2Cor 7:12 Therefore, although I wrote to you, I did not do it for the sake of him who had done the wrong, nor for the sake of him who suffered wrong, but that our care for you *in the sight of God* might appear to you
Gal 3:11 But that no one is justified by the law *in the sight of God* is evident, for
1Tim 2:3 For this is good and acceptable *in the sight of God* our Savior
1Tim 6:13 I urge you *in the sight of God* who gives life to all things, and before Christ Jesus who witnessed the good confession before Pontius Pilate
1Pet 3:4 but let it be the hidden person of the heart, with the incorruptible ornament of a gentle and quiet spirit, which is very precious *in the sight of God*

IN THE SIGHT OF THE LORD
Gen 38:7 But Er, Judah's firstborn, was wicked *in the sight of the Lord*, and the Lord killed him
Lev 10:19 If I had eaten the sin offering today, would it have been accepted *in the sight of the Lord*
Num 32:13 So the Lord's anger was aroused against Israel, and He made them wander in the wilderness forty years, until all the generation that had done evil *in the sight of the Lord* was gone
Deut 4:25 When you beget children and grandchildren and have grown old in the land, act corruptly and make a carved image in the form of anything, and do evil *in the sight of the Lord* your God to provoke Him to anger
Deut 6:18 And you shall do what is right and good *in the sight of the Lord*, that it may be well with you, and that you may go in and possess the good land of which the Lord swore to your fathers
Deut 9:18 I neither ate bread nor drank water, because of all your sin which you committed in doing wickedly *in the sight of the Lord*, to provoke Him to anger
Deut 12:25 You shall not eat it, that it may go well with you and your children after you, when you do what is right *in the sight of the Lord*
Deut 12:28 Observe and obey all these words which I command you, that it may go well with you and your children after you forever, when you do what is good and right *in the sight of the Lord* your God
Deut 17:2 If there is found among you, within any of your gates which the Lord your God gives you, a man or a woman who has been wicked *in the sight of the Lord* your God, in transgressing His covenant
Deut 21:9 So you shall put away the guilt of innocent blood from among you when you do what is right *in the sight of the Lord*
Deut 31:29 and evil will befall you in the latter days, because you will do evil *in the sight of the Lord*, to provoke Him to anger through the work of your hands
Judg 2:11 Then the children of Israel did evil *in the sight of the Lord*, and served the Baals
Judg 3:7 So the children of Israel did evil *in the sight of the Lord*
Judg 3:12 And the children of Israel again did evil *in the sight of the Lord*. So the Lord strengthened Eglon king of Moab against Israel, because they had done evil *in the sight of the Lord*
Judg 4:1 When Ehud was dead, the children of Israel again did evil *in the sight of the Lord*
Judg 6:1 And the children of Israel did evil *in the sight of the Lord*
Judg 10:6 Then the children of Israel again did evil *in the sight of the Lord*, and served the Baals and the Ashtoreths, the gods of Syria, the gods of Sidon, the gods of Moab, the gods of the people of Ammon, and the gods of the Philistines
Judg 13:1 Again the children of Israel did evil *in the sight of the Lord*, and the Lord delivered them into the hand of the Philistines for forty years
1Sam 12:17 I will call to the Lord, and He will send thunder and rain, that you may perceive and see that your wickedness is great, which you have done *in the sight of the Lord*, in asking a king for yourselves
1Sam 15:19 Why did you swoop down on the spoil, and do evil *in the sight of the Lord*
1Kin 11:6 Solomon did evil *in the sight of the Lord*, and did not fully follow the Lord, as did his father David
1Kin 14:22 Now Judah did evil *in the sight of the Lord*, and they provoked Him to jealousy with their sins which they committed, more than all that their fathers had done
1Kin 15:26 And he did evil *in the sight of the Lord*, and walked in the way of his father, and in his sin by which he had made Israel sin
1Kin 15:34 He did evil *in the sight of the Lord*, and walked in the way of Jeroboam, and in his sin by which he had made Israel sin
1Kin 16:7 And also the word of the Lord came by the prophet Jehu the son of Hanani against Baasha and his house, because of all the evil that he did *in the sight of the Lord* in provoking Him to anger with the work of his hands, in being like the house of Jeroboam, and because he killed them
1Kin 16:19 because of the sins which he had sinned in doing evil *in the sight of the Lord*, in walking in the way of Jeroboam, and in his sin which he had committed to make Israel sin
1Kin 16:30 Now Ahab the son of Omri did evil *in the sight of the Lord*, more than all who were before him
1Kin 21:20 And he answered, "I have found you, because you have sold yourself to do evil *in the sight of the Lord*
1Kin 21:25 But there was no one like Ahab who sold himself to do wickedness *in the sight of the Lord*, because Jezebel his wife stirred him up
1Kin 22:52 He did evil *in the sight of the Lord*, and walked in the way of his father and in the way of

his mother and in the way of Jeroboam the son of Nebat, who had made Israel sin
2Kin 3:2 And he did evil *in the sight of the Lord*, but not like his father and mother
2Kin 3:18 And this is but a trivial thing *in the sight of the Lord*
2Kin 8:18 and he did evil *in the sight of the Lord*
2Kin 8:27 And he walked in the way of the house of Ahab, and did evil *in the sight of the Lord*, as the house of Ahab had done, for he was the son-in-law of the house of Ahab
2Kin 12:2 Jehoash did what was right *in the sight of the Lord* all the days in which Jehoiada the priest instructed him
2Kin 13:2 And he did evil *in the sight of the Lord*, and followed the sins of Jeroboam the son of Nebat, who had made Israel sin
2Kin 13:11 And he did evil *in the sight of the Lord*
2Kin 14:3 And he did what was right *in the sight of the Lord*, yet not like his father David
2Kin 14:24 And he did evil *in the sight of the Lord*
2Kin 15:3 And he did what was right *in the sight of the Lord*, according to all that his father Amaziah had done
2Kin 15:9 And he did evil *in the sight of the Lord*, as his fathers had done
2Kin 15:18 And he did evil *in the sight of the Lord*
2Kin 15:24 And he did evil *in the sight of the Lord*
2Kin 15:28 And he did evil *in the sight of the Lord*
2Kin 15:34 And he did what was right *in the sight of the Lord*
2Kin 16:2 and he did not do what was right *in the sight of the Lord* his God, as his father David had done
2Kin 17:2 And he did evil *in the sight of the Lord*, but not as the kings of Israel who were before him
2Kin 17:17 And they caused their sons and daughters to pass through the fire, practiced witchcraft and soothsaying, and sold themselves to do evil *in the sight of the Lord*, to provoke Him to anger
2Kin 18:3 And he did what was right *in the sight of the Lord*, according to all that his father David had done
2Kin 21:2 And he did evil *in the sight of the Lord*, according to the abominations of the nations whom the Lord had cast out before the children of Israel
2Kin 21:6 He did much evil *in the sight of the Lord*, to provoke Him to anger
2Kin 21:16 Moreover Manasseh shed very much innocent blood, till he had filled Jerusalem from one end to another, besides his sin with which he made Judah sin, in doing evil *in the sight of the Lord*
2Kin 21:20 And he did evil *in the sight of the Lord*, as his father Manasseh had done
2Kin 22:2 And he did what was right *in the sight of the Lord*, and walked in all the ways of his father David
2Kin 23:32 And he did evil *in the sight of the Lord*, according to all that his fathers had done
2Kin 23:37 And he did evil *in the sight of the Lord*, according to all that his fathers had done
2Kin 24:9 And he did evil *in the sight of the Lord*, according to all that his father had done
2Kin 24:19 He also did evil *in the sight of the Lord*, according to all that Jehoiakim had done
1Chr 2:3 Er, the firstborn of Judah, was wicked *in the sight of the Lord*
2Chr 20:32 And he walked in the way of his father Asa, and did not turn aside from it, doing what was right *in the sight of the Lord*
2Chr 21:6 and he did evil *in the sight of the Lord*
2Chr 22:4 Therefore he did evil *in the sight of the Lord*, like the house of Ahab
2Chr 24:2 Joash did what was right *in the sight of the Lord* all the days of Jehoiada the priest
2Chr 25:2 And he did what was right *in the sight of the Lord*, but not with a loyal heart
2Chr 26:4 And he did what was right *in the sight of the Lord*, according to all that his father Amaziah had done
2Chr 27:2 And he did what was right *in the sight of the Lord*, according to all that his father Uzziah had done (although he did not enter the temple of the Lord
2Chr 28:1 and he did not do what was right *in the sight of the Lord*, as his father David had done
2Chr 29:2 And he did what was right *in the sight of the Lord*, according to all that his father David had done
2Chr 33:2 But he did evil *in the sight of the Lord*, according to the abominations of the nations whom the Lord had cast out before the children of Israel
2Chr 33:6 He did much evil *in the sight of the Lord*, to provoke Him to anger
2Chr 33:22 But he did evil *in the sight of the Lord*, as his father Manasseh had done
2Chr 34:2 And he did what was right *in the sight of the Lord*, and walked in the ways of his father David
2Chr 36:5 And he did evil *in the sight of the Lord* his God
2Chr 36:9 And he did evil *in the sight of the Lord*
2Chr 36:12 He also did evil *in the sight of the Lord* his God, and did not humble himself before Jeremiah the prophet, who spoke from the mouth of the Lord
Ps 116:15 Precious *in the sight of the Lord* is the death of His saints
Jer 52:2 He also did evil *in the sight of the Lord*, according to all that Jehoiakim had done
Mal 2:17 In that you say, "Everyone who does evil is good *in the sight of the Lord*, and He delights in them
Luke 1:15 For he will be great *in the sight of the Lord*, and shall drink neither wine nor strong drink
2Cor 8:21 providing honorable things, not only *in the sight of the Lord*, but also in the sight of men
Jas 4:10 Humble yourselves *in the sight of the Lord*, and He will lift you up

IN THE SPIRIT
Ezek 37:1 The hand of the Lord came upon me and brought me out *in the Spirit* of the Lord, and set me down in the midst of the valley
Matt 22:43 He said to them, "How then does David *in the Spirit* call Him
Luke 1:17 He will also go before Him *in the spirit* and power of Elijah
Luke 10:21 In that hour Jesus rejoiced *in the Spirit* and said
John 11:33 Therefore, when Jesus saw her weeping, and the Jews who came with her weeping, He groaned *in the spirit* and was troubled
Acts 19:21 When these things were accomplished, Paul purposed *in the Spirit*, when he had passed through Macedonia and Achaia, to go to Jerusalem, saying
Acts 20:22 And see, now I go bound *in the spirit* to Jerusalem, not knowing the things that will happen to me there
Rom 2:29 but he is a Jew who is one inwardly, and circumcision is that of the heart, *in the Spirit*, and not in the letter
Rom 8:9 But you are not in the flesh but *in the Spirit*, if indeed the Spirit of God dwells in you
1Cor 14:2 For he who speaks in a tongue does not speak to men but to God, for no one understands him; however, *in the spirit* he speaks mysteries
Gal 3:3 Having begun *in the Spirit*, are you now being made perfect by the flesh

Gal 5:16 Walk *in the Spirit*, and you shall not fulfill the lust of the flesh
Gal 5:25 If we live *in the Spirit*, let us also walk *in the Spirit*
Eph 2:22 in whom you also are being built together for a habitation of God *in the Spirit*
Eph 4:23 and be renewed *in the spirit* of your mind
Eph 6:18 praying always with all prayer and supplication *in the Spirit*, being watchful to this end with all perseverance and supplication for all the saints
Phil 3:3 For we are the circumcision, who worship God *in the Spirit*, rejoice in Christ Jesus, and have no confidence in the flesh
Col 1:8 who also declared to us your love *in the Spirit*
1Tim 3:16 God was manifested in the flesh, justified *in the Spirit*, seen by angels, preached among the Gentiles, believed on in the world, received up in glory
1Pet 4:6 For this reason the gospel was preached also to those who are dead, that they might be judged according to men in the flesh, but live according to God *in the spirit*
Rev 1:10 I was *in the Spirit* on the Lord's Day, and I heard behind me a loud voice, as of a trumpet
Rev 4:2 Immediately I was *in the Spirit;* and behold, a throne set in heaven, and One sat on the throne
Rev 17:3 So he carried me away *in the Spirit* into the wilderness
Rev 21:10 And he carried me away *in the Spirit* to a great and high mountain, and showed me the great city, the holy Jerusalem, descending out of heaven from God

IN THE WILDERNESS
Gen 16:7 Now the Angel of the Lord found her by a spring of water *in the wilderness*, by the spring on the way to Shur
Gen 21:14 Then she departed and wandered *in the Wilderness* of Beersheba
Gen 21:20 and he grew and dwelt *in the wilderness*, and became an archer
Gen 21:21 He dwelt *in the Wilderness* of Paran; and his mother took a wife for him from the land of Egypt
Gen 36:24 This was the Anah who found the water *in the wilderness* as he pastured the donkeys of his father Zibeon
Gen 37:22 And Reuben said to them, "Shed no blood, but cast him into this pit which is *in the wilderness*, and do not lay a hand on him
Ex 5:1 Let My people go, that they may hold a feast to Me *in the wilderness*
Ex 7:16 And you shall say to him, 'The Lord God of the Hebrews has sent me to you, saying, "Let My people go, that they may serve Me *in the wilderness*
Ex 8:28 And Pharaoh said, "I will let you go, that you may sacrifice to the Lord your God *in the wilderness*
Ex 14:11 Then they said to Moses, "Because there were no graves in Egypt, have you taken us away to die *in the wilderness*
Ex 14:12 For it would have been better for us to serve the Egyptians than that we should die *in the wilderness*
Ex 15:22 And they went three days *in the wilderness* and found no water
Ex 16:2 Then the whole congregation of the children of Israel complained against Moses and Aaron *in the wilderness*
Ex 16:32 Fill an omer with it, to be kept for your generations, that they may see the bread with which I fed you *in the wilderness*, when I brought you out of the land of Egypt
Ex 18:5 and Jethro, Moses' father-in-law, came with his sons and his wife to Moses *in the wilderness*, where he was encamped at the mountain of God
Ex 19:2 For they had departed from Rephidim, had come to the Wilderness of Sinai, and camped *in the wilderness*
Lev 7:38 which the Lord commanded Moses on Mount Sinai, on the day when He commanded the children of Israel to offer their offerings to the Lord *in the Wilderness* of Sinai
Lev 16:22 The goat shall bear on itself all their iniquities to an uninhabited land; and he shall release the goat *in the wilderness*
Num 1:1 Now the Lord spoke to Moses *in the Wilderness* of Sinai, in the tabernacle of meeting, on the first day of the second month, in the second year after they had come out of the land of Egypt, saying
Num 1:19 As the Lord commanded Moses, so he numbered them *in the Wilderness* of Sinai
Num 3:4 Nadab and Abihu had died before the Lord when they offered profane fire before the Lord *in the Wilderness* of Sinai
Num 3:14 Then the Lord spoke to Moses *in the Wilderness* of Sinai, saying
Num 9:1 Now the Lord spoke to Moses *in the Wilderness* of Sinai, in the first month of the second year after they had come out of the land of Egypt, saying
Num 9:5 And they kept the Passover on the fourteenth day of the first month, at twilight, *in the Wilderness* of Sinai
Num 10:12 then the cloud settled down *in the Wilderness* of Paran
Num 10:31 So Moses said, "Please do not leave, inasmuch as you know how we are to camp *in the wilderness*, and you can be our eyes
Num 12:16 And afterward the people moved from Hazeroth and camped *in the Wilderness* of Paran
Num 13:26 So they departed and came back to Moses and Aaron and all the congregation of the children of Israel *in the Wilderness* of Paran, at Kadesh
Num 14:16 Because the Lord was not able to bring this people to the land which He swore to give them, therefore He killed them *in the wilderness*
Num 14:22 because all these men who have seen My glory and the signs which I did in Egypt and *in the wilderness*, and have put Me to the test now these ten times, and have not heeded My voice
Num 14:33 And your sons shall be shepherds *in the wilderness* forty years, and bear the brunt of your infidelity, until your carcasses are consumed *in the wilderness*
Num 15:32 Now while the children of Israel were *in the wilderness*, they found a man gathering sticks on the Sabbath day
Num 16:13 Is it a small thing that you have brought us up out of a land flowing with milk and honey, to kill us *in the wilderness*, that you should keep acting like a prince over us
Num 21:5 Why have you brought us up out of Egypt to die *in the wilderness*
Num 21:11 And they journeyed from Oboth and camped at Ije Abarim, *in the wilderness* which is east of Moab, toward the sunrise
Num 21:13 From there they moved and camped on the other side of the Arnon, which is *in the wilderness* that extends from the border of the Amorites
Num 21:23 So Sihon gathered all his people together and went out against Israel *in the wilderness* , and he came to Jahaz and fought against Israel
Num 26:64 But among these there was not a man of those who were numbered by Moses and

Aaron the priest when they numbered the children of Israel *in the Wilderness* of Sinai
Num 26:65 For the Lord had said of them, "They shall surely die *in the wilderness*
Num 27:3 Our father died *in the wilderness;* but he was not in the company of those who gathered together against the Lord, in company with Korah, but he died in his own sin
Num 27:14 For *in the Wilderness* of Zin, during the strife of the congregation, you rebelled against My command to hallow Me at the waters before their eyes." (These are the waters of Meribah, at Kadesh *in the Wilderness* of Zin
Num 32:13 So the Lord's anger was aroused against Israel, and He made them wander *in the wilderness* forty years, until all the generation that had done evil in the sight of the Lord was gone
Num 32:15 For if you turn away from following Him, He will once again leave them *in the wilderness*, and you will destroy all these people
Num 33:8 They departed from before Hahiroth and passed through the midst of the sea into the wilderness, went three days' journey *in the Wilderness* of Etham, and camped at Marah
Num 33:11 They moved from the Red Sea and camped *in the Wilderness* of Sin
Num 33:15 They departed from Rephidim and camped *in the Wilderness* of Sinai
Num 33:36 They moved from Ezion Geber and camped *in the Wilderness* of Zin, which is Kadesh
Deut 1:1 These are the words which Moses spoke to all Israel on this side of the Jordan *in the wilderness*, in the plain opposite Suph, between Paran, Tophel, Laban, Hazeroth, and Dizahab
Deut 1:31 and *in the wilderness* where you saw how the Lord your God carried you, as a man carries his son, in all the way that you went until you came to this place
Deut 4:43 Bezer *in the wilderness* on the plateau for the Reubenites, Ramoth in Gilead for the Gadites, and Golan in Bashan for the Manassites
Deut 8:2 And you shall remember that the Lord your God led you all the way these forty years *in the wilderness*, to humble you and test you, to know what was in your heart, whether you would keep His commandments or not
Deut 8:16 who fed you *in the wilderness* with manna, which your fathers did not know, that He might humble you and that He might test you, to do you good in the end
Deut 9:7 Remember and do not forget how you provoked the Lord your God to wrath *in the wilderness*
Deut 9:28 lest the land from which You brought us should say, "Because the Lord was not able to bring them to the land which He promised them, and because He hated them, He has brought them out to kill them *in the wilderness*
Deut 11:5 what He did for you *in the wilderness* until you came to this place
Deut 29:5 And I have led you forty years *in the wilderness*
Deut 32:51 because you trespassed against Me among the children of Israel at the waters of Meribah Kadesh, *in the Wilderness* of Zin, because you did not hallow Me in the midst of the children of Israel
Josh 5:4 All the people who came out of Egypt who were males, all the men of war, had died *in the wilderness* on the way, after they had come out of Egypt
Josh 5:5 For all the people who came out had been circumcised, but all the people who were born *in the wilderness* on the way as they came out of Egypt had not been circumcised
Josh 5:6 For the children of Israel walked forty years *in the wilderness*, till all the people who were men of war, who came out of Egypt, were consumed, because they did not obey the voice of the Lord to whom the Lord swore that He would not show them the land which the Lord had sworn to their fathers that He would give us
Josh 8:24 And it came to pass when Israel had made an end of slaying all the inhabitants of Ai in the field, *in the wilderness* where they pursued them, and when they all had fallen by the edge of the sword until they were consumed, that all the Israelites returned to Ai and struck it with the edge of the sword
Josh 12:8 in the mountain country, in the lowlands, in the Jordan plain, in the slopes, *in the wilderness*, and in the South the Hittites, the Amorites, the Canaanites, the Perizzites, the Hivites, and the Jebusites
Josh 14:10 And now, behold, the Lord has kept me alive, as He said, these forty-five years, ever since the Lord spoke this word to Moses while Israel wandered *in the wilderness*
Josh 15:61 *In the wilderness:* Beth Arabah Middin, Secacah
Josh 20:8 And on the other side of the Jordan, by Jericho eastward, they assigned Bezer *in the wilderness* on the plain, from the tribe of Reuben, Ramoth in Gilead, from the tribe of Gad, and Golan in Bashan, from the tribe of Manasseh
Josh 24:7 And your eyes saw what I did in Egypt. Then you dwelt *in the wilderness* a long time
1Sam 4:8 These are the gods who struck the Egyptians with all the plagues *in the wilderness*
1Sam 17:28 And with whom have you left those few sheep *in the wilderness*
1Sam 23:14 And David stayed in strongholds *in the wilderness*, and remained in the mountains *in the Wilderness* of Ziph
1Sam 23:15 And David was *in the Wilderness* of Ziph in a forest
1Sam 23:24 But David and his men were *in the Wilderness* of Maon, in the plain on the south of Jeshimon
1Sam 23:25 Therefore he went down to the rock, and stayed *in the Wilderness* of Maon. And when Saul heard that, he pursued David *in the Wilderness* of Maon
1Sam 24:1 Now it happened, when Saul had returned from following the Philistines, that it was told him, saying, "Take note! David is *in the Wilderness* of En Gedi
1Sam 25:4 When David heard *in the wilderness* that Nabal was shearing his sheep
1Sam 25:21 Now David had said, "Surely in vain I have protected all that this fellow has *in the wilderness*, so that nothing was missed of all that belongs to him
1Sam 26:2 Then Saul arose and went down to the Wilderness of Ziph, having three thousand chosen men of Israel with him, to seek David *in the Wilderness* of Ziph
1Sam 26:3 But David stayed *in the wilderness*, and he saw that Saul came after him into the wilderness
2Sam 16:2 So Ziba said, "The donkeys are for the king's household to ride on, the bread and summer fruit for the young men to eat, and the wine for those who are faint *in the wilderness* to drink
2Sam 17:29 For they said, "The people are hungry and weary and thirsty *in the wilderness*
1Kin 2:34 and he was buried in his own house *in the wilderness*
1Kin 9:18 Baalath, and Tadmor *in the wilderness*, in the land of Judah
1Chr 6:78 Bezer *in the wilderness* with its common-lands, Jahzah with its common-lands
1Chr 12:8 Some Gadites joined David at the stronghold *in the wilderness*, mighty men of

valor, men trained for battle, who could handle shield and spear, whose faces were like the faces of lions, and were as swift as gazelles on the mountains

1Chr 21:29 For the tabernacle of the Lord and the altar of the burnt offering, which Moses had made *in the wilderness*, were at that time at the high place in Gibeon

2Chr 1:3 for the tabernacle of meeting with God was there, which Moses the servant of the Lord had made *in the wilderness*

2Chr 8:4 He also built Tadmor *in the wilderness*, and all the storage cities which he built in Hamath

2Chr 24:9 And they made a proclamation throughout Judah and Jerusalem to bring to the Lord the collection that Moses the servant of God had imposed on Israel *in the wilderness*

Neh 9:19 Yet in Your manifold mercies You did not forsake them *in the wilderness*

Neh 9:21 Forty years You sustained them *in the wilderness*, so that they lacked nothing

Ps 55:7 Indeed, I would wander far off, and remain *in the wilderness*

Ps 72:9 Those who dwell *in the wilderness* will bow before Him, and His enemies will lick the dust

Ps 78:15 He split the rocks *in the wilderness*, and gave them drink in abundance like the depths

Ps 78:17 But they sinned even more against Him by rebelling against the Most High *in the wilderness*

Ps 78:19 They said, "Can God prepare a table *in the wilderness*

Ps 78:40 How often they provoked Him *in the wilderness*, and grieved Him in the desert

Ps 78:52 But He made His own people go forth like sheep, and guided them *in the wilderness* like a flock

Ps 95:8 Do not harden your hearts, as in the rebellion, and as in the day of trial *in the wilderness*

Ps 106:14 But lusted exceedingly *in the wilderness*, and tested God in the desert

Ps 106:26 Therefore He lifted up His hand in an oath against them, to overthrow them *in the wilderness*

Ps 107:4 They wandered *in the wilderness* in a desolate way; they found no city to dwell in

Ps 107:40 He pours contempt on princes, and causes them to wander *in the wilderness* where there is no way

Prov 21:19 It is better to dwell *in the wilderness*, than with a contentious and angry woman

Is 32:16 Then justice will dwell *in the wilderness*, and righteousness remain in the fruitful field

Is 35:6 For waters shall burst forth *in the wilderness*, and streams in the desert

Is 40:3 The voice of one crying *in the wilderness:* "Prepare the way of the Lord

Is 41:19 I will plant *in the wilderness* the cedar and the acacia tree, the myrtle and the oil tree

Is 43:19 I will even make a road *in the wilderness* and rivers in the desert

Is 43:20 The beast of the field will honor Me, the jackals and the ostriches, because I give waters *in the wilderness* and rivers in the desert, to give drink to My people, My chosen

Is 63:13 Who led them through the deep, as a horse *in the wilderness*, that they might not stumble

Jer 2:2 I remember you, the kindness of your youth, the love of your betrothal, when you went after Me *in the wilderness*, in a land that was not sown

Jer 3:2 By the road you have sat for them like an Arabian *in the wilderness*

Jer 4:11 At that time it will be said to this people and to Jerusalem, "A dry wind of the desolate heights blows *in the wilderness* toward the daughter of My people not to fan or to cleanse

Jer 9:2 Oh, that I had *in the wilderness* a lodging place for wayfaring men

Jer 9:26 Egypt, Judah, Edom, the people of Ammon, Moab, and all who are in the farthest corners, who dwell *in the wilderness*

Jer 12:12 The plunderers have come on all the desolate heights *in the wilderness*, for the sword of the Lord shall devour from one end of the land to the other end of the land

Jer 17:6 For he shall be like a shrub in the desert, and shall not see when good comes, but shall inhabit the parched places *in the wilderness*, in a salt land which is not inhabited

Jer 31:2 The people who survived the sword found grace *in the wilderness* Israel, when I went to give him rest

Jer 48:6 Flee, save your lives! And be like the juniper *in the wilderness*

Lam 4:3 but the daughter of my people has become cruel, like ostriches *in the wilderness*

Lam 4:19 They pursued us on the mountains and lay in wait for us *in the wilderness*

Lam 5:9 We get our bread at the risk of our lives, because of the sword *in the wilderness*

Ezek 19:13 And now she is planted *in the wilderness*, in a dry and thirsty land

Ezek 20:13 Yet the house of Israel rebelled against Me *in the wilderness;* they did not walk in My statutes; they despised My judgments, which, if a man does, he shall live by them; and they greatly defiled My Sabbaths. Then I said I would pour out My fury on them *in the wilderness*, to consume them

Ezek 20:15 So I also lifted My hand in an oath to them *in the wilderness*, that I would not bring them into the land which I had given them, flowing with milk and honey, the glory of all lands

Ezek 20:17 I did not make an end of them *in the wilderness*

Ezek 20:18 But I said to their children *in the wilderness*, 'Do not walk in the statutes of your fathers, nor observe their judgments, nor defile yourselves with their idols

Ezek 20:21 Then I said I would pour out My fury on them and fulfill My anger against them *in the wilderness*

Ezek 20:23 Also I lifted My hand in an oath to those *in the wilderness*, that I would scatter them among the Gentiles and disperse them throughout the countries

Ezek 20:36 Just as I pleaded My case with your fathers *in the wilderness* of the land of Egypt, so I will plead My case with you

Ezek 29:5 I will leave you *in the wilderness*, you and all the fish of your rivers

Ezek 34:25 and they will dwell safely *in the wilderness* and sleep in the woods

Hos 9:10 I found Israel like grapes *in the wilderness;* I saw your fathers as the firstfruits on the fig tree in its first season

Hos 13:5 I knew you *in the wilderness*, in the land of great drought

Amos 5:25 Did you offer Me sacrifices and offerings *in the wilderness* forty years, O house of Israel

Matt 3:1 In those days John the Baptist came preaching *in the wilderness* of Judea

Matt 3:3 The voice of one crying *in the wilderness:* 'Prepare the way of the Lord, make His paths straight

Matt 15:33 Then His disciples said to Him, "Where could we get enough bread *in the wilderness* to fill such a great multitude

Mark 1:3 The voice of one crying *in the wilderness:* 'Prepare the way of the Lord, make His paths straight

Mark 1:4 John came baptizing *in the wilderness* and preaching a baptism of repentance for the remission of sins
Mark 1:13 And He was there *in the wilderness* forty days, tempted by Satan, and was with the wild beasts
Mark 8:4 Then His disciples answered Him, "How can one satisfy these people with bread here *in the wilderness*
Luke 3:2 Annas and Caiaphas being high priests, the word of God came to John the son of Zacharias *in the wilderness*
Luke 3:4 The voice of one crying *in the wilderness:* 'Prepare the way of the Lord, make His paths straight
Luke 15:4 What man of you, having a hundred sheep, if he loses one of them, does not leave the ninety-nine *in the wilderness*, and go after the one which is lost until he finds it
John 1:23 I am 'The voice of one crying *in the wilderness*
John 3:14 And as Moses lifted up the serpent *in the wilderness*, even so must the Son of Man be lifted up
John 6:49 Your fathers ate the manna *in the wilderness*, and are dead
Acts 7:30 And when forty years had passed, an Angel of the Lord appeared to him in a flame of fire in a bush, *in the wilderness* of Mount Sinai
Acts 7:36 He brought them out, after he had shown wonders and signs in the land of Egypt, and in the Red Sea, and *in the wilderness* forty years
Acts 7:38 This is he who was in the congregation *in the wilderness* with the Angel who spoke to him on Mount Sinai, and with our fathers, the one who received the living oracles to give to us
Acts 7:42 Did you offer Me slaughtered animals and sacrifices during forty years *in the wilderness*, O house of Israel
Acts 7:44 Our fathers had the tabernacle of witness *in the wilderness*, as He appointed, instructing Moses to make it according to the pattern that he had seen
Acts 13:18 Now for a time of about forty years He put up with their ways *in the wilderness*
1Cor 10:5 But with most of them God was not well pleased, for their bodies were scattered *in the wilderness*
2Cor 11:26 in journeys often, in perils of waters, in perils of robbers, in perils of my own countrymen, in perils of the Gentiles, in perils in the city, in perils *in the wilderness*, in perils in the sea, in perils among false brethren
Heb 3:8 do not harden your hearts as in the rebellion, in the day of trial *in the wilderness*
Heb 3:17 Was it not with those who sinned, whose corpses fell *in the wilderness*

IN THE WORLD
John 1:10 He was *in the world*, and the world was made through Him, and the world did not know Him
John 9:5 As long as I am *in the world*, I am the light of the world
John 13:1 Now before the feast of the Passover, when Jesus knew that His hour had come that He should depart from this world to the Father, having loved His own who were *in the world*, He loved them to the end
John 16:33 *In the world* you will have tribulation; but be of good cheer, I have overcome the world
John 17:11 Now I am no longer *in the world*, but these are *in the world*, and I come to You
John 17:12 While I was with them *in the world*, I kept them in Your name
John 17:13 But now I come to You, and these things I speak *in the world*, that they may have My joy fulfilled in themselves
Rom 5:13 (For until the law sin was *in the world*, but sin is not imputed when there is no law
1Cor 8:4 Therefore concerning the eating of things offered to idols, we know that an idol is nothing *in the world*, and that there is no other God but one
1Cor 14:10 There are, it may be, so many kinds of languages *in the world*, and none of them is without significance
2Cor 1:12 the testimony of our conscience that we conducted ourselves *in the world* in simplicity and godly sincerity, not with fleshly wisdom but by the grace of God, and more abundantly toward you
Eph 2:12 that at that time you were without Christ, being aliens from the commonwealth of Israel and strangers from the covenants of promise, having no hope and without God *in the world*
Phil 2:15 that you may become blameless and harmless, children of God without fault in the midst of a crooked and perverse generation, among whom you shine as lights *in the world*
Col 2:20 Therefore, if you died with Christ from the basic principles of the world, why, as though living *in the world*, do you subject yourselves to regulations
1Tim 3:16 God was manifested in the flesh, justified in the Spirit, seen by angels, preached among the Gentiles, believed on *in the world*, received up in glory
1Pet 5:9 Resist him, steadfast in the faith, knowing that the same sufferings are experienced by your brotherhood *in the world*
2Pet 1:4 by which have been given to us exceedingly great and precious promises, that through these you may be partakers of the divine nature, having escaped the corruption that is *in the world* through lust
1Jn 2:15 Do not love the world or the things *in the world*
1Jn 2:16 For all that is *in the world* the lust of the flesh, the lust of the eyes, and the pride of life is not of the Father but is of the world
1Jn 4:3 And this is the spirit of the Antichrist, which you have heard was coming, and is now already *in the world*
1Jn 4:4 You are of God, little children, and have overcome them, because He who is in you is greater than he who is *in the world*

IN THEIR GENERATIONS (KJV)
(See *THROUGHOUT THEIR GENERATIONS*)

IN THESE LAST DAYS
Heb 1:2 has *in these last days* spoken to us by His Son, whom He has appointed heir of all things, through whom also He made the worlds

IN THOSE DAYS
Gen 6:4 There were giants on the earth *in those days*, and also afterward, when the sons of God came in to the daughters of men and they bore children to them
Ex 2:11 Now it came to pass *in those days*, when Moses was grown, that he went out to his brethren and looked at their burdens
Deut 17:9 and you shall come to the priests, the Levites, and to the judge there *in those days*, and inquire of them
Deut 19:17 then both men in the controversy shall stand before the Lord, before the priests and the judges who serve *in those days*
Deut 26:3 And you shall go to the one who is priest *in those days*, and say to him
Josh 20:6 And he shall dwell in that city until he stands before the congregation for judgment, and

until the death of the one who is high priest *in those days*

Judg 17:6 *In those days* there was no king in Israel; everyone did what was right in his own eyes

Judg 18:1 *In those days* there was no king in Israel. And *in those days* the tribe of the Danites was seeking an inheritance for itself to dwell in

Judg 19:1 And it came to pass *in those days*, when there was no king in Israel, that there was a certain Levite sojourning in the remote mountains of Ephraim

Judg 20:27 So the children of Israel inquired of the Lord (the ark of the covenant of God was there *in those days*

Judg 20:28 and Phinehas the son of Eleazar, the son of Aaron, stood before it *in those days*

Judg 21:25 *In those days* there was no king in Israel; everyone did what was right in his own eyes

1Sam 3:1 And the word of the Lord was rare *in those days*

1Sam 28:1 Now it happened *in those days* that the Philistines gathered their armies together for war, to fight with Israel

2Sam 16:23 And the counsel of Ahithophel, which he gave *in those days*, was as if one had inquired at the oracle of God

2Kin 10:32 *In those days* the Lord began to cut off parts of Israel

2Kin 15:37 *In those days* the Lord began to send Rezin king of Syria and Pekah the son of Remaliah against Judah

2Kin 20:1 *In those days* Hezekiah was sick and near death. And Isaiah the prophet, the son of Amoz, went to him and said to him

2Chr 32:24 *In those days* Hezekiah was sick and near death, and he prayed to the Lord

Neh 6:17 Moreover *in those days* the nobles of Judah sent many letters to Tobiah, and the letters of Tobiah came to them

Neh 13:15 *In those days* I saw in Judah some people treading wine presses on the Sabbath, and bringing in sheaves, and loading donkeys with wine, grapes, figs, and all kinds of burdens, which they brought into Jerusalem on the Sabbath day

Neh 13:23 *In those days* I also saw Jews who had married women of Ashdod, Ammon, and Moab

Esth 1:2 *in those days* when King Ahasuerus sat on the throne of his kingdom, which was in Shushan the citadel

Esth 2:21 *In those days*, while Mordecai sat within the king's gate, two of the king's eunuchs, Bigthan and Teresh, doorkeepers, became furious and sought to lay hands on King Ahasuerus

Is 38:1 *In those days* Hezekiah was sick and near death. And Isaiah the prophet, the son of Amoz, went to him and said to him

Jer 3:16 Then it shall come to pass, when you are multiplied and increased in the land *in those days*

Jer 3:18 *In those days* the house of Judah shall walk with the house of Israel, and they shall come together out of the land of the north to the land that I have given as an inheritance to your fathers

Jer 5:18 Nevertheless *in those days*," says the Lord, "I will not make a complete end of you

Jer 31:29 *In those days* they shall say no more: 'The fathers have eaten sour grapes, and the children's teeth are set on edge

Jer 33:15 *In those days* and at that time I will cause to grow up to David a Branch of righteousness

Jer 33:16 *In those days* Judah will be saved, and Jerusalem will dwell safely

Jer 50:4 *In those days* and in that time," says the Lord

Jer 50:20 *In those days* and in that time," says the Lord

Ezek 38:17 Are you he of whom I have spoken in former days by My servants the prophets of Israel, who prophesied for years *in those days* that I would bring you against them

Dan 10:2 *In those days* I, Daniel, was mourning three full weeks

Joel 2:29 And also on My menservants and on My maidservants I will pour out My Spirit *in those days*

Joel 3:1 For behold, *in those days* and at that time, when I bring back the captives of Judah and Jerusalem

Zech 8:23 *In those days* ten men from every language of the nations shall grasp the sleeve of a Jewish man, saying

Matt 3:1 *In those days* John the Baptist came preaching in the wilderness of Judea

Matt 24:19 But woe to those who are pregnant and to those with nursing babies *in those days*

Mark 1:9 It came to pass *in those days* that Jesus came from Nazareth of Galilee, and was baptized by John in the Jordan

Mark 2:20 But the days will come when the bridegroom will be taken away from them, and then they will fast *in those days*

Mark 8:1 *In those days*, the multitude being very great and having nothing to eat, Jesus called His disciples to Him and said to them

Mark 13:17 But woe to those who are pregnant and to those with nursing babies *in those days*

Mark 13:19 For *in those days* there will be tribulation, such as has not been from the beginning of creation which God created until this time, nor ever shall be

Mark 13:24 But *in those days*, after that tribulation, the sun will be darkened, and the moon will not give its light

Luke 1:39 Now Mary arose *in those days* and went into the hill country with haste, to a city of Judah

Luke 2:1 And it came to pass *in those days* that a decree went out from Caesar Augustus that all the world should be registered

Luke 4:2 And *in those days* He ate nothing, and afterward, when they had ended, He was hungry

Luke 5:35 But the days will come when the bridegroom will be taken away from them; then they will fast *in those days*

Luke 6:12 Now it came to pass *in those days* that He went out to the mountain to pray, and continued all night in prayer to God

Luke 9:36 But they kept quiet, and told no one *in those days* any of the things they had seen

Luke 21:23 But woe to those who are pregnant and to those who are nursing babies *in those days*

Acts 1:15 And *in those days* Peter stood up in the midst of the disciples (altogether the number of names was about a hundred and twenty

Acts 2:18 and on My menservants and on My maidservants I will pour out My Spirit *in those days*

Acts 6:1 Now *in those days*, when the number of the disciples was multiplying, there arose a murmuring against the Hebrews by the Hellenists, because their widows were neglected in the daily distribution

Acts 7:41 And they made a calf *in those days*, offered sacrifices to the idol, and rejoiced in the works of their own hands

Acts 9:37 But it happened *in those days* that she became sick and died

Rev 9:6 *In those days* men will seek death and will not find it

IN THREE DAYS

Matt 26:61 and said, "This fellow said, 'I am able to destroy the temple of God and to build it *in three days*

Matt 27:40 and saying, "You who destroy the temple and build it *in three days*, save Yourself
Mark 15:29 You who destroy the temple and build it *in three days*
John 2:19 Jesus answered and said to them, "Destroy this temple, and *in three days* I will raise it up
John 2:20 Then the Jews said, "It has taken forty-six years to build this temple, and will You raise it up *in three days*

IN TIME OF TROUBLE
Ps 41:1 Blessed is he who considers the poor; the Lord will deliver him *in time of trouble*
Prov 25:19 Confidence in an unfaithful man *in time of trouble* is like a bad tooth and a foot out of joint
Jer 14:8 O the Hope of Israel, his Savior *in time of trouble*, why should You be like a stranger in the land, and like a wayfaring man who turns aside to tarry for a night

IN TORMENT WITHIN (NIV)
(See *SOUL IS TROUBLED*)

IN WHOM I AM WELL PLEASED
Matt 3:17 And suddenly a voice came from heaven, saying, "This is My beloved Son, *in whom I am well pleased*
Matt 17:5 and suddenly a voice came out of the cloud, saying, "This is My beloved Son, *in whom I am well pleased*
Mark 1:11 Then a voice came from heaven, "You are My beloved Son, *in whom I am well pleased*
2Pet 1:17 This is My beloved Son, *in whom I am well pleased*

IN WRATH REMEMBER MERCY
Hab 3:2 in the midst of the years make it known; *in wrath remember mercy*

IN YOUR PRESENCE (NIV)
(See *BEFORE YOUR FACE*)

IN YOUR SEED
Gen 22:18 *In your seed* all the nations of the earth shall be blessed, because you have obeyed My voice
Gen 26:4 and *in your seed* all the nations of the earth shall be blessed
Gen 28:14 and in you and *in your seed* all the families of the earth shall be blessed
Acts 3:25 You are sons of the prophets, and of the covenant which God made with our fathers, saying to Abraham, 'And *in your seed* all the families of the earth shall be blessed

IN ZION
Ps 9:11 Sing praises to the Lord, who dwells *in Zion!* Declare His deeds among the people
Ps 65:1 Praise is awaiting You, O God, *in Zion;* and to You the vow shall be performed
Ps 76:2 In Salem also is His tabernacle, and His dwelling place *in Zion*
Ps 84:7 They go from strength to strength; every one of them appears before God *in Zion*
Ps 99:2 The Lord is great *in Zion*, and He is high above all the peoples
Ps 102:21 To declare the name of the Lord *in Zion*, and His praise in Jerusalem
Is 4:3 And it shall come to pass that he who is left *in Zion* and he who remains in Jerusalem will be called holy everyone who is recorded among the living in Jerusalem
Is 10:24 O My people, who dwell *in Zion*, do not be afraid of the Assyrian
Is 28:16 Behold, I lay *in Zion* a stone for a foundation, a tried stone, a precious cornerstone, a sure foundation
Is 30:19 For the people shall dwell *in Zion* at Jerusalem; you shall weep no more
Is 31:9 He shall cross over to his stronghold for fear, and his princes shall be afraid of the banner," says the Lord, whose fire is *in Zion* and whose furnace is in Jerusalem
Is 33:14 The sinners *in Zion* are afraid; fearfulness has seized the hypocrites
Is 46:13 And I will place salvation *in Zion*, for Israel My glory
Is 61:3 to console those who mourn *in Zion*, to give them beauty for ashes, the oil of joy for mourning, the garment of praise for the spirit of heaviness
Jer 8:19 Is not the Lord *in Zion?* Is not her King in her
Jer 50:28 The voice of those who flee and escape from the land of Babylon declares *in Zion* the vengeance of the Lord our God, the vengeance of His temple
Jer 51:10 Come and let us declare *in Zion* the work of the Lord our God
Jer 51:24 And I will repay Babylon and all the inhabitants of Chaldea for all the evil they have done *in Zion* in your sight
Lam 2:6 the Lord has caused the appointed feasts and Sabbaths to be forgotten *in Zion*
Lam 4:11 He kindled a fire *in Zion*, and it has devoured its foundations
Lam 5:11 They ravished the women *in Zion*, the maidens in the cities of Judah
Joel 2:1 Blow the trumpet *in Zion*, and sound an alarm in My holy mountain
Joel 2:15 Blow the trumpet *in Zion*, consecrate a fast, call a sacred assembly
Joel 3:17 So you shall know that I am the Lord your God, dwelling *in Zion* My holy mountain
Joel 3:21 For I will acquit them of bloodguilt, whom I had not acquitted; for the Lord dwells *in Zion*
Amos 6:1 Woe to you who are at ease *in Zion*, and trust in Mount Samaria, notable persons in the chief nation, to whom the house of Israel comes
Rom 9:33 Behold, I lay *in Zion* a stumbling stone and rock of offense, and whoever believes on Him will not be put to shame
1Pet 2:6 Therefore it is also contained in the Scripture, "Behold, I lay *in Zion* a chief cornerstone, elect, precious, and he who believes on Him will by no means be put to shame

INCLINE YOUR EAR
2Kin 19:16 *Incline Your ear*, O Lord, and hear; open Your eyes, O Lord, and see
Ps 17:6 I have called upon You, for You will hear me, O God; *incline Your ear* to me, and hear my speech
Ps 45:10 Listen, O daughter, consider and *incline your ear;* forget your own people also, and your father's house
Ps 71:2 Deliver me in Your righteousness, and cause me to escape; *incline Your ear* to me, and save me
Ps 88:2 Let my prayer come before You; *incline Your ear* to my cry
Ps 102:2 *Incline Your ear* to me; in the day that I call, answer me speedily
Prov 2:2 so that you *incline your ear* to wisdom, and apply your heart to understanding
Prov 4:20 My son, give attention to my words; *incline your ear* to my sayings
Prov 22:17 *Incline your ear* and hear the words of the wise, and apply your heart to my knowledge
Is 37:17 *Incline Your ear*, O Lord, and hear; open Your eyes, O Lord, and see

Is 55:3 *Incline your ear*, and come to Me. Hear, and your soul shall live
Dan 9:18 O my God, *incline Your ear* and hear; open Your eyes and see our desolations, and the city which is called by Your name

INCLINE YOUR HEART
Josh 24:23 Now therefore," he said, "put away the foreign gods which are among you, and *incline your heart* to the Lord God of Israel

INCREASE KNOWLEDGE (NIV)
(See *KNOWLEDGE SHALL INCREASE*)

INCREASE OUR FAITH
Luke 17:5 And the apostles said to the Lord, "*Increase our faith*

INCREASE YOUR DESCENDANTS (NIV)
(See *MULTIPLY YOUR DESCENDANTS*)

INCREASE YOUR PAINS (NIV)
(See *MULTIPLY YOUR SORROW*)

INCREASED IN WISDOM AND STATURE
Luke 2:52 And Jesus *increased in wisdom and stature*, and in favor with God and men

INCURABLE WOUND (NIV)
(See *MY WOUND IS INCURABLE*)

INDULGE THE SINFUL NATURE (NIV)
(See *OPPORTUNITY FOR THE FLESH*)

INDULGENCE OF THE FLESH
Col 2:23 These things indeed have an appearance of wisdom in self-imposed religion, false humility, and neglect of the body, but are of no value against the *indulgence of the flesh*

INEXPRESSIBLE AND GLORIOUS JOY (NIV)
(See *JOY INEXPRESSIBLE*)

INFANTS WHO NEVER SAW LIGHT
Job 3:16 or why was I not hidden like a stillborn child, like *infants who never saw light*

INFERIOR TO THE MOST EMINENT APOSTLES
2Cor 11:5 For I consider that I am not at all *inferior to the most eminent apostles*

INFIRMITIES OF THE WEAK (KJV)
(See *SCRUPLES OF THE WEAK*)

INFLAMING YOURSELVES WITH GODS
Is 57:5 *inflaming yourselves with gods* under every green tree, slaying the children in the valleys, under the clefts of the rocks

INFLICT PUNISHMENT (NIV)
(See *EXECUTE JUDGMENTS*)

INHABITANTS OF JERUSALEM
Josh 15:63 As for the Jebusites, the *inhabitants of Jerusalem*, the children of Judah could not drive them out
2Kin 23:2 And the king went up to the house of the Lord with all the men of Judah, and with him all the *inhabitants of Jerusalem* the priests and the prophets and all the people, both small and great
2Chr 20:15 and he said, "Listen, all you of Judah and you *inhabitants of Jerusalem*, and you, King Jehoshaphat
2Chr 20:18 And Jehoshaphat bowed his head with his face to the ground, and all Judah and the *inhabitants of Jerusalem* bowed before the Lord, worshiping the Lord
2Chr 20:20 and as they went out, Jehoshaphat stood and said, "Hear me, O Judah and you *inhabitants of Jerusalem*
2Chr 21:11 Moreover he made high places in the mountains of Judah, and caused the *inhabitants of Jerusalem* to commit harlotry, and led Judah astray
2Chr 21:13 but have walked in the way of the kings of Israel, and have made Judah and the *inhabitants of Jerusalem* to play the harlot like the harlotry of the house of Ahab, and also have killed your brothers, those of your father's household, who were better than yourself
2Chr 22:1 Then the *inhabitants of Jerusalem* made Ahaziah his youngest son king in his place, for the raiders who came with the Arabians into the camp had killed all the older sons
2Chr 32:22 Thus the Lord saved Hezekiah and the *inhabitants of Jerusalem* from the hand of Sennacherib the king of Assyria, and from the hand of all others, and guided them on every side
2Chr 32:26 Then Hezekiah humbled himself for the pride of his heart, he and the *inhabitants of Jerusalem*, so that the wrath of the Lord did not come upon them in the days of Hezekiah
2Chr 32:33 and all Judah and the *inhabitants of Jerusalem* honored him at his death
2Chr 33:9 So Manasseh seduced Judah and the *inhabitants of Jerusalem* to do more evil than the nations whom the Lord had destroyed before the children of Israel
2Chr 34:30 And the king went up to the house of the Lord, with all the men of Judah and the *inhabitants of Jerusalem*
2Chr 34:32 So the *inhabitants of Jerusalem* did according to the covenant of God, the God of their fathers
2Chr 35:18 and none of the kings of Israel had kept such a Passover as Josiah kept, with the priests and the Levites, all Judah and Israel who were present, and the *inhabitants of Jerusalem*
Neh 7:3 and appoint guards from among the *inhabitants of Jerusalem*, one at his watch station and another in front of his own house
Is 5:3 And now, O *inhabitants of Jerusalem* and men of Judah, judge, please, between Me and My vineyard
Is 8:14 He will be as a sanctuary, but a stone of stumbling and a rock of offense to both the houses of Israel, as a trap and a snare to the *inhabitants of Jerusalem*
Is 22:21 He shall be a father to the *inhabitants of Jerusalem* and to the house of Judah
Jer 4:4 Circumcise yourselves to the Lord, and take away the foreskins of your hearts, you men of Judah and *inhabitants of Jerusalem*, lest My fury come forth like fire, and burn so that no one can quench it, because of the evil of your doings
Jer 8:1 At that time," says the Lord, "they shall bring out the bones of the kings of Judah, and the bones of its princes, and the bones of the priests, and the bones of the prophets, and the bones of the *inhabitants of Jerusalem*, out of their graves
Jer 11:2 Hear the words of this covenant, and speak to the men of Judah and to the *inhabitants of Jerusalem*
Jer 11:9 And the Lord said to me, "A conspiracy has been found among the men of Judah and among the *inhabitants of Jerusalem*
Jer 11:12 Then the cities of Judah and the *inhabitants of Jerusalem* will go and cry out to the gods to whom they offer incense, but they will not save them at all in the time of their trouble
Jer 13:13 Behold, I will fill all the inhabitants of this land even the kings who sit on David's throne, the priests, the prophets, and all the *inhabitants of Jerusalem* with drunkenness
Jer 17:20 and say to them, 'Hear the word of the

Lord, you kings of Judah, and all Judah, and all the *inhabitants of Jerusalem*, who enter by these gates

Jer 17:25 then shall enter the gates of this city kings and princes sitting on the throne of David, riding in chariots and on horses, they and their princes, accompanied by the men of Judah and the *inhabitants of Jerusalem*

Jer 18:11 Now therefore, speak to the men of Judah and to the *inhabitants of Jerusalem*, saying

Jer 19:3 and say, 'Hear the word of the Lord, O kings of Judah and *inhabitants of Jerusalem*

Jer 25:2 which Jeremiah the prophet spoke to all the people of Judah and to all the *inhabitants of Jerusalem*, saying

Jer 32:32 because of all the evil of the children of Israel and the children of Judah, which they have done to provoke Me to anger they, their kings, their princes, their priests, their prophets, the men of Judah, and the *inhabitants of Jerusalem*

Jer 35:13 Go and tell the men of Judah and the *inhabitants of Jerusalem*

Jer 35:17 Behold, I will bring on Judah and on all the *inhabitants of Jerusalem* all the doom that I have pronounced against them

Jer 36:31 and I will bring on them, on the *inhabitants of Jerusalem*, and on the men of Judah all the doom that I have pronounced against them

Jer 42:18 As My anger and My fury have been poured out on the *inhabitants of Jerusalem*, so will My fury be poured out on you when you enter Egypt

Ezek 11:15 Son of man, your brethren, your relatives, your kinsmen, and all the house of Israel in its entirety, are those about whom the *inhabitants of Jerusalem* have said

Ezek 12:19 And say to the people of the land, 'Thus says the Lord God to the *inhabitants of Jerusalem* and to the land of Israel

Ezek 15:6 Like the wood of the vine among the trees of the forest, which I have given to the fire for fuel, so I will give up the *inhabitants of Jerusalem*

Dan 9:7 O Lord, righteousness belongs to You, but to us shame of face, as it is this day to the men of Judah, to the *inhabitants of Jerusalem* and all Israel, those near and those far off in all the countries to which You have driven them, because of the unfaithfulness which they have committed against You

Zeph 1:4 I will stretch out My hand against Judah, and against all the *inhabitants of Jerusalem*

Zech 12:5 And the governors of Judah shall say in their heart, 'The *inhabitants of Jerusalem* are my strength in the Lord of hosts, their God

Zech 12:7 The Lord will save the tents of Judah first, so that the glory of the house of David and the glory of the *inhabitants of Jerusalem* shall not become greater than that of Judah

Zech 12:8 In that day the Lord will defend the *inhabitants of Jerusalem*

Zech 12:10 And I will pour on the house of David and on the *inhabitants of Jerusalem* the Spirit of grace and supplication

Zech 13:1 In that day a fountain shall be opened for the house of David and for the *inhabitants of Jerusalem*, for sin and for uncleanness

INHABITANTS OF THE EARTH

Ps 33:14 From the place of His habitation He looks on all the *inhabitants of the earth*

Is 24:6 Therefore the *inhabitants of the earth* are burned, and few men are left

Is 26:21 For behold, the Lord comes out of His place to punish the *inhabitants of the earth* for their iniquity

Jer 25:29 You shall not be unpunished, for I will call for a sword on all the *inhabitants of the earth*

Jer 25:30 He will give a shout, as those who tread the grapes, against all the *inhabitants of the earth*

Dan 4:35 All the *inhabitants of the earth* are reputed as nothing; He does according to His will in the army of heaven and among the *inhabitants of the earth*

Rev 8:13 And I looked, and I heard an angel flying through the midst of heaven, saying with a loud voice, "Woe, woe, woe to the *inhabitants of the earth*, because of the remaining blasts of the trumpet of the three angels who are about to sound

Rev 12:12 Woe to the *inhabitants of the earth* and the sea

Rev 17:2 with whom the kings of the earth committed fornication, and the *inhabitants of the earth* were made drunk with the wine of her fornication

INHABITANTS OF THE WORLD

Ps 33:8 Let all the *inhabitants of the world* stand in awe of Him

Ps 49:1 Hear this, all you peoples; give ear, all you *inhabitants of the world*

Is 18:3 All *inhabitants of the world* and dwellers on the earth

Is 26:9 for when Your judgments are in the earth, the *inhabitants of the world* will learn righteousness

Is 26:18 we have not accomplished any deliverance in the earth, nor have the *inhabitants of the world* fallen

Is 38:11 I shall observe man no more among the *inhabitants of the world*

Lam 4:12 The kings of the earth, and all *inhabitants of the world*, would not have believed that the adversary and the enemy could enter the gates of Jerusalem

INHERIT ETERNAL LIFE

Mark 10:17 Now as He was going out on the road, one came running, knelt before Him, and asked Him, "Good Teacher, what shall I do that I may *inherit eternal life*

Luke 10:25 And behold, a certain lawyer stood up and tested Him, saying, "Teacher, what shall I do to *inherit eternal life*

Luke 18:18 Now a certain ruler asked Him, saying, "Good Teacher, what shall I do to *inherit eternal life*

INHERIT ONLY WIND (NIV)
(See *INHERIT THE WIND*)

INHERIT THE BLESSING

Heb 12:17 For you know that afterward, when he wanted to *inherit the blessing*, he was rejected, for he found no place for repentance, though he sought it diligently with tears

INHERIT THE EARTH

Ps 25:13 He himself shall dwell in prosperity, and his descendants shall *inherit the earth*

Ps 37:9 But those who wait on the Lord, they shall *inherit the earth*

Ps 37:11 But the meek shall *inherit the earth*, and shall delight themselves in the abundance of peace

Ps 37:22 For those who are blessed by Him shall *inherit the earth*, but those who are cursed by Him shall be cut off

Matt 5:5 Blessed are the meek, for they shall *inherit the earth*

INHERIT THE KINGDOM (NIV)
(See *HEIRS OF THE KINGDOM*)

INHERIT THE LAND
Gen 28:4 and give you the blessing of Abraham, to you and your descendants with you, that you may *inherit the land* in which you are a stranger, which God gave to Abraham
Ex 23:30 Little by little I will drive them out from before you, until you have increased, and you *inherit the land*
Deut 3:28 for he shall go over before this people, and he shall cause them to *inherit the land* which you will see
Deut 16:20 You shall follow what is altogether just, that you may live and *inherit the land* which the Lord your God is giving you
Ps 37:29 The righteous shall *inherit the land*, and dwell in it forever
Ps 37:34 Wait on the Lord, and keep His way, and He shall exalt you to *inherit the land*
Is 60:21 they shall *inherit the land* forever, the branch of My planting, the work of My hands, that I may be glorified

INHERIT THE WIND
Prov 11:29 He who troubles his own house will *inherit the wind*, and the fool will be servant to the wise of heart

INHERITANCE OF THE
Num 36:3 Now if they are married to any of the sons of the other tribes of the children of Israel, then their inheritance will be taken from the inheritance of our fathers, and it will be added to the *inheritance of the* tribe into which they marry
Num 36:4 And when the Jubilee of the children of Israel comes, then their inheritance will be added to the *inheritance of the* tribe into which they marry; so their inheritance will be taken away from the *inheritance of the* tribe of our fathers
Num 36:7 So the *inheritance of the* children of Israel shall not change hands from tribe to tribe, for every one of the children of Israel shall keep the *inheritance of the* tribe of his fathers
Josh 13:23 This was the *inheritance of the* children of Reuben according to their families, the cities and their villages
Josh 13:28 This is the *inheritance of the* children of Gad according to their families, the cities and their villages
Josh 14:3 For Moses had given the *inheritance of the* two tribes and the half-tribe on the other side of the Jordan
Josh 15:20 This was the *inheritance of the* tribe of the children of Judah according to their families
Josh 16:8 This was the *inheritance of the* tribe of the children of Ephraim according to their families
Josh 16:9 The separate cities for the children of Ephraim were among the *inheritance of the* children of Manasseh, all the cities with their villages
Josh 18:20 This was the *inheritance of the* children of Benjamin, according to its boundaries all around, according to their families
Josh 18:28 This was the *inheritance of the* children of Benjamin according to their families
Josh 19:1 And their inheritance was within the *inheritance of the* children of Judah
Josh 19:8 This was the *inheritance of the* tribe of the children of Simeon according to their families
Josh 19:9 The *inheritance of the* children of Simeon was included in the portion of the children of Judah, for the portion of the children of Judah was too much for them
Josh 19:16 This was the *inheritance of the* children of Zebulun according to their families, these cities with their villages
Josh 19:23 This was the *inheritance of the* tribe of the children of Issachar according to their families, the cities and their villages
Josh 19:31 This was the *inheritance of the* tribe of the children of Asher according to their families, these cities with their villages
Josh 19:39 This was the *inheritance of the* tribe of the children of Naphtali according to their families, the cities and their villages
Josh 19:48 This is the *inheritance of the* tribe of the children of Dan according to their families, these cities with their villages
Josh 24:32 The bones of Joseph, which the children of Israel had brought up out of Egypt, they buried at Shechem, in the plot of ground which Jacob had bought from the sons of Hamor the father of Shechem for one hundred pieces of silver, and which had become an *inheritance of the* children of Joseph
1Sam 26:19 But if it is the children of men, may they be cursed before the Lord, for they have driven me out this day from abiding in the *inheritance of the* Lord, saying
2Sam 20:19 Why would you swallow up the *inheritance of the* Lord
2Sam 21:3 And with what shall I make atonement, that you may bless the *inheritance of the* Lord
Job 31:2 For what is the allotment of God from above, and the *inheritance of the* Almighty from on high
Ezek 35:15 As you rejoiced because the *inheritance of the* house of Israel was desolate, so I will do to you
Col 1:12 giving thanks to the Father who has qualified us to be partakers of the *inheritance of the* saints in the light

INHERITANCE OF THE LORD
1Sam 26:19 But if it is the children of men, may they be cursed before the Lord, for they have driven me out this day from abiding in the *inheritance of the Lord*, saying
2Sam 20:19 Why would you swallow up the *inheritance of the Lord*
2Sam 21:3 And with what shall I make atonement, that you may bless the *inheritance of the Lord*

INHERITED THE BLESSING (KJV)
(See *INHERIT THE BLESSING*)

INIQUITIES HAVE SEPARATED YOU
Is 59:2 But your *iniquities have separated you* from your God; and your sins have hidden His face from you, so that He will not hear

INIQUITIES OF MY YOUTH
Job 13:26 For You write bitter things against me, and make me inherit the *iniquities of my youth*

INIQUITY OF THE FATHER (KJV, RSV)
(See *GUILT OF THE FATHER*)

INIQUITY OF THE FATHERS
Ex 20:5 For I, the Lord your God, am a jealous God, visiting the *iniquity of the fathers* on the children to the third and fourth generations of those who hate Me
Ex 34:7 keeping mercy for thousands, forgiving iniquity and transgression and sin, by no means clearing the guilty, visiting the *iniquity of the fathers* upon the children and the children's children to the third and the fourth generation
Num 14:18 but He by no means clears the guilty, visiting the *iniquity of the fathers* on the children to the third and fourth generation
Deut 5:9 For I, the Lord your God, am a jealous God, visiting the *iniquity of the fathers* upon the

children to the third and fourth generations of those who hate Me
Jer 32:18 You show lovingkindness to thousands, and repay the *iniquity of the fathers* into the bosom of their children after them the Great, the Mighty God, whose name is the Lord of hosts

INIQUITY TO BE PUNISHED (KJV, RSV)
(See *WORTHY OF JUDGMENT*)

INNOCENT AS DOVES (NAS, NIV, RSV)
(See *HARMLESS AS DOVES*)

INNOCENT BLOOD
Deut 19:10 lest *innocent blood* be shed in the midst of your land which the Lord your God is giving you as an inheritance, and thus bloodguiltiness be upon you
Deut 19:13 Your eye shall not pity him, but you shall put away the guilt of *innocent blood* from Israel, that it may go well with you
Deut 21:8 Provide atonement, O Lord, for Your people Israel, whom You have redeemed, and do not lay *innocent blood* to the charge of Your people Israel
Deut 21:9 So you shall put away the guilt of *innocent blood* from among you when you do what is right in the sight of the Lord
1Sam 19:5 Why then will you sin against *innocent blood*, to kill David without a cause
1Kin 2:31 And the king said to him, "Do as he has said, and strike him down and bury him, that you may take away from me and from the house of my father the *innocent blood* which Joab shed
2Kin 21:16 Moreover Manasseh shed very much *innocent blood*, till he had filled Jerusalem from one end to another, besides his sin with which he made Judah sin
2Kin 24:4 and also because of the *innocent blood* that he had shed; for he had filled Jerusalem with *innocent blood*, which the Lord would not pardon
Ps 94:21 They gather together against the life of the righteous, and condemn *innocent blood*
Ps 106:38 And shed *innocent blood*, even the blood of their sons and daughters, whom they sacrificed to the idols of Canaan
Prov 6:17 A proud look, a lying tongue, hands that shed *innocent blood*
Is 59:7 Their feet run to evil, and they make haste to shed *innocent blood*
Jer 7:6 if you do not oppress the stranger, the fatherless, and the widow, and do not shed *innocent blood* in this place, or walk after other gods to your hurt
Jer 22:3 Do no wrong and do no violence to the stranger, the fatherless, or the widow, nor shed *innocent blood* in this place
Jer 22:17 Yet your eyes and your heart are for nothing but your covetousness, for shedding *innocent blood*, and practicing oppression and violence
Jer 26:15 But know for certain that if you put me to death, you will surely bring *innocent blood* on yourselves, on this city, and on its inhabitants
Joel 3:19 Egypt shall be a desolation, and Edom a desolate wilderness, because of violence against the people of Judah, for they have shed *innocent blood* in their land
Jon 1:14 Therefore they cried out to the Lord and said, "We pray, O Lord, please do not let us perish for this man's life, and do not charge us with *innocent blood*
Matt 27:4 saying, "I have sinned by betraying *innocent blood*." And they said

INQUIRE OF THE LORD
Gen 25:22 and she said, "If all is well, why am I this way?" So she went to *inquire of the Lord*
1Kin 22:8 So the king of Israel said to Jehoshaphat, "There is still one man, Micaiah the son of Imlah, by whom we may *inquire of the Lord*
2Kin 3:11 But Jehoshaphat said, "Is there no prophet of the Lord here, that we may *inquire of the Lord* by him
2Kin 8:8 And the king said to Hazael, "Take a present in your hand, and go to meet the man of God, and *inquire of the Lord* by him, saying
2Kin 22:13 Go, *inquire of the Lord* for me, for the people and for all Judah, concerning the words of this book that has been found
2Kin 22:18 But to the king of Judah, who sent you to *inquire of the Lord*, in this manner you shall speak to him
1Chr 10:14 But he did not *inquire of the Lord;* therefore He killed him, and turned the kingdom over to David the son of Jesse
2Chr 18:7 So the king of Israel said to Jehoshaphat, "There is still one man by whom we may *inquire of the Lord*
2Chr 34:21 Go, *inquire of the Lord* for me, and for those who are left in Israel and Judah, concerning the words of the book that is found
2Chr 34:26 And as for the king of Judah, who sent you to *inquire of the Lord*, in this manner you shall speak to him
Jer 21:2 Please *inquire of the Lord* for us, for Nebuchadnezzar king of Babylon makes war against us
Ezek 20:1 It came to pass in the seventh year, in the fifth month, on the tenth day of the month, that certain of the elders of Israel came to *inquire of the Lord*, and sat before me

INQUIRED OF THE LORD
Judg 20:27 So the children of Israel *inquired of the Lord* (the ark of the covenant of God was there in those days
1Sam 10:22 Therefore they *inquired of the Lord* further, "Has the man come here yet
1Sam 22:10 And he *inquired of the Lord* for him, gave him provisions, and gave him the sword of Goliath the Philistine
1Sam 23:2 Therefore David *inquired of the Lord*, saying, "Shall I go and attack these Philistines
1Sam 23:4 Then David *inquired of the Lord* once again. And the Lord answered him and said
1Sam 28:6 And when Saul *inquired of the Lord*, the Lord did not answer him, either by dreams or by Urim or by the prophets
1Sam 30:8 So David *inquired of the Lord*, saying, "Shall I pursue this troop
2Sam 2:1 It happened after this that David *inquired of the Lord*, saying
2Sam 5:19 And David *inquired of the Lord*, saying, "Shall I go up against the Philistines
2Sam 5:23 And when David *inquired of the Lord*, He said, "You shall not go up
2Sam 21:1 and David *inquired of the Lord*. And the Lord answered

INQUIRING OF THE LORD (NIV)
(See *SOUGHT THE LORD*)

INSIDE THE FISH (NIV)
(See *BELLY OF THE FISH*)

INSIDE THE VEIL
Lev 16:2 Tell Aaron your brother not to come at simply any time into the Holy Place *inside the veil*, before the mercy seat which is on the ark, lest he die
Lev 16:12 Then he shall take a censer full of burning coals of fire from the altar before the Lord,

with his hands full of sweet incense beaten fine, and bring it *inside the veil*
Lev 16:15 Then he shall kill the goat of the sin offering, which is for the people, bring its blood *inside the veil*, do with that blood as he did with the blood of the bull, and sprinkle it on the mercy seat and before the mercy seat

INSPIRATION OF GOD
2Tim 3:16 All Scripture is given by *inspiration of God*, and is profitable for doctrine, for reproof, for correction, for instruction in righteousness

INSPIRED BY GOD (NAS, RSV)
(See *INSPIRATION OF GOD*)

INSTRUCTED TONGUE (NIV)
(See *SPEAK A WORD*)

INSTRUCTION IN RIGHTEOUSNESS
2Tim 3:16 All Scripture is given by inspiration of God, and is profitable for doctrine, for reproof, for correction, for *instruction in righteousness*

INSTRUCTION OF YOUR FATHER
Prov 1:8 My son, hear the *instruction of your father*, and do not forsake the law of your mother

INSTRUMENTS FOR MUSIC TO THE LORD (RSV)
(See *MUSIC OF THE LORD*)

INSTRUMENTS OF DEATH
Ps 7:13 He also prepares for Himself *instruments of death;* He makes His arrows into fiery shafts

INSTRUMENTS OF RIGHTEOUSNESS
Rom 6:13 And do not present your members as instruments of unrighteousness to sin, but present yourselves to God as being alive from the dead, and your members as *instruments of righteousness* to God

INSULTED THE POOR (NIV)
(See *DISHONORED THE POOR MAN*)

INSULTS HIS MAKER (RSV)
(See *REPROACHES HIS MAKER*)

INTEGRITY OF YOUR HEART
Gen 20:6 And God said to him in a dream, "Yes, I know that you did this in the *integrity of your heart*

INTENTS OF THE HEART
Heb 4:12 For the word of God is living and powerful, and sharper than any two-edged sword, piercing even to the division of soul and spirit, and of joints and marrow, and is a discerner of the thoughts and *intents of the heart*

INTERCEDE WITH (NIV)
(See *ENTREAT THE FAVOR*)

INTEREST ON MONEY
Deut 23:19 You shall not charge interest to your brother *interest on money* or food or anything that is lent out at interest

INTERPRETATION OF TONGUES
1Cor 12:10 to another the working of miracles, to another prophecy, to another discerning of spirits, to another different kinds of tongues, to another the *interpretation of tongues*

INTO A FAR COUNTRY
Matt 21:33 And he leased it to vinedressers and went *into a far country*
Mark 12:1 And he leased it to vinedressers and went *into a far country*
Luke 19:12 A certain nobleman went *into a far country* to receive for himself a kingdom and to return
Luke 20:9 A certain man planted a vineyard, leased it to vinedressers, and went *into a far country* for a long time

INTO HELL
Ps 9:17 The wicked shall be turned *into hell*, and all the nations that forget God
Ps 55:15 Let them go down alive *into hell*, for wickedness is in their dwellings and among them
Amos 9:2 Though they dig *into hell*, from there my hand shall take them
Matt 5:29 for it is more profitable for you that one of your members perish, than for your whole body to be cast *into hell*
Matt 5:30 for it is more profitable for you that one of your members perish, than for your whole body to be cast *into hell*
Matt 18:9 It is better for you to enter into life with one eye, rather than having two eyes, to be cast *into hell* fire
Mark 9:45 It is better for you to enter life lame, than having two feet, to be cast *into hell*, into the fire that shall never be quenched
Mark 9:47 It is better for you to enter the kingdom of God with one eye, than having two eyes, to be cast *into hell* fire
Luke 12:5 Fear Him who, after He has killed, has power to cast *into hell*

INTO HIS RIGHT HAND (NIV, RSV)
(See *IN HIS RIGHT HAND*)

INTO SMOKE THEY SHALL VANISH AWAY
Ps 37:20 And the enemies of the Lord, Like the splendor of the meadows, shall vanish. *Into smoke they shall vanish away*

INTO YOUR HANDS
Deut 20:13 And when the Lord your God delivers it *into your hands*, you shall strike every male in it with the edge of the sword
Judg 8:3 God has delivered *into your hands* the princes of Midian, Oreb and Zeeb
Judg 18:10 For God has given it *into your hands*, a place where there is no lack of anything that is on the earth
2Kin 10:24 Now Jehu had appointed for himself eighty men on the outside, and had said, "If any of the men whom I have brought *into your hands* escapes, whoever lets him escape, it shall be his life for the life of the other
Luke 23:46 And when Jesus had cried out with a loud voice, He said, "Father, '*into Your hands* I commend My spirit

INTOXICATED WITH THE WINE (NIV)
(See *DRUNK WITH THE WINE*)

INWARD MAN
Rom 7:22 For I delight in the law of God according to the *inward man*
2Cor 4:16 Even though our outward man is perishing, yet the *inward man* is being renewed day by day

IRON SCEPTER (NIV)
(See *ROD OF IRON*)

IRON SHARPENS IRON
Prov 27:17 As *iron sharpens iron*, so a man sharpens the countenance of his friend

IS CHRIST DIVIDED
1Cor 1:13 *Is Christ divided?* Was Paul crucified for you? Or were you baptized in the name of Paul

IS IT LAWFUL
Matt 12:10 And they asked Him, saying, "*Is it lawful* to heal on the Sabbath
Matt 19:3 The Pharisees also came to Him, testing Him, and saying to Him, "*Is it lawful* for a man to divorce his wife for just any reason
Matt 22:17 *Is it lawful* to pay taxes to Caesar, or not
Mark 3:4 And He said to them, "*Is it lawful* on the Sabbath to do good or to do evil, to save life or to kill
Mark 10:2 The Pharisees came and asked Him, "*Is it lawful* for a man to divorce his wife
Mark 12:14 *Is it lawful* to pay taxes to Caesar, or not
Luke 6:9 *Is it lawful* on the Sabbath to do good or to do evil, to save life or to destroy it
Luke 14:3 And Jesus, answering, spoke to the lawyers and Pharisees, saying, "*Is it lawful* to heal on the Sabbath
Luke 20:22 *Is it lawful* for us to pay taxes to Caesar or not
Acts 22:25 And as they bound him with thongs, Paul said to the centurion who stood by, "*Is it lawful* for you to scourge a man who is a Roman, and uncondemned

IS SAUL ALSO AMONG THE PROPHETS
1Sam 10:11 And it happened, when all who knew him formerly saw that he indeed prophesied among the prophets, that the people said to one another, "What is this that has come upon the son of Kish? *Is Saul also among the prophets*
1Sam 10:12 Therefore it became a proverb: *Is Saul also among the prophets*
1Sam 19:24 And he also stripped off his clothes and prophesied before Samuel in like manner, and lay down naked all that day and all that night. Therefore they say, "*Is Saul also among the prophets*

ISRAEL HAD NO KING (NIV)
(See *NO KING IN ISRAEL*)

ISRAEL MY INHERITANCE
Is 19:25 whom the Lord of hosts shall bless, saying, "Blessed is Egypt My people, and Assyria the work of My hands, and *Israel My inheritance*

ISRAEL OF GOD
Gal 6:16 And as many as walk according to this rule, peace and mercy be upon them, and upon the *Israel of God*

ISRAEL'S ARROGANCE (NIV)
(See *PRIDE OF ISRAEL*)

ISRAEL'S JUDGES (NIV)
(See *JUDGES OF ISRAEL*)

ISRAEL'S SINGER OF SONGS (NIV)
(See *SWEET PSALMIST OF ISRAEL*)

ISRAEL'S SONS (NIV)
(See *SONS OF ISRAEL*)

ISSUE OF BLOOD (KJV)
(See *FLOW OF BLOOD*)

ISSUES OF LIFE
Prov 4:23 Keep your heart with all diligence, for out of it spring the *issues of life*

IT IS AN EVIL TIME
Amos 5:13 Therefore the prudent keep silent at that time, for *it is an evil time*

IT IS BEYOND UNDERSTANDING (NIV)
(See *IT IS WONDERFUL*)

IT IS FINISHED
John 19:30 So when Jesus had received the sour wine, He said, "*It is finished*

IT IS FOR HIS LIFE (KJV)
(See *TAKE HIS LIFE*)

IT IS I
1Kin 18:8 And he answered him, "*It is I*. Go, tell your master
Is 52:6 therefore they shall know in that day that I am He who speaks: 'Behold, *it is I*
Matt 14:27 But immediately Jesus spoke to them, saying, "Be of good cheer! *It is I;* do not be afraid
Mark 6:50 And immediately He talked with them and said to them, "Be of good cheer! *It is I;* do not be afraid
Luke 24:39 Behold My hands and My feet, that *it is I* Myself
John 6:20 But He said to them, "*It is I;* do not be afraid

IT IS IMPOSSIBLE
Mark 10:27 But looking at them, Jesus said, "With men *it is impossible*, but not with God
Luke 17:1 Then He said to the disciples, "*It is impossible* that no offenses should come, but woe to him through whom they do come
Heb 6:4 For *it is impossible* for those who were once enlightened, and have tasted the heavenly gift, and have become partakers of the Holy Spirit
Heb 6:18 that by two immutable things, in which *it is impossible* for God to lie, we might have strong consolation, who have fled for refuge to lay hold of the hope set before us
Heb 11:6 But without faith *it is impossible* to please Him, for he who comes to God must believe that He is, and that He is a rewarder of those who diligently seek Him

IT IS MINE TO AVENGE (NIV)
(See *VENGEANCE IS MINE*)

IT IS SECRET (KJV)
(See *IT IS WONDERFUL*)

IT IS THE LORD
1Sam 3:18 And he said, "*It is the Lord*. Let Him do what seems good to Him
1Sam 12:6 And Samuel said to the people, "*It is the Lord* who raised up Moses and Aaron, and who brought your fathers up from the land of Egypt
John 21:7 Therefore that disciple whom Jesus loved said to Peter, "*It is the Lord*

IT IS WONDERFUL
Judg 13:18 And the Angel of the Lord said to him, "Why do you ask My name, seeing *it is wonderful*

IT IS WRITTEN
Josh 8:31 as Moses the servant of the Lord had commanded the children of Israel, as *it is written* in the Book of the Law of Moses
2Sam 1:18 and he told them to teach the children of Judah the Song of the Bow; indeed *it is written* in the Book of Jasher
1Kin 2:3 to walk in His ways, to keep His statutes, His commandments, His judgments, and His testimonies, as *it is written* in the Law of Moses,

that you may prosper in all that you do and wherever you turn
2Kin 23:21 Then the king commanded all the people, saying, "Keep the Passover to the Lord your God, as *it is written* in this Book of the Covenant
2Chr 23:18 Also Jehoiada appointed the oversight of the house of the Lord to the hand of the priests, the Levites, whom David had assigned in the house of the Lord, to offer the burnt offerings of the Lord, as *it is written* in the Law of Moses, with rejoicing and with singing, as it was established by David
2Chr 25:4 However he did not execute their children, but did as *it is written* in the Law in the Book of Moses, where the Lord commanded, saying
2Chr 31:3 for the morning and evening burnt offerings, the burnt offerings for the Sabbaths and the New Moons and the set feasts, as *it is written* in the Law of the Lord
2Chr 35:12 Then they removed the burnt offerings that they might give them to the divisions of the fathers' houses of the lay people, to offer to the Lord, as *it is written* in the Book of Moses
Ezra 3:2 Then Jeshua the son of Jozadak and his brethren the priests, and Zerubbabel the son of Shealtiel and his brethren, arose and built the altar of the God of Israel, to offer burnt offerings on it, as *it is written* in the Law of Moses the man of God
Ezra 3:4 They also kept the Feast of Tabernacles, as *it is written*, and offered the daily burnt offerings in the number required by ordinance for each day
Ezra 6:18 They assigned the priests to their divisions and the Levites to their divisions, over the service of God in Jerusalem, as *it is written* in the Book of Moses
Neh 8:15 and that they should announce and proclaim in all their cities and in Jerusalem, saying, "Go out to the mountain, and bring olive branches, branches of oil trees, myrtle branches, palm branches, and branches of leafy trees, to make booths, as *it is written*
Neh 10:34 We cast lots among the priests, the Levites, and the people, for bringing the wood offering into the house of our God, according to our fathers' houses, at the appointed times year by year, to burn on the altar of the Lord our God as *it is written* in the Law
Neh 10:36 to bring the firstborn of our sons and our cattle, as *it is written* in the Law, and the firstlings of our herds and our flocks, to the house of our God, to the priests who minister in the house of our God
Ps 40:7 In the scroll of the Book *it is written* of me
Is 65:6 Behold, *it is written* before Me: I will not keep silence, but will repay even repay into their bosom
Dan 9:13 As *it is written* in the Law of Moses, all this disaster has come upon us
Matt 2:5 So they said to him, "In Bethlehem of Judea, for thus *it is written* by the prophet
Matt 4:4 But He answered and said, "*It is written*, 'Man shall not live by bread alone, but by every word that proceeds from the mouth of God
Matt 4:6 For *it is written:* 'He shall give His angels charge concerning you
Matt 4:7 Jesus said to him, "*It is written* again, 'You shall not tempt the Lord your God
Matt 4:10 For *it is written*, 'You shall worship the Lord your God, and Him only you shall serve
Matt 11:10 For this is he of whom *it is written:* 'Behold, I send My messenger before Your face, who will prepare Your way before You
Matt 21:13 And He said to them, "*It is written*, 'My house shall be called a house of prayer
Matt 26:24 The Son of Man goes as *it is written* of Him, but woe to that man by whom the Son of Man is betrayed
Matt 26:31 Then Jesus said to them, "All of you will be made to stumble because of Me this night, for *it is written*
Mark 1:2 As *it is written* in the Prophets: "Behold, I send My messenger before Your face, who will prepare Your way before You
Mark 7:6 He answered and said to them, "Well did Isaiah prophesy of you hypocrites, as *it is written*
Mark 9:13 But I say to you that Elijah has also come, and they did to him whatever they wished, as *it is written* of him
Mark 14:21 The Son of Man indeed goes just as *it is written* of Him, but woe to that man by whom the Son of Man is betrayed
Mark 14:27 Then Jesus said to them, "All of you will be made to stumble because of Me this night, for *it is written*
Luke 2:23 (as *it is written* in the law of the Lord
Luke 3:4 as *it is written* in the book of the words of Isaiah the prophet, saying
Luke 4:4 But Jesus answered him, saying, "*It is written*, 'Man shall not live by bread alone, but by every word of God
Luke 4:8 For *it is written*, 'You shall worship the Lord your God, and Him only you shall serve
Luke 4:10 For *it is written:* 'He shall give His angels charge over You, to keep You
Luke 7:27 This is he of whom *it is written:* 'Behold, I send My messenger before Your face, who will prepare Your way before You
Luke 19:46 saying to them, "*It is written*, 'My house is a house of prayer
Luke 24:46 Then He said to them, "Thus *it is written*, and thus it was necessary for the Christ to suffer and to rise from the dead the third day
John 6:31 as *it is written*, 'He gave them bread from heaven to eat
John 6:45 *It is written* in the prophets, 'And they shall all be taught by God
John 12:14 Then Jesus, when He had found a young donkey, sat on it; as *it is written*
Acts 1:20 For *it is written* in the book of Psalms: 'Let his habitation be desolate, and let no one live in it
Acts 7:42 Then God turned and gave them up to worship the host of heaven, as *it is written* in the book of the Prophets
Acts 15:15 And with this the words of the prophets agree, just as *it is written*
Acts 23:5 for *it is written*, 'You shall not speak evil of the ruler of your people
Rom 1:17 as *it is written*, "The just shall live by faith
Rom 2:24 For "The name of God is blasphemed among the Gentiles because of you," as *it is written*
Rom 3:4 As *it is written:* "That you may be justified in Your words, and may overcome when You are judged
Rom 3:10 As *it is written:* "There is none righteous, no, not one
Rom 4:17 (as *it is written*, "I have made you a father of many nations
Rom 8:36 As *it is written:* "For your sake we are killed all day long
Rom 9:13 As *it is written*, "Jacob I have loved, but Esau I have hated
Rom 9:33 As *it is written:* "Behold, I lay in Zion a stumbling stone and rock of offense, and whoever believes on Him will not be put to shame
Rom 10:15 As *it is written:* "How beautiful are the feet of those who preach the gospel of peace, who bring glad tidings of good things
Rom 11:8 Just as *it is written:* "God has given them a spirit of stupor, eyes that they should not

see and ears that they should not hear, to this very day
Rom 11:26 And so all Israel will be saved, as *it is written*
Rom 12:19 for *it is written*, "Vengeance is Mine, I will repay
Rom 14:11 For *it is written:* "As I live says the Lord, every knee shall bow to Me, and every tongue shall confess to God
Rom 15:3 but as *it is written*, "The reproaches of those who reproached You fell on Me
Rom 15:9 and that the Gentiles might glorify God for His mercy, as *it is written*
Rom 15:21 but as *it is written:* "To whom He was not announced, they shall see
1Cor 1:19 For *it is written:* "I will destroy the wisdom of the wise, and bring to nothing the understanding of the prudent
1Cor 1:31 that, as *it is written*, "He who glories, let him glory in the Lord
1Cor 2:9 But as *it is written:* "Eye has not seen, nor ear heard, nor have entered into the heart of man the things which God has prepared for those who love Him
1Cor 3:19 For *it is written*, "He catches the wise in their own craftiness
1Cor 9:9 For *it is written* in the law of Moses, "You shall not muzzle an ox while it treads out the grain
1Cor 10:7 As *it is written*, "The people sat down to eat and drink, and rose up to play
1Cor 14:21 In the law *it is written:* "With men of other tongues and other lips I will speak to this people
1Cor 15:45 And so *it is written*, "The first man Adam became a living being
2Cor 8:15 As *it is written*, "He who gathered much had nothing left over, and he who gathered little had no lack
2Cor 9:9 As *it is written:* "He has dispersed abroad, He has given to the poor
Gal 3:10 for *it is written*, "Cursed is everyone who does not continue in all things which are written in the book of the law, to do them
Gal 3:13 Christ has redeemed us from the curse of the law, having become a curse for us (for *it is written*
Gal 4:22 For *it is written* that Abraham had two sons: the one by a bondwoman, the other by a freewoman
Gal 4:27 For *it is written:* "Rejoice, O barren, you who do not bear
Heb 10:7 Then I said, 'Behold, I have come in the volume of the book *it is written* of Me to do Your will, O God
1Pet 1:16 because *it is written*, "Be holy, for I am holy

IT REPENTED THE LORD (KJV)
(See *LORD WAS MOVED TO PITY*)

IT WAS GOOD
Gen 1:4 And God saw the light, that *it was good;* and God divided the light from the darkness
Gen 1:10 And God called the dry land Earth, and the gathering together of the waters He called Seas. And God saw that *it was good*
Gen 1:12 And the earth brought forth grass, the herb that yields seed according to its kind, and the tree that yields fruit, whose seed is in itself according to its kind. And God saw that *it was good*
Gen 1:18 and to rule over the day and over the night, and to divide the light from the darkness. And God saw that *it was good*
Gen 1:21 So God created great sea creatures and every living thing that moves, with which the waters abounded, according to their kind, and every winged bird according to its kind. And God saw that *it was good*
Gen 1:25 And God made the beast of the earth according to its kind, cattle according to its kind, and everything that creeps on the earth according to its kind. And God saw that *it was good*

IT WILL BE FORGIVEN
Is 33:24 the people who dwell in *it will be forgiven* their iniquity
Matt 12:32 Anyone who speaks a word against the Son of Man, *it will be forgiven* him
Luke 12:10 And anyone who speaks a word against the Son of Man, *it will be forgiven* him

IT'S ALL RIGHT (NIV)
(See *PEACE BE WITH YOU*)

IVORY PALACES
Ps 45:8 All Your garments are scented with myrrh and aloes and cassia, out of the *ivory palaces*, by which they have made You glad

IVORY TOWER
Song 7:4 Your neck is like an *ivory tower*, your eyes like the pools in Heshbon by the gate of Bath Rabbim

J

JACOB I HAVE LOVED
Mal 1:2 "Was not Esau Jacob's brother?" says the Lord. "Yet *Jacob I have loved*
Rom 9:13 As it is written, "*Jacob I have loved*, but Esau I have hated

JAR OF OIL
1Kin 17:14 The bin of flour shall not be used up, nor shall the *jar of oil* run dry, until the day the Lord sends rain on the earth
1Kin 17:16 The bin of flour was not used up, nor did the *jar of oil* run dry, according to the word of the Lord which He spoke by Elijah
2Kin 4:2 And she said, "Your maidservant has nothing in the house but a *jar of oil*

JAWBONE OF A DONKEY
Judg 15:15 He found a fresh *jawbone of a donkey*, reached out his hand and took it, and killed a thousand men with it
Judg 15:16 With the *jawbone of a donkey*, heaps upon heaps, with the *jawbone of a donkey* I have slain a thousand men

JEALOUS FOR JERUSALEM (KJV, NAS, NIV, RSV)
(See *ZEALOUS FOR JERUSALEM*)

JEALOUS GOD
Ex 20:5 For I, the Lord your God, am a *jealous God*, visiting the iniquity of the fathers on the children to the third and fourth generations of those who hate Me
Ex 34:14 (for you shall worship no other god, for the Lord, whose name is Jealous, is a *jealous God*
Deut 4:24 For the Lord your God is a consuming fire, a *jealous God*
Deut 5:9 For I, the Lord your God, am a *jealous God*, visiting the iniquity of the fathers upon the children to the third and fourth generations of those who hate Me
Deut 6:15 (for the Lord your God is a *jealous God* among you
Josh 24:19 He is a *jealous God;* He will not forgive your transgressions nor your sins

JEALOUSY SLAYS (RSV)
(See *ENVY SLAYS*)

JERUSALEM ABOVE IS FREE
Gal 4:26 but the *Jerusalem above is free*, which is the mother of us all

JERUSALEM SURROUNDED BY ARMIES
Luke 21:20 But when you see *Jerusalem surrounded by armies*, then know that its desolation is near

JESUS CHRIST
Matt 1:1 The book of the genealogy of *Jesus Christ*, the Son of David, the Son of Abraham
Matt 1:18 Now the birth of *Jesus Christ* was as follows: After His mother Mary was betrothed to Joseph, before they came together, she was found with child of the Holy Spirit
Mark 1:1 The beginning of the gospel of *Jesus Christ*, the Son of God
John 1:17 For the law was given through Moses, but grace and truth came through *Jesus Christ*
John 17:3 And this is eternal life, that they may know You, the only true God, and *Jesus Christ* whom You have sent
Acts 2:38 Then Peter said to them, "Repent, and let every one of you be baptized in the name of *Jesus Christ* for the remission of sins
Acts 3:6 In the name of *Jesus Christ* of Nazareth, rise up and walk
Acts 3:20 and that He may send *Jesus Christ*, who was preached to you before
Acts 4:10 let it be known to you all, and to all the people of Israel, that by the name of *Jesus Christ* of Nazareth, whom you crucified, whom God raised from the dead, by Him this man stands here before you whole
Acts 8:12 But when they believed Philip as he preached the things concerning the kingdom of God and the name of *Jesus Christ*, both men and women were baptized
Acts 8:37 And he answered and said, "I believe that *Jesus Christ* is the Son of God
Acts 10:36 The word which God sent to the children of Israel, preaching peace through *Jesus Christ* He is Lord of all
Acts 11:17 If therefore God gave them the same gift as He gave us when we believed on the Lord *Jesus Christ*, who was I that I could withstand God
Acts 15:11 But we believe that through the grace of the Lord *Jesus Christ* we shall be saved in the same manner as they
Acts 15:26 men who have risked their lives for the name of our Lord *Jesus Christ*
Acts 16:18 But Paul, greatly annoyed, turned and said to the spirit, "I command you in the name of *Jesus Christ* to come out of her
Acts 16:31 So they said, "Believe on the Lord *Jesus Christ*, and you will be saved, you and your household
Acts 20:21 testifying to Jews, and also to Greeks, repentance toward God and faith toward our Lord *Jesus Christ*
Acts 28:31 preaching the kingdom of God and teaching the things which concern the Lord *Jesus Christ* with all confidence, no one forbidding him
Rom 1:1 Paul, a servant of *Jesus Christ*, called to be an apostle, separated to the gospel of God
Rom 1:3 concerning His Son *Jesus Christ* our Lord, who was born of the seed of David according to the flesh
Rom 1:6 among whom you also are the called of *Jesus Christ*
Rom 1:7 Grace to you and peace from God our Father and the Lord *Jesus Christ*
Rom 1:8 First, I thank my God through *Jesus Christ* for you all, that your faith is spoken of throughout the whole world
Rom 2:16 in the day when God will judge the secrets of men by *Jesus Christ*, according to my gospel
Rom 3:22 even the righteousness of God which is through faith in *Jesus Christ* to all and on all who believe
Rom 5:1 Therefore, having been justified by faith, we have peace with God through our Lord *Jesus Christ*
Rom 5:11 And not only that, but we also rejoice in God through our Lord *Jesus Christ*, through whom we have now received the reconciliation
Rom 5:15 For if by the one man's offense many died, much more the grace of God and the gift by the grace of the one Man, *Jesus Christ*, abounded to many
Rom 5:17 For if by the one man's offense death reigned through the one, much more those who receive abundance of grace and of the gift of righteousness will reign in life through the One, *Jesus Christ*
Rom 5:21 so that as sin reigned in death, even so grace might reign through righteousness to eternal life through *Jesus Christ* our Lord
Rom 7:25 I thank God through *Jesus Christ* our Lord! So then, with the mind I myself serve the law of God, but with the flesh the law of sin
Rom 13:14 But put on the Lord *Jesus Christ*, and make no provision for the flesh, to fulfill its lusts
Rom 15:6 that you may with one mind and one mouth glorify the God and Father of our Lord *Jesus Christ*
Rom 15:8 Now I say that *Jesus Christ* has become a servant to the circumcision for the truth of God, to confirm the promises made to the fathers
Rom 15:16 that I might be a minister of *Jesus Christ* to the Gentiles, ministering the gospel of God, that the offering of the Gentiles might be acceptable, sanctified by the Holy Spirit
Rom 15:30 Now I beg you, brethren, through the Lord *Jesus Christ*, and through the love of the Spirit, that you strive together with me in your prayers to God for me
Rom 16:18 For those who are such do not serve our Lord *Jesus Christ*, but their own belly, and by smooth words and flattering speech deceive the hearts of the simple
Rom 16:20 The grace of our Lord *Jesus Christ* be with you
Rom 16:24 The grace of our Lord *Jesus Christ* be with you all
Rom 16:25 Now to Him who is able to establish you according to my gospel and the preaching of *Jesus Christ*, according to the revelation of the mystery which was kept secret since the world began
Rom 16:27 to God, alone wise, be glory through *Jesus Christ* forever
1Cor 1:1 Paul, called to be an apostle of *Jesus Christ* through the will of God, and Sosthenes our brother
1Cor 1:2 To the church of God which is at Corinth, to those who are sanctified in Christ Jesus, called to be saints, with all who in every place call on the name of *Jesus Christ* our Lord, both theirs and ours
1Cor 1:3 Grace to you and peace from God our Father and the Lord *Jesus Christ*
1Cor 1:7 so that you come short in no gift, eagerly waiting for the revelation of our Lord *Jesus Christ*
1Cor 1:8 who will also confirm you to the end, that you may be blameless in the day of our Lord *Jesus Christ*
1Cor 1:9 God is faithful, by whom you were called

into the fellowship of His Son, *Jesus Christ* our Lord
1Cor 1:10 Now I plead with you, brethren, by the name of our Lord *Jesus Christ*, that you all speak the same thing, and that there be no divisions among you, but that you be perfectly joined together in the same mind and in the same judgment
1Cor 2:2 For I determined not to know anything among you except *Jesus Christ* and Him crucified
1Cor 3:11 For no other foundation can anyone lay than that which is laid, which is *Jesus Christ*
1Cor 5:4 In the name of our Lord *Jesus Christ*, when you are gathered together, along with my spirit, with the power of our Lord *Jesus Christ*
1Cor 8:6 and one Lord *Jesus Christ*, through whom are all things, and through whom we live
1Cor 9:1 Have I not seen *Jesus Christ* our Lord? Are you not my work in the Lord
1Cor 15:57 But thanks be to God, who gives us the victory through our Lord *Jesus Christ*
1Cor 16:22 If anyone does not love the Lord *Jesus Christ*, let him be accursed
1Cor 16:23 The grace of our Lord *Jesus Christ* be with you
2Cor 1:1 Paul, an apostle of *Jesus Christ* by the will of God, and Timothy our brother, to the church of God which is at Corinth, with all the saints who are in all Achaia
2Cor 1:2 Grace to you and peace from God our Father and the Lord *Jesus Christ*
2Cor 1:3 Blessed be the God and Father of our Lord *Jesus Christ*, the Father of mercies and God of all comfort
2Cor 1:19 For the Son of God, *Jesus Christ*, who was preached among you by us by me, Silvanus, and Timothy was not Yes and No, but in Him was Yes
2Cor 4:6 For it is the God who commanded light to shine out of darkness who has shone in our hearts to give the light of the knowledge of the glory of God in the face of *Jesus Christ*
2Cor 5:18 Now all things are of God, who has reconciled us to Himself through *Jesus Christ*, and has given us the ministry of reconciliation
2Cor 8:9 For you know the grace of our Lord *Jesus Christ*, that though He was rich, yet for your sakes He became poor, that you through His poverty might become rich
2Cor 11:31 The God and Father of our Lord *Jesus Christ*, who is blessed forever, knows that I am not lying
2Cor 13:5 Do you not know yourselves, that *Jesus Christ* is in you
2Cor 13:14 The grace of the Lord *Jesus Christ*, and the love of God, and the communion of the Holy Spirit be with you all
Gal 1:1 Paul, an apostle (not from men nor through man, but through *Jesus Christ* and God the Father who raised Him from the dead
Gal 1:3 Grace to you and peace from God the Father and our Lord *Jesus Christ*
Gal 1:12 For I neither received it from man, nor was I taught it, but it came through the revelation of *Jesus Christ*
Gal 2:16 knowing that a man is not justified by the works of the law but by faith in *Jesus Christ*, even we have believed in Christ Jesus, that we might be justified by faith in Christ and not by the works of the law
Gal 3:1 Who has bewitched you that you should not obey the truth, before whose eyes *Jesus Christ* was clearly portrayed among you as crucified
Gal 3:22 But the Scripture has confined all under sin, that the promise by faith in *Jesus Christ* might be given to those who believe
Gal 6:14 But God forbid that I should glory except in the cross of our Lord *Jesus Christ*, by whom the world has been crucified to me, and I to the world
Gal 6:18 Brethren, the grace of our Lord *Jesus Christ* be with your spirit
Eph 1:1 Paul, an apostle of *Jesus Christ* by the will of God, to the saints who are in Ephesus, and faithful in Christ Jesus
Eph 1:2 Grace to you and peace from God our Father and the Lord *Jesus Christ*
Eph 1:3 Blessed be the God and Father of our Lord *Jesus Christ*, who has blessed us with every spiritual blessing in the heavenly places in Christ
Eph 1:5 having predestined us to adoption as sons by *Jesus Christ* to Himself, according to the good pleasure of His will
Eph 1:17 that the God of our Lord *Jesus Christ*, the Father of glory, may give to you the spirit of wisdom and revelation in the knowledge of Him
Eph 2:20 having been built on the foundation of the apostles and prophets, *Jesus Christ* Himself being the chief cornerstone
Eph 3:1 For this reason I, Paul, the prisoner of *Jesus Christ* for you Gentiles
Eph 3:9 and to make all people see what is the fellowship of the mystery, which from the beginning of the ages has been hidden in God who created all things through *Jesus Christ*
Eph 3:14 For this reason I bow my knees to the Father of our Lord *Jesus Christ*
Eph 5:20 giving thanks always for all things to God the Father in the name of our Lord *Jesus Christ*
Eph 6:23 Peace to the brethren, and love with faith, from God the Father and the Lord *Jesus Christ*
Eph 6:24 Grace be with all those who love our Lord *Jesus Christ* in sincerity
Phil 1:1 Paul and Timothy, servants of *Jesus Christ*, to all the saints in Christ Jesus who are in Philippi, with the bishops and deacons
Phil 1:2 Grace to you and peace from God our Father and the Lord *Jesus Christ*
Phil 1:6 being confident of this very thing, that He who has begun a good work in you will complete it until the day of *Jesus Christ*
Phil 1:8 For God is my witness, how greatly I long for you all with the affection of *Jesus Christ*
Phil 1:11 being filled with the fruits of righteousness which are by *Jesus Christ*, to the glory and praise of God
Phil 1:19 For I know that this will turn out for my salvation through your prayer and the supply of the Spirit of *Jesus Christ*
Phil 1:26 that your rejoicing for me may be more abundant in *Jesus Christ* by my coming to you again
Phil 2:11 and that every tongue should confess that *Jesus Christ* is Lord, to the glory of God the Father
Phil 3:20 For our citizenship is in heaven, from which we also eagerly wait for the Savior, the Lord *Jesus Christ*
Phil 4:23 The grace of our Lord *Jesus Christ* be with you all
Col 1:1 Paul, an apostle of *Jesus Christ* by the will of God, and Timothy our brother
Col 1:2 Grace to you and peace from God our Father and the Lord *Jesus Christ*
Col 1:3 We give thanks to the God and Father of our Lord *Jesus Christ*, praying always for you
1Th 1:1 Paul, Silvanus, and Timothy, to the church of the Thessalonians in God the Father and the Lord *Jesus Christ:* Grace to you and peace from God our Father and the Lord *Jesus Christ*
1Th 1:3 remembering without ceasing your work of faith, labor of love, and patience of hope in our

Lord *Jesus Christ* in the sight of our God and Father
1Th 2:19 Is it not even you in the presence of our Lord *Jesus Christ* at His coming
1Th 3:11 Now may our God and Father Himself, and our Lord *Jesus Christ*, direct our way to you
1Th 3:13 so that He may establish your hearts blameless in holiness before our God and Father at the coming of our Lord *Jesus Christ* with all His saints
1Th 5:9 For God did not appoint us to wrath, but to obtain salvation through our Lord *Jesus Christ*
1Th 5:23 and may your whole spirit, soul, and body be preserved blameless at the coming of our Lord *Jesus Christ*
1Th 5:28 The grace of our Lord *Jesus Christ* be with you
2Th 1:1 Paul, Silvanus, and Timothy, to the church of the Thessalonians in God our Father and the Lord *Jesus Christ*
2Th 1:2 Grace to you and peace from God our Father and the Lord *Jesus Christ*
2Th 1:8 in flaming fire taking vengeance on those who do not know God, and on those who do not obey the gospel of our Lord *Jesus Christ*
2Th 1:12 that the name of our Lord *Jesus Christ* may be glorified in you, and you in Him, according to the grace of our God and the Lord *Jesus Christ*
2Th 2:1 Now, brethren, concerning the coming of our Lord *Jesus Christ* and our gathering together to Him, we ask you
2Th 2:14 to which He called you by our gospel, for the obtaining of the glory of our Lord *Jesus Christ*
2Th 2:16 Now may our Lord *Jesus Christ* Himself, and our God and Father, who has loved us and given us everlasting consolation and good hope by grace
2Th 3:6 But we command you, brethren, in the name of our Lord *Jesus Christ*, that you withdraw from every brother who walks disorderly and not according to the tradition which he received from us
2Th 3:12 Now those who are such we command and exhort through our Lord *Jesus Christ* that they work in quietness and eat their own bread
2Th 3:18 The grace of our Lord *Jesus Christ* be with you all
1Tim 1:1 Paul, an apostle of *Jesus Christ*, by the commandment of God our Savior and the Lord *Jesus Christ*, our hope
1Tim 1:2 Grace, mercy, and peace from God our Father and *Jesus Christ* our Lord
1Tim 1:16 However, for this reason I obtained mercy, that in me first *Jesus Christ* might show all longsuffering, as a pattern to those who are going to believe on Him for everlasting life
1Tim 4:6 If you instruct the brethren in these things, you will be a good minister of *Jesus Christ*, nourished in the words of faith and of the good doctrine which you have carefully followed
1Tim 5:21 I charge you before God and the Lord *Jesus Christ* and the elect angels that you observe these things without prejudice, doing nothing with partiality
1Tim 6:3 If anyone teaches otherwise and does not consent to wholesome words, even the words of our Lord *Jesus Christ*, and to the doctrine which is according to godliness
2Tim 1:1 Paul, an apostle of *Jesus Christ* by the will of God, according to the promise of life which is in Christ Jesus
2Tim 1:10 but has now been revealed by the appearing of our Savior *Jesus Christ*, who has abolished death and brought life and immortality to light through the gospel
2Tim 2:3 You therefore must endure hardship as a good soldier of *Jesus Christ*
2Tim 2:8 Remember that *Jesus Christ*, of the seed of David, was raised from the dead according to my gospel
2Tim 4:1 I charge you therefore before God and the Lord *Jesus Christ*, who will judge the living and the dead at His appearing and His kingdom
2Tim 4:22 The Lord *Jesus Christ* be with your spirit. Grace be with you
Tit 1:1 Paul, a servant of God and an apostle of *Jesus Christ*, according to the faith of God's elect and the acknowledgment of the truth which is according to godliness
Tit 1:4 Grace, mercy, and peace from God the Father and the Lord *Jesus Christ* our Savior
Tit 2:13 looking for the blessed hope and glorious appearing of our great God and Savior *Jesus Christ*
Tit 3:6 whom He poured out on us abundantly through *Jesus Christ* our Savior
Phm 3 Grace to you and peace from God our Father and the Lord *Jesus Christ*
Phm 9 yet for love's sake I rather appeal to you being such a one as Paul, the aged, and now also a prisoner of *Jesus Christ*
Phm 25 The grace of our Lord *Jesus Christ* be with your spirit
Heb 10:10 By that will we have been sanctified through the offering of the body of *Jesus Christ* once for all
Heb 13:8 *Jesus Christ* is the same yesterday, today, and forever
Heb 13:21 make you complete in every good work to do His will, working in you what is well pleasing in His sight, through *Jesus Christ*, to whom be glory forever and ever
Jas 1:1 James, a servant of God and of the Lord *Jesus Christ*, to the twelve tribes which are scattered abroad
Jas 2:1 My brethren, do not hold the faith of our Lord *Jesus Christ*, the Lord of glory, with partiality
1Pet 1:1 Peter, an apostle of *Jesus Christ*, to the pilgrims of the Dispersion in Pontus, Galatia, Cappadocia, Asia, and Bithynia
1Pet 1:2 elect according to the foreknowledge of God the Father, in sanctification of the Spirit, for obedience and sprinkling of the blood of *Jesus Christ*
1Pet 1:3 Blessed be the God and Father of our Lord *Jesus Christ*, who according to His abundant mercy has begotten us again to a living hope through the resurrection of *Jesus Christ* from the dead
1Pet 1:7 that the genuineness of your faith, being much more precious than gold that perishes, though it is tested by fire, may be found to praise, honor, and glory at the revelation of *Jesus Christ*
1Pet 1:13 Therefore gird up the loins of your mind, be sober, and rest your hope fully upon the grace that is to be brought to you at the revelation of *Jesus Christ*
1Pet 2:5 you also, as living stones, are being built up a spiritual house, a holy priesthood, to offer up spiritual sacrifices acceptable to God through *Jesus Christ*
1Pet 3:21 There is also an antitype which now saves us, namely baptism (not the removal of the filth of the flesh, but the answer of a good conscience toward God), through the resurrection of *Jesus Christ*
1Pet 4:11 If anyone ministers, let him do it as with the ability which God supplies, that in all things God may be glorified through *Jesus Christ*, to whom belong the glory and the dominion forever and ever
2Pet 1:1 Simon Peter, a servant and apostle of

Jesus Christ, to those who have obtained like precious faith with us by the righteousness of our God and Savior *Jesus Christ*
2Pet 1:8 For if these things are yours and abound, you will be neither barren nor unfruitful in the knowledge of our Lord *Jesus Christ*
2Pet 1:11 for so an entrance will be supplied to you abundantly into the everlasting kingdom of our Lord and Savior *Jesus Christ*
2Pet 1:14 knowing that shortly I must put off my tent, just as our Lord *Jesus Christ* showed me
2Pet 1:16 For we did not follow cunningly devised fables when we made known to you the power and coming of our Lord *Jesus Christ*, but were eyewitnesses of His majesty
2Pet 2:20 For if, after they have escaped the pollutions of the world through the knowledge of the Lord and Savior *Jesus Christ*, they are again entangled in them and overcome, the latter end is worse for them than the beginning
2Pet 3:18 but grow in the grace and knowledge of our Lord and Savior *Jesus Christ*
1Jn 1:3 and truly our fellowship is with the Father and with His Son *Jesus Christ*
1Jn 1:7 But if we walk in the light as He is in the light, we have fellowship with one another, and the blood of *Jesus Christ* His Son cleanses us from all sin
1Jn 2:1 And if anyone sins, we have an Advocate with the Father, *Jesus Christ* the righteous
1Jn 3:23 that we should believe on the name of His Son *Jesus Christ* and love one another, as He gave us commandment
1Jn 4:2 Every spirit that confesses that *Jesus Christ* has come in the flesh is of God
1Jn 4:3 and every spirit that does not confess that *Jesus Christ* has come in the flesh is not of God
1Jn 5:6 This is He who came by water and blood *Jesus Christ*
1Jn 5:20 and we are in Him who is true, in His Son *Jesus Christ*
2Jn 3 Grace, mercy, and peace will be with you from God the Father and from the Lord *Jesus Christ*, the Son of the Father, in truth and love
2Jn 7 For many deceivers have gone out into the world who do not confess *Jesus Christ* as coming in the flesh
Jude 1 Jude, a servant of *Jesus Christ*, and brother of James, to those who are called, sanctified by God the Father, and preserved in *Jesus Christ*
Jude 4 For certain men have crept in unnoticed, who long ago were marked out for this condemnation, ungodly men, who turn the grace of our God into licentiousness and deny the only Lord God and our Lord *Jesus Christ*
Jude 17 But you, beloved, remember the words which were spoken before by the apostles of our Lord *Jesus Christ*
Jude 21 keep yourselves in the love of God, looking for the mercy of our Lord *Jesus Christ* unto eternal life
Rev 1:1 The Revelation of *Jesus Christ*, which God gave Him to show His servants things which must shortly take place
Rev 1:2 who bore witness to the word of God, and to the testimony of *Jesus Christ*, and to all things that he saw
Rev 1:5 and from *Jesus Christ*, the faithful witness, the firstborn from the dead, and the ruler over the kings of the earth
Rev 1:9 I, John, both your brother and companion in tribulation, and in the kingdom and patience of *Jesus Christ*, was on the island that is called Patmos for the word of God and for the testimony of *Jesus Christ*
Rev 12:17 And the dragon was enraged with the woman, and he went to make war with the rest of her offspring, who keep the commandments of God and have the testimony of *Jesus Christ*
Rev 22:21 The grace of our Lord *Jesus Christ* be with you all

JESUS CHRIST THE RIGHTEOUS
1Jn 2:1 And if anyone sins, we have an Advocate with the Father, *Jesus Christ the righteous*

JESUS CRIED OUT
Matt 27:46 And about the ninth hour *Jesus cried out* with a loud voice, saying
Mark 15:34 And at the ninth hour *Jesus cried out* with a loud voice, saying
Mark 15:37 And *Jesus cried out* with a loud voice, and breathed His last
John 7:28 Then *Jesus cried out*, as He taught in the temple, saying
John 12:44 Then *Jesus cried out* and said, "He who believes in Me, believes not in Me but in Him who sent Me

JESUS DID MANY OTHER THINGS (NIV)
(See *MANY OTHER THINGS THAT JESUS DID*)

JESUS IS LORD
1Cor 12:3 Therefore I make known to you that no one speaking by the Spirit of God calls Jesus accursed, and no one can say that *Jesus is Lord* except by the Holy Spirit

JESUS IS THE CHRIST
John 20:31 but these are written that you may believe that *Jesus is the Christ*, the Son of God, and that believing you may have life in His name
Acts 9:22 But Saul increased all the more in strength, and confounded the Jews who dwelt in Damascus, proving that this *Jesus is the Christ*
Acts 18:5 When Silas and Timothy had come from Macedonia, Paul was constrained by the Spirit, and testified to the Jews that *Jesus is the Christ*
Acts 18:28 for he vigorously refuted the Jews publicly, showing from the Scriptures that *Jesus is the Christ*
1Jn 2:22 Who is a liar but he who denies that *Jesus is the Christ*
1Jn 5:1 Whoever believes that *Jesus is the Christ* is born of God, and everyone who loves Him who begot also loves him who is begotten of Him

JESUS OF NAZARETH
Matt 26:71 And when he had gone out to the gateway, another girl saw him and said to those who were there, "This fellow also was with *Jesus of Nazareth*
Mark 1:24 What have we to do with You, *Jesus of Nazareth*
Mark 10:47 And when he heard that it was *Jesus of Nazareth*, he began to cry out and say
Mark 14:67 And when she saw Peter warming himself, she looked at him and said, "You also were with *Jesus of Nazareth*
Mark 16:6 You seek *Jesus of Nazareth*, who was crucified. He is risen
Luke 4:34 What have we to do with You, *Jesus of Nazareth*
Luke 18:37 So they told him that *Jesus of Nazareth* was passing by
Luke 24:19 And they said to Him, "The things concerning *Jesus of Nazareth*, who was a Prophet mighty in deed and word before God and all the people
John 1:45 Philip found Nathanael and said to him, "We have found Him of whom Moses in the law, and also the prophets, wrote *Jesus of Nazareth*, the son of Joseph

John 18:5 They answered Him, "*Jesus of Nazareth.*" Jesus said to them
John 18:7 Then He asked them again, "Whom are you seeking?" And they said, "*Jesus of Nazareth*
John 19:19 And the writing was: Jesus of Nazareth, the King of the Jews,
Acts 2:22 *Jesus of Nazareth*, a Man attested by God to you by miracles, wonders, and signs which God did through Him in your midst, as you yourselves also know
Acts 6:14 for we have heard him say that this *Jesus of Nazareth* will destroy this place and change the customs which Moses delivered to us
Acts 10:38 how God anointed *Jesus of Nazareth* with the Holy Spirit and with power, who went about doing good and healing all who were oppressed by the devil, for God was with Him
Acts 22:8 And He said to me, 'I am *Jesus of Nazareth*, whom you are persecuting
Acts 26:9 Indeed, I myself thought I must do many things contrary to the name of *Jesus of Nazareth*

JESUS SAID
Matt 4:7 *Jesus said* to him, "It is written again, 'You shall not tempt the Lord your God
Matt 4:10 Then *Jesus said* to him, "Away with you, Satan! For it is written
Matt 8:4 And *Jesus said* to him, "See that you tell no one
Matt 8:7 And *Jesus said* to him, "I will come and heal him
Matt 8:13 Then *Jesus said* to the centurion, "Go your way; and as you have believed, so let it be done for you
Matt 8:20 And *Jesus said* to him, "Foxes have holes and birds of the air have nests, but the Son of Man has nowhere to lay His head
Matt 8:22 But *Jesus said* to him, "Follow Me, and let the dead bury their own dead
Matt 9:15 And *Jesus said* to them, "Can the friends of the bridegroom mourn as long as the bridegroom is with them
Matt 9:28 And *Jesus said* to them, "Do you believe that I am able to do this
Matt 13:51 *Jesus said* to them, "Have you understood all these things
Matt 13:57 But *Jesus said* to them, "A prophet is not without honor except in his own country and in his own house
Matt 14:16 But *Jesus said* to them, "They do not need to go away
Matt 15:16 So *Jesus said*, "Are you also still without understanding
Matt 15:34 *Jesus said* to them, "How many loaves do you have
Matt 16:6 Then *Jesus said* to them, "Take heed and beware of the leaven of the Pharisees and the Sadducees
Matt 16:24 Then *Jesus said* to His disciples, "If anyone desires to come after Me, let him deny himself, and take up his cross, and follow Me
Matt 17:20 So *Jesus said* to them, "Because of your unbelief; for assuredly, I say to you, if you have faith as a mustard seed, you will say to this mountain
Matt 17:22 Now while they were staying in Galilee, *Jesus said* to them
Matt 17:26 Peter said to Him, "From strangers." *Jesus said* to him, "Then the sons are free
Matt 18:22 *Jesus said* to him, "I do not say to you, up to seven times, but up to seventy times seven
Matt 19:14 But *Jesus said*, "Let the little children come to Me, and do not forbid them
Matt 19:18 *Jesus said*, "'You shall not murder,' 'You shall not commit adultery
Matt 19:21 *Jesus said* to him, "If you want to be perfect, go, sell what you have and give to the poor, and you will have treasure in heaven
Matt 19:23 Then *Jesus said* to His disciples, "Assuredly, I say to you that it is hard for a rich man to enter the kingdom of heaven
Matt 19:28 So *Jesus said* to them, "Assuredly I say to you, that in the regeneration, when the Son of Man sits on the throne of His glory, you who have followed Me will also sit on twelve thrones, judging the twelve tribes of Israel
Matt 21:16 And *Jesus said* to them, "Yes. Have you never read
Matt 21:31 *Jesus said* to them, "Assuredly, I say to you that tax collectors and harlots enter the kingdom of God before you
Matt 21:42 *Jesus said* to them, "Did you never read in the Scriptures
Matt 22:37 *Jesus said* to him, "'You shall love the Lord your God with all your heart, with all your soul, and with all your mind
Matt 24:2 And *Jesus said* to them, "Do you not see all these things
Matt 26:31 Then *Jesus said* to them, "All of you will be made to stumble because of Me this night, for it is written
Matt 26:34 *Jesus said* to him, "Assuredly, I say to you that this night, before the rooster crows, you will deny Me three times
Matt 26:50 And *Jesus said* to him, "Friend, why have you come
Matt 26:52 Then *Jesus said* to him, "Put your sword in its place, for all who take the sword will perish by the sword
Matt 26:55 In that hour *Jesus said* to the multitudes, "Have you come out, as against a robber, with swords and clubs to take Me
Matt 26:64 *Jesus said* to him, "It is as you said. Nevertheless, I say to you, hereafter you will see the Son of Man sitting at the right hand of the Power, and coming on the clouds of heaven
Matt 27:11 So *Jesus said* to him, "It is as you say
Matt 28:10 Then *Jesus said* to them, "Do not be afraid. Go and tell My brethren to go to Galilee, and there they will see Me
Mark 1:17 Then *Jesus said* to them, "Come after Me, and I will make you become fishers of men
Mark 2:19 So *Jesus said* to them, "Can the friends of the bridegroom fast while the bridegroom is with them
Mark 6:4 But *Jesus said* to them, "A prophet is not without honor except in his own country, among his own relatives, and in his own house
Mark 7:27 But *Jesus said* to her, "Let the children be filled first, for it is not good to take the children's bread and throw it to the little dogs
Mark 9:23 *Jesus said* to him, "If you can believe, all things are possible to him who believes
Mark 9:39 But *Jesus said*, "Do not forbid him, for no one who works a miracle in My name can soon afterward speak evil of Me
Mark 10:18 So *Jesus said* to him, "Why do you call Me good
Mark 10:27 But looking at them, *Jesus said*, "With men it is impossible, but not with God
Mark 10:38 But *Jesus said* to them, "You do not know what you ask
Mark 10:39 And *Jesus said* to them, "You will indeed drink the cup that I drink, and with the baptism I am baptized with you will be baptized
Mark 10:52 Then *Jesus said* to him, "Go your way; your faith has made you well
Mark 11:14 In response *Jesus said* to it, "Let no one eat fruit from you ever again
Mark 14:6 But *Jesus said*, "Let her alone. Why do you trouble her
Mark 14:18 Now as they sat and ate, *Jesus said*, "Assuredly, I say to you, one of you who eats with Me will betray Me

Mark 14:27 Then *Jesus said* to them, "All of you will be made to stumble because of Me this night, for it is written
Mark 14:30 And *Jesus said* to him, "Assuredly, I say to you that today, even this night, before the rooster crows twice, you will deny Me three times
Mark 14:62 And *Jesus said*, "I am. And you will see the Son of Man sitting at the right hand of the Power, and coming with the clouds of heaven
Luke 5:10 And *Jesus said* to Simon, "Do not be afraid. From now on you will catch men
Luke 6:9 Then *Jesus said* to them, "I will ask you one thing
Luke 8:45 And *Jesus said*, "Who touched Me?" When all denied it, Peter and those with him said
Luke 8:46 But *Jesus said*, "Somebody touched Me, for I perceived power going out from Me
Luke 9:50 But *Jesus said* to him, "Do not forbid him, for he who is not against us is for us
Luke 9:58 And *Jesus said* to him, "Foxes have holes and birds of the air have nests, but the Son of Man has nowhere to lay His head
Luke 9:60 *Jesus said* to him, "Let the dead bury their own dead, but you go and preach the kingdom of God
Luke 9:62 But *Jesus said* to him, "No one, having put his hand to the plow, and looking back, is fit for the kingdom of God
Luke 10:37 And he said, "He who showed mercy on him." Then *Jesus said* to him, "Go and do likewise
Luke 18:19 So *Jesus said* to him, "Why do you call Me good
Luke 18:42 Then *Jesus said* to him, "Receive your sight; your faith has saved you
Luke 19:9 And *Jesus said* to him, "Today salvation has come to this house, because he also is a son of Abraham
Luke 20:8 And *Jesus said* to them, "Neither will I tell you by what authority I do these things
Luke 22:48 But *Jesus said* to him, "Judas, are you betraying the Son of Man with a kiss
Luke 22:52 Then *Jesus said* to the chief priests, captains of the temple, and the elders who had come to Him
Luke 23:34 Then *Jesus said*, "Father, forgive them, for they do not know what they do
Luke 23:43 And *Jesus said* to him, "Assuredly, I say to you, today you will be with Me in Paradise
John 2:3 And when they ran out of wine, the mother of *Jesus said* to Him
John 2:4 *Jesus said* to her, "Woman, what does your concern have to do with Me
John 2:7 *Jesus said* to them, "Fill the waterpots with water." And they filled them up to the brim
John 4:7 A woman of Samaria came to draw water. *Jesus said* to her, "Give Me a drink
John 4:16 *Jesus said* to her, "Go, call your husband, and come here
John 4:17 *Jesus said* to her, "You have well said, 'I have no husband
John 4:21 *Jesus said* to her, "Woman, believe Me, the hour is coming when you will neither on this mountain, nor in Jerusalem, worship the Father
John 4:26 *Jesus said* to her, "I who speak to you am He
John 4:34 *Jesus said* to them, "My food is to do the will of Him who sent Me, and to finish His work
John 4:48 Then *Jesus said* to him, "Unless you people see signs and wonders, you will by no means believe
John 4:50 *Jesus said* to him, "Go your way; your son lives
John 4:53 So the father knew that it was at the same hour in which *Jesus said* to him
John 5:8 *Jesus said* to him, "Rise, take up your bed and walk
John 6:10 Then *Jesus said*, "Make the people sit down." Now there was much grass in the place
John 6:32 Then *Jesus said* to them, "Most assuredly, I say to you, Moses did not give you the bread from heaven, but My Father gives you the true bread from heaven
John 6:35 And *Jesus said* to them, "I am the bread of life
John 6:53 Then *Jesus said* to them, "Most assuredly, I say to you, unless you eat the flesh of the Son of Man and drink His blood, you have no life in you
John 6:67 Then *Jesus said* to the twelve, "Do you also want to go away
John 7:6 Then *Jesus said* to them, "My time has not yet come, but your time is always ready
John 7:33 Then *Jesus said* to them, "I shall be with you a little while longer, and then I go to Him who sent Me
John 8:11 And *Jesus said* to her, "Neither do I condemn you
John 8:21 Then *Jesus said* to them again, "I am going away, and you will seek Me, and will die in your sin
John 8:25 And *Jesus said* to them, "Just what I have been saying to you from the beginning
John 8:28 Then *Jesus said* to them, "When you lift up the Son of Man, then you will know that I am He, and that I do nothing of Myself
John 8:31 Then *Jesus said* to those Jews who believed Him, "If you abide in My word, you are My disciples indeed
John 8:39 *Jesus said* to them, "If you were Abraham's children, you would do the works of Abraham
John 8:42 *Jesus said* to them, "If God were your Father, you would love Me, for I proceeded forth and came from God
John 8:58 *Jesus said* to them, "Most assuredly, I say to you, before Abraham was, I AM
John 9:37 And *Jesus said* to him, "You have both seen Him and it is He who is talking with you
John 9:39 And *Jesus said*, "For judgment I have come into this world, that those who do not see may see, and that those who see may be made blind
John 9:41 *Jesus said* to them, "If you were blind, you would have no sin
John 10:7 Then *Jesus said* to them again, "Most assuredly, I say to you, I am the door of the sheep
John 11:14 Then *Jesus said* to them plainly, "Lazarus is dead
John 11:23 *Jesus said* to her, "Your brother will rise again
John 11:25 *Jesus said* to her, "I am the resurrection and the life
John 11:39 *Jesus said*, "Take away the stone." Martha, the sister of him who was dead, said to Him
John 11:40 *Jesus said* to her, "Did I not say to you that if you would believe you would see the glory of God
John 11:44 *Jesus said* to them, "Loose him, and let him go
John 12:7 Then *Jesus said*, "Let her alone; she has kept this for the day of My burial
John 12:35 Then *Jesus said* to them, "A little while longer the light is with you
John 13:10 *Jesus said* to him, "He who is bathed needs only to wash his feet, but is completely clean
John 13:27 Then *Jesus said* to him, "What you do, do quickly
John 13:31 So, when he had gone out, *Jesus said*, "Now the Son of Man is glorified, and God is glorified in Him
John 14:6 *Jesus said* to him, "I am the way, the truth, and the life

John 14:9 *Jesus said* to him, "Have I been with you so long, and yet you have not known Me, Philip
John 18:5 *Jesus said* to them, "I am He." And Judas, who betrayed Him, also stood with them
John 18:11 Then *Jesus said* to Peter, "Put your sword into the sheath
John 20:15 *Jesus said* to her, "Woman, why are you weeping? Whom are you seeking
John 20:16 *Jesus said* to her, "Mary!" She turned and said to Him
John 20:17 *Jesus said* to her, "Do not cling to Me, for I have not yet ascended to My Father
John 20:21 Then *Jesus said* to them again, "Peace to you! As the Father has sent Me, I also send you
John 20:29 *Jesus said* to him, "Thomas, because you have seen Me, you have believed
John 21:5 Then *Jesus said* to them, "Children, have you any food
John 21:10 *Jesus said* to them, "Bring some of the fish which you have just caught
John 21:12 *Jesus said* to them, "Come and eat breakfast." Yet none of the disciples dared ask Him
John 21:15 So when they had eaten breakfast, *Jesus said* to Simon Peter
John 21:17 You know that I love You." *Jesus said* to him, "Feed My sheep
John 21:22 *Jesus said* to him, "If I will that he remain till I come, what is that to you

JESUS THE MEDIATOR
Heb 12:24 to *Jesus the Mediator* of the new covenant, and to the blood of sprinkling that speaks better things than that of Abel

JESUS WEPT
John 11:35 *Jesus wept*

JESUS' MOTHER (NIV)
(See *MOTHER OF JESUS*)

JEW FIRST AND ALSO FOR THE GREEK
Rom 1:16 For I am not ashamed of the gospel of Christ, for it is the power of God to salvation for everyone who believes, for the *Jew first and also for the Greek*

JEWEL OF KINGDOMS (NIV)
(See *GLORY OF KINGDOMS*)

JEWISH PASSOVER (NIV)
(See *PASSOVER OF THE JEWS*)

JEWISH SYNAGOGUE (NIV, RSV)
(See *SYNAGOGUE OF THE JEWS*)

JEWS AND GREEKS
Acts 18:4 And he reasoned in the synagogue every Sabbath, and persuaded both *Jews and Greeks*
Acts 19:10 And this continued for two years, so that all who dwelt in Asia heard the word of the Lord Jesus, both *Jews and Greeks*
Acts 19:17 This became known both to all *Jews and Greeks* dwelling in Ephesus
Rom 3:9 For we have previously charged both *Jews and Greeks* that they are all under sin
1Cor 1:24 but to those who are called, both *Jews and Greeks*, Christ the power of God and the wisdom of God

JEWS' ENEMY (KJV)
(See *ENEMY OF THE JEWS*)

JEWS' PASSOVER (KJV)
(See *PASSOVER OF THE JEWS*)

JOHN'S TESTIMONY (NIV)
(See *TESTIMONY OF JOHN*)

JOINT HEIRS WITH CHRIST
Rom 8:17 and if children, then heirs—heirs of God and *joint heirs with Christ*, if indeed we suffer with Him, that we may also be glorified together

JOURNEYED TO A FAR COUNTRY
Luke 15:13 And not many days after, the younger son gathered all together, *journeyed to a far country*, and there wasted his possessions with prodigal living

JOY AND GLADNESS
Deut 28:47 Because you did not serve the Lord your God with *joy and gladness* of heart, for the abundance of all things
Esth 8:17 And in every province and city, wherever the king's command and decree came, the Jews had *joy and gladness*, a feast and a holiday
Ps 51:8 Make me to hear *joy and gladness*, That the bones which You have broken may rejoice
Is 22:13 But instead, *joy and gladness*, slaying oxen and killing sheep, eating meat and drinking wine
Is 35:10 They shall obtain *joy and gladness*, and sorrow and sighing shall flee away
Is 51:3 *joy and gladness* will be found in it, thanksgiving and the voice of melody
Is 51:11 They shall obtain *joy and gladness*, and sorrow and sighing shall flee away
Jer 48:33 *Joy and gladness* are taken from the plentiful field and from the land of Moab
Joel 1:16 Is not the food cut off before our eyes, *joy and gladness* from the house of our God
Zech 8:19 The fast of the fourth month, the fast of the fifth, the fast of the seventh, and the fast of the tenth, shall be *joy and gladness* and cheerful feasts for the house of Judah
Luke 1:14 And you will have *joy and gladness*, and many will rejoice at his birth

JOY INEXPRESSIBLE
1Pet 1:8 Though now you do not see Him, yet believing, you rejoice with *joy inexpressible* and full of glory

JOY MAY BE FULL
John 15:11 These things I have spoken to you, that My joy may remain in you, and that your *joy may be full*
John 16:24 Ask, and you will receive, that your *joy may be full*
1Jn 1:4 And these things we write to you that your *joy may be full*
2Jn 12 but I hope to come to you and speak face to face, that our *joy may be full*

JOY OF ALL THE EARTH (RSV)
(See *JOY OF THE WHOLE EARTH*)

JOY OF THE HOLY SPIRIT
1Th 1:6 And you became followers of us and of the Lord, having received the word in much affliction, with *joy of the Holy Spirit*

JOY OF THE LORD
Neh 8:10 Do not sorrow, for the *joy of the Lord* is your strength

JOY OF THE WHOLE EARTH
Ps 48:2 Beautiful in elevation, the *joy of the whole earth*, is Mount Zion on the sides of the north, the city of the great King
Lam 2:15 Is this the city that is called 'the perfection of beauty, the *joy of the whole earth*

JOY OF TITUS
2Cor 7:13 And we rejoiced exceedingly more for the *joy of Titus*, because his spirit has been refreshed by you all

JOY UNSPEAKABLE (KJV)
(See *JOY INEXPRESSIBLE*)

JOYFUL SHOUT
Job 3:7 Oh, may that night be barren! May no *joyful shout* come into it
Ps 66:1 Make a *joyful shout* to God, all the earth
Ps 81:1 Sing aloud to God our strength; make a *joyful shout* to the God of Jacob
Ps 100:1 Make a *joyful shout* to the Lord, all you lands

JOYFULLY AND GLADLY (NIV)
(See *JOY AND GLADNESS*)

JOYFULNESS, AND WITH GLADNESS (KJV)
(See *JOY AND GLADNESS*)

JUDAH AND JERUSALEM
2Kin 18:22 But if you say to me, 'We trust in the Lord our God,' is it not He whose high places and whose altars Hezekiah has taken away, and said to *Judah and Jerusalem*
2Kin 23:1 Then the king sent them to gather all the elders of *Judah and Jerusalem* to him
1Chr 6:15 Jehozadak went into captivity when the Lord carried *Judah and Jerusalem* into captivity by the hand of Nebuchadnezzar
2Chr 2:7 Therefore send me at once a man skillful to work in gold and silver, in bronze and iron, in purple and crimson and blue, who has skill to engrave with the skillful men who are with me in *Judah and Jerusalem*, whom David my father provided
2Chr 11:14 For the Levites left their common-lands and their possessions and came to *Judah and Jerusalem*, for Jeroboam and his sons had rejected them from serving as priests to the Lord
2Chr 20:5 Then Jehoshaphat stood in the congregation of *Judah and Jerusalem*, in the house of the Lord, before the new court
2Chr 20:17 Position yourselves, stand still and see the salvation of the Lord, who is with you, O *Judah and Jerusalem*
2Chr 20:27 Then they returned, every man of *Judah and Jerusalem*, with Jehoshaphat in front of them, to go back to Jerusalem with joy, for the Lord had made them rejoice over their enemies
2Chr 24:9 And they made a proclamation throughout *Judah and Jerusalem* to bring to the Lord the collection that Moses the servant of God had imposed on Israel in the wilderness
2Chr 24:18 and wrath came upon *Judah and Jerusalem* because of their trespass
2Chr 24:23 and they came to *Judah and Jerusalem*, and destroyed all the leaders of the people from among the people, and sent all their spoil to the king of Damascus
2Chr 28:10 And now you propose to force the children of *Judah and Jerusalem* to be your male and female slaves
2Chr 29:8 Therefore the wrath of the Lord fell upon *Judah and Jerusalem*, and He has given them up to trouble, to astonishment, and to jeering, as you see with your eyes
2Chr 32:12 Has not the same Hezekiah taken away His high places and His altars, and commanded *Judah and Jerusalem*, saying
2Chr 32:25 therefore wrath was looming over him and over *Judah and Jerusalem*
2Chr 34:3 and in the twelfth year he began to purge *Judah and Jerusalem* of the high places, the wooden images, the carved images, and the molded images
2Chr 34:5 He also burned the bones of the priests on their altars, and cleansed *Judah and Jerusalem*
2Chr 34:29 Then the king sent and gathered all the elders of *Judah and Jerusalem*
2Chr 35:24 So he died, and was buried in one of the tombs of his fathers. And all *Judah and Jerusalem* mourned for Josiah
2Chr 36:4 Then the king of Egypt made his brother Eliakim king over *Judah and Jerusalem*, and changed his name to Jehoiakim
2Chr 36:10 At the turn of the year King Nebuchadnezzar summoned him and took him to Babylon, with the costly articles from the house of the Lord, and made Zedekiah, Jehoiakim's brother, king over *Judah and Jerusalem*
Ezra 4:6 Now in the reign of Ahasuerus, in the beginning of his reign, they wrote an accusation against the inhabitants of *Judah and Jerusalem*
Ezra 5:1 Then the prophet Haggai and Zechariah the son of Iddo, prophets, prophesied to the Jews who were in *Judah and Jerusalem*, in the name of the God of Israel, who was over them
Ezra 7:14 And whereas you are being sent by the king and his seven counselors to inquire concerning *Judah and Jerusalem*, with regard to the Law of your God which is in your hand
Ezra 9:9 but He extended mercy to us in the sight of the kings of Persia, to revive us, to repair the house of our God, to rebuild its ruins, and to give us a wall in *Judah and Jerusalem*
Ezra 10:7 And they issued a proclamation throughout *Judah and Jerusalem* to all the descendants of the captivity, that they must gather at Jerusalem
Is 1:1 The vision of Isaiah the son of Amoz, which he saw concerning *Judah and Jerusalem* in the days of Uzziah, Jotham, Ahaz, and Hezekiah, kings of Judah
Is 2:1 The word that Isaiah the son of Amoz saw concerning *Judah and Jerusalem*
Is 36:7 But if you say to me, 'We trust in the Lord our God,' is it not He whose high places and whose altars Hezekiah has taken away, and said to *Judah and Jerusalem*
Jer 4:3 For thus says the Lord to the men of *Judah and Jerusalem*
Jer 19:7 And I will make void the counsel of *Judah and Jerusalem* in this place, and I will cause them to fall by the sword before their enemies and by the hands of those who seek their lives
Jer 27:20 which Nebuchadnezzar king of Babylon did not take, when he carried away captive Jeconiah the son of Jehoiakim, king of Judah, from Jerusalem to Babylon, and all the nobles of *Judah and Jerusalem*
Jer 29:2 (This happened after Jeconiah the king, the queen mother, the eunuchs, the princes of *Judah and Jerusalem*, the craftsmen, and the smiths had departed from Jerusalem
Joel 3:1 For behold, in those days and at that time, when I bring back the captives of *Judah and Jerusalem*
Zech 12:2 Behold, I will make Jerusalem a cup of drunkenness to all the surrounding peoples, when they lay siege against *Judah and Jerusalem*
Mal 3:4 Then the offering of *Judah and Jerusalem* will be pleasant to the Lord, as in the days of old, as in former years

JUDAH BECAME STRONG AMONG HIS BROTHERS (RSV)
(See *JUDAH PREVAILED OVER HIS BROTHERS*)

JUDAH PREVAILED OVER HIS BROTHERS
1Chr 5:2 yet *Judah prevailed over his brothers*, and from him came a ruler, although the birthright was Joseph's

JUDAH WAS THE STRONGEST OF HIS BROTHERS (NIV)
(See *JUDAH PREVAILED OVER HIS BROTHERS*)

JUDGE ACCORDING TO THE FLESH
John 8:15 You *judge according to the flesh;* I judge no one

JUDGE ME (KJV)
(See *VINDICATE ME*)

JUDGE OF THE EARTH
Ps 94:2 Rise up, O *Judge of the earth;* render punishment to the proud

JUDGE OF THE WIDOWS (KJV)
(See *DEFENDER OF WIDOWS*)

JUDGE THE FATHERLESS (KJV)
(See *DEFEND THE FATHERLESS*)

JUDGE THE POOR (KJV)
(See *JUSTICE TO THE POOR*)

JUDGE THE WORLD IN RIGHTEOUSNESS
Ps 9:8 He shall *judge the world in righteousness*, and He shall administer judgment for the peoples in uprightness
Acts 17:31 because He has appointed a day on which He will *judge the world in righteousness* by the Man whom He has ordained

JUDGE WITH RIGHTEOUS JUDGMENT
John 7:24 Do not judge according to appearance, but *judge with righteous judgment*

JUDGED BY THE LAW
Rom 2:12 For as many as have sinned without law will also perish without law, and as many as have sinned in the law will be *judged by the law*
Jas 2:12 So speak and so do as those who will be *judged by the law* of liberty

JUDGED THE CAUSE OF THE POOR
Jer 22:16 He *judged the cause of the poor* and needy; then it was well

JUDGES OF ISRAEL
Num 25:5 So Moses said to the *judges of Israel*, "Every one of you kill his men who were joined to Baal of Peor
1Chr 17:6 Wherever I have moved about with all Israel, have I ever spoken a word to any of the *judges of Israel*, whom I commanded to shepherd My people, saying

JUDGES OF THE EARTH
Ps 2:10 Now therefore, be wise, O kings; be instructed, you *judges of the earth*
Ps 148:11 Kings of the earth and all peoples; princes and all *judges of the earth*
Prov 8:16 By me princes rule, and nobles, all the *judges of the earth*
Is 40:23 He brings the princes to nothing; He makes the *judges of the earth* useless

JUDGES THE THOUGHTS (NIV)
(See *DISCERNER OF THE THOUGHTS*)

JUDGING THE TWELVE TRIBES
Matt 19:28 So Jesus said to them, "Assuredly I say to you, that in the regeneration, when the Son of Man sits on the throne of His glory, you who have followed Me will also sit on twelve thrones, *judging the twelve tribes* of Israel
Luke 22:30 that you may eat and drink at My table in My kingdom, and sit on thrones *judging the twelve tribes* of Israel

JUDGMENT AND JUSTICE (KJV)
(See *JUSTICE AND RIGHTEOUSNESS*)

JUDGMENT OF GOD
Rom 1:32 who, knowing the righteous *judgment of God*, that those who practice such things are worthy of death, not only do the same but also approve of those who practice them
Rom 2:2 But we know that the *judgment of God* is according to truth against those who practice such things
Rom 2:3 And do you think this, O man, you who judge those practicing such things, and doing the same, that you will escape the *judgment of God*
Rom 2:5 But in accordance with your hardness and your impenitent heart you are treasuring up for yourself wrath in the day of wrath and revelation of the righteous *judgment of God*
2Th 1:5 which is manifest evidence of the righteous *judgment of God*, that you may be counted worthy of the kingdom of God, for which you also suffer

JUDGMENT OF THIS WORLD (NIV, RSV)
(See *RULER OF THIS WORLD*)

JUDGMENT SEAT OF CHRIST
Rom 14:10 For we shall all stand before the *judgment seat of Christ*
2Cor 5:10 For we must all appear before the *judgment seat of Christ*, that each one may receive the things done in the body, according to what he has done, whether good or bad

JUDGMENT TO THE GENTILES (KJV)
(See *JUSTICE TO THE GENTILES*)

JUDGMENTS OF THE LORD
Ps 19:9 The *judgments of the Lord* are true and righteous altogether

JUDGMENTS OF THE NATIONS
Ezek 5:7 Because you have multiplied disobedience more than the nations that are all around you, and have not walked in My statutes, nor kept My judgments, nor even done according to the *judgments of the nations* that are all around you

JUDGMENTS SO RIGHTEOUS (KJV)
(See *RIGHTEOUS JUDGMENTS*)

JUG OF OIL (NIV)
(See *JAR OF OIL*)

JUMPED UP AND BEGAN TO WALK (NIV)
(See *LEAPED AND WALKED*)

JUNCTION OF THE TWO ROADS (NIV)
(See *FORK OF THE TWO ROADS*)

JUST AND RIGHT FOR ALL HIS PEOPLE (NIV)
(See *JUSTICE TO ALL HIS PEOPLE*)

JUST AS HE IS PURE
1Jn 3:3 And everyone who has this hope in Him purifies himself, *just as He is pure*

JUST AS HE IS RIGHTEOUS
1Jn 3:7 He who practices righteousness is righteous, *just as He is righteous*

JUST AS THE LORD HAD SAID
Ex 8:19 But Pharaoh's heart grew hard, and he did not heed them, *just as the Lord had said*
Num 16:40 to be a memorial to the children of Israel that no outsider, who is not a descendant of Aaron, should come near to offer incense before the Lord, that he might not become like Korah and his companions, *just as the Lord had said* to him through Moses

JUST BALANCE
Job 31:6 Let me be weighed in a *just balance*, that God may know my integrity

JUST BALANCES
Lev 19:36 You shall have *just balances*, just weights, a just ephah, and a just hin
Ezek 45:10 You shall have *just balances*, a just ephah, and a just bath

JUST DECREES OF THE LORD (RSV)
(See *JUSTICE OF THE LORD*)

JUST ORDINANCES
Neh 9:13 You came down also on Mount Sinai, and spoke with them from heaven, and gave them *just ordinances* and true laws, good statutes and commandments

JUST REWARD
Is 49:4 yet surely my *just reward* is with the Lord, and my work with my God
Heb 2:2 For if the word spoken through angels proved steadfast, and every transgression and disobedience received a *just reward*

JUST SHALL LIVE BY FAITH
Rom 1:17 as it is written, "The *just shall live by faith*
Gal 3:11 But that no one is justified by the law in the sight of God is evident, for "The *just shall live by faith*
Heb 10:38 Now the *just shall live by faith;* but if anyone draws back, my soul has no pleasure in him

JUST SHALL LIVE BY HIS FAITH
Hab 2:4 Behold the proud, his soul is not upright in him; but the *just shall live by his faith*

JUST WEIGHT
Deut 25:15 You shall have a perfect and *just weight*, a perfect and just measure, that your days may be lengthened in the land which the Lord your God is giving you
Prov 11:1 A false balance is an abomination to the Lord, but a *just weight* is His delight
Prov 16:11 A *just weight* and balance are the Lord's; all the weights in the bag are His work

JUST WEIGHTS
Lev 19:36 You shall have just balances, *just weights*, a just ephah, and a just hin

JUSTICE AND JUDGMENT (KJV)
(See *RIGHTEOUSNESS AND JUSTICE*)

JUSTICE AND RIGHTEOUSNESS
1Kin 10:9 Because the Lord has loved Israel forever, therefore He made you king, to do *justice and righteousness*
2Chr 9:8 Because your God has loved Israel, to establish them forever, therefore He made you king over them, to do *justice and righteousness*
Ps 99:4 You have established equity; You have executed *justice and righteousness* in Jacob
Ps 119:121 I have done *justice and righteousness;* do not leave me to my oppressors
Eccl 5:8 If you see the oppression of the poor, and the violent perversion of *justice and righteousness* in a province, do not marvel at the matter
Is 33:5 The Lord is exalted, for He dwells on high; He has filled Zion with *justice and righteousness*
Jer 22:15 Did not your father eat and drink, and do *justice and righteousness*
Ezek 45:9 Remove violence and plundering, execute *justice and righteousness*, and stop dispossessing My people

JUSTICE AT THE GATE
Amos 5:12 You afflict the just and take bribes; you divert the poor from *justice at the gate*

JUSTICE FOR THE NEEDY (RSV)
(See *JUSTICE FOR THE POOR*)

JUSTICE FOR THE POOR
Ps 140:12 I know that the Lord will maintain the cause of the afflicted, and *justice for the poor*

JUSTICE GOES FORTH PERVERTED (RSV)
(See *PERVERSE JUDGMENT PROCEEDS*)

JUSTICE IN THE COURTS (NIV)
(See *JUSTICE AT THE GATE*)

JUSTICE IS PERVERTED (NIV)
(See *PERVERSE JUDGMENT PROCEEDS*)

JUSTICE OF THE LORD
Deut 33:21 He administered the *justice of the Lord*, and His judgments with Israel

JUSTICE TO ALL HIS PEOPLE
2Sam 8:15 and David administered judgment and *justice to all his people*
1Chr 18:14 So David reigned over all Israel, and administered judgment and *justice to all his people*

JUSTICE TO THE AFFLICTED
Ps 82:3 Defend the poor and fatherless; do *justice to the afflicted* and needy

JUSTICE TO THE GENTILES
Is 42:1 I have put My Spirit upon Him; He will bring forth *justice to the Gentiles*
Matt 12:18 I will put My Spirit upon Him, and He will declare *justice to the Gentiles*

JUSTICE TO THE NATIONS (NAS, NIV, RSV)
(See *JUSTICE TO THE GENTILES*)

JUSTICE TO THE OPPRESSED
Job 36:6 He does not preserve the life of the wicked, but gives *justice to the oppressed*

JUSTICE TO THE POOR
Ps 72:4 He will bring *justice to the poor* of the people

JUSTIFICATION OF LIFE
Rom 5:18 Therefore, as through one man's offense judgment came to all men, resulting in condemnation, even so through one Man's righteous act the free gift came to all men, resulting in *justification of life*

JUSTIFIED BY CHRIST
Gal 2:17 But if, while we seek to be *justified by Christ*, we ourselves also are found sinners, is Christ therefore a minister of sin

JUSTIFIED BY FAITH
Rom 3:28 Therefore we conclude that a man is *justified by faith* apart from the deeds of the law

Rom 5:1 Therefore, having been *justified by faith*, we have peace with God through our Lord Jesus Christ
Gal 2:16 knowing that a man is not justified by the works of the law but by faith in Jesus Christ, even we have believed in Christ Jesus, that we might be *justified by faith* in Christ and not by the works of the law
Gal 3:24 Therefore the law was our tutor to bring us to Christ, that we might be *justified by faith*

JUSTIFIED BY HIS GRACE AS A GIFT (RSV)
(See *JUSTIFIED FREELY*)

JUSTIFIED BY THE LAW
Acts 13:39 and by Him everyone who believes is justified from all things from which you could not be *justified by the law* of Moses
Gal 3:11 But that no one is *justified by the law* in the sight of God is evident, for

JUSTIFIED BY WORKS
Rom 4:2 For if Abraham was *justified by works*, he has something of which to boast, but not before God
Jas 2:21 Was not Abraham our father *justified by works* when he offered Isaac his son on the altar
Jas 2:24 You see then that a man is *justified by works*, and not by faith only
Jas 2:25 Likewise, was not Rahab the harlot also *justified by works* when she received the messengers and sent them out another way

JUSTIFIED FREELY
Rom 3:24 being *justified freely* by His grace through the redemption that is in Christ Jesus

K

KEEP ALL MY COMMANDMENTS
Deut 5:29 Oh, that they had such a heart in them that they would fear Me and always *keep all My commandments*, that it might be well with them and with their children forever
1Kin 6:12 Concerning this temple which you are building, if you walk in My statutes, execute My judgments, *keep all My commandments*, and walk in them, then I will perform My word with you, which I spoke to your father David

KEEP ALL MY DECREES (NIV)
(See *KEEP ALL MY STATUTES*)

KEEP ALL MY STATUTES
Lev 20:22 You shall therefore *keep all My statutes* and all My judgments, and perform them, that the land where I am bringing you to dwell may not vomit you out

KEEP HIMSELF UNSPOTTED (KJV)
(See *KEEP ONESELF UNSPOTTED*)

KEEP HIS COMMANDMENTS
Deut 7:9 Therefore know that the Lord your God, He is God, the faithful God who keeps covenant and mercy for a thousand generations with those who love Him and *keep His commandments*
Deut 8:2 And you shall remember that the Lord your God led you all the way these forty years in the wilderness, to humble you and test you, to know what was in your heart, whether you would *keep His commandments* or not
Deut 13:4 You shall walk after the Lord your God and fear Him, and *keep His commandments* and obey His voice, and you shall serve Him and hold fast to Him
Deut 28:45 Moreover all these curses shall come upon you and pursue and overtake you, until you are destroyed, because you did not obey the voice of the Lord your God, to *keep His commandments* and His statutes which He commanded you
Deut 30:10 if you obey the voice of the Lord your God, to *keep His commandments* and His statutes which are written in this Book of the Law, and if you turn to the Lord your God with all your heart and with all your soul
Deut 30:16 in that I command you today to love the Lord your God, to walk in His ways, and to *keep His commandments*, His statutes, and His judgments, that you may live and multiply
Josh 22:5 But take diligent heed to do the commandment and the law which Moses the servant of the Lord commanded you, to love the Lord your God, to walk in all His ways, to *keep His commandments*, to hold fast to Him, and to serve Him with all your heart and with all your soul
1Kin 8:58 that He may incline our hearts to Himself, to walk in all His ways, and to *keep His commandments* and His statutes and His judgments, which He commanded our fathers
1Kin 8:61 Let your heart therefore be loyal to the Lord our God, to walk in His statutes and *keep His commandments*, as at this day
2Kin 23:3 Then the king stood by a pillar and made a covenant before the Lord, to follow the Lord and to *keep His commandments* and His testimonies and His statutes, with all his heart and all his soul, to perform the words of this covenant that were written in this book
2Chr 34:31 Then the king stood in his place and made a covenant before the Lord, to follow the Lord, and to *keep His commandments* and His testimonies and His statutes with all his heart and all his soul, to perform the words of the covenant that were written in this book
Ps 78:7 That they may set their hope in God, and not forget the works of God, but *keep His commandments*
Eccl 12:13 Fear God and *keep His commandments*, for this is the whole duty of man
Dan 9:4 And I prayed to the Lord my God, and made confession, and said, "O Lord, great and awesome God, who keeps His covenant and mercy with those who love Him, and with those who *keep His commandments*
1Jn 2:3 Now by this we know that we know Him, if we *keep His commandments*
1Jn 2:4 He who says, "I know Him," and does not *keep His commandments*, is a liar, and the truth is not in him
1Jn 3:22 And whatever we ask we receive from Him, because we *keep His commandments* and do those things that are pleasing in His sight
1Jn 5:2 By this we know that we love the children of God, when we love God and *keep His commandments*
1Jn 5:3 For this is the love of God, that we *keep His commandments*

KEEP IT FOR THE GENERATIONS (NIV)
(See *KEPT FOR YOUR GENERATIONS*)

KEEP IT HOLY
Ex 20:8 Remember the Sabbath day, to *keep it holy*
Deut 5:12 Observe the Sabbath day, to *keep it holy*, as the Lord your God commanded you

KEEP MY COMMANDMENTS
Ex 16:28 And the Lord said to Moses, "How long do you refuse to *keep My commandments* and My laws

Ex 20:6 but showing mercy to thousands, to those who love Me and *keep My commandments*
Lev 22:31 Therefore you shall *keep My commandments*, and perform them
Lev 26:3 If you walk in My statutes and *keep My commandments*, and perform them
Deut 5:10 but showing mercy to thousands, to those who love Me and *keep My commandments*
1Kin 9:6 But if you or your sons at all turn from following Me, and do not *keep My commandments* and My statutes which I have set before you, but go and serve other gods and worship them
2Kin 17:13 Yet the Lord testified against Israel and against Judah, by all of His prophets, namely every seer, saying, "Turn from your evil ways, and *keep My commandments* and My statutes, according to all the law which I commanded your fathers, and which I sent to you by My servants the prophets
Neh 1:9 but if you return to Me, and *keep My commandments* and do them, though some of you were cast out to the farthest part of the heavens, yet I will gather them from there, and bring them to the place which I have chosen as a dwelling for My name
Ps 89:31 If they break My statutes and do not *keep My commandments*
John 14:15 If you love Me, *keep My commandments*
John 15:10 If you *keep My commandments*, you will abide in My love, just as I have kept My Father's commandments and abide in His love

KEEP MY COVENANT
Gen 17:9 As for you, you shall *keep My covenant*, you and your descendants after you throughout their generations
Ex 19:5 Now therefore, if you will indeed obey My voice and *keep My covenant*, then you shall be a special treasure to Me above all people
Ps 132:12 If your sons will *keep My covenant* and My testimony which I shall teach them, their sons also shall sit upon your throne forevermore

KEEP MY DECREES (NIV)
(See *KEEP MY STATUTES*)

KEEP MY SAYING (KJV)
(See *KEEPS MY WORD*)

KEEP MY STATUTES
Lev 18:5 You shall therefore *keep My statutes* and My judgments, which if a man does, he shall live by them
Lev 18:26 You shall therefore *keep My statutes* and My judgments, and shall not commit any of these abominations, either any of your own nation or any stranger who sojourns among you
Lev 19:19 You shall *keep My statutes*. You shall not let your livestock breed with another kind
Lev 20:8 And you shall *keep My statutes*, and perform them
1Kin 3:14 So if you walk in My ways, to *keep My statutes* and My commandments, as your father David walked, then I will lengthen your days
1Kin 9:4 Now if you walk before Me as your father David walked, in integrity of heart and in uprightness, to do according to all that I have commanded you, and if you *keep My statutes* and My judgments
1Kin 11:33 because they have forsaken Me, and worshiped Ashtoreth the goddess of the Sidonians, Chemosh the god of the Moabites, and Milcom the god of the people of Ammon, and have not walked in My ways to do what is right in My eyes and *keep My statutes* and My judgments, as did his father David
1Kin 11:38 Then it shall be, if you heed all that I command you, walk in My ways, and do what is right in My sight, to *keep My statutes* and My commandments, as My servant David did, then I will be with you and build for you an enduring house, as I built for David, and will give Israel to you
2Chr 7:17 As for you, if you walk before Me as your father David walked, and do according to all that I have commanded you, and if you *keep My statutes* and My judgments

KEEP MY TONGUE FROM SIN (NIV)
(See *SIN WITH MY TONGUE*)

KEEP MY WORDS
Prov 7:1 My son, *keep my words*, and treasure my commands within you
John 14:24 He who does not love Me does not *keep My words*

KEEP ON BABBLING (NIV)
(See *VAIN REPETITIONS*)

KEEP ONESELF FROM BEING POLLUTED (NIV)
(See *KEEP ONESELF UNSPOTTED*)

KEEP ONESELF UNSPOTTED
Jas 1:27 to visit orphans and widows in their trouble, and to *keep oneself unspotted* from the world

KEEP SILENCE BEFORE HIM
Hab 2:20 But the Lord is in His holy temple. Let all the earth *keep silence before Him*

KEEP SILENT
2Kin 2:3 And the sons of the prophets who were at Bethel came out to Elisha, and said to him, "Do you know that the Lord will take away your master from over you today?" And he said, "Yes, I know; *keep silent*
2Kin 2:5 And the sons of the prophets who were at Jericho came to Elisha and said to him, "Do you know that the Lord will take away your master from over you today?" So he answered, "Yes, I know; *keep silent*
Ps 50:3 Our God shall come, and shall not *keep silent;* a fire shall devour before Him, and it shall be very tempestuous all around Him
Ps 83:1 Do not *keep silent*, O God! Do not hold Your peace, and do not be still, O God
Ps 109:1 Do not *keep silent*, O God of my praise
Is 62:6 You who make mention of the Lord, do not *keep silent*
Lam 3:28 Let him sit alone and *keep silent*, because God has laid it on him
Amos 5:13 Therefore the prudent *keep silent* at that time, for it is an evil time
Luke 19:40 But He answered and said to them, "I tell you that if these should *keep silent*, the stones would immediately cry out
Acts 12:17 But motioning to them with his hand to *keep silent*, he declared to them how the Lord had brought him out of the prison
Acts 18:9 Now the Lord spoke to Paul in the night by a vision, "Do not be afraid, but speak, and do not *keep silent*
1Cor 14:28 But if there is no interpreter, let him *keep silent* in church, and let him speak to himself and to God
1Cor 14:30 But if anything is revealed to another who sits by, let the first *keep silent*
1Cor 14:34 Let your women *keep silent* in the churches, for they are not permitted to speak

KEEP THE LAW
1Chr 22:12 Only may the Lord give you wisdom and understanding, and give you charge concerning Israel, that you may *keep the law* of the Lord your God
Prov 28:4 Those who forsake the law praise the wicked, but such as *keep the law* contend with them
Acts 15:5 But some of the sect of the Pharisees who believed rose up, saying, "It is necessary to circumcise them, and to command them to *keep the law* of Moses
Acts 15:24 Since we have heard that some who went out from us have troubled you with words, unsettling your souls, saying, 'You must be circumcised and *keep the law*
Acts 21:24 Take them and be purified with them, and pay their expenses so that they may shave their heads, and that all may know that those things of which they were informed concerning you are nothing, but that you yourself also walk orderly and *keep the law*
Rom 2:25 For circumcision is indeed profitable if you *keep the law*
Gal 6:13 For not even those who are circumcised *keep the law*, but they desire to have you circumcised that they may glory in your flesh

KEEP THE PASSOVER
Ex 12:48 And when a stranger dwells with you and wants to *keep the Passover* to the Lord, let all his males be circumcised, and then let him come near and keep it
Num 9:2 Let the children of Israel *keep the Passover* at its appointed time
Num 9:4 So Moses told the children of Israel that they should *keep the Passover*
Num 9:6 Now there were certain men who were defiled by the dead body of a man, so that they could not *keep the Passover* on that day
Num 9:13 But the man who is clean and is not on a journey, and ceases to *keep the Passover*, that same person shall be cut off from among his people, because he did not bring the offering of the Lord at its appointed time
Deut 16:1 Observe the month of Abib, and *keep the Passover* to the Lord your God, for in the month of Abib the Lord your God brought you out of Egypt by night
2Kin 23:21 Then the king commanded all the people, saying, "*Keep the Passover* to the Lord your God, as it is written in this Book of the Covenant
2Chr 30:1 And Hezekiah sent to all Israel and Judah, and also wrote letters to Ephraim and Manasseh, that they should come to the house of the Lord at Jerusalem, to *keep the Passover* to the Lord God of Israel
2Chr 30:2 For the king and his leaders and all the congregation in Jerusalem had agreed to *keep the Passover* in the second month
2Chr 30:5 So they resolved to make a proclamation throughout all Israel, from Beersheba to Dan, that they should come to *keep the Passover* to the Lord God of Israel at Jerusalem, since they had not done it for a long time in the prescribed manner
2Chr 35:16 So all the service of the Lord was prepared the same day, to *keep the Passover* and to offer burnt offerings on the altar of the Lord, according to the command of King Josiah
Matt 26:18 I will *keep the Passover* at your house with My disciples

KEEP THE SABBATH
Ex 31:14 You shall *keep the Sabbath*, therefore, for it is holy to you
Ex 31:16 Therefore the children of Israel shall *keep the Sabbath*, to observe the Sabbath throughout their generations as a perpetual covenant
Deut 5:15 therefore the Lord your God commanded you to *keep the Sabbath* day
John 9:16 Therefore some of the Pharisees said, "This Man is not from God, because He does not *keep the Sabbath*

KEEP THE WHOLE LAW
Gal 5:3 And I testify again to every man who becomes circumcised that he is a debtor to *keep the whole law*
Jas 2:10 For whoever shall *keep the whole law*, and yet stumble in one point, he is guilty of all

KEEP THEM AND DO THEM (RSV)
(See *CAREFUL TO OBSERVE*)

KEEP THY FOOT (KJV)
(See *WALK PRUDENTLY*)

KEEP WATCH
Ps 141:3 Set a guard, O Lord, over my mouth; *keep watch* over the door of my lips

KEEP YOUR HEARTS (KJV, RSV)
(See *GUARD YOUR HEARTS*)

KEEPER OF SHEEP
Gen 4:2 Now Abel was a *keeper of sheep*, but Cain was a tiller of the ground

KEEPING WATCH OVER THEIR FLOCK
Luke 2:8 Now there were in the same country shepherds living out in the fields, *keeping watch over their flock* by night

KEEPING WITH REPENTANCE (NAS, NIV)
(See *WORTHY OF REPENTANCE*)

KEEPS MY WORD
John 8:51 Most assuredly, I say to you, if anyone *keeps My word* he shall never see death
John 8:52 and You say, 'If anyone *keeps My word* he shall never taste death

KEPT ALL THESE THINGS IN HER HEART
Luke 2:51 Then He went down with them and came to Nazareth, and was subject to them, but His mother *kept all these things in her heart*

KEPT BOUND WITH CHAINS (KJV)
(See *KEPT UNDER GUARD*)

KEPT FLOCKS (NIV)
(See *KEEPER OF SHEEP*)

KEPT FOR YOUR GENERATIONS
Ex 16:32 Fill an omer with it, to be *kept for your generations*, that they may see the bread with which I fed you in the wilderness, when I brought you out of the land of Egypt
Ex 16:33 And Moses said to Aaron, "Take a pot and put an omer of manna in it, and lay it up before the Lord, to be *kept for your generations*

KEPT IN HEAVEN (NIV, RSV)
(See *RESERVED IN HEAVEN*)

KEPT MY COMMAND
Rev 3:10 Because you have *kept My command* to persevere, I also will keep you from the hour of trial which shall come upon the whole world, to test those who dwell on the earth

KEPT THE COMMANDMENT
1Sam 13:13 You have not *kept the commandment* of the Lord your God, which He commanded you

1Kin 13:21 Because you have disobeyed the word of the Lord, and have not *kept the commandment* which the Lord your God commanded you

KEPT THE FAITH
2Tim 4:7 I have fought the good fight, I have finished the race, I have *kept the faith*

KEPT THE LAWS (NIV)
(See *WALK IN HIS LAWS*)

KEPT THE WORD (KJV, NAS)
(See *KEPT MY COMMAND*)

KEPT THROUGHOUT YOUR GENERATIONS (NAS, RSV)
(See *KEPT FOR YOUR GENERATIONS*)

KEPT UNDER GUARD
Luke 8:29 For it had often seized him, and he was *kept under guard*, bound with chains and shackles
Gal 3:23 But before faith came, we were *kept under guard* by the law, kept for the faith which would afterward be revealed

KEPT UNTIL THE JUDGMENT (RSV)
(See *RESERVED FOR JUDGMENT*)

KEY OF DAVID
Rev 3:7 And to the angel of the church in Philadelphia write, 'These things says He who is holy, He who is true, "He who has the *key of David*, He who opens and no one shuts, and shuts and no one opens

KEYS OF HADES
Rev 1:18 And I have the *keys of Hades* and of Death

KEYS OF HELL (KJV)
(See *KEYS OF HADES*)

KEYS OF THE KINGDOM
Matt 16:19 And I will give you the *keys of the kingdom* of heaven, and whatever you bind on earth will be bound in heaven, and whatever you loose on earth will be loosed in heaven

KICK AGAINST THE GOADS
Acts 9:5 It is hard for you to *kick against the goads*
Acts 26:14 It is hard for you to *kick against the goads*

KILL AND EAT
Acts 10:13 And a voice came to him, "Rise, Peter; *kill and eat*
Acts 11:7 And I heard a voice saying to me, 'Rise, Peter; *kill and eat*

KILLED THE FATTED CALF
Luke 15:27 And he said to him, 'Your brother has come, and because he has received him safe and sound, your father has *killed the fatted calf*
Luke 15:30 But as soon as this son of yours came, who has devoured your livelihood with harlots, you *killed the fatted calf* for him

KIND TO THE NEEDY (NIV, RSV)
(See *MERCY ON THE NEEDY*)

KIND TO THE POOR (RSV)
(See *MERCY ON THE POOR*)

KINDLED HIS WRATH
Job 19:11 He has also *kindled His wrath* against me, and He counts me as one of His enemies

KINDNESS AND FAITHFULNESS (NIV)
(See *MERCY AND TRUTH*)

KINDNESS OF GOD
2Sam 9:3 Then the king said, "Is there not still someone of the house of Saul, to whom I may show the *kindness of God*

KINDNESS OF THE LORD
1Sam 20:14 And you shall not only show me the *kindness of the Lord* while I still live, that I may not die

KING OF GLORY
Ps 24:7 And be lifted up, you everlasting doors! And the *King of glory* shall come in
Ps 24:8 Who is this *King of glory?* The Lord strong and mighty, the Lord mighty in battle
Ps 24:9 And lift them up, you everlasting doors! And the *King of glory* shall come in
Ps 24:10 Who is this *King of glory?* The Lord of hosts, He is the *King of glory*

KING OF ISRAEL
1Sam 24:14 After whom has the *king of Israel* come out? Whom do you pursue
1Sam 26:20 For the *king of Israel* has come out to seek a flea, as when one hunts a partridge in the mountains
1Sam 29:3 And Achish said to the princes of the Philistines, "Is this not David, the servant of Saul *king of Israel*, who has been with me these days, or these years
2Sam 6:20 And Michal the daughter of Saul came out to meet David, and said, "How glorious was the *king of Israel* today, uncovering himself today in the eyes of the maids of his servants, as one of the base fellows shamelessly uncovers himself
1Kin 15:9 In the twentieth year of Jeroboam *king of Israel*, Asa became king over Judah
1Kin 15:16 Now there was war between Asa and Baasha *king of Israel* all their days
1Kin 15:17 And Baasha *king of Israel* came up against Judah, and built Ramah, that he might let none go out or come in to Asa king of Judah
1Kin 15:19 Come and break your treaty with Baasha *king of Israel*, so that he will withdraw from me
1Kin 15:32 And there was war between Asa and Baasha *king of Israel* all their days
1Kin 20:2 Then he sent messengers into the city to Ahab *king of Israel*, and said to him
1Kin 20:4 And the *king of Israel* answered and said, "My lord, O king, just as you say, I and all that I have are yours
1Kin 20:7 Then the *king of Israel* called all the elders of the land, and said
1Kin 20:11 So the *king of Israel* answered and said, "Tell him
1Kin 20:13 Suddenly a prophet approached Ahab *king of Israel*, saying, "Thus says the Lord
1Kin 20:21 Then the *king of Israel* went out and attacked the horses and chariots, and killed the Syrians with a great slaughter
1Kin 20:22 And the prophet came to the *king of Israel* and said to him
1Kin 20:28 Then a man of God came and spoke to the *king of Israel*, and said
1Kin 20:31 Please, let us put sackcloth around our waists and ropes around our heads, and go out to the *king of Israel*
1Kin 20:32 So they wore sackcloth around their waists and put ropes around their heads, and came to the *king of Israel* and said
1Kin 20:40 And the *king of Israel* said to him, "So shall your judgment be

1Kin 20:41 and the *king of Israel* recognized him as one of the prophets
1Kin 20:43 So the *king of Israel* went to his house sullen and displeased, and came to Samaria
1Kin 21:18 Arise, go down to meet Ahab *king of Israel*, who lives in Samaria
1Kin 22:2 Then it came to pass, in the third year, that Jehoshaphat the king of Judah went down to visit the *king of Israel*
1Kin 22:3 And the *king of Israel* said to his servants, "Do you know that Ramoth in Gilead is ours, but we hesitate to take it out of the hand of the king of Syria
1Kin 22:4 And Jehoshaphat said to the *king of Israel*, "I am as you are, my people as your people, my horses as your horses
1Kin 22:5 And Jehoshaphat said to the *king of Israel*, "Please inquire for the word of the Lord today
1Kin 22:6 Then the *king of Israel* gathered the prophets together, about four hundred men, and said to them
1Kin 22:8 So the *king of Israel* said to Jehoshaphat, "There is still one man, Micaiah the son of Imlah, by whom we may inquire of the Lord
1Kin 22:9 Then the *king of Israel* called an officer and said
1Kin 22:10 The *king of Israel* and Jehoshaphat the king of Judah, having put on their robes, sat each on his throne, at a threshing floor at the entrance of the gate of Samaria
1Kin 22:18 And the *king of Israel* said to Jehoshaphat, "Did I not tell you that he would not prophesy good concerning me, but evil
1Kin 22:26 Then the *king of Israel* said, "Take Micaiah, and return him to Amon the governor of the city and to Joash the king's son
1Kin 22:29 So the *king of Israel* and Jehoshaphat the king of Judah went up to Ramoth Gilead
1Kin 22:30 And the *king of Israel* said to Jehoshaphat, "I will disguise myself and go into battle; but you put on your robes." So the *king of Israel* disguised himself and went into battle
1Kin 22:31 Now the king of Syria had commanded the thirty-two captains of his chariots, saying, "Fight with no one small or great, but only with the *king of Israel*
1Kin 22:32 So it was, when the captains of the chariots saw Jehoshaphat, that they said, "Surely it is the *king of Israel*
1Kin 22:33 And it happened, when the captains of the chariots saw that it was not the *king of Israel*, that they turned back from pursuing him
1Kin 22:34 Now a certain man drew a bow at random, and struck the *king of Israel* between the joints of his armor
1Kin 22:41 Now Jehoshaphat the son of Asa had become king over Judah in the fourth year of Ahab *king of Israel*
1Kin 22:44 Also Jehoshaphat made peace with the *king of Israel*
2Kin 3:4 Now Mesha king of Moab was a sheepbreeder, and he regularly paid the *king of Israel* one hundred thousand lambs and the wool of one hundred thousand rams
2Kin 3:5 But it happened, when Ahab died, that the king of Moab rebelled against the *king of Israel*
2Kin 3:9 So the *king of Israel* went with the king of Judah and the king of Edom, and they marched on that roundabout route seven days
2Kin 3:10 And the *king of Israel* said, "Alas! For the Lord has called these three kings together to deliver them into the hand of Moab
2Kin 3:11 And one of the servants of the *king of Israel* answered and said
2Kin 3:12 So the *king of Israel* and Jehoshaphat and the king of Edom went down to him
2Kin 3:13 Then Elisha said to the *king of Israel*, "What have I to do with you? Go to the prophets of your father and the prophets of your mother." And the *king of Israel* said to him
2Kin 5:5 So the king of Syria said, "Go now, and I will send a letter to the *king of Israel*
2Kin 5:6 Then he brought the letter to the *king of Israel*, which said
2Kin 5:7 And it happened, when the *king of Israel* read the letter, that he tore his clothes and said
2Kin 5:8 So it was, when Elisha the man of God heard that the *king of Israel* had torn his clothes, that he sent to the king, saying
2Kin 6:9 And the man of God sent to the *king of Israel*, saying
2Kin 6:10 Then the *king of Israel* sent someone to the place of which the man of God had told him
2Kin 6:11 and he called his servants and said to them, "Will you not show me which of us is for the *king of Israel*
2Kin 6:12 but Elisha, the prophet who is in Israel, tells the *king of Israel* the words that you speak in your bedroom
2Kin 6:21 Now when the *king of Israel* saw them, he said to Elisha
2Kin 6:26 Then, as the *king of Israel* was passing by on the wall, a woman cried out to him, saying
2Kin 7:6 so they said to one another, "Look, the *king of Israel* has hired against us the kings of the Hittites and the kings of the Egyptians to attack us
2Kin 8:16 Now in the fifth year of Joram the son of Ahab, *king of Israel*, Jehoshaphat having been king of Judah, Jehoram the son of Jehoshaphat began to reign as king of Judah
2Kin 8:25 In the twelfth year of Joram the son of Ahab, *king of Israel*, Ahaziah the son of Jehoram, king of Judah, began to reign
2Kin 8:26 His mother's name was Athaliah the granddaughter of Omri, *king of Israel*
2Kin 9:21 Then Joram *king of Israel* and Ahaziah king of Judah went out, each in his chariot
2Kin 13:14 Then Joash the *king of Israel* came down to him, and wept over his face, and said
2Kin 13:16 Then he said to the *king of Israel*, "Put your hand on the bow
2Kin 13:18 And he said to the *king of Israel*, "Strike the ground
2Kin 14:1 In the second year of Joash the son of Jehoahaz, *king of Israel*, Amaziah the son of Joash, king of Judah, became king
2Kin 14:8 Then Amaziah sent messengers to Jehoash the son of Jehoahaz, the son of Jehu, *king of Israel*, saying
2Kin 14:9 And Jehoash *king of Israel* sent to Amaziah king of Judah, saying
2Kin 14:11 Therefore Jehoash *king of Israel* went out; so he and Amaziah king of Judah faced one another at Beth Shemesh, which belongs to Judah
2Kin 14:13 Then Jehoash *king of Israel* captured Amaziah king of Judah, the son of Jehoash, the son of Ahaziah, at Beth Shemesh
2Kin 14:17 Amaziah the son of Joash, king of Judah, lived fifteen years after the death of Jehoash the son of Jehoahaz, *king of Israel*
2Kin 14:23 In the fifteenth year of Amaziah the son of Joash, king of Judah, Jeroboam the son of Joash, *king of Israel*, became king in Samaria, and reigned forty-one years
2Kin 15:1 In the twenty-seventh year of Jeroboam *king of Israel*, Azariah the son of Amaziah, king of Judah, became king
2Kin 15:29 In the days of Pekah *king of Israel*, Tiglath-Pileser king of Assyria came and took Ijon, Abel Beth Maachah, Janoah, Kedesh, Hazor, Gilead, and Galilee, all the land of Naphtali
2Kin 15:32 In the second year of Pekah the son of

Remaliah, *king of Israel*, Jotham the son of Uzziah, king of Judah, began to reign

2Kin 16:5 Then Rezin king of Syria and Pekah the son of Remaliah, *king of Israel*, came up to Jerusalem to make war

2Kin 16:7 Come up and save me from the hand of the king of Syria and from the hand of the *king of Israel*, who rise up against me

2Kin 17:1 In the twelfth year of Ahaz king of Judah, Hoshea the son of Elah became *king of Israel* in Samaria, and he reigned nine years

2Kin 18:1 Now it came to pass in the third year of Hoshea the son of Elah, *king of Israel*, that Hezekiah the son of Ahaz, king of Judah, began to reign

2Kin 18:9 Now it came to pass in the fourth year of King Hezekiah, which was the seventh year of Hoshea the son of Elah, *king of Israel*, that Shalmaneser king of Assyria came up against Samaria and besieged it

2Kin 18:10 In the sixth year of Hezekiah, that is, the ninth year of Hoshea *king of Israel*, Samaria was taken

2Kin 21:3 he raised up altars for Baal, and made a wooden image, as Ahab *king of Israel* had done

2Kin 23:13 Then the king defiled the high places that were east of Jerusalem, which were on the south of the Mount of Corruption, which Solomon *king of Israel* had built for Ashtoreth the abomination of the Sidonians, for Chemosh the abomination of the Moabites, and for Milcom the abomination of the people of Ammon

2Kin 24:13 And he carried out from there all the treasures of the house of the Lord and the treasures of the king's house, and he cut in pieces all the articles of gold which Solomon *king of Israel* had made in the temple of the Lord, as the Lord had said

1Chr 5:17 All these were registered by genealogies in the days of Jotham king of Judah, and in the days of Jeroboam *king of Israel*

2Chr 8:11 Now Solomon brought the daughter of Pharaoh up from the City of David to the house he had built for her, for he said, "My wife shall not dwell in the house of David *king of Israel*, because the places to which the ark of the Lord has come are holy

2Chr 16:1 In the thirty-sixth year of the reign of Asa, Baasha *king of Israel* came up against Judah and built Ramah, that he might let none go out or come in to Asa king of Judah

2Chr 16:3 come, break your treaty with Baasha *king of Israel*, so that he will withdraw from me

2Chr 18:3 So Ahab *king of Israel* said to Jehoshaphat king of Judah

2Chr 18:4 And Jehoshaphat said to the *king of Israel*, "Please inquire for the word of the Lord today

2Chr 18:5 Then the *king of Israel* gathered the prophets together, four hundred men, and said to them

2Chr 18:7 So the *king of Israel* said to Jehoshaphat, "There is still one man by whom we may inquire of the Lord

2Chr 18:8 Then the *king of Israel* called one of his officers and said

2Chr 18:9 And the *king of Israel* and Jehoshaphat king of Judah, clothed in their robes, sat each on his throne

2Chr 18:17 And the *king of Israel* said to Jehoshaphat, "Did I not tell you that he would not prophesy good concerning me, but evil

2Chr 18:19 And the Lord said, 'Who will persuade Ahab *king of Israel* to go up, that he may fall at Ramoth Gilead

2Chr 18:25 Then the *king of Israel* said, "Take Micaiah, and return him to Amon the governor of the city and to Joash the king's son

2Chr 18:28 So the *king of Israel* and Jehoshaphat the king of Judah went up to Ramoth Gilead

2Chr 18:29 And the *king of Israel* said to Jehoshaphat, "I will disguise myself and go into battle; but you put on your robes." So the *king of Israel* disguised himself, and they went into battle

2Chr 18:30 Now the king of Syria had commanded the captains of the chariots who were with him, saying, "Fight with no one small or great, but only with the *king of Israel*

2Chr 18:31 So it was, when the captains of the chariots saw Jehoshaphat, that they said, "It is the *king of Israel*

2Chr 18:32 For so it was, when the captains of the chariots saw that it was not the *king of Israel*, that they turned back from pursuing him

2Chr 18:33 Now a certain man drew a bow at random, and struck the *king of Israel* between the joints of his armor

2Chr 18:34 The battle increased that day, and the *king of Israel* propped himself up in his chariot facing the Syrians until evening

2Chr 20:35 After this Jehoshaphat king of Judah allied himself with Ahaziah *king of Israel*, who acted very wickedly

2Chr 21:2 all these were the sons of Jehoshaphat *king of Israel*

2Chr 22:5 He also walked in their counsel, and went with Jehoram the son of Ahab *king of Israel* to make war against Hazael king of Syria at Ramoth Gilead

2Chr 25:17 Then Amaziah king of Judah took counsel and sent to Joash the son of Jehoahaz, the son of Jehu, *king of Israel*, saying

2Chr 25:18 And Joash *king of Israel* sent to Amaziah king of Judah, saying

2Chr 25:21 So Joash *king of Israel* went out; and he and Amaziah king of Judah faced one another at Beth Shemesh, which belongs to Judah

2Chr 25:23 Then Joash the *king of Israel* captured Amaziah king of Judah, the son of Joash, the son of Jehoahaz, at Beth Shemesh

2Chr 25:25 Amaziah the son of Joash, king of Judah, lived fifteen years after the death of Joash the son of Jehoahaz, *king of Israel*

2Chr 28:5 Then he was also delivered into the hand of the *king of Israel*, who defeated him with a great slaughter

2Chr 28:19 For the Lord brought Judah low because of Ahaz *king of Israel*, for he had encouraged moral decline in Judah and had been continually unfaithful to the Lord

2Chr 29:27 And when the burnt offering began, the song of the Lord also began, with the trumpets and with the instruments of David *king of Israel*

2Chr 30:26 So there was great joy in Jerusalem, for since the time of Solomon the son of David, *king of Israel*, there had been nothing like this in Jerusalem

2Chr 35:3 Put the holy ark in the house which Solomon the son of David, *king of Israel*, built

2Chr 35:4 Prepare yourselves according to your fathers' houses, according to your divisions, following the written instruction of David *king of Israel* and the written instruction of Solomon his son

Ezra 3:10 When the builders laid the foundation of the temple of the Lord, the priests stood in their apparel with trumpets, and the Levites, the sons of Asaph, with cymbals, to praise the Lord, according to the ordinance of David *king of Israel*

Ezra 5:11 We are the servants of the God of heaven and earth, and we are rebuilding the temple that was built many years ago, which a great *king of Israel* built and completed

Neh 13:26 Did not Solomon *king of Israel* sin by these things

Prov 1:1 The proverbs of Solomon the son of David, *king of Israel*
Is 7:1 Now it came to pass in the days of Ahaz the son of Jotham, the son of Uzziah, king of Judah, that Rezin king of Syria and Pekah the son of Remaliah, *king of Israel*, went up to Jerusalem to make war against it, but could not prevail against it
Is 44:6 Thus says the Lord, the *King of Israel*, and his Redeemer, the Lord of hosts
Jer 41:9 Now the pit into which Ishmael had cast all the dead bodies of the men whom he had slain, because of Gedaliah, was the same one Asa the king had made for fear of Baasha *king of Israel*
Hos 1:1 The word of the Lord that came to Hosea the son of Beeri, in the days of Uzziah, Jotham, Ahaz, and Hezekiah, kings of Judah, and in the days of Jeroboam the son of Joash, *king of Israel*
Hos 10:15 In a morning the *king of Israel* shall be cut off utterly
Amos 1:1 The words of Amos, who was among the herdsmen of Tekoa, which he saw concerning Israel in the days of Uzziah king of Judah, and in the days of Jeroboam the son of Joash, *king of Israel*, two years before the earthquake
Amos 7:10 Then Amaziah the priest of Bethel sent to Jeroboam *king of Israel*, saying
Zeph 3:15 the *King of Israel*, the Lord, is in your midst
Matt 27:42 If He is the *King of Israel*, let Him now come down from the cross, and we will believe Him
Mark 15:32 Let the Christ, the *King of Israel*, descend now from the cross, that we may see and believe
John 1:49 Nathanael answered and said to Him, "Rabbi, You are the Son of God! You are the *King of Israel*
John 12:13 Blessed is He who comes in the name of the Lord!' The *King of Israel*

KING OF JUDAH
1Kin 12:23 Speak to Rehoboam the son of Solomon, *king of Judah*, to all the house of Judah and Benjamin, and to the rest of the people, saying
1Kin 12:27 If these people go up to offer sacrifices in the house of the Lord at Jerusalem, then the heart of this people will turn back to their lord, Rehoboam *king of Judah*, and they will kill me and go back to Rehoboam *king of Judah*
1Kin 15:17 And Baasha king of Israel came up against Judah, and built Ramah, that he might let none go out or come in to Asa *king of Judah*
1Kin 15:25 Now Nadab the son of Jeroboam became king over Israel in the second year of Asa *king of Judah*, and he reigned over Israel two years
1Kin 15:28 Baasha killed him in the third year of Asa *king of Judah*, and reigned in his place
1Kin 15:33 In the third year of Asa *king of Judah*, Baasha the son of Ahijah became king over all Israel in Tirzah, and reigned twenty-four years
1Kin 16:8 In the twenty-sixth year of Asa *king of Judah*, Elah the son of Baasha became king over Israel, and reigned two years in Tirzah
1Kin 16:10 and Zimri went in and struck him and killed him in the twenty-seventh year of Asa *king of Judah*, and reigned in his place
1Kin 16:15 In the twenty-seventh year of Asa *king of Judah*, Zimri had reigned in Tirzah seven days
1Kin 16:23 In the thirty-first year of Asa *king of Judah*, Omri became king over Israel, and reigned twelve years
1Kin 16:29 In the thirty-eighth year of Asa *king of Judah*, Ahab the son of Omri became king over Israel
1Kin 22:2 Then it came to pass, in the third year, that Jehoshaphat the *king of Judah* went down to visit the king of Israel
1Kin 22:10 The king of Israel and Jehoshaphat the *king of Judah*, having put on their robes, sat each on his throne, at a threshing floor at the entrance of the gate of Samaria
1Kin 22:29 So the king of Israel and Jehoshaphat the *king of Judah* went up to Ramoth Gilead
1Kin 22:51 Ahaziah the son of Ahab became king over Israel in Samaria in the seventeenth year of Jehoshaphat *king of Judah*, and reigned two years over Israel
2Kin 1:17 Because he had no son, Jehoram became king in his place, in the second year of Jehoram the son of Jehoshaphat, *king of Judah*
2Kin 3:1 Now Jehoram the son of Ahab became king over Israel at Samaria in the eighteenth year of Jehoshaphat *king of Judah*, and reigned twelve years
2Kin 3:7 Then he went and sent to Jehoshaphat *king of Judah*, saying
2Kin 3:9 So the king of Israel went with the *king of Judah* and the king of Edom, and they marched on that roundabout route seven days
2Kin 3:14 And Elisha said, "As the Lord of hosts lives, before whom I stand, surely were it not that I regard the presence of Jehoshaphat *king of Judah*, I would not look at you, nor see you
2Kin 8:16 Now in the fifth year of Joram the son of Ahab, king of Israel, Jehoshaphat having been *king of Judah*, Jehoram the son of Jehoshaphat began to reign as *king of Judah*
2Kin 8:25 In the twelfth year of Joram the son of Ahab, king of Israel, Ahaziah the son of Jehoram, *king of Judah*, began to reign
2Kin 8:29 And Ahaziah the son of Jehoram, *king of Judah*, went down to see Joram the son of Ahab in Jezreel, because he was sick
2Kin 9:16 and Ahaziah *king of Judah* had come down to see Joram
2Kin 9:21 Then Joram king of Israel and Ahaziah *king of Judah* went out, each in his chariot
2Kin 9:27 But when Ahaziah *king of Judah* saw this, he fled by the road to Beth Haggan
2Kin 10:13 Jehu met with the brothers of Ahaziah *king of Judah*, and said
2Kin 12:18 And Jehoash *king of Judah* took all the sacred things that his fathers, Jehoshaphat and Jehoram and Ahaziah, kings of Judah, had dedicated, and his own sacred things, and all the gold found in the treasuries of the house of the Lord and in the king's house, and sent them to Hazael king of Syria
2Kin 13:1 In the twenty-third year of Joash the son of Ahaziah, *king of Judah*, Jehoahaz the son of Jehu became king over Israel in Samaria, and reigned seventeen years
2Kin 13:10 In the thirty-seventh year of Joash *king of Judah*, Jehoash the son of Jehoahaz became king over Israel in Samaria, and reigned sixteen years
2Kin 13:12 Now the rest of the acts of Joash, all that he did, and his might with which he fought against Amaziah *king of Judah*, are they not written in the book of the chronicles of the kings of Israel
2Kin 14:1 In the second year of Joash the son of Jehoahaz, king of Israel, Amaziah the son of Joash, *king of Judah*, became king
2Kin 14:9 And Jehoash king of Israel sent to Amaziah *king of Judah*, saying
2Kin 14:11 so he and Amaziah *king of Judah* faced one another at Beth Shemesh, which belongs to Judah
2Kin 14:13 Then Jehoash king of Israel captured Amaziah *king of Judah*, the son of Jehoash, the son of Ahaziah, at Beth Shemesh
2Kin 14:15 Now the rest of the acts of Jehoash

which he did his might, and how he fought with Amaziah *king of Judah* are they not written in the book of the chronicles of the kings of Israel

2Kin 14:17 Amaziah the son of Joash, *king of Judah*, lived fifteen years after the death of Jehoash the son of Jehoahaz, king of Israel

2Kin 14:23 In the fifteenth year of Amaziah the son of Joash, *king of Judah*, Jeroboam the son of Joash, king of Israel, became king in Samaria, and reigned forty-one years

2Kin 15:1 In the twenty-seventh year of Jeroboam king of Israel, Azariah the son of Amaziah, *king of Judah*, became king

2Kin 15:8 In the thirty-eighth year of Azariah *king of Judah*, Zechariah the son of Jeroboam reigned over Israel in Samaria six months

2Kin 15:13 Shallum the son of Jabesh became king in the thirty-ninth year of Uzziah *king of Judah*

2Kin 15:17 In the thirty-ninth year of Azariah *king of Judah*, Menahem the son of Gadi became king over Israel, and reigned ten years in Samaria

2Kin 15:23 In the fiftieth year of Azariah *king of Judah*, Pekahiah the son of Menahem became king over Israel in Samaria, and reigned two years

2Kin 15:27 In the fifty-second year of Azariah *king of Judah*, Pekah the son of Remaliah became king over Israel in Samaria, and reigned twenty years

2Kin 15:32 In the second year of Pekah the son of Remaliah, king of Israel, Jotham the son of Uzziah, *king of Judah*, began to reign

2Kin 16:1 In the seventeenth year of Pekah the son of Remaliah, Ahaz the son of Jotham, *king of Judah*, began to reign

2Kin 17:1 In the twelfth year of Ahaz *king of Judah*, Hoshea the son of Elah became king of Israel in Samaria, and he reigned nine years

2Kin 18:1 Now it came to pass in the third year of Hoshea the son of Elah, king of Israel, that Hezekiah the son of Ahaz, *king of Judah*, began to reign

2Kin 18:14 Then Hezekiah *king of Judah* sent to the king of Assyria at Lachish, saying, "I have done wrong; turn away from me; whatever you impose on me I will pay." And the king of Assyria assessed Hezekiah *king of Judah* three hundred talents of silver and thirty talents of gold

2Kin 18:16 At that time Hezekiah stripped the gold from the doors of the temple of the Lord, and from the pillars which Hezekiah *king of Judah* had overlaid, and gave it to the king of Assyria

2Kin 19:10 Thus you shall speak to Hezekiah *king of Judah*, saying

2Kin 21:11 Because Manasseh *king of Judah* has done these abominations (he has acted more wickedly than all the Amorites who were before him, and has also made Judah sin with his idols

2Kin 22:16 Behold, I will bring calamity on this place and on its inhabitants all the words of the book which the *king of Judah* has read

2Kin 22:18 But to the *king of Judah*, who sent you to inquire of the Lord, in this manner you shall speak to him

2Kin 24:12 Then Jehoiachin *king of Judah*, his mother, his servants, his princes, and his officers went out to the king of Babylon

2Kin 25:27 Now it came to pass in the thirty-seventh year of the captivity of Jehoiachin *king of Judah*, in the twelfth month, on the twenty-seventh day of the month, that Evil-Merodach king of Babylon, in the year that he began to reign, released Jehoiachin *king of Judah* from prison

1Chr 4:41 These recorded by name came in the days of Hezekiah *king of Judah*

1Chr 5:17 All these were registered by genealogies in the days of Jotham *king of Judah*, and in the days of Jeroboam king of Israel

2Chr 11:3 Speak to Rehoboam the son of Solomon, *king of Judah*, and to all Israel in Judah and Benjamin, saying

2Chr 16:1 In the thirty-sixth year of the reign of Asa, Baasha king of Israel came up against Judah and built Ramah, that he might let none go out or come in to Asa *king of Judah*

2Chr 16:7 And at that time Hanani the seer came to Asa *king of Judah*, and said to him

2Chr 18:3 So Ahab king of Israel said to Jehoshaphat *king of Judah*

2Chr 18:9 And the king of Israel and Jehoshaphat *king of Judah*, clothed in their robes, sat each on his throne

2Chr 18:28 So the king of Israel and Jehoshaphat the *king of Judah* went up to Ramoth Gilead

2Chr 19:1 Then Jehoshaphat the *king of Judah* returned safely to his house in Jerusalem

2Chr 20:35 After this Jehoshaphat *king of Judah* allied himself with Ahaziah king of Israel, who acted very wickedly

2Chr 21:12 Because you have not walked in the ways of Jehoshaphat your father, or in the ways of Asa *king of Judah*

2Chr 22:1 So Ahaziah the son of Jehoram, *king of Judah*, reigned

2Chr 22:6 And Azariah the son of Jehoram, *king of Judah*, went down to see Jehoram the son of Ahab in Jezreel, because he was sick

2Chr 25:17 Then Amaziah *king of Judah* took counsel and sent to Joash the son of Jehoahaz, the son of Jehu, king of Israel, saying

2Chr 25:18 And Joash king of Israel sent to Amaziah *king of Judah*, saying

2Chr 25:21 and he and Amaziah *king of Judah* faced one another at Beth Shemesh, which belongs to Judah

2Chr 25:23 Then Joash the king of Israel captured Amaziah *king of Judah*, the son of Joash, the son of Jehoahaz, at Beth Shemesh

2Chr 25:25 Amaziah the son of Joash, *king of Judah*, lived fifteen years after the death of Joash the son of Jehoahaz, king of Israel

2Chr 30:24 For Hezekiah *king of Judah* gave to the congregation a thousand bulls and seven thousand sheep, and the leaders gave to the congregation a thousand bulls and ten thousand sheep

2Chr 32:8 And the people were strengthened by the words of Hezekiah *king of Judah*

2Chr 32:9 to Hezekiah *king of Judah*, and to all Judah who were in Jerusalem, saying

2Chr 32:23 And many brought gifts to the Lord at Jerusalem, and presents to Hezekiah *king of Judah*, so that he was exalted in the sight of all nations thereafter

2Chr 34:24 Behold, I will bring calamity on this place and on its inhabitants, all the curses that are written in the book which they have read before the *king of Judah*

2Chr 34:26 And as for the *king of Judah*, who sent you to inquire of the Lord, in this manner you shall speak to him

2Chr 35:21 But he sent messengers to him, saying, "What have I to do with you, *king of Judah*

Esth 2:6 Kish had been carried away from Jerusalem with the captives who had been captured with Jeconiah *king of Judah*, whom Nebuchadnezzar the king of Babylon had carried away

Prov 25:1 These also are proverbs of Solomon which the men of Hezekiah *king of Judah* copied

Is 7:1 Now it came to pass in the days of Ahaz the son of Jotham, the son of Uzziah, *king of Judah*, that Rezin king of Syria and Pekah the son of Remaliah, king of Israel, went up to Jerusalem to make war against it, but could not prevail against it

Is 37:10 Thus you shall speak to Hezekiah *king of Judah*, saying
Is 38:9 This is the writing of Hezekiah *king of Judah*, when he had been sick and had recovered from his sickness
Jer 1:2 to whom the word of the Lord came in the days of Josiah the son of Amon, *king of Judah*, in the thirteenth year of his reign
Jer 1:3 It came also in the days of Jehoiakim the son of Josiah, *king of Judah*, until the end of the eleventh year of Zedekiah the son of Josiah, *king of Judah*, until the carrying away of Jerusalem captive in the fifth month
Jer 15:4 I will hand them over to trouble, to all kingdoms of the earth, because of Manasseh the son of Hezekiah, *king of Judah*, for what he did in Jerusalem
Jer 21:7 And afterward," says the Lord, "I will deliver Zedekiah *king of Judah*, his servants and the people, and such as are left in this city from the pestilence and the sword and the famine, into the hand of Nebuchadnezzar king of Babylon, into the hand of their enemies, and into the hand of those who seek their life
Jer 21:11 And concerning the house of the *king of Judah*, say
Jer 22:1 Go down to the house of the *king of Judah*, and there speak this word
Jer 22:2 and say, 'Hear the word of the Lord, O *king of Judah*, you who sit on the throne of David, you and your servants and your people who enter these gates
Jer 22:6 For thus says the Lord to the house of the *king of Judah*
Jer 22:11 For thus says the Lord concerning Shallum the son of Josiah, *king of Judah*, who reigned instead of Josiah his father, who went from this place
Jer 22:18 Therefore thus says the Lord concerning Jehoiakim the son of Josiah, *king of Judah*
Jer 22:24 As I live," says the Lord, "though Coniah the son of Jehoiakim, *king of Judah*, were the signet on My right hand, yet I would pluck you off
Jer 24:1 The Lord showed me, and there were two baskets of figs set before the temple of the Lord, after Nebuchadnezzar king of Babylon had carried away captive Jeconiah the son of Jehoiakim, *king of Judah*, and the princes of Judah with the craftsmen and smiths, from Jerusalem, and had brought them to Babylon
Jer 24:8 And as the bad figs which cannot be eaten, they are so bad' surely thus says the Lord 'so will I give up Zedekiah the *king of Judah*, his princes, the residue of Jerusalem who remain in this land, and those who dwell in the land of Egypt
Jer 25:1 The word that came to Jeremiah concerning all the people of Judah, in the fourth year of Jehoiakim the son of Josiah, *king of Judah* (which was the first year of Nebuchadnezzar king of Babylon
Jer 25:3 From the thirteenth year of Josiah the son of Amon, *king of Judah*, even to this day, this is the twenty-third year in which the word of the Lord has come to me
Jer 26:1 In the beginning of the reign of Jehoiakim the son of Josiah, *king of Judah*, this word came from the Lord, saying
Jer 26:18 Micah of Moresheth prophesied in the days of Hezekiah *king of Judah*, and spoke to all the people of Judah, saying
Jer 26:19 Did Hezekiah *king of Judah* and all Judah ever put him to death
Jer 27:1 In the beginning of the reign of Jehoiakim the son of Josiah, *king of Judah*, this word came to Jeremiah from the Lord, saying
Jer 27:3 and send them to the king of Edom, the king of Moab, the king of the Ammonites, the king of Tyre, and the king of Sidon, by the hand of the messengers who come to Jerusalem to Zedekiah *king of Judah*
Jer 27:12 I also spoke to Zedekiah *king of Judah* according to all these words, saying
Jer 27:18 But if they are prophets, and if the word of the Lord is with them, let them now make intercession to the Lord of hosts, that the vessels which are left in the house of the Lord, in the house of the *king of Judah*, and at Jerusalem, do not go to Babylon
Jer 27:20 which Nebuchadnezzar king of Babylon did not take, when he carried away captive Jeconiah the son of Jehoiakim, *king of Judah*, from Jerusalem to Babylon, and all the nobles of Judah and Jerusalem
Jer 27:21 yes, thus says the Lord of hosts, the God of Israel, concerning the vessels that remain in the house of the Lord, and in the house of the *king of Judah* and of Jerusalem
Jer 28:1 And it happened in the same year, at the beginning of the reign of Zedekiah *king of Judah*, in the fourth year and in the fifth month, that Hananiah the son of Azur the prophet, who was from Gibeon, spoke to me in the house of the Lord in the presence of the priests and of all the people, saying
Jer 28:4 And I will bring back to this place Jeconiah the son of Jehoiakim, *king of Judah*, with all the captives of Judah who went to Babylon
Jer 29:3 The letter was sent by the hand of Elasah the son of Shaphan, and Gemariah the son of Hilkiah, whom Zedekiah *king of Judah* sent to Babylon, to Nebuchadnezzar king of Babylon, saying
Jer 32:1 The word that came to Jeremiah from the Lord in the tenth year of Zedekiah *king of Judah*, which was the eighteenth year of Nebuchadnezzar
Jer 32:3 For Zedekiah *king of Judah* had shut him up, saying
Jer 32:4 and Zedekiah *king of Judah* shall not escape from the hand of the Chaldeans, but shall surely be delivered into the hand of the king of Babylon, and shall speak with him face to face, and see him eye to eye
Jer 34:2 Go and speak to Zedekiah *king of Judah* and tell him
Jer 34:4 Yet hear the word of the Lord, O Zedekiah *king of Judah*
Jer 34:6 Then Jeremiah the prophet spoke all these words to Zedekiah *king of Judah* in Jerusalem
Jer 34:21 And I will give Zedekiah *king of Judah* and his princes into the hand of their enemies, into the hand of those who seek their life, and into the hand of the king of Babylon's army which has gone back from you
Jer 35:1 The word which came to Jeremiah from the Lord in the days of Jehoiakim the son of Josiah, *king of Judah*, saying
Jer 36:1 Now it came to pass in the fourth year of Jehoiakim the son of Josiah, *king of Judah*, that this word came to Jeremiah from the Lord, saying
Jer 36:9 Now it came to pass in the fifth year of Jehoiakim the son of Josiah, *king of Judah*, in the ninth month, that they proclaimed a fast before the Lord to all the people in Jerusalem, and to all the people who came from the cities of Judah to Jerusalem
Jer 36:28 Take yet another scroll, and write on it all the former words that were in the first scroll which Jehoiakim the *king of Judah* has burned
Jer 36:29 And you shall say to Jehoiakim *king of Judah*, 'Thus says the Lord
Jer 36:30 Therefore thus says the Lord concerning Jehoiakim *king of Judah*

Jer 36:32 Then Jeremiah took another scroll and gave it to Baruch the scribe, the son of Neriah, who wrote on it at the instruction of Jeremiah all the words of the book which Jehoiakim *king of Judah* had burned in the fire
Jer 37:7 Thus says the Lord, the God of Israel, 'Thus you shall say to the *king of Judah*, who sent you to Me to inquire of Me
Jer 39:1 In the ninth year of Zedekiah *king of Judah*, in the tenth month, Nebuchadnezzar king of Babylon and all his army came against Jerusalem, and besieged it
Jer 39:4 So it was, when Zedekiah the *king of Judah* and all the men of war saw them, that they fled and went out of the city by night, by way of the king's garden, by the gate between the two walls
Jer 44:30 Behold, I will give Pharaoh Hophra king of Egypt into the hand of his enemies and into the hand of those who seek his life, as I gave Zedekiah *king of Judah* into the hand of Nebuchadnezzar king of Babylon, his enemy who sought his life
Jer 45:1 The word that Jeremiah the prophet spoke to Baruch the son of Neriah, when he had written these words in a book at the instruction of Jeremiah, in the fourth year of Jehoiakim the son of Josiah, *king of Judah*, saying
Jer 46:2 Concerning the army of Pharaoh Necho, king of Egypt, which was by the River Euphrates in Carchemish, and which Nebuchadnezzar king of Babylon defeated in the fourth year of Jehoiakim the son of Josiah, *king of Judah*
Jer 49:34 The word of the Lord that came to Jeremiah the prophet against Elam, in the beginning of the reign of Zedekiah *king of Judah*, saying
Jer 51:59 The word which Jeremiah the prophet commanded Seraiah the son of Neriah, the son of Mahseiah, when he went with Zedekiah the *king of Judah* to Babylon in the fourth year of his reign
Jer 52:31 Now it came to pass in the thirty-seventh year of the captivity of Jehoiachin *king of Judah*, in the twelfth month, on the twenty-fifth day of the month, that Evil-Merodach king of Babylon, in the first year of his reign, lifted up the head of Jehoiachin *king of Judah* and brought him out of prison
Dan 1:1 In the third year of the reign of Jehoiakim *king of Judah*, Nebuchadnezzar king of Babylon came to Jerusalem and besieged it
Dan 1:2 And the Lord gave Jehoiakim *king of Judah* into his hand, with some of the articles of the house of God, which he carried into the land of Shinar to the house of his god
Amos 1:1 The words of Amos, who was among the herdsmen of Tekoa, which he saw concerning Israel in the days of Uzziah *king of Judah*, and in the days of Jeroboam the son of Joash, king of Israel, two years before the earthquake
Zeph 1:1 The word of the Lord which came to Zephaniah the son of Cushi, the son of Gedaliah, the son of Amariah, the son of Hezekiah, in the days of Josiah the son of Amon, *king of Judah*
Zech 14:5 Yes, you shall flee as you fled from the earthquake in the days of Uzziah *king of Judah*

KING OF KINGS
Ezra 7:12 Artaxerxes, *king of kings*, to Ezra the priest, a scribe of the Law of the God of heaven
Ezek 26:7 Behold, I will bring against Tyre from the north Nebuchadnezzar king of Babylon, *king of kings*, with horses, with chariots, and with horsemen, and an army with many people
Dan 2:37 You, O king, are a *king of kings*. For the God of heaven has given you a kingdom, power, strength, and glory
1Tim 6:15 which He will manifest in His own time, He who is the blessed and only Potentate, the *King of kings* and Lord of lords
Rev 17:14 These will make war with the Lamb, and the Lamb will overcome them, for He is Lord of lords and *King of kings*
Rev 19:16 And He has on His robe and on His thigh a name written: *KING OF KINGS* and LORD OF LORDS

KING OF RIGHTEOUSNESS
Heb 7:2 to whom also Abraham gave a tenth part of all, first being translated "*king of righteousness*

KING OF THE JEWS
Matt 2:2 saying, "Where is He who has been born *King of the Jews*
Matt 27:11 And the governor asked Him, saying, "Are You the *King of the Jews*
Matt 27:29 And they bowed the knee before Him and mocked Him, saying, "Hail, *King of the Jews*
Matt 27:37 And they put up over His head the accusation written against Him: THIS IS JESUS, *KING OF THE JEWS*
Mark 15:2 Then Pilate asked Him, "Are You the *King of the Jews*
Mark 15:9 But Pilate answered them, saying, "Do you want me to release to you the *King of the Jews*
Mark 15:12 And Pilate answered and said to them again, "What then do you want me to do with Him whom you call the *King of the Jews*
Mark 15:18 and began to salute Him, "Hail, *King of the Jews*
Mark 15:26 And the inscription of His accusation was written above: THE *KING OF THE JEWS*
Luke 23:3 So Pilate asked Him, saying, "Are You the *King of the Jews*
Luke 23:37 and saying, "If You are the *King of the Jews*, save Yourself
Luke 23:38 And an inscription also was written over Him in letters of Greek, Latin, and Hebrew: THIS IS THE *KING OF THE JEWS*
John 18:33 Then Pilate entered the Praetorium again, called Jesus, and said to Him, "Are You the *King of the Jews*
John 18:39 Do you therefore want me to release to you the *King of the Jews*
John 19:3 Then they said, "Hail, *King of the Jews!*" And they struck Him with their hands
John 19:19 And the writing was: The *King of the Jews*
John 19:21 Then the chief priests of the Jews said to Pilate, "Do not write, 'The *King of the Jews*,' but, 'He said, "I am the *King of the Jews*

KING OVER ISRAEL
1Sam 15:17 And did not the Lord anoint you *king over Israel*
1Sam 15:26 But Samuel said to Saul, "I will not return with you, for you have rejected the word of the Lord, and the Lord has rejected you from being *king over Israel*
1Sam 15:35 Nevertheless Samuel mourned for Saul, and the Lord regretted that He had made Saul *king over Israel*
1Sam 23:17 You shall be *king over Israel*, and I shall be next to you
2Sam 5:3 So all the elders of Israel came to the king at Hebron, and King David made a covenant with them at Hebron before the Lord. And they anointed David *king over Israel*
2Sam 5:12 So David knew that the Lord had established him as *king over Israel*, and that He had exalted His kingdom for His people Israel's sake
2Sam 5:17 Now when the Philistines heard that

they had anointed David *king over Israel*, all the Philistines went up to search for David
2Sam 12:7 I anointed you *king over Israel*, and I delivered you from the hand of Saul
2Sam 19:22 For do I not know that today I am *king over Israel*
1Kin 1:34 There let Zadok the priest and Nathan the prophet anoint him *king over Israel*
1Kin 11:37 So I will take you, and you shall reign over all your heart desires, and you shall be *king over Israel*
1Kin 14:14 Moreover the Lord will raise up for Himself a *king over Israel* who shall cut off the house of Jeroboam
1Kin 15:25 Now Nadab the son of Jeroboam became *king over Israel* in the second year of Asa king of Judah, and he reigned over Israel two years
1Kin 16:8 In the twenty-sixth year of Asa king of Judah, Elah the son of Baasha became *king over Israel*, and reigned two years in Tirzah
1Kin 16:16 So all Israel made Omri, the commander of the army, *king over Israel* that day in the camp
1Kin 16:23 In the thirty-first year of Asa king of Judah, Omri became *king over Israel*, and reigned twelve years
1Kin 16:29 In the thirty-eighth year of Asa king of Judah, Ahab the son of Omri became *king over Israel*
1Kin 19:16 Also you shall anoint Jehu the son of Nimshi as *king over Israel*
1Kin 22:51 Ahaziah the son of Ahab became *king over Israel* in Samaria in the seventeenth year of Jehoshaphat king of Judah, and reigned two years over Israel
2Kin 3:1 Now Jehoram the son of Ahab became *king over Israel* at Samaria in the eighteenth year of Jehoshaphat king of Judah, and reigned twelve years
2Kin 9:3 I have anointed you *king over Israel*." Then open the door and flee, and do not delay
2Kin 9:12 So he said, "Thus and thus he spoke to me, saying, 'Thus says the Lord: "I have anointed you *king over Israel*
2Kin 13:1 In the twenty-third year of Joash the son of Ahaziah, king of Judah, Jehoahaz the son of Jehu became *king over Israel* in Samaria, and reigned seventeen years
2Kin 13:10 In the thirty-seventh year of Joash king of Judah, Jehoash the son of Jehoahaz became *king over Israel* in Samaria, and reigned sixteen years
2Kin 15:17 In the thirty-ninth year of Azariah king of Judah, Menahem the son of Gadi became *king over Israel*, and reigned ten years in Samaria
2Kin 15:23 In the fiftieth year of Azariah king of Judah, Pekahiah the son of Menahem became *king over Israel* in Samaria, and reigned two years
2Kin 15:27 In the fifty-second year of Azariah king of Judah, Pekah the son of Remaliah became *king over Israel* in Samaria, and reigned twenty years
1Chr 11:3 Then they anointed David *king over Israel*, according to the word of the Lord by Samuel
1Chr 14:2 And David perceived that the Lord had established him as *king over Israel*, for his kingdom was highly exalted because of His people Israel
1Chr 23:1 So when David was old and full of days, he made his son Solomon *king over Israel*
1Chr 28:4 However the Lord God of Israel chose me above all the house of my father to be *king over Israel* forever, for He has chosen Judah to be the ruler
Eccl 1:12 I, the Preacher, was *king over Israel* in Jerusalem

KING OVER JUDAH
1Kin 15:1 Now in the eighteenth year of King Jeroboam the son of Nebat, Abijam became *king over Judah*
1Kin 15:9 In the twentieth year of Jeroboam king of Israel, Asa became *king over Judah*
1Kin 22:41 Now Jehoshaphat the son of Asa had become *king over Judah* in the fourth year of Ahab king of Israel
2Kin 9:29 In the eleventh year of Joram the son of Ahab, Ahaziah had become *king over Judah*
2Chr 13:1 In the eighteenth year of King Jeroboam, Abijah became *king over Judah*
2Chr 20:31 So Jehoshaphat was *king over Judah*. He was thirty-five years old when he became king, and he reigned twenty-five years in Jerusalem
2Chr 36:4 Then the king of Egypt made his brother Eliakim *king over Judah* and Jerusalem, and changed his name to Jehoiakim
2Chr 36:10 At the turn of the year King Nebuchadnezzar summoned him and took him to Babylon, with the costly articles from the house of the Lord, and made Zedekiah, Jehoiakim's brother, *king over Judah* and Jerusalem

KING'S HIGHWAY
Num 20:17 we will go along the *King's Highway;* we will not turn aside to the right hand or to the left until we have passed through your territory
Num 21:22 but we will go by the *King's Highway* until we have passed through your territory

KING'S TABLE
1Sam 20:29 Therefore he has not come to the *king's table*
2Sam 9:13 So Mephibosheth dwelt in Jerusalem, for he ate continually at the *king's table*

KINGDOM AGAINST KINGDOM
Is 19:2 everyone will fight against his brother, and everyone against his neighbor, city against city, *kingdom against kingdom*
Matt 24:7 For nation will rise against nation, and *kingdom against kingdom*
Mark 13:8 For nation will rise against nation, and *kingdom against kingdom*
Luke 21:10 Then He said to them, "Nation will rise against nation, and *kingdom against kingdom*

KINGDOM AND PRIESTS TO SERVE HIS GOD AND FATHER (NIV)
(See *KINGS AND PRIESTS TO HIS GOD AND FATHER*)

KINGDOM DIVIDED AGAINST ITSELF
Matt 12:25 Every *kingdom divided against itself* is brought to desolation, and every city or house divided against itself will not stand
Luke 11:17 Every *kingdom divided against itself* is brought to desolation, and a house divided against a house falls

KINGDOM OF GOD
Matt 6:33 But seek first the *kingdom of God* and His righteousness, and all these things shall be added to you
Matt 12:28 But if I cast out demons by the Spirit of God, surely the *kingdom of God* has come upon you
Matt 19:24 And again I say to you, it is easier for a camel to go through the eye of a needle than for a rich man to enter the *kingdom of God*
Matt 21:31 Jesus said to them, "Assuredly, I say

to you that tax collectors and harlots enter the *kingdom of God* before you
Matt 21:43 Therefore I say to you, the *kingdom of God* will be taken from you and given to a nation bearing the fruits of it
Mark 1:14 Now after John was put in prison, Jesus came to Galilee, preaching the gospel of the *kingdom of God*
Mark 1:15 and saying, "The time is fulfilled, and the *kingdom of God* is at hand
Mark 4:11 And He said to them, "To you it has been given to know the mystery of the *kingdom of God*
Mark 4:26 And He said, "The *kingdom of God* is as if a man should scatter seed on the ground
Mark 4:30 And He said, "To what shall we liken the *kingdom of God*
Mark 9:1 And He said to them, "Assuredly, I say to you that there are some standing here who will not taste death till they see the *kingdom of God* present with power
Mark 9:47 It is better for you to enter the *kingdom of God* with one eye, than having two eyes, to be cast into hell fire
Mark 10:14 But when Jesus saw it, He was greatly displeased and said to them, "Let the little children come to Me, and do not forbid them; for of such is the *kingdom of God*
Mark 10:15 Assuredly, I say to you, whoever does not receive the *kingdom of God* as a little child will by no means enter it
Mark 10:23 Then Jesus looked around and said to His disciples, "How hard it is for those who have riches to enter the *kingdom of God*
Mark 10:24 But Jesus answered again and said to them, "Children, how hard it is for those who trust in riches to enter the *kingdom of God*
Mark 10:25 It is easier for a camel to go through the eye of a needle than for a rich man to enter the *kingdom of God*
Mark 12:34 So when Jesus saw that he answered wisely, He said to him, "You are not far from the *kingdom of God*
Mark 14:25 Assuredly, I say to you, I will no longer drink of the fruit of the vine until that day when I drink it new in the *kingdom of God*
Mark 15:43 Joseph of Arimathea, a prominent council member, who was himself waiting for the *kingdom of God*, coming and taking courage, went in to Pilate and asked for the body of Jesus
Luke 4:43 but He said to them, "I must preach the *kingdom of God* to the other cities also, because for this purpose I have been sent
Luke 6:20 Blessed are you poor, for yours is the *kingdom of God*
Luke 7:28 but he who is least in the *kingdom of God* is greater than he
Luke 8:1 Now it came to pass, afterward, that He went through every city and village, preaching and bringing the glad tidings of the *kingdom of God*
Luke 8:10 And He said, "To you it has been given to know the mysteries of the *kingdom of God*, but to the rest it is given in parables, that
Luke 9:2 He sent them to preach the *kingdom of God* and to heal the sick
Luke 9:11 and He received them and spoke to them about the *kingdom of God*, and healed those who had need of healing
Luke 9:27 But I tell you truly, there are some standing here who shall not taste death till they see the *kingdom of God*
Luke 9:60 Jesus said to him, "Let the dead bury their own dead, but you go and preach the *kingdom of God*
Luke 9:62 But Jesus said to him, "No one, having put his hand to the plow, and looking back, is fit for the *kingdom of God*
Luke 10:9 And heal the sick who are there, and say to them, 'The *kingdom of God* has come near to you
Luke 10:11 Nevertheless know this, that the *kingdom of God* has come near you
Luke 11:20 But if I cast out demons with the finger of God, surely the *kingdom of God* has come upon you
Luke 12:31 But seek the *kingdom of God*, and all these things shall be added to you
Luke 13:18 Then He said, "What is the *kingdom of God* like
Luke 13:20 And again He said, "To what shall I liken the *kingdom of God*
Luke 13:28 There will be weeping and gnashing of teeth, when you see Abraham and Isaac and Jacob and all the prophets in the *kingdom of God*, and yourselves thrust out
Luke 13:29 They will come from the east and the west, from the north and the south, and sit down in the *kingdom of God*
Luke 14:15 Now when one of those who sat at the table with Him heard these things, he said to Him, "Blessed is he who shall eat bread in the *kingdom of God*
Luke 16:16 Since that time the *kingdom of God* has been preached, and everyone is pressing into it
Luke 17:20 Now when He was asked by the Pharisees when the *kingdom of God* would come, He answered them and said, "The *kingdom of God* does not come with observation
Luke 17:21 For indeed, the *kingdom of God* is within you
Luke 18:16 But Jesus called them to Him and said, "Let the little children come to Me, and do not forbid them; for of such is the *kingdom of God*
Luke 18:17 Assuredly, I say to you, whoever does not receive the *kingdom of God* as a little child will by no means enter it
Luke 18:24 And when Jesus saw that he became very sorrowful, He said, "How hard it is for those who have riches to enter the *kingdom of God*
Luke 18:25 For it is easier for a camel to go through a needle's eye than for a rich man to enter the *kingdom of God*
Luke 18:29 So He said to them, "Assuredly, I say to you, there is no one who has left house or parents or brothers or wife or children, for the sake of the *kingdom of God*
Luke 19:11 Now as they heard these things, He spoke another parable, because He was near Jerusalem and because they thought the *kingdom of God* would appear immediately
Luke 21:31 So you, likewise, when you see these things happening, know that the *kingdom of God* is near
Luke 22:16 for I say to you, I will no longer eat of it until it is fulfilled in the *kingdom of God*
Luke 22:18 for I say to you, I will not drink of the fruit of the vine until the *kingdom of God* comes
Luke 23:51 He was from Arimathea, a city of the Jews, who himself was also waiting for the *kingdom of God*
John 3:3 Jesus answered and said to him, "Most assuredly, I say to you, unless one is born again, he cannot see the *kingdom of God*
John 3:5 Jesus answered, "Most assuredly, I say to you, unless one is born of water and the Spirit, he cannot enter the *kingdom of God*
Acts 1:3 to whom He also presented Himself alive after His suffering by many infallible proofs, being seen by them during forty days and speaking of the things pertaining to the *kingdom of God*
Acts 8:12 But when they believed Philip as he preached the things concerning the *kingdom of God* and the name of Jesus Christ, both men and women were baptized

Acts 14:22 strengthening the souls of the disciples, exhorting them to continue in the faith, and saying, "We must through many tribulations enter the *kingdom of God*
Acts 19:8 And he went into the synagogue and spoke boldly for three months, reasoning and persuading concerning the things of the *kingdom of God*
Acts 20:25 And indeed, now I know that you all, among whom I have gone preaching the *kingdom of God*, will see my face no more
Acts 28:23 So when they had appointed him a day, many came to him at his lodging, to whom he explained and solemnly testified of the *kingdom of God*, persuading them concerning Jesus from both the Law of Moses and the Prophets, from morning till evening
Acts 28:31 preaching the *kingdom of God* and teaching the things which concern the Lord Jesus Christ with all confidence, no one forbidding him
Rom 14:17 for the *kingdom of God* is not food and drink, but righteousness and peace and joy in the Holy Spirit
1Cor 4:20 For the *kingdom of God* is not in word but in power
1Cor 6:9 Do you not know that the unrighteous will not inherit the *kingdom of God*
1Cor 6:10 nor thieves, nor covetous, nor drunkards, nor revilers, nor extortioners will inherit the *kingdom of God*
1Cor 15:50 Now this I say, brethren, that flesh and blood cannot inherit the *kingdom of God*
Gal 5:21 of which I tell you beforehand, just as I also told you in time past, that those who practice such things will not inherit the *kingdom of God*
Col 4:11 These are my only fellow workers for the *kingdom of God* who are of the circumcision
2Th 1:5 which is manifest evidence of the righteous judgment of God, that you may be counted worthy of the *kingdom of God*, for which you also suffer

KINGDOM OF GOD BELONGS TO SUCH AS THESE (NAS, NIV)
(See *SUCH IS THE KINGDOM OF GOD*)

KINGDOM OF GOD HAS BEEN PREACHED
Luke 16:16 Since that time the *kingdom of God has been preached*, and everyone is pressing into it

KINGDOM OF GOD IS AT HAND
Mark 1:15 and saying, "The time is fulfilled, and the *kingdom of God is at hand*

KINGDOM OF GOD IS NEAR
Luke 21:31 So you, likewise, when you see these things happening, know that the *kingdom of God is near*

KINGDOM OF HEAVEN
Matt 3:2 and saying, "Repent, for the *kingdom of heaven* is at hand
Matt 4:17 From that time Jesus began to preach and to say, "Repent, for the *kingdom of heaven* is at hand
Matt 5:3 Blessed are the poor in spirit, for theirs is the *kingdom of heaven*
Matt 5:10 Blessed are those who are persecuted for righteousness' sake, for theirs is the *kingdom of heaven*
Matt 5:19 Whoever therefore breaks one of the least of these commandments, and teaches men so, shall be called least in the *kingdom of heaven;* but whoever does and teaches them, he shall be called great in the *kingdom of heaven*
Matt 5:20 For I say to you, that unless your righteousness exceeds the righteousness of the scribes and Pharisees, you will by no means enter the *kingdom of heaven*
Matt 7:21 Not everyone who says to Me, 'Lord, Lord,' shall enter the *kingdom of heaven*, but he who does the will of My Father in heaven
Matt 8:11 And I say to you that many will come from east and west, and sit down with Abraham, Isaac, and Jacob in the *kingdom of heaven*
Matt 10:7 And as you go, preach, saying, 'The *kingdom of heaven* is at hand
Matt 11:11 but he who is least in the *kingdom of heaven* is greater than he
Matt 11:12 And from the days of John the Baptist until now the *kingdom of heaven* suffers violence, and the violent take it by force
Matt 13:11 He answered and said to them, "Because it has been given to you to know the mysteries of the *kingdom of heaven*, but to them it has not been given
Matt 13:24 The *kingdom of heaven* is like a man who sowed good seed in his field
Matt 13:31 The *kingdom of heaven* is like a mustard seed, which a man took and sowed in his field
Matt 13:33 The *kingdom of heaven* is like leaven, which a woman took and hid in three measures of meal till it was all leavened
Matt 13:44 Again, the *kingdom of heaven* is like treasure hidden in a field, which a man found and hid
Matt 13:45 Again, the *kingdom of heaven* is like a merchant seeking beautiful pearls
Matt 13:47 Again, the *kingdom of heaven* is like a dragnet that was cast into the sea and gathered some of every kind
Matt 13:52 Then He said to them, "Therefore every scribe instructed concerning the *kingdom of heaven* is like a householder who brings out of his treasure things new and old
Matt 16:19 And I will give you the keys of the *kingdom of heaven*, and whatever you bind on earth will be bound in heaven, and whatever you loose on earth will be loosed in heaven
Matt 18:1 At that time the disciples came to Jesus, saying, "Who then is greatest in the *kingdom of heaven*
Matt 18:3 and said, "Assuredly, I say to you, unless you are converted and become as little children, you will by no means enter the *kingdom of heaven*
Matt 18:4 Therefore whoever humbles himself as this little child is the greatest in the *kingdom of heaven*
Matt 18:23 Therefore the *kingdom of heaven* is like a certain king who wanted to settle accounts with his servants
Matt 19:14 But Jesus said, "Let the little children come to Me, and do not forbid them; for of such is the *kingdom of heaven*
Matt 19:23 Then Jesus said to His disciples, "Assuredly, I say to you that it is hard for a rich man to enter the *kingdom of heaven*
Matt 20:1 For the *kingdom of heaven* is like a landowner who went out early in the morning to hire laborers for his vineyard
Matt 22:2 The *kingdom of heaven* is like a certain king who arranged a marriage for his son
Matt 23:13 For you shut up the *kingdom of heaven* against men
Matt 25:1 Then the *kingdom of heaven* shall be likened to ten virgins who took their lamps and went out to meet the bridegroom
Matt 25:14 For the *kingdom of heaven* is like a man traveling to a far country, who called his own servants and delivered his goods to them

KINGDOM OF OUR FATHER DAVID
Mark 11:10 Blessed is the *kingdom of our father David* that comes in the name of the Lord

KINGDOM OF PRIESTS
Ex 19:6 And you shall be to Me a *kingdom of priests* and a holy nation

KINGDOMS OF OUR LORD
Rev 11:15 And there were loud voices in heaven, saying, "The kingdoms of this world have become the *kingdoms of our Lord* and of His Christ, and He shall reign forever and ever

KINGDOMS OF THE EARTH
Deut 28:25 and you shall become troublesome to all the *kingdoms of the earth*
2Kin 19:15 O Lord God of Israel, the One who dwells between the cherubim, You are God, You alone, of all the *kingdoms of the earth*
2Kin 19:19 Now therefore, O Lord our God, I pray, save us from his hand, that all the *kingdoms of the earth* may know that You are the Lord God, You alone
2Chr 36:23 All the *kingdoms of the earth* the Lord God of heaven has given me
Ezra 1:2 All the *kingdoms of the earth* the Lord God of heaven has given me
Ps 68:32 Sing to God, you *kingdoms of the earth;* oh, sing praises to the Lord
Is 37:16 O Lord of hosts, God of Israel, the One who dwells between the cherubim, You are God, You alone, of all the *kingdoms of the earth*
Is 37:20 Now therefore, O Lord our God, save us from his hand, that all the *kingdoms of the earth* may know that You are the Lord, You alone
Jer 15:4 I will hand them over to trouble, to all *kingdoms of the earth*, because of Manasseh the son of Hezekiah, king of Judah, for what he did in Jerusalem
Jer 24:9 I will deliver them to trouble into all the *kingdoms of the earth*, for their harm, to be a reproach and a byword, a taunt and a curse, in all places where I shall drive them
Jer 29:18 and I will deliver them to trouble among all the *kingdoms of the earth* to be a curse, an astonishment, a hissing, and a reproach among all the nations where I have driven them
Jer 34:1 The word which came to Jeremiah from the Lord, when Nebuchadnezzar king of Babylon and all his army, all the *kingdoms of the earth* under his dominion, and all the people, fought against Jerusalem and all its cities, saying
Jer 34:17 And I will deliver you to trouble among all the *kingdoms of the earth*

KINGDOMS OF THE WORLD
Is 23:17 She will return to her pay, and commit fornication with all the *kingdoms of the world* on the face of the earth
Jer 25:26 and all the *kingdoms of the world* which are on the face of the earth
Matt 4:8 Again, the devil took Him up on an exceedingly high mountain, and showed Him all the *kingdoms of the world* and their glory
Luke 4:5 Then the devil, taking Him up on a high mountain, showed Him all the *kingdoms of the world* in a moment of time

KINGDOMS ON EARTH (NIV)
(See *KINGDOMS OF THE EARTH*)

KINGDOMS ON THE FACE OF THE EARTH (NIV)
(See *KINGDOMS OF THE WORLD*)

KINGS AND PRIESTS TO HIS GOD AND FATHER
Rev 1:6 and has made us *kings and priests to His God and Father*, to Him be glory and dominion forever and ever

KINGS OF THE EARTH
1Kin 4:34 And men of all nations, from all the *kings of the earth* who had heard of his wisdom, came to hear the wisdom of Solomon
1Kin 10:23 So King Solomon surpassed all the *kings of the earth* in riches and wisdom
2Chr 9:22 So King Solomon surpassed all the *kings of the earth* in riches and wisdom
2Chr 9:23 And all the *kings of the earth* sought the presence of Solomon to hear his wisdom, which God had put in his heart
Ps 2:2 The *kings of the earth* set themselves, and the rulers take counsel together, against the Lord and against His Anointed, saying
Ps 76:12 He shall cut off the spirit of princes; He is awesome to the *kings of the earth*
Ps 89:27 Also I will make him My firstborn, the highest of the *kings of the earth*
Ps 102:15 So the nations shall fear the name of the Lord, and all the *kings of the earth* Your glory
Ps 138:4 All the *kings of the earth* shall praise You, O Lord, when they hear the words of Your mouth
Ps 148:11 Kings of the earth and all peoples; princes and all judges of the earth
Is 24:21 It shall come to pass in that day that the Lord will punish on high the host of exalted ones, and on the earth the *kings of the earth*
Lam 4:12 The *kings of the earth*, and all inhabitants of the world, would not have believed that the adversary and the enemy could enter the gates of Jerusalem
Ezek 27:33 you enriched the *kings of the earth* with your many luxury goods and your merchandise
Matt 17:25 From whom do the *kings of the earth* take customs or taxes, from their own sons or from strangers
Acts 4:26 the *kings of the earth* took their stand, and the rulers were gathered together against the Lord and against His Christ
Rev 1:5 and from Jesus Christ, the faithful witness, the firstborn from the dead, and the ruler over the *kings of the earth*
Rev 6:15 And the *kings of the earth*, the great men, the rich men, the commanders, the mighty men, every slave and every free man, hid themselves in the caves and in the rocks of the mountains
Rev 16:14 For they are spirits of demons, performing signs, which go out to the *kings of the earth* and of the whole world, to gather them to the battle of that great day of God Almighty
Rev 17:2 with whom the *kings of the earth* committed fornication, and the inhabitants of the earth were made drunk with the wine of her fornication
Rev 17:18 And the woman whom you saw is that great city which reigns over the *kings of the earth*
Rev 18:3 For all the nations have drunk of the wine of the wrath of her fornication, the *kings of the earth* have committed fornication with her, and the merchants of the earth have become rich through the abundance of her luxury
Rev 18:9 And the *kings of the earth* who committed fornication and lived luxuriously with her will weep and lament for her, when they see the smoke of her burning
Rev 19:19 And I saw the beast, the *kings of the earth*, and their armies, gathered together to

make war against Him who sat on the horse and against His army
Rev 21:24 And the nations of those who are saved shall walk in its light, and the *kings of the earth* bring their glory and honor into it

KINGS OF THE GENTILES
Luke 22:25 And He said to them, "The *kings of the Gentiles* exercise lordship over them, and those who exercise authority over them are called

KINGS OF THE WORLD (NIV)
(See *KINGS OF THE EARTH*)

KISS OF CHARITY (KJV)
(See *KISS OF LOVE*)

KISS OF LOVE
1Pet 5:14 Greet one another with a *kiss of love*. Peace to you all who are in Christ Jesus

KISSED EACH OTHER
Ps 85:10 Mercy and truth have met together; righteousness and peace have *kissed each other*

KISSES OF AN ENEMY
Prov 27:6 Faithful are the wounds of a friend, but the *kisses of an enemy* are deceitful

KNELT DOWN AND PRAYED
Luke 22:41 And He was withdrawn from them about a stone's throw, and He *knelt down and prayed*
Acts 9:40 But Peter put them all out, and *knelt down and prayed*
Acts 20:36 And when he had said these things, he *knelt down and prayed* with them all

KNEW NO SIN
2Cor 5:21 For He made Him who *knew no sin* to be sin for us, that we might become the righteousness of God in Him

KNEW THEIR THOUGHTS
Matt 12:25 But Jesus *knew their thoughts*, and said to them: "Every kingdom divided against itself is brought to desolation, and every city or house divided against itself will not stand
Luke 6:8 But He *knew their thoughts*, and said to the man who had the withered hand

KNIT TOGETHER IN LOVE
Col 2:2 that their hearts may be encouraged, being *knit together in love*, and attaining to all riches of the full assurance of understanding, to the knowledge of the mystery of God, both of the Father and of Christ

KNOW GOOD AND EVIL
Gen 3:22 Then the Lord God said, "Behold, the man has become like one of Us, to *know good and evil*

KNOW IN PART
1Cor 13:9 For we *know in part* and we prophesy in part
1Cor 13:12 Now I *know in part*, but then I shall know just as I also am known

KNOW THAT I AM THE LORD
Ex 6:7 Then you shall *know that I am the Lord* your God who brings you out from under the burdens of the Egyptians
Ex 7:5 And the Egyptians shall *know that I am the Lord*, when I stretch out My hand on Egypt and bring out the children of Israel from among them
Ex 7:17 By this you shall *know that I am the Lord*
Ex 8:22 And in that day I will set apart the land of Goshen, in which My people dwell, that no swarms of flies shall be there, in order that you may *know that I am the Lord* in the midst of the land
Ex 10:2 and that you may tell in the hearing of your son and your son's son the mighty things I have done in Egypt, and My signs which I have done among them, that you may *know that I am the Lord*
Ex 14:4 and I will gain honor over Pharaoh and over all his army, that the Egyptians may *know that I am the Lord*
Ex 14:18 Then the Egyptians shall *know that I am the Lord*, when I have gained honor for Myself over Pharaoh, his chariots, and his horsemen
Ex 16:12 And you shall *know that I am the Lord* your God
Ex 29:46 And they shall *know that I am the Lord* their God, who brought them up out of the land of Egypt, that I may dwell among them
Ex 31:13 Surely My Sabbaths you shall keep, for it is a sign between Me and you throughout your generations, that you may *know that I am the Lord* who sanctifies you
Deut 29:6 that you may *know that I am the Lord* your God
1Kin 20:13 Behold, I will deliver it into your hand today, and you shall *know that I am the Lord*
1Kin 20:28 Because the Syrians have said, "The Lord is God of the hills, but He is not God of the valleys," therefore I will deliver all this great multitude into your hand, and you shall *know that I am the Lord*
Is 49:23 Then you will *know that I am the Lord*, for they shall not be ashamed who wait for Me
Ezek 6:7 The slain shall fall in your midst, and you shall *know that I am the Lord*
Ezek 6:10 And they shall *know that I am the Lord*, and that I have not said in vain that I would bring this calamity upon them
Ezek 6:13 Then you shall *know that I am the Lord*, when their slain men are among their idols all around their altars, on every high hill, on all the mountaintops, under every green tree, and under every thick oak, wherever they offered sweet incense to all their idols
Ezek 6:14 So I will stretch out My hand against them and make the land desolate, yes, more desolate than the wilderness toward Diblah, in all their habitations. Then they shall *know that I am the Lord*
Ezek 7:4 but I will repay your ways, and your abominations shall be in your midst; then you shall *know that I am the Lord*
Ezek 7:9 Then you will *know that I am the Lord* who strikes
Ezek 7:27 I will do to them according to their way, and according to what they deserve I will judge them; then they shall *know that I am the Lord*
Ezek 11:10 I will judge you at the border of Israel. Then you shall *know that I am the Lord*
Ezek 11:12 And you shall *know that I am the Lord;* for you have not walked in My statutes nor executed My judgments, but have done according to the customs of the Gentiles which are all around you
Ezek 12:15 Then they shall *know that I am the Lord*, when I scatter them among the nations and disperse them throughout the countries
Ezek 12:16 But I will spare a few of their men from the sword, from famine, and from pestilence, that they may declare all their abominations among the Gentiles wherever they go. Then they shall *know that I am the Lord*
Ezek 12:20 Then the cities that are inhabited shall

be laid waste, and the land shall become desolate; and you shall *know that I am the Lord*
Ezek 13:9 Then you shall *know that I am the Lord* God
Ezek 13:14 it will fall, and you shall be consumed in the midst of it. Then you shall *know that I am the Lord*
Ezek 13:21 I will also tear off your veils and deliver My people out of your hand, and they shall no longer be as prey in your hand. Then you shall *know that I am the Lord*
Ezek 13:23 for I will deliver My people out of your hand, and you shall *know that I am the Lord*
Ezek 14:8 I will set My face against that man and make him a sign and a proverb, and I will cut him off from the midst of My people. Then you shall *know that I am the Lord*
Ezek 15:7 Then you shall *know that I am the Lord*, when I set My face against them
Ezek 16:62 And I will establish My covenant with you. Then you shall *know that I am the Lord*
Ezek 20:12 Moreover I also gave them My Sabbaths, to be a sign between them and Me, that they might *know that I am the Lord* who sanctifies them
Ezek 20:20 hallow My Sabbaths, and they will be a sign between Me and you, that you may *know that I am the Lord* your God
Ezek 20:26 and I pronounced them unclean because of their ritual gifts, in that they caused all their firstborn to pass through the fire, that I might make them desolate and that they might *know that I am the Lord*
Ezek 20:38 I will bring them out of the country where they sojourn, but they shall not enter the land of Israel. Then you will *know that I am the Lord*
Ezek 20:42 Then you shall *know that I am the Lord*, when I bring you into the land of Israel, into the country for which I lifted My hand in an oath to give to your fathers
Ezek 20:44 Then you shall *know that I am the Lord*, when I have dealt with you for My name's sake, not according to your wicked ways nor according to your corrupt doings, O house of Israel
Ezek 22:16 You shall defile yourself in the sight of the nations; then you shall *know that I am the Lord*
Ezek 23:49 Then you shall *know that I am the Lord* God
Ezek 24:24 and when this comes, you shall *know that I am the Lord* God
Ezek 24:27 Thus you will be a sign to them, and they will *know that I am the Lord*
Ezek 25:5 And I will make Rabbah a stable for camels and Ammon a resting place for flocks. Then you shall *know that I am the Lord*
Ezek 25:7 I will destroy you, and you shall *know that I am the Lord*
Ezek 25:11 And I will execute judgments upon Moab, and they shall *know that I am the Lord*
Ezek 25:17 and they shall *know that I am the Lord*, when I lay My vengeance upon them
Ezek 26:6 Also her daughter villages which are in the fields shall be slain by the sword. Then they shall *know that I am the Lord*
Ezek 28:22 and they shall *know that I am the Lord*, when I execute judgments in her and am hallowed in her
Ezek 28:23 the wounded shall be judged in her midst by the sword against her on every side; then they shall *know that I am the Lord*
Ezek 28:24 Then they shall *know that I am the Lord* God
Ezek 28:26 Then they shall *know that I am the Lord* their God
Ezek 29:6 Then all the inhabitants of Egypt shall *know that I am the Lord*, because they have been a staff of reed to the house of Israel
Ezek 29:9 then they will *know that I am the Lord*, because he said
Ezek 29:16 Then they shall *know that I am the Lord* God
Ezek 29:21 In that day I will cause the horn of the house of Israel to spring forth, and I will open your mouth to speak in their midst. Then they shall *know that I am the Lord*
Ezek 30:8 Then they will *know that I am the Lord*, when I have set a fire in Egypt and all her helpers are destroyed
Ezek 30:19 Thus I will execute judgments on Egypt, then they shall *know that I am the Lord*
Ezek 30:25 they shall *know that I am the Lord*, when I put My sword into the hand of the king of Babylon and he stretches it out against the land of Egypt
Ezek 30:26 I will scatter the Egyptians among the nations and disperse them throughout the countries. Then they shall *know that I am the Lord*
Ezek 32:15 When I make the land of Egypt desolate, and the country is destitute of all that once filled it, when I strike all who dwell in it, then they shall *know that I am the Lord*
Ezek 33:29 Then they shall *know that I am the Lord*, when I have made the land most desolate because of all their abominations which they have committed
Ezek 34:27 and they shall *know that I am the Lord*, when I have broken the bands of their yoke and delivered them from the hand of those who enslaved them
Ezek 35:4 I shall lay your cities waste, and you shall be desolate. Then you shall *know that I am the Lord*
Ezek 35:9 I will make you perpetually desolate, and your cities shall be uninhabited; then you shall *know that I am the Lord*
Ezek 35:12 Then you shall *know that I am the Lord*. I have heard all your blasphemies which you have spoken against the mountains of Israel, saying
Ezek 35:15 you shall be desolate, O Mount Seir, as well as all of Edom all of it! Then they shall *know that I am the Lord*
Ezek 36:11 I will make you inhabited as in former times, and do better for you than at your beginnings. Then you shall *know that I am the Lord*
Ezek 36:23 and the nations shall *know that I am the Lord*
Ezek 36:38 Like a flock offered as holy sacrifices, like the flock at Jerusalem on its feast days, so shall the ruined cities be filled with flocks of men. Then they shall *know that I am the Lord*
Ezek 37:6 and you shall live. Then you shall *know that I am the Lord*
Ezek 37:13 Then you shall *know that I am the Lord*, when I have opened your graves, O My people, and brought you up from your graves
Ezek 38:23 Thus I will magnify Myself and sanctify Myself, and I will be known in the eyes of many nations. Then they shall *know that I am the Lord*
Ezek 39:6 And I will send fire on Magog and on those who live in security in the coastlands. Then they shall *know that I am the Lord*
Ezek 39:7 Then the nations shall *know that I am the Lord*, the Holy One in Israel
Ezek 39:22 So the house of Israel shall *know that I am the Lord* their God from that day forward
Ezek 39:28 then they shall *know that I am the Lord* their God, who sent them into captivity among the nations, but also brought them back to their own land, and left none of them captive any longer

Joel 3:17 So you shall *know that I am the Lord* your God, dwelling in Zion My holy mountain

KNOW THE LORD
Ex 5:2 I do not *know the Lord*, nor will I let Israel go
Judg 2:10 When all that generation had been gathered to their fathers, another generation arose after them who did not *know the Lord* nor the work which He had done for Israel
1Sam 2:12 Now the sons of Eli were corrupt; they did not *know the Lord*
1Sam 3:7 (Now Samuel did not yet *know the Lord*, nor was the word of the Lord yet revealed to him
Is 19:21 Then the Lord will be known to Egypt, and the Egyptians will *know the Lord* in that day, and will make sacrifice and offering
Jer 31:34 No more shall every man teach his neighbor, and every man his brother, saying, '*Know the Lord*
Hos 2:20 I will betroth you to Me in faithfulness, and you shall *know the Lord*
Hos 5:4 They do not direct their deeds toward turning to their God, for the spirit of harlotry is in their midst, and they do not *know the Lord*
Heb 8:11 None of them shall teach his neighbor, and none his brother, saying, '*Know the Lord*

KNOW THE TRUE MEANING (NIV)
(See *KNOW THE TRUTH*)

KNOW THE TRUTH
Dan 7:19 Then I wished to *know the truth* about the fourth beast, which was different from all the others, exceedingly dreadful, with its teeth of iron and its nails of bronze, which devoured, broke in pieces, and trampled the residue with its feet
John 8:32 And you shall *know the truth*, and the truth shall make you free
1Tim 4:3 forbidding to marry, and commanding to abstain from foods which God created to be received with thanksgiving by those who believe and *know the truth*
2Tim 2:25 in humility correcting those who are in opposition, if God perhaps will grant them repentance, so that they may *know the truth*
1Jn 2:21 I have not written to you because you do not *know the truth*, but because you know it, and that no lie is of the truth

KNOW THEREFORE THIS DAY (KJV, RSV)
(See *KNOW THIS DAY*)

KNOW THIS DAY
Deut 4:39 Therefore *know this day*, and consider it in your heart, that the Lord Himself is God in heaven above and on the earth beneath

KNOWEST THOU NOT (KJV)
(See *DO YOU NOT KNOW*)

KNOWING GOOD AND EVIL (NAS, NIV, RSV)
(See *KNOW GOOD AND EVIL*)

KNOWING THEIR THOUGHTS
Matt 9:4 But Jesus, *knowing their thoughts*, said, "Why do you think evil in your hearts
Luke 11:17 But He, *knowing their thoughts*, said to them: "Every kingdom divided against itself is brought to desolation, and a house divided against a house falls

KNOWLEDGE AND GOOD JUDGMENT (NIV)
(See *GOOD JUDGMENT AND KNOWLEDGE*)

KNOWLEDGE FROM THE MOST HIGH (NIV)
(See *KNOWLEDGE OF THE MOST HIGH*)

KNOWLEDGE OF GOD
Prov 2:5 then you will understand the fear of the Lord, and find the *knowledge of God*
Hos 4:1 There is no truth or mercy or *knowledge of God* in the land
Hos 6:6 For I desire mercy and not sacrifice, and the *knowledge of God* more than burnt offerings
Rom 11:33 Oh, the depth of the riches both of the wisdom and *knowledge of God*
1Cor 15:34 for some do not have the *knowledge of God*. I speak this to your shame
2Cor 10:5 casting down arguments and every high thing that exalts itself against the *knowledge of God*, bringing every thought into captivity to the obedience of Christ
Col 1:10 that you may have a walk worthy of the Lord, fully pleasing Him, being fruitful in every good work and increasing in the *knowledge of God*
2Pet 1:2 Grace and peace be multiplied to you in the *knowledge of God* and of Jesus our Lord

KNOWLEDGE OF GOOD AND EVIL
Gen 2:9 The tree of life was also in the midst of the garden, and the tree of the *knowledge of good and evil*
Gen 2:17 but of the tree of the *knowledge of good and evil* you shall not eat, for in the day that you eat of it you shall surely die
Deut 1:39 Moreover your little ones and your children, who you say will be victims, who today have no *knowledge of good and evil*, they shall go in there

KNOWLEDGE OF OUR LORD
2Pet 1:8 For if these things are yours and abound, you will be neither barren nor unfruitful in the *knowledge of our Lord* Jesus Christ
2Pet 3:18 but grow in the grace and *knowledge of our Lord* and Savior Jesus Christ

KNOWLEDGE OF THE LORD
2Chr 30:22 And Hezekiah gave encouragement to all the Levites who taught the good *knowledge of the Lord*
Is 11:9 They shall not hurt nor destroy in all My holy mountain, for the earth shall be full of the *knowledge of the Lord* as the waters cover the sea
Hos 6:3 Let us know, let us pursue the *knowledge of the Lord*
2Pet 2:20 For if, after they have escaped the pollutions of the world through the *knowledge of the Lord* and Savior Jesus Christ, they are again entangled in them and overcome, the latter end is worse for them than the beginning

KNOWLEDGE OF THE MOST HIGH
Num 24:16 the utterance of him who hears the words of God, and knows the *knowledge of the Most High*, who sees the vision of the Almighty, who falls down, with eyes opened wide

KNOWLEDGE OF THE TRUTH
1Tim 2:4 who desires all men to be saved and to come to the *knowledge of the truth*
2Tim 3:7 always learning and never able to come to the *knowledge of the truth*
Heb 10:26 For if we sin willfully after we have received the *knowledge of the truth*, there no longer remains a sacrifice for sins

KNOWLEDGE PUFFS UP
1Cor 8:1 We know that we all have knowledge. *Knowledge puffs up*, but love edifies

KNOWLEDGE SHALL INCREASE
Dan 12:4 many shall run to and fro, and *knowledge shall increase*

KNOWN ABOUT GOD (NAS)
(See *KNOWN OF GOD*)

KNOWN AMONG THE GENTILES
Is 61:9 Their descendants shall be *known among the Gentiles*, and their offspring among the people

KNOWN AMONG THE NATIONS (NAS)
(See *KNOWN AMONG THE GENTILES*)

KNOWN BY ITS FRUIT
Matt 12:33 Either make the tree good and its fruit good, or else make the tree bad and its fruit bad; for a tree is *known by its fruit*

KNOWN IN ALL THE EARTH
Is 12:5 Sing to the Lord, for He has done excellent things; this is *known in all the earth*

KNOWN IN THE GATES
Prov 31:23 Her husband is *known in the gates*, when he sits among the elders of the land

KNOWN OF GOD
Rom 1:19 because what may be *known of God* is manifest in them, for God has shown it to them

KNOWN TO ALL THE WORLD (NIV)
(See *KNOWN IN ALL THE EARTH*)

KNOWS GOD
1Jn 4:6 He who *knows God* hears us; he who is not of God does not hear us
1Jn 4:7 and everyone who loves is born of God and *knows God*

KNOWS HOW WE ARE FORMED (NIV)
(See *KNOWS OUR FRAME*)

KNOWS OUR FRAME
Ps 103:14 For He *knows our frame;* He remembers that we are dust

L

LABOR IN VAIN
Job 9:29 If I am condemned, why then do I *labor in vain*
Ps 127:1 Unless the Lord builds the house, they *labor in vain* who build it
Is 65:23 They shall not *labor in vain*, nor bring forth children for trouble
Jer 51:58 the people will *labor in vain*, and the nations, because of the fire

LABOR OF FOOLS
Eccl 10:15 The *labor of fools* wearies them, for they do not even know how to go to the city

LABOR OF LOVE
1Th 1:3 remembering without ceasing your work of faith, *labor of love*, and patience of hope in our Lord Jesus Christ in the sight of our God and Father
Heb 6:10 For God is not unjust to forget your work and *labor of love* which you have shown toward His name, in that you have ministered to the saints, and do minister

LABOR OF MY HANDS
Gen 31:42 God has seen my affliction and the *labor of my hands*, and rebuked you last night

LABOR OF OUR FATHERS
Jer 3:24 For shame has devoured the *labor of our fathers* from our youth their flocks and their herds, their sons and their daughters

LABOR PROMPTED BY LOVE (NIV)
(See *LABOR OF LOVE*)

LABORED IN VAIN
Is 49:4 Then I said, 'I have *labored in vain*, I have spent my strength for nothing and in vain
Phil 2:16 holding fast the word of life, so that I may rejoice in the day of Christ that I have not run in vain or *labored in vain*

LABORED TO NO PURPOSE (NIV)
(See *LABORED IN VAIN*)

LABORER IS WORTHY
Luke 10:7 And remain in the same house, eating and drinking such things as they give, for the *laborer is worthy* of his wages
1Tim 5:18 For the Scripture says, "You shall not muzzle an ox while it treads out the grain," and, "The *laborer is worthy* of his wages

LABORERS ARE FEW
Matt 9:37 Then He said to His disciples, "The harvest truly is plentiful, but the *laborers are few*
Luke 10:2 Then He said to them, "The harvest truly is great, but the *laborers are few*

LACK OF KNOWLEDGE (KJV, NAS, NIV, RSV)
(See *REJECTED KNOWLEDGE*)

LACK ONE THING (RSV)
(See *ONE THING YOU LACK*)

LACKED JUDGMENT (NIV)
(See *DEVOID OF UNDERSTANDING*)

LADEN WITH INIQUITY
Is 1:4 Alas, sinful nation, a people *laden with iniquity*, a brood of evildoers, children who are corrupters

LAID DOWN HIS LIFE
1Jn 3:16 By this we know love, because He *laid down His life* for us

LAID HIM IN A TOMB
Mark 15:46 And he *laid Him in a tomb* which had been hewn out of the rock, and rolled a stone against the door of the tomb
Acts 13:29 Now when they had fulfilled all that was written concerning Him, they took Him down from the tree and *laid Him in a tomb*

LAID HIS HANDS ON
Num 27:23 And he *laid his hands on* him and inaugurated him, just as the Lord commanded by the hand of Moses
Deut 34:9 Now Joshua the son of Nun was full of the spirit of wisdom, for Moses had *laid his hands on* him
Matt 19:15 And He *laid His hands on* them and departed from there
Mark 6:5 Now He could do no mighty work there, except that He *laid His hands on* a few sick people and healed them

Luke 4:40 and He *laid His hands on* every one of them and healed them
Luke 13:13 And He *laid His hands on* her, and immediately she was made straight, and glorified God
Acts 28:8 Paul went in to him and prayed, and he *laid his hands on* him and healed him

LAID IN THE BALANCE (KJV)
(See *WEIGHED IN THE BALANCES*)

LAID THE EARTH'S FOUNDATION (NIV)
(See *LAID THE FOUNDATIONS*)

LAID THE FOUNDATION
Ezra 3:10 When the builders *laid the foundation* of the temple of the Lord, the priests stood in their apparel with trumpets, and the Levites, the sons of Asaph, with cymbals, to praise the Lord, according to the ordinance of David king of Israel
Ezra 5:16 Then the same Sheshbazzar came and *laid the foundation* of the house of God which is in Jerusalem
Ps 102:25 Of old You *laid the foundation* of the earth, and the heavens are the work of Your hands
Is 48:13 Indeed My hand has *laid the foundation* of the earth, and My right hand has stretched out the heavens
Zech 4:9 The hands of Zerubbabel have *laid the foundation* of this temple
Luke 6:48 He is like a man building a house, who dug deep and *laid the foundation* on the rock
Luke 14:29 lest, after he has *laid the foundation*, and is not able to finish it, all who see it begin to mock him
1Cor 3:10 According to the grace of God which was given to me, as a wise master builder I have *laid the foundation*, and another builds on it
Heb 1:10 You, Lord, in the beginning *laid the foundation* of the earth, and the heavens are the work of Your hands

LAID THE FOUNDATIONS
Job 38:4 Where were you when I *laid the foundations* of the earth
Ps 104:5 You who *laid the foundations* of the earth, so that it should not be moved forever
Is 51:13 And you forget the Lord your Maker, Who stretched out the heavens and *laid the foundations* of the earth

LAID THEIR HANDS ON
Lev 8:14 Then Aaron and his sons *laid their hands on* the head of the bull for the sin offering
Lev 8:18 And Aaron and his sons *laid their hands on* the head of the ram
Lev 8:22 Then Aaron and his sons *laid their hands on* the head of the ram
2Chr 29:23 Then they brought out the male goats for the sin offering before the king and the congregation, and they *laid their hands on* them
Mark 14:46 Then they *laid their hands on* Him and took Him
Acts 5:18 and *laid their hands on* the apostles and put them in the common prison

LAID UP FOR YOU IN HEAVEN
Col 1:5 because of the hope which is *laid up for you in heaven*, of which you heard before in the word of the truth of the gospel

LAKE OF FIRE
Rev 19:20 These two were cast alive into the *lake of fire* burning with brimstone
Rev 20:10 And the devil, who deceived them, was cast into the *lake of fire* and brimstone where the beast and the false prophet are
Rev 20:14 Then Death and Hades were cast into the *lake of fire*
Rev 20:15 And anyone not found written in the Book of Life was cast into the *lake of fire*

LAMB FOR A BURNT OFFERING
Gen 22:7 And he said, "Look, the fire and the wood, but where is the *lamb for a burnt offering*
Gen 22:8 And Abraham said, "My son, God will provide for Himself the *lamb for a burnt offering*

LAMB OF GOD
John 1:29 The *Lamb of God* who takes away the sin of the world
John 1:36 And looking at Jesus as He walked, he said, "Behold the *Lamb of God*

LAMB TO THE SLAUGHTER
Is 53:7 He was led as a *lamb to the slaughter*, and as a sheep before its shearers is silent, so He opened not his mouth

LAMB WITHOUT BLEMISH
1Pet 1:19 but with the precious blood of Christ, as of a *lamb without blemish* and without spot

LAMBS AMONG WOLVES
Luke 10:3 Go your way; behold, I send you out as *lambs among wolves*

LAMENT LIKE A VIRGIN
Joel 1:8 *Lament like a virgin* girded with sackcloth for the husband of her youth

LAMP OF GOD
1Sam 3:3 and before the *lamp of God* went out in the tabernacle of the Lord where the ark of God was, and while Samuel was lying down to sleep

LAMP OF ISRAEL
2Sam 21:17 Then the men of David swore to him, saying, "You shall go out no more with us to battle, lest you quench the *lamp of Israel*

LAMP OF ISRAEL WILL NOT BE EXTINGUISHED (NIV)
(See *QUENCH THE LAMP OF ISRAEL*)

LAMP OF THE BODY
Matt 6:22 The *lamp of the body* is the eye. If therefore your eye is good, your whole body will be full of light
Luke 11:34 The *lamp of the body* is the eye. Therefore, when your eye is good, your whole body also is full of light

LAMP OF THE WICKED
Job 21:17 How often is the *lamp of the wicked* put out
Prov 13:9 The light of the righteous rejoices, but the *lamp of the wicked* will be put out
Prov 24:20 for there will be no prospect for the evil man; the *lamp of the wicked* will be put out

LAMP TO MY FEET
Ps 119:105 Your word is a *lamp to my feet* and a light to my path

LAND AS A HERITAGE
Ps 135:12 And gave their *land as a heritage*, a heritage to Israel His people
Ps 136:21 And gave their *land as a heritage*, for His mercy endures forever

LAND FLOWING WITH MILK AND HONEY
Ex 3:8 So I have come down to deliver them out of the hand of the Egyptians, and to bring them

up from that land to a good and large land, to a *land flowing with milk and honey*, to the place of the Canaanites and the Hittites and the Amorites and the Perizzites and the Hivites and the Jebusites

Ex 3:17 and I have said I will bring you up out of the affliction of Egypt to the land of the Canaanites and the Hittites and the Amorites and the Perizzites and the Hivites and the Jebusites, to a *land flowing with milk and honey*

Ex 13:5 And it shall be, when the Lord brings you into the land of the Canaanites and the Hittites and the Amorites and the Hivites and the Jebusites, which He swore to your fathers to give you, a *land flowing with milk and honey*, that you shall keep this service in this month

Ex 33:3 Go up to a *land flowing with milk and honey*

Lev 20:24 But I have said to you, "You shall inherit their land, and I will give it to you to possess, a *land flowing with milk and honey*

Num 16:13 Is it a small thing that you have brought us up out of a *land flowing with milk and honey*, to kill us in the wilderness, that you should keep acting like a prince over us

Num 16:14 Moreover you have not brought us into a *land flowing with milk and honey*, nor given us inheritance of fields and vineyards

Deut 6:3 Therefore hear, O Israel, and be careful to observe it, that it may be well with you, and that you may multiply greatly as the Lord God of your fathers has promised you' a *land flowing with milk and honey*

Deut 11:9 and that you may prolong your days in the land which the Lord swore to give your fathers, to them and their descendants, 'a *land flowing with milk and honey*

Deut 26:9 He has brought us to this place and has given us this land, "a *land flowing with milk and honey*

Deut 26:15 Look down from Your holy habitation, from heaven, and bless Your people Israel and the land which You have given us, just as You swore to our fathers, "a *land flowing with milk and honey*

Deut 27:3 You shall write on them all the words of this law, when you have crossed over, that you may enter the land which the Lord your God is giving you, 'a *land flowing with milk and honey*

Deut 31:20 When I have brought them to the *land flowing with milk and honey*, of which I swore to their fathers, and they have eaten and filled themselves and grown fat, then they will turn to other gods and serve them

Josh 5:6 For the children of Israel walked forty years in the wilderness, till all the people who were men of war, who came out of Egypt, were consumed, because they did not obey the voice of the Lord to whom the Lord swore that He would not show them the land which the Lord had sworn to their fathers that He would give us, "a *land flowing with milk and honey*

Jer 11:5 that I may establish the oath which I have sworn to your fathers, to give them a *land flowing with milk and honey*, as it is this day

Jer 32:22 You have given them this land, of which You swore to their fathers to give them "a *land flowing with milk and honey*

LAND HE PROMISED THEM ON OATH (NIV)
(See *LAND WHICH HE SWORE TO GIVE*)

LAND I SWORE WITH UPLIFTED HAND TO GIVE (NIV)
(See *LAND WHICH I SWORE TO GIVE*)

LAND MOURNS AND LANGUISHES (RSV)
(See *EARTH MOURNS AND LANGUISHES*)

LAND MOURNS AND WASTES AWAY (NIV)
(See *EARTH MOURNS AND LANGUISHES*)

LAND OF CANAAN

Gen 11:31 And Terah took his son Abram and his grandson Lot, the son of Haran, and his daughter-in-law Sarai, his son Abram's wife, and they went out with them from Ur of the Chaldeans to go to the *land of Canaan*

Gen 12:5 Then Abram took Sarai his wife and Lot his brother's son, and all their possessions that they had gathered, and the people whom they had acquired in Haran, and they departed to go to the *land of Canaan*. So they came to the *land of Canaan*

Gen 13:12 Abram dwelt in the *land of Canaan*, and Lot dwelt in the cities of the plain and pitched his tent even as far as Sodom

Gen 16:3 Then Sarai, Abram's wife, took Hagar her maid, the Egyptian, and gave her to her husband Abram to be his wife, after Abram had dwelt ten years in the *land of Canaan*

Gen 17:8 Also I give to you and your descendants after you the land in which you are a stranger, all the *land of Canaan*, as an everlasting possession

Gen 23:2 in the *land of Canaan*, and Abraham came to mourn for Sarah and to weep for her

Gen 23:19 And after this, Abraham buried Sarah his wife in the cave of the field of Machpelah, before Mamre (that is, Hebron) in the *land of Canaan*

Gen 31:18 And he carried away all his livestock and all his possessions which he had gained, his acquired livestock which he had gained in Padan Aram, to go to his father Isaac in the *land of Canaan*

Gen 33:18 Then Jacob came safely to the city of Shechem, which is in the *land of Canaan*, when he came from Padan Aram

Gen 35:6 which is in the *land of Canaan*, he and all the people who were with him

Gen 36:5 These were the sons of Esau who were born to him in the *land of Canaan*

Gen 36:6 Then Esau took his wives, his sons, his daughters, and all the persons of his household, his cattle and all his animals, and all his goods which he had gained in the *land of Canaan*, and went to a country away from the presence of his brother Jacob

Gen 37:1 Now Jacob dwelt in the land where his father was a stranger, in the *land of Canaan*

Gen 42:5 And the sons of Israel went to buy grain among those who journeyed, for the famine was in the *land of Canaan*

Gen 42:7 And they said, "From the *land of Canaan* to buy food

Gen 42:13 And they said, "Your servants are twelve brothers, the sons of one man in the *land of Canaan*

Gen 42:29 Then they went to Jacob their father in the *land of Canaan* and told him all that had happened to them, saying

Gen 42:32 one is no more, and the youngest is with our father this day in the *land of Canaan*

Gen 44:8 Look, we brought back to you from the *land of Canaan* the money which we found in the mouth of our sacks

Gen 45:17 Load your animals and depart; go to the *land of Canaan*

Gen 45:25 Then they went up out of Egypt, and came to the *land of Canaan* to Jacob their father

Gen 46:6 So they took their livestock and their goods, which they had acquired in the *land of*

Canaan, and went to Egypt, Jacob and all his descendants with him

Gen 46:12 The sons of Judah were Er, Onan, Shelah, Perez, and Zerah (but Er and Onan died in the *land of Canaan*

Gen 46:31 Then Joseph said to his brothers and to his father's household, "I will go up and tell Pharaoh, and say to him, 'My brothers and those of my father's house, who were in the *land of Canaan*, have come to me

Gen 47:1 Then Joseph went and told Pharaoh, and said, "My father and my brothers, their flocks and their herds and all that they possess, have come from the *land of Canaan*

Gen 47:4 And they said to Pharaoh, "We have come to dwell in the land, because your servants have no pasture for their flocks, for the famine is severe in the *land of Canaan*

Gen 47:13 for the famine was very severe, so that the land of Egypt and all the *land of Canaan* languished because of the famine

Gen 47:14 And Joseph gathered up all the money that was found in the land of Egypt and in the *land of Canaan*, for the grain which they bought

Gen 47:15 So when the money failed in the land of Egypt and in the *land of Canaan*, all the Egyptians came to Joseph and said

Gen 48:3 God Almighty appeared to me at Luz in the *land of Canaan* and blessed me

Gen 48:7 But as for me, when I came from Padan, Rachel died beside me in the *land of Canaan* on the way, when there was but a little distance to go to Ephrath

Gen 49:30 in the cave that is in the field of Machpelah, which is before Mamre in the *land of Canaan*, which Abraham bought with the field of Ephron the Hittite as a possession for a burial place

Gen 50:5 in my grave which I dug for myself in the *land of Canaan*, there you shall bury me

Gen 50:13 For his sons carried him to the *land of Canaan*, and buried him in the cave of the field of Machpelah, before Mamre, which Abraham bought with the field from Ephron the Hittite as property for a burial place

Ex 6:4 I have also established My covenant with them, to give them the *land of Canaan*, the land of their pilgrimage, in which they were strangers

Ex 16:35 they ate manna until they came to the border of the *land of Canaan*

Lev 14:34 When you have come into the *land of Canaan*, which I give you as a possession, and I put the leprous plague in a house in the land of your possession

Lev 18:3 and according to the doings of the *land of Canaan*, where I am bringing you, you shall not do

Lev 25:38 I am the Lord your God, who brought you out of the land of Egypt, to give you the *land of Canaan* and to be your God

Num 13:2 Send men to spy out the *land of Canaan*, which I am giving to the children of Israel

Num 13:17 So Moses sent them to spy out the *land of Canaan*, and said to them

Num 26:19 and Er and Onan died in the *land of Canaan*

Num 32:30 But if they do not cross over armed with you, they shall have possessions among you in the *land of Canaan*

Num 32:32 We will cross over armed before the Lord into the *land of Canaan*, but the possession of our inheritance shall remain with us on this side of the Jordan

Num 33:40 Now the king of Arad, the Canaanite, who dwelt in the South in the *land of Canaan*, heard of the coming of the children of Israel

Num 33:51 When you have crossed the Jordan into the *land of Canaan*

Num 34:2 When you come into the *land of Canaan*, this is the land that shall fall to you as an inheritance the *land of Canaan* to its boundaries

Num 34:29 These are the ones the Lord commanded to divide the inheritance among the children of Israel in the *land of Canaan*

Num 35:10 When you cross the Jordan into the *land of Canaan*

Num 35:14 You shall appoint three cities on this side of the Jordan, and three cities you shall appoint in the *land of Canaan*, which will be cities of refuge

Deut 32:49 view the *land of Canaan*, which I give to the children of Israel as a possession

Josh 5:12 and the children of Israel no longer had manna, but they ate the food of the *land of Canaan* that year

Josh 14:1 These are the areas which the children of Israel inherited in the *land of Canaan*, which Eleazar the priest, Joshua the son of Nun, and the heads of the fathers of the tribes of the children of Israel distributed as an inheritance to them

Josh 21:2 And they spoke to them at Shiloh in the *land of Canaan*, saying

Josh 22:9 So the children of Reuben, the children of Gad, and half the tribe of Manasseh returned, and departed from the children of Israel at Shiloh, which is in the *land of Canaan*, to go to the country of Gilead, to the land of their possession, which they possessed according to the word of the Lord by the hand of Moses

Josh 22:10 And when they came to the region of the Jordan which is in the *land of Canaan*, the children of Reuben, the children of Gad, and half the tribe of Manasseh built an altar there by the Jordan a great, impressive altar

Josh 22:11 Now the children of Israel heard someone say, "Behold, the children of Reuben, the children of Gad, and half the tribe of Manasseh have built an altar on the frontier of the *land of Canaan*, in the region of the Jordan, on the side occupied by the children of Israel

Josh 22:32 And Phinehas the son of Eleazar the priest, and the rulers, returned from the children of Reuben and the children of Gad, from the land of Gilead to the *land of Canaan*, to the children of Israel, and brought back word to them

Josh 24:3 Then I took your father Abraham from the other side of the River, led him throughout all the *land of Canaan*, and multiplied his descendants and gave him Isaac

Judg 21:12 and they brought them to the camp at Shiloh, which is in the *land of Canaan*

1Chr 16:18 saying, "To you I will give the *land of Canaan* as the allotment of your inheritance

Ps 105:11 Saying, "To you I will give the *land of Canaan* as the allotment of your inheritance

Ezek 16:3 Your birth and your nativity are from the *land of Canaan*

Acts 13:19 And when He had destroyed seven nations in the *land of Canaan*, He distributed their land to them by allotment

LAND OF FORGETFULNESS

Ps 88:12 Shall Your wonders be known in the dark? And Your righteousness in the *land of forgetfulness*

LAND OF GOSHEN

Gen 45:10 You shall dwell in the *land of Goshen*, and you shall be near to me, you and your children, your children's children, your flocks and your herds, and all that you have

Gen 46:28 Then he sent Judah before him to Joseph, to point out before him the way to Goshen. And they came to the *land of Goshen*
Gen 46:34 that you shall say, 'Your servants' occupation has been with livestock from our youth even till now, both we and also our fathers,' that you may dwell in the *land of Goshen*
Gen 47:1 Then Joseph went and told Pharaoh, and said, "My father and my brothers, their flocks and their herds and all that they possess, have come from the land of Canaan; and indeed they are in the *land of Goshen*
Gen 47:4 Now therefore, please let your servants dwell in the *land of Goshen*
Gen 47:6 let them dwell in the *land of Goshen*. And if you know any competent men among them, then make them chief herdsmen over my livestock
Gen 50:8 Only their little ones, their flocks, and their herds they left in the *land of Goshen*
Ex 8:22 And in that day I will set apart the *land of Goshen*, in which My people dwell, that no swarms of flies shall be there, in order that you may know that I am the Lord in the midst of the land
Ex 9:26 Only in the *land of Goshen*, where the children of Israel were, there was no hail
Josh 11:16 the mountain country, all the South, all the *land of Goshen*, the lowland, and the Jordan plain the mountains of Israel and its lowlands

LAND OF ISRAEL
1Sam 13:19 Now there was no blacksmith to be found throughout all the *land of Israel*, for the Philistines said
2Kin 5:2 And the Syrians had gone out on raids, and had brought back captive a young girl from the *land of Israel*
2Kin 5:4 And Naaman went in and told his master, saying, "Thus and thus said the girl who is from the *land of Israel*
2Kin 6:23 So the bands of Syrian raiders came no more into the *land of Israel*
1Chr 13:2 And David said to all the congregation of Israel, "If it seems good to you, and if it is of the Lord our God, let us send out to our brethren everywhere who are left in all the *land of Israel*, and with them to the priests and Levites who are in their cities and their common-lands, that they may gather together to us
1Chr 22:2 So David commanded to gather the aliens who were in the *land of Israel*
2Chr 2:17 Then Solomon numbered all the aliens who were in the *land of Israel*, after the census in which David his father had numbered them
2Chr 30:25 The whole congregation of Judah rejoiced, also the priests and Levites, all the congregation that came from Israel, the sojourners who came from the *land of Israel*, and those who dwelt in Judah
2Chr 34:7 When he had broken down the altars and the wooden images, had beaten the carved images into powder, and cut down all the incense altars throughout all the *land of Israel*, he returned to Jerusalem
Ezek 7:2 And you, son of man, thus says the Lord God to the *land of Israel*
Ezek 11:17 I will gather you from the peoples, assemble you from the countries where you have been scattered, and I will give you the *land of Israel*
Ezek 12:19 And say to the people of the land, 'Thus says the Lord God to the inhabitants of Jerusalem and to the *land of Israel*
Ezek 12:22 Son of man, what is this proverb that you people have about the *land of Israel*, which says
Ezek 13:9 they shall not be in the assembly of My people, nor be written in the record of the house of Israel, nor shall they enter into the *land of Israel*
Ezek 18:2 What do you mean when you use this proverb concerning the *land of Israel*, saying
Ezek 20:38 I will bring them out of the country where they sojourn, but they shall not enter the *land of Israel*
Ezek 20:42 Then you shall know that I am the Lord, when I bring you into the *land of Israel*, into the country for which I lifted My hand in an oath to give to your fathers
Ezek 21:2 Son of man, set your face toward Jerusalem, preach against the holy places, and prophesy against the *land of Israel*
Ezek 21:3 and say to the *land of Israel*, 'Thus says the Lord
Ezek 25:3 against My sanctuary when it was profaned, and against the *land of Israel* when it was desolate, and against the house of Judah when they went into captivity
Ezek 25:6 Because you clapped your hands, stamped your feet, and rejoiced in heart with all your disdain for the *land of Israel*
Ezek 27:17 Judah and the *land of Israel* were your traders. They traded for your merchandise wheat of Minnith, millet, honey, oil, and balm
Ezek 33:24 Son of man, they who inhabit those ruins in the *land of Israel* are saying
Ezek 36:6 Therefore prophesy concerning the *land of Israel*, and say to the mountains, the hills, the rivers, and the valleys
Ezek 37:12 Behold, O My people, I will open your graves and cause you to come up from your graves, and bring you into the *land of Israel*
Ezek 38:18 And it will come to pass at the same time, when Gog comes against the *land of Israel*
Ezek 38:19 Surely in that day there shall be a great earthquake in the *land of Israel*
Ezek 40:2 In the visions of God He took me into the *land of Israel* and set me on a very high mountain
Ezek 47:18 On the east side you shall mark out the border from between Hauran and Damascus, and between Gilead and the *land of Israel*, along the Jordan, and along the eastern side of the sea
Matt 2:20 saying, "Arise, take the young Child and His mother, and go to the *land of Israel*, for those who sought the young Child's life are dead
Matt 2:21 Then he arose, took the young Child and His mother, and came into the *land of Israel*

LAND OF OBLIVION (NIV)
(See *LAND OF FORGETFULNESS*)

LAND OF SLAVERY (NIV)
(See *HOUSE OF BONDAGE*)

LAND OF THE LIVING
Job 28:13 Man does not know its value, nor is it found in the *land of the living*
Ps 27:13 I would have lost heart, unless I had believed That I would see the goodness of the Lord in the *land of the living*
Ps 52:5 He shall take you away, and pluck you out of your dwelling place, and uproot you from the *land of the living*
Ps 116:9 I will walk before the Lord in the *land of the living*
Ps 142:5 I said, "You are my refuge, my portion in the *land of the living*

Is 38:11 I said, "I shall not see YAH, the Lord in the *land of the living*
Is 53:8 For He was cut off from the *land of the living*
Jer 11:19 and I did not know that they had devised schemes against me, saying, "Let us destroy the tree with its fruit, and let us cut him off from the *land of the living*, that his name may be remembered no more
Ezek 26:20 and I shall establish glory in the *land of the living*
Ezek 32:23 Her graves are set in the recesses of the Pit, and her company is all around her grave, all of them slain, fallen by the sword, who caused terror in the *land of the living*
Ezek 32:24 There is Elam and all her multitude, all around her grave, all of them slain, fallen by the sword, who have gone down uncircumcised to the lower parts of the earth, who caused their terror in the *land of the living*
Ezek 32:25 though their terror was caused in the *land of the living*, yet they bear their shame with those who go down to the Pit
Ezek 32:26 There are Meshech and Tubal and all their multitudes, with all their graves around it, all of them uncircumcised, slain by the sword, though they caused their terror in the *land of the living*
Ezek 32:27 they have laid their swords under their heads, but their iniquities will be on their bones, because of the terror of the mighty in the *land of the living*
Ezek 32:32 For I have caused My terror in the *land of the living*

LAND OF YOUR FATHERS
Gen 31:3 Then the Lord said to Jacob, "Return to the *land of your fathers* and to your family, and I will be with you
Gen 48:21 Then Israel said to Joseph, "Behold, I am dying, but God will be with you and bring you back to the *land of your fathers*

LAND WAS DESECRATED (NIV)
(See *LAND WAS POLLUTED*)

LAND WAS POLLUTED
Ps 106:38 And shed innocent blood, even the blood of their sons and daughters, whom they sacrificed to the idols of Canaan; and the *land was polluted* with blood

LAND WHICH FLOWS WITH MILK AND HONEY
Num 14:8 If the Lord delights in us, then He will bring us into this land and give it to us,' a *land which flows with milk and honey*

LAND WHICH HE SWORE TO GIVE
Num 14:16 Because the Lord was not able to bring this people to the *land which He swore to give* them, therefore He killed them in the wilderness

LAND WHICH I HAVE GIVEN YOU
Deut 9:23 Likewise, when the Lord sent you from Kadesh Barnea, saying, 'Go up and possess the *land which I have given you*
Jer 35:15 then you will dwell in the *land which I have given you* and your fathers

LAND WHICH I SWORE TO GIVE
Ex 6:8 And I will bring you into the *land which I swore to give* to Abraham, Isaac, and Jacob

LANGUISHING SOUL (RSV)
(See *ANGUISH OF SOUL*)

LARGE CROWD (NIV)
(See *COMMON PEOPLE*)

LARGE CROWDS (NIV)
(See *GREAT MULTITUDES*)

LARGE MEETING (NIV)
(See *GREAT ASSEMBLY*)

LAST DAY
Neh 8:18 Also day by day, from the first day until the *last day*, he read from the Book of the Law of God
John 6:39 This is the will of the Father who sent Me, that of all He has given Me I should lose nothing, but should raise it up at the *last day*
John 6:40 and I will raise him up at the *last day*
John 6:44 and I will raise him up at the *last day*
John 6:54 Whoever eats My flesh and drinks My blood has eternal life, and I will raise him up at the *last day*
John 7:37 On the *last day*, that great day of the feast, Jesus stood and cried out, saying
John 11:24 Martha said to Him, "I know that he will rise again in the resurrection at the *last day*
John 12:48 He who rejects Me, and does not receive My words, has that which judges him the word that I have spoken will judge him in the *last day*

LAST DAYS
Gen 49:1 And Jacob called his sons and said, "Gather together, that I may tell you what shall befall you in the *last days*
Acts 2:17 And it shall come to pass in the *last days*, says God, that I will pour out of My Spirit on all flesh
2Tim 3:1 But know this, that in the *last days* perilous times will come
Heb 1:2 has in these *last days* spoken to us by His Son, whom He has appointed heir of all things, through whom also He made the worlds
Jas 5:3 Your gold and silver are corroded, and their corrosion will be a witness against you and will eat your flesh like fire. You have heaped up treasure in the *last days*
2Pet 3:3 that scoffers will come in the *last days*, walking according to their own lusts

LAST HOUR
1Jn 2:18 Little children, it is the *last hour;* and as you have heard that the Antichrist is coming, even now many antichrists have come, by which we know that it is the *last hour*

LAST WILL BE FIRST
Matt 20:16 So the *last will be first*, and the first last

LASTING COVENANT (NIV)
(See *PERPETUAL COVENANT*)

LASTING ORDINANCE (NIV)
(See *EVERLASTING ORDINANCE*)

LATER RAIN (RSV)
(See *LATTER RAIN*)

LATTER DAYS
Num 24:14 Come, I will advise you what this people will do to your people in the *latter days*
Deut 4:30 When you are in distress, and all these things come upon you in the *latter days*, when you turn to the Lord your God and obey His voice
Deut 31:29 and evil will befall you in the *latter*

days, because you will do evil in the sight of the Lord, to provoke Him to anger through the work of your hands
Job 42:12 Now the Lord blessed the *latter days* of Job more than his beginning
Prov 19:20 Listen to counsel and receive instruction, that you may be wise in your *latter days*
Is 2:2 Now it shall come to pass in the *latter days* that the mountain of the Lord's house shall be established on the top of the mountains, and shall be exalted above the hills
Jer 23:20 The anger of the Lord will not turn back until He has executed and performed the thoughts of His heart. In the *latter days* you will understand it perfectly
Jer 30:24 The fierce anger of the Lord will not return until He has done it, and until He has performed the intents of His heart. In the *latter days* you will consider it
Jer 48:47 Yet I will bring back the captives of Moab in the *latter days*
Jer 49:39 But it shall come to pass in the *latter days*
Ezek 38:16 It will be in the *latter days* that I will bring you against My land, so that the nations may know Me, when I am hallowed in you, O Gog, before their eyes
Dan 2:28 But there is a God in heaven who reveals secrets, and He has made known to King Nebuchadnezzar what will be in the *latter days*
Dan 10:14 Now I have come to make you understand what will happen to your people in the *latter days*, for the vision refers to many days yet to come
Hos 3:5 Afterward the children of Israel shall return, seek the Lord their God and David their king, and fear the Lord and His goodness in the *latter days*
Mic 4:1 Now it shall come to pass in the *latter days* that the mountain of the Lord's house shall be established on the top of the mountains, and shall be exalted above the hills

LATTER RAIN
Deut 11:14 then I will give you the rain for your land in its season, the early rain and the *latter rain*, that you may gather in your grain, your new wine, and your oil
Prov 16:15 In the light of the king's face is life, and his favor is like a cloud of the *latter rain*
Jer 3:3 Therefore the showers have been withheld, and there has been no *latter rain*
Joel 2:23 for He has given you the former rain faithfully, and He will cause the rain to come down for you the former rain, and the *latter rain* in the first month
Zech 10:1 Ask the Lord for rain in the time of the *latter rain*
Jas 5:7 See how the farmer waits for the precious fruit of the earth, waiting patiently for it until it receives the early and *latter rain*

LAW AND THE PROPHETS
Matt 7:12 Therefore, whatever you want men to do to you, do also to them, for this is the *Law and the Prophets*
Matt 22:40 On these two commandments hang all the *Law and the Prophets*
Luke 16:16 The *law and the prophets* were until John. Since that time the kingdom of God has been preached, and everyone is pressing into it
Acts 13:15 And after the reading of the *Law and the Prophets*, the rulers of the synagogue sent to them, saying
Rom 3:21 But now the righteousness of God apart from the law is revealed, being witnessed by the *Law and the Prophets*

LAW AT WORK IN THE MEMBERS (NIV)
(See *LAW IN MY MEMBERS*)

LAW IN MY MEMBERS
Rom 7:23 But I see another *law in my members*, warring against the law of my mind, and bringing me into captivity to the law of sin which is in my members

LAW IS GOOD
1Tim 1:8 But we know that the *law is good* if one uses it lawfully

LAW IS HOLY
Rom 7:12 Therefore the *law is holy*, and the commandment holy and just and good

LAW IS LIGHT
Prov 6:23 For the commandment is a lamp, and the *law is light*

LAW IS SPIRITUAL
Rom 7:14 For we know that the *law is spiritual*, but I am carnal, sold under sin

LAW OF CHRIST
Gal 6:2 Bear one another's burdens, and so fulfill the *law of Christ*

LAW OF FAITH
Rom 3:27 By what law? Of works? No, but by the *law of faith*

LAW OF GOD
Josh 24:26 Then Joshua wrote these words in the Book of the *Law of God*
Neh 8:8 So they read distinctly from the book, in the *Law of God*
Neh 8:18 Also day by day, from the first day until the last day, he read from the Book of the *Law of God*
Neh 10:28 Now the rest of the people (the priests, the Levites, the gatekeepers, the singers, the Nethinim, and all those who had separated themselves from the peoples of the lands to the *Law of God*, their wives, their sons, and their daughters, everyone who had knowledge and understanding
Rom 7:22 For I delight in the *law of God* according to the inward man
Rom 7:25 So then, with the mind I myself serve the *law of God*, but with the flesh the law of sin
Rom 8:7 for it is not subject to the *law of God*, nor indeed can be

LAW OF LEPROSY
Lev 14:57 to teach when it is unclean and when it is clean. This is the *law of leprosy*

LAW OF LIBERTY
Jas 1:25 But he who looks into the perfect *law of liberty* and continues in it, and is not a forgetful hearer but a doer of the work, this one will be blessed in what he does
Jas 2:12 So speak and so do as those who will be judged by the *law of liberty*

LAW OF MOSES
Josh 8:31 as Moses the servant of the Lord had commanded the children of Israel, as it is written in the Book of the *Law of Moses*
Josh 8:32 And there, in the presence of the children of Israel, he wrote on the stones a copy of the *law of Moses*, which he had written
Josh 23:6 Therefore be very courageous to keep and to do all that is written in the Book of the *Law of Moses*, lest you turn aside from it to the right hand or to the left
1Kin 2:3 to walk in His ways, to keep His statutes,

His commandments, His judgments, and His testimonies, as it is written in the *Law of Moses*, that you may prosper in all that you do and wherever you turn

2Kin 14:6 But the children of the murderers he did not execute, according to what is written in the Book of the *Law of Moses*, in which the Lord commanded, saying

2Kin 23:25 Now before him there was no king like him, who turned to the Lord with all his heart, with all his soul, and with all his might, according to all the *Law of Moses*

2Chr 23:18 Also Jehoiada appointed the oversight of the house of the Lord to the hand of the priests, the Levites, whom David had assigned in the house of the Lord, to offer the burnt offerings of the Lord, as it is written in the *Law of Moses*, with rejoicing and with singing, as it was established by David

2Chr 30:16 They stood in their place according to their custom, according to the *Law of Moses* the man of God

Ezra 3:2 Then Jeshua the son of Jozadak and his brethren the priests, and Zerubbabel the son of Shealtiel and his brethren, arose and built the altar of the God of Israel, to offer burnt offerings on it, as it is written in the *Law of Moses* the man of God

Ezra 7:6 and he was a skilled scribe in the *Law of Moses*, which the Lord God of Israel had given

Neh 8:1 and they told Ezra the scribe to bring the Book of the *Law of Moses*, which the Lord had commanded Israel

Dan 9:11 therefore the curse and the oath written in the *Law of Moses* the servant of God have been poured out on us, because we have sinned against Him

Dan 9:13 As it is written in the *Law of Moses*, all this disaster has come upon us

Mal 4:4 Remember the *Law of Moses*, My servant, which I commanded him in Horeb for all Israel, with the statutes and judgments

Luke 2:22 Now when the days of her purification according to the *law of Moses* were completed, they brought Him to Jerusalem to present Him to the Lord

Luke 24:44 Then He said to them, "These are the words which I spoke to you while I was still with you, that all things must be fulfilled which were written in the *Law of Moses* and the Prophets and the Psalms concerning Me

John 7:23 If a man receives circumcision on the Sabbath, so that the *law of Moses* should not be broken, are you angry with Me because I made a man completely well on the Sabbath

Acts 13:39 and by Him everyone who believes is justified from all things from which you could not be justified by the *law of Moses*

Acts 15:5 But some of the sect of the Pharisees who believed rose up, saying, "It is necessary to circumcise them, and to command them to keep the *law of Moses*

Acts 28:23 So when they had appointed him a day, many came to him at his lodging, to whom he explained and solemnly testified of the kingdom of God, persuading them concerning Jesus from both the *Law of Moses* and the Prophets, from morning till evening

1Cor 9:9 For it is written in the *law of Moses*, "You shall not muzzle an ox while it treads out the grain

LAW OF RIGHTEOUSNESS

Rom 9:31 but Israel, pursuing the *law of righteousness*, has not attained to the *law of righteousness*

LAW OF SIN

Rom 7:23 But I see another law in my members, warring against the law of my mind, and bringing me into captivity to the *law of sin* which is in my members

Rom 7:25 So then, with the mind I myself serve the law of God, but with the flesh the *law of sin*

Rom 8:2 For the law of the Spirit of life in Christ Jesus has made me free from the *law of sin* and death

LAW OF THE LORD

2Kin 10:31 But Jehu took no heed to walk in the *law of the Lord* God of Israel with all his heart

1Chr 16:40 to offer burnt offerings to the Lord on the altar of burnt offering regularly morning and evening, and to do according to all that is written in the *Law of the Lord* which He commanded Israel

1Chr 22:12 Only may the Lord give you wisdom and understanding, and give you charge concerning Israel, that you may keep the *law of the Lord* your God

2Chr 12:1 Now it came to pass, when Rehoboam had established the kingdom and had strengthened himself, that he forsook the *law of the Lord*, and all Israel along with him

2Chr 17:9 So they taught in Judah, and had the Book of the *Law of the Lord* with them

2Chr 31:3 for the morning and evening burnt offerings, the burnt offerings for the Sabbaths and the New Moons and the set feasts, as it is written in the *Law of the Lord*

2Chr 31:4 Moreover he commanded the people who dwelt in Jerusalem to contribute support for the priests and the Levites, that they might devote themselves to the *Law of the Lord*

2Chr 34:14 Now when they brought out the money that was brought into the house of the Lord, Hilkiah the priest found the Book of the *Law of the Lord* given by Moses

2Chr 35:26 Now the rest of the acts of Josiah and his goodness, according to what was written in the *Law of the Lord*

Ezra 7:10 For Ezra had prepared his heart to seek the *Law of the Lord*, and to do it, and to teach statutes and ordinances in Israel

Neh 9:3 And they stood up in their place and read from the Book of the *Law of the Lord* their God for one-fourth of the day

Ps 1:2 But his delight is in the *law of the Lord*, and in His law he meditates day and night

Ps 19:7 The *law of the Lord* is perfect, converting the soul

Ps 119:1 Blessed are the undefiled in the way, who walk in the *law of the Lord*

Is 5:24 because they have rejected the *law of the Lord* of hosts, and despised the word of the Holy One of Israel

Is 30:9 that this is a rebellious people, lying children, children who will not hear the *law of the Lord*

Jer 8:8 How can you say, 'We are wise, and the *law of the Lord* is with us

Amos 2:4 For three transgressions of Judah, and for four, I will not turn away its punishment, because they have despised the *law of the Lord*, and have not kept His commandments

Luke 2:23 (as it is written in the *law of the Lord*

Luke 2:24 and to offer a sacrifice according to what is said in the *law of the Lord*

Luke 2:39 So when they had performed all things according to the *law of the Lord*, they returned to Galilee, to their own city, Nazareth

LAW OF THE NAZIRITE

Num 6:13 Now this is the *law of the Nazirite:* When the days of his separation are fulfilled, he shall be brought to the door of the tabernacle of meeting

Num 6:21 This is the *law of the Nazirite* who vows to the Lord the offering for his separation, and besides that, whatever else his hand is able to provide

LAW OF THE SPIRIT
Rom 8:2 For the *law of the Spirit* of life in Christ Jesus has made me free from the law of sin and death

LAW SHALL GO FORTH
Mic 4:2 For out of Zion the *law shall go forth*, and the word of the Lord from Jerusalem

LAW THAT GIVES FREEDOM (NIV)
(See *LAW OF LIBERTY*)

LAW WAS GIVEN THROUGH MOSES
John 1:17 For the *law was given through Moses*, but grace and truth came through Jesus Christ

LAW WILL GO OUT (NIV)
(See *LAW SHALL GO FORTH*)

LAW WRITTEN IN THEIR HEARTS
Rom 2:15 who show the work of the *law written in their hearts*, their conscience also bearing witness, and between themselves their thoughts accusing or else excusing them

LAW'S REQUIREMENTS (NIV)
(See *RIGHTEOUS REQUIREMENTS OF THE LAW*)

LAWLESS ONE
2Th 2:8 And then the *lawless one* will be revealed, whom the Lord will consume with the breath of His mouth and destroy with the brightness of His coming

2Th 2:9 The coming of the *lawless one* is according to the working of Satan, with all power, signs, and lying wonders

LAWS OF YOUR GOD
Ezra 7:25 And you, Ezra, according to your God-given wisdom, set magistrates and judges who may judge all the people who are in the region beyond the River, all such as know the *laws of your God*

LAY A STONE IN ZION (NIV)
(See *LAY IN ZION A STONE*)

LAY A STONE IN ZION, A CHOSEN AND PRECIOUS CORNERSTONE (NIV)
(See *LAY IN ZION A CHIEF CORNERSTONE*)

LAY ASIDE
Ezek 26:16 Then all the princes of the sea will come down from their thrones, *lay aside* their robes, and take off their embroidered garments

Heb 12:1 Therefore we also, since we are surrounded by so great a cloud of witnesses, let us *lay aside* every weight, and the sin which so easily ensnares us, and let us run with endurance the race that is set before us

Jas 1:21 Therefore *lay aside* all filthiness and overflow of wickedness, and receive with meekness the implanted word, which is able to save your souls

LAY BY TO BE KEPT (RSV)
(See *LAY UP FOR YOURSELVES*)

LAY DOWN MY LIFE
John 10:15 As the Father knows Me, even so I know the Father; and I *lay down My life* for the sheep

John 10:17 Therefore My Father loves Me, because I *lay down My life* that I may take it again

John 13:37 Peter said to Him, "Lord, why can I not follow You now? I will *lay down my life* for Your sake

LAY HOLD ON ETERNAL LIFE
1Tim 6:12 Fight the good fight of faith, *lay hold on eternal life*, to which you were also called and have confessed the good confession in the presence of many witnesses

1Tim 6:19 storing up for themselves a good foundation for the time to come, that they may *lay hold on eternal life*

LAY IN ZION A CHIEF CORNERSTONE
1Pet 2:6 Therefore it is also contained in the Scripture, "Behold, I *lay in Zion a chief cornerstone* , elect, precious, and he who believes on Him will by no means be put to shame

LAY IN ZION A STONE
Is 28:16 Behold, I *lay in Zion a stone* for a foundation, a tried stone, a precious cornerstone, a sure foundation

LAY IT TO HEART (RSV)
(See *COME TO THEMSELVES*)

LAY UP FOR YOURSELVES
Ex 16:23 and *lay up for yourselves* all that remains, to be kept until morning

Matt 6:19 Do not *lay up for yourselves* treasures on earth, where moth and rust destroy and where thieves break in and steal

Matt 6:20 but *lay up for yourselves* treasures in heaven, where neither moth nor rust destroys and where thieves do not break in and steal

LAYETH IT TO HEART (KJV)
(See *TAKES IT TO HEART*)

LAYING ASIDE ALL MALICE
1Pet 2:1 Therefore, *laying aside all malice*, all guile, hypocrisy, envy, and all evil speaking

LAYING IN ZION A STONE, A CORNERSTONE (RSV)
(See *LAY IN ZION A CHIEF CORNERSTONE*)

LAYING IN ZION FOR A FOUNDATION A STONE (RSV)
(See *LAY IN ZION A STONE*)

LAYING ON OF HANDS
Heb 6:2 of the doctrine of baptisms, of *laying on of hands*, of resurrection of the dead, and of eternal judgment

LAYING ON OF THE APOSTLES' HANDS
Acts 8:18 Now when Simon saw that through the *laying on of the apostles' hands* the Holy Spirit was given, he offered them money

LAYS IT TO HEART (RSV)
(See *TAKES IT TO HEART*)

LAZARUS, COME FORTH
John 11:43 Now when He had said these things, He cried with a loud voice, "*Lazarus, come forth*

LAZY MAN (NIV)
(See *SLOTHFUL MAN*)

LEAD A QUIET LIFE
1Th 4:11 that you also aspire to *lead a quiet life*, to mind your own business, and to work with your own hands, as we commanded you

LEAD MY PEOPLE ASTRAY
(See *SEDUCED MY PEOPLE*)

LEADING CAPTIVES IN THY TRAIN (RSV)
(See *LED CAPTIVITY CAPTIVE*)

LEADS TO DEATH (NIV)
(See *WAY OF DEATH*)

LEADS TO LIFE
Prov 10:16 The labor of the righteous *leads to life*, the wages of the wicked to sin
Prov 11:19 As righteousness *leads to life*, so he who pursues evil pursues it to his own death
Prov 19:23 The fear of the Lord *leads to life*, and he who has it will abide in satisfaction
Matt 7:14 Because narrow is the gate and difficult is the way which *leads to life*, and there are few who find it

LEADS TO POVERTY
Prov 11:24 and there is one who withholds more than is right, but it *leads to poverty*

LEADS US IN TRIUMPH
2Cor 2:14 Now thanks be to God who always *leads us in triumph* in Christ, and through us diffuses the fragrance of His knowledge in every place

LEAN ON THE LORD
Mic 3:11 yet they *lean on the Lord*, and say, "Is not the Lord among us

LEANING ON THE TOP OF HIS STAFF
Heb 11:21 By faith Jacob, when he was dying, blessed each of the sons of Joseph, and worshiped, *leaning on the top of his staff*

LEAP FOR JOY
Luke 6:23 Rejoice in that day and *leap for joy!* for indeed your reward is great in heaven, for in like manner their fathers did to the prophets

LEAPED AND WALKED
Acts 14:10 said with a loud voice, "Stand up straight on your feet!" And he *leaped and walked*

LEAPED IN HER WOMB
Luke 1:41 And it happened, when Elizabeth heard the greeting of Mary, that the babe *leaped in her womb*

LEARN IN SILENCE
1Tim 2:11 Let a woman *learn in silence* with all submission

LEARNED OBEDIENCE
Heb 5:8 though He was a Son, yet He *learned obedience* by the things which He suffered

LEAST AMONG YOU
Luke 9:48 For he who is *least among you* all will be great

LEAST OF THESE
Matt 5:19 Whoever therefore breaks one of the *least of these* commandments, and teaches men so, shall be called least in the kingdom of heaven
Matt 25:40 And the King will answer and say to them, 'Assuredly, I say to you, inasmuch as you did it to one of the *least of these* My brethren, you did it to Me
Matt 25:45 Then He will answer them, saying, 'Assuredly, I say to you, inasmuch as you did not do it to one of the *least of these*, you did not do it to Me

LEAVE ME (NIV)
(See *DEPART FROM ME*)

LEAVE YOUR COUNTRY (NIV)
(See *GET OUT OF YOUR COUNTRY*)

LEAVEN LEAVENS THE WHOLE LUMP
1Cor 5:6 Do you not know that a little *leaven leavens the whole lump*
Gal 5:9 A little *leaven leavens the whole lump*

LEAVEN OF THE PHARISEES
Matt 16:6 Then Jesus said to them, "Take heed and beware of the *leaven of the Pharisees* and the Sadducees
Matt 16:11 but you should beware of the *leaven of the Pharisees* and Sadducees
Mark 8:15 Then He charged them, saying, "Take heed, beware of the *leaven of the Pharisees* and the leaven of Herod
Luke 12:1 In the meantime, when an innumerable multitude of people had gathered together, so that they trampled one another, He began to say to His disciples first of all, "Beware of the *leaven of the Pharisees*, which is hypocrisy

LED BY THE SPIRIT
Luke 4:1 Then Jesus, being filled with the Holy Spirit, returned from the Jordan and was *led by the Spirit* into the wilderness
Rom 8:14 For as many as are *led by the Spirit* of God, these are sons of God
Gal 5:18 But if you are *led by the Spirit*, you are not under the law

LED CAPTIVES IN YOUR TRAIN (NIV)
(See *LED CAPTIVITY CAPTIVE*)

LED CAPTIVITY CAPTIVE
Ps 68:18 You have ascended on high, You have *led captivity captive*
Eph 4:8 When He ascended on high, He *led captivity captive*, and gave gifts to men

LED MY PEOPLE ISRAEL ASTRAY (NAS, NIV, RSV)
(See *CAUSED MY PEOPLE ISRAEL TO ERR*)

LED YOU UP FROM EGYPT
Judg 2:1 I *led you up from Egypt* and brought you to the land of which I swore to your fathers

LEND, HOPING FOR NOTHING IN RETURN
Luke 6:35 But love your enemies, do good, and *lend, hoping for nothing in return*

LENDS TO THE LORD
Prov 19:17 He who has pity on the poor *lends to the Lord*, and He will pay back what he has given

LENGTH OF THE ARK
Gen 6:15 The *length of the ark* shall be three hundred cubits, its width fifty cubits, and its height thirty cubits

LENGTHEN YOUR CORDS
Is 54:2 do not spare; *lengthen your cords*, and strengthen your stakes

LENGTHEN YOUR DAYS
1Kin 3:14 So if you walk in My ways, to keep My statutes and My commandments, as your father David walked, then I will *lengthen your days*

LENGTHENING OF YOUR PROSPERITY
Dan 4:27 break off your sins by being righteous, and your iniquities by showing mercy to the poor. Perhaps there may be a *lengthening of your prosperity*

LENGTHENING OF YOUR TRANQUILITY (RSV)
(See *LENGTHENING OF YOUR PROSPERITY*)

LENTIL STEW (NAS, NIV)
(See *STEW OF LENTILS*)

LESS THAN NOTHING
Is 40:17 All nations before Him are as nothing, and they are counted by Him *less than nothing* and worthless

LET ALL THE EARTH KEEP SILENCE
Hab 2:20 But the Lord is in His holy temple. *Let all the earth keep silence* before Him

LET DOWN YOUR NETS
Luke 5:4 Now when He had stopped speaking, He said to Simon, "Launch out into the deep and *let down your nets* for a catch

LET HIM HEAR
Jer 20:16 *Let him hear* the cry in the morning and the shouting at noon
Ezek 3:27 He who hears, *let him hear;* and he who refuses, let him refuse
Matt 11:15 He who has ears to hear, *let him hear*
Matt 13:9 He who has ears to hear, *let him hear*
Matt 13:43 Then the righteous will shine forth as the sun in the kingdom of their Father. He who has ears to hear, *let him hear*
Mark 4:9 And He said to them, "He who has ears to hear, *let him hear*
Mark 4:23 If anyone has ears to hear, *let him hear*
Mark 7:16 If anyone has ears to hear, *let him hear*
Luke 8:8 When He had said these things He cried, "He who has ears to hear, *let him hear*
Luke 14:35 It is neither fit for the land nor for the dunghill, but men throw it out. He who has ears to hear, *let him hear*
Rev 2:7 He who has an ear, *let him hear* what the Spirit says to the churches
Rev 2:11 He who has an ear, *let him hear* what the Spirit says to the churches
Rev 2:17 He who has an ear, *let him hear* what the Spirit says to the churches
Rev 2:29 He who has an ear, *let him hear* what the Spirit says to the churches
Rev 3:6 He who has an ear, *let him hear* what the Spirit says to the churches
Rev 3:13 He who has an ear, *let him hear* what the Spirit says to the churches
Rev 3:22 He who has an ear, *let him hear* what the Spirit says to the churches
Rev 13:9 If anyone has an ear, *let him hear*

LET HIM WHO IS WITHOUT SIN (RSV)
(See *HE WHO IS WITHOUT SIN*)

LET IT REST ON THE HEAD
2Sam 3:29 *Let it rest on the head* of Joab and on all his father's house

LET JUSTICE RUN DOWN LIKE WATER
Amos 5:24 But *let justice run down like water*, and righteousness like a mighty stream

LET MARRIAGE BE HELD IN HONOR (RSV)
(See *MARRIAGE IS HONORABLE*)

LET MY PEOPLE GO
Ex 5:1 *Let My people go*, that they may hold a feast to Me in the wilderness
Ex 7:16 And you shall say to him, 'The Lord God of the Hebrews has sent me to you, saying, "*Let My people go*, that they may serve Me in the wilderness
Ex 8:1 And the Lord spoke to Moses, "Go to Pharaoh and say to him, 'Thus says the Lord: *Let My people go*, that they may serve Me
Ex 8:20 Then say to him, 'Thus says the Lord: *Let My people go*, that they may serve Me
Ex 8:21 Or else, if you will not *let My people go*, behold, I will send swarms of flies on you and your servants, on your people and into your houses
Ex 9:1 Then the Lord said to Moses, "Go in to Pharaoh and tell him, 'Thus says the Lord God of the Hebrews: "*Let My people go* that they may serve Me
Ex 9:13 Then the Lord said to Moses, "Rise early in the morning and stand before Pharaoh, and say to him, 'Thus says the Lord God of the Hebrews: *Let My people go* that they may serve Me
Ex 10:3 How long will you refuse to humble yourself before Me? *Let My people go*, that they may serve Me
Ex 10:4 Or else, if you refuse to *let My people go*, behold, tomorrow I will bring locusts into your territory

LET NO DEBT REMAIN OUTSTANDING (NIV)
(See *OWE NO ONE ANYTHING*)

LET NOT YOUR HEART BE TROUBLED
John 14:1 *Let not your heart be troubled;* you believe in God, believe also in Me
John 14:27 *Let not your heart be troubled*, neither let it be afraid

LET THE LITTLE CHILDREN COME
Matt 19:14 But Jesus said, "*Let the little children come* to Me, and do not forbid them
Mark 10:14 But when Jesus saw it, He was greatly displeased and said to them, "*Let the little children come* to Me, and do not forbid them
Luke 18:16 But Jesus called them to Him and said, "*Let the little children come* to Me, and do not forbid them

LET THE LORD JUDGE BETWEEN YOU AND ME
1Sam 24:12 *Let the Lord judge between you and me*, and let the Lord avenge me on you

LET THE READER UNDERSTAND
Mark 13:14 But when you see the 'abomination of desolation,' spoken of by Daniel the prophet, standing where it ought not" (*let the reader understand*

LET THERE BE
Gen 1:3 Then God said, "*Let there be* light"; and there was light
Gen 1:6 Then God said, "*Let there be* a firmament in the midst of the waters, and let it divide the waters from the waters
Gen 1:14 Then God said, "*Let there be* lights in the firmament of the heavens to divide the day from the night
Gen 13:8 So Abram said to Lot, "Please *let there be* no strife between you and me, and between my herdsmen and your herdsmen
Judg 6:39 let it now be dry only on the fleece, but on all the ground *let there be* dew

2Sam 1:21 O mountains of Gilboa, *let there be* no dew, nor *let there be* rain upon you, nor fields of offerings
1Kin 15:19 *Let there be* a treaty between you and me, as there was between my father and your father
2Chr 16:3 *Let there be* a treaty between you and me, as there was between my father and your father
Job 6:29 Turn now, *let there be* no injustice; yes, turn again, my righteousness still stands
Ps 79:10 *Let there be* known among the nations in our sight the avenging of the blood of Your servants which has been shed
Ps 109:12 *Let there be* none to extend mercy to him, nor *let there be* any to favor his fatherless children
1Cor 14:27 If anyone speaks in a tongue, *let there be* two or at the most three, each in turn, and let one interpret

LET THIS THING BE DONE FOR ME
Judg 11:37 Then she said to her father, "*Let this thing be done for me*

LET US
Gen 1:26 Then God said, "*Let Us* make man in Our image, according to Our likeness
Gen 11:3 Then they said to one another, "Come, *let us* make bricks and bake them thoroughly
Gen 11:4 And they said, "Come, *let us* build ourselves a city, and a tower whose top is in the heavens; *let us* make a name for ourselves, lest we be scattered abroad over the face of the whole earth
Gen 11:7 Come, *let Us* go down and there confuse their language, that they may not understand one another's speech
Gen 19:32 Come, *let us* make our father drink wine, and we will lie with him, that we may preserve the lineage of our father
Gen 19:34 *let us* make him drink wine tonight also, and you go in and lie with him, that we may preserve the lineage of our father
Gen 26:28 So we said, 'Let there now be an oath between us, between you and us; and *let us* make a covenant with you
Gen 31:44 Now therefore, come, *let us* make a covenant, you and I, and let it be a witness between you and me
Gen 33:12 Then Esau said, "*Let us* take our journey; *let us* go, and I will go before you
Gen 34:21 *Let us* take their daughters to us as wives, and *let us* give them our daughters
Gen 34:23 Only *let us* consent to them, and they will dwell with us
Gen 35:3 Then *let us* arise and go up to Bethel; and I will make an altar there to God, who answered me in the day of my distress and has been with me in the way which I have gone
Gen 37:17 And the man said, "They have departed from here, for I heard them say, '*Let us* go to Dothan
Gen 37:20 Come therefore, *let us* now kill him and cast him into some pit
Gen 37:21 But Reuben heard it, and he delivered him out of their hands, and said, "*Let us* not kill him
Gen 37:27 Come and *let us* sell him to the Ishmaelites, and let not our hand be upon him, for he is our brother and our flesh
Gen 47:25 *let us* find favor in the sight of my lord, and we will be Pharaoh's servants
Ex 1:10 come, *let us* deal shrewdly with them, lest they multiply, and it happen, in the event of war, that they also join our enemies and fight against us, and so go up out of the land
Ex 3:18 and now, please, *let us* go three days' journey into the wilderness, that we may sacrifice to the Lord our God
Ex 5:3 Please, *let us* go three days' journey into the desert and sacrifice to the Lord our God, lest He fall upon us with pestilence or with the sword
Ex 5:8 therefore they cry out, saying, '*Let us* go and sacrifice to our God
Ex 5:17 Therefore you say, '*Let us* go and sacrifice to the Lord
Ex 14:12 Is this not the word that we told you in Egypt, saying, '*Let us* alone that we may serve the Egyptians
Ex 14:25 and the Egyptians said, "*Let us* flee from the face of Israel, for the Lord fights for them against the Egyptians
Num 13:30 Then Caleb quieted the people before Moses, and said, "*Let us* go up at once and take possession, for we are well able to overcome it
Num 14:4 So they said to one another, "*Let us* select a leader and return to Egypt
Num 20:17 Please *let us* pass through your country. We will not pass through fields or vineyards, nor will we drink water from wells
Deut 1:22 And everyone of you came near to me and said, '*Let us* send men before us, and let them search out the land for us, and bring back word to us of the way by which we should go up, and of the cities into which we shall come
Deut 2:30 But Sihon king of Heshbon would not *let us* pass through, for the Lord your God hardened his spirit and made his heart obstinate, that He might deliver him into your hand, as it is this day
Deut 13:2 and the sign or the wonder of which he spoke to you comes to pass, saying, '*Let us* go after other gods which you have not known, and *let us* serve them
Deut 13:6 If your brother, the son of your mother, your son or your daughter, the wife of your bosom, or your friend who is as your own soul, secretly entices you, saying, '*Let us* go and serve other gods
Deut 13:13 Certain corrupt men have gone out from among you and enticed the inhabitants of their city, saying, "*Let us* go and serve other gods
Josh 2:18 unless, when we come into the land, you bind this line of scarlet cord in the window through which you *let us* down, and unless you bring your father, your mother, your brothers, and all your father's household to your own home
Josh 22:26 Therefore we said, '*Let us* now prepare to build ourselves an altar, not for burnt offering nor for sacrifice
Judg 11:19 and Israel said to him, "Please *let us* pass through your land into our place
Judg 13:15 Then Manoah said to the Angel of the Lord, "Please *let us* detain You, and we will prepare a young goat for You
Judg 18:9 So they said, "Arise, *let us* go up against them
Judg 19:11 and the servant said to his master, "Come, please, and *let us* turn aside into this city of the Jebusites and lodge in it
Judg 19:13 So he said to his servant, "Come, *let us* draw near to one of these places, and spend the night in Gibeah or in Ramah
Judg 19:28 And he said to her, "Get up and *let us* be going
Judg 20:32 But the children of Israel said, "*Let us* flee and draw them away from the city to the highways
1Sam 4:3 *Let us* bring the ark of the covenant of the Lord from Shiloh to us, that when it comes among us it may save us from the hand of our enemies
1Sam 9:5 When they had come to the land of Zuph, Saul said to his servant who was with him,

"Come, *let us* return, lest my father cease caring about the donkeys and become worried about us
1Sam 9:6 So *let us* go there; perhaps he can show us the way that we should go
1Sam 9:9 Come, *let us* go to the seer"; for he who is now called a prophet was formerly called a seer
1Sam 9:10 come, *let us* go." So they went to the city where the man of God was
1Sam 11:14 Then Samuel said to the people, "Come, *let us* go to Gilgal and renew the kingdom there
1Sam 14:1 Now it happened one day that Jonathan the son of Saul said to the young man who bore his armor, "Come, *let us* go over to the Philistines
1Sam 14:6 Then Jonathan said to the young man who bore his armor, "Come, *let us* go over to the garrison of these uncircumcised
1Sam 14:8 Then Jonathan said, "Very well, *let us* cross over to these men, and we will show ourselves to them
1Sam 14:36 And Saul said, "*Let us* go down after the Philistines by night, and plunder them until the morning light; and *let us* not leave a man of them." And they said, "Do whatever seems good to you." Then the priest said, "*Let us* draw near to God here
1Sam 20:11 And Jonathan said to David, "Come, and *let us* go out into the field
1Sam 26:11 But please, take now the spear and the jug of water that are by his head, and *let us* go
2Sam 10:12 Be of good courage, and *let us* be strong for our people and for the cities of our God
2Sam 13:25 But the king said to Absalom, "No, my son, *let us* not all go now, lest we be a burden to you
2Sam 15:14 So David said to all his servants who were with him at Jerusalem, "Arise, and *let us* flee
2Sam 17:5 Then Absalom said, "Now call Hushai the Archite also, and *let us* hear what he says too
2Sam 24:14 Please *let us* fall into the hand of the Lord, for His mercies are great
1Kin 20:31 Please, *let us* put sackcloth around our waists and ropes around our heads, and go out to the king of Israel
2Kin 4:10 Please, *let us* make a small upper room on the wall; and *let us* put a bed for him there, and a table and a chair and a lampstand
2Kin 6:2 Please, *let us* go to the Jordan, and let every man take a beam from there, and *let us* make there a place where we may dwell
2Kin 7:4 Now therefore, come, *let us* surrender to the army of the Syrians
2Kin 7:9 Now therefore, come, *let us* go and tell the king's household
2Kin 7:13 or indeed, I say, they may become like all the multitude of Israel left from those who are consumed; so *let us* send them and see
2Kin 14:8 Then Amaziah sent messengers to Jehoash the son of Jehoahaz, the son of Jehu, king of Israel, saying, "Come, *let us* face one another in battle
1Chr 13:2 And David said to all the congregation of Israel, "If it seems good to you, and if it is of the Lord our God, *let us* send out to our brethren everywhere who are left in all the land of Israel, and with them to the priests and Levites who are in their cities and their common-lands, that they may gather together to us
1Chr 13:3 and *let us* bring the ark of our God back to us, for we have not inquired at it since the days of Saul
1Chr 19:13 Be of good courage, and *let us* be strong for our people and for the cities of our God
2Chr 14:7 Therefore he said to Judah, "*Let us* build these cities and make walls around them, and towers, gates, and bars, while the land is yet before us, because we have sought the Lord our God
2Chr 25:17 Then Amaziah king of Judah took counsel and sent to Joash the son of Jehoahaz, the son of Jehu, king of Israel, saying, "Come, *let us* face one another in battle
Ezra 4:2 they came to Zerubbabel and the heads of the fathers' houses, and said to them, "*Let us* build with you, for we seek your God as you do
Ezra 10:3 Now therefore, *let us* make a covenant with our God to put away all these wives and those who have been born to them, according to the counsel of my master and of those who tremble at the commandment of our God
Neh 2:17 Come and *let us* build the wall of Jerusalem, that we may no longer be a reproach
Neh 2:18 So they said, "*Let us* rise up and build." Then they set their hands to do this good work
Neh 5:2 therefore *let us* get grain for them, that we may eat and live
Neh 5:10 I also, with my brethren and my servants, am lending them money and grain. Please, *let us* stop this usury
Neh 6:2 that Sanballat and Geshem sent to me, saying, "Come, *let us* meet together in one of the villages in the plain of Ono
Neh 6:7 Now these matters will be reported to the king. So come, therefore, and *let us* take counsel together
Neh 6:10 and he said, "*Let us* meet together in the house of God, within the temple, and *let us* close the doors of the temple, for they are coming to kill you
Job 34:4 *Let us* choose justice for ourselves; *let us* know among ourselves what is good
Ps 2:3 *Let us* break their bonds in pieces and cast away their cords from us
Ps 34:3 Oh, magnify the Lord with me, and *let us* exalt His name together
Ps 74:8 They said in their hearts, "*Let us* destroy them altogether
Ps 83:4 They have said, "Come, and *let us* cut them off from being a nation, that the name of Israel may be remembered no more
Ps 83:12 Who said, "*Let us* take for ourselves the pastures of God for a possession
Ps 95:1 Oh come, *let us* sing to the Lord! *Let us* shout joyfully to the Rock of our salvation
Ps 95:2 *Let us* come before His presence with thanksgiving; *let us* shout joyfully to Him with psalms
Ps 95:6 Oh come, *let us* worship and bow down; *let us* kneel before the Lord our Maker
Ps 122:1 I was glad when they said to me, "*Let us* go into the house of the Lord
Ps 132:7 *Let us* go into His tabernacle; *let us* worship at His footstool
Prov 1:11 If they say, "Come with us, *let us* lie in wait to shed blood; *let us* lurk secretly for the innocent without cause
Prov 1:12 *let us* swallow them alive like Sheol, and whole, like those who go down to the Pit
Prov 1:14 cast in your lot among us, *let us* all have one purse
Prov 7:18 Come, *let us* take our fill of love until morning; *let us* delight ourselves with love
Eccl 12:13 *Let us* hear the conclusion of the whole matter: Fear God and keep His commandments, for this is the whole duty of man
Song 7:11 Come, my beloved, *let us* go forth to the field; *let us* lodge in the villages
Song 7:12 *Let us* get up early to the vineyards; *let us* see if the vine has budded, whether the grape blossoms are open, and the pomegranates are in bloom
Is 1:18 Come now, and *let us* reason together," says the Lord

Is 2:3 Many people shall come and say, "Come, and *let us* go up to the mountain of the Lord, to the house of the God of Jacob
Is 2:5 O house of Jacob, come and *let us* walk in the light of the Lord
Is 4:1 only *let us* be called by your name, to take away our reproach
Is 7:6 *Let us* go up against Judah and trouble it, and *let us* make a gap in its wall for ourselves, and set a king over them, the son of Tabeel
Is 22:13 But instead, joy and gladness, slaying oxen and killing sheep, eating meat and drinking wine: "*Let us* eat and drink, for tomorrow we die
Is 41:1 Let them come near, then let them speak; *let us* come near together for judgment
Is 43:26 *let us* contend together; state your case, that you may be acquitted
Is 50:8 *Let us* stand together. Who is My adversary? Let him come near Me
Jer 4:5 cry, 'Gather together,' and say, 'Assemble yourselves, and *let us* go into the fortified cities
Jer 5:24 They do not say in their heart, "*Let us* now fear the Lord our God, Who gives rain, both the former and the latter, in its season
Jer 6:4 arise, and *let us* go up at noon. Woe to us, for the day goes away, for the shadows of the evening are lengthening
Jer 6:5 Arise, and *let us* go by night, and *let us* destroy her palaces
Jer 8:14 Assemble yourselves, and *let us* enter the fortified cities, and *let us* be silent there
Jer 11:19 and I did not know that they had devised schemes against me, saying, "*Let us* destroy the tree with its fruit, and *let us* cut him off from the land of the living, that his name may be remembered no more
Jer 18:18 Then they said, "Come and *let us* devise plans against Jeremiah; for the law shall not perish from the priest, nor counsel from the wise, nor the word from the prophet. Come and *let us* attack him with the tongue, and *let us* not give heed to any of his words
Jer 31:6 For there shall be a day when the watchmen will cry on Mount Ephraim, 'Arise, and *let us* go up to Zion, to the Lord our God
Jer 35:11 But it came to pass, when Nebuchadnezzar king of Babylon came up into the land, that we said, 'Come, *let us* go to Jerusalem for fear of the army of the Chaldeans and for fear of the army of the Syrians
Jer 46:16 *Let us* go back to our own people and to the land of our nativity from the oppressing sword
Jer 48:2 Come, and *let us* cut her off as a nation
Jer 50:5 They shall ask the way to Zion, with their faces toward it, saying, 'Come and *let us* join ourselves to the Lord in a perpetual covenant that will not be forgotten
Jer 51:9 Forsake her, and *let us* go everyone to his own country
Jer 51:10 Come and *let us* declare in Zion the work of the Lord our God
Lam 3:40 *Let us* search out and examine our ways, and turn back to the Lord
Lam 3:41 *let us* lift our hearts and hands to God in heaven
Ezek 44:6 O house of Israel, *let us* have no more of all your abominations
Hos 6:1 Come, and *let us* return to the Lord; for He has torn, but He will heal us
Hos 6:3 *Let us* know, *let us* pursue the knowledge of the Lord
Amos 4:1 Hear this word, you cows of Bashan, who are on the mountain of Samaria, who oppress the poor, who crush the needy, who say to your husbands, "Bring wine, *let us* drink
Obad 1 Thus says the Lord God concerning Edom (We have heard a report from the Lord, and a messenger has been sent among the nations, saying, "Arise, and *let us* rise up against her for battle
Jon 1:7 And they said to one another, "Come, *let us* cast lots, that we may know for whose cause this trouble has come upon us
Jon 1:14 Therefore they cried out to the Lord and said, "We pray, O Lord, please do not *let us* perish for this man's life, and do not charge us with innocent blood
Mic 4:2 Many nations shall come and say, "Come, and *let us* go up to the mountain of the Lord, to the house of the God of Jacob
Zech 8:21 the inhabitants of one city shall go to another, saying, "*Let us* continue to go and pray before the Lord, and seek the Lord of hosts
Zech 8:23 In those days ten men from every language of the nations shall grasp the sleeve of a Jewish man, saying, "*Let us* go with you, for we have heard that God is with you
Matt 17:4 if You wish, *let us* make here three tabernacles: one for You, one for Moses, and one for Elijah
Matt 21:38 But when the vinedressers saw the son, they said among themselves, 'This is the heir. Come, *let us* kill him and seize his inheritance
Matt 26:46 Rise, *let us* be going. See, he who betrays Me is at hand
Matt 27:49 *let us* see if Elijah will come to save Him
Mark 1:24 saying, "*Let us* alone! What have we to do with You, Jesus of Nazareth
Mark 1:38 But He said to them, "*Let us* go into the next towns, that I may preach there also, because for this purpose I have come forth
Mark 4:35 On the same day, when evening had come, He said to them, "*Let us* cross over to the other side
Mark 9:5 and *let us* make three tabernacles: one for You, one for Moses, and one for Elijah
Mark 12:7 Come, *let us* kill him, and the inheritance will be ours
Mark 14:42 Rise up, *let us* go. See, My betrayer is at hand
Mark 15:36 *let us* see if Elijah will come to take Him down
Luke 2:15 So it was, when the angels had gone away from them into heaven, that the shepherds said to one another, "*Let us* now go to Bethlehem and see this thing that has come to pass, which the Lord has made known to us
Luke 4:34 saying, "*Let us* alone! What have we to do with You, Jesus of Nazareth
Luke 8:22 And He said to them, "*Let us* go over to the other side of the lake
Luke 9:33 and *let us* make three tabernacles: one for You, one for Moses, and one for Elijah
Luke 15:23 And bring the fatted calf here and kill it, and *let us* eat and be merry
Luke 20:14 Come, *let us* kill him, that the inheritance may be ours
John 11:7 Then after this He said to the disciples, "*Let us* go to Judea again
John 11:15 And I am glad for your sakes that I was not there, that you may believe. Nevertheless *let us* go to him
John 11:16 Then Thomas, who is called Didymus, said to his fellow disciples, "*Let us* also go, that we may die with Him
John 14:31 But that the world may know that I love the Father, and as the Father gave Me commandment, so I do. Arise, *let us* go from here
John 19:24 They said therefore among themselves, "*Let us* not tear it, but cast lots for it, whose it shall be
Acts 4:17 But so that it spreads no further among the people, *let us* severely threaten them, that from now on they speak to no man in this name

Acts 15:36 Then after some days Paul said to Barnabas, "*Let us* now go back and visit our brethren in every city where we have preached the word of the Lord, and see how they are doing
Acts 23:9 but if a spirit or an angel has spoken to him, *let us* not fight against God
Rom 3:8 And why not say, "*Let us* do evil that good may come
Rom 12:6 Having then gifts differing according to the grace that is given to us, *let us* use them: if prophecy, let us prophesy in proportion to our faith
Rom 12:7 or ministry, *let us* use it in our ministering; he who teaches, in teaching
Rom 13:12 Therefore *let us* cast off the works of darkness, and *let us* put on the armor of light
Rom 13:13 *Let us* walk properly, as in the day, not in revelry and drunkenness, not in licentiousness and lewdness, not in strife and envy
Rom 14:13 Therefore *let us* not judge one another anymore, but rather resolve this, not to put a stumbling block or a cause to fall in our brother's way
Rom 14:19 Therefore *let us* pursue the things which make for peace and the things by which one may edify another
1Cor 5:8 Therefore *let us* keep the feast, not with old leaven, nor with the leaven of malice and wickedness, but with the unleavened bread of sincerity and truth
1Cor 10:8 Nor *let us* commit sexual immorality, as some of them did, and in one day twenty-three thousand fell
1Cor 10:9 nor *let us* tempt Christ, as some of them also tempted, and were destroyed by serpents
1Cor 15:32 If the dead do not rise, "*Let us* eat and drink, for tomorrow we die
2Cor 7:1 Therefore, having these promises, beloved, *let us* cleanse ourselves from all filthiness of the flesh and spirit, perfecting holiness in the fear of God
Gal 5:25 If we live in the Spirit, *let us* also walk in the Spirit
Gal 5:26 *Let us* not become conceited, provoking one another, envying one another
Gal 6:9 And *let us* not grow weary while doing good, for in due season we shall reap if we do not lose heart
Gal 6:10 Therefore, as we have opportunity, *let us* do good to all, especially to those who are of the household of faith
Phil 3:15 Therefore *let us*, as many as are mature, have this mind
Phil 3:16 Nevertheless, to the degree that we have already attained, *let us* walk by the same rule, *let us* be of the same mind
1Th 5:6 Therefore *let us* not sleep, as others do, but *let us* watch and be sober
1Th 5:8 But *let us* who are of the day be sober, putting on the breastplate of faith and love, and as a helmet the hope of salvation
Heb 4:1 Therefore, since a promise remains of entering His rest, *let us* fear lest any of you seem to have come short of it
Heb 4:11 *Let us* therefore be diligent to enter that rest, lest anyone fall after the same example of disobedience
Heb 4:14 Seeing then that we have a great High Priest who has passed through the heavens, Jesus the Son of God, *let us* hold fast our confession
Heb 4:16 *Let us* therefore come boldly to the throne of grace, that we may obtain mercy and find grace to help in time of need
Heb 6:1 Therefore, leaving the discussion of the elementary principles of Christ, *let us* go on to perfection, not laying again the foundation of repentance from dead works and of faith toward God
Heb 10:22 *let us* draw near with a true heart in full assurance of faith, having our hearts sprinkled from an evil conscience and our bodies washed with pure water
Heb 10:23 *Let us* hold fast the confession of our hope without wavering, for He who promised is faithful
Heb 10:24 And *let us* consider one another in order to stir up love and good works
Heb 12:1 Therefore we also, since we are surrounded by so great a cloud of witnesses, *let us* lay aside every weight, and the sin which so easily ensnares us, and *let us* run with endurance the race that is set before us
Heb 12:28 Therefore, since we are receiving a kingdom which cannot be shaken, *let us* have grace, by which we may serve God acceptably with reverence and godly fear
Heb 13:13 Therefore *let us* go forth to Him, outside the camp, bearing His reproach
Heb 13:15 Therefore by Him *let us* continually offer the sacrifice of praise to God, that is, the fruit of our lips, giving thanks to His name
1Jn 3:18 My little children, *let us* not love in word or in tongue, but in deed and in truth
1Jn 4:7 Beloved, *let us* love one another, for love is of God
Rev 19:7 *Let us* be glad and rejoice and give Him glory, for the marriage of the Lamb has come, and His wife has made herself ready

LET US BUILD
Gen 11:4 And they said, "Come, *let us build* ourselves a city, and a tower whose top is in the heavens
2Chr 14:7 Therefore he said to Judah, "*Let us build* these cities and make walls around them, and towers, gates, and bars, while the land is yet before us, because we have sought the Lord our God
Ezra 4:2 they came to Zerubbabel and the heads of the fathers' houses, and said to them, "*Let us build* with you, for we seek your God as you do
Neh 2:17 Come and *let us build* the wall of Jerusalem, that we may no longer be a reproach

LET US EAT AND DRINK
Is 22:13 But instead, joy and gladness, slaying oxen and killing sheep, eating meat and drinking wine: "*Let us eat and drink,* for tomorrow we die
1Cor 15:32 If the dead do not rise, "*Let us eat and drink*, for tomorrow we die

LET US MAKE MAN
Gen 1:26 Then God said, "*Let Us make man* in Our image, according to Our likeness

LET US REASON TOGETHER
Is 1:18 Come now, and *let us reason together*," says the Lord

LET YOUR LIGHT SO SHINE
Matt 5:16 *Let your light so shine* before men, that they may see your good works and glorify your Father in heaven

LEVEL PATHS (NIV)
(See *STRAIGHT PATHS*)

LEVIATHAN THE FLEEING SERPENT
Is 27:1 In that day the Lord with His severe sword, great and strong, will punish *Leviathan the fleeing serpent*, Leviathan that twisted serpent

LEVIATHAN THE GLIDING SERPENT (NIV)
(See *LEVIATHAN THE FLEEING SERPENT*)

LEVIATHAN THE PIERCING SERPENT (KJV)
(See *LEVIATHAN THE FLEEING SERPENT*)

LIABLE TO DESTRUCTION (NIV)
(See *DOOMED TO DESTRUCTION*)

LIBERTY OF THE CHILDREN OF GOD
Rom 8:21 because the creation itself also will be delivered from the bondage of corruption into the glorious *liberty of the children of God*

LIBERTY WHICH WE HAVE IN CHRIST
Gal 2:4 But this occurred because of false brethren secretly brought in (who came in by stealth to spy out our *liberty which we have in Christ* Jesus, that they might bring us into bondage

LICK THE DUST
Ps 72:9 Those who dwell in the wilderness will bow before Him, and His enemies will *lick the dust*
Mic 7:17 They shall *lick the dust* like a serpent; they shall crawl from their holes like snakes of the earth

LIE DOWN IN GREEN PASTURES
Ps 23:2 He makes me to *lie down in green pastures;* He leads me beside the still waters

LIE DOWN IN THE DUST
Job 7:21 For now I will *lie down in the dust*, and You will seek me diligently, but I will no longer be

LIE TO THE HOLY SPIRIT
Acts 5:3 But Peter said, "Ananias, why has Satan filled your heart to *lie to the Holy Spirit* and keep back part of the price of the land for yourself

LIES DOWN AS A LION
Gen 49:9 He bows down, he *lies down as a lion;* and as a lion, who shall rouse him
Num 24:9 He bows down, he *lies down as a lion;* and as a lion, who will rouse him

LIFE FROM THE DEAD
Rom 11:15 For if their being cast away is the reconciling of the world, what will their acceptance be but *life from the dead*

LIFE IN CHRIST JESUS
Rom 6:23 For the wages of sin is death, but the gift of God is eternal *life in Christ Jesus* our Lord
Rom 8:2 For the law of the Spirit of *life in Christ Jesus* has made me free from the law of sin and death

LIFE IS A BREATH
Job 7:7 Oh, remember that my *life is a breath!* My eye will never again see good

LIFE IS BUT A BREATH (NIV)
(See *LIFE IS A BREATH*)

LIFE IS MORE THAN FOOD
Luke 12:23 *Life is more than food*, and the body is more than clothing

LIFE IS WIND (KJV)
(See *LIFE IS A BREATH*)

LIFE MORE THAN FOOD
Matt 6:25 Is not *life more than food* and the body more than clothing

LIFE OF GOD
Eph 4:18 having their understanding darkened, being alienated from the *life of God*, because of the ignorance that is in them, because of the hardening of their heart

LIFE OF JESUS
2Cor 4:10 always carrying about in the body the dying of the Lord Jesus, that the *life of Jesus* also may be manifested in our body
2Cor 4:11 For we who live are always delivered to death for Jesus' sake, that the *life of Jesus* also may be manifested in our mortal flesh

LIFE OF THE WORLD
John 6:51 and the bread that I shall give is My flesh, which I shall give for the *life of the world*

LIFE WAS THE LIGHT OF MEN
John 1:4 In Him was life, and the *life was the light of men*

LIFE WHICH IS IN CHRIST
2Tim 1:1 Paul, an apostle of Jesus Christ by the will of God, according to the promise of *life which is in Christ* Jesus

LIFE WHICH WAS WITH THE FATHER
1Jn 1:2 the life was manifested, and we have seen, and bear witness, and declare to you that eternal *life which was with the Father* and was manifested to us

LIFE WILL BE SAVED (RSV)
(See *SOUL SHALL LIVE*)

LIFE WILL BE SPARED (NIV)
(See *SOUL SHALL LIVE*)

LIFE WORTHY OF GOD (RSV)
(See *WALK WORTHY OF GOD*)

LIFT UP HIS EYES (NAS, RSV)
(See *LIFTED UP HIS EYES*)

LIFT UP MY EYES
Ps 121:1 I will *lift up my eyes* to the hills from whence comes my help
Ps 123:1 Unto You I *lift up my eyes*, O You who dwell in the heavens

LIFT UP MY SOUL
Ps 25:1 To You, O Lord, I *lift up my soul*
Ps 86:4 Rejoice the soul of Your servant, for to You, O Lord, I *lift up my soul*
Ps 143:8 Cause me to know the way in which I should walk, for I *lift up my soul* to You

LIFT UP THE HORN
Ps 75:4 I said to the boastful, 'Do not deal boastfully,' And to the wicked, 'Do not *lift up the horn*

LIFT UP THE SON OF MAN
John 8:28 Then Jesus said to them, "When you *lift up the Son of Man*, then you will know that I am He, and that I do nothing of Myself

LIFT UP YOUR EYES
Is 40:26 *Lift up your eyes* on high, and see who has created these things, Who brings out their host by number
Is 49:18 *Lift up your eyes*, look around and see; all these gather together and come to you
Is 51:6 *Lift up your eyes* to the heavens, and look on the earth beneath
Is 60:4 *Lift up your eyes* all around, and see: They all gather together, they come to you

Jer 3:2 *Lift up your eyes* to the desolate heights and see
Jer 13:20 *Lift up your eyes* and see those who come from the north
Ezek 33:25 You eat meat with blood, you *lift up your eyes* toward your idols, and shed blood
John 4:35 Behold, I say to you, *lift up your eyes* and look at the fields, for they are already white for harvest

LIFT UP YOUR HEADS
Ps 24:7 *Lift up your heads*, O you gates! And be lifted up, you everlasting doors
Ps 24:9 *Lift up your heads*, O you gates! And lift them up, you everlasting doors
Luke 21:28 Now when these things begin to happen, look up and *lift up your heads*, because your redemption draws near

LIFT UP YOUR HORN
Ps 75:5 Do not *lift up your horn* on high; do not speak with a stiff neck

LIFT UP YOUR VOICE
Job 38:34 Can you *lift up your voice* to the clouds, that an abundance of water may cover you
Prov 2:3 yes, if you cry out for discernment, and *lift up your voice* for understanding
Is 10:30 *Lift up your voice*, O daughter of Gallim! Cause it to be heard as far as Laish O poor Anathoth
Is 40:9 O Jerusalem, you who bring good tidings, *lift up your voice* with strength, lift it up, be not afraid
Is 58:1 *lift up your voice* like a trumpet; tell My people their transgression, and the house of Jacob their sins
Jer 22:20 Go up to Lebanon, and cry out, and *lift up your voice* in Bashan

LIFT YOUR SKIRTS OVER YOUR FACE
Nah 3:5 I will *lift your skirts over your face*, I will show the nations your nakedness, and the kingdoms your shame

LIFTED UP
Gen 7:17 The waters increased and *lifted up* the ark, and it rose high above the earth
Gen 27:38 Bless me, even me also, O my father!" And Esau *lifted up* his voice and wept
Gen 29:11 Then Jacob kissed Rachel, and *lifted up* his voice and wept
Gen 40:20 and he *lifted up* the head of the chief butler and of the chief baker among his servants
Ex 7:20 So he *lifted up* the rod and struck the waters that were in the river, in the sight of Pharaoh and in the sight of his servants
Num 14:1 Then all the congregation *lifted up* their voices and cried, and the people wept that night
Num 18:30 When you have *lifted up* the best of it, then the rest shall be accounted to the Levites as the produce of the threshing floor and as the produce of the winepress
Num 18:32 And you shall bear no sin because of it, when you have *lifted up* the best of it
Deut 8:14 when your heart is *lifted up*, and you forget the Lord your God who brought you out of the land of Egypt, from the house of bondage
Judg 2:4 And so it was, when the Angel of the Lord spoke these words to all the children of Israel, that the people *lifted up* their voice and wept
Judg 21:2 Then the people came to the house of God, and remained there before God till evening. They *lifted up* their voices and wept bitterly
Ruth 1:9 Then she kissed them, and they *lifted up* their voices and wept
Ruth 1:14 Then they *lifted up* their voices and wept again; and Orpah kissed her mother-in-law, but Ruth clung to her
1Sam 11:4 And all the people *lifted up* their voices and wept
1Sam 30:4 Then David and the people who were with him *lifted up* their voices and wept, until they had no more power to weep
2Sam 3:32 and the king *lifted up* his voice and wept at the grave of Abner, and all the people wept
2Sam 13:36 So it was, as soon as he had finished speaking, that the king's sons indeed came, and they *lifted up* their voice and wept
2Kin 19:22 Against whom have you raised your voice, and *lifted up* your eyes on high
1Chr 11:11 he had *lifted up* his spear against three hundred, killed by him at one time
1Chr 11:20 He had *lifted up* his spear against three hundred men and killed them, and won a name among these three
2Chr 5:13 indeed it came to pass, when the trumpeters and singers were as one, to make one sound to be heard in praising and thanking the Lord, and when they *lifted up* their voice with the trumpets and cymbals and instruments of music, and praised the Lord, saying
2Chr 25:19 Indeed you say that you have defeated the Edomites, and your heart is *lifted up* to boast
2Chr 26:16 But when he was strong his heart was *lifted up*, to his destruction, for he transgressed against the Lord his God by entering the temple of the Lord to burn incense on the altar of incense
2Chr 32:25 But Hezekiah did not repay according to the favor shown him, for his heart was *lifted up*
Ps 24:4 He who has clean hands and a pure heart, who has not *lifted up* his soul to an idol, nor sworn deceitfully
Ps 24:7 And be *lifted up*, you everlasting doors! And the King of glory shall come in
Ps 27:6 And now my head shall be *lifted up* above my enemies all around me
Ps 41:9 Even my own familiar friend in whom I trusted, who ate my bread, has *lifted up* his heel against me
Ps 83:2 And those who hate You have *lifted up* their head
Ps 93:3 The floods have *lifted up*, O Lord, the floods have *lifted up* their voice
Ps 106:26 Therefore He *lifted up* His hand in an oath against them, to overthrow them in the wilderness
Prov 30:13 There is a generation oh, how lofty are their eyes! And their eyelids are *lifted up*
Is 2:12 For the day of the Lord of hosts shall come upon everything proud and lofty, upon everything *lifted up* and it shall be brought low
Is 2:13 upon all the cedars of Lebanon that are high and *lifted up*, and upon all the oaks of Bashan
Is 2:14 upon all the high mountains, and upon all the hills that are *lifted up*
Is 6:1 In the year that King Uzziah died, I saw the Lord sitting on a throne, high and *lifted up*, and the train of His robe filled the temple
Is 26:11 Lord, when Your hand is *lifted up*, they will not see
Is 37:23 Against whom have you raised your voice, and *lifted up* your eyes on high
Jer 51:9 for her judgment reaches to heaven and is *lifted up* to the skies
Jer 52:31 Now it came to pass in the thirty-seventh year of the captivity of Jehoiachin king of Judah, in the twelfth month, on the twenty-fifth day of the month, that Evil-Merodach king of Babylon, in the first year of his reign, *lifted up* the

head of Jehoiachin king of Judah and brought him out of prison

Ezek 1:19 and when the living creatures were *lifted up* from the earth, the wheels were *lifted up*

Ezek 1:21 and when those were *lifted up* from the earth, the wheels were *lifted up* together with them, for the spirit of the living creatures was in the wheels

Ezek 10:15 And the cherubim were *lifted up*. This was the living creature I saw by the River Chebar

Ezek 10:17 When the cherubim stood still, the wheels stood still, and when one was *lifted up*, the other lifted itself up, for the spirit of the living creature was in them

Ezek 11:22 Then the cherubim *lifted up* their wings, with the wheels beside them, and the glory of the God of Israel was high above them

Ezek 18:6 if he has not eaten on the mountains, nor *lifted up* his eyes to the idols of the house of Israel, nor defiled his neighbor's wife, nor approached a woman during her impurity

Ezek 28:2 Because your heart is *lifted up*, and you say, 'I am a god, I sit in the seat of gods, in the midst of the seas

Ezek 28:5 by your great wisdom in trade you have increased your riches, and your heart is *lifted up* because of your riches

Ezek 28:17 Your heart was *lifted up* because of your beauty; you corrupted your wisdom for the sake of your splendor

Ezek 31:10 Because you have increased in height, and it set its top among the thick boughs, and its heart was *lifted up* in its height

Dan 5:20 But when his heart was *lifted up*, and his spirit was hardened in pride, he was deposed from his kingly throne, and they took his glory from him

Dan 7:4 and it was *lifted up* from the earth and made to stand on two feet like a man, and a man's heart was given to it

Dan 11:12 When he has taken away the multitude, his heart will be *lifted up*

Zech 1:21 but the craftsmen are coming to terrify them, to cast out the horns of the nations that *lifted up* their horn against the land of Judah to scatter it

Zech 5:7 Here is a lead disc *lifted up*, and this is a woman sitting inside the basket

Zech 5:9 for they had wings like the wings of a stork, and they *lifted up* the basket between earth and heaven

Matt 17:8 And when they had *lifted up* their eyes, they saw no one but Jesus only

Luke 6:20 Then He *lifted up* His eyes toward His disciples, and said

Luke 16:23 And being in torments in Hades, he *lifted up* his eyes and saw Abraham afar off, and Lazarus in his bosom

Luke 17:13 And they *lifted up* their voices and said, "Jesus, Master, have mercy on us

Luke 24:50 And He led them out as far as Bethany, and He *lifted up* His hands and blessed them

John 3:14 And as Moses *lifted up* the serpent in the wilderness, even so must the Son of Man be *lifted up*

John 6:5 Then Jesus *lifted up* His eyes, and seeing a great multitude coming toward Him, He said to Philip

John 11:41 And Jesus *lifted up* His eyes and said, "Father, I thank You that You have heard Me

John 12:32 And I, if I am *lifted up* from the earth, will draw all peoples to Myself

John 12:34 and how can You say, 'The Son of Man must be *lifted up*

John 13:18 but that the Scripture may be fulfilled, 'He who eats bread with Me has *lifted up* his heel against Me

John 17:1 Jesus spoke these words, *lifted up* His eyes to heaven, and said

Rev 10:5 And the angel whom I saw standing on the sea and on the land *lifted up* his hand to heaven

LIFTED UP FROM THE EARTH

Ezek 1:19 and when the living creatures were *lifted up from the earth*, the wheels were lifted up

Ezek 1:21 and when those were *lifted up from the earth*, the wheels were lifted up together with them, for the spirit of the living creatures was in the wheels

Dan 7:4 and it was *lifted up from the earth* and made to stand on two feet like a man, and a man's heart was given to it

John 12:32 And I, if I am *lifted up from the earth*, will draw all peoples to Myself

LIFTED UP HIS EYES

Ezek 18:6 if he has not eaten on the mountains, nor *lifted up his eyes* to the idols of the house of Israel, nor defiled his neighbor's wife, nor approached a woman during her impurity

Luke 6:20 Then He *lifted up His eyes* toward His disciples, and said

Luke 16:23 And being in torments in Hades, he *lifted up his eyes* and saw Abraham afar off, and Lazarus in his bosom

John 6:5 Then Jesus *lifted up His eyes*, and seeing a great multitude coming toward Him, He said to Philip

John 11:41 And Jesus *lifted up His eyes* and said, "Father, I thank You that You have heard Me

John 17:1 Jesus spoke these words, *lifted up His eyes* to heaven, and said

LIFTED UP HIS HEEL

Ps 41:9 Even my own familiar friend in whom I trusted, who ate my bread, has *lifted up his heel* against me

John 13:18 but that the Scripture may be fulfilled, 'He who eats bread with Me has *lifted up his heel* against Me

LIFTED UP THE SERPENT

John 3:14 And as Moses *lifted up the serpent* in the wilderness, even so must the Son of Man be lifted up

LIFTED UP THE SON OF MAN (KJV, NIV, RSV)
(See *LIFT UP THE SON OF MAN*)

LIFTED UP THEIR VOICE

Judg 2:4 And so it was, when the Angel of the Lord spoke these words to all the children of Israel, that the people *lifted up their voice* and wept

2Sam 13:36 So it was, as soon as he had finished speaking, that the king's sons indeed came, and they *lifted up their voice* and wept

2Chr 5:13 indeed it came to pass, when the trumpeters and singers were as one, to make one sound to be heard in praising and thanking the Lord, and when they *lifted up their voice* with the trumpets and cymbals and instruments of music, and praised the Lord, saying

Ps 93:3 The floods have lifted up, O Lord, the floods have *lifted up their voice*

LIFTED UP THEIR VOICES

Num 14:1 Then all the congregation *lifted up their voices* and cried, and the people wept that night

Judg 21:2 Then the people came to the house of God, and remained there before God till evening. They *lifted up their voices* and wept bitterly

Ruth 1:9 Then she kissed them, and they *lifted up their voices* and wept

Ruth 1:14 Then they *lifted up their voices* and wept again; and Orpah kissed her mother-in-law, but Ruth clung to her
1Sam 11:4 And all the people *lifted up their voices* and wept
1Sam 30:4 Then David and the people who were with him *lifted up their voices* and wept, until they had no more power to weep
Luke 17:13 And they *lifted up their voices* and said, "Jesus, Master, have mercy on us

LIGHT FROM HEAVEN
Acts 22:6 Now it happened, as I journeyed and came near Damascus at about noon, suddenly a great *light from heaven* shone around me
Acts 26:13 at midday, O king, along the road I saw a *light from heaven*, brighter than the sun, shining around me and those who journeyed with me

LIGHT HAS COME INTO THE WORLD
John 3:19 And this is the condemnation, that the *light has come into the world*, and men loved darkness rather than light, because their deeds were evil

LIGHT OF ISRAEL
Is 10:17 So the *Light of Israel* will be for a fire, and his Holy One for a flame

LIGHT OF LIFE
Job 33:30 To bring back his soul from the Pit, that he may be enlightened with the *light of life*
John 8:12 He who follows Me shall not walk in darkness, but have the *light of life*

LIGHT OF THE BODY (KJV)
(See *LAMP OF THE BODY*)

LIGHT OF THE GOSPEL
2Cor 4:4 whose minds the god of this age has blinded, who do not believe, lest the *light of the gospel* of the glory of Christ, who is the image of God, should shine on them

LIGHT OF THE LIVING (KJV)
(See *LIGHT OF LIFE*)

LIGHT OF THE LORD
Is 2:5 O house of Jacob, come and let us walk in the *light of the Lord*

LIGHT OF THE PEOPLES
Is 51:4 for law will proceed from Me, and I will make My justice rest as a *light of the peoples*

LIGHT OF THE WORLD
Matt 5:14 You are the *light of the world*. A city that is set on a hill cannot be hidden
John 8:12 Then Jesus spoke to them again, saying, "I am the *light of the world*
John 9:5 As long as I am in the world, I am the *light of the world*

LIGHT OF THIS WORLD
John 11:9 If anyone walks in the day, he does not stumble, because he sees the *light of this world*

LIGHT OF YOUR COUNTENANCE
Ps 4:6 Lord, lift up the *light of Your countenance* upon us
Ps 44:3 But it was Your right hand, Your arm, and the *light of Your countenance*, because You favored them
Ps 89:15 They walk, O Lord, in the *light of Your countenance*
Ps 90:8 You have set our iniquities before You, our secret sins in the *light of Your countenance*

LIGHT OF YOUR FACE (NIV)
(See *LIGHT OF YOUR COUNTENANCE*)

LIGHT SHINES IN THE DARKNESS
John 1:5 And the *light shines in the darkness*, and the darkness did not comprehend it

LIGHT TO GOVERN THE DAY (NAS, NIV)
(See *LIGHT TO RULE THE DAY*)

LIGHT TO MY PATH
Ps 119:105 Your word is a lamp to my feet and a *light to my path*

LIGHT TO RULE THE DAY
Gen 1:16 the greater *light to rule the day*, and the lesser light to rule the night

LIGHT TO THE GENTILES
Is 42:6 I will keep You and give You as a covenant to the people, as a *light to the Gentiles*
Is 49:6 I will also give You as a *light to the Gentiles*, that You should be My salvation to the ends of the earth
Acts 13:47 I have set you to be a *light to the Gentiles* , that you should be for salvation to the ends of the earth

LIGHT TO THE NATIONS (NAS, RSV)
(See *LIGHT TO THE GENTILES*)

LIGHTEN THE YOKE
1Kin 12:9 How should we answer this people who have spoken to me, saying, '*Lighten the yoke* which your father put on us
2Chr 10:9 How should we answer this people who have spoken to me, saying, '*Lighten the yoke* which your father put on us

LIKE A CHILD (NAS, RSV)
(See *AS A LITTLE CHILD*)

LIKE A CLOUD
Job 30:15 they pursue my honor as the wind, and my prosperity has passed *like a cloud*
Prov 16:15 In the light of the king's face is life, and his favor is *like a cloud* of the latter rain
Is 18:4 For so the Lord said to me, "I will take My rest, and I will look from My dwelling place like clear heat in sunshine, *like a cloud* of dew in the heat of harvest
Is 44:22 I have blotted out, like a thick cloud, your transgressions, and *like a cloud*, your sins
Is 60:8 Who are these who fly *like a cloud*, and like doves to their roosts
Ezek 38:9 You will ascend, coming like a storm, covering the land *like a cloud*, you and all your troops and many peoples with you
Ezek 38:16 You will come up against My people Israel *like a cloud*, to cover the land

LIKE A DOVE
Ps 55:6 And I said, "Oh, that I had wings *like a dove*
Is 38:14 I mourned *like a dove;* my eyes fail from looking upward
Hos 11:11 they shall come trembling like a bird from Egypt, *like a dove* from the land of Assyria
Matt 3:16 and behold, the heavens were opened to Him, and He saw the Spirit of God descending *like a dove* and alighting upon Him
Mark 1:10 And immediately, coming up from the water, He saw the heavens parting and the Spirit descending upon Him *like a dove*
Luke 3:22 And the Holy Spirit descended in bodily form *like a dove* upon Him, and a voice came from heaven which said
John 1:32 And John bore witness, saying, "I saw

the Spirit descending from heaven *like a dove*, and He remained upon Him

LIKE A DRUNKEN MAN
Job 12:25 They grope in the dark without light, and He makes them stagger *like a drunken man*
Ps 107:27 They reel to and fro, and stagger *like a drunken man*, and are at their wits
Jer 23:9 I am *like a drunken man*, and like a man whom wine has overcome, because of the Lord, and because of His holy words

LIKE A FLEETING SHADOW (NIV)
(See *LIKE A PASSING SHADOW*)

LIKE A LION HE CROUCHES (NIV)
(See *LIES DOWN AS A LION*)

LIKE A PASSING SHADOW
Ps 144:4 Man is like a breath; his days are *like a passing shadow*

LIKE A REFINER'S FIRE
Mal 3:2 For He is *like a refiner's fire* and like fuller's soap

LIKE A ROARING LION
Prov 28:15 *Like a roaring lion* and a charging bear is a wicked ruler over poor people
Ezek 22:25 The conspiracy of her prophets in her midst is *like a roaring lion* tearing the prey
1Pet 5:8 because your adversary the devil walks about *like a roaring lion*, seeking whom he may devour

LIKE A TRAVAILING WOMAN (KJV)
(See *LIKE A WOMAN IN LABOR*)

LIKE A TREE PLANTED BY THE RIVERS
Ps 1:3 He shall be *like a tree planted by the rivers* of water, that brings forth its fruit in its season, whose leaf also shall not wither

LIKE A WAVE
Jas 1:6 But let him ask in faith, with no doubting, for he who doubts is *like a wave* of the sea driven and tossed by the wind

LIKE A WOMAN IN LABOR
Is 42:14 Now I will cry *like a woman in labor*, I will pant and gasp at once
Jer 13:21 Will not pangs seize you, *like a woman in labor*
Jer 30:6 So why do I see every man with his hands on his loins *like a woman in labor*, and all faces turned pale
Jer 49:24 Anguish and sorrows have taken her *like a woman in labor*
Mic 4:9 For pangs have seized you *like a woman in labor*

LIKE A WOMAN IN TRAVAIL (RSV)
(See *AS A WOMAN IN CHILDBIRTH*)

LIKE LIGHTNING FROM HEAVEN
Luke 10:18 And He said to them, "I saw Satan fall *like lightning from heaven*

LIKE MELCHIZEDEK (NIV)
(See *LIKENESS OF MELCHIZEDEK*)

LIKE SMOKE THEY VANISH AWAY (NAS, RSV)
(See *INTO SMOKE THEY SHALL VANISH AWAY*)

LIKE SNOW (NIV)
(See *WHITE AS SNOW*)

LIKE THE ANGELS (NIV)
(See *EQUAL TO THE ANGELS*)

LIKE THE DEW THAT GOES AWAY EARLY (NAS)
(See *LIKE THE EARLY DEW*)

LIKE THE EARLY DEW
Hos 6:4 For your faithfulness is like a morning cloud, and *like the early dew* it goes away
Hos 13:3 Therefore they shall be like the morning cloud and *like the early dew* that passes away, like chaff blown off from a threshing floor and like smoke from a chimney

LIKE THE TROUBLED SEA
Is 57:20 But the wicked are *like the troubled sea*, when it cannot rest, whose waters cast up mire and dirt

LIKENESS OF GOD
Gen 5:1 In the day that God created man, He made him in the *likeness of God*

LIKENESS OF HIS DEATH
Rom 6:5 For if we have been united together in the *likeness of His death*, certainly we also shall be in the likeness of His resurrection

LIKENESS OF HIS RESURRECTION
Rom 6:5 For if we have been united together in the likeness of His death, certainly we also shall be in the *likeness of His resurrection*

LIKENESS OF HIS SON (NIV)
(See *IMAGE OF HIS SON*)

LIKENESS OF MELCHIZEDEK
Heb 7:15 And it is yet far more evident if, in the *likeness of Melchizedek*, there arises another priest

LILIES OF THE FIELD
Matt 6:28 Consider the *lilies of the field*, how they grow

LILY AMONG THORNS
Song 2:2 Like a *lily among thorns*, so is my love among the daughters

LILY OF THE VALLEYS
Song 2:1 I am the rose of Sharon, and the *lily of the valleys*

LIMITS OF THE ALMIGHTY
Job 11:7 Can you search out the deep things of God? Can you find out the *limits of the Almighty*

LINE UPON LINE
Is 28:10 For precept must be upon precept, precept upon precept, *line upon line*, *line upon line*, here a little, there a little
Is 28:13 But the word of the Lord was to them, "Precept upon precept, precept upon precept, *line upon line*, *line upon line*, here a little, there a little

LINEAGE OF DAVID
Luke 2:4 And Joseph also went up from Galilee, out of the city of Nazareth, into Judea, to the city of David, which is called Bethlehem, because he was of the house and *lineage of David*

LINGER LONG AT THE WINE
Prov 23:30 Those who *linger long at the wine*, those who go in search of mixed wine

LION HAS ROARED
Amos 3:8 A *lion has roared!* Who will not fear? The Lord God has spoken

LION OF THE TRIBE OF JUDAH
Rev 5:5 Behold, the *Lion of the tribe of Judah*, the Root of David, has prevailed to open the scroll and to loose its seven seals

LION'S DEN (NIV)
(See *DEN OF LIONS*)

LIPS FREE OF DECEIT (RSV)
(See *DECEITFUL LIPS*)

LISTEN, MY SON, TO YOUR FATHER'S INSTRUCTION (NIV)
(See *MY SON, HEAR THE INSTRUCTION*)

LISTEN TO HIM (NAS, NIV, RSV)
(See *HEAR HIM*)

LISTEN TO ME
Gen 23:15 My lord, *listen to me;* the land is worth four hundred shekels of silver
Num 23:18 Rise up, Balak, and hear! *Listen to me*, son of Zippor
Deut 3:26 But the Lord was angry with me on your account, and would not *listen to me*
Judg 9:7 *Listen to me*, you men of Shechem, that God may listen to you
Job 32:10 Therefore I say, '*Listen to me*, I also will declare my opinion
Job 33:31 Give ear, Job, *listen to me;* hold your peace, and I will speak
Job 33:33 If not, *listen to me;* hold your peace, and I will teach you wisdom
Job 34:10 Therefore *listen to me*, you men of understanding: Far be it from God to do wickedness, and from the Almighty to commit iniquity
Job 34:34 Men of understanding say to me, wise men who *listen to me*
Ps 34:11 Come, you children, *listen to me;* I will teach you the fear of the Lord
Ps 81:8 Hear, O My people, and I will admonish you! O Israel, if you will *listen to Me*
Ps 81:13 Oh, that My people would *listen to Me*, that Israel would walk in My ways
Prov 7:24 Now therefore, *listen to me*, my children; pay attention to the words of my mouth
Prov 8:32 Now therefore, *listen to me*, my children, for blessed are those who keep my ways
Is 46:3 *Listen to Me*, O house of Jacob, and all the remnant of the house of Israel, who have been upheld by Me from birth, who have been carried from the womb
Is 46:12 *Listen to Me*, you stubborn-hearted, who are far from righteousness
Is 48:12 *Listen to Me*, O Jacob, and Israel, My called: I am He, I am the First, I am also the Last
Is 51:1 *Listen to Me*, you who follow after righteousness, you who seek the Lord
Is 51:4 *Listen to Me*, My people; and give ear to Me, O My nation
Is 51:7 *Listen to Me*, you who know righteousness, you people in whose heart is My law
Jer 26:4 If you will not *listen to Me*, to walk in My law which I have set before you
Jer 38:15 And if I give you counsel, you will not *listen to me*
Ezek 3:7 But the house of Israel will not listen to you, because they will not *listen to Me*
Acts 15:13 And after they had become silent, James answered, saying, "Men and brethren, *listen to me*

LISTEN TO MY CRY (NIV)
(See *ATTEND TO MY CRY*)

LISTEN TO MY PRAYER (NIV, RSV)
(See *ATTEND TO MY PRAYER*)

LISTEN TO MY VOICE
Ex 4:1 Then Moses answered and said, "But suppose they will not believe me or *listen to my voice*

LITTLE CHILD
1Kin 3:7 Now, O Lord my God, You have made Your servant king instead of my father David, but I am a *little child*
1Kin 11:17 that Hadad fled to go to Egypt, he and certain Edomites of his father's servants with him. Hadad was still a *little child*
2Kin 5:14 and his flesh was restored like the flesh of a *little child*, and he was clean
Is 11:6 The wolf also shall dwell with the lamb, the leopard shall lie down with the young goat, the calf and the young lion and the fatling together; and a *little child* shall lead them
Matt 18:2 And Jesus called a *little child* to Him, set him in the midst of them
Matt 18:4 Therefore whoever humbles himself as this *little child* is the greatest in the kingdom of heaven
Matt 18:5 And whoever receives one *little child* like this in My name receives Me
Mark 9:36 Then He took a *little child* and set him in the midst of them
Mark 10:15 Assuredly, I say to you, whoever does not receive the kingdom of God as a *little child* will by no means enter it
Luke 9:47 And Jesus, perceiving the thought of their heart, took a *little child* and set him by Him
Luke 9:48 and said to them, "Whoever receives this *little child* in My name receives Me
Luke 18:17 Assuredly, I say to you, whoever does not receive the kingdom of God as a *little child* will by no means enter it

LITTLE CHILDREN
Num 16:27 and Dathan and Abiram came out and stood at the door of their tents, with their wives, their sons, and their *little children*
Esth 3:13 And the letters were sent by couriers into all the king's provinces, to destroy, to kill, and to annihilate all the Jews, both young and old, *little children* and women, in one day, on the thirteenth day of the twelfth month, which is the month of Adar, and to plunder their possessions
Esth 8:11 By these letters the king permitted the Jews who were in every city to gather together and protect their lives to destroy, kill, and annihilate all the forces of any people or province that would assault them, both *little children* and women, and to plunder their possessions
Ezek 9:6 Utterly slay old and young men, maidens and *little children* and women
Matt 18:3 and said, "Assuredly, I say to you, unless you are converted and become as *little children*, you will by no means enter the kingdom of heaven
Matt 19:13 Then *little children* were brought to Him that He might put His hands on them and pray, but the disciples rebuked them
Matt 19:14 But Jesus said, "Let the *little children* come to Me, and do not forbid them
Mark 9:37 Whoever receives one of these *little children* in My name receives Me
Mark 10:14 But when Jesus saw it, He was greatly

displeased and said to them, "Let the *little children* come to Me, and do not forbid them
Luke 18:16 But Jesus called them to Him and said, "Let the *little children* come to Me, and do not forbid them
John 13:33 *Little children*, I shall be with you a little while longer
Gal 4:19 My *little children*, for whom I labor in birth again until Christ is formed in you
1Jn 2:1 My *little children*, these things I write to you, that you may not sin
1Jn 2:12 I write to you, *little children*, because your sins are forgiven you for His name's sake
1Jn 2:13 I write to you, *little children*, because you have known the Father
1Jn 2:18 *Little children*, it is the last hour; and as you have heard that the Antichrist is coming, even now many antichrists have come, by which we know that it is the last hour
1Jn 2:28 And now, *little children*, abide in Him, that when He appears, we may have confidence and not be ashamed before Him at His coming
1Jn 3:7 *Little children*, let no one deceive you. He who practices righteousness is righteous, just as He is righteous
1Jn 3:18 My *little children*, let us not love in word or in tongue, but in deed and in truth
1Jn 4:4 You are of God, *little children*, and have overcome them, because He who is in you is greater than he who is in the world
1Jn 5:21 *Little children*, keep yourselves from idols. Amen

LITTLE FAITH
Matt 6:30 Now if God so clothes the grass of the field, which today is, and tomorrow is thrown into the oven, will He not much more clothe you, O you of *little faith*
Matt 8:26 But He said to them, "Why are you fearful, O you of *little faith*
Matt 14:31 And immediately Jesus stretched out His hand and caught him, and said to him, "O you of *little faith*, why did you doubt
Matt 16:8 But when Jesus perceived it, He said to them, "O you of *little faith*, why do you reason among yourselves because you have brought no bread
Luke 12:28 If then God so clothes the grass, which today is in the field and tomorrow is thrown into the oven, how much more will He clothe you, O you of *little faith*

LITTLE HILLS LIKE LAMBS
Ps 114:4 The mountains skipped like rams, the *little hills like lambs*

LITTLE HORN
Dan 8:9 And out of one of them came a *little horn* which grew exceedingly great toward the south, toward the east, and toward the Glorious Land

LITTLE LESS THAN GOD (RSV)
(See *LOWER THAN THE ANGELS*)

LITTLE ONES
Gen 34:29 All their *little ones* and their wives they took captive
Gen 43:8 Then Judah said to Israel his father, "Send the lad with me, and we will arise and go, that we may live and not die, both we and you and also our *little ones*
Gen 45:19 Take carts out of the land of Egypt for your *little ones* and your wives
Gen 46:5 and the sons of Israel carried their father Jacob, their *little ones*, and their wives, in the carts which Pharaoh had sent to carry him
Gen 47:24 Four-fifths shall be your own, as seed for the field and for your food, for those of your households and as food for your *little ones*
Gen 50:8 Only their *little ones*, their flocks, and their herds they left in the land of Goshen
Gen 50:21 I will provide for you and your *little ones*." And he comforted them and spoke kindly to them
Ex 10:10 Then he said to them, "The Lord had better be with you when I let you and your *little ones* go
Ex 10:24 only let your flocks and your herds be kept back. Let your *little ones* also go with you
Num 14:31 But your *little ones*, whom you said would be victims, I will bring in, and they shall know the land which you have despised
Num 31:9 And the children of Israel took all the women of Midian captive, with their *little ones*, and took as spoil all their cattle, all their flocks, and all their goods
Num 31:17 Now therefore, kill every male among the *little ones*, and kill every woman who has known a man intimately
Num 32:16 We will build sheepfolds here for our livestock, and cities for our *little ones*
Num 32:17 and our *little ones* will dwell in the fortified cities because of the inhabitants of the land
Num 32:24 Build cities for your *little ones* and folds for your sheep, and do what has proceeded out of your mouth
Num 32:26 Our *little ones*, our wives, our flocks, and all our livestock will be there in the cities of Gilead
Deut 1:39 Moreover your *little ones* and your children, who you say will be victims, who today have no knowledge of good and evil, they shall go in there
Deut 2:34 We took all his cities at that time, and we utterly destroyed the men, women, and *little ones* of every city
Deut 3:19 But your wives, your *little ones*, and your livestock (I know that you have much livestock
Deut 20:14 But the women, the *little ones*, the livestock, and all that is in the city, all its spoil, you shall plunder for yourself
Deut 29:11 your *little ones* and your wives also the stranger who is in your camp, from the one who cuts your wood to the one who draws your water
Deut 31:12 Gather the people together, men and women and *little ones*, and the stranger who is within your gates, that they may hear and that they may learn to fear the Lord your God and carefully observe all the words of this law
Josh 1:14 Your wives, your *little ones*, and your livestock shall remain in the land which Moses gave you on this side of the Jordan
Josh 8:35 There was not a word of all that Moses had commanded which Joshua did not read before all the congregation of Israel, with the women, the *little ones*, and the strangers who were living among them
Judg 18:21 Then they turned and departed, and put the *little ones*, the livestock, and the goods in front of them
2Sam 15:22 Then Ittai the Gittite and all his men and all the *little ones* who were with him crossed over
2Chr 20:13 Now all Judah, with their *little ones*, their wives, and their children, stood before the Lord
2Chr 31:18 and to all who were written in the genealogy their *little ones* and their wives, their sons and daughters, the whole company of them for in their faithfulness they sanctified themselves in holiness
Ezra 8:21 Then I proclaimed a fast there at the

river of Ahava, that we might humble ourselves before our God, to seek from Him the right way for us and our *little ones* and all our possessions

Job 21:11 They send forth their *little ones* like a flock, and their children dance

Ps 137:9 Happy shall he be who takes and dashes Your *little ones* against the rock

Jer 48:4 her *little ones* have caused a cry to be heard

Zech 13:7 then I will turn My hand against the *little ones*

Matt 10:42 And whoever gives one of these *little ones* only a cup of cold water in the name of a disciple, assuredly, I say to you, he shall by no means lose his reward

Matt 18:6 But whoever causes one of these *little ones* who believe in Me to sin, it would be better for him if a millstone were hung around his neck, and he were drowned in the depth of the sea

Matt 18:10 Take heed that you do not despise one of these *little ones*, for I say to you that in heaven their angels always see the face of My Father who is in heaven

Matt 18:14 Even so it is not the will of your Father who is in heaven that one of these *little ones* should perish

Mark 9:42 And whoever causes one of these *little ones* who believe in Me to stumble, it would be better for him if a millstone were hung around his neck, and he were thrown into the sea

Luke 17:2 It would be better for him if a millstone were hung around his neck, and he were thrown into the sea, than that he should offend one of these *little ones*

LITTLE SLEEP

Prov 6:10 A *little sleep*, a little slumber, a little folding of the hands to sleep

Prov 24:33 a *little sleep*, a little slumber, a little folding of the hands to rest

LIVE ACCORDING TO GOD

1Pet 4:6 For this reason the gospel was preached also to those who are dead, that they might be judged according to men in the flesh, but *live according to God* in the spirit

LIVE ACCORDING TO THE FLESH

Rom 8:5 For those who *live according to the flesh* set their minds on the things of the flesh, but those who live according to the Spirit, the things of the Spirit

Rom 8:12 Therefore, brethren, we are debtors not to the flesh, to *live according to the flesh*

Rom 8:13 For if you *live according to the flesh* you will die

LIVE ACCORDING TO THE SINFUL NATURE (NIV)

(See *LIVE ACCORDING TO THE FLESH*)

LIVE ACCORDING TO THE SPIRIT

Rom 8:5 For those who live according to the flesh set their minds on the things of the flesh, but those who *live according to the Spirit*, the things of the Spirit

LIVE AT PEACE WITH EVERYONE (NIV)

(See *LIVE PEACEABLY WITH ALL MEN*)

LIVE BY FAITH

Rom 1:17 as it is written, "The just shall *live by faith*

Gal 2:20 and the life which I now live in the flesh I *live by faith* in the Son of God, who loved me and gave Himself for me

Gal 3:11 But that no one is justified by the law in the sight of God is evident, for "The just shall *live by faith*

Heb 10:38 Now the just shall *live by faith;* but if anyone draws back, my soul has no pleasure in him

LIVE BY THE SPIRIT (NAS, RSV)

(See *LIVE IN THE SPIRIT*)

LIVE FOREVER

Gen 3:22 And now, lest he put out his hand and take also of the tree of life, and eat, and *live forever*

Deut 32:40 For I lift My hand to heaven, and say, "As I *live forever*

1Kin 1:31 Then Bathsheba bowed with her face to the earth, and did homage to the king, and said, "Let my lord King David *live forever*

Neh 2:3 and said to the king, "May the king *live forever*

Job 7:16 I would not *live forever*. Let me alone, for my days are but a breath

Ps 22:26 Those who seek Him will praise the Lord. Let your heart *live forever*

Dan 2:4 Then the Chaldeans spoke to the king in Aramaic, "O king, *live forever*

Dan 3:9 They spoke and said to King Nebuchadnezzar, "O king, *live forever*

Dan 5:10 And the queen spoke, saying, "O king, *live forever!* Do not let your thoughts trouble you, nor let your countenance change

Dan 6:6 So these governors and satraps thronged before the king, and said thus to him: "King Darias, *live forever*

Dan 6:21 Then Daniel said to the king, "O king, *live forever*

Zech 1:5 Your fathers, where are they? And the prophets, do they *live forever*

John 6:51 If anyone eats of this bread, he will *live forever*

John 6:58 This is the bread which came down from heaven not as your fathers ate the manna, and are dead. He who eats this bread will *live forever*

LIVE IN ACCORDANCE WITH THE SPIRIT (NIV)

(See *LIVE ACCORDING TO THE SPIRIT*)

LIVE IN OUR LAND (NIV)

(See *DWELL IN THE LAND*)

LIVE IN PEACE

2Cor 13:11 Be of good comfort, be of one mind, *live in peace*

LIVE IN THE SPIRIT

Gal 5:25 If we *live in the Spirit*, let us also walk in the Spirit

LIVE IN THE SPIRIT LIKE GOD (RSV)

(See *LIVE ACCORDING TO GOD*)

LIVE LONG IN THE LAND (NIV)

(See *THAT YOU MAY PROLONG YOUR DAYS*)

LIVE PEACEABLY WITH ALL MEN

Rom 12:18 If it is possible, as much as depends on you, *live peaceably with all men*

LIVED FOR A WHILE AMONG US (NIV)

(See *DWELT AMONG US*)

LIVELY HOPE (KJV)

(See *LIVING HOPE*)

LIVELY STONES (KJV)

(See *LIVING STONES*)

LIVES FOREVER AND EVER

Rev 4:9 Whenever the living creatures give glory and honor and thanks to Him who sits on the throne, who *lives forever and ever*

Rev 4:10 the twenty-four elders fall down before Him who sits on the throne and worship Him who *lives forever and ever*, and cast their crowns before the throne, saying
Rev 5:14 And the twenty-four elders fell down and worshiped Him who *lives forever and ever*
Rev 10:6 and swore by Him who *lives forever and ever*, who created heaven and the things that are in it, the earth and the things that are in it, and the sea and the things that are in it, that there should be delay no longer
Rev 15:7 Then one of the four living creatures gave to the seven angels seven golden bowls full of the wrath of God who *lives forever and ever*

LIVES WORTHY OF GOD (NIV)
(See *WALK WORTHY OF GOD*)

LIVING AMONG THE DEAD
Luke 24:5 Then, as they were afraid and bowed their faces to the earth, they said to them, "Why do you seek the *living among the dead*

LIVING BREAD
John 6:51 I am the *living bread* which came down from heaven

LIVING CREATURE
Gen 1:24 Then God said, "Let the earth bring forth the *living creature* according to its kind
Gen 2:19 And whatever Adam called each *living creature*, that was its name
Gen 9:10 and with every *living creature* that is with you: the birds, the cattle, and every beast of the earth with you, of all that go out of the ark, every beast of the earth
Gen 9:12 This is the sign of the covenant which I make between Me and you, and every *living creature* that is with you, for perpetual generations
Gen 9:15 and I will remember My covenant which is between Me and you and every *living creature* of all flesh
Gen 9:16 The rainbow shall be in the cloud, and I will look on it to remember the everlasting covenant between God and every *living creature* of all flesh that is on the earth
Lev 11:46 This is the law of the beasts and the birds and every *living creature* that moves in the waters, and of every creature that creeps on the earth
Ezek 1:15 Now as I looked at the living creatures, behold, a wheel was on the earth beside each *living creature* with its four faces
Ezek 10:15 This was the *living creature* I saw by the River Chebar
Ezek 10:17 When the cherubim stood still, the wheels stood still, and when one was lifted up, the other lifted itself up, for the spirit of the *living creature* was in them
Ezek 10:20 This is the *living creature* I saw under the God of Israel by the River Chebar, and I knew they were cherubim
Rev 4:7 The first *living creature* was like a lion, the second *living creature* like a calf, the third *living creature* had a face like a man, and the fourth *living creature* was like a flying eagle
Rev 6:3 When He opened the second seal, I heard the second *living creature* saying
Rev 6:5 When He opened the third seal, I heard the third *living creature* say
Rev 6:7 When He opened the fourth seal, I heard the voice of the fourth *living creature* saying
Rev 16:3 Then the second angel poured out his bowl on the sea, and it became blood as of a dead man; and every *living creature* in the sea died

LIVING CREATURES
Gen 1:20 Then God said, "Let the waters abound with an abundance of *living creatures*, and let birds fly above the earth across the face of the firmament of the heavens
Ezek 1:5 Also from within it came the likeness of four *living creatures*
Ezek 1:13 As for the likeness of the *living creatures* , their appearance was like burning coals of fire, and like the appearance of torches. Fire was going back and forth among the *living creatures*
Ezek 1:14 And the *living creatures* ran back and forth, in appearance like a flash of lightning
Ezek 1:15 Now as I looked at the *living creatures*, behold, a wheel was on the earth beside each living creature with its four faces
Ezek 1:19 When the *living creatures* went, the wheels went beside them; and when the *living creatures* were lifted up from the earth, the wheels were lifted up
Ezek 1:20 and the wheels were lifted together with them, for the spirit of the *living creatures* was in the wheels
Ezek 1:21 and when those were lifted up from the earth, the wheels were lifted up together with them, for the spirit of the *living creatures* was in the wheels
Ezek 1:22 The likeness of the firmament above the heads of the *living creatures* was like the color of an awesome crystal, stretched out over their heads
Ezek 3:13 I also heard the noise of the wings of the *living creatures* that touched one another, and the noise of the wheels beside them, and a great thunderous noise
Rev 4:6 And in the midst of the throne, and around the throne, were four *living creatures* full of eyes in front and in back
Rev 4:8 And the four *living creatures*, each having six wings, were full of eyes around and within
Rev 4:9 Whenever the *living creatures* give glory and honor and thanks to Him who sits on the throne, who lives forever and ever
Rev 5:6 And I looked, and behold, in the midst of the throne and of the four *living creatures* , and in the midst of the elders, stood a Lamb as though it had been slain, having seven horns and seven eyes, which are the seven Spirits of God sent out into all the earth
Rev 5:8 Now when He had taken the scroll, the four *living creatures* and the twenty-four elders fell down before the Lamb, each having a harp, and golden bowls full of incense, which are the prayers of the saints
Rev 5:11 Then I looked, and I heard the voice of many angels around the throne, the *living creatures*, and the elders
Rev 5:14 Then the four *living creatures* said, "Amen!" And the twenty-four elders fell down and worshiped Him who lives forever and ever
Rev 6:1 and I heard one of the four *living creatures* saying with a voice like thunder
Rev 6:6 And I heard a voice in the midst of the four *living creatures* saying
Rev 7:11 And all the angels stood around the throne and the elders and the four *living creatures* , and fell on their faces before the throne and worshiped God
Rev 8:9 and a third of the *living creatures* in the sea died, and a third of the ships were destroyed
Rev 14:3 And they sang as it were a new song before the throne, before the four *living creatures,* and the elders
Rev 15:7 Then one of the four *living creatures* gave to the seven angels seven golden bowls full of the wrath of God who lives forever and ever
Rev 19:4 And the twenty-four elders and the four *living creatures* fell down and worshiped God who sat on the throne, saying

LIVING GOD
Deut 5:26 For who is there of all flesh who has heard the voice of the *living God* speaking from the midst of the fire, as we have, and lived
Josh 3:10 And Joshua said, "By this you shall know that the *living God* is among you, and that He will without fail drive out from before you the Canaanites and the Hittites and the Hivites and the Perizzites and the Girgashites and the Amorites and the Jebusites
1Sam 17:26 For who is this uncircumcised Philistine, that he should defy the armies of the *living God*
1Sam 17:36 and this uncircumcised Philistine will be like one of them, seeing he has defied the armies of the *living God*
2Kin 19:4 It may be that the Lord your God will hear all the words of the Rabshakeh, whom his master the king of Assyria has sent to reproach the *living God*, and will reprove the words which the Lord your God has heard
2Kin 19:16 and hear the words of Sennacherib, which he has sent to reproach the *living God*
Ps 42:2 My soul thirsts for God, for the *living God*. When shall I come and appear before God
Ps 84:2 My heart and my flesh cry out for the *living God*
Is 37:4 It may be that the Lord your God will hear the words of the Rabshakeh, whom his master the king of Assyria has sent to reproach the *living God*, and will reprove the words which the Lord your God has heard
Is 37:17 and hear all the words of Sennacherib, who has sent to reproach the *living God*
Jer 10:10 He is the *living God* and the everlasting King. At His wrath the earth will tremble, and the nations will not be able to abide His indignation
Jer 23:36 For every man's word will be his oracle, for you have perverted the words of the *living God*, the Lord of hosts, our God
Dan 6:20 The king spoke, saying to Daniel, "Daniel, servant of the *living God*, has your God, whom you serve continually, been able to deliver you from the lions
Dan 6:26 For He is the *living God*, and steadfast forever; His kingdom is the one which shall not be destroyed, and His dominion shall endure to the end
Hos 1:10 And it shall come to pass in the place where it was said to them, 'You are not My people,' there it shall be said to them, 'You are the sons of the *living God*
Matt 16:16 And Simon Peter answered and said, "You are the Christ, the Son of the *living God*
Matt 26:63 And the high priest answered and said to Him, "I adjure You by the *living God* that You tell us if You are the Christ, the Son of God
John 6:69 Also we have come to believe and know that You are the Christ, the Son of the *living God*
Acts 14:15 We also are men with the same nature as you, and preach to you that you should turn from these vain things to the *living God*, who made the heaven, the earth, the sea, and all things that are in them
Rom 9:26 And it shall come to pass in the place where it was said to them, 'You are not My people,' there they will be called sons of the *living God*
2Cor 3:3 you are manifestly an epistle of Christ, ministered by us, written not with ink but by the Spirit of the *living God*, not on tablets of stone but on tablets of flesh, that is, of the heart
2Cor 6:16 For you are the temple of the *living God*. As God has said
1Tim 3:15 but if I am delayed, I write so that you may know how you ought to conduct yourself in the house of God, which is the church of the *living God*, the pillar and ground of the truth
1Tim 4:10 For to this end we both labor and suffer reproach, because we trust in the *living God*, who is the Savior of all men, especially of those who believe
1Tim 6:17 Command those who are rich in this present age not to be haughty, nor to trust in uncertain riches but in the *living God*, who gives us richly all things to enjoy
Heb 3:12 Beware, brethren, lest there be in any of you an evil heart of unbelief in departing from the *living God*
Heb 9:14 how much more shall the blood of Christ, who through the eternal Spirit offered Himself without spot to God, purge your conscience from dead works to serve the *living God*
Heb 10:31 It is a fearful thing to fall into the hands of the *living God*
Heb 12:22 But you have come to Mount Zion and to the city of the *living God*, the heavenly Jerusalem, to an innumerable company of angels
Rev 7:2 Then I saw another angel ascending from the east, having the seal of the *living God*

LIVING HOPE
1Pet 1:3 Blessed be the God and Father of our Lord Jesus Christ, who according to His abundant mercy has begotten us again to a *living hope* through the resurrection of Jesus Christ from the dead

LIVING IN DARKNESS (NIV)
(See *SIT IN DARKNESS*)

LIVING SACRIFICE
Rom 12:1 I beseech you therefore, brethren, by the mercies of God, that you present your bodies a *living sacrifice*, holy, acceptable to God, which is your reasonable service

LIVING STONE
1Pet 2:4 Coming to Him as to a *living stone*, rejected indeed by men, but chosen by God and precious

LIVING STONES
1Pet 2:5 you also, as *living stones*, are being built up a spiritual house, a holy priesthood, to offer up spiritual sacrifices acceptable to God through Jesus Christ

LIVING WATER
John 4:10 Jesus answered and said to her, "If you knew the gift of God, and who it is who says to you, 'Give Me a drink,' you would have asked Him, and He would have given you *living water*
John 4:11 The woman said to Him, "Sir, You have nothing to draw with, and the well is deep. Where then do You get that *living water*
John 7:38 He who believes in Me, as the Scripture has said, out of his heart will flow rivers of *living water*

LOADED WITH GUILT (NIV)
(See *LADEN WITH INIQUITY*)

LOAF OF BREAD
Ex 29:23 one *loaf of bread*, one cake made with oil, and one wafer from the basket of the unleavened bread that is before the Lord
2Sam 6:19 Then he distributed among all the people, among the whole multitude of Israel, both the women and the men, to everyone a *loaf of bread*, a piece of meat, and a cake of raisins
1Chr 16:3 Then he distributed to everyone of Israel, both man and woman, to everyone a *loaf of bread*, a piece of meat, and a cake of raisins

LOATHE MY LIFE (RSV)
(See *DESPISE MY LIFE*)

LOAVES OF BREAD
Judg 8:5 Then he said to the men of Succoth, "Please give *loaves of bread* to the people who follow me, for they are exhausted, and I am pursuing Zebah and Zalmunna, kings of Midian
1Sam 10:3 There three men going up to God at Bethel will meet you, one carrying three young goats, another carrying three *loaves of bread*, and another carrying a skin of wine
1Sam 10:4 And they will greet you and give you two *loaves of bread*, which you shall receive from their hands
1Sam 21:3 Give me five *loaves of bread* in my hand, or whatever can be found
1Sam 25:18 Then Abigail made haste and took two hundred *loaves of bread*, two skins of wine, five sheep already dressed, five seahs of roasted grain, one hundred clusters of raisins, and two hundred cakes of figs, and loaded them on donkeys
2Sam 16:1 When David was a little past the top of the mountain, there was Ziba the servant of Mephibosheth, who met him with a couple of saddled donkeys, and on them two hundred *loaves of bread*, one hundred clusters of raisins, one hundred summer fruits, and a skin of wine

LOCUST SWARMS
Amos 7:1 Behold, He formed *locust swarms* at the beginning of the late crop

LOFTY AND LIFTED UP (NAS, RSV)
(See *HIGH AND LIFTED UP*)

LOG THAT IS IN YOUR OWN EYE (NAS, RSV)
(See *PLANK IN YOUR OWN EYE*)

LOINS GIRT ABOUT WITH TRUTH (KJV)
(See *GIRDED YOUR WAIST WITH TRUTH*)

LONELY PLACE (NAS, RSV)
(See *DESERTED PLACE*)

LONG FOR THE PURE SPIRITUAL MILK (RSV)
(See *DESIRE THE PURE MILK*)

LONG LIVE THE KING
1Sam 10:24 So all the people shouted and said, "*Long live the king*
2Sam 16:16 And so it was, when Hushai the Archite, David's friend, came to Absalom, that Hushai said to Absalom, "*Long live the king! Long live the king*
2Kin 11:12 they made him king and anointed him, and they clapped their hands and said, "*Long live the king*
2Chr 23:11 Then Jehoiada and his sons anointed him, and said, "*Long live the king*

LONG ROBE WITH SLEEVES (RSV)
(See *TUNIC OF MANY COLORS*)

LONGSUFFERING OF GOD
1Pet 3:20 who formerly were disobedient, when once the *longsuffering of God* waited in the days of Noah, while the ark was being prepared, in which a few, that is, eight souls, were saved through water

LOOK AFTER ORPHANS AND WIDOWS (NIV)
(See *VISIT ORPHANS AND WIDOWS*)

LOOK DOWN FROM HEAVEN
Ps 80:14 *Look down from heaven* and see, and visit this vine
Ps 85:11 Truth shall spring out of the earth, and righteousness shall *look down from heaven*
Is 63:15 *Look down from heaven*, and see from Your habitation, holy and glorious

LOOK ON HIM (RSV)
(See *LOOK ON ME*)

LOOK ON ME
Zech 12:10 then they will *look on Me* whom they have pierced

LOOKED ON MY AFFLICTION
Gen 29:32 for she said, "The Lord has surely *looked on my affliction*

LOOKED ON OUR AFFLICTION
Deut 26:7 Then we cried out to the Lord God of our fathers, and the Lord heard our voice and *looked on our affliction* and our labor and our oppression

LOOKED ON THEIR AFFLICTION
Ex 4:31 and when they heard that the Lord had visited the children of Israel and that He had *looked on their affliction*, then they bowed their heads and worshiped

LOOKED UP (NIV)
(See *LIFTED UP*)

LOOKING INTO HEAVEN (RSV)
(See *GAZING UP INTO HEAVEN*)

LOOKING INTO THE SKY (NAS, NIV)
(See *GAZING UP INTO HEAVEN*)

LOOKING UNTO JESUS
Heb 12:2 *looking unto Jesus*, the author and finisher of our faith, who for the joy that was set before Him endured the cross, despising the shame, and has sat down at the right hand of the throne of God

LOOSED IN HEAVEN
Matt 16:19 And I will give you the keys of the kingdom of heaven, and whatever you bind on earth will be bound in heaven, and whatever you loose on earth will be *loosed in heaven*
Matt 18:18 Assuredly, I say to you, whatever you bind on earth will be bound in heaven, and whatever you loose on earth will be *loosed in heaven*

LOOSED THE PAINS OF DEATH
Acts 2:24 whom God raised up, having *loosed the pains of death*, because it was not possible that He should be held by it

LORD ALMIGHTY
2Cor 6:18 I will be a Father to you, and you shall be My sons and daughters, says the *Lord Almighty*

LORD ALMIGHTY HAS A DAY (NIV)
(See *DAY OF THE LORD*)

LORD ALSO OF THE SABBATH (KJV)
(See *LORD OF THE SABBATH*)

LORD APPEARED IN THE CLOUD
Ex 16:10 Now it came to pass, as Aaron spoke to the whole congregation of the children of Israel, that they looked toward the wilderness, and behold, the glory of the *Lord appeared in the cloud*

LORD APPEARED TO
Gen 12:7 Then the *Lord appeared to* Abram and said, "To your descendants I will give this land

Gen 17:1 When Abram was ninety-nine years old, the *Lord appeared to* Abram and said to him
Gen 18:1 Then the *Lord appeared to* him by the terebinth trees of Mamre, as he was sitting in the tent door in the heat of the day
Gen 26:2 Then the *Lord appeared to* him and said
Gen 26:24 And the *Lord appeared to* him the same night and said
Ex 3:2 And the Angel of the *Lord appeared to* him in a flame of fire from the midst of a bush
Lev 9:23 Then the glory of the *Lord appeared to* all the people
Num 16:19 Then the glory of the *Lord appeared to* all the congregation
Num 20:6 So Moses and Aaron went from the presence of the assembly to the door of the tabernacle of meeting, and they fell on their faces. And the glory of the *Lord appeared to* them
Judg 6:12 And the Angel of the *Lord appeared to* him, and said to him
Judg 13:3 And the Angel of the *Lord appeared to* the woman and said to her
1Kin 3:5 At Gibeon the *Lord appeared to* Solomon in a dream by night
1Kin 9:2 that the *Lord appeared to* Solomon the second time, as He had appeared to him at Gibeon
2Chr 7:12 Then the *Lord appeared to* Solomon by night, and said to him
Matt 1:20 But while he thought about these things, behold, an angel of the *Lord appeared to* him in a dream, saying
Matt 2:13 Now when they had departed, behold, an angel of the *Lord appeared to* Joseph in a dream, saying
Luke 1:11 Then an angel of the *Lord appeared to* him, standing on the right side of the altar of incense
Acts 7:30 And when forty years had passed, an Angel of the *Lord appeared to* him in a flame of fire in a bush, in the wilderness of Mount Sinai

LORD BE EXALTED (NIV)
(See *LORD BE MAGNIFIED*)

LORD BE MAGNIFIED
Ps 35:27 And let them say continually, "Let the *Lord be magnified*, Who has pleasure in the prosperity of His servant
Ps 40:16 Let such as love Your salvation say continually, "The *Lord be magnified*

LORD BE WITH YOU
Judg 18:6 May the presence of the *Lord be with you* on your way
Ruth 2:4 Now behold, Boaz came from Bethlehem, and said to the reapers, "The *Lord be with you*
1Sam 17:37 And Saul said to David, "Go, and the *Lord be with you*
1Sam 20:13 And the *Lord be with you* as He has been with my father
1Chr 22:11 Now, my son, may the *Lord be with you;* and may you prosper, and build the house of the Lord your God, as He has said to you
1Chr 22:16 Arise and begin working, and the *Lord be with you*
2Th 3:16 Now may the Lord of peace Himself give you peace always in every way. The *Lord be with you* all

LORD BLESS YOU
Num 6:24 The *Lord bless you* and keep you
Ruth 2:4 Now behold, Boaz came from Bethlehem, and said to the reapers, "The Lord be with you!" And they answered him, "The *Lord bless you*
Ps 128:5 The *Lord bless you* out of Zion, and may you see the good of Jerusalem all the days of your life
Jer 31:23 The *Lord bless you*, O habitation of justice, and mountain of holiness

LORD BLESSED THE SABBATH
Ex 20:11 Therefore the *Lord blessed the Sabbath* day and hallowed it

LORD BRINGS DEATH AND MAKES ALIVE (NIV)
(See *LORD KILLS AND MAKES ALIVE*)

LORD BUILDS UP JERUSALEM
Ps 147:2 The *Lord builds up Jerusalem;* He gathers together the outcasts of Israel

LORD BURNED (NIV)
(See *LORD WAS AROUSED*)

LORD BY FIRE (NIV)
(See *FIRE TO THE LORD*)

LORD CAME DOWN IN THE CLOUD (NIV)
(See *LORD DESCENDED IN THE CLOUD*)

LORD COMMANDED
Gen 7:5 And Noah did according to all that the *Lord commanded* him
Ex 7:6 Then Moses and Aaron did so; just as the *Lord commanded* them, so they did
Ex 7:10 So Moses and Aaron went in to Pharaoh, and they did so, just as the *Lord commanded*
Ex 7:20 And Moses and Aaron did so, just as the *Lord commanded*
Ex 12:50 as the *Lord commanded* Moses and Aaron, so they did
Ex 16:34 As the *Lord commanded* Moses, so Aaron laid it up before the Testimony, to be kept
Ex 19:7 So Moses came and called for the elders of the people, and laid before them all these words which the *Lord commanded* him
Ex 35:4 And Moses spoke to all the congregation of the children of Israel, saying, "This is the thing which the *Lord commanded*, saying
Ex 36:5 and they spoke to Moses, saying, "The people bring much more than enough for the service of the work which the *Lord commanded* us to do
Lev 7:36 The *Lord commanded* this to be given to them by the children of Israel, on the day that He anointed them, by a statute forever throughout their generations
Lev 7:38 which the *Lord commanded* Moses on Mount Sinai, on the day when He commanded the children of Israel to offer their offerings to the Lord in the Wilderness of Sinai
Lev 8:4 So Moses did as the *Lord commanded* him. And the assembly was gathered together at the door of the tabernacle of meeting
Lev 8:5 And Moses said to the congregation, "This is what the *Lord commanded* to be done
Lev 9:6 Then Moses said, "This is the thing which the *Lord commanded* you to do, and the glory of the Lord will appear to you
Lev 9:7 Offer the offering of the people, and make atonement for them, as the *Lord commanded*
Lev 16:34 This shall be an everlasting statute for you, to make atonement for the children of Israel, for all their sins, once a year." And he did as the *Lord commanded* Moses
Lev 24:23 So the children of Israel did as the *Lord commanded* Moses
Lev 27:34 These are the commandments which the *Lord commanded* Moses for the children of Israel on Mount Sinai
Num 1:19 As the *Lord commanded* Moses, so he numbered them in the Wilderness of Sinai
Num 1:54 according to all that the *Lord commanded* Moses, so they did

Num 2:33 But the Levites were not numbered among the children of Israel, just as the *Lord commanded* Moses
Num 2:34 Thus the children of Israel did according to all that the *Lord commanded* Moses
Num 3:42 So Moses numbered all the firstborn among the children of Israel, as the *Lord commanded* him
Num 3:51 And Moses gave their redemption money to Aaron and his sons, according to the word of the Lord, as the *Lord commanded* Moses
Num 4:49 thus were they numbered by him, as the *Lord commanded* Moses
Num 8:3 he arranged the lamps to face toward the front of the lampstand, as the *Lord commanded* Moses
Num 8:20 according to all that the *Lord commanded* Moses concerning the Levites, so the children of Israel did to them
Num 8:22 as the *Lord commanded* Moses concerning the Levites, so they did to them
Num 9:5 according to all that the *Lord commanded* Moses, so the children of Israel did
Num 15:36 So, as the *Lord commanded* Moses, all the congregation brought him outside the camp and stoned him with stones, and he died
Num 20:27 So Moses did just as the *Lord commanded*, and they went up to Mount Hor in the sight of all the congregation
Num 26:4 Take a census of the people from twenty years old and above, just as the *Lord commanded* Moses and the children of Israel who came out of the land of Egypt
Num 27:11 And it shall be to the children of Israel a statute of judgment, just as the *Lord commanded* Moses
Num 27:22 So Moses did as the *Lord commanded* him. He took Joshua and set him before Eleazar the priest and before all the congregation
Num 27:23 And he laid his hands on him and inaugurated him, just as the *Lord commanded* by the hand of Moses
Num 29:40 So Moses told the children of Israel everything, just as the *Lord commanded* Moses
Num 30:16 These are the statutes which the *Lord commanded* Moses, between a man and his wife, and between a father and his daughter in her youth in her father's house
Num 31:7 And they warred against the Midianites, just as the *Lord commanded* Moses, and they killed all the males
Num 31:21 Then Eleazar the priest said to the men of war who had gone to the battle, "This is the ordinance of the law which the *Lord commanded* Moses
Num 31:31 So Moses and Eleazar the priest did as the *Lord commanded* Moses
Num 31:41 So Moses gave the tribute which was the Lord's heave offering to Eleazar the priest, as the *Lord commanded* Moses
Num 31:47 and from the children of Israel's half Moses took one of every fifty, drawn from man and beast, and gave them to the Levites, who kept charge of the tabernacle of the Lord, as the *Lord commanded* Moses
Num 34:29 These are the ones the *Lord commanded* to divide the inheritance among the children of Israel in the land of Canaan
Num 36:2 The *Lord commanded* my lord Moses to give the land as an inheritance by lot to the children of Israel, and my lord was commanded by the Lord to give the inheritance of our brother Zelophehad to his daughters
Num 36:10 Just as the *Lord commanded* Moses, so did the daughters of Zelophehad
Num 36:13 These are the commandments and the judgments which the *Lord commanded* the children of Israel by the hand of Moses in the plains of Moab by the Jordan, across from Jericho
Deut 4:14 And the *Lord commanded* me at that time to teach you statutes and judgments, that you might observe them in the land which you cross over to possess
Deut 6:24 And the *Lord commanded* us to observe all these statutes, to fear the Lord our God, for our good always, that He might preserve us alive, as it is this day
Deut 10:5 and there they are, just as the *Lord commanded* me
Deut 29:1 These are the words of the covenant which the *Lord commanded* Moses to make with the children of Israel in the land of Moab, besides the covenant which He made with them in Horeb
Josh 1:13 Remember the word which Moses the servant of the *Lord commanded* you, saying
Josh 17:4 And they came near before Eleazar the priest, before Joshua the son of Nun, and before the rulers, saying, "The *Lord commanded* Moses to give us an inheritance among our brothers
Josh 21:2 And they spoke to them at Shiloh in the land of Canaan, saying, "The *Lord commanded* through Moses to give us cities to dwell in, with their common-lands for our livestock
Josh 22:2 You have kept all that Moses the servant of the *Lord commanded* you, and have obeyed my voice in all that I commanded you
Josh 22:5 But take diligent heed to do the commandment and the law which Moses the servant of the *Lord commanded* you, to love the Lord your God, to walk in all His ways, to keep His commandments, to hold fast to Him, and to serve Him with all your heart and with all your soul
1Sam 13:14 The Lord has sought for Himself a man after His own heart, and the Lord has commanded him to be commander over His people, because you have not kept what the *Lord commanded* you
2Sam 5:25 And David did so, as the *Lord commanded* him; and he drove back the Philistines from Geba as far as Gezer
2Sam 24:19 So David, according to the word of Gad, went up as the *Lord commanded*
2Kin 14:6 But the children of the murderers he did not execute, according to what is written in the Book of the Law of Moses, in which the *Lord commanded*, saying
1Chr 21:18 Then the angel of the *Lord commanded* Gad to say to David that David should go and erect an altar to the Lord on the threshing floor of Ornan the Jebusite
1Chr 21:27 Then the *Lord commanded* the angel, and he returned his sword to its sheath
2Chr 25:4 However he did not execute their children, but did as it is written in the Law in the Book of Moses, where the *Lord commanded*, saying
Job 42:9 So Eliphaz the Temanite and Bildad the Shuhite and Zophar the Naamathite went and did as the *Lord commanded* them
Ps 133:3 It is like the dew of Hermon, descending upon the mountains of Zion; for there the *Lord commanded* the blessing life forevermore
Jer 13:5 So I went and hid it by the Euphrates, as the *Lord commanded* me
Matt 1:24 Then Joseph, being aroused from sleep, did as the angel of the *Lord commanded* him and took to him his wife

LORD DESCENDED IN THE CLOUD
Ex 34:5 Then the *Lord descended in the cloud* and stood with him there, and proclaimed the name of the Lord

LORD DWELLS IN ZION
Joel 3:21 For I will acquit them of bloodguilt, whom I had not acquitted; for the *Lord dwells in Zion*

LORD EVEN OF THE SABBATH (NAS, NIV, RSV)
(See *LORD OF THE SABBATH*)

LORD FILLED THE HOUSE (KJV, NAS)
(See *LORD FILLED THE TEMPLE*)

LORD FILLED THE TEMPLE
2Chr 7:1 Now when Solomon had finished praying, fire came down from heaven and consumed the burnt offering and the sacrifices; and the glory of the *Lord filled the temple*
Ezek 43:5 and behold, the glory of the *Lord filled the temple*

LORD FORBID
1Sam 24:6 And he said to his men, "The *Lord forbid* that I should do this thing to my master, the Lord's anointed, to stretch out my hand against him, seeing he is the anointed of the Lord
1Sam 26:11 The *Lord forbid* that I should stretch out my hand against the Lord's anointed
1Kin 21:3 And Naboth said to Ahab, "The *Lord forbid* that I should give the inheritance of my fathers to you

LORD GAVE THEM REST
Josh 21:44 The *Lord gave them rest* all around, according to all that He had sworn to their fathers
2Chr 15:15 and He was found by them, and the *Lord gave them rest* all around

LORD GIVES YOU REST
Is 14:3 It shall come to pass in the day the *Lord gives you rest* from your sorrow, and from your fear and the hard bondage in which you were made to serve

LORD GOD OF HOSTS
2Sam 5:10 So David went on and became great, and the *Lord God of hosts* was with him
1Kin 19:10 So he said, "I have been very zealous for the *Lord God of hosts*
1Kin 19:14 So he said, "I have been very zealous for the *Lord God of hosts*
Ps 59:5 You therefore, O *Lord God of hosts*, the God of Israel, awake to punish all the nations
Ps 69:6 Let not those who wait for You, O *Lord God of hosts*, be ashamed because of me
Ps 80:4 O *Lord God of hosts*, how long will You be angry against the prayer of Your people
Ps 80:19 Restore us, O *Lord God of hosts;* cause Your face to shine, and we shall be saved
Ps 84:8 O *Lord God of hosts*, hear my prayer; give ear, O God of Jacob
Ps 89:8 O *Lord God of hosts*, Who is mighty like You, O Lord
Is 3:15 What do you mean by crushing My people and grinding the faces of the poor?" says the *Lord God of hosts*
Is 10:23 For the *Lord God of hosts* will make a determined end in the midst of all the land
Is 10:24 Therefore thus says the *Lord God of hosts:* "O My people, who dwell in Zion, do not be afraid of the Assyrian
Is 22:5 For it is a day of trouble and treading down and perplexity by the *Lord God of hosts* in the Valley of Vision breaking down the walls and of crying to the mountain
Is 22:12 And in that day the *Lord God of hosts* called for weeping and for mourning, for baldness and for girding with sackcloth
Is 22:14 Then it was revealed in my hearing by the Lord of hosts, "Surely for this iniquity there will be no atonement for you, even to your death," says the *Lord God of hosts*
Is 22:15 Thus says the *Lord God of hosts:* Go, proceed to this steward, to Shebna, who is over the house, and say
Is 28:22 for I have heard from the *Lord God of hosts*, a destruction determined even upon the whole earth
Jer 2:19 Know therefore and see that it is an evil and bitter thing that you have forsaken the Lord your God, and the fear of Me is not in you," says the *Lord God of hosts*
Jer 5:14 Therefore thus says the *Lord God of hosts:* "Because you speak this word, behold, I will make My words in your mouth fire, and this people wood, and it shall devour them
Jer 15:16 for I am called by Your name, O *Lord God of hosts*
Jer 35:17 Therefore thus says the *Lord God of hosts*, the God of Israel
Jer 46:10 For this is the day of the *Lord God of hosts*, a day of vengeance, that He may avenge Himself on His adversaries. The sword shall devour; it shall be satiated and made drunk with their blood; for the *Lord God of hosts* has a sacrifice in the north country by the River Euphrates
Jer 49:5 Behold, I will bring fear upon you," says the *Lord God of hosts*
Jer 50:25 For this is the work of the *Lord God of hosts* in the land of the Chaldeans
Jer 50:31 says the *Lord God of hosts;* "For your day has come, the time that I will punish you
Hos 12:5 that is, the *Lord God of hosts*. The Lord is His memorial
Amos 4:13 For behold, He who forms mountains, and creates the wind, who declares to man what his thought is, and makes the morning darkness, who treads the high places of the earth the *Lord God of hosts* is His name
Amos 5:14 so the *Lord God of hosts* will be with you, as you have spoken
Amos 5:15 It may be that the *Lord God of hosts* will be gracious to the remnant of Joseph
Amos 5:16 Therefore the *Lord God of hosts*, the Lord, says this
Amos 6:8 The Lord God has sworn by Himself, the *Lord God of hosts* says
Amos 6:14 But, behold, I will raise up a nation against you, O house of Israel," says the *Lord God of hosts*
Amos 9:5 The *Lord God of hosts*, He who touches the earth and it melts, and all who dwell there mourn

LORD GOD OF ISRAEL
Ex 5:1 Afterward Moses and Aaron went in and told Pharaoh, "Thus says the *Lord God of Israel*
Ex 32:27 And he said to them, "Thus says the *Lord God of Israel*
Ex 34:23 Three times in the year all your men shall appear before the Lord, the *Lord God of Israel*
Josh 7:13 Get up, sanctify the people, and say, 'Sanctify yourselves for tomorrow, because thus says the *Lord God of Israel*
Josh 7:19 So Joshua said to Achan, "My son, I beg you, give glory to the *Lord God of Israel*, and make confession to Him, and tell me now what you have done
Josh 7:20 And Achan answered Joshua and said, "Indeed I have sinned against the *Lord God of Israel*, and this is what I have done
Josh 8:30 Now Joshua built an altar to the *Lord God of Israel* in Mount Ebal
Josh 9:18 But the children of Israel did not attack

them, because the rulers of the congregation had sworn to them by the *Lord God of Israel*
Josh 9:19 Then all the rulers said to all the congregation, "We have sworn to them by the *Lord God of Israel*
Josh 10:40 he left none remaining, but utterly destroyed all that breathed, as the *Lord God of Israel* had commanded
Josh 10:42 All these kings and their land Joshua took at one time, because the *Lord God of Israel* fought for Israel
Josh 13:14 the sacrifices of the *Lord God of Israel* made by fire are their inheritance, as He said to them
Josh 13:33 the *Lord God of Israel* was their inheritance, as He had said to them
Josh 14:14 Hebron therefore became the inheritance of Caleb the son of Jephunneh the Kenizzite to this day, because he wholly followed the *Lord God of Israel*
Josh 22:24 But in fact we have done it for fear, for a reason, saying, 'In time to come your descendants may speak to our descendants, saying, "What have you to do with the *Lord God of Israel*
Josh 24:2 And Joshua said to all the people, "Thus says the *Lord God of Israel*
Josh 24:23 Now therefore," he said, "put away the foreign gods which are among you, and incline your heart to the *Lord God of Israel*
Judg 4:6 Then she sent and called for Barak the son of Abinoam from Kedesh in Naphtali, and said to him, "Has not the *Lord God of Israel* commanded, saying
Judg 5:3 I will sing praise to the *Lord God of Israel*
Judg 5:5 the mountains gushed before the Lord, this Sinai, before the *Lord God of Israel*
Judg 6:8 that the Lord sent a prophet to the children of Israel, who said to them, "Thus says the *Lord God of Israel*
Judg 11:21 And the *Lord God of Israel* delivered Sihon and all his people into the hand of Israel, and they defeated them
Judg 11:23 So now the *Lord God of Israel* has dispossessed the Amorites from before His people Israel
Judg 21:3 and said, "O *Lord God of Israel*, why has this come to pass in Israel, that today there should be one tribe missing in Israel
Ruth 2:12 The Lord repay your work, and a full reward be given you by the *Lord God of Israel*, under whose wings you have come for refuge
1Sam 2:30 Therefore the *Lord God of Israel* says: "I said indeed that your house and the house of your father would walk before Me forever
1Sam 10:18 and said to the children of Israel, "Thus says the *Lord God of Israel*
1Sam 14:41 Therefore Saul said to the *Lord God of Israel*, "Give a perfect lot
1Sam 20:12 The *Lord God of Israel* is witness! When I have sounded out my father sometime tomorrow, or the third day, and indeed there is good toward David, and I do not send to you and tell you
1Sam 23:10 Then David said, "O *Lord God of Israel*, Your servant has certainly heard that Saul seeks to come to Keilah to destroy the city for my sake
1Sam 23:11 O *Lord God of Israel*, I pray, tell Your servant
1Sam 25:32 Blessed be the *Lord God of Israel*, who sent you this day to meet me
1Sam 25:34 For indeed, as the *Lord God of Israel* lives, who has kept me back from hurting you, unless you had hastened and come to meet me, surely by morning light no males would have been left to Nabal
2Sam 12:7 Thus says the *Lord God of Israel:* I anointed you king over Israel, and I delivered you from the hand of Saul
1Kin 1:30 just as I swore to you by the *Lord God of Israel*, saying
1Kin 1:48 Also the king said thus, 'Blessed be the *Lord God of Israel*, who has given one to sit on my throne this day, while my eyes see it
1Kin 8:15 Blessed be the *Lord God of Israel*, who spoke with His mouth to my father David, and with His hand has fulfilled it, saying
1Kin 8:17 Now it was in the heart of my father David to build a house for the name of the *Lord God of Israel*
1Kin 8:20 and I have built a house for the name of the *Lord God of Israel*
1Kin 8:23 *Lord God of Israel*, there is no God in heaven above or on earth below like You, who keep Your covenant and mercy with Your servants who walk before You with all their heart
1Kin 8:25 Therefore, *Lord God of Israel*, now keep what You promised Your servant David my father, saying
1Kin 11:9 So the Lord became angry with Solomon, because his heart had turned from the *Lord God of Israel*, who had appeared to him twice
1Kin 14:7 Go, tell Jeroboam, 'Thus says the *Lord God of Israel*
1Kin 14:13 And all Israel shall mourn for him and bury him, for he is the only one of Jeroboam who shall come to the grave, because in him there is found something good toward the *Lord God of Israel* in the house of Jeroboam
1Kin 15:30 because of the sins of Jeroboam, which he had sinned and by which he had made Israel sin, because of his provocation with which he had provoked the *Lord God of Israel* to anger
1Kin 16:13 for all the sins of Baasha and the sins of Elah his son, by which they had sinned and by which they had made Israel sin, in provoking the *Lord God of Israel* to anger with their idols
1Kin 16:26 For he walked in all the ways of Jeroboam the son of Nebat, and in his sin by which he had made Israel sin, provoking the *Lord God of Israel* to anger with their idols
1Kin 16:33 Ahab did more to provoke the *Lord God of Israel* to anger than all the kings of Israel who were before him
1Kin 17:1 And Elijah the Tishbite, of the inhabitants of Gilead, said to Ahab, "As the *Lord God of Israel* lives, before whom I stand, there shall not be dew nor rain these years, except at my word
1Kin 17:14 For thus says the *Lord God of Israel:* 'The bin of flour shall not be used up, nor shall the jar of oil run dry, until the day the Lord sends rain on the earth
1Kin 22:53 for he served Baal and worshiped him, and provoked the *Lord God of Israel* to anger, according to all that his father had done
2Kin 9:6 And he poured the oil on his head, and said to him, "Thus says the *Lord God of Israel*
2Kin 10:31 But Jehu took no heed to walk in the law of the *Lord God of Israel* with all his heart
2Kin 14:25 He restored the territory of Israel from the entrance of Hamath to the Sea of the Arabah, according to the word of the *Lord God of Israel*, which He had spoken through His servant Jonah the son of Amittai, the prophet who was from Gath Hepher
2Kin 18:5 He trusted in the *Lord God of Israel*, so that after him was none like him among all the kings of Judah, nor any who were before him
2Kin 19:15 O *Lord God of Israel*, the One who dwells between the cherubim, You are God, You alone, of all the kingdoms of the earth
2Kin 19:20 Then Isaiah the son of Amoz sent to

Hezekiah, saying, "Thus says the *Lord God of Israel*
2Kin 21:12 therefore thus says the *Lord God of Israel:* "Behold, I am bringing such calamity upon Jerusalem and Judah, that whoever hears of it, both his ears will tingle
2Kin 22:15 Then she said to them, "Thus says the *Lord God of Israel*
2Kin 22:18 But to the king of Judah, who sent you to inquire of the Lord, in this manner you shall speak to him, 'Thus says the *Lord God of Israel*
1Chr 15:12 sanctify yourselves, you and your brethren, that you may bring up the ark of the *Lord God of Israel* to the place I have prepared for it
1Chr 15:14 So the priests and the Levites sanctified themselves to bring up the ark of the *Lord God of Israel*
1Chr 16:4 And he appointed some of the Levites to minister before the ark of the Lord, to commemorate, to thank, and to praise the *Lord God of Israel*
1Chr 16:36 Blessed be the *Lord God of Israel* from everlasting to everlasting
1Chr 22:6 Then he called for his son Solomon, and charged him to build a house for the *Lord God of Israel*
1Chr 23:25 For David said, "The *Lord God of Israel* has given rest to His people, that they may dwell in Jerusalem forever
1Chr 24:19 This was the schedule of their service for coming into the house of the Lord according to their ordinance by the hand of Aaron their father, as the *Lord God of Israel* had commanded him
1Chr 28:4 However the *Lord God of Israel* chose me above all the house of my father to be king over Israel forever, for He has chosen Judah to be the ruler
1Chr 29:10 Blessed are You, *Lord God of Israel*, our Father, forever and ever
2Chr 2:12 Blessed be the *Lord God of Israel*, who made heaven and earth, for He has given King David a wise son, endowed with prudence and understanding, who will build a temple for the Lord and a royal house for himself
2Chr 6:4 Blessed be the *Lord God of Israel*, who has fulfilled with His hands what He spoke with His mouth to my father David, saying
2Chr 6:7 Now it was in the heart of my father David to build a temple for the name of the *Lord God of Israel*
2Chr 6:10 and I have built the temple for the name of the *Lord God of Israel*
2Chr 6:14 *Lord God of Israel*, there is no God in heaven or on earth like You, who keep Your covenant and mercy with Your servants who walk before You with all their hearts
2Chr 6:16 Therefore, *Lord God of Israel*, now keep what You promised Your servant David my father, saying
2Chr 6:17 Now then, O *Lord God of Israel*, let Your word come true, which You have spoken to Your servant David
2Chr 11:16 And after the Levites left, those from all the tribes of Israel, such as set their heart to seek the *Lord God of Israel*, came to Jerusalem to sacrifice to the Lord God of their fathers
2Chr 13:5 Should you not know that the *Lord God of Israel* gave the dominion over Israel to David forever, to him and his sons, by a covenant of salt
2Chr 15:4 but when in their trouble they turned to the *Lord God of Israel*, and sought Him, He was found by them
2Chr 15:13 and whoever would not seek the *Lord God of Israel* was to be put to death, whether small or great, whether man or woman
2Chr 20:19 Then the Levites of the children of the Kohathites and of the children of the Korahites stood up to praise the *Lord God of Israel* with voices loud and high
2Chr 29:10 Now it is in my heart to make a covenant with the *Lord God of Israel*, that His fierce wrath may turn away from us
2Chr 30:1 And Hezekiah sent to all Israel and Judah, and also wrote letters to Ephraim and Manasseh, that they should come to the house of the Lord at Jerusalem, to keep the Passover to the *Lord God of Israel*
2Chr 30:5 So they resolved to make a proclamation throughout all Israel, from Beersheba to Dan, that they should come to keep the Passover to the *Lord God of Israel* at Jerusalem, since they had not done it for a long time in the prescribed manner
2Chr 32:17 He also wrote letters to revile the *Lord God of Israel*, and to speak against Him, saying
2Chr 33:16 He also repaired the altar of the Lord, sacrificed peace offerings and thank offerings on it, and commanded Judah to serve the *Lord God of Israel*
2Chr 33:18 Now the rest of the acts of Manasseh, his prayer to his God, and the words of the seers who spoke to him in the name of the *Lord God of Israel*, indeed they are written in the book of the kings of Israel
2Chr 34:23 Then she answered them, "Thus says the *Lord God of Israel*
2Chr 34:26 And as for the king of Judah, who sent you to inquire of the Lord, in this manner you shall speak to him, 'Thus says the *Lord God of Israel*
2Chr 36:13 but he stiffened his neck and hardened his heart against turning to the *Lord God of Israel*
Ezra 1:3 Now let him go up to Jerusalem, which is in Judah, and build the house of the *Lord God of Israel* (He is God
Ezra 4:1 Now when the adversaries of Judah and Benjamin heard that the descendants of the captivity were building the temple of the *Lord God of Israel*
Ezra 4:3 but we alone will build to the *Lord God of Israel*, as King Cyrus the king of Persia has commanded us
Ezra 6:21 Then the children of Israel who had returned from the captivity ate together with all who had separated themselves from the filth of the nations of the land in order to seek the *Lord God of Israel*
Ezra 7:6 and he was a skilled scribe in the Law of Moses, which the *Lord God of Israel* had given
Ezra 9:15 O *Lord God of Israel*, You are righteous, for we are left as a remnant, as it is this day
Ps 41:13 Blessed be the *Lord God of Israel* from everlasting to everlasting
Ps 106:48 Blessed be the *Lord God of Israel* from everlasting to everlasting
Is 17:6 Yet gleaning grapes will be left in it, like the shaking of an olive tree, two or three olives at the top of the uppermost bough, four or five in its most fruitful branches," says the *Lord God of Israel*
Is 21:17 and the remainder of the number of archers, the mighty men of the people of Kedar, will be diminished; for the *Lord God of Israel* has spoken it
Is 24:15 Therefore glorify the Lord in the dawning light, the name of the *Lord God of Israel* in the coastlands of the sea
Is 37:21 Then Isaiah the son of Amoz sent to Hezekiah, saying, "Thus says the *Lord God of Israel*
Jer 11:3 and say to them, 'Thus says the *Lord God of Israel*
Jer 13:12 Thus says the *Lord God of Israel:* Every bottle shall be filled with wine

Jer 21:4 Thus says the *Lord God of Israel:* Behold, I will turn back the weapons of war that are in your hands, with which you fight against the king of Babylon and the Chaldeans who besiege you outside the walls
Jer 23:2 Therefore thus says the *Lord God of Israel* against the shepherds who feed My people
Jer 25:15 For thus says the *Lord God of Israel* to me
Jer 30:2 Thus speaks the *Lord God of Israel*, saying: "Write in a book for yourself all the words that I have spoken to you
Ezek 44:2 it shall not be opened, and no man shall enter by it, because the *Lord God of Israel* has entered by it
Mal 2:16 For the *Lord God of Israel* says that He hates divorce, for it covers one's garment with violence
Luke 1:68 Blessed is the *Lord God of Israel*, for He has visited and redeemed His people

LORD GOD PLANTED A GARDEN
Gen 2:8 The *Lord God planted a garden* eastward in Eden, and there He put the man whom He had formed

LORD HAD CLOSED HER WOMB
1Sam 1:5 But to Hannah he would give a double portion, for he loved Hannah, although the *Lord had closed her womb*
1Sam 1:6 And her rival also provoked her severely, to make her miserable, because the *Lord had closed her womb*

LORD HAD COMPASSION (NIV)
(See *LORD WAS MOVED TO PITY*)

LORD HAD SHUT UP HER WOMB (KJV)
(See *LORD HAD CLOSED HER WOMB*)

LORD HARDENED PHARAOH'S HEART
Ex 10:20 But the *Lord hardened Pharaoh's heart*, and he did not let the children of Israel go
Ex 10:27 But the *Lord hardened Pharaoh's heart*, and he would not let them go
Ex 11:10 and the *Lord hardened Pharaoh's heart*, and he did not let the children of Israel go out of his land

LORD HAS AVENGED YOU
Judg 11:36 So she said to him, "My father, if you have given your word to the Lord, do to me according to what has gone out of your mouth, because the *Lord has avenged you* of your enemies, the people of Ammon
2Sam 18:31 For the *Lord has avenged you* this day of all those who rose against you

LORD HAS CHOSEN YOU
Deut 14:2 For you are a holy people to the Lord your God, and the *Lord has chosen you* to be a people for Himself, a special treasure above all the peoples who are on the face of the earth
1Chr 28:10 Consider now, for the *Lord has chosen you* to build a house for the sanctuary
2Chr 29:11 My sons, do not be negligent now, for the *Lord has chosen you* to stand before Him, to serve Him, and that you should minister to Him and burn incense

LORD HAS DIRECTED (NIV)
(See *LORD HAS SPOKEN*)

LORD HAS DONE GREAT THINGS
Ps 126:2 Then they said among the nations, "The *Lord has done great things* for them
Ps 126:3 The *Lord has done great things* for us, whereof we are glad

LORD HAS GIVEN YOU REST (RSV)
(See *LORD GIVES YOU REST*)

LORD HAS PROSPERED MY WAY
Gen 24:56 And he said to them, "Do not hinder me, since the *Lord has prospered my way*

LORD HAS RISEN (NAS, RSV)
(See *LORD IS RISEN*)

LORD HAS SPOKEN
Gen 24:51 take her and go, and let her be your master's son's wife, as the *Lord has spoken*
Ex 19:8 Then all the people answered together and said, "All that the *Lord has spoken* we will do
Lev 10:11 and that you may teach the children of Israel all the statutes which the *Lord has spoken* to them by the hand of Moses
Num 15:22 And if you sin unintentionally, and do not observe all these commandments which the *Lord has spoken* to Moses
Deut 6:19 to cast out all your enemies from before you, as the *Lord has spoken*
2Sam 3:18 For the *Lord has spoken* of David, saying, 'By the hand of My servant David, I will save My people Israel from the hand of the Philistines and the hand of all their enemies
1Kin 13:3 And he gave a sign the same day, saying, "This is the sign which the *Lord has spoken*
1Kin 14:11 The dogs shall eat whoever belongs to Jeroboam and dies in the city, and the birds of the air shall eat whoever dies in the field; for the *Lord has spoken* it
2Kin 19:21 This is the word which the *Lord has spoken* concerning him
2Chr 2:15 Now therefore, the wheat, the barley, the oil, and the wine which my *lord has spoken* of, let him send to his servants
Is 1:2 For the *Lord has spoken:* "I have nourished and brought up children, and they have rebelled against Me
Is 1:20 but if you refuse and rebel, you shall be devoured by the sword"; for the mouth of the *Lord has spoken*
Is 16:13 This is the word which the *Lord has spoken* concerning Moab since that time
Is 16:14 But now the *Lord has spoken*, saying, "Within three years, as the years of a hired man, the glory of Moab will be despised with all that great multitude, and the remnant will be very small and feeble
Is 22:25 In that day,' says the Lord of hosts, 'the peg that is fastened in the secure place will be removed and be cut down and fall, and the burden that was on it will be cut off; for the *Lord has spoken*
Is 24:3 The land shall be entirely emptied and utterly plundered, for the *Lord has spoken* this word
Is 25:8 the rebuke of His people He will take away from all the earth; for the *Lord has spoken*
Is 31:4 For thus the *Lord has spoken* to me: As a lion roars, and a young lion over his prey (when a multitude of shepherds is summoned against him, he will not be afraid of their voice nor be disturbed by their noise
Is 37:22 this is the word which the *Lord has spoken* concerning him
Is 40:5 the glory of the Lord shall be revealed, and all flesh shall see it together; for the mouth of the *Lord has spoken*
Is 58:14 and I will cause you to ride on the high hills of the earth, and feed you with the heritage of Jacob your father. The mouth of the *Lord has spoken*
Jer 9:12 And who is he to whom the mouth of the *Lord has spoken*, that he may declare it

Jer 13:15 Hear and give ear: the *Lord has spoken*
Jer 27:13 Why will you die, you and your people, by the sword, by the famine, and by the pestilence, as the *Lord has spoken* against the nation that will not serve the king of Babylon
Jer 48:8 The valley also shall perish, and the plain shall be destroyed, as the *Lord has spoken*
Joel 3:8 I will sell your sons and your daughters into the hand of the people of Judah, and they will sell them to the Sabeans, to a people far off; for the *Lord has spoken*
Amos 3:1 Hear this word that the *Lord has spoken* against you, O children of Israel, against the whole family which I brought up from the land of Egypt, saying
Obad 18 they shall kindle them and devour them, and no survivor shall remain of the house of Esau," for the *Lord has spoken*

LORD HAS SWORN
Ex 17:16 for he said, "Because the *Lord has sworn:* the Lord will have war with Amalek from generation to generation
Deut 31:7 Then Moses called Joshua and said to him in the sight of all Israel, "Be strong and of good courage, for you must go with this people to the land which the *Lord has sworn* to their fathers to give them, and you shall cause them to inherit it
2Sam 3:9 May God do so to Abner, and more also, if I do not do for David as the *Lord has sworn* to him
Ps 110:4 The *Lord has sworn* and will not relent, "You are a priest forever according to the order of Melchizedek
Ps 132:11 The *Lord has sworn* in truth to David; He will not turn from it
Is 62:8 The *Lord has sworn* by His right hand and by the arm of His strength
Amos 8:7 The *Lord has sworn* by the pride of Jacob: "Surely I will never forget any of their works
Heb 7:21 The *Lord has sworn* and will not relent, 'You are a priest forever according to the order of Melchizedek

LORD HATH TAKEN VENGEANCE (KJV)
(See *LORD HAS AVENGED YOU*)

LORD, HE IS GOD
1Kin 18:39 and they said, "The *Lord, He is God!* The *Lord, He is God*
Ps 100:3 Know that the *Lord, He is God;* it is He who has made us, and not we ourselves

LORD IS A MAN OF WAR
Ex 15:3 The *Lord is a man of war;* the Lord is His name

LORD IS A WARRIOR (NAS, NIV)
(See *MAN OF WAR*)

LORD IS AT YOUR RIGHT HAND
Ps 110:5 The *Lord is at Your right hand;* He shall execute kings in the day of His wrath

LORD IS GOOD
Ps 34:8 Oh, taste and see that the *Lord is good;* blessed is the man who trusts in Him
Ps 100:5 For the *Lord is good;* His mercy is everlasting, and His truth endures to all generations
Ps 135:3 Praise the Lord, for the *Lord is good;* Sing praises to His name, for it is pleasant
Ps 145:9 The *Lord is good* to all, and His tender mercies are over all His works
Jer 33:11 Praise the Lord of hosts, for the *Lord is good*, for His mercy endures forever
Lam 3:25 The *Lord is good* to those who wait for Him, to the soul who seeks Him
Nah 1:7 The *Lord is good*, a stronghold in the day of trouble

LORD IS GREAT
1Chr 16:25 For the *Lord is great* and greatly to be praised
Ps 96:4 For the *Lord is great* and greatly to be praised
Ps 99:2 The *Lord is great* in Zion, and He is high above all the peoples
Ps 135:5 For I know that the *Lord is great*, and our Lord is above all gods
Joel 2:11 For the day of the *Lord is great* and very terrible

LORD IS HIS NAME
Ex 15:3 The Lord is a man of war; the *Lord is His name*
Jer 33:2 Thus says the Lord who made it, the Lord who formed it to establish it (the *Lord is His name*
Amos 5:8 He calls for the waters of the sea and pours them out on the face of the earth; the *Lord is His name*
Amos 9:6 who calls for the waters of the sea, and pours them out on the face of the earth the *Lord is His name*

LORD IS HIS REFUGE
Ps 14:6 You shame the counsel of the poor, but the *Lord is his refuge*

LORD IS IN HIS HOLY TEMPLE
Ps 11:4 The *Lord is in His holy temple*, the Lord's throne is in heaven
Hab 2:20 But the *Lord is in His holy temple*. Let all the earth keep silence before Him

LORD IS KING
Ps 10:16 The *Lord is King* forever and ever; the nations have perished out of His land

LORD IS MY ROCK
2Sam 22:2 The *Lord is my rock*, my fortress and my deliverer
Ps 18:2 The *Lord is my rock* and my fortress and my deliverer

LORD IS MY SHEPHERD
Ps 23:1 The *Lord is my shepherd;* I shall not want

LORD IS MY STRENGTH
Ex 15:2 The *Lord is my strength* and song, and He has become my salvation
Ps 28:7 The *Lord is my strength* and my shield; my heart trusted in Him, and I am helped
Ps 118:14 The *Lord is my strength* and song, and He has become my salvation

LORD IS OUR JUDGE
Is 33:22 (for the *Lord is our Judge*, the Lord is our Lawgiver, the Lord is our King

LORD IS OUR LAWGIVER
Is 33:22 (for the Lord is our Judge, the *Lord is our Lawgiver*, the Lord is our King

LORD IS OUR RIGHTEOUSNESS (RSV)
(See *LORD OUR RIGHTEOUSNESS*)

LORD IS OUR RULER (RSV)
(See *LORD IS OUR LAWGIVER*)

LORD IS PERFECT
Ps 19:7 The law of the *Lord is perfect*, converting the soul

LORD IS RIGHTEOUS
Ex 9:27 The *Lord is righteous*, and my people and I are wicked
2Chr 12:6 So the leaders of Israel and the king humbled themselves; and they said, "The *Lord is righteous*
Ps 11:7 For the *Lord is righteous*, He loves righteousness; His countenance beholds the upright
Ps 129:4 The *Lord is righteous;* He has cut in pieces the cords of the wicked
Ps 145:17 The *Lord is righteous* in all His ways, gracious in all His works
Lam 1:18 The *Lord is righteous*, for I rebelled against His commandment
Zeph 3:5 The *Lord is righteous*, He is in her midst, He will do no unrighteousness

LORD IS RISEN
Is 60:1 and the glory of the *Lord is risen* upon you
Luke 24:34 saying, "The *Lord is risen* indeed, and has appeared to Simon

LORD IS THEIR REFUGE (NIV)
(See *LORD IS HIS REFUGE*)

LORD IS THERE
Ezek 48:35 and the name of the city from that day shall be: THE *LORD IS THERE*

LORD IS WITNESS
1Sam 12:5 Then he said to them, "The *Lord is witness* against you, and His anointed is witness this day, that you have not found anything in my hand

LORD IS YOUR WAY (KJV)
(See *LORD BE WITH YOU*)

LORD JESUS CHRIST
Acts 11:17 If therefore God gave them the same gift as He gave us when we believed on the *Lord Jesus Christ*, who was I that I could withstand God
Acts 15:11 But we believe that through the grace of the *Lord Jesus Christ* we shall be saved in the same manner as they
Acts 15:26 men who have risked their lives for the name of our *Lord Jesus Christ*
Acts 16:31 So they said, "Believe on the *Lord Jesus Christ*, and you will be saved, you and your household
Acts 20:21 testifying to Jews, and also to Greeks, repentance toward God and faith toward our *Lord Jesus Christ*
Acts 28:31 preaching the kingdom of God and teaching the things which concern the *Lord Jesus Christ* with all confidence, no one forbidding him
Rom 1:7 Grace to you and peace from God our Father and the *Lord Jesus Christ*
Rom 5:1 Therefore, having been justified by faith, we have peace with God through our *Lord Jesus Christ*
Rom 5:11 And not only that, but we also rejoice in God through our *Lord Jesus Christ*, through whom we have now received the reconciliation
Rom 13:14 But put on the *Lord Jesus Christ*, and make no provision for the flesh, to fulfill its lusts
Rom 15:6 that you may with one mind and one mouth glorify the God and Father of our *Lord Jesus Christ*
Rom 15:30 Now I beg you, brethren, through the *Lord Jesus Christ*, and through the love of the Spirit, that you strive together with me in your prayers to God for me
Rom 16:18 For those who are such do not serve our *Lord Jesus Christ*, but their own belly, and by smooth words and flattering speech deceive the hearts of the simple
Rom 16:20 The grace of our *Lord Jesus Christ* be with you
Rom 16:24 The grace of our *Lord Jesus Christ* be with you all
1Cor 1:3 Grace to you and peace from God our Father and the *Lord Jesus Christ*
1Cor 1:7 so that you come short in no gift, eagerly waiting for the revelation of our *Lord Jesus Christ*
1Cor 1:8 who will also confirm you to the end, that you may be blameless in the day of our *Lord Jesus Christ*
1Cor 1:10 Now I plead with you, brethren, by the name of our *Lord Jesus Christ*, that you all speak the same thing, and that there be no divisions among you, but that you be perfectly joined together in the same mind and in the same judgment
1Cor 5:4 In the name of our *Lord Jesus Christ*, when you are gathered together, along with my spirit, with the power of our *Lord Jesus Christ*
1Cor 8:6 and one *Lord Jesus Christ*, through whom are all things, and through whom we live
1Cor 15:57 But thanks be to God, who gives us the victory through our *Lord Jesus Christ*
1Cor 16:22 If anyone does not love the *Lord Jesus Christ*, let him be accursed
1Cor 16:23 The grace of our *Lord Jesus Christ* be with you
2Cor 1:2 Grace to you and peace from God our Father and the *Lord Jesus Christ*
2Cor 1:3 Blessed be the God and Father of our *Lord Jesus Christ*, the Father of mercies and God of all comfort
2Cor 8:9 For you know the grace of our *Lord Jesus Christ*, that though He was rich, yet for your sakes He became poor, that you through His poverty might become rich
2Cor 11:31 The God and Father of our *Lord Jesus Christ*, who is blessed forever, knows that I am not lying
2Cor 13:14 The grace of the *Lord Jesus Christ*, and the love of God, and the communion of the Holy Spirit be with you all
Gal 1:3 Grace to you and peace from God the Father and our *Lord Jesus Christ*
Gal 6:14 But God forbid that I should glory except in the cross of our *Lord Jesus Christ*, by whom the world has been crucified to me, and I to the world
Gal 6:18 Brethren, the grace of our *Lord Jesus Christ* be with your spirit
Eph 1:2 Grace to you and peace from God our Father and the *Lord Jesus Christ*
Eph 1:3 Blessed be the God and Father of our *Lord Jesus Christ*, who has blessed us with every spiritual blessing in the heavenly places in Christ
Eph 1:17 that the God of our *Lord Jesus Christ*, the Father of glory, may give to you the spirit of wisdom and revelation in the knowledge of Him
Eph 3:14 For this reason I bow my knees to the Father of our *Lord Jesus Christ*
Eph 5:20 giving thanks always for all things to God the Father in the name of our *Lord Jesus Christ*
Eph 6:23 Peace to the brethren, and love with faith, from God the Father and the *Lord Jesus Christ*
Eph 6:24 Grace be with all those who love our *Lord Jesus Christ* in sincerity
Phil 1:2 Grace to you and peace from God our Father and the *Lord Jesus Christ*
Phil 3:20 For our citizenship is in heaven, from which we also eagerly wait for the Savior, the *Lord Jesus Christ*
Phil 4:23 The grace of our *Lord Jesus Christ* be with you all

Col 1:2 Grace to you and peace from God our Father and the *Lord Jesus Christ*
Col 1:3 We give thanks to the God and Father of our *Lord Jesus Christ*, praying always for you
1Th 1:1 Paul, Silvanus, and Timothy, to the church of the Thessalonians in God the Father and the *Lord Jesus Christ:* Gráce to you and peace from God our Father and the *Lord Jesus Christ*
1Th 1:3 remembering without ceasing your work of faith, labor of love, and patience of hope in our *Lord Jesus Christ* in the sight of our God and Father
1Th 2:19 Is it not even you in the presence of our *Lord Jesus Christ* at His coming
1Th 3:11 Now may our God and Father Himself, and our *Lord Jesus Christ*, direct our way to you
1Th 3:13 so that He may establish your hearts blameless in holiness before our God and Father at the coming of our *Lord Jesus Christ* with all His saints
1Th 5:9 For God did not appoint us to wrath, but to obtain salvation through our *Lord Jesus Christ*
1Th 5:23 and may your whole spirit, soul, and body be preserved blameless at the coming of our *Lord Jesus Christ*
1Th 5:28 The grace of our *Lord Jesus Christ* be with you
2Th 1:1 Paul, Silvanus, and Timothy, To the church of the Thessalonians in God our Father and the *Lord Jesus Christ*
2Th 1:2 Grace to you and peace from God our Father and the *Lord Jesus Christ*
2Th 1:8 in flaming fire taking vengeance on those who do not know God, and on those who do not obey the gospel of our *Lord Jesus Christ*
2Th 1:12 that the name of our *Lord Jesus Christ* may be glorified in you, and you in Him, according to the grace of our God and the *Lord Jesus Christ*
2Th 2:1 Now, brethren, concerning the coming of our *Lord Jesus Christ* and our gathering together to Him, we ask you
2Th 2:14 to which He called you by our gospel, for the obtaining of the glory of our *Lord Jesus Christ*
2Th 2:16 Now may our *Lord Jesus Christ* Himself, and our God and Father, who has loved us and given us everlasting consolation and good hope by grace
2Th 3:6 But we command you, brethren, in the name of our *Lord Jesus Christ*, that you withdraw from every brother who walks disorderly and not according to the tradition which he received from us
2Th 3:12 Now those who are such we command and exhort through our *Lord Jesus Christ* that they work in quietness and eat their own bread
2Th 3:18 The grace of our *Lord Jesus Christ* be with you all
1Tim 1:1 Paul, an apostle of Jesus Christ, by the commandment of God our Savior and the *Lord Jesus Christ*, our hope
1Tim 5:21 I charge you before God and the *Lord Jesus Christ* and the elect angels that you observe these things without prejudice, doing nothing with partiality
1Tim 6:3 If anyone teaches otherwise and does not consent to wholesome words, even the words of our *Lord Jesus Christ*, and to the doctrine which is according to godliness
2Tim 4:1 I charge you therefore before God and the *Lord Jesus Christ*, who will judge the living and the dead at His appearing and His kingdom
2Tim 4:22 The *Lord Jesus Christ* be with your spirit. Grace be with you
Tit 1:4 Grace, mercy, and peace from God the Father and the *Lord Jesus Christ* our Savior
Phm 3 Grace to you and peace from God our Father and the *Lord Jesus Christ*
Phm 25 The grace of our *Lord Jesus Christ* be with your spirit
Jas 1:1 James, a servant of God and of the *Lord Jesus Christ*, to the twelve tribes which are scattered abroad
Jas 2:1 My brethren, do not hold the faith of our *Lord Jesus Christ*, the Lord of glory, with partiality
1Pet 1:3 Blessed be the God and Father of our *Lord Jesus Christ*, who according to His abundant mercy has begotten us again to a living hope through the resurrection of Jesus Christ from the dead
2Pet 1:8 For if these things are yours and abound, you will be neither barren nor unfruitful in the knowledge of our *Lord Jesus Christ*
2Pet 1:14 knowing that shortly I must put off my tent, just as our *Lord Jesus Christ* showed me
2Pet 1:16 For we did not follow cunningly devised fables when we made known to you the power and coming of our *Lord Jesus Christ*, but were eyewitnesses of His majesty
2Jn 3 Grace, mercy, and peace will be with you from God the Father and from the *Lord Jesus Christ*, the Son of the Father, in truth and love
Jude 4 For certain men have crept in unnoticed, who long ago were marked out for this condemnation, ungodly men, who turn the grace of our God into licentiousness and deny the only Lord God and our *Lord Jesus Christ*
Jude 17 But you, beloved, remember the words which were spoken before by the apostles of our *Lord Jesus Christ*
Jude 21 keep yourselves in the love of God, looking for the mercy of our *Lord Jesus Christ* unto eternal life
Rev 22:21 The grace of our *Lord Jesus Christ* be with you all

LORD JESUS HAS GIVEN (NIV)
(See *RECEIVED FROM THE LORD*)

LORD JUDGE BETWEEN
Gen 16:5 and when she saw that she had conceived, I became despised in her eyes. The *Lord judge between* you and me
1Sam 24:12 Let the *Lord judge between* you and me, and let the Lord avenge me on you

LORD KILLS AND MAKES ALIVE
1Sam 2:6 The *Lord kills and makes alive;* He brings down to the grave and brings up

LORD LOOKS FROM HEAVEN
Ps 33:13 The *Lord looks from heaven;* He sees all the sons of men

LORD, LORD
Matt 7:21 Not everyone who says to Me, '*Lord, Lord*,' shall enter the kingdom of heaven, but he who does the will of My Father in heaven
Matt 7:22 Many will say to Me in that day, '*Lord, Lord*, have we not prophesied in Your name, cast out demons in Your name, and done many wonders in Your name
Matt 25:11 Afterward the other virgins came also, saying, '*Lord, Lord*, open to us
Luke 6:46 But why do you call Me '*Lord, Lord*,' and do not do the things which I say
Luke 13:25 When once the Master of the house has risen up and shut the door, and you begin to stand outside and knock at the door, saying,' *Lord, Lord*, open for us

LORD LOVES JUSTICE
Ps 37:28 For the *Lord loves justice*, and does not forsake His saints

LORD LOVES THE JUST (NIV)
(See *LORD LOVES JUSTICE*)

LORD LOVES THE RIGHTEOUS
Ps 146:8 The Lord raises those who are bowed down; the *Lord loves the righteous*

LORD MAKE HIS FACE SHINE UPON YOU
Num 6:25 the *Lord make His face shine upon you*, and be gracious to you

LORD MIGHTY IN BATTLE
Ps 24:8 The Lord strong and mighty, the *Lord mighty in battle*

LORD MOST HIGH
Ps 7:17 I will praise the Lord according to His righteousness, and will sing praise to the name of the *Lord Most High*
Ps 47:2 For the *Lord Most High* is awesome; He is a great King over all the earth

LORD OF GLORY
1Cor 2:8 for had they known, they would not have crucified the *Lord of glory*
Jas 2:1 My brethren, do not hold the faith of our Lord Jesus Christ, the *Lord of glory*, with partiality

LORD OF HEAVEN AND EARTH
Matt 11:25 At that time Jesus answered and said, "I thank You, Father, *Lord of heaven and earth*, because You have hidden these things from the wise and prudent and have revealed them to babes
Luke 10:21 In that hour Jesus rejoiced in the Spirit and said, "I praise You, Father, *Lord of heaven and earth*, that You have hidden these things from the wise and prudent and revealed them to babes
Acts 17:24 God, who made the world and everything in it, since He is *Lord of heaven and earth*, does not dwell in temples made with hands

LORD OF HOSTS
1Sam 1:3 This man went up from his city yearly to worship and sacrifice to the *Lord of hosts* in Shiloh
1Sam 1:11 Then she made a vow and said, "O *Lord of hosts*, if You will indeed look on the affliction of your maidservant and remember me, and not forget your maidservant, but will give your maidservant a male child, then I will give him to the Lord all the days of his life, and no razor shall come upon his head
1Sam 4:4 So the people sent to Shiloh, that they might bring from there the ark of the covenant of the *Lord of hosts*, who dwells between the cherubim
1Sam 15:2 Thus says the *Lord of hosts:* "I will punish what Amalek did to Israel, how he laid wait for him on the way when he came up from Egypt
1Sam 17:45 But I come to you in the name of the *Lord of hosts*, the God of the armies of Israel, whom you have defied
2Sam 6:2 And David arose and went with all the people who were with him from Baale Judah to bring up from there the ark of God, whose name is called by the Name, the *Lord of Hosts*, who dwells between the cherubim
2Sam 6:18 And when David had finished offering burnt offerings and peace offerings, he blessed the people in the name of the *Lord of hosts*
2Sam 7:8 Now therefore, thus shall you say to My servant David, 'Thus says the *Lord of hosts*
2Sam 7:26 So let Your name be magnified forever, saying, 'The *Lord of hosts* is the God over Israel
2Sam 7:27 For You, O *Lord of hosts*, God of Israel, have revealed this to Your servant, saying
1Kin 18:15 Then Elijah said, "As the *Lord of hosts* lives, before whom I stand, I will surely present myself to him today
2Kin 3:14 And Elisha said, "As the *Lord of hosts* lives, before whom I stand, surely were it not that I regard the presence of Jehoshaphat king of Judah, I would not look at you, nor see you
2Kin 19:31 The zeal of the *Lord of hosts* shall do this
1Chr 11:9 Then David went on and became great, and the *Lord of hosts* was with him
1Chr 17:7 Now therefore, thus shall you say to My servant David, 'Thus says the *Lord of hosts*
1Chr 17:24 So let it be established, that Your name may be magnified forever, saying, 'The *Lord of hosts*, the God of Israel, is Israel's God
Ps 24:10 The *Lord of hosts*, He is the King of glory
Ps 46:7 The *Lord of hosts* is with us; the God of Jacob is our refuge
Ps 46:11 The *Lord of hosts* is with us; the God of Jacob is our refuge
Ps 48:8 As we have heard, so we have seen in the city of the *Lord of hosts*, in the city of our God
Ps 84:1 How lovely is Your tabernacle, O *Lord of hosts*
Ps 84:3 Even the sparrow has found a home, and the swallow a nest for herself, where she may lay her young even Your altars, O *Lord of hosts*, my King and my God
Ps 84:12 O *Lord of hosts*, blessed is the man who trusts in You
Is 1:9 Unless the *Lord of hosts* had left to us a very small remnant, we would have become like Sodom, we would have been made like Gomorrah
Is 1:24 Therefore the Lord says, the *Lord of hosts*, the Mighty One of Israel
Is 2:12 For the day of the *Lord of hosts* shall come upon everything proud and lofty, upon everything lifted up and it shall be brought low
Is 3:1 For behold, the Lord, the *Lord of hosts*, takes away from Jerusalem and from Judah the stock and the store, the whole supply of bread and the whole supply of water
Is 5:7 For the vineyard of the *Lord of hosts* is the house of Israel, and the men of Judah are His pleasant plant
Is 5:9 In my hearing the *Lord of hosts* said, "Truly, many houses shall be desolate, great and beautiful ones, without inhabitant
Is 5:16 But the *Lord of hosts* shall be exalted in judgment, and God who is holy shall be hallowed in righteousness
Is 5:24 because they have rejected the law of the *Lord of hosts*, and despised the word of the Holy One of Israel
Is 6:3 Holy, holy, holy is the *Lord of hosts;* the whole earth is full of His glory
Is 6:5 for my eyes have seen the King, the *Lord of hosts*
Is 8:13 The *Lord of hosts*, Him you shall hallow; let Him be your fear, and let Him be your dread
Is 8:18 We are for signs and wonders in Israel from the *Lord of hosts*, Who dwells in Mount Zion
Is 9:7 The zeal of the *Lord of hosts* will perform this
Is 9:13 For the people do not turn to Him who strikes them, nor do they seek the *Lord of hosts*
Is 9:19 Through the wrath of the *Lord of hosts* the land is burned up, and the people shall be as fuel for the fire

Is 10:16 Therefore the Lord, the *Lord of hosts*, will send leanness among his fat ones
Is 10:26 And the *Lord of hosts* will stir up a scourge for him like the slaughter of Midian at the rock of Oreb
Is 10:33 Behold, the Lord, the *Lord of hosts*, will lop off the bough with terror
Is 13:4 A tumultuous noise of the kingdoms of nations gathered together! The *Lord of hosts* musters the army for battle
Is 13:13 Therefore I will shake the heavens, and the earth will move out of her place, in the wrath of the *Lord of hosts* and in the day of His fierce anger
Is 14:22 For I will rise up against them," says the *Lord of hosts*
Is 14:23 I will sweep it with the broom of destruction," says the *Lord of hosts*
Is 14:24 The *Lord of hosts* has sworn, saying, "Surely, as I have thought, so it shall come to pass, and as I have purposed, so it shall stand
Is 14:27 For the *Lord of hosts* has purposed, and who will annul it
Is 17:3 they will be as the glory of the children of Israel," says the *Lord of hosts*
Is 18:7 In that time a present will be brought to the *Lord of hosts* from a people tall and smooth of skin, and from a people terrible from their beginning onward, a nation powerful and treading down, whose land the rivers divide to the place of the name of the *Lord of hosts*, to Mount Zion
Is 19:4 And the Egyptians I will give into the hand of a cruel master, and a fierce king will rule over them," says the Lord, the *Lord of hosts*
Is 19:12 Let them tell you now, and let them know what the *Lord of hosts* has purposed against Egypt
Is 19:16 In that day Egypt will be like women, and will be afraid and fear because of the waving of the hand of the *Lord of hosts*, which He waves over it
Is 19:17 everyone who makes mention of it will be afraid in himself, because of the counsel of the *Lord of hosts* which He has determined against it
Is 19:18 In that day five cities in the land of Egypt will speak the language of Canaan and swear by the *Lord of hosts*
Is 19:20 And it will be for a sign and for a witness to the *Lord of hosts* in the land of Egypt
Is 19:25 whom the *Lord of hosts* shall bless, saying, "Blessed is Egypt My people, and Assyria the work of My hands, and Israel My inheritance
Is 21:10 That which I have heard from the *Lord of hosts*, the God of Israel, I have declared to you
Is 22:14 Then it was revealed in my hearing by the *Lord of hosts*
Is 22:25 In that day,' says the *Lord of hosts*, 'the peg that is fastened in the secure place will be removed and be cut down and fall, and the burden that was on it will be cut off
Is 23:9 The *Lord of hosts* has purposed it, to bring to dishonor the pride of all glory, and to bring into contempt all the honorable of the earth
Is 24:23 for the *Lord of hosts* will reign on Mount Zion and in Jerusalem and before His elders, gloriously
Is 25:6 And in this mountain the *Lord of hosts* will make for all people a feast of choice pieces, a feast of wines on the lees, of fat things full of marrow, of well-refined wines on the lees
Is 28:5 In that day the *Lord of hosts* will be for a crown of glory and a diadem of beauty to the remnant of His people
Is 28:29 This also comes from the *Lord of hosts*, Who is wonderful in counsel and excellent in guidance
Is 29:6 You will be punished by the *Lord of hosts* with thunder and earthquake and great noise, with storm and tempest And the flame of devouring fire
Is 31:4 so the *Lord of hosts* will come down to fight for Mount Zion and for its hill
Is 31:5 Like birds flying about, so will the *Lord of hosts* defend Jerusalem
Is 37:16 O *Lord of hosts*, God of Israel, the One who dwells between the cherubim, You are God, You alone, of all the kingdoms of the earth
Is 37:32 The zeal of the *Lord of hosts* will do this
Is 39:5 Then Isaiah said to Hezekiah, "Hear the word of the *Lord of hosts*
Is 44:6 Thus says the Lord, the King of Israel, and his Redeemer, the *Lord of hosts*
Is 45:13 he shall build My city and let My exiles go free, not for price nor reward," says the *Lord of hosts*
Is 47:4 As for our Redeemer, the *Lord of hosts* is His name, the Holy One of Israel
Is 48:2 for they call themselves after the holy city, and lean on the God of Israel; the *Lord of hosts* is His name
Is 51:15 But I am the Lord your God, who divided the sea whose waves roared the *Lord of hosts* is His name
Is 54:5 For your Maker is your husband, the *Lord of hosts* is His name
Jer 6:6 For thus has the *Lord of hosts* said: Hew down trees, and build a mound against Jerusalem
Jer 6:9 Thus says the *Lord of hosts:* They shall thoroughly glean as a vine the remnant of Israel
Jer 7:3 Thus says the *Lord of hosts*, the God of Israel
Jer 7:21 Thus says the *Lord of hosts*, the God of Israel
Jer 8:3 Then death shall be chosen rather than life by all the residue of those who remain of this evil family, who remain in all the places where I have driven them," says the *Lord of hosts*
Jer 9:7 Therefore thus says the *Lord of hosts:* "Behold, I will refine them and try them
Jer 9:15 therefore thus says the *Lord of hosts*, the God of Israel
Jer 9:17 Thus says the *Lord of hosts:* Consider and call for the mourning women, that they may come
Jer 10:16 The Portion of Jacob is not like them, for He is the Maker of all things, and Israel is the tribe of His inheritance; the *Lord of hosts* is His name
Jer 11:17 For the *Lord of hosts*, who planted you, has pronounced doom against you for the evil of the house of Israel and of the house of Judah, which they have done against themselves to provoke Me to anger in offering incense to Baal
Jer 11:20 But, O *Lord of hosts*, you who judge righteously, testing the mind and the heart, let me see Your vengeance on them, for to You I have revealed my cause
Jer 11:22 therefore thus says the *Lord of hosts:* 'Behold, I will punish them
Jer 16:9 For thus says the *Lord of hosts*, the God of Israel
Jer 19:3 Thus says the *Lord of hosts*, the God of Israel
Jer 19:11 and say to them, 'Thus says the *Lord of hosts*
Jer 19:15 Thus says the *Lord of hosts*, the God of Israel
Jer 20:12 But, O *Lord of hosts*, You who test the righteous, and see the mind and heart, let me see Your vengeance on them
Jer 23:15 Therefore thus says the *Lord of hosts* concerning the prophets
Jer 23:16 Thus says the *Lord of hosts:* Do not listen to the words of the prophets who prophesy to you
Jer 23:36 For every man's word will be his oracle,

for you have perverted the words of the living God, the *Lord of hosts*, our God

Jer 25:8 Therefore thus says the *Lord of hosts:* 'Because you have not heard My words

Jer 25:27 Therefore you shall say to them, 'Thus says the *Lord of hosts*, the God of Israel

Jer 25:28 And it shall be, if they refuse to take the cup from your hand to drink, then you shall say to them, 'Thus says the *Lord of hosts*

Jer 25:29 You shall not be unpunished, for I will call for a sword on all the inhabitants of the earth," says the *Lord of hosts*

Jer 25:32 Thus says the *Lord of hosts:* Behold, disaster shall go forth from nation to nation, and a great whirlwind shall be raised up from the farthest parts of the earth

Jer 26:18 Micah of Moresheth prophesied in the days of Hezekiah king of Judah, and spoke to all the people of Judah, saying, 'Thus says the *Lord of hosts*

Jer 27:4 And command them to say to their masters, "Thus says the *Lord of hosts*, the God of Israel thus you shall say to your masters

Jer 27:18 But if they are prophets, and if the word of the Lord is with them, let them now make intercession to the *Lord of hosts*, that the vessels which are left in the house of the Lord, in the house of the king of Judah, and at Jerusalem, do not go to Babylon

Jer 27:19 For thus says the *Lord of hosts* concerning the pillars, concerning the Sea, concerning the carts, and concerning the remainder of the vessels that remain in this city

Jer 27:21 yes, thus says the *Lord of hosts*, the God of Israel, concerning the vessels that remain in the house of the Lord, and in the house of the king of Judah and of Jerusalem

Jer 28:2 Thus speaks the *Lord of hosts*, the God of Israel, saying

Jer 28:14 For thus says the *Lord of hosts*, the God of Israel

Jer 29:4 Thus says the *Lord of hosts*, the God of Israel, to all who were carried away captive, whom I have caused to be carried away from Jerusalem to Babylon

Jer 29:8 For thus says the *Lord of hosts*, the God of Israel

Jer 29:17 thus says the *Lord of hosts:* I will send on them the sword, the famine, and the pestilence, and will make them like rotten figs that cannot be eaten, they are so bad

Jer 29:21 Thus says the *Lord of hosts*, the God of Israel, concerning Ahab the son of Kolaiah, and Zedekiah the son of Maaseiah, who prophesy a lie to you in My name

Jer 29:25 Thus speaks the *Lord of hosts*, the God of Israel, saying

Jer 30:8 For it shall come to pass in that day,' says the *Lord of hosts*

Jer 31:23 Thus says the *Lord of hosts*, the God of Israel

Jer 31:35 Thus says the Lord, Who gives the sun for a light by day, and the ordinances of the moon and the stars for a light by night, Who disturbs the sea, and its waves roar (the *Lord of hosts* is His name

Jer 32:14 Thus says the *Lord of hosts*, the God of Israel

Jer 32:15 For thus says the *Lord of hosts*, the God of Israel

Jer 32:18 You show lovingkindness to thousands, and repay the iniquity of the fathers into the bosom of their children after them the Great, the Mighty God, whose name is the *Lord of hosts*

Jer 33:11 Praise the *Lord of hosts*, for the Lord is good, for His mercy endures forever

Jer 33:12 Thus says the *Lord of hosts:* this place which is desolate, without man and without beast, and in all its cities, there shall again be a habitation of shepherds causing their flocks to lie down

Jer 35:13 Thus says the *Lord of hosts*, the God of Israel

Jer 35:18 And Jeremiah said to the house of the Rechabites, "Thus says the *Lord of hosts*, the God of Israel

Jer 35:19 therefore thus says the *Lord of hosts*, the God of Israel

Jer 39:16 Go and speak to Ebed-Melech the Ethiopian, saying, 'Thus says the *Lord of hosts*, the God of Israel

Jer 42:15 Thus says the *Lord of hosts*, the God of Israel

Jer 42:18 For thus says the *Lord of hosts*, the God of Israel

Jer 43:10 and say to them, 'Thus says the *Lord of hosts*, the God of Israel

Jer 44:2 Thus says the *Lord of hosts*, the God of Israel

Jer 44:11 Therefore thus says the *Lord of hosts*, the God of Israel

Jer 44:25 Thus says the *Lord of hosts*, the God of Israel, saying

Jer 46:18 As I live," says the King, whose name is the *Lord of hosts*

Jer 46:25 The *Lord of hosts*, the God of Israel, says: "I will bring punishment on Amon of No, and Pharaoh and Egypt, with their gods and their kings Pharaoh and those who trust in him

Jer 48:1 Thus says the *Lord of hosts*, the God of Israel

Jer 48:15 Her chosen young men have gone down to the slaughter," says the King, Whose name is the *Lord of hosts*

Jer 49:7 Thus says the *Lord of hosts:* Is wisdom no more in Teman

Jer 49:26 Therefore her young men shall fall in her streets, and all the men of war shall be cut off in that day," says the *Lord of hosts*

Jer 49:35 Thus says the *Lord of hosts:* "Behold, I will break the bow of Elam, the foremost of their might

Jer 50:18 Therefore thus says the *Lord of hosts*, the God of Israel

Jer 50:33 Thus says the *Lord of hosts:* The children of Israel were oppressed, along with the children of Judah

Jer 50:34 the *Lord of hosts* is His name. He will thoroughly plead their case, that He may give rest to the land, and disquiet the inhabitants of Babylon

Jer 51:5 For Israel is not forsaken, nor Judah, by his God, the *Lord of hosts*, though their land was filled with sin against the Holy One of Israel

Jer 51:14 The *Lord of hosts* has sworn by Himself: "Surely I will fill you with men, as with locusts, and they shall lift up a shout against you

Jer 51:19 and Israel is the tribe of His inheritance. The *Lord of hosts* is His name

Jer 51:33 For thus says the *Lord of hosts*, the God of Israel

Jer 51:57 and they shall sleep a perpetual sleep and not awake," says the King, Whose name is the *Lord of hosts*

Jer 51:58 Thus says the *Lord of hosts:* The broad walls of Babylon shall be utterly broken, and her high gates shall be burned with fire

Mic 4:4 for the mouth of the *Lord of hosts* has spoken

Nah 2:13 Behold, I am against you," says the *Lord of hosts*

Nah 3:5 Behold, I am against you," says the *Lord of hosts*

Hab 2:13 Behold, is it not of the *Lord of hosts* that the peoples labor to feed the fire, and nations weary themselves in vain

Zeph 2:9 Therefore, as I live," says the *Lord of hosts*, the God of Israel
Zeph 2:10 This they shall have for their pride, because they have reproached and made arrogant threats against the people of the *Lord of hosts*
Hag 1:2 Thus speaks the *Lord of hosts*, saying: 'This people says
Hag 1:5 Now therefore, thus says the *Lord of hosts:* Consider your ways
Hag 1:7 Thus says the *Lord of hosts:* Consider your ways
Hag 1:9 says the *Lord of hosts*. "Because of My house that is in ruins, while every one of you runs to his own house
Hag 1:14 and they came and worked on the house of the *Lord of hosts*, their God
Hag 2:4 for I am with you,' says the *Lord of hosts*
Hag 2:6 For thus says the *Lord of hosts:* Once more (it is a little while
Hag 2:7 and I will shake all nations, and they shall come to the Desire of All Nations, and I will fill this temple with glory,' says the *Lord of hosts*
Hag 2:8 The silver is Mine, and the gold is Mine,' says the *Lord of hosts*
Hag 2:9 The glory of this latter temple shall be greater than the former,' says the *Lord of hosts*. 'And in this place I will give peace,' says the *Lord of hosts*
Hag 2:11 Thus says the *Lord of hosts:* "Now ask the priests concerning the law, saying
Hag 2:23 In that day,' says the *Lord of hosts*, 'I will take you, Zerubbabel My servant, the son of Shealtiel,' says the Lord, 'and will make you as a signet ring; for I have chosen you,' says the *Lord of hosts*
Zech 1:3 Therefore say to them, 'Thus says the *Lord of hosts:* "Return to me," says the *Lord of hosts*, "and I will return to you," says the *Lord of hosts*
Zech 1:4 Do not be like your fathers, to whom the former prophets preached, saying, 'Thus says the *Lord of hosts*
Zech 1:6 Just as the *Lord of hosts* determined to do to us, according to our ways and according to our deeds, so He has dealt with us
Zech 1:12 Then the Angel of the Lord answered and said, "O *Lord of hosts*, how long will You not have mercy on Jerusalem and on the cities of Judah, against which You were angry these seventy years
Zech 1:14 So the angel who spoke with me said to me, "Proclaim, saying, 'Thus says the *Lord of hosts*
Zech 1:16 my house shall be built in it," says the *Lord of hosts*
Zech 1:17 Again proclaim, saying, 'Thus says the *Lord of hosts:* "My cities shall again spread out through prosperity
Zech 2:8 For thus says the *Lord of hosts:* He sent Me after glory, to the nations which plunder you
Zech 2:9 Then you will know that the *Lord of hosts* has sent Me
Zech 2:11 Then you will know that the *Lord of hosts* has sent Me to you
Zech 3:7 Thus says the *Lord of hosts:* "If you will walk in My ways, and if you will keep My command, then you shall also judge My house, and likewise have charge of My courts
Zech 3:9 Behold, I will engrave its inscription,' says the *Lord of hosts*
Zech 3:10 In that day,' says the *Lord of hosts*, 'Everyone will invite his neighbor under his vine and under his fig tree
Zech 4:6 Not by might nor by power, but by My Spirit,' says the *Lord of hosts*
Zech 4:9 Then you will know that the *Lord of hosts* has sent Me to you
Zech 5:4 I will send out the curse," says the *Lord of hosts*
Zech 6:12 Then speak to him, saying, 'Thus says the *Lord of hosts*, saying
Zech 6:15 Then you shall know that the *Lord of hosts* has sent Me to you
Zech 7:3 and to ask the priests who were in the house of the *Lord of hosts*, and the prophets, saying
Zech 7:4 Then the word of the *Lord of hosts* came to me, saying
Zech 7:9 Thus says the *Lord of hosts:* 'Execute true justice, show mercy and compassion everyone to his brother
Zech 7:12 Yes, they made their hearts like flint, refusing to hear the law and the words which the *Lord of hosts* had sent by His Spirit through the former prophets. Thus great wrath came from the *Lord of hosts*
Zech 7:13 Therefore it happened, that just as He proclaimed and they would not hear, so they called out and I would not listen," says the *Lord of hosts*
Zech 8:1 Again the word of the *Lord of hosts* came, saying
Zech 8:2 Thus says the *Lord of hosts:* "I am zealous for Zion with great zeal
Zech 8:3 Jerusalem shall be called the City of Truth, the Mountain of the *Lord of hosts*, the Holy Mountain
Zech 8:4 Thus says the *Lord of hosts:* 'old men and old women shall again sit in the streets of Jerusalem, each one with his staff in his hand because of great age
Zech 8:6 Thus says the *Lord of hosts:* 'If it is marvelous in the eyes of the remnant of this people in these days, will it also be marvelous in My eyes?' says the *Lord of hosts*
Zech 8:7 Thus says the *Lord of hosts:* "Let I will save My people from the land of the east and from the land of the west
Zech 8:9 Thus says the *Lord of hosts:* 'Let your hands be strong, you who have been hearing in these days these words by the mouth of the prophets, who were in the day that the foundation was laid for the house of the *Lord of hosts*, that the temple might be built
Zech 8:11 But now I will not treat the remnant of this people as in the former days,' says the *Lord of hosts*
Zech 8:14 For thus says the *Lord of hosts:* Just as I determined to punish you when your fathers provoked Me to wrath,' says the *Lord of hosts*
Zech 8:18 Then the word of the *Lord of hosts* came to me, saying
Zech 8:19 Thus says the *Lord of hosts:* 'The fast of the fourth month, the fast of the fifth, the fast of the seventh, and the fast of the tenth, shall be joy and gladness and cheerful feasts for the house of Judah
Zech 8:20 Thus says the *Lord of hosts:* "Peoples shall yet come, inhabitants of many cities
Zech 8:21 the inhabitants of one city shall go to another, saying, "Let us continue to go and pray before the Lord, and seek the *Lord of hosts*
Zech 8:22 Yes, many peoples and strong nations shall come to seek the *Lord of hosts* in Jerusalem, and to pray before the Lord
Zech 8:23 Thus says the *Lord of hosts:* 'In those days ten men from every language of the nations shall grasp the sleeve of a Jewish man, saying
Zech 9:15 The *Lord of hosts* will defend them; they shall devour and subdue with sling stones
Zech 10:3 For the *Lord of hosts* will visit His flock, the house of Judah, and will make them as His royal horse in the battle
Zech 12:5 And the governors of Judah shall say in

their heart, 'The inhabitants of Jerusalem are my strength in the *Lord of hosts*, their God
Zech 13:2 It shall be in that day," says the *Lord of hosts*
Zech 13:7 Awake, O sword, against My Shepherd, against the Man who is My Companion," says the *Lord of hosts*
Zech 14:16 And it shall come to pass that everyone who is left of all the nations which came against Jerusalem shall go up from year to year to worship the King, the *Lord of hosts*, and to keep the Feast of Tabernacles
Zech 14:17 And it shall be that whichever of the families of the earth do not come up to Jerusalem to worship the King, the *Lord of hosts*, on them there will be no rain
Zech 14:21 Yes, every pot in Jerusalem and Judah shall be holiness to the *Lord of hosts*. Everyone who sacrifices shall come and take them and cook in them. In that day there shall no longer be a Canaanite in the house of the *Lord of hosts*
Mal 1:4 Even though Edom has said, "We have been impoverished, but we will return and build the desolate places," thus says the *Lord of hosts*
Mal 1:6 Says the *Lord of hosts* to you priests who despise My name
Mal 1:8 Would he accept you favorably?" says the *Lord of hosts*
Mal 1:9 While this is being done by your hands, will He accept you favorably?" says the *Lord of hosts*
Mal 1:10 I have no pleasure in you," says the *Lord of hosts*
Mal 1:11 For My name shall be great among the nations," says the *Lord of hosts*
Mal 1:13 and you sneer at it," says the *Lord of hosts*
Mal 1:14 But cursed be the deceiver who has in his flock a male, and makes a vow, but sacrifices to the Lord what is blemished for I am a great King," says the *Lord of hosts*
Mal 2:2 If you will not hear, and if you will not take it to heart, to give glory to My name," says the *Lord of hosts*
Mal 2:4 Then you shall know that I have sent this commandment to you, that My covenant with Levi may continue," says the *Lord of hosts*
Mal 2:7 for he is the messenger of the *Lord of hosts*
Mal 2:8 You have corrupted the covenant of Levi," says the *Lord of hosts*
Mal 2:12 May the Lord cut off from the tents of Jacob the man who does this, being awake and aware, and who brings an offering to the *Lord of hosts*
Mal 2:16 For the Lord God of Israel says that He hates divorce, for it covers one's garment with violence," says the *Lord of hosts*
Mal 3:1 And the Lord, whom you seek, will suddenly come to His temple, even the Messenger of the covenant, in whom you delight. Behold, He is coming," says the *Lord of hosts*
Mal 3:5 I will be a swift witness against sorcerers, against adulterers, against perjurers, against those who exploit wage earners and widows and the fatherless, and against those who turn away an alien because they do not fear Me," says the *Lord of hosts*
Mal 3:7 Return to Me, and I will return to you," says the *Lord of hosts*
Mal 3:10 Bring all the tithes into the storehouse, that there may be food in My house, and prove Me now in this," says the *Lord of hosts*
Mal 3:11 And I will rebuke the devourer for your sakes, so that he will not destroy the fruit of your ground, nor shall the vine fail to bear fruit for you in the field," says the *Lord of hosts*
Mal 3:12 And all nations will call you blessed, for you will be a delightful land," says the *Lord of hosts*
Mal 3:14 what profit is it that we have kept His ordinance, and that we have walked as mourners before the *Lord of hosts*
Mal 3:17 They shall be Mine," says the *Lord of hosts*, "On the day that I make them My jewels
Mal 4:1 And the day which is coming shall burn them up," says the *Lord of hosts*
Mal 4:3 You shall trample the wicked, for they shall be ashes under the soles of your feet on the day that I do this," says the *Lord of hosts*

LORD OF HOSTS HAS A DAY (RSV)
(See *DAY OF THE LORD*)

LORD OF LORDS
Deut 10:17 For the Lord your God is God of gods and *Lord of lords*, the great God, mighty and awesome, who shows no partiality nor takes a bribe
Ps 136:3 Oh, give thanks to the *Lord of lords!* For His mercy endures forever
1Tim 6:15 which He will manifest in His own time, He who is the blessed and only Potentate, the King of kings and *Lord of lords*
Rev 17:14 These will make war with the Lamb, and the Lamb will overcome them, for He is *Lord of lords* and King of kings
Rev 19:16 And He has on His robe and on His thigh a name written: KING OF KINGS AND *LORD OF LORDS*

LORD OF THE HARVEST
Matt 9:38 Therefore pray the *Lord of the harvest* to send out laborers into His harvest
Luke 10:2 therefore pray the *Lord of the harvest* to send out laborers into His harvest

LORD OF THE SABBATH
Mark 2:28 Therefore the Son of Man is also *Lord of the Sabbath*
Luke 6:5 And He said to them, "The Son of Man is also *Lord of the Sabbath*

LORD OUR RIGHTEOUSNESS
Jer 23:6 now this is His name by which He will be called: THE *LORD OUR RIGHTEOUSNESS*
Jer 33:16 And this is the name by which she will be called:THE *LORD OUR RIGHTEOUSNESS*

LORD PONDERETH THE HEARTS (KJV)
(See *LORD WEIGHS THE HEARTS*)

LORD PRESERVES ALL WHO LOVE HIM
Ps 145:20 The *Lord preserves all who love Him*, but all the wicked He will destroy

LORD PRESERVES THE FAITHFUL
Ps 31:23 For the *Lord preserves the faithful*, and fully repays the proud person

LORD PRESERVES THE SIMPLE
Ps 116:6 The *Lord preserves the simple;* I was brought low, and He saved me

LORD REDEEMS THE LIFE (RSV)
(See *LORD REDEEMS THE SOUL*)

LORD REDEEMS THE SOUL
Ps 34:22 The *Lord redeems the soul* of His servants, and none of those who trust in Him shall be condemned

LORD REIGNS
1Chr 16:31 and let them say among the nations, "The *Lord reigns*
Ps 93:1 The *Lord reigns*, He is clothed with maj-

esty; the Lord is clothed, He has girded Himself with strength
Ps 96:10 Say among the nations, "The *Lord reigns;* the world also is firmly established, it shall not be moved
Ps 97:1 The *Lord reigns;* let the earth rejoice; let the multitude of isles be glad
Ps 99:1 The *Lord reigns;* let the peoples tremble! He dwells between the cherubim

LORD RISES (NIV)
(See *LORD IS RISEN*)

LORD ROARS FROM ZION
Amos 1:2 The *Lord roars from Zion*, and utters His voice from Jerusalem

LORD SAID
Gen 4:6 So the *Lord said* to Cain, "Why are you angry
Gen 4:9 Then the *Lord said* to Cain, "Where is Abel your brother
Gen 4:15 And the *Lord said* to him, "Therefore, whoever kills Cain, vengeance shall be taken on him sevenfold
Gen 6:3 And the *Lord said*, "My Spirit shall not strive with man forever, for he is indeed flesh
Gen 6:7 So the *Lord said*, "I will destroy man whom I have created from the face of the earth, both man and beast, creeping thing and birds of the air, for I am sorry that I have made them
Gen 7:1 Then the *Lord said* to Noah, "Come into the ark, you and all your household, because I have seen that you are righteous before Me in this generation
Gen 8:21 Then the *Lord said* in His heart, "I will never again curse the ground for man's sake, although the imagination of man's heart is evil from his youth
Gen 11:6 And the *Lord said*, "Indeed the people are one and they all have one language, and this is what they begin to do
Gen 13:14 And the *Lord said* to Abram, after Lot had separated from him
Gen 16:9 So the Angel of the *Lord said* to her, "Return to your mistress, and submit yourself under her hand
Gen 16:10 Then the Angel of the *Lord said* to her, "I will multiply your descendants exceedingly, so that they shall not be counted for multitude
Gen 16:11 And the Angel of the *Lord said* to her: shall bear a son
Gen 18:13 And the *Lord said* to Abraham, "Why did Sarah laugh, saying
Gen 18:17 And the *Lord said*, "Shall I hide from Abraham what I am doing
Gen 18:20 And the *Lord said*, "Because the outcry against Sodom and Gomorrah is great, and because their sin is very grave
Gen 18:26 And the *Lord said*, "If I find in Sodom fifty righteous within the city, then I will spare all the place for their sakes
Gen 25:23 And the *Lord said* to her: "Two nations are in your womb, two peoples shall be separated from your body
Gen 31:3 Then the *Lord said* to Jacob, "Return to the land of your fathers and to your family, and I will be with you
Ex 3:7 And the *Lord said:* "I have surely seen the oppression of My people who are in Egypt, and have heard their cry because of their taskmasters, for I know their sorrows
Ex 4:2 So the *Lord said* to him, "What is that in your hand
Ex 4:4 Then the *Lord said* to Moses, "Reach out your hand and take it by the tail
Ex 4:6 Furthermore the *Lord said* to him, "Now put your hand in your bosom
Ex 4:11 So the *Lord said* to him, "Who has made man's mouth
Ex 4:19 And the *Lord said* to Moses in Midian, "Go, return to Egypt
Ex 4:21 And the *Lord said* to Moses, "When you go back to Egypt, see that you do all those wonders before Pharaoh which I have put in your hand
Ex 4:27 And the *Lord said* to Aaron, "Go into the wilderness to meet Moses
Ex 6:1 Then the *Lord said* to Moses, "Now you shall see what I will do to Pharaoh
Ex 6:26 These are the same Aaron and Moses to whom the *Lord said*
Ex 7:1 So the *Lord said* to Moses: I have made you as God to Pharaoh, and Aaron your brother shall be your prophet
Ex 7:14 So the *Lord said* to Moses: "Pharaoh's heart is hard
Ex 8:16 So the *Lord said* to Moses, "Say to Aaron, 'Stretch out your rod, and strike the dust of the land, so that it may become lice throughout all the land of Egypt
Ex 8:20 And the *Lord said* to Moses, "Rise early in the morning and stand before Pharaoh as he comes out to the water
Ex 9:1 Then the *Lord said* to Moses, "Go in to Pharaoh and tell him
Ex 9:8 So the *Lord said* to Moses and Aaron, "Take for yourselves handfuls of ashes from a furnace, and let Moses scatter it toward the heavens in the sight of Pharaoh
Ex 9:13 Then the *Lord said* to Moses, "Rise early in the morning and stand before Pharaoh, and say to him
Ex 9:22 Then the *Lord said* to Moses, "Stretch out your hand toward heaven, that there may be hail in all the land of Egypt on man, on beast, and on every herb of the field, throughout the land of Egypt
Ex 10:1 Now the *Lord said* to Moses, "Go in to Pharaoh
Ex 10:12 Then the *Lord said* to Moses, "Stretch out your hand over the land of Egypt for the locusts, that they may come upon the land of Egypt, and eat every herb of the land all that the hail has left
Ex 10:21 Then the *Lord said* to Moses, "Stretch out your hand toward heaven, that there may be darkness over the land of Egypt, darkness which may even be felt
Ex 11:1 And the *Lord said* to Moses, "I will bring yet one more plague on Pharaoh and on Egypt
Ex 11:9 But the *Lord said* to Moses, "Pharaoh will not heed you, so that My wonders may be multiplied in the land of Egypt
Ex 12:43 And the *Lord said* to Moses and Aaron, "This is the ordinance of the Passover
Ex 14:15 And the *Lord said* to Moses, "Why do you cry to Me
Ex 14:26 Then the *Lord said* to Moses, "Stretch out your hand over the sea, that the waters may come back upon the Egyptians, on their chariots, and on their horsemen
Ex 16:4 Then the *Lord said* to Moses, "Behold, I will rain bread from heaven for you
Ex 16:28 And the *Lord said* to Moses, "How long do you refuse to keep My commandments and My laws
Ex 17:5 And the *Lord said* to Moses, "Go on before the people, and take with you some of the elders of Israel
Ex 17:14 Then the *Lord said* to Moses, "Write this for a memorial in the book and recount it in the hearing of Joshua, that I will utterly blot out the remembrance of Amalek from under heaven
Ex 19:9 And the *Lord said* to Moses, "Behold, I come to you in the thick cloud, that the people

may hear when I speak with you, and believe you forever
Ex 19:10 Then the *Lord said* to Moses, "Go to the people and consecrate them today and tomorrow, and let them wash their clothes
Ex 19:21 And the *Lord said* to Moses, "Go down and warn the people, lest they break through to gaze at the Lord, and many of them perish
Ex 19:24 Then the *Lord said* to him, "Away! Get down and then come up, you and Aaron with you
Ex 20:22 Then the *Lord said* to Moses, "Thus you shall say to the children of Israel
Ex 24:12 Then the *Lord said* to Moses, "Come up to Me on the mountain and be there
Ex 30:34 And the *Lord said* to Moses: "Take sweet spices, stacte and onycha and galbanum, and pure frankincense with these sweet spices
Ex 32:7 And the *Lord said* to Moses, "Go, get down! For your people whom you brought out of the land of Egypt have corrupted themselves
Ex 32:9 And the *Lord said* to Moses, "I have seen this people, and indeed it is a stiff-necked people
Ex 32:33 And the *Lord said* to Moses, "Whoever has sinned against Me, I will blot him out of My book
Ex 33:1 Then the *Lord said* to Moses, "Depart and go up from here, you and the people whom you have brought out of the land of Egypt, to the land of which I swore to Abraham, Isaac, and Jacob, saying
Ex 33:17 Then the *Lord said* to Moses, "I will also do this thing that you have spoken
Ex 33:21 And the *Lord said*, "Here is a place by Me, and you shall stand on the rock
Ex 34:1 And the *Lord said* to Moses, "Cut two tablets of stone like the first ones, and I will write on these tablets the words that were on the first tablets which you broke
Ex 34:27 Then the *Lord said* to Moses, "Write these words, for according to the tenor of these words I have made a covenant with you and with Israel
Lev 16:2 and the *Lord said* to Moses: "Tell Aaron your brother not to come at simply any time into the Holy Place inside the veil, before the mercy seat which is on the ark, lest he die
Lev 21:1 And the *Lord said* to Moses, "Speak to the priests, the sons of Aaron, and say to them
Num 3:40 Then the *Lord said* to Moses: Number all the firstborn males of the children of Israel from a month old and above, and take the number of their names
Num 7:11 For the *Lord said* to Moses, "They shall offer their offering, one leader each day, for the dedication of the altar
Num 10:29 Now Moses said to Hobab the son of Reuel the Midianite, Moses' father-in-law, "We are setting out for the place of which the *Lord said*
Num 11:16 So the *Lord said* to Moses: "Gather to Me seventy men of the elders of Israel, whom you know to be the elders of the people and officers over them
Num 11:23 And the *Lord said* to Moses, "Has the Lord's arm been shortened
Num 12:4 Suddenly the *Lord said* to Moses, Aaron, and Miriam, "Come out, you three, to the tabernacle of meeting
Num 12:14 Then the *Lord said* to Moses, "If her father had but spit in her face, would she not be shamed seven days
Num 14:11 And the *Lord said* to Moses: "How long will these people reject Me
Num 14:20 Then the *Lord said:* 'I have pardoned according to your word
Num 15:35 Then the *Lord said* to Moses, "The man must surely be put to death
Num 17:10 And the *Lord said* to Moses, "Bring Aaron's rod back before the Testimony, to be kept as a sign against the rebels, that you may put their murmurings away from Me, lest they die
Num 18:1 Then the *Lord said* to Aaron: You and your sons and your father's house with you shall bear the iniquity related to the sanctuary, and you and your sons with you shall bear the iniquity associated with your priesthood
Num 18:20 Then the *Lord said* to Aaron: You shall have no inheritance in their land, nor shall you have any portion among them
Num 21:8 Then the *Lord said* to Moses, "Make a fiery serpent, and set it on a pole
Num 21:16 And from there they went to Beer, which is the well where the *Lord said* to Moses
Num 21:34 Then the *Lord said* to Moses, "Do not fear him, for I have delivered him into your hand, with all his people and his land
Num 22:32 And the Angel of the *Lord said* to him, "Why have you struck your donkey these three times
Num 22:35 Then the Angel of the *Lord said* to Balaam, "Go with the men, but only the word that I speak to you, that you shall speak
Num 25:4 Then the *Lord said* to Moses, "Take all the leaders of the people and hang the offenders before the Lord, out in the sun, that the fierce anger of the Lord may turn away from Israel
Num 27:12 Now the *Lord said* to Moses: "Go up into this Mount Abarim, and see the land which I have given to the children of Israel
Num 27:18 And the *Lord said* to Moses: "Take Joshua the son of Nun with you, a man in whom is the Spirit, and lay your hand on him
Deut 1:42 And the *Lord said* to me, 'Tell them, "Do not go up nor fight, for I am not among you
Deut 2:9 Then the *Lord said* to me, 'Do not harass Moab, nor contend with them in battle, for I will not give you any of their land as a possession, because I have given Ar to the descendants of Lot as a possession
Deut 2:31 And the *Lord said* to me, 'See, I have begun to give Sihon and his land over to you
Deut 3:2 And the *Lord said* to me, 'Do not fear him, for I have delivered him and all his people and his land into your hand
Deut 3:26 So the *Lord said* to me: "Enough of that! Speak no more to Me of this matter
Deut 4:10 especially concerning the day you stood before the Lord your God in Horeb, when the *Lord said* to me
Deut 5:28 Then the Lord heard the voice of your words when you spoke to me, and the *Lord said* to me
Deut 9:12 Then the *Lord said* to me, 'Arise, go down quickly from here, for your people whom you brought out of Egypt have acted corruptly
Deut 10:1 At that time the *Lord said* to me, 'Hew for yourself two tablets of stone like the first, and come up to Me on the mountain and make yourself an ark of wood
Deut 10:11 Then the *Lord said* to me, 'Arise, begin your journey before the people, that they may go in and possess the land which I swore to their fathers to give them
Deut 18:17 And the *Lord said* to me: "What you have spoken is good
Deut 31:14 Then the *Lord said* to Moses, "Behold, the days approach when you must die
Deut 31:16 And the *Lord said* to Moses: you will rest with your fathers
Deut 34:4 Then the *Lord said* to him, "This is the land of which I swore to give Abraham, Isaac, and Jacob, saying
Josh 3:7 And the *Lord said* to Joshua, "This day I will begin to magnify you in the sight of all Israel,

that they may know that, as I was with Moses, so I will be with you
Josh 5:2 At that time the *Lord said* to Joshua, "Make flint knives for yourself, and circumcise the sons of Israel again the second time
Josh 5:9 Then the *Lord said* to Joshua, "This day I have rolled away the reproach of Egypt from you
Josh 6:2 And the *Lord said* to Joshua: See! I have given Jericho into your hand, its king, and the mighty men of valor
Josh 7:10 So the *Lord said* to Joshua: "Get up! Why do you lie thus on your face
Josh 8:1 Then the *Lord said* to Joshua: Do not be afraid, nor be dismayed
Josh 8:18 Then the *Lord said* to Joshua, "Stretch out the spear that is in your hand toward Ai, for I will give it into your hand
Josh 10:8 And the *Lord said* to Joshua, "Do not fear them, for I have delivered them into your hand
Josh 11:6 But the *Lord said* to Joshua, "Do not be afraid because of them, for tomorrow about this time I will deliver all of them slain before Israel
Josh 13:1 And the *Lord said* to him: "You are old, advanced in years, and there remains very much land yet to be possessed
Josh 14:6 You know the word which the *Lord said* to Moses the man of God concerning you and me in Kadesh Barnea
Josh 14:12 It may be that the Lord will be with me, and I shall be able to drive them out as the *Lord said*
Judg 1:2 And the *Lord said*, "Judah shall go up. Indeed I have delivered the land into his hand
Judg 6:16 And the *Lord said* to him, "Surely I will be with you, and you shall defeat the Midianites as one man
Judg 6:23 Then the *Lord said* to him, "Peace be with you
Judg 6:25 Now it came to pass the same night that the *Lord said* to him
Judg 7:2 And the *Lord said* to Gideon, "The people who are with you are too many for Me to give the Midianites into their hands, lest Israel claim glory for itself against Me, saying
Judg 7:4 And the *Lord said* to Gideon, "The people are still too many
Judg 7:5 And the *Lord said* to Gideon, "Everyone who laps from the water with his tongue, as a dog laps, you shall set apart by himself
Judg 7:7 Then the *Lord said* to Gideon, "By the three hundred men who lapped I will save you, and deliver the Midianites into your hand
Judg 7:9 And it happened on the same night that the *Lord said* to him
Judg 10:11 So the *Lord said* to the children of Israel, "Did I not deliver you from the Egyptians and from the Amorites and from the people of Ammon and from the Philistines
Judg 13:13 So the Angel of the *Lord said* to Manoah, "Of all that I said to the woman let her be careful
Judg 13:16 And the Angel of the *Lord said* to Manoah, "Though you detain Me, I will not eat your food
Judg 13:18 And the Angel of the *Lord said* to him, "Why do you ask My name, seeing it is wonderful
Judg 20:18 They said, "Which of us shall go up first to battle against the children of Benjamin?" And the *Lord said*, "Judah shall go up first
Judg 20:23 Then the children of Israel went up and wept before the Lord until evening, and asked counsel of the Lord, saying, "Shall I again draw near for battle against the children of my brother Benjamin?" And the *Lord said*, "Go up against him
Judg 20:28 And the *Lord said*, "Go up, for tomorrow I will deliver them into your hand
1Sam 3:11 Then the *Lord said* to Samuel: Behold, I will do something in Israel at which both ears of everyone who hears it will tingle
1Sam 8:7 And the *Lord said* to Samuel, "Heed the voice of the people in all that they say to you
1Sam 8:22 So the *Lord said* to Samuel, "Heed their voice, and make them a king
1Sam 9:17 And when Samuel saw Saul, the *Lord said* to him
1Sam 15:16 And I will tell you what the *Lord said* to me last night
1Sam 16:1 Then the *Lord said* to Samuel, "How long will you mourn for Saul, seeing I have rejected him from reigning over Israel
1Sam 16:2 And the *Lord said*, "Take a heifer with you, and say
1Sam 16:4 So Samuel did what the *Lord said*, and went to Bethlehem
1Sam 16:7 But the *Lord said* to Samuel, "Do not look at his appearance or at the height of his stature, because I have refused him
1Sam 16:12 And the *Lord said*, "Arise, anoint him; for this is the one
1Sam 23:2 And the *Lord said* to David, "Go and attack the Philistines, and save Keilah
1Sam 23:11 O Lord God of Israel, I pray, tell Your servant." And the *Lord said*, "He will come down
1Sam 23:12 Then David said, "Will the men of Keilah deliver me and my men into the hand of Saul?" And the *Lord said*, "They will deliver you
1Sam 24:4 Then the men of David said to him, "This is the day of which the *Lord said* to you
2Sam 2:1 And the *Lord said* to him, "Go up." David said
2Sam 5:2 and the *Lord said* to you, 'You shall shepherd My people Israel, and be ruler over Israel
2Sam 5:19 And the *Lord said* to David, "Go up, for I will doubtless deliver the Philistines into your hand
1Kin 8:12 The *Lord said* He would dwell in the dark cloud
1Kin 8:18 But the *Lord said* to my father David, 'Whereas it was in your heart to build a house for My name, you did well that it was in your heart
1Kin 9:3 And the *Lord said* to him: "I have heard your prayer and your supplication that you have made before Me
1Kin 11:11 Therefore the *Lord said* to Solomon, "Because you have done this, and have not kept My covenant and My statutes, which I have commanded you, I will surely tear the kingdom away from you and give it to your servant
1Kin 13:22 but you came back, ate bread, and drank water in the place of which the *Lord said* to you
1Kin 19:15 Then the *Lord said* to him: "Go, return on your way to the Wilderness of Damascus
1Kin 22:17 And the *Lord said*, 'These have no master. Let each return to his house in peace
1Kin 22:20 And the *Lord said*, 'Who will persuade Ahab to go up, that he may fall at Ramoth Gilead
1Kin 22:22 The *Lord said* to him, 'In what way?' So he said
2Kin 1:3 But the angel of the *Lord said* to Elijah the Tishbite
2Kin 1:15 And the angel of the *Lord said* to Elijah, "Go down with him
2Kin 10:30 And the *Lord said* to Jehu, "Because you have done well in doing what is right in My sight, and have done to the house of Ahab all that was in My heart, your sons shall sit on the throne of Israel to the fourth generation
2Kin 18:25 The *Lord said* to me, 'Go up against this land, and destroy it
2Kin 23:27 And the *Lord said*, "I will also remove

Judah from My sight, as I have removed Israel, and will cast off this city Jerusalem which I have chosen, and the house of which I said
1Chr 14:10 And the *Lord said* to him, "Go up, for I will deliver them into your hand
2Chr 6:1 The *Lord said* He would dwell in the dark cloud
2Chr 6:8 But the *Lord said* to my father David, 'Whereas it was in your heart to build a temple for My name, you did well in that it was in your heart
2Chr 18:16 And the *Lord said*, 'These have no master. Let each return to his house in peace
2Chr 18:19 And the *Lord said*, 'Who will persuade Ahab king of Israel to go up, that he may fall at Ramoth Gilead
2Chr 18:20 Then a spirit came forward and stood before the Lord, and said, 'I will persuade him.' The *Lord said* to him, 'In what way
2Chr 18:21 And the *Lord said*, 'You shall persuade him and also prevail
Job 1:7 And the *Lord said* to Satan, "From where do you come
Job 1:8 Then the *Lord said* to Satan, "Have you considered My servant Job, that there is none like him on the earth, a blameless and upright man, one who fears God and shuns evil
Job 1:12 So the *Lord said* to Satan, "Behold, all that he has is in your power
Job 2:2 And the *Lord said* to Satan, "From where do you come
Job 2:3 Then the *Lord said* to Satan, "Have you considered My servant Job, that there is none like him on the earth, a blameless and upright man, one who fears God and shuns evil
Job 2:6 So the *Lord said* to Satan, "Behold, he is in your hand, but spare his life
Job 42:7 And so it was, after the Lord had spoken these words to Job, that the *Lord said* to Eliphaz the Temanite
Ps 68:22 The *Lord said*, "I will bring back from Bashan, I will bring them back from the depths of the sea
Ps 110:1 The *Lord said* to my Lord, "Sit at My right hand, till I make Your enemies Your footstool
Is 7:3 Then the *Lord said* to Isaiah, "Go out now to meet Ahaz, you and Shear-Jashub your son, at the end of the aqueduct from the upper pool, on the highway to the Fuller's Field
Is 8:1 Moreover the *Lord said* to me, "Take a large scroll, and write on it with a man's pen concerning Maher-Shalal-Hash-Baz
Is 8:3 Then the *Lord said* to me, "Call his name Maher-Shalal-Hash-Baz
Is 18:4 For so the *Lord said* to me, "I will take My rest, and I will look from My dwelling place like clear heat in sunshine, like a cloud of dew in the heat of harvest
Is 20:3 Then the *Lord said*, "Just as My servant Isaiah has walked naked and barefoot three years for a sign and a wonder against Egypt and Ethiopia
Is 21:6 For thus has the *Lord said* to me: Go, set a watchman, let him declare what he sees
Is 29:13 Therefore the *Lord said:* "Inasmuch as these people draw near to Me with their mouths and honor Me with their lips, but have removed their hearts far from Me, and their fear toward Me is taught by the commandment of men
Is 36:10 The *Lord said* to me, 'Go up against this land, and destroy it
Jer 1:7 But the *Lord said* to me: "Do not say, 'I am a youth
Jer 1:9 Then the Lord put forth His hand and touched my mouth, and the *Lord said* to me
Jer 1:12 Then the *Lord said* to me, "You have seen well, for I am ready to perform My word
Jer 1:14 Then the *Lord said* to me: "Out of the north calamity shall break forth on all the inhabitants of the land
Jer 3:6 The *Lord said* also to me in the days of Josiah the king
Jer 3:11 Then the *Lord said* to me, "Backsliding Israel has shown herself more righteous than treacherous Judah
Jer 9:13 And the *Lord said*, "Because they have forsaken My law which I set before them, and have not obeyed My voice, nor walked according to it
Jer 11:6 Then the *Lord said* to me, "Proclaim all these words in the cities of Judah and in the streets of Jerusalem, saying
Jer 11:9 And the *Lord said* to me, "A conspiracy has been found among the men of Judah and among the inhabitants of Jerusalem
Jer 13:1 Thus the *Lord said* to me: get yourself a linen sash, and put it around your waist, but do not put it in water
Jer 13:6 And it came to pass after many days that the *Lord said* to me
Jer 14:11 Then the *Lord said* to me, "Do not pray for this people, for their good
Jer 14:14 And the *Lord said* to me, "The prophets prophesy lies in My name
Jer 15:1 Then the *Lord said* to me, "Though Moses and Samuel stood before Me, yet My mind could not be favorable toward this people
Jer 15:11 The *Lord said:* "Surely it will be well with your remnant
Jer 17:19 Thus the *Lord said* to me: stand in the gate of the children of the people, by which the kings of Judah come in and by which they go out, and in all the gates of Jerusalem
Jer 24:3 Then the *Lord said* to me, "What do you see, Jeremiah
Ezek 4:13 Then the *Lord said*, "So shall the children of Israel eat their defiled bread among the Gentiles, where I will drive them
Ezek 9:4 and the *Lord said* to him, "Go through the midst of the city, through the midst of Jerusalem, and put a mark on the foreheads of the men who sigh and cry over all the abominations that are done within it
Ezek 44:2 And the *Lord said* to me, "This gate shall be shut
Ezek 44:5 And the *Lord said* to me, "Son of man, mark well, see with your eyes and hear with your ears, all that I say to you concerning all the ordinances of the house of the Lord and all its laws
Hos 1:2 When the Lord began to speak by Hosea, the *Lord said* to Hosea
Hos 1:4 Then the *Lord said* to him: "Call his name Jezreel, for in a little while I will avenge the bloodshed of Jezreel on the house of Jehu, and bring an end to the kingdom of the house of Israel
Hos 3:1 Then the *Lord said* to me, "Go again, love a woman who is loved by a lover and is committing adultery, just like the love of the Lord for the children of Israel, who look to other gods and love the raisin cakes of the pagans
Amos 7:8 And the *Lord said* to me, "Amos, what do you see?" And I said, "A plumb line." Then the *Lord said*
Amos 7:15 Then the Lord took me as I followed the flock, and the *Lord said* to me
Amos 8:2 Then the *Lord said* to me: "The end has come upon my people Israel
Jon 4:4 Then the *Lord said*, "Is it right for you to be angry
Jon 4:10 But the *Lord said*, "You have had pity on the plant for which you have not labored, nor made it grow, which came up in a night and perished in a night

Zech 3:2 And the *Lord said* to Satan, "The Lord rebuke you, Satan
Zech 11:13 And the *Lord said* to me, "Throw it to the potter
Zech 11:15 And the *Lord said* to me, "Next, take for yourself the implements of a foolish shepherd
Matt 22:44 The *Lord said* to my Lord, "Sit at My right hand, till I make Your enemies Your footstool
Matt 25:21 His *lord said* to him, 'Well done, good and faithful servant
Matt 25:23 His *lord said* to him, 'Well done, good and faithful servant
Mark 12:36 The *Lord said* to my Lord, "Sit at My right hand, till I make Your enemies Your footstool
Luke 7:31 And the *Lord said*, "To what then shall I liken the men of this generation, and what are they like
Luke 11:39 But the *Lord said* to him, "Now you Pharisees make the outside of the cup and dish clean, but your inward part is full of greed and wickedness
Luke 12:42 And the *Lord said*, "Who then is that faithful and wise steward, whom his master will make ruler over his household, to give them their portion of food in due season
Luke 17:6 So the *Lord said*, "If you have faith as a mustard seed, you can say to this mulberry tree
Luke 18:6 Then the *Lord said*, "Hear what the unjust judge said
Luke 20:42 Now David himself said in the Book of Psalms, 'The *Lord said* to my Lord
Luke 22:31 And the *Lord said*, "Simon, Simon! Indeed, Satan has asked for you, that he may sift you as wheat
Acts 2:34 The *Lord said* to my Lord, "Sit at My right hand
Acts 7:33 Then the *Lord said* to him, "Take your sandals off your feet, for the place where you stand is holy ground
Acts 9:5 And the *Lord said*, "I am Jesus, whom you are persecuting
Acts 9:6 And the *Lord said* to him, "Arise and go into the city, and you will be told what you must do
Acts 9:10 and to him the *Lord said* in a vision, "Ananias
Acts 9:11 So the *Lord said* to him, "Arise and go to the street called Straight, and inquire at the house of Judas for one called Saul of Tarsus, for behold, he is praying
Acts 9:15 But the *Lord said* to him, "Go, for he is a chosen vessel of Mine to bear My name before Gentiles, kings, and the children of Israel
Acts 22:10 And the *Lord said* to me, 'Arise and go into Damascus, and there you will be told all things which are appointed for you to do

LORD SEARCHES ALL HEARTS
1Chr 28:9 for the *Lord searches all hearts* and understands all the intent of the thoughts

LORD SENT ME
Josh 14:7 I was forty years old when Moses the servant of the *Lord sent me* from Kadesh Barnea to spy out the land, and I brought back word to him as it was in my heart
1Sam 15:1 Samuel also said to Saul, "The *Lord sent me* to anoint you king over His people, over Israel
1Sam 15:20 And Saul said to Samuel, "But I have obeyed the voice of the Lord, and gone on the mission on which the *Lord sent me*, and brought back Agag king of Amalek
Jer 26:12 The *Lord sent me* to prophesy against this house and against this city with all the words that you have heard

LORD SHALL
Gen 28:21 so that I come back to my father's house in peace, then the *Lord shall* be my God
Gen 30:24 So she called his name Joseph, and said, "The *Lord shall* add to me another son
Ex 15:18 The *Lord shall* reign forever and ever
Ex 22:11 then an oath of the *Lord shall* be between them both, that he has not put his hand into his neighbor's goods
Lev 2:11 No grain offering which you bring to the *Lord shall* be made with leaven, for you shall burn no leaven nor any honey in any offering to the Lord made by fire
Lev 7:29 He who offers the sacrifice of his peace offering to the *Lord shall* bring his offering to the Lord from the sacrifice of his peace offering
Lev 24:16 And whoever blasphemes the name of the *Lord shall* surely be put to death, and all the congregation shall certainly stone him, the stranger as well as him who is born in the land
Lev 27:9 And if it is a beast such as men may bring as an offering to the Lord, all such that any man gives to the *Lord shall* be holy
Num 15:4 then he who presents his offering to the *Lord shall* bring a grain offering of one-tenth of an ephah of fine flour mixed with one-fourth of a hin of oil
Num 28:15 Also one kid of the goats as a sin offering to the *Lord shall* be offered, besides the regular burnt offering and its drink offering
Deut 33:12 The beloved of the *Lord shall* dwell in safety by Him, Who shelters him all the day long
Judg 5:11 then the people of the *Lord shall* go down to the gates
Judg 8:23 But Gideon said to them, "I will not rule over you, nor shall my son rule over you; the *Lord shall* rule over you
1Sam 2:10 The adversaries of the *Lord shall* be broken in pieces
1Sam 25:29 Yet a man has risen to pursue you and seek your life, but the life of my *lord shall* be bound in the bundle of the living with the Lord your God
1Sam 26:10 David said furthermore, "As the Lord lives, the *Lord shall* strike him, or his day shall come to die, or he shall go out to battle and perish
2Sam 3:39 The *Lord shall* repay the evildoer according to his wickedness
2Sam 22:29 For You are my lamp, O Lord; the *Lord shall* enlighten my darkness
Ps 2:4 He who sits in the heavens shall laugh; the *Lord shall* hold them in derision
Ps 7:8 The *Lord shall* judge the peoples; judge me, O Lord, according to my righteousness, and according to my integrity within me
Ps 9:7 But the *Lord shall* endure forever; He has prepared His throne for judgment
Ps 21:9 The *Lord shall* swallow them up in His wrath, and the fire shall devour them
Ps 34:10 But those who seek the *Lord shall* not lack any good thing
Ps 37:40 And the *Lord shall* help them and deliver them; He shall deliver them from the wicked, and save them, because they trust in Him
Ps 55:16 As for me, I will call upon God, and the *Lord shall* save me
Ps 92:13 Those who are planted in the house of the *Lord shall* flourish in the courts of our God
Ps 102:16 For the *Lord shall* build up Zion; He shall appear in His glory
Ps 110:2 The *Lord shall* send the rod of Your strength out of Zion
Ps 121:7 The *Lord shall* preserve you from all evil; He shall preserve your soul
Ps 121:8 The *Lord shall* preserve your going out and your coming in from this time forth, and even forevermore
Ps 125:5 As for such as turn aside to their crooked

ways, the *Lord shall* lead them away with the workers of iniquity
Ps 146:10 The *Lord shall* reign forever Your God, O Zion, to all generations
Prov 29:25 The fear of man brings a snare, but whoever trusts in the *Lord shall* be safe
Is 1:28 The destruction of transgressors and of sinners shall be together, and those who forsake the *Lord shall* be consumed
Is 4:2 In that day the Branch of the *Lord shall* be beautiful and glorious
Is 9:11 Therefore the *Lord shall* set up the adversaries of Rezin against him, and spur his enemies on
Is 11:2 The Spirit of the *Lord shall* rest upon Him, the Spirit of wisdom and understanding, the Spirit of counsel and might, the Spirit of knowledge and of the fear of the Lord
Is 11:11 It shall come to pass in that day that the *Lord shall* set His hand again the second time to recover the remnant of His people who are left, from Assyria and Egypt, from Pathros and Cush, from Elam and Shinar, from Hamath and the islands of the sea
Is 35:10 And the ransomed of the *Lord shall* return, and come to Zion with singing, with everlasting joy on their heads
Is 40:5 the glory of the *Lord shall* be revealed, and all flesh shall see it together
Is 40:31 But those who wait on the *Lord shall* renew their strength
Is 42:13 The *Lord shall* go forth like a mighty man; He shall stir up His zeal like a man of war
Is 51:11 So the ransomed of the *Lord shall* return, and come to Zion with singing, with everlasting joy on their heads
Is 53:10 When You make His soul an offering for sin, He shall see His seed, He shall prolong His days, and the pleasure of the *Lord shall* prosper in His hand
Is 58:8 the glory of the *Lord shall* be your rear guard
Is 66:14 the hand of the *Lord shall* be known to His servants, and His indignation to His enemies
Is 66:16 For by fire and by His sword the Lord will judge all flesh; and the slain of the *Lord shall* be many
Jer 12:12 The plunderers have come on all the desolate heights in the wilderness, for the sword of the *Lord shall* devour from one end of the land to the other end of the land
Jer 25:33 And at that day the slain of the *Lord shall* be from one end of the earth even to the other end of the earth
Jer 47:4 for the *Lord shall* plunder the Philistines, the remnant of the country of Caphtor
Jer 51:29 for every purpose of the *Lord shall* be performed against Babylon, to make the land of Babylon a desolation without inhabitant
Ezek 42:13 Then he said to me, "The north chambers and the south chambers, which are opposite the separating courtyard, are the holy chambers where the priests who approach the *Lord shall* eat the most holy offerings
Ezek 48:9 The district that you shall set apart for the *Lord shall* be twenty-five thousand cubits in length and ten thousand in width
Ezek 48:10 The sanctuary of the *Lord shall* be in the center
Hos 13:15 the wind of the *Lord shall* come up from the wilderness
Joel 2:32 And it shall come to pass that whoever calls on the name of the *Lord shall* be saved
Zech 14:9 And the *Lord shall* be King over all the earth
Acts 2:21 And it shall come to pass that whoever calls on the name of the *Lord shall* be saved
Rom 4:8 blessed is the man to whom the *Lord shall* not impute sin
Rom 10:13 For "whoever calls upon the name of the *Lord shall* be saved

LORD SHALL GIVE THEE REST (KJV)
(See *LORD GIVES YOU REST*)

LORD TESTS THE HEARTS
Prov 17:3 The refining pot is for silver and the furnace for gold, but the *Lord tests the hearts*

LORD THAT DOTH SANCTIFY (KJV)
(See *LORD WHO SANCTIFIES*)

LORD THUNDERED
1Sam 7:10 But the *Lord thundered* with a loud thunder upon the Philistines that day, and so confused them that they were overcome before Israel
2Sam 22:14 The *Lord thundered* from heaven, and the Most High uttered His voice

LORD, TO WHOM SHALL WE GO
John 6:68 Then Simon Peter answered Him, "*Lord, to whom shall we go*

LORD TRIES HEARTS (RSV)
(See *LORD TESTS THE HEARTS*)

LORD TRIETH THE HEARTS (KJV)
(See *LORD TESTS THE HEARTS*)

LORD WAS ANGRY
Deut 3:26 But the *Lord was angry* with me on your account, and would not listen to me
Deut 4:21 Furthermore the *Lord was angry* with me for your sakes, and swore that I would not cross over the Jordan, and that I would not enter the good land which the Lord your God is giving you as an inheritance
Deut 9:8 Also in Horeb you provoked the Lord to wrath, so that the *Lord was angry* enough with you to have destroyed you
Deut 9:19 For I was afraid of the anger and hot displeasure with which the *Lord was angry* with you, to destroy you

LORD WAS ANGRY ENOUGH (NAS, NIV)
(See *LORD WAS VERY ANGRY*)

LORD WAS AROUSED
Num 11:33 But while the meat was still between their teeth, before it was chewed, the wrath of the *Lord was aroused* against the people, and the Lord struck the people with a very great plague
Num 12:9 So the anger of the *Lord was aroused* against them, and He departed
Num 25:3 So Israel was joined to Baal of Peor, and the anger of the *Lord was aroused* against Israel
Deut 29:27 Then the anger of the *Lord was aroused* against this land, to bring on it every curse that is written in this book
2Sam 6:7 Then the anger of the *Lord was aroused* against Uzzah, and God struck him there for his error
2Sam 24:1 Again the anger of the *Lord was aroused* against Israel, and He moved David against them to say
2Kin 13:3 Then the anger of the *Lord was aroused* against Israel, and He delivered them into the hand of Hazael king of Syria, and into the hand of Ben-Hadad the son of Hazael, all their days
1Chr 13:10 Then the anger of the *Lord was aroused* against Uzza, and He struck him because he put his hand to the ark
2Chr 25:15 Therefore the anger of the *Lord was aroused* against Amaziah, and He sent him a prophet who said to him

LORD WAS KINDLED (KJV, NAS, RSV)
(See *LORD WAS AROUSED*)

LORD WAS MOVED TO PITY
Judg 2:18 for the *Lord was moved to pity* by their groaning because of those who oppressed them and harassed them

LORD WAS SO ANGRY (RSV)
(See *LORD WAS VERY ANGRY*)

LORD WAS VERY ANGRY
Deut 9:20 And the *Lord was very angry* with Aaron and would have destroyed him
2Kin 17:18 Therefore the *Lord was very angry* with Israel, and removed them from His sight

LORD WAS WITH HIM
Gen 39:3 And his master saw that the *Lord was with him* and that the Lord made all he did to prosper in his hand
Gen 39:23 The keeper of the prison did not look into anything that was under Joseph's hand, because the *Lord was with him*
1Sam 3:19 So Samuel grew, and the *Lord was with him* and let none of his words fall to the ground
1Sam 18:12 Now Saul was afraid of David, because the *Lord was with him*, but had departed from Saul
1Sam 18:14 And David behaved wisely in all his ways, and the *Lord was with him*
2Kin 18:7 The *Lord was with him;* he prospered wherever he went
1Chr 9:20 And Phinehas the son of Eleazar had been the officer over them in time past; the *Lord was with him*
Luke 1:66 And all those who heard them kept them in their hearts, saying, "What kind of child will this be?" And the hand of the *Lord was with him*

LORD WAS WITH THEM
Judg 1:22 And the house of Joseph also went up against Bethel, and the *Lord was with them*
Acts 11:21 And the hand of the *Lord was with them*, and a great number believed and turned to the Lord

LORD WAS WROTH (KJV)
(See *LORD WAS ANGRY*)

LORD WATCHES OVER ALL WHO LOVE HIM (NIV)
(See *LORD PRESERVES ALL WHO LOVE HIM*)

LORD WEIGHS THE HEARTS
Prov 21:2 Every way of a man is right in his own eyes, but the *Lord weighs the hearts*

LORD WENT BEFORE THEM
Ex 13:21 And the *Lord went before them* by day in a pillar of cloud to lead the way, and by night in a pillar of fire to give them light, so as to go by day and night
Num 10:33 and the ark of the covenant of the *Lord went before them* for the three days

LORD, WHO HAD APPEARED TO
Gen 12:7 And there he built an altar to the *Lord, who had appeared to* him

LORD WHO SANCTIFIES
Ex 31:13 Surely My Sabbaths you shall keep, for it is a sign between Me and you throughout your generations, that you may know that I am the *Lord who sanctifies* you
Lev 20:8 And you shall keep My statutes, and perform them: I am the *Lord who sanctifies* you
Lev 22:32 You shall not profane My holy name, but I will be hallowed among the children of Israel. I am the *Lord who sanctifies* you
Ezek 20:12 Moreover I also gave them My Sabbaths, to be a sign between them and Me, that they might know that I am the *Lord who sanctifies* them

LORD WILL FIGHT FOR YOU
Ex 14:14 The *Lord will fight for you*, and you shall hold your peace

LORD WILL NOT CAST AWAY (RSV)
(See *LORD WILL NOT FORSAKE*)

LORD WILL NOT FORSAKE
1Sam 12:22 For the *Lord will not forsake* His people, for His great name's sake, because it has pleased the Lord to make you His people

LORD WILL NOT REJECT (NIV)
(See *LORD WILL NOT FORSAKE*)

LORD WILL ROAR FROM ZION (KJV)
(See *LORD ROARS FROM ZION*)

LORD WILL SCATTER YOU
Deut 4:27 And the *Lord will scatter you* among the peoples, and you will be left few in number among the nations where the Lord will drive you
Deut 28:64 Then the *Lord will scatter you* among all peoples, from one end of the earth to the other, and there you shall serve other gods, which neither you nor your fathers have known wood and stone

LORD YOUR GOD HAS CHOSEN YOU
Deut 7:6 the *Lord your God has chosen you* to be a people for Himself, a special treasure above all the peoples on the face of the earth

LORD'S ANOINTED
1Sam 16:6 So it was, when they came, that he looked at Eliab and said, "Surely the *Lord's anointed* is before Him
1Sam 24:6 And he said to his men, "The Lord forbid that I should do this thing to my master, the *Lord's anointed*, to stretch out my hand against him, seeing he is the anointed of the Lord
1Sam 24:10 But my eye spared you, and I said, 'I will not stretch out my hand against my lord, for he is the *Lord's anointed*
1Sam 26:9 for who can stretch out his hand against the *Lord's anointed*, and be guiltless
1Sam 26:11 The Lord forbid that I should stretch out my hand against the *Lord's anointed*
1Sam 26:16 As the Lord lives, you are worthy to die, because you have not guarded your master, the *Lord's anointed*
1Sam 26:23 for the Lord delivered you into my hand today, but I would not stretch out my hand against the *Lord's anointed*
2Sam 1:14 And David said to him, "How was it you were not afraid to put forth your hand to destroy the *Lord's anointed*
2Sam 1:16 So David said to him, "Your blood is on your own head, for your own mouth has testified against you, saying, 'I have killed the *Lord's anointed*
2Sam 19:21 But Abishai the son of Zeruiah answered and said, "Shall not Shimei be put to death for this, because he cursed the *Lord's anointed*

LORD'S APPROVAL (NIV)
(See *LORD BE WITH YOU*)

LORD'S ARM
Num 11:23 And the Lord said to Moses, "Has the *Lord's arm* been shortened

LORD'S BATTLES (NIV)
(See *BATTLES OF THE LORD*)

LORD'S COMMAND (NIV)
(See *COMMAND OF THE LORD*)

LORD'S DWELLING PLACE (NIV)
(See *HABITATION OF THE LORD*)

LORD'S HAND (KJV, RSV)
(See *LORD'S ARM*)

LORD'S HOUSE
Gen 40:7 So he asked Pharaoh's officers who were with him in the custody of his *lord's house*, saying
Gen 44:8 How then could we steal silver or gold from your *lord's house*
2Chr 7:2 And the priests could not enter the house of the Lord, because the glory of the Lord had filled the *Lord's house*
Ps 116:19 In the courts of the *Lord's house*, in the midst of you, O Jerusalem
Is 2:2 Now it shall come to pass in the latter days that the mountain of the *Lord's house* shall be established on the top of the mountains, and shall be exalted above the hills
Jer 7:2 Stand in the gate of the *Lord's house*, and proclaim there this word, and say
Jer 19:14 and he stood in the court of the *Lord's house* and said to all the people
Jer 26:2 Stand in the court of the *Lord's house*, and speak to all the cities of Judah, which come to worship in the *Lord's house*, all the words that I command you to speak to them
Jer 26:10 When the princes of Judah heard these things, they came up from the king's house to the house of the Lord and sat down in the entry of the new gate of the *Lord's house*
Jer 27:16 Do not listen to the words of your prophets who prophesy to you, saying, "Behold, the vessels of the *Lord's house* will now shortly be brought back from Babylon
Jer 28:3 Within two full years I will bring back to this place all the vessels of the *Lord's house*, that Nebuchadnezzar king of Babylon took away from this place and carried to Babylon
Jer 28:6 the Lord perform your words which you have prophesied, to bring back the vessels of the *Lord's house* and all who were carried away captive, from Babylon to this place
Jer 36:6 You go, therefore, and read from the scroll which you have written at my instruction, the words of the Lord, in the hearing of the people in the *Lord's house* on the day of fasting
Jer 36:8 And Baruch the son of Neriah did according to all that Jeremiah the prophet commanded him, reading from the book the words of the Lord in the *Lord's house*
Jer 36:10 Then Baruch read from the book the words of Jeremiah in the house of the Lord, in the chamber of Gemariah the son of Shaphan the scribe, in the upper court at the entry of the New Gate of the *Lord's house*, in the hearing of all the people
Jer 51:51 Shame has covered our faces, for strangers have come into the sanctuaries of the *Lord's house*
Ezek 8:14 So He brought me to the door of the north gate of the *Lord's house*
Ezek 8:16 So He brought me into the inner court of the *Lord's house*
Ezek 10:19 and they stood at the door of the east gate of the *Lord's house*, and the glory of the God of Israel was above them
Ezek 11:1 Then the Spirit lifted me up and brought me to the east gate of the *Lord's house*, which faces eastward
Mic 4:1 Now it shall come to pass in the latter days that the mountain of the *Lord's house* shall be established on the top of the mountains, and shall be exalted above the hills
Hag 1:2 This people says, "The time has not come, the time that the *Lord's house* should be built
Zech 14:20 The pots in the *Lord's house* shall be like the bowls before the altar

LORD'S INHERITANCE (NIV)
(See *INHERITANCE OF THE LORD*)

LORD'S MUSICAL INSTRUMENTS (NIV)
(See *MUSIC OF THE LORD*)

LORD'S PEOPLE (NAS, NIV)
(See *PEOPLE OF THE LORD*)

LORD'S RIGHTEOUS WILL (NIV)
(See *JUSTICE OF THE LORD*)

LORD'S SERVANT (NIV)
(See *MAIDSERVANT OF THE LORD*)

LORD'S SERVANTS (NIV)
(See *SERVANTS OF THE LORD*)

LORD'S SUPPER
1Cor 11:20 Therefore when you come together in one place, it is not to eat the *Lord's Supper*

LORD'S SUPPER THAT YOU EAT (RSV)
(See *EAT THE LORD'S SUPPER*)

LORD'S WILL (NIV)
(See *WILL OF THE LORD*)

LORDS OF THE PHILISTINES
Josh 13:3 the five *lords of the Philistines* the Gazites, the Ashdodites, the Ashkelonites, the Gittites, and the Ekronites
Judg 3:3 namely, five *lords of the Philistines*, all the Canaanites, the Sidonians, and the Hivites who dwelt in Mount Lebanon, from Mount Baal Hermon to the entrance of Hamath
Judg 16:5 And the *lords of the Philistines* came up to her and said to her
Judg 16:8 So the *lords of the Philistines* brought up to her seven fresh bowstrings, not yet dried, and she bound him with them
Judg 16:18 When Delilah saw that he had told her all his heart, she sent and called for the *lords of the Philistines*, saying, "Come up once more, for he has told me all his heart." So the *lords of the Philistines* came up to her and brought the money in their hand
Judg 16:23 Now the *lords of the Philistines* gathered together to offer a great sacrifice to Dagon their god, and to rejoice
Judg 16:27 all the *lords of the Philistines* were there. In fact, there were about three thousand men and women on the roof who watched while Samson performed
1Sam 5:8 Therefore they sent and gathered to themselves all the *lords of the Philistines*, and said
1Sam 5:11 So they sent and gathered together all the *lords of the Philistines*, and said
1Sam 6:4 They answered, "Five golden tumors

and five golden rats, according to the number of the *lords of the Philistines*
1Sam 6:12 And the *lords of the Philistines* went after them to the border of Beth Shemesh
1Sam 6:16 So when the five *lords of the Philistines* had seen it, they returned to Ekron the same day
1Sam 7:7 Now when the Philistines heard that the children of Israel had gathered together at Mizpah, the *lords of the Philistines* went up against Israel
1Sam 29:2 And the *lords of the Philistines* passed in review by hundreds and by thousands, but David and his men passed in review at the rear with Achish
1Sam 29:7 Therefore return now, and go in peace, that you may not displease the *lords of the Philistines*
1Chr 12:19 but they did not help them, for the *lords of the Philistines* sent him away by counsel, saying

LOSE HEART
Luke 18:1 Then He spoke a parable to them, that men always ought to pray and not *lose heart*
2Cor 4:1 Therefore, since we have this ministry, as we have received mercy, we do not *lose heart*
2Cor 4:16 Therefore we do not *lose heart*. Even though our outward man is perishing, yet the inward man is being renewed day by day
Gal 6:9 And let us not grow weary while doing good, for in due season we shall reap if we do not *lose heart*
Eph 3:13 Therefore I ask that you do not *lose heart* at my tribulations for you, which is your glory

LOST MY FOOTHOLD (NIV)
(See *STEPS HAD NEARLY SLIPPED*)

LOST SHEEP
Ps 119:176 I have gone astray like a *lost sheep;* seek Your servant, for I do not forget Your commandments
Jer 50:6 My people have been *lost sheep*. Their shepherds have led them astray
Matt 10:6 But go rather to the *lost sheep* of the house of Israel
Matt 15:24 But He answered and said, "I was not sent except to the *lost sheep* of the house of Israel

LOST SHEEP OF THE HOUSE OF ISRAEL
Matt 10:6 But go rather to the *lost sheep of the house of Israel*
Matt 15:24 But He answered and said, "I was not sent except to the *lost sheep of the house of Israel*

LOUD TRUMPET BLAST (NIV, RSV)
(See *SOUND OF THE TRUMPET*)

LOVE AND JUSTICE (NIV)
(See *MERCY AND JUSTICE*)

LOVE BUILDS UP (NIV, RSV)
(See *LOVE EDIFIES*)

LOVE CAREFULLY CONCEALED
Prov 27:5 Open rebuke is better than *love carefully concealed*

LOVE CASTS OUT FEAR
1Jn 4:18 but perfect *love casts out fear*, because fear involves torment

LOVE COVERS ALL SINS
Prov 10:12 Hatred stirs up strife, but *love covers all sins*

LOVE DOES NOT ENVY
1Cor 13:4 *love does not envy;* love does not parade itself, is not puffed up

LOVE DRIVES OUT FEAR (NIV)
(See *LOVE CASTS OUT FEAR*)

LOVE EDIFIES
1Cor 8:1 We know that we all have knowledge. Knowledge puffs up, but *love edifies*

LOVE ENDURES FOREVER (NIV, RSV)
(See *MERCY ENDURES FOREVER*)

LOVE IS AS STRONG AS DEATH
Song 8:6 for *love is as strong as death*, jealousy as cruel as the grave

LOVE IS NOT JEALOUS (RSV)
(See *LOVE DOES NOT ENVY*)

LOVE IS PATIENT (NAS, NIV, RSV)
(See *LOVE SUFFERS LONG*)

LOVE ME AND KEEP MY COMMANDMENTS
Ex 20:6 but showing mercy to thousands, to those who *love Me and keep My commandments*
Deut 5:10 but showing mercy to thousands, to those who *love Me and keep My commandments*

LOVE NEVER ENDS (RSV)
(See *LOVE NEVER FAILS*)

LOVE NEVER FAILS
1Cor 13:8 *Love never fails*. But whether there are prophecies, they will fail

LOVE OF CHRIST
Rom 8:35 Who shall separate us from the *love of Christ?* Shall tribulation, or distress, or persecution, or famine, or nakedness, or peril, or sword
2Cor 5:14 For the *love of Christ* constrains us, because we judge thus
Eph 3:19 to know the *love of Christ* which passes knowledge; that you may be filled with all the fullness of God

LOVE OF GOD
Luke 11:42 For you tithe mint and rue and all manner of herbs, and pass by justice and the *love of God*
John 5:42 But I know you, that you do not have the *love of God* in you
Rom 5:5 Now hope does not disappoint, because the *love of God* has been poured out in our hearts by the Holy Spirit who was given to us
Rom 8:39 nor height nor depth, nor any other created thing, shall be able to separate us from the *love of God* which is in Christ Jesus our Lord
2Cor 13:14 The grace of the Lord Jesus Christ, and the *love of God*, and the communion of the Holy Spirit be with you all
2Th 3:5 Now may the Lord direct your hearts into the *love of God* and into the patience of Christ
Tit 3:4 But when the kindness and the *love of God* our Savior toward man appeared
1Jn 2:5 But whoever keeps His word, truly the *love of God* is perfected in him
1Jn 3:17 But whoever has this world's goods, and sees his brother in need, and shuts up his heart from him, how does the *love of God* abide in him
1Jn 4:9 In this the *love of God* was manifested toward us, that God has sent His only begotten

Son into the world, that we might live through Him

1Jn 5:3 For this is the *love of God*, that we keep His commandments

Jude 21 keep yourselves in the *love of God*, looking for the mercy of our Lord Jesus Christ unto eternal life

LOVE OF MONEY

1Tim 6:10 For the *love of money* is a root of all kinds of evil, for which some have strayed from the faith in their greediness, and pierced themselves through with many sorrows

LOVE ONE ANOTHER

John 13:34 A new commandment I give to you, that you *love one another;* as I have loved you, that you also *love one another*

John 15:12 This is My commandment, that you *love one another* as I have loved you

John 15:17 These things I command you, that you *love one another*

Rom 13:8 Owe no one anything except to *love one another*, for he who loves another has fulfilled the law

1Th 4:9 But concerning brotherly love you have no need that I should write to you, for you yourselves are taught by God to *love one another*

1Pet 1:22 Since you have purified your souls in obeying the truth through the Spirit in sincere love of the brethren, *love one another* fervently with a pure heart

1Jn 3:11 For this is the message that you heard from the beginning, that we should *love one another*

1Jn 3:23 that we should believe on the name of His Son Jesus Christ and *love one another*, as He gave us commandment

1Jn 4:7 Beloved, let us *love one another*, for love is of God

1Jn 4:11 Beloved, if God so loved us, we also ought to *love one another*

1Jn 4:12 If we *love one another*, God abides in us, and His love has been perfected in us

2Jn 5 And now I plead with you, lady, not as though I wrote a new commandment to you, but that which we have had from the beginning: that we *love one another*

LOVE SUFFERS LONG

1Cor 13:4 *Love suffers long* and is kind; love does not envy

LOVE THE LORD YOUR GOD

Deut 6:5 You shall *love the Lord your God* with all your heart, with all your soul, and with all your might

Deut 11:1 Therefore you shall *love the Lord your God*, and keep His charge, His statutes, His judgments, and His commandments always

Deut 11:13 And it shall be that if you diligently obey My commandments which I command you today, to *love the Lord your God* and serve Him with all your heart and with all your soul

Deut 11:22 For if you carefully keep all these commandments which I command you to do to *love the Lord your God*, to walk in all His ways, and to hold fast to Him

Deut 13:3 you shall not listen to the words of that prophet or that dreamer of dreams, for the Lord your God is testing you to know whether you *love the Lord your God* with all your heart and with all your soul

Deut 19:9 and if you keep all these commandments and do them, which I command you today, to *love the Lord your God* and to walk always in His ways, then you shall add three more cities for yourself besides these three

Deut 30:6 And the Lord your God will circumcise your heart and the heart of your descendants, to *love the Lord your God* with all your heart and with all your soul, that you may live

Deut 30:16 in that I command you today to *love the Lord your God*, to walk in His ways, and to keep His commandments, His statutes, and His judgments, that you may live and multiply

Deut 30:20 that you may *love the Lord your God*, that you may obey His voice, and that you may cling to Him, for He is your life and the length of your days

Josh 22:5 But take diligent heed to do the commandment and the law which Moses the servant of the Lord commanded you, to *love the Lord your God*, to walk in all His ways, to keep His commandments, to hold fast to Him, and to serve Him with all your heart and with all your soul

Josh 23:11 Therefore take diligent heed to yourselves, that you *love the Lord your God*

Matt 22:37 Jesus said to him, "'You shall *love the Lord your God* with all your heart, with all your soul, and with all your mind

Mark 12:30 And you shall *love the Lord your God* with all your heart, with all your soul, with all your mind, and with all your strength

Luke 10:27 So he answered and said, "'You shall *love the Lord your God* with all your heart, with all your soul, with all your strength, and with all your mind

LOVE YOUR ENEMIES

2Sam 19:6 in that you *love your enemies* and hate your friends

Matt 5:44 But I say to you, *love your enemies*, bless those who curse you, do good to those who hate you, and pray for those who spitefully use you and persecute you

Luke 6:27 *Love your enemies*, do good to those who hate you

Luke 6:35 But *love your enemies*, do good, and lend, hoping for nothing in return

LOVE YOUR LAW

Ps 119:97 Oh, how I *love Your law!* It is my meditation all the day

Ps 119:113 I hate the double-minded, but I *love Your law*

Ps 119:163 I hate and abhor lying, but I *love Your law*

Ps 119:165 Great peace have those who *love Your law*, and nothing causes them to stumble

LOVE YOUR NEIGHBOR

Lev 19:18 You shall not take vengeance, nor bear any grudge against the children of your people, but you shall *love your neighbor* as yourself

Matt 5:43 You have heard that it was said, 'You shall *love your neighbor* and hate your enemy

Matt 19:19 Honor your father and your mother,' and, 'You shall *love your neighbor* as yourself

Matt 22:39 And the second is like it: *Love your neighbor* as yourself

Mark 12:31 You shall *love your neighbor* as yourself.' There is no other commandment greater than these

Rom 13:9 For the commandments, "You shall not commit adultery," "You shall not murder," "You shall not steal," "You shall not bear false witness," "You shall not covet," and if there is any other commandment, are all summed up in this saying, namely, "You shall *love your neighbor* as yourself

Gal 5:14 For all the law is fulfilled in one word, even in this: *Love your neighbor* as yourself

Jas 2:8 If you really fulfill the royal law according to the Scripture, "You shall *love your neighbor* as yourself

LOVED BY MY FATHER
John 14:21 And he who loves Me will be *loved by My Father*, and I will love him and manifest Myself to him

LOVED HIM AS HIMSELF (NAS, NIV)
(See *LOVED HIM AS HIS OWN SOUL*)

LOVED HIM AS HIS OWN SOUL
1Sam 18:1 And it was so, when he had finished speaking to Saul, that the soul of Jonathan was knit to the soul of David, and Jonathan *loved him as his own soul*
1Sam 18:3 Then Jonathan and David made a covenant, because he *loved him as his own soul*

LOVED MONEY (NIV)
(See *LOVERS OF MONEY*)

LOVED YOU WITH AN EVERLASTING LOVE
Jer 31:3 Yes, I have *loved you with an everlasting love;* therefore with lovingkindness I have drawn you

LOVER OF GOOD (KJV)
(See *LOVER OF WHAT IS GOOD*)

LOVER OF GOODNESS (RSV)
(See *LOVER OF WHAT IS GOOD*)

LOVER OF MONEY (NIV, RSV)
(See *GREEDY FOR MONEY*)

LOVER OF WHAT IS GOOD
Tit 1:8 but hospitable, a *lover of what is good*, sober-minded, just, holy, self-controlled

LOVERS OF MONEY
Luke 16:14 Now the Pharisees, who were *lovers of money*, also heard all these things, and they derided Him
2Tim 3:2 For men will be lovers of themselves, *lovers of money*, boasters, proud, blasphemers, disobedient to parents, unthankful, unholy

LOVERS OF PLEASURE
2Tim 3:4 traitors, headstrong, haughty, *lovers of pleasure* rather than lovers of God

LOVEST THOU ME (KJV)
(See *DO YOU LOVE ME*)

LOW AND HIGH
Ps 49:2 Both *low and high*, rich and poor together

LOW ESTATE OF HIS HANDMAIDEN (KJV, RSV)
(See *LOWLY STATE OF HIS MAIDSERVANT*)

LOWER PARTS OF THE EARTH
Ps 63:9 But those who seek my life, to destroy it, shall go into the *lower parts of the earth*
Is 44:23 Shout, you *lower parts of the earth;* break forth into singing, you mountains, O forest, and every tree in it
Ezek 32:24 There is Elam and all her multitude, all around her grave, all of them slain, fallen by the sword, who have gone down uncircumcised to the *lower parts of the earth*, who caused their terror in the land of the living
Eph 4:9 (Now this, "He ascended" what does it mean but that He also first descended into the *lower parts of the earth*

LOWER THAN THE ANGELS
Ps 8:5 For You have made him a little *lower than the angels*, and You have crowned him with glory and honor
Heb 2:7 You made him a little *lower than the angels;* You crowned him with glory and honor, and set him over the works of Your hands
Heb 2:9 But we see Jesus, who was made a little *lower than the angels*, for the suffering of death crowned with glory and honor, that He, by the grace of God, might taste death for everyone

LOWEST HELL (KJV)
(See *DEPTHS OF SHEOL*)

LOWLY, AND SITTING ON A DONKEY
Matt 21:5 Tell the daughter of Zion, 'Behold, your King is coming to you, *lowly, and sitting on a donkey*, a colt, the foal of a donkey

LOWLY IN HEART
Matt 11:29 Take My yoke upon you and learn from Me, for I am gentle and *lowly in heart*, and you will find rest for your souls

LOWLY STATE OF HIS MAIDSERVANT
Luke 1:48 For He has regarded the *lowly state of His maidservant*

LOYAL LOVE OF THE LORD (RSV)
(See *KINDNESS OF THE LORD*)

LOYALTY AND OF JUSTICE (RSV)
(See *MERCY AND JUSTICE*)

LUKE THE BELOVED PHYSICIAN
Col 4:14 *Luke the beloved physician* and Demas greet you

LUST OF THE EYES
1Jn 2:16 For all that is in the world the lust of the flesh, the *lust of the eyes*, and the pride of life is not of the Father but is of the world

LUST OF THE FLESH
Gal 5:16 Walk in the Spirit, and you shall not fulfill the *lust of the flesh*
1Jn 2:16 For all that is in the world the *lust of the flesh*, the lust of the eyes, and the pride of life is not of the Father but is of the world

LUSTS OF THEIR HEARTS
Rom 1:24 Therefore God also gave them up to uncleanness, in the *lusts of their hearts*, to dishonor their bodies among themselves

LYING IN A MANGER
Luke 2:12 You will find a Babe wrapped in swaddling cloths, *lying in a manger*
Luke 2:16 And they came with haste and found Mary and Joseph, and the Babe *lying in a manger*

LYING SPIRIT
1Kin 22:22 So he said, 'I will go out and be a *lying spirit* in the mouth of all his prophets
1Kin 22:23 The Lord has put a *lying spirit* in the mouth of all these prophets of yours, and the Lord has declared disaster against you
2Chr 18:21 So he said, 'I will go out and be a *lying spirit* in the mouth of all his prophets
2Chr 18:22 The Lord has put a *lying spirit* in the mouth of these prophets of yours, and the Lord has declared disaster against you

M

MADE A COVENANT
Gen 15:18 On the same day the Lord *made a covenant* with Abram, saying

Gen 21:27 So Abraham took sheep and oxen and gave them to Abimelech, and the two of them *made a covenant*
Gen 21:32 Thus they *made a covenant* at Beersheba. So Abimelech rose with Phichol, the commander of his army, and they returned to the land of the Philistines
Ex 34:27 Then the Lord said to Moses, "Write these words, for according to the tenor of these words I have *made a covenant* with you and with Israel
Deut 5:2 The Lord our God *made a covenant* with us in Horeb
Josh 9:15 So Joshua made peace with them, and *made a covenant* with them to let them live
Josh 9:16 And it happened at the end of three days, after they had *made a covenant* with them, that they heard that they were their neighbors who dwelt near them
Josh 24:25 So Joshua *made a covenant* with the people that day, and made for them a statute and an ordinance in Shechem
1Sam 18:3 Then Jonathan and David *made a covenant*, because he loved him as his own soul
1Sam 20:16 So Jonathan *made a covenant* with the house of David, saying
1Sam 22:8 All of you have conspired against me, and there is no one who reveals to me that my son has *made a covenant* with the son of Jesse
1Sam 23:18 So the two of them *made a covenant* before the Lord
2Sam 5:3 So all the elders of Israel came to the king at Hebron, and King David *made a covenant* with them at Hebron before the Lord
1Kin 8:9 There was nothing in the ark except the two tablets of stone which Moses put there at Horeb, when the Lord *made a covenant* with the children of Israel, when they came out of the land of Egypt
2Kin 11:4 And he *made a covenant* with them and took an oath from them in the house of the Lord, and showed them the king's son
2Kin 11:17 Then Jehoiada *made a covenant* between the Lord, the king, and the people, that they should be the Lord's people, and also between the king and the people
2Kin 17:35 with whom the Lord had *made a covenant* and charged them, saying
2Kin 23:3 Then the king stood by a pillar and *made a covenant* before the Lord, to follow the Lord and to keep His commandments and His testimonies and His statutes, with all his heart and all his soul, to perform the words of this covenant that were written in this book
1Chr 11:3 Therefore all the elders of Israel came to the king at Hebron, and David *made a covenant* with them at Hebron before the Lord
2Chr 5:10 There was nothing in the ark except the two tablets which Moses put there at Horeb, when the Lord *made a covenant* with the children of Israel, when they had come out of Egypt
2Chr 23:1 In the seventh year Jehoiada strengthened himself, and *made a covenant* with the captains of hundreds
2Chr 23:3 Then all the congregation *made a covenant* with the king in the house of God
2Chr 23:16 Then Jehoiada *made a covenant* between himself, the people, and the king, that they should be the Lord's people
2Chr 34:31 Then the king stood in his place and *made a covenant* before the Lord, to follow the Lord, and to keep His commandments and His testimonies and His statutes with all his heart and all his soul, to perform the words of the covenant that were written in this book
Neh 9:8 You found his heart faithful before You, and *made a covenant* with him to give the land of the Canaanites, the Hittites, the Amorites, the Perizzites, the Jebusites, and the Girgashites to give it to his descendants
Job 31:1 I have *made a covenant* with my eyes; why then should I look upon a young woman
Ps 50:5 Gather My saints together to Me, those who have *made a covenant* with Me by sacrifice
Ps 89:3 I have *made a covenant* with My chosen, I have sworn to My servant David
Is 28:15 because you have said, "We have *made a covenant* with death, and with Sheol we are in agreement
Is 57:8 you have enlarged your bed and *made a covenant* with them
Jer 34:8 This is the word that came to Jeremiah from the Lord, after King Zedekiah had *made a covenant* with all the people who were at Jerusalem to proclaim liberty to them
Jer 34:13 I *made a covenant* with your fathers in the day that I brought them out of the land of Egypt, out of the house of bondage, saying
Jer 34:15 and you *made a covenant* before Me in the house which is called by My name
Ezek 17:13 And he took the king's offspring, *made a covenant* with him, and put him under oath

MADE A VOW
Gen 28:20 Then Jacob *made a vow*, saying, "If God will be with me, and keep me in this way that I am going, and give me bread to eat and clothing to put on
Gen 31:13 I am the God of Bethel, where you anointed the pillar and where you *made a vow* to Me
Num 21:2 So Israel *made a vow* to the Lord, and said
Judg 11:30 And Jephthah *made a vow* to the Lord, and said
1Sam 1:11 Then she *made a vow* and said, "O Lord of hosts, if You will indeed look on the affliction of your maidservant and remember me, and not forget your maidservant, but will give your maidservant a male child, then I will give him to the Lord all the days of his life, and no razor shall come upon his head

MADE HIMSELF OF NO REPUTATION
Phil 2:7 but *made Himself of no reputation*, taking the form of a servant, and coming in the likeness of men

MADE INTERCESSION
Is 53:12 Therefore I will divide Him a portion with the great, and He shall divide the spoil with the strong, because He poured out His soul unto death, and He was numbered with the transgressors, and He bore the sin of many, and *made intercession* for the transgressors

MADE PERFECT IN LOVE
1Jn 4:18 But he who fears has not been *made perfect in love*

MADE PERFECT IN WEAKNESS
2Cor 12:9 And He said to me, "My grace is sufficient for you, for My strength is *made perfect in weakness*

MADE THE HEART OF THE PEOPLE MELT
Josh 14:8 Nevertheless my brethren who went up with me *made the heart of the people melt*, but I wholly followed the Lord my God

MADE THEMSELVES COVERINGS
Gen 3:7 and they sewed fig leaves together and *made themselves coverings*

MADE UNDER THE LAW (KJV)
(See *BORN UNDER THE LAW*)

MADE YOU TO GO UP OUT OF EGYPT (KJV)
(See *LED YOU UP FROM EGYPT*)

MADNESS AND FOLLY
Eccl 1:17 And I set my heart to know wisdom and to know *madness and folly*
Eccl 2:12 Then I turned myself to consider wisdom and *madness and folly*

MADNESS OF THE PROPHET
2Pet 2:16 a dumb donkey speaking with a man's voice restrained the *madness of the prophet*

MAGNIFIED IN MY BODY
Phil 1:20 according to my earnest expectation and hope that in nothing I shall be ashamed, but that with all boldness, as always, so now also Christ will be *magnified in my body*, whether by life or by death

MAGNIFY THE LORD
Ps 34:3 Oh, *magnify the Lord* with me, and let us exalt His name together

MAIDENS OF JERUSALEM (RSV)
(See *VIRGINS OF JERUSALEM*)

MAIDSERVANT OF THE LORD
Luke 1:38 Then Mary said, "Behold the *maidservant of the Lord!* Let it be to me according to your word

MAINTAIN GOOD WORKS
Tit 3:8 This is a faithful saying, and these things I want you to affirm constantly, that those who have believed in God should be careful to *maintain good works*
Tit 3:14 And let our people also learn to *maintain good works*, to meet urgent needs, that they may not be unfruitful

MAINTAIN JUSTICE (NIV)
(See *ESTABLISH JUSTICE*)

MAINTAIN JUSTICE AND RIGHTEOUSNESS (NIV)
(See *DO JUSTICE AND RIGHTEOUSNESS*)

MAINTAIN THE NAME OF THE DEAD (NIV)
(See *RAISE UP THE NAME OF THE DEAD*)

MAINTAIN THE RIGHT OF THE AFFLICTED (RSV)
(See *JUSTICE TO THE AFFLICTED*)

MAJESTIC IS THY NAME (NAS, RSV)
(See *EXCELLENT IS YOUR NAME*)

MAJESTY IN HEAVEN (NIV)
(See *MAJESTY ON HIGH*)

MAJESTY OF GOD
Luke 9:43 And they were all amazed at the *majesty of God*

MAJESTY ON HIGH
Heb 1:3 who being the brightness of His glory and the express image of His person, and upholding all things by the word of His power, when He had by Himself purged our sins, sat down at the right hand of the *Majesty on high*

MAKE A CAREFUL SEARCH (NIV)
(See *SEARCH DILIGENTLY*)

MAKE A COVENANT
Gen 26:28 So we said, 'Let there now be an oath between us, between you and us; and let us *make a covenant* with you
Gen 31:44 Now therefore, come, let us *make a covenant* , you and I, and let it be a witness between you and me
Ex 34:10 Behold, I *make a covenant*. Before all your people I will do marvels such as have not been done in all the earth, nor in any nation
Ex 34:12 Take heed to yourself, lest you *make a covenant* with the inhabitants of the land where you are going, lest it be a snare in your midst
Ex 34:15 lest you *make a covenant* with the inhabitants of the land, and they play the harlot with their gods and make sacrifice to their gods, and one of them invites you and you eat of his sacrifice
Josh 9:6 And they went to Joshua, to the camp at Gilgal, and said to him and to the men of Israel, "We have come from a far country; now therefore, *make a covenant* with us
Josh 9:7 But the men of Israel said to the Hivites, "Perhaps you dwell among us; so how can we *make a covenant* with you
Josh 9:11 Therefore our elders and all the inhabitants of our country spoke to us, saying, 'Take provisions with you for the journey, and go to meet them, and say to them, "We are your servants; now therefore, *make a covenant* with us
1Sam 11:1 and all the men of Jabesh said to Nahash, "*Make a covenant* with us, and we will serve you
1Sam 11:2 And Nahash the Ammonite answered them, "On this condition I will *make a covenant* with you, that I may put out all your right eyes, and bring reproach on all Israel
2Sam 3:13 And David said, "Good, I will *make a covenant* with you
2Sam 3:21 Then Abner said to David, "I will arise and go, and gather all Israel to my lord the king, that they may *make a covenant* with you, and that you may reign over all that your heart desires
2Chr 29:10 Now it is in my heart to *make a covenant* with the Lord God of Israel, that His fierce wrath may turn away from us
Ezra 10:3 Now therefore, let us *make a covenant* with our God to put away all these wives and those who have been born to them, according to the counsel of my master and of those who tremble at the commandment of our God
Job 41:4 Will he *make a covenant* with you? Will you take him as a servant forever
Ezek 34:25 I will *make a covenant* of peace with them, and cause wild beasts to cease from the land
Ezek 37:26 Moreover I will *make a covenant* of peace with them, and it shall be an everlasting covenant with them
Hos 2:18 In that day I will *make a covenant* for them with the beasts of the field, with the birds of the air, and with the creeping things of the ground
Hos 12:1 Also they *make a covenant* with the Assyrians, and oil is carried to Egypt

MAKE A JOYFUL NOISE (KJV, RSV)
(See *SHOUT JOYFULLY*)

MAKE A RIGHT JUDGMENT (NIV)
(See *JUDGE WITH RIGHTEOUS JUDGMENT*)

MAKE ATONEMENT FOR
Ex 29:36 You shall cleanse the altar when you *make atonement for* it, and you shall anoint it to sanctify it

Ex 29:37 Seven days you shall *make atonement for* the altar and sanctify it
Ex 30:15 The rich shall not give more and the poor shall not give less than half a shekel, when you give an offering to the Lord, to *make atonement for* yourselves
Ex 30:16 And you shall take the atonement money of the children of Israel, and shall appoint it for the service of the tabernacle of meeting, that it may be a memorial for the children of Israel before the Lord, to *make atonement for* yourselves
Ex 32:30 So now I will go up to the Lord; perhaps I can *make atonement for* your sin
Lev 1:4 Then he shall put his hand on the head of the burnt offering, and it will be accepted on his behalf to *make atonement for* him
Lev 4:20 So the priest shall *make atonement for* them, and it shall be forgiven them
Lev 4:26 So the priest shall *make atonement for* him concerning his sin, and it shall be forgiven him
Lev 4:31 So the priest shall *make atonement for* him, and it shall be forgiven him
Lev 4:35 So the priest shall *make atonement for* his sin that he has committed, and it shall be forgiven him
Lev 5:6 So the priest shall *make atonement for* him concerning his sin
Lev 5:13 The priest shall *make atonement for* him, for his sin that he has sinned in any of these matters
Lev 5:16 So the priest shall *make atonement for* him with the ram of the trespass offering, and it shall be forgiven him
Lev 5:18 So the priest shall *make atonement for* him regarding his ignorance in which he erred and did not know it, and it shall be forgiven him
Lev 6:7 So the priest shall *make atonement for* him before the Lord, and he shall be forgiven for any one of these things that he may have done in which he trespasses
Lev 8:15 and he poured the blood at the base of the altar, and sanctified it, to *make atonement for* it
Lev 8:34 As he has done this day, so the Lord has commanded to do, to *make atonement for* you
Lev 9:7 And Moses said to Aaron, "Go to the altar, offer your sin offering and your burnt offering, and *make atonement for* yourself and for the people. Offer the offering of the people, and *make atonement for* them, as the Lord commanded
Lev 10:17 Why have you not eaten the sin offering in a holy place, since it is most holy, and God has given it to you to bear the guilt of the congregation, to *make atonement for* them before the Lord
Lev 12:7 Then he shall offer it before the Lord, and *make atonement for* her
Lev 12:8 So the priest shall *make atonement for* her, and she will be clean
Lev 14:18 So the priest shall *make atonement for* him before the Lord
Lev 14:19 Then the priest shall offer the sin offering, and *make atonement for* him who is to be cleansed from his uncleanness
Lev 14:20 So the priest shall *make atonement for* him, and he shall be clean
Lev 14:21 But if he is poor and cannot afford it, then he shall take one male lamb as a trespass offering to be waved, to *make atonement for* him, one-tenth of an ephah of fine flour mixed with oil as a grain offering, a log of oil
Lev 14:29 The rest of the oil that is in the priest's hand he shall put on the head of him who is to be cleansed, to *make atonement for* him before the Lord
Lev 14:31 So the priest shall *make atonement for* him who is to be cleansed before the Lord
Lev 14:53 Then he shall let the living bird loose outside the city in the open field, and *make atonement for* the house, and it shall be clean
Lev 15:15 So the priest shall *make atonement for* him before the Lord because of his discharge
Lev 15:30 Then the priest shall offer the one as a sin offering and the other as a burnt offering, and the priest shall *make atonement for* her before the Lord for the discharge of her uncleanness
Lev 16:6 Aaron shall offer the bull as a sin offering, which is for himself, and *make atonement for* himself and for his house
Lev 16:11 And Aaron shall bring the bull of the sin offering, which is for himself, and *make atonement for* himself and for his house, and shall kill the bull as the sin offering which is for himself
Lev 16:16 So he shall *make atonement for* the Holy Place, because of the uncleanness of the children of Israel, and because of their transgressions, for all their sins
Lev 16:17 There shall be no man in the tabernacle of meeting when he goes in to make atonement in the Holy Place, until he comes out, that he may *make atonement for* himself, for his household, and for all the congregation of Israel
Lev 16:18 And he shall go out to the altar that is before the Lord, and *make atonement for* it, and shall take some of the blood of the bull and some of the blood of the goat, and put it on the horns of the altar all around
Lev 16:24 And he shall wash his body with water in a holy place, put on his garments, come out and offer his burnt offering and the burnt offering of the people, and *make atonement for* himself and for the people
Lev 16:30 For on that day the priest shall *make atonement for* you, to cleanse you, that you may be clean from all your sins before the Lord
Lev 16:33 then he shall *make atonement for* the Holy Sanctuary, and he shall *make atonement for* the tabernacle of meeting and for the altar, and he shall *make atonement for* the priests and for all the people of the congregation
Lev 16:34 This shall be an everlasting statute for you, to *make atonement for* the children of Israel, for all their sins, once a year
Lev 17:11 For the life of the flesh is in the blood, and I have given it to you upon the altar to *make atonement for* your souls
Lev 19:22 The priest shall *make atonement for* him with the ram of the trespass offering before the Lord for his sin which he has done
Lev 23:28 And you shall do no work on that same day, for it is the Day of Atonement, to *make atonement for* you before the Lord your God
Num 6:11 and the priest shall offer one as a sin offering and the other as a burnt offering, and *make atonement for* him, because he sinned by reason of the dead body
Num 8:12 Then the Levites shall lay their hands on the heads of the young bulls, and you shall offer one as a sin offering and the other as a burnt offering to the Lord, to *make atonement for* the Levites
Num 8:19 And I have given the Levites as a gift to Aaron and his sons from among the children of Israel, to do the work for the children of Israel in the tabernacle of meeting, and to *make atonement for* the children of Israel, that there be no plague among the children of Israel when the children of Israel come near the sanctuary
Num 15:25 So the priest shall *make atonement for* the whole congregation of the children of Israel, and it shall be forgiven them, for it was unintentional
Num 15:28 So the priest shall *make atonement for* the person who sins unintentionally, when he

sins unintentionally before the Lord, to *make atonement for* him
Num 16:46 So Moses said to Aaron, "Take a censer and put fire in it from the altar, put incense on it, and take it quickly to the congregation and *make atonement for* them
Num 28:22 also one goat as a sin offering, to *make atonement for* you
Num 28:30 also one kid of the goats, to *make atonement for* you
Num 29:5 also one kid of the goats as a sin offering, to *make atonement for* you
Num 31:50 armlets and bracelets and signet rings and earrings and necklaces, to *make atonement for* ourselves before the Lord
1Chr 6:49 But Aaron and his sons offered sacrifices on the altar of burnt offering and on the altar of incense, for all the work of the Most Holy Place, and to *make atonement for* Israel, according to all that Moses the servant of God had commanded
Neh 10:33 for the holy things, for the sin offerings to *make atonement for* Israel, and all the work of the house of our God
Ezek 43:20 thus you shall cleanse it and *make atonement for* it
Ezek 43:26 Seven days they shall *make atonement for* the altar and purify it, and so consecrate it
Ezek 45:15 These shall be for grain offerings, burnt offerings, and peace offerings, to *make atonement for* them
Ezek 45:17 He shall prepare the sin offering, the grain offering, the burnt offering, and the peace offerings to *make atonement for* the house of Israel
Ezek 45:20 And so you shall do on the seventh day of the month for everyone who has sinned unintentionally or in ignorance. Thus you shall *make atonement for* the temple

MAKE EVERY EFFORT TO LIVE IN PEACE (NIV)
(See *PURSUE PEACE*)

MAKE FRIENDS QUICKLY WITH YOUR ACCUSER (RSV)
(See *AGREE WITH YOUR ADVERSARY*)

MAKE HASTE TO SHED INNOCENT BLOOD
Is 59:7 Their feet run to evil, and they *make haste to shed innocent blood*

MAKE HIM A GREAT NATION
Gen 17:20 He shall beget twelve princes, and I will *make him a great nation*
Gen 21:18 Arise, lift up the lad and hold him with your hand, for I will *make him a great nation*

MAKE HIS PATHS STRAIGHT
Matt 3:3 Prepare the way of the Lord, *make His paths straight*
Mark 1:3 Prepare the way of the Lord, *make His paths straight*
Luke 3:4 Prepare the way of the Lord, *make His paths straight*

MAKE ME TO KNOW THY WAYS (RSV)
(See *SHOW ME YOUR WAYS*)

MAKE MUSIC TO YOUR NAME (NIV)
(See *SING PRAISES TO YOUR NAME*)

MAKE MY BED IN HELL
Ps 139:8 If I *make my bed in hell*, behold, You are there

MAKE MY BED IN SHEOL (NAS, RSV)
(See *MAKE MY BED IN HELL*)

MAKE MY BED IN THE DEPTHS (NIV)
(See *MAKE MY BED IN HELL*)

MAKE OUR YOKE LIGHTER (NIV)
(See *LIGHTEN THE YOKE*)

MAKE STRAIGHT PATHS FOR HIM (NIV)
(See *MAKE HIS PATHS STRAIGHT*)

MAKE SURE (NIV)
(See *TAKE HEED*)

MAKE THE MOST OF EVERY OPPORTUNITY (NIV)
(See *REDEEMING THE TIME*)

MAKE THE TRUMPET TO SOUND
Lev 25:9 on the Day of Atonement you shall *make the trumpet to sound* throughout all your land

MAKE THEM COME IN (NIV)
(See *COMPEL THEM TO COME IN*)

MAKE THEM KNOWN TO YOUR CHILDREN (RSV)
(See *TEACH THEM TO YOUR CHILDREN*)

MAKE UP FOR (NIV)
(See *SUPPLY WHAT WAS LACKING*)

MAKE WAR (KJV, NAS)
(See *WAGE WAR*)

MAKE YOU A GREAT NATION
Gen 12:2 I will *make you a great nation;* I will bless you and make your name great

MAKE YOUR ENEMIES YOUR FOOTSTOOL
Ps 110:1 The Lord said to my Lord, "Sit at My right hand, till I *make Your enemies Your footstool*
Matt 22:44 The Lord said to my Lord, "Sit at My right hand, till I *make Your enemies Your footstool*
Mark 12:36 The Lord said to my Lord, "Sit at My right hand, till I *make Your enemies Your footstool*
Luke 20:43 till I *make Your enemies Your footstool*
Acts 2:35 till I *make Your enemies Your footstool*
Heb 1:13 Sit at My right hand, till I *make Your enemies Your footstool*

MAKE YOUR THRONE FIRM (NIV)
(See *BUILD UP YOUR THRONE*)

MAKER OF HEAVEN AND EARTH (RSV)
(See *POSSESSOR OF HEAVEN AND EARTH*)

MAKING MANY BOOKS THERE IS NO END
Eccl 12:12 Of *making many books there is no end*, and much study is wearisome to the flesh

MAKING MENTION OF YOU
Eph 1:16 do not cease to give thanks for you, *making mention of you* in my prayers
1Th 1:2 We give thanks to God always for you all, *making mention of you* in our prayers
Phm 4 I thank my God, *making mention of you* always in my prayers

MAKING THE MOST OF THE TIME (RSV)
(See *REDEEMING THE TIME*)

MAKING WISE THE SIMPLE
Ps 19:7 The testimony of the Lord is sure, *making wise the simple*

MALE AND FEMALE
Gen 1:27 in the image of God He created him; *male and female* He created them
Gen 5:2 He created them *male and female*, and blessed them and called them Mankind in the day they were created
Gen 6:19 And of every living thing of all flesh you shall bring two of every sort into the ark, to keep them alive with you; they shall be *male and female*
Gen 7:3 also seven each of birds of the air, *male and female*, to keep the species alive on the face of all the earth
Gen 7:9 two by two they went into the ark to Noah, *male and female*, as God had commanded Noah
Gen 7:16 So those that entered, *male and female* of all flesh, went in as God had commanded him
Gen 12:16 He had sheep, oxen, male donkeys, *male and female* servants, female donkeys, and camels
Gen 20:14 Then Abimelech took sheep, oxen, and *male and female* servants, and gave them to Abraham
Gen 24:35 and He has given him flocks and herds, silver and gold, *male and female* servants, and camels and donkeys
Gen 32:5 I have oxen, donkeys, flocks, and *male and female* servants
Lev 25:44 And as for your *male and female* slaves whom you may have from the nations that are around you, from them you may buy *male and female* slaves
Num 5:3 You shall put out both *male and female;* you shall put them outside the camp, that they may not defile their camps in the midst of which I dwell
Deut 28:68 And there you shall be offered for sale to your enemies as *male and female* slaves, but no one will buy you
2Kin 5:26 Is it time to receive money and to receive clothing, olive groves and vineyards, sheep and oxen, *male and female* servants
2Chr 28:10 And now you propose to force the children of Judah and Jerusalem to be your *male and female* slaves
Ezra 2:65 besides their *male and female* servants, of whom there were seven thousand three hundred and thirty-seven
Neh 7:67 besides their *male and female* servants, of whom there were seven thousand three hundred and thirty-seven
Esth 7:4 Had we been sold as *male and female* slaves, I would have held my tongue, although the enemy could never compensate for the king's loss
Eccl 2:7 I acquired *male and female* servants, and had servants born in my house
Eccl 2:8 I acquired *male and female* singers, the delights of the sons of men, and musical instruments of all kinds
Jer 34:9 that every man should set free his *male and female* slave a Hebrew man or woman that no one should keep a Jewish brother in bondage
Jer 34:10 Now when all the princes and all the people, who had entered into the covenant, heard that everyone should set free his *male and female* slaves, that no one should keep them in bondage anymore, they obeyed and let them go
Jer 34:11 But afterward they changed their minds and made the *male and female* slaves return, whom they had set free, and brought them into subjection as *male and female* slaves
Jer 34:16 Then you turned around and profaned My name, and every one of you brought back his *male and female* slaves, whom he had set at liberty, at their pleasure, and brought them back into subjection, to be your *male and female* slaves
Matt 19:4 And He answered and said to them, "Have you not read that He who made them at the beginning 'made them *male and female*
Mark 10:6 But from the beginning of the creation, God 'made them *male and female*

MALE CULT PROSTITUTES (NAS, RSV)
(See *PERVERTED PERSONS*)

MALE OR FEMALE
Ex 21:20 And if a man beats his *male or female* servant with a rod, so that he dies under his hand, he shall surely be punished
Ex 21:26 If a man strikes the eye of his *male or female* servant, and destroys it, he shall let him go free for the sake of his eye
Ex 21:27 And if he knocks out the tooth ofhis *male or female* servant, he shall let him go free for the sake of his tooth
Ex 21:32 If the ox gores a *male or female* servant, he shall give to their master thirty shekels of silver, and the ox shall be stoned
Lev 3:1 When his offering is a sacrifice of a peace offering, if he offers it of the herd, whether *male or female*, he shall offer it without blemish before the Lord
Lev 3:6 If his offering as a sacrifice of a peace offering to the Lord is of the flock, whether *male or female*, he shall offer it without blemish
Deut 4:16 lest you act corruptly and make for yourselves a carved image in the form of any figure: the likeness of *male or female*
Deut 7:14 there shall not be a *male or female* barren among you or among your livestock

MALE SHRINE PROSTITUTES (NIV)
(See *PERVERTED PERSONS*)

MAMMON OF UNRIGHTEOUSNESS (KJV, NAS)
(See *UNRIGHTEOUS MAMMON*)

MAN AFTER HIS OWN HEART
1Sam 13:14 The Lord has sought for Himself a *man after His own heart*, and the Lord has commanded him to be commander over His people, because you have not kept what the Lord commanded you

MAN AFTER MY OWN HEART
Acts 13:22 And when He had removed him, He raised up for them David as king, to whom also He gave testimony and said, 'I have found David the son of Jesse, a *man after My own heart*, who will do all My will

MAN AND BEAST
Gen 6:7 So the Lord said, "I will destroy man whom I have created from the face of the earth, both *man and beast*, creeping thing and birds of the air, for I am sorry that I have made them
Ex 8:17 For Aaron stretched out his hand with his rod and struck the dust of the earth, and it became lice on *man and beast*
Ex 8:18 Now the magicians so worked with their enchantments to bring forth lice, but they could not. So there were lice on *man and beast*
Ex 9:9 And it will become fine dust in all the land of Egypt, and it will cause boils that break out in sores on *man and beast* throughout all the land of Egypt

Ex 9:10 And they caused boils that break out in sores on *man and beast*
Ex 9:25 And the hail struck throughout the whole land of Egypt, all that was in the field, both *man and beast*
Ex 12:12 For I will pass through the land of Egypt on that night, and will strike all the firstborn in the land of Egypt, both *man and beast*
Ex 13:2 Consecrate to Me all the firstborn, whatever opens the womb among the children of Israel, both of *man and beast*
Lev 27:28 Nevertheless no devoted offering that a man may devote to the Lord of all that he has, both *man and beast*, or the field of his possession, shall be sold or redeemed
Num 3:13 On the day that I struck all the firstborn in the land of Egypt, I sanctified to Myself all the firstborn in Israel, both *man and beast*
Num 8:17 For all the firstborn among the children of Israel are Mine, both *man and beast*
Num 31:11 And they took all the spoil and all the booty, both of *man and beast*
Num 31:26 Count up the plunder that was taken, both of *man and beast*, you and Eleazar the priest and the chief fathers of the congregation
Num 31:47 and from the children of Israel's half Moses took one of every fifty, drawn from *man and beast*, and gave them to the Levites, who kept charge of the tabernacle of the Lord, as the Lord commanded Moses
Ps 36:6 Your judgments are a great deep; O Lord, You preserve *man and beast*
Ps 135:8 He destroyed the firstborn of Egypt, both of *man and beast*
Jer 21:6 I will strike the inhabitants of this city, both *man and beast*
Jer 36:29 You have burned this scroll, saying, 'Why have you written in it that the king of Babylon will certainly come and destroy this land, and cause *man and beast* to cease from here
Jer 50:3 They shall move, they shall depart, both *man and beast*
Ezek 14:13 I will cut off its supply of bread, send famine on it, and cut off *man and beast* from it
Ezek 14:17 Or if I bring a sword on that land, and say, 'Sword, go through the land,' and I cut off *man and beast* from it
Ezek 14:19 Or if I send a pestilence into that land and pour out My fury on it in blood, and cut off from it *man and beast*
Ezek 14:21 How much more it shall be when I send My four severe judgments on Jerusalem the sword and famine and wild beasts and pestilence to cut off *man and beast* from it
Ezek 25:13 I will also stretch out My hand against Edom, cut off *man and beast* from it, and make it desolate from Teman
Ezek 29:8 Surely I will bring a sword upon you and cut off from you *man and beast*
Ezek 36:11 I will multiply upon you *man and beast;* and they shall increase and bear young
Jon 3:8 But let *man and beast* be covered with sackcloth, and cry mightily to God
Zeph 1:3 I will consume *man and beast;* I will consume the birds of the heavens, the fish of the sea, and the stumbling blocks along with the wicked

MAN BECAME A LIVING BEING
Gen 2:7 And the Lord God formed man of the dust of the ground, and breathed into his nostrils the breath of life; and *man became a living being*

MAN DIGS A PIT (NIV)
(See *WHOEVER DIGS A PIT*)

MAN FROM HEAVEN (NIV)
(See *HEAVENLY MAN*)

MAN FULL OF FAITH
Acts 6:5 And they chose Stephen, a *man full of faith* and the Holy Spirit, and Philip, Prochorus, Nicanor, Timon, Parmenas, and Nicolas, a proselyte from Antioch

MAN IS BORN TO TROUBLE
Job 5:7 yet *man is born to trouble*, as the sparks fly upward

MAN IS LIKE A BREATH
Ps 144:4 *Man is like a breath;* his days are like a passing shadow

MAN IS LIKE TO VANITY (KJV)
(See *MAN IS LIKE A BREATH*)

MAN NOR BEAST
Jer 51:62 then you shall say, 'O Lord, You have spoken against this place to cut it off, so that none shall remain in it, neither *man nor beast*, but it shall be desolate forever
Jon 3:7 And he caused it to be proclaimed and published throughout Nineveh by the decree of the king and his nobles, saying, "Let neither *man nor beast*, herd nor flock, taste anything

MAN OF DISCRETION (RSV)
(See *MAN OF UNDERSTANDING*)

MAN OF DUST
1Cor 15:48 As was the *man of dust*, so also are those who are made of dust
1Cor 15:49 And as we have borne the image of the *man of dust*, we shall also bear the image of the heavenly Man

MAN OF GOD
Deut 33:1 Now this is the blessing with which Moses the *man of God* blessed the children of Israel before his death
Josh 14:6 You know the word which the Lord said to Moses the *man of God* concerning you and me in Kadesh Barnea
Judg 13:6 So the woman came and told her husband, saying, "A *Man of God* came to me, and His countenance was like the countenance of the Angel of God, very awesome
Judg 13:8 Then Manoah prayed to the Lord, and said, "O my Lord, please let the *Man of God* whom You sent come to us again and teach us what we shall do for the child who will be born
1Sam 2:27 Then a *man of God* came to Eli and said to him
1Sam 9:6 And he said to him, "Look now, there is in this city a *man of God*, and he is an honorable man
1Sam 9:7 For the bread in our vessels is all gone, and there is no present to bring to the *man of God*
1Sam 9:8 I will give that to the *man of God*, to tell us our way
1Sam 9:10 So they went to the city where the *man of God* was
1Kin 12:22 But the word of God came to Shemaiah the *man of God*, saying
1Kin 13:1 And behold, a *man of God* went from Judah to Bethel by the word of the Lord, and Jeroboam stood by the altar to burn incense
1Kin 13:4 So it came to pass when King Jeroboam heard the saying of the *man of God*, who cried out against the altar in Bethel, that he stretched out his hand from the altar, saying
1Kin 13:5 The altar also was split apart, and the ashes poured out from the altar, according to the sign which the *man of God* had given by the word of the Lord

1Kin 13:6 Then the king answered and said to the *man of God*, "Please entreat the favor of the Lord your God, and pray for me, that my hand may be restored to me." So the *man of God* entreated the Lord, and the king's hand was restored to him, and became as it was before
1Kin 13:7 Then the king said to the *man of God*, "Come home with me and refresh yourself, and I will give you a reward
1Kin 13:8 But the *man of God* said to the king, "If you were to give me half your house, I would not go in with you
1Kin 13:11 Now an old prophet dwelt in Bethel, and his sons came and told him all the works that the *man of God* had done that day in Bethel
1Kin 13:12 For his sons had seen which way the *man of God* went who came from Judah
1Kin 13:14 and went after the *man of God*, and found him sitting under an oak. Then he said to him, "Are you the *man of God* who came from Judah
1Kin 13:21 and he cried out to the *man of God* who came from Judah, saying
1Kin 13:26 So when the prophet who had brought him back from the way heard it, he said, "It is the *man of God* who was disobedient to the word of the Lord
1Kin 13:29 And the prophet took up the corpse of the *man of God*, laid it on the donkey, and brought it back
1Kin 13:31 So it was, after he had buried him, that he spoke to his sons, saying, "When I am dead, then bury me in the tomb where the *man of God* is buried
1Kin 17:18 So she said to Elijah, "What have I to do with you, O *man of God*
1Kin 17:24 Then the woman said to Elijah, "Now by this I know that you are a *man of God*, and that the word of the Lord in your mouth is the truth
1Kin 20:28 Then a *man of God* came and spoke to the king of Israel, and said
2Kin 1:9 And he spoke to him: "*Man of God*, the king has said, 'Come down
2Kin 1:10 So Elijah answered and said to the captain of fifty, "If I am a *man of God*, then let fire come down from heaven and consume you and your fifty men
2Kin 1:11 *Man of God*, thus has the king said, 'Come down quickly
2Kin 1:12 So Elijah answered and said to them, "If I am a *man of God*, let fire come down from heaven and consume you and your fifty men
2Kin 1:13 *Man of God*, please let my life and the life of these fifty servants of yours be precious in your sight
2Kin 4:7 Then she came and told the *man of God*. And he said
2Kin 4:9 And she said to her husband, "Look now, I know that this is a holy *man of God*, who passes by us regularly
2Kin 4:16 And she said, "No, my lord. *Man of God*, do not lie to your maidservant
2Kin 4:21 And she went up and laid him on the bed of the *man of God*, shut the door upon him, and went out
2Kin 4:22 Then she called to her husband, and said, "Please send me one of the young men and one of the donkeys, that I may run to the *man of God* and come back
2Kin 4:25 So she departed, and went to the *man of God* at Mount Carmel. And so it was, when the *man of God* saw her afar off, that he said to his servant Gehazi
2Kin 4:27 Now when she came to the *man of God* at the hill, she caught him by the feet, but Gehazi came near to push her away. But the *man of God* said
2Kin 4:40 Now it happened, as they were eating the stew, that they cried out and said, "O *man of God*, there is death in the pot
2Kin 4:42 Then a man came from Baal Shalisha, and brought the *man of God* bread of the first-fruits, twenty loaves of barley bread, and newly ripened grain in his knapsack
2Kin 5:8 So it was, when Elisha the *man of God* heard that the king of Israel had torn his clothes, that he sent to the king, saying
2Kin 5:14 So he went down and dipped seven times in the Jordan, according to the saying of the *man of God*
2Kin 5:15 Then he returned to the *man of God*, he and all his aides, and came and stood before him
2Kin 5:20 But Gehazi, the servant of Elisha the *man of God*, said
2Kin 6:6 And the *man of God* said, "Where did it fall
2Kin 6:9 And the *man of God* sent to the king of Israel, saying
2Kin 6:10 Then the king of Israel sent someone to the place of which the *man of God* had told him
2Kin 6:15 And when the servant of the *man of God* arose early and went out, there was an army, surrounding the city with horses and chariots
2Kin 7:2 So an officer on whose hand the king leaned answered the *man of God* and said
2Kin 7:17 But the people trampled him in the gate, and he died, just as the *man of God* had said, who spoke when the king came down to him
2Kin 7:18 So it happened just as the *man of God* had spoken to the king, saying
2Kin 7:19 Then that officer had answered the *man of God*, and said
2Kin 8:2 So the woman arose and did according to the saying of the *man of God*, and she went with her household and sojourned in the land of the Philistines seven years
2Kin 8:4 Then the king talked with Gehazi, the servant of the *man of God*, saying
2Kin 8:7 and it was told him, saying, "The *man of God* has come here
2Kin 8:8 And the king said to Hazael, "Take a present in your hand, and go to meet the *man of God*, and inquire of the Lord by him, saying
2Kin 8:11 Then he set his countenance in a stare until he was ashamed; and the *man of God* wept
2Kin 13:19 And the *man of God* was angry with him, and said
2Kin 23:16 And he sent and took the bones out of the tombs and burned them on the altar, and defiled it according to the word of the Lord which the *man of God* proclaimed, who proclaimed these words
2Kin 23:17 And the men of the city told him, "It is the tomb of the *man of God* who came from Judah and proclaimed these things which you have done against the altar of Bethel
1Chr 23:14 Now the sons of Moses the *man of God* were reckoned to the tribe of Levi
2Chr 8:14 as the duty of each day required, and the gatekeepers by their divisions at each gate; for so David the *man of God* had commanded
2Chr 11:2 But the word of the Lord came to Shemaiah the *man of God*, saying
2Chr 25:7 But a *man of God* came to him, saying, "O king, do not let the army of Israel go with you, for the Lord is not with Israel not with any of the children of Ephraim
2Chr 25:9 Then Amaziah said to the *man of God*,

"But what shall we do about the hundred talents which I have given to the troops of Israel?" And the *man of God* answered

2Chr 30:16 They stood in their place according to their custom, according to the Law of Moses the *man of God*

Ezra 3:2 Then Jeshua the son of Jozadak and his brethren the priests, and Zerubbabel the son of Shealtiel and his brethren, arose and built the altar of the God of Israel, to offer burnt offerings on it, as it is written in the Law of Moses the *man of God*

Neh 12:24 And the heads of the Levites were Hashabiah, Sherebiah, and Jeshua the son of Kadmiel, with their brothers across from them, to praise and give thanks, group alternating with group, according to the command of David the *man of God*

Neh 12:36 and his brethren, Shemaiah, Azarel, Milalai, Gilalai, Maai, Nethaneal, Judah, and Hanani, with the musical instruments of David the *man of God*

Jer 35:4 and I brought them into the house of the Lord, into the chamber of the sons of Hanan the son of Igdaliah, a *man of God*, which was by the chamber of the princes, above the chamber of Maaseiah the son of Shallum, the keeper of the door

1Tim 6:11 But you, O *man of God*, flee these things and pursue righteousness, godliness, faith, love, patience, gentleness

2Tim 3:17 that the *man of God* may be complete, thoroughly equipped for every good work

MAN OF HEAVEN (RSV)
(See *HEAVENLY MAN*)

MAN OF INTEGRITY (NIV)
(See *FAITHFUL MAN*)

MAN OF SORROWS

Is 53:3 He is despised and rejected by men, a *man of sorrows* and acquainted with grief

MAN OF UNCLEAN LIPS

Is 6:5 Because I am a *man of unclean lips*, and I dwell in the midst of a people of unclean lips

MAN OF UNDERSTANDING

Ezra 8:18 Then, by the good hand of our God upon us, they brought us a *man of understanding*, of the sons of Mahli the son of Levi, the son of Israel, namely Sherebiah, with his sons and brothers, eighteen men

Prov 1:5 A wise man will hear and increase learning, and a *man of understanding* will attain wise counsel

Prov 10:23 To do evil is like sport to a fool, but a *man of understanding* has wisdom

Prov 11:12 He who is devoid of wisdom despises his neighbor, but a *man of understanding* holds his peace

Prov 15:21 Folly is joy to him who is destitute of discernment, but a *man of understanding* walks uprightly

Prov 17:27 He who has knowledge spares his words, and a *man of understanding* is of a calm spirit

Prov 20:5 Counsel in the heart of man is like deep water, but a *man of understanding* will draw it out

Prov 28:2 but by a *man of understanding* and knowledge right will be prolonged

MAN OF WAR

Ex 15:3 The Lord is a *man of war;* the Lord is His name

Josh 17:1 namely for Machir the firstborn of Manasseh, the father of Gilead, because he was a *man of war*

1Sam 16:18 Then one of the servants answered and said, "Look, I have seen a son of Jesse the Bethlehemite, who is skillful in playing, a mighty man of valor, a *man of war*, prudent in speech, and a handsome person

1Sam 17:33 for you are but a youth, and he a *man of war* from his youth

2Sam 17:8 and your father is a *man of war*, and will not camp with the people

1Chr 28:3 But God said to me, 'You shall not build a house for My name, because you have been a *man of war* and have shed blood

Is 3:2 the mighty man and the *man of war*, the judge and the prophet, and the diviner and the elder

Is 42:13 He shall stir up His zeal like a *man of war*

MAN OF WISDOM (NIV)
(See *WISE MAN*)

MAN REAPS WHAT HE SOWS (NIV)
(See *WHATEVER A MAN SOWS*)

MAN SENT FROM GOD

John 1:6 There was a *man sent from God*, whose name was John

MAN SHALL NOT LIVE BY BREAD ALONE

Deut 8:3 So He humbled you, allowed you to hunger, and fed you with manna which you did not know nor did your fathers know, that He might make you know that *man shall not live by bread alone*

Matt 4:4 But He answered and said, "It is written, '*Man shall not live by bread alone*, but by every word that proceeds from the mouth of God

Luke 4:4 But Jesus answered him, saying, "It is written, '*Man shall not live by bread alone*, but by every word of God

MAN WHO IS A ROMAN

Acts 22:25 And as they bound him with thongs, Paul said to the centurion who stood by, "Is it lawful for you to scourge a *man who is a Roman*, and uncondemned

MAN WHO IS BORN OF WOMAN

Job 14:1 *Man who is born of woman* is of few days and full of trouble

MAN WHO IS WEAK IN FAITH, WELCOME HIM (RSV)
(See *RECEIVE ONE WHO IS WEAK*)

MANIFESTATION OF THE SPIRIT

1Cor 12:7 But the *manifestation of the Spirit* is given to each one for the profit of all

MANIFESTED IN THE FLESH

1Tim 3:16 God was *manifested in the flesh*, justified in the Spirit, seen by angels, preached among the Gentiles, believed on in the world, received up in glory

MANIFOLD WISDOM OF GOD

Eph 3:10 to the intent that now the *manifold wisdom of God* might be made known by the church to the principalities and powers in the heavenly places

MANTLE OF ELIJAH

2Kin 2:13 He also took up the *mantle of Elijah* that had fallen from him, and went back and stood by the bank of the Jordan

2Kin 2:14 Then he took the *mantle of Elijah* that

had fallen from him, and struck the water, and said

MANY ARE CALLED, BUT FEW ARE CHOSEN
Matt 22:14 For *many are called, but few are chosen*

MANY OTHER THINGS THAT JESUS DID
John 21:25 And there are also *many other things that Jesus did*, which if they were written one by one, I suppose that even the world itself could not contain the books that would be written

MANY TIMES AND IN VARIOUS WAYS (NIV)
(See *VARIOUS TIMES AND IN DIFFERENT WAYS*)

MARCHED AROUND THE CITY
Josh 6:14 And the second day they *marched around the city* once and returned to the camp
Josh 6:15 But it came to pass on the seventh day that they rose early, about the dawning of the day, and *marched around the city* seven times in the same manner. On that day only they *marched around the city* seven times

MARITAL UNFAITHFULNESS (NIV)
(See *SEXUAL IMMORALITY*)

MARK OF THE BEAST
Rev 16:2 So the first went and poured out his bowl upon the earth, and a foul and loathsome sore came upon the men who had the *mark of the beast* and those who worshiped his image
Rev 19:20 Then the beast was captured, and with him the false prophet who worked signs in his presence, by which he deceived those who received the *mark of the beast* and those who worshiped his image

MARK ON YOUR HAND (RSV)
(See *SIGN ON YOUR HAND*)

MARRIAGE FEAST (RSV)
(See *WEDDING FEAST*)

MARRIAGE IS HONORABLE
Heb 13:4 *Marriage is honorable* among all, and the bed undefiled; but fornicators and adulterers God will judge

MARRIAGE SUPPER OF THE LAMB
Rev 19:9 Blessed are those who are called to the *marriage supper of the Lamb*

MARVELOUS IN OUR EYES
Ps 118:23 This was the Lord's doing; it is *marvelous in our eyes*
Matt 21:42 This was the Lord's doing, and it is *marvelous in our eyes*
Mark 12:11 This was the Lord's doing, and it is *marvelous in our eyes*

MASTER IN HEAVEN
Col 4:1 Masters, give your servants what is just and fair, knowing that you also have a *Master in heaven*

MASTER OF THE HOUSE
Ex 22:8 If the thief is not found, then the *master of the house* shall be brought to the judges to see whether he has put his hand into his neighbor's goods
Judg 19:22 They spoke to the *master of the house*, the old man, saying
Judg 19:23 But the man, the *master of the house*, went out to them and said to them
Matt 10:25 If they have called the *master of the house* Beelzebub, how much more will they call those of his household
Matt 24:43 But know this, that if the *master of the house* had known what hour the thief would come, he would have watched and not allowed his house to be broken into
Mark 13:35 Watch therefore, for you do not know when the *master of the house* is coming in the evening, at midnight, at the crowing of the rooster, or in the morning
Mark 14:14 And wherever he goes in, say to the *master of the house*
Luke 12:39 But know this, that if the *master of the house* had known what hour the thief would come, he would have watched and not allowed his house to be broken into
Luke 13:25 When once the *Master of the house* has risen up and shut the door, and you begin to stand outside and knock at the door, saying
Luke 14:21 Then the *master of the house*, being angry, said to his servant
Luke 22:11 Then you shall say to the *master of the house*

MASTER'S HOUSE (NAS, NIV, RSV)
(See *LORD'S HOUSE*)

MATURE MANHOOD (RSV)
(See *PERFECT MAN*)

MAY THE LORD JUDGE BETWEEN ME AND YOU (RSV)
(See *LET THE LORD JUDGE BETWEEN YOU AND ME*)

MAY THE LORD REWARD YOU
1Sam 24:19 Therefore *may the Lord reward you* with good for what you have done to me this day

MAY THIS NEVER BE (NIV)
(See *CERTAINLY NOT*)

MAY YOU PROSPER GREATLY (NIV)
(See *PEACE BE MULTIPLIED TO YOU*)

MEANINGLESS! MEANINGLESS (NIV)
(See *VANITY OF VANITIES*)

MEASURE OF FAITH
Rom 12:3 For I say, through the grace given to me, to everyone who is among you, not to think of himself more highly than he ought to think, but to think soberly, as God has dealt to each one a *measure of faith*

MEASURE YOU GIVE (RSV)
(See *WITH THE SAME MEASURE*)

MEASURED THE WATERS
Is 40:12 Who has *measured the waters* in the hollow of his hand, measured heaven with a span and calculated the dust of the earth in a measure

MEASURING LINE
2Kin 21:13 And I will stretch over Jerusalem the *measuring line* of Samaria and the plummet of the house of Ahab
Is 28:17 Also I will make justice the *measuring line*, and righteousness the plummet
Is 34:17 He has cast the lot for them, and His hand has divided it among them with a *measuring line*
Jer 52:21 the height of one pillar was eighteen cubits, a *measuring line* of twelve cubits could measure its circumference, and its thickness was four fingers
Zech 2:1 Then I raised my eyes and looked, and behold, a man with a *measuring line* in his hand

MEAT COMMENDETH US NOT (KJV)
(See *FOOD DOES NOT COMMEND US*)

MEAT WHICH PERISHETH (KJV)
(See *FOOD WHICH PERISHES*)

MEATS OFFERED TO IDOLS (KJV)
(See *THINGS OFFERED TO IDOLS*)

MEDIATOR BETWEEN GOD AND MEN
1Tim 2:5 For there is one God and one *Mediator between God and men*, the Man Christ Jesus

MEDIATOR OF THE NEW COVENANT
Heb 9:15 And for this reason He is the *Mediator of the new covenant*, by means of death, for the redemption of the transgressions under the first covenant, that those who are called may receive the promise of the eternal inheritance
Heb 12:24 to Jesus the *Mediator of the new covenant*, and to the blood of sprinkling that speaks better things than that of Abel

MEDITATE IN THY STATUTES (KJV)
(See *MEDITATE ON YOUR WORD*)

MEDITATE ON THESE THINGS
Phil 4:8 Finally, brethren, whatever things are true, whatever things are noble, whatever things are just, whatever things are pure, whatever things are lovely, whatever things are of good report, if there is any virtue and if there is anything praiseworthy *meditate on these things*
1Tim 4:15 *Meditate on these things;* give yourself entirely to them, that your progress may be evident to all

MEDITATE ON YOUR DECREES (NIV)
(See *MEDITATE ON YOUR WORD*)

MEDITATE ON YOUR PRECEPTS
Ps 119:15 I will *meditate on Your precepts*, and contemplate Your ways
Ps 119:78 Let the proud be ashamed, for they treated me wrongfully with falsehood; but I will *meditate on Your precepts*

MEDITATE ON YOUR WORD
Ps 119:148 My eyes are awake through the night watches, that I may *meditate on Your word*

MEDIUMS AND SPIRITISTS
2Kin 23:24 Moreover Josiah put away those who consulted *mediums and spiritists*, the household gods and idols, all the abominations that were seen in the land of Judah and in Jerusalem, that he might perform the words of the law which were written in the book that Hilkiah the priest found in the house of the Lord
2Chr 33:6 he practiced soothsaying, used witchcraft and sorcery, and consulted *mediums and spiritists*

MEDIUMS AND THE WIZARDS (RSV)
(See *MEDIUMS AND SPIRITISTS*)

MEEK AND LOWLY IN HEART (KJV)
(See *GENTLE AND LOWLY IN HEART*)

MEEK, AND SITTING UPON AN ASS (KJV)
(See *LOWLY, AND SITTING ON A DONKEY*)

MEEK OF THE EARTH
Is 11:4 but with righteousness He shall judge the poor, and decide with equity for the *meek of the earth*
Zeph 2:3 Seek the Lord, all you *meek of the earth*, who have upheld His justice

MEEK SHALL INHERIT THE EARTH
Ps 37:11 But the *meek shall inherit the earth*, and shall delight themselves in the abundance of peace

MEET ALL YOUR NEEDS (NIV)
(See *SUPPLY ALL YOUR NEED*)

MEET FOR REPENTANCE (KJV)
(See *WORTHY OF REPENTANCE*)

MEET THE LORD IN THE AIR
1Th 4:17 Then we who are alive and remain shall be caught up together with them in the clouds to *meet the Lord in the air*

MEET WITH GOD (NIV)
(See *APPEAR BEFORE GOD*)

MELT LIKE WAX
Ps 97:5 The mountains *melt like wax* at the presence of the Lord, at the presence of the Lord of the whole earth

MELT WITH FERVENT HEAT
2Pet 3:10 But the day of the Lord will come as a thief in the night, in which the heavens will pass away with a great noise, and the elements will *melt with fervent heat*
2Pet 3:12 looking for and hastening the coming of the day of God, because of which the heavens will be dissolved being on fire, and the elements will *melt with fervent heat*

MEMBER OF THE COMMUNITY (NIV)
(See *COMMON PEOPLE*)

MEMBERS OF CHRIST
1Cor 6:15 Do you not know that your bodies are *members of Christ?* Shall I then take the *members of Christ* and make them members of a harlot

MEMBERS OF HIS BODY
Eph 5:30 For we are *members of His body*, of His flesh and of His bones

MEMBERS OF ONE ANOTHER
Rom 12:5 so we, being many, are one body in Christ, and individually *members of one another*
Eph 4:25 Therefore, putting away lying, each one speak truth with his neighbor, for we are *members of one another*

MEMBERS OF THE BODY
1Cor 12:22 No, much rather, those *members of the body* which seem to be weaker are necessary
1Cor 12:23 And those *members of the body* which we think to be less honorable, on these we bestow greater honor

MEN AND ANIMALS (NIV)
(See *MAN AND BEAST*)

MEN AND BRETHREN
Acts 1:16 *Men and brethren*, this Scripture had to be fulfilled, which the Holy Spirit spoke before by the mouth of David concerning Judas, who became a guide to those who arrested Jesus
Acts 2:29 *Men and brethren*, let me speak freely to you of the patriarch David, that he is both dead and buried, and his tomb is with us to this day
Acts 2:37 Now when they heard this, they were cut to the heart, and said to Peter and the rest of the apostles, "*Men and brethren*, what shall we do
Acts 7:2 And he said, "*Men and brethren* and fa-

thers, listen: The God of glory appeared to our father Abraham when he was in Mesopotamia, before he dwelt in Haran
Acts 13:15 And after the reading of the Law and the Prophets, the rulers of the synagogue sent to them, saying, "*Men and brethren*, if you have any word of exhortation for the people, say on
Acts 13:26 *Men and brethren*, sons of the family of Abraham, and those among you who fear God, to you the word of this salvation has been sent
Acts 15:7 *Men and brethren*, you know that a good while ago God chose among us, that by my mouth the Gentiles should hear the word of the gospel and believe
Acts 15:13 And after they had become silent, James answered, saying, "*Men and brethren*, listen to me
Acts 23:1 Then Paul, looking earnestly at the council, said, "*Men and brethren*, I have lived in all good conscience before God until this day
Acts 23:6 But when Paul perceived that one part were Sadducees and the other Pharisees, he cried out in the council, "*Men and brethren*, I am a Pharisee, the son of a Pharisee
Acts 28:17 *Men and brethren*, though I have done nothing against our people or the customs of our fathers, yet I was delivered as a prisoner from Jerusalem into the hands of the Romans

MEN OF CORRUPT MINDS
1Tim 6:5 useless wranglings of *men of corrupt minds* and destitute of the truth, who suppose that godliness is a means of gain
2Tim 3:8 Now as Jannes and Jambres resisted Moses, so do these also resist the truth: *men of corrupt minds*, disapproved concerning the faith

MEN OF ISRAEL
Num 13:24 The place was called the Valley of Eshcol, because of the cluster which the *men of Israel* cut down there
Deut 27:14 And the Levites shall speak with a loud voice and say to all the *men of Israel*
Deut 29:10 your leaders and your tribes and your elders and your officers, all the *men of Israel*
Josh 9:6 And they went to Joshua, to the camp at Gilgal, and said to him and to the *men of Israel*
Josh 9:7 But the *men of Israel* said to the Hivites, "Perhaps you dwell among us
Josh 9:14 Then the *men of Israel* took some of their provisions
Josh 10:24 So it was, when they brought out those kings to Joshua, that Joshua called for all the *men of Israel*, and said to the captains of the men of war who went with him
Judg 7:23 And the *men of Israel* gathered together from Naphtali, Asher, and all Manasseh, and pursued the Midianites
Judg 8:22 Then the *men of Israel* said to Gideon, "Rule over us, both you and your son, and your grandson also
Judg 9:55 And when the *men of Israel* saw that Abimelech was dead, they departed, every man to his own place
Judg 20:11 So all the *men of Israel* were gathered against the city, united together as one man
Judg 20:17 Now besides Benjamin, the *men of Israel* numbered four hundred thousand men who drew the sword
Judg 20:20 And the *men of Israel* went out to battle against Benjamin, and the *men of Israel* put themselves in battle array to fight against them at Gibeah
Judg 20:22 And the people, that is, the *men of Israel*, encouraged themselves and again formed the battle line at the place where they had put themselves in array on the first day
Judg 20:31 They began to strike down and kill some of the people, as at the other times, in the highways (one of which goes up to Bethel and the other to Gibeah) and in the field, about thirty *men of Israel*
Judg 20:33 So all the *men of Israel* rose from their place and put themselves in battle array at Baal Tamar
Judg 20:36 The *men of Israel* had given ground to the Benjamites, because they relied on the men in ambush whom they had set against Gibeah
Judg 20:38 Now the appointed signal between the *men of Israel* and the men in ambush was that they would make a great cloud of smoke rise up from the city
Judg 20:39 whereupon the *men of Israel* would turn in battle. Now Benjamin had begun to strike and kill about thirty of the *men of Israel*
Judg 20:41 And when the *men of Israel* turned back, the men of Benjamin panicked, for they saw that disaster had come upon them
Judg 20:42 Therefore they turned their backs before the *men of Israel* in the direction of the wilderness
Judg 20:48 And the *men of Israel* turned back against the children of Benjamin, and struck them down with the edge of the sword from every city, men and beasts, all who were found
Judg 21:1 Now the *men of Israel* had sworn an oath at Mizpah, saying
1Sam 7:11 And the *men of Israel* went out of Mizpah and pursued the Philistines, and drove them back as far as below Beth Car
1Sam 8:22 And Samuel said to the *men of Israel*, "Every man go to his city
1Sam 11:15 There they made sacrifices of peace offerings before the Lord, and there Saul and all the *men of Israel* rejoiced greatly
1Sam 13:2 Saul chose for himself three thousand *men of Israel*. Two thousand were with Saul in Michmash and in the mountains of Bethel, and a thousand were with Jonathan in Gibeah of Benjamin
1Sam 13:6 When the *men of Israel* saw that they were in danger (for the people were distressed
1Sam 14:22 Likewise all the *men of Israel* who had hidden in the mountains of Ephraim, when they heard that the Philistines fled, they also followed hard after them in the battle
1Sam 14:24 And the *men of Israel* were distressed that day, for Saul had placed the people under oath, saying
1Sam 17:2 And Saul and the *men of Israel* were gathered together, and they encamped in the Valley of Elah, and drew up in battle array against the Philistines
1Sam 17:19 Now Saul and they and all the *men of Israel* were in the Valley of Elah, fighting with the Philistines
1Sam 17:24 And all the *men of Israel*, when they saw the man, fled from him and were dreadfully afraid
1Sam 17:25 So the *men of Israel* said, "Have you seen this man who has come up
1Sam 17:52 Now the *men of Israel* and Judah arose and shouted, and pursued the Philistines as far as the entrance of the valley and to the gates of Ekron
1Sam 26:2 Then Saul arose and went down to the Wilderness of Ziph, having three thousand chosen *men of Israel* with him, to seek David in the Wilderness of Ziph
1Sam 31:1 and the *men of Israel* fled from before the Philistines, and fell slain on Mount Gilboa
1Sam 31:7 And when the *men of Israel* who were on the other side of the valley, and those who were on the other side of the Jordan, saw that the *men of Israel* had fled and that Saul and his sons were dead, they forsook the cities and fled

2Sam 2:17 So there was a very fierce battle that day, and Abner and the *men of Israel* were beaten before the servants of David
2Sam 6:1 Again David gathered all the choice *men of Israel*, thirty thousand
2Sam 10:9 When Joab saw that the battle line was against him before and behind, he chose some of the choice *men of Israel* and put them in battle array against the Syrians
2Sam 15:6 So Absalom stole the hearts of the *men of Israel*
2Sam 15:13 And a messenger came to David, saying, "The hearts of the *men of Israel* are with Absalom
2Sam 16:15 Meanwhile Absalom and all the people, the *men of Israel*, came to Jerusalem
2Sam 16:18 And Hushai said to Absalom, "No, but whom the Lord and this people and all the *men of Israel* choose, his I will be, and with him I will remain
2Sam 17:14 So Absalom and all the *men of Israel* said, "The counsel of Hushai the Archite is better than the counsel of Ahithophel
2Sam 17:24 And Absalom crossed over the Jordan, he and all the *men of Israel* with him
2Sam 19:41 Just then all the *men of Israel* came to the king, and said to the king
2Sam 19:42 So all the men of Judah answered the *men of Israel*
2Sam 19:43 And the *men of Israel* answered the men of Judah, and said, "We have ten shares in the king; therefore we also have more right to David than you. Why then do you despise us were we not the first to advise bringing back our king?" Yet the words of the men of Judah were fiercer than the words of the *men of Israel*
2Sam 23:9 And after him was Eleazar the son of Dodo, the Ahohite, one of the three mighty men with David when they defied the Philistines who were gathered there for battle, and the *men of Israel* had retreated
1Kin 8:2 And all the *men of Israel* assembled to King Solomon at the feast in the month of Ethanim, which is the seventh month
1Chr 10:1 and the *men of Israel* fled from before the Philistines, and fell slain on Mount Gilboa
1Chr 10:7 And when all the *men of Israel* who were in the valley saw that they had fled and that Saul and his sons were dead, they forsook their cities and fled
1Chr 19:10 When Joab saw that the battle line was set against him before and behind, he chose some of the choice *men of Israel*, and put them in battle array against the Syrians
1Chr 21:14 So the Lord sent a plague upon Israel, and seventy thousand *men of Israel* fell
2Chr 5:3 Therefore all the *men of Israel* assembled together with the king at the feast, which was in the seventh month
2Chr 13:17 so five hundred thousand choice *men of Israel* fell slain
Ezra 7:28 and I gathered chief *men of Israel* to go up with me
Ps 78:31 The wrath of God came against them, and slew the stoutest of them, and struck down the choice *men of Israel*
Is 41:14 Fear not, you worm Jacob, you *men of Israel!* I will help you
Acts 2:22 *Men of Israel*, hear these words: Jesus of Nazareth, a Man attested by God to you by miracles, wonders, and signs which God did through Him in your midst, as you yourselves also know
Acts 3:12 *Men of Israel*, why do you marvel at this? Or why look so intently at us, as though by our own power or godliness we had made this man walk
Acts 5:35 *Men of Israel*, take heed to yourselves what you intend to do regarding these men
Acts 13:16 Then Paul stood up, and motioning with his hand said, "*Men of Israel*, and you who fear God, listen
Acts 21:28 crying out, "*Men of Israel*, help! This is the man who teaches all men everywhere against the people, the law, and this place

MEN OF LITTLE FAITH (NAS, RSV)
(See *YOU OF LITTLE FAITH*)

MEN OF OLD (NIV)
(See *FORMER THINGS*)

MEN OF SODOM
Gen 13:13 But the *men of Sodom* were exceedingly wicked and sinful against the Lord
Gen 19:4 Now before they lay down, the men of the city, the *men of Sodom*, both old and young, all the people from every quarter, surrounded the house

MEN OF VALOR (KJV, RSV)
(See *MIGHTY MEN OF VALOR*)

MEN OF WAR
Num 31:21 Then Eleazar the priest said to the *men of war* who had gone to the battle
Num 31:28 And levy a tribute for the Lord on the *men of war* who went out to battle
Num 31:32 And the booty remaining from the plunder, which the *men of war* had taken, was six hundred and seventy-five thousand sheep
Num 31:49 and they said to Moses, "Your servants have taken a count of the *men of war* who are under our command, and not a man of us is missing
Num 31:53 (The *men of war* had taken spoil, every man for himself
Deut 2:14 And the time we took to come from Kadesh Barnea until we crossed over the Valley of the Zered was thirty-eight years, until all the generation of the *men of war* was consumed from the midst of the camp, just as the Lord had sworn to them
Deut 2:16 So it was, when all the *men of war* had finally perished from among the people
Josh 5:4 All the people who came out of Egypt who were males, all the *men of war*, had died in the wilderness on the way, after they had come out of Egypt
Josh 5:6 For the children of Israel walked forty years in the wilderness, till all the people who were *men of war*, who came out of Egypt, were consumed, because they did not obey the voice of the Lord to whom the Lord swore that He would not show them the land which the Lord had sworn to their fathers that He would give us
Josh 6:3 You shall march around the city, all you *men of war*
Josh 10:24 So it was, when they brought out those kings to Joshua, that Joshua called for all the men of Israel, and said to the captains of the *men of war* who went with him
Judg 20:17 Now besides Benjamin, the men of Israel numbered four hundred thousand men who drew the sword; all of these were *men of war*
1Sam 18:5 And Saul set him over the *men of war*, and he was accepted in the sight of all the people and also in the sight of Saul's servants
1Kin 9:22 But of the children of Israel Solomon made no forced laborers, because they were *men of war* and his servants
2Kin 25:4 Then the city wall was broken through, and all the *men of war* fled at night by way of the gate between two walls, which was by the king's

garden, even though the Chaldeans were still encamped all around against the city

2Kin 25:19 He also took out of the city an officer who had charge of the *men of war*, five men of the king's close associates who were found in the city, the principal scribe of the army who mustered the people of the land, and sixty men of the people of the land who were found in the city

1Chr 12:38 All these *men of war*, who could keep ranks, came to Hebron with a loyal heart, to make David king over all Israel

2Chr 8:9 Some were *men of war*, captains of his officers, captains of his chariots, and his cavalry

2Chr 17:13 and the *men of war*, mighty men of valor, were in Jerusalem

Jer 6:23 and they ride on horses, as *men of war* set in array against you, O daughter of Zion

Jer 38:4 Therefore the princes said to the king, "Please, let this man be put to death, for thus he weakens the hands of the *men of war* who remain in this city, and the hands of all the people, by speaking such words to them

Jer 39:4 So it was, when Zedekiah the king of Judah and all the *men of war* saw them, that they fled and went out of the city by night, by way of the king's garden, by the gate between the two walls

Jer 41:3 Ishmael also struck down all the Jews who were with him, that is, with Gedaliah at Mizpah, and the Chaldeans who were found there, the *men of war*

Jer 41:16 Then Johanan the son of Kareah, and all the captains of the forces that were with him, took from Mizpah all the rest of the people whom he had recovered from Ishmael the son of Nethaniah after he had murdered Gedaliah the son of Ahikam the mighty *men of war* and the women and the children and the eunuchs, whom he had brought back from Gibeon

Jer 49:26 Therefore her young men shall fall in her streets, and all the *men of war* shall be cut off in that day

Jer 50:30 Therefore her young men shall fall in the streets, and all her *men of war* shall be cut off in that day

Jer 51:32 The passages are blocked, the reeds they have burned with fire, and the *men of war* are terrified

Jer 52:7 Then the city wall was broken through, and all the *men of war* fled and went out of the city at night by way of the gate between the two walls, which was by the king's garden, even though the Chaldeans were near the city all around

Jer 52:25 He also took out of the city an officer who had charge of the *men of war*, seven men of the king's close associates who were found in the city, the principal scribe of the army who mustered the people of the land, and sixty men of the people of the land who were found in the midst of the city

Ezek 27:10 Those from Persia, Lydia, and Libya were in your army as *men of war*

Ezek 27:27 Your riches, wares, and merchandise, your mariners and pilots, your caulkers and merchandisers, all your *men of war* who are in you, and the entire company which is in your midst, will fall into the midst of the seas on the day of your ruin

Ezek 39:20 You shall be filled at My table with horses and riders, with mighty men and with all the *men of war*

Joel 2:7 They run like mighty men, they climb the wall like *men of war*

Joel 3:9 Wake up the mighty men, let all the *men of war* draw near, let them come up

Luke 23:11 Then Herod, with his *men of war*, treated Him with contempt and mocked Him, arrayed Him in a gorgeous robe, and sent Him back to Pilate

MEN WHO ARE DEPRAVED IN MIND (RSV)
(See *MEN OF CORRUPT MINDS*)

MEN WILL HATE YOU (NIV)
(See *HATED BY ALL*)

MENSERVANTS AND MAIDSERVANTS

Luke 12:45 But if that servant says in his heart, 'My master is delaying his coming,' and begins to beat the *menservants and maidservants*, and to eat and drink and be drunk

MERCIES OF GOD

Rom 12:1 I beseech you therefore, brethren, by the *mercies of God*, that you present your bodies a living sacrifice, holy, acceptable to God, which is your reasonable service

MERCY AND JUSTICE

Ps 101:1 I will sing of *mercy and justice;* to You, O Lord, I will sing praises

Hos 12:6 observe *mercy and justice*, and wait on your God continually

MERCY AND NOT SACRIFICE

Hos 6:6 For I desire *mercy and not sacrifice*, and the knowledge of God more than burnt offerings

Matt 9:13 I desire *mercy and not sacrifice*.' For I did not come to call the righteous, but sinners, to repentance

Matt 12:7 But if you had known what this means, 'I desire *mercy and not sacrifice*

MERCY AND TRUTH

2Sam 15:20 Return, and take your brethren back. *Mercy and truth* be with you

Ps 25:10 All the paths of the Lord are *mercy and truth*, to such as keep His covenant and His testimonies

Ps 61:7 He shall abide before God forever. Oh, prepare *mercy and truth*, which may preserve him

Ps 85:10 *Mercy and truth* have met together; righteousness and peace have kissed each other

Ps 86:15 But You, O Lord, are a God full of compassion, and gracious, longsuffering and abundant in *mercy and truth*

Ps 89:14 Righteousness and justice are the foundation of Your throne; *mercy and truth* go before Your face

Prov 3:3 let not *mercy and truth* forsake you; bind them around your neck, write them on the tablet of your heart

Prov 14:22 but *mercy and truth* belong to those who devise good

Prov 16:6 In *mercy and truth* atonement is provided for iniquity; and by the fear of the Lord one departs from evil

Prov 20:28 *Mercy and truth* preserve the king, and by lovingkindness he upholds his throne

MERCY ENDURES FOREVER

1Chr 16:34 Oh, give thanks to the Lord, for He is good! For His *mercy endures forever*

1Chr 16:41 and with them Heman and Jeduthun and the rest who were chosen, who were designated by name, to give thanks to the Lord, because His *mercy endures forever*

2Chr 5:13 For He is good, for His *mercy endures forever*," that the house, the house of the Lord, was filled with a cloud

2Chr 7:3 When all the children of Israel saw how the fire came down, and the glory of the Lord on the temple, they bowed their faces to the ground on the pavement, and worshiped and praised the

Lord, saying: "For He is good, for His *mercy endures forever*

2Chr 7:6 the Levites also with instruments of the music of the Lord, which King David had made to praise the Lord, saying, "For His *mercy endures forever*

2Chr 20:21 And when he had consulted with the people, he appointed those who should sing to the Lord, and who should praise the beauty of holiness, as they went out before the army and were saying: "Praise the Lord, for His *mercy endures forever*

Ezra 3:11 For He is good, for His *mercy endures forever* toward Israel

Ps 106:1 Oh, give thanks to the Lord, for He is good! For His *mercy endures forever*

Ps 107:1 Oh, give thanks to the Lord, for He is good! For His *mercy endures forever*

Ps 118:1 Oh, give thanks to the Lord, for He is good! Because His *mercy endures forever*

Ps 118:2 Let Israel now say, "His *mercy endures forever*

Ps 118:3 Let the house of Aaron now say, "His *mercy endures forever*

Ps 118:4 Let those who fear the Lord now say, "His *mercy endures forever*

Ps 118:29 Oh, give thanks to the Lord, for He is good! For His *mercy endures forever*

Ps 136:1 Oh, give thanks to the Lord, for He is good! For His *mercy endures forever*

Ps 136:2 Oh, give thanks to the God of gods! For His *mercy endures forever*

Ps 136:3 Oh, give thanks to the Lord of lords! For His *mercy endures forever*

Ps 136:4 To Him who alone does great wonders, for His *mercy endures forever*

Ps 136:5 To Him who by wisdom made the heavens, for His *mercy endures forever*

Ps 136:6 To Him who laid out the earth above the waters, for His *mercy endures forever*

Ps 136:7 To Him who made great lights, for His *mercy endures forever*

Ps 136:8 The sun to rule by day, for His *mercy endures forever*

Ps 136:9 The moon and stars to rule by night, for His *mercy endures forever*

Ps 136:10 To Him who struck Egypt in their firstborn, for His *mercy endures forever*

Ps 136:11 And brought out Israel from among them, for His *mercy endures forever*

Ps 136:12 With a strong hand, and with an outstretched arm, for His *mercy endures forever*

Ps 136:13 To Him who divided the Red Sea in two, for His *mercy endures forever*

Ps 136:14 And made Israel pass through the midst of it, for His *mercy endures forever*

Ps 136:15 But overthrew Pharaoh and his army in the Red Sea, for His *mercy endures forever*

Ps 136:16 To Him who led His people through the wilderness, for His *mercy endures forever*

Ps 136:17 To Him who struck down great kings, for His *mercy endures forever*

Ps 136:18 And slew famous kings, for His *mercy endures forever*

Ps 136:19 Sihon king of the Amorites, for His *mercy endures forever*

Ps 136:20 And Og king of Bashan, for His *mercy endures forever*

Ps 136:21 And gave their land as a heritage, for His *mercy endures forever*

Ps 136:22 A heritage to Israel His servant, for His *mercy endures forever*

Ps 136:23 Who remembered us in our lowly state, for His *mercy endures forever*

Ps 136:24 And rescued us from our enemies, for His *mercy endures forever*

Ps 136:25 Who gives food to all flesh, for His *mercy endures forever*

Ps 136:26 Oh, give thanks to the God of heaven! For His *mercy endures forever*

Jer 33:11 Praise the Lord of hosts, for the Lord is good, for His *mercy endures forever*

MERCY OF GOD

Ps 52:8 I trust in the *mercy of God* forever and ever

MERCY ON THE NEEDY

Prov 14:31 He who oppresses the poor reproaches his Maker, but he who honors Him has *mercy on the needy*

MERCY ON THE POOR

Prov 14:21 but he who has *mercy on the poor*, happy is he

MERCY REJOICETH AGAINST JUDGMENT (KJV)

(See *MERCY TRIUMPHS OVER JUDGMENT*)

MERCY SEAT

Ex 25:17 You shall make a *mercy seat* of pure gold; two and a half cubits shall be its length and a cubit and a half its width

Ex 25:18 of hammered work you shall make them at the two ends of the *mercy seat*

Ex 25:19 you shall make the cherubim at the two ends of it of one piece with the *mercy seat*

Ex 25:20 And the cherubim shall stretch out their wings above, covering the *mercy seat* with their wings, and they shall face one another; the faces of the cherubim shall be toward the *mercy seat*

Ex 25:21 You shall put the *mercy seat* on top of the ark, and in the ark you shall put the Testimony that I will give you

Ex 25:22 And there I will meet with you, and I will speak with you from above the *mercy seat*, from between the two cherubim which are on the ark of the Testimony, of all things which I will give you in commandment to the children of Israel

Ex 26:34 You shall put the *mercy seat* upon the ark of the Testimony in the Most Holy

Ex 30:6 And you shall put it before the veil that is before the ark of the Testimony, before the *mercy seat* that is over the Testimony, where I will meet with you

Ex 31:7 the tabernacle of meeting, the ark of the Testimony and the *mercy seat* that is on it, and all the furniture of the tabernacle

Ex 35:12 the ark and its poles, with the *mercy seat*, and the veil of the covering

Ex 37:6 He also made the *mercy seat* of pure gold; two and a half cubits was its length and a cubit and a half its width

Ex 37:7 he made them of one piece at the two ends of the *mercy seat*

Ex 37:8 He made the cherubim at the two ends of one piece with the *mercy seat*

Ex 37:9 The cherubim spread out their wings above, and covered the *mercy seat* with their wings. They faced one another; the faces of the cherubim were toward the *mercy seat*

Ex 39:35 the ark of the Testimony with its poles, and the *mercy seat*

Ex 40:20 He took the Testimony and put it into the ark, inserted the poles through the rings of the ark, and put the *mercy seat* on top of the ark

Lev 16:2 Tell Aaron your brother not to come at simply any time into the Holy Place inside the veil, before the *mercy seat* which is on the ark, lest he die; for I will appear in the cloud above the *mercy seat*

Lev 16:13 And he shall put the incense on the fire before the Lord, that the cloud of incense may cover the *mercy seat* that is on the Testimony, lest he die

Lev 16:14 He shall take some of the blood of the bull and sprinkle it with his finger on the *mercy seat* on the east side; and before the *mercy seat* he shall sprinkle some of the blood with his finger seven times
Lev 16:15 Then he shall kill the goat of the sin offering, which is for the people, bring its blood inside the veil, do with that blood as he did with the blood of the bull, and sprinkle it on the *mercy seat* and before the *mercy seat*
Num 7:89 Now when Moses went into the tabernacle of meeting to speak with Him, he heard the voice of One speaking to him from above the *mercy seat* that was on the ark of the Testimony, from between the two cherubim
1Chr 28:11 Then David gave his son Solomon the plans for the vestibule, its houses, its treasuries, its upper chambers, its inner chambers, and the place of the *mercy seat*
Heb 9:5 and above it were the cherubim of glory overshadowing the *mercy seat*

MERCY TRIUMPHS OVER JUDGMENT
Jas 2:13 For judgment is without mercy to the one who has shown no mercy. *Mercy triumphs over judgment*

MESSAGE FROM GOD (NIV)
(See *WORD OF GOD*)

MESSAGE OF RECONCILIATION (NIV, RSV)
(See *WORD OF RECONCILIATION*)

MESSENGER OF GOOD TIDINGS (NIV)
(See *ONE WHO BRINGS GOOD TIDINGS*)

MESSENGER OF THE COVENANT
Mal 3:1 And the Lord, whom you seek, will suddenly come to His temple, even the *Messenger of the covenant*, in whom you delight

METE OUT THE WATERS BY MEASURE
Job 28:25 to establish a weight for the wind, and *mete out the waters by measure*

MIDST OF THE NATIONS
Ezek 5:5 I have set her in the *midst of the nations* and the countries all around her

MIGHTY ACTS
Ps 106:2 Who can utter the *mighty acts* of the Lord? Or can declare all His praise
Ps 145:4 One generation shall praise Your works to another, and shall declare Your *mighty acts*
Ps 145:12 To make known to the sons of men His *mighty acts*, and the glorious majesty of His kingdom
Ps 150:2 Praise Him for His *mighty acts;* praise Him according to His excellent greatness

MIGHTY ACTS OF JUDGMENT (NIV)
(See *GREAT JUDGMENTS*)

MIGHTY AGAINST HIS FOES (RSV)
(See *PREVAIL AGAINST HIS ENEMIES*)

MIGHTY ANGEL
Rev 10:1 And I saw still another *mighty angel* coming down from heaven, clothed with a cloud
Rev 18:21 Then a *mighty angel* took up a stone like a great millstone and threw it into the sea, saying

MIGHTY DEEDS (NAS, RSV)
(See *STRENGTH OF THE LORD*)

MIGHTY DOINGS (RSV)
(See *MIGHTY ACTS*)

MIGHTY GOD
Gen 49:24 But his bow remained in strength, and the arms of his hands were made strong by the hands of the *Mighty God* of Jacob (from there is the Shepherd, the Stone of Israel
Ps 132:2 How he swore to the Lord, and vowed to the *Mighty God* of Jacob
Ps 132:5 Until I find a place for the Lord, a dwelling place for the *Mighty God* of Jacob
Is 9:6 And His name will be called Wonderful, Counselor, *Mighty God*, Everlasting Father, Prince of Peace
Is 10:21 The remnant will return, the remnant of Jacob, to the *Mighty God*
Jer 32:18 You show lovingkindness to thousands, and repay the iniquity of the fathers into the bosom of their children after them the Great, the *Mighty God*, whose name is the Lord of hosts

MIGHTY GOD AND TERRIBLE (KJV)
(See *GREAT AND AWESOME GOD*)

MIGHTY HAND AND AN OUTSTRETCHED ARM
Deut 4:34 Or did God ever try to go and take for Himself a nation from the midst of another nation, by trials, by signs, by wonders, by war, by a *mighty hand and an outstretched arm*, and by great terrors, according to all that the Lord your God did for you in Egypt before your eyes

MIGHTY HUNTER BEFORE THE LORD
Gen 10:9 He was a *mighty hunter before the Lord;* therefore it is said, "Like Nimrod the *mighty hunter before the Lord*

MIGHTY MAN OF VALOR
Judg 6:12 And the Angel of the Lord appeared to him, and said to him, "The Lord is with you, you *mighty man of valor*
Judg 11:1 Now Jephthah the Gileadite was a *mighty man of valor*, but he was the son of a harlot
1Sam 16:18 Then one of the servants answered and said, "Look, I have seen a son of Jesse the Bethlehemite, who is skillful in playing, a *mighty man of valor*, a man of war, prudent in speech, and a handsome person
1Kin 11:28 The man Jeroboam was a *mighty man of valor;* and Solomon, seeing that the young man was industrious, made him the officer over all the labor force of the house of Joseph
2Kin 5:1 He was also a *mighty man of valor*, but he was a leper
2Chr 17:17 Eliada a *mighty man of valor*, and with him two hundred thousand men armed with bow and shield
2Chr 32:21 Then the Lord sent an angel who cut down every *mighty man of valor*, leader, and captain in the camp of the king of Assyria

MIGHTY MEN OF VALOR
Josh 1:14 But you shall pass before your brethren armed, all your *mighty men of valor*, and help them
Josh 6:2 I have given Jericho into your hand, its king, and the *mighty men of valor*
Josh 8:3 and Joshua chose thirty thousand *mighty men of valor* and sent them away by night
Josh 10:7 So Joshua ascended from Gilgal, he and all the people of war with him, and all the *mighty men of valor*

2Kin 24:14 all the captains and all the *mighty men of valor*, ten thousand captives, and all the craftsmen and smiths
1Chr 5:24 They were *mighty men of valor*, famous men, and heads of their fathers' houses
1Chr 7:2 The sons of Tola were *mighty men of valor* in their generations
1Chr 7:5 Now their brethren among all the families of Issachar were *mighty men of valor*, listed by their genealogies, eighty-seven thousand in all
1Chr 7:7 They were heads of their fathers' houses, and they were listed by their genealogies, twenty-two thousand and thirty-four *mighty men of valor*
1Chr 7:9 And they were recorded by genealogy according to their generations, heads of their fathers' houses, twenty thousand two hundred *mighty men of valor*
1Chr 7:11 there were seventeen thousand two hundred *mighty men of valor* fit to go out for war and battle
1Chr 7:40 All these were the children of Asher, heads of their fathers' houses, choice men, *mighty men of valor*, chief leaders
1Chr 8:40 The sons of Ulam were *mighty men of valor* archers
1Chr 12:8 Some Gadites joined David at the stronghold in the wilderness, *mighty men of valor*, men trained for battle, who could handle shield and spear, whose faces were like the faces of lions, and were as swift as gazelles on the mountains
1Chr 12:21 And they helped David against the bands of raiders, for they were all *mighty men of valor*, and they were captains in the army
1Chr 12:25 of the children of Simeon, *mighty men of valor* fit for war, seven thousand one hundred
1Chr 12:30 of the children of Ephraim twenty thousand eight hundred, *mighty men of valor*, famous men throughout their father's house
1Chr 28:1 the officers of the tribes and the captains of the divisions who served the king, the captains over thousands and captains over hundreds, and the stewards over all the substance and possessions of the king and of his sons, with the officials, the valiant men, and all the *mighty men of valor*
2Chr 13:3 Jeroboam also drew up in battle formation against him with eight hundred thousand choice men, *mighty men of valor*
2Chr 14:8 And Asa had an army of three hundred thousand men from Judah who carried shields and spears, and from Benjamin two hundred and eighty thousand men who carried shields and drew bows; all these were *mighty men of valor*
2Chr 17:13 and the men of war, *mighty men of valor*, were in Jerusalem
2Chr 17:14 Adnah the captain, and with him three hundred thousand *mighty men of valor*
2Chr 17:16 and next to him was Amasiah the son of Zichri, who willingly offered himself to the Lord, and with him two hundred thousand *mighty men of valor*
2Chr 25:6 He also hired one hundred thousand *mighty men of valor* from Israel for one hundred talents of silver
2Chr 26:12 The total number of chief officers of the *mighty men of valor* was two thousand six hundred
Neh 11:14 and their brethren, *mighty men of valor*, were one hundred and twenty-eight
Dan 3:20 And he commanded certain *mighty men of valor* who were in his army to bind Shadrach, Meshach, and Abed-Nego, and cast them into the burning fiery furnace

MIGHTY ONE (NAS, NIV, RSV)
(See *MIGHTY GOD*)

MIGHTY POWER OF GOD (KJV)
(See *MAJESTY OF GOD*)

MIGHTY SIGNS AND WONDERS
Rom 15:19 in *mighty signs and wonders*, by the power of the Spirit of God, so that from Jerusalem and round about to Illyricum I have fully preached the gospel of Christ

MIGHTY TO SAVE
Is 63:1 Who is this who comes from Edom, with dyed garments from Bozrah, this One who is glorious in His apparel, traveling in the greatness of His strength? "I who speak in righteousness, *mighty to save*

MIGHTY WARRIOR (NIV)
(See *MIGHTY MAN OF VALOR*)

MIGHTY WATERS
Ex 15:10 You blew with Your wind, the sea covered them; they sank like lead in the *mighty waters*
Neh 9:11 and their persecutors You threw into the deep, as a stone into the *mighty waters*
Is 17:12 Woe to the multitude of many people who make a noise like the roar of the seas, and to the rushing of nations that make a rushing like the rushing of *mighty waters*
Is 28:2 Behold, the Lord has a mighty and strong one, like a tempest of hail and a destroying storm, like a flood of *mighty waters* overflowing, who will bring them down to the earth with His hand
Is 43:16 Thus says the Lord, who makes a way in the sea and a path through the *mighty waters*

MIGHTY WORKS
Matt 11:20 Then He began to upbraid the cities in which most of His *mighty works* had been done, because they did not repent
Matt 11:21 For if the *mighty works* which were done in you had been done in Tyre and Sidon, they would have repented long ago in sackcloth and ashes
Matt 11:23 for if the *mighty works* which were done in you had been done in Sodom, it would have remained until this day
Matt 13:54 And when He had come to His own country, He taught them in their synagogue, so that they were astonished and said, "Where did this Man get this wisdom and these *mighty works*
Matt 13:58 And He did not do many *mighty works* there because of their unbelief
Mark 6:2 And what wisdom is this which is given to Him, that such *mighty works* are performed by His hands
Luke 10:13 For if the *mighty works* which were done in you had been done in Tyre and Sidon, they would have repented a great while ago, sitting in sackcloth and ashes
Luke 19:37 Then, as He was now drawing near the descent of the Mount of Olives, the whole multitude of the disciples began to rejoice and praise God with a loud voice for all the *mighty works* they had seen

MILK AND HONEY
Ex 3:8 So I have come down to deliver them out of the hand of the Egyptians, and to bring them up from that land to a good and large land, to a land flowing with *milk and honey*, to the place of the Canaanites and the Hittites and the Amorites and the Perizzites and the Hivites and the Jebusites

Ex 3:17 and I have said I will bring you up out of the affliction of Egypt to the land of the Canaanites and the Hittites and the Amorites and the Perizzites and the Hivites and the Jebusites, to a land flowing with *milk and honey*
Ex 13:5 And it shall be, when the Lord brings you into the land of the Canaanites and the Hittites and the Amorites and the Hivites and the Jebusites, which He swore to your fathers to give you, a land flowing with *milk and honey*, that you shall keep this service in this month
Ex 33:3 Go up to a land flowing with *milk and honey*
Lev 20:24 But I have said to you, "You shall inherit their land, and I will give it to you to possess, a land flowing with *milk and honey*
Num 13:27 It truly flows with *milk and honey*, and this is its fruit
Num 14:8 If the Lord delights in us, then He will bring us into this land and give it to us, 'a land which flows with *milk and honey*
Num 16:13 Is it a small thing that you have brought us up out of a land flowing with *milk and honey*, to kill us in the wilderness, that you should keep acting like a prince over us
Num 16:14 Moreover you have not brought us into a land flowing with *milk and honey*, nor given us inheritance of fields and vineyards
Deut 6:3 Therefore hear, O Israel, and be careful to observe it, that it may be well with you, and that you may multiply greatly as the Lord God of your fathers has promised you' a land flowing with *milk and honey*
Deut 11:9 and that you may prolong your days in the land which the Lord swore to give your fathers, to them and their descendants, 'a land flowing with *milk and honey*
Deut 26:9 He has brought us to this place and has given us this land, "a land flowing with *milk and honey*
Deut 26:15 Look down from Your holy habitation, from heaven, and bless Your people Israel and the land which You have given us, just as You swore to our fathers, "a land flowing with *milk and honey*
Deut 27:3 You shall write on them all the words of this law, when you have crossed over, that you may enter the land which the Lord your God is giving you, 'a land flowing with *milk and honey*
Deut 31:20 When I have brought them to the land flowing with *milk and honey*, of which I swore to their fathers, and they have eaten and filled themselves and grown fat, then they will turn to other gods and serve them
Josh 5:6 For the children of Israel walked forty years in the wilderness, till all the people who were men of war, who came out of Egypt, were consumed, because they did not obey the voice of the Lord to whom the Lord swore that He would not show them the land which the Lord had sworn to their fathers that He would give us, "a land flowing with *milk and honey*
Jer 11:5 that I may establish the oath which I have sworn to your fathers, to give them a land flowing with *milk and honey*, as it is this day
Jer 32:22 You have given them this land, of which You swore to their fathers to give them "a land flowing with *milk and honey*
Ezek 20:6 On that day I lifted My hand in an oath to them, to bring them out of the land of Egypt into a land that I had searched out for them, flowing with *milk and honey*, the glory of all lands
Ezek 20:15 So I also lifted My hand in an oath to them in the wilderness, that I would not bring them into the land which I had given them, flowing with *milk and honey*, the glory of all lands

MIND CONTROLLED BY THE SPIRIT (NIV)
(See *SPIRITUALLY MINDED*)

MIND COULD NOT REST (RSV)
(See *REST IN MY SPIRIT*)

MIND OF CHRIST
1Cor 2:16 For "Who has known the mind of the Lord that he may instruct Him?" But we have the *mind of Christ*

MIND OF SINFUL MAN (NIV)
(See *CARNALLY MINDED*)

MIND OF THE LORD
Lev 24:12 Then they put him in custody, that the *mind of the Lord* might be shown to them
Rom 11:34 For who has known the *mind of the Lord?* Or who has become His counselor
1Cor 2:16 For "Who has known the *mind of the Lord* that he may instruct Him

MIND ON THE FLESH (RSV)
(See *CARNALLY MINDED*)

MIND WAS TROUBLED (NIV)
(See *SPIRIT WAS TROUBLED*)

MINDFUL OF HIS COVENANT FOR EVER (RSV)
(See *REMEMBER HIS COVENANT ALWAYS*)

MINDS OF FOOLS (RSV)
(See *HEART OF THE FOOL*)

MINE HOUR IS NOT YET COME (KJV)
(See *MY HOUR HAS NOT YET COME*)

MINGLED WITH GALL
Matt 27:34 they gave Him sour wine *mingled with gall* to drink

MINISTER AS PRIESTS
Ex 31:10 the garments of ministry, the holy garments for Aaron the priest and the garments of his sons, to *minister as priests*
Ex 35:19 the garments of ministry, for ministering in the holy place the holy garments for Aaron the priest and the garments of his sons, to *minister as priests*
Ex 39:41 the holy garments for Aaron the priest, and his sons' garments, to *minister as priests*
Num 3:3 These are the names of the sons of Aaron, the anointed priests, whom he consecrated to *minister as priests*

MINISTER BY NIGHT IN THE HOUSE OF THE LORD (NIV)
(See *STAND IN THE HOUSE OF THE LORD*)

MINISTER IN THE HOLY PLACE
Ex 28:43 They shall be on Aaron and on his sons when they come into the tabernacle of meeting, or when they come near the altar to *minister in the holy place*, that they do not incur iniquity and die
Ex 29:30 That son who becomes priest in his place shall put them on for seven days, when he enters the tabernacle of meeting to *minister in the holy place*
Ex 39:41 and the garments of ministry, to *minister in the holy place*

MINISTER IN THE PRIEST'S OFFICE (KJV)
(See *MINISTER AS PRIESTS*)

MINISTER IN THE SANCTUARY
Num 4:12 Then they shall take all the utensils of service with which they *minister in the sanctuary*, put them in a blue cloth, cover them with a covering of badger skins, and put them on a carrying beam
Ezek 44:27 And on the day that he goes to the sanctuary to *minister in the sanctuary*, he must offer his sin offering in the inner court

MINISTER OF CHRIST
Col 1:7 as you also learned from Epaphras, our dear fellow servant, who is a faithful *minister of Christ* on your behalf

MINISTER OF GOD
1Th 3:2 and sent Timothy, our brother and *minister of God*, and our fellow laborer in the gospel of Christ, to establish you and encourage you concerning your faith

MINISTER TO THE LORD
Lev 7:35 This is the consecrated portion for Aaron and his sons, from the offerings made by fire to the Lord, on the day when Moses presented them to *minister to the Lord* as priests
2Chr 13:10 and the priests who *minister to the Lord* are the sons of Aaron, and the Levites attend to their duties
Ezek 45:4 It shall be a holy portion of the land, belonging to the priests, the ministers of the sanctuary, who come near to *minister to the Lord*
Joel 1:9 The grain offering and the drink offering have been cut off from the house of the Lord; the priests mourn, who *minister to the Lord*
Joel 2:17 Let the priests, who *minister to the Lord*, weep between the porch and the altar

MINISTERING IN THE HOLY PLACE
Ex 35:19 the garments of ministry, for *ministering in the holy place* the holy garments for Aaron the priest and the garments of his sons, to minister as priests
Ex 39:1 Of the blue, purple, and scarlet thread they made garments of ministry, for *ministering in the holy place*, and made the holy garments for Aaron, as the Lord had commanded Moses

MINISTERING IN THE HOUSE OF THE LORD (RSV)
(See *SERVE IN THE HOUSE OF THE LORD*)

MINISTERING IN THE SANCTUARY (NIV)
(See *MINISTER IN THE SANCTUARY*)

MINISTERING IN THE TEMPLE OF THE LORD (NIV)
(See *SERVE IN THE HOUSE OF THE LORD*)

MINISTERS OF CHRIST (KJV)
(See *SERVANTS OF CHRIST*)

MINISTERS OF GOD (RSV)
(See *GOD'S MINISTERS*)

MINISTERS OF THE NEW COVENANT
2Cor 3:6 who also made us sufficient as *ministers of the new covenant*, not of the letter but of the Spirit

MINISTRATION OF THE SPIRIT (KJV)
(See *MINISTRY OF THE SPIRIT*)

MINISTRY OF RECONCILIATION
2Cor 5:18 Now all things are of God, who has reconciled us to Himself through Jesus Christ, and has given us the *ministry of reconciliation*

MINISTRY OF THE SAINTS
1Cor 16:15 I urge you, brethren you know the household of Stephanas, that it is the firstfruits of Achaia, and that they have devoted themselves to the *ministry of the saints*

MINISTRY OF THE SPIRIT
2Cor 3:8 how will the *ministry of the Spirit* not be more glorious

MINISTRY OF THE WORD
Acts 6:4 but we will give ourselves continually to prayer and to the *ministry of the word*

MIRACULOUS POWERS (NIV)
(See *WORKING OF MIRACLES*)

MISERY OF MY PEOPLE (NIV)
(See *OPPRESSION OF MY PEOPLE*)

MISLED MY PEOPLE (NAS, RSV)
(See *SEDUCED MY PEOPLE*)

MISSED THE MARK AS REGARDS THE FAITH (RSV)
(See *STRAYED CONCERNING THE FAITH*)

MISUSE THE NAME OF THE LORD (NIV)
(See *TAKE THE NAME OF THE LORD YOUR GOD IN VAIN*)

MISUSES HIS NAME (NIV)
(See *TAKES HIS NAME IN VAIN*)

MIXED WITH GALL (NIV)
(See *MINGLED WITH GALL*)

MOAN LIKE DOVES (NIV)
(See *VOICE OF DOVES*)

MOANING LIKE DOVES (RSV)
(See *VOICE OF DOVES*)

MODEST APPAREL
1Tim 2:9 in like manner also, that the women adorn themselves in *modest apparel*, with propriety and moderation, not with braided hair or gold or pearls or costly clothing

MOLDED IMAGE
Deut 9:12 they have quickly turned aside from the way which I commanded them; they have made themselves a *molded image*
Deut 27:15 Cursed is the one who makes any carved or *molded image*, an abomination to the Lord, the work of the hands of the craftsman, and sets it up in secret
Judg 17:3 So when he had returned the eleven hundred shekels of silver to his mother, his mother said, "I had wholly dedicated the silver from my hand to the Lord for my son, to make a carved image and a *molded image*
Judg 17:4 Then his mother took two hundred shekels of silver and gave them to the silversmith, and he made it into a carved image and a *molded image*
Judg 18:14 Then the five men who had gone to spy out the country of Laish answered and said to their brethren, "Do you know that there are in

these houses an ephod, household idols, a carved image, and a *molded image*

Judg 18:17 Then the five men who had gone to spy out the land went up, and entering there, they took the carved image, the ephod, the household idols, and the *molded image*

Judg 18:18 When these went into Micah's house and took the graven image, the ephod, the household idols, and the *molded image*, the priest said to them

2Kin 17:16 So they left all the commandments of the Lord their God, made for themselves a *molded image* and two calves, made a wooden image and worshiped all the host of heaven, and served Baal

Ps 106:19 They made a calf in Horeb, and worshiped the *molded image*

Is 48:5 before it came to pass I proclaimed it to you, lest you should say, 'My idol has done them, and my carved image and my *molded image* have commanded them

Jer 10:14 for his *molded image* is falsehood, and there is no breath in them

Jer 51:17 for his *molded image* is falsehood, and there is no breath in them

Nah 1:14 Out of the house of your gods I will cut off the carved image and the *molded image*

Hab 2:18 What profit is the image, that its maker should carve it, the *molded image*, a teacher of lies, that the maker of its mold should trust in it, to make mute idols

MOLTEN IMAGE (KJV, NAS, RSV)
(See *MOLDED IMAGE*)

MONSTER OF THE DEEP (NIV)
(See *SEA SERPENT*)

MORE ACCEPTABLE SACRIFICE (RSV)
(See *MORE EXCELLENT SACRIFICE*)

MORE BLESSED TO GIVE

Acts 20:35 And remember the words of the Lord Jesus, that He said, 'It is *more blessed to give* than to receive

MORE EXCELLENT SACRIFICE

Heb 11:4 By faith Abel offered to God a *more excellent sacrifice* than Cain, through which he obtained witness that he was righteous, God testifying of his gifts

MORE THAN CONQUERORS

Rom 8:37 Yet in all these things we are *more than conquerors* through Him who loved us

MORE WONDERFUL THAN THAT OF WOMEN (NIV)
(See *SURPASSING THE LOVE OF WOMEN*)

MORNING AFTER MORNING (NAS, NIV)
(See *MORNING BY MORNING*)

MORNING AND EVENING

1Sam 17:16 And the Philistine drew near and presented himself forty days, *morning and evening*

1Chr 16:40 to offer burnt offerings to the Lord on the altar of burnt offering regularly *morning and evening*, and to do according to all that is written in the Law of the Lord which He commanded Israel

2Chr 2:4 Behold, I am building a temple for the name of the Lord my God, to dedicate it to Him, to burn before Him sweet incense, for the continual showbread, for the burnt offerings *morning and evening*, on the Sabbaths, on the New Moons, and on the set feasts of the Lord our God

2Chr 31:3 for the *morning and evening* burnt offerings, the burnt offerings for the Sabbaths and the New Moons and the set feasts, as it is written in the Law of the Lord

Ezra 3:3 and they offered burnt offerings on it to the Lord, both the *morning and evening* burnt offerings

Ps 65:8 You make the outgoings of the *morning and evening* rejoice

MORNING BY MORNING

Is 28:19 for *morning by morning* it will pass over, and by day and by night

Is 50:4 He awakens me *morning by morning*, he awakens my ear to hear as the learned

MORNING MIST (NIV)
(See *EARLY DEW*)

MORNING STAR

2Pet 1:19 We also have the prophetic word made more sure, which you do well to heed as a light that shines in a dark place, until the day dawns and the *morning star* rises in your hearts

Rev 2:28 and I will give him the *morning star*

Rev 22:16 I am the Root and the Offspring of David, the Bright and *Morning Star*

MORNING STARS

Job 38:7 when the *morning stars* sang together, and all the sons of God shouted for joy

MORTAL BODIES

Rom 8:11 But if the Spirit of Him who raised Jesus from the dead dwells in you, He who raised Christ from the dead will also give life to your *mortal bodies* through His Spirit who dwells in you

MORTAL BODY

Rom 6:12 Therefore do not let sin reign in your *mortal body*, that you should obey it in its lusts

MOSES AND THE PROPHETS

Luke 16:29 Abraham said to him, 'They have *Moses and the prophets*

Luke 16:31 But he said to him, 'If they do not hear *Moses and the prophets*, neither will they be persuaded though one rise from the dead

Luke 24:44 Then He said to them, "These are the words which I spoke to you while I was still with you, that all things must be fulfilled which were written in the Law of *Moses and the Prophets* and the Psalms concerning Me

Acts 28:23 So when they had appointed him a day, many came to him at his lodging, to whom he explained and solemnly testified of the kingdom of God, persuading them concerning Jesus from both the Law of *Moses and the Prophets*, from morning till evening

MOST ASSUREDLY, I SAY TO YOU

John 1:51 And He said to him, "*Most assuredly, I say to you*, hereafter you shall see heaven open, and the angels of God ascending and descending upon the Son of Man

John 3:3 Jesus answered and said to him, "*Most assuredly, I say to you*, unless one is born again, he cannot see the kingdom of God

John 3:5 Jesus answered, "*Most assuredly, I say to you*, unless one is born of water and the Spirit, he cannot enter the kingdom of God

John 3:11 *Most assuredly, I say to you*, We speak what We know and testify what We have seen, and you do not receive Our witness

John 5:19 Then Jesus answered and said to them, "*Most assuredly, I say to you*, the Son can do nothing of Himself, but what He sees the Father do

John 5:24 *Most assuredly, I say to you*, he who

hears My word and believes in Him who sent Me has everlasting life, and shall not come into judgment, but has passed from death into life
John 5:25 *Most assuredly, I say to you*, the hour is coming, and now is, when the dead will hear the voice of the Son of God
John 6:26 Jesus answered them and said, "*Most assuredly, I say to you*, you seek Me, not because you saw the signs, but because you ate of the loaves and were filled
John 6:32 Then Jesus said to them, "*Most assuredly, I say to you*, Moses did not give you the bread from heaven, but My Father gives you the true bread from heaven
John 6:47 *Most assuredly, I say to you*, he who believes in Me has everlasting life
John 6:53 Then Jesus said to them, "*Most assuredly, I say to you*, unless you eat the flesh of the Son of Man and drink His blood, you have no life in you
John 8:34 Jesus answered them, "*Most assuredly, I say to you*, whoever commits sin is a slave of sin
John 8:51 *Most assuredly, I say to you*, if anyone keeps My word he shall never see death
John 8:58 Jesus said to them, "*Most assuredly, I say to you*, before Abraham was, I AM
John 10:1 *Most assuredly, I say to you*, he who does not enter the sheepfold by the door, but climbs up some other way, the same is a thief and a robber
John 10:7 Then Jesus said to them again, "*Most assuredly, I say to you*, I am the door of the sheep
John 12:24 *Most assuredly, I say to you*, unless a grain of wheat falls into the ground and dies, it remains alone
John 13:16 *Most assuredly, I say to you*, a servant is not greater than his master
John 13:20 *Most assuredly, I say to you*, he who receives whomever I send receives Me
John 13:21 When Jesus had said these things, He was troubled in spirit, and testified and said, "*Most assuredly, I say to you*, one of you will betray Me
John 13:38 *Most assuredly, I say to you*, the rooster shall not crow till you have denied Me three times
John 14:12 *Most assuredly, I say to you*, he who believes in Me, the works that I do he will do also
John 16:20 *Most assuredly, I say to you* that you will weep and lament, but the world will rejoice
John 16:23 *Most assuredly, I say to you*, whatever you ask the Father in My name He will give you
John 21:18 *Most assuredly, I say to you*, when you were younger, you girded yourself and walked where you wished

MOST BEAUTIFUL OF WOMEN (NIV)
(See *FAIREST AMONG WOMEN*)

MOST EXCELLENT
Luke 1:3 it seemed good to me also, having had perfect understanding of all things from the very first, to write to you an orderly account, *most excellent* Theophilus
Acts 23:26 Claudius Lysias, to the *most excellent* governor Felix: Greetings

MOST HIGH
Gen 14:18 Then Melchizedek king of Salem brought out bread and wine; he was the priest of God *Most High*
Gen 14:19 Blessed be Abram of God *Most High*, Possessor of heaven and earth
Gen 14:20 And blessed be God *Most High*, Who has delivered your enemies into your hand
Gen 14:22 But Abram said to the king of Sodom, "I have lifted my hand to the Lord, God *Most High*, the Possessor of heaven and earth
Num 24:16 the utterance of him who hears the words of God, and knows the knowledge of the *Most High*, who sees the vision of the Almighty, who falls down, with eyes opened wide
Deut 32:8 when the *Most High* divided their inheritance to the nations, when He separated the sons of Adam, He set the boundaries of the peoples according to the number of the children of Israel
2Sam 22:14 The Lord thundered from heaven, and the *Most High* uttered His voice
Ps 7:17 I will praise the Lord according to His righteousness, and will sing praise to the name of the Lord *Most High*
Ps 9:2 I will sing praise to Your name, O *Most High*
Ps 18:13 The Lord also thundered in the heavens, and the *Most High* uttered His voice, hailstones and coals of fire
Ps 21:7 For the king trusts in the Lord, and through the mercy of the *Most High* he shall not be moved
Ps 46:4 There is a river whose streams shall make glad the city of God, the holy place of the tabernacle of the *Most High*
Ps 47:2 For the Lord *Most High* is awesome; He is a great King over all the earth
Ps 50:14 Offer to God thanksgiving, and pay your vows to the *Most High*
Ps 56:2 My enemies would hound me all day, for there are many who fight against me, O *Most High*
Ps 57:2 I will cry out to God *Most High*, to God who performs all things for me
Ps 73:11 And they say, "How does God know? And is there knowledge in the *Most High*
Ps 77:10 But I will remember the years of the right hand of the *Most High*
Ps 78:17 But they sinned even more against Him by rebelling against the *Most High* in the wilderness
Ps 78:35 Then they remembered that God was their rock, and the *Most High* God their redeemer
Ps 78:56 Yet they tested and provoked the *Most High* God, and did not keep His testimonies
Ps 82:6 I said, "You are gods, and all of you are children of the *Most High*
Ps 83:18 That men may know that You, whose name alone is the Lord, are the *Most High* over all the earth
Ps 87:5 And of Zion it will be said, "This one and that one were born in her; and the *Most High* Himself shall establish her
Ps 91:1 He who dwells in the secret place of the *Most High* shall abide under the shadow of the Almighty
Ps 91:9 Because you have made the Lord, who is my refuge, even the *Most High*, your habitation
Ps 92:1 It is good to give thanks to the Lord, and to sing praises to Your name, O *Most High*
Ps 97:9 For You, Lord, are *most high* above all the earth
Ps 107:11 Because they rebelled against the words of God, and despised the counsel of the *Most High*
Is 14:14 I will ascend above the heights of the clouds, I will be like the *Most High*
Lam 3:35 to turn aside the justice due a man before the face of the *Most High*
Lam 3:38 Is it not from the mouth of the *Most High* that woe and well-being proceed
Dan 3:26 Then Nebuchadnezzar went near the mouth of the burning fiery furnace and spoke, saying, "Shadrach, Meshach, and Abed-Nego,

servants of the *Most High* God, come out, and come here
Dan 4:2 I thought it good to declare the signs and wonders that the *Most High* God has worked for me
Dan 4:17 This decision is by the decree of the watchers, and the sentence by the word of the holy ones, in order that the living may know that the *Most High* rules in the kingdom of men, gives it to whomever He will, and sets over it the lowest of men
Dan 4:24 this is the interpretation, O king, and this is the decree of the *Most High*, which has come upon my lord the king
Dan 4:25 They shall wet you with the dew of heaven, and seven times shall pass over you, till you know that the *Most High* rules in the kingdom of men, and gives it to whomever He chooses
Dan 4:32 and seven times shall pass over you, until you know that the *Most High* rules in the kingdom of men, and gives it to whomever He chooses
Dan 4:34 and I blessed the *Most High* and praised and honored Him who lives forever
Dan 5:18 O king, the *Most High* God gave Nebuchadnezzar your father a kingdom and majesty, glory and honor
Dan 5:21 They fed him with grass like oxen, and his body was wet with the dew of heaven, till he knew that the *Most High* God rules in the kingdom of men, and appoints over it whomever He chooses
Dan 7:18 But the saints of the *Most High* shall receive the kingdom, and possess the kingdom forever, even forever and ever
Dan 7:22 until the Ancient of Days came, and a judgment was made in favor of the saints of the *Most High*, and the time came for the saints to possess the kingdom
Dan 7:25 He shall speak pompous words against the *Most High*, shall persecute the saints of the *Most High*, and shall intend to change times and law
Dan 7:27 Then the kingdom and dominion, and the greatness of the kingdoms under the whole heaven, shall be given to the people, the saints of the *Most High*
Hos 7:16 They return, but not to the *Most High;* they are like a deceitful bow
Hos 11:7 Though they call to the *Most High*, none at all exalt Him
Mark 5:7 And he cried out with a loud voice and said, "What have I to do with You, Jesus, Son of the *Most High* God
Luke 8:28 When he saw Jesus, he cried out, fell down before Him, and with a loud voice said, "What have I to do with You, Jesus, Son of the *Most High* God
Acts 7:48 However, the *Most High* does not dwell in temples made with hands, as the prophet says
Acts 16:17 This girl followed Paul and us, and cried out, saying, "These men are the servants of the *Most High* God, who proclaim to us the way of salvation
Heb 7:1 For this Melchizedek, king of Salem, priest of the *Most High* God, who met Abraham returning from the slaughter of the kings and blessed him

MOST HIGH GOD
Ps 78:35 Then they remembered that God was their rock, and the *Most High God* their redeemer
Ps 78:56 Yet they tested and provoked the *Most High God*, and did not keep His testimonies
Dan 3:26 Then Nebuchadnezzar went near the mouth of the burning fiery furnace and spoke, saying, "Shadrach, Meshach, and Abed-Nego, servants of the *Most High God*, come out, and come here
Dan 4:2 I thought it good to declare the signs and wonders that the *Most High God* has worked for me
Dan 5:18 O king, the *Most High God* gave Nebuchadnezzar your father a kingdom and majesty, glory and honor
Dan 5:21 They fed him with grass like oxen, and his body was wet with the dew of heaven, till he knew that the *Most High God* rules in the kingdom of men, and appoints over it whomever He chooses
Mark 5:7 And he cried out with a loud voice and said, "What have I to do with You, Jesus, Son of the *Most High God*
Luke 8:28 When he saw Jesus, he cried out, fell down before Him, and with a loud voice said, "What have I to do with You, Jesus, Son of the *Most High God*
Acts 16:17 This girl followed Paul and us, and cried out, saying, "These men are the servants of the *Most High God*, who proclaim to us the way of salvation
Heb 7:1 For this Melchizedek, king of Salem, priest of the *Most High God*, who met Abraham returning from the slaughter of the kings and blessed him

MOST HOLY PLACE
Num 18:10 In a *most holy place* you shall eat it; every male shall eat it
1Kin 6:16 he built it inside as the inner sanctuary, as the *Most Holy Place*
1Kin 7:50 and the hinges of gold, both for the doors of the inner room (the *Most Holy Place*
1Kin 8:6 Then the priests brought in the ark of the covenant of the Lord to its place, into the inner sanctuary of the temple, to the *Most Holy Place*, under the wings of the cherubim
1Chr 6:49 But Aaron and his sons offered sacrifices on the altar of burnt offering and on the altar of incense, for all the work of the *Most Holy Place*, and to make atonement for Israel, according to all that Moses the servant of God had commanded
2Chr 3:8 And he made the *Most Holy Place*. Its length was according to the width of the house, twenty cubits, and its width twenty cubits
2Chr 3:10 In the *Most Holy Place* he made two cherubim, fashioned by carving, and overlaid them with gold
2Chr 4:22 As for the entry of the sanctuary, its inner doors to the *Most Holy Place*, and the doors of the main hall of the temple, were of gold
2Chr 5:7 Then the priests brought in the ark of the covenant of the Lord to its place, into the inner sanctuary of the temple, to the *Most Holy Place*, under the wings of the cherubim
2Chr 5:11 And it came to pass when the priests came out of the *Most Holy Place* (for all the priests who were present had sanctified themselves, without keeping to their divisions
Ezek 41:4 and he said to me, "This is the *Most Holy Place*
Ezek 44:13 And they shall not come near Me to minister to Me as priest, nor come near any of My holy things, nor into the *Most Holy Place*
Ezek 45:3 in it shall be the sanctuary, the *Most Holy Place*
Heb 9:12 Not with the blood of goats and calves, but with His own blood He entered the *Most Holy Place* once for all, having obtained eternal redemption
Heb 9:25 not that He should offer Himself often, as the high priest enters the *Most Holy Place* every year with blood of another

MOTE THAT IS IN THY BROTHER'S EYE (KJV)
(See *SPECK IN YOUR BROTHER'S EYE*)

MOTH WILL EAT THEM UP
Is 50:9 Indeed they will all grow old like a garment; the *moth will eat them up*
Is 51:8 For the *moth will eat them up* like a garment, and the worm will eat them like wool

MOTHER OF JESUS
John 2:1 On the third day there was a wedding in Cana of Galilee, and the *mother of Jesus* was there
John 2:3 And when they ran out of wine, the *mother of Jesus* said to Him
Acts 1:14 These all continued with one accord in prayer and supplication, with the women and Mary the *mother of Jesus*, and with His brothers

MOTHS HAVE EATEN YOUR CLOTHES (NIV)
(See *GARMENTS ARE MOTH-EATEN*)

MOUNT EPHRAIM (KJV)
(See *MOUNTAINS OF EPHRAIM*)

MOUNT OF OLIVES
2Sam 15:30 So David went up by the ascent of the *Mount of Olives*, and wept as he went up
Zech 14:4 And in that day His feet will stand on the *Mount of Olives*, which faces Jerusalem on the east. And the *Mount of Olives* shall be split in two, from east to west, making a very large valley
Matt 21:1 Now when they drew near to Jerusalem, and came to Bethphage, at the *Mount of Olives*, then Jesus sent two disciples
Matt 24:3 Now as He sat on the *Mount of Olives*, the disciples came to Him privately, saying
Matt 26:30 And when they had sung a hymn, they went out to the *Mount of Olives*
Mark 11:1 Now when they came near Jerusalem, to Bethphage and Bethany, at the *Mount of Olives*, He sent out two of His disciples
Mark 13:3 Now as He sat on the *Mount of Olives* opposite the temple, Peter, James, John, and Andrew asked Him privately
Mark 14:26 And when they had sung a hymn, they went out to the *Mount of Olives*
Luke 19:37 Then, as He was now drawing near the descent of the *Mount of Olives*, the whole multitude of the disciples began to rejoice and praise God with a loud voice for all the mighty works they had seen
Luke 22:39 And coming out, He went to the *Mount of Olives*, as He was accustomed, and His disciples also followed Him
John 8:1 But Jesus went to the *Mount of Olives*

MOUNT OF THE LORD (KJV, NAS, RSV)
(See *MOUNTAIN OF THE LORD*)

MOUNT OLIVET (KJV)
(See *MOUNT OF OLIVES*)

MOUNT SINAI
Ex 19:11 For on the third day the Lord will come down upon *Mount Sinai* in the sight of all the people
Ex 19:18 Now *Mount Sinai* was completely in smoke, because the Lord descended upon it in fire
Ex 19:20 Then the Lord came down upon *Mount Sinai*, on the top of the mountain
Ex 19:23 And Moses said to the Lord, "The people cannot come up to *Mount Sinai*
Ex 24:16 Now the glory of the Lord rested on *Mount Sinai*, and the cloud covered it six days
Ex 31:18 And when He had made an end of speaking with him on *Mount Sinai*, He gave Moses two tablets of the Testimony, tablets of stone, written with the finger of God
Ex 34:2 So be ready in the morning, and come up in the morning to *Mount Sinai*, and present yourself to Me there on the top of the mountain
Ex 34:4 Then Moses rose early in the morning and went up *Mount Sinai*, as the Lord had commanded him
Ex 34:29 Now it was so, when Moses came down from *Mount Sinai* (and the two tablets of the Testimony were in Moses' hand when he came down from the mountain
Ex 34:32 Afterward all the children of Israel came near, and he gave them as commandments all that the Lord had spoken with him on *Mount Sinai*
Lev 7:38 which the Lord commanded Moses on *Mount Sinai*, on the day when He commanded the children of Israel to offer their offerings to the Lord in the Wilderness of Sinai
Lev 25:1 And the Lord spoke to Moses on *Mount Sinai*, saying
Lev 26:46 These are the statutes and judgments and laws which the Lord made between Himself and the children of Israel on *Mount Sinai* by the hand of
Lev 27:34 These are the commandments which the Lord commanded Moses for the children of Israel on *Mount Sinai*
Num 3:1 Now these are the records of Aaron and Moses when the Lord spoke with Moses on *Mount Sinai*
Num 28:6 It is a regular burnt offering which was ordained at *Mount Sinai* for a sweet aroma, an offering made by fire to the Lord
Neh 9:13 You came down also on *Mount Sinai*, and spoke with them from heaven, and gave them just ordinances and true laws, good statutes and commandments
Acts 7:30 And when forty years had passed, an Angel of the Lord appeared to him in a flame of fire in a bush, in the wilderness of *Mount Sinai*
Acts 7:38 This is he who was in the congregation in the wilderness with the Angel who spoke to him on *Mount Sinai*, and with our fathers, the one who received the living oracles to give to us
Gal 4:24 the one from *Mount Sinai* which gives birth to bondage, which is Hagar
Gal 4:25 for this Hagar is *Mount Sinai* in Arabia, and corresponds to Jerusalem which now is, and is in bondage with her children

MOUNT ZION
2Kin 19:31 For out of Jerusalem shall go a remnant, and those who escape from *Mount Zion*
Ps 48:2 Beautiful in elevation, the joy of the whole earth, is *Mount Zion* on the sides of the north, the city of the great King
Ps 48:11 Let *Mount Zion* rejoice, let the daughters of Judah be glad, because of Your judgments
Ps 74:2 Remember Your congregation, which You have purchased of old, the tribe of Your inheritance, which You have redeemed this *Mount Zion* where You have dwelt
Ps 78:68 But chose the tribe of Judah, *Mount Zion* which He loved
Ps 125:1 Those who trust in the Lord are like *Mount Zion*, which cannot be moved, but abides forever
Is 4:5 then the Lord will create above every dwelling place of *Mount Zion*, and above her assemblies, a cloud and smoke by day and the shining of a flaming fire by night
Is 8:18 We are for signs and wonders in Israel from the Lord of hosts, Who dwells in *Mount Zion*
Is 10:12 Therefore it shall come to pass, when the

Lord has performed all His work on *Mount Zion* and on Jerusalem, that He will say

Is 18:7 In that time a present will be brought to the Lord of hosts from a people tall and smooth of skin, and from a people terrible from their beginning onward, a nation powerful and treading down, whose land the rivers divide to the place of the name of the Lord of hosts, to *Mount Zion*

Is 24:23 for the Lord of hosts will reign on *Mount Zion* and in Jerusalem and before His elders, gloriously

Is 29:8 so the multitude of all the nations shall be, who fight against *Mount Zion*

Is 31:4 so the Lord of hosts will come down to fight for *Mount Zion* and for its hill

Is 37:32 For out of Jerusalem shall go a remnant, and those who escape from *Mount Zion*

Lam 5:18 because of *Mount Zion* which is desolate, with foxes walking about on it

Joel 2:32 For in *Mount Zion* and in Jerusalem there shall be deliverance, as the Lord has said, among the remnant whom the Lord calls

Obad 17 But on *Mount Zion* there shall be deliverance, and there shall be holiness

Obad 21 Then saviors shall come to *Mount Zion* to judge the mountains of Esau, and the kingdom shall be the Lord's

Mic 4:7 so the Lord will reign over them in *Mount Zion* from now on, even forever

Heb 12:22 But you have come to *Mount Zion* and to the city of the living God, the heavenly Jerusalem, to an innumerable company of angels

Rev 14:1 Then I looked, and behold, a Lamb standing on *Mount Zion*, and with Him one hundred and forty-four thousand, having His Father's name written on their foreheads

MOUNTAIN OF GOD

Ex 3:1 And he led the flock to the back of the desert, and came to Horeb, the *mountain of God*

Ex 4:27 So he went and met him on the *mountain of God*, and kissed him

Ex 18:5 and Jethro, Moses' father-in-law, came with his sons and his wife to Moses in the wilderness, where he was encamped at the *mountain of God*

Ex 24:13 So Moses arose with his assistant Joshua, and Moses went up to the *mountain of God*

1Kin 19:8 and he went in the strength of that food forty days and forty nights as far as Horeb, the *mountain of God*

Ps 68:15 A *mountain of God* is the mountain of Bashan; a mountain of many peaks is the mountain of Bashan

Ezek 28:14 you were on the holy *mountain of God;* you walked back and forth in the midst of fiery stones

Ezek 28:16 therefore I cast you as a profane thing out of the *mountain of God*

MOUNTAIN OF THE LORD

Num 10:33 So they departed from the *mountain of the Lord* on a journey of three days

Is 2:3 Many people shall come and say, "Come, and let us go up to the *mountain of the Lord*, to the house of the God of Jacob

Is 30:29 You shall have a song as in the night when a holy festival is kept, and gladness of heart as when one goes with a flute, to come into the *mountain of the Lord*, to the Mighty One of Israel

Mic 4:2 Many nations shall come and say, "Come, and let us go up to the *mountain of the Lord*, to the house of the God of Jacob

Zech 8:3 Jerusalem shall be called the City of Truth, the *Mountain of the Lord* of hosts, the Holy Mountain

MOUNTAINS MELT LIKE WAX

Ps 97:5 The *mountains melt like wax* at the presence of the Lord, at the presence of the Lord of the whole earth

MOUNTAINS OF EPHRAIM

Josh 17:15 So Joshua answered them, "If you are a great people, then go up to the forest country and clear a place for yourself there in the land of the Perizzites and the giants, since the *mountains of Ephraim* are too confined for you

Josh 19:50 According to the word of the Lord they gave him the city which he asked for, Timnath Serah in the *mountains of Ephraim*

Josh 20:7 So they appointed Kedesh in Galilee, in the mountains of Naphtali, Shechem in the *mountains of Ephraim*, and Kirjath Arba (which is Hebron

Josh 21:21 For they gave them Shechem with its common-land in the *mountains of Ephraim* (a city of refuge for the slayer

Josh 24:30 And they buried him within the border of his inheritance at Timnath Serah, which is in the *mountains of Ephraim*, on the north side of Mount Gaash

Josh 24:33 and they buried him in a hill that belonged to Phinehas his son, which was given to him in the *mountains of Ephraim*

Judg 2:9 And they buried him within the border of his inheritance at Timnath Heres, in the *mountains of Ephraim*, on the north side of Mount Gaash

Judg 3:27 And it happened, when he arrived, that he blew the trumpet in the *mountains of Ephraim*, and the children of Israel went down with him from the mountains

Judg 4:5 And she would sit under the palm tree of Deborah between Ramah and Bethel in the *mountains of Ephraim*

Judg 7:24 Then Gideon sent messengers throughout all the *mountains of Ephraim*, saying

Judg 10:1 and he dwelt in Shamir in the *mountains of Ephraim*

Judg 17:1 Now there was a man from the *mountains of Ephraim*, whose name was Micah

Judg 17:8 Then he came to the *mountains of Ephraim*, to the house of Micah, as he journeyed

Judg 18:2 So they went to the *mountains of Ephraim*, to the house of Micah, and lodged there

Judg 18:13 And they passed from there to the *mountains of Ephraim*, and came to the house of Micah

Judg 19:1 And it came to pass in those days, when there was no king in Israel, that there was a certain Levite sojourning in the remote *mountains of Ephraim*

Judg 19:16 Just then an old man came in from his work in the field at evening, who also was from the *mountains of Ephraim*

Judg 19:18 So he said to him, "We are passing from Bethlehem in Judah toward the remote *mountains of Ephraim*

1Sam 1:1 Now there was a certain man of Ramathaim Zophim, of the *mountains of Ephraim*, and his name was Elkanah the son of Jeroham, the son of Elihu, the son of Tohu, the son of Zuph, an Ephraimite

1Sam 9:4 So he passed through the *mountains of Ephraim* and through the land of Shalisha, but they did not find them

1Sam 14:22 Likewise all the men of Israel who had hidden in the *mountains of Ephraim*, when they heard that the Philistines fled, they also followed hard after them in the battle

2Sam 20:21 But a man from the *mountains of Ephraim*, Sheba the son of Bichri by name, has raised his hand against the king, against David

1Kin 4:8 These are their names: Ben-Hur, in the *mountains of Ephraim*
1Kin 12:25 Then Jeroboam built Shechem in the *mountains of Ephraim*, and dwelt there
2Kin 5:22 My master has sent me, saying, 'Indeed, just now two young men of the sons of the prophets have come to me from the *mountains of Ephraim*
1Chr 6:67 And they gave them one of the cities of refuge, Shechem with its common-lands, in the *mountains of Ephraim*, also Gezer with its common-lands
2Chr 13:4 Then Abijah stood on Mount Zemaraim, which is in the *mountains of Ephraim*, and said
2Chr 15:8 And when Asa heard these words and the prophecy of Oded the prophet, he took courage, and removed the abominable idols from all the land of Judah and Benjamin and from the cities which he had taken in the *mountains of Ephraim*
2Chr 19:4 and he went out again among the people from Beersheba to the *mountains of Ephraim*, and brought them back to the Lord God of their fathers

MOUNTAINS SKIPPED LIKE RAMS
Ps 114:4 The *mountains skipped like rams*, the little hills like lambs

MOUNTED ON AN ASS (RSV)
(See *SITTING ON A DONKEY*)

MOURN LIKE A VIRGIN (NIV)
(See *LAMENT LIKE A VIRGIN*)

MOUTH OF FOOLS
Prov 15:2 The tongue of the wise uses knowledge rightly, but the *mouth of fools* pours forth foolishness
Prov 15:14 The heart of him who has understanding seeks knowledge, but the *mouth of fools* feeds on foolishness
Prov 26:7 Like the legs of the lame that hang limp is a proverb in the *mouth of fools*
Prov 26:9 Like a thorn that goes into the hand of a drunkard is a proverb in the *mouth of fools*

MOUTH OF GOD
2Chr 35:22 Nevertheless Josiah would not turn his face from him, but disguised himself so that he might fight with him, and did not heed the words of Necho from the *mouth of God*
Matt 4:4 But He answered and said, "It is written, 'Man shall not live by bread alone, but by every word that proceeds from the *mouth of God*

MOUTH OF HIS HOLY PROPHETS
Luke 1:70 as He spoke by the *mouth of His holy prophets*, who have been since the world began

MOUTH OF SHEOL (NAS, RSV)
(See *MOUTH OF THE GRAVE*)

MOUTH OF THE CAVE
Josh 10:18 So Joshua said, "Roll large stones against the *mouth of the cave*, and set men by it to guard them
Josh 10:22 Then Joshua said, "Open the *mouth of the cave*, and bring out those five kings to me from the cave

MOUTH OF THE GRAVE
Ps 141:7 Our bones are scattered at the *mouth of the grave*, as when one plows and breaks up the earth

MOUTH OF THE LORD
Deut 8:3 but man lives by every word that proceeds from the *mouth of the Lord*
2Chr 36:12 He also did evil in the sight of the Lord his God, and did not humble himself before Jeremiah the prophet, who spoke from the *mouth of the Lord*
Is 1:20 but if you refuse and rebel, you shall be devoured by the sword"; for the *mouth of the Lord* has spoken
Is 40:5 the glory of the Lord shall be revealed, and all flesh shall see it together; for the *mouth of the Lord* has spoken
Is 58:14 and I will cause you to ride on the high hills of the earth, and feed you with the heritage of Jacob your father. The *mouth of the Lord* has spoken
Is 62:2 You shall be called by a new name, which the *mouth of the Lord* will name
Jer 9:12 And who is he to whom the *mouth of the Lord* has spoken, that he may declare it
Jer 23:16 they speak a vision of their own heart, not from the *mouth of the Lord*
Mic 4:4 for the *mouth of the Lord* of hosts has spoken

MOUTH OF THE PROPHETS
Zech 8:9 Let your hands be strong, you who have been hearing in these days these words by the *mouth of the prophets*, who were in the day that the foundation was laid for the house of the Lord of hosts, that the temple might be built

MOUTH OF THE WICKED
Ps 109:2 For the *mouth of the wicked* and the mouth of the deceitful have opened against me
Prov 10:6 Blessings are on the head of the righteous, but violence covers the *mouth of the wicked*
Prov 10:11 The mouth of the righteous is a well of life, but violence covers the *mouth of the wicked*
Prov 10:32 The lips of the righteous know what is acceptable, but the *mouth of the wicked* what is perverse
Prov 11:11 By the blessing of the upright the city is exalted, but it is overthrown by the *mouth of the wicked*
Prov 15:28 The heart of the righteous studies how to answer, but the *mouth of the wicked* pours forth evil
Prov 19:28 A disreputable witness scorns justice, and the *mouth of the wicked* devours iniquity

MOUTH OF TWO WITNESSES, OR THREE WITNESSES (KJV)
(See *TESTIMONY OF TWO OR THREE WITNESSES*)

MOVED WITH COMPASSION
Matt 9:36 But when He saw the multitudes, He was *moved with compassion* for them, because they were weary and scattered, like sheep having no shepherd
Matt 14:14 and He was *moved with compassion* for them, and healed their sick
Matt 18:27 Then the master of that servant was *moved with compassion*, released him, and forgave him the debt
Mark 1:41 And Jesus, *moved with compassion*, put out His hand and touched him, and said to him
Mark 6:34 And Jesus, when He came out, saw a great multitude and was *moved with compassion* for them, because they were like sheep not having a shepherd

MUCH LEARNING IS DRIVING YOU MAD
Acts 26:24 Now as he thus made his defense, Festus said with a loud voice, "Paul, you are beside yourself! *Much learning is driving you mad*

MUCH STUDY IS WEARISOME
Eccl 12:12 Of making many books there is no end, and *much study is wearisome* to the flesh

MULTIPLY MY DAYS AS THE SAND
Job 29:18 Then I said, 'I shall die in my nest, and *multiply my days as the sand*

MULTIPLY THY SEED (KJV)
(See *MULTIPLY YOUR DESCENDANTS*)

MULTIPLY YOUR DESCENDANTS
Gen 16:10 Then the Angel of the Lord said to her, "I will *multiply your descendants* exceedingly, so that they shall not be counted for multitude
Gen 22:17 in blessing I will bless you, and in multiplying I will *multiply your descendants* as the stars of the heaven and as the sand which is on the seashore
Gen 26:24 I will bless you and *multiply your descendants* for My servant Abraham's sake
Ex 32:13 Remember Abraham, Isaac, and Israel, Your servants, to whom You swore by Your own self, and said to them, 'I will *multiply your descendants* as the stars of heaven

MULTIPLY YOUR PAIN (NAS, RSV)
(See *MULTIPLY YOUR SORROW*)

MULTIPLY YOUR SORROW
Gen 3:16 I will greatly *multiply your sorrow* and your conception; in pain you shall bring forth children

MULTITUDE OF SINS
Jas 5:20 let him know that he who turns a sinner from the error of his way will save a soul from death and cover a *multitude of sins*
1Pet 4:8 And above all things have fervent love for one another, for "love will cover a *multitude of sins*

MULTITUDE OF THE HEAVENLY HOST
Luke 2:13 And suddenly there was with the angel a *multitude of the heavenly host* praising God and saying

MULTITUDE OF YOUR INIQUITIES
Jer 30:14 for I have wounded you with the wound of an enemy, with the chastisement of a cruel one, for the *multitude of your iniquities*, because your sins have increased
Jer 30:15 Because of the *multitude of your iniquities*, because your sins have increased, I have done these things to you
Ezek 28:18 You defiled your sanctuaries by the *multitude of your iniquities*, by the iniquity of your trading

MURMURED AGAINST MOSES
Num 14:2 And all the children of Israel *murmured against Moses* and Aaron, and the whole congregation said to them
Num 16:41 On the next day all the congregation of the children of Israel *murmured against Moses* and Aaron, saying

MUSIC OF THE LORD
2Chr 7:6 the Levites also with instruments of the *music of the Lord*, which King David had made to praise the Lord, saying

MUZZLE AN OX
Deut 25:4 You shall not *muzzle an ox* while it treads out the grain
1Cor 9:9 For it is written in the law of Moses, "You shall not *muzzle an ox* while it treads out the grain
1Tim 5:18 For the Scripture says, "You shall not *muzzle an ox* while it treads out the grain

MY BELOVED SON
Matt 3:17 And suddenly a voice came from heaven, saying, "This is *My beloved Son*, in whom I am well pleased
Matt 17:5 and suddenly a voice came out of the cloud, saying, "This is *My beloved Son*, in whom I am well pleased
Mark 1:11 Then a voice came from heaven, "You are *My beloved Son*, in whom I am well pleased
Mark 9:7 and a voice came out of the cloud, saying, "This is *My beloved Son*
Luke 3:22 And the Holy Spirit descended in bodily form like a dove upon Him, and a voice came from heaven which said, "You are *My beloved Son*
Luke 9:35 Then a voice came out of the cloud, saying, "This is *My beloved Son*
Luke 20:13 I will send *my beloved son*. Probably they will respect him when they see him
2Tim 1:2 To Timothy, *my beloved son:* Grace, mercy, and peace from God the Father and Christ Jesus our Lord
2Pet 1:17 This is *My beloved Son*, in whom I am well pleased

MY BETRAYER IS AT HAND
Mark 14:42 Rise up, let us go. See, *My betrayer is at hand*

MY BLOOD
1Sam 26:20 Now therefore, do not let *my blood* fall to the earth before the face of the Lord
Job 16:18 O earth, do not cover *my blood*, and let my cry have no resting place
Ps 30:9 What profit is there in *my blood*, when I go down to the pit
Jer 51:35 And *my blood* be upon the inhabitants of Chaldea!" Jerusalem will say
Matt 26:28 For this is *My blood* of the new covenant, which is shed for many for the remission of sins
Mark 14:24 And He said to them, "This is *My blood* of the new covenant, which is shed for many
Luke 22:20 Likewise He also took the cup after supper, saying, "This cup is the new covenant in *My blood*, which is shed for you
John 6:54 Whoever eats My flesh and drinks *My blood* has eternal life, and I will raise him up at the last day
John 6:55 For My flesh is food indeed, and *My blood* is drink indeed
John 6:56 He who eats My flesh and drinks *My blood* abides in Me, and I in him
1Cor 11:25 In the same manner He also took the cup after supper, saying, "This cup is the new covenant in *My blood*

MY BONE AND MY FLESH
Gen 29:14 And Laban said to him, "Surely you are *my bone and my flesh*
2Sam 19:12 You are my brethren, you are *my bone and my flesh*
2Sam 19:13 And say to Amasa, 'Are you not *my bone and my flesh*

MY BROTHER'S KEEPER
Gen 4:9 And he said, "I do not know. Am I *my brother's keeper*

MY BURDEN IS LIGHT
Matt 11:30 For My yoke is easy and *My burden is light*

MY CATTLE (KJV)
(See *MY FLOCK*)

MY CHILDREN
Gen 30:26 Give me my wives and *my children* for whom I have served you, and let me go
Gen 31:43 And Laban answered and said to Jacob, "These daughters are my daughters, and these children are *my children*, and this flock is my flock
Ex 21:5 But if the servant plainly says, 'I love my master, my wife, and *my children*
1Kin 20:7 Then the king of Israel called all the elders of the land, and said, "Notice, please, and see how this man seeks trouble, for he sent to me for my wives, *my children*, my silver, and my gold
Job 29:5 when the Almighty was yet with me, when *my children* were around me
Prov 4:1 Hear, *my children*, the instruction of a father, and give attention to know understanding
Prov 5:7 Therefore hear me now, *my children*, and do not depart from the words of my mouth
Prov 7:24 Now therefore, listen to me, *my children;* pay attention to the words of my mouth
Prov 8:32 Now therefore, listen to me, *my children*, for blessed are those who keep my ways
Is 49:21 Then you will say in your heart, 'Who has begotten these for me, since I have lost *my children* and am desolate, a captive, and wandering to and fro
Jer 10:20 *my children* have gone from me, and they are no more
Lam 1:16 because the comforter, who should restore my life, is far from me. *My children* are desolate because the enemy prevailed
Ezek 16:21 that you have slain *My children* and offered them up to them by causing them to pass through the fire
Luke 11:7 the door is now shut, and *my children* are with me in bed
3Jn 4 I have no greater joy than to hear that *my children* walk in truth

MY COMMANDMENTS AND MY STATUTES
1Kin 9:6 But if you or your sons at all turn from following Me, and do not keep *My commandments and My statutes* which I have set before you, but go and serve other gods and worship them
1Kin 11:34 However I will not take the whole kingdom out of his hand, because I have made him ruler all the days of his life for the sake of My servant David, whom I chose because he kept *My commandments and My statutes*
2Kin 17:13 Yet the Lord testified against Israel and against Judah, by all of His prophets, namely every seer, saying, "Turn from your evil ways, and keep *My commandments and My statutes*, according to all the law which I commanded your fathers, and which I sent to you by My servants the prophets

MY COVENANT
Gen 6:18 But I will establish *My covenant* with you; and you shall go into the ark you, your sons, your wife, and your sons' wives with you
Gen 9:9 And as for Me, behold, I establish *My covenant* with you and with your descendants after you
Gen 9:11 Thus I establish *My covenant* with you: Never again shall all flesh be cut off by the waters of the flood
Gen 9:15 and I will remember *My covenant* which is between Me and you and every living creature of all flesh
Gen 17:2 And I will make *My covenant* between Me and you, and will multiply you exceedingly
Gen 17:4 As for Me, behold, *My covenant* is with you, and you shall be a father of many nations
Gen 17:7 And I will establish *My covenant* between Me and you and your descendants after you in their generations, for an everlasting covenant, to be God to you and your descendants after you
Gen 17:9 As for you, you shall keep *My covenant*, you and your descendants after you throughout their generations
Gen 17:10 This is *My covenant* which you shall keep, between Me and you and your descendants after you
Gen 17:13 He who is born in your house and he who is bought with your money must be circumcised, and *My covenant* shall be in your flesh for an everlasting covenant
Gen 17:14 And the uncircumcised male child, who is not circumcised in the flesh of his foreskin, that person shall be cut off from his people; he has broken *My covenant*
Gen 17:19 I will establish *My covenant* with him for an everlasting covenant, and with his descendants after him
Gen 17:21 But *My covenant* I will establish with Isaac, whom Sarah shall bear to you at this set time next year
Ex 6:4 I have also established *My covenant* with them, to give them the land of Canaan, the land of their pilgrimage, in which they were strangers
Ex 6:5 And I have also heard the groaning of the children of Israel whom the Egyptians keep in bondage, and I have remembered *My covenant*
Ex 19:5 Now therefore, if you will indeed obey My voice and keep *My covenant*, then you shall be a special treasure to Me above all people
Lev 26:9 For I will look on you favorably and make you fruitful, multiply you and confirm *My covenant* with you
Lev 26:15 and if you despise My statutes, or if your soul abhors My judgments, so that you do not perform all My commandments, but break *My covenant*
Lev 26:25 And I will bring a sword against you that will execute the vengeance of *My covenant*
Lev 26:42 then I will remember *My covenant* with Jacob, and *My covenant* with Isaac and *My covenant* with Abraham I will remember
Lev 26:44 Yet for all that, when they are in the land of their enemies, I will not cast them away, nor shall I abhor them, to utterly destroy them and break *My covenant* with them
Num 25:12 Therefore say, 'Behold, I give to him *My covenant* of peace
Deut 31:16 and this people will rise and play the harlot with the gods of the foreigners of the land, where they go to be among them, and they will forsake Me and break *My covenant* which I have made with them
Deut 31:20 When I have brought them to the land flowing with milk and honey, of which I swore to their fathers, and they have eaten and filled themselves and grown fat, then they will turn to other gods and serve them; and they will provoke Me and break *My covenant*
Josh 7:11 Israel has sinned, and they have also transgressed *My covenant* which I commanded them
Judg 2:1 and I said, 'I will never break *My covenant* with you
Judg 2:20 and He said, "Because this nation has transgressed *My covenant* which I commanded their fathers, and has not heeded My voice
1Kin 11:11 Therefore the Lord said to Solomon,

"Because you have done this, and have not kept *My covenant* and My statutes, which I have commanded you, I will surely tear the kingdom away from you and give it to your servant

Ps 50:16 What right have you to declare My statutes, or take *My covenant* in your mouth

Ps 89:28 My mercy I will keep for him forever, and *My covenant* shall stand firm with him

Ps 89:34 *My covenant* I will not break, nor alter the word that has gone out of My lips

Ps 132:12 If your sons will keep *My covenant* and My testimony which I shall teach them, their sons also shall sit upon your throne forevermore

Is 54:10 For the mountains shall depart and the hills be removed, but My kindness shall not depart from you, nor shall *My covenant* of peace be removed

Is 56:4 To the eunuchs who keep My Sabbaths, and choose what pleases Me, and hold fast *My covenant*

Is 56:6 Also the sons of the foreigner who join themselves to the Lord, to serve Him, and to love the name of the Lord, to be His servants everyone who keeps from defiling the Sabbath, and holds fast *My covenant*

Is 59:21 As for Me," says the Lord, "this is *My covenant* with them

Jer 11:10 the house of Israel and the house of Judah have broken *My covenant* which I made with their fathers

Jer 31:32 not according to the covenant that I made with their fathers in the day that I took them by the hand to bring them out of the land of Egypt, *My covenant* which they broke, though I was a husband to them

Jer 33:20 If you can break *My covenant* with the day and *My covenant* with the night, so that there will not be day and night in their season

Jer 33:21 then *My covenant* may also be broken with David My servant, so that he shall not have a son to reign on his throne, and with the Levites, the priests, My ministers

Jer 33:25 If *My covenant* is not with day and night, and if I have not appointed the ordinances of heaven and earth

Jer 34:18 And I will give the men who have transgressed *My covenant*, who have not performed the words of the covenant which they made before Me, when they cut the calf in two and passed between the parts of it

Ezek 16:60 Nevertheless I will remember *My covenant* with you in the days of your youth, and I will establish an everlasting covenant with you

Ezek 16:61 for I will give them to you for daughters, but not because of *My covenant* with you

Ezek 16:62 And I will establish *My covenant* with you. Then you shall know that I am the Lord

Ezek 17:19 As I live, surely My oath which he despised, and *My covenant* which he broke, I will recompense on his own head

Ezek 44:7 When you brought in foreigners, uncircumcised in heart and uncircumcised in flesh, to be in My sanctuary to defile it My house and when you offered My food, the fat and the blood, then they broke *My covenant* because of all your abominations

Hos 8:1 He shall come like an eagle against the house of the Lord, because they have transgressed *My covenant* and rebelled against My law

Mal 2:4 Then you shall know that I have sent this commandment to you, that *My covenant* with Levi may continue

Mal 2:5 *My covenant* was with him, one of life and peace, and I gave them to him that he might fear Me

Rom 11:27 For this is *My covenant* with them, when I take away their sins

Heb 8:9 because they did not continue in *My covenant* , and I disregarded them

MY CUP RUNS OVER

Ps 23:5 You anoint my head with oil; *my cup runs over*

MY DECISIONS ARE RIGHT (NIV)
(See *MY JUDGMENT IS TRUE*)

MY DECREES AND LAWS (NIV)
(See *MY STATUTES AND MY JUDGMENTS*)

MY FATHER

Gen 19:34 It happened on the next day that the firstborn said to the younger, "Indeed I lay with *my father* last night

Gen 20:12 She is the daughter of *my father*, but not the daughter of my mother

Gen 22:7 But Isaac spoke to Abraham his father and said, "*My father*

Gen 27:12 Perhaps *my father* will feel me, and I shall seem to be a deceiver to him

Gen 27:18 So he went to his father and said, "*My father*

Gen 27:31 He also had made savory food, and brought it to his father, and said to his father, "Let *my father* arise and eat of his son's game, that your soul may bless me

Gen 27:34 When Esau heard the words of his father, he cried with an exceedingly great and bitter cry, and said to his father, "Bless me, even me also, O *my father*

Gen 27:38 And Esau said to his father, "Have you only one blessing, *my father?* Bless me, even me also, O *my father*

Gen 27:41 So Esau hated Jacob because of the blessing with which his father blessed him, and Esau said in his heart, "The days of mourning for *my father* are at hand

Gen 31:5 but the God of *my father* has been with me

Gen 31:42 Unless the God of *my father*, the God of Abraham and the Fear of Isaac, had been with me, surely now you would have sent me away empty-handed

Gen 32:9 Then Jacob said, "O God of *my father* Abraham and God of *my father* Isaac, the Lord who said to me

Gen 44:24 So it was, when we went up to your servant *my father*, that we told him the words of my lord

Gen 44:27 Then your servant *my father* said to us, 'You know that my wife bore me two sons

Gen 44:30 Now therefore, when I come to your servant *my father*, and the lad is not with us, since his life is bound up in the lad's life

Gen 44:32 For your servant became surety for the lad to *my father*, saying, 'If I do not bring him back to you, then I shall bear the blame before *my father* forever

Gen 44:34 For how shall I go up to *my father* if the lad is not with me, lest perhaps I see the evil that would come upon *my father*

Gen 45:3 does *my father* still live?" But his brothers could not answer him, for they were dismayed in his presence

Gen 45:9 Hurry and go up to *my father*, and say to him

Gen 45:13 So you shall tell *my father* of all my glory in Egypt, and of all that you have seen; and you shall hurry and bring *my father* down here

Gen 47:1 Then Joseph went and told Pharaoh, and said, "*My father* and my brothers, their flocks and their herds and all that they possess, have come from the land of Canaan

Gen 48:18 And Joseph said to his father, "Not so, *my father*, for this one is the firstborn

Gen 50:5 *My father* made me swear, saying, "Behold, I am dying; in my grave which I dug for myself in the land of Canaan, there you shall bury me." Now therefore, please let me go up and bury *my father*, and I will come back
Ex 18:4 and the name of the other was Eliezer (for he said, "The God of *my father* was my help, and delivered me from the sword of Pharaoh
Deut 26:5 *My father* was a Syrian, about to perish, and he went down to Egypt and sojourned there, few in number
Josh 2:13 and spare *my father*, my mother, my brothers, my sisters, and all that they have, and deliver our lives from death
Judg 9:17 for *my father* fought for you, risked his life, and delivered you out of the hand of Midian
Judg 11:36 So she said to him, "*My father*, if you have given your word to the Lord, do to me according to what has gone out of your mouth, because the Lord has avenged you of your enemies, the people of Ammon
Judg 14:16 And he said to her, "Look, I have not explained it to *my father* or my mother
1Sam 9:5 When they had come to the land of Zuph, Saul said to his servant who was with him, "Come, let us return, lest *my father* cease caring about the donkeys and become worried about us
1Sam 14:29 But Jonathan said, "*My father* has troubled the land. Look now, how my countenance has brightened because I tasted a little of this honey
1Sam 19:2 So Jonathan told David, saying, "*My father* Saul seeks to kill you
1Sam 19:3 And I will go out and stand beside *my father* in the field where you are, and I will speak with *my father* about you
1Sam 20:2 Indeed, *my father* will do nothing either great or small without first telling me. And why should *my father* hide this thing from me
1Sam 20:9 For if I knew certainly that evil was determined by *my father* to come upon you, then would I not tell you
1Sam 20:12 When I have sounded out *my father* sometime tomorrow, or the third day, and indeed there is good toward David, and I do not send to you and tell you
1Sam 20:13 But if it pleases *my father* to do you evil, then I will report it to you and send you away, that you may go in safety. And the Lord be with you as He has been with *my father*
1Sam 22:3 and he said to the king of Moab, "Please let *my father* and mother come here with you, till I know what God will do for me
1Sam 22:15 Let not the king impute anything to his servant, or to any in the house of *my father*
1Sam 23:17 And he said to him, "Do not fear, for the hand of Saul *my father* shall not find you. You shall be king over Israel, and I shall be next to you. Even *my father* Saul knows that
1Sam 24:11 Moreover, *my father*, see! Yes, see the corner of your robe in my hand
2Sam 16:3 And Ziba said to the king, "Indeed he is staying in Jerusalem, for he said, 'Today the house of Israel will restore the kingdom of *my father* to me
2Sam 19:37 Please let your servant turn back again, that I may die in my own city, and be buried by the grave of *my father* and mother
1Kin 2:24 Now therefore, as the Lord lives, who has established me and set me on the throne of David *my father*, and who has made me a house, as He promised, Adonijah shall be put to death today
1Kin 2:26 but I will not put you to death at this time, because you carried the ark of the Lord God before *my father* David, and because you were afflicted every time *my father* was afflicted
1Kin 2:31 And the king said to him, "Do as he has said, and strike him down and bury him, that you may take away from me and from the house of *my father* the innocent blood which Joab shed
1Kin 2:32 So the Lord will return his blood on his head, because he struck down two men more righteous and better than he, and killed them with the sword Abner the son of Ner, the commander of the army of Israel, and Amasa the son of Jether, the commander of the army of Judah though *my father* David did not know it
1Kin 2:44 The king said moreover to Shimei, "You know, as your heart acknowledges, all the wickedness that you did to *my father* David
1Kin 3:6 You have shown great mercy to your servant David *my father*, because he walked before You in truth, in righteousness, and in uprightness of heart with You
1Kin 3:7 Now, O Lord my God, You have made Your servant king instead of *my father* David, but I am a little child
1Kin 5:3 You know how *my father* David could not build a house for the name of the Lord his God because of the wars which were fought against him on every side, until the Lord put his foes under the soles of his feet
1Kin 5:5 And behold, I propose to build a house for the name of the Lord my God, as the Lord spoke to *my father* David, saying
1Kin 8:15 Blessed be the Lord God of Israel, who spoke with His mouth to *my father* David, and with His hand has fulfilled it, saying
1Kin 8:17 Now it was in the heart of *my father* David to build a house for the name of the Lord God of Israel
1Kin 8:18 But the Lord said to *my father* David, 'Whereas it was in your heart to build a house for My name, you did well that it was in your heart
1Kin 8:20 and I have filled the position of *my father* David, and sit on the throne of Israel, as the Lord promised
1Kin 8:24 You have kept what You promised Your servant David *my father*
1Kin 8:25 Therefore, Lord God of Israel, now keep what You promised Your servant David *my father*, saying
1Kin 8:26 And now I pray, O God of Israel, let Your word come true, which You have spoken to Your servant David *my father*
1Kin 12:11 And now, whereas *my father* laid a heavy yoke on you, I will add to your yoke; *my father* chastised you with whips, but I will chastise you with scourges
1Kin 12:14 and he spoke to them according to the counsel of the young men, saying, "*My father* made your yoke heavy, but I will add to your yoke; *my father* chastised you with whips, but I will chastise you with scourges
1Kin 15:19 Let there be a treaty between you and me, as there was between *my father* and your father
1Kin 19:20 And he left the oxen and ran after Elijah, and said, "Please let me kiss *my father* and my mother, and then I will follow you
1Kin 20:34 Then Ben-Hadad said to him, "The cities which *my father* took from your father I will restore; and you may set up marketplaces for yourself in Damascus, as *my father* did in Samaria
2Kin 2:12 Now Elisha saw it, and he cried out, "*My father*, *my father*, the chariot of Israel and its horsemen
2Kin 5:13 And his servants came near and spoke to him, and said, "*My father*, if the prophet had told you to do something great, would you not have done it
2Kin 6:21 Now when the king of Israel saw them, he said to Elisha, "*My father*, shall I kill them
2Kin 13:14 Then Joash the king of Israel came

down to him, and wept over his face, and said, "O *my father*, *my father*, the chariots of Israel and their horsemen

1Chr 28:4 However the Lord God of Israel chose me above all the house of *my father* to be king over Israel forever, for He has chosen Judah to be the ruler; and of the house of Judah, the house of *my father*, and among the sons of *my father*, He was pleased with me to make me king over all Israel

2Chr 1:8 You have shown great mercy to David *my father*, and have made me king in his place

2Chr 1:9 Now, O Lord God, let Your promise to David *my father* be established, for You have made me king over a people like the dust of the earth in multitude

2Chr 2:3 As you have dealt with David *my father*, and sent him cedars to build himself a house to dwell in, so deal with me

2Chr 2:7 Therefore send me at once a man skillful to work in gold and silver, in bronze and iron, in purple and crimson and blue, who has skill to engrave with the skillful men who are with me in Judah and Jerusalem, whom David *my father* provided

2Chr 6:4 Blessed be the Lord God of Israel, who has fulfilled with His hands what He spoke with His mouth to *my father* David, saying

2Chr 6:7 Now it was in the heart of *my father* David to build a temple for the name of the Lord God of Israel

2Chr 6:8 But the Lord said to *my father* David, 'Whereas it was in your heart to build a temple for My name, you did well in that it was in your heart

2Chr 6:10 So the Lord has fulfilled His word which He spoke, and I have filled the position of *my father* David, and sit on the throne of Israel, as the Lord promised

2Chr 6:15 You have kept what You promised Your servant David *my father*

2Chr 6:16 Therefore, Lord God of Israel, now keep what You promised Your servant David *my father*, saying

2Chr 10:11 And now, whereas *my father* put a heavy yoke on you, I will add to your yoke; *my father* chastised you with whips, but I will chastise you with scourges

2Chr 10:14 and he spoke to them according to the counsel of the young men, saying, "*My father* made your yoke heavy, but I will add to it; *my father* chastised you with whips, but I will chastise you with scourges

2Chr 16:3 Let there be a treaty between you and me, as there was between *my father* and your father

Job 17:14 if I say to corruption, 'You are *my father*,' and to the worm

Ps 27:10 When *my father* and my mother forsake me, then the Lord will take care of me

Ps 89:26 He shall cry to Me, 'You are *my Father*, My God, and the rock of my salvation

Is 8:4 for before the child shall have knowledge to cry '*My father*

Jer 2:27 Saying to a tree, 'You are *my father*,' and to a stone

Jer 3:4 Will you not from this time cry to Me, '*My father*, You are the guide of my youth

Jer 3:19 You shall call Me, "*My Father*," and not turn away from Me

Jer 20:15 Let the man be cursed who brought news to *my father*, saying

Dan 5:13 And the king spoke, and said to Daniel, "Are you that Daniel who is one of the captives from Judah, whom *my father* the king brought from Judah

Matt 7:21 Not everyone who says to Me, 'Lord, Lord,' shall enter the kingdom of heaven, but he who does the will of *My Father* in heaven

Matt 8:21 Then another of His disciples said to Him, "Lord, let me first go and bury *my father*

Matt 10:32 Therefore whoever confesses Me before men, him I will also confess before *My Father* who is in heaven

Matt 10:33 But whoever denies Me before men, him I will also deny before *My Father* who is in heaven

Matt 11:27 All things have been delivered to Me by *My Father*, and no one knows the Son except the Father

Matt 12:50 For whoever does the will of *My Father* in heaven is My brother and sister and mother

Matt 16:17 Jesus answered and said to him, "Blessed are you, Simon Bar-Jonah, for flesh and blood has not revealed this to you, but *My Father* who is in heaven

Matt 18:10 Take heed that you do not despise one of these little ones, for I say to you that in heaven their angels always see the face of *My Father* who is in heaven

Matt 18:19 Again I say to you that if two of you agree on earth concerning anything that they ask, it will be done for them by *My Father* in heaven

Matt 20:23 but to sit on My right hand and on My left is not Mine to give, but it is for those for whom it is prepared by *My Father*

Matt 24:36 But of that day and hour no one knows, no, not even the angels of heaven, but *My Father* only

Matt 25:34 Then the King will say to those on His right hand, 'Come, you blessed of *My Father*, inherit the kingdom prepared for you from the foundation of the world

Matt 26:39 He went a little farther and fell on His face, and prayed, saying, "O *My Father*, if it is possible, let this cup pass from Me

Matt 26:42 He went away again a second time and prayed, saying, "O *My Father*, if this cup cannot pass away from Me unless I drink it, Your will be done

Matt 26:53 Or do you think that I cannot now pray to *My Father*, and He will provide Me with more than twelve legions of angels

Luke 9:59 But he said, "Lord, let me first go and bury *my father*

Luke 10:22 All things have been delivered to Me by *My Father*, and no one knows who the Son is but the Father, and who the Father is but the Son, and the one to whom the Son wills to reveal Him

Luke 15:18 I will arise and go to *my father*, and will say to him

Luke 22:29 And I bestow upon you a kingdom, just as *My Father* bestowed one upon Me

Luke 24:49 Behold, I send the Promise of *My Father* upon you

John 5:17 But Jesus answered them, "*My Father* has been working until now, and I have been working

John 6:32 Then Jesus said to them, "Most assuredly, I say to you, Moses did not give you the bread from heaven, but *My Father* gives you the true bread from heaven

John 6:65 And He said, "Therefore I have said to you that no one can come to Me unless it has been granted to him by *My Father*

John 8:19 Jesus answered, "You know neither Me nor *My Father*. If you had known Me, you would have known *My Father* also

John 8:28 but as *My Father* taught Me, I speak these things

John 8:38 I speak what I have seen with *My Fa-*

ther, and you do what you have seen with your father
John 8:49 Jesus answered, "I do not have a demon; but I honor *My Father*, and you dishonor Me
John 8:54 It is *My Father* who honors Me, of whom you say that He is your God
John 10:17 Therefore *My Father* loves Me, because I lay down My life that I may take it again
John 10:18 I have power to lay it down, and I have power to take it again. This command I have received from *My Father*
John 10:29 *My Father*, who has given them to Me, is greater than all
John 10:30 I and *My Father* are one
John 10:32 Jesus answered them, "Many good works I have shown you from *My Father*
John 10:37 If I do not do the works of *My Father*, do not believe Me
John 12:26 and where I am, there My servant will be also. If anyone serves Me, him *My Father* will honor
John 14:7 If you had known Me, you would have known *My Father* also
John 14:12 and greater works than these he will do, because I go to *My Father*
John 14:20 At that day you will know that I am in *My Father*, and you in Me, and I in you
John 14:21 And he who loves Me will be loved by *My Father*, and I will love him and manifest Myself to him
John 14:23 and *My Father* will love him, and We will come to him and make Our home with him
John 14:28 If you loved Me, you would rejoice because I said, 'I am going to the Father,' for *My Father* is greater than I
John 15:1 I am the true vine, and *My Father* is the vinedresser
John 15:8 By this *My Father* is glorified, that you bear much fruit
John 15:15 but I have called you friends, for all things that I heard from *My Father* I have made known to you
John 15:23 He who hates Me hates *My Father* also
John 15:24 but now they have seen and also hated both Me and *My Father*
John 16:10 of righteousness, because I go to *My Father* and you see Me no more
John 18:11 Shall I not drink the cup which *My Father* has given Me
John 20:17 Jesus said to her, "Do not cling to Me, for I have not yet ascended to *My Father;* but go to My brethren and say to them, 'I am ascending to *My Father* and your Father, and to My God and your God
Rev 2:27 as the potter's vessels shall be broken to pieces as I also have received from *My Father*
Rev 3:5 but I will confess his name before *My Father* and before His angels
Rev 3:21 To him who overcomes I will grant to sit with Me on My throne, as I also overcame and sat down with *My Father* on His throne

MY FATHER IN HEAVEN
Matt 7:21 Not everyone who says to Me, 'Lord, Lord,' shall enter the kingdom of heaven, but he who does the will of *My Father in heaven*
Matt 12:50 For whoever does the will of *My Father in heaven* is My brother and sister and mother
Matt 18:19 Again I say to you that if two of you agree on earth concerning anything that they ask, it will be done for them by *My Father in heaven*

MY FATHER IS GLORIFIED
John 15:8 By this *My Father is glorified*, that you bear much fruit

MY FATHER WHO IS IN HEAVEN (NAS, NIV, RSV)
(See *MY FATHER IN HEAVEN*)

MY FATHER'S BUSINESS
Luke 2:49 Did you not know that I must be about *My Father's business*

MY FATHER'S HOUSE
Gen 20:13 And it came to pass, when God caused me to wander from *my father's house*, that I said to her
Gen 24:7 The Lord God of heaven, who took me from *my father's house* and from the land of my family, and who spoke to me and swore to me, saying
Gen 24:38 but you shall go to *my father's house* and to my family, and take a wife for my son
Gen 24:40 and you shall take a wife for my son from my family and from *my father's house*
Gen 28:21 so that I come back to *my father's house* in peace, then the Lord shall be my God
Gen 41:51 For God has made me forget all my toil and all *my father's house*
Gen 46:31 Then Joseph said to his brothers and to his father's household, "I will go up and tell Pharaoh, and say to him, 'My brothers and those of *my father's house*, who were in the land of Canaan, have come to me
Josh 2:12 Now therefore, I beg you, swear to me by the Lord, since I have shown you kindness, that you also will show kindness to *my father's house*, and give me a true token
Judg 6:15 Indeed my clan is the weakest in Manasseh, and I am the least in *my father's house*
Judg 9:18 but you have risen up against *my father's house* this day, and killed his seventy sons on one stone, and made Abimelech, the son of his maidservant, king over the men of Shechem, because he is your brother
Judg 11:7 So Jephthah said to the elders of Gilead, "Did you not hate me, and expel me from *my father's house*
1Sam 24:21 Therefore swear now to me by the Lord that you will not cut off my descendants after me, and that you will not destroy my name from *my father's house*
2Sam 14:9 And the woman of Tekoa said to the king, "My lord, O king, let the iniquity be on me and on *my father's house*, and the king and his throne be guiltless
2Sam 19:28 For all of *my father's house* were but dead men before my lord the king
2Sam 24:17 Let Your hand, I pray, be against me and against *my father's house*
1Chr 21:17 Let Your hand, I pray, O Lord my God, be against me and *my father's house*, but not against Your people that they should be plagued
Neh 1:6 please let Your ear be attentive and Your eyes open, that You may hear the prayer of Your servant which I pray before You now, day and night, for the children of Israel Your servants, and confess the sins of the children of Israel which we have sinned against You. Both *my father's house* and I have sinned
Luke 16:27 Then he said, 'I beg you therefore, father, that you would send him to *my father's house*
John 2:16 Do not make *My Father's house* a house of merchandise
John 14:2 In *My Father's house* are many mansions; if it were not so, I would have told you

MY FLESH
Gen 2:23 This is now bone of my bones and flesh of *my flesh*
Gen 29:14 And Laban said to him, "Surely you are my bone and *my flesh*

2Sam 19:12 You are my brethren, you are my bone and *my flesh*
2Sam 19:13 And say to Amasa, 'Are you not my bone and *my flesh*
Job 6:12 Is my strength the strength of stones? Or is *my flesh* bronze
Job 7:5 *My flesh* is caked with worms and dust, my skin is cracked and breaks out afresh
Job 13:14 Why do I take *my flesh* in my teeth, and put my life in my hands
Job 19:20 My bone clings to my skin and to *my flesh*, and I have escaped by the skin of my teeth
Job 19:22 Why do you persecute me as God does, and are not satisfied with *my flesh*
Job 19:26 and after my skin is destroyed, this I know, that in *my flesh* I shall see God
Job 21:6 Even when I remember I am terrified, and trembling takes hold of *my flesh*
Ps 16:9 Therefore my heart is glad, and my glory rejoices; *my flesh* also will rest in hope
Ps 27:2 When the wicked came against me to eat up *my flesh*, my enemies and foes, they stumbled and fell
Ps 38:3 There is no soundness in *my flesh* because of Your anger, nor is there any health in my bones because of my sin
Ps 38:7 For my loins are full of inflammation, and there is no soundness in *my flesh*
Ps 63:1 *My flesh* longs for You in a dry and thirsty land where there is no water
Ps 73:26 *My flesh* and my heart fail; but God is the strength of my heart and my portion forever
Ps 84:2 My heart and *my flesh* cry out for the living God
Ps 109:24 My knees are weak through fasting, and *my flesh* is feeble from lack of fatness
Ps 119:120 *My flesh* trembles for fear of You, and I am afraid of Your judgments
Eccl 2:3 I searched in my heart how to gratify *my flesh* with wine, while guiding my heart with wisdom, and how to lay hold on folly, till I might see what was good for the sons of men to do under heaven all the days of their lives
Jer 51:35 Let the violence done to me and *my flesh* be upon Babylon
Lam 3:4 He has aged *my flesh* and my skin, and broken my bones
John 6:51 and the bread that I shall give is *My flesh*, which I shall give for the life of the world
John 6:54 Whoever eats *My flesh* and drinks My blood has eternal life, and I will raise him up at the last day
John 6:55 For *My flesh* is food indeed, and My blood is drink indeed
John 6:56 He who eats *My flesh* and drinks My blood abides in Me, and I in him
Acts 2:26 therefore my heart rejoiced, and my tongue was glad; moreover *my flesh* will also rest in hope
Rom 7:18 For I know that in me (that is, in *my flesh*
Rom 11:14 if by any means I may provoke to jealousy those who are *my flesh* and save some of them
Gal 4:14 And my trial which was in *my flesh* you did not despise or reject, but you received me as an angel of God, even as Christ Jesus
Col 1:24 I now rejoice in my sufferings for you, and fill up in *my flesh* what is lacking in the afflictions of Christ, for the sake of His body, which is the church

MY FLOCK
Gen 31:43 And Laban answered and said to Jacob, "These daughters are my daughters, and these children are my children, and this flock is *my flock*
Job 30:1 But now they mock at me, men younger than I, whose fathers I disdained to put with the dogs of *my flock*
Jer 23:2 You have scattered *My flock*, driven them away, and not attended to them
Jer 23:3 But I will gather the remnant of *My flock* out of all countries where I have driven them, and bring them back to their folds
Ezek 34:6 yes, *My flock* was scattered over the whole face of the earth, and no one was seeking or searching for them
Ezek 34:8 as I live," says the Lord God, "surely because *My flock* became a prey, and *My flock* became food for every beast of the field, because there was no shepherd, nor did My shepherds search for *My flock*, but the shepherds fed themselves and did not feed *My flock*
Ezek 34:10 Behold, I am against the shepherds, and I will require *My flock* at their hand; I will cause them to cease feeding the sheep, and the shepherds shall feed themselves no more; for I will deliver *My flock* from their mouths, that they may no longer be food for them
Ezek 34:15 I will feed *My flock*, and I will make them lie down
Ezek 34:17 And as for you, O *My flock*, thus says the Lord God
Ezek 34:19 And as for *My flock*, they eat what you have trampled with your feet, and they drink what you have fouled with your feet
Ezek 34:22 therefore I will save *My flock*, and they shall no longer be a prey
Ezek 34:31 You are *My flock*, the flock of My pasture; you are men, and I am your God

MY FORTRESS
2Sam 22:2 The Lord is my rock, *my fortress* and my deliverer
Ps 18:2 The Lord is my rock and *my fortress* and my deliverer
Ps 31:3 For You are my rock and *my fortress;* therefore, for Your name's sake, lead me and guide me
Ps 71:3 You have given the commandment to save me, for You are my rock and *my fortress*
Ps 91:2 I will say of the Lord, "He is my refuge and *my fortress*
Ps 144:2 My lovingkindness and *my fortress*, my high tower and my deliverer, my shield and the One in whom I take refuge, Who subdues my people under me
Jer 16:19 O Lord, my strength and *my fortress*, my refuge in the day of affliction, the Gentiles shall come to You from the ends of the earth and say

MY GOD, MY GOD
Ps 22:1 *My God, My God*, why have You forsaken Me
Matt 27:46 that is, "*My God, My God*, why have You forsaken Me
Mark 15:34 which is translated, "*My God, My God*, why have You forsaken Me

MY GRACE IS SUFFICIENT
2Cor 12:9 And He said to me, "*My grace is sufficient* for you, for My strength is made perfect in weakness

MY HOLY HILL
Ps 2:6 Yet I have set My King on *My holy hill* of Zion

MY HOUR HAS NOT YET COME
John 2:4 Jesus said to her, "Woman, what does your concern have to do with Me? *My hour has not yet come*

MY JOY IS THE JOY OF YOU ALL
2Cor 2:3 And I wrote this very thing to you, lest, when I came, I should have sorrow over those from whom I ought to have joy, having confidence in you all that *my joy is the joy of you all*

MY JUDGMENT IS TRUE
John 8:16 And yet if I do judge, *My judgment is true*

MY KINGDOM IS NOT OF THIS WORLD
John 18:36 Jesus answered, "*My kingdom is not of this world*. If My kingdom were of this world, My servants would fight, so that I should not be delivered to the Jews

MY LEGS TREMBLED (NIV)
(See *TREMBLED IN MYSELF*)

MY LIGHT AND MY SALVATION
Ps 27:1 The Lord is *my light and my salvation;* whom shall I fear

MY LORD AND MY GOD
John 20:28 And Thomas answered and said to Him, "*My Lord and my God*

MY LORD THE KING
1Sam 24:8 David also arose afterward, went out of the cave, and called out to Saul, saying, "*My lord the king*
1Sam 26:19 Now therefore, please, let *my lord the king* hear the words of his servant
1Sam 29:8 And to this day what have you found in your servant as long as I have been with you, that I may not go and fight against the enemies of *my lord the king*
2Sam 3:21 Then Abner said to David, "I will arise and go, and gather all Israel to *my lord the king*, that they may make a covenant with you, and that you may reign over all that your heart desires
2Sam 4:8 and the Lord has avenged *my lord the king* this day of Saul and his descendants
2Sam 9:11 Then Ziba said to the king, "According to all that *my lord the king* has commanded his servant, so will your servant do
2Sam 13:33 Now therefore, let not *my lord the king* take the thing to his heart, to think that all the king's sons are dead
2Sam 14:12 Then the woman said, "Please, let your maidservant speak another word to *my lord the king*
2Sam 14:15 Now therefore, I have come to speak of this thing to *my lord the king* because the people have made me afraid
2Sam 14:17 Your maidservant said, 'The word of *my lord the king* will now be comforting; for as the angel of God, so is *my lord the king* in discerning good and evil
2Sam 14:18 And the woman said, "Please, let *my lord the king* speak
2Sam 14:19 And the woman answered and said, "As you live, *my lord the king*, no one can turn to the right hand or to the left from anything that *my lord the king* has spoken
2Sam 15:15 And the king's servants said to the king, "We are your servants, ready to do whatever *my lord the king* commands
2Sam 15:21 And Ittai answered the king and said, "As the Lord lives, and as *my lord the king* lives, surely in whatever place *my lord the king* shall be, whether in death or life, even there also your servant will be
2Sam 16:9 Then Abishai the son of Zeruiah said to the king, "Why should this dead dog curse *my lord the king*
2Sam 18:28 Then he bowed down with his face to the earth before the king, and said, "Blessed be the Lord your God, who has delivered up the men who raised their hand against *my lord the king*
2Sam 18:31 Just then the Cushite came, and the Cushite said, "There is good news, *my lord the king*
2Sam 18:32 And the Cushite answered, "May the enemies of *my lord the king*, and all who rise against you to do you harm, be as that young man is
2Sam 19:19 Then he said to the king, "Do not let my lord impute iniquity to me, or remember what wrong your servant did on the day that *my lord the king* left Jerusalem, that the king should take it to heart
2Sam 19:20 Therefore here I am, the first to come today of all the house of Joseph to go down to meet *my lord the king*
2Sam 19:27 And he has slandered your servant to *my lord the king*, but *my lord the king* is like the angel of God
2Sam 19:28 For all of my father's house were but dead men before *my lord the king*
2Sam 19:30 Then Mephibosheth said to the king, "Rather, let him take it all, inasmuch as *my lord the king* has come back in peace to his own house
2Sam 19:35 Why then should your servant be a further burden to *my lord the king*
2Sam 19:37 let him cross over with *my lord the king*, and do for him what seems good to you
2Sam 24:3 And Joab said to the king, "Now may the Lord your God add to the people a hundredfold more than there are, and may the eyes of *my lord the king* see it. But why does *my lord the king* desire this thing
2Sam 24:21 Then Araunah said, "Why has *my lord the king* come to his servant
2Sam 24:22 Now Araunah said to David, "Let *my lord the king* take and offer up whatever seems good to him
1Kin 1:18 and now, *my lord the king*, you do not know about it
1Kin 1:20 And as for you, my lord, O king, the eyes of all Israel are on you, that you should tell them who will sit on the throne of *my lord the king* after him
1Kin 1:21 Otherwise it will happen, when *my lord the king* rests with his fathers, that I and my son Solomon will be counted as offenders
1Kin 1:27 Has this thing been done by *my lord the king*, and you have not told your servant who should sit on the throne of *my lord the king* after him
1Kin 1:36 May the Lord God of *my lord the king* say so too
1Kin 1:37 As the Lord has been with *my lord the king*, even so may He be with Solomon, and make his throne greater than the throne of my lord King David
1Kin 2:38 As *my lord the king* has said, so your servant will do
1Kin 20:9 Therefore he said to the messengers of Ben-Hadad, "Tell *my lord the king*
1Chr 21:3 But, *my lord the king*, are they not all my lord's servants
1Chr 21:23 And Ornan said to David, "Take it to yourself, and let *my lord the king* do what is good in his eyes
Jer 37:20 Therefore please hear now, O *my lord the king*. Please, let my petition be accepted before you, and do not make me return to the house of Jonathan the scribe, lest I die there
Jer 38:9 *My lord the king*, these men have done evil in all that they have done to Jeremiah the prophet, whom they have cast into the dungeon, and he is likely to die from hunger in the place where he is

Dan 1:10 And the chief of the eunuchs said to Daniel, "I fear *my lord the king*, who has appointed your food and drink
Dan 4:24 this is the interpretation, O king, and this is the decree of the Most High, which has come upon *my lord the king*

MY MOTHER'S WOMB
Judg 16:17 that he told her all his heart, and said to her, "No razor has ever come upon my head, for I have been a Nazirite to God from *my mother's womb*
Job 1:21 Naked I came from *my mother's womb*, and naked shall I return there
Job 3:10 because it did not shut up the doors of *my mother's womb*, nor hide sorrow from my eyes
Job 31:18 (But from my youth I reared him as a father, and from *my mother's womb* I guided the widow
Ps 22:10 I was cast upon You from birth. From *My mother's womb* You have been My God
Ps 71:6 You are He who took me out of *my mother's womb*
Ps 139:13 For You have formed my inward parts; You have covered me in *my mother's womb*
Gal 1:15 But when it pleased God, who separated me from *my mother's womb* and called me through His grace

MY NAME IS LEGION
Mark 5:9 And he answered, saying, "*My name is Legion;* for we are many

MY OWN FLESH AND BLOOD (NIV)
(See *MY BONE AND MY FLESH*)

MY PEOPLE
Gen 23:11 I give it to you in the presence of the sons of *my people*
Gen 41:40 You shall be over my house, and all *my people* shall be ruled according to your word
Gen 49:29 I am to be gathered to *my people;* bury me with my fathers in the cave that is in the field of Ephron the Hittite
Ex 3:7 I have surely seen the oppression of *My people* who are in Egypt, and have heard their cry because of their taskmasters, for I know their sorrows
Ex 3:10 Come now, therefore, and I will send you to Pharaoh that you may bring *My people*, the children of Israel, out of Egypt
Ex 5:1 Let *My people* go, that they may hold a feast to Me in the wilderness
Ex 6:7 I will take you as *My people*, and I will be your God
Ex 7:4 But Pharaoh will not heed you, so that I may lay My hand on Egypt and bring My armies and *My people*, the children of Israel, out of the land of Egypt by great judgments
Ex 7:16 And you shall say to him, 'The Lord God of the Hebrews has sent me to you, saying, "Let *My people* go, that they may serve Me in the wilderness
Ex 8:1 And the Lord spoke to Moses, "Go to Pharaoh and say to him, 'Thus says the Lord: "Let *My people* go, that they may serve Me
Ex 8:8 Then Pharaoh called for Moses and Aaron, and said, "Entreat the Lord that He may take away the frogs from me and from *my people*
Ex 8:20 Then say to him, 'Thus says the Lord: "Let *My people* go, that they may serve Me
Ex 8:21 Or else, if you will not let *My people* go, behold, I will send swarms of flies on you and your servants, on your people and into your houses
Ex 8:22 And in that day I will set apart the land of Goshen, in which *My people* dwell, that no swarms of flies shall be there, in order that you may know that I am the Lord in the midst of the land
Ex 8:23 I will make a difference between *My people* and your people
Ex 9:1 Then the Lord said to Moses, "Go in to Pharaoh and tell him, 'Thus says the Lord God of the Hebrews: "Let *My people* go, that they may serve Me
Ex 9:13 Then the Lord said to Moses, "Rise early in the morning and stand before Pharaoh, and say to him, 'Thus says the Lord God of the Hebrews: "Let *My people* go, that they may serve Me
Ex 9:17 As yet you exalt yourself against *My people* in that you will not let them go
Ex 9:27 The Lord is righteous, and *my people* and I are wicked
Ex 10:3 How long will you refuse to humble yourself before Me? Let *My people* go, that they may serve Me
Ex 10:4 Or else, if you refuse to let *My people* go, behold, tomorrow I will bring locusts into your territory
Ex 12:31 Then he called for Moses and Aaron by night, and said, "Rise and go out from among *my people*, both you and the children of Israel
Ex 22:25 If you lend money to any of *My people* who are poor among you, you shall not be like a moneylender to him
Lev 26:12 I will walk among you and be your God, and you shall be *My people*
Num 24:14 And now, indeed, I am going to *my people*. Come, I will advise you what this people will do to your people in the latter days
Judg 12:2 And Jephthah said to them, "*My people* and I were in a great struggle with the people of Ammon
Judg 14:3 Then his father and mother said to him, "Is there no woman among the daughters of your brethren, or among all *my people*, that you must go and get a wife from the uncircumcised Philistines
Judg 14:16 You have posed a riddle to the sons of *my people*, but you have not explained it to me
Ruth 1:16 your people shall be *my people*, and your God, my God
Ruth 4:4 And I thought to inform you, saying, 'Buy it back in the presence of the inhabitants and the elders of *my people*
1Sam 2:29 Why do you kick at My sacrifice and My offering which I have commanded in My habitation, and honor your sons more than Me, to make yourselves fat with the best of all the offerings of Israel *My people*
1Sam 9:16 Tomorrow about this time I will send you a man from the land of Benjamin, and you shall anoint him commander over *My people* Israel, that he may save *My people* from the hand of the Philistines; for I have looked upon *My people*, because their cry has come to me
1Sam 9:17 And when Samuel saw Saul, the Lord said to him, "There he is, the man of whom I spoke to you. This one shall reign over *My people*
1Sam 15:30 yet honor me now, please, before the elders of *my people* and before Israel, and return with me, that I may worship the Lord your God
2Sam 3:18 For the Lord has spoken of David, saying, 'By the hand of My servant David, I will save *My people* Israel from the hand of the Philistines and the hand of all their enemies
2Sam 5:2 and the Lord said to you, 'You shall shepherd *My people* Israel, and be ruler over Israel
2Sam 7:7 In all the places where I have walked with all the children of Israel, have I ever spoken a word to anyone from the tribes of Israel, whom

I commanded to shepherd *My people* Israel, saying
2Sam 7:8 I took you from the sheepfold, from following the sheep, to be ruler over *My people*, over Israel
2Sam 7:10 Moreover I will appoint a place for *My people* Israel, and will plant them, that they may dwell in a place of their own and move no more
2Sam 7:11 since the time that I commanded judges to be over *My people* Israel, and have caused you to rest from all your enemies
2Sam 22:44 You have also delivered me from the strivings of *my people*
1Kin 6:13 And I will dwell among the children of Israel, and will not forsake *My people* Israel
1Kin 8:16 Since the day that I brought *My people* Israel out of Egypt, I have chosen no city from any tribe of Israel in which to build a house, that My name might be there; but I chose David to be over *My people* Israel
1Kin 14:7 Because I exalted you from among the people, and made you ruler over *My people* Israel
1Kin 16:2 Inasmuch as I lifted you out of the dust and made you ruler over *My people* Israel, and you have walked in the way of Jeroboam, and have made *My people* Israel sin, to provoke Me to anger with their sins
1Kin 22:4 And Jehoshaphat said to the king of Israel, "I am as you are, *my people* as your people, my horses as your horses
2Kin 3:7 I am as you are, *my people* as your people, my horses as your horses
2Kin 20:5 Return and tell Hezekiah the leader of *My people*, 'Thus says the Lord, the God of David your father
1Chr 11:2 and the Lord your God said to you, 'You shall shepherd *My people* Israel, and be ruler over *My people* Israel
1Chr 17:6 Wherever I have moved about with all Israel, have I ever spoken a word to any of the judges of Israel, whom I commanded to shepherd *My people*, saying
1Chr 17:7 I took you from the sheepfold, from following the sheep, that you should be ruler over *My people* Israel
1Chr 17:9 Moreover I will appoint a place for *My people* Israel, and will plant them, that they may dwell in a place of their own and move no more
1Chr 17:10 since the time that I commanded judges to be over *My people* Israel
1Chr 28:2 Then King David rose to his feet and said, "Hear me, my brethren and *my people*
1Chr 29:14 But who am I, and who are *my people*, that we should be able to offer so willingly as this
2Chr 1:11 Because this was in your heart, and you have not asked riches or wealth or honor or the life of your enemies, nor have you asked long life but have asked wisdom and knowledge for yourself, that you may judge *My people* over whom I have made you king
2Chr 6:5 Since the day that I brought *My people* out of the land of Egypt, I have chosen no city from any tribe of Israel in which to build a house, that My name might be there, nor did I choose any man to be a ruler over *My people* Israel
2Chr 6:6 and I have chosen David to be over *My people* Israel
2Chr 7:13 When I shut up heaven and there is no rain, or command the locusts to devour the land, or send pestilence among *My people*
2Chr 7:14 if *My people* who are called by My name will humble themselves, and pray and seek My face, and turn from their wicked ways, then I will hear from heaven, and will forgive their sin and heal their land
2Chr 18:3 And he answered him, "I am as you are, and *my people* as your people
Esth 7:3 Then Queen Esther answered and said, "If I have found favor in your sight, O king, and if it pleases the king, let my life be given me at my petition, and *my people* at my request
Esth 7:4 For we have been sold, *my people* and I, to be destroyed, to be killed, and to be annihilated
Esth 8:6 For how can I endure to see the evil that will come to *my people*
Ps 14:4 Have all the workers of iniquity no knowledge, who eat up *my people* as they eat bread, and do not call on the Lord
Ps 50:7 Hear, O *My people*, and I will speak, O Israel, and I will testify against you
Ps 53:4 Have the workers of iniquity no knowledge, who eat up *my people* as they eat bread, and do not call upon God
Ps 59:11 Do not slay them, lest *my people* forget; scatter them by Your power, and bring them down, O Lord our shield
Ps 78:1 Give ear, O *my people*, to my law; incline your ears to the words of my mouth
Ps 81:8 Hear, O *My people*, and I will admonish you! O Israel, if you will listen to Me
Ps 81:11 But *My people* would not heed My voice, and Israel would have none of Me
Ps 81:13 Oh, that *My people* would listen to Me, that Israel would walk in My ways
Ps 144:2 My lovingkindness and my fortress, my high tower and my deliverer, my shield and the One in whom I take refuge, Who subdues *my people* under me
Is 1:3 but Israel does not know, *My people* do not consider
Is 3:12 As for *My people*, children are their oppressors, and women rule over them. O *My people*
Is 3:15 What do you mean by crushing *My people* and grinding the faces of the poor
Is 5:13 Therefore *my people* have gone into captivity, because they have no knowledge
Is 10:2 to rob the needy of justice, and to take what is right from the poor of *My people*, that widows may be their prey, and that they may rob the fatherless
Is 10:24 O *My people*, who dwell in Zion, do not be afraid of the Assyrian
Is 19:25 whom the Lord of hosts shall bless, saying, "Blessed is Egypt *My people*, and Assyria the work of My hands, and Israel My inheritance
Is 22:4 do not labor to comfort me because of the plundering of the daughter of *my people*
Is 26:20 Come, *my people*, enter your chambers, and shut your doors behind you
Is 32:13 On the land of *my people* will come up thorns and briers, yes, on all the happy homes in the joyous city
Is 32:18 *My people* will dwell in a peaceful habitation, in secure dwellings, and in quiet resting places
Is 40:1 Comfort, yes, comfort *My people!*" says your God
Is 43:20 The beast of the field will honor Me, the jackals and the ostriches, because I give waters in the wilderness and rivers in the desert, to give drink to *My people*, My chosen
Is 47:6 I was angry with *My people;* I have profaned My inheritance, and given them into your hand
Is 51:4 Listen to Me, *My people;* and give ear to Me, O My nation
Is 51:16 I have covered you with the shadow of My hand, that I may plant the heavens, lay the foundations of the earth, and say to Zion, 'You are *My people*
Is 52:4 *My people* went down at first into Egypt to sojourn there
Is 52:5 Now therefore, what have I here," says the Lord, "that *My people* are taken away for nothing

Is 52:6 Therefore *My people* shall know My name; therefore they shall know in that day that I am He who speaks
Is 53:8 For He was cut off from the land of the living; for the transgressions of *My people* He was stricken
Is 57:14 Prepare the way, take the stumbling block out of the way of *My people*
Is 58:1 tell *My people* their transgression, and the house of Jacob their sins
Is 63:8 For He said, "Surely they are *My people*, children who will not lie
Is 65:10 Sharon shall be a fold of flocks, and the Valley of Achor a place for herds to lie down, for *My people* who have sought Me
Is 65:19 I will rejoice in Jerusalem, and joy in *My people*
Is 65:22 for as the days of a tree, so shall be the days of *My people*, and My elect shall long enjoy the work of their hands
Jer 2:11 But *My people* have changed their glory for what does not profit
Jer 2:13 For *My people* have committed two evils: they have forsaken Me, the fountain of living waters, and hewn themselves cisterns broken cisterns that can hold no water
Jer 2:31 Why do *My people* say, 'We are lords; we will come no more to You
Jer 2:32 Can a virgin forget her ornaments, or a bride her attire? Yet *My people* have forgotten Me days without number
Jer 4:11 At that time it will be said to this people and to Jerusalem, "A dry wind of the desolate heights blows in the wilderness toward the daughter of *My people* not to fan or to cleanse
Jer 4:22 For *My people* are foolish, they have not known Me
Jer 5:26 For among *My people* are found wicked men; they lie in wait as one who sets snares
Jer 5:31 and *My people* love to have it so. But what will you do in the end
Jer 6:14 They have also healed the hurt of *My people* slightly, saying
Jer 6:26 O daughter of *my people*, clothe yourself with sackcloth, and roll about in ashes
Jer 6:27 I have set you as an assayer and a fortress among *My people*, that you may know and test their way
Jer 7:12 But go now to My place which was in Shiloh, where I set My name at the first, and see what I did to it because of the wickedness of *My people* Israel
Jer 7:23 But this is what I commanded them, saying, 'Obey My voice, and I will be your God, and you shall be *My people*
Jer 8:7 But *My people* do not know the judgment of the Lord
Jer 8:11 For they have healed the hurt of the daughter of *My people* slightly, saying
Jer 8:19 The voice, the cry of the daughter of *my people* from a far country
Jer 8:21 For the hurt of the daughter of *my people* I am hurt
Jer 8:22 Why then is there no recovery for the health of the daughter of *my people*
Jer 9:1 Oh, that my head were waters, and my eyes a fountain of tears, that I might weep day and night for the slain of the daughter of *my people*
Jer 9:2 that I might leave *my people*, and go from them
Jer 9:7 for how shall I deal with the daughter of *My people*
Jer 11:4 so shall you be *My people*, and I will be your God
Jer 12:14 Against all My evil neighbors who touch the inheritance which I have caused *My people* Israel to inherit behold, I will pluck them out of their land and pluck out the house of Judah from among them
Jer 12:16 And it shall be, if they will diligently learn the ways of *My people*, to swear by My name, 'As the Lord lives,' as they taught *My people* to swear by Baal, then they shall be established in the midst of *My people*
Jer 13:11 For as the sash clings to the waist of a man, so I have caused the whole house of Israel and the whole house of Judah to cling to Me,' says the Lord, 'that they may become *My people*, for renown, for praise, and for glory
Jer 14:17 for the virgin daughter of *my people* has been broken with a mighty stroke, with a very severe blow
Jer 15:7 I will destroy *My people*, since they do not return from their ways
Jer 18:15 Because *My people* have forgotten Me, they have burned incense to worthless idols
Jer 23:2 Therefore thus says the Lord God of Israel against the shepherds who feed *My people*
Jer 23:13 they prophesied by Baal and caused *My people* Israel to err
Jer 23:22 But if they had stood in My counsel, and had caused *My people* to hear My words, then they would have turned them from their evil way and from the evil of their doings
Jer 23:27 who try to make *My people* forget My name by their dreams which everyone tells his neighbor, as their fathers forgot My name for Baal
Jer 23:32 Behold, I am against those who prophesy false dreams," says the Lord, "and tell them, and cause *My people* to err by their lies and by their recklessness
Jer 24:7 and they shall be *My people*, and I will be their God, for they shall return to Me with their whole heart
Jer 29:32 he shall not have anyone to dwell among this people, nor shall he see the good that I will do for *My people*
Jer 30:3 For behold, the days are coming,' says the Lord, 'that I will bring back from captivity *My people* Israel and Judah
Jer 30:22 You shall be *My people*, and I will be your God
Jer 31:1 At the same time," says the Lord, "I will be the God of all the families of Israel, and they shall be *My people*
Jer 31:14 I will satiate the soul of the priests with abundance, and *My people* shall be satisfied with My goodness
Jer 31:33 and I will be their God, and they shall be *My people*
Jer 32:38 They shall be *My people*, and I will be their God
Jer 33:24 Thus they have despised *My people*, as if they should no more be a nation before them
Jer 50:6 *My people* have been lost sheep. Their shepherds have led them astray
Jer 51:45 *My people*, go out of the midst of her! And let everyone deliver himself from the fierce anger of the Lord
Lam 2:11 my bile is poured on the ground because of the destruction of the daughter of *my people*, because the children and the infants faint in the streets of the city
Lam 3:14 I have become the ridicule of all *my people*, and their taunting song all the day
Lam 3:48 My eyes overflow with rivers of water for the destruction of the daughter of *my people*
Lam 4:3 but the daughter of *my people* has become cruel, like ostriches in the wilderness
Lam 4:6 The punishment of the iniquity of the daughter of *my people* is greater than the punishment of the sin of Sodom, which was overthrown in a moment, with no hand to help her

Lam 4:10 they became food for them in the destruction of the daughter of *my people*
Ezek 11:20 and they shall be *My people*, and I will be their God
Ezek 13:9 they shall not be in the assembly of *My people*, nor be written in the record of the house of Israel, nor shall they enter into the land of Israel
Ezek 13:10 Because, indeed, because they have seduced *My people*, saying, 'Peace
Ezek 13:18 Will you hunt the souls of *My people*, and keep yourselves alive
Ezek 13:19 And will you profane Me among *My people* for handfuls of barley and for pieces of bread, killing people who should not die, and keeping people alive who should not live, by your lying to *My people* who listen to lies
Ezek 13:21 I will also tear off your veils and deliver *My people* out of your hand, and they shall no longer be as prey in your hand
Ezek 13:23 for I will deliver *My people* out of your hand, and you shall know that I am the Lord
Ezek 14:8 I will set My face against that man and make him a sign and a proverb, and I will cut him off from the midst of *My people*
Ezek 14:9 And if the prophet is induced to speak anything, I the Lord have induced that prophet, and I will stretch out My hand against him and destroy him from among *My people* Israel
Ezek 14:11 that the house of Israel may no longer stray from Me, nor be profaned anymore with all their transgressions, but that they may be *My people* and I may be their God
Ezek 21:12 for it will be against *My people*, against all the princes of Israel. Terrors including the sword will be against *My people*
Ezek 25:14 I will lay My vengeance on Edom by the hand of *My people* Israel, that they may do in Edom according to My anger and according to My fury
Ezek 33:31 So they come to you as people do, they sit before you as *My people*, and they hear your words, but they do not do them
Ezek 34:30 Thus they shall know that I, the Lord their God, am with them, and that they, the house of Israel, are *My people*
Ezek 36:8 But you, O mountains of Israel, you shall shoot forth your branches and yield your fruit to *My people* Israel, for they are about to come
Ezek 36:12 Yes, I will cause men to walk on you, *My people* Israel
Ezek 36:28 you shall be *My people*, and I will be your God
Ezek 37:12 Behold, O *My people*, I will open your graves and cause you to come up from your graves, and bring you into the land of Israel
Ezek 37:13 Then you shall know that I am the Lord, when I have opened your graves, O *My people*, and brought you up from your graves
Ezek 37:23 Then they shall be *My people*, and I will be their God
Ezek 37:27 indeed I will be their God, and they shall be *My people*
Ezek 38:14 On that day when *My people* Israel dwell safely, will you not know it
Ezek 38:16 You will come up against *My people* Israel like a cloud, to cover the land
Ezek 39:7 So I will make My holy name known in the midst of *My people* Israel, and I will not let them profane My holy name anymore
Ezek 44:23 And they shall teach *My people* the difference between the holy and the unholy, and cause them to discern between the unclean and the clean
Ezek 45:8 and My princes shall no more oppress *My people*, but they shall give the rest of the land to the house of Israel, according to their tribes
Ezek 45:9 Remove violence and plundering, execute justice and righteousness, and stop dispossessing *My people*
Ezek 46:18 he shall provide an inheritance for his sons from his own property, so that none of *My people* may be scattered from his property
Dan 9:20 Now while I was speaking, praying, and confessing my sin and the sin of *my people* Israel, and presenting my supplication before the Lord my God for the holy mountain of my God
Hos 1:9 Call his name Lo-Ammi, for you are not *My people*, and I will not be your God
Hos 1:10 And it shall come to pass in the place where it was said to them, 'You are not *My people*
Hos 2:1 Say to your brethren, '*My people*,' and to your sisters
Hos 2:23 then I will say to those who were not *My people*, 'You are *My people*
Hos 4:6 *My people* are destroyed for lack of knowledge. Because you have rejected knowledge, I also will reject you from being priest for Me
Hos 4:8 They eat up the sin of *My people;* they set their heart on their iniquity
Hos 4:12 *My people* ask counsel from their wooden idols, and their staff informs them
Hos 6:11 Also, O Judah, a harvest is appointed for you, when I return the captives of *My people*
Hos 11:7 *My people* are bent on backsliding from Me. Though they call to the Most High, none at all exalt Him
Joel 2:26 You shall eat in plenty and be satisfied, and praise the name of the Lord your God, who has dealt wondrously with you; and *My people* shall never be put to shame
Joel 2:27 Then you shall know that I am in the midst of Israel, and that I am the Lord your God and there is no other. *My people* shall never be put to shame
Joel 3:2 and I will enter into judgment with them there on account of *My people*, My heritage Israel, whom they have scattered among the nations
Joel 3:3 They have cast lots for *My people*, have given a boy in exchange for a harlot, and sold a girl for wine, that they may drink
Amos 7:8 Behold, I am setting a plumb line in the midst of *My people* Israel
Amos 7:15 Then the Lord took me as I followed the flock, and the Lord said to me, 'Go, prophesy to *My people* Israel
Amos 8:2 The end has come upon *my people* Israel; I will not pass by them anymore
Amos 9:10 All the sinners of *My people* shall die by the sword, who say
Amos 9:14 I will bring back the captives of *My people* Israel
Obad 13 You should not have entered the gate of *My people* in the day of their calamity
Mic 1:9 it has come to the gate of *My people*, even to Jerusalem
Mic 2:4 He has changed the heritage of *my people;* how He has removed it from me
Mic 2:8 Lately *My people* have risen up as an enemy you pull off the robe with the garment from those who trust you, as they pass by, like men returned from war
Mic 2:9 The women of *My people* you cast out from their pleasant houses
Mic 3:2 who strip the skin from *My people*, and the flesh from their bones
Mic 3:3 Who also eat the flesh of *My people*, flay their skin from them, break their bones, and chop them in pieces like meat for the pot, like flesh in the caldron
Mic 3:5 Thus says the Lord concerning the prophets who make *my people* stray

Mic 6:3 O *My people*, what have I done to you? And how have I wearied you
Mic 6:5 O *My people*, remember now what Balak king of Moab counseled, and what Balaam the son of Beor answered him, from Acacia Grove to Gilgal, that you may know the righteousness of the Lord
Mic 6:16 and you walk in their counsels, that I may make you a desolation, and your inhabitants a hissing. Therefore you shall bear the reproach of *My people*
Zeph 2:8 I have heard the reproach of Moab, and the revilings of the people of Ammon, with which they have reproached *My people*, and made arrogant threats against their borders
Zeph 2:9 the residue of *My people* shall plunder them, and the remnant of *My people* shall possess them
Zech 2:11 Many nations shall be joined to the Lord in that day, and they shall become *My people*
Zech 8:7 Behold, I will save *My people* from the land of the east and from the land of the west
Zech 8:8 They shall be *My people* and I will be their God, in truth and righteousness
Zech 13:9 I will say, 'This is *My people*'; and each one will say
Matt 2:6 for out of you shall come a Ruler who will shepherd *My people* Israel
Acts 7:34 I have certainly seen the oppression of *my people* who are in Egypt
Rom 9:25 I will call them *My people*, who were not *My people*, and her beloved, who was not beloved
Rom 9:26 And it shall come to pass in the place where it was said to them, 'You are not *My people*
2Cor 6:16 I will be their God, and they shall be *My people*
Heb 8:10 and I will be their God, and they shall be *My people*
Rev 18:4 And I heard another voice from heaven saying, "Come out of her, *my people*, lest you share in her sins, and lest you receive of her plagues

MY RECORD IS TRUE (KJV)
(See *MY WITNESS IS TRUE*)

MY REFUGE AND MY FORTRESS
Ps 91:2 I will say of the Lord, "He is *my refuge and my fortress*

MY RIGHT HAND
Job 30:12 At *my right hand* the rabble arises; they push away my feet, and they raise against me their ways of destruction
Ps 16:8 Because He is at *my right hand* I shall not be moved
Ps 73:23 Nevertheless I am continually with You; You hold me by *my right hand*
Ps 110:1 The Lord said to my Lord, "Sit at *My right hand*, till I make Your enemies Your footstool
Ps 137:5 If I forget you, O Jerusalem, let *my right hand* forget her skill
Ps 142:4 Look on *my right hand* and see, for there is no one who acknowledges me
Is 44:20 and he cannot deliver his soul, nor say, "Is there not a lie in *my right hand*
Is 48:13 Indeed My hand has laid the foundation of the earth, and *My right hand* has stretched out the heavens
Jer 22:24 As I live," says the Lord, "though Coniah the son of Jehoiakim, king of Judah, were the signet on *My right hand*, yet I would pluck you off
Matt 20:23 but to sit on *My right hand* and on My left is not Mine to give, but it is for those for whom it is prepared by My Father
Matt 22:44 The Lord said to my Lord, "Sit at *My right hand*, till I make Your enemies Your footstool
Mark 10:40 but to sit on *My right hand* and on My left is not Mine to give, but it is for those for whom it is prepared
Mark 12:36 The Lord said to my Lord, "Sit at *My right hand*, till I make Your enemies Your footstool
Luke 20:42 Now David himself said in the Book of Psalms, 'The Lord said to my Lord, "sit at *My right hand*
Acts 2:25 I foresaw the Lord always before my face, for He is at *my right hand*, that I may not be shaken
Acts 2:34 The Lord said to my Lord, "Sit at *My right hand*
Heb 1:13 Sit at *My right hand*, till I make Your enemies Your footstool
Rev 1:20 The mystery of the seven stars which you saw in *My right hand*, and the seven golden lampstands

MY SALVATION
Ex 15:2 The Lord is my strength and song, and He has become *my salvation*
2Sam 22:3 the God of my strength, in Him I will trust, my shield and the horn of *my salvation*, my stronghold and my refuge
2Sam 22:47 Blessed be my Rock! Let God be exalted, the Rock of *my salvation*
2Sam 23:5 For this is all *my salvation* and all my desire
Job 13:16 He also shall be *my salvation*, for a hypocrite could not come before Him
Ps 18:2 My shield and the horn of *my salvation*, my stronghold
Ps 18:46 Blessed be my Rock! Let the God of *my salvation* be exalted
Ps 25:5 Lead me in Your truth and teach me, for You are the God of *my salvation*
Ps 27:1 The Lord is my light and *my salvation;* whom shall I fear
Ps 27:9 Do not leave me nor forsake me, O God of *my salvation*
Ps 38:22 Make haste to help me, O Lord, *my salvation*
Ps 51:14 Deliver me from bloodguiltiness, O God, the God of *my salvation*, and my tongue shall sing aloud of Your righteousness
Ps 62:1 Truly my soul silently waits for God; from Him comes *my salvation*
Ps 62:2 He only is my rock and *my salvation;* He is my defense
Ps 62:6 He only is my rock and *my salvation;* He is my defense
Ps 62:7 In God is *my salvation* and my glory; the rock of my strength, and my refuge, is in God
Ps 88:1 O Lord, God of *my salvation*, I have cried out day and night before You
Ps 89:26 He shall cry to Me, 'You are my Father, My God, and the rock of *my salvation*
Ps 91:16 With long life I will satisfy him, and show him *My salvation*
Ps 118:14 The Lord is my strength and song, and He has become *my salvation*
Ps 118:21 I will praise You, for You have answered me, and have become *my salvation*
Ps 140:7 O God the Lord, the strength of *my salvation*, You have covered my head in the day of battle
Is 12:2 Behold, God is *my salvation*, I will trust and not be afraid; for YAH, the Lord, is my strength and my song; He also has become *my salvation*

Is 46:13 *My salvation* shall not linger. And I will place salvation in Zion, for Israel My glory
Is 49:6 I will also give You as a light to the Gentiles, that You should be *My salvation* to the ends of the earth
Is 51:5 My righteousness is near, *My salvation* has gone forth, and My arms will judge the peoples
Is 51:6 but *My salvation* will be forever, and My righteousness will not be abolished
Is 51:8 but My righteousness will be forever, and *My salvation* from generation to generation
Is 56:1 Keep justice, and do righteousness, for *My salvation* is about to come, and My righteousness to be revealed
Mic 7:7 I will wait for the God of *my salvation;* my God will hear me
Hab 3:18 Yet I will rejoice in the Lord, I will joy in the God of *my salvation*
Phil 1:19 For I know that this will turn out for *my salvation* through your prayer and the supply of the Spirit of Jesus Christ

MY SERVANT THE BRANCH
Zech 3:8 for behold, I am bringing forth *My Servant the BRANCH*

MY SERVANTS THE PROPHETS
2Kin 9:7 You shall strike down the house of Ahab your master, that I may avenge the blood of *My servants the prophets*, and the blood of all the servants of the Lord, at the hand of Jezebel
2Kin 17:13 Yet the Lord testified against Israel and against Judah, by all of His prophets, namely every seer, saying, "Turn from your evil ways, and keep My commandments and My statutes, according to all the law which I commanded your fathers, and which I sent to you by *My servants the prophets*
Jer 7:25 Since the day that your fathers came out of the land of Egypt until this day, I have even sent to you all *My servants the prophets*, daily rising up early and sending them
Jer 26:5 to heed the words of *My servants the prophets* whom I sent to you, both rising up early and sending them (but you have not heeded
Jer 29:19 because they have not heeded My words, says the Lord, which I sent to them by *My servants the prophets*, rising up early and sending them
Jer 35:15 I have also sent to you all *My servants the prophets*, rising up early and sending them, saying
Jer 44:4 However I have sent to you all *My servants the prophets*, rising early and sending them, saying
Ezek 38:17 Are you he of whom I have spoken in former days by *My servants the prophets* of Israel, who prophesied for years in those days that I would bring you against them
Zech 1:6 Yet surely My words and My statutes, which I commanded *My servants the prophets*, did they not overtake your fathers

MY SHIELD
2Sam 22:3 the God of my strength, in Him I will trust, *my shield* and the horn of my salvation, my stronghold and my refuge
Ps 18:2 *My shield* and the horn of my salvation, my stronghold
Ps 28:7 The Lord is my strength and *my shield;* my heart trusted in Him, and I am helped
Ps 119:114 You are my hiding place and *my shield;* I hope in Your word
Ps 144:2 My lovingkindness and my fortress, my high tower and my deliverer, *my shield* and the One in whom I take refuge, Who subdues my people under me

MY SISTER, MY SPOUSE
Song 4:9 You have ravished my heart, *my sister, my spouse*
Song 4:10 How fair is your love, *my sister, my spouse*
Song 4:12 A garden enclosed is *my sister, my spouse*, a spring shut up, a fountain sealed
Song 5:1 I have come to my garden, *my sister, my spouse*

MY SON, HEAR THE INSTRUCTION
Prov 1:8 *My son, hear the instruction* of your father, and do not forsake the law of your mother

MY SON, WHOM I LOVE (NIV)
(See *MY BELOVED SON*)

MY SOUL IS CAST DOWN
Ps 42:6 O my God, *my soul is cast down* within me

MY SOUL IS EXCEEDINGLY SORROWFUL
Matt 26:38 Then He said to them, "*My soul is exceedingly sorrowful*, even to death
Mark 14:34 Then He said to them, "*My soul is exceedingly sorrowful*, even to death

MY SOUL IS OVERWHELMED WITH SORROW (NIV)
(See *MY SOUL IS EXCEEDINGLY SORROWFUL*)

MY SOUL IS VERY SORROWFUL (RSV)
(See *MY SOUL IS EXCEEDINGLY SORROWFUL*)

MY SOUL MAGNIFIES THE LORD
Luke 1:46 And Mary said: *My soul magnifies the Lord*

MY SOUL PRAISES THE LORD (NIV)
(See *MY SOUL MAGNIFIES THE LORD*)

MY SOUL THIRSTS FOR GOD
Ps 42:2 *My soul thirsts for God*, for the living God. When shall I come and appear before God

MY STATUTES AND MY COMMANDMENTS
1Kin 3:14 So if you walk in My ways, to keep *My statutes and My commandments*, as your father David walked, then I will lengthen your days
1Kin 11:38 Then it shall be, if you heed all that I command you, walk in My ways, and do what is right in My sight, to keep *My statutes and My commandments*, as My servant David did, then I will be with you and build for you an enduring house, as I built for David, and will give Israel to you
2Chr 7:19 But if you turn away and forsake *My statutes and My commandments* which I have set before you, and go and serve other gods, and worship them

MY STATUTES AND MY JUDGMENTS
Lev 18:5 You shall therefore keep *My statutes and My judgments*, which if a man does, he shall live by them
Lev 18:26 You shall therefore keep *My statutes and My judgments*, and shall not commit any of these abominations, either any of your own nation or any stranger who sojourns among you
1Kin 9:4 Now if you walk before Me as your father David walked, in integrity of heart and in uprightness, to do according to all that I have commanded you, and if you keep *My statutes and My judgments*
1Kin 11:33 because they have forsaken Me, and worshiped Ashtoreth the goddess of the Sidonians, Chemosh the god of the Moabites, and Mil-

com the god of the people of Ammon, and have not walked in My ways to do what is right in My eyes and keep *My statutes and My judgments*, as did his father David

2Chr 7:17 As for you, if you walk before Me as your father David walked, and do according to all that I have commanded you, and if you keep *My statutes and My judgments*

MY STRENGTH FAILS
Ps 31:10 *My strength fails* because of my iniquity, and my bones waste away
Ps 38:10 My heart pants, *my strength fails* me; as for the light of my eyes, it also has gone from me
Ps 71:9 Do not cast me off in the time of old age; do not forsake me when *my strength fails*

MY TESTIMONY IS TRUE (RSV)
(See *MY WITNESS IS TRUE*)

MY TESTIMONY IS VALID (NIV)
(See *MY WITNESS IS TRUE*)

MY THOUGHTS ARE NOT YOUR THOUGHTS
Is 55:8 For *My thoughts are not your thoughts*, nor are your ways My ways

MY TIME HAS NOT YET COME
John 7:6 Then Jesus said to them, "*My time has not yet come*, but your time is always ready

MY VOWS I WILL PAY (RSV)
(See *PAY MY VOWS*)

MY WITNESS IS TRUE
John 8:14 Jesus answered and said to them, "Even if I bear witness of Myself, *My witness is true*, for I know where I came from and where I am going

MY WOUND IS INCURABLE
Job 34:6 Should I lie concerning my right? *My wound is incurable*, though I am without transgression

MY YOKE IS EASY
Matt 11:30 For *My yoke is easy* and My burden is light

MY ZEAL HAS CONSUMED ME
Ps 119:139 *My zeal has consumed me*, because my enemies have forgotten Your words

MYRRH AND ALOES
Ps 45:8 All Your garments are scented with *myrrh and aloes* and cassia, out of the ivory palaces, by which they have made You glad
Song 4:14 spikenard and saffron, calamus and cinnamon, with all trees of frankincense, *myrrh and aloes*, with all the chief spices
John 19:39 And Nicodemus, who at first came to Jesus by night, also came, bringing a mixture of *myrrh and aloes*, about a hundred pounds

MYSTERIES OF GOD (NIV)
(See *DEEP THINGS OF GOD*)

MYSTERY OF CHRIST
Eph 3:4 by which, when you read, you may understand my knowledge in the *mystery of Christ*
Col 4:3 meanwhile praying also for us, that God would open to us a door for the word, to speak the *mystery of Christ*, for which I am also in chains

MYSTERY OF GOD
Col 2:2 that their hearts may be encouraged, being knit together in love, and attaining to all riches of the full assurance of understanding, to the knowledge of the *mystery of God*, both of the Father and of Christ
Rev 10:7 but in the days of the sounding of the seventh angel, when he is about to sound, the *mystery of God* would be finished, as He declared to His servants the prophets

MYSTERY OF GODLINESS
1Tim 3:16 And without controversy great is the *mystery of godliness:* God was manifested in the flesh, justified in the Spirit, seen by angels, preached among the Gentiles, believed on in the world, received up in glory

MYSTERY OF INIQUITY (KJV)
(See *MYSTERY OF LAWLESSNESS*)

MYSTERY OF LAWLESSNESS
2Th 2:7 For the *mystery of lawlessness* is already at work; only He who now restrains will do so until He is taken out of the way

MYSTERY OF OUR RELIGION (RSV)
(See *MYSTERY OF GODLINESS*)

MYSTERY OF THE GOSPEL
Eph 6:19 and for me, that utterance may be given to me, that I may open my mouth boldly to make known the *mystery of the gospel*

MYSTERY OF THE KINGDOM OF GOD
Mark 4:11 And He said to them, "To you it has been given to know the *mystery of the kingdom of God*

N

NAILS AND HAMMERS
Jer 10:4 they fasten it with *nails and hammers* so that it will not topple

NAKED AND BARE
Ezek 16:7 Your breasts were formed, your hair grew, but you were *naked and bare*
Ezek 16:22 And in all your abominations and acts of harlotry you did not remember the days of your youth, when you were *naked and bare*, struggling in your blood
Ezek 16:39 They shall also strip you of your clothes, take your beautiful jewelry, and leave you *naked and bare*
Ezek 23:29 They will deal hatefully with you, take away all you have worked for, and leave you *naked and bare*

NAKED AND BAREFOOT
Is 20:2 at the same time the Lord spoke by Isaiah the son of Amoz, saying, "Go, and remove the sackcloth from your body, and take your sandals off your feet." And he did so, walking *naked and barefoot*
Is 20:3 Then the Lord said, "Just as My servant Isaiah has walked *naked and barefoot* three years for a sign and a wonder against Egypt and Ethiopia
Is 20:4 so shall the king of Assyria lead away the Egyptians as prisoners and the Ethiopians as captives, young and old, *naked and barefoot*, with their buttocks uncovered, to the shame of Egypt

NAKEDNESS OF HIS FATHER
Gen 9:22 And Ham, the father of Canaan, saw the *nakedness of his father*, and told his two brothers outside

NAKEDNESS OF THEIR FATHER (KJV, NAS, RSV)
(See *FATHER'S NAKEDNESS*)

NAME AND A PRAISE (KJV)
(See *FAME AND PRAISE*)

NAME OF GOD
Ps 69:30 I will praise the *name of God* with a song, and will magnify Him with thanksgiving
Dan 2:20 Blessed be the *name of God* forever and ever, for wisdom and might are His
Rom 2:24 For "The *name of God* is blasphemed among the Gentiles because of you
1Tim 6:1 Let as many servants as are under the yoke count their own masters worthy of all honor, so that the *name of God* and His doctrine may not be blasphemed
Rev 16:9 And men were scorched with great heat, and they blasphemed the *name of God* who has power over these plagues

NAME OF JESUS CHRIST OF NAZARETH
Acts 3:6 In the *name of Jesus Christ of Nazareth*, rise up and walk
Acts 4:10 let it be known to you all, and to all the people of Israel, that by the *name of Jesus Christ of Nazareth*, whom you crucified, whom God raised from the dead, by Him this man stands here before you whole

NAME OF OUR LORD JESUS CHRIST
Acts 15:26 men who have risked their lives for the *name of our Lord Jesus Christ*
1Cor 1:10 Now I plead with you, brethren, by the *name of our Lord Jesus Christ*, that you all speak the same thing, and that there be no divisions among you, but that you be perfectly joined together in the same mind and in the same judgment
1Cor 5:4 In the *name of our Lord Jesus Christ*, when you are gathered together, along with my spirit, with the power of our Lord Jesus Christ
Eph 5:20 giving thanks always for all things to God the Father in the *name of our Lord Jesus Christ*
2Th 1:12 that the *name of our Lord Jesus Christ* may be glorified in you, and you in Him, according to the grace of our God and the Lord Jesus Christ
2Th 3:6 But we command you, brethren, in the *name of our Lord Jesus Christ*, that you withdraw from every brother who walks disorderly and not according to the tradition which he received from us

NAME OF THAT PLACE WAS CALLED
Num 21:3 And the Lord listened to the voice of Israel and delivered up the Canaanites, and they utterly destroyed them and their cities. So the *name of that place was called* Hormah
2Chr 20:26 therefore the *name of that place was called* The Valley of Berachah until this day

NAME OF THE LORD
Gen 4:26 Then men began to call on the *name of the Lord*
Gen 12:8 there he built an altar to the Lord and called on the *name of the Lord*
Gen 13:4 And there Abram called on the *name of the Lord*
Gen 16:13 Then she called the *name of the Lord* who spoke to her, You-Are-the-God-Who-Sees
Gen 21:33 Then Abraham planted a tamarisk tree in Beersheba, and there called on the *name of the Lord*, the Everlasting God
Gen 26:25 So he built an altar there and called on the *name of the Lord*, and he pitched his tent there
Ex 20:7 You shall not take the *name of the Lord* your God in vain, for the Lord will not hold him guiltless who takes His name in vain
Ex 33:19 Then He said, "I will make all My goodness pass before you, and I will proclaim the *name of the Lord* before you
Ex 34:5 Then the Lord descended in the cloud and stood with him there, and proclaimed the *name of the Lord*
Lev 24:11 And the Israelite woman's son blasphemed the *name of the Lord* and cursed
Lev 24:16 And whoever blasphemes the *name of the Lord* shall surely be put to death, and all the congregation shall certainly stone him, the stranger as well as him who is born in the land. When he blasphemes the *name of the Lord*, he shall be put to death
Deut 5:11 You shall not take the *name of the Lord* your God in vain, for the Lord will not hold him guiltless who takes His name in vain
Deut 18:5 For the Lord your God has chosen him out of all your tribes to stand to minister in the *name of the Lord*, him and his sons forever
Deut 18:7 then he may serve in the *name of the Lord* his God as all his brethren the Levites do, who stand there before the Lord
Deut 18:22 when a prophet speaks in the *name of the Lord*, if the thing does not happen or come to pass, that is the thing which the Lord has not spoken
Deut 21:5 Then the priests, the sons of Levi, shall come near, for the Lord your God has chosen them to minister to Him and to bless in the *name of the Lord*
Deut 28:10 Then all peoples of the earth shall see that you are called by the *name of the Lord*, and they shall be afraid of you
Deut 32:3 For I proclaim the *name of the Lord:* ascribe greatness to our God
Josh 9:9 From a very far country your servants have come, because of the *name of the Lord* your God
1Sam 17:45 But I come to you in the *name of the Lord* of hosts, the God of the armies of Israel, whom you have defied
1Sam 20:42 Then Jonathan said to David, "Go in peace, since we have both sworn in the *name of the Lord*, saying
2Sam 6:18 And when David had finished offering burnt offerings and peace offerings, he blessed the people in the *name of the Lord* of hosts
1Kin 3:2 Meanwhile the people sacrificed at the high places, because there was no house built for the *name of the Lord* until those days
1Kin 5:3 You know how my father David could not build a house for the *name of the Lord* his God because of the wars which were fought against him on every side, until the Lord put his foes under the soles of his feet
1Kin 5:5 And behold, I propose to build a house for the *name of the Lord* my God, as the Lord spoke to my father David, saying
1Kin 8:17 Now it was in the heart of my father David to build a house for the *name of the Lord* God of Israel
1Kin 8:20 and I have built a house for the *name of the Lord* God of Israel
1Kin 10:1 Now when the queen of Sheba heard of the fame of Solomon concerning the *name of the Lord*, she came to test him with hard questions
1Kin 18:24 Then you call on the name of your gods, and I will call on the *name of the Lord*
1Kin 18:32 Then with the stones he built an altar in the *name of the Lord*
1Kin 22:16 So the king said to him, "How many

times shall I make you swear that you tell me nothing but the truth in the *name of the Lord*
2Kin 2:24 So he turned around and looked at them, and pronounced a curse on them in the *name of the Lord*
2Kin 5:11 But Naaman became furious, and went away and said, "Indeed, I said to myself, 'He will surely come out to me, and stand and call on the *name of the Lord* his God, and wave his hand over the place, and heal the leprosy
1Chr 16:2 And when David had finished offering the burnt offerings and the peace offerings, he blessed the people in the *name of the Lord*
1Chr 21:19 So David went up at the word of Gad, which he had spoken in the *name of the Lord*
1Chr 22:7 My son, as for me, it was in my mind to build a house to the *name of the Lord* my God
1Chr 22:19 Therefore arise and build the sanctuary of the Lord God, to bring the ark of the covenant of the Lord and the holy articles of God into the house that is to be built for the *name of the Lord*
2Chr 2:1 Then Solomon determined to build a temple for the *name of the Lord*, and a royal house for himself
2Chr 2:4 Behold, I am building a temple for the *name of the Lord* my God, to dedicate it to Him, to burn before Him sweet incense, for the continual showbread, for the burnt offerings morning and evening, on the Sabbaths, on the New Moons, and on the set feasts of the Lord our God
2Chr 6:7 Now it was in the heart of my father David to build a temple for the *name of the Lord* God of Israel
2Chr 6:10 and I have built the temple for the *name of the Lord* God of Israel
2Chr 18:15 So the king said to him, "How many times shall I make you swear that you tell me nothing but the truth in the *name of the Lord*
2Chr 33:18 Now the rest of the acts of Manasseh, his prayer to his God, and the words of the seers who spoke to him in the *name of the Lord* God of Israel, indeed they are written in the book of the kings of Israel
Job 1:21 The Lord gave, and the Lord has taken away; blessed be the *name of the Lord*
Ps 7:17 I will praise the Lord according to His righteousness, and will sing praise to the *name of the Lord* Most High
Ps 20:7 But we will remember the *name of the Lord* our God
Ps 102:15 So the nations shall fear the *name of the Lord*, and all the kings of the earth Your glory
Ps 102:21 To declare the *name of the Lord* in Zion, and His praise in Jerusalem
Ps 113:1 Praise, O servants of the Lord, praise the *name of the Lord*
Ps 113:2 Blessed be the *name of the Lord* from this time forth and forevermore
Ps 116:4 Then I called upon the *name of the Lord:* "O Lord, I implore You, deliver my soul
Ps 116:13 I will take up the cup of salvation, and call upon the *name of the Lord*
Ps 116:17 I will offer to You the sacrifice of thanksgiving, and will call upon the *name of the Lord*
Ps 118:10 All nations surrounded me, but in the *name of the Lord* I will destroy them
Ps 118:11 But in the *name of the Lord* I will destroy them
Ps 118:12 For in the *name of the Lord* I will destroy them
Ps 118:26 Blessed is he who comes in the *name of the Lord*
Ps 122:4 Where the tribes go up, the tribes of the Lord, to the Testimony of Israel, to give thanks to the *name of the Lord*
Ps 124:8 Our help is in the *name of the Lord*, Who made heaven and earth
Ps 129:8 Neither let those who pass by them say, "The blessing of the Lord be upon you; we bless you in the *name of the Lord*
Ps 135:1 Praise the *name of the Lord;* praise Him, O you servants of the Lord
Ps 148:5 Let them praise the *name of the Lord*, for He commanded and they were created
Ps 148:13 Let them praise the *name of the Lord*, for His name alone is exalted
Prov 18:10 The *name of the Lord* is a strong tower; the righteous run to it and are safe
Is 18:7 In that time a present will be brought to the Lord of hosts from a people tall and smooth of skin, and from a people terrible from their beginning onward, a nation powerful and treading down, whose land the rivers divide to the place of the *name of the Lord* of hosts, to Mount Zion
Is 24:15 Therefore glorify the Lord in the dawning light, the *name of the Lord* God of Israel in the coastlands of the sea
Is 30:27 Behold, the *name of the Lord* comes from afar, burning with His anger, and His burden is heavy
Is 48:1 who swear by the *name of the Lord*, and make mention of the God of Israel, but not in truth or in righteousness
Is 50:10 Let him trust in the *name of the Lord* and rely upon his God
Is 56:6 Also the sons of the foreigner who join themselves to the Lord, to serve Him, and to love the *name of the Lord*, to be His servants everyone who keeps from defiling the Sabbath, and holds fast My covenant
Is 59:19 So shall they fear the *name of the Lord* from the west, and His glory from the rising of the sun
Is 60:9 and the ships of Tarshish will come first, to bring your sons from afar, their silver and their gold with them, to the *name of the Lord* your God, and to the Holy One of Israel, because He has glorified you
Jer 3:17 At that time Jerusalem shall be called The Throne of the Lord, and all the nations shall be gathered to it, to the *name of the Lord*, to Jerusalem
Jer 11:21 Therefore thus says the Lord concerning the men of Anathoth who seek your life, saying, 'Do not prophesy in the *name of the Lord*, lest you die by our hand
Jer 26:9 Why have you prophesied in the *name of the Lord*, saying
Jer 26:16 For he has spoken to us in the *name of the Lord* our God
Jer 26:20 Now there was also a man who prophesied in the *name of the Lord*, Urijah the son of Shemaiah of Kirjath Jearim, who prophesied against this city and against this land according to all the words of Jeremiah
Jer 44:16 As for the word that you have spoken to us in the *name of the Lord*, we will not listen to you
Joel 2:26 You shall eat in plenty and be satisfied, and praise the *name of the Lord* your God, who has dealt wondrously with you
Joel 2:32 And it shall come to pass that whoever calls on the *name of the Lord* shall be saved
Amos 6:10 For we dare not mention the *name of the Lord*
Mic 4:5 For all people walk each in the name of his god, but we will walk in the *name of the Lord* our God forever and ever
Mic 5:4 And He shall stand and feed His flock in the strength of the Lord, in the majesty of the *name of the Lord* His God
Zeph 3:9 For then I will restore to the peoples a

pure language, that they all may call on the *name of the Lord*, to serve Him with one accord
Zeph 3:12 I will leave in your midst a meek and humble people, and they shall trust in the *name of the Lord*
Zech 13:3 It shall come to pass that if anyone still prophesies, then his father and mother who begot him will say to him, 'You shall not live, because you have spoken lies in the *name of the Lord*
Matt 21:9 Blessed is He who comes in the *name of the Lord*
Matt 23:39 for I say to you, you shall see Me no more till you say, 'Blessed is He who comes in the *name of the Lord*
Mark 11:9 Blessed is He who comes in the *name of the Lord*
Mark 11:10 Blessed is the kingdom of our father David that comes in the *name of the Lord*
Luke 13:35 and assuredly, I say to you, you shall not see Me until the time comes when you say, 'Blessed is He who comes in the *name of the Lord*
Luke 19:38 Blessed is the King who comes in the *name of the Lord*
John 12:13 Blessed is He who comes in the *name of the Lord*
Acts 2:21 And it shall come to pass that whoever calls on the *name of the Lord* shall be saved
Acts 8:16 They had only been baptized in the *name of the Lord* Jesus
Acts 9:29 And he spoke boldly in the *name of the Lord* Jesus and disputed against the Hellenists, but they attempted to kill him
Acts 10:48 And he commanded them to be baptized in the *name of the Lord*
Acts 19:5 When they heard this, they were baptized in the *name of the Lord* Jesus
Acts 19:13 Then some of the itinerant Jewish exorcists took it upon themselves to call the *name of the Lord* Jesus over those who had evil spirits, saying
Acts 19:17 and fear fell on them all, and the *name of the Lord* Jesus was magnified
Acts 21:13 For I am ready not only to be bound, but also to die at Jerusalem for the *name of the Lord* Jesus
Acts 22:16 Arise and be baptized, and wash away your sins, calling on the *name of the Lord*
Rom 10:13 For "whoever calls upon the *name of the Lord* shall be saved
1Cor 6:11 But you were washed, but you were sanctified, but you were justified in the *name of the Lord* Jesus and by the Spirit of our God
Col 3:17 And whatever you do in word or deed, do all in the *name of the Lord* Jesus, giving thanks to God the Father through Him
Jas 5:10 My brethren, take the prophets, who spoke in the *name of the Lord*, as an example of suffering and patience
Jas 5:14 Let him call for the elders of the church, and let them pray over him, anointing him with oil in the *name of the Lord*

NARROW IS THE GATE
Matt 7:14 Because *narrow is the gate* and difficult is the way which leads to life, and there are few who find it

NATION WILL RISE AGAINST NATION
Matt 24:7 For *nation will rise against nation*, and kingdom against kingdom
Mark 13:8 For *nation will rise against nation*, and kingdom against kingdom
Luke 21:10 Then He said to them, "*Nation will rise against nation*, and kingdom against kingdom

NATIONS OF THE EARTH
Gen 18:18 since Abraham shall surely become a great and mighty nation, and all the *nations of the earth* shall be blessed in him
Gen 22:18 In your seed all the *nations of the earth* shall be blessed, because you have obeyed My voice
Gen 26:4 and in your seed all the *nations of the earth* shall be blessed
Deut 28:1 Now it shall come to pass, if you diligently obey the voice of the Lord your God, to observe carefully all His commandments which I command you today, that the Lord your God will set you high above all *nations of the earth*
Jer 26:6 then I will make this house like Shiloh, and will make this city a curse to all the *nations of the earth*
Jer 33:9 Then it shall be to Me a name of joy, a praise, and an honor before all *nations of the earth*, who shall hear all the good that I do to them
Jer 44:8 in that you provoke Me to wrath with the works of your hands, burning incense to other gods in the land of Egypt where you have gone to dwell, that you may cut yourselves off and be a curse and a reproach among all the *nations of the earth*
Zech 12:3 all who would heave it away will surely be cut in pieces, though all *nations of the earth* are gathered against it

NATIONS THE LORD HAD DRIVEN OUT (NIV)
(See *NATIONS WHOM THE LORD HAD CAST OUT*)

NATIONS WHOM THE LORD HAD CAST OUT
2Kin 16:3 indeed he made his son pass through the fire, according to the abominations of the *nations whom the Lord had cast out* from before the children of Israel
2Kin 17:8 and had walked in the statutes of the *nations whom the Lord had cast out* from before the children of Israel, and of the kings of Israel, which they had made
2Kin 21:2 And he did evil in the sight of the Lord, according to the abominations of the *nations whom the Lord had cast out* before the children of Israel
2Chr 28:3 He burned incense in the Valley of the Son of Hinnom, and burned his children in the fire, according to the abominations of the *nations whom the Lord had cast out* before the children of Israel
2Chr 33:2 But he did evil in the sight of the Lord, according to the abominations of the *nations whom the Lord had cast out* before the children of Israel

NATURE OF A SERVANT (NIV)
(See *FORM OF A SERVANT*)

NEED A DOCTOR (NIV)
(See *NEED OF A PHYSICIAN*)

NEED NOT A PHYSICIAN (KJV)
(See *NEED OF A PHYSICIAN*)

NEED OF A PHYSICIAN
Matt 9:12 But when Jesus heard that, He said to them, "Those who are well have no *need of a physician*, but those who are sick
Mark 2:17 When Jesus heard it, He said to them, "Those who are well have no *need of a physician*, but those who are sick

NEED TO BE BAPTIZED
Matt 3:14 And John tried to prevent Him, saying, "I have *need to be baptized* by You, and are You coming to me

NEEDY WILL NOT ALWAYS BE FORGOTTEN (NAS, NIV)
(See *EXPECTATION OF THE POOR*)

NEGLECTED THE MORE IMPORTANT MATTERS (NIV)
(See *NEGLECTED THE WEIGHTIER MATTERS*)

NEGLECTED THE WEIGHTIER MATTERS
Matt 23:23 For you pay tithe of mint and anise and cumin, and have *neglected the weightier matters* of the law

NEIGHBOR'S BOUNDARY STONE (NIV)
(See *NEIGHBOR'S LANDMARK*)

NEIGHBOR'S LANDMARK
Deut 19:14 You shall not remove your *neighbor's landmark*, which the men of old have set, in your inheritance which you will inherit in the land that the Lord your God is giving you to possess
Deut 27:17 Cursed is the one who moves his *neighbor's landmark*.' And all the people shall say

NEITHER CIRCUMCISION NOR UNCIRCUMCISION
Gal 5:6 For in Christ Jesus *neither circumcision nor uncircumcision* avails anything, but faith working through love
Gal 6:15 For in Christ Jesus *neither circumcision nor uncircumcision* avails anything, but a new creation

NEITHER COLD NOR HOT
Rev 3:15 I know your works, that you are *neither cold nor hot*
Rev 3:16 So then, because you are lukewarm, and *neither cold nor hot*, I will spew you out of My mouth

NEITHER GREEK NOR JEW
Col 3:11 where there is *neither Greek nor Jew*, circumcised nor uncircumcised, barbarian, Scythian, slave nor free, but Christ is all and in all

NEITHER JEW NOR GREEK
Gal 3:28 There is *neither Jew nor Greek*, there is neither slave nor free, there is neither male nor female

NEITHER MALE NOR FEMALE
Gal 3:28 There is neither Jew nor Greek, there is neither slave nor free, there is *neither male nor female*

NEITHER MARRY NOR ARE GIVEN IN MARRIAGE
Matt 22:30 For in the resurrection they *neither marry nor are given in marriage*, but are like angels of God in heaven
Mark 12:25 For when they rise from the dead, they *neither marry nor are given in marriage*, but are like angels in heaven
Luke 20:35 But those who are counted worthy to attain that age, and the resurrection from the dead, *neither marry nor are given in marriage*

NEITHER POVERTY NOR RICHES
Prov 30:8 give me *neither poverty nor riches* feed me with the food You prescribe for me

NEITHER SHADOW OF TURNING (KJV)
(See *VARIATION OR SHADOW OF TURNING*)

NEITHER TURN UNTO THE RIGHT HAND NOR TO THE LEFT (KJV)
(See *TURN NEITHER TO THE RIGHT NOR TO THE LEFT*)

NETHER PART OF THE MOUNT (KJV)
(See *FOOT OF THE MOUNTAIN*)

NETHER PARTS OF THE EARTH (KJV)
(See *DEPTHS OF THE EARTH*)

NETHER WORLD (RSV)
(See *DEPTHS OF THE EARTH*)

NEVER AGAIN PASS BY THEM (RSV)
(See *NOT PASS BY THEM ANYMORE*)

NEVER FAIL (NIV)
(See *STAND FIRM*)

NEVER FAIL YOU NOR FORSAKE YOU (RSV)
(See *NEVER LEAVE YOU NOR FORSAKE YOU*)

NEVER LEAVE YOU NOR FORSAKE YOU
Heb 13:5 For He Himself has said, "I will *never leave you nor forsake you*

NEVER RISE AGAIN
Amos 8:14 and, 'As the way of Beersheba lives!' They shall fall and *never rise again*

NEW COMMANDMENT
John 13:34 A *new commandment* I give to you, that you love one another
1Jn 2:7 Brethren, I write no *new commandment* to you, but an old commandment which you have had from the beginning
1Jn 2:8 Again, a *new commandment* I write to you, which thing is true in Him and in you, because the darkness is passing away, and the true light is already shining
2Jn 5 And now I plead with you, lady, not as though I wrote a *new commandment* to you, but that which we have had from the beginning

NEW COVENANT
Jer 31:31 Behold, the days are coming," says the Lord, "when I will make a *new covenant* with the house of Israel and with the house of Judah
Matt 26:28 For this is My blood of the *new covenant*, which is shed for many for the remission of sins
Mark 14:24 And He said to them, "This is My blood of the *new covenant*, which is shed for many
Luke 22:20 Likewise He also took the cup after supper, saying, "This cup is the *new covenant* in My blood, which is shed for you
1Cor 11:25 In the same manner He also took the cup after supper, saying, "This cup is the *new covenant* in My blood
2Cor 3:6 who also made us sufficient as ministers of the *new covenant*, not of the letter but of the Spirit
Heb 8:8 Behold, the days are coming," says the Lord, "when I will make a *new covenant* with the house of Israel and with the house of Judah
Heb 8:13 In that He says, "A *new covenant*," He has made the first obsolete
Heb 9:15 And for this reason He is the Mediator of the *new covenant*, by means of death, for the redemption of the transgressions under the first covenant, that those who are called may receive the promise of the eternal inheritance

Heb 12:24 to Jesus the Mediator of the *new covenant*, and to the blood of sprinkling that speaks better things than that of Abel

NEW COVENANT IN MY BLOOD
Luke 22:20 Likewise He also took the cup after supper, saying, "This cup is the *new covenant in My blood*, which is shed for you
1Cor 11:25 In the same manner He also took the cup after supper, saying, "This cup is the *new covenant in My blood*

NEW CREATION
2Cor 5:17 Therefore, if anyone is in Christ, he is a *new creation*
Gal 6:15 For in Christ Jesus neither circumcision nor uncircumcision avails anything, but a *new creation*

NEW CREATURE (KJV, NAS)
(See *NEW CREATION*)

NEW DOCTRINE
Mark 1:27 What *new doctrine* is this? For with authority He commands even the unclean spirits, and they obey Him
Acts 17:19 And they took him and brought him to the Areopagus, saying, "May we know what this *new doctrine* is of which you speak

NEW HEAVENS AND A NEW EARTH
Is 65:17 For behold, I create *new heavens and a new earth*
2Pet 3:13 Nevertheless we, according to His promise, look for *new heavens and a new earth* in which righteousness dwells

NEW JERUSALEM
Rev 3:12 And I will write on him the name of My God and the name of the city of My God, the *New Jerusalem*, which comes down out of heaven from My God
Rev 21:2 Then I, John, saw the holy city, *New Jerusalem*, coming down out of heaven from God, prepared as a bride adorned for her husband

NEW MAN
Eph 2:15 having abolished in His flesh the enmity, that is, the law of commandments contained in ordinances, so as to create in Himself one *new man* from the two, thus making peace
Eph 4:24 and that you put on the *new man* which was created according to God, in righteousness and true holiness
Col 3:10 and have put on the *new man* who is renewed in knowledge according to the image of Him who created him

NEW MOON
Num 29:6 besides the burnt offering with its grain offering for the *New Moon*, the regular burnt offering with its grain offering, and their drink offerings, according to their ordinance, as a sweet aroma, an offering made by fire to the Lord
1Sam 20:5 And David said to Jonathan, "Indeed tomorrow is the *New Moon*, and I should not fail to sit with the king to eat
1Sam 20:18 Then Jonathan said to David, "Tomorrow is the *New Moon*
1Sam 20:24 And when the *New Moon* had come, the king sat down to eat the feast
2Kin 4:23 It is neither the *New Moon* nor the Sabbath." And she said
Ps 81:3 Blow the trumpet at the time of the *New Moon*, at the full moon, on our solemn feast day
Is 66:23 And it shall come to pass that from one *New Moon* to another, and from one Sabbath to another, all flesh shall come to worship before Me
Ezek 46:1 but on the Sabbath it shall be opened, and on the day of the *New Moon* it shall be opened
Ezek 46:6 On the day of the *New Moon* it shall be a young bull without blemish, six lambs, and a ram
Hos 5:7 Now a *New Moon* shall devour them and their heritage
Amos 8:5 When will the *New Moon* be past, that we may sell grain
Col 2:16 Therefore let no one judge you in food or in drink, or regarding a festival or a *new moon* or sabbaths

NEW MOONS
1Chr 23:31 and at every presentation of a burnt offering to the Lord on the Sabbaths and on the *New Moons* and on the set feasts, by number according to the ordinance governing them, regularly before the Lord
2Chr 2:4 Behold, I am building a temple for the name of the Lord my God, to dedicate it to Him, to burn before Him sweet incense, for the continual showbread, for the burnt offerings morning and evening, on the Sabbaths, on the *New Moons*, and on the set feasts of the Lord our God
2Chr 8:13 according to the daily rate, offering according to the commandment of Moses, for the Sabbaths, the *New Moons*, and the three appointed yearly feasts the Feast of Unleavened Bread, the Feast of Weeks, and the Feast of Tabernacles
2Chr 31:3 for the morning and evening burnt offerings, the burnt offerings for the Sabbaths and the *New Moons* and the set feasts, as it is written in the Law of the Lord
Ezra 3:5 and afterward they offered the regular burnt offering, and those for *New Moons* and for all the appointed feasts of the Lord that were consecrated, and those of everyone who willingly offered a freewill offering to the Lord
Neh 10:33 for the showbread, for the regular grain offering, for the regular burnt offering of the Sabbaths, the *New Moons*, and the set feasts
Is 1:13 The *New Moons*, the Sabbaths, and the calling of assemblies I cannot endure iniquity and the sacred meeting
Is 1:14 Your *New Moons* and your appointed feasts my soul hates
Ezek 45:17 Then it shall be the prince's part to give burnt offerings, grain offerings, and drink offerings, at the feasts, the *New Moons*, the Sabbaths, and at all the appointed seasons of the house of Israel
Ezek 46:3 Likewise the people of the land shall worship at the entrance to this gateway before the Lord on the Sabbaths and the *New Moons*
Hos 2:11 I will also cause all her mirth to cease, her feast days, her *New Moons*, her Sabbaths all her appointed feasts

NEW SONG
Ps 33:3 Sing to Him a *new song;* play skillfully with a shout of joy
Ps 40:3 He has put a *new song* in my mouth. Praise to our God
Ps 96:1 Oh, sing to the Lord a *new song!* Sing to the Lord, all the earth
Ps 98:1 Oh, sing to the Lord a *new song!* For He has done marvelous things
Ps 144:9 I will sing a *new song* to You, O God
Ps 149:1 Sing to the Lord a *new song*, and His praise in the congregation of saints
Is 42:10 Sing to the Lord a *new song*, and His praise from the ends of the earth, you who go down to the sea, and all that is in it, you coastlands and you inhabitants of them

Rev 5:9 And they sang a *new song*, saying: "You are worthy to take the scroll, and to open its seals
Rev 14:3 And they sang as it were a *new song* before the throne, before the four living creatures, and the elders

NEW TEACHING (NAS, NIV, RSV)
(See *NEW DOCTRINE*)

NEW TESTAMENT IN MY BLOOD (KJV)
(See *NEW COVENANT IN MY BLOOD*)

NEW THINGS
Is 42:9 Behold, the former things have come to pass, and *new things* I declare
Is 48:6 I have made you hear *new things* from this time, even hidden things, and you did not know them

NEW TOMB
Matt 27:60 and laid it in his *new tomb* which he had hewn out of the rock
John 19:41 Now in the place where He was crucified there was a garden, and in the garden a *new tomb* in which no one had yet been laid

NEW WINE
Num 18:12 All the best of the oil, all the best of the *new wine* and the grain, their firstfruits which they offer to the Lord, I have given them to you
Deut 7:13 He will also bless the fruit of your womb and the fruit of your land, your grain and your *new wine* and your oil, the increase of your cattle and the offspring of your flock, in the land of which He swore to your fathers to give you
Deut 11:14 then I will give you the rain for your land in its season, the early rain and the latter rain, that you may gather in your grain, your *new wine*, and your oil
Deut 12:17 You may not eat within your gates the tithe of your grain or your *new wine* or your oil, of the firstlings of your herd or your flock, of any of your offerings which you vow, of your freewill offerings, or of the heave offering of your hand
Deut 14:23 And you shall eat before the Lord your God, in the place where He chooses to make His name abide, the tithe of your grain and your *new wine* and your oil, of the firstlings of your herds and your flocks, that you may learn to fear the Lord your God always
Deut 18:4 The firstfruits of your grain and your *new wine* and your oil, and the first of the fleece of your sheep, you shall give him
Deut 28:51 they shall not leave you grain or *new wine* or oil, or the increase of your cattle or the offspring of your flocks, until they have destroyed you
Deut 33:28 Then Israel shall dwell in safety, the fountain of Jacob alone, in a land of grain and *new wine*
Judg 9:13 But the vine said to them, 'Should I cease my *new wine*, which cheers both God and men, and go to sway over trees
2Kin 18:32 until I come and take you away to a land like your own land, a land of grain and *new wine*, a land of bread and vineyards, a land of olive groves and honey, that you may live and not die
Neh 5:11 Restore now to them, even this day, their lands, their vineyards, their olive groves, and their houses, also the hundredth part of the money and the grain, the *new wine* and the oil, that you have charged them
Neh 10:37 to bring the firstfruits of our dough, our offerings, the fruit from all kinds of trees, the *new wine* and oil, to the priests, to the storerooms of the house of our God
Neh 10:39 For the children of Israel and the children of Levi shall bring the offering of the grain, of the *new wine* and the oil, to the storerooms where the articles of the sanctuary are, where the priests who minister and the gatekeepers and the singers are
Neh 13:5 And he had prepared for him a large room, where previously they had stored the grain offerings, the frankincense, the articles, the tithes of grain, the *new wine* and oil, which were commanded to be given to the Levites and singers and gatekeepers, and the offerings for the priests
Neh 13:12 Then all Judah brought the tithe of the grain and the *new wine* and the oil to the storehouse
Prov 3:10 so your barns will be filled with plenty, and your vats will overflow with *new wine*
Is 24:7 The *new wine* fails, the vine languishes, all the merry-hearted sigh
Is 36:17 until I come and take you away to a land like your own land, a land of grain and *new wine*, a land of bread and vineyards
Is 62:8 and the sons of the foreigner shall not drink your *new wine*, for which you have labored
Is 65:8 As the *new wine* is found in the cluster, and one says
Jer 31:12 Therefore they shall come and sing in the height of Zion, streaming to the goodness of the Lord for wheat and *new wine* and oil, for the young of the flock and the herd
Hos 2:8 For she did not know that I gave her grain, *new wine*, and oil, and multiplied her silver and gold which they prepared for Baal
Hos 2:9 Therefore I will return and take away my grain in its time and My *new wine* in its season, and will take back My wool and My linen, given to cover her nakedness
Hos 2:22 The earth shall answer with grain, with *new wine*, and with oil
Hos 4:11 Harlotry, wine, and *new wine* enslave the heart
Hos 7:14 They assemble together for grain and *new wine*, they rebel against Me
Hos 9:2 The threshing floor and the winepress shall not feed them, and the *new wine* shall fail in her
Joel 1:5 and wail, all you drinkers of wine, because of the *new wine*, for it has been cut off from your mouth
Joel 1:10 for the grain is ruined, the *new wine* is dried up, the oil fails
Joel 2:19 The Lord will answer and say to His people, "Behold, I will send you grain and *new wine* and oil, and you will be satisfied by them
Joel 2:24 The threshing floors shall be full of wheat, and the vats shall overflow with *new wine* and oil
Joel 3:18 And it will come to pass in that day that the mountains shall drip with *new wine*, the hills shall flow with milk, and all the brooks of Judah shall be flooded with water
Hag 1:11 For I called for a drought on the land and the mountains, on the grain and the *new wine* and the oil, on whatever the ground brings forth, on men and livestock, and on all the labor of your hands
Zech 9:17 Grain shall make the young men thrive, and *new wine* the young women
Matt 9:17 Nor do people put *new wine* into old wineskins, or else the wineskins break, the wine is spilled, and the wineskins are ruined. But they put *new wine* into new wineskins, and both are preserved
Mark 2:22 And no one puts *new wine* into old wineskins; or else the *new wine* bursts the wineskins, the wine is spilled, and the wineskins are ruined. But *new wine* must be put into new wineskins
Luke 5:37 And no one puts *new wine* into old

wineskins; or else the *new wine* will burst the wineskins and be spilled, and the wineskins will be ruined
Luke 5:38 But *new wine* must be put into new wineskins, and both are preserved
Acts 2:13 Others mocking said, "They are full of *new wine*

NEW WINE INTO OLD WINESKINS
Matt 9:17 Nor do people put *new wine into old wineskins*, or else the wineskins break, the wine is spilled, and the wineskins are ruined
Mark 2:22 And no one puts *new wine into old wineskins;* or else the new wine bursts the wineskins, the wine is spilled, and the wineskins are ruined
Luke 5:37 And no one puts *new wine into old wineskins;* or else the new wine will burst the wineskins and be spilled, and the wineskins will be ruined

NIGHT AND DAY
1Sam 25:16 They were a wall to us both by *night and day*, all the time we were with them keeping the sheep
1Kin 8:29 that Your eyes may be open toward this temple *night and day*, toward the place of which You said
Is 27:3 lest any hurt it, I keep it *night and day*
Jer 14:17 Let my eyes flow with tears *night and day*, and let them not cease
Mark 5:5 And always, *night and day*, he was in the mountains and in the tombs, crying out and cutting himself with stones
Luke 2:37 and this woman was a widow of about eighty-four years, who did not depart from the temple, but served God with fastings and prayers *night and day*
Acts 20:31 Therefore watch, and remember that for three years I did not cease to warn everyone *night and day* with tears
Acts 26:7 To this promise our twelve tribes, earnestly serving God *night and day*, hope to attain
1Th 2:9 for laboring *night and day*, that we might not be a burden to any of you, we preached to you the gospel of God
1Th 3:10 *night and day* praying exceedingly that we may see your face and perfect what is lacking in your faith
2Th 3:8 nor did we eat anyone's bread free of charge, but worked with labor and toil *night and day*, that we might not be a burden to any of you
1Tim 5:5 Now she who is really a widow, and left alone, trusts in God and continues in supplications and prayers *night and day*
2Tim 1:3 I thank God, whom I serve with a pure conscience, as my forefathers did, as without ceasing I remember you in my prayers *night and day*

NIGHT VISIONS
Dan 7:7 After this I saw in the *night visions*, and behold, a fourth beast, dreadful and terrible, exceedingly strong
Dan 7:13 I was watching in the *night visions*, and behold, One like the Son of Man, coming with the clouds of heaven

NIGHT WATCHES
Ps 63:6 When I remember You on my bed, I meditate on You in the *night watches*
Ps 119:148 My eyes are awake through the *night watches*, that I may meditate on Your word

NO BEAUTY OR MAJESTY (NIV)
(See *NO FORM OR COMELINESS*)

NO CLOAK FOR THEIR SIN (KJV)
(See *NO EXCUSE*)

NO EXCUSE
John 15:22 If I had not come and spoken to them, they would have no sin, but now they have *no excuse* for their sin

NO EYE HAS SEEN (NIV, RSV)
(See *EYE HAS NOT SEEN*)

NO FORM OR COMELINESS
Is 53:2 He has *no form or comeliness;* and when we see Him, there is no beauty that we should desire Him

NO GREEK OR JEW (NIV)
(See *NEITHER GREEK NOR JEW*)

NO KING IN ISRAEL
Judg 17:6 In those days there was *no king in Israel;* everyone did what was right in his own eyes
Judg 18:1 In those days there was *no king in Israel*. And in those days the tribe of the Danites was seeking an inheritance for itself to dwell in
Judg 19:1 And it came to pass in those days, when there was *no king in Israel*, that there was a certain Levite sojourning in the remote mountains of Ephraim
Judg 21:25 In those days there was *no king in Israel;* everyone did what was right in his own eyes

NO MAN HATH SEEN GOD (KJV)
(See *NO ONE HAS SEEN GOD*)

NO ONE CAN SERVE TWO MASTERS
Matt 6:24 *No one can serve two masters;* for either he will hate the one and love the other, or else he will be loyal to the one and despise the other

NO ONE COMES TO THE FATHER
John 14:6 Jesus said to him, "I am the way, the truth, and the life. *No one comes to the Father* except through Me

NO ONE HAS SEEN GOD
John 1:18 *No one has seen God* at any time. The only begotten Son, who is in the bosom of the Father, He has declared Him
1Jn 4:12 *No one has seen God* at any time. If we love one another, God abides in us, and His love has been perfected in us

NO ONE LIKE YOU (NIV)
(See *NONE LIKE YOU*)

NO ONE RIGHTEOUS, NOT EVEN ONE (NIV)
(See *NONE RIGHTEOUS, NO, NOT ONE*)

NO ONE SEEKS FOR GOD (RSV)
(See *NONE WHO SEEKS AFTER GOD*)

NO ONE TO HELP YOU (RSV)
(See *NO ONE TO RESCUE THEM*)

NO ONE TO RESCUE THEM
Deut 28:31 your sheep shall be given to your enemies, and you shall have *no one to rescue them*

NO ONE WHO SEEKS GOD (NIV)
(See *NONE WHO SEEKS AFTER GOD*)

NO ORDINARY CHILD (NIV)
(See *PLEASING TO GOD*)

NO OTHER GODS
Ex 20:3 You shall have *no other gods* before Me
Deut 5:7 You shall have *no other gods* before Me

NO PEACE
2Chr 15:5 And in those times there was *no peace* to the one who went out, nor to the one who came in, but great turmoil was on all the inhabitants of the lands
Prov 29:9 If a wise man contends with a foolish man, whether the fool rages or laughs, there is *no peace*
Is 48:22 There is *no peace*," says the Lord, "for the wicked
Is 57:21 There is *no peace*," says my God, "for the wicked
Jer 6:14 They have also healed the hurt of My people slightly, saying, 'Peace, peace!' When there is *no peace*
Jer 8:11 For they have healed the hurt of the daughter of My people slightly, saying, 'Peace, peace!' When there is *no peace*
Ezek 13:10 when there is *no peace* and one builds a boundary wall, and they plaster it with untempered mortar
Ezek 13:16 that is, the prophets of Israel who prophesy concerning Jerusalem, and who see visions of peace for her when there is *no peace*
Zech 8:10 there was *no peace* from the enemy for whoever went out or came in

NO PLACE FOR THEM (RSV)
(See *NO ROOM FOR THEM*)

NO PLACE TO LAY HIS HEAD (NIV)
(See *NOWHERE TO LAY HIS HEAD*)

NO PROFIT UNDER THE SUN
Eccl 2:11 and indeed all was vanity and grasping for the wind. There was *no profit under the sun*

NO ROOM FOR THEM
Luke 2:7 And she brought forth her firstborn Son, and wrapped Him in swaddling cloths, and laid Him in a manger, because there was *no room for them* in the inn

NOAH LIVED (NIV)
(See *DAYS OF NOAH*)

NOISE OF THE SEAS
Ps 65:7 You who still the *noise of the seas*, the noise of their waves, and the tumult of the peoples

NOISE OF THEIR WAVES
Ps 65:7 You who still the noise of the seas, the *noise of their waves*, and the tumult of the peoples

NOISOME PESTILENCE (KJV)
(See *PERILOUS PESTILENCE*)

NONE LIKE YOU
2Sam 7:22 For there is *none like You*, nor is there any God besides You, according to all that we have heard with our ears
1Chr 17:20 O Lord, there is *none like You*, nor is there any God besides You, according to all that we have heard with our ears
Ps 86:8 Among the gods there is *none like You*, O Lord
Jer 10:6 Inasmuch as there is *none like You*, O Lord (You are great, and Your name is great in might
Jer 10:7 For this is Your rightful due, for among all the wise men of the nations, and in all their kingdoms, there is *none like You*

NONE OF HIS STEPS SHALL SLIDE
Ps 37:31 The law of his God is in his heart; *none of his steps shall slide*

NONE RIGHTEOUS, NO, NOT ONE
Rom 3:10 As it is written: "There is *none righteous, no, not one*

NONE TO RESCUE THEM (KJV)
(See *NO ONE TO RESCUE THEM*)

NONE WHO SEEKS AFTER GOD
Rom 3:11 there is none who understands; there is *none who seeks after God*

NOT A MAN WAS LEFT
Judg 4:16 But Barak pursued the chariots and the army as far as Harosheth Hagoyim, and all the army of Sisera fell by the edge of the sword; *not a man was left*

NOT A WHIT BEHIND THE VERY CHEIFEST APOSTLES (KJV)
(See *INFERIOR TO THE MOST EMINENT APOSTLES*)

NOT ASHAMED OF THE GOSPEL
Rom 1:16 For I am *not ashamed of the gospel* of Christ, for it is the power of God to salvation for everyone who believes, for the Jew first and also for the Greek

NOT AT ALL (NIV)
(See *CERTAINLY NOT*)

NOT BY MIGHT NOR BY POWER
Zech 4:6 *Not by might nor by power*, but by My Spirit

NOT DESERVING OF DEATH (NIV)
(See *WORTHY OF DEATH*)

NOT GIVE UP (NIV)
(See *LOSE HEART*)

NOT I BUT THE LORD
1Cor 7:10 Now to the married I command, yet *not I but the Lord*

NOT MY WILL, BUT YOURS
Luke 22:42 saying, "Father, if it is Your will, remove this cup from Me; nevertheless *not My will, but Yours*, be done

NOT OF THE WORLD
John 15:19 Yet because you are *not of the world*, but I chose you out of the world, therefore the world hates you
John 17:14 and the world has hated them because they are *not of the world*, just as I am *not of the world*
John 17:16 They are *not of the world*, just as I am *not of the world*

NOT ONE STONE
Matt 24:2 Assuredly, I say to you, *not one stone* shall be left here upon another, that shall not be thrown down
Mark 13:2 *Not one stone* shall be left upon another, that shall not be thrown down
Luke 21:6 As for these things which you see, the

days will come in which *not one stone* shall be left upon another that shall not be thrown down

NOT PASS BY THEM ANYMORE
Amos 7:8 Behold, I am setting a plumb line in the midst of My people Israel; I will *not pass by them anymore*
Amos 8:2 The end has come upon my people Israel; I will *not pass by them anymore*

NOT PERFECTED IN LOVE (NAS, RSV)
(See *MADE PERFECT IN LOVE*)

NOT SAFE TO TRAVEL (NIV)
(See *NO PEACE*)

NOT TO FAINT (KJV)
(See *LOSE HEART*)

NOT TURN ASIDE TO THE RIGHT OR TO THE LEFT (NAS, NIV)
(See *TURN NEITHER TO THE RIGHT NOR TO THE LEFT*)

NOTHING TO BE GAINED UNDER THE SUN (RSV)
(See *NO PROFIT UNDER THE SUN*)

NOTHING WAS GAINED UNDER THE SUN (NIV)
(See *NO PROFIT UNDER THE SUN*)

NOTHING WILL BE IMPOSSIBLE
Matt 17:20 for assuredly, I say to you, if you have faith as a mustard seed, you will say to this mountain, 'Move from here to there,' and it will move; and *nothing will be impossible* for you
Luke 1:37 For with God *nothing will be impossible*

NOTHING WILL HINDER YOUR PRAYERS (NIV)
(See *PRAYERS MAY NOT BE HINDERED*)

NOTHING WILL SHAKE ME (NIV)
(See *I SHALL NOT BE MOVED*)

NOURISHED IN THE WORDS OF FAITH
1Tim 4:6 If you instruct the brethren in these things, you will be a good minister of Jesus Christ, *nourished in the words of faith* and of the good doctrine which you have carefully followed

NOW CONCERNING
Deut 4:32 For ask *now concerning* the days that are past, which were before you, since the day that God created man on the earth, and ask from one end of heaven to the other, whether any great thing like this has happened, or anything like it has been heard
2Chr 24:27 *Now concerning* his sons, and the many oracles about him, and the repairing of the house of God, indeed they are written in the annals of the book of the kings
Jer 52:21 *Now concerning* the pillars: the height of one pillar was eighteen cubits, a measuring line of twelve cubits could measure its circumference, and its thickness was four fingers
1Cor 7:1 *Now concerning* the things of which you wrote to me
1Cor 7:25 *Now concerning* virgins: I have no commandment from the Lord
1Cor 8:1 *Now concerning* things offered to idols: We know that we all have knowledge
1Cor 12:1 *Now concerning* spiritual gifts, brethren, I do not want you to be ignorant
1Cor 16:1 *Now concerning* the collection for the saints, as I have given orders to the churches of Galatia, so you must do also
1Cor 16:12 *Now concerning* our brother Apollos, I strongly urged him to come to you with the brethren, but he was quite unwilling to come at this time
2Cor 9:1 *Now concerning* the ministering to the saints, it is superfluous for me to write to you
Gal 1:20 *(Now concerning* the things which I write to you, indeed, before God, I do not lie

NOWHERE TO LAY HIS HEAD
Matt 8:20 And Jesus said to him, "Foxes have holes and birds of the air have nests, but the Son of Man has *nowhere to lay His head*
Luke 9:58 And Jesus said to him, "Foxes have holes and birds of the air have nests, but the Son of Man has *nowhere to lay His head*

NUMBER OUR DAYS
Ps 90:12 So teach us to *number our days*, that we may gain a heart of wisdom

O

O GOD
Gen 32:9 Then Jacob said, "*O God* of my father Abraham and God of my father Isaac, the Lord who said to me
Num 12:13 So Moses cried out to the Lord, saying, "Please heal her, *O God*, I pray
Num 16:22 Then they fell on their faces, and said, "*O God*, the God of the spirits of all flesh, shall one man sin, and You be angry with all the congregation
Judg 16:28 Strengthen me, I pray, just this once, *O God*, that I may with one blow take vengeance on the Philistines for my two eyes
1Kin 8:26 And now I pray, *O God* of Israel, let Your word come true, which You have spoken to Your servant David my father
1Chr 16:35 And say, "Save us, *O God* of our salvation; gather us together, and deliver us from the Gentiles, to give thanks to Your holy name, to triumph in Your praise
1Chr 17:17 And yet this was a small thing in Your sight, *O God*
Neh 6:9 For they all were trying to make us afraid, saying, "Their hands will be weakened in the work, and it will not be done." Now therefore, *O God*, strengthen my hands
Ps 4:1 Hear me when I call, *O God* of my righteousness
Ps 5:10 Pronounce them guilty, *O God!* Let them fall by their own counsels
Ps 10:12 *O God*, lift up Your hand! Do not forget the humble
Ps 16:1 Preserve me, *O God*, for in You I put my trust
Ps 17:6 I have called upon You, for You will hear me, *O God*
Ps 25:22 Redeem Israel, *O God*, out of all their troubles
Ps 27:9 Do not leave me nor forsake me, *O God* of my salvation
Ps 36:7 How precious is Your lovingkindness, *O God!* Therefore the children of men put their trust under the shadow of Your wings
Ps 42:1 As the deer pants for the water brooks, so pants my soul for You, *O God*
Ps 43:1 Vindicate me, *O God*, and plead my cause against an ungodly nation
Ps 43:4 And on the harp I will praise You, *O God*, my God
Ps 44:1 We have heard with our ears, *O God*, our

fathers have told us, what deeds You did in their days, in days of old
Ps 44:4 You are my King, *O God;* command victories for Jacob
Ps 45:6 Your throne, *O God*, is forever and ever; a scepter of righteousness is the scepter of Your kingdom
Ps 48:9 We have thought, *O God*, on Your lovingkindness, in the midst of Your temple
Ps 48:10 According to Your name, *O God*, so is Your praise to the ends of the earth
Ps 51:1 Have mercy upon me, *O God*, according to Your lovingkindness
Ps 51:10 Create in me a clean heart, *O God*, and renew a steadfast spirit within me
Ps 51:14 Deliver me from bloodguiltiness, *O God*, the God of my salvation, and my tongue shall sing aloud of Your righteousness
Ps 51:17 The sacrifices of God are a broken spirit, a broken and a contrite heart. These, *O God*, You will not despise
Ps 54:1 Save me, *O God*, by Your name, and vindicate me by Your strength
Ps 54:2 Hear my prayer, *O God;* give ear to the words of my mouth
Ps 55:1 Give ear to my prayer, *O God*, and do not hide Yourself from my supplication
Ps 55:23 But You, *O God*, shall bring them down to the pit of destruction
Ps 56:1 Be merciful to me, *O God*, for man would swallow me up
Ps 56:7 Shall they escape by iniquity? In anger cast down the peoples, *O God*
Ps 56:12 Vows made to You are binding upon me, *O God*
Ps 57:1 Be merciful to me, *O God*, be merciful to me
Ps 57:5 Be exalted, *O God*, above the heavens; let Your glory be above all the earth
Ps 57:7 My heart is steadfast, *O God*, my heart is steadfast
Ps 57:11 Be exalted, *O God*, above the heavens; let Your glory be above all the earth
Ps 58:6 Break their teeth in their mouth, *O God!* Break out the fangs of the young lions, O Lord
Ps 60:1 *O God*, You have cast us off; You have broken us down
Ps 60:10 Is it not You, *O God*, who cast us off? And You, *O God*, who did not go out with our armies
Ps 61:1 Hear my cry, *O God;* attend to my prayer
Ps 61:5 For You, *O God*, have heard my vows; You have given me the heritage of those who fear Your name
Ps 63:1 *O God*, You are my God; early will I seek You
Ps 64:1 Hear my voice, *O God*, in my meditation; preserve my life from fear of the enemy
Ps 65:1 Praise is awaiting You, *O God*, in Zion; and to You the vow shall be performed
Ps 65:5 By awesome deeds in righteousness You will answer us, *O God* of our salvation, You who are the confidence of all the ends of the earth, and of the far-off seas
Ps 66:10 For You, *O God*, have proved us; You have refined us as silver is refined
Ps 67:3 Let the peoples praise You, *O God;* let all the peoples praise You
Ps 67:5 Let the peoples praise You, *O God;* let all the peoples praise You
Ps 68:7 *O God*, when You went out before Your people, when You marched through the wilderness
Ps 68:9 You, *O God*, sent a plentiful rain, whereby You confirmed Your inheritance, when it was weary
Ps 68:10 You, *O God*, provided from Your goodness for the poor
Ps 68:24 They have seen Your procession, *O God*, the procession of my God, my King, into the sanctuary
Ps 68:28 Your God has commanded your strength; strengthen, *O God*, what You have done for us
Ps 68:35 *O God*, You are more awesome than Your holy places
Ps 69:1 Save me, *O God!* For the waters have come up to my neck
Ps 69:5 *O God*, You know my foolishness; and my sins are not hidden from You
Ps 69:6 Let not those who seek You be confounded because of me, *O God* of Israel
Ps 69:13 *O God*, in the multitude of Your mercy, hear me in the truth of Your salvation
Ps 69:29 Let Your salvation, *O God*, set me up on high
Ps 70:1 Make haste, *O God*, to deliver me! Make haste to help me, O Lord
Ps 70:5 Make haste to me, *O God!* You are my help and my deliverer
Ps 71:12 *O God*, do not be far from me; O my God, make haste to help me
Ps 71:17 *O God*, You have taught me from my youth; and to this day I declare Your wondrous works
Ps 71:18 Now also when I am old and grayheaded, *O God*, do not forsake me, until I declare Your strength to this generation, Your power to everyone who is to come
Ps 71:19 Also Your righteousness, *O God*, is very high, You who have done great things; *O God*, who is like You
Ps 72:1 Give the king Your judgments, *O God*, and Your righteousness to the king's Son
Ps 74:1 *O God*, why have You cast us off forever? Why does Your anger smoke against the sheep of Your pasture
Ps 74:10 *O God*, how long will the adversary reproach? Will the enemy blaspheme Your name forever
Ps 74:22 Arise, *O God*, plead Your own cause; remember how the foolish man reproaches You daily
Ps 75:1 We give thanks to You, *O God*, we give thanks
Ps 76:6 At Your rebuke, *O God* of Jacob, both the chariot and horse were cast into a dead sleep
Ps 77:13 Your way, *O God*, is in the sanctuary; who is so great a God as our God
Ps 77:16 The waters saw You, *O God;* the waters saw You, they were afraid
Ps 79:1 *O God*, the nations have come into Your inheritance; Your holy temple they have defiled
Ps 79:9 Help us, *O God* of our salvation, for the glory of Your name
Ps 80:3 Restore us, *O God;* cause Your face to shine, and we shall be saved
Ps 80:7 Restore us, *O God* of hosts; cause Your face to shine, and we shall be saved
Ps 80:14 Return, we beseech You, *O God* of hosts; look down from heaven and see, and visit this vine
Ps 82:8 Arise, *O God*, judge the earth; for You shall inherit all nations
Ps 83:1 Do not keep silent, *O God!* Do not hold Your peace, and do not be still, *O God*
Ps 84:8 O Lord God of hosts, hear my prayer; give ear, *O God* of Jacob
Ps 84:9 *O God*, behold our shield, and look upon the face of Your anointed
Ps 85:4 Restore us, *O God* of our salvation, and cause Your anger toward us to cease
Ps 86:14 *O God*, the proud have risen against me, and a mob of violent men have sought my life, and have not set You before them
Ps 94:1 O Lord God, to whom vengeance belongs *O God*, to whom vengeance belongs, shine forth

Ps 108:1 *O God*, my heart is steadfast; I will sing and give praise, even with my glory
Ps 108:5 Be exalted, *O God*, above the heavens, and Your glory above all the earth
Ps 108:11 Is it not You, *O God*, who cast us off? And You, *O God*, who did not go out with our armies
Ps 109:1 Do not keep silent, *O God* of my praise
Ps 109:21 But You, *O God* the Lord, deal with me for Your name's sake
Ps 139:17 How precious also are Your thoughts to me, *O God*
Ps 139:19 Oh, that You would slay the wicked, *O God!* Depart from me, therefore, you bloodthirsty men
Ps 139:23 Search me, *O God*, and know my heart; try me, and know my anxieties
Ps 140:7 *O God* the Lord, the strength of my salvation, You have covered my head in the day of battle
Ps 141:8 But my eyes are upon You, *O God* the Lord
Ps 144:9 I will sing a new song to You, *O God*
Is 45:15 Truly You are God, who hide Yourself, *O God* of Israel, the Savior
Dan 2:23 I thank You and praise You, *O God* of my fathers
Heb 1:8 Your throne, *O God*, is forever and ever; a scepter of righteousness is the scepter of Your Kingdom
Heb 10:7 Then I said, 'Behold, I have come in the volume of the book it is written of Me to do Your will, *O God*
Heb 10:9 then He said, "Behold, I have come to do Your will, *O God*

O GRAVE, I WILL BE YOUR DESTRUCTION
Hos 13:14 *O grave, I will be your destruction!* Pity is hidden from My eyes

O JERUSALEM, JERUSALEM
Matt 23:37 *O Jerusalem, Jerusalem*, the one who kills the prophets and stones those who are sent to her
Luke 13:34 *O Jerusalem, Jerusalem*, the one who kills the prophets and stones those who are sent to her

O LORD, BE GRACIOUS
Is 33:2 *O Lord, be gracious* to us; we have waited for You

O LORD MY GOD
1Kin 3:7 Now, *O Lord my God*, You have made Your servant king instead of my father David, but I am a little child
1Kin 8:28 Yet regard the prayer of Your servant and his supplication, *O Lord my God*, and listen to the cry and the prayer which Your servant is praying before You today
1Kin 17:20 Then he cried out to the Lord and said, "*O Lord my God*, have You also brought tragedy on the widow with whom I lodge, by killing her son
1Kin 17:21 And he stretched himself out on the child three times, and cried out to the Lord and said, "*O Lord my God*, I pray, let this child's soul come back to him
1Chr 21:17 Let Your hand, I pray, *O Lord my God*, be against me and my father's house, but not against Your people that they should be plagued
2Chr 6:19 Yet regard the prayer of Your servant and his supplication, *O Lord my God*, and listen to the cry and to the prayer which Your servant is praying before You
Ps 7:1 *O Lord my God*, in You I put my trust
Ps 7:3 *O Lord my God*, if I have done this: if there is iniquity in my hands
Ps 13:3 Consider and hear me, *O Lord my God;* enlighten my eyes, lest I sleep the sleep of death
Ps 30:2 *O Lord my God*, I cried out to You, and You have healed me
Ps 30:12 *O Lord my God*, I will give thanks to You forever
Ps 35:24 Vindicate me, *O Lord my God*, according to Your righteousness
Ps 38:15 For in You, O Lord, I hope; You will hear, *O Lord my God*
Ps 40:5 Many, *O Lord my God*, are Your wonderful works which You have done
Ps 86:12 I will praise You, *O Lord my God*, with all my heart, and I will glorify Your name forevermore
Ps 104:1 *O Lord my God*, You are very great: You are clothed with honor and majesty
Ps 109:26 Help me, *O Lord my God!* Oh, save me according to Your mercy
Hab 1:12 Are You not from everlasting, *O Lord my God*, my Holy One

O SHEOL, WHERE IS YOUR DESTRUCTION (RSV)
(See *O GRAVE, I WILL BE YOUR DESTRUCTION*)

OAKS OF BASHAN
Is 2:13 upon all the cedars of Lebanon that are high and lifted up, and upon all the *oaks of Bashan*
Zech 11:2 Wail, O *oaks of Bashan*, for the thick forest has come down

OATH BETWIXT US (KJV)
(See *MAKE A COVENANT*)

OATH WHICH HE SWORE
Deut 7:8 but because the Lord loves you, and because He would keep the *oath which He swore* to your fathers, the Lord has brought you out with a mighty hand, and redeemed you from the house of bondage, from the hand of Pharaoh king of Egypt
Luke 1:73 the *oath which He swore* to our father Abraham

OBEDIENCE THAT COMES FROM FAITH (NIV)
(See *OBEDIENCE TO THE FAITH*)

OBEDIENCE TO RIGHTEOUSNESS
Rom 6:16 Do you not know that to whom you present yourselves slaves to obey, you are that one's slaves whom you obey, whether of sin to death, or of *obedience to righteousness*

OBEDIENCE TO THE FAITH
Rom 1:5 through whom we have received grace and apostleship for *obedience to the faith* among all nations for His name
Rom 16:26 but now has been made manifest, and by the prophetic Scriptures has been made known to all nations, according to the commandment of the everlasting God, for *obedience to the faith*

OBEDIENCE, WHICH LEADS TO RIGHTEOUSNESS (NIV, RSV)
(See *OBEDIENCE TO RIGHTEOUSNESS*)

OBEDIENT CHILDREN
1Pet 1:14 as *obedient children*, not conforming yourselves to the former lusts, as in your ignorance

OBEDIENT IN ALL THINGS
2Cor 2:9 For to this end I also wrote, that I might put you to the test, whether you are *obedient in all things*

OBEDIENT TO THE POINT OF DEATH
Phil 2:8 And being found in appearance as a man, He humbled Himself and became *obedient to the point of death*, even the death of the cross

OBEDIENT TO THEIR OWN HUSBANDS
Tit 2:5 to be discreet, chaste, homemakers, good, *obedient to their own husbands*, that the word of God may not be blasphemed

OBEDIENT TO THEIR OWN MASTERS
Tit 2:9 Exhort servants to be *obedient to their own masters*, to be well pleasing in all things, not answering back

OBEDIENT UNTO DEATH (KJV, RSV)
(See *OBEDIENT TO THE POINT OF DEATH*)

OBEY GOD RATHER THAN MEN
Acts 5:29 Then Peter and the other apostles answered and said: "We ought to *obey God rather than men*

OBEY MY VOICE
Gen 27:8 Now therefore, my son, *obey my voice* according to what I command you
Gen 27:13 only *obey my voice*, and go, get them for me
Gen 27:43 Now therefore, my son, *obey my voice:* arise, flee to my brother Laban in Haran
Ex 19:5 Now therefore, if you will indeed *obey My voice* and keep My covenant, then you shall be a special treasure to Me above all people
2Kin 10:6 If you are for me, and if you will *obey my voice*, take the heads of the men, your master's sons, and come to me at Jezreel by this time tomorrow
Jer 7:23 But this is what I commanded them, saying, '*Obey My voice*, and I will be your God, and you shall be My people
Jer 11:4 which I commanded your fathers in the day that I brought them out of the land of Egypt, from the iron furnace, saying, '*Obey My voice*, and do according to all that I command you
Jer 11:7 For I earnestly exhorted your fathers in the day that I brought them up out of the land of Egypt, until this day, rising early and exhorting, saying, "*Obey My voice*
Jer 18:10 if it does evil in My sight so that it does not *obey My voice*, then I will relent concerning the good with which I said I would benefit it
Jer 22:21 This has been your manner from your youth, that you did not *obey My voice*

OBEY MY WORD (RSV)
(See *OBEY MY VOICE*)

OBEY THE COMMANDMENTS OF THE LORD
Deut 11:27 the blessing, if you *obey the commandments of the Lord* your God which I command you today
Deut 11:28 and the curse, if you do not *obey the commandments of the Lord* your God, but turn aside from the way which I command you today, to go after other gods which you have not known
Judg 3:4 And they were left, that He might test Israel by them, to know whether they would *obey the commandments of the Lord*, which He had commanded their fathers by the hand of Moses

OBEY THE TRUTH (KJV)
(See *OBEYING THE TRUTH*)

OBEY THE VOICE OF THE LORD
Deut 15:5 only if you carefully *obey the voice of the Lord* your God, to observe with care all these commandments which I command you today
Deut 27:10 Therefore you shall *obey the voice of the Lord* your God, and observe His commandments and His statutes which I command you today
Deut 28:1 Now it shall come to pass, if you diligently *obey the voice of the Lord* your God, to observe carefully all His commandments which I command you today, that the Lord your God will set you high above all nations of the earth
Deut 28:2 And all these blessings shall come upon you and overtake you, because you *obey the voice of the Lord* your God
Deut 28:15 But it shall come to pass, if you do not *obey the voice of the Lord* your God, to observe carefully all His commandments and His statutes which I command you today, that all these curses will come upon you and overtake you
Deut 28:45 Moreover all these curses shall come upon you and pursue and overtake you, until you are destroyed, because you did not *obey the voice of the Lord* your God, to keep His commandments and His statutes which He commanded you
Deut 28:62 You shall be left few in number, whereas you were as the stars of heaven in multitude, because you would not *obey the voice of the Lord* your God
Deut 30:8 And you will again *obey the voice of the Lord* and do all His commandments which I command you today
Deut 30:10 if you *obey the voice of the Lord* your God, to keep His commandments and His statutes which are written in this Book of the Law, and if you turn to the Lord your God with all your heart and with all your soul
Josh 5:6 For the children of Israel walked forty years in the wilderness, till all the people who were men of war, who came out of Egypt, were consumed, because they did not *obey the voice of the Lord* to whom the Lord swore that He would not show them the land which the Lord had sworn to their fathers that He would give us
1Sam 12:15 However, if you do not *obey the voice of the Lord*, but rebel against the commandment of the Lord, then the hand of the Lord will be against you, as it was against your fathers
1Sam 15:19 Why then did you not *obey the voice of the Lord*
1Sam 28:18 Because you did not *obey the voice of the Lord* nor execute His fierce wrath upon Amalek, therefore the Lord has done this thing to you this day
2Kin 18:12 because they did not *obey the voice of the Lord* their God, but transgressed His covenant and all that Moses the servant of the Lord had commanded
Jer 7:28 So you shall say to them, 'This is a nation that does not *obey the voice of the Lord* their God nor receive correction
Jer 26:13 Now therefore, amend your ways and your doings, and *obey the voice of the Lord* your God
Jer 38:20 Please, *obey the voice of the Lord* which I speak to you
Jer 42:6 Whether it is pleasing or displeasing, we will *obey the voice of the Lord* our God to whom we send you, that it may be well with us when we *obey the voice of the Lord* our God
Jer 43:4 So Johanan the son of Kareah, all the captains of the forces, and all the people would not

obey the voice of the Lord, to remain in the land of Judah

Jer 43:7 So they went to the land of Egypt, for they did not *obey the voice of the Lord*

Zech 6:15 And this shall come to pass if you diligently *obey the voice of the Lord* your God

OBEY THE WHOLE LAW (NIV)
(See *KEEP THE WHOLE LAW*)

OBEY YOUR PARENTS

Eph 6:1 Children, *obey your parents* in the Lord, for this is right

Col 3:20 Children, *obey your parents* in all things, for this is well pleasing to the Lord

OBEYED MY VOICE

Gen 22:18 In your seed all the nations of the earth shall be blessed, because you have *obeyed My voice*

Gen 26:5 because Abraham *obeyed My voice* and kept My charge, My commandments, My statutes, and My laws

Josh 22:2 You have kept all that Moses the servant of the Lord commanded you, and have *obeyed my voice* in all that I commanded you

Judg 2:2 But you have not *obeyed My voice*. Why have you done this

Judg 6:10 do not fear the gods of the Amorites, in whose land you dwell. But you have not *obeyed My voice*

Jer 3:13 Only acknowledge your iniquity, that you have transgressed against the Lord your God, and have scattered your charms to alien deities under every green tree, and you have not *obeyed My voice*

Jer 9:13 And the Lord said, "Because they have forsaken My law which I set before them, and have not *obeyed My voice*, nor walked according to it

OBEYING THE TRUTH

Gal 5:7 You ran well. Who hindered you from *obeying the truth*

1Pet 1:22 Since you have purified your souls in *obeying the truth* through the Spirit in sincere love of the brethren, love one another fervently with a pure heart

OBJECT OF YOUR AFFECTION (NIV)
(See *DELIGHT OF YOUR SOUL*)

OBJECTS OF HIS MERCY (NIV)
(See *VESSELS OF MERCY*)

OBJECTS OF HIS WRATH (NIV)
(See *VESSELS OF WRATH*)

OBSERVE THE SABBATH

Ex 31:16 Therefore the children of Israel shall keep the Sabbath, to *observe the Sabbath* throughout their generations as a perpetual covenant

Deut 5:12 *Observe the Sabbath* day, to keep it holy, as the Lord your God commanded you

OBSERVE THEM CAREFULLY (NIV)
(See *CAREFUL TO OBSERVE*)

OBSERVING THE LAW (NIV)
(See *DEEDS OF THE LAW*)

OBTAIN MERCY

Matt 5:7 Blessed are the merciful, for they shall *obtain mercy*

Rom 11:31 even so these also have now been disobedient, that through the mercy shown you they also may *obtain mercy*

Heb 4:16 Let us therefore come boldly to the throne of grace, that we may *obtain mercy* and find grace to help in time of need

OBTAIN THE GLORY (RSV)
(See *OBTAINING OF THE GLORY*)

OBTAINED MERCY

Hos 2:23 Then I will sow her for Myself in the earth, and I will have mercy on her who had not *obtained mercy*

Rom 11:30 For as you were once disobedient to God, yet have now *obtained mercy* through their disobedience

1Tim 1:13 but I *obtained mercy* because I did it ignorantly in unbelief

1Tim 1:16 However, for this reason I *obtained mercy*, that in me first Jesus Christ might show all longsuffering, as a pattern to those who are going to believe on Him for everlasting life

1Pet 2:10 who once were not a people but are now the people of God, who had not *obtained mercy* but now have *obtained mercy*

OBTAINED WITH THE BLOOD OF HIS OWN SON (RSV)
(See *PURCHASED WITH HIS OWN BLOOD*)

OBTAINING OF THE GLORY

2Th 2:14 to which He called you by our gospel, for the *obtaining of the glory* of our Lord Jesus Christ

OCCASION TO THE FLESH (KJV)
(See *OPPORTUNITY FOR THE FLESH*)

OF THE CIRCUMCISION

Ex 4:26 Then she said, "You are a husband of blood!" because *of the circumcision*

Acts 10:45 And those *of the circumcision* who believed were astonished, as many as came with Peter, because the gift of the Holy Spirit had been poured out on the Gentiles also

Acts 11:2 And when Peter came up to Jerusalem, those *of the circumcision* contended with him

Rom 4:12 and the father of circumcision to those who not only are *of the circumcision*, but who also walk in the steps of the faith which our father Abraham had while still uncircumcised

Gal 2:12 but when they came, he withdrew and separated himself, fearing those who were *of the circumcision*

Col 4:11 These are my only fellow workers for the kingdom of God who are *of the circumcision*

Tit 1:10 For there are many insubordinate, both idle talkers and deceivers, especially those *of the circumcision*

OF THE EARTH (NIV)
(See *OF THE WORLD*)

OF THE FLESH

Ex 12:46 you shall not carry any *of the flesh* outside the house, nor shall you break one of its bones

Ex 29:34 And if any *of the flesh* of the consecration offerings, or of the bread, remains until the morning, then you shall burn the remainder with fire

Lev 7:17 the remainder *of the flesh* of the sacrifice on the third day must be burned with fire

Lev 7:18 And if any *of the flesh* of the sacrifice of his peace offering is eaten at all on the third day, it shall not be accepted, nor shall it be imputed to him

Lev 8:32 What remains *of the flesh* and of the bread you shall burn with fire

Lev 17:11 For the life *of the flesh* is in the blood,

and I have given it to you upon the altar to make atonement for your souls
John 1:13 who were born, not of blood, nor of the will *of the flesh*, nor of the will of man, but of God
John 3:6 That which is born *of the flesh* is flesh, and that which is born of the Spirit is spirit
Rom 8:5 For those who live according to the flesh set their minds on the things *of the flesh*, but those who live according to the Spirit, the things of the Spirit
Rom 9:8 That is, those who are the children *of the flesh*, these are not the children of God
1Cor 5:5 deliver such a one to Satan for the destruction *of the flesh*, that his spirit may be saved in the day of the Lord Jesus
2Cor 7:1 Therefore, having these promises, beloved, let us cleanse ourselves from all filthiness *of the flesh* and spirit, perfecting holiness in the fear of God
Gal 5:16 Walk in the Spirit, and you shall not fulfill the lust *of the flesh*
Gal 5:19 Now the works *of the flesh* are evident, which are
Gal 6:8 For he who sows to his flesh will *of the flesh* reap corruption, but he who sows to the Spirit will of the Spirit reap everlasting life
Eph 2:3 among whom also we all once conducted ourselves in the lusts of our flesh, fulfilling the desires *of the flesh* and of the mind, and were by nature children of wrath, just as the others
Col 2:11 In Him you were also circumcised with the circumcision made without hands, by putting off the body of the sins *of the flesh*, by the circumcision of Christ
Col 2:23 These things indeed have an appearance of wisdom in self-imposed religion, false humility, and neglect of the body, but are of no value against the indulgence *of the flesh*
Heb 9:13 For if the blood of bulls and goats and the ashes of a heifer, sprinkling the unclean, sanctifies for the purifying *of the flesh*
1Pet 3:21 There is also an antitype which now saves us, namely baptism (not the removal of the filth *of the flesh*, but the answer of a good conscience toward God
2Pet 2:18 For when they speak great swelling words of emptiness, they allure through the lusts *of the flesh*, through licentiousness, the ones who have actually escaped from those who live in error
1Jn 2:16 For all that is in the world the lust *of the flesh*, the lust of the eyes, and the pride of life is not of the Father but is of the world

OF THE MONTH (KJV)
(See *NEW MOON*)

OF THE WORLD
2Sam 22:16 Then the channels of the sea were seen, the foundations *of the world* were uncovered, at the rebuke of the Lord, at the blast of the breath of His nostrils
Job 18:18 He is driven from light into darkness, and chased out *of the world*
Ps 17:14 With Your hand from men, O Lord, from men *of the world* who have their portion in this life, and whose belly You fill with Your hidden treasure
Ps 18:15 Then the channels of waters were seen, and the foundations *of the world* were uncovered at Your rebuke, O Lord, at the blast of the breath of Your nostrils
Ps 19:4 Their line has gone out through all the earth, and their words to the end *of the world*
Ps 22:27 All the ends *of the world* shall remember and turn to the Lord, and all the families of the nations shall worship before You
Ps 33:8 Let all the inhabitants *of the world* stand in awe of Him
Ps 49:1 Hear this, all you peoples; give ear, all you inhabitants *of the world*
Prov 8:26 while as yet He had not made the earth or the fields, or the primeval dust *of the world*
Is 14:21 Prepare slaughter for his children because of the iniquity of their fathers, lest they rise up and possess the land, and fill the face *of the world* with cities
Is 18:3 All inhabitants *of the world* and dwellers on the earth
Is 23:17 She will return to her pay, and commit fornication with all the kingdoms *of the world* on the face of the earth
Is 26:9 for when Your judgments are in the earth, the inhabitants *of the world* will learn righteousness
Is 26:18 we have not accomplished any deliverance in the earth, nor have the inhabitants *of the world* fallen
Is 27:6 Israel shall blossom and bud, and fill the face *of the world* with fruit
Is 38:11 I shall observe man no more among the inhabitants *of the world*
Is 62:11 Indeed the Lord has proclaimed to the end *of the world*
Is 64:4 For since the beginning *of the world* men have not heard nor perceived by the ear, nor has the eye seen any God besides You, Who acts for the one who waits for Him
Jer 25:26 and all the kingdoms *of the world* which are on the face of the earth
Lam 4:12 The kings of the earth, and all inhabitants *of the world*, would not have believed that the adversary and the enemy could enter the gates of Jerusalem
Matt 4:8 Again, the devil took Him up on an exceedingly high mountain, and showed Him all the kingdoms *of the world* and their glory
Matt 5:14 You are the light *of the world*. A city that is set on a hill cannot be hidden
Matt 13:35 I will utter things which have been kept secret from the foundation *of the world*
Matt 24:21 For then there will be great tribulation, such as has not been since the beginning *of the world* until this time, no, nor ever shall be
Matt 25:34 Then the King will say to those on His right hand, 'Come, you blessed of My Father, inherit the kingdom prepared for you from the foundation *of the world*
Luke 4:5 Then the devil, taking Him up on a high mountain, showed Him all the kingdoms *of the world* in a moment of time
Luke 11:50 that the blood of all the prophets which was shed from the foundation *of the world* may be required of this generation
Luke 12:30 For all these things the nations *of the world* seek after, and your Father knows that you need these things
John 1:29 The Lamb of God who takes away the sin *of the world*
John 4:42 Then they said to the woman, "Now we believe, not because of what you said, for we have heard for ourselves and know that this is indeed the Christ, the Savior *of the world*
John 6:51 and the bread that I shall give is My flesh, which I shall give for the life *of the world*
John 8:12 Then Jesus spoke to them again, saying, "I am the light *of the world*
John 9:5 As long as I am in the world, I am the light *of the world*
John 15:19 If you were *of the world*, the world would love its own. Yet because you are not *of the world*, but I chose you out *of the world*, therefore the world hates you
John 17:6 I have manifested Your name to the men whom You have given Me out *of the world*

John 17:14 and the world has hated them because they are not *of the world,* just as I am not *of the world*
John 17:15 I do not pray that You should take them out *of the world,* but that You should keep them from the evil one
John 17:16 They are not *of the world,* just as I am not *of the world*
John 17:24 for You loved Me before the foundation *of the world*
Rom 1:20 For since the creation *of the world* His invisible attributes are clearly seen, being understood by the things that are made, even His eternal power and Godhead, so that they are without excuse
Rom 4:13 For the promise that he would be the heir *of the world* was not to Abraham or to his seed through the law, but through the righteousness of faith
Rom 10:18 Their sound has gone out to all the earth, and their words to the ends *of the world*
Rom 11:15 For if their being cast away is the reconciling *of the world,* what will their acceptance be but life from the dead
1Cor 1:27 But God has chosen the foolish things *of the world* to put to shame the wise, and God has chosen the weak things *of the world* to put to shame the things which are mighty
1Cor 1:28 and the base things *of the world* and the things which are despised God has chosen, and the things which are not, to bring to nothing the things that are
1Cor 2:12 Now we have received, not the spirit *of the world,* but the Spirit who is from God, that we might know the things that have been freely given to us by God
1Cor 4:13 We have been made as the filth *of the world,* the offscouring of all things until now
1Cor 5:10 Yet I certainly did not mean with the sexually immoral people of this world, or with the covetous, or extortioners, or idolaters, since then you would need to go out *of the world*
1Cor 7:33 But he who is married cares about the things *of the world* how he may please his wife
1Cor 7:34 But she who is married cares about the things *of the world* how she may please her husband
2Cor 7:10 For godly sorrow produces repentance to salvation, not to be regretted; but the sorrow *of the world* produces death
Gal 4:3 Even so we, when we were children, were in bondage under the elements *of the world*
Eph 1:4 just as He chose us in Him before the foundation *of the world,* that we should be holy and without blame before Him in love
Col 2:8 Beware lest anyone cheat you through philosophy and empty deceit, according to the tradition of men, according to the basic principles *of the world,* and not according to Christ
Col 2:20 Therefore, if you died with Christ from the basic principles *of the world,* why, as though living in the world, do you subject yourselves to regulations
Heb 4:3 So I swore in My wrath, they shall not enter My rest," although the works were finished from the foundation *of the world*
Heb 9:26 He then would have had to suffer often since the foundation *of the world*
Jas 4:4 Whoever therefore wants to be a friend *of the world* makes himself an enemy of God
1Pet 1:20 He indeed was foreordained before the foundation *of the world,* but was manifest in these last times for you
2Pet 2:20 For if, after they have escaped the pollutions *of the world* through the knowledge of the Lord and Savior Jesus Christ, they are again entangled in them and overcome, the latter end is worse for them than the beginning
1Jn 2:16 For all that is in the world the lust of the flesh, the lust of the eyes, and the pride of life is not of the Father but is *of the world*
1Jn 4:5 They are *of the world.* Therefore they speak as *of the world,* and the world hears them
1Jn 4:14 And we have seen and testify that the Father has sent the Son as Savior *of the world*
Rev 13:8 And all who dwell on the earth will worship him, whose names have not been written in the Book of Life of the Lamb slain from the foundation *of the world*
Rev 17:8 And those who dwell on the earth will marvel, whose names are not written in the Book of Life from the foundation *of the world,* when they see the beast that was, and is not, and yet is

OF THIS LIFE (NIV)
(See *OF THIS WORLD*)

OF THIS WORLD
Matt 13:22 Now he who received seed among the thorns is he who hears the word, and the cares *of this world* and the deceitfulness of riches choke the word, and he becomes unfruitful
Mark 4:19 and the cares *of this world,* the deceitfulness of riches, and the desires for other things entering in choke the word, and it becomes unfruitful
Luke 16:8 For the sons *of this world* are more shrewd in their generation than the sons of light
John 8:23 You are *of this world;* I am not *of this world*
John 11:9 If anyone walks in the day, he does not stumble, because he sees the light *of this world*
John 12:31 Now is the judgment *of this world;* now the ruler *of this world* will be cast out
John 14:30 I will no longer talk much with you, for the ruler *of this world* is coming, and he has nothing in Me
John 16:11 of judgment, because the ruler *of this world* is judged
John 18:36 Jesus answered, "My kingdom is not *of this world.* If My kingdom were *of this world,* My servants would fight, so that I should not be delivered to the Jews
1Cor 1:20 Has not God made foolish the wisdom *of this world*
1Cor 3:19 For the wisdom *of this world* is foolishness with God
1Cor 5:10 Yet I certainly did not mean with the sexually immoral people *of this world,* or with the covetous, or extortioners, or idolaters, since then you would need to go out of the world
1Cor 7:31 and those who use this world as not misusing it. For the form *of this world* is passing away
Eph 2:2 in which you once walked according to the course *of this world,* according to the prince of the power of the air, the spirit who now works in the sons of disobedience
Jas 2:5 Has God not chosen the poor *of this world* to be rich in faith and heirs of the kingdom which He promised to those who love Him
Rev 11:15 And there were loud voices in heaven, saying, "The kingdoms *of this world* have become the kingdoms of our Lord and of His Christ, and He shall reign forever and ever

OFFER A SIN OFFERING FOR THE ALTAR (RSV)
(See *CLEANSE THE ALTAR*)

OFFER FOOD (NIV)
(See *BREAK BREAD*)

OFFER SACRIFICE
2Kin 17:36 but the Lord, who brought you up from the land of Egypt with great power and an out-

stretched arm, Him you shall fear, Him you shall worship, and to Him you shall *offer sacrifice*
Is 57:7 On a lofty and high mountain you have set your bed; even there you went up to *offer sacrifice*

OFFER SACRIFICES
Deut 33:19 there they shall *offer sacrifices* of righteousness; for they shall partake of the abundance of the seas and of treasures hidden in the sand
1Kin 12:27 If these people go up to *offer sacrifices* in the house of the Lord at Jerusalem, then the heart of this people will turn back to their lord, Rehoboam king of Judah, and they will kill me and go back to Rehoboam king of Judah
2Kin 10:24 So they went in to *offer sacrifices* and burnt offerings
Ezra 6:10 that they may *offer sacrifices* of sweet aroma to the God of heaven, and pray for the life of the king and his sons
Neh 4:2 Will they *offer sacrifices?* Will they complete it in a day
Ps 27:6 Therefore I will *offer sacrifices* of joy in His tabernacle
Hos 4:13 They *offer sacrifices* on the mountaintops, and burn incense on the hills, under oaks, poplars, and terebinths, because their shade is good
Hos 4:14 for the men themselves go apart with harlots, and *offer sacrifices* with a ritual harlot

OFFER UP SPIRITUAL SACRIFICES
1Pet 2:5 you also, as living stones, are being built up a spiritual house, a holy priesthood, to *offer up spiritual sacrifices* acceptable to God through Jesus Christ

OFFER YOUR BODIES (NIV)
(See *PRESENT YOUR BODIES*)

OFFERED SACRIFICES
Gen 46:1 So Israel took his journey with all that he had, and came to Beersheba, and *offered sacrifices* to the God of his father Isaac
2Sam 15:12 Then Absalom sent for Ahithophel the Gilonite, David's counselor, from his city, namely from Giloh, while he *offered sacrifices*
1Kin 8:62 Then the king and all Israel with him *offered sacrifices* before the Lord
1Kin 12:32 Jeroboam ordained a feast on the fifteenth day of the eighth month, like the feast that was in Judah, and *offered sacrifices* on the altar
1Kin 12:33 And he ordained a feast for the children of Israel, and *offered sacrifices* on the altar and burned incense
1Kin 22:43 Nevertheless the high places were not taken away, for the people *offered sacrifices* and burned incense on the high places
1Chr 6:49 But Aaron and his sons *offered sacrifices* on the altar of burnt offering and on the altar of incense, for all the work of the Most Holy Place, and to make atonement for Israel, according to all that Moses the servant of God had commanded
2Chr 7:4 Then the king and all the people *offered sacrifices* before the Lord
Ezra 6:3 Let the house be rebuilt, the place where they *offered sacrifices*
Ezra 6:17 And they *offered sacrifices* at the dedication of this house of God, one hundred bulls, two hundred rams, four hundred lambs, and as a sin offering for all Israel twelve male goats, according to the number of the tribes of Israel
Acts 7:41 And they made a calf in those days, *offered sacrifices* to the idol, and rejoiced in the works of their own hands

OFFERED UP ISAAC
Heb 11:17 By faith Abraham, when he was tested, *offered up Isaac*, and he who had received the promises offered up his only begotten son

OFFERING BY FIRE (NAS, RSV)
(See *OFFERING MADE BY FIRE*)

OFFERING FOR SIN
Is 53:10 When You make His soul an *offering for sin*, He shall see His seed, He shall prolong His days, and the pleasure of the Lord shall prosper in His hand
Heb 10:18 Now where there is remission of these, there is no longer an *offering for sin*

OFFERING MADE BY FIRE
Ex 29:18 it is a sweet aroma, an *offering made by fire* to the Lord
Ex 29:25 It is an *offering made by fire* to the Lord
Ex 29:41 and you shall offer with it the grain offering and the drink offering, as in the morning, for a sweet aroma, an *offering made by fire* to the Lord
Ex 30:20 When they go into the tabernacle of meeting, or when they come near the altar to minister, to burn an *offering made by fire* to the Lord, they shall wash with water, lest they die
Lev 1:9 And the priest shall burn all on the altar as a burnt sacrifice, an *offering made by fire*, a sweet aroma to the Lord
Lev 1:13 it is a burnt sacrifice, an *offering made by fire*, a sweet aroma to the Lord
Lev 1:17 It is a burnt sacrifice, an *offering made by fire*, a sweet aroma to the Lord
Lev 2:2 And the priest shall burn it as a memorial on the altar, an *offering made by fire*, a sweet aroma to the Lord
Lev 2:9 It is an *offering made by fire*, a sweet aroma to the Lord
Lev 2:16 part of its beaten grain and part of its oil, with all the frankincense, as an *offering made by fire* to the Lord
Lev 3:3 Then he shall offer from the sacrifice of the peace offering an *offering made by fire* to the Lord
Lev 3:5 and Aaron's sons shall burn it on the altar upon the burnt sacrifice, which is on the wood that is on the fire, as an *offering made by fire*, a sweet aroma to the Lord
Lev 3:9 Then he shall offer from the sacrifice of the peace offering, as an *offering made by fire* to the Lord, its fat and the whole fat tail which he shall remove close to the backbone
Lev 3:11 and the priest shall burn them on the altar as food, an *offering made by fire* to the Lord
Lev 3:14 Then he shall offer from it his offering, as an *offering made by fire* to the Lord
Lev 3:16 and the priest shall burn them on the altar as food, an *offering made by fire* for a sweet aroma
Lev 7:5 and the priest shall burn them on the altar as an *offering made by fire* to the Lord
Lev 7:25 For whoever eats the fat of the beast of which men offer an *offering made by fire* to the Lord, the person who eats it shall be cut off from his people
Lev 8:21 It was a burnt sacrifice for a sweet aroma, and an *offering made by fire* to the Lord, as the Lord had commanded Moses
Lev 8:28 That was an *offering made by fire* to the Lord
Lev 22:27 and from the eighth day and thereafter it shall be accepted as an *offering made by fire* to the Lord
Lev 23:8 But you shall offer an *offering made by fire* to the Lord for seven days
Lev 23:13 Its grain offering shall be two-tenths of

an ephah of fine flour mixed with oil, an *offering made by fire* to the Lord, for a sweet aroma

Lev 23:18 They shall be as a burnt offering to the Lord, with their grain offering and their drink offerings, an *offering made by fire* for a sweet aroma to the Lord

Lev 23:25 and you shall offer an *offering made by fire* to the Lord

Lev 23:27 you shall afflict your souls, and offer an *offering made by fire* to the Lord

Lev 23:36 For seven days you shall offer an *offering made by fire* to the Lord. On the eighth day you shall have a holy convocation, and you shall offer an *offering made by fire* to the Lord

Lev 23:37 These are the feasts of the Lord which you shall proclaim to be holy convocations, to offer an *offering made by fire* to the Lord, a burnt offering and a grain offering, a sacrifice and drink offerings, everything on its day

Lev 24:7 And you shall put pure frankincense on each row, that it may be on the bread for a memorial, an *offering made by fire* to the Lord

Num 15:10 and you shall bring as the drink offering half a hin of wine as an *offering made by fire*, a sweet aroma to the Lord

Num 15:13 All who are native-born shall do these things in this manner, in presenting an *offering made by fire*, a sweet aroma to the Lord

Num 15:14 And if a stranger sojourns with you, or whoever is among you throughout your generations, and would present an *offering made by fire*, a sweet aroma to the Lord, just as you do, so shall he do

Num 15:25 they shall bring their offering, an *offering made by fire* to the Lord, and their sin offering before the Lord, for their unintended sin

Num 18:17 You shall sprinkle their blood on the altar, and burn their fat as an *offering made by fire* for a sweet aroma to the Lord

Num 28:3 And you shall say to them, 'This is the *offering made by fire* which you shall offer to the Lord

Num 28:6 It is a regular burnt offering which was ordained at Mount Sinai for a sweet aroma, an *offering made by fire* to the Lord

Num 28:8 as the morning grain offering and its drink offering, you shall offer it as an *offering made by fire*, a sweet aroma to the Lord

Num 28:13 and one-tenth of an ephah of fine flour, mixed with oil, as a grain offering for each lamb, as a burnt offering of sweet aroma, an *offering made by fire* to the Lord

Num 28:19 And you shall present an *offering made by fire* as a burnt offering to the Lord

Num 28:24 In this manner you shall offer the food of the *offering made by fire* daily for seven days, as a sweet aroma to the Lord

Num 29:6 besides the burnt offering with its grain offering for the New Moon, the regular burnt offering with its grain offering, and their drink offerings, according to their ordinance, as a sweet aroma, an *offering made by fire* to the Lord

Num 29:13 You shall present a burnt offering, an *offering made by fire* as a sweet aroma to the Lord

Num 29:36 You shall present a burnt offering, an *offering made by fire* as a sweet aroma to the Lord

OFFERING OF THE GENTILES

Rom 15:16 that I might be a minister of Jesus Christ to the Gentiles, ministering the gospel of God, that the *offering of the Gentiles* might be acceptable, sanctified by the Holy Spirit

OFFERING SPIRITUAL SACRIFICES (NIV)
(See *OFFER UP SPIRITUAL SACRIFICES*)

OFFSPRING OF ABRAHAM (RSV)
(See *SEED OF ABRAHAM*)

OFFSPRING OF GOD

Acts 17:29 Therefore, since we are the *offspring of God*, we ought not to think that the Divine Nature is like gold or silver or stone, something shaped by art and man's devising

OIL OF GLADNESS (NAS, NIV, RSV)
(See *OIL OF JOY*)

OIL OF JOY

Is 61:3 to console those who mourn in Zion, to give them beauty for ashes, the *oil of joy* for mourning, the garment of praise for the spirit of heaviness

OLD AND FULL OF DAYS

Gen 35:29 So Isaac breathed his last and died, and was gathered to his people, being *old and full of days*

1Chr 23:1 So when David was *old and full of days*, he made his son Solomon king over Israel

Job 42:17 So Job died, *old and full of days*

OLD AND FULL OF YEARS (NIV)
(See *OLD AND FULL OF DAYS*)

OLD AND GRAYHEADED

1Sam 12:2 and I am *old and grayheaded*, and look, my sons are with you

OLD COVENANT (NAS, NIV, RSV)
(See *OLD TESTAMENT*)

OLD MAN

Gen 25:8 Then Abraham breathed his last and died in a good old age, an *old man* and full of years, and was gathered to his people

Gen 43:27 Then he asked them about their well-being, and said, "Is your father well, the *old man* of whom you spoke

Gen 44:20 And we said to my lord, 'We have a father, an *old man*, and a child of his old age, who is young

Lev 19:32 You shall rise before the gray headed and honor the presence of an *old man*, and fear your God

Judg 19:16 Just then an *old man* came in from his work in the field at evening, who also was from the mountains of Ephraim

Judg 19:17 and the *old man* said, "Where are you going, and where do you come from

Judg 19:20 And the *old man* said, "Peace be with you! However, let all your needs be my responsibility

Judg 19:22 They spoke to the master of the house, the *old man*, saying

1Sam 2:31 Behold, the days are coming that I will cut off your arm and the arm of your father's house, so that there will not be an *old man* in your house

1Sam 2:32 And there shall not be an *old man* in your house forever

1Sam 28:14 And she said, "An *old man* is coming up, and he is covered with a mantle

Is 65:20 No more shall an infant from there live but a few days, nor an *old man* who has not fulfilled his days

Luke 1:18 For I am an *old man*, and my wife is well advanced in years

Rom 6:6 knowing this, that our *old man* was crucified with Him, that the body of sin might be

done away with, that we should no longer be slaves of sin
Eph 4:22 that you put off, concerning your former conduct, the *old man* which grows corrupt according to the deceitful lusts
Col 3:9 Do not lie to one another, since you have put off the *old man* with his deeds

OLD ORDER OF THINGS (NIV)
(See *FORMER THINGS*)

OLD SERPENT (KJV)
(See *SERPENT OF OLD*)

OLD TESTAMENT
2Cor 3:14 For until this day the same veil remains unlifted in the reading of the *Old Testament*, because the veil is taken away in Christ

OLD WAY OF THE WRITTEN CODE (NIV)
(See *OLDNESS OF THE LETTER*)

OLD WINESKINS
Josh 9:4 And they took old sacks on their donkeys, *old wineskins* torn and mended
Matt 9:17 Nor do people put new wine into *old wineskins*, or else the wineskins break, the wine is spilled, and the wineskins are ruined
Mark 2:22 And no one puts new wine into *old wineskins;* or else the new wine bursts the wineskins, the wine is spilled, and the wineskins are ruined
Luke 5:37 And no one puts new wine into *old wineskins;* or else the new wine will burst the wineskins and be spilled, and the wineskins will be ruined

OLD WRITTEN CODE (RSV)
(See *OLDNESS OF THE LETTER*)

OLDNESS OF THE LETTER
Rom 7:6 But now we have been delivered from the law, having died to what we were held by, so that we should serve in the newness of the Spirit and not in the *oldness of the letter*

OMITTED THE WEIGHTIER MATTERS (KJV)
(See *NEGLECTED THE WEIGHTIER MATTERS*)

ON ACCOUNT OF HIS NAME (NIV)
(See *FOR HIS NAME'S SAKE*)

ON ACCOUNT OF ME (NIV)
(See *FOR MY SAKE*)

ON BREAD ALONE (NIV)
(See *BY BREAD ALONE*)

ON EARTH
Deut 3:24 O Lord God, You have begun to show Your servant Your greatness and Your mighty hand, for what god is there in heaven or *on earth* who can do anything like Your works and Your mighty deeds
Deut 4:36 *on earth* He showed you His great fire, and you heard His words out of the midst of the fire
Josh 2:11 neither did there remain any more courage in anyone because of you, for the Lord your God, He is God in heaven above and *on earth* beneath
1Kin 8:23 Lord God of Israel, there is no God in heaven above or *on earth* below like You, who keep Your covenant and mercy with Your servants who walk before You with all their heart
1Chr 29:15 our days *on earth* are as a shadow, and without hope
2Chr 6:14 Lord God of Israel, there is no God in heaven or *on earth* like You, who keep Your covenant and mercy with Your servants who walk before You with all their hearts
Job 7:1 Is there not a time of hard service for man *on earth*
Job 8:9 for we are but of yesterday, and know nothing, because our days *on earth* are a shadow
Job 20:4 Do you not know this of old, since man was placed *on earth*
Job 41:33 *On earth* there is nothing like him, which is made without fear
Ps 67:2 That Your way may be known *on earth*, Your salvation among all nations
Ps 67:4 For You shall judge the people righteously, and govern the nations *on earth*
Ps 112:2 His descendants will be mighty *on earth;* the generation of the upright will be blessed
Ps 119:87 They almost made an end of me *on earth*, but I did not forsake Your precepts
Eccl 5:2 For God is in heaven, and you *on earth;* therefore let your words be few
Eccl 7:20 For there is not a just man *on earth* who does good and does not sin
Eccl 8:14 There is a vanity which occurs *on earth*, that there are just men to whom it happens according to the work of the wicked
Eccl 8:16 When I applied my heart to know wisdom and to see the business that is done *on earth*, even though one sees no sleep day or night
Dan 2:10 The Chaldeans answered the king, and said, "There is not a man *on earth* who can tell the king's matter
Dan 6:27 He delivers and rescues, and He works signs and wonders in heaven and *on earth*, Who has delivered Daniel from the power of the lions
Dan 7:23 The fourth beast shall be a fourth kingdom *on earth*, which shall be different from all other kingdoms, and shall devour the whole earth, trample it and break it in pieces
Matt 6:10 Your will be done *on earth* as it is in heaven
Matt 6:19 Do not lay up for yourselves treasures *on earth*, where moth and rust destroy and where thieves break in and steal
Matt 9:6 But that you may know that the Son of Man has power *on earth* to forgive sins
Matt 10:34 Do not think that I came to bring peace *on earth*
Matt 16:19 And I will give you the keys of the kingdom of heaven, and whatever you bind *on earth* will be bound in heaven, and whatever you loose *on earth* will be loosed in heaven
Matt 18:18 Assuredly, I say to you, whatever you bind *on earth* will be bound in heaven, and whatever you loose *on earth* will be loosed in heaven
Matt 18:19 Again I say to you that if two of you agree *on earth* concerning anything that they ask, it will be done for them by My Father in heaven
Matt 23:9 Do not call anyone *on earth* your father; for One is your Father, He who is in heaven
Matt 28:18 Then Jesus came and spoke to them, saying, "All authority has been given to Me in heaven and *on earth*
Mark 2:10 But that you may know that the Son of Man has power *on earth* to forgive sins
Mark 4:31 It is like a mustard seed which, when it is sown on the ground, is smaller than all the seeds *on earth*
Mark 9:3 His clothes became shining, exceedingly white, like snow, such as no launderer *on earth* can whiten them
Luke 2:14 Glory to God in the highest, and *on earth* peace, good will toward men
Luke 5:24 But that you may know that the Son of Man has power *on earth* to forgive sins

Luke 11:2 Your will be done *On earth* as it is in heaven
Luke 12:51 Do you suppose that I came to give peace *on earth*
1Cor 8:5 For even if there are so-called gods, whether in heaven or *on earth* (as there are many gods and many lords
Eph 1:10 that in the dispensation of the fullness of the times He might gather together in one all things in Christ, both which are in heaven and which are *on earth* in Him
Phil 2:10 that at the name of Jesus every knee should bow, of those in heaven, and of those *on earth*, and of those under the earth
Col 1:16 For by Him all things were created that are in heaven and that are *on earth*, visible and invisible, whether thrones or dominions or principalities or powers
Col 1:20 and by Him to reconcile all things to Himself, by Him, whether things *on earth* or things in heaven, having made peace through the blood of His cross
Heb 8:4 For if He were *on earth*, He would not be a priest, since there are priests who offer the gifts according to the law
Heb 12:25 For if they did not escape who refused Him who spoke *on earth*, much more shall we not escape if we turn away from Him who speaks from heaven
1Jn 5:8 And there are three that bear witness *on earth:* the Spirit, the water, and the blood

ON EARTH PEACE
Luke 2:14 Glory to God in the highest, and *on earth peace*, good will toward men

ON OUR BEHALF
2Cor 1:11 you also helping together in prayer for us, that thanks may be given by many persons *on our behalf* for the gift granted to us through many
2Cor 5:12 For we do not commend ourselves again to you, but give you opportunity to glory *on our behalf*, that you may have something to answer those who glory in appearance and not in heart

ON THAT DAY
Gen 7:11 In the six hundredth year of Noah's life, in the second month, the seventeenth day of the month, *on that day* all the fountains of the great deep were broken up, and the windows of heaven were opened
Lev 16:30 For *on that day* the priest shall make atonement for you, to cleanse you, that you may be clean from all your sins before the Lord
Lev 23:12 And you shall offer *on that day*, when you wave the sheaf, a male lamb of the first year, without blemish, as a burnt offering to the Lord
Lev 27:23 then the priest shall reckon to him the worth of your valuation, up to the Year of Jubilee, and he shall give your valuation *on that day* as a holy offering to the Lord
Num 9:6 Now there were certain men who were defiled by the dead body of a man, so that they could not keep the Passover *on that day*
Num 32:10 So the Lord's anger was aroused *on that day*, and He swore an oath, saying
Josh 4:14 *On that day* the Lord magnified Joshua in the sight of all Israel
Josh 6:15 *On that day* only they marched around the city seven times
Josh 10:28 *On that day* Joshua took Makkedah, and struck it and its king with the edge of the sword
Josh 10:35 They took it *on that day* and struck it with the edge of the sword
Josh 14:9 So Moses swore *on that day*, saying, 'Surely the land where your foot has trodden shall be your inheritance and your children's forever, because you have wholly followed the Lord my God
Judg 4:23 So *on that day* God subdued Jabin king of Canaan in the presence of the children of Israel
Judg 5:1 Then Deborah and Barak the son of Abinoam sang *on that day*, saying
Judg 6:32 Therefore *on that day* he called him Jerubbaal, saying, "Let Baal plead against him, because he has torn down his altar
Judg 20:21 Then the children of Benjamin came out of Gibeah, and *on that day* cut down to the ground twenty-two thousand men of the Israelites
1Sam 22:18 So Doeg the Edomite turned and struck the priests, and killed *on that day* eighty-five men who wore a linen ephod
2Sam 5:8 Now David said *on that day*, "Whoever climbs up by way of the water shaft and defeats the Jebusites (the lame and the blind, who are hated by David's soul
1Kin 22:25 And Micaiah said, "Indeed, you shall see *on that day* when you go into an inner chamber to hide
1Chr 16:7 And *on that day* David first delivered this psalm into the hand of Asaph and his brethren, to thank the Lord
1Chr 29:22 So they ate and drank before the Lord with great gladness *on that day*
2Chr 18:24 And Micaiah said, "Indeed you shall see *on that day* when you go into an inner chamber to hide
Neh 13:1 *On that day* they read from the Book of Moses in the hearing of the people, and in it was found written that no Ammonite or Moabite should ever come into the congregation of God
Esth 8:1 *On that day* King Ahasuerus gave Queen Esther the house of Haman, the enemy of the Jews
Esth 8:13 A copy of the document was to be issued as a decree in every province and published to all people, so that the Jews would be ready *on that day* to avenge themselves on their enemies
Esth 9:11 *On that day* the number of those who were killed in Shushan the citadel was brought to the king
Jer 48:41 the mighty men's hearts in Moab *on that day* shall be like the heart of a woman in birth pangs
Ezek 20:6 *On that day* I lifted My hand in an oath to them, to bring them out of the land of Egypt into a land that I had searched out for them, flowing with milk and honey, the glory of all lands
Ezek 24:26 *on that day* one who escapes will come to you to let you hear it with your ears
Ezek 24:27 *on that day* your mouth will be opened to him who has escaped
Ezek 30:9 *On that day* messengers shall go forth from Me in ships to make the careless Ethiopians afraid, and great anguish shall come upon them, as on the day of Egypt
Ezek 38:10 *On that day* it shall come to pass that thoughts will arise in your mind, and you will make an evil plan
Ezek 38:14 *On that day* when My people Israel dwell safely, will you not know it
Ezek 45:22 And *on that day* the prince shall prepare for himself and for all the people of the land a bull for a sin offering
Amos 9:11 *On that day* I will raise up the tabernacle of David, which has fallen down, and repair its damages
Zeph 1:10 And there shall be *on that day*," says the Lord
Zech 11:11 So it was broken *on that day*. Thus the

poor of the flock, who were watching me, knew that it was the word of the Lord

2Tim 4:8 Finally, there is laid up for me the crown of righteousness, which the Lord, the righteous Judge, will give to me *on that Day*, and not to me only but also to all who have loved His appearing

ON THE FIRST DAY OF THE WEEK

Mark 16:2 Very early in the morning, *on the first day of the week*, they came to the tomb when the sun had risen

Mark 16:9 Now when He rose early *on the first day of the week*, He appeared first to Mary Magdalene, out of whom He had cast seven demons

Luke 24:1 Now *on the first day of the week*, very early in the morning, they, and certain other women with them, came to the tomb bringing the spices which they had prepared

John 20:1 *On the first day of the week* Mary Magdalene came to the tomb early, while it was still dark, and saw that the stone had been taken away from the tomb

Acts 20:7 Now *on the first day of the week*, when the disciples came together to break bread, Paul, ready to depart the next day, spoke to them and continued his message until midnight

1Cor 16:2 *On the first day of the week* let each one of you lay something aside, storing up as he may prosper, that there be no collections when I come

ON THE MOUNTAIN FROM THE MIDST OF THE FIRE

Deut 5:4 The Lord talked with you face to face *on the mountain from the midst of the fire*

Deut 9:10 Then the Lord delivered to me two tablets of stone written with the finger of God, and on them were all the words which the Lord had spoken to you *on the mountain from the midst of the fire* in the day of the assembly

ON THE RIGHT HAND OF GOD (KJV)
(See *AT THE RIGHT HAND OF GOD*)

ON THE RIGHT ROAD (NIV)
(See *WAY OF TRUTH*)

ON THE SABBATH

Ex 31:15 Whoever does any work *on the Sabbath* day, he shall surely be put to death

Ex 35:3 You shall kindle no fire throughout your dwellings *on the Sabbath* day

Num 15:32 Now while the children of Israel were in the wilderness, they found a man gathering sticks *on the Sabbath* day

Num 28:9 And *on the Sabbath* day two lambs in their first year, without blemish, and two-tenths of an ephah of fine flour as a grain offering, mixed with oil, with its drink offering

2Kin 11:5 One-third of you who come on duty *on the Sabbath* shall be keeping watch over the king's house

2Kin 11:7 The two contingents of you who go off duty *on the Sabbath* shall keep the watch of the house of the Lord for the king

2Kin 11:9 Each of them took his men who were to be on duty *on the Sabbath*, with those who were going off duty *on the Sabbath*, and came to Jehoiada the priest

2Chr 23:4 One-third of you entering *on the Sabbath*, of the priests and the Levites, shall be keeping watch over the doors

2Chr 23:8 And each man took his men who were to be on duty *on the Sabbath*, with those who were going off duty *on the Sabbath*

Neh 10:31 that if the peoples of the land bring wares or any grain to sell *on the Sabbath* day, we would not buy it from them *on the Sabbath*, or on a holy day

Neh 13:15 In those days I saw in Judah some people treading wine presses *on the Sabbath*, and bringing in sheaves, and loading donkeys with wine, grapes, figs, and all kinds of burdens, which they brought into Jerusalem *on the Sabbath* day

Neh 13:16 Men of Tyre dwelt there also, who brought in fish and all kinds of goods, and sold them *on the Sabbath* to the children of Judah, and in Jerusalem

Neh 13:19 Then I posted some of my servants at the gates, so that no burdens would be brought in *on the Sabbath* day

Neh 13:21 From that time on they came no more *on the Sabbath*

Jer 17:21 Take heed to yourselves, and bear no burden *on the Sabbath* day, nor bring it in by the gates of Jerusalem

Jer 17:22 nor carry a burden out of your houses *on the Sabbath* day, nor do any work, but hallow the Sabbath day, as I commanded your fathers

Jer 17:24 And it shall be, if you diligently heed Me," says the Lord, "to bring no burden through the gates of this city *on the Sabbath* day, but hallow the Sabbath day, to do no work in it

Jer 17:27 But if you will not heed Me to hallow the Sabbath day, such as not carrying a burden when entering the gates of Jerusalem *on the Sabbath* day, then I will kindle a fire in its gates, and it shall devour the palaces of Jerusalem, and it shall not be quenched

Ezek 46:1 but *on the Sabbath* it shall be opened, and on the day of the New Moon it shall be opened

Ezek 46:4 The burnt offering that the prince offers to the Lord *on the Sabbath* day shall be six lambs without blemish, and a ram without blemish

Ezek 46:12 and he shall prepare his burnt offering and his peace offerings as he did *on the Sabbath* day

Matt 12:1 At that time Jesus went through the grainfields *on the Sabbath*

Matt 12:2 But when the Pharisees saw it, they said to Him, "Look, Your disciples are doing what is not lawful to do *on the Sabbath*

Matt 12:5 Or have you not read in the law that *on the Sabbath* the priests in the temple profane the Sabbath, and are blameless

Matt 12:10 And they asked Him, saying, "Is it lawful to heal *on the Sabbath*

Matt 12:11 Then He said to them, "What man is there among you who has one sheep, and if it falls into a pit *on the Sabbath*, will not lay hold of it and lift it out

Matt 12:12 Therefore it is lawful to do good *on the Sabbath*

Matt 24:20 And pray that your flight may not be in winter or *on the Sabbath*

Mark 1:21 Then they went into Capernaum, and immediately *on the Sabbath* He entered the synagogue and taught

Mark 2:23 Now it happened that He went through the grainfields *on the Sabbath*

Mark 2:24 And the Pharisees said to Him, "Look, why do they do what is not lawful *on the Sabbath*

Mark 3:2 And they watched Him closely, whether He would heal him *on the Sabbath*, so that they might accuse Him

Mark 3:4 And He said to them, "Is it lawful *on the Sabbath* to do good or to do evil, to save life or to kill

Luke 4:16 And as His custom was, He went into the synagogue *on the Sabbath* day, and stood up to read

Luke 6:2 And some of the Pharisees said to them,

"Why are you doing what is not lawful to do *on the Sabbath*

Luke 6:7 And the scribes and Pharisees watched Him closely, whether He would heal *on the Sabbath*, that they might find an accusation against Him

Luke 6:9 Is it lawful *on the Sabbath* to do good or to do evil, to save life or to destroy it

Luke 13:10 Now He was teaching in one of the synagogues *on the Sabbath*

Luke 13:14 But the ruler of the synagogue answered with indignation, because Jesus had healed *on the Sabbath;* and he said to the crowd, "There are six days on which men ought to work; therefore come and be healed on them, and not *on the Sabbath* day

Luke 13:15 Does not each one of you *on the Sabbath* loose his ox or his donkey from the stall, and lead it away to water it

Luke 13:16 So ought not this woman, being a daughter of Abraham, whom Satan has bound think of it for eighteen years, be loosed from this bond *on the Sabbath*

Luke 14:1 Now it happened, as He went into the house of one of the rulers of the Pharisees to eat bread *on the Sabbath*, that they watched Him closely

Luke 14:3 And Jesus, answering, spoke to the lawyers and Pharisees, saying, "Is it lawful to heal *on the Sabbath*

Luke 14:5 Then He answered them, saying, "Which of you, having a donkey or an ox that has fallen into a pit, will not immediately pull him out *on the Sabbath* day

Luke 23:56 And they rested *on the Sabbath* according to the commandment

John 5:16 For this reason the Jews persecuted Jesus, and sought to kill Him, because He had done these things *on the Sabbath*

John 7:22 Moses therefore gave you circumcision (not that it is from Moses, but from the fathers), and you circumcise a man *on the Sabbath*

John 7:23 If a man receives circumcision *on the Sabbath*, so that the law of Moses should not be broken, are you angry with Me because I made a man completely well *on the Sabbath*

John 19:31 Therefore, because it was the Preparation Day, that the bodies should not remain on the cross *on the Sabbath* (for that Sabbath was a high day

Acts 13:14 But when they departed from Perga, they came to Antioch in Pisidia, and went into the synagogue *on the Sabbath* day and sat down

Acts 16:13 And *on the Sabbath* day we went out of the city to the riverside, where prayer was customarily made

ON THE SABBATH DAY TO SELL (KJV, NAS, RSV)
(See *SELL ON THE SABBATH DAY*)

ON THE SEVENTH DAY HE RESTED (NIV)
(See *RESTED ON THE SEVENTH DAY*)

ON THE THIRD DAY

Gen 22:4 Then *on the third day* Abraham lifted his eyes and saw the place afar off

Gen 31:22 And Laban was told *on the third day* that Jacob had fled

Gen 34:25 Now it came to pass *on the third day*, when they were in pain, that two of the sons of Jacob, Simeon and Levi, Dinah's brothers, each took his sword and came boldly upon the city and killed all the males

Gen 40:20 Now it came to pass *on the third day*, which was Pharaoh's birthday, that he made a feast for all his servants

Ex 19:11 For *on the third day* the Lord will come down upon Mount Sinai in the sight of all the people

Ex 19:16 Then it came to pass *on the third day*, in the morning, that there were thunderings and lightnings, and a thick cloud on the mountain

Lev 7:17 the remainder of the flesh of the sacrifice *on the third day* must be burned with fire

Lev 7:18 And if any of the flesh of the sacrifice of his peace offering is eaten at all *on the third day*, it shall not be accepted, nor shall it be imputed to him

Lev 19:7 And if it is eaten at all *on the third day*, it is an abomination

Num 7:24 *On the third day* Eliab the son of Helon, leader of the children of Zebulun, presented an offering

Num 19:12 He shall purify himself with the water *on the third day* and on the seventh day; then he will be clean. But if he does not purify himself *on the third day* and on the seventh day, he will not be clean

Num 19:19 The clean person shall sprinkle the unclean *on the third day* and on the seventh day

Num 29:20 *On the third day* present eleven bulls, two rams, fourteen lambs in their first year without blemish

Num 31:19 whoever has killed any person, and whoever has touched any slain, purify yourselves and your captives *on the third day* and on the seventh day

Josh 9:17 Then the children of Israel journeyed and came to their cities *on the third day*

Judg 20:30 And the children of Israel went up against the children of Benjamin *on the third day*, and put themselves in battle array against Gibeah as at the other times

1Sam 30:1 Now it happened, when David and his men came to Ziklag, *on the third day*, that the Amalekites had invaded the South and Ziklag, attacked Ziklag and burned it with fire

2Sam 1:2 *on the third day*, behold, it happened that a man came from Saul's camp with his clothes torn and dust on his head

2Kin 20:5 *On the third day* you shall go up to the house of the Lord

2Chr 10:12 So Jeroboam and all the people came to Rehoboam *on the third day*, as the king had appointed, saying

Ezra 6:15 Now the temple was finished *on the third day* of the month of Adar, which was in the sixth year of the reign of King Darius

Esth 5:1 Now it happened *on the third day* that Esther put on her royal robes and stood in the inner court of the king's palace, across from the king's house, while the king sat on his royal throne in the royal house, facing the entrance of the house

Hos 6:2 *on the third day* He will raise us up, that we may live in His sight

John 2:1 *On the third day* there was a wedding in Cana of Galilee, and the mother of Jesus was there

Acts 10:40 Him God raised up *on the third day*, and showed Him openly

Acts 27:19 *On the third day* we threw the ship's tackle overboard with our own hands

ON THIS ROCK

Judg 6:20 The Angel of God said to him, "Take the meat and the unleavened bread and lay them *on this rock*, and pour out the broth

Matt 16:18 And I also say to you that you are Peter, and *on this rock* I will build My church, and the gates of Hades shall not prevail against it

ONCE FOR ALL

Rom 6:10 For the death that He died, He died to sin *once for all*

Heb 7:27 who does not need daily, as those high priests, to offer up sacrifices, first for His own sins and then for the people's, for this He did *once for all* when He offered up Himself
Heb 9:12 Not with the blood of goats and calves, but with His own blood He entered the Most Holy Place *once for all*, having obtained eternal redemption
Heb 10:10 By that will we have been sanctified through the offering of the body of Jesus Christ *once for all*
Jude 3 Beloved, while I was very diligent to write to you concerning our common salvation, I found it necessary to write to you exhorting you to contend earnestly for the faith which was *once for all* delivered to the saints

ONE FATHER
Mal 2:10 Have we not all *one Father?* Has not one God created us
John 8:41 Then they said to Him, "We were not born of fornication; we have *one Father* God

ONE FLESH
Gen 2:24 Therefore a man shall leave his father and mother and be joined to his wife, and they shall become *one flesh*
Matt 19:5 and said, 'For this reason a man shall leave his father and mother and be joined to his wife, and the two shall become *one flesh*
Matt 19:6 So then, they are no longer two but *one flesh*
Mark 10:8 and the two shall become *one flesh*'; so then they are no longer two, but *one flesh*
1Cor 6:16 Or do you not know that he who is joined to a harlot is one body with her? For "The two," He says, "shall become *one flesh*
Eph 5:31 For this reason a man shall leave his father and mother and be joined to his wife, and the two shall become *one flesh*

ONE FLOCK AND ONE SHEPHERD
John 10:16 them also I must bring, and they will hear My voice; and there will be *one flock and one shepherd*

ONE FOLD, AND ONE SHEPHERD (KJV)
(See *ONE FLOCK AND ONE SHEPHERD*)

ONE OF THE LEAST OF THESE
Matt 5:19 Whoever therefore breaks *one of the least of these* commandments, and teaches men so, shall be called least in the kingdom of heaven
Matt 25:40 And the King will answer and say to them, 'Assuredly, I say to you, inasmuch as you did it to *one of the least of these* My brethren, you did it to Me
Matt 25:45 Then He will answer them, saying, 'Assuredly, I say to you, inasmuch as you did not do it to *one of the least of these*, you did not do it to Me

ONE OF THESE LITTLE ONES
Matt 10:42 And whoever gives *one of these little ones* only a cup of cold water in the name of a disciple, assuredly, I say to you, he shall by no means lose his reward
Matt 18:6 But whoever causes *one of these little ones* who believe in Me to sin, it would be better for him if a millstone were hung around his neck, and he were drowned in the depth of the sea
Matt 18:10 Take heed that you do not despise *one of these little ones*, for I say to you that in heaven their angels always see the face of My Father who is in heaven
Matt 18:14 Even so it is not the will of your Father who is in heaven that *one of these little ones* should perish
Mark 9:42 And whoever causes *one of these little ones* who believe in Me to stumble, it would be better for him if a millstone were hung around his neck, and he were thrown into the sea
Luke 17:2 It would be better for him if a millstone were hung around his neck, and he were thrown into the sea, than that he should offend *one of these little ones*

ONE OF YOU WILL BETRAY ME
Matt 26:21 Now as they were eating, He said, "Assuredly, I say to you, *one of you will betray Me*
John 13:21 When Jesus had said these things, He was troubled in spirit, and testified and said, "Most assuredly, I say to you, *one of you will betray Me*

ONE SINNER WHO REPENTS
Luke 15:7 I say to you that likewise there will be more joy in heaven over *one sinner who repents* than over ninety-nine just persons who need no repentance
Luke 15:10 Likewise, I say to you, there is joy in the presence of the angels of God over *one sinner who repents*

ONE SPIRIT TO DRINK (NIV)
(See *DRINK INTO ONE SPIRIT*)

ONE STONE UPON ANOTHER
Luke 19:44 and they will not leave in you *one stone upon another*, because you did not know the time of your visitation

ONE THING IS NEEDED
Luke 10:42 But *one thing is needed*, and Mary has chosen that good part, which will not be taken away from her

ONE THING YOU LACK
Mark 10:21 Then Jesus, looking at him, loved him, and said to him, "*One thing you lack*

ONE WHO BRINGS GOOD TIDINGS
Is 41:27 and I will give to Jerusalem *one who brings good tidings*

ONE WHO FEARED GOD
Job 1:1 and that man was blameless and upright, and *one who feared God* and shunned evil
Acts 10:2 a devout man and *one who feared God* with all his household, who gave alms generously to the people, and prayed to God always

ONE WHO HAS A DEMON
John 10:21 Others said, "These are not the words of *one who has a demon*

ONE WHO IS BORN IN HIS HOUSE
Lev 22:11 and *one who is born in his house* may eat his food

ONE WHO LOVES WHAT IS GOOD (NIV)
(See *LOVER OF WHAT IS GOOD*)

ONE WHO SENT ME (NIV)
(See *HE WHO SENT ME*)

ONLY BEGOTTEN OF THE FATHER
John 1:14 And the Word became flesh and dwelt among us, and we beheld His glory, the glory as of the *only begotten of the Father*, full of grace and truth

ONLY BEGOTTEN SON
John 1:18 The *only begotten Son*, who is in the bosom of the Father, He has declared Him

ONLY SON

John 3:16 For God so loved the world that He gave His *only begotten Son*, that whoever believes in Him should not perish but have everlasting life
John 3:18 but he who does not believe is condemned already, because he has not believed in the name of the *only begotten Son* of God
Heb 11:17 By faith Abraham, when he was tested, offered up Isaac, and he who had received the promises offered up his *only begotten son*
1Jn 4:9 In this the love of God was manifested toward us, that God has sent His *only begotten Son* into the world, that we might live through Him

ONLY SON (NIV, RSV)
(See *ONLY BEGOTTEN SON*)

ONLY SON FROM THE FATHER (RSV)
(See *ONLY BEGOTTEN OF THE FATHER*)

ONLY SUFFERS WANT (RSV)
(See *LEADS TO POVERTY*)

OPEN COUNTRY
Ezek 36:5 Surely I have spoken in My burning jealousy against the rest of the nations and against all Edom, who gave My land to themselves as a possession, with whole-hearted joy and spiteful minds, in order to plunder its *open country*
Hos 4:16 now the Lord will let them forage like a lamb in *open country*

OPEN DOOR
Rev 3:8 See, I have set before you an *open door*, and no one can shut it

OPEN, LORD, THINE EYES (KJV)
(See *OPEN YOUR EYES*)

OPEN REBUKE IS BETTER
Prov 27:5 *Open rebuke is better* than love carefully concealed

OPEN YOUR EYES
2Kin 19:16 *open Your eyes*, O Lord, and see; and hear the words of Sennacherib, which he has sent to reproach the living God
Job 14:3 And do You *open Your eyes* on such a one, and bring me to judgment with Yourself
Prov 20:13 *open your eyes*, and you will be satisfied with bread
Is 37:17 *open Your eyes*, O Lord, and see; and hear all the words of Sennacherib, who has sent to reproach the living God
Dan 9:18 *open Your eyes* and see our desolations, and the city which is called by Your name
John 9:26 Then they said to him again, "What did He do to you? How did He *open your eyes*

OPEN YOUR HAND
Deut 15:8 but you shall *open your hand* wide to him and willingly lend him sufficient for his need, whatever he needs
Deut 15:11 therefore I command you, saying, 'You shall *open your hand* wide to your brother, to your poor and your needy, in your land
Ps 104:28 What You give them they gather in; You *open Your hand*, they are filled with good
Ps 145:16 You *open Your hand* and satisfy the desire of every living thing

OPENED THE SCRIPTURES
Luke 24:32 And they said to one another, "Did not our heart burn within us while He talked with us on the road, and while He *opened the Scriptures* to us

OPPORTUNE TIME
Luke 4:13 Now when the devil had ended every temptation, he departed from Him until an *opportune time*

OPPORTUNITY FOR THE FLESH
Gal 5:13 only do not use liberty as an *opportunity for the flesh*, but through love serve one another

OPPRESS NOT THE STRANGER (KJV)
(See *OPPRESS THE STRANGER*)

OPPRESS NOT THE WIDOW (KJV)
(See *OPPRESS THE WIDOW*)

OPPRESS THE ALIEN (NAS, NIV, RSV)
(See *OPPRESS THE STRANGER*)

OPPRESS THE POOR
Amos 4:1 Hear this word, you cows of Bashan, who are on the mountain of Samaria, who *oppress the poor*, who crush the needy, who say to your husbands

OPPRESS THE STRANGER
Jer 7:6 if you do not *oppress the stranger*, the fatherless, and the widow, and do not shed innocent blood in this place, or walk after other gods to your hurt
Ezek 22:29 The people of the land have used oppressions, committed robbery, and mistreated the poor and needy; and they wrongfully *oppress the stranger*

OPPRESS THE WIDOW
Zech 7:10 Do not *oppress the widow* or the fatherless, the alien or the poor

OPPRESSED BY THE DEVIL
Acts 10:38 how God anointed Jesus of Nazareth with the Holy Spirit and with power, who went about doing good and healing all who were *oppressed by the devil*, for God was with Him

OPPRESSES THE POOR
Prov 14:31 He who *oppresses the poor* reproaches his Maker, but he who honors Him has mercy on the needy
Prov 22:16 He who *oppresses the poor* to increase his riches, and he who gives to the rich, will surely come to poverty
Prov 28:3 A poor man who *oppresses the poor* is like a driving rain which leaves no food

OPPRESSING ISRAEL (NIV)
(See *OPPRESSION OF ISRAEL*)

OPPRESSION DESTROYS
Eccl 7:7 Surely *oppression destroys* a wise man's reason, and a bribe debases the heart

OPPRESSION OF ISRAEL
2Kin 13:4 for He saw the *oppression of Israel*, because the king of Syria oppressed them

OPPRESSION OF MY PEOPLE
Ex 3:7 I have surely seen the *oppression of My people* who are in Egypt, and have heard their cry because of their taskmasters, for I know their sorrows
Acts 7:34 I have certainly seen the *oppression of my people* who are in Egypt

OPPRESSION OF THE POOR
Ps 12:5 For the *oppression of the poor*, for the sighing of the needy, now I will arise
Eccl 5:8 If you see the *oppression of the poor*, and

the violent perversion of justice and righteousness in a province, do not marvel at the matter

OPPRESSION OF THE WEAK (NIV)
(See *OPPRESSION OF THE POOR*)

ORACLE CONCERNING (NAS, NIV, RSV)
(See *BURDEN AGAINST*)

ORACLE OF THE LORD
Jer 23:33 So when these people or the prophet or the priest ask you, saying, 'What is the *oracle of the Lord*
Jer 23:34 And as for the prophet and the priest and the people who say, 'The *oracle of the Lord*
Jer 23:36 And the *oracle of the Lord* you shall mention no more
Jer 23:38 But since you say, 'The *oracle of the Lord!*' therefore thus says the Lord: 'Because you say this word, "The *oracle of the Lord!*" and I have sent to you, saying, "Do not say, 'The *oracle of the Lord*

ORACLES OF GOD
Rom 3:2 Chiefly because to them were committed the *oracles of God*
Heb 5:12 For though by this time you ought to be teachers, you need someone to teach you again the first principles of the *oracles of God*
1Pet 4:11 If anyone speaks, let him speak as the *oracles of God*

ORDAIN THEM (NAS, NIV, RSV)
(See *SANCTIFY THEM*)

ORDAINED YOURSELVES (RSV)
(See *CONSECRATE YOURSELVES*)

ORDER OF MELCHIZEDEK
Ps 110:4 The Lord has sworn and will not relent, "You are a priest forever according to the *order of Melchizedek*
Heb 5:6 You are a priest forever according to the *order of Melchizedek*
Heb 5:10 called by God as High Priest "according to the *order of Melchizedek*
Heb 6:20 where the forerunner has entered for us, even Jesus, having become High Priest forever according to the *order of Melchizedek*
Heb 7:11 what further need was there that another priest should rise according to the *order of Melchizedek*, and not be called according to the order of Aaron
Heb 7:17 You are a priest forever according to the *order of Melchizedek*
Heb 7:21 The Lord has sworn and will not relent, 'You are a priest forever according to the *order of Melchizedek*

ORDINANCE FOREVER
Num 10:8 and these shall be to you as an *ordinance forever* throughout your generations
Num 15:15 One ordinance shall be for you of the congregation and for the stranger who sojourns with you, an *ordinance forever* throughout your generations
Num 18:8 I have given them as a portion to you and your sons, as an *ordinance forever*
Num 18:11 I have given them to you, and your sons and daughters with you, as an *ordinance forever*
Num 18:19 All the heave offerings of the holy things, which the children of Israel offer to the Lord, I have given to you and your sons and daughters with you as an *ordinance forever*
2Chr 2:4 Behold, I am building a temple for the name of the Lord my God, to dedicate it to Him, to burn before Him sweet incense, for the continual showbread, for the burnt offerings morning and evening, on the Sabbaths, on the New Moons, and on the set feasts of the Lord our God. This is an *ordinance forever* to Israel

ORDINANCE OF GOD
Rom 13:2 Therefore whoever resists the authority resists the *ordinance of God*, and those who resist will bring judgment on themselves

ORDINANCES OF THE LORD (NIV, RSV)
(See *JUDGMENTS OF THE LORD*)

ORDINANCES OF THE NATIONS (NAS, RSV)
(See *JUDGMENTS OF THE NATIONS*)

OTHER GODS
Ex 20:3 You shall have no *other gods* before Me
Ex 23:13 And in all that I have said to you, be circumspect and make no mention of the name of *other gods*, nor let it be heard from your mouth
Deut 5:7 You shall have no *other gods* before Me
Deut 6:14 You shall not go after *other gods*, the gods of the peoples who are all around you
Deut 7:4 For they will turn your sons away from following Me, to serve *other gods*
Deut 8:19 Then it shall be, if you by any means forget the Lord your God, and follow *other gods*, and serve them and worship them, I testify against you this day that you shall surely perish
Deut 11:16 Take heed to yourselves, lest your heart be deceived, and you turn aside and serve *other gods* and worship them
Deut 11:28 and the curse, if you do not obey the commandments of the Lord your God, but turn aside from the way which I command you today, to go after *other gods* which you have not known
Deut 13:2 and the sign or the wonder of which he spoke to you comes to pass, saying, 'Let us go after *other gods* which you have not known, and let us serve them
Deut 13:6 If your brother, the son of your mother, your son or your daughter, the wife of your bosom, or your friend who is as your own soul, secretly entices you, saying, 'Let us go and serve *other gods*
Deut 13:13 Certain corrupt men have gone out from among you and enticed the inhabitants of their city, saying, "Let us go and serve *other gods*
Deut 17:3 who has gone and served *other gods* and worshiped them, either the sun or moon or any of the host of heaven, which I have not commanded
Deut 18:20 But the prophet who presumes to speak a word in My name, which I have not commanded him to speak, or who speaks in the name of *other gods*, that prophet shall die
Deut 28:14 So you shall not turn aside from any of the words which I command you this day, to the right hand or to the left, to go after *other gods* to serve them
Deut 28:36 The Lord will bring you and the king whom you set over you to a nation which neither you nor your fathers have known, and there you shall serve *other gods* wood and stone
Deut 28:64 Then the Lord will scatter you among all peoples, from one end of the earth to the other, and there you shall serve *other gods*, which neither you nor your fathers have known wood and stone
Deut 29:26 for they went and served *other gods* and worshiped them, gods that they did not know and that He had not given to them
Deut 30:17 But if your heart turns away so that you do not hear, and are drawn away, and worship *other gods* and serve them
Deut 31:18 And I will surely hide My face in that

day because of all the evil which they have done, in that they have turned to *other gods*

Deut 31:20 When I have brought them to the land flowing with milk and honey, of which I swore to their fathers, and they have eaten and filled themselves and grown fat, then they will turn to *other gods* and serve them

Josh 23:16 When you have transgressed the covenant of the Lord your God, which He commanded you, and have gone and served *other gods*, and bowed down to them, then the anger of the Lord will burn against you, and you shall perish quickly from the good land which He has given you

Josh 24:2 Your fathers, including Terah, the father of Abraham and the father of Nahor, dwelt on the other side of the River in old times; and they served *other gods*

Josh 24:16 Far be it from us that we should forsake the Lord to serve *other gods*

Judg 2:12 and they followed *other gods* from among the gods of the people who were all around them, and they bowed down to them

Judg 2:17 Yet they would not listen to their judges, but they played the harlot with *other gods*, and bowed down to them

Judg 2:19 And it came to pass, when the judge was dead, that they reverted and behaved more corruptly than their fathers, by following *other gods*, to serve them and bow down to them

Judg 10:13 Yet you have forsaken Me and served *other gods*. Therefore I will deliver you no more

1Sam 8:8 According to all the works which they have done since the day that I brought them up out of Egypt, even to this day with which they have forsaken Me and served *other gods* so they are doing to you also

1Sam 26:19 But if it is the children of men, may they be cursed before the Lord, for they have driven me out this day from abiding in the inheritance of the Lord, saying, 'Go, serve *other gods*

1Kin 9:6 But if you or your sons at all turn from following Me, and do not keep My commandments and My statutes which I have set before you, but go and serve *other gods* and worship them

1Kin 9:9 Then they will answer, 'Because they forsook the Lord their God, who brought their fathers out of the land of Egypt, and have embraced *other gods*, and worshiped them and served them

1Kin 11:4 For it was so, when Solomon was old, that his wives turned his heart after *other gods*

1Kin 11:10 and had commanded him concerning this thing, that he should not go after *other gods*

1Kin 14:9 but you have done more evil than all who were before you, for you have gone and made for yourself *other gods* and molded images to provoke Me to anger, and have cast Me behind your back

2Kin 5:17 for your servant will no longer offer either burnt offering or sacrifice to *other gods*, but to the Lord

2Kin 17:7 For so it was that the children of Israel had sinned against the Lord their God, who had brought them up out of the land of Egypt, from under the hand of Pharaoh king of Egypt; and they had feared *other gods*

2Kin 17:35 You shall not fear *other gods*, nor bow down to them nor serve them nor sacrifice to them

2Kin 17:37 And the statutes, the ordinances, the law, and the commandment which He wrote for you, you shall be careful to observe forever; you shall not fear *other gods*

2Kin 17:38 And the covenant that I have made with you, you shall not forget, nor shall you fear *other gods*

2Kin 22:17 because they have forsaken Me and burned incense to *other gods*, that they might provoke Me to anger with all the works of their hands

2Chr 7:19 But if you turn away and forsake My statutes and My commandments which I have set before you, and go and serve *other gods*, and worship them

2Chr 7:22 Then they will answer, 'Because they forsook the Lord God of their fathers, who brought them out of the land of Egypt, and embraced *other gods*, and worshiped them and served them

2Chr 28:25 And in every single city of Judah he made high places to burn incense to *other gods*, and provoked to anger the Lord God of his fathers

2Chr 34:25 because they have forsaken Me and burned incense to *other gods*, that they might provoke Me to anger with all the works of their hands

Jer 1:16 I will utter My judgments against them concerning all their wickedness, because they have forsaken Me, burned incense to *other gods*, and worshiped the works of their own hands

Jer 7:6 if you do not oppress the stranger, the fatherless, and the widow, and do not shed innocent blood in this place, or walk after *other gods* to your hurt

Jer 7:9 Will you steal, murder, commit adultery, swear falsely, burn incense to Baal, and walk after *other gods* whom you do not know

Jer 7:18 and they pour out drink offerings to *other gods*, that they may provoke Me to anger

Jer 11:10 They have turned back to the iniquities of their forefathers who refused to hear My words, and they have gone after *other gods* to serve them

Jer 13:10 This evil people, who refuse to hear My words, who walk in the imagination of their heart, and walk after *other gods* to serve them and worship them, shall be just like this sash which is profitable for nothing

Jer 16:11 they have walked after *other gods* and have served them and worshiped them, and have forsaken Me and not kept My law

Jer 16:13 and there you shall serve *other gods* day and night, where I will not show you favor

Jer 19:4 Because they have forsaken Me and made this an alien place, because they have burned incense in it to *other gods* whom neither they, their fathers, nor the kings of Judah have known, and have filled this place with the blood of the innocents

Jer 19:13 And the houses of Jerusalem and the houses of the kings of Judah shall be defiled like the place of Tophet, because of all the houses on whose roofs they have burned incense to all the host of heaven, and poured out drink offerings to *other gods*

Jer 22:9 Then they will answer, 'Because they have forsaken the covenant of the Lord their God, and worshiped *other gods* and served them

Jer 25:6 Do not go after *other gods* to serve them and worship them, and do not provoke Me to anger with the works of your hands

Jer 32:29 And the Chaldeans who fight against this city shall come and set fire to this city and burn it, with the houses on whose roofs they have offered incense to Baal and poured out drink offerings to *other gods*, to provoke Me to anger

Jer 35:15 I have also sent to you all My servants the prophets, rising up early and sending them, saying, 'Turn now everyone from his evil way, amend your doings, and do not go after *other gods* to serve them

Jer 44:3 because of their wickedness which they have committed to provoke Me to anger, in that they went to burn incense and to serve *other gods* whom they did not know, they nor you nor your fathers

Jer 44:5 But they did not listen or incline their ear to turn from their wickedness, to burn no incense to *other gods*

Jer 44:8 in that you provoke Me to wrath with the works of your hands, burning incense to *other gods* in the land of Egypt where you have gone to dwell, that you may cut yourselves off and be a curse and a reproach among all the nations of the earth

Jer 44:15 Then all the men who knew that their wives had burned incense to *other gods*, with all the women who stood by, a great multitude, and all the people who dwelt in the land of Egypt, in Pathros, answered Jeremiah, saying

Hos 3:1 Then the Lord said to me, "Go again, love a woman who is loved by a lover and is committing adultery, just like the love of the Lord for the children of Israel, who look to *other gods* and love the raisin cakes of the pagans

OTHER SHEEP I HAVE

John 10:16 And *other sheep I have* which are not of this fold

OTHER SIDE OF THE JORDAN

Num 32:19 For we will not inherit with them on the *other side of the Jordan* and beyond, because our inheritance has fallen to us on this eastern side of the Jordan

Deut 11:30 Are they not on the *other side of the Jordan*, toward the setting sun, in the land of the Canaanites who dwell in the plain opposite Gilgal, beside the terebinth trees of Moreh

Josh 2:10 For we have heard how the Lord dried up the water of the Red Sea for you when you came out of Egypt, and what you did to the two kings of the Amorites who were on the *other side of the Jordan*, Sihon and Og, whom you utterly destroyed

Josh 7:7 Oh, that we had been content, and dwelt on the *other side of the Jordan*

Josh 12:1 These are the kings of the land whom the children of Israel defeated, and whose land they possessed on the *other side of the Jordan* toward the rising of the sun, from the River Arnon to Mount Hermon, and all the eastern Jordan plain

Josh 13:27 and in the valley Beth Haram, Beth Nimrah, Succoth, and Zaphon, the rest of the kingdom of Sihon king of Heshbon, with the Jordan as its border, as far as the edge of the Sea of Chinnereth, on the *other side of the Jordan* eastward

Josh 13:32 These are the areas which Moses had distributed as an inheritance in the plains of Moab on the *other side of the Jordan*, by Jericho eastward

Josh 14:3 For Moses had given the inheritance of the two tribes and the half-tribe on the *other side of the Jordan*

Josh 17:5 Ten portions fell to Manasseh, besides the land of Gilead and Bashan, which were on the *other side of the Jordan*

Josh 20:8 And on the *other side of the Jordan*, by Jericho eastward, they assigned Bezer in the wilderness on the plain, from the tribe of Reuben, Ramoth in Gilead, from the tribe of Gad, and Golan in Bashan, from the tribe of Manasseh

Josh 22:4 now therefore, return and go to your tents and to the land of your possession, which Moses the servant of the Lord gave you on the *other side of the Jordan*

Josh 24:8 And I brought you into the land of the Amorites, who dwelt on the *other side of the Jordan*, and they fought with you

Judg 7:25 They pursued Midian and brought the heads of Oreb and Zeeb to Gideon on the *other side of the Jordan*

Judg 10:8 From that year they harassed and oppressed the children of Israel for eighteen years all the children of Israel who were on the *other side of the Jordan* in the land of the Amorites, in Gilead

1Sam 31:7 And when the men of Israel who were on the other side of the valley, and those who were on the *other side of the Jordan*, saw that the men of Israel had fled and that Saul and his sons were dead, they forsook the cities and fled

1Chr 6:78 And on the *other side of the Jordan*, across from Jericho, on the east side of the Jordan, they were given from the tribe of Reuben

1Chr 12:37 of the Reubenites and the Gadites and the half-tribe of Manasseh, from the *other side of the Jordan*, one hundred and twenty thousand armed for battle with every kind of weapon of war

Mark 10:1 Then He arose from there and came to the region of Judea by the *other side of the Jordan*

OUR DEAR FRIEND LUKE, THE DOCTOR (NIV)

(See *LUKE THE BELOVED PHYSICIAN*)

OUR FATHER IN HEAVEN

Matt 6:9 In this manner, therefore, pray: *Our Father in heaven*, hallowed be Your name

Luke 11:2 *Our Father in heaven*, hallowed be Your name. Your kingdom come

OUR HELP

Ps 33:20 Our soul waits for the Lord; He is *our help* and our shield

Ps 44:26 Arise for *our help*, and redeem us for Your mercies' sake

Ps 124:8 *Our help* is in the name of the Lord, Who made heaven and earth

Lam 4:17 Still our eyes failed us, watching vainly for *our help*

OUR LORD AND SAVIOR

2Pet 1:11 for so an entrance will be supplied to you abundantly into the everlasting kingdom of *our Lord and Savior* Jesus Christ

2Pet 3:18 but grow in the grace and knowledge of *our Lord and Savior* Jesus Christ

OUR SHIELD

Ps 33:20 Our soul waits for the Lord; He is our help and *our shield*

Ps 59:11 Scatter them by Your power, and bring them down, O Lord *our shield*

Ps 84:9 O God, behold *our shield*, and look upon the face of Your anointed

Ps 89:18 For *our shield* belongs to the Lord, and our king to the Holy One of Israel

OUR TESTIMONY IS TRUE

3Jn 12 And we also bear witness, and you know that *our testimony is true*

OUR YEARS COME TO AN END LIKE A SIGH (RSV)

(See *FINISH OUR YEARS LIKE A SIGH*)

OUT OF DARKNESS

Job 12:22 He uncovers deep things *out of darkness*, and brings the shadow of death to light

Ps 107:14 He brought them *out of darkness* and the shadow of death, and broke their chains in pieces

Is 29:18 In that day the deaf shall hear the words of the book, and the eyes of the blind shall see out of obscurity and *out of darkness*

2Cor 4:6 For it is the God who commanded light to shine *out of darkness* who has shone in our hearts to give the light of the knowledge of the glory of God in the face of Jesus Christ

1Pet 2:9 But you are a chosen generation, a royal priesthood, a holy nation, His own special people, that you may proclaim the praises of Him who called you *out of darkness* into His marvelous light

OUT OF EGYPT

Gen 45:25 Then they went up *out of Egypt*, and came to the land of Canaan to Jacob their father

Gen 47:30 you shall carry me *out of Egypt* and bury me in their burial place

Ex 3:10 Come now, therefore, and I will send you to Pharaoh that you may bring My people, the children of Israel, *out of Egypt*

Ex 3:11 But Moses said to God, "Who am I that I should go to Pharaoh, and that I should bring the children of Israel *out of Egypt*

Ex 3:12 When you have brought the people *out of Egypt*, you shall serve God on this mountain

Ex 12:39 And they baked unleavened cakes of the dough which they had brought *out of Egypt;* for it was not leavened, because they were driven *out of Egypt* and could not wait, nor had they prepared provisions for themselves

Ex 13:3 Remember this day in which you went *out of Egypt*, out of the house of bondage

Ex 13:9 for with a strong hand the Lord has brought you *out of Egypt*

Ex 13:14 that you shall say to him, 'By strength of hand the Lord brought us *out of Egypt*, out of the house of bondage

Ex 13:16 It shall be as a sign on your hand and as frontlets between your eyes, for by strength of hand the Lord brought us *out of Egypt*

Ex 14:11 Why have you so dealt with us, to bring us up *out of Egypt*

Ex 17:3 And the people thirsted there for water, and the people complained against Moses, and said, "Why is it you have brought us up *out of Egypt*, to kill us and our children and our livestock with thirst

Ex 18:1 And Jethro, the priest of Midian, Moses' father-in-law, heard of all that God had done for Moses and for Israel His people that the Lord had brought Israel *out of Egypt*

Ex 23:15 You shall keep the Feast of Unleavened Bread (you shall eat unleavened bread seven days, as I commanded you, at the time appointed in the month of Abib, for in it you came *out of Egypt*

Num 11:20 but for a whole month, until it comes out of your nostrils and becomes loathsome to you, because you have despised the Lord who is among you, and have wept before Him, saying, "Why did we ever come up *out of Egypt*

Num 20:5 And why have you made us come up *out of Egypt*, to bring us to this evil place

Num 20:16 When we cried out to the Lord, He heard our voice and sent the Angel and brought us up *out of Egypt*

Num 21:5 Why have you brought us up *out of Egypt* to die in the wilderness

Num 22:11 Look, a people has come *out of Egypt*, and they cover the face of the earth

Num 23:22 God brings them *out of Egypt;* He has strength like a wild ox

Num 24:8 God brings him *out of Egypt;* He has strength like a wild ox

Deut 4:20 But the Lord has taken you and brought you out of the iron furnace, *out of Egypt*, to be His people, His inheritance, as you are this day

Deut 4:37 and He brought you *out of Egypt* with His Presence, with His mighty power

Deut 4:45 These are the testimonies, the statutes, and the judgments which Moses spoke to the children of Israel after they came *out of Egypt*

Deut 4:46 on this side of the Jordan, in the valley opposite Beth Peor, in the land of Sihon king of the Amorites, who dwelt at Heshbon, whom Moses and the children of Israel defeated after they came *out of Egypt*

Deut 6:21 We were slaves of Pharaoh in Egypt, and the Lord brought us *out of Egypt* with a mighty hand

Deut 9:12 Then the Lord said to me, 'Arise, go down quickly from here, for your people whom you brought *out of Egypt* have acted corruptly

Deut 9:26 O Lord God, do not destroy Your people and Your inheritance whom You have redeemed through Your greatness, whom You have brought *out of Egypt* with a mighty hand

Deut 16:1 Observe the month of Abib, and keep the Passover to the Lord your God, for in the month of Abib the Lord your God brought you *out of Egypt* by night

Deut 16:6 but at the place where the Lord your God chooses to make His name abide, there you shall sacrifice the Passover at twilight, at the going down of the sun, at the time you came *out of Egypt*

Deut 23:4 because they did not meet you with bread and water on the road when you came *out of Egypt*, and because they hired against you Balaam the son of Beor from Pethor of Mesopotamia, to curse you

Deut 24:9 Remember what the Lord your God did to Miriam on the way when you came *out of Egypt*

Deut 25:17 Remember what Amalek did to you on the way as you were coming *out of Egypt*

Deut 26:8 So the Lord brought us *out of Egypt* with a mighty hand and with an outstretched arm, with great terror and with signs and wonders

Josh 2:10 For we have heard how the Lord dried up the water of the Red Sea for you when you came *out of Egypt*, and what you did to the two kings of the Amorites who were on the other side of the Jordan, Sihon and Og, whom you utterly destroyed

Josh 5:4 All the people who came *out of Egypt* who were males, all the men of war, had died in the wilderness on the way, after they had come *out of Egypt*

Josh 5:5 For all the people who came out had been circumcised, but all the people who were born in the wilderness on the way as they came *out of Egypt* had not been circumcised

Josh 5:6 For the children of Israel walked forty years in the wilderness, till all the people who were men of war, who came *out of Egypt*, were consumed, because they did not obey the voice of the Lord to whom the Lord swore that He would not show them the land which the Lord had sworn to their fathers that He would give us

Josh 24:6 Then I brought your fathers *out of Egypt*, and you came to the sea

Josh 24:32 The bones of Joseph, which the children of Israel had brought up *out of Egypt*, they buried at Shechem, in the plot of ground which Jacob had bought from the sons of Hamor the father of Shechem for one hundred pieces of silver, and which had become an inheritance of the children of Joseph

Judg 11:13 And the king of the people of Ammon answered the messengers of Jephthah, "Because Israel took away my land when they came up *out of Egypt*, from the Arnon as far as the Jabbok, and to the Jordan

1Sam 8:8 According to all the works which they have done since the day that I brought them up *out of Egypt*, even to this day with which they have forsaken Me and served other gods so they are doing to you also

1Sam 10:18 I brought up Israel *out of Egypt*, and delivered you from the hand of the Egyptians and from the hand of all kingdoms and from those who oppressed you

1Sam 12:8 When Jacob had gone into Egypt, and your fathers cried out to the Lord, then the Lord sent Moses and Aaron, who brought your fathers *out of Egypt* and made them dwell in this place

1Sam 15:6 For you showed kindness to all the children of Israel when they came up *out of Egypt*

1Kin 8:16 Since the day that I brought My people Israel *out of Egypt*, I have chosen no city from any tribe of Israel in which to build a house, that My name might be there

1Kin 8:51 (for they are Your people and Your inheritance, whom You brought *out of Egypt*, out of the iron furnace

1Kin 8:53 For You separated them from among all the peoples of the earth to be Your inheritance, as You spoke by the hand of Your servant Moses, when You brought our fathers *out of Egypt*, O Lord God

2Kin 21:15 because they have done evil in My sight, and have provoked Me to anger since the day their fathers came *out of Egypt*, even to this day

2Chr 5:10 There was nothing in the ark except the two tablets which Moses put there at Horeb, when the Lord made a covenant with the children of Israel, when they had come *out of Egypt*

2Chr 12:3 with twelve hundred chariots, sixty thousand horsemen, and people without number who came with him *out of Egypt* the Lubim and the Sukkiim and the Ethiopians

Neh 9:18 Even when they made a molded calf for themselves, and said, 'This is your god that brought you up *out of Egypt*

Ps 68:31 Envoys will come *out of Egypt;* Ethiopia will quickly stretch out her hands to God

Ps 80:8 You have brought a vine *out of Egypt;* You have cast out the nations, and planted it

Ps 114:1 When Israel went *out of Egypt*, the house of Jacob from a people of strange language

Hos 11:1 When Israel was a child, I loved him, and *out of Egypt* I called My son

Hos 12:13 By a prophet the Lord brought Israel *out of Egypt*, and by a prophet he was preserved

Hag 2:5 According to the word that I covenanted with you when you came *out of Egypt*, so My Spirit remains among you

Matt 2:15 and was there until the death of Herod, that it might be fulfilled which was spoken by the Lord through the prophet, saying, "*Out of Egypt* I called My Son

Heb 3:16 Indeed, was it not all who came *out of Egypt*, led by Moses

OUT OF THE DEPTHS

Ps 130:1 *Out of the depths* I have cried to You, O Lord

OUT OF THE FIRE ON THE MOUNTAIN (NIV)

(See *ON THE MOUNTAIN FROM THE MIDST OF THE FIRE*)

OUT OF THE HEART

Matt 15:19 For *out of the heart* proceed evil thoughts, murders, adulteries, fornications, thefts, false witness, blasphemies

Mark 7:21 For from within, *out of the heart* of men, proceed evil thoughts, adulteries, fornications, murders

OUT OF THE IRON FURNACE

Deut 4:20 But the Lord has taken you and brought you *out of the iron furnace*, out of Egypt, to be His people, His inheritance, as you are this day

1Kin 8:51 (for they are Your people and Your inheritance, whom You brought out of Egypt, *out of the iron furnace*

OUT OF THE IVORY PALACES

Ps 45:8 All Your garments are scented with myrrh and aloes and cassia, *out of the ivory palaces*, by which they have made You glad

OUT OF THE MOUTH OF BABES

Ps 8:2 *Out of the mouth of babes* and infants You have ordained strength, because of Your enemies, that You may silence the enemy and the avenger

Matt 21:16 Have you never read, '*Out of the mouth of babes* and nursing infants You have perfected praise

OUT OF ZION

Ps 14:7 Oh, that the salvation of Israel would come *out of Zion*

Ps 20:2 May He send you help from the sanctuary, and strengthen you *out of Zion*

Ps 50:2 *Out of Zion*, the perfection of beauty, God will shine forth

Ps 53:6 Oh, that the salvation of Israel would come *out of Zion*

Ps 110:2 The Lord shall send the rod of Your strength *out of Zion*

Ps 128:5 The Lord bless you *out of Zion*, and may you see the good of Jerusalem all the days of your life

Ps 135:21 Blessed be the Lord *out of Zion*, Who dwells in Jerusalem

Is 2:3 For *out of Zion* shall go forth the law, and the word of the Lord from Jerusalem

Mic 4:2 For *out of Zion* the law shall go forth, and the word of the Lord from Jerusalem

Rom 11:26 The Deliverer will come *out of Zion*, and He will turn away ungodliness from Jacob

OUT ON THE SEA IN SHIPS (NIV)

(See *DOWN TO THE SEA IN SHIPS*)

OUTCASTS OF ISRAEL

Ps 147:2 The Lord builds up Jerusalem; He gathers together the *outcasts of Israel*

Is 11:12 He will set up a banner for the nations, and will assemble the *outcasts of Israel*, and gather together the dispersed of Judah from the four corners of the earth

Is 56:8 The Lord God, who gathers the *outcasts of Israel*, says

OUTER DARKNESS

Matt 8:12 But the sons of the kingdom will be cast out into *outer darkness*

Matt 22:13 Then the king said to the servants, 'Bind him hand and foot, take him away, and cast him into *outer darkness*

Matt 25:30 And cast the unprofitable servant into the *outer darkness*. There will be weeping and gnashing of teeth

OUTER NATURE (RSV)

(See *OUTWARD MAN*)

OUTSIDE THE CAMP

Ex 29:14 But the flesh of the bull, with its skin and its offal, you shall burn with fire *outside the camp*

Ex 33:7 Moses took his tent and pitched it *outside the camp*, far from the camp, and called it the tabernacle of meeting. And it came to pass that everyone who sought the Lord went out to the tabernacle of meeting which was *outside the camp*

Lev 4:12 the whole bull he shall carry *outside the camp* to a clean place, where the ashes are poured out, and burn it on wood with fire

Lev 4:21 Then he shall carry the bull *outside the camp*, and burn it as he burned the first bull

Lev 6:11 Then he shall take off his garments, put on other garments, and carry the ashes *outside the camp* to a clean place

Lev 8:17 But the bull, its hide, its flesh, and its offal, he burned with fire *outside the camp*, as the Lord had commanded Moses

Lev 9:11 The flesh and the hide he burned with fire *outside the camp*

Lev 13:46 He is unclean, and he shall dwell alone; his habitation shall be *outside the camp*

Lev 16:27 The bull for the sin offering and the goat for the sin offering, whose blood was brought in to make atonement in the Holy Place, shall be carried *outside the camp*

Lev 17:3 Whatever man of the house of Israel, kills an ox or lamb or goat in the camp, or who kills it *outside the camp*

Lev 24:14 Take *outside the camp* him who has cursed; then let all who heard him lay their hands on his head, and let all the congregation stone him

Lev 24:23 and they took *outside the camp* him who had cursed, and stoned him with stones

Num 5:3 you shall put them *outside the camp*, that they may not defile their camps in the midst of which I dwell

Num 5:4 And the children of Israel did so, and put them *outside the camp*

Num 15:35 all the congregation shall stone him with stones *outside the camp*

Num 15:36 So, as the Lord commanded Moses, all the congregation brought him *outside the camp* and stoned him with stones, and he died

Num 19:3 You shall give it to Eleazar the priest, that he may take it *outside the camp*, and it shall be slaughtered before him

Num 19:9 Then a man who is clean shall gather up the ashes of the heifer, and store them *outside the camp* in a clean place

Num 31:13 And Moses, Eleazar the priest, and all the leaders of the congregation, went to meet them *outside the camp*

Num 31:19 And as for you, remain *outside the camp* seven days

Deut 23:10 If there is any man among you who becomes unclean by some occurrence in the night, then he shall go *outside the camp*

Deut 23:12 Also you shall have a place *outside the camp*, where you may go out

Josh 6:23 So they brought out all her relatives and left them *outside the camp* of Israel

Heb 13:11 For the bodies of those beasts, whose blood is brought into the sanctuary by the high priest for sin, are burned *outside the camp*

Heb 13:13 Therefore let us go forth to Him, *outside the camp*, bearing His reproach

OUTSTRETCHED ARM

Ex 6:6 I will bring you out from under the burdens of the Egyptians, I will rescue you from their bondage, and I will redeem you with an *outstretched arm* and with great judgments

Deut 4:34 Or did God ever try to go and take for Himself a nation from the midst of another nation, by trials, by signs, by wonders, by war, by a mighty hand and an *outstretched arm*, and by great terrors, according to all that the Lord your God did for you in Egypt before your eyes

Deut 5:15 And remember that you were a slave in the land of Egypt, and that the Lord your God brought you out from there by a mighty hand and by an *outstretched arm*

Deut 7:19 the great trials which your eyes saw, the signs and the wonders, the mighty hand and the *outstretched arm*, by which the Lord your God brought you out

Deut 9:29 Yet they are Your people and Your inheritance, whom You brought out by Your mighty power and by Your *outstretched arm*

Deut 11:2 Know today that I do not speak with your children, who have not known and who have not seen the chastening of the Lord your God, His greatness and His mighty hand and His *outstretched arm*

Deut 26:8 So the Lord brought us out of Egypt with a mighty hand and with an *outstretched arm*, with great terror and with signs and wonders

1Kin 8:42 (for they will hear of Your great name and Your strong hand and Your *outstretched arm*

2Kin 17:36 but the Lord, who brought you up from the land of Egypt with great power and an *outstretched arm*, Him you shall fear, Him you shall worship, and to Him you shall offer sacrifice

2Chr 6:32 Moreover, concerning a foreigner, who is not of Your people Israel, but who comes from a far country for the sake of Your great name and Your mighty hand and Your *outstretched arm*, when they come and pray in this temple

Ps 136:12 With a strong hand, and with an *outstretched arm*, for His mercy endures forever

Jer 27:5 I have made the earth, the man and the beast that are on the ground, by My great power and by My *outstretched arm*, and have given it to whom it seemed proper to Me

Jer 32:17 Behold, You have made the heavens and the earth by Your great power and *outstretched arm*

Jer 32:21 You have brought Your people Israel out of the land of Egypt with signs and wonders, with a strong hand and an *outstretched arm*, and with great terror

Ezek 20:33 As I live," says the Lord God, "surely with a mighty hand, with an *outstretched arm*, and with fury poured out, I will rule over you

Ezek 20:34 I will bring you out from the peoples and gather you out of the countries where you are scattered, with a mighty hand, with an *outstretched arm*, and with fury poured out

OUTWARD APPEARANCE

1Sam 16:7 for man looks at the *outward appearance*, but the Lord looks at the heart

2Cor 10:7 Do you look at things according to the *outward appearance*

OUTWARD MAN

2Cor 4:16 Even though our *outward man* is perishing, yet the inward man is being renewed day by day

OVER AGAINST (KJV)

(See *SIDE BY SIDE*)

OVERCOME THE WICKED ONE

1Jn 2:13 I write to you, young men, because you have *overcome the wicked one*

1Jn 2:14 I have written to you, young men, because you are strong, and the word of God abides in you, and you have *overcome the wicked one*

OVERCOME THE WORLD

John 16:33 but be of good cheer, I have *overcome the world*

1Jn 5:4 And this is the victory that has *overcome the world* our faith

OVERCOMES THE WORLD
1Jn 5:4 For whatever is born of God *overcomes the world*. And this is the victory that has overcome the world our faith
1Jn 5:5 Who is he who *overcomes the world*, but he who believes that Jesus is the Son of God

OVERFLOW OF THE HEART (NIV)
(See *ABUNDANCE OF THE HEART*)

OVERTAKE THE REAPER
Amos 9:13 Behold, the days are coming," says the Lord, "When the plowman shall *overtake the reaper*, and the treader of grapes him who sows seed

OVERTHREW THE TABLES (KJV)
(See *OVERTURNED THE TABLES*)

OVERTURNED THE TABLES
Matt 21:12 Then Jesus went into the temple of God and drove out all those who bought and sold in the temple, and *overturned the tables* of the moneychangers and the seats of those who sold doves
Mark 11:15 And Jesus went into the temple and began to drive out those who bought and sold in the temple, and *overturned the tables* of the moneychangers and the seats of those who sold doves
John 2:15 When He had made a whip of cords, He drove them all out of the temple, with the sheep and the oxen, and poured out the changers' money and *overturned the tables*

OWE NO ONE ANYTHING
Rom 13:8 *Owe no one anything* except to love one another, for he who loves another has fulfilled the law

OWN POSSESSION (NAS, RSV)
(See *SPECIAL TREASURE*)

OWN SON AFTER THE COMMON FAITH (KJV)
(See *TRUE SON IN OUR COMMON FAITH*)

OWNER OF THE HOUSE (NAS, NIV, RSV)
(See *MASTER OF THE HOUSE*)

P

PAID THE LAST PENNY
Matt 5:26 Assuredly, I say to you, you will by no means get out of there till you have *paid the last penny*

PAID THE UTTERMOST FARTHING (KJV)
(See *PAID THE LAST PENNY*)

PAID THE VERY LAST MITE
Luke 12:59 I tell you, you shall not depart from there till you have *paid the very last mite*

PAIN OF HEART (RSV)
(See *SORROW OF HEART*)

PALACES ADORNED WITH IVORY (NIV)
(See *IVORY PALACES*)

PALACES OF JERUSALEM
Jer 17:27 But if you will not heed Me to hallow the Sabbath day, such as not carrying a burden when entering the gates of Jerusalem on the Sabbath day, then I will kindle a fire in its gates, and it shall devour the *palaces of Jerusalem*, and it shall not be quenched
Amos 2:5 but I will send a fire upon Judah, and it shall devour the *palaces of Jerusalem*

PALM BRANCH AND BULRUSH
Is 9:14 Therefore the Lord will cut off head and tail from Israel, *palm branch and bulrush* in one day

PALM BRANCH AND REED (NIV, RSV)
(See *PALM BRANCH AND BULRUSH*)

PALMS OF MY HANDS
Is 49:16 See, I have inscribed you on the *palms of My hands*
Dan 10:10 Then, suddenly, a hand touched me, which made me tremble on my knees and on the *palms of my hands*

PANGS OF DEATH
Ps 18:4 The *pangs of death* encompassed me, and the floods of ungodliness made me afraid

PANGS OF SHEOL
Ps 116:3 The pains of death encompassed me, and the *pangs of Sheol* laid hold of me

PARABLE IN THE MOUTH OF FOOLS (KJV)
(See *PROVERB IN THE MOUTH OF FOOLS*)

PART IN THE LORD
Josh 22:25 You have no *part in the Lord*." So your descendants would make our descendants cease fearing the Lord
Josh 22:27 that your descendants may not say to our descendants in time to come, "You have no *part in the Lord*

PART MY GARMENTS (KJV)
(See *DIVIDE MY GARMENTS*)

PARTAKERS OF HIS HOLINESS
Heb 12:10 For they indeed for a few days chastened us as seemed best to them, but He for our profit, that we may be *partakers of His holiness*

PARTED HIS GARMENTS (KJV)
(See *DIVIDED HIS GARMENTS*)

PARTED MY GARMENTS (KJV)
(See *DIVIDED MY GARMENTS*)

PARTED THE HEAVENS (NIV)
(See *BOWED THE HEAVENS*)

PARTICIPATION IN THE BLOOD (NIV, RSV)
(See *COMMUNION OF THE BLOOD*)

PARTICIPATION IN THE BODY (NIV, RSV)
(See *COMMUNION OF THE BODY*)

PARTS OF THE BODY (NIV, RSV)
(See *MEMBERS OF THE BODY*)

PASS BY THEM
Ps 129:8 Neither let those who *pass by them* say, "The blessing of the Lord be upon you
Ezek 37:2 Then He caused me to *pass by them* all around, and behold, there were very many in the open valley
Amos 7:8 Behold, I am setting a plumb line in the midst of My people Israel; I will not *pass by them* anymore
Amos 8:2 The end has come upon my people Israel; I will not *pass by them* anymore

PASSED FROM DEATH TO LIFE
1Jn 3:14 We know that we have *passed from death to life*, because we love the brethren

PASSING THE LOVE OF WOMEN (KJV, RSV)
(See *SURPASSING THE LOVE OF WOMEN*)

PASSION MAKES THE BONES ROT (RSV)
(See *ENVY IS ROTTENNESS*)

PASSOVER OF THE JEWS
John 2:13 Now the *Passover of the Jews* was at hand, and Jesus went up to Jerusalem
John 11:55 And the *Passover of the Jews* was near, and many went from the country up to Jerusalem before the Passover, to purify themselves

PATH IN THE MIGHTY WATERS (KJV, RSV)
(See *PATH THROUGH THE MIGHTY WATERS*)

PATH OF LIFE
Ps 16:11 You will show me the *path of life;* in Your presence is fullness of joy
Prov 5:6 Lest you ponder her *path of life* her ways are unstable

PATH THROUGH THE MIGHTY WATERS
Is 43:16 Thus says the Lord, who makes a way in the sea and a *path through the mighty waters*

PATHS OF JUSTICE
Prov 2:8 He guards the *paths of justice*, and preserves the way of His saints
Prov 8:20 I traverse the way of righteousness, in the midst of the *paths of justice*

PATHS OF RIGHTEOUSNESS
Ps 23:3 He leads me in the *paths of righteousness* for His name's sake
Prov 2:20 so you may walk in the way of goodness, and keep to the *paths of righteousness*

PATIENT IN AFFLICTION (NIV)
(See *PATIENT IN TRIBULATION*)

PATIENT IN TRIBULATION
Rom 12:12 rejoicing in hope, *patient in tribulation*, continuing steadfastly in prayer

PATROL THE EARTH (NAS, RSV)
(See *THROUGHOUT THE EARTH*)

PAY ATTENTION (NIV)
(See *GIVE EAR*)

PAY MY VOWS
Ps 22:25 I will *pay My vows* before those who fear Him
Ps 116:14 I will *pay my vows* to the Lord now in the presence of all His people
Ps 116:18 I will *pay my vows* to the Lord now in the presence of all His people

PAY TAXES TO CAESAR
Matt 22:17 Is it lawful to *pay taxes to Caesar*, or not
Mark 12:14 Is it lawful to *pay taxes to Caesar*, or not
Luke 20:22 Is it lawful for us to *pay taxes to Caesar* or not
Luke 23:2 And they began to accuse Him, saying, "We found this fellow perverting the nation, and forbidding to *pay taxes to Caesar*, saying that He Himself is Christ, a King

PEACE ABOUND (RSV)
(See *ABUNDANCE OF PEACE*)

PEACE AND EQUITY
Mal 2:6 He walked with Me in *peace and equity*, and turned many away from iniquity

PEACE AND SECURITY (NIV, RSV)
(See *PEACE AND TRUTH*)

PEACE AND TRUTH
2Kin 20:19 For he said, "Will there not be *peace and truth* at least in my days
Esth 9:30 And Mordecai sent letters to all the Jews, to the one hundred and twenty-seven provinces of the kingdom of Ahasuerus, with words of *peace and truth*
Is 39:8 For he said, "At least there will be *peace and truth* in my days
Jer 33:6 I will heal them and reveal to them the abundance of *peace and truth*

PEACE AND UPRIGHTNESS (NAS, NIV)
(See *PEACE AND EQUITY*)

PEACE BE IN ISRAEL (RSV)
(See *PEACE BE UPON ISRAEL*)

PEACE BE MULTIPLIED TO YOU
Dan 4:1 Nebuchadnezzar the king, to all peoples, nations and languages that dwell in all the earth: *Peace be multiplied to you*
Dan 6:25 To all peoples, nations, and languages that dwell in all the earth: *Peace be multiplied to you*
2Pet 1:2 Grace and *peace be multiplied to you* in the knowledge of God and of Jesus our Lord

PEACE, BE STILL
Mark 4:39 Then He arose and rebuked the wind, and said to the sea, "*Peace, be still*

PEACE BE UPON ISRAEL
Ps 125:5 As for such as turn aside to their crooked ways, the Lord shall lead them away with the workers of iniquity. *Peace be upon Israel*
Ps 128:6 Yes, may you see your children's children. *Peace be upon Israel*

PEACE BE WITH YOU
Gen 43:23 But he said, "*Peace be with you*, do not be afraid
Judg 6:23 Then the Lord said to him, "*Peace be with you*
Judg 19:20 And the old man said, "*Peace be with you!* However, let all your needs be my responsibility
John 20:19 Then, the same day at evening, being the first day of the week, when the doors were shut where the disciples were assembled, for fear of the Jews, Jesus came and stood in the midst, and said to them, "*Peace be with you*
Rom 15:33 Now the God of *peace be with you* all. Amen

PEACE FROM GOD OUR FATHER
Rom 1:7 Grace to you and *peace from God our Father* and the Lord Jesus Christ
1Cor 1:3 Grace to you and *peace from God our Father* and the Lord Jesus Christ
2Cor 1:2 Grace to you and *peace from God our Father* and the Lord Jesus Christ
Eph 1:2 Grace to you and *peace from God our Father* and the Lord Jesus Christ
Phil 1:2 Grace to you and *peace from God our Father* and the Lord Jesus Christ
Col 1:2 Grace to you and *peace from God our Father* and the Lord Jesus Christ

1Th 1:1 Grace to you and *peace from God our Father* and the Lord Jesus Christ
2Th 1:2 Grace to you and *peace from God our Father* and the Lord Jesus Christ
1Tim 1:2 Grace, mercy, and *peace from God our Father* and Jesus Christ our Lord
Phm 3 Grace to you and *peace from God our Father* and the Lord Jesus Christ

PEACE OF GOD
Phil 4:7 and the *peace of God*, which surpasses all understanding, will guard your hearts and minds through Christ Jesus
Col 3:15 And let the *peace of God* rule in your hearts, to which also you were called in one body

PEACE OF JERUSALEM
Ps 122:6 Pray for the *peace of Jerusalem:* "May they prosper who love you

PEACE OFFERING
Lev 3:1 When his offering is a sacrifice of a *peace offering*, if he offers it of the herd, whether male or female, he shall offer it without blemish before the Lord
Lev 3:3 Then he shall offer from the sacrifice of the *peace offering* an offering made by fire to the Lord
Lev 3:6 If his offering as a sacrifice of a *peace offering* to the Lord is of the flock, whether male or female, he shall offer it without blemish
Lev 3:9 Then he shall offer from the sacrifice of the *peace offering*, as an offering made by fire to the Lord, its fat and the whole fat tail which he shall remove close to the backbone
Lev 4:10 as it was taken from the bull of the sacrifice of the *peace offering*
Lev 4:26 And he shall burn all its fat on the altar, like the fat of the sacrifice of the *peace offering*
Lev 4:31 He shall remove all its fat, as fat is removed from the sacrifice of the *peace offering*
Lev 4:35 He shall remove all its fat, as the fat of the lamb is removed from the sacrifice of the *peace offering*
Lev 7:13 Besides the cakes, as his offering he shall offer leavened bread with the sacrifice of thanksgiving of his *peace offering*
Lev 7:14 It shall belong to the priest who sprinkles the blood of the *peace offering*
Lev 7:15 The flesh of the sacrifice of his *peace offering* for thanksgiving shall be eaten the same day it is offered
Lev 7:18 And if any of the flesh of the sacrifice of his *peace offering* is eaten at all on the third day, it shall not be accepted, nor shall it be imputed to him
Lev 7:20 But the person who eats the flesh of the sacrifice of the *peace offering* that belongs to the Lord, while he is unclean, that person shall be cut off from his people
Lev 7:21 Moreover the person who touches any unclean thing, such as human uncleanness, any unclean beast, or any abominable unclean thing, and who eats the flesh of the sacrifice of the *peace offering* that belongs to the Lord, that person shall be cut off from his people
Lev 7:29 He who offers the sacrifice of his *peace offering* to the Lord shall bring his offering to the Lord from the sacrifice of his *peace offering*
Lev 7:33 He among the sons of Aaron, who offers the blood of the *peace offering*, and the fat, shall have the right thigh for his part
Lev 7:37 This is the law of the burnt offering, the grain offering, the sin offering, the trespass offering, the consecrations, and the sacrifice of the *peace offering*
Lev 19:5 And if you offer a sacrifice of *peace offering* to the Lord, you shall offer it of your own free will
Lev 22:21 And whoever offers a sacrifice of *peace offering* to the Lord, to fulfill his vow, or a freewill offering from the cattle or the sheep, it must be perfect to be accepted
Lev 23:19 Then you shall sacrifice one kid of the goats as a sin offering, and two male lambs of the first year as a sacrifice of *peace offering*
Num 6:14 one male lamb in its first year without blemish as a burnt offering, one ewe lamb in its first year without blemish as a sin offering, one ram without blemish as a *peace offering*
Num 6:17 and he shall offer the ram as a sacrifice of *peace offering* to the Lord, with the basket of unleavened bread
Num 6:18 Then the Nazirite shall shave his consecrated head at the door of the tabernacle of meeting, and shall take the hair from his consecrated head and put it on the fire which is under the sacrifice of the *peace offering*
Num 15:8 And when you prepare a young bull as a burnt offering, or as a sacrifice to fulfill a vow, or as a *peace offering* to the Lord
Ezek 46:12 Now when the prince makes a voluntary burnt offering or voluntary *peace offering* to the Lord, the gate that faces toward the east shall then be opened for him

PEACE OFFERINGS
Ex 20:24 An altar of earth you shall make for Me, and you shall sacrifice on it your burnt offerings and your *peace offerings*, your sheep and your oxen
Ex 24:5 Then he sent young men of the children of Israel, who offered burnt offerings and sacrificed *peace offerings* of oxen to the Lord
Ex 29:28 it shall be a heave offering from the children of Israel from the sacrifices of their *peace offerings*, that is, their heave offering to the Lord
Ex 32:6 Then they rose early on the next day, offered burnt offerings, and brought *peace offerings*
Lev 6:12 and he shall burn on it the fat of the *peace offerings*
Lev 7:11 This is the law of the sacrifice of *peace offerings* which he shall offer to the Lord
Lev 7:32 Also the right thigh you shall give to the priest as a heave offering from the sacrifices of your *peace offerings*
Lev 7:34 For the breast of the wave offering and the thigh of the heave offering I have taken from the children of Israel, from the sacrifices of their *peace offerings*, and I have given them to Aaron the priest and to his sons from the children of Israel by a statute forever
Lev 9:4 also a bull and a ram as *peace offerings*, to sacrifice before the Lord, and a grain offering mixed with oil
Lev 9:18 He also killed the bull and the ram as sacrifices of *peace offerings*, which were for the people
Lev 9:22 Then Aaron lifted his hand toward the people, blessed them, and came down from offering the sin offering, the burnt offering, and *peace offerings*
Lev 10:14 for they are your due and your sons' due, which are given from the sacrifices of *peace offerings* of the children of Israel
Lev 17:5 to the end that the children of Israel may bring their sacrifices which they offer in the open field, that they may bring them to the Lord at the door of the tabernacle of meeting, to the priest, and offer them as *peace offerings* to the Lord
Num 7:17 and for the sacrifice of *peace offerings:* two oxen, five rams, five male goats, and five male lambs in their first year
Num 7:23 and as the sacrifice of *peace offerings:*

two oxen, five rams, five male goats, and five male lambs in their first year

Num 7:29 and for the sacrifice of *peace offerings:* two oxen, five rams, five male goats, and five male lambs in their first year

Num 7:35 and as the sacrifice of *peace offerings:* two oxen, five rams, five male goats, and five male lambs in their first year

Num 7:41 and as the sacrifice of *peace offerings:* two oxen, five rams, five male goats, and five male lambs in their first year

Num 7:47 and as the sacrifice of *peace offerings:* two oxen, five rams, five male goats, and five male lambs in their first year

Num 7:53 and as the sacrifice of *peace offerings:* two oxen, five rams, five male goats, and five male lambs in their first year

Num 7:59 and as the sacrifice of *peace offerings:* two oxen, five rams, five male goats, and five male lambs in their first year

Num 7:65 and as the sacrifice of *peace offerings:* two oxen, five rams, five male goats, and five male lambs in their first year

Num 7:71 and as the sacrifice of *peace offerings:* two oxen, five rams, five male goats, and five male lambs in their first year

Num 7:77 and as the sacrifice of *peace offerings:* two oxen, five rams, five male goats, and five male lambs in their first year

Num 7:83 and as the sacrifice of *peace offerings:* two oxen, five rams, five male goats, and five male lambs in their first year

Num 7:88 And all the oxen for the sacrifice of *peace offerings* were twenty-four bulls, the rams sixty, the male goats sixty, and the lambs in their first year sixty

Num 10:10 Also in the day of your gladness, in your appointed feasts, and at the beginning of your months, you shall blow the trumpets over your burnt offerings and over the sacrifices of your *peace offerings*

Num 29:39 as your burnt offerings and your grain offerings, as your drink offerings and your *peace offerings*

Deut 27:7 You shall offer *peace offerings*, and shall eat there, and rejoice before the Lord your God

Josh 8:31 And they offered on it burnt offerings to the Lord, and sacrificed *peace offerings*

Josh 22:23 If we have built ourselves an altar to turn from following the Lord, or if to offer on it burnt offerings or grain offerings, or if to offer *peace offerings* on it, let the Lord Himself require an account

Josh 22:27 but that it may be a witness between you and us and our generations after us, that we may perform the service of the Lord before Him with our burnt offerings, with our sacrifices, and with our *peace offerings*

Judg 20:26 and they offered burnt offerings and *peace offerings* before the Lord

Judg 21:4 So it was, on the next morning, that the people rose early and built an altar there, and offered burnt offerings and *peace offerings*

1Sam 10:8 and surely I will come down to you to offer burnt offerings and make sacrifices of *peace offerings*

1Sam 11:15 There they made sacrifices of *peace offerings* before the Lord, and there Saul and all the men of Israel rejoiced greatly

1Sam 13:9 So Saul said, "Bring a burnt offering and *peace offerings* here to me

2Sam 6:17 Then David offered burnt offerings and *peace offerings* before the Lord

2Sam 6:18 And when David had finished offering burnt offerings and *peace offerings*, he blessed the people in the name of the Lord of hosts

2Sam 24:25 And David built there an altar to the Lord, and offered burnt offerings and *peace offerings*

1Kin 3:15 And he came to Jerusalem and stood before the ark of the covenant of the Lord, offered up burnt offerings, offered *peace offerings*, and made a feast for all his servants

1Kin 8:63 And Solomon offered a sacrifice of *peace offerings*, which he offered to the Lord, twenty-two thousand bulls and one hundred and twenty thousand sheep

1Kin 8:64 for there he offered burnt offerings, grain offerings, and the fat of the *peace offerings*, because the bronze altar that was before the Lord was too small to receive the burnt offerings, the grain offerings, and the fat of the *peace offerings*

1Kin 9:25 Now three times a year Solomon offered burnt offerings and *peace offerings* on the altar which he had built for the Lord, and he burned incense with them on the altar that was before the Lord

2Kin 16:13 and he poured his drink offering and sprinkled the blood of his *peace offerings* on the altar

1Chr 16:1 Then they offered burnt offerings and *peace offerings* before God

1Chr 16:2 And when David had finished offering the burnt offerings and the *peace offerings*, he blessed the people in the name of the Lord

1Chr 21:26 And David built there an altar to the Lord, and offered burnt offerings and *peace offerings*, and called on the Lord

2Chr 7:7 for there he offered burnt offerings and the fat of the *peace offerings*, because the bronze altar which Solomon had made was not able to receive the burnt offerings, the grain offerings, and the fat

2Chr 29:35 Also the burnt offerings were in abundance, with the fat of the *peace offerings* and with the drink offerings for every burnt offering

2Chr 30:22 and they ate throughout the feast seven days, offering *peace offerings* and making confession to the Lord God of their fathers

2Chr 31:2 And Hezekiah appointed the divisions of the priests and the Levites according to their divisions, each man according to his service, the priests and Levites for burnt offerings and *peace offerings*, to serve, to give thanks, and to praise in the gates of the camp of the Lord

2Chr 33:16 He also repaired the altar of the Lord, sacrificed *peace offerings* and thank offerings on it, and commanded Judah to serve the Lord God of Israel

Prov 7:14 I have *peace offerings* with me; today I have paid my vows

Ezek 43:27 When these days are over it shall be, on the eighth day and thereafter, that the priests shall offer your burnt offerings and your *peace offerings* on the altar

Ezek 45:15 These shall be for grain offerings, burnt offerings, and *peace offerings*, to make atonement for them

Ezek 45:17 He shall prepare the sin offering, the grain offering, the burnt offering, and the *peace offerings* to make atonement for the house of Israel

Ezek 46:2 The priests shall prepare his burnt offering and his *peace offerings*

Ezek 46:12 and he shall prepare his burnt offering and his *peace offerings* as he did on the Sabbath day

Amos 5:22 Though you offer Me burnt offerings and your grain offerings, I will not accept them, Nor will I regard your fattened *peace offerings*

PEACE ON EARTH

Matt 10:34 Do not think that I came to bring *peace on earth*

Luke 12:51 Do you suppose that I came to give *peace on earth*

PEACE, PEACE
1Chr 12:18 *Peace, peace* to you, and peace to your helpers
Is 57:19 *peace, peace* to him who is far off and to him who is near
Jer 6:14 They have also healed the hurt of My people slightly, saying, '*Peace, peace*
Jer 8:11 For they have healed the hurt of the daughter of My people slightly, saying, '*Peace, peace*

PEACE SHALL BE UPON ISRAEL (KJV)
(See *PEACE BE UPON ISRAEL*)

PEACE TO THE EARTH (NIV)
(See *PEACE ON EARTH*)

PEACE TO THE NATIONS
Zech 9:10 He shall speak *peace to the nations;* His dominion shall be

PEACE TO THIS HOUSE
Luke 10:5 But whatever house you enter, first say, '*Peace to this house*

PEACE TO YOU
1Chr 12:18 Peace, *peace to you*, and peace to your helpers! For your God helps you
Luke 24:36 Now as they said these things, Jesus Himself stood in the midst of them, and said to them, "*Peace to you*
John 20:21 Then Jesus said to them again, "*Peace to you!* As the Father has sent Me, I also send you
John 20:26 Jesus came, the doors being shut, and stood in the midst, and said, "*Peace to you*
Eph 2:17 And He came and preached *peace to you* who were afar off and to those who were near
1Pet 5:14 *Peace to you* all who are in Christ Jesus. Amen
3Jn 14 *Peace to you*. Our friends greet you. Greet the friends by name

PEACE UNTO THE HEATHEN (KJV)
(See *PEACE TO THE NATIONS*)

PEACE WITH GOD
Rom 5:1 Therefore, having been justified by faith, we have *peace with God* through our Lord Jesus Christ

PEACEFUL FOLDS (NAS, RSV)
(See *PEACEFUL HABITATIONS*)

PEACEFUL HABITATIONS
Jer 25:37 and the *peaceful habitations* are cut down because of the fierce anger of the Lord

PEACEFUL MEADOWS (NIV)
(See *PEACEFUL HABITATIONS*)

PEARL OF GREAT PRICE
Matt 13:46 who, when he had found one *pearl of great price*, went and sold all that he had and bought it

PEARLS BEFORE SWINE
Matt 7:6 nor cast your *pearls before swine*, lest they trample them under their feet, and turn and tear you in pieces

PECULIAR PEOPLE (KJV)
(See *SPECIAL PEOPLE*)

PECULIAR TREASURE (KJV)
(See *SPECIAL TREASURE*)

PEOPLE COMPLAINED
Ex 15:24 And the *people complained* against Moses, saying, "What shall we drink
Ex 17:3 And the people thirsted there for water, and the *people complained* against Moses, and said
Num 11:1 Now when the *people complained*, it displeased the Lord; for the Lord heard it, and His anger was aroused

PEOPLE FOR HIS OWN POSSESSION (RSV)
(See *SPECIAL PEOPLE*)

PEOPLE, HIS TREASURED POSSESSION (NIV)
(See *SPECIAL PEOPLE*)

PEOPLE OF GOD
Judg 20:2 And the leaders of all the people, all the tribes of Israel, presented themselves in the assembly of the *people of God*, four hundred thousand foot soldiers who drew the sword
2Sam 14:13 Why then have you schemed such a thing against the *people of God*
Heb 4:9 There remains therefore a rest for the *people of God*
Heb 11:25 choosing rather to suffer affliction with the *people of God* than to enjoy the passing pleasures of sin
1Pet 2:10 who once were not a people but are now the *people of God*, who had not obtained mercy but now have obtained mercy

PEOPLE OF ISRAEL
Num 21:6 So the Lord sent fiery serpents among the people, and they bit the people; and many of the *people of Israel* died
Josh 8:33 Half of them were in front of Mount Gerizim and half of them in front of Mount Ebal, as Moses the servant of the Lord had commanded before, that they should bless the *people of Israel*
2Sam 18:7 The *people of Israel* were overthrown there before the servants of David, and a great slaughter of twenty thousand men took place there that day
2Sam 19:40 And all the people of Judah escorted the king, and also half the *people of Israel*
2Sam 24:4 So Joab and the captains of the army went out from the presence of the king to count the *people of Israel*
1Kin 16:21 Then the *people of Israel* were divided into two parts
Ezra 2:2 The number of the men of the *people of Israel*
Ezra 7:13 I issue a decree that all those of the *people of Israel* and the priests and Levites in my realm, who volunteer to go up to Jerusalem, may go with you
Ezra 9:1 When these things were done, the leaders came to me, saying, "The *people of Israel* and the priests and the Levites have not separated themselves from the peoples of the lands, with respect to the abominations of the Canaanites, the Hittites, the Perizzites, the Jebusites, the Ammonites, the Moabites, the Egyptians, and the Amorites
Neh 7:7 The number of the men of the *people of Israel*
Acts 4:10 let it be known to you all, and to all the *people of Israel*, that by the name of Jesus Christ of Nazareth, whom you crucified, whom God raised from the dead, by Him this man stands here before you whole

Acts 4:27 For truly against Your holy Servant Jesus, whom You anointed, both Herod and Pontius Pilate, with the Gentiles and the *people of Israel*, were gathered together
Acts 13:24 after John had first preached, before His coming, the baptism of repentance to all the *people of Israel*

PEOPLE OF THE LAND
Gen 23:7 Then Abraham stood up and bowed himself to the *people of the land*, the sons of Heth
Gen 23:12 Then Abraham bowed himself down before the *people of the land*
Gen 23:13 and he spoke to Ephron in the hearing of the *people of the land*, saying
Gen 42:6 and it was he who sold to all the *people of the land*
Ex 5:5 And Pharaoh said, "Look, the *people of the land* are many now, and you make them rest from their labor
Lev 20:2 The *people of the land* shall stone him with stones
Lev 20:4 And if the *people of the land* should in any way hide their eyes from the man, when he gives some of his descendants to Molech, and they do not kill him
Num 14:9 Only do not rebel against the Lord, nor fear the *people of the land*, for they are our bread
1Sam 14:25 Now all the *people of the land* came to a forest
2Kin 11:14 All the *people of the land* were rejoicing and blowing trumpets
2Kin 11:18 And all the *people of the land* went to the temple of Baal, and tore it down
2Kin 11:19 Then he took the captains of hundreds, the bodyguards, the escorts, and all the *people of the land*
2Kin 11:20 So all the *people of the land* rejoiced; and the city was quiet, for they had slain Athaliah with the sword in the king's house
2Kin 15:5 And Jotham the king's son was over the royal house, judging the *people of the land*
2Kin 16:15 Then King Ahaz commanded Urijah the priest, saying, "On the great new altar burn the morning burnt offering, the evening grain offering, the king's burnt sacrifice, and his grain offering, with the burnt offering of all the *people of the land*, their grain offering, and their drink offerings
2Kin 21:24 But the *people of the land* executed all those who had conspired against King Amon. Then the *people of the land* made his son Josiah king in his place
2Kin 23:30 And the *people of the land* took Jehoahaz the son of Josiah, anointed him, and made him king in his father's place
2Kin 23:35 he exacted the silver and gold from the *people of the land*, from every one according to his assessment, to give it to Pharaoh Necho
2Kin 24:14 all the captains and all the mighty men of valor, ten thousand captives, and all the craftsmen and smiths. None remained except the poorest *people of the land*
2Kin 25:3 By the ninth day of the fourth month the famine had become so severe in the city that there was no food for the *people of the land*
2Kin 25:19 He also took out of the city an officer who had charge of the men of war, five men of the king's close associates who were found in the city, the principal scribe of the army who mustered the *people of the land*, and sixty men of the *people of the land* who were found in the city
2Chr 23:13 There were all the *people of the land*, rejoicing and blowing trumpets, also the singers with instruments of music, and those who led in praise
2Chr 23:20 Then he took the captains of hundreds, the nobles, the governors of the people, and all the *people of the land*, and brought the king down from the house of the Lord
2Chr 23:21 So all the *people of the land* rejoiced; and the city was quiet, for they had slain Athaliah with the sword
2Chr 26:21 Then Jotham his son was over the king's house, judging the *people of the land*
2Chr 33:25 But the *people of the land* executed all those who had conspired against King Amon. Then the *people of the land* made his son Josiah king in his place
2Chr 36:1 Then the *people of the land* took Jehoahaz the son of Josiah, and made him king in his father's place in Jerusalem
Ezra 4:4 Then the *people of the land* tried to discourage the people of Judah
Neh 9:24 you subdued before them the inhabitants of the land, the Canaanites, and gave them into their hands, with their kings and the *people of the land*, that they might do with them as they would
Esth 8:17 Then many of the *people of the land* became Jews, because fear of the Jews fell upon them
Jer 1:18 For behold, I have made you this day a fortified city and an iron pillar, and bronze walls against the whole land against the kings of Judah, against its princes, against its priests, and against the *people of the land*
Jer 34:19 the princes of Judah, the princes of Jerusalem, the eunuchs, the priests, and all the *people of the land* who passed between the parts of the calf
Jer 37:2 But neither he nor his servants nor the *people of the land* gave heed to the words of the Lord which He spoke by the prophet Jeremiah
Jer 44:21 The incense that you burned in the cities of Judah and in the streets of Jerusalem, you and your fathers, your kings and your princes, and the *people of the land*, did not the Lord remember them, and did it not come into His mind
Jer 52:6 By the fourth month, on the ninth day of the month, the famine had become so severe in the city that there was no food for the *people of the land*
Jer 52:25 He also took out of the city an officer who had charge of the men of war, seven men of the king's close associates who were found in the city, the principal scribe of the army who mustered the *people of the land*, and sixty men of the *people of the land* who were found in the midst of the city
Ezek 12:19 And say to the *people of the land*, 'Thus says the Lord God to the inhabitants of Jerusalem and to the land of Israel
Ezek 22:29 The *people of the land* have used oppressions, committed robbery, and mistreated the poor and needy
Ezek 33:2 When I bring the sword upon a land, and the *people of the land* take a man from their territory and make him their watchman
Ezek 39:13 Indeed all the *people of the land* will be burying them, and they will gain renown for it on the day that I am glorified
Ezek 45:16 All the *people of the land* shall give this offering for the prince in Israel
Ezek 45:22 And on that day the prince shall prepare for himself and for all the *people of the land* a bull for a sin offering
Ezek 46:3 Likewise the *people of the land* shall worship at the entrance to this gateway before the Lord on the Sabbaths and the New Moons
Ezek 46:9 But when the *people of the land* come before the Lord on the appointed feast days, whoever enters by way of the north gate to worship shall go out by way of the south gate
Dan 9:6 Neither have we heeded Your servants the prophets, who spoke in Your name to our

kings and our princes, to our fathers and all the *people of the land*
Hag 2:4 and be strong, all you *people of the land,'* says the Lord
Zech 7:5 Say to all the *people of the land*, and to the priests

PEOPLE OF THE LIGHT (NIV)
(See *SONS OF LIGHT*)

PEOPLE OF THE LORD
Num 16:41 On the next day all the congregation of the children of Israel murmured against Moses and Aaron, saying, "You have killed the *people of the Lord*
Deut 27:9 This day you have become the *people of the Lord* your God
Judg 5:11 then the *people of the Lord* shall go down to the gates
2Sam 1:12 And they mourned and wept and fasted until evening for Saul and for Jonathan his son, for the *people of the Lord* and for the house of Israel, because they had fallen by the sword
2Sam 6:21 So David said to Michal, "It was before the Lord, who chose me instead of your father and all his house, to appoint me ruler over the *people of the Lord*, over Israel
2Kin 9:6 I have anointed you king over the *people of the Lord*, over Israel
Ezek 36:20 When they came to the nations, wherever they went, they profaned My holy name when they said of them, 'These are the *people of the Lord*, and yet they have gone out of His land
Zeph 2:10 This they shall have for their pride, because they have reproached and made arrogant threats against the *people of the Lord* of hosts

PEOPLE OF THIS AGE (NIV)
(See *SONS OF THIS AGE*)

PEOPLE OF THIS WORLD (NIV)
(See *SONS OF THIS WORLD*)

PEOPLES OF THE LAND
1Chr 5:25 And they were unfaithful to the God of their fathers, and played the harlot after the gods of the *peoples of the land*, whom God had destroyed before them
Ezra 10:2 And Shechaniah the son of Jehiel, one of the sons of Elam, spoke up and said to Ezra, "We have trespassed against our God, and have taken pagan wives from the *peoples of the land*
Ezra 10:11 separate yourselves from the *peoples of the land*, and from the pagan wives
Neh 10:30 that we would not give our daughters as wives to the *peoples of the land*, nor take their daughters for our sons
Neh 10:31 that if the *peoples of the land* bring wares or any grain to sell on the Sabbath day, we would not buy it from them on the Sabbath, or on a holy day

PEOPLES ON EARTH (NIV)
(See *FAMILIES OF THE EARTH*)

PERADVENTURE THERE BE FIFTY RIGHTEOUS (KJV)
(See *SUPPOSE THERE WERE FIFTY RIGHTEOUS*)

PERFECT IN BEAUTY
Ezek 27:3 O Tyre, you have said, 'I am *perfect in beauty*
Ezek 28:12 You were the seal of perfection, full of wisdom and *perfect in beauty*

PERFECT LOVE
1Jn 4:18 but *perfect love* casts out fear, because fear involves torment

PERFECT MAN
Eph 4:13 till we all come to the unity of the faith and the knowledge of the Son of God, to a *perfect man*, to the measure of the stature of the fullness of Christ
Jas 3:2 If anyone does not stumble in word, he is a *perfect man*, able also to bridle the whole body

PERFECT PEACE
Ezra 7:12 Artaxerxes, king of kings, to Ezra the priest, a scribe of the Law of the God of heaven: *Perfect peace*, and so forth
Is 26:3 You will keep him in *perfect peace*, whose mind is stayed on You, because he trusts in You

PERFECTER OF OUR FAITH (NIV)
(See *FINISHER OF OUR FAITH*)

PERFORM SIGNS (NIV)
(See *SHOW SIGNS*)

PERILOUS PESTILENCE
Ps 91:3 Surely He shall deliver you from the snare of the fowler and from the *perilous pestilence*

PERISH BY THE SWORD
Job 36:12 But if they do not obey, they shall *perish by the sword*, and they shall die without knowledge
Matt 26:52 Then Jesus said to him, "Put your sword in its place, for all who take the sword will *perish by the sword*

PERPETUAL COVENANT
Ex 31:16 Therefore the children of Israel shall keep the Sabbath, to observe the Sabbath throughout their generations as a *perpetual covenant*
Jer 50:5 They shall ask the way to Zion, with their faces toward it, saying, 'come and let us join ourselves to the Lord in a *perpetual covenant* that will not be forgotten

PERPETUAL DESOLATIONS
Ps 74:3 Lift up Your feet to the *perpetual desolations*. The enemy has damaged everything in the sanctuary
Jer 25:9 behold, I will send and take all the families of the north,' says the Lord, 'and Nebuchadnezzar the king of Babylon, My servant, and will bring them against this land, against its inhabitants, and against these nations all around, and will utterly destroy them, and make them an astonishment, a hissing, and *perpetual desolations*

PERPETUAL RUINS (RSV)
(See *PERPETUAL DESOLATIONS*)

PERPETUAL STATUTE
Ex 29:9 The priesthood shall be theirs for a *perpetual statute*. So you shall consecrate Aaron and his sons
Lev 3:17 This shall be a *perpetual statute* throughout your generations in all your dwellings
Lev 24:9 for it is most holy to him from the offerings of the Lord made by fire, by a *perpetual statute*
Num 19:21 It shall be a *perpetual statute* for them. He who sprinkles the water of purification shall wash his clothes

PERSECUTED THE CHURCH OF GOD
1Cor 15:9 For I am the least of the apostles, who am not worthy to be called an apostle, because I *persecuted the church of God*
Gal 1:13 For you have heard of my former conduct in Judaism, how I *persecuted the church of God* beyond measure and tried to destroy it

PERSECUTED THE POOR
Ps 109:16 Because he did not remember to show mercy, but *persecuted the poor* and needy man, that he might even slay the broken in heart

PERSECUTION FOR THE CROSS OF CHRIST
Gal 6:12 As many as desire to make a good showing in the flesh, these try to compel you to be circumcised, only that they may not suffer *persecution for the cross of Christ*

PERSUADE HER (NIV)
(See *SPEAK KINDLY TO*)

PERSUADED BETTER THINGS (KJV)
(See *CONFIDENT OF BETTER THINGS*)

PERSUASIVE WORDS
1Cor 2:4 And my speech and my preaching were not with *persuasive words* of human wisdom, but in demonstration of the Spirit and of power
Col 2:4 Now this I say lest anyone should deceive you with *persuasive words*

PERVERSE GENERATION
Deut 32:20 I will hide My face from them, I will see what their end will be, for they are a *perverse generation*, children in whom is no faith
Matt 17:17 Then Jesus answered and said, "O faithless and *perverse generation*, how long shall I be with you
Luke 9:41 Then Jesus answered and said, "O faithless and *perverse generation*, how long shall I be with you and bear with you
Acts 2:40 And with many other words he testified and exhorted them, saying, "Be saved from this *perverse generation*
Phil 2:15 that you may become blameless and harmless, children of God without fault in the midst of a crooked and *perverse generation*, among whom you shine as lights in the world

PERVERSE JUDGMENT PROCEEDS
Hab 1:4 For the wicked surround the righteous; therefore *perverse judgment proceeds*

PERVERT JUSTICE
Ex 23:2 nor shall you testify in a dispute so as to turn aside after many to *pervert justice*
Deut 16:19 You shall not *pervert justice;* you shall not show partiality, nor take a bribe, for a bribe blinds the eyes of the wise and twists the words of the righteous
Deut 24:17 You shall not *pervert justice* due the stranger or the fatherless, nor take a widow's garment as a pledge
Job 8:3 Does God subvert judgment? Or does the Almighty *pervert justice*
Job 34:12 Surely God will never do wickedly, nor will the Almighty *pervert justice*

PERVERTED PERSONS
1Kin 14:24 And there were also *perverted persons* in the land. They did according to all the abominations of the nations which the Lord had cast out before the children of Israel
1Kin 15:12 And he banished the *perverted persons* from the land, and removed all the idols that his fathers had made
1Kin 22:46 And the rest of the *perverted persons*, who remained in the days of his father Asa, he banished from the land
2Kin 23:7 Then he tore down the ritual booths of the *perverted persons* that were in the house of the Lord, where the women wove hangings for the wooden image
Job 36:14 They die in youth, and their life ends among the *perverted persons*

PHARAOH HARDENED HIS HEART
Ex 8:32 But *Pharaoh hardened his heart* at this time also; neither would he let the people go

PHARAOH'S HEART GREW HARD
Ex 7:13 And *Pharaoh's heart grew hard*, and he did not heed them, as the Lord had said
Ex 7:22 and *Pharaoh's heart grew hard*, and he did not heed them, as the Lord had said
Ex 8:19 But *Pharaoh's heart grew hard*, and he did not heed them, just as the Lord had said

PHARISEES AND DOCTORS OF THE LAW (KJV)
(See *PHARISEES AND TEACHERS OF THE LAW*)

PHARISEES AND TEACHERS OF THE LAW
Luke 5:17 Now it happened on a certain day, as He was teaching, that there were *Pharisees and teachers of the law* sitting by, who had come out of every town of Galilee, Judea, and Jerusalem

PHILISTINE RULERS (NIV)
(See *LORDS OF THE PHILISTINES*)

PHILOSOPHER OF THIS AGE (NIV)
(See *DISPUTER OF THIS AGE*)

PHYSICAL IS OF SOME VALUE (NIV)
(See *BODILY EXERCISE PROFITS A LITTLE*)

PHYSICIAN, HEAL YOURSELF
Luke 4:23 And He said to them, "You will surely say this proverb to Me, '*Physician, heal yourself*

PICK UP SERPENTS (NAS, RSV)
(See *TAKE UP SERPENTS*)

PICTURES OF SILVER (KJV)
(See *SETTINGS OF SILVER*)

PIECES OF SILVER (KJV)
(See *SHEKELS OF SILVER*)

PIERCED FOR OUR TRANSGRESSIONS (NIV)
(See *WOUNDED FOR OUR TRANSGRESSIONS*)

PIERCED HIS SIDE
John 19:34 But one of the soldiers *pierced His side* with a spear, and immediately blood and water came out

PIERCED JESUS' SIDE (NIV)
(See *PIERCED HIS SIDE*)

PIERCED MY HANDS AND MY FEET
Ps 22:16 The assembly of the wicked has enclosed Me. They *pierced My hands and My feet*

PILGRIMS ON THE EARTH
Heb 11:13 These all died in faith, not having received the promises, but having seen them afar off were assured of them, embraced them, and confessed that they were strangers and *pilgrims on the earth*

PILLAR OF CLOUD
Ex 13:21 And the Lord went before them by day in a *pillar of cloud* to lead the way, and by night in a pillar of fire to give them light, so as to go by day and night
Ex 13:22 He did not take away the *pillar of cloud* by day or the pillar of fire by night from before the people
Ex 14:19 and the *pillar of cloud* went from before them and stood behind them
Ex 33:9 And it came to pass, when Moses entered the tabernacle, that the *pillar of cloud* descended and stood at the door of the tabernacle, and the Lord talked with Moses
Ex 33:10 All the people saw the *pillar of cloud* standing at the tabernacle door, and all the people rose and worshiped, each man in his tent door
Num 12:5 Then the Lord came down in the *pillar of cloud* and stood in the door of the tabernacle, and called Aaron and Miriam
Num 14:14 and You go before them in a *pillar of cloud* by day and in a pillar of fire by night
Deut 31:15 Now the Lord appeared at the tabernacle in a *pillar of cloud*, and the *pillar of cloud* stood above the door of the tabernacle

PILLAR OF FIRE
Ex 13:21 And the Lord went before them by day in a pillar of cloud to lead the way, and by night in a *pillar of fire* to give them light, so as to go by day and night
Ex 13:22 He did not take away the pillar of cloud by day or the *pillar of fire* by night from before the people
Ex 14:24 Now it came to pass, in the morning watch, that the Lord looked down upon the army of the Egyptians through the *pillar of fire* and cloud, and He troubled the army of the Egyptians
Num 14:14 and You go before them in a pillar of cloud by day and in a *pillar of fire* by night
Neh 9:12 Moreover You led them by day with a cloudy pillar, and by night with a *pillar of fire*, to give them light on the road which they should travel
Neh 9:19 nor the *pillar of fire* by night, to show them light, and the way they should go

PILLAR OF SALT
Gen 19:26 But his wife looked back behind him, and she became a *pillar of salt*

PINNACLE OF THE TEMPLE
Matt 4:5 Then the devil took Him up into the holy city, set Him on the *pinnacle of the temple*
Luke 4:9 Then he brought Him to Jerusalem, set Him on the *pinnacle of the temple*, and said to Him

PIONEER AND PERFECTER OF OUR FAITH (RSV)
(See *AUTHOR AND FINISHER OF OUR FAITH*)

PIT OF CORRUPTION
Is 38:17 but You have lovingly delivered my soul from the *pit of corruption*, for You have cast all my sins behind Your back

PIT OF DESTRUCTION (NIV, RSV)
(See *PIT OF CORRUPTION*)

PITCHED HIS TENT
Gen 12:8 And he moved from there to the mountain east of Bethel, and he *pitched his tent* with Bethel on the west and Ai on the east
Gen 13:12 Abram dwelt in the land of Canaan, and Lot dwelt in the cities of the plain and *pitched his tent* even as far as Sodom
Gen 26:17 Then Isaac departed from there and *pitched his tent* in the Valley of Gerar, and dwelt there
Gen 26:25 So he built an altar there and called on the name of the Lord, and he *pitched his tent* there
Gen 31:25 Now Jacob had *pitched his tent* in the mountains, and Laban with his brethren pitched in the mountains of Gilead
Gen 33:18 Then Jacob came safely to the city of Shechem, which is in the land of Canaan, when he came from Padan Aram; and he *pitched his tent* before the city
Gen 33:19 And he bought the parcel of land, where he had *pitched his tent*, from the children of Hamor, Shechem's father, for one hundred pieces of money
Gen 35:21 Then Israel journeyed and *pitched his tent* beyond the tower of Eder
Judg 4:11 Now Heber the Kenite, of the children of Hobab the father-in-law of Moses, had separated himself from the Kenites and *pitched his tent* near the terebinth tree at Zaanaim, which is beside Kedesh

PITY THE MAN (NIV)
(See *WOE TO HIM*)

PLACE THE LORD WILL CHOOSE (NIV)
(See *PLACE WHICH THE LORD CHOOSES*)

PLACE WHERE THE LORD YOUR GOD CHOOSES
Deut 12:5 But you shall seek the *place where the Lord your God chooses*, out of all your tribes, to put His name for His habitation
Deut 12:11 then there will be the *place where the Lord your God chooses* to make His name abide
Deut 12:21 If the *place where the Lord your God chooses* to put His name is too far from you, then you may slaughter from your herd and from your flock which the Lord has given you, just as I have commanded you, and you may eat within your gates as much as your heart desires
Deut 14:24 But if the journey is too long for you, so that you are not able to carry the tithe, or if the *place where the Lord your God chooses* to put His name is too far from you, when the Lord your God has blessed you
Deut 16:6 but at the *place where the Lord your God chooses* to make His name abide, there you shall sacrifice the Passover at twilight, at the going down of the sun, at the time you came out of Egypt
Deut 16:11 You shall rejoice before the Lord your God, you and your son and your daughter, your manservant and your maidservant, the Levite who is within your gates, the stranger and the fatherless and the widow who are among you, at the *place where the Lord your God chooses* to make His name abide
Deut 26:2 that you shall take some of the first of all the produce of the ground, which you shall bring from your land that the Lord your God is giving you, and put it in a basket and go to the *place where the Lord your God chooses* to make His name abide

PLACE WHICH THE LORD CHOOSES
Deut 12:14 but in the *place which the Lord chooses*, in one of your tribes, there you shall offer your burnt offerings, and there you shall do all that I command you
Deut 12:26 Only the holy things which you have, and your vowed offerings, you shall take and go to the *place which the Lord chooses*
Deut 15:20 You and your household shall eat it

before the Lord your God year by year in the *place which the Lord chooses*

Deut 16:15 Seven days you shall keep a sacred feast to the Lord your God in the *place which the Lord chooses*, because the Lord your God will bless you in all your produce and in all the work of your hands, so that you surely rejoice

Deut 17:10 You shall do according to the sentence which they pronounce upon you in that *place which the Lord chooses*

Deut 18:6 And if a Levite comes from any of your gates, from where he sojourns among all Israel, and comes with all the desire of his mind to the *place which the Lord chooses*

PLACED IT IN A TOMB (NIV)
(See *LAID HIM IN A TOMB*)

PLAIN OF MEGIDDO

Zech 12:11 In that day there shall be a great mourning in Jerusalem, like the mourning at Hadad Rimmon in the *plain of Megiddo*

PLAN EVIL (RSV)
(See *DEVISE EVIL*)

PLAN FOR THE FULNESS (RSV)
(See *DISPENSATION OF THE FULLNESS*)

PLANK IN YOUR OWN EYE

Matt 7:3 And why do you look at the speck in your brother's eye, but do not consider the *plank in your own eye*

Luke 6:41 And why do you look at the speck in your brother's eye, but do not perceive the *plank in your own eye*

PLANNED EVIL (NIV)
(See *DEVISED EVIL*)

PLANT VINEYARDS

Deut 28:39 You shall *plant vineyards* and tend them, but you shall neither drink of the wine nor gather the grapes

2Kin 19:29 also in the third year sow and reap, *plant vineyards* and eat the fruit of them

Ps 107:37 And sow fields and *plant vineyards*, that they may yield a fruitful harvest

Is 37:30 also in the third year sow and reap, *plant vineyards*, and eat the fruit of them

Is 65:21 They shall build houses and inhabit them; they shall *plant vineyards* and eat their fruit

Ezek 28:26 And they will dwell safely there, build houses, and *plant vineyards*

Amos 9:14 they shall *plant vineyards* and drink wine from them; they shall also make gardens and eat fruit from them

Zeph 1:13 They shall build houses, but not inhabit them; they shall *plant vineyards*, but not drink their wine

PLANTED TOGETHER IN THE LIKENESS OF (KJV)
(See *UNITED TOGETHER IN THE LIKENESS OF*)

PLAUSIBLE WORDS (RSV)
(See *PERSUASIVE WORDS*)

PLAY THE HARLOT

Ex 34:15 lest you make a covenant with the inhabitants of the land, and they *play the harlot* with their gods and make sacrifice to their gods, and one of them invites you and you eat of his sacrifice

Ex 34:16 and you take of his daughters for your sons, and his daughters *play the harlot* with their gods and make your sons *play the harlot* with their gods

Deut 22:21 then they shall bring out the young woman to the door of her father's house, and the men of her city shall stone her to death with stones, because she has done a disgraceful thing in Israel, to *play the harlot* in her father's house

Deut 31:16 and this people will rise and *play the harlot* with the gods of the foreigners of the land, where they go to be among them, and they will forsake Me and break My covenant which I have made with them

2Chr 21:13 but have walked in the way of the kings of Israel, and have made Judah and the inhabitants of Jerusalem to *play the harlot* like the harlotry of the house of Ahab, and also have killed your brothers, those of your father's household, who were better than yourself

Ezek 6:9 Then those of you who escape will remember Me among the nations where they are carried captive, because I was crushed by their adulterous heart which has departed from Me, and by their eyes which *play the harlot* after their idols

Hos 3:3 you shall not *play the harlot*, nor shall you have a man

Hos 4:15 Though you, Israel, *play the harlot*, let not Judah offend

PLAYED THE FOOL

1Sam 26:21 For I will harm you no more, because my life was precious in your eyes this day. Indeed I have *played the fool* and erred exceedingly

PLAYED THE HARLOT

Gen 38:24 And it came to pass, about three months after, that Judah was told, saying, "Tamar your daughter-in-law has *played the harlot*

Lev 17:7 They shall no more offer their sacrifices to demons, after whom they have *played the harlot*

Judg 2:17 Yet they would not listen to their judges, but they *played the harlot* with other gods, and bowed down to them

Judg 8:27 And all Israel *played the harlot* with it there. It became a snare to Gideon and to his house

Judg 8:33 And it was so, as soon as Gideon was dead, that the children of Israel again *played the harlot* with the Baals, and made Baal-Berith their god

Judg 19:2 But his concubine *played the harlot* against him, and went away from him to her father's house at Bethlehem in Judah, and was there four whole months

1Chr 5:25 And they were unfaithful to the God of their fathers, and *played the harlot* after the gods of the peoples of the land, whom God had destroyed before them

Ps 106:39 Thus they were defiled by their own works, and *played the harlot* by their own deeds

Jer 3:1 But you have *played the harlot* with many lovers; yet return to Me

Jer 3:6 She has gone up on every high mountain and under every green tree, and there *played the harlot*

Jer 3:8 yet her treacherous sister Judah did not fear, but went and *played the harlot* also

Ezek 16:15 But you trusted in your own beauty, *played the harlot* because of your fame, and poured out your harlotry on everyone passing by who would have it

Ezek 16:16 You took some of your garments and adorned multicolored high places for yourself, and *played the harlot* on them

Ezek 16:17 You have also taken your beautiful jewelry from My gold and My silver, which I had

given you, and made for yourself male images and *played the harlot* with them
Ezek 16:28 You also *played the harlot* with the Assyrians, because you were insatiable; indeed you *played the harlot* with them and still were not satisfied
Ezek 23:5 Oholah *played the harlot* even though she was Mine; and she lusted for her lovers, the neighboring Assyrians
Ezek 23:19 Yet she multiplied her harlotry in calling to remembrance the days of her youth, when she had *played the harlot* in the land of Egypt
Hos 2:5 For their mother has *played the harlot;* she who conceived them has done shamefully
Hos 4:12 For the spirit of harlotry has caused them to stray, and they have *played the harlot* against their God
Hos 9:1 Do not rejoice, O Israel, with joy like other peoples, for you have *played the harlot* against your God

PLEAD FOR THE WIDOW
Is 1:17 seek justice, reprove the oppressor; defend the fatherless, *plead for the widow*

PLEAD MY CASE
1Sam 24:15 Therefore let the Lord be judge, and judge between you and me, and see and *plead my case*, and deliver me out of your hand
Jer 2:35 Behold, I will *plead My case* against you, because you say
Ezek 20:35 And I will bring you into the wilderness of the peoples, and there I will *plead My case* with you face to face
Ezek 20:36 Just as I pleaded My case with your fathers in the wilderness of the land of Egypt, so I will *plead My case* with you

PLEAD YOUR CASE
Jer 51:36 Behold, I will *plead your case* and take vengeance for you
Mic 6:1 Arise, *plead your case* before the mountains, and let the hills hear your voice

PLEADED THE CASE
Lam 3:58 O Lord, You have *pleaded the case* for my soul

PLEADED WITH GOD
2Sam 12:16 David therefore *pleaded with God* for the child, and David fasted and went in and lay all night on the ground

PLEADED WITH THE LORD
Gen 25:21 Now Isaac *pleaded with the Lord* for his wife, because she was barren
Ex 32:11 Then Moses *pleaded with the Lord* his God, and said
Deut 3:23 Then I *pleaded with the Lord* at that time, saying
2Kin 13:4 So Jehoahaz *pleaded with the Lord*, and the Lord listened to him
2Cor 12:8 Concerning this thing I *pleaded with the Lord* three times that it might depart from me

PLEADS MY CASE
Mic 7:9 I will bear the indignation of the Lord, because I have sinned against Him, until He *pleads my case* and executes justice for me

PLEASANT LAND (KJV)
(See *GLORIOUS LAND*)

PLEASANT TO THE EYES
Gen 3:6 So when the woman saw that the tree was good for food, that it was *pleasant to the eyes*, and a tree desirable to make one wise, she took of its fruit and ate

PLEASANT VINEYARD (RSV)
(See *VINEYARD OF RED WINE*)

PLEASING ODOR (RSV)
(See *SWEET INCENSE*)

PLEASING ODOR TO THE LORD (RSV)
(See *SWEET AROMA TO THE LORD*)

PLEASING TO GOD
Acts 7:20 At this time Moses was born, and was well *pleasing to God*
Phil 4:18 I am full, having received from Epaphroditus the things which were sent from you, a sweet-smelling aroma, an acceptable sacrifice, well *pleasing to God*

PLEASING TO THE EYE (NIV)
(See *PLEASANT TO THE EYES*)

PLEASING TO THE LORD (RSV)
(See *ACCEPTABLE TO THE LORD*)

PLEASURE OF THE LORD
Is 53:10 When You make His soul an offering for sin, He shall see His seed, He shall prolong His days, and the *pleasure of the Lord* shall prosper in His hand

PLEASURES OF SIN
Heb 11:25 choosing rather to suffer affliction with the people of God than to enjoy the passing *pleasures of sin*

PLENTEOUS IN MERCY (KJV)
(See *ABOUNDING IN MERCY*)

PLIGHTED MY TROTH TO YOU (RSV)
(See *SWORE AN OATH TO*)

PLOT HARM (NIV)
(See *DEVISE EVIL*)

PLOWED WITH MY HEIFER
Judg 14:18 If you had not *plowed with my heifer*, you would not have solved my riddle

PLOWSHARES INTO SWORDS
Joel 3:10 Beat your *plowshares into swords* and your pruninghooks into spears

PLUCK THEM OUT OF MY HAND (KJV)
(See *SNATCH THEM OUT OF MY HAND*)

PLUCKED OFF THE HAIR (KJV)
(See *PLUCKED OUT THE BEARD*)

PLUCKED OUT THE BEARD
Is 50:6 I gave My back to those who struck Me, and My cheeks to those who *plucked out the beard*

PLUMB LINE
Amos 7:7 Behold, the Lord stood on a wall made with a *plumb line*, with a *plumb line* in His hand
Amos 7:8 And I said, "A *plumb line*." Then the Lord said: "Behold, I am setting a *plumb line* in the midst of My people Israel
Zech 4:10 for these seven rejoice to see the *plumb line* in the hand of Zerubbabel

PLUNDER THE EGYPTIANS
Ex 3:22 and you shall put them on your sons and on your daughters. So you shall *plunder the Egyptians*

PLUNDERING OF THE DAUGHTER OF MY PEOPLE
Is 22:4 do not labor to comfort me because of the *plundering of the daughter of my people*

POINT OF DEATH
Judg 5:18 Zebulun is a people who jeopardized their lives to the *point of death*, Naphtali also, on the heights of the battlefield
Mark 5:23 and begged Him earnestly, saying, "My little daughter lies at the *point of death*
John 4:47 When he heard that Jesus had come out of Judea into Galilee, he went to Him and implored Him to come down and heal his son, for he was at the *point of death*
Phil 2:8 And being found in appearance as a man, He humbled Himself and became obedient to the *point of death*, even the death of the cross

POLLUTE THE LAND
Num 35:33 So you shall not *pollute the land* where you are

POLLUTE THE SANCTUARY (KJV)
(See *DEFILE THE SANCTUARY*)

POLLUTED BY THE WORLD (NIV)
(See *UNSPOTTED FROM THE WORLD*)

POLLUTED MY SABBATHS (KJV)
(See *PROFANED MY SABBATHS*)

POLLUTES THE LAND (NAS, RSV)
(See *DEFILES THE LAND*)

POLLUTIONS OF THE WORLD
2Pet 2:20 For if, after they have escaped the *pollutions of the world* through the knowledge of the Lord and Savior Jesus Christ, they are again entangled in them and overcome, the latter end is worse for them than the beginning

PONDERED THEM IN HER HEART
Luke 2:19 But Mary kept all these things and *pondered them in her heart*

PONDERS IT IN HIS HEART (NIV)
(See *TAKES IT TO HEART*)

POOR ALWAYS YE HAVE WITH YOU (KJV)
(See *POOR YOU HAVE WITH YOU*)

POOR AND NEEDY
Deut 24:14 You shall not oppress a hired servant who is *poor and needy*, whether one of your brethren or one of the aliens who is in your land within your gates
Job 24:14 he kills the *poor and needy;* and in the night he is like a thief
Ps 37:14 The wicked have drawn the sword and have bent their bow, to cast down the *poor and needy*, to slay those who are of upright conduct
Ps 40:17 But I am *poor and needy;* yet the Lord thinks upon me
Ps 70:5 But I am *poor and needy;* make haste to me, O God
Ps 72:13 He will spare the *poor and needy*, and will save the souls of the needy
Ps 74:21 Oh, do not let the oppressed return ashamed! Let the *poor and needy* praise Your name
Ps 82:4 Deliver the *poor and needy;* free them from the hand of the wicked
Ps 86:1 Bow down Your ear, O Lord, hear me; for I am *poor and needy*
Ps 109:16 Because he did not remember to show mercy, but persecuted the *poor and needy* man, that he might even slay the broken in heart
Ps 109:22 For I am *poor and needy*, and my heart is wounded within me
Prov 31:9 Open your mouth, judge righteously, and plead the cause of the *poor and needy*
Is 41:17 When the *poor and needy* seek water, and there is none, and their tongues fail for thirst, I, the Lord, will hear them
Jer 22:16 He judged the cause of the *poor and needy;* then it was well
Ezek 16:49 neither did she strengthen the hand of the *poor and needy*
Ezek 18:12 if he has oppressed the *poor and needy*, robbed by violence, not restored the pledge, lifted his eyes to the idols, or committed abomination
Ezek 22:29 The people of the land have used oppressions, committed robbery, and mistreated the *poor and needy*

POOR AND THE MAIMED
Luke 14:21 Then the master of the house, being angry, said to his servant, 'Go out quickly into the streets and lanes of the city, and bring in here the *poor and the maimed* and the lame and the blind

POOR ARE DESPOILED (RSV)
(See *OPPRESSION OF THE POOR*)

POOR HAVE HOPE
Job 5:16 So the *poor have hope*, and injustice shuts her mouth

POOR IN THE EYES OF THE WORLD (NIV)
(See *POOR OF THIS WORLD*)

POOR MAN PLEADS (NIV)
(See *POOR MAN USES ENTREATIES*)

POOR MAN USES ENTREATIES
Prov 18:23 The *poor man uses entreaties*, but the rich answers roughly

POOR OF THE EARTH (NIV)
(See *MEEK OF THE EARTH*)

POOR OF THE LAND
2Kin 25:12 But the captain of the guard left some of the *poor of the land* as vinedressers and farmers
Job 24:4 They push the needy off the road, so that the *poor of the land* are forced to hide
Jer 52:16 But Nebuzaradan the captain of the guard left some of the *poor of the land* as vinedressers and farmers
Amos 8:4 Hear this, you who swallow up the needy, and make the *poor of the land* fail

POOR OF THIS WORLD
Jas 2:5 Has God not chosen the *poor of this world* to be rich in faith and heirs of the kingdom which He promised to those who love Him

POOR USETH ENTREATIES (KJV)
(See *POOR MAN USES ENTREATIES*)

POOR WIDOW
Mark 12:42 Then one *poor widow* came and threw in two mites, which make a quadrans
Mark 12:43 So He called His disciples to Him and said to them, "Assuredly, I say to you that this *poor widow* has put in more than all those who have given to the treasury
Luke 21:2 and He saw also a certain *poor widow* putting in two mites
Luke 21:3 So He said, "Truly I say to you that this *poor widow* has put in more than all

POOR WILL NEVER CEASE
Deut 15:11 For the *poor will never cease* from the land; therefore I command you, saying

POOR YOU HAVE WITH YOU
John 12:8 For the *poor you have with you* always, but Me you do not have always

POOREST OF THE POOR (NIV)
(See *FIRSTBORN OF THE POOR*)

POOREST PEOPLE OF THE LAND (NIV)
(See *POOR OF THE LAND*)

PORTION IN THE LORD (NAS, RSV)
(See *PART IN THE LORD*)

PORTION OF JACOB
Jer 10:16 The *Portion of Jacob* is not like them, for He is the Maker of all things, and Israel is the tribe of His inheritance
Jer 51:19 The *Portion of Jacob* is not like them, for He is the Maker of all things

POSSESS THE LAND
Deut 1:8 go in and *possess the land* which the Lord swore to your fathers to Abraham, Isaac, and Jacob to give to them and their descendants after them
Deut 3:20 until the Lord has given rest to your brethren as to you, and they also *possess the land* which the Lord your God is giving them beyond the Jordan
Deut 4:1 Now, O Israel, listen to the statutes and the judgments which I teach you to observe, that you may live, and go in and *possess the land* which the Lord God of your fathers is giving you
Deut 8:1 Every commandment which I command you today you must be careful to observe, that you may live and multiply, and go in and *possess the land* of which the Lord swore to your fathers
Deut 9:23 Likewise, when the Lord sent you from Kadesh Barnea, saying, 'Go up and *possess the land* which I have given you
Deut 10:11 Then the Lord said to me, 'Arise, begin your journey before the people, that they may go in and *possess the land* which I swore to their fathers to give them
Deut 11:8 Therefore you shall keep every commandment which I command you today, that you may be strong, and go in and *possess the land* which you cross over to possess
Deut 11:31 For you will cross over the Jordan and go in to *possess the land* which the Lord your God is giving you, and you will possess it and dwell in it
Josh 1:11 Pass through the camp and command the people, saying, 'Prepare provisions for yourselves, for within three days you will cross over this Jordan, to go in to *possess the land* which the Lord your God is giving you to possess
Josh 18:3 How long will you neglect to go and *possess the land* which the Lord God of your fathers has given you
Judg 2:6 And when Joshua had dismissed the people, the children of Israel went each to his own inheritance to *possess the land*
Judg 18:9 Do not hesitate to go, that you may enter to *possess the land*
Neh 9:15 You gave them bread from heaven for their hunger, and brought them water out of the rock for their thirst, and told them to go in to *possess the land* which You had sworn to give them
Is 14:21 Prepare slaughter for his children because of the iniquity of their fathers, lest they rise up and *possess the land*, and fill the face of the world with cities
Is 57:13 But he who puts his trust in Me shall *possess the land*, and shall inherit My holy mountain
Ezek 33:25 You eat meat with blood, you lift up your eyes toward your idols, and shed blood. Should you then *possess the land*
Ezek 33:26 You rely on your sword, you commit abominations, and you defile one another's wives. Should you then *possess the land*
Amos 2:10 Also it was I who brought you up from the land of Egypt, and led you forty years through the wilderness, to *possess the land* of the Amorite
Obad 20 And the captives of this host of the children of Israel shall *possess the land* of the Canaanites as far as Zarephath

POSSESS THEIR LAND
Deut 9:5 It is not because of your righteousness or the uprightness of your heart that you go in to *possess their land*, but because of the wickedness of these nations that the Lord your God drives them out from before you, and that He may fulfill the word which the Lord swore to your fathers, to Abraham, Isaac, and Jacob
Josh 23:5 So you shall *possess their land*, as the Lord your God has promised you
Josh 24:8 But I gave them into your hand, that you might *possess their land*, and I destroyed them from before you

POSSESSED BY A DEMON (NIV)
(See *ONE WHO HAS A DEMON*)

POSSESSED HIS LAND (KJV)
(See *TOOK POSSESSION OF HIS LAND*)

POSSESSED THE LAND
Neh 9:24 So the people went in and *possessed the land;* you subdued before them the inhabitants of the land, the Canaanites, and gave them into their hands, with their kings and the people of the land, that they might do with them as they would
Job 22:8 But the mighty man *possessed the land*, and the honorable man dwelt in it

POSSESSION OF THE LAND (NIV)
(See *POSSESSED THE LAND*)

POSSESSION OF THEIR LAND (NIV)
(See *POSSESS THEIR LAND*)

POSSESSOR OF HEAVEN AND EARTH
Gen 14:19 Blessed be Abram of God Most High, *Possessor of heaven and earth*
Gen 14:22 But Abram said to the king of Sodom, "I have lifted my hand to the Lord, God Most High, the *Possessor of heaven and earth*

POTTAGE OF LENTILS (KJV, RSV)
(See *STEW OF LENTILS*)

POTTERY FOR NOBLE PURPOSES (NIV)
(See *VESSEL FOR HONOR*)

POUR OUT MY SPIRIT
Prov 1:23 Surely I will *pour out my spirit* on you; I will make my words known to you
Joel 2:28 And it shall come to pass afterward that I will *pour out My Spirit* on all flesh
Joel 2:29 And also on My menservants and on My maidservants I will *pour out My Spirit* in those days
Acts 2:18 and on My menservants and on My maidservants I will *pour out My Spirit* in those days

POUR OUT MY WRATH
Hos 5:10 I will *pour out my wrath* on them like water

POUR OUT YOUR WRATH
Ps 79:6 *Pour out Your wrath* on the nations that do not know You, and on the kingdoms that do not call on Your name

POURED OUT FOR MANY (NAS, NIV, RSV)
(See *SHED FOR MANY*)

POURED OUT FOR YOU (NAS, NIV, RSV)
(See *SHED FOR YOU*)

POURED OUT HIS BOWL
Rev 16:2 So the first went and *poured out his bowl* upon the earth, and a foul and loathsome sore came upon the men who had the mark of the beast and those who worshiped his image
Rev 16:3 Then the second angel *poured out his bowl* on the sea, and it became blood as of a dead man
Rev 16:4 Then the third angel *poured out his bowl* on the rivers and springs of water, and they became blood
Rev 16:8 Then the fourth angel *poured out his bowl* on the sun, and power was given to him to scorch men with fire
Rev 16:10 Then the fifth angel *poured out his bowl* on the throne of the beast, and his kingdom became full of darkness
Rev 16:12 Then the sixth angel *poured out his bowl* on the great river Euphrates, and its water was dried up, so that the way of the kings from the east might be prepared
Rev 16:17 Then the seventh angel *poured out his bowl* into the air, and a loud voice came out of the temple of heaven, from the throne, saying

POURED OUT INNOCENT BLOOD (RSV)
(See *SHED INNOCENT BLOOD*)

POURED OUT MY FURY
Ezek 22:22 then you shall know that I, the Lord, have *poured out My fury* on you
Ezek 36:18 Therefore I *poured out My fury* on them for the blood they had shed on the land, and for their idols with which they had defiled it

POWER AGAINST UNCEAN SPIRITS (KJV)
(See *POWER OVER UNCLEAN SPIRITS*)

POWER AND MIGHT
1Chr 29:12 In Your hand is *power and might;* in Your hand it is to make great and to give strength to all
2Chr 20:6 O Lord God of our fathers, are You not God in heaven, and do You not rule over all the kingdoms of the nations, and in Your hand is there not *power and might*, so that no one is able to withstand You
Eph 1:21 far above all principality and *power and might* and dominion, and every name that is named, not only in this age but also in that which is to come
2Pet 2:11 whereas angels, who are greater in *power and might*, do not bring a reviling accusation against them before the Lord
Rev 7:12 Blessing and glory and wisdom, thanksgiving and honor and *power and might*, be to our God forever and ever

POWER BELONGS TO GOD
Ps 62:11 God has spoken once, twice I have heard this: That *power belongs to God*

POWER FROM ON HIGH
Luke 24:49 but tarry in the city of Jerusalem until you are endued with *power from on high*

POWER IS MADE PERFECT (NIV, RSV)
(See *STRENGTH IS MADE PERFECT*)

POWER OF CHRIST
2Cor 12:9 Therefore most gladly I will rather boast in my infirmities, that the *power of Christ* may rest upon me

POWER OF DARKNESS
Luke 22:53 But this is your hour, and the *power of darkness*
Col 1:13 He has delivered us from the *power of darkness* and translated us into the kingdom of the Son of His love

POWER OF GOD
Matt 22:29 Jesus answered and said to them, "You are mistaken, not knowing the Scriptures nor the *power of God*
Mark 12:24 Jesus answered and said to them, "Are you not therefore mistaken, because you do not know the Scriptures nor the *power of God*
Luke 22:69 Hereafter the Son of Man will sit on the right hand of the *power of God*
Acts 8:10 to whom they all gave heed, from the least to the greatest, saying, "This man is the great *power of God*
Rom 1:16 For I am not ashamed of the gospel of Christ, for it is the *power of God* to salvation for everyone who believes, for the Jew first and also for the Greek
1Cor 1:18 For the message of the cross is foolishness to those who are perishing, but to us who are being saved it is the *power of God*
1Cor 1:24 but to those who are called, both Jews and Greeks, Christ the *power of God* and the wisdom of God
1Cor 2:5 that your faith should not be in the wisdom of men but in the *power of God*
2Cor 6:7 by the word of truth, by the *power of God*, by the armor of righteousness on the right hand and on the left
2Cor 13:4 For though He was crucified in weakness, yet He lives by the *power of God*. For we also are weak in Him, but we shall live with Him by the *power of God* toward you
2Tim 1:8 Therefore do not be ashamed of the testimony of our Lord, nor of me His prisoner, but share with me in the sufferings for the gospel according to the *power of God*
1Pet 1:5 who are kept by the *power of God* through faith for salvation ready to be revealed in the last time

POWER OF HIS RESURRECTION
Phil 3:10 that I may know Him and the *power of His resurrection*, and the fellowship of His sufferings, being conformed to His death

POWER OF SHEOL (NAS, RSV)
(See *POWER OF THE GRAVE*)

POWER OF SIGNS AND MIRACLES (NIV)
(See *MIGHTY SIGNS AND WONDERS*)

POWER OF THE GRAVE
Ps 49:15 But God will redeem my soul from the *power of the grave*, for He shall receive me
Ps 89:48 Can he deliver his life from the *power of the grave*
Hos 13:14 I will ransom them from the *power of the grave*

POWER OF THE HIGHEST
Luke 1:35 And the angel answered and said to her, "The Holy Spirit will come upon you, and the *power of the Highest* will overshadow you

POWER OF THE LORD
Luke 5:17 And the *power of the Lord* was present to heal them

POWER OF THE MOST HIGH (NAS, NIV, RSV)
(See *POWER OF THE HIGHEST*)

POWER OF THE SPIRIT
Luke 4:14 Then Jesus returned in the *power of the Spirit* to Galilee, and news of Him went out through all the surrounding region
Rom 15:19 in mighty signs and wonders, by the *power of the Spirit* of God, so that from Jerusalem and round about to Illyricum I have fully preached the gospel of Christ

POWER ON EARTH
Matt 9:6 But that you may know that the Son of Man has *power on earth* to forgive sins
Mark 2:10 But that you may know that the Son of Man has *power on earth* to forgive sins
Luke 5:24 But that you may know that the Son of Man has *power on earth* to forgive sins

POWER OVER UNCLEAN SPIRITS
Matt 10:1 And when He had called His twelve disciples to Him, He gave them *power over unclean spirits*, to cast them out, and to heal all kinds of sickness and all kinds of disease
Mark 6:7 And He called the twelve to Him, and began to send them out two by two, and gave them *power over unclean spirits*

POWER TO CRUCIFY
John 19:10 Do You not know that I have *power to crucify* You, and power to release You

POWERS OF DEATH (RSV)
(See *GATES OF HADES*)

POWERS OF THIS DARK WORLD (NIV)
(See *RULERS OF THE DARKNESS OF THIS AGE*)

PRACTICE HOSPITALITY (NIV, RSV)
(See *GIVEN TO HOSPITALITY*)

PRAISE AND FAME
Zeph 3:19 I will appoint them for *praise and fame* in every land where they were put to shame

PRAISE AND HONOR (NIV)
(See *PRAISE AND FAME*)

PRAISE AND THANKSGIVING
Neh 12:46 For in the days of David and Asaph of old there were chiefs of the singers, and songs of *praise and thanksgiving* to God

PRAISE BE TO THE GOD (NIV)
(See *BLESSED BE THE GOD*)

PRAISE BE TO THE LORD (NIV)
(See *BLESSED BE THE LORD*)

PRAISE GOD
Ps 150:1 *Praise God* in His sanctuary; praise Him in His mighty firmament
Luke 19:37 Then, as He was now drawing near the descent of the Mount of Olives, the whole multitude of the disciples began to rejoice and *praise God* with a loud voice for all the mighty works they had seen

PRAISE OF HIS GLORY
Eph 1:12 that we who first trusted in Christ should be to the *praise of His glory*
Eph 1:14 who is the guarantee of our inheritance until the redemption of the purchased possession, to the *praise of His glory*

PRAISE THE LORD
Gen 29:35 And she conceived again and bore a son, and said, "Now I will *praise the Lord*
1Chr 16:4 And he appointed some of the Levites to minister before the ark of the Lord, to commemorate, to thank, and to *praise the Lord* God of Israel
1Chr 23:30 to stand every morning to thank and *praise the Lord*, and likewise at evening
1Chr 25:3 Gedaliah, Zeri, Jeshaiah, Shimei, Hashabiah, and Mattithiah, six, under the direction of their father Jeduthun, who prophesied with a harp to give thanks and to *praise the Lord*
2Chr 7:6 the Levites also with instruments of the music of the Lord, which King David had made to *praise the Lord*, saying
2Chr 20:19 Then the Levites of the children of the Kohathites and of the children of the Korahites stood up to *praise the Lord* God of Israel with voices loud and high
2Chr 20:21 And when he had consulted with the people, he appointed those who should sing to the Lord, and who should praise the beauty of holiness, as they went out before the army and were saying: "*Praise the Lord*, for His mercy endures forever
Ezra 3:10 When the builders laid the foundation of the temple of the Lord, the priests stood in their apparel with trumpets, and the Levites, the sons of Asaph, with cymbals, to *praise the Lord*, according to the ordinance of David king of Israel
Ps 7:17 I will *praise the Lord* according to His righteousness, and will sing praise to the name of the Lord Most High
Ps 22:26 Those who seek Him will *praise the Lord*. Let your heart live forever
Ps 33:2 *Praise the Lord* with the harp; make melody to Him with an instrument of ten strings
Ps 102:18 This will be written for the generation to come, that a people yet to be created may *praise the Lord*
Ps 104:35 May sinners be consumed from the earth, and the wicked be no more. Bless the Lord, O my soul! *Praise the Lord*
Ps 105:45 That they might observe His statutes and keep His laws. *Praise the Lord*
Ps 106:1 *Praise the Lord!* Oh, give thanks to the Lord, for He is good
Ps 106:48 And let all the people say, "Amen!" *Praise the Lord*
Ps 109:30 I will greatly *praise the Lord* with my mouth; yes, I will praise Him among the multitude
Ps 111:1 *Praise the Lord!* I will *praise the Lord* with my whole heart, in the assembly of the upright and in the congregation
Ps 112:1 *Praise the Lord!* Blessed is the man who fears the Lord, who delights greatly in His commandments
Ps 113:1 *Praise the Lord!* Praise, O servants of the Lord, praise the name of the Lord
Ps 113:9 He grants the barren woman a home, like a joyful mother of children. *Praise the Lord*
Ps 115:17 The dead do not *praise the Lord*, nor any who go down into silence
Ps 115:18 But we will bless the Lord from this time forth and forevermore. *Praise the Lord*
Ps 116:19 In the courts of the Lord's house, in the midst of you, O Jerusalem. *Praise the Lord*
Ps 117:1 Oh, *praise the Lord*, all you Gentiles! Laud Him, all you peoples

Ps 117:2 For His merciful kindness is great toward us, and the truth of the Lord endures forever. *Praise the Lord*
Ps 118:19 I will go through them, and I will *praise the Lord*
Ps 135:1 *Praise the Lord!* Praise the name of the Lord; praise Him, O you servants of the Lord
Ps 135:3 *Praise the Lord*, for the Lord is good; sing praises to His name, for it is pleasant
Ps 135:21 Blessed be the Lord out of Zion, Who dwells in Jerusalem! *Praise the Lord*
Ps 146:1 *Praise the Lord! Praise the Lord*, O my soul
Ps 146:2 While I live I will *praise the Lord;* I will sing praises to my God while I have my being
Ps 146:10 The Lord shall reign forever Your God, O Zion, to all generations. *Praise the Lord*
Ps 147:1 *Praise the Lord!* For it is good to sing praises to our God
Ps 147:12 *Praise the Lord*, O Jerusalem! Praise your God, O Zion
Ps 147:20 And as for His judgments, they have not known them. *Praise the Lord*
Ps 148:1 *Praise the Lord! Praise the Lord* from the heavens
Ps 148:7 *Praise the Lord* from the earth, you great sea creatures and all the depths
Ps 148:14 And He has exalted the horn of His people, the praise of all His saints of the children of Israel, a people near to Him. *Praise the Lord*
Ps 149:1 *Praise the Lord!* Sing to the Lord a new song, and His praise in the congregation of saints
Ps 149:9 To execute on them the written judgment this honor have all His saints. *Praise the Lord*
Ps 150:1 *Praise the Lord!* Praise God in His sanctuary; praise Him in His mighty firmament
Ps 150:6 Let everything that has breath *praise the Lord. Praise the Lord*
Is 12:4 *Praise the Lord*, call upon His name; declare His deeds among the peoples, make mention that His name is exalted
Is 62:9 But those who have gathered it shall eat it, and *praise the Lord*
Jer 20:13 *Praise the Lord!* For He has delivered the life of the poor from the hand of evildoers
Jer 33:11 *Praise the Lord* of hosts, for the Lord is good, for His mercy endures forever
Rom 15:11 *Praise the Lord*, all you Gentiles! laud Him, all you peoples

PRAISED GOD (NIV)
(See *GLORIFIED GOD*)

PRAISED THE LORD
1Chr 16:36 And all the people said, "Amen!" and *praised the Lord*
1Chr 23:5 four thousand were gatekeepers, and four thousand *praised the Lord* with musical instruments
2Chr 5:13 indeed it came to pass, when the trumpeters and singers were as one, to make one sound to be heard in praising and thanking the Lord, and when they lifted up their voice with the trumpets and cymbals and instruments of music, and *praised the Lord*, saying
2Chr 7:3 When all the children of Israel saw how the fire came down, and the glory of the Lord on the temple, they bowed their faces to the ground on the pavement, and worshiped and *praised the Lord*, saying
2Chr 30:21 and the Levites and the priests *praised the Lord* day by day, singing to the Lord, accompanied by loud instruments
Ezra 3:11 Then all the people shouted with a great shout, when they *praised the Lord*, because the foundation of the house of the Lord was laid
Neh 5:13 and *praised the Lord*. Then the people did according to this promise

PRAISES OF THE LORD
Ps 78:4 We will not hide them from their children, telling to the generation to come the *praises of the Lord*, and His strength and His wonderful works that He has done
Is 60:6 they shall bring gold and incense, and they shall proclaim the *praises of the Lord*
Is 63:7 I will mention the lovingkindnesses of the Lord and the *praises of the Lord*, according to all that the Lord has bestowed on us, and the great goodness toward the house of Israel, which He has bestowed on them according to His mercies, according to the multitude of His lovingkindnesses

PRAISEWORTHY DEEDS OF THE LORD (NIV)
(See *PRAISES OF THE LORD*)

PRAISING GOD (NIV)
(See *GLORIFYING GOD*)

PRAY FOR
Gen 20:7 for he is a prophet, and he will *pray for* you and you shall live
1Sam 12:19 And all the people said to Samuel, "*Pray for* your servants to the Lord your God, that we may not die
1Sam 12:23 Moreover, as for me, far be it from me that I should sin against the Lord in ceasing to *pray for* you
1Kin 13:6 Then the king answered and said to the man of God, "Please entreat the favor of the Lord your God, and *pray for* me, that my hand may be restored to me
Ezra 6:10 that they may offer sacrifices of sweet aroma to the God of heaven, and *pray for* the life of the king and his sons
Job 42:8 and My servant Job shall *pray for* you. For I will accept him, lest I deal with you according to your folly
Ps 122:6 *Pray for* the peace of Jerusalem: "May they prosper who love you
Jer 7:16 Therefore do not *pray for* this people, nor lift up a cry or prayer for them, nor make intercession to Me
Jer 11:14 Therefore do not *pray for* this people, or lift up a cry or prayer for them
Jer 14:11 Then the Lord said to me, "Do not *pray for* this people, for their good
Jer 42:2 and said to Jeremiah the prophet, "Please, let our petition be acceptable to you, and *pray for* us to the Lord your God, for all this remnant (since we are left but a few of many, as you can see
Jer 42:20 For you were hypocrites in your hearts when you sent me to the Lord your God, saying, '*Pray for* us to the Lord our God, and according to all that the Lord your God says, so declare to us and we will do it
Matt 5:44 But I say to you, love your enemies, bless those who curse you, do good to those who hate you, and *pray for* those who spitefully use you and persecute you
Luke 6:28 bless those who curse you, and *pray for* those who spitefully use you
John 17:9 I *pray for* them. I do not *pray for* the world but for those whom You have given Me, for they are Yours
John 17:20 I do not *pray for* these alone, but also for those who will believe in Me through their word
Rom 8:26 For we do not know what we should *pray for* as we ought, but the Spirit Himself makes intercession for us with groanings which cannot be uttered

Col 1:9 For this reason we also, since the day we heard it, do not cease to *pray for* you, and to ask that you may be filled with the knowledge of His will in all wisdom and spiritual understanding
1Th 5:25 Brethren, *pray for* us
2Th 3:1 Finally, brethren, *pray for* us, that the word of the Lord may have free course and be glorified, just as it is with you
Heb 13:18 *Pray for* us; for we are confident that we have a good conscience, in all things desiring to live honorably
Jas 5:16 Confess your trespasses to one another, and *pray for* one another, that you may be healed

PRAY FOR EACH OTHER (NIV)
(See *PRAY FOR ONE ANOTHER*)

PRAY FOR ONE ANOTHER
Jas 5:16 Confess your trespasses to one another, and *pray for one another*, that you may be healed

PRAY FOR THE PEACE OF JERUSALEM
Ps 122:6 *Pray for the peace of Jerusalem:* "May they prosper who love you

PRAY IN A TONGUE
1Cor 14:14 For if I *pray in a tongue*, my spirit prays, but my understanding is unfruitful

PRAY IN THE HOLY SPIRIT (NIV, RSV)
(See *PRAYING IN THE HOLY SPIRIT*)

PRAY TO THE LORD (NIV)
(See *ENTREAT THE LORD*)

PRAY WITH THE SPIRIT
1Cor 14:15 I will *pray with the spirit*, and I will also pray with the understanding

PRAY WITHOUT CEASING
1Th 5:17 *pray without ceasing*

PRAYED TO THE LORD
Num 11:2 Then the people cried out to Moses, and when Moses *prayed to the Lord*, the fire was quenched
Deut 9:26 Therefore I *prayed to the Lord*, and said: "O Lord God, do not destroy Your people and Your inheritance whom You have redeemed through Your greatness, whom You have brought out of Egypt with a mighty hand
Judg 13:8 Then Manoah *prayed to the Lord*, and said, "O my Lord, please let the Man of God whom You sent come to us again and teach us what we shall do for the child who will be born
1Sam 1:10 And she was in bitterness of soul, and *prayed to the Lord* and wept in anguish
1Sam 8:6 But the thing displeased Samuel when they said, "Give us a king to judge us." So Samuel *prayed to the Lord*
2Kin 4:33 He went in therefore, shut the door behind the two of them, and *prayed to the Lord*
2Kin 6:18 So when the Syrians came down to him, Elisha *prayed to the Lord*, and said
2Kin 20:2 Then he turned his face toward the wall, and *prayed to the Lord*, saying
2Chr 32:24 In those days Hezekiah was sick and near death, and he *prayed to the Lord*
Is 37:15 Then Hezekiah *prayed to the Lord*, saying
Is 38:2 Then Hezekiah turned his face toward the wall, and *prayed to the Lord*
Jer 32:16 Now when I had delivered the purchase deed to Baruch the son of Neriah, I *prayed to the Lord*, saying
Dan 9:4 And I *prayed to the Lord* my God, and made confession, and said
Jon 2:1 Then Jonah *prayed to the Lord* his God from the fish's belly
Jon 4:2 So he *prayed to the Lord*, and said, "Ah, Lord, was not this what I said when I was still in my country

PRAYER AND FASTING
Matt 17:21 However, this kind does not go out except by *prayer and fasting*
Mark 9:29 So He said to them, "This kind can come out by nothing but *prayer and fasting*

PRAYER OF A RIGHTEOUS MAN
Jas 5:16 The effective, fervent *prayer of a righteous man* avails much

PRAYERS MAY NOT BE HINDERED
1Pet 3:7 Likewise you husbands, dwell with them with understanding, giving honor to the wife, as to the weaker vessel, and as being heirs together of the grace of life, that your *prayers may not be hindered*

PRAYERS OF THE SAINTS
Rev 5:8 Now when He had taken the scroll, the four living creatures and the twenty-four elders fell down before the Lamb, each having a harp, and golden bowls full of incense, which are the *prayers of the saints*
Rev 8:4 And the smoke of the incense, with the *prayers of the saints*, ascended before God from the angel's hand

PRAYING IN THE HOLY SPIRIT
Jude 20 But you, beloved, building yourselves up on your most holy faith, *praying in the Holy Spirit*

PREACH CHRIST
1Cor 1:23 but we *preach Christ* crucified, to the Jews a stumbling block and to the Greeks foolishness
Phil 1:15 Some indeed *preach Christ* even from envy and strife, and some also from good will
Phil 1:16 The former *preach Christ* from selfish ambition, not sincerely, supposing to add affliction to my chains

PREACH DELIVERANCE
Luke 4:18 He has sent Me to heal the brokenhearted, to *preach deliverance* to the captives and recovery of sight to the blind, to set at liberty those who are oppressed

PREACH GOOD TIDINGS
Is 61:1 The Spirit of the Lord God is upon Me, because the Lord has anointed Me to *preach good tidings* to the poor

PREACH THE ACCEPTABLE YEAR
Luke 4:19 to *preach the acceptable year* of the Lord

PREACH THE GOOD NEWS (NIV)
(See *PREACH THE GOSPEL*)

PREACH THE GOSPEL
Mark 16:15 And He said to them, "Go into all the world and *preach the gospel* to every creature
Luke 4:18 The Spirit of the Lord is upon Me, because He has anointed Me to *preach the gospel* to the poor
Acts 16:10 Now after he had seen the vision, immediately we sought to go to Macedonia, concluding that the Lord had called us to *preach the gospel* to them
Rom 1:15 So, as much as is in me, I am ready to *preach the gospel* to you who are in Rome also
Rom 10:15 How beautiful are the feet of those

who *preach the gospel* of peace, who bring glad tidings of good things

Rom 15:20 And so I have made it my aim to *preach the gospel*, not where Christ was named, lest I should build on another man's foundation

1Cor 1:17 For Christ did not send me to baptize, but to *preach the gospel*, not with wisdom of words, lest the cross of Christ should be made of no effect

1Cor 9:14 Even so the Lord has commanded that those who *preach the gospel* should live from the gospel

1Cor 9:16 For if I *preach the gospel*, I have nothing to boast of, for necessity is laid upon me; yes, woe is me if I do not *preach the gospel*

1Cor 9:18 That when I *preach the gospel*, I may present the gospel of Christ without charge, that I may not abuse my authority in the gospel

2Cor 10:16 to *preach the gospel* in the regions beyond you, and not to boast in another man's sphere of accomplishment

PREACH THE WORD

Acts 16:6 Now when they had gone through Phrygia and the region of Galatia, they were forbidden by the Holy Spirit to *preach the word* in Asia

2Tim 4:2 *Preach the word!* Be ready in season and out of season

PREACHED THE GOSPEL

Luke 20:1 Now it happened on one of those days, as He taught the people in the temple and *preached the gospel*, that the chief priests and the scribes, together with the elders, confronted Him

Acts 14:21 And when they had *preached the gospel* to that city and made many disciples, they returned to Lystra, Iconium, and Antioch

Rom 15:19 in mighty signs and wonders, by the power of the Spirit of God, so that from Jerusalem and round about to Illyricum I have fully *preached the gospel* of Christ

2Cor 11:7 Did I commit sin in abasing myself that you might be exalted, because I *preached the gospel* of God to you free of charge

Gal 3:8 And the Scripture, foreseeing that God would justify the nations by faith, *preached the gospel* to Abraham beforehand, saying

Gal 4:13 You know that because of physical infirmity I *preached the gospel* to you at the first

1Pet 1:12 To them it was revealed that, not to themselves, but to us they were ministering the things which now have been reported to you through those who have *preached the gospel* to you by the Holy Spirit sent from heaven things which angels desire to look into

PREACHER OF RIGHTEOUSNESS

2Pet 2:5 and did not spare the ancient world, but saved Noah, one of eight people, a *preacher of righteousness*, bringing in the flood on the world of the ungodly

PREACHING BOLDLY (RSV)
(See *SPOKE BOLDLY*)

PREACHING THE GOSPEL

Matt 4:23 Now Jesus went about all Galilee, teaching in their synagogues, *preaching the gospel* of the kingdom, and healing all kinds of sickness and all kinds of disease among the people

Matt 9:35 And Jesus went about all the cities and villages, teaching in their synagogues, *preaching the gospel* of the kingdom, and healing every sickness and every disease among the people

Mark 1:14 Now after John was put in prison, Jesus came to Galilee, *preaching the gospel* of the kingdom of God

Luke 9:6 So they departed and went through the towns, *preaching the gospel* and healing everywhere

Acts 8:25 So when they had testified and preached the word of the Lord, they returned to Jerusalem, *preaching the gospel* in many villages of the Samaritans

Acts 14:7 And they were *preaching the gospel* there

PRECEPT UPON PRECEPT

Is 28:10 For precept must be upon precept, *precept upon precept*, line upon line, line upon line, here a little, there a little

Is 28:13 But the word of the Lord was to them, "*Precept upon precept, precept upon precept*, line upon line, line upon line, here a little, there a little

PRECEPTS OF THE LAW (RSV)
(See *RIGHTEOUS REQUIREMENTS OF THE LAW*)

PRECIOUS CORNERSTONE

Is 28:16 Behold, I lay in Zion a stone for a foundation, a tried stone, a *precious cornerstone*, a sure foundation

PRECIOUS IN THE SIGHT OF THE LORD

Ps 116:15 *Precious in the sight of the Lord* is the death of His saints

PRECIOUS OIL (NAS, RSV)
(See *PRECIOUS OINTMENT*)

PRECIOUS OINTMENT

2Kin 20:13 And Hezekiah was attentive to them, and showed them all the house of his treasures the silver and gold, the spices and *precious ointment*, and all his armory all that was found among his treasures

Eccl 7:1 A good name is better than *precious ointment*, and the day of death than the day of one's birth

Is 39:2 And Hezekiah was pleased with them, and showed them the house of his treasures the silver and gold, the spices and *precious ointment*, and all his armory all that was found among his treasures

PREDESTINED TO BE CONFORMED

Rom 8:29 For whom He foreknew, He also *predestined to be conformed* to the image of His Son, that He might be the firstborn among many brethren

PREPARATIONS FOR US TO EAT THE PASSOVER (NIV)
(See *PREPARE THE PASSOVER*)

PREPARE A PLACE

John 14:2 if it were not so, I would have told you. I go to *prepare a place* for you

John 14:3 And if I go and *prepare a place* for you, I will come again and receive you to Myself

PREPARE A TABLE

Ps 23:5 You *prepare a table* before me in the presence of my enemies

Ps 78:19 They said, "Can God *prepare a table* in the wilderness

Is 65:11 But you are those who forsake the Lord, who forget My holy mountain, who *prepare a table* for Gad, and who furnish a drink offering for Meni

PREPARE FOR BATTLE (NIV)
(See *GIRD YOURSELVES*)

PREPARE THE PASSOVER
Luke 22:8 And He sent Peter and John, saying, "Go and *prepare the Passover* for us, that we may eat

PREPARE THE WAY
Is 40:3 *Prepare the way* of the Lord; make straight in the desert a highway for our God
Is 57:14 *Prepare the way*, take the stumbling block out of the way of My people
Is 62:10 *Prepare the way* for the people; build up, build up the highway
Mal 3:1 Behold, I send My messenger, and he will *prepare the way* before Me
Matt 3:3 *Prepare the way* of the Lord, make His paths straight
Mark 1:3 *Prepare the way* of the Lord, make His paths straight
Luke 3:4 *Prepare the way* of the Lord, make His paths straight

PREPARE THEIR FOOD IN THE SUMMER
Prov 30:25 the ants are a people not strong, yet they *prepare their food in the summer*

PREPARE TO MEET YOUR GOD
Amos 4:12 and because I will do this to you, *prepare to meet your God*, O Israel

PREPARE YOUR MINDS (NIV)
(See *GIRD UP THE LOINS*)

PREPARE YOUR WAY
Matt 11:10 Behold, I send My messenger before Your face, who will *prepare Your way* before You
Mark 1:2 Behold, I send My messenger before Your face, who will *prepare Your way* before You
Luke 7:27 Behold, I send My messenger before Your face, who will *prepare Your way* before You

PREPARED FOR BATTLE (NIV)
(See *EXPERT IN WAR*)

PREPARED HIS THRONE
Ps 9:7 But the Lord shall endure forever; He has *prepared His throne* for judgment

PRESENCE OF GOD
Ps 68:2 As wax melts before the fire, so let the wicked perish at the *presence of God*
Ps 68:8 The heavens also dropped rain at the *presence of God;* Sinai itself was moved at the *presence of God*, the God of Israel
Luke 1:19 And the angel answered and said to him, "I am Gabriel, who stands in the *presence of God*, and was sent to speak to you and bring you these glad tidings
Heb 9:24 For Christ has not entered the holy places made with hands, which are copies of the true, but into heaven itself, now to appear in the *presence of God* for us

PRESENCE OF MY ENEMIES
Ps 23:5 You prepare a table before me in the *presence of my enemies*

PRESENCE OF THE LORD
Gen 3:8 And they heard the sound of the Lord God walking in the garden in the cool of the day, and Adam and his wife hid themselves from the *presence of the Lord* God among the trees of the garden
Gen 4:16 Then Cain went out from the *presence of the Lord* and dwelt in the land of Nod on the east of Eden
Gen 27:7 Bring me game and make savory food for me, that I may eat it and bless you in the *presence of the Lord* before my death
Judg 18:6 May the *presence of the Lord* be with you on your way
Job 1:12 Then Satan went out from the *presence of the Lord*
Job 2:7 Then Satan went out from the *presence of the Lord*, and struck Job with painful boils from the sole of his foot to the crown of his head
Ps 97:5 The mountains melt like wax at the *presence of the Lord*, at the *presence of the Lord* of the whole earth
Ps 114:7 Tremble, O earth, at the *presence of the Lord*, at the presence of the God of Jacob
Jer 4:26 I beheld, and indeed the fruitful land was a wilderness, and all its cities were broken down at the *presence of the Lord*, by His fierce anger
Jon 1:3 But Jonah arose to flee to Tarshish from the *presence of the Lord*. He went down to Joppa, and found a ship going to Tarshish; so he paid the fare, and went down into it, to go with them to Tarshish from the *presence of the Lord*
Jon 1:10 For the men knew that he fled from the *presence of the Lord*, because he had told them
Zeph 1:7 Be silent in the *presence of the Lord* God; for the day of the Lord is at hand, for the Lord has prepared a sacrifice
Hag 1:12 Then Zerubbabel the son of Shealtiel, and Joshua the son of Jehozadak, the high priest, with all the remnant of the people, obeyed the voice of the Lord their God, and the words of Haggai the prophet, as the Lord their God had sent him; and the people feared the *presence of the Lord*
Acts 3:19 Repent therefore and be converted, that your sins may be blotted out, so that times of refreshing may come from the *presence of the Lord*
2Th 1:9 These shall be punished with everlasting destruction from the *presence of the Lord* and from the glory of His power

PRESENT YOUR BODIES
Rom 12:1 I beseech you therefore, brethren, by the mercies of God, that you *present your bodies* a living sacrifice, holy, acceptable to God, which is your reasonable service

PRESENT YOUR CASE
Is 41:21 *Present your case*," says the Lord."Bring forth your strong reasons

PRESSED DOWN, SHAKEN TOGETHER
Luke 6:38 good measure, *pressed down, shaken together*, and running over will be put into your bosom

PRESSED IN THE SPIRIT (KJV)
(See *CONSTRAINED BY THE SPIRIT*)

PREVAIL AGAINST HIS ENEMIES
Is 42:13 He shall cry out, yes, shout aloud; He shall *prevail against His enemies*

PREVIOUS DAYS (NIV)
(See *FORMER DAYS*)

PRICE OF WISDOM
Job 28:18 No mention shall be made of coral or quartz, for the *price of wisdom* is above rubies
Prov 17:16 Why is there in the hand of a fool the purchase *price of wisdom*, since he has no heart for it

PRIDE GOES BEFORE DESTRUCTION
Prov 16:18 *Pride goes before destruction*, and a haughty spirit before a fall

PRIDE OF ISRAEL
Hos 5:5 The *pride of Israel* testifies to his face; therefore Israel and Ephraim stumble in their iniquity
Hos 7:10 And the *pride of Israel* testifies to his face, but they do not return to the Lord their God, nor seek Him for all this

PRIDE OF LIFE
1Jn 2:16 For all that is in the world the lust of the flesh, the lust of the eyes, and the *pride of life* is not of the Father but is of the world

PRIEST FOREVER
Ps 110:4 The Lord has sworn and will not relent, "You are a *priest forever* according to the order of Melchizedek
Heb 5:6 You are a *priest forever* according to the order of Melchizedek
Heb 6:20 where the forerunner has entered for us, even Jesus, having become High *Priest forever* according to the order of Melchizedek
Heb 7:17 You are a *priest forever* according to the order of Melchizedek
Heb 7:21 The Lord has sworn and will not relent, 'You are a *priest forever* according to the order of Melchizedek

PRIEST OF BAAL
2Kin 11:18 They thoroughly broke in pieces its altars and images, and killed Mattan the *priest of Baal* before the altars
2Chr 23:17 They broke in pieces its altars and images, and killed Mattan the *priest of Baal* before the altars

PRIESTHOOD PERMANENTLY (NAS, RSV)
(See *UNCHANGEABLE PRIESTHOOD*)

PRIESTS AND LEVITES
1Chr 13:2 And David said to all the congregation of Israel, "If it seems good to you, and if it is of the Lord our God, let us send out to our brethren everywhere who are left in all the land of Israel, and with them to the *priests and Levites* who are in their cities and their common-lands, that they may gather together to us
1Chr 24:6 And the scribe, Shemaiah the son of Nethaneel, one of the Levites, wrote them down before the king, the leaders, Zadok the priest, Ahimelech the son of Abiathar, and the heads of the fathers' houses of the *priests and Levites*, one father's house taken for Eleazar and one for Ithamar
1Chr 24:31 These also cast lots just as their brothers the sons of Aaron did, in the presence of King David, Zadok, Ahimelech, and the heads of the fathers' houses of the *priests and Levites*
2Chr 8:15 They did not depart from the command of the king to the *priests and Levites* concerning any matter or concerning the treasuries
2Chr 30:25 The whole congregation of Judah rejoiced, also the *priests and Levites*, all the congregation that came from Israel, the sojourners who came from the land of Israel, and those who dwelt in Judah
2Chr 31:2 And Hezekiah appointed the divisions of the priests and the Levites according to their divisions, each man according to his service, the *priests and Levites* for burnt offerings and peace offerings, to serve, to give thanks, and to praise in the gates of the camp of the Lord
Ezra 3:12 But many of the *priests and Levites* and heads of the fathers' houses, who were old men, who had seen the first temple, wept with a loud voice when the foundation of this temple was laid before their eyes
Ezra 7:13 I issue a decree that all those of the people of Israel and the *priests and Levites* in my realm, who volunteer to go up to Jerusalem, may go with you
Neh 8:13 Now on the second day the heads of the fathers' houses of all the people, with the *priests and Levites*, were gathered to Ezra the scribe, in order to understand the words of the Law
Neh 11:20 And the rest of Israel, of the *priests and Levites*, were in all the cities of Judah, everyone in his own inheritance
Neh 12:30 Then the *priests and Levites* purified themselves, and purified the people, the gates, and the wall
Neh 12:44 And at the same time some were appointed over the rooms of the storehouse for the offerings, the firstfruits, and the tithes, to gather into them from the fields of the cities the portions specified by the Law for the *priests and Levites;* for Judah rejoiced over the *priests and Levites* who ministered
Is 66:21 And I will also take some of them for *priests and Levites*
John 1:19 Now this is the testimony of John, when the Jews sent *priests and Levites* from Jerusalem to ask him

PRIME OF LIFE (NAS, NIV)
(See *FLOWER OF THEIR AGE*)

PRINCE AND A JUDGE
Ex 2:14 Then he said, "Who made you a *prince and a judge* over us

PRINCE OF LIFE
Acts 3:15 and killed the *Prince of life*, whom God raised from the dead, of which we are witnesses

PRINCE OF PEACE
Is 9:6 And His name will be called Wonderful, Counselor, Mighty God, Everlasting Father, *Prince of Peace*

PRINCIPALITIES AND POWERS
Eph 3:10 to the intent that now the manifold wisdom of God might be made known by the church to the *principalities and powers* in the heavenly places
Col 2:15 Having disarmed *principalities and powers*, He made a public spectacle of them, triumphing over them in it

PRISONER OF CHRIST JESUS
Phm 1 Paul, a *prisoner of Christ Jesus*, and Timothy our brother, to Philemon our beloved friend and fellow laborer

PRISONER OF JESUS CHRIST
Eph 3:1 For this reason I, Paul, the *prisoner of Jesus Christ* for you Gentiles
Phm 9 yet for love's sake I rather appeal to you being such a one as Paul, the aged, and now also a *prisoner of Jesus Christ*

PRIZE OF THE UPWARD CALL
Phil 3:14 I press toward the goal for the *prize of the upward call* of God in Christ Jesus

PROCESSION OF MY GOD
Ps 68:24 They have seen Your procession, O God, the *procession of my God*, my King, into the sanctuary

PROCESSION OF PROPHETS (NIV)
(See *GROUP OF PROPHETS*)

PROCLAIM A FAST
1Kin 21:9 And she wrote in the letters, saying, "*Proclaim a fast*, and seat Naboth with high honor among the people

PROCLAIM A SOLEMN ASSEMBLY
2Kin 10:20 And Jehu said, "*Proclaim a solemn assembly* for Baal." So they proclaimed it

PROCLAIM FREEDOM (NIV)
(See *PREACH DELIVERANCE*)

PROCLAIM LIBERTY
Lev 25:10 And you shall consecrate the fiftieth year, and *proclaim liberty* throughout all the land to all its inhabitants
Is 61:1 He has sent Me to heal the brokenhearted, to *proclaim liberty* to the captives, and the opening of the prison to those who are bound
Jer 34:8 This is the word that came to Jeremiah from the Lord, after King Zedekiah had made a covenant with all the people who were at Jerusalem to *proclaim liberty* to them
Jer 34:17 Behold, I *proclaim liberty* to you,' says the Lord 'to the sword, to pestilence, and to famine

PROCLAIM RELEASE (NAS, RSV)
(See *PREACH DELIVERANCE*)

PROCLAIM THE ACCEPTABLE YEAR
Is 61:2 to *proclaim the acceptable year* of the Lord, and the day of vengeance of our God

PROCLAIM THE LORD'S DEATH
1Cor 11:26 For as often as you eat this bread and drink this cup, you *proclaim the Lord's death* till He comes

PROCLAIM THE WORKS OF GOD (NIV)
(See *DECLARE THE WORK OF GOD*)

PROCLAIM THE YEAR OF THE LORDS FAVOR (NIV)
(See *PROCLAIM THE ACCEPTABLE YEAR*)

PROCLAIMED A FAST
1Kin 21:12 They *proclaimed a fast*, and seated Naboth with high honor among the people
2Chr 20:3 And Jehoshaphat feared, and set himself to seek the Lord, and *proclaimed a fast* throughout all Judah
Ezra 8:21 Then I *proclaimed a fast* there at the river of Ahava, that we might humble ourselves before our God, to seek from Him the right way for us and our little ones and all our possessions
Jer 36:9 Now it came to pass in the fifth year of Jehoiakim the son of Josiah, king of Judah, in the ninth month, that they *proclaimed a fast* before the Lord to all the people in Jerusalem, and to all the people who came from the cities of Judah to Jerusalem
Jon 3:5 So the people of Nineveh believed God, *proclaimed a fast*, and put on sackcloth, from the greatest to the least of them

PROCLAIMED ON THE HOUSETOPS
Luke 12:3 Therefore whatever you have spoken in the dark will be heard in the light, and what you have spoken in the ear in inner rooms will be *proclaimed on the housetops*

PRODUCE YOUR CAUSE (KJV)
(See *PRESENT YOUR CASE*)

PROFANE MY HOLY NAME
Lev 20:3 I will set My face against that man, and will cut him off from his people, because he has given some of his descendants to Molech, to defile My sanctuary and *profane My holy name*
Lev 22:2 Speak to Aaron and his sons, that they separate themselves from the holy things of the children of Israel, and that they do not *profane My holy name* in those things which they sanctify to Me
Lev 22:32 You shall not *profane My holy name*, but I will be hallowed among the children of Israel
Ezek 20:39 but *profane My holy name* no more with your gifts and your idols
Ezek 39:7 So I will make My holy name known in the midst of My people Israel, and I will not let them *profane My holy name* anymore

PROFANE THE NAME
Lev 18:21 And you shall not let any of your descendants pass through the fire to Molech, nor shall you *profane the name* of your God
Lev 19:12 And you shall not swear by My name falsely, nor shall you *profane the name* of your God
Lev 21:6 They shall be holy to their God and not *profane the name* of their God, for they offer the offerings of the Lord made by fire, and the bread of their God
Prov 30:9 Or lest I be poor and steal, and *profane the name* of my God

PROFANE THE SABBATH
Neh 13:17 Then I contended with the nobles of Judah, and said to them, "What evil thing is this that you do, by which you *profane the Sabbath* day
Matt 12:5 Or have you not read in the law that on the Sabbath the priests in the temple *profane the Sabbath*, and are blameless

PROFANE THE TEMPLE (RSV)
(See *DEFILE THE SANCTUARY*)

PROFANED MY SABBATHS
Ezek 20:16 because they despised My judgments and did not walk in My statutes, but *profaned My Sabbaths*
Ezek 20:21 but they *profaned My Sabbaths*. Then I said I would pour out My fury on them and fulfill My anger against them in the wilderness
Ezek 20:24 because they had not executed My judgments, but had despised My statutes, *profaned My Sabbaths*, and their eyes were fixed on their fathers' idols
Ezek 22:8 You have despised My holy things and *profaned My Sabbaths*
Ezek 23:38 They have defiled My sanctuary on the same day and *profaned My Sabbaths*

PROFANING THE SABBATH (NAS, RSV)
(See *PROFANE THE SABBATH*)

PROFESSING TO BE WISE
Rom 1:22 *Professing to be wise*, they became fools

PROMISE OF GOD
Rom 4:20 He did not waver at the *promise of God* through unbelief, but was strengthened in faith, giving glory to God

PROMISE OF HIS COMING
2Pet 3:4 and saying, "Where is the *promise of His coming?* For since the fathers fell asleep, all

things continue as they were from the beginning of creation

PROMISE OF THE HOLY SPIRIT
Acts 2:33 Therefore being exalted to the right hand of God, and having received from the Father the *promise of the Holy Spirit*, He poured out this which you now see and hear

PROMISE OF THE SPIRIT
Gal 3:14 that the blessing of Abraham might come upon the Gentiles in Christ Jesus, that we might receive the *promise of the Spirit* through faith

PROMISE TO DAVID
2Chr 1:9 Now, O Lord God, let Your *promise to David* my father be established, for You have made me king over a people like the dust of the earth in multitude

PROMISE WAS STATED (NIV)
(See *WORD OF PROMISE*)

PROMISES OF GOD
2Cor 1:20 For all the *promises of God* in Him are Yes, and in Him Amen, to the glory of God through us
Gal 3:21 Is the law then against the *promises of God?* Certainly not

PROOF TO THE PEOPLE (RSV)
(See *TESTIMONY TO THEM*)

PROPHECY IS IMPERFECT (RSV)
(See *PROPHESY IN PART*)

PROPHESY IN PART
1Cor 13:9 For we know in part and we *prophesy in part*

PROPHESY LIES
Jer 14:14 And the Lord said to me, "The prophets *prophesy lies* in My name
Jer 23:25 I have heard what the prophets have said who *prophesy lies* in My name, saying
Jer 23:26 How long will this be in the heart of the prophets who *prophesy lies*

PROPHESY TO THESE BONES
Ezek 37:4 Again He said to me, "*Prophesy to these bones*, and say to them

PROPHET IS NOT WITHOUT HONOR
Matt 13:57 But Jesus said to them, "A *prophet is not without honor* except in his own country and in his own house
Mark 6:4 But Jesus said to them, "A *prophet is not without honor* except in his own country, among his own relatives, and in his own house

PROPHET LIKE ME
Deut 18:15 The Lord your God will raise up for you a *Prophet like me* from your midst, from your brethren
Acts 3:22 For Moses truly said to the fathers, 'The Lord your God will raise up for you a *prophet like me* from your brethren
Acts 7:37 This is that Moses who said to the children of Israel, 'The Lord your God will raise up for you a *prophet like me* from your brethren

PROPHET OF THE LORD
1Sam 3:20 And all Israel from Dan to Beersheba knew that Samuel had been established as a *prophet of the Lord*
1Kin 18:22 Then Elijah said to the people, "I alone am left a *prophet of the Lord*
1Kin 22:7 And Jehoshaphat said, "Is there not still a *prophet of the Lord* here, that we may inquire of Him
2Kin 3:11 But Jehoshaphat said, "Is there no *prophet of the Lord* here, that we may inquire of the Lord by him
2Chr 18:6 But Jehoshaphat said, "Is there not still a *prophet of the Lord* here, that we may inquire of Him
2Chr 28:9 But a *prophet of the Lord* was there, whose name was Oded

PROPHET TO THE NATIONS
Jer 1:5 before you were born I sanctified you; and I ordained you a *prophet to the nations*

PROPHET WITHOUT HONOR (NIV)
(See *PROPHET IS NOT WITHOUT HONOR*)

PROPHET'S MADNESS (NIV, RSV)
(See *MADNESS OF THE PROPHET*)

PROPHET'S SON (KJV, NIV, RSV)
(See *SON OF A PROPHET*)

PROPHETS OF BAAL
1Kin 18:19 Now therefore, send and gather all Israel to me on Mount Carmel, the four hundred and fifty *prophets of Baal*, and the four hundred prophets of Asherah, who eat at Jezebel's table
1Kin 18:25 Now Elijah said to the *prophets of Baal*, "Choose one bull for yourselves and prepare it first, for you are many
1Kin 18:40 And Elijah said to them, "Seize the *prophets of Baal*
2Kin 10:19 Now therefore, call to me all the *prophets of Baal*, all his servants, and all his priests

PROPHETS OF GOD
Ezra 5:2 and the *prophets of God* were with them, helping them

PROPHETS OF THE LORD
1Kin 18:4 For so it was, while Jezebel massacred the *prophets of the Lord*, that Obadiah had taken one hundred prophets and hidden them, fifty to a cave, and had fed them with bread and water
1Kin 18:13 Was it not reported to my lord what I did when Jezebel killed the *prophets of the Lord*, how I hid one hundred men of the Lord's prophets, fifty to a cave, and fed them with bread and water

PROPITIATION BY HIS BLOOD
Rom 3:25 whom God set forth to be a *propitiation by His blood*, through faith, to demonstrate His righteousness, because in His forbearance God had passed over the sins that were previously committed

PROPITIATION FOR OUR SINS
1Jn 2:2 And He Himself is the *propitiation for our sins*, and not for ours only but also for the whole world
1Jn 4:10 In this is love, not that we loved God, but that He loved us and sent His Son to be the *propitiation for our sins*

PROPITIATION THROUGH FAITH IN HIS BLOOD (KJV)
(See *PROPITIATION BY HIS BLOOD*)

PROPOSE YOUR PLAN (NIV)
(See *SPEAK THE WORD*)

PROSPERITY OF THE WICKED
Ps 73:3 For I was envious of the boastful, when I saw the *prosperity of the wicked*

PROSPERITY WILL ABOUND (NIV)
(See *ABUNDANCE OF PEACE*)

PROSPERITY WILL CONTINUE (NIV)
(See *LENGTHENING OF YOUR PROSPERITY*)

PROSTITUTE THEMSELVES (NIV)
(See *PLAY THE HARLOT*)

PROTECTOR OF WIDOWS (RSV)
(See *DEFENDER OF WIDOWS*)

PROUD IN SPIRIT
Eccl 7:8 The end of a thing is better than its beginning, and the patient in spirit is better than the *proud in spirit*

PROVE ALL THINGS (KJV)
(See *TEST ALL THINGS*)

PROVERB IN THE MOUTH OF FOOLS
Prov 26:7 Like the legs of the lame that hang limp is a *proverb in the mouth of fools*
Prov 26:9 Like a thorn that goes into the hand of a drunkard is a *proverb in the mouth of fools*

PROVERBS OF SOLOMON
Prov 1:1 The *proverbs of Solomon* the son of David, king of Israel
Prov 10:1 The *Proverbs of Solomon:* A wise son makes a glad father, but a foolish son is the grief of his mother
Prov 25:1 These also are *proverbs of Solomon* which the men of Hezekiah king of Judah copied

PROVIDE ATONEMENT
Deut 21:8 *Provide atonement*, O Lord, for Your people Israel, whom You have redeemed, and do not lay innocent blood to the charge of Your people Israel
Deut 32:43 He will *provide atonement* for His land and His people
2Chr 30:18 But Hezekiah prayed for them, saying, "May the good Lord *provide atonement* for everyone
Ps 65:3 As for our transgressions, You will *provide atonement* for them
Ps 79:9 And deliver us, and *provide atonement* for our sins, for Your name's sake

PROVIDE THEIR FOOD IN THE SUMMER (RSV)
(See *PREPARE THEIR FOOD IN THE SUMMER*)

PROVIDES CLOTHING FOR THE NAKED (NIV)
(See *COVERED THE NAKED WITH CLOTHING*)

PROVOKE HIM
Ex 23:21 do not *provoke Him*, for He will not pardon your transgressions
Deut 4:25 When you beget children and grandchildren and have grown old in the land, act corruptly and make a carved image in the form of anything, and do evil in the sight of the Lord your God to *provoke Him* to anger
Deut 9:18 I neither ate bread nor drank water, because of all your sin which you committed in doing wickedly in the sight of the Lord, to *provoke Him* to anger
Deut 31:29 and evil will befall you in the latter days, because you will do evil in the sight of the Lord, to *provoke Him* to anger through the work of your hands
2Kin 17:17 And they caused their sons and daughters to pass through the fire, practiced witchcraft and soothsaying, and sold themselves to do evil in the sight of the Lord, to *provoke Him* to anger
2Kin 21:6 He did much evil in the sight of the Lord, to *provoke Him* to anger
2Chr 33:6 He did much evil in the sight of the Lord, to *provoke Him* to anger

PROVOKE ME
Deut 31:20 When I have brought them to the land flowing with milk and honey, of which I swore to their fathers, and they have eaten and filled themselves and grown fat, then they will turn to other gods and serve them; and they will *provoke Me* and break My covenant
1Kin 14:9 but you have done more evil than all who were before you, for you have gone and made for yourself other gods and molded images to *provoke Me* to anger, and have cast Me behind your back
1Kin 16:2 Inasmuch as I lifted you out of the dust and made you ruler over My people Israel, and you have walked in the way of Jeroboam, and have made My people Israel sin, to *provoke Me* to anger with their sins
2Kin 22:17 because they have forsaken Me and burned incense to other gods, that they might *provoke Me* to anger with all the works of their hands
2Chr 34:25 because they have forsaken Me and burned incense to other gods, that they might *provoke Me* to anger with all the works of their hands
Is 65:3 a people who *provoke Me* to anger continually to My face
Jer 7:18 and they pour out drink offerings to other gods, that they may *provoke Me* to anger
Jer 7:19 Do they *provoke Me* to anger?" says the Lord. "Do they not provoke themselves, to the shame of their own faces
Jer 11:17 For the Lord of hosts, who planted you, has pronounced doom against you for the evil of the house of Israel and of the house of Judah, which they have done against themselves to *provoke Me* to anger in offering incense to Baal
Jer 25:6 Do not go after other gods to serve them and worship them, and do not *provoke Me* to anger with the works of your hands
Jer 25:7 Yet you have not listened to Me," says the Lord, "that you might *provoke Me* to anger with the works of your hands to your own hurt
Jer 32:29 And the Chaldeans who fight against this city shall come and set fire to this city and burn it, with the houses on whose roofs they have offered incense to Baal and poured out drink offerings to other gods, to *provoke Me* to anger
Jer 32:32 because of all the evil of the children of Israel and the children of Judah, which they have done to *provoke Me* to anger they, their kings, their princes, their priests, their prophets, the men of Judah, and the inhabitants of Jerusalem
Jer 44:3 because of their wickedness which they have committed to *provoke Me* to anger, in that they went to burn incense and to serve other gods whom they did not know, they nor you nor your fathers
Jer 44:8 in that you *provoke Me* to wrath with the works of your hands, burning incense to other gods in the land of Egypt where you have gone to dwell, that you may cut yourselves off and be a curse and a reproach among all the nations of the earth
Ezek 8:17 then they have returned to *provoke Me* to anger. Indeed they put the branch to their nose
Ezek 16:26 You also committed harlotry with the Egyptians, your very fleshly neighbors, and increased your acts of harlotry to *provoke Me* to anger

PROVOKED THE LORD
Deut 9:7 Remember and do not forget how you *provoked the Lord* your God to wrath in the wilderness
Deut 9:8 Also in Horeb you *provoked the Lord* to wrath, so that the Lord was angry enough with you to have destroyed you
Deut 9:22 Also at Taberah and Massah and Kibroth Hattaavah you *provoked the Lord* to wrath
Judg 2:12 and they followed other gods from among the gods of the people who were all around them, and they bowed down to them; and they *provoked the Lord* to anger
1Kin 15:30 because of the sins of Jeroboam, which he had sinned and by which he had made Israel sin, because of his provocation with which he had *provoked the Lord* God of Israel to anger
1Kin 22:53 for he served Baal and worshiped him, and *provoked the Lord* God of Israel to anger, according to all that his father had done

PRUDENT MAN
Prov 12:16 A fool's wrath is known at once, but a *prudent man* covers shame
Prov 12:23 A *prudent man* conceals knowledge, but the heart of fools proclaims foolishness
Prov 13:16 Every *prudent man* acts with knowledge, but a fool lays open his folly
Prov 14:15 The simple believes every word, but the *prudent man* considers well his steps
Prov 22:3 A *prudent man* foresees evil and hides himself, but the simple pass on and are punished
Prov 27:12 A *prudent man* foresees evil and hides himself; the simple pass on and are punished

PRUNINGHOOKS INTO SPEARS
Joel 3:10 Beat your plowshares into swords and your *pruninghooks into spears*

PUBLICANS AND SINNERS (KJV)
(See *TAX COLLECTORS AND SINNERS*)

PUBLICANS AND THE HARLOTS (KJV)
(See *TAX COLLECTORS AND HARLOTS*)

PULL DOWN MY BARNS
Luke 12:18 I will *pull down my barns* and build greater, and there I will store all my crops and my goods

PULL OUT THE MOTE (KJV)
(See *REMOVE THE SPECK*)

PULLED OUT MY BEARD (NIV)
(See *PLUCKED OUT THE BEARD*)

PUNISH THEIR SINS
Jer 14:10 He will remember their iniquity now, and *punish their sins*
Hos 8:13 Now He will remember their iniquity and *punish their sins*
Hos 9:9 He will remember their iniquity; He will *punish their sins*

PUNISHING THE CHILDREN FOR THE SIN OF THE FATHERS (NIV)
(See *VISITING THE INIQUITY OF THE FATHERS*)

PUNISHMENT TO FOOLS (NIV)
(See *CORRECTION OF FOOLS*)

PURCHASED WITH HIS OWN BLOOD
Acts 20:28 Therefore take heed to yourselves and to all the flock, among which the Holy Spirit has made you overseers, to shepherd the church of God which He *purchased with His own blood*

PURE CANDLESTICK (KJV)
(See *GOLD LAMPSTAND*)

PURE HEART
Ps 24:4 He who has clean hands and a *pure heart*, who has not lifted up his soul to an idol, nor sworn deceitfully
1Tim 1:5 Now the purpose of the commandment is love from a *pure heart*, from a good conscience, and from sincere faith
2Tim 2:22 but pursue righteousness, faith, love, peace with those who call on the Lord out of a *pure heart*
1Pet 1:22 Since you have purified your souls in obeying the truth through the Spirit in sincere love of the brethren, love one another fervently with a *pure heart*

PURE IN HEART
Ps 73:1 Truly God is good to Israel, to such as are *pure in heart*
Matt 5:8 Blessed are the *pure in heart*, for they shall see God

PURE MILK OF THE WORD
1Pet 2:2 as newborn babes, desire the *pure milk of the word*, that you may grow thereby

PURGE ME WITH HYSSOP
Ps 51:7 *Purge me with hyssop*, and I shall be clean; wash me, and I shall be whiter than snow

PURGE OUT THE OLD LEAVEN
1Cor 5:7 Therefore *purge out the old leaven*, that you may be a new lump, since you truly are unleavened

PURGE THE EVIL (NAS, NIV, RSV)
(See *PUT AWAY THE EVIL*)

PURGED OUR SINS
Heb 1:3 who being the brightness of His glory and the express image of His person, and upholding all things by the word of His power, when He had by Himself *purged our sins*, sat down at the right hand of the Majesty on high

PURIFICATION FOR SINS (NIV)
(See *PURGED OUR SINS*)

PURIFIED WITH THE WATER
Num 31:23 and it shall be *purified with the water* of purification

PURIFIED YOUR SOULS
1Pet 1:22 Since you have *purified your souls* in obeying the truth through the Spirit in sincere love of the brethren, love one another fervently with a pure heart

PURIFY THE ALTAR (NAS, NIV)
(See *CLEANSE THE ALTAR*)

PURIFY YOUR HEARTS
Jas 4:8 Cleanse your hands, you sinners; and *purify your hearts*, you double-minded

PURIFY YOURSELVES
Gen 35:2 And Jacob said to his household and to all who were with him, "Put away the foreign gods that are among you, *purify yourselves*, and change your garments
Num 31:19 whoever has killed any person, and whoever has touched any slain, *purify yourselves* and your captives on the third day and on the seventh day

PURPOSE OF GOD
Rom 9:11 (for the children not yet being born, nor having done any good or evil, that the *purpose of God* according to election might stand, not of works but of Him who calls

PURSUE PEACE
Heb 12:14 *Pursue peace* with all men, and holiness, without which no one will see the Lord

PURSUE RIGHTEOUSNESS
Rom 9:30 That Gentiles, who did not *pursue righteousness*, have attained to righteousness, even the righteousness of faith
1Tim 6:11 But you, O man of God, flee these things and *pursue righteousness*, godliness, faith, love, patience, gentleness
2Tim 2:22 but *pursue righteousness*, faith, love, peace with those who call on the Lord out of a pure heart

PURSUE THEM WITH DRAWN SWORD (NIV)
(See *DRAW OUT A SWORD AFTER THEM*)

PURSUED THE POOR (RSV)
(See *PERSECUTED THE POOR*)

PUT AN OBSTACLE IN THE WAY OF THE GOSPEL (RSV)
(See *HINDER THE GOSPEL*)

PUT ASIDE (NIV)
(See *PUT OFF*)

PUT AWAY ALL MALICE (RSV)
(See *LAYING ASIDE ALL MALICE*)

PUT AWAY THE EVIL
Deut 13:5 So you shall *put away the evil* from your midst
Deut 17:7 So you shall *put away the evil* person from among you
Deut 17:12 So you shall *put away the evil* person from Israel
Deut 19:19 so you shall *put away the evil* person from among you
Deut 21:21 so you shall *put away the evil* person from among you, and all Israel shall hear and fear
Deut 22:21 so you shall *put away the evil* person from among you
Deut 22:22 so you shall *put away the evil* person from Israel
Deut 22:24 so you shall *put away the evil* person from among you
Deut 24:7 and you shall *put away the evil* person from among you
Is 1:16 *put away the evil* of your doings from before My eyes

PUT FORTH (KJV)
(See *REACH OUT*)

PUT FORTH HIS HAND (RSV)
(See *STRETCHED OUT HIS HAND*)

PUT HIM TO AN OPEN SHAME
Heb 6:6 if they fall away, to renew them again to repentance, since they crucify again for themselves the Son of God, and *put Him to an open shame*

PUT HIM UNDER OATH
Ezek 17:13 And he took the king's offspring, made a covenant with him, and *put him under oath*

PUT HIS LIFE IN HIS HAND (KJV)
(See *TOOK HIS LIFE IN HIS HANDS*)

PUT HIS NAME THERE
1Kin 14:21 He reigned seventeen years in Jerusalem, the city which the Lord had chosen out of all the tribes of Israel, to *put His name there*
2Chr 12:13 and he reigned seventeen years in Jerusalem, the city which the Lord had chosen out of all the tribes of Israel, to *put His name there*

PUT IN TRUST WITH THE GOSPEL (KJV)
(See *ENTRUSTED WITH THE GOSPEL*)

PUT IT OUT OF HIS MIND (NIV)
(See *TAKE IT TO HEART*)

PUT MY LAW IN THEIR MINDS
Jer 31:33 After those days, says the Lord, I will *put My law in their minds*, and write it on their hearts

PUT MY LIFE IN MY HANDS (KJV)
(See *TOOK MY LIFE IN MY HANDS*)

PUT NEW WINE INTO OLD BOTTLES (KJV)
(See *NEW WINE INTO OLD WINESKINS*)

PUT OFF
Deut 21:13 She shall *put off* the clothes of her captivity, remain in your house, and mourn her father and her mother a full month
Job 9:27 If I say, 'I will forget my complaint, I will *put off* my sad face and wear a smile
Ps 30:11 You have *put off* my sackcloth and clothed me with gladness
Eph 4:22 that you *put off*, concerning your former conduct, the old man which grows corrupt according to the deceitful lusts
Col 3:8 But now you must also *put off* all these: anger, wrath, malice, blasphemy, filthy language out of your mouth
Col 3:9 Do not lie to one another, since you have *put off* the old man with his deeds
2Pet 1:14 knowing that shortly I must *put off* my tent, just as our Lord Jesus Christ showed me

PUT ON
Gen 28:20 Then Jacob made a vow, saying, "If God will be with me, and keep me in this way that I am going, and give me bread to eat and clothing to *put on*
Gen 38:19 So she arose and went away, and laid aside her veil and *put on* the garments of her widowhood
Ex 33:4 And when the people heard this bad news, they mourned, and no one *put on* his ornaments
Lev 6:10 And the priest shall *put on* his linen garment, and his linen trousers he shall *put on* his body, and take up the ashes of the burnt offering which the fire has consumed on the altar, and he shall put them beside the altar
Lev 6:11 Then he shall take off his garments, *put on* other garments, and carry the ashes outside the camp to a clean place
Lev 11:38 But if any water is *put on* the seed, and if a part of any such carcass falls on it, it becomes unclean to you
Lev 14:18 The rest of the oil that is in the priest's hand he shall *put on* the head of him who is to be cleansed
Lev 14:29 The rest of the oil that is in the priest's hand he shall *put on* the head of him who is to be cleansed, to make atonement for him before the Lord
Lev 16:23 Then Aaron shall come into the tabernacle of meeting, shall take off the linen gar-

ments which he *put on* when he went into the Holy Place, and shall leave them there
Lev 16:24 And he shall wash his body with water in a holy place, *put on* his garments, come out and offer his burnt offering and the burnt offering of the people, and make atonement for himself and for the people
Lev 16:32 And the priest, who is anointed and consecrated to minister as priest in his father's place, shall make atonement, and *put on* the linen clothes, the holy garments
Num 4:6 Then they shall *put on* it a covering of badger skins, and spread over that a cloth entirely of blue
Num 4:7 On the table of showbread they shall spread a blue cloth, and *put on* it the dishes, the pans, the bowls, and the pitchers for pouring
Num 4:14 They shall *put on* it all its implements with which they minister there the firepans, the forks, the shovels, the basins, and all the utensils of the altar and they shall spread on it a covering of badger skins, and insert its poles
Num 19:17 And for an unclean person they shall take some of the ashes of the heifer burnt for purification from sin, and running water shall be *put on* them in a vessel
Deut 22:5 A woman shall not wear anything that pertains to a man, nor shall a man *put on* a woman's garment, for all who do so are an abomination to the Lord your God
Ruth 3:3 Therefore wash yourself and anoint yourself, *put on* your best garment and go down to the threshing floor
1Sam 28:8 So Saul disguised himself and *put on* other clothes, and he went, and two men with him
2Sam 14:2 And Joab sent to Tekoa and brought from there a wise woman, and said to her, "Please pretend to be a mourner, and *put on* mourning apparel
1Kin 12:4 now therefore, lighten the burdensome service of your father, and his heavy yoke which he *put on* us, and we will serve you
1Kin 12:9 How should we answer this people who have spoken to me, saying, 'Lighten the yoke which your father *put on* us
1Kin 22:10 The king of Israel and Jehoshaphat the king of Judah, having *put on* their robes, sat each on his throne, at a threshing floor at the entrance of the gate of Samaria
1Kin 22:30 but you *put on* your robes." So the king of Israel disguised himself and went into battle
2Kin 4:38 and he said to his servant, "*Put on* the large pot, and boil stew for the sons of the prophets
2Chr 10:4 now therefore, lighten the burdensome service of your father and his heavy yoke which he *put on* us, and we will serve you
2Chr 10:9 How should we answer this people who have spoken to me, saying, 'Lighten the yoke which your father *put on* us
2Chr 18:29 but you *put on* your robes." So the king of Israel disguised himself, and they went into battle
Esth 4:1 When Mordecai learned all that had happened, he tore his clothes and *put on* sackcloth and ashes, and went out into the midst of the city
Esth 5:1 Now it happened on the third day that Esther *put on* her royal robes and stood in the inner court of the king's palace, across from the king's house, while the king sat on his royal throne in the royal house, facing the entrance of the house
Job 29:14 I *put on* righteousness, and it clothed me; my justice was like a robe and a turban
Is 51:9 Awake, awake, *put on* strength, O arm of the Lord
Is 52:1 *Put on* your strength, O Zion; *put on* your beautiful garments, O Jerusalem, the holy city
Is 59:17 For He *put on* righteousness as a breastplate, and a helmet of salvation on His head; He *put on* the garments of vengeance for clothing, and was clad with zeal as a cloak
Jer 46:4 Stand forth with your helmets, polish the spears, *put on* the armor
Ezek 24:3 *Put on* a pot, set it on, and also pour water into it
Ezek 30:21 and see, it has not been bandaged for healing, nor a splint *put on* to bind it, to make it strong enough to hold a sword
Ezek 42:14 They shall *put on* other garments; then they may approach that which is for the people
Ezek 44:17 And it shall be, whenever they enter the gates of the inner court, that they shall *put on* linen garments
Ezek 44:19 When they go out to the outer court, to the outer court to the people, they shall take off their garments in which they have ministered, leave them in the holy chambers, and *put on* other garments
Jon 3:5 So the people of Nineveh believed God, proclaimed a fast, and *put on* sackcloth, from the greatest to the least of them
Matt 6:25 nor about your body, what you will *put on*. Is not life more than food and the body more than clothing
Mark 6:9 but to wear sandals, and not to *put on* two tunics
Luke 12:22 And He said to His disciples, "Therefore I say to you, do not worry about your life, what you will eat; nor about the body, what you will *put on*
John 19:2 And the soldiers twisted a crown of thorns and put it on His head, and they *put on* Him a purple robe
John 21:7 Now when Simon Peter heard that it was the Lord, he *put on* his outer garment (for he had removed it
Acts 12:8 And he said to him, "*Put on* your garment and follow me
Rom 13:12 Therefore let us cast off the works of darkness, and let us *put on* the armor of light
Rom 13:14 But *put on* the Lord Jesus Christ, and make no provision for the flesh, to fulfill its lusts
1Cor 15:53 For this corruptible must *put on* incorruption, and this mortal must *put on* immortality
1Cor 15:54 So when this corruptible has *put on* incorruption, and this mortal has *put on* immortality, then shall be brought to pass the saying that is written
Gal 3:27 For as many of you as were baptized into Christ have *put on* Christ
Eph 4:24 and that you *put on* the new man which was created according to God, in righteousness and true holiness
Eph 6:11 *Put on* the whole armor of God, that you may be able to stand against the wiles of the devil
Eph 6:14 Stand therefore, having girded your waist with truth, having *put on* the breastplate of righteousness
Col 3:10 and have *put on* the new man who is renewed in knowledge according to the image of Him who created him
Col 3:12 Therefore, as the elect of God, holy and beloved, *put on* tender mercies, kindness, humbleness of mind, meekness, longsuffering
Col 3:14 But above all these things *put on* love, which is the bond of perfection
Rev 2:24 But to you I say, and to the rest in Thyatira, as many as do not have this doctrine, and who have not known the depths of Satan, as they call them, I will *put on* you no other burden

PUT ON IMMORTALITY
1Cor 15:53 For this corruptible must put on incorruption, and this mortal must *put on immortality*
1Cor 15:54 So when this corruptible has put on incorruption, and this mortal has *put on immortality*, then shall be brought to pass the saying that is written

PUT OUT (RSV)
(See *REACH OUT*)

PUT OUT OF THE SYNAGOGUE
John 9:22 His parents said these things because they feared the Jews, for the Jews had agreed already that if anyone confessed that He was Christ, he would be *put out of the synagogue*
John 12:42 Nevertheless even among the rulers many believed in Him, but because of the Pharisees they did not confess Him, lest they should be *put out of the synagogue*

PUT THE LORD TO THE TEST (NIV)
(See *TEMPT THE LORD*)

PUT TO DEATH
Gen 26:11 So Abimelech charged all his people, saying, "He who touches this man or his wife shall surely be *put to death*
Ex 19:12 Whoever touches the mountain shall surely be *put to death*
Ex 21:12 He who strikes a man so that he dies shall surely be *put to death*
Ex 21:15 And he who strikes his father or his mother shall surely be *put to death*
Ex 21:16 He who kidnaps a man and sells him, or if he is found in his hand, shall surely be *put to death*
Ex 21:17 And he who curses his father or his mother shall surely be *put to death*
Ex 21:29 But if the ox tended to thrust with its horn in times past, and it has been made known to his owner, and he has not kept it confined, so that it has killed a man or a woman, the ox shall be stoned and its owner also shall be *put to death*
Ex 22:19 Whoever lies with an animal shall surely be *put to death*
Ex 31:14 Everyone who profanes it shall surely be *put to death*
Ex 31:15 Whoever does any work on the Sabbath day, he shall surely be *put to death*
Ex 35:2 Whoever does any work on it shall be *put to death*
Lev 19:20 but they shall not be *put to death*, because she was not free
Lev 20:2 Whoever of the children of Israel, or of the strangers who sojourn in Israel, who gives any of his descendants to Molech, he shall surely be *put to death*
Lev 20:9 For everyone who curses his father or his mother shall surely be *put to death*
Lev 20:10 The man who commits adultery with another man's wife, he who commits adultery with his neighbor's wife, the adulterer and the adulteress, shall surely be *put to death*
Lev 20:11 both of them shall surely be *put to death*. Their blood shall be upon them
Lev 20:12 If a man lies with his daughter-in-law, both of them shall surely be *put to death*
Lev 20:13 They shall surely be *put to death*. Their blood shall be upon them
Lev 20:15 If a man mates with a beast, he shall surely be *put to death*, and you shall kill the beast
Lev 20:16 They shall surely be *put to death*. Their blood is upon them
Lev 20:27 A man or a woman who is a medium, or who has familiar spirits, shall surely be *put to death*
Lev 24:16 And whoever blasphemes the name of the Lord shall surely be *put to death*, and all the congregation shall certainly stone him, the stranger as well as him who is born in the land. When he blasphemes the name of the Lord, he shall be *put to death*
Lev 24:17 Whoever kills any man shall surely be *put to death*
Lev 24:21 but whoever kills a man shall be *put to death*
Lev 27:29 No person under the ban, who may become doomed to destruction among men, shall be redeemed, but shall surely be *put to death*
Num 1:51 The outsider who comes near shall be *put to death*
Num 3:10 but the outsider who comes near shall be *put to death*
Num 3:38 but the outsider who came near was to be *put to death*
Num 15:35 Then the Lord said to Moses, "The man must surely be *put to death*
Num 18:7 I give your priesthood to you as a gift for service, but the outsider who comes near shall be *put to death*
Num 35:16 But if he strikes him with an iron implement, so that he dies, he is a murderer; the murderer shall surely be *put to death*
Num 35:17 And if he strikes him with a stone in the hand, by which one could die, and he does die, he is a murderer; the murderer shall surely be *put to death*
Num 35:18 Or if he strikes him with a wooden hand weapon, by which one could die, and he does die, he is a murderer; the murderer shall surely be *put to death*
Num 35:21 or in enmity he strikes him with his hand so that he dies, the one who struck him shall surely be *put to death*, for he is a murderer
Num 35:30 Whoever kills a person, the murderer shall be *put to death* on the testimony of witnesses
Num 35:31 Moreover you shall take no ransom for the life of a murderer who is guilty of death, but he shall surely be *put to death*
Deut 13:5 But that prophet or that dreamer of dreams shall be *put to death*, because he has spoken in order to turn you away from the Lord your God, who brought you out of the land of Egypt and redeemed you from the house of bondage, to entice you from the way in which the Lord your God commanded you to walk
Deut 17:6 Whoever is worthy of death shall be *put to death* on the testimony of two or three witnesses, but he shall not be *put to death* on the testimony of one witness
Deut 21:22 If a man has committed a sin worthy of death, and he is *put to death*, and you hang him on a tree
Deut 24:16 The fathers shall not be *put to death* for their children, nor shall the children be *put to death* for their fathers; a person shall be *put to death* for his own sin
Josh 1:18 Whoever rebels against your command and does not heed your words, in all that you command him, shall be *put to death*
Judg 6:31 Let the one who would plead for him be *put to death* by morning
Judg 21:5 For they had made a great oath concerning anyone who had not come up to the Lord at Mizpah, saying, "He shall surely be *put to death*
1Sam 11:13 But Saul said, "Not a man shall be *put to death* this day, for today the Lord has accomplished salvation in Israel
2Sam 8:2 With two lines he measured off those to be *put to death*, and with one full line those to be kept alive
2Sam 19:21 But Abishai the son of Zeruiah answered and said, "Shall not Shimei be *put to*

death for this, because he cursed the Lord's anointed
2Sam 19:22 Shall any man be *put to death* today in Israel
2Sam 21:9 So they fell, all seven together, and were *put to death* in the days of harvest, in the first days, in the beginning of barley harvest
1Kin 2:24 Now therefore, as the Lord lives, who has established me and set me on the throne of David my father, and who has made me a house, as He promised, Adonijah shall be *put to death* today
2Kin 11:8 and whoever comes within range, let him be *put to death*
2Kin 14:6 But the children of the murderers he did not execute, according to what is written in the Book of the Law of Moses, in which the Lord commanded, saying, "The fathers shall not be *put to death* for the children, nor shall the children be *put to death* for the fathers; but a person shall be *put to death* for his own sin
2Chr 15:13 and whoever would not seek the Lord God of Israel was to be *put to death*, whether small or great, whether man or woman
2Chr 23:7 and whoever comes into the house, let him be *put to death*
2Chr 25:4 However he did not execute their children, but did as it is written in the Law in the Book of Moses, where the Lord commanded, saying, "The fathers shall not be *put to death* for their children, nor shall the children be *put to death* for their fathers
Jer 18:21 Let their men be *put to death*, their young men be slain by the sword in battle
Jer 38:4 Therefore the princes said to the king, "Please, let this man be *put to death*, for thus he weakens the hands of the men of war who remain in this city, and the hands of all the people, by speaking such words to them
Matt 2:16 and he sent forth and *put to death* all the male children who were in Bethlehem and in all its districts, from two years old and under, according to the time which he had determined from the wise men
Matt 10:21 and children will rise up against parents and cause them to be *put to death*
Matt 15:4 and, 'He who curses father or mother, let him be *put to death*
Mark 7:10 and, 'He who curses father or mother, let him be *put to death*
Mark 13:12 and children will rise up against parents and cause them to be *put to death*
Luke 23:32 There were also two others, criminals, led with Him to be *put to death*
Acts 2:23 Him, being delivered by the determined counsel and foreknowledge of God, you have taken by lawless hands, have crucified, and *put to death*
Acts 12:19 But when Herod had searched for him and not found him, he examined the guards and commanded that they should be *put to death*
Acts 13:28 And though they found no cause for death in Him, they asked Pilate that He should be *put to death*
Acts 26:10 and when they were *put to death*, I cast my vote against them
Rom 8:13 but if by the Spirit you *put to death* the deeds of the body, you will live
Col 3:5 Therefore *put to death* your members which are on the earth
1Pet 3:18 For Christ also suffered once for sins, the just for the unjust, that He might bring us to God, being *put to death* in the flesh but made alive by the Spirit

PUT TO SHAME
Ps 35:4 Let those be *put to shame* and brought to dishonor who seek after my life
Ps 44:7 But You have saved us from our enemies, and have *put to shame* those who hated us
Ps 71:1 In You, O Lord, I put my trust; let me never be *put to shame*
Ps 83:17 Let them be confounded and dismayed forever; yes, let them be *put to shame* and perish
Ps 97:7 Let all be *put to shame* who serve carved images, who boast of idols
Ps 129:5 Let all those who hate Zion be *put to shame* and turned back
Is 54:4 nor be disgraced, for you will not be *put to shame*
Jer 10:14 every metalsmith is *put to shame* by the graven image
Jer 17:18 Let them be ashamed who persecute me, but do not let me be *put to shame*
Jer 51:17 every metalsmith is *put to shame* by the carved image
Joel 2:26 You shall eat in plenty and be satisfied, and praise the name of the Lord your God, who has dealt wondrously with you; and My people shall never be *put to shame*
Joel 2:27 Then you shall know that I am in the midst of Israel, and that I am the Lord your God and there is no other. My people shall never be *put to shame*
Zeph 3:19 I will appoint them for praise and fame in every land where they were *put to shame*
Zech 10:5 They shall fight because the Lord is with them, and the riders on horses shall be *put to shame*
Luke 13:17 And when He said these things, all His adversaries were *put to shame*
Rom 9:33 Behold, I lay in Zion a stumbling stone and rock of offense, and whoever believes on Him will not be *put to shame*
Rom 10:11 For the Scripture says, "Whoever believes on Him will not be *put to shame*
1Cor 1:27 But God has chosen the foolish things of the world to *put to shame* the wise, and God has chosen the weak things of the world to *put to shame* the things which are mighty
1Pet 2:6 Therefore it is also contained in the Scripture, "Behold, I lay in Zion a chief cornerstone, elect, precious, and he who believes on Him will by no means be *put to shame*

PUT YOU OUT OF THE SYNAGOGUES
John 16:2 They will *put you out of the synagogues;* yes, the time is coming that whoever kills you will think that he offers God service

PUT YOUR HOUSE IN ORDER (NIV)
(See *SET YOUR HOUSE IN ORDER*)

PUTTING HIM UNDER OATH (NAS, NIV, RSV)
(See *PUT HIM UNDER OATH*)

Q

QUEEN OF HEAVEN
Jer 7:18 The children gather wood, the fathers kindle the fire, and the women knead their dough, to make cakes for the *queen of heaven*
Jer 44:17 But we will certainly do whatever has gone out of our own mouth, to burn incense to the *queen of heaven* and pour out drink offerings to her, as we have done, we and our fathers, our kings and our princes, in the cities of Judah and in the streets of Jerusalem
Jer 44:18 But since we stopped burning incense to the *queen of heaven* and pouring out drink offerings to her, we have lacked everything and have been consumed by the sword and by famine
Jer 44:19 The women also said, "And when we

burned incense to the *queen of heaven* and poured out drink offerings to her, did we make cakes for her, to worship her, and pour out drink offerings to her without our husbands' permission
Jer 44:25 You and your wives have spoken with your mouths and fulfilled with your hands, saying, "We will surely perform our vows that we have made, to burn incense to the *queen of heaven* and pour out drink offerings to her

QUEEN OF SHEBA
1Kin 10:1 Now when the *queen of Sheba* heard of the fame of Solomon concerning the name of the Lord, she came to test him with hard questions
1Kin 10:4 And when the *queen of Sheba* had seen all the wisdom of Solomon, the house that he had built
1Kin 10:10 There never again came such abundance of spices as the *queen of Sheba* gave to King Solomon
1Kin 10:13 And King Solomon gave the *queen of Sheba* all she desired, whatever she asked, besides what Solomon had given her according to the royal bounty
2Chr 9:1 Now when the *queen of Sheba* heard of the fame of Solomon, she came to Jerusalem to test Solomon with hard questions, having a very great retinue, camels that bore spices, gold in abundance, and precious stones
2Chr 9:3 And when the *queen of Sheba* had seen the wisdom of Solomon, the house that he had built
2Chr 9:9 there never were any spices such as those the *queen of Sheba* gave to King Solomon
2Chr 9:12 Now King Solomon gave to the *queen of Sheba* all she desired, whatever she asked, much more than she had brought to the king

QUEEN OF THE SOUTH
Matt 12:42 The *queen of the South* will rise up in the judgment with this generation and condemn it, for she came from the ends of the earth to hear the wisdom of Solomon
Luke 11:31 The *queen of the South* will rise up in the judgment with the men of this generation and condemn them, for she came from the ends of the earth to hear the wisdom of Solomon

QUENCH THE LAMP OF ISRAEL
2Sam 21:17 Then the men of David swore to him, saying, "You shall go out no more with us to battle, lest you *quench the lamp of Israel*

QUENCH THE SPIRIT
1Th 5:19 Do not *quench the Spirit*

QUESTION FOR CONSCIENCE' SAKE
1Cor 10:27 If any of those who do not believe invites you to dinner, and you desire to go, eat whatever is set before you, asking no *question for conscience' sake*

QUICKENED BY THE SPIRIT (KJV)
(See *ALIVE BY THE SPIRIT*)

QUICKENED TOGETHER WITH HIM (KJV)
(See *ALIVE TOGETHER WITH HIM*)

QUICKENETH THE DEAD (KJV)
(See *GIVES LIFE TO THE DEAD*)

QUIET! BE STILL (NIV)
(See *PEACE, BE STILL*)

QUIETNESS AND CONFIDENCE SHALL BE YOUR STRENGTH
Is 30:15 in *quietness and confidence shall be your strength*." But you would not

R

RACE IS NOT TO THE SWIFT
Eccl 9:11 I returned and saw under the sun that the *race is not to the swift*, nor the battle to the strong, nor bread to the wise, nor riches to men of understanding, nor favor to men of skill

RACHEL WEEPING FOR HER CHILDREN
Jer 31:15 A voice was heard in Ramah, lamentation and bitter weeping, *Rachel weeping for her children*, refusing to be comforted for her children, because they are no more
Matt 2:18 A voice was heard in Ramah, lamentation, weeping, and great mourning, *Rachel weeping for her children*, refusing to be comforted, because they were no more

RAIMENT TO PLEDGE (KJV)
(See *GARMENT AS A PLEDGE*)

RAIN BREAD FROM HEAVEN
Ex 16:4 Then the Lord said to Moses, "Behold, I will *rain bread from heaven* for you

RAIN SALVATION UPON YOU (RSV)
(See *RAINS RIGHTEOUSNESS ON YOU*)

RAINBOW IN THE CLOUD
Gen 9:13 I set My *rainbow in the cloud*, and it shall be for the sign of the covenant between Me and the earth

RAINED BRIMSTONE
Gen 19:24 Then the Lord *rained brimstone* and fire on Sodom and Gomorrah, from the Lord out of the heavens

RAINED DOWN BURNING SULFUR (NIV)
(See *RAINED BRIMSTONE*)

RAINS RIGHTEOUSNESS ON YOU
Hos 10:12 break up your fallow ground, for it is time to seek the Lord, till He comes and *rains righteousness on you*

RAISE A LAMENTATION (RSV)
(See *TAKE UP A LAMENTATION*)

RAISE HIM UP
2Sam 12:17 So the elders of his house arose and went to him, to *raise him up* from the ground
Jer 50:32 The most proud shall stumble and fall, and no one will *raise him up*
John 6:40 and I will *raise him up* at the last day
John 6:44 and I will *raise him up* at the last day
John 6:54 Whoever eats My flesh and drinks My blood has eternal life, and I will *raise him up* at the last day
Heb 11:19 accounting that God was able to *raise him up*, even from the dead, from which he also received him in a figurative sense
Jas 5:15 And the prayer of faith will save the sick, and the Lord will *raise him up*

RAISE THE DEAD
Matt 10:8 Heal the sick, cleanse the lepers, *raise the dead*, cast out demons

RAISE UP FOR THEM A PROPHET
Deut 18:18 I will *raise up for them a Prophet* like you from among their brethren, and will put My words in His mouth, and He shall speak to them all that I command Him

RAISE UP THE AGE-OLD FOUNDATIONS (NAS, NIV)
(See *BUILD THE OLD WASTE PLACES*)

RAISE UP THE NAME OF THE DEAD
Ruth 4:5 Then Boaz said, "On the day you buy the field from the hand of Naomi, you must also buy it from Ruth the Moabitess, the wife of the dead, to *raise up the name of the dead* on his inheritance
Ruth 4:10 Moreover, Ruth the Moabitess, the wife of Mahlon, I have acquired as my wife, to *raise up the name of the dead* on his inheritance, that the name of the dead may not be cut off from among his brethren and from the gate of his place

RAISE YOUR VOICE (NIV)
(See *LIFT UP YOUR VOICE*)

RAISED A LOUD CRY (RSV)
(See *LIFTED UP THEIR VOICES*)

RAISED AGAIN
Matt 16:21 From that time Jesus began to show to His disciples that He must go to Jerusalem, and suffer many things from the elders and chief priests and scribes, and be killed, and be *raised again* the third day

RAISED FROM THE DEAD
Mark 6:16 But when Herod heard, he said, "This is John, whom I beheaded; he has been *raised from the dead*
John 12:1 Then, six days before the Passover, Jesus came to Bethany, where Lazarus was who had been dead, whom He had *raised from the dead*
John 12:9 and they came, not for Jesus' sake only, but that they might also see Lazarus, whom He had *raised from the dead*
John 21:14 This is now the third time Jesus showed Himself to His disciples after He was *raised from the dead*
Acts 3:15 and killed the Prince of life, whom God *raised from the dead*, of which we are witnesses
Acts 4:10 let it be known to you all, and to all the people of Israel, that by the name of Jesus Christ of Nazareth, whom you crucified, whom God *raised from the dead*, by Him this man stands here before you whole
Rom 6:4 Therefore we were buried with Him through baptism into death, that just as Christ was *raised from the dead* by the glory of the Father, even so we also should walk in newness of life
Rom 6:9 knowing that Christ, having been *raised from the dead*, dies no more
Rom 7:4 Therefore, my brethren, you also have become dead to the law through the body of Christ, that you may be married to another, even to Him who was *raised from the dead*, that we should bear fruit to God
1Cor 15:12 Now if Christ is preached that He has been *raised from the dead*, how do some among you say that there is no resurrection of the dead
1Th 1:10 and to wait for His Son from heaven, whom He *raised from the dead*, even Jesus who delivers us from the wrath to come
2Tim 2:8 Remember that Jesus Christ, of the seed of David, was *raised from the dead* according to my gospel

RAISED HIM FROM THE DEAD
John 12:17 Therefore the people, who were with Him when He called Lazarus out of his tomb and *raised him from the dead*, bore witness
Acts 13:30 But God *raised Him from the dead*
Acts 13:34 And that He *raised Him from the dead*, no more to return to corruption, He has spoken thus
Rom 10:9 that if you confess with your mouth the Lord Jesus and believe in your heart that God has *raised Him from the dead*, you will be saved
Gal 1:1 Paul, an apostle (not from men nor through man, but through Jesus Christ and God the Father who *raised Him from the dead*
Eph 1:20 which He worked in Christ when He *raised Him from the dead* and seated Him at His right hand in the heavenly places
Col 2:12 buried with Him in baptism, in which you also were raised with Him through faith in the working of God, who *raised Him from the dead*
1Pet 1:21 who through Him believe in God, who *raised Him from the dead* and gave Him glory, so that your faith and hope are in God

RAISED IN INCORRUPTION
1Cor 15:42 The body is sown in corruption, it is *raised in incorruption*

RAISED IS IMPERISHABLE (RSV)
(See *RAISED IN INCORRUPTION*)

RAISED ON THE THIRD DAY (NAS, NIV, RSV)
(See *ROSE AGAIN THE THIRD DAY*)

RAISED THE THIRD DAY
Luke 9:22 saying, "The Son of Man must suffer many things, and be rejected by the elders and chief priests and scribes, and be killed, and be *raised the third day*

RAISED THEIR VOICES (NIV)
(See *LIFTED UP THEIR VOICES*)

RAISED TO LIFE
Heb 11:35 Women received their dead *raised to life* again. And others were tortured, not accepting deliverance, that they might obtain a better resurrection

RAISED UP A DELIVERER
Judg 3:9 When the children of Israel cried out to the Lord, the Lord *raised up a deliverer* for the children of Israel, who delivered them
Judg 3:15 And when the children of Israel cried out to the Lord, the Lord *raised up a deliverer* for them

RAISED UP JUDGES
Judg 2:16 Then the Lord *raised up judges* who delivered them out of the hand of those who plundered them
Judg 2:18 And when the Lord *raised up judges* for them, the Lord was with the judge and delivered them out of the hand of their enemies all the days of the judge

RAISED UP PROPHETS
Jer 29:15 Because you have said, "The Lord has *raised up prophets* for us in Babylon

RAISING HIM FROM THE DEAD (NIV)
(See *RAISED HIM FROM THE DEAD*)

RAN HIM THROUGH (NIV)
(See *THRUST HIM THROUGH*)

RANSOM FOR MANY
Matt 20:28 just as the Son of Man did not come to be served, but to serve, and to give His life a *ransom for many*
Mark 10:45 For even the Son of Man did not come to be served, but to serve, and to give His life a *ransom for many*

RANSOMED OF THE LORD
Is 35:10 And the *ransomed of the Lord* shall return, and come to Zion with singing, with everlasting joy on their heads
Is 51:11 So the *ransomed of the Lord* shall return, and come to Zion with singing, with everlasting joy on their heads

RAZOR SHALL COME UPON HIS HEAD
Num 6:5 All the days of the vow of his separation no *razor shall come upon his head*
Judg 13:5 And no *razor shall come upon his head*, for the child shall be a Nazirite to God from the womb
1Sam 1:11 Then she made a vow and said, "O Lord of hosts, if You will indeed look on the affliction of your maidservant and remember me, and not forget your maidservant, but will give your maidservant a male child, then I will give him to the Lord all the days of his life, and no *razor shall come upon his head*

REACH OUT
Ex 4:4 Then the Lord said to Moses, "*Reach out* your hand and take it by the tail
Ps 125:3 For the scepter of wickedness shall not rest on the land allotted to the righteous, lest the righteous *reach out* their hands to iniquity

REACHED OUT HIS HAND (NIV)
(See *STRETCHED OUT HIS HAND*)

REACHED THEIR FULFILLMENT (NIV)
(See *DISPENSATION OF THE FULLNESS*)

READ FROM THE BOOK
Neh 8:18 Also day by day, from the first day until the last day, he *read from the Book* of the Law of God
Neh 9:3 And they stood up in their place and *read from the Book* of the Law of the Lord their God for one-fourth of the day
Neh 13:1 On that day they *read from the Book* of Moses in the hearing of the people, and in it was found written that no Ammonite or Moabite should ever come into the congregation of God
Jer 36:10 Then Baruch *read from the book* the words of Jeremiah in the house of the Lord, in the chamber of Gemariah the son of Shaphan the scribe, in the upper court at the entry of the New Gate of the Lord's house, in the hearing of all the people

REAP EVERLASTING LIFE
Gal 6:8 For he who sows to his flesh will of the flesh reap corruption, but he who sows to the Spirit will of the Spirit *reap everlasting life*

REAP IN JOY
Ps 126:5 Those who sow in tears shall *reap in joy*

REAP LIFE EVERLASTING (KJV)
(See *REAP EVERLASTING LIFE*)

REAP THE WHIRLWIND
Hos 8:7 They sow the wind, and *reap the whirlwind*. The stalk has no bud

REAP WITH SHOUTS OF JOY (RSV)
(See *REAP IN JOY*)

REAP WITH SONGS OF JOY (NIV)
(See *REAP IN JOY*)

REAPER WILL BE OVERTAKEN (NIV)
(See *OVERTAKE THE REAPER*)

REAPING WHAT I DID NOT SOW
Luke 19:22 You knew that I was an austere man, collecting what I did not deposit and *reaping what I did not sow*

REASONABLE SERVICE
Rom 12:1 I beseech you therefore, brethren, by the mercies of God, that you present your bodies a living sacrifice, holy, acceptable to God, which is your *reasonable service*

REBEL AGAINST HIM (NIV, RSV)
(See *PROVOKE HIM*)

REBEL AGAINST THE LORD
Num 14:9 Only do not *rebel against the Lord*, nor fear the people of the land, for they are our bread
Josh 22:19 but do not *rebel against the Lord*, nor rebel against us, by building yourselves an altar besides the altar of the Lord our God
Josh 22:29 Far be it from us that we should *rebel against the Lord*, and turn from following the Lord this day, to build an altar for burnt offerings, for grain offerings, or for sacrifices, besides the altar of the Lord our God which is before His tabernacle

REBELLED AGAINST THE LORD (NIV)
(See *CONTENDED AGAINST THE LORD*)

REBELLING AGAINST WHAT GOD HAS INSTITUTED (NIV)
(See *RESISTS THE ORDINANCE OF GOD*)

REBELLION AGAINST THE LORD
Jer 28:16 This year you shall die, because you have taught *rebellion against the Lord*
Jer 29:32 he shall not have anyone to dwell among this people, nor shall he see the good that I will do for My people," says the Lord,"because he has taught *rebellion against the Lord*

REBELLIOUS HOUSE
Ezek 2:5 As for them, whether they hear or whether they refuse for they are a *rebellious house* yet they will know that a prophet has been among them
Ezek 2:6 do not be afraid of their words or dismayed by their looks, though they are a *rebellious house*
Ezek 2:8 Do not be rebellious like that *rebellious house;* open your mouth and eat what I give you
Ezek 3:9 do not be afraid of them, nor be dismayed at their looks, though they are a *rebellious house*
Ezek 3:26 I will make your tongue cling to the roof of your mouth, so that you shall be mute and not be a reprover to them, for they are a *rebellious house*
Ezek 3:27 and he who refuses, let him refuse; for they are a *rebellious house*
Ezek 12:2 Son of man, you dwell in the midst of a *rebellious house*, which has eyes to see but does not see, and ears to hear but does not hear; for they are a *rebellious house*
Ezek 12:3 It may be that they will consider, though they are a *rebellious house*
Ezek 12:9 Son of man, has not the house of Israel, the *rebellious house*, said to you
Ezek 12:25 for in your days, O *rebellious house*, I will say the word and perform it
Ezek 17:12 Say now to the *rebellious house:* 'Do you not know what these things mean
Ezek 24:3 And utter a parable to the *rebellious house*, and say to them

REBUILT THE WALL
Neh 6:1 Now it happened when Sanballat, Tobiah, Geshem the Arab, and the rest of our enemies heard that I had *rebuilt the wall*, and that there were no breaks left in it (though at that time I had not hung the doors in the gates

REBUKE A WISE MAN
Prov 9:8 Do not reprove a scoffer, lest he hate you; *rebuke a wise man*, and he will love you

RECEDED AS A SCROLL
Rev 6:14 Then the sky *receded as a scroll* when it is rolled up, and every mountain and island was moved out of its place

RECEIVE A HUNDREDFOLD
Matt 19:29 And everyone who has left houses or brothers or sisters or father or mother or wife or children or lands, for My name's sake, shall *receive a hundredfold*, and inherit everlasting life
Mark 10:30 who shall not *receive a hundredfold* now in this time houses and brothers and sisters and mothers and children and lands, with persecutions and in the age to come, eternal life

RECEIVE MY INSTRUCTION
Prov 8:10 *Receive my instruction*, and not silver, and knowledge rather than choice gold

RECEIVE MY PRAYER
Ps 6:9 The Lord has heard my supplication; the Lord will *receive my prayer*

RECEIVE MY SAYINGS
Prov 4:10 Hear, my son, and *receive my sayings*, and the years of your life will be many

RECEIVE ONE WHO IS WEAK
Rom 14:1 *Receive one who is weak* in the faith, but not to disputes over doubtful things

RECEIVE THE CROWN OF LIFE
Jas 1:12 for when he has been proved, he will *receive the crown of life* which the Lord has promised to those who love Him

RECEIVE THE HOLY SPIRIT
John 20:22 And when He had said this, He breathed on them, and said to them, "*Receive the Holy Spirit*
Acts 8:15 who, when they had come down, prayed for them that they might *receive the Holy Spirit*
Acts 8:19 saying, "Give me this power also, that anyone on whom I lay hands may *receive the Holy Spirit*
Acts 19:2 he said to them, "Did you *receive the Holy Spirit* when you believed

RECEIVE THE KINGDOM
Dan 7:18 But the saints of the Most High shall *receive the kingdom*, and possess the kingdom forever, even forever and ever
Mark 10:15 Assuredly, I say to you, whoever does not *receive the kingdom* of God as a little child will by no means enter it
Luke 18:17 Assuredly, I say to you, whoever does not *receive the kingdom* of God as a little child will by no means enter it

RECEIVE THE SPIRIT
Rom 8:15 For you did not *receive the spirit* of bondage again to fear, but you received the Spirit of adoption by whom we cry out
Gal 3:2 Did you *receive the Spirit* by the works of the law, or by the hearing of faith

RECEIVED FROM THE LORD
Acts 20:24 nor do I count my life dear to myself, so that I may finish my race with joy, and the ministry which I *received from the Lord* Jesus, to testify to the gospel of the grace of God
1Cor 11:23 For I *received from the Lord* that which I also delivered to you

RECEIVED MERCY (NIV, RSV)
(See *OBTAINED MERCY*)

RECEIVED THE HOLY SPIRIT
Acts 8:17 Then they laid hands on them, and they *received the Holy Spirit*
Acts 10:47 Can anyone forbid water, that these should not be baptized who have *received the Holy Spirit* just as we have

RECEIVED THE SPIRIT
Rom 8:15 For you did not receive the spirit of bondage again to fear, but you *received the Spirit* of adoption by whom we cry out

RECEIVED UP IN GLORY
1Tim 3:16 God was manifested in the flesh, justified in the Spirit, seen by angels, preached among the Gentiles, believed on in the world, *received up in glory*

RECEIVED WITH THANKSGIVING
1Tim 4:3 forbidding to marry, and commanding to abstain from foods which God created to be *received with thanksgiving* by those who believe and know the truth
1Tim 4:4 For every creature of God is good, and nothing is to be refused if it is *received with thanksgiving*

RECEIVING OF THE LAW (NIV)
(See *GIVING OF THE LAW*)

RECKONED TO HIM (NAS, RSV)
(See *ACCOUNTED TO HIM*)

RECKONED TO US (RSV)
(See *IMPUTED TO US*)

RECOGNIZED BY ITS FRUIT (NIV)
(See *KNOWN BY ITS FRUIT*)

RECOGNIZING THE BODY OF THE LORD (NIV)
(See *DISCERNING THE LORD'S BODY*)

RECONCILE ALL THINGS TO HIMSELF
Col 1:20 and by Him to *reconcile all things to Himself*, by Him, whether things on earth or things in heaven, having made peace through the blood of His cross

RECONCILING THE WORLD TO HIMSELF
2Cor 5:19 that is, that God was in Christ *reconciling the world to Himself*, not imputing their trespasses to them, and has committed to us the word of reconciliation

RECORD IS TRUE (KJV)
(See *TESTIMONY IS TRUE*)

RECORD OF JOHN (KJV)
(See *TESTIMONY OF JOHN*)

RECORDED IN THE BOOK (RSV)
(See *WRITTEN IN THE BOOK*)

RECORDED IN THIS BOOK OF THE LAW (NIV)
(See *WRITTEN IN THE BOOK*)

RECOVERY OF SIGHT TO THE BLIND
Luke 4:18 He has sent Me to heal the brokenhearted, to preach deliverance to the captives and *recovery of sight to the blind*, to set at liberty those who are oppressed

REDEEM FOR HIMSELF AS A PEOPLE
2Sam 7:23 And who is like Your people, like Israel, the one nation on the earth whom God went

to *redeem for Himself as a people*, to make for Himself a name and to do for You great and awesome deeds for Your land before Your people whom You redeemed for Yourself from Egypt, from the nations and their gods

1Chr 17:21 And who is like Your people Israel, the one nation on the earth whom God went to *redeem for Himself as a people* to make for Yourself a name by great and awesome deeds, by driving out nations from before Your people whom You redeemed from Egypt

REDEEM ME

Job 6:23 or, 'Deliver me from the enemy's hand'? or, '*Redeem me* from the hand of oppressors

Ps 26:11 But as for me, I will walk in my integrity; *redeem me* and be merciful to me

Ps 119:134 *Redeem me* from the oppression of man, that I may keep Your precepts

Ps 119:154 Plead my cause and *redeem me;* revive me according to Your word

REDEEM TO BE HIS PEOPLE (RSV)
(See *REDEEM FOR HIMSELF AS A PEOPLE*)

REDEEM YOU WITH AN OUTSTRETCHED ARM

Ex 6:6 I will bring you out from under the burdens of the Egyptians, I will rescue you from their bondage, and I will *redeem you with an outstretched arm* and with great judgments

REDEEMED OF THE LORD

Ps 107:2 Let the *redeemed of the Lord* say so, whom He has redeemed from the hand of the enemy

Is 62:12 And they shall call them the Holy People, the *Redeemed of the Lord*

REDEEMED YOU FROM THE HOUSE OF BONDAGE

Deut 7:8 but because the Lord loves you, and because He would keep the oath which He swore to your fathers, the Lord has brought you out with a mighty hand, and *redeemed you from the house of bondage*, from the hand of Pharaoh king of Egypt

Deut 13:5 But that prophet or that dreamer of dreams shall be put to death, because he has spoken in order to turn you away from the Lord your God, who brought you out of the land of Egypt and *redeemed you from the house of bondage*, to entice you from the way in which the Lord your God commanded you to walk

Mic 6:4 For I brought you up from the land of Egypt, I *redeemed you from the house of bondage*

REDEEMED YOU FROM THE LAND OF SLAVERY (NIV)
(See *REDEEMED YOU FROM THE HOUSE OF BONDAGE*)

REDEEMING THE TIME

Eph 5:16 *redeeming the time*, because the days are evil

Col 4:5 Walk in wisdom toward those who are outside, *redeeming the time*

REDEMPTION OF OUR BODY

Rom 8:23 And not only they, but we also who have the firstfruits of the Spirit, even we ourselves groan within ourselves, eagerly waiting for the adoption, the *redemption of our body*

REDEMPTION OF THE LAND

Lev 25:24 And in all the land of your possession you shall grant *redemption of the land*

REDEMPTION THAT IS IN CHRIST

Rom 3:24 being justified freely by His grace through the *redemption that is in Christ* Jesus

REDEMPTION THROUGH HIS BLOOD

Eph 1:7 In Him we have *redemption through His blood*, the forgiveness of sins, according to the riches of His grace

Col 1:14 in whom we have *redemption through His blood*, the forgiveness of sins

REDUCED TO SKIN AND BONES (NIV)
(See *BONES CLING TO MY SKIN*)

REED SHAKEN BY THE WIND

Matt 11:7 What did you go out into the wilderness to see? A *reed shaken by the wind*

Luke 7:24 What did you go out into the wilderness to see? A *reed shaken by the wind*

REEL TO AND FRO LIKE A DRUNKARD

Is 24:20 The earth shall *reel to and fro like a drunkard*, and shall totter like a hut

REFINED US AS SILVER

Ps 66:10 For You, O God, have proved us; You have *refined us as silver* is refined

REFRAIN FROM (NAS, NIV, RSV)
(See *ABSTAIN FROM*)

REFRAIN MY MOUTH (KJV)
(See *RESTRAIN MY MOUTH*)

REFRESH MY HEART IN THE LORD

Phm 20 Yes, brother, let me have joy from you in the Lord; *refresh my heart in the Lord*

REFRESHED MY SPIRIT

1Cor 16:18 For they *refreshed my spirit* and yours; therefore acknowledge such men

REFUGE IN TIMES OF TROUBLE

Ps 9:9 The Lord also will be a refuge for the oppressed, a *refuge in times of trouble*

REGARD THE PRAYER

1Kin 8:28 Yet *regard the prayer* of Your servant and his supplication, O Lord my God, and listen to the cry and the prayer which Your servant is praying before You today

2Chr 6:19 Yet *regard the prayer* of Your servant and his supplication, O Lord my God, and listen to the cry and to the prayer which Your servant is praying before You

Ps 102:17 He shall *regard the prayer* of the destitute, and shall not despise their prayer

REGION OF GOSHEN (NIV)
(See *LAND OF GOSHEN*)

REGULATIONS AND LAWS THAT ARE JUST (NIV)
(See *JUST ORDINANCES*)

REGULATIONS FOR INFECTIOUS SKIN DISEASES (NIV)
(See *LAW OF LEPROSY*)

REIGN OVER JUDAH (RSV)
(See *KING OVER JUDAH*)

REIGN OVER THE HOUSE OF JACOB

Luke 1:33 And He will *reign over the house of Jacob* forever, and of His kingdom there will be no end

REIGNED WITH CHRIST
Rev 20:4 And they lived and *reigned with Christ* for a thousand years

REJECT MY DECREES (NIV)
(See *DESPISE MY STATUTES*)

REJECTED KNOWLEDGE
Hos 4:6 Because you have *rejected knowledge*, I also will reject you from being priest for Me

REJECTED THE LAW (NAS, NIV, RSV)
(See *DESPISED THE LAW*)

REJECTED YOUR GOD
1Sam 10:19 But you have today *rejected your God*, who Himself saved you out of all your adversities and your tribulations

REJECTING ME (NIV)
(See *PROVOKE ME*)

REJOICE AND BE GLAD
Ps 40:16 Let all those who seek You *rejoice and be glad* in You
Ps 70:4 Let all those who seek You *rejoice and be glad* in You
Ps 90:14 Oh, satisfy us early with Your mercy, that we may *rejoice and be glad* all our days
Ps 118:24 This is the day which the Lord has made; we will *rejoice and be glad* in it
Lam 4:21 *Rejoice and be glad*, O daughter of Edom, you who dwell in the land of Uz

REJOICE BEFORE THE LORD
Lev 23:40 and you shall *rejoice before the Lord* your God for seven days
Deut 12:12 And you shall *rejoice before the Lord* your God, you and your sons and your daughters, your menservants and your maidservants, and the Levite who is within your gates, since he has no portion nor inheritance with you
Deut 12:18 and you shall *rejoice before the Lord* your God in all to which you put your hands
Deut 16:11 You shall *rejoice before the Lord* your God, you and your son and your daughter, your manservant and your maidservant, the Levite who is within your gates, the stranger and the fatherless and the widow who are among you, at the place where the Lord your God chooses to make His name abide
Deut 27:7 You shall offer peace offerings, and shall eat there, and *rejoice before the Lord* your God
1Chr 16:33 Then the trees of the woods shall *rejoice before the Lord*, for He is coming to judge the earth
Ps 96:12 Then all the trees of the woods will *rejoice before the Lord*

REJOICE IN THE GLADNESS
Ps 106:5 That I may see the benefit of Your chosen ones, that I may *rejoice in the gladness* of Your nation, that I may glory with Your inheritance

REJOICE IN THE LORD
Ps 33:1 *Rejoice in the Lord*, O you righteous! For praise from the upright is beautiful
Ps 97:12 *Rejoice in the Lord*, you righteous, and give thanks at the remembrance of His holy name
Is 41:16 you shall *rejoice in the Lord*, and glory in the Holy One of Israel
Is 61:10 I will greatly *rejoice in the Lord*, my soul shall be joyful in my God
Joel 2:23 Be glad then, you children of Zion, and *rejoice in the Lord* your God
Hab 3:18 Yet I will *rejoice in the Lord*, I will joy in the God of my salvation
Zech 10:7 Yes, their children shall see it and be glad; their heart shall *rejoice in the Lord*
Phil 3:1 Finally, my brethren, *rejoice in the Lord*. For me to write the same things to you is not tedious, but for you it is safe
Phil 4:4 *Rejoice in the Lord* always. Again I will say, rejoice

REJOICE WHO SEEK THE LORD
1Chr 16:10 let the hearts of those *rejoice who seek the Lord*
Ps 105:3 Let the hearts of those *rejoice who seek the Lord*

REJOICED IN THE SPIRIT
Luke 10:21 In that hour Jesus *rejoiced in the Spirit* and said

REJOICES IN THE RIGHT (RSV)
(See *REJOICES IN THE TRUTH*)

REJOICES IN THE TRUTH
1Cor 13:6 does not rejoice in iniquity, but *rejoices in the truth*

RELEASE TO THE CAPTIVES (NAS, RSV)
(See *DELIVERANCE TO THE CAPTIVES*)

RELEASED FROM THIS OATH
Gen 24:8 And if the woman is not willing to follow you, then you will be *released from this oath*

RELIEVE THE OPPRESSED (KJV)
(See *REPROVE THE OPPRESSOR*)

RELIEVES THE FATHERLESS AND WIDOW
Ps 146:9 He *relieves the fatherless and widow;* but the way of the wicked He turns upside down

RELY ON HORSES
Is 31:1 Woe to those who go down to Egypt for help, and *rely on horses*, who trust in chariots because they are many, and in horsemen because they are very strong, but who do not look to the Holy One of Israel, nor seek the Lord

RELY ON THE LORD (RSV)
(See *TRUST IN THE LORD*)

REMAIN ALIVE UNTIL I RETURN (NIV)
(See *REMAIN TILL I COME*)

REMAIN TILL I COME
John 21:22 Jesus said to him, "If I will that he *remain till I come*, what is that to you
John 21:23 Yet Jesus did not say to him that he would not die, but, "If I will that he *remain till I come*, what is that to you

REMAIN UNMARRIED
1Cor 7:11 But even if she does depart, let her *remain unmarried* or be reconciled to her husband

REMAINS A PRIEST CONTINUALLY
Heb 7:3 without father, without mother, without genealogy, having neither beginning of days nor end of life, but made like the Son of God, *remains a priest continually*

REMEMBER HIM (NIV)
(See *REMEMBER YOUR CREATOR*)

REMEMBER HIS COVENANT ALWAYS
1Chr 16:15 *Remember His covenant always*, the word which He commanded, for a thousand generations

REMEMBER HIS HOLY COVENANT
Luke 1:72 to perform the mercy promised to our fathers and to *remember His holy covenant*

REMEMBER LOT'S WIFE
Luke 17:32 *Remember Lot's wife*

REMEMBER ME
Gen 40:14 But *remember me* when it is well with you, and please show kindness to me
Judg 16:28 Then Samson called to the Lord, saying, "O Lord God, *remember me*, I pray
1Sam 1:11 Then she made a vow and said, "O Lord of hosts, if You will indeed look on the affliction of your maidservant and *remember me*, and not forget your maidservant, but will give your maidservant a male child, then I will give him to the Lord all the days of his life, and no razor shall come upon his head
Neh 5:19 *Remember me*, my God, for good, according to all that I have done for this people
Neh 13:14 *Remember me*, O my God, concerning this, and do not wipe out my good deeds that I have done for the house of my God, and for its services
Neh 13:22 *Remember me*, O my God, concerning this also, and spare me according to the greatness of Your mercy
Neh 13:31 and to bringing the wood offering and the firstfruits at appointed times. *Remember me*, O my God, for good
Job 14:13 Oh, that You would hide me in the grave, that You would conceal me until Your wrath is past, that You would appoint me a set time, and *remember me*
Ps 25:7 According to Your mercy *remember me*, for Your goodness' sake, O Lord
Ps 106:4 *Remember me*, O Lord, with the favor You have toward Your people
Jer 15:15 *remember me* and visit me, and take vengeance for me on my persecutors
Ezek 6:9 Then those of you who escape will *remember Me* among the nations where they are carried captive, because I was crushed by their adulterous heart which has departed from Me, and by their eyes which play the harlot after their idols
Zech 10:9 I will sow them among the peoples, and they shall *remember Me* in far countries
Luke 23:42 Then he said to Jesus, "Lord, *remember me* when You come into Your kingdom
1Cor 11:2 Now I praise you, brethren, that you *remember me* in all things and keep the traditions as I delivered them to you

REMEMBER MY COVENANT
Gen 9:15 and I will *remember My covenant* which is between Me and you and every living creature of all flesh
Lev 26:42 then I will *remember My covenant* with Jacob, and My covenant with Isaac and My covenant with Abraham I will remember
Ezek 16:60 Nevertheless I will *remember My covenant* with you in the days of your youth, and I will establish an everlasting covenant with you

REMEMBER THAT YOU WERE A SLAVE
Deut 5:15 And *remember that you were a slave* in the land of Egypt, and that the Lord your God brought you out from there by a mighty hand and by an outstretched arm
Deut 15:15 You shall *remember that you were a slave* in the land of Egypt, and the Lord your God redeemed you
Deut 16:12 And you shall *remember that you were a slave* in Egypt, and you shall be careful to observe these statutes
Deut 24:18 But you shall *remember that you were a slave* in Egypt, and the Lord your God redeemed you from there
Deut 24:22 And you shall *remember that you were a slave* in the land of Egypt

REMEMBER THE LORD
Deut 8:18 And you shall *remember the Lord* your God, for it is He who gives you power to get wealth, that He may establish His covenant which He swore to your fathers, as it is this day
Judg 8:34 Thus the children of Israel did not *remember the Lord* their God, who had delivered them from the hands of all their enemies on every side
2Sam 14:11 Then she said, "Please let the king *remember the Lord* your God, and do not permit the avenger of blood to destroy anymore, lest they destroy my son
Neh 4:14 *Remember the Lord*, great and awesome, and fight for your brethren, your sons, your daughters, your wives, and your houses
Jer 51:50 *Remember the Lord* afar off, and let Jerusalem come to your mind

REMEMBER THE SABBATH DAY
Ex 20:8 *Remember the Sabbath day*, to keep it holy

REMEMBER YOUR CREATOR
Eccl 12:6 *Remember your Creator* before the silver cord is loosed, or the golden bowl is broken, or the pitcher shattered at the fountain, or the wheel broken at the well

REMEMBERED HIS COVENANT
Ex 2:24 So God heard their groaning, and God *remembered His covenant* with Abraham, with Isaac, and with Jacob
Ps 105:8 He has *remembered His covenant* forever, the word which He commanded, for a thousand generations
Ps 106:45 And for their sake He *remembered His covenant*, and relented according to the multitude of His mercies

REMEMBERED NOT THE LORD (KJV)
(See *DID NOT REMEMBER THE LORD*)

REMEMBERING TO BE MERCIFUL (NIV)
(See *REMEMBRANCE OF HIS MERCY*)

REMEMBERING YOU (NIV, RSV)
(See *MAKING MENTION OF YOU*)

REMEMBRANCE OF HIS MERCY
Luke 1:54 He has helped His servant Israel, in *remembrance of His mercy*

REMIND YOU (NIV)
(See *BRING TO YOUR REMEMBRANCE*)

REMISSION OF SINS
Matt 26:28 For this is My blood of the new covenant, which is shed for many for the *remission of sins*
Mark 1:4 John came baptizing in the wilderness and preaching a baptism of repentance for the *remission of sins*
Luke 3:3 And he went into all the region around the Jordan, preaching a baptism of repentance for the *remission of sins*
Luke 24:47 and that repentance and *remission of sins* should be preached in His name to all nations, beginning at Jerusalem
Acts 2:38 Then Peter said to them, "Repent, and let every one of you be baptized in the name of Jesus Christ for the *remission of sins*
Acts 10:43 To Him all the prophets witness that,

through His name, whoever believes in Him will receive *remission of sins*

REMNANT OF HIS PEOPLE
Is 11:11 It shall come to pass in that day that the Lord shall set His hand again the second time to recover the *remnant of His people* who are left, from Assyria and Egypt, from Pathros and Cush, from Elam and Shinar, from Hamath and the islands of the sea
Is 11:16 There will be a highway for the *remnant of His people* who will be left from Assyria, as it was for Israel in the day that he came up from the land of Egypt
Is 28:5 In that day the Lord of hosts will be for a crown of glory and a diadem of beauty to the *remnant of His people*

REMNANT OF ISRAEL
2Chr 34:9 When they came to Hilkiah the high priest, they delivered the money that was brought into the house of God, which the Levites who kept the doors had gathered from the hand of Manasseh and Ephraim, from all the *remnant of Israel*, from all Judah and Benjamin, and which they had brought back to Jerusalem
Is 10:20 And it shall come to pass in that day that the *remnant of Israel*, and such as have escaped of the house of Jacob, will never again depend on him who defeated them, but will depend on the Lord, the Holy One of Israel, in truth
Jer 6:9 They shall thoroughly glean as a vine the *remnant of Israel*
Jer 31:7 proclaim, give praise, and say, 'O Lord, save Your people, the *remnant of Israel*
Ezek 9:8 Will You destroy all the *remnant of Israel* in pouring out Your fury on Jerusalem
Ezek 11:13 Will You make a complete end of the *remnant of Israel*
Mic 2:12 I will surely assemble all of you, O Jacob, I will surely gather the *remnant of Israel*
Zeph 3:13 The *remnant of Israel* shall do no unrighteousness and speak no lies, nor shall a deceitful tongue be found in their mouth

REMNANT OF JACOB
Is 10:21 The remnant will return, the *remnant of Jacob*, to the Mighty God
Mic 5:7 Then the *remnant of Jacob* shall be in the midst of many peoples, like dew from the Lord, like showers on the grass, that tarry for no man nor wait for the sons of men
Mic 5:8 And the *remnant of Jacob* shall be among the Gentiles, in the midst of many peoples, like a lion among the beasts of the forest, like a young lion among flocks of sheep, who, if he passes through, both treads down and tears in pieces, and none can deliver

REMNANT OF MY PEOPLE (KJV, NAS, NIV, RSV)
(See *RESIDUE OF MY PEOPLE*)

REMNANT OF THEM WILL BE SAVED (RSV)
(See *REMNANT WILL BE SAVED*)

REMNANT THAT IS LEFT OF HIS PEOPLE (NIV)
(See *REMNANT OF HIS PEOPLE*)

REMNANT WILL BE SAVED
Rom 9:27 Though the number of the children of Israel be as the sand of the sea, the *remnant will be saved*

REMNANT WILL RETURN
Is 10:21 The *remnant will return*, the remnant of Jacob, to the Mighty God

REMOTE PLACE (NIV)
(See *DESERTED PLACE*)

REMOVE THE SPECK
Matt 7:4 Or how can you say to your brother, 'Let me *remove the speck* out of your eye
Matt 7:5 First remove the plank from your own eye, and then you will see clearly to *remove the speck* out of your brother's eye
Luke 6:42 Or how can you say to your brother, 'Brother, let me *remove the speck* that is in your eye,' when you yourself do not see the plank that is in your own eye? Hypocrite! First remove the plank from your own eye, and then you will see clearly to *remove the speck* that is in your brother's eye

REMOVE THIS CUP
Luke 22:42 saying, "Father, if it is Your will, *remove this cup* from Me

REMOVED LIKE A COTTAGE (KJV)
(See *TOTTER LIKE A HUT*)

REMOVED THEIR HEARTS FAR FROM ME
Is 29:13 Inasmuch as these people draw near to Me with their mouths and honor Me with their lips, but have *removed their hearts far from Me*, and their fear toward Me is taught by the commandment of men

REND YOUR HEART
Joel 2:13 So *rend your heart*, and not your garments; return to the Lord your God, for He is gracious and merciful, slow to anger, and of great kindness

RENDER EVIL FOR GOOD
Ps 38:20 Those also who *render evil for good*, they are my adversaries, because I follow what is good

RENDER TO CAESAR
Mark 12:17 Then Jesus answered and said to them, "*Render to Caesar* the things that are Caesar's, and to God the things that are God's

RENDER TO EACH ONE
Ps 62:12 For You *render to each one* according to his work
Rom 2:6 who "will *render to each one* according to his deeds

RENDER TO THE LORD
Ps 116:12 What shall I *render to the Lord* for all His benefits toward me

RENEW THEIR STRENGTH
Is 40:31 But those who wait on the Lord shall *renew their strength*
Is 41:1 Keep silence before Me, O coastlands, and let the people *renew their strength*

RENEWING OF THE HOLY SPIRIT
Tit 3:5 not by works of righteousness which we have done, but according to His mercy He saved us, through the washing of regeneration and *renewing of the Holy Spirit*

RENOWNED AND PRAISED (RSV)
(See *FAME AND PRAISE*)

RENT HIS CLOTHES (KJV, RSV)
(See *TORE HIS CLOTHES*)

RENT THEIR CLOTHES (NIV)
(See *TORE THEIR CLOTHES*)

REPAID EVIL FOR GOOD
Gen 44:4 and when you overtake them, say to them, 'Why have you *repaid evil for good*

REPAIRED THE WALL
Neh 3:15 he built it, covered it, hung its doors with its bolts and bars, and *repaired the wall* of the Pool of Shelah by the King's Garden, as far as the stairs that go down from the City of David

REPAY ME EVIL FOR GOOD (NAS, NIV)
(See *REWARD ME EVIL FOR GOOD*)

REPAY MY GOOD WITH EVIL (NIV)
(See *RENDER EVIL FOR GOOD*)

REPAY THE LORD (NIV)
(See *RENDER TO THE LORD*)

REPAY THEM FOR THEIR DEEDS (NIV)
(See *GIVE TO THEM ACCORDING TO THEIR DEEDS*)

REPENT, AND LET EVERY ONE OF YOU BE BAPTIZED
Acts 2:38 Then Peter said to them, "*Repent, and let every one of you be baptized* in the name of Jesus Christ for the remission of sins

REPENT THEREFORE AND BE CONVERTED
Acts 3:19 *Repent therefore and be converted*, that your sins may be blotted out, so that times of refreshing may come from the presence of the Lord

REPENTANCE BY THEIR DEEDS (NIV)
(See *WORKS BEFITTING REPENTANCE*)

REPENTANCE TOWARD GOD
Acts 20:21 testifying to Jews, and also to Greeks, *repentance toward God* and faith toward our Lord Jesus Christ

REPROACH AND A BYWORD
Jer 24:9 I will deliver them to trouble into all the kingdoms of the earth, for their harm, to be a *reproach and a byword*, a taunt and a curse, in all places where I shall drive them

REPROACH AND A PROVERB (KJV, NAS)
(See *REPROACH AND A BYWORD*)

REPROACH OF MEN
Ps 22:6 But I am a worm, and no man; a *reproach of men*, and despised of the people
Is 51:7 do not fear the *reproach of men*, nor be afraid of their revilings

REPROACHES HIS MAKER
Prov 14:31 He who oppresses the poor *reproaches his Maker*, but he who honors Him has mercy on the needy
Prov 17:5 He who mocks the poor *reproaches his Maker;* he who is glad at calamity will not go unpunished

REPROVE A WISE MAN (NAS, RSV)
(See *REBUKE A WISE MAN*)

REPROVE THE OPPRESSOR
Is 1:17 seek justice, *reprove the oppressor;* defend the fatherless, plead for the widow

REPROVE THE WORLD OF SIN (KJV)
(See *CONVICT THE WORLD OF SIN*)

REQUIRE THE LIFE OF MAN
Gen 9:5 From the hand of every man's brother I will *require the life of man*

REQUITE A MAN (RSV)
(See *RENDER TO EACH ONE*)

REQUITE ME EVIL FOR GOOD (RSV)
(See *REWARD ME EVIL FOR GOOD*)

RESCUE ME
Ps 35:17 *Rescue me* from their destructions, my precious life from the lions
Ps 144:7 *Rescue me* and deliver me out of great waters, from the hand of foreigners
Ps 144:11 *Rescue me* and deliver me from the hand of foreigners, whose mouth speaks vain words, and whose right hand is a right hand of falsehood

RESCUE MY SOUL (KJV, NAS)
(See *RESCUE ME*)

RESERVED FOR JUDGMENT
2Pet 2:4 For if God did not spare the angels who sinned, but cast them down to hell and delivered them into chains of darkness, to be *reserved for judgment*

RESERVED IN HEAVEN
1Pet 1:4 to an inheritance incorruptible and undefiled and that does not fade away, *reserved in heaven* for you

RESIDUE OF MY PEOPLE
Zeph 2:9 the *residue of My people* shall plunder them, and the remnant of My people shall possess them

RESIST THE DEVIL
Jas 4:7 Therefore submit to God. *Resist the devil* and he will flee from you

RESISTS THE ORDINANCE OF GOD
Rom 13:2 Therefore whoever resists the authority *resists the ordinance of God*, and those who resist will bring judgment on themselves

RESPECT PERSONS IN JUDGMENT (KJV)
(See *SHOW PARTIALITY*)

RESPECT UNTO THE PRAYER (KJV)
(See *REGARD THE PRAYER*)

RESPECTED AT THE CITY GATE (NIV)
(See *KNOWN IN THE GATES*)

REST ASSURED (RSV)
(See *PEACE BE WITH YOU*)

REST IN MY SPIRIT
2Cor 2:13 I had no *rest in my spirit*, because I did not find Titus my brother

REST OF THE HOLY SABBATH (KJV)
(See *SABBATH REST*)

RESTED ON THE SABBATH
Luke 23:56 And they *rested on the Sabbath* according to the commandment

RESTED ON THE SEVENTH DAY
Gen 2:2 And on the seventh day God ended His work which He had done, and He *rested on the seventh day* from all His work which He had done
Ex 16:30 So the people *rested on the seventh day*
Heb 4:4 And God *rested on the seventh day* from all His works

RESTED THE SABBATH DAY (KJV)
(See *RESTED ON THE SABBATH*)

RESTED WITH HIS FATHERS
1Kin 2:10 So David *rested with his fathers*, and was buried in the City of David
1Kin 11:21 Now when Hadad heard in Egypt that David *rested with his fathers*, and that Joab the commander of the army was dead, Hadad said to Pharaoh
1Kin 11:43 Then Solomon *rested with his fathers*, and was buried in the City of David his father

1Kin 14:20 So he *rested with his fathers*. Then Nadab his son reigned in his place
1Kin 14:31 So Rehoboam *rested with his fathers*, and was buried with his fathers in the City of David
1Kin 15:8 So Abijam *rested with his fathers*, and they buried him in the City of David
1Kin 15:24 So Asa *rested with his fathers*, and was buried with his fathers in the City of David his father
1Kin 16:6 So Baasha *rested with his fathers* and was buried in Tirzah
1Kin 16:28 So Omri *rested with his fathers* and was buried in Samaria
1Kin 22:40 So Ahab *rested with his fathers*. Then Ahaziah his son reigned in his place
1Kin 22:50 And Jehoshaphat *rested with his fathers*, and was buried with his fathers in the City of David his father
2Kin 8:24 So Joram *rested with his fathers*, and was buried with his fathers in the City of David
2Kin 10:35 So Jehu *rested with his fathers*, and they buried him in Samaria
2Kin 13:9 So Jehoahaz *rested with his fathers*, and they buried him in Samaria
2Kin 13:13 So Joash *rested with his fathers*. Then Jeroboam sat on his throne
2Kin 14:16 So Jehoash *rested with his fathers*, and was buried in Samaria with the kings of Israel
2Kin 14:22 He built Elath and restored it to Judah, after the king *rested with his fathers*
2Kin 14:29 So Jeroboam *rested with his fathers*, the kings of Israel
2Kin 15:7 So Azariah *rested with his fathers*, and they buried him with his fathers in the City of David
2Kin 15:22 So Menahem *rested with his fathers*. Then Pekahiah his son reigned in his place
2Kin 15:38 So Jotham *rested with his fathers*, and was buried with his fathers in the City of David his father
2Kin 16:20 So Ahaz *rested with his fathers*, and was buried with his fathers in the City of David
2Kin 20:21 So Hezekiah *rested with his fathers*. Then Manasseh his son reigned in his place
2Kin 21:18 So Manasseh *rested with his fathers*, and was buried in the garden of his own house, in the garden of Uzza
2Kin 24:6 So Jehoiakim *rested with his fathers*. Then Jehoiachin his son reigned in his place
2Chr 9:31 Then Solomon *rested with his fathers*, and was buried in the City of David his father
2Chr 12:16 So Rehoboam *rested with his fathers*, and was buried in the City of David
2Chr 14:1 So Abijah *rested with his fathers*, and they buried him in the City of David
2Chr 16:13 So Asa *rested with his fathers;* he died in the forty-first year of his reign
2Chr 21:1 And Jehoshaphat *rested with his fathers*, and was buried with his fathers in the City of David
2Chr 26:2 He built Elath and restored it to Judah, after the king *rested with his fathers*
2Chr 26:23 So Uzziah *rested with his fathers*, and they buried him with his fathers in the field of burial which belonged to the kings, for they said
2Chr 27:9 So Jotham *rested with his fathers*, and they buried him in the City of David
2Chr 28:27 So Ahaz *rested with his fathers*, and they buried him in the city, in Jerusalem
2Chr 32:33 So Hezekiah *rested with his fathers*, and they buried him in the upper tombs of the sons of David
2Chr 33:20 So Manasseh *rested with his fathers*, and they buried him in his own house

RESTITUTION OF ALL THINGS (KJV)
(See *RESTORATION OF ALL THINGS*)

RESTORATION OF ALL THINGS
Acts 3:21 whom heaven must receive until the times of *restoration of all things*, which God has spoken by the mouth of all His holy prophets since the world began

RESTORE OUR FORTUNES (NIV, RSV)
(See *BRING BACK OUR CAPTIVITY*)

RESTORE THE FORTUNES (NAS, NIV, RSV)
(See *BRING BACK THE CAPTIVITY*)

RESTORE THE KINGDOM TO ISRAEL
Acts 1:6 Therefore, when they had come together, they asked Him, saying, "Lord, will You at this time *restore the kingdom to Israel*

RESTORE THE NAME OF THE DEAD (RSV)
(See *RAISE UP THE NAME OF THE DEAD*)

RESTORED TO LIFE
2Kin 8:1 Then Elisha spoke to the woman whose son he had *restored to life*, saying
2Kin 8:5 Now it happened, as he was telling the king how he had restored the dead to life, that there was the woman whose son he had *restored to life*, appealing to the king for her house and for her land. And Gehazi said, "My lord, O king, this is the woman, and this is her son whom Elisha *restored to life*

RESTORES MY SOUL
Ps 23:3 He *restores my soul;* He leads me in the paths of righteousness for His name's sake

RESTRAIN MY MOUTH
Job 7:11 Therefore I will not *restrain my mouth;* I will speak in the anguish of my spirit
Ps 39:1 I will *restrain my mouth* with a muzzle, while the wicked are before me

RESTRAIN YOUR HAND
2Sam 24:16 now *restrain Your hand*." And the angel of the Lord was by the threshing floor of Araunah the Jebusite
1Chr 21:15 now *restrain your hand*." And the angel of the Lord stood by the threshing floor of Ornan the Jebusite

RESTRAINED NOT HIS HAND (RSV)
(See *WITHDRAWN HIS HAND*)

RESURRECTION OF CONDEMNATION
John 5:29 and come forth those who have done good, to the resurrection of life, and those who have done evil, to the *resurrection of condemnation*

RESURRECTION OF DAMNATION (KJV)
(See *RESURRECTION OF CONDEMNATION*)

RESURRECTION OF JESUS CHRIST
1Pet 1:3 Blessed be the God and Father of our Lord Jesus Christ, who according to His abundant mercy has begotten us again to a living hope through the *resurrection of Jesus Christ* from the dead
1Pet 3:21 There is also an antitype which now saves us, namely baptism (not the removal of the filth of the flesh, but the answer of a good conscience toward God), through the *resurrection of Jesus Christ*

RESURRECTION OF JUDGMENT (NAS, RSV)
(See *RESURRECTION OF CONDEMNATION*)

RESURRECTION OF LIFE
John 5:29 and come forth those who have done good, to the *resurrection of life*, and those who have done evil, to the resurrection of condemnation

RESURRECTION OF THE DEAD
Matt 22:31 But concerning the *resurrection of the dead*, have you not read what was spoken to you by God, saying
Acts 17:32 And when they heard of the *resurrection of the dead*, some mocked, while others said
Acts 23:6 concerning the hope and *resurrection of the dead* I am being judged
Acts 24:15 I have hope in God, which they themselves also accept, that there will be a *resurrection of the dead*, both of the just and the unjust
Acts 24:21 unless it is for this one statement which I cried out, standing among them, 'Concerning the *resurrection of the dead* I am being judged by you this day
1Cor 15:12 Now if Christ is preached that He has been raised from the dead, how do some among you say that there is no *resurrection of the dead*
1Cor 15:13 But if there is no *resurrection of the dead*, then Christ is not risen
1Cor 15:21 For since by man came death, by Man also came the *resurrection of the dead*
1Cor 15:42 So also is the *resurrection of the dead*. The body is sown in corruption, it is raised in incorruption
Heb 6:2 of the doctrine of baptisms, of laying on of hands, of *resurrection of the dead*, and of eternal judgment

RESURRECTION OF THE JUST
Luke 14:14 for you shall be repaid at the *resurrection of the just*

RESURRECTION OF THE LORD JESUS
Acts 4:33 And with great power the apostles gave witness to the *resurrection of the Lord Jesus*

RETURN SAFELY (NAS, NIV)
(See *COME IN PEACE*)

RETURN TO DUST
Job 34:15 All flesh would perish together, and man would *return to dust*
Eccl 3:20 all are from the dust, and all *return to dust*

RETURN TO ME VOID
Is 55:11 it shall not *return to Me void*, but it shall accomplish what I please, and it shall prosper in the thing for which I sent it

RETURN TO THE GRAVE (NIV)
(See *INTO HELL*)

RETURN TO THE LORD
Deut 30:2 and you *return to the Lord* your God and obey His voice, according to all that I command you today, you and your children, with all your heart and with all your soul
1Sam 7:3 Then Samuel spoke to all the house of Israel, saying, "If you *return to the Lord* with all your hearts, then put away the foreign gods and the Ashtoreths from among you, and prepare your hearts for the Lord, and serve Him only
2Chr 30:6 Children of Israel, *return to the Lord* God of Abraham, Isaac, and Israel
2Chr 30:9 For if you *return to the Lord*, your brethren and your children will be treated with compassion by those who lead them captive, so that they may come back to this land
Is 19:22 they will *return to the Lord*, and He will be entreated by them and heal them
Is 55:7 let him *return to the Lord*, and He will have mercy on him
Hos 6:1 Come, and let us *return to the Lord;* for He has torn, but He will heal us
Hos 7:10 And the pride of Israel testifies to his face, but they do not *return to the Lord* their God, nor seek Him for all this
Hos 14:1 O Israel, *return to the Lord* your God, for you have stumbled because of your iniquity
Hos 14:2 Take words with you, and *return to the Lord*. Say to Him
Joel 2:13 *return to the Lord* your God, for He is gracious and merciful, slow to anger, and of great kindness

RETURNED EVIL FOR GOOD (RSV)
(See *REPAID EVIL FOR GOOD*)

REVEAL HIS SON IN ME
Gal 1:16 to *reveal His Son in me*, that I might preach Him among the Gentiles, I did not immediately confer with flesh and blood

REVEALED BY THE SPIRIT
Eph 3:5 which in other ages was not made known to the sons of men, as it has now been *revealed by the Spirit* to His holy apostles and prophets

REVEALED FROM HEAVEN
Rom 1:18 For the wrath of God is *revealed from heaven* against all ungodliness and unrighteousness of men, who suppress the truth in unrighteousness
2Th 1:7 and to give you who are troubled rest with us when the Lord Jesus is *revealed from heaven* with His mighty angels

REVELATION OF JESUS CHRIST
Gal 1:12 For I neither received it from man, nor was I taught it, but it came through the *revelation of Jesus Christ*
1Pet 1:7 that the genuineness of your faith, being much more precious than gold that perishes, though it is tested by fire, may be found to praise, honor, and glory at the *revelation of Jesus Christ*
1Pet 1:13 Therefore gird up the loins of your mind, be sober, and rest your hope fully upon the grace that is to be brought to you at the *revelation of Jesus Christ*
Rev 1:1 The *Revelation of Jesus Christ*, which God gave Him to show His servants things which must shortly take place

REVELATION OF THE MYSTERY
Rom 16:25 Now to Him who is able to establish you according to my gospel and the preaching of Jesus Christ, according to the *revelation of the mystery* which was kept secret since the world began

REVELATIONS OF THE LORD
2Cor 12:1 I will come to visions and *revelations of the Lord*

REVENUES WITHOUT JUSTICE
Prov 16:8 Better is a little with righteousness, than vast *revenues without justice*

REVERENCE CHRIST AS LORD (RSV)
(See *SANCTIFY THE LORD*)

REVIVE US AGAIN
Ps 85:6 Will You not *revive us again*, that Your people may rejoice in You

REWARD EACH PERSON (NIV)
(See *RENDER TO EACH ONE*)

REWARD IN HEAVEN
Matt 5:12 Rejoice and be exceedingly glad, for great is your *reward in heaven*, for so they persecuted the prophets who were before you

REWARD ME EVIL FOR GOOD
Ps 35:12 They *reward me evil for good*, to the sorrow of my soul

REWARDED EVIL FOR GOOD (KJV)
(See *REPAID EVIL FOR GOOD*)

REWARDER OF THOSE WHO DILIGENTLY SEEK HIM
Heb 11:6 But without faith it is impossible to please Him, for he who comes to God must believe that He is, and that He is a *rewarder of those who diligently seek Him*

REWARDS THOSE WHO SEEK HIM (RSV)
(See *REWARDER OF THOSE WHO DILIGENTLY SEEK HIM*)

RICH AND POOR
Ps 49:2 Both low and high, *rich and poor* together
Rev 13:16 And he causes all, both small and great, *rich and poor*, free and slave, to receive a mark on their right hand or on their foreheads

RICH IN FAITH
Jas 2:5 Has God not chosen the poor of this world to be *rich in faith* and heirs of the kingdom which He promised to those who love Him

RICH IN GOOD WORKS
1Tim 6:18 Let them do good, that they be *rich in good works*, ready to give, willing to share

RICH IN MERCY
Eph 2:4 But God, who is *rich in mercy*, because of His great love with which He loved us

RICHES AND HONOR
1Kin 3:13 both *riches and honor*, so that there shall not be anyone like you among the kings all your days
1Chr 29:12 Both *riches and honor* come from You, and You reign over all
1Chr 29:28 So he died in a good old age, full of days and *riches and honor*
2Chr 17:5 and all Judah gave presents to Jehoshaphat, and he had *riches and honor* in abundance
2Chr 18:1 Jehoshaphat had *riches and honor* in abundance; and by marriage he allied himself with Ahab
2Chr 32:27 Hezekiah had very great *riches and honor*. And he made himself treasuries for silver, for gold, for precious stones, for spices, for shields, and for all kinds of desirable items
Prov 3:16 Length of days is in her right hand, in her left hand *riches and honor*
Prov 8:18 *Riches and honor* are with me, enduring riches and righteousness
Prov 22:4 By humility and the fear of the Lord are *riches and honor* and life

RICHES, AND PLEASURES OF LIFE
Luke 8:14 And the ones that fell among thorns are those who, when they have heard, go out and are choked with cares, *riches, and pleasures of life*, and bring no fruit to maturity

RICHES IN GLORY
Phil 4:19 And my God shall supply all your need according to His *riches in glory* by Christ Jesus

RICHES OF GOD'S GRACE (NIV)
(See *RICHES OF HIS GRACE*)

RICHES OF HIS GLORY
Rom 9:23 and that He might make known the *riches of His glory* on the vessels of mercy, which He had prepared beforehand for glory
Eph 3:16 that He would grant you, according to the *riches of His glory*, to be strengthened with might through His Spirit in the inner man

RICHES OF HIS GRACE
Eph 1:7 In Him we have redemption through His blood, the forgiveness of sins, according to the *riches of His grace*
Eph 2:7 that in the ages to come He might show the exceeding *riches of His grace* in His kindness toward us in Christ Jesus

RICHLY ORNAMENTED ROBE (NIV)
(See *TUNIC OF MANY COLORS*)

RID YOURSELVES OF ALL MALICE (NIV)
(See *LAYING ASIDE ALL MALICE*)

RIDES ON A SWIFT CLOUD
Is 19:1 Behold, the Lord *rides on a swift cloud*, and will come into Egypt

RIDES ON THE CLOUDS
Ps 68:4 Extol Him who *rides on the clouds*, by His name YAH, and rejoice before Him

RIDICULE TO ALL THE NATIONS (NIV)
(See *BYWORD AMONG ALL NATIONS*)

RIGHT AND JUST (NIV)
(See *RIGHTEOUSNESS AND JUSTICE*)

RIGHT HAND
Gen 24:49 And if not, tell me, that I may turn to the *right hand* or to the left
Gen 48:13 And Joseph took them both, Ephraim with his *right hand* toward Israel's left hand, and Manasseh with his left hand toward Israel's *right hand*, and brought them near him
Gen 48:14 Then Israel stretched out his *right hand* and laid it on Ephraim's head, who was the younger, and his left hand on Manasseh's head, guiding his hands knowingly, for Manasseh was the firstborn
Gen 48:17 Now when Joseph saw that his father laid his *right hand* on the head of Ephraim, it displeased him
Gen 48:18 And Joseph said to his father, "Not so, my father, for this one is the firstborn; put your *right hand* on his head
Ex 14:22 So the children of Israel went into the midst of the sea on the dry ground, and the waters were a wall to them on their *right hand* and on their left
Ex 14:29 But the children of Israel had walked on dry land in the midst of the sea, and the waters were a wall to them on their *right hand* and on their left
Ex 15:6 Your *right hand*, O Lord, has become glorious in power; Your *right hand*, O Lord, has dashed the enemy in pieces
Ex 15:12 You stretched out Your *right hand;* the earth swallowed them
Ex 29:20 Then you shall kill the ram, and take some of its blood and put it on the tip of the right ear of Aaron and on the tip of the right ear of his sons, on the thumb of their *right hand* and on the big toe of their right foot, and sprinkle the blood all around on the altar
Lev 8:23 And he took some of its blood and put it

on the tip of Aaron's right ear, on the thumb of his *right hand*, and on the big toe of his right foot
Lev 14:14 The priest shall take some of the blood of the trespass offering, and the priest shall put it on the tip of the right ear of him who is to be cleansed, on the thumb of his *right hand*, and on the big toe of his right foot
Lev 14:17 And of the rest of the oil in his hand, the priest shall put some on the tip of the right ear of him who is to be cleansed, on the thumb of his *right hand*, and on the big toe of his right foot, on the blood of the trespass offering
Lev 14:25 Then he shall kill the lamb of the trespass offering, and the priest shall take some of the blood of the trespass offering and put it on the tip of the right ear of him who is to be cleansed, on the thumb of his *right hand*, and on the big toe of his right foot
Lev 14:28 And the priest shall put some of the oil that is in his hand on the tip of the right ear of him who is to be cleansed, on the thumb of the *right hand*, and on the big toe of his right foot, on the place of the blood of the trespass offering
Num 20:17 we will not turn aside to the *right hand* or to the left until we have passed through your territory
Num 22:26 Then the Angel of the Lord went further, and stood in a narrow place where there was no way to turn either to the *right hand* or to the left
Deut 5:32 you shall not turn aside to the *right hand* or to the left
Deut 17:11 you shall not turn aside to the *right hand* or to the left from the sentence which they pronounce upon you
Deut 17:20 that his heart may not be lifted above his brethren, that he may not turn aside from the commandment to the *right hand* or to the left, and that he may prolong his days in his kingdom, he and his children in the midst of Israel
Deut 28:14 So you shall not turn aside from any of the words which I command you this day, to the *right hand* or to the left, to go after other gods to serve them
Deut 33:2 from His *right hand* came a fiery law for them
Josh 1:7 do not turn from it to the *right hand* or to the left, that you may prosper wherever you go
Josh 23:6 Therefore be very courageous to keep and to do all that is written in the Book of the Law of Moses, lest you turn aside from it to the *right hand* or to the left
Judg 5:26 She stretched her hand to the tent peg, her *right hand* to the workmen's hammer
1Sam 6:12 Then the cows headed straight for the road to Beth Shemesh, and went along the highway, lowing as they went, and did not turn aside to the *right hand* or the left
2Sam 2:19 So Asahel pursued Abner, and in going he did not turn to the *right hand* or to the left from following Abner
2Sam 2:21 And Abner said to him, "Turn aside to your *right hand* or to your left, and lay hold on one of the young men and take his armor for yourself
2Sam 14:19 And the woman answered and said, "As you live, my lord the king, no one can turn to the *right hand* or to the left from anything that my lord the king has spoken
2Sam 16:6 And all the people and all the mighty men were on his *right hand* and on his left
2Sam 20:9 And Joab took Amasa by the beard with his *right hand* to kiss him
1Kin 2:19 And the king rose up to meet her and bowed down to her, and sat down on his throne and had a throne set for the king's mother; so she sat at his *right hand*
1Kin 22:19 I saw the Lord sitting on His throne, and all the host of heaven standing by, on His *right hand* and on His left
2Kin 22:2 he did not turn aside to the *right hand* or to the left
1Chr 6:39 And his brother Asaph, who stood at his *right hand*, was Asaph the son of Berachiah, the son of Shimea
1Chr 12:2 armed with bows, using both the *right hand* and the left in hurling stones and shooting arrows with the bow
2Chr 3:17 Then he set up the pillars before the temple, one on the *right hand* and the other on the left; he called the name of the one on the *right hand* Jachin, and the name of the one on the left Boaz
2Chr 18:18 I saw the Lord sitting on His throne, and all the host of heaven standing on His *right hand* and on His left
2Chr 34:2 he did not turn aside to the *right hand* or to the left
Neh 8:4 and beside him, at his *right hand*, stood Mattithiah, Shema, Anaiah, Urijah, Hilkiah, and Maaseiah
Neh 12:31 So I brought the leaders of Judah up on the wall, and appointed two large thanksgiving choirs, one of which went to the *right hand* on the wall toward the Refuse Gate
Job 23:9 when He turns to the *right hand*, I cannot see Him
Job 30:12 At my *right hand* the rabble arises; they push away my feet, and they raise against me their ways of destruction
Job 40:14 Then I will also confess to you that your own *right hand* can save you
Ps 16:8 Because He is at my *right hand* I shall not be moved
Ps 16:11 In Your presence is fullness of joy; at Your *right hand* are pleasures forevermore
Ps 17:7 Show Your marvelous lovingkindness by Your *right hand*, O You who save those who trust in You from those who rise up against them
Ps 18:35 Your *right hand* has held me up, your gentleness has made me great
Ps 20:6 He will answer him from His holy heaven with the saving strength of His *right hand*
Ps 21:8 Your hand will find all Your enemies; Your *right hand* will find those who hate You
Ps 26:10 In whose hands is a sinister scheme, and whose *right hand* is full of bribes
Ps 44:3 But it was Your *right hand*, Your arm, and the light of Your countenance, because You favored them
Ps 45:4 And in Your majesty ride prosperously because of truth, humility, and righteousness; and Your *right hand* shall teach You awesome things
Ps 45:9 At Your *right hand* stands the queen in gold from Ophir
Ps 48:10 According to Your name, O God, so is Your praise to the ends of the earth; Your *right hand* is full of righteousness
Ps 60:5 That Your beloved may be delivered, save with Your *right hand*, and hear me
Ps 63:8 My soul follows close behind You; Your *right hand* upholds me
Ps 73:23 Nevertheless I am continually with You; You hold me by my *right hand*
Ps 74:11 Why do You withdraw Your hand, even Your *right hand*
Ps 77:10 But I will remember the years of the *right hand* of the Most High
Ps 78:54 And He brought them to His holy border, this mountain which His *right hand* had acquired
Ps 80:15 And the vineyard which Your *right hand* has planted, and the branch that You made strong for Yourself
Ps 80:17 Let Your hand be upon the man of Your *right hand*, upon the son of man whom You made strong for Yourself

Ps 89:13 Strong is Your hand, and high is Your *right hand*
Ps 89:25 Also I will set his hand over the sea, and his *right hand* over the rivers
Ps 89:42 You have exalted the *right hand* of his adversaries; You have made all his enemies rejoice
Ps 91:7 A thousand may fall at your side, and ten thousand at your *right hand*
Ps 98:1 His *right hand* and His holy arm have gained Him the victory
Ps 108:6 That Your beloved may be delivered, save with Your *right hand*, and hear me
Ps 109:6 Set a wicked man over him, and let an accuser stand at his *right hand*
Ps 109:31 For He shall stand at the *right hand* of the poor, to save him from those who condemn him
Ps 110:1 The Lord said to my Lord, "Sit at My *right hand*, till I make Your enemies Your footstool
Ps 110:5 The Lord is at Your *right hand;* He shall execute kings in the day of His wrath
Ps 118:15 The voice of rejoicing and salvation is in the tents of the righteous; the *right hand* of the Lord does valiantly
Ps 118:16 The *right hand* of the Lord is exalted; the *right hand* of the Lord does valiantly
Ps 121:5 The Lord is your keeper; the Lord is your shade at your *right hand*
Ps 137:5 If I forget you, O Jerusalem, let my *right hand* forget her skill
Ps 138:7 You will stretch out Your hand against the wrath of my enemies, and Your *right hand* will save me
Ps 139:10 Even there Your hand shall lead me, and Your *right hand* shall hold me
Ps 142:4 Look on my *right hand* and see, for there is no one who acknowledges me
Ps 144:8 Whose mouth speaks vain words, and whose *right hand* is a *right hand* of falsehood
Ps 144:11 Rescue me and deliver me from the hand of foreigners, whose mouth speaks vain words, and whose *right hand* is a *right hand* of falsehood
Prov 3:16 Length of days is in her *right hand*, in her left hand riches and honor
Prov 27:16 whoever restrains her restrains the wind, and grasps oil with his *right hand*
Eccl 10:2 A wise man's heart is at his *right hand*, but a fool's heart at his left
Song 2:6 His left hand is under my head, and his *right hand* embraces me
Song 8:3 His left hand is under my head, and his *right hand* embraces me
Is 9:20 And he shall snatch on the *right hand* and be hungry
Is 30:21 Your ears shall hear a word behind you, saying, "This is the way, walk in it," whenever you turn to the *right hand* or whenever you turn to the left
Is 41:10 I will strengthen you, yes, I will help you, I will uphold you with My righteous *right hand*
Is 41:13 For I, the Lord your God, will hold your *right hand*, saying to you
Is 44:20 and he cannot deliver his soul, nor say, "Is there not a lie in my *right hand*
Is 45:1 Thus says the Lord to His anointed, to Cyrus, whose *right hand* I have held to subdue nations before him and loose the armor of kings, to open before him the double doors, so that the gates will not be shut
Is 48:13 Indeed My hand has laid the foundation of the earth, and My *right hand* has stretched out the heavens
Is 62:8 The Lord has sworn by His *right hand* and by the arm of His strength
Is 63:12 Who led them by the *right hand* of Moses, with His glorious arm, dividing the water before them to make for Himself an everlasting name
Jer 22:24 As I live," says the Lord, "though Coniah the son of Jehoiakim, king of Judah, were the signet on My *right hand*, yet I would pluck you off
Lam 2:3 He has drawn back His *right hand* from before the enemy
Lam 2:4 with His *right hand*, like an adversary, He has slain all who were pleasing to His eye
Ezek 21:22 In his *right hand* is the divination for Jerusalem: To set up battering rams, to call for a slaughter, to lift the voice with shouting, to set battering rams against the gates, to heap up a siege mound, and to build a wall
Ezek 39:3 Then I will knock the bow out of your left hand, and cause the arrows to fall out of your *right hand*
Dan 12:7 Then I heard the man clothed in linen, who was above the waters of the river, when he held up his *right hand* and his left hand to heaven, and swore by Him who lives forever, that it shall be for a time, times, and half a time
Jon 4:11 And should I not pity Nineveh, that great city, in which are more than one hundred and twenty thousand persons who cannot discern between their *right hand* and their left, and also much livestock
Hab 2:16 The cup of the Lord's *right hand* will be turned against you, and utter shame will be on your glory
Zech 3:1 Then he showed me Joshua the high priest standing before the Angel of the Lord, and Satan standing at his *right hand* to oppose him
Zech 12:6 they shall devour all the surrounding peoples on the *right hand* and on the left, but Jerusalem shall be inhabited again in her own place Jerusalem
Matt 5:30 And if your *right hand* causes you to sin, cut it off and cast it from you
Matt 6:3 But when you do a charitable deed, do not let your left hand know what your *right hand* is doing
Matt 20:21 She said to Him, "Grant that these two sons of mine may sit, one on Your *right hand* and the other on the left, in Your kingdom
Matt 20:23 but to sit on My *right hand* and on My left is not Mine to give, but it is for those for whom it is prepared by My Father
Matt 22:44 The Lord said to my Lord, "Sit at My *right hand*, till I make Your enemies Your footstool
Matt 25:33 And He will set the sheep on His *right hand*, but the goats on the left
Matt 25:34 Then the King will say to those on His *right hand*
Matt 26:64 Nevertheless, I say to you, hereafter you will see the Son of Man sitting at the *right hand* of the Power, and coming on the clouds of heaven
Matt 27:29 When they had twisted a crown of thorns, they put it on His head, and a reed in His *right hand*
Mark 10:37 They said to Him, "Grant us that we may sit, one on Your *right hand* and the other on Your left, in Your glory
Mark 10:40 but to sit on My *right hand* and on My left is not Mine to give, but it is for those for whom it is prepared
Mark 12:36 The Lord said to my Lord, "Sit at My *right hand*, till I make Your enemies Your footstool
Mark 14:62 And you will see the Son of Man sitting at the *right hand* of the Power, and coming with the clouds of heaven
Mark 16:19 So then, after the Lord had spoken to them, He was received up into heaven, and sat down at the *right hand* of God

Luke 6:6 And a man was there whose *right hand* was withered
Luke 20:42 Now David himself said in the Book of Psalms, 'The Lord said to my Lord, "sit at My *right hand*
Luke 22:69 Hereafter the Son of Man will sit on the *right hand* of the power of God
Luke 23:33 And when they had come to the place called Calvary, there they crucified Him, and the criminals, one on the *right hand* and the other on the left
Acts 2:25 I foresaw the Lord always before my face, for He is at my *right hand*, that I may not be shaken
Acts 2:33 Therefore being exalted to the *right hand* of God, and having received from the Father the promise of the Holy Spirit, He poured out this which you now see and hear
Acts 2:34 The Lord said to my Lord, "Sit at My *right hand*
Acts 3:7 And he took him by the *right hand* and lifted him up, and immediately his feet and ankle bones received strength
Acts 5:31 Him God has exalted to His *right hand* to be Prince and Savior, to give repentance to Israel and forgiveness of sins
Acts 7:55 But he, being full of the Holy Spirit, gazed into heaven and saw the glory of God, and Jesus standing at the *right hand* of God
Acts 7:56 I see the heavens opened and the Son of Man standing at the *right hand* of God
Rom 8:34 It is Christ who died, and furthermore is also risen, who is even at the *right hand* of God, who also makes intercession for us
2Cor 6:7 by the word of truth, by the power of God, by the armor of righteousness on the *right hand* and on the left
Gal 2:9 and when James, Cephas, and John, who seemed to be pillars, perceived the grace that had been given to me, they gave me and Barnabas the *right hand* of fellowship, that we should go to the Gentiles and they to the circumcised
Eph 1:20 which He worked in Christ when He raised Him from the dead and seated Him at His *right hand* in the heavenly places
Col 3:1 If then you were raised with Christ, seek those things which are above, where Christ is, sitting at the *right hand* of God
Heb 1:3 who being the brightness of His glory and the express image of His person, and upholding all things by the word of His power, when He had by Himself purged our sins, sat down at the *right hand* of the Majesty on high
Heb 1:13 Sit at My *right hand*, till I make Your enemies Your footstool
Heb 8:1 We have such a High Priest, who is seated at the *right hand* of the throne of the Majesty in the heavens
Heb 10:12 But this Man, after He had offered one sacrifice for sins forever, sat down at the *right hand* of God
Heb 12:2 looking unto Jesus, the author and finisher of our faith, who for the joy that was set before Him endured the cross, despising the shame, and has sat down at the *right hand* of the throne of God
1Pet 3:22 who has gone into heaven and is at the *right hand* of God, angels and authorities and powers having been made subject to Him
Rev 1:16 He had in His *right hand* seven stars, out of His mouth went a sharp two-edged sword, and His countenance was like the sun shining in its strength
Rev 1:17 But He laid His *right hand* on me, saying to me
Rev 1:20 The mystery of the seven stars which you saw in My *right hand*, and the seven golden lampstands
Rev 2:1 To the angel of the church of Ephesus write, 'These things says He who holds the seven stars in His *right hand*, who walks in the midst of the seven golden lampstands
Rev 5:1 And I saw in the *right hand* of Him who sat on the throne a scroll written inside and on the back, sealed with seven seals
Rev 5:7 Then He came and took the scroll out of the *right hand* of Him who sat on the throne
Rev 13:16 And he causes all, both small and great, rich and poor, free and slave, to receive a mark on their *right hand* or on their foreheads

RIGHT HAND OF GOD
Mark 16:19 So then, after the Lord had spoken to them, He was received up into heaven, and sat down at the *right hand of God*
Acts 2:33 Therefore being exalted to the *right hand of God*, and having received from the Father the promise of the Holy Spirit, He poured out this which you now see and hear
Acts 7:55 But he, being full of the Holy Spirit, gazed into heaven and saw the glory of God, and Jesus standing at the *right hand of God*
Acts 7:56 I see the heavens opened and the Son of Man standing at the *right hand of God*
Rom 8:34 It is Christ who died, and furthermore is also risen, who is even at the *right hand of God*, who also makes intercession for us
Col 3:1 If then you were raised with Christ, seek those things which are above, where Christ is, sitting at the *right hand of God*
Heb 10:12 But this Man, after He had offered one sacrifice for sins forever, sat down at the *right hand of God*
1Pet 3:22 who has gone into heaven and is at the *right hand of God*, angels and authorities and powers having been made subject to Him

RIGHT HAND UPHOLDS ME
Ps 63:8 My soul follows close behind You; Your *right hand upholds me*

RIGHT IN HIS OWN EYES
Deut 12:8 You shall not at all do as we are doing here today every man doing whatever is *right in his own eyes*
Judg 17:6 In those days there was no king in Israel; everyone did what was *right in his own eyes*
Judg 21:25 In those days there was no king in Israel; everyone did what was *right in his own eyes*
Prov 12:15 The way of a fool is *right in his own eyes*, but he who heeds counsel is wise
Prov 21:2 Every way of a man is *right in his own eyes*, but the Lord weighs the hearts

RIGHT JUDGMENTS (KJV)
(See *JUST ORDINANCES*)

RIGHT OF THE FIRSTBORN
Deut 21:17 But he shall acknowledge the son of the unloved wife as the firstborn by giving him a double portion of all that he has, for he is the beginning of his strength; the *right of the firstborn* is his

RIGHT OF THE POOR (KJV)
(See *JUSTICE FOR THE POOR*)

RIGHT ORDINANCES (RSV)
(See *JUST ORDINANCES*)

RIGHT TIME FOR ME HAS NOT YET COME (NIV)
(See *MY TIME HAS NOT YET COME*)

RIGHT TO THE POOR (KJV)
(See *JUSTICE TO THE OPPRESSED*)

RIGHTEOUS ACTS ARE LIKE FILTHY RAGS (NIV)
(See *RIGHTEOUSNESSES ARE LIKE FILTHY RAGS*)

RIGHTEOUS ACTS OF THE LORD
Judg 5:11 Far from the noise of the archers, among the watering places, there they shall recount the *righteous acts of the Lord*, the righteous acts for His villagers in Israel
1Sam 12:7 Now therefore, stand still, that I may reason with you before the Lord concerning all the *righteous acts of the Lord* which He did to you and your fathers

RIGHTEOUS BRANCH (KJV, NAS, NIV, RSV)
(See *BRANCH OF RIGHTEOUSNESS*)

RIGHTEOUS DECREES (NIV)
(See *RIGHTEOUS JUDGMENTS*)

RIGHTEOUS DEEDS ARE LIKE A POLLUTED GARMENT (RSV)
(See *RIGHTEOUSNESSES ARE LIKE FILTHY RAGS*)

RIGHTEOUS JUDGMENTS
Deut 4:8 And what great nation is there that has such statutes and *righteous judgments* as are in all this law which I set before you this day
Ps 119:7 I will praise You with uprightness of heart, when I learn Your *righteous judgments*
Ps 119:62 At midnight I will rise to give thanks to You, because of Your *righteous judgments*
Ps 119:106 I have sworn and confirmed that I will keep Your *righteous judgments*
Ps 119:160 The entirety of Your word is truth, and every one of Your *righteous judgments* endures forever
Ps 119:164 Seven times a day I praise You, because of Your *righteous judgments*

RIGHTEOUS MAN
Ps 37:16 A little that a *righteous man* has is better than the riches of many wicked
Prov 12:10 A *righteous man* regards the life of his animal, but the tender mercies of the wicked are cruel
Prov 13:5 A *righteous man* hates lying, but a wicked man is loathsome and comes to shame
Prov 20:7 The *righteous man* walks in his integrity; his children are blessed after him
Prov 24:16 for a *righteous man* may fall seven times and rise again, but the wicked shall fall by calamity
Prov 25:26 A *righteous man* who falters before the wicked is like a murky spring and a polluted well
Is 5:23 who justify the wicked for a bribe, and take away justice from the *righteous man*
Ezek 3:20 Again, when a *righteous man* turns from his righteousness and commits iniquity, and I lay a stumbling block before him, he shall die
Ezek 3:21 Nevertheless if you warn the *righteous man* that the righteous should not sin, and he does not sin, he shall surely live because he took warning
Ezek 18:24 But when a *righteous man* turns away from his righteousness and commits iniquity, and does according to all the abominations that the wicked man does, shall he live
Ezek 18:26 When a *righteous man* turns away from his righteousness, commits iniquity, and dies in it, it is because of the iniquity which he has done that he dies
Ezek 33:12 The righteousness of the *righteous man* shall not deliver him in the day of his transgression
Matt 10:41 And he who receives a *righteous man* in the name of a *righteous man* shall receive a righteous man's reward
Luke 23:47 Now when the centurion saw what had happened, he glorified God, saying, "Certainly this was a *righteous Man*
Rom 5:7 For scarcely for a *righteous man* will one die; yet perhaps for a good man someone would even dare to die
Jas 5:16 The effective, fervent prayer of a *righteous man* avails much
2Pet 2:8 (for that *righteous man*, dwelling among them, tormented his righteous soul from day to day by seeing and hearing their lawless deeds

RIGHTEOUS ONE
1Pet 4:18 Now "If the *righteous one* is scarcely saved, where will the ungodly and the sinner appear

RIGHTEOUS REQUIREMENTS OF THE LAW
Rom 2:26 Therefore, if an uncircumcised man keeps the *righteous requirements of the law*, will not his uncircumcision be counted as circumcision

RIGHTEOUSNESS AND JUSTICE
Gen 18:19 For I have known him, in order that he may command his children and his household after him, that they keep the way of the Lord, to do *righteousness and justice*, that the Lord may bring to Abraham what He has spoken to him
Ps 33:5 He loves *righteousness and justice;* the earth is full of the goodness of the Lord
Ps 89:14 *Righteousness and justice* are the foundation of Your throne; mercy and truth go before Your face
Ps 97:2 Clouds and darkness surround Him; *righteousness and justice* are the foundation of His throne
Ps 103:6 The Lord executes *righteousness and justice* for all who are oppressed
Prov 2:9 Then you will understand *righteousness and justice*, equity and every good path
Prov 21:3 To do *righteousness and justice* is more acceptable to the Lord than sacrifice
Hos 2:19 yes, I will betroth you to Me in *righteousness and justice*, in lovingkindness and mercy

RIGHTEOUSNESS AND KINDNESS (RSV)
(See *RIGHTEOUSNESS AND MERCY*)

RIGHTEOUSNESS AND LOVE (NIV)
(See *RIGHTEOUSNESS AND MERCY*)

RIGHTEOUSNESS AND MERCY
Prov 21:21 He who follows *righteousness and mercy* finds life, righteousness and honor

RIGHTEOUSNESS AND PEACE
Ps 85:10 Mercy and truth have met together; *righteousness and peace* have kissed each other
Rom 14:17 for the kingdom of God is not food and drink, but *righteousness and peace* and joy in the Holy Spirit

RIGHTEOUSNESS EXALTS A NATION
Prov 14:34 *Righteousness exalts a nation*, but sin is a reproach to any people

RIGHTEOUSNESS GOES FORTH
Is 62:1 For Zion's sake I will not hold My peace, and for Jerusalem's sake I will not rest, until her

righteousness goes forth as brightness, and her salvation as a lamp that burns

RIGHTEOUSNESS LIKE A MIGHTY STREAM
Amos 5:24 But let justice run down like water, and *righteousness like a mighty stream*

RIGHTEOUSNESS OF FAITH
Rom 4:13 For the promise that he would be the heir of the world was not to Abraham or to his seed through the law, but through the *righteousness of faith*
Rom 9:30 That Gentiles, who did not pursue righteousness, have attained to righteousness, even the *righteousness of faith*
Rom 10:6 But the *righteousness of faith* speaks in this way, "Do not say in your heart

RIGHTEOUSNESS OF GOD
Rom 1:17 For in it the *righteousness of God* is revealed from faith to faith
Rom 3:5 But if our unrighteousness demonstrates the *righteousness of God*, what shall we say
Rom 3:21 But now the *righteousness of God* apart from the law is revealed, being witnessed by the Law and the Prophets
Rom 3:22 even the *righteousness of God* which is through faith in Jesus Christ to all and on all who believe
Rom 10:3 For they being ignorant of God's righteousness, and seeking to establish their own righteousness, have not submitted to the *righteousness of God*
2Cor 5:21 For He made Him who knew no sin to be sin for us, that we might become the *righteousness of God* in Him
Jas 1:20 for the wrath of man does not produce the *righteousness of God*

RIGHTEOUSNESS OF THE LAW (KJV)
(See *RIGHTEOUS REQUIREMENTS OF THE LAW*)

RIGHTEOUSNESS SHINES OUT (NIV)
(See *RIGHTEOUSNESS GOES FORTH*)

RIGHTEOUSNESS THAT COMES BY FAITH (NIV)
(See *RIGHTEOUSNESS OF FAITH*)

RIGHTEOUSNESSES ARE LIKE FILTHY RAGS
Is 64:6 But we are all like an unclean thing, and all our *righteousnesses are like filthy rags*

RIGHTLY DIVIDING THE WORD OF TRUTH
2Tim 2:15 Be diligent to present yourself approved to God, a worker who does not need to be ashamed, *rightly dividing the word of truth*

RIGHTLY HANDLING THE WORD OF TRUTH (RSV)
(See *RIGHTLY DIVIDING THE WORD OF TRUTH*)

RIGHTS OF THE POOR (NAS, RSV)
(See *CAUSE OF THE POOR*)

RINGS OF GOLD
Ex 25:12 You shall cast four *rings of gold* for it, and put them in its four corners
Ex 25:26 And you shall make for it four *rings of gold*, and put the rings on the four corners that are at its four legs
Ex 26:29 You shall overlay the boards with gold, make their *rings of gold* as holders for the bars, and overlay the bars with gold
Ex 28:23 And you shall make two *rings of gold* for the breastplate, and put the two rings on the two ends of the breastplate
Ex 28:26 You shall make two *rings of gold*, and put them on the two ends of the breastplate, on the edge of it, which is on the inner side of the ephod
Ex 28:27 And two other *rings of gold* you shall make, and put them on the two shoulder straps, underneath the ephod toward its front, right at the seam above the intricately woven band of the ephod
Ex 36:34 He overlaid the boards with gold, made their *rings of gold* to be holders for the bars, and overlaid the bars with gold
Ex 37:3 And he cast for it four *rings of gold* to be set in its four corners
Ex 37:13 And he cast for it four *rings of gold*, and put the rings on the four corners that were at its four legs
Ex 37:27 He made two *rings of gold* for it under its molding, by its two corners on both sides, as holders for the poles with which to bear it
Ex 39:19 And they made two *rings of gold* and put them on the two ends of the breastplate, on the edge of it, which was on the inward side of the ephod

RIPE FOR HARVEST (NIV)
(See *WHITE FOR HARVEST*)

RISE FROM THE DEAD
Mark 12:25 For when they *rise from the dead*, they neither marry nor are given in marriage, but are like angels in heaven
Luke 16:31 But he said to him, 'If they do not hear Moses and the prophets, neither will they be persuaded though one *rise from the dead*
Luke 24:46 Then He said to them, "Thus it is written, and thus it was necessary for the Christ to suffer and to *rise from the dead* the third day
Acts 26:23 that the Christ would suffer, that He would be the first to *rise from the dead*, and would proclaim light to the Jewish people and to the Gentiles

RISE UP, O LORD
Num 10:35 *Rise up, O Lord!* Let Your enemies be scattered, and let those who hate You flee before You

RISEN FROM THE DEAD (KJV)
(See *RAISED FROM THE DEAD*)

RISING AGAINST THE SKY (NIV)
(See *ASCENDED INTO HEAVEN*)

RISKED THEIR LIVES
Acts 15:26 men who have *risked their lives* for the name of our Lord Jesus Christ

RIVER OF WATER OF LIFE
Rev 22:1 And he showed me a pure *river of water of life*, clear as crystal, proceeding from the throne of God and of the Lamb

RIVERS IN THE DESERT
Is 43:19 I will even make a road in the wilderness and *rivers in the desert*
Is 43:20 The beast of the field will honor Me, the jackals and the ostriches, because I give waters in the wilderness and *rivers in the desert*, to give drink to My people, My chosen

RIVERS OF LIVING WATER
John 7:38 He who believes in Me, as the Scripture has said, out of his heart will flow *rivers of living water*

RIVERS OF WATER
Deut 10:7 From there they journeyed to Gudgodah, and from Gudgodah to Jotbathah, a land of *rivers of water*
Ps 1:3 He shall be like a tree planted by the *rivers of water*, that brings forth its fruit in its season, whose leaf also shall not wither
Ps 119:136 *Rivers of water* run down from my eyes, because men do not keep Your law
Prov 21:1 The king's heart is in the hand of the Lord, like the *rivers of water*
Is 32:2 A man will be as a hiding place from the wind, and a cover from the tempest, as *rivers of water* in a dry place, as the shadow of a great rock in a weary land
Lam 3:48 My eyes overflow with *rivers of water* for the destruction of the daughter of my people

ROAD IN THE WILDERNESS
Is 43:19 I will even make a *road in the wilderness* and rivers in the desert

ROAD THAT LEADS TO LIFE (NIV)
(See *WAY WHICH LEADS TO LIFE*)

ROADS AND COUNTRY LANES (NIV)
(See *HIGHWAYS AND HEDGES*)

ROAR LIKE A LION
Hos 11:10 He will *roar like a lion*. When He roars, then His sons shall come trembling from the west

ROAR LIKE THE SEA
Jer 50:42 Their voice shall *roar like the sea;* they shall ride on horses, set in array, like a man for the battle, against you, O daughter of Babylon

ROARING OF A LION
Prov 19:12 The king's wrath is like the *roaring of a lion*, but his favor is like dew on the grass
Prov 20:2 The wrath of a king is like the *roaring of a lion*

ROARING OF THE SEA
Is 5:30 In that day they will roar against them like the *roaring of the sea*

ROARING OF THE SEAS (NIV, RSV)
(See *NOISE OF THEIR WAVES*)

ROBBED OTHER CHURCHES
2Cor 11:8 I *robbed other churches*, taking wages from them to minister to you

ROBE FILLED THE TEMPLE
Is 6:1 In the year that King Uzziah died, I saw the Lord sitting on a throne, high and lifted up, and the train of His *robe filled the temple*

ROBE OF RIGHTEOUSNESS
Is 61:10 for He has clothed me with the garments of salvation, He has covered me with the *robe of righteousness*, as a bridegroom decks himself with ornaments, and as a bride adorns herself with her jewels

ROBED IN MAJESTY (NIV, RSV)
(See *CLOTHED WITH MAJESTY*)

ROCK, MY SAVIOR (NIV)
(See *ROCK OF MY SALVATION*)

ROCK OF MY SALVATION
2Sam 22:47 Blessed be my Rock! Let God be exalted, the *Rock of my salvation*
Ps 89:26 He shall cry to Me, 'You are my Father, my God, and the *rock of my salvation*

ROCK OF STUMBLING (RSV)
(See *STONE OF STUMBLING*)

ROCK THAT FOLLOWED THEM
1Cor 10:4 For they drank of that spiritual *Rock that followed them*, and that Rock was Christ

ROD OF CORRECTION
Prov 22:15 Foolishness is bound up in the heart of a child, but the *rod of correction* will drive it far from him

ROD OF GOD
Ex 4:20 And Moses took the *rod of God* in his hand
Ex 17:9 Tomorrow I will stand on the top of the hill with the *rod of God* in my hand
Job 21:9 Their houses are safe from fear, neither is the *rod of God* upon them

ROD OF HIS WRATH
Lam 3:1 I am the man who has seen affliction by the *rod of His wrath*

ROD OF IRON
Ps 2:9 You shall break them with a *rod of iron;* You shall dash them in pieces like a potter's vessel
Rev 2:27 He shall rule them with a *rod of iron;* as the potter's vessels shall be broken to pieces
Rev 12:5 And she bore a male Child who was to rule all nations with a *rod of iron*
Rev 19:15 And He Himself will rule them with a *rod of iron*

ROD OF MY ANGER
Is 10:5 Woe to Assyria, the *rod of My anger* and the staff in whose hand is My indignation

ROLLED UP LIKE A SCROLL
Is 34:4 All the host of heaven shall be dissolved, and the heavens shall be *rolled up like a scroll*

ROMAN CITIZEN (NIV, RSV)
(See *MAN WHO IS A ROMAN*)

ROOF CHAMBER (NAS, RSV)
(See *UPPER ROOM*)

ROOT OF ALL KINDS OF EVIL
1Tim 6:10 For the love of money is a *root of all kinds of evil*, for which some have strayed from the faith in their greediness, and pierced themselves through with many sorrows

ROOT OF JESSE
Is 11:10 And in that day there shall be a *Root of Jesse*, who shall stand as a banner to the people
Rom 15:12 There shall be a *root of Jesse;* and He who shall rise to reign over the Gentiles, in Him the Gentiles shall hope

ROOTS OF THE SEA (RSV)
(See *DEPTHS OF THE SEA*)

ROSE AGAIN THE THIRD DAY
1Cor 15:4 and that He was buried, and that He *rose again the third day* according to the Scriptures

ROSE FROM THE EARTH (NAS, RSV)
(See *LIFTED UP FROM THE EARTH*)

ROSE FROM THE GROUND (NIV)
(See *LIFTED UP FROM THE EARTH*)

ROSE OF SHARON
Song 2:1 I am the *rose of Sharon*, and the lily of the valleys

ROTTENNESS IN HIS BONES
Prov 12:4 an excellent wife is the crown of her husband, but she who causes shame is like *rottenness in his bones*

ROYAL PRIESTHOOD
1Pet 2:9 But you are a chosen generation, a *royal priesthood*, a holy nation, His own special people, that you may proclaim the praises of Him who called you out of darkness into His marvelous light

RUBBED WITH SALT
Ezek 16:4 you were not *rubbed with salt* nor swathed in swaddling cloths

RUDIMENTS OF THE WORLD (KJV)
(See *BASIC PRINCIPLES OF THE WORLD*)

RUINS GOOD MORALS (RSV)
(See *CORRUPTS GOOD HABITS*)

RULE MY PEOPLE (KJV)
(See *SHEPHERD MY PEOPLE*)

RULE OVER (NAS, NIV)
(See *HAVE DOMINION OVER*)

RULE THEM WITH AN IRON SCEPTER (NIV)
(See *BREAK THEM WITH A ROD OF IRON*)

RULER AND JUDGE (NIV)
(See *PRINCE AND A JUDGE*)

RULER OF THE SYNAGOGUE
Mark 5:36 As soon as Jesus heard the word that was spoken, He said to the *ruler of the synagogue*
Mark 5:38 Then He came to the house of the *ruler of the synagogue*, and saw a tumult and those who wept and wailed loudly
Luke 8:41 And behold, there came a man named Jairus, and he was a *ruler of the synagogue*
Luke 13:14 But the *ruler of the synagogue* answered with indignation, because Jesus had healed on the Sabbath
Acts 18:8 Then Crispus, the *ruler of the synagogue*, believed on the Lord with all his household
Acts 18:17 Then all the Greeks took Sosthenes, the *ruler of the synagogue*, and beat him before the judgment seat

RULER OF THIS WORLD
John 12:31 now the *ruler of this world* will be cast out
John 14:30 I will no longer talk much with you, for the *ruler of this world* is coming, and he has nothing in Me
John 16:11 of judgment, because the *ruler of this world* is judged

RULERS AND AUTHORITIES
Tit 3:1 Remind them to be subject to *rulers and authorities*, to obey, to be ready for every good work

RULERS OF THE DARKNESS OF THIS AGE
Eph 6:12 For we do not wrestle against flesh and blood, but against principalities, against powers, against the *rulers of the darkness of this age*, against spiritual hosts of wickedness in the heavenly places

RULERS OF THE EARTH (NIV, RSV)
(See *JUDGES OF THE EARTH*)

RULERS OF THE PHILISTINES (RSV)
(See *LORDS OF THE PHILISTINES*)

RULES OVER THE NATIONS
Ps 22:28 For the kingdom is the Lord's, and He *rules over the nations*

RUN IN VAIN
Phil 2:16 holding fast the word of life, so that I may rejoice in the day of Christ that I have not *run in vain* or labored in vain

RUN OR LABOR FOR NOTHING (NIV)
(See *RUN IN VAIN*)

RUSHING MIGHTY WIND
Acts 2:2 And suddenly there came a sound from heaven, as of a *rushing mighty wind*, and it filled the whole house where they were sitting

S

SABBATH DAY
Ex 20:8 Remember the *Sabbath day*, to keep it holy
Ex 20:11 Therefore the Lord blessed the *Sabbath day* and hallowed it
Ex 31:15 Whoever does any work on the *Sabbath day*, he shall surely be put to death
Ex 35:3 You shall kindle no fire throughout your dwellings on the *Sabbath day*
Num 15:32 Now while the children of Israel were in the wilderness, they found a man gathering sticks on the *Sabbath day*
Num 28:9 And on the *Sabbath day* two lambs in their first year, without blemish, and two-tenths of an ephah of fine flour as a grain offering, mixed with oil, with its drink offering
Deut 5:12 Observe the *Sabbath day*, to keep it holy, as the Lord your God commanded you
Deut 5:15 therefore the Lord your God commanded you to keep the *Sabbath day*
Neh 10:31 that if the peoples of the land bring wares or any grain to sell on the *Sabbath day*, we would not buy it from them on the Sabbath, or on a holy day
Neh 13:15 In those days I saw in Judah some people treading wine presses on the Sabbath, and bringing in sheaves, and loading donkeys with wine, grapes, figs, and all kinds of burdens, which they brought into Jerusalem on the *Sabbath day*
Neh 13:17 Then I contended with the nobles of Judah, and said to them, "What evil thing is this that you do, by which you profane the *Sabbath day*
Neh 13:19 Then I posted some of my servants at the gates, so that no burdens would be brought in on the *Sabbath day*
Neh 13:22 And I commanded the Levites that they should cleanse themselves, and that they should go and guard the gates, to sanctify the *Sabbath day*
Jer 17:21 Take heed to yourselves, and bear no burden on the *Sabbath day*, nor bring it in by the gates of Jerusalem
Jer 17:22 nor carry a burden out of your houses on the *Sabbath day*, nor do any work, but hallow the *Sabbath day*, as I commanded your fathers
Jer 17:24 And it shall be, if you diligently heed Me," says the Lord, "to bring no burden through the gates of this city on the *Sabbath day*, but hallow the *Sabbath day*, to do no work in it
Jer 17:27 But if you will not heed Me to hallow the *Sabbath day*, such as not carrying a burden when entering the gates of Jerusalem on the *Sabbath day*, then I will kindle a fire in its gates, and it shall devour the palaces of Jerusalem, and it shall not be quenched
Ezek 46:4 The burnt offering that the prince offers to the Lord on the *Sabbath day* shall be six lambs without blemish, and a ram without blemish

Ezek 46:12 and he shall prepare his burnt offering and his peace offerings as he did on the *Sabbath day*
Luke 4:16 And as His custom was, He went into the synagogue on the *Sabbath day*, and stood up to read
Luke 13:14 therefore come and be healed on them, and not on the *Sabbath day*
Luke 14:5 Then He answered them, saying, "Which of you, having a donkey or an ox that has fallen into a pit, will not immediately pull him out on the *Sabbath day*
Acts 13:14 But when they departed from Perga, they came to Antioch in Pisidia, and went into the synagogue on the *Sabbath day* and sat down
Acts 16:13 And on the *Sabbath day* we went out of the city to the riverside, where prayer was customarily made

SABBATH DAY'S JOURNEY
Acts 1:12 Then they returned to Jerusalem from the Mount called Olivet, which is near Jerusalem, a *Sabbath day's journey*

SABBATH OF SOLEMN REST
Lev 16:31 It is a *sabbath of solemn rest* for you, and you shall afflict your souls
Lev 23:3 Six days shall work be done, but the seventh day is a *Sabbath of solemn rest*, a holy convocation
Lev 23:32 It shall be to you a *sabbath of solemn rest*, and you shall afflict your souls
Lev 25:4 but in the seventh year there shall be a *sabbath of solemn rest* for the land, a sabbath to the Lord

SABBATH OF THE LORD
Ex 20:10 but the seventh day is the *Sabbath of the Lord* your God
Lev 23:3 it is the *Sabbath of the Lord* in all your dwellings
Deut 5:14 but the seventh day is the *Sabbath of the Lord* your God

SABBATH REST
Ex 16:23 Tomorrow is a *Sabbath rest*, a holy Sabbath to the Lord

SABBATH THEY RESTED (NAS, RSV)
(See *RESTED ON THE SABBATH*)

SACKCLOTH AND ASHES
Esth 4:1 When Mordecai learned all that had happened, he tore his clothes and put on *sackcloth and ashes*, and went out into the midst of the city
Esth 4:3 And in every province where the king's command and decree arrived, there was great mourning among the Jews, with fasting, weeping, and wailing; and many lay in *sackcloth and ashes*
Is 58:5 Is it to bow down his head like a bulrush, and to spread out *sackcloth and ashes*
Matt 11:21 For if the mighty works which were done in you had been done in Tyre and Sidon, they would have repented long ago in *sackcloth and ashes*
Luke 10:13 For if the mighty works which were done in you had been done in Tyre and Sidon, they would have repented a great while ago, sitting in *sackcloth and ashes*

SACRED ASSEMBLY
Lev 23:36 It is a *sacred assembly*, and you shall do no customary work on it
Num 29:35 On the eighth day you shall have a *sacred assembly*
Deut 16:8 Six days you shall eat unleavened bread, and on the seventh day there shall be a *sacred assembly* to the Lord your God
2Chr 7:9 And on the eighth day they held a *sacred assembly*, for they observed the dedication of the altar seven days, and the feast seven days
Neh 8:18 and on the eighth day there was a *sacred assembly*, according to the prescribed manner
Joel 1:14 Consecrate a fast, call a *sacred assembly;* gather the elders and all the inhabitants of the land into the house of the Lord your God, and cry out to the Lord
Joel 2:15 Blow the trumpet in Zion, consecrate a fast, call a *sacred assembly*

SACRED TO THE LORD (NIV, RSV)
(See *CONSECRATED TO THE LORD*)

SACRIFICE ACCEPTABLE TO GOD (RSV)
(See *SACRIFICES OF GOD*)

SACRIFICE FOR SINS
Heb 10:12 But this Man, after He had offered one *sacrifice for sins* forever, sat down at the right hand of God
Heb 10:26 For if we sin willfully after we have received the knowledge of the truth, there no longer remains a *sacrifice for sins*

SACRIFICE OF PEACE OFFERINGS
Lev 7:11 This is the law of the *sacrifice of peace offerings* which he shall offer to the Lord
Num 7:17 and for the *sacrifice of peace offerings:* two oxen, five rams, five male goats, and five male lambs in their first year
Num 7:23 and as the *sacrifice of peace offerings:* two oxen, five rams, five male goats, and five male lambs in their first year
Num 7:29 and for the *sacrifice of peace offerings:* two oxen, five rams, five male goats, and five male lambs in their first year
Num 7:35 and as the *sacrifice of peace offerings:* two oxen, five rams, five male goats, and five male lambs in their first year
Num 7:41 and as the *sacrifice of peace offerings:* two oxen, five rams, five male goats, and five male lambs in their first year
Num 7:47 and as the *sacrifice of peace offerings:* two oxen, five rams, five male goats, and five male lambs in their first year
Num 7:53 and as the *sacrifice of peace offerings:* two oxen, five rams, five male goats, and five male lambs in their first year
Num 7:59 and as the *sacrifice of peace offerings:* two oxen, five rams, five male goats, and five male lambs in their first year
Num 7:65 and as the *sacrifice of peace offerings:* two oxen, five rams, five male goats, and five male lambs in their first year
Num 7:71 and as the *sacrifice of peace offerings:* two oxen, five rams, five male goats, and five male lambs in their first year
Num 7:77 and as the *sacrifice of peace offerings:* two oxen, five rams, five male goats, and five male lambs in their first year
Num 7:83 and as the *sacrifice of peace offerings:* two oxen, five rams, five male goats, and five male lambs in their first year
Num 7:88 And all the oxen for the *sacrifice of peace offerings* were twenty-four bulls, the rams sixty, the male goats sixty, and the lambs in their first year sixty
1Kin 8:63 And Solomon offered a *sacrifice of peace offerings*, which he offered to the Lord, twenty-two thousand bulls and one hundred and twenty thousand sheep

SACRIFICE OF PRAISE
Jer 33:11 Praise the Lord of hosts, for the Lord is good, for His mercy endures forever" and of those

who will bring the *sacrifice of praise* into the house of the Lord
Heb 13:15 Therefore by Him let us continually offer the *sacrifice of praise* to God, that is, the fruit of our lips, giving thanks to His name

SACRIFICE OF THE PEACE OFFERING
Lev 3:3 Then he shall offer from the *sacrifice of the peace offering* an offering made by fire to the Lord
Lev 3:9 Then he shall offer from the *sacrifice of the peace offering*, as an offering made by fire to the Lord, its fat and the whole fat tail which he shall remove close to the backbone
Lev 4:10 as it was taken from the bull of the *sacrifice of the peace offering*
Lev 4:26 And he shall burn all its fat on the altar, like the fat of the *sacrifice of the peace offering*
Lev 4:31 He shall remove all its fat, as fat is removed from the *sacrifice of the peace offering*
Lev 4:35 He shall remove all its fat, as the fat of the lamb is removed from the *sacrifice of the peace offering*
Lev 7:20 But the person who eats the flesh of the *sacrifice of the peace offering* that belongs to the Lord, while he is unclean, that person shall be cut off from his people
Lev 7:21 Moreover the person who touches any unclean thing, such as human uncleanness, any unclean beast, or any abominable unclean thing, and who eats the flesh of the *sacrifice of the peace offering* that belongs to the Lord, that person shall be cut off from his people
Lev 7:37 This is the law of the burnt offering, the grain offering, the sin offering, the trespass offering, the consecrations, and the *sacrifice of the peace offering*
Num 6:18 Then the Nazirite shall shave his consecrated head at the door of the tabernacle of meeting, and shall take the hair from his consecrated head and put it on the fire which is under the *sacrifice of the peace offering*

SACRIFICE YOUR CHILDREN IN THE RAVINES (NIV)
(See *SLAYING THE CHILDREN IN THE VALLEYS*)

SACRIFICES FOR SIN
Heb 10:6 In burnt offerings and *sacrifices for sin* you had no pleasure

SACRIFICES OF GOD
Ps 51:17 The *sacrifices of God* are a broken spirit, a broken and a contrite heart these, O God, You will not despise

SAFE THROUGH CHILDBIRTH (NIV)
(See *SAVED IN CHILDBEARING*)

SAFE UNDER THE SHELTER (RSV)
(See *TRUST IN THE SHELTER*)

SAKE OF OUR LORD JESUS CHRIST (RSV)
(See *NAME OF OUR LORD JESUS CHRIST*)

SALT OF THE EARTH
Matt 5:13 You are the *salt of the earth;* but if the salt loses its flavor, how shall it be seasoned

SALTED WITH SALT (KJV)
(See *SEASONED WITH SALT*)

SALVATION BELONGS TO OUR GOD
Rev 7:10 and crying out with a loud voice, saying, "*Salvation belongs to our God* who sits on the throne, and to the Lamb

SALVATION BELONGS TO THE LORD
Ps 3:8 *Salvation belongs to the Lord*. Your blessing is upon Your people

SALVATION COMES FROM THE LORD (NIV)
(See *SALVATION IS OF THE LORD*)

SALVATION IS OF THE LORD
Jon 2:9 I will pay what I have vowed. *Salvation is of the Lord*

SALVATION OF THE LORD
Ex 14:13 Stand still, and see the *salvation of the Lord*, which He will accomplish for you today
2Chr 20:17 Position yourselves, stand still and see the *salvation of the Lord*, who is with you, O Judah and Jerusalem
Lam 3:26 It is good that one should hope and wait quietly for the *salvation of the Lord*

SALVATION TO OUR GOD (KJV, NAS)
(See *SALVATION BELONGS TO OUR GOD*)

SALVATION WHICH IS IN CHRIST JESUS
2Tim 2:10 Therefore I endure all things for the sake of the elect, that they also may obtain the *salvation which is in Christ Jesus* with eternal glory

SAMARITAN WOMAN (NIV)
(See *WOMAN OF SAMARIA*)

SAME DAY (KJV, NAS)
(See *ON THAT DAY*)

SAME SPIRIT
1Cor 12:4 Now there are diversities of gifts, but the *same Spirit*
1Cor 12:8 for to one is given the word of wisdom through the Spirit, to another the word of knowledge through the *same Spirit*
1Cor 12:9 to another faith by the *same Spirit*, to another gifts of healings by the *same Spirit*
1Cor 12:11 But one and the *same Spirit* works all these things, distributing to each one individually as He wills
2Cor 4:13 But since we have the *same spirit* of faith, according to what is written
2Cor 12:18 Did we not walk in the *same spirit?* Did we not walk in the same steps

SANCTIFICATION BY THE SPIRIT
2Th 2:13 But we are bound to give thanks to God always for you, brethren beloved by the Lord, because God from the beginning chose you for salvation through *sanctification by the Spirit* and belief in the truth

SANCTIFICATION OF THE SPIRIT
1Pet 1:2 elect according to the foreknowledge of God the Father, in *sanctification of the Spirit*, for obedience and sprinkling of the blood of Jesus Christ

SANCTIFIED IN CHRIST JESUS
1Cor 1:2 To the church of God which is at Corinth, to those who are *sanctified in Christ Jesus*, called to be saints, with all who in every place call on the name of Jesus Christ our Lord, both theirs and ours

SANCTIFY A SOLEMN ASSEMBLY (RSV, NAS)
(See *PROCLAIM A SOLEMN ASSEMBLY*)

SANCTIFY THE LORD
1Pet 3:15 But *sanctify the Lord* God in your hearts, and always be ready to give a defense to

everyone who asks you a reason for the hope that is in you, with meekness and fear

SANCTIFY THEM
Ex 28:41 You shall anoint them, consecrate them, and *sanctify them*, that they may minister to Me as priests
Ex 29:33 They shall eat those things with which the atonement was made, to consecrate and to *sanctify them*
Lev 8:11 He sprinkled some of it on the altar seven times, anointed the altar and all its utensils, and the laver and its base, to *sanctify them*
Lev 21:23 only he shall not go near the veil or approach the altar, because he has a defect, lest he profane My sanctuaries; for I the Lord *sanctify them*
Lev 22:9 They shall therefore keep My ordinance, lest they bear sin for it and die thereby, if they profane it: I the Lord *sanctify them*
Lev 22:16 or allow them to bear the guilt of trespass when they eat their holy offerings; for I the Lord *sanctify them*
2Chr 30:17 therefore the Levites had charge of the slaughter of the Passover lambs for everyone who was not clean, to *sanctify them* to the Lord
Job 1:5 So it was, when the days of feasting had run their course, that Job would send and *sanctify them*, and he would rise early in the morning and offer burnt offerings according to the number of them all
John 17:17 *Sanctify them* by Your truth. Your word is truth

SANCTIFY YOURSELVES
Lev 11:44 You shall therefore *sanctify yourselves*, and you shall be holy
Lev 20:7 *Sanctify yourselves* therefore, and be holy, for I am the Lord your God
Num 11:18 Then you shall say to the people, *'Sanctify yourselves* for tomorrow, and you shall eat meat
Josh 3:5 And Joshua said to the people, *'Sanctify yourselves*, for tomorrow the Lord will do wonders among you
Josh 7:13 Get up, sanctify the people, and say, *'Sanctify yourselves* for tomorrow, because thus says the Lord God of Israel
1Sam 16:5 *Sanctify yourselves*, and come with me to the sacrifice." Then he sanctified Jesse and his sons, and invited them to the sacrifice
1Chr 15:12 *sanctify yourselves*, you and your brethren, that you may bring up the ark of the Lord God of Israel to the place I have prepared for it
2Chr 29:5 Now *sanctify yourselves*, sanctify the house of the Lord God of your fathers, and carry out the rubbish from the holy place
2Chr 35:6 So slaughter the Passover offerings, *sanctify yourselves*, and prepare them for your brethren, that they may do according to the word of the Lord by the hand of Moses

SANCTIFYING WORK OF THE SPIRIT (NIV)
(See *SANCTIFICATION BY THE SPIRIT*)

SAND OF THE SEA
Gen 32:12 For You said, 'I will surely treat you well, and make your descendants as the *sand of the sea*, which cannot be numbered for multitude
Gen 41:49 Joseph gathered very much grain, as the *sand of the sea*, until he stopped counting, for it was without number
Job 6:3 For then it would be heavier than the *sand of the sea* therefore my words have been rash
Is 10:22 For though your people, O Israel, be as the *sand of the sea*, yet a remnant of them will return
Jer 33:22 As the host of heaven cannot be numbered, nor the *sand of the sea* measured, so will I multiply the descendants of David My servant and the Levites who minister to Me
Hos 1:10 Yet the number of the children of Israel shall be as the *sand of the sea*, which cannot be measured or numbered
Rom 9:27 Though the number of the children of Israel be as the *sand of the sea*, the remnant will be saved
Rev 13:1 Then I stood on the *sand of the sea*. And I saw a beast rising up out of the sea, having seven heads and ten horns, and on his horns ten crowns, and on his heads a blasphemous name
Rev 20:8 and will go out to deceive the nations which are in the four corners of the earth, Gog and Magog, to gather them together to battle, whose number is as the *sand of the sea*

SAND ON THE SEASHORE
1Kin 4:29 And God gave Solomon wisdom and exceedingly great understanding, and largeness of heart like the *sand on the seashore*

SANG A NEW SONG
Rev 5:9 And they *sang a new song*, saying: You are worthy to take the scroll, and to open its seals

SATAN ENTERED JUDAS
Luke 22:3 Then *Satan entered Judas*, surnamed Iscariot, who was numbered among the twelve

SATED WITH BLOOD (RSV)
(See *FILLED WITH BLOOD*)

SATISFYING OF THE FLESH (KJV)
(See *INDULGENCE OF THE FLESH*)

SAUL HAS SLAIN HIS THOUSANDS
1Sam 18:7 *Saul has slain his thousands*, and David his ten thousands
1Sam 21:11 *Saul has slain his thousands*, and David his ten thousands
1Sam 29:5 *Saul has slain his thousands*, and David his ten thousands

SAVAGE WOLVES
Acts 20:29 For I know this, that after my departure *savage wolves* will come in among you, not sparing the flock

SAVE A SOUL FROM DEATH
Jas 5:20 let him know that he who turns a sinner from the error of his way will *save a soul from death* and cover a multitude of sins

SAVE HIS LIFE (KJV)
(See *SPARE HIS LIFE*)

SAVE LIFE OR TO DESTROY IT
Luke 6:9 Is it lawful on the Sabbath to do good or to do evil, to *save life or to destroy it*

SAVE ME
2Sam 22:3 the God of my strength, in Him I will trust, my shield and the horn of my salvation, my stronghold and my refuge; my Savior, You *save me* from violence
2Kin 16:7 Come up and *save me* from the hand of the king of Syria and from the hand of the king of Israel, who rise up against me
Ps 3:7 *Save me*, O my God! For You have struck all my enemies on the cheekbone
Ps 6:4 Return, O Lord, deliver me! Oh, *save me* for Your mercies' sake
Ps 7:1 *Save me* from all those who persecute me; and deliver me

Ps 22:21 *Save Me* from the lion's mouth and from the horns of the wild oxen
Ps 31:2 Be my rock of refuge, a fortress of defense to *save me*
Ps 31:16 Make Your face shine upon Your servant; *save me* for Your mercies' sake
Ps 44:6 For I will not trust in my bow, nor shall my sword *save me*
Ps 54:1 *Save me*, O God, by Your name, and vindicate me by Your strength
Ps 55:16 As for me, I will call upon God, and the Lord shall *save me*
Ps 57:3 He shall send from heaven and *save me;* He reproaches the one who would swallow me up
Ps 59:2 Deliver me from the workers of iniquity, and *save me* from bloodthirsty men
Ps 69:1 *Save me*, O God! For the waters have come up to my neck
Ps 71:2 Deliver me in Your righteousness, and cause me to escape; incline Your ear to me, and *save me*
Ps 71:3 You have given the commandment to *save me*, for You are my rock and my fortress
Ps 109:26 Help me, O Lord my God! Oh, *save me* according to Your mercy
Ps 119:94 I am Yours, *save me;* for I have sought Your precepts
Ps 119:146 I cry out to You; *save me*, and I will keep Your testimonies
Ps 138:7 You will stretch out Your hand against the wrath of my enemies, and Your right hand will *save me*
Is 38:20 The Lord was ready to *save me;* therefore we will sing my songs with stringed instruments all the days of our life, in the house of the Lord
Jer 17:14 *save me*, and I shall be saved, for You are my praise
Matt 14:30 and beginning to sink he cried out, saying, "Lord, *save me*
John 12:27 Father, *save Me* from this hour'? But for this purpose I came to this hour

SAVE THAT WHICH WAS LOST
Matt 18:11 For the Son of Man has come to *save that which was lost*
Luke 19:10 for the Son of Man has come to seek and to *save that which was lost*

SAVE WHATEVER IS LEFT (NIV)
(See *LAY UP FOR YOURSELVES*)

SAVE WITH YOUR RIGHT HAND
Ps 60:5 That Your beloved may be delivered, *save with Your right hand*, and hear me
Ps 108:6 That Your beloved may be delivered, *save with Your right hand*, and hear me

SAVE YOURSELF
Matt 27:40 and saying, "You who destroy the temple and build it in three days, *save Yourself*
Mark 15:30 *save Yourself*, and come down from the cross
Luke 23:37 and saying, "If You are the King of the Jews, *save Yourself*
Luke 23:39 Then one of the criminals who were hanged blasphemed Him, saying, "If You are the Christ, *save Yourself* and us

SAVED BY HIS LIFE
Rom 5:10 For if when we were enemies we were reconciled to God through the death of His Son, much more, having been reconciled, we shall be *saved by His life*

SAVED IN CHILDBEARING
1Tim 2:15 Nevertheless she will be *saved in childbearing* if they continue in faith, love, and holiness, with self-control

SAVED THROUGH FAITH
Eph 2:8 For by grace you have been *saved through faith*, and that not of yourselves

SAVIOR OF THE WORLD
John 4:42 Then they said to the woman, "Now we believe, not because of what you said, for we have heard for ourselves and know that this is indeed the Christ, the *Savior of the world*
1Jn 4:14 And we have seen and testify that the Father has sent the Son as *Savior of the world*

SAW AND BELIEVED
John 20:8 Then the other disciple, who came to the tomb first, went in also; and he *saw and believed*

SAW OUR AFFLICTION (NAS, RSV)
(See *LOOKED ON OUR AFFLICTION*)

SAW OUR MISERY (NIV)
(See *LOOKED ON OUR AFFLICTION*)

SAW THE LORD
1Kin 22:19 I *saw the Lord* sitting on His throne, and all the host of heaven standing by, on His right hand and on His left
2Chr 18:18 I *saw the Lord* sitting on His throne, and all the host of heaven standing on His right hand and on His left
Is 6:1 In the year that King Uzziah died, I *saw the Lord* sitting on a throne, high and lifted up, and the train of His robe filled the temple
Amos 9:1 I *saw the Lord* standing by the altar, and He said
John 20:20 Then the disciples were glad when they *saw the Lord*

SAY ANYTHING BAD ABOUT ME (NIV)
(See *SPEAK EVIL OF ME*)

SAY OF ME IN MALICE (NIV, RSV)
(See *SPEAK EVIL OF ME*)

SAY THE WORD (NAS, NIV, RSV)
(See *SPEAK A WORD*)

SAYING IS SURE AND WORTHY (RSV)
(See *FAITHFUL SAYING*)

SAYINGS AND RIDDLES OF THE WISE (NIV)
(See *WORDS OF THE WISE*)

SAYS THE LORD
Gen 22:16 By Myself I have sworn, *says the Lord*, because you have done this thing, and have not withheld your son, your only son
Ex 4:22 Then you shall say to Pharaoh, 'Thus *says the Lord*
Ex 5:1 Afterward Moses and Aaron went in and told Pharaoh, "Thus *says the Lord* God of Israel
Ex 7:17 Thus *says the Lord:* "By this you shall know that I am the Lord
Ex 8:1 And the Lord spoke to Moses, "Go to Pharaoh and say to him, 'Thus *says the Lord*
Ex 8:20 Then say to him, 'Thus *says the Lord:* "Let My people go, that they may serve Me
Ex 9:1 Then the Lord said to Moses, "Go in to Pharaoh and tell him, 'Thus *says the Lord* God of the Hebrews
Ex 9:13 Then the Lord said to Moses, "Rise early in the morning and stand before Pharaoh, and say to him, 'Thus *says the Lord* God of the Hebrews
Ex 10:3 So Moses and Aaron came in to Pharaoh and said to him, "Thus *says the Lord* God of the Hebrews
Ex 11:4 Then Moses said, "Thus *says the Lord:*

'About midnight I will go out into the midst of Egypt
Ex 32:27 And he said to them, "Thus *says the Lord* God of Israel
Num 14:28 Say to them, 'As I live,' *says the Lord*
Josh 7:13 Get up, sanctify the people, and say, 'Sanctify yourselves for tomorrow, because thus *says the Lord* God of Israel
Josh 24:2 And Joshua said to all the people, "Thus *says the Lord* God of Israel
Judg 6:8 that the Lord sent a prophet to the children of Israel, who said to them, "Thus *says the Lord* God of Israel
1Sam 2:27 Then a man of God came to Eli and said to him, "Thus *says the Lord*
1Sam 10:18 and said to the children of Israel, "Thus *says the Lord* God of Israel
1Sam 15:2 Thus *says the Lord* of hosts: "I will punish what Amalek did to Israel, how he laid wait for him on the way when he came up from Egypt
2Sam 7:5 Go and tell My servant David, 'Thus *says the Lord*
2Sam 7:8 Now therefore, thus shall you say to My servant David, 'Thus *says the Lord* of hosts
2Sam 12:7 Thus *says the Lord* God of Israel: I anointed you king over Israel, and I delivered you from the hand of Saul
2Sam 12:11 Thus *says the Lord:* "Behold, I will raise up adversity against you from your own house
2Sam 24:12 Go and tell David, 'Thus *says the Lord:* "I offer you three things
1Kin 11:31 And he said to Jeroboam, "Take for yourself ten pieces, for thus *says the Lord*, the God of Israel
1Kin 12:24 Thus *says the Lord:* "You shall not go up nor fight against your brethren the children of Israel
1Kin 13:2 Thus *says the Lord:* "Behold, a child, Josiah by name, shall be born to the house of David
1Kin 13:21 and he cried out to the man of God who came from Judah, saying, "Thus *says the Lord*
1Kin 14:7 Go, tell Jeroboam, 'Thus *says the Lord* God of Israel
1Kin 17:14 For thus *says the Lord* God of Israel: 'The bin of flour shall not be used up, nor shall the jar of oil run dry, until the day the Lord sends rain on the earth
1Kin 20:13 Suddenly a prophet approached Ahab king of Israel, saying, "Thus *says the Lord*
1Kin 20:14 And he said, "Thus *says the Lord:* By the young leaders of the provinces
1Kin 20:28 Then a man of God came and spoke to the king of Israel, and said, "Thus *says the Lord*
1Kin 20:42 And he said to him, "Thus *says the Lord:* 'Because you have let slip out of your hand a man whom I appointed to utter destruction, therefore your life shall go for his life, and your people for his people
1Kin 21:19 You shall speak to him, saying, 'Thus *says the Lord:* "Have you murdered and also taken possession?"' And you shall speak to him, saying, 'Thus *says the Lord*
1Kin 22:11 and he said, "Thus *says the Lord:* With these you shall gore the Syrians until they are destroyed
2Kin 1:4 Now therefore, thus *says the Lord:* You shall not come down from the bed to which you have gone up, but you shall surely die
2Kin 1:6 So they said to him, "A man came up to meet us, and said to us, 'Go, return to the king who sent you, and say to him, "Thus *says the Lord*
2Kin 1:16 Then he said to him, "Thus *says the Lord:* 'Because you have sent messengers to inquire of Baal-Zebub, the god of Ekron, is it because there is no God in Israel to inquire of His word
2Kin 2:21 Then he went out to the source of the water, and cast in the salt there, and said, "Thus *says the Lord*
2Kin 3:16 And he said, "Thus *says the Lord:* Make this valley full of ditches
2Kin 3:17 For thus *says the Lord:* "You shall not see wind, nor shall you see rain
2Kin 4:43 for thus *says the Lord:* "They shall eat and have some left over
2Kin 7:1 Thus *says the Lord:* "Tomorrow about this time a seah of fine flour shall be sold for a shekel, and two seahs of barley for a shekel, at the gate of Samaria
2Kin 9:3 Then take the flask of oil, and pour it on his head, and say, 'Thus *says the Lord*
2Kin 9:6 And he poured the oil on his head, and said to him, "Thus *says the Lord* God of Israel
2Kin 9:12 So he said, "Thus and thus he spoke to me, saying, 'Thus *says the Lord*
2Kin 9:26 Surely I saw yesterday the blood of Naboth and the blood of his sons,' *says the Lord*, 'and I will repay you in this plot,' *says the Lord*
2Kin 19:6 And Isaiah said to them, "Thus you shall say to your master, 'Thus *says the Lord*
2Kin 19:20 Then Isaiah the son of Amoz sent to Hezekiah, saying, "Thus *says the Lord* God of Israel
2Kin 19:32 Therefore thus *says the Lord* concerning the king of Assyria
2Kin 19:33 and he shall not come into this city,' *says the Lord*
2Kin 20:1 And Isaiah the prophet, the son of Amoz, went to him and said to him, "Thus *says the Lord*
2Kin 20:5 Return and tell Hezekiah the leader of My people, 'Thus *says the Lord*, the God of David your father
2Kin 20:17 Behold, the days are coming when all that is in your house, and what your fathers have accumulated until this day, shall be carried to Babylon; nothing shall be left,' *says the Lord*
2Kin 21:12 therefore thus *says the Lord* God of Israel: "Behold, I am bringing such calamity upon Jerusalem and Judah, that whoever hears of it, both his ears will tingle
2Kin 22:15 Then she said to them, "Thus *says the Lord* God of Israel
2Kin 22:16 Thus *says the Lord:* "Behold, I will bring calamity on this place and on its inhabitants all the words of the book which the king of Judah has read
2Kin 22:18 But to the king of Judah, who sent you to inquire of the Lord, in this manner you shall speak to him, 'Thus *says the Lord* God of Israel
2Kin 22:19 because your heart was tender, and you humbled yourself before the Lord when you heard what I spoke against this place and against its inhabitants, that they would become a desolation and a curse, and you tore your clothes and wept before Me, I also have heard you," *says the Lord*
1Chr 17:4 Go and tell My servant David, 'Thus *says the Lord*
1Chr 17:7 Now therefore, thus shall you say to My servant David, 'Thus *says the Lord* of hosts
1Chr 21:10 Go and tell David, saying, 'Thus *says the Lord:* "I offer you three things
1Chr 21:11 So Gad came to David and said to him, "Thus *says the Lord*
2Chr 11:4 Thus *says the Lord:* "You shall not go up or fight against your brethren
2Chr 12:5 Then Shemaiah the prophet came to Rehoboam and the leaders of Judah, who were gathered together in Jerusalem because of Shishak, and said to them, "Thus *says the Lord*

2Chr 18:10 and he said, "Thus *says the Lord:* With these you shall gore the Syrians until they are destroyed
2Chr 20:15 Thus *says the Lord* to you: 'Do not be afraid nor dismayed because of this great multitude, for the battle is not yours, but God's
2Chr 21:12 And a letter came to him from Elijah the prophet, saying, Thus *says the Lord* God of your father David
2Chr 34:23 Then she answered them, "Thus *says the Lord* God of Israel
2Chr 34:24 Thus *says the Lord:* 'Behold, I will bring calamity on this place and on its inhabitants, all the curses that are written in the book which they have read before the king of Judah
2Chr 34:26 And as for the king of Judah, who sent you to inquire of the Lord, in this manner you shall speak to him, 'Thus *says the Lord* God of Israel
2Chr 34:27 because your heart was tender, and you humbled yourself before God when you heard His words against this place and against its inhabitants, and you humbled yourself before Me, and you tore your clothes and wept before Me, I also have heard you," *says the Lord*
Ps 12:5 For the oppression of the poor, for the sighing of the needy, now I will arise," *says the Lord*
Is 1:11 *says the Lord.* "I have had enough of burnt offerings of rams and the fat of fed cattle
Is 1:18 Come now, and let us reason together," *says the Lord*
Is 3:15 What do you mean by crushing My people and grinding the faces of the poor?" *says the Lord* God of hosts
Is 7:7 thus *says the Lord* God: "It shall not stand, nor shall it come to pass
Is 10:24 Therefore thus *says the Lord* God of hosts: "O My people, who dwell in Zion, do not be afraid of the Assyrian
Is 14:22 For I will rise up against them," *says the Lord* of hosts, "And cut off from Babylon the name and remnant, and offspring and posterity," *says the Lord*
Is 14:23 I will sweep it with the broom of destruction," *says the Lord* of hosts
Is 17:3 they will be as the glory of the children of Israel," *says the Lord* of hosts
Is 17:6 Yet gleaning grapes will be left in it, like the shaking of an olive tree, two or three olives at the top of the uppermost bough, four or five in its most fruitful branches," *says the Lord* God of Israel
Is 19:4 And the Egyptians I will give into the hand of a cruel master, and a fierce king will rule over them," *says the Lord*, the Lord of hosts
Is 22:14 Then it was revealed in my hearing by the Lord of hosts, "Surely for this iniquity there will be no atonement for you, even to your death," *says the Lord* God of hosts
Is 22:15 Thus *says the Lord* God of hosts: Go, proceed to this steward, to Shebna, who is over the house, and say
Is 22:25 In that day,' *says the Lord* of hosts, 'the peg that is fastened in the secure place will be removed and be cut down and fall, and the burden that was on it will be cut off
Is 28:16 Therefore thus *says the Lord* God: Behold, I lay in Zion a stone for a foundation, a tried stone, a precious cornerstone, a sure foundation
Is 29:22 Therefore thus *says the Lord*, who redeemed Abraham, concerning the house of Jacob
Is 30:1 Woe to the rebellious children," *says the Lord*, "who take counsel, but not of Me, and who devise plans, but not of My Spirit, that they may add sin to sin
Is 30:15 For thus *says the Lord* God, the Holy One of Israel
Is 31:9 He shall cross over to his stronghold for fear, and his princes shall be afraid of the banner," *says the Lord*, whose fire is in Zion and whose furnace is in Jerusalem
Is 33:10 Now I will rise," *says the Lord;* "now I will be exalted, now I will lift Myself up
Is 37:6 And Isaiah said to them, "Thus shall you say to your master, 'Thus *says the Lord*
Is 37:21 Then Isaiah the son of Amoz sent to Hezekiah, saying, "Thus *says the Lord* God of Israel
Is 37:33 Therefore thus *says the Lord* concerning the king of Assyria
Is 37:34 and he shall not come into this city,' *says the Lord*
Is 38:1 And Isaiah the prophet, the son of Amoz, went to him and said to him, "Thus *says the Lord*
Is 38:5 Go and say to Hezekiah, 'Thus *says the Lord*, the God of David your father
Is 39:6 Behold, the days are coming when all that is in your house, and what your fathers have accumulated until this day, shall be carried to Babylon; nothing shall be left,' *says the Lord*
Is 41:14 I will help you," *says the Lord* and your Redeemer, the Holy One of Israel
Is 41:21 Present your case," *says the Lord.* "Bring forth your strong reasons
Is 43:1 But now, thus *says the Lord*, who created you, O Jacob, and He who formed you, O Israel
Is 43:10 You are My witnesses," *says the Lord*, "And My servant whom I have chosen, that you may know and believe Me, and understand that I am He
Is 43:12 therefore you are My witnesses," *says the Lord*, "that I am God
Is 43:14 Thus *says the Lord*, your Redeemer, the Holy One of Israel
Is 43:16 Thus *says the Lord*, who makes a way in the sea and a path through the mighty waters
Is 44:2 Thus *says the Lord* who made you and formed you from the womb, who will help you
Is 44:6 Thus *says the Lord*, the King of Israel, and his Redeemer, the Lord of hosts
Is 44:24 Thus *says the Lord*, your Redeemer, and He who formed you from the womb
Is 45:1 Thus *says the Lord* to His anointed, to Cyrus, whose right hand I have held to subdue nations before him and loose the armor of kings, to open before him the double doors, so that the gates will not be shut
Is 45:11 Thus *says the Lord*, the Holy One of Israel, and his Maker
Is 45:13 he shall build My city and let My exiles go free, not for price nor reward," *says the Lord* of hosts
Is 45:14 Thus *says the Lord:* "The labor of Egypt and merchandise of Cush and of the Sabeans, men of stature, shall come over to you, and they shall be yours
Is 45:18 For thus *says the Lord*, Who created the heavens, Who is God, Who formed the earth and made it, Who has established it, Who did not create it in vain, Who formed it to be inhabited
Is 48:17 Thus *says the Lord*, your Redeemer, the Holy One of Israel
Is 48:22 There is no peace," *says the Lord*, "for the wicked
Is 49:7 Thus *says the Lord*, the Redeemer of Israel, their Holy One, to Him whom man despises, to Him whom the nation abhors, to the Servant of rulers
Is 49:8 Thus *says the Lord:* "In an acceptable time I have heard You, and in the day of salvation I have helped You
Is 49:18 As I live," *says the Lord*, "you shall surely clothe yourselves with them all as an ornament, and bind them on you as a bride does
Is 49:22 Thus *says the Lord* God: "Behold, I will

lift My hand in an oath to the nations, and set up My standard for the peoples
Is 49:25 But thus *says the Lord:* "Even the captives of the mighty shall be taken away, and the prey of the terrible be delivered
Is 50:1 Thus *says the Lord:* "Where is the certificate of your mother's divorce, whom I have put away
Is 52:3 For thus *says the Lord:* "You have sold yourselves for nothing, and you shall be redeemed without money
Is 52:4 For thus *says the Lord* God: "My people went down at first into Egypt to sojourn there
Is 52:5 Now therefore, what have I here," *says the Lord,* "That My people are taken away for nothing? Those who rule over them make them wail," *says the Lord*
Is 54:1 For more are the children of the desolate than the children of the married woman," *says the Lord*
Is 54:8 but with everlasting kindness I will have mercy on you," *says the Lord,* your Redeemer
Is 54:10 For the mountains shall depart and the hills be removed, but My kindness shall not depart from you, nor shall My covenant of peace be removed," *says the Lord,* who has mercy on you
Is 54:17 This is the heritage of the servants of the Lord, and their righteousness is from Me," *says the Lord*
Is 55:8 For My thoughts are not your thoughts, nor are your ways My ways," *says the Lord*
Is 56:1 Thus *says the Lord:* "Keep justice, and do righteousness, for My salvation is about to come, and My righteousness to be revealed
Is 56:4 For thus *says the Lord:* "To the eunuchs who keep My Sabbaths, and choose what pleases Me, and hold fast My covenant
Is 57:19 peace, peace to him who is far off and to him who is near," *says the Lord*
Is 59:20 The Redeemer will come to Zion, and to those who turn from transgression in Jacob," *says the Lord*
Is 59:21 As for Me," *says the Lord,* "this is My covenant with them: My Spirit who is upon you, and My words which I have put in your mouth, shall not depart from your mouth, nor from the mouth of your descendants, nor from the mouth of your descendants' descendants," *says the Lord*
Is 65:7 your iniquities and the iniquities of your fathers together," *says the Lord*
Is 65:8 Thus *says the Lord:* "As the new wine is found in the cluster, and one says
Is 65:13 Therefore thus *says the Lord* God: Behold, My servants shall eat, but you shall be hungry
Is 65:25 They shall not hurt nor destroy in all My holy mountain," *says the Lord*
Is 66:1 Thus *says the Lord:* "Heaven is My throne, and earth is My footstool
Is 66:2 For all those things My hand has made, and all those things exist," *says the Lord*
Is 66:9 *says the Lord.* "Shall I who cause delivery shut up the womb
Is 66:12 For thus *says the Lord:* "Behold, I will extend peace to her like a river, and the glory of the Gentiles like a flowing stream
Is 66:17 Those who sanctify themselves and purify themselves, to go to the gardens after an idol in the midst, eating swine's flesh and the abomination and the mouse, shall be consumed together," *says the Lord*
Is 66:20 Then they shall bring all your brethren for an offering to the Lord out of all nations, on horses and in chariots and in litters, on mules and on camels, to My holy mountain Jerusalem," *says the Lord*
Is 66:21 And I will also take some of them for priests and Levites," *says the Lord*
Is 66:22 For as the new heavens and the new earth which I will make shall remain before Me," *says the Lord*
Is 66:23 And it shall come to pass that from one New Moon to another, and from one Sabbath to another, all flesh shall come to worship before Me," *says the Lord*
Jer 1:8 Do not be afraid of their faces, for I am with you to deliver you," *says the Lord*
Jer 1:15 For behold, I am calling all the families of the kingdoms of the north," *says the Lord*
Jer 1:19 For I am with you," *says the Lord,* "to deliver you
Jer 2:2 Go and cry in the hearing of Jerusalem, saying, 'Thus *says the Lord*
Jer 2:3 All that devour him will offend; disaster will come upon them," *says the Lord*
Jer 2:5 Thus *says the Lord:* "What injustice have your fathers found in Me, that they have gone far from Me, have followed idols, and have become idolaters
Jer 2:9 Therefore I will yet bring charges against you," *says the Lord*
Jer 2:12 Be astonished, O heavens, at this, and be horribly afraid; be very desolate," *says the Lord*
Jer 2:19 Know therefore and see that it is an evil and bitter thing that you have forsaken the Lord your God, and the fear of Me is not in you," *says the Lord* God of hosts
Jer 2:22 For though you wash yourself with lye, and use much soap, yet your iniquity is marked before Me," *says the Lord* God
Jer 2:29 Why will you plead with Me? You all have transgressed against Me," *says the Lord*
Jer 3:1 But you have played the harlot with many lovers; yet return to Me," *says the Lord*
Jer 3:10 And yet for all this her treacherous sister Judah has not turned to Me with her whole heart, but in pretense," *says the Lord*
Jer 3:12 Return, backsliding Israel,' *says the Lord,* 'and I will not cause My anger to fall on you; for I am merciful,' *says the Lord*
Jer 3:13 Only acknowledge your iniquity, that you have transgressed against the Lord your God, and have scattered your charms to alien deities under every green tree, and you have not obeyed My voice,' *says the Lord*
Jer 3:14 Return, O backsliding children," *says the Lord;* "for I am married to you
Jer 3:16 Then it shall come to pass, when you are multiplied and increased in the land in those days," *says the Lord*
Jer 3:20 Surely, as a wife treacherously departs from her husband, so have you dealt treacherously with Me, O house of Israel," *says the Lord*
Jer 4:1 If you will return, O Israel," *says the Lord,* "return to Me
Jer 4:3 For thus *says the Lord* to the men of Judah and Jerusalem
Jer 4:9 And it shall come to pass in that day," *says the Lord*
Jer 4:17 Like keepers of a field they are against her all around, because she has been rebellious against Me," *says the Lord*
Jer 4:27 For thus *says the Lord:* "The whole land shall be desolate
Jer 5:9 *says the Lord.* "And shall I not avenge Myself on such a nation as this
Jer 5:11 For the house of Israel and the house of Judah have dealt very treacherously with Me," *says the Lord*
Jer 5:14 Therefore thus *says the Lord* God of hosts: "Because you speak this word, behold, I will make My words in your mouth fire, and this people wood, and it shall devour them
Jer 5:15 Behold, I will bring a nation against you from afar, O house of Israel," *says the Lord*

Jer 5:18 Nevertheless in those days," *says the Lord,* "I will not make a complete end of you
Jer 5:22 *says the Lord.* 'Will you not tremble at My presence, Who have placed the sand as the bound of the sea, by a perpetual decree, that it cannot pass beyond it
Jer 5:29 *says the Lord.* 'Shall I not avenge Myself on such a nation as this
Jer 6:9 Thus *says the Lord* of hosts: They shall thoroughly glean as a vine the remnant of Israel
Jer 6:12 for I will stretch out My hand against the inhabitants of the land," *says the Lord*
Jer 6:15 at the time I punish them, they shall be cast down," *says the Lord*
Jer 6:16 Thus *says the Lord:* "Stand in the ways and see, and ask for the old paths, where the good way is, and walk in it
Jer 6:21 Therefore thus *says the Lord:* "Behold, I will lay stumbling blocks before this people, and the fathers and the sons together shall fall on them
Jer 6:22 Thus *says the Lord:* "Behold, a people comes from the north country, and a great nation will be raised from the farthest parts of the earth
Jer 7:3 Thus *says the Lord* of hosts, the God of Israel
Jer 7:11 Behold, I, even I, have seen it," *says the Lord*
Jer 7:13 And now, because you have done all these works," *says the Lord*
Jer 7:19 *says the Lord.* "Do they not provoke themselves, to the shame of their own faces
Jer 7:20 Therefore thus *says the Lord* God: Behold, My anger and My fury will be poured out on this place on man and on beast, on the trees of the field and on the fruit of the ground
Jer 7:21 Thus *says the Lord* of hosts, the God of Israel
Jer 7:30 For the children of Judah have done evil in My sight," *says the Lord*
Jer 7:32 Therefore behold, the days are coming," *says the Lord,* "when it will no more be called Tophet, or the Valley of the Son of Hinnom, but the Valley of Slaughter
Jer 8:1 At that time," *says the Lord,* "they shall bring out the bones of the kings of Judah, and the bones of its princes, and the bones of the priests, and the bones of the prophets, and the bones of the inhabitants of Jerusalem, out of their graves
Jer 8:3 Then death shall be chosen rather than life by all the residue of those who remain of this evil family, who remain in all the places where I have driven them," *says the Lord* of hosts
Jer 8:4 Moreover you shall say to them, 'Thus *says the Lord*
Jer 8:12 in the time of their punishment they shall be cast down," *says the Lord*
Jer 8:13 I will surely consume them," *says the Lord.* "There shall be no grapes on the vine, nor figs on the fig tree, and the leaf shall fade
Jer 8:17 For behold, I will send serpents among you, vipers which cannot be charmed, and they shall bite you," *says the Lord*
Jer 9:3 For they proceed from evil to evil, and they do not know Me," *says the Lord*
Jer 9:6 through deceit they refuse to know Me," *says the Lord*
Jer 9:7 Therefore thus *says the Lord* of hosts: "Behold, I will refine them and try them
Jer 9:9 *says the Lord.* "Shall I not avenge Myself on such a nation as this
Jer 9:15 therefore thus *says the Lord* of hosts, the God of Israel
Jer 9:17 Thus *says the Lord* of hosts: Consider and call for the mourning women, that they may come
Jer 9:22 Speak, "Thus *says the Lord:* 'Even the carcasses of men shall fall as refuse on the open field, like cuttings after the harvester, and no one shall gather them
Jer 9:23 Thus *says the Lord:* "Let not the wise man glory in his wisdom, let not the mighty man glory in his might, nor let the rich man glory in his riches
Jer 9:24 but let him who glories glory in this, that he understands and knows Me, that I am the Lord, exercising lovingkindness, judgment, and righteousness in the earth. For in these I delight," *says the Lord*
Jer 9:25 Behold, the days are coming," *says the Lord,* "that I will punish all those who are circumcised with the uncircumcised
Jer 10:2 Thus *says the Lord:* "Do not learn the way of the Gentiles
Jer 10:18 For thus *says the Lord:* "Behold, I will throw out at this time the inhabitants of the land, and will distress them, that they may find it so
Jer 11:3 and say to them, 'Thus *says the Lord* God of Israel
Jer 11:11 Therefore thus *says the Lord:* "Behold, I will surely bring calamity on them which they will not be able to escape
Jer 11:21 Therefore thus *says the Lord* concerning the men of Anathoth who seek your life, saying
Jer 11:22 therefore thus *says the Lord* of hosts: 'Behold, I will punish them
Jer 12:14 Thus *says the Lord:* "Against all My evil neighbors who touch the inheritance which I have caused My people Israel to inherit behold, I will pluck them out of their land and pluck out the house of Judah from among them
Jer 12:17 But if they do not obey, I will utterly pluck up and destroy that nation," *says the Lord*
Jer 13:9 Thus *says the Lord:* 'In this manner I will ruin the pride of Judah and the great pride of Jerusalem
Jer 13:11 For as the sash clings to the waist of a man, so I have caused the whole house of Israel and the whole house of Judah to cling to Me,' *says the Lord*
Jer 13:12 Thus *says the Lord* God of Israel: Every bottle shall be filled with wine
Jer 13:13 Then you shall say to them, 'Thus *says the Lord*
Jer 13:14 And I will dash them one against another, even the fathers and the sons together," *says the Lord*
Jer 13:25 This is your lot, the portion of your measures from Me," *says the Lord*
Jer 14:10 Thus *says the Lord* to this people: Thus they have loved to wander
Jer 14:15 Therefore thus *says the Lord* concerning the prophets who prophesy in My name, whom I did not send, and who say
Jer 15:2 then you shall tell them, 'Thus *says the Lord*
Jer 15:3 And I will appoint over them four forms of destruction," *says the Lord*
Jer 15:6 You have forsaken Me," *says the Lord,* "you have gone backward
Jer 15:9 And the remnant of them I will deliver to the sword before their enemies," *says the Lord*
Jer 15:19 Therefore thus *says the Lord:* "If you return, then I will bring you back
Jer 15:20 for I am with you to save you and deliver you," *says the Lord*
Jer 16:3 For thus *says the Lord* concerning the sons and daughters who are born in this place, and concerning their mothers who bore them and their fathers who begot them in this land
Jer 16:5 For thus *says the Lord:* "Do not enter the house of mourning, nor go to lament or bemoan them; for I have taken away My peace from this people," *says the Lord*
Jer 16:9 For thus *says the Lord* of hosts, the God of Israel

Jer 16:11 then you shall say to them, 'Because your fathers have forsaken Me,' *says the Lord*
Jer 16:14 Therefore behold, the days are coming," *says the Lord*, "that it shall no more be said
Jer 16:16 Behold, I will send for many fishermen," *says the Lord*
Jer 17:5 Thus *says the Lord:* "Cursed is the man who trusts in man and makes flesh his strength, whose heart departs from the Lord
Jer 17:21 Thus *says the Lord:* "Take heed to yourselves, and bear no burden on the Sabbath day, nor bring it in by the gates of Jerusalem
Jer 17:24 And it shall be, if you diligently heed Me," *says the Lord*
Jer 18:6 *says the Lord*. "Look, as the clay is in the potter's hand, so are you in My hand, O house of Israel
Jer 18:11 Now therefore, speak to the men of Judah and to the inhabitants of Jerusalem, saying, 'Thus *says the Lord*
Jer 18:13 Therefore thus *says the Lord:* "Ask now among the Gentiles, who has heard such things
Jer 19:1 Thus *says the Lord:* "Go and get a potter's earthen flask, and take some of the elders of the people and some of the elders of the priests
Jer 19:3 Thus *says the Lord* of hosts, the God of Israel
Jer 19:6 therefore behold, the days are coming," *says the Lord*, "that this place shall no more be called Tophet or the Valley of the Son of Hinnom, but the Valley of Slaughter
Jer 19:11 and say to them, 'Thus *says the Lord* of hosts
Jer 19:12 Thus I will do to this place," *says the Lord*
Jer 19:15 Thus *says the Lord* of hosts, the God of Israel
Jer 20:4 For thus *says the Lord:* 'Behold, I will make you a terror to yourself and to all your friends
Jer 21:4 Thus *says the Lord* God of Israel: Behold, I will turn back the weapons of war that are in your hands, with which you fight against the king of Babylon and the Chaldeans who besiege you outside the walls
Jer 21:7 And afterward," *says the Lord*, "I will deliver Zedekiah king of Judah, his servants and the people, and such as are left in this city from the pestilence and the sword and the famine, into the hand of Nebuchadnezzar king of Babylon, into the hand of their enemies, and into the hand of those who seek their life
Jer 21:8 Now you shall say to this people, 'Thus *says the Lord*
Jer 21:10 For I have set My face against this city for adversity and not for good," *says the Lord*
Jer 21:12 Thus *says the Lord:* "Execute judgment in the morning; and deliver him who is plundered out of the hand of the oppressor, lest My fury go out like fire and burn so that no one can quench it, because of the evil of your doings
Jer 21:13 Behold, I am against you, O inhabitant of the valley, and rock of the plain," *says the Lord*
Jer 21:14 But I will punish you according to the fruit of your doings," *says the Lord*
Jer 22:1 Thus *says the Lord:* "Go down to the house of the king of Judah, and there speak this word
Jer 22:3 Thus *says the Lord:* "Execute judgment and righteousness, and deliver the plundered out of the hand of the oppressor
Jer 22:5 But if you will not hear these words, I swear by Myself," *says the Lord*
Jer 22:6 For thus *says the Lord* to the house of the king of Judah
Jer 22:11 For thus *says the Lord* concerning Shallum the son of Josiah, king of Judah, who reigned instead of Josiah his father, who went from this place
Jer 22:16 then it was well. Was not this knowing Me?" *says the Lord*
Jer 22:18 Therefore thus *says the Lord* concerning Jehoiakim the son of Josiah, king of Judah
Jer 22:24 As I live," *says the Lord*, "though Coniah the son of Jehoiakim, king of Judah, were the signet on My right hand, yet I would pluck you off
Jer 22:30 Thus *says the Lord:* "Write this man down as childless, a man who shall not prosper in his days
Jer 23:1 Woe to the shepherds who destroy and scatter the sheep of My pasture!" *says the Lord*
Jer 23:2 Therefore thus *says the Lord* God of Israel against the shepherds who feed My people: "You have scattered My flock, driven them away, and not attended to them. Behold, I will attend to you for the evil of your doings," *says the Lord*
Jer 23:4 and they shall fear no more, nor be dismayed, nor shall they be lacking," *says the Lord*
Jer 23:5 Behold, the days are coming," *says the Lord*, "That I will raise to David a Branch of righteousness
Jer 23:7 Therefore, behold, the days are coming," *says the Lord*, "that they shall no longer say
Jer 23:11 yes, in My house I have found their wickedness," *says the Lord*
Jer 23:12 for I will bring disaster on them, the year of their punishment," *says the Lord*
Jer 23:15 Therefore thus *says the Lord* of hosts concerning the prophets
Jer 23:16 Thus *says the Lord* of hosts: Do not listen to the words of the prophets who prophesy to you
Jer 23:23 Am I a God near at hand," *says the Lord*
Jer 23:24 *says the Lord;* "do I not fill heaven and earth?" *says the Lord*
Jer 23:28 What is the chaff to the wheat?" *says the Lord*
Jer 23:29 *says the Lord*, "And like a hammer that breaks the rock in pieces
Jer 23:30 Therefore behold, I am against the prophets," *says the Lord*
Jer 23:31 Behold, I am against the prophets," *says the Lord*, "who use their tongues and say
Jer 23:32 Behold, I am against those who prophesy false dreams," *says the Lord*, "and tell them, and cause My people to err by their lies and by their recklessness. Yet I did not send them or command them; therefore they shall not profit this people at all," *says the Lord*
Jer 23:33 you shall then say to them, 'What oracle?' I will even forsake you," *says the Lord*
Jer 23:38 therefore thus *says the Lord:* Because you say this word
Jer 24:5 Thus *says the Lord*, the God of Israel: 'Like these good figs, so will I acknowledge those who are carried away captive from Judah, whom I have sent out of this place for their own good, into the land of the Chaldeans
Jer 24:8 And as the bad figs which cannot be eaten, they are so bad' surely thus *says the Lord*
Jer 25:7 Yet you have not listened to Me," *says the Lord*
Jer 25:8 Therefore thus *says the Lord* of hosts: 'Because you have not heard My words
Jer 25:9 behold, I will send and take all the families of the north,' *says the Lord*
Jer 25:12 Then it will come to pass, when seventy years are completed, that I will punish the king of Babylon and that nation, the land of the Chaldeans, for their iniquity,' *says the Lord*
Jer 25:15 For thus *says the Lord* God of Israel to me
Jer 25:27 Therefore you shall say to them, 'Thus *says the Lord* of hosts, the God of Israel

Jer 25:28 And it shall be, if they refuse to take the cup from your hand to drink, then you shall say to them, 'Thus *says the Lord* of hosts
Jer 25:29 You shall not be unpunished, for I will call for a sword on all the inhabitants of the earth," *says the Lord* of hosts
Jer 25:31 He will give those who are wicked to the sword,' *says the Lord*
Jer 25:32 Thus *says the Lord* of hosts: Behold, disaster shall go forth from nation to nation, and a great whirlwind shall be raised up from the farthest parts of the earth
Jer 26:2 Thus *says the Lord:* 'Stand in the court of the Lord's house, and speak to all the cities of Judah, which come to worship in the Lord's house, all the words that I command you to speak to them
Jer 26:4 And you shall say to them, 'Thus *says the Lord*
Jer 26:18 Micah of Moresheth prophesied in the days of Hezekiah king of Judah, and spoke to all the people of Judah, saying, 'Thus *says the Lord* of hosts
Jer 27:2 Thus *says the Lord* to me: 'Make for yourselves bonds and yokes, and put them on your neck
Jer 27:4 And command them to say to their masters, "Thus *says the Lord* of hosts, the God of Israel thus you shall say to your masters
Jer 27:8 And it shall be, that the nation and kingdom which will not serve Nebuchadnezzar the king of Babylon, and which will not put its neck under the yoke of the king of Babylon, that nation I will punish,' *says the Lord*
Jer 27:11 But the nations that bring their necks under the yoke of the king of Babylon and serve him, I will let them remain in their own land,' *says the Lord*
Jer 27:15 for I have not sent them," *says the Lord*, "yet they prophesy a lie in My name, that I may drive you out, and that you may perish, you and the prophets who prophesy to you
Jer 27:16 Also I spoke to the priests and to all this people, saying, "Thus *says the Lord*
Jer 27:19 For thus *says the Lord* of hosts concerning the pillars, concerning the Sea, concerning the carts, and concerning the remainder of the vessels that remain in this city
Jer 27:21 yes, thus *says the Lord* of hosts, the God of Israel, concerning the vessels that remain in the house of the Lord, and in the house of the king of Judah and of Jerusalem
Jer 27:22 They shall be carried to Babylon, and there they shall be until the day that I visit them,' *says the Lord*
Jer 28:4 And I will bring back to this place Jeconiah the son of Jehoiakim, king of Judah, with all the captives of Judah who went to Babylon,' *says the Lord*
Jer 28:11 And Hananiah spoke in the presence of all the people, saying, "Thus *says the Lord*
Jer 28:13 Go and tell Hananiah, saying, 'Thus *says the Lord:* "You have broken the yokes of wood, but you have made in their place yokes of iron
Jer 28:14 For thus *says the Lord* of hosts, the God of Israel
Jer 28:16 Therefore thus *says the Lord:* "Behold, I will cast you from the face of the earth
Jer 29:4 Thus *says the Lord* of hosts, the God of Israel, to all who were carried away captive, whom I have caused to be carried away from Jerusalem to Babylon
Jer 29:8 For thus *says the Lord* of hosts, the God of Israel
Jer 29:9 For they prophesy falsely to you in My name; I have not sent them, *says the Lord*
Jer 29:10 For thus *says the Lord:* After seventy years are completed at Babylon, I will visit you and perform My good word toward you, and cause you to return to this place
Jer 29:11 For I know the thoughts that I think toward you, *says the Lord*, thoughts of peace and not of evil, to give you a future and a hope
Jer 29:14 I will be found by you, *says the Lord*, and I will bring you back from your captivity; I will gather you from all the nations and from all the places where I have driven you, *says the Lord*, and I will bring you to the place from which I cause you to be carried away captive
Jer 29:16 therefore thus *says the Lord* concerning the king who sits on the throne of David, concerning all the people who dwell in this city, and concerning your brethren who have not gone out with you into captivity
Jer 29:17 thus *says the Lord* of hosts: Behold, I will send on them the sword, the famine, and the pestilence, and will make them like rotten figs that cannot be eaten, they are so bad
Jer 29:19 because they have not heeded My words, *says the Lord*, which I sent to them by My servants the prophets, rising up early and sending them; neither would you heed, *says the Lord*
Jer 29:21 Thus *says the Lord* of hosts, the God of Israel, concerning Ahab the son of Kolaiah, and Zedekiah the son of Maaseiah, who prophesy a lie to you in My name
Jer 29:23 Indeed I know, and am a witness, *says the Lord*
Jer 29:31 Send to all those in captivity, saying, 'Thus *says the Lord* concerning Shemaiah the Nehelamite
Jer 29:32 therefore thus *says the Lord:* Behold, I will punish Shemaiah the Nehelamite and his family: he shall not have anyone to dwell among this people, nor shall he see the good that I will do for My people," *says the Lord*
Jer 30:3 For behold, the days are coming,' *says the Lord*, 'that I will bring back from captivity My people Israel and Judah,' *says the Lord*
Jer 30:5 For thus *says the Lord:* 'We have heard a voice of trembling, of fear, and not of peace
Jer 30:8 For it shall come to pass in that day,' *says the Lord* of hosts
Jer 30:10 Therefore do not fear, O My servant Jacob,' *says the Lord*
Jer 30:11 For I am with you,' *says the Lord*, 'to save you
Jer 30:12 For thus *says the Lord:* 'Your affliction is incurable, your wound is severe
Jer 30:17 For I will restore health to you and heal you of your wounds,' *says the Lord*
Jer 30:18 Thus *says the Lord:* 'Behold, I will bring back the captivity of Jacob's tents, and have mercy on his dwelling places
Jer 30:21 for who is this who pledged his heart to approach Me?' *says the Lord*
Jer 31:1 At the same time," *says the Lord*, "I will be the God of all the families of Israel, and they shall be My people
Jer 31:2 Thus *says the Lord:* "The people who survived the sword found grace in the wilderness Israel, when I went to give him rest
Jer 31:7 For thus *says the Lord:* "Sing with gladness for Jacob, and shout among the chief of the nations
Jer 31:14 I will satiate the soul of the priests with abundance, and My people shall be satisfied with My goodness," *says the Lord*
Jer 31:15 Thus *says the Lord:* "A voice was heard in Ramah, lamentation and bitter weeping, Rachel weeping for her children, refusing to be comforted for her children, because they are no more
Jer 31:16 Thus *says the Lord:* "Refrain your voice from weeping, and your eyes from tears; for your work shall be rewarded," *says the Lord*
Jer 31:17 There is hope in your future," *says the*

Lord, "that your children shall come back to their own border
Jer 31:20 I will surely have mercy on him," *says the Lord*
Jer 31:23 Thus *says the Lord* of hosts, the God of Israel
Jer 31:27 Behold, the days are coming," *says the Lord*, "that I will sow the house of Israel and the house of Judah with the seed of man and the seed of beast
Jer 31:28 And it shall come to pass, that as I have watched over them to pluck up, to break down, to throw down, to destroy, and to afflict, so I will watch over them to build and to plant," *says the Lord*
Jer 31:31 Behold, the days are coming," *says the Lord*, "when I will make a new covenant with the house of Israel and with the house of Judah
Jer 31:32 not according to the covenant that I made with their fathers in the day that I took them by the hand to bring them out of the land of Egypt, My covenant which they broke, though I was a husband to them," *says the Lord*
Jer 31:33 After those days, *says the Lord*, I will put My law in their minds, and write it on their hearts
Jer 31:34 No more shall every man teach his neighbor, and every man his brother, saying, 'Know the Lord,' for they all shall know Me, from the least of them to the greatest of them," *says the Lord*
Jer 31:35 Thus *says the Lord*, Who gives the sun for a light by day, and the ordinances of the moon and the stars for a light by night, Who disturbs the sea, and its waves roar (the Lord of hosts is His name
Jer 31:36 If those ordinances depart from before Me," *says the Lord*
Jer 31:37 Thus *says the Lord:* "If heaven above can be measured, and the foundations of the earth searched out beneath, I will also cast off all the seed of Israel for all that they have done," *says the Lord*
Jer 31:38 Behold, the days are coming," *says the Lord*, "that the city shall be built for the Lord from the Tower of Hananeel to the Corner Gate
Jer 32:3 For Zedekiah king of Judah had shut him up, saying, "Why do you prophesy and say, 'Thus *says the Lord*
Jer 32:5 then he shall lead Zedekiah to Babylon, and there he shall be until I visit him," *says the Lord*
Jer 32:14 Thus *says the Lord* of hosts, the God of Israel
Jer 32:15 For thus *says the Lord* of hosts, the God of Israel
Jer 32:28 Therefore thus *says the Lord:* "Behold, I will give this city into the hand of the Chaldeans, into the hand of Nebuchadnezzar king of Babylon, and he shall take it
Jer 32:30 For the children of Israel have provoked Me only to anger with the work of their hands," *says the Lord*
Jer 32:36 Now therefore, thus *says the Lord*, the God of Israel, concerning this city of which you say
Jer 32:42 For thus *says the Lord:* 'Just as I have brought all this great calamity on this people, so I will bring on them all the good that I have promised them
Jer 32:44 for I will cause their captives to return,' *says the Lord*
Jer 33:2 Thus *says the Lord* who made it, the Lord who formed it to establish it (the Lord is His name
Jer 33:4 For thus *says the Lord*, the God of Israel, concerning the houses of this city and the houses of the kings of Judah, which have been pulled down to fortify against the siege mounds and the sword
Jer 33:10 Thus *says the Lord:* 'Again there shall be heard in this place of which you say
Jer 33:11 For I will cause the captives of the land to return as at the first,' *says the Lord*
Jer 33:12 Thus *says the Lord* of hosts: 'In this place which is desolate, without man and without beast, and in all its cities, there shall again be a habitation of shepherds causing their flocks to lie down
Jer 33:13 In the cities of the mountains, in the cities of the lowland, in the cities of the South, in the land of Benjamin, in the places around Jerusalem, and in the cities of Judah, the flocks shall again pass under the hands of him who counts them,' *says the Lord*
Jer 33:14 Behold, the days are coming,' *says the Lord*, 'that I will perform that good thing which I have promised to the house of Israel and to the house of Judah
Jer 33:17 For thus *says the Lord:* 'David shall never lack a man to sit on the throne of the house of Israel
Jer 33:20 Thus *says the Lord:* 'If you can break My covenant with the day and My covenant with the night, so that there will not be day and night in their season
Jer 33:25 Thus *says the Lord:* 'If My covenant is not with day and night, and if I have not appointed the ordinances of heaven and earth
Jer 34:2 Thus *says the Lord*, the God of Israel: 'Go and speak to Zedekiah king of Judah and tell him, "Thus *says the Lord*
Jer 34:4 Thus *says the Lord* concerning you: You shall not die by the sword
Jer 34:5 For I have pronounced the word," *says the Lord*
Jer 34:13 Thus *says the Lord*, the God of Israel: 'I made a covenant with your fathers in the day that I brought them out of the land of Egypt, out of the house of bondage, saying
Jer 34:17 Therefore thus *says the Lord:* "You have not obeyed Me in proclaiming liberty, every one to his brother and every one to his neighbor. Behold, I proclaim liberty to you,' *says the Lord*
Jer 34:22 Behold, I will command,' *says the Lord*, 'and cause them to return to this city
Jer 35:13 Thus *says the Lord* of hosts, the God of Israel: 'Go and tell the man of Judah and the inhabitants of Jerusalem, "Will you not receive instruction to obey My words?" *says the Lord*
Jer 35:17 Therefore thus *says the Lord* God of hosts, the God of Israel
Jer 35:18 And Jeremiah said to the house of the Rechabites, "Thus *says the Lord* of hosts, the God of Israel
Jer 35:19 therefore thus *says the Lord* of hosts, the God of Israel
Jer 36:29 And you shall say to Jehoiakim king of Judah, 'Thus *says the Lord*
Jer 36:30 Therefore thus *says the Lord* concerning Jehoiakim king of Judah
Jer 37:7 Thus *says the Lord*, the God of Israel, 'Thus you shall say to the king of Judah, who sent you to Me to inquire of Me
Jer 37:9 Thus *says the Lord:* 'Do not deceive yourselves, saying, "The Chaldeans will surely depart from us
Jer 38:2 Thus *says the Lord:* 'He who remains in this city shall die by the sword, by famine, and by pestilence
Jer 38:3 Thus *says the Lord:* 'This city shall surely be given into the hand of the king of Babylon's army, which shall take it
Jer 38:17 Then Jeremiah said to Zedekiah, "Thus *says the Lord*, the God of hosts, the God of Israel
Jer 39:16 Go and speak to Ebed-Melech the Ethi-

opian, saying, 'Thus *says the Lord* of hosts, the God of Israel
Jer 39:17 But I will deliver you in that day," *says the Lord*
Jer 39:18 but your life shall be as a prize to you, because you have put your trust in Me," *says the Lord*
Jer 42:9 and said to them, "Thus *says the Lord*, the God of Israel, to whom you sent me to present your petition before Him
Jer 42:11 do not be afraid of him,' *says the Lord*
Jer 42:15 Thus *says the Lord* of hosts, the God of Israel
Jer 42:18 For thus *says the Lord* of hosts, the God of Israel
Jer 43:10 and say to them, 'Thus *says the Lord* of hosts, the God of Israel
Jer 44:2 Thus *says the Lord* of hosts, the God of Israel
Jer 44:7 Now therefore, thus *says the Lord*, the God of hosts, the God of Israel
Jer 44:11 Therefore thus *says the Lord* of hosts, the God of Israel
Jer 44:25 Thus *says the Lord* of hosts, the God of Israel, saying
Jer 44:26 Behold, I have sworn by My great name,' *says the Lord*
Jer 44:29 And this shall be a sign to you,' *says the Lord*
Jer 44:30 Thus *says the Lord:* 'Behold, I will give Pharaoh Hophra king of Egypt into the hand of his enemies and into the hand of those who seek his life, as I gave Zedekiah king of Judah into the hand of Nebuchadnezzar king of Babylon, his enemy who sought his life
Jer 45:2 Thus *says the Lord*, the God of Israel, to you, O Baruch
Jer 45:4 Thus you shall say to him, 'Thus *says the Lord*
Jer 45:5 for behold, I will bring adversity on all flesh," *says the Lord*
Jer 46:5 They have speedily fled, and did not look back, for fear was all around," *says the Lord*
Jer 46:23 They shall cut down her forest," *says the Lord*, "though it cannot be searched, because they are innumerable, and more numerous than grasshoppers
Jer 46:26 Afterward it shall be inhabited as in the days of old," *says the Lord*
Jer 46:28 Do not fear, O Jacob My servant," *says the Lord*
Jer 47:2 Thus *says the Lord:* "Behold, waters rise out of the north, and shall be an overflowing flood
Jer 48:1 Thus *says the Lord* of hosts, the God of Israel
Jer 48:12 Therefore behold, the days are coming," *says the Lord*, "that I shall send him wine-workers who will tip him over and empty his vessels and break the bottles
Jer 48:25 The horn of Moab is cut off, and his arm is broken," *says the Lord*
Jer 48:30 I know his wrath," *says the Lord*, "but it is not right
Jer 48:35 Moreover," *says the Lord*, "I will cause to cease in Moab the one who offers sacrifices in the high places and burns incense to his gods
Jer 48:38 for I have broken Moab like a vessel in which is no pleasure," *says the Lord*
Jer 48:40 For thus *says the Lord:* "Behold, one shall fly like an eagle, and spread his wings over Moab
Jer 48:43 Fear and the pit and the snare shall be upon you, O inhabitant of Moab," *says the Lord*
Jer 48:44 For upon Moab, upon it I will bring the year of their punishment," *says the Lord*
Jer 48:47 Yet I will bring back the captives of Moab in the latter days," *says the Lord*
Jer 49:1 Thus *says the Lord:* "Has Israel no sons? Has he no heir
Jer 49:2 Therefore behold, the days are coming," *says the Lord*, "that I will cause to be heard an alarm of war in Rabbah of the Ammonites; it shall be a desolate mound, and her villages shall be burned with fire. Then Israel shall take possession of his inheritance," *says the Lord*
Jer 49:5 Behold, I will bring fear upon you," *says the Lord* God of hosts
Jer 49:6 But afterward I will bring back the captives of the people of Ammon," *says the Lord*
Jer 49:7 Thus *says the Lord* of hosts: Is wisdom no more in Teman
Jer 49:12 For thus *says the Lord:* "Behold, those whose judgment was not to drink of the cup have assuredly drunk
Jer 49:13 For I have sworn by Myself," *says the Lord*, "that Bozrah shall become a desolation, a reproach, a waste, and a curse
Jer 49:16 Though you make your nest as high as the eagle, I will bring you down from there," *says the Lord*
Jer 49:18 As in the overthrow of Sodom and Gomorrah and their neighboring cities," *says the Lord*
Jer 49:26 Therefore her young men shall fall in her streets, and all the men of war shall be cut off in that day," *says the Lord* of hosts
Jer 49:28 Thus *says the Lord:* "Arise, go up to Kedar, and devastate the men of the East
Jer 49:30 *says the Lord.* "For Nebuchadnezzar king of Babylon has taken counsel against you, and has conceived a plan against you
Jer 49:31 Arise, go up to the wealthy nation that dwells securely," *says the Lord*
Jer 49:32 I will scatter to all winds those in the farthest corners, and I will bring their calamity from all its sides," *says the Lord*
Jer 49:35 Thus *says the Lord* of hosts: 'Behold, I will break the bow of Elam, the foremost of their might
Jer 49:37 I will bring disaster upon them, my fierce anger,' *says the Lord*
Jer 49:38 I will set My throne in Elam, and will destroy from there the king and the princes,' *says the Lord*
Jer 49:39 I will bring back the captives of Elam,' *says the Lord*
Jer 50:4 In those days and in that time," *says the Lord*
Jer 50:10 all who plunder her shall be satisfied," *says the Lord*
Jer 50:18 Therefore thus *says the Lord* of hosts, the God of Israel
Jer 50:20 In those days and in that time," *says the Lord*
Jer 50:21 Waste and utterly destroy them," *says the Lord*, "and do according to all that I have commanded you
Jer 50:30 Therefore her young men shall fall in the streets, and all her men of war shall be cut off in that day," *says the Lord*
Jer 50:31 *says the Lord* God of hosts; "For your day has come, the time that I will punish you
Jer 50:33 Thus *says the Lord* of hosts: The children of Israel were oppressed, along with the children of Judah
Jer 50:35 A sword is against the Chaldeans," *says the Lord*, "against the inhabitants of Babylon, and against her princes and her wise men
Jer 50:40 As God overthrew Sodom and Gomorrah and their neighboring cities," *says the Lord*
Jer 51:1 Thus *says the Lord:* "Behold, I will raise up against Babylon, against those who dwell in Leb Kamai, a destroying wind
Jer 51:24 And I will repay Babylon and all the in-

habitants of Chaldea for all the evil they have done in Zion in your sight," *says the Lord*
Jer 51:25 Behold, I am against you, O destroying mountain, who destroys all the earth," *says the Lord*
Jer 51:26 They shall not take from you a stone for a corner nor a stone for a foundation, but you shall be desolate forever," *says the Lord*
Jer 51:33 For thus *says the Lord* of hosts, the God of Israel
Jer 51:36 Therefore thus *says the Lord:* "Behold, I will plead your case and take vengeance for you
Jer 51:39 I will make them drunk, that they may rejoice, and sleep a perpetual sleep and not awake," *says the Lord*
Jer 51:48 for the plunderers shall come to her from the north," *says the Lord*
Jer 51:52 Therefore behold, the days are coming," *says the Lord*, "that I will bring judgment on her carved images, and throughout all her land the wounded shall groan
Jer 51:53 Though Babylon were to mount up to heaven, and though she were to fortify the height of her strength, yet from Me plunderers would come to her," *says the Lord*
Jer 51:58 Thus *says the Lord* of hosts: The broad walls of Babylon shall be utterly broken, and her high gates shall be burned with fire
Ezek 2:4 I am sending you to them, and you shall say to them, 'Thus *says the Lord* God
Ezek 3:11 And go, get to the captives, to the children of your people, and speak to them and tell them, 'Thus *says the Lord* God
Ezek 3:27 But when I speak with you, I will open your mouth, and you shall say to them, 'Thus *says the Lord* God
Ezek 5:5 Thus *says the Lord* God: 'This is Jerusalem; I have set her in the midst of the nations and the countries all around her
Ezek 5:7 Therefore thus *says the Lord* God: Because you have multiplied disobedience more than the nations that are all around you, and have not walked in My statutes, nor kept My judgments, nor even done according to the judgments of the nations that are all around you
Ezek 5:8 therefore thus *says the Lord* God: Indeed I, even I, am against you and will execute judgments in your midst in the sight of the nations
Ezek 5:11 Therefore, as I live,' *says the Lord* God, 'surely, because you have defiled My sanctuary with all your detestable things and with all your abominations, therefore I will also diminish you
Ezek 6:3 Thus *says the Lord* God to the mountains, to the hills, to the ravines, and to the valleys
Ezek 6:11 Thus *says the Lord* God: "Pound your fists and stamp your feet, and say
Ezek 7:2 And you, son of man, thus *says the Lord* God to the land of Israel
Ezek 7:5 Thus *says the Lord* God: 'A disaster, a singular disaster
Ezek 11:5 Thus *says the Lord:* "Thus you have said, O house of Israel
Ezek 11:7 Therefore thus *says the Lord* God: Your slain whom you have laid in its midst, they are the meat, and this city is the caldron
Ezek 11:8 and I will bring a sword upon you," *says the Lord* God
Ezek 11:16 Therefore say, 'Thus *says the Lord* God: "Although I have cast them far off among the Gentiles, and although I have scattered them among the countries, yet I shall be a little sanctuary for them in the countries where they have gone
Ezek 11:17 Therefore say, 'Thus *says the Lord* God: "I will gather you from the peoples, assemble you from the countries where you have been scattered, and I will give you the land of Israel
Ezek 11:21 But as for those whose hearts walk after the heart of their detestable things and their abominations, I will recompense their deeds on their own heads," *says the Lord* God
Ezek 12:10 Say to them, 'Thus *says the Lord* God: "This burden concerns the prince in Jerusalem and all the house of Israel who are among them
Ezek 12:19 And say to the people of the land, 'Thus *says the Lord* God to the inhabitants of Jerusalem and to the land of Israel
Ezek 12:23 Tell them therefore, 'Thus *says the Lord* God: "I will lay this proverb to rest, and they shall no more use it as a proverb in Israel
Ezek 12:25 for in your days, O rebellious house, I will say the word and perform it," *says the Lord* God
Ezek 12:28 Therefore say to them, 'Thus *says the Lord* God: "None of My words will be postponed any more, but the word which I speak will be done," *says the Lord* God
Ezek 13:3 Thus *says the Lord* God: "Woe to the foolish prophets, who follow their own spirit and have seen nothing
Ezek 13:6 They have envisioned futility and false divination, saying, 'Thus *says the Lord*
Ezek 13:8 Therefore thus *says the Lord* God: Because you have spoken nonsense and envisioned lies, therefore I am indeed against you," *says the Lord* God
Ezek 13:13 Therefore thus *says the Lord* God: I will cause a stormy wind to break forth in My fury
Ezek 13:16 that is, the prophets of Israel who prophesy concerning Jerusalem, and who see visions of peace for her when there is no peace,'" *says the Lord* God
Ezek 13:18 and say, 'Thus *says the Lord* God: Woe to the women who sew magic charms on their sleeves and make veils for the heads of people of every height to hunt souls
Ezek 13:20 Therefore thus *says the Lord* God: Behold, I am against your magic charms by which you hunt souls there like birds
Ezek 14:4 Therefore speak to them, and say to them, 'Thus *says the Lord* God
Ezek 14:6 Therefore say to the house of Israel, 'Thus *says the Lord* God
Ezek 14:11 that the house of Israel may no longer stray from Me, nor be profaned anymore with all their transgressions, but that they may be My people and I may be their God," *says the Lord* God
Ezek 14:14 Though these three men, Noah, Daniel, and Job, were in it, they would deliver only themselves by their righteousness," *says the Lord* God
Ezek 14:16 even though these three men were in it, as I live," *says the Lord* God
Ezek 14:18 even though these three men were in it, as I live," *says the Lord* God
Ezek 14:20 even though Noah, Daniel, and Job were in it, as I live," *says the Lord* God
Ezek 14:21 For thus *says the Lord* God: "How much more it shall be when I send My four severe judgments on Jerusalem the sword and famine and wild beasts and pestilence to cut off man and beast from it
Ezek 14:23 and you shall know that I have done nothing without cause that I have done in it," *says the Lord* God
Ezek 15:6 Therefore thus *says the Lord* God: Like the wood of the vine among the trees of the forest, which I have given to the fire for fuel, so I will give up the inhabitants of Jerusalem
Ezek 15:8 Thus I will make the land desolate, because they have persisted in unfaithfulness,' *says the Lord* God
Ezek 16:3 and say, 'Thus *says the Lord* God to

Jerusalem: "Your birth and your nativity are from the land of Canaan
Ezek 16:8 Yes, I swore an oath to you and entered into a covenant with you, and you became Mine," *says the Lord* God
Ezek 16:14 Your fame went out among the nations because of your beauty, for it was perfect through My splendor which I had bestowed on you," *says the Lord* God
Ezek 16:19 Also My food which I gave you the pastry of fine flour, oil, and honey which I fed you you set it before them as sweet incense; and so it was," *says the Lord* God
Ezek 16:23 Then it was so, after all your wickedness 'Woe, woe to you!' *says the Lord* God
Ezek 16:30 *says the Lord* God, "seeing you do all these things, the deeds of a brazen harlot
Ezek 16:36 Thus *says the Lord* God: "Because your filthiness was poured out and your nakedness uncovered in your harlotry with your lovers, and with all your abominable idols, and because of the blood of your children which you gave to them
Ezek 16:43 Because you did not remember the days of your youth, but agitated Me with all these things, surely I will also recompense your deeds on your own head," *says the Lord* God
Ezek 16:48 As I live," *says the Lord* God, "neither your sister Sodom nor her daughters have done as you and your daughters have done
Ezek 16:58 You have paid for your lewdness and your abominations," *says the Lord*
Ezek 16:59 For thus *says the Lord* God: "I will deal with you as you have done, who despised the oath by breaking the covenant
Ezek 16:63 that you may remember and be ashamed, and never open your mouth anymore because of your shame, when I provide you an atonement for all you have done," *says the Lord* God
Ezek 17:3 and say, 'Thus *says the Lord* God: A great eagle with large wings and long pinions, full of feathers of various colors, came to Lebanon and took from the cedar the highest branch
Ezek 17:9 Say, 'Thus *says the Lord* God: Will it thrive? Will he not pull up its roots, cut off its fruit, and leave it to wither
Ezek 17:16 As I live,' *says the Lord* God, 'surely in the place where the king dwells who made him king, whose oath he despised and whose covenant he broke with him in the midst of Babylon he shall die
Ezek 17:19 Therefore thus *says the Lord* God: As I live, surely My oath which he despised, and My covenant which he broke, I will recompense on his own head
Ezek 17:22 Thus *says the Lord* God: "I will take also one of the highest branches of the high cedar and set it out
Ezek 18:3 As I live," *says the Lord* God, "you shall no longer use this proverb in Israel
Ezek 18:9 if he has walked in My statutes and kept My judgments faithfully he is just; he shall surely live!" *says the Lord* God
Ezek 18:23 *says the Lord* God, "and not that he should turn from his ways and live
Ezek 18:30 Therefore I will judge you, O house of Israel, every one according to his ways," *says the Lord* God
Ezek 18:32 For I have no pleasure in the death of one who dies," *says the Lord* God
Ezek 20:3 Son of man, speak to the elders of Israel, and say to them, 'Thus *says the Lord* God: "Have you come to inquire of Me? As I live," *says the Lord* God
Ezek 20:5 Say to them, 'Thus *says the Lord* God: "On the day when I chose Israel and lifted My hand in an oath to the descendants of the house of Jacob, and made Myself known to them in the land of Egypt, I lifted My hand in an oath to them, saying
Ezek 20:27 Therefore, son of man, speak to the house of Israel, and say to them, 'Thus *says the Lord* God
Ezek 20:30 Therefore say to the house of Israel, 'Thus *says the Lord* God
Ezek 20:31 As I live," *says the Lord* God, "I will not be inquired of by you
Ezek 20:33 As I live," *says the Lord* God, "surely with a mighty hand, with an outstretched arm, and with fury poured out, I will rule over you
Ezek 20:36 Just as I pleaded My case with your fathers in the wilderness of the land of Egypt, so I will plead My case with you," *says the Lord* God
Ezek 20:39 As for you, O house of Israel," thus *says the Lord* God
Ezek 20:40 For on My holy mountain, on the mountain height of Israel," *says the Lord* God
Ezek 20:44 Then you shall know that I am the Lord, when I have dealt with you for My name's sake, not according to your wicked ways nor according to your corrupt doings, O house of Israel," *says the Lord* God
Ezek 20:47 Thus *says the Lord* God: "Behold, I will kindle a fire in you, and it shall devour every green tree and every dry tree in you
Ezek 21:3 and say to the land of Israel, 'Thus *says the Lord*
Ezek 21:7 Behold, it is coming and shall be brought to pass,' *says the Lord* God
Ezek 21:9 Son of man, prophesy and say, 'Thus *says the Lord*
Ezek 21:13 The scepter shall be no more," *says the Lord* God
Ezek 21:24 Therefore thus *says the Lord* God: Because you have made your iniquity to be remembered, in that your transgressions are uncovered, so that in all your doings your sins appear because you have come to remembrance, you shall be taken in hand
Ezek 21:26 thus *says the Lord* God: 'Remove the turban, and take off the crown
Ezek 21:28 And you, son of man, prophesy and say, 'Thus *says the Lord* God concerning the Ammonites and concerning their reproach
Ezek 22:3 Then say, 'Thus *says the Lord* God: The city sheds blood in her own midst, that her time may come
Ezek 22:12 you have made profit from your neighbors by extortion, and have forgotten Me," *says the Lord* God
Ezek 22:19 Therefore thus *says the Lord* God: Because you have all become dross, therefore behold, I will gather you into the midst of Jerusalem
Ezek 22:28 Her prophets plastered them with untempered mortar, seeing false visions, and divining lies for them, saying, 'Thus *says the Lord* God
Ezek 22:31 and I have recompensed their deeds on their own heads," *says the Lord* God
Ezek 23:22 Therefore, Oholibah, thus *says the Lord* God: 'Behold, I will stir up your lovers against you, from whom you have alienated yourself, and I will bring them against you from every side
Ezek 23:28 For thus *says the Lord* God: 'Surely I will deliver you into the hand of those whom you hate, into the hand of those from whom you alienated yourself
Ezek 23:32 Thus *says the Lord* God: 'You shall drink of your sister's cup, the deep and wide one
Ezek 23:34 You shall drink and drain it, you shall break its shards, and tear at your own breasts; for I have spoken,' *says the Lord* God
Ezek 23:35 Therefore thus *says the Lord* God: Because you have forgotten Me and cast Me behind

your back, therefore you shall bear the penalty of your lewdness and your harlotry
Ezek 23:46 For thus *says the Lord* God: 'Bring up an assembly against them, give them up to trouble and plunder
Ezek 24:3 And utter a parable to the rebellious house, and say to them, 'Thus *says the Lord* God
Ezek 24:6 Therefore thus *says the Lord* God: Woe to the bloody city, to the pot whose scum is in it, and whose scum is not gone from it
Ezek 24:9 Therefore thus *says the Lord* God: Woe to the bloody city
Ezek 24:14 according to your ways and according to your deeds they will judge you," *says the Lord* God
Ezek 24:21 Speak to the house of Israel, "Thus *says the Lord* God
Ezek 25:3 Thus *says the Lord* God: "Because you said, 'Aha!' against My sanctuary when it was profaned, and against the land of Israel when it was desolate, and against the house of Judah when they went into captivity
Ezek 25:6 For thus *says the Lord* God: "Because you clapped your hands, stamped your feet, and rejoiced in heart with all your disdain for the land of Israel
Ezek 25:8 Thus *says the Lord* God: "Because Moab and Seir say
Ezek 25:12 Thus *says the Lord* God: "Because of what Edom did against the house of Judah by taking vengeance, and has greatly offended by avenging itself on them
Ezek 25:13 therefore thus *says the Lord* God: I will also stretch out My hand against Edom, cut off man and beast from it, and make it desolate from Teman
Ezek 25:14 and they shall know My vengeance," *says the Lord* God
Ezek 25:15 Thus *says the Lord* God: "Because the Philistines dealt vengefully and took vengeance with a spiteful heart, to destroy because of the old hatred
Ezek 25:16 therefore thus *says the Lord* God: I will stretch out My hand against the Philistines, and I will cut off the Cherethites and destroy the remnant of the seacoast
Ezek 26:3 Therefore thus *says the Lord* God: Behold, I am against you, O Tyre, and will cause many nations to come up against you, as the sea causes its waves to come up
Ezek 26:5 It shall be a place for spreading nets in the midst of the sea, for I have spoken,' *says the Lord* God
Ezek 26:7 For thus *says the Lord* God: 'Behold, I will bring against Tyre from the north Nebuchadnezzar king of Babylon, king of kings, with horses, with chariots, and with horsemen, and an army with many people
Ezek 26:14 you shall be a place for spreading nets, and you shall never be rebuilt, for I the Lord have spoken,' *says the Lord* God
Ezek 26:15 Thus *says the Lord* God to Tyre: Will the coastlands not shake at the sound of your fall, when the wounded cry, when slaughter is made in the midst of you
Ezek 26:19 For thus *says the Lord* God: 'When I make you a desolate city, like cities that are not inhabited, when I bring the deep upon you, and great waters cover you
Ezek 26:21 though you are sought for, you will never be found again,' *says the Lord* God
Ezek 27:3 and say to Tyre, 'You who are situated at the entrance of the sea, merchant of the peoples on many coastlands, thus *says the Lord* God
Ezek 28:2 Son of man, say to the prince of Tyre, 'Thus *says the Lord* God
Ezek 28:6 Therefore thus *says the Lord* God: Because you have set your heart as the heart of a god
Ezek 28:10 You shall die the death of the uncircumcised by the hand of aliens; for I have spoken," *says the Lord* God
Ezek 28:12 Son of man, take up a lamentation for the king of Tyre, and say to him, 'Thus *says the Lord* God
Ezek 28:22 and say, 'Thus *says the Lord* God: Behold, I am against you, O Sidon
Ezek 28:25 Thus *says the Lord* God: "When I have gathered the house of Israel from the peoples among whom they are scattered, and am hallowed in them in the sight of the Gentiles, then they will dwell in their own land which I gave to My servant Jacob
Ezek 29:3 Speak, and say, 'Thus *says the Lord* God: "Behold, I am against you, O Pharoah king of Egypt, O great monster who lies in the midst of his rivers, who has said
Ezek 29:8 Therefore thus *says the Lord* God: Surely I will bring a sword upon you and cut off from you man and beast
Ezek 29:13 Yet, thus *says the Lord* God: At the end of forty years I will gather the Egyptians from the peoples among whom they were scattered
Ezek 29:19 Therefore thus *says the Lord* God: Surely I will give the land of Egypt to Nebuchadnezzar king of Babylon
Ezek 29:20 I have given him the land of Egypt for his labor, because they worked for Me,' *says the Lord* God
Ezek 30:2 Son of man, prophesy and say, 'Thus *says the Lord* God
Ezek 30:6 Thus *says the Lord:* "Those who uphold Egypt shall fall, and the pride of her power shall come down. From Migdol to Syene those within her shall fall by the sword," *says the Lord* God
Ezek 30:10 Thus *says the Lord* God: "I will also make a multitude of Egypt to cease by the hand of Nebuchadnezzar king of Babylon
Ezek 30:13 Thus *says the Lord* God: "I will also destroy the idols, and cause the images to cease from Noph
Ezek 30:22 Therefore thus *says the Lord* God: Surely I am against Pharaoh king of Egypt, and will break his arms, both the strong one and the one that was broken
Ezek 31:10 Therefore thus *says the Lord* God: Because you have increased in height, and it set its top among the thick boughs, and its heart was lifted up in its height
Ezek 31:15 Thus *says the Lord* God: 'In the day when it went down to hell, I caused mourning
Ezek 31:18 This is Pharaoh and all his multitude,' *says the Lord* God
Ezek 32:3 Thus *says the Lord* God: therefore spread My net over you with a company of many people, and they will draw you up in My net
Ezek 32:8 All the bright lights of the heavens I will make dark over you, and bring darkness upon your land,' *says the Lord* God
Ezek 32:11 For thus *says the Lord* God: 'The sword of the king of Babylon shall come upon you
Ezek 32:14 Then I will make their waters clear, and make their rivers run like oil,' *says the Lord* God
Ezek 32:16 they shall lament for her, for Egypt, and for all her multitude,' *says the Lord* God
Ezek 32:31 Pharaoh will see them and be comforted over all his multitude, Pharaoh and all his army, slain by the sword," *says the Lord* God
Ezek 32:32 and he shall be placed in the midst of the uncircumcised with those slain by the sword,

Pharaoh and all his multitude," *says the Lord* God
Ezek 33:11 As I live,' *says the Lord* God, 'I have no pleasure in the death of the wicked, but that the wicked turn from his way and live
Ezek 33:25 Therefore say to them, 'Thus *says the Lord* God: "You eat meat with blood, you lift up your eyes toward your idols, and shed blood
Ezek 33:27 Say thus to them, 'Thus *says the Lord* God: "As I live, surely those who are in the ruins shall fall by the sword, and the one who is in the open field I will give to the beasts to be devoured, and those who are in the strongholds and caves shall die of the pestilence
Ezek 34:2 Son of man, prophesy against the shepherds of Israel, prophesy and say to them, 'Thus *says the Lord* God to the shepherds
Ezek 34:8 as I live," *says the Lord* God, "surely because My flock became a prey, and My flock became food for every beast of the field, because there was no shepherd, nor did My shepherds search for My flock, but the shepherds fed themselves and did not feed My flock
Ezek 34:10 Thus *says the Lord* God: "Behold, I am against the shepherds, and I will require My flock at their hand
Ezek 34:11 For thus *says the Lord* God: "Indeed I Myself will search for My sheep and seek them out
Ezek 34:15 I will feed My flock, and I will make them lie down," *says the Lord* God
Ezek 34:17 And as for you, O My flock, thus *says the Lord* God
Ezek 34:20 Therefore thus *says the Lord* God to them: "Behold, I Myself will judge between the fat and the lean sheep
Ezek 34:30 Thus they shall know that I, the Lord their God, am with them, and that they, the house of Israel, are My people," *says the Lord* God
Ezek 34:31 you are men, and I am your God," *says the Lord* God
Ezek 35:3 and say to it, 'Thus *says the Lord* God: "Behold, O Mount Seir, I am against you
Ezek 35:6 therefore, as I live," *says the Lord* God, "I will prepare you for blood, and blood shall pursue you
Ezek 35:11 therefore, as I live," *says the Lord* God, "I will do according to your anger and according to the envy which you showed in your hatred against them
Ezek 35:14 Thus *says the Lord* God: "The whole earth will rejoice when I make you desolate
Ezek 36:2 Thus *says the Lord* God: "Because the enemy has said of you
Ezek 36:3 therefore prophesy, and say, 'Thus *says the Lord* God: "Because they made you desolate and swallowed you up on every side, so that you became the possession of the rest of the nations, and you are taken up by the lips of talkers and slandered by the people
Ezek 36:4 Thus *says the Lord* God to the mountains, the hills, the rivers, the valleys, the desolate wastes, and the cities that have been forsaken, which became plunder and mockery to the rest of the nations all around
Ezek 36:5 therefore thus *says the Lord* God: Surely I have spoken in My burning jealousy against the rest of the nations and against all Edom, who gave My land to themselves as a possession, with whole-hearted joy and spiteful minds, in order to plunder its open country
Ezek 36:6 Therefore prophesy concerning the land of Israel, and say to the mountains, the hills, the rivers, and the valleys, 'Thus *says the Lord* God
Ezek 36:7 Therefore thus *says the Lord* God: I have lifted My hand in an oath that surely the nations that are around you shall bear their own shame
Ezek 36:13 Thus *says the Lord* God: "Because they say to you
Ezek 36:14 therefore you shall devour men no more, nor bereave your nation anymore," *says the Lord* God
Ezek 36:15 Nor will I let you hear the taunts of the nations anymore, nor bear the reproach of the peoples anymore, nor shall you cause your nation to stumble anymore," *says the Lord* God
Ezek 36:22 Therefore say to the house of Israel, 'Thus *says the Lord* God
Ezek 36:23 and the nations shall know that I am the Lord," *says the Lord* God
Ezek 36:32 Not for your sake do I do this," *says the Lord* God
Ezek 36:33 Thus *says the Lord* God: "On the day that I cleanse you from all your iniquities, I will also enable you to dwell in the cities, and the ruins shall be rebuilt
Ezek 36:37 Thus *says the Lord* God: "I will also let the house of Israel inquire of Me to do this for them
Ezek 37:5 Thus *says the Lord* God to these bones: "Surely I will cause breath to enter into you, and you shall live
Ezek 37:9 Then He said to me, "Prophesy to the breath, prophesy, son of man, and say to the breath, 'Thus *says the Lord* God
Ezek 37:12 Therefore prophesy and say to them, 'Thus *says the Lord* God
Ezek 37:14 Then you shall know that I, the Lord, have spoken it and performed it," *says the Lord*
Ezek 37:19 say to them, 'Thus *says the Lord* God: "Surely I will take the stick of Joseph, which is in the hand of Ephraim, and the tribes of Israel, his companions
Ezek 37:21 Then say to them, 'Thus *says the Lord* God: "Surely I will take the children of Israel from among the nations, wherever they have gone, and will gather them from every side and bring them into their own land
Ezek 38:3 and say, 'Thus *says the Lord* God: Behold, I am against you, O Gog, the prince of Rosh, Meshech, and Tubal
Ezek 38:10 Thus *says the Lord* God: "On that day it shall come to pass that thoughts will arise in your mind, and you will make an evil plan
Ezek 38:14 Therefore, son of man, prophesy and say to Gog, 'Thus *says the Lord* God
Ezek 38:17 Thus *says the Lord* God: "Are you he of whom I have spoken in former days by My servants the prophets of Israel, who prophesied for years in those days that I would bring you against them
Ezek 38:18 And it will come to pass at the same time, when Gog comes against the land of Israel," *says the Lord* God
Ezek 38:21 I will call for a sword against Gog throughout all My mountains," *says the Lord* God
Ezek 39:1 And you, son of man, prophesy against Gog, and say, 'Thus *says the Lord* God
Ezek 39:5 You shall fall on the open field; for I have spoken," *says the Lord* God
Ezek 39:8 Surely it is coming, and it shall be done," *says the Lord* God
Ezek 39:10 and they will plunder those who plundered them, and pillage those who pillaged them," *says the Lord* God
Ezek 39:13 Indeed all the people of the land will be burying them, and they will gain renown for it on the day that I am glorified," *says the Lord* God
Ezek 39:17 And as for you, son of man, thus *says the Lord* God
Ezek 39:20 You shall be filled at My table with

horses and riders, with mighty men and with all the men of war," *says the Lord* God
Ezek 39:25 Therefore thus *says the Lord* God: Now I will bring back the captives of Jacob, and have mercy on the whole house of Israel
Ezek 39:29 for I shall have poured out My Spirit on the house of Israel,' *says the Lord* God
Ezek 43:18 And He said to me, "Son of man, thus *says the Lord* God
Ezek 43:19 You shall give a young bull for a sin offering to the priests, the Levites, who are of the seed of Zadok, who approach Me to minister to Me,' *says the Lord* God
Ezek 43:27 and I will accept you,' *says the Lord* God
Ezek 44:6 Now say to the rebellious, to the house of Israel, 'Thus *says the Lord* God
Ezek 44:9 Thus *says the Lord* God: "No foreigner, uncircumcised in heart or uncircumcised in flesh, shall enter My sanctuary, including any foreigner who is among the children of Israel
Ezek 44:12 Because they ministered to them before their idols and caused the house of Israel to fall into iniquity, therefore I have lifted My hand in an oath against them," *says the Lord* God
Ezek 44:15 and they shall stand before Me to offer to Me the fat and the blood," *says the Lord* God
Ezek 44:27 And on the day that he goes to the sanctuary to minister in the sanctuary, he must offer his sin offering in the inner court," *says the Lord* God
Ezek 45:9 Thus *says the Lord* God: "Enough, O princes of Israel! Remove violence and plundering, execute justice and righteousness, and stop dispossessing My people," *says the Lord* God
Ezek 45:15 These shall be for grain offerings, burnt offerings, and peace offerings, to make atonement for them," *says the Lord* God
Ezek 45:18 Thus *says the Lord* God: "In the first month, on the first day of the month, you shall take a young bull without blemish and cleanse the sanctuary
Ezek 46:1 Thus *says the Lord* God: "The gateway of the inner court that faces toward the east shall be shut the six working days
Ezek 46:16 Thus *says the Lord* God: "If the prince gives a gift of some of his inheritance to any of his sons, it shall belong to his sons
Ezek 47:13 Thus *says the Lord* God: "These are the borders by which you shall divide the land as an inheritance among the twelve tribes of Israel
Ezek 47:23 And it shall be that in whatever tribe the stranger sojourns, there you shall give him his inheritance," *says the Lord* God
Ezek 48:29 This is the land which you shall divide by lot as an inheritance among the tribes of Israel, and these are their portions," *says the Lord* God
Hos 2:13 She decked herself with her earrings and jewelry, and went after her lovers. Then she forgot Me," *says the Lord*
Hos 2:16 And it shall be, in that day," *says the Lord*
Hos 2:21 It shall come to pass in that day that I will answer," *says the Lord*
Hos 11:11 And I will let them dwell in their houses," *says the Lord*
Joel 2:12 Now, therefore," *says the Lord*, "turn to me with all your heart, with fasting, with weeping, and with mourning
Amos 1:3 Thus *says the Lord:* "For three transgressions of Damascus, and for four, I will not turn away its punishment, because they have threshed Gilead with implements of iron
Amos 1:5 the people of Syria shall go captive to Kir," *says the Lord*
Amos 1:6 Thus *says the Lord:* "For three transgressions of Gaza, and for four, I will not turn away its punishment, because they took captive the whole captivity to deliver them up to Edom
Amos 1:8 I will turn My hand against Ekron, and the remnant of the Philistines shall perish," *says the Lord* God
Amos 1:9 Thus *says the Lord:* "For three transgressions of Tyre, and for four, I will not turn away its punishment, because they delivered up the whole captivity to Edom, and did not remember the covenant of brotherhood
Amos 1:11 Thus *says the Lord:* "For three transgressions of Edom, and for four, I will not turn away its punishment, because he pursued his brother with the sword, and cast off all pity
Amos 1:13 Thus *says the Lord:* "For three transgressions of the people of Ammon, and for four, I will not turn away its punishment, because they ripped open the women with child in Gilead, that they might enlarge their territory
Amos 1:15 Their king shall go into captivity, he and his princes together," *says the Lord*
Amos 2:1 Thus *says the Lord:* "For three transgressions of Moab, and for four, I will not turn away its punishment, because he burned the bones of the king of Edom to lime
Amos 2:3 And I will cut off the judge from its midst, and slay all its princes with him," *says the Lord*
Amos 2:4 Thus *says the Lord:* "For three transgressions of Judah, and for four, I will not turn away its punishment, because they have despised the law of the Lord, and have not kept His commandments
Amos 2:6 Thus *says the Lord:* "For three transgressions of Israel, and for four, I will not turn away its punishment, because they sell the righteous for silver, and the poor for a pair of sandals
Amos 2:11 Is it not so, O you children of Israel?" *says the Lord*
Amos 2:16 The most courageous men of might shall flee naked in that day," *says the Lord*
Amos 3:10 For they do not know to do right,' *says the Lord*
Amos 3:11 Therefore thus *says the Lord* God: An adversary shall be all around the land
Amos 3:12 Thus *says the Lord:* "As a shepherd takes from the mouth of a lion two legs or a piece of an ear, so shall the children of Israel be taken out who dwell in Samaria in the corner of a bed and on the edge of a couch
Amos 3:13 Hear and testify against the house of Jacob," *says the Lord* God, the God of hosts
Amos 3:15 the houses of ivory shall perish, and the great houses shall have an end," *says the Lord*
Amos 4:3 You will go out through broken walls, each one straight ahead of her, and you will be cast into Harmon," *says the Lord*
Amos 4:5 for this you love, you children of Israel!" *says the Lord* God
Amos 4:6 yet you have not returned to Me," *says the Lord*
Amos 4:8 yet you have not returned to Me," *says the Lord*
Amos 4:9 yet you have not returned to Me," *says the Lord*
Amos 4:10 yet you have not returned to Me," *says the Lord*
Amos 4:11 yet you have not returned to Me," *says the Lord*
Amos 5:3 For thus *says the Lord* God: "The city that goes out by a thousand shall have a hundred left, and that which goes out by a hundred shall have ten left to the house of Israel
Amos 5:4 For thus *says the Lord* to the house of Israel
Amos 5:17 In all vineyards there shall be wailing, for I will pass through you," *says the Lord*

Amos 5:27 Therefore I will send you into captivity beyond Damascus," *says the Lord*, whose name is the God of hosts
Amos 6:14 But, behold, I will raise up a nation against you, O house of Israel," *says the Lord* God of hosts
Amos 7:17 Therefore thus *says the Lord:* "Your wife shall be a harlot in the city
Amos 8:3 And the songs of the temple shall be wailing in that day," *says the Lord* God
Amos 8:9 And it shall come to pass in that day," *says the Lord* God
Amos 8:11 Behold, the days are coming," *says the Lord* God, "that I will send a famine on the land, not a famine of bread, nor a thirst for water, but of hearing the words of the Lord
Amos 9:7 *says the Lord*. "Did I not bring up Israel from the land of Egypt, the Philistines from Caphtor, and the Syrians from Kir
Amos 9:8 yet I will not utterly destroy the house of Jacob," *says the Lord*
Amos 9:12 that they may possess the remnant of Edom, and all the Gentiles who are called by My name," *says the Lord* who does this thing
Amos 9:13 Behold, the days are coming," *says the Lord*, "when the plowman shall overtake the reaper, and the treader of grapes him who sows seed
Amos 9:15 I will plant them in their land, and no longer shall they be pulled up from the land I have given them," *says the Lord* your God
Obad 1 Thus *says the Lord* God concerning Edom (We have heard a report from the Lord, and a messenger has been sent among the nations, saying
Obad 4 Though you exalt yourself as high as the eagle, and though you set your nest among the stars, from there I will bring you down," *says the Lord*
Obad 8 Will I not in that day," *says the Lord*, "even destroy the wise men from Edom, and understanding from the mountains of Esau
Mic 2:3 Therefore thus *says the Lord:* "Behold, against this family I am devising disaster, from which you cannot remove your necks
Mic 3:5 Thus *says the Lord* concerning the prophets who make my people stray
Mic 4:6 In that day," *says the Lord*, "I will assemble the lame, I will gather the outcast and those whom I have afflicted
Mic 5:10 And it shall be in that day," *says the Lord*
Nah 1:12 Thus *says the Lord:* "Though they are safe, and likewise many, yet in this manner they will be cut down when he passes through
Nah 2:13 Behold, I am against you," *says the Lord* of hosts
Nah 3:5 Behold, I am against you," *says the Lord* of hosts
Zeph 1:2 I will utterly consume all things from the face of the land," *says the Lord*
Zeph 1:3 I will cut off man from the face of the land," *says the Lord*
Zeph 1:10 And there shall be on that day," *says the Lord*
Zeph 2:9 Therefore, as I live," *says the Lord* of hosts, the God of Israel
Zeph 3:8 Therefore wait for Me," *says the Lord*, "until the day I rise up for plunder
Zeph 3:20 for I will give you fame and praise among all the peoples of the earth, when I return your captives before your eyes," *says the Lord*
Hag 1:5 Now therefore, thus *says the Lord* of hosts: "Consider your ways
Hag 1:7 Thus *says the Lord* of hosts: "Consider your ways
Hag 1:8 Go up to the mountains and bring wood and build the temple, that I may take pleasure in it and be glorified," *says the Lord*
Hag 1:9 *says the Lord* of hosts. "Because of My house that is in ruins, while every one of you runs to his own house
Hag 1:13 Then Haggai, the Lord's messenger, spoke the Lord's message to the people, saying, "I am with you, *says the Lord*
Hag 2:4 Yet now be strong, Zerubbabel,' *says the Lord;* 'and be strong, Joshua, son of Jehozadak, the high priest; and be strong, all you people of the land,' *says the Lord*, 'and work; for I am with you,' *says the Lord* of hosts
Hag 2:6 For thus *says the Lord* of hosts: Once more (it is a little while
Hag 2:7 and I will shake all nations, and they shall come to the Desire of All Nations, and I will fill this temple with glory,' *says the Lord* of hosts
Hag 2:8 The silver is Mine, and the gold is Mine,' *says the Lord* of hosts
Hag 2:9 The glory of this latter temple shall be greater than the former,' *says the Lord* of hosts. 'And in this place I will give peace,' *says the Lord* of hosts
Hag 2:11 Thus *says the Lord* of hosts: 'Now, ask the priests concerning the law, saying
Hag 2:14 Then Haggai answered and said, "'So is this people, and so is this nation before Me,' *says the Lord*
Hag 2:17 yet you did not turn to Me,' *says the Lord*
Hag 2:23 In that day,' *says the Lord* of hosts, 'I will take you, Zerubbabel My servant, the son of Shealtiel,' *says the Lord*, 'and will make you as a signet ring; for I have chosen you,' *says the Lord* of hosts
Zech 1:3 Therefore say to them, 'Thus *says the Lord* of hosts: "Return to Me," *says the Lord* of hosts, "and I will return to you," *says the Lord* of hosts
Zech 1:4 Do not be like your fathers, to whom the former prophets preached, saying, 'Thus *says the Lord* of hosts: "Turn now from your evil ways and your evil deeds."' But they did not hear nor heed Me," *says the Lord*
Zech 1:14 So the angel who spoke with me said to me, "Proclaim, saying, 'Thus *says the Lord* of hosts
Zech 1:16 Therefore thus *says the Lord:* "I am returning to Jerusalem with mercy; my house shall be built in it," *says the Lord* of hosts
Zech 1:17 Again proclaim, saying, 'Thus *says the Lord* of hosts: "My cities shall again spread out through prosperity
Zech 2:5 For I,' *says the Lord*, 'will be a wall of fire all around her, and I will be the glory in her midst
Zech 2:6 Flee from the land of the north," *says the Lord;* "for I have spread you abroad like the four winds of heaven," *says the Lord*
Zech 2:8 For thus *says the Lord* of hosts: He sent Me after glory, to the nations which plunder you
Zech 2:10 For behold, I am coming and I will dwell in your midst," *says the Lord*
Zech 3:7 Thus *says the Lord* of hosts: 'If you will walk in My ways, and if you will keep My command, then you shall also judge My house, and likewise have charge of My courts
Zech 3:9 Behold, I will engrave its inscription,' *says the Lord* of hosts
Zech 3:10 In that day,' *says the Lord* of hosts, 'everyone will invite his neighbor under his vine and under his fig tree
Zech 4:6 Not by might nor by power, but by My Spirit,' *says the Lord* of hosts
Zech 5:4 I will send out the curse," *says the Lord* of hosts
Zech 6:12 Then speak to him, saying, 'Thus *says the Lord* of hosts, saying

Zech 7:9 Thus *says the Lord* of hosts: 'Execute true justice, show mercy and compassion everyone to his brother
Zech 7:13 Therefore it happened, that just as He proclaimed and they would not hear, so they called out and I would not listen," *says the Lord* of hosts
Zech 8:2 Thus *says the Lord* of hosts: 'I am zealous for Zion with great zeal
Zech 8:3 Thus *says the Lord:* 'I will return to Zion, and dwell in the midst of Jerusalem
Zech 8:4 Thus *says the Lord* of hosts: 'Old men and old women shall again sit in the streets of Jerusalem, each one with his staff in his hand because of great age
Zech 8:6 Thus *says the Lord* of hosts: 'If it is marvelous in the eyes of the remnant of this people in these days, will it also be marvelous in My eyes?' *says the Lord* of hosts
Zech 8:7 Thus *says the Lord* of hosts: 'Behold, I will save My people from the land of the east and from the land of the west
Zech 8:9 Thus *says the Lord* of hosts: 'Let your hands be strong, you who have been hearing in these days these words by the mouth of the prophets, who were in the day that the foundation was laid for the house of the Lord of hosts, that the temple might be built
Zech 8:11 But now I will not treat the remnant of this people as in the former days,' *says the Lord* of hosts
Zech 8:14 For thus *says the Lord* of hosts: Just as I determined to punish you when your fathers provoked Me to wrath,' *says the Lord* of hosts
Zech 8:17 For all these are things that I hate,' *says the Lord*
Zech 8:19 Thus *says the Lord* of hosts: 'The fast of the fourth month, the fast of the fifth, the fast of the seventh, and the fast of the tenth, shall be joy and gladness and cheerful feasts for the house of Judah
Zech 8:20 Thus *says the Lord* of hosts: 'Peoples shall yet come, inhabitants of many cities
Zech 8:23 Thus *says the Lord* of hosts: 'In those days ten men from every language of the nations shall grasp the sleeve of a Jewish man, saying
Zech 10:12 So I will strengthen them in the Lord, and they shall walk up and down in His name," *says the Lord*
Zech 11:4 Thus *says the Lord* my God, "Feed the flock for slaughter
Zech 11:6 For I will no longer pity the inhabitants of the land," *says the Lord*
Zech 12:1 Thus *says the Lord*, who stretches out the heavens, lays the foundation of the earth, and forms the spirit of man within him
Zech 12:4 In that day," *says the Lord*, "I will strike every horse with confusion, and its rider with madness
Zech 13:2 It shall be in that day," *says the Lord* of hosts
Zech 13:7 Awake, O sword, against My Shepherd, against the Man who is My Companion," *says the Lord* of hosts
Zech 13:8 And it shall come to pass in all the land," *says the Lord*
Mal 1:2 I have loved you," *says the Lord*. "Yet you say, 'In what way have You loved us?' "Was not Esau Jacob's brother?" *says the Lord*
Mal 1:4 Even though Edom has said, "We have been impoverished, but we will return and build the desolate places," thus *says the Lord* of hosts
Mal 1:6 *Says the Lord* of hosts to you priests who despise My name
Mal 1:8 Would he accept you favorably?" *says the Lord* of hosts
Mal 1:9 While this is being done by your hands, will He accept you favorably?" *says the Lord* of hosts
Mal 1:10 I have no pleasure in you," *says the Lord* of hosts
Mal 1:11 For My name shall be great among the nations," *says the Lord* of hosts
Mal 1:13 and you sneer at it," *says the Lord* of hosts. "And you bring the stolen, the lame, and the sick; thus you bring an offering! Should I accept this from your hand?" *says the Lord*
Mal 1:14 But cursed be the deceiver who has in his flock a male, and makes a vow, but sacrifices to the Lord what is blemished for I am a great King," *says the Lord* of hosts
Mal 2:2 If you will not hear, and if you will not take it to heart, to give glory to My name," *says the Lord* of hosts
Mal 2:4 Then you shall know that I have sent this commandment to you, that My covenant with Levi may continue," *says the Lord* of hosts
Mal 2:8 You have corrupted the covenant of Levi," *says the Lord* of hosts
Mal 2:16 For the Lord God of Israel says that He hates divorce, for it covers one's garment with violence," *says the Lord* of hosts
Mal 3:1 And the Lord, whom you seek, will suddenly come to His temple, even the Messenger of the covenant, in whom you delight. Behold, He is coming," *says the Lord* of hosts
Mal 3:5 I will be a swift witness against sorcerers, against adulterers, against perjurers, against those who exploit wage earners and widows and the fatherless, and against those who turn away an alien because they do not fear Me," *says the Lord* of hosts
Mal 3:7 Return to Me, and I will return to you," *says the Lord* of hosts
Mal 3:10 Bring all the tithes into the storehouse, that there may be food in My house, and prove Me now in this," *says the Lord* of hosts
Mal 3:11 And I will rebuke the devourer for your sakes, so that he will not destroy the fruit of your ground, nor shall the vine fail to bear fruit for you in the field," *says the Lord* of hosts
Mal 3:12 And all nations will call you blessed, for you will be a delightful land," *says the Lord* of hosts
Mal 3:13 Your words have been harsh against Me," *says the Lord*
Mal 3:17 They shall be Mine," *says the Lord* of hosts, "on the day that I make them My jewels
Mal 4:1 And the day which is coming shall burn them up," *says the Lord* of hosts
Mal 4:3 You shall trample the wicked, for they shall be ashes under the soles of your feet on the day that I do this," *says the Lord* of hosts
Acts 7:49 *says the Lord*, or what is the place of My rest
Acts 15:17 so that the rest of mankind may seek the Lord, even all the Gentiles who are called by My name, *says the Lord* who does all these things
Rom 12:19 for it is written, "Vengeance is Mine, I will repay," *says the Lord*
Rom 14:11 As I live, *says the Lord*, every knee shall bow to Me, and every tongue shall confess to God
1Cor 14:21 and yet, for all that, they will not hear Me," *says the Lord*
2Cor 6:17 Therefore "Come out from among them and be separate, *says the Lord*
2Cor 6:18 I will be a Father to you, and you shall be My sons and daughters, *says the Lord* Almighty
Heb 8:8 Behold, the days are coming," *says the Lord*, "when I will make a new covenant with the house of Israel and with the house of Judah
Heb 8:9 because they did not continue in My covenant, and I disregarded them," *says the Lord*

Heb 8:10 After those days," *says the Lord*, "I will put My laws in their mind and write them on their hearts
Heb 10:16 This is the covenant that I will make with them after those days, *says the Lord*
Heb 10:30 I will repay, *says the Lord*." And again, "The Lord will judge His people
Rev 1:8 I am the Alpha and the Omega, the Beginning and the End," *says the Lord*

SCARLET CORD
Josh 2:18 unless, when we come into the land, you bind this line of *scarlet cord* in the window through which you let us down, and unless you bring your father, your mother, your brothers, and all your father's household to your own home
Josh 2:21 And she sent them away, and they departed. And she bound the *scarlet cord* in the window

SCATTER THE SHEEP
Jer 23:1 Woe to the shepherds who destroy and *scatter the sheep* of My pasture

SCATTER THEM AMONG THE NATIONS
Ezek 12:15 Then they shall know that I am the Lord, when I *scatter them among the nations* and disperse them throughout the countries

SCATTER TO EVERY WIND
Ezek 12:14 I will *scatter to every wind* all who are around him to help him, and all his troops

SCATTERED ABROAD
Gen 11:4 let us make a name for ourselves, lest we be *scattered abroad* over the face of the whole earth
Ex 5:12 So the people were *scattered abroad* throughout all the land of Egypt to gather stubble instead of straw
John 11:52 and not for that nation only, but also that He would gather together in one the children of God who were *scattered abroad*
Jas 1:1 James, a servant of God and of the Lord Jesus Christ, To the twelve tribes which are *scattered abroad*

SCATTERED OVER THE FACE OF THE WHOLE EARTH (NIV)
(See *SCATTERED ABROAD*)

SCATTERED SALT OVER IT (NIV)
(See *SOWED IT WITH SALT*)

SCATTERED SHEEP
Jer 50:17 Israel is like *scattered sheep;* the lions have driven him away
Ezek 34:12 As a shepherd seeks out his flock on the day he is among his *scattered sheep*, so will I seek out My sheep and deliver them from all the places where they were scattered on a cloudy and dark day

SCATTERED THE PROUD
Luke 1:51 he has *scattered the proud* in the imagination of their hearts

SCATTERED THEM ABROAD
Gen 11:8 So the Lord *scattered them abroad* from there over the face of all the earth, and they ceased building the city
Gen 11:9 and from there the Lord *scattered them abroad* over the face of all the earth
Ezek 34:21 Because you have pushed with side and shoulder, butted all the weak ones with your horns, and *scattered them abroad*

SCATTERS ABROAD
Is 24:1 Behold, the Lord makes the earth empty and makes it waste, distorts its surface and *scatters abroad* its inhabitants
Matt 12:30 He who is not with Me is against Me, and he who does not gather with Me *scatters abroad*

SCEPTER SHALL RISE
Num 24:17 A *Scepter shall rise* out of Israel, and batter the brow of Moab, and destroy all the sons of tumult

SCOFFERS WILL COME
2Pet 3:3 that *scoffers will come* in the last days, walking according to their own lusts

SCORNED BY MEN (NIV, RSV)
(See *REPROACH OF MEN*)

SCORNING ITS SHAME (NIV)
(See *DESPISING THE SHAME*)

SCORNS INSTRUCTION (NIV)
(See *DESPISES THE WORD*)

SCOURGE OF SMALL CORDS (KJV)
(See *WHIP OF CORDS*)

SCRIBES AND PHARISEES
Matt 5:20 For I say to you, that unless your righteousness exceeds the righteousness of the *scribes and Pharisees*, you will by no means enter the kingdom of heaven
Matt 12:38 Then some of the *scribes and Pharisees* answered, saying, "Teacher, we want to see a sign from You
Matt 15:1 Then the *scribes and Pharisees* who were from Jerusalem came to Jesus, saying
Matt 23:13 But woe to you, *scribes and Pharisees*, hypocrites! For you shut up the kingdom of heaven against men
Matt 23:14 Woe to you, *scribes and Pharisees*, hypocrites! For you devour widows' houses, and for a pretense make long prayers
Matt 23:15 Woe to you, *scribes and Pharisees*, hypocrites! For you travel land and sea to win one proselyte, and when he is won, you make him twice as much a son of hell as yourselves
Matt 23:23 Woe to you, *scribes and Pharisees*, hypocrites! For you pay tithe of mint and anise and cumin, and have neglected the weightier matters of the law
Matt 23:25 Woe to you, *scribes and Pharisees*, hypocrites! For you cleanse the outside of the cup and dish, but inside they are full of extortion and self-indulgence
Matt 23:27 Woe to you, *scribes and Pharisees*, hypocrites! For you are like whitewashed tombs which indeed appear beautiful outwardly, but inside are full of dead men's bones and all uncleanness
Matt 23:29 Woe to you, *scribes and Pharisees*, hypocrites! Because you build the tombs of the prophets and adorn the monuments of the righteous
Mark 2:16 And when the *scribes and Pharisees* saw Him eating with the tax collectors and sinners, they said to His disciples
Luke 6:7 And the *scribes and Pharisees* watched Him closely, whether He would heal on the Sabbath, that they might find an accusation against Him
Luke 11:44 Woe to you, *scribes and Pharisees*, hypocrites! For you are like graves which are not seen, and the men who walk over them are not aware of them

John 8:3 Then the *scribes and Pharisees* brought to Him a woman caught in adultery

SCRIPTURE CANNOT BE BROKEN
John 10:35 If He called them gods, to whom the word of God came (and the *Scripture cannot be broken*

SCRIPTURE HAD TO BE FULFILLED
Acts 1:16 Men and brethren, this *Scripture had to be fulfilled*, which the Holy Spirit spoke before by the mouth of David concerning Judas, who became a guide to those who arrested Jesus

SCRIPTURE MAY BE FULFILLED
John 13:18 but that the *Scripture may be fulfilled*, 'He who eats bread with Me has lifted up his heel against Me

SCRIPTURE MIGHT BE FULFILLED
John 17:12 and none of them is lost except the son of perdition, that the *Scripture might be fulfilled*
John 19:24 They said therefore among themselves, "Let us not tear it, but cast lots for it, whose it shall be," that the *Scripture might be fulfilled* which says
John 19:28 After this, Jesus, knowing that all things were now accomplished, that the *Scripture might be fulfilled*, said

SCRIPTURE SAYS
John 19:37 And again another *Scripture says*, "They shall look on Him whom they pierced
Rom 9:17 For the *Scripture says* to Pharaoh, "Even for this same purpose I have raised you up, that I might show My power in you, and that My name might be declared in all the earth
Rom 10:11 For the *Scripture says*, "Whoever believes on Him will not be put to shame
Rom 11:2 Or do you not know what the *Scripture says* of Elijah, how he pleads with God against Israel, saying
1Tim 5:18 For the *Scripture says*, "You shall not muzzle an ox while it treads out the grain
Jas 4:5 Or do you think that the *Scripture says* in vain

SCRIPTURE SHOULD BE FULFILLED
John 19:36 For these things were done that the *Scripture should be fulfilled*

SCRIPTURE WAS FULFILLED
Mark 15:28 So the *Scripture was fulfilled* which says, "And He was numbered with the transgressors
Jas 2:23 And the *Scripture was fulfilled* which says, "Abraham believed God, and it was accounted to him for righteousness

SCRIPTURE WOULD BE FULFILLED (NIV)
(See *SCRIPTURE SHOULD BE FULFILLED*)

SCRUPLES OF THE WEAK
Rom 15:1 We then who are strong ought to bear with the *scruples of the weak*, and not to please ourselves

SEA MONSTER (NAS, RSV)
(See *SEA SERPENT*)

SEA OF GLASS
Rev 4:6 Before the throne there was a *sea of glass*, like crystal
Rev 15:2 And I saw something like a *sea of glass* mingled with fire, and those who have the victory over the beast, over his image and over his mark and over the number of his name, standing on the *sea of glass*, having harps of God

SEA SERPENT
Job 7:12 Am I a sea, or a *sea serpent*, that You set a guard over me

SEAL OF GOD
Rev 9:4 They were commanded not to harm the grass of the earth, or any green thing, or any tree, but only those men who do not have the *seal of God* on their foreheads

SEAL THE BOOK
Dan 12:4 But you, Daniel, shut up the words, and *seal the book* until the time of the end

SEAL THE WORDS OF THE SCROLL (NIV)
(See *SEAL THE BOOK*)

SEAL UP
Dan 8:26 therefore *seal up* the vision, for it refers to many days in the future
Dan 9:24 Seventy weeks are determined for your people and for your holy city, to finish the transgression, to make an end of sins, to make reconciliation for iniquity, to bring in everlasting righteousness, to *seal up* vision and prophecy, and to anoint the Most Holy
Rev 10:4 but I heard a voice from heaven saying to me, "*Seal up* the things which the seven thunders uttered, and do not write them

SEALED IT
Esth 8:10 And he wrote in the name of King Ahasuerus, *sealed it* with the king's signet ring, and sent letters by couriers on horseback, riding on royal horses bred from swift steeds
Jer 32:10 And I signed the deed and *sealed it*, took witnesses, and weighed the money in the balances
Dan 6:17 Then a stone was brought and laid on the mouth of the den, and the king *sealed it* with his own signet ring and with the signets of his lords, that the purpose concerning Daniel might not be changed

SEALED THE DEED (NIV)
(See *SEALED IT*)

SEALED THE DISPATCHES (NIV)
(See *SEALED IT*)

SEALED WITH THE HOLY SPIRIT
Eph 1:13 in whom also, having believed, you were *sealed with the Holy Spirit* of promise

SEARCH DILIGENTLY
Matt 2:8 And he sent them to Bethlehem and said, "Go and *search diligently* for the young Child, and when you have found Him, bring back word to me, that I may come and worship Him also

SEARCH JERUSALEM WITH LAMPS
Zeph 1:12 And it shall come to pass at that time that I will *search Jerusalem with lamps*, and punish the men who are settled in complacency, who say in their heart

SEARCH ME, O GOD
Ps 139:23 *Search me, O God*, and know my heart; Try me, and know my anxieties

SEARCH THE SCRIPTURES
John 5:39 You *search the Scriptures*, for in them you think you have eternal life

SEARCHED THE LAND (KJV)
(See *SPIED OUT THE LAND*)

SEARCHED THE SCRIPTURES DAILY
Acts 17:11 These were more fair-minded than those in Thessalonica, in that they received the word with all readiness, and *searched the Scriptures daily* to find out whether these things were so

SEASON FOR EVERY ACTIVITY UNDER HEAVEN (NIV)
(See *TIME FOR EVERY PURPOSE UNDER HEAVEN*)

SEASONED WITH SALT
Mark 9:49 For everyone will be seasoned with fire, and every sacrifice will be *seasoned with salt*
Col 4:6 Let your speech always be with grace, *seasoned with salt*, that you may know how you ought to answer each one

SEATED AT THE RIGHT HAND (RSV)
(See *SITTING AT THE RIGHT HAND*)

SEATED ON HIGH (RSV)
(See *DWELLS ON HIGH*)

SEATED ON THE THRONE (RSV)
(See *SITS ON THE THRONE*)

SECOND DEATH
Rev 2:11 He who overcomes shall not be hurt by the *second death*
Rev 20:6 Over such the *second death* has no power, but they shall be priests of God and of Christ, and shall reign with Him a thousand years
Rev 20:14 Then Death and Hades were cast into the lake of fire. This is the *second death*
Rev 21:8 But the cowardly, unbelieving, abominable, murderers, sexually immoral, sorcerers, idolaters, and all liars shall have their part in the lake which burns with fire and brimstone, which is the *second death*

SECOND MAN
1Cor 15:47 The first man was of the earth, made of dust; the *second Man* is the Lord from heaven

SECRET LOVE (KJV)
(See *LOVE CAREFULLY CONCEALED*)

SECRET OF THE KINGDOM OF GOD (NIV, RSV)
(See *MYSTERY OF THE KINGDOM OF GOD*)

SECRET PLACE OF THE MOST HIGH
Ps 91:1 He who dwells in the *secret place of the Most High* shall abide under the shadow of the Almighty

SECRET POWER OF LAWLESSNESS (NIV)
(See *MYSTERY OF LAWLESSNESS*)

SECRET SINS
Ps 90:8 You have set our iniquities before You, our *secret sins* in the light of Your countenance

SECRET THINGS BELONG TO THE LORD
Deut 29:29 The *secret things belong to the Lord* our God, but those things which are revealed belong to us and to our children forever, that we may do all the words of this law

SECRETS OF THE HEART
Ps 44:21 Would not God search this out? For He knows the *secrets of the heart*

SEDUCED MY PEOPLE
Ezek 13:10 Because, indeed, because they have *seduced My people*, saying, 'Peace

SEE AND BE ASHAMED
Is 26:11 But they will *see and be ashamed* for their envy of people
Mic 7:16 The nations shall *see and be ashamed* of all their might

SEE AND BE CONFOUNDED (KJV)
(See *SEE AND BE ASHAMED*)

SEE YOUR ZEAL FOR YOUR PEOPLE AND BE PUT TO SHAME (NIV)
(See *SEE AND BE ASHAMED*)

SEED OF ABRAHAM
Ps 105:6 O *seed of Abraham* His servant, you children of Jacob, His chosen ones
Rom 9:7 nor are they all children because they are the *seed of Abraham*
Rom 11:1 For I also am an Israelite, of the *seed of Abraham*, of the tribe of Benjamin
2Cor 11:22 So am I. Are they the *seed of Abraham?* So am I
Heb 2:16 For indeed He does not give aid to angels, but He does give aid to the *seed of Abraham*

SEED OF DAVID
John 7:42 Has not the Scripture said that the Christ comes from the *seed of David* and from the town of Bethlehem, where David was
Rom 1:3 concerning His Son Jesus Christ our Lord, who was born of the *seed of David* according to the flesh
2Tim 2:8 Remember that Jesus Christ, of the *seed of David*, was raised from the dead according to my gospel

SEEDTIME AND HARVEST
Gen 8:22 While the earth remains, *seedtime and harvest*, and cold and heat, and winter and summer, and day and night shall not cease

SEEK AFTER THE LORD (KJV)
(See *SEEK THE LORD*)

SEEK, AND YOU WILL FIND
Matt 7:7 *seek, and you will find;* knock, and it will be opened to you
Luke 11:9 *seek, and you will find;* knock, and it will be opened to you

SEEK FIRST THE KINGDOM OF GOD
Matt 6:33 But *seek first the kingdom of God* and His righteousness, and all these things shall be added to you

SEEK JUDGMENT (KJV)
(See *SEEK JUSTICE*)

SEEK JUSTICE
Is 1:17 *seek justice*, reprove the oppressor; defend the fatherless, plead for the widow

SEEK ME AND FIND ME
Jer 29:13 And you will *seek Me and find Me*, when you search for Me with all your heart

SEEK MY LIFE
Ps 38:12 Those also who *seek my life* lay snares for me
Ps 63:9 But those who *seek my life*, to destroy it, shall go into the lower parts of the earth
Ps 70:2 Let them be ashamed and confounded who *seek my life*
Rom 11:3 Lord, they have killed Your prophets

and torn down Your altars, and I alone am left, and they *seek my life*

SEEK MY SOUL (KJV)
(See *SEEK MY LIFE*)

SEEK PEACE
Ps 34:14 Depart from evil, and do good; *seek peace*, and pursue it
Ezek 7:25 Destruction comes; they will *seek peace*, but there shall be none
1Pet 3:11 let him turn away from evil and do good; let him *seek peace* and pursue it

SEEK THE FAVOR (RSV)
(See *ENTREAT THE FAVOR*)

SEEK THE LORD
Deut 4:29 But from there you will *seek the Lord* your God, and you will find Him if you seek Him with all your heart and with all your soul
1Chr 16:10 let the hearts of those rejoice who *seek the Lord*
1Chr 16:11 *Seek the Lord* and His strength; seek His face evermore
1Chr 22:19 Now set your heart and your soul to *seek the Lord* your God
2Chr 11:16 And after the Levites left, those from all the tribes of Israel, such as set their heart to *seek the Lord* God of Israel, came to Jerusalem to sacrifice to the Lord God of their fathers
2Chr 12:14 And he did evil, because he did not prepare his heart to *seek the Lord*
2Chr 14:4 He commanded Judah to *seek the Lord* God of their fathers, and to observe the law and the commandment
2Chr 15:12 Then they entered into a covenant to *seek the Lord* God of their fathers with all their heart and with all their soul
2Chr 15:13 and whoever would not *seek the Lord* God of Israel was to be put to death, whether small or great, whether man or woman
2Chr 16:12 yet in his disease he did not *seek the Lord*, but the physicians
2Chr 20:3 And Jehoshaphat feared, and set himself to *seek the Lord*, and proclaimed a fast throughout all Judah
2Chr 20:4 and from all the cities of Judah they came to *seek the Lord*
Ezra 6:21 Then the children of Israel who had returned from the captivity ate together with all who had separated themselves from the filth of the nations of the land in order to *seek the Lord* God of Israel
Ps 34:10 But those who *seek the Lord* shall not lack any good thing
Ps 105:3 Let the hearts of those rejoice who *seek the Lord*
Ps 105:4 *Seek the Lord* and His strength; seek His face evermore
Prov 28:5 Evil men do not understand justice, but those who *seek the Lord* understand all
Is 9:13 For the people do not turn to Him who strikes them, nor do they *seek the Lord* of hosts
Is 31:1 Woe to those who go down to Egypt for help, and rely on horses, who trust in chariots because they are many, and in horsemen because they are very strong, but who do not look to the Holy One of Israel, nor *seek the Lord*
Is 51:1 Listen to Me, you who follow after righteousness, you who *seek the Lord*
Is 55:6 *Seek the Lord* while He may be found, call upon Him while He is near
Jer 50:4 with continual weeping they shall come, and *seek the Lord* their God
Hos 3:5 Afterward the children of Israel shall return, *seek the Lord* their God and David their king, and fear the Lord and His goodness in the latter days
Hos 5:6 With their flocks and herds they shall go to *seek the Lord*, but they will not find Him
Hos 10:12 break up your fallow ground, for it is time to *seek the Lord*, till He comes and rains righteousness on you
Amos 5:6 *Seek the Lord* and live, lest He break out like fire in the house of Joseph, and devour it, with no one to quench it in Bethel
Zeph 2:3 *Seek the Lord*, all you meek of the earth, who have upheld His justice
Zech 8:21 the inhabitants of one city shall go to another, saying, "Let us continue to go and pray before the Lord, and *seek the Lord* of hosts
Zech 8:22 Yes, many peoples and strong nations shall come to *seek the Lord* of hosts in Jerusalem, and to pray before the Lord
Acts 15:17 so that the rest of mankind may *seek the Lord*, even all the Gentiles who are called by My name, Says the Lord who does all these things
Acts 17:27 so that they should *seek the Lord*, in the hope that they might grope for Him and find Him, though He is not far from each one of us

SEEK THE LORD AND LIVE
Amos 5:6 *Seek the Lord and live*, lest He break out like fire in the house of Joseph, and devour it, with no one to quench it in Bethel

SEEMED GOOD IN YOUR SIGHT
Matt 11:26 Even so, Father, for so it *seemed good in Your sight*
Luke 10:21 Even so, Father, for so it *seemed good in Your sight*

SEEN BY ANGELS
1Tim 3:16 God was manifested in the flesh, justified in the Spirit, *seen by angels*, preached among the Gentiles, believed on in the world, received up in glory

SEEN MY MISERY (NIV)
(See *LOOKED ON MY AFFLICTION*)

SEEN THEIR AFFLICTION (NAS, RSV)
(See *LOOKED ON THEIR AFFLICTION*)

SEEN THEIR MISERY (NIV)
(See *LOOKED ON THEIR AFFLICTION*)

SELL ALL THAT YOU HAVE
Luke 18:22 *Sell all that you have* and distribute to the poor, and you will have treasure in heaven

SELL ON THE SABBATH DAY
Neh 10:31 that if the peoples of the land bring wares or any grain to *sell on the Sabbath day*, we would not buy it from them on the Sabbath, or on a holy day

SELL THE RIGHTEOUS FOR SILVER
Amos 2:6 For three transgressions of Israel, and for four, I will not turn away its punishment, because they *sell the righteous for silver*, and the poor for a pair of sandals

SELL WHAT YOU HAVE
Matt 19:21 Jesus said to him, "If you want to be perfect, go, *sell what you have* and give to the poor, and you will have treasure in heaven
Luke 12:33 *Sell what you have* and give alms; provide yourselves money bags which do not grow old, a treasure in the heavens that does not fail, where no thief approaches nor moth destroys

SELLING HIS BIRTHRIGHT (NIV)
(See *SOLD HIS BIRTHRIGHT*)

SELLING THEIR POSSESSIONS (NIV)
(See *SOLD THEIR POSSESSIONS*)

SEND A FIRE
Amos 1:4 But I will *send a fire* into the house of Hazael, which shall devour the palaces of Ben-Hadad
Amos 1:7 But I will *send a fire* upon the wall of Gaza, which shall devour its palaces
Amos 1:10 But I will *send a fire* upon the wall of Tyre, which shall devour its palaces
Amos 1:12 But I will *send a fire* upon Teman, which shall devour the palaces of Bozrah
Amos 2:2 But I will *send a fire* upon Moab, and it shall devour the palaces of Kerioth
Amos 2:5 but I will *send a fire* upon Judah, and it shall devour the palaces of Jerusalem

SEND ABROAD THE LOUD TRUMPET (RSV)
(See *MAKE THE TRUMPET TO SOUND*)

SEND AN ANGEL (KJV, NAS, NIV, RSV)
(See *SEND MY ANGEL*)

SEND FIRE ON THE EARTH
Luke 12:49 I came to *send fire on the earth*, and how I wish it were already kindled

SEND FORTH YOUR SPIRIT
Ps 104:30 You *send forth Your Spirit*, they are created; and You renew the face of the earth

SEND HIS ANGEL
Gen 24:7 The Lord God of heaven, who took me from my father's house and from the land of my family, and who spoke to me and swore to me, saying, 'To your descendants I give this land,' He will *send His angel* before you, and you shall take a wife for my son from there
Gen 24:40 But he said to me, 'The Lord, before whom I walk, will *send His angel* with you and prosper your way

SEND ME
Gen 24:54 Then they arose in the morning, and he said, *"Send me* away to my master
Gen 24:56 *send me* away so that I may go to my master
Gen 30:25 And it came to pass, when Rachel had borne Joseph, that Jacob said to Laban, *"Send me* away, that I may go to my own place and to my country
1Sam 16:19 Therefore Saul sent messengers to Jesse, and said, *"Send me* your son David, who is with the sheep
2Sam 11:6 Then David sent to Joab, saying, *"Send me* Uriah the Hittite
2Sam 15:36 and by them you shall *send me* everything you hear
2Kin 4:22 Then she called to her husband, and said, "Please *send me* one of the young men and one of the donkeys, that I may run to the man of God and come back
2Chr 2:7 Therefore *send me* at once a man skillful to work in gold and silver, in bronze and iron, in purple and crimson and blue, who has skill to engrave with the skillful men who are with me in Judah and Jerusalem, whom David my father provided
2Chr 2:8 Also *send me* cedar and cypress and algum logs from Lebanon, for I know that your servants have skill to cut timber in Lebanon
Neh 2:5 And I said to the king, "If it pleases the king, and if your servant has found favor in your sight, I ask that you *send me* to Judah, to the city of my fathers' tombs, that I may rebuild it
Neh 2:6 So it pleased the king to *send me;* and I set him a time
Is 6:8 Whom shall I send, and who will go for Us?" Then I said, "Here am I! *Send me*
1Cor 1:17 For Christ did not *send me* to baptize, but to preach the gospel, not with wisdom of words, lest the cross of Christ should be made of no effect
1Cor 16:6 But it may be that I will remain, or even spend the winter with you, that you may *send me* on my journey, wherever I go

SEND MY ANGEL
Ex 33:2 And I will *send My Angel* before you, and I will drive out the Canaanite and the Amorite and the Hittite and the Perizzite and the Hivite and the Jebusite

SEND MY MESSENGER
Mal 3:1 Behold, I *send My messenger*, and he will prepare the way before Me
Matt 11:10 Behold, I *send My messenger* before Your face, who will prepare Your way before You
Mark 1:2 Behold, I *send My messenger* before Your face, who will prepare Your way before You
Luke 7:27 Behold, I *send My messenger* before Your face, who will prepare Your way before You

SEND MY MESSENGER BEFORE YOUR FACE
Matt 11:10 Behold, I *send My messenger before Your face*, who will prepare Your way before You
Mark 1:2 Behold, I *send My messenger before Your face*, who will prepare Your way before You
Luke 7:27 Behold, I *send My messenger before Your face*, who will prepare Your way before You

SEND YOU ELIJAH THE PROPHET
Mal 4:5 Behold, I will *send you Elijah the prophet* before the coming of the great and dreadful day of the Lord

SENDS RAIN ON THE JUST AND ON THE UNJUST
Matt 5:45 for He makes His sun rise on the evil and on the good, and *sends rain on the just and on the unjust*

SENSES EXERCISED TO DISCERN BOTH GOOD AND EVIL
Heb 5:14 But solid food belongs to those who are of full age, that is, those who by reason of use have their *senses exercised to discern both good and evil*

SENSUAL INDULGENCE (NIV)
(See *INDULGENCE OF THE FLESH*)

SENT FROM GOD
John 1:6 There was a man *sent from God*, whose name was John

SENT SIGNS AND WONDERS
Ps 135:9 He *sent signs and wonders* into the midst of you, O Egypt, upon Pharaoh and all his servants

SENTENCE OF DEATH
2Cor 1:9 Yes, we had the *sentence of death* in ourselves, that we should not trust in ourselves but in God who raises the dead

SENTENCED TO DEATH (NIV)
(See *DESERVES TO DIE*)

SEPARATE THE DAY FROM THE NIGHT (NAS, NIV, RSV)
(See *DIVIDE THE DAY FROM THE NIGHT*)

SEPARATE THE HOLY AREAS FROM THE COMMON
Ezek 42:20 it had a wall all around, five hundred cubits long and five hundred wide, to *separate the holy areas from the common*

SEPARATE TO ME
Acts 13:2 As they ministered to the Lord and fasted, the Holy Spirit said, "Now *separate to Me* Barnabas and Saul for the work to which I have called them

SEPARATED ME FROM
Is 56:3 Do not let the son of the foreigner who has joined himself to the Lord speak, saying, "The Lord has utterly *separated me from* His people
Gal 1:15 But when it pleased God, who *separated me from* my mother's womb and called me through His grace

SEPARATED THE WATER (NIV)
(See *DIVIDED THE WATERS*)

SEPARATED TO THE GOSPEL OF GOD
Rom 1:1 Paul, a servant of Jesus Christ, called to be an apostle, *separated to the gospel of God*

SEPARATION BETWEEN THE HOLY AND THE COMMON (RSV)
(See *SEPARATE THE HOLY AREAS FROM THE COMMON*)

SEPARATION BETWEEN THE SANCTUARY AND THE PROFANE PLACE (KJV)
(See *SEPARATE THE HOLY AREAS FROM THE COMMON*)

SEPULCHRES OF THE KINGS (KJV)
(See *TOMBS OF THE KINGS*)

SERPENT DECEIVED EVE
2Cor 11:3 But I fear, lest somehow, as the *serpent deceived Eve* by his craftiness, so your minds may be corrupted from the simplicity that is in Christ

SERPENT DECEIVED ME
Gen 3:13 And the woman said, "The *serpent deceived me*, and I ate

SERPENT INSTEAD OF A FISH
Luke 11:11 Or if he asks for a fish, will he give him a *serpent instead of a fish*

SERPENT OF OLD
Rev 12:9 So the great dragon was cast out, that *serpent of old*, called the Devil and Satan, who deceives the whole world
Rev 20:2 He laid hold of the dragon, that *serpent of old*, who is the Devil and Satan, and bound him for a thousand years

SERPENT WAS MORE CUNNING
Gen 3:1 Now the *serpent was more cunning* than any beast of the field which the Lord God had made

SERVANT IS NOT GREATER
John 13:16 Most assuredly, I say to you, a *servant is not greater* than his master
John 15:20 Remember the word that I said to you, 'A *servant is not greater* than his master

SERVANT OF CHRIST
Gal 1:10 For if I still pleased men, I would not be a *servant of Christ*
Col 4:12 Epaphras, who is one of you, a *servant of Christ*, greets you, always laboring fervently for you in prayers, that you may stand perfect and complete in all the will of God

SERVANT OF GOD
1Chr 6:49 But Aaron and his sons offered sacrifices on the altar of burnt offering and on the altar of incense, for all the work of the Most Holy Place, and to make atonement for Israel, according to all that Moses the *servant of God* had commanded
2Chr 24:9 And they made a proclamation throughout Judah and Jerusalem to bring to the Lord the collection that Moses the *servant of God* had imposed on Israel in the wilderness
Neh 10:29 they joined with their brethren, their nobles, and entered into a curse and an oath to walk in God's Law, which was given by Moses the *servant of God*, and to observe and do all the commandments of the Lord our Lord, and His ordinances and His statutes
Dan 9:11 therefore the curse and the oath written in the Law of Moses the *servant of God* have been poured out on us, because we have sinned against Him
Tit 1:1 Paul, a *servant of God* and an apostle of Jesus Christ, according to the faith of God's elect and the acknowledgment of the truth which is according to godliness
Jas 1:1 James, a *servant of God* and of the Lord Jesus Christ, To the twelve tribes which are scattered abroad
Rev 15:3 And they sing the song of Moses, the *servant of God*, and the song of the Lamb, saying

SERVANT OF JESUS CHRIST
Rom 1:1 Paul, a *servant of Jesus Christ*, called to be an apostle, separated to the gospel of God
Jude 1 Jude, a *servant of Jesus Christ*, and brother of James, to those who are called, sanctified by God the Father, and preserved in Jesus Christ

SERVANT OF SIN (KJV)
(See *SLAVE OF SIN*)

SERVANT OF THE LORD
Deut 34:5 So Moses the *servant of the Lord* died there in the land of Moab, according to the word of the Lord
Josh 1:1 After the death of Moses the *servant of the Lord*, it came to pass that the Lord spoke to Joshua the son of Nun, Moses' assistant
Josh 1:13 Remember the word which Moses the *servant of the Lord* commanded you, saying
Josh 8:31 as Moses the *servant of the Lord* had commanded the children of Israel, as it is written in the Book of the Law of Moses
Josh 8:33 Half of them were in front of Mount Gerizim and half of them in front of Mount Ebal, as Moses the *servant of the Lord* had commanded before, that they should bless the people of Israel
Josh 11:12 He utterly destroyed them, as Moses the *servant of the Lord* had commanded
Josh 12:6 These Moses the *servant of the Lord* and the children of Israel had conquered; and Moses the *servant of the Lord* had given it as a possession to the Reubenites, the Gadites, and half the tribe of Manasseh
Josh 13:8 With the other half tribe the Reubenites and the Gadites received their inheritance, which

Moses had given them, beyond the Jordan eastward, as Moses the *servant of the Lord* had given them
Josh 14:7 I was forty years old when Moses the *servant of the Lord* sent me from Kadesh Barnea to spy out the land, and I brought back word to him as it was in my heart
Josh 18:7 And Gad, Reuben, and half the tribe of Manasseh have received their inheritance beyond the Jordan on the east, which Moses the *servant of the Lord* gave them
Josh 22:2 You have kept all that Moses the *servant of the Lord* commanded you, and have obeyed my voice in all that I commanded you
Josh 22:4 now therefore, return and go to your tents and to the land of your possession, which Moses the *servant of the Lord* gave you on the other side of the Jordan
Josh 22:5 But take diligent heed to do the commandment and the law which Moses the *servant of the Lord* commanded you, to love the Lord your God, to walk in all His ways, to keep His commandments, to hold fast to Him, and to serve Him with all your heart and with all your soul
Josh 24:29 Now it came to pass after these things that Joshua the son of Nun, the *servant of the Lord*, died, being one hundred and ten years old
Judg 2:8 Now Joshua the son of Nun, the *servant of the Lord*, died when he was one hundred and ten years old
2Kin 18:12 because they did not obey the voice of the Lord their God, but transgressed His covenant and all that Moses the *servant of the Lord* had commanded
2Chr 1:3 for the tabernacle of meeting with God was there, which Moses the *servant of the Lord* had made in the wilderness
2Chr 24:6 So the king called Jehoiada the chief priest, and said to him, "Why have you not required the Levites to bring in from Judah and from Jerusalem the collection, according to the commandment of Moses the *servant of the Lord* and of the congregation of Israel, for the tabernacle of witness
2Tim 2:24 And a *servant of the Lord* must not quarrel but be gentle to all, able to teach, patient

SERVANT'S MISERY (NIV)
(See *AFFLICTION OF YOUR MAIDSERVANT*)

SERVANTS OF CHRIST
1Cor 4:1 Let a man so consider us, as *servants of Christ* and stewards of the mysteries of God
Eph 6:6 not with eyeservice, as men-pleasers, but as *servants of Christ*, doing the will of God from the heart

SERVANTS OF GOD
1Pet 2:16 as free, yet not using your liberty as a cloak for vice, but as *servants of God*

SERVANTS OF RIGHTEOUSNESS (KJV)
(See *SLAVES OF RIGHTEOUSNESS*)

SERVANTS OF SIN (KJV)
(See *SLAVES OF SIN*)

SERVANTS OF THE LORD
2Kin 9:7 You shall strike down the house of Ahab your master, that I may avenge the blood of My servants the prophets, and the blood of all the *servants of the Lord*, at the hand of Jezebel
2Kin 10:23 Then Jehu and Jehonadab the son of Rechab went into the temple of Baal, and said to the worshipers of Baal, "Search and see that no *servants of the Lord* are here with you, but only the worshipers of Baal
Ps 113:1 Praise, O *servants of the Lord*, praise the name of the Lord
Ps 134:1 Behold, bless the Lord, all you *servants of the Lord*, who by night stand in the house of the Lord
Ps 135:1 Praise the name of the Lord; praise Him, O you *servants of the Lord*
Is 54:17 This is the heritage of the *servants of the Lord*, and their righteousness is from Me

SERVANTS TO GOD (KJV)
(See *SLAVES OF GOD*)

SERVE AS PRIESTS (NIV)
(See *MINISTER AS PRIESTS*)

SERVE AS PRIESTS OF THE LORD (RSV)
(See *MINISTER TO THE LORD*)

SERVE GOD AND MAMMON
Matt 6:24 for either he will hate the one and love the other, or else he will be loyal to the one and despise the other. You cannot *serve God and mammon*
Luke 16:13 for either he will hate the one and love the other, or else he will be loyal to the one and despise the other. You cannot *serve God and mammon*

SERVE IN THE HOUSE OF THE LORD
1Chr 26:12 Among these were the divisions of the gatekeepers, among the chief men, having duties just like their brethren, to *serve in the house of the Lord*

SERVE OTHER GODS
Deut 7:4 For they will turn your sons away from following Me, to *serve other gods*
Deut 11:16 Take heed to yourselves, lest your heart be deceived, and you turn aside and *serve other gods* and worship them
Deut 13:6 If your brother, the son of your mother, your son or your daughter, the wife of your bosom, or your friend who is as your own soul, secretly entices you, saying, 'Let us go and *serve other gods*
Deut 13:13 Certain corrupt men have gone out from among you and enticed the inhabitants of their city, saying, "Let us go and *serve other gods*
Deut 28:36 The Lord will bring you and the king whom you set over you to a nation which neither you nor your fathers have known, and there you shall *serve other gods* wood and stone
Deut 28:64 Then the Lord will scatter you among all peoples, from one end of the earth to the other, and there you shall *serve other gods*, which neither you nor your fathers have known wood and stone
Josh 24:16 Far be it from us that we should forsake the Lord to *serve other gods*
1Sam 26:19 But if it is the children of men, may they be cursed before the Lord, for they have driven me out this day from abiding in the inheritance of the Lord, saying, 'Go, *serve other gods*
1Kin 9:6 But if you or your sons at all turn from following Me, and do not keep My commandments and My statutes which I have set before you, but go and *serve other gods* and worship them
2Chr 7:19 But if you turn away and forsake My statutes and My commandments which I have set before you, and go and *serve other gods*, and worship them
Jer 16:13 and there you shall *serve other gods* day and night, where I will not show you favor
Jer 44:3 because of their wickedness which they have committed to provoke Me to anger, in that

they went to burn incense and to *serve other gods* whom they did not know, they nor you nor your fathers

SERVE SIN (KJV)
(See *SLAVES OF SIN*)

SERVE THE LORD
Ex 10:7 Let the men go, that they may *serve the Lord* their God
Ex 10:8 So Moses and Aaron were brought again to Pharaoh, and he said to them, "Go, *serve the Lord* your God
Ex 10:11 Go now, you who are men, and *serve the Lord*, for that is what you desired
Ex 10:24 Then Pharaoh called to Moses and said, "Go, *serve the Lord*
Ex 10:26 For we must take some of them to *serve the Lord* our God, and even we do not know with what we must *serve the Lord* until we arrive there
Ex 12:31 Then he called for Moses and Aaron by night, and said, "Rise and go out from among my people, both you and the children of Israel. And go, *serve the Lord* as you have said
Ex 23:25 So you shall *serve the Lord* your God, and He will bless your bread and your water
Deut 10:12 And now, Israel, what does the Lord your God require of you, but to fear the Lord your God, to walk in all His ways and to love Him, to *serve the Lord* your God with all your heart and with all your soul
Deut 28:47 Because you did not *serve the Lord* your God with joy and gladness of heart, for the abundance of all things
Josh 24:14 Now therefore, fear the Lord, serve Him in sincerity and in truth, and put away the gods which your fathers served on the other side of the River and in Egypt. *Serve the Lord*
Josh 24:15 And if it seems evil to you to *serve the Lord*, choose for yourselves this day whom you will serve, whether the gods which your fathers served that were on the other side of the River, or the gods of the Amorites, in whose land you dwell. But as for me and my house, we will *serve the Lord*
Josh 24:18 We also will *serve the Lord*, for He is our God
Josh 24:19 But Joshua said to the people, "You cannot *serve the Lord*, for He is a holy God
Josh 24:21 And the people said to Joshua, "No, but we will *serve the Lord*
1Sam 12:20 yet do not turn aside from following the Lord, but *serve the Lord* with all your heart
2Sam 15:8 For your servant vowed a vow while I dwelt at Geshur in Syria, saying, 'If the Lord indeed brings me back to Jerusalem, then I will *serve the Lord*
2Chr 30:8 and enter His sanctuary, which He has sanctified forever, and *serve the Lord* your God, that the fierceness of His wrath may turn away from you
2Chr 33:16 He also repaired the altar of the Lord, sacrificed peace offerings and thank offerings on it, and commanded Judah to *serve the Lord* God of Israel
2Chr 34:33 Thus Josiah removed all the abominations from all the country that belonged to the children of Israel, and made all who were present in Israel diligently *serve the Lord* their God
2Chr 35:3 Now *serve the Lord* your God and His people Israel
Ps 2:11 *Serve the Lord* with fear, and rejoice with trembling
Ps 100:2 *Serve the Lord* with gladness; come before His presence with singing
Ps 102:22 When the peoples are gathered together, and the kingdoms, to *serve the Lord*
Jer 30:9 But they shall *serve the Lord* their God, and David their king, whom I will raise up for them
1Cor 7:35 And this I say for your own profit, not that I may put a leash on you, but for what is proper, and that you may *serve the Lord* without distraction
Col 3:24 knowing that from the Lord you will receive the reward of the inheritance; for you *serve the Lord* Christ

SERVE THE LORD WITH GLADNESS
Ps 100:2 *Serve the Lord with gladness;* come before His presence with singing

SERVE TWO MASTERS
Matt 6:24 No one can *serve two masters;* for either he will hate the one and love the other, or else he will be loyal to the one and despise the other
Luke 16:13 No servant can *serve two masters;* for either he will hate the one and love the other, or else he will be loyal to the one and despise the other

SERVED CREATED THINGS (NIV)
(See *SERVED THE CREATURE*)

SERVED OTHER GODS (NIV)
(See *WORSHIPED OTHER GODS*)

SERVED THE CREATURE
Rom 1:25 who exchanged the truth of God for the lie, and worshiped and *served the creature* rather than the Creator, who is blessed forever

SERVICE AS PRIESTS (RSV)
(See *MINISTER AS PRIESTS*)

SERVICE IN THE HOLY PLACE (KJV)
(See *MINISTERING IN THE HOLY PLACE*)

SERVICE OF GOD
Ezra 6:18 They assigned the priests to their divisions and the Levites to their divisions, over the *service of God* in Jerusalem, as it is written in the Book of Moses
Rom 9:4 who are Israelites, to whom pertain the adoption, the glory, the covenants, the giving of the law, the *service of God*, and the promises

SERVICE OF THE LORD (NIV, RSV)
(See *KNOWLEDGE OF THE LORD*)

SERVICE OF THE SAINTS (NIV, RSV)
(See *MINISTRY OF THE SAINTS*)

SET A GUARD (NAS, NIV, RSV)
(See *KEEP WATCH*)

SET A WATCH (KJV)
(See *KEEP WATCH*)

SET APART
Ex 8:22 And in that day I will *set apart* the land of Goshen, in which My people dwell, that no swarms of flies shall be there, in order that you may know that I am the Lord in the midst of the land
Ex 13:12 that you shall *set apart* to the Lord all that open the womb, that is, every firstborn that comes from an animal which you have
Lev 15:19 If a woman has a discharge, and the discharge from her body is blood, she shall be *set apart* seven days
Deut 4:41 Then Moses *set apart* three cities on this side of the Jordan, toward the rising of the sun

Judg 7:5 And the Lord said to Gideon, "Everyone who laps from the water with his tongue, as a dog laps, you shall *set apart* by himself
1Sam 9:24 It was *set apart* for you. Eat; for until this time it has been kept for you, since I said I invited the people
1Chr 23:13 and Aaron was *set apart*, he and his sons forever, that he should sanctify the most holy things, to burn incense before the Lord, to minister to Him, and to give the blessing in His name forever
Ezra 10:16 And Ezra the priest, with certain heads of the fathers' households, were *set apart* by the fathers' households, each of them by name
Ps 4:3 But know that the Lord has *set apart* for Himself him who is godly
Is 23:18 Her gain and her pay will be *set apart* for the Lord
Ezek 22:10 in you they violate women who are *set apart* during their impurity
Ezek 39:14 They will *set apart* men regularly employed, with the help of a search party, to pass through the land and bury those bodies remaining on the ground, in order to cleanse it
Ezek 45:1 Moreover, when you divide the land by lot into inheritance, you shall *set apart* a district for the Lord, a holy portion of the land
Ezek 48:8 by the border of Judah, from the east side to the west, shall be the district which you shall *set apart*, twenty-five thousand cubits in width, and in length the same as one of the other portions, from the east side to the west, with the sanctuary in the center
Ezek 48:9 The district that you shall *set apart* for the Lord shall be twenty-five thousand cubits in length and ten thousand in width
Ezek 48:12 And this district of land that is *set apart* shall be to them a thing most holy by the border of the Levites
Ezek 48:20 You shall *set apart* the holy district with the property of the city

SET APART CHRIST AS LORD (NIV)
(See *SANCTIFY THE LORD*)

SET APART FOR ME (NAS, NIV, RSV)
(See *SEPARATE TO ME*)

SET APART FOR THE GOSPEL OF GOD (NAS, NIV, RSV)
(See *SEPARATED TO THE GOSPEL OF GOD*)

SET AT LIBERTY
Jer 34:16 Then you turned around and profaned My name, and every one of you brought back his male and female slaves, whom he had *set at liberty*, at their pleasure, and brought them back into subjection, to be your male and female slaves
Luke 4:18 He has sent Me to heal the brokenhearted, to preach deliverance to the captives and recovery of sight to the blind, to *set at liberty* those who are oppressed

SET FORTH YOUR CASE (RSV)
(See *PRESENT YOUR CASE*)

SET FREE TO GO WHERE THEY WISHED (NIV)
(See *SET AT LIBERTY*)

SET ME APART (NIV, RSV)
(See *SEPARATED ME FROM*)

SET MY FEET UPON A ROCK
Ps 40:2 He also brought me up out of a horrible pit, out of the miry clay, and *set my feet upon a rock*, and established my steps

SET MY NAME THERE (KJV)
(See *DWELLING FOR MY NAME*)

SET OFF FOR A DISTANT COUNTRY (NIV)
(See *JOURNEYED TO A FAR COUNTRY*)

SET ON FIRE
Deut 32:22 it shall consume the earth with her increase, and *set on fire* the foundations of the mountains
2Kin 8:12 Their strongholds you will *set on fire*, and their young men you will kill with the sword
Ps 57:4 I lie among the sons of men who are *set on fire*, whose teeth are spears and arrows, and their tongue a sharp sword
Ezek 39:9 Then those who dwell in the cities of Israel will go out and *set on fire* and burn the weapons, both the shields and bucklers, the bows and arrows, the javelins and spears
Jas 3:6 The tongue is so set among our members that it defiles the whole body, and sets on fire the course of nature; and it is *set on fire* by hell

SET YOUR FACE AGAINST
Ezek 4:3 *Set your face against* it, and it shall be besieged, and you shall lay siege against it
Ezek 13:17 Likewise, son of man, *set your face against* the daughters of your people, who prophesy out of their own heart
Ezek 25:2 Son of man, *set your face against* the Ammonites, and prophesy against them
Ezek 29:2 Son of man, *set your face against* Pharaoh king of Egypt, and prophesy against him, and against all Egypt
Ezek 35:2 Son of man, *set your face against* Mount Seir and prophesy against it
Ezek 38:2 Son of man, *set your face against* Gog, of the land of Magog, the prince of Rosh, Meshech, and Tubal, and prophesy against him

SET YOUR HOUSE IN ORDER
2Kin 20:1 *Set your house in order*, for you shall die, and not live
Is 38:1 *Set your house in order*, for you shall die and not live

SETTINGS OF SILVER
Prov 25:11 A word fitly spoken is like apples of gold in *settings of silver*

SETTLED IN HEAVEN
Ps 119:89 Forever, O Lord, Your word is *settled in heaven*

SETTLED THERE (NAS, NIV, RSV)
(See *DWELT THERE*)

SEVEN CHURCHES
Rev 1:4 John, to the *seven churches* which are in Asia: Grace to you and peace from Him who is and who was and who is to come, and from the seven Spirits who are before His throne
Rev 1:11 saying, "I am the Alpha and the Omega, the First and the Last," and, "What you see, write in a book and send it to the *seven churches* which are in Asia
Rev 1:20 The seven stars are the angels of the *seven churches*, and the seven lampstands which you saw are the *seven churches*

SEVEN GOLDEN LAMPSTANDS
Rev 1:12 Then I turned to see the voice that spoke with me. And having turned I saw *seven golden lampstands*
Rev 1:20 The mystery of the seven stars which you saw in My right hand, and the *seven golden lampstands*
Rev 2:1 To the angel of the church of Ephesus

write, 'These things says He who holds the seven stars in His right hand, who walks in the midst of the *seven golden lampstands*

SEVEN SONS

Ruth 4:15 for your daughter-in-law, who loves you, who is better to you than *seven sons*, has borne him

Job 1:2 And *seven sons* and three daughters were born to him

Job 42:13 He also had *seven sons* and three daughters

Acts 19:14 Also there were *seven sons* of Sceva, a Jewish chief priest, who did so

SEVEN SPIRITS OF GOD

Rev 3:1 And to the angel of the church in Sardis write, 'These things says He who has the *seven Spirits of God* and the seven stars

Rev 4:5 And there were seven lamps of fire burning before the throne, which are the *seven Spirits of God*

Rev 5:6 And I looked, and behold, in the midst of the throne and of the four living creatures, and in the midst of the elders, stood a Lamb as though it had been slain, having seven horns and seven eyes, which are the *seven Spirits of God* sent out into all the earth

SEVEN TIMES

Gen 33:3 Then he crossed over before them and bowed himself to the ground *seven times*, until he came near to his brother

Lev 4:6 The priest shall dip his finger in the blood and sprinkle some of the blood *seven times* before the Lord, in front of the veil of the sanctuary

Lev 4:17 Then the priest shall dip his finger in the blood and sprinkle it *seven times* before the Lord, in front of the veil

Lev 8:11 He sprinkled some of it on the altar *seven times*, anointed the altar and all its utensils, and the laver and its base, to sanctify them

Lev 14:7 And he shall sprinkle it *seven times* on him who is to be cleansed from the leprosy, and shall pronounce him clean, and shall let the living bird loose in the open field

Lev 14:16 Then the priest shall dip his right finger in the oil that is in his left hand, and shall sprinkle some of the oil with his finger *seven times* before the Lord

Lev 14:27 Then the priest shall sprinkle with his right finger some of the oil that is in his left hand *seven times* before the Lord

Lev 14:51 and he shall take the cedar wood, the hyssop, the scarlet, and the living bird, and dip them in the blood of the slain bird and in the running water, and sprinkle the house *seven times*

Lev 16:14 and before the mercy seat he shall sprinkle some of the blood with his finger *seven times*

Lev 16:19 Then he shall sprinkle some of the blood on it with his finger *seven times*, cleanse it, and sanctify it from the uncleanness of the children of Israel

Lev 25:8 And you shall count seven sabbaths of years for yourself, *seven times* seven years

Lev 26:18 And after all this, if you do not obey Me, then I will punish you *seven times* more for your sins

Lev 26:21 Then, if you walk contrary to Me, and are not willing to obey Me, I will bring on you *seven times* more plagues, according to your sins

Lev 26:24 then I also will walk contrary to you, and I will punish you yet *seven times* for your sins

Lev 26:28 and I, even I, will chastise you *seven times* for your sins

Num 19:4 and Eleazar the priest shall take some of its blood with his finger, and sprinkle some of its blood *seven times* directly in front of the tabernacle of meeting

Josh 6:4 But the seventh day you shall march around the city *seven times*, and the priests shall blow the trumpets

Josh 6:15 But it came to pass on the seventh day that they rose early, about the dawning of the day, and marched around the city *seven times* in the same manner. On that day only they marched around the city *seven times*

1Kin 18:43 So he went up and looked, and said, "There is nothing." And *seven times* he said, "Go again

2Kin 4:35 then the child sneezed *seven times*, and the child opened his eyes

2Kin 5:10 And Elisha sent a messenger to him, saying, "Go and wash in the Jordan *seven times*, and your flesh shall be restored to you, and you shall be clean

2Kin 5:14 So he went down and dipped *seven times* in the Jordan, according to the saying of the man of God

Ps 12:6 The words of the Lord are pure words, like silver tried in a furnace of earth, purified *seven times*

Ps 119:164 *Seven times* a day I praise You, because of Your righteous judgments

Prov 24:16 for a righteous man may fall *seven times* and rise again, but the wicked shall fall by calamity

Dan 3:19 Therefore he spoke and commanded that they heat the furnace *seven times* more than it was usually heated

Dan 4:16 Let his heart be changed from that of a man, let him be given the heart of an animal, and let *seven times* pass over him

Dan 4:23 let it be wet with the dew of heaven, and let him graze with the beasts of the field, till *seven times* pass over him

Dan 4:25 They shall wet you with the dew of heaven, and *seven times* shall pass over you, till you know that the Most High rules in the kingdom of men, and gives it to whomever He chooses

Dan 4:32 and *seven times* shall pass over you, until you know that the Most High rules in the kingdom of men, and gives it to whomever He chooses

Matt 18:21 Then Peter came to Him and said, "Lord, how often shall my brother sin against me, and I forgive him? Up to *seven times*

Matt 18:22 Jesus said to him, "I do not say to you, up to *seven times*, but up to seventy times seven

Luke 17:4 And if he sins against you *seven times* in a day, and *seven times* in a day returns to you, saying

SEVEN TIMES SEVEN

Lev 25:8 And you shall count seven sabbaths of years for yourself, *seven times seven* years

SEVENTH DAY

Gen 2:2 And on the *seventh day* God ended His work which He had done, and He rested on the *seventh day* from all His work which He had done

Gen 2:3 Then God blessed the *seventh day* and sanctified it, because in it He rested from all His work which God had created and made

Ex 12:15 For whoever eats leavened bread from the first day until the *seventh day*, that person shall be cut off from Israel

Ex 12:16 On the first day there shall be a holy convocation, and on the *seventh day* there shall be a holy convocation for you

Ex 13:6 Seven days you shall eat unleavened

bread, and on the *seventh day* there shall be a feast to the Lord
Ex 16:26 Six days you shall gather it, but on the *seventh day*, which is the Sabbath, there will be none
Ex 16:27 Now it happened that some of the people went out on the *seventh day* to gather, but they found none
Ex 16:29 let no man go out of his place on the *seventh day*
Ex 16:30 So the people rested on the *seventh day*
Ex 20:10 but the *seventh day* is the Sabbath of the Lord your God
Ex 20:11 For in six days the Lord made the heavens and the earth, the sea, and all that is in them, and rested the *seventh day*
Ex 23:12 Six days you shall do your work, and on the *seventh day* you shall rest, that your ox and your donkey may rest, and the son of your female servant and the stranger may be refreshed
Ex 24:16 And on the *seventh day* He called to Moses out of the midst of the cloud
Ex 31:17 for in six days the Lord made the heavens and the earth, and on the *seventh day* He rested and was refreshed
Ex 34:21 Six days you shall work, but on the *seventh day* you shall rest
Ex 35:2 Work shall be done for six days, but the *seventh day* shall be a holy day for you, a Sabbath of rest to the Lord
Lev 13:5 And the priest shall look at him on the *seventh day*
Lev 13:6 Then the priest shall look at him again on the *seventh day*
Lev 13:27 And the priest shall look at him on the *seventh day*
Lev 13:32 And on the *seventh day* the priest shall look at the sore
Lev 13:34 On the *seventh day* the priest shall look at the scall
Lev 13:51 And he shall look at the plague on the *seventh day*
Lev 14:9 But on the *seventh day* he shall shave all the hair off his head and his beard and his eyebrows all his hair he shall shave off
Lev 14:39 And the priest shall come again on the *seventh day* and look
Lev 23:3 Six days shall work be done, but the *seventh day* is a Sabbath of solemn rest, a holy convocation
Lev 23:8 The *seventh day* shall be a holy convocation; you shall do no customary work on it
Num 6:9 And if anyone dies very suddenly beside him, and he defiles his consecrated head, then he shall shave his head on the day of his cleansing; on the *seventh day* he shall shave it
Num 7:48 On the *seventh day* Elishama the son of Ammihud, leader of the children of Ephraim, presented an offering
Num 19:12 He shall purify himself with the water on the third day and on the *seventh day;* then he will be clean. But if he does not purify himself on the third day and on the *seventh day*, he will not be clean
Num 19:19 The clean person shall sprinkle the unclean on the third day and on the *seventh day;* and on the *seventh day* he shall purify himself, wash his clothes, and bathe in water
Num 28:25 And on the *seventh day* you shall have a holy convocation
Num 29:32 On the *seventh day* present seven bulls, two rams, and fourteen lambs in their first year without blemish
Num 31:19 whoever has killed any person, and whoever has touched any slain, purify yourselves and your captives on the third day and on the *seventh day*
Num 31:24 And you shall wash your clothes on the *seventh day* and be clean, and afterward you may come into the camp
Deut 5:14 but the *seventh day* is the Sabbath of the Lord your God
Deut 16:8 Six days you shall eat unleavened bread, and on the *seventh day* there shall be a sacred assembly to the Lord your God
Josh 6:4 But the *seventh day* you shall march around the city seven times, and the priests shall blow the trumpets
Josh 6:15 But it came to pass on the *seventh day* that they rose early, about the dawning of the day, and marched around the city seven times in the same manner
Judg 14:15 So it came to pass on the *seventh day* that they said to Samson's wife
Judg 14:17 And it happened on the *seventh day* that he told her, because she pressed him so much
Judg 14:18 So the men of the city said to him on the *seventh day* before the sun went down
2Sam 12:18 Then on the *seventh day* it came to pass that the child died
1Kin 20:29 So it was that on the *seventh day* the battle was joined
2Kin 25:8 Now in the fifth month, on the *seventh day* of the month (which was the nineteenth year of King Nebuchadnezzar king of Babylon
Esth 1:10 On the *seventh day*, when the heart of the king was merry with wine, he commanded Mehuman, Biztha, Harbona, Bigtha, Abagtha, Zethar, and Carcas, seven eunuchs who served in the presence of King Ahasuerus
Ezek 30:20 And it came to pass in the eleventh year, in the first month, on the *seventh day* of the month, that the word of the Lord came to me, saying
Ezek 45:20 And so you shall do on the *seventh day* of the month for everyone who has sinned unintentionally or in ignorance
Heb 4:4 For He has spoken in a certain place of the *seventh day* in this way: "And God rested on the *seventh day* from all His works

SEVENTH YEAR
Ex 23:11 but the *seventh year* you shall let it rest and lie fallow, that the poor of your people may eat
Lev 25:4 but in the *seventh year* there shall be a sabbath of solemn rest for the land, a sabbath to the Lord
Lev 25:20 And if you say, "What shall we eat in the *seventh year*, since we shall not sow nor gather in our produce
Deut 15:9 Beware lest there be a wicked thought in your heart, saying, 'The *seventh year*, the year of release, is at hand
Deut 15:12 If your brother, a Hebrew man, or a Hebrew woman, is sold to you and serves you six years, then in the *seventh year* you shall let him go free from you
2Kin 11:4 In the *seventh year* Jehoiada sent and brought the captains of hundreds, of the bodyguards and the escorts, and brought them into the house of the Lord to him
2Kin 12:1 In the *seventh year* of Jehu, Jehoash became king, and he reigned forty years in Jerusalem
2Kin 18:9 Now it came to pass in the fourth year of King Hezekiah, which was the *seventh year* of Hoshea the son of Elah, king of Israel, that Shalmaneser king of Assyria came up against Samaria and besieged it
2Chr 23:1 In the *seventh year* Jehoiada strengthened himself, and made a covenant with the captains of hundreds
Ezra 7:7 Some of the children of Israel, the priests, the Levites, the singers, the gatekeepers, and the

Nethinim came up to Jerusalem in the *seventh year* of King Artaxerxes
Ezra 7:8 And Ezra came to Jerusalem in the fifth month, which was in the *seventh year* of the king
Esth 2:16 So Esther was taken to King Ahasuerus, into his royal palace, in the tenth month, which is the month of Tebeth, in the *seventh year* of his reign
Jer 52:28 These are the people whom Nebuchadnezzar carried away captive: in the *seventh year*, three thousand and twenty-three Jews
Ezek 20:1 It came to pass in the *seventh year*, in the fifth month, on the tenth day of the month, that certain of the elders of Israel came to inquire of the Lord, and sat before me

SEVENTY SONS
Judg 8:30 Gideon had *seventy sons* who were his own offspring, for he had many wives
Judg 9:5 Then he went to his father's house at Ophrah and killed his brothers, the *seventy sons* of Jerubbaal, on one stone
Judg 9:18 but you have risen up against my father's house this day, and killed his *seventy sons* on one stone, and made Abimelech, the son of his maidservant, king over the men of Shechem, because he is your brother
Judg 9:24 that the crime done to the *seventy sons* of Jerubbaal might be settled and their blood be laid on Abimelech their brother, who killed them, and on the men of Shechem, who aided him in the killing of his brothers
2Kin 10:1 Now Ahab had *seventy sons* in Samaria. And Jehu wrote letters and sent them to Samaria, to the rulers of Jezreel, to the elders, and to those who reared Ahab's sons, saying

SEVENTY YEARS
Gen 5:12 Cainan lived *seventy years*, and begot Mahalalel
Gen 11:26 Now Terah lived *seventy years*, and begot Abram, Nahor, and Haran
2Chr 36:21 As long as she lay desolate she kept Sabbath, to fulfill *seventy years*
Ps 90:10 The days of our lives are *seventy years;* and if by reason of strength they are eighty years, yet their boast is only labor and sorrow
Is 23:15 Now it shall come to pass in that day that Tyre will be forgotten *seventy years*, according to the days of one king. At the end of *seventy years* it will happen to Tyre as in the song of the harlot
Is 23:17 And it shall be, at the end of *seventy years*, that the Lord will visit Tyre
Jer 25:11 And this whole land shall be a desolation and an astonishment, and these nations shall serve the king of Babylon *seventy years*
Jer 25:12 Then it will come to pass, when *seventy years* are completed, that I will punish the king of Babylon and that nation, the land of the Chaldeans, for their iniquity
Jer 29:10 After *seventy years* are completed at Babylon, I will visit you and perform My good word toward you, and cause you to return to this place
Dan 9:2 in the first year of his reign I, Daniel, understood by the books the number of the years specified by the word of the Lord, given through Jeremiah the prophet, that He would accomplish *seventy years* in the desolations of Jerusalem
Zech 1:12 Then the Angel of the Lord answered and said, "O Lord of hosts, how long will You not have mercy on Jerusalem and on the cities of Judah, against which You were angry these *seventy years*
Zech 7:5 When you fasted and mourned in the fifth and seventh months during those *seventy years*, did you really fast for Me—for Me

SEWED FIG LEAVES TOGETHER
Gen 3:7 and they *sewed fig leaves together* and made themselves coverings

SEXUAL IMMORALITY
Matt 5:32 But I say to you that whoever divorces his wife for any reason except *sexual immorality* causes her to commit adultery
Matt 19:9 And I say to you, whoever divorces his wife, except for *sexual immorality*, and marries another, commits adultery
Acts 15:20 but that we write to them to abstain from things polluted by idols, from *sexual immorality*, from things strangled, and from blood
Acts 15:29 that you abstain from things offered to idols, from blood, from things strangled, and from *sexual immorality*
Acts 21:25 But concerning the Gentiles who believe, we have written and decided that they should observe no such thing, except that they should keep themselves from things offered to idols, from blood, from things strangled, and from *sexual immorality*
Rom 1:29 being filled with all unrighteousness, *sexual immorality*, wickedness, covetousness, maliciousness
1Cor 5:1 It is actually reported that there is *sexual immorality* among you, and such *sexual immorality* as is not even named among the Gentiles that a man has his father's wife
1Cor 6:13 Now the body is not for *sexual immorality* but for the Lord, and the Lord for the body
1Cor 6:18 Flee *sexual immorality*. Every sin that a man does is outside the body, but he who commits *sexual immorality* sins against his own body
1Cor 7:2 Nevertheless, because of *sexual immorality*, let each man have his own wife, and let each woman have her own husband
1Cor 10:8 Nor let us commit *sexual immorality*, as some of them did, and in one day twenty-three thousand fell
1Th 4:3 For this is the will of God, your sanctification: that you should abstain from *sexual immorality*
Jude 7 as Sodom and Gomorrah, and the cities around them in a similar manner to these, having given themselves over to *sexual immorality* and gone after strange flesh, are set forth as an example, suffering the vengeance of eternal fire
Rev 2:14 But I have a few things against you, because you have there those who hold the doctrine of Balaam, who taught Balak to put a stumbling block before the children of Israel, to eat things sacrificed to idols, and to commit *sexual immorality*
Rev 2:20 Nevertheless I have a few things against you, because you allow that woman Jezebel, who calls herself a prophetess, to teach and beguile My servants to commit *sexual immorality* and to eat things sacrificed to idols
Rev 2:21 And I gave her time to repent of her *sexual immorality*, and she did not repent
Rev 9:21 and they did not repent of their murders or their sorceries or their *sexual immorality* or their thefts

SEXUAL RELATIONS (NIV)
(See *UNCOVER HER NAKEDNESS*)

SHADE OF ITS BRANCHES (NAS, NIV, RSV)
(See *SHADOW OF ITS BRANCHES*)

SHADOW OF DEATH
Job 3:5 May darkness and the *shadow of death* claim it; may a cloud settle on it
Job 10:21 Before I go to the place from which I shall not return, to the land of darkness and the *shadow of death*

Job 10:22 a land as dark as darkness itself, as the *shadow of death*, without any order, where even the light is like darkness
Job 12:22 He uncovers deep things out of darkness, and brings the *shadow of death* to light
Job 16:16 My face is flushed from weeping, and on my eyelids is the *shadow of death*
Job 24:17 For the morning is the same to them as the *shadow of death;* if someone recognizes them, they are in the terrors of the *shadow of death*
Job 28:3 Man puts an end to darkness, and searches every recess for ore in the darkness and the *shadow of death*
Job 34:22 There is no darkness nor *shadow of death* where the workers of iniquity may hide themselves
Job 38:17 Or have you seen the doors of the *shadow of death*
Ps 23:4 Yea, though I walk through the valley of the *shadow of death*, I will fear no evil
Ps 44:19 But You have severely broken us in the place of jackals, and covered us with the *shadow of death*
Ps 107:10 Those who sat in darkness and in the *shadow of death*, bound in affliction and irons
Ps 107:14 He brought them out of darkness and the *shadow of death*, and broke their chains in pieces
Is 9:2 those who dwelt in the land of the *shadow of death*, upon them a light has shined
Jer 2:6 Neither did they say, 'Where is the Lord, Who brought us up out of the land of Egypt, Who led us through the wilderness, through a land of deserts and pits, through a land of drought and the *shadow of death*, through a land that no one crossed and where no one dwelt
Jer 13:16 Give glory to the Lord your God before He causes darkness, and before your feet stumble on the dark mountains, and while you are looking for light, He turns it into the *shadow of death* and makes it dense darkness
Amos 5:8 he turns the *shadow of death* into morning and makes the day dark as night
Matt 4:16 the people who sat in darkness saw a great light, and upon those who sat in the region and *shadow of death* light has dawned
Luke 1:79 to give light to those who sit in darkness and the *shadow of death*, to guide our feet into the way of peace

SHADOW OF ITS BRANCHES
Ezek 17:23 Under it will dwell birds of every sort; in the *shadow of its branches* they will dwell

SHADOW OF THE ALMIGHTY
Ps 91:1 He who dwells in the secret place of the Most High shall abide under the *shadow of the Almighty*

SHADOW OF YOUR WINGS
Ps 17:8 Keep me as the apple of Your eye; hide me under the *shadow of Your wings*
Ps 36:7 Therefore the children of men put their trust under the *shadow of Your wings*
Ps 57:1 And in the *shadow of Your wings* I will make my refuge, until these calamities have passed by
Ps 63:7 Because You have been my help, therefore in the *shadow of Your wings* I will rejoice

SHADOW THAT PASSETH AWAY (KJV)
(See *LIKE A PASSING SHADOW*)

SHAFT OF THE ABYSS (NIV)
(See *BOTTOMLESS PIT*)

SHAKE OFF THE DUST
Matt 10:14 And whoever will not receive you nor hear your words, when you depart from that house or city, *shake off the dust* from your feet
Mark 6:11 And whoever will not receive you nor hear you, when you depart from there, *shake off the dust* under your feet as a testimony against them

SHAKE THEIR HEADS
Ps 109:25 I also have become a reproach to them; when they look at me, they *shake their heads*
Lam 2:15 they hiss and *shake their heads* at the daughter of Jerusalem

SHAKES THE NATIONS (NIV)
(See *SIFT THE NATIONS*)

SHALL NOT PITY
Deut 19:13 Your eye *shall not pity* him, but you shall put away the guilt of innocent blood from Israel, that it may go well with you
Deut 19:21 Your eye *shall not pity;* but life shall be for life, eye for eye, tooth for tooth, hand for hand, foot for foot
Deut 25:12 then you shall cut off her hand; your eye *shall not pity* her

SHARE IN HIS GUILT (NIV)
(See *BEAR SIN BECAUSE OF HIM*)

SHARE IN HIS HOLINESS (NIV)
(See *PARTAKERS OF HIS HOLINESS*)

SHARE IN THE GLORY (NIV)
(See *OBTAINING OF THE GLORY*)

SHARE IN THE HERITAGE OF THE LORD (RSV)
(See *INHERITANCE OF THE LORD*)

SHARE IN THE JOY (NIV)
(See *REJOICE IN THE GLADNESS*)

SHARE IN THE LORD (NIV)
(See *PART IN THE LORD*)

SHARE IN YOUR SALVATION (NIV)
(See *COME INTO YOUR RIGHTEOUSNESS*)

SHARE YOUR BREAD
Is 58:7 Is it not to *share your bread* with the hungry, and that you bring to your house the poor who are cast out

SHARP TWO-EDGED SWORD
Rev 1:16 He had in His right hand seven stars, out of His mouth went a *sharp two-edged sword*, and His countenance was like the sun shining in its strength
Rev 2:12 And to the angel of the church in Pergamos write, 'These things says He who has the *sharp two-edged sword*

SHARPER THAN ANY TWO-EDGED SWORD
Heb 4:12 For the word of God is living and powerful, and *sharper than any two-edged sword*, piercing even to the division of soul and spirit, and of joints and marrow, and is a discerner of the thoughts and intents of the heart

SHE FORGOT ME
Hos 2:13 She decked herself with her earrings and jewelry, and went after her lovers. Then *she forgot Me,"* says the Lord

SHE HAD SEEN THE LORD
John 20:18 Mary Magdalene came and told the disciples that *she had seen the Lord*, and that He had spoken these things to her

SHE WAS BARREN
Gen 25:21 Now Isaac pleaded with the Lord for his wife, because *she was barren*

SHED BLOOD
Lev 17:4 He has *shed blood;* and that man shall be cut off from among his people
1Sam 25:31 that this will be no grief to you, nor offense of heart to my lord, either that you have *shed blood* without cause, or that my lord has avenged himself
1Chr 28:3 But God said to me, 'You shall not build a house for My name, because you have been a man of war and have *shed blood*
Prov 1:11 If they say, "Come with us, let us lie in wait to *shed blood*
Prov 1:16 for their feet run to evil, and they make haste to *shed blood*
Ezek 16:38 And I will judge you as women who break wedlock or *shed blood* are judged
Ezek 22:6 each one has used his power to *shed blood* in you
Ezek 22:12 In you they take bribes to *shed blood;* you take usury and increase
Ezek 22:27 Her princes in her midst are like wolves tearing the prey, to *shed blood*, to destroy people, and to get dishonest gain
Ezek 23:45 But righteous men will judge them after the manner of adulteresses, and after the manner of women who *shed blood*, because they are adulteresses, and blood is on their hands
Ezek 33:25 You eat meat with blood, you lift up your eyes toward your idols, and *shed blood*
Rom 3:15 Their feet are swift to *shed blood*

SHED FOR MANY
Matt 26:28 For this is My blood of the new covenant, which is *shed for many* for the remission of sins
Mark 14:24 And He said to them, "This is My blood of the new covenant, which is *shed for many*

SHED FOR YOU
Luke 22:20 Likewise He also took the cup after supper, saying, "This cup is the new covenant in My blood, which is *shed for you*

SHED INNOCENT BLOOD
Ps 106:38 And *shed innocent blood*, even the blood of their sons and daughters, whom they sacrificed to the idols of Canaan
Prov 6:17 A proud look, a lying tongue, hands that *shed innocent blood*
Is 59:7 Their feet run to evil, and they make haste to *shed innocent blood*
Jer 7:6 if you do not oppress the stranger, the fatherless, and the widow, and do not *shed innocent blood* in this place, or walk after other gods to your hurt
Jer 22:3 Do no wrong and do no violence to the stranger, the fatherless, or the widow, nor *shed innocent blood* in this place
Joel 3:19 Egypt shall be a desolation, and Edom a desolate wilderness, because of violence against the people of Judah, for they have *shed innocent blood* in their land

SHEDDING OF BLOOD
Heb 9:22 And according to the law almost all things are purged with blood, and without *shedding of blood* there is no remission

SHEEP BEFORE ITS SHEARERS
Is 53:7 He was led as a lamb to the slaughter, and as a *sheep before its shearers* is silent, so He opened not his mouth

SHEEP DRIVEN AWAY (RSV)
(See *SCATTERED SHEEP*)

SHEEP FOR THE SLAUGHTER
Ps 44:22 Yet for Your sake we are killed all day long; we are accounted as *sheep for the slaughter*
Jer 12:3 Pull them out like *sheep for the slaughter*, and prepare them for the day of slaughter
Rom 8:36 For Your sake we are killed all day long; we are accounted as *sheep for the slaughter*

SHEEP GOING ASTRAY
Deut 22:1 You shall not see your brother's ox or his *sheep going astray*, and hide yourself from them
1Pet 2:25 For you were like *sheep going astray*, but have now returned to the Shepherd and Overseer of your souls

SHEEP HEAR HIS VOICE
John 10:3 To him the doorkeeper opens, and the *sheep hear his voice*

SHEEP MAY BE SCATTERED (NAS, RSV)
(See *SHEEP WILL BE SCATTERED*)

SHEEP NOT HAVING A SHEPHERD
Mark 6:34 And Jesus, when He came out, saw a great multitude and was moved with compassion for them, because they were like *sheep not having a shepherd*

SHEEP OF HIS PASTURE
Ps 100:3 We are His people and the *sheep of His pasture*

SHEEP OF MY PASTURE
Jer 23:1 Woe to the shepherds who destroy and scatter the *sheep of My pasture*

SHEEP OF YOUR PASTURE
Ps 74:1 Why does Your anger smoke against the *sheep of Your pasture*
Ps 79:13 So we, Your people and *sheep of Your pasture*, will give You thanks forever

SHEEP SHALL BE SCATTERED (KJV)
(See *SHEEP WILL BE SCATTERED*)

SHEEP STRAYING (NAS, NIV)
(See *SHEEP GOING ASTRAY*)

SHEEP THAT HAVE NO SHEPHERD
1Kin 22:17 Then he said, "I saw all Israel scattered on the mountains, as *sheep that have no shepherd*
2Chr 18:16 Then he said, "I saw all Israel scattered on the mountains, as *sheep that have no shepherd*

SHEEP TO BE SLAUGHTERED (NAS, NIV)
(See *SHEEP FOR THE SLAUGHTER*)

SHEEP WILL BE SCATTERED
Zech 13:7 Strike the Shepherd, and the *sheep will be scattered;* then I will turn My hand against the little ones
Mark 14:27 I will strike the Shepherd, and the *sheep will be scattered*

SHEEP WITHOUT A SHEPHERD (NAS, NIV, RSV)
(See *SHEEP NOT HAVING A SHEPHERD*)

SHEEP'S CLOTHING
Matt 7:15 Beware of false prophets, who come to you in *sheep's clothing*, but inwardly they are ravenous wolves

SHEKELS OF SILVER
Gen 23:15 the land is worth four hundred *shekels of silver*. What is that between you and me
Gen 23:16 and Abraham weighed out the silver for Ephron which he had named in the hearing of the sons of Heth, four hundred *shekels of silver*, currency of the merchants
Gen 37:28 so the brothers pulled Joseph up and lifted him out of the pit, and sold him to the Ishmaelites for twenty *shekels of silver*
Ex 21:32 If the ox gores a male or female servant, he shall give to their master thirty *shekels of silver*, and the ox shall be stoned
Lev 5:15 If a person commits a trespass, and sins unintentionally in regard to the holy things of the Lord, then he shall bring to the Lord as his trespass offering a ram without blemish from the flocks, with your valuation in *shekels of silver* according to the shekel of the sanctuary, as a trespass offering
Lev 27:3 if your valuation is of a male from twenty years old up to sixty years old, then your valuation shall be fifty *shekels of silver*, according to the shekel of the sanctuary
Lev 27:6 and if from a month old up to five years old, then your valuation for a male shall be five *shekels of silver*, and for a female your valuation shall be three *shekels of silver*
Lev 27:16 A homer of barley seed shall be valued at fifty *shekels of silver*
Num 18:16 And those redeemed of the devoted things you shall redeem when one month old, according to your valuation, for five *shekels of silver*, according to the shekel of the sanctuary, which is twenty gerahs
Deut 22:19 and they shall fine him one hundred *shekels of silver* and give them to the father of the young woman, because he has brought a bad name on a virgin of Israel
Deut 22:29 then the man who lay with her shall give to the young woman's father fifty *shekels of silver*, and she shall be his wife because he has humbled her
Josh 7:21 When I saw among the spoils a beautiful Babylonian garment, two hundred *shekels of silver*, and a wedge of gold weighing fifty shekels, I coveted them and took them
Judg 9:4 So they gave him seventy *shekels of silver* from the temple of Baal-Berith, with which Abimelech hired worthless and reckless men
Judg 17:2 And he said to his mother, "The eleven hundred *shekels of silver* that were taken from you, and on which you put a curse, even saying it in my ears here is the silver with me
Judg 17:3 So when he had returned the eleven hundred *shekels of silver* to his mother, his mother said
Judg 17:4 Then his mother took two hundred *shekels of silver* and gave them to the silversmith, and he made it into a carved image and a molded image
Judg 17:10 Micah said to him, "Dwell with me, and be a father and a priest to me, and I will give you ten *shekels of silver* per year, a suit of clothes, and your sustenance
2Sam 18:11 I would have given you ten *shekels of silver* and a belt
2Sam 18:12 But the man said to Joab, "Though I were to receive a thousand *shekels of silver* in my hand, I would not raise my hand against the king's son
2Sam 24:24 So David bought the threshing floor and the oxen for fifty *shekels of silver*
1Kin 10:29 Now a chariot that was imported from Egypt cost six hundred *shekels of silver*, and a horse one hundred and fifty
2Kin 6:25 and indeed they besieged it until a donkey's head was sold for eighty *shekels of silver*, and one-fourth of a kab of dove droppings for five *shekels of silver*
2Kin 15:20 And Menahem exacted the money from Israel, from all the very wealthy, from each man fifty *shekels of silver*, to give to the king of Assyria
2Chr 1:17 They also acquired and imported from Egypt a chariot for six hundred *shekels of silver*, and a horse for one hundred and fifty
Neh 5:15 But the former governors who had been before me laid burdens on the people, and took from them bread and wine, besides forty *shekels of silver*
Is 7:23 It shall happen in that day, that wherever there could be a thousand vines worth a thousand *shekels of silver*, it will be for briers and thorns
Jer 32:9 So I bought the field from Hanameel, the son of my uncle who was in Anathoth, and weighed out to him the money seventeen *shekels of silver*
Hos 3:2 So I bought her for myself for fifteen *shekels of silver*, and one and one-half homers of barley

SHELTER OF THE MOST HIGH (NAS, NIV)
(See *SECRET PLACE OF THE MOST HIGH*)

SHELTER OF YOUR WINGS
Ps 61:4 I will trust in the *shelter of Your wings*

SHEOL AND ABADDON (NAS, RSV)
(See *HELL AND DESTRUCTION*)

SHEPHERD MY PEOPLE
2Sam 5:2 and the Lord said to you, 'You shall *shepherd My people* Israel, and be ruler over Israel
2Sam 7:7 In all the places where I have walked with all the children of Israel, have I ever spoken a word to anyone from the tribes of Israel, whom I commanded to *shepherd My people* Israel, saying
1Chr 11:2 and the Lord your God said to you, 'You shall *shepherd My people* Israel, and be ruler over My people Israel
1Chr 17:6 Wherever I have moved about with all Israel, have I ever spoken a word to any of the judges of Israel, whom I commanded to *shepherd My people*, saying
Matt 2:6 for out of you shall come a Ruler who will *shepherd My people* Israel

SHEPHERD OF THE SHEEP
John 10:2 But he who enters by the door is the *shepherd of the sheep*
Heb 13:20 Now may the God of peace who brought up our Lord Jesus from the dead, that great *Shepherd of the sheep*, through the blood of the everlasting covenant

SHEPHERD THE FLOCK OF GOD
1Pet 5:2 *Shepherd the flock of God* which is among you, serving as overseers, not by constraint but willingly, not for dishonest gain but eagerly

SHEPHERDS LIVING OUT IN THE FIELDS
Luke 2:8 Now there were in the same country *shepherds living out in the fields*, keeping watch over their flock by night

SHEPHERDS OF ISRAEL
Ezek 34:2 Son of man, prophesy against the *shepherds of Israel*, prophesy and say to them, 'Thus says the Lord God to the shepherds: "Woe to the *shepherds of Israel* who feed themselves

SHEPHERDS OF TEKOA (NIV, RSV)
(See *AMONG THE HERDSMEN OF TEKOA*)

SHIELD OF FAITH
Eph 6:16 above all, taking the *shield of faith* with which you will be able to quench all the fiery darts of the wicked one

SHIELD OF VICTORY (NIV)
(See *SHIELD OF YOUR SALVATION*)

SHIELD OF YOUR SALVATION
2Sam 22:36 You have also given me the *shield of Your salvation*, and Your gentleness has made me great
Ps 18:35 You have also given me the *shield of Your salvation*

SHIELDS MY HEAD (NIV)
(See *COVERED MY HEAD*)

SHIPS OF TARSHISH
Ps 48:7 as when You break the *ships of Tarshish* with an east wind
Is 2:16 upon all the *ships of Tarshish*, and upon all the beautiful sloops
Is 23:1 Wail, you *ships of Tarshish!* For it is laid waste, so that there is no house, no harbor
Is 23:14 Wail, you *ships of Tarshish!* For your strength is laid waste
Is 60:9 and the *ships of Tarshish* will come first, to bring your sons from afar, their silver and their gold with them, to the name of the Lord your God, and to the Holy One of Israel, because He has glorified you
Ezek 27:25 The *ships of Tarshish* were carriers of your merchandise. You were filled and very glorious in the midst of the seas

SHOD YOUR FEET WITH THE PREPARATION OF THE GOSPEL OF PEACE
Eph 6:15 and having *shod your feet with the preparation of the gospel of peace*

SHOUT ALOUD (NIV)
(See *SHOUT JOYFULLY*)

SHOUT JOYFULLY
Ps 95:1 Let us *shout joyfully* to the Rock of our salvation
Ps 95:2 Let us come before His presence with thanksgiving; let us *shout joyfully* to Him with psalms
Ps 98:4 *Shout joyfully* to the Lord, all the earth; break forth in song, rejoice, and sing praises
Ps 98:6 With trumpets and the sound of a horn; *shout joyfully* before the Lord, the King

SHOUT OF JOY (NIV)
(See *JOYFUL SHOUT*)

SHOW COMPASSION
Lam 3:32 Though He causes grief, yet He will *show compassion* according to the multitude of His mercies

SHOW FAVORITISM (NIV)
(See *SHOW PARTIALITY*)

SHOW FORTH ALL THY MARVELLOUS WORKS (KJV)
(See *TELL OF ALL YOUR MARVELOUS WORKS*)

SHOW GOD'S RIGHTEOUSNESS (RSV)
(See *DEMONSTRATE HIS RIGHTEOUSNESS*)

SHOW HIM NO PITY (NIV)
(See *SHALL NOT PITY*)

SHOW KINDNESS
Gen 24:12 Then he said, "O Lord God of my master Abraham, please give me success this day, and *show kindness* to my master Abraham
Gen 40:14 But remember me when it is well with you, and please *show kindness* to me
Josh 2:12 Now therefore, I beg you, swear to me by the Lord, since I have shown you kindness, that you also will *show kindness* to my father's house, and give me a true token
Judg 8:35 nor did they *show kindness* to the house of Jerubbaal (that is, Gideon
2Sam 2:6 And now may the Lord *show kindness* and truth to you
2Sam 10:2 Then David said, "I will *show kindness* to Hanun the son of Nahash, as his father showed kindness to me
1Kin 2:7 But *show kindness* to the sons of Barzillai the Gileadite, and let them be among those who eat at your table, for so they came to me when I fled from Absalom your brother
1Chr 19:2 Then David said, "I will *show kindness* to Hanun the son of Nahash, because his father showed kindness to me

SHOW ME A SIGN
Judg 6:17 Then he said to Him, "If now I have found favor in Your sight, then *show me a sign* that it is You who talk with me
Ps 86:17 *Show me a sign* for good, that those who hate me may see it and be ashamed, because You, Lord, have helped me and comforted me

SHOW ME YOUR FAITH
Jas 2:18 *Show me your faith* without your works, and I will show you my faith by my works

SHOW ME YOUR WAYS
Ps 25:4 *Show me Your ways*, O Lord; teach me Your paths

SHOW MERCY
Deut 7:2 You shall make no covenant with them nor *show mercy* to them
Ps 109:16 Because he did not remember to *show mercy*, but persecuted the poor and needy man, that he might even slay the broken in heart
Jer 50:42 they are cruel and shall not *show mercy*. Their voice shall roar like the sea
Zech 7:9 Execute true justice, *show mercy* and compassion everyone to his brother

SHOW PARTIALITY
Ex 23:3 You shall not *show partiality* to a poor man in his dispute
Deut 1:17 You shall not *show partiality* in judgment; you shall hear the small as well as the great
Deut 16:19 you shall not *show partiality*, nor take a bribe, for a bribe blinds the eyes of the wise and twists the words of the righteous
Job 13:8 Will you *show partiality* for Him? Will you contend for God
Job 13:10 He will surely reprove you if you secretly *show partiality*
Job 32:21 Let me not, I pray, *show partiality* to anyone; nor let me flatter any man
Ps 82:2 How long will you judge unjustly, and *show partiality* to the wicked
Prov 18:5 It is not good to *show partiality* to the wicked, or to overthrow the righteous in judgment

Prov 24:23 These things also belong to the wise: It is not good to *show partiality* in judgment
Prov 28:21 To *show partiality* is not good, because for a piece of bread a man will transgress
Jas 2:9 but if you *show partiality*, you commit sin, and are convicted by the law as transgressors

SHOW SIGNS
Mark 13:22 For false christs and false prophets will rise and *show signs* and wonders to deceive, if possible, even the elect

SHOW STEADFAST LOVE (RSV)
(See *SHOW KINDNESS*)

SHOW THE LORD'S DEATH (KJV)
(See *PROCLAIM THE LORD'S DEATH*)

SHOW THEM NO MERCY (NIV)
(See *SHOW MERCY*)

SHOW US THE FATHER
John 14:8 Philip said to Him, "Lord, *show us the Father*, and it is sufficient for us
John 14:9 He who has seen Me has seen the Father; so how can you say, '*Show us the Father*

SHOWERS OF BLESSING
Ezek 34:26 and I will cause showers to come down in their season; there shall be *showers of blessing*

SHOWERS RIGHTEOUSNESS ON YOU (NIV)
(See *RAINS RIGHTEOUSNESS ON YOU*)

SHOWING LOVE (NIV)
(See *SHOWING MERCY*)

SHOWING MERCY
Ex 20:6 but *showing mercy* to thousands, to those who love Me and keep My commandments
Deut 5:10 but *showing mercy* to thousands, to those who love Me and keep My commandments
Dan 4:27 break off your sins by being righteous, and your iniquities by *showing mercy* to the poor

SHOWING STEADFAST LOVE (RSV)
(See *SHOWING MERCY*)

SHOWN MERCY (NIV)
(See *OBTAIN MERCY*)

SHOWS CONTEMPT FOR THEIR MAKER (NIV)
(See *REPROACHES HIS MAKER*)

SHOWS NO PARTIALITY (RSV)
(See *THERE IS NO PARTIALITY*)

SHRIVEL UP LIKE A LEAF (NIV)
(See *FADE AS A LEAF*)

SHUN EVIL (NIV)
(See *DEPART FROM EVIL*)

SHUN THE WORSHIP OF IDOLS (RSV)
(See *FLEE FROM IDOLATRY*)

SHUT THOU UP (KJV)
(See *SEAL UP*)

SICKNESS IS NOT UNTO DEATH
John 11:4 When Jesus heard that, He said, "This *sickness is not unto death*, but for the glory of God, that the Son of God may be glorified through it

SIDE BY SIDE
Ezek 45:7 and bordering on the holy district and the city's property, extending westward on the west side and eastward on the east side, the length shall be *side by side* with one of the tribal portions, from the west border to the east border

SIDES OF THE EARTH (KJV)
(See *FARTHEST PARTS OF THE EARTH*)

SIDES OF THE NORTH
Ps 48:2 Beautiful in elevation, the joy of the whole earth, is Mount Zion on the *sides of the north*, the city of the great King
Is 14:13 I will also sit on the mount of the congregation on the farthest *sides of the north*

SIDES OF THE PIT (KJV)
(See *DEPTHS OF THE PIT*)

SIFT THE NATIONS
Is 30:28 His breath is like an overflowing stream, which reaches up to the neck, to *sift the nations* with the sieve of futility

SIGN DEEDS AND SEAL THEM
Jer 32:44 Men will buy fields for money, *sign deeds and seal them*, and take witnesses, in the land of Benjamin, in the places around Jerusalem, in the cities of Judah, in the cities of the mountains, in the cities of the lowland, and in the cities of the South

SIGN FROM HEAVEN
Matt 16:1 Then the Pharisees and Sadducees came, and testing Him asked that He would show them a *sign from heaven*
Mark 8:11 And the Pharisees came out and began to dispute with Him, seeking from Him a *sign from heaven*, testing Him
Luke 11:16 And others, testing Him, sought from Him a *sign from heaven*

SIGN OF JONAH THE PROPHET
Luke 11:29 It seeks a sign, and no sign will be given to it except the *sign of Jonah the prophet*

SIGN OF THE COVENANT
Gen 9:12 This is the *sign of the covenant* which I make between Me and you, and every living creature that is with you, for perpetual generations
Gen 9:13 I set My rainbow in the cloud, and it shall be for the *sign of the covenant* between Me and the earth
Gen 9:17 And God said to Noah, "This is the *sign of the covenant* which I have established between Me and all flesh that is on the earth
Gen 17:11 and you shall be circumcised in the flesh of your foreskins, and it shall be a *sign of the covenant* between Me and you

SIGN OF THE PROPHET JONAH
Matt 12:39 But He answered and said to them, "An evil and adulterous generation seeks after a sign, and no sign will be given to it except the *sign of the prophet Jonah*
Matt 16:4 A wicked and adulterous generation seeks after a sign, and no sign shall be given to it except the *sign of the prophet Jonah*

SIGN ON YOUR HAND
Ex 13:16 It shall be as a *sign on your hand* and as frontlets between your eyes, for by strength of hand the Lord brought us out of Egypt
Deut 6:8 You shall bind them as a *sign on your hand*, and they shall be as frontlets between your eyes
Deut 11:18 Therefore you shall lay up these words of mine in your heart and in your soul, and bind them as a *sign on your hand*, and they shall be as frontlets between your eyes

SIGN TO YOU

Ex 3:12 And this shall be a *sign to you* that I have sent you

Ex 13:9 It shall be as a *sign to you* on your hand and as a memorial between your eyes, that the Lord's law may be in your mouth

1Sam 2:34 Now this shall be a *sign to you* that will come upon your two sons, on Hophni and Phinehas

2Kin 19:29 This shall be a *sign to you:* You shall eat this year such as grows of itself, and in the second year what springs from the same

2Kin 20:9 Then Isaiah said, "This is the *sign to you* from the Lord, that the Lord will do the thing which He has spoken

Is 37:30 This shall be a *sign to you:* You shall eat this year such as grows of itself, and the second year what springs from the same

Is 38:7 And this is the *sign to you* from the Lord, that the Lord will do this thing which He has spoken

Jer 44:29 And this shall be a *sign to you,'* says the Lord

Ezek 12:11 Say, 'I am a *sign to you*. As I have done, so shall it be done to them

Ezek 24:24 Thus Ezekiel is a *sign to you;* according to all that he has done you shall do

Luke 2:12 And this will be the *sign to you:* You will find a Babe wrapped in swaddling cloths, lying in a manger

SIGNS AND WONDERS

Deut 6:22 and the Lord showed *signs and wonders* before our eyes, great and severe, against Egypt, Pharaoh, and all his household

Deut 26:8 So the Lord brought us out of Egypt with a mighty hand and with an outstretched arm, with great terror and with *signs and wonders*

Deut 34:11 in all the *signs and wonders* which the Lord sent him to do in the land of Egypt, before Pharaoh, before all his servants, and in all his land

Neh 9:10 You showed *signs and wonders* against Pharaoh, against all his servants, and against all the people of his land

Ps 135:9 He sent *signs and wonders* into the midst of you, O Egypt, upon Pharaoh and all his servants

Is 8:18 We are for *signs and wonders* in Israel from the Lord of hosts, who dwells in Mount Zion

Jer 32:20 You have set *signs and wonders* in the land of Egypt, to this day, and in Israel and among other men

Jer 32:21 You have brought Your people Israel out of the land of Egypt with *signs and wonders*, with a strong hand and an outstretched arm, and with great terror

Dan 4:2 I thought it good to declare the *signs and wonders* that the Most High God has worked for me

Dan 6:27 He delivers and rescues, and He works *signs and wonders* in heaven and on earth, Who has delivered Daniel from the power of the lions

Matt 24:24 For false christs and false prophets will arise and show great *signs and wonders*, so as to deceive, if possible, even the elect

Mark 13:22 For false christs and false prophets will rise and show *signs and wonders* to deceive, if possible, even the elect

John 4:48 Then Jesus said to him, "Unless you people see *signs and wonders*, you will by no means believe

Acts 4:30 by stretching out Your hand to heal, and that *signs and wonders* may be done through the name of Your holy Servant Jesus

Acts 5:12 And through the hands of the apostles many *signs and wonders* were done among the people

Acts 14:3 Therefore they stayed there a long time, speaking boldly in the Lord, who was bearing witness to the word of His grace, granting *signs and wonders* to be done by their hands

Rom 15:19 in mighty *signs and wonders*, by the power of the Spirit of God, so that from Jerusalem and round about to Illyricum I have fully preached the gospel of Christ

2Cor 12:12 Truly the signs of an apostle were accomplished among you with all perseverance, in *signs and wonders* and mighty deeds

Heb 2:4 God also bearing witness both with *signs and wonders*, with various miracles, and gifts of the Holy Spirit, according to His own will

SIGNS OF A TRUE APOSTLE (NAS, RSV)
(See *SIGNS OF AN APOSTLE*)

SIGNS OF AN APOSTLE

2Cor 12:12 Truly the *signs of an apostle* were accomplished among you with all perseverance, in signs and wonders and mighty deeds

SIGNS OF THE TIMES

Matt 16:3 You know how to discern the face of the sky, but you cannot discern the *signs of the times*

SILVER AND GOLD

Gen 24:35 and He has given him flocks and herds, *silver and gold*, male and female servants, and camels and donkeys

Num 22:18 Then Balaam answered and said to the servants of Balak, "Though Balak were to give me his house full of *silver and gold*, I could not go beyond the word of the Lord my God, to do less or more

Num 24:13 Though Balak were to give me his house full of *silver and gold*, I could not go beyond the word of the Lord, to do either good or bad of my own will

Deut 17:17 nor shall he greatly multiply *silver and gold* for himself

Deut 29:17 and you saw their abominations and their idols which were among them wood and stone and *silver and gold*

Josh 6:19 But all the *silver and gold*, and vessels of bronze and iron, are consecrated to the Lord

Josh 6:24 Only the *silver and gold*, and the vessels of bronze and iron, they put into the treasury of the house of the Lord

2Sam 8:11 King David dedicated these to the Lord, along with the *silver and gold* that he had dedicated from all the nations which he had subdued

1Kin 10:25 articles of *silver and gold*, garments, armor, spices, horses, and mules, at a set rate year by year

1Kin 15:15 He also brought into the house of the Lord the things which his father had dedicated, and the things which he himself had dedicated: *silver and gold* and utensils

1Kin 15:18 Then Asa took all the *silver and gold* that was left in the treasuries of the house of the Lord and the treasuries of the king's house, and delivered them into the hand of his servants

1Kin 15:19 See, I have sent you a present of *silver and gold*

2Kin 7:8 And when these lepers came to the outskirts of the camp, they went into one tent and ate and drank, and carried from it *silver and gold* and clothing, and went and hid them

2Kin 16:8 And Ahaz took the *silver and gold* that was found in the house of the Lord, and in the treasuries of the king's house, and sent it as a present to the king of Assyria

2Kin 20:13 And Hezekiah was attentive to them, and showed them all the house of his treasures the *silver and gold*, the spices and precious ointment, and all his armory all that was found among his treasures
2Kin 23:35 So Jehoiakim gave the *silver and gold* to Pharaoh; but he taxed the land to give money according to the commandment of Pharaoh; he exacted the *silver and gold* from the people of the land, from every one according to his assessment, to give it to Pharaoh Necho
1Chr 18:11 King David also dedicated these to the Lord, along with the *silver and gold* that he had brought from all these nations from Edom, from Moab, from the people of Ammon, from the Philistines, and from Amalek
2Chr 1:15 Also the king made *silver and gold* as common in Jerusalem as stones, and he made cedars as abundant as the sycamores which are in the lowland
2Chr 9:24 articles of *silver and gold*, garments, armor, spices, horses, and mules, at a set rate year by year
2Chr 15:18 He also brought into the house of God the things that his father had dedicated and that he himself had dedicated: *silver and gold* and utensils
2Chr 16:2 Then Asa brought *silver and gold* from the treasuries of the house of the Lord and of the king's house, and sent to Ben-Hadad king of Syria, who dwelt in Damascus, saying
2Chr 16:3 Here, I have sent you *silver and gold;* come, break your treaty with Baasha king of Israel, so that he will withdraw from me
2Chr 21:3 Their father gave them great gifts of *silver and gold* and precious things, with fortified cities in Judah
Ezra 1:4 And whoever remains in any place where he sojourns, let the men of his place help him with *silver and gold*, with goods and livestock, besides the freewill offerings for the house of God which is in Jerusalem
Ezra 1:6 And all those who were around them encouraged them with articles of *silver and gold*, with goods and livestock, and with precious things, besides all that was willingly offered
Ezra 7:15 and whereas you are to carry the *silver and gold* which the king and his counselors have freely offered to the God of Israel, whose dwelling is in Jerusalem
Ezra 7:16 and whereas all the *silver and gold* that you may find in all the province of Babylon, along with the freewill offering of the people and the priests, are to be freely offered for the house of their God in Jerusalem
Ps 105:37 He also brought them out with *silver and gold*, and there was none feeble among His tribes
Ps 115:4 Their idols are *silver and gold*, the work of men's hands
Ps 135:15 The idols of the nations are *silver and gold*, the work of men's hands
Prov 22:1 A good name is to be chosen rather than great riches, loving favor rather than *silver and gold*
Eccl 2:8 I also gathered for myself *silver and gold* and the special treasures of kings and of the provinces
Is 2:7 Their land is also full of *silver and gold*, and there is no end to their treasures
Is 39:2 And Hezekiah was pleased with them, and showed them the house of his treasures the *silver and gold*, the spices and precious ointment, and all his armory all that was found among his treasures
Jer 10:4 They decorate it with *silver and gold;* they fasten it with nails and hammers so that it will not topple
Ezek 38:13 Have you gathered your army to take booty, to carry away *silver and gold*, to take away livestock and goods, to take great plunder
Dan 5:23 And you have praised the gods of *silver and gold*, bronze and iron, wood and stone, which do not see or hear or know
Dan 11:8 And he shall also carry their gods captive to Egypt, with their princes and their precious articles of *silver and gold*
Hos 2:8 For she did not know that I gave her grain, new wine, and oil, and multiplied her *silver and gold* which they prepared for Baal
Hos 8:4 From their *silver and gold* they made idols for themselves that they might be cut off
Zech 6:11 Take the *silver and gold*, make an elaborate crown, and set it on the head of Joshua the son of Jehozadak, the high priest
Acts 3:6 Then Peter said, "*Silver and gold* I do not have, but what I do have I give you

SILVER REFINED IN A FURNACE (NIV, RSV)
(See *SILVER TRIED IN A FURNACE*)

SILVER TRIED IN A FURNACE
Ps 12:6 The words of the Lord are pure words, like *silver tried in a furnace* of earth, purified seven times

SIMILITUDE OF MELCHIZEDEK (KJV)
(See *LIKENESS OF MELCHIZEDEK*)

SIMPLICITY THAT IS IN CHRIST
2Cor 11:3 But I fear, lest somehow, as the serpent deceived Eve by his craftiness, so your minds may be corrupted from the *simplicity that is in Christ*

SIN AGAINST
Gen 39:9 How then can I do this great wickedness, and *sin against* God
Gen 42:22 And Reuben answered them, saying, "Did I not speak to you, saying, 'Do not *sin against* the boy
Ex 23:33 They shall not dwell in your land, lest they make you *sin against* Me
Deut 20:18 lest they teach you to do according to all their abominations which they have done for their gods, and you *sin against* the Lord your God
1Sam 12:23 Moreover, as for me, far be it from me that I should *sin against* the Lord in ceasing to pray for you
1Sam 14:34 and do not *sin against* the Lord by eating with the blood
1Sam 19:4 Now Jonathan spoke well of David to Saul his father, and said to him, "Let not the king *sin against* his servant, against David, because he has not sinned against you, and because his works have been very good toward you
1Sam 19:5 Why then will you *sin against* innocent blood, to kill David without a cause
1Kin 8:46 When they *sin against* You (for there is no one who does not sin
2Chr 6:36 When they *sin against* You (for there is no one who does not sin
Ps 119:11 Your word I have hidden in my heart, that I might not *sin against* You
Jer 51:5 For Israel is not forsaken, nor Judah, by his God, the Lord of hosts, though their land was filled with *sin against* the Holy One of Israel
Matt 18:21 Then Peter came to Him and said, "Lord, how often shall my brother *sin against* me, and I forgive him
1Cor 8:12 But when you thus *sin against* the brethren, and wound their weak conscience, you *sin against* Christ

SIN AGAINST GOD
Gen 39:9 How then can I do this great wickedness, and *sin against God*

SIN AGAINST THE LORD
Deut 20:18 lest they teach you to do according to all their abominations which they have done for their gods, and you *sin against the Lord* your God
1Sam 12:23 Moreover, as for me, far be it from me that I should *sin against the Lord* in ceasing to pray for you
1Sam 14:34 and do not *sin against the Lord* by eating with the blood

SIN ENTERED THE WORLD
Rom 5:12 Therefore, just as through one man *sin entered the world*, and death through sin, and thus death spread to all men, because all sinned

SIN HATH REIGNED UNTO DEATH (KJV)
(See *SIN REIGNED IN DEATH*)

SIN INDEED WAS IN THE WORLD (RSV)
(See *SIN WAS IN THE WORLD*)

SIN IS CROUCHING AT YOUR DOOR (NIV)
(See *SIN LIES AT THE DOOR*)

SIN IS LAWLESSNESS
1Jn 3:4 Whoever commits sin also commits lawlessness, and *sin is lawlessness*

SIN IS THE TRANSGRESSION OF THE LAW (KJV)
(See *SIN IS LAWLESSNESS*)

SIN LEADING TO DEATH
1Jn 5:16 There is *sin leading to death*. I do not say that he should pray about that

SIN LIES AT THE DOOR
Gen 4:7 And if you do not do well, *sin lies at the door*

SIN LIVING IN ME (NIV)
(See *SIN THAT DWELLS IN ME*)

SIN NOT LEADING TO DEATH
1Jn 5:16 If anyone sees his brother sinning a sin which does not lead to death, he will ask, and He will give him life for those who commit *sin not leading to death*
1Jn 5:17 All unrighteousness is sin, and there is *sin not leading to death*

SIN NOT WITH MY TONGUE (KJV)
(See *SIN WITH MY TONGUE*)

SIN OF THE FATHERS (NIV)
(See *INIQUITY OF THE FATHERS*)

SIN OF THE WORLD
John 1:29 The Lamb of God who takes away the *sin of the world*

SIN OFFERING
Ex 29:14 But the flesh of the bull, with its skin and its offal, you shall burn with fire outside the camp. It is a *sin offering*
Ex 29:36 And you shall offer a bull every day as a *sin offering* for atonement
Ex 30:10 And Aaron shall make atonement upon its horns once a year with the blood of the *sin offering* of atonement
Lev 4:3 if the anointed priest sins, bringing guilt on the people, then let him offer to the Lord for his sin which he has sinned a young bull without blemish as a *sin offering*
Lev 4:8 He shall take from it all the fat of the bull as the *sin offering*
Lev 4:20 And he shall do with the bull as he did with the bull as a *sin offering*
Lev 4:21 Then he shall carry the bull outside the camp, and burn it as he burned the first bull. It is a *sin offering* for the assembly
Lev 4:24 And he shall lay his hand on the head of the goat, and kill it at the place where they kill the burnt offering before the Lord. It is a *sin offering*
Lev 4:25 The priest shall take some of the blood of the *sin offering* with his finger, put it on the horns of the altar of burnt offering, and pour its blood at the base of the altar of burnt offering
Lev 4:29 And he shall lay his hand on the head of the *sin offering*, and kill the *sin offering* at the place of the burnt offering
Lev 4:32 If he brings a lamb as his *sin offering*, he shall bring a female without blemish
Lev 4:33 Then he shall lay his hand on the head of the *sin offering*, and kill it as a *sin offering* at the place where they kill the burnt offering
Lev 4:34 The priest shall take some of the blood of the *sin offering* with his finger, put it on the horns of the altar of burnt offering, and pour all the remaining blood at the base of the altar
Lev 5:6 and he shall bring his trespass offering to the Lord for his sin which he has committed, a female from the flock, a lamb or a kid of the goats as a *sin offering*
Lev 5:7 one as a *sin offering* and the other as a burnt offering
Lev 5:8 And he shall bring them to the priest, who shall offer that which is for the *sin offering* first, and wring off its head from its neck, but shall not divide it completely
Lev 5:9 Then he shall sprinkle some of the blood of the *sin offering* on the side of the altar, and the rest of the blood shall be drained out at the base of the altar. It is a *sin offering*
Lev 5:11 But if he is not able to bring two turtledoves or two young pigeons, then he who sinned shall bring for his offering one-tenth of an ephah of fine flour as a *sin offering*. He shall put no oil on it, nor shall he put any frankincense on it, for it is a *sin offering*
Lev 5:12 Then he shall bring it to the priest, and the priest shall take his handful of it as a memorial portion, and burn it on the altar according to the offerings made by fire to the Lord. It is a *sin offering*
Lev 6:17 it is most holy, like the *sin offering* and the trespass offering
Lev 6:25 Speak to Aaron and to his sons, saying, 'This is the law of the *sin offering:* In the place where the burnt offering is killed, the *sin offering* shall be killed before the Lord
Lev 6:30 But no *sin offering* from which any of the blood is brought into the tabernacle of meeting, to make atonement in the holy place, shall be eaten
Lev 7:7 The trespass offering is like the *sin offering;* there is one law for them both
Lev 7:37 This is the law of the burnt offering, the grain offering, the *sin offering*, the trespass offering, the consecrations, and the sacrifice of the peace offering
Lev 8:2 Take Aaron and his sons with him, and the garments, the anointing oil, a bull as the *sin offering*, two rams, and a basket of unleavened bread
Lev 8:14 And he brought the bull for the *sin offering*. Then Aaron and his sons laid their hands on the head of the bull for the *sin offering*
Lev 9:2 And he said to Aaron, "Take for yourself a young bull as a *sin offering* and a ram as a burnt offering, without blemish, and offer them before the Lord
Lev 9:3 And to the children of Israel you shall speak, saying, 'Take a kid of the goats as a *sin*

offering, and a calf and a lamb, both of the first year, without blemish, as a burnt offering

Lev 9:7 And Moses said to Aaron, "Go to the altar, offer your *sin offering* and your burnt offering, and make atonement for yourself and for the people

Lev 9:8 Aaron therefore went to the altar and killed the calf of the *sin offering*, which was for himself

Lev 9:10 But the fat, the kidneys, and the fatty lobe from the liver of the *sin offering* he burned on the altar, as the Lord had commanded Moses

Lev 9:15 Then he brought the people's offering, and took the goat, which was the *sin offering* for the people, and killed it and offered it for sin, like the first one

Lev 9:22 Then Aaron lifted his hand toward the people, blessed them, and came down from offering the *sin offering*, the burnt offering, and peace offerings

Lev 10:16 Then Moses diligently made inquiry about the goat of the *sin offering*, and there it was, burned up

Lev 10:17 Why have you not eaten the *sin offering* in a holy place, since it is most holy, and God has given it to you to bear the guilt of the congregation, to make atonement for them before the Lord

Lev 10:19 And Aaron said to Moses, "Look, this day they have offered their *sin offering* and their burnt offering before the Lord, and such things have befallen me! If I had eaten the *sin offering* today, would it have been accepted in the sight of the Lord

Lev 12:6 When the days of her purification are fulfilled, whether for a son or a daughter, she shall bring to the priest a lamb of the first year as a burnt offering, and a young pigeon or a turtledove as a *sin offering*, to the door of the tabernacle of meeting

Lev 12:8 And if she is not able to bring a lamb, then she may bring two turtledoves or two young pigeons one as a burnt offering and the other as a *sin offering*

Lev 14:13 Then he shall kill the lamb in the place where he kills the *sin offering* and the burnt offering, in a holy place; for as the *sin offering* is the priest's, so is the trespass offering

Lev 14:19 Then the priest shall offer the *sin offering*, and make atonement for him who is to be cleansed from his uncleanness

Lev 14:22 one shall be a *sin offering* and the other a burnt offering

Lev 14:31 such as he is able to afford, the one as a *sin offering* and the other as a burnt offering, with the grain offering

Lev 15:15 Then the priest shall offer them, the one as a *sin offering* and the other as a burnt offering

Lev 15:30 Then the priest shall offer the one as a *sin offering* and the other as a burnt offering, and the priest shall make atonement for her before the Lord for the discharge of her uncleanness

Lev 16:3 with the blood of a young bull as a *sin offering*, and of a ram as a burnt offering

Lev 16:5 And he shall take from the congregation of the children of Israel two kids of the goats as a *sin offering*, and one ram as a burnt offering

Lev 16:6 Aaron shall offer the bull as a *sin offering*, which is for himself, and make atonement for himself and for his house

Lev 16:9 And Aaron shall bring the goat on which the Lord's lot fell, and offer it as a *sin offering*

Lev 16:11 And Aaron shall bring the bull of the *sin offering*, which is for himself, and make atonement for himself and for his house, and shall kill the bull as the *sin offering* which is for himself

Lev 16:15 Then he shall kill the goat of the *sin offering*, which is for the people, bring its blood inside the veil, do with that blood as he did with the blood of the bull, and sprinkle it on the mercy seat and before the mercy seat

Lev 16:25 The fat of the *sin offering* he shall burn on the altar

Lev 16:27 The bull for the *sin offering* and the goat for the *sin offering*, whose blood was brought in to make atonement in the Holy Place, shall be carried outside the camp

Lev 23:19 Then you shall sacrifice one kid of the goats as a *sin offering*, and two male lambs of the first year as a sacrifice of peace offering

Num 6:11 and the priest shall offer one as a *sin offering* and the other as a burnt offering, and make atonement for him, because he sinned by reason of the dead body

Num 6:14 one male lamb in its first year without blemish as a burnt offering, one ewe lamb in its first year without blemish as a *sin offering*, one ram without blemish as a peace offering

Num 6:16 Then the priest shall bring them before the Lord and offer his *sin offering* and his burnt offering

Num 7:16 one kid of the goats as a *sin offering*

Num 7:22 one kid of the goats as a *sin offering*

Num 7:28 one kid of the goats as a *sin offering*

Num 7:34 one kid of the goats as a *sin offering*

Num 7:40 one kid of the goats as a *sin offering*

Num 7:46 one kid of the goats as a *sin offering*

Num 7:52 one kid of the goats as a *sin offering*

Num 7:58 one kid of the goats as a *sin offering*

Num 7:64 one kid of the goats as a *sin offering*

Num 7:70 one kid of the goats as a *sin offering*

Num 7:76 one kid of the goats as a *sin offering*

Num 7:82 one kid of the goats as a *sin offering*

Num 7:87 All the oxen for the burnt offering were twelve young bulls, the rams twelve, the male lambs in their first year twelve, with their grain offering, and the kids of the goats as a *sin offering* twelve

Num 8:8 Then let them take a young bull with its grain offering of fine flour mixed with oil, and you shall take another young bull as a *sin offering*

Num 8:12 Then the Levites shall lay their hands on the heads of the young bulls, and you shall offer one as a *sin offering* and the other as a burnt offering to the Lord, to make atonement for the Levites

Num 15:24 then it will be, if it is unintentionally committed, without the knowledge of the congregation, that the whole congregation shall offer one young bull as a burnt offering, as a sweet aroma to the Lord, with its grain offering and its drink offering, according to the ordinance, and one kid of the goats as a *sin offering*

Num 15:25 they shall bring their offering, an offering made by fire to the Lord, and their *sin offering* before the Lord, for their unintended sin

Num 15:27 And if a person sins unintentionally, then he shall bring a female goat in its first year as a *sin offering*

Num 18:9 every offering of theirs, every grain offering and every *sin offering* and every trespass offering which they render to Me, shall be most holy for you and your sons

Num 28:15 Also one kid of the goats as a *sin offering* to the Lord shall be offered, besides the regular burnt offering and its drink offering

Num 28:22 also one goat as a *sin offering*, to make atonement for you

Num 29:5 also one kid of the goats as a *sin offering*, to make atonement for you

Num 29:11 also one kid of the goats as a *sin offering*, besides the *sin offering* for atonement, the regular burnt offering with its grain offering, and their drink offerings

Num 29:16 also one kid of the goats as a *sin offer-*

ing, besides the regular burnt offering, its grain offering, and its drink offering
Num 29:19 also one kid of the goats as a *sin offering*, besides the regular burnt offering with its grain offering, and their drink offerings
Num 29:22 also one goat as a *sin offering*, besides the regular burnt offering, its grain offering, and its drink offering
Num 29:25 also one kid of the goats as a *sin offering*, besides the regular burnt offering, its grain offering, and its drink offering
Num 29:28 also one goat as a *sin offering*, besides the regular burnt offering, its grain offering, and its drink offering
Num 29:31 also one goat as a *sin offering*, besides the regular burnt offering, its grain offering, and its drink offering
Num 29:34 also one goat as a *sin offering*, besides the regular burnt offering, its grain offering, and its drink offering
Num 29:38 also one goat as a *sin offering*, besides the regular burnt offering, its grain offering, and its drink offering
2Chr 29:21 And they brought seven bulls, seven rams, seven lambs, and seven male goats for a *sin offering* for the kingdom, for the sanctuary, and for Judah
2Chr 29:23 Then they brought out the male goats for the *sin offering* before the king and the congregation, and they laid their hands on them
2Chr 29:24 and they presented their blood on the altar as a *sin offering* to make an atonement for all Israel, for the king commanded that the burnt offering and the *sin offering* be made for all Israel
Ezra 6:17 And they offered sacrifices at the dedication of this house of God, one hundred bulls, two hundred rams, four hundred lambs, and as a *sin offering* for all Israel twelve male goats, according to the number of the tribes of Israel
Ezra 8:35 twelve bulls for all Israel, ninety-six rams, seventy-seven lambs, and twelve male goats as a *sin offering*
Ps 40:6 my ears You have opened; burnt offering and *sin offering* You did not require
Ezek 40:39 In the vestibule of the gateway were two tables on this side and two tables on that side, on which to slay the burnt offering, the *sin offering*, and the trespass offering
Ezek 42:13 There they shall lay the most holy offerings the grain offering, the *sin offering*, and the trespass offering for the place is holy
Ezek 43:19 You shall give a young bull for a *sin offering* to the priests, the Levites, who are of the seed of Zadok, who approach Me to minister to Me
Ezek 43:21 Then you shall also take the bull of the *sin offering*, and burn it in the appointed place of the temple, outside the sanctuary
Ezek 43:22 On the second day you shall offer a kid of the goats without blemish for a *sin offering*
Ezek 43:25 Every day for seven days you shall prepare a goat for a *sin offering*
Ezek 44:27 And on the day that he goes to the sanctuary to minister in the sanctuary, he must offer his *sin offering* in the inner court
Ezek 44:29 They shall eat the grain offering, the *sin offering*, and the trespass offering
Ezek 45:17 He shall prepare the *sin offering*, the grain offering, the burnt offering, and the peace offerings to make atonement for the house of Israel
Ezek 45:19 The priest shall take some of the blood of the *sin offering* and put it on the doorposts of the temple, on the four corners of the ledge of the altar, and on the gateposts of the gate of the inner court
Ezek 45:22 And on that day the prince shall prepare for himself and for all the people of the land a bull for a *sin offering*
Ezek 45:23 On the seven days of the feast he shall prepare a burnt offering to the Lord, seven bulls and seven rams without blemish, daily for seven days, and a kid of the goats daily for a *sin offering*
Ezek 45:25 In the seventh month, on the fifteenth day of the month, at the feast, he shall do likewise for seven days, according to the *sin offering*, the burnt offering, the grain offering, and the oil
Ezek 46:20 And he said to me, "This is the place where the priests shall boil the trespass offering and the *sin offering*, and where they shall bake the grain offering, so that they do not bring them out into the outer court to sanctify the people

SIN OFFERINGS (NIV, RSV)
(See *SACRIFICES FOR SIN*)

SIN REIGNED IN DEATH
Rom 5:21 so that as *sin reigned in death*, even so grace might reign through righteousness to eternal life through Jesus Christ our Lord

SIN REVIVED
Rom 7:9 I was alive once without the law, but when the commandment came, *sin revived* and I died

SIN SPRANG TO LIFE (NIV)
(See *SIN REVIVED*)

SIN THAT DWELLS IN ME
Rom 7:17 But now, it is no longer I who do it, but *sin that dwells in me*
Rom 7:20 Now if I do what I will not to do, it is no longer I who do it, but *sin that dwells in me*

SIN THEY HAVE COMMITTED AGAINST ME (NIV)
(See *SINNED AGAINST ME*)

SIN THROUGH IGNORANCE (KJV)
(See *SINS UNINTENTIONALLY*)

SIN UNINTENTIONALLY
Num 15:22 And if you *sin unintentionally*, and do not observe all these commandments which the Lord has spoken to Moses

SIN UNTO DEATH (KJV)
(See *SIN LEADING TO DEATH*)

SIN WAS IN THE WORLD
Rom 5:13 (For until the law *sin was in the world*, but sin is not imputed when there is no law

SIN WE HAVE SO FOOLISHLY COMMITTED (NIV)
(See *WE HAVE SINNED*)

SIN WHICH DWELLS WITHIN ME (NAS, RSV)
(See *SIN THAT DWELLS IN ME*)

SIN WHICH IS MORTAL (RSV)
(See *SIN LEADING TO DEATH*)

SIN WITH MY TONGUE
Ps 39:1 I said, "I will guard my ways, lest I *sin with my tongue*

SINCE BIRTH (NIV)
(See *MY MOTHER'S WOMB*)

SINCE GOD SO LOVED US (NIV)
(See *IF GOD SO LOVED US*)

SINCE MY NAME (NAS, NIV)
(See *FOR MY NAME*)

SINCERE AND PURE DEVOTION TO CHRIST (NIV, RSV)
(See *SIMPLICITY THAT IS IN CHRIST*)

SINCERE FAITH
1Tim 1:5 Now the purpose of the commandment is love from a pure heart, from a good conscience, and from *sincere faith*

SINCERE MILK OF THE WORD (KJV)
(See *PURE MILK OF THE WORD*)

SINFUL DESIRES OF THEIR HEARTS (NIV)
(See *LUSTS OF THEIR HEARTS*)

SING A NEW SONG
Ps 144:9 I will *sing a new song* to You, O God

SING AND MAKE MELODY TO THE LORD (RSV)
(See *SING PRAISES TO THE LORD*)

SING AND MAKE MUSIC TO THE LORD (NIV)
(See *SING PRAISES TO THE LORD*)

SING FOR GLADNESS (RSV)
(See *SING FOR JOY*)

SING FOR JOY
Job 29:13 The blessing of a perishing man came upon me, and I caused the widow's heart to *sing for joy*
Ps 67:4 Oh, let the nations be glad and *sing for joy*
Is 65:14 behold, My servants shall *sing for joy* of heart, but you shall cry for sorrow of heart, and wail for grief of spirit

SING JOYFULLY TO THE LORD (NIV)
(See *REJOICE IN THE LORD*)

SING PRAISE TO YOUR NAME
Ps 9:2 I will *sing praise to Your name*, O Most High
Ps 61:8 So I will *sing praise to Your name* forever, that I may daily perform my vows

SING PRAISES TO THE LORD
Ps 9:11 *Sing praises to the Lord*, who dwells in Zion! Declare His deeds among the people
Ps 27:6 I will sing, yes, I will *sing praises to the Lord*
Ps 68:32 Sing to God, you kingdoms of the earth; oh, *sing praises to the Lord*

SING PRAISES TO YOUR NAME
2Sam 22:50 Therefore I will give thanks to You, O Lord, among the Gentiles, and *sing praises to Your name*
Ps 18:49 Therefore I will give thanks to You, O Lord, among the Gentiles, and *sing praises to Your name*
Ps 66:4 All the earth shall worship You and sing praises to You; they shall *sing praises to Your name*
Ps 92:1 It is good to give thanks to the Lord, and to *sing praises to Your name*, O Most High

SING TO THE LORD
Ex 15:1 I will *sing to the Lord*, for He has triumphed gloriously
Ex 15:21 *Sing to the Lord*, for He has triumphed gloriously! The horse and its rider He has thrown into the sea
Judg 5:3 I, even I, will *sing to the Lord;* I will sing praise to the Lord God of Israel
1Chr 16:23 *Sing to the Lord*, all the earth; proclaim the good news of His salvation from day to day
2Chr 20:21 And when he had consulted with the people, he appointed those who should *sing to the Lord*, and who should praise the beauty of holiness, as they went out before the army and were saying
Ps 13:6 I will *sing to the Lord*, because He has dealt bountifully with me
Ps 95:1 Oh come, let us *sing to the Lord!* Let us shout joyfully to the Rock of our salvation
Ps 96:1 Oh, *sing to the Lord* a new song! *Sing to the Lord*, all the earth
Ps 96:2 *Sing to the Lord*, bless His name; proclaim the good news of His salvation from day to day
Ps 98:1 Oh, *sing to the Lord* a new song! For He has done marvelous things
Ps 98:5 *Sing to the Lord* with the harp, with the harp and the sound of a psalm
Ps 104:33 I will *sing to the Lord* as long as I live
Ps 147:7 *Sing to the Lord* with thanksgiving; sing praises on the harp to our God
Ps 149:1 *Sing to the Lord* a new song, and His praise in the congregation of saints
Is 12:5 *Sing to the Lord*, for He has done excellent things
Is 42:10 *Sing to the Lord* a new song, and His praise from the ends of the earth, you who go down to the sea, and all that is in it, you coastlands and you inhabitants of them
Jer 20:13 *Sing to the Lord!* Praise the Lord! For He has delivered the life of the poor from the hand of evildoers

SINK AND NOT RISE
Jer 51:64 Then you shall say, 'Thus Babylon shall *sink and not rise* from the catastrophe that I will bring upon her

SINK TO RISE NO MORE (NIV, RSV)
(See *SINK AND NOT RISE*)

SINNED AGAINST HEAVEN
Luke 15:18 I will arise and go to my father, and will say to him, "Father, I have *sinned against heaven* and before you
Luke 15:21 And the son said to him, 'Father, I have *sinned against heaven* and in your sight, and am no longer worthy to be called your son

SINNED AGAINST ME
Ex 32:33 And the Lord said to Moses, "Whoever has *sinned against Me*, I will blot him out of My book
Jer 33:8 I will cleanse them from all their iniquity by which they have *sinned against Me*, and I will pardon all their iniquities by which they have sinned and by which they have transgressed against Me
Hos 4:7 The more they increased, the more they *sinned against Me*

SINNED AGAINST THE LORD
Ex 10:16 Then Pharaoh called for Moses and Aaron in haste, and said, "I have *sinned against the Lord* your God and against you
Num 32:23 But if you do not do so, then take note, you have *sinned against the Lord*

Deut 1:41 Then you answered and said to me, 'We have *sinned against the Lord*
Deut 9:16 And I looked, and there, you had *sinned against the Lord* your God, and had made for yourselves a molded calf
Josh 7:20 And Achan answered Joshua and said, "Indeed I have *sinned against the Lord* God of Israel, and this is what I have done
1Sam 7:6 And they fasted that day, and said there, "We have *sinned against the Lord*
2Sam 12:13 Then David said to Nathan, "I have *sinned against the Lord*
2Kin 17:7 For so it was that the children of Israel had *sinned against the Lord* their God, who had brought them up out of the land of Egypt, from under the hand of Pharaoh king of Egypt
Jer 3:25 For we have *sinned against the Lord* our God, we and our fathers, from our youth even to this day, and have not obeyed the voice of the Lord our God
Jer 8:14 For the Lord our God has put us to silence and given us water of gall to drink, because we have *sinned against the Lord*
Jer 40:3 Because you people have *sinned against the Lord*, and not obeyed His voice, therefore this thing has come upon you
Jer 44:23 Because you have burned incense and because you have *sinned against the Lord*, and have not obeyed the voice of the Lord or walked in His law, in His statutes or in His testimonies, therefore this calamity has happened to you, as at this day
Jer 50:7 and their adversaries said, 'We have not offended, because they have *sinned against the Lord*, the habitation of justice, the Lord, the hope of their fathers
Jer 50:14 shoot at her, spare no arrows, for she has *sinned against the Lord*
Zeph 1:17 I will bring distress upon men, and they shall walk like blind men, because they have *sinned against the Lord*

SINNED AGAINST YOU
Judg 10:10 And the children of Israel cried out to the Lord, saying, "We have *sinned against You*, because we have both forsaken our God and served the Baals
Judg 11:27 Therefore I have not *sinned against you*, but you wronged me by fighting against me
1Sam 19:4 Now Jonathan spoke well of David to Saul his father, and said to him, "Let not the king sin against his servant, against David, because he has not *sinned against you*, and because his works have been very good toward you
1Sam 24:11 For in that I cut off the corner of your robe, and did not kill you, know and see that there is neither evil nor rebellion in my hand, and I have not *sinned against you*
1Kin 8:33 When Your people Israel are defeated before an enemy because they have *sinned against You*, and when they turn back to You and confess Your name, and pray and make supplication to You in this temple
1Kin 8:35 When the heavens are shut up and there is no rain because they have *sinned against You*, when they pray toward this place and confess Your name, and turn from their sin because You afflict them
1Kin 8:50 and forgive Your people who have *sinned against You*, and all their transgressions which they have transgressed against You
2Chr 6:24 Or if Your people Israel are defeated before an enemy because they have *sinned against You*, and return and confess Your name, and pray and make supplication before You in this temple
2Chr 6:26 When heaven is shut up and there is no rain because they have *sinned against You*, when they pray toward this place and confess Your name, and turn from their sin because You afflict them
2Chr 6:39 then hear from heaven Your dwelling place their prayer and their supplications, and maintain their cause, and forgive Your people who have *sinned against You*
Neh 1:6 please let Your ear be attentive and Your eyes open, that You may hear the prayer of Your servant which I pray before You now, day and night, for the children of Israel Your servants, and confess the sins of the children of Israel which we have *sinned against You*
Ps 41:4 I said, "Lord, be merciful to me; heal my soul, for I have *sinned against You*
Jer 14:7 for our backslidings are many, we have *sinned against You*
Jer 14:20 We acknowledge, O Lord, our wickedness and the iniquity of our fathers, for we have *sinned against You*
Dan 9:8 O Lord, to us belongs shame of face, to our kings, our princes, and our fathers, because we have *sinned against You*

SINS AGAINST HIS OWN BODY
1Cor 6:18 Every sin that a man does is outside the body, but he who commits sexual immorality *sins against his own body*

SINS ARE LIKE SCARLET
Is 1:18 Come now, and let us reason together," says the Lord, "Though your *sins are like scarlet*, they shall be as white as snow

SINS BE AS SCARLET (KJV)
(See *SINS ARE LIKE SCARLET*)

SINS BEHIND YOUR BACK
Is 38:17 but You have lovingly delivered my soul from the pit of corruption, for You have cast all my *sins behind Your back*

SINS HAVE HIDDEN HIS FACE
Is 59:2 and your *sins have hidden His face* from you, so that He will not hear

SINS OF HIS FATHER
1Kin 15:3 And he walked in all the *sins of his father*, which he had done before him

SINS OF JEROBOAM
1Kin 14:16 And He will give Israel up because of the *sins of Jeroboam*, who sinned and who made Israel sin
1Kin 15:30 because of the *sins of Jeroboam*, which he had sinned and by which he had made Israel sin, because of his provocation with which he had provoked the Lord God of Israel to anger
1Kin 16:31 And it came to pass, as though it had been a trivial thing for him to walk in the *sins of Jeroboam* the son of Nebat, that he took as wife Jezebel the daughter of Ethbaal, king of the Sidonians
2Kin 3:3 Nevertheless he persisted in the *sins of Jeroboam* the son of Nebat, who had made Israel sin
2Kin 10:29 However Jehu did not turn away from the *sins of Jeroboam* the son of Nebat, who had made Israel sin, that is, from the golden calves that were at Bethel and Dan
2Kin 10:31 for he did not depart from the *sins of Jeroboam*, who had made Israel sin
2Kin 13:2 And he did evil in the sight of the Lord, and followed the *sins of Jeroboam* the son of Nebat, who had made Israel sin
2Kin 13:11 he did not depart from all the *sins of Jeroboam* the son of Nebat, who had made Israel sin

2Kin 14:24 he did not depart from all the *sins of Jeroboam* the son of Nebat, who had made Israel sin
2Kin 15:9 he did not depart from the *sins of Jeroboam* the son of Nebat, who had made Israel sin
2Kin 15:18 he did not depart all his days from the *sins of Jeroboam* the son of Nebat, who had made Israel sin
2Kin 15:24 he did not depart from the *sins of Jeroboam* the son of Nebat, who had made Israel sin
2Kin 15:28 he did not depart from the *sins of Jeroboam* the son of Nebat, who had made Israel sin
2Kin 17:22 For the children of Israel walked in all the *sins of Jeroboam* which he did

SINS OF MY YOUTH
Ps 25:7 Do not remember the *sins of my youth*, nor my transgressions

SINS TO BE JUDGED (NIV)
(See *WORTHY OF JUDGMENT*)

SINS UNINTENTIONALLY
Lev 4:2 If a person *sins unintentionally* against any of the commandments of the Lord in anything which ought not to be done, and does any of them
Lev 4:13 Now if the whole congregation of Israel *sins unintentionally*, and the thing is hidden from the eyes of the assembly, and they have done something against any of the commandments of the Lord in anything which should not be done, and are guilty
Lev 4:27 If anyone of the common people *sins unintentionally* by doing something against any of the commandments of the Lord in anything which ought not to be done, and is guilty
Lev 5:15 If a person commits a trespass, and *sins unintentionally* in regard to the holy things of the Lord, then he shall bring to the Lord as his trespass offering a ram without blemish from the flocks, with your valuation in shekels of silver according to the shekel of the sanctuary, as a trespass offering
Num 15:27 And if a person *sins unintentionally*, then he shall bring a female goat in its first year as a sin offering
Num 15:28 So the priest shall make atonement for the person who *sins unintentionally*, when he *sins unintentionally* before the Lord, to make atonement for him
Num 15:29 You shall have one law for him who *sins unintentionally*, both for him who is native-born among the children of Israel and for the stranger who sojourns among them

SINS WHICH HIS FATHER DID (RSV)
(See *SINS OF HIS FATHER*)

SIT AT MY RIGHT HAND
Ps 110:1 The Lord said to my Lord, "*Sit at My right hand*, till I make Your enemies Your footstool
Matt 22:44 The Lord said to my Lord, "*Sit at My right hand*, till I make Your enemies Your footstool
Mark 12:36 The Lord said to my Lord, "*Sit at My right hand*, till I make Your enemies Your footstool
Luke 20:42 Now David himself said in the Book of Psalms, 'The Lord said to my Lord, "*Sit at My right hand*
Acts 2:34 The Lord said to my Lord, "*Sit at My right hand*
Heb 1:13 *Sit at My right hand*, till I make Your enemies Your footstool

SIT IN DARKNESS
Is 42:7 To open blind eyes, to bring out prisoners from the prison, those who *sit in darkness* from the prison house
Mic 7:8 when I *sit in darkness*, the Lord will be a light to me
Luke 1:79 to give light to those who *sit in darkness* and the shadow of death, to guide our feet into the way of peace

SIT ON DAVID'S THRONE
Jer 13:13 Behold, I will fill all the inhabitants of this land even the kings who *sit on David's throne*, the priests, the prophets, and all the inhabitants of Jerusalem with drunkenness

SIT THOU ON MY RIGHT HAND (KJV)
(See *SIT AT MY RIGHT HAND*)

SITS ON THE THRONE
Deut 17:18 Also it shall be, when he *sits on the throne* of his kingdom, that he shall write for himself a copy of this law in a book, from the one before the priests, the Levites
1Kin 1:46 Also Solomon *sits on the throne* of the kingdom
Prov 20:8 A king who *sits on the throne* of judgment scatters all evil with his eyes
Jer 29:16 therefore thus says the Lord concerning the king who *sits on the throne* of David, concerning all the people who dwell in this city, and concerning your brethren who have not gone out with you into captivity
Matt 19:28 So Jesus said to them, "Assuredly I say to you, that in the regeneration, when the Son of Man *sits on the throne* of His glory, you who have followed Me will also sit on twelve thrones, judging the twelve tribes of Israel
Rev 4:9 Whenever the living creatures give glory and honor and thanks to Him who *sits on the throne*, who lives forever and ever
Rev 4:10 the twenty-four elders fall down before Him who *sits on the throne* and worship Him who lives forever and ever, and cast their crowns before the throne, saying
Rev 5:13 Blessing and honor and glory and power be to Him who *sits on the throne*, and to the Lamb, forever and ever
Rev 6:16 and said to the mountains and rocks, "Fall on us and hide us from the face of Him who *sits on the throne* and from the wrath of the Lamb
Rev 7:10 and crying out with a loud voice, saying, "Salvation belongs to our God who *sits on the throne*, and to the Lamb
Rev 7:15 And He who *sits on the throne* will dwell among them

SITTING AT THE RIGHT HAND
Matt 26:64 Nevertheless, I say to you, hereafter you will see the Son of Man *sitting at the right hand* of the Power, and coming on the clouds of heaven
Mark 14:62 And you will see the Son of Man *sitting at the right hand* of the Power, and coming with the clouds of heaven
Col 3:1 If then you were raised with Christ, seek those things which are above, where Christ is, *sitting at the right hand* of God

SITTING ON A DONKEY
Matt 21:5 Tell the daughter of Zion, 'Behold, your King is coming to you, lowly, and *sitting on a donkey*, a colt, the foal of a donkey

SITTING UNDER AN OAK
1Kin 13:14 and went after the man of God, and found him *sitting under an oak*

SITTING UPON AN ASS (KJV)
(See *SITTING ON A DONKEY*)

SIX DAYS
Ex 16:26 *Six days* you shall gather it, but on the seventh day, which is the Sabbath, there will be none
Ex 20:9 *Six days* you shall labor and do all your work
Ex 20:11 For in *six days* the Lord made the heavens and the earth, the sea, and all that is in them, and rested the seventh day
Ex 23:12 *Six days* you shall do your work, and on the seventh day you shall rest, that your ox and your donkey may rest, and the son of your female servant and the stranger may be refreshed
Ex 24:16 Now the glory of the Lord rested on Mount Sinai, and the cloud covered it *six days*
Ex 31:15 Work shall be done for *six days*, but the seventh is the Sabbath of rest, holy to the Lord
Ex 31:17 for in *six days* the Lord made the heavens and the earth, and on the seventh day He rested and was refreshed
Ex 34:21 *Six days* you shall work, but on the seventh day you shall rest
Ex 35:2 Work shall be done for *six days*, but the seventh day shall be a holy day for you, a Sabbath of rest to the Lord
Lev 23:3 *Six days* shall work be done, but the seventh day is a Sabbath of solemn rest, a holy convocation
Deut 5:13 *Six days* you shall labor and do all your work
Deut 16:8 *Six days* you shall eat unleavened bread, and on the seventh day there shall be a sacred assembly to the Lord your God
Josh 6:3 you shall go all around the city once. This you shall do *six days*
Josh 6:14 And the second day they marched around the city once and returned to the camp. So they did *six days*
Matt 17:1 Now after *six days* Jesus took Peter, James, and John his brother, brought them up on a high mountain by themselves
Mark 9:2 Now after *six days* Jesus took Peter, James, and John, and led them up on a high mountain apart by themselves
Luke 13:14 and he said to the crowd, "There are *six days* on which men ought to work
John 12:1 Then, *six days* before the Passover, Jesus came to Bethany, where Lazarus was who had been dead, whom He had raised from the dead

SIXTH HOUR
Matt 27:45 Now from the *sixth hour* until the ninth hour there was darkness over all the land
Mark 15:33 Now when the *sixth hour* had come, there was darkness over the whole land until the ninth hour
Luke 23:44 And it was about the *sixth hour*, and there was darkness over all the earth until the ninth hour
John 4:6 Jesus therefore, being wearied from His journey, sat thus by the well. It was about the *sixth hour*
John 19:14 Now it was the Preparation Day of the Passover, and about the *sixth hour*
Acts 10:9 The next day, as they went on their journey and drew near the city, Peter went up on the housetop to pray, about the *sixth hour*

SKIES BECAME FAIR (NIV)
(See *ADORNED THE HEAVENS*)

SKILLFUL PLAYER ON THE HARP
1Sam 16:16 Let our master now command your servants, who are before you, to seek out a man who is a *skillful player on the harp*

SKIN FOR SKIN
Job 2:4 So Satan answered the Lord and said, *"Skin for skin*

SKIN OF MY TEETH
Job 19:20 My bone clings to my skin and to my flesh, and I have escaped by the *skin of my teeth*

SLAVE OF SIN
John 8:34 Jesus answered them, "Most assuredly, I say to you, whoever commits sin is a *slave of sin*

SLAVE OR FREE (NIV)
(See *BOND AND FREE*)

SLAVE WOMAN'S SON (NIV)
(See *SON OF THE BONDWOMAN*)

SLAVES OF CHRIST (NAS, NIV)
(See *SERVANTS OF CHRIST*)

SLAVES OF GOD
Rom 6:22 But now having been set free from sin, and having become *slaves of God*, you have your fruit to holiness, and the end, everlasting life

SLAVES OF RIGHTEOUSNESS
Rom 6:18 And having been set free from sin, you became *slaves of righteousness*
Rom 6:19 For just as you presented your members as slaves of uncleanness, and of lawlessness leading to more lawlessness, so now present your members as *slaves of righteousness* for holiness

SLAVES OF SIN
Rom 6:6 knowing this, that our old man was crucified with Him, that the body of sin might be done away with, that we should no longer be *slaves of sin*
Rom 6:17 But God be thanked that though you were *slaves of sin*, yet you obeyed from the heart that form of doctrine to which you were delivered
Rom 6:20 For when you were *slaves of sin*, you were free in regard to righteousness

SLAYING THE CHILDREN IN THE VALLEYS
Is 57:5 inflaming yourselves with gods under every green tree, *slaying the children in the valleys*, under the clefts of the rocks

SLEEP IN THE DUST (KJV)
(See *LIE DOWN IN THE DUST*)

SLEEP OF A LABORING MAN
Eccl 5:12 The *sleep of a laboring man* is sweet, whether he eats little or much

SLEPT WITH HIS FATHERS (KJV, NAS, RSV)
(See *RESTED WITH HIS FATHERS*)

SLOTHFUL MAN
Prov 12:27 The *slothful man* does not roast what he took in hunting, but diligence is man's precious possession
Prov 15:19 The way of the *slothful man* is like a hedge of thorns, but the way of the upright is a highway
Prov 19:24 A *slothful man* buries his hand in the bowl, and will not so much as bring it to his mouth again
Prov 22:13 The *slothful man* says, "There is a lion outside! I shall be slain in the streets
Prov 26:13 The *slothful man* says, "There is a lion in the road
Prov 26:15 The *slothful man* buries his hand in the bowl; it wearies him to bring it back to his mouth

SLOW OF SPEECH
Ex 4:10 but I am *slow of speech* and slow of tongue

SLOW TO ANGER
Neh 9:17 But You are God, ready to pardon, gracious and merciful, *slow to anger*, abundant in kindness, and did not forsake them
Ps 103:8 The Lord is merciful and gracious, *slow to anger*, and abounding in mercy
Ps 145:8 The Lord is gracious and full of compassion, *slow to anger* and great in mercy
Prov 15:18 A wrathful man stirs up strife, but he who is *slow to anger* allays contention
Prov 16:32 He who is *slow to anger* is better than the mighty, and he who rules his spirit than he who takes a city
Prov 19:11 The discretion of a man makes him *slow to anger*, and it is to his glory to overlook a transgression
Joel 2:13 return to the Lord your God, for He is gracious and merciful, *slow to anger*, and of great kindness
Jon 4:2 for I know that You are a gracious and merciful God, *slow to anger* and abundant in lovingkindness, One who relents from doing harm
Nah 1:3 the Lord is *slow to anger* and great in power, and will not at all acquit the wicked

SLOW TO LEARN (NIV)
(See *DULL OF HEARING*)

SLUMBER OR SLEEP
Is 5:27 No one will be weary or stumble among them, no one will *slumber or sleep*

SMALL AND GREAT
Gen 19:11 And they struck the men who were at the doorway of the house with blindness, both *small and great*, so that they became weary trying to find the door
1Sam 5:9 and He struck the men of the city, both *small and great*, and tumors broke out on them
2Kin 23:2 And the king went up to the house of the Lord with all the men of Judah, and with him all the inhabitants of Jerusalem the priests and the prophets and all the people, both *small and great*
2Kin 25:26 And all the people, *small and great*, and the captains of the armies, arose and went to Egypt
Job 3:19 The *small and great* are there, and the servant is free from his master
Ps 104:25 This great and wide sea, in which are innumerable teeming things, living things both *small and great*
Ps 115:13 He will bless those who fear the Lord, both *small and great*
Acts 26:22 Therefore, having obtained help from God, to this day I stand, witnessing both to *small and great*, saying no other things than those which the prophets and Moses said would come
Rev 11:18 The nations were angry, and Your wrath has come, and the time of the dead, that they should be judged, and that You should reward Your servants the prophets and the saints, and those who fear Your name, *small and great*, and should destroy those who destroy the earth
Rev 13:16 And he causes all, both *small and great*, rich and poor, free and slave, to receive a mark on their right hand or on their foreheads
Rev 19:5 Then a voice came from the throne, saying, "Praise our God, all you His servants and those who fear Him, both *small and great*
Rev 19:18 that you may eat the flesh of kings, the flesh of captains, the flesh of mighty men, the flesh of horses and of those who sit on them, and the flesh of all people, free and slave, both *small and great*
Rev 20:12 And I saw the dead, *small and great*, standing before God, and books were opened

SMALL IS THE GATE (NIV)
(See *NARROW IS THE GATE*)

SMASHED THE SACRED STONES (NIV)
(See *BROKE DOWN THE SACRED PILLARS*)

SMITE THE EARTH WITH A CURSE (KJV)
(See *STRIKE THE EARTH WITH A CURSE*)

SMITE WITH THE SWORD (KJV)
(See *STRIKE WITH THE SWORD*)

SMOKE OF A FURNACE
Gen 19:28 and he saw, and behold, the smoke of the land which went up like the *smoke of a furnace*
Ex 19:18 Its smoke ascended like the *smoke of a furnace*, and the whole mountain quaked greatly

SMOKE OF A KILN (RSV)
(See *SMOKE OF A FURNACE*)

SMOKING FLAX
Is 42:3 A bruised reed He will not break, and *smoking flax* He will not quench
Matt 12:20 A bruised reed He will not break, and *smoking flax* He will not quench, till He sends forth justice to victory

SMOLDERING WICK (NAS, NIV)
(See *SMOKING FLAX*)

SMOTE THE ROCK (KJV)
(See *STRUCK THE ROCK*)

SNARE OF A FOWLER (KJV)
(See *FOWLER'S SNARE*)

SNARE OF THE DEVIL
1Tim 3:7 Moreover he must have a good testimony among those who are outside, lest he fall into reproach and the *snare of the devil*
2Tim 2:26 and that they may come to their senses and escape the *snare of the devil*, having been taken captive by him to do his will

SNARE TO YOU
Ex 23:33 For if you serve their gods, it will surely be a *snare to you*
Deut 7:16 nor shall you serve their gods, for that will be a *snare to you*
Judg 2:3 but they shall be thorns in your side, and their gods shall be a *snare to you*

SNARES OF DEATH
2Sam 22:6 the sorrows of Sheol surrounded me, the *snares of death* confronted me
Ps 18:5 The sorrows of Sheol surrounded me; the *snares of death* confronted me
Prov 13:14 The law of the wise is a fountain of life, to turn one away from the *snares of death*
Prov 14:27 The fear of the Lord is a fountain of life, to avoid the *snares of death*

SNATCH THEM OUT OF MY HAND
John 10:28 And I give them eternal life, and they shall never perish; neither shall anyone *snatch them out of My hand*

SO GREAT A SALVATION
Heb 2:3 how shall we escape if we neglect *so great a salvation*, which at the first began to be spoken by the Lord, and was confirmed to us by those who heard Him

SO THE PLACE WAS NAMED (NIV)
(See *NAME OF THAT PLACE WAS CALLED*)

SOAKED WITH BLOOD
Is 34:7 their land shall be *soaked with blood*, and their dust saturated with fatness

SODOM AND GOMORRAH
Gen 13:10 And Lot lifted his eyes and saw all the plain of Jordan, that it was well watered everywhere (before the Lord destroyed *Sodom and Gomorrah*
Gen 14:10 and the kings of *Sodom and Gomorrah* fled; some fell there, and the remainder fled to the mountains
Gen 14:11 Then they took all the goods of *Sodom and Gomorrah*, and all their provisions, and went their way
Gen 18:20 And the Lord said, "Because the outcry against *Sodom and Gomorrah* is great, and because their sin is very grave
Gen 19:24 Then the Lord rained brimstone and fire on *Sodom and Gomorrah*, from the Lord out of the heavens
Gen 19:28 Then he looked toward *Sodom and Gomorrah*, and toward all the land of the plain
Deut 29:23 it is not sown, nor does it bear, nor does any grass grow there, like the overthrow of *Sodom and Gomorrah*, Admah, and Zeboim, which the Lord overthrew in His anger and His wrath
Is 13:19 And Babylon, the glory of kingdoms, the beauty of the Chaldeans' pride, will be as when God overthrew *Sodom and Gomorrah*
Jer 49:18 As in the overthrow of *Sodom and Gomorrah* and their neighboring cities
Jer 50:40 As God overthrew *Sodom and Gomorrah* and their neighboring cities
Amos 4:11 I overthrew some of you, as God overthrew *Sodom and Gomorrah*, and you were like a firebrand plucked from the burning
Matt 10:15 Assuredly, I say to you, it will be more tolerable for the land of *Sodom and Gomorrah* in the day of judgment than for that city
Mark 6:11 Assuredly, I say to you, it will be more tolerable for *Sodom and Gomorrah* in the day of judgment than for that city
2Pet 2:6 and turning the cities of *Sodom and Gomorrah* into ashes, condemned them to destruction, making them an example to those who afterward would live ungodly
Jude 7 as *Sodom and Gomorrah*, and the cities around them in a similar manner to these, having given themselves over to sexual immorality and gone after strange flesh, are set forth as an example, suffering the vengeance of eternal fire

SOFT ANSWER
Prov 15:1 A *soft answer* turns away wrath, but a harsh word stirs up anger

SOJOURNER IN A FOREIGN LAND (NAS, RSV)
(See *STRANGER IN A FOREIGN LAND*)

SOLD HIS BIRTHRIGHT
Gen 25:33 So he swore to him, and *sold his birthright* to Jacob
Heb 12:16 lest there be any fornicator or profane person like Esau, who for one morsel of food *sold his birthright*

SOLD THEIR POSSESSIONS
Acts 2:45 and *sold their possessions* and goods, and divided them among all, as anyone had need

SOLD THEM INTO THE HANDS OF THEIR ENEMIES
Judg 2:14 and He *sold them into the hands of their enemies* all around, so that they could no longer stand before their enemies

SOLDIER OF JESUS CHRIST
2Tim 2:3 You therefore must endure hardship as a good *soldier of Jesus Christ*

SOLDIERS WHO HAD GONE INTO BATTLE (NIV)
(See *MEN OF WAR*)

SOLEMN ASSEMBLY (KJV, NAS, RSV)
(See *SACRED ASSEMBLY*)

SOLEMN OATH (NIV)
(See *SWORE AN OATH TO*)

SOLEMN REST (RSV)
(See *SABBATH REST*)

SOLES OF HIS FEET
1Kin 5:3 You know how my father David could not build a house for the name of the Lord his God because of the wars which were fought against him on every side, until the Lord put his foes under the *soles of his feet*

SOLES OF YOUR FEET
Is 60:14 Also the sons of those who afflicted you shall come bowing to you, and all those who despised you shall fall prostrate at the *soles of your feet*
Mal 4:3 You shall trample the wicked, for they shall be ashes under the *soles of your feet* on the day that I do this

SOLITARY PLACE (NIV)
(See *DESERTED PLACE*)

SOLOMON'S WISDOM (NIV)
(See *WISDOM OF SOLOMON*)

SOMEONE WHO CAN PLAY THE HARP (NIV)
(See *SKILLFUL PLAYER ON THE HARP*)

SON MAKES YOU FREE
John 8:36 Therefore if the *Son makes you free*, you shall be free indeed

SON OF A PROPHET
Amos 7:14 I was no prophet, nor was I a *son of a prophet*, but I was a herdsman and a tender of sycamore fruit

SON OF DAVID
2Sam 13:1 Now after this it was so that Absalom the *son of David* had a lovely sister, whose name was Tamar; and Amnon the *son of David* loved her
1Chr 29:22 And they made Solomon the *son of David* king the second time, and anointed him before the Lord to be the leader, and Zadok to be priest
2Chr 1:1 Now Solomon the *son of David* was strengthened in his kingdom, and the Lord his God was with him and exalted him exceedingly
2Chr 11:18 Then Rehoboam took for himself as wife Mahalath the daughter of Jerimoth the *son of David*, and of Abihail the daughter of Eliah the son of Jesse
2Chr 13:6 Yet Jeroboam the son of Nebat, the servant of Solomon the *son of David*, rose up and rebelled against his lord
2Chr 30:26 So there was great joy in Jerusalem, for since the time of Solomon the *son of David*,

king of Israel, there had been nothing like this in Jerusalem
2Chr 35:3 Put the holy ark in the house which Solomon the *son of David*, king of Israel, built
Prov 1:1 The proverbs of Solomon the *son of David*, king of Israel
Eccl 1:1 The words of the Preacher, the *son of David*, king in Jerusalem
Matt 1:1 The book of the genealogy of Jesus Christ, the *Son of David*, the Son of Abraham
Matt 1:20 But while he thought about these things, behold, an angel of the Lord appeared to him in a dream, saying, "Joseph, *son of David*, do not be afraid to take to you Mary your wife, for that which is conceived in her is of the Holy Spirit
Matt 9:27 When Jesus departed from there, two blind men followed Him, crying out and saying, "*Son of David*, have mercy on us
Matt 12:23 And all the multitudes were amazed and said, "Could this be the *Son of David*
Matt 15:22 And behold, a woman of Canaan came from that region and cried out to Him, saying, "Have mercy on me, O Lord, *Son of David*
Matt 20:30 And behold, two blind men sitting by the road, when they heard that Jesus was passing by, cried out, saying, "Have mercy on us, O Lord, *Son of David*
Matt 20:31 but they cried out all the more, saying, "Have mercy on us, O Lord, *Son of David*
Matt 21:9 Hosanna to the *Son of David!* 'Blessed is He who comes in the name of the Lord
Matt 21:15 But when the chief priests and scribes saw the wonderful things that He did, and the children crying out in the temple and saying, "Hosanna to the *Son of David*
Matt 22:42 Whose Son is He?" They said to Him, "The *Son of David*
Mark 10:47 And when he heard that it was Jesus of Nazareth, he began to cry out and say, "Jesus, *Son of David*, have mercy on me
Mark 10:48 but he cried out all the more, "*Son of David*, have mercy on me
Mark 12:35 Then Jesus answered and said, while He taught in the temple, "How is it that the scribes say that the Christ is the *Son of David*
Luke 3:31 the son of Melea, the son of Menan, the son of Mattathah, the son of Nathan, the *son of David*
Luke 18:38 And he cried out, saying, "Jesus, *Son of David*, have mercy on me
Luke 18:39 but he cried out all the more, "*Son of David*, have mercy on me

SON OF GOD
Dan 3:25 and they are not hurt, and the form of the fourth is like the *Son of God*
Matt 4:3 Now when the tempter came to Him, he said, "If You are the *Son of God*, command that these stones become bread
Matt 4:6 and said to Him, "If You are the *Son of God*, throw Yourself down
Matt 8:29 And suddenly they cried out, saying, "What have we to do with You, Jesus, You *Son of God*
Matt 14:33 Then those who were in the boat came and worshiped Him, saying, "Truly You are the *Son of God*
Matt 26:63 And the high priest answered and said to Him, "I adjure You by the living God that You tell us if You are the Christ, the *Son of God*
Matt 27:40 If You are the *Son of God*, come down from the cross
Matt 27:43 let Him deliver Him now if He will have Him; for He said, 'I am the *Son of God*
Matt 27:54 Now when the centurion and those with him, who were guarding Jesus, saw the earthquake and the things that had happened, they feared greatly, saying, "Truly this was the *Son of God*
Mark 1:1 The beginning of the gospel of Jesus Christ, the *Son of God*
Mark 3:11 And the unclean spirits, whenever they saw Him, fell down before Him and cried out, saying, "You are the *Son of God*
Mark 15:39 Now when the centurion, who stood opposite Him, saw that He cried out like this and breathed His last, he said, "Truly this Man was the *Son of God*
Luke 1:35 therefore, also, that Holy One who is to be born will be called the *Son of God*
Luke 3:38 the son of Enos, the son of Seth, the son of Adam, the *son of God*
Luke 4:3 And the devil said to Him, "If You are the *Son of God*, command this stone to become bread
Luke 4:9 Then he brought Him to Jerusalem, set Him on the pinnacle of the temple, and said to Him, "If You are the *Son of God*, throw Yourself down from here
Luke 4:41 And demons also came out of many, crying out and saying, "You are the Christ, the *Son of God*
Luke 22:70 Then they all said, "Are You then the *Son of God*
John 1:34 And I have seen and testified that this is the *Son of God*
John 1:49 Nathanael answered and said to Him, "Rabbi, You are the *Son of God*
John 3:18 but he who does not believe is condemned already, because he has not believed in the name of the only begotten *Son of God*
John 5:25 Most assuredly, I say to you, the hour is coming, and now is, when the dead will hear the voice of the *Son of God*
John 9:35 and when He had found him, He said to him, "Do you believe in the *Son of God*
John 10:36 do you say of Him whom the Father sanctified and sent into the world, 'You are blaspheming,' because I said, 'I am the *Son of God*
John 11:4 When Jesus heard that, He said, "This sickness is not unto death, but for the glory of God, that the *Son of God* may be glorified through it
John 11:27 She said to Him, "Yes, Lord, I believe that You are the Christ, the *Son of God*, who is to come into the world
John 19:7 The Jews answered him, "We have a law, and according to our law He ought to die, because He made Himself the *Son of God*
John 20:31 but these are written that you may believe that Jesus is the Christ, the *Son of God*, and that believing you may have life in His name
Acts 8:37 And he answered and said, "I believe that Jesus Christ is the *Son of God*
Acts 9:20 Immediately he preached the Christ in the synagogues, that He is the *Son of God*
Rom 1:4 and declared to be the *Son of God* with power, according to the Spirit of holiness, by the resurrection from the dead
2Cor 1:19 For the *Son of God*, Jesus Christ, who was preached among you by us by me, Silvanus, and Timothy was not Yes and No, but in Him was Yes
Gal 2:20 and the life which I now live in the flesh I live by faith in the *Son of God*, who loved me and gave Himself for me
Eph 4:13 till we all come to the unity of the faith and the knowledge of the *Son of God*, to a perfect man, to the measure of the stature of the fullness of Christ
Heb 4:14 Seeing then that we have a great High Priest who has passed through the heavens, Jesus the *Son of God*, let us hold fast our confession
Heb 6:6 if they fall away, to renew them again to repentance, since they crucify again for them-

selves the *Son of God*, and put Him to an open shame
Heb 7:3 without father, without mother, without genealogy, having neither beginning of days nor end of life, but made like the *Son of God*, remains a priest continually
Heb 10:29 Of how much worse punishment, do you suppose, will he be thought worthy who has trampled the *Son of God* underfoot, counted the blood of the covenant by which he was sanctified a common thing, and insulted the Spirit of grace
1Jn 3:8 For this purpose the *Son of God* was manifested, that He might destroy the works of the devil
1Jn 4:15 Whoever confesses that Jesus is the *Son of God*, God abides in him, and he in God
1Jn 5:5 Who is he who overcomes the world, but he who believes that Jesus is the *Son of God*
1Jn 5:10 He who believes in the *Son of God* has the witness in himself
1Jn 5:12 he who does not have the *Son of God* does not have life
1Jn 5:13 These things I have written to you who believe in the name of the *Son of God*, that you may know that you have eternal life, and that you may continue to believe in the name of the *Son of God*
1Jn 5:20 And we know that the *Son of God* has come and has given us an understanding, that we may know Him who is true
Rev 2:18 And to the angel of the church in Thyatira write, 'These things says the *Son of God*, who has eyes like a flame of fire, and His feet like fine brass

SON OF MAN

Num 23:19 God is not a man, that He should lie, nor a *son of man*, that He should repent
Job 25:6 how much less man, who is a maggot, and a *son of man*, who is a worm
Job 35:8 Your wickedness affects a man such as you, and your righteousness a *son of man*
Ps 8:4 What is man that You are mindful of him, and the *son of man* that You visit him
Ps 80:17 Let Your hand be upon the man of Your right hand, upon the *son of man* whom You made strong for Yourself
Ps 144:3 Or the *son of man*, that You are mindful of him
Ps 146:3 Do not put your trust in princes, nor in a *son of man*, in whom there is no help
Is 56:2 Blessed is the man who does this, and the *son of man* who lays hold on it
Jer 49:18 As in the overthrow of Sodom and Gomorrah and their neighboring cities," says the Lord, "No one shall abide there, nor shall a *son of man* dwell in it
Jer 49:33 no one shall reside there, nor *son of man* dwell in it
Jer 50:40 As God overthrew Sodom and Gomorrah and their neighboring cities," says the Lord, "So no one shall reside there, nor *son of man* dwell in it
Jer 51:43 Her cities are a desolation, a dry land and a wilderness, a land where no one dwells, through which no *son of man* passes
Ezek 2:1 And He said to me, *"Son of man*, stand on your feet, and I will speak to you
Ezek 2:3 *Son of man*, I am sending you to the children of Israel, to a rebellious nation that has rebelled against Me
Ezek 2:6 And you, *son of man*, do not be afraid of them nor be afraid of their words, though briers and thorns are with you and you dwell among scorpions
Ezek 2:8 But you, *son of man*, hear what I say to you
Ezek 3:1 Moreover He said to me, *"Son of man*, eat what you find
Ezek 3:3 And He said to me, *"Son of man*, feed your belly, and fill your stomach with this scroll that I give you
Ezek 3:4 *Son of man*, go to the house of Israel and speak with My words to them
Ezek 3:10 *Son of man*, receive into your heart all My words that I speak to you, and hear with your ears
Ezek 3:17 *Son of man*, I have made you a watchman for the house of Israel
Ezek 3:25 And you, O *son of man*, surely they will put ropes on you and bind you with them, so that you cannot go out among them
Ezek 4:1 You also, *son of man*, take a clay tablet and lay it before you, and portray on it a city, Jerusalem
Ezek 4:16 Moreover He said to me, *"Son of man*, surely I will cut off the supply of bread in Jerusalem
Ezek 5:1 And you, *son of man*, take a sharp sword, take it as a barber's razor, and pass it over your head and your beard
Ezek 6:2 *Son of man*, set your face toward the mountains of Israel, and prophesy against them
Ezek 7:2 And you, *son of man*, thus says th- Lord God to the land of Israel
Ezek 8:5 Then He said to me, *"Son of man*, lift your eyes now toward the north
Ezek 8:6 Furthermore He said to me, *"Son of man*, do you see what they are doing, the great abominations that the house of Israel commits here, to make Me go far away from My sanctuary
Ezek 8:8 Then He said to me, *"Son of man*, dig into the wall
Ezek 8:12 Then He said to me, *"Son of man*, have you seen what the elders of the house of Israel do in the dark, every man in the room of his idols
Ezek 8:15 Then He said to me, "Have you seen this, O *son of man*
Ezek 8:17 Then He said to me, "Have you seen this, O *son of man*
Ezek 11:2 *Son of man*, these are the men who devise iniquity and give wicked counsel in this city
Ezek 11:4 Therefore prophesy against them, prophesy, O *son of man*
Ezek 11:15 *Son of man*, your brethren, your relatives, your kinsmen, and all the house of Israel in its entirety, are those about whom the inhabitants of Jerusalem have said
Ezek 12:2 *Son of man*, you dwell in the midst of a rebellious house, which has eyes to see but does not see, and ears to hear but does not hear
Ezek 12:3 Therefore, *son of man*, prepare your belongings for captivity, and go into captivity by day in their sight
Ezek 12:9 *Son of man*, has not the house of Israel, the rebellious house, said to you
Ezek 12:18 *Son of man*, eat your bread with quaking, and drink your water with trembling and anxiety
Ezek 12:22 *Son of man*, what is this proverb that you people have about the land of Israel, which says
Ezek 12:27 *Son of man*, look, the house of Israel is saying
Ezek 13:2 *Son of man*, prophesy against the prophets of Israel who prophesy, and say to those who prophesy out of their own heart
Ezek 13:17 Likewise, *son of man*, set your face against the daughters of your people, who prophesy out of their own heart
Ezek 14:3 *Son of man*, these men have set up their idols in their hearts, and put before them that which causes them to stumble into iniquity
Ezek 14:13 *Son of man*, when a land sins against

Me by persistent unfaithfulness, I will stretch out My hand against it
Ezek 15:2 *Son of man*, how is the wood of the vine better than any other wood, the vine branch which is among the trees of the forest
Ezek 16:2 *Son of man*, cause Jerusalem to know her abominations
Ezek 17:2 *Son of man*, pose a riddle, and speak a parable to the house of Israel
Ezek 20:3 *Son of man*, speak to the elders of Israel, and say to them
Ezek 20:4 Will you judge them, *son of man*, will you judge them
Ezek 20:27 Therefore, *son of man*, speak to the house of Israel, and say to them
Ezek 20:46 *Son of man*, set your face toward the south; preach against the south and prophesy against the forest land, the South
Ezek 21:2 *Son of man*, set your face toward Jerusalem, preach against the holy places, and prophesy against the land of Israel
Ezek 21:6 Sigh therefore, *son of man*, with a breaking heart, and sigh with bitterness before their eyes
Ezek 21:9 *Son of man*, prophesy and say, 'Thus says the Lord
Ezek 21:12 Cry and wail, *son of man;* for it will be against My people, against all the princes of Israel
Ezek 21:14 You therefore, *son of man*, prophesy, and strike your hands together
Ezek 21:19 And *son of man*, appoint for yourself two ways for the sword of the king of Babylon to go
Ezek 21:28 And you, *son of man*, prophesy and say, 'Thus says the Lord God concerning the Ammonites and concerning their reproach
Ezek 22:2 Now, *son of man*, will you judge, will you judge the bloody city
Ezek 22:18 *Son of man*, the house of Israel has become dross to Me
Ezek 22:24 *Son of man*, say to her: 'You are a land that is not cleansed or rained on in the day of indignation
Ezek 23:2 *Son of man*, there were two women, the daughters of one mother
Ezek 23:36 *Son of man*, will you judge Oholah and Oholibah? Then declare to them their abominations
Ezek 24:2 *Son of man*, write down the name of the day, this very day the king of Babylon started his siege against Jerusalem this very day
Ezek 24:16 *Son of man*, behold, I take away from you the desire of your eyes with one stroke
Ezek 24:25 And you, *son of man* will it not be in the day when I take from them their stronghold, their joy and their glory, the desire of their eyes, and that on which they set their minds, their sons and their daughters
Ezek 25:2 *Son of man*, set your face against the Ammonites, and prophesy against them
Ezek 26:2 *Son of man*, because Tyre has said against Jerusalem, 'Aha
Ezek 27:2 Now, *son of man*, take up a lamentation for Tyre
Ezek 28:2 *Son of man*, say to the prince of Tyre, 'Thus says the Lord God
Ezek 28:12 *Son of man*, take up a lamentation for the king of Tyre, and say to him
Ezek 28:21 *Son of man*, set your face toward Sidon, and prophesy against her
Ezek 29:2 *Son of man*, set your face against Pharaoh king of Egypt, and prophesy against him, and against all Egypt
Ezek 29:18 *Son of man*, Nebuchadnezzar king of Babylon caused his army to labor strenuously against Tyre
Ezek 30:2 *Son of man*, prophesy and say, 'Thus says the Lord God
Ezek 30:21 *Son of man*, I have broken the arm of Pharaoh king of Egypt
Ezek 31:2 *Son of man*, say to Pharaoh king of Egypt and to his multitude
Ezek 32:2 *Son of man*, take up a lamentation for Pharaoh king of Egypt, and say to him
Ezek 32:18 *Son of man*, wail over the multitude of Egypt, and cast them down to the depths of the earth, her and the daughters of the famous nations, with those who go down to the Pit
Ezek 33:2 *Son of man*, speak to the children of your people, and say to them
Ezek 33:7 So you, *son of man:* I have made you a watchman for the house of Israel
Ezek 33:10 Therefore you, O *son of man*, say to the house of Israel
Ezek 33:12 Therefore you, O *son of man*, say to the children of your people
Ezek 33:24 *Son of man*, they who inhabit those ruins in the land of Israel are saying
Ezek 33:30 As for you, *son of man*, the children of your people are talking about you beside the walls and in the doors of the houses
Ezek 34:2 *Son of man*, prophesy against the shepherds of Israel, prophesy and say to them
Ezek 35:2 *Son of man*, set your face against Mount Seir and prophesy against it
Ezek 36:1 And you, *son of man*, prophesy to the mountains of Israel, and say
Ezek 36:17 *Son of man*, when the house of Israel dwelt in their own land, they defiled it by their own ways and deeds
Ezek 37:3 And He said to me, "*Son of man*, can these bones live
Ezek 37:9 Then He said to me, "Prophesy to the breath, prophesy, *son of man*, and say to the breath
Ezek 37:11 Then He said to me, "*Son of man*, these bones are the whole house of Israel
Ezek 37:16 As for you, *son of man*, take a stick for yourself and write on it
Ezek 38:2 *Son of man*, set your face against Gog, of the land of Magog, the prince of Rosh, Meshech, and Tubal, and prophesy against him
Ezek 38:14 Therefore, *son of man*, prophesy and say to Gog, 'Thus says the Lord God
Ezek 39:1 And you, *son of man*, prophesy against Gog, and say
Ezek 39:17 And as for you, *son of man*, thus says the Lord God
Ezek 40:4 And the man said to me, *"Son of man*, look with your eyes and hear with your ears, and fix your mind on everything I show you
Ezek 43:7 And He said to me, *"Son of man*, this is the place of My throne and the place of the soles of My feet, where I will dwell in the midst of the children of Israel forever
Ezek 43:10 *Son of man*, describe the temple to the house of Israel, that they may be ashamed of their iniquities
Ezek 43:18 And He said to me, *"Son of man*, thus says the Lord God
Ezek 44:5 And the Lord said to me, *"Son of man*, mark well, see with your eyes and hear with your ears, all that I say to you concerning all the ordinances of the house of the Lord and all its laws
Ezek 47:6 He said to me, *"Son of man*, have you seen this
Dan 7:13 I was watching in the night visions, and behold, One like the *Son of Man*, coming with the clouds of heaven
Dan 8:17 but he said to me, "Understand, *son of man*, that the vision refers to the time of the end
Matt 8:20 And Jesus said to him, "Foxes have holes and birds of the air have nests, but the *Son of Man* has nowhere to lay His head

Matt 9:6 But that you may know that the *Son of Man* has power on earth to forgive sins
Matt 10:23 For assuredly, I say to you, you will not have gone through the cities of Israel before the *Son of Man* comes
Matt 11:19 The *Son of Man* came eating and drinking, and they say
Matt 12:8 For the *Son of Man* is Lord even of the Sabbath
Matt 12:32 Anyone who speaks a word against the *Son of Man*, it will be forgiven him
Matt 12:40 For as Jonah was three days and three nights in the belly of the great fish, so will the *Son of Man* be three days and three nights in the heart of the earth
Matt 13:37 He who sows the good seed is the *Son of Man*
Matt 13:41 The *Son of Man* will send out His angels, and they will gather out of His kingdom all things that offend, and those who practice lawlessness
Matt 16:13 When Jesus came into the region of Caesarea Philippi, He asked His disciples, saying, "Who do men say that I, the *Son of Man*, am
Matt 16:27 For the *Son of Man* will come in the glory of His Father with His angels, and then He will reward each according to his works
Matt 16:28 Assuredly, I say to you, there are some standing here who shall not taste death till they see the *Son of Man* coming in His kingdom
Matt 17:9 Now as they came down from the mountain, Jesus commanded them, saying, "Tell the vision to no one until the *Son of Man* is risen from the dead
Matt 17:12 Likewise the *Son of Man* is also about to suffer at their hands
Matt 17:22 Now while they were staying in Galilee, Jesus said to them, "The *Son of Man* is about to be betrayed into the hands of men
Matt 18:11 For the *Son of Man* has come to save that which was lost
Matt 19:28 So Jesus said to them, "Assuredly I say to you, that in the regeneration, when the *Son of Man* sits on the throne of His glory, you who have followed Me will also sit on twelve thrones, judging the twelve tribes of Israel
Matt 20:18 Behold, we are going up to Jerusalem, and the *Son of Man* will be betrayed to the chief priests and to the scribes
Matt 20:28 just as the *Son of Man* did not come to be served, but to serve, and to give His life a ransom for many
Matt 24:27 For as the lightning comes from the east and flashes to the west, so also will the coming of the *Son of Man* be
Matt 24:30 Then the sign of the *Son of Man* will appear in heaven, and then all the tribes of the earth will mourn, and they will see the *Son of Man* coming on the clouds of heaven with power and great glory
Matt 24:37 But as the days of Noah were, so also will the coming of the *Son of Man* be
Matt 24:39 and did not know until the flood came and took them all away, so also will the coming of the *Son of Man* be
Matt 24:44 Therefore you also be ready, for the *Son of Man* is coming at an hour when you do not expect Him
Matt 25:13 Watch therefore, for you know neither the day nor the hour in which the *Son of Man* is coming
Matt 25:31 When the *Son of Man* comes in His glory, and all the holy angels with Him, then He will sit on the throne of His glory
Matt 26:2 You know that after two days is the Passover, and the *Son of Man* will be delivered up to be crucified
Matt 26:24 The *Son of Man* goes as it is written of Him, but woe to that man by whom the *Son of Man* is betrayed
Matt 26:45 Behold, the hour is at hand, and the *Son of Man* is being betrayed into the hands of sinners
Matt 26:64 Nevertheless, I say to you, hereafter you will see the *Son of Man* sitting at the right hand of the Power, and coming on the clouds of heaven
Mark 2:10 But that you may know that the *Son of Man* has power on earth to forgive sins
Mark 2:28 Therefore the *Son of Man* is also Lord of the Sabbath
Mark 8:31 And He began to teach them that the *Son of Man* must suffer many things, and be rejected by the elders and chief priests and scribes, and be killed, and after three days rise again
Mark 8:38 For whoever is ashamed of Me and My words in this adulterous and sinful generation, of him the *Son of Man* also will be ashamed when He comes in the glory of His Father with the holy angels
Mark 9:9 Now as they came down from the mountain, He commanded them that they should tell no one the things they had seen, till the *Son of Man* had risen from the dead
Mark 9:12 And how is it written concerning the *Son of Man*, that He must suffer many things and be treated with contempt
Mark 9:31 For He taught His disciples and said to them, "The *Son of Man* is being delivered into the hands of men, and they will kill Him
Mark 10:33 Behold, we are going up to Jerusalem, and the *Son of Man* will be delivered to the chief priests and to the scribes, and they will condemn Him to death and deliver Him to the Gentiles
Mark 10:45 For even the *Son of Man* did not come to be served, but to serve, and to give His life a ransom for many
Mark 13:26 Then they will see the *Son of Man* coming in the clouds with great power and glory
Mark 14:21 The *Son of Man* indeed goes just as it is written of Him, but woe to that man by whom the *Son of Man* is betrayed
Mark 14:41 behold, the *Son of Man* is being betrayed into the hands of sinners
Mark 14:62 And you will see the *Son of Man* sitting at the right hand of the Power, and coming with the clouds of heaven
Luke 5:24 But that you may know that the *Son of Man* has power on earth to forgive sins
Luke 6:5 And He said to them, "The *Son of Man* is also Lord of the Sabbath
Luke 7:34 The *Son of Man* has come eating and drinking, and you say
Luke 9:22 saying, "The *Son of Man* must suffer many things, and be rejected by the elders and chief priests and scribes, and be killed, and be raised the third day
Luke 9:26 For whoever is ashamed of Me and My words, of him the *Son of Man* will be ashamed when He comes in His own glory, and in His Father's, and of the holy angels
Luke 9:44 Let these words sink down into your ears, for the *Son of Man* is about to be delivered into the hands of men
Luke 9:56 For the *Son of Man* did not come to destroy men's lives but to save them
Luke 9:58 And Jesus said to him, "Foxes have holes and birds of the air have nests, but the *Son of Man* has nowhere to lay His head
Luke 11:30 For as Jonah became a sign to the Ninevites, so also the *Son of Man* will be to this generation
Luke 12:8 Also I say to you, whoever confesses Me before men, him the *Son of Man* also will confess before the angels of God

Luke 12:10 And anyone who speaks a word against the *Son of Man*, it will be forgiven him
Luke 12:40 Therefore you also be ready, for the *Son of Man* is coming at an hour you do not expect
Luke 17:22 Then He said to the disciples, "The days will come when you will desire to see one of the days of the *Son of Man*, and you will not see it
Luke 17:24 For as the lightning that flashes out of one part under heaven shines to the other part under heaven, so also the *Son of Man* will be in His day
Luke 17:26 And as it was in the days of Noah, so it will be also in the days of the *Son of Man*
Luke 17:30 Even so will it be in the day when the *Son of Man* is revealed
Luke 18:8 Nevertheless, when the *Son of Man* comes, will He really find faith on the earth
Luke 18:31 Then He took the twelve aside and said to them, "Behold, we are going up to Jerusalem, and all things that are written by the prophets concerning the *Son of Man* will be accomplished
Luke 19:10 for the *Son of Man* has come to seek and to save that which was lost
Luke 21:27 Then they will see the *Son of Man* coming in a cloud with power and great glory
Luke 21:36 Watch therefore, and pray always that you may be counted worthy to escape all these things that will come to pass, and to stand before the *Son of Man*
Luke 22:22 And truly the *Son of Man* goes as it has been determined, but woe to that man by whom He is betrayed
Luke 22:48 But Jesus said to him, "Judas, are you betraying the *Son of Man* with a kiss
Luke 22:69 Hereafter the *Son of Man* will sit on the right hand of the power of God
Luke 24:7 saying, 'The *Son of Man* must be delivered into the hands of sinful men, and be crucified, and the third day rise again
John 1:51 And He said to him, "Most assuredly, I say to you, hereafter you shall see heaven open, and the angels of God ascending and descending upon the *Son of Man*
John 3:13 No one has ascended to heaven but He who came down from heaven, that is, the *Son of Man* who is in heaven
John 3:14 And as Moses lifted up the serpent in the wilderness, even so must the *Son of Man* be lifted up
John 5:27 and has given Him authority to execute judgment also, because He is the *Son of Man*
John 6:27 Do not labor for the food which perishes, but for the food which endures to everlasting life, which the *Son of Man* will give you, because God the Father has set His seal on Him
John 6:53 Then Jesus said to them, "Most assuredly, I say to you, unless you eat the flesh of the *Son of Man* and drink His blood, you have no life in you
John 6:62 What then if you should see the *Son of Man* ascend where He was before
John 8:28 Then Jesus said to them, "When you lift up the *Son of Man*, then you will know that I am He, and that I do nothing of Myself
John 12:23 But Jesus answered them, saying, "The hour has come that the *Son of Man* should be glorified
John 12:34 and how can You say, 'The *Son of Man* must be lifted up'? Who is this *Son of Man*
John 13:31 So, when he had gone out, Jesus said, "Now the *Son of Man* is glorified, and God is glorified in Him
Acts 7:56 I see the heavens opened and the *Son of Man* standing at the right hand of God
Heb 2:6 What is man that You are mindful of him, or the *son of man* that You take care of him
Rev 1:13 and in the midst of the seven lampstands One like the *Son of Man*, clothed with a garment down to the feet and girded about the chest with a golden band
Rev 14:14 And I looked, and behold, a white cloud, and on the cloud sat One like the *Son of Man*, having on His head a golden crown, and in His hand a sharp sickle

SON OF PERDITION
John 17:12 and none of them is lost except the *son of perdition*, that the Scripture might be fulfilled
2Th 2:3 for that Day will not come unless the falling away comes first, and the man of sin is revealed, the *son of perdition*

SON OF THE BONDWOMAN
Gen 21:13 Yet I will also make a nation of the *son of the bondwoman*, because he is your seed
Gal 4:30 Cast out the bondwoman and her son, for the *son of the bondwoman* shall not be heir with the son of the freewoman

SON OF THE FREEWOMAN
Gal 4:30 Cast out the bondwoman and her son, for the son of the bondwoman shall not be heir with the *son of the freewoman*

SON OF THE GODS (NAS, NIV, RSV)
(See *SON OF GOD*)

SON OF THE MAIDSERVANT (NIV)
(See *SON OF THE BONDWOMAN*)

SON OF THE SLAVE WOMAN (RSV)
(See *SON OF THE BONDWOMAN*)

SON SETS YOU FREE (NIV)
(See *SON MAKES YOU FREE*)

SON THEREFORE SHALL MAKE YOU FREE (KJV)
(See *SON MAKES YOU FREE*)

SON, WHOM I LOVE (NIV)
(See *BELOVED SON*)

SONG OF MOSES
Rev 15:3 And they sing the *song of Moses*, the servant of God, and the song of the Lamb, saying

SONG OF THE LAMB
Rev 15:3 And they sing the song of Moses, the servant of God, and the *song of the Lamb*, saying

SONGS IN THE NIGHT
Job 35:10 But no one says, 'Where is God my Maker, Who gives *songs in the night*

SONGS OF THANKSGIVING (NAS, NIV, RSV)
(See *THANKSGIVING PSALMS*)

SONGS OF ZION
Ps 137:3 For there those who carried us away captive required of us a song, and those who plundered us required of us mirth, saying, "Sing us one of the *songs of Zion*

SONS ARE A HERITAGE (NIV, RSV)
(See *CHILDREN ARE A HERITAGE*)

SONS DID NOT WALK IN HIS WAYS
1Sam 8:3 But his *sons did not walk in his ways;* they turned aside after dishonest gain, took bribes, and perverted justice

SONS OF DAVID

1Chr 3:1 Now these were the *sons of David* who were born to him in Hebron

1Chr 3:9 These were all the *sons of David*, besides the sons of the concubines, and Tamar their sister

2Chr 13:8 And now you think to withstand the kingdom of the Lord, which is in the hand of the *sons of David*

2Chr 23:3 And he said to them, "Behold, the king's son shall reign, as the Lord has said of the *sons of David*

2Chr 32:33 So Hezekiah rested with his fathers, and they buried him in the upper tombs of the *sons of David*

Ezra 8:2 of the sons of Ithamar, Daniel; of the *sons of David*, Hattush

SONS OF DISOBEDIENCE

Eph 2:2 in which you once walked according to the course of this world, according to the prince of the power of the air, the spirit who now works in the *sons of disobedience*

Eph 5:6 Let no one deceive you with empty words, for because of these things the wrath of God comes upon the *sons of disobedience*

Col 3:6 Because of these things the wrath of God is coming upon the *sons of disobedience*

SONS OF GOD

Gen 6:2 that the *sons of God* saw the daughters of men, that they were beautiful

Gen 6:4 There were giants on the earth in those days, and also afterward, when the *sons of God* came in to the daughters of men and they bore children to them

Job 1:6 Now there was a day when the *sons of God* came to present themselves before the Lord, and Satan also came among them

Job 2:1 Again there was a day when the *sons of God* came to present themselves before the Lord, and Satan came also among them to present himself before the Lord

Job 38:7 when the morning stars sang together, and all the *sons of God* shouted for joy

Matt 5:9 Blessed are the peacemakers, for they shall be called *sons of God*

Luke 20:36 nor can they die anymore, for they are equal to the angels and are *sons of God*, being sons of the resurrection

Rom 8:14 For as many as are led by the Spirit of God, these are *sons of God*

Rom 8:19 For the earnest expectation of the creation eagerly waits for the revealing of the *sons of God*

Gal 3:26 For you are all *sons of God* through faith in Christ Jesus

SONS OF ISRAEL

Gen 42:5 And the *sons of Israel* went to buy grain among those who journeyed, for the famine was in the land of Canaan

Gen 45:21 Then the *sons of Israel* did so; and Joseph gave them carts, according to the command of Pharaoh, and he gave them provisions for the journey

Gen 46:5 and the *sons of Israel* carried their father Jacob, their little ones, and their wives, in the carts which Pharaoh had sent to carry him

Ex 28:9 Then you shall take two onyx stones and engrave on them the names of the *sons of Israel*

Ex 28:11 With the work of an engraver in stone, like the engravings of a signet, you shall engrave the two stones with the names of the *sons of Israel*

Ex 28:12 And you shall put the two stones on the shoulders of the ephod as memorial stones for the *sons of Israel*

Ex 28:21 And the stones shall have the names of the *sons of Israel*, twelve according to their names, like the engravings of a signet, each one with its own name

Ex 28:29 So Aaron shall bear the names of the *sons of Israel* on the breastplate of judgment over his heart, when he goes into the holy place, as a memorial before the Lord continually

Ex 39:6 they were engraved, as signets are engraved, with the names of the *sons of Israel*

Ex 39:7 He put them on the shoulders of the ephod, that they should be stones for a memorial for the *sons of Israel*, as the Lord had commanded Moses

Ex 39:14 There were twelve stones according to the names of the *sons of Israel*

Deut 23:17 There shall be no ritual harlot of the daughters of Israel, or a perverted one of the *sons of Israel*

Josh 5:2 At that time the Lord said to Joshua, "Make flint knives for yourself, and circumcise the *sons of Israel* again the second time

Josh 5:3 So Joshua made flint knives for himself, and circumcised the *sons of Israel* at the hill of the foreskins

1Chr 2:1 These were the *sons of Israel:* Reuben, Simeon, Levi, Judah, Issachar, Zebulun

SONS OF LEVI

Gen 46:11 The *sons of Levi* were Gershon, Kohath, and Merari

Ex 6:16 These are the names of the *sons of Levi* according to their generations

Ex 32:26 And all the *sons of Levi* gathered themselves together to him

Ex 32:28 So the *sons of Levi* did according to the word of Moses

Num 3:17 These were the *sons of Levi* by their names: Gershon, Kohath, and Merari

Num 16:7 You take too much upon yourselves, you *sons of Levi*

Num 16:8 Then Moses said to Korah, "Hear now, you *sons of Levi*

Num 16:10 and that He has brought you near to Himself, you and all your brethren, the *sons of Levi*, with you

Deut 21:5 Then the priests, the *sons of Levi*, shall come near, for the Lord your God has chosen them to minister to Him and to bless in the name of the Lord

Deut 31:9 So Moses wrote this law and delivered it to the priests, the *sons of Levi*, who bore the ark of the covenant of the Lord, and to all the elders of Israel

1Kin 12:31 He made shrines on the high places, and made priests from every class of people, who were not of the *sons of Levi*

1Chr 6:1 The *sons of Levi* were Gershon, Kohath, and Merari

1Chr 6:16 The *sons of Levi* were Gershon, Kohath, and Merari

1Chr 23:6 And David divided them into divisions among the *sons of Levi*

1Chr 23:24 These were the *sons of Levi* by their fathers' houses the heads of the fathers' houses as they were counted individually by the number of their names, who did the work for the service of the house of the Lord, from the age of twenty years and above

1Chr 24:20 Now the rest of the *sons of Levi:* of the sons of Amram, Shubael

Ezra 8:15 And I looked among the people and the priests, and found none of the *sons of Levi* there

Neh 12:23 The *sons of Levi*, the heads of the fathers' houses until the days of Johanan the son of Eliashib, were written in the book of the chronicles

Ezek 40:46 these are the sons of Zadok, from the

sons of Levi, who come near the Lord to minister to Him

Mal 3:3 He will purify the *sons of Levi*, and purge them as gold and silver, that they may offer to the Lord an offering in righteousness

Heb 7:5 And indeed those who are of the *sons of Levi*, who receive the priesthood, have a commandment to receive tithes from the people according to the law, that is, from their brethren, though they have come from the loins of Abraham

SONS OF LIGHT

Luke 16:8 For the sons of this world are more shrewd in their generation than the *sons of light*

John 12:36 While you have the light, believe in the light, that you may become *sons of light*

1Th 5:5 You are all *sons of light* and sons of the day

SONS OF MEN

Gen 11:5 But the Lord came down to see the city and the tower which the *sons of men* had built

2Sam 7:14 If he commits iniquity, I will chasten him with the rod of men and with the blows of the *sons of men*

1Kin 8:39 then hear in heaven Your dwelling place, and forgive, and act, and give to everyone according to all his ways, whose heart You know (for You, only You, know the hearts of all the *sons of men*

2Chr 6:30 then hear from heaven Your dwelling place, and forgive, and give to everyone according to all his ways, whose heart You know (for You alone know the hearts of the *sons of men*

Ps 4:2 How long, O you *sons of men*, will you turn my glory to shame

Ps 11:4 His eyes behold, His eyelids test the *sons of men*

Ps 12:1 For the faithful disappear from among the *sons of men*

Ps 12:8 The wicked prowl on every side, when vileness is exalted among the *sons of men*

Ps 21:10 Their offspring You shall destroy from the earth, and their descendants from among the *sons of men*

Ps 31:19 Oh, how great is Your goodness, which You have laid up for those who fear You, which You have prepared for those who trust in You in the presence of the *sons of men*

Ps 33:13 The Lord looks from heaven; He sees all the *sons of men*

Ps 45:2 You are fairer than the *sons of men;* grace is poured upon Your lips

Ps 57:4 I lie among the *sons of men* who are set on fire, whose teeth are spears and arrows, and their tongue a sharp sword

Ps 58:1 Do you indeed speak righteousness, you silent ones? Do you judge uprightly, you *sons of men*

Ps 66:5 He is awesome in His doing toward the *sons of men*

Ps 145:12 To make known to the *sons of men* His mighty acts, and the glorious majesty of His kingdom

Prov 8:4 To you, O men, I call, and my voice is to the *sons of men*

Prov 8:31 rejoicing in His inhabited world, and my delight was with the *sons of men*

Prov 15:11 so how much more the hearts of the *sons of men*

Eccl 2:3 I searched in my heart how to gratify my flesh with wine, while guiding my heart with wisdom, and how to lay hold on folly, till I might see what was good for the *sons of men* to do under heaven all the days of their lives

Eccl 2:8 I acquired male and female singers, the delights of the *sons of men*, and musical instruments of all kinds

Eccl 3:10 I have seen the God-given task with which the *sons of men* are to be occupied

Eccl 3:18 I said in my heart, "Concerning the estate of the *sons of men*, God tests them, that they may see that they themselves are like beasts

Eccl 3:19 For what happens to the *sons of men* also happens to beasts

Eccl 3:21 Who knows the spirit of the *sons of men*, which goes upward, and the spirit of the beast, which goes down to the earth

Eccl 8:11 Because the sentence against an evil work is not executed speedily, therefore the heart of the *sons of men* is fully set in them to do evil

Eccl 9:3 Truly the hearts of the *sons of men* are full of evil

Eccl 9:12 Like fish taken in a cruel net, like birds caught in a snare, so the *sons of men* are snared in an evil time, when it falls suddenly upon them

Is 52:14 Just as many were astonished at you, so His visage was marred more than any man, and His form more than the *sons of men*

Jer 32:19 You are great in counsel and mighty in work, for your eyes are open to all the ways of the *sons of men*, to give everyone according to his ways and according to the fruit of his doings

Dan 5:21 Then he was driven from the *sons of men*, his heart was made like the beasts, and his dwelling was with the wild donkeys

Dan 10:16 And suddenly, one having the likeness of the *sons of men* touched my lips

Joel 1:12 surely joy has withered away from the *sons of men*

Mic 5:7 Then the remnant of Jacob shall be in the midst of many peoples, like dew from the Lord, like showers on the grass, that tarry for no man nor wait for the *sons of men*

Mark 3:28 Assuredly, I say to you, all sins will be forgiven the *sons of men*, and whatever blasphemies they may utter

Eph 3:5 which in other ages was not made known to the *sons of men*, as it has now been revealed by the Spirit to His holy apostles and prophets

SONS OF THE PROPHETS

1Kin 20:35 Now a certain man of the *sons of the prophets* said to his neighbor by the word of the Lord

2Kin 2:3 And the *sons of the prophets* who were at Bethel came out to Elisha, and said to him

2Kin 2:5 And the *sons of the prophets* who were at Jericho came to Elisha and said to him

2Kin 2:7 And fifty men of the *sons of the prophets* went and stood facing them at a distance, while the two of them stood by the Jordan

2Kin 2:15 Now when the *sons of the prophets* who were from Jericho saw him, they said

2Kin 4:1 A certain woman of the wives of the *sons of the prophets* cried out to Elisha, saying

2Kin 4:38 Now the *sons of the prophets* were sitting before him; and he said to his servant, "Put on the large pot, and boil stew for the *sons of the prophets*

2Kin 5:22 My master has sent me, saying, 'Indeed, just now two young men of the *sons of the prophets* have come to me from the mountains of Ephraim

2Kin 6:1 And the *sons of the prophets* said to Elisha, "See now, the place where we dwell with you is too small for us

2Kin 9:1 And Elisha the prophet called one of the *sons of the prophets*, and said to him

Acts 3:25 You are *sons of the prophets*, and of the covenant which God made with our fathers, saying to Abraham

SONS OF THE RESURRECTION
Luke 20:36 nor can they die anymore, for they are equal to the angels and are sons of God, being *sons of the resurrection*

SONS OF THIS AGE
Luke 20:34 And Jesus answered and said to them, "The *sons of this age* marry and are given in marriage

SONS OF THIS WORLD
Luke 16:8 For the *sons of this world* are more shrewd in their generation than the sons of light

SONS OF THUNDER
Mark 3:17 James the son of Zebedee and John the brother of James, to whom He gave the name Boanerges, that is, *"Sons of Thunder*

SONS OF ZEBEDEE
Matt 26:37 And He took with Him Peter and the two *sons of Zebedee*, and He began to be sorrowful and deeply distressed
Mark 10:35 Then James and John, the *sons of Zebedee*, came to Him, saying
Luke 5:10 and so also were James and John, the *sons of Zebedee*, who were partners with Simon
John 21:2 Simon Peter, Thomas called Didymus, Nathanael of Cana in Galilee, the *sons of Zebedee*, and two others of His disciples were together

SONS WALKED NOT IN HIS WAYS (KJV)
(See *SONS DID NOT WALK IN HIS WAYS*)

SORROW AND MOURNING SHALL FLEE AWAY (KJV)
(See *SORROW AND SIGHING SHALL FLEE AWAY*)

SORROW AND SIGHING SHALL FLEE AWAY
Is 35:10 They shall obtain joy and gladness, and *sorrow and sighing shall flee away*
Is 51:11 They shall obtain joy and gladness, and *sorrow and sighing shall flee away*

SORROW OF HEART
Lev 26:16 I will even appoint terror over you, wasting disease and fever which shall consume the eyes and cause *sorrow of heart*
Neh 2:2 This is nothing but *sorrow of heart"*. Then I became dreadfully afraid
Is 65:14 behold, My servants shall sing for joy of heart, but you shall cry for *sorrow of heart*, and wail for grief of spirit

SORROW TO HIS MOTHER (RSV)
(See *GRIEF OF HIS MOTHER*)

SORROWS OF DEATH (KJV)
(See *PANGS OF DEATH*)

SORROWS OF HELL (KJV)
(See *SORROWS OF SHEOL*)

SORROWS OF SHEOL
2Sam 22:6 the *sorrows of Sheol* surrounded me, the snares of death confronted me
Ps 18:5 The *sorrows of Sheol* surrounded me; the snares of death confronted me

SOUGHT THE LORD
Ex 33:7 And it came to pass that everyone who *sought the Lord* went out to the tabernacle of meeting which was outside the camp
2Chr 14:7 Therefore he said to Judah, "Let us build these cities and make walls around them, and towers, gates, and bars, while the land is yet before us, because we have *sought the Lord* our God
2Chr 22:9 When they had killed him, they buried him, "because," they said, "he is the son of Jehoshaphat, who *sought the Lord* with all his heart
2Chr 26:5 and as long as he *sought the Lord*, God made him prosper
Ps 34:4 I *sought the Lord*, and He heard me, and delivered me from all my fears
Ps 77:2 In the day of my trouble I *sought the Lord*
Jer 10:21 For the shepherds have become dull-hearted, and have not *sought the Lord*
Zeph 1:6 those who have turned back from following the Lord, and have not *sought the Lord*, nor inquired of Him

SOUGHT THE LORD'S FAVOR (NIV)
(See *SUPPLICATION TO THE LORD*)

SOUL IS TROUBLED
Lam 1:20 my *soul is troubled;* my heart is overturned within me, for I have been very rebellious
John 12:27 Now My *soul is troubled*, and what shall I say

SOUL SHALL LIVE
Gen 19:20 please let me escape there (is it not a little one?) and my *soul shall live*
Is 55:3 Hear, and your *soul shall live;* and I will make an everlasting covenant with you the sure mercies of David
Jer 38:17 If you surely surrender to the king of Babylon's princes, then your *soul shall live*
Jer 38:20 So it shall be well with you, and your *soul shall live*

SOUL THIRSTS FOR GOD
Ps 42:2 My *soul thirsts for God*, for the living God. When shall I come and appear before God

SOUL WAITS FOR THE LORD
Ps 33:20 Our *soul waits for the Lord;* He is our help and our shield
Ps 130:6 My *soul waits for the Lord* more than those who watch for the morning I say, more than those who watch for the morning

SOUL WHO SINS
Ezek 18:4 the soul of the father as well as the soul of the son is Mine; the *soul who sins* shall die
Ezek 18:20 The *soul who sins* shall die. The son shall not bear the guilt of the father, nor the father bear the guilt of the son

SOUND DOCTRINE
1Tim 1:10 for fornicators, for sodomites, for kidnappers, for liars, for perjurers, and if there is any other thing that is contrary to *sound doctrine*
2Tim 4:3 For the time will come when they will not endure *sound doctrine*, but according to their own desires, because they have itching ears, they will heap up for themselves teachers
Tit 1:9 holding fast the faithful word as he has been taught, that he may be able, by *sound doctrine*, both to exhort and convict those who contradict
Tit 2:1 But as for you, speak the things which are proper for *sound doctrine*

SOUND INSTRUCTION (NIV)
(See *WHOLESOME WORDS*)

SOUND LIKE THE ROARING SEA (NIV)
(See *ROAR LIKE THE SEA*)

SOUND OF THE TRUMPET
Ex 19:16 and the *sound of the trumpet* was very loud, so that all the people who were in the camp trembled

Ex 20:18 Now all the people witnessed the thunderings, the lightning flashes, the *sound of the trumpet*, and the mountain smoking
Josh 6:5 Then it shall come to pass, when they make a long blast with the ram's horn, and when you hear the *sound of the trumpet*, that all the people shall shout with a great shout
Josh 6:20 And it happened when the people heard the *sound of the trumpet*, and the people shouted with a great shout, that the wall fell down flat
2Sam 6:15 So David and all the house of Israel brought up the ark of the Lord with shouting and with the *sound of the trumpet*
2Sam 15:10 Then Absalom sent spies throughout all the tribes of Israel, saying, "As soon as you hear the *sound of the trumpet*, then you shall say
Neh 4:20 Therefore, wherever you hear the *sound of the trumpet*, rally to us there
Ps 150:3 Praise Him with the *sound of the trumpet;* praise Him with the lute and harp
Jer 4:19 I cannot hold my peace, because you have heard, O my soul, the *sound of the trumpet*, the alarm of war
Jer 4:21 How long will I see the standard, and hear the *sound of the trumpet*
Jer 6:17 Also, I set watchmen over you, saying, 'listen to the *sound of the trumpet*
Jer 42:14 saying, 'No, but we will go to the land of Egypt where we shall see no war, nor hear the *sound of the trumpet*, nor be hungry for bread, and there we will dwell
Ezek 33:4 then whoever hears the *sound of the trumpet* and does not take warning, if the sword comes and takes him away, his blood shall be on his own head
Ezek 33:5 He heard the *sound of the trumpet*, but did not take warning

SOUND TEACHING (NAS)
(See *SOUND DOCTRINE*)

SOUND THE ALARM
2Chr 13:12 Now look, God Himself is with us as our head, and His priests with sounding trumpets to *sound the alarm* against you

SOUND THE TRUMPET (NIV)
(See *MAKE THE TRUMPET TO SOUND*)

SOUND WORDS (NAS, RSV)
(See *WHOLESOME WORDS*)

SOUNDED THE TRUMPET
Neh 4:18 And the one who *sounded the trumpet* was beside me

SOUNDING TRUMPETS TO CRY ALARM (KJV)
(See *SOUND THE ALARM*)

SOUNDS OF JOY AND GLADNESS (NIV)
(See *VOICE OF GLADNESS*)

SOUR GRAPES
Jer 31:29 The fathers have eaten *sour grapes*, and the children's teeth are set on edge
Jer 31:30 every man who eats the *sour grapes*, his teeth shall be set on edge
Ezek 18:2 The fathers have eaten *sour grapes*, and the children's teeth are set on edge

SOW IN TEARS
Ps 126:5 Those who *sow in tears* shall reap in joy

SOW THE WIND
Hos 8:7 They *sow the wind*, and reap the whirlwind. The stalk has no bud

SOWED IT WITH SALT
Judg 9:45 and he demolished the city and *sowed it with salt*

SOWN IN CORRUPTION
1Cor 15:42 The body is *sown in corruption*, it is raised in incorruption

SOWS DISCORD
Prov 6:14 perversity is in his heart, he devises evil continually, he *sows discord*
Prov 6:19 a false witness who speaks lies, and one who *sows discord* among brethren

SPARE HIS LIFE
Job 2:6 So the Lord said to Satan, "Behold, he is in your hand, but *spare his life*

SPARE THE POOR AND NEEDY
Ps 72:13 He will *spare the poor and needy*, and will save the souls of the needy

SPARE THEM NO LONGER (NAS, NIV)
(See *NOT PASS BY THEM ANYMORE*)

SPARES HIS ROD
Prov 13:24 He who *spares his rod* hates his son, but he who loves him disciplines him promptly

SPARKLES IN THE CUP
Prov 23:31 Do not look on the wine when it is red, when it *sparkles in the cup*, when it swirls around smoothly

SPEAK A WORD
Gen 44:18 O my lord, please let your servant *speak a word* in my lord's hearing, and do not let your anger burn against your servant
Deut 18:20 But the prophet who presumes to *speak a word* in My name, which I have not commanded him to speak, or who speaks in the name of other gods, that prophet shall die
Is 50:4 The Lord God has given me the tongue of the learned, that I should know how to *speak a word* in season to him who is weary
Matt 8:8 But only *speak a word*, and my servant will be healed

SPEAK AS THE ORACLES OF GOD
1Pet 4:11 If anyone speaks, let him *speak as the oracles of God*

SPEAK BOLDLY
Acts 18:26 So he began to *speak boldly* in the synagogue. When Aquila and Priscilla heard him, they took him aside and explained to him the way of God more accurately
Eph 6:20 that in it I may *speak boldly*, as I ought to speak

SPEAK EVIL OF ME
Ps 41:5 My enemies *speak evil of me:* "When will he die, and his name perish
Mark 9:39 But Jesus said, "Do not forbid him, for no one who works a miracle in My name can soon afterward *speak evil of Me*

SPEAK FRIENDLY UNTO (KJV)
(See *SPEAK KINDLY TO*)

SPEAK IN OTHER TONGUES (NIV, RSV)
(See *SPEAK WITH OTHER TONGUES*)

SPEAK IN TONGUES (NIV, RSV)
(See *SPOKE WITH TONGUES*)

SPEAK KINDLY TO
Judg 19:3 Then her husband arose and went after her, to *speak kindly to* her and bring her back, having his servant and a couple of donkeys with him

SPEAK THE WORD
Is 8:10 *speak the word*, but it will not stand, for God is with us

Phil 1:14 and most of the brethren in the Lord, having become confident by my chains, are much more bold to *speak the word* without fear

SPEAK WITH OTHER TONGUES
Acts 2:4 And they were all filled with the Holy Spirit and began to *speak with other tongues*, as the Spirit gave them utterance

SPEAK WITH TONGUES
Acts 10:46 For they heard them *speak with tongues* and magnify God
1Cor 12:30 Do all have gifts of healings? Do all *speak with tongues?* Do all interpret
1Cor 14:18 I thank my God I *speak with tongues* more than you all
1Cor 14:23 Therefore if the whole church comes together in one place, and all *speak with tongues*, and there come in those who are uninformed or unbelievers, will they not say that you are out of your mind
1Cor 14:39 Therefore, brethren, desire earnestly to prophesy, and do not forbid to *speak with tongues*

SPEAKETH IN AN UNKNOWN TONGUE (KJV)
(See *SPEAKS IN A TONGUE*)

SPEAKING BOLDLY
Acts 14:3 Therefore they stayed there a long time, *speaking boldly* in the Lord, who was bearing witness to the word of His grace, granting signs and wonders to be done by their hands

SPEAKING IN TONGUES (NIV, RSV)
(See *SPEAK WITH TONGUES*)

SPEAKING OPENLY (RSV)
(See *SPEAKS BOLDLY*)

SPEAKING PUBLICLY (NAS, NIV)
(See *SPEAKS BOLDLY*)

SPEAKING THE VERY WORDS OF GOD (NIV)
(See *SPEAK AS THE ORACLES OF GOD*)

SPEAKS BOLDLY
John 7:26 He *speaks boldly*, and they say nothing to Him. Do the rulers know indeed that this is truly the Christ

SPEAKS IN A TONGUE
1Cor 14:2 For he who *speaks in a tongue* does not speak to men but to God, for no one understands him
1Cor 14:4 He who *speaks in a tongue* edifies himself, but he who prophesies edifies the church
1Cor 14:13 Therefore let him who *speaks in a tongue* pray that he may interpret
1Cor 14:27 If anyone *speaks in a tongue*, let there be two or at the most three, each in turn, and let one interpret

SPEAKS WITH TONGUES
1Cor 14:5 for he who prophesies is greater than he who *speaks with tongues*, unless indeed he interprets, that the church may receive edification

SPECIAL PEOPLE
Deut 26:18 Also today the Lord has proclaimed you to be His *special people*, just as He has promised you, that you should keep all His commandments
Tit 2:14 who gave Himself for us, that He might redeem us from every lawless deed and purify for Himself His own *special people*, zealous for good works
1Pet 2:9 But you are a chosen generation, a royal priesthood, a holy nation, His own *special people*, that you may proclaim the praises of Him who called you out of darkness into His marvelous light

SPECIAL TREASURE
Ex 19:5 Now therefore, if you will indeed obey My voice and keep My covenant, then you shall be a *special treasure* to Me above all people
Deut 7:6 the Lord your God has chosen you to be a people for Himself, a *special treasure* above all the peoples on the face of the earth
Deut 14:2 For you are a holy people to the Lord your God, and the Lord has chosen you to be a people for Himself, a *special treasure* above all the peoples who are on the face of the earth
1Chr 29:3 Moreover, because I have set my affection on the house of my God, I have given to the house of my God, over and above all that I have prepared for the holy house, my own *special treasure* of gold and silver
Ps 135:4 For the Lord has chosen Jacob for Himself, Israel for His *special treasure*

SPECK IN YOUR BROTHER'S EYE
Matt 7:3 And why do you look at the *speck in your brother's eye*, but do not consider the plank in your own eye
Luke 6:41 And why do you look at the *speck in your brother's eye*, but do not perceive the plank in your own eye

SPECK OF SAWDUST IN YOUR BROTHER'S EYE (NIV)
(See *SPECK IN YOUR BROTHER'S EYE*)

SPECTACLE TO THE WORLD
1Cor 4:9 for we have been made a *spectacle to the world*, both to angels and to men

SPEND OUR YEARS AS A TALE THAT IS TOLD (KJV)
(See *FINISH OUR YEARS LIKE A SIGH*)

SPEND THE NIGHT
Gen 19:2 And he said, "Here now, my lords, please turn in to your servant's house and *spend the night*, and wash your feet; then you may rise early and go on your way." And they said, "No, but we will *spend the night* in the open square
Judg 19:9 please *spend the night*. See, the day is coming to an end
Judg 19:13 So he said to his servant, "Come, let us draw near to one of these places, and *spend the night* in Gibeah or in Ramah
Judg 19:15 And when he went in, he sat down in the open square of the city, for no one would take them into his house to *spend the night*
Judg 19:20 only do not *spend the night* in the open square
Judg 20:4 So the Levite, the husband of the woman who was murdered, answered and said, "My concubine and I went into Gibeah, which belongs to Benjamin, to *spend the night*
Neh 13:21 So I warned them, and said to them, "Why do you *spend the night* around the wall
Job 24:7 They *spend the night* naked, without clothing, and have no covering in the cold
Is 65:4 Who sit among the graves, and *spend the night* in the tombs

SPEW YOU OUT
Rev 3:16 So then, because you are lukewarm, and neither cold nor hot, I will *spew you out* of My mouth

SPIED OUT THE LAND
Num 13:21 So they went up and *spied out the land* from the Wilderness of Zin as far as Rehob, near the entrance of Hamath
Num 14:6 And Joshua the son of Nun and Caleb the son of Jephunneh, who were among those who had *spied out the land*, tore their clothes
Num 14:34 According to the number of the days in which you *spied out the land*, forty days, for each day you shall bear your guilt one year, namely forty years, and you shall know My rejection

SPIRIT AND TRUTH
John 4:23 But the hour is coming, and now is, when the true worshipers will worship the Father in *spirit and truth*
John 4:24 God is Spirit, and those who worship Him must worship in *spirit and truth*

SPIRIT AS A GUARANTEE
2Cor 5:5 Now He who has prepared us for this very thing is God, who also has given us the *Spirit as a guarantee*

SPIRIT CLEARLY SAYS (NIV)
(See *SPIRIT EXPRESSLY SAYS*)

SPIRIT COME DOWN (NIV)
(See *SPIRIT DESCENDING*)

SPIRIT DESCENDED
Luke 3:22 And the Holy *Spirit descended* in bodily form like a dove upon Him, and a voice came from heaven which said

SPIRIT DESCENDING
Mark 1:10 And immediately, coming up from the water, He saw the heavens parting and the *Spirit descending* upon Him like a dove
John 1:32 And John bore witness, saying, "I saw the *Spirit descending* from heaven like a dove, and He remained upon Him
John 1:33 I did not know Him, but He who sent me to baptize with water said to me, 'Upon whom you see the *Spirit descending*, and remaining on Him, this is He who baptizes with the Holy Spirit

SPIRIT EXPRESSLY SAYS
1Tim 4:1 Now the *Spirit expressly says* that in latter times some will depart from the faith, giving heed to deceiving spirits and doctrines of demons

SPIRIT GIVES LIFE (NIV)
(See *SPIRIT WHO GIVES LIFE*)

SPIRIT HIMSELF MAKES INTERCESSION
Rom 8:26 For we do not know what we should pray for as we ought, but the *Spirit Himself makes intercession* for us with groanings which cannot be uttered

SPIRIT IN OUR HEARTS
2Cor 1:22 who also has sealed us and given us the *Spirit in our hearts* as a deposit

SPIRIT IN OUR HEARTS AS A DEPOSIT
2Cor 1:22 who also has sealed us and given us the *Spirit in our hearts as a deposit*

SPIRIT IS LIFE
Rom 8:10 And if Christ is in you, the body is dead because of sin, but the *Spirit is life* because of righteousness

SPIRIT LIFTED ME UP
Ezek 3:12 Then the *Spirit lifted me up*, and I heard behind me a great thunderous voice
Ezek 3:14 So the *Spirit lifted me up* and took me away, and I went in bitterness, in the heat of my spirit
Ezek 8:3 and the *Spirit lifted me up* between earth and heaven, and brought me in visions of God to Jerusalem, to the door of the north gate of the inner court, where the seat of the image of jealousy was, which provokes to jealousy
Ezek 11:1 Then the *Spirit lifted me up* and brought me to the east gate of the Lord's house, which faces eastward
Ezek 43:5 The *Spirit lifted me up* and brought me into the inner court

SPIRIT LIKE A DOVE DESCENDING (KJV, NAS)
(See *SPIRIT DESCENDING*)

SPIRIT OF ADOPTION
Rom 8:15 For you did not receive the spirit of bondage again to fear, but you received the *Spirit of adoption* by whom we cry out

SPIRIT OF BONDAGE
Rom 8:15 For you did not receive the *spirit of bondage* again to fear, but you received the Spirit of adoption by whom we cry out

SPIRIT OF GOD
Gen 1:2 And the *Spirit of God* was hovering over the face of the waters
Gen 41:38 And Pharaoh said to his servants, "Can we find such a one as this, a man in whom is the *Spirit of God*
Ex 31:3 And I have filled him with the *Spirit of God*, in wisdom, in understanding, in knowledge, and in all manner of workmanship
Ex 35:31 and He has filled him with the *Spirit of God*, in wisdom and understanding, in knowledge and all manner of workmanship
Num 24:2 And Balaam raised his eyes, and saw Israel encamped according to their tribes; and the *Spirit of God* came upon him
1Sam 10:10 then the *Spirit of God* came upon him, and he prophesied among them
1Sam 11:6 Then the *Spirit of God* came upon Saul when he heard this news, and his anger was greatly aroused
1Sam 19:20 And when they saw the group of prophets prophesying, and Samuel standing as leader over them, the *Spirit of God* came upon the messengers of Saul, and they also prophesied
1Sam 19:23 Then the *Spirit of God* was upon him also, and he went on and prophesied until he came to Naioth in Ramah
2Chr 15:1 Now the *Spirit of God* came upon Azariah the son of Oded
2Chr 24:20 Then the *Spirit of God* came upon Zechariah the son of Jehoiada the priest, who stood above the people, and said to them
Job 33:4 The *Spirit of God* has made me, and the breath of the Almighty gives me life
Ezek 11:24 Then the Spirit took me up and brought me in a vision by the *Spirit of God* into Chaldea, to those in captivity
Dan 5:14 I have heard of you, that the *Spirit of God* is in you, and that light and understanding and excellent wisdom are found in you
Matt 3:16 and behold, the heavens were opened to Him, and He saw the *Spirit of God* descending like a dove and alighting upon Him
Matt 12:28 But if I cast out demons by the *Spirit of God*, surely the kingdom of God has come upon you
Rom 8:9 But you are not in the flesh but in the Spirit, if indeed the *Spirit of God* dwells in you
Rom 8:14 For as many as are led by the *Spirit of God*, these are sons of God
Rom 15:19 in mighty signs and wonders, by the

power of the *Spirit of God*, so that from Jerusalem and round about to Illyricum I have fully preached the gospel of Christ

1Cor 2:11 Even so no one knows the things of God except the *Spirit of God*

1Cor 2:14 But the natural man does not receive the things of the *Spirit of God*, for they are foolishness to him

1Cor 3:16 Do you not know that you are the temple of God and that the *Spirit of God* dwells in you

1Cor 7:40 But she is happier if she remains as she is, according to my judgment and I think I also have the *Spirit of God*

1Cor 12:3 Therefore I make known to you that no one speaking by the *Spirit of God* calls Jesus accursed, and no one can say that Jesus is Lord except by the Holy Spirit

Eph 4:30 And do not grieve the Holy *Spirit of God*, by whom you were sealed for the day of redemption

1Jn 4:2 By this you know the *Spirit of God:* Every spirit that confesses that Jesus Christ has come in the flesh is of God

SPIRIT OF GOD DESCENDING

Matt 3:16 and behold, the heavens were opened to Him, and He saw the *Spirit of God descending* like a dove and alighting upon Him

SPIRIT OF IMPURITY (NIV)
(See *UNCLEAN SPIRIT*)

SPIRIT OF LIFE

Gen 7:22 All in whose nostrils was the breath of the *spirit of life*, all that was on the dry land, died

Rom 8:2 For the law of the *Spirit of life* in Christ Jesus has made me free from the law of sin and death

SPIRIT OF MAN

Zech 12:1 Thus says the Lord, who stretches out the heavens, lays the foundation of the earth, and forms the *spirit of man* within him

SPIRIT OF SLAVERY (NAS, RSV)
(See *SPIRIT OF BONDAGE*)

SPIRIT OF SONSHIP (NIV, RSV)
(See *SPIRIT OF ADOPTION*)

SPIRIT OF THE LIVING GOD

2Cor 3:3 you are manifestly an epistle of Christ, ministered by us, written not with ink but by the *Spirit of the living God*, not on tablets of stone but on tablets of flesh, that is, of the heart

SPIRIT OF THE LORD

Judg 3:10 The *Spirit of the Lord* came upon him, and he judged Israel

Judg 6:34 But the *Spirit of the Lord* came upon Gideon; then he blew the trumpet, and the Abiezrites gathered behind him

Judg 11:29 Then the *Spirit of the Lord* came upon Jephthah, and he passed through Gilead and Manasseh, and passed through Mizpah of Gilead

Judg 13:25 And the *Spirit of the Lord* began to move upon him at Mahaneh Dan between Zorah and Eshtaol

Judg 14:6 And the *Spirit of the Lord* came mightily upon him, and he tore the lion apart as one would have torn apart a young goat, though he had nothing in his hand

Judg 14:19 Then the *Spirit of the Lord* came upon him mightily, and he went down to Ashkelon and killed thirty of their men, took their apparel, and gave the changes of clothing to those who had explained the riddle

Judg 15:14 Then the *Spirit of the Lord* came mightily upon him

1Sam 10:6 Then the *Spirit of the Lord* will come upon you, and you will prophesy with them and be turned into another man

1Sam 16:13 and the *Spirit of the Lord* came upon David from that day forward

1Sam 16:14 But the *Spirit of the Lord* departed from Saul, and a distressing spirit from the Lord troubled him

2Sam 23:2 The *Spirit of the Lord* spoke by me, and His word was on my tongue

1Kin 18:12 And it shall come to pass, as soon as I am gone from you, that the *Spirit of the Lord* will carry you to a place I do not know

2Kin 2:16 Please let them go and search for your master, lest perhaps the *Spirit of the Lord* has taken him up and cast him upon some mountain or into some valley

2Chr 20:14 Then the *Spirit of the Lord* came upon Jahaziel the son of Zechariah, the son of Benaiah, the son of Jeiel, the son of Mattaniah, a Levite of the sons of Asaph, in the midst of the congregation

Is 11:2 The *Spirit of the Lord* shall rest upon Him, the Spirit of wisdom and understanding, the Spirit of counsel and might, the Spirit of knowledge and of the fear of the Lord

Is 40:13 Who has directed the *Spirit of the Lord*, or as His counselor has taught Him

Is 59:19 when the enemy comes in like a flood, the *Spirit of the Lord* will lift up a standard against him

Is 61:1 The *Spirit of the Lord* God is upon Me, because the Lord has anointed Me to preach good tidings to the poor

Is 63:14 As a beast goes down into the valley, And the *Spirit of the Lord* causes him to rest, so You lead Your people, to make Yourself a glorious name

Ezek 11:5 Then the *Spirit of the Lord* fell upon me, and said to me

Ezek 37:1 The hand of the Lord came upon me and brought me out in the *Spirit of the Lord*, and set me down in the midst of the valley

Mic 2:7 Is the *Spirit of the Lord* restricted? Are these His doings

Mic 3:8 But truly I am full of power by the *Spirit of the Lord*, and of justice and might, to declare to Jacob his transgression and to Israel his sin

Luke 4:18 The *Spirit of the Lord* is upon Me, because He has anointed Me to preach the gospel to the poor

Acts 5:9 Then Peter said to her, "How is it that you have agreed together to test the *Spirit of the Lord*

Acts 8:39 Now when they came up out of the water, the *Spirit of the Lord* caught Philip away, so that the eunuch saw him no more

2Cor 3:17 and where the *Spirit of the Lord* is, there is liberty

2Cor 3:18 But we all, with unveiled face, beholding as in a mirror the glory of the Lord, are being transformed into the same image from glory to glory, just as by the *Spirit of the Lord*

SPIRIT OF TRUTH

John 14:17 even the *Spirit of truth*, whom the world cannot receive, because it neither sees Him nor knows Him

John 15:26 But when the Helper comes, whom I shall send to you from the Father, the *Spirit of truth* who proceeds from the Father, He will testify of Me

John 16:13 However, when He, the *Spirit of truth*, has come, He will guide you into all truth

1Jn 4:6 By this we know the *spirit of truth* and the spirit of error

SPIRIT SEARCHES ALL THINGS
1Cor 2:10 For the *Spirit searches all things*, yes, the deep things of God

SPIRIT SPEAKETH EXPRESSLY (KJV)
(See *SPIRIT EXPRESSLY SAYS*)

SPIRIT THAT DWELLETH IN YOU (KJV)
(See *SPIRIT WHO DWELLS IN YOU*)

SPIRIT THAT GIVES LIFE (RSV)
(See *SPIRIT WHO GIVES LIFE*)

SPIRIT THAT MAKES YOU A SLAVE AGAIN (NIV)
(See *SPIRIT OF BONDAGE*)

SPIRIT THAT QUICKENETH (KJV)
(See *SPIRIT WHO GIVES LIFE*)

SPIRIT TOOK ME UP (KJV)
(See *SPIRIT LIFTED ME UP*)

SPIRIT WAS TROUBLED
Gen 41:8 Now it came to pass in the morning that his *spirit was troubled*, and he sent and called for all the magicians of Egypt and all its wise men

SPIRIT WHO DWELLS IN YOU
Rom 8:11 But if the Spirit of Him who raised Jesus from the dead dwells in you, He who raised Christ from the dead will also give life to your mortal bodies through His *Spirit who dwells in you*

SPIRIT WHO GIVES LIFE
John 6:63 It is the *Spirit who gives life;* the flesh profits nothing

SPIRIT, WHO LIVES IN YOU (NIV)
(See *SPIRIT WHO DWELLS IN YOU*)

SPIRITS IN PRISON
1Pet 3:19 by whom also He went and preached to the *spirits in prison*

SPIRITS OF THE PROPHETS
1Cor 14:32 And the *spirits of the prophets* are subject to the prophets

SPIRITUAL GIFTS
1Cor 12:1 Now concerning *spiritual gifts*, brethren, I do not want you to be ignorant
1Cor 14:1 Pursue love, and desire *spiritual gifts*, but especially that you may prophesy
1Cor 14:12 Even so you, since you are zealous for *spiritual gifts*, let it be for the edification of the church that you seek to excel

SPIRITUAL SACRIFICES
1Pet 2:5 you also, as living stones, are being built up a spiritual house, a holy priesthood, to offer up *spiritual sacrifices* acceptable to God through Jesus Christ

SPIRITUAL WORSHIP (NIV, RSV)
(See *REASONABLE SERVICE*)

SPIRITUALLY MINDED
Rom 8:6 For to be carnally minded is death, but to be *spiritually minded* is life and peace

SPIT YOU OUT (NAS, NIV)
(See *SPEW YOU OUT*)

SPLENDOR AND MAJESTY (NAS, NIV)
(See *HONOR AND MAJESTY*)

SPLENDOR OF HIS HOLINESS (NIV)
(See *BEAUTY OF HOLINESS*)

SPLENDOR OF HIS MAJESTY (NAS, NIV)
(See *GLORY OF HIS MAJESTY*)

SPOILING OF THE DAUGHTER OF MY PEOPLE (KJV)
(See *PLUNDERING OF THE DAUGHTER OF MY PEOPLE*)

SPOKE BOLDLY
Acts 9:29 And he *spoke boldly* in the name of the Lord Jesus and disputed against the Hellenists, but they attempted to kill him
Acts 19:8 And he went into the synagogue and *spoke boldly* for three months, reasoning and persuading concerning the things of the kingdom of God

SPOKE WITH TONGUES
Acts 19:6 And when Paul had laid hands on them, the Holy Spirit came upon them, and they *spoke with tongues* and prophesied
1Cor 14:5 I wish you all *spoke with tongues*, but even more that you prophesied

SPOKEN BY ISAIAH
Matt 4:14 that it might be fulfilled which was *spoken by Isaiah* the prophet, saying
Matt 8:17 that it might be fulfilled which was *spoken by Isaiah* the prophet, saying
Matt 12:17 that it might be fulfilled which was *spoken by Isaiah* the prophet, saying

SPOKEN BY THE PROPHET
Matt 13:35 that it might be fulfilled which was *spoken by the prophet*, saying
Matt 21:4 All this was done that it might be fulfilled which was *spoken by the prophet*, saying
Matt 27:35 Then they crucified Him, and divided His garments, casting lots, that it might be fulfilled which was *spoken by the prophet*
Acts 2:16 But this is what was *spoken by the prophet* Joel

SPOKEN BY THE PROPHETS (NIV)
(See *MOUTH OF THE PROPHETS*)

SPOTS IN YOUR LOVE FEASTS
Jude 12 These are *spots in your love feasts*, while they feast with you without fear, serving only themselves

SPRANG UP AND WALKED (RSV)
(See *LEAPED AND WALKED*)

SPREAD A NET
Ps 140:5 They have *spread a net* by the wayside; they have set traps for me
Lam 1:13 He has *spread a net* for my feet and turned me back

SPREAD ABROAD HIS HANDS (KJV)
(See *SPREAD OUT HIS HANDS*)

SPREAD FORTH HIS HANDS (KJV, RSV)
(See *SPREAD OUT HIS HANDS*)

SPREAD LIKE CANCER
2Tim 2:17 And their message will *spread like cancer*. Hymenaeus and Philetus are of this sort

SPREAD OUT HIS HANDS
Ex 9:33 So Moses went out of the city from Pharaoh and *spread out his hands* to the Lord
1Kin 8:22 Then Solomon stood before the altar of the Lord in the presence of all the congregation of Israel, and *spread out his hands* toward heaven
2Chr 6:12 Then Solomon stood before the altar of the Lord in the presence of all the congregation of Israel, and *spread out his hands*
2Chr 6:13 and he stood on it, knelt down on his knees before all the congregation of Israel, and *spread out his hands* toward heaven
Is 25:11 And He will *spread out His hands* in their midst as he who swims spreads out his hands to swim, and He will bring down their pride together with the trickery of their hands

SPREAD OUT MY HANDS (NAS, NIV, RSV)
(See *STRETCHED OUT MY HANDS*)

SPREAD OUT THE CORDS OF THEIR NET (NIV)
(See *SPREAD A NET*)

SPREAD WITH OIL (NAS, RSV)
(See *ANOINTED WITH OIL*)

SPRING OF LIVING WATER (NIV)
(See *FOUNTAIN OF LIVING WATERS*)

SPRINGS OF LIFE (NAS, RSV)
(See *ISSUES OF LIFE*)

SPRINKLE DUST ON THEIR HEADS (NIV)
(See *CAST DUST ON THEIR HEADS*)

SPRINKLE ITS BLOOD
Lev 1:11 and the priests, Aaron's sons, shall *sprinkle its blood* all around on the altar
Lev 3:8 and Aaron's sons shall *sprinkle its blood* all around on the altar
Lev 3:13 and the sons of Aaron shall *sprinkle its blood* all around on the altar

SPRINKLE THE BLOOD
Ex 29:20 Then you shall kill the ram, and take some of its blood and put it on the tip of the right ear of Aaron and on the tip of the right ear of his sons, on the thumb of their right hand and on the big toe of their right foot, and *sprinkle the blood* all around on the altar
Lev 1:5 and the priests, Aaron's sons, shall bring the blood and *sprinkle the blood* all around on the altar that is by the door of the tabernacle of meeting
Lev 3:2 and Aaron's sons, the priests, shall *sprinkle the blood* all around on the altar
Lev 17:6 And the priest shall *sprinkle the blood* on the altar of the Lord at the door of the tabernacle of meeting, and burn the fat for a sweet aroma to the Lord

SPRINKLE THEIR BLOOD
Num 18:17 You shall *sprinkle their blood* on the altar, and burn their fat as an offering made by fire for a sweet aroma to the Lord

SPRINKLED BLOOD (NAS, NIV, RSV)
(See *BLOOD OF SPRINKLING*)

SPRINKLED DUST ON THEIR HEADS (NIV)
(See *THROW DUST ON THEIR HEADS*)

SPRINKLED ON THE ALTAR
Ex 24:6 And Moses took half the blood and put it in basins, and half the blood he *sprinkled on the altar*

SPRINKLED THE BLOOD
Lev 8:19 Then he *sprinkled the blood* all around on the altar
Lev 8:24 And Moses *sprinkled the blood* all around on the altar
2Kin 16:13 and he poured his drink offering and *sprinkled the blood* of his peace offerings on the altar
2Chr 29:22 Likewise they killed the rams and *sprinkled the blood* on the altar. They also killed the lambs and *sprinkled the blood* on the altar
2Chr 30:16 the priests *sprinkled the blood* which they received from the hand of the Levites
2Chr 35:11 and the priests *sprinkled the blood* with their hands, while the Levites skinned the animals

SPRINKLING OF BLOOD
Heb 11:28 By faith he kept the Passover and the *sprinkling of blood*, lest he who destroyed the firstborn should touch them

SPURN MY STATUTES (RSV)
(See *DESPISE MY STATUTES*)

SPY OUT THE COUNTRY
Josh 7:2 Now Joshua sent men from Jericho to Ai, which is beside Beth Aven, on the east side of Bethel, and spoke to them, saying, "Go up and *spy out the country*
Judg 18:14 Then the five men who had gone to *spy out the country* of Laish answered and said to their brethren

SPY OUT THE LAND
Num 13:2 Send men to *spy out the land* of Canaan, which I am giving to the children of Israel
Num 13:16 These are the names of the men whom Moses sent to *spy out the land*
Num 13:17 So Moses sent them to *spy out the land* of Canaan, and said to them
Num 14:36 And the men whom Moses sent to *spy out the land*, who returned and made all the congregation murmur against him by bringing a bad report of the land
Num 14:38 But Joshua the son of Nun and Caleb the son of Jephunneh remained alive, of the men who went to *spy out the land*
Josh 14:7 I was forty years old when Moses the servant of the Lord sent me from Kadesh Barnea to *spy out the land*, and I brought back word to him as it was in my heart
Judg 18:2 So the children of Dan sent five men of their family from their territory, men of valor from Zorah and Eshtaol, to *spy out the land* and search it
Judg 18:17 Then the five men who had gone to *spy out the land* went up, and entering there, they took the carved image, the ephod, the household idols, and the molded image
1Chr 19:3 Did his servants not come to you to search and to overthrow and to *spy out the land*

STAFF OF GOD (NAS, NIV)
(See *ROD OF GOD*)

STAGGER LIKE A DRUNKEN MAN
Job 12:25 They grope in the dark without light, and He makes them *stagger like a drunken man*
Ps 107:27 They reel to and fro, and *stagger like a drunken man*, and are at their wits

STAGGERS LIKE A DRUNKEN MAN (RSV)
(See *REEL TO AND FRO LIKE A DRUNKARD*)

STALKS IN THE DARKNESS (NIV)
(See *WALKS IN DARKNESS*)

STAMP YOUR FEET
Ezek 6:11 Pound your fists and *stamp your feet*, and say, 'Alas, for all the evil abominations of the house of Israel

STAND BEFORE THE LORD
Deut 10:8 At that time the Lord separated the tribe of Levi to bear the ark of the covenant of the Lord, to *stand before the Lord* to minister to Him and to bless in His name, to this day
Deut 19:17 then both men in the controversy shall *stand before the Lord*, before the priests and the judges who serve in those days

STAND BY NIGHT IN THE HOUSE OF THE LORD (RSV)
(See *STAND IN THE HOUSE OF THE LORD*)

STAND FAST (KJV)
(See *STAND FIRM*)

STAND FAST IN THE FAITH
1Cor 16:13 Watch, *stand fast in the faith*, be brave, be strong

STAND FIRM
Job 39:24 nor does he *stand firm*, because the trumpet has sounded
Ps 89:28 My mercy I will keep for him forever, and My covenant shall *stand firm* with him

STAND FIRM IN THE FAITH (NAS, NIV)
(See *STAND FAST IN THE FAITH*)

STAND IN AWE
Ps 33:8 Let all the inhabitants of the world *stand in awe* of Him

STAND IN THE HOUSE OF THE LORD
Ps 134:1 Behold, bless the Lord, all you servants of the Lord, who by night *stand in the house of the Lord*
Ps 135:2 You who *stand in the house of the Lord*, in the courts of the house of our God

STAND STILL (NAS, NIV, RSV)
(See *STAND FIRM*)

STANDARDS OF THE NATIONS (NIV)
(See *JUDGMENTS OF THE NATIONS*)

STANDING AT THE RIGHT HAND OF GOD
Acts 7:55 But he, being full of the Holy Spirit, gazed into heaven and saw the glory of God, and Jesus *standing at the right hand of God*
Acts 7:56 I see the heavens opened and the Son of Man *standing at the right hand of God*

STANDING BEFORE THE LORD (NAS, NIV)
(See *STOOD BEFORE THE LORD*)

STANDS FIRM IN THE HEAVENS (NIV)
(See *SETTLED IN HEAVEN*)

STANDS IN AWE
Ps 119:161 Princes persecute me without a cause, but my heart *stands in awe* of Your word

STAR IN THE EAST
Matt 2:2 For we have seen His *star in the East* and have come to worship Him

STARS IN THE UNIVERSE (NIV)
(See *AS LIGHTS IN THE WORLD*)

STARS OF HEAVEN
Gen 26:4 And I will make your descendants multiply as the *stars of heaven*
Ex 32:13 Remember Abraham, Isaac, and Israel, Your servants, to whom You swore by Your own self, and said to them, 'I will multiply your descendants as the *stars of heaven*
Deut 1:10 The Lord your God has multiplied you, and here you are today, as the *stars of heaven* in multitude
Deut 10:22 Your fathers went down to Egypt with seventy persons, and now the Lord your God has made you as the *stars of heaven* in multitude
Deut 28:62 You shall be left few in number, whereas you were as the *stars of heaven* in multitude, because you would not obey the voice of the Lord your God
Neh 9:23 You also multiplied their children as the *stars of heaven*, and brought them into the land which You had told their fathers to go in and possess
Is 13:10 For the *stars of heaven* and their constellations will not give their light
Nah 3:16 You have multiplied your merchants more than the *stars of heaven*
Mark 13:25 the *stars of heaven* will fall, and the powers in heaven will be shaken
Rev 6:13 And the *stars of heaven* fell to the earth, as a fig tree drops its late figs when it is shaken by a mighty wind
Rev 12:4 His tail drew a third of the *stars of heaven* and threw them to the earth

STATUTE AND AN ORDINANCE
Ex 15:25 There He made a *statute and an ordinance* for them
Josh 24:25 So Joshua made a covenant with the people that day, and made for them a *statute and an ordinance* in Shechem
1Sam 30:25 he made it a *statute and an ordinance* for Israel to this day

STATUTE FOREVER
Ex 27:21 It shall be a *statute forever* to their generations on behalf of the children of Israel
Ex 28:43 It shall be a *statute forever* to him and his descendants after him
Ex 29:28 It shall be from the children of Israel for Aaron and his sons by a *statute forever*
Ex 30:21 And it shall be a *statute forever* to them to him and his descendants throughout their generations
Lev 6:18 It shall be a *statute forever* in your generations concerning the offerings made by fire to the Lord
Lev 6:22 It is a *statute forever* to the Lord. It shall be wholly burned
Lev 7:34 For the breast of the wave offering and the thigh of the heave offering I have taken from the children of Israel, from the sacrifices of their peace offerings, and I have given them to Aaron the priest and to his sons from the children of Israel by a *statute forever*
Lev 7:36 The Lord commanded this to be given to them by the children of Israel, on the day that He anointed them, by a *statute forever* throughout their generations
Lev 10:9 Do not drink wine or intoxicating drink, you, nor your sons with you, when you go into the tabernacle of meeting, lest you die. It shall be a *statute forever* throughout your generations
Lev 10:15 And it shall be yours and your sons' with you, by a *statute forever*, as the Lord has commanded
Lev 16:29 This shall be a *statute forever* for you: In the seventh month, on the tenth day of the month, you shall afflict your souls, and do no work at all, whether a native of your own country or a stranger who sojourns among you
Lev 16:31 It is a sabbath of solemn rest for you, and you shall afflict your souls. It is a *statute forever*
Lev 17:7 This shall be a *statute forever* for them throughout their generations
Lev 23:14 it shall be a *statute forever* throughout your generations in all your dwellings
Lev 23:21 It shall be a *statute forever* in all your dwellings throughout your generations

Lev 23:31 it shall be a *statute forever* throughout your generations in all your dwellings
Lev 23:41 It shall be a *statute forever* in your generations. You shall celebrate it in the seventh month
Lev 24:3 Outside the veil of the Testimony, in the tabernacle of meeting, Aaron shall be in charge of it from evening until morning before the Lord continually; it shall be a *statute forever* in your generations
Num 18:23 it shall be a *statute forever*, throughout your generations, that among the children of Israel they shall have no inheritance
Num 19:10 It shall be a *statute forever* to the children of Israel and to the stranger who sojourns among them

STATUTES AND JUDGMENTS
Lev 26:46 These are the *statutes and judgments* and laws which the Lord made between Himself and the children of Israel on Mount Sinai by the hand of
Deut 4:5 Surely I have taught you *statutes and judgments*, just as the Lord my God commanded me, that you should act according to them in the land which you go to possess
Deut 4:14 And the Lord commanded me at that time to teach you *statutes and judgments*, that you might observe them in the land which you cross over to possess
Deut 5:1 Hear, O Israel, the *statutes and judgments* which I speak in your hearing today, that you may learn them and be careful to observe them
Deut 6:1 Now this is the commandment, and these are the *statutes and judgments* which the Lord your God has commanded to teach you, that you may observe them in the land which you are crossing over to possess
Deut 11:32 And you shall be careful to observe all the *statutes and judgments* which I set before you today
Deut 12:1 These are the *statutes and judgments* which you shall be careful to observe in the land which the Lord God of your fathers is giving you to possess, all the days that you live on the earth
Deut 26:16 This day the Lord your God commands you to observe these *statutes and judgments*
1Chr 22:13 Then you will prosper, if you take care to fulfill the *statutes and judgments* with which the Lord charged Moses concerning Israel
Mal 4:4 Remember the Law of Moses, My servant, which I commanded him in Horeb for all Israel, with the *statutes and judgments*

STATUTES AND ORDINANCES (NAS, RSV)
(See *STATUTES AND JUDGMENTS*)

STATUTES WHICH I COMMAND
Deut 8:11 Beware that you do not forget the Lord your God by not keeping His commandments, His judgments, and His *statutes which I command* you today
Deut 10:13 and to keep the commandments of the Lord and His *statutes which I command* you today for your good
Deut 27:10 Therefore you shall obey the voice of the Lord your God, and observe His commandments and His *statutes which I command* you today
Deut 28:15 But it shall come to pass, if you do not obey the voice of the Lord your God, to observe carefully all His commandments and His *statutes which I command* you today, that all these curses will come upon you and overtake you

STAY IN THE CITY (NAS, NIV, RSV)
(See *TARRY IN THE CITY OF JERUSALEM*)

STAY ON HORSES (KJV)
(See *RELY ON HORSES*)

STAY YOUR HAND (RSV)
(See *RESTRAIN YOUR HAND*)

STEADFAST LOVE (RSV)
(See *YOUR LOVINGKINDNESS*)

STEADFAST LOVE AND FAITHFULNESS (RSV)
(See *MERCY AND TRUTH*)

STEADFAST LOVE AND NOT SACRIFICE (RSV)
(See *MERCY AND NOT SACRIFICE*)

STEADFAST LOVE OF GOD (RSV)
(See *MERCY OF GOD*)

STEEPED IN SIN AT BIRTH (NIV)
(See *BORN IN SINS*)

STEM OF JESSE
Is 11:1 There shall come forth a Rod from the *stem of Jesse*, and a Branch shall grow out of his roots

STEPS HAD NEARLY SLIPPED
Ps 73:2 But as for me, my feet had almost stumbled; my *steps had nearly slipped*

STEPS TOTTER BENEATH ME (RSV)
(See *TREMBLED IN MYSELF*)

STEW OF LENTILS
Gen 25:34 And Jacob gave Esau bread and *stew of lentils;* then he ate and drank, arose, and went his way

STIFF-NECKED PEOPLE
Ex 32:9 And the Lord said to Moses, "I have seen this people, and indeed it is a *stiff-necked people*
Ex 33:3 for I will not go up in your midst, lest I consume you on the way for you are a *stiff-necked people*
Ex 33:5 For the Lord had said to Moses, "Say to the children of Israel, 'You are a *stiff-necked people*
Ex 34:9 Then he said, "If now I have found grace in Your sight, O Lord, let my Lord, I pray, go among us, even though we are a *stiff-necked people*
Deut 9:6 Therefore understand that the Lord your God is not giving you this good land to possess because of your righteousness, for you are a *stiff-necked people*
Deut 9:13 Furthermore the Lord spoke to me, saying, 'I have seen this people, and indeed they are a *stiff-necked people*

STILL SMALL VOICE
1Kin 19:12 and after the earthquake a fire, but the Lord was not in the fire; and after the fire a *still small voice*

STING OF DEATH
1Cor 15:56 The *sting of death* is sin, and the strength of sin is the law

STIRS UP DISSENSION (NIV)
(See *SOWS DISCORD*)

STIRS UP STRIFE
Prov 10:12 Hatred *stirs up strife*, but love covers all sins

Prov 15:18 A wrathful man *stirs up strife*, but he who is slow to anger allays contention
Prov 28:25 He who is of a proud heart *stirs up strife*, but he who trusts in the Lord will be prospered
Prov 29:22 An angry man *stirs up strife*, and a furious man abounds in transgression

STOCK OF ABRAHAM (KJV)
(See *FAMILY OF ABRAHAM*)

STOLE THE HEARTS
2Sam 15:6 So Absalom *stole the hearts* of the men of Israel

STOLEN WATER IS SWEET
Prov 9:17 *Stolen water is sweet*, and bread eaten in secret is pleasant

STONE HER TO DEATH
Deut 22:21 then they shall bring out the young woman to the door of her father's house, and the men of her city shall *stone her to death* with stones, because she has done a disgraceful thing in Israel, to play the harlot in her father's house

STONE HIM TO DEATH
Deut 21:21 Then all the men of his city shall *stone him to death* with stones

STONE OF STUMBLING
Is 8:14 He will be as a sanctuary, but a *stone of stumbling* and a rock of offense to both the houses of Israel, as a trap and a snare to the inhabitants of Jerusalem
1Pet 2:8 and "A *stone of stumbling* and a rock of offense

STONE TO DEATH
Deut 17:5 then you shall bring out to your gates that man or woman who has committed that wicked thing, and shall *stone to death* that man or woman with stones

STONE WHICH THE BUILDERS REJECTED
Ps 118:22 The *stone which the builders rejected* has become the chief cornerstone
Matt 21:42 The *stone which the builders rejected* has become the chief cornerstone
Mark 12:10 The *stone which the builders rejected* has become the chief cornerstone
Luke 20:17 The *stone which the builders rejected* has become the chief cornerstone
1Pet 2:7 but to those who are disobedient, "The *stone which the builders rejected* has become the chief cornerstone

STONED HIM WITH STONES
Lev 24:23 and they took outside the camp him who had cursed, and *stoned him with stones*
Num 15:36 So, as the Lord commanded Moses, all the congregation brought him outside the camp and *stoned him with stones*, and he died
Josh 7:25 So all Israel *stoned him with stones;* and they burned them with fire after they had stoned them with stones
1Kin 12:18 but all Israel *stoned him with stones*, and he died
1Kin 21:13 Then they took him outside the city and *stoned him with stones*, so that he died
2Chr 10:18 but the children of Israel *stoned him with stones*, and he died
2Chr 24:21 So they conspired against him, and at the commandment of the king they *stoned him with stones* in the court of the house of the Lord

STOOD BEFORE THE LORD
Gen 18:22 Then the men turned away from there and went toward Sodom, but Abraham still *stood before the Lord*
Gen 19:27 And Abraham went early in the morning to the place where he had *stood before the Lord*
Lev 9:5 And all the congregation drew near and *stood before the Lord*
Deut 4:10 especially concerning the day you *stood before the Lord* your God in Horeb, when the Lord said to me
1Kin 22:21 Then a spirit came forward and *stood before the Lord*, and said
2Chr 18:20 Then a spirit came forward and *stood before the Lord*, and said
2Chr 20:13 Now all Judah, with their little ones, their wives, and their children, *stood before the Lord*

STORE AWAY IN BARNS (NIV)
(See *GATHER INTO BARNS*)

STORE UP THEIR FOOD IN THE SUMMER (NIV)
(See *PREPARE THEIR FOOD IN THE SUMMER*)

STORE UP WRATH
Job 36:13 But the hypocrites in heart *store up wrath;* they do not cry for help when He binds them

STORED UP FOR YOU IN HEAVEN (NIV)
(See *LAID UP FOR YOU IN HEAVEN*)

STRAIGHT PATHS
Heb 12:13 and make *straight paths* for your feet, so that what is lame may not be dislocated, but rather be healed

STRAIGHT STREET (NIV)
(See *STREET CALLED STRAIGHT*)

STRAIN OUT A GNAT
Matt 23:24 Blind guides, who *strain out a gnat* and swallow a camel

STRAINING OUT A GNAT (RSV)
(See *STRAIN OUT A GNAT*)

STRAIT IS THE GATE (KJV)
(See *NARROW IS THE GATE*)

STRANGE GODS (KJV)
(See *FOREIGN GODS*)

STRANGER IN A FOREIGN LAND
Ex 2:22 for he said, "I have been a *stranger in a foreign land*
Ex 18:3 with her two sons, of whom the name of one was Gershom (for he said, "I have been a *stranger in a foreign land*

STRANGER THAT SOJOURNETH AMONG YOU (KJV)
(See *STRANGER WHO DWELLS AMONG YOU*)

STRANGER WHO DWELLS AMONG YOU
Ex 12:49 One law shall be for the native-born and for the *stranger who dwells among you*
Lev 19:34 But the *stranger who dwells among you* shall be to you as one born among you, and you shall love him as yourself

STRANGER WHO SOJOURNS AMONG YOU
Lev 16:29 In the seventh month, on the tenth day of the month, you shall afflict your souls, and do

no work at all, whether a native of your own country or a *stranger who sojourns among you*
Lev 17:12 Therefore I said to the children of Israel, 'No one among you shall eat blood, nor shall any *stranger who sojourns among you* eat blood
Lev 18:26 You shall therefore keep My statutes and My judgments, and shall not commit any of these abominations, either any of your own nation or any *stranger who sojourns among you*

STRANGERS AND PILGRIMS
Heb 11:13 These all died in faith, not having received the promises, but having seen them afar off were assured of them, embraced them, and confessed that they were *strangers and pilgrims* on the earth

STRANGERS ON EARTH (NIV)
(See *PILGRIMS ON THE EARTH*)

STRANGERS WHO SOJOURN AMONG YOU
Lev 17:8 Whatever man of the house of Israel, or of the *strangers who sojourn among you*, who offers a burnt offering or sacrifice
Lev 17:10 And whatever man of the house of Israel, or of the *strangers who sojourn among you*, who eats any blood, I will set My face against that person who eats blood, and will cut him off from among his people
Lev 17:13 And whatever man of the children of Israel, or of the *strangers who sojourn among you*, who hunts and catches any animal or bird that may be eaten, he shall pour out its blood and cover it with dust
Lev 25:45 Moreover you may buy the children of the *strangers who sojourn among you*, and their families who are with you, which they beget in your land
Ezek 47:22 It shall be that you will divide it by lot as an inheritance for yourselves, and for the *strangers who sojourn among you* and who bear children among you

STRAW TO MAKE BRICK
Ex 5:7 You shall no longer give the people *straw to make brick* as before

STRAYED CONCERNING THE FAITH
1Tim 6:21 by professing it, some have *strayed concerning the faith*. Grace be with you

STRAYED CONCERNING THE TRUTH
2Tim 2:18 who have *strayed concerning the truth*, saying that the resurrection is already past

STREAMS IN THE DESERT
Is 35:6 For waters shall burst forth in the wilderness, and *streams in the desert*

STREAMS IN THE NEGEV (NIV)
(See *STREAMS IN THE SOUTH*)

STREAMS IN THE SOUTH
Ps 126:4 Bring back our captivity, O Lord, as the *streams in the South*

STREAMS IN THE WASTELAND (NIV)
(See *RIVERS IN THE DESERT*)

STREAMS OF LIVING WATER (NIV)
(See *RIVERS OF LIVING WATER*)

STREAMS OF WATER (NIV)
(See *RIVERS OF WATER*)

STREET CALLED STRAIGHT
Acts 9:11 So the Lord said to him, "Arise and go to the *street called Straight*, and inquire at the house of Judas for one called Saul of Tarsus, for behold, he is praying

STRENGTH AND POWER (NIV)
(See *POWER AND MIGHT*)

STRENGTH FAILETH (KJV)
(See *STRENGTH FAILS*)

STRENGTH FAILS
Ps 31:10 My *strength fails* because of my iniquity, and my bones waste away
Ps 38:10 My heart pants, my *strength fails* me; as for the light of my eyes, it also has gone from me
Ps 71:9 Do not cast me off in the time of old age; do not forsake me when my *strength fails*
Is 44:12 even so, he is hungry, and his *strength fails;* he drinks no water and is faint

STRENGTH IS MADE PERFECT
2Cor 12:9 And He said to me, "My grace is sufficient for you, for My *strength is made perfect* in weakness

STRENGTH OF THE HORSE
Ps 147:10 He does not delight in the *strength of the horse*

STRENGTH OF THE LORD
Ps 71:16 I will go in the *strength of the Lord* God
Mic 5:4 And He shall stand and feed His flock in the *strength of the Lord*, in the majesty of the name of the Lord His God

STRENGTHEN THE WEAK HANDS
Is 35:3 *Strengthen the weak hands*, and make firm the feeble knees

STRENGTHEN YOUR BRETHREN
Luke 22:32 and when you have returned to Me, *strengthen your brethren*

STRENGTHEN YOUR HEART
Ps 27:14 Be of good courage, and He shall *strengthen your heart*
Ps 31:24 Be of good courage, and He shall *strengthen your heart*, all you who hope in the Lord

STRENGTHEN YOUR STAKES
Is 54:2 do not spare; lengthen your cords, and *strengthen your stakes*

STRETCH OUT MY HAND
Ex 3:20 So I will *stretch out My hand* and strike Egypt with all My wonders which I will do in its midst
Ex 7:5 And the Egyptians shall know that I am the Lord, when I *stretch out My hand* on Egypt and bring out the children of Israel from among them
1Sam 24:6 And he said to his men, "The Lord forbid that I should do this thing to my master, the Lord's anointed, to *stretch out my hand* against him, seeing he is the anointed of the Lord
1Sam 24:10 But my eye spared you, and I said, 'I will not *stretch out my hand* against my lord, for he is the Lord's anointed
1Sam 26:11 The Lord forbid that I should *stretch out my hand* against the Lord's anointed
1Sam 26:23 for the Lord delivered you into my hand today, but I would not *stretch out my hand* against the Lord's anointed
Jer 6:12 for I will *stretch out My hand* against the inhabitants of the land
Jer 15:6 Therefore I will *stretch out My hand* against you and destroy you
Jer 51:25 And I will *stretch out My hand* against

you, roll you down from the rocks, and make you a burnt mountain
Ezek 6:14 So I will *stretch out My hand* against them and make the land desolate, yes, more desolate than the wilderness toward Diblah, in all their habitations
Ezek 14:9 And if the prophet is induced to speak anything, I the Lord have induced that prophet, and I will *stretch out My hand* against him and destroy him from among My people Israel
Ezek 14:13 Son of man, when a land sins against Me by persistent unfaithfulness, I will *stretch out My hand* against it
Ezek 25:7 indeed, therefore, I will *stretch out My hand* against you, and give you as plunder to the nations
Ezek 25:13 I will also *stretch out My hand* against Edom, cut off man and beast from it, and make it desolate from Teman
Ezek 25:16 I will *stretch out My hand* against the Philistines, and I will cut off the Cherethites and destroy the remnant of the seacoast
Ezek 35:3 I will *stretch out My hand* against you, and make you most desolate
Zeph 1:4 I will *stretch out My hand* against Judah, and against all the inhabitants of Jerusalem

STRETCHED FORTH HIS HAND (KJV)
(See *STRETCHED OUT HIS HAND*)

STRETCHED FORTH MY HANDS (KJV)
(See *STRETCHED OUT MY HANDS*)

STRETCHED OUT ARM (KJV)
(See *OUTSTRETCHED ARM*)

STRETCHED OUT HIS HAND (RSV)
Gen 22:10 And Abraham *stretched out his hand* and took the knife to slay his son
Ex 8:6 So Aaron *stretched out his hand* over the waters of Egypt, and the frogs came up and covered the land of Egypt
Ex 8:17 For Aaron *stretched out his hand* with his rod and struck the dust of the earth, and it became lice on man and beast
Ex 10:22 So Moses *stretched out his hand* toward heaven, and there was thick darkness in all the land of Egypt three days
Ex 14:21 Then Moses *stretched out his hand* over the sea; and the Lord caused the sea to go back by a strong east wind all that night, and made the sea into dry land, and the waters were divided
Ex 14:27 And Moses *stretched out his hand* over the sea; and when the morning appeared, the sea returned to its full depth, while the Egyptians were fleeing into it
Josh 8:19 they ran as soon as he had *stretched out his hand*, and they entered the city and took it, and hastened to set the city on fire
2Sam 24:16 And when the angel *stretched out His hand* over Jerusalem to destroy it, the Lord relented from the destruction, and said to the angel who was destroying the people
1Kin 13:4 So it came to pass when King Jeroboam heard the saying of the man of God, who cried out against the altar in Bethel, that he *stretched out his hand* from the altar, saying
Is 5:25 he has *stretched out His hand* against them and stricken them, and the hills trembled
Is 23:11 He *stretched out His hand* over the sea, He shook the kingdoms
Ezek 10:7 And the cherub *stretched out his hand* from among the cherubim to the fire that was among the cherubim, and took some of it and put it into the hands of the man clothed with linen, who took it and went out
Hos 7:5 In the day of our king princes have made him sick, inflamed with wine; He *stretched out his hand* with scoffers
Matt 12:49 And He *stretched out His hand* toward His disciples and said
Matt 14:31 And immediately Jesus *stretched out His hand* and caught him, and said to him
Matt 26:51 And suddenly, one of those who were with Jesus *stretched out his hand* and drew his sword, struck the servant of the high priest, and cut off his ear
Acts 12:1 Now about that time Herod the king *stretched out his hand* to harass some from the church
Acts 26:1 So Paul *stretched out his hand* and answered for himself

STRETCHED OUT HIS HANDS (RSV)
(See *SPREAD OUT HIS HANDS*)

STRETCHED OUT MY HANDS
Ps 88:9 Lord, I have called daily upon You; I have *stretched out my hands* to You
Is 65:2 I have *stretched out My hands* all day long to a rebellious people, who walk in a way that is not good, according to their own thoughts
Rom 10:21 All day long I have *stretched out My hands* to a disobedient and contrary people

STRICKEN IN YEARS (KJV)
(See *ADVANCED IN YEARS*)

STRIKE HIS HEEL (NIV)
(See *BRUISE HIS HEEL*)

STRIKE THE
Zech 13:7 *Strike the Shepherd*, and the sheep will be scattered; then I will turn My hand against the little ones
Matt 26:31 I will *strike the Shepherd*, and the sheep of the flock will be scattered
Mark 14:27 I will *strike the Shepherd*, and the sheep will be scattered

STRIKE THE EARTH WITH A CURSE
Mal 4:6 And he will turn the hearts of the fathers to the children, and the hearts of the children to their fathers, lest I come and *strike the earth with a curse*

STRIKE THE LAND WITH A CURSE (NIV)
(See *STRIKE THE EARTH WITH A CURSE*)

STRIKE WITH THE SWORD
Luke 22:49 When those around Him saw what was going to happen, they said to Him, "Lord, shall we *strike with the sword*

STRIPPED AND BAREFOOT (NIV)
(See *NAKED AND BAREFOOT*)

STRIVE FOR PEACE (RSV)
(See *PURSUE PEACE*)

STRIVE WITH MAN
Gen 6:3 And the Lord said, "My Spirit shall not *strive with man* forever, for he is indeed flesh

STRIVEN WITH GOD (NAS, RSV)
(See *STRUGGLED WITH GOD*)

STRIVING AFTER WIND (NAS, RSV)
(See *GRASPING FOR THE WIND*)

STRONG CITY (KJV)
(See *FORTIFIED CITY*)

STRONGHOLD IN TIMES OF TROUBLE (NAS, NIV, RSV)
(See *REFUGE IN TIMES OF TROUBLE*)

STROVE AGAINST THE LORD (KJV)
(See *CONTENDED AGAINST THE LORD*)

STROVE WITH GOD (RSV)
(See *STRUGGLED WITH GOD*)

STRUCK THE ROCK
Num 20:11 Then Moses lifted his hand and *struck the rock* twice with his rod
Ps 78:20 Behold, He *struck the rock*, so that the waters gushed out, and the streams overflowed

STRUGGLE IN VAIN (NIV)
(See *LABOR IN VAIN*)

STRUGGLE IS NOT AGAINST FLESH (NAS, NIV)
(See *WRESTLE AGAINST FLESH*)

STRUGGLED WITH GOD
Gen 32:28 for you have *struggled with God* and with men, and have prevailed
Hos 12:3 He took his brother by the heel in the womb, and in his strength he *struggled with God*

STUBBORN REFUSAL (NIV)
(See *HARDNESS OF HEART*)

STUBBORNLY FOLLOW THEIR OWN EVIL HEART (RSV)
(See *STUBBORNNESS OF THEIR EVIL HEART*)

STUBBORNNESS OF THEIR EVIL HEART
Jer 3:17 they shall walk no more after the *stubbornness of their evil heart*

STUDY TO BE QUIET (KJV)
(See *LEAD A QUIET LIFE*)

STUMBLING BLOCK
Is 57:14 Prepare the way, take the *stumbling block* out of the way of My people
Ezek 3:20 Again, when a righteous man turns from his righteousness and commits iniquity, and I lay a *stumbling block* before him, he shall die
Ezek 7:19 they will not satisfy their souls, nor fill their stomachs, because it became their *stumbling block* of iniquity
Rom 11:9 Let their table become a snare and a trap, a *stumbling block* and a recompense to them
Rom 14:13 Therefore let us not judge one another anymore, but rather resolve this, not to put a *stumbling block* or a cause to fall in our brother's way
1Cor 1:23 but we preach Christ crucified, to the Jews a *stumbling block* and to the Greeks foolishness
1Cor 8:9 But beware lest somehow this liberty of yours become a *stumbling block* to those who are weak
Rev 2:14 But I have a few things against you, because you have there those who hold the doctrine of Balaam, who taught Balak to put a *stumbling block* before the children of Israel, to eat things sacrificed to idols, and to commit sexual immorality

STUMP OF JESSE (NIV, RSV)
(See *STEM OF JESSE*)

SUBDUE THE PEOPLES
Ps 47:3 He will *subdue the peoples* under us, and the nations under our feet

SUBJECT TO BLEEDING (NIV)
(See *FLOW OF BLOOD*)

SUBJECT TO VANITY (KJV)
(See *SUBJECTED TO FUTILITY*)

SUBJECTED IT IN HOPE
Rom 8:20 For the creation was subjected to futility, not willingly, but because of Him who *subjected it in hope*

SUBJECTED TO FUTILITY
Rom 8:20 For the creation was *subjected to futility*, not willingly, but because of Him who subjected it in hope

SUBJECTING HIM TO PUBLIC DISGRACE (NIV)
(See *PUT HIM TO AN OPEN SHAME*)

SUBMISSIVE TO YOUR OWN HUSBANDS
1Pet 3:1 Likewise you wives, be *submissive to your own husbands*, that even if some do not obey the word, they, without a word, may be won by the conduct of their wives

SUBMIT TO
Deut 33:29 Your enemies shall *submit to* you, and you shall tread down their high places
2Sam 22:45 The foreigners *submit to* me; as soon as they hear, they obey me
Ps 18:44 As soon as they hear of me they obey me; the foreigners *submit to* me
1Cor 16:16 that you also *submit to* such, and to everyone who works and labors with us
Eph 5:22 Wives, *submit to* your own husbands, as to the Lord
Col 3:18 Wives, *submit to* your own husbands, as is fitting in the Lord
Jas 4:7 Therefore *submit to* God. Resist the devil and he will flee from you

SUBSCRIBE EVIDENCES, AND SEAL THEM (KJV)
(See *SIGN DEEDS AND SEAL THEM*)

SUBSTANCE OF THINGS
Heb 11:1 Now faith is the *substance of things* hoped for, the evidence of things not seen

SUCCESS, SUCCESS (NIV)
(See *PEACE, PEACE*)

SUCH A GREAT SALVATION (NIV, RSV)
(See *SO GREAT A SALVATION*)

SUCH IS THE KINGDOM OF GOD
Mark 10:14 But when Jesus saw it, He was greatly displeased and said to them, "Let the little children come to Me, and do not forbid them; for of *such is the kingdom of God*
Luke 18:16 But Jesus called them to Him and said, "Let the little children come to Me, and do not forbid them; for of *such is the kingdom of God*

SUFFER FOR YOUR SINS (NIV)
(See *BEAR YOUR GUILT*)

SUFFER MANY THINGS
Matt 16:21 From that time Jesus began to show to His disciples that He must go to Jerusalem, and *suffer many things* from the elders and chief priests and scribes, and be killed, and be raised again the third day
Mark 8:31 And He began to teach them that the Son of Man must *suffer many things*, and be rejected by the elders and chief priests and scribes, and be killed, and after three days rise again

Mark 9:12 And how is it written concerning the Son of Man, that He must *suffer many things* and be treated with contempt
Luke 9:22 saying, "The Son of Man must *suffer many things*, and be rejected by the elders and chief priests and scribes, and be killed, and be raised the third day
Luke 17:25 But first He must *suffer many things* and be rejected by this generation

SUFFER SIN UPON HIM (KJV)
(See *BEAR SIN BECAUSE OF HIM*)

SUFFERED A GREAT DEAL (NIV)
(See *SUFFERED MANY THINGS*)

SUFFERED FOR SINS (KJV)
(See *SUFFERED ONCE FOR SINS*)

SUFFERED FROM A HEMORRHAGE (RSV)
(See *FLOW OF BLOOD*)

SUFFERED MANY THINGS
Matt 27:19 While he was sitting on the judgment seat, his wife sent to him, saying, "Have nothing to do with that just Man, for I have *suffered many things* today in a dream because of Him
Mark 5:26 and had *suffered many things* from many physicians. She had spent all that she had and was no better, but rather grew worse

SUFFERED ONCE FOR SINS
1Pet 3:18 For Christ also *suffered once for sins*, the just for the unjust, that He might bring us to God, being put to death in the flesh but made alive by the Spirit

SUFFERED OUTSIDE THE GATE
Heb 13:12 Therefore Jesus also, that He might sanctify the people with His own blood, *suffered outside the gate*

SUFFERINGS OF CHRIST
2Cor 1:5 For as the *sufferings of Christ* abound in us, so our consolation also abounds through Christ
1Pet 1:11 searching what, or what manner of time, the Spirit of Christ who was in them was indicating when He testified beforehand the *sufferings of Christ* and the glories that would follow
1Pet 5:1 The elders who are among you I exhort, I who am a fellow elder and a witness of the *sufferings of Christ*, and also a partaker of the glory that will be revealed

SUFFICIENT FOR THE DAY
Matt 6:34 Therefore do not worry about tomorrow, for tomorrow will worry about its own things. *Sufficient for the day* is its own trouble

SUMMER AND WINTER
Ps 74:17 You have set all the borders of the earth; You have made *summer and winter*
Zech 14:8 And in that day it shall be that living waters shall flow from Jerusalem, half of them toward the eastern sea and half of them toward the western sea; in both *summer and winter* it shall occur

SUN ALSO RISES
Eccl 1:5 The *sun also rises*, and the sun goes down, and hastens to the place where it arose

SUN OF RIGHTEOUSNESS
Mal 4:2 But to you who fear My name the *Sun of Righteousness* shall arise with healing in His wings

SUN RISES (NAS, NIV, RSV)
(See *SUN ALSO RISES*)

SUN SHALL BE DARKENED (KJV)
(See *SUN WILL BE DARKENED*)

SUN STOOD STILL
Josh 10:13 So the *sun stood still*, and the moon stopped, till the people had revenge upon their enemies. Is this not written in the Book of Jasher? So the *sun stood still* in the midst of heaven, and did not hasten to go down for about a whole day

SUN STOPPED SHINING (NIV)
(See *SUN WAS DARKENED*)

SUN WAS DARKENED
Luke 23:45 Then the *sun was darkened*, and the veil of the temple was torn in two

SUN WILL BE DARKENED
Is 13:10 the *sun will be darkened* in its going forth, and the moon will not cause its light to shine
Matt 24:29 Immediately after the tribulation of those days the *sun will be darkened*, and the moon will not give its light
Mark 13:24 But in those days, after that tribulation, the *sun will be darkened*, and the moon will not give its light

SUN'S LIGHT FAILED (RSV)
(See *SUN WAS DARKENED*)

SUNDRY TIMES AND IN DIVERS MANNERS (KJV)
(See *VARIOUS TIMES AND IN DIFFERENT WAYS*)

SUPPLEMENT YOUR FAITH (RSV)
(See *ADD TO YOUR FAITH*)

SUPPLICATION TO THE LORD
1Sam 13:12 then I said, 'The Philistines will now come down on me at Gilgal, and I have not made *supplication to the Lord*
1Kin 8:54 And so it was, when Solomon had finished praying all this prayer and *supplication to the Lord*, that he arose from before the altar of the Lord, from kneeling on his knees with his hands spread up to heaven

SUPPLY ALL YOUR NEED
Phil 4:19 And my God shall *supply all your need* according to His riches in glory by Christ Jesus

SUPPLY WHAT WAS LACKING
Phil 2:30 because for the work of Christ he came close to death, not regarding his life, to *supply what was lacking* in your service toward me

SUPPOSE THERE WERE FIFTY RIGHTEOUS
Gen 18:24 *Suppose there were fifty righteous* within the city; would You also destroy the place and not spare it for the fifty righteous that were in it

SURE BLESSINGS PROMISED TO DAVID (NIV)
(See *SURE MERCIES OF DAVID*)

SURE LOVE FOR DAVID (RSV)
(See *SURE MERCIES OF DAVID*)

SURE MERCIES OF DAVID
Is 55:3 and I will make an everlasting covenant with you the *sure mercies of David*
Acts 13:34 And that He raised Him from the dead,

no more to return to corruption, He has spoken thus: 'I will give you the sure mercies of David

SURE OF BETTER THINGS (RSV)
(See *CONFIDENT OF BETTER THINGS*)

SURFACE OF THE DEEP (NAS, NIV)
(See *FACE OF THE DEEP*)

SURPASSING THE LOVE OF WOMEN
2Sam 1:26 Your love to me was wonderful, *surpassing the love of women*

SURRENDER ME (NIV, RSV)
(See *DELIVER ME*)

SUSPENDS THE EARTH OVER NOTHING (NIV)
(See *HANGS THE EARTH ON NOTHING*)

SUSTAINING ALL THINGS (NIV)
(See *UPHOLDING ALL THINGS*)

SUSTAINS THE FATHERLESS AND THE WIDOW (NIV)
(See *RELIEVES THE FATHERLESS AND WIDOW*)

SWADDLING CLOTHS
Ezek 16:4 you were not rubbed with salt nor swathed in *swaddling cloths*
Luke 2:7 And she brought forth her firstborn Son, and wrapped Him in *swaddling cloths*, and laid Him in a manger, because there was no room for them in the inn
Luke 2:12 You will find a Babe wrapped in *swaddling cloths*, lying in a manger

SWALLOW A CAMEL
Matt 23:24 Blind guides, who strain out a gnat and *swallow a camel*

SWALLOW UP DEATH
Is 25:8 He will *swallow up death* forever, and the Lord God will wipe away tears from all faces

SWARE UNTO THEE (KJV)
(See *SWORE AN OATH TO*)

SWARMS OF LOCUSTS (NIV)
(See *LOCUST SWARMS*)

SWATHED WITH BANDS (RSV)
(See *SWADDLING CLOTHS*)

SWAYS LIKE A HUT (NIV, RSV)
(See *TOTTER LIKE A HUT*)

SWEAR ALLEGIANCE TO THE LORD (NIV, RSV)
(See *SWEAR BY THE LORD*)

SWEAR AN OATH
2Chr 36:13 And he also rebelled against King Nebuchadnezzar, who had made him *swear an oath* by God
Ezra 10:5 Then Ezra arose, and made the leaders of the priests, the Levites, and all Israel *swear an oath* that they would do according to this word
Ps 102:8 My enemies reproach me all day long, and those who deride me *swear an oath* against me
Hos 4:15 Do not come up to Gilgal, nor go up to Beth Aven, nor *swear an oath*

SWEAR BY GOD
Neh 13:25 So I contended with them and cursed them, struck some of them and pulled out their hair, and made them *swear by God*

SWEAR BY HIS NAME (KJV, NAS, RSV)
(See *TAKE OATHS*)

SWEAR BY THE LORD
Gen 24:3 and I will make you *swear by the Lord*, the God of heaven and the God of the earth, that you will not take a wife for my son from the daughters of the Canaanites, among whom I dwell
2Sam 19:7 For I *swear by the Lord*, if you do not go out, not one will stay with you this night
1Kin 2:42 Then the king sent and called for Shimei, and said to him, "Did I not make you *swear by the Lord*, and warn you, saying
Is 19:18 In that day five cities in the land of Egypt will speak the language of Canaan and *swear by the Lord* of hosts

SWEAR FALSELY
Jer 5:2 Though they say, 'As the Lord lives,' surely they *swear falsely*
Jer 7:9 Will you steal, murder, commit adultery, *swear falsely*, burn incense to Baal, and walk after other gods whom you do not know
Matt 5:33 Again you have heard that it was said to those of old, 'You shall not *swear falsely*, but shall perform your oaths to the Lord

SWEAR TO ME
Gen 21:23 Now therefore, *swear to me* by God that you will not deal falsely with me, with my offspring, or with my posterity
Gen 25:33 Then Jacob said, *"Swear to me* as of this day
Gen 47:31 Then he said, *"Swear to me."* And he swore to him
Josh 2:12 Now therefore, I beg you, *swear to me* by the Lord, since I have shown you kindness, that you also will show kindness to my father's house, and give me a true token
Judg 15:12 Then Samson said to them, *"Swear to me* that you will not kill me yourselves
1Sam 30:15 And he said, *"Swear to me* by God that you will neither kill me nor deliver me into the hands of my master, and I will take you down to this troop
1Kin 1:51 for look, he has taken hold of the horns of the altar, saying, 'Let King Solomon *swear to me* today that he will not put his servant to death with the sword

SWEAR TO THE LORD (KJV)
(See *SWEAR BY THE LORD*)

SWEAT BECAME LIKE GREAT DROPS
Luke 22:44 And His *sweat became like great drops* of blood falling down to the ground

SWEAT OF YOUR FACE
Gen 3:19 In the *sweat of your face* you shall eat bread till you return to the ground, for out of it you were taken

SWEAT WAS AS IT WERE GREAT DROPS (KJV)
(See *SWEAT BECAME LIKE GREAT DROPS*)

SWEET AROMA TO THE LORD
Lev 1:9 And the priest shall burn all on the altar as a burnt sacrifice, an offering made by fire, a *sweet aroma to the Lord*
Lev 1:13 it is a burnt sacrifice, an offering made by fire, a *sweet aroma to the Lord*
Lev 1:17 It is a burnt sacrifice, an offering made by fire, a *sweet aroma to the Lord*
Lev 2:2 And the priest shall burn it as a memorial on the altar, an offering made by fire, a *sweet aroma to the Lord*

Lev 2:9 It is an offering made by fire, a *sweet aroma to the Lord*
Lev 3:5 and Aaron's sons shall burn it on the altar upon the burnt sacrifice, which is on the wood that is on the fire, as an offering made by fire, a *sweet aroma to the Lord*
Lev 4:31 and the priest shall burn it on the altar for a *sweet aroma to the Lord*
Lev 6:21 And the baked pieces of the grain offering you shall offer for a *sweet aroma to the Lord*
Lev 17:6 And the priest shall sprinkle the blood on the altar of the Lord at the door of the tabernacle of meeting, and burn the fat for a *sweet aroma to the Lord*
Lev 23:18 They shall be as a burnt offering to the Lord, with their grain offering and their drink offerings, an offering made by fire for a *sweet aroma to the Lord*
Num 15:3 and you make an offering by fire to the Lord, a burnt offering or a sacrifice, to fulfill a vow or as a freewill offering or in your appointed feasts, to make a *sweet aroma to the Lord*, from the herd or the flock
Num 15:7 and as a drink offering you shall offer one-third of a hin of wine as a *sweet aroma to the Lord*
Num 15:10 and you shall bring as the drink offering half a hin of wine as an offering made by fire, a *sweet aroma to the Lord*
Num 15:13 All who are native-born shall do these things in this manner, in presenting an offering made by fire, a *sweet aroma to the Lord*
Num 15:14 And if a stranger sojourns with you, or whoever is among you throughout your generations, and would present an offering made by fire, a *sweet aroma to the Lord*, just as you do, so shall he do
Num 15:24 then it will be, if it is unintentionally committed, without the knowledge of the congregation, that the whole congregation shall offer one young bull as a burnt offering, as a *sweet aroma to the Lord*, with its grain offering and its drink offering, according to the ordinance, and one kid of the goats as a sin offering
Num 18:17 You shall sprinkle their blood on the altar, and burn their fat as an offering made by fire for a *sweet aroma to the Lord*
Num 28:8 as the morning grain offering and its drink offering, you shall offer it as an offering made by fire, a *sweet aroma to the Lord*
Num 28:24 In this manner you shall offer the food of the offering made by fire daily for seven days, as a *sweet aroma to the Lord*
Num 28:27 You shall present a burnt offering as a *sweet aroma to the Lord*
Num 29:2 You shall offer a burnt offering as a *sweet aroma to the Lord*
Num 29:13 You shall present a burnt offering, an offering made by fire as a *sweet aroma to the Lord*
Num 29:36 You shall present a burnt offering, an offering made by fire as a *sweet aroma to the Lord*

SWEET AS HONEY
Rev 10:9 and it will make your stomach bitter, but it will be as *sweet as honey* in your mouth
Rev 10:10 And I took the little book out of the angel's hand and ate it, and it was as *sweet as honey* in my mouth

SWEET INCENSE
Ex 25:6 oil for the light, and spices for the anointing oil and for the *sweet incense*
Ex 30:7 Aaron shall burn on it *sweet incense* every morning; when he tends the lamps, he shall burn incense on it
Ex 31:11 and the anointing oil and *sweet incense* for the holy place
Ex 35:8 oil for the light, and spices for the anointing oil and for the *sweet incense*
Ex 35:15 the incense altar, its poles, the anointing oil, the *sweet incense*, and the screen for the door at the entrance of the tabernacle
Ex 35:28 and spices and oil for the light, for the anointing oil, and for the *sweet incense*
Ex 39:38 the gold altar, the anointing oil, and the *sweet incense*
Ex 40:27 and he burned *sweet incense* on it, as the Lord had commanded Moses
Lev 4:7 And the priest shall put some of the blood on the horns of the altar of *sweet incense* before the Lord, which is in the tabernacle of meeting
Lev 16:12 Then he shall take a censer full of burning coals of fire from the altar before the Lord, with his hands full of *sweet incense* beaten fine, and bring it inside the veil
Num 4:16 The appointed duty of Eleazar the son of Aaron the priest is the oil for the light, the *sweet incense*, the daily grain offering, the anointing oil, the oversight of all the tabernacle, of all that is in it, with the sanctuary and its furnishings
2Chr 2:4 Behold, I am building a temple for the name of the Lord my God, to dedicate it to Him, to burn before Him *sweet incense*, for the continual showbread, for the burnt offerings morning and evening, on the Sabbaths, on the New Moons, and on the set feasts of the Lord our God
2Chr 13:11 And they burn to the Lord every morning and every evening burnt sacrifices and *sweet incense*
Ezek 6:13 Then you shall know that I am the Lord, when their slain men are among their idols all around their altars, on every high hill, on all the mountaintops, under every green tree, and under every thick oak, wherever they offered *sweet incense* to all their idols
Ezek 16:19 Also My food which I gave you the pastry of fine flour, oil, and honey which I fed you you set it before them as *sweet incense*

SWEET PSALMIST OF ISRAEL
2Sam 23:1 thus says the man raised up on high, the anointed of the God of Jacob, and the *sweet psalmist of Israel*

SWEET SAVOR (KJV)
(See *SWEET INCENSE*)

SWEET SAVOR UNTO THE LORD (KJV)
(See *SWEET AROMA TO THE LORD*)

SWERVE TO THE RIGHT OR TO THE LEFT (RSV)
(See *TURN TO THE RIGHT OR THE LEFT*)

SWERVED FROM THE TRUTH (RSV)
(See *STRAYED CONCERNING THE TRUTH*)

SWIFT TO SHED BLOOD
Rom 3:15 Their feet are *swift to shed blood*

SWIFT TO SHED INNOCENT BLOOD (NIV)
(See *MAKE HASTE TO SHED INNOCENT BLOOD*)

SWIFTER THAN A WEAVER'S SHUTTLE
Job 7:6 My days are *swifter than a weaver's shuttle*, and are spent without hope

SWINE'S FLESH
Is 65:4 who eat *swine's flesh*, and the broth of abominable things is in their vessels
Is 66:17 Those who sanctify themselves and purify

themselves, to go to the gardens after an idol in the midst, eating *swine's flesh* and the abomination and the mouse, shall be consumed together

SWORD OF MY MOUTH
Rev 2:16 Repent, or else I will come to you quickly and will fight against them with the *sword of My mouth*

SWORD OF THE LORD
Judg 7:18 When I blow the trumpet, I and all who are with me, then you also blow the trumpets on every side of the whole camp, and say, 'The *sword of the Lord* and of Gideon
Judg 7:20 Then the three companies blew the trumpets and broke the pitchers they held the torches in their left hands and the trumpets in their right hands for blowing and they cried, "The *sword of the Lord* and of Gideon
1Chr 21:12 either three years of famine, or three months to be defeated by your foes with the sword of your enemies overtaking you, or else for three days the *sword of the Lord* the plague in the land, with the angel of the Lord destroying throughout all the territory of Israel
Is 34:6 The *sword of the Lord* is filled with blood, it is made overflowing with fatness, and with the blood of lambs and goats, with the fat of the kidneys of rams
Jer 12:12 The plunderers have come on all the desolate heights in the wilderness, for the *sword of the Lord* shall devour from one end of the land to the other end of the land
Jer 47:6 O you *sword of the Lord*, how long until you are quiet

SWORD OF THE SPIRIT
Eph 6:17 And take the helmet of salvation, and the *sword of the Spirit*, which is the word of God

SWORD SHALL NEVER DEPART
2Sam 12:10 Now therefore, the *sword shall never depart* from your house, because you have despised Me, and have taken the wife of Uriah the Hittite to be your wife

SWORDS INTO PLOWSHARES
Is 2:4 they shall beat their *swords into plowshares*, and their spears into pruning hooks
Mic 4:3 they shall beat their *swords into plowshares*, and their spears into pruning hooks

SWORE AN OATH TO
Ezek 16:8 Yes, I *swore an oath to* you and entered into a covenant with you, and you became Mine

SWORE TO YOUR FATHERS
Ex 13:5 And it shall be, when the Lord brings you into the land of the Canaanites and the Hittites and the Amorites and the Hivites and the Jebusites, which He *swore to your fathers* to give you, a land flowing with milk and honey, that you shall keep this service in this month
Deut 1:8 go in and possess the land which the Lord *swore to your fathers* to Abraham, Isaac, and Jacob to give to them and their descendants after them
Deut 6:10 And it shall be, when the Lord your God brings you into the land of which He *swore to your fathers*, to Abraham, Isaac, and Jacob, to give you large and beautiful cities which you did not build
Deut 6:18 And you shall do what is right and good in the sight of the Lord, that it may be well with you, and that you may go in and possess the good land of which the Lord *swore to your fathers*
Deut 7:8 but because the Lord loves you, and because He would keep the oath which He *swore to your fathers*, the Lord has brought you out with a mighty hand, and redeemed you from the house of bondage, from the hand of Pharaoh king of Egypt
Deut 7:12 Then it shall come to pass, because you listen to these judgments, and keep and do them, that the Lord your God will keep with you the covenant and the mercy which He *swore to your fathers*
Deut 7:13 He will also bless the fruit of your womb and the fruit of your land, your grain and your new wine and your oil, the increase of your cattle and the offspring of your flock, in the land of which He *swore to your fathers* to give you
Deut 8:1 Every commandment which I command you today you must be careful to observe, that you may live and multiply, and go in and possess the land of which the Lord *swore to your fathers*
Deut 8:18 And you shall remember the Lord your God, for it is He who gives you power to get wealth, that He may establish His covenant which He *swore to your fathers*, as it is this day
Deut 9:5 It is not because of your righteousness or the uprightness of your heart that you go in to possess their land, but because of the wickedness of these nations that the Lord your God drives them out from before you, and that He may fulfill the word which the Lord *swore to your fathers*, to Abraham, Isaac, and Jacob
Deut 11:21 that your days and the days of your children may be multiplied in the land of which the Lord *swore to your fathers* to give them, like the days of the heavens above the earth
Deut 13:17 So none of the accursed things shall remain in your hand, that the Lord may turn from the fierceness of His anger and show you mercy, have compassion on you and multiply you, just as He *swore to your fathers*
Deut 19:8 Now if the Lord your God enlarges your territory, as He *swore to your fathers*, and gives you the land which He promised to give to your fathers
Deut 28:11 And the Lord will grant you plenty of goods, in the fruit of your body, in the increase of your livestock, and in the produce of your ground, in the land of which the Lord *swore to your fathers* to give you
Deut 30:20 and that you may dwell in the land which the Lord *swore to your fathers*, to Abraham, Isaac, and Jacob, to give them
Judg 2:1 I led you up from Egypt and brought you to the land of which I *swore to your fathers*

SWORN AGREEMENT (NIV)
(See *MAKE A COVENANT*)

SWORN BY MY HOLINESS
Ps 89:35 Once I have *sworn by My holiness;* I will not lie to David

SYMBOL ON YOUR FOREHEAD (NIV)
(See *FRONTLETS BETWEEN YOUR EYES*)

SYMBOLS ON YOUR HANDS (NIV)
(See *SIGN ON YOUR HAND*)

SYNAGOGUE OF SATAN
Rev 2:9 and I know the blasphemy of those who say they are Jews and are not, but are a *synagogue of Satan*
Rev 3:9 Indeed I will make those of the *synagogue of Satan*, who say they are Jews and are not, but lie indeed I will make them come and worship before your feet, and to know that I have loved you

SYNAGOGUE OF THE JEWS
Acts 14:1 Now it happened in Iconium that they went together to the *synagogue of the Jews*, and so spoke that a great multitude both of the Jews and of the Greeks believed
Acts 17:1 Now when they had passed through Amphipolis and Apollonia, they came to Thessalonica, where there was a *synagogue of the Jews*
Acts 17:10 When they arrived, they went into the *synagogue of the Jews*

SYNAGOGUE RULER (NIV)
(See *RULER OF THE SYNAGOGUE*)

T

TABERNACLE OF THE LORD
Lev 17:4 and does not bring it to the door of the tabernacle of meeting, to offer an offering to the Lord before the *tabernacle of the Lord*, bloodguilt shall be imputed to that man
Num 16:9 Is it a small thing to you that the God of Israel has separated you from the congregation of Israel, to bring you near to Himself, to do the work of the *tabernacle of the Lord*, and to stand before the congregation to serve them
Num 17:13 Whoever even comes near the *tabernacle of the Lord* must die
Num 19:13 Whoever touches the body of anyone who has died, and does not purify himself, defiles the *tabernacle of the Lord*
Num 31:30 And from the children of Israel's half you shall take one of every fifty, drawn from the persons, the cattle, the donkeys, and the sheep, from all the livestock, and give them to the Levites who keep charge of the *tabernacle of the Lord*
Num 31:47 and from the children of Israel's half Moses took one of every fifty, drawn from man and beast, and gave them to the Levites, who kept charge of the *tabernacle of the Lord*, as the Lord commanded Moses
1Sam 1:9 Now Eli the priest was sitting on the seat by the doorpost of the *tabernacle of the Lord*
1Sam 3:3 and before the lamp of God went out in the *tabernacle of the Lord* where the ark of God was, and while Samuel was lying down to sleep
1Kin 2:28 So Joab fled to the *tabernacle of the Lord*, and took hold of the horns of the altar
1Kin 2:29 And King Solomon was told, "Joab has fled to the *tabernacle of the Lord*
1Kin 2:30 So Benaiah went to the *tabernacle of the Lord*, and said to him
1Chr 16:39 and Zadok the priest and his brethren the priests, before the *tabernacle of the Lord* at the high place that was at Gibeon
1Chr 21:29 For the *tabernacle of the Lord* and the altar of the burnt offering, which Moses had made in the wilderness, were at that time at the high place in Gibeon
2Chr 1:5 Now the bronze altar that Bezaleel the son of Uri, the son of Hur, had made, he put before the *tabernacle of the Lord*

TABERNACLE OF THE TESTIMONY
Ex 38:21 This is the inventory of the tabernacle, the *tabernacle of the Testimony*, which was counted according to the commandment of Moses, for the service of the Levites, by the hand of Ithamar, son of Aaron the priest
Num 1:50 but you shall appoint the Levites over the *tabernacle of the Testimony*, over all its furnishings, and over all things that belong to it
Num 1:53 but the Levites shall camp around the *tabernacle of the Testimony*, that there may be no wrath on the congregation of the children of Israel; and the Levites shall keep charge of the *tabernacle of the Testimony*
Num 10:11 Now it came to pass on the twentieth day of the second month, in the second year, that the cloud was taken up from above the *tabernacle of the Testimony*
Rev 15:5 After these things I looked, and behold, the temple of the *tabernacle of the testimony* in heaven was opened

TABLE OF SHOWBREAD
Num 4:7 On the *table of showbread* they shall spread a blue cloth, and put on it the dishes, the pans, the bowls, and the pitchers for pouring

TABLE OF THE BREAD OF THE PRESENCE (NAS,RSV)
(See *TABLE OF SHOWBREAD*)

TABLE OF THE LORD
Mal 1:7 By saying, 'The *table of the Lord* is contemptible
Mal 1:12 But you profane it, in that you say, 'The *table of the Lord* is defiled

TABLE OF THE PRESENCE (NIV)
(See *TABLE OF SHOWBREAD*)

TABLES OF THE MONEYCHANGERS
Matt 21:12 Then Jesus went into the temple of God and drove out all those who bought and sold in the temple, and overturned the *tables of the moneychangers* and the seats of those who sold doves
Mark 11:15 And Jesus went into the temple and began to drive out those who bought and sold in the temple, and overturned the *tables of the moneychangers* and the seats of those who sold doves

TABLET OF THEIR HEART
Jer 17:1 with the point of a diamond it is engraved on the *tablet of their heart*, and on the horns of your altars

TABLET OF YOUR HEART
Prov 3:3 bind them around your neck, write them on the *tablet of your heart*
Prov 7:3 Bind them on your fingers; write them on the *tablet of your heart*

TABLETS OF STONE
Ex 24:12 and I will give you *tablets of stone*, and the law and commandments which I have written, that you may teach them
Ex 31:18 And when He had made an end of speaking with him on Mount Sinai, He gave Moses two tablets of the Testimony, *tablets of stone*, written with the finger of God
Ex 34:1 And the Lord said to Moses, "Cut two *tablets of stone* like the first ones, and I will write on these tablets the words that were on the first tablets which you broke
Ex 34:4 So he cut two *tablets of stone* like the first ones. Then Moses rose early in the morning and went up Mount Sinai, as the Lord had commanded him; and he took in his hand the two *tablets of stone*
Deut 4:13 So He declared to you His covenant which He commanded you to perform, that is, the Ten Commandments; and He wrote them on two *tablets of stone*
Deut 5:22 And He wrote them on two *tablets of stone* and gave them to me
Deut 9:9 When I went up into the mountain to receive the *tablets of stone*, the tablets of the covenant which the Lord made with you, then I

stayed on the mountain forty days and forty nights

Deut 9:10 Then the Lord delivered to me two *tablets of stone* written with the finger of God, and on them were all the words which the Lord had spoken to you on the mountain from the midst of the fire in the day of the assembly

Deut 9:11 And it came to pass, at the end of forty days and forty nights, that the Lord gave me the two *tablets of stone*, the tablets of the covenant

Deut 10:1 At that time the Lord said to me, 'Hew for yourself two *tablets of stone* like the first, and come up to Me on the mountain and make yourself an ark of wood

Deut 10:3 So I made an ark of acacia wood, hewed two *tablets of stone* like the first, and went up the mountain, having the two tablets in my hand

1Kin 8:9 There was nothing in the ark except the two *tablets of stone* which Moses put there at Horeb, when the Lord made a covenant with the children of Israel, when they came out of the land of Egypt

2Cor 3:3 you are manifestly an epistle of Christ, ministered by us, written not with ink but by the Spirit of the living God, not on *tablets of stone* but on tablets of flesh, that is, of the heart

TABLETS OF THE COVENANT

Deut 9:9 When I went up into the mountain to receive the tablets of stone, the *tablets of the covenant* which the Lord made with you, then I stayed on the mountain forty days and forty nights

Deut 9:11 And it came to pass, at the end of forty days and forty nights, that the Lord gave me the two tablets of stone, the *tablets of the covenant*

Deut 9:15 and the two *tablets of the covenant* were in my two hands

Heb 9:4 which had the golden altar of incense and the ark of the covenant overlaid on all sides with gold, in which were the golden pot that had the manna, Aaron's rod that budded, and the *tablets of the covenant*

TABLETS OF THE TESTIMONY

Ex 31:18 And when He had made an end of speaking with him on Mount Sinai, He gave Moses two *tablets of the Testimony*, tablets of stone, written with the finger of God

Ex 32:15 And Moses turned and went down from the mountain, and the two *tablets of the Testimony* were in his hand

Ex 34:29 Now it was so, when Moses came down from Mount Sinai (and the two *tablets of the Testimony* were in Moses' hand when he came down from the mountain

TAKE A CENSUS

Num 1:2 *Take a census* of all the congregation of the children of Israel, by their families, by their fathers' houses, according to the number of names, every male individually

Num 1:49 Only the tribe of Levi you shall not number, nor *take a census* of them among the children of Israel

Num 4:2 *Take a census* of the sons of Kohath from among the children of Levi, by their families, by their fathers' house

Num 4:22 Also *take a census* of the sons of Gershon, by their fathers' house, by their families

Num 26:2 *Take a census* of all the congregation of the children of Israel from twenty years old and above, by their fathers' houses, all who are able to go to war in Israel

Num 26:4 *Take a census* of the people from twenty years old and above, just as the Lord commanded Moses and the children of Israel who came out of the land of Egypt

TAKE A LOWLY SEAT (NAS,RSV)
(See *HUMBLE YOURSELVES*)

TAKE AN OATH

1Kin 8:31 When anyone sins against his neighbor, and is forced to *take an oath*, and comes and takes an oath before Your altar in this temple

2Chr 6:22 If anyone sins against his neighbor, and is forced to *take an oath*, and comes and takes an oath before Your altar in this temple

Is 45:23 the word has gone out of My mouth in righteousness, and shall not return, that to Me every knee shall bow, every tongue shall *take an oath*

TAKE AN OATH IN GOD'S NAME (NIV)
(See *SWEAR BY GOD*)

TAKE AND EAT

Rev 10:9 And he said to me, "*Take and eat* it; and it will make your stomach bitter, but it will be as sweet as honey in your mouth

TAKE AWAY SINS

Heb 10:4 For it is not possible that the blood of bulls and goats could *take away sins*

Heb 10:11 And every priest stands ministering daily and offering repeatedly the same sacrifices, which can never *take away sins*

TAKE AWAY THE GUILT (NIV)
(See *BEAR THE GUILT*)

TAKE CARE OF MY SHEEP (NIV)
(See *TEND MY SHEEP*)

TAKE, EAT

Matt 26:26 And as they were eating, Jesus took bread, blessed it and broke it, and gave it to the disciples and said, "*Take, eat*

Mark 14:22 And as they were eating, Jesus took bread, blessed it and broke it, and gave it to them and said, "*Take, eat*

1Cor 11:24 and when He had given thanks, He broke it and said, "*Take, eat*

TAKE HEART (NIV)
(See *BE OF GOOD COURAGE*)

TAKE HEED

Ex 10:28 *Take heed* to yourself and see my face no more

Ex 19:12 You shall set bounds for the people all around, saying, '*Take heed* to yourselves that you do not go up to the mountain or touch its base

Ex 34:12 *Take heed* to yourself, lest you make a covenant with the inhabitants of the land where you are going, lest it be a snare in your midst

Num 23:12 So he answered and said, "Must I not *take heed* to speak what the Lord has put in my mouth

Deut 4:9 Only *take heed* to yourself, and diligently keep yourself, lest you forget the things your eyes have seen, and lest they depart from your heart all the days of your life

Deut 4:19 And *take heed*, lest you lift your eyes to heaven, and when you see the sun, the moon, and the stars, all the host of heaven, you feel driven to worship them and serve them, which the Lord your God has given to all the peoples under the whole heaven as a heritage

Deut 4:23 *Take heed* to yourselves, lest you forget the covenant of the Lord your God which He made with you, and make for yourselves a carved image in the form of anything which the Lord your God has forbidden you

Deut 11:16 *Take heed* to yourselves, lest your

heart be deceived, and you turn aside and serve other gods and worship them
Deut 12:13 *Take heed* to yourself that you do not offer your burnt offerings in every place that you see
Deut 12:19 *Take heed* to yourself that you do not forsake the Levite as long as you live in your land
Deut 12:30 *take heed* to yourself that you are not ensnared to follow them, after they are destroyed from before you, and that you do not inquire after their gods, saying
Deut 24:8 *Take heed* in an outbreak of leprosy, that you diligently observe and do according to all that the priests, the Levites, shall teach you
Deut 27:9 Then Moses and the priests, the Levites, spoke to all Israel, saying, "*Take heed* and listen, O Israel
1Kin 2:4 that the Lord may fulfill His word which He spoke concerning me, saying, 'If your sons *take heed* to their way, to walk before Me in truth with all their heart and with all their soul
1Kin 8:25 Therefore, Lord God of Israel, now keep what You promised Your servant David my father, saying, 'You shall not fail to have a man sit before Me on the throne of Israel, only if your sons *take heed* to their way, that they walk before Me as you have walked before Me
1Kin 22:28 Then Micaiah said, "If you ever return in peace, the Lord has not spoken by me." And he said, "*Take heed*, all you people
2Chr 6:16 Therefore, Lord God of Israel, now keep what You promised Your servant David my father, saying, 'You shall not fail to have a man sit before Me on the throne of Israel, only if your sons *take heed* to their way, to walk in My law as you have walked before Me
2Chr 18:27 Then Micaiah said, "If you ever return in peace, the Lord has not spoken by me." And he said, "*Take heed*, all you people
2Chr 19:6 and said to the judges, "*Take heed* to what you are doing, for you do not judge for man but for the Lord, who is with you in the judgment
Ezra 4:22 *Take heed* now that you do not fail to do this
Job 36:21 *Take heed*, do not turn to iniquity, for you have chosen this rather than affliction
Is 7:4 *Take heed*, and be quiet; do not fear or be fainthearted for these two stubs of smoking firebrands, for the fierce anger of Rezin and Syria, and the son of Remaliah
Is 49:1 Listen, O coastlands, to Me, and *take heed*, you peoples from afar
Jer 9:4 Everyone *take heed* to his neighbor, and do not trust any brother
Jer 17:21 *Take heed* to yourselves, and bear no burden on the Sabbath day, nor bring it in by the gates of Jerusalem
Hos 5:1 *Take heed*, O house of Israel! Give ear, O house of the king
Mal 2:15 Therefore *take heed* to your spirit, and let none deal treacherously with the wife of his youth
Mal 2:16 Therefore *take heed* to your spirit, that you do not deal treacherously
Matt 6:1 *Take heed* that you do not do your charitable deeds before men, to be seen by them
Matt 16:6 Then Jesus said to them, "*Take heed* and beware of the leaven of the Pharisees and the Sadducees
Matt 18:10 *Take heed* that you do not despise one of these little ones, for I say to you that in heaven their angels always see the face of My Father who is in heaven
Matt 24:4 And Jesus answered and said to them: "*Take heed* that no one deceives you
Mark 4:24 And He said to them, "*Take heed* what you hear
Mark 8:15 Then He charged them, saying, "*Take heed*, beware of the leaven of the Pharisees and the leaven of Herod
Mark 13:5 And Jesus, answering them, began to say: "*Take heed* that no one deceives you
Mark 13:23 But *take heed;* see, I have told you all things beforehand
Mark 13:33 *Take heed*, watch and pray; for you do not know when the time is
Luke 8:18 Therefore *take heed* how you hear. For whoever has, to him more will be given
Luke 11:35 Therefore *take heed* that the light which is in you is not darkness
Luke 12:15 And He said to them, "*Take heed* and beware of covetousness, for one's life does not consist in the abundance of the things he possesses
Luke 17:3 *Take heed* to yourselves. If your brother sins against you, rebuke him
Luke 21:8 *Take heed* that you not be deceived. For many, will come in My name, saying
Luke 21:34 But *take heed* to yourselves, lest your hearts be weighed down with carousing, drunkenness, and cares of this life, and that Day come on you unexpectedly
Acts 5:35 Men of Israel, *take heed* to yourselves what you intend to do regarding these men
Acts 20:28 Therefore *take heed* to yourselves and to all the flock, among which the Holy Spirit has made you overseers, to shepherd the church of God which He purchased with His own blood
1Cor 3:10 But let each one *take heed* how he builds on it
1Cor 10:12 Therefore let him who thinks he stands *take heed* lest he fall
Col 4:17 And say to Archippus, "*Take heed* to the ministry which you have received in the Lord, that you may fulfill it
1Tim 4:16 *Take heed* to yourself and to the doctrine. Continue in them, for in doing this you will save both yourself and those who hear you

TAKE HEED TO YOURSELF (RSV)
(See *BE ON YOUR GUARD*)

TAKE HIS LIFE
Prov 7:23 As a bird hastens to the snare, he did not know it would *take his life*

TAKE HOLD OF THE ETERNAL LIFE (NAS, NIV, RSV)
(See *LAY HOLD ON ETERNAL LIFE*)

TAKE IT, AND EAT IT (KJV, NAS, NIV)
(See *TAKE AND EAT*)

TAKE IT AWAY FROM ME (NIV)
(See *DEPART FROM ME*)

TAKE IT TO HEART
2Sam 19:19 Then he said to the king, "Do not let my lord impute iniquity to me, or remember what wrong your servant did on the day that my lord the king left Jerusalem, that the king should *take it to heart*
Eccl 7:2 It is better to go to the house of mourning than to go to the house of feasting, for that is the end of all men; and the living will *take it to heart*
Is 42:25 and it burned him, yet he did not *take it to heart*
Mal 2:2 If you will not hear, and if you will not *take it to heart*, to give glory to My name," says the Lord of hosts, "I will send a curse upon you, and I will curse your blessings. Yes, I have cursed them already, because you do not *take it to heart*

TAKE ITS BLOOD AND SPRINKLE IT
Ex 29:16 and you shall kill the ram, and you shall *take its blood and sprinkle it* all around on the altar

TAKE ITS BLOOD AND THROW IT (RSV)
(See *TAKE ITS BLOOD AND SPRINKLE IT*)

TAKE MY INSTRUCTION (NAS, RSV)
(See *RECEIVE MY INSTRUCTION*)

TAKE MY YOKE
Matt 11:29 *Take My yoke* upon you and learn from Me, for I am gentle and lowly in heart, and you will find rest for your souls

TAKE NO BRIBE
Ex 23:8 And you shall *take no bribe*, for a bribe blinds the discerning and perverts the words of the righteous

TAKE NO GIFT (KJV)
(See *TAKE NO BRIBE*)

TAKE OATHS
Deut 6:13 You shall fear the Lord your God and serve Him, and shall *take oaths* in His name
Deut 10:20 you shall serve Him, and to Him you shall hold fast, and *take oaths* in His name

TAKE PITY ON THE WEAK AND THE NEEDY (NIV)
(See *SPARE THE POOR AND NEEDY*)

TAKE PLEASURE IN (RSV)
(See *ENJOY THE GOOD*)

TAKE REFUGE IN THE SHELTER (NAS, NIV)
(See *TRUST IN THE SHELTER*)

TAKE REFUGE IN THEE (NAS, RSV)
(See *TRUST IN YOU*)

TAKE REFUGE IN YOU (NIV)
(See *TRUST IN YOU*)

TAKE THE KINGDOM (KJV)
(See *RECEIVE THE KINGDOM*)

TAKE THE NAME OF THE LORD YOUR GOD IN VAIN
Ex 20:7 You shall not *take the name of the Lord your God in vain*, for the Lord will not hold him guiltless who takes His name in vain
Deut 5:11 You shall not *take the name of the Lord your God in vain*, for the Lord will not hold him guiltless who takes His name in vain

TAKE THE SPECK (NAS, NIV, RSV)
(See *REMOVE THE SPECK*)

TAKE THEM OUT OF THE WORLD
John 17:15 I do not pray that You should *take them out of the world*, but that You should keep them from the evil one

TAKE THIS CUP
Mark 14:36 *Take this cup* away from Me; nevertheless, not what I will, but what You will

TAKE UP A LAMENTATION
Jer 7:29 Cut off your hair and cast it away, and *take up a lamentation* on the desolate heights
Ezek 19:1 Moreover *take up a lamentation* for the princes of Israel
Ezek 26:17 And they will *take up a lamentation* for you, and say to you
Ezek 27:2 Now, son of man, *take up a lamentation* for Tyre
Ezek 27:32 In their wailing for you they will *take up a lamentation*, and lament for you
Ezek 28:12 Son of man, *take up a lamentation* for the king of Tyre, and say to him
Ezek 32:2 Son of man, *take up a lamentation* for Pharaoh king of Egypt, and say to him

TAKE UP HIS CROSS
Matt 16:24 Then Jesus said to His disciples, "If anyone desires to come after Me, let him deny himself, and *take up his cross*, and follow Me
Mark 8:34 And when He had called the people to Him, with His disciples also, He said to them, "Whoever desires to come after Me, let him deny himself, and *take up his cross*, and follow Me
Luke 9:23 Then He said to them all, "If anyone desires to come after Me, let him deny himself, and *take up his cross* daily, and follow Me

TAKE UP SERPENTS
Mark 16:18 they will *take up serpents;* and if they drink anything deadly, it will by no means hurt them

TAKE UP THE CROSS
Mark 10:21 Go your way, sell whatever you have and give to the poor, and you will have treasure in heaven; and come, *take up the cross*, and follow Me

TAKE UP YOUR BED AND WALK
Mark 2:9 Which is easier, to say to the paralytic, 'Your sins are forgiven you,' or to say, 'Arise, *take up your bed and walk*
John 5:8 Jesus said to him, "Rise, *take up your bed and walk*
John 5:11 He answered them, "He who made me well said to me, '*Take up your bed and walk*
John 5:12 Then they asked him, "Who is the Man who said to you, '*Take up your bed and walk*

TAKE UP YOUR PALLET AND WALK (RSV)
(See *TAKE UP YOUR BED AND WALK*)

TAKE YE THE SUM (KJV)
(See *TAKE A CENSUS*)

TAKE YOUR HOLY SPIRIT
Ps 51:11 Do not cast me away from Your presence, and do not *take Your Holy Spirit* from me

TAKE YOUR MAT AND WALK (NIV)
(See *TAKE UP YOUR BED AND WALK*)

TAKEN UNDER THE SUN (KJV)
(See *TOILED UNDER THE SUN*)

TAKEN UP IN GLORY (NAS, NIV, RSV)
(See *RECEIVED UP IN GLORY*)

TAKEN UP MY CAUSE (RSV)
(See *PLEADED THE CASE*)

TAKES AWAY THE
John 1:29 The Lamb of God who *takes away the sin of the world*

TAKES HIS NAME IN VAIN
Ex 20:7 You shall not take the name of the Lord your God in vain, for the Lord will not hold him guiltless who *takes His name in vain*
Deut 5:11 You shall not take the name of the Lord your God in vain, for the Lord will not hold him guiltless who *takes His name in vain*

TAKES IT TO HEART
Is 57:1 The righteous perishes, and no man *takes it to heart*
Jer 12:11 the whole land is made desolate, because no one *takes it to heart*

TAKES THE THRONE (NIV)
(See *SITS ON THE THRONE*)

TALENTS OF SILVER
Ex 38:27 And from the hundred *talents of silver* were cast the sockets of the sanctuary and the bases of the veil
1Kin 16:24 And he bought the hill of Samaria from Shemer for two *talents of silver*
2Kin 5:5 So he departed and took with him ten *talents of silver*, six thousand shekels of gold, and ten changes of clothing
2Kin 5:23 And he urged him, and bound two *talents of silver* in two bags, with two changes of garments, and handed them to two of his servants
2Kin 15:19 and Menahem gave Pul a thousand *talents of silver*, that his hand might be with him to strengthen the kingdom in his hand
2Kin 18:14 And the king of Assyria assessed Hezekiah king of Judah three hundred *talents of silver* and thirty talents of gold
2Kin 23:33 and he imposed on the land a tribute of one hundred *talents of silver* and a talent of gold
1Chr 19:6 When the people of Ammon saw that they had made themselves repulsive to David, Hanun and the people of Ammon sent a thousand *talents of silver* to hire for themselves chariots and horsemen from Mesopotamia, from Syrian Maachah, and from Zobah
1Chr 22:14 Indeed I have taken much trouble to prepare for the house of the Lord one hundred thousand talents of gold and one million *talents of silver*, and bronze and iron beyond measure, for it is so abundant
1Chr 29:7 They gave for the work of the house of God five thousand talents and ten thousand darics of gold, ten thousand *talents of silver*, eighteen thousand talents of bronze, and one hundred thousand talents of iron
2Chr 25:6 He also hired one hundred thousand mighty men of valor from Israel for one hundred *talents of silver*
2Chr 27:5 And the people of Ammon gave him in that year one hundred *talents of silver*, ten thousand kors of wheat, and ten thousand of barley
2Chr 36:3 and he imposed on the land a tribute of one hundred *talents of silver* and a talent of gold
Ezra 7:22 up to one hundred *talents of silver*, one hundred kors of wheat, one hundred baths of wine, one hundred baths of oil, and salt without prescribed limit
Ezra 8:26 I even weighed into their hand six hundred and fifty *talents of silver*, silver articles weighing one hundred talents, one hundred talents of gold
Esth 3:9 If it pleases the king, let a decree be written that they be destroyed, and I will pay ten thousand *talents of silver* into the hands of those who do the work, to bring it into the king's treasuries

TALKED AND DEBATED (NIV)
(See *SPOKE BOLDLY*)

TALL AND LOFTY (NIV)
(See *HIGH AND LIFTED UP*)

TAME THE TONGUE
Jas 3:8 But no man can *tame the tongue*. It is an unruly evil, full of deadly poison

TARES OF THE FIELD
Matt 13:36 And His disciples came to Him, saying, "Explain to us the parable of the *tares of the field*

TARRY ALL NIGHT (KJV)
(See *SPEND THE NIGHT*)

TARRY IN THE CITY OF JERUSALEM
Luke 24:49 but *tarry in the city of Jerusalem* until you are endued with power from on high

TARRY LONG OVER WINE (RSV)
(See *LINGER LONG AT THE WINE*)

TARRY TILL I COME (KJV)
(See *REMAIN TILL I COME*)

TASTE AND SEE
Ps 34:8 Oh, *taste and see* that the Lord is good; blessed is the man who trusts in Him

TASTE DEATH
Matt 16:28 Assuredly, I say to you, there are some standing here who shall not *taste death* till they see the Son of Man coming in His kingdom
Mark 9:1 And He said to them, "Assuredly, I say to you that there are some standing here who will not *taste death* till they see the kingdom of God present with power
Luke 9:27 But I tell you truly, there are some standing here who shall not *taste death* till they see the kingdom of God
John 8:52 and You say, 'If anyone keeps My word he shall never *taste death*
Heb 2:9 But we see Jesus, who was made a little lower than the angels, for the suffering of death crowned with glory and honor, that He, by the grace of God, might *taste death* for everyone

TASTED THE HEAVENLY GIFT
Heb 6:4 For it is impossible for those who were once enlightened, and have *tasted the heavenly gift*, and have become partakers of the Holy Spirit

TAUGHT DAILY IN THE TEMPLE (KJV)
(See *TEACHING DAILY IN THE TEMPLE*)

TAX COLLECTOR
Matt 10:3 Thomas and Matthew the *tax collector;* James the son of Alphaeus, and Lebbaeus, whose surname was Thaddaeus
Matt 18:17 But if he refuses even to hear the church, let him be to you like a heathen and a *tax collector*
Luke 5:27 After these things He went out and saw a *tax collector* named Levi, sitting at the tax office
Luke 18:10 Two men went up to the temple to pray, one a Pharisee and the other a *tax collector*
Luke 18:11 The Pharisee stood and prayed thus with himself, 'God, I thank You that I am not like other men extortioners, unjust, adulterers, or even as this *tax collector*
Luke 18:13 And the *tax collector*, standing afar off, would not so much as raise his eyes to heaven, but beat his breast, saying
Luke 19:2 Now behold, there was a man named Zacchaeus who was a chief *tax collector*, and he was rich

TAX COLLECTORS AND HARLOTS
Matt 21:31 Jesus said to them, "Assuredly, I say to you that *tax collectors and harlots* enter the kingdom of God before you
Matt 21:32 but *tax collectors and harlots* believed him; and when you saw it, you did not afterward relent and believe him

TAX COLLECTORS AND SINNERS
Matt 9:10 And so it was, as Jesus sat at the table in the house, that behold, many *tax collectors and sinners* came and sat down with Him and His disciples
Matt 9:11 And when the Pharisees saw it, they said to His disciples, "Why does your Teacher eat with *tax collectors and sinners*
Matt 11:19 The Son of Man came eating and drinking, and they say, 'Look, a gluttonous man and a winebibber, a friend of *tax collectors and sinners*
Mark 2:15 Now it happened, as He was dining in Levi's house, that many *tax collectors and sinners* also sat together with Jesus and His disciples
Mark 2:16 And when the scribes and Pharisees saw Him eating with the *tax collectors and sinners*, they said to His disciples, "How is it that He eats and drinks with *tax collectors and sinners*
Luke 5:30 But their scribes and the Pharisees murmured against His disciples, saying, "Why do You eat and drink with *tax collectors and sinners*
Luke 7:34 The Son of Man has come eating and drinking, and you say, 'Look, a glutton and a winebibber, a friend of *tax collectors and sinners*

TEACH AND EXHORT
1Tim 6:2 And those who have believing masters, let them not despise them because they are brethren, but rather serve them because those who are benefited are believers and beloved. *Teach and exhort* these things

TEACH HIS NEIGHBOR
Jer 31:34 No more shall every man *teach his neighbor*, and every man his brother, saying
Heb 8:11 None of them shall *teach his neighbor*, and none his brother, saying

TEACH ME
Job 6:24 *Teach me*, and I will hold my tongue; cause me to understand wherein I have erred
Job 34:32 *teach me* what I do not see; if I have done iniquity, I will do no more
Ps 25:4 Show me Your ways, O Lord; *teach me* Your paths
Ps 25:5 Lead me in Your truth and *teach me*, for You are the God of my salvation
Ps 27:11 *Teach me* Your way, O Lord, and lead me in a smooth path, because of my enemies
Ps 86:11 *Teach me* Your way, O Lord; I will walk in Your truth
Ps 119:12 Blessed are You, O Lord! *Teach me* Your statutes
Ps 119:26 I have declared my ways, and You answered me; *teach me* Your statutes
Ps 119:33 *Teach me*, O Lord, the way of Your statutes, and I shall keep it to the end
Ps 119:64 The earth, O Lord, is full of Your mercy; *teach me* Your statutes
Ps 119:66 *teach me* good judgment and knowledge, for I believe Your commandments
Ps 119:68 You are good, and do good; *teach me* Your statutes
Ps 119:108 Accept, I pray, the freewill offerings of my mouth, O Lord, and *teach me* Your judgments
Ps 119:124 Deal with Your servant according to Your mercy, and *teach me* Your statutes
Ps 119:135 Make Your face shine upon Your servant, and *teach me* Your statutes
Ps 119:171 My lips shall utter praise, for You *teach me* Your statutes
Ps 143:10 *Teach me* to do Your will, for You are my God

TEACH THEIR CHILDREN
Deut 4:10 especially concerning the day you stood before the Lord your God in Horeb, when the Lord said to me, 'Gather the people to Me, and I will let them hear My words, that they may learn to fear Me all the days they live on the earth, and that they may *teach their children*

TEACH THEM TO YOUR CHILDREN
Deut 4:9 Only take heed to yourself, and diligently keep yourself, lest you forget the things your eyes have seen, and lest they depart from your heart all the days of your life. And *teach them to your children* and your grandchildren
Deut 11:19 You shall *teach them to your children*, speaking of them when you sit in your house, when you walk by the way, when you lie down, and when you rise up

TEACH US
Judg 13:8 Then Manoah prayed to the Lord, and said, "O my Lord, please let the Man of God whom You sent come to us again and *teach us* what we shall do for the child who will be born
Job 37:19 *Teach us* what we should say to Him, for we can prepare nothing because of the darkness
Ps 90:12 So *teach us* to number our days, that we may gain a heart of wisdom
Is 2:3 he will *teach us* His ways, and we shall walk in His paths
Mic 4:2 He will *teach us* His ways, and we shall walk in His paths
Luke 11:1 And it came to pass, as He was praying in a certain place, when He ceased, that one of His disciples said to Him, "Lord, *teach us* to pray, as John also taught his disciples

TEACHERS OF THE LAW
Luke 5:17 Now it happened on a certain day, as He was teaching, that there were Pharisees and *teachers of the law* sitting by, who had come out of every town of Galilee, Judea, and Jerusalem
1Tim 1:7 desiring to be *teachers of the law*, understanding neither what they say nor the things which they affirm

TEACHING DAILY IN THE TEMPLE
Luke 19:47 And He was *teaching daily in the temple*. But the chief priests, the scribes, and the leaders of the people sought to destroy Him

TEACHING IS A LIGHT (NIV)
(See *LAW IS LIGHT*)

TEACHING OF CHRIST (NAS, NIV)
(See *DOCTRINE OF CHRIST*)

TEAR DOWN MY BARNS (NAS, NIV)
(See *PULL DOWN MY BARNS*)

TEAR DOWN THEIR ALTARS (NAS, RSV)
(See *DESTROY THEIR ALTARS*)

TEETH ARE LIKE A FLOCK
Song 4:2 Your *teeth are like a flock* of shorn sheep which have come up from the washing, every one of which bears twins, and none is barren among them
Song 6:6 Your *teeth are like a flock* of sheep which have come up from the washing

TELL IT NOT IN GATH
2Sam 1:20 *Tell it not in Gath*, proclaim it not in the streets of Ashkelon lest the daughters of the Philistines rejoice, lest the daughters of the uncircumcised triumph

Mic 1:10 *Tell it not in Gath*, weep not at all in Beth Aphrah, roll yourself in the dust

TELL IT TO YOUR CHILDREN (NIV)
(See *TELL YOUR CHILDREN ABOUT IT*)

TELL OF ALL YOUR MARVELOUS WORKS
Ps 9:1 I will praise You, O Lord, with my whole heart; I will *tell of all Your marvelous works*

TELL WHAT GOD HAS WROUGHT (RSV)
(See *DECLARE THE WORK OF GOD*)

TELL WHAT THE RIDDLE WAS (RSV)
(See *EXPLAIN THE RIDDLE*)

TELL YOUR CHILDREN ABOUT IT
Joel 1:3 *Tell your children about it*, let your children tell their children, and their children another generation

TEMPLE OF BAAL
1Kin 16:32 Then he set up an altar for Baal in the *temple of Baal*, which he had built in Samaria
2Kin 10:21 So they came into the *temple of Baal*, and the *temple of Baal* was full from one end to the other
2Kin 10:23 Then Jehu and Jehonadab the son of Rechab went into the *temple of Baal*, and said to the worshipers of Baal
2Kin 10:25 then the guards and the officers threw them out, and went into the inner room of the *temple of Baal*
2Kin 10:26 And they brought the sacred pillars out of the *temple of Baal* and burned them
2Kin 10:27 Then they broke down the sacred pillar of Baal, and tore down the *temple of Baal* and made it a refuse dump to this day
2Kin 11:18 And all the people of the land went to the *temple of Baal*, and tore it down
2Chr 23:17 And all the people went to the *temple of Baal*, and tore it down

TEMPLE OF GOD
2Chr 23:9 And Jehoiada the priest gave to the captains of hundreds the spears and the large and small shields which had been King David's, that were in the *temple of God*
Matt 21:12 Then Jesus went into the *temple of God* and drove out all those who bought and sold in the temple, and overturned the tables of the moneychangers and the seats of those who sold doves
Matt 26:61 and said, "This fellow said, 'I am able to destroy the *temple of God* and to build it in three days
1Cor 3:16 Do you not know that you are the *temple of God* and that the Spirit of God dwells in you
1Cor 3:17 If anyone defiles the *temple of God*, God will destroy him. For the *temple of God* is holy, which temple you are
2Cor 6:16 And what agreement has the *temple of God* with idols
2Th 2:4 who opposes and exalts himself above all that is called God or that is worshiped, so that he sits as God in the *temple of God*, showing himself that he is God
Rev 11:1 And the angel stood, saying, "Rise and measure the *temple of God*, the altar, and those who worship there
Rev 11:19 Then the *temple of God* was opened in heaven, and the ark of His covenant was seen in His temple

TEMPLE OF THE HOLY SPIRIT
1Cor 6:19 Or do you not know that your body is the *temple of the Holy Spirit* who is in you, whom you have from God, and you are not your own

TEMPLE OF THE LORD
2Kin 11:10 And the priest gave the captains of hundreds the spears and shields which had belonged to King David, that were in the *temple of the Lord*
2Kin 11:13 Now when Athaliah heard the noise of the escorts and the people, she came to the people, into the *temple of the Lord*
2Kin 18:16 At that time Hezekiah stripped the gold from the doors of the *temple of the Lord*, and from the pillars which Hezekiah king of Judah had overlaid, and gave it to the king of Assyria
2Kin 23:4 And the king commanded Hilkiah the high priest, the priests of the second order, and the doorkeepers, to bring out of the *temple of the Lord* all the articles that were made for Baal, for Asherah, and for all the host of heaven
2Kin 24:13 And he carried out from there all the treasures of the house of the Lord and the treasures of the king's house, and he cut in pieces all the articles of gold which Solomon king of Israel had made in the *temple of the Lord*, as the Lord had said
2Chr 23:12 Now when Athaliah heard the noise of the people running and praising the king, she came to the people in the *temple of the Lord*
2Chr 26:16 But when he was strong his heart was lifted up, to his destruction, for he transgressed against the Lord his God by entering the *temple of the Lord* to burn incense on the altar of incense
2Chr 27:2 And he did what was right in the sight of the Lord, according to all that his father Uzziah had done (although he did not enter the *temple of the Lord*
2Chr 29:16 Then the priests went into the inner part of the house of the Lord to cleanse it, and brought out all the debris that they found in the *temple of the Lord* to the court of the house of the Lord
Ezra 3:6 But the foundation of the *temple of the Lord* had not yet been laid
Ezra 3:10 When the builders laid the foundation of the *temple of the Lord*, the priests stood in their apparel with trumpets, and the Levites, the sons of Asaph, with cymbals, to praise the Lord, according to the ordinance of David king of Israel
Ezra 4:1 Now when the adversaries of Judah and Benjamin heard that the descendants of the captivity were building the *temple of the Lord* God of Israel
Jer 7:4 Do not trust in these lying words, saying, 'The *temple of the Lord*, the *temple of the Lord*, the *temple of the Lord* are these
Jer 24:1 The Lord showed me, and there were two baskets of figs set before the *temple of the Lord*, after Nebuchadnezzar king of Babylon had carried away captive Jeconiah the son of Jehoiakim, king of Judah, and the princes of Judah with the craftsmen and smiths, from Jerusalem, and had brought them to Babylon
Ezek 8:16 and there, at the door of the *temple of the Lord*, between the porch and the altar, were about twenty-five men with their backs toward the *temple of the Lord* and their faces toward the east, and they were worshiping the sun toward the east
Hag 2:15 from before stone was laid upon stone in the *temple of the Lord*
Zech 6:12 From His place He shall branch out, and He shall build the *temple of the Lord*
Zech 6:13 yes, He shall build the *temple of the Lord*. He shall bear the glory, and shall sit and rule on His throne

TEMPLE WORSHIP

Zech 6:14 Now the elaborate crown shall be for a memorial in the *temple of the Lord* for Helem, Tobijah, Jedaiah, and Hen the son of Zephaniah
Zech 6:15 Even those who are far away shall come and build the *temple of the Lord*
Luke 1:9 according to the custom of the priesthood, his lot fell to burn incense when he went into the *temple of the Lord*

TEMPLE WORSHIP (NIV)
(See *SERVICE OF GOD*)

TEMPT THE LORD
Ex 17:2 And Moses said to them, "Why do you contend with me? Why do you *tempt the Lord*
Deut 6:16 You shall not *tempt the Lord* your God as you tempted Him in Massah
Matt 4:7 Jesus said to him, "It is written again, 'You shall not *tempt the Lord* your God
Luke 4:12 And Jesus answered and said to him, "It has been said, 'You shall not *tempt the Lord* your God

TEMPTED AS WE ARE
Heb 4:15 For we do not have a High Priest who cannot sympathize with our weaknesses, but was in all points *tempted as we are*, yet without sin

TEMPTED BY SATAN
Mark 1:13 And He was there in the wilderness forty days, *tempted by Satan*, and was with the wild beasts

TEMPTED BY THE DEVIL
Matt 4:1 Then Jesus was led up by the Spirit into the wilderness to be *tempted by the devil*

TEMPTED GOD (KJV, NAS)
(See *TESTED GOD*)

TEMPTED IN EVERY WAY (NIV)
(See *TEMPTED AS WE ARE*)

TEN COMMANDMENTS
Ex 34:28 And He wrote on the tablets the words of the covenant, the *Ten Commandments*
Deut 4:13 So He declared to you His covenant which He commanded you to perform, that is, the *Ten Commandments*
Deut 10:4 And He wrote on the tablets according to the first writing, the *Ten Commandments*, which the Lord had spoken to you in the mountain from the midst of the fire in the day of the assembly

TEN THOUSAND WORDS IN A TONGUE
1Cor 14:19 yet in the church I would rather speak five words with my understanding, that I may teach others also, than *ten thousand words in a tongue*

TEND MY SHEEP
John 21:16 You know that I love You." He said to him, "*Tend My sheep*

TEND THE FLOCK OF GOD (RSV)
(See *SHEPHERD THE FLOCK OF GOD*)

TENDER MERCIES
Ps 25:6 Remember, O Lord, Your *tender mercies* and Your lovingkindnesses, for they have been from of old
Ps 40:11 Do not withhold Your *tender mercies* from me, O Lord
Ps 51:1 According to the multitude of Your *tender mercies*, blot out my transgressions
Ps 69:16 Turn to me according to the multitude of Your *tender mercies*
Ps 77:9 Has He in anger shut up His *tender mercies*
Ps 79:8 Let Your *tender mercies* come speedily to meet us, for we have been brought very low
Ps 103:4 Who redeems your life from destruction, Who crowns you with lovingkindness and *tender mercies*
Ps 119:77 Let Your *tender mercies* come to me, that I may live
Ps 119:156 Great are Your *tender mercies*, O Lord; revive me according to Your judgments
Ps 145:9 The Lord is good to all, and His *tender mercies* are over all His works
Prov 12:10 A righteous man regards the life of his animal, but the *tender mercies* of the wicked are cruel
Col 3:12 Therefore, as the elect of God, holy and beloved, put on *tender mercies*, kindness, humbleness of mind, meekness, longsuffering

TENDER MERCY
Luke 1:78 Through the *tender mercy* of our God, with which the Dayspring from on high has visited us

TENDETH TO LIFE (KJV)
(See *LEADS TO LIFE*)

TENDETH TO POVERTY (KJV)
(See *LEADS TO POVERTY*)

TENT OF MEETING
Ex 39:32 Thus all the work of the tabernacle of the *tent of meeting* was finished
Ex 39:40 all the utensils for the service of the tabernacle, for the *tent of meeting*
Ex 40:2 On the first day of the first month you shall set up the tabernacle of the *tent of meeting*
Ex 40:6 Then you shall set the altar of the burnt offering before the door of the tabernacle of the *tent of meeting*
Ex 40:29 And he put the altar of burnt offering before the door of the tabernacle of the *tent of meeting*, and offered upon it the burnt offering and the grain offering, as the Lord had commanded Moses

TENT OF THE CONGREGATION (KJV)
(See *TENT OF MEETING*)

TENT OF THE TESTIMONY
Num 9:15 And on the day that the tabernacle was raised up, the cloud covered the tabernacle, the *tent of the Testimony*

TENTH GENERATION
Deut 23:2 even to the *tenth generation* none of his descendants shall enter the congregation of the Lord
Deut 23:3 even to the *tenth generation* none of his descendants shall enter the congregation of the Lord forever

TENTH OF YOUR MINT, RUE AND ALL OTHER KINDS OF GARDEN HERBS (NIV)
(See *TITHE MINT AND RUE AND ALL MANNER OF HERBS*)

TENTS OF THE WICKED (NIV)
(See *DWELLING PLACE OF THE WICKED*)

TERROR AND PIT AND SNARE (NAS, NIV)
(See *FEAR AND THE PIT AND THE SNARE*)

TERROR OF CALAMITY FROM GOD (RSV)
(See *GOD IS A TERROR*)

TERROR OF THE LORD
Is 2:10 Enter into the rock, and hide in the dust, from the *terror of the Lord* and the glory of His majesty

Is 2:19 They shall go into the holes of the rocks, and into the caves of the earth, from the *terror of the Lord* and the glory of His majesty, when He arises to shake the earth mightily
Is 2:21 to go into the clefts of the rocks, and into the crags of the rugged rocks, from the *terror of the Lord* and the glory of His majesty, when He arises to shake the earth mightily
2Cor 5:11 Knowing, therefore, the *terror of the Lord*, we persuade men

TERROR ON EVERY SIDE (NIV, RSV)
(See *FEAR IS ON EVERY SIDE*)

TEST ALL THINGS
1Th 5:21 *Test all things;* hold fast what is good

TEST EVERYTHING (NIV, RSV)
(See *TEST ALL THINGS*)

TEST THE HEART
1Chr 29:17 I know also, my God, that You *test the heart* and have pleasure in uprightness

TEST THE LORD (NAS, NIV)
(See *TEMPT THE LORD*)

TEST THE SPIRITS
1Jn 4:1 Beloved, do not believe every spirit, but *test the spirits*, whether they are of God

TESTED GOD
Ps 78:18 And they *tested God* in their heart by asking for the food of their fancy
Ps 106:14 But lusted exceedingly in the wilderness, and *tested God* in the desert

TESTIFY CONCERNING (NIV)
(See *BEAR WITNESS*)

TESTIMONY IS TRUE
John 19:35 And he who has seen has testified, and his *testimony is true*
John 21:24 This is the disciple who testifies of these things, and wrote these things; and we know that his *testimony is true*
Tit 1:13 This *testimony is true*. Therefore rebuke them sharply, that they may be sound in the faith
3Jn 12 And we also bear witness, and you know that our *testimony is true*

TESTIMONY OF GOD
1Cor 2:1 And I, brethren, when I came to you, did not come with excellence of speech or of wisdom declaring to you the *testimony of God*

TESTIMONY OF JESUS
Rev 1:2 who bore witness to the word of God, and to the *testimony of Jesus* Christ, and to all things that he saw
Rev 1:9 I, John, both your brother and companion in tribulation, and in the kingdom and patience of Jesus Christ, was on the island that is called Patmos for the word of God and for the *testimony of Jesus* Christ
Rev 12:17 And the dragon was enraged with the woman, and he went to make war with the rest of her offspring, who keep the commandments of God and have the *testimony of Jesus* Christ
Rev 19:10 I am your fellow servant, and of your brethren who have the *testimony of Jesus*. Worship God! For the *testimony of Jesus* is the spirit of prophecy

TESTIMONY OF JOHN
John 1:19 Now this is the *testimony of John*, when the Jews sent priests and Levites from Jerusalem to ask him

TESTIMONY OF THE LORD
Ps 19:7 The *testimony of the Lord* is sure, making wise the simple

TESTIMONY OF TWO OR THREE WITNESSES
Deut 17:6 Whoever is worthy of death shall be put to death on the *testimony of two or three witnesses*, but he shall not be put to death on the testimony of one witness
Heb 10:28 Anyone who has rejected Moses' law dies without mercy on the *testimony of two or three witnesses*

TESTIMONY TO JESUS (RSV)
(See *WITNESS TO JESUS*)

TESTIMONY TO THEM
Matt 8:4 but go your way, show yourself to the priest, and offer the gift that Moses commanded, as a *testimony to them*
Matt 10:18 And you will be brought before governors and kings for My sake, as a *testimony to them* and to the Gentiles
Mark 1:44 but go your way, show yourself to the priest, and offer for your cleansing those things which Moses commanded, as a *testimony to them*
Mark 13:9 And you will be brought before rulers and kings for My sake, for a *testimony to them*
Luke 5:14 And He charged him to tell no one, "But go and show yourself to the priest, and make an offering for your cleansing, as a *testimony to them*, just as Moses commanded

THANK OFFERINGS (NIV, RSV)
(See *SACRIFICE OF PRAISE*)

THANK THE LORD
1Chr 16:7 And on that day David first delivered this psalm into the hand of Asaph and his brethren, to *thank the Lord*

THANKS BE TO GOD
1Cor 15:57 But *thanks be to God*, who gives us the victory through our Lord Jesus Christ
2Cor 2:14 Now *thanks be to God* who always leads us in triumph in Christ, and through us diffuses the fragrance of His knowledge in every place
2Cor 8:16 But *thanks be to God* who puts the same earnest care for you into the heart of Titus
2Cor 9:15 *Thanks be to God* for His indescribable gift

THANKSGIVING BE SUNG TO THE LORD (RSV)
(See *THANK THE LORD*)

THANKSGIVING PSALMS
Neh 12:8 Moreover the Levites were Jeshua, Binnui, Kadmiel, Sherebiah, Judah, and Mattaniah who led the *thanksgiving psalms*, he and his brethren

THAT BELIEVETH ON HIM (KJV)
(See *WHO BELIEVES IN HIM*)

THAT IT MAY GO WELL WITH YOU
Deut 4:40 You shall therefore keep His statutes and His commandments which I command you today, *that it may go well with you* and with your children after you, and that you may prolong your days in the land which the Lord your God is giving you for all time
Deut 12:25 You shall not eat it, *that it may go well with you* and your children after you, when you do what is right in the sight of the Lord
Deut 12:28 Observe and obey all these words which I command you, *that it may go well with you* and your children after you forever, when you do what is good and right in the sight of the Lord your God
Deut 19:13 Your eye shall not pity him, but you

shall put away the guilt of innocent blood from Israel, *that it may go well with you*

THAT IT MIGHT BE FULFILLED
Matt 1:22 Now all this was done *that it might be fulfilled* which was spoken by the Lord through the prophet, saying
Matt 2:15 and was there until the death of Herod, *that it might be fulfilled* which was spoken by the Lord through the prophet, saying
Matt 2:23 And he came and dwelt in a city called Nazareth, *that it might be fulfilled* which was spoken by the prophets
Matt 4:14 *that it might be fulfilled* which was spoken by Isaiah the prophet
Matt 8:17 *that it might be fulfilled* which was spoken by Isaiah the prophet
Matt 12:17 *that it might be fulfilled* which was spoken by Isaiah the prophet
Matt 13:35 *that it might be fulfilled* which was spoken by the prophet
Matt 21:4 All this was done *that it might be fulfilled* which was spoken by the prophet
Matt 27:35 Then they crucified Him, and divided His garments, casting lots, *that it might be fulfilled* which was spoken by the prophet

THAT THEY ALL MAY BE ONE
John 17:21 *that they all may be one*, as You, Father, are in Me, and I in You

THAT THEY MAY BE ONE
John 17:11 Holy Father, keep through Your name those whom You have given Me, *that they may be one* as We are
John 17:22 And the glory which You gave Me I have given them, *that they may be one* just as We are one

THAT THEY MAY BELIEVE
Ex 4:5 *that they may believe* that the Lord God of their fathers, the God of Abraham, the God of Isaac, and the God of Jacob, has appeared to you
Ex 4:8 Then it will be, if they do not believe you, nor heed the message of the first sign, *that they may believe* the message of the latter sign
John 11:42 And I know that You always hear Me, but because of the people who are standing by I said this, *that they may believe* that You sent Me

THAT WHICH IS GOOD (KJV)
(See *WHAT IS GOOD*)

THAT WHICH YOUR SOUL PITIETH (KJV)
(See *DELIGHT OF YOUR SOUL*)

THAT YOU MAY BELIEVE
John 11:15 And I am glad for your sakes that I was not there, *that you may believe*
John 19:35 and he knows that he is telling the truth, so *that you may believe*
John 20:31 but these are written *that you may believe* that Jesus is the Christ, the Son of God, and that believing you may have life in His name

THAT YOU MAY PROLONG YOUR DAYS
Deut 4:40 You shall therefore keep His statutes and His commandments which I command you today, that it may go well with you and with your children after you, and *that you may prolong your days* in the land which the Lord your God is giving you for all time
Deut 5:33 You shall walk in all the ways which the Lord your God has commanded you, that you may live and that it may be well with you, and *that you may prolong your days* in the land which you shall possess
Deut 11:9 and *that you may prolong your days* in the land which the Lord swore to give your fathers, to them and their descendants
Deut 22:7 you shall surely let the mother go, and take the young for yourself, that it may be well with you and *that you may prolong your days*

THAT YOUR JOY MAY BE FULL
John 15:11 These things I have spoken to you, that My joy may remain in you, and *that your joy may be full*
John 16:24 Ask, and you will receive, *that your joy may be full*
1Jn 1:4 And these things we write to you *that your joy may be full*

THE CIRCUMCISION PARTY (RSV)
(See *THOSE WHO WERE OF THE CIRCUMCISION*)

THE TWELVE
Gen 49:28 All these are *the twelve* tribes of Israel, and this is what their father spoke to them
Ex 24:4 And he rose early in the morning, and built an altar at the foot of the mountain, and twelve pillars according to *the twelve* tribes of Israel
Ex 28:21 And the stones shall have the names of the sons of Israel, twelve according to their names, like the engravings of a signet, each one with its own name; they shall be according to *the twelve* tribes
Ex 39:14 according to their names, engraved like a signet, each one with its own name according to *the twelve* tribes
Num 7:86 *The twelve* gold pans full of incense weighed ten shekels apiece, according to the shekel of the sanctuary
Josh 4:4 Then Joshua called *the twelve* men whom he had appointed from the children of Israel, one man from every tribe
Jer 52:20 The two pillars, one Sea, *the twelve* bronze bulls which were under it, and the carts, which King Solomon had made for the house of the Lord the bronze of all these articles was beyond measure
Ezek 47:13 These are the borders by which you shall divide the land as an inheritance among *the twelve* tribes of Israel
Dan 4:29 At the end of *the twelve* months he was walking about the royal palace of Babylon
Matt 10:2 Now the names of *the twelve* apostles are these: first, Simon, who is called Peter, and Andrew his brother
Matt 19:28 So Jesus said to them, "Assuredly I say to you, that in the regeneration, when the Son of Man sits on the throne of His glory, you who have followed Me will also sit on twelve thrones, judging *the twelve* tribes of Israel
Matt 20:17 Then Jesus, going up to Jerusalem, took *the twelve* disciples aside on the road and said to them
Matt 26:14 Then one of *the twelve*, called Judas Iscariot, went to the chief priests
Matt 26:20 Now when evening had come, He sat down with *the twelve*
Matt 26:47 And while He was still speaking, behold, Judas, one of *the twelve*, with a great multitude with swords and clubs, came from the chief priests and elders of the people
Mark 4:10 But when He was alone, those around Him with *the twelve* asked Him about the parable
Mark 6:7 And He called *the twelve* to Him, and began to send them out two by two, and gave them power over unclean spirits
Mark 9:35 And He sat down, called *the twelve*, and said to them
Mark 10:32 Then He took *the twelve* aside again

and began to tell them the things that would happen to Him
Mark 11:11 So when He had looked around at all things, as the hour was already late, He went out to Bethany with *the twelve*
Mark 14:10 Then Judas Iscariot, one of *the twelve*, went to the chief priests to betray Him to them
Mark 14:17 In the evening He came with *the twelve*
Mark 14:20 Then He answered and said to them, "It is one of *the twelve*, who dips with Me in the dish
Mark 14:43 And immediately, while He was still speaking, Judas, one of *the twelve*, with a great multitude with swords and clubs, came from the chief priests and the scribes and the elders
Luke 8:1 Now it came to pass, afterward, that He went through every city and village, preaching and bringing the glad tidings of the kingdom of God. And *the twelve* were with Him
Luke 9:12 When the day began to wear away, *the twelve* came and said to Him
Luke 18:31 Then He took *the twelve* aside and said to them
Luke 22:3 Then Satan entered Judas, surnamed Iscariot, who was numbered among *the twelve*
Luke 22:14 And when the hour had come, He sat down, and *the twelve* apostles with Him
Luke 22:30 that you may eat and drink at My table in My kingdom, and sit on thrones judging *the twelve* tribes of Israel
Luke 22:47 and he who was called Judas, one of *the twelve*, went before them and drew near to Jesus to kiss Him
John 6:67 Then Jesus said to *the twelve*, "Do you also want to go away
John 6:70 Jesus answered them, "Did I not choose you, *the twelve*, and one of you is a devil
John 6:71 He spoke of Judas Iscariot, the son of Simon, for it was he who would betray Him, being one of *the twelve*
John 20:24 But Thomas, called Didymus, one of *the twelve*, was not with them when Jesus came
Acts 6:2 Then *the twelve* summoned the multitude of the disciples and said
Acts 7:8 and Isaac begot Jacob, and Jacob begot *the twelve* patriarchs
1Cor 15:5 and that He was seen by Cephas, then by *the twelve*
Jas 1:1 James, a servant of God and of the Lord Jesus Christ, to *the twelve* tribes which are scattered abroad
Rev 21:12 Also she had a great and high wall with twelve gates, and twelve angels at the gates, and names written on them, which are the names of *the twelve* tribes of the children of Israel
Rev 21:14 Now the wall of the city had twelve foundations, and on them were the names of *the twelve* apostles of the Lamb
Rev 21:21 And *the twelve* gates were twelve pearls: each individual gate was of one pearl

THERE IS A TIME FOR EVERYTHING (NIV)
(See *TO EVERYTHING THERE IS A SEASON*)

THERE IS NO DIFFERENCE
Rom 3:22 even the righteousness of God which is through faith in Jesus Christ to all and on all who believe. For *there is no difference*

THERE IS NO OTHER
Deut 4:39 Therefore know this day, and consider it in your heart, that the Lord Himself is God in heaven above and on the earth beneath; *there is no other*
1Sam 21:9 For *there is no other* except that one here." And David said
1Kin 8:60 that all the peoples of the earth may know that the Lord is God; *there is no other*
Is 44:8 Indeed *there is no other* Rock; I know not one
Is 45:5 I am the Lord, and *there is no other;* there is no God besides Me
Is 45:6 That they may know from the rising of the sun to its setting that there is none besides Me. I am the Lord, and *there is no other*
Is 45:14 They will make supplication to you, saying, 'Surely God is in you, and *there is no other; there is no other* God
Is 45:18 For thus says the Lord, Who created the heavens, Who is God, Who formed the earth and made it, Who has established it, Who did not create it in vain, Who formed it to be inhabited: "I am the Lord, and *there is no other*
Is 45:21 And *there is no other* God besides Me, a just God and a Savior
Is 45:22 Look to Me, and be saved, all you ends of the earth! For I am God, and *there is no other*
Is 46:9 Remember the former things of old, for I am God, and *there is no other*
Dan 2:11 It is a difficult thing that the king requires, and *there is no other* who can tell it to the king except the gods, whose dwelling is not with flesh
Dan 3:29 because *there is no other* God who can deliver like this
Joel 2:27 Then you shall know that I am in the midst of Israel, and that I am the Lord your God and *there is no other*
Mark 12:31 You shall love your neighbor as yourself.' *There is no other* commandment greater than these
Mark 12:32 You have spoken the truth, for there is one God, and *there is no other* but He
Acts 4:12 Nor is there salvation in any other, for *there is no other* name under heaven given among men by which we must be saved
1Cor 8:4 Therefore concerning the eating of things offered to idols, we know that an idol is nothing in the world, and that *there is no other* God but one

THERE IS NO PARTIALITY
Rom 2:11 For *there is no partiality* with God
Eph 6:9 And you, masters, do the same things to them, giving up threatening, knowing that your own Master also is in heaven, and *there is no partiality* with Him
Col 3:25 But he who does wrong will be repaid for the wrong which he has done, and *there is no partiality*

THERE IS NO RESPECT OF PERSONS (KJV)
(See *THERE IS NO PARTIALITY*)

THERE IS NONE BESIDES ME
Is 45:6 That they may know from the rising of the sun to its setting that *there is none besides Me*
Is 45:21 And there is no other God besides Me, a just God and a Savior; *there is none besides Me*
Zeph 2:15 This is the rejoicing city that dwelt securely, that said in her heart, "I am it, and *there is none besides me*

THERE WAS NO KING IN ISRAEL
Judg 17:6 In those days *there was no king in Israel;* everyone did what was right in his own eyes
Judg 18:1 In those days *there was no king in Israel*. And in those days the tribe of the Danites was seeking an inheritance for itself to dwell in
Judg 19:1 And it came to pass in those days, when *there was no king in Israel*, that there was a certain Levite sojourning in the remote mountains of Ephraim

Judg 21:25 In those days *there was no king in Israel;* everyone did what was right in his own eyes

THERE WE SAT DOWN
Ps 137:1 By the rivers of Babylon, *there we sat down*, yea, we wept when we remembered Zion

THEREFORE KEEP WATCH (NIV)
(See *WATCH THEREFORE*)

THESE ARE THE NAMES OF
Ex 1:1 Now *these are the names of* the children of Israel who came to Egypt
Ex 6:16 *These are the names of* the sons of Levi according to their generations
Num 1:5 *These are the names of* the men who shall stand with you
Num 3:2 And *these are the names of* the sons of Aaron
Num 3:3 *These are the names of* the sons of Aaron, the anointed priests, whom he consecrated to minister as priests
Num 3:18 And *these are the names of* the sons of Gershon by their families
Num 13:16 *These are the names of* the men whom Moses sent to spy out the land
Num 34:17 *These are the names of* the men who shall divide the land among you as an inheritance
Num 34:19 *These are the names of* the men: from the tribe of Judah, Caleb the son of Jephunneh
Josh 17:3 And *these are the names of* his daughters: Mahlah, Noah, Hoglah, Milcah, and Tirzah
2Sam 5:14 Now *these are the names of* those who were born to him in Jerusalem
2Sam 23:8 *These are the names of* the mighty men whom David had
1Chr 6:17 *These are the names of* the sons of Gershon: Libni and Shimei
1Chr 14:4 And *these are the names of* his children whom he had in Jerusalem
Ezek 48:1 Now *these are the names of* the tribes: From the northern border along the road to Hethlon at the entrance of Hamath, to Hazar Enan, the border of Damascus northward, in the direction of Hamath, there shall be one portion for Dan from its east to its west side

THEY
Gen 42:28 Then their hearts failed them and *they were afraid*, saying to one another
Gen 42:35 and when they and their father saw the bundles of money, *they were afraid*
Ex 34:30 So when Aaron and all the children of Israel saw Moses, behold, the skin of his face shone, and *they were afraid* to come near him
1Sam 7:7 And when the children of Israel heard of it, *they were afraid* of the Philistines
2Kin 25:26 And all the people, small and great, and the captains of the armies, arose and went to Egypt; for *they were afraid* of the Chaldeans
Ps 77:16 The waters saw You, *they were afraid;* the depths also trembled
Jer 41:18 for *they were afraid* of them, because Ishmael the son of Nethaniah had murdered Gedaliah the son of Ahikam, whom the king of Babylon had made governor in the land
Mark 5:15 Then they came to Jesus, and saw the one who had been demon-possessed and had the legion, sitting and clothed and in his right mind. And *they were afraid*
Mark 10:32 And as they followed *they were afraid*. Then He took the twelve aside again and began to tell them the things that would happen to Him
Mark 16:8 And they said nothing to anyone, for *they were afraid*
Luke 8:25 And *they were afraid*, and marveled, saying to one another
Luke 8:35 Then they went out to see what had happened, and came to Jesus, and found the man from whom the demons had departed, sitting at the feet of Jesus, clothed and in his right mind. And *they were afraid*
Luke 9:45 and *they were afraid* to ask Him about this saying
Luke 24:5 Then, as *they were afraid* and bowed their faces to the earth, they said to them
John 6:19 So when they had rowed about three or four miles, they saw Jesus walking on the sea and drawing near the boat; and *they were afraid*
Acts 16:38 And the officers told these words to the magistrates, and *they were afraid* when they heard that they were Romans

THEY ALSO WHICH ARE FALLEN ASLEEP (KJV)
(See *THOSE WHO HAVE FALLEN ASLEEP*)

THEY ARE DECEASED
Is 26:14 *they are deceased*, they will not rise. Therefore You have punished and destroyed them, and made all their memory to perish

THEY ARE REBELLIOUS
Ezek 2:7 You shall speak My words to them, whether they hear or whether they refuse, for *they are rebellious*

THEY ARE WORTHY
Rev 3:4 and they shall walk with Me in white, for *they are worthy*

THEY BROKE MY COVENANT (NIV)
(See *COVENANT WHICH THEY BROKE*)

THEY FORGOT ME
Hos 13:6 they were filled and their heart was exalted; therefore *they forgot Me*

THEY HAVE THEIR REWARD
Matt 6:2 Therefore, when you do a charitable deed, do not sound a trumpet before you as the hypocrites do in the synagogues and in the streets, that they may have glory from men. Assuredly, I say to you, *they have their reward*
Matt 6:5 For they love to pray standing in the synagogues and on the corners of the streets, that they may be seen by men. Assuredly, I say to you, *they have their reward*
Matt 6:16 For they disfigure their faces that they may appear to men to be fasting. Assuredly, I say to you, *they have their reward*

THEY REMEMBERED
Ps 78:35 Then *they remembered* that God was their rock, and the Most High God their redeemer
Luke 24:8 And *they remembered* His words
John 12:16 but when Jesus was glorified, then *they remembered* that these things were written about Him and that they had done these things to Him

THEY SHALL REIGN (RSV)
(See *WE SHALL REIGN*)

THEY SHALL RISE
Josh 18:4 *they shall rise* and go through the land, survey it according to their inheritance, and come back to me

THEY THAT ARE AFTER THE FLESH (KJV)
(See *LIVE ACCORDING TO THE FLESH*)

THEY THAT ARE AFTER THE SPIRIT (KJV)
(See *LIVE ACCORDING TO THE SPIRIT*)

THEY WERE ACCURSED (KFV)
(See *DOOMED TO DESTRUCTION*)

THEY WERE AMAZED
Mark 10:32 and *they were amazed*. And as they followed they were afraid
Luke 2:48 So when they saw Him, *they were amazed;* and His mother said to Him

THEY WERE DIVIDED (NIV)
(See *DIVISION AMONG THEM*)

THEY WHICH DO HUNGER AND THIRST (KJV)
(See *THOSE WHO HUNGER AND THIRST FOR RIGHTEOUSNESS*)

THEY WILL KNOW THAT I AM THE LORD
Ezek 24:27 Thus you will be a sign to them, and *they will know that I am the Lord*
Ezek 29:9 then *they will know that I am the Lord*, because he said
Ezek 30:8 Then *they will know that I am the Lord*, when I have set a fire in Egypt and all her helpers are destroyed

THEY WILL REIGN (NAS, NIV)
(See *WE SHALL REIGN*)

THICK CLOUD
Ex 19:9 And the Lord said to Moses, "Behold, I come to you in the *thick cloud*, that the people may hear when I speak with you, and believe you forever
Ex 19:16 Then it came to pass on the third day, in the morning, that there were thunderings and lightnings, and a *thick cloud* on the mountain
Is 44:22 I have blotted out, like a *thick cloud*, your transgressions, and like a cloud, your sins
Ezek 8:11 Each man had a censer in his hand, and a *thick cloud* of incense went up

THIEF IN THE NIGHT
1Th 5:2 For you yourselves know perfectly that the day of the Lord so comes as a *thief in the night*
2Pet 3:10 But the day of the Lord will come as a *thief in the night*, in which the heavens will pass away with a great noise, and the elements will melt with fervent heat

THIEVES AND ROBBERS
John 10:8 All who ever came before Me are *thieves and robbers*, but the sheep did not hear them

THINE ENEMIES (KJV)
(See *YOUR ENEMY*)

THING FOR DESTRUCTION (RSV)
(See *DOOMED TO DESTRUCTION*)

THINGS OF GOD
Job 11:7 Can you search out the deep *things of God?* Can you find out the limits of the Almighty
Matt 16:23 You are an offense to Me, for you are not mindful of the *things of God*, but the things of men
Mark 8:33 For you are not mindful of the *things of God*, but the things of men
1Cor 2:10 For the Spirit searches all things, yes, the deep *things of God*
1Cor 2:11 Even so no one knows the *things of God* except the Spirit of God

THINGS OF MEN
Matt 16:23 You are an offense to Me, for you are not mindful of the things of God, but the *things of men*
Mark 8:33 For you are not mindful of the things of God, but the *things of men*

THINGS OFFERED TO IDOLS
Acts 15:29 that you abstain from *things offered to idols*, from blood, from things strangled, and from sexual immorality
Acts 21:25 But concerning the Gentiles who believe, we have written and decided that they should observe no such thing, except that they should keep themselves from *things offered to idols*, from blood, from things strangled, and from sexual immorality
1Cor 8:1 Now concerning *things offered to idols:* We know that we all have knowledge
1Cor 8:4 Therefore concerning the eating of *things offered to idols*, we know that an idol is nothing in the world, and that there is no other God but one
1Cor 8:10 For if anyone sees you who have knowledge eating in an idol's temple, will not the conscience of him who is weak be emboldened to eat those *things offered to idols*

THINGS SACRIFICED TO IDOLS
Rev 2:14 But I have a few things against you, because you have there those who hold the doctrine of Balaam, who taught Balak to put a stumbling block before the children of Israel, to eat *things sacrificed to idols*, and to commit sexual immorality
Rev 2:20 Nevertheless I have a few things against you, because you allow that woman Jezebel, who calls herself a prophetess, to teach and beguile My servants to commit sexual immorality and to eat *things sacrificed to idols*

THINGS THAT ARE CAESAR'S
Matt 22:21 And He said to them, "Render therefore to Caesar the *things that are Caesar's*, and to God the things that are God's
Mark 12:17 Then Jesus answered and said to them, "Render to Caesar the *things that are Caesar's*, and to God the things that are God's
Luke 20:25 And He said to them, "Render therefore to Caesar the *things that are Caesar's*, and to God the things that are God's

THINGS THAT COME OUT OF THE MOUTH (NIV)
(See *THINGS WHICH PROCEED OUT OF THE MOUTH*)

THINGS THAT MARK AN APOSTLE (NIV)
(See *SIGNS OF AN APOSTLE*)

THINGS WHICH ARE SEEN
2Cor 4:18 while we do not look at the *things which are seen*, but at the things which are not seen. For the *things which are seen* are temporary, but the things which are not seen are eternal
Heb 11:3 By faith we understand that the worlds were framed by the word of God, so that the *things which are seen* were not made of things which are visible

THINGS WHICH PERTAIN TO GOD
Rom 15:17 Therefore I have reason to glory in Christ Jesus in the *things which pertain to God*

THINGS WHICH PROCEED OUT OF THE MOUTH
Matt 15:18 But those *things which proceed out of the mouth* come from the heart, and they defile a man

THINK ABOUT SUCH THINGS (NIV)
(See *MEDITATE ON THESE THINGS*)

THINK ON ME (KJV)
(See *REMEMBER ME*)

THINK ON THESE THINGS (KJV)
(See *MEDITATE ON THESE THINGS*)

THIRD AND FOURTH GENERATION
Num 14:18 but He by no means clears the guilty, visiting the iniquity of the fathers on the children to the *third and fourth generation*

THIRD DAY
Gen 1:13 So the evening and the morning were the *third day*
Gen 22:4 Then on the *third day* Abraham lifted his eyes and saw the place afar off
Gen 31:22 And Laban was told on the *third day* that Jacob had fled
Gen 34:25 Now it came to pass on the *third day*, when they were in pain, that two of the sons of Jacob, Simeon and Levi, Dinah's brothers, each took his sword and came boldly upon the city and killed all the males
Gen 40:20 Now it came to pass on the *third day*, which was Pharaoh's birthday, that he made a feast for all his servants
Gen 42:18 Then Joseph said to them the *third day*, "Do this and live, for I fear God
Ex 19:11 And let them be ready for the *third day*. For on the *third day* the Lord will come down upon Mount Sinai in the sight of all the people
Ex 19:15 And he said to the people, "Be ready for the *third day*
Ex 19:16 Then it came to pass on the *third day*, in the morning, that there were thunderings and lightnings, and a thick cloud on the mountain
Lev 7:17 the remainder of the flesh of the sacrifice on the *third day* must be burned with fire
Lev 7:18 And if any of the flesh of the sacrifice of his peace offering is eaten at all on the *third day*, it shall not be accepted, nor shall it be imputed to him
Lev 19:6 And if any remains until the *third day*, it shall be burned in the fire
Lev 19:7 And if it is eaten at all on the *third day*, it is an abomination
Num 7:24 On the *third day* Eliab the son of Helon, leader of the children of Zebulun, presented an offering
Num 19:12 He shall purify himself with the water on the *third day* and on the seventh day; then he will be clean. But if he does not purify himself on the *third day* and on the seventh day, he will not be clean
Num 19:19 The clean person shall sprinkle the unclean on the *third day* and on the seventh day
Num 29:20 On the *third day* present eleven bulls, two rams, fourteen lambs in their first year without blemish
Num 31:19 whoever has killed any person, and whoever has touched any slain, purify yourselves and your captives on the *third day* and on the seventh day
Josh 9:17 Then the children of Israel journeyed and came to their cities on the *third day*
Judg 20:30 And the children of Israel went up against the children of Benjamin on the *third day*, and put themselves in battle array against Gibeah as at the other times
1Sam 20:5 But let me go, that I may hide in the field until the *third day* at evening
1Sam 20:12 When I have sounded out my father sometime tomorrow, or the *third day*, and indeed there is good toward David, and I do not send to you and tell you
1Sam 30:1 Now it happened, when David and his men came to Ziklag, on the *third day*, that the Amalekites had invaded the South and Ziklag, attacked Ziklag and burned it with fire
2Sam 1:2 on the *third day*, behold, it happened that a man came from Saul's camp with his clothes torn and dust on his head
1Kin 3:18 Then it happened, the *third day* after I had given birth, that this woman also gave birth
1Kin 12:12 So Jeroboam and all the people came to Rehoboam the *third day*, as the king directed, saying, "Come back to me the *third day*
2Kin 20:5 On the *third day* you shall go up to the house of the Lord
2Kin 20:8 And Hezekiah said to Isaiah, "What is the sign that the Lord will heal me, and that I shall go up to the house of the Lord the *third day*
2Chr 10:12 So Jeroboam and all the people came to Rehoboam on the *third day*, as the king had appointed, saying, "Come back to me the *third day*
Ezra 6:15 Now the temple was finished on the *third day* of the month of Adar, which was in the sixth year of the reign of King Darius
Esth 5:1 Now it happened on the *third day* that Esther put on her royal robes and stood in the inner court of the king's palace, across from the king's house, while the king sat on his royal throne in the royal house, facing the entrance of the house
Hos 6:2 on the *third day* He will raise us up, that we may live in His sight
Matt 16:21 From that time Jesus began to show to His disciples that He must go to Jerusalem, and suffer many things from the elders and chief priests and scribes, and be killed, and be raised again the *third day*
Matt 17:23 and they will kill Him, and the *third day* He will be raised up
Matt 20:19 and deliver Him to the Gentiles to mock and to scourge and to crucify. And the *third day* He will rise again
Matt 27:64 Therefore command that the tomb be made secure until the *third day*, lest His disciples come by night and steal Him away, and say to the people
Mark 9:31 And after He is killed, He will rise the *third day*
Mark 10:34 and they will mock Him, and scourge Him, and spit on Him, and kill Him. And the *third day* He will rise again
Luke 9:22 saying, "The Son of Man must suffer many things, and be rejected by the elders and chief priests and scribes, and be killed, and be raised the *third day*
Luke 13:32 And He said to them, "Go, tell that fox, 'Behold, I cast out demons and perform cures today and tomorrow, and the *third day* I shall be perfected
Luke 18:33 And they will scourge Him and put Him to death. And the *third day* He will rise again
Luke 24:7 saying, 'The Son of Man must be delivered into the hands of sinful men, and be crucified, and the *third day* rise again
Luke 24:21 Indeed, besides all this, today is the *third day* since these things happened
Luke 24:46 Then He said to them, "Thus it is writ-

ten, and thus it was necessary for the Christ to suffer and to rise from the dead the *third day*
John 2:1 On the *third day* there was a wedding in Cana of Galilee, and the mother of Jesus was there
Acts 10:40 Him God raised up on the *third day*, and showed Him openly
Acts 27:19 On the *third day* we threw the ship's tackle overboard with our own hands
1Cor 15:4 and that He was buried, and that He rose again the *third day* according to the Scriptures

THIRD DAY BE RAISED (NIV, RSV)
(See *RAISED THE THIRD DAY*)

THIRD GENERATION
Gen 50:23 Joseph saw Ephraim's children to the *third generation*. The children of Machir, the son of Manasseh, were also brought up on Joseph's knees
Deut 23:8 The children of the *third generation* born to them may enter the congregation of the Lord

THIRTY PIECES OF SILVER
Zech 11:12 So they weighed out for my wages *thirty pieces of silver*
Zech 11:13 So I took the *thirty pieces of silver* and threw them into the house of the Lord for the potter
Matt 26:15 And they counted out to him *thirty pieces of silver*
Matt 27:3 Then Judas, His betrayer, seeing that He had been condemned, was remorseful and brought back the *thirty pieces of silver* to the chief priests and elders
Matt 27:9 Then was fulfilled what was spoken by Jeremiah the prophet, saying, "And they took the *thirty pieces of silver*, the value of Him who was priced, whom they of the children of Israel priced

THIRTY SHEKELS OF SILVER
Ex 21:32 If the ox gores a male or female servant, he shall give to their master *thirty shekels of silver*, and the ox shall be stoned

THIS CUP
Matt 26:39 He went a little farther and fell on His face, and prayed, saying, "O My Father, if it is possible, let *this cup* pass from Me
Matt 26:42 He went away again a second time and prayed, saying, "O My Father, if *this cup* cannot pass away from Me unless I drink it, Your will be done
Mark 14:36 Take *this cup* away from Me; nevertheless, not what I will, but what You will
Luke 22:20 Likewise He also took the cup after supper, saying, "*This cup* is the new covenant in My blood, which is shed for you
Luke 22:42 saying, "Father, if it is Your will, remove *this cup* from Me
1Cor 11:25 In the same manner He also took the cup after supper, saying, "*This cup* is the new covenant in My blood
1Cor 11:26 For as often as you eat this bread and drink *this cup*, you proclaim the Lord's death till He comes
1Cor 11:27 Therefore whoever eats this bread or drinks *this cup* of the Lord in an unworthy manner will be guilty of the body and blood of the Lord

THIS DAY HAVE I BEGOTTEN YOU (KJV)
(See *TODAY I HAVE BEGOTTEN YOU*)

THIS DO, AND LIVE (KJV)
(See *DO THIS AND LIVE*)

THIS GENERATION
Gen 7:1 Then the Lord said to Noah, "Come into the ark, you and all your household, because I have seen that you are righteous before Me in *this generation*
Ps 12:7 You shall keep them, O Lord, You shall preserve them from *this generation* forever
Ps 71:18 Now also when I am old and grayheaded, O God, do not forsake me, until I declare Your strength to *this generation*, Your power to everyone who is to come
Matt 11:16 But to what shall I liken *this generation?* It is like children sitting in the marketplaces and calling to their companions
Matt 12:41 The men of Nineveh will rise in the judgment with *this generation* and condemn it, because they repented at the preaching of Jonah
Matt 12:42 The queen of the South will rise up in the judgment with *this generation* and condemn it, for she came from the ends of the earth to hear the wisdom of Solomon
Matt 23:36 Assuredly, I say to you, all these things will come upon *this generation*
Matt 24:34 Assuredly, I say to you, *this generation* will by no means pass away till all these things are fulfilled
Mark 8:12 But He sighed deeply in His spirit, and said, "Why does *this generation* seek a sign? Assuredly, I say to you, no sign shall be given to *this generation*
Mark 13:30 Assuredly, I say to you, *this generation* will by no means pass away till all these things take place
Luke 7:31 And the Lord said, "To what then shall I liken the men of *this generation*, and what are they like
Luke 11:30 For as Jonah became a sign to the Ninevites, so also the Son of Man will be to *this generation*
Luke 11:31 The queen of the South will rise up in the judgment with the men of *this generation* and condemn them, for she came from the ends of the earth to hear the wisdom of Solomon
Luke 11:32 The men of Nineveh will rise up in the judgment with *this generation* and condemn it, for they repented at the preaching of Jonah
Luke 11:50 that the blood of all the prophets which was shed from the foundation of the world may be required of *this generation*
Luke 11:51 Yes, I say to you, it shall be required of *this generation*
Luke 17:25 But first He must suffer many things and be rejected by *this generation*
Luke 21:32 Assuredly, I say to you, *this generation* will by no means pass away till all things are fulfilled

THIS HOLY PLACE
Acts 6:13 They also set up false witnesses who said, "This man does not cease to speak blasphemous words against *this holy place* and the law
Acts 21:28 and furthermore he also brought Greeks into the temple and has defiled *this holy place*

THIS IS MY BODY
Matt 26:26 And as they were eating, Jesus took bread, blessed it and broke it, and gave it to the disciples and said, "Take, eat; *this is My body*
Mark 14:22 And as they were eating, Jesus took bread, blessed it and broke it, and gave it to them and said, "Take, eat; *this is My body*

THIS IS TO MY FATHER'S GLORY

Luke 22:19 And He took bread, gave thanks and broke it, and gave it to them, saying, "*This is My body* which is given for you

1Cor 11:24 *this is My body* which is broken for you; do this in remembrance of Me

THIS IS TO MY FATHER'S GLORY (NIV)
(See *MY FATHER IS GLORIFIED*)

THIS IS WHAT THE LORD SAYS (NIV)
(See *THUS SAYS THE LORD*)

THIS VERY DAY

Deut 29:4 Yet the Lord has not given you a heart to perceive and eyes to see and ears to hear, to *this very day*

Josh 10:27 So it was at the time of the going down of the sun that Joshua commanded, and they took them down from the trees, cast them into the cave where they had been hidden, and laid large stones against the cave's mouth, which remain until *this very day*

Esth 1:18 *This very day* the noble ladies of Persia and Media will say to all the king's officials that they have heard of the behavior of the queen

Ezek 2:3 they and their fathers have transgressed against Me to *this very day*

Ezek 24:2 Son of man, write down the name of the day, *this very day* the king of Babylon started his siege against Jerusalem *this very day*

Rom 11:8 God has given them a spirit of stupor, eyes that they should not see and ears that they should not hear, to *this very day*

THIS WILL BE A SIGN

1Sam 14:10 For the Lord has delivered them into our hand, and *this will be a sign* to us

Ezek 4:3 *This will be a sign* to the house of Israel

THIS WILL BE THE SIGN

Luke 2:12 And *this will be the sign* to you: You will find a Babe wrapped in swaddling cloths, lying in a manger

THORN IN THE FLESH

2Cor 12:7 And lest I should be exalted above measure by the abundance of the revelations, a *thorn in the flesh* was given to me, a messenger of Satan to buffet me, lest I be exalted above measure

THORNS AND THISTLES

Gen 3:18 Both *thorns and thistles* it shall bring forth for you, and you shall eat the herb of the field

THOSE THAT ARE BORN IN HIS HOUSE (RSV)
(See *ONE WHO IS BORN IN HIS HOUSE*)

THOSE WHO ARE DISOBEDIENT

1Pet 2:7 but to *those who are disobedient*, "The stone which the builders rejected has become the chief cornerstone

THOSE WHO ARE PERISHING

1Cor 1:18 For the message of the cross is foolishness to *those who are perishing*, but to us who are being saved it is the power of God

2Cor 2:15 For we are to God the fragrance of Christ among those who are being saved and among *those who are perishing*

2Cor 4:3 But even if our gospel is veiled, it is veiled to *those who are perishing*

THOSE WHO DO NOT BELIEVE (NIV, RSV)
(See *THOSE WHO ARE DISOBEDIENT*)

THOSE WHO DO WRONG (NIV)
(See *WORKERS OF INIQUITY*)

THOSE WHO GRIEVE IN ZION (NIV)
(See *THOSE WHO MOURN IN ZION*)

THOSE WHO HAVE FALLEN ASLEEP

1Cor 15:18 Then also *those who have fallen asleep* in Christ have perished

1Cor 15:20 But now Christ is risen from the dead, and has become the firstfruits of *those who have fallen asleep*

1Th 4:13 But I do not want you to be ignorant, brethren, concerning *those who have fallen asleep*, lest you sorrow as others who have no hope

THOSE WHO HUNGER AND THIRST FOR RIGHTEOUSNESS

Matt 5:6 Blessed are *those who hunger and thirst for righteousness*, for they shall be filled

THOSE WHO MOURN IN ZION

Is 61:3 to console *those who mourn in Zion*, to give them beauty for ashes, the oil of joy for mourning, the garment of praise for the spirit of heaviness

THOSE WHO SIT IN DARKNESS

Is 42:7 To open blind eyes, to bring out prisoners from the prison, *those who sit in darkness* from the prison house

Luke 1:79 to give light to *those who sit in darkness* and the shadow of death, to guide our feet into the way of peace

THOSE WHO SLEEP IN JESUS

1Th 4:14 For if we believe that Jesus died and rose again, even so God will bring with Him *those who sleep in Jesus*

THOSE WHO WERE OF THE CIRCUMCISION

Gal 2:12 but when they came, he withdrew and separated himself, fearing *those who were of the circumcision*

THOU ANOINTEST MY HEAD WITH OIL (KJV, RSV)
(See *YOU ANOINT MY HEAD WITH OIL*)

THOU, O GOD, ART MY FORTRESS (RSV)
(See *GOD IS MY DEFENSE*)

THOU SHALT NOT KILL (KJV)
(See *YOU SHALL NOT MURDER*)

THOU SHALT SURELY DIE (KJV)
(See *YOU WILL SURELY DIE*)

THOU WHO TRIEST THE MINDS AND HEARTS (RSV)
(See *GOD TESTS THE HEARTS*)

THOUGH YOUR SINS ARE LIKE SCARLET

Is 1:18 Come now, and let us reason together," says the Lord, "*though your sins are like scarlet*, they shall be as white as snow

THOUGHT AS A CHILD

1Cor 13:11 When I was a child, I spoke as a child, I understood as a child, I *thought as a child*

THOUGHT EVIL (KJV)
(See *DEVISED EVIL*)

THOUSAND GENERATIONS
Deut 7:9 Therefore know that the Lord your God, He is God, the faithful God who keeps covenant and mercy for a *thousand generations* with those who love Him and keep His commandments
1Chr 16:15 Remember His covenant always, the word which He commanded, for a *thousand generations*
Ps 105:8 He has remembered His covenant forever, the word which He commanded, for a *thousand generations*

THOUSAND YEARS
Ps 90:4 For a *thousand years* in Your sight are like yesterday when it is past, and like a watch in the night
Eccl 6:6 even if he lives a *thousand years* twice over but has not seen goodness
2Pet 3:8 But, beloved, do not forget this one thing, that with the Lord one day is as a *thousand years*, and a *thousand years* as one day
Rev 20:2 He laid hold of the dragon, that serpent of old, who is the Devil and Satan, and bound him for a *thousand years*
Rev 20:3 and he cast him into the bottomless pit, and shut him up, and set a seal on him, so that he should deceive the nations no more till the *thousand years* were finished
Rev 20:4 And they lived and reigned with Christ for a *thousand years*
Rev 20:5 But the rest of the dead did not live again until the *thousand years* were finished
Rev 20:6 Over such the second death has no power, but they shall be priests of God and of Christ, and shall reign with Him a *thousand years*
Rev 20:7 Now when the *thousand years* have expired, Satan will be released from his prison

THREE DAYS
Gen 40:12 And Joseph said to him, "This is the interpretation of it: The three branches are *three days*
Gen 40:13 Now within *three days* Pharaoh will lift up your head and restore you to your place, and you will put Pharaoh's cup in his hand according to the former manner, when you were his butler
Gen 40:18 So Joseph answered and said, "This is the interpretation of it: The three baskets are *three days*
Gen 40:19 Within *three days* Pharaoh will lift off your head from you and hang you on a tree
Gen 42:17 So he put them all together in prison *three days*
Ex 10:22 So Moses stretched out his hand toward heaven, and there was thick darkness in all the land of Egypt *three days*
Ex 10:23 nor did anyone rise from his place for *three days*
Ex 15:22 And they went *three days* in the wilderness and found no water
Num 10:33 So they departed from the mountain of the Lord on a journey of *three days;* and the ark of the covenant of the Lord went before them for the *three days*
Josh 1:11 Pass through the camp and command the people, saying, 'Prepare provisions for yourselves, for within *three days* you will cross over this Jordan, to go in to possess the land which the Lord your God is giving you to possess
Josh 2:16 Hide there *three days*, until the pursuers have returned. Afterward you may go your way
Josh 2:22 Then they departed and went to the mountain, and stayed there *three days* until the pursuers returned
Josh 3:2 So it was, after *three days*, that the officers went through the camp
Josh 9:16 And it happened at the end of *three days*, after they had made a covenant with them, that they heard that they were their neighbors who dwelt near them
Judg 14:14 Now for *three days* they could not explain the riddle
Judg 19:4 and he stayed with him *three days*. So they ate and drank and lodged there
1Sam 9:20 But as for your donkeys that were lost *three days* ago, do not be anxious about them, for they have been found
1Sam 20:19 And when you have stayed *three days*, go down quickly and come to the place where you hid on the day of the deed
1Sam 21:5 Then David answered the priest, and said to him, "Truly, women have been kept from us about *three days* since I came out
1Sam 30:12 for he had eaten no bread nor drunk any water for *three days* and three nights
1Sam 30:13 and my master left me behind, because *three days* ago I fell sick
2Sam 20:4 Then the king said to Amasa, "Assemble the men of Judah for me within *three days*, and be present here yourself
1Kin 12:5 So he said to them, "Depart for *three days*, then come back to me
2Kin 2:17 Therefore they sent fifty men, and they searched for *three days* but did not find him
1Chr 12:39 And they were there with David *three days*, eating and drinking, for their brethren had prepared for them
1Chr 21:12 either three years of famine, or three months to be defeated by your foes with the sword of your enemies overtaking you, or else for *three days* the sword of the Lord the plague in the land, with the angel of the Lord destroying throughout all the territory of Israel
2Chr 10:5 So he said to them, "Come back to me after *three days*
2Chr 20:25 and they were *three days* gathering the spoil because there was so much
Ezra 8:15 Now I gathered them by the river that flows to Ahava, and we camped there *three days*
Ezra 8:32 So we came to Jerusalem, and stayed there *three days*
Ezra 10:8 and that whoever would not come within *three days*, according to the counsel of the leaders and elders, all his property would be confiscated, and he himself would be separated from the congregation of those from the captivity
Ezra 10:9 So all the men of Judah and Benjamin gathered at Jerusalem within *three days*
Neh 2:11 So I came to Jerusalem and was there *three days*
Esth 4:16 neither eat nor drink for *three days*, night or day
Amos 4:4 bring your sacrifices every morning, your tithes every *three days*
Jon 1:17 And Jonah was in the belly of the fish *three days* and three nights
Matt 12:40 For as Jonah was *three days* and three nights in the belly of the great fish, so will the Son of Man be *three days* and three nights in the heart of the earth
Matt 15:32 Then Jesus called His disciples to Him and said, "I have compassion on the multitude, because they have now continued with Me *three days* and have nothing to eat
Matt 26:61 and said, "This fellow said, 'I am able to destroy the temple of God and to build it in *three days*
Matt 27:40 and saying, "You who destroy the temple and build it in *three days*, save Yourself
Matt 27:63 saying, "Sir, we remember, while He was still alive, how that deceiver said, 'After *three days* I will rise

Mark 8:2 I have compassion on the multitude, because they have now been with Me *three days* and have nothing to eat
Mark 8:31 And He began to teach them that the Son of Man must suffer many things, and be rejected by the elders and chief priests and scribes, and be killed, and after *three days* rise again
Mark 14:58 We heard Him say, 'I will destroy this temple that is made with hands, and within *three days* I will build another made without hands
Mark 15:29 You who destroy the temple and build it in *three days*
Luke 2:46 Now so it was that after *three days* they found Him in the temple, sitting in the midst of the teachers, both listening to them and asking them questions
John 2:19 Jesus answered and said to them, "Destroy this temple, and in *three days* I will raise it up
John 2:20 Then the Jews said, "It has taken forty-six years to build this temple, and will You raise it up in *three days*
Acts 9:9 And he was *three days* without sight, and neither ate nor drank
Acts 25:1 Now when Festus had come to the province, after *three days* he went up from Caesarea to Jerusalem
Acts 28:7 Now in that region there was an estate of the leading citizen of the island, whose name was Publius, who received us and entertained us courteously for *three days*
Acts 28:12 And landing at Syracuse, we stayed *three days*
Acts 28:17 And it came to pass after *three days* that Paul called the leaders of the Jews together

THREE DAYS AND THREE NIGHTS

1Sam 30:12 for he had eaten no bread nor drunk any water for *three days and three nights*
Jon 1:17 And Jonah was in the belly of the fish *three days and three nights*
Matt 12:40 For as Jonah was *three days and three nights* in the belly of the great fish, so will the Son of Man be *three days and three nights* in the heart of the earth

THREE DAYS' JOURNEY

Gen 30:36 Then he put *three days' journey* between himself and Jacob, and Jacob fed the rest of Laban's flocks
Ex 3:18 and now, please, let us go *three days' journey* into the wilderness, that we may sacrifice to the Lord our God
Ex 5:3 Please, let us go *three days' journey* into the desert and sacrifice to the Lord our God, lest He fall upon us with pestilence or with the sword
Ex 8:27 We will go *three days' journey* into the wilderness and sacrifice to the Lord our God as He will command us
Num 33:8 They departed from before Hahiroth and passed through the midst of the sea into the wilderness, went *three days' journey* in the Wilderness of Etham, and camped at Marah

THREE TIMES

Ex 23:14 *Three times* you shall keep a feast to Me in the year
Ex 23:17 *Three times* in the year all your males shall appear before the Lord God
Ex 34:23 *Three times* in the year all your men shall appear before the Lord, the Lord God of Israel
Ex 34:24 neither will any man covet your land when you go up to appear before the Lord your God *three times* in the year
Num 22:28 Then the Lord opened the mouth of the donkey, and she said to Balaam, "What have I done to you, that you have struck me these *three times*
Num 22:32 And the Angel of the Lord said to him, "Why have you struck your donkey these *three times*
Num 22:33 The donkey saw Me and turned aside from Me these *three times*
Num 24:10 and Balak said to Balaam, "I called you to curse my enemies, and look, you have bountifully blessed them these *three times*
Deut 16:16 *Three times* a year all your males shall appear before the Lord your God in the place which He chooses
Judg 16:15 You have mocked me these *three times*, and have not told me where your great strength lies
1Sam 20:41 Now as soon as the lad had gone, David arose from a place toward the south, fell on his face to the ground, and bowed down *three times*
1Kin 9:25 Now *three times* a year Solomon offered burnt offerings and peace offerings on the altar which he had built for the Lord, and he burned incense with them on the altar that was before the Lord
1Kin 17:21 And he stretched himself out on the child *three times*, and cried out to the Lord and said
2Kin 13:18 And he said to the king of Israel, "Strike the ground"; so he struck *three times*, and stopped
2Kin 13:19 then you would have struck Syria till you had destroyed it. But now you will strike Syria only *three times*
2Kin 13:25 *Three times* Joash defeated him and recaptured the cities of Israel
Job 33:29 Behold, God works all these things, twice, in fact, *three times* with a man
Dan 6:10 And in his upper room, with his windows open toward Jerusalem, he knelt down on his knees *three times* that day, and prayed and gave thanks before his God, as was his custom since early days
Dan 6:13 So they answered and said before the king, "That Daniel, who is one of the captives from Judah, does not show due regard for you, O king, or for the decree that you have signed, but makes his petition *three times* a day
Matt 26:34 Jesus said to him, "Assuredly, I say to you that this night, before the rooster crows, you will deny Me *three times*
Matt 26:75 And Peter remembered the word of Jesus who had said to him, "Before the rooster crows, you will deny Me *three times*
Mark 14:30 And Jesus said to him, "Assuredly, I say to you that today, even this night, before the rooster crows twice, you will deny Me *three times*
Mark 14:72 And Peter called to mind the word that Jesus had said to him, "Before the rooster crows twice, you will deny Me *three times*
Luke 22:34 Then He said, "I tell you, Peter, the rooster will not crow this day before you will deny *three times* that you know Me
Luke 22:61 And Peter remembered the word of the Lord, how He had said to him, "Before the rooster crows, you will deny Me *three times*
John 13:38 Most assuredly, I say to you, the rooster shall not crow till you have denied Me *three times*
Acts 10:16 This was done *three times*. And the object was taken up into heaven again
Acts 11:10 Now this was done *three times*, and all were drawn up again into heaven
2Cor 11:25 *Three times* I was beaten with rods; once I was stoned; *three times* I was shipwrecked
2Cor 12:8 Concerning this thing I pleaded with the Lord *three times* that it might depart from me

THREE TIMES A YEAR
Deut 16:16 *Three times a year* all your males shall appear before the Lord your God in the place which He chooses
1Kin 9:25 Now *three times a year* Solomon offered burnt offerings and peace offerings on the altar which he had built for the Lord, and he burned incense with them on the altar that was before the Lord

THREE WHO BEAR WITNESS
1Jn 5:7 For there are *three who bear witness* in heaven: the Father, the Word, and the Holy Spirit

THREESCORE AND TEN SONS (KJV)
(See *SEVENTY SONS*)

THREESCORE AND TEN YEARS (KJV)
(See *SEVENTY YEARS*)

THREW AGAINST THE ALTAR (RSV)
(See *SPRINKLED ON THE ALTAR*)

THREW THE BLOOD (RSV)
(See *SPRINKLED THE BLOOD*)

THROAT IS AN OPEN TOMB
Ps 5:9 Their *throat is an open tomb;* they flatter with their tongue
Rom 3:13 Their *throat is an open tomb;* with their tongues they have practiced deceit

THRONE OF DAVID
2Sam 3:10 to transfer the kingdom from the house of Saul, and set up the *throne of David* over Israel and over Judah, from Dan to Beersheba
1Kin 2:24 Now therefore, as the Lord lives, who has established me and set me on the *throne of David* my father, and who has made me a house, as He promised, Adonijah shall be put to death today
1Kin 2:45 But King Solomon shall be blessed, and the *throne of David* shall be established before the Lord forever
Is 9:7 Of the increase of His government and peace there will be no end, upon the *throne of David* and over His kingdom, to order it and establish it with judgment and justice from that time forward, even forever
Jer 17:25 then shall enter the gates of this city kings and princes sitting on the *throne of David*, riding in chariots and on horses, they and their princes, accompanied by the men of Judah and the inhabitants of Jerusalem
Jer 22:2 and say, 'Hear the word of the Lord, O king of Judah, you who sit on the *throne of David*, you and your servants and your people who enter these gates
Jer 22:4 For if you indeed do this thing, then shall enter the gates of this house, riding on horses and in chariots, accompanied by servants and people, kings who sit on the *throne of David*
Jer 22:30 for none of his descendants shall prosper, sitting on the *throne of David*, and ruling anymore in Judah
Jer 29:16 therefore thus says the Lord concerning the king who sits on the *throne of David*, concerning all the people who dwell in this city, and concerning your brethren who have not gone out with you into captivity
Jer 36:30 He shall have no one to sit on the *throne of David*, and his dead body shall be cast out to the heat of the day and the frost of the night

THRONE OF GOD
Matt 23:22 And he who swears by heaven, swears by the *throne of God* and by Him who sits on it
Heb 12:2 looking unto Jesus, the author and finisher of our faith, who for the joy that was set before Him endured the cross, despising the shame, and has sat down at the right hand of the *throne of God*
Rev 7:15 Therefore they are before the *throne of God*, and serve Him day and night in His temple
Rev 14:5 And in their mouth was found no guile, for they are without fault before the *throne of God*
Rev 22:1 And he showed me a pure river of water of life, clear as crystal, proceeding from the *throne of God* and of the Lamb
Rev 22:3 And there shall be no more curse, but the *throne of God* and of the Lamb shall be in it, and His servants shall serve Him

THRONE OF HIS KINGDOM
Deut 17:18 Also it shall be, when he sits on the *throne of his kingdom*, that he shall write for himself a copy of this law in a book, from the one before the priests, the Levites
2Sam 7:13 He shall build a house for My name, and I will establish the *throne of his kingdom* forever
1Chr 22:10 and I will establish the *throne of his kingdom* over Israel forever
Esth 1:2 in those days when King Ahasuerus sat on the *throne of his kingdom*, which was in Shushan the citadel

THRONE OF THE LORD
1Chr 29:23 Then Solomon sat on the *throne of the Lord* as king instead of David his father, and prospered
Jer 3:17 At that time Jerusalem shall be called The *Throne of the Lord*, and all the nations shall be gathered to it, to the name of the Lord, to Jerusalem

THROUGH A NEEDLE'S EYE
Luke 18:25 For it is easier for a camel to go *through a needle's eye* than for a rich man to enter the kingdom of God

THROUGH HIS HOLY PROPHETS (NIV)
(See *MOUTH OF HIS HOLY PROPHETS*)

THROUGH THE RED SEA
Heb 11:29 By faith they passed *through the Red Sea* as by dry land, whereas the Egyptians, attempting to do so, were drowned

THROUGH THE RIGHTEOUSNESS OF FAITH
Rom 4:13 For the promise that he would be the heir of the world was not to Abraham or to his seed through the law, but *through the righteousness of faith*

THROUGH THE SPIRIT
Acts 21:4 They told Paul *through the Spirit* not to go up to Jerusalem
1Cor 12:8 for to one is given the word of wisdom *through the Spirit*, to another the word of knowledge through the same Spirit
Gal 5:5 For we *through the Spirit* eagerly wait for the hope of righteousness by faith
1Pet 1:22 Since you have purified your souls in obeying the truth *through the Spirit* in sincere love of the brethren, love one another fervently with a pure heart

THROUGH YOUR OFFSPRING (NIV)
(See *IN YOUR SEED*)

THROUGHOUT ALL GENERATIONS
Ps 72:5 They shall fear You as long as the sun and moon endure, *throughout all generations*
Ps 102:24 I said, "O my God, do not take me away

in the midst of my days; Your years are *throughout all generations*

Ps 135:13 Your name, O Lord, endures forever, Your fame, O Lord, *throughout all generations*

Ps 145:13 Your kingdom is an everlasting kingdom, and Your dominion endures *throughout all generations*

THROUGHOUT THE EARTH

Zech 1:10 And the man who stood among the myrtle trees answered and said, "These are the ones whom the Lord has sent to walk to and fro *throughout the earth*

Zech 1:11 So they answered the Angel of the Lord, who stood among the myrtle trees, and said, "We have walked to and fro *throughout the earth*, and behold, all the earth is resting quietly

Zech 5:6 He also said, "This is their resemblance *throughout the earth*

Zech 6:7 Then the strong steeds went out, eager to go, that they might walk to and fro *throughout the earth*. And He said, "Go, walk to and fro *throughout the earth*." So they walked to and fro *throughout the earth*

THROUGHOUT THEIR GENERATIONS

Gen 17:9 As for you, you shall keep My covenant, you and your descendants after you *throughout their generations*

Ex 12:42 This is that night of the Lord, a solemn observance for all the children of Israel *throughout their generations*

Ex 30:21 And it shall be a statute forever to them to him and his descendants *throughout their generations*

Ex 31:16 Therefore the children of Israel shall keep the Sabbath, to observe the Sabbath *throughout their generations* as a perpetual covenant

Ex 40:15 for their anointing shall surely be an everlasting priesthood *throughout their generations*

Lev 7:36 The Lord commanded this to be given to them by the children of Israel, on the day that He anointed them, by a statute forever *throughout their generations*

Lev 17:7 This shall be a statute forever for them *throughout their generations*

Num 15:38 Tell them to make tassels on the corners of their garments *throughout their generations*, and to put a blue thread in the tassels of the corners

1Chr 9:34 These heads of the fathers' houses of the Levites were heads *throughout their generations*

THROW DUST ON THEIR HEADS

Lam 2:10 they *throw dust on their heads* and gird themselves with sackcloth

THROW ITS BLOOD (RSV)

(See *SPRINKLE ITS BLOOD*)

THROW THE BLOOD (RSV)

(See *SPRINKLE THE BLOOD*)

THROWN INTO THE FIRE

Ezek 15:4 Instead, it is *thrown into the fire* for fuel; the fire devours both ends of it, and its middle is burned

Matt 3:10 Therefore every tree which does not bear good fruit is cut down and *thrown into the fire*

Matt 7:19 Every tree that does not bear good fruit is cut down and *thrown into the fire*

Luke 3:9 Therefore every tree which does not bear good fruit is cut down and *thrown into the fire*

THROWN ON THE FIRE (NIV)

(See *THROWN INTO THE FIRE*)

THROWN OUTSIDE, INTO THE DARKNESS (NIV)

(See *OUTER DARKNESS*)

THRUST HIM THROUGH

Judg 9:54 So his young man *thrust him through*, and he died

Zech 13:3 And his father and mother who begot him shall *thrust him through* when he prophesies

THUS SAYS THE LORD

Ex 4:22 Then you shall say to Pharaoh, '*Thus says the Lord*

Ex 5:1 Afterward Moses and Aaron went in and told Pharaoh, "*Thus says the Lord* God of Israel

Ex 7:17 *Thus says the Lord:* "By this you shall know that I am the Lord

Ex 8:1 And the Lord spoke to Moses, "Go to Pharaoh and say to him, '*Thus says the Lord*

Ex 8:20 Then say to him, '*Thus says the Lord:* "Let My people go, that they may serve Me

Ex 9:1 Then the Lord said to Moses, "Go in to Pharaoh and tell him, '*Thus says the Lord* God of the Hebrews

Ex 9:13 Then the Lord said to Moses, "Rise early in the morning and stand before Pharaoh, and say to him, '*Thus says the Lord* God of the Hebrews

Ex 10:3 So Moses and Aaron came in to Pharaoh and said to him, "*Thus says the Lord* God of the Hebrews

Ex 11:4 Then Moses said, "*Thus says the Lord:* 'About midnight I will go out into the midst of Egypt

Ex 32:27 And he said to them, "*Thus says the Lord* God of Israel

Josh 7:13 Get up, sanctify the people, and say, 'Sanctify yourselves for tomorrow, because *thus says the Lord* God of Israel

Josh 24:2 And Joshua said to all the people, "*Thus says the Lord* God of Israel

Judg 6:8 that the Lord sent a prophet to the children of Israel, who said to them, "*Thus says the Lord* God of Israel

1Sam 2:27 Then a man of God came to Eli and said to him, "*Thus says the Lord*

1Sam 10:18 and said to the children of Israel, "*Thus says the Lord* God of Israel

1Sam 15:2 *Thus says the Lord* of hosts: 'I will punish what Amalek did to Israel, how he laid wait for him on the way when he came up from Egypt

2Sam 7:5 Go and tell My servant David, '*Thus says the Lord*

2Sam 7:8 Now therefore, thus shall you say to My servant David, '*Thus says the Lord* of hosts

2Sam 12:7 *Thus says the Lord* God of Israel: 'I anointed you king over Israel, and I delivered you from the hand of Saul

2Sam 12:11 *Thus says the Lord:* 'Behold, I will raise up adversity against you from your own house

2Sam 24:12 Go and tell David, '*Thus says the Lord:* "I offer you three things

1Kin 11:31 And he said to Jeroboam, "Take for yourself ten pieces, for *thus says the Lord*, the God of Israel

1Kin 12:24 *Thus says the Lord:* "You shall not go up nor fight against your brethren the children of Israel

1Kin 13:2 *Thus says the Lord:* 'Behold, a child, Josiah by name, shall be born to the house of David

1Kin 13:21 and he cried out to the man of God who came from Judah, saying, "*Thus says the Lord*

1Kin 14:7 Go, tell Jeroboam, '*Thus says the Lord* God of Israel
1Kin 17:14 For *thus says the Lord* God of Israel: 'The bin of flour shall not be used up, nor shall the jar of oil run dry, until the day the Lord sends rain on the earth
1Kin 20:13 Suddenly a prophet approached Ahab king of Israel, saying, "*Thus says the Lord*
1Kin 20:14 And he said, "*Thus says the Lord:* 'By the young leaders of the provinces
1Kin 20:28 Then a man of God came and spoke to the king of Israel, and said, "*Thus says the Lord*
1Kin 20:42 And he said to him, "*Thus says the Lord:* 'Because you have let slip out of your hand a man whom I appointed to utter destruction, therefore your life shall go for his life, and your people for his people
1Kin 21:19 You shall speak to him, saying, '*Thus says the Lord:* "Have you murdered and also taken possession?"' And you shall speak to him, saying, '*Thus says the Lord*
1Kin 22:11 and he said, "*Thus says the Lord:* 'With these you shall gore the Syrians until they are destroyed
2Kin 1:4 Now therefore, *thus says the Lord:* 'You shall not come down from the bed to which you have gone up, but you shall surely die
2Kin 1:6 So they said to him, "A man came up to meet us, and said to us, 'Go, return to the king who sent you, and say to him, "*Thus says the Lord*
2Kin 1:16 Then he said to him, "*Thus says the Lord:* 'Because you have sent messengers to inquire of Baal-Zebub, the god of Ekron, is it because there is no God in Israel to inquire of His word
2Kin 2:21 Then he went out to the source of the water, and cast in the salt there, and said, "*Thus says the Lord*
2Kin 3:16 And he said, "*Thus says the Lord:* 'Make this valley full of ditches
2Kin 3:17 For *thus says the Lord:* 'You shall not see wind, nor shall you see rain
2Kin 4:43 for *thus says the Lord:* 'They shall eat and have some left over
2Kin 7:1 *Thus says the Lord:* 'Tomorrow about this time a seah of fine flour shall be sold for a shekel, and two seahs of barley for a shekel, at the gate of Samaria
2Kin 9:3 Then take the flask of oil, and pour it on his head, and say, '*Thus says the Lord*
2Kin 9:6 And he poured the oil on his head, and said to him, "*Thus says the Lord* God of Israel
2Kin 9:12 So he said, "Thus and thus he spoke to me, saying, '*Thus says the Lord*
2Kin 19:6 And Isaiah said to them, "Thus you shall say to your master, '*Thus says the Lord*
2Kin 19:20 Then Isaiah the son of Amoz sent to Hezekiah, saying, "*Thus says the Lord* God of Israel
2Kin 19:32 Therefore *thus says the Lord* concerning the king of Assyria
2Kin 20:1 And Isaiah the prophet, the son of Amoz, went to him and said to him, "*Thus says the Lord*
2Kin 20:5 Return and tell Hezekiah the leader of My people, '*Thus says the Lord*, the God of David your father
2Kin 21:12 therefore *thus says the Lord* God of Israel: 'Behold, I am bringing such calamity upon Jerusalem and Judah, that whoever hears of it, both his ears will tingle
2Kin 22:15 Then she said to them, "*Thus says the Lord* God of Israel
2Kin 22:16 *Thus says the Lord:* 'Behold, I will bring calamity on this place and on its inhabitants all the words of the book which the king of Judah has read
2Kin 22:18 But to the king of Judah, who sent you to inquire of the Lord, in this manner you shall speak to him, '*Thus says the Lord* God of Israel
1Chr 17:4 Go and tell My servant David, '*Thus says the Lord*
1Chr 17:7 Now therefore, thus shall you say to My servant David, '*Thus says the Lord* of hosts
1Chr 21:10 Go and tell David, saying, '*Thus says the Lord:* "I offer you three things
1Chr 21:11 So Gad came to David and said to him, "*Thus says the Lord*
2Chr 11:4 *Thus says the Lord:* "You shall not go up or fight against your brethren
2Chr 12:5 Then Shemaiah the prophet came to Rehoboam and the leaders of Judah, who were gathered together in Jerusalem because of Shishak, and said to them, "*Thus says the Lord*
2Chr 18:10 and he said, "*Thus says the Lord:* 'With these you shall gore the Syrians until they are destroyed
2Chr 20:15 *Thus says the Lord* to you: 'Do not be afraid nor dismayed because of this great multitude, for the battle is not yours, but God's
2Chr 21:12 And a letter came to him from Elijah the prophet, saying, *Thus says the Lord* God of your father David
2Chr 34:23 Then she answered them, "*Thus says the Lord* God of Israel
2Chr 34:24 *Thus says the Lord:* 'Behold, I will bring calamity on this place and on its inhabitants, all the curses that are written in the book which they have read before the king of Judah
2Chr 34:26 And as for the king of Judah, who sent you to inquire of the Lord, in this manner you shall speak to him, '*Thus says the Lord* God of Israel
Is 7:7 *thus says the Lord* God: "It shall not stand, nor shall it come to pass
Is 10:24 Therefore *thus says the Lord* God of hosts: "O My people, who dwell in Zion, do not be afraid of the Assyrian
Is 22:15 *Thus says the Lord* God of hosts: "Go, proceed to this steward, to Shebna, who is over the house, and say
Is 28:16 Therefore *thus says the Lord* God: "Behold, I lay in Zion a stone for a foundation, a tried stone, a precious cornerstone, a sure foundation
Is 29:22 Therefore *thus says the Lord*, who redeemed Abraham, concerning the house of Jacob
Is 30:15 For *thus says the Lord* God, the Holy One of Israel
Is 37:6 And Isaiah said to them, "Thus shall you say to your master, '*Thus says the Lord*
Is 37:21 Then Isaiah the son of Amoz sent to Hezekiah, saying, "*Thus says the Lord* God of Israel
Is 37:33 Therefore *thus says the Lord* concerning the king of Assyria
Is 38:1 And Isaiah the prophet, the son of Amoz, went to him and said to him, "*Thus says the Lord*
Is 38:5 Go and say to Hezekiah, '*Thus says the Lord*, the God of David your father
Is 43:1 But now, *thus says the Lord*, who created you, O Jacob, and He who formed you, O Israel
Is 43:14 *Thus says the Lord*, your Redeemer, the Holy One of Israel
Is 43:16 *Thus says the Lord*, who makes a way in the sea and a path through the mighty waters
Is 44:2 *Thus says the Lord* who made you and formed you from the womb, who will help you
Is 44:6 *Thus says the Lord*, the King of Israel, and his Redeemer, the Lord of hosts
Is 44:24 *Thus says the Lord*, your Redeemer, and He who formed you from the womb
Is 45:1 *Thus says the Lord* to His anointed, to Cyrus, whose right hand I have held to subdue nations before him and loose the armor of kings, to

open before him the double doors, so that the gates will not be shut

Is 45:11 *Thus says the Lord*, the Holy One of Israel, and his Maker

Is 45:14 *Thus says the Lord:* "The labor of Egypt and merchandise of Cush and of the Sabeans, men of stature, shall come over to you, and they shall be yours

Is 45:18 For *thus says the Lord*, Who created the heavens, Who is God, Who formed the earth and made it, Who has established it, Who did not create it in vain, Who formed it to be inhabited

Is 48:17 *Thus says the Lord*, your Redeemer, the Holy One of Israel

Is 49:7 *Thus says the Lord*, the Redeemer of Israel, their Holy One, to Him whom man despises, to Him whom the nation abhors, to the Servant of rulers

Is 49:8 *Thus says the Lord:* "In an acceptable time I have heard You, and in the day of salvation I have helped You

Is 49:22 *Thus says the Lord* God: "Behold, I will lift My hand in an oath to the nations, and set up My standard for the peoples

Is 49:25 But *thus says the Lord:* "Even the captives of the mighty shall be taken away, and the prey of the terrible be delivered

Is 50:1 *Thus says the Lord:* "Where is the certificate of your mother's divorce, whom I have put away

Is 52:3 For *thus says the Lord:* "You have sold yourselves for nothing, and you shall be redeemed without money

Is 52:4 For *thus says the Lord* God: "My people went down at first into Egypt to sojourn there

Is 56:1 *Thus says the Lord:* "Keep justice, and do righteousness, for My salvation is about to come, and My righteousness to be revealed

Is 56:4 For *thus says the Lord:* "To the eunuchs who keep My Sabbaths, and choose what pleases Me, and hold fast My covenant

Is 65:8 *Thus says the Lord:* "As the new wine is found in the cluster, and one says

Is 65:13 Therefore *thus says the Lord* God: "Behold, My servants shall eat, but you shall be hungry

Is 66:1 *Thus says the Lord:* "Heaven is My throne, and earth is My footstool

Is 66:12 For *thus says the Lord:* "Behold, I will extend peace to her like a river, and the glory of the Gentiles like a flowing stream

Jer 2:2 Go and cry in the hearing of Jerusalem, saying, '*Thus says the Lord*

Jer 2:5 *Thus says the Lord:* "What injustice have your fathers found in Me, that they have gone far from Me, have followed idols, and have become idolaters

Jer 4:3 For *thus says the Lord* to the men of Judah and Jerusalem

Jer 4:27 For *thus says the Lord:* "The whole land shall be desolate

Jer 5:14 Therefore *thus says the Lord* God of hosts: "Because you speak this word, behold, I will make My words in your mouth fire, and this people wood, and it shall devour them

Jer 6:9 *Thus says the Lord* of hosts: "They shall thoroughly glean as a vine the remnant of Israel

Jer 6:16 *Thus says the Lord:* "Stand in the ways and see, and ask for the old paths, where the good way is, and walk in it

Jer 6:21 Therefore *thus says the Lord:* "Behold, I will lay stumbling blocks before this people, and the fathers and the sons together shall fall on them

Jer 6:22 *Thus says the Lord:* "Behold, a people comes from the north country, and a great nation will be raised from the farthest parts of the earth

Jer 7:3 *Thus says the Lord* of hosts, the God of Israel

Jer 7:20 Therefore *thus says the Lord* God: "Behold, My anger and My fury will be poured out on this place on man and on beast, on the trees of the field and on the fruit of the ground

Jer 7:21 *Thus says the Lord* of hosts, the God of Israel

Jer 8:4 Moreover you shall say to them, '*Thus says the Lord*

Jer 9:7 Therefore *thus says the Lord* of hosts: "Behold, I will refine them and try them

Jer 9:15 therefore *thus says the Lord* of hosts, the God of Israel

Jer 9:17 *Thus says the Lord* of hosts: "Consider and call for the mourning women, that they may come

Jer 9:22 Speak, "*Thus says the Lord:* 'Even the carcasses of men shall fall as refuse on the open field, like cuttings after the harvester, and no one shall gather them

Jer 9:23 *Thus says the Lord:* "Let not the wise man glory in his wisdom, let not the mighty man glory in his might, nor let the rich man glory in his riches

Jer 10:2 *Thus says the Lord:* "Do not learn the way of the Gentiles

Jer 10:18 For *thus says the Lord:* "Behold, I will throw out at this time the inhabitants of the land, and will distress them, that they may find it so

Jer 11:3 and say to them, '*Thus says the Lord* God of Israel

Jer 11:11 Therefore *thus says the Lord:* "Behold, I will surely bring calamity on them which they will not be able to escape

Jer 11:21 Therefore *thus says the Lord* concerning the men of Anathoth who seek your life, saying

Jer 11:22 therefore *thus says the Lord* of hosts: 'Behold, I will punish them

Jer 12:14 *Thus says the Lord:* "Agaist all My evil neighbors who touch the inheritance which I have caused My people Israel to inherit behold, I will pluck them out of their land and pluck out the house of Judah from among them

Jer 13:9 *Thus says the Lord:* 'In this manner I will ruin the pride of Judah and the great pride of Jerusalem

Jer 13:12 *Thus says the Lord* God of Israel: "Every bottle shall be filled with wine

Jer 13:13 Then you shall say to them, '*Thus says the Lord*

Jer 14:10 *Thus says the Lord* to this people: "Thus they have loved to wander

Jer 14:15 Therefore *thus says the Lord* concerning the prophets who prophesy in My name, whom I did not send, and who say

Jer 15:2 then you shall tell them, '*Thus says the Lord*

Jer 15:19 Therefore *thus says the Lord:* "If you return, then I will bring you back

Jer 16:3 For *thus says the Lord* concerning the sons and daughters who are born in this place, and concerning their mothers who bore them and their fathers who begot them in this land

Jer 16:5 For *thus says the Lord:* "Do not enter the house of mourning, nor go to lament or bemoan them

Jer 16:9 For *thus says the Lord* of hosts, the God of Israel

Jer 17:5 *Thus says the Lord:* "Cursed is the man who trusts in man and makes flesh his strength, whose heart departs from the Lord

Jer 17:21 *Thus says the Lord:* "Take heed to yourselves, and bear no burden on the Sabbath day, nor bring it in by the gates of Jerusalem

Jer 18:11 Now therefore, speak to the men of Judah and to the inhabitants of Jerusalem, saying, '*Thus says the Lord*

Jer 18:13 Therefore *thus says the Lord:* "Ask now among the Gentiles, who has heard such things
Jer 19:1 *Thus says the Lord:* "Go and get a potter's earthen flask, and take some of the elders of the people and some of the elders of the priests
Jer 19:3 *Thus says the Lord* of hosts, the God of Israel
Jer 19:11 and say to them, '*Thus says the Lord* of hosts
Jer 19:15 *Thus says the Lord* of hosts, the God of Israel
Jer 20:4 For *thus says the Lord:* 'Behold, I will make you a terror to yourself and to all your friends
Jer 21:4 *Thus says the Lord* God of Israel: "Behold, I will turn back the weapons of war that are in your hands, with which you fight against the king of Babylon and the Chaldeans who besiege you outside the walls
Jer 21:8 Now you shall say to this people, '*Thus says the Lord*
Jer 21:12 *Thus says the Lord:* "Execute judgment in the morning; and deliver him who is plundered out of the hand of the oppressor, lest My fury go out like fire and burn so that no one can quench it, because of the evil of your doings
Jer 22:1 *Thus says the Lord:* "Go down to the house of the king of Judah, and there speak this word
Jer 22:3 *Thus says the Lord:* "Execute judgment and righteousness, and deliver the plundered out of the hand of the oppressor
Jer 22:6 For *thus says the Lord* to the house of the king of Judah
Jer 22:11 For *thus says the Lord* concerning Shallum the son of Josiah, king of Judah, who reigned instead of Josiah his father, who went from this place
Jer 22:18 Therefore *thus says the Lord* concerning Jehoiakim the son of Josiah, king of Judah
Jer 22:30 *Thus says the Lord:* 'Write this man down as childless, a man who shall not prosper in his days
Jer 23:2 Therefore *thus says the Lord* God of Israel against the shepherds who feed My people
Jer 23:15 Therefore *thus says the Lord* of hosts concerning the prophets
Jer 23:16 *Thus says the Lord* of hosts: "Do not listen to the words of the prophets who prophesy to you
Jer 23:38 therefore *thus says the Lord:* 'Because you say this word
Jer 24:5 *Thus says the Lord*, the God of Israel: 'Like these good figs, so will I acknowledge those who are carried away captive from Judah, whom I have sent out of this place for their own good, into the land of the Chaldeans
Jer 24:8 And as the bad figs which cannot be eaten, they are so bad surely *thus says the Lord*
Jer 25:8 Therefore *thus says the Lord* of hosts: 'Because you have not heard My words
Jer 25:15 For *thus says the Lord* God of Israel to me
Jer 25:27 Therefore you shall say to them, '*Thus says the Lord* of hosts, the God of Israel
Jer 25:28 And it shall be, if they refuse to take the cup from your hand to drink, then you shall say to them, '*Thus says the Lord* of hosts
Jer 25:32 *Thus says the Lord* of hosts: "Behold, disaster shall go forth from nation to nation, and a great whirlwind shall be raised up from the farthest parts of the earth
Jer 26:2 *Thus says the Lord:* 'Stand in the court of the Lord's house, and speak to all the cities of Judah, which come to worship in the Lord's house, all the words that I command you to speak to them
Jer 26:4 And you shall say to them, '*Thus says the Lord*
Jer 26:18 Micah of Moresheth prophesied in the days of Hezekiah king of Judah, and spoke to all the people of Judah, saying, '*Thus says the Lord* of hosts
Jer 27:2 *Thus says the Lord* to me: 'Make for yourselves bonds and yokes, and put them on your neck
Jer 27:4 And command them to say to their masters, "*Thus says the Lord* of hosts, the God of Israel thus you shall say to your masters
Jer 27:16 Also I spoke to the priests and to all this people, saying, "*Thus says the Lord*
Jer 27:19 For *thus says the Lord* of hosts concerning the pillars, concerning the Sea, concerning the carts, and concerning the remainder of the vessels that remain in this city
Jer 27:21 yes, *thus says the Lord* of hosts, the God of Israel, concerning the vessels that remain in the house of the Lord, and in the house of the king of Judah and of Jerusalem
Jer 28:11 And Hananiah spoke in the presence of all the people, saying, "*Thus says the Lord*
Jer 28:13 Go and tell Hananiah, saying, '*Thus says the Lord:* "You have broken the yokes of wood, but you have made in their place yokes of iron
Jer 28:14 For *thus says the Lord* of hosts, the God of Israel
Jer 28:16 Therefore *thus says the Lord:* 'Behold, I will cast you from the face of the earth
Jer 29:4 *Thus says the Lord* of hosts, the God of Israel, to all who were carried away captive, whom I have caused to be carried away from Jerusalem to Babylon
Jer 29:8 For *thus says the Lord* of hosts, the God of Israel
Jer 29:10 For *thus says the Lord:* After seventy years are completed at Babylon, I will visit you and perform My good word toward you, and cause you to return to this place
Jer 29:16 therefore *thus says the Lord* concerning the king who sits on the throne of David, concerning all the people who dwell in this city, and concerning your brethren who have not gone out with you into captivity
Jer 29:17 *thus says the Lord* of hosts: Behold, I will send on them the sword, the famine, and the pestilence, and will make them like rotten figs that cannot be eaten, they are so bad
Jer 29:21 *Thus says the Lord* of hosts, the God of Israel, concerning Ahab the son of Kolaiah, and Zedekiah the son of Maaseiah, who prophesy a lie to you in My name
Jer 29:31 Send to all those in captivity, saying, '*Thus says the Lord* concerning Shemaiah the Nehelamite
Jer 29:32 therefore *thus says the Lord:* "Behold, I will punish Shemaiah the Nehelamite and his family
Jer 30:5 For *thus says the Lord:* 'We have heard a voice of trembling, of fear, and not of peace
Jer 30:12 For *thus says the Lord:* 'Your affliction is incurable, your wound is severe
Jer 30:18 *Thus says the Lord:* 'Behold, I will bring back the captivity of Jacob's tents, and have mercy on his dwelling places
Jer 31:2 *Thus says the Lord:* "The people who survived the sword found grace in the wilderness Israel, when I went to give him rest
Jer 31:7 For *thus says the Lord:* "Sing with gladness for Jacob, and shout among the chief of the nations
Jer 31:15 *Thus says the Lord:* "A voice was heard in Ramah, lamentation and bitter weeping, Rachel weeping for her children, refusing to be comforted for her children, because they are no more

Jer 31:16 *Thus says the Lord:* "Refrain your voice from weeping, and your eyes from tears
Jer 31:23 *Thus says the Lord* of hosts, the God of Israel
Jer 31:35 *Thus says the Lord*, Who gives the sun for a light by day, and the ordinances of the moon and the stars for a light by night, Who disturbs the sea, and its waves roar (the Lord of hosts is His name
Jer 31:37 *Thus says the Lord:* "If heaven above can be measured, and the foundations of the earth searched out beneath, I will also cast off all the seed of Israel for all that they have done
Jer 32:3 For Zedekiah king of Judah had shut him up, saying, "Why do you prophesy and say, '*Thus says the Lord*
Jer 32:14 *Thus says the Lord* of hosts, the God of Israel
Jer 32:15 For *thus says the Lord* of hosts, the God of Israel
Jer 32:28 Therefore *thus says the Lord:* "Behold, I will give this city into the hand of the Chaldeans, into the hand of Nebuchadnezzar king of Babylon, and he shall take it
Jer 32:36 Now therefore, *thus says the Lord*, the God of Israel, concerning this city of which you say
Jer 32:42 For *thus says the Lord:* 'Just as I have brought all this great calamity on this people, so I will bring on them all the good that I have promised them
Jer 33:2 *Thus says the Lord* who made it, the Lord who formed it to establish it (the Lord is His name
Jer 33:4 For *thus says the Lord*, the God of Israel, concerning the houses of this city and the houses of the kings of Judah, which have been pulled down to fortify against the siege mounds and the sword
Jer 33:10 *Thus says the Lord:* "Again there shall be heard in this place of which you say
Jer 33:12 *Thus says the Lord* of hosts: In this place which is desolate, without man and without beast, and in all its cities, there shall again be a habitation of shepherds causing their flocks to lie down
Jer 33:17 For *thus says the Lord:* "David shall never lack a man to sit on the throne of the house of Israel
Jer 33:20 *Thus says the Lord:* 'If you can break My covenant with the day and My covenant with the night, so that there will not be day and night in their season
Jer 33:25 *Thus says the Lord:* If My covenant is not with day and night, and if I have not appointed the ordinances of heaven and earth
Jer 34:2 *Thus says the Lord*, the God of Israel: 'Go and speak to Zedekiah king of Judah and tell him, "*Thus says the Lord*
Jer 34:4 *Thus says the Lord* concerning you: 'You shall not die by the sword
Jer 34:13 *Thus says the Lord*, the God of Israel: 'I made a covenant with your fathers in the day that I brought them out of the land of Egypt, out of the house of bondage, saying
Jer 34:17 Therefore *thus says the Lord:* 'You have not obeyed Me in proclaiming liberty, every one to his brother and every one to his neighbor
Jer 35:13 *Thus says the Lord* of hosts, the God of Israel
Jer 35:17 Therefore *thus says the Lord* God of hosts, the God of Israel
Jer 35:18 And Jeremiah said to the house of the Rechabites, "*Thus says the Lord* of hosts, the God of Israel
Jer 35:19 therefore *thus says the Lord* of hosts, the God of Israel
Jer 36:29 And you shall say to Jehoiakim king of Judah, '*Thus says the Lord*
Jer 36:30 Therefore *thus says the Lord* concerning Jehoiakim king of Judah
Jer 37:7 *Thus says the Lord*, the God of Israel, 'Thus you shall say to the king of Judah, who sent you to Me to inquire of Me
Jer 37:9 *Thus says the Lord:* 'Do not deceive yourselves, saying, "The Chaldeans will surely depart from us
Jer 38:2 *Thus says the Lord:* 'He who remains in this city shall die by the sword, by famine, and by pestilence
Jer 38:3 *Thus says the Lord:* 'This city shall surely be given into the hand of the king of Babylon's army, which shall take it
Jer 38:17 Then Jeremiah said to Zedekiah, "*Thus says the Lord*, the God of hosts, the God of Israel
Jer 39:16 Go and speak to Ebed-Melech the Ethiopian, saying, '*Thus says the Lord* of hosts, the God of Israel
Jer 42:9 and said to them, "*Thus says the Lord*, the God of Israel, to whom you sent me to present your petition before Him
Jer 42:15 *Thus says the Lord* of hosts, the God of Israel
Jer 42:18 For *thus says the Lord* of hosts, the God of Israel
Jer 43:10 and say to them, '*Thus says the Lord* of hosts, the God of Israel
Jer 44:2 *Thus says the Lord* of hosts, the God of Israel
Jer 44:7 Now therefore, *thus says the Lord*, the God of hosts, the God of Israel
Jer 44:11 Therefore *thus says the Lord* of hosts, the God of Israel
Jer 44:25 *Thus says the Lord* of hosts, the God of Israel, saying
Jer 44:30 *Thus says the Lord:* 'Behold, I will give Pharaoh Hophra king of Egypt into the hand of his enemies and into the hand of those who seek his life, as I gave Zedekiah king of Judah into the hand of Nebuchadnezzar king of Babylon, his enemy who sought his life
Jer 45:2 *Thus says the Lord*, the God of Israel, to you, O Baruch
Jer 45:4 Thus you shall say to him, '*Thus says the Lord*
Jer 47:2 *Thus says the Lord:* "Behold, waters rise out of the north, and shall be an overflowing flood
Jer 48:1 *Thus says the Lord* of hosts, the God of Israel
Jer 48:40 For *thus says the Lord:* "Behold one shall fly like an eagle, and spread his wings over Moab
Jer 49:1 *Thus says the Lord:* "Has Israel no sons? Has he no heir
Jer 49:7 *Thus says the Lord* of hosts: "Is wisdom no more in Teman
Jer 49:12 For *thus says the Lord:* "Behold, those whose judgment was not to drink of the cup have assuredly drunk
Jer 49:28 *Thus says the Lord:* "Arise, go up to Kedar, and devastate the men of the East
Jer 49:35 *Thus says the Lord* of hosts: 'Behold, I will break the bow of Elam, the foremost of their might
Jer 50:18 Therefore *thus says the Lord* of hosts, the God of Israel
Jer 50:33 *Thus says the Lord* of hosts: "The children of Israel were oppressed, along with the children of Judah
Jer 51:1 *Thus says the Lord:* "Behold, I will raise up against Babylon, against those who dwell in Leb Kamai, a destroying wind
Jer 51:33 For *thus says the Lord* of hosts, the God of Israel

Jer 51:36 Therefore *thus says the Lord:* "Behold, I will plead your case and take vengeance for you
Jer 51:58 *Thus says the Lord* of hosts: "The broad walls of Babylon shall be utterly broken, and her high gates shall be burned with fire
Ezek 2:4 I am sending you to them, and you shall say to them, '*Thus says the Lord* God
Ezek 3:11 And go, get to the captives, to the children of your people, and speak to them and tell them, '*Thus says the Lord* God
Ezek 3:27 But when I speak with you, I will open your mouth, and you shall say to them, '*Thus says the Lord* God
Ezek 5:5 *Thus says the Lord* God: 'This is Jerusalem; I have set her in the midst of the nations and the countries all around her
Ezek 5:7 Therefore *thus says the Lord* God: 'Because you have multiplied disobedience more than the nations that are all around you, and have not walked in My statutes, nor kept My judgments, nor even done according to the judgments of the nations that are all around you
Ezek 5:8 therefore *thus says the Lord* God: 'Indeed I, even I, am against you and will execute judgments in your midst in the sight of the nations
Ezek 6:3 *Thus says the Lord* God to the mountains, to the hills, to the ravines, and to the valleys
Ezek 6:11 *Thus says the Lord* God: "Pound your fists and stamp your feet, and say
Ezek 7:2 And you, son of man, *thus says the Lord* God to the land of Israel
Ezek 7:5 *Thus says the Lord* God: 'A disaster, a singular disaster
Ezek 11:5 *Thus says the Lord:* "Thus you have said, O house of Israel
Ezek 11:7 Therefore *thus says the Lord* God: "Your slain whom you have laid in its midst, they are the meat, and this city is the caldron
Ezek 11:16 Therefore say, '*Thus says the Lord* God: "Although I have cast them far off among the Gentiles, and although I have scattered them among the countries, yet I shall be a little sanctuary for them in the countries where they have gone
Ezek 11:17 Therefore say, '*Thus says the Lord* God: "I will gather you from the peoples, assemble you from the countries where you have been scattered, and I will give you the land of Israel
Ezek 12:10 Say to them, '*Thus says the Lord* God: "This burden concerns the prince in Jerusalem and all the house of Israel who are among them
Ezek 12:19 And say to the people of the land, '*Thus says the Lord* God to the inhabitants of Jerusalem and to the land of Israel
Ezek 12:23 Tell them therefore, '*Thus says the Lord* God: "I will lay this proverb to rest, and they shall no more use it as a proverb in Israel
Ezek 12:28 Therefore say to them, '*Thus says the Lord* God: "None of My words will be postponed any more, but the word which I speak will be done
Ezek 13:3 *Thus says the Lord* God: "Woe to the foolish prophets, who follow their own spirit and have seen nothing
Ezek 13:6 They have envisioned futility and false divination, saying, '*Thus says the Lord*
Ezek 13:8 Therefore *thus says the Lord* God: "Because you have spoken nonsense and envisioned lies, therefore I am indeed against you
Ezek 13:13 Therefore *thus says the Lord* God: "I will cause a stormy wind to break forth in My fury
Ezek 13:18 and say, '*Thus says the Lord* God: "Woe to the women who sew magic charms on their sleeves and make veils for the heads of people of every height to hunt souls
Ezek 13:20 Therefore *thus says the Lord* God: "Behold, I am against your magic charms by which you hunt souls there like birds
Ezek 14:4 Therefore speak to them, and say to them, '*Thus says the Lord* God
Ezek 14:6 Therefore say to the house of Israel, '*Thus says the Lord* God
Ezek 14:21 For *thus says the Lord* God: "How much more it shall be when I send My four severe judgments on Jerusalem the sword and famine and wild beasts and pestilence to cut off man and beast from it
Ezek 15:6 Therefore *thus says the Lord* God: 'Like the wood of the vine among the trees of the forest, which I have given to the fire for fuel, so I will give up the inhabitants of Jerusalem
Ezek 16:3 and say, '*Thus says the Lord* God to Jerusalem: "Your birth and your nativity are from the land of Canaan
Ezek 16:36 *Thus says the Lord* God: "Because your filthiness was poured out and your nakedness uncovered in your harlotry with your lovers, and with all your abominable idols, and because of the blood of your children which you gave to them
Ezek 16:59 For *thus says the Lord* God: "I will deal with you as you have done, who despised the oath by breaking the covenant
Ezek 17:3 and say, '*Thus says the Lord* God: "A great eagle with large wings and long pinions, full of feathers of various colors, came to Lebanon and took from the cedar the highest branch
Ezek 17:9 Say, '*Thus says the Lord* God: "Will it thrive? Will he not pull up its roots, cut off its fruit, and leave it to wither
Ezek 17:19 Therefore *thus says the Lord* God: "As I live, surely My oath which he despised, and My covenant which he broke, I will recompense on his own head
Ezek 17:22 *Thus says the Lord* God: "I will take also one of the highest branches of the high cedar and set it out
Ezek 20:3 Son of man, speak to the elders of Israel, and say to them, '*Thus says the Lord* God
Ezek 20:5 Say to them, '*Thus says the Lord* God: "On the day when I chose Israel and lifted My hand in an oath to the descendants of the house of Jacob, and made Myself known to them in the land of Egypt, I lifted My hand in an oath to them, saying
Ezek 20:27 Therefore, son of man, speak to the house of Israel, and say to them, '*Thus says the Lord* God
Ezek 20:30 Therefore say to the house of Israel, '*Thus says the Lord* God
Ezek 20:39 As for you, O house of Israel," *thus says the Lord* God
Ezek 20:47 *Thus says the Lord* God: "Behold, I will kindle a fire in you, and it shall devour every green tree and every dry tree in you
Ezek 21:3 and say to the land of Israel, '*Thus says the Lord*
Ezek 21:9 Son of man, prophesy and say, '*Thus says the Lord*
Ezek 21:24 Therefore *thus says the Lord* God: 'Because you have made your iniquity to be remembered, in that your transgressions are uncovered, so that in all your doings your sins appear because you have come to remembrance, you shall be taken in hand
Ezek 21:26 *thus says the Lord* God: 'Remove the turban, and take off the crown
Ezek 21:28 And you, son of man, prophesy and say, '*Thus says the Lord* God concerning the Ammonites and concerning their reproach
Ezek 22:3 Then say, '*Thus says the Lord* God: "The city sheds blood in her own midst, that her time may come

Ezek 22:19 Therefore *thus says the Lord* God: 'Because you have all become dross, therefore behold, I will gather you into the midst of Jerusalem
Ezek 22:28 Her prophets plastered them with untempered mortar, seeing false visions, and divining lies for them, saying, '*Thus says the Lord* God
Ezek 23:22 Therefore, Oholibah, *thus says the Lord* God: 'Behold, I will stir up your lovers against you, from whom you have alienated yourself, and I will bring them against you from every side
Ezek 23:28 For *thus says the Lord* God: 'Surely I will deliver you into the hand of those whom you hate, into the hand of those from whom you alienated yourself
Ezek 23:32 *Thus says the Lord* God: 'You shall drink of your sister's cup, the deep and wide one
Ezek 23:35 Therefore *thus says the Lord* God: 'Because you have forgotten Me and cast Me behind your back, therefore you shall bear the penalty of your lewdness and your harlotry
Ezek 23:46 For *thus says the Lord* God: 'Bring up an assembly against them, give them up to trouble and plunder
Ezek 24:3 And utter a parable to the rebellious house, and say to them, '*Thus says the Lord* God
Ezek 24:6 Therefore *thus says the Lord* God: "Woe to the bloody city, to the pot whose scum is in it, and whose scum is not gone from it
Ezek 24:9 Therefore *thus says the Lord* God: "Woe to the bloody city
Ezek 24:21 Speak to the house of Israel, "*Thus says the Lord* God
Ezek 25:3 *Thus says the Lord* God: "Because you said, 'Aha!' against My sanctuary when it was profaned, and against the land of Israel when it was desolate, and against the house of Judah when they went into captivity
Ezek 25:6 For *thus says the Lord* God: "Because you clapped your hands, stamped your feet, and rejoiced in heart with all your disdain for the land of Israel
Ezek 25:8 *Thus says the Lord* God: "Because Moab and Seir say
Ezek 25:12 *Thus says the Lord* God: "Because of what Edom did against the house of Judah by taking vengeance, and has greatly offended by avenging itself on them
Ezek 25:13 therefore *thus says the Lord* God: "I will also stretch out My hand against Edom, cut off man and beast from it, and make it desolate from Teman
Ezek 25:15 *Thus says the Lord* God: "Because the Philistines dealt vengefully and took vengeance with a spiteful heart, to destroy because of the old hatred
Ezek 25:16 therefore *thus says the Lord* God: "I will stretch out My hand against the Philistines, and I will cut off the Cherethites and destroy the remnant of the seacoast
Ezek 26:3 Therefore *thus says the Lord* God: 'Behold, I am against you, O Tyre, and will cause many nations to come up against you, as the sea causes its waves to come up
Ezek 26:7 For *thus says the Lord* God: 'Behold, I will bring against Tyre from the north Nebuchadnezzar king of Babylon, king of kings, with horses, with chariots, and with horsemen, and an army with many people
Ezek 26:15 *Thus says the Lord* God to Tyre: 'Will the coastlands not shake at the sound of your fall, when the wounded cry, when slaughter is made in the midst of you
Ezek 26:19 For *thus says the Lord* God: 'When I make you a desolate city, like cities that are not inhabited, when I bring the deep upon you, and great waters cover you
Ezek 27:3 and say to Tyre, 'You who are situated at the entrance of the sea, merchant of the peoples on many coastlands, *thus says the Lord* God
Ezek 28:2 Son of man, say to the prince of Tyre, '*Thus says the Lord* God
Ezek 28:6 Therefore *thus says the Lord* God: "Because you have set your heart as the heart of a god
Ezek 28:12 Son of man, take up a lamentation for the king of Tyre, and say to him, '*Thus says the Lord* God
Ezek 28:22 and say, '*Thus says the Lord* God: "Behold, I am against you, O Sidon
Ezek 28:25 *Thus says the Lord* God: "When I have gathered the house of Israel from the peoples among whom they are scattered, and am hallowed in them in the sight of the Gentiles, then they will dwell in their own land which I gave to My servant Jacob
Ezek 29:3 Speak, and say, '*Thus says the Lord* God: "Behold, I am against you, O Pharaoh king of Egypt, O great monster who lies in the midst of his rivers, who has said
Ezek 29:8 Therefore *thus says the Lord* God: "Surely I will bring a sword upon you and cut off from you man and beast
Ezek 29:13 Yet, *thus says the Lord* God: "At the end of forty years I will gather the Egyptians from the peoples among whom they were scattered
Ezek 29:19 Therefore *thus says the Lord* God: "Surely I will give the land of Egypt to Nebuchadnezzar king of Babylon
Ezek 30:2 Son of man, prophesy and say, '*Thus says the Lord* God
Ezek 30:6 *Thus says the Lord:* "Those who uphold Egypt shall fall, and the pride of her power shall come down
Ezek 30:10 *Thus says the Lord* God: "I will also make a multitude of Egypt to cease by the hand of Nebuchadnezzar king of Babylon
Ezek 30:13 *Thus says the Lord* God: "I will also destroy the idols, and cause the images to cease from Noph
Ezek 30:22 Therefore *thus says the Lord* God: "Surely I am against Pharaoh king of Egypt, and will break his arms, both the strong one and the one that was broken
Ezek 31:10 Therefore *thus says the Lord* God: "Because you have increased in height, and it set its top among the thick boughs, and its heart was lifted up in its height
Ezek 31:15 *Thus says the Lord* God: 'In the day when it went down to hell, I caused mourning
Ezek 32:3 *Thus says the Lord* God: 'I will therefore spread My net over you with a company of many people, And they will draw you up in My net
Ezek 32:11 For *thus says the Lord* God: 'The sword of the king of Babylon shall come upon you
Ezek 33:25 Therefore say to them, '*Thus says the Lord* God: "You eat meat with blood, you lift up your eyes toward your idols, and shed blood
Ezek 33:27 Say thus to them, '*Thus says the Lord* God: "As I live, surely those who are in the ruins shall fall by the sword, and the one who is in the open field I will give to the beasts to be devoured, and those who are in the strongholds and caves shall die of the pestilence
Ezek 34:2 Son of man, prophesy against the shepherds of Israel, prophesy and say to them, '*Thus says the Lord* God to the shepherds
Ezek 34:10 *Thus says the Lord* God: "Behold, I am against the shepherds, and I will require My flock at their hand
Ezek 34:11 For *thus says the Lord* God: "Indeed I Myself will search for My sheep and seek them out

Ezek 34:17 And as for you, O My flock, *thus says the Lord* God
Ezek 34:20 Therefore *thus says the Lord* God to them: "Behold, I Myself will judge between the fat and the lean sheep
Ezek 35:3 and say to it, '*Thus says the Lord* God: "Behold, O Mount Seir, I am against you
Ezek 35:14 *Thus says the Lord* God: "The whole earth will rejoice when I make you desolate
Ezek 36:2 *Thus says the Lord* God: "Because the enemy has said of you
Ezek 36:3 therefore prophesy, and say, '*Thus says the Lord* God: Because they made you desolate and swallowed you up on every side, so that you became the possession of the rest of the nations, and you are taken up by the lips of talkers and slandered by the people
Ezek 36:4 *Thus says the Lord* God to the mountains, the hills, the rivers, the valleys, the desolate wastes, and the cities that have been forsaken, which became plunder and mockery to the rest of the nations all around
Ezek 36:5 therefore *thus says the Lord* God: "Surely I have spoken in My burning jealousy against the rest of the nations and against all Edom, who gave My land to themselves as a possession, with whole-hearted joy and spiteful minds, in order to plunder its open country
Ezek 36:6 Therefore prophesy concerning the land of Israel, and say to the mountains, the hills, the rivers, and the valleys, '*Thus says the Lord* God
Ezek 36:7 Therefore *thus says the Lord* God: "I have lifted My hand in an oath that surely the nations that are around you shall bear their own shame
Ezek 36:13 *Thus says the Lord* God: "Because they say to you
Ezek 36:22 Therefore say to the house of Israel, '*Thus says the Lord* God
Ezek 36:33 *Thus says the Lord* God: "On the day that I cleanse you from all your iniquities, I will also enable you to dwell in the cities, and the ruins shall be rebuilt
Ezek 36:37 *Thus says the Lord* God: "I will also let the house of Israel inquire of Me to do this for them
Ezek 37:5 *Thus says the Lord* God to these bones: "Surely I will cause breath to enter into you, and you shall live
Ezek 37:9 Then He said to me, "Prophesy to the breath, prophesy, son of man, and say to the breath, '*Thus says the Lord* God
Ezek 37:12 Therefore prophesy and say to them, '*Thus says the Lord* God
Ezek 37:19 say to them, '*Thus says the Lord* God: "Surely I will take the stick of Joseph, which is in the hand of Ephraim, and the tribes of Israel, his companions
Ezek 37:21 Then say to them, '*Thus says the Lord* God: "Surely I will take the children of Israel from among the nations, wherever they have gone, and will gather them from every side and bring them into their own land
Ezek 38:3 and say, '*Thus says the Lord* God: "Behold, I am against you, O Gog, the prince of Rosh, Meshech, and Tubal
Ezek 38:10 *Thus says the Lord* God: "On that day it shall come to pass that thoughts will arise in your mind, and you will make an evil plan
Ezek 38:14 Therefore, son of man, prophesy and say to Gog, '*Thus says the Lord* God
Ezek 38:17 *Thus says the Lord* God: "Are you he of whom I have spoken in former days by My servants the prophets of Israel, who prophesied for years in those days that I would bring you against them
Ezek 39:1 And you, son of man, prophesy against Gog, and say, '*Thus says the Lord* God
Ezek 39:17 And as for you, son of man, *thus says the Lord* God
Ezek 39:25 Therefore *thus says the Lord* God: "Now I will bring back the captives of Jacob, and have mercy on the whole house of Israel
Ezek 43:18 And He said to me, "Son of man, *thus says the Lord* God
Ezek 44:6 Now say to the rebellious, to the house of Israel, '*Thus says the Lord* God
Ezek 44:9 *Thus says the Lord* God: "No foreigner, uncircumcised in heart or uncircumcised in flesh, shall enter My sanctuary, including any foreigner who is among the children of Israel
Ezek 45:9 *Thus says the Lord* God: "Enough, O princes of Israel
Ezek 45:18 *Thus says the Lord* God: "In the first month, on the first day of the month, you shall take a young bull without blemish and cleanse the sanctuary
Ezek 46:1 *Thus says the Lord* God: "The gateway of the inner court that faces toward the east shall be shut the six working days
Ezek 46:16 *Thus says the Lord* God: "If the prince gives a gift of some of his inheritance to any of his sons, it shall belong to his sons
Ezek 47:13 *Thus says the Lord* God: "These are the borders by which you shall divide the land as an inheritance among the twelve tribes of Israel
Amos 1:3 *Thus says the Lord:* "For three transgressions of Damascus, and for four, I will not turn away its punishment, because they have threshed Gilead with implements of iron
Amos 1:6 *Thus says the Lord:* "For three transgressions of Gaza, and for four, I will not turn away its punishment, because they took captive the whole captivity to deliver them up to Edom
Amos 1:9 *Thus says the Lord:* "For three transgressions of Tyre, and for four, I will not turn away its punishment, because they delivered up the whole captivity to Edom, and did not remember the covenant of brotherhood
Amos 1:11 *Thus says the Lord:* "For three transgressions of Edom, and for four, I will not turn away its punishment, because he pursued his brother with the sword, and cast off all pity
Amos 1:13 *Thus says the Lord:* "For three transgressions of the people of Ammon, and for four, I will not turn away its punishment, because they ripped open the women with child in Gilead, that they might enlarge their territory
Amos 2:1 *Thus says the Lord:* "For three transgressions of Moab, and for four, I will not turn away its punishment, because he burned the bones of the king of Edom to lime
Amos 2:4 *Thus says the Lord:* "For three transgressions of Judah, and for four, I will not turn away its punishment, because they have despised the law of the Lord, and have not kept His commandments
Amos 2:6 *Thus says the Lord:* "For three transgressions of Israel, and for four, I will not turn away its punishment, because they sell the righteous for silver, and the poor for a pair of sandals
Amos 3:11 Therefore *thus says the Lord* God: "An adversary shall be all around the land
Amos 3:12 *Thus says the Lord:* "As a shepherd takes from the mouth of a lion two legs or a piece of an ear, so shall the children of Israel be taken out who dwell in Samaria in the corner of a bed and on the edge of a couch
Amos 5:3 For *thus says the Lord* God: "The city that goes out by a thousand shall have a hundred left, and that which goes out by a hundred shall have ten left to the house of Israel
Amos 5:4 For *thus says the Lord* to the house of Israel
Amos 7:17 Therefore *thus says the Lord:* "Your wife shall be a harlot in the city

Obad 1 *Thus says the Lord* God concerning Edom (We have heard a report from the Lord, and a messenger has been sent among the nations, saying
Mic 2:3 Therefore *thus says the Lord:* "Behold, against this family I am devising disaster, from which you cannot remove your necks
Mic 3:5 *Thus says the Lord* concerning the prophets who make my people stray
Nah 1:12 *Thus says the Lord:* "Though they are safe, and likewise many, yet in this manner they will be cut down when he passes through
Hag 1:5 Now therefore, *thus says the Lord* of hosts: "Consider your ways
Hag 1:7 *Thus says the Lord* of hosts: "Consider your ways
Hag 2:6 For *thus says the Lord* of hosts: "Once more (it is a little while
Hag 2:11 *Thus says the Lord* of hosts: 'Now ask the priests concerning the law, saying
Zech 1:3 Therefore say to them, '*Thus says the Lord* of hosts
Zech 1:4 Do not be like your fathers, to whom the former prophets preached, saying, '*Thus says the Lord* of hosts
Zech 1:14 So the angel who spoke with me said to me, "Proclaim, saying, '*Thus says the Lord* of hosts
Zech 1:16 Therefore *thus says the Lord:* "I am returning to Jerusalem with mercy
Zech 1:17 Again proclaim, saying, '*Thus says the Lord* of hosts: "My cities shall again spread out through prosperity
Zech 2:8 For *thus says the Lord* of hosts: "He sent Me after glory, to the nations which plunder you
Zech 3:7 *Thus says the Lord* of hosts: 'If you will walk in My ways, and if you will keep My command, then you shall also judge My house, and likewise have charge of My courts
Zech 6:12 Then speak to him, saying, '*Thus says the Lord* of hosts, saying
Zech 7:9 *Thus says the Lord* of hosts: 'Execute true justice, show mercy and compassion everyone to his brother
Zech 8:2 *Thus says the Lord* of hosts: 'I am zealous for Zion with great zeal
Zech 8:3 *Thus says the Lord:* 'I will return to Zion, and dwell in the midst of Jerusalem
Zech 8:4 *Thus says the Lord* of hosts: 'Old men and old women shall again sit in the streets of Jerusalem, each one with his staff in his hand because of great age
Zech 8:6 *Thus says the Lord* of hosts: 'If it is marvelous in the eyes of the remnant of this people in these days, will it also be marvelous in My eyes
Zech 8:7 *Thus says the Lord* of hosts: 'Behold, I will save My people from the land of the east and from the land of the west
Zech 8:9 *Thus says the Lord* of hosts: 'Let your hands be strong, you who have been hearing in these days these words by the mouth of the prophets, who were in the day that the foundation was laid for the house of the Lord of hosts, that the temple might be built
Zech 8:14 For *thus says the Lord* of hosts: 'Just as I determined to punish you when your fathers provoked Me to wrath
Zech 8:19 *Thus says the Lord* of hosts: 'The fast of the fourth month, the fast of the fifth, the fast of the seventh, and the fast of the tenth, shall be joy and gladness and cheerful feasts for the house of Judah
Zech 8:20 *Thus says the Lord* of hosts: 'Peoples shall yet come, inhabitants of many cities
Zech 8:23 *Thus says the Lord* of hosts: 'In those days ten men from every language of the nations shall grasp the sleeve of a Jewish man, saying
Zech 11:4 *Thus says the Lord* my God, "Feed the flock for slaughter
Zech 12:1 *Thus says the Lord,* who stretches out the heavens, lays the foundation of the earth, and forms the spirit of man within him
Mal 1:4 Even though Edom has said, "We have been impoverished, but we will return and build the desolate places," *thus says the Lord* of hosts

THY HOLY CHILD JESUS (KJV)
(See *YOUR HOLY SERVANT JESUS*)

THY KINGDOM COME (KJV, NAS, RSV)
(See *YOUR KINGDOM COME*)

THY ROD AND THY STAFF (KJV, NAS, RSV)
(See *YOUR ROD AND YOUR STAFF*)

TIE THEM AS SYMBOLS (NIV)
(See *BIND THEM AS A SIGN*)

TILLER OF THE GROUND
Gen 4:2 Now Abel was a keeper of sheep, but Cain was a *tiller of the ground*

TIME FOR ESTABLISHING ALL (RSV)
(See *RESTORATION OF ALL THINGS*)

TIME FOR EVERY MATTER UNDER HEAVEN (RSV)
(See *TIME FOR EVERY PURPOSE UNDER HEAVEN*)

TIME FOR EVERY PURPOSE UNDER HEAVEN
Eccl 3:1 To everything there is a season, a *time for every purpose under heaven*

TIME HAS COME (NIV)
(See *TIME IS FULFILLED*)

TIME IS COMING
John 16:2 yes, the *time is coming* that whoever kills you will think that he offers God service
John 16:25 but the *time is coming* when I will no longer speak to you in figurative language, but I will tell you plainly about the Father

TIME IS FAR PAST (KJV)
(See *HOUR IS LATE*)

TIME IS FULFILLED
Mark 1:15 and saying, "The *time is fulfilled*, and the kingdom of God is at hand

TIME IS NOW PAST (KJV)
(See *HOUR IS ALREADY LATE*)

TIME OF GOD'S FAVOR (NIV)
(See *ACCEPTED TIME*)

TIME OF PRAYER (NIV)
(See *HOUR OF PRAYER*)

TIME OF PUNISHMENT (NIV)
(See *DAYS OF VENGEANCE*)

TIME OF THE END
Dan 8:17 but he said to me, "Understand, son of man, that the vision refers to the *time of the end*
Dan 11:35 And some of those of understanding shall fall, to refine them, purge them, and make them white, until the *time of the end*
Dan 11:40 At the *time of the end* the king of the South shall attack him
Dan 12:4 But you, Daniel, shut up the words, and seal the book until the *time of the end*
Dan 12:9 And he said, "Go your way, Daniel, for

the words are closed up and sealed till the *time of the end*

TIME OF THE OFFERING OF THE OBLATION (RSV)
(See *EVENING SACRIFICE*)

TIME OF THEIR PUNISHMENT
Jer 8:12 in the *time of their punishment* they shall be cast down
Jer 10:15 They are futile, a work of errors; in the *time of their punishment* they shall perish
Jer 46:21 They did not stand, for the day of their calamity had come upon them, the *time of their punishment*
Jer 50:27 for their day has come, the *time of their punishment*
Jer 51:18 They are futile, a work of errors; in the *time of their punishment* they shall perish

TIME OF TROUBLE
Job 38:23 Which I have reserved for the *time of trouble*, for the day of battle and war
Ps 27:5 For in the *time of trouble* He shall hide me in His pavilion
Ps 37:39 But the salvation of the righteous is from the Lord; He is their strength in the *time of trouble*
Ps 41:1 Blessed is he who considers the poor; the Lord will deliver him in *time of trouble*
Prov 25:19 Confidence in an unfaithful man in *time of trouble* is like a bad tooth and a foot out of joint
Is 33:2 Be their arm every morning, our salvation also in the *time of trouble*
Jer 14:8 O the Hope of Israel, his Savior in *time of trouble*, why should You be like a stranger in the land, and like a wayfaring man who turns aside to tarry for a night
Dan 12:1 And there shall be a *time of trouble*, such as never was since there was a nation, even to that time

TIME TO COME
Gen 30:33 So my righteousness will answer for me in *time to come*, when the subject of my wages comes before you
Ex 13:14 So it shall be, when your son asks you in *time to come*, saying
Deut 6:20 When your son asks you in *time to come*, saying
Josh 4:6 that this may be a sign among you when your children ask in *time to come*, saying
Josh 4:21 When your children ask their fathers in *time to come*, saying
Josh 22:24 But in fact we have done it for fear, for a reason, saying, 'In *time to come* your descendants may speak to our descendants, saying
Josh 22:27 that your descendants may not say to our descendants in *time to come*
Josh 22:28 Therefore we said that it will be, when they say this to us or to our generations in *time to come*, that we may say
Prov 31:25 Strength and honor are her clothing; she shall rejoice in *time to come*
Is 30:8 Now go, write it before them on a tablet, and note it on a scroll, that it may be for *time to come*, forever and ever
Is 42:23 Who will listen and hear for the *time to come*
1Tim 6:19 storing up for themselves a good foundation for the *time to come*, that they may lay hold on eternal life

TIME TO DIE
Eccl 3:2 A time to be born, and a *time to die*

TIME TO LAUGH
Eccl 3:4 a time to weep, and a *time to laugh;* a time to mourn, and a time to dance

TIME TO WEEP
Eccl 3:4 a *time to weep*, and a time to laugh; a time to mourn, and a time to dance

TIMES OF IGNORANCE
Acts 17:30 Truly, these *times of ignorance* God overlooked, but now commands all men everywhere to repent

TIMES OF THE GENTILES
Luke 21:24 And Jerusalem will be trampled by Gentiles until the *times of the Gentiles* are fulfilled

TIMES OF TROUBLE
Ps 9:9 The Lord also will be a refuge for the oppressed, a refuge in *times of trouble*
Ps 10:1 Why do You stand afar off, O Lord? Why do You hide Yourself in *times of trouble*

TIMES WILL HAVE REACHED THEIR FULFILLMENT (NIV)
(See *FULLNESS OF THE TIMES*)

TIRED AND WEARY
Deut 25:18 how he met you on the way and attacked your rear ranks, all the stragglers at your rear, when you were *tired and weary*

TITHE MINT AND RUE AND ALL MANNER OF HERBS
Luke 11:42 For you *tithe mint and rue and all manner of herbs*, and pass by justice and the love of God

TITHES AND OFFERINGS
Mal 3:8 But you say, 'In what way have we robbed You?' In *tithes and offerings*

TO BRING PRAISE TO GOD (NIV)
(See *TO THE GLORY OF GOD*)

TO DIE IS GAIN
Phil 1:21 For to me, to live is Christ, and *to die is gain*

TO DUST ALL RETURN (NIV)
(See *ALL RETURN TO DUST*)

TO DUST YOU SHALL RETURN
Gen 3:19 for dust you are, and *to dust you shall return*

TO EVERYTHING THERE IS A SEASON
Eccl 3:1 *To everything there is a season*, a time for every purpose under heaven

TO FULFILL THE SCRIPTURE (RSV)
(See *SCRIPTURE MIGHT BE FULFILLED*)

TO HIM WHO CONQUERS (RSV)
(See *TO HIM WHO OVERCOMES*)

TO HIM WHO OVERCOMES
Rev 2:7 *To him who overcomes* I will give to eat from the tree of life, which is in the midst of the Paradise of God
Rev 2:17 *To him who overcomes* I will give some of the hidden manna to eat
Rev 3:21 *To him who overcomes* I will grant to sit with Me on My throne, as I also overcame and sat down with My Father on His throne

TO ME BELONGETH VENGEANCE (KJV)
(See *VENGEANCE IS MINE*)

TO OBEY IS BETTER THAN SACRIFICE
1Sam 15:22 Behold, *to obey is better than sacrifice*, and to heed than the fat of rams

TO SEEK AND TO SAVE
Luke 19:10 for the Son of Man has come *to seek and to save* that which was lost

TO THE GLORY OF GOD
Rom 15:7 Therefore receive one another, just as Christ also received us, *to the glory of God*
1Cor 10:31 Therefore, whether you eat or drink, or whatever you do, do all *to the glory of God*
2Cor 1:20 For all the promises of God in Him are Yes, and in Him Amen, *to the glory of God* through us
2Cor 4:15 For all things are for your sakes, that grace, having spread through the many, may cause thanksgiving to abound *to the glory of God*
Phil 2:11 and that every tongue should confess that Jesus Christ is Lord, *to the glory of God* the Father

TO THE HUMBLE HE SHOWS FAVOR (RSV)
(See *GIVES GRACE TO THE HUMBLE*)

TO THE INTENT YE MAY BELIEVE (KJV)
(See *THAT YOU MAY BELIEVE*)

TO THE LAW AND TO THE TESTIMONY
Is 8:20 *To the law and to the testimony!* If they do not speak according to this word, it is because there is no light in them

TO THE LORD
Gen 4:3 And in the process of time it came to pass that Cain brought an offering of the fruit of the ground *to the Lord*
Gen 4:13 And Cain said *to the Lord*, "My punishment is greater than I can bear
Gen 8:20 Then Noah built an altar *to the Lord*, and took of every clean animal and of every clean bird, and offered burnt offerings on the altar
Gen 12:7 And there he built an altar *to the Lord*, who had appeared to him
Gen 12:8 there he built an altar *to the Lord* and called on the name of the Lord
Gen 13:18 Then Abram moved his tent, and went and dwelt by the terebinth trees of Mamre, which are in Hebron, and built an altar there *to the Lord*
Gen 14:22 But Abram said to the king of Sodom, "I have lifted my hand *to the Lord*, God Most High, the Possessor of heaven and earth
Gen 18:27 Then Abraham answered and said, "Indeed now, I who am but dust and ashes have taken it upon myself to speak *to the Lord*
Gen 18:31 Then he said, "Indeed now, I have taken it upon myself to speak *to the Lord*
Ex 3:18 and now, please, let us go three days' journey into the wilderness, that we may sacrifice *to the Lord* our God
Ex 4:10 Then Moses said *to the Lord*, "O my Lord, I am not eloquent, neither before nor since You have spoken to Your servant
Ex 5:3 Please, let us go three days' journey into the desert and sacrifice *to the Lord* our God, lest He fall upon us with pestilence or with the sword
Ex 5:17 Therefore you say, 'Let us go and sacrifice *to the Lord*
Ex 5:22 So Moses returned *to the Lord* and said, "Lord, why have You brought trouble on this people
Ex 8:8 and I will let the people go, that they may sacrifice *to the Lord*
Ex 8:12 And Moses cried out *to the Lord* concerning the frogs which He had brought against Pharaoh
Ex 8:26 And Moses said, "It is not right to do so, for we would be sacrificing the abomination of the Egyptians *to the Lord* our God
Ex 8:27 We will go three days' journey into the wilderness and sacrifice *to the Lord* our God as He will command us
Ex 8:28 And Pharaoh said, "I will let you go, that you may sacrifice *to the Lord* your God in the wilderness
Ex 8:29 But let Pharaoh not deal deceitfully anymore in not letting the people go to sacrifice *to the Lord*
Ex 9:29 And Moses said to him, "As soon as I have gone out of the city, I will spread out my hands *to the Lord*
Ex 9:33 So Moses went out of the city from Pharaoh and spread out his hands *to the Lord*
Ex 10:9 with our sons and our daughters, with our flocks and our herds we will go, for we must hold a feast *to the Lord*
Ex 10:25 But Moses said, "You must also give us sacrifices and burnt offerings, that we may sacrifice *to the Lord* our God
Ex 12:14 and you shall keep it as a feast *to the Lord* throughout your generations
Ex 12:42 It is a night of solemn observance *to the Lord* for bringing them out of the land of Egypt
Ex 12:48 And when a stranger dwells with you and wants to keep the Passover *to the Lord*, let all his males be circumcised, and then let him come near and keep it
Ex 13:6 Seven days you shall eat unleavened bread, and on the seventh day there shall be a feast *to the Lord*
Ex 13:12 that you shall set apart *to the Lord* all that open the womb, that is, every firstborn that comes from an animal which you have
Ex 13:15 Therefore I sacrifice *to the Lord* all males that open the womb, but all the firstborn of my sons I redeem
Ex 14:10 So they were very afraid, and the children of Israel cried out *to the Lord*
Ex 15:1 Then Moses and the children of Israel sang this song *to the Lord*, and spoke, saying: "I will sing *to the Lord*, for He has triumphed gloriously
Ex 15:21 Sing *to the Lord*, for He has triumphed gloriously! The horse and its rider He has thrown into the sea
Ex 15:25 So he cried out *to the Lord*, and the Lord showed him a tree
Ex 16:23 Tomorrow is a Sabbath rest, a holy Sabbath *to the Lord*
Ex 16:25 Then Moses said, "Eat that today, for today is a Sabbath *to the Lord*
Ex 17:4 So Moses cried out *to the Lord*, saying, "What shall I do with this people
Ex 19:8 So Moses brought back the words of the people *to the Lord*
Ex 19:9 So Moses told the words of the people *to the Lord*
Ex 19:23 And Moses said *to the Lord*, "The people cannot come up to Mount Sinai
Ex 19:24 But do not let the priests and the people break through to come up *to the Lord*, lest He break out against them
Ex 22:20 He who sacrifices to any god, except *to the Lord* only, he shall be utterly destroyed
Ex 24:1 Now He said to Moses, "Come up *to the Lord*, you and Aaron, Nadab and Abihu, and seventy of the elders of Israel, and worship from afar
Ex 24:5 Then he sent young men of the children of Israel, who offered burnt offerings and sacrificed peace offerings of oxen *to the Lord*
Ex 28:36 You shall also make a plate of pure gold and engrave on it, like the engraving of a signet: HOLINESS *TO THE LORD*
Ex 29:18 It is a burnt offering *to the Lord;* it is a sweet aroma, an offering made by fire *to the Lord*
Ex 29:25 It is an offering made by fire *to the Lord*
Ex 29:28 it shall be a heave offering from the chil-

dren of Israel from the sacrifices of their peace offerings, that is, their heave offering *to the Lord*
Ex 29:41 and you shall offer with it the grain offering and the drink offering, as in the morning, for a sweet aroma, an offering made by fire *to the Lord*
Ex 30:10 once a year he shall make atonement upon it throughout your generations. It is most holy *to the Lord*
Ex 30:12 When you take the census of the children of Israel for their number, then every man shall give a ransom for himself *to the Lord*, when you number them, that there may be no plague among them when you number them
Ex 30:13 half a shekel according to the shekel of the sanctuary (a shekel is twenty gerahs). The half-shekel shall be an offering *to the Lord*
Ex 30:14 Everyone included among those who are numbered, from twenty years old and above, shall give an offering *to the Lord*
Ex 30:15 The rich shall not give more and the poor shall not give less than half a shekel, when you give an offering *to the Lord*, to make atonement for yourselves
Ex 30:20 When they go into the tabernacle of meeting, or when they come near the altar to minister, to burn an offering made by fire *to the Lord*, they shall wash with water, lest they die
Ex 31:15 Work shall be done for six days, but the seventh is the Sabbath of rest, holy *to the Lord*
Ex 32:5 And Aaron made a proclamation and said, "Tomorrow is a feast *to the Lord*
Ex 32:29 Then Moses said, "Consecrate yourselves today *to the Lord*, that He may bestow on you a blessing this day, for every man has opposed his son and his brother
Ex 32:30 So now I will go up *to the Lord;* perhaps I can make atonement for your sin
Ex 32:31 Then Moses returned *to the Lord* and said, "Oh, these people have committed a great sin, and have made for themselves a god of gold
Ex 33:12 Then Moses said *to the Lord*, "See, You say to me
Ex 35:2 Work shall be done for six days, but the seventh day shall be a holy day for you, a Sabbath of rest *to the Lord*
Ex 35:5 Take from among you an offering *to the Lord*. Whoever is of a willing heart, let him bring it as an offering *to the Lord*
Ex 35:22 They came, both men and women, as many as had a willing heart, and brought earrings and nose rings, rings and necklaces, all jewelry of gold, that is, every man who offered an offering of gold *to the Lord*
Ex 35:29 The children of Israel brought a freewill offering *to the Lord*, all the men and women whose hearts were willing to bring material for all kinds of work which the Lord, by the hand of Moses, had commanded to be done
Ex 39:30 Then they made the plate of the holy crown of pure gold, and wrote on it an inscription like the engraving of a signet: HOLINESS *TO THE LORD*
Lev 1:2 When any one of you brings an offering *to the Lord*, you shall bring your offering of the livestock of the herd and of the flock
Lev 1:9 And the priest shall burn all on the altar as a burnt sacrifice, an offering made by fire, a sweet aroma *to the Lord*
Lev 1:13 it is a burnt sacrifice, an offering made by fire, a sweet aroma *to the Lord*
Lev 1:14 And if the burnt sacrifice of his offering *to the Lord* is of birds, then he shall bring his offering of turtledoves or young pigeons
Lev 1:17 It is a burnt sacrifice, an offering made by fire, a sweet aroma *to the Lord*
Lev 2:1 When anyone offers a grain offering *to the Lord*, his offering shall be of fine flour
Lev 2:2 And the priest shall burn it as a memorial on the altar, an offering made by fire, a sweet aroma *to the Lord*
Lev 2:3 It is a most holy offering of the offerings *to the Lord* made by fire
Lev 2:8 You shall bring the grain offering that is made of these things *to the Lord*
Lev 2:9 It is an offering made by fire, a sweet aroma *to the Lord*
Lev 2:10 It is a most holy offering of the offerings *to the Lord* made by fire
Lev 2:11 No grain offering which you bring *to the Lord* shall be made with leaven, for you shall burn no leaven nor any honey in any offering *to the Lord* made by fire
Lev 2:12 As for the offering of the firstfruits, you shall offer them *to the Lord*, but they shall not be burned on the altar for a sweet aroma
Lev 2:14 If you offer a grain offering of your firstfruits *to the Lord*, you shall offer for the grain offering of your firstfruits green heads of grain roasted on the fire, grain beaten from full heads
Lev 2:16 part of its beaten grain and part of its oil, with all the frankincense, as an offering made by fire *to the Lord*
Lev 3:3 Then he shall offer from the sacrifice of the peace offering an offering made by fire *to the Lord*
Lev 3:5 and Aaron's sons shall burn it on the altar upon the burnt sacrifice, which is on the wood that is on the fire, as an offering made by fire, a sweet aroma *to the Lord*
Lev 3:6 If his offering as a sacrifice of a peace offering *to the Lord* is of the flock, whether male or female, he shall offer it without blemish
Lev 3:9 Then he shall offer from the sacrifice of the peace offering, as an offering made by fire *to the Lord*, its fat and the whole fat tail which he shall remove close to the backbone
Lev 3:11 and the priest shall burn them on the altar as food, an offering made by fire *to the Lord*
Lev 3:14 Then he shall offer from it his offering, as an offering made by fire *to the Lord*
Lev 4:3 if the anointed priest sins, bringing guilt on the people, then let him offer *to the Lord* for his sin which he has sinned a young bull without blemish as a sin offering
Lev 4:31 and the priest shall burn it on the altar for a sweet aroma *to the Lord*
Lev 4:35 Then the priest shall burn it on the altar, according to the offerings made by fire *to the Lord*
Lev 5:6 and he shall bring his trespass offering *to the Lord* for his sin which he has committed, a female from the flock, a lamb or a kid of the goats as a sin offering
Lev 5:7 If he is not able to bring a lamb, then he shall bring *to the Lord*, for his trespass which he has committed, two turtledoves or two young pigeons
Lev 5:12 Then he shall bring it to the priest, and the priest shall take his handful of it as a memorial portion, and burn it on the altar according to the offerings made by fire *to the Lord*
Lev 5:15 If a person commits a trespass, and sins unintentionally in regard to the holy things of the Lord, then he shall bring *to the Lord* as his trespass offering a ram without blemish from the flocks, with your valuation in shekels of silver according to the shekel of the sanctuary, as a trespass offering
Lev 6:6 And he shall bring his trespass offering *to the Lord*, a ram without blemish from the flock, with your valuation, as a trespass offering, to the priest
Lev 6:15 He shall take from it his handful of the fine flour of the grain offering, with its oil, and all the frankincense which is on the grain offering,

and shall burn it on the altar for a sweet aroma, as a memorial *to the Lord*
Lev 6:18 It shall be a statute forever in your generations concerning the offerings made by fire *to the Lord*
Lev 6:20 This is the offering of Aaron and his sons, which they shall offer *to the Lord*, beginning on the day when he is anointed
Lev 6:21 And the baked pieces of the grain offering you shall offer for a sweet aroma *to the Lord*
Lev 6:22 It is a statute forever *to the Lord*. It shall be wholly burned
Lev 7:5 and the priest shall burn them on the altar as an offering made by fire *to the Lord*
Lev 7:11 This is the law of the sacrifice of peace offerings which he shall offer *to the Lord*
Lev 7:14 And from it he shall offer one cake from each offering as a heave offering *to the Lord*
Lev 7:20 But the person who eats the flesh of the sacrifice of the peace offering that belongs *to the Lord*, while he is unclean, that person shall be cut off from his people
Lev 7:21 Moreover the person who touches any unclean thing, such as human uncleanness, any unclean beast, or any abominable unclean thing, and who eats the flesh of the sacrifice of the peace offering that belongs *to the Lord*, that person shall be cut off from his people
Lev 7:25 For whoever eats the fat of the beast of which men offer an offering made by fire *to the Lord*, the person who eats it shall be cut off from his people
Lev 7:29 He who offers the sacrifice of his peace offering *to the Lord* shall bring his offering *to the Lord* from the sacrifice of his peace offering
Lev 7:30 His own hands shall bring the offerings made by fire *to the Lord*
Lev 7:35 This is the consecrated portion for Aaron and his sons, from the offerings made by fire *to the Lord*, on the day when Moses presented them to minister *to the Lord* as priests
Lev 7:38 which the Lord commanded Moses on Mount Sinai, on the day when He commanded the children of Israel to offer their offerings *to the Lord* in the Wilderness of Sinai
Lev 8:21 It was a burnt sacrifice for a sweet aroma, and an offering made by fire *to the Lord*, as the Lord had commanded Moses
Lev 8:28 That was an offering made by fire *to the Lord*
Lev 10:12 Take the grain offering that remains of the offerings made by fire *to the Lord*, and eat it without leaven beside the altar
Lev 10:13 And you shall eat it in a holy place, because it is your due and your sons' due, of the sacrifices made by fire *to the Lord*
Lev 17:4 and does not bring it to the door of the tabernacle of meeting, to offer an offering *to the Lord* before the tabernacle of the Lord, bloodguilt shall be imputed to that man
Lev 17:5 to the end that the children of Israel may bring their sacrifices which they offer in the open field, that they may bring them *to the Lord* at the door of the tabernacle of meeting, to the priest, and offer them as peace offerings *to the Lord*
Lev 17:6 And the priest shall sprinkle the blood on the altar of the Lord at the door of the tabernacle of meeting, and burn the fat for a sweet aroma *to the Lord*
Lev 17:9 and does not bring it to the door of the tabernacle of meeting, to offer it *to the Lord*, that man shall be cut off from among his people
Lev 19:5 And if you offer a sacrifice of peace offering *to the Lord*, you shall offer it of your own free will
Lev 19:21 And he shall bring his trespass offering *to the Lord*, to the door of the tabernacle of meeting, a ram as a trespass offering
Lev 19:24 But in the fourth year all its fruit shall be holy, a praise *to the Lord*
Lev 21:21 No man of the descendants of Aaron the priest, who has a defect, shall come near to offer the offerings made by fire *to the Lord*
Lev 22:3 Whoever of all your descendants throughout your generations, who goes near the holy things which the children of Israel sanctify *to the Lord*, while he has uncleanness upon him, that person shall be cut off from My presence
Lev 22:15 They shall not profane the holy offerings of the children of Israel, which they offer *to the Lord*
Lev 22:18 Whatever man of the house of Israel, or of the strangers in Israel, who offers his sacrifice for any of his vows or for any of his freewill offerings, which they offer *to the Lord* as a burnt offering
Lev 22:21 And whoever offers a sacrifice of peace offering *to the Lord*, to fulfill his vow, or a freewill offering from the cattle or the sheep, it must be perfect to be accepted
Lev 22:22 Those that are blind or broken or maimed, or have an ulcer or eczema or scabs, you shall not offer *to the Lord*, nor make an offering by fire of them on the altar *to the Lord*
Lev 22:24 You shall not offer *to the Lord* what is bruised or crushed, or torn or cut
Lev 22:27 and from the eighth day and thereafter it shall be accepted as an offering made by fire *to the Lord*
Lev 22:29 And when you offer a sacrifice of thanksgiving *to the Lord*, offer it of your own free will
Lev 23:6 And on the fifteenth day of the same month is the Feast of Unleavened Bread *to the Lord*
Lev 23:8 But you shall offer an offering made by fire *to the Lord* for seven days
Lev 23:12 And you shall offer on that day, when you wave the sheaf, a male lamb of the first year, without blemish, as a burnt offering *to the Lord*
Lev 23:13 Its grain offering shall be two-tenths of an ephah of fine flour mixed with oil, an offering made by fire *to the Lord*, for a sweet aroma
Lev 23:16 then you shall offer a new grain offering *to the Lord*
Lev 23:17 they shall be baked with leaven. They are the firstfruits *to the Lord*
Lev 23:18 They shall be as a burnt offering *to the Lord*, with their grain offering and their drink offerings, an offering made by fire for a sweet aroma *to the Lord*
Lev 23:20 They shall be holy *to the Lord* for the priest
Lev 23:25 and you shall offer an offering made by fire *to the Lord*
Lev 23:27 you shall afflict your souls, and offer an offering made by fire *to the Lord*
Lev 23:34 The fifteenth day of this seventh month shall be the Feast of Tabernacles for seven days *to the Lord*
Lev 23:36 For seven days you shall offer an offering made by fire *to the Lord*. On the eighth day you shall have a holy convocation, and you shall offer an offering made by fire *to the Lord*
Lev 23:37 These are the feasts of the Lord which you shall proclaim to be holy convocations, to offer an offering made by fire *to the Lord*, a burnt offering and a grain offering, a sacrifice and drink offerings, everything on its day
Lev 23:38 besides the Sabbaths of the Lord, besides your gifts, besides all your vows, and besides all your freewill offerings which you give *to the Lord*
Lev 23:41 You shall keep it as a feast *to the Lord* for seven days in the year
Lev 24:7 And you shall put pure frankincense on

each row, that it may be on the bread for a memorial, an offering made by fire *to the Lord*
Lev 25:2 When you come into the land which I give you, then the land shall keep a sabbath *to the Lord*
Lev 25:4 but in the seventh year there shall be a sabbath of solemn rest for the land, a sabbath *to the Lord*
Lev 27:2 When a man consecrates by a vow certain persons *to the Lord*, according to your valuation
Lev 27:9 And if it is a beast such as men may bring as an offering *to the Lord*, all such that any man gives *to the Lord* shall be holy
Lev 27:11 If it is an unclean beast which they do not offer as a sacrifice *to the Lord*, then he shall present the beast before the priest
Lev 27:14 And when a man sanctifies his house to be holy *to the Lord*, then the priest shall set a value for it, whether it is good or bad
Lev 27:16 And if a man sanctifies *to the Lord* some part of a field of his possession, then your valuation shall be according to the seed for it
Lev 27:21 but the field, when it is released in the Jubilee, shall be holy *to the Lord*, as a devoted field
Lev 27:22 And if a man sanctifies *to the Lord* a field which he has bought, which is not the field of his possession
Lev 27:23 then the priest shall reckon to him the worth of your valuation, up to the Year of Jubilee, and he shall give your valuation on that day as a holy offering *to the Lord*
Lev 27:28 Nevertheless no devoted offering that a man may devote *to the Lord* of all that he has, both man and beast, or the field of his possession, shall be sold or redeemed; every devoted offering is most holy *to the Lord*
Lev 27:30 And all the tithe of the land, whether of the seed of the land or of the fruit of the tree, is the Lord's. It is holy *to the Lord*
Lev 27:32 And concerning the tithe of the herd or the flock, of whatever passes under the rod, the tenth one shall be holy *to the Lord*
Num 5:8 But if the man has no kinsman to whom restitution may be made for the wrong, the restitution for the wrong must go *to the Lord* for the priest, in addition to the ram of the atonement with which atonement is made for him
Num 6:2 When either a man or woman consecrates an offering to take the vow of a Nazirite, to separate himself *to the Lord*
Num 6:5 until the days are fulfilled for which he separated himself *to the Lord*, he shall be holy
Num 6:6 All the days that he separates himself *to the Lord* he shall not go near a dead body
Num 6:8 All the days of his separation he shall be holy *to the Lord*
Num 6:12 He shall consecrate *to the Lord* the days of his separation, and bring a male lamb in its first year as a trespass offering
Num 6:14 And he shall present his offering *to the Lord:* one male lamb in its first year without blemish as a burnt offering, one ewe lamb in its first year without blemish as a sin offering, one ram without blemish as a peace offering
Num 6:17 and he shall offer the ram as a sacrifice of peace offering *to the Lord*, with the basket of unleavened bread
Num 6:21 This is the law of the Nazirite who vows *to the Lord* the offering for his separation, and besides that, whatever else his hand is able to provide
Num 8:12 Then the Levites shall lay their hands on the heads of the young bulls, and you shall offer one as a sin offering and the other as a burnt offering *to the Lord*, to make atonement for the Levites
Num 8:13 And you shall stand the Levites before Aaron and his sons, and then offer them as though a wave offering *to the Lord*
Num 11:2 Then the people cried out to Moses, and when Moses prayed *to the Lord*, the fire was quenched
Num 11:11 So Moses said *to the Lord*, "Why have You afflicted Your servant
Num 12:13 So Moses cried out *to the Lord*, saying, "Please heal her, O God, I pray
Num 14:13 And Moses said *to the Lord:* 'Then the Egyptians will hear it, for by Your might You brought these people up from among them
Num 15:3 and you make an offering by fire *to the Lord*, a burnt offering or a sacrifice, to fulfill a vow or as a freewill offering or in your appointed feasts, to make a sweet aroma *to the Lord*, from the herd or the flock
Num 15:4 then he who presents his offering *to the Lord* shall bring a grain offering of one-tenth of an ephah of fine flour mixed with one-fourth of a hin of oil
Num 15:7 and as a drink offering you shall offer one-third of a hin of wine as a sweet aroma *to the Lord*
Num 15:8 And when you prepare a young bull as a burnt offering, or as a sacrifice to fulfill a vow, or as a peace offering *to the Lord*
Num 15:10 and you shall bring as the drink offering half a hin of wine as an offering made by fire, a sweet aroma *to the Lord*
Num 15:13 All who are native-born shall do these things in this manner, in presenting an offering made by fire, a sweet aroma *to the Lord*
Num 15:14 And if a stranger sojourns with you, or whoever is among you throughout your generations, and would present an offering made by fire, a sweet aroma *to the Lord*, just as you do, so shall he do
Num 15:19 then it will be, when you eat of the bread of the land, that you shall offer up a heave offering *to the Lord*
Num 15:21 Of the first of your ground meal you shall give *to the Lord* a heave offering throughout your generations
Num 15:24 then it will be, if it is unintentionally committed, without the knowledge of the congregation, that the whole congregation shall offer one young bull as a burnt offering, as a sweet aroma *to the Lord*, with its grain offering and its drink offering, according to the ordinance, and one kid of the goats as a sin offering
Num 15:25 they shall bring their offering, an offering made by fire *to the Lord*, and their sin offering before the Lord, for their unintended sin
Num 16:15 Then Moses was very angry, and said *to the Lord*
Num 18:12 All the best of the oil, all the best of the new wine and the grain, their firstfruits which they offer *to the Lord*, I have given them to you
Num 18:13 Whatever first ripe fruit is in their land, which they bring *to the Lord*, shall be yours
Num 18:15 Everything that first opens the womb of all flesh, which they bring *to the Lord*, whether man or beast, shall be yours
Num 18:17 You shall sprinkle their blood on the altar, and burn their fat as an offering made by fire for a sweet aroma *to the Lord*
Num 18:19 All the heave offerings of the holy things, which the children of Israel offer *to the Lord*, I have given to you and your sons and daughters with you as an ordinance forever
Num 18:24 For the tithes of the children of Israel, which they offer up as a heave offering *to the Lord*, I have given to the Levites as an inheritance
Num 18:26 When you take from the children of Israel the tithes which I have given you from

them as your inheritance, then you shall offer up a heave offering of it *to the Lord*, a tenth of the tithe
Num 18:28 Thus you shall also offer a heave offering *to the Lord* from all your tithes which you receive from the children of Israel, and you shall give the Lord's heave offering from it to Aaron the priest
Num 18:29 Of all your gifts you shall offer up every heave offering due *to the Lord*, from all the best of them, the sanctified part of them
Num 20:16 When we cried out *to the Lord*, He heard our voice and sent the Angel and brought us up out of Egypt
Num 21:2 So Israel made a vow *to the Lord*, and said
Num 21:7 pray *to the Lord* that He take away the serpents from us
Num 27:15 Then Moses spoke *to the Lord*, saying
Num 28:3 And you shall say to them, 'This is the offering made by fire which you shall offer *to the Lord*
Num 28:6 It is a regular burnt offering which was ordained at Mount Sinai for a sweet aroma, an offering made by fire *to the Lord*
Num 28:7 in a holy place you shall pour out the drink *to the Lord* as an offering
Num 28:8 as the morning grain offering and its drink offering, you shall offer it as an offering made by fire, a sweet aroma *to the Lord*
Num 28:11 At the beginnings of your months you shall present a burnt offering *to the Lord*
Num 28:13 and one-tenth of an ephah of fine flour, mixed with oil, as a grain offering for each lamb, as a burnt offering of sweet aroma, an offering made by fire *to the Lord*
Num 28:15 Also one kid of the goats as a sin offering *to the Lord* shall be offered, besides the regular burnt offering and its drink offering
Num 28:19 And you shall present an offering made by fire as a burnt offering *to the Lord*
Num 28:24 In this manner you shall offer the food of the offering made by fire daily for seven days, as a sweet aroma *to the Lord*
Num 28:26 Also on the day of the firstfruits, when you bring a new grain offering *to the Lord* at your Feast of Weeks, you shall have a holy convocation
Num 28:27 You shall present a burnt offering as a sweet aroma *to the Lord*
Num 29:2 You shall offer a burnt offering as a sweet aroma *to the Lord*
Num 29:6 besides the burnt offering with its grain offering for the New Moon, the regular burnt offering with its grain offering, and their drink offerings, according to their ordinance, as a sweet aroma, an offering made by fire *to the Lord*
Num 29:8 You shall present a burnt offering *to the Lord* as a sweet aroma
Num 29:12 You shall do no customary work, and you shall keep a feast *to the Lord* seven days
Num 29:13 You shall present a burnt offering, an offering made by fire as a sweet aroma *to the Lord*
Num 29:36 You shall present a burnt offering, an offering made by fire as a sweet aroma *to the Lord*
Num 29:39 These things you shall present *to the Lord* at your appointed feasts (besides your vowed offerings and your freewill offerings
Num 30:2 If a man vows a vow *to the Lord*, or swears an oath to bind himself by some agreement, he shall not break his word
Num 30:3 Or if a woman vows a vow *to the Lord*, and binds herself by some agreement while in her father's house in her youth
Num 31:29 take it from their half, and give it to Eleazar the priest as a heave offering *to the Lord*
Num 31:52 And all the gold of the offering that they offered *to the Lord*, from the captains of thousands and captains of hundreds, was sixteen thousand seven hundred and fifty shekels
Deut 4:4 But you who held fast *to the Lord* your God are alive today, every one of you
Deut 4:30 When you are in distress, and all these things come upon you in the latter days, when you turn *to the Lord* your God and obey His voice
Deut 7:6 For you are a holy people *to the Lord* your God
Deut 7:25 for it is an abomination *to the Lord* your God
Deut 9:26 Therefore I prayed *to the Lord*, and said: 'O Lord God, do not destroy Your people and Your inheritance whom You have redeemed through Your greatness, whom You have brought out of Egypt with a mighty hand
Deut 10:14 Indeed heaven and the highest heavens belong *to the Lord* your God, also the earth with all that is in it
Deut 12:11 your burnt offerings, your sacrifices, your tithes, the heave offerings of your hand, and all your choice offerings which you vow *to the Lord*
Deut 12:31 for every abomination *to the Lord* which He hates they have done to their gods
Deut 14:2 For you are a holy people *to the Lord* your God, and the Lord has chosen you to be a people for Himself, a special treasure above all the peoples who are on the face of the earth
Deut 14:21 for you are a holy people *to the Lord* your God
Deut 15:9 Beware lest there be a wicked thought in your heart, saying, 'The seventh year, the year of release, is at hand,' and your eye be evil against your poor brother and you give him nothing, and he cry out *to the Lord* against you, and it become sin among you
Deut 15:19 All the firstborn males that come from your herd and your flock you shall sanctify *to the Lord* your God
Deut 15:21 But if there is any defect in it, if it is lame or blind or has any serious defect, you shall not sacrifice it *to the Lord* your God
Deut 16:1 Observe the month of Abib, and keep the Passover *to the Lord* your God, for in the month of Abib the Lord your God brought you out of Egypt by night
Deut 16:2 Therefore you shall sacrifice the Passover *to the Lord* your God, from the flock and the herd, in the place where the Lord chooses to put His name
Deut 16:8 Six days you shall eat unleavened bread, and on the seventh day there shall be a sacred assembly *to the Lord* your God
Deut 16:10 Then you shall keep the Feast of Weeks *to the Lord* your God with the tribute of a freewill offering from your hand, which you shall give as the Lord your God blesses you
Deut 16:15 Seven days you shall keep a sacred feast *to the Lord* your God in the place which the Lord chooses, because the Lord your God will bless you in all your produce and in all the work of your hands, so that you surely rejoice
Deut 16:21 You shall not plant for yourself any tree, as a wooden image, near the altar which you build for yourself *to the Lord* your God
Deut 17:1 You shall not sacrifice *to the Lord* your God a bull or sheep which has any blemish or defect, for that is an abomination *to the Lord* your God
Deut 18:12 For all who do these things are an abomination *to the Lord*, and because of these abominations the Lord your God drives them out from before you
Deut 22:5 A woman shall not wear anything that

pertains to a man, nor shall a man put on a woman's garment, for all who do so are an abomination *to the Lord* your God

Deut 23:18 You shall not bring the hire of a harlot or the price of a dog to the house of the Lord your God for any vowed offering, for both of these are an abomination *to the Lord* your God

Deut 23:21 When you make a vow *to the Lord* your God, you shall not delay to pay it

Deut 23:23 That which has gone from your lips you shall keep and perform, for you voluntarily vowed *to the Lord* your God what you have promised with your mouth

Deut 24:15 lest he cry out against you *to the Lord*, and it be sin to you

Deut 25:16 For all who do such things, and all who behave unrighteously, are an abomination *to the Lord* your God

Deut 26:3 And you shall go to the one who is priest in those days, and say to him, 'I declare today *to the Lord* your God that I have come to the country which the Lord swore to our fathers to give us

Deut 26:7 Then we cried out *to the Lord* God of our fathers, and the Lord heard our voice and looked on our affliction and our labor and our oppression

Deut 26:19 and that He will set you high above all nations which He has made, in praise, in name, and in honor, and that you may be a holy people *to the Lord* your God, just as He has spoken

Deut 27:5 And there you shall build an altar *to the Lord* your God, an altar of stones

Deut 27:6 You shall build with whole stones the altar of the Lord your God, and offer burnt offerings on it *to the Lord* your God

Deut 27:15 Cursed is the one who makes any carved or molded image, an abomination *to the Lord*, the work of the hands of the craftsman, and sets it up in secret

Deut 29:29 The secret things belong *to the Lord* our God, but those things which are revealed belong to us and to our children forever, that we may do all the words of this law

Deut 30:2 and you return *to the Lord* your God and obey His voice, according to all that I command you today, you and your children, with all your heart and with all your soul

Deut 30:10 if you obey the voice of the Lord your God, to keep His commandments and His statutes which are written in this Book of the Law, and if you turn *to the Lord* your God with all your heart and with all your soul

Josh 6:19 But all the silver and gold, and vessels of bronze and iron, are consecrated *to the Lord*

Josh 7:19 So Joshua said to Achan, "My son, I beg you, give glory *to the Lord* God of Israel, and make confession to Him, and tell me now what you have done

Josh 8:30 Now Joshua built an altar *to the Lord* God of Israel in Mount Ebal

Josh 8:31 And they offered on it burnt offerings *to the Lord*, and sacrificed peace offerings

Josh 10:12 Then Joshua spoke *to the Lord* in the day when the Lord delivered up the Amorites before the children of Israel, and he said in the sight of Israel

Josh 23:8 but you shall hold fast *to the Lord* your God, as you have done to this day

Josh 24:7 So they cried out *to the Lord;* and He put darkness between you and the Egyptians, brought the sea upon them, and covered them

Josh 24:23 Now therefore," he said, "put away the foreign gods which are among you, and incline your heart *to the Lord* God of Israel

Judg 2:5 Then they called the name of that place Bochim; and they sacrificed there *to the Lord*

Judg 3:9 When the children of Israel cried out *to the Lord*, the Lord raised up a deliverer for the children of Israel, who delivered them

Judg 3:15 And when the children of Israel cried out *to the Lord*, the Lord raised up a deliverer for them

Judg 4:3 And the children of Israel cried out *to the Lord*

Judg 5:3 I, even I, will sing *to the Lord;* I will sing praise *to the Lord* God of Israel

Judg 6:6 So Israel was greatly impoverished because of the Midianites, and the children of Israel cried out *to the Lord*

Judg 6:7 And it came to pass, when the children of Israel cried out *to the Lord* because of the Midianites

Judg 6:24 So Gideon built an altar there *to the Lord*, and called it The-Lord-Shalom

Judg 6:26 and build an altar *to the Lord* your God on top of this rock in the proper arrangement, and take the second bull and offer a burnt sacrifice with the wood of the image which you shall cut down

Judg 10:10 And the children of Israel cried out *to the Lord*, saying

Judg 10:15 Then the children of Israel said *to the Lord*, "We have sinned

Judg 11:30 And Jephthah made a vow *to the Lord*, and said

Judg 11:35 For I have given my word *to the Lord*, and I cannot go back on it

Judg 11:36 So she said to him, "My father, if you have given your word *to the Lord*, do to me according to what has gone out of your mouth, because the Lord has avenged you of your enemies, the people of Ammon

Judg 13:8 Then Manoah prayed *to the Lord*, and said, "O my Lord, please let the Man of God whom You sent come to us again and teach us what we shall do for the child who will be born

Judg 13:16 But if you offer a burnt offering, you must offer it *to the Lord*

Judg 13:19 So Manoah took the young goat with the grain offering, and offered it upon the rock *to the Lord*

Judg 15:18 so he cried out *to the Lord* and said, "You have given this great deliverance by the hand of Your servant

Judg 16:28 Then Samson called *to the Lord*, saying, "O Lord God, remember me, I pray

Judg 17:3 So when he had returned the eleven hundred shekels of silver to his mother, his mother said, "I had wholly dedicated the silver from my hand *to the Lord* for my son, to make a carved image and a molded image

Judg 21:5 The children of Israel said, "Who is there among all the tribes of Israel who did not come up with the assembly *to the Lord?*" For they had made a great oath concerning anyone who had not come up *to the Lord* at Mizpah, saying

Judg 21:8 And they said, "What one is there from the tribes of Israel who did not come up to Mizpah *to the Lord*

1Sam 1:3 This man went up from his city yearly to worship and sacrifice *to the Lord* of hosts in Shiloh

1Sam 1:10 And she was in bitterness of soul, and prayed *to the Lord* and wept in anguish

1Sam 1:11 Then she made a vow and said, "O Lord of hosts, if You will indeed look on the affliction of your maidservant and remember me, and not forget your maidservant, but will give your maidservant a male child, then I will give him *to the Lord* all the days of his life, and no razor shall come upon his head

1Sam 1:21 And the man Elkanah and all his house went up to offer *to the Lord* the yearly sacrifice and his vow

1Sam 1:26 As your soul lives, my lord, I am the woman who stood by you here, praying *to the Lord*
1Sam 1:28 Therefore I also have lent him *to the Lord;* as long as he lives he shall be lent *to the Lord*
1Sam 2:11 But the child ministered *to the Lord* before Eli the priest
1Sam 2:20 And Eli would bless Elkanah and his wife, and say, "The Lord give you descendants from this woman for the loan that was lent *to the Lord*
1Sam 3:1 Then the boy Samuel ministered *to the Lord* before Eli
1Sam 6:14 So they split the wood of the cart and offered the cows as a burnt offering *to the Lord*
1Sam 6:15 Then the men of Beth Shemesh offered burnt offerings and made sacrifices the same day *to the Lord*
1Sam 6:17 Now these are the gold tumors which the Philistines returned as a trespass offering *to the Lord*
1Sam 7:3 Then Samuel spoke to all the house of Israel, saying, "If you return *to the Lord* with all your hearts, then put away the foreign gods and the Ashtoreths from among you, and prepare your hearts for the Lord, and serve Him only
1Sam 7:5 And Samuel said, "Gather all Israel to Mizpah, and I will pray *to the Lord* for you
1Sam 7:8 So the children of Israel said to Samuel, "Do not cease to cry out *to the Lord* our God for us, that He may save us from the hand of the Philistines
1Sam 7:9 And Samuel took a suckling lamb and offered it as a whole burnt offering *to the Lord*. Then Samuel cried out *to the Lord* for Israel, and the Lord answered him
1Sam 7:17 There he judged Israel, and there he built an altar *to the Lord*
1Sam 8:6 But the thing displeased Samuel when they said, "Give us a king to judge us." So Samuel prayed *to the Lord*
1Sam 10:17 Then Samuel called the people together *to the Lord* at Mizpah
1Sam 12:8 When Jacob had gone into Egypt, and your fathers cried out *to the Lord*, then the Lord sent Moses and Aaron, who brought your fathers out of Egypt and made them dwell in this place
1Sam 12:10 Then they cried out *to the Lord*, and said, 'We have sinned, because we have forsaken the Lord and served the Baals and Ashtoreths
1Sam 12:17 I will call *to the Lord*, and He will send thunder and rain, that you may perceive and see that your wickedness is great, which you have done in the sight of the Lord, in asking a king for yourselves
1Sam 12:18 So Samuel called *to the Lord*, and the Lord sent thunder and rain that day
1Sam 12:19 And all the people said to Samuel, "Pray for your servants *to the Lord* your God, that we may not die
1Sam 13:12 then I said, 'The Philistines will now come down on me at Gilgal, and I have not made supplication *to the Lord*
1Sam 14:35 Then Saul built an altar *to the Lord*. This was the first altar that he built *to the Lord*
1Sam 14:41 Therefore Saul said *to the Lord* God of Israel, "Give a perfect lot
1Sam 15:11 And it grieved Samuel, and he cried out *to the Lord* all night
1Sam 15:15 for the people spared the best of the sheep and the oxen, to sacrifice *to the Lord* your God
1Sam 15:21 But the people took of the plunder, sheep and oxen, the best of the things which should have been utterly destroyed, to sacrifice *to the Lord* your God in Gilgal
1Sam 16:2 And the Lord said, "Take a heifer with you, and say, 'I have come to sacrifice *to the Lord*
1Sam 16:5 I have come to sacrifice *to the Lord*. Sanctify yourselves, and come with me to the sacrifice
2Sam 8:11 King David dedicated these *to the Lord*, along with the silver and gold that he had dedicated from all the nations which he had subdued
2Sam 15:7 And it came to pass after forty years that Absalom said to the king, "Please, let me go to Hebron and pay the vow which I vowed *to the Lord*
2Sam 22:1 Then David spoke *to the Lord* the words of this song, on the day when the Lord had delivered him from the hand of all his enemies, and from the hand of Saul
2Sam 22:42 even *to the Lord*, but He did not answer them
2Sam 23:16 Nevertheless he would not drink it, but poured it out *to the Lord*
2Sam 24:10 So David said *to the Lord*, "I have sinned greatly in what I have done
2Sam 24:17 Then David spoke *to the Lord* when he saw the angel who was striking the people, and said
2Sam 24:18 And Gad came that day to David and said to him, "Go up, erect an altar *to the Lord* on the threshing floor of Araunah the Jebusite
2Sam 24:21 And David said, "To buy the threshing floor from you, to build an altar *to the Lord*, that the plague may be withdrawn from the people
2Sam 24:24 nor will I offer burnt offerings *to the Lord* my God with that which costs me nothing
2Sam 24:25 And David built there an altar *to the Lord*, and offered burnt offerings and peace offerings
1Kin 2:27 So Solomon removed Abiathar from being priest *to the Lord*, that he might fulfill the word of the Lord which He spoke concerning the house of Eli at Shiloh
1Kin 8:44 When Your people go out to battle against their enemy, wherever You send them, and when they pray *to the Lord* toward the city which You have chosen and toward the temple which I have built for Your name
1Kin 8:54 And so it was, when Solomon had finished praying all this prayer and supplication *to the Lord*, that he arose from before the altar of the Lord, from kneeling on his knees with his hands spread up to heaven
1Kin 8:61 Let your heart therefore be loyal *to the Lord* our God, to walk in His statutes and keep His commandments, as at this day
1Kin 8:63 And Solomon offered a sacrifice of peace offerings, which he offered *to the Lord*, twenty-two thousand bulls and one hundred and twenty thousand sheep
1Kin 11:4 and his heart was not loyal *to the Lord* his God, as was the heart of his father David
1Kin 15:3 his heart was not loyal *to the Lord* his God, as was the heart of his father David
1Kin 15:14 Nevertheless Asa's heart was loyal *to the Lord* all his days
1Kin 17:20 Then he cried out *to the Lord* and said, "O Lord my God, have You also brought tragedy on the widow with whom I lodge, by killing her son
1Kin 17:21 And he stretched himself out on the child three times, and cried out *to the Lord* and said
2Kin 4:33 He went in therefore, shut the door behind the two of them, and prayed *to the Lord*
2Kin 5:17 for your servant will no longer offer either burnt offering or sacrifice to other gods, but *to the Lord*

2Kin 6:18 So when the Syrians came down to him, Elisha prayed *to the Lord*, and said
2Kin 18:6 For he held fast *to the Lord;* he did not depart from following Him, but kept His commandments, which the Lord had commanded Moses
2Kin 20:2 Then he turned his face toward the wall, and prayed *to the Lord*, saying
2Kin 20:11 So Isaiah the prophet cried out *to the Lord*, and He brought the shadow ten degrees backward, by which it had gone down on the sundial of Ahaz
2Kin 23:21 Then the king commanded all the people, saying, "Keep the Passover *to the Lord* your God, as it is written in this Book of the Covenant
2Kin 23:25 Now before him there was no king like him, who turned *to the Lord* with all his heart, with all his soul, and with all his might, according to all the Law of Moses
1Chr 11:18 Nevertheless David would not drink it, but poured it out *to the Lord*
1Chr 16:8 Oh, give thanks *to the Lord!* Call upon His name
1Chr 16:23 Sing *to the Lord*, all the earth; proclaim the good news of His salvation from day to day
1Chr 16:28 Give *to the Lord*, O kindreds of the peoples, give *to the Lord* glory and strength
1Chr 16:29 Give *to the Lord* the glory due His name; bring an offering, and come before Him
1Chr 16:34 Oh, give thanks *to the Lord*, for He is good
1Chr 16:40 to offer burnt offerings *to the Lord* on the altar of burnt offering regularly morning and evening, and to do according to all that is written in the Law of the Lord which He commanded Israel
1Chr 16:41 and with them Heman and Jeduthun and the rest who were chosen, who were designated by name, to give thanks *to the Lord*, because His mercy endures forever
1Chr 18:11 King David also dedicated these *to the Lord*, along with the silver and gold that he had brought from all these nations from Edom, from Moab, from the people of Ammon, from the Philistines, and from Amalek
1Chr 21:18 Then the angel of the Lord commanded Gad to say to David that David should go and erect an altar *to the Lord* on the threshing floor of Ornan the Jebusite
1Chr 21:22 Then David said to Ornan, "Grant me the place of this threshing floor, that I may build an altar on it *to the Lord*
1Chr 21:26 And David built there an altar *to the Lord*, and offered burnt offerings and peace offerings, and called on the Lord
1Chr 23:31 and at every presentation of a burnt offering *to the Lord* on the Sabbaths and on the New Moons and on the set feasts, by number according to the ordinance governing them, regularly before the Lord
1Chr 29:5 Who then is willing to consecrate himself this day *to the Lord*
1Chr 29:9 Then the people rejoiced, for they had offered willingly, because with a loyal heart they had offered willingly *to the Lord*
1Chr 29:21 And they made sacrifices *to the Lord* and offered burnt offerings *to the Lord* on the next day
2Chr 8:12 Then Solomon offered burnt offerings *to the Lord* on the altar of the Lord which he had built before the vestibule
2Chr 11:14 For the Levites left their commonlands and their possessions and came to Judah and Jerusalem, for Jeroboam and his sons had rejected them from serving as priests *to the Lord*
2Chr 11:16 And after the Levites left, those from all the tribes of Israel, such as set their heart to seek the Lord God of Israel, came to Jerusalem to sacrifice *to the Lord* God of their fathers
2Chr 13:10 and the priests who minister *to the Lord* are the sons of Aaron, and the Levites attend to their duties
2Chr 13:11 And they burn *to the Lord* every morning and every evening burnt sacrifices and sweet incense
2Chr 13:14 and they cried out *to the Lord*, and the priests sounded the trumpets
2Chr 14:11 And Asa cried out *to the Lord* his God, and said
2Chr 15:4 but when in their trouble they turned *to the Lord* God of Israel, and sought Him, He was found by them
2Chr 15:11 And they offered *to the Lord* at that time seven hundred bulls and seven thousand sheep from the spoil which they had brought
2Chr 17:16 and next to him was Amasiah the son of Zichri, who willingly offered himself *to the Lord*, and with him two hundred thousand mighty men of valor
2Chr 19:4 and he went out again among the people from Beersheba to the mountains of Ephraim, and brought them back *to the Lord* God of their fathers
2Chr 20:21 And when he had consulted with the people, he appointed those who should sing *to the Lord*, and who should praise the beauty of holiness, as they went out before the army and were saying
2Chr 24:9 And they made a proclamation throughout Judah and Jerusalem to bring *to the Lord* the collection that Moses the servant of God had imposed on Israel in the wilderness
2Chr 24:19 Yet He sent prophets to them, to bring them back *to the Lord*
2Chr 26:18 And they withstood King Uzziah, and said to him, "It is not for you, Uzziah, to burn incense *to the Lord*, but for the priests, the sons of Aaron, who are consecrated to burn incense
2Chr 28:19 For the Lord brought Judah low because of Ahaz king of Israel, for he had encouraged moral decline in Judah and had been continually unfaithful *to the Lord*
2Chr 28:22 Now in the time of his distress King Ahaz became increasingly unfaithful *to the Lord*
2Chr 29:30 Moreover King Hezekiah and the leaders commanded the Levites to sing praise *to the Lord* with the words of David and of Asaph the seer
2Chr 29:31 Then Hezekiah answered and said, "Now that you have consecrated yourselves *to the Lord*, come near, and bring sacrifices and thank offerings into the house of the Lord
2Chr 29:32 all these were for a burnt offering *to the Lord*
2Chr 30:1 And Hezekiah sent to all Israel and Judah, and also wrote letters to Ephraim and Manasseh, that they should come to the house of the Lord at Jerusalem, to keep the Passover *to the Lord* God of Israel
2Chr 30:5 So they resolved to make a proclamation throughout all Israel, from Beersheba to Dan, that they should come to keep the Passover *to the Lord* God of Israel at Jerusalem, since they had not done it for a long time in the prescribed manner
2Chr 30:6 Children of Israel, return *to the Lord* God of Abraham, Isaac, and Israel
2Chr 30:8 Now do not be stiffnecked, as your fathers were, but yield yourselves *to the Lord*
2Chr 30:9 For if you return *to the Lord*, your brethren and your children will be treated with compassion by those who lead them captive, so that they may come back to this land
2Chr 30:17 therefore the Levites had charge of the

slaughter of the Passover lambs for everyone who was not clean, to sanctify them *to the Lord*
2Chr 30:21 and the Levites and the priests praised the Lord day by day, singing *to the Lord*, accompanied by loud instruments
2Chr 30:22 and they ate throughout the feast seven days, offering peace offerings and making confession *to the Lord* God of their fathers
2Chr 31:6 also the tithe of holy things which were consecrated *to the Lord* their God they laid in heaps
2Chr 32:23 And many brought gifts *to the Lord* at Jerusalem, and presents to Hezekiah king of Judah, so that he was exalted in the sight of all nations thereafter
2Chr 32:24 In those days Hezekiah was sick and near death, and he prayed *to the Lord*
2Chr 33:17 Nevertheless the people still sacrificed on the high places, but only *to the Lord* their God
2Chr 35:1 Now Josiah kept a Passover *to the Lord* in Jerusalem, and they slaughtered the Passover lambs on the fourteenth day of the first month
2Chr 35:3 Then he said to the Levites who taught all Israel, who were holy *to the Lord*
2Chr 35:12 Then they removed the burnt offerings that they might give them to the divisions of the fathers' houses of the lay people, to offer *to the Lord*, as it is written in the Book of Moses
2Chr 36:13 but he stiffened his neck and hardened his heart against turning *to the Lord* God of Israel
Ezra 3:3 and they offered burnt offerings on it *to the Lord*, both the morning and evening burnt offerings
Ezra 3:5 and afterward they offered the regular burnt offering, and those for New Moons and for all the appointed feasts of the Lord that were consecrated, and those of everyone who willingly offered a freewill offering *to the Lord*
Ezra 3:6 From the first day of the seventh month they began to offer burnt offerings *to the Lord*
Ezra 3:11 And they sang responsively, praising and giving thanks *to the Lord*
Ezra 4:3 but we alone will build *to the Lord* God of Israel, as King Cyrus the king of Persia has commanded us
Ezra 8:28 And I said to them, "You are holy *to the Lord;* the articles are holy also; and the silver and the gold are a freewill offering *to the Lord* God of your fathers
Ezra 8:35 twelve bulls for all Israel, ninety-six rams, seventy-seven lambs, and twelve male goats as a sin offering. All this was a burnt offering *to the Lord*
Ezra 9:5 and having torn my garment and my robe, I fell on my knees and spread out my hands *to the Lord* my God
Ezra 10:11 Now therefore, make confession *to the Lord* God of your fathers, and do His will
Neh 8:9 And Nehemiah, who was the governor, Ezra the priest and scribe, and the Levites who taught the people said to all the people, "This day is holy *to the Lord* your God
Neh 9:4 Then Jeshua, Bani, Kadmiel, Shebaniah, Bunni, Sherebiah, Bani, and Chenani stood on the stairs of the Levites and cried out with a loud voice *to the Lord* their God
Ps 3:4 I cried *to the Lord* with my voice, and He heard me from His holy hill
Ps 3:8 Salvation belongs *to the Lord*. Your blessing is upon Your people
Ps 9:11 Sing praises *to the Lord*, who dwells in Zion! Declare His deeds among the people
Ps 13:6 I will sing *to the Lord*, because He has dealt bountifully with me
Ps 16:2 O my soul, you have said *to the Lord*, "You are my Lord, My goodness is nothing apart from You
Ps 18:41 They cried out, but there was none to save them, even *to the Lord*, but He did not answer them
Ps 22:27 All the ends of the world shall remember and turn *to the Lord*, and all the families of the nations shall worship before You
Ps 27:6 I will sing, yes, I will sing praises *to the Lord*
Ps 30:4 Sing praise *to the Lord*, You saints of His, and give thanks at the remembrance of His holy name
Ps 30:8 I cried out to You, O Lord; and *to the Lord* I made supplication
Ps 32:5 I said, "I will confess my transgressions *to the Lord*
Ps 37:5 Commit your way *to the Lord*, trust also in Him, and He shall bring it to pass
Ps 68:32 Sing to God, you kingdoms of the earth; Oh, sing praises *to the Lord*
Ps 76:11 Make vows *to the Lord* your God, and pay them
Ps 89:6 For who in the heavens can be compared *to the Lord?* Who among the sons of the mighty can be likened *to the Lord*
Ps 89:18 For our shield belongs *to the Lord*, and our king to the Holy One of Israel
Ps 92:1 It is good to give thanks *to the Lord*, and to sing praises to Your name, O Most High
Ps 95:1 Oh come, let us sing *to the Lord!* Let us shout joyfully to the Rock of our salvation
Ps 96:1 Oh, sing *to the Lord* a new song! Sing *to the Lord*, all the earth
Ps 96:2 Sing *to the Lord*, bless His name; proclaim the good news of His salvation from day to day
Ps 96:7 Give *to the Lord*, O kindreds of the peoples, give *to the Lord* glory and strength
Ps 96:8 Give *to the Lord* the glory due His name; bring an offering, and come into His courts
Ps 98:1 Oh, sing *to the Lord* a new song! For He has done marvelous things
Ps 98:4 Shout joyfully *to the Lord*, all the earth; break forth in song, rejoice, and sing praises
Ps 98:5 Sing *to the Lord* with the harp, with the harp and the sound of a psalm
Ps 100:1 Make a joyful shout *to the Lord*, all you lands
Ps 104:33 I will sing *to the Lord* as long as I live
Ps 105:1 Oh, give thanks *to the Lord!* Call upon His name
Ps 106:1 Oh, give thanks *to the Lord*, for He is good
Ps 107:1 Oh, give thanks *to the Lord*, for He is good
Ps 107:6 Then they cried out *to the Lord* in their trouble, and He delivered them out of their distresses
Ps 107:8 Oh, that men would give thanks *to the Lord* for His goodness, and for His wonderful works to the children of men
Ps 107:13 Then they cried out *to the Lord* in their trouble, and He saved them out of their distresses
Ps 107:15 Oh, that men would give thanks *to the Lord* for His goodness, and for His wonderful works to the children of men
Ps 107:19 Then they cried out *to the Lord* in their trouble, and He saved them out of their distresses
Ps 107:21 Oh, that men would give thanks *to the Lord* for His goodness, and for His wonderful works to the children of men
Ps 107:28 Then they cry out *to the Lord* in their trouble, and He brings them out of their distresses
Ps 107:31 Oh, that men would give thanks *to the Lord* for His goodness, and for His wonderful works to the children of men
Ps 116:12 What shall I render *to the Lord* for all His benefits toward me

Ps 116:14 I will pay my vows *to the Lord* now in the presence of all His people
Ps 116:18 I will pay my vows *to the Lord* now in the presence of all His people
Ps 118:1 Oh, give thanks *to the Lord*, for He is good
Ps 118:29 Oh, give thanks *to the Lord*, for He is good
Ps 120:1 In my distress I cried *to the Lord*, and He heard me
Ps 123:2 Behold, as the eyes of servants look to the hand of their masters, as the eyes of a maid to the hand of her mistress, so our eyes look *to the Lord* our God, until He has mercy on us
Ps 132:2 How he swore *to the Lord*, and vowed to the Mighty God of Jacob
Ps 136:1 Oh, give thanks *to the Lord*, for He is good
Ps 136:3 Oh, give thanks *to the Lord* of lords! For His mercy endures forever
Ps 140:6 I said *to the Lord:* "You are my God; hear the voice of my supplications, O Lord
Ps 142:1 I cry out *to the Lord* with my voice; with my voice *to the Lord* I make my supplication
Ps 147:7 Sing *to the Lord* with thanksgiving; sing praises on the harp to our God
Ps 149:1 Sing *to the Lord* a new song, and His praise in the congregation of saints
Prov 3:32 for the perverse person is an abomination *to the Lord*, but His secret counsel is with the upright
Prov 11:1 A false balance is an abomination *to the Lord*, but a just weight is His delight
Prov 11:20 Those who are of a perverse heart are an abomination *to the Lord*, but such as are blameless in their ways are His delight
Prov 12:22 Lying lips are an abomination *to the Lord*, but those who deal truthfully are His delight
Prov 15:8 The sacrifice of the wicked is an abomination *to the Lord*, but the prayer of the upright is His delight
Prov 15:9 The way of the wicked is an abomination *to the Lord*, but He loves him who follows righteousness
Prov 15:26 The thoughts of the wicked are an abomination *to the Lord*, but the words of the pure are pleasant
Prov 16:3 Commit your works *to the Lord*, and your thoughts will be established
Prov 16:5 Everyone who is proud in heart is an abomination *to the Lord*
Prov 17:15 He who justifies the wicked, and he who condemns the just, both of them alike are an abomination *to the Lord*
Prov 19:17 He who has pity on the poor lends *to the Lord*, and He will pay back what he has given
Prov 20:10 Diverse weights and diverse measures, they are both alike, an abomination *to the Lord*
Prov 20:23 Diverse weights are an abomination *to the Lord*, and a false balance is not good
Prov 21:3 To do righteousness and justice is more acceptable *to the Lord* than sacrifice
Is 12:5 Sing *to the Lord*, for He has done excellent things
Is 18:7 In that time a present will be brought *to the Lord* of hosts from a people tall and smooth of skin, and from a people terrible from their beginning onward, a nation powerful and treading down, whose land the rivers divide to the place of the name of the Lord of hosts, to Mount Zion
Is 19:19 In that day there will be an altar *to the Lord* in the midst of the land of Egypt, and a pillar *to the Lord* at its border
Is 19:20 And it will be for a sign and for a witness *to the Lord* of hosts in the land of Egypt; for they will cry *to the Lord* because of the oppressors, and He will send them a Savior and a Mighty One, and He will deliver them
Is 19:21 yes, they will make a vow *to the Lord* and perform it
Is 19:22 they will return *to the Lord*, and He will be entreated by them and heal them
Is 37:15 Then Hezekiah prayed *to the Lord*, saying
Is 38:2 Then Hezekiah turned his face toward the wall, and prayed *to the Lord*
Is 42:10 Sing *to the Lord* a new song, and His praise from the ends of the earth, you who go down to the sea, and all that is in it, you coastlands and you inhabitants of them
Is 42:12 Let them give glory *to the Lord*, and declare His praise in the coastlands
Is 55:7 let him return *to the Lord*, and He will have mercy on him
Is 55:13 and it shall be *to the Lord* for a name, for an everlasting sign that shall not be cut off
Is 56:3 Do not let the son of the foreigner who has joined himself *to the Lord* speak, saying
Is 56:6 Also the sons of the foreigner who join themselves *to the Lord*, to serve Him, and to love the name of the Lord, to be His servants everyone who keeps from defiling the Sabbath, and holds fast My covenant
Is 58:5 Would you call this a fast, and an acceptable day *to the Lord*
Is 66:20 Then they shall bring all your brethren for an offering *to the Lord* out of all nations, on horses and in chariots and in litters, on mules and on camels, to My holy mountain Jerusalem
Jer 2:3 Israel was holiness *to the Lord*, the firstfruits of His increase
Jer 4:4 Circumcise yourselves *to the Lord*, and take away the foreskins of your hearts, you men of Judah and inhabitants of Jerusalem, lest My fury come forth like fire, and burn so that no one can quench it, because of the evil of your doings
Jer 13:16 Give glory *to the Lord* your God before He causes darkness, and before your feet stumble on the dark mountains, and while you are looking for light, He turns it into the shadow of death and makes it dense darkness
Jer 20:13 Sing *to the Lord!* Praise the Lord! For He has delivered the life of the poor from the hand of evildoers
Jer 27:18 But if they are prophets, and if the word of the Lord is with them, let them now make intercession *to the Lord* of hosts, that the vessels which are left in the house of the Lord, in the house of the king of Judah, and at Jerusalem, do not go to Babylon
Jer 29:7 And seek the peace of the city where I have caused you to be carried away captive, and pray *to the Lord* for it
Jer 31:6 For there shall be a day when the watchmen will cry on Mount Ephraim, 'Arise, and let us go up to Zion, *to the Lord* our God
Jer 31:40 And the whole valley of the dead bodies and of the ashes, and all the fields as far as the Brook Kidron, to the corner of the Horse Gate toward the east, shall be holy *to the Lord*
Jer 32:16 Now when I had delivered the purchase deed to Baruch the son of Neriah, I prayed *to the Lord*, saying
Jer 37:3 And Zedekiah the king sent Jehucal the son of Shelemiah, and Zephaniah the son of Maaseiah, the priest, to the prophet Jeremiah, saying, "Pray now *to the Lord* our God for us
Jer 42:2 and said to Jeremiah the prophet, "Please, let our petition be acceptable to you, and pray for us *to the Lord* your God, for all this remnant (since we are left but a few of many, as you can see
Jer 42:4 Indeed, I will pray *to the Lord* your God according to your words, and it shall be, that

whatever the Lord answers you, I will declare it to you
Jer 42:20 For you were hypocrites in your hearts when you sent me *to the Lord* your God, saying, 'Pray for us *to the Lord* our God, and according to all that the Lord your God says, so declare to us and we will do it
Jer 50:5 They shall ask the way to Zion, with their faces toward it, saying, 'come and let us join ourselves *to the Lord* in a perpetual covenant that will not be forgotten
Lam 2:18 Their heart cried out *to the Lord*, "O wall of the daughter of Zion, let tears run down like a river day and night
Lam 3:40 Let us search out and examine our ways, and turn back *to the Lord*
Ezek 43:24 When you offer them before the Lord, the priests shall throw salt on them, and they will offer them up as a burnt offering *to the Lord*
Ezek 45:4 It shall be a holy portion of the land, belonging to the priests, the ministers of the sanctuary, who come near to minister *to the Lord*
Ezek 45:23 On the seven days of the feast he shall prepare a burnt offering *to the Lord*, seven bulls and seven rams without blemish, daily for seven days, and a kid of the goats daily for a sin offering
Ezek 46:4 The burnt offering that the prince offers *to the Lord* on the Sabbath day shall be six lambs without blemish, and a ram without blemish
Ezek 46:12 Now when the prince makes a voluntary burnt offering or voluntary peace offering *to the Lord*, the gate that faces toward the east shall then be opened for him
Ezek 46:13 You shall daily make a burnt offering *to the Lord* of a lamb of the first year without blemish
Ezek 46:14 This grain offering is a perpetual ordinance, to be made regularly *to the Lord*
Ezek 48:14 they may not alienate this best part of the land, for it is holy *to the Lord*
Dan 9:4 And I prayed *to the Lord* my God, and made confession, and said
Dan 9:9 *To the Lord* our God belong mercy and forgiveness, though we have rebelled against Him
Hos 6:1 Come, and let us return *to the Lord;* for He has torn, but He will heal us
Hos 7:10 And the pride of Israel testifies to his face, but they do not return *to the Lord* their God, nor seek Him for all this
Hos 9:4 They shall not offer wine offerings *to the Lord*, nor shall their sacrifices be pleasing to Him
Hos 14:1 O Israel, return *to the Lord* your God, for you have stumbled because of your iniquity
Hos 14:2 Take words with you, and return *to the Lord*. Say to Him
Joel 1:9 The grain offering and the drink offering have been cut off from the house of the Lord; the priests mourn, who minister *to the Lord*
Joel 1:14 gather the elders and all the inhabitants of the land into the house of the Lord your God, and cry out *to the Lord*
Joel 2:13 return *to the Lord* your God, for He is gracious and merciful, slow to anger, and of great kindness
Joel 2:17 Let the priests, who minister *to the Lord*, weep between the porch and the altar
Jon 1:14 Therefore they cried out *to the Lord* and said, "We pray, O Lord, please do not let us perish for this man's life, and do not charge us with innocent blood
Jon 1:16 Then the men feared the Lord exceedingly, and offered a sacrifice *to the Lord* and made vows
Jon 2:1 Then Jonah prayed *to the Lord* his God from the fish's belly
Jon 2:2 I cried out *to the Lord* because of my affliction, and He answered me
Jon 4:2 So he prayed *to the Lord*, and said, "Ah, Lord, was not this what I said when I was still in my country
Mic 3:4 Then they will cry *to the Lord*, but He will not hear them
Mic 4:13 I will consecrate their gain *to the Lord*, and their substance *to the Lord* of the whole earth
Mic 7:7 Therefore I will look *to the Lord;* I will wait for the God of my salvation
Zech 2:11 Many nations shall be joined *to the Lord* in that day, and they shall become My people
Zech 14:7 It shall be one day which is known *to the Lord* neither day nor night
Zech 14:20 In that day "HOLINESS *TO THE LORD*" shall be engraved on the bells of the horses
Zech 14:21 Yes, every pot in Jerusalem and Judah shall be holiness *to the Lord* of hosts
Mal 1:14 But cursed be the deceiver who has in his flock a male, and makes a vow, but sacrifices *to the Lord* what is blemished for I am a great King
Mal 2:12 May the Lord cut off from the tents of Jacob the man who does this, being awake and aware, and who brings an offering *to the Lord* of hosts
Mal 3:3 He will purify the sons of Levi, and purge them as gold and silver, that they may offer *to the Lord* an offering in righteousness
Mal 3:4 Then the offering of Judah and Jerusalem will be pleasant *to the Lord*, as in the days of old, as in former years
Matt 5:33 Again you have heard that it was said to those of old, 'You shall not swear falsely, but shall perform your oaths *to the Lord*
Luke 1:16 And he will turn many of the children of Israel *to the Lord* their God
Luke 2:22 Now when the days of her purification according to the law of Moses were completed, they brought Him to Jerusalem to present Him *to the Lord*
Luke 2:23 (as it is written in the law of the Lord, "Every male who opens the womb shall be called holy *to the Lord*
Luke 2:38 And coming in that instant she gave thanks *to the Lord*, and spoke of Him to all those who looked for redemption in Jerusalem
Luke 17:5 And the apostles said *to the Lord*, "Increase our faith
Luke 19:8 Then Zacchaeus stood and said *to the Lord*, "Look, Lord, I give half of my goods to the poor
Acts 5:14 And believers were increasingly added *to the Lord*, multitudes of both men and women
Acts 8:24 Then Simon answered and said, "Pray *to the Lord* for me, that none of the things which you have spoken may come upon me
Acts 9:35 So all who dwelt at Lydda and Sharon saw him and turned *to the Lord*
Acts 11:21 And the hand of the Lord was with them, and a great number believed and turned *to the Lord*
Acts 11:24 And a great many people were added *to the Lord*
Acts 13:2 As they ministered *to the Lord* and fasted, the Holy Spirit said
Acts 14:23 So when they had appointed elders in every church, and prayed with fasting, they commended them *to the Lord* in whom they had believed
Acts 16:15 And when she and her household were baptized, she begged us, saying, "If you have judged me to be faithful *to the Lord*, come to my house and stay
Rom 14:6 He who observes the day, observes it *to the Lord;* and he who does not observe the day, *to the Lord* he does not observe it. He who eats,

eats *to the Lord*, for he gives God thanks; and he who does not eat, *to the Lord* he does not eat, and gives God thanks

Rom 14:8 For if we live, we live *to the Lord;* and if we die, we die *to the Lord*

1Cor 6:17 But he who is joined *to the Lord* is one spirit with Him

1Cor 7:32 He who is unmarried cares for the things that belong *to the Lord* how he may please the Lord

2Cor 3:16 Nevertheless when one turns *to the Lord*, the veil is taken away

2Cor 8:5 And this they did, not as we had hoped, but first gave themselves *to the Lord*, and then to us by the will of God

2Cor 11:17 What I speak, I speak not according *to the Lord*, but as it were, foolishly, in this confidence of boasting

Eph 5:10 proving what is acceptable *to the Lord*

Eph 5:19 speaking to one another in psalms and hymns and spiritual songs, singing and making melody in your heart *to the Lord*

Eph 5:22 Wives, submit to your own husbands, as *to the Lord*

Eph 6:7 with good will doing service, as *to the Lord*, and not to men

Col 3:16 Let the word of Christ dwell in you richly in all wisdom, teaching and admonishing one another in psalms and hymns and spiritual songs, singing with grace in your hearts *to the Lord*

Col 3:20 Children, obey your parents in all things, for this is well pleasing *to the Lord*

Col 3:23 And whatever you do, do it heartily, as *to the Lord* and not to men

Rev 19:1 Salvation and glory and honor and power *to the Lord* our God

TO THE TEACHING AND TO THE TESTIMONY (RSV)

(See *TO THE LAW AND TO THE TESTIMONY*)

TO THIS DAY

Gen 19:37 he is the father of the Moabites *to this day*

Gen 19:38 he is the father of the people of Ammon *to this day*

Gen 22:14 as it is said *to this day*, "In the Mount of The Lord it shall be provided

Gen 26:33 Therefore the name of the city is Beersheba *to this day*

Gen 32:32 Therefore *to this day* the children of Israel do not eat the muscle that shrank, which is on the hip socket, because He touched the socket of Jacob's hip in the muscle that shrank

Gen 35:20 And Jacob set a pillar on her grave, which is the pillar of Rachel's grave *to this day*

Gen 47:26 And Joseph made it a law over the land of Egypt *to this day*, that Pharaoh should have one-fifth, except for the land of the priests only, which did not become Pharaoh's

Gen 48:15 God, before whom my fathers Abraham and Isaac walked, the God who has fed me all my life long *to this day*

Ex 10:6 They shall fill your houses, the houses of all your servants, and the houses of all the Egyptians which neither your fathers nor your fathers' fathers have seen, since the day that they were on the earth *to this day*

Num 22:30 So the donkey said to Balaam, "Am I not your donkey on which you have ridden, ever since I became yours, *to this day*

Deut 2:22 They dispossessed them and dwelt in their place, even *to this day*

Deut 3:14 Jair the son of Manasseh took all the region of Argob, as far as the border of the Geshurites and the Maacathites, and called Bashan after his own name, Havoth Jair, *to this day*

Deut 10:8 At that time the Lord separated the tribe of Levi to bear the ark of the covenant of the Lord, to stand before the Lord to minister to Him and to bless in His name, *to this day*

Deut 11:4 how He made the waters of the Red Sea overflow them as they pursued you, and how the Lord has destroyed them *to this day*

Deut 34:6 And He buried him in a valley in the land of Moab, opposite Beth Peor; but no one knows his grave *to this day*

Josh 4:9 Then Joshua set up twelve stones in the midst of the Jordan, in the place where the feet of the priests who bore the ark of the covenant stood; and they are there *to this day*

Josh 5:9 Therefore the name of the place is called Gilgal *to this day*

Josh 6:25 So she dwells in Israel *to this day*, because she hid the messengers whom Joshua sent to spy out Jericho

Josh 7:26 Then they raised over him a great heap of stones, still there *to this day*. So the Lord turned from the fierceness of His anger. Therefore the name of that place has been called the Valley of Achor *to this day*

Josh 8:28 So Joshua burned Ai and made it a heap forever, a desolation *to this day*

Josh 8:29 And as soon as the sun was down, Joshua commanded that they should take his corpse down from the tree, cast it at the entrance of the gate of the city, and raise over it a great heap of stones that remains *to this day*

Josh 9:27 And that day Joshua made them woodcutters and water carriers for the congregation and for the altar of the Lord, in the place which He would choose, even *to this day*

Josh 14:14 Hebron therefore became the inheritance of Caleb the son of Jephunneh the Kenizzite *to this day*, because he wholly followed the Lord God of Israel

Josh 15:63 but the Jebusites dwell with the children of Judah at Jerusalem *to this day*

Josh 16:10 but the Canaanites dwell among the Ephraimites *to this day* and have become forced laborers

Josh 22:3 You have not left your brethren these many days, up *to this day*, but have kept the charge of the commandment of the Lord your God

Josh 23:8 but you shall hold fast to the Lord your God, as you have done *to this day*

Josh 23:9 but as for you, no one has been able to stand against you *to this day*

Judg 1:21 so the Jebusites dwell with the children of Benjamin in Jerusalem *to this day*

Judg 1:26 And the man went to the land of the Hittites, built a city, and called its name Luz, which is its name *to this day*

Judg 6:24 *To this day* it is still in Ophrah of the Abiezrites

Judg 10:4 they also had thirty towns, which are called"Havoth Jair" *to this day*, which are in the land of Gilead

Judg 15:19 Therefore he called its name En Hakkore, which is in Lehi *to this day*

Judg 18:12 (Therefore they call that place Mahaneh Dan *to this day*

1Sam 5:5 Therefore neither the priests of Dagon nor any who come into Dagon's temple tread on the threshold of Dagon in Ashdod *to this day*

1Sam 6:18 and the gold rats, according to the number of all the cities of the Philistines belonging to the five lords, both fortified cities and country villages, even as far as the large stone of Abel on which they set the ark of the Lord, which stone remains *to this day* in the field of Joshua of Beth Shemesh

1Sam 8:8 According to all the works which they have done since the day that I brought them up out of Egypt, even *to this day* with which they

have forsaken Me and served other gods so they are doing to you also
1Sam 12:2 I have walked before you from my childhood *to this day*
1Sam 27:6 Therefore Ziklag has belonged to the kings of Judah *to this day*
1Sam 29:3 And *to this day* I have found no fault in him since he defected to me
1Sam 29:6 For *to this day* I have not found evil in you since the day of your coming to me
1Sam 29:8 And *to this day* what have you found in your servant as long as I have been with you, that I may not go and fight against the enemies of my lord the king
1Sam 30:25 he made it a statute and an ordinance for Israel *to this day*
2Sam 6:8 and he called the name of the place Perez Uzzah *to this day*
2Sam 7:6 For I have not dwelt in a house since the time that I brought the children of Israel up from Egypt, even *to this day*, but have moved about in a tent and in a tabernacle
2Sam 18:18 He called the pillar after his own name. And *to this day* it is called Absalom's Monument
1Kin 8:8 but they could not be seen from outside. So they are there *to this day*
1Kin 9:13 And he called them the land of Cabul, as they are *to this day*
1Kin 9:21 that is, their descendants who were left in the land after them, whom the children of Israel had not been able to destroy completely from these Solomon raised forced labor, as it is *to this day*
1Kin 10:12 There never again came such almug wood, nor has the like been seen *to this day*
1Kin 12:19 So Israel has been in rebellion against the house of David *to this day*
2Kin 2:22 So the water remains healed *to this day*, according to the saying of Elisha which he spoke
2Kin 8:22 Thus Edom has been in revolt against Judah's authority *to this day*
2Kin 10:27 Then they broke down the sacred pillar of Baal, and tore down the temple of Baal and made it a refuse dump *to this day*
2Kin 14:7 He killed ten thousand Edomites in the Valley of Salt, and took Sela by war, and called its name Joktheel *to this day*
2Kin 16:6 Then the Edomites went to Elath, and dwell there *to this day*
2Kin 17:23 So Israel was carried away from their own land to Assyria, as it is *to this day*
2Kin 17:34 *To this day* they continue practicing the former rituals; they do not fear the Lord, nor do they follow their statutes or their ordinances, or the law and commandment which the Lord had commanded the children of Jacob, whom He named Israel
2Kin 17:41 also their children and their children's children have continued doing as their fathers did, even *to this day*
2Kin 21:15 because they have done evil in My sight, and have provoked Me to anger since the day their fathers came out of Egypt, even *to this day*
1Chr 4:41 and they attacked their tents and the Meunites who were found there, and utterly destroyed them, as it is *to this day*
1Chr 4:43 And they defeated the rest of the Amalekites who had escaped. They have dwelt there *to this day*
1Chr 5:26 He took them to Halah, Habor, Hara, and the river of Gozan *to this day*
1Chr 13:11 therefore that place is called Perez Uzza *to this day*
1Chr 17:5 For I have not dwelt in a house since the time that I brought up Israel, even *to this day*, but have gone from tent to tent, and from one tabernacle to another
2Chr 5:9 but they could not be seen from outside. And they are there *to this day*
2Chr 8:8 from these Solomon raised forced labor, as it is *to this day*
2Chr 10:19 So Israel has been in rebellion against the house of David *to this day*
2Chr 21:10 Thus the Edomites have been in revolt against Judah's authority *to this day*
2Chr 35:25 And *to this day* all the singing men and the singing women speak of Josiah in their lamentations
Ezra 9:7 Since the days of our fathers *to this day* we have been very guilty, and for our iniquities we, our kings, and our priests have been delivered into the hand of the kings of the lands, to the sword, to captivity, to plunder, and to humiliation, as it is this day
Ps 71:17 O God, You have taught me from my youth; and *to this day* I declare Your wondrous works
Jer 3:25 For we have sinned against the Lord our God, we and our fathers, from our youth even *to this day*, and have not obeyed the voice of the Lord our God
Jer 25:3 From the thirteenth year of Josiah the son of Amon, king of Judah, even *to this day*, this is the twenty-third year in which the word of the Lord has come to me
Jer 32:20 You have set signs and wonders in the land of Egypt, *to this day*, and in Israel and among other men
Jer 32:31 For this city has been to Me a provocation of My anger and My fury from the day that they built it, even *to this day*
Jer 35:14 for *to this day* they drink none, and obey their father's commandment
Jer 36:2 Take a scroll of a book and write on it all the words that I have spoken to you against Israel, against Judah, and against all the nations, from the day I spoke to you, from the days of Josiah even *to this day*
Jer 44:10 They have not been humbled, *to this day*, nor have they feared
Ezek 20:29 So its name is called Bamah *to this day*
Ezek 20:31 For when you offer your gifts and make your sons pass through the fire, you defile yourselves with all your idols, even *to this day*
Matt 27:8 Therefore that field has been called the Field of Blood *to this day*
Acts 2:29 Men and brethren, let me speak freely to you of the patriarch David, that he is both dead and buried, and his tomb is with us *to this day*
Acts 26:22 Therefore, having obtained help from God, *to this day* I stand, witnessing both to small and great, saying no other things than those which the prophets and Moses said would come
2Cor 3:15 But even *to this day*, when Moses is read, a veil lies on their heart

TO WHOM IT SHALL BE IMPUTED (KJV)
(See *IMPUTED TO US*)

TO WHOM THEN WILL YOU LIKEN GOD
Is 40:18 *To whom then will you liken God?* Or what likeness will you compare to Him

TO WHOM THEN WILL YOU LIKEN ME
Is 40:25 *To whom then will you liken Me*, or to whom shall I be equal

TODAY I HAVE BECOME YOUR FATHER (NIV)
(See *TODAY I HAVE BEGOTTEN YOU*)

TODAY I HAVE BEGOTTEN YOU
Ps 2:7 The Lord has said to Me, "You are My Son, *today I have begotten You*

Acts 13:33 As it is also written in the second Psalm: 'You are My Son, *today I have begotten You*
Heb 1:5 You are My Son, *today I have begotten You*"? And again
Heb 5:5 So also Christ did not glorify Himself to become High Priest, but it was He who said to Him: "You are My Son, today I have begotten You

TODAY YOU WILL BE WITH ME
Luke 23:43 And Jesus said to him, "Assuredly, I say to you, *today you will be with Me* in Paradise

TOIL OF A FOOL (NAS, RSV)
(See *LABOR OF FOOLS*)

TOIL OF MY HANDS (NAS, NIV)
(See *LABOR OF MY HANDS*)

TOILED UNDER THE SUN
Eccl 2:18 Then I hated all my labor in which I had *toiled under the sun*, because I must leave it to the man who will come after me
Eccl 2:20 Therefore I turned my heart and despaired of all the labor in which I had *toiled under the sun*
Eccl 2:22 For what has man for all his labor, and for the striving of his heart with which he has *toiled under the sun*

TOILING FOR FOOD (NIV)
(See *BREAD OF SORROWS*)

TOKEN OF THE COVENANT (KJV)
(See *SIGN OF THE COVENANT*)

TOKEN UPON THINE HAND (KJV)
(See *SIGN ON YOUR HAND*)

TOKENS AND WONDERS (KJV)
(See *SIGNS AND WONDERS*)

TOMB OF HIS FATHER
Judg 16:31 And his brothers and all his father's household came down and took him, and brought him up and buried him between Zorah and Eshtaol in the *tomb of his father* Manoah

TOMBS OF THE KINGS
2Chr 21:20 However they buried him in the City of David, but not in the *tombs of the kings*
2Chr 24:25 And they buried him in the City of David, but they did not bury him in the *tombs of the kings*
2Chr 28:27 but they did not bring him into the *tombs of the kings* of Israel

TONGUE CAN NO MAN TAME (KJV)
(See *TAME THE TONGUE*)

TONGUE CLEAVES TO MY JAWS (NAS, RSV)
(See *TONGUE CLINGS TO MY JAWS*)

TONGUE CLINGS TO MY JAWS
Ps 22:15 My strength is dried up like a potsherd, and My *tongue clings to My jaws*

TONGUE HATH SPOKEN IN MY MOUTH (KJV)
(See *TONGUE SPEAKS IN MY MOUTH*)

TONGUE IN MY MOUTH SPEAKS (NAS, RSV)
(See *TONGUE SPEAKS IN MY MOUTH*)

TONGUE IS A FIRE
Jas 3:6 And the *tongue is a fire*, a world of iniquity

TONGUE IS AN ARROW SHOT OUT
Jer 9:8 Their *tongue is an arrow shot out;* it speaks deceit

TONGUE LIKE A SWORD
Ps 64:3 Who sharpen their *tongue like a sword*, and bend their bows to shoot their arrows bitter words

TONGUE OF THOSE WHO ARE TAUGHT (RSV)
(See *SPEAK A WORD*)

TONGUE SPEAKS IN MY MOUTH
Job 33:2 Now, I open my mouth; my *tongue speaks in my mouth*

TONGUE STICKS TO THE ROOF OF MY MOUTH (NIV)
(See *TONGUE CLINGS TO MY JAWS*)

TONGUES, AS OF FIRE
Acts 2:3 Then there appeared to them divided *tongues, as of fire*, and one sat upon each of them

TONGUES LIKE SWORDS (NIV, RSV)
(See *TONGUE LIKE A SWORD*)

TOOK AN OATH
Gen 50:25 Then Joseph *took an oath* from the children of Israel, saying
Deut 1:34 And the Lord heard the sound of your words, and was angry, and *took an oath*, saying
1Sam 20:3 Then David *took an oath* again, and said, "Your father certainly knows that I have found favor in your eyes, and he says
2Sam 3:35 And when all the people came to persuade David to eat food while it was still day, David *took an oath*, saying
1Kin 1:29 And the king *took an oath* and said, "As the Lord lives, who has redeemed my life from every distress
1Kin 18:10 and when they said, 'He is not here,' he *took an oath* from the kingdom or nation that they could not find you
2Kin 11:4 And he made a covenant with them and *took an oath* from them in the house of the Lord, and showed them the king's son
2Kin 25:24 And Gedaliah *took an oath* before them and their men, and said to them
2Chr 15:14 Then they *took an oath* before the Lord with a loud voice, with shouting and trumpets and rams' horns
Jer 40:9 And Gedaliah the son of Ahikam, the son of Shaphan, *took an oath* before them and their men, saying

TOOK BREAD
Gen 21:14 So Abraham rose early in the morning, and *took bread* and a skin of water
Matt 26:26 And as they were eating, Jesus *took bread*, blessed it and broke it, and gave it to the disciples and said
Mark 14:22 And as they were eating, Jesus *took bread*, blessed it and broke it, and gave it to them and said
Luke 22:19 And He *took bread*, gave thanks and broke it, and gave it to them, saying
Luke 24:30 Now it came to pass, as He sat at the table with them, that He *took bread*, blessed and broke it, and gave it to them
Acts 27:35 And when he had said these things, he *took bread* and gave thanks to God in the presence of them all
1Cor 11:23 that the Lord Jesus on the same night in which He was betrayed *took bread*

TOOK HIS LIFE IN HIS HANDS
1Sam 19:5 For he *took his life in his hands* and killed the Philistine, and the Lord brought about a great salvation for all Israel

TOOK MY LIFE IN MY HANDS
Judg 12:3 So when I saw that you would not deliver me, I *took my life in my hands* and crossed over against the people of Ammon

TOOK OUR INFIRMITIES
Matt 8:17 that it might be fulfilled which was spoken by Isaiah the prophet, saying: "He Himself *took our infirmities* and bore our sicknesses

TOOK OVER HIS LAND (NIV)
(See *TOOK POSSESSION OF HIS LAND*)

TOOK POSSESSION OF HIS LAND
Num 21:24 Then Israel defeated him with the edge of the sword, and *took possession of his land* from the Arnon to the Jabbok, as far as the people of Ammon
Num 21:35 So they defeated him, his sons, and all his people, until there was no survivor left him; and they *took possession of his land*
Deut 4:47 And they *took possession of his land* and the land of Og king of Bashan, two kings of the Amorites, who were on this side of the Jordan, toward the rising of the sun

TOOK THE CUP AFTER SUPPER
Luke 22:20 Likewise He also *took the cup after supper*, saying, "This cup is the new covenant in My blood, which is shed for you
1Cor 11:25 In the same manner He also *took the cup after supper*, saying

TOOK UP MY CASE (NIV)
(See *PLEADED THE CASE*)

TOOTH FOR A TOOTH
Matt 5:38 You have heard that it was said, 'An eye for an eye and a *tooth for a tooth*

TOP OF EVERY STREET (KJV)
(See *HEAD OF EVERY STREET*)

TORE DOWN THE ALTARS (NAS, NIV)
(See *BROKEN DOWN THE ALTARS*)

TORE HIS CLOTHES
Gen 37:29 Then Reuben returned to the pit, and indeed Joseph was not in the pit; and he *tore his clothes*
Gen 37:34 Then Jacob *tore his clothes*, put sackcloth on his waist, and mourned for his son many days
Josh 7:6 Then Joshua *tore his clothes*, and fell to the earth on his face before the ark of the Lord until evening, both he and the elders of Israel
Judg 11:35 And it came to pass, when he saw her, that he *tore his clothes*, and said
1Kin 21:27 So it was, when Ahab heard those words, that he *tore his clothes* and put sackcloth on his body, and fasted and lay in sackcloth, and went about mourning
2Kin 5:7 And it happened, when the king of Israel read the letter, that he *tore his clothes* and said
2Kin 6:30 Now it happened, when the king heard the words of the woman, that he *tore his clothes*
2Kin 19:1 And so it was, when King Hezekiah heard it, that he *tore his clothes*, covered himself with sackcloth, and went into the house of the Lord
2Kin 22:11 Now it happened, when the king heard the words of the Book of the Law, that he *tore his clothes*
2Chr 34:19 Now it happened, when the king heard the words of the Law, that he *tore his clothes*
Esth 4:1 When Mordecai learned all that had happened, he *tore his clothes* and put on sackcloth and ashes, and went out into the midst of the city
Is 37:1 And so it was, when King Hezekiah heard it, that he *tore his clothes*, covered himself with sackcloth, and went into the house of the Lord
Matt 26:65 Then the high priest *tore his clothes*, saying, "He has spoken blasphemy
Mark 14:63 Then the high priest *tore his clothes* and said, "What further need do we have of witnesses

TORE THEIR CLOTHES
Gen 44:13 Then they *tore their clothes*, and each man loaded his donkey and returned to the city
Num 14:6 And Joshua the son of Nun and Caleb the son of Jephunneh, who were among those who had spied out the land, *tore their clothes*
Acts 14:14 But when the apostles Barnabas and Paul heard this, they *tore their clothes* and ran in among the multitude, crying out

TORMENTED IN THIS FLAME
Luke 16:24 Then he cried and said, 'Father Abraham, have mercy on me, and send Lazarus that he may dip the tip of his finger in water and cool my tongue; for I am *tormented in this flame*

TOSSED TO AND FRO
Eph 4:14 that we should no longer be children, *tossed to and fro* and carried about with every wind of doctrine, by the trickery of men, in the cunning craftiness by which they lie in wait to deceive

TOTTER LIKE A HUT
Is 24:20 The earth shall reel to and fro like a drunkard, and shall *totter like a hut*

TOUCH NO UNCLEAN THING
Is 52:11 Go out from there, *touch no unclean thing;* go out from the midst of her, be clean, you who bear the vessels of the Lord

TOUCH THE EDGE OF HIS CLOAK (NIV)
(See *TOUCH THE HEM OF HIS GARMENT*)

TOUCH THE FRINGE OF HIS GARMENT (RSV)
(See *TOUCH THE HEM OF HIS GARMENT*)

TOUCH THE HEM OF HIS GARMENT
Matt 14:36 and begged Him that they might only *touch the hem of His garment*

TOWARD JERUSALEM
Ezek 21:2 Son of man, set your face *toward Jerusalem*, preach against the holy places, and prophesy against the land of Israel
Dan 6:10 And in his upper room, with his windows open *toward Jerusalem*, he knelt down on his knees three times that day, and prayed and gave thanks before his God, as was his custom since early days
Luke 13:22 And He went through the cities and villages, teaching, and journeying *toward Jerusalem*

TOWER OF IVORY (KJV, NAS)
(See *IVORY TOWER*)

TRADING SHIP (NIV)
(See *SHIPS OF TARSHISH*)

TRADITION OF MEN
Mark 7:8 For laying aside the commandment of God, you hold the *tradition of men* the washing of pitchers and cups, and many other such things you do
Col 2:8 Beware lest anyone cheat you through philosophy and empty deceit, according to the *tradition of men*, according to the basic principles of the world, and not according to Christ

TRADITION OF THE ELDERS
Matt 15:2 Why do Your disciples transgress the *tradition of the elders*

Mark 7:3 For the Pharisees and all the Jews do not eat unless they wash their hands in a special way, holding the *tradition of the elders*
Mark 7:5 Then the Pharisees and scribes asked Him, "Why do Your disciples not walk according to the *tradition of the elders*, but eat bread with unwashed hands

TRAIN FILLED THE TEMPLE (KJV, RSV)
(See *ROBE FILLED THE TEMPLE*)

TRAIN OF HIS ROBE
Is 6:1 In the year that King Uzziah died, I saw the Lord sitting on a throne, high and lifted up, and the *train of His robe* filled the temple

TRAINED THEMSELVES TO DISTINGUISH GOOD FROM EVIL (NIV)
(See *SENSES EXERCISED TO DISCERN BOTH GOOD AND EVIL*)

TRAINING IN RIGHTEOUSNESS (NAS, NIV, RSV)
(See *INSTRUCTION IN RIGHTEOUSNESS*)

TRAMPLED UNDER FOOT
Is 28:3 The crown of pride, the drunkards of Ephraim, will be *trampled under foot*
Dan 8:13 and another holy one said to that certain one who was speaking, "How long will the vision be, concerning the daily sacrifices and the transgression of desolation, the giving of both the sanctuary and the host to be *trampled under foot*
Matt 5:13 It is then good for nothing but to be thrown out and *trampled under foot* by men

TRAMPLED UNDERFOOT
Lam 1:15 The Lord has *trampled underfoot* all my mighty men in my midst

TRANSGRESSED SORE AGAINST THE LORD (KJV)
(See *UNFAITHFUL TO THE LORD*)

TRANSGRESSED THE COVENANT
Josh 7:15 Then it shall be that he who is taken with the accursed thing shall be burned with fire, he and all that he has, because he has *transgressed the covenant* of the Lord, and because he has done a disgraceful thing in Israel
Josh 23:16 When you have *transgressed the covenant* of the Lord your God, which He commanded you, and have gone and served other gods, and bowed down to them, then the anger of the Lord will burn against you, and you shall perish quickly from the good land which He has given you
Hos 6:7 But like men they *transgressed the covenant*; there they dealt treacherously with Me

TRAP OF THE DEVIL (NIV)
(See *SNARE OF THE DEVIL*)

TREASURE HIDDEN IN A FIELD
Matt 13:44 Again, the kingdom of heaven is like *treasure hidden in a field*, which a man found and hid

TREASURE IN HEAVEN
Matt 19:21 Jesus said to him, "If you want to be perfect, go, sell what you have and give to the poor, and you will have *treasure in heaven*
Mark 10:21 Go your way, sell whatever you have and give to the poor, and you will have *treasure in heaven*
Luke 18:22 Sell all that you have and distribute to the poor, and you will have *treasure in heaven*

TREASURED ALL THESE THINGS IN HER HEART (NAS, NIV)
(See *KEPT ALL THESE THINGS IN HER HEART*)

TREASURED POSSESSION (NIV)
(See *SPECIAL TREASURE*)

TREASURES IN HEAVEN
Matt 6:20 but lay up for yourselves *treasures in heaven*, where neither moth nor rust destroys and where thieves do not break in and steal

TREASURES OF ALL NATIONS (RSV)
(See *DESIRE OF ALL NATIONS*)

TREASURES ON EARTH
Matt 6:19 Do not lay up for yourselves *treasures on earth*, where moth and rust destroy and where thieves break in and steal

TREATY OF BROTHERHOOD (NIV)
(See *COVENANT OF BROTHERHOOD*)

TREE OF LIFE
Gen 2:9 The *tree of life* was also in the midst of the garden, and the tree of the knowledge of good and evil
Gen 3:22 And now, lest he put out his hand and take also of the *tree of life*, and eat, and live forever
Gen 3:24 and He placed cherubim at the east of the garden of Eden, and a flaming sword which turned every way, to guard the way to the *tree of life*
Prov 3:18 She is a *tree of life* to those who take hold of her, and happy are all who retain her
Prov 11:30 The fruit of the righteous is a *tree of life*, and he who wins souls is wise
Prov 13:12 Hope deferred makes the heart sick, but when the desire comes, it is a *tree of life*
Prov 15:4 A wholesome tongue is a *tree of life*, but perverseness in it breaks the spirit
Rev 2:7 To him who overcomes I will give to eat from the *tree of life*, which is in the midst of the Paradise of God
Rev 22:2 In the middle of its street, and on either side of the river, was the *tree of life*, which bore twelve fruits, each tree yielding its fruit every month
Rev 22:14 Blessed are those who do His commandments, that they may have the right to the *tree of life*, and may enter through the gates into the city

TREE PLANTED BY THE RIVERS
Ps 1:3 He shall be like a *tree planted by the rivers* of water, that brings forth its fruit in its season, whose leaf also shall not wither

TREMBLE BEFORE HIM
1Chr 16:30 *Tremble before Him*, all the earth. The world also is firmly established, it shall not be moved
Esth 5:9 but when Haman saw Mordecai in the king's gate, and that he did not stand or *tremble before him*, he was filled with indignation against Mordecai
Ps 96:9 Oh, worship the Lord in the beauty of holiness! *Tremble before Him*, all the earth

TREMBLED IN MYSELF
Hab 3:16 and I *trembled in myself*, that I might rest in the day of trouble

TRESPASS OFFERING
Lev 5:6 and he shall bring his *trespass offering* to the Lord for his sin which he has committed, a

female from the flock, a lamb or a kid of the goats as a sin offering
Lev 5:15 If a person commits a trespass, and sins unintentionally in regard to the holy things of the Lord, then he shall bring to the Lord as his *trespass offering* a ram without blemish from the flocks, with your valuation in shekels of silver according to the shekel of the sanctuary, as a *trespass offering*
Lev 5:16 So the priest shall make atonement for him with the ram of the *trespass offering*, and it shall be forgiven him
Lev 5:18 And he shall bring to the priest a ram without blemish from the flock, with your valuation, as a *trespass offering*
Lev 5:19 It is a *trespass offering;* he has certainly trespassed against the Lord
Lev 6:5 He shall restore its full value, add one-fifth more to it, and give it to whomever it belongs, on the day of his *trespass offering*
Lev 6:6 And he shall bring his *trespass offering* to the Lord, a ram without blemish from the flock, with your valuation, as a *trespass offering*, to the priest
Lev 6:17 it is most holy, like the sin offering and the *trespass offering*
Lev 7:1 Likewise this is the law of the *trespass offering* (it is most holy
Lev 7:2 In the place where they kill the burnt offering they shall kill the *trespass offering*
Lev 7:5 and the priest shall burn them on the altar as an offering made by fire to the Lord. It is a *trespass offering*
Lev 7:7 The *trespass offering* is like the sin offering; there is one law for them both
Lev 7:37 This is the law of the burnt offering, the grain offering, the sin offering, the *trespass offering*, the consecrations, and the sacrifice of the peace offering
Lev 14:12 And the priest shall take one male lamb and offer it as a *trespass offering*, and the log of oil, and wave them as a wave offering before the Lord
Lev 14:13 for as the sin offering is the priest's, so is the *trespass offering*
Lev 14:14 The priest shall take some of the blood of the *trespass offering*, and the priest shall put it on the tip of the right ear of him who is to be cleansed, on the thumb of his right hand, and on the big toe of his right foot
Lev 14:17 And of the rest of the oil in his hand, the priest shall put some on the tip of the right ear of him who is to be cleansed, on the thumb of his right hand, and on the big toe of his right foot, on the blood of the *trespass offering*
Lev 14:21 But if he is poor and cannot afford it, then he shall take one male lamb as a *trespass offering* to be waved, to make atonement for him, one-tenth of an ephah of fine flour mixed with oil as a grain offering, a log of oil
Lev 14:24 And the priest shall take the lamb of the *trespass offering* and the log of oil, and the priest shall wave them as a wave offering before the Lord
Lev 14:25 Then he shall kill the lamb of the *trespass offering*, and the priest shall take some of the blood of the *trespass offering* and put it on the tip of the right ear of him who is to be cleansed, on the thumb of his right hand, and on the big toe of his right foot
Lev 14:28 And the priest shall put some of the oil that is in his hand on the tip of the right ear of him who is to be cleansed, on the thumb of the right hand, and on the big toe of his right foot, on the place of the blood of the *trespass offering*
Lev 19:21 And he shall bring his *trespass offering* to the Lord, to the door of the tabernacle of meeting, a ram as a *trespass offering*
Lev 19:22 The priest shall make atonement for him with the ram of the *trespass offering* before the Lord for his sin which he has done
Num 6:12 He shall consecrate to the Lord the days of his separation, and bring a male lamb in its first year as a *trespass offering*
Num 18:9 every offering of theirs, every grain offering and every sin offering and every *trespass offering* which they render to Me, shall be most holy for you and your sons
1Sam 6:3 but by all means return it to Him with a *trespass offering*
1Sam 6:4 Then they said, "What is the *trespass offering* which we shall return to Him
1Sam 6:8 and put the articles of gold which you are returning to Him as a *trespass offering* in a chest by its side
1Sam 6:17 Now these are the gold tumors which the Philistines returned as a *trespass offering* to the Lord
Ezra 10:19 and being guilty, they presented a ram of the flock as their *trespass offering*
Ezek 40:39 In the vestibule of the gateway were two tables on this side and two tables on that side, on which to slay the burnt offering, the sin offering, and the *trespass offering*
Ezek 42:13 There they shall lay the most holy offerings the grain offering, the sin offering, and the *trespass offering* for the place is holy
Ezek 44:29 They shall eat the grain offering, the sin offering, and the *trespass offering*
Ezek 46:20 And he said to me, "This is the place where the priests shall boil the *trespass offering* and the sin offering, and where they shall bake the grain offering, so that they do not bring them out into the outer court to sanctify the people

TRESPASSED AGAINST THE LORD
Lev 5:19 It is a trespass offering; he has certainly *trespassed against the Lord*
2Chr 30:7 And do not be like your fathers and your brethren, who *trespassed against the Lord* God of their fathers, so that He gave them up to astonishment, as you see

TRIAL OF YOUR FAITH (KJV)
(See *GENUINENESS OF YOUR FAITH*)

TRIBES OF ISRAEL
Gen 49:16 Dan shall judge his people as one of the *tribes of Israel*
Gen 49:28 All these are the twelve *tribes of Israel*, and this is what their father spoke to them
Ex 24:4 And he rose early in the morning, and built an altar at the foot of the mountain, and twelve pillars according to the twelve *tribes of Israel*
Num 31:4 A thousand from each tribe of all the *tribes of Israel* you shall send to the war
Deut 29:21 And the Lord would separate him from all the *tribes of Israel* for adversity, according to all the curses of the covenant that are written in this Book of the Law
Deut 33:5 And He was King in Jeshurun, when the leaders of the people were gathered, all the *tribes of Israel* together
Josh 3:12 Now therefore, take for yourselves twelve men from the *tribes of Israel*, one man from every tribe
Josh 12:7 And these are the kings of the country which Joshua and the children of Israel conquered on this side of the Jordan, on the west, from Baal Gad in the Valley of Lebanon as far as Mount Halak and the ascent to Seir, which Joshua gave to the *tribes of Israel* as a possession according to their divisions
Josh 24:1 Then Joshua gathered all the *tribes of Israel* to Shechem and called for the elders of Is-

rael, for their heads, for their judges, and for their officers
Judg 18:1 for until that day their whole inheritance among the *tribes of Israel* had not yet fallen to them
Judg 20:2 And the leaders of all the people, all the *tribes of Israel*, presented themselves in the assembly of the people of God, four hundred thousand foot soldiers who drew the sword
Judg 20:10 We will take ten men out of every hundred throughout all the *tribes of Israel*, a hundred out of every thousand, and a thousand out of every ten thousand, to make provisions for the people, that when they come to Gibeah in Benjamin, they may repay all the vileness that they have done in Israel
Judg 20:12 Then the *tribes of Israel* sent men through all the tribe of Benjamin, saying
Judg 21:5 The children of Israel said, "Who is there among all the *tribes of Israel* who did not come up with the assembly to the Lord
Judg 21:8 And they said, "What one is there from the *tribes of Israel* who did not come up to Mizpah to the Lord
Judg 21:15 And the people grieved for Benjamin, because the Lord had made a void in the *tribes of Israel*
1Sam 2:28 Did I not choose him out of all the *tribes of Israel* to be My priest, to offer upon My altar, to burn incense, and to wear an ephod before Me
1Sam 9:21 And Saul answered and said, "Am I not a Benjamite, of the smallest of the *tribes of Israel*, and my family the least of all the families of the tribe of Benjamin
1Sam 10:20 And when Samuel had caused all the *tribes of Israel* to come near, the tribe of Benjamin was chosen
1Sam 15:17 So Samuel said, "When you were little in your own eyes, were you not head of the *tribes of Israel*
2Sam 5:1 Then all the *tribes of Israel* came to David at Hebron and spoke, saying
2Sam 7:7 In all the places where I have walked with all the children of Israel, have I ever spoken a word to anyone from the *tribes of Israel*, whom I commanded to shepherd My people Israel, saying
2Sam 15:10 Then Absalom sent spies throughout all the *tribes of Israel*, saying
2Sam 19:9 Now all the people were in a dispute throughout all the *tribes of Israel*, saying
2Sam 20:14 And he went through all the *tribes of Israel* to Abel and Beth Maachah and all the Berites
2Sam 24:2 So the king said to Joab the commander of the army who was with him, "Now go throughout all the *tribes of Israel*, from Dan to Beersheba, and count the people, that I may know the number of the people
1Kin 11:32 (but he shall have one tribe for the sake of My servant David, and for the sake of Jerusalem, the city which I have chosen out of all the *tribes of Israel*
1Kin 14:21 He reigned seventeen years in Jerusalem, the city which the Lord had chosen out of all the *tribes of Israel*, to put His name there
2Kin 21:7 He even set a carved image of Asherah that he had made, in the house of which the Lord had said to David and to Solomon his son, "In this house and in Jerusalem, which I have chosen out of all the *tribes of Israel*, I will put My name forever
1Chr 27:16 Furthermore, over the *tribes of Israel:* the officer over the Reubenites was Eliezer the son of Zichri
1Chr 27:22 over Dan, Azarel the son of Jeroham. These were the leaders of the *tribes of Israel*
1Chr 29:6 Then the leaders of the fathers' houses, leaders of the *tribes of Israel*, the captains of thousands and of hundreds, with the officers over the king's work, offered willingly
2Chr 11:16 And after the Levites left, those from all the *tribes of Israel*, such as set their heart to seek the Lord God of Israel, came to Jerusalem to sacrifice to the Lord God of their fathers
2Chr 12:13 and he reigned seventeen years in Jerusalem, the city which the Lord had chosen out of all the *tribes of Israel*, to put His name there
2Chr 33:7 He even set a carved image, the idol which he had made, in the house of God, of which God had said to David and to Solomon his son, "In this house and in Jerusalem, which I have chosen out of all the *tribes of Israel*, I will put My name forever
Ezra 6:17 And they offered sacrifices at the dedication of this house of God, one hundred bulls, two hundred rams, four hundred lambs, and as a sin offering for all Israel twelve male goats, according to the number of the *tribes of Israel*
Ps 78:55 He also drove out the nations before them, allotted them an inheritance by survey, and made the *tribes of Israel* dwell in their tents
Ezek 37:19 Surely I will take the stick of Joseph, which is in the hand of Ephraim, and the *tribes of Israel*, his companions
Ezek 47:13 These are the borders by which you shall divide the land as an inheritance among the twelve *tribes of Israel*
Ezek 47:21 Thus you shall divide this land among yourselves according to the *tribes of Israel*
Ezek 47:22 they shall have an inheritance with you among the *tribes of Israel*
Ezek 48:19 The workers of the city, from all the *tribes of Israel*, shall cultivate it
Ezek 48:29 This is the land which you shall divide by lot as an inheritance among the *tribes of Israel*, and these are their portions
Ezek 48:31 (the gates of the city shall be named after the *tribes of Israel*
Hos 5:9 among the *tribes of Israel* I make known what is sure
Zech 9:1 The burden of the word of the Lord against the land of Hadrach, and Damascus its resting place (for the eyes of men and all the *tribes of Israel* are on the Lord
Matt 19:28 So Jesus said to them, "Assuredly I say to you, that in the regeneration, when the Son of Man sits on the throne of His glory, you who have followed Me will also sit on twelve thrones, judging the twelve *tribes of Israel*
Luke 22:30 that you may eat and drink at My table in My kingdom, and sit on thrones judging the twelve *tribes of Israel*

TRIED US AS SILVER (RSV)
(See *REFINED US AS SILVER*)

TRIEST THE HEART (KJV, NAS, RSV)
(See *TEST THE HEART*)

TRIUMPH IN CHRIST
2Cor 2:14 Now thanks be to God who always leads us in *triumph in Christ*, and through us diffuses the fragrance of His knowledge in every place

TRIUMPH OVER HIS ENEMIES (NIV)
(See *PREVAIL AGAINST HIS ENEMIES*)

TRIUMPHAL PROCESSION IN CHRIST (NIV)
(See *TRIUMPH IN CHRIST*)

TRIUMPHS OF THE LORD (RSV)
(See *RIGHTEOUS ACTS OF THE LORD*)

TRODDEN THE WINEPRESS
Is 63:3 I have *trodden the winepress* alone, and from the peoples no one was with Me

TRODDEN UNDERFOOT (KJV)
(See *TRAMPLED UNDERFOOT*)

TROUBLED IN SPIRIT
John 13:21 When Jesus had said these things, He was *troubled in spirit*, and testified and said

TRUE AND FAITHFUL
Jer 42:5 Then they said to Jeremiah, "Let the Lord be a *true and faithful* witness between us, if we do not do according to everything which the Lord your God sends us by you
Rev 21:5 And He said to me, "Write, for these words are *true and faithful*

TRUE CHILD IN A COMMON FAITH (NAS, RSV)
(See *TRUE SON IN OUR COMMON FAITH*)

TRUE GOD
2Chr 15:3 For a long time Israel has been without the *true God*, without a teaching priest, and without law
Jer 10:10 But the Lord is the *true God;* He is the living God and the everlasting King
John 17:3 And this is eternal life, that they may know You, the only *true God*, and Jesus Christ whom You have sent
1Th 1:9 For they themselves declare concerning us what manner of entry we had to you, and how you turned to God from idols to serve the living and *true God*
1Jn 5:20 and we are in Him who is true, in His Son Jesus Christ. This is the *true God* and eternal life

TRUE LIGHT
John 1:9 That was the *true Light* which gives light to every man who comes into the world
1Jn 2:8 Again, a new commandment I write to you, which thing is true in Him and in you, because the darkness is passing away, and the *true light* is already shining

TRUE SON IN OUR COMMON FAITH
Tit 1:4 To Titus, my *true son in our common faith:* Grace, mercy, and peace from God the Father and the Lord Jesus Christ our Savior

TRUE VINE
John 15:1 I am the *true vine*, and My Father is the vinedresser

TRULY, I SAY TO YOU (NAS, RSV)
(See *ASSUREDLY, I SAY TO YOU*)

TRULY, TRULY, I SAY TO YOU (NAS, RSV)
(See *MOST ASSUREDLY, I SAY TO YOU*)

TRUMPET EXCEEDING LOUD (KJV)
(See *SOUND OF THE TRUMPET*)

TRUMPET OF GOD
1Th 4:16 For the Lord Himself will descend from heaven with a shout, with the voice of an archangel, and with the *trumpet of God*

TRUST IN GOD'S UNFAILING LOVE (NIV)
(See *TRUST IN THE MERCY OF GOD*)

TRUST IN THE COVERT (KJV)
(See *TRUST IN THE SHELTER*)

TRUST IN THE LORD
2Kin 18:22 But if you say to me, 'We *trust in the Lord* our God
2Kin 18:30 nor let Hezekiah make you *trust in the Lord*, saying
Ps 4:5 Offer the sacrifices of righteousness, and put your *trust in the Lord*
Ps 31:6 I have hated those who regard vain idols; but I *trust in the Lord*
Ps 37:3 *Trust in the Lord*, and do good; dwell in the land, and feed on His faithfulness
Ps 40:3 Many will see it and fear, and will *trust in the Lord*
Ps 73:28 I have put my *trust in the Lord* God, that I may declare all Your works
Ps 115:9 O Israel, *trust in the Lord;* He is their help and their shield
Ps 115:10 O house of Aaron, *trust in the Lord;* He is their help and their shield
Ps 115:11 You who fear the Lord, *trust in the Lord;* He is their help and their shield
Ps 118:8 It is better to *trust in the Lord* than to put confidence in man
Ps 118:9 It is better to *trust in the Lord* than to put confidence in princes
Ps 125:1 Those who *trust in the Lord* are like Mount Zion, which cannot be moved, but abides forever
Prov 3:5 *Trust in the Lord* with all your heart, and lean not on your own understanding
Is 26:4 *Trust in the Lord* forever, for in YAH, the Lord, is everlasting strength
Is 36:7 But if you say to me, 'We *trust in the Lord* our God
Is 36:15 nor let Hezekiah make you *trust in the Lord*, saying
Phil 2:19 But I *trust in the Lord* Jesus to send Timothy to you shortly, that I also may be encouraged when I know your state
Phil 2:24 But I *trust in the Lord* that I myself shall also come shortly

TRUST IN THE MERCY OF GOD
Ps 52:8 I *trust in the mercy of God* forever and ever

TRUST IN THE SHELTER
Ps 61:4 I will *trust in the shelter* of Your wings

TRUST IN THE STEADFAST LOVE OF GOD (RSV)
(See *TRUST IN THE MERCY OF GOD*)

TRUST IN VANITY (KJV)
(See *EMPTY WORDS*)

TRUST IN YOU
Ps 5:11 But let all those rejoice who put their *trust in You*
Ps 9:10 And those who know Your name will put their *trust in You*
Ps 17:7 Show Your marvelous lovingkindness by Your right hand, O You who save those who *trust in You* from those who rise up against them
Ps 25:2 O my God, I *trust in You;* let me not be ashamed
Ps 25:20 Let me not be ashamed, for I put my *trust in You*
Ps 31:14 But as for me, I *trust in You*, O Lord
Ps 31:19 Oh, how great is Your goodness, which You have laid up for those who fear You, which You have prepared for those who *trust in You* in the presence of the sons of men
Ps 55:23 Bloodthirsty and deceitful men shall not live out half their days; but I will *trust in You*
Ps 56:3 Whenever I am afraid, I will *trust in You*

TRUSTED IN GOD (NIV)
(See *BELIEVED IN GOD*)

TRUSTED IN THE LORD
2Kin 18:5 He *trusted in the Lord* God of Israel, so that after him was none like him among all the kings of Judah, nor any who were before him

Ps 22:8 He *trusted in the Lord*, let Him rescue Him; let Him deliver Him, since He delights in Him
Ps 26:1 I have also *trusted in the Lord;* I shall not slip
Zeph 3:2 she has not *trusted in the Lord*, she has not drawn near to her God

TRUSTS IN THE LORD
Ps 21:7 For the king *trusts in the Lord*, and through the mercy of the Most High he shall not be moved
Ps 32:10 But he who *trusts in the Lord*, mercy shall surround him
Prov 16:20 He who heeds the word wisely will find good, and whoever *trusts in the Lord*, happy is he
Prov 28:25 He who is of a proud heart stirs up strife, but he who *trusts in the Lord* will be prospered
Prov 29:25 The fear of man brings a snare, but whoever *trusts in the Lord* shall be safe
Jer 17:7 Blessed is the man who *trusts in the Lord*, and whose hope is the Lord

TRUSTWORTHY SAYING (NIV)
(See *FAITHFUL SAYING*)

TRUTH CAME THROUGH JESUS CHRIST
John 1:17 For the law was given through Moses, but grace and *truth came through Jesus Christ*

TRUTH OF THE GOSPEL
Gal 2:5 to whom we did not yield submission even for an hour, that the *truth of the gospel* might continue with you
Gal 2:14 But when I saw that they were not straightforward about the *truth of the gospel*, I said to Peter before them all
Col 1:5 because of the hope which is laid up for you in heaven, of which you heard before in the word of the *truth of the gospel*

TRUTH SHALL MAKE YOU FREE
John 8:32 And you shall know the truth, and the *truth shall make you free*

TRY THE SPIRITS (KJV)
(See *TEST THE SPIRITS*)

TRYING TO KILL ME (NIV)
(See *SEEK MY LIFE*)

TUNIC OF MANY COLORS
Gen 37:3 Now Israel loved Joseph more than all his children, because he was the son of his old age. Also he made him a *tunic of many colors*
Gen 37:23 So it came to pass, when Joseph had come to his brothers, that they stripped Joseph of his tunic, the *tunic of many colors* that was on him
Gen 37:32 Then they sent the *tunic of many colors*, and they brought it to their father and said

TURN AGAIN UNTO DUST (KJV)
(See *RETURN TO DUST*)

TURN ASIDE
Ex 3:3 Then Moses said, "I will now *turn aside* and see this great sight, why the bush does not burn
Ex 23:2 nor shall you testify in a dispute so as to *turn aside* after many to pervert justice
Num 20:17 we will not *turn aside* to the right hand or to the left until we have passed through your territory
Num 21:22 We will not *turn aside* into fields or vineyards; we will not drink water from wells
Deut 5:32 you shall not *turn aside* to the right hand or to the left
Deut 11:16 Take heed to yourselves, lest your heart be deceived, and you *turn aside* and serve other gods and worship them
Deut 11:28 and the curse, if you do not obey the commandments of the Lord your God, but *turn aside* from the way which I command you today, to go after other gods which you have not known
Deut 17:11 you shall not *turn aside* to the right hand or to the left from the sentence which they pronounce upon you
Deut 17:20 that his heart may not be lifted above his brethren, that he may not *turn aside* from the commandment to the right hand or to the left, and that he may prolong his days in his kingdom, he and his children in the midst of Israel
Deut 28:14 So you shall not *turn aside* from any of the words which I command you this day, to the right hand or to the left, to go after other gods to serve them
Deut 31:29 For I know that after my death you will become utterly corrupt, and *turn aside* from the way which I have commanded you
Josh 23:6 Therefore be very courageous to keep and to do all that is written in the Book of the Law of Moses, lest you *turn aside* from it to the right hand or to the left
Judg 4:18 And Jael went out to meet Sisera, and said to him, "*Turn aside*, my lord, *turn aside* to me
Judg 19:11 and the servant said to his master, "Come, please, and let us *turn aside* into this city of the Jebusites and lodge in it
Judg 19:12 But his master said to him, "We will not *turn aside* here into a city of foreigners, who are not of the children of Israel
1Sam 6:12 Then the cows headed straight for the road to Beth Shemesh, and went along the highway, lowing as they went, and did not *turn aside* to the right hand or the left
1Sam 12:20 yet do not *turn aside* from following the Lord, but serve the Lord with all your heart
1Sam 12:21 And do not *turn aside;* for then you would go after empty things which cannot profit or deliver, for they are nothing
2Sam 2:21 And Abner said to him, "*Turn aside* to your right hand or to your left, and lay hold on one of the young men and take his armor for yourself." But Asahel would not *turn aside* from following him
2Sam 2:22 So Abner said again to Asahel, "*Turn aside* from following me
2Sam 2:23 However, he refused to *turn aside*. Therefore Abner struck him in the stomach with the blunt end of the spear, so that the spear came out of his back
2Sam 18:30 And the king said, "*Turn aside* and stand here." So he turned aside and stood still
1Kin 22:43 He did not *turn aside* from them, doing what was right in the eyes of the Lord
2Kin 22:2 he did not *turn aside* to the right hand or to the left
2Chr 20:32 And he walked in the way of his father Asa, and did not *turn aside* from it, doing what was right in the sight of the Lord
2Chr 34:2 he did not *turn aside* to the right hand or to the left
Job 6:18 The paths of their way *turn aside*, they go nowhere and perish
Ps 40:4 Blessed is that man who makes the Lord his trust, and does not respect the proud, nor such as *turn aside* to lies
Ps 119:51 The proud have me in great derision, yet I do not *turn aside* from Your law
Ps 125:5 As for such as *turn aside* to their crooked ways, the Lord shall lead them away with the workers of iniquity
Prov 7:25 Do not let your heart *turn aside* to her ways, do not stray into her paths

Is 29:21 who make a man an offender by a word, and lay a snare for him who reproves in the gate, and *turn aside* the just for a thing of naught
Is 30:11 Get out of the way, *turn aside* from the path, cause the Holy One of Israel to cease from before us
Jer 15:5 Or who will *turn aside* to ask how you are doing
Lam 3:35 to *turn aside* the justice due a man before the face of the Most High
Ezek 1:17 When they went, they went toward any one of four directions; they did not *turn aside* when they went
Ezek 10:11 they did not *turn aside* when they went, but followed in the direction the head was facing. They did not *turn aside* when they went

TURN ASIDE NEITHER TO THE RIGHT NOR TO THE LEFT (RSV)
(See *TURN NEITHER TO THE RIGHT NOR TO THE LEFT*)

TURN ASIDE TO FALSE GODS (NIV)
(See *TURN ASIDE TO LIES*)

TURN ASIDE TO LIES
Ps 40:4 Blessed is that man who makes the Lord his trust, and does not respect the proud, nor such as *turn aside to lies*

TURN ASIDE TO THE RIGHT HAND OR TO THE LEFT
Num 20:17 we will not *turn aside to the right hand or to the left* until we have passed through your territory
Deut 5:32 you shall not *turn aside to the right hand or to the left*
Deut 17:11 you shall not *turn aside to the right hand or to the left* from the sentence which they pronounce upon you
2Kin 22:2 he did not *turn aside to the right hand or to the left*
2Chr 34:2 he did not *turn aside to the right hand or to the left*

TURN AWAY ITS PUNISHMENT
Amos 1:3 For three transgressions of Damascus, and for four, I will not *turn away its punishment*, because they have threshed Gilead with implements of iron
Amos 1:6 For three transgressions of Gaza, and for four, I will not *turn away its punishment*, because they took captive the whole captivity to deliver them up to Edom
Amos 1:9 For three transgressions of Tyre, and for four, I will not *turn away its punishment*, because they delivered up the whole captivity to Edom, and did not remember the covenant of brotherhood
Amos 1:11 For three transgressions of Edom, and for four, I will not *turn away its punishment*, because he pursued his brother with the sword, and cast off all pity
Amos 1:13 For three transgressions of the people of Ammon, and for four, I will not *turn away its punishment*, because they ripped open the women with child in Gilead, that they might enlarge their territory
Amos 2:1 For three transgressions of Moab, and for four, I will not *turn away its punishment*, because he burned the bones of the king of Edom to lime
Amos 2:4 For three transgressions of Judah, and for four, I will not *turn away its punishment*, because they have despised the law of the Lord, and have not kept His commandments
Amos 2:6 For three transgressions of Israel, and for four, I will not *turn away its punishment*, because they sell the righteous for silver, and the poor for a pair of sandals

TURN AWAY YOUR HEARTS
1Kin 11:2 For surely they will *turn away your hearts* after their gods

TURN BACK MY WRATH (NIV)
(See *TURN AWAY ITS PUNISHMENT*)

TURN FROM THEIR SIN
1Kin 8:35 When the heavens are shut up and there is no rain because they have sinned against You, when they pray toward this place and confess Your name, and *turn from their sin* because You afflict them
2Chr 6:26 When heaven is shut up and there is no rain because they have sinned against You, when they pray toward this place and confess Your name, and *turn from their sin* because You afflict them

TURN NEITHER TO THE RIGHT NOR TO THE LEFT
Deut 2:27 I will keep strictly to the road, and I will *turn neither to the right nor to the left*

TURN NOT TO THE RIGHT HAND NOR TO THE LEFT (KJV)
(See *TURN TO THE RIGHT OR THE LEFT*)

TURN THE HEARTS OF THE FATHERS
Mal 4:6 And he will *turn the hearts of the fathers* to the children, and the hearts of the children to their fathers, lest I come and strike the earth with a curse
Luke 1:17 He will also go before Him in the spirit and power of Elijah, 'to *turn the hearts of the fathers* to the children

TURN TO GOD IN REPENTANCE (NIV)
(See *REPENTANCE TOWARD GOD*)

TURN TO OTHER GODS
Deut 31:20 When I have brought them to the land flowing with milk and honey, of which I swore to their fathers, and they have eaten and filled themselves and grown fat, then they will *turn to other gods* and serve them

TURN TO THE LORD
Deut 4:30 When you are in distress, and all these things come upon you in the latter days, when you *turn to the Lord* your God and obey His voice
Deut 30:10 if you obey the voice of the Lord your God, to keep His commandments and His statutes which are written in this Book of the Law, and if you *turn to the Lord* your God with all your heart and with all your soul
Ps 22:27 All the ends of the world shall remember and *turn to the Lord*, and all the families of the nations shall worship before You

TURN TO THE RIGHT OR THE LEFT
Prov 4:27 Do not *turn to the right or the left;* remove your foot from evil

TURN YOUR EAR (NIV)
(See *BOW DOWN YOUR EAR*)

TURN YOUR FACE TOWARD (NIV)
(See *SET YOUR FACE AGAINST*)

TURN YOUR HEARTS (NIV)
(See *TURN AWAY YOUR HEARTS*)

TURNED HIS HEART AFTER OTHER GODS
1Kin 11:4 For it was so, when Solomon was old, that his wives *turned his heart after other gods*

TURNED TO THE LORD
2Kin 23:25 Now before him there was no king like him, who *turned to the Lord* with all his heart, with all his soul, and with all his might, according to all the Law of Moses
2Chr 15:4 but when in their trouble they *turned to the Lord* God of Israel, and sought Him, He was found by them
Acts 9:35 So all who dwelt at Lydda and Sharon saw him and *turned to the Lord*
Acts 11:21 And the hand of the Lord was with them, and a great number believed and *turned to the Lord*

TWAIN SHALL BE ONE FLESH (KJV)
(See *TWO SHALL BECOME ONE FLESH*)

TWELVE APOSTLES
Matt 10:2 Now the names of the *twelve apostles* are these: first, Simon, who is called Peter, and Andrew his brother
Luke 22:14 And when the hour had come, He sat down, and the *twelve apostles* with Him
Rev 21:14 Now the wall of the city had twelve foundations, and on them were the names of the *twelve apostles* of the Lamb

TWELVE DISCIPLES
Matt 10:1 And when He had called His *twelve disciples* to Him, He gave them power over unclean spirits, to cast them out, and to heal all kinds of sickness and all kinds of disease
Matt 11:1 Now it came to pass, when Jesus finished commanding His *twelve disciples*, that He departed from there to teach and to preach in their cities
Matt 20:17 Then Jesus, going up to Jerusalem, took the *twelve disciples* aside on the road and said to them
Luke 9:1 Then He called His *twelve disciples* together and gave them power and authority over all demons, and to cure diseases

TWELVE HOURS IN THE DAY
John 11:9 Jesus answered, "Are there not *twelve hours in the day*

TWELVE THOUSAND
Num 31:5 So there were recruited from the divisions of Israel one thousand from each tribe, *twelve thousand* armed for war
Josh 8:25 So it was that all who fell that day, both men and women, were *twelve thousand* all the people of Ai
Judg 21:10 So the congregation sent out there *twelve thousand* of their most valiant men, and commanded them, saying
2Sam 10:6 and from King Maacah one thousand men, and from Ish-Tob *twelve thousand* men
2Sam 17:1 Moreover Ahithophel said to Absalom, "Now let me choose *twelve thousand* men, and I will arise and pursue David tonight
1Kin 4:26 Solomon had forty thousand stalls of horses for his chariots, and *twelve thousand* horsemen
1Kin 10:26 he had one thousand four hundred chariots and *twelve thousand* horsemen, whom he stationed in the chariot cities and with the king in Jerusalem
2Chr 1:14 he had one thousand four hundred chariots and *twelve thousand* horsemen, whom he stationed in the chariot cities and with the king in Jerusalem
2Chr 9:25 Solomon had four thousand stalls for horses and chariots, and *twelve thousand* horsemen whom he stationed in the chariot cities and with the king at Jerusalem
Rev 7:5 of the tribe of Judah *twelve thousand* were sealed; of the tribe of Reuben *twelve thousand* were sealed; of the tribe of Gad *twelve thousand* were sealed
Rev 7:6 of the tribe of Asher *twelve thousand* were sealed; of the tribe of Naphtali *twelve thousand* were sealed; of the tribe of Manasseh *twelve thousand* were sealed
Rev 7:7 of the tribe of Simeon *twelve thousand* were sealed; of the tribe of Levi *twelve thousand* were sealed; of the tribe of Issachar *twelve thousand* were sealed
Rev 7:8 of the tribe of Zebulun *twelve thousand* were sealed; of the tribe of Joseph *twelve thousand* were sealed; of the tribe of Benjamin *twelve thousand* were sealed
Rev 21:16 *twelve thousand* furlongs. Its length, breadth, and height are equal

TWELVE TRIBES
Gen 49:28 All these are the *twelve tribes* of Israel, and this is what their father spoke to them
Ex 24:4 And he rose early in the morning, and built an altar at the foot of the mountain, and twelve pillars according to the *twelve tribes* of Israel
Ex 28:21 And the stones shall have the names of the sons of Israel, twelve according to their names, like the engravings of a signet, each one with its own name; they shall be according to the *twelve tribes*
Ex 39:14 according to their names, engraved like a signet, each one with its own name according to the *twelve tribes*
Ezek 47:13 These are the borders by which you shall divide the land as an inheritance among the *twelve tribes* of Israel
Matt 19:28 So Jesus said to them, "Assuredly I say to you, that in the regeneration, when the Son of Man sits on the throne of His glory, you who have followed Me will also sit on twelve thrones, judging the *twelve tribes* of Israel
Luke 22:30 that you may eat and drink at My table in My kingdom, and sit on thrones judging the *twelve tribes* of Israel
Acts 26:7 To this promise our *twelve tribes*, earnestly serving God night and day, hope to attain
Jas 1:1 James, a servant of God and of the Lord Jesus Christ, to the *twelve tribes* which are scattered abroad
Rev 21:12 Also she had a great and high wall with twelve gates, and twelve angels at the gates, and names written on them, which are the names of the *twelve tribes* of the children of Israel

TWENTY-FOUR ELDERS
Rev 4:4 Around the throne were twenty-four thrones, and on the thrones I saw *twenty-four elders* sitting, clothed in white robes
Rev 4:10 the *twenty-four elders* fall down before Him who sits on the throne and worship Him who lives forever and ever, and cast their crowns before the throne, saying
Rev 5:8 Now when He had taken the scroll, the four living creatures and the *twenty-four elders* fell down before the Lamb, each having a harp, and golden bowls full of incense, which are the prayers of the saints
Rev 5:14 And the *twenty-four elders* fell down and worshiped Him who lives forever and ever
Rev 11:16 And the *twenty-four elders* who sat before God on their thrones fell on their faces and worshiped God
Rev 19:4 And the *twenty-four elders* and the four living creatures fell down and worshiped God who sat on the throne, saying

TWICE DEAD
Jude 12 late autumn trees without fruit, *twice dead*, pulled up by the roots

TWINKLING OF AN EYE
1Cor 15:52 in a moment, in the *twinkling of an eye*, at the last trumpet

TWO BY TWO
Gen 7:9 *two by two* they went into the ark to Noah, male and female, as God had commanded Noah
Gen 7:15 And they went into the ark to Noah, *two by two*, of all flesh in which is the breath of life
1Chr 26:17 On the east were six Levites, on the north four each day, on the south four each day, and for the storehouse *two by two*
Mark 6:7 And He called the twelve to Him, and began to send them out *two by two*, and gave them power over unclean spirits
Luke 10:1 After these things the Lord appointed seventy others also, and sent them *two by two* before His face into every city and place where He Himself was about to go

TWO COPPER COINS (RSV)
(See *TWO MITES*)

TWO MITES
Mark 12:42 Then one poor widow came and threw in *two mites*, which make a quadrans
Luke 21:2 and He saw also a certain poor widow putting in *two mites*

TWO SHALL BECOME ONE FLESH
Matt 19:5 and said, 'For this reason a man shall leave his father and mother and be joined to his wife, and the *two shall become one flesh*
Mark 10:8 and the *two shall become one flesh*'; so then they are no longer two, but one flesh
Eph 5:31 For this reason a man shall leave his father and mother and be joined to his wife, and the *two shall become one flesh*

TWO TABLETS
Ex 31:18 And when He had made an end of speaking with him on Mount Sinai, He gave Moses *two tablets* of the Testimony, tablets of stone, written with the finger of God
Ex 32:15 And Moses turned and went down from the mountain, and the *two tablets* of the Testimony were in his hand
Ex 34:1 And the Lord said to Moses, "Cut *two tablets* of stone like the first ones, and I will write on these tablets the words that were on the first tablets which you broke
Ex 34:4 So he cut *two tablets* of stone like the first ones. Then Moses rose early in the morning and went up Mount Sinai, as the Lord had commanded him; and he took in his hand the *two tablets* of stone
Ex 34:29 Now it was so, when Moses came down from Mount Sinai (and the *two tablets* of the Testimony were in Moses' hand when he came down from the mountain
Deut 4:13 So He declared to you His covenant which He commanded you to perform, that is, the Ten Commandments; and He wrote them on *two tablets* of stone
Deut 5:22 And He wrote them on *two tablets* of stone and gave them to me
Deut 9:10 Then the Lord delivered to me *two tablets* of stone written with the finger of God, and on them were all the words which the Lord had spoken to you on the mountain from the midst of the fire in the day of the assembly
Deut 9:11 And it came to pass, at the end of forty days and forty nights, that the Lord gave me the *two tablets* of stone, the tablets of the covenant
Deut 9:15 and the *two tablets* of the covenant were in my two hands
Deut 9:17 Then I took the *two tablets* and threw them out of my two hands and broke them before your eyes
Deut 10:1 At that time the Lord said to me, 'Hew for yourself *two tablets* of stone like the first, and come up to Me on the mountain and make yourself an ark of wood
Deut 10:3 So I made an ark of acacia wood, hewed *two tablets* of stone like the first, and went up the mountain, having the *two tablets* in my hand
1Kin 8:9 There was nothing in the ark except the *two tablets* of stone which Moses put there at Horeb, when the Lord made a covenant with the children of Israel, when they came out of the land of Egypt
2Chr 5:10 There was nothing in the ark except the *two tablets* which Moses put there at Horeb, when the Lord made a covenant with the children of Israel, when they had come out of Egypt

TWO VERY SMALL COPPER COINS (NIV)
(See *TWO MITES*)

TWO-EDGED SWORD
Ps 149:6 Let the high praises of God be in their mouth, and a *two-edged sword* in their hand
Prov 5:4 but in the end she is bitter as wormwood, sharp as a *two-edged sword*
Heb 4:12 For the word of God is living and powerful, and sharper than any *two-edged sword*, piercing even to the division of soul and spirit, and of joints and marrow, and is a discerner of the thoughts and intents of the heart
Rev 1:16 He had in His right hand seven stars, out of His mouth went a sharp *two-edged sword*, and His countenance was like the sun shining in its strength
Rev 2:12 And to the angel of the church in Pergamos write, 'These things says He who has the sharp *two-edged sword*

U

UNCHANGEABLE PRIESTHOOD
Heb 7:24 But He, because He continues forever, has an *unchangeable priesthood*

UNCIRCUMCISED HEARTS
Lev 26:41 if their *uncircumcised hearts* are humbled, and they accept their guilt

UNCIRCUMCISED IN
Ezek 44:7 When you brought in foreigners, *uncircumcised in heart* and uncircumcised in flesh, to be in My sanctuary to defile it My house and when you offered My food, the fat and the blood, then they broke My covenant because of all your abominations
Ezek 44:9 No foreigner, *uncircumcised in heart* or uncircumcised in flesh, shall enter My sanctuary, including any foreigner who is among the children of Israel
Acts 7:51 You stiffnecked and *uncircumcised in heart* and ears! You always resist the Holy Spirit

UNCIRCUMCISED IN THE HEART
Jer 9:26 For all these nations are uncircumcised, and all the house of Israel are *uncircumcised in the heart*

UNCIRCUMCISED LIPS
Ex 6:12 How then shall Pharaoh heed me, for I am of *uncircumcised lips*
Ex 6:30 But Moses said before the Lord, "Behold, I am of *uncircumcised lips*, and how shall Pharaoh heed me

UNCIRCUMCISED PHILISTINES
Judg 14:3 Then his father and mother said to him, "Is there no woman among the daughters of your brethren, or among all my people, that you must go and get a wife from the *uncircumcised Philistines*

UNCLEAN AND CLEAN
Lev 10:10 that you may distinguish between holy and unholy, and between *unclean and clean*

UNCLEAN AND THE CLEAN
Lev 11:47 To distinguish between the *unclean and the clean*, and between the animal that may be eaten and the animal that may not be eaten
Deut 12:15 the *unclean and the clean* may eat of it, of the gazelle and the deer alike
Deut 12:22 Just as the gazelle and the deer are eaten, so you may eat them; the *unclean and the clean* alike may eat them
Deut 15:22 the *unclean and the clean* person alike may eat it, as if it were a gazelle or a deer
Ezek 22:26 they have not distinguished between the holy and unholy, nor have they made known the difference between the *unclean and the clean*
Ezek 44:23 And they shall teach My people the difference between the holy and the unholy, and cause them to discern between the *unclean and the clean*

UNCLEAN SPIRIT
Zech 13:2 I will also cause the prophets and the *unclean spirit* to depart from the land
Matt 12:43 When an *unclean spirit* goes out of a man, he goes through dry places, seeking rest, and finds none
Mark 1:23 Now there was a man in their synagogue with an *unclean spirit*
Mark 1:26 And when the *unclean spirit* had convulsed him and cried out with a loud voice, he came out of him
Mark 3:30 because they said, "He has an *unclean spirit*
Mark 5:2 And when He had come out of the boat, immediately there met Him out of the tombs a man with an *unclean spirit*
Mark 5:8 For He said to him, "Come out of the man, *unclean spirit*
Mark 7:25 For a woman whose young daughter had an *unclean spirit* heard about Him, and she came and fell at His feet
Mark 9:25 When Jesus saw that the people came running together, He rebuked the *unclean spirit*, saying to him
Luke 8:29 For He had commanded the *unclean spirit* to come out of the man
Luke 9:42 Then Jesus rebuked the *unclean spirit*, healed the child, and gave him back to his father
Luke 11:24 When an *unclean spirit* goes out of a man, he goes through dry places, seeking rest

UNCLEAN SPIRITS
Matt 10:1 And when He had called His twelve disciples to Him, He gave them power over *unclean spirits*, to cast them out, and to heal all kinds of sickness and all kinds of disease
Mark 1:27 For with authority He commands even the *unclean spirits*, and they obey Him
Mark 3:11 And the *unclean spirits*, whenever they saw Him, fell down before Him and cried out, saying
Mark 5:13 Then the *unclean spirits* went out and entered the swine (there were about two thousand
Mark 6:7 And He called the twelve to Him, and began to send them out two by two, and gave them power over *unclean spirits*
Luke 4:36 For with authority and power He commands the *unclean spirits*, and they come out
Luke 6:18 as well as those who were tormented with *unclean spirits*
Acts 5:16 Also a multitude gathered from the surrounding cities to Jerusalem, bringing sick people and those who were tormented by *unclean spirits*, and they were all healed
Acts 8:7 For *unclean spirits*, crying with a loud voice, came out of many who were possessed
Rev 16:13 And I saw three *unclean spirits* like frogs coming out of the mouth of the dragon, out of the mouth of the beast, and out of the mouth of the false prophet

UNCLEAN TO YOU
Lev 11:4 the camel, because it chews the cud but does not have cloven hooves, is *unclean to you*
Lev 11:5 the rock hyrax, because it chews the cud but does not have cloven hooves, is *unclean to you*
Lev 11:6 the hare, because it chews the cud but does not have cloven hooves, is *unclean to you*
Lev 11:7 and the swine, though it divides the hoof, having cloven hooves, yet does not chew the cud, is *unclean to you*
Lev 11:8 Their flesh you shall not eat, and their carcasses you shall not touch. They are *unclean to you*
Lev 11:26 The carcass of any beast which divides the foot, but is not cloven-hoofed or does not chew the cud, is *unclean to you*
Lev 11:27 And whatever goes on its paws, among all kinds of animals that go on all fours, those are *unclean to you*
Lev 11:28 Whoever carries any such carcass shall wash his clothes and be unclean until evening. It is *unclean to you*
Lev 11:29 These also shall be *unclean to you* among the creeping things that creep on the earth
Lev 11:31 These are *unclean to you* among all that creep. Whoever touches them when they are dead shall be unclean until evening
Lev 11:35 for they are unclean, and shall be *unclean to you*
Lev 11:38 But if any water is put on the seed, and if a part of any such carcass falls on it, it becomes *unclean to you*

UNCOVER HER NAKEDNESS
Lev 18:7 She is your mother; you shall not *uncover her nakedness*
Lev 18:11 The nakedness of your father's wife's daughter, begotten by your father she is your sister you shall not *uncover her nakedness*
Lev 18:15 You shall not uncover the nakedness of your daughter-in-law she is your son's wife you shall not *uncover her nakedness*
Lev 18:17 You shall not uncover the nakedness of a woman and her daughter, nor shall you take her son's daughter or her daughter's daughter, to *uncover her nakedness*
Lev 18:18 Nor shall you take a woman as a rival to her sister, to *uncover her nakedness* while the other is alive
Lev 18:19 Also you shall not approach a woman to *uncover her nakedness* as long as she is in her customary impurity

UNCOVER HIS NAKEDNESS
Lev 18:6 None of you shall approach anyone who is near of kin to him, to *uncover his nakedness*

UNDEFILED RELIGION BEFORE GOD
Jas 1:27 Pure and *undefiled religion before God* and the Father is this

UNDER EVERY GREEN TREE
Deut 12:2 You shall utterly destroy all the places where the nations which you shall dispossess served their gods, on the high mountains and on the hills and *under every green tree*
1Kin 14:23 For they also built for themselves high places, sacred pillars, and wooden images on every high hill and *under every green tree*
2Kin 16:4 And he sacrificed and burned incense on the high places, on the hills, and *under every green tree*
2Kin 17:10 They set up for themselves sacred pillars and wooden images on every high hill and *under every green tree*
2Chr 28:4 And he sacrificed and burned incense on the high places, on the hills, and *under every green tree*
Is 57:5 inflaming yourselves with gods *under every green tree*, slaying the children in the valleys, under the clefts of the rocks
Jer 2:20 and you said, 'I will not transgress,' when on every high hill and *under every green tree* you lay down, playing the harlot
Jer 3:6 She has gone up on every high mountain and *under every green tree*, and there played the harlot
Jer 3:13 Only acknowledge your iniquity, that you have transgressed against the Lord your God, and have scattered your charms to alien deities *under every green tree*, and you have not obeyed My voice
Ezek 6:13 Then you shall know that I am the Lord, when their slain men are among their idols all around their altars, on every high hill, on all the mountaintops, *under every green tree*, and under every thick oak, wherever they offered sweet incense to all their idols

UNDER EVERY SPREADING TREE (NIV)
(See *UNDER EVERY GREEN TREE*)

UNDER GAMALIEL (NAS, NIV)
(See *AT THE FEET OF GAMALIEL*)

UNDER GRACE
Rom 6:14 For sin shall not have dominion over you, for you are not under law but *under grace*
Rom 6:15 Shall we sin because we are not under law but *under grace*

UNDER HIS FEET
Ex 24:10 And there was *under His feet* as it were a paved work of sapphire stone, and it was like the very heavens in its clarity
2Sam 22:10 He bowed the heavens also, and came down with darkness *under His feet*
Ps 8:6 You have made him to have dominion over the works of Your hands; You have put all things *under his feet*
Ps 18:9 He bowed the heavens also, and came down with darkness *under His feet*
Lam 3:34 To crush *under His feet* all the prisoners of the earth
1Cor 15:25 For He must reign till He has put all enemies *under His feet*
1Cor 15:27 For "He has put all things *under His feet*." But when He says
Eph 1:22 And He put all things *under His feet*, and gave Him to be head over all things to the church
Heb 2:8 You have put all things in subjection *under his feet*

UNDER HIS FIG TREE
Mic 4:4 But everyone shall sit under his vine and *under his fig tree*, and no one shall make them afraid
Zech 3:10 In that day,' says the Lord of hosts, 'Everyone will invite his neighbor under his vine and *under his fig tree*

UNDER HIS WINGS
Ps 91:4 He shall cover you with His feathers, and *under His wings* you shall take refuge

UNDER LAW
Rom 6:14 For sin shall not have dominion over you, for you are not *under law* but under grace
Rom 6:15 Shall we sin because we are not *under law* but under grace
1Cor 9:21 to those who are without law, as without law (not being without law toward God, but *under law* toward Christ

UNDER THE EYE OF THE LORD (RSV)
(See *LORD BE WITH YOU*)

UNDER THE HILL (KJV)
(See *FOOT OF THE MOUNTAIN*)

UNDER THE LAW
Rom 3:19 Now we know that whatever the law says, it says to those who are *under the law*, that every mouth may be stopped, and all the world may become guilty before God
1Cor 9:20 to those who are *under the law*, as *under the law*, that I might win those who are *under the law*
Gal 4:4 But when the fullness of the time had come, God sent forth His Son, born of a woman, born *under the law*
Gal 4:5 to redeem those who were *under the law*, that we might receive the adoption as sons
Gal 4:21 Tell me, you who desire to be *under the law*, do you not hear the law
Gal 5:18 But if you are led by the Spirit, you are not *under the law*

UNDER THE POWER OF THE DEVIL (NIV)
(See *OPPRESSED BY THE DEVIL*)

UNDER THE SUN
Eccl 1:3 What profit has a man from all his labor in which he toils *under the sun*
Eccl 1:9 That which has been is what will be, that which is done is what will be done, and there is nothing new *under the sun*
Eccl 1:14 I have seen all the works that are done *under the sun*
Eccl 2:11 and indeed all was vanity and grasping for the wind. there was no profit *under the sun*
Eccl 2:17 Therefore I hated life because the work that was done *under the sun* was grievous to me, for all is vanity and grasping for the wind
Eccl 2:18 Then I hated all my labor in which I had toiled *under the sun*, because I must leave it to the man who will come after me
Eccl 2:19 Yet he will rule over all my labor in which I toiled and in which I have shown myself wise *under the sun*
Eccl 2:20 Therefore I turned my heart and despaired of all the labor in which I had toiled *under the sun*
Eccl 2:22 For what has man for all his labor, and for the striving of his heart with which he has toiled *under the sun*
Eccl 3:16 Moreover I saw *under the sun:* In the place of judgment, wickedness was there
Eccl 4:1 Then I returned and considered all the oppression that is done *under the sun*
Eccl 4:3 Yet, better than both is he who has never existed, who has not seen the evil work that is done *under the sun*
Eccl 4:7 Then I returned, and I saw vanity *under the sun*

Eccl 4:15 I saw all the living who walk *under the sun*
Eccl 5:13 There is a severe evil which I have seen *under the sun*
Eccl 5:18 It is good and fitting for one to eat and drink, and to enjoy the good of all his labor in which he toils *under the sun* all the days of his life which God gives him
Eccl 6:1 There is an evil which I have seen *under the sun*, and it is common among men
Eccl 6:12 Who can tell a man what will happen after him *under the sun*
Eccl 8:9 All this I have seen, and applied my heart to every work that is done *under the sun*
Eccl 8:15 So I commended enjoyment, because a man has nothing better *under the sun* than to eat, drink, and be merry; for this will remain with him in his labor for the days of his life which God gives him *under the sun*
Eccl 8:17 then I saw all the work of God, that a man cannot find out the work that is done *under the sun*
Eccl 9:3 This is an evil in all that is done *under the sun*
Eccl 9:6 nevermore will they have a share in anything done *under the sun*
Eccl 9:9 Live joyfully with the wife whom you love all the days of your vain life which He has given you *under the sun*, all your days of vanity; for that is your portion in life, and in the labor which you perform *under the sun*
Eccl 9:11 I returned and saw *under the sun* that The race is not to the swift, nor the battle to the strong, nor bread to the wise, nor riches to men of understanding, nor favor to men of skill
Eccl 9:13 This wisdom I have also seen *under the sun*, and it seemed great to me
Eccl 10:5 There is an evil I have seen *under the sun*, as an error proceeding from the ruler

UNDERNEATH ARE THE EVERLASTING ARMS
Deut 33:27 The eternal God is your refuge, and *underneath are the everlasting arms*

UNDERSTANDING OF THE SERVICE OF THE LORD (NIV)
(See *KNOWLEDGE OF THE LORD*)

UNEQUALLY YOKED
2Cor 6:14 Do not be *unequally yoked* together with unbelievers. For what fellowship has righteousness with lawlessness

UNFAILING KINDNESS LIKE THAT OF THE LORD (NIV)
(See *KINDNESS OF THE LORD*)

UNFAITHFUL TO THE LORD
2Chr 28:19 For the Lord brought Judah low because of Ahaz king of Israel, for he had encouraged moral decline in Judah and had been continually *unfaithful to the Lord*
2Chr 28:22 Now in the time of his distress King Ahaz became increasingly *unfaithful to the Lord*

UNFRUITFUL WORKS OF DARKNESS
Eph 5:11 And have no fellowship with the *unfruitful works of darkness*, but rather expose them

UNINTENTIONALLY FAIL (NIV)
(See *SIN UNINTENTIONALLY*)

UNITED IN LOVE (NIV)
(See *KNIT TOGETHER IN LOVE*)

UNITED TOGETHER IN THE LIKENESS OF
Rom 6:5 For if we have been *united together in the likeness of* His death, certainly we also shall be in the likeness of His resurrection

UNITED WITH HIM IN HIS DEATH (NIV)
(See *LIKENESS OF HIS DEATH*)

UNITED WITH HIM IN A RESURRECTION (RSV)
(See *LIKENESS OF HIS RESURRECTION*)

UNITY OF THE FAITH
Eph 4:13 till we all come to the *unity of the faith* and the knowledge of the Son of God, to a perfect man, to the measure of the stature of the fullness of Christ

UNJUST STEWARD
Luke 16:8 So the master commended the *unjust steward* because he had dealt shrewdly

UNKNOWN GOD
Acts 17:23 to the *unknown God*. Therefore, the One whom you worship without knowing, Him I proclaim to you

UNLEAVENED BREAD
Gen 19:3 Then he made them a feast, and baked *unleavened bread*, and they ate
Ex 12:8 roasted in fire, with *unleavened bread* and with bitter herbs they shall eat it
Ex 12:15 Seven days you shall eat *unleavened bread*. On the first day you shall remove leaven from your houses
Ex 12:17 So you shall observe the Feast of *Unleavened Bread*, for on this same day I will have brought your armies out of the land of Egypt
Ex 12:18 In the first month, on the fourteenth day of the month at evening, you shall eat *unleavened bread*, until the twenty-first day of the month at evening
Ex 12:20 You shall eat nothing leavened; in all your dwellings you shall eat *unleavened bread*
Ex 13:6 Seven days you shall eat *unleavened bread*, and on the seventh day there shall be a feast to the Lord
Ex 13:7 *Unleavened bread* shall be eaten seven days. And no leavened bread shall be seen among you, nor shall leaven be seen among you in all your quarters
Ex 23:15 You shall keep the Feast of *Unleavened Bread* (you shall eat *unleavened bread* seven days, as I commanded you, at the time appointed in the month of Abib, for in it you came out of Egypt
Ex 29:2 and *unleavened bread*, unleavened cakes mixed with oil, and unleavened wafers anointed with oil (you shall make them of wheat flour
Ex 29:23 one loaf of bread, one cake made with oil, and one wafer from the basket of the *unleavened bread* that is before the Lord
Ex 34:18 The Feast of *Unleavened Bread* you shall keep. Seven days you shall eat *unleavened bread*, as I commanded you, in the appointed time of the month of Abib
Lev 6:16 with *unleavened bread* it shall be eaten in a holy place
Lev 8:2 Take Aaron and his sons with him, and the garments, the anointing oil, a bull as the sin offering, two rams, and a basket of *unleavened bread*
Lev 8:26 and from the basket of *unleavened bread* that was before the Lord he took one unleavened cake, a cake of bread anointed with oil, and one wafer, and put them on the fat and on the right thigh
Lev 23:6 And on the fifteenth day of the same month is the Feast of *Unleavened Bread* to the Lord; seven days you must eat *unleavened bread*
Num 6:15 a basket of *unleavened bread*, cakes of fine flour mixed with oil, unleavened wafers anointed with oil, and their grain offering with their drink offerings

Num 6:17 and he shall offer the ram as a sacrifice of peace offering to the Lord, with the basket of *unleavened bread*
Num 9:11 They shall eat it with *unleavened bread* and bitter herbs
Num 28:17 And on the fifteenth day of this month is the feast; *unleavened bread* shall be eaten for seven days
Deut 16:3 seven days you shall eat *unleavened bread* with it, that is, the bread of affliction (for you came out of the land of Egypt in haste
Deut 16:8 Six days you shall eat *unleavened bread*, and on the seventh day there shall be a sacred assembly to the Lord your God
Deut 16:16 at the Feast of *Unleavened Bread*, at the Feast of Weeks, and at the Feast of Tabernacles
Josh 5:11 And they ate of the produce of the land on the day after the Passover, *unleavened bread* and parched grain on the very same day
Judg 6:19 Then Gideon went in and prepared a young goat, and *unleavened bread* from an ephah of flour
Judg 6:20 The Angel of God said to him, "Take the meat and the *unleavened bread* and lay them on this rock, and pour out the broth
Judg 6:21 Then the Angel of the Lord put out the end of the staff that was in His hand, and touched the meat and the *unleavened bread;* and fire rose out of the rock and consumed the meat and the *unleavened bread*
1Sam 28:24 And she took flour and kneaded it, and baked *unleavened bread* from it
2Kin 23:9 Nevertheless the priests of the high places did not come up to the altar of the Lord in Jerusalem, but they ate *unleavened bread* among their brethren
2Chr 8:13 according to the daily rate, offering according to the commandment of Moses, for the Sabbaths, the New Moons, and the three appointed yearly feasts the Feast of *Unleavened Bread*, the Feast of Weeks, and the Feast of Tabernacles
2Chr 30:13 Now many people, a very great congregation, assembled at Jerusalem to keep the Feast of *Unleavened Bread* in the second month
2Chr 30:21 So the children of Israel who were present at Jerusalem kept the Feast of *Unleavened Bread* seven days with great gladness
2Chr 35:17 And the children of Israel who were present kept the Passover at that time, and the Feast of *Unleavened Bread* for seven days
Ezra 6:22 And they kept the Feast of *Unleavened Bread* seven days with joy
Ezek 45:21 In the first month, on the fourteenth day of the month, you shall observe the Passover, a feast of seven days; *unleavened bread* shall be eaten
Matt 26:17 Now on the first day of the Feast of the *Unleavened Bread* the disciples came to Jesus, saying to Him
Mark 14:1 After two days it was the Passover and the Feast of *Unleavened Bread*
Mark 14:12 Now on the first day of *Unleavened Bread*, when they killed the Passover lamb, His disciples said to Him
Luke 22:1 Now the Feast of *Unleavened Bread* drew near, which is called Passover
Luke 22:7 Then came the Day of *Unleavened Bread*, when the Passover must be killed
Acts 12:3 And because he saw that it pleased the Jews, he proceeded further to seize Peter also. Now it was during the Days of *Unleavened Bread*
Acts 20:6 But we sailed away from Philippi after the Days of *Unleavened Bread*, and in five days joined them at Troas, where we stayed seven days
1Cor 5:8 Therefore let us keep the feast, not with old leaven, nor with the leaven of malice and wickedness, but with the *unleavened bread* of sincerity and truth

UNLESS A GRAIN OF WHEAT FALLS
John 12:24 Most assuredly, I say to you, *unless a grain of wheat falls* into the ground and dies, it remains alone

UNLESS THE LORD BUILDS THE HOUSE
Ps 127:1 *Unless the Lord builds the house*, they labor in vain who build it

UNLESS YOU ARE CONVERTED
Matt 18:3 and said, "Assuredly, I say to you, *unless you are converted* and become as little children, you will by no means enter the kingdom of heaven

UNLESS YOU CHANGE (NIV)
(See *UNLESS YOU ARE CONVERTED*)

UNLESS YOU REPENT
Luke 13:3 I tell you, no; but *unless you repent* you will all likewise perish
Luke 13:5 I tell you, no; but *unless you repent* you will all likewise perish
Rev 2:5 repent and do the first works, or else I will come to you quickly and remove your lampstand from its place *unless you repent*

UNLESS YOU TURN (RSV)
(See *UNLESS YOU ARE CONVERTED*)

UNPROFITABLE SERVANTS
Luke 17:10 So likewise you, when you have done all those things which you are commanded, say, 'We are *unprofitable servants*

UNQUENCHABLE FIRE
Matt 3:12 but He will burn up the chaff with *unquenchable fire*
Luke 3:17 His winnowing fan is in His hand, and He will thoroughly purge His threshing floor, and gather the wheat into His barn; but the chaff He will burn with *unquenchable fire*

UNRELIABLE STREAM
Jer 15:18 Will You surely be to me like an *unreliable stream*, as waters that fail

UNRIGHTEOUS MAMMON
Luke 16:9 And I say to you, make friends for yourselves by *unrighteous mammon*, that when you fail, they may receive you into everlasting habitations
Luke 16:11 Therefore if you have not been faithful in the *unrighteous mammon*, who will commit to your trust the true riches

UNSHEATH THE SWORD (RSV)
(See *DRAW OUT A SWORD AFTER THEM*)

UNSPOTTED FROM THE WORLD
Jas 1:27 to visit orphans and widows in their trouble, and to keep oneself *unspotted from the world*

UNSTAINED FROM THE WORLD (RSV)
(See *UNSPOTTED FROM THE WORLD*)

UNTIL THIS DAY
Josh 13:13 Nevertheless the children of Israel did not drive out the Geshurites or the Maachathites, but the Geshurites and the Maachathites dwell among the Israelites *until this day*
Josh 22:17 Is the iniquity of Peor not enough for us, from which we are not cleansed *until this day*,

although there was a plague in the congregation of the Lord
Judg 19:30 And so it was that all who saw it said, "No such deed has been done or seen from the day that the children of Israel came up from the land of Egypt *until this day*
2Sam 4:3 because the Beerothites fled to Gittaim and have been sojourners there *until this day*
2Kin 20:17 Behold, the days are coming when all that is in your house, and what your fathers have accumulated *until this day*, shall be carried to Babylon
2Chr 20:26 therefore the name of that place was called The Valley of Berachah *until this day*
Neh 9:32 do not let all the trouble seem small before You that has come upon us, our kings and our princes, our priests and our prophets, our fathers and on all Your people, from the days of the kings of Assyria *until this day*
Is 39:6 Behold, the days are coming when all that is in your house, and what your fathers have accumulated *until this day*, shall be carried to Babylon
Jer 7:25 Since the day that your fathers came out of the land of Egypt *until this day*, I have even sent to you all My servants the prophets, daily rising up early and sending them
Jer 11:7 For I earnestly exhorted your fathers in the day that I brought them up out of the land of Egypt, *until this day*, rising early and exhorting, saying
Matt 11:23 for if the mighty works which were done in you had been done in Sodom, it would have remained *until this day*
Matt 28:15 and this saying is commonly reported among the Jews *until this day*
Acts 23:1 Then Paul, looking earnestly at the council, said, "Men and brethren, I have lived in all good conscience before God *until this day*
2Cor 3:14 For *until this day* the same veil remains unlifted in the reading of the Old Testament, because the veil is taken away in Christ

UNTIMELY BORN (NAS, RSV)
(See *BORN OUT OF DUE TIME*)

UNTO THE DEATH (KJV)
(See *POINT OF DEATH*)

UNTO US A CHILD IS BORN
Is 9:6 For *unto us a Child is born*, unto us a Son is given

UNUTTERABLE AND EXALTED JOY (RSV)
(See *JOY INEXPRESSIBLE*)

UNWASHED HANDS
Matt 15:20 These are the things which defile a man, but to eat with *unwashed hands* does not defile a man
Mark 7:2 Now when they saw some of His disciples eat bread with defiled, that is, with *unwashed hands*, they found fault
Mark 7:5 Then the Pharisees and scribes asked Him, "Why do Your disciples not walk according to the tradition of the elders, but eat bread with *unwashed hands*

UNWORTHY SERVANTS (NIV, RSV)
(See *UNPROFITABLE SERVANTS*)

UP TO HALF MY KINGDOM
Esth 5:3 It shall be given to you *up to half my kingdom*
Esth 5:6 What is your request, *up to half my kingdom*? It shall be done
Esth 7:2 And what is your request, *up to half my kingdom*

UPHOLDING ALL THINGS
Heb 1:3 who being the brightness of His glory and the express image of His person, and *upholding all things* by the word of His power, when He had by Himself purged our sins, sat down at the right hand of the Majesty on high

UPHOLDING THE UNIVERSE (RSV)
(See *UPHOLDING ALL THINGS*)

UPHOLDS THE WIDOW AND FATHERLESS (RSV)
(See *RELIEVES THE FATHERLESS AND WIDOW*)

UPON ZION
Is 33:20 Look *upon Zion*, the city of our appointed feasts; your eyes will see Jerusalem, a quiet habitation, a tabernacle that will not be taken down
Mic 4:11 Now also many nations have gathered against you, who say, "Let her be defiled, and let our eye look *upon Zion*

UPPER ROOM
Judg 3:23 Then Ehud went out through the porch and shut the doors of the *upper room* behind him and locked them
Judg 3:24 When he had gone out, Eglon's servants came to look, and to their surprise, the doors of the *upper room* were locked
Judg 3:25 So they waited till they were embarrassed, and still he had not opened the doors of the *upper room*
1Kin 17:19 So he took him out of her arms and carried him to the *upper room* where he was staying, and laid him on his own bed
1Kin 17:23 And Elijah took the child and brought him down from the *upper room* into the house, and gave him to his mother
2Kin 1:2 Now Ahaziah fell through the lattice of his *upper room* in Samaria, and was injured
2Kin 4:10 Please, let us make a small *upper room* on the wall
2Kin 4:11 And it happened one day that he came there, and he turned in to the *upper room* and lay down there
Neh 3:31 After him Malchijah, one of the goldsmiths, made repairs as far as the house of the Nethinim and of the merchants, in front of the Miphkad Gate, and as far as the *upper room* at the corner
Neh 3:32 And between the *upper room* at the corner, as far as the Sheep Gate, the goldsmiths and the merchants made repairs
Dan 6:10 And in his *upper room*, with his windows open toward Jerusalem, he knelt down on his knees three times that day, and prayed and gave thanks before his God, as was his custom since early days
Mark 14:15 Then he will show you a large *upper room*, furnished and prepared
Luke 22:12 Then he will show you a large, furnished *upper room*
Acts 1:13 And when they had entered, they went up into the *upper room* where they were staying
Acts 9:37 When they had washed her, they laid her in an *upper room*
Acts 9:39 When he had come, they brought him to the *upper room*
Acts 20:8 There were many lamps in the *upper room* where they were gathered together

UPRIGHT IN HEART
Ps 7:10 My defense is of God, Who saves the *upright in heart*
Ps 11:2 The wicked bend their bow, they make ready their arrow on the string, that they may shoot secretly at the *upright in heart*

Ps 32:11 Be glad in the Lord and rejoice, you righteous; and shout for joy, all you *upright in heart*
Ps 36:10 Oh, continue Your lovingkindness to those who know You, and Your righteousness to the *upright in heart*
Ps 64:10 The righteous shall be glad in the Lord, and trust in Him. And all the *upright in heart* shall glory
Ps 94:15 But judgment will return to righteousness, and all the *upright in heart* will follow it
Ps 97:11 Light is sown for the righteous, and gladness for the *upright in heart*

URIM AND THUMMIM
Ezra 2:63 And the governor said to them that they should not eat of the most holy things till a priest could consult with the *Urim and Thummim*
Neh 7:65 And the governor said to them that they should not eat of the most holy things till a priest could consult with the *Urim and Thummim*

USED IN THE SANCTUARY (RSV)
(See *MINISTER IN THE SANCTUARY*)

UTMOST HEIGHTS (NIV)
(See *SIDES OF THE NORTH*)

UTTERMOST PART OF HEAVEN (KJV)
(See *FARTHEST PART OF HEAVEN*)

UTTERMOST PART OF THE HEAVEN (KJV)
(See *FARTHEST PART OF THE HEAVENS*)

UTTERS ORACLES OF GOD (RSV)
(See *SPEAK AS THE ORACLES OF GOD*)

V

VAIN REPETITIONS
Matt 6:7 But when you pray, do not use *vain repetitions* as the heathen do

VALLEY OF DECISION
Joel 3:14 Multitudes, multitudes in the *valley of decision!* For the day of the Lord is near in the *valley of decision*

VALLEY OF HINNOM
Josh 15:8 The border went up to the top of the mountain that lies before the *Valley of Hinnom* westward, which is at the end of the Valley of Rephaim northward
Josh 18:16 Then the border came down to the end of the mountain that lies before the Valley of the Son of Hinnom, which is in the Valley of the Rephaim on the north, descended to the *Valley of Hinnom*, to the side of the Jebusite city on the south, and descended to En Rogel
Neh 11:30 in Azekah and its villages. They dwelt from Beersheba to the *Valley of Hinnom*

VALLEY OF JEZREEL
Josh 17:16 and all the Canaanites who dwell in the land of the valley have chariots of iron, both those who are of Beth Shean and its towns and those who are of the *Valley of Jezreel*
Judg 6:33 and they crossed over and encamped in the *Valley of Jezreel*
Hos 1:5 It shall come to pass in that day that I will break the bow of Israel in the *Valley of Jezreel*

VALLEY OF THE SHADOW OF DEATH
Ps 23:4 Yea, though I walk through the *valley of the shadow of death*, I will fear no evil

VANISH LIKE SMOKE (NAS, NIV, RSV)
(See *INTO SMOKE THEY SHALL VANISH AWAY*)

VANISHED LIKE A SCROLL (RSV)
(See *RECEDED AS A SCROLL*)

VANITY OF VANITIES
Eccl 1:2 *Vanity of vanities*," says the Preacher; "*Vanity of vanities*, all is vanity
Eccl 12:8 *Vanity of vanities*," says the Preacher, "All is vanity

VARIATION OR SHADOW OF TURNING
Jas 1:17 Every good gift and every perfect gift is from above, and comes down from the Father of lights, with whom there is no *variation or shadow of turning*

VARIETIES OF GIFTS (NAS, RSV)
(See *DIVERSITIES OF GIFTS*)

VARIOUS TIMES AND IN DIFFERENT WAYS
Heb 1:1 God, who at *various times and in different ways* spoke in time past to the fathers by the prophets

VARIOUS WAYS (NIV, RSV)
(See *VARIOUS TIMES AND IN DIFFERENT WAYS*)

VAULTED HEAVENS (NIV)
(See *CIRCLE OF HEAVEN*)

VEIL OF THE TEMPLE
Matt 27:51 And behold, the *veil of the temple* was torn in two from top to bottom
Mark 15:38 Then the *veil of the temple* was torn in two from top to bottom
Luke 23:45 Then the sun was darkened, and the *veil of the temple* was torn in two

VEIL OVER HIS FACE
2Cor 3:13 unlike Moses, who put a *veil over his face* so that the children of Israel could not look steadily at the end of what was passing away

VENGEANCE IS MINE
Deut 32:35 *Vengeance is Mine*, and recompense; their foot shall slip in due time
Rom 12:19 for it is written, "*Vengeance is Mine*, I will repay
Heb 10:30 For we know Him who said, "*Vengeance is Mine;* I will repay, says the Lord

VENGEANCE OF THE LORD
Jer 50:15 for it is the *vengeance of the Lord*. Take vengeance on her
Jer 50:28 The voice of those who flee and escape from the land of Babylon declares in Zion the *vengeance of the Lord* our God, the vengeance of His temple
Jer 51:11 For His plan is against Babylon to destroy it, because it is the *vengeance of the Lord*, the vengeance for His temple

VENGEANCE ON HIS FOES (NIV)
(See *AVENGE HIMSELF ON HIS ADVERSARIES*)

VERILY, I SAY UNTO YOU (KJV)
(See *ASSUREDLY, I SAY TO YOU*)

VERILY, VERILY, I SAY UNTO YOU (KJV)
(See *MOST ASSUREDLY, I SAY TO YOU*)

VESSEL FOR BEAUTY (RSV)
(See *VESSEL FOR HONOR*)

VESSEL FOR HONOR
Rom 9:21 Does not the potter have power over the clay, from the same lump to make one *vessel for honor* and another for dishonor

2Tim 2:21 Therefore if anyone cleanses himself from the latter, he will be a *vessel for honor*, sanctified and useful for the Master, prepared for every good work

VESSELS OF MERCY
Rom 9:23 and that He might make known the riches of His glory on the *vessels of mercy*, which He had prepared beforehand for glory

VESSELS OF WRATH
Rom 9:22 What if God, wanting to show His wrath and to make His power known, endured with much longsuffering the *vessels of wrath* prepared for destruction

VEXATION OF SPIRIT (KJV)
(See *GRASPING FOR THE WIND*)

VICTORY OF THE LORD (RSV)
(See *SALVATION OF THE LORD*)

VICTORY RESTS WITH THE LORD (NIV)
(See *DELIVERANCE IS OF THE LORD*)

VIEW THE COUNTRY (KJV)
(See *SPY OUT THE COUNTRY*)

VINDICATE ME
Ps 26:1 *Vindicate me*, O Lord, for I have walked in my integrity
Ps 35:24 *Vindicate me*, O Lord my God, according to Your righteousness
Ps 43:1 *Vindicate me*, O God, and plead my cause against an ungodly nation
Ps 54:1 Save me, O God, by Your name, and *vindicate me* by Your strength

VINDICATION GOES FORTH (RSV)
(See *RIGHTEOUSNESS GOES FORTH*)

VINE OF SIBMAH
Is 16:8 For the fields of Heshbon languish, and the *vine of Sibmah*
Is 16:9 Therefore I will bewail the *vine of Sibmah*, with the weeping of Jazer
Jer 48:32 O *vine of Sibmah!* I will weep for you with the weeping of Jazer

VINEYARD OF NABOTH
1Kin 21:7 I will give you the *vineyard of Naboth* the Jezreelite
1Kin 21:15 And it came to pass, when Jezebel heard that Naboth had been stoned and was dead, that Jezebel said to Ahab, "Arise, take possession of the *vineyard of Naboth* the Jezreelite, which he refused to give you for money
1Kin 21:16 So it was, when Ahab heard that Naboth was dead, that Ahab got up and went down to take possession of the *vineyard of Naboth* the Jezreelite
1Kin 21:18 There he is, in the *vineyard of Naboth*, where he has gone down to take possession of it

VINEYARD OF RED WINE
Is 27:2 In that day sing to her, "A *vineyard of red wine*

VIOLATE MY COVENANT (NIV)
(See *BREAK MY COVENANT*)

VIOLATED THE COVENANT (NIV)
(See *TRANSGRESSED THE COVENANT*)

VIOLENCE IN THE LAND
Jer 51:46 And lest your heart faint, and you fear for the rumor that will be heard in the land (a rumor will come one year, and after that, in another year a rumor will come, and *violence in the land*, ruler against ruler

VIRGIN DAUGHTER OF ZION
Lam 2:13 what shall I compare with you, that I may comfort you, O *virgin daughter of Zion*

VIRGIN SHALL CONCEIVE
Is 7:14 Behold, the *virgin shall conceive* and bear a Son, and shall call His name Immanuel

VIRGINS OF JERUSALEM
Lam 2:10 The *virgins of Jerusalem* bow their heads to the ground

VIRTUOUS WOMAN
Ruth 3:11 I will do for you all that you request, for all the people of my town know that you are a *virtuous woman*

VISION AT NIGHT (NIV)
(See *NIGHT VISIONS*)

VISION OF ISAIAH
2Chr 32:32 Now the rest of the acts of Hezekiah, and his goodness, indeed they are written in the *vision of Isaiah* the prophet, the son of Amoz, and in the book of the kings of Judah and Israel
Is 1:1 The *vision of Isaiah* the son of Amoz, which he saw concerning Judah and Jerusalem in the days of Uzziah, Jotham, Ahaz, and Hezekiah, kings of Judah

VISIONS OF GOD
2Chr 26:5 He sought God in the days of Zechariah, who had understanding in the *visions of God*
Ezek 1:1 Now it came to pass in the thirtieth year, in the fourth month, on the fifth day of the month, as I was among the captives by the River Chebar, that the heavens were opened and I saw *visions of God*
Ezek 8:3 and the Spirit lifted me up between earth and heaven, and brought me in *visions of God* to Jerusalem, to the door of the north gate of the inner court, where the seat of the image of jealousy was, which provokes to jealousy
Ezek 40:2 In the *visions of God* He took me into the land of Israel and set me on a very high mountain

VISIT ORPHANS AND WIDOWS
Jas 1:27 to *visit orphans and widows* in their trouble, and to keep oneself unspotted from the world

VISIT THEIR SINS (KJV)
(See *PUNISH THEIR SINS*)

VISITING THE INIQUITY OF THE FATHERS
Ex 20:5 For I, the Lord your God, am a jealous God, *visiting the iniquity of the fathers* on the children to the third and fourth generations of those who hate Me
Ex 34:7 keeping mercy for thousands, forgiving iniquity and transgression and sin, by no means clearing the guilty, *visiting the iniquity of the fathers* upon the children and the children's children to the third and the fourth generation
Num 14:18 but He by no means clears the guilty, *visiting the iniquity of the fathers* on the children to the third and fourth generation
Deut 5:9 For I, the Lord your God, am a jealous God, *visiting the iniquity of the fathers* upon the children to the third and fourth generations of those who hate Me

VOICE OF DOVES
Nah 2:7 and her maidservants shall lead her as with the *voice of doves*, beating their breasts

VOICE OF GLADNESS
Jer 7:34 Then I will cause to cease from the cities of Judah and from the streets of Jerusalem the

voice of mirth and the *voice of gladness*, the voice of the bridegroom and the voice of the bride

Jer 16:9 Behold, I will cause to cease from this place, before your eyes and in your days, the voice of mirth and the *voice of gladness*, the voice of the bridegroom and the voice of the bride

Jer 25:10 Moreover I will take from them the voice of mirth and the *voice of gladness*, the voice of the bridegroom and the voice of the bride, the sound of the millstones and the light of the lamp

Jer 33:11 the voice of joy and the *voice of gladness*, the voice of the bridegroom and the voice of the bride, the voice of those who will say

VOICE OF ONE CRYING IN THE WILDERNESS

Is 40:3 The *voice of one crying in the wilderness:* "Prepare the way of the Lord

Matt 3:3 The *voice of one crying in the wilderness:* 'Prepare the way of the Lord, make His paths straight

Mark 1:3 The *voice of one crying in the wilderness:* 'Prepare the way of the Lord, make His paths straight

Luke 3:4 The *voice of one crying in the wilderness:* 'Prepare the way of the Lord, make His paths straight

John 1:23 I am 'The *voice of one crying in the wilderness*

VOICE OF THE BRIDEGROOM

Jer 7:34 Then I will cause to cease from the cities of Judah and from the streets of Jerusalem the voice of mirth and the voice of gladness, the *voice of the bridegroom* and the voice of the bride

Jer 16:9 Behold, I will cause to cease from this place, before your eyes and in your days, the voice of mirth and the voice of gladness, the *voice of the bridegroom* and the voice of the bride

Jer 25:10 Moreover I will take from them the voice of mirth and the voice of gladness, the *voice of the bridegroom* and the voice of the bride, the sound of the millstones and the light of the lamp

Jer 33:11 the voice of joy and the voice of gladness, the *voice of the bridegroom* and the voice of the bride, the voice of those who will say

VOICE OF THE LORD

Ex 15:26 and said, "If you diligently heed the *voice of the Lord* your God and do what is right in His sight, give ear to His commandments and keep all His statutes, I will put none of the diseases on you which I have brought on the Egyptians

Deut 5:25 if we hear the *voice of the Lord* our God anymore, then we shall die

Deut 8:20 As the nations which the Lord destroys before you, so you shall perish, because you would not be obedient to the *voice of the Lord* your God

Deut 13:18 because you have listened to the *voice of the Lord* your God, to keep all His commandments which I command you today, to do what is right in the eyes of the Lord your God

Deut 15:5 only if you carefully obey the *voice of the Lord* your God, to observe with care all these commandments which I command you today

Deut 18:16 according to all you desired of the Lord your God in Horeb in the day of the assembly, saying, 'Let me not hear again the *voice of the Lord* my God, nor let me see this great fire anymore, lest I die

Deut 26:14 I have obeyed the *voice of the Lord* my God, and have done according to all that You have commanded me

Deut 27:10 Therefore you shall obey the *voice of the Lord* your God, and observe His commandments and His statutes which I command you today

Deut 28:1 Now it shall come to pass, if you diligently obey the *voice of the Lord* your God, to observe carefully all His commandments which I command you today, that the Lord your God will set you high above all nations of the earth

Deut 28:2 And all these blessings shall come upon you and overtake you, because you obey the *voice of the Lord* your God

Deut 28:15 But it shall come to pass, if you do not obey the *voice of the Lord* your God, to observe carefully all His commandments and His statutes which I command you today, that all these curses will come upon you and overtake you

Deut 28:45 Moreover all these curses shall come upon you and pursue and overtake you, until you are destroyed, because you did not obey the *voice of the Lord* your God, to keep His commandments and His statutes which He commanded you

Deut 28:62 You shall be left few in number, whereas you were as the stars of heaven in multitude, because you would not obey the *voice of the Lord* your God

Deut 30:8 And you will again obey the *voice of the Lord* and do all His commandments which I command you today

Deut 30:10 if you obey the *voice of the Lord* your God, to keep His commandments and His statutes which are written in this Book of the Law, and if you turn to the Lord your God with all your heart and with all your soul

Josh 5:6 For the children of Israel walked forty years in the wilderness, till all the people who were men of war, who came out of Egypt, were consumed, because they did not obey the *voice of the Lord* to whom the Lord swore that He would not show them the land which the Lord had sworn to their fathers that He would give us

1Sam 12:15 However, if you do not obey the *voice of the Lord*, but rebel against the commandment of the Lord, then the hand of the Lord will be against you, as it was against your fathers

1Sam 15:19 Why then did you not obey the *voice of the Lord*

1Sam 15:20 And Saul said to Samuel, "But I have obeyed the *voice of the Lord*, and gone on the mission on which the Lord sent me, and brought back Agag king of Amalek

1Sam 15:22 Has the Lord as great delight in burnt offerings and sacrifices, as in obeying the *voice of the Lord*

1Sam 28:18 Because you did not obey the *voice of the Lord* nor execute His fierce wrath upon Amalek, therefore the Lord has done this thing to you this day

1Kin 20:36 Then he said to him, "Because you have not obeyed the *voice of the Lord*, surely, as soon as you depart from me, a lion shall kill you

2Kin 18:12 because they did not obey the *voice of the Lord* their God, but transgressed His covenant and all that Moses the servant of the Lord had commanded

Ps 29:3 The *voice of the Lord* is over the waters; the God of glory thunders

Ps 29:4 The *voice of the Lord* is powerful; the *voice of the Lord* is full of majesty

Ps 29:5 The *voice of the Lord* breaks the cedars, yes, the Lord splinters the cedars of Lebanon

Ps 29:7 The *voice of the Lord* divides the flames of fire

Ps 29:8 The *voice of the Lord* shakes the wilderness; the Lord shakes the Wilderness of Kadesh

Ps 29:9 The *voice of the Lord* makes the deer give birth, and strips the forests bare

Ps 106:25 But murmured in their tents, and did not heed the *voice of the Lord*

Is 6:8 Also I heard the *voice of the Lord*, saying: "Whom shall I send, and who will go for Us
Is 30:31 For through the *voice of the Lord* Assyria will be beaten down, who struck with a rod
Is 66:6 The *voice of the Lord*, Who fully repays His enemies
Jer 3:25 For we have sinned against the Lord our God, we and our fathers, from our youth even to this day, and have not obeyed the *voice of the Lord* our God
Jer 7:28 So you shall say to them, 'This is a nation that does not obey the *voice of the Lord* their God nor receive correction
Jer 26:13 Now therefore, amend your ways and your doings, and obey the *voice of the Lord* your God
Jer 38:20 Please, obey the *voice of the Lord* which I speak to you
Jer 42:6 Whether it is pleasing or displeasing, we will obey the *voice of the Lord* our God to whom we send you, that it may be well with us when we obey the *voice of the Lord* our God
Jer 42:13 But if you say, 'We will not dwell in this land,' disobeying the *voice of the Lord* your God
Jer 42:21 And I have this day declared it to you, but you have not obeyed the *voice of the Lord* your God, or anything which He has sent you by me
Jer 43:4 So Johanan the son of Kareah, all the captains of the forces, and all the people would not obey the *voice of the Lord*, to remain in the land of Judah
Jer 43:7 So they went to the land of Egypt, for they did not obey the *voice of the Lord*
Jer 44:23 Because you have burned incense and because you have sinned against the Lord, and have not obeyed the *voice of the Lord* or walked in His law, in His statutes or in His testimonies, therefore this calamity has happened to you, as at this day
Dan 9:10 We have not obeyed the *voice of the Lord* our God, to walk in His laws, which He set before us by His servants the prophets
Hag 1:12 Then Zerubbabel the son of Shealtiel, and Joshua the son of Jehozadak, the high priest, with all the remnant of the people, obeyed the *voice of the Lord* their God, and the words of Haggai the prophet, as the Lord their God had sent him
Zech 6:15 And this shall come to pass if you diligently obey the *voice of the Lord* your God
Acts 7:31 and as he drew near to observe, the *voice of the Lord* came to him

VOID OF UNDERSTANDING (KJV)
(See *DEVOID OF UNDERSTANDING*)

VOW TO THE LORD
Num 21:2 So Israel made a *vow to the Lord*, and said
Num 30:2 If a man vows a *vow to the Lord*, or swears an oath to bind himself by some agreement, he shall not break his word
Num 30:3 Or if a woman vows a *vow to the Lord*, and binds herself by some agreement while in her father's house in her youth
Deut 12:11 your burnt offerings, your sacrifices, your tithes, the heave offerings of your hand, and all your choice offerings which you *vow to the Lord*
Deut 23:21 When you make a *vow to the Lord* your God, you shall not delay to pay it
Judg 11:30 And Jephthah made a *vow to the Lord*, and said
Is 19:21 yes, they will make a *vow to the Lord* and perform it

VOWED A VOW (KJV)
(See *MADE A VOW*)

W

WAGE THE GOOD WARFARE
1Tim 1:18 This charge I commit to you, son Timothy, according to the prophecies previously made concerning you, that by them you may *wage the good warfare*

WAGE WAR
Prov 20:18 Every purpose is established by counsel; by wise counsel *wage war*

WAILING AND GNASHING
Matt 13:42 and will cast them into the furnace of fire. There will be *wailing and gnashing* of teeth
Matt 13:50 and cast them into the furnace of fire. There will be *wailing and gnashing* of teeth

WAIT EAGERLY FOR OUR ADOPTION (NIV)
(See *WAITING FOR THE ADOPTION*)

WAIT FOR THE LORD (RSV)
(See *HOPE IN THE LORD*)

WAIT IN HOPE FOR THE LORD (NIV)
(See *WAITS FOR THE LORD*)

WAIT ON THE LORD
Ps 27:14 *Wait on the Lord;* be of good courage, and He shall strengthen your heart
Ps 37:9 But those who *wait on the Lord*, they shall inherit the earth
Ps 37:34 *Wait on the Lord*, and keep His way, and He shall exalt you to inherit the land
Is 8:17 And I will *wait on the Lord*, Who hides His face from the house of Jacob
Is 40:31 But those who *wait on the Lord* shall renew their strength

WAITED PATIENTLY FOR THE LORD
Ps 40:1 I *waited patiently for the Lord;* and He inclined to me, and heard my cry

WAITING FOR THE ADOPTION
Rom 8:23 And not only they, but we also who have the firstfruits of the Spirit, even we ourselves groan within ourselves, eagerly *waiting for the adoption*, the redemption of our body

WAITS FOR THE LORD
Ps 33:20 Our soul *waits for the Lord;* He is our help and our shield
Ps 130:6 My soul *waits for the Lord* more than those who watch for the morning I say, more than those who watch for the morning

WALK BEFORE GOD
Ps 56:13 Have You not delivered my feet from falling, that I may *walk before God* in the light of the living

WALK HUMBLY WITH YOUR GOD
Mic 6:8 and what does the Lord require of you but to do justly, to love mercy, and to *walk humbly with your God*

WALK IN ALL HIS WAYS
Deut 10:12 And now, Israel, what does the Lord your God require of you, but to fear the Lord your God, to *walk in all His ways* and to love Him, to serve the Lord your God with all your heart and with all your soul

Deut 11:22 For if you carefully keep all these commandments which I command you to do to love the Lord your God, to *walk in all His ways*, and to hold fast to Him
Josh 22:5 But take diligent heed to do the commandment and the law which Moses the servant of the Lord commanded you, to love the Lord your God, to *walk in all His ways*, to keep His commandments, to hold fast to Him, and to serve Him with all your heart and with all your soul
1Kin 8:58 that He may incline our hearts to Himself, to *walk in all His ways*, and to keep His commandments and His statutes and His judgments, which He commanded our fathers

WALK IN DARK WAYS (NIV)
(See *WALK IN THE WAYS OF*)

WALK IN DARKNESS
Lam 3:2 He has led me and made me *walk in darkness* and not in light
John 8:12 He who follows Me shall not *walk in darkness*, but have the light of life
1Jn 1:6 If we say that we have fellowship with Him, and *walk in darkness*, we lie and do not practice the truth

WALK IN HIS LAWS
Dan 9:10 We have not obeyed the voice of the Lord our God, to *walk in His laws*, which He set before us by His servants the prophets

WALK IN HIS WAYS
Deut 8:6 Therefore you shall keep the commandments of the Lord your God, to *walk in His ways* and to fear Him
Deut 26:17 Today you have proclaimed the Lord to be your God, and that you will *walk in His ways* and keep His statutes, His commandments, and His judgments, and that you will obey His voice
Deut 28:9 The Lord will establish you as a holy people to Himself, just as He has sworn to you, if you keep the commandments of the Lord your God and *walk in His ways*
Deut 30:16 in that I command you today to love the Lord your God, to *walk in His ways*, and to keep His commandments, His statutes, and His judgments, that you may live and multiply
1Sam 8:3 But his sons did not *walk in his ways;* they turned aside after dishonest gain, took bribes, and perverted justice
1Kin 2:3 to *walk in His ways*, to keep His statutes, His commandments, His judgments, and His testimonies, as it is written in the Law of Moses, that you may prosper in all that you do and wherever you turn
Ps 119:3 They also do no iniquity; they *walk in His ways*
Is 42:24 For they would not *walk in His ways*, nor were they obedient to His law

WALK IN MY STATUTES
Lev 26:3 If you *walk in My statutes* and keep My commandments, and perform them
1Kin 6:12 Concerning this temple which you are building, if you *walk in My statutes*, execute My judgments, keep all My commandments, and walk in them, then I will perform My word with you, which I spoke to your father David
Ezek 11:20 that they may *walk in My statutes* and keep My judgments and do them
Ezek 20:13 they did not *walk in My statutes;* they despised My judgments, which, if a man does, he shall live by them
Ezek 20:16 because they despised My judgments and did not *walk in My statutes*, but profaned My Sabbaths
Ezek 20:19 *Walk in My statutes*, keep My judgments, and do them
Ezek 20:21 they did not *walk in My statutes*, and were not careful to observe My judgments
Ezek 36:27 I will put My Spirit within you and cause you to *walk in My statutes*, and you will keep My judgments and do them

WALK IN THE LIGHT
Is 2:5 O house of Jacob, come and let us *walk in the light* of the Lord
Is 50:11 *walk in the light* of your fire and in the sparks you have kindled this you shall have from My hand
1Jn 1:7 But if we *walk in the light* as He is in the light, we have fellowship with one another, and the blood of Jesus Christ His Son cleanses us from all sin

WALK IN THE SPIRIT
Gal 5:16 *Walk in the Spirit*, and you shall not fulfill the lust of the flesh
Gal 5:25 If we live in the Spirit, let us also *walk in the Spirit*

WALK IN THE TRUTH
3Jn 3 For I rejoiced greatly when brethren came and testified of the truth that is in you, just as you *walk in the truth*

WALK IN THE WAY OF
2Kin 21:22 He forsook the Lord God of his fathers, and did not *walk in the way of* the Lord
Prov 2:20 so you may *walk in the way of* goodness, and keep to the paths of righteousness
Prov 4:14 Do not enter the path of the wicked, and do not *walk in the way of* evil
Is 8:11 For the Lord spoke thus to me with a strong hand, and instructed me that I should not *walk in the way of* this people, saying

WALK IN THE WAYS OF
Prov 2:13 from those who leave the paths of uprightness to *walk in the ways of* darkness
Eccl 11:9 *walk in the ways of* your heart, and in the sight of your eyes

WALK PRUDENTLY
Eccl 5:1 *Walk prudently* when you go to the house of God

WALK WORTHY OF GOD
1Th 2:12 that you would have a *walk worthy of God* who calls you into His own kingdom and glory

WALKED IN THE WAY OF
1Kin 15:26 And he did evil in the sight of the Lord, and *walked in the way of* his father, and in his sin by which he had made Israel sin
1Kin 15:34 He did evil in the sight of the Lord, and *walked in the way of* Jeroboam, and in his sin by which he had made Israel sin
1Kin 16:2 Inasmuch as I lifted you out of the dust and made you ruler over My people Israel, and you have *walked in the way of* Jeroboam, and have made My people Israel sin, to provoke Me to anger with their sins
1Kin 22:52 He did evil in the sight of the Lord, and *walked in the way of* his father and in the way of his mother and in the way of Jeroboam the son of Nebat, who had made Israel sin
2Kin 8:18 And he *walked in the way of* the kings of Israel, just as the house of Ahab had done, for the daughter of Ahab was his wife
2Kin 8:27 And he *walked in the way of* the house of Ahab, and did evil in the sight of the Lord, as

the house of Ahab had done, for he was the son-in-law of the house of Ahab
2Kin 16:3 But he *walked in the way of* the kings of Israel
2Chr 11:17 So they strengthened the kingdom of Judah, and made Rehoboam the son of Solomon strong for three years, because they *walked in the way of* David and Solomon for three years
2Chr 20:32 And he *walked in the way of* his father Asa, and did not turn aside from it, doing what was right in the sight of the Lord
2Chr 21:6 And he *walked in the way of* the kings of Israel, just as the house of Ahab had done, for he had the daughter of Ahab as a wife
2Chr 21:13 but have *walked in the way of* the kings of Israel, and have made Judah and the inhabitants of Jerusalem to play the harlot like the harlotry of the house of Ahab, and also have killed your brothers, those of your father's household, who were better than yourself
Ezek 23:31 You have *walked in the way of* your sister; therefore I will put her cup in your hand

WALKED IN THE WAYS OF
2Chr 21:12 Because you have not *walked in the ways of* Jehoshaphat your father, or in the ways of Asa king of Judah
2Chr 22:3 He also *walked in the ways of* the house of Ahab, for his mother counseled him to do wickedly
2Chr 28:2 For he *walked in the ways of* the kings of Israel, and made molded images for the Baals
2Chr 34:2 And he did what was right in the sight of the Lord, and *walked in the ways of* his father David

WALKED WITH GOD
Gen 5:22 After he begot Methuselah, Enoch *walked with God* three hundred years, and begot sons and daughters
Gen 5:24 And Enoch *walked with God;* and he was not, for God took him
Gen 6:9 Noah was a just man, perfect in his generations. Noah *walked with God*

WALKING IN THE GARDEN
Gen 3:8 And they heard the sound of the Lord God *walking in the garden* in the cool of the day, and Adam and his wife hid themselves from the presence of the Lord God among the trees of the garden

WALKING ON THE LAKE (NIV)
(See *WALKING ON THE SEA*)

WALKING ON THE SEA
Matt 14:25 Now in the fourth watch of the night Jesus went to them, *walking on the sea*
Matt 14:26 And when the disciples saw Him *walking on the sea*, they were troubled, saying
Mark 6:48 And about the fourth watch of the night He came to them, *walking on the sea*, and would have passed them by
Mark 6:49 But when they saw Him *walking on the sea*, they supposed it was a ghost, and cried out
John 6:19 So when they had rowed about three or four miles, they saw Jesus *walking on the sea* and drawing near the boat

WALKS IN DARKNESS
Ps 91:6 Nor of the pestilence that *walks in darkness*, nor of the destruction that lays waste at noonday
Eccl 2:14 The wise man's eyes are in his head, but the fool *walks in darkness*
Is 50:10 Who *walks in darkness* and has no light? Let him trust in the name of the Lord and rely upon his God
John 12:35 he who *walks in darkness* does not know where he is going
1Jn 2:11 But he who hates his brother is in darkness and *walks in darkness*, and does not know where he is going, because the darkness has blinded his eyes

WALL OF FIRE
Zech 2:5 For I,' says the Lord, 'will be a *wall of fire* all around her, and I will be the glory in her midst

WALLOWING IN THE MIRE
2Pet 2:22 A dog returns to his own vomit," and, "a sow, having washed, to her *wallowing in the mire*

WALLS OF JERUSALEM
2Kin 25:10 And all the army of the Chaldeans who were with the captain of the guard broke down the *walls of Jerusalem* all around
Neh 2:13 And I went out by night through the Valley Gate to the Serpent Well and the Refuse Gate, and viewed the *walls of Jerusalem* which were broken down and its gates which were burned with fire
Neh 4:7 Now it happened, when Sanballat, Tobiah, the Arabs, the Ammonites, and the Ashdodites heard that the *walls of Jerusalem* were being restored and the gaps were beginning to be closed, that they became very angry
Ps 51:18 Do good in Your good pleasure to Zion; build the *walls of Jerusalem*
Jer 39:8 And the Chaldeans burned the king's house and the houses of the people with fire, and broke down the *walls of Jerusalem*
Jer 52:14 And all the army of the Chaldeans who were with the captain of the guard broke down all the *walls of Jerusalem* all around

WANDERED AWAY FROM THE TRUTH (NIV)
(See *STRAYED CONCERNING THE TRUTH*)

WANDERED FROM THE FAITH (NIV)
(See *STRAYED CONCERNING THE FAITH*)

WANDERED IN THE WILDERNESS
Gen 21:14 Then she departed and *wandered in the Wilderness* of Beersheba
Josh 14:10 And now, behold, the Lord has kept me alive, as He said, these forty-five years, ever since the Lord spoke this word to Moses while Israel *wandered in the wilderness*
Ps 107:4 They *wandered in the wilderness* in a desolate way; they found no city to dwell in

WANTONLY TREACHEROUS (RSV)
(See *DEAL TREACHEROUSLY*)

WAR A GOOD WARFARE (KJV)
(See *WAGE THE GOOD WARFARE*)

WARS AND RUMORS OF WARS
Matt 24:6 And you will hear of *wars and rumors of wars*
Mark 13:7 And when you hear of *wars and rumors of wars*, do not be troubled

WAS HAD IN ABOMINATION (KJV)
(See *BECOME AN ABOMINATION*)

WASH AWAY YOUR SINS
Acts 22:16 Arise and be baptized, and *wash away your sins*, calling on the name of the Lord

WASH THE DISCIPLES' FEET
John 13:5 After that, He poured water into a basin and began to *wash the disciples' feet*, and to wipe them with the towel with which He was girded

WASH THE FEET
1Sam 25:41 Then she arose, bowed her face to the earth, and said, "Here is your maidservant, a servant to *wash the feet* of the servants of my lord

WASHED MY FEET
Song 5:3 I have *washed my feet;* how can I defile them
Luke 7:44 you gave Me no water for My feet, but she has *washed My feet* with her tears and wiped them with the hair of her head

WASHED THEIR FEET
Gen 43:24 So the man brought the men into Joseph's house and gave them water, and they *washed their feet*
Judg 19:21 So he brought him into his house, and gave fodder to the donkeys. And they *washed their feet*, and ate and drank
John 13:12 So when He had *washed their feet*, taken His garments, and sat down again, He said to them

WASHED WITH PURE WATER
Heb 10:22 let us draw near with a true heart in full assurance of faith, having our hearts sprinkled from an evil conscience and our bodies *washed with pure water*

WASHING OF REGENERATION
Tit 3:5 not by works of righteousness which we have done, but according to His mercy He saved us, through the *washing of regeneration* and renewing of the Holy Spirit

WAST NOT SALTED (KJV)
(See *RUBBED WITH SALT*)

WASTE AND DESOLATE GROUND (RSV)
(See *DESOLATE WASTE*)

WATCH AND PRAY
Matt 26:41 *Watch and pray*, lest you enter into temptation. The spirit indeed is willing, but the flesh is weak
Mark 13:33 Take heed, *watch and pray;* for you do not know when the time is
Mark 14:38 *Watch and pray*, lest you enter into temptation. The spirit truly is ready, but the flesh is weak

WATCH THEREFORE
Matt 24:42 *Watch therefore*, for you do not know what hour your Lord is coming
Matt 25:13 *Watch therefore*, for you know neither the day nor the hour in which the Son of Man is coming
Mark 13:35 *Watch therefore*, for you do not know when the master of the house is coming in the evening, at midnight, at the crowing of the rooster, or in the morning
Luke 21:36 *Watch therefore*, and pray always that you may be counted worthy to escape all these things that will come to pass, and to stand before the Son of Man

WATCHES OF THE NIGHT (NIV, RSV)
(See *NIGHT WATCHES*)

WATCHMAN OVER EPHRAIM (NIV)
(See *FOWLER'S SNARE*)

WATCHMAN, WHAT OF THE NIGHT
Is 21:11 He calls to me out of Seir, "*Watchman, what of the night? Watchman, what of the night*

WATER AND BLOOD
1Jn 5:6 This is He who came by *water and blood* Jesus Christ; not only by water, but by *water and blood*

WATER MY COUCH WITH MY TEARS (KJV)
(See *DRENCH MY COUCH WITH MY TEARS*)

WATER OF AFFLICTION
1Kin 22:27 Put this fellow in prison, and feed him with bread of affliction and *water of affliction* , until I come in peace
2Chr 18:26 Put this fellow in prison, and feed him with bread of affliction and *water of affliction* until I return in peace
Is 30:20 And though the Lord gives you the bread of adversity and the *water of affliction*, yet your teachers will not be moved into a corner anymore, but your eyes shall see your teachers

WATER OF LIFE
Rev 21:6 I will give of the fountain of the *water of life* freely to him who thirsts
Rev 22:1 And he showed me a pure river of *water of life*, clear as crystal, proceeding from the throne of God and of the Lamb
Rev 22:17 And whoever desires, let him take the *water of life* freely

WATERCOURSES IN THE NEGEB (RSV)
(See *STREAMS IN THE SOUTH*)

WATERS CLOSED IN OVER ME (RSV)
(See *WATERS ENCOMPASSED ME*)

WATERS ENCOMPASSED ME
Jon 2:5 The *waters encompassed me*, even to my soul; the deep closed around me

WATERS OF MERIBAH
Num 27:14 (These are the *waters of Meribah*, at Kadesh in the Wilderness of Zin
Deut 32:51 because you trespassed against Me among the children of Israel at the *waters of Meribah* Kadesh, in the Wilderness of Zin, because you did not hallow Me in the midst of the children of Israel
Deut 33:8 Let Your Thummim and Your Urim be with Your holy one, whom You tested at Massah, and with whom You contended at the *waters of Meribah*
Ps 81:7 I answered you in the secret place of thunder; I proved you at the *waters of Meribah*
Ezek 47:19 The south side, toward the South, shall be from Tamar to the *waters of Meribah* by Kadesh, along the brook to the Great Sea
Ezek 48:28 by the border of Gad, on the south side, toward the South, the border shall be from Tamar to the *waters of Meribah* by Kadesh, along the brook to the Great Sea

WATERS WERE DIVIDED
Ex 14:21 and the Lord caused the sea to go back by a strong east wind all that night, and made the sea into dry land, and the *waters were divided*

WAVE OFFERING
Ex 29:24 and you shall put all these in the hands of Aaron and in the hands of his sons, and you shall wave them as a *wave offering* before the Lord
Ex 29:26 Then you shall take the breast of the ram of Aaron's consecration and wave it as a *wave offering* before the Lord
Ex 29:27 And from the ram of the consecration you shall consecrate the breast of the *wave offering* which is waved, and the thigh of the heave

offering which is raised, of that which is for Aaron and of that which is for his sons
Lev 7:30 The fat with the breast he shall bring, that the breast may be waved as a *wave offering* before the Lord
Lev 7:34 For the breast of the *wave offering* and the thigh of the heave offering I have taken from the children of Israel, from the sacrifices of their peace offerings, and I have given them to Aaron the priest and to his sons from the children of Israel by a statute forever
Lev 8:27 and he put all these in Aaron's hands and in his sons' hands, and waved them as a *wave offering* before the Lord
Lev 8:29 And Moses took the breast and waved it as a *wave offering* before the Lord
Lev 9:21 but the breasts and the right thigh Aaron waved as a *wave offering* before the Lord, as Moses had commanded
Lev 10:14 The breast of the *wave offering* and the thigh of the heave offering you shall eat in a clean place, you, your sons, and your daughters with you
Lev 10:15 The thigh of the heave offering and the breast of the *wave offering* they shall bring with the offerings of fat made by fire, to offer as a *wave offering* before the Lord
Lev 14:12 And the priest shall take one male lamb and offer it as a trespass offering, and the log of oil, and wave them as a *wave offering* before the Lord
Lev 14:24 And the priest shall take the lamb of the trespass offering and the log of oil, and the priest shall wave them as a *wave offering* before the Lord
Lev 23:15 And you shall count for yourselves from the day after the Sabbath, from the day that you brought the sheaf of the *wave offering*
Lev 23:20 The priest shall wave them with the bread of the firstfruits as a *wave offering* before the Lord, with the two lambs
Num 6:20 and the priest shall wave them as a *wave offering* before the Lord; they are holy for the priest, together with the breast of the *wave offering* and the thigh of the heave offering
Num 8:11 and Aaron shall offer the Levites before the Lord, as though a *wave offering* from the children of Israel, that they may perform the work of the Lord
Num 8:13 And you shall stand the Levites before Aaron and his sons, and then offer them as though a *wave offering* to the Lord
Num 8:15 So you shall cleanse them and offer them, as though a *wave offering*
Num 8:21 then Aaron presented them, as though a *wave offering* before the Lord, and Aaron made atonement for them to cleanse them

WAVE THE SHEAF
Lev 23:11 He shall *wave the sheaf* before the Lord, to be accepted on your behalf
Lev 23:12 And you shall offer on that day, when you *wave the sheaf*, a male lamb of the first year, without blemish, as a burnt offering to the Lord

WAVER BETWEEN TWO OPINIONS (NIV)
(See *FALTER BETWEEN TWO OPINIONS*)

WAVES OF THE SEA
Job 9:8 He alone spreads out the heavens, and treads on the *waves of the sea*
Ps 93:4 The Lord on high is mightier than the noise of many waters, than the mighty *waves of the sea*
Ps 107:25 For He commands and raises the stormy wind, which lifts up the *waves of the sea*
Is 48:18 Then your peace would have been like a river, and your righteousness like the *waves of the sea*
Zech 10:11 He shall pass through the sea with affliction, and strike the *waves of the sea*
Jude 13 raging *waves of the sea*, foaming up their own shame

WAX OLD LIKE A GARMENT (KJV)
(See *GROW OLD LIKE A GARMENT*)

WAY IN THE DESERT (NIV)
(See *ROAD IN THE WILDERNESS*)

WAY IN THE WILDERNESS (KJV, RSV)
(See *ROAD IN THE WILDERNESS*)

WAY OF A FOOL
Prov 12:15 The *way of a fool* is right in his own eyes, but he who heeds counsel is wise

WAY OF A MAN WITH A MAIDEN (NIV, RSV)
(See *WAY OF A MAN WITH A VIRGIN*)

WAY OF A MAN WITH A VIRGIN
Prov 30:19 the way of an eagle in the air, the way of a serpent on a rock, the way of a ship in the midst of the sea, and the *way of a man with a virgin*

WAY OF ALL THE EARTH
Josh 23:14 Behold, this day I am going the *way of all the earth*
1Kin 2:2 I go the *way of all the earth;* be strong, therefore, and prove yourself a man

WAY OF CAIN
Jude 11 For they have gone in the *way of Cain*, have run greedily in the error of Balaam for profit, and perished in the rebellion of Korah

WAY OF DEATH
Prov 14:12 There is a way which seems right to a man, but its end is the *way of death*
Prov 16:25 There is a way that seems right to a man, but its end is the *way of death*
Jer 21:8 Behold, I set before you the way of life and the *way of death*

WAY OF GOD
Matt 22:16 And they sent to Him their disciples with the Herodians, saying, "Teacher, we know that You are true, and teach the *way of God* in truth
Mark 12:14 for You do not regard the person of men, but teach the *way of God* in truth
Luke 20:21 And they asked Him, saying, "Teacher, we know that You say and teach rightly, and You do not show personal favoritism, but teach the *way of God* truly
Acts 18:26 When Aquila and Priscilla heard him, they took him aside and explained to him the *way of God* more accurately

WAY OF HIS FATHER
1Kin 15:26 And he did evil in the sight of the Lord, and walked in the *way of his father*, and in his sin by which he had made Israel sin
1Kin 22:52 He did evil in the sight of the Lord, and walked in the *way of his father* and in the way of his mother and in the way of Jeroboam the son of Nebat, who had made Israel sin
2Chr 20:32 And he walked in the *way of his father* Asa, and did not turn aside from it, doing what was right in the sight of the Lord

WAY OF HOLINESS (KJV, NIV)
(See *HIGHWAY OF HOLINESS*)

WAY OF LIFE
Prov 6:23 For the commandment is a lamp, and the law is light; reproofs of instruction are the *way of life*
Prov 10:17 He who keeps instruction is in the *way of life*, but he who refuses reproof goes astray
Prov 15:24 The *way of life* winds upward for the wise, that he may turn away from hell below
Jer 21:8 Behold, I set before you the *way of life* and the way of death

WAY OF PEACE
Is 59:8 The *way of peace* they have not known, and there is no justice in their ways
Luke 1:79 to give light to those who sit in darkness and the shadow of death, to guide our feet into the *way of peace*
Rom 3:17 and the *way of peace* they have not known

WAY OF RIGHTEOUSNESS
Prov 8:20 I traverse the *way of righteousness*, in the midst of the paths of justice
Prov 12:28 In the *way of righteousness* is life, and in its pathway there is no death
Prov 16:31 The silver-haired head is a crown of glory, if it is found in the *way of righteousness*
Matt 21:32 For John came to you in the *way of righteousness*, and you did not believe him
2Pet 2:21 For it would have been better for them not to have known the *way of righteousness*, than having known it, to turn from the holy commandment delivered to them

WAY OF THE LORD
Gen 18:19 For I have known him, in order that he may command his children and his household after him, that they keep the *way of the Lord*, to do righteousness and justice, that the Lord may bring to Abraham what He has spoken to him
2Kin 21:22 He forsook the Lord God of his fathers, and did not walk in the *way of the Lord*
Prov 10:29 The *way of the Lord* is strength for the upright, but destruction will come to the workers of iniquity
Is 40:3 Prepare the *way of the Lord;* make straight in the desert a highway for our God
Jer 5:4 for they do not know the *way of the Lord*, the judgment of their God
Jer 5:5 I will go to the great men and speak to them, for they have known the *way of the Lord*, the judgment of their God
Ezek 18:25 Yet you say, 'The *way of the Lord* is not fair
Ezek 18:29 Yet the house of Israel says, 'The *way of the Lord* is not fair
Ezek 33:17 Yet the children of your people say, 'The *way of the Lord* is not fair
Ezek 33:20 Yet you say, 'The *way of the Lord* is not fair
Matt 3:3 Prepare the *way of the Lord*, make His paths straight
Mark 1:3 Prepare the *way of the Lord*, make His paths straight
Luke 3:4 Prepare the *way of the Lord*, make His paths straight
John 1:23 Make straight the *way of the Lord*,' as the prophet Isaiah said
Acts 18:25 This man had been instructed in the *way of the Lord*

WAY OF THE RIGHTEOUS
Ps 1:6 For the Lord knows the *way of the righteous*, but the way of the ungodly shall perish

WAY OF THE SEA
Is 9:1 Nevertheless the gloom will not be upon her who is distressed, as when at first He lightly esteemed the land of Zebulun and the land of Naphtali, and afterward more heavily oppressed her, by the *way of the sea*, beyond the Jordan, in Galilee of the Gentiles
Matt 4:15 The land of Zebulun and the land of Naphtali, the *way of the sea*, beyond the Jordan, Galilee of the Gentiles

WAY OF THE WICKED
Ps 146:9 But the *way of the wicked* He turns upside down
Prov 4:19 The *way of the wicked* is like darkness; they do not know what makes them stumble
Prov 12:26 The righteous should choose his friends carefully, for the *way of the wicked* leads them astray
Prov 15:9 The *way of the wicked* is an abomination to the Lord, but He loves him who follows righteousness
Jer 12:1 Why does the *way of the wicked* prosper? Why are those happy who deal so treacherously

WAY OF TRUTH
Gen 24:48 And I bowed my head and worshiped the Lord, and blessed the Lord God of my master Abraham, who had led me in the *way of truth* to take the daughter of my master's brother for his son
Ps 119:30 I have chosen the *way of truth;* Your judgments I have laid before me
2Pet 2:2 And many will follow their destructive ways, because of whom the *way of truth* will be blasphemed

WAY THAT SEEMS RIGHT TO A MAN
Prov 16:25 There is a *way that seems right to a man*, but its end is the way of death

WAY WHICH LEADS TO LIFE
Matt 7:14 Because narrow is the gate and difficult is the *way which leads to life*, and there are few who find it

WAYS OF JEROBOAM
1Kin 16:26 For he walked in all the *ways of Jeroboam* the son of Nebat, and in his sin by which he had made Israel sin, provoking the Lord God of Israel to anger with their idols

WAYS OF THE LORD
Judg 2:22 so that through them I may test Israel, whether they will keep the *ways of the Lord*, to walk in them as their fathers kept them, or not
2Sam 22:22 For I have kept the *ways of the Lord*, and have not wickedly departed from my God
2Chr 17:6 And his heart took delight in the *ways of the Lord*
Ps 18:21 For I have kept the *ways of the Lord*, and have not wickedly departed from my God
Ps 138:5 Yes, they shall sing of the *ways of the Lord*, for great is the glory of the Lord
Hos 14:9 For the *ways of the Lord* are right; the righteous walk in them, but transgressors stumble in them
Acts 13:10 and said, "O full of all deceit and all fraud, you son of the devil, you enemy of all righteousness, will you not cease perverting the straight *ways of the Lord*

WAYS OF THIS WORLD (NIV)
(See *COURSE OF THIS WORLD*)

WE ALL, LIKE SHEEP (NIV)
(See *ALL WE LIKE SHEEP*)

WE ARE THE CLAY
Is 64:8 *we are the clay*, and You our potter; and all we are the work of Your hand

WE ARE WITNESSES
Josh 24:22 So Joshua said to the people, "You are witnesses against yourselves that you have chosen the Lord for yourselves, to serve Him." And they said, "*We are witnesses*
Ruth 4:11 And all the people who were at the gate, and the elders, said, "*We are witnesses*
Acts 3:15 and killed the Prince of life, whom God raised from the dead, of which *we are witnesses*
Acts 10:39 And *we are witnesses* of all things which He did both in the land of the Jews and in Jerusalem, whom they killed by hanging on a tree

WE BEHELD HIS GLORY
John 1:14 And the Word became flesh and dwelt among us, and *we beheld His glory*, the glory as of the only begotten of the Father, full of grace and truth

WE BROUGHT NOTHING INTO THIS WORLD
1Tim 6:7 For *we brought nothing into this world*, and it is certain we can carry nothing out

WE COMMEND OURSELVES
2Cor 6:4 But in all things *we commend ourselves* as ministers of God

WE HAVE SEEN HIS GLORY (NIV)
(See *WE BEHELD HIS GLORY*)

WE HAVE SEEN HIS STAR
Matt 2:2 For *we have seen His star* in the East and have come to worship Him

WE HAVE SINNED
Num 12:11 Please do not lay this sin on us, in which we have done foolishly and in which *we have sinned*
Num 14:40 And they rose early in the morning and went up to the top of the mountain, saying, "Here we are, and we will go up to the place which the Lord has promised, for *we have sinned*
Num 21:7 Therefore the people came to Moses, and said, "*We have sinned*, for we have spoken against the Lord and against you
Deut 1:41 Then you answered and said to me, '*We have sinned* against the Lord
Judg 10:10 And the children of Israel cried out to the Lord, saying, "*We have sinned* against You, because we have both forsaken our God and served the Baals
Judg 10:15 Then the children of Israel said to the Lord, "*We have sinned*
1Sam 7:6 And they fasted that day, and said there, "*We have sinned* against the Lord
1Sam 12:10 Then they cried out to the Lord, and said, '*We have sinned*, because we have forsaken the Lord and served the Baals and Ashtoreths
1Kin 8:47 yet when they come to themselves in the land where they were carried captive, and repent, and make supplication to You in the land of those who took them captive, saying, '*We have sinned* and done wrong, we have committed wickedness
2Chr 6:37 yet when they come to themselves in the land where they were carried captive, and repent, and make supplication to You in the land of their captivity, saying, '*We have sinned*, we have done wrong, and have acted wickedly
Neh 1:6 please let Your ear be attentive and Your eyes open, that You may hear the prayer of Your servant which I pray before You now, day and night, for the children of Israel Your servants, and confess the sins of the children of Israel which *we have sinned* against You
Ps 106:6 *We have sinned* with our fathers, we have committed iniquity, we have done wickedly
Is 42:24 Was it not the Lord, He against whom *we have sinned*
Is 64:5 You are indeed angry, for *we have sinned* in these ways we continue
Jer 3:25 For *we have sinned* against the Lord our God, we and our fathers, from our youth even to this day, and have not obeyed the voice of the Lord our God
Jer 8:14 For the Lord our God has put us to silence and given us water of gall to drink, because *we have sinned* against the Lord
Jer 14:7 for our backslidings are many, *we have sinned* against You
Jer 14:20 We acknowledge, O Lord, our wickedness and the iniquity of our fathers, for *we have sinned* against You
Lam 5:16 The crown has fallen from our head. Woe to us, for *we have sinned*
Dan 9:5 *we have sinned* and committed iniquity, we have done wickedly and rebelled, even by departing from Your precepts and Your judgments
Dan 9:8 O Lord, to us belongs shame of face, to our kings, our princes, and our fathers, because *we have sinned* against You
Dan 9:11 therefore the curse and the oath written in the Law of Moses the servant of God have been poured out on us, because *we have sinned* against Him
Dan 9:15 And now, O Lord our God, who brought Your people out of the land of Egypt with a mighty hand, and made Yourself a name, as it is this day *we have sinned*, we have done wickedly

WE SAW HIS STAR (NAS, NIV)
(See *WE HAVE SEEN HIS STAR*)

WE SHALL ALL BE CHANGED
1Cor 15:51 We shall not all sleep, but *we shall all be changed*

WE SHALL REIGN
Rev 5:10 and have made us kings and priests to our God; and *we shall reign* on the earth

WE WAIT IN HOPE FOR THE LORD (NIV)
(See *SOUL WAITS FOR THE LORD*)

WE WILL OBEY
Josh 24:24 And the people said to Joshua, "The Lord our God we will serve, and His voice *we will obey*
Jer 42:6 Whether it is pleasing or displeasing, *we will obey* the voice of the Lord our God to whom we send you, that it may be well with us when we obey the voice of the Lord our God

WEAK CONSCIENCE
1Cor 8:12 But when you thus sin against the brethren, and wound their *weak conscience*, you sin against Christ

WEAK HANDS
Job 4:3 Surely you have instructed many, and you have strengthened *weak hands*
Is 35:3 Strengthen the *weak hands*, and make firm the feeble knees

WEAK IN FAITH
Rom 4:19 And not being *weak in faith*, he did not consider his own body, already dead (since he was about a hundred years old

WEAK KNEES (NIV, RSV)
(See *FEEBLE KNEES*)

WEAKER SEX (RSV)
(See *WEAKER VESSEL*)

WEAKER VESSEL
1Pet 3:7 Likewise you husbands, dwell with them with understanding, giving honor to the wife, as

to the *weaker vessel*, and as being heirs together of the grace of life, that your prayers may not be hindered

WEAKNESS OF GOD
1Cor 1:25 Because the foolishness of God is wiser than men, and the *weakness of God* is stronger than men

WEALTH BRINGS MANY NEW FRIENDS (RSV)
(See *WEALTH MAKES MANY FRIENDS*)

WEALTH MAKES MANY FRIENDS
Prov 19:4 *Wealth makes many friends*, but the poor is separated from his friend

WEAPONS OF WAR
Deut 1:41 And when everyone of you had girded on his *weapons of war*, you were ready to go up into the mountain
Judg 18:11 And six hundred men of the family of the Danites went from there, from Zorah and Eshtaol, armed with *weapons of war*
Judg 18:16 The six hundred men armed with their *weapons of war*, who were of the children of Dan, stood by the entrance of the gate
Judg 18:17 The priest stood at the entrance of the gate with the six hundred men who were armed with *weapons of war*
1Sam 8:12 He will appoint captains over his thousands and captains over his fifties, will set some to plow his ground and reap his harvest, and some to make his *weapons of war* and equipment for his chariots
2Sam 1:27 How the mighty have fallen, and the *weapons of war* perished
1Chr 12:33 of Zebulun there were fifty thousand who went out to battle, expert in war with all *weapons of war*, stouthearted men who could keep ranks
Eccl 9:18 Wisdom is better than *weapons of war;* but one sinner destroys much good
Jer 21:4 Behold, I will turn back the *weapons of war* that are in your hands, with which you fight against the king of Babylon and the Chaldeans who besiege you outside the walls
Jer 51:20 You are My battle-ax and *weapons of war:* for with you I will break the nation in pieces
Ezek 32:27 They do not lie with the mighty who are fallen of the uncircumcised, who have gone down to hell with their *weapons of war*

WEAR OUT LIKE A GARMENT (NAS, NIV, RSV)
(See *GROW OLD LIKE A GARMENT*)

WEARY AND WORN OUT (NIV)
(See *TIRED AND WEARY*)

WEARY WITH MY CRYING
Ps 69:3 I am *weary with my crying;* my throat is dry

WEARY WITH MY GROANING
Ps 6:6 I am *weary with my groaning;* all night I make my bed swim

WEDDING FEAST
Luke 14:8 When you are invited by anyone to a *wedding feast*, do not sit down in the best place, lest one more honorable than you be invited by him

WEDDING SUPPER OF THE LAMB (NIV)
(See *MARRIAGE SUPPER OF THE LAMB*)

WEEDS IN THE FIELD (NIV)
(See *TARES OF THE FIELD*)

WEEP AND GNASH (RSV)
(See *WAILING AND GNASHING*)

WEEP AND WAIL (NIV)
(See *WEEPING AND WAILING*)

WEEP NOT FOR THE DEAD
Jer 22:10 *Weep not for the dead*, nor bemoan him; but weep bitterly for him who goes away, for he shall return no more, nor see his native country

WEEPING AND FOR MOURNING
Is 22:12 And in that day the Lord God of hosts called for *weeping and for mourning*, for baldness and for girding with sackcloth

WEEPING AND GNASHING (NAS, NIV)
(See *WAILING AND GNASHING*)

WEEPING AND GNASHING OF TEETH
Matt 8:12 But the sons of the kingdom will be cast out into outer darkness. There will be *weeping and gnashing of teeth*
Matt 22:13 Then the king said to the servants, 'Bind him hand and foot, take him away, and cast him into outer darkness; there will be *weeping and gnashing of teeth*
Matt 24:51 and will cut him in two and appoint him his portion with the hypocrites. There shall be *weeping and gnashing of teeth*
Matt 25:30 And cast the unprofitable servant into the outer darkness. There will be *weeping and gnashing of teeth*
Luke 13:28 There will be *weeping and gnashing of teeth*, when you see Abraham and Isaac and Jacob and all the prophets in the kingdom of God, and yourselves thrust out

WEEPING AND WAILING
Jer 9:10 I will take up a *weeping and wailing* for the mountains, and for the habitations of the wilderness a lamentation, because they are burned up, so that no one can pass through them
Rev 18:15 The merchants of these things, who became rich by her, will stand at a distance for fear of her torment, *weeping and wailing*
Rev 18:19 And they threw dust on their heads and cried out, *weeping and wailing*, and saying

WEEPING BITTERLY (NIV)
(See *WEPT BITTERLY*)

WEIGHED IN THE BALANCES
Ps 62:9 If they are *weighed in the balances*, they are altogether lighter than vapor
Dan 5:27 You have been *weighed in the balances*, and found wanting

WEIGHETH THE WATERS BY MEASURE (KJV)
(See *METE OUT THE WATERS BY MEASURE*)

WEIGHTIER MATTERS OF THE LAW
Matt 23:23 For you pay tithe of mint and anise and cumin, and have neglected the *weightier matters of the law*

WELL ADVANCED IN YEARS
Luke 1:7 But they had no child, because Elizabeth was barren, and they were both *well advanced in years*
Luke 1:18 For I am an old man, and my wife is *well advanced in years*

WELL DID ISAIAH PROPHESY
Matt 15:7 Hypocrites! *Well did Isaiah prophesy* about you, saying
Mark 7:6 He answered and said to them, "*Well did Isaiah prophesy* of you hypocrites, as it is written

WELL STRICKEN IN YEARS (KJV)
(See *WELL ADVANCED IN YEARS*)

WELLSPRING OF LIFE
Prov 16:22 Understanding is a *wellspring of life* to him who has it

WENT AWAY ON A JOURNEY (NIV)
(See *INTO A FAR COUNTRY*)

WENT INTO ANOTHER COUNTRY (RSV)
(See *INTO A FAR COUNTRY*)

WENT INTO THE SYNAGOGUE AND BEGAN TO TEACH (NIV)
(See *ENTERED THE SYNAGOGUE AND TAUGHT*)

WENT TO AND FRO (RSV)
(See *GOING TO AND FRO*)

WENT UP TO HEAVEN (RSV)
(See *ASCENDED TO HEAVEN*)

WEPT ALOUD (NIV, RSV)
(See *WEPT WITH A LOUD VOICE*)

WEPT BITTERLY
Judg 21:2 Then the people came to the house of God, and remained there before God till evening. They lifted up their voices and *wept bitterly*
2Kin 20:3 Remember now, O Lord, I pray, how I have walked before You in truth and with a loyal heart, and have done what was good in Your sight." And Hezekiah *wept bitterly*
Is 38:3 and said, "Remember now, O Lord, I pray, how I have walked before You in truth and with a loyal heart, and have done what is good in Your sight." And Hezekiah *wept bitterly*
Matt 26:75 And Peter remembered the word of Jesus who had said to him, "Before the rooster crows, you will deny Me three times." Then he went out and *wept bitterly*
Luke 22:62 Then Peter went out and *wept bitterly*

WEPT WITH A LOUD VOICE
2Sam 15:23 And all the country *wept with a loud voice*, and all the people crossed over
Ezra 3:12 But many of the priests and Levites and heads of the fathers' houses, who were old men, who had seen the first temple, *wept with a loud voice* when the foundation of this temple was laid before their eyes

WHAT COMES OUT OF THE MOUTH PROCEEDS (RSV)
(See *THINGS WHICH PROCEED OUT OF THE MOUTH*)

WHAT DO YOU SEE
Jer 1:11 Moreover the word of the Lord came to me, saying, "Jeremiah, *what do you see*
Jer 1:13 And the word of the Lord came to me the second time, saying, "*What do you see*
Jer 24:3 Then the Lord said to me, "*What do you see*, Jeremiah
Amos 7:8 And the Lord said to me, "Amos, *what do you see*
Amos 8:2 And He said, "Amos, *what do you see?*" So I said
Zech 4:2 And he said to me, "*What do you see?*" So I said
Zech 5:2 And he said to me, "*What do you see?*" So I answered

WHAT DOES THE LORD REQUIRE
Mic 6:8 and *what does the Lord require* of you but to do justly, to love mercy, and to walk humbly with your God

WHAT GOD HAS JOINED TOGETHER
Matt 19:6 Therefore *what God has joined together*, let not man separate
Mark 10:9 Therefore *what God has joined together*, let not man separate

WHAT GOOD IS IT FOR A MAN (NIV)
(See *WHAT WILL IT PROFIT A MAN*)

WHAT HAS BEEN SACRIFICED TO IDOLS (RSV)
(See *THINGS OFFERED TO IDOLS*)

WHAT I HAVE WRITTEN
John 19:22 Pilate answered, "*What I have written*, I have written

WHAT IF THERE ARE FIFTY RIGHTEOUS (NIV)
(See *SUPPOSE THERE WERE FIFTY RIGHTEOUS*)

WHAT IS GOOD
Deut 12:28 Observe and obey all these words which I command you, that it may go well with you and your children after you forever, when you do *what is good* and right in the sight of the Lord your God
2Sam 19:27 And he has slandered your servant to my lord the king, but my lord the king is like the angel of God. Therefore do *what is good* in your eyes
2Kin 10:5 but we will not make anyone king. Do *what is good* in your sight
1Chr 19:13 And may the Lord do *what is good* in His sight
1Chr 21:23 And Ornan said to David, "Take it to yourself, and let my lord the king do *what is good* in his eyes
Job 34:4 Let us choose justice for ourselves; let us know among ourselves *what is good*
Ps 38:20 Those also who render evil for good, they are my adversaries, because I follow *what is good*
Ps 85:12 Yes, the Lord will give *what is good;* and our land will yield its increase
Eccl 6:12 For who knows *what is good* for man in life, all the days of his vain life which he passes like a shadow
Is 38:3 and said, "Remember now, O Lord, I pray, how I have walked before You in truth and with a loyal heart, and have done *what is good* in Your sight
Is 55:2 Listen diligently to Me, and eat *what is good*, and let your soul delight itself in abundance
Mic 6:8 He has shown you, O man, *what is good;* and what does the Lord require of you but to do justly, to love mercy, and to walk humbly with your God
Rom 2:10 but glory, honor, and peace to everyone who works *what is good*, to the Jew first and also to the Greek
Rom 7:13 Has then *what is good* become death to me? Certainly not! But sin, that it might appear sin, was producing death in me through *what is good*, so that sin through the commandment might become exceedingly sinful

Rom 7:18 for to will is present with me, but how to perform *what is good* I do not find
Rom 12:9 Let love be without hypocrisy. Abhor what is evil. Cling to *what is good*
Rom 13:3 Do *what is good*, and you will have praise from the same
Rom 16:19 but I want you to be wise in *what is good*, and simple concerning evil
Eph 4:28 Let him who stole steal no longer, but rather let him labor, working with his hands *what is good*, that he may have something to give him who has need
Eph 4:29 Let no corrupt communication proceed out of your mouth, but *what is good* for necessary edification, that it may impart grace to the hearers
1Th 5:15 See that no one renders evil for evil to anyone, but always pursue *what is good* both for yourselves and for all
1Th 5:21 Test all things; hold fast *what is good*
Tit 1:8 but hospitable, a lover of *what is good*, sober-minded, just, holy, self-controlled
1Pet 3:13 And who is he who will harm you if you become followers of *what is good*
3Jn 11 Beloved, do not imitate what is evil, but *what is good*

WHAT IS MAN
Job 7:17 *What is man*, that You should magnify him, that You should set Your heart on him
Job 15:14 *What is man*, that he could be pure? And he who is born of a woman, that he could be righteous
Ps 8:4 *What is man* that You are mindful of him, and the son of man that You visit him
Ps 144:3 Lord, *what is man*, that You take knowledge of him
Heb 2:6 *What is man* that You are mindful of him, or the son of man that You take care of him

WHAT IS SEEN (NAS, NIV)
(See *THINGS WHICH ARE SEEN*)

WHAT IS TRUTH
John 18:38 Pilate said to Him, "*What is truth?*" And when he had said this, he went out again to the Jews, and said to them

WHAT IS WRITTEN (NIV)
(See *AS IT IS WRITTEN*)

WHAT SHALL WE DO
Judg 21:7 *What shall we do* for wives for those who remain, seeing we have sworn by the Lord that we will not give them our daughters as wives
Judg 21:16 Then the elders of the congregation said, "*What shall we do* for wives for those who remain, since the women of Benjamin have been destroyed
1Sam 5:8 Therefore they sent and gathered to themselves all the lords of the Philistines, and said, "*What shall we do* with the ark of the God of Israel
1Sam 6:2 And the Philistines called for the priests and the diviners, saying, "*What shall we do* with the ark of the Lord
2Kin 6:15 And his servant said to him, "Alas, my master! *What shall we do*
2Chr 25:9 Then Amaziah said to the man of God, "But *what shall we do* about the hundred talents which I have given to the troops of Israel
Esth 1:15 *What shall we do* to Queen Vashti, according to law, because she did not obey the command of King Ahasuerus brought to her by the eunuchs
Song 8:8 *What shall we do* for our sister in the day when she is spoken for
Jon 1:11 Then they said to him, "*What shall we do* to you that the sea may be calm for us
Luke 3:10 So the people asked him, saying, "*What shall we do* then
Luke 3:12 Then tax collectors also came to be baptized, and said to him, "Teacher, *what shall we do*
Luke 3:14 Likewise the soldiers asked him, saying, "And *what shall we do*
John 6:28 Then they said to Him, "*What shall we do*, that we may work the works of God
John 11:47 Then the chief priests and the Pharisees gathered a council and said, "*What shall we do*
Acts 2:37 Now when they heard this, they were cut to the heart, and said to Peter and the rest of the apostles, "Men and brethren, *what shall we do*
Acts 4:16 saying, "*What shall we do* to these men? For, indeed, that a notable miracle has been done through them is evident to all who dwell in Jerusalem, and we cannot deny it

WHAT THE PROMISE SAID (RSV)
(See *WORD OF PROMISE*)

WHAT WAS RIGHT IN HIS OWN EYES
Judg 17:6 In those days there was no king in Israel; everyone did *what was right in his own eyes*
Judg 21:25 In those days there was no king in Israel; everyone did *what was right in his own eyes*

WHAT WAS SAID THROUGH THE PROPHET ISAIAH (NIV)
(See *SPOKEN BY ISAIAH*)

WHAT WILL IT PROFIT A MAN
Mark 8:36 For *what will it profit a man* if he gains the whole world, and loses his own soul

WHATEVER A MAN SOWS
Gal 6:7 for *whatever a man sows*, that he will also reap

WHATEVER YOU BIND ON EARTH
Matt 16:19 And I will give you the keys of the kingdom of heaven, and *whatever you bind on earth* will be bound in heaven, and whatever you loose on earth will be loosed in heaven
Matt 18:18 Assuredly, I say to you, *whatever you bind on earth* will be bound in heaven, and whatever you loose on earth will be loosed in heaven

WHATEVER YOU LOOSE ON EARTH
Matt 16:19 And I will give you the keys of the kingdom of heaven, and whatever you bind on earth will be bound in heaven, and *whatever you loose on earth* will be loosed in heaven
Matt 18:18 Assuredly, I say to you, whatever you bind on earth will be bound in heaven, and *whatever you loose on earth* will be loosed in heaven

WHATEVER YOUR HAND FINDS TO DO
Eccl 9:10 *Whatever your hand finds to do*, do it with your might

WHATSOEVER A MAN SOWETH (KJV)
(See *WHATEVER A MAN SOWS*)

WHEAT AND BARLEY
Deut 8:8 a land of *wheat and barley*, of vines and fig trees and pomegranates, a land of olive oil and honey

WHEEL IN THE MIDDLE OF A WHEEL
Ezek 1:16 The appearance of their works was, as it were, a *wheel in the middle of a wheel*

Ezek 10:10 As for their appearance, all four looked alike as it were, a *wheel in the middle of a wheel*

WHEN GOODS INCREASE
Eccl 5:11 *When goods increase*, they increase who eat them; So what profit have the owners except to see them with their eyes

WHEN HE COMES (NIV)
(See *AT HIS COMING*)

WHEN HE HAD FINISHED SPEAKING
Judg 15:17 And so it was, *when he had finished speaking*, that he threw the jawbone from his hand, and called that place Ramath Lehi
1Sam 18:1 And it was so, *when he had finished speaking* to Saul, that the soul of Jonathan was knit to the soul of David, and Jonathan loved him as his own soul

WHEN HE TAKES REVENGE (NIV, RSV)
(See *DAY OF VENGEANCE*)

WHEN HE WAS REVILED
1Pet 2:23 who, *when He was reviled*, did not revile in return

WHEN I PUNISH THEM (RSV)
(See *TIME OF THEIR PUNISHMENT*)

WHEN OUR LORD JESUS COMES (NIV)
(See *AT THE COMING*)

WHEN THE GRINDERS CEASE
Eccl 12:3 *when the grinders cease* because they are few, and those that look through the windows grow dim

WHEN THE HOUR CAME (NIV, RSV)
(See *WHEN THE HOUR HAD COME*)

WHEN THE HOUR HAD COME
Luke 22:14 And *when the hour had come*, He sat down, and the twelve apostles with Him

WHEN THEY ARE PUNISHED (NIV)
(See *TIME OF THEIR PUNISHMENT*)

WHEN THEY HURLED THEIR INSULTS AT HIM (NIV)
(See *WHEN HE WAS REVILED*)

WHEN THEY MET HIM (NIV)
(See *AT HIS COMING*)

WHEN YOU REAP
Lev 19:9 *When you reap* the harvest of your land, you shall not wholly reap the corners of your field, nor shall you gather the gleanings of your harvest
Lev 23:22 *When you reap* the harvest of your land, you shall not wholly reap the corners of your field *when you reap*, nor shall you gather any gleaning from your harvest
Deut 24:19 *When you reap* your harvest in your field, and forget a sheaf in the field, you shall not go back to get it

WHENEVER OUR HEARTS CONDEMN US (NIV, RSV)
(See *IF OUR HEART CONDEMNS US*)

WHERE ARE YOU GOING
Gen 16:8 And He said, "Hagar, Sarai's maid, where have you come from, and *where are you going*
Gen 32:17 And he commanded the first one, saying, "When Esau my brother meets you and asks you, saying, 'To whom do you belong, and *where are you going*
Judg 19:17 and the old man said, "*Where are you going*, and where do you come from
Zech 2:2 So I said, "*Where are you going?*" And he said to me
John 13:36 Simon Peter said to Him, "Lord, *where are You going*
John 16:5 But now I go away to Him who sent Me, and none of you asks Me, '*Where are You going*

WHERE GOD WAS WORSHIPED (NAS, RSV)
(See *WORSHIPED GOD*)

WHERE IS THEIR GOD
Ps 79:10 Why should the nations say, "*Where is their God?*" Let there be known among the nations in our sight The avenging of the blood of Your servants which has been shed
Joel 2:17 Why should they say among the peoples, '*Where is their God*

WHERE NEITHER MOTH NOR RUST DESTROYS
Matt 6:20 but lay up for yourselves treasures in heaven, *where neither moth nor rust destroys* and where thieves do not break in and steal

WHERE, O GRAVE, IS YOUR DESTRUCTION (NIV)
(See *O GRAVE, I WILL BE YOUR DESTRUCTION*)

WHERE PRAYER WAS CUSTOMARILY MADE
Acts 16:13 And on the Sabbath day we went out of the city to the riverside, *where prayer was customarily made*

WHERE SATAN DWELLS
Rev 2:13 And you hold fast to My name, and did not deny My faith even in the days in which Antipas was My faithful martyr, who was killed among you, *where Satan dwells*

WHERE WE EXPECTED TO FIND A PLACE OF PRAYER (NIV)
(See *WHERE PRAYER WAS CUSTOMARILY MADE*)

WHERE WE SUPPOSED THERE WAS A PLACE OF PRAYER (RSV)
(See *WHERE PRAYER WAS CUSTOMARILY MADE*)

WHEREFORE THE LORD REWARD THEE (KJV)
(See *MAY THE LORD REWARD YOU*)

WHICH BEING INTERPRETED IS (KJV)
(See *WHICH IS TRANSLATED*)

WHICH HAVE BROUGHT THEE OUT OF THE LAND OF EGYPT (KJV)
(See *WHO BROUGHT YOU OUT OF THE LAND OF EGYPT*)

WHICH I SWORE
Gen 26:3 for to you and your descendants I give all these lands, and I will perform the oath *which I swore* to Abraham your father
Ex 6:8 And I will bring you into the land *which I swore* to give to Abraham, Isaac, and Jacob
Ex 33:1 Then the Lord said to Moses, "Depart and go up from here, you and the people whom you have brought out of the land of Egypt, to the land of *which I swore* to Abraham, Isaac, and Jacob, saying
Num 14:23 they certainly shall not see the land of

which I swore to their fathers, nor shall any of those who rejected Me see it
Num 14:30 Except for Caleb the son of Jephunneh and Joshua the son of Nun, you shall by no means enter the land *which I swore* I would make you dwell in
Num 32:11 Surely none of the men who came up from Egypt, from twenty years old and above, shall see the land of *which I swore* to Abraham, Isaac, and Jacob, because they have not wholly followed Me
Deut 1:35 Surely not one of these men of this evil generation shall see that good land of *which I swore* to give to your fathers
Deut 10:11 Then the Lord said to me, 'Arise, begin your journey before the people, that they may go in and possess the land *which I swore* to their fathers to give them
Deut 31:20 When I have brought them to the land flowing with milk and honey, of *which I swore* to their fathers, and they have eaten and filled themselves and grown fat, then they will turn to other gods and serve them
Deut 31:21 for it will not be forgotten in the mouths of their descendants, for I know the inclination of their behavior today, even before I have brought them to the land of *which I swore* to give them
Deut 31:23 for you shall bring the children of Israel into the land of *which I swore* to them, and I will be with you
Deut 34:4 Then the Lord said to him, "This is the land of *which I swore* to give Abraham, Isaac, and Jacob, saying
Josh 1:6 Be strong and of good courage, for to this people you shall divide as an inheritance the land *which I swore* to their fathers to give them
Judg 2:1 I led you up from Egypt and brought you to the land of *which I swore* to your fathers

WHICH IS TRANSLATED
Matt 1:23 Behold, a virgin shall be with child, and bear a Son, and they shall call His name Immanuel," *which is translated*
Mark 5:41 Then He took the child by the hand, and said to her, "Talitha, cumi," *which is translated*
Mark 15:22 And they brought Him to the place Golgotha, *which is translated*, Place of a Skull
Mark 15:34 *which is translated*, "My God, My God, why have You forsaken Me
John 1:41 He first found his own brother Simon, and said to him, "We have found the Messiah" (*which is translated*, the Christ
John 1:42 You shall be called Cephas" (*which is translated*, A Stone
John 9:7 And He said to him, "Go, wash in the pool of Siloam" (*which is translated*, Sent
Acts 4:36 And Joses, who was also named Barnabas by the apostles (*which is translated* Son of Encouragement
Acts 9:36 At Joppa there was a certain disciple named Tabitha, *which is translated* Dorcas

WHICH SLEEP IN JESUS (KJV)
(See *THOSE WHO SLEEP IN JESUS*)

WHICH WAS, AND IS, AND IS TO COME (KJV)
(See *WHO WAS AND IS AND IS TO COME*)

WHILE THEIR HEARTS ARE FAR FROM ME (RSV)
(See *REMOVED THEIR HEARTS FAR FROM ME*)

WHIP OF CORDS
John 2:15 When He had made a *whip of cords*, He drove them all out of the temple, with the sheep and the oxen, and poured out the changers' money and overturned the tables

WHITE ALREADY TO HARVEST (KJV)
(See *WHITE FOR HARVEST*)

WHITE AS SNOW
Num 12:10 And when the cloud departed from above the tabernacle, suddenly Miriam became leprous, as *white as snow*
2Kin 5:27 And he went out from his presence leprous, as *white as snow*
Ps 68:14 When the Almighty scattered kings in it, it was *white as snow* in Zalmon
Is 1:18 Come now, and let us reason together," says the Lord, "Though your sins are like scarlet, they shall be as *white as snow*
Dan 7:9 His garment was *white as snow*, and the hair of His head was like pure wool
Matt 28:3 His countenance was like lightning, and his clothing as *white as snow*
Rev 1:14 His head and His hair were white like wool, as *white as snow*, and His eyes like a flame of fire

WHITE FOR HARVEST
John 4:35 Behold, I say to you, lift up your eyes and look at the fields, for they are already *white for harvest*

WHITED SEPULCHRES (KJV)
(See *WHITEWASHED TOMBS*)

WHITEWASHED TOMBS
Matt 23:27 For you are like *whitewashed tombs* which indeed appear beautiful outwardly, but inside are full of dead men's bones and all uncleanness

WHITHER WILT THOU GO (KJV)
(See *WHERE ARE YOU GOING*)

WHO AM I, O LORD
2Sam 7:18 *Who am I, O Lord* God? And what is my house, that You have brought me this far
1Chr 17:16 *Who am I, O Lord* God? And what is my house, that You have brought me this far

WHO BELIEVES IN HIM
John 3:18 He *who believes in Him* is not condemned; but he who does not believe is condemned already, because he has not believed in the name of the only begotten Son of God

WHO BELIEVES IN THE SON
John 3:36 He *who believes in the Son* has everlasting life; and he who does not believe the Son shall not see life, but the wrath of God abides on him
1Jn 5:10 He *who believes in the Son* of God has the witness in himself

WHO BELIEVES ON HIM
1Pet 2:6 Therefore it is also contained in the Scripture, "Behold, I lay in Zion a chief cornerstone, elect, precious, and he *who believes on Him* will by no means be put to shame

WHO BROUGHT YOU OUT OF THE LAND OF EGYPT
Ex 20:2 I am the Lord your God, *who brought you out of the land of Egypt*, out of the house of bondage
Lev 19:36 I am the Lord your God, *who brought you out of the land of Egypt*
Lev 22:33 *who brought you out of the land of Egypt*, to be your God
Lev 25:38 I am the Lord your God, *who brought*

you out of the land of Egypt, to give you the land of Canaan and to be your God
Lev 26:13 I am the Lord your God, *who brought you out of the land of Egypt*, that you should not be their slaves
Num 15:41 I am the Lord your God, *who brought you out of the land of Egypt*, to be your God
Deut 5:6 I am the Lord your God *who brought you out of the land of Egypt*, out of the house of bondage
Deut 6:12 then beware, lest you forget the Lord *who brought you out of the land of Egypt*, from the house of bondage
Deut 8:14 when your heart is lifted up, and you forget the Lord your God *who brought you out of the land of Egypt*, from the house of bondage
Deut 13:5 But that prophet or that dreamer of dreams shall be put to death, because he has spoken in order to turn you away from the Lord your God, *who brought you out of the land of Egypt* and redeemed you from the house of bondage, to entice you from the way in which the Lord your God commanded you to walk
Deut 13:10 And you shall stone him with stones until he dies, because he sought to entice you away from the Lord your God, *who brought you out of the land of Egypt*, from the house of bondage
Ps 81:10 I am the Lord your God, *Who brought you out of the land of Egypt*

WHO CAME FROM THE FATHER (NIV)
(See *ONLY BEGOTTEN OF THE FATHER*)

WHO CAN FORGIVE SINS
Mark 2:7 Why does this Man speak blasphemies like this? *Who can forgive sins* but God alone
Luke 5:21 And the scribes and the Pharisees began to reason, saying, "Who is this who speaks blasphemies? *Who can forgive sins* but God alone

WHO DIGS A PIT (NAS, RSV)
(See *WHOEVER DIGS A PIT*)

WHO HAD DONE GREAT THINGS
Ps 106:21 They forgot God their Savior, *Who had done great things* in Egypt

WHO HAS BELIEVED OUR MESSAGE (NAS, NIV)
(See *WHO HAS BELIEVED OUR REPORT*)

WHO HAS BELIEVED OUR REPORT
Is 53:1 *Who has believed our report?* And to whom has the arm of the Lord been revealed
John 12:38 Lord, *who has believed our report?* And to whom has the arm of the Lord been revealed
Rom 10:16 But they have not all obeyed the gospel. For Isaiah says, "Lord, *who has believed our report*

WHO HAS BELIEVED WHAT WE HAVE HEARD (RSV)
(See *WHO HAS BELIEVED OUR REPORT*)

WHO HAVE DONE GREAT THINGS
Ps 71:19 Also Your righteousness, O God, is very high, You *who have done great things*

WHO HAVE FALLEN ASLEEP IN HIM (NIV)
(See *THOSE WHO SLEEP IN JESUS*)

WHO IS MY NEIGHBOR
Luke 10:29 But he, wanting to justify himself, said to Jesus, "And *who is my neighbor*

WHO SEEK THE LORD REJOICE (NIV, RSV)
(See *REJOICE WHO SEEK THE LORD*)

WHO SHALL SEPARATE US
Rom 8:35 *Who shall separate us* from the love of Christ? Shall tribulation, or distress, or persecution, or famine, or nakedness, or peril, or sword

WHO TESTIFIES (NIV)
(See *BEARS WITNESS*)

WHO THROUGH FAITH IS RIGHTEOUS SHALL LIVE (RSV)
(See *LIVE BY FAITH*)

WHO TRUSTS IN HIM (NIV)
(See *WHO BELIEVES ON HIM*)

WHO WAS AND IS AND IS TO COME
Rev 4:8 Holy, holy, holy, Lord God Almighty, *Who was and is and is to come*

WHOEVER BELIEVES (NIV)
(See *HE WHO BELIEVES*)

WHOEVER BELIEVES IN HIM
John 3:15 that *whoever believes in Him* should not perish but have eternal life
John 3:16 For God so loved the world that He gave His only begotten Son, that *whoever believes in Him* should not perish but have everlasting life
Acts 10:43 To Him all the prophets witness that, through His name, *whoever believes in Him* will receive remission of sins

WHOEVER BELIEVES IN THE SON (NIV)
(See *WHO BELIEVES IN THE SON*)

WHOEVER BELIEVES ON HIM
Rom 9:33 Behold, I lay in Zion a stumbling stone and rock of offense, and *whoever believes on Him* will not be put to shame
Rom 10:11 For the Scripture says, "*Whoever believes on Him* will not be put to shame

WHOEVER DESIRES TO BE FIRST
Matt 20:27 And *whoever desires to be first* among you, let him be your slave

WHOEVER DESIRES TO COME
Mark 8:34 And when He had called the people to Him, with His disciples also, He said to them, "*Whoever desires to come* after Me, let him deny himself, and take up his cross, and follow Me

WHOEVER DESIRES TO SAVE
Matt 16:25 For *whoever desires to save* his life will lose it, and whoever loses his life for My sake will find it
Mark 8:35 For *whoever desires to save* his life will lose it, but whoever loses his life for My sake and the gospel's will save it
Luke 9:24 For *whoever desires to save* his life will lose it, but whoever loses his life for My sake will save it

WHOEVER DIGS A PIT
Prov 26:27 *Whoever digs a pit* will fall into it, and he who rolls a stone will have it roll back on him

WHOEVER EATS MY FLESH
John 6:54 *Whoever eats My flesh* and drinks My blood has eternal life, and I will raise him up at the last day

WHOEVER HATES HIS BROTHER (NIV)
(See *HE WHO HATES HIS BROTHER*)

WHOEVER LOSES HIS LIFE (NIV)
(See *HE WHO LOSES HIS LIFE*)

WHOEVER LOSES HIS LIFE FOR MY SAKE
Matt 16:25 For whoever desires to save his life will lose it, and *whoever loses his life for My sake* will find it
Mark 8:35 For whoever desires to save his life will lose it, but *whoever loses his life for My sake* and the gospel's will save it
Luke 9:24 For whoever desires to save his life will lose it, but *whoever loses his life for My sake* will save it

WHOEVER RECEIVES ONE LITTLE CHILD
Matt 18:5 And *whoever receives one little child* like this in My name receives Me

WHOEVER SEEKS TO SAVE HIS LIFE
Luke 17:33 *Whoever seeks to save his life* will lose it, and whoever loses his life will preserve it

WHOEVER SERVES ME (NIV)
(See *IF ANYONE SERVES ME*)

WHOEVER SHEDS MAN'S BLOOD
Gen 9:6 *Whoever sheds man's blood*, by man his blood shall be shed

WHOEVER TRIES TO KEEP HIS LIFE (NIV)
(See *WHOEVER SEEKS TO SAVE HIS LIFE*)

WHOEVER WANTS TO BE FIRST (NIV)
(See *WHOEVER DESIRES TO BE FIRST*)

WHOEVER WANTS TO SAVE (NIV)
(See *WHOEVER DESIRES TO SAVE*)

WHOEVER WELCOMES A LITTLE CHILD (NIV)
(See *WHOEVER RECEIVES ONE LITTLE CHILD*)

WHOEVER WOULD BE FIRST (RSV)
(See *WHOEVER DESIRES TO BE FIRST*)

WHOEVER WOULD SAVE (RSV)
(See *WHOEVER DESIRES TO SAVE*)

WHOLE ARMOR OF GOD
Eph 6:11 Put on the *whole armor of God*, that you may be able to stand against the wiles of the devil
Eph 6:13 Therefore take up the *whole armor of God*, that you may be able to withstand in the evil day, and having done all, to stand

WHOLE CHURCH
Acts 15:22 Then it pleased the apostles and elders, with the *whole church*, to send chosen men of their own company to Antioch with Paul and Barnabas, namely, Judas who was also named Barsabas, and Silas, leading men among the brethren
Rom 16:23 Gaius, my host and the host of the *whole church*, greets you
1Cor 14:23 Therefore if the *whole church* comes together in one place, and all speak with tongues, and there come in those who are uninformed or unbelievers, will they not say that you are out of your mind

WHOLE COUNSEL OF GOD
Acts 20:27 For I have not shunned to declare to you the *whole counsel of God*

WHOLE DUTY OF MAN
Eccl 12:13 Fear God and keep His commandments, for this is the *whole duty of man*

WHOLE EARTH
Gen 8:9 But the dove found no resting place for the sole of her foot, and she returned into the ark to him, for the waters were on the face of the *whole earth*
Gen 9:19 These three were the sons of Noah, and from these the *whole earth* was populated
Gen 11:1 Now the *whole earth* had one language and one speech
Gen 11:4 let us make a name for ourselves, lest we be scattered abroad over the face of the *whole earth*
Ex 10:15 For they covered the face of the *whole earth*, so that the land was darkened
2Chr 16:9 For the eyes of the Lord run to and fro throughout the *whole earth*, to show Himself strong on behalf of those whose heart is loyal to Him
Job 37:12 and they swirl about, being turned by His guidance, that they may do whatever He commands them on the face of the *whole earth*
Ps 48:2 Beautiful in elevation, the joy of the *whole earth*, is Mount Zion on the sides of the north, the city of the great King
Ps 72:19 And let the *whole earth* be filled with His glory
Ps 97:5 The mountains melt like wax at the presence of the Lord, at the presence of the Lord of the *whole earth*
Is 6:3 Holy, holy, holy is the Lord of hosts; the *whole earth* is full of His glory
Is 14:7 The *whole earth* is at rest and quiet; they break forth into singing
Is 14:26 This is the purpose that is purposed against the *whole earth*, and this is the hand that is stretched out over all the nations
Is 28:22 for I have heard from the Lord God of hosts, a destruction determined even upon the *whole earth*
Is 54:5 and your Redeemer is the Holy One of Israel; He is called the God of the *whole earth*
Jer 15:10 Woe is me, my mother, that you have borne me, a man of strife and a man of contention to the *whole earth*
Jer 50:23 How the hammer of the *whole earth* has been cut apart and broken
Jer 51:41 Oh, how the praise of the *whole earth* is seized
Lam 2:15 Is this the city that is called'the perfection of beauty, the joy of the *whole earth*
Ezek 32:4 And with you I will fill the beasts of the *whole earth*
Ezek 35:14 The *whole earth* will rejoice when I make you desolate
Dan 2:35 And the stone that struck the image became a great mountain and filled the *whole earth*
Dan 7:23 The fourth beast shall be a fourth kingdom on earth, which shall be different from all other kingdoms, and shall devour the *whole earth*, trample it and break it in pieces
Dan 8:5 And as I was considering, suddenly a male goat came from the west, across the surface of the *whole earth*, without touching the ground
Mic 4:13 I will consecrate their gain to the Lord, and their substance to the Lord of the *whole earth*
Zech 4:10 They are the eyes of the Lord, which scan to and fro throughout the *whole earth*
Zech 4:14 So he said, "These are the two anointed ones, who stand beside the Lord of the *whole earth*
Zech 5:3 Then he said to me, "This is the curse that goes out over the face of the *whole earth*

Luke 21:35 For it will come as a snare on all those who dwell on the face of the *whole earth*

WHOLE HEAD IS SICK
Is 1:5 The *whole head is sick*, and the whole heart faints

WHOLE ISRAELITE COMMUNITY (NIV)
(See *CONGREGATION OF THE CHILDREN OF ISRAEL*)

WHOLE WILL OF GOD (NIV)
(See *WHOLE COUNSEL OF GOD*)

WHOLESOME WORDS
1Tim 6:3 If anyone teaches otherwise and does not consent to *wholesome words*, even the words of our Lord Jesus Christ, and to the doctrine which is according to godliness

WHOM HAVE I IN HEAVEN
Ps 73:25 *Whom have I in heaven* but You? And there is none upon earth that I desire besides You

WHOSE SIN IS NOT MORTAL (RSV)
(See *SIN NOT LEADING TO DEATH*)

WHOSESOEVER SINS YE REMIT (KJV)
(See *IF YOU FORGIVE THE SINS*)

WHOSESOEVER SINS YE RETAIN (KJV)
(See *IF YOU RETAIN THE SINS*)

WHOSO SHALL RECEIVE ONE SUCH LITTLE CHILD (KJV)
(See *WHOEVER RECEIVES ONE LITTLE CHILD*)

WHOSOEVER WILL BE CHIEF (KJV)
(See *WHOEVER DESIRES TO BE FIRST*)

WHOSOEVER WILL COME (KJV)
(See *WHOEVER DESIRES TO COME*)

WHOSOEVER WILL LOSE HIS LIFE FOR MY SAKE (KJV)
(See *WHOEVER LOSES HIS LIFE FOR MY SAKE*)

WHOSOEVER WILL SAVE (KJV)
(See *WHOEVER DESIRES TO SAVE*)

WHY ARE YOU TROUBLED
Luke 24:38 And He said to them, "*Why are you troubled*? And why do doubts arise in your hearts

WHY ARE YOU WEEPING
John 20:13 Then they said to her, "Woman, *why are you weeping*
John 20:15 Jesus said to her, "Woman, *why are you weeping?* Whom are you seeking

WHY DO THE HEATHEN RAGE (KJV)
(See *WHY DO THE NATIONS RAGE*)

WHY DO THE NATIONS CONSPIRE (RSV)
(See *WHY DO THE NATIONS RAGE*)

WHY DO THE NATIONS RAGE
Ps 2:1 *Why do the nations rage*, and the people plot a vain thing

WHY DO YOU CAST OFF MY SOUL
Ps 88:14 Lord, *why do You cast off my soul?* Why do You hide Your face from me

WHY DO YOU SEEK THE LIVING
Luke 24:5 Then, as they were afraid and bowed their faces to the earth, they said to them, "*Why do you seek the living* among the dead

WHY DO YOU SLEEP, O LORD
Ps 44:23 *Why do You sleep, O Lord?* Arise! Do not cast us off forever

WHY, O LORD, DO YOU REJECT ME (NIV)
(See *WHY DO YOU CAST OFF MY SOUL*)

WHY SLEEPEST THOU, O LORD (KJV, RSV)
(See *WHY DO YOU SLEEP, O LORD*)

WHY WEEPEST THOU (KJV)
(See *WHY ARE YOU WEEPING*)

WHY WILL YOU DIE
Jer 27:13 *Why will you die*, you and your people, by the sword, by the famine, and by the pestilence, as the Lord has spoken against the nation that will not serve the king of Babylon

WICKED AND ADULTEROUS GENERATION (NIV)
(See *EVIL AND ADULTEROUS GENERATION*)

WICKED AND DECEITFUL MOUTHS (RSV)
(See *MOUTH OF THE WICKED*)

WICKED FLEE WHEN NO ONE PURSUES
Prov 28:1 The *wicked flee when no one pursues*, but the righteous are bold as a lion

WIDOWS WHO ARE REALLY WIDOWS
1Tim 5:3 Honor *widows who are really widows*

WIFE OF HIS NEIGHBOR (NIV, RSV)
(See *ANOTHER MAN'S WIFE*)

WILD ANIMALS (NIV)
(See *BEAST OF THE EARTH*)

WILDERNESS OF JUDAH
Judg 1:16 Now the children of the Kenite, Moses' father-in-law, went up from the city of palms with the children of Judah into the *Wilderness of Judah*, which lies in the South near Arad

WILES OF THE DEVIL
Eph 6:11 Put on the whole armor of God, that you may be able to stand against the *wiles of the devil*

WILL A MAN ROB GOD
Mal 3:8 *Will a man rob God?* Yet you have robbed Me

WILL BE SAVED
Num 10:9 When you go to war in your land against the enemy who oppresses you, then you shall sound an alarm with the trumpets, and you will be remembered before the Lord your God, and you *will be saved* from your enemies
Prov 28:18 Whoever walks blamelessly *will be saved*, but he who is perverse in his ways will fall at once
Jer 23:6 In His days Judah *will be saved*, and Israel will dwell safely
Jer 33:16 In those days Judah *will be saved*, and Jerusalem will dwell safely
Matt 10:22 But he who endures to the end *will be saved*
Mark 16:16 He who believes and is baptized *will be saved;* but he who does not believe will be condemned

John 10:9 If anyone enters by Me, he *will be saved*, and will go in and out and find pasture
Acts 11:14 who will tell you words by which you and all your household *will be saved*
Acts 16:31 So they said, "Believe on the Lord Jesus Christ, and you *will be saved*, you and your household
Rom 9:27 Though the number of the children of Israel be as the sand of the sea, the remnant *will be saved*
Rom 10:9 that if you confess with your mouth the Lord Jesus and believe in your heart that God has raised Him from the dead, you *will be saved*
Rom 11:26 And so all Israel *will be saved*, as it is written
1Cor 3:15 but he himself *will be saved*, yet so as through fire
1Tim 2:15 Nevertheless she *will be saved* in childbearing if they continue in faith, love, and holiness, with self-control

WILL HE FOR A FISH GIVE HIM A SERPENT (KJV)
(See *SERPENT INSTEAD OF A FISH*)

WILL NEVER LEAVE YOU NOR FORSAKE YOU (NIV)
(See *WILL NOT LEAVE YOU NOR FORSAKE YOU*)

WILL NOT CLING (NIV)
(See *FALL AWAY*)

WILL NOT FAIL THEE, NOR FORSAKE THEE (KJV)
(See *WILL NOT LEAVE YOU NOR FORSAKE YOU*)

WILL NOT GO UNPUNISHED
Prov 11:21 Though they join forces, the wicked *will not go unpunished*
Prov 17:5 he who is glad at calamity *will not go unpunished*
Prov 19:5 A false witness *will not go unpunished*, and he who speaks lies will not escape
Prov 19:9 A false witness *will not go unpunished*, and he who speaks lies shall perish
Prov 28:20 A faithful man will abound with blessings, but he who hastens to be rich *will not go unpunished*

WILL NOT LEAVE YOU NOR FORSAKE YOU
Deut 31:6 for the Lord your God, He is the One who goes with you. He *will not leave you nor forsake you*
Deut 31:8 He will be with you, He *will not leave you nor forsake you*
Josh 1:5 as I was with Moses, so I will be with you. I *will not leave you nor forsake you*
1Chr 28:20 He *will not leave you nor forsake you*, until you have finished all the work for the service of the house of the Lord

WILL NOT REVOKE THE PUNISHMENT (RSV)
(See *TURN AWAY ITS PUNISHMENT*)

WILL OF GOD
Mark 3:35 For whoever does the *will of God* is My brother and My sister and mother
Acts 13:36 For David, after he had served his own generation by the *will of God*, fell asleep, was buried with his fathers, and saw corruption
Rom 1:10 making request if, by some means, now at last I may find a way in the *will of God* to come to you
Rom 8:27 Now He who searches the hearts knows what the mind of the Spirit is, because He makes intercession for the saints according to the *will of God*
Rom 12:2 And do not be conformed to this world, but be transformed by the renewing of your mind, that you may prove what is that good and acceptable and perfect *will of God*
Rom 15:32 that I may come to you with joy by the *will of God*, and may be refreshed together with you
1Cor 1:1 Paul, called to be an apostle of Jesus Christ through the *will of God*, and Sosthenes our brother
2Cor 1:1 Paul, an apostle of Jesus Christ by the *will of God*, and Timothy our brother, To the church of God which is at Corinth, with all the saints who are in all Achaia
2Cor 8:5 And this they did, not as we had hoped, but first gave themselves to the Lord, and then to us by the *will of God*
Eph 1:1 Paul, an apostle of Jesus Christ by the *will of God*, To the saints who are in Ephesus, and faithful in Christ Jesus
Eph 6:6 not with eyeservice, as men-pleasers, but as servants of Christ, doing the *will of God* from the heart
Col 1:1 Paul, an apostle of Jesus Christ by the *will of God*, and Timothy our brother
Col 4:12 Epaphras, who is one of you, a servant of Christ, greets you, always laboring fervently for you in prayers, that you may stand perfect and complete in all the *will of God*
1Th 4:3 For this is the *will of God*, your sanctification: that you should abstain from sexual immorality
1Th 5:18 for this is the *will of God* in Christ Jesus for you
2Tim 1:1 Paul, an apostle of Jesus Christ by the *will of God*, according to the promise of life which is in Christ Jesus
Heb 10:36 For you have need of endurance, so that after you have done the *will of God*, you may receive the promise
1Pet 2:15 For this is the *will of God*, that by doing good you may put to silence the ignorance of foolish men
1Pet 3:17 For it is better, if it is the *will of God*, to suffer for doing good than for doing evil
1Pet 4:2 that he no longer should live the rest of his time in the flesh for the lusts of men, but for the *will of God*
1Pet 4:19 Therefore let those who suffer according to the *will of God* commit their souls to Him in doing good, as to a faithful Creator
1Jn 2:17 but he who does the *will of God* abides forever

WILL OF MAN
John 1:13 who were born, not of blood, nor of the will of the flesh, nor of the *will of man*, but of God
2Pet 1:21 for prophecy never came by the *will of man*, but holy men of God spoke as they were moved by the Holy Spirit

WILL OF THE FLESH
John 1:13 who were born, not of blood, nor of the *will of the flesh*, nor of the will of man, but of God
Gal 6:8 For he who sows to his flesh *will of the flesh* reap corruption, but he who sows to the Spirit will of the Spirit reap everlasting life

WILL OF THE LORD
Acts 21:14 So when he would not be persuaded, we ceased, saying, "The *will of the Lord* be done
Eph 5:17 Therefore do not be unwise, but understand what the *will of the Lord* is

WILL THE LORD CAST OFF
Ps 77:7 *Will the Lord cast off* forever? And will He be favorable no more

WILL YOU BE ANGRY
Ps 79:5 *Will You be angry* forever? Will Your jealousy burn like fire
Ps 80:4 O Lord God of hosts, how long *will You be angry* against the prayer of Your people
Ps 85:5 *Will You be angry* with us forever? Will You prolong Your anger to all generations

WIN CHRIST (KJV)
(See *GAIN CHRIST*)

WIND BLOWS WHERE IT WISHES
John 3:8 The *wind blows where it wishes*, and you hear the sound of it, but cannot tell where it comes from and where it goes

WIND OUT OF HIS TREASURIES
Ps 135:7 He makes lightning for the rain; He brings the *wind out of His treasuries*
Jer 10:13 He makes lightning for the rain, He brings the *wind out of His treasuries*
Jer 51:16 He makes lightnings for the rain; He brings the *wind out of His treasuries*

WINDOWS FROM ON HIGH
Is 24:18 for the *windows from on high* are open, and the foundations of the earth are shaken

WINDOWS OF HEAVEN
Gen 7:11 In the six hundredth year of Noah's life, in the second month, the seventeenth day of the month, on that day all the fountains of the great deep were broken up, and the *windows of heaven* were opened
Gen 8:2 The fountains of the deep and the *windows of heaven* were also stopped, and the rain from heaven was restrained
Mal 3:10 Bring all the tithes into the storehouse, that there may be food in My house, and prove Me now in this," says the Lord of hosts, "If I will not open for you the *windows of heaven* And pour out for you such blessing That there will not be room enough to receive it

WINE AND OIL
1Chr 12:40 Moreover those who were near to them, from as far away as Issachar and Zebulun and Naphtali, were bringing food on donkeys and camels, on mules and oxen provisions of flour and cakes of figs and cakes of raisins, *wine and oil* and oxen and sheep abundantly, for there was joy in Israel
Neh 10:37 to bring the firstfruits of our dough, our offerings, the fruit from all kinds of trees, the new *wine and oil*, to the priests, to the storerooms of the house of our God
Neh 13:5 And he had prepared for him a large room, where previously they had stored the grain offerings, the frankincense, the articles, the tithes of grain, the new *wine and oil*, which were commanded to be given to the Levites and singers and gatekeepers, and the offerings for the priests
Prov 21:17 he who loves *wine and oil* will not be rich
Jer 31:12 Therefore they shall come and sing in the height of Zion, streaming to the goodness of the Lord for wheat and new *wine and oil*, for the young of the flock and the herd
Joel 2:19 The Lord will answer and say to His people, "Behold, I will send you grain and new *wine and oil*, and you will be satisfied by them
Joel 2:24 The threshing floors shall be full of wheat, and the vats shall overflow with new *wine and oil*
Rev 18:13 and cinnamon and incense, fragrant oil and frankincense, *wine and oil*, fine flour and wheat, cattle and sheep, horses and chariots, and bodies and souls of men

WINE BOTTLES, OLD AND RENT (KJV)
(See *OLD WINESKINS*)

WINE GLADDENS LIFE (RSV)
(See *WINE MAKES MERRY*)

WINE IS A MOCKER
Prov 20:1 *Wine is a mocker*, intoxicating drink arouses brawling, and whoever is led astray by it is not wise

WINE MAKES MERRY
Eccl 10:19 A feast is made for laughter, and *wine makes merry*

WINE TO DRINK (NAS, RSV)
(See *DRINK THE WINE*)

WINEPRESS OF THE WRATH OF GOD
Rev 14:19 So the angel thrust his sickle into the earth and gathered the vine of the earth, and threw it into the great *winepress of the wrath of God*

WINESKINS, WORN-OUT AND TORN AND MENDED (NAS, RSV)
(See *OLD WINESKINS*)

WINGS OF THE CHERUBIM
1Kin 6:27 and they stretched out the *wings of the cherubim* so that the wing of the one touched one wall, and the wing of the other cherub touched the other wall
1Kin 8:6 Then the priests brought in the ark of the covenant of the Lord to its place, into the inner sanctuary of the temple, to the Most Holy Place, under the *wings of the cherubim*
2Chr 3:11 The *wings of the cherubim* were twenty cubits in overall length
2Chr 5:7 Then the priests brought in the ark of the covenant of the Lord to its place, into the inner sanctuary of the temple, to the Most Holy Place, under the *wings of the cherubim*
Ezek 10:5 And the sound of the *wings of the cherubim* was heard even in the outer court, like the voice of Almighty God when He speaks

WINGS OF THE WIND
2Sam 22:11 and He was seen upon the *wings of the wind*
Ps 18:10 And He rode upon a cherub, and flew; He flew upon the *wings of the wind*
Ps 104:3 He lays the beams of His upper chambers in the waters, Who makes the clouds His chariot, Who walks on the *wings of the wind*

WINNOWING FAN
Jer 15:7 And I will winnow them with a *winnowing fan* in the gates of the land
Matt 3:12 His *winnowing fan* is in His hand, and He will thoroughly purge His threshing floor, and gather His wheat into the barn
Luke 3:17 His *winnowing fan* is in His hand, and He will thoroughly purge His threshing floor, and gather the wheat into His barn

WINNOWING FORK (NAS, NIV, RSV)
(See *WINNOWING FAN*)

WISDOM AND KNOWLEDGE
2Chr 1:10 Now give me *wisdom and knowledge*, that I may go out and come in before this people
2Chr 1:11 Because this was in your heart, and you

have not asked riches or wealth or honor or the life of your enemies, nor have you asked long life but have asked *wisdom and knowledge* for yourself, that you may judge My people over whom I have made you king

2Chr 1:12 *wisdom and knowledge* are granted to you; and I will give you riches and wealth and honor, such as none of the kings have had who have been before you, nor shall any after you have the like

Eccl 1:16 I communed with my heart, saying, "Look, I have attained greatness, and have gained more wisdom than all who were before me in Jerusalem. My heart has understood great *wisdom and knowledge*

Eccl 2:26 For God gives *wisdom and knowledge* and joy to a man who is good in His sight

Is 33:6 *Wisdom and knowledge* will be the stability of your times, and the strength of salvation

Rom 11:33 Oh, the depth of the riches both of the *wisdom and knowledge* of God

Col 2:3 in whom are hidden all the treasures of *wisdom and knowledge*

WISDOM HAS BUILT HER HOUSE

Prov 9:1 *Wisdom has built her house*, she has hewn out her seven pillars

WISDOM IS BETTER THAN

Prov 8:11 for *wisdom is better than* rubies, and all the things one may desire cannot be compared with her

Eccl 9:16 *Wisdom is better than* strength. Nevertheless the poor man's wisdom is despised, and his words are not heard

Eccl 9:18 *Wisdom is better than* weapons of war; but one sinner destroys much good

WISDOM IS JUSTIFIED

Matt 11:19 The Son of Man came eating and drinking, and they say, 'Look, a gluttonous man and a winebibber, a friend of tax collectors and sinners!' But *wisdom is justified* by her children

Luke 7:35 But *wisdom is justified* by all her children

WISDOM IS MORE PRECIOUS THAN (NIV)
(See *WISDOM IS BETTER THAN*)

WISDOM IS PROFOUND (NIV)
(See *WISE IN HEART*)

WISDOM IS PROVED RIGHT (NIV)
(See *WISDOM IS JUSTIFIED*)

WISDOM OF GOD

1Kin 3:28 and they feared the king, for they saw that the *wisdom of God* was in him to administer justice

Luke 11:49 Therefore the *wisdom of God* also said, 'I will send them prophets and apostles, and some of them they will kill and persecute

1Cor 1:21 For since, in the *wisdom of God*, the world through wisdom did not know God, it pleased God through the foolishness of the message preached to save those who believe

1Cor 1:24 but to those who are called, both Jews and Greeks, Christ the power of God and the *wisdom of God*

1Cor 2:7 But we speak the *wisdom of God* in a mystery, the hidden wisdom which God ordained before the ages for our glory

Eph 3:10 to the intent that now the manifold *wisdom of God* might be made known by the church to the principalities and powers in the heavenly places

WISDOM OF SOLOMON

1Kin 4:34 And men of all nations, from all the kings of the earth who had heard of his wisdom, came to hear the *wisdom of Solomon*

1Kin 10:4 And when the queen of Sheba had seen all the *wisdom of Solomon*, the house that he had built

2Chr 9:3 And when the queen of Sheba had seen the *wisdom of Solomon*, the house that he had built

Matt 12:42 The queen of the South will rise up in the judgment with this generation and condemn it, for she came from the ends of the earth to hear the *wisdom of Solomon*

Luke 11:31 The queen of the South will rise up in the judgment with the men of this generation and condemn them, for she came from the ends of the earth to hear the *wisdom of Solomon*

WISDOM OF THIS WORLD

1Cor 1:20 Has not God made foolish the *wisdom of this world*

1Cor 3:19 For the *wisdom of this world* is foolishness with God

WISE COUNSEL

Prov 1:5 A wise man will hear and increase learning, and a man of understanding will attain *wise counsel*

Prov 20:18 Every purpose is established by counsel; by *wise counsel* wage war

Prov 24:6 for by *wise counsel* you will wage your own war, and in a multitude of counselors there is safety

WISE IN HEART

Job 9:4 God is *wise in heart* and mighty in strength. Who has hardened himself against Him and prospered

Prov 10:8 The *wise in heart* will receive commands, but a prating fool will fall

Prov 16:21 The *wise in heart* will be called prudent, and sweetness of the lips increases learning

WISE IN THEIR OWN CONCEIT (RSV)
(See *WISE OF HEART*)

WISE IN YOUR OWN EYES

Prov 3:7 Do not be *wise in your own eyes;* fear the Lord and depart from evil

WISE MAN

Gen 41:33 Now therefore, let Pharaoh select a discerning and *wise man*, and set him over the land of Egypt

1Kin 2:9 Now therefore, do not hold him guiltless, for you are a *wise man* and know what you ought to do to him

1Chr 27:32 Also Jehonathan, David's uncle, was a counselor, a *wise man*, and a scribe

Job 15:2 Should a *wise man* answer with empty knowledge, and fill himself with the east wind

Job 17:10 But please, come back again, all of you, for I shall not find one *wise man* among you

Prov 1:5 A *wise man* will hear and increase learning, and a man of understanding will attain wise counsel

Prov 9:8 Do not reprove a scoffer, lest he hate you; rebuke a *wise man*, and he will love you

Prov 9:9 Give instruction to a *wise man*, and he will be still wiser

Prov 14:16 A *wise man* fears and departs from evil, but a fool rages and is self-confident

Prov 16:14 As messengers of death is the king's wrath, but a *wise man* will appease it

Prov 17:10 Reproof is more effective for a *wise man* than a hundred blows on a fool

Prov 21:22 A *wise man* scales the city of the mighty, and brings down the trusted stronghold
Prov 24:5 A *wise man* is strong, yes, a man of knowledge increases strength
Prov 29:9 If a *wise man* contends with a foolish man, whether the fool rages or laughs, there is no peace
Prov 29:11 A fool vents all his feelings, but a *wise man* holds them back
Eccl 2:16 and how does a *wise man* die? As the fool
Eccl 2:19 And who knows whether he will be a *wise man* or a fool
Eccl 6:8 For what more has the *wise man* than the fool
Eccl 8:1 Who is like a *wise man?* and who knows the interpretation of a thing
Eccl 8:17 moreover, though a *wise man* attempts to know it, he will not be able to find it
Eccl 9:15 Now there was found in it a poor *wise man*, and he by his wisdom delivered the city
Jer 9:12 Who is the *wise man* who may understand this? And who is he to whom the mouth of the Lord has spoken, that he may declare it
Jer 9:23 Let not the *wise man* glory in his wisdom, let not the mighty man glory in his might, nor let the rich man glory in his riches
Matt 7:24 Therefore whoever hears these sayings of Mine, and does them, I will liken him to a *wise man* who built his house on the rock
1Cor 6:5 Is it so, that there is not a *wise man* among you, not even one, who will be able to judge between his brethren

WISE MEN
Gen 41:8 Now it came to pass in the morning that his spirit was troubled, and he sent and called for all the magicians of Egypt and all its *wise men*
Ex 7:11 But Pharaoh also called the *wise men* and the sorcerers
Esth 1:13 Then the king said to the *wise men* who understood the times (for this was the king's manner toward all who knew law and justice
Esth 6:13 When Haman told his wife Zeresh and all his friends everything that had happened to him, his *wise men* and his wife Zeresh said to him
Job 15:18 what *wise men* have told, not hiding anything received from their fathers
Job 34:2 Hear my words, you *wise men;* give ear to me, you who have knowledge
Job 34:34 Men of understanding say to me, *wise men* who listen to me
Ps 49:10 For he sees that *wise men* die; likewise the fool and the senseless person perish, and leave their wealth to others
Prov 13:20 He who walks with *wise men* will be wise, but the companion of fools will be destroyed
Prov 29:8 Scoffers ensnare a city, but *wise men* turn away wrath
Is 19:12 Where are your *wise men?* Let them tell you now, and let them know what the Lord of hosts has purposed against Egypt
Is 29:14 for the wisdom of their *wise men* shall perish, and the understanding of their prudent men shall be hidden
Is 44:25 Who turns *wise men* backward, and makes their knowledge foolishness
Jer 8:9 The *wise men* are ashamed, they are dismayed and taken
Jer 10:7 For this is Your rightful due, for among all the *wise men* of the nations, and in all their kingdoms, there is none like You
Jer 50:35 A sword is against the Chaldeans," says the Lord, "against the inhabitants of Babylon, and against her princes and her *wise men*
Jer 51:57 And I will make drunk her princes and *wise men*, her governors, her deputies, and her mighty men
Ezek 27:8 your own *wise men*, O Tyre, were in you; they became your pilots
Ezek 27:9 Elders of Gebal and its *wise men* were in you to caulk your seams
Dan 2:12 For this reason the king was angry and very furious, and gave a command to destroy all the *wise men* of Babylon
Dan 2:13 So the decree went out, and they began killing the *wise men*
Dan 2:14 Then with counsel and wisdom Daniel answered Arioch, the captain of the king's guard, who had gone out to kill the *wise men* of Babylon
Dan 2:18 that they might seek mercies from the God of heaven concerning this secret, so that Daniel and his companions might not perish with the rest of the *wise men* of Babylon
Dan 2:24 Therefore Daniel went to Arioch, whom the king had appointed to destroy the *wise men* of Babylon. He went and said thus to him: "Do not destroy the wise men of Babylon
Dan 2:27 Daniel answered in the presence of the king, and said, "The secret which the king has demanded, the *wise men*, the astrologers, the magicians, and the soothsayers cannot declare to the king
Dan 2:48 and he made him ruler over the whole province of Babylon, and chief administrator over all the *wise men* of Babylon
Dan 4:6 Therefore I issued a decree to bring in all the *wise men* of Babylon before me, that they might make known to me the interpretation of the dream
Dan 4:18 Now you, Belteshazzar, declare its interpretation, since all the *wise men* of my kingdom are not able to make known to me the interpretation
Dan 5:7 And the king spoke, saying to the *wise men* of Babylon
Dan 5:8 Now all the king's *wise men* came, but they could not read the writing, or make known to the king its interpretation
Dan 5:15 Now the *wise men*, the astrologers, have been brought in before me, that they should read this writing and make known to me its interpretation, but they could not give the interpretation of the thing
Obad 8 Will I not in that day," says the Lord, "Even destroy the *wise men* from Edom, and understanding from the mountains of Esau
Matt 2:1 Now after Jesus was born in Bethlehem of Judea in the days of Herod the king, behold, *wise men* from the East came to Jerusalem
Matt 2:7 Then Herod, when he had secretly called the *wise men*, determined from them what time the star appeared
Matt 2:16 Then Herod, when he saw that he was deceived by the *wise men*, was exceedingly angry; and he sent forth and put to death all the male children who were in Bethlehem and in all its districts, from two years old and under, according to the time which he had determined from the *wise men*
Matt 23:34 Therefore, indeed, I send you prophets, *wise men*, and scribes
1Cor 10:15 I speak as to *wise men;* judge for yourselves what I say

WISE OF HEART
Job 37:24 He shows no partiality to any who are *wise of heart*
Prov 11:29 He who troubles his own house will inherit the wind, and the fool will be servant to the *wise of heart*

WISE WOMAN
2Sam 14:2 And Joab sent to Tekoa and brought from there a *wise woman*, and said to her

2Sam 20:16 Then a *wise woman* cried out from the city, "Hear, Hear
Prov 14:1 Every *wise woman* builds her house, but the foolish pulls it down with her hands

WITH A MIGHTY HAND AND WITH AN OUTSTRETCHED ARM
Deut 26:8 So the Lord brought us out of Egypt *with a mighty hand and with an outstretched arm*, with great terror and with signs and wonders

WITH ALL YOUR HEART
Deut 4:29 But from there you will seek the Lord your God, and you will find Him if you seek Him *with all your heart* and with all your soul
Deut 6:5 You shall love the Lord your God *with all your heart*, with all your soul, and with all your might
Deut 10:12 And now, Israel, what does the Lord your God require of you, but to fear the Lord your God, to walk in all His ways and to love Him, to serve the Lord your God *with all your heart* and with all your soul
Deut 11:13 And it shall be that if you diligently obey My commandments which I command you today, to love the Lord your God and serve Him *with all your heart* and with all your soul
Deut 13:3 you shall not listen to the words of that prophet or that dreamer of dreams, for the Lord your God is testing you to know whether you love the Lord your God *with all your heart* and with all your soul
Deut 26:16 therefore you shall be careful to observe them *with all your heart* and with all your soul
Deut 30:2 and you return to the Lord your God and obey His voice, according to all that I command you today, you and your children, *with all your heart* and with all your soul
Deut 30:6 And the Lord your God will circumcise your heart and the heart of your descendants, to love the Lord your God *with all your heart* and with all your soul, that you may live
Deut 30:10 if you obey the voice of the Lord your God, to keep His commandments and His statutes which are written in this Book of the Law, and if you turn to the Lord your God *with all your heart* and with all your soul
Josh 22:5 But take diligent heed to do the commandment and the law which Moses the servant of the Lord commanded you, to love the Lord your God, to walk in all His ways, to keep His commandments, to hold fast to Him, and to serve Him *with all your heart* and with all your soul
1Sam 12:20 yet do not turn aside from following the Lord, but serve the Lord *with all your heart*
1Sam 12:24 Only fear the Lord, and serve Him in truth *with all your heart*
Prov 3:5 Trust in the Lord *with all your heart*, and lean not on your own understanding
Jer 29:13 And you will seek Me and find Me, when you search for Me *with all your heart*
Joel 2:12 Now, therefore," says the Lord, "Turn to me *with all your heart*, with fasting, with weeping, and with mourning
Zeph 3:14 Be glad and rejoice *with all your heart*, O daughter of Jerusalem
Matt 22:37 Jesus said to him, "'You shall love the Lord your God *with all your heart*, with all your soul, and with all your mind
Mark 12:30 And you shall love the Lord your God *with all your heart*, with all your soul, with all your mind, and with all your strength
Luke 10:27 So he answered and said, "'You shall love the Lord your God *with all your heart*, with all your soul, with all your strength, and with all your mind
Acts 8:37 Then Philip said, "If you believe *with all your heart*, you may

WITH ALL YOUR SOUL
Deut 4:29 But from there you will seek the Lord your God, and you will find Him if you seek Him with all your heart and *with all your soul*
Deut 6:5 You shall love the Lord your God with all your heart, *with all your soul*, and with all your might
Deut 10:12 And now, Israel, what does the Lord your God require of you, but to fear the Lord your God, to walk in all His ways and to love Him, to serve the Lord your God with all your heart and *with all your soul*
Deut 11:13 And it shall be that if you diligently obey My commandments which I command you today, to love the Lord your God and serve Him with all your heart and *with all your soul*
Deut 13:3 you shall not listen to the words of that prophet or that dreamer of dreams, for the Lord your God is testing you to know whether you love the Lord your God with all your heart and *with all your soul*
Deut 26:16 therefore you shall be careful to observe them with all your heart and *with all your soul*
Deut 30:2 and you return to the Lord your God and obey His voice, according to all that I command you today, you and your children, with all your heart and *with all your soul*
Deut 30:6 And the Lord your God will circumcise your heart and the heart of your descendants, to love the Lord your God with all your heart and *with all your soul*, that you may live
Deut 30:10 if you obey the voice of the Lord your God, to keep His commandments and His statutes which are written in this Book of the Law, and if you turn to the Lord your God with all your heart and *with all your soul*
Josh 22:5 But take diligent heed to do the commandment and the law which Moses the servant of the Lord commanded you, to love the Lord your God, to walk in all His ways, to keep His commandments, to hold fast to Him, and to serve Him with all your heart and *with all your soul*
Matt 22:37 Jesus said to him, "'You shall love the Lord your God with all your heart, *with all your soul*, and with all your mind
Mark 12:30 And you shall love the Lord your God with all your heart, *with all your soul*, with all your mind, and with all your strength
Luke 10:27 So he answered and said, "'You shall love the Lord your God with all your heart, *with all your soul*, with all your strength, and with all your mind

WITH AUTHORITY
Mark 1:27 For *with authority* He commands even the unclean spirits, and they obey Him
Luke 4:32 And they were astonished at His teaching, for His word was *with authority*
Luke 4:36 For *with authority* and power He commands the unclean spirits, and they come out
Acts 26:12 While thus occupied, as I journeyed to Damascus *with authority* and commission from the chief priests

WITH BLOOD
Deut 32:42 I will make My arrows drunk *with blood*, and My sword shall devour flesh, with the blood of the slain and the captives, from the heads of the leaders of the enemy
1Kin 2:9 but bring his gray hair down to the grave *with blood*
Ps 106:38 And shed innocent blood, even the blood of their sons and daughters, whom they sacrificed

to the idols of Canaan; and the land was polluted *with blood*
Is 34:6 The sword of the Lord is filled *with blood*, it is made overflowing with fatness, and with the blood of lambs and goats, with the fat of the kidneys of rams
Is 34:7 their land shall be soaked *with blood*, and their dust saturated with fatness
Is 59:3 For your hands are defiled *with blood*, and your fingers with iniquity
Lam 4:14 they have defiled themselves *with blood*, so that no one would touch their garments
Ezek 33:25 You eat meat *with blood*, you lift up your eyes toward your idols, and shed blood
Hos 6:8 Gilead is a city of evildoers, and is defiled *with blood*
Zech 9:15 they shall be filled *with blood* like basins, like the corners of the altar
Heb 9:21 Then likewise he sprinkled *with blood* both the tabernacle and all the vessels of the ministry
Heb 9:22 And according to the law almost all things are purged *with blood*, and without shedding of blood there is no remission
Heb 9:25 not that He should offer Himself often, as the high priest enters the Most Holy Place every year *with blood* of another
Rev 8:7 And hail and fire followed, mingled *with blood*, and they were thrown to the earth

WITH GOD
Gen 5:22 After he begot Methuselah, Enoch walked *with God* three hundred years, and begot sons and daughters
Gen 5:24 And Enoch walked *with God;* and he was not, for God took him
Gen 6:9 Noah was a just man, perfect in his generations. Noah walked *with God*
Gen 32:28 for you have struggled *with God* and with men, and have prevailed
Ex 19:17 And Moses brought the people out of the camp to meet *with God*, and they stood at the foot of the mountain
1Sam 14:45 As the Lord lives, not one hair of his head shall fall to the ground, for he has worked *with God* this day
2Sam 12:16 David therefore pleaded *with God* for the child, and David fasted and went in and lay all night on the ground
2Sam 23:5 Although my house is not so *with God*, yet He has made with me an everlasting covenant, ordered in all things and secure
2Chr 1:3 for the tabernacle of meeting *with God* was there, which Moses the servant of the Lord had made in the wilderness
2Chr 35:21 Refrain from meddling *with God*, who is with me, lest He destroy you
Job 13:3 But I would speak to the Almighty, and I desire to reason *with God*
Job 16:21 Oh, that one might plead for a man *with God*, as a man pleads for his neighbor
Job 27:13 This is the portion of a wicked man *with God*, and the heritage of oppressors, received from the Almighty
Job 37:22 He comes from the north as golden splendor; *with God* is awesome majesty
Hos 11:12 but Judah still walks *with God*, even with the Holy One who is faithful
Hos 12:3 He took his brother by the heel in the womb, and in his strength he struggled *with God*
Matt 19:26 But Jesus looked at them and said to them, "With men this is impossible, but *with God* all things are possible
Mark 10:27 But looking at them, Jesus said, "With men it is impossible, but not *with God;* for *with God* all things are possible
Luke 1:30 Then the angel said to her, "Do not be afraid, Mary, for you have found favor *with God*
Luke 1:37 For *with God* nothing will be impossible
Luke 2:52 And Jesus increased in wisdom and stature, and in favor *with God* and men
Luke 18:27 But He said, "The things which are impossible with men are possible *with God*
John 1:1 In the beginning was the Word, and the Word was *with God*, and the Word was God
John 1:2 He was in the beginning *with God*
John 5:18 Therefore the Jews sought all the more to kill Him, because He not only broke the Sabbath, but also said that God was His Father, making Himself equal *with God*
Rom 2:11 For there is no partiality *with God*
Rom 5:1 Therefore, having been justified by faith, we have peace *with God* through our Lord Jesus Christ
Rom 9:14 What shall we say then? Is there unrighteousness *with God?* Certainly not
Rom 11:2 Or do you not know what the Scripture says of Elijah, how he pleads *with God* against Israel, saying
1Cor 3:19 For the wisdom of this world is foolishness *with God*
1Cor 7:24 Brethren, let each one remain *with God* in that calling in which he was called
Phil 2:6 who, being in the form of God, did not consider it robbery to be equal *with God*
2Th 1:6 since it is a righteous thing *with God* to repay with tribulation those who trouble you
Jas 4:4 Do you not know that friendship with the world is enmity *with God*

WITH HIS STRIPES WE ARE HEALED (KJV, RSV)
(See *BY HIS STRIPES WE ARE HEALED*)

WITH MY SPIRIT
Rom 1:9 For God is my witness, whom I serve *with my spirit* in the gospel of His Son, that without ceasing I make mention of you always in my prayers
1Cor 5:4 In the name of our Lord Jesus Christ, when you are gathered together, along *with my spirit*, with the power of our Lord Jesus Christ

WITH MY WHOLE HEART (NIV)
(See *WITH MY SPIRIT*)

WITH ONE ACCORD
Josh 9:2 that they gathered together to fight with Joshua and Israel *with one accord*
1Kin 22:13 Then the messenger who had gone to call Micaiah spoke to him, saying, "Now listen, the words of the prophets *with one accord* encourage the king
2Chr 18:12 Then the messenger who had gone to call Micaiah spoke to him, saying, "Now listen, the words of the prophets *with one accord* encourage the king
Zeph 3:9 For then I will restore to the peoples a pure language, that they all may call on the name of the Lord, to serve Him *with one accord*
Luke 14:18 But they all *with one accord* began to make excuses
Acts 1:14 These all continued *with one accord* in prayer and supplication, with the women and Mary the mother of Jesus, and with His brothers
Acts 2:1 Now when the Day of Pentecost had fully come, they were all *with one accord* in one place
Acts 2:46 So continuing daily *with one accord* in the temple, and breaking bread from house to house, they ate their food with gladness and simplicity of heart
Acts 4:24 So when they heard that, they raised their voice to God *with one accord* and said
Acts 5:12 And they were all *with one accord* in Solomon's Porch

Acts 7:57 Then they cried out with a loud voice, stopped their ears, and ran at him *with one accord*
Acts 8:6 And the multitudes *with one accord* heeded the things spoken by Philip, hearing and seeing the miracles which he did
Acts 12:20 but they came to him *with one accord*, and having made Blastus the king's chamberlain their friend, they asked for peace, because their country was supplied with food by the king's country
Acts 15:25 it seemed good to us, being assembled *with one accord*, to send chosen men to you with our beloved Barnabas and Paul
Acts 18:12 Now when Gallio was proconsul of Achaia, the Jews *with one accord* rose up against Paul and brought him to the judgment seat
Acts 19:29 So the whole city was filled with confusion, and rushed into the theater *with one accord*, having seized Gaius and Aristarchus, Macedonians, Paul's travel companions

WITH OUR HEARTS SPRINKLED (RSV)
(See *HAVING OUR HEARTS SPRINKLED*)

WITH THE HEART
Rom 10:10 For *with the heart* one believes to righteousness, and with the mouth confession is made to salvation

WITH THE HOLY SPIRIT AND FIRE
Matt 3:11 He will baptize you *with the Holy Spirit and fire*

WITH THE SAME MEASURE
Matt 7:2 and *with the same measure* you use, it will be measured back to you
Mark 4:24 *With the same measure* you use, it will be measured to you
Luke 6:38 For *with the same measure* that you use, it will be measured back to you

WITH THE SWORD (RSV)
(See *EDGE OF THE SWORD*)

WITH THE SWORD, FAMINE AND PLAGUE (NIV)
(See *BY THE SWORD, BY THE FAMINE, AND BY THE PESTILENCE*)

WITH THEIR LIPS DO HONOR ME (KJV)
(See *HONOR ME WITH THEIR LIPS*)

WITH WHOM I AM WELL PLEASED (RSV)
(See *IN WHOM I AM WELL PLEASED*)

WITHDRAW YOUR HAND
1Sam 14:19 Now it happened, while Saul talked to the priest, that the noise which was in the camp of the Philistines continued to increase; so Saul said to the priest, "*Withdraw your hand*
Job 13:21 *Withdraw Your hand* far from me, and let not the dread of You make me afraid
Ps 74:11 Why do You *withdraw Your hand*, even Your right hand

WITHDRAWN HIS HAND
Lam 2:8 He has not *withdrawn His hand* from destroying; therefore He has caused the rampart and wall to lament
Ezek 18:8 if he has not exacted usury nor taken any increase, but has *withdrawn his hand* from iniquity and executed true judgment between man and man
Ezek 18:17 who has *withdrawn his hand* from the poor and not received usury or increase, but has executed My judgments and walked in My statutes he shall not die for the iniquity of his father

WITHDREW INTO THE WILDERNESS
Luke 5:16 So He Himself often *withdrew into the wilderness* and prayed

WITHHOLD HIS HAND (NIV)
(See *WITHDRAWN HIS HAND*)

WITHIN THE VEIL (KJV, RSV)
(See *INSIDE THE VEIL*)

WITHOUT BLEMISH
Ex 12:5 Your lamb shall be *without blemish*, a male of the first year
Ex 29:1 And this is what you shall do to them to hallow them for ministering to Me as priests: Take one young bull and two rams *without blemish*
Lev 1:3 If his offering is a burnt sacrifice of the herd, let him offer a male *without blemish*
Lev 1:10 And if his offering is of the flocks of the sheep or of the goats as a burnt sacrifice, he shall bring a male *without blemish*
Lev 3:1 When his offering is a sacrifice of a peace offering, if he offers it of the herd, whether male or female, he shall offer it *without blemish* before the Lord
Lev 3:6 If his offering as a sacrifice of a peace offering to the Lord is of the flock, whether male or female, he shall offer it *without blemish*
Lev 4:3 if the anointed priest sins, bringing guilt on the people, then let him offer to the Lord for his sin which he has sinned a young bull *without blemish* as a sin offering
Lev 4:23 or if his sin which he has committed comes to his knowledge, he shall bring as his offering a kid of the goats, a male *without blemish*
Lev 4:28 or if his sin which he has committed comes to his knowledge, then he shall bring as his offering a kid of the goats, a female *without blemish*, for his sin which he has committed
Lev 4:32 If he brings a lamb as his sin offering, he shall bring a female *without blemish*
Lev 5:15 If a person commits a trespass, and sins unintentionally in regard to the holy things of the Lord, then he shall bring to the Lord as his trespass offering a ram *without blemish* from the flocks, with your valuation in shekels of silver according to the shekel of the sanctuary, as a trespass offering
Lev 5:18 And he shall bring to the priest a ram *without blemish* from the flock, with your valuation, as a trespass offering
Lev 6:6 And he shall bring his trespass offering to the Lord, a ram *without blemish* from the flock, with your valuation, as a trespass offering, to the priest
Lev 9:2 And he said to Aaron, "Take for yourself a young bull as a sin offering and a ram as a burnt offering, *without blemish*, and offer them before the Lord
Lev 9:3 And to the children of Israel you shall speak, saying, 'Take a kid of the goats as a sin offering, and a calf and a lamb, both of the first year, *without blemish*, as a burnt offering
Lev 14:10 And on the eighth day he shall take two male lambs *without blemish*, one ewe lamb of the first year *without blemish*, three-tenths of an ephah of fine flour mixed with oil as a grain offering, and one log of oil
Lev 22:19 you shall offer of your own free will a male *without blemish* from the cattle, from the sheep, or from the goats
Lev 23:12 And you shall offer on that day, when you wave the sheaf, a male lamb of the first year, *without blemish*, as a burnt offering to the Lord
Lev 23:18 And you shall offer with the bread seven lambs of the first year, *without blemish*, one young bull, and two rams

Num 6:14 one male lamb in its first year *without blemish* as a burnt offering, one ewe lamb in its first year *without blemish* as a sin offering, one ram *without blemish* as a peace offering
Num 19:2 Speak to the children of Israel, that they bring you a red heifer *without blemish*, in which there is no defect and on which a yoke has never come
Num 28:3 two male lambs in their first year *without blemish*, day by day, as a regular burnt offering
Num 28:9 And on the Sabbath day two lambs in their first year, *without blemish*, and two-tenths of an ephah of fine flour as a grain offering, mixed with oil, with its drink offering
Num 28:11 two young bulls, one ram, and seven lambs in their first year, *without blemish*
Num 28:19 two young bulls, one ram, and seven lambs in their first year. Be sure they are *without blemish*
Num 28:31 Be sure they are *without blemish*. You shall present them with their drink offerings, besides the regular burnt offering with its grain offering
Num 29:2 one young bull, one ram, and seven lambs in their first year, *without blemish*
Num 29:8 one young bull, one ram, and seven lambs in their first year. Be sure they are *without blemish*
Num 29:13 thirteen young bulls, two rams, and fourteen lambs in their first year. They shall be *without blemish*
Num 29:17 On the second day present twelve young bulls, two rams, fourteen lambs in their first year *without blemish*
Num 29:20 On the third day present eleven bulls, two rams, fourteen lambs in their first year *without blemish*
Num 29:23 On the fourth day present ten bulls, two rams, and fourteen lambs in their first year, *without blemish*
Num 29:26 On the fifth day present nine bulls, two rams, and fourteen lambs in their first year *without blemish*
Num 29:29 On the sixth day present eight bulls, two rams, and fourteen lambs in their first year *without blemish*
Num 29:32 On the seventh day present seven bulls, two rams, and fourteen lambs in their first year *without blemish*
Num 29:36 one bull, one ram, seven lambs in their first year *without blemish*
Ezek 43:22 On the second day you shall offer a kid of the goats *without blemish* for a sin offering
Ezek 43:23 When you have finished cleansing it, you shall offer a young bull *without blemish*, and a ram from the flock *without blemish*
Ezek 43:25 they shall also prepare a young bull and a ram from the flock, both *without blemish*
Ezek 45:18 In the first month, on the first day of the month, you shall take a young bull *without blemish* and cleanse the sanctuary
Ezek 45:23 On the seven days of the feast he shall prepare a burnt offering to the Lord, seven bulls and seven rams *without blemish*, daily for seven days, and a kid of the goats daily for a sin offering
Ezek 46:4 The burnt offering that the prince offers to the Lord on the Sabbath day shall be six lambs *without blemish*, and a ram *without blemish*
Ezek 46:6 On the day of the New Moon it shall be a young bull *without blemish*, six lambs, and a ram; they shall be *without blemish*
Ezek 46:13 You shall daily make a burnt offering to the Lord of a lamb of the first year *without blemish*
Eph 5:27 that He might present it to Himself a glorious church, not having spot or wrinkle or any such thing, but that it should be holy and *without blemish*
1Pet 1:19 but with the precious blood of Christ, as of a lamb *without blemish* and without spot

WITHOUT BLOOD
Heb 9:7 But into the second part the high priest went alone once a year, not *without blood*, which he offered for himself and for the people's sins committed in ignorance
Heb 9:18 Therefore not even the first covenant was dedicated *without blood*

WITHOUT DEFECT (NAS, NIV)
(See *WITHOUT BLEMISH*)

WITHOUT FORM, AND VOID
Gen 1:2 The earth was *without form, and void;* and darkness was on the face of the deep
Jer 4:23 I beheld the earth, and indeed it was *without form, and void*

WITHOUT GRUMBLING
1Pet 4:9 Be hospitable to one another *without grumbling*

WITHOUT KNOWLEDGE HE MULTIPLIES WORDS (NIV)
(See *WORDS WITHOUT KNOWLEDGE*)

WITHOUT MONEY AND WITHOUT PRICE
Is 55:1 Yes, come, buy wine and milk *without money and without price*

WITHOUT SENSE (RSV)
(See *DEVOID OF UNDERSTANDING*)

WITHOUT SIN
John 8:7 So when they continued asking Him, He raised Himself up and said to them, "He who is *without sin* among you, let him throw a stone at her first
Heb 4:15 For we do not have a High Priest who cannot sympathize with our weaknesses, but was in all points tempted as we are, yet *without sin*

WITHOUT THE CAMP (KJV)
(See *OUTSIDE THE CAMP*)

WITHOUT THE LAW (KJV)
(See *APART FROM THE LAW*)

WITNESS AGAINST YOU
Deut 4:26 I call heaven and earth to *witness against you* this day, that you will soon utterly perish from the land which you cross over the Jordan to possess
Deut 31:26 Take this Book of the Law, and put it beside the ark of the covenant of the Lord your God, that it may be there as a *witness against you*
1Sam 12:5 Then he said to them, "The Lord is *witness against you*, and His anointed is witness this day, that you have not found anything in my hand
Mic 1:2 Let the Lord God be a *witness against you*, the Lord from His holy temple
Jas 5:3 Your gold and silver are corroded, and their corrosion will be a *witness against you* and will eat your flesh like fire

WITNESS BETWEEN YOU AND ME
Gen 31:44 Now therefore, come, let us make a covenant, you and I, and let it be a *witness between you and me*
Gen 31:48 And Laban said, "This heap is a *witness between you and me* this day
Gen 31:50 If you afflict my daughters, or if you

take other wives besides my daughters, although no man is with us see, God is *witness between you and me*

WITNESS TO JESUS

Rev 20:4 And I saw the souls of those who had been beheaded for their *witness to Jesus* and for the word of God, who had not worshiped the beast or his image, and had not received his mark on their foreheads or on their hands

WOE IS ME

Ps 120:5 *Woe is me*, that I sojourn in Meshech, That I dwell among the tents of Kedar

Is 6:5 *Woe is me*, for I am undone! Because I am a man of unclean lips, and I dwell in the midst of a people of unclean lips

Jer 4:31 For I have heard a voice as of a woman in labor, the anguish as of her who brings forth her first child, the voice of the daughter of Zion bewailing herself, who spreads her hands, saying, '*Woe is me* now, for my soul is weary because of murderers

Jer 10:19 *Woe is me* for my hurt! My wound is severe

Jer 15:10 *Woe is me*, my mother, that you have borne me, a man of strife and a man of contention to the whole earth

Jer 45:3 You said, "*Woe is me* now! For the Lord has added grief to my sorrow

Mic 7:1 *Woe is me!* For I am like those who gather summer fruits, like those who glean vintage grapes

1Cor 9:16 yes, *woe is me* if I do not preach the gospel

WOE TO ARIEL

Is 29:1 *Woe to Ariel*, to Ariel, the city where David dwelt

WOE TO HIM

Eccl 4:10 But *woe to him* who is alone when he falls, for he has no one to help him up

Is 45:9 *Woe to him* who strives with his Maker! Let the potsherd strive with the potsherds of the earth

Is 45:10 *Woe to him* who says to his father, 'What are you begetting

Jer 22:13 *Woe to him* who builds his house by unrighteousness and his chambers by injustice, who uses his neighbor's service without wages and gives him nothing for his work

Hab 2:6 Shall not all these take up a proverb against him, and a taunting riddle against him, and say, '*Woe to him* who increases what is not his how long

Hab 2:9 *Woe to him* who covets evil gain for his house, that he may set his nest on high, that he may be delivered from the power of disaster

Hab 2:12 *Woe to him* who builds a town with bloodshed, who establishes a city by iniquity

Hab 2:15 *Woe to him* who gives drink to his neighbor, pressing him to your bottle, even to make him drunk, that you may look on his nakedness

Hab 2:19 *Woe to him* who says to wood, 'Awake!' to silent stone

Luke 17:1 Then He said to the disciples, "It is impossible that no offenses should come, but *woe to him* through whom they do come

WOE TO ME

Job 10:15 If I am wicked, *woe to me;* even if I am righteous, I cannot lift up my head

Is 24:16 *Woe to me!* The treacherous dealers have dealt treacherously, indeed, the treacherous dealers have dealt very treacherously

WOE TO THE BLOODY CITY

Ezek 24:6 *Woe to the bloody city*, to the pot whose scum is in it, and whose scum is not gone from it

Ezek 24:9 *Woe to the bloody city!* I too will make the pyre great

Nah 3:1 *Woe to the bloody city!* It is all full of lies and robbery

WOE TO THOSE

Is 5:8 *Woe to those* who join house to house, who add field to field, till there is no place Where they may dwell alone in the midst of the land

Is 5:11 *Woe to those* who rise early in the morning, that they may follow intoxicating drink

Is 5:18 *Woe to those* who draw iniquity with cords of vanity, and sin as if with a cart rope

Is 5:20 *Woe to those* who call evil good, and good evil

Is 5:21 *Woe to those* who are wise in their own eyes, and prudent in their own sight

Is 10:1 *Woe to those* who decree unrighteous decrees, who write misfortune, which they have prescribed

Is 29:15 *Woe to those* who seek deep to hide their counsel far from the Lord, and their works are in the dark

Is 31:1 *Woe to those* who go down to Egypt for help, and rely on horses, who trust in chariots because they are many, and in horsemen because they are very strong, but who do not look to the Holy One of Israel, nor seek the Lord

Mic 2:1 *Woe to those* who devise iniquity, and work out evil on their beds

Matt 24:19 But *woe to those* who are pregnant and to those with nursing babies in those days

Mark 13:17 But *woe to those* who are pregnant and to those with nursing babies in those days

Luke 21:23 But *woe to those* who are pregnant and to those who are nursing babies in those days

WOE TO YOU

Num 21:29 *Woe to you*, Moab! You have perished, O people of Chemosh

Eccl 10:16 *Woe to you*, O land, when your king is a child, and your princes feast in the morning

Is 33:1 *Woe to you* who plunder, though you have not been plundered

Jer 13:27 *Woe to you*, O Jerusalem! Will you still not be made clean

Jer 48:46 *Woe to you*, O Moab! The people of Chemosh perish

Ezek 16:23 Then it was so, after all your wickedness' Woe, *woe to you*

Amos 5:18 *Woe to you* who desire the day of the Lord

Amos 6:1 *Woe to you* who are at ease in Zion, and trust in Mount Samaria, notable persons in the chief nation, to whom the house of Israel comes

Amos 6:3 *Woe to you* who put far off the day of doom, who cause the seat of violence to come near

Matt 11:21 *Woe to you*, Chorazin! *Woe to you*, Bethsaida

Matt 23:13 But *woe to you*, scribes and Pharisees, hypocrites! For you shut up the kingdom of heaven against men

Matt 23:14 *Woe to you*, scribes and Pharisees, hypocrites! For you devour widows' houses, and for a pretense make long prayers

Matt 23:15 *Woe to you*, scribes and Pharisees, hypocrites! For you travel land and sea to win one proselyte, and when he is won, you make him twice as much a son of hell as yourselves

Matt 23:16 *Woe to you*, blind guides, who say, 'Whoever swears by the temple, it is nothing

Matt 23:23 *Woe to you*, scribes and Pharisees, hypocrites! For you pay tithe of mint and anise

and cumin, and have neglected the weightier matters of the law
Matt 23:25 *Woe to you*, scribes and Pharisees, hypocrites! For you cleanse the outside of the cup and dish, but inside they are full of extortion and self-indulgence
Matt 23:27 *Woe to you*, scribes and Pharisees, hypocrites! For you are like whitewashed tombs which indeed appear beautiful outwardly, but inside are full of dead men's bones and all uncleanness
Matt 23:29 *Woe to you*, scribes and Pharisees, hypocrites! Because you build the tombs of the prophets and adorn the monuments of the righteous
Luke 6:24 But *woe to you* who are rich, for you have received your consolation
Luke 6:25 *Woe to you* who are full, for you shall hunger. *Woe to you* who laugh now, for you shall mourn and weep
Luke 6:26 *Woe to you* when all men speak well of you, for so did their fathers to the false prophets
Luke 10:13 *Woe to you*, Chorazin! *Woe to you*, Bethsaida
Luke 11:42 But *woe to you* Pharisees! For you tithe mint and rue and all manner of herbs, and pass by justice and the love of God
Luke 11:43 *Woe to you* Pharisees! For you love the best seats in the synagogues and greetings in the marketplaces
Luke 11:44 *Woe to you*, scribes and Pharisees, hypocrites! For you are like graves which are not seen, and the men who walk over them are not aware of them
Luke 11:46 And He said, "*Woe to you* also, you lawyers! For you load men with burdens hard to bear, and you yourselves do not touch the burdens with one of your fingers
Luke 11:47 *Woe to you!* For you build the tombs of the prophets, and your fathers killed them
Luke 11:52 *Woe to you* lawyers! For you have taken away the key of knowledge

WOE UNTO THEM (KJV)
(See *WOE TO THOSE*)

WOLF AND THE LAMB
Is 65:25 The *wolf and the lamb* shall feed together, the lion shall eat straw like the ox, and dust shall be the serpent's food

WOLVES AT DUSK (NIV)
(See *EVENING WOLVES*)

WOLVES WILL COME IN AMONG YOU
Acts 20:29 For I know this, that after my departure savage *wolves will come in among you*, not sparing the flock

WOMAN, BEHOLD YOUR SON
John 19:26 When Jesus therefore saw His mother, and the disciple whom He loved standing by, He said to His mother, "*Woman, behold your son*

WOMAN CAUGHT IN ADULTERY
John 8:3 Then the scribes and Pharisees brought to Him a *woman caught in adultery*

WOMAN, HERE IS YOUR SON (NIV)
(See *WOMAN, BEHOLD YOUR SON*)

WOMAN IN BIRTH PANGS
Jer 48:41 the mighty men's hearts in Moab on that day shall be like the heart of a *woman in birth pangs*
Jer 49:22 The heart of the mighty men of Edom in that day shall be like the heart of a *woman in birth pangs*
Mic 4:10 Be in pain, and labor to bring forth, O daughter of Zion, like a *woman in birth pangs*

WOMAN IN LABOR
Is 21:3 pangs have taken hold of me, like the pangs of a *woman in labor*
Is 42:14 Now I will cry like a *woman in labor*, I will pant and gasp at once
Jer 4:31 For I have heard a voice as of a *woman in labor*, the anguish as of her who brings forth her first child, the voice of the daughter of Zion bewailing herself, who spreads her hands, saying
Jer 6:24 Anguish has taken hold of us, pain as of a *woman in labor*
Jer 13:21 Will not pangs seize you, like a *woman in labor*
Jer 22:23 O inhabitant of Lebanon, making your nest in the cedars, how gracious will you be when pangs come upon you, like the pain of a *woman in labor*
Jer 30:6 So why do I see every man with his hands on his loins like a *woman in labor*, and all faces turned pale
Jer 49:24 Anguish and sorrows have taken her like a *woman in labor*
Mic 4:9 For pangs have seized you like a *woman in labor*

WOMAN IN TRAVAIL
Ps 48:6 Fear took hold of them there, and pain, as of a *woman in travail*

WOMAN OF NOBLE CHARACTER (NIV)
(See *VIRTUOUS WOMAN*)

WOMAN OF SAMARIA
John 4:7 A *woman of Samaria* came to draw water. Jesus said to her
John 4:9 Then the *woman of Samaria* said to Him, "How is it that You, being a Jew, ask a drink from me, a Samaritan woman

WOMAN OF WORTH (RSV)
(See *VIRTUOUS WOMAN*)

WOMAN TAKEN IN ADULTERY (KJV)
(See *WOMAN CAUGHT IN ADULTERY*)

WOMAN THAT TRAVAILETH (KJV)
(See *WOMAN IN LABOR*)

WOMAN WHO HAD A FLOW OF BLOOD
Matt 9:20 And suddenly, a *woman who had a flow of blood* for twelve years came from behind and touched the hem of His garment

WONDERFUL ACTS (NIV)
(See *WONDROUS WORKS*)

WONDERFUL THINGS (NIV)
(See *GLORIOUS THINGS*)

WONDERFUL WORKS
Ps 40:5 Many, O Lord my God, are Your *wonderful works* which You have done
Ps 78:4 We will not hide them from their children, telling to the generation to come the praises of the Lord, and His strength and His *wonderful works* that He has done
Ps 107:8 Oh, that men would give thanks to the Lord for His goodness, and for His *wonderful works* to the children of men
Ps 107:15 Oh, that men would give thanks to the Lord for His goodness, and for His *wonderful works* to the children of men
Ps 107:21 Oh, that men would give thanks to the Lord for His goodness, and for His *wonderful works* to the children of men

Ps 107:31 Oh, that men would give thanks to the Lord for His goodness, and for His *wonderful works* to the children of men
Ps 111:4 He has made His *wonderful works* to be remembered; the Lord is gracious and full of compassion
Jer 21:2 Perhaps the Lord will deal with us according to all His *wonderful works*, that the king may go away from us
Acts 2:11 Cretans and Arabs we hear them speaking in our own tongues the *wonderful works* of God

WONDERS HE HAS DONE (NIV)
(See *WORKS THAT HE HAS DONE*)

WONDERS WHICH HE HAS WROUGHT (RSV)
(See *WORKS THAT HE HAS DONE*)

WONDROUS DEEDS (RSV)
(See *WONDERFUL WORKS*)

WONDROUS WORKS
1Chr 16:9 Sing to Him, sing psalms to Him; talk of all His *wondrous works*
Job 37:14 Listen to this, O Job; stand still and consider the *wondrous works* of God
Job 37:16 Do you know the balance of clouds, those *wondrous works* of Him who is perfect in knowledge
Ps 26:7 That I may proclaim with the voice of thanksgiving, and tell of all Your *wondrous works*
Ps 71:17 O God, You have taught me from my youth; and to this day I declare Your *wondrous works*
Ps 75:1 For Your *wondrous works* declare that Your name is near
Ps 78:32 In spite of this they still sinned, and did not believe in His *wondrous works*
Ps 105:2 Sing to Him, sing psalms to Him; talk of all His *wondrous works*
Ps 106:22 *Wondrous works* in the land of Ham, awesome things by the Red Sea
Ps 119:27 Make me understand the way of Your precepts; so shall I meditate on Your *wondrous works*
Ps 145:5 I will meditate on the glorious splendor of Your majesty, and on Your *wondrous works*

WOODEN ASHERAH POLE (NIV)
(See *WOODEN IMAGE*)

WOODEN IMAGE
Deut 16:21 You shall not plant for yourself any tree, as a *wooden image*, near the altar which you build for yourself to the Lord your God
Judg 6:25 Now it came to pass the same night that the Lord said to him, "Take your father's young bull, the second bull of seven years old, and tear down the altar of Baal that your father has, and cut down the *wooden image* that is beside it
Judg 6:28 and the *wooden image* that was beside it was cut down, and the second bull was being offered on the altar which had been built
Judg 6:30 Then the men of the city said to Joash, "Bring out your son, that he may die, because he has torn down the altar of Baal, and because he has cut down the *wooden image* that was beside it
1Kin 16:33 And Ahab made a *wooden image*. Ahab did more to provoke the Lord God of Israel to anger than all the kings of Israel who were before him
2Kin 17:16 So they left all the commandments of the Lord their God, made for themselves a molded image and two calves, made a *wooden image* and worshiped all the host of heaven, and served Baal
2Kin 21:3 he raised up altars for Baal, and made a *wooden image*, as Ahab king of Israel had done
2Kin 23:6 And he brought out the *wooden image* from the house of the Lord, to the Brook Kidron outside Jerusalem, burned it at the Brook Kidron and ground it to ashes, and threw its ashes on the graves of the common people
2Kin 23:7 Then he tore down the ritual booths of the perverted persons that were in the house of the Lord, where the women wove hangings for the *wooden image*
2Kin 23:15 and he burned the high place and crushed it to powder, and burned the *wooden image*

WOODEN IMAGES
Ex 34:13 But you shall destroy their altars, break their sacred pillars, and cut down their *wooden images*
Deut 7:5 you shall destroy their altars, and break down their sacred pillars, and cut down their *wooden images*, and burn their carved images with fire
Deut 12:3 And you shall destroy their altars, break their sacred pillars, and burn their *wooden images* with fire
1Kin 14:15 He will uproot Israel from this good land which He gave to their fathers, and will scatter them beyond the River, because they have made their *wooden images*, provoking the Lord to anger
1Kin 14:23 For they also built for themselves high places, sacred pillars, and *wooden images* on every high hill and under every green tree
2Kin 13:6 Nevertheless they did not depart from the sins of the house of Jeroboam, who had made Israel sin, but walked in them; and the *wooden images* also remained in Samaria
2Kin 17:10 They set up for themselves sacred pillars and *wooden images* on every high hill and under every green tree
2Kin 18:4 He removed the high places and broke the sacred pillars, cut down the *wooden images* and broke in pieces the bronze serpent that Moses had made
2Kin 23:14 And he broke in pieces the sacred pillars and cut down the *wooden images*, and filled their places with the bones of men
2Chr 14:3 for he removed the altars of the foreign gods and the high places, and broke down the sacred pillars and cut down the *wooden images*
2Chr 17:6 moreover he removed the high places and *wooden images* from Judah
2Chr 19:3 Nevertheless good things are found in you, in that you have removed the *wooden images* from the land, and have prepared your heart to seek God
2Chr 24:18 Therefore they left the house of the Lord God of their fathers, and served *wooden images* and idols
2Chr 31:1 Now when all this was finished, all Israel who were present went out to the cities of Judah and broke the sacred pillars in pieces, cut down the *wooden images*, and threw down the high places and the altars from all Judah, Benjamin, Ephraim, and Manasseh until they had utterly destroyed them all
2Chr 33:3 he raised up altars for the Baals, and made *wooden images*
2Chr 33:19 Also his prayer and how God received his entreaty, and all his sin and trespass, and the sites where he built high places and set up *wooden images* and carved images, before he was humbled, indeed they are written among the sayings of Hozai
2Chr 34:3 and in the twelfth year he began to

purge Judah and Jerusalem of the high places, the *wooden images*, the carved images, and the molded images
2Chr 34:4 and the *wooden images*, the carved images, and the molded images he broke in pieces, and made dust of them and scattered it on the graves of those who had sacrificed to them
2Chr 34:7 When he had broken down the altars and the *wooden images*, had beaten the carved images into powder, and cut down all the incense altars throughout all the land of Israel, he returned to Jerusalem
Is 17:8 he will not respect what his fingers have made, nor the *wooden images* nor the incense altars
Is 27:9 when he makes all the stones of the altar like chalkstones that are beaten to dust, when *wooden images* and incense altars do not stand up
Jer 17:2 while their children remember their altars and their *wooden images* by the green trees on the high hills
Mic 5:14 I will pluck your *wooden images* from your midst; thus I will destroy your cities

WORD APTLY SPOKEN (NIV)
(See *WORD FITLY SPOKEN*)

WORD BECAME FLESH
John 1:14 And the *Word became flesh* and dwelt among us, and we beheld His glory, the glory as of the only begotten of the Father, full of grace and truth

WORD FITLY SPOKEN
Prov 25:11 A *word fitly spoken* is like apples of gold in settings of silver

WORD OF EXHORTATION
Acts 13:15 And after the reading of the Law and the Prophets, the rulers of the synagogue sent to them, saying, "Men and brethren, if you have any *word of exhortation* for the people, say on
Heb 13:22 And I appeal to you, brethren, bear with the *word of exhortation*, for I have written to you in few words

WORD OF FAITH
Rom 10:8 The word is near you, even in your mouth and in your heart" (that is, the *word of faith* which we preach

WORD OF GOD
1Sam 9:27 But you stand here awhile, that I may announce to you the *word of God*
1Kin 12:22 But the *word of God* came to Shemaiah the man of God, saying
1Chr 17:3 But it happened that night that the *word of God* came to Nathan, saying
Prov 30:5 Every *word of God* is pure; He is a shield to those who put their trust in Him
Mark 7:13 making the *word of God* of no effect through your tradition which you have handed down
Luke 3:2 Annas and Caiaphas being high priests, the *word of God* came to John the son of Zacharias in the wilderness
Luke 4:4 But Jesus answered him, saying, "It is written, 'Man shall not live by bread alone, but by every *word of God*
Luke 5:1 Now so it was, as the multitude pressed about Him to hear the *word of God*, that He stood by the Lake of Gennesaret
Luke 8:11 Now the parable is this: The seed is the *word of God*
Luke 8:21 But He answered and said to them, "My mother and My brothers are these who hear the *word of God* and do it
Luke 11:28 But He said, "More than that, blessed are those who hear the *word of God* and keep it
John 10:35 If He called them gods, to whom the *word of God* came (and the Scripture cannot be broken
Acts 4:31 and they were all filled with the Holy Spirit, and they spoke the *word of God* with boldness
Acts 6:2 Then the twelve summoned the multitude of the disciples and said, "It is not desirable that we should leave the *word of God* and serve tables
Acts 6:7 And the *word of God* spread, and the number of the disciples multiplied greatly in Jerusalem, and a great many of the priests were obedient to the faith
Acts 8:14 Now when the apostles who were at Jerusalem heard that Samaria had received the *word of God*, they sent Peter and John to them
Acts 11:1 Now the apostles and brethren who were in Judea heard that the Gentiles had also received the *word of God*
Acts 12:24 But the *word of God* grew and multiplied
Acts 13:5 And when they arrived in Salamis, they preached the *word of God* in the synagogues of the Jews
Acts 13:7 This man called for Barnabas and Saul and sought to hear the *word of God*
Acts 13:44 And the next Sabbath almost the whole city came together to hear the *word of God*
Acts 13:46 Then Paul and Barnabas grew bold and said, "It was necessary that the *word of God* should be spoken to you first
Acts 17:13 But when the Jews from Thessalonica learned that the *word of God* was preached by Paul at Berea, they came there also and stirred up the crowds
Acts 18:11 And he continued there a year and six months, teaching the *word of God* among them
Rom 9:6 But it is not that the *word of God* has taken no effect
Rom 10:17 So then faith comes by hearing, and hearing by the *word of God*
1Cor 14:36 Or did the *word of God* come originally from you
2Cor 2:17 For we are not, as so many, peddling the *word of God*
2Cor 4:2 But we have renounced the hidden things of shame, not walking in craftiness nor handling the *word of God* deceitfully, but by manifestation of the truth commending ourselves to every man's conscience in the sight of God
Eph 6:17 And take the helmet of salvation, and the sword of the Spirit, which is the *word of God*
Col 1:25 of which I became a minister according to the stewardship from God which was given to me for you, to fulfill the *word of God*
1Th 2:13 For this reason we also thank God without ceasing, because when you received the *word of God* which you heard from us, you welcomed it not as the word of men, but as it is in truth, the *word of God*, which also effectively works in you who believe
1Tim 4:5 for it is sanctified by the *word of God* and prayer
2Tim 2:9 for which I suffer trouble as an evildoer, even to the point of chains; but the *word of God* is not chained
Tit 2:5 to be discreet, chaste, homemakers, good, obedient to their own husbands, that the *word of God* may not be blasphemed
Heb 4:12 For the *word of God* is living and powerful, and sharper than any two-edged sword, piercing even to the division of soul and spirit, and of joints and marrow, and is a discerner of the thoughts and intents of the heart

Heb 6:5 and have tasted the good *word of God* and the powers of the age to come
Heb 11:3 By faith we understand that the worlds were framed by the *word of God*, so that the things which are seen were not made of things which are visible
Heb 13:7 Remember those who rule over you, who have spoken the *word of God* to you, whose faith follow, considering the outcome of their conduct
1Pet 1:23 having been born again, not of corruptible seed but incorruptible, through the *word of God* which lives and abides forever
2Pet 3:5 that by the *word of God* the heavens were of old, and the earth standing out of water and in the water
1Jn 2:14 I have written to you, young men, because you are strong, and the *word of God* abides in you, and you have overcome the wicked one
Rev 1:2 who bore witness to the *word of God*, and to the testimony of Jesus Christ, and to all things that he saw
Rev 1:9 I, John, both your brother and companion in tribulation, and in the kingdom and patience of Jesus Christ, was on the island that is called Patmos for the *word of God* and for the testimony of Jesus Christ
Rev 6:9 When He opened the fifth seal, I saw under the altar the souls of those who had been slain for the *word of God* and for the testimony which they held
Rev 19:13 He was clothed with a robe dipped in blood, and His name is called The *Word of God*
Rev 20:4 And I saw the souls of those who had been beheaded for their witness to Jesus and for the *word of God*, who had not worshiped the beast or his image, and had not received his mark on their foreheads or on their hands

WORD OF LIFE
Phil 2:16 holding fast the *word of life*, so that I may rejoice in the day of Christ that I have not run in vain or labored in vain
1Jn 1:1 That which was from the beginning, which we have heard, which we have seen with our eyes, which we have looked upon, and our hands have handled, concerning the *Word of life*

WORD OF OUR GOD STANDS FOREVER
Is 40:8 The grass withers, the flower fades, but the *word of our God stands forever*

WORD OF PROMISE
Rom 9:9 For this is the *word of promise:* "At this time I will come and Sarah shall have a son

WORD OF RECONCILIATION
2Cor 5:19 that is, that God was in Christ reconciling the world to Himself, not imputing their trespasses to them, and has committed to us the *word of reconciliation*

WORD OF THE LORD
Gen 15:1 After these things the *word of the Lord* came to Abram in a vision, saying
Gen 15:4 And behold, the *word of the Lord* came to him, saying
Ex 9:20 He who feared the *word of the Lord* among the servants of Pharaoh made his servants and his livestock flee to the houses
Ex 9:21 But he who did not regard the *word of the Lord* left his servants and his livestock in the field
Num 3:16 So Moses numbered them according to the *word of the Lord*, as he was commanded
Num 3:51 And Moses gave their redemption money to Aaron and his sons, according to the *word of the Lord*, as the Lord commanded Moses
Num 4:45 These are the ones who were numbered of the families of the sons of Merari, whom Moses and Aaron numbered according to the *word of the Lord* by the hand of Moses
Num 15:31 Because he has despised the *word of the Lord*, and has broken His commandment, that person shall be completely cut off
Num 22:18 Then Balaam answered and said to the servants of Balak, "Though Balak were to give me his house full of silver and gold, I could not go beyond the *word of the Lord* my God, to do less or more
Num 24:13 Though Balak were to give me his house full of silver and gold, I could not go beyond the *word of the Lord*, to do either good or bad of my own will
Num 36:5 Then Moses commanded the children of Israel according to the *word of the Lord*, saying
Deut 5:5 I stood between the Lord and you at that time, to declare to you the *word of the Lord*
Deut 34:5 So Moses the servant of the Lord died there in the land of Moab, according to the *word of the Lord*
Josh 8:27 Only the livestock and the spoil of that city Israel took as booty for themselves, according to the *word of the Lord* which He had commanded Joshua
Josh 19:50 According to the *word of the Lord* they gave him the city which he asked for, Timnath Serah in the mountains of Ephraim
Josh 22:9 So the children of Reuben, the children of Gad, and half the tribe of Manasseh returned, and departed from the children of Israel at Shiloh, which is in the land of Canaan, to go to the country of Gilead, to the land of their possession, which they possessed according to the *word of the Lord* by the hand of Moses
1Sam 3:1 And the *word of the Lord* was rare in those days
1Sam 3:7 (Now Samuel did not yet know the Lord, nor was the *word of the Lord* yet revealed to him
1Sam 3:21 For the Lord revealed Himself to Samuel in Shiloh by the *word of the Lord*
1Sam 15:10 Now the *word of the Lord* came to Samuel, saying
1Sam 15:23 Because you have rejected the *word of the Lord*, He also has rejected you from being king
1Sam 15:26 But Samuel said to Saul, "I will not return with you, for you have rejected the *word of the Lord*, and the Lord has rejected you from being king over Israel
2Sam 7:4 But it happened that night that the *word of the Lord* came to Nathan, saying
2Sam 22:31 the *word of the Lord* is proven; he is a shield to all who trust in Him
2Sam 24:11 Now when David arose in the morning, the *word of the Lord* came to the prophet Gad, David's seer, saying
1Kin 2:27 So Solomon removed Abiathar from being priest to the Lord, that he might fulfill the *word of the Lord* which He spoke concerning the house of Eli at Shiloh
1Kin 6:11 Then the *word of the Lord* came to Solomon, saying
1Kin 12:24 Therefore they obeyed the *word of the Lord*, and turned back, according to the *word of the Lord*
1Kin 13:1 And behold, a man of God went from Judah to Bethel by the *word of the Lord*, and Jeroboam stood by the altar to burn incense
1Kin 13:2 Then he cried out against the altar by the *word of the Lord*, and said
1Kin 13:5 The altar also was split apart, and the ashes poured out from the altar, according to the sign which the man of God had given by the *word of the Lord*
1Kin 13:9 For so it was commanded me by the *word of the Lord*, saying

1Kin 13:17 For I have been told by the *word of the Lord*
1Kin 13:18 He said to him, "I too am a prophet as you are, and an angel spoke to me by the *word of the Lord*, saying
1Kin 13:20 Now it happened, as they sat at the table, that the *word of the Lord* came to the prophet who had brought him back
1Kin 13:21 Because you have disobeyed the *word of the Lord*, and have not kept the commandment which the Lord your God commanded you
1Kin 13:26 So when the prophet who had brought him back from the way heard it, he said, "It is the man of God who was disobedient to the *word of the Lord*. Therefore the Lord has delivered him to the lion, which has torn him and killed him, according to the *word of the Lord* which He spoke to him
1Kin 13:32 For the saying which he cried out by the *word of the Lord* against the altar in Bethel, and against all the shrines on the high places which are in the cities of Samaria, will surely come to pass
1Kin 14:18 and all Israel mourned for him, according to the *word of the Lord* which He spoke through His servant Ahijah the prophet
1Kin 15:29 He did not leave to Jeroboam anyone that breathed, until he had destroyed him, according to the *word of the Lord* which He had spoken by His servant Ahijah the Shilonite
1Kin 16:1 Then the *word of the Lord* came to Jehu the son of Hanani, against Baasha, saying
1Kin 16:7 And also the *word of the Lord* came by the prophet Jehu the son of Hanani against Baasha and his house, because of all the evil that he did in the sight of the Lord in provoking Him to anger with the work of his hands, in being like the house of Jeroboam, and because he killed them
1Kin 16:12 Thus Zimri destroyed all the household of Baasha, according to the *word of the Lord*, which He spoke against Baasha by Jehu the prophet
1Kin 16:34 He laid its foundation with Abiram his firstborn, and with his youngest son Segub he set up its gates, according to the *word of the Lord*, which He had spoken through Joshua the son of Nun
1Kin 17:2 Then the *word of the Lord* came to him, saying
1Kin 17:5 So he went and did according to the *word of the Lord*, for he went and stayed by the Brook Cherith, which flows into the Jordan
1Kin 17:8 Then the *word of the Lord* came to him, saying
1Kin 17:16 The bin of flour was not used up, nor did the jar of oil run dry, according to the *word of the Lord* which He spoke by Elijah
1Kin 17:24 Then the woman said to Elijah, "Now by this I know that you are a man of God, and that the *word of the Lord* in your mouth is the truth
1Kin 18:1 Now it came to pass after many days that the *word of the Lord* came to Elijah, in the third year, saying
1Kin 18:31 And Elijah took twelve stones, according to the number of the tribes of the sons of Jacob, to whom the *word of the Lord* had come, saying
1Kin 19:9 and behold, the *word of the Lord* came to him, and He said to him
1Kin 20:35 Now a certain man of the sons of the prophets said to his neighbor by the *word of the Lord*
1Kin 21:17 Then the *word of the Lord* came to Elijah the Tishbite, saying
1Kin 21:28 And the *word of the Lord* came to Elijah the Tishbite, saying
1Kin 22:5 And Jehoshaphat said to the king of Israel, "Please inquire for the *word of the Lord* today
1Kin 22:19 Then Micaiah said, "Therefore hear the *word of the Lord*
1Kin 22:38 Then someone washed the chariot at a pool in Samaria, and the dogs licked up his blood while the harlots bathed, according to the *word of the Lord* which He had spoken
2Kin 1:17 So Ahaziah died according to the *word of the Lord* which Elijah had spoken
2Kin 3:12 And Jehoshaphat said, "The *word of the Lord* is with him
2Kin 4:44 and they ate and had some left over, according to the *word of the Lord*
2Kin 7:1 Then Elisha said, "Hear the *word of the Lord*. Thus says the Lord
2Kin 7:16 So a seah of fine flour was sold for a shekel, and two seahs of barley for a shekel, according to the *word of the Lord*
2Kin 9:26 Now therefore, take and throw him on the plot of ground, according to the *word of the Lord*
2Kin 9:36 And he said, "This is the *word of the Lord*, which He spoke by His servant Elijah the Tishbite, saying
2Kin 10:10 Know now that nothing shall fall to the earth of the *word of the Lord* which the Lord spoke concerning the house of Ahab
2Kin 10:17 And when he came to Samaria, he killed all who remained to Ahab in Samaria, till he had destroyed them, according to the *word of the Lord* which He spoke to Elijah
2Kin 14:25 He restored the territory of Israel from the entrance of Hamath to the Sea of the Arabah, according to the *word of the Lord* God of Israel, which He had spoken through His servant Jonah the son of Amittai, the prophet who was from Gath Hepher
2Kin 15:12 This was the *word of the Lord* which He spoke to Jehu, saying
2Kin 20:4 Then it happened, before Isaiah had gone out into the middle court, that the *word of the Lord* came to him, saying
2Kin 20:16 Then Isaiah said to Hezekiah, "Hear the *word of the Lord*
2Kin 20:19 Then Hezekiah said to Isaiah, "The *word of the Lord* which you have spoken is good
2Kin 23:16 And he sent and took the bones out of the tombs and burned them on the altar, and defiled it according to the *word of the Lord* which the man of God proclaimed, who proclaimed these words
2Kin 24:2 He sent them against Judah to destroy it, according to the *word of the Lord* which He had spoken by His servants the prophets
1Chr 10:13 So Saul died for his unfaithfulness which he had committed against the Lord, because he did not keep the *word of the Lord*, and also because he consulted a medium for guidance
1Chr 11:3 Then they anointed David king over Israel, according to the *word of the Lord* by Samuel
1Chr 11:10 Now these were the heads of the mighty men whom David had, who strengthened themselves with him in his kingdom, with all Israel, to make him king, according to the *word of the Lord* concerning Israel
1Chr 12:23 Now these were the numbers of the divisions that were equipped for the war, and came to David at Hebron to turn over the kingdom of Saul to him, according to the *word of the Lord*
1Chr 15:15 And the children of the Levites bore the ark of God on their shoulders, by its poles, as Moses had commanded according to the *word of the Lord*

1Chr 22:8 but the *word of the Lord* came to me, saying
2Chr 11:2 But the *word of the Lord* came to Shemaiah the man of God, saying
2Chr 12:7 Now when the Lord saw that they humbled themselves, the *word of the Lord* came to Shemaiah, saying
2Chr 18:4 And Jehoshaphat said to the king of Israel, "Please inquire for the *word of the Lord* today
2Chr 18:18 Then Micaiah said, "Therefore hear the *word of the Lord*
2Chr 30:12 Also the hand of God was on Judah to give them singleness of heart to do the commandment of the king and the leaders, at the *word of the Lord*
2Chr 34:21 for great is the wrath of the Lord that is poured out on us, because our fathers have not kept the *word of the Lord*, to do according to all that is written in this book
2Chr 35:6 So slaughter the Passover offerings, sanctify yourselves, and prepare them for your brethren, that they may do according to the *word of the Lord* by the hand of Moses
2Chr 36:21 to fulfill the *word of the Lord* by the mouth of Jeremiah, until the land had enjoyed her Sabbaths
2Chr 36:22 Now in the first year of Cyrus king of Persia, that the *word of the Lord* spoken by the mouth of Jeremiah might be fulfilled, the Lord stirred up the spirit of Cyrus king of Persia, so that he made a proclamation throughout all his kingdom, and also put it in writing, saying
Ezra 1:1 Now in the first year of Cyrus king of Persia, that the *word of the Lord* spoken by the mouth of Jeremiah might be fulfilled, the Lord stirred up the spirit of Cyrus king of Persia, so that he made a proclamation throughout all his kingdom, and also put it in writing, saying
Ps 18:30 The *word of the Lord* is proven; He is a shield to all who trust in Him
Ps 33:4 For the *word of the Lord* is right, and all His work is done in truth
Ps 33:6 By the *word of the Lord* the heavens were made, and all the host of them by the breath of His mouth
Ps 105:19 Until the time that his word came to pass, the *word of the Lord* tested him
Is 1:10 Hear the *word of the Lord*, you rulers of Sodom
Is 2:3 For out of Zion shall go forth the law, and the *word of the Lord* from Jerusalem
Is 28:13 But the *word of the Lord* was to them, "Precept upon precept, precept upon precept, line upon line, line upon line, here a little, there a little
Is 28:14 Therefore hear the *word of the Lord*, you scornful men, who rule this people who are in Jerusalem
Is 38:4 Then the *word of the Lord* came to Isaiah, saying
Is 39:5 Then Isaiah said to Hezekiah, "Hear the *word of the Lord* of hosts
Is 39:8 Then Hezekiah said to Isaiah, "The *word of the Lord* which you have spoken is good
Is 66:5 Hear the *word of the Lord*, you who tremble at His word
Jer 1:2 to whom the *word of the Lord* came in the days of Josiah the son of Amon, king of Judah, in the thirteenth year of his reign
Jer 1:4 Then the *word of the Lord* came to me, saying
Jer 1:11 Moreover the *word of the Lord* came to me, saying
Jer 1:13 And the *word of the Lord* came to me the second time, saying
Jer 2:1 Moreover the *word of the Lord* came to me, saying
Jer 2:4 Hear the *word of the Lord*, O house of Jacob and all the families of the house of Israel
Jer 2:31 O generation, see the *word of the Lord!* Have I been a wilderness to Israel, Or a land of darkness
Jer 6:10 Behold, the *word of the Lord* is a reproach to them
Jer 7:2 Stand in the gate of the Lord's house, and proclaim there this word, and say, 'Hear the *word of the Lord*, all you of Judah who enter in at these gates to worship the Lord
Jer 8:9 Behold, they have rejected the *word of the Lord;* so what wisdom do they have
Jer 9:20 Yet hear the *word of the Lord*, O women, and let your ear receive the word of His mouth
Jer 13:2 So I got a sash according to the *word of the Lord*, and put it around my waist
Jer 13:3 And the *word of the Lord* came to me the second time, saying
Jer 13:8 Then the *word of the Lord* came to me, saying
Jer 14:1 The *word of the Lord* that came to Jeremiah concerning the droughts
Jer 16:1 The *word of the Lord* also came to me, saying
Jer 17:15 Indeed they say to me, "Where is the *word of the Lord*
Jer 17:20 and say to them, 'Hear the *word of the Lord*, you kings of Judah, and all Judah, and all the inhabitants of Jerusalem, who enter by these gates
Jer 18:5 Then the *word of the Lord* came to me, saying
Jer 19:3 and say, 'Hear the *word of the Lord*, O kings of Judah and inhabitants of Jerusalem
Jer 20:8 Because the *word of the Lord* was made to me a reproach and a derision daily
Jer 21:11 And concerning the house of the king of Judah, say, 'Hear the *word of the Lord*
Jer 22:2 and say, 'Hear the *word of the Lord*, O king of Judah, you who sit on the throne of David, you and your servants and your people who enter these gates
Jer 22:29 O earth, earth, earth, hear the *word of the Lord*
Jer 24:4 Again the *word of the Lord* came to me, saying
Jer 25:3 From the thirteenth year of Josiah the son of Amon, king of Judah, even to this day, this is the twenty-third year in which the *word of the Lord* has come to me
Jer 27:18 But if they are prophets, and if the *word of the Lord* is with them, let them now make intercession to the Lord of hosts, that the vessels which are left in the house of the Lord, in the house of the king of Judah, and at Jerusalem, do not go to Babylon
Jer 28:12 Then the *word of the Lord* came to Jeremiah, after Hananiah the prophet had broken the yoke from the neck of the prophet Jeremiah, saying
Jer 29:20 Therefore hear the *word of the Lord*, all you of the captivity, whom I have sent from Jerusalem to Babylon
Jer 29:30 Then the *word of the Lord* came to Jeremiah, saying
Jer 31:10 Hear the *word of the Lord*, O nations, and declare it in the isles afar off, and say
Jer 32:6 And Jeremiah said, "The *word of the Lord* came to me, saying
Jer 32:8 Then Hanameel my uncle's son came to me in the court of the prison according to the *word of the Lord*, and said to me, 'Please buy my field that is in Anathoth, which is in the country of Benjamin; for the right of inheritance is yours, and the redemption yours; buy it for yourself.' Then I knew that this was the *word of the Lord*

Jer 32:26 Then the *word of the Lord* came to Jeremiah, saying
Jer 33:1 Moreover the *word of the Lord* came to Jeremiah a second time, while he was still shut up in the court of the prison, saying
Jer 33:19 And the *word of the Lord* came to Jeremiah, saying
Jer 33:23 Moreover the *word of the Lord* came to Jeremiah, saying
Jer 34:4 Yet hear the *word of the Lord*, O Zedekiah king of Judah
Jer 34:12 Therefore the *word of the Lord* came to Jeremiah from the Lord, saying
Jer 35:12 Then came the *word of the Lord* to Jeremiah, saying
Jer 36:27 Now after the king had burned the scroll with the words which Baruch had written at the instruction of Jeremiah, the *word of the Lord* came to Jeremiah, saying
Jer 37:6 And the *word of the Lord* came to the prophet Jeremiah, saying
Jer 39:15 Now the *word of the Lord* had come to Jeremiah while he was shut up in the court of the prison, saying
Jer 42:7 And it happened after ten days that the *word of the Lord* came to Jeremiah
Jer 42:15 Then hear now the *word of the Lord*, O remnant of Judah
Jer 43:8 Then the *word of the Lord* came to Jeremiah in Tahpanhes, saying
Jer 44:24 Moreover Jeremiah said to all the people and to all the women, "Hear the *word of the Lord*, all Judah who are in the land of Egypt
Jer 44:26 Therefore hear the *word of the Lord*, all Judah who dwell in the land of Egypt
Jer 46:1 The *word of the Lord* which came to Jeremiah the prophet against the nations
Jer 47:1 The *word of the Lord* that came to Jeremiah the prophet against the Philistines, before Pharaoh attacked Gaza
Jer 49:34 The *word of the Lord* that came to Jeremiah the prophet against Elam, in the beginning of the reign of Zedekiah king of Judah, saying
Ezek 1:3 the *word of the Lord* came expressly to Ezekiel the priest, the son of Buzi, in the land of the Chaldeans by the River Chebar
Ezek 3:16 Now it came to pass at the end of seven days that the *word of the Lord* came to me, saying
Ezek 6:1 Now the *word of the Lord* came to me, saying
Ezek 6:3 and say, 'O mountains of Israel, hear the *word of the Lord* God
Ezek 7:1 Moreover the *word of the Lord* came to me, saying
Ezek 11:14 Again the *word of the Lord* came to me, saying
Ezek 12:1 Now the *word of the Lord* came to me, saying
Ezek 12:8 And in the morning the *word of the Lord* came to me, saying
Ezek 12:17 Moreover the *word of the Lord* came to me, saying
Ezek 12:21 And the *word of the Lord* came to me, saying
Ezek 12:26 Again the *word of the Lord* came to me, saying
Ezek 13:1 And the *word of the Lord* came to me, saying
Ezek 13:2 Son of man, prophesy against the prophets of Israel who prophesy, and say to those who prophesy out of their own heart, 'Hear the *word of the Lord*
Ezek 14:2 And the *word of the Lord* came to me, saying
Ezek 14:12 The *word of the Lord* came again to me, saying
Ezek 15:1 Then the *word of the Lord* came to me, saying
Ezek 16:1 Again the *word of the Lord* came to me, saying
Ezek 16:35 Now then, O harlot, hear the *word of the Lord*
Ezek 17:1 And the *word of the Lord* came to me, saying
Ezek 17:11 Moreover the *word of the Lord* came to me, saying
Ezek 18:1 The *word of the Lord* came to me again, saying
Ezek 20:2 Then the *word of the Lord* came to me, saying
Ezek 20:45 Furthermore the *word of the Lord* came to me, saying
Ezek 20:47 and say to the forest of the South, 'Hear the *word of the Lord*
Ezek 21:1 And the *word of the Lord* came to me, saying
Ezek 21:8 Again the *word of the Lord* came to me, saying
Ezek 21:18 The *word of the Lord* came to me again, saying
Ezek 22:1 Moreover the *word of the Lord* came to me, saying
Ezek 22:17 The *word of the Lord* came to me, saying
Ezek 22:23 And the *word of the Lord* came to me, saying
Ezek 23:1 The *word of the Lord* came again to me, saying
Ezek 24:1 Again, in the ninth year, in the tenth month, on the tenth day of the month, the *word of the Lord* came to me, saying
Ezek 24:15 Also the *word of the Lord* came to me, saying
Ezek 24:20 Then I answered them, "The *word of the Lord* came to me, saying
Ezek 25:1 The *word of the Lord* came to me, saying
Ezek 25:3 Say to the Ammonites, 'Hear the *word of the Lord* God
Ezek 26:1 And it came to pass in the eleventh year, on the first day of the month, that the *word of the Lord* came to me, saying
Ezek 27:1 The *word of the Lord* came again to me, saying
Ezek 28:1 The *word of the Lord* came to me again, saying
Ezek 28:11 Moreover the *word of the Lord* came to me, saying
Ezek 28:20 Then the *word of the Lord* came to me, saying
Ezek 29:1 In the tenth year, in the tenth month, on the twelfth day of the month, the *word of the Lord* came to me, saying
Ezek 29:17 And it came to pass in the twenty-seventh year, in the first month, on the first day of the month, that the *word of the Lord* came to me, saying
Ezek 30:1 The *word of the Lord* came to me again, saying
Ezek 30:20 And it came to pass in the eleventh year, in the first month, on the seventh day of the month, that the *word of the Lord* came to me, saying
Ezek 31:1 Now it came to pass in the eleventh year, in the third month, on the first day of the month, that the *word of the Lord* came to me, saying
Ezek 32:1 And it came to pass in the twelfth year, in the twelfth month, on the first day of the month, that the *word of the Lord* came to me, saying
Ezek 32:17 It came to pass also in the twelfth year, on the fifteenth day of the month, that the *word of the Lord* came to me, saying

Ezek 33:1 Again the *word of the Lord* came to me, saying
Ezek 33:23 Then the *word of the Lord* came to me, saying
Ezek 34:1 And the *word of the Lord* came to me, saying
Ezek 34:7 Therefore, you shepherds, hear the *word of the Lord*
Ezek 34:9 therefore, O shepherds, hear the *word of the Lord*
Ezek 35:1 Moreover the *word of the Lord* came to me, saying
Ezek 36:1 And you, son of man, prophesy to the mountains of Israel, and say, 'O mountains of Israel, hear the *word of the Lord*
Ezek 36:4 therefore, O mountains of Israel, hear the *word of the Lord* God
Ezek 36:16 Moreover the *word of the Lord* came to me, saying
Ezek 37:4 Again He said to me, "Prophesy to these bones, and say to them, 'O dry bones, hear the *word of the Lord*
Ezek 37:15 Again the *word of the Lord* came to me, saying
Ezek 38:1 Now the *word of the Lord* came to me, saying
Dan 9:2 in the first year of his reign I, Daniel, understood by the books the number of the years specified by the *word of the Lord*, given through Jeremiah the prophet, that He would accomplish seventy years in the desolations of Jerusalem
Hos 1:1 The *word of the Lord* that came to Hosea the son of Beeri, in the days of Uzziah, Jotham, Ahaz, and Hezekiah, kings of Judah, and in the days of Jeroboam the son of Joash, king of Israel
Hos 4:1 Hear the *word of the Lord*, you children of Israel, for the Lord brings a charge against the inhabitants of the land
Joel 1:1 The *word of the Lord* that came to Joel the son of Pethuel
Amos 7:16 Now therefore, hear the *word of the Lord:* you say
Amos 8:12 they shall run to and fro, seeking the *word of the Lord*, but shall not find it
Jon 1:1 Now the *word of the Lord* came to Jonah the son of Amittai, saying
Jon 3:1 Now the *word of the Lord* came to Jonah the second time, saying
Jon 3:3 So Jonah arose and went to Nineveh, according to the *word of the Lord*
Mic 1:1 The *word of the Lord* that came to Micah of Moresheth in the days of Jotham, Ahaz, and Hezekiah, kings of Judah, which he saw concerning Samaria and Jerusalem
Mic 4:2 For out of Zion the law shall go forth, and the *word of the Lord* from Jerusalem
Zeph 1:1 The *word of the Lord* which came to Zephaniah the son of Cushi, the son of Gedaliah, the son of Amariah, the son of Hezekiah, in the days of Josiah the son of Amon, king of Judah
Zeph 2:5 The *word of the Lord* is against you, O Canaan, land of the Philistines
Hag 1:1 In the second year of King Darius, in the sixth month, on the first day of the month, the *word of the Lord* came by Haggai the prophet to Zerubbabel the son of Shealtiel, governor of Judah, and to Joshua the son of Jehozadak, the high priest, saying
Hag 1:3 Then the *word of the Lord* came by Haggai the prophet, saying
Hag 2:1 In the seventh month, on the twenty-first day of the month, the *word of the Lord* came by Haggai the prophet, saying
Hag 2:10 On the twenty-fourth day of the ninth month, in the second year of Darius, the *word of the Lord* came by Haggai the prophet, saying
Hag 2:20 And again the *word of the Lord* came to Haggai on the twenty-fourth day of the month, saying
Zech 1:1 In the eighth month of the second year of Darius, the *word of the Lord* came to Zechariah the son of Berechiah, the son of Iddo the prophet, saying
Zech 1:7 On the twenty-fourth day of the eleventh month, which is the month Shebat, in the second year of Darius, the *word of the Lord* came to Zechariah the son of Berechiah, the son of Iddo the prophet
Zech 4:6 This is the *word of the Lord* to Zerubbabel: 'Not by might nor by power, but by My Spirit
Zech 4:8 Moreover the *word of the Lord* came to me, saying
Zech 6:9 Then the *word of the Lord* came to me, saying
Zech 7:1 Now in the fourth year of King Darius it came to pass that the *word of the Lord* came to Zechariah, on the fourth day of the ninth month, which is Chislev
Zech 7:4 Then the *word of the Lord* of hosts came to me, saying
Zech 7:8 Then the *word of the Lord* came to Zechariah, saying
Zech 8:1 Again the *word of the Lord* of hosts came, saying
Zech 8:18 Then the *word of the Lord* of hosts came to me, saying
Zech 9:1 The burden of the *word of the Lord* against the land of Hadrach, and Damascus its resting place (for the eyes of men and all the tribes of Israel are on the Lord
Zech 11:11 Thus the poor of the flock, who were watching me, knew that it was the *word of the Lord*
Zech 12:1 The burden of the *word of the Lord* against Israel
Mal 1:1 The burden of the *word of the Lord* to Israel by Malachi
Luke 22:61 And Peter remembered the *word of the Lord*, how He had said to him
Acts 8:25 So when they had testified and preached the *word of the Lord*, they returned to Jerusalem, preaching the gospel in many villages of the Samaritans
Acts 11:16 Then I remembered the *word of the Lord*, how He said
Acts 13:48 Now when the Gentiles heard this, they were glad and glorified the *word of the Lord*
Acts 13:49 And the *word of the Lord* was being spread throughout all the region
Acts 15:35 Paul and Barnabas also remained in Antioch, teaching and preaching the *word of the Lord*, with many others also
Acts 15:36 Then after some days Paul said to Barnabas, "Let us now go back and visit our brethren in every city where we have preached the *word of the Lord*, and see how they are doing
Acts 16:32 Then they spoke the *word of the Lord* to him and to all who were in his house
Acts 19:10 And this continued for two years, so that all who dwelt in Asia heard the *word of the Lord* Jesus, both Jews and Greeks
Acts 19:20 So the *word of the Lord* grew mightily and prevailed
1Th 1:8 For from you the *word of the Lord* has sounded forth, not only in Macedonia and Achaia, but also in every place
1Th 4:15 For this we say to you by the *word of the Lord*, that we who are alive and remain until the coming of the Lord will by no means precede those who are asleep
2Th 3:1 Finally, brethren, pray for us, that the *word of the Lord* may have free course and be glorified, just as it is with you
1Pet 1:25 but the *word of the Lord* endures for-

ever." Now this is the word which by the gospel was preached to you

WORD OF TRUTH
Ps 119:43 And take not the *word of truth* utterly out of my mouth, for I have hoped in Your ordinances
2Cor 6:7 by the *word of truth*, by the power of God, by the armor of righteousness on the right hand and on the left
Eph 1:13 In Him you also trusted, after you heard the *word of truth*, the gospel of your salvation
2Tim 2:15 Be diligent to present yourself approved to God, a worker who does not need to be ashamed, rightly dividing the *word of truth*
Jas 1:18 Of His own will He brought us forth by the *word of truth*, that we might be a kind of firstfruits of His creatures

WORD WAS GOD
John 1:1 In the beginning was the Word, and the Word was with God, and the *Word was God*

WORD WAS MADE FLESH (KJV)
(See *WORD BECAME FLESH*)

WORD WAS WITH GOD
John 1:1 In the beginning was the Word, and the *Word was with God*, and the Word was God

WORDS ARE ON THE TIP OF MY TONGUE (NIV)
(See *TONGUE SPEAKS IN MY MOUTH*)

WORDS FALL TO THE GROUND
1Sam 3:19 So Samuel grew, and the Lord was with him and let none of his *words fall to the ground*

WORDS OF ETERNAL LIFE
John 6:68 Then Simon Peter answered Him, "Lord, to whom shall we go? You have the *words of eternal life*

WORDS OF GOD
Num 24:4 the utterance of him who hears the *words of God*, who sees the vision of the Almighty, who falls down, with eyes opened wide
Num 24:16 the utterance of him who hears the *words of God*, and knows the knowledge of the Most High, who sees the vision of the Almighty, who falls down, with eyes opened wide
1Chr 25:5 All these were the sons of Heman the king's seer in the *words of God*, to exalt his horn
Ps 107:11 Because they rebelled against the *words of God*, and despised the counsel of the Most High
John 3:34 For He whom God has sent speaks the *words of God*, for God does not give the Spirit by measure
Rev 17:17 For God has put it into their hearts to fulfill His purpose, to be of one mind, and to give their kingdom to the beast, until the *words of God* are fulfilled

WORDS OF OUR LORD JESUS
1Tim 6:3 If anyone teaches otherwise and does not consent to wholesome words, even the *words of our Lord Jesus* Christ, and to the doctrine which is according to godliness

WORDS OF THE COVENANT
Ex 34:28 And He wrote on the tablets the *words of the covenant*, the Ten Commandments
Deut 29:1 These are the *words of the covenant* which the Lord commanded Moses to make with the children of Israel in the land of Moab, besides the covenant which He made with them in Horeb
2Chr 34:31 Then the king stood in his place and made a covenant before the Lord, to follow the Lord, and to keep His commandments and His testimonies and His statutes with all his heart and all his soul, to perform the *words of the covenant* that were written in this book
Jer 34:18 And I will give the men who have transgressed My covenant, who have not performed the *words of the covenant* which they made before Me, when they cut the calf in two and passed between the parts of it

WORDS OF THE LORD
Ex 4:28 So Moses told Aaron all the *words of the Lord* who had sent him, and all the signs which He had commanded him
Ex 24:3 So Moses came and told the people all the *words of the Lord* and all the judgments
Ex 24:4 And Moses wrote all the *words of the Lord*. And he rose early in the morning, and built an altar at the foot of the mountain, and twelve pillars according to the twelve tribes of Israel
Num 11:24 So Moses went out and told the people the *words of the Lord*, and he gathered the seventy men of the elders of the people and placed them around the tabernacle
Josh 3:9 So Joshua said to the children of Israel, "Come here, and hear the *words of the Lord* your God
Josh 24:27 And Joshua said to all the people, "Behold, this stone shall be a witness to us, for it has heard all the *words of the Lord* which He spoke to us
1Sam 8:10 So Samuel told all the *words of the Lord* to the people who asked him for a king
1Sam 15:1 Now therefore, heed the voice of the *words of the Lord*
2Chr 11:4 "' Therefore they obeyed the *words of the Lord*, and turned back from attacking Jeroboam
2Chr 29:15 And they gathered their brethren, sanctified themselves, and went according to the commandment of the king, at the *words of the Lord*, to cleanse the house of the Lord
Ps 12:6 The *words of the Lord* are pure words, like silver tried in a furnace of earth, purified seven times
Jer 36:4 and Baruch wrote on a scroll of a book, at the instruction of Jeremiah, all the *words of the Lord* which He had spoken to him
Jer 36:6 You go, therefore, and read from the scroll which you have written at my instruction, the *words of the Lord*, in the hearing of the people in the Lord's house on the day of fasting
Jer 36:8 And Baruch the son of Neriah did according to all that Jeremiah the prophet commanded him, reading from the book the *words of the Lord* in the Lord's house
Jer 36:11 When Michaiah the son of Gemariah, the son of Shaphan, heard all the *words of the Lord* from the book
Jer 37:2 But neither he nor his servants nor the people of the land gave heed to the *words of the Lord* which He spoke by the prophet Jeremiah
Jer 43:1 Now it happened, when Jeremiah had stopped speaking to all the people all the *words of the Lord* their God, for which the Lord their God had sent him to them, all these words
Amos 8:11 Behold, the days are coming," says the Lord God, "that I will send a famine on the land, not a famine of bread, nor a thirst for water, but of hearing the *words of the Lord*
Acts 20:35 And remember the *words of the Lord* Jesus, that He said

WORDS OF THE WISE
Prov 1:6 to understand a proverb and an enigma, the *words of the wise* and their riddles

Prov 22:17 Incline your ear and hear the *words of the wise*, and apply your heart to my knowledge
Eccl 9:17 *Words of the wise*, spoken quietly, should be heard rather than the shout of a ruler of fools
Eccl 12:11 The *words of the wise* are like goads, and the words of scholars are like well-driven nails, given by one Shepherd

WORDS OF THIS BOOK
2Kin 22:13 Go, inquire of the Lord for me, for the people and for all Judah, concerning the *words of this book* that has been found; for great is the wrath of the Lord that is aroused against us, because our fathers have not obeyed the *words of this book*, to do according to all that is written concerning us
Rev 22:9 For I am your fellow servant, and of your brethren the prophets, and of those who keep the *words of this book*

WORDS WITHOUT KNOWLEDGE
Job 35:16 Therefore Job opens his mouth in vain; he multiplies *words without knowledge*
Job 38:2 Who is this who darkens counsel by *words without knowledge*

WORK OF GOD
Ex 32:16 Now the tablets were the *work of God*, and the writing was the writing of God engraved on the tablets
Ps 64:9 All men shall fear, and shall declare the *work of God*
Eccl 7:13 Consider the *work of God;* for who can make straight what He has made crooked
Eccl 8:17 then I saw all the *work of God*, that a man cannot find out the work that is done under the sun
John 6:29 Jesus answered and said to them, "This is the *work of God*, that you believe in Him whom He sent
Rom 14:20 Do not destroy the *work of God* for the sake of food

WORK OF MEN'S HANDS
Deut 4:28 And there you will serve gods, the *work of men's hands*, wood and stone, which neither see nor hear nor eat nor smell
2Kin 19:18 for they were not gods, but the *work of men's hands* wood and stone
2Chr 32:19 And they spoke against the God of Jerusalem, as against the gods of the people of the earth the *work of men's hands*
Ps 115:4 Their idols are silver and gold, the *work of men's hands*
Ps 135:15 The idols of the nations are silver and gold, the *work of men's hands*
Is 37:19 for they were not gods, but the *work of men's hands* wood and stone

WORK OF OUR HANDS
Ps 90:17 And let the beauty of the Lord our God be upon us, and establish the *work of our hands* for us; yes, establish the *work of our hands*
Hos 14:3 Assyria shall not save us, we will not ride on horses, nor will we say anymore to the *work of our hands*

WORK OF THE LORD
Ex 34:10 and all the people among whom you are shall see the *work of the Lord*
Num 8:11 and Aaron shall offer the Levites before the Lord, as though a wave offering from the children of Israel, that they may perform the *work of the Lord*
Is 5:12 but they do not regard the *work of the Lord*, nor consider the operation of His hands
Jer 48:10 Cursed is he who does the *work of the Lord* deceitfully, and cursed is he who keeps back his sword from blood
Jer 50:25 For this is the *work of the Lord* God of hosts in the land of the Chaldeans
Jer 51:10 Come and let us declare in Zion the *work of the Lord* our God
1Cor 15:58 Therefore, my beloved brethren, be steadfast, immovable, always abounding in the *work of the Lord*, knowing that your labor is not in vain in the Lord
1Cor 16:10 for he does the *work of the Lord*, as I also do

WORK OF YOUR HANDS
Deut 16:15 Seven days you shall keep a sacred feast to the Lord your God in the place which the Lord chooses, because the Lord your God will bless you in all your produce and in all the *work of your hands*, so that you surely rejoice
Deut 24:19 it shall be for the stranger, the fatherless, and the widow, that the Lord your God may bless you in all the *work of your hands*
Deut 31:29 and evil will befall you in the latter days, because you will do evil in the sight of the Lord, to provoke Him to anger through the *work of your hands*
Job 10:3 Does it seem good to You that You should oppress, that You should despise the *work of Your hands*, and shine on the counsel of the wicked
Job 14:15 You shall call, and I will answer You; You shall desire the *work of Your hands*
Ps 102:25 Of old You laid the foundation of the earth, and the heavens are the *work of Your hands*
Ps 143:5 I meditate on all Your works; I muse on the *work of Your hands*
Eccl 5:6 Why should God be angry at your excuse and destroy the *work of your hands*
Mic 5:13 you shall no more worship the *work of your hands*
Heb 1:10 You, Lord, in the beginning laid the foundation of the earth, and the heavens are the *work of Your hands*

WORKED THE SOIL (NIV)
(See *TILLER OF THE GROUND*)

WORKER DESERVES (NIV)
(See *LABORER IS WORTHY*)

WORKERS ARE FEW (NAS, NIV)
(See *LABORERS ARE FEW*)

WORKERS OF INIQUITY
Job 31:3 Is it not destruction for the wicked, and disaster for the *workers of iniquity*
Job 34:8 who goes in company with the *workers of iniquity*, and walks with wicked men
Job 34:22 There is no darkness nor shadow of death where the *workers of iniquity* may hide themselves
Ps 5:5 The boastful shall not stand in Your sight; You hate all *workers of iniquity*
Ps 6:8 Depart from me, all you *workers of iniquity*; for the Lord has heard the voice of my weeping
Ps 14:4 Have all the *workers of iniquity* no knowledge, who eat up my people as they eat bread, and do not call on the Lord
Ps 28:3 Do not take me away with the wicked and with the *workers of iniquity*, who speak peace to their neighbors, but evil is in their hearts
Ps 36:12 There the *workers of iniquity* have fallen; they have been cast down and are not able to rise
Ps 37:1 Do not fret because of evildoers, nor be envious of the *workers of iniquity*
Ps 53:4 Have the *workers of iniquity* no knowl-

edge, who eat up my people as they eat bread, and do not call upon God
Ps 59:2 Deliver me from the *workers of iniquity*, and save me from bloodthirsty men
Ps 64:2 Hide me from the secret counsel of the wicked, from the insurrection of the *workers of iniquity*
Ps 92:7 When the wicked spring up like grass, and when all the *workers of iniquity* flourish, it is that they may be destroyed forever
Ps 92:9 For behold, Your enemies, O Lord, for behold, Your enemies shall perish; all the *workers of iniquity* shall be scattered
Ps 94:4 They utter speech, and speak insolent things; all the *workers of iniquity* boast in themselves
Ps 94:16 Who will stand up for me against the *workers of iniquity*
Ps 125:5 As for such as turn aside to their crooked ways, the Lord shall lead them away with the *workers of iniquity*
Ps 141:9 Keep me from the snares which they have laid for me, and from the traps of the *workers of iniquity*
Prov 10:29 The way of the Lord is strength for the upright, but destruction will come to the *workers of iniquity*
Prov 21:15 It is a joy for the just to do justice, but destruction will come to the *workers of iniquity*
Luke 13:27 But He will say, 'I tell you I do not know you, where you are from. Depart from Me, all you *workers of iniquity*

WORKERS OF MIRACLES
1Cor 12:29 Are all prophets? Are all teachers? Are all *workers of miracles*

WORKERS WITH FAMILIAR SPIRITS, AND THE WIZARDS (KJV)
(See *MEDIUMS AND SPIRITISTS*)

WORKING OF MIRACLES
1Cor 12:10 to another the *working of miracles*, to another prophecy, to another discerning of spirits, to another different kinds of tongues, to another the interpretation of tongues

WORKS BEFITTING REPENTANCE
Acts 26:20 but declared first to those in Damascus and in Jerusalem, and throughout all the region of Judea, and then to the Gentiles, that they should repent, turn to God, and do *works befitting repentance*

WORKS OF GOD
Job 37:14 Listen to this, O Job; stand still and consider the wondrous *works of God*
Ps 66:5 Come and see the *works of God;* He is awesome in His doing toward the sons of men
Ps 78:7 That they may set their hope in God, and not forget the *works of God*, but keep His commandments
Eccl 11:5 As you do not know what is the way of the wind, or how the bones grow in the womb of her who is with child, so you do not know the *works of God* who makes all things
John 6:28 Then they said to Him, "What shall we do, that we may work the *works of God*
John 9:3 Jesus answered, "Neither this man nor his parents sinned, but that the *works of God* should be revealed in him
Acts 2:11 Cretans and Arabs we hear them speaking in our own tongues the wonderful *works of God*

WORKS OF THE FLESH
Gal 5:19 Now the *works of the flesh* are evident, which are

WORKS OF THE LAW
Rom 9:32 Because they did not seek it by faith, but as it were, by the *works of the law*
Gal 2:16 knowing that a man is not justified by the *works of the law* but by faith in Jesus Christ, even we have believed in Christ Jesus, that we might be justified by faith in Christ and not by the *works of the law;* for by the *works of the law* no flesh shall be justified
Gal 3:2 Did you receive the Spirit by the *works of the law*, or by the hearing of faith
Gal 3:5 Therefore He who supplies the Spirit to you and works miracles among you, does He do it by the *works of the law*, or by the hearing of faith
Gal 3:10 For as many as are of the *works of the law* are under the curse

WORKS OF THE LORD
Josh 24:31 Israel served the Lord all the days of Joshua, and all the days of the elders who outlived Joshua, who had known all the *works of the Lord* which He had done for Israel
Judg 2:7 So the people served the Lord all the days of Joshua, and all the days of the elders who outlived Joshua, who had seen all the great *works of the Lord* which He had done for Israel
Ps 28:5 Because they do not regard the *works of the Lord*, nor the operation of His hands, He shall destroy them and not build them up
Ps 46:8 Come, behold the *works of the Lord*, Who has made desolations in the earth
Ps 77:11 I will remember the *works of the Lord;* surely I will remember Your wonders of old
Ps 107:24 They see the *works of the Lord*, and His wonders in the deep
Ps 111:2 The *works of the Lord* are great, studied by all who have pleasure in them
Ps 118:17 I shall not die, but live, and declare the *works of the Lord*

WORKS RIGHTEOUSNESS
Ps 15:2 He who walks uprightly, and *works righteousness*, and speaks the truth in his heart
Acts 10:35 But in every nation whoever fears Him and *works righteousness* is accepted by Him

WORKS THAT HE HAS DONE
Ps 78:4 We will not hide them from their children, telling to the generation to come the praises of the Lord, and His strength and His wonderful *works that He has done*

WORLD IS PASSING AWAY
1Cor 7:31 and those who use this world as not misusing it. For the form of this *world is passing away*
1Jn 2:17 And the *world is passing away*, and the lust of it

WORLD ITSELF COULD NOT CONTAIN THE BOOKS
John 21:25 And there are also many other things that Jesus did, which if they were written one by one, I suppose that even the *world itself could not contain the books* that would be written

WORLD TO COME
Heb 2:5 For He has not put the *world to come*, of which we speak, in subjection to angels

WORLD WOULD NOT HAVE ROOM FOR THE BOOKS (NIV)
(See *WORLD ITSELF COULD NOT CONTAIN THE BOOKS*)

WORLDLY WEALTH (NIV)
(See *UNRIGHTEOUS MAMMON*)

WORM DOES NOT DIE
Is 66:24 For their *worm does not die*, and their fire is not quenched
Mark 9:44 where 'their *worm does not die* and the fire is not quenched
Mark 9:46 where 'their *worm does not die* and the fire is not quenched
Mark 9:48 where 'their *worm does not die* and the fire is not quenched

WORN OUT CALLING FOR HELP (NIV)
(See *WEARY WITH MY CRYING*)

WORN OUT FROM GROANING (NIV)
(See *WEARY WITH MY GROANING*)

WORRIES OF THIS LIFE (NIV)
(See *CARES OF THIS WORLD*)

WORSHIP GOD
Acts 18:13 saying, "This fellow persuades men to *worship God* contrary to the law
1Cor 14:25 and so, falling down on his face, he will *worship God* and report that God is truly among you
Phil 3:3 For we are the circumcision, who *worship God* in the Spirit, rejoice in Christ Jesus, and have no confidence in the flesh
Rev 19:10 *Worship God!* For the testimony of Jesus is the spirit of prophecy
Rev 22:9 For I am your fellow servant, and of your brethren the prophets, and of those who keep the words of this book. *Worship God*

WORSHIP THE FATHER
John 4:21 Jesus said to her, "Woman, believe Me, the hour is coming when you will neither on this mountain, nor in Jerusalem, *worship the Father*
John 4:23 But the hour is coming, and now is, when the true worshipers will *worship the Father* in spirit and truth

WORSHIP THE LORD
Deut 12:4 You shall not *worship the Lord* your God with such things
Deut 12:31 You shall not *worship the Lord* your God in that way
1Sam 15:25 Now therefore, please pardon my sin, and return with me, that I may *worship the Lord*
1Sam 15:30 yet honor me now, please, before the elders of my people and before Israel, and return with me, that I may *worship the Lord* your God
1Chr 16:29 bring an offering, and come before Him. oh, *worship the Lord* in the beauty of holiness
Ps 29:2 Give unto the Lord the glory due to His name; *worship the Lord* in the beauty of holiness
Ps 96:9 Oh, *worship the Lord* in the beauty of holiness! Tremble before Him, all the earth
Is 27:13 they will come, who are about to perish in the land of Assyria, and they who are outcasts in the land of Egypt, and shall *worship the Lord* in the holy mount at Jerusalem
Jer 7:2 Stand in the gate of the Lord's house, and proclaim there this word, and say, 'Hear the word of the Lord, all you of Judah who enter in at these gates to *worship the Lord*
Matt 4:10 For it is written, 'You shall *worship the Lord* your God, and Him only you shall serve
Luke 4:8 For it is written, 'You shall *worship the Lord* your God, and Him only you shall serve

WORSHIPED GOD
2Sam 15:32 Now it happened when David had come to the top of the mountain, where he *worshiped God*, that there was Hushai the Archite, coming to meet him with his robe torn and dust on his head
Acts 16:14 She was a seller of purple from the city of Thyatira, who *worshiped God*
Acts 18:7 And he departed from there and entered the house of a certain man named Justus, one who *worshiped God*, whose house was next door to the synagogue
Rev 7:11 And all the angels stood around the throne and the elders and the four living creatures, and fell on their faces before the throne and *worshiped God*
Rev 11:16 And the twenty-four elders who sat before God on their thrones fell on their faces and *worshiped God*
Rev 19:4 And the twenty-four elders and the four living creatures fell down and *worshiped God* who sat on the throne, saying

WORSHIPED OTHER GODS
Jer 22:9 Then they will answer, 'Because they have forsaken the covenant of the Lord their God, and *worshiped other gods* and served them

WORSHIPED THE LORD
Gen 24:26 Then the man bowed down his head and *worshiped the Lord*
Gen 24:48 And I bowed my head and *worshiped the Lord*, and blessed the Lord God of my master Abraham, who had led me in the way of truth to take the daughter of my master's brother for his son
Gen 24:52 And it came to pass, when Abraham's servant heard their words, that he *worshiped the Lord*, bowing himself to the earth
1Sam 1:28 as long as he lives he shall be lent to the Lord." So they *worshiped the Lord* there
1Sam 15:31 So Samuel turned back after Saul, and Saul *worshiped the Lord*
Neh 8:6 And they bowed their heads and *worshiped the Lord* with their faces to the ground
Neh 9:3 and for another fourth they confessed and *worshiped the Lord* their God

WORSHIPER OF GOD
John 9:31 but if anyone is a *worshiper of God* and does His will, He hears him

WORSHIPING OTHER GODS (NIV)
(See *SERVE OTHER GODS*)

WORTHLESS IDOLS
Jer 18:15 Because My people have forgotten Me, they have burned incense to *worthless idols*
Jon 2:8 Those who regard *worthless idols* forsake their own Mercy

WORTHY IS THE LAMB
Rev 5:12 *Worthy is the Lamb* who was slain to receive power and riches and wisdom, and strength and honor and glory and blessing

WORTHY OF DEATH
Deut 17:6 Whoever is *worthy of death* shall be put to death on the testimony of two or three witnesses, but he shall not be put to death on the testimony of one witness
Deut 19:6 lest the avenger of blood, while his anger is hot, pursue the manslayer and overtake him, because the way is long, and kill him, though he was not *worthy of death*, since he had not hated the victim in time past
Deut 21:22 If a man has committed a sin *worthy of death*, and he is put to death, and you hang him on a tree
Deut 22:26 there is in the young woman no sin *worthy of death*, for just as when a man rises

against his neighbor and kills him, even so is this matter
1Kin 2:26 And to Abiathar the priest the king said, "Go to Anathoth, to your own fields, for you are *worthy of death*
Mark 14:64 And they all condemned Him to be *worthy of death*
Luke 23:15 and indeed nothing *worthy of death* has been done by Him
Acts 23:29 I found out that he was accused concerning questions of their law, but had nothing charged against him *worthy of death* or chains
Acts 25:11 For if I am an offender, or have committed anything *worthy of death*, I do not object to dying
Acts 25:25 But when I found that he had committed nothing *worthy of death*, and that he himself had appealed to Augustus, I decided to send him
Acts 26:31 and when they had gone aside, they talked among themselves, saying, "This man is doing nothing *worthy of death* or chains
Rom 1:32 who, knowing the righteous judgment of God, that those who practice such things are *worthy of death*, not only do the same but also approve of those who practice them

WORTHY OF JUDGMENT
Job 31:11 For that would be wickedness; yes, it would be iniquity *worthy of judgment*
Job 31:28 this also would be an iniquity *worthy of judgment*, for I would have denied God who is above

WORTHY OF ME
Matt 10:37 He who loves father or mother more than Me is not *worthy of Me*. And he who loves son or daughter more than Me is not *worthy of Me*
Matt 10:38 And he who does not take his cross and follow after Me is not *worthy of Me*

WORTHY OF REPENTANCE
Matt 3:8 Therefore bear fruits *worthy of repentance*
Luke 3:8 Therefore bear fruits *worthy of repentance*, and do not begin to say to yourselves

WORTHY TO BREAK (NIV)
(See *WORTHY TO OPEN*)

WORTHY TO DIE (KJV)
(See *DESERVES TO DIE*)

WORTHY TO OPEN
Rev 5:2 Then I saw a strong angel proclaiming with a loud voice, "Who is *worthy to open* the scroll and to loose its seals
Rev 5:4 So I wept much, because no one was found *worthy to open* and read the scroll, or to look at it

WOULD ALL SHARE MY JOY (NIV)
(See *MY JOY IS THE JOY OF YOU ALL*)

WOUND FOR WOUND
Ex 21:25 burn for burn, *wound for wound*, stripe for stripe

WOUNDED FOR OUR TRANSGRESSIONS
Is 53:5 But He was *wounded for our transgressions*, He was bruised for our iniquities

WRAPPED HIM IN SWADDLING CLOTHS
Luke 2:7 And she brought forth her firstborn Son, and *wrapped Him in swaddling cloths*, and laid Him in a manger, because there was no room for them in the inn

WRAPPED IN CLOTH (NIV)
(See *SWADDLING CLOTHS*)

WRATH OF GOD
Ps 78:31 The *wrath of God* came against them, and slew the stoutest of them, and struck down the choice men of Israel
John 3:36 and he who does not believe the Son shall not see life, but the *wrath of God* abides on him
Rom 1:18 For the *wrath of God* is revealed from heaven against all ungodliness and unrighteousness of men, who suppress the truth in unrighteousness
Eph 5:6 Let no one deceive you with empty words, for because of these things the *wrath of God* comes upon the sons of disobedience
Col 3:6 Because of these things the *wrath of God* is coming upon the sons of disobedience
Rev 14:10 he himself shall also drink of the wine of the *wrath of God*, which is poured out full strength into the cup of His indignation
Rev 14:19 So the angel thrust his sickle into the earth and gathered the vine of the earth, and threw it into the great winepress of the *wrath of God*
Rev 15:1 seven angels having the seven last plagues, for in them the *wrath of God* is complete
Rev 15:7 Then one of the four living creatures gave to the seven angels seven golden bowls full of the *wrath of God* who lives forever and ever
Rev 16:1 Then I heard a loud voice from the temple saying to the seven angels, "Go and pour out the bowls of the *wrath of God* on the earth

WRATH OF THE LORD
Num 11:33 But while the meat was still between their teeth, before it was chewed, the *wrath of the Lord* was aroused against the people, and the Lord struck the people with a very great plague
2Kin 22:13 for great is the *wrath of the Lord* that is aroused against us, because our fathers have not obeyed the words of this book, to do according to all that is written concerning us
2Chr 12:12 When he humbled himself, the *wrath of the Lord* turned from him, so as not to destroy him completely
2Chr 19:2 And Jehu the son of Hanani the seer went out to meet him, and said to King Jehoshaphat, "Should you help the wicked and love those who hate the Lord? Therefore the *wrath of the Lord* is upon you
2Chr 28:11 Now hear me, therefore, and return the captives, whom you have taken captive from your brethren, for the fierce *wrath of the Lord* is upon you
2Chr 29:8 Therefore the *wrath of the Lord* fell upon Judah and Jerusalem, and He has given them up to trouble, to astonishment, and to jeering, as you see with your eyes
2Chr 32:26 Then Hezekiah humbled himself for the pride of his heart, he and the inhabitants of Jerusalem, so that the *wrath of the Lord* did not come upon them in the days of Hezekiah
2Chr 34:21 for great is the *wrath of the Lord* that is poured out on us, because our fathers have not kept the word of the Lord, to do according to all that is written in this book
2Chr 36:16 But they mocked the messengers of God, despised His words, and scoffed at His prophets, until the *wrath of the Lord* arose against His people, till there was no remedy
Ps 106:40 Therefore the *wrath of the Lord* was kindled against His people, so that He abhorred His own inheritance
Is 9:19 Through the *wrath of the Lord* of hosts the land is burned up, and the people shall be as fuel for the fire

WRATH TO COME

Is 13:13 Therefore I will shake the heavens, and the earth will move out of her place, in the *wrath of the Lord* of hosts and in the day of His fierce anger
Jer 50:13 Because of the *wrath of the Lord* she shall not be inhabited, but she shall be wholly desolate
Ezek 7:19 their silver and their gold will not be able to deliver them in the day of the *wrath of the Lord*

WRATH TO COME
Matt 3:7 Who has warned you to flee from the *wrath to come*
Luke 3:7 Who warned you to flee from the *wrath to come*
1Th 1:10 and to wait for His Son from heaven, whom He raised from the dead, even Jesus who delivers us from the *wrath to come*

WREST JUDGMENT (KJV)
(See *PERVERT JUSTICE*)

WRESTLE AGAINST FLESH
Eph 6:12 For we do not *wrestle against flesh* and blood, but against principalities, against powers, against the rulers of the darkness of this age, against spiritual hosts of wickedness in the heavenly places

WRETCHED MAN THAT I AM
Rom 7:24 O *wretched man that I am!* Who will deliver me from this body of death

WRITE IN A BOOK
Jer 30:2 *Write in a book* for yourself all the words that I have spoken to you
Rev 1:11 saying, "I am the Alpha and the Omega, the First and the Last," and, "What you see, *write in a book* and send it to the seven churches which are in Asia

WRITE ON IT
Is 8:1 Moreover the Lord said to me, "Take a large scroll, and *write on it* with a man's pen concerning Maher-Shalal-Hash-Baz
Jer 36:2 Take a scroll of a book and *write on it* all the words that I have spoken to you against Israel, against Judah, and against all the nations, from the day I spoke to you, from the days of Josiah even to this day
Jer 36:28 Take yet another scroll, and *write on it* all the former words that were in the first scroll which Jehoiakim the king of Judah has burned
Ezek 37:16 As for you, son of man, take a stick for yourself and *write on it:* 'For Judah and for the children of Israel, his companions.' Then take another stick and *write on it*

WRITTEN BY THE PROPHETS
Luke 18:31 Then He took the twelve aside and said to them, "Behold, we are going up to Jerusalem, and all things that are *written by the prophets* concerning the Son of Man will be accomplished

WRITTEN IN THE BOOK
Deut 28:61 Also every sickness and every plague, which is not *written in the book* of this law, will the Lord bring upon you until you are destroyed
Josh 8:31 as Moses the servant of the Lord had commanded the children of Israel, as it is *written in the Book* of the Law of Moses
Josh 8:34 And afterward he read all the words of the law, the blessings and the cursings, according to all that is *written in the Book* of the Law
Josh 10:13 Is this not *written in the Book* of Jasher? So the sun stood still in the midst of heaven, and did not hasten to go down for about a whole day
Josh 23:6 Therefore be very courageous to keep and to do all that is *written in the Book* of the Law of Moses, lest you turn aside from it to the right hand or to the left
2Sam 1:18 and he told them to teach the children of Judah the Song of the Bow; indeed it is *written in the Book* of Jasher
1Kin 11:41 Now the rest of the acts of Solomon, all that he did, and his wisdom, are they not *written in the book* of the acts of Solomon
1Kin 14:19 Now the rest of the acts of Jeroboam, how he made war and how he reigned, indeed they are *written in the book* of the chronicles of the kings of Israel
1Kin 14:29 Now the rest of the acts of Rehoboam, and all that he did, are they not *written in the book* of the chronicles of the kings of Judah
1Kin 15:7 Now the rest of the acts of Abijam, and all that he did, are they not *written in the book* of the chronicles of the kings of Judah
1Kin 15:23 The rest of all the acts of Asa, all his might, all that he did, and the cities which he built, are they not *written in the book* of the chronicles of the kings of Judah
1Kin 15:31 Now the rest of the acts of Nadab, and all that he did, are they not *written in the book* of the chronicles of the kings of Israel
1Kin 16:5 Now the rest of the acts of Baasha, what he did, and his might, are they not *written in the book* of the chronicles of the kings of Israel
1Kin 16:14 Now the rest of the acts of Elah, and all that he did, are they not *written in the book* of the chronicles of the kings of Israel
1Kin 16:20 Now the rest of the acts of Zimri, and the treason he committed, are they not *written in the book* of the chronicles of the kings of Israel
1Kin 16:27 Now the rest of the acts of Omri which he did, and the might that he showed, are they not *written in the book* of the chronicles of the kings of Israel
1Kin 22:39 Now the rest of the acts of Ahab and all that he did, the ivory house which he built and all the cities that he built, are they not *written in the book* of the chronicles of the kings of Israel
1Kin 22:45 Now the rest of the acts of Jehoshaphat, the might that he showed, and how he made war, are they not *written in the book* of the chronicles of the kings of Judah
2Kin 1:18 Now the rest of the acts of Ahaziah which he did, are they not *written in the book* of the chronicles of the kings of Israel
2Kin 8:23 Now the rest of the acts of Joram, and all that he did, are they not *written in the book* of the chronicles of the kings of Judah
2Kin 10:34 Now the rest of the acts of Jehu, all that he did, and all his might, are they not *written in the book* of the chronicles of the kings of Israel
2Kin 12:19 Now the rest of the acts of Joash, and all that he did, are they not *written in the book* of the chronicles of the kings of Judah
2Kin 13:8 Now the rest of the acts of Jehoahaz, all that he did, and his might, are they not *written in the book* of the chronicles of the kings of Israel
2Kin 13:12 Now the rest of the acts of Joash, all that he did, and his might with which he fought against Amaziah king of Judah, are they not *written in the book* of the chronicles of the kings of Israel
2Kin 14:6 But the children of the murderers he did not execute, according to what is *written in the Book* of the Law of Moses, in which the Lord commanded, saying
2Kin 14:15 Now the rest of the acts of Jehoash which he did his might, and how he fought with

Amaziah king of Judah are they not *written in the book* of the chronicles of the kings of Israel

2Kin 14:18 Now the rest of the acts of Amaziah, are they not *written in the book* of the chronicles of the kings of Judah

2Kin 14:28 Now the rest of the acts of Jeroboam, and all that he did his might, how he made war, and how he recaptured for Israel, from Damascus and Hamath, what had belonged to Judah are they not *written in the book* of the chronicles of the kings of Israel

2Kin 15:6 Now the rest of the acts of Azariah, and all that he did, are they not *written in the book* of the chronicles of the kings of Judah

2Kin 15:11 Now the rest of the acts of Zechariah, indeed they are *written in the book* of the chronicles of the kings of Israel

2Kin 15:15 Now the rest of the acts of Shallum, and the conspiracy which he led, indeed they are *written in the book* of the chronicles of the kings of Israel

2Kin 15:21 Now the rest of the acts of Menahem, and all that he did, are they not *written in the book* of the chronicles of the kings of Israel

2Kin 15:26 Now the rest of the acts of Pekahiah, and all that he did, indeed they are *written in the book* of the chronicles of the kings of Israel

2Kin 15:31 Now the rest of the acts of Pekah, and all that he did, indeed they are *written in the book* of the chronicles of the kings of Israel

2Kin 15:36 Now the rest of the acts of Jotham, and all that he did, are they not *written in the book* of the chronicles of the kings of Judah

2Kin 16:19 Now the rest of the acts of Ahaz which he did, are they not *written in the book* of the chronicles of the kings of Judah

2Kin 20:20 Now the rest of the acts of Hezekiah all his might, and how he made a pool and a tunnel and brought water into the city are they not *written in the book* of the chronicles of the kings of Judah

2Kin 21:17 Now the rest of the acts of Manasseh all that he did, and the sin that he committed are they not *written in the book* of the chronicles of the kings of Judah

2Kin 21:25 Now the rest of the acts of Amon which he did, are they not *written in the book* of the chronicles of the kings of Judah

2Kin 23:24 Moreover Josiah put away those who consulted mediums and spiritists, the household gods and idols, all the abominations that were seen in the land of Judah and in Jerusalem, that he might perform the words of the law which were *written in the book* that Hilkiah the priest found in the house of the Lord

2Kin 23:28 Now the rest of the acts of Josiah, and all that he did, are they not *written in the book* of the chronicles of the kings of Judah

2Kin 24:5 Now the rest of the acts of Jehoiakim, and all that he did, are they not *written in the book* of the chronicles of the kings of Judah

1Chr 29:29 Now the acts of King David, first and last, indeed they are *written in the book* of Samuel the seer, in the book of Nathan the prophet, and in the book of Gad the seer

2Chr 9:29 Now the rest of the acts of Solomon, first and last, are they not *written in the book* of Nathan the prophet, in the prophecy of Ahijah the Shilonite, and in the visions of Iddo the seer concerning Jeroboam the son of Nebat

2Chr 12:15 The acts of Rehoboam, first and last, are they not *written in the book* of Shemaiah the prophet, and of Iddo the seer concerning genealogies

2Chr 16:11 Note that the acts of Asa, first and last, are indeed *written in the book* of the kings of Judah and Israel

2Chr 20:34 Now the rest of the acts of Jehoshaphat, first and last, indeed they are *written in the book* of Jehu the son of Hanani, which is mentioned in the book of the kings of Israel

2Chr 25:26 Now the rest of the acts of Amaziah, from first to last, indeed are they not *written in the book* of the kings of Judah and Israel

2Chr 27:7 Now the rest of the acts of Jotham, and all his wars and his ways, indeed they are *written in the book* of the kings of Israel and Judah

2Chr 28:26 Now the rest of his acts and all his ways, from first to last, indeed they are *written in the book* of the kings of Judah and Israel

2Chr 33:18 Now the rest of the acts of Manasseh, his prayer to his God, and the words of the seers who spoke to him in the name of the Lord God of Israel, indeed they are *written in the book* of the kings of Israel

2Chr 34:24 Behold, I will bring calamity on this place and on its inhabitants, all the curses that are *written in the book* which they have read before the king of Judah

2Chr 35:12 Then they removed the burnt offerings that they might give them to the divisions of the fathers' houses of the lay people, to offer to the Lord, as it is *written in the Book* of Moses

2Chr 35:27 and his deeds from first to last, indeed they are *written in the book* of the kings of Israel and Judah

2Chr 36:8 Now the rest of the acts of Jehoiakim, the abominations which he did, and what was found against him, indeed they are *written in the book* of the kings of Israel and Judah

Ezra 6:18 They assigned the priests to their divisions and the Levites to their divisions, over the service of God in Jerusalem, as it is *written in the Book* of Moses

Neh 12:23 The sons of Levi, the heads of the fathers' houses until the days of Johanan the son of Eliashib, were *written in the book* of the chronicles

Esth 2:23 and it was *written in the book* of the chronicles in the presence of the king

Esth 10:2 Now all the acts of his power and his might, and the account of the greatness of Mordecai, to which the king advanced him, are they not *written in the book* of the chronicles of the kings of Media and Persia

Dan 12:1 and at that time your people shall be delivered, every one who is found *written in the book*

Luke 3:4 as it is *written in the book* of the words of Isaiah the prophet, saying

Acts 1:20 For it is *written in the book* of Psalms: "Let his habitation be desolate and let no one live in it

Acts 7:42 Then God turned and gave them up to worship the host of heaven, as it is *written in the book* of the Prophets

Gal 3:10 for it is written, "Cursed is everyone who does not continue in all things which are *written in the book* of the law, to do them

Rev 13:8 And all who dwell on the earth will worship him, whose names have not been *written in the Book* of Life of the Lamb slain from the foundation of the world

Rev 17:8 And those who dwell on the earth will marvel, whose names are not *written in the Book* of Life from the foundation of the world, when they see the beast that was, and is not, and yet is

Rev 20:15 And anyone not found *written in the Book* of Life was cast into the lake of fire

WRITTEN IN THE PROPHETS

Mark 1:2 As it is *written in the Prophets:* "Behold, I send My messenger before Your face, who will prepare Your way before You

John 6:45 It is *written in the prophets*, 'And they shall all be taught by God

WRONG JUDGMENT PROCEEDETH (KJV)
(See *PERVERSE JUDGMENT PROCEEDS*)

WRONGDOING AGAINST THE LORD (NIV)
(See *TRESPASSED AGAINST THE LORD*)

WRONGED YOU (NIV)
(See *SINNED AGAINST YOU*)

WROUGHT FOLLY (KJV, RSV)
(See *DISGRACEFUL THING*)

Y

YEAR OF JUBILEE
Lev 25:13 In this *Year of Jubilee*, each of you shall return to his possession
Lev 25:28 But if he is not able to have it restored to himself, then what was sold shall remain in the hand of him who bought it until the *Year of Jubilee*
Lev 25:33 And if a man purchases a house from the Levites, then the house that was sold in the city of his possession shall be released in the *Year of Jubilee*
Lev 25:40 But as a hired servant and a sojourner he shall be with you, and shall serve you until the *Year of Jubilee*
Lev 25:50 The price of his release shall be according to the number of years, from the year that he was sold to him until the *Year of Jubilee*
Lev 25:52 And if there remain but a few years until the *Year of Jubilee*, then he shall reckon with him, and according to his years he shall repay him the price of his redemption
Lev 25:54 And if he is not redeemed in these years, then he shall be released in the *Year of Jubilee*, both he and his children with him
Lev 27:17 If he sanctifies his field from the *Year of Jubilee*, according to your valuation it shall stand
Lev 27:18 But if he sanctifies his field after the Jubilee, then the priest shall reckon to him the money due according to the years that remain till the *Year of Jubilee*, and it shall be deducted from your valuation
Lev 27:23 then the priest shall reckon to him the worth of your valuation, up to the *Year of Jubilee*, and he shall give your valuation on that day as a holy offering to the Lord
Lev 27:24 In the *Year of Jubilee* the field shall return to him from whom it was bought, to the one who owned the land as a possession

YEAR OF RELEASE
Deut 15:9 Beware lest there be a wicked thought in your heart, saying, 'The seventh year, the *year of release*, is at hand
Deut 31:10 At the end of every seven years, at the appointed time in the *year of release*, at the Feast of Tabernacles

YEAR OF THE LORD
Is 61:2 to proclaim the acceptable *year of the Lord*, and the day of vengeance of our God
Luke 4:19 to preach the acceptable *year of the Lord*

YEAR OF THE LORD'S FAVOR (NIV, RSV)
(See *ACCEPTABLE YEAR*)

YEAST OF THE PHARISEES (NIV)
(See *LEAVEN OF THE PHARISEES*)

YEAST WORKS THROUGH THE WHOLE BATCH (NIV)
(See *LEAVEN LEAVENS THE WHOLE LUMP*)

YET YOU HAVE NOT RETURNED
Amos 4:6 *yet you have not returned* to Me," says the Lord
Amos 4:8 *yet you have not returned* to Me," says the Lord
Amos 4:9 *yet you have not returned* to Me," says the Lord
Amos 4:10 *yet you have not returned* to Me," says the Lord
Amos 4:11 *yet you have not returned* to Me," says the Lord

YIELD YOUR HEARTS (NIV)
(See *INCLINE YOUR HEART*)

YOKE OF BONDAGE
Gal 5:1 Stand fast therefore in the liberty by which Christ has made us free, and do not be entangled again with a *yoke of bondage*

YONDER SIDE JORDAN (KJV)
(See *OTHER SIDE OF THE JORDAN*)

YOU AND YOUR MEN DESERVE TO DIE (NIV)
(See *YOU ARE WORTHY*)

YOU ANOINT MY HEAD WITH OIL
Ps 23:5 *You anoint my head with oil;* my cup runs over

YOU ARE DUST (RSV)
(See *FOR DUST YOU ARE*)

YOU ARE MY FRIENDS
John 15:14 *You are My friends* if you do whatever I command you

YOU ARE MY WITNESSES
Is 43:10 *You are My witnesses*," says the Lord, "And My servant whom I have chosen, that you may know and believe Me, and understand that I am He
Is 43:12 therefore *you are My witnesses*," says the Lord, "that I am God
Is 44:8 *You are My witnesses*. Is there a God besides Me

YOU ARE THE BRANCHES
John 15:5 I am the vine, *you are the branches*. He who abides in Me, and I in him, bears much fruit

YOU ARE THE CHRIST
Matt 16:16 And Simon Peter answered and said, "*You are the Christ*, the Son of the living God
Matt 26:63 And the high priest answered and said to Him, "I adjure You by the living God that You tell us if *You are the Christ*, the Son of God
Mark 8:29 And Peter answered and said to Him, "*You are the Christ*
Luke 4:41 And demons also came out of many, crying out and saying, "*You are the Christ*, the Son of God
Luke 22:67 If *You are the Christ*, tell us." But He said to them
Luke 23:39 Then one of the criminals who were hanged blasphemed Him, saying, "If *You are the Christ*, save Yourself and us
John 6:69 Also we have come to believe and know that *You are the Christ*, the Son of the living God
John 10:24 Then the Jews surrounded Him and said to Him, "How long do You keep us in doubt? If *You are the Christ*, tell us plainly
John 11:27 She said to Him, "Yes, Lord, I believe that *You are the Christ*, the Son of God, who is to come into the world

YOU ARE THE MAN
2Sam 12:7 Then Nathan said to David, "*You are the man!* Thus says the Lord God of Israel

YOU ARE WITNESSES
Josh 24:22 So Joshua said to the people, "*You are witnesses* against yourselves that you have chosen the Lord for yourselves, to serve Him

Ruth 4:9 And Boaz said to the elders and to all the people, "*You are witnesses* this day that I have bought all that was Elimelech's, and all that was Chilion's and Mahlon's, from the hand of Naomi
Ruth 4:10 Moreover, Ruth the Moabitess, the wife of Mahlon, I have acquired as my wife, to raise up the name of the dead on his inheritance, that the name of the dead may not be cut off from among his brethren and from the gate of his place. *You are witnesses* this day
Matt 23:31 Therefore *you are witnesses* against yourselves that you are sons of those who murdered the prophets
Luke 24:48 And *you are witnesses* of these things
1Th 2:10 *You are witnesses*, and God also, how devoutly and justly and blamelessly we behaved ourselves among you who believe

YOU ARE WORTHY
1Sam 26:16 As the Lord lives, *you are worthy* to die, because you have not guarded your master, the Lord's anointed
1Kin 2:26 And to Abiathar the priest the king said, "Go to Anathoth, to your own fields, for *you are worthy* of death
Rev 4:11 *You are worthy*, O Lord, to receive glory and honor and power
Rev 5:9 *You are worthy* to take the scroll, and to open its seals

YOU HAVE BEEN SET APART (NIV)
(See *CONSECRATE YOURSELVES*)

YOU HAVE HEARD THAT IT WAS SAID
Matt 5:21 *You have heard that it was said* to those of old
Matt 5:27 *You have heard that it was said* to those of old
Matt 5:33 Again *you have heard that it was said* to those of old
Matt 5:38 *You have heard that it was said*, 'An eye for an eye and a tooth for a tooth
Matt 5:43 *You have heard that it was said*, 'You shall love your neighbor and hate your enemy

YOU HYPOCRITES
Matt 22:18 But Jesus perceived their wickedness, and said, "Why do you test Me, *you hypocrites*
Mark 7:6 He answered and said to them, "Well did Isaiah prophesy of *you hypocrites*, as it is written

YOU, ISRAEL, ARE MY SERVANT
Is 41:8 But *you, Israel, are My servant*, Jacob, whom I have chosen, the descendants of Abraham My friend

YOU MUST BE BORN AGAIN
John 3:7 Do not marvel that I said to you, '*You must be born again*

YOU MUST DIE (NAS, NIV)
(See *YOU WILL SURELY DIE*)

YOU, O GOD, ARE MY FORTRESS (NIV)
(See *GOD IS MY DEFENSE*)

YOU, O GOD, ARE STRONG (NIV)
(See *POWER BELONGS TO GOD*)

YOU OF LITTLE FAITH
Matt 6:30 Now if God so clothes the grass of the field, which today is, and tomorrow is thrown into the oven, will He not much more clothe you, O *you of little faith*
Matt 8:26 But He said to them, "Why are you fearful, O *you of little faith*
Matt 14:31 And immediately Jesus stretched out His hand and caught him, and said to him, "O *you of little faith*, why did you doubt
Matt 16:8 But when Jesus perceived it, He said to them, "O *you of little faith*, why do you reason among yourselves because you have brought no bread
Luke 12:28 If then God so clothes the grass, which today is in the field and tomorrow is thrown into the oven, how much more will He clothe you, O *you of little faith*

YOU SHALL DIE (RSV)
(See *YOU WILL SURELY DIE*)

YOU SHALL NOT KILL (RSV)
(See *YOU SHALL NOT MURDER*)

YOU SHALL NOT MURDER
Ex 20:13 *You shall not murder*
Deut 5:17 *You shall not murder*
Matt 5:21 You have heard that it was said to those of old, '*You shall not murder*
Matt 19:18 Jesus said, "'*You shall not murder*,' 'You shall not commit adultery
Rom 13:9 For the commandments, "You shall not commit adultery," "*You shall not murder*

YOU WILL SURELY DIE
Jer 26:8 Now it happened, when Jeremiah had made an end of speaking all that the Lord had commanded him to speak to all the people, that the priests and the prophets and all the people seized him, saying, "*You will surely die*

YOUNG AND OLD
Josh 6:21 And they utterly destroyed all that was in the city, both man and woman, *young and old*, ox and sheep and donkey, with the edge of the sword
Esth 3:13 And the letters were sent by couriers into all the king's provinces, to destroy, to kill, and to annihilate all the Jews, both *young and old*, little children and women, in one day, on the thirteenth day of the twelfth month, which is the month of Adar, and to plunder their possessions
Is 20:4 so shall the king of Assyria lead away the Egyptians as prisoners and the Ethiopians as captives, *young and old*, naked and barefoot, with their buttocks uncovered, to the shame of Egypt
Lam 2:21 *Young and old* lie on the ground in the streets

YOUNG WOMAN SHALL CONCEIVE (RSV)
(See *VIRGIN SHALL CONCEIVE*)

YOUNG WOMEN OF JERUSALEM (NIV)
(See *VIRGINS OF JERUSALEM*)

YOUR BROTHER JACOB
Obad 10 For your violence against *your brother Jacob*, shame shall cover you, and you shall be cut off forever

YOUR DWELLING PLACE
Num 24:21 Firm is *your dwelling place*, and your nest is set in the rock
1Kin 8:30 When they pray toward this place, then hear in heaven *Your dwelling place*
1Kin 8:39 then hear in heaven *Your dwelling place*, and forgive, and act, and give to everyone according to all his ways, whose heart You know (for You, only You, know the hearts of all the sons of men
1Kin 8:43 hear in heaven *Your dwelling place*, and do according to all for which the foreigner calls to You, that all peoples of the earth may know Your name and fear You, as do Your people Israel, and

that they may know that this temple which I have built is called by Your name
1Kin 8:49 then hear in heaven *Your dwelling place* their prayer and their supplication, and maintain their cause
2Kin 19:27 But I know *your dwelling place*, your going out and your coming in, and your rage against Me
2Chr 6:21 hear from *Your dwelling place*, in heaven; and when You hear, forgive
2Chr 6:30 then hear from heaven *Your dwelling place*, and forgive, and give to everyone according to all his ways, whose heart You know (for You alone know the hearts of the sons of men
2Chr 6:33 then hear from heaven *Your dwelling place*, and do according to all for which the foreigner calls to You, that all people of the earth may know Your name and fear You, as do Your people Israel, and that they may know that this temple which I have built is called by Your name
2Chr 6:39 then hear from heaven *Your dwelling place* their prayer and their supplications, and maintain their cause, and forgive Your people who have sinned against You
Ps 52:5 He shall take you away, and pluck you out of *your dwelling place*, and uproot you from the land of the living
Is 37:28 But I know *your dwelling place*, your going out and your coming in, and your rage against Me

YOUR ENEMY
Deut 28:53 You shall eat the fruit of your own body, the flesh of your sons and your daughters whom the Lord your God has given you, in the siege and desperate straits in which *your enemy* shall distress you
Deut 28:55 so that he will not give any of them the flesh of his children whom he will eat, because he has nothing left in the siege and desperate straits in which *your enemy* shall distress you at all your gates
Deut 28:57 for she will eat them secretly for lack of all things in the siege and desperate straits in which *your enemy* shall distress you at all your gates
1Sam 24:4 Then the men of David said to him, "This is the day of which the Lord said to you, 'Behold, I will deliver *your enemy* into your hand, that you may do to him as it seems good to you
1Sam 26:8 Then Abishai said to David, "God has delivered *your enemy* into your hand this day
1Sam 28:16 Why then do you ask me, seeing the Lord has departed from you and has become *your enemy*
2Sam 4:8 And they brought the head of Ishbosheth to David at Hebron, and said to the king, "Here is the head of Ishbosheth, the son of Saul *your enemy*, who sought your life
Job 13:24 Why do You hide Your face, and regard me as *Your enemy*
Prov 24:17 Do not rejoice when *your enemy* falls, and do not let your heart be glad when he stumbles
Prov 25:21 If *your enemy* is hungry, give him bread to eat
Lam 2:17 He has thrown down and has not pitied, and He has caused *your enemy* to rejoice over you
Zeph 3:15 The Lord has taken away your judgments, he has cast out *your enemy*
Matt 5:43 You have heard that it was said, 'You shall love your neighbor and hate *your enemy*
Rom 12:20 Therefore if *your enemy* hungers, feed him; if he thirsts, give him a drink
Gal 4:16 Have I therefore become *your enemy* because I tell you the truth

YOUR FATHER ABRAHAM (NAS, NIV)
(See *ABRAHAM YOUR FATHER*)

YOUR FATHER'S INSTRUCTION (NIV, RSV)
(See *INSTRUCTION OF YOUR FATHER*)

YOUR FEET FITTED WITH THE READINESS THAT COMES FROM THE GOSPEL OF PEACE (NIV)
(See *SHOD YOUR FEET WITH THE PREPARATION OF THE GOSPEL OF PEACE*)

YOUR FOOTSTOOL
Ps 110:1 The Lord said to my Lord, "Sit at My right hand, till I make Your enemies *Your footstool*
Matt 22:44 The Lord said to my Lord, "Sit at My right hand, till I make Your enemies *Your footstool*
Mark 12:36 The Lord said to my Lord, "Sit at My right hand, till I make Your enemies *Your footstool*
Luke 20:43 till I make Your enemies *Your footstool*
Acts 2:35 till I make Your enemies *Your footstool*
Heb 1:13 Sit at My right hand, till I make Your enemies *Your footstool*

YOUR HOLY SERVANT JESUS
Acts 4:27 For truly against *Your holy Servant Jesus*, whom You anointed, both Herod and Pontius Pilate, with the Gentiles and the people of Israel, were gathered together
Acts 4:30 by stretching out Your hand to heal, and that signs and wonders may be done through the name of *Your holy Servant Jesus*

YOUR JOY MAY BE FULL
John 15:11 These things I have spoken to you, that My joy may remain in you, and that *your joy may be full*
John 16:24 Ask, and you will receive, that *your joy may be full*
1Jn 1:4 And these things we write to you that *your joy may be full*

YOUR KINGDOM COME
Matt 6:10 *Your kingdom come*. Your will be done on earth as it is in heaven
Luke 11:2 *Your kingdom come*. Your will be done On earth as it is in heaven

YOUR LAW IS MY DELIGHT
Ps 119:77 Let Your tender mercies come to me, that I may live; for *Your law is my delight*
Ps 119:174 I long for Your salvation, O Lord, and *Your law is my delight*

YOUR LOVINGKINDNESS
Ps 26:3 For *Your lovingkindness* is before my eyes, and I have walked in Your truth
Ps 36:7 How precious is *Your lovingkindness*, O God! Therefore the children of men put their trust under the shadow of Your wings
Ps 36:10 Oh, continue *Your lovingkindness* to those who know You, and Your righteousness to the upright in heart
Ps 40:10 I have not concealed *Your lovingkindness* and Your truth from the great congregation
Ps 40:11 Do not withhold Your tender mercies from me, O Lord; let *Your lovingkindness* and Your truth continually preserve me
Ps 48:9 We have thought, O God, on *Your lovingkindness*, in the midst of Your temple
Ps 51:1 Have mercy upon me, O God, according to *Your lovingkindness*
Ps 63:3 Because *Your lovingkindness* is better than life, my lips shall praise You

Ps 69:16 Hear me, O Lord, for *Your lovingkindness* is good; turn to me according to the multitude of Your tender mercies
Ps 88:11 Shall *Your lovingkindness* be declared in the grave? Or Your faithfulness in the place of destruction
Ps 92:2 To declare *Your lovingkindness* in the morning, and Your faithfulness every night
Ps 119:88 Revive me according to *Your lovingkindness*, so that I may keep the testimony of Your mouth
Ps 119:149 Hear my voice according to *Your lovingkindness;* O Lord, revive me according to Your justice
Ps 119:159 Consider how I love Your precepts; revive me, O Lord, according to *Your lovingkindness*
Ps 138:2 I will worship toward Your holy temple, and praise Your name for *Your lovingkindness* and Your truth
Ps 143:8 Cause me to hear *Your lovingkindness* in the morning, for in You do I trust

YOUR PEOPLE SHALL BE MY PEOPLE
Ruth 1:16 *your people shall be my people*, and your God, my God

YOUR PRAYER IS HEARD
Luke 1:13 But the angel said to him, "Do not be afraid, Zacharias, for *your prayer is heard*

YOUR REDEMPTION DRAWS NEAR
Luke 21:28 Now when these things begin to happen, look up and lift up your heads, because *your redemption draws near*

YOUR ROD AND YOUR STAFF
Ps 23:4 For You are with me; *Your rod and Your staff*, they comfort me

YOUR SERVANTS THE PROPHETS
Ezra 9:11 which You have commanded by *Your servants the prophets*, saying
Dan 9:6 Neither have we heeded *Your servants the prophets*, who spoke in Your name to our kings and our princes, to our fathers and all the people of the land
Rev 11:18 The nations were angry, and Your wrath has come, and the time of the dead, that they should be judged, and that You should reward *Your servants the prophets* and the saints, and those who fear Your name, small and great, and should destroy those who destroy the earth

YOUR SIN WILL FIND YOU OUT
Num 32:23 But if you do not do so, then take note, you have sinned against the Lord; and be sure *your sin will find you out*

YOUR SINS ARE FORGIVEN YOU
Matt 9:2 And Jesus, seeing their faith, said to the paralytic, "Son, be of good cheer; *your sins are forgiven you*
Matt 9:5 For which is easier, to say, '*Your sins are forgiven you*
Mark 2:5 When Jesus saw their faith, He said to the paralytic, "Son, *your sins are forgiven you*
Mark 2:9 Which is easier, to say to the paralytic, '*Your sins are forgiven you*
Luke 5:20 So when He saw their faith, He said to him, "Man, *your sins are forgiven you*
Luke 5:23 Which is easier, to say, '*Your sins are forgiven you*
1Jn 2:12 I write to you, little children, because *your sins are forgiven you* for His name's sake

YOUR WORD IS TRUTH
Ps 119:160 The entirety of *Your word is truth*, and every one of Your righteous judgments endures forever
John 17:17 Sanctify them by Your truth. *Your word is truth*

YOUTH IS RENEWED
Ps 103:5 Who satisfies your mouth with good things, so that your *youth is renewed* like the eagle's

Z

ZEAL FOR GOD
Rom 10:2 For I bear them witness that they have a *zeal for God*, but not according to knowledge

ZEAL FOR YOUR HOUSE
Ps 69:9 Because *zeal for Your house* has eaten me up, and the reproaches of those who reproach You have fallen on me
John 2:17 Then His disciples remembered that it was written, "*Zeal for Your house* has eaten Me up

ZEAL OF THE LORD
2Kin 19:31 The *zeal of the Lord* of hosts shall do this
Is 9:7 The *zeal of the Lord* of hosts will perform this
Is 37:32 The *zeal of the Lord* of hosts will do this

ZEAL OF THINE HOUSE (KJV)
(See *ZEAL FOR YOUR HOUSE*)

ZEALOUS FOR GOD (NIV)
(See *ZEAL FOR GOD*)

ZEALOUS FOR GOOD WORKS
Tit 2:14 who gave Himself for us, that He might redeem us from every lawless deed and purify for Himself His own special people, *zealous for good works*

ZEALOUS FOR JERUSALEM
Zech 1:14 I am *zealous for Jerusalem* and for Zion with great zeal

ZEALOUS FOR THE LAW
Acts 21:20 And they said to him, "You see, brother, how many myriads of Jews there are who have believed, and they are all *zealous for the law*

ZION, MY HOLY HILL (NIV, RSV)
(See *HILL OF ZION*)

KEY WORD INDEX

for locating specific phrases
in the

Phrase Concordance
of the Bible

This Key Word Index contains almost 400 significant words which appear frequently in the Bible. Under each one of these words are listed all the phrases in this concordance that contain that particular word. If you can recall only one word of a specific biblical phrase which you are searching for, look under that word in this Index. It should help you find the specific phrase you have in mind.

B

D

DAY (continued)
In the day of trouble
Know therefore this day
Know this day
Last day
Light to govern the day
Light to rule the day
Lord Almighty has a day
Lord of hosts has a day
Night and day
On that day
On the first day of the week
On the Sabbath day to sell
On the seventh day He rested
On the third day
Raised on the third day
Raised the third day
Remember the Sabbath day
Rested on the seventh day
Rested the Sabbath day
Rose again the third day
Sabbath day
Same day
Sell on the Sabbath day
Separate the day from the night
Seventh day
Sufficient for the day
Third day
Third day be raised
This day have I begotten you
This very day
To this day
Twelve hours in the day
Until this day

DEAD
As good as dead
Baptized for the dead
Dead in Christ
Dead in trespasses
Dead in your transgressions
Dead rise
Dead shall live
Dead through the trespasses
Dead to the law
Dead with Christ
Firstborn from the dead
Gives life to the dead
God of the dead
If the dead do not rise
Life from the dead
Living among the dead
Maintain the name of the dead
Quickeneth the dead
Raise the dead
Raise up the name of the dead
Raised from the dead
Raised him from the dead
Raising him from the dead
Restore the name of the dead
Resurrection of the dead
Rise from the dead
Risen from the dead
Twice dead
Weep not for the dead

DEATH
After the death of
Baptism into death
Be put to death
Becoming like Him in death
Conformed to His death
Cords of death
Covenant with death
Day of His death
Day of their death
Death and destruction
Death is swallowed up
Death of His saints
Death of the one who made it
Death of the testator
Death reigned from Adam to Moses
Death shall not prevail
Destruction and death
Dust of death
Faithful, even to the point of death
Faithful until death
Fear of death
Freeing him from the agony of death
Gates of death
Guilty of death
Have no pleasure in the death
Hounded to death the poor
Illness is not unto death
Instruments of death
Leads to death
Likeness of His death
Loosed the pains of death
Lord brings death and makes alive
Love is as strong as death
Not deserving of death
Obedient to the point of death
Obedient unto death
Pangs of death
Passed from death to life
Point of death
Powers of death
Proclaim the Lord's death
Put to death
Save a soul from death
Second death
Sentence of death
Sentenced to death
Shadow of death
Show the Lord's death
Sickness is not unto death
Sin hath reigned unto death
Sin leading to death
Sin not leading to death
Sin reigned in death
Sin unto death
Snares of death
Sorrows of death
Sting of death
Stone her to death
Stone him to death
Stone to death
Swallow up death
Taste death
United with Him in death
Unto the death
Valley of the shadow of death
Way of death
Worthy of death

DELIVERANCE
Deliverance belongs to the Lord
Deliverance is of the Lord
Deliverance the Lord will bring
Deliverance to the captives
From the Lord comes deliverance
God rests my deliverance
Great deliverance
Preach deliverance

E

F

FACE
Before your face
Behold the face of God
Discover thy skirts upon thy face
Entreat now the face
Face of an angel
Face of God
Face of the deep
Face of the earth
Face of the Lord
Face shine upon you
Face to face
Fell down on his face
Fell on my face
Hid my face
Hidden his face
Hidden my face
Hide his face
Hide my face
Hide your face
Hides his face
Kingdoms on the face of the earth
Lift your skirts over your face
Light of your face
Lord make His face shine upon you
Scattered over the face of the whole earth
Send my messenger before your face
Set your face against
Sins have hidden His face
Sweat of your face
Turn your face toward
Veil over his face

FAITH
Accept him whose faith is weak
According to your faith
Add to your faith
Atonement through faith in His blood
Author and finisher of our faith
Brought up in the truths of faith
By faith
Contend earnestly for the faith
Continue in faith
Continue in the faith
Erred concerning the faith
Faith as a mustard seed
Faith comes by
Faith from first to last
Faith has made you well
Faith has no value
Faith has saved you
Faith, hope, love
Faith in Christ
Faith in God
Faith in Jesus
Faith in the Lord
Faith is made void
Faith is null
Faith to faith
Faith unfeigned
Faith without works
Finisher of our faith
Genuineness of your faith
Great faith
Have faith
Hearing of faith
Him that is weak in the faith receive ye
Household of faith
In the faith
Increase our faith
Just shall live by faith
Just shall live by his faith
Justified by faith
Kept the faith
Law of faith
Little faith
Live by faith
Man full of faith
Man who is weak in faith, welcome him
Measure of faith
Men of little faith
Missed the mark as regards the faith
Nourished in the words of faith
Obedience that comes from faith
Obedience to the faith
Own son after the common faith
Perfecter of our faith
Pioneer and perfecter of our faith
Propitiation through faith in His blood
Rich in faith
Righteousness of faith
Righteousness that comes by faith
Saved through faith
Shield of faith
Show me your faith
Sincere faith
Stand fast in the faith
Stand firm in the faith
Strayed concerning the faith
Supplement your faith
Through the righteousness of faith
Trial of your faith
True child in a common faith
True son in our common faith
Unity of the faith
Wandered from the faith
Weak in faith
Who through faith is righteous shall live
Word of faith
You of little faith

FAITHFUL
Faithful and true
Faithful and wise servant
Faithful, even to the point of death
Faithful love promised to David
Faithful man
Faithful saying
Faithful until death
Faithful witness
God is faithful
Good and faithful servant
Lord preserves the faithful
True and faithful

FAMILY
Come from David's family
Family of Abraham
Family of believers
Head of a family

FASTING
Fasting and lamenting
Prayer and fasting

FATHER
Abba, Father
Abraham your father

G

Guilt is so great
In a great strait
In great distress
Lord has done great things
Lord is great
Make him a great nation
Make you a great nation
Pearl of great price
Small and great
So great a salvation
Such a great salvation
Suffered a great deal
Sweat became like great drops
Sweat was as it were great drops
Who had done great things
Who have done great things

H

HANDS
Behold My hands and My feet
Betrayed into the hands of
Betrayed into the hands of men
Blood is on their hands
Clap your hands
Claps his hands
Clean hands
Delivered into the hands of
Delivered into the hands of men
Feeble hands
Fell into the hands of robbers
Hands of the living God
Hands over the kingdom
Held out my hands
Into Your hands
Labor of my hands
Laid His hands on
Laid their hands on
Laying on of hands
Laying on of the apostles' hands
Palms of My hands
Pierced My hands and My feet
Put My life in My hands
Sold them into the hands of their enemies
Spread abroad His hands
Spread forth His hands
Spread out His hands
Spread out my hands
Strengthen the weak hands
Stretched forth My hands
Stretched out His hands
Stretched out My hands
Symbols on your hands
Toil of my hands
Took His life in His hands
Took my life in my hands
Unwashed hands
Weak hands
Work of men's hands
Work of our hands
Work of your hands

HAPPY
Happy is he
Happy is the man

HATE
Hate discipline
Hate evil
Hate instruction
Hate your enemy
Men will hate you

HEAL
Heal my soul
Heal on the Sabbath
Heal the brokenhearted
Heal the sick
Physician, heal yourself

HEALED
By His stripes we are healed
With His stripes we are healed

HEART
Abundance of the heart
Acknowledge and take to heart this day
Anguish of heart
Apply your heart
Attitudes of the heart
Be strong and let your heart take courage
Be strong and take heart
Believe in your heart
Bribe debases the heart
Broken and a contrite heart
Change of heart
Circumcise your heart
Clean heart
Deceit of their heart
Deceives his own heart
Despairing heart
Do not lose heart
Err in heart
Gentle and lowly in heart
Hardened Pharaoh's heart
Hardness of heart
Haughtiness of his heart
Heart burn within us
Heart condemns us
Heart exults
Heart fails me
Heart greatly rejoices
Heart grows faint
Heart has turned to wax
Heart is deceitful
Heart is faint
Heart is far from me
Heart is like wax
Heart is overwhelmed
Heart is sick
Heart is troubled
Heart leaps for joy
Heart of a child
Heart of flesh
Heart of fools
Heart of stone
Heart of the fool
Heart of the foolish
Heart pounded
Heart was hardened
Humble in heart
If our heart condemns us
Imagination of their evil heart
Incline your heart
Integrity of your heart
Intents of the heart
Kept all these things in her heart
Lay it to heart
Layeth it to heart
Lays it to heart
Let not your heart be troubled
Lord hardened Pharaoh's heart
Lose heart

I

J

K

L

LIGHT

LORD

M

N

O

P

R

T

U

Y

Z